WEBSTER'S

AMERICAN

BIOGRAPHIES

WEBSTER'S AMERICAN BIOGRAPHIES

Charles Van Doren, EDITOR

Robert McHenry, ASSOCIATE EDITOR

A Merriam-Webster ®

MERRIAM-WEBSTER INC., *Publishers*

SPRINGFIELD, MASSACHUSETTS

Copyright © 1984 by Merriam-Webster Inc.

Philippines Copyright 1984 by Merriam-Webster Inc.

Library of Congress Cataloging in Publication Data

Main entry under title:

Webster's American biographies.

   Includes indexes.
    1. United States—Biography. I. Van Doren, Charles Lincoln, 1926–   . II. McHenry, Robert.
CT213.W43   1984   920'.073   83-26706
ISBN 0-87779-253-4

Webster's American Biographies principal copyright 1974

The quotation on page 761 is from a poem © 1930 by Ogden Nash that originally appeared in *The New Yorker*. It is used with the permission of Little, Brown and Company, the publisher of *Verses From 1929 On* by Ogden Nash.

Printed and bound in the United States of America

9RRD89

M. V. D.

1894–1972

Contents

Introduction

WEBSTER'S AMERICAN BIOGRAPHIES is a collection of full-scale biographies of more than 3000 notable Americans. By a "full-scale" biography is meant an account of a person's life that provides something more than the basic facts—birth and death dates, titles of works, names of offices held, and so forth. The basic facts are indeed here, but we tried also to provide something more. Within the compass of an average of 350 words, we sought wherever possible to describe the shape of a life, to place it in juxtaposition to other, similar lives, and to set it in the context of surrounding events. In the case of scientists and inventors, for example, the attempt was made to describe in some detail the individual's significant contribution to his field of research or to an industry; in the case of political figures, to describe in as much detail as possible the individual's actions together with their motivation and effects; and in the case of artists and literary figures, to assess the importance and influence of a person's work.

To that end, the biographies account for almost all of the years, and all of the mature and productive years, of their subjects. Thus, the typical biography describes the character of a subject's early and formative experience—his education; his first, often tentative, assays at a career, together with his initial failures, if any; and then his mature works and achievements, together with mention of the places where they occurred, and of the associates with whom they were done, where relevant; finally, the activities of his last years. Such extended descriptions are supplemented by lists of works—literary or other—which, although usually not complete, at least try to include the major items. Honors such as Nobel prizes, Pulitzer prizes, National Book awards, Spingarn medals, and membership in the Hall of Fame for Great Americans are also mentioned.

The 3082 biographical subjects treated in this book represent what is, after all, only a very small sample of all the Americans who have ever lived (and are still living). The editors are aware that it is almost inevitable that readers will question the inclusion of some subjects, and regret the exclusion of others. The editors sought the best advice they could find, and often accepted it. In the task of choosing subjects to be considered for inclusion within particular fields or occupations the editors were greatly aided by a panel of consultants that included Stephen Ambrose of Louisiana State University (military history), Matthew Baigell of Rutgers University (art history), Saul Benison of the University of Cincinnati (history of science), Russel B. Nye of Michigan State University (literary and intellectual history), Milton Schafer of John Jay College, CUNY (music), Harry Scheiber of the University of California at San Diego (business and economic history), and Donald M. Scott of the University of Chicago (religious and social history). But the final choice had to be the editors', and they take responsibility for it. It is therefore desirable to state the criteria used to decide who should be treated.

The most important criterion may be called "significant contribution;" that is, no subject was included who has not, in the opinion of the editors, made a contribution of note to American life and American history. The judgment of whom to include was not always easy to make, and it would often have been inordinately difficult if a single scale, ranging from the most important figure in American history (whoever that may be) at the one end, to the least important at the other, had been used. Instead, multiple scales were employed, which allowed the editors the freedom to ignore arguments about whether music, for example, is more or less important than politics, or finance more or less significant than sports. Thus, although a certain number of subjects were included because of their undoubted, indisputable, and overall significance in the general life and history of the nation, others were included because of their significance within a particular field.

Another criterion may be called "look-up-ableness." The editors asked themselves, in drawing up the list of subjects to be included, whether each nominee was likely to be of interest to contemporary readers. This was always an important consideration, and it partly accounts for the fact that the book contains proportionally more biographies of living subjects than many other biographical reference works of this kind. It also helps to account for the fact that it contains many biographies of representatives of the "popular," as opposed to the "high" or "formal," culture—entertainers, sports figures, and the like. Such persons, although a century ago they might not have been thought worthy of inclusion, are now of great interest to many readers. And indeed, why should they not be?

One example will perhaps be illuminating. Six subjects named Kelly are treated in the book. Ellsworth Kelly, the noted modern painter and sculptor, and William Kelly, the inventor of the so-called Bessemer process for manufacturing steel (therein lies a historical injustice that this book will probably not correct), are representatives of the "high" culture. Emmett Kelly, the great clown, and Walt Kelly, the cartoonist and creator of Pogo, are representatives of a more "popular" culture. Grace Kelly is almost sui generis; a fine young movie actress, this princess of the silver screen became a real-life princess as well. Finally, there is "Shipwreck" Kelly, the flagpole sitter, whose most remarkable feat was remaining on top of a flagpole in Atlantic City for 49 days in the summer of 1930. A hundred years hence no one may remember this, but now people do, and so we have provided the facts about this strange, brave man.

Still another criterion for inclusion may be called "catholicity." Thus, a special attempt was made to cover geographical regions and groups within the American population that, on the whole, are not very well represented in other general biographical reference works. Among such often neglected groups of subjects are women, Afro-Americans, American Indians, scientists (including social scientists), persons associated with the Southwestern and Western frontiers (as opposed to those associated with the New England and Midwestern frontiers), and businessmen and industrialists. However, it should be noted that traditional categories of subjects, such as political and military figures, remain inevitably large.

Certain persons gained inclusion "ex officio." Thus, all presidents of the United States, all Supreme Court justices, all Speakers of the House of Representatives, and all U.S. Nobel Prize winners were automatically included.

Still another criterion requires comment. A subject had to have spent some time in the United States (or in North America before 1776) to be considered. But it was not required that a subject either have been born here or have died here. America was and to an extent still is a nation of immigrants, and some immigrants come and stay for a while and then leave again. To insist on a narrow nativism would have defeated the book's purpose. Hence, it was not required that a nominated immigrant have become a naturalized citizen, although if he did (or did not) this was sometimes taken into consideration in deciding whether to include or exclude him.

Most subjects are treated in separate biographies, even if closely related, since that is most convenient for readers. However, in a small number of cases, where members of the same immediate family—parent and child, siblings, or husband and wife—followed very similar or parallel careers, they are treated within the same biographical entry. Thus, for example, the Harper brothers, publishers, and the Thomas J. Watsons, entrepreneurial father and son, are treated jointly. A few pairs of persons are treated together even though not related—for example, Nathaniel Currier and James Merritt Ives, Freeman Fisher Gosden ("Amos") and Charles J. Correll ("Andy"), and Nicola Sacco and Bartolomeo Vanzetti. In these and a few other cases the pair had made the "significant contribution" that was the reason for inclusion. It would be difficult and indeed self-defeating to separate them.

Because the biographies of such persons as Ives and Vanzetti do not occur in alphabetical order in the text, there are cross references from their names to the pages on which their biographies actually appear. There are also cross references from well-known nicknames or pseudonyms—for example, "F.P.A.," "David Grayson," and "Mark Twain." For the most part, biographies are entered in the alphabetical order under the best known name of the subject, but this is not always the subject's formal name. In such cases, cross references under the formal name send the reader to the biography. The system of cross references is extensive and the editors hope that no reader will ever fail to find the biography he is looking for.

It has been noted that the average length of the biographies is about 350 words. But there is considerable range. The three longest biographies, not surprisingly, are of Benjamin Franklin, Abraham Lincoln, and George Washington, a fact that reflects their importance in American history together with the wide range of activities in which they (and especially Franklin) engaged. On the whole, there is a relationship between the importance of a subject and the length of his biography, but judgments of importance are not always to be derived solely from the length of an entry.

Besides the 3082 entries and more than 370 cross references, the book contains two indexes that, it is hoped, will be useful and interesting to readers. A careers and professions index lists subjects alphabetically under a variety of different professions or occupations, which are themselves arranged in alphabetical order, with cross references. Every subject appears in at least one of these lists, and many appear in more than one.

A geographical index lists subjects alphabetically under place, including the 50 states and the District of Columbia and other lands, such as England, Scotland, Wales, Ireland, Germany, Austria, Poland, Russia, China, Italy, Jamaica, and Yugoslavia. A subject was listed under a U.S. state or territory if he was born there or lived a considerable part of his life in it or is in some way memorably associated with it; thus, subjects may appear in more than one geographical category. The listings under other countries is, in general, limited to a person's place of birth. Some places subtend many names—Illinois, Massachusetts, and New York, for example, among the states; England, France, and Germany, among the foreign countries. Others subtend only a single subject, for example, Australia (Harry Bridges) and Senegal (Phillis Wheatley). The placement of subjects under this or that occupational or geographical heading, like the choice of subjects, remains (for good or ill) the responsibility of the editors.

A book of this size and scope is necessarily the product of many minds and hands. A very great debt is owed to George Ducas and Wayne Moquin, who wrote drafts of many of the biographies; to Marlys A. Buswell, who carried out with ability and dispatch a large number of necessary clerical tasks, many of them onerous, and also directed the useful labors of a clerical staff that included Caroline Hedlund and Renée Rendler; to Susan Campbell, who checked most of the biographies with great skill; to Mrs. Helen Witty, who edited the final manuscript, providing not only a consistency of style but also a degree of accuracy that would have been otherwise unobtainable; and to Mortimer J. Adler, who provided much useful advice and was always available to help out when crises occurred—as they frequently did.

Many others lent a hand, but perhaps it would be unjust to mention any names lest someone else's contribution go unacknowledged. The editor must, however, acknowledge his debt to two men without whom the book could never have existed. One is the associate editor, Robert McHenry, who wrote more than half the biographies, rewrote many of the others, and answered the great majority of the copy editor's queries. Even more important, perhaps, he could always find something to smile about when things seemed most gloomy. The other is Robert Feldman, general reference editor at G. & C. Merriam, whose knowledge, combined with patience, is perhaps unparalleled in his field.

Charles Van Doren
Chicago
December 1973

WEBSTER'S

AMERICAN

BIOGRAPHIES

A

Aaron, Henry Louis (1934–   ), "Hank," baseball player. Born in Mobile, Alabama, on February 5, 1934, Aaron began playing amateur baseball while in high school and, after starring against them in a game, signed with the Indianapolis Clowns of the Negro National League in 1952. Later in the same year he was bought by the Milwaukee Braves and, after two fine years with farm clubs, was brought up to the parent club for the 1954 season. He was moved from shortstop to the outfield and, despite an injury that cut the season short for him, batted .280 while hitting 13 home runs. The next year he batted .314 and in 1956 won the National League batting championship with a .328 average while hitting 26 home runs. He won it again in 1959 with a .355 average and 39 homers, led the league in runs batted in in 1957 (132), in 1960 (126), and in 1963 (130), and in 1957, the year the Braves won the World Series, he was voted the league's most valuable player. Beginning in 1955 Aaron was a regular choice for the National League's all-star team, but it was only after 1966, when the Braves moved to Atlanta and he led the league in homers with 44, that he began to be recognized as the genuine superstar that in fact he was. By the end of the 1973 season, his twentieth in the big leagues, he was very close to the all-time leaders in many batting categories, including runs scored, total bases, runs batted in, and particularly Babe Ruth's lifetime record of 714 home runs. He hit his 715th home run in Atlanta, Georgia, April 8, 1974.

Abbe, Cleveland (1838–1916), astronomer and meteorologist. Born in New York City on December 3, 1838, Abbe graduated from the Free Academy there (later the College of the City of New York) in 1857 and, after three years of teaching at Trinity Latin School in New York City, at Michigan Agricultural College, and at the University of Michigan, received his M.A. degree from the Free Academy. Disqualified from service in the Civil War because of poor eyesight, he spent the years 1861–1864 in Cambridge, Massachusetts, working for the U.S. Coast Survey. From 1864 to 1866 he was a guest astronomer at the observatory in Pulkovo, Russia; upon his return to the United States he briefly held a position at the Naval Observatory and then, in 1868, became director of the Cincinnati Observatory. For the observatory, which served principally as a mildly educational place of public entertainment, he projected an ambitious program of serious research. While most of his ideas were far beyond the means at hand, he was successful in recruiting a corps of weather observers who reported to him by telegraph. The system of reporting he developed enabled him to construct weather maps and to issue storm warnings and, beginning in 1869, to make regular forecasts. Partly as a result of this work, a national weather service was established within the U.S. Signal Service the following year. Abbe joined it early in 1871, remaining until his retirement in 1916. He contributed greatly to the spread of interest in and knowledge of meteorology and was also an effective proponent of the adoption of a standard time system. He edited many publications of the Weather Service (after 1891, the Weather Bureau) and was professor of meteorology at Columbian (now The George Washington) University from 1886 to 1905 and lecturer at The Johns Hopkins University from 1896 to 1914. Abbe died in Chevy Chase, Maryland, on October 28, 1916.

Abbey, Edwin Austin (1852–1911), illustrator and painter. Born on April 1, 1852, in Philadelphia, Abbey ended his regular schooling at sixteen and began the full-time study of drawing, first with private teachers and later at the Pennsylvania Academy of the Fine Arts. In 1870 his illustration "The Puritans' First Thanksgiving" was published in *Harper's Weekly*, and the following year he joined the regular staff of Harper & Brothers in New York. He remained there doing mainly routine illustration work for several years except for a brief period as a free-lance artist, during which he illustrated his first book, Dickens's *Christmas Stories*, in 1875. In 1878 Harper's sent him to England to gather background for illustrating an article on Stratford-upon-Avon and then for a series of poems by Robert Herrick. The latter appeared in book form in 1882; Abbey followed with drawings for Oliver Goldsmith's *She Stoops to Conquer*, 1887; *Old Songs*, 1889; *The Quiet Life*, 1890; and the comedies of Shakespeare, 1896, all of which contributed to his reputation as the finest book illustrator of his time. Through these years he developed an interest in painting that continued to grow until it largely displaced his drawing. His early work had won him election to the Royal Institute of Painters in Water-Colours in 1883, and soon he was fully established in England, where he mainly lived thereafter and became a friend of fellow expatriates John Singer Sargent and Henry James. In 1890 he for the first time exhibited an oil, "Mayday Morning," at the Royal Academy and in the same year was commissioned to do a series of murals for the Boston Public Library. Twelve years in the making, the series depicting the legendary quest for the Holy Grail earned him honorary membership in the Institute of American Architects. Abbey now began to be widely honored; elected to the Royal Academy of Arts in 1896, he became an academician in 1898, was given numerous awards in France, including the Legion of Honor, and in 1901 was named to the U.S. National Academy of Design. Among his many commissions in his later years were his official coronation portrait of Edward VII in 1902 and his great murals for the Pennsylvania state capitol in Harrisburg. These, together with his supervision of the decoration of the peers' corridor in the Houses of Parliament, occupied him until his death in London on August 1, 1911.

Abbot, Francis Ellingwood (1836–1903), religious leader and philosopher. Born in Boston on November 6, 1836, Abbot graduated from Harvard in 1859 and attended its divinity school for a year before going to Meadville, Pennsylvania, to take charge of a girls' school and to complete his studies at Meadville Theological Seminary. He graduated in 1863 and became pastor of the Unitarian Church in Dover, New Hampshire. He wrote philosophical articles for the *North American Review* that were greatly admired. His radical religious views, however, led him to join in forming the Free Religious Association—based on the view that "God in Christ" must be replaced by "God in humanity"—that caused a split in his Dover congregation in 1869. Chairs of philosophy at Cornell and Harvard were denied him, despite strong recommendations, because of theological opposition. He finally accepted the Unitarian pastorate in Toledo, Ohio; the congregation changed its name to the Independent Church and offered funds for the publication of a weekly journal of Free Religion. He edited the *Index* for ten years and also organized the National Liberal League (1876) to support religious freedom. Returning to Harvard, he took his doctorate in 1881; a version of his thesis, *Scientific Theism*, soon ran through three editions and a German translation won him European attention. In 1888 he substituted for Josiah Royce at Harvard, but his lectures (published as *The Way Out of Agnosticism*, 1890) were publicly attacked by Royce upon his return. Abbot, whose belief in the unity of reason and experience was to become acceptable 20 years later, was embittered by the controversy and withdrew into solitude to prepare his major work, *The Syllogistic Philosophy*, 1906. When it was completed, just ten years after his wife's death, he committed suicide by taking poison at her grave, on October 23, 1903.

Abbott, Grace (1878–1939), social reformer. Born in Grand Island, Nebraska, on November 17, 1878, Miss Abbott graduated from Grand Island College in 1898 and thereafter did graduate work at the University of Nebraska while teaching in the high school in her native town. She went to Chicago in 1908 to work at Jane Addams's Hull House and in that year was made director of the

Immigrants' Protective League. She continued her graduate studies at the University of Chicago, receiving her Ph.M. in political science in 1909 and joining the faculty of the Chicago School of Civics and Philanthropy the next year. She was active in connection with Hull House until 1915; she severed her connections with the Immigrants' Protective League and the Chicago School of Civics and Philanthropy in 1917 to enter government service. She was director of the child-labor division of the Children's Bureau, Washington, D.C., from 1917 to 1919; an adviser to the War Labor Policies Board in 1918; executive secretary of the Illinois Immigrants' Commission in 1920–1921; chief of the U.S. Children's Bureau from 1921 to 1934; and professor of public welfare at the University of Chicago from 1934 until her death. During 1909–1910 she wrote a series of weekly articles, under the title "Within the City's Gates," for the *Chicago Evening Post*, exposing the exploitation of immigrants, and she revealed further aspects of exploitation in articles in the *Journal of Criminal Law and Criminology*, 1911 and 1915, and in a book, *The Immigrant and the Community*, 1917. During her first stint with the Children's Bureau, during and after World War I, she administered the first federal child-labor law. As director of the bureau during the 1920s and early 1930s she administered the Maternity and Infancy Act from 1922 to 1929. While serving as a professor at the University of Chicago she edited the *Social Service Review*, 1934–1939, and completed the research for what is probably her best-known and most influential work, *The Child and the State*, two volumes, 1938. A collection of her papers, *From Relief to Social Security*, was published in 1940, after her death in Chicago on June 19, 1939.

Abbott, Lyman (1835–1922), religious leader and editor. Born in Roxbury, Massachusetts, on December 18, 1835, Abbott was raised in Farmington, Maine, and in New York City. Upon graduation, from New York University, in 1853 he joined his brothers' law firm in New York. By 1859 he was earning a good income as a lawyer, but his boyhood aspiration to the ministry revived and he returned to Farmington, where he was ordained in 1860. He was pastor of the Congregational Church in Terre Haute, Indiana, during the Civil War, and in 1865 returned to New York to serve as corresponding secretary of the American Union Commission, a group of ministers and laymen formed to help in the task of Southern reconstruction. He held this post for four years and was simultaneously pastor of the New England Congregational Church in New York City. His book reviews for *Harper's Magazine* led the American Tract Society to appoint him editor of the *Illustrated Christian Weekly* in 1870. He joined Henry Ward Beecher in the editorship of the *Christian Union* in 1876 and became editor in chief in 1881. He also succeeded Beecher as pastor of Plymouth Church in Brooklyn, but he resigned in 1899 to devote himself entirely to editing. The *Christian Union*, renamed the *Outlook* in 1893, became a powerful exponent of progressive and practical Christianity. Although Abbott's books ranged from sympathetic interpretations of modern science to widely read works of devotion, the bulk of his writings, from *Christianity and Social Problems*, 1897, to *America in the Making*, 1911, made him a major proponent of the social gospel, the attempt to apply Christianity to the problems of the industrial world. His middle-of-the-road views opposed both socialism and laissez-faire economics. He died in New York City on October 22, 1922.

Abbott, Robert Sengstacke (1868–1940), newspaper editor and publisher. Born on St. Simons Island, Georgia, on November 28, 1868, Abbott was the son of former slaves. He was educated at Hampton Institute, graduating in 1896 as a trained printer. He moved to Chicago and in 1899 received a law degree from Kent College of Law, but the difficulties that confronted a Negro lawyer forced him to seek another career. After a few years of false starts, he fell back on his Hampton training and some past newspaper experience and on May 15, 1905, issued the first number of the *Chicago Defender*. With the slogan American Race Prejudice Must Be Destroyed on its masthead, the *Defender* quickly became a leading voice in the battle for just treatment for black Americans. Abbott used the paper to launch a massive campaign to induce Southern Negroes to move to the North, where there were fewer racial restrictions and more jobs; the campaign, coinciding with the industrial boom of World War I, was highly successful. Within ten years of publication, the *Defender's* circulation was nearly a quarter-million. Abbott died in Chicago on February 29, 1940.

Abell, Arunah Shepherdson (1806–1888), newspaper editor and publisher. Born in East Providence, Rhode Island, on August 10, 1806, Abell left school at fourteen and worked as a clerk until 1822, when he became an apprentice in the office of the *Providence Patriot*. Upon completing his apprenticeship he worked for a few years as a journeyman printer in Boston and New York City. In 1836 he and two partners began the *Philadelphia Public Ledger*, a penny daily modeled on Benjamin H. Day's *New York Sun*. The success of the paper led to the establishment a year later of the *Baltimore Sun*; Abell took charge of the *Sun*, leaving his partners to manage the *Ledger*. Under his guidance the *Sun* provided its readers with comprehensive, impartial news coverage and developed a strong, independent, though temperate editorial policy; and it maintained an unshakable soundness in both its journalistic and financial spects. A pioneer in systematic news gathering and classification, Abell sought constantly for speed in distributing information. He used pony express riders, establishing regular routes to Boston and New Orleans. The New Orleans system brought news of the Mexican War in 60 hours, beating both the U.S. mail and the government's own dispatches. For shorter distances, Abell used a flock of carrier pigeons. He worked with Samuel F. B. Morse and was an enthusiastic promoter and user of Morse's newly developed telegraph. The *Public Ledger* and the *Sun* were also among the first newspapers to install Richard M. Hoe's rotary presses. The *Public Ledger* was sold in 1864 and four years later, his partners having died, Abell became sole owner of the *Sun*. He continued to direct its operations until his death in Baltimore on April 19, 1888.

Acheson, Dean Gooderham (1893–1971), lawyer, public official, and diplomat. Born in Middletown, Connecticut, on April 11, 1893, Acheson received his B.A. from Yale in 1915 and his LL.B. from Harvard in 1918. He was private secretary to U.S. Supreme Court Justice Louis D. Brandeis from 1919 to 1921 and practiced with a Washington law firm until 1933, when President Franklin D. Roosevelt appointed him undersecretary of the treasury. As a Depression measure, the administration sought to depart from the international gold standard through a gold-purchase plan, but Acheson considered this plan illegal and was emphatic in his view. After he had served six months in the Treasury, Roosevelt asked for his resignation. Acheson resumed his successful Washington law practice until the attorney general named him to direct a study of administrative tribunals in 1939. The report on "judicial fair play," 1941, was considered a landmark in administrative reform. Long active in promoting aid to Great Britain, Acheson was then appointed assistant secretary of state by Roosevelt. He also served as undersecretary from 1945 to 1947 before becoming President Harry S. Truman's secretary of state in 1949. Never outspokenly hostile to the Soviet Union, he was accused by some during the second Truman administration of being "soft on Communism" despite his commitment to a vigorous policy of containment of the U.S.S.R. During his service in the cabinet he was influential in the development of the International Bank for Reconstruction and Development (IBRD), the United Nations Relief and Rehabilitation Administration (UNRRA), the Baruch Plan for the international control of atomic energy, and the Marshall Plan for European economic recovery. He gave invaluable support to President Truman during the Korean conflict and was a principal architect of the North Atlantic Treaty Organization (NATO) and the independent, rearmed Federal Republic of Germany, both of which he saw as essential elements of the containment policy. He resumed his Washington law practice in 1953 and also served as an adviser on foreign policy to the Democratic National Committee and to successive U.S. presidents. His books include *Power and Diplomacy*, 1958; the autobiographical *Morning and Noon*, 1965; and *Present at the Creation*, 1969, which won a Pulitzer Prize. Acheson died at his farm in Sandy Spring, Maryland, on October 12, 1971.

Adams, Abigail (1744–1818), First Lady and letter writer. Born in Weymouth, Massachusetts, on November 11 (old style), 1744, Abigail Smith was a delicate child who spent much of her time living quietly with her grandparents in Mount Wollaston. Although she received no formal schooling, her broad-mindedness and intelligence found ample scope. In 1764 she married John Adams, a practicing lawyer in Boston. Their four children were born in the next ten years: John Quincy, Thomas, Charles, and Abby. Mrs. Adams resolutely supported her husband in his insistence on colonial independence and brought to his cause a loyal zeal. During the early days of the Revolution her husband was much in Philadelphia and she had entire care of the family. Her letters, written during her husband's long absences, conveyed a vivid picture of the times. After the signing of the peace treaty in 1783, she joined her husband in Paris the next year; after eight months they moved to London, where he served as the first American minister to the court of George III. Despite suffering social discourtesies, "England," she wrote later, "is the country of my greatest partiality." In 1789 her husband was elected vice-president and in 1796 president. One of the most admired of First Ladies, Mrs. Adams returned with her husband to Quincy, Massachusetts, in 1801 to live as tranquilly "as that bald old fellow, called Time" would permit. Shortly before her death from typhoid fever on October 28, 1818, she had laughed at proposals to publish her letters. A vital source of social history, they have been repeatedly republished.

Adams, Andy (1859–1935), cowboy and author. Born in Whitley County, Indiana, on May 3, 1859, Adams received an elementary education before leaving home and making his way to Texas. Through the great era of the cattle drives he rode the trail and learned the cowboy life "from the hurricane deck," as he later wrote, "of a Texas horse." When the extension of the railroads ended the drives, Adams made an unsuccessful venture into mining during the Cripple Creek boom in Colorado, then settled in Colorado Springs about 1892. The growing popularity of stories about the West—and the often remarkable ignorance of many who wrote them—moved him to try his hand at describing Western life as he had known it. A number of his short stories were published in magazines and in 1903 appeared a semi-autobiographical novel, *The Log of a Cowboy*. It was followed by *The Texas Matchmaker*, 1904; *The Outlet*, 1905; *Cattle Brands*, 1906, a collection of his earlier stories; and others. Adams made a valuable contribution to American letters and did much to offset the romanticized images of the West in popular literature. He died in Colorado Springs on September 26, 1935.

Adams, Ansel (1902–   ), photographer. Born in San Francisco on February 20, 1902, Adams was educated principally by special studies in literature, the sciences, and music. From 1920 to 1930 he taught piano and performed as a pianist, but an interest in photography grew until it occupied his full attention; his love of the Yosemite Valley and other spectacular wilderness areas led him to the subject matter that he was to make his own. Among his early exhibitions were a show at the De Young Memorial Museum in San Francisco in 1932 and one at Alfred Stieglitz's "An American Place" gallery in New York City in 1936. In 1939 he became director of the photography department of the Art Center School in Los Angeles and in 1940 supervised the "Pageant of Photography" exhibition at San Francisco's Golden Gate International Exposition. From 1940 to 1942 he was vice-chairman of the photography department of the Museum of Modern Art in New York City and from 1946 to 1949 director of the photography department of the California School of Fine Arts, having been a founder of both. Adams's first portfolio, *Parmelian Prints of the High Sierras*, 1928, was prepared for the Sierra Club, of which he had been a member since 1917 and would become a director in 1936. In 1930 he published *Taos Pueblo*, with text by Mary Austin; this was followed by *Sierra Nevada: The John Muir Trail*, 1938; *Born Free and Equal*, 1944 (a photographic study of Japanese-Americans interned in the Manzanar relocation center); *My Camera in Yosemite Valley*, 1949; *My Camera in the National Parks*, 1950; and a number of books with text by Nancy Newhall: *Death Valley*, 1954; *Mission San Xavier del Bac*, 1954; *Yosemite Valley*, 1959; *This Is the American Earth*, 1960; and *This We Inherit: America's Parklands*, 1962. He also wrote technical works on photography, including the five-volume *Basic Photo Series*, 1957–1969. His later exhibitions included "This Is the American Earth," 1955, and "The Eloquent Light," 1963, both in collaboration with Nancy Newhall; "A Nation of Nations" for the U.S. Information Agency, 1957; and retrospective shows in San Francisco in 1963 and in Boston in 1967. Beginning in 1955 he conducted an annual photography workshop in Yosemite Valley. One of the foremost photographic artists of his time, Adams was virtually without peer in his own special field of nature and landscape photography, to which he brought a deep and intelligent concern for the preservation of Wilderness areas.

Adams, Brooks (1848–1927), historian. Born in Quincy, Massachusetts, on June 24, 1848, Brooks Adams was a grandson of John Quincy Adams, son of Charles Francis Adams, and a brother of Charles Francis Adams, Jr., and Henry Adams. He graduated from Harvard in 1870 and after a year at its law school served as secretary to his diplomat father during the *Alabama* claims arbitration in Geneva. He then returned to Boston and practiced law until 1881. He traveled extensively in Europe, the Middle East, and India, and began an exchange of letters with his brother Henry, also a historian, in which they developed the then revolutionary idea that American democracy was foredoomed to degradation and decay. His first work, *The Emancipation of Massachusetts*, 1887, was a protest against the ancestor worship common in previous New England historiography. *The Law of Civilization and Decay*, 1895, developed his theory that civilizations rise and fall according to a predetermined pattern of industrial and commercial growth and decline. *America's Economic Supremacy*, 1900, and *New Empire*, 1902, developed the theory further and predicted that in 50 years there would be only two powers in the world, Russia and the United States, with the United States having economic supremacy. Adams's study of the defects of the American form of government, *The Theory of Social Revolutions*, 1913, concluded that the immediate danger lay in the fact that the very wealthy exerted tremendous private power but shirked public responsibility. In 1920 he saw his late brother Henry's book, *The Degradation of the Democratic Dogma*, through the press, adding to it a prefatory family chronicle going back to President John Adams and ending with a renunciation of "democratic dogma" by his two grandsons. Although Brooks never held public office, he was elected to the Massachusetts constitutional convention in 1917. World War I, for him, fulfilled his prediction of the collapse of modern Western civilization. He died in Boston on February 13, 1927.

Adams, Charles Francis (1807–1886), diplomat and public official. Born in Boston on August 18, 1807, Adams was the grandson of John Adams and son of John Quincy Adams. At the age of two he went with his father to Russia and lived in St. Petersburg for six years. His regular schooling began in England and continued in Boston. He graduated from Harvard in 1825 and went to live in the White House during the last two years of his father's term, studying law and moving among the statesmen of the capital. Returning to Boston, he completed his law studies under Daniel Webster and was admitted to the bar in 1829. He took over the management of his father's financial affairs so that the former president could return to Washington as a congressman. Although he disapproved of his father's second career and did not yet agree with the measures he adopted in behalf of the antislavery cause, he campaigned for him and supported his pro-abolitionist views. He also practiced law and wrote articles on American history for the *North American Review*. In 1835 his series of newspaper articles was reprinted as the widely read pamphlet, *An Appeal from the New to the Old Whigs, by a Whig of the Old School*. By 1837 the attacks against the abolitionists had converted him fully to their cause. During his five years in the state legislature, 1840–1845, he put Massachusetts on record as being abolitionist in sentiment despite a lack of party support. He founded the *Boston Whig* in 1846 and edited it until 1848, when he became vice-presidential candidate of the Free-Soil party. With the formation of the Republican party, he represented his father's old district in

Congress, 1859–1861, and became a party leader. Lincoln's election brought demands that Adams be given a cabinet post, but the delicacy of diplomatic relations with Great Britain led to his appointment as minister to the Court of St. James. Before Adams could disembark the English had acknowledged the belligerency of the Southern states; and they threatened, for the next few years, to recognize the Confederacy as an independent nation, an action tantamount to believing in the ultimate defeat of the Union. His wisdom and dignity in the face of aristocratic sympathy for the South and of the British need for cotton were instrumental in maintaining the continued neutrality of Great Britain. In 1868 he returned to America, where he found a changed political scene and declined the only post he was offered —the presidency of Harvard—and settled in Quincy, Massachusetts. His last public service was as the U.S. member of the five-man tribunal that met in Geneva, 1871–1872, to adjudicate the *Alabama* claims. American success in the case was wholly attributed to his skillful diplomacy. Adams received support for the presidential nomination at the 1872 Liberal Republican party convention, but lost to Horace Greeley. He published numerous political pamphlets and addresses and edited many family papers. He died in Boston on November 21, 1886.

Adams, Charles Francis, Jr. (1835–1915), historian and civic leader. Born in Boston on May 27, 1835, Adams was a grandson of John Quincy Adams, son of Charles Francis Adams, and the elder brother of Henry and Brooks Adams. He graduated from Harvard in 1856, entered a Boston law firm, and was admitted to the bar in 1858. Not caring for the law, he was glad when family circumstances allowed him to join the Union army. He served for three and a half years, fighting in the battles of Antietam and Gettysburg and rising from first lieutenant to colonel. He declined a high staff position so that he could stay with his Negro regiment, the 5th Massachusetts Cavalry. In June 1865 he was mustered out as a brigadier general and for a year toured Europe to regain his health. He then turned to the study of American railroads, which were at the time overbuilt, corruptly financed, and the objects of uncontrolled stock speculation and manipulation. Parts of his *Chapters of Erie and Other Essays*, 1871; *Railroads: Their Origin and Problems*, 1878; and *Notes on American Railroad Accidents*, 1879, first appeared in periodicals. His exposés led to the formation of the Massachusetts Board of Railroad Commissioners; Adams was appointed its youngest member in 1869 and served as chairman from 1872 to 1879. He also became chairman of the government directors of the Union Pacific in 1878 and was named the railroad's president in 1884, a position from which he was ousted in 1890 by Jay Gould. He devoted himself to civic affairs in his family's home town of Quincy, Massachusetts, putting its budget in the black, arranging for its first public library, and reorganizing its antiquated school system. His *New Departure in the Common Schools of Quincy,* 1879, went through six editions, and the "Quincy system," substituting a problems approach for rote memorization, was widely adopted. He served on the Harvard Board of Overseers for 24 years and was president of the Massachusetts Historical Society from 1895 until his death on May 20, 1915, in Washington, D.C.

Adams, Franklin Pierce (1881–1960), "F.P.A.," journalist and humorist. Born in Chicago on November 15, 1881, Adams graduated from Armour Scientific Academy in 1899, attended the University of Michigan, and "almost completed my freshman year." He then worked for an insurance company as a supply clerk and salesman until he joined the staff of the *Chicago Journal* in 1903. He conducted a column and wrote a daily weather story. The following year he went to New York City to do a column for the *Evening Mail,* "Always in Good Humor." In 1913 he moved to the *New York Tribune* with the column "The Conning Tower." He served in military intelligence during World War I: "I didn't fight and I didn't shoot/ But, General, how I did salute!" He also wrote an occasional column, "The Listening Post," for *Stars and Stripes.* After the armistice, he returned to the *Tribune,* staying until 1923, when he set up his "Conning Tower" at the *New York World.* He returned to the *Tribune*—by now the *Herald Tribune*—in 1931, and the column, signed, as were most of his writings, with his initials "F.P.A.," was syndicated in six newspapers. His trenchant comments on the American scene were supplemented by his "mocking and impudent" poems, and the column often included contributions from notable people he knew. In 1938 he became a regular panelist on the radio program "Information Please." He moved "The Conning Tower" to the *New York Post* in 1938, but stopped writing it in 1941. In *The Melancholy Lute,* 1936, he collected ten books of his verse. A two-volume collection of his writings, *The Diary of Our Own Samuel Pepys: 1911–1934,* appeared in 1935. Adams died in New York City on March 23, 1960.

Adams, Henry Brooks (1838–1918), historian. Born in Boston on February 16, 1838, a grandson of John Quincy Adams, a son of Charles Francis Adams, and the brother of Charles Francis Adams, Jr., and Brooks Adams, Henry Adams graduated from Harvard in 1858. He went to Berlin to study civil law but soon decided to tour Germany and Italy instead. In Italy he secured an interview with Garibaldi that was published in the *Boston Courier.* A few months later he returned to Boston and became secretary to his father, then a congressman and later, during the Civil War, minister to Great Britain. His first historical articles began appearing in the *North American Review* before his return to the United States in 1868. He took up residence in Washington, D.C., but the quality of President Ulysses S.

Grant's cabinet appointments soon dashed his hopes for political reform and he accepted Harvard's offer to teach history in 1870, becoming at the same time editor of the *Review.* In his medieval history course, he introduced seminar teaching to the United States and his joint researches with students resulted in his first book, *Essays in Anglo-Saxon Law,* 1876. After seven years of teaching, he left the "laborious banishment" and returned to Washington in order to write and be with old friends, including Secretary of State William M. Evarts and John Hay. He produced *Documents Relating to New England Federalism, 1800–1815,* 1877; biographies of Albert Gallatin, 1879, and John Randolph, 1882; and two novels, *Democracy,* 1880, and *Esther,* 1884. He also began his nine-volume *History of the United States of America from 1801 to 1817,* 1889–1891, a monumental work interrupted by the death of his wife and subsequent travels to Mexico and the Caribbean, the South Seas, the Orient, Russia, and Europe. Adams was chosen president of the American Historical Association in 1894. He privately printed *Mont-Saint-Michel and Chartres* in 1904, but the wide appeal of this study of medieval life, art, and philosophy gave rise to its reprinting in 1913. In similar fashion its sequel, the autobiographical *Education of Henry Adams,* was privately printed in 1906 and published in 1918. In the *Education,* while dealing with many other subjects, he developed his dynamic theory of history. His other writings include *A Letter to American Teachers of History,* 1910, and *The Degradation of the Democratic Dogma,* 1919. He died in Washington on March 27, 1918.

Adams, Herbert Baxter (1850–1901), historian. Born on April 16, 1850, in Shutesbury, Massachusetts, Adams graduated from Amherst College at the head of the class of 1872. He pursued his studies in Germany at the universities of Göttingen, Berlin, and Heidelberg, taking his Ph.D. *summa cum laude* at Heidelberg in 1876. He was immediately appointed to the faculty of the new Johns Hopkins University in Baltimore and remained there for the rest of his career, after 1891 as professor of American and institutional history. In 1882 he inaugurated the Johns Hopkins Studies in Historical and Political Science, the first such series published in the United States. In 1887 he began editing for the U.S. Office of Education the series Contributions to American Educational History. He contributed to both series, especially the latter. In 1884 he took the lead in the founding of the American Historical Association and served as its secretary until 1900. Adams was known primarily as a teacher and as a promoter of historical research; his devoted graduate students included Woodrow Wilson, Frederick Jackson Turner, Charles M. Andrews, and many others. Among his numerous publications were *Maryland's Influence in Founding a National Commonwealth,* 1877; *Methods of Historical Study,* 1884; *Maryland's Influence upon Land Cessions to the United States,* 1885; *Thomas*

Jefferson and the University of Virginia, 1888; and *Life and Writings of Jared Sparks*, 1893. Adams died in Amherst, Massachusetts, on July 30, 1901.

Adams, James Truslow (1878–1949), historian. Born on October 18, 1878, in Brooklyn, New York, Adams graduated from the Polytechnic Institute of Brooklyn in 1898 and two years later received an M.A. from Yale. He originally planned an academic career but was prevented by family circumstances. He took a job in a New York stock brokerage office and rose quickly to a partnership in the firm; by 1912 he had accumulated a fortune that allowed him to return to intellectual pursuits. During World War I he served in military intelligence and in 1919 was on the staff of the U.S. delegation to the Versailles peace conference. Returning to private life, he began producing a steady flow of books that were well received both popularly and critically. Among them were *The Founding of New England*, 1921, which won a Pulitzer Prize; *Revolutionary New England, 1691–1776*, 1923; *New England in the Republic, 1776–1850*, 1926; *Provincial Society, 1690–1763*, 1927; *Hamiltonian Principles*, 1928; *Jeffersonian Principles*, 1928; *Our Business Civilization*, 1929; *The Adams Family*, 1930, about the Massachusetts Adamses, to whom he was not closely related; the widely translated *The Epic of America*, 1931; *The March of Democracy*, two volumes, 1932–1933; *America's Tragedy*, 1935; *The American*, 1943; and *Frontiers of American Culture*, 1944. Adams served as editor in chief of the *Dictionary of American History*, six volumes, 1940; *The Atlas of American History*, 1943; and *The Album of American History*, four volumes, 1944–1948. A gifted generalist, he was a champion of what he believed to be the cardinal American virtues—work, morality, individualism, fiscal responsibility, and dedication to duty. A contributor to the *Encyclopaedia Britannica*, the *Dictionary of American Biography*, and many periodicals, he served on the Pulitzer Prize history jury from 1924 to 1932, the last two years as chairman. He died in Westport, Connecticut, on May 18, 1949.

Adams, John (1735–1826), second president of the United States. Born in Braintree (later Quincy), Massachusetts, on October 19 (old style), 1735, Adams graduated from Harvard in 1755 and three years later, having taught school for a time before taking up the study of law, was admitted to the bar. Prominence came first in 1765 when, in protest against the Stamp Act, he drafted the instructions to Braintree's representatives in the legislature; these were used as models by many other Massachusetts towns. Later that year he published a series of articles in the *Boston Gazette* that were issued in book form in 1768 as *A Dissertation on the Canon and Feudal Law*. Moving to Boston in 1768, he included among his legal cases a defense of John Hancock against a charge of smuggling; but his most famous appearance before the bar came in 1770 when he

displayed integrity and courage by defending the British soldiers accused of murder in the Boston Massacre. The following year he was elected to the legislature. He consistently opposed the harsh measures imposed by England on the colonies and in 1774 was sent as a Massachusetts delegate to the Continental Congress. He gradually became convinced of the necessity for American independence and in June 1776 seconded Richard Henry Lee's motion to that effect. He served on the committee charged with drafting the Declaration of Independence and, although Thomas Jefferson wrote the document, Adams was its leading advocate in debate. He continued in Congress, serving on several major committees, until 1778, when he joined Benjamin Franklin and Arthur Lee in a mission to the French government. On his recommendation Congress soon named Franklin the sole representative; Adams returned home in June 1779 and was immediately elected to the Massachusetts constitutional convention, for which he wrote most of the first draft of the new instrument. In November he sailed again for France, this time secretly empowered to negotiate peace with Great Britain. He was extremely distrustful of the French government and at length persuaded his colleagues—John Jay and Franklin—to disregard their instructions from Congress and to initiate direct talks with the British without first consulting the French. The preliminary treaty was signed in November 1782; in the meantime Adams, appointed minister to the Netherlands in 1780, had secured from that country diplomatic recognition, a loan, and a commercial treaty. He remained based in Holland until his appointment as the first U.S. minister to Great Britain in 1785. Returning to America in 1788, he was elected the first vice-president under the new Constitution the next year. His eight years in the office were unpleasant: "My country has in its wisdom contrived for me the most insignificant office that ever the invention of man contrived or his imagination conceived." Nonetheless he emerged as one of the principal leaders of the Federalists and in 1796 was elected president. He took office at a time of serious problems in foreign affairs; Jay's Treaty had antagonized France, and a conciliatory commission sent by Adams was refused a hearing until a bribe was paid to agents known only as X, Y, and Z. The affair inflamed Congress and the American public, and the Federalists began calling for war; Adams endorsed defensive military preparations but ignored party pressure by continuing to seek a peaceful solution to the diplomatic impasse. He assented to the passage of the Alien and Sedition Acts in 1798 and appointed George Washington to the command of the newly mobilized army. France finally relented and indicated a willingness to receive a minister; Adams enraged Alexander Hamilton and other Federalists by sending an envoy and averting war. Hamilton's opposition, combined with popular dislike of the alien and sedition laws, swung support away from Adams, and in the presidential election of 1800 he was defeated by Thomas Jefferson. Among his final official acts were a number of last-minute, or "midnight," appointments to the federal judiciary, concurred in by an earlier appointee, Chief Justice John Marshall. Retiring to Quincy, Adams lived out his life quietly; he removed himself from public affairs and devoted much time to correspondence. Through the agency of Benjamin Rush, he and Jefferson were eventually reconciled. Between them passed a series of remarkable epistolary observations and speculations on man and government, published in a new edition in 1959 as *The Adams–Jefferson Letters*. Adams died at home on July 4, 1826, the fiftieth anniversary of the Declaration of Independence, uttering with his last breath the words "Thomas Jefferson still lives"; but Jefferson had died a few hours earlier. Adams was elected to the Hall of Fame in 1900.

Adams, John Quincy (1767–1848), sixth president of the United States. Born in Braintree (later Quincy), Massachusetts, on July 11, 1767, the eldest son of John and Abigail Adams, John Quincy Adams received some of his schooling in Europe, where he accompanied his father on diplomatic missions. In 1781 he traveled to Russia as private secretary to the U.S. representative there, and a year later joined his father in Paris. When the elder Adams was named minister to Great Britain in 1785, the son returned to Massachusetts and entered Harvard, from which he graduated in 1787. Three years later he was admitted to the bar. A series of newspaper articles supporting President George Washington's policy of neutrality led to his appointment as minister to the Netherlands in 1794; after two years of valuable service there he was named minister to Portugal, but before he was able to assume the post his father was elected president and changed his assignment to Berlin. He returned to the United States in 1801; in 1802 he was elected to the Massachusetts legislature, which in turn sent him to the U.S. Senate the next year. Although nominally a Federalist, he steered a completely independent course during his five years in the Senate, particularly in supporting the Louisiana Purchase appropriations and, in 1807, President Thomas Jefferson's embargo proposal. His resignation was finally forced in 1808 by angered New England Federalists. Retaining his independence, he formed connections with the Republicans and in 1809 was named minister to Russia by President James Madison. In 1811, while in Russia, he declined an appointment to the Supreme Court. Adams was the chief U.S. negotiator at the talks that resulted in the Treaty of Ghent in 1814, and soon afterward was made minister to Great Britain. There he remained until 1817, when he became President James Monroe's secretary of state. During his eight years in that office he brought his considerable skill and experience to bear on a number of problems and scored brilliant successes, notably in a treaty with Great Britain in 1818 extending the U.S.–Canadian border

westward to the Rockies along the 49th parallel; in arranging for future arbitration of the Oregon boundary question; and in a treaty with Spain in 1819 that ceded Florida to the U.S. in return for a renunciation of U.S. claims to Texas. The Monroe Doctrine, announced by the president in 1823, was largely the work of Adams. In the presidential election of 1824 he was a leading contender; the electoral vote failed to yield a majority for any of the candidates, however, and the choice went to the House of Representatives. Henry Clay, who had run fourth, controlled the deciding block of votes, and he favored Adams over Andrew Jackson as the lesser of two evils. Jackson's followers quickly raised the charge of a "corrupt bargain" that, while unfounded, seemed more credible when Adams named Clay his secretary of state. The next four years were notable primarily for the growth of a new party alignment and the unrestrained antagonism between the Jacksonians and the National Republicans. Adams himself commanded little personal following and could accomplish nothing of importance. Defeated by Jackson in 1828, he retired to Quincy upon leaving office in March 1829. In the next year he began the final phase of his career with his election to the House of Representatives, where he served until his death. His independence of party policy became more pronounced than ever and was a source of confusion to those of less spirit and breadth of view. His principal efforts centered on presenting to the House the increasing flow of antislavery petitions from individuals, groups, and even state legislatures. (Adams himself was strongly antislavery in sentiment, although not, strictly speaking, an abolitionist.) The petitions increased in number to the point that in 1836 proslavery elements in the House invoked a gag rule, prohibiting discussion of the matter. Despite Adams's ardent exertions the rule was retained until 1844. In 1839 he defied its provisions by offering resolutions for a scheme of gradual elimination of slavery, and on many occasions he was threatened with censure for his insistence on the right to petition the Congress. His defense of the antislavery cause and of himself earned him the nickname "Old Man Eloquent." In 1841 he appeared before the Supreme Court and successfully defended the African mutineers of the slave ship *Amistad*. He fervently opposed both the annexation of Texas and the Mexican War as unconstitutional and unjustifiable means of extending the domain of slavery, and he was still protesting when he suffered a stroke and collapsed in the House. He died two days later, on February 23, 1848. His *Memoirs* were edited and published by his son, Charles Francis Adams (1807–1886), in 1874–1877. He was elected to the Hall of Fame in 1905.

Adams, Maude (1872–1953), actress. Born on November 11, 1872, in Salt Lake City, Utah, Maude Kiskadden began her theatrical career at the age of nine months, when she was carried on stage in a production of *The Lost Child.* She began playing actual roles as soon as she could talk, adopting her actress mother's maiden name (Adams) for the stage. At five she attracted considerable attention in San Francisco in *Fritz,* and at sixteen she joined Edward H. Sothern's company in New York City. Soon after her appearance in *A Midnight Bell* she moved to Charles Frohman's company where, from 1892 to 1897, she regularly played opposite John Drew. She first won top billing as Lady Babbie in James M. Barrie's *The Little Minister* in 1897. Although she played a wide range of roles, including several of Shakespeare's great heroines, it was her portrayals of Barrie characters that brought her acclaim and the devotion of audiences. Her greatest successes were in *Quality Street,* in 1902 and again in 1915–1916; *What Every Woman Knows,* 1908–1909; *A Kiss for Cinderella,* 1916–1918; and especially *Peter Pan,* in which she starred in more than 1500 performances in 1905–1907, 1913, and 1918. Other plays in which she appeared included *Romeo and Juliet,* 1899; *L'Aiglon,* 1900–1901; Schiller's *Joan of Arc,* 1909; and *Chantecler,* 1910–1911. In 1918, though still a dazzling beauty, she retired from the stage and for a time worked with Charles P. Steinmetz on improving stage lighting. In 1931 she played opposite Otis Skinner in *The Merchant of Venice* and in 1934 made her last appearance, in *Twelfth Night.* From 1937 to 1943 she was chairman of the drama department of Stephens College in Columbia, Missouri. She had always kept her private life from public view and she lived quietly in retirement until her death in Tannersville, New York, on July 17, 1953.

Adams, Roger (1889–1971), chemist. Born in Boston on January 2, 1889, Adams graduated from Harvard in 1909 and received his A.M. from that university in 1910 and his Ph.D. in 1912. After further studies at the University of Berlin, 1912–1913, and at the Kaiser Wilhelm Institute, 1913, he joined the faculties of Harvard and of Radcliffe College as an instructor in organic chemistry in 1913. He left in 1916 for the University of Illinois, with which he was associated for the rest of his career, serving as assistant professor, 1916–1919; as professor from 1919; as head of the department of chemistry and chemical engineering from 1926 until 1954; and as research professor from the latter year until his retirement in 1957. One of the foremost organic chemists of the twentieth century, he did important research into the constitution of many natural substances, among them chaulmoogra oil, gossypol, marijuana, and numerous alkaloids. He also did research in stereochemistry, the synthesis of medicinal compounds, and platinum catalysts. He was a valued adviser to government bodies and industrial firms and was awarded many prizes and medals, including the Gibbs Medal, 1936; the Davy Medal, 1944; the Priestley Medal, 1946; and the Franklin Medal, 1960. He was a member of almost every important U.S. chemical and scientific society and of many foreign ones as well.

He edited *Organic Reactions* from 1941 until 1968; in that journal, and in others in his field, he published influential research papers. He died in Champaign, Illinois, on July 6, 1971.

Adams, Samuel (1722–1803), Revolutionary leader. Born in Boston on September 27, 1722, Adams was a second cousin of John Adams. He graduated from Harvard College in 1740 and studied law for a time. His life from 1740 to 1756 was marked by financial difficulties attributable mainly to his own incompetent management of several business ventures; a stint as Boston's tax collector from 1756 to 1764 was a similar failure, leaving him heavily in debt. He had dabbled in politics before 1764, but the passage of the Sugar Act in that year marked the beginning of his rise to power and influence. Adams led the condemnation of the act, and he was elected to the Massachusetts legislature, in which he served until 1774. The Stamp Act of 1765 roused the public to elect a controlling number of popular-radical members to that body, and Adams quickly became a central figure. He helped instigate the Stamp Act riots in Boston, and in reaction to the Townshend Acts he organized the Non-Importation Association in 1768. He stirred up antagonism against British troops sent to Boston in 1768, and after the Boston Massacre in 1770 he led the agitation for their removal. When the duties were repealed in 1770, except for a largely symbolic one on tea, Adams continued to condemn that tax despite the cooling of public sentiment and the dwindling power of the radicals for whom he spoke. By this time he had evidently fixed upon American independence as his goal. His fierce polemics against the British were constantly in the newspapers during the lull from 1770 to 1773 as he hounded them on issue after issue. He was responsible for the formation of Boston's Committee of Correspondence in 1772 and for the formation of similar committees throughout the colony. The declaration of rights published by the Boston committee was his work and, like others of his writings, it anticipated the Declaration of Independence on many points. The Tea Act of 1773 reawakened popular resentment of the British, and Adams was ready at hand as a leader in the events that culminated in the Boston Tea Party. He led the resistance to the Coercive Acts that followed and was active in the adoption by Massachusetts of the Suffolk Resolves. He was a member of the first and second Continental Congresses and, with John Hancock, was excepted from the pardon to rebels offered by General Thomas Gage. He was a signer of the Declaration of Independence, which he had strongly supported. After 1776 Adams began to recede from prominence as the times increasingly required abilities other than his: his greatest contributions had been as a tireless and powerful polemicist and agitator. He continued as a member of Congress until 1781 and was thereafter engaged in state politics, serving as governor of Massachusetts from 1794 to 1797. He died in Boston on

October 2, 1803. His *Writings* were edited and published by H. A. Cushing in four volumes in 1904–1908.

Adams, Samuel Hopkins (1871–1958), author. Born on January 26, 1871, in Dunkirk, New York, Adams graduated from Hamilton College in 1891 and immediately joined the staff of the *New York Sun*. Nine years later he moved to the McClure Syndicate, where he held a number of editorial and business positions for five years. In 1905 he wrote a series of articles for *Collier's Weekly* in which, in the best muckraker tradition, he exposed chicanery in the patent-medicine business; the series led to the publication of *The Great American Fraud*, 1906, which helped to achieve passage of the Pure Food and Drug Act of that year. During the next 50 years he produced books at a rate of more than one a year, including works in a wide range of forms. Many of his novels, such as *Canal Town*, 1944, had historical settings, and he wrote history as well: in 1926 he published *Revelry*, a fictionalized version of the scandalous years of the Harding administration. Charges of exaggeration and inaccuracy in that book were later refuted by his factual account of the period, entitled *The Incredible Era*, 1939. *The Godlike Daniel*, 1930, was a biography of Webster, and Adams received critical acclaim for his treatment of his fellow Hamilton College alumnus in *A. Woollcott: His Life and His World*, 1945. Others of his books included *Average Jones*, a detective novel, 1911; *The Secret of Lonesome Cove*, 1913; *The Clarion*, 1914; *Our Square and the People In It*, 1917; *Success*, 1921; *The Flagrant Years*, 1929; *The World Goes Smash*, 1938; *The Harvey Girls*, 1942; *The Pony Express*, 1950; *The Santa Fe Trail*, 1952; and *The Erie Canal*, 1953. A number of his stories were made into motion pictures, most notable the Academy Award-winning *It Happened One Night*, based on his novelette *Night Bus*. His last book, *Grandfather Stories*, appeared in 1955. Adams died in Beaufort, South Carolina, on November 15, 1958.

Adams, Walter Sydney (1876–1956), astronomer. Born on December 20, 1876, in Antioch (Antakya), Turkey, of American missionary parents, Adams was brought to the United States at the age of eight. He graduated from Dartmouth in 1898 and pursued graduate studies at the universities of Chicago and Munich. In 1901 he joined the staff of the Yerkes Observatory in Wisconsin and three years later was invited to move to the Carnegie Institution of Washington's newly established observatory on Mt. Wilson near Pasadena, California. There he carried out a wide program of research and served as director from 1923 to 1946. His astronomical investigations dealt mainly with stellar spectra. In 1914 he and an associate, Arnold Kolschutter, were able to determine the luminosity, or absolute brightness, of a star from its spectrum; this led Adams to develop a method of determining the distance of a star from earth by comparing its luminosity to its apparent brightness. During his career he ascertained the velocities and distances of thousands of stars. In 1925 he contributed to the confirmation of Einstein's general theory of relativity by demonstrating that the light emitted by the immensely dense companion star to Sirius was, as the theory predicted, shifted toward the red end of the spectrum. Adams also studied the spectra of sunspots, measured spectrally the differential rotation of the sun at various solar latitudes, investigated interstellar gas, and discovered that the atmosphere of Venus contains large amounts of carbon dioxide. He was widely honored for his work and served as president of the American Astronomical Society from 1931 to 1934. He played a prominent role in the planning and development of Mt. Palomar Observatory northwest of San Diego, California, with its 200-inch telescope installed in 1947–1948. Adams died in Pasadena on May 11, 1956.

Adams, William Taylor (1822–1897), "Oliver Optic," author. Born in Bellingham, Massachusetts, on July 30, 1822, Adams grew up there and on a farm in West Roxbury, completing his schooling at the cost of much effort. After a period of travel and of work in his father's tavern, he began teaching in Dorchester, now a part of Boston, in 1845. He loved writing and turned out pieces with increasing frequency for various periodicals. His first book, *Hatchie, the Guardian Slave*, appeared in 1853; his third, *The Boat Club*, 1854, went through several editions and established him as a highly successful writer. *The Boat Club* was extended to a six-volume series and several other series followed, including Onward and Upward; Riverdale Story Books; Woodville Stories; Army and Navy; Blue and Gray; Starry Flag; and Great Western. In 1865 Adams began to devote full time to writing and in all produced about 125 books and more than 1000 stories, all published under pseudonyms, principally "Oliver Optic" but also including "Irving Brown," "Clingham Hunter, M.D.," and "Old Stager." His works, with their mixture of adventure, patriotism, and realistic detail, were immensely popular with boys. He also edited a number of periodicals including *The Student and Schoolmate*, in which he published *Ragged Dick*, Horatio Alger's first and best-known novel; *Our Little Ones*; and *Oliver Optic's Magazine for Boys and Girls*. In 1869, at the height of his career, he served a term in the Massachusetts legislature. Adams died in Dorchester on March 27, 1897.

Addams, Charles Samuel (1912–   ), cartoonist. Born on January 7, 1912, in Westfield, New Jersey, Addams was a doodler from childhood. After spending a year each at Colgate University and the University of Pennsylvania and two years at the Grand Central School of Art in New York City, he decided in 1932 to be an illustrator and cartoonist. He worked for a short time on one of Bernarr Macfadden's pulp magazines and then forsook regular employment. His free-lance career began in 1935 with the sale of a cartoon to the *New Yorker*, and he became closely associated with that magazine, where his macabre, involuted, and quietly mad form of humor found a perfect home. One of his most popular cartoons, published in 1940, depicted a female skier whose twin tracks led to a large tree, passed unswervingly one on either side, and continued beyond. Addams was best known for the creation of a cartoon family whose various members were ghoulish, vampirish, ogreish, and Frankensteinian, and who inhabited a world locked in perennial Hallowe'en. During World War II he worked as an illustrator and animator for the Army Signal Corps. After the war he continued to turn out drawings that appeared in the *New Yorker*. His cartoons were exhibited in a number of gallery shows and were collected in *New Yorker* albums as well as in *Drawn and Quartered*, 1942; *Addams and Evil*, 1947; *Monster Rally*, 1950; *Home Bodies*, 1954; *Nightcrawlers*, 1957; *Black Maria*, 1960; *The Charles Addams Mother Goose*, 1967; and others. His work also inspired "The Addams Family," a television comedy series that was popular during the 1960s.

Addams, Jane (1860–1935), social reformer. Born on September 6, 1860, in Cedarville, Illinois, Miss Addams graduated from Rockford College in 1881, studied medicine briefly, and for several years traveled and studied in search of a vocation. In London in 1888 she visited Toynbee Hall, a pioneer settlement house, and determined to devote herself to the betterment of life among the urban poor. Returning to Chicago in 1889, she established in a slum neighborhood the settlement she called Hull House, aided by her companion, Ellen Gates Starr. She attracted a number of socially minded artists and educators to Hull House and together they instituted a number of pioneering programs. Through personal contacts and with the income from extensive writings she was able to maintain the settlement on a firm financial basis. Her deep interest in reform led her into the labor, woman suffrage, and pacifist movements. She worked for the improvement of social and welfare services and participated in Theodore Roosevelt's Progressive party campaign in 1912. She was chairman of the 1915 International Congress of Women and president of the subsequently established Women's International League for Peace and Freedom. In 1931 she was awarded the Nobel Peace Prize jointly with Nicholas Murray Butler. Her major written work, the autobiographical *Twenty Years at Hull House*, 1910, became a classic in social reform. Its sequel was *The Second Twenty Years at Hull House*, 1930. After several years of ill health, she died in Chicago on May 21, 1935. She was elected to the Hall of Fame in 1965.

Ade, George (1866–1944), humorist and playwright. Born in Kentland, Indiana, on February 9, 1866, Ade graduated from Purdue University in 1887 and joined the staff of the *Chicago Record* in 1890. His humorous column, produced in collaboration with the artist John T. McCutcheon, evolved into the popular *Fables in Slang*, published in 1899. The book, a best seller, was followed by 11 subsequent volumes of short humorous fables in which Ade gently lampooned the follies and foibles of his countrymen. His work was notable for its facile use of the vernacular, and he created what many thought to be masterful portraits of the common man. He turned to the theater with equal success and at one point had three plays running simultaneously in New York. He wrote a number of early movie scripts and, in the midst of the Prohibition era, he wrote another popular book, *The Old Time Saloon*, 1936. He died at his estate near Brook, Indiana, on May 16, 1944.

Adler, Cyrus (1863–1940), religious leader and educator. Born on September 13, 1863, in Van Buren, Arkansas, Adler was raised from the age of three by an uncle in Philadelphia who oversaw the boy's education in a yeshiva and under several noted rabbis. He earned his B.A. and M.A. degrees from the University of Pennsylvania in 1883 and 1886 and received a Ph.D. in Semitics from The Johns Hopkins University in 1887. He remained at Hopkins, teaching Semitic languages, until 1893. In 1889 he became a curator at the United States National Museum, supervising collections relating to Oriental antiquity, historical archeology, and historical religion, until 1908. He also became librarian at the Smithsonian Institution in Washington, D.C., in 1892 and was assistant secretary from 1905 to 1908, when he resigned to become president of the new Dropsie College for Hebrew and Cognate Learning in Philadelphia. That post, which he held until his death, made him an important lay leader of American Jews. He established the United Synagogue of America in 1913, but resigned in 1917 because of its adoption of Zionist principles, which he opposed together with the influence of Rabbi Stephen S. Wise and his group, the American Jewish Congress. Adler later cooperated with the Zionists on several occasions, however. Despite the fact that he was not a rabbi, Adler was named acting president of the Jewish Theological Seminary in New York City, becoming its president in 1924. He largely planned and directed the publication of the *Jewish Encyclopedia*, the *American Jewish Year-Book*, the *Jewish Quarterly Review*, the Jewish Classics series, and an English translation of the Hebrew Scriptures. He was active in the affairs of the Jewish Agency for Palestine, the Hebrew University in Jerusalem, and the U.S. Jewish Welfare Board. He attended the peace conference in Versailles in 1919 and made a plea for the social and economics rights of all minority groups which was incorporated into the final draft of the peace treaty. He had helped to found the American Jewish Committee in 1906 and was its president in 1929. A major force in conservative Judaism, he died in Philadelphia on April 7, 1940.

Adler, Dankmar (1844–1900), architect. Born on July 3, 1844, in Stadtlengsfeld, Germany, Adler emigrated to the United States with his father in 1854 and settled in Detroit. He studied architecture in Detroit and Chicago and from 1862 to 1865 served in the Civil War with an Illinois artillery regiment. Returning to Chicago, he worked for a succession of architectural firms and designed his first major building, the Central Music Hall, which was noted for its fine acoustics. In 1881 he and Louis H. Sullivan formed a partnership that was to have a profound influence on modern architecture. With Sullivan as planner and artist and Adler as engineer and administrator, the firm produced designs for the famed Auditorium Theater, the Transportation Building at the World's Columbian Exposition (1893), and the Gage Building, all in Chicago; the Wainwright Building in St. Louis (1890), generally credited with being the first true skyscraper; the Guaranty Building in Buffalo, New York; the Opera House in Pueblo, Colorado; and many others. The partnership was dissolved in 1895, and Adler did no further architectural work of note, but in 1896 he published the most important of his many technical papers, "The Influence of Steel Construction and Plate Glass Upon the Development of Modern Style." He died in Chicago on April 16, 1900.

Adler, Felix (1851–1933), educator. Born on August 13, 1851, in Alzey, Germany, Adler was brought to New York City at the age of six. He graduated from Columbia in 1870 and pursued graduate studies in Germany at the universities of Berlin and Heidelberg, taking his Ph.D. *summa cum laude* at Heidelberg in 1873. Unable to fit his critical spirit and his view of the modern world into the frame of Jewish tradition, he decided against entering the rabbinate and instead joined the faculty of Cornell University in 1874 as professor of Hebrew and Oriental literature. Two years later he returned to New York and established the Society for Ethical Culture. A nonsectarian organization devoted to realizing the highest moral potential of man, the society embraced no creed, although members were free to follow whatever religious teachings they might choose. Adler, who viewed Ethical Culture as an evolutionary step beyond all received religious tradition, directed the society toward practical rather than ideological concerns. Within a few years sister societies sprang up in other cities and in Europe. In 1877 he founded a free kindergarten and in 1880 the Manhattan Trade School for Girls and the Workingmen's School, which, called the Ethical Culture School after 1895, combined excellent general schooling with manual training and moral instruction. Adler was active in many reform movements, including those promoting model tenement housing, the abolition of child labor, the organization of cooperatives, and the formation of good-government clubs. From 1902 until his death he was professor of political and social ethics at Columbia University. Among his many books were *Creed and Deed*, 1877; *The Moral Instruction of Children*, 1892; *The Religion of Duty*, 1905; *An Ethical Philosophy of Life*, 1918; and *The Reconstruction of the Spiritual Ideal*, 1924. Adler died on April 24, 1933, in New York City.

Adler, Mortimer Jerome (1902–   ), philosopher and educator. Born on December 28, 1902, in New York City, Adler studied philosophy and psychology at Columbia University. He left without a degree in 1923 and began to teach at Columbia and at the People's Institute. His first book, *Dialectic*, 1927, gained him a reputation as a somewhat controversial young philosopher. He received his Ph.D. from Columbia in 1928 and went to the University of Chicago in 1930 as professor of the philosophy of law and as an adviser to the president, Robert M. Hutchins. Hutchins and Adler instituted important changes at the university, reorganizing the curriculum and emphasizing reading and discussion of the classics of the Western tradition. Out of these activities came the 54-volume *Great Books of the Western World*, 1952, which they edited. In 1952 Adler founded in San Francisco the Institute for Philosophical Research, which undertook to take stock of Western thought on subjects that have been of continuing interest since the advent of philosophy. The first "great idea" to be treated was that of freedom; the results of research by a large staff were incorporated by Adler in *The Idea of Freedom*, two volumes, 1958 and 1961. Adler returned to Chicago in 1964 and served as editor of or editorial consultant for a number of works, including the 20-volume *Annals of America*, 1969. Several series of his lectures at the University of Chicago in the 1960s were developed into books, including *The Conditions of Philosophy*, 1965; *The Difference of Man and the Difference It Makes*, 1969; *The Time of Our Lives*, 1970; and *The Common Sense of Politics*, 1971. Among his other works were *Art and Prudence*, 1937; *What Man Has Made of Man*, 1938; *A Dialectic of Morals*, 1941; and, with Louis O. Kelso, *The Capitalist Manifesto*, 1958. He was also the author of the best seller *How to Read a Book*, 1940, which appeared in a revised edition written with Charles Van Doren in 1972. Adler's career as an editor of massive reference works was crowned in 1974 by the appearance of the 15th edition of the *Encyclopedia Britannica*, the novel arrangement of whose contents he had largely planned.

Adoian, Vosdanig Manoog, *see* Gorky, Arshile

Agassiz, Alexander (1835–1910), marine zoologist and mining entrepreneur. Born on December 17, 1835, in Neuchâtel, Switzerland, Agassiz was the son of Louis Agassiz. In 1849 he sailed for the United States to rejoin his father, who was already established at Harvard's Lawrence Scientific School. He graduated from Harvard in 1855 and two years later took a B.S. in engineering from Lawrence. He also did postgraduate work in chemistry and sociology and received a B.S. in natural history from Harvard in 1862 while teaching in the girls' school founded by his stepmother, Elizabeth Cabot Cary Agassiz. In 1859 he joined the U.S. Coast Survey and while surveying in Washington Territory collected marine specimens from the Pacific coastal waters and Puget Sound. In 1865 he published three works, *North American Acalephae, Embryology of the Starfish,* and, with his stepmother, the popular *Seaside Studies in Natural History.* In the 1860s he became interested in mining and was a developer and ultimately the president of the Calumet and Hecla copper mines on Lake Superior, an enterprise that yielded him a fortune. In 1872–1874 he published the two-volume *Revision of the Echini,* based on his assisting Sir Charles Wyville Thomson in studying and classifying the collections of the *Challenger* expedition; but the work, projected to be much more extensive, was cut short by the sudden deaths of his father and of his wife within eight days of one another. In 1874 Agassiz was made curator of Harvard's Museum of Comparative Zoology, founded by his father, to which he ultimately gave more than a million dollars; he held the position until 1885, and from 1902 until his death was the director. He explored in South America in 1875, examining copper mines and charting Lake Titicaca, and between 1877 and 1904 he made a great number of oceanographic expeditions to the Caribbean and the Pacific. His activities ranged from collecting new specimens for the museum to making detailed surveys of the Gulf Stream and the Humboldt Current and to gathering the evidence that gave rise to his theory of the origin of coral atolls and barrier reefs, which opposed that of Darwin. Others of his books included *Marine Animals of Massachusetts Bay,* 1871; and *North American Starfishes,* 1877. Agassiz died on March 27, 1910, while returning to the United States from England aboard the *Adriatic.*

Agassiz, Louis (1807–1873), naturalist, geologist, and educator. Born in Môtier-en-Vully, Switzerland, on May 28, 1807, Jean Louis Rodolphe Agassiz studied at a number of European universities, taking a Ph.D. at Erlangen in 1829 and an M.D. at Munich in 1830. His first major work, on the fishes of Brazil, was published in 1829. Moving to Paris, then the center of zoological research, in 1832, he published a monumental five-volume work on fossil fish, *Recherches sur les poissons fossiles,* 1833–1844. He met the great naturalist and explorer Baron Alexander von Humboldt, whose influence won Agassiz a professorship at the University of Neuchâtel, Switzerland, a post he held from 1832 until 1846. During this time he continued his researches in zoology, publishing a number of major works. In 1836 he began a series of pioneer studies on glaciation that were to establish the occurrence of the ice age in geological history, publishing his early findings in *Études sur les glaciers,* 1840. In 1846 he journeyed to the United States to study

and lecture. He accepted the chair of natural history at the newly established Lawrence Scientific School at Harvard in 1848. His many expeditions led him to publish *Lake Superior,* 1850, and four of the originally projected ten volumes of *Contributions to the Natural History of the United States,* 1857–1862. In 1859 he founded Harvard's comprehensive Museum of Comparative Zoology. His naturalization as an American citizen ended the chance that recognition in Europe might draw him back there; he remained in the United States for the rest of his life. His major accomplishments were the stimulating of interest in natural history and the introduction of vivid and effective teaching methods that left a lasting impression on American education. With the aid of a generous gift from an admirer in New York, he established the Anderson School of Natural History in 1873 to train teachers in the use of his methods. His achievements as an educator stand unchallenged, whereas much of his later scientific work was marred by his opposition to Darwin's theory of natural selection and by a tendency toward a teleological interpretation of evolution. He died on December 12, 1873, in Cambridge, Massachusetts. He was elected to the Hall of Fame in 1915.

Agee, James (1909–1955), author and screenwriter. Born on November 27, 1909, in Knoxville, Tennessee, Agee graduated from Harvard in 1932. His first work, a book of verse called *Permit Me Voyage,* was published two years later. He joined the editorial staff of *Fortune* magazine in 1932, wrote film criticism for *Time* magazine, 1939–1943, and contributed to the *Nation, Partisan Review, Harper's,* and the *Forum.* His reporting was perceptive, illuminating social issues with warmth and concern. Sent with photographer Walker Evans by *Fortune* to investigate the situation of sharecroppers in Alabama, he became deeply concerned about their plight and went beyond his assignment to produce *Let Us Now Praise Famous Men,* 1941, a moving text and picture book. After 1948 he worked mainly in the medium of film. He wrote and narrated *The Quiet One,* about an underprivileged Harlem boy, and wrote scripts for *The African Queen, Night of the Hunter, Mr. Lincoln,* and *The Bride Comes to Yellow Sky,* based on a story by Stephen Crane. In 1951 he published a novella, *The Morning Watch,* a sensitive study of a schoolboy. His only novel, *A Death in the Family,* a young boy's view of his family after the death of his father, was published posthumously and awarded a Pulitzer Prize in 1958. He died on May 16, 1955, in New York City. A collection of his film criticism and screenplays was published in two volumes as *Agee on Film,* 1958–1960. His *Collected Poems* appeared in 1968.

Agnew, David Hayes (1818–1892), surgeon and educator. Born in Lancaster County, Pennsylvania, on November 24, 1818, Agnew attended Moscow College and Delaware College and graduated from the University of Pennsylvania with a medical degree in 1838. For the next several years he carried on a general medical practice in country districts. In 1848 he moved to Philadelphia and four years later bought the Philadelphia School of Anatomy, revitalizing the institution and gaining a reputation as a brilliant lecturer and demonstrator in anatomy and surgery during his ten years there. He was appointed to a surgical and teaching post at the Pennsylvania Hospital in 1854 and served in several Union military hospitals during the Civil War. In 1870 he became professor of surgery in the medical department of the University of Pennsylvania. His skill and reputation were such that he was chosen chief medical consultant when President James A. Garfield was shot and mortally wounded in 1881. Foremost among his many publications was the three-volume *Treatise on the Principles and Practice of Surgery*, 1878–1883. In 1889 he retired from the university and was elected president of the Philadelphia College of Physicians, and in the same year Thomas Eakins completed his famous painting "The Agnew Clinic." Agnew died in Philadelphia on March 22, 1892.

Agnew, Spiro Theodore (1918–   ), vice-president. Born in Baltimore on November 9, 1918, Agnew, whose Greek immigrant father had shortened the family name from the original **Anagnostopoulos**, studied for three years at The Johns Hopkins University and then, while working for several insurance companies, attended night classes at the Baltimore Law School. After serving in France and Germany during World War II he returned to take his law degree in 1947. He gained a local reputation as a lawyer specializing in labor cases and in 1957 was appointed as a Republican to the Zoning Board of Appeals of Baltimore County. In 1962 he became the first Republican since 1895 to serve as county executive of Baltimore County. In 1966 he ran for governor of Maryland. Attracting the support of blacks and liberals mainly because his opponent was an outspoken segregationist, he was elected by a large margin. Later, particularly after Baltimore suffered a violent racial disturbance in April 1968, he began moving to a more conservative position and strongly denounced student protesters and militant civil-rights leaders. He criticized the Poor People's March on Washington in 1968 and took up the "law and order" cry. A supporter of New York's Governor Nelson A. Rockefeller for the 1968 Republican presidential nomination until Rockefeller withdrew from the race, Agnew switched his support to Richard M. Nixon and at the party's convention placed his name in nomination. Agnew, although little known outside Maryland, was chosen as Nixon's running mate. Elected by a narrow popular margin, he continued his swing to the right and soon became the Nixon administration's principal traveling representative and political phrasemaker, rousing considerable controversy, particularly with strong criticisms of the news media. In 1972 he was reelected with Nixon, but on October 10, 1973, he resigned the vice-presidency amid charges of illegal financial dealings while in office in Maryland. He pleaded no contest to charges of federal income tax violations and was found guilty.

Ahern, James, *see* Herne, James A.

Aiken, Conrad Potter (1889–1973), poet, novelist, and critic. Born on August 5, 1889, in Savannah, Georgia, Aiken was taken to live with relatives in Massachusetts at the age of eleven, following his father's murder of his wife and subsequent suicide. He attended Harvard, where he was a close friend of T.S. Eliot, and received his degree in 1912. After a few volumes of minor verse he devoted the years 1915–1920 to the writing of five poetic "symphonies," including *The Jig of Forslin*, 1916; *The Charnel Rose*, 1918; and *The House of Dust*, 1920, in which he sought to capture the purity and form of music. Following a period, 1917–1919, as a contributing editor of the *Dial* he published *Scepticisms*, 1919, a collection of critical essays on contemporary poets. His own poetry ranged from the lyricism of the "symphonies" to intense and often lengthy psychological studies and meditations. Among his many volumes of poetry were *Priapus and the Pool*, 1922; *Senlin, a Biography*, 1925; *John Deth*, 1930; *Preludes for Memnon*, 1931; *Time in the Rock*, 1936; *And in the Human Heart*, 1940; *Brownstone Eclogues*, 1942; *The Soldier*, 1944; *The Kid*, 1947; *Skylight One*, 1949; *A Letter from Li Po*, 1955; and *The Morning Song of Lord Zero*, 1963. His *Selected Poems*, 1929, won a Pulitzer Prize, but not until the appearance of *Collected Poems*, 1953, which won a National Book Award, did he become a widely known figure in modern letters. Aiken also wrote a number of novels, including *Blue Voyage*, 1927; *Great Circle*, 1933; *King Coffin*, 1935; and *Conversation; or, Pilgrim's Progress*, 1940, in which the theme of self-discovery was predominant. He also wrote plays, including *Mr. Arcularis* (with Diana Hamilton), 1949; short stories, collected in, among others, *The Short Stories of Conrad Aiken*, 1950; and an autobiographical "essay," *Ushant*, 1952. He lived much in England, writing from London for the *New Yorker*, until 1947. He died in Savannah on August 17, 1973.

Aimee, Sister, *see* McPherson, Aimee Semple

Akeley, Carl Ethan (1864–1926), naturalist and sculptor. Born in Orleans County, New York, on May 19, 1864, Akeley became interested in nature study and taxidermy at an early age and at nineteen became an apprentice in Ward's Natural Science Establishment in Rochester, New York. In 1887 he moved to Milwaukee, where he divided his time between working at the museum and operating his own taxidermy shop. Eight years later he joined the Field Museum of Natural History in Chicago and expanded the technique of constructing large habitat groups, showing animals in their natural surroundings, that he had developed in Milwaukee. In 1896 he made the first of five trips to Africa to study and collect animals. On his second trip, in 1905, he collected the specimens that became his "Fighting Bulls" elephant group in the Field Museum. He devised a greatly improved method of taxidermy in which the skin was laid on a finely modeled form, thereby achieving unprecedented realism. In 1909 Akeley moved to the American Museum of Natural History in New York City and made his third African expedition. In 1916 he patented the Akeley motion-picture camera, designed for naturalists in the field; he used it in 1921–1922 to make the first films of gorillas in their natural habitat. He was also the inventor of the Akeley cement gun, widely used for modeling; was the sculptor of several notable pieces depicting lions, elephants, and Nandi tribesmen; and was the author of *In Brightest Africa*, 1923. An indefatigable student of African wildlife, he once killed an attacking leopard with his bare hands; and in 1926, at the age of sixty-two, he climbed Mt. Mikeno to make observations in preparation for mounting a gorilla group. He died during this expedition, on November 17, 1926, and was buried in Albert National Park, in the establishment of which he had played a major role.

Albee, Edward Franklin (1928–   ), playwright. Born on March 12, 1928, in Washington D.C., Albee was adopted as an infant by Reed A. Albee, the son of Edward Franklin Albee, a founder of the Keith–Albee vaudeville circuit. Raised in New York City, he decided to be a writer after two years at Trinity College in Hartford, Connecticut, and subsequently supported himself with jobs ranging from minor writing for radio to being a Western Union delivery man. During these years he was working on plays, the first of which, *The Zoo Story*, was staged in 1958. *The Death of Bessie Smith*, 1959, concerned the staff of a Southern hospital where blues singer Bessie Smith, brought in critical condition before her death, was refused treatment because of her race. With *The American Dream*, 1960, Albee began to acquire a reputation as a capable playwright with the ability to sustain dramatic tension while at the same time voicing scathing social criticism, a reputation that was confirmed in 1962 when *Who's Afraid of Virginia Woolf?* opened on Broadway. It became a smash hit, and later a powerful film. Among his other plays were *The Sandbox*, 1959; *Tiny Alice*, 1964; *A Delicate Balance*, 1966, which won a Pulitzer Prize the next year; *The Box* and *Quotations from Chairman Mao Tsetung*, both 1968; *All Over*, 1971; *Seascape*, another Pulitzer Prize winner, 1975; *The Lady from Dubuque*, 1977; and *Lolita*, 1979.

Albers, Josef (1888–1976), painter and designer. Born on March 19, 1888, in Bottrop, Germany, Albers graduated from the teachers college in Büren in 1908 and for five years taught elementary school. He studied at the Royal Art School in Berlin for two years, then moved to the School of Applied Art in Essen; in 1919–1920 he was at the Munich Art Academy, and in 1920 he joined the Bauhaus school in Weimar. Completing his studies in 1923, he remained at the Bauhaus as a teacher until 1933, when the school was closed by the Nazi regime. The next year Albers joined the faculty of the highly experimental Black Mountain College in North Carolina. He remained there for 16 years, becoming a U.S. citizen in 1939. In 1950 he was appointed chairman of Yale's newly organized Department of Design, a position he held together with a regular professorship until 1958, when he retired. He also lectured widely and was much in demand as a visiting teacher of painting and design. His own paintings won critical acclaim; the first of his more than 100 one-man shows was in 1936, and he earned through the years an impressive number of prizes and decorations. His canvases were designed with care and executed with great precision; almost wholly straight-line constructions, they exhibited none of the improvisational or accidental character of many abstract works. A close student of the interrelationships of light and color, Albers never attempted to conceal the calculation that lay behind his paintings, which were important in laying the theoretical groundwork for the Op art movement. The seeming simplicity of his designs is suggested by the fact that many of his works formed a long experimental series entitled "Homage to the Square." In 1958 he published *Poems and Drawings*, and in 1963 *Interaction of Color*. He died in New Haven, Connecticut, on March 25, 1976.

Albert, Carl Bert (1908–   ), public official. Born on May 10, 1908, in McAlester, Oklahoma, Albert graduated from the University of Oklahoma in 1931 and studied for three years at Oxford on a Rhodes scholarship, taking two law degrees. Admitted to the bar in 1935, he practiced in Oklahoma City for five years. In 1940 he joined the legal department of the Ohio Oil Company, but the following year enlisted as a private in the army. He was discharged in 1946 as a lieutenant colonel and in the same year ran successfully for the House of Representatives from his home district. A staunch Democrat, he was reelected regularly and at the opening of the 84th Congress in 1955 was elected majority whip. In the second session of the 87th Congress he became majority leader. In 1968 he was chairman of the Democratic national convention and in 1971, at the opening of the 92nd Congress, he was chosen speaker of the House. He retired in 1976.

Albright, Ivan Le Lorraine (1897–   ), painter. Born in North Harvey, Illinois, a Chicago suburb, on February 20, 1897, Albright was one of twin boys who both became painters. He studied for a year each at Northwestern University and the University of Illinois and then served in the American Expeditionary Force in World War I. His painstaking drawings of wounds and injuries, undertaken on his own, led to his appointment as a medical draftsman for a military hospital in Nantes. Upon his return to the United States he studied at the Art Institute of Chicago in 1919–1923, at the Pennsylvania Academy of the Fine Arts in 1923, and at the National Academy of Design in New York in 1924. He then settled in Warrenville, Illinois, to devote himself to painting. Financially secure by inheritance, Albright was able to invest as much as ten years' work in a single canvas and not concern himself with sales; and, although he won many prizes and honors and was represented in a number of galleries and museums, his work appealed to few collectors. His intricately detailed paintings often portrayed the ghastly or macabre or reflected his fascination with the gruesome and downright ugly. This often shocked viewers, as did his choice of colors and his use of texture. The titles of his works tended to heighten the effect—"Into the World There Came a Soul Called Ida" (a repulsive prostitute), "That Which I Should Have Done I Did Not Do" (a mortuary scene), "Poor Room—There Is No Time, No End, No Today, No Yesterday, No Tomorrow, Only the Forever, and Forever, and Forever, Without End" (a still life).

Albright, Jacob (1759–1808), religious leader. Born near Pottstown, Pennsylvania, on May 1, 1759, Albright was the son of German immigrant parents whose name was originally Albrecht. Largely uneducated, he followed his father's trade of brickmaker, carrying it on after moving to Lancaster County. Although he had been reared a Lutheran, he was not a notably religious man until 1790, when the deaths of several of his children struck him deeply. He took up the Methodist creed and in 1796 began to preach. Traveling throughout southeastern Pennsylvania and in Maryland and Virginia, he preached to other German settlers and slowly attracted a scattering of followers whom he formed into classes and by whom he was ordained a minister in 1803. Four years later the small sect elected Albright bishop of "The Newly Formed Methodist Conference." A short time thereafter, on May 18, 1808, he died at his home in Lancaster County, Pennsylvania. The organization he had created continued to grow, changing its name to "The so-called Albrights," later to the Evangelical Association, and finally to the Evangelical Church, which in 1946 merged with the Church of the United Brethren in Christ to form the Evangelical United Brethren Church. Albright College, in Reading, Pennsylvania, is named after him.

Albright, William Foxwell (1891–1971), archaeologist and educator. Born on May 24, 1891, in Coquimbo, Chile, the son of Methodist missionaries, Albright was brought to the United States in 1903. He graduated from Upper Iowa University in 1912 and, after a year of teaching school, entered The Johns Hopkins University, from which he received his Ph.D. in 1916. After service in World War I he studied at the American School of Oriental Research in Jerusalem.

He served as acting director of the school in 1920 and director in 1921–1929 and again in 1933–1936. He pursued an active program of archaeological excavations in Palestine and Jordan. In 1929 he was named W. W. Spence Professor of Semitic Languages at Johns Hopkins, a chair he held until his retirement in 1958. In 1947 he was chief archaeologist for the University of California's expedition in Sinai, and in 1950–1951 he held a similar post with the American Foundation for the Study of Man at several sites in Arabia. A leading authority on biblical languages, Albright aided the study of biblical history by stressing the use of linguistic and archaeological findings, and greatly advanced archaeology itself by his accurate—often inspired—identification and dating of pottery and potsherds. He was a leading consultant and commentator on the Dead Sea Scrolls after their discovery in 1947. Among his many writings were *The Archaeology of Palestine and the Bible*, 1932; *The Excavation of Tell Beit Mirsim*, in several volumes, 1932–1943; *From the Stone Age to Christianity*, 1940; *Archaeology and the Religion of Israel*, 1942; *The Bible and the Ancient Near East*, 1961; and *Yahweh and the Gods of Canaan*, 1968. He also served as senior editor of the Anchor Bible, launched in 1964, and contributed one volume in the monumental series himself—*Matthew*, 1971, with C. S. Mann. Albright was a member of many U.S. and international scientific and learned organizations. He died in Baltimore on September 19, 1971.

Alcott, Amos Bronson (1799–1888), educator and social reformer. Born near Wolcott, Connecticut, on November 29, 1799, Bronson Alcott (he changed the name from the original Alcox) received little formal education and, unable to attend Yale because of the need to help support his family, spent the years 1818–1823 as a farmer, a factory worker, and an itinerant peddler in Virginia and the Carolinas. For the next ten years he taught in a number of schools in the Northeast, but his educational theories, when put into practice, usually aroused opposition that led to his dismissal. His manner of teaching aimed at development of the whole child and combined gymnastics, conversation, and an emphasis on learning as a pleasant end in itself. Alcott attempted to stimulate the child's capacity for independent thought and, while firm, he was consistently gentle with his charges, dispensing with corporal punishment and referring disciplinary judgments to the class as a whole. In 1834 he opened his Temple School in Boston; but public opposition, bolstered by suspicions of unorthodox religious beliefs and his acceptance of a black pupil, forced him to close it in 1839. He moved to Concord, Massachusetts, in 1840 and became an intimate of Ralph Waldo Emerson and a member of the Transcendentalist circle; more loftily spiritual and mystical even than they, he won their love and admiration and often their financial aid, as his complete impracticality made the support of his wife and children difficult. To the *Dial* he contributed a great number of his "Orphic Sayings." Following a visit, at Emerson's expense, to England in 1842 to observe the methods of the Alcott House School, an experimental school named in his honor, he established in northern Massachusetts a utopian community, Fruitlands, in 1844. There practical necessities were neglected for talk and for work with various reform movements, and Fruitlands was deserted by its nearly starved remaining members within a few months. After moving from town to town in New England, Alcott and his family returned to Concord in 1857. After 1853 he made numerous lecture tours during which, rather than actually lecturing, he conversed on stage, often vaguely, sometimes completely obscurely, but always brilliantly. In 1859 he became superintendent of the Concord schools and successfully introduced many of his educational ideas. He remained cheerfully improvident, aided by his adoring family and by friends who included most of the notable intellectual figures of the day. Financial security came at last with the publication in 1868 of *Little Women* by his daughter, Louisa May Alcott. In 1879 he founded the Concord School of Philosophy, a summer school, which continued until his death in Boston on March 4, 1888. His *Journals* were edited and published by Odell Shepard in 1938.

Alcott, Louisa May (1832–1888), author. Born on November 29, 1832, in Germantown, Pennsylvania, the daughter of Amos Bronson Alcott, Louisa was raised in Boston and nearby Concord and was educated primarily by her father, with tutoring from her neighbor, Henry David Thoreau, and guidance from Ralph Waldo Emerson and Theodore Parker. Her first book, *Flower Fables*, a collection of fairy tales, was not published until 1855, six years after she wrote it; so she attempted to earn money for her family by sewing and teaching until, at seventeen, she was attracted by the theater and wrote several plays, one of which was sold to the Boston Theater but never performed. Continuing to write poems and short stories, she contributed regularly to magazines and in 1860 was published in the *Atlantic Monthly*. As a nurse during the Civil War, she wrote letters to her family which were compiled in *Hospital Sketches*, 1863. Public notice followed and she published her first novel, *Moods*, in 1864. After traveling to Europe she edited the children's magazine, *Merry's Museum*. She published the two volumes of *Little Women* in 1868 and 1869; its warmth and sensibility had a universal appeal. The book, for which she drew on the life of the Alcott family, was soon successful enough to make her family comfortable and was translated into several languages. Thereafter, she participated in women's-rights and temperance movements, settled in Boston, and wrote other enormously successful autobiographical novels, among them *An Old Fashioned Girl*, 1870; *Little Men*, 1871; and *Jo's Boys*, 1886. She died in Boston, on March 6, 1888, two days after her father's death.

Alden, John (1599?–1687), Pilgrim leader. Born in England about 1599, Alden was hired by William Bradford in 1620 to serve on the *Mayflower* as a cooper during the Pilgrims' voyage to America. He was a signer of the Mayflower Compact but, contrary to tradition, was not the first to set foot on Plymouth Rock. A founder of the settlement of Duxbury, Massachusetts, he became one of the Plymouth Colony's more substantial citizens and held numerous public offices. He was the governor's assistant from 1633 to 1641 and from 1650 to 1686 and was on occasion acting governor of the colony. Alden is remembered because of a popular legend, taken up by Henry Wadsworth Longfellow in his poem *The Courtship of Miles Standish*, in which he is said to have been importuned by the shy Standish to court Priscilla Mullins (or Molines) for him. The legend is baseless, although Alden and Standish were indeed friends and Alden did marry Priscilla, as in the story, in 1623. The last surviving signer of the Mayflower Compact and the last surviving male member of the *Mayflower* company, Alden died in Duxbury on September 12, 1687.

Aldrich, Nelson Wilmarth (1841–1915), public official. Born on November 6, 1841, in Foster, Rhode Island, Aldrich went to work at seventeen and within seven years, with time out for brief service in the Civil War, was a junior partner in a substantial wholesale grocery business. Beginning in 1869 he served for six years on the Providence common council and in the state legislature for two terms. In 1878 he was elected to the House of Representatives. He was reelected in 1880, but before Congress reconvened he sought and won the Senate seat made vacant by the death of Gen. Ambrose E. Burnside. Aldrich soon established himself as an authority on financial and fiscal policy, a staunch protectionist Republican, and a superlative parliamentarian. While working steadily to maintain and raise tariff levels, he succeeded in modifying the 1887 Interstate Commerce Act and the 1890 Sherman Anti-Trust Act to make them less unpalatable to business. The management of the unpopular Republican measures of 1890—principally the McKinley Tariff—was largely in his hands; and the security with which he held his seat was evidenced in 1892, when he was reelected in the face of a strong Democratic sweep of Congress. From that time on, he was a member of the inmost circle of Republican leadership and after the Republican resurgence in 1896 was one of the "Big Four" coterie—the other members were O. H. Platt, J. C. Spooner, and W. B. Allison—that virtually ruled the Senate. Legislation fitted his purposes of protection, fiscal stability, and party unity or it did not pass. It was Aldrich who drew the sharpest teeth of the Hepburn Rate Bill of 1906, and in 1908 he sponsored the Aldrich–Vreeland Act, a measure designed to introduce flexibility into the national monetary system. That act also created the National Monetary Commission for bank reform, of which Aldrich became chairman. Retiring from the Senate in 1911, he remained with the commission. His Aldrich Plan influenced the organization of the Federal Reserve System in 1913. Having made throughout his life extensive investments in banking, sugar, electricity, gas, and other fields, he left a fortune upon his death in New York City on April 16, 1915.

Aldrich, Thomas Bailey (1836–1907), author and editor. Born in Portsmouth, New Hampshire, on November 11, 1836, Aldrich left school at thirteen upon the death of his father. After a time he moved to New York City and, while working as a clerk, wrote verse in his spare time. After the publication of a collection, *The Bells,* in 1855, he devoted himself entirely to literary pursuits, becoming junior literary critic for the *Evening Mirror* and then subeditor of Nathaniel Parker Willis's *Home Journal.* A companion of many of New York's literary lights and bohemians, he joined some of them in 1858 in publishing the short-lived *Saturday Press.* Following a brief period as a Civil War correspondent and passing involvements with a number of New York periodicals and publishers, Aldrich moved to Boston in 1865. His reputation as an editor and as author of the long poems *Judith and Holofernes* and *Friar Jerome's Beautiful Book,* both 1862, soon won him the editorship of *Every Saturday,* a post he held for seven years. In 1870 he published his best-known work, the autobiographical *Story of a Bad Boy. Marjorie Daw and Other People,* 1873, showed him to be at his best in the short-story form. This collection was followed by the novels *Prudence Palfrey,* 1874; *The Queen of Sheba,* 1877; and *The Stillwater Tragedy,* 1880. In 1881 he succeeded William Dean Howells as editor of the *Atlantic Monthly,* filling the position with distinction for nine years. Although most successful in prose, Aldrich wrote verse throughout his career, publishing among other volumes *Cloth of Gold,* 1874; *Flower and Thorn,* 1877; *Mercedes and Later Lyrics,* 1884; and *Windham Towers,* 1890. Collections of his essays and stories were *An Old Town by the Sea,* 1893; *Two Bites at a Cherry,* 1894; *A Sea Turn and Others Matters,* 1902; and *Ponkapog Papers,* 1903. Aldrich dramatized for the stage both *Mercedes* and the early *Judith and Holofernes.* His last work was a poem written for the Longfellow centennial in 1907. He died that year, in Boston, on March 19th.

Aldridge, Ira Frederick (1804?–1867), actor. Born around 1804, probably in New York City, Aldridge apparently got his start in acting at the African Theater there. He went to England around 1824 and made his English debut the next year. A protégé of Edmund Kean, he soon became one of the leading tragedians of his time, appearing notably in such roles as Othello, Lear, and Macbeth; he was known as the "African Roscius." It is not known whether he ever returned to the United States, but if he did, it was during the 1830s. After 1853 he played primarily on the Continent, where he was enormously popular.

He amassed a fortune and received numerous honors, including tributes from the Austrian emperor and the king of Prussia. He became a British subject in 1863. He died at Lodz, Poland, on August 7, 1867, while on his way to fulfill an engagement in Russia.

Alexanderson, Ernst Frederik Werner (1878–1975), electrical engineer and inventor. Born on January 25, 1878, in Uppsala, Sweden, Alexanderson studied at the University of Lund, then graduated from the Royal Institute of Technology in Stockholm in 1900. After further study at the Royal Technical Institute in Berlin he came to the United States in 1901. The following year he fulfilled his ambition of working with Charles P. Steinmetz, taking a job under him at the General Electric Company in Schenectady, New York. His first major accomplishment was the design and construction of a powerful high-frequency alternator for use in radio experiments being made by Reginald A. Fessenden. With further improvements by the inventor, the Alexanderson alternator made possible reliable transoceanic radio communication. He became a U.S. citizen in 1908. When the Radio Corporation of America (RCA) was organized in 1919, Alexanderson was loaned to the new company, serving as its chief engineer for five years. He returned to General Electric in 1924 and over the next four decades made a large number of important contributions in various fields of research, including a selective tuning system, an amplidyne motor control system, and a system for electronic amplification, and he was a pioneer in railroad electrification. He was also one of the earliest to achieve practical results in the field of television. He transmitted the first transatlantic facsimile message in 1924; three years later he had a working home television receiver, which he demonstrated publicly in 1928; and in 1930 he demonstrated a complete television system, including the projection of a large picture on a theater screen. He retired from General Electric in 1948 but continued to work for the company as a consultant. In 1952 he rejoined RCA in a similar capacity and there developed a color television receiver. Alexanderson was the recipient of numerous awards and was granted more than 300 patents. He died in Schenectady, New York, on May 14, 1975.

Alger, Cyrus (1781–1856), industrialist and inventor. Born in Bridgewater, Massachusetts, on November 11, 1781, Alger early learned the foundry business in one of his father's establishments. In 1809 he set up his own works in South Boston, and government contracts for cannonballs during the War of 1812 put the business on a firm financial footing. In 1827 he organized the South Boston Iron Company, which soon became the largest in the United States. Alger was an imaginative inventor and an experimenter in metallurgy. He designed the first cylinder stoves and the first gun with a rifled barrel, and he made improvements in many other items of hardware and ordnance;

he also made several innovations in foundry processes, including a method of purifying and strengthening cast iron. He was a leader in the development of South Boston and was active in Boston public affairs throughout his career. He died in Boston on February 4, 1856.

Alger, Horatio (1832–1899), author. Born in Revere, Massachusetts, on January 13, 1832, Alger was the son of a stern Unitarian minister who intended that his son should follow in his footsteps. "Holy Horatio," as his schoolmates called him, graduated from Harvard in 1852 and after a few years with a Boston newspaper and as a tutor entered Harvard Divinity School. Graduating in 1860, he used an unexpected legacy to finance a year in Paris where he pursued the bohemian life despite painful conflicts with his Puritan conscience. After his return to the United States he tried unsuccessfully to enlist in the Union army for Civil War service and finally, in 1864, gave himself over to conscience by assuming the ministry of a Unitarian church in Brewster, Massachusetts. Determined still, however, that literature was to be his life, he submitted several stories and plot outlines to William T. Adams ("Oliver Optic"), an author and publisher of juvenile fiction, from whom he received encouragement. In 1866 Alger resigned his pulpit and went to New York City. The next year his first successful novel, *Ragged Dick, or Street Life in New York*, was serialized in Adams's *Student and Schoolmate*. The hero, Dick Hunter, is a New York bootblack, a boy of the streets who, by pluck, honesty, hard work, and a little luck, rises to become, in the course of several sequels, a rich man. The pattern set in *Ragged Dick* was followed with little variation in more than 100 Alger books during the next thirty years. The books were from the outset enormously popular; capturing the imagination of American youth in a period of great industrial growth and the making of huge personal fortunes, Alger communicated something of Herbert Spencer's philosophy of laissez-faire while entertaining, rather than exercising, his readers. The appeal of his single story idea is indicated by the fact that he became the most popular author of his generation with a series of books whose literary quality was consistently and outrageously bad. For many years he was the chief benefactor, adviser, and hero of the Newsboys' Lodging House in New York City. Except for two Western trips to gather material for books, he remained in the city until 1895, when he moved to Peekskill, New York. After a brief and fruitless romance that led him to Paris and a nervous breakdown, he returned to the United States and lived with his sister in Natick, Massachusetts, until his death on July 18, 1899.

Ali, Muhammad (1942–   ), boxer. Born Cassius Marcellus Clay, Jr., on January 18, 1942, in Louisville, Kentucky, Ali was educated in the local schools. At twelve a local policeman encouraged him to learn boxing; he trained for six weeks and boxed on the television program "Champions of Tomorrow" and won. He continued fighting as an amateur for 6 years, winning 100 of 108 matches and 6 Golden Gloves titles in Kentucky. Accepted for the U.S. Olympic team in 1960, he won the gold medal in the light-heavyweight competition. Turning professional, he was trained by Archie Moore and Angelo Dundee. He won his first professional fight on October 29, 1960, and began attracting nationwide attention not only for his dazzling performances in the ring but also for his much-publicized boasting and his doggerel verse, in which he predicted, sometimes correctly, the round in which he would knock out his opponent. By 1963 he had fought 19 professional fights and won all of them. In August of that year he made a record album entitled *I Am the Greatest!* in which he claimed he would beat heavyweight champion Sonny Liston in the eighth round. This and other publicity stunts led to record-breaking attendance and nationwide closed-circuit television coverage of the match on February 25, 1964. He scored a technical knockout against the heavily favored Liston in the seventh round. The next day he announced that henceforth his name was Muhammad Ali and his religion was Islam as practiced by the Black Muslim sect. The World Boxing Association (WBA) withdrew its recognition of him as champion in March 1964 because of his behavior before the Liston fight, which included making an arrangement for the promotion of future fights. Despite the association's ban, a rematch was fought on May 25, 1965. Liston was knocked out in one minute of the first round, making the bout the shortest in championship history. Ali, who successfully defended his title eight more times over the next two years, was hailed as one of the finest boxers of the twentieth century. He refused induction into the army in 1967; denied reclassification as a conscientious objector, he was convicted of draft evasion in June 1967. With much attendant controversy, he was stripped of his world championship title by the WBA and the New York State Athletic Commission. Still considered the champion by much of the boxing public, he withdrew from competition for a time. In March 1971, before a huge audience that included viewers of closed-circuit and satellite-transmitted television, he met Joe Frazier, who had emerged from the scramble for the vacated title. Ali lost by a unanimous decision, but his purse was a record $2.5 million. Three months later his 1967 conviction was overturned on technical grounds by the U.S. Supreme Court. On October 30, 1974, he became the second boxer ever to regain the heavyweight title by beating George Foreman in Kinshasa, Zaire. After several defenses of it, he lost the title to Leon Spinks on February 15, 1978. On September 15, 1978, he beat Spinks and became the first heavyweight ever to hold the title three times.

Alinsky, Saul David (1909–1972), social reformer. Born in Chicago on January 30, 1909, Alinsky graduated from the University of Chicago in 1930 and remained there for two additional years studying criminology. While employed as a social worker dealing with juvenile delinquents, and, from 1933 to 1936, as a criminologist with the Illinois state penal system, he gained first-hand understanding of the roots of social pathology —discrimination, disease, unemployment, poor housing—and the workings of the poverty cycle. He had already done much fund raising and organizational work for various reform movements when he decided in 1938 to make a career of such work. Moving to the Back of the Yards district of Chicago—a poor working-class area near the stockyards—he enlisted the aid of labor and religious leaders in forming the Back of the Yards Council, a citizens' organization whose purpose was to act as a pressure bloc for social improvement. Using peaceful direct-action tactics, the council succeeded in vastly improving conditions in the neighborhood and, more importantly, in demonstrating to all who participated the realities of political and economic power and their own ability to use power to achieve their own legitimate ends. In 1940 Alinsky established the Industrial Areas Foundation (IAF) to serve as a reservoir of money, manpower, and expertise for community organizing. After serving as a consultant to various government agencies during World War II, he returned to the IAF and undertook community organizing in scores of poor and powerless neighborhoods across the country. Working always at the invitation of local groups, he concentrated on developing indigenous leadership and on instilling the notion of self-help. Firmly opposed to paternalism either on the part of the powerful or of that of self-seeking "reformers," he was a passionate and controversial exponent of radical democracy. Among the groups that benefited from his tireless and fearless efforts were Mexican Americans in California, black citizens of ghetto neighborhoods in Chicago, Detroit, Kansas City, Missouri, and Rochester and Buffalo, New York; and, in later years, residents of numerous white middle-class neighborhoods. His success was attested to both by the number of his ardent admirers and by the vehemence of the attacks made on him by those opposed to change. Among his published works were *Reveille for Radicals*, 1947, and *Rules for Radicals: A Pragmatic Primer for Realistic Radicals*, 1971. Alinsky died at his home in Carmel, California, on June 12, 1972.

Allen, Ethan (1738–1789), Revolutionary soldier. Born on January 21, 1738 in Litchfield, Connecticut, Allen was prevented from completing his education by the death of his father in 1755, after which he assumed financial responsibility for his family. During his youth he became intrigued by the ideas of a young rationalist, Thomas Young, and later wrote a book based on them, *Reason, the Only Oracle of Man*, 1784. After serving in the French and Indian Wars in 1757 he acquired, with his brothers, large land holdings in the region, then known as the New Hampshire Grants, that was to become the state of Vermont.

Jurisdiction over the Grants was being disputed by New York and New Hampshire. Eager to control the region themselves, the Allens formed the Green Mountain Boys, a group that harassed New Yorkers in the area and eventually grew so notorious that the governor of New York offered a £100 reward for Ethan's capture. Allen intended to petition the king to confer separate status on the disputed area, but the outbreak of the Revolution interrupted his efforts. In 1775 he was instructed by the Connecticut Assembly to capture Fort Ticonderoga and, with the able assistance of Col. Benedict Arnold and a body of militia, Allen and his patriot band succeeded triumphantly. Emboldened by this success, he attempted to take Montreal but was promptly captured and imprisoned by the British. In 1778 he was released in exchange for a British prisoner. The honorary rank of colonel was conferred on him when he was released from prison, but he returned to his own affairs in Vermont. His *Narrative of Colonel Ethan Allen's Captivity*, 1779, omitted mention of Arnold's aid in capturing Fort Ticonderoga. With his brothers, he resumed his activities in behalf of the region and appealed to his former captors, the British in Canada, to annex Vermont to Canada or, at the least, to aid Vermont to obtain separate status. He died in Burlington on February 11, 1789. Two years later Vermont achieved statehood and under its tax laws, the Allens lost all of their land.

Allen, Fred (1894–1956), humorist. Born on May 31, 1894, in Cambridge, Massachusetts, John Florence Sullivan started his career on the vaudeville stage as a juggler. One evening when the audience was decidedly unappreciative, the theater manager stepped onto the stage and asked him, yet a boy, just where he had learned to juggle. He quipped, "I took a correspondence course in baggage smashing," and his career as a humorist was on its way. He toured vaudeville theaters for ten years, at $25 a week. During World War I he was in the army, then returned to the stage as "Freddie James, World's Worst Juggler." An agent named Allen suggested the professional name that he finally adopted. He began to rely on the dry humor and the singsong, nasal delivery that became his trademarks. For his material, which was frequently topical, he studied newspapers and magazines. In 1932, he began the radio program "Allen's Alley," with his wife, Portland Hoffa. The show continued until 1949, and at its peak had 20,000,000 listeners. Characters populating the "Alley," included Senator Claghorn, Titus Moody, Mrs. Nussbaum, and Ajax Cassidy. Allen's withering criticisms of Hollywood, Madison Avenue, and the banal world of broadcasting did not exclude his own sponsors and such network executives as "the vice president in charge of waving fingers at comedians." Allen philosophized that "a conference of radio executives is a meeting at which a group of men who, singly, can do nothing, agree collectively that nothing can be done." He wrote nearly all the material for his show and for his frequent guest appearances. In 1954 appeared *Treadmill to Oblivion*, a book about his years in radio. He appeared in movies, twice with Jack Benny (*Love Thy Neighbor* and *It's in the Bag*), with whom he conducted a comic "feud" for many years. In 1955 he became a regular panel member on the television quiz show "What's My Line?" He was writing his autobiography at the time of his death in New York City on March 17, 1956.

Allen, Frederick Lewis (1890–1954), editor and historian. Born in Boston on July 5, 1890, Allen graduated from Harvard in 1912 and taught English there for two years, taking his M.A. in 1913. From 1914 to 1916 he was associate editor of the *Atlantic Monthly* and from 1916 to 1917 was managing editor of the *Century*. During World War I he served on the Council of National Defense and afterward returned to Harvard as secretary to the Corporation. In 1923 he joined *Harper's Magazine*, of which he became associate editor in 1931 and editor in 1941. In 1931 he published the first of his two best-known works, *Only Yesterday*, a fascinating social history of the United States during the 1920s; that book, together with *Since Yesterday*, 1940, which treated in similar fashion the Depression decade of the thirties, provided a richly flavored account of one of the most interesting periods of American history. Among Allen's other works were *The Lords of Creation*, 1935, the story of American business and finance in the years 1900–1935; *The Great Pierpont Morgan*, 1949, and *The Big Change*, 1952, a summary of U.S. social history of the first half of the twentieth century. Allen retired from *Harper's* in 1953 and died in New York City on February 13, 1954.

Allen, Henry Watkins (1820–1866), soldier and public official. Born on April 29, 1820, in Prince Edward County, Virginia, Allen grew up there and, after 1833, in present-day Lafayette County, Missouri. After two years at Marion College he moved to Grand Gulf, Mississippi, where he taught school, studied law, and was admitted to the bar. He suspended his practice briefly to respond to Sam Houston's appeal for volunteers for the Texas army in 1842. After the death of his wife he left Mississippi for Louisiana, settling in 1852 in West Baton Rouge. He was elected to the legislature the next year and, despite his going to Harvard to study law and then sailing suddenly to Italy to join Garibaldi's forces (he arrived too late), he was reelected in absentia for a second term. At the outbreak of the Civil War Allen, by that time a popular figure in the state, enlisted as a private and was quickly commissioned a lieutenant colonel. He was a brave and capable commander; he was in action at Shiloh, Vicksburg, and elsewhere, was twice seriously wounded, and by 1863 had risen to brigadier general. Late in that year he was elected governor of Louisiana, emerging, in his year and a half in the post, as the best administrator in the Con-

federacy. To relieve the widespread suffering of the people, he set up a system of state stores and factories which made and distributed needed goods and helped to restore the value of the state's money. He rigidly controlled exports and imports, bringing in necessities from Mexico and banning luxuries; the sale of alcoholic beverages was stopped and an active program of relief for the needy and for disabled soldiers was established. After Gen. Robert E. Lee's surrender in April 1865, Gen. Edmund Kirby-Smith, Confederate commander in Louisiana, was prepared to continue his resistance, particularly since his army at that time was as strong or stronger than it had ever been. Allen, however, finally persuaded Kirby-Smith to surrender, thus preventing the death and destruction that would otherwise have been inevitable. Following the surrender Allen fled to Mexico and started an English-language newspaper. However, his popularity in Louisiana remained such that late in 1865, in spite of his fugitive status, he was widely suggested for governor. His health having suffered greatly from his battle wounds, he died in Mexico City on April 22, 1866.

Allen, Horatio (1802–1889), engineer. Born on May 10, 1802, in Schenectady, New York, Allen graduated from Columbia College in 1823 and took up the study of law. He soon found his interest captured by engineering, however, and after working for a year for the Chesapeake & Delaware Canal Company he became an engineer for the Delaware & Hudson Company. His work was of such caliber that in 1828 he was sent to England by the company to purchase the first locomotives ever brought to the United States; and the following year he himself tested one of them at Honesdale, Pennsylvania, in the first steam-railway run made in America. Later in 1829 he became chief engineer of the South Carolina Railroad Company, for which he directed track construction and which he persuaded to use locomotives rather than horses. He subsequently designed and supervised construction at the West Point Foundry of the *Best Friend of Charleston*, the first locomotive built for sale in the United States, and saw it into service in 1830. In designing a second locomotive, he hit upon the important idea of mounting it on pivoted trucks rather than fixed axles, thus enabling it to negotiate sharp curves with greater safety. After several years spent in travel, Allen moved to New York City and served in engineering positions with the builders of the Croton Aqueduct and with the New York & Erie Railroad. In 1842 he became a partner in a company building steam engines for ships. He was made president of the New York & Erie in 1843. He continued to serve as an engineering consultant even after his retirement in 1870, notably on the construction of the Brooklyn Bridge and the Panama Railroad. In 1872 he served as president of the American Society of Civil Engineers and he was a founder of both the Union League Club of New York and the New

York Gallery of Art. Allen died at his home near South Orange, New Jersey, on December 31, 1889.

Allen, John (1810–1892), dentist. Born in Broome County, New York, on November 4, 1810, Allen grew up there and in Ohio. At nineteen he began a year of study with a dentist in Chillicothe, Ohio, and then started his own practice in Cincinnati, where he also continued to study in the medical college, eventually receiving an M.D. In 1845 he was awarded a patent for a device that, when attached to false teeth, filled out the face where the shrinking of tissue had altered the original contours. He then set about making improved dentures. He discarded gold for platinum in the base plate, thus making possible the use of harder and more acid-resistant porcelain for the teeth. He then covered the plate with a porcelain "continuous gum" in which the teeth might be set in any desired arrangement, at the same time being sealed against the seepage of oral fluids. His perfected denture, the product of several years of experimentation, was patented in 1851 and is the type still in use. In 1845 he was a founder of the Ohio College of Dental Surgery, the second such school in the world, and, having moved to New York City about 1853, was later a founder of the New York College of Dentistry. Allen died on March 8, 1892, in Plainfield, New Jersey.

Allen, Richard (1760–1831), religious leader. Born in Philadelphia on February 14, 1760, Allen was the son of slave parents, together with whom he was sold to a Delaware farmer soon after his birth. Of a religious nature from an early age, he joined the Methodist Episcopal Church at seventeen, and five years later he was licensed to preach. By 1786 he had saved enough money to buy his freedom and he moved back to Philadelphia. Joining St. George's Methodist Church, he was permitted to preach to a black congregation until its growing numbers aroused the ire of white members. Allen thereupon withdrew, converted an old blacksmith shop into a church, and organized the Free African Society, the first Negro church in America. In 1794 the society built a new church which was affiliated with the Methodist Episcopal Church and dedicated by Bishop Francis Asbury. Five years later Allen became the first Negro to be regularly ordained in the Methodist Church. He was one of the moving spirits in the organization of the African Methodist Episcopal Church by 16 independent Negro congregations in 1816 and was chosen its first bishop. He remained in that office, working with great effect, until his death in Philadelphia on March 26, 1831.

Allen, Steve (1921–   ), entertainer. Born in New York City on December 26, 1921, Stephen Valentine Patrick William Allen was the son of vaudeville performers. His father died soon after his birth and Allen grew up in the homes of relatives all over the country. He briefly attended both Drake University and Arizona State Teachers College and in 1942 got his first job, as a radio announcer in Phoenix, Arizona. After serving in the army in World War II he worked for a number of stations in California until 1950, when he moved to New York City and originated the highly popular "Tonight" show on NBC television. His later "Steve Allen Show" on television usually had the format of a talk and variety show and featured Allen's unique and largely ad-lib style of humor. A highly versatile man, Allen composed more than 2000 songs, including his theme, "This Could Be the Start of Something Big;" "Pretend You Don't See Her;" "Gravy Waltz;" and the theme songs for several motion pictures, including *On the Beach, Picnic, Houseboat,* and *Bell, Book and Candle.* He starred in the motion pictures *I'll Get By,* 1950, and *The Benny Goodman Story,* 1956, and wrote the music and lyrics for a Broadway musical, *Sophie,* 1963. Among his many books were *Fourteen for Tonight,* a collection of stories, 1955; *Wry on the Rocks,* 1956, a book of verse; *Mark It and Strike It,* 1960, an autobiography; *Letter to a Conservative,* 1965; and *Bigger than a Breadbox,* 1967. Allen also interested himself in numerous political and social causes.

Allison, William Boyd (1829–1908), public official. Born on March 2, 1829, near Ashland, Ohio, Allison was educated at Wooster Academy, Allegheny College, and Western Reserve College, from the last of which he graduated in 1849. He was admitted to the bar in the same year and practiced in Ashland while becoming involved in politics. He abandoned his early Whiggism to join the disaffected Democrats who founded the Ohio Republican party in 1855, and he helped to elect Salmon P. Chase governor while himself losing the race for attorney general. The next year he was a delegate to the Know-Nothing convention. In 1857 he moved to Dubuque, Iowa, resumed the practice of law, and soon became active in promoting Republican interests there. At the Republican convention in Chicago in 1860 he supported Abraham Lincoln over his old friend Chase. Two years later Allison was elected to the House of Representatives, where he served four terms and was known as a conciliator of conflicting class and sectional interests. He was somewhat tainted by the Crédit Mobilier scandal of 1870, and for that and other reasons he failed to win election to the Senate in that year. He won in 1872, however, and remained in the Senate for the rest of his life. A fiscal conservative, he kept the support of his Western constituents largely by taking a moderate stand on the tariff. As a member of the finance committee, chairman of the appropriations committee from 1881, and chairman of the Senate Republican caucus after 1897, Allison was of the inner councils of his party, particularly after 1890, when he, N. W. Aldrich, O. H. Platt, and J. C. Spooner constituted the "Big Four," known as the masters of the Senate. His role was that of a moderate and a compromiser: his best-known legislative work was the Bland-Allison Silver Act of 1878, in which he balanced conservative and inflationist demands by skillfully weakening a House bill for the remonetization of silver. In 1906 he served as the conciliator in a dispute between Aldrich and President Theodore Roosevelt over the Hepburn Rate Bill. Although he was the oldest member of the Senate, Allison was renominated for his seat in Iowa's first senatorial primary in 1908, but he died in Dubuque shortly thereafter, on August 4, 1908.

Allouez, Claude Jean (1622–1689), Jesuit missionary. Born on June 6, 1622, in St.-Didier, France, Allouez entered the Society of Jesus at Toulouse in 1639. He was ordained in 1655 and three years later sailed for Quebec, where for five years he ministered to settlements along the St. Lawrence River. In 1663 he was appointed Jesuit vicar-general of the Northwest, with responsibility for conducting missions to the various Indian tribes, for regulating their relations with traders, and for extending the domain of the Church. He traveled extensively in the Great Lakes region, first preceding and then later collaborating with Jacques Marquette, for whom he composed a book of prayers in the French and Illinois languages. He was effective in conciliating intertribal disputes and founded many new missions, notably that at the present De Pere, Wisconsin. Allouez continued Marquette's work among the Illinois after the latter's death in 1675, spending most of his latter years in that tribe's region and among the Miamis of southeastern Michigan. He died during the night of August 27–28, 1689, near the site of present-day Niles, Michigan.

Allport, Gordon Willard (1897–1967), psychologist. Born on November 11, 1897, in Montezuma, Indiana, Allport grew up there and in Cleveland. He graduated from Harvard in 1919 and after a year spent in teaching English at Robert College in Istanbul, Turkey, he returned to Harvard to take his Ph.D. in 1922. He pursued further studies at the universities of Berlin and Hamburg in 1922–1923 and at Cambridge University in 1923–1924 and then joined the Harvard faculty. Two years later he moved to Dartmouth College but in 1930 returned to Harvard, with which he was associated for the rest of his life, becoming a full professor of psychology in 1942 and Richard Clarke Cabot Professor of Social Ethics in 1966. His major work was the development of a theory of personality that steered between the poles of Freudianism and behaviorism. In a number of books—among them *Personality: A Psychological Interpretation*, 1937; *The Nature of Personality*, 1950; *Becoming*, 1955; *Pattern and Growth in Personality*, 1961; and *The Person in Psychology*, 1968—he evolved a concept of personality as a real, identifiable, and unique organization that grows out of but becomes independent of infantile drives and is the basis of identity and inner continuity. Allport rejected both the mythological tendencies of the Freudians and the radically positivistic attitudes of the behaviorists, following instead a careful "empiricism restrained by reason." This position attained considerable influence, as did its therapeutic corollary—treating real, present problems instead of concentrating on the search for childhood traumas. Among his other works were *The Psychology of Rumor* (with L. Postman), 1947; the widely read and praised *Nature of Prejudice*, 1954; and *Personality and Social Encounter*, 1960. He was editor of the *Journal of Abnormal and Social Psychology* from 1937 to 1949. Allport died on October 9, 1967, in Cambridge, Massachusetts.

Allston, Robert Francis Withers (1801–1864), agriculturist and public official. Born on April 21, 1801, in All Saints' Parish, South Carolina, Allston graduated from West Point in 1821. He was assigned to duty making harbor surveys at Plymouth and Provincetown, Massachusetts, and at Mobile Bay, Alabama but resigned his commission after a year to take charge of the family plantation. He used his training in engineering to construct a system of drainage ditches and embankments which made it possible to reclaim and cultivate rice on a large amount of marshland. While emerging as one of South Carolina's leading planters he served two terms as surveyor general and from 1828 to 1832 was in the lower house of the state legislature. From 1832 to 1856 he served in the state senate, the last nine years as its president. A states'-rights advocate in the pre–Civil War period, he nonetheless opposed precipitate and unilateral action on the part of South Carolina, counseling instead a policy of cooperation with other Southern states. He was a delegate to the 1850 Nashville Convention called to discuss a general movement of secession. He served a single term as governor, 1856–1858, during which he devoted himself to the improvement of public education and of agriculture. His own contributions to agricultural development were his most important work; the example of his plantation was of great influence through his writings, *A Memoir of the Introduction and Planting of Rice in South Carolina*, 1843, and *An Essay on Sea Coast Crops*, 1854. Allston died on April 7, 1864, near Georgetown, South Carolina.

Allston, Washington (1779–1843), painter. Born on his family's plantation in Georgetown County, South Carolina, on November 5, 1779, Allston early displayed a talent for drawing and painting. He was schooled in Newport, Rhode Island, and graduated from Harvard in 1800. The next year he sailed to England to study at the Royal Academy school under Benjamin West; in 1803 he went on to Paris and then to Italy, where he studied the old masters and formed close friendships with Samuel Taylor Coleridge and Washington Irving. In 1808 he went to Boston to marry Ann, the sister of a Harvard classmate, William Ellery Channing. Three years later he returned to England with his pupil, Samuel F. B. Morse, and set about producing his finest paintings, among them a portrait of Coleridge and "Dead Man Revived by Touching the Bones of the Prophet Elisha," "The Angel Liberating St. Peter from Prison," "Uriel in the Sun," "Jacob's Ladder," "Elijah in the Desert," and "The Agony of Judas." He considered the "Agony" his best painting but destroyed it for fear of its being misunderstood. Allston's canvases were distinguished by their highly dramatic content and the characteristically romantic treatment of light, while his color was often compared to that of Titian. During his years in England he also published a book of verse, *The Sylphs of the Seasons with Other Poems*, 1813. In 1818 he returned to the United States, establishing his studio first in Boston and later in Cambridgeport, Massachusetts. His first wife having died, he married in 1830 Martha Dana, the sister of Richard Henry Dana. Among the major works of his last years were "Moonlit Landscape," "The Flight of Florimell," and "Belshazzar's Feast," a huge painting that he had begun in 1817 and that, despite almost continual work, he left unfinished at his death. None of the works of this period seemed to fulfill the promise of his youth, but he had nonetheless a secure position in American art. In 1841 he published a novel, *Monaldi*. Allston died in Cambridgeport on July 9, 1843.

Alter, David (1807–1881), physicist and physician. Born in Westmoreland County, Pennsylvania, on December 3, 1807, Alter graduated in 1832 from the Reformed Medical College in New York City. Although he was a physician by profession, his true enthusiasm throughout his life was experimenting with electricity and other phenomena, an interest originally aroused by a youthful reading of a biography of Benjamin Franklin. Using mostly equipment that he made himself, he devised an electric clock, a model electric locomotive, and in 1836 an electric telegraph that was, however, cumbersome to operate; apparently because it was considered absurd, it was declared unpatentable. In the field of chemistry he developed a method of purifying bromine and a means of extracting coal oil from coal, the latter a discovery that might have had great commercial potential but for the fact that a more economical source of kerosine appeared with the drilling of the first oil well in 1859. Alter's major achievement was in spectroscopy: almost simultaneously with Swedish physicist A. J. Ångström, who is generally given credit, he published his discovery of the principal, later known as Kirchhoff's Second Law, that every elemental gas, when heated to incandescence, emits light with a unique and characteristic spectrum, thus making relatively simple the identification of any sample of gas. Alter died at his home in Westmoreland County, Pennsylvania, on September 18, 1881.

Altgeld, John Peter (1847–1902), public official. Born in Nassau, Germany, on December 30, 1847, the young Altgeld emigrated with his family to a farm in Richland County, Ohio, where he remained until he was twenty-one. Growing up in poverty, he received little formal education and his years on the farm were interrupted only by brief service in the Civil War. In 1869 he left Ohio and for five years worked as a farm laborer, taught school, and studied law. In 1874, living in Savannah, Missouri, he was elected prosecuting attorney for Andrew County. He resigned the following year and moved to Chicago. He lost a bid for the House of Representatives in 1884, but in 1886 he was elected superior court judge in Cook County. He resigned from the court in 1891 after having become its chief judge. In 1892 he was elected the first Democratic governor of Illinois since the Civil War; within a short time after taking office he became a center of great controversy when, upon the urging of Clarence Darrow and others, he pardoned three of the men convicted as the "conspirators" responsible for the Haymarket riot of 1886. Although his decision now seems to have been fully justified, he drew the immediate and bitter condemnation of Republicans, of the great capitalists, and of the press. The furor was revived in July 1894 when, during the Pullman strike, he protested to President Grover Cleveland the sending of regular army troops to Illinois, basing his protest on the unconstitutionality of the action and on the fact that the disorders, which had been exaggerated by the press, were of small scale and entirely within the ability of local government to control. Altgeld was defeated for reelection in 1896. He died in Joliet, Illinois, still a figure of scorn to his many opponents, on March 12, 1902. Later, partly because of a number of literary works about his life and career, he became a hero to many for his championship of liberal causes and the rights of the individual.

Altman, Benjamin (1840–1913), businessman and art collector. Born on July 12, 1840, on the Lower East Side of New York City, Altman was the son of German Jewish immigrant parents. He had little formal schooling and, beginning in his father's shop, worked in a succession of small retail stores. By the age of twenty-five he had opened his own dry-goods store. The business grew steadily and in 1906, by then known as B. Altman & Company, it moved uptown to Fifth Avenue and 34th Street, pioneering in what soon became a general northward movement of commerce in New York City. By 1914 the store covered a full city block. Altman, possessing great organizational ability and capacity for hard work, broke new ground in employee relations, supplying various amenities and medical-service benefits and establishing the Altman Foundation for his employee's welfare and for other philanthropic ends. He was an avid and astute collector of art. As early as 1882 he began collecting Chinese enamels and porcelains and later, on several European trips, he acquired paintings by such artists as Botticelli, Filippo Lippi, Holbein, and Rembrandt. At the time of his death in New York City on October 7, 1913, his collection, including a large art library, was appraised at $20 million; it was left to the Metropolitan Museum of Art, together with a cash bequest for its maintenance. The National Academy of Design also received a substantial gift from his estate.

Alvarez, Luis Walter (1911–   ), physicist. Born on June 13, 1911, in San Francisco, Alvarez grew up there and in Rochester, Minnesota. He graduated from the University of Chicago in 1932 and remained there for graduate studies in physics, taking his Ph.D. in 1936. He joined the faculty of the University of California at Berkeley in that year as a research assistant. In 1940 he took leave from the university to do research for the army, first at the Radiation Laboratory of the Massachusetts Institute of Technology, where he worked on radar and devised (with Lawrence Johnston) a ground-controlled-approach system that made possible all-weather aircraft landing. From 1943 to 1945 he was at the Los Alamos atomic-bomb project. In 1945 he was awarded the Collier Trophy by President Harry S. Truman for his radar work, and in that year he returned to the University of California at Berkeley as professor of physics. Thereafter he devoted himself to the development of linear accelerators for subatomic particles and of bubble chambers for their detection. This work led to the discovery, by him and others, of a large number of subatomic events, resonance states that, as time went on, came more and more commonly to be interpreted as subatomic particles. For his revolutionary researches in this important area of nucelar physics, Alvarez received the Albert Einstein Award in 1961 and the Nobel Prize for Physics in 1968.

Ames, Fisher (1758–1808), public official and political leader. Born in Dedham, Massachusetts, on April 9, 1758, Ames graduated from Harvard College at the age of sixteen. From 1774 to 1781 he studied on his own; in 1779 he turned from the classics to law and in 1781 was admitted to the bar. His published essays on Shays's Rebellion and in support of a federal constitutional convention brought him to public notice. He was elected to the Massachusetts ratifying convention in 1787 and to the House of Representatives in 1789. A brilliant Federalist theoretician and speaker, he remained a member of the House until 1797 and was a staunch supporter of Alexander Hamilton. Beset by ill health, he roused himself in April 1796 to deliver his greatest speech, favoring the enabling appropriation bill for Jay's Treaty. He declined reelection in 1796 and the presidency of Harvard in 1805. His last years were spent at home, where he continued to write in support of the Federalist view of government. He died in Dedham on July 4, 1808.

Ames, Oakes (1804–1873), businessman and public official. Born in Easton, Massachusetts, on January 10, 1804, Ames attended school until he was sixteen and then went to work in his father's shovel factory. In 1844 he and his brother Oliver took over the management of the factory and by 1860, aided by the gold rushes to California and Australia, they had built it into a $4 million business. In 1862 Ames was elected as a Republican to the House of Representatives, and he held the seat for the rest of his life. In 1865 he and Oliver, with T. C. Durant and others, organized the Crédit Mobilier of America, a construction company established to promote and build the Union Pacific Railroad and to keep the profits in the hands of a few insiders. By means of vastly inflated construction contracts let to Ames and then sublet by him to seven trustees, Union Pacific assets were converted into personal fortunes. Early in 1868, when it seemed that Congress might investigate such dubious transactions involving its substantial grants to the Union Pacific, Ames sold Crédit Mobilier stock to several key political figures at a fraction of their market value, hoping thereby to induce them to use their influence to forestall an inquiry. The details of this action were revealed in 1872 and Congress promptly investigated. As a result the "Crédit Mobilier scandal" came to be a symbol of the corruption that was rampant during the presidency of Ulysses S. Grant. Ames and Representative James Brooks of New York were formally censured by Congress in 1873. Among those absolved of wrongdoing but nonetheless tainted with suspicion were Vice-President Schuyler Colfax and James A. Garfield, who was then a Congressman. Soon after being censured, Ames returned home to Easton and died there on May 8, 1873.

Amos 'n' Andy, *see* Gosden, Freeman Fisher

Anderson, Carl David (1905–   ), physicist. Born in New York City on September 3, 1905, Anderson grew up mainly in Los Angeles and attended the California Institute of Technology. After graduating in 1927 he stayed on to study under Robert A. Millikan and to assist him in his investigations of cosmic rays. Anderson received his Ph.D. in 1930. In 1932 he announced that he and his colleague, Seth Neddermeyer, had found in a cloud chamber definite evidence of the existence of a subatomic particle equal in mass to the electron but positively charged; he named it the positron and by 1933 was able to produce it artificially by gamma-ray bombardment. For this achievement he was awarded the 1936 Nobel Prize for Physics jointly with V. F. Hess of Austria. Shortly thereafter he published his experimental confirmation, again with Neddermeyer, of the existence of yet another particle that had been predicted theoretically by Hideki Yukawa in 1935. This particle he named the mesotron; it was later called the meson and, later still, renamed the mu meson, or muon. In 1939 Anderson became a full professor at Caltech and in 1962 was made chairman of the division of physics, mathematics, and astronomy.

Anderson, Joseph Reid (1813–1892), industrialist and soldier. Born in Botetourt County, Virginia, on February 6, 1813, Anderson graduated from West Point in 1836. He was commissioned a second lieutenant of artillery but was soon transferred to the Corps of Engineers, where he assisted in the construction of Fort Pulaski, Georgia, before resigning his commission in 1837. After a brief period as assistant engineer for the state of Virginia, he became chief engineer of the Valley Turnpike Company. In 1841 he became an agent for the Tredegar Iron Works in Richmond and by 1848 was the owner. While directing the growing company, which manufactured locomotives for Southern railroads as well as ordnance and machinery for the federal government, he became interested in public affairs, serving in the legislature from 1852 to 1855. When secession appeared imminent in 1860 Anderson contracted to supply ordnance to several Southern state militias and obtained a brigadier general's commission in the Confederate army. He took part in the Peninsular Campaign and performed creditably, but in July 1862 he resigned to return to the Tredegar Works, whose importance to the Confederacy was such as to have been largely responsible for Richmond's becoming the capital. For most of the war, Tredegar was virtually the only producer of heavy artillery for the Confederacy and also manufactured most of the other Confederate ordnance, along with railroad and naval equipment. In the face of seemingly insuperable difficulties with manpower, materials, transportation, and money, Anderson maintained Tredegar's output until the fall of Richmond in April 1865. The works were confiscated and held by the U.S. government until 1867, when the company was reorganized with Anderson as president. He retained that post, except during 1876–1878 when Tredegar was in receivership, until his death on one of the Isles of Shoals, New Hampshire, on September 7, 1892.

Anderson, Margaret (1893?–1973), editor. Born in Indianapolis about 1893, Miss Anderson grew up in a middle-class atmosphere that she rejected at the earliest possible moment. While still in her teens she traveled to Chicago, determined to make the richest life she could for herself, and found the means in the arts. In 1914 she founded the *Little Review*, a magazine of the arts that announced itself as devoted to "Life for Art's sake" and that succeeded in becoming foremost in its field. With her long-time associate, Jane Heap, Miss Anderson managed to publish the magazine regularly with no ascertainable resources and to attract the best writers in the country, although they were paid nothing. As the organ of the "Chicago school," the *Little Review* published contributions by Carl Sandburg, Maxwell Bodenheim, Ben Hecht, and Sherwood Anderson, among others, and dealt with movements ranging from anarchism to psychoanalysis to feminism and with thinkers from Neitzsche to Bergson to Emma Goldman. Miss Anderson excelled as a literary impresario, and by a combination of luck, energy, and a fascination with anything novel,

she produced a magazine of legendary quality. Once, to protest the temporary lack of exciting new works, she issued 64 blank pages between covers. Other writers who contributed to the *Review* included William Carlos Williams, Amy Lowell, Ford Maddox Ford, Wallace Stevens, and Malcolm Cowley. In 1917 Ezra Pound became foreign editor and through his influence the *Review* published works by William Butler Yeats, T. S. Eliot, Hart Crane and James Joyce, whose *Ulysses* was serialized beginning in 1918, when the magazine moved to New York City. Four issues were seized and burned by postal authorities during the three-year serialization of *Ulysses* and the matter became a cause célèbre when a charge of obscenity was sustained in court. In 1924 Miss Anderson moved to Paris and the *Little Review* was published until 1929, championing Cubism, Dada, and Surrealism. She published three volumes of autobiography—*My Thirty Years' War*, 1930; *The Fiery Fountains*, 1950; and *The Strange Necessity*, 1969—before her death at Le Cannet, France, on October 18, 1973.

Anderson, Marian (1902–   ), singer. Born on February 17, 1902, in Philadelphia, Miss Anderson displayed vocal talent as a child, but her family could not afford to pay for formal training. From the age of six she was tutored in the choir of the Union Baptist Church, where she sang parts written for bass, alto, tenor, and soprano voices. Members of the congregation raised funds for her to attend a music school for a year. At nineteen she became a pupil of Giuseppe Boghetti, who was so impressed by her talent that he gave her free lessons for a year. In 1925 she entered a contest with 300 competitors and won first prize, a series of recitals including one in New York City with the New York Philharmonic Orchestra. Although many concert opportunities were closed to her because of her race, she toured black Southern college campuses and appeared at New York City's Town Hall. In 1933 she made a successful European tour. Still relatively unknown in the United States, she received scholarships to study abroad and appeared before the crowned heads of Sweden, Norway, Denmark, and England and sang at the Salzburg music festival in 1935. On hearing her sing, the Finnish composer Jean Sibelius wrote "Solitude" for her. Her pure vocal quality and tremendous range made her, in the opinion of many, the world's greatest contralto. In 1939 she attempted to rent concert facilities in Washington's Constitution Hall owned by the Daughters of the American Revolution (DAR), but was refused because of her race. This produced widespread protest from many people, including Eleanor Roosevelt, who resigned from the DAR. Arrangements were made for Miss Anderson to appear at the Lincoln Memorial on Easter Sunday, and she drew an audience of 75,000. She was awarded the Spingarn Medal for high achievement by a member of her race in 1939 and she received the $10,000 Bok Award in 1940. By 1941 she and Paul Robeson were the highest-paid black concert artists in the country. On January 7, 1955, she became the first Negro to perform at the Metropolitan Opera in New York City. Before she began to sing her role of Ulrica in Verdi's *The Masked Ball*, she was given a standing ovation by the audience. In 1957 she made a 12-nation, 35,000–mile tour that was sponsored by the Department of State, the American National Theatre and Academy, and Edward R. Murrow's television series "See It Now." Her role as a goodwill ambassador for the United States was formalized in September 1958 when she was made a delegate to the United Nations. Miss Anderson was awarded the Presidential Medal of Freedom in 1963 by President Lyndon B. Johnson, and she was the recipient of numerous honorary degrees. She made farewell tours of the world and the United States in 1964–1965.

Anderson, Maxwell (1888–1959), playwright. Born on December 15, 1888, in Atlantic, Pennsylvania, Anderson received his B.A. from the University of North Dakota in 1911 and his M.A. from Stanford in 1914. He taught school in North Dakota and California and began a career in journalism in those states, then worked on newspapers in New York City until the success of his first play, *White Desert*, in 1923. Thenceforth he devoted himself to the drama. His themes were philosophical, portraying the dual existence of both good and evil in men. His dramas were consistently provocative and outstanding. With Laurence Stallings he wrote *What Price Glory?*, 1924, a World War I drama; *First Flight*, 1925, about the youth of Andrew Jackson; and *The Buccaneer*, 1925, about the pirate Sir Henry Morgan. Turning to verse drama, he drew upon history for *Elizabeth the Queen*, 1930. *Both Your Houses*, a political satire in prose, won a Pulitzer Prize in 1933. Anderson returned to verse in a series of notable dramas, including *Mary of Scotland*, 1933; *Valley Forge*, 1934; *Winterset*, 1935, inspired by the Sacco–Vanzetti case; and *High Tor*, 1936. *Winterset* and *High Tor* won New York Drama Critics' Circle Awards. Other plays included *The Star Wagon*, 1937; *Knickerbocker Holiday*, 1938, a musical written with Kurt Weill; *Key Largo*, 1939; *Anne of the Thousand Days*, 1948; and *Barefoot in Athens*, 1951. Anderson's work was generally acclaimed by critics, but he shared with other playwrights a dislike for the traditional role of the critic in determining the fate of a play. He was one of the founders of the Playwrights Company in 1938. One of his last works was the adaptation for the stage in 1954 of William March's novel *The Bad Seed*; the play was the basis of the Academy Award-winning movie of 1957. Anderson died on February 28, 1959, in Stamford, Connecticut.

Anderson, Rasmus Björn (1846–1936), educator and businessman. Born on January 12, 1846, in Albion, Wisconsin, Anderson graduated from Luther College in 1866. After three years of teaching Greek and modern languages at Albion

Academy he joined the faculty of the University of Wisconsin, where until 1883 he was professor of Scandinavian languages and literature. From 1885 to 1889 he served as U.S. minister to Denmark. In 1895 he became president of the Wisconsin Life Insurance Company, a position he held until 1922, and from 1904 until his death he was president of the Wisconsin Rubber Company. His major achievement, however, was in his writings and translations, which brought to the public a new awareness of Scandinavian life, history, and contributions to America. Among his works were *America Not Discovered by Columbus*, 1874; *Norse Mythology*, 1875; *Viking Tales of the North*, 1877; and *The Younger Edda*, 1880. From 1898 to 1922 he was publisher and editor of the Scandinavian weekly *Amerika*. His autobiography appeared in 1915. He died in Madison, Wisconsin, on March 2, 1936.

Anderson, Sherwood (1876–1941), author. Born in Camden, Ohio, on September 13, 1876, Anderson grew up in poverty and at fourteen left school for a succession of petty jobs that eventually took him to Chicago. In 1898 he joined the National Guard and served for a while in Cuba; in 1899 he returned and spent a year in a preparatory school. He became an advertising copywriter and in 1907 organized his own business, a small paint factory in Elyria, Ohio. After five years as a businessman, he suddenly moved back to Chicago and sought a literary life. He became a member of the Chicago circle of Carl Sandburg, Theodore Dreiser, Edgar Lee Masters, and Ben Hecht, contributed to Margaret Anderson's *Little Review* and other little magazines, and published his first two novels, *Windy McPherson's Son*, 1916, and *Marching Men*, 1917. In 1919 he published his most famous book, a collection of interrelated short stories and sketches entitled *Winesburg, Ohio*. This was followed by two similar volumes, *Poor White*, 1920, and *The Triumph of the Egg*, 1921; the three books constitute his best work and are the basis for his claim to lasting reputation. Returning to the novel form, he produced a number of social and autobiographical works, including *Dark Laughter*, 1925; *Tar, a Midwest Childhood*, 1926; *Beyond Desire*, 1932; and *Kit Brandon*, 1936; but these were distinctly minor efforts. His short stories were primarily concerned with the frustrations and narrowness of life in the small towns of the Midwest and the deforming effect of that life on human beings. In 1925 he moved to Marion, Virginia, and became the publisher of two country newspapers. He died while visting Panama on March 8, 1941. His *Memoirs* appeared posthumously in 1942, a collection of his letters in 1953.

Andreassen, Anders, *see* Furuseth, Andrew

Andretti, Mario Gabriel (1940–   ), automobile racer. Born on February 28, 1940, in Montona, Italy, Andretti early developed a love of cars and racing and was especially inspired by the great

Italian driver Alberto Ascari. Together with his brother he studied auto mechanics and, in spite of his family's disapproval, began racing formula junior cars. In 1955 he moved with his family to the United States, where they settled in Nazareth, Pennsylvania. He dropped out of high school, took a job in a garage, and raced in a number of stock-car events. In 1961 he decided to devote full time to racing, and after three seasons of midget and sprint-car racing had compiled a record sufficiently impressive to win professional backing. In 1964 he joined the United States Auto Club (USAC), the sanctioning authority for the most important U.S. races. A highly aggressive and confident driver, Andretti won the USAC national championship the next year after a season highlighted by a third-place finish in his first Indianapolis 500 race. The following year he again captured the USAC championship with wins in eight races, in one of which, the Atlanta 300, he performed the unprecedented feat of leading all the way from start to finish. In 1967 he tried his hand at big-time stock-car racing and won the top event, the Daytona 500; in that year, too, he was named Martini and Rossi Driver of the Year. In 1969 he added the Indianapolis 500 to his string of victories and again took the USAC title. After only a decade in the professional ranks Andretti was, by virtue of his winnings and the income from testimonials and test-driving contracts, one of the world's wealthiest sports figures.

Andrew, John Albion (1818–1867), public official. Born on May 31, 1818, in Windham, Maine, Andrew graduated from Bowdoin College in 1837. He moved to Boston, studied law, and in 1840 was admitted to the bar. While building up his practice he involved himself deeply in the antislavery movement and took part in a number of fugitive-slave cases. As an opponent of the Mexican War he was associated with the "conscience Whigs," and with them he joined the Free-Soil party in 1848. Six years later he was an organizer of the Republican party in Massachusetts and on their ticket was elected to the legislature in 1857. He came to wide public notice and popularity at the time of his vigorous defense in 1859 of John Brown of Harpers Ferry fame and his subsequent appearance before a Senate investigating committee in Washington. In 1860 he led the Massachusetts delegation to the Republican national convention in Chicago, and later in the year he was elected governor by the largest popular majority recorded in his state up to that time. Immediately upon taking office Andrew secured from the legislature an emergency appropriation for the raising and training of a substantial militia; as a result of his foresight, Massachusetts troops were the first to respond to President Lincoln's call for volunteers in April 1861 and were the first to arrive for the defense of Washington, D.C. One of the strongest and most effective of the Union war governors, he was reelected regularly until he retired from office

at the end of 1866. The achievement in which he took the greatest pride was winning authorization from Secretary of War Edwin M. Stanton to organize Negro troops in 1863; in May of that year the 54th Massachusetts Regiment became the first black unit (although it had white officers) to enter the war. In 1865 Andrew presided over the first national convention of the Unitarian Church. In 1866 he resumed his law practice and worked for the reform of divorce and usury laws. But the war years had worn him out, and he died in Boston on October 30, 1867.

Andrews, Charles McLean (1863–1943), historian. Born on February 22, 1863, in Wethersfield, Connecticut, Andrews graduated from Trinity College in 1884 and after two years as a high-school principal went on to The Johns Hopkins University, where he took his Ph.D. in 1889. He joined the faculty of Bryn Mawr College and taught there until 1907, when he returned to Johns Hopkins; in 1910 he moved to Yale, with which he was associated for the rest of his career. His early work was in the field of European history and he published, among other books, *The Old English Manor*, 1892; the two-volume *Historical Development of Modern Europe, 1815–1897*, 1896–1898; *Contemporary Europe, Asia, and Africa, 1871–1901*, 1902; and *A History of England*, 1903, a text for schools. His interest shifted gradually to American colonial history, however, and he became recognized as preeminent in the field. He was a leader of the "imperial school," which held that the focus of colonial history ought to be not the colonies themselves but the mother country, England. This interpretation is developed in many of his books, including *Colonial Self-Government, 1652–1689*, 1904; *British Commissions, Councils, and Committees, 1622–1675*, 1908; *The Colonial Period*, 1912; *The Boston Merchants and the Non-Importation Movement*, 1917; *Fathers of New England*, 1919; *Colonial Folkways*, 1919; *The Colonial Background of the American Revolution*, 1924; and the four-volume *Colonial Period of American History*, 1934–1937, the first volume of which won a Pulitzer Prize in 1935. Andrews also published a number of highly useful guides to documentary materials on colonial America in British archives. In 1924–1925 he was president of the American Historical Association. He retired from his Yale professorship in 1931 but continued for two years to edit the Yale Historical Publications series. He died in New Haven, Connecticut, on September 9, 1943.

Andrews, Frank Maxwell (1884–1943), air force officer. Born on February 3, 1884, in Nashville, Tennessee, Andrews graduated from West Point in 1906 and was commissioned in the cavalry. After service in Hawaii and the Philippines he transferred to the new aviation section of the Signal Corps in 1917 and by 1919 was a lieutenant colonel. In the post-World War I years he served in Germany, at Kelly Field in Texas, and with the General Staff. In 1935 he was given the rank of brigadier general and named commander of General Headquarters Air Force, the first U.S. independent strategic air unit. The successful organization of that unit, which was succeeded by the Army Air Corps of World War II, was credited to him, as was a large role in the development of the B-17 bomber. In the early years of World War II he was stationed in the Caribbean, first as air commander and later as commander in chief of the entire theater, the first air officer to achieve that status. In 1941 he was promoted to lieutenant general and in February 1943 was made commander of all U.S. forces in Europe, replacing Gen. Dwight D. Eisenhower, who had been sent to North Africa as Supreme Allied Commander. A short time later, on May 3, 1943, Andrews was killed in an airplane accident in Iceland.

Andrews, Roy Chapman (1884–1960), naturalist and explorer. Born in Beloit, Wisconsin, on January 26, 1884, Andrews graduated from Beloit College in 1906 and immediately took a job with the American Museum of Natural History in New York City. For eight years thereafter he specialized in the study of whales, making trips to Alaska in 1908 and 1913, to the East Indies as the museum's representative on the voyage of the *Albatross* in 1909–1910, and to Korea and Japan in 1911 and 1912. In the course of those years he became the world's foremost cetologist. In 1914 Andrews was made the head of the museum's division of Asian exploration and from then until 1932 he led a number of expeditions into Korea, Manchuria, Tibet, China, Central Asia, Borneo, and Burma. He was particularly interested in the largely unexplored and uncharted Gobi region of Central Asia, where on one trip he found perfectly preserved dinsosaur eggs. Other discoveries of his various expeditions included new geological formations, rich fossil fields, and remains of the *Baluchitherium*, the largest known land mammal. From 1935 until his retirement at the end of 1941, he was director of the museum. He wrote a number of popular books describing his work, including *Whale Hunting with Gun and Camera*, 1916; *Camps and Trails in China*, 1918; *Across Mongolian Plains*, 1921; *On the Trail of Ancient Man*, 1926–1927; *Ends of the Earth*, 1929; *The New Conquest of Central Asia*, 1933; *This Amazing Planet*, 1940; and *Heart of Asia*, 1951. *Under a Lucky Star*, 1943, *An Explorer Comes Home*, 1947, and *Beyond Adventure*, 1954, were largely autobiographical. Andrews died in Carmel, California, on March 11, 1960.

Andrews, Stephen Pearl (1812–1886), social reformer and philosopher. Born in Templeton, Massachusetts, on March 22, 1812, Andrews moved to New Orleans when he was nineteen, studied law, and was admitted to the bar. A zealous abolitionist, he devised a plan for freeing slaves that involved the establishment of a government-managed fund for their purchase. In 1839 he moved to the Republic of Texas, but his abolitionism aroused the ire of his Houston neighbors and in 1843 he and his family were forced to flee. Andrews then sailed to England and attempted to secure backing from the British government for his manumission fund. Failing in that because of diplomatic pressure from Texas, he became interested in the new method of shorthand writing devised by Sir Isaac Pitman, and upon his return to the United States he opened a shorthand school in Boston. He soon moved to New York and embraced spelling reform, which he tried to popularize by editing two magazines printed in a phonetic alphabet. With A. F. Boyle he published two textbooks on shorthand, *The Comprehensive Phonographic Class-Book* and *The Phonographic Reader*, both in 1845. He was also interested in promoting the study of languages—he was said to be master of 32—and published a Chinese text in 1854 and a *Primary Grammar of Alwato*, an international language he devised himself, in 1877. By far his most ambitious work was *The Basic Outline of Universology*, 1877, in which he attempted to construct a comprehensive, deductive science of the universe. "Pantarchy," the social scheme he outlined in the book, was a semianarchistic system that enjoyed a certain vogue that drew him into the leadership of various related radical movements. Still firm in the belief that he had paved the way for an imminent reformation of society, Andrews died in New York City on May 21, 1886.

Andros, Sir Edmund (1637–1714), colonial governor. Born in London on December 6, 1637, Andros was of the feudal aristocracy of the island of Guernsey. He was reared as a page in the royal household and soon after the Restoration began to win preferment. After military service in the West Indies he acquired extensive holdings in the Carolinas and in 1674 succeeded his father as royal bailiff of Guernsey. In the same year he was appointed governor of New York by his friend and patron, the Duke of York. His administration was efficient but he was lacking in sympathy and tact and he was recalled in 1681. He was still favored by the king, however, and was knighted. Chosen largely for his military abilities in the face of pressing needs for defense against the Indians and the French, he returned to America in 1686—the Duke of York having acceded to the throne as James II—as governor of the Dominion of New England, a province newly formed by the consolidation of the colonies of Massachusetts, Maine, Plymouth, Connecticut, Rhode Island, and New Hampshire. The traditions of local and popular government, already deeply rooted, were brusquely ignored under Andros, provoking widespread resentment. The new governor's conservative and aristocratic manner, along with his imposition of the Anglican form of worship in Congregational Boston and his vigorous enforcement of unpopular laws and taxes, further alienated the colonists. By 1688, when New York and the Jerseys were added to the Dominion, plans were being made by colonial leaders in Boston, notably Cotton Mather, to rebel. When news came of the events of 1688 in England—the landing of William of Orange and the flight of James II—the Bostonians rose up and arrested Andros and many other officials. He was sent to England for trial and the former colonies resumed self-government. Acquitted and still in royal favor, Andros was appointed in 1692 governor of Virginia, a post he filled capably until 1697. In later years he served as lieutenant governor of Guernsey, 1704–1706. He died in London on February 24, 1714.

Anfinsen, Christian Boehmer (1916–   ), biochemist. Born in Monessen, Pennsylvania, on March 26, 1916, Anfinsen attended Swarthmore College and the University of Pennsylvania before receiving a Ph.D. from Harvard in 1943. After World War II he did research at the Medical Nobel Institute in Stockholm before accepting, in 1948, a post in biological chemistry at Harvard Medical School. In 1950 he began a long association with the National Institutes of Health in Bethesda, Maryland; he served as chief of the laboratory of cellular physiology and metabolism of the National Heart and Lung Institute for 12 years, and then returned to Harvard for a year as professor of biochemistry. In 1963 he was appointed head of the chemical biology laboratory of the National Institute of Arthritis and Metabolic Diseases. His book, *The Molecular Basis of Evolution*, was published in 1959. In the early 1950s Anfinsen directed his research toward answering some of the fundamental questions about the chemical basis of life. Concentrating on an analysis of protein structure, especially the enzyme ribonuclease, he was able to obtain knowledge of how the enzyme was formed in a living cell and to make intelligible the relationship between the structure of proteins and their genetic function. His work established him as one among only a handful of experts in the field and bridged a wide gap in the knowledge of the chemistry of living organisms. In 1972 he shared, with Stanford Moore and William H. Stein, the Nobel Prize for Chemistry for his contribution to the study of enzymes.

Angell, James Burrill (1829–1916), educator, diplomat, and journalist. Born on January 7, 1829, near Scituate, Rhode Island, Angell graduated in 1849 from Brown University, then under the progressive administration of Francis Wayland. After graduation he journeyed through the South, coming into contact with the workings of slavery, and then worked briefly as a civil engineer. He spent nearly two years in Europe, studying modern languages and literature, and in 1852 was invited by Wayland to join the faculty of Brown. In 1853 he introduced a course in modern languages, but after Wayland's resignation in 1855 and the university's return to a conservative curriculum, he turned to other occupations. Angell contributed to the *North American Review*, revised and edited Chambers's *Handbook of French*

Literature in 1857, and wrote editorials for the *Providence Journal*, of which be became editor in 1860. With the *Journal* until 1866, he was an unwavering Unionist and a strong supporter of President Abraham Lincoln, and he exhibited a flair for understanding and writing about world politics and matters involving international law. He was unsuccessful in attempts to buy the paper, however, and in 1866 accepted the presidency of the University of Vermont. There he succeeded in making substantial improvements in the impoverished institution. In 1871 he was elected president of the University of Michigan, in Ann Arbor, where he developed further his concepts of the relationships of the state university to the state and to the larger academic world. He also taught international law and the history of treaties, was dean of the College, and served as the registrar. He instituted lasting changes in the curriculum, raised academic standards while making the university more accessible to prospective students, and effectively promoted improved secondary education in the state. His attempts to separate the school into a basic two-year junior university and a more advanced two-year university and to broaden the graduate program were too far ahead of his time to be accepted. He was named U.S. minister to China by President Rutherford B. Hayes in 1880 and was charged with negotiating a new immigration treaty; he retained the post until 1881 and then returned to his university duties in Ann Arbor. In 1897 President William McKinley appointed him minister to Turkey, where he served for a year. A founder of the American Historical Association in 1884, he was its president in 1893–1894. He retired from the presidency of the university in 1909 and died in Ann Arbor on April 1, 1916.

Ann, Mother, *see* Lee, Ann

Anson, Adrian Constantine (1851–1922), "Cap," baseball player and manager. Born on April 11, 1851, in Marshalltown, Iowa, Anson first came to notice in 1871 when the Philadelphia Athletics of the National Association (predecessor of the National League) acquired him from a baseball team in Rockford, Illinois. He remained with the Athletics from 1872 through 1875, playing every position except pitcher. In 1876 his friend Albert G. Spalding, a pitcher for Boston, became manager of the Chicago club of the newly organized National League and signed Anson as player and captain. Anson succeeded Spalding as manager in 1879 and thereafter played mostly at first base, although he even pitched a few games. He won league batting championships in 1879, 1881, 1887, and 1888, and during 27 playing seasons—the longest career of any major-leaguer—compiled a lifetime batting average of .339, amassing over 3500 hits (a record that put him in third place on the all-time list, behind Ty Cobb and Stan Musial). "Cap," as he was called until he became "Pop" in his later years, steered the Chicago club to league pennants in 1880, 1881, 1882, 1885, and 1886, and he took his team on a world tour in 1889–1890, playing exhibition games against a team made up of other National League players. He retired from the Chicago club in 1897 and, after a year as non-playing manager of a New York team, left baseball for good. From 1905 to 1907 he served in the elected post of clerk of the city of Chicago, where he lived until his death on April 14, 1922. He was elected to the National Baseball Hall of Fame in 1939.

Anthony, Susan Brownell (1820–1906), social reformer. Born to a Quaker family in Adams, Massachusetts, on February 15, 1820, Miss Anthony grew up independent, strong-willed, and extremely severe in her moral outlook. She received an unusually good education for a woman of her time, and from 1835 to 1849 she taught school in New York State. Returning home in 1850, she became acquainted with the circle of leading abolitionists who met regularly in her father's home; she also met the women who were to be her companions in the woman-suffrage movement—Elizabeth Cady Stanton, Lucretia Mott, Amelia Bloomer, and Lucy Stone. In 1852 her first efforts to work actively for temperance were rebuffed because of her sex, whereupon she organized a separate temperance group for women. From 1856 until the Civil War she was an agent for the American Anti-Slavery Society. She was an early advocate of Negro suffrage and attempted to have the Fourteenth Amendment extended to include women. From 1868 to 1870 she helped publish a radical New York City weekly, the *Revolution*. In November 1872 she challenged the law by voting; before she was brought to trial she voted again the following March. Although she was convicted, she steadfastly refused to pay the fine imposed. As an officer of the National Woman Suffrage Association from its founding in 1869 and as vice-president and president of the National American Woman Suffrage Association from 1890 until 1900, Miss Anthony wrote and lectured ceaselessly, both in the United States and Europe, in the face of constant opposition, ridicule, and vituperation; and she organized associations to promote her cause throughout the world. She died in Rochester, New York, on March 13, 1906. She was elected to the Hall of Fame in 1950.

Antin, Mary (1881–1949), author. Born in Polotsk, Russia, in 1881, Miss Antin emigrated to the United States with her parents in 1894. She studied at Teachers College and Barnard College of Columbia University from 1901 to 1904. Her first book about her experiences as an immigrant, *From Polotzk to Boston*, was written in Yiddish; it was published in an English translation in 1899. Her subsequent books, *The Promised Land*, 1912, and *They Who Knock at Our Gates*, 1914, also dealt with immigrants, their hopes, characters, and experiences. In 1901 she married Amadeus William Grabau, a paleontologist and professor at Columbia University. She lectured for a number of years on the subject of immigration and campaigned against proposals in Congress to adopt restrictive immigration legislation. She was widely acclaimed for her efforts to secure understanding and the realization of the American promise for the immigrant. She died in Suffern, New York, on May 15, 1949.

Anza, Juan Bautista de (1735– ?), explorer and colonial official. Born in Fronteras, Mexico, in 1735, Anza joined the Spanish army at an early age and in 1760 became captain of the presidio at Tubac, south of the present Tucson, Arizona. Following the founding of Mission San Carlos Borromeo at Monterey, California, in 1770, Anza conceived the idea of bringing supplies to it by land rather than by sea. With permission from Antonio M. Bucareli, viceroy of New Spain, he set out from Tubac early in 1774 and, after much hardship in the Colorado Desert, reached first Mission San Gabriel and then Monterey. Soon after his return to Tubac he was promoted to lieutenant colonel for establishing a land route to Spain's northern outposts and thus helping to secure them against Russian and English advances. In 1775 Anza again left Tubac with a large party, bearing instructions to explore and secure the region around San Francisco Bay. He reached his goal in the spring of 1776, chose a site for a settlement, and set out for Mexico City, leaving his subordinate, Lt. José Joaquin Moraga, to actually found, on September 17, 1776, the presidio around which San Francisco was to grow. The Mission San Francisco de Asís (later known as Mission Dolores) was established shortly afterward, on October 9. The following year Anza was made governor of New Mexico; in 1788 he was relieved of the office and no further record of him has been found.

Apostle to the Indians, *see* Eliot, John

Appleby, John Francis (1840–1917), inventor. Born in Westmoreland, New York, on May 23, 1840, Appleby was the son of English immigrant parents who in 1845 moved to a farm in Wisconsin. There he received an elementary education while working on the farm. One day in 1859, when he was still only eighteen, the idea of a mechanical binder came to him as he was busy binding sheaves as they came from a new reaper. He built a working model of a twine knotter but had no money with which to pursue the project. He served in the Union army during the Civil War and while at Vicksburg devised a magazine and automatic feeder for rifle cartridges; with $500 from the sale of this invention, patented in 1864, he returned home to develop his binder. In 1872 he unveiled a wire binder that was, however, rejected by farmers who mistrusted wire. In 1874 he oragnized the Appleby Reaper Works and continued to work on his twine binder. Two years later he succeeded and produced a knotter and binder which were patented in 1878 and 1879. Manufacturing licenses were sold to leading producers of reapers and the Appleby knotter came into general use throughout the world. He died at Mazomanie, Wisconsin, on November 8, 1917.

Applegate, Jesse (1811–1888), surveyor, cattleman, and author. Born in Kentucky on July 5, 1811, Applegate grew up in Missouri. Following a period of study at Rock Spring Seminary in Illinois, he taught school and then became a clerk in the surveyor general's office in St. Louis. He advanced to deputy surveyor general and until 1843 also farmed and did field work in Missouri. In that year he joined the movement westward, leading the cattle column of an Oregon-bound wagon train. His description of the experience, "A Day with the Cow-Column," 1876, became a classic in the literature of Western settlement. In 1845 he led the party that opened the southern route into Oregon. A capable and persuasive writer and a powerful personality, Applegate became a political leader in Oregon. He reorganized the pre-territorial provisional government and succeeded in unifying the English and American settlements in the region. He was successful at raising cattle on his ranch in Yoncalla, from which he wrote occasional newspaper essays on public issues. Politically a Whig and then, with the dissolution of that party, a Republican, Applegate was an influential supporter of President Abraham Lincoln and the Union. He died in Oregon on April 22, 1888.

Appleseed, Johnny, see Chapman, John

Appleton, Victor, see Stratemeyer, Edward

Arcaro, George Edward (1916–   ), "Eddie," jockey. Born in Cincinnati on February 19, 1916, Arcaro grew up there and in Southgate, Kentucky. He entered his first race in 1931 but it took 45 more outings before he rode his first winner, Eagle Bird, early in 1932. In 1935 he rode in the first of his 21 Kentucky Derbies on Nellie Flag; three years later he won the Derby on Lawrin and went on to establish a record by finishing first four more times—in 1941, 1945, 1948, and 1952—in the most famous U.S. horse race. He won the other two stakes classics for three-year-olds, the Preakness Stakes and the Belmont Stakes, six times each; and in 1941, on Whirlaway, and in 1948, on Citation, he swept the Triple Crown, the first jockey to win all three races twice. In 31 years of riding Arcaro entered more than 24,000 races and won 4779, a total surpassed only by Johnny Longden and England's Sir Gordon Richards. His mounts won more than $30 million in prize money, and Arcaro's share of about ten percent amounted to a considerable fortune. He retired from the track in 1962 and thereafter devoted himself to various business interests.

Arden, Elizabeth (1884–1966), businesswoman. Born on December 31, 1884, in Woodbridge, Ontario, Florence Nightingale Graham briefly pursued nurse's training, was a secretary, and held various other jobs before moving from Canada to New York City about 1908. She became assistant to a beauty specialist, Eleanor Adair, and in 1910 went into partnership with Elizabeth Hubbard in a beauty salon on Fifth Avenue, investing about $1000 in the venture. The partnership split up and Miss Graham decided to continue under the corporate name of Elizabeth Arden. In 1914 she hired chemists to produce a fluffy face cream and an astringent lotion, the first products in a cosmetics line which eventually included about 300 items. A pioneer in the advertising of beauty aids, she stressed her products' acceptable, "ladylike" qualities in an age when makeup and beauty aids were thought of mainly in connection with "low women." In 1915 she began to market her cosmetics internationally, selling them wholesale to pharmacies and department stores. As scrupulous as she was ambitious, she ruled over all aspects of her business, from the tone of advertisements to the names given her products. By the time of her death there were 100 Elizabeth Arden beauty salons throughout the world, offering hairdressing, facial treatments, exercise, steam baths, massage, manicures, pedicures, and many other luxury services. She operated Maine Chance beauty spas in Mount Vernon, Maine, and in Scottsdale, Arizona, where a one-week stay cost about $750. Her clientele included socialities, politicians, European royalty, and movie stars. One of the nation's foremost racehorse owners, she operated stables near Lexington, Kentucky from which came Jet Pilot, winner of the 1947 Kentucky Derby. She bolstered her own image of ageless beauty by successfully concealing her age, which was not divulged until her death on October 18, 1966, in New York City.

Arendt, Hannah (1906–1975), political scientist. Born on October 14, 1906, in Hannover, Germany, Miss Arendt grew up there and in Königsberg (now Kaliningrad, U.S.S.R.). She studied at the universities of Marburg, Freiburg, and Heidelberg, taking her Ph.D. in philosophy at Heidelberg in 1928. With the rise of the Nazi regime in 1933 she left Germany for Paris, where she continued to study and for four years did social work with Jewish orphans. In 1940 she came to the United States and ten years later became a citizen. From 1944 to 1946 she served as research director for the Conference on Jewish Relations and from 1946 to 1948 was chief editor of Schocken Books. During this period, and while serving as executive secretary of Jewish Cultural Reconstruction, 1949–1952, she published a number of articles that pointed toward her first major book, *The Origins of Totalitarianism*, 1951, in which she traced the roots of modern totalitarianism, particularly as manifested in Nazism and Communism, back to the imperialism and anti-Semitism of the nineteenth century. Miss Arendt was awarded a Guggenheim fellowship in 1952 and lectured at Princeton in 1952–1953. In 1955 she was at the University of California at Berkeley, and in 1956 she delivered the Walgreen Lectures at the University of Chicago. These were later published as *The Human Condition*, 1958. She became the first woman to hold full professorial rank at Princeton when she was appointed visiting professor of political science in 1959. She was visiting professor at Columbia in 1960; from 1963 to 1967 she was professor of political science at the University of Chicago, and in 1967 she joined the faculty of the New School for Social Research in New York City. Others of her books, in which a strain of pessimism was evident in her penetrating analyses of history and of political man, included *On Revolution*, 1963; *Eichmann in Jerusalem*, 1963; *Men in Dark Times*, 1968; *On Violence*, 1970; and *Crises of the Republic*, 1972. She died in New York City on December 4, 1975.

Arlen, Harold (1905–   ), composer. Born Hyman Arluck on February 15, 1905, in Buffalo, New York, Arlen was introduced to music at the age of seven by way of piano lessons and singing in a synagogue choir. By the age of fifteen he had organized a trio and was playing professional dates around Buffalo; with success the band grew to 15 pieces, and in 1927 the group made its way to New York City. The band did not last long, but Arlen soon found work as a pianist-arranger for the 1927 production of George White's *Scandals*. Other such jobs followed and in 1930, while rehearsing a musical, he dashed off a lively tune that attracted much attention; with lyrics by Ted Koehler, it became "Get Happy," a show-stopping hit in the *9:15 Review* that year. For the next four years he and Koehler wrote revues for the fashionable Cotton Club in Harlem, producing such songs as "I've Got the World on a String," "Between the Devil and the Deep Blue Sea" (introduced by Bill Robinson), "Stormy Weather" (introduced by Ethel Waters), and "I Love a Parade." During that period they also wrote for the 1930 and 1932 productions of Earl Carroll's *Vanities*, composing, most notably, "I Gotta Right to Sing the Blues." In 1933 Arlen and Koehler wrote the title song for *Let's Fall in Love*, their first film assignment. Arlen's "It's Only a Paper Moon," written with E. Y. Harburg and Billy Rose, was used in *The Great Magoo*, 1933. For the next several years Arlen was one of the busiest composers in show business. For Broadway he worked on, among other shows, *Life Begins at 8:40* ("You're a Builder Upper"), with Harburg and Ira Gershwin, 1934; *Cabin in the Sky* ("Happiness is a Thing Called Joe"), with Harburg, 1940; *Bloomer Girl* ("I Got a Song"), again with Harburg, 1944; *St. Louis Woman* ("Any Place I Hang My Hat Is Home," "Come Rain or Come Shine"), with Johnny Mercer, 1946; and *House of Flowers* ("A Sleepin' Bee"), with Truman Capote, 1954. For Hollywood he worked on *The Wizard of Oz* ("Somewhere Over the Rainbow"), with Harburg, 1939; and with Mercer on *Blues in the Night*, 1941; *Star Spangled Rhythm* ("That Old Black Magic"),

1942; *The Sky's the Limit* ("One for My Baby"), 1943; and *Here Come the Waves* ("Ac-cent-tchu-ate the Positive"), 1944. He continued to contribute songs to movies and musicals, notably *Jamaica*, 1957, which starred Lena Horne on Broadway, but his earlier compositions remained his most popular; many were revived on Broadway in *The Harold Arlen Songbook*, 1967. In 1971 he was among the first ten popular composers to be elected to the newly established Songwriters' Hall of Fame.

Arluck, Hyman, *see* Arlen, Harold

Armour, Philip Danforth (1832–1901), businessman. Born on May 16, 1832, in Stockbridge, New York, Armour was a miner, a farmer, and a wholesale grocer before entering the meat packing and grain business in Milwaukee with John Plankinton in 1863. During the last months of Civil War, confident that the price of pork would fall as Union victory approached, Armour went to New York City and offered barrels of pork at $30 to $40 for future delivery. When the price dropped, as he expected, he purchased for $18 what he had already sold at the higher prices and netted nearly $2 million. Returning to Milwaukee, he invested in a grain commission house opened in Chicago by his brother Herman. With the addition of a meat-packing plant, the firm was reorganized in 1870 as a partnership of Philip, Herman, and another brother, Andrew; in 1875 Philip moved to Chicago to assume control of the business. Among his pioneer ventures, soon to be imitated by competitors, were shipping live hogs to the Chicago stockyards for slaughtering, and using waste materials for innumerable by-products. With little competition, he made Chicago the major pork-packing city in the nation. He began to can meat and export it to Europe. With the development of refrigeration, he purchased his own railroad cars and shipped fresh meat to eastern cities, where he established distribution plants. Armour became known for his spectacular trades and winnings on the stock exchange. During 1898–1899 he became involved, along with other meat packers, in the "embalmed beef" scandals, arising from charges that chemically treated meat had been supplied to the armed forces, and fed to the troops. Protesting that graft, if it existed elsewhere, had never touched Armour and Company, he nevertheless did not recover from the shock of the charges and subsequent inquiries and died on January 29, 1901, in Pasadena, California. His wealth was estimated at $50 million at the time of his death. His son, J. Ogden, became president of the company upon his death. When J. Ogden retired in 1923, Armour and Company were the world's largest meat packers.

Armstrong Edwin Howard (1890–1954), engineer and inventor. Born in New York City on December 18, 1890, Armstrong was educated at Columbia University and before his graduation in 1913

had invented the regenerative or feedback circuit that virtually revolutionized the then still primitive field of radio. Similar and nearly simultaneous work by Lee De Forest and Irving Langmuir in the United States and Alexander Meissner in Germany led to patent litigation that was not settled until 1934, when in spite of Armstrong's apparent priority the Supreme Court decided the legal issue in favor of De Forest. After graduating, Armstrong remained at Columbia as an assistant to Michael I. Pupin. During World War I he served as a major in the Army Signal Corps in France and developed the superheterodyne circuit that greatly increased the selectivity and sensitivity of radio receivers over a wide band of frequencies and became the basic design for amplitude modulation (AM) radios. Returning to Columbia after the war, he went on to develop in 1920 the superregenerative circuit that came into wide use in short-wave police and amateur radio. In 1934 he assumed the professorship of electrical engineering vacated in 1931 by Pupin's retirement and held the chair for the rest of his life. Armstrong's greatest achievement was the result of several years of experimentation: in 1933 he demonstrated his system of frequency modulation (FM) radio transmission that completely eliminated static interference and that, by using a wider band than AM, made possible extremely high-fidelity broadcasts. It was six years before FM receivers were commercially available, by which time Armstrong had lost patience with the radio industry's slowness in exploiting the new medium and had built his own broadcasting station on the New Jersey Palisades. Much of his time in his remaining years was spent in litigation—with the Federal Communications Commission over licensing for FM stations, and with various companies in the industry over patent questions. His last major contribution to radio was a method of broadcasting more than one FM program on the same frequency, the multiplexing system that made possible the rental broadcast of background music to stores, restaurants, and factories and, later, the broadcast of programs in stereophonic sound. Major Armstrong, as he was usually called, took his own life on February 1, 1954, in New York City.

Armstrong, John (1755–1816), soldier and explorer. Born in New Jersey on April 20, 1755, Armstrong served with distinction in the Pennsylvania militia during the Revolution and in 1783–1784 was an officer in the force sent to quiet the Pennsylvania–Connecticut land-claims dispute in the Wyoming Valley of Pennsylvania. In 1784 he was given an army commission and sent to the Ohio frontier. In 1785–1786 he commanded Fort Pitt and during that period began the exploits and adventures that were to make him a near-legendary figure. In 1790 he was chosen to make secret explorations into Spanish territory to the west; little is known of his trip beyond the fact that he went alone and that, although he intended to follow the Missouri River and cross the

Rockies, as Meriwether Lewis and William Clark were to do 14 years later, he was forced by Indian wars to turn back some distance beyond St. Louis; he then explored much of what is now Indiana. Later in the same year he commanded the regulars in Gen. Josiah Harmar's expedition to pacify the Indians in the Maumee Valley; his escape after the militia deserted added to his reputation. He also took part in Gen. Arthur St. Clair's 1791 expedition against the Indians. In 1793 he resigned from the army and settled in Columbia, near Cincinnati, and three years later became treasurer of the Northwest Territory. In 1814 he moved to Armstrong's Station in what is now Indiana and died there on February 4, 1816.

Armstrong, John (1758–1843), soldier and public official. Born in Carlisle, Pennsylvania, on November 25, 1758, Armstrong entered the College of New Jersey (now Princeton) but left in 1775 to take part in the Revolution. He served with Gen. Hugh Mercer and Gen. Horatio Gates and was a major on Gates's staff at the end of the war. When Congress failed to appropriate money to pay its soldiers, discontent spread rapidly through the Continental army, particularly among the officers, and in March 1783 Armstrong circulated the unsigned "Newburgh Letters," urging the men to reject further promises and to take decisive action to force Congress to meet its obligations. The threat was ended by Gen. George Washington's speech to his officers on March 15. Armstrong returned to Pennsylvania and was appointed secretary to the state's Supreme Executive Council. In 1784 he commanded a militia force sent to the Wyoming Valley of Pennsylvania to quell a dispute over land claims between Pennsylvania and Connecticut settlers and in spite of, or perhaps because of, his unfair treatment of the Connecticut party, he soon became state adjutant general. He was elected to Congress in 1787. Two years later he moved to New York and, by his marriage to Alida, the sister of Robert R. Livingston, formed an alliance with the dominant political force in the state, among the leaders of which were George and De Witt Clinton. In 1800 the Republican victory of the Livingston–Clinton group brought Armstrong a Senate seat. He resigned in 1802 in favor of De Witt Clinton but resumed the seat in 1803 when Clinton became mayor of New York City. He resigned again in 1804 to succeed Livingston as U.S. minister to France. During six years in Paris he enjoyed little success and in fact failed to perceive a course of events in 1810 which led to war with England two years later. Armstrong won a brigadier general's commission and command of New York City when the War of 1812 broke out and in 1813 was appointed secretary of war by President James Madison. His administration of the War Department was mixed, but on balance it was a failure; he did well in promoting and supporting such officers as Winfield Scott and Andrew Jackson, but he shared responsibility for the disastrous Montreal campaign and especially for the fall of the city of Washington. He resigned under pressure in September 1814 and retired to his home in Red Hook, New York, where he died on April 1, 1843.

Armstrong, Louis Daniel (1900–1971), musician. Born on July 4, 1900, in New Orleans, Armstrong admired the cornet playing of Buck Jones as a child, but could not afford an instrument. At thirteen he was sent to the Colored Waifs' Home for Boys, a reform school, for firing a shot into a New Year's Day parade. There he found a cornet and taught himself to play it. He was leader of the reform-school band until his release 18 months later. Then he worked as a coalman, a milkman, and a rag-and-bones man, having persuaded his idol, Joe "King" Oliver, to give him cornet lessons in the evenings. When Oliver left for Chicago in 1917, Armstrong replaced him in Kid Ory's band. He joined Oliver's Creole Jazz Band in Chicago in 1922, and Fletcher Henderson's orchestra in New York in 1924. Nicknamed "Dippermouth" and later "Satchmo," short for "Satchelmouth," he introduced "scat" singing, using his gravelly voice as a musical instrument and singing nonsense syllables instead of words. In Chicago in 1925 with Erskine Tate's orchestra, he switched instruments and was often billed thereafter as the "World's Greatest Trumpeter." He formed his own band, the Hot Five, later the Hot Seven, in 1926. Their records, many now considered collector's items, were made with the finest jazz performers and blues singers of the time. Possessed of an instinctive musicianship, Armstrong did much to mellow the brass-band sound of early jazz. Whether in delicately melodious passages or in driving, raucous riffs, he displayed a genius for improvisation that inspired succeeding generations of jazzmen. Through the years "Satchmo" changed his style very little. His sure tone, endless capacity for creating new melodies, and lively, joyous quality brought an appreciation for New Orleans jazz to audiences throughout the world. He was also known as a comedian and movie performer after 1930. A jovial goodwill ambassador, he toured Europe in the 1930s and played before King George VI, to whom he dedicated a number with the words, "This one's for you, Rex!" Filmed highlights of his tour of Europe and Africa in 1956 were released under the title *Satchmo the Great*. His more famous recordings include "Shine," "Chinatown," "Tiger Rag," "Tight Like That," "Potato Head Blues," "When It's Sleepy Time Down South," "I Can't Give You Anything But Love," "Ain't Misbehavin'," "C'est si bon," and "I'll Walk Alone." His compositions include "Sister Kate" and "If We Never Meet Again." Armstrong died in New York City on July 6, 1971.

Armstrong, Neil Alden (1930–   ), astronaut. Born on August 5, 1930, near Wapakoneta, Ohio, Armstrong early developed an interest in aviation and received his pilot's license on his sixteenth birthday. In 1947 he entered Purdue University as a naval air cadet. Two years later he was called to active duty; during service in the Korean War he flew 78 combat missions and was awarded the Air Medal three times. Returning to Purdue, he graduated in 1955 and joined the staff of the National Advisory Committee for Aeronautics as a civilian test pilot. During the next seven years he tested several new types of aircraft, including the X-15 rocket plane, and in 1962 was accepted into the astronaut training program of the National Aeronautics and Space Administration (NASA). His first space flight came in March 1966 when he commanded *Gemini VIII*; he performed the first manual docking maneuver in space and successfully dealt with trouble in the thruster-control system that threatened to wreck the mission. On July 16, 1969, in command of *Apollo XI*, Armstrong, with astronauts Edwin Aldrin and Michael Collins, headed for the moon. Four days later he piloted the lunar landing module *Eagle* to the moon's surface, landing at the edge of the Sea of Tranquility. When he descended a ladder and set foot on the moon as an automatic television camera beamed the event back to earth, he spoke the words, "That's one small step for a man, one giant leap for mankind." Armstrong and Aldrin, who had followed him onto the moon, set up scientific observations on the lunar surface before returning to the *Eagle* with a quantity of moon material for later study. The next day they rocketed back to the command ship, which had remained in lunar orbit, and began the return trip. After splashdown in the Pacific on July 24th they were met by President Richard M. Nixon on board the aircraft carrier *Hornet* before beginning an 18-day period of quarantine to guard against the possible consequences of dangerous microorganisms that they might have come in contact with on the moon. In 1970 Armstrong was appointed chairman of the Peace Corps National Advisory Council. In the same year he retired from the astronaut corps to become an administrator of NASA, but resigned the next year to join the faculty of the University of Cincinnati.

Armstrong, Samuel Chapman (1839–1893), educator. Born on January 30, 1839, on Maui in the Hawaiian Islands, Armstrong was the son of American missionaries. He studied at Oahu College and in 1860 entered Williams College, but soon left to accept a captain's commission in a New York regiment. He saw action at Gettysburg and elsewhere during the Civil War, and in 1864 was made colonel of the 9th Regiment, a unit of the newly organized Negro troops. He was successful in training and leading his men and at the end of the war he held the rank of brigadier general. Feeling a deep interest in the fate of the former slaves, he became an agent of the Freedmen's Bureau and in 1866 took charge of a Negro encampment at Hampton, Virginia. The need for educating the Negroes for their new life quickly became apparent, and, inspired by recollections of the Hilo Manual Labor School in his native

Hawaii, Armstrong persuaded the American Missionary Association and a number of private benefactors to provide funds to purchase a large estate in Hampton and establish the Hampton Normal and Agricultural Institute (now the Hampton Institute), opened in 1868. He spent the rest of his life as principal of the institute, building it into a great and influential school dedicated to both academic and vocational education. Armstrong died in Hampton on May 11, 1893.

Arno, Peter (1904–1968), cartoonist. Born on January 8, 1904, in New York City, Curtis Arnoux Peters entered Yale in 1922, but left two years later to make his way as an illustrator and designer under the name Peter Arno. He succeeded in selling a cartoon to the *New Yorker* in 1925 and his career was launched. He quickly became a regular contributor to the *New Yorker* and his cartoons became almost a trademark of the magazine. Rendered in a bold line and with telling accuracy in the suggestion of subtle nuances of attitude, they were bitingly satirical comments on the whims and foibles and aspirations of society, both café and high. The aesthete, the clubman, the dowager, the roué—all were skewered with the most graceful and sophisticated wit, to the immense delight of Arno's legion of admirers. His cartoons were collected in several books, including *Whoops Dearie*, 1927; *Hullabaloo*, 1930; *For Members Only*, 1935; *Man in the Shower*, 1944; *Sizzling Platter*, 1949; and *Hell of a Way to Run a Railroad*, 1957. Something of a bon vivant and socialite himself, Arno wrote a number of musical revues, enjoyed a number of one-man shows of his work, and in 1941 was voted the best-dressed man in America. He continued to contribute to the *New Yorker* and drew for many other periodicals and for advertisements until his death in Port Chester, New York, on February 22, 1968.

Arnold, Benedict (1741–1801), Revolutionary soldier and traitor. Born in Norwich, Connecticut, on January 14, 1741, to an eminent Rhode Island family, Arnold served at sixteen with the colonial militia in the French and Indian Wars. On his return home he completed an apprenticeship to a druggist and in 1762 moved to New Haven, where he operated a drug and book shop. The business prospered and he began investing in merchant voyages in the Canadian and West Indian trade. In April 1775 Arnold, who had been for some months captain of the local militia, set out immediately with his men on hearing of the battle of Lexington. When he reached Cambridge, Massachusetts, he proposed to the Committee of Safety an expedition to Fort Ticonderoga to capture ordnance stored there. He was commissioned colonel and dispatched on the mission, but soon encountered Ethan Allen, sent by Connecticut for the same purpose; they agreed to joint command of the merged expedition, although Allen assumed a measure of precedence. Ticonderoga was taken in May and Arnold embarked with his men on a rapid trip up Lake Champlain and captured St. Johns, Quebec. He then returned to Connecticut briefly, in part to attend to his personal affairs and in part because his successes had been somewhat ignored by Massachusetts authorities and by Congress. He was soon in Cambridge again, where he proposed to Gen. George Washington a march on Quebec city. He left with 700 men in September 1775, made a heroic journey through the Maine woods, and was joined before Quebec by a second force under Gen. Richard Montgomery, who had advanced from Ticonderoga, capturing Montreal en route. The attack on Quebec on the snowy night of December 31, 1775, was a failure; Montgomery was killed and Arnold, severely wounded, settled in for a seige, during which he was promoted by Congress to brigadier general. In the spring he was forced to retire by the approach of British reinforcements bound for Quebec and thence Albany, but he fought a brilliant retreat, inflicting heavy losses on a superior enemy force in a battle on Lake Champlain (October 1776) and thus succeeded in forestalling the invasion of New York. Spending the winter of 1776–1777 at home, Arnold came close to resigning his commission when, in February, Congress for political reasons promoted five brigadiers who were junior to him to major general. Washington prevailed upon him to remain in the army. In April his prompt and courageous action routed a British attack on Danbury, Connecticut, an exploit that forced Congress to promote him to major general, although his seniority was not restored. Washington had again to intervene personally to keep Arnold from resigning. In July he marched north to join Gen. Philip J. Schuyler above Albany to meet a British advance from Canada; with remarkable quickness he raised the siege of Fort Stanwix, sending Col. Barry St. Leger into hasty retreat, and swung back to Saratoga to join Gen. Horatio Gates in the two battles that ended Gen. John Burgoyne's advance. Arnold performed brilliantly in the second battle, on October 7, and was seriously wounded. His seniority was at last restored by Congress and, after recuperating from his wound, he was placed in command of Philadelphia in June 1778. There he led a highly social life and, in his attempts to keep up with the previous British occupiers of the city, incurred heavy debts, for his pay as a Continental officer could not support his style of life. He still had enemies in Congress, and they managed to bring a number of charges of impropriety against him; always sensitive to the slightest criticism, he responded to the charges with indignation. His marriage in April 1779 to Margaret (Peggy) Shippen, the daughter of a wealthy merchant who had earlier moved easily in Loyalist circles, probably increased his already growing disaffection with the American cause, for in May 1779 he initiated a secret correspondence with Sir Henry Clinton, the British commander in chief, in which he offered military information in return for a considerable sum of money. This first phase of the famous traitorous correspondence only lasted for a few months, ending in the fall of 1779 when Arnold apparently had reason to believe that the charges still pending against him would be dropped or nullified. He was finally court-martialed in December 1779 and most of the charges were dropped, but on two minor ones he had to undergo a mild reprimand by Washington. Evidently infuriated by this rebuke, he then reopened the correspondence with Clinton, providing much valuable information the extent of which was not known until the relevant British military papers were brought to the United States in the 1920s. Around June 1780 Arnold learned that he was to be appointed commandant of West Point, and in July of that year he proposed to betray that vital American fort to Clinton for £20,000. In September 1780 Maj. John André was sent by Clinton under a false flag of truce to arrange the details with Arnold. But André was captured more or less by accident, the plot was discovered through some papers hidden in his stocking, and Arnold fled to New York City on a British warship. André, who had disobeyed Clinton's orders and attired himself in civilian clothes, was hanged as a spy. Given the rank of brigadier general of provincial troops by the British, Arnold commanded marauding expeditions into Virginia in December 1780 and into Connecticut in September 1781. On the latter occasion he burned New London, an act that was never forgiven by his one-time neighbors, colleagues, and friends. In November 1781 he sailed for England. Given a small pension, he was widely scorned as a traitor and became deeply embittered. He engaged without success in trade in Canada and the West Indies until his death in London on June 14, 1801. His wife remained his loyal friend and supporter until the end.

Arnold, Henry Harley (1886–1950), "Hap," soldier and airman. Born on June 25, 1886, in Gladwyne, Pennsylvania, Arnold graduated from West Point in 1907 and was assigned to the infantry. He later transferred to the aviation section of the Army Signal Corps, and in 1911 received his pilot's license after taking instruction from Orville Wright. During World War I he served in Panama organizing air defenses, then was commanding officer at various airfields. In 1929 he graduated from the army's Command and General Staff School and in 1936 became assistant chief of the Army Air Corps; he became its chief two years later. Throughout the 1920s and 1930s Arnold was a leading advocate of military air power and supported Gen. William (Billy) Mitchell in pressing for increased appropriations, better equipment and training, and more independence for the service. With the approach of World War II he arranged for the training of military pilots at private flying schools, a program that Congress later approved and paid for. In 1941 he was promoted to major general and later to lieutenant general and named deputy chief of staff of the army, becoming the first air officer to serve on the general staff; and in 1942 he became commanding general of the Army Air Forces, being promoted to full general the next year. Serving also on the Allied combined chiefs of staff, he was instrumental in planning overall strategy. His major achievement, however, was in developing, refining, and successfully applying air power as both a strategic and tactical weapon. He planned the massive air strikes against Germany and later Japan, and in 1944 he took a major step toward the eventual creation of an air force independent of the other services by forming the 20th Air Force, which, unlike other such groups, was retained under his immediate command instead of being assigned to a theater or group commander, and which was used as an independent strike force. In December 1944 he was promoted to the five-star rank of general of the army; the commission was changed in 1949 to general of the air force, the first such rank ever conferred. In 1946 he retired to a farm near Sonoma, California, where he died on January 15, 1950.

Arnold, Thurman Wesley (1891–1969), lawyer. Born in Laramie, Wyoming, on June 2, 1891, Arnold graduated from Princeton in 1911 and three years later took his law degree from Harvard. He practiced for a short time in Chicago and then served in the artillery during World War I. In 1919 he returned to Laramie, resumed the practice of law, and took up sheep ranching. He also developed an interest in politics, serving in the state legislature in 1921 and as mayor of Laramie in 1923–1924, as well as an interest in teaching. He was a lecturer in law at the University of Wyoming from 1921 to 1926, and in 1927 he accepted the position of dean of the law college at West Virginia University. Three years later he joined the law faculty at Yale. During seven years there he served as counsel to the federal government for a number of New Deal programs, and in 1938 he entered full-time public service as U.S. assistant attorney general in charge of antitrust litigation. Between that year and 1943 he filed a total of 230 suits—a record number—involving monopoly or restraint of trade, not only against the common run of corporate targets but also against labor organizations, the American Medical Association, and, in what proved to be a landmark case, the Associated Press. In 1943 he was appointed to the U.S. Court of Appeals for the District of Columbia. Resigning in 1945, he organized the legal firm of Arnold, Fortas and Porter. In consonance with his Jeffersonian viewpoint, he took a special interest in cases involving personal liberty and civil rights. He was the author of several books, including the well-known *The Folklore of Capitalism*, 1937. He continued to practice law until his death in Alexandria, Virginia, on November 7, 1969.

Arp, Bill, *see* Smith, Charles Henry

Arrow, Kenneth Joseph (1921–   ), economist. Born in New York City on August 23, 1921,

Arrow graduated from the College of the City of New York (CCNY) in 1940 and after taking his M.A. the following year at Columbia joined the army air force for service in World War II. After his discharge he resumed the study of economics at Columbia, serving on the staff of the Cowles Commission for Research in Economics and accepting an appointment to the faculty of Stanford University in 1949, two years before receiving his Ph.D. from Columbia. By 1953 he had advanced to a full professorship at Stanford and was beginning to attract considerable notice in professional circles as a highly original and productive thinker in the field of mathematical economics. Dealing with abstract notions rather than with the more immediately practical concerns of "marketplace" economists, Arrow led in developing general approaches to such complex problems as the possibility of predicting trends from among the innumerable concrete options operating in the economy; outlining a coherent understanding of risk-taking; and evolving a theory of welfare. Outstanding among his achievements, and one with implications beyond economics, was his "impossibility theorem," by which he was able to demonstrate, in a brilliant and inventive mathematical proof, that a perfect system of democratic choice-making is in principle impossible. Arrow moved to Harvard in 1968 and in 1972 was awarded the Swedish National Bank's Nobel Memorial Prize for Economics, jointly with Sir John R. Hicks of Great Britain, for "pioneering contributions to general economic equilibrium theory and welfare theory." Among Arrow's published works were *Social Choice and Individual Values*, 1951; *Studies in Linear and Nonlinear Programming*, 1958; and *Essays in the Theory of Risk-Bearing*, 1971.

Arthur, Chester Alan (1829–1886), twenty-first president of the United States. Born on October 5, 1829, in Fairfield, Vermont, the son of an Irish immigrant who became a Baptist minister, Arthur lived in both the United States and Canada during his childhood. He graduated from Union College in Schenectady, New York, in 1848; then, while teaching school, he studied law, winning admission to the bar in 1854. His legal career in New York City was noted for two cases—one in which he secured the freedom of Negro slaves in New York who were traveling between two slave states, and another in which he secured equal rights for Negroes in seating and in service on city transportation. He threw himself into Republican politics, participating in the national convention of 1854, involving himself locally in partisan affairs, and serving under Gov. Edwin P. Morgan as engineer in chief of New York during the Civil War. Upon Morgan's retirement Arthur returned to his law practice, having distinguished himself as a competent executive. In 1871 he was appointed collector of customs for the port of New York by President Ulysses S. Grant. President Rutherford B. Hayes, bent on civil-service reform, removed Arthur from the post despite the fact that he had exercised prudence in this previously notorious patronage position; this removal won Senate approval in 1879. At the 1880 Republican convention he worked for the nomination of Grant for a third term. When James A. Garfield was nominated instead, Arthur was chosen as the vice-presidential nominee to placate the "Stalwart" faction of the party. After winning the election, he openly opposed President Garfield on the issue of New York patronage. When Garfield was assassinated in 1881 there was much consternation over Arthur's succession, in view of his reputation as a spoilsman. But in his inaugural address he assured the public that he would avoid party prejudice in his administration. To the amazement of his critics, he was true to his word. His selections for government office were irreproachable. He proceeded against post-office officials involved in the "star route" frauds, vetoed the 1882 Chinese exclusion act, strongly supported the Pendleton Act of 1883, which created a civil-service commission to regulate government hiring, and secured increased funds for national defense. In 1884, in the secret knowledge that he was dying, he declined to campaign vigorously and lost the nomination to James G. Blaine, who was defeated by Grover Cleveland despite Arthur's loyal support. Retiring to New York City, Arthur died on November 18, 1886.

Arthur, Timothy Shay (1809–1885), author and editor. Born near Newburgh, New York, on June 6, 1809, Arthur grew up there and in Baltimore. He did poorly in school but became an avid reader and this, combined with work as a watchmaker's apprentice, seriously damaged his eyesight. He was employed for a time as a clerk and then as a bank agent; then, about 1833, he began writing and thereafter held a succession of editorial posts with the *Baltimore Athenaeum*, the *Baltimore Saturday Visitor*, the *Baltimore Book*, the *Baltimore Literary Magazine*, and the *Baltimore Merchant*. He had for some time been contributing stories to various magazines when in 1841 he moved to Philadelphia and began devoting full time to writing. His stories, nearly always moralizing in tone, and, like his books, often reflecting his interest in the temperance movement, appeared regularly in *Godey's Lady's Book*, *Graham's Magazine*, and other periodicals, and in 1842 he published *Six Nights with the Washingtonians: A Series of Original Temperance Tales.* In 1845 he began the short-lived *Arthur's Ladies' Magazine* and published *Married and Single: Or Marriage and Celibacy Contrasted*, a work that cast discredit on the single state. *The Lady at Home*, 1847, and *The Maiden*, 1848, followed, and in 1850 he established the successful weekly *Arthur's Home Gazette* (after 1853 the monthly *Arthur's Home Magazine*), which he edited for the rest of his life. He published at other times several more magazines with varying success; they included *Children's Hour, Once A Month,* and *The Workingman.* Didactic stories and novels continued to issue from his pen and in 1854 he published his greatest success, *Ten Nights in a Barroom and What I Saw There*, a lurid tale of drunkenness and degradation that was second only to *Uncle Tom's Cabin* in sales and became a highly popular play as well. Among his many later books were *Three Years in a Mantrap*, 1872; *Woman to the Rescue*, 1874; and *The Strike at Tivoli Mills*, 1879, each concerned with the evils of strong drink. Arthur died in Philadelphia on March 6, 1885.

Asbury, Francis (1745–1816), religious leader. Born on August 20, 1745, near Birmingham, England, Asbury became a Methodist preacher after brief schooling. He traveled for four years as a preacher for the Wesleyan conference. In August 1771 he and other English preachers volunteered to become missionaries in America. Arriving in Philadelphia that October, he embarked on trips the next month through the colonies and, eventually, to the Mississippi territory. He was made superintendent of the American Methodists in 1772; succeeded in 1773 by Thomas Rankin, he wrangled with his new superior and was summoned back to England in 1775. But he refused to go, convinced of the inevitability of American independence, and was left as the only English missionary in New England at the outbreak of the Revolution. He united lay preachers under John Wesley's code and developed the system of circuit riders who traveled on horseback preaching to settlers on the Western frontier. A powerful preacher and excellent organizer, he conferred with Northern and Southern Methodists and established himself as leader of the organization in 1782. In 1784 Wesley sent Thomas Coke to act as joint superintendent of the recently organized Methodist Episcopal Church in America with him, but Asbury refused to accept second place without the assent of the preachers. Voted and consecrated superintendent, he called himself bishop and subordinated Coke to his rule. Thereafter he traveled thousands of miles every year, expanding three Methodist groups into a league of 412 societies and 214,235 adherents. He ordained more than 4000 ministers and established Methodism as one of the principal U.S. denominations, especially in the South. His journals and letters, published in three volumes in 1821, contain valuable materials for the social history of the early frontier. He died in Virginia after a long illness on March 31, 1816.

Ashburner, Charles Edward (1870–1932), engineer and public official. Born in 1870 in Bombay, India, the son of a British army officer, Ashburner was educated in England, France, and Germany and took a degree in engineering from the University of Heidelberg. He came to the United States around 1900 and for several years worked as an engineer on highway, river, and railroad projects. He also worked occasionally as an independent consultant and contractor and it was in that capacity that he was approached by the city council of Staunton, Virginia, about some needed dam repairs. Ashburner had the repairs done for less than a fifth of a local contractor's original estimate and as a consequence the city council created the post of city manager—the first to be established in the country—and gave Ashburner complete control of the city's affairs. In three years in the post, 1908–1911, he succeeded, despite difficulties, in defining and setting high standards for an entirely new form of municipal organization. He returned to engineering work until 1914, when he agreed to serve as city manager of Springfield, Ohio. By that time cities across the country were adopting the city-manager system in increasing numbers. Ashburner left Springfield in 1918 to become manager of Norfolk, Virginia, where he promoted a highly ambitious but in some respects disappointing plan of development. In 1923 he accepted the city manager's post in Stockton, California. He resigned in 1929 and returned to Norfolk, where he engaged in investment banking and the insurance business until his death on October 26, 1932.

Ashe, Arthur Robert, Jr. (1943–   ), tennis player. Born on July 10, 1943, in Richmond, Virginia, Ashe became interested in tennis at the age of eight. Through the intercession of a patron of promising young black players, who had assisted Althea Gibson several years before, he received a solid grounding in the game. By 1960 he had progressed enough to win the U.S. junior indoor singles title. He won the championship again in 1961 and after a year spent in special schooling in St. Louis he entered the University of California at Los Angeles in 1962 on a tennis scholarship. There, in addition to his regular varsity coaching, he received help from Richard (Pancho) Gonzales. He was named to the Davis Cup team in 1963. By the end of 1965 Ashe was the second-ranked player in the ratings of the U.S. Lawn Tennis Association, and the next year he won the National Collegiate Athletic Association (NCAA) singles and doubles titles. On graduating from UCLA in 1966 he joined the army reserve. His service left him ample time for tennis, and in 1968 he won the U.S. national men's singles championship at Forest Hills—the first American to have held the title in 13 years and the first black player to win it. He followed this feat with a dazzling performance at the first U.S. Open tournament later in the year, turning in a brilliant final set to win the championship. In 1969 he gave up his amateur standing and became a professional player. Noted for his powerful serve and his extraordinary composure on the court, Ashe was the first black player ever to rise to top ranking in men's competition. In 1975 he defeated the heavily favored Jimmy Connors to win the men's singles title at Wimbledon.

Ashley, William Henry (1778?–1838), fur trader and public official. Born about 1778 in Powhatan County, Virginia, Ashley was already a capable businessman when he moved to Missouri in 1802. For some twenty years he engaged in saltpeter and lead mining and gunpowder manufacturing. He became Missouri's first lieutenant governor in 1820 and brigadier general of militia in 1821. In 1822, in partnership with Andrew Henry, he began a fur-trading operation, leading trapping parties up the Missouri River to the Yellowstone country in 1822 and 1823. Troubles with hostile Indians forced the partners to abandon the river route and Henry withdrew from the business in 1824, but Ashley continued the trade, using overland transportation. He initiated one of the most colorful of early Western institutions, the rendezvous, where the trappers—by this time permanent wilderness denizens known as "mountain men"— would gather and trade their year's or two years' fur catch for supplies brought west by the company. Ashley himself led his supply and collection party from St. Louis in 1824, reaching the Green River the following spring and making the first voyage down that difficult waterway to the first rendezvous of the fur traders, held at Henry's Fork. After an expedition in 1826 that almost reached the Great Salt Lake, he retired from the fur trade. He had continued to be interested in politics in the meanwhile; he ran unsuccessfully for governor in 1824, for the Senate in 1829, and again for governor in 1836, but won election to the House of Representatives in 1831 and remained there until 1837. He died near Boonville, Missouri, on March 26, 1838.

Ashmun, Jehudi (1794–1828), colonial agent. Born in Champlain, New York, on April 21, 1794, Ashmun studied at Middlebury College for three years and then transferred to Burlington College (now the University of Vermont), from which he graduated in 1816. He was ordained in the Congregational Church and for two years headed the Maine Charity School in Hampden, Maine. After a brief period in Baltimore, he found a job in Washington, D.C., as editor of the Episcopal Church publication *Theological Repertory*. Ashmun became deeply interested in the work of the American Colonization Society, founded in 1817 and funded by Congress in 1819 to send contraband slaves and other Negroes from the United States to the African colony of Liberia, and in 1822 he was appointed by the government to accompany a party there. Upon his arrival he found the colony in dire straits, ravaged by disease, threatened by hostile tribesmen, and deserted by the Society's agents. He immediately decided to remain and, despite his own illness and the death of his wife, he succeeded in restoring order and organizing a defense against attack. His position was, however, unofficial and in 1823 a new agent arrived and attempted to undermine Ashmun's position. The newcomer, however, soon found Africa not to his liking and departed, and in 1824 an investigator for the society cleared Ashmun of a number of baseless charges and secured his appointment as agent. Ashmun remained in Liberia until his health failed in 1828; he sailed to the West Indies and then to Boston, where he died on August 25, 1828.

Asimov, Isaac (1920–   ), biochemist and author. Born on January 2, 1920, in Petrovichi, U.S.S.R., Asimov emigrated to the United States with his parents in 1923 and settled in Brooklyn. He took a degree in chemistry from Columbia University in 1939 and received his M.A. two years later; after working at the Naval Air Experimental Station in Philadelphia and serving in the army in 1945–1946, he returned to Columbia to take his Ph.D. in 1948. In the following year he joined the faculty of the Boston University Medical School as an instructor in biochemistry, becoming associate professor in 1955. From an early age he had felt the urge to write and his first published story, a science-fiction piece entitled "Marooned Off Vesta," appeared in *Amazing Stories* in 1939, while he was still an undergraduate. He continued to write and to publish with increasing frequency in all the major science-fiction magazines, and his first book, *Pebble in the Sky*, was issued in 1950. Others quickly followed, including *I, Robot*, 1950; *The Stars Like Dust*, 1951; *The Currents of Space*, 1952; *The Caves of Steel*, 1954; *The Naked Sun*, 1957; *Earth Is Room Enough*, 1957; and his *Foundation* trilogy—*Foundation, Foundation and Empire*, and *Second Foundation*, 1951–1953—which won a Hugo Award, the most prized in science fiction. After writing a biochemistry textbook with two of his colleagues at Boston University in 1952, Asimov developed a growing interest in science writing as well, and he became highly adept at explaining scientific concepts to the layman, often in amusing terms. Among such works were *The Chemicals of Life*, 1954; *Inside the Atom*, 1956; *Building Blocks of the Universe*, 1957; *The World of Nitrogen*, 1958; *The Living River*, 1959; *Life and Energy*, 1962; *The Human Brain*, 1964; and *Photosynthesis*, 1969. He also wrote science fiction and books on science for young people, as well as a highly varied collection of works on history, etymology, literature, the Bible, and other subjects. His rate of production was such that by the 1980s he had published more than 200 books. His later titles included *Asimov's Guide to Shakespeare*, 1970; *Asimov's Guide to Science*, 1972; *Asimov on Physics*, 1976; *The Thirteen Crimes of Science Fiction*, 1979.

Astaire, Fred (1899–   ), dancer and actor. Born in Omaha, Nebraska, on May 10, 1899, Astaire, originally Fred Austerlitz, was dancing almost as soon as he could walk. With his sister Adele he began touring in vaudeville in 1906 and they became an instant Broadway hit in Sigmund Romberg's musical *Over the Top*. A succession of increasingly popular shows followed, including *For Goodness' Sake, Apple Blossoms, Lady Be Good, Funny Face*, and *The Band Wagon*, and Fred and Adele were the toasts of New York and London. Adele married and left show business in 1932, and it was doubted by many that Fred could continue without her; but in 1933 he starred with Ginger Rogers in *Flying Down to Rio*, a movie that introduced both a dance called the Carioca and the most successful dance team in Hollywood history. Astaire and Rogers subsequently appeared in a string of movie classics—*The Gay Divorcee*, 1934; *Roberta*, 1935; *Top Hat*, 1935; *Follow the Fleet*, 1936; *Swing Time*, 1936; *Shall We Dance*, 1937; *Carefree*, 1938; and *The Story of Vernon and Irene Castle*, 1939. After 1939 Astaire, with other partners, continued to attract avid audiences to such films as *Damsel in Distress*, 1939; *Broadway Melody of 1940*, 1939; *Holiday Inn*, 1942; *You Were Never Lovelier*, 1942; *The Sky's the Limit*, 1943; *Blue Skies*, 1946; *Easter Parade*, 1948; *The Barkleys of Broadway* (in which Ginger Rogers returned), 1949; *Three Little Words*, 1950; *Let's Dance*, 1950; *Daddy Long Legs*, 1955; *Funny Face*, 1956; *Silk Stockings*, 1957; *Notorious Landlady*, 1962; and *Finian's Rainbow*, 1967. In 1949 he was given a special Academy Award for his unique contribution to motion pictures. In 1959 he appeared in a dramatic role in *On the Beach*, and he was often on television, his "Evening with Fred Astaire" in 1958 winning nine Emmy awards and leading to similar shows in 1959 and 1968.

Astor, John Jacob (1763–1848), businessman. Born on July 17, 1763, near Heidelberg, Germany, the son of a butcher, Astor left home at the age of seventeen, following the death of his mother and his father's remarriage. He knew how to read and write and had resolved, according to a story about him, never to cheat, gamble, or be idle. He earned money working on a timber raft, then sailed to England. There he joined a brother, saved money, and learned English in preparation for his intended journey to America. On his way in 1783, he befriended a German immigrant who was well versed in fur trading with the American Indians. By the time he reached New York City in 1784 he had settled on fur trading as his occupation. He owned his own shop by 1786. He traveled constantly to the nearby frontiers, made an arrangement in Montreal for importing furs after the Jay Treaty, and through his shrewd business sense was a prominent man in the industry by 1800, having amassed a fortune of $250,000. Subsequently he gained access to the foreign ports controlled by the East India Company and prospered enormously in trade at Canton and other places. He began also to invest in real estate in New York City. After the Louisiana Purchase he extended his trade into the West and in 1808 combined all of his holdings into the American Fur Company. His plans to control the entire fur trade in the Far West suffered unforeseen disasters and were halted by the War of 1812. But his real estate soared in value and during the war, especially after 1813, he loaned money to the government at enormous rates of interest. After the war he again attained dominance of the trade west of the Mississippi, but his ambitious plans were affected by Indian raids and a decline in the fur market. He sold his interests in 1834 and retired, the richest man in America, to manage his fortune. He died in New York City on March 29, 1848, leaving funds to establish the Astor Library, now part of the New York Public Library. The Astor family continued to acquire property and wealth and for the next three-quarters of a century was one of the most talked-about clans in the country. Some of its members attained distinction apart from their wealth. William Backhouse Astor (1792–1875) inherited both the estate and the reputation as the richest man in America from his father, the original John Jacob Astor. He added greatly to the family fortune by astute investments in New York City real estate and expanded the Astor Library. His grandson, John Jacob Astor IV (1864–1912), served ably in the Spanish-American War and experimented with various inventions, including a bicycle brake. He built the Astoria section of what later became the Waldorf-Astoria Hotel in New York City and died in the sinking of the *Titanic* on April 15, 1912. His cousin, William Waldorf Astor (1848–1919), established the British branch of the family. He built the Waldorf section of the Waldorf-Astoria Hotel and served as U.S. minister to Italy from 1882 to 1885, but by 1890 he had developed a strong distaste for the United States, largely because of his inability to realize his political ambitions, and in that year he went to England, becoming a British subject in 1899. He bought the *Pall Mall Gazette* and established the *Pall Mall Magazine*, restored ancient castles at great expense, and in 1916 was raised to the peerage as Baron Astor, becoming Viscount Astor the next year. His eldest son, Waldorf Astor (1879–1952), was elected to Parliament in 1910 and during World War I served as private secretary to Prime Minister David Lloyd George and as parliamentary secretary to the ministry of foods. In 1915 he bought *The Observer*. He succeeded to the title of Viscount Astor in 1919 and later served as chairman of the Royal Institute of International Affairs, from 1935 to 1949. He was the husband of Lady Nancy Astor. His younger brother, John Jacob Astor (1886–1971), also enjoyed a political career, as aide-de-camp to the viceroy of India, 1911–1914, and as a member of Parliament. In 1912 he became the chief owner of the London *Times*. He was created a baron in his own right in 1956.

Atchison, David Rice (1807–1886), lawyer and public official. Born in Frogtown, Kentucky, on August 11, 1807, Atchison graduated from Transylvania University in 1828 and, although intended by his parents for the ministry, took up the study of law. He was admitted to the Kentucky bar in 1830 but soon thereafter moved to Missouri, where he practiced law and entered politics. He served in the Missouri legislature from 1834 to 1838. Named to a federal judgeship in Platte County, Missouri, in 1841, he was appointed to the U.S. Senate in the fall of 1843 and elected to a full term in 1849. Between August 1846 and November 1854 he was elected president pro tem of the Senate 16 times. He held that office in the spring of 1849, when a unique occurrence in the history of the U.S. presidency brought him to the attention of historians. The Inauguration day of Zachary Taylor, elected president the previous fall, was, under the Constitution, to be March 4, 1849. But that was a Sunday, and Taylor elected to take the oath of office on the following day. At the time it was felt by many that Atchison, by virtue of his senatorial position, had therefore been president of the United States for one day, but it was later shown that either the outgoing James K. Polk or Taylor had actually been president for that day. Defeated for reelection to the Senate in 1855, Atchison returned to Missouri and became a leader of the "border ruffians" who conducted raids into Kansas. He spent the Civil War in Texas and then returned home and farmed until his death in Gower, Missouri, on January 26, 1886.

Atkinson, Brooks (1894–   ), journalist and critic. Born in Melrose, Massachusetts, on November 28, 1894, Justin Brooks Atkinson graduated from Harvard in 1917 and, after a year of teaching at Dartmouth and a short stint on the *Springfield Daily News*, joined the staff of the *Boston Transcript*. He moved to the *New York Times* in 1922, working as a book reviewer and then as editor of the Sunday book-review section until being made theater critic in 1925. Combining a strong sense of artistic integrity with a sharp eye and ear for theater, he became the most influential critic in America, the "autocrat of the aisle seat" who, it was said, could kill a new show single-handedly with a bad review. During World War II, in an amazing change of pace, he served as *New York Times* correspondent in China and later in Moscow; his series of reports on the Soviet Union won him a Pulitzer Prize in 1947. He returned to his critic's chair in 1946 and held it until his retirement in 1960, an event marked by extraordinary displays of respect, including the renaming of the Mansfield Theater in his honor and the granting of a lifetime pass to all Broadway productions. During his career he wrote a number of books, including *Henry Thoreau, Cosmic Yankee*, 1927; *Cingalese Prince*, 1934; *Broadway Scrapbook*, 1947; *Once Around the Sun*, 1951; *Tuesdays and Fridays*, 1963; *Brief Chronicles*, 1966; and *Broadway*, 1970. He also edited collections of the writings of Thoreau and Emerson. From 1960 to 1965 he wrote an occasional "Critic at Large" column for the *Times*; thereafter he contributed articles, often on nature and conservation, to various periodicals.

Atkinson, Henry (1782–1842), soldier. Born in North Carolina in 1782, Atkinson entered the army in 1808; of his childhood and youth there is no record. Commissioned a captain upon enlistment, he advanced to colonel during the War of 1812, at the end of which he was placed in command of the 6th Infantry regiment. In 1819 Secretary of War John C. Calhoun proposed that a strong expeditionary force be sent to the Yel-

lowstone country as a demonstration of U.S. interest to the Indians and the British traders there. Atkinson was put in charge but, through no fault of his own, the trip ended at Old Council Bluffs in what is now Nebraska. In 1820, while stationed in St. Louis, he was promoted to brigadier general in joint command of the Western Department but an army reorganization the following year returned him to his previous rank. In 1825 he led a second expedition to the West and this time succeeded in reaching the mouth of the Yellowstone, treating with a number of Indian tribes along the way and also meeting trader William H. Ashley, who was returning from the first rendezvous of the "mountain men," as the fur trappers were known. The two parties joined for the return to St. Louis. In 1826 Atkinson chose the site for Jefferson Barracks, an army post south of St. Louis, and the following year he sent Col. Henry Leavenworth to establish a post—Fort Leavenworth—on the Kansas frontier. Later in 1827 he traveled north to Prairie du Chien to pacify the Winnebago Indians. Atkinson commanded the U.S. volunteers in the Black Hawk War in 1832 and was field commander during the decisive battle at Bad Axe. In 1840 he was in charge of the removal of the Winnebagos from Wisconsin to Iowa, where the next year Fort Atkinson was built. He returned to Jefferson Barracks, where he died on June 14, 1842.

Atkinson, Justin Brooks, *see* Atkinson, Brooks

Atlas, Charles (1894–1972), physical culturist. Born on October 30, 1894, in Acri, Italy, Angelo Siciliano moved with his family to the United States in 1904 and settled in Brooklyn. Anemic and morose as a youth, he actually was a "97-pound weakling," as he later was to describe himself. A statue of Hercules in a museum inspired him, however, and he began working out at a YMCA gymnasium, at first with standard exercises and then, when they failed to accomplish much, with a system which he developed after watching a lion stretch and ripple his muscles at the zoo. The method of pitting one muscle against another—which he later called "dynamic tension"—yielded spectacular results. A friend remarked one day on his resemblance to a statue of Atlas, and he adopted the name as his own. After high school he worked as a strong man and janitor at Coney Island until a sculptor invited him to be a model. He was soon much in demand and he posed for such works as the statue of George Washington in Washington Square, New York; the "Dawn of Glory" in Prospect Park, Brooklyn, and the statue of Alexander Hamilton at the Treasury Building in Washington, D.C. In 1922 he won the title of "World's Most Perfectly Developed Man" in a contest sponsored by Bernarr Macfadden and his *Physical Culture* magazine. Soon afterward, on the advice of sculptor friends, Atlas opened a gymnasium in New York to teach his system to others. He then worked out a program of mail-order lessons that was a huge success; he closed the gymnasium and, advertising heavily throughout the United States and the world, continued to build bodies by mail at the rate of tens of thousands a year. He died on December 23, 1972, in Long Beach, New York.

Attucks, Crispus (1723?–1770), Revolutionary patriot. Born about 1723, Attucks is believed to have been a mulatto, but nothing is known of his early life. He may well have been a runaway slave, for an advertisement for a slave named Crispus was published in a Boston newspaper in 1750. He may also have been at some time a sailor. All that is definitely known of him concerns the Boston Massacre on March 5, 1770. Toward evening on that day a crowd of colonists gathered and began taunting a small group of British soldiers. Tension mounted rapidly, and when one of the soldiers was struck the others opened fire. Attucks, described as a huge man "whose looks was enough to terrify any person," was shot, and he died almost immediately. Of the five victims of the fray, Attucks was the only one whose name was widely remembered, possibly because of the irony of the fact that one of the first men to shed blood in the cause of American independence was one whose personal rights were not secure and would not have been secure after the Revolution. A statue of him by Augustus Saint-Gaudens was unveiled on Boston Common in 1888.

Atwater, Wilbur Olin (1844–1907), chemist and agriculturalist. Born on May 3, 1844, in Johnsburg, New York, Atwater graduated from Wesleyan University in Middletown, Connecticut, in 1865 and then went to Yale to study agricultural chemistry. After taking his Ph.D. in 1869 he spent two years in further study in Germany at the universities of Leipzig and Berlin. In 1871 he began a teaching career at the University of Tennessee, moving the next year to Maine State College of Agriculture and the Mechanic Arts (now the University of Maine), and the following year to Wesleyan. He was in large part responsible for the founding in 1875 of the country's first state agricultural experiment station, and he served as its director until it was moved from Middletown to New Haven two years later. In 1887 he provided the main impetus for the passage of the act by which Congress provided money for the maintenance of such stations in every state. The next year he founded and assumed the directorship of the U.S. Department of Agriculture's Office of Experiment Stations, a post he held, together with his professorship at Wesleyan, for the rest of his life. In addition to fostering large-scale research in agricultural and nutritional chemistry, he carried on his own investigations as well. His first major discovery, the result of experiments with fertilizers, was announced in 1881; he had found that leguminous

plants were able to "fix" atmospheric nitrogen and thus return that vital and easily depleted element to the soil. In 1892, in collaboration with Wesleyan physicist E. B. Rosa, he began work on the Atwater-Rosa-Benedict calorimeter. With this device, perfected only after five years of work, the inventors were able to show that the heat-energy output of the human body exactly equals the heat-energy potential of the foods taken in. In 1896 Atwater published tables, still widely in use, showing the caloric potential of a large number of foods. With funds from the Carnegie Institution, Atwater was actively organizing an ambitious study on an international scale of the relationships among diet, labor output, and national health and productivity, when he died in Middletown on September 22, 1907.

Auden, Wystan Hugh (1907–1973), poet. Born in York, England, on February 21, 1907, Auden took a degree at Christ Church, Oxford, in 1928 and for a time taught school. His first book of poems was published privately in 1928. During the next several years he continued to write and publish poetry—including *Poems*, 1930, and *Look, Stranger!*, 1936— and, with Christopher Isherwood, verse plays. He was awarded King George's Gold Medal for poetry in 1937. His poetry of the 1930s was greatly concerned with social issues and reflected the influence of Freudianism and certain aspects of Marxism. He married Erika Mann, daughter of the German novelist Thomas Mann, in 1936; in 1939 he came to the United States, becoming a citizen in 1946. His poetry began to turn, largely under the influence of Sören Kierkegaard's thought, to religious and existential themes. He published, among other volumes in this period, *The Age of Anxiety*, 1947, and *Nones*, 1951. In 1948 he was awarded the Pulitzer Prize for poetry. He continued to work occasionally with musicians and in 1951 he collaborated on the libretto for Igor Stravinsky's opera *The Rake's Progress*. His later publications include *The Shield of Achilles*, 1955, which won a National Book Award; *The Enchafèd Flood: The Romantic Iconography of the Sea*, 1950; *Homage to Clio*, 1960; *The Dyer's Hand and Other Essays*, 1962; *About the House*, 1965; *Secondary Worlds*, 1969; *City Without Walls and Other Poems*, 1970; and *A Certain World*, 1970. From 1956 to 1961 he was professor of poetry at Oxford. He continued to maintain a residence in the United States until 1972, when he returned to England. In his later years he was generally considered to be one of the best poets in the English language. He died in Vienna on September 28, 1973.

Audubon, John James (1785–1851), artist and naturalist. Born on April 26, 1785, in what is now Haiti, on a plantation owned by his father, a French naval officer, Audubon was taken to France in 1789, his Creole mother probably having died soon after his birth, and was cared for until he was eighteen by an indulgent foster mother. His formal education may have been somewhat scanty, but he early developed an abiding interest in nature and in drawing. He came to the United States in 1803 and for a while lived the life of a dandyish aristocrat. He left, spent a year in France, and returned in 1806, this time to enter business. He tried a number of occupations and finally, in partnership with a friend, operated a series of general stores in Kentucky. In 1808 he married, bringing his wife to Kentucky with him where, neglectful of business, he spent a great deal of his time exploring the woods and making drawings of birds. His last business venture ended in bankruptcy and after 1820, with his wife's financial support, he devoted himself to his ornithological and zoological interests. In 1826 he took his collection of drawings to Great Britain to seek a publisher; his genius was immediately recognized and in 1827 he was elected to the Royal Society of Edinburgh. His drawings, although occasionally falling short of complete scientific accuracy, were hailed as masterworks. Financed by subscription, the large-format *The Birds of America* began to appear in parts in London in 1827 and publication was completed 11 years later. The text, issued separately in five volumes as *Ornithological Biography*, occupied Audubon from 1831 to 1839; in the latter year he also published an index to the work. The years after 1826 were spent shuttling back and forth between America and Europe; in 1839 he returned to the United States permanently, issued a smaller edition of *Birds*, and began his next work, *Viviparous Quadrupeds of North America*, which was completed by his sons and his collaborator, John Bachman, and published in 30 parts (plates) and 3 volumes of text between 1842 and 1854. Audubon died in New York City on January 27, 1851. He was elected to the Hall of Fame in 1900.

August, John, *see* De Voto, Bernard Augustine

Austerlitz, Fred, *see* Astaire, Fred

Austin, Frank, *see* Faust, Frederick Schiller

Austin, Mary (1868–1934), author. Born on September 9, 1868, in Carlinville, Illinois, Mary Hunter graduated from Blackburn College in 1888 and soon afterward moved with her family to Bakersfield, California. She married Stafford W. Austin in 1891 and for several years they lived in various towns in the Owens Valley; Mrs. Austin soon learned to love the desert and the Indians who lived in it, and both figured in her first book, *The Land of Little Rain*, 1903, which was a success and which was followed by a collection of stories, *The Basket Woman*, 1904. In 1905 she separated from her husband and moved to Carmel, California. She later traveled to Italy, France, and England, where meeting H. G. Wells and other intellectuals strengthened her feminist ideas and added a deep commitment to socialism to her own tendency toward mysticism. Returning to New York City, she became associated with John Reed, Walter Lippmann, and others of the group of writers and artists whose center was Mabel Dodge. *The Arrow Maker*, 1911, a play, and her best novel, *A Woman of Genius*, 1912, were the product of those New York years, as were scores of rather didactic articles on socialism, women's rights, and a variety of other topics. In 1924 she settled in Santa Fe, New Mexico. She published in that year *The Land of Journey's End* and followed it with, among other books, *Children Sing in the Far West*, 1928 (like her earlier *American Rhythm*, 1923, a collection of Indian songs and original poems inspired by them); *Starry Adventure*, 1931; *Experiences Facing Death*, 1931; and an autobiography, *Earth Horizon*, 1932. Her best writing, that which was concerned with nature or Indian life, was reminiscent of Ralph Waldo Emerson and John Muir in its transcendental tone and occasional primitivist leanings. Mrs. Austin died in Santa Fe on August 13, 1934.

Austin, Stephen Fuller (1793–1836), colonizer and political leader. Born in Austinville, Virginia, on November 3, 1793, Austin grew up on the Missouri frontier, where his father, Moses, had taken the family in 1798. Stephen received a remarkably good education. Before 1820 he had served five years in the territorial legislature. The financial panic of 1819 prompted the elder Austin to colonize in Texas, where he died a short time later; Stephen Austin hesitated until July 1821 before following in his father's footsteps and moving to Texas. Giving himself loyally to Mexican citizenship, he confirmed his father's land grant and in 1822 founded a colony, the first settlement of Anglo-Americans to be made legally in the region. Required to go to Mexico City to reconfirm his father's grant, he returned armed with effective dictatorial powers. Under a state law passed by the Coahuila legislature in 1825, colonization of Texas by U.S. citizens expanded rapidly. Austin remained the major leader of the new settlements; his connections in Mexico City, combined with considerable diplomatic skill and membership in the state legislature, enabled him to fend off an attempt to bar slavery from Texas. His major accomplishment during those years was the extremely difficult double task of holding in check the growing American colonies while allaying Mexican suspicions that U.S. colonization might be a subtle prelude to U.S. annexation of Texas. In 1833 his efforts in Mexico City to have Texas separated from Coahuila and made a state of the Mexican confederation brought about his imprisonment; when he was released and returned to Texas in July 1835 revolution was too close to be prevented, and fighting broke out in October. Austin was sent to secure help from the United States; he returned in June 1836, shortly after the revolution ended, and, losing the presidency of the new Republic of Texas to Sam Houston, served briefly as its secretary of state. He died at home, in Austin, Texas, on December 27, 1836.

Axelrod, Julius (1912–   ), biochemist. Born in New York City on May 30, 1912, Axelrod graduated from the College of the City of New York in 1933 but, as a Jew, was unable to enter medical school because of restrictive admissions policies. He worked as a biochemist in New York City's Laboratory of Industrial Hygiene from 1935 to 1946, meanwhile taking his M.S. from New York University in 1941. From 1946 to 1949 he worked for hospitals in New York City and in 1949 joined the staff of the National Heart and Lung Institute of the National Institutes of Health (NIH). In 1955 he received a Ph.D. from The George Washington University and in the same year was appointed head of the pharmacology section of the NIH National Institute of Mental Health. In the course of research into the mechanism of nerve-impulse transmission, in particular the action of noradrenaline, the key chemical in the process, he discovered the means by which the chemical is reabsorbed or inactivated after performing its function. Such reabsorption or inactivation, he found, is vital to the maintenance of stability in the nervous system and consequently affects such autonomically controlled functions as mental states and blood pressure. His researches thus raised hopes that eventually pharmacological treatments for a number of ailments usually diagnosed as mental disorders might be developed. For his work Axelrod shared the 1970 Nobel Prize for Medicine and Physiology with Sir Bernard Katz of Great Britain and Ulf von Euler of Sweden, both of whom had made important contributions in this field. In 1971 Axelrod received the Albert Einstein Commemorative Award and was elected to membership in the National Academy of Sciences.

Ayer, Francis Wayland (1848–1923), pioneer advertising man. Born in Lee, Massachusetts, on February 4, 1848, Ayer was the son of an itinerant schoolteacher. He taught school for a few years, studied for a year at the University of Rochester, and in 1869 moved to Philadelphia. There, after a few months spent working as an advertising solicitor for the *National Baptist,* he opened his own advertising firm, naming it N. W. Ayer & Son after his father. At a time when advertising was considered at best a calling of doubtful respectability, Ayer brought to the business an ethical approach that worked a revolution in methods and standards. He changed the role of the agent from that of middleman between advertiser and publisher to one of adviser to the advertiser; he developed an open form of contract that promised the client optimal use of his advertising budget, supported his billings with an itemized account of expenses, and charged a flat commission fee for the service, thus initiating a system that has since become customary. His firm was the first to provide the client with advertising copy and the first to conduct market research. As an additional service it issued the *American Newspaper Annual and Directory,* which became a standard reference work. Ayer pioneered in the use of trademarks, slogans, and other now common advertising devices, and the great reputation for integrity that he enjoyed—he refused, for example, to represent useless or fraudulent products —did much to establish advertising as a necessary and reputable adjunct to business. From 1895 to 1910 he headed the Merchants' National Bank of Philadelphia and later gave much time to his New York State dairy farm. He died in Camden, New Jersey, on March 5, 1923.

B

Baade, Walter (1893–1960), astronomer. Born on March 24, 1893, in Schröttinghausen, Germany, Baade studied at the universities of Münster and Göttingen, taking his Ph.D. from Göttingen in 1919. From that year until 1931 he was on the staff of the observatory of the University of Hamburg. In 1931 he came to the United States and joined the staff of the Mt. Wilson Observatory in Pasadena, California. Working there and also, after 1948, at nearby Mt. Palomar Observatory, Baade concentrated mainly on investigations of galactic and extragalactic scope, although he did important theoretical work on stellar interiors as well. He was interested in supernovas and variable stars, and discovered that the luminosities of a particular class of variable stars used as yardsticks in gauging extragalactic distances had been wrongly estimated. His revision led in 1952 to a doubling of the believed size of the observable universe and of all the extragalactic distances in it. Retiring from the observatory in 1958, he returned to Germany in 1959 to become Gauss Professor at Göttingen, He died there on June 25, 1960.

Babbitt, Irving (1865–1933), educator and author. Born on August 2, 1865, in Dayton, Ohio, Babbitt held various jobs as a boy. He attended high school in Cincinnati, and graduated from Harvard in 1889. As an instructor at the University of Montana for two years, he earned enough for a year of study at the Sorbonne, in Paris, then entered the Harvard graduate school and earned his master's degree in Oriental studies in 1893. A fellow student was Paul Elmer More, who later became his close friend and associate in the neo-humanist movement. In 1894 Babbitt became a teacher of French and comparative literature at Harvard; he was made an assistant professor in 1902 and professor in 1912. At Harvard and as a guest lecturer at universities and colleges in the United States and abroad, his lectures on the romantic movement, especially in English, French, and German literature, were widely popular. He urged a return to the rational values of the classics and a turning away from the emotionalism of his time, advocating the development of a new humanism consistent with the modern spirit. A widely publicized controversy developed in 1929–1930 between the humanists and the anti-humanists led by H. L. Mencken, who argued that the artist should present an unembellished picture of life. Babbitt's books on literature and various social and political phenomena included *Literature and the American College*, 1908; *The New Lao-koön*, 1910; *The Masters of Modern French Criti-cism*, 1912; *Rousseau and Romanticism*, 1919; and *On Being Creative and Other Essays*, 1932. He died in Cambridge, Massachusetts, on July 15, 1933.

Babbitt, Isaac (1799–1862), inventor. Born in Taunton, Massachusetts, on July 26, 1799, Babbitt received little formal education but was trained as a goldsmith. In experimenting with various metals and alloys he produced in 1824 the first britannia-metal ware made in the United States and for a number of years devoted himself to its manufacture. With a partner he built a factory in Taunton in 1827, but within a few years they sold out to their apprentices, who later, as Reed & Barton, were highly successful manufacturers of silverware. In 1834 Babbitt moved to Boston and took a job in Cyrus Alger's South Boston Iron Works. There he continued his experiments and in 1839 patented an improved bearing housing of a type known as a journal box. In the patent specification he noted incidentally that a good lining for the box could be made by mixing tin, antimony, and copper in a particular ratio. The device itself received slight attention, but the white-metal alloy was a major contribution to bearing engineering and was soon universally known, in its numerous variations, as Babbitt metal. On behalf of the navy, Congress awarded him $20,000 for the right to use his journal box and the Babbitt-metal formula. Babbitt died in a mental hospital at Somerville, Massachusetts, on May 26, 1862.

Babbitt, Milton Byron (1916–   ), composer. Born on May 10, 1916, in Philadelphia, Babbitt grew up in Jackson, Mississippi. He became interested in both music and mathematics at an early age and studied both at New York University, from which he graduated in 1935. While pursuing graduate studies at Princeton, he was strongly influenced by Roger H. Sessions. He became an instructor in music in 1938, taking his M.F.A. four years later. Remaining on the Princeton faculty, he began exploring the possibilities of the twelve-tone music of Arnold Schönberg and Anton von Webern and developed means whereby the set and series principles used to construct harmonic and tonal patterns could be expanded to apply to such other musical components as rhythm, register, timbre, and dynamics, producing a "totally organized" music. Employing this complex and highly mathematical approach, Babbitt composed a number of advanced and much noted works, including *Three Compositions for Piano*, 1947; *Composition for Four In-*

struments, 1948; *Composition for Twelve Instruments*, 1948; *Composition for Viola and Piano*, 1950; *Woodwind Quartet*, 1953; *Du*, 1954, a song cycle; *All Set*, 1957; and *Composition for Tenor and Six Instruments*, 1960. He had long been interested in the new field of electronically produced music when, in 1959, he became, with Sessions, Otto C. Luening, and Vladimir A. Ussachevsky, a director of the Columbia–Princeton Electronic Music Center. Using the center's electronic synthesizer, he created such revolutionary pieces as *Composition for Synthesizer*, 1961, and *Vision and Prayer*, 1961, for soprano and synthesizer. Others of Babbitt's works included *Ensembles*, 1962; *Philomel*, 1964; *Relata II*, 1969; and a string quartet, 1970. In 1966 he became William Shubael Conant Professor of Music at Princeton.

Babcock, Stephen Moulton (1843–1931), agricultural chemist. Born in Bridgewater, New York, on October 22, 1843, Babcock graduated from Tufts College in 1866, studied at Cornell, and took his Ph.D. from the University of Göttingen in 1879. He taught at Cornell in 1881–1882 and for five years thereafter worked as a chemist for the New York State agricultural experiment station there. In 1887 he joined the faculty of the University of Wisconsin, where he was professor of agricultural chemistry until his retirement in 1913. Among Babcock's important contributions to agricultural science, foremost was a simple test for the butterfat content of milk. When sulfuric acid was added to a measured amount of milk, thus liberating the fat, and the sample was centrifuged to bring the fat to the top quickly, the butterfat content could be read from a gauge. The device, simple enough to be used anywhere, greatly discouraged the watering down of milk, made possible a realistic scale of payments to farmers based on milk quality, and provided strong impetus for the improvement of dairy herds. Babcock also invented an improved viscosimeter, used to measure the viscosity of milk and other liquids, and undertook researches into the nutritional value of various feeds that eventually led others to the discovery of vitamin A. He patented none of his inventions, hoping thereby to speed their acceptance and use. Babcock died in Madison, Wisconsin, on July 2, 1931.

Babson, Roger Ward (1875–1967), statistician and economist. Born on July 6, 1875, in Gloucester, Massachusetts, Babson graduated from the Massachusetts Institute of Technology in 1898. He engaged in the securities business for a few years, made profitable personal investments, and became vice-president of the Adirondack Light and Power Company. His real interest, however, was in statistics and their application to business and investment and, having moved to Wellesley Hills, Massachusetts, he incorporated the Babson Business Statistical Organization in 1904 to provide statistical summaries and analyses of business conditions to investors. In 1907 he developed

his "Babsonchart," a graphic representation of the movements of the stock market, with projections of future trends based on his own theory of business cycles, which was based on Newton's law of action and reaction. He began writing articles on investment in 1910 and during World War I served as director general of information and education in the Department of Labor, producing in 1917 *Why Are We Fighting?*, a pamphlet distributed to the armed forces. He later wrote for the Scripps Syndicate and in 1923 organized his own syndicate, the Publishers Financial Bureau, to serve newspapers throughout the country. His economic predictions, sometimes wrong but more often right, gained considerable credence when his forecast in September 1929 of an imminent sharp drop in stock prices proved all too correct within two months. Babson was deeply interested in promoting peace, good business practices, education, religion, temperance— he was the Prohibition party's presidential candidate in 1940—and other causes. In 1919 he founded at Babson Park, near Boston, the Babson Institute, a two-year school devoted to sound business training; eight years later a similar school for women, Webber College, was established with his wife's help at their ranch in Polk County, Florida. In 1946 he founded Utopia College at Eureka, Kansas. In addition to his regular reports and his syndicated column, he wrote a great number of books, including *Washington and the Revolutionists*, 1934; *Actions and Reactions*, 1935, an autobiography; *Can These Dry Bones Live?*, 1945, with D. Zuver; and many works on business and finance. Babson died in Mountain Lake, Florida, on March 5, 1967.

Bacharach, Burt (1929–   ), composer. Born in Kansas City, Missouri, on May 12, 1929, Bacharach grew up there and in New York City. He took up the piano at an early age and after graduating from high school began playing in hotels and clubs and on USO tours. He later studied music and composition at McGill University, the New School for Social Research, and the Music Academy of the West. After serving in the army in 1950–1952, he worked for several years as an accompanist to a number of popular singers, including Vic Damone, Georgia Gibbs, the Ames Brothers, and Marlene Dietrich. He began to experiment with songwriting and by 1962 had a contract with a small recording company. In collaboration with lyricist Hal David he produced songs, many for singer Dionne Warwick, that began appearing on the popularity charts, among them "Don't Make Me Over," "Walk on By," "Trains and Boats and Planes," and "What the World Needs Now." At the same time Bacharach was writing music for such motion pictures as *The Man Who Shot Liberty Valance*, *Wives and Lovers*, *What's New Pussycat?*, and *Alfie*. His title songs for the last two won Academy Award nominations in 1965 and 1966 as did "The Look of Love" from *Casino Royale* in 1967. With their low-keyed and often lush sound, his songs were at odds with the dominant harshness of most contemporary popular music, but he nevertheless commanded a following in the millions both in the singles record market and in the movies and Broadway shows with which he was involved. Much of the appeal of his music doubtless lay in his uniquely unorthodox use of chord and time-signature changes. In 1967–1968, with David, he wrote the score for Neil Simon's Broadway musical *Promises, Promises* and received unanimously high praise from audience and critics alike. In 1970 he won an Academy Award for his score for *Butch Cassidy and the Sundance Kid* and shared another with David for a song from that film, "Raindrops Keep Fallin' on My Head."

Bache, Alexander Dallas (1806–1867), physicist and educator. Born in Philadelphia on July 19, 1806, Bache was a great-grandson of Benjamin Franklin, a grandson of Alexander J. Dallas, and a nephew of Benjamin F. Bache. A brilliant student, he entered West Point at fifteen and graduated with highest honors in 1925. He taught for a time at West Point and then served with the army engineers. Upon his appointment as professor of natural philosophy and chemistry at the University of Pennsylvania in 1828 he resigned his commission. He became active in the work of the Franklin Institute and of the American Philosophical Society. In 1836 he was named the first president of Girard College. In preparation for the schools' opening he traveled in Europe for two years studying educational practices and published *Education in Europe* on his return in 1839; he then reorganized the Philadelphia public schools into a model system and in 1842, the college not yet having opened, he returned to his post at the University of Pennsylvania. The following year he succeeded Ferdinand R. Hassler as head of the U.S. Coast Survey. He held this position for the rest of his life, serving also from 1846 as regent of the Smithsonian Institution. Under his leadership the Survey won expanded appropriations from Congress and greatly expanded its work, particularly in Bache's own special field of interest, that of terrestrial magnetism. He took the lead in organizing the National Academy of Sciences, chartered by Congress in 1863, and was its first president. Bache died in Newport, Rhode Island, on February 17, 1867.

Bache, Benjamin Franklin (1769–1798), journalist. Born in Philadelphia on August 12, 1769, Bache was a grandson of Benjamin Franklin. With his grandfather he traveled in Europe as a boy, beginning his education there and continuing it later in Philadelphia. He also learned printing and in 1790 founded the *General Advertiser* in his native city. The paper, later known as the *Aurora*, was from the first a highly partisan organ of the Republicans, and when Philip M. Freneau's *National Gazette* ceased publication in 1793 it became the leading voice of the Jeffersonians. Under Bache's editorial leadership the *Aurora* carried the common journalistic vices of the

time—exaggeration, vituperation, and blatant disregard of truth—to their utmost limits; his attacks on George Washington were particularly violent and unfair. The details of Jay's Treaty were printed in the *Aurora* before President Washington wished them to be made public and Bache played a central role in stirring up public resentment against it. He continued his anti-Federalist tirades against President John Adams and in the excitement that followed the XYZ Affair—much publicized in the *Aurora*—he and his newspaper were among the main targets of the administration's Sedition Act of 1798. Under that act he was arrested for libeling the president. Released on parole, he died of yellow fever soon after, on September 10, 1798, in Philadelphia.

Backus, Isaac (1724–1806), religious leader. Born in Norwich, Connecticut, on January 9, 1724, to a prosperous family long active in church affairs in Connecticut, Backus was an indifferent church member until 1741, when in the wave of enthusiasm known as the Great Awakening he underwent conversion. In 1746 he was among those who withdrew from the liberal Congregational church in Norwich to found a New Light church upon the older principles espoused by the Puritans. Later in the same year he felt the call to preach and, although he had had only a rudimentary education and no formal theological training, he began to travel to other towns in Connecticut and Massachusetts. In 1748 he drew up articles of faith for a new church in Titicut, Massachusetts, and was elected its minister. He became convinced that baptism was required by Scripture to be an adult experience and one of total immersion and in 1751 he converted to the Baptist Church. A major controversy ensued, both with his own parishioners and with other New Light leaders, and in 1756 he organized a new Baptist congregation in Middleborough, Massachusetts. He remained pastor of that church for the rest of his life. Backus continued to travel widely on behalf of the Baptist Church, ranging throughout New England and in 1789 as far as Virginia and North Carolina. He was the leading spokesman of the Baptists in Massachusetts and during the years of the New Light movement and later was a staunch defender of religious freedom. He lobbied at the first Continental Congress in 1774 and in 1780 fought the retention of a provision for an established church in the Massachusetts constitution. A member of the Massachusetts convention called to consider ratifying the federal Constitution in 1788, he broke with the majority of his Baptist colleagues and voted for ratification because of the separation of church and state that the document guaranteed. During his travels he had gathered a wealth of information and documentation on church and New England history, and his researches bore fruit in his *History of New England, with Particular Reference to the Denomination of Christians Called Baptists*, which appeared in three volumes (1777–1796). Backus died in Middleborough on November 20, 1806.

Bacon, Delia Salter (1811–1859), author. Born on February 2, 1811, in what soon became Tallmadge, Ohio, Miss Bacon grew up there and in Hartford, Connecticut, where she attended Catharine E. Beecher's school for girls. She tried and failed to establish her own school in several places and she turned to writing—*Tales of the Puritans*, 1831, and *The Bride of Fort Edward*, 1839 —and also lectured on literary and historical topics. She gradually evolved a theory that the works attributed to Shakespeare had in fact been written by a coterie of writers led by Francis Bacon and including Edmund Spenser and Sir Walter Raleigh, and were credited by them to the relatively obscure actor and theater manager William Shakespeare largely for political reasons. Becoming thoroughly convinced of the notion, and with some encouragement from Ralph Waldo Emerson, she traveled to England in 1853 to seek proof. For three years she lived in poverty while she developed her thesis; in 1856, for reasons unknown, she abandoned on the brink of fruition her plan of opening Shakespeare's grave to look for certain documents she believed would support her position. Nathaniel Hawthorne, at that time U.S. consul in Liverpool, took pity on her, lent her money, and arranged for the publication of her book, *The Philosophy of the Plays of Shakespeare Unfolded,* 1857. Immediately after the appearance of the book she went insane and never learned that it had met with little but ridicule. She was brought back to the United States in 1858; she died in Hartford on September 2, 1859. The idea that had obsessed her assumed a life of its own and the theory continued to have its adherents throughout the years.

Bacon, Nathaniel (1647–1676), colonial leader. Born on January 2, 1647, in the county of Suffolk, England, Bacon was a kinsman of Francis Bacon. He studied at Cambridge and at Gray's Inn. In 1673 he emigrated to Virginia, established two plantations, and within a year was appointed to the governor's council. He was soon at odds with Governor Sir William Berkeley, principally because Berkeley was reluctant to authorize reprisals against the Indians who were raiding frontier settlements and Bacon was strongly in sympathy with the inhabitants who demanded action. In 1676 an expeditionary force was organized in defiance of Berkeley and Bacon was chosen to lead it. Raids were launched against the Pamunkey, Susquehanna, and Occaneechi tribes, while Berkeley denounced Bacon and his followers as rebels. The colonists, who by this time were demanding governmental reforms as well as protection from the Indians, forced the governor to back down, however, and through the weight of public opinion, Bacon returned to the council. He soon organized another raiding party and was again denounced by Berkeley. Bacon and his supporters then occupied Jamestown, the capital, and Berkeley fled. When Bacon left the town to move again against Pamunkey villages, the governor returned. Bacon led his force back to Jamestown

and, after a sharp battle, burned it while the governor once again fled. By this time Bacon was in control of virtually all of Virginia; he withdrew to Green Spring to consolidate his power, but in October 1676 he died suddenly, and Bacon's Rebellion quickly collapsed.

Badin, Stephen Theodore (1768–1853), religious leader and missionary. Born on July 17, 1768, in Orléans, France, Badin was educated in Paris and began studying for the priesthood in his native city. Fleeing revolutionary France for America in 1792, he finished his studies in Baltimore and in May 1793, with Bishop John Carroll officiating, became the first Roman Catholic priest to be ordained in the United States. Sent to minister to the scattered Roman Catholics in Kentucky, he spent 26 years there, riding from settlement to settlement and establishing log-cabin chapels in several places, as well as more substantial ones in Louisville and Lexington in 1811 and 1812. In 1819 he returned to France, where for nine years he served in various parishes and collected money for American missions. He was called back to America in 1822 to carry on missions among the French Canadians and the Potawatomi Indians of Michigan. About 1832 he obtained the land upon which was founded the University of Notre Dame ten years later. In his latter years Father Badin was something of an itinerant priest, serving and visiting parishes all over the Midwest. He died in Cincinnati on April 19, 1853.

Baekeland, Leo Hendrik (1863–1944), chemist and inventor. Born in Ghent, Belgium, on November 14, 1863, Baekeland graduated from the University of Ghent in 1882, remaining there to take his doctorate with highest honors in 1884 and to teach chemistry. In 1889 he visited the United States and decided to remain. He worked briefly for a manufacturer of photographic materials in New York City and then began experimenting on his own with photographic papers. He invented a paper that could be developed in artificial light, named it Velox, and organized the Nepera Chemical Company to produce it. In 1899 the company was bought by George Eastman of the Eastman Kodak Company for a sum of around a million dollars. Independently wealthy as a result, Baekeland equipped a laboratory and began a systematic program of experiments in making synthetic resins. The reaction of phenol and formaldehyde particularly interested him and he eventually found that by using high temperatures and pressures and controlling the reaction closely, he could produce a hard, insoluble, acid-resistant material capable of being molded into any desired shape. In its liquid phase it could be used to coat canvas or to impregnate wood or other fibers, rendering them hard and durable. Any number of products could be made from the substance; it could be used in precision casting, would sustain machining, and was an excellent electrical insulator. Baekeland demonstrated the material in 1907, gave it the name Bakelite, and the following year founded the Bakelite Corporation to manufacture it. He served as president of the company until his retirement in 1939. He was Chandler Lecturer at Columbia University in 1914 and honorary professor of chemical engineering there from 1917 until his death. The recipient of many awards and honors, he was also a member of a great number of national and international scientific organizations. He died in Beacon, New York, on February 23, 1944.

Baer, Arthur (1886–1969), "Bugs," journalist. Born in 1886 in Philadelphia, Baer left school at fourteen but later studied art and joined the *Philadelphia Public Ledger* around 1906 as a staff artist. From there he moved to the *Washington (D.C.) Times*, where he worked as a sports cartoonist and columnist. He drew strange little insects into his cartoons and thus earned a nickname; he was thereafter known exclusively as "Bugs" Baer. Joining the *New York World* before World War I, he wrote a feature column that attracted a growing audience and in 1919 was hired away by William Randolph Hearst's *New York American*, from which his column was distributed by King Features Syndicate to reach more than 15 million readers daily. Full of quips, pungent comments, and a worldly-wise view of life, the column remained a staple item for a host of followers until the late 1960s. Baer's observations ranged from the difficulty of stealing second base ("His head was full of larceny but his feet were too honest") to international affairs ("We must make the world pay for the last war to prevent it from affording the next one"), and from the vagaries of politics ("Europe is where they name a street after you one day and chase you down it the next") to the injustice of it all ("Alimony is like buying oats for a dead horse"). He died in New York City on May 17, 1969.

Baer, George Frederick (1842–1914), lawyer and businessman. Born on September 26, 1842, near Lavansville, Pennsylvania, Baer left school at thirteen to work in the office of a local newspaper, the *Somerset Democrat*, but later studied at Franklin and Marshall College. With his brother he bought the newspaper in 1861 and while managing it began to study law. He organized and commanded an infantry company during the Civil War, and although he served for only a year he saw action at the second battle of Bull Run and at Antietam, Fredericksburg, and Chancellorsville. Discharged as a major in 1863, he resumed the study of law and was admitted to the bar in 1864. For several years he conducted a successful practice in Reading, Pennsylvania, and in 1870 joined the legal staff of the Philadelphia & Reading Railway Company. He had many business interests and became local agent for J. P. Morgan. The railroad was bought by Morgan and in the reorganization of 1901 Baer became president of the Philadelphia & Reading Railway, the Philadelphia & Reading Coal and Iron Company, and the Central Railroad Company of New Jersey.

In 1902, when the newly organized United Mine Workers of America went on strike, he became the leader of the business forces opposed to yielding to the union's demand for negotiations. In July of that year he wrote a letter to a Mr. Clark of Wilkes-Barre that was published in newspapers across the country and aroused a torrent of indignation, for in it he said that "the rights and interests of the laboring man will be protected and cared for—not by the labor agitators, but by the Christian men to whom God in His infinite wisdom has given the control of the property interests of the country. . . ." Coming at a time when the power of unfettered capital was under attack from many quarters, the letter summarized perfectly the arrogant attitude that lay at the root of the growing popular resentment of business. The strike was settled shortly afterward and Baer himself continued to pursue his business interests and to live quietly in Reading until his death on April 26, 1914.

Baez, Joan (1941–   ), singer. Born on January 9, 1941, on Staten Island in New York City, Miss Baez grew up there and in other Eastern cities and, after graduation from high school, moved with her family to Boston. She attended Boston University briefly and then began singing in coffeehouses in Boston and Cambridge. Her strong, direct renditions of traditional folk songs and ballads, backed by her simple but sure guitar playing, soon attracted a considerable local following and in 1959, after an appearance in Chicago, she was invited to sing at the Folk Festival in Newport, Rhode Island. The audience there received her enthusiastically and she returned for the festival in 1960. A recording contract resulted and her first album, titled simply *Joan Baez*, was a great success, as were the many that followed. Drawing her repertoire from old English ballads, Southern and country music, and increasingly from the modern canon of protest songs, she made a concert tour in 1961 that evoked high praise from audiences and critics for her clear soprano voice and her straightforward manner. Other tours—of Europe and Japan, and of campuses and concert halls across the United States—increased her popularity and she soon ranked with Bob Dylan at the top of her field. Miss Baez became deeply involved in Civil Rights activities during the early 1960s, giving concerts in the South that brought her great popularity. In the later 1960s she became involved in the opposition to the Vietnam War and was in particular a supporter of the movement resisting the military draft. In 1965 she founded an institute for the study of nonviolence, and in her concert and television appearances she continued to mix performing with pleas for nonviolent opposition to war and injustice.

Bagley, William Chandler (1874–1946), educator. Born on March 15, 1874, in Detroit, Bagley graduated from Michigan Agricultural College (now Michigan State University) in 1895. After two years of teaching school he began graduate studies at the University of Wisconsin, took his M.S. in 1898, and then moved to Cornell University, where he received his Ph.D. in 1900. He returned to teaching in normal schools until 1908, when he became professor of education at the University of Illinois. In 1917 he joined the faculty of Teachers College of Columbia University, where he remained until his retirement in 1940. Bagley was active in the National Education Association, serving as editor of its journal in 1920–1925 and as president of its National Council of Education in 1931–1937. He was a prolific writer on various problems and aspects of American education, publishing, among other works, *The Educative Process*, 1905; *Classroom Management*, 1907; *Craftsmanship in Teaching*, 1911; *School Discipline*, 1915; *Determinism in Education*, 1925; *Education, Crime, and Social Progress*, 1931; *Education and Emergent Man*, 1934; and *A Century of the Universal School*, 1937. He collaborated with historian Charles A. Beard on several books, notably *A History of the American People*, 1918, and *Our Old World Background*, 1922. During the 1930s Bagley emerged as a prominent and outspoken critic of the practices, in large part derived from the writings of John Dewey, commonly referred to as "progressive" education. Seeing in progressive theory the threat of schooling that was simply poor and trivial, he advocated in opposition to it a rigorous curriculum similar to that traditional in European schools. From their insistence upon the teaching of a core of essential knowledge and on developing intellectual skills, Bagley and his followers became known as the "essentialist" school of pedagogues. He was editor of *School and Society* from 1939 until his death on July 1, 1946, in New York City.

Bailey, F. Lee (1933–   ), lawyer. Born in Waltham, Massachusetts, on June 10, 1933, Francis Lee Bailey entered Harvard in 1950 but left after two years to join the navy. He transferred to the Marines and, although he had no legal training, served on the legal staff of the Marine air base at Cherry Point, North Carolina. His experience there later enabled him to enter the Boston University Law School without the usual prerequisites and he graduated at the top of his class in 1960. While in law school he had organized and run a detective agency, and the investigative experience he gained from it was later as valuable as his formal education in his chosen field of criminal law. He made himself an expert in the electronic techniques used in criminal investigation and in polygraphy ("lie detecting"). It was as an authority on polygraphy that he was originally called into his first major case, that of Dr. Samuel Sheppard of Cleveland, who had been convicted in 1954, amid blaring publicity, of murdering his wife. Bailey helped to force a review of the trial all the way to the Supreme Court, which ruled in 1966 that the pretrial publicity may have prejudiced the jury. In a retrial, completed in 1966, Bailey secured Sheppard's acquittal and thus became one of the country's leading trial lawyers. Other spectacular involvements followed, including murder trials in New Jersey and Florida, a $1.5 million mail robbery case in Massachusetts, and representation of the confessed "Boston Strangler." In 1969 Bailey successfully defended a U.S. Special Forces ("Green Beret") officer accused of executing a double agent in Vietnam, and in 1971 won an acquittal in the court-martial of Capt. Ernest L. Medina, charged with responsibility for the massacre of civilians by U.S. troops at My Lai, South Vietnam. Employing tactics that bordered at times on the flamboyant, Bailey was on a few occasions censured formally for his trial conduct, but his method of tirelessly pursuing every possible line of investigation and legal action made him one of the most sought-after legal defenders in the country.

Bailey, Frederick Augustus Washington, *see* Douglass, Frederick

Bailey, Gamaliel (1807–1859), editor and social reformer. Born in Mount Holly, New Jersey, on December 3, 1807, Bailey grew up in Philadelphia and graduated from Jefferson Medical College in 1827. He made numerous false starts on a career, working for a short period as a school teacher, shipping on a merchant vessel to China, practicing medicine briefly, and serving as editor of the short-lived *Methodist Protestant*. In 1831, after an ill-fated atttempt to emigrate to Oregon, he was in Cincinnati when a cholera epidemic led him to resume medical practice. In 1834 he was a lecturer on physiology at Lane Theological Seminary when a fierce debate over slavery that racked the school that year converted him to the abolitionist cause. Two years later he joined James G. Birney's antislavery paper, the Cincinnati *Philanthropist*, as assistant editor; and on Birney's departure in 1837 Bailey succeeded to the editorship, a post he retained, through three sackings of the office by aroused mobs, until 1843, when he began the daily *Herald*. In 1847 the American and Foreign Anti-Slavery Society called him from Cincinnati to Washington, D.C., to take charge of its newly founded journal, the *National Era*. Under his editorship the *National Era* quickly became one of the foremost abolitionist periodicals in the country, combining moral fervor with high literary quality and publishing contributions from such authors as Nathaniel Hawthorne, John Greenleaf Whittier, and Theodore Parker. It was in the *Era* that, during 1851–1852, Harriet Beecher Stowe's *Uncle Tom's Cabin* first appeared, in serial form. In declining health for several years, Bailey sailed to Europe in 1859 to seek relief, but he died at sea on June 5, 1859.

Bailey, Liberty Hyde (1858–1954), botanist, horticulturist, and educator. Born in South Haven, Michigan, on March 15, 1858, Bailey graduated from Michigan Agricultural College (now Michigan State University) in 1882. For two years he worked as an assistant to Asa Gray at Harvard and in 1884 was appointed professor of horticulture at his alma mater, organizing there the nation's first college department of horticulture. In 1888 he moved to Cornell University where, two years later, he organized the New York State College of Agriculture. He served as dean of the agricultural college and head of the associated agricultural experiment station from 1903 to 1913, expanding their work rapidly in many directions. Recognized as the leading U.S. authority on and practitioner of agricultural education, Bailey was chosen to head President Theodore Roosevelt's Commission on Country Life in 1908. He wrote scores of books on horticulture and related topics; edited several periodicals at various times; edited four encyclopedic works in the fields of botany, horticulture, and agriculture; and published two volumes of poetry as well as works on religion, philosophy, rural sociology, and other subjects. After his retirement from teaching in 1913 he continued his research at Cornell; he was an expert in the taxonomy of such difficult genera as *Carex*, *Rubus*, *Prunus*, and *Brassica* and on the palms of the Western Hemisphere. In 1920 he founded the world's first botanical institution devoted to studying the classification and identification of cultivated plants, the Bailey Hortorium. In 1935 he arranged for the Hortorium—a term of his own devising—to become a part of Cornell University, and he served as its director from then until 1951. He died in Ithaca, New York, on December 25, 1954.

Bainbridge, William (1774–1833), naval officer. Born in Princeton, New Jersey, on May 7, 1774, Bainbridge received a thorough schooling and at the age of fifteen went to sea on a merchant ship. Before he was twenty he was in command of his own vessel. In 1796, while engaged in trade between Europe and the West Indies at a time when England was conducting an undeclared war at sea against the United States, Bainbridge made a name for himself by defeating a British privateer with twice his firepower that had attacked his ship without warning. Later, after one of his men had been impressed by a heavily armed cruiser, he immediately seized a replacement from a British merchantman. In 1798, when the Department of the Navy was organized in the face of the need to defend shipping against the French and the Barbary pirates, Bainbridge was commissioned lieutenant commandant and given command of the 14-gun *Retaliation*. Captured by the French, he was imprisoned for a time on Guadeloupe; upon his release he was promoted and given a larger ship. His success in defending a large convoy of merchant craft bound from the West Indies to the United States led to his promotion to captain, then the highest rank in the navy, in 1800. That same year, in command of the *George Washington*, he undertook the extremely difficult mission of bearing tribute to Algiers, and while scoring diplomatic gains for the United States he rescued several French citizens from slavery. In 1803 he commanded the *Philadelphia* in Commodore Edward Preble's squadron operating against Tripoli in the U.S. war against the Barbary pirates. When his ship ran aground and he and the crew were taken prisoner, it was at his suggestion that the *Philadelphia* was burned in a daring raid into the harbor by Stephen Decatur. Released in 1805 after having taken an important part in the peace negotiations with Tripoli, Bainbridge reentered the merchant service. He was recalled to active duty as a commodore during 1808–1810 and again at the outbreak of the War of 1812. He succeeded Isaac Hull as commander of the *Constitution* and won a notable victory over the British frigate *Java*. He made two more voyages to the Mediterranean, in 1815 and 1820, helping to maintain there a strong American guard against a resumption of piracy by the Barbary states. Upon his return in 1821 he served on the board of naval commissioners and organized the first U.S. school for naval officers. Bainbridge died in Philadelphia on July 27, 1833.

Baird, Spencer Fullerton (1823–1887), naturalist. Born on February 3, 1823, in Reading, Pennsylvania, Baird early developed a love of nature, and while still a student at Dickinson College attracted the notice and friendship of John James Audubon. After graduating in 1840 he studied medicine briefly, but soon returned to his growing collection of birds, reptiles, and other fauna. In 1845 he was appointed professor of natural history at Dickinson, becoming also a professor of chemistry three years later. In 1850 he was named assistant to Joseph Henry, secretary of the Smithsonian Institution, and his huge collection became the nucleus of the Smithsonian's natural-history museum. He directed a vigorous program of research and collecting, traveling widely himself and enlisting the aid of interested observers everywhere, including army officers on the frontier. The results of this wide-ranging work were collected and edited in 13 volumes of reports; these, together with Baird's own classic monographs—*Birds*, 1858; *Mammals of North America*, 1859; and *History of North American Birds*, 1875–1884 (with T. M. Brewer and R. Ridgway)—ushered in a new era of scientific nature study in America. In 1871 he was appointed Commissioner of Fish and Fisheries, at the head of a commission created by Congress largely at his urging. He served without pay, setting up research programs that served as models for many other nations and establishing an important marine biological laboratory at Woods Hole, Massachusetts. In 1878 he succeeded Henry as secretary of the Smithsonian, and he continued to direct both that institution and the Fish Commission until his death on August 19, 1887, at the Woods Hole station.

Baker, George (1877–1965), "Father Divine," religious leader. Born in 1877 near Savannah, Georgia, Baker began preaching about 1900, first in the South, then in Baltimore, and, from about

1915, in New York City. There in 1919 he organized the Peace Mission movement and adopted the name Father Divine. Establishing themselves first in a communal settlement in Sayville on Long Island, New York, the followers of the movement were soon forced to leave and they returned to New York City. There and in Philadelphia Father Divine attracted a growing number of followers that eventually ran to many thousands. The central tenets of the movement were renunciation of personal property in communal living, a strict moral code that included celibacy and total bans on liquor, tobacco, cosmetics, and movies, and complete racial equality. In the settlements—each of which was called a "heaven" and which at one time numbered more than 170—informal religious services were held and "Peace" was the universal greeting. Although Baker neither affirmed nor denied its truth, the slogan of the movement, sincerely accepted by many, perhaps most, of its adherents (called angels), was "Father Divine is God." The members were predominantly black, but an estimated one-third to one-fourth were white. The movement dwindled quickly after Father Divine's death near Philadelphia on September 10, 1965.

Baker, George (1915–1975), cartoonist. Born on May 22, 1915, in Lowell, Massachusetts, Baker grew up there, in Rockford, Illinois, and in Chicago. After attending an art school briefly he became a commercial artist. In 1937, on the brink of joining a West Coast minor-league baseball team, he instead took a job with the Walt Disney studios in Hollywood. He worked on a number of Disney cartoon features until 1941, when he was drafted into the army. Assigned to duty at Fort Monmouth, New Jersey, he was attached to the Signal Corps to do animations for information films; while there he toyed with a cartoon series depicting army life as seen from the bottom of the heap. A few of his strips were published in *Life,* and in 1942, when *Yank* magazine was organized, he became an original member of the staff. Baker's cartoon series, starring a well-meaning but thoroughly inept private known only as "The Sad Sack," became *Yank's* most enduring and popular feature. Followed by an estimated 10 million servicemen throughout the world, the Sad Sack's adventures reflected and magnified the experiences of every enlisted man who ever faced red tape, KP, sergeants, officers, and duty details. The Sack, who never spoke, became probably the best-known fictional figure of the war (his only competitors being Bill Mauldin's Joe and Willie) and was credited with being one of the army's most effective morale builders. Collections of strips from *Yank* were published in 1944 and 1946, and after the war Baker continued to draw the Sad Sack for a newspaper syndicate and later for a comic-book series. He died in Los Angeles on May 7, 1975.

Baker, George Fisher (1840–1931), financier and philanthropist. Born on March 27, 1840, in Troy, New York, Baker became a clerk in the state banking department at the age of sixteen. He quickly demonstrated ability in this work and in 1863 was invited to help found the First National Bank of New York City (later the First National City Bank). He bought a small number of shares in the bank and began work as its teller and bookkeeper. Within two years he was cashier and chief operating officer of the institution and was being frequently consulted by the U.S. secretary of the treasury. He convinced the bank's president that they should remain in business during the financial panic of 1873 and four years later he himself became president. Under his direction the bank developed firm connections with other major financial and commercial establishments and, although it remained relatively small, the bank and Baker became central factors in American finance. In 1908 he founded the First Security Corporation to deal (as the bank legally could not) in the securities market. From 1909 until his death Baker was chairman of the board of the bank and served additionally as director of more than 80 corporations. After 1912 he devoted much time to philanthropy; among his benefactions, which totaled more than $19 million, were a $6 million gift to Harvard for the establishment of the Graduate School of Business Administration, large grants to the Metropolitan Museum of Art and the American Red Cross, and others to colleges, hospitals, libraries, museums, and other institutions. Columbia University's Baker Field is named after him. One of the most canny financial manipulators of his or any time, he made large sums in the stock market even during the Crash of 1929. He died on May 2, 1931, in New York City.

Baker, George Pierce (1866–1935), educator. Born in Providence, Rhode Island, on April 4, 1866, Baker graduated from Harvard in 1887 and the following year joined its faculty as an instructor in English. He began a pioneer course in oral debate in 1889 and was coach of the Harvard debating team for many years. In 1905, the year he became a full professor, he tried a new course in practical playwriting at Radcliffe College and the next year introduced it at Harvard. Although not a playwright himself, he was an excellent teacher and critic and an inspiration to many of his students; in the classroom of English 47, as the course was designated, and more importantly as the director of the 47 Workshop, where the students' dramatic efforts were produced, he guided such future literary luminaries as Eugene O'Neill, Sidney Howard, George Abbott, and Thomas Wolfe. By emphasizing the practical aspects of playwriting in the workshop, Baker was in large part responsible for the general improvement of the U.S. theater that marked the period after World War I and for the establishment of dramatic-arts courses in colleges across the country. In 1924 he left Harvard for Yale, where he served as professor of history and technique of drama. He established the Yale school of drama and directed the University Theater. He was active also in the Little Theater movement and in the American Folk Dance Society; he introduced to the United States much of current European thought on drama, edited collections of plays, and wrote extensively on various aspects of the theater, notably in *The Development of Shakespeare as a Dramatist*, 1907, and *Dramatic Technique*, 1919. Baker retired from Yale in 1933 and died in New York City on January 6, 1935.

Baker, Josephine (1906–1975), entertainer. Born in St. Louis on June 3, 1906, Miss Baker grew up fatherless and in poverty. Between the ages of eight and ten she was out of school, helping to support her family. She was early attracted to things theatrical and as an adolescent danced occasionally in local vaudeville houses. At sixteen she joined a Philadelphia-based traveling dance troupe and shortly afterward, in 1923, won a spot in the chorus line of *Shuffle Along* on Broadway. She next appeared in *Chocolate Dandies* and at the plush Plantation Club in Harlem. In 1925 she accepted an offer to appear in the Paris show *La Revue Nègre;* she rose to stardom on the wave of French enthusiasm for jazz and everything connected with it and was soon receiving top billing at the Folies Bergère, where she became celebrated across Europe for her G-string ornamented with bananas. She opened her own Paris club in 1926 and became the darling of café society; given to eccentricities, she created a sensation by walking a leashed leopard on the Champs Élysées. She began to sing professionally in 1930 and thereby added a new and, if possible, more exciting dimension to her performances. During the 1930s she appeared in several French movies and in *La Créole*, a light opera with music by Jacques Offenbach. Miss Baker became a naturalized French citizen in 1937. At the outbreak of World War II she did volunteer work with the Red Cross and when France was invaded in 1940, joined the Resistance. After the war she starred again at the Folies and later made a number of world tours, including visits to the United States, where she performed and took part in civil-rights activities. She maintained a large estate in the south of France, where she raised a large "rainbow family" of adopted children of various colors and nationalities. In 1968 the estate was sold to satisfy accumulated debts. She died in Paris on April 12, 1975, during the fiftieth anniversary of her Parisian debut.

Baker, Newton Diehl (1871–1937), lawyer and public official. Born on December 3, 1871, in Martinsburg, West Virginia, Baker attended The Johns Hopkins University, where one of his teachers was Woodrow Wilson. He graduated in 1892 and entered Washington and Lee University, earning his law degree in 1894. He returned to Martinsburg to practice, spending his evenings studying foreign languages. In 1896 he was called to Washington to become secretary to the postmaster general. He moved his practice to Cleveland about 1898, and there became assistant director of the city's law department, city solicitor, and the principal adviser to the municipal administration under reform mayor Tom L. Johnson. In 1911 he was elected mayor of Cleveland, winning reelection in 1913. An ardent supporter of Wilson, he became a prominent national figure in the presidential campaign of 1912. In 1916 President Wilson appointed him secretary of war. During his first year of service, faced with the Pancho Villa guerrilla war in Mexico and the war in Europe, he did surprisingly little to strengthen the military forces, but when the United States entered the war he presented a plan for conscription that enlarged the army from 95,000 to 4,000,000 men. He supported Gen. John J. Pershing's policy of keeping U.S. troops in a separate fighting force and he shared President Wilson's liberal, intellectual outlook. He was, however, sharply criticized by some of his contemporaries. Shortages of equipment and food were blamed on his administration; as a pacifist, he was accused of letting the military bear the conduct of the war; and a Senate probe begun in 1917 forced him to remove inexperienced, bureaucratic generals from the War Department. After the war, he returned to his law practice in Cleveland. He supported American entry into the League of Nations in the 1920s and was appointed to the Permanent Court of Arbitration at The Hague in 1928. His views became more conservative as he grew older, and in 1936 he was considered for political office by both Republicans and conservative Democrats. But poor health forced his retirement, and he died in Shaker Heights, Ohio, on December 25, 1937.

Baker, Norma Jean, *see* Monroe, Marilyn

Baker, Ray Stannard (1870–1946), "David Grayson," journalist and author. Born on April 17, 1870, in Lansing, Michigan, Baker was raised from the age of five in northwestern Wisconsin, then frontier territory. He graduated from Michigan Agricultural College in 1889 and entered law school at the University of Michigan, but soon switched to literature. At twenty-two he became a stringer for the *Chicago Record;* his first major story concerned a Chicago restaurant strike and earned him a regular staff job. Assigned to report on coal thefts, he demonstrated an ability to probe below the surface of news events; he discovered that the culprits lived in run-down, unheated shacks and earned such low wages that they could not afford heat. His coverage of the march of "Coxey's Army" in 1894 earned him an editorship on the *Chicago Record*, but *McClure's* hired him away as an editor in 1897. From 1899 to 1905 he was associate editor of *McClure's Magazine*, working there with other noted muckraking journalists, including Ida M. Tarbell, Lincoln Steffens, and William Allen White. Together this group founded the *American Magazine* in 1906, which Baker coedited from then until 1915. He met Woodrow Wilson in Paris in 1919 while serving as director of the press bureau of the American Commission to Negotiate Peace. They developed a close friendship, from which emerged 18 books by Baker, including an eight-volume authorized biography, *Woodrow Wilson—Life and Letters*, 1927–1939, which won a Pulitzer Prize in 1940. He wrote other books on a wide range of subjects, including *Seen in Germany*, 1901; *Following the Color Line*, 1908; *The Spiritual Unrest*, 1910; and *The New Industrial Unrest*, 1920. Under the pseudonym David Grayson, he wrote collections of immensely popular philosophical essays. Baker's autobiography, in three volumes, appeared in 1941–1945. He died on July 12, 1946, at his home in Amherst, Massachusetts.

Balanchine, George (1904–1983), choreographer. Born Georgi Melitonovitch Balanchivadze on January 9, 1904, in St. Petersburg (now Leningrad), Russia, the son of composer Meliton Balanchivadze, Balanchine was trained at the Imperial Ballet School in St. Petersburg from the age of ten and graduated in 1921, by which time it had become the Soviet State Ballet School. He continued his studies at the Conservatory of Music in Moscow and joined the Soviet State Dancers. He toured with them to Paris in 1924 and decided to remain, joining the Ballet Russe of Sergei Diaghilev, who suggested the French version of his name that he used thereafter. Balanchine worked more frequently as a choreographer than a dancer because of his slight build. By 1929, when Diaghilev died and his troupe disbanded, Balanchine had choreographed *Enigma*, *La Chatte*, and *Apollo*. He went to London and arranged the dances for Cole Porter's *Wake Up and Dream*, then became ballet master of the Royal Danish Ballet in Copenhagen. In 1932 he helped to organize the Ballet Russe de Monte Carlo, and the next year in Paris formed his own company, Les Ballets. During this period he composed *Cotillon* and *La Concurrence*. Stressing visual pattern and movement rather than an intricate plot, his dances were precise variations on themes of classic ballet. In 1933 Lincoln Kirstein, a Boston philanthropist, invited him to America to establish a school for U.S. dancers. Together they founded in 1934 the School of American Ballet, which produced a throng of good dancers to staff the companies Kirstein and Balanchine subsequently formed: the American Ballet Company, Ballet Caravan, Ballet Society, and the New York City Ballet, which Balanchine headed after its founding in 1948. Balanchine choreographed some 200 ballets, among them *Concerto Barocco*, *Le Bourgeois Gentilhomme*, *Danses Concertantes*, *Symphonies Concertantes*, *Waltz Academy*, *The Four Temperaments*, *The Triumph of Bacchus*, *Orpheus*, *Serenade*, *Le Baiser de la Fée*, *Agon*, *Firebird*, *Swan Lake*, *Nutcracker Suite*, and *Ruslan and Ludmilla*; in 1962 he collaborated with composer Igor Stravinsky on the televised premiere of *Noah and the Flood*. For the musical-comedy stage he arranged the dances for such productions as *Babes in Arms*, 1937; *I Married an Angel*, 1938; *Cabin in the Sky*, 1940; *Louisiana Purchase*, 1940; *Song of Norway*, 1944; and *Courtin' Time*,

1951. Regarded by many observers as the outstanding choreographer of the 20th century, he died in New York City on April 30, 1983.

Balch, Emily Greene (1867–1961), economist and social reformer. Born on January 8, 1867, in Jamaica Plain, Massachusetts, Miss Balch was in the first class to graduate from Bryn Mawr College, in 1889. She pursued further studies in Paris and Berlin and at the University of Chicago and received training in social work from followers of Jacob Riis in New York City and in a settlement house in Boston. In 1897 she began her teaching career at Wellesley College, becoming in 1913 professor of political economy and political and social science. She continued her interest in the settlement-house movement, working with Jane Addams's Hull House in Chicago, was active in promoting various child-welfare reforms, and served on the Massachusetts commissions on industrial education (1908–1909) and immigration (1913–1914) and on the Boston city planning board, 1914–1917. A member of the Society of Friends, Miss Balch became increasingly committed to the cause of peace and, following her attendance at the International Congress of Women at The Hague in 1915, she devoted her major efforts to that cause. Pacificism being an unpopular position in the United States at that time, she was relieved of her post at Wellesley in 1918. She helped found the Women's International League for Peace and Freedom in Zurich the following year and served as its secretary until 1922, when ill health forced her resignation; she resumed the post again briefly in 1934–1935 and in 1936 was elected honorary international president. In 1926 she was appointed to a committee sent to study conditions in Haiti, and the committee's report, of which she was the principal author, was credited with hastening the withdrawal of U.S. forces from the country. Her work for peace finally achieved its due recognition in 1946, when, with John R. Mott, she shared the Nobel Peace Prize. Among her many writings were *Our Slavic Fellow Citizens*, 1910, a thorough and sympathetic study of Slavic immigrants; *Approaches to the Great Settlement*, 1918; *Refugees as Assets*, 1939; *One Europe*, 1947; and *Toward Human Unity, or Beyond Nationalism*, 1952. Miss Balch died in Cambridge, Massachusetts, on January 9, 1961.

Baldwin, Henry (1780–1844), justice of the Supreme Court. Born on January 14, 1780, in New Haven, Connecticut, Baldwin graduated from Yale in 1797 and took up the study of law under Alexander J. Dallas. He began his practice in Pittsburgh and soon attained a high reputation both as an attorney and as a legal scholar. In 1816 he was elected to the House of Representatives, where he remained until forced by ill health to resign in 1822. A strong supporter of Andrew Jackson in the presidential election of 1828, he was appointed by Jackson to the Supreme Court two years later. On the Court Baldwin was at first a follower of John Marshall, but he soon began to seek a middle course between the loose- and strict-constructionist views of the Constitution, a course he attempted to define in *A General View of the Origin and Nature of the Constitution and Government of the United States,* 1837. The practical outcome of his rather vague judicial principles was, however, a marked degree of unpredictability in his decisions. His most important opinion came in 1832 in *U.S.* v. *Arredondo,* a case concerning a Spanish land grant made in Florida prior to the acquisition of the territory by the United States under the Adams-Onís Treaty of 1819 (ratified by the United States in 1821). In his opinion Baldwin made strict adherence to treaties the fundamental element of the government's public-land policy. His last years were a period of some financial difficulty, and at the same time his behavior became so erratic as to verge at times on insanity. Baldwin died in Philadelphia on April 21, 1844.

Baldwin, James (1924–   ), author. Born in New York City on August 2, 1924, Baldwin grew up under the strict guidance of his strongly religious father and at fourteen was preaching in storefront churches in Harlem. In high school his interest turned to writing, and, leaving home at seventeen, he spent several years alternating between holding menial jobs and writing with the support of a series of fellowships. None of this early work was published at the time. In 1948 he went to Paris where, in an atmosphere relatively free of racial prejudice and tension, he remained for nearly ten years. In Paris he lived in poverty but continued to write, receiving encouragement from Richard Wright. His first published novel, *Go Tell It on the Mountain,* appeared in 1953; in 1955 appeared a volume of essays, *Notes of a Native Son.* Both received good critical notices but their sales were small. Popular success came after his return to the United States in 1957: *Nobody Knows My Name,* another collection of essays published in 1961, and the novel *Another Country,* 1962, established him not only as a leading black spokesman but also as a major figure in contemporary American literature. He followed with *The Fire Next Time,* essays, in 1963 and two modestly successful plays, *Blues for Mister Charlie* and *The Amen Corner.* In 1965 he published a volume of short stories, *Going to Meet the Man,* in 1968 another novel, *Tell Me How Long the Train's Been Gone,* and in 1972 a fourth collection of essays, *No Name in the Street.*

Baldwin, Loammi (1745–1807), engineer. Born in North Woburn, Massachusetts, on January 10, 1745, Baldwin became an apprentice cabinetmaker at an early age but studied physics and mathematics on his own and with his friend, Benjamin Thompson, with whom he often attended lectures at Harvard. He began working as a surveyor and, as his self-education progressed, as a civil engineer. During the Revolution he commanded a regiment that served in Boston and, under Gen. George Washington, in New York and New Jersey. He resigned in 1777 because of ill health, returned home, and the next year was elected to the Massachusetts legislature. He was also high sheriff of Middlesex County for several years and again served in the legislature from 1800 to 1804. From 1794 to 1804 he planned and supervised the construction of the Middlesex Canal, which connected the Charles and Merrimack rivers. He continued to work as an engineer until his death and he collected a large library of books on the subject. He is best remembered, however, for his development of the Baldwin apple, a hardy and satisfying variety that became the most widely cultivated winter apple in the East. Baldwin died on October 20, 1807, in Woburn.

Baldwin, Loammi (1780–1838), engineer and lawyer. Born in North Woburn, Massachusetts, on May 16, 1780, the son of Loammi Baldwin (1745–1807), the younger Baldwin graduated from Harvard in 1800. Prevented by the cost of apprenticeship from becoming an instrument maker, he instead studied law. In 1802 he designed and built a fire engine for the town of Groton, Massachusetts, where he was studying. The fire engine was still being used in the 1890s. He practiced law from 1804 to 1807, but upon the death of his father in 1807 he turned to engineering. After making a tour of inspection of public works in Europe, he opened an office in Charlestown, Massachusetts. He built Fort Strong in Boston Harbor (1814), worked for a time on projects in Virginia, and in 1819 became engineer of improvements for the city of Boston. In 1821 he began planning and supervising the construction of the Union Canal from Reading to Middletown, Pennsylvania, which included the largest dam yet built in this country. His specifications for the dam were disregarded at first, whereupon he resigned from the project; but he was later vindicated when expensive alterations were found to be necessary. Other projects in which Baldwin was involved included the designing of the Bunker Hill Monument, surveying a route for a canal from Boston Harbor to the Hudson River that would have opened a shipping route to the Erie Canal, and constructing dry docks at the naval yards in Charlestown and in Norfolk, Virginia. He also drew plans for dry docks in New York Harbor and planned an extensive inland navigation system for Georgia and a marine railroad for Pensacola, Florida; none of the projects were built until after his death. He died in Charlestown on June 30, 1838.

Baldwin, Matthias William (1795–1866), businessman. Born in Elizabethtown, New Jersey, on December 10, 1795, Baldwin became an apprentice jewelry maker in Philadelphia after finishing school. Following his apprenticeship he conducted his own jewelry manufacturing business for six years, but in 1826 he took in a partner and began making tools and textile-printing machinery. By 1827 he had begun manufacturing steam engines. In 1831 he built a full-scale model locomotive and the next year constructed a real one, named *Old Ironsides*, for the Philadelphia & Germantown Railroad. He continued to build steam engines and locomotives for ten years and then devoted himself entirely to locomotives, in which he introduced a great many improvements: his steam-tight metal joint, for example, enabled his locomotives to operate at twice the steam pressure that had previously been used. The M. W. Baldwin Company, later the world-famous Baldwin Locomotive Works, one of the great manufacturing establishments of Philadelphia, built more than 1500 locomotives during his lifetime. Baldwin was also interested in various philanthropies, particularly those concerned with the welfare of Negroes, and his abolitionist sympathies led to a boycott of his locomotives by Southern railroads for some years. He had been one of the founders of Philadelphia's Franklin Institute in 1824. He died in Philadelphia on September 7, 1866.

Baline, Israel, *see* Berlin, Irving

Ball, Lucille (1911–   ), actress. Born on August 6, 1911, in Jamestown, New York, Miss Ball determined at an early age to become an actress and left high school at fifteen to enroll in a drama school in New York City. Her early attempts to find a place in the theater all met with rebuffs and she took a job as a model under the name Diane Belmont. She was moderately successful as a model, and a poster on which she appeared won her a spot in Samuel Goldwyn's *Roman Scandals* in 1934. She remained in Hollywood to appear in increasingly larger roles in a string of movies—*Roberta, The Girl from Paris, Dance, Girl, Dance,* and in 1940 *Too Many Girls,* in which she starred and which also featured Desi Arnaz, whom she married a few months later. For ten years they conducted separate careers, he as a band leader who took occasional small parts in movies and she as a movie actress who was usually seen in B-grade comedies. She won major roles in *The Big Street, Du Barry Was a Lady, Best Foot Forward, Meet the People,* and *Easy to Wed,* all comedies which were box-office successes, but she was less fortunate in dramatic parts. In 1950 she and her husband formed Desilu Productions which, after experimenting with a radio program, launched in 1951 a television comedy series entitled "I Love Lucy." Starring the two of them in a comedy version of their real lives, the show was an instant hit, and for six years during which fresh episodes were produced it remained at or near the top of the TV ratings. "I Love Lucy" won an Emmy award in 1956 and, released into syndicated distribution, was still being seen by millions in reruns 20 years after it had begun. Meanwhile Desilu began producing other shows for television and became one of the major companies in a highly competitive field. Miss Ball and Arnaz were divorced in 1960 and

two years later she succeeded him as president of Desilu. She starred in the Broadway show *Wildcat* in 1961 and in the late 1960s returned to television in "The Lucy Show," a popular comedy series which won an Emmy award in 1968.

Ballou, Adin (1803–1890), religious leader and social reformer. Born in Cumberland, Rhode Island, on April 23, 1903, Ballou, a distant cousin of Hosea Ballou, developed early interests in both scholarship and religion. He began to preach locally at the age of eighteen and, reversing his original opinion of Universalism, he joined that sect and began active work on its behalf in 1823. He withdrew because of a theological dispute and in 1831 formed his own splinter Universalist group, which lasted for ten years. He was active in a number of reform movements, particularly those directed toward peace, temperance, and the abolition of slavery. In 1840, in order to expound his own views on society and the imperative call to establish the Kingdom of God on earth, he began to publish the *Practical Christian,* a biweekly newspaper that continued for 20 years. His social and religious ideas came to fruition almost immediately when in 1841, with 31 associates, he founded the Hopedale Community, a self-contained religious society based on what he called "fraternal communism." Actually a joint-stock company, the group purchased 250 acres of land near Milford, Massachusetts, and prospered for several years. Presiding over the community until 1856, Ballou retired with full confidence in the success of his experiment. However, three years later, when the community was dissolved by two brothers who had acquired a controlling interest in the stock, Ballou blamed the failure on a lack of wholehearted moral dedication among the members. He remained as pastor of the Hopedale Unitarian Parish which succeeded the community until 1880. He died on August 5, 1890.

Ballou, Hosea (1771–1852), religious leader. Born in Richmond, New Hampshire, on April 30, 1771, Ballou grew up in poverty and acquired an education largely on his own. Brought up in the Baptist Church, he formally joined that church at eighteen, but he was already beginning to think along unorthodox lines, and his conviction that salvation was open to all men led to his excommunication by the Baptists in 1791. In that year he made his first attempt at preaching. He began traveling in Rhode Island and Massachusetts, expounding his views and supporting himself by teaching school, and in 1794 he was ordained in the Universalist Church. Through close study of the Bible and his reading of deistic works, particularly Ethan Allen's *Reason, the Only Oracle of Man,* he began applying the same form of critique to other doctrines as he had to the Calvinistic belief in an elect, and he gradually evolved a positive theology for Universalism. His liberalism went farther than many other Universalist leaders wished, for he dismissed the

Trinitarian thesis, original sin, Christ's full deity, and the prevailing interpretation of Christ's sacrifice, discussing the last in his most important book, *A Treatise on the Atonement*, 1805. Ballou, an indefatigable circuit rider, was based from 1795 to 1803 in Dana, Massachusetts, and from 1803 to 1809 in Barnard, Vermont. He made trips to western New York in 1806 and 1807 and in 1809 he assumed the Universalist pastorate in Portsmouth, New Hampshire. In 1815 he moved to Salem, Massachusetts, and in 1817 to Boston, where he remained for the rest of his life. By this time the leading figure in the Universalist movement, he edited the *Universalist Magazine* from 1819 to 1828 and the *Universalist Expositor* from 1830 to 1840. About 1817 he had begun to develop his most radical contribution to Universalist theology, the doctrine that there is no punishment after death for sin, but that the soul is purified immediately and received into heaven. He presented this position fully in *An Examination of the Doctrine of Future Retribution*, 1834, but took no major role in the controversy over the idea that arose with the schismatic "Restorationists." Ballou also published several volumes of sermons during his career. He died in Boston on June 7, 1852, having served as pastor of the Second Universalist Society there for 35 years.

Baltimore, Baron *see* Calvert, Charles; Calvert, George.

Bancroft, Edward (1744–1821), secret agent. Born in Westfield, Massachusetts, on January 9, 1744, Bancroft received little or no formal education. Possessed of an adventurous and inquiring spirit, he was for a time a sailor, and then a settler in Dutch Guiana (Surinam). At length he moved to England, where, having acquired an education, he became a physician. He wrote numerous articles about America for the *Monthly Review* and published several books, including *Essay on the Natural History of Guiana*, 1769, and *Remarks on the Review of the Controversy between Great Britain and Her Colonies*, 1769. After the outbreak of the Revolution he volunteered his services as a spy to Benjamin Franklin, who was then representing the American colonies in Paris, and he subsequently formed a close association with Franklin's colleague, Silas Deane. Through Deane he was paid by Congress for his work as a confidential agent. At the same time he was in the pay of the British government, to whom he sent, through his fellow spy Paul Wentworth, details of the various French-American agreements and treaties and advance notice of the movement of supplies, ships, and troops from France to America. He was never discovered by Franklin or Deane. After the war, he remained in England and interested himself in the manufacture of textile dyes, making some notable discoveries. He died in Margate on September 8, 1821.

Bancroft, George (1800–1891), historian, public official, and diplomat. Born in Worcester, Massa-

chusetts, on October 3, 1800, Bancroft graduated from Harvard in 1817. He studied theology for a year and then, in 1818, with financial support arranged by President Kirkland of Harvard, he continued his studies in Germany. With a Ph.D. from Göttingen, in 1820 he returned to Harvard in 1822 to teach for a year. He then established, with Joseph Cogswell, the Round Hill School in Northampton, Massachusetts. He remained with the school for eight years, during which time he began, through writing articles and pamphlets, to enter political affairs. He also began his great work, the *History of the United States*, publishing the first three volumes in 1834, 1837, and 1840. Written in florid prose and with a marked democratic and nationalist bias, the work established Bancroft as the nation's foremost historian. He gained influence in the Democratic party and upon Martin Van Buren's election to the presidency in 1836, he was appointed collector of the port of Boston. In 1845 he became President James K. Polk's secretary of the navy and promoted the establishment of the Naval Academy; he directed the occupation of California and, as acting secretary of war, issued the order that sent Gen. Zachary Taylor across the U.S.–Texas border and led directly to the Mexican War. In 1846 he became minister to England and while in that post he continued research for his *History*. He returned in 1849 and devoted the next 18 years to his massive project, ultimately publishing six more volumes. In 1867 he became minister to Prussia and in 1871 minister to the German imperial court, in which position he represented the United States in the arbitration of the Oregon boundary dispute with Great Britain. He returned again to the United States in 1874, published the tenth volume of the *History* shortly thereafter, and prepared the revised six-volume Centenary Edition. In 1882, he published a two-volume work on the formation of the Constitution; four years later it was included in the final revised edition of the *History*. He continued to publish books and articles until his death in Washington, D.C., on January 17, 1891. He was elected to the Hall of Fame in 1910.

Bancroft, Hubert Howe (1832–1918), historian and editor. Born in Granville, Ohio, on May 5, 1832, Bancroft chose business over college upon finishing school and took a job in a bookstore in Buffalo, New York. In 1852 he sailed to California, where he worked as a miner and at other jobs until 1856, when he opened his own bookstore in San Francisco. In 1859 he began collecting works on California history; his interest gradually expanded to include the entire western part of the continent, from Central America to Alaska. As the collection grew to an eventual 60,000 volumes, he began to organize the wealth of material it contained with the aim of producing a definitive history of the region. Employing a staff of assistants who researched and indexed the library, sought out original documents from all over the Pacific Coast, interviewed old settlers, and did much of the draft writing, he supervised a huge outpouring of historical works, among them *The Native Races of the Pacific States*, 1874–1875, 5 volumes; *Chronicles of the Builders*, 1891–1892, 8 volumes; *Book of the Fair*, 1893, 5 volumes; and *Book of Wealth*, 1896–1908, 10 volumes. Although Bancroft did write portions of the books, his principal function was that of editing and unifying the work of others; nonetheless, all appeared under his name (he published them all himself), with no credit being given to his team of assistants. This did not detract from the value of the works, however, and Bancroft's collection itself provided a basic source for the study of the history of western America. He presented his library to the University of California in 1905. He continued to write, producing volumes of essays that included the autobiographical *Literary Industries*, 1890; *The New Pacific*, 1900; *Retrospection, Political and Personal*, 1912; and *In These Latter Days*, 1917. Bancroft died on March 2, 1918, in Walnut Creek, California.

Bandelier, Adolph Francis Alphonse (1840–1914), archaeologist and anthropologist. Born on August 6, 1840, in Bern, Switzerland, Bandelier emigrated with his family to a farm near Highland, Illinois, in 1848. After finishing his schooling at home he returned briefly to Switzerland to study geology at the University of Bern. He then took an uncongenial job in a bank in Highland and pursued an extensive program of reading in history and ethnology. He came under the influence of Lewis H. Morgan and published a series of studies on Aztec society that paralleled Morgan's work on the Iroquois Indians. The studies included *On the Art of War and Mode of Warfare . . . Among the Ancient Mexicans*, 1877; *Distribution and Tenure of Lands Among the Ancient Mexicans*, 1878; and *On the Social Organization . . . of the Ancient Mexicans*, 1879. Although later superseded by the less dogmatic work of others, the works won Bandelier considerable attention and the sponsorship of the Archaeological Institute of America, under whose auspices he traveled to the Southwest in 1880. During the decade he spent there he did a vast amount of field work, living for a time with the Pueblo Indians, and supplementing his observations with detailed archival research. The resulting works, *Final Report of Investigations Among the Indians of the Southwestern United States*, 1890–1892, and *Contributions to the History of the Southwestern Portion of the United States*, 1890, were landmark studies that remained of significant value. In 1892, sponsored by Henry Villard, he went to South America and for 11 years observed and did research on the Indians of Peru and Bolivia, producing later *The Indians and Aboriginal Ruins of Chachapoyas, Peru*, 1907, and most importantly, *The Islands of Titicaca and Koati*, 1910. He returned to the United States in 1903 and settled in New York City, where he was on the staff of the American Museum of Natural History and, from 1904 to 1911, was a lecturer on Spanish-American literature at Columbia University. He became a member of the Hispanic Society of America in 1906, and in 1911 he was appointed to the staff of the Carnegie Institution of Washington, by which he was sent to conduct research in Spain. He died in Seville on March 18, 1914.

Bankhead, Tallulah Brockman (1903–1968), actress. Born in Huntsville, Alabama, on January 31, 1903, Miss Bankhead was the daughter of William B. Bankhead. She was educated in convent schools and at fifteen, having won a movie-magazine beauty contest, went to New York to become an actress. She made her first Broadway appearance in *Squab Farm* in 1918; during the next four years she played a number of roles, none particularly memorable, while becoming a member of the "Algonquin set"—a group that included Alexander Woollcott, Dorothy Parker, Robert Benchley, and Harpo and Groucho Marx—and a figure about town. In 1923 she starred in the London production of *The Dancers* and, thereafter remained in London for eight years, appearing in more than a dozen plays and becoming a celebrity's celebrity. Between 1931 and 1933 she made several movies and then returned to Broadway in a series of productions that failed to engage her unique talents. Finally, in 1939, she appeared in *The Little Foxes* and gave a performance that won the year's top acting award from the New York Drama Critics' Circle. She won the award again three years later for her performance in Thornton Wilder's *The Skin of Our Teeth* and in 1944 took the New York Film Critics' highest award for her role in Alfred Hitchcock's *Lifeboat*. Such successes established her as a star whose name could underwrite any production; her deep voice, lush beauty, and mysterious manner, to say nothing of her singular name, fascinated millions. She continued to play on Broadway in, among other productions, *Foolish Notion*, *Private Lives*, a 1956 revival of *Streetcar Named Desire*, and *Eugenia*, while appearing occasionally in movies and later on television. In 1950–1952 she conducted a combined variety show and talk program on radio. In 1952 she published *Tallulah, My Autobiography*. Tallulah—her last name had for years been entirely superfluous—died in New York City on December 12, 1968.

Bankhead, William Brockman (1874–1940), public official. Born in Moscow, Alabama, on April 12, 1874, Bankhead graduated from the University of Alabama in 1893 and two years later took a law degree from Georgetown University. He began his practice in Huntsville, Alabama, but soon moved to New York City, where, discouraged in his ambition to be an actor (his daughter Tallulah was to succeed where he had failed), he became involved in Tammany politics. He continued his political activity after his return to Alabama in 1900 and held a number of local and state offices in Huntsville and, after 1905, in Jasper. In 1914 he ran unsuccessfully for the House of Representatives, but two years later, with the aid of his politically influential family, he was elected to the seat which he held for the rest of his life. Bankhead served as a loyal Democrat, which led him after 1932 to be a loyal New Dealer as well. He was elected House majority leader in 1934 and two years later was chosen to succeed Joseph W. Byrns as speaker of the House. At the 1940 Democratic national convention he gave the keynote address and was promoted by many for the vice-presidency. He died a short time later, on September 15, 1940, in Bethesda, Maryland.

Banks, Nathaniel Prentiss (1816–1894), public official and soldier. Born on January 30, 1816, in Waltham, Massachusetts, Banks was largely self-educated. He read widely, practiced public speaking, and after a brief dalliance with the Boston stage took up the study of law. He was admitted to the bar in 1839 but never practiced, instead taking a job in the Boston customhouse and, for three years, publishing the weekly *Middlesex Reporter*. After several unsuccessful campaigns he won election to the Massachusetts house of representatives in 1849 and served for four years, the last two as speaker. In 1853 he presided over the state constitutional convention and in the same year entered the U.S. House of Representatives as a Democrat. He was reelected in 1854 as a Know-Nothing and thereupon waged a long and arduous battle for the speakership of the House, winning it on the 133rd ballot. He conducted the office in an eminently fair and tactful manner and was widely respected for his parliamentary skill. In 1857 he was elected governor of Massachusetts as a moderate Republican. During his three years in that office he was an efficient administrator, and he is often given credit for making possible the immediate response of his successor, John A. Andrew, to President Lincoln's call for troops in 1861. By that time Banks had gone to Chicago to replace George B. McClellan as president of the Illinois Central Railroad, but he soon resigned to accept an army commission as major general; he was put in command of the Department of Annapolis. Early in 1862, in command of a corps detached from Gen. George B. McClellan's Army of the Potomac, he faced Gen. T. J. (Stonewall) Jackson in the Shenandoah Valley and after an initial success was forced to retreat. Later, leading a unit of Gen. John Pope's Army of Virginia, he attacked and was again outfought by Jackson at Cedar Mountain. After a brief period in command of the defense of Washington, D.C., he was sent to New Orleans to succeed Gen. Benjamin F. Butler as commander of the Department of the Gulf. In 1863 he captured Alexandria and laid siege to Port Hudson, which surrendered after the fall of Vicksburg, thus earning Banks a congressional commendation. In 1864 he commanded an ill-conceived joint expedition up the Red River with a river fleet under Adm. David D. Porter. The combined force suffered serious reverses at Sabine Crossroads on April 8 and at Pleasant Hill the next day; Banks was forced to withdraw and

Porter's fleet escaped only with great difficulty. Banks resigned in 1865, returned to Waltham, and was immediately elected again, as a Republican, to the House of Representatives. He served in Congress until his defeat on the Liberal Republican ticket in 1872. He was then elected to the Massachusetts senate, but was returned to the House as a Democrat in 1874 and as a Republican in 1876. From 1879 to 1888 he served as federal marshal for Massachusetts, and in 1888 was once again elected to the House as a Republican. Ill health forced his retirement in 1891 and he died in Waltham on September 1, 1894.

Banneker, Benjamin (1731–1806), mathematician. Born on November 9, 1731, in Ellicott, Maryland, Banneker was the son of a slave father and a free mother. Free himself, he attended a local school, where he early displayed a talent for mathematics, and afterward continued to study a wide range of subjects in books borrowed from a friendly white neighbor. In his youth he constructed a wooden clock, apparently the first to be made in America, which struck the hours and kept remarkably accurate time for many years. His interests ranged from the habits of bees and seventeen-year locusts to astronomy, and it was in the latter field that he was to do his most notable work. He came to the attention of Thomas Jefferson, who in 1790 secured him a position with the surveying team appointed to lay out the District of Columbia and the site of the city of Washington. When the chief architect and city planner, Pierre L'Enfant, was dismissed in 1792 and departed, taking with him his detailed maps, Banneker was able to reproduce L'Enfant's plan from memory. In 1791 he published an almanac containing the results of his astronomical observations and calculations. He sent a copy to Jefferson, who was sufficiently impressed by the work, and by Banneker's accompanying letter defending the intellectual equality of the Negro, to forward it to the French Academy of Sciences. Editions of the almanac continued to appear regularly until 1802. Banneker died in 1806 in Baltimore County.

Bara, Theda (1890–1955), actress. Born in Cincinnati on July 20, 1890, Theodosia Goodman began her movie career in 1915 with William Fox, who built his motion-picture empire on her films. She appeared first in *A Fool There Was* and created a nationwide sensation; this film, together with a huge outpouring of studio publicity, some of it bordering on the farcical, made her one of the most magnetic stars of the silent-movie era. In five years she made some 40 films, including *Cleopatra, Salome,* and *The Vampire*, the last giving rise to the term "vamp" through her playing of a role that was perfectly suited to her sultry, heavy-lidded manner and often semiclad person. Her screen appearances were of such an arousing nature that on several occasions she was denounced from the pulpit. She changed her name legally to Theda Bara at the outset of her career and the Fox publicity department had a field day telling the nation that her first name was an anagram for "death" and her second was "Arab" spelled backward; she was, they suggested darkly, the daughter of a French artist and an Arabian princess and had been born somewhere in the Sahara. Others of her films included *Madame Du Barry, The Tiger Woman, Forbidden Path,* and *The Rose of Blood,* all with titles designed to convey the mysterious allure of the star. Miss Bara left the movies in 1920, made one unsuccessful attempt on Broadway in *The Blue Flame,* and retired to live quietly in Los Angeles until her death there on April 7, 1955.

Baraka, Imamu Amiri (1934–   ), poet and playwright. Born Everett LeRoi Jones on October 7, 1934, in Newark, New Jersey, the son of a postman, Baraka graduated from Howard University in Washington, D.C., in 1954, at age nineteen. He served in the air force from 1954 to 1957, after which he studied German literature at Columbia and philosophy at the New School for Social Research, interrupting his studies from time to time for travel in Europe, Africa, and the Middle East. He began writing in the later 1950s and published his first book of poems, *Preface to a Twenty-Volume Suicide Note,* in 1961. In 1960–1961 a John Hay Whitney Fellowship helped him to continue his writing, and he also taught during the next few years at the New School. His play *The Dutchman* was produced off-Broadway in 1964 and won the Obie Award as the best off-Broadway play of the 1963–1964 season. It was released in a film version in 1967. Notable among his other plays were *The Toilet,* produced off-Broadway in 1964, and *The Slave,* which won second prize in drama at the first World Festival of Negro Arts in Dakar, Senegal, in 1966. Among his nondramatic works were *Blues People: Negro Music in White America,* 1963; an autobiographical novel, *The System of Dante's Hell,* 1965; a collection of "social essays," *Home,* 1966; a collection of stories, *Tales,* 1967; and a collection of essays on and reviews of jazz performers and performances, *Black Music,* 1968. He changed his name toward the end of the 1960s and at that time became active in organizing black people for social and political action.

Barber, Samuel (1910–1981), composer. Born on March 9, 1910, in West Chester, Pennsylvania, Barber had composed an opera at seven and decided on a musical career at the age of eight. He was one of the first students at the Curtis Institute of Music in Philadelphia, studying piano, voice, and conducting from 1924 to 1934. Before graduation he wrote a musical setting for "Dover Beach," for voice and string quartet, an overture to *The School for Scandal,* and *Music for a Scene from Shelley,* the last two of which established his reputation. Thereafter his work became popular in Europe as well as in the United States, where he ranked as a leading composer. His *Symphony in One Movement,* 1936, was the first piece by an American to be played at the Salz-burg music festival in Austria. From his *String Quartet,* 1936, the second movement, called, *Adagio for Strings,* became his most popular lyrical work. During World War II while serving in the army, he wrote his *Second Symphony,* commissioned by and dedicated to the Army Air Force. It was premiered in 1944. His other compositions include *Essays for Orchestra,* 1937 and 1942; *Violin Concerto,* 1939; *Cello Concerto,* 1945; *Piano Sonata,* 1948; music for the ballet *Medea,* 1946; and the opera *Vanessa,* 1958, which won a Pulitzer Prize. Although Barber's later works, such as the *Pianoforte Sonata,* 1951, often made use of dissonance and the twelve-tone scale, his work was eminently melodic and listenable. The harmonies were pure and strong, as in the popular *Adagio,* and often reached thrilling climaxes, as in the *Violin Concerto.* In 1963 his *First Piano Concerto* was awarded a Pulitzer Prize, making Barber the first composer to win the prize twice. Other works included *A Hand of Bridge,* 1960, an opera with libretto by Gian-Carlo Menotti; *Antony and Cleopatra,* 1966, commissioned by the Metropolitan Opera for the opening of its new home at the Lincoln Center for the Performing Arts; *Mutations from Bach,* 1968; and *Fadograph of a Yestern Scene,* 1971. He died in New York City on January 23, 1981.

Barbour, Philip Pendleton (1783–1841), public official and justice of the Supreme Court. Born in Barboursville, Virginia, on May 25, 1783, Barbour, whose family was prominent but not wealthy, received little formal education beyond that provided by a local school. He was nonetheless possessed of an inquiring mind, and after reading law and practicing briefly in Kentucky in 1800–1801 he enrolled for a short time in the College of William and Mary. He returned to law practice in 1802 in his native state and became highly successful. In 1812 he was elected to the state legislature and two years later was sent to the House of Representatives, remaining until 1825 and serving as speaker from 1821 to 1823. A conservative and strict constructionist, he opposed the nationalistic proposals of Henry Clay and his followers and stood zealously for states' rights. He served in 1821 as counsel for Virginia before the Supreme Court in *Cohens* v. *Virginia* and argued strongly against the right of the Supreme Court to review the decision of a state court. From 1825 to 1827 he was a member of the general court of Virginia, but in the latter year returned to Congress to continue his fight against the growth of national power under President John Quincy Adams and Chief Justice John Marshall. Barbour replaced the ailing James Monroe as president of the Virginia constitutional convention in 1829–1830 and President Andrew Jackson appointed him a federal district judge in Virginia in 1830. In 1836 he was named to the Supreme Court and along with Chief Justice Roger B. Taney, set out to try to reverse the tide of Marshall's nationalism, reflected in a number of decisions of the Court under the late chief justice that had supported federal power as against that of the states. His one major opinion, in *New York* v. *Miln* in 1837, upheld the use of state power in certain commercial activities that were felt by nationalists to fall under federal jurisdiction. Although he gave every evidence of possessing the ability to develop high judicial competence, Barbour was on the bench for too short a time to be of great influence. He died in Washington, D.C., on February 25, 1841.

Bard, John (1716–1799), physician. Born in Burlington, New Jersey, on February 1, 1716, Bard was apprenticed at fifteen to a physician in Philadelphia. He studied in that city for seven years, forming during that time a close friendship with Benjamin Franklin. It was on Franklin's advice that Bard moved to New York City in 1746, after seven years of independent practice in Philadelphia. There he became a popular and successful physician and took great interest in the prevention of epidemics, persuading the authorities to establish a quarantine station on Bedloe's Island and serving as the city's first health officer. In 1750 he performed, with Peter Middleton, the first recorded dissection of a human body for the instruction of medical students in America and in 1759 made the first report of an extrauterine pregnancy. He also wrote a number of papers on yellow fever. In 1778, soon after the outbreak of the Revolution, Bard, who had Loyalist sympathies, retired to his farm at Hyde Park, New York. After the Revolution, in 1783, he returned to his city practice and five years later was elected the first president of the Medical Society of the State of New York. He retired from practice in 1798 and died at his farm on March 30, 1799.

Bard, Samuel (1742–1821), physician. Born on April 1, 1742, in Philadelphia, the son of John Bard, Samuel grew up there and, from 1746, in New York. He graduated from King's College (later Columbia) in 1760 and then set sail for England to study medicine. His ship was captured by a French privateer and he was imprisoned for five months. His father's friend, Benjamin Franklin, secured his release and he continued to London and took up his studies there and later at the University of Edinburgh, where he was awarded his medical degree in 1765. Returning to New York, he began to practice with his father, whom he soon surpassed in popularity; his specialty was midwifery, on which he wrote a widely used textbook. He took an active role in establishing the medical school of King's College in 1767 and served it as a professor. A Loyalist, he moved from New York to Shrewsbury, New Jersey, when the Revolution began, and he returned when the city was occupied by the British. After the war he remained to become George Washington's personal physician when the city became the seat of the new federal government. Bard was a leader in founding New York Hospital in 1791 and the next year became dean of the

faculty of its medical school. He was also active in the establishment of the New York Dispensary and the public library. He retired to his father's farm in Hyde Park, New York, in 1798. In 1811 he was elected president of the College of Physicians and Surgeons and held that post until his death on May 24, 1821, in Hyde Park.

Bard, William (1778–1853), businessman. Born in Philadelphia on April 4, 1778, Bard was the son of Samuel Bard. He graduated from Columbia College in 1797 and became a businessman, but little is known of his activities before 1830, when he organized the New York Life Insurance and Trust Company, the first company to make life insurance its primary business rather than a sideline. Faced at first by a mixture of public distrust and apathy, Bard made considerable headway by means of advertising and pamphleteering and devised the agency system for the sale of policies. The company was highly successful until it began to meet strong competition in the late 1840s; Bard then retired. He died in Staten Island, New York, on October 17, 1853.

Bardeen, John (1908–   ), physicist. Born on May 23, 1908, in Madison, Wisconsin, Bardeen graduated from the University of Wisconsin in 1928 and remained there to take his M.S. the following year. From 1930 to 1933 he worked as a geophysicist in Pittsburgh and then returned to graduate school, earning a Ph.D. in physics and mathematics at Princeton University in 1936. Between 1935 and 1938 he was also a junior fellow in the Society of Fellows at Harvard. In 1938 he was appointed assistant professor of physics at the University of Minnesota; he remained there until 1941, when he began work as chief physicist for the Naval Ordnance Laboratory in Washington, D.C. At the end of World War II he joined the Bell Telephone Laboratories, where William B. Shockley and Walter H. Brattain were already experimenting with semiconductor materials and their possible applications in electronic technology. Bardeen joined the team and served as its theorist, evolving a hypothesis on the nature of electron behavior that pointed the way to the perfection of a solid-state device that could replace the bulky, fragile, and inefficient vaccum tube. The name of the device, at first "transfer resistor," was quickly shortened to "transistor." For their invention the three shared the 1956 Nobel Prize for Physics. Bardeen left Bell in 1951 to become professor of physics and electrical engineering at the University of Illinois. His later researches involved deeper investigations into semiconductors and on the superconductivity of materials at extremely low temperatures. To the latter field he made especially important contributions and in 1972 he was again awarded the Nobel Prize for Physics, jointly with Leon N. Cooper and John R. Schrieffer, becoming the first man to win two Nobel prizes in the same field. He was the recipient of numerous other honors and awards, and was for many years associate editor of the *Physical Review*. A member of many leading scientific organizations, he served on the President's Science Advisory Committee from 1959 to 1962.

Barkley, Alben William (1877–1956), vice-president. Born on November 24, 1877, in Graves County, Kentucky, Barkley graduated from Marvin College in 1897, studied law briefly at Emory College, and then worked as a law clerk to finance his studies at the University of Virginia Law School. Admitted to the bar in 1901, he practiced successfully in Paducah, Kentucky, and soon entered politics. He was elected county prosecuting attorney in 1905, judge of the county court in 1909, and in 1912 won a seat in the House of Representatives. He served seven terms in the House and in 1926 was elected to the Senate. His amiability and party loyalty earned him increasing influence and in 1937, during his second Senate term, he began a period of ten years as majority leader which was interrupted only briefly in 1945, when, in a disagreement with President Franklin D. Roosevelt over a tax bill, he resigned but was promptly reelected by his colleagues. He was an early convert to the New Deal and was responsible for seeing much of its legislation through the Senate. In 1947, when a Republican majority organized the Senate, he continued to head his party as minority leader. A prominent figure at Democratic national conventions from 1920 onward, Barkley was mentioned as a vice-presidential possibility in 1940 and 1944; he won the nomination in 1948 and was elected vice-president on the ticket headed by Harry S. Truman. In 1952 he gave some thought to seeking the presidential nomination but at length decided not to, primarily because of his age. Two years later he was reelected to the Senate and served there until his death on April 30, 1956, in Lexington, Virginia.

Barlow, Joel (1754–1812), poet, author, and diplomat. Born in Redding, Connecticut, on March 24, 1754, Barlow graduated from Yale in 1778, firmly determined to win literary fame. He served for three years as a chaplain with the Revolutionary army; in 1786, after several years spent in various occupations, he was admitted to the bar. He was a leading member of the circle of Yale men known as the Connecticut Wits and was all the while hard at work on a projected philosophical epic of America. This he published as *The Vision of Columbus* in 1787; although of less than epic merit, the work won recognition by its energy and optimistic nationalism. In 1788 Barlow sailed to France as a land-company agent, then went to London for a lengthy stay. Exposed to the thinking of the European Enlightenment, he became more and more radical in his political views. He was a friend of Thomas Paine and in 1792, in reply to Edmund Burke's tract on the French Revolution, he wrote *Advice to the Privileged Orders*, a radically democratic document that, together with other writings, won him citizenship

in France and proscription in England. The following year, while living in France, he wrote his best-remembered poetical work, *The Hasty-Pudding*, a humorous pastoral evocation of New England. From 1795 to 1797 he was in Algiers as U.S. consul, arranging the release of American prisoners and negotiating treaties. He returned to the United States in 1805 and two years later published a revised and expanded version of his epic poem, now entitled *The Columbiad*. In 1811 he was sent to negotiate a commercial treaty with France. Scheduled to meet with Napoleon, who was in Russia with his troops, Barlow was caught up in the disastrous retreat from Moscow and died of exposure at Zarnowiec, Poland, on December 24, 1812.

Barnard, Edward Emerson (1857–1923), astronomer. Born in Nashville, Tennessee, on December 16, 1857, Barnard went to work as a photographer's assistant at the age of nine. During the next 16 years he became expert in photographic optics and procedures while at the same time studying astronomy and mathematics on his own. In 1881 he discovered the first of 16 comets credited to his observations. Two years later he entered Vanderbilt University and in 1887, at the age of thirty, he graduated. He was immediately appointed astronomer at Lick Observatory (Mt. Hamilton, California), where he undertook a photographic survey of the Milky Way. By using a wide-angle camera lens he was able to capture the structural details of the galaxy over large spans; the nebular features exhibited by his photographs opened a new field of study in astronomy and his basic survey technique was widely adopted. In 1892 he discovered Jupiter V, the first new satellite of the planet to be observed since Galileo found the four major ones. In 1895 he became professor of practical astronomy at the University of Chicago and astronomer at Yerkes Observatory, posts he held until his death. Barnard's visual and photographic studies extended to a wide range of subjects—planets, comets, globular clusters, novae, and nebulae. In 1916 he found what is still known as Barnard's star, the one with the greatest known angular motion relative to the earth. He published nearly a thousand papers and was for some time associate editor of the *Astronomical Journal*. Not a great theoretical astronomer, he was nevertheless widely honored for his many important observations which aided the work of other researchers. He died at Williams Bay, Wisconsin, on February 6, 1923.

Barnard, Frederick Augustus Porter (1809–1889), educator. Born on May 5, 1809, in Sheffield, Massachusetts, Barnard graduated from Yale in 1828 and taught for several years, principally in schools for deaf-mutes. In 1838 he was appointed professor of mathematics and natural history at the University of Alabama and later added teaching chemistry to his duties. In 1854 he became professor of mathematics and natural philosophy at the University of Mississippi; two years later he was chosen president and in 1858 chancellor, a position he held until 1861, when, an ardent Unionist, he resigned upon the outbreak of the Civil War. He accepted the presidency of Columbia College in New York City in 1864. Although he had earlier been an adherent of the traditional classics-based college curriculum, Barnard had already begun to modify his position when he went to Columbia, and during 25 years there he encouraged a great widening in scope of the programs and courses offered. The School of Mines, already being planned, was opened early in his administration, and professional training in a number of other fields was added over the years. He introduced an elective system similar to that established by Charles W. Eliot at Harvard, a system that aimed at producing not only disciplined minds but also cultivated ones. His major contribution to Columbia was his long and successful effort to extend higher education to women in a separate college that would share Columbia's faculty. The new college opened shortly after his death, and in recognition of his role in making it possible was named Barnard College. Further, his efforts in transforming a local college into a major university were tangibly recognized with the official establishment of Columbia University in 1896. He was a prolific writer, notably on education, science, politics, and economics, and was among the founders of the National Academy of Sciences and the American Association for the Advancement of Science. Barnard died in New York City on April 27, 1889.

Barnard, George Grey (1863–1938), sculptor. Born in Bellefonte, Pennsylvania, on May 24, 1863, Barnard was apprenticed to a jeweler at thirteen and while learning that craft began studying sculpture on his own. By 1880 he had earned enough money to obtain formal training at the Art Institute of Chicago, and three years later he traveled to Paris to enter the École des Beaux-Arts and the studio of Pierre Jules Cavelier. In 1887 he established his own studio in Paris and soon enjoyed a measure of success. His first public show, at the Salon of 1894, was a popular and critical sensation and gave him an immediate reputation; among the works that particularly delighted the viewers was the huge marble, "Struggle of the Two Natures in Man." To be received so warmly in Paris art circles was unusual for an American artist of Barnard's day, a fact that made the impact of the show all the greater and aided his quick rise to worldwide fame. In subsequent exhibitions—at the expositions in Paris in 1900, in Buffalo in 1901, and in St. Louis in 1904, and again at the Paris Salon of 1910—he confirmed the promise of his first show; at the 1910 Salon he unveiled what was probably his *magnum opus*, two colossal groups commissioned for the Pennsylvania state capitol at Harrisburg. In 1917 he completed for Lytle Park, Cincinnati, a statue of Abraham Lincoln that, although marked by great vitality, aroused re-

markably violent controversy by portraying the man as outwardly common and simple. Barnard was an avid collector of early Gothic and medieval sculpture, paintings, and fragments of architectural decoration, and in 1925 his collection was purchased and presented to the Metropolitan Museum of Art by John D. Rockefeller, Jr., and it formed the nucleus of the famed collection of the museum's branch, The Cloisters, in Fort Tryon Park, New York City. Barnard's last major work, a great memorial "Rainbow Arch" that was to be placed in a new art center overlooking the Hudson River, was unfinished at the time of his death in New York City on April 24, 1938.

Barnard, Henry (1811–1900), educator. Born on January 24, 1811, in Hartford, Connecticut, Barnard was enrolled as a child in a district school but found the conditions so intolerable that he planned to run away to sea. His father then enrolled him in private schools, where he prepared for college, entering Yale in 1826. While participating in the "bread and butter rebellion," a student strike for better food in 1828 and 1829, he visited schools in several cities and wrote about them in the *New England Review*. Graduating from Yale in 1830, he taught school and attended Yale Law School, gaining admission to the bar in 1835. Strongly interested in education, he toured Europe during 1835–1836, meeting prominent men and becoming acquainted with advanced educational theories. In 1837 he was elected to the Connecticut state legislature. In 1838 he campaigned successfully for a bill providing better administration of common schools. Barnard was chosen secretary of the board of school commissioners established by the bill and made effective efforts to stimulate the reform of deplorable school conditions. He visited schools, wrote letters and sent questionnaires to parents, made extensive reports to the legislature, and founded a teacher-training institute and the *Connecticut Common School Journal*. In 1843 he moved to Rhode Island as the state's first commissioner of public schools and implemented a similar program. Forced to retire because of ill health in 1849, he returned to Connecticut later that year as the state superintendent of schools. From 1858 to 1860 he was chancellor of the University of Wisconsin, in 1866–1867 president of St. John's College, Annapolis, Maryland, and from 1867 to 1870 was the first U.S. commissioner of education. His reports, which created a new literature of education, were surveys of the history of educational legislation or summaries of investigations of actual conditions. He founded and edited the *American Journal of Education* whose 32 volumes appeared irregularly from 1855 to 1882. He died in Hartford on July 5, 1900.

Barnett, Ida Wells, *see* Wells, Ida Bell

Barney, Joshua (1759–1818), naval officer. Born in Baltimore on July 6, 1759, Barney went to sea at the age of eleven. Four years later, when the captain of the ship on which he was serving died suddenly in mid-Atlantic, he took command, successfully completed the voyage and handled the business details upon reaching port, and returned to Baltimore. He joined the colonial navy in 1775; the next year he was at the capture of New Providence in the Bahamas, and performed with sufficient distinction to earn a commission as lieutenant. He served on a number of ships during the Revolution, captured many prizes, and was three times captured and imprisoned by the British, the last time for a year in England, whence he escaped to France and then to America. In 1782 he took command of the Pennsylvania ship *Hyder-Ally,* a small converted merchant vessel, and set out to convoy a merchant fleet down Delaware Bay; at Cape May he was set upon by a much more heavily armed British force. Barney covered the retreat of the merchantmen and then brilliantly outmaneuvered and captured the *General Monk,* an action for which he was widely celebrated. Barney retired from active service in 1784 and for ten years engaged in various enterprises. In 1794 he was assigned to active duty as captain of a ship to be sent against the Barbary pirates, but he balked at what he considered an insultingly low rank and resigned. He returned to the merchant service, where he served until 1796, when he accepted a commission in the French navy; he served for six years and then returned to Baltimore. During the War of 1812, he equipped and commanded a number of privateer vessels that operated against British shipping. In 1814 he was called to aid in the defense of Washington, D.C. With a fleet of armed barges he held off the British advance up Chesapeake Bay for some weeks and, when the enemy eventually eluded him and threatened the capital, he abandoned the barges and marched his small force back to Bladensburg, Maryland, and placed his men, armed with a few ship's guns mounted on carriages, at the center of Gen. William H. Winder's position. The battle was a serious defeat for the Americans, who were saved from utter disgrace only by the valiant resistance offered by Barney's small command. Barney, wounded in the battle, had performed his last public service; he died in Pittsburgh on December 1, 1818.

Barnum, Phineas Taylor (1810–1891), showman. Born on July 5, 1810, in Bethel, Connecticut, Barnum held various jobs in his youth, from editing an abolitionist newspaper to selling tickets for a Philadelphia theater. In Philadelphia in 1835 he saw Joice Heth, an old Negro woman, being exhibited as the 160-year-old nurse of George Washington. The show was obviously phony but the woman's performance caught Barnum's fancy. Wondering just how far he could stretch the public imagination, he bought Joice Heth and displayed her in the role of Washington's old nurse against a background of patriotic notices, billboards proclaiming her 100-year association with the Baptist Church, and artificially antiqued purchase sheets signed by Washington's father.

When she died he buried her, amid well-publicized mourning, in his own family plot, then ran anonymous newspaper articles attacking her authenticity and other articles defending his patriotic intentions. Convinced by now that there was no limit to the public's gullibility, he purchased Scudder's American Museum in New York City in 1841 and renamed it Barnum's American Museum. It became a house of curiosities; on the premises were woolly horses, bearded ladies, a Fiji mermaid, and the dwarf, "General Tom Thumb." Not the least of the attractions was a door marked "Egress," which many patrons flocked to see, only to find themselves outside. In a serious gesture, Barnum brought Swedish singer Jenny Lind to the United States in 1850 and made a celebrity of her and a wealthier man of himself. To offset the artistic seriousness of Miss Lind's tour, Barnum presented New York City with its first live hippopotamus. During a period of retirement from show business, he served in the Connecticut legislature, 1867–1869, and in 1875 was mayor of Bridgeport, where he developed an exemplary workers' community and lived in the grotesque mansion he called "Iranistan." In 1871 he proclaimed with extravagant publicity the opening of the "Greatest Show on Earth," a circus that he quickly developed into a three-ring extravaganza. He combined forces with his chief competitor, James A. Bailey, in 1881 to form the great Barnum and Bailey Circus. The next year he purchased Jumbo, a huge African elephant, from the Royal Zoological Society in London and proceeded to advertise the beast as the world's only surviving mastodon. Barnum professed the belief that Americans wanted to be "humbugged" and thus diverted from reality, and he always presented a show that was worth more than the price of admission despite its deceptive advertising. Reputedly the man who said "There's a sucker born every minute," Barnum possessed a genius for showmanship that reaped him a fortune and brought entertainment to millions of people. Among his candid writings were an autobiography, 1855, and *Humbugs of the World,* 1865. He died in Philadelphia on April 7, 1891.

Barron, Clarence Walker (1855–1928), editor and publisher. Born in Boston on July 2, 1855, Barron early determined on a newspaper career and in 1875 joined the staff of the *Boston Evening Transcript,* in which he later inaugurated a section on financial news. Convinced of the value to businessmen of reliable, up-to-the-minute information, he struck out on his own in 1887 and founded the Boston News Bureau, whose early bulletins and dispatches evolved in time into a full newspaper devoted to financial matters. In 1895 he established the *Philadelphia Financial News* (two years later converted to the Philadelphia News Bureau) on the same plan. He bought out Dow Jones & Company in 1901, thus becoming the publisher of its daily *Wall Street Journal* and completing his system of news services for the entire Eastern financial establishment. In 1921 he expanded his readership by beginning publication of *Barron's National Business and Financial Weekly,* later simply *Barron's Financial Weekly.* Barron wrote innumerable articles, editorials, and pamphlets and a number of books, including *The Federal Reserve Act,* 1914; *The Audacious War,* 1915; *War Finance,* 1919; and *A World Remaking,* 1920. He died on October 2, 1928, in Battle Creek, Michigan.

Barron, James (1768–1851), naval officer. Born on September 15, 1768, probably in Norfolk, Virginia, Barron was the son of a merchant captain, and as his father's apprentice he saw some naval action late in the Revolution. He continued to follow the sea after the war and in 1798 was commissioned a lieutenant in the navy and assigned to the *United States* under Commodore John Barry. The next year he was promoted to captain and given command of the *Essex* and then the *President,* serving in the Mediterranean fleet until 1805. In 1807, with the rank of commodore, he assumed command of the hastily activated *Chesapeake* and was en route to the Mediterranean when, off Cape Henry, Virginia, he was stopped by the British frigate *Leopard,* which demanded the return of several alleged deserters from the British navy who were claimed to be aboard. When Barron refused to allow a search of his ship the *Leopard* opened fire with devastating effect; Barron's unprepared and ill-trained men were thrown into confusion and he surrendered the ship to prevent its complete destruction. The *Leopard* then seized four men, at least two of whom were American citizens, and left the *Chesapeake* to limp home to Hampton Roads severely damaged and with three men dead and a score wounded, including Barron. The incident inflamed the American public and proved to be the most serious of the period preceding the declaration of war in 1812. Barron was found guilty of negligence in the affair but was acquitted of charges of cowardice and was suspended from duty for five years, during which time he served in the French navy. When he returned to active U.S. service he found himself blocked from promotion and sea duty; his frustration grew until, in 1820, he accused Commodore Stephen Decatur of leading an intrigue against him and challenged him to a duel. Decatur was killed in the exchange on March 22nd and Barron, badly wounded, found himself universally condemned. For the rest of his life he was on inactive status and, at his death in Norfolk, on April 21, 1851, he was the senior but probably the most unpopular officer in the navy.

Barrow, Joseph Louis, *see* Louis, Joe

Barry, John (1745?–1803), naval officer. Born in County Wexford, Ireland, about 1745, Barry went to sea at an early age and by 1760 had settled in Philadelphia. A successful merchant captain, he was also an ardent patriot and in March 1776 was commissioned captain in the Continental navy and placed in command of the *Lexington.* A month later he captured the British sloop *Edward* in the first American naval victory of the Revolution. He later commanded the *Effingham,* but his ship was kept in Philadelphia by the British blockade of Delaware Bay; during that period he fought with the army in Philadelphia and at Trenton and Princeton. In the winter of 1777–1778 he was forced to scuttle the *Effingham* to keep it from the hands of the British occupying Philadelphia, but he was able to lead a daring boat foray down the Delaware and capture a British schooner, several transports, and many supplies. In 1778 he sailed the *Raleigh* out of Boston but lost it in a sea battle against a much superior British naval force in Penobscot Bay. Two years later he was placed in command of the *Alliance.* On his first voyage, while conveying John Laurens to France, he captured a number of prizes on the way and defeated two sloops of war off Newfoundland on the return trip. After the American victory at Yorktown Barry made a second trip to France, this time to carry the Marquis de Lafayette home. In 1782 he put out for the West Indies on his final wartime cruise; he captured several prizes and four British ships of the line, and on his return from Havana with a load of bullion repelled an attack by three frigates, damaging one of them severely in the last Revolutionary naval engagement of note. Barry returned to the merchant trade briefly and then retired; in 1794 he was recalled, named senior captain of the navy, and sent with the *United States* to the West Indies as commander of all U.S. ships in those waters. After a trip to France carrying diplomatic envoys, he assumed command of the naval station at Guadeloupe in the West Indies. He returned home to Philadelphia in 1801 and was senior officer of the navy when he died on September 13, 1803, in that city.

Barry, Leonora Marie Kearney (1849–1930), "Mother Lake," labor leader and social reformer. Born on August 13, 1849, in County Cork, Ireland, Miss Kearney emigrated with her family to the United States in 1852, settling in St. Lawrence County, New York. After several years of teaching school she married W. E. Barry in 1871; he died ten years later and Mrs. Barry, left with two children to support, took a menial job in a clothing factory in Amsterdam, New York. Typically for the time, working conditions in the factory were poor and the pay was exceedingly low, and in 1884 Mrs. Barry joined a women's branch of the Knights of Labor. She rose rapidly to the post of master workman of the local branch and in 1886, at the national convention of the Knights, she was elected to take charge of the newly created department of women's work. During four years in that post she worked tirelessly to improve wages and working conditions for women throughout the country, traveling widely to organize, inspire, and investigate. Her annual reports were detailed and vigorous indictments of the effects of the factory system on women and children and contributed greatly to the passage of a factory-inspection law in Pennsylvania in 1889. She resigned from her position in 1890 upon her marriage to O. R. Lake, but, by then living in St. Louis, she continued to travel and speak on behalf of woman suffrage, temperance, and other movements. During this period and later, after moving to Minooka, Illinois, in 1916, she was active in the Woman's Christian Temperance Union and the Catholic Total Abstinence Union of America and, as a popular lecturer on the Chautauqua and Redpath circuits until 1928, she roused much public support for Prohibition. Mrs. Barry, sometimes known in later life as Mrs. Barry-Lake or Mother Lake, died in Minooka on July 15, 1930.

Barry-Lake, Mrs. see Barry, Leonora Marie Kearney.

Barrymore, Ethel (1879–1959), actress. Born in Philadelphia on August 15, 1879, the daughter of Maurice and Georgiana Drew Barrymore and the sister of Lionel and John Barrymore, Ethel Barrymore, attended the Convent of the Sacred Heart in Philadelphia and, after first intending to be a pianist, made her stage debut at fourteen in a New York City production of R. B. Sheridan's *The Rivals*, which also featured Lionel and her grandmother, Louisa Drew. She next appeared with her uncle, John Drew, in *The Bauble Shop* and then went to London, playing in *Secret Service*, *The Bells*, and *Peter the Great* in 1897–1898. Returning to Broadway, she starred in the Charles Frohman production of *Captain Jinks of the Horse Marines* in 1901. Subsequent roles in *A Doll's House* and *Alice-Sit-by-the-Fire*, both 1905; *Sunday*, 1906; *Mid-Channel*, 1910; *Trelawney of the Wells*, 1911; *Déclassée*, 1919; *The Second Mrs. Tanqueray*, 1924; *The Kingdom of God*, 1928, in which she opened the Ethel Barrymore Theatre in New York City; *The Constant Wife*, also 1928; *Scarlet Sister Mary*, 1931; *Whiteoaks*, 1938; and *The Corn Is Green*, 1942, won her a lasting reputation in the theater. She also played in vaudeville, on radio, on television, and in motion pictures, appearing with both of her brothers in *Rasputin and the Empress*, 1932. Her performance in *None but the Lonely Heart*, 1944, won her an Academy Award. She published *Memories* in 1955 and died in Hollywood, California, on June 18, 1959.

Barrymore, John (1882–1942), actor. Born in Philadelphia on February 15, 1882, John was the son of Maurice and Georgiana Drew Barrymore and the younger brother of Lionel and Ethel Barrymore. He first appeared on the stage in 1903 in *Magda*, in Chicago, and in *Glad of It* in New York City. In London in 1905 he played in *The Dictator*, and in that year appeared with William Collier's company. He toured in *The Boys of Company B* and returned to Chicago in 1908 to play in *A Stubborn Cinderella*. He appeared on the Broadway stage in, among many others, *The*

Jest (with Lionel), 1919, and *My Dear Children*, 1939, and starred there in 1920 as Richard III; in New York in 1922–1923 and in London in 1924, he starred as Hamlet; his Hamlet was considered among the greatest of all time. Dubbed the "Great Profile," he was a matinee idol in his earlier years. After about 1925 he appeared mostly in films, starring in *Rasputin and the Empress* (with Lionel and Ethel), *The Dictator, Sherlock Holmes, The Test of Honor, Beau Brummel, Don Juan, Dinner at Eight, Grand Hotel,* and *Counsellor-at-Law,* among others. He died in Hollywood, California, on May 29, 1942, after a tempestuous life which was in marked contrast to the quiet lives of Lionel and Ethel.

Barrymore, Lionel (1878–1954), actor. Born on April 28, 1878, in Philadelphia, the son of Maurice and Georgiana Drew Barrymore and the elder brother of Ethel and John Barrymore, Lionel first appeared on the stage at the age of six. He returned at fifteen in R. B. Sheridan's *The Rivals* with his grandmother, Louisa Drew, and Ethel, but then went to Paris and studied painting for three years. He appeared with his uncle, John Drew, in *Second in Command*, and after another visit to Paris turned finally to acting as a career. He made a few motion pictures at the Biograph studios under D. W. Griffith, including *The New York Hat* with Mary Pickford. His greatest stage triumphs were in *Peter Ibbetson* in 1917, *The Copperhead* in 1918, and *The Jest* in 1919, with his brother, John. After 1925 he starred in numerous motion pictures, including *Free Soul*, for which he won an Academy Award in 1931; *Rasputin and the Empress* (with both Ethel and John), 1932; and *None but the Lonely Heart* (with Ethel), 1944. Subsequently he played Scrooge in an annual radio broadcast of Charles Dickens's *A Christmas Carol* and starred in the "Dr. Kildare" movie and radio series. He published *We Barrymores* (with C. Schipp), 1951, and *Mr. Cantonwine: A Moral Tale*, 1953, and in his later years was well known as a composer. He died in Van Nuys, California, on November 15, 1954.

Barrymore, Maurice (1847–1905), actor. Born in 1847 in Fort Agra, India, where his father was employed by the East India Company, Herbert Blythe was educated in England at Harrow and Oxford. He abandoned a prospective law career to be an actor, first appearing in 1872 in London in a revival of *The London Assurance* and in E. G. Bulwer-Lytton's *Money*. In 1875 he came to the United States and made a Boston debut in *Under the Gaslight*. Subsequently he joined Augustin Daly's summer stock company and met Georgiana Emma Drew, the daughter of the distinguished actors John and Louisa Lane Drew, and married her on December 31, 1876. The couple were both prominent in Daly's company, appearing with such actors as Fanny Davenport and Joseph Jefferson. They formed their own road company with Georgiana's brother, John Drew, and toured in 1878 and 1879; and they appeared individually or together in A. M. Palmer's company (she at various times with Edwin Booth, Lawrence Barrett, and John McCullough). Barrymore also joined Lester Wallach's company and made a notable appearance as Captain Absolute in R. B. Sheridan's *The Rivals*. After 1881 he appeared in London opposite Mme Helena Modjeska, for whom he wrote the play *Nadjeska*. They again starred together in *Romeo and Juliet* in New York City in the last performance given in the Booth Theatre (1883). Mrs. Barrymore gave her final performances in Boston in *Settled Out of Court* and *The Sportsman*, both in 1892, and died in Santa Barbara, California, on July 2, 1893. Maurice played in David Belasco's *Heart of Maryland* in New York in 1895 and in London in 1898, and was again featured in Palmer's company and various vaudeville theaters. He died in Amityville, New York, on March 26, 1905. Their three children—Lionel, Ethel, and John, who were raised in the tradition of the theater—became known as the "royal family" of the American stage.

Barth, John Simmons (1930–   ), author. Born on May 27, 1930, in Cambridge, Maryland, Barth attended the Juilliard School of Music in New York City for a brief period and then transferred to The Johns Hopkins University, from which he graduated in 1951; he took an M.A. there in 1952. In 1953 he joined the department of English at Pennsylvania State University, where he remained for 12 years. He had begun writing while still in college, and in 1956 he published his first book, *The Floating Opera*, an existentialist novel that won wide notice and was a runner-up for a National Book Award. *The End of the Road* followed in 1958; like his first novel, it took as its central theme the inability of a modern intellectual to decide on or commit himself to anything at all. Barth abandoned the realistic novel in his third book, *The Sot-Weed Factor*, which was an elaborate picaresque story set in early colonial Maryland. A parody of Elizabethan literature that displayed great technical skill, the book was crammed with witticisms and ribald adventures and was a best seller as well as a critical success. In *Giles Goat-Boy*, 1966, Barth constructed an allegorical tale of Swiftian proportions and further solidified his position as one of the most inventive and challenging U.S. writers. In 1968 he published *Lost in the Funhouse*, a collection of stories and experimental pieces. *Chimera* appeared in 1972. In 1965 he joined the English department at the State University of New York at Buffalo and during the following years published "revised editions" of some of his earlier works.

Bartlett, John (1820–1905), editor and publisher. Born in Plymouth, Massachusetts, on June 14, 1820, Bartlett found employment in the University Book Store in Cambridge when he was sixteen. He there became an avid reader and lover of books, gaining such extensive knowledge of them that "ask John Bartlett" became common advice to Harvard students and teachers with difficult questions about books and quotations. In order to maintain his reputation he began keeping a notebook of references which evolved into his *Familiar Quotations*, first published in 1855. He had become the owner of the store in 1849 and in 1863 he joined the publishing firm of Little, Brown & Company, becoming senior partner 15 years later. *Familiar Quotations* went through nine editions during Bartlett's lifetime and has continued to be a standard reference work, a centennial thirteenth edition appearing in 1955. Bartlett wrote on other subjects as well, including chess and fishing, and in 1894 produced his valuable *Complete Concordance to Shakespeare's Dramatic Works and Poems*. Long a popular and admired figure in Cambridge, he died there on December 3, 1905.

Bartlett, John Russell (1805–1886), bibliographer. Born on October 23, 1805, in Providence, Rhode Island, Bartlett grew up in Kingston, Ontario, and returned to Providence in 1824. While working in a dry-goods store and later in a bank, he pursued interests in natural science and history and in 1831 joined in the founding of the Providence Athenaeum. In 1836 he moved to New York City, where for several years he was a partner in a bookstore and publishing firm. He was a prominent member of The New-York Historical Society and in 1842 aided Albert Gallatin in the organization of the American Ethnological Society; his interest in the races of man led also to his *Progress of Ethnology*, 1847. In 1848 he published his valuable *Dictionary of Americanisms: a Glossary of Words and Phrases Usually Regarded as Peculiar to the United States*, which went through four editions and was translated into Dutch and German. President Zachary Taylor appointed him in 1850 U.S. commissioner for the survey of the boundary between the United States and Mexico specified in the Treaty of Guadalupe Hidalgo. He described his three years' work and observations in *A Personal Narrative of Explorations and Incidents in Texas, New Mexico, California, Sonora and Chihuahua*, two volumes, 1854. In 1855 Bartlett was elected secretary of state of Rhode Island, a post he retained for 17 years by annual reelections. He undertook to arrange, catalog, and bind the accumulated papers of the state and published the 10-volume *Records of the Colony of Rhode Island, 1636–1792*; the 12-volume *Index to the Acts, Resolves and Reports of Rhode Island, from 1758 to 1862*, 1856–1863; a *Bibliography of Rhode Island*, 1864; and other aids to the study of history. For many years he assisted John Carter Brown in assembling and classifying the huge collection of early Americana that became the John Carter Brown Library of Brown University in Providence. He compiled and published the *John Carter Brown Catalogue*, four volumes, 1865–1882, itself a valuable reference source. Bartlett died in Providence on May 28, 1886.

Bartlett, Robert Abram (1875–1946), explorer. Born on August 15, 1875, in Brigus, Newfoundland, Bob Bartlett attended Methodist College in

St. John's. He began his arctic explorations with Robert E. Peary at the Kane Basin in 1897 and, after several years spent in various other activities, including four years as master of a Newfoundland sealing ship, he returned to the Arctic as captain of Peary's ship *Roosevelt* in 1905–1906 and 1908–1909. It was on the second of these trips that Peary reached the North Pole. In 1913–1914 Bartlett commanded the *Karluk* in the Canadian government's arctic expedition under Vilhjalmur Stefansson. The ship was caught in ice off Point Barrow and drifted until it was crushed near Wrangel Island in January 1914; Bartlett got the survivors to the island and then, accompanied only by a single Eskimo, made his way over the ice to Siberia to find help, returning to Wrangel Island in September 1914 and bringing the survivors into Nome, Alaska, a year later. In 1917 he commanded the third Crocker Land Relief Expedition to northern Greenland. Eight years later he traveled to northern Alaska and the Arctic Ocean to make biological and oceanographic observations for the National Geographic Society, at the same time looking for sites for aircraft bases. Under the auspices of various U.S. scientific organizations he headed expeditions to, among other regions, Greenland and Ellesmere Island, 1926; Baffin Island, 1927 and 1934; Siberia, 1928; Labrador, 1929; and Greenland again, in 1930, 1931, and 1932. From 1942 to 1945, with the rank of lieutenant commander in the naval reserve, he commanded his own ship, the *Morrissey*, and made a series of voyages seeking sites for U.S. military and naval bases in the Arctic. He was the recipient of a great many honors and awards for his work and during his lifetime he published *The Last Voyage of the Karluk*, 1916; *The Log of Bob Bartlett*, 1928; and *Sails over Ice*, 1934. Bartlett died in New York City on April 28, 1946.

Barton, Bruce (1886–1967), advertising man and author. Born on August 5, 1886, in Robbins, Tennessee, Barton grew up there and in Oak Park, Illinois. After a year at Berea College he transferred to Amherst and graduated in 1907. Later in that year he became managing editor of the *Home World* magazine in Chicago, a position he held until going over to the *Housekeeper* in 1910. In 1912 he moved to New York City and was employed for two years as assistant sales manager for a publishing company and then until 1918 as editor of *Every Week* magazine. With two partners he organized an advertising agency in 1919, serving as its president until 1928, when he became chairman of the board of the merged and reorganized company, Batten, Barton, Durstine & Osborn, Incorporated. BBD&O soon became one of the giants of the advertising business. Barton was president of the company from 1939 to 1946 and then resumed the chairmanship. A man of wide interests, he wrote editorials, magazine articles, a newspaper column, and several books in addition to advertising copy; among his books were *More Power to You*, 1917; *It's a Good*

Old World, 1920; and two best sellers, *The Man Nobody Knows*, 1925 (which presented Jesus in terms of a highly successful modern advertiser and salesman), and *The Book Nobody Knows*, 1926, about the Bible. In 1936 Barton won election to the House of Representatives and during two terms there was a leading Republican opponent of the New Deal. During an unsuccessful campaign for the Senate in 1940 he was one of those referred to in President Franklin D. Roosevelt's famous disparaging phrase, "Martin, Barton, and Fish." Widely honored by the industry he had helped create, Barton retired in 1961 and died on July 5, 1967, in New York City.

Barton, Clara (1821–1912), founder of the American Red Cross. Born on December 25, 1821 in Oxford, Massachusetts, Clarissa Harlowe Barton was the youngest of five children. She was educated at home and grew up willful and independent, with a love for outdoor sports. She began an 18-year career of teaching at the age of fifteen. In 1851 she attended the Liberal Institute at Clinton, New York, then established in New Jersey a free school that became so large that the townsmen would no longer allow a woman to run it. Rather than subordinate herself to a male principal, she resigned. She was employed by the U.S. Patent Office from 1854 to 1861. In 1861 she showed characteristic initiative in organizing facilities to recover soldiers' lost baggage and in securing medicine and supplies for men wounded in the first battle of Bull Run. She gained permission to pass through the battle lines to distribute supplies, search for the missing, and nurse the wounded. She carried on this work through the remainder of the Civil War, traveling with the army as far south as Charleston. In 1869 she went abroad and did relief work in the Franco-Prussian War. Learning of the activities of the International Red Cross recently organized in Geneva, Switzerland, she campaigned and lobbied vigorously upon her return home, with the result that the United States became a signatory of the Geneva Convention in 1882. In 1881 she organized the American National Red Cross and served as its president until 1904. She supervised the organization's activities so closely that finally charges of authoritarianism were brought against her by members of her executive council. Public contributions to the organization diminished, and only congressional intercession in 1904 kept it from dissolving. It was agreed that she was a poor business manager; this did not, however, negate the enormous value of her contributions, which encompassed relief work in the United States, in Armenia, and in Cuba during times of war, and which included the successful advocacy of the "American amendment" to the Geneva Convention, a provision that permitted the Red Cross to provide relief in times of natural disasters and calamities as well as in wartime. She was planning to establish a Red Cross in Mexico at the time of her death in Glen Echo, Maryland, on April 12, 1912.

Bartram, John (1699–1777), botanist. Born on May 23, 1699, in Chester County, Pennsylvania, near Philadelphia, Bartram had little formal education but was interested in botany from the age of ten. In 1728 he purchased land near the Schuylkill River, at Kingsessing, Pennsylvania, for the purpose of conducting experiments in hybridization. Excited by his achievements in this work, he began a correspondence with Peter Collinson, an English horticulturist, around 1733, and the two exchanged notes and specimens. His circle of admirers grew and soon he was corresponding with Carolus Linnaeus, who considered Bartram a great natural botanist. Through Collinson's influence he became botanist in the American colonies for King George III in 1765. His garden, within easy reach of Philadelphia, became a favorite place of recreation for Benjamin Franklin, George Washington, and other noted men. Bartram traveled to the frontiers to collect bulbs, seeds, and new plants, and he recorded his experiences in journals, the best known being *Observations on the Inhabitants, Climate, Soil, etc. . . . from Pennsylvania to . . . Lake Ontario,* published in 1751. Among the plants he discovered was the tree *Franklinia alatamaha,* named for Franklin, and the moss *Bartramia,* named for himself. America's first important botanist, he died in Kingsessing on September 22, 1777.

Bartram, William (1739–1823), botanist, ornithologist, and author. Born in Kingsessing, Pennsylvania, on February 9, 1739, Bartram earned praise in his youth for drawings of specimens gathered by his father, the botanist John Bartram, and he tended the Bartram garden and added to its collections of rare plants. He spent much of the 1780s in the Carolinas, Georgia, and Florida, investigating, cataloging, and describing the animals and plants he saw, and he prepared the most complete list of American birds compiled up to his time. He is best known for his journal, *Travels Through North and South Carolina, Georgia, East and West Florida, the Cherokee Country, etc.,* published in 1791 and many times subsequently reprinted in various editions. The work made singificant contributions to science, but it is read now because of the strong effect that its descriptions of wild scenery had on English literature of the romantic period. Wordsworth and Coleridge were both assiduous readers of the book, as were later Romantics. Bartram spent most of the last 30 years of his life at his birthplace, near Philadelphia, and died there on July 22, 1823.

Baruch, Bernard Mannes (1870–1965), financier and public official. Born in Camden, South Carolina, on August 19, 1870, Baruch graduated from the College of the City of New York in 1889 and soon thereafter entered a Wall Street brokerage firm. His canny management of stock dealings enabled him to open his own office in 1903 and within 10 years after his first appearance on Wall Street he had accumulated a large fortune. In 1916 President Woodrow Wilson appointed him, over the protests of several congressmen and senators who objected to Baruch's reputation as a financial speculator, to the advisory commission of the Council of National Defense; he advanced to the chairmanship of the War Industries Board in March 1918. After World War I he was a member of the Supreme Economic Council at the Versailles Peace Conference and also served in numerous other advisory capacities on economic matters. Although he thereafter held no major administrative post—not even during World War II, when he was active in government economic and industrial mobilization work—he was widely known as a friend, adviser, and confidante of every U.S. president from Wilson to John F. Kennedy. In 1946 he represented the United States on the UN Atomic Energy Commission, to which he presented a proposal for the international development and control of atomic energy that, although developed largely by Dean Acheson and David Lilienthal, became known as the Baruch Plan. For many of his later years Baruch was a familiar sight in Washington, D.C., where he particularly favored a bench in Lafayette Square, opposite the White House; there he presided as a popular sage and regularly received mail deliveries. He published two volumes of memoirs, *Baruch: My Own Story,* 1957, and *Baruch: The Public Years,* 1960. In 1964 he presented his papers to the Princeton University library as a nucleus for the collection of the Center for Studies in Twentieth-Century American Statecraft and Public Policy. He died in New York City on June 20, 1965.

Barzun, Jacques Martin (1907–   ), historian and educator. Born on November 30, 1907, in Créteil, France, Barzun grew up in an intellectual atmosphere. He was brought to the United States by his parents in 1919; they settled in New York City, and Barzun graduated from Columbia University in 1927 at the head of his class. He remained at Columbia as an instructor in history, took his Ph.D. in 1932, and by 1945 was a full professor. He had become a U.S. citizen in 1933. Early attracted to the artists and thinkers of the nineteenth-century romanic movement, Barzun presented them in his writings as the flowering of a centuries-old tradition of liberal education and free thought, contrasting their works sharply with the products of modern scientific mechanism and political absolutism. His studies, scholarly and literate in the highest sense, include *Of Human Freedom,* 1939; *Darwin, Marx, Wagner: Critique of a Heritage,* 1941; *Romanticism and the Modern Ego,* 1943; *Berlioz and the Romantic Century,* 1950; *Energies of Art,* 1956; *The House of Intellect,* 1959; and *Science: The Glorious Entertainment,* 1964. An ardent advocate of the liberal arts as opposed to vocational and overspecialized courses, he produced a number of widely read and often controversial works critical of the modern university, notably *Teacher in America,* 1945, and *The American University,* 1968. In 1955 Barzun became dean of the graduate faculties at Columbia and three years later was made dean of faculties and provost, posts he held until 1967. From 1960 to 1967 he was Seth Low Professor of History and in 1967 became University Professor, Columbia's highest-ranking teaching position.

Basie, William (1904–   ), "Count," musician. Born in Red Bank, New Jersey, on August 21, 1904, William Basie was musically inclined from childhood. In his teens he studied piano, for a time with Fats Waller, who also taught him to play the organ and got him into vaudeville as an accompanist. For a few years he played on the East Coast and then worked his way west until he was stranded in Kansas City, Missouri. There he joined Walter Page's "Blue Devils" and then Benny Moten's band, at the time the leading jazz group in the Midwest. Soon after Moten's death in 1935, Basie formed his own band with Page, Freddy Green, Jo Jones, Lester Young, and others. The band played at the Reno Club in Kansas City and, although it was short on formal arrangements, soon attracted a considerable following with its driving rhythm and brilliant solo work. A chance hearing of one of their local radio broadcasts by an influential jazz enthusiast led to their traveling to New York City in 1936 and to a recording contract the following year. Engagements at a series of fashionable clubs, theaters, and hotels quickly established the band as one of the most popular in the country and recordings spread their fame throughout the world. A succession of great soloists—among them Buck Clayton, Dickie Wells, Illinois Jacquet, J. J. Johnson, and Don Byas—and vocalists such as Jimmy Rushing and Joe Williams helped to keep the appeal of Count Basie's music growing; always it was characterized by the trademark "jumping" beat and the contrapuntal accents of Basie's own piano. The band broke up in 1950 and for a year or so Basie toured with a small combo that featured Clark Terry, Buddy DeFranco, and Wardell Gray. In 1951 he organized a new big band and immediately surpassed his earlier success in a number of tours across the country and in Europe. In later years he appeared often in movies and on television and remained one of the world's most popular bandleaders.

Baskin, Leonard (1922–   ), artist. Born on August 15, 1922, in New Brunswick, New Jersey, Baskin grew up there and in New York City. After several years of Talmudic studies he gave up thought of the rabbinate and turned to sculpture, studying first in a private studio, then at the New York University School of Architecture and Fine Arts, and from 1941 to 1943 at the Yale School of the Fine Arts. During World War II he served in the navy and in the merchant marine and then resumed his education, graduating from the New School for Social Research in 1949. During 1950–1951 he studied in Paris and in Florence, where he had his first one-man show of sculpture. Other exhibitions followed in Princeton, New Jersey, and at Mount Holyoke College in Massa-

chusetts, both in 1952. By 1953, when he joined the faculty of Smith College, he had become interested in print-making and his work in that medium attracted much attention and won him a Guggenheim fellowship in that year. Critical estimation of his sculpture rose rapidly as he exhibited regularly in New York City and elsewhere; both his sculpture and his graphic works revealed a mastery of technique and a deeply humanistic outlook, occasionally with social and political overtones. Baskin's art conveyed strong convictions of nobility, dignity, vulnerability, and mortality, suggesting that such qualities were fundamental to and interdependent in man. In his insistence on imparting such meanings to his work he stood out as a prominent opponent of the dominant mode of abstractionism in contemporary art. He was also noted as a book illustrator and he founded Gehenna Press, a producer of limited editions. Among major shows of his works were an exhibition assembled by the Museum of Modern Art that visited several European cities in 1961 and a large exhibition at Bowdoin College in 1962. Baskin is represented in many major U.S. galleries and museums.

Bass, Sam (1851–1878), outlaw. Born near Mitchell, Indiana, on July 21, 1851, Bass was orphaned by the time he was thirteen and received little or no schooling. At eighteen he began to roam, moving to St. Louis, to Mississippi, and then to Denton, Texas, working at various jobs from mill-hand to deputy sheriff. He was accounted an honest man in this period and not until 1875 did he begin, for reasons not certainly known, a brief but spectacular career as a Western badman. A horse-stealing raid on Indian herds was followed by a cattle drive to Kansas, a legitimate activity except that he and a friend absconded with the proceeds. Moving to the newly built mining town of Deadwood, South Dakota, Bass, Bud Collins, and their gang began preying on stagecoaches and in September 1877, at Big Springs, Nebraska, they took $65,000 in gold and other valuables from a Union Pacific train. Bass lost several of his companions in the ensuing flight through Kansas and Missouri but he himself survived to gather a new gang in Denton early in 1878. Four more train robberies in the region around Dallas followed in quick succession. The Texas Rangers finally persuaded one of Bass's men, who had been captured, to serve as an informant; with his aid a trap was ready when an attempt was made to rob the bank at Round Rock and in the gunfight that ensued, Bass was mortally wounded, dying two days later on July 21, 1878, his twenty-seventh birthday.

Bateman, Ellen *see under* Bateman, Hezekiah Linthicum

Bateman, Hezekiah Linthicum (1812–1875), theatrical manager. Born in Baltimore on December 6, 1812, Bateman began an acting career at the age of twenty and played in various repertory companies until the middle 1840s, when he turned to managing the careers of his two small daughters, Kate and Ellen, who, as the Bateman Children, began touring as child prodigies. In New York in 1849 they played the male and female leads in a number of plays, including *Richard III*, *Macbeth*, and *The Merchant of Venice*. In 1850–1851 the children performed in England under the management of P. T. Barnum and then rejoined their father to tour as far west as San Francisco. Bateman managed a St. Louis theater in 1855 and then moved to New York City. Ellen left the stage early, but Bateman continued to direct Kate's career and in 1863 produced her great success, *Leah the Forsaken*, Augustin Daly's adaptation of S. H. Mosenthal's *Deborah*. Kate went on to become a popular star in London, and Bateman remained in New York to introduce the opéra bouffe of Jacques Offenbach to American audiences in 1867–1869. In 1871 he leased the Lyceum Theatre in London and produced a series of plays that won high praise for their consistently good quality and lofty moral tone. He engaged Henry Irving, who at that time was accounted by most a mediocre actor, and made him a great star in *The Bells*. Irving later appeared opposite Kate Bateman in a number of successful productions. Bateman died suddenly in London on March 22, 1875. His wife, Sidney F. Cowell Bateman, an actress and playwright, continued to manage the Lyceum until 1878 and later took over the Sadler's Wells Theatre.

Bateman, Kate *see under* Bateman, Hezekiah Linthicum

Bateman, Sidney F. Cowell *see under* Bateman, Hezekiah Linthicum

Bates, Edward (1793–1869), public official. Born on September 4, 1793, in Goochland County, Virginia, Bates received his education largely at home. After service in the militia in 1813 he followed his elder brother Frederick to Missouri, studied law, and began to practice in St. Louis in 1816. He soon became interested in politics, serving in the state constitutional convention in 1820, as state attorney general, and in the legislature. Elected as a Whig to the House of Representatives in 1826, he served only one term, the Jacksonian fever blocking his hopes of reelection or of running for the Senate. He remained nonetheless the leading Whig in Missouri and again served in the legislature during 1830–1834. In 1847 he came to national attention as president of the River and Harbor Improvement Convention in Chicago. Personal problems caused him to decline President Millard Fillmore's offer of the post of secretary of war in 1850, but he continued to rise in prominence as he spoke and wrote widely on the issues of the day. Bates had long since taken a strong stand on slavery—he had freed his own slaves—and he opposed both the repeal of the Missouri Compromise and the admission of Kansas as a slave state. Although he presided over the Whig convention in Baltimore in 1856, he perceived that the party was by then clearly moribund and began to establish ties with the newly organized Republicans. In the months before the Republican convention of 1860 there was considerable talk of nominating Bates for president on the theory that the election of a Southern-born candidate from a border state who held free-soil opinions could prevent secession. He received little support in Chicago, however, and lost the nomination to Abraham Lincoln. When Lincoln offered him a cabinet post he chose that of attorney general and became the first cabinet officer from west of the Mississippi. Devoted to the preservation of law and civil rights, he opposed the admission of West Virginia and much of the administration's military policy, but in a cabinet dominated by William H. Seward and Edwin M. Stanton his efforts had little effect. In frustration he resigned in 1864 and returned to Missouri to fight the growing power of the Radical Republicans, whom he considered enemies of good government. After a period of ill health he died in St. Louis on March 25, 1869.

Bates, Katharine Lee (1859–1929), educator and author. Born on August 12, 1859, in Falmouth, Massachusetts, Miss Bates graduated from Wellesley College in 1880. After a few years of teaching school she returned to Wellesley in 1885 as an instructor in English. She was made a professor in 1891 and remained with the college for 40 years in all, retiring as professor emeritus in 1925. During her long career as a teacher she also wrote volumes of poetry, travel books, and scholarly works, among them *The College Beautiful and Other Poems*, 1887; *Rose and Thorn*, 1888; *English Religious Drama*, 1893; *Spanish Highways and Byways*, 1900; *From Gretna Green to Land's End*, 1907; *The Story of Chaucer's Canterbury Tales Re-told for Children*, 1909; *Fairy Gold*, 1916; *The Retinue and Other Poems*, 1918; *Sigurd*, 1919; *Yellow Clover*, 1922; and *The Pilgrim Ship*, 1926. While on a western tour in 1893 she climbed Pike's Peak and was inspired by the view to write a poem entitled "America the Beautiful." She first published it in 1895; it appeared in a revised version in 1904 and in its final form in 1911. Set to the music of Samuel A. Ward's "Materna," the poem became, unofficially but indisputably, the national hymn. Miss Bates died in Wellesley, Massachusetts, on March 28, 1929.

Baugh, Samuel Adrian (1914–   ), "Sammy," football player. Born on March 17, 1914, in Temple, Texas, Baugh moved with his family to Sweetwater when he was sixteen and there he starred in high-school athletics. In 1933 he entered Texas Christian University in and, although baseball actually attracted him more than football, he quickly became an outstanding player on the gridiron; during his junior year, 1935, he led the team to a Southwest Conference championship and was named quarterback of Grantland Rice's All-American team, an honor he won again in 1936. After graduating in 1937 and quarterbacking the All-Star team of college players to victory over the Green Bay Packers he signed with the Washington Redskins at a salary remarkably high for the time—$8000. In his first professional season he singlehandedly laid to rest all doubts as to the usefulness of the still novel forward pass, taking the Redskins to a division title and then clinching the National Football League championship by throwing three touchdown passes against the Chicago Bears. At a time when there were no special rules protecting the passer from ambitious—or vicious—linemen, "Slingin' Sammy" made the pass a vital offensive weapon and in the course of his career was the top passer in the league in six seasons—1937, 1940, 1943, 1945, 1947, and 1949. He led the Redskins to five division titles and another league championship in 1942. He was also a great defensive player, leading the league in interceptions in 1943 and holding most of the punting records. On retiring at the end of the 1952 season after a then-record 16 years in professional football Baugh held an enormous number of league records, including: Passes attempted (3016); passes attempted in a season (354); passes completed (1709); passes completed in a season (210); yards gained passing (22,085); yards gained passing in a season (2938—1947); yards gained passing in a game (446—1948); touchdown passes (187); passing average (56.6 percent); passing average in a season (70.3 percent—1945); punting average (44.9 yards); and punting average in a season (48.7 yards—1942). After a time spent on his farm near Rotan, Texas, he became head football coach at Hardin-Simmons University, a post he held in 1955–1959. A member of the Football Hall of Fame, he was on the coaching staffs of the New York Titans (now the Jets) in 1960–1961, of the Houston Oilers in 1964, and of the Detroit Lions in 1966.

Baum, Lyman Frank (1856–1919), author. Born on May 15, 1856, in Chittenango, New York, Baum was educated at an academy in Syracuse. He was editor of the *Dakota Pioneer* at Aberdeen, South Dakota, from 1888 to 1890, and of *Chicago Show Window*, a trade magazine for window decorators, from 1897 to 1902. His first book was an instantly successful children's story, *Father Goose: His Book*, 1899. He thereupon submitted a draft of a book called *Wizard of Oz* to his publisher. It appeared in 1900 as *The Wonderful Wizard of Oz* and its potential for stage production being obvious, it was produced in Chicago in 1901 as a musical extravaganza. (Later the story became a motion picture, with Bert Lahr and Ray Bolger, in which Judy Garland, as Dorothy, sang "Over the Rainbow.") After the enormous success of the book and play, Baum traveled in Europe, spending some of the time writing. He moved to Pasadena, California, upon his return from Europe in 1902, into a large house with a flower garden in which he kept an enormous cage full of rare songbirds. He continued to write Oz stories, including the *Woggle Bug Book*, 1905, and *The Tik-*

Tok Man of Oz, 1914. He wrote fourteen Oz books in all; singly and as a series they have become classics of children's literature. Other stories included *The Life and Adventures of Santa Claus*, 1902; *Enchanted Isle of Yew*, 1903; *The Magical Monarch of Mo*, 1903; *The Daring Twins*, 1910; and *Sky Island*, 1912. He wrote under other names besides his own, including "Schuyler Staunton," "Floyd Akers," and "Edith Van Dyne." Eight of his books were adapted for the stage. He died on May 6, 1919, in Hollywood, California. After his death the Oz series was continued by R. P. Thompson.

Baxter, George Owen, *see* Faust, Frederick Schiller

Bayard, Thomas Francis (1828–1898), public official and diplomat. Born in Wilmington, Delaware, on October 29, 1828, to a family long prominent in public affairs, Bayard received his schooling in Flushing, New York. He worked for a time in New York City as a clerk, but in 1848 he returned to Wilmington to study law. He was admitted to the bar three years later and soon built up a large practice. During 1853–1854 he served as U.S. attorney for Delaware. A peace Democrat, he opposed both secession and the Civil War and after his election to the Senate in 1869—to a seat held by his father and his grandfather before him —he was a leading opponent of Radical Reconstruction policies. Possessed of great ability and integrity, he was an active member of several important committees and of the Electoral Commission in 1877 and was widely mentioned as a presidential possibility in 1880 and 1884. Upon the election to the presidency of Grover Cleveland in 1884 Bayard resigned his Senate seat to become secretary of state. During four years in that office, 1885–1889, he dealt with international disputes concerning North Atlantic fisheries, fur sealing in the Pacific, and the problems of Samoa, and the Alaskan boundary. Although he failed to finally resolve any of the disputes, he won high regard for his devotion to the principle of peaceful arbitration. In 1893, during Cleveland's second administration, Bayard was appointed U.S. ambassador to Great Britain, the first man to hold ambassadorial rank (previously, U.S. representatives abroad had been ministers). He was popular in London and worked steadily to cement Anglo-American friendship; some of his speeches, however, were badly received in the United States and in 1896 the House of Representatives, incensed by his criticism of the tariff in a speech in Edinburgh, voted a resolution censuring him. After a period of failing health he resigned in 1897 and left London for Dedham, Massachusetts, where he died on September 28, 1898.

Bayes, Nora (1880–1928), singer and actress. Born in Los Angeles in 1880, Dora Goldberg went on the stage at eighteen, taking the name Nora Bayes. For a time she performed with a San Francisco repertory company, then about 1900 entered vaudeville and became a star in 1902 at the

Orpheum Theatre in Brooklyn with her rendition of "Down Where the Wurzburger Flows," a song she introduced and with which she was long identified. From 1904 to 1907 she toured in variety shows and musical comedies in Europe and then returned to appear in the first edition of the *Ziegfeld Follies*. Thereafter she was an eminently successful fixture on the Broadway and London musical stages. Among the other songs that she introduced or made popular were "Take Me Out to the Ball Game," "Japanese Sandman," George M. Cohan's great song of World War I "Over There" and the song that became her theme and that was always associated with her memory, "Shine On Harvest Moon," written by her and Jack Norwood. Miss Bayes died in New York City on March 19, 1928.

Bayley, Richard (1745–1801), physician. Born in 1745 in Fairfield, Connecticut, Bayley studied medicine in New York City and, from 1769 to 1771, in London under the great English physician and anatomist William Hunter. On his return to New York City he began practice and made a significant contribution to medicine in the diphtheria epidemic of 1774, when by close observation and making autopsies he learned to distinguish the disease from other ailments producing similar symptoms and succeeded in reducing the mortality rate by half. He was again working with Hunter in London for a time in 1775–1776 and returned to America as a surgeon with reinforcements for the army of Gen. Sir William Howe. In 1777 he reentered private practice in New York City. His anatomical research, together with his use of dissection in teaching, aroused considerable public opposition that culminated in the wrecking of his laboratory by a mob in 1788. He joined the Columbia College medical faculty in 1792 and was a founder of the New York Dispensary. His research in later years was concerned primarily with yellow fever; he performed heroic service in the epidemic of that disease in New York City in 1795, made and published valuable observations on it, and later was instrumental in securing the passage of quarantine laws. Himself a victim of yellow fever, he died in Staten Island, New York, on August 17, 1801.

Beach, Alfred Ely (1826–1896), inventor and journalist. Born in Springfield, Massachusetts, on September 1, 1826, Alfred Ely Beach was the son of Moses Yale Beach. He learned journalism by working for his father on the *New York Sun* and in 1845 became a partner in the *Sun's* parent company. The next year he joined with Orson D. Munn and Salem H. Wales in organizing Munn & Company, which bought the six-month-old *Scientific American* magazine from Rufus Porter and built it over the years into a great and unique periodical. Beach's principal interest was in inventions and, although he was for a time the magazine's editor, he devoted himself mainly to aiding and advising inventors and to working on his own ideas. He patented, among other things,

a typewriter, a typewriter for the blind, a cable railway system, and pneumatic tube systems for transporting mail and people. Each of his patents contributed to the final evolution of a practical device. He built a demonstration pneumatic passenger subway under Broadway in New York City, but the project was eventually abandoned. Beach died on January 1, 1896, in New York City.

Beach, Frederick Converse (1848–1918), business man and editor. Born on March 27, 1848, in Brooklyn, New York, the son of Alfred Ely Beach, Frederick Converse Beach graduated from Yale's Sheffield Scientific School in 1868. He entered Munn & Company, taking, like his father, a special interest in inventions and patents, and in 1896 became a director of the Scientific American Company. He had various other business interests as well and was active in promoting the establishment of the U.S. parcel-post system. An early and noted amateur photographer, he founded in 1889 the *American Amateur Photographer* (later *American Photography*) and served as its editor. From 1902 he was also editor in chief of the *Encyclopedia Americana*. Beach died on June 18, 1918, in Stratford, Connecticut.

Beach, Moses Sperry (1822–1892), inventor and journalist. Born in Springfield, Massachusetts, on October 5, 1822, Moses Sperry Beach was the son of Moses Yale Beach. He learned journalism in the printing shop and editorial office of the *New York Sun* and in 1845, after a brief connection with the *Boston Daily Times*, joined with his father and his brother, Alfred Ely Beach, in forming Moses Y. Beach & Sons, the *Sun's* parent company. Three years later the elder Beach retired and in 1852 Alfred withdrew from the firm to pursue other interests, leaving Moses S. in full command. He continued the *Sun* on a successful basis for 16 years, with the exception of a brief period in 1860–1861 when, in hopes of an early retirement, he leased it to a group who nearly destroyed it in an attempt to make it into a religious journal. Beach had, like his father, a talent for things mechanical; he invented both a web press and a cutting device that made possible printing on a continuous roll of paper instead of precut sheets. He was also apparently the first to print both sides of the paper at once. In 1868 he sold the *Sun* to a group headed by Charles A. Dana and retired to his estate in Peekskill, New York, where he died on July 25, 1892.

Beach, Moses Yale (1800–1868), inventor and journalist. Born in Wallingford, Connecticut, on January 15, 1800, Beach grew up on the family's farm and early developed a flair for mechanics. At fourteen he was apprenticed to a cabinetmaker; he paid off his indenture four years later and began to work on his own, moving gradually from his trade to promising but expensive experiments with gunpowder engines, steam engines, and rag-cutting machinery; his rag-cutter is still used. In 1834 he took a job with the *New*

York Sun, begun the year before by his brother-in-law, Benjamin H. Day. By 1838 he had bought out Day and begun an enterprising and successful career in journalism. Faced with bold competition from James Gordon Bennett's *New York Herald*, Beach sought constantly for faster means of gathering the news: he sent out boats to meet incoming ships bearing news from Europe, and at various other times he employed pony-express riders, chartered trains, and carrier pigeons. Edgar Allan Poe satirized the speed mania in his "Balloon-Hoax" that, like the "Moon-Hoax" published by Day in 1835, appeared as news in the *Sun* on April 13, 1844. In both cases, Beach was in on the joke. Under Beach the *Sun* greatly expanded its coverage of national and international events while maintaining the appeal to the working man which it had possessed from the start. He is credited with originating the syndicated news story and establishing the first European edition of a U.S. paper (the *American Sun*, a weekly begun in 1848). In the midst of the difficuties of news gathering during the Mexican War, he eliminated much wasteful competition by organizing among the leading journals of the city the New York Associated Press. The *Sun* had a circulation of 50,000 in 1848 when Beach retired and turned the paper over to his sons, Moses S. Beach and Alfred E. Beach. He lived quietly in Wallingford, where he died on July 19, 1868.

Beadle, Erastus Flavel (1821–1894), publisher. Born near Cooperstown, New York, on September 11, 1821, Beadle grew up on a farm there and later in Michigan. He served an apprenticeship to a miller and in 1841 took a job in a printshop. He moved to Buffalo with his brother Irwin about 1850 and in 1852 they opened a printing business that soon undertook publishing as well, beginning the magazine *Youth's Casket* in 1852 and *Home, a Fireside Monthly* (later *Beadle's Home Monthly*) in 1856. In 1856 Robert Adams joined the company, which became Beadle & Adams, and two years later the entire operation was moved to New York City. Success with the experimental issue of a ten-cent paperbound songbook led to dime joke books, dime etiquette books, and in 1860 to the first dime novel, a story by Anne S. Stephens entitled *Malaeska: The Indian Wife of the White Hunter* that was a runaway best seller. Beadle immediately arranged for more such books and the Beadle Dime Novel series was launched. Hiring a stable of writers, mostly hacks and all prolific, and putting them in charge of editor Orville J. Victor, Beadle & Adams began turning out dozens and then hundreds of dime novels in several series. Victor's wife Metta produced *Maum Guinea and Her Plantation "Children"* in 1861 and sales of that book alone reached half a million. The Dime Novel series ran to 631 titles; subsequent series were even larger, the Dime Library reaching 1103 titles and the Half Dime Library 1168. The books, full of bloodshed and high adventure, were enormously popular with boys and men alike; during the Civil War wagonloads were hauled to army camps for distribution to the soldiers. Although many were Westerns, all manner of settings and characters were employed in the various series, which included the Deadwood Dick and Nick Carter series, and all used essentially the same plot formula and the same improbable sort of dialogue and narrative language. Violence and suspense were paramount in the dime novel, where virtue invariably triumphed and immorality was nonexistent. Several other firms entered the field to flood the country with yet more millions of the cheap books, but Beadle & Adams retained the lead and the distinction of having invented the most popular and characteristic U.S. literary form of the nineteenth century. Beadle himself retired a millionaire in 1889 to his Cooperstown estate and died there on December 18, 1894.

Beadle, George Wells (1903–), geneticist. Born on October 22, 1903, in Wahoo, Nebraska, Beadle graduated from the University of Nebraska in 1926, remained to take his M.S. the following year, and then moved to Cornell University, where he received his Ph.D. in 1931. His graduate research had been on the genetics of Indian corn, and for the next several years he studied at the California Institute of Technology with Thomas Hunt Morgan, who had performed the classic genetic work with the fruit fly *Drosophila* that established the existence of the gene as the basic unit of heredity. In 1935 Beadle went to Paris where, with Boris Ephrussi, he investigated the mechanism of gene action and was able to demonstrate that a hereditary defect in the eye pigment of *Drosophila* was the result of the chemical properties of specific genes. After teaching at Harvard for a year he became professor of biology at Stanford University in 1937. There, with Edward L. Tatum, he continued his research into gene action. Technical difficulties forced them to abandon *Drosophila* for *Neurospora crassa*, a red bread mold, and over the next several years they showed that the function of the genes was to determine and regulate the synthesis of vitamins, amino acids, and proteins in the cell and thus to control its metabolism. For this work Beadle and Tatum were awarded, with Joshua Lederberg, the 1958 Nobel Prize for Physiology and Medicine. Beadle left Stanford in 1946 to succeed Morgan as chairman of the biology division at Caltech. In 1961 he became chancellor and then president of the University of Chicago. Seven years later he retired as president emeritus and Wrather Distinguished Service Professor and assumed the directorship of the Institute for Biomedical Research of the American Medical Association.

Bean, Roy (1825?–1903), frontier figure. Born in Mason County, Kentucky, about 1825, Bean worked at various jobs, sought gold in the West, and traded in Mexico before eventually making his way to Texas about 1875 and settling in San Antonio. In 1882 he moved to a barren spot known as Vinegaroon on the lower Pecos River and opened another in the series of saloons he had been operating for construction men working on the Southern Pacific Railroad. He soon became, more or less officially, the local justice of the peace. He held court sessions in the saloon, where he dispensed rough and ready justice and hung up a sign designating him "the law west of the Pecos," a phrase that became a part of Western legend. In 1898, avoiding a ban by the state of Texas, he picked a sandbar in the middle of the Rio Grande—the border between Texas and Mexico—to hold a boxing match that featured heavyweight champion Robert P. Fitzsimmons. Bean died at his settlement—which he had renamed Langtry, after the actress Lillie Langtry, "The Jersey Lily"—on March 16, 1903.

Beard, Charles Austin (1874–1948), political scientist and historian. Born near Knightstown, Indiana, on November 27, 1874, Beard graduated from DePauw University in 1898 and spent the next four years abroad, studying for a year at Oxford. He returned to the United States to continue his studies at Cornell and at Columbia, from which he received his Ph.D. in 1904. He taught history and politics at Columbia from 1907 to 1917; during that time his interest shifted from the history of Europe to that of America. His early and influential works, *The Development of Modern Europe* (with J. H. Robinson), 1907; *The Supreme Court and the Constitution*, 1912; *An Economic Interpretation of the Constitution of the United States*, 1913; and *The Economic Origins of Jeffersonian Democracy*, 1915, while not explicitly embracing economic determinism, did much to foster that approach to history among other historians. Beard was an influential leader of the Progressive movement and one of its intellectual mainstays. In 1917 he resigned from Columbia in protest against the university's policy concerning academic freedom under President Nicholas Murray Butler. He became a director of the Training School for Public Service in that year, helped found (with Robinson, John Dewey, Alvin A. Johnson, and others) the New School for Social Research in 1919, and thereafter was from time to time an adviser to the governments of Japan and Yugoslavia. With his wife Mary, a distinguished historian in her own right, he produced *The Rise of American Civilization* in four parts, beginning in 1927 and concluding with *America in Midpassage*, 1939; *The American Spirit*, 1942; and *A Basic History of the United States*, 1944, long a standard text. During the 1930s and 1940s Beard was deeply concerned with U.S. foreign policy, publishing *The Idea of National Interest*, 1934, and *The Open Door at Home*, 1934, both with G. H. E. Smith. His outlook tended toward isolationism, and in *American Foreign Policy in the Making, 1932–1940*, 1946, and *President Roosevelt and the Coming of War 1941*, 1948, he severely criticized President Franklin D. Roosevelt's policies in the period leading to World War II. Beard died on September 1, 1948, in New Haven, Connecticut.

Beard, Daniel Carter (1850–1941), artist, outdoorsman, and author. Born on June 21, 1850, in Cincinnati, Dan Beard attended school in Covington, Kentucky, and from 1880 to 1884 studied at the Art Students League in New York. He was a successful illustrator, his work appearing in leading magazines and in many books. His interest in woodcraft and outdoor life led him to write numerous books on the subject, including *American Boys' Handy Book*, 1882; *Outdoor Handy Book*, 1900; *Boy Pioneers and Sons of Daniel Boone*, 1909; *The Buckskin Book*, 1911; *Shelters, Shacks, and Shanties*, 1914; *American Boys' Book of Wild Animals*, 1921; and *Wisdom of the Woods*, 1927. From 1893 to 1900 he taught at the Woman's School of Applied Design, inaugurating the first class in animal drawing in the world. He edited *Recreation* magazine in 1905–1906. In 1905 he founded the Sons of Daniel Boone; in 1910 the society was merged with the newly chartered Boy Scouts of America, patterned after the movement begun in England by Robert Baden-Powell. Beard became national commissioner of the Scouts and, in recognition of his leadership in promoting and establishing scouting in the United States, was given the only Golden Eagle medal ever awarded by the organization. From 1911 to 1914 he organized and headed the department of woodcraft at Culver Military Academy in Indiana. For many years he served as associate editor of the Boy Scout magazine, *Boys' Life*. He died in Suffern, New York, on June 11, 1941. Mt. Beard, adjoining Mt. McKinley in Alaska, is named for him.

Beaumont, William (1785–1853), surgeon. Born on November 21, 1785, in Lebanon, Connecticut, Beaumont was apprenticed in 1810 to a Vermont surgeon and was licensed to practice medicine two years later. He served in the army during the War of 1812, and after four years of private practice in Plattsburgh, New York, he enlisted for a second time in 1819 and was sent to Fort Mackinac Territory in Michigan as post surgeon. In 1822 he treated a young Canadian trapper, Alexis St. Martin, for a gunshot wound that left a permanent opening into his stomach. He restored the man to health but was unable to close the wound. About 1825 it occurred to Beaumont to take advantage of St. Martin's condition to study the action of the stomach in a living man. Soon after he began his observations, however, St. Martin ran away and it was not until 1829 that Beaumont, then at Fort Crawford, in Wisconsin Territory, located him and persuaded him to return. There, and later in Washington, D.C., Beaumont pursued his investigations. To his earlier findings —on the movements of the stomach during digestion, the relative digestibility of various foods, and the ability of gastric juice to digest food even outside the body—he added further knowledge of the nature of the gastric juice itself. A collaborator, Professor Robley Dunglison of the University of Virginia, determined that the principal constituent was free hydrochloric acid and suggested the presence of another chemical (later shown to be pepsin) that then defied analysis. Beaumont's work was summed up in his classic *Experiments and Observations on the Gastric Juice and the Physiology of Digestion*, 1833. In 1834 St. Martin returned to Canada and thereafter refused to participate in further experiments; in the same year Beaumont was transferred to St. Louis. He resigned from the army in 1840 and carried on a private practice until his death in St. Louis on April 25, 1853.

Beauregard, Pierre Gustave Toutant (1818–1893), soldier. Born near New Orleans on May 28, 1818, Beauregard graduated from West Point in 1838 and was commissioned in the Corps of Engineers. In the Mexican War he saw action at Veracruz, Cerro Gordo, Contreras, and Mexico City and was twice rewarded by brevet promotions. He was then stationed in Louisiana until his appointment as superintendent of West Point. He served less than a week in that post, resigning his commission in February 1861 to become a brigadier general in the Confederate army. Placed in command of Charleston, South Carolina, he gave the order for the firing on Fort Sumter in April. He was then made second in command, under Gen. Joseph E. Johnston, of the Confederate forces in Virginia and was on the field at the first victory of Manassas (Bull Run). Promoted to full general, he joined Gen. Albert S. Johnston in Tennessee in 1862 and at Shiloh succeeded to command upon Johnston's death. After a period of illness he took charge of the coastal defense of Georgia and South Carolina and through 1863 and into 1864 successfully repelled Union attacks, particularly at Charleston. Beauregard was then sent to defend Richmond against Gen. Benjamin F. Butler, whom he defeated, and then finally against Gen. Ulysses S. Grant, against whom he set up defenses at Petersburg. He turned his forces over to Lee at that point, served again for a time in the West, and at the end of the war was with Joseph Johnston's army in the Carolinas. After the war he was for five years president of the New Orleans, Jackson & Mississippi Railway and thereafter served variously as manager of the Louisiana lottery, commissioner of public works for New Orleans, and state adjutant general. He wrote numerous books and articles on military affairs, including *Principles and Maxims of the Art of War*, 1863; *Report on the Defense of Charleston*, 1864; and *A Commentary on the Campaign and Battle of Manassas*, 1891. Beauregard died in New Orleans on February 20, 1893.

Becker, Carl Lotus (1873–1945), historian. Born on September 7, 1873, near Waterloo, Iowa, Becker attended Cornell College in Iowa and graduated in 1896 from the University of Wisconsin, where he remained to take his Ph.D. in 1907. He was a fellow in constitutional law at Columbia during 1898–1899, an instructor in history and political science at Pennsylvania State College from 1899 to 1901, instructor in history at Dartmouth in 1901–1902, and a professor at the University of

Kansas until 1916 and at the University of Minnesota in 1916–1917. He went to Cornell University as professor of European history in 1917. He was a popular lecturer and found time to write essays on aspects of American, French, and modern European history. The style for which he became known blended great learning with an easy popular quality. His broad analyses of historical institutions reflected his apprenticeship under Frederick Jackson Turner at the University of Wisconsin; his views on subjective historical interpretation were the subject of his notable presidential address, "Every Man His Own Historian," to the American Historical Association in 1931. He wrote many books, among them *The Declaration of Independence*, 1922, (revised edition, 1942); *Our Great Experiment in Democracy*, 1924; *Modern History*, 1931; *The Heavenly City of the Eighteenth-Century Philosophers*, 1932; *Progress and Power*, 1936; and *How New Will the Better World Be?*, 1944. He retired in 1941 and died in Ithaca, New York, on April 10, 1945.

Becker, George Ferdinand (1847–1919), geologist. Born on January 5, 1847, in New York City, Becker grew up there and in Cambridge, Massachusetts. He early developed a passion for nature study and added interests in chemistry and mathematics at Harvard. Graduating in 1868, he took his Ph.D. the next year from the University of Heidelberg and, after a year as a correspondent for the *New York Herald* reporting on the Franco-Prussian War, he pursued further studies at the Royal Academy of Mines in Berlin. He returned to the United States, worked for a time as a construction engineer in Illinois, and in 1874 became an instructor in mining and metallurgy at the University of California at Berkeley. There he met Clarence King, who in 1879 became director of the newly consolidated U.S. Geological Survey and immediately appointed Becker to the staff. For the Survey he undertook a number of geological investigations of a highly technical and comprehensive nature. His reports on them included *Geology of the Comstock Lode and Washoe District*, 1882; *Statistics and Technology of the Precious Metals*, with Samuel F. Emmons, 1885 (a nationwide study performed for the 1880 census), *Geology of the Quicksilver Deposits of the Pacific Slope*, 1888; and *Finite Homogeneous Strain, Flow and Rupture of Rocks*, 1893, a theoretical work that reflected Becker's principal interest, the study of the physical and chemical properties of rocks and minerals. To the end of placing the more descriptive phases of geology on a sound theoretical basis, he organized a geophysical laboratory within the Survey. In 1896 he traveled to South Africa to examine gold and diamond fields and during 1898–1899 was attached as geologist to the U.S. forces occupying the Philippines. Becker died on April 20, 1919, in Washington, D.C.

Becknell, William (1796?–1865), trader and explorer. Born about 1796 in Amherst County, Virginia, Becknell later moved to Missouri and settled at Arrow Rock. In 1821, while on a trading journey to the southern Rockies, he received word that American traders were at last welcome in Santa Fe, the Spanish authorities having been ousted. He immediately turned south to follow the Arkansas River nearly to its source, then struck south to Taos and Santa Fe, where he sold his goods at a huge profit. The following year he set out for Santa Fe from Franklin, Missouri, with several wagons; instead of following the Arkansas to its upper reaches, he left it near what is now Cimarron, Kansas, just west of Dodge City, and turned south to the Cimarron River, the main fork of which he then followed upstream to the Rockies and thence descended through Raton Pass to Santa Fe. The 1821 journey had been the first by an American trader; that of 1822 established the standard trading route that became known as the Santa Fe Trail, central to the commerce of the Southwest for nearly 50 years and to Western legend forever. Becknell moved to Texas about 1834, served in the revolutionary forces there, and later joined the Texas Rangers. He died on April 30, 1865.

Bee, Barnard Elliott (1824–1861), soldier. Born early in 1824 in Charleston, South Carolina, Bee moved with his family to Texas in 1835. He graduated from West Point in 1845, was commissioned in the infantry, and was off almost immediately to the Mexican War. He saw action under Gen. Zachary Taylor at Palo Alto and Resaca de la Palma and under Gen. Winfield Scott at Cerro Gordo, Chapultepec, and Mexico City, and was twice given brevet promotions for distinguished conduct. After the war he was on frontier duty until 1861, when he resigned his commission and was appointed a major and then a brigadier general in the Confederate army. In July of that year he was in command of a brigade of Gen. Joseph E. Johnston's army at the first battle of Manassas (Bull Run); his inexperienced men faced the heaviest part of the first Union attack and, in a desperate effort to maintain their courage, Bee pointed to a nearby brigade and its commander, saying "Let us determine to die here, and we will conquer. There is Jackson standing like a stone wall. Rally behind the Virginians!" The second sentence gave Gen. Thomas J. Jackson the nickname by which he was afterwards known. Bee was seriously wounded a short time later and died the next day, July 22, 1861.

Beebe, Charles William, see Beebe, William

Beebe, Lucius Morris (1902–1966), journalist and author. Born in Wakefield, Massachusetts, on December 9, 1902, Beebe attended Yale, which he left in a dispute with the Divinity School over Prohibition, and Harvard, from which he graduated in 1927. He remained at Harvard for another year, writing a thesis on Edwin Arlington Robinson, and then joined the staff of the *Boston Evening Transcript.* In 1929 he moved to the *New York Herald Tribune,* where his penchant for

covering fires in morning dress and other such eccentricities won him promotion from reporter to second-string drama critic. In 1933 he began a syndicated column, "This New York," in which for 11 years he chronicled, in rococo prose, the comings and goings of café society. His own style of living of which elegance was the keynote, was perfectly attuned to the "purlieus of magnificence" that he frequented in order to ferret out all the wonderfully inconsequential details of life with the "500." Beebe was, paradoxically enough, also an imaginative and irrepressible practical joker and an authority on railroading, particularly that of the age of steam. This interest resulted in a great many books, including *High Iron,* 1938; *Highliners,* 1940; *Highball,* 1945; *Mansions on Rails,* 1959; *The 20th Century Limited,* 1962; and *The Overland Limited,* 1963. He also wrote numerous books on Western history, among them *The U.S. West: The Saga of Wells Fargo,* 1949; *Legends of the Comstock Lode,* 1950; *The American West,* 1955; and *San Francisco's Golden Era,* 1960. He discontinued his column in 1944 but remained with the *Herald Tribune* until 1950. From 1950 to 1960 he was publisher of the *Territorial Enterprise,* Mark Twain's old newspaper in Virginia City, Nevada, and in 1960 he moved to San Francisco and began to write the column "This Wild West" for the *Chronicle.* Beebe died at his home near San Mateo, California, on February 4, 1966.

Beebe, William (1877–1962), naturalist and author. Born in Brooklyn, New York, on July 29, 1877, Charles William Beebe graduated from Columbia University in 1898, pursued postgraduate studies there for a year, and in 1899 was appointed curator of ornithology at the Bronx Zoo. For the New York Zoological Society he undertook a long series of research trips to Mexico, British Guiana, Venezuela, the Galápagos Islands, the West Indies, and the Far East, studying a variety of animals ranging from pheasants to fish. From 1919 onward he was director of the society's department of tropical research. Beebe wrote numerous valuable scientific articles and monographs and in addition produced popular books that were highly praised not only for their wealth of information and insight into nature but also for their literary quality. Among the latter were *Jungle Peace,* 1918; *Jungle Days,* 1925; *Arcturus Adventure,* 1926; *Beneath Tropic Seas,* 1928; *Nonesuch: Land of Water,* 1932; *Book of Naturalists,* 1944; *High Jungle,* 1949; and *Unseen Life of New York,* 1953. In 1934 he made a descent into the ocean in the specially designed bathysphere, which he had constructed in association with Otis Barton, reaching a then-record depth of 3028 feet and recording his experience in *Half Mile Down,* 1934. He was also a noted lecturer and the recipient of many honors and awards. Beebe died on June 4, 1962, in Trinidad in the West Indies.

Beecher, Catharine Esther (1800–1878), educator. Born in East Hampton, New York, on September

6, 1800, Miss Beecher was the eldest daughter in one of the nineteenth century's most remarkable families. Daughter of Lyman Beecher and sister of Edward and Henry Ward Beecher and Harriet Beecher Stowe, to name only the three most prominent of her siblings, she grew up in an atmosphere of learning but was hindered by her sex from receiving much formal education. She attended schools for young ladies conducted in the fashion of the day while independently studying Latin, philosophy, and mathematics. In 1824 she established the Hartford Female Seminary in Hartford, Connecticut, an advanced school for girls in which she introduced calisthenics in a course of physical education. Moving with her father to Cincinnati, in 1832, she opened the Western Female Institute; financial difficulties closed the school five years later. The rest of her life was devoted to the promotion of equal educational opportunities for women. She inspired the founding of several women's colleges in the Midwest, and her writings did much to introduce domestic science into the American school curriculum. Though in sympathy with much of the reformist spirit of the century, she stoutly opposed woman suffrage. She died on May 12, 1878, in Elmira, New York.

Beecher, Edward (1803–1895), religious leader and educator. Born in East Hampton, New York, on August 27, 1803, Beecher was the third child of Lyman Beecher and a member of the illustrious family that included also Henry Ward and Catharine Beecher and Harriet Beecher Stowe. Graduating at the head of his Yale class of 1822, he taught and studied by turns until 1826, when he became pastor of the Park Street Church in Boston. In 1830 he became the first president of Illinois College at Jacksonville, the state's first institution of higher learning. While leading the college to distinction in spite of financial troubles, Beecher became involved in the abolitionist movement. He was a close associate of Elijah P. Lovejoy, whose death in the Alton riots in 1837 created a furor in the North. Beecher's *Narrative of Riots at Alton,* which appeared the next year, became an important document of the period. In 1844 he resigned his college presidency and returned to the ministry in Boston, where he was a founder and, from 1849 to 1853, editor of the *Congregationalist.* From 1855 to 1871 he was again in Illinois as pastor of a church in Galesburg. In 1871 he moved to Brooklyn, New York, where his brother Henry was an immensely popular preacher; there he remained, for a few years as pastor of a small Congregational church in nearby Parkville, until his death on July 28, 1895.

Beecher, Henry Ward (1813–1887), religious leader and social reformer. Born on June 24, 1813, in Litchfield, Connecticut, one of 13 children of clergyman Lyman Beecher, he graduated from Amherst in 1834. He studied for three years at Lane Theological Seminary in Cincinnati while his father was its president and in 1837 became pastor of a small church at Lawrenceburg Indiana. Two years later, he transferred to the Second Presbyterian Church of Indianapolis. He developed a forceful, imaginative style of delivering his sermons, intending to affect his parishioners emotionally and thereby to improve their characters. His own manner and dress were noticeably independent and unorthodox and his large congregation became as interested in his personality and conduct as in his gospel. By 1847, his reputation as an orator and a writer won him the pastorate of the Plymouth (Congregational) Church in Brooklyn, New York. There he involved himself in social and political issues, opposing slavery, campaigning for political candidates, and supporting the Civil War and moderate Reconstruction policies. In general he used his ebullient oratory to support the opinions of other men rather than to offer ideas of his own. He edited the Congregationalist *Independent* in the 1860s and later was editor of the *Christian Union.* In a sensational scandal in 1874, he was brought to trial on charges of adultery. The jury could not agree on a verdict and he was acquitted, returned to lecture and to preach at the Plymouth Church. His writings included *Seven Lectures to Young Men,* 1844; *Evolution and Religion,* 1885; and *Life of Jesus the Christ,* 1871–1891. He died in Brooklyn on March 8, 1887. He was elected to the Hall of Fame in 1900.

Beecher, Lyman (1775–1863), religious leader and social reformer. Born on October 12, 1775, in New Haven, Connecticut, the son and grandson of blacksmiths, Beecher attended Yale, where he was profoundly influenced by its president, theologian Timothy Dwight. He graduated in 1797 and entered Yale's divinity school; he was ordained by Dwight in 1799. He established himself at the Presbyterian Church in East Hampton, New York, during 1799–1810. His reputation for fiery preaching reached Litchfield, Connecticut, a center of wealth in New England, and he was called in 1810 to become pastor there. He conducted "continuous revivals," railing at intemperance, Roman Catholicism, and religious tolerance. He brought about the passage of blue laws, formed a society to educate men for the ministry, and published vigorous sermons on intemperance in the *Connecticut Observer* that were later translated into foreign languages. When the new Hanover Street Church was founded in Boston in 1826, he was asked to become its minister. His influence on the town was profound; unfortunately his denunciations of Catholicism became an incentive for townsmen to plunder the Ursuline Convent in 1831. He accepted an offer to become president of the new Lane Theological Seminary in Cincinnati and moved there in 1832. His Calvinist doctrines were violently attacked by conservatives for being too "moderate" and he was tried for heresy soon after his arrival. Eager to affect the religious development of the West, he was stunned by this response, and when acquitted, faced yet another battle at the seminary, where rules had been passed during his absence forbidding students to discuss the slavery issue. An abolitionist, he fought for revision of the rules, but nevertheless lost most of his students to Oberlin College. He resigned in 1850 after being for nearly two decades a highly controversial figure and went to live with his son Henry in Brooklyn, New York, where he died on January 10, 1863. He married three times and raised 13 extremely gifted children, the majority of whom attained either contemporary or lasting fame. Notable among them were Harriet Beecher Stowe, Henry Ward Beecher, Catharine E. Beecher, and Edward Beecher.

Beers, Clifford Whittingham (1876–1943), social reformer. Born on March 30, 1876, in New Haven, Connecticut, Beers graduated from the Sheffield Scientific School of Yale University in 1897 and went into business in New York City. He suffered a breakdown in 1906, the culmination of mental illness that had been growing steadily worse for several years, and during the next two years was confined to a series of institutions. He was appalled to find that such institutions offered their inmates no therapy, no aid, nor even comfort, but only abuse and neglect. On gaining his release in 1908 he wrote an autobiography detailing his experiences and published it later that year as *A Mind That Found Itself*. The book was highly successful—by 1939 it had gone through 24 printings—and launched Beers on the work in behalf of mental hygiene to which he devoted the rest of his life. In 1908 he organized the Connecticut Society for Mental Hygiene, the first such organization in the world. The following year he founded the National Commission for Mental Hygiene, of which he served as secretary. Similar societies soon sprang up in other states and in 1918 he helped organize the Canadian National Committee for Mental Hygiene. From its founding in 1928 until his death he was secretary of the American Foundation for Mental Hygiene. During 1923 he traveled extensively in Europe, conferring with and giving advice to leaders in mental hygiene, and in 1930 he organized the first International Congress on Mental Hygiene and helped found the International Commission for Mental Hygiene. He served as secretary of the commission and of the International Foundation for Mental Hygiene, founded in 1931. During 1933, the 25th anniversary of his first steps as a pioneer in the field of public health, Beers was widely honored for his work, being awarded membership in the French Legion of Honor and a gold medal of the National Institute of Social Sciences. *Twenty-Five Years After—Sidelights on the Mental Hygiene Movement and Its Founder*, a commemorative volume with many distinguished contributors, was published in 1934. Beers died in Providence, Rhode Island, on July 9, 1943.

Beery, Wallace (1886–1949), actor. Born on April 1, 1886, in Kansas City, Missouri, Beery ran away from home in his youth and joined the Ringling Brothers Circus, where he became an elephant trainer. Later he joined his brother Noah on the musical-comedy stage and for several years was a popular figure on Broadway and in touring stock companies. He made his first film appearance about 1913 for the Essaness Studios in Chicago; two years later he moved to Hollywood and in 1917 won his first major movie role in *Behind the Door*. With Mack Sennett's Keystone Company he made dozens of short silents, generally playing villains, for which his massive physique and his scowling face well suited him. Later, however, at Metro-Goldwyn-Mayer, his versatility enabled him to take on other sorts of roles and gradually he developed the screen character of a sentimental, bumbling, awkward, and occasionally alcoholic old fellow, irresponsible but lovable. In just such a role he won an Academy Award for *The Champ*, 1931, and he gained great popularity in memorable performances opposite Marie Dressler, notably in *Min and Bill*, 1931, and *Tugboat Annie*, 1933. Others of his best movies included *Dinner at Eight*, 1934; *Viva Villa*, 1934, for which he won a gold medal at the Venice International Motion Picture Exposition; and the film version of Eugene O'Neill's *Ah! Wilderness*, 1935. A veteran of some 250 movies, Beery died in Beverly Hills, California, on April 15, 1949.

Beiderbecke, Leon Bismarck (1903–1931), "Bix," musician. Born on March 10, 1903, in Davenport, Iowa, Beiderbecke taught himself as a child to play the piano and cornet. After a year at Lake Forest Academy in Illinois he joined a jazz group called the Wolverines, with whom he played cornet around the Midwest and finally in New York. During the rest of his brief career he played intermittently with a number of bands, some, like that of Frankie Trumbauer, devoted to real jazz, and others of a more commercial nature, such as those of Jean Goldkette, Paul Whiteman, and Glen Gray. Although he often sat in with such top jazzmen as Joe "King" Oliver and Louis Armstrong, Beiderbecke's recordings were all made with groups—his own or Trumbauer's—of lesser ability. It was partly for this reason that during his lifetime he was little known outside of a small coterie of fellow musicians and jazz aficionados. He died on August 7, 1931, in New York City. His recordings gradually became collectors' items and with the publication of Dorothy Baker's *Young Man With a Horn*, 1938, a novel inspired loosely by his music and, contrary claims notwithstanding, not at all by his life, he came to be more widely known. It is said that his best playing was never recorded; nevertheless, his unique legato phrasing, clear tone, and use of often highly unorthodox harmonies were preserved in such classic recordings as "Singin' the Blues," "I'm Comin' Virginia," "Fidgety Feet," "Since My Best Girl Turned Me Down," "The Love Nest," and "In a Mist," the last of which he wrote and on which he played piano. Many later jazz musicians were strongly influenced by his style, and he came to be recognized as one of jazz's greatest exponents.

Beissel, Johann Conrad (1690–1768), religious leader. Born in April 1690 in Eberbach, Germany, Beissel was early orphaned and apprenticed to a baker. He was for many years a journeyman baker, but his conversion to a strongly pietistic form of Christianity led him to emigrate to America in 1720. He lived in various places in Pennsylvania as his religious thinking turned toward the beliefs of the Dunkard sect. About 1730 he founded a retreat called "Economy" at Ephrata and was soon joined by a number of followers, both men (Solitary Brethren) and women (Order of Spiritual Virgins). The community of Seventh-Day Baptists became known as the Ephrata Cloisters and it grew to include several hundred members. A strictly celibate, semimonastic rule was maintained, the members wearing hoods and the women veils as well. Printing was the principal vocation, along with the making of illuminated manuscripts. The community was also noted for its music, for which Beissel, a prolific and unorthodox hymn writer, was largely responsible. His *Göttliche Liebes und Lobes Gethöne*, printed by Benjamin Franklin in 1730, was the first Pennsylvania German hymnal. Others of his compositions appeared in *Turtel-Taube*, 1747. After his death in Ephrata on July 6, 1768, the Cloisters began a slow decline, but the community's influence on music persisted for a century or more, and its customs continued to be practiced in isolated places in Pennsylvania until the middle of the 19th century.

Békésy, Georg von (1899–1972), physicist. Born on June 3, 1899, in Budapest, Hungary, Békésy was educated at the universities of Bern, Switzerland, and Budapest, taking a Ph.D. from Budapest in 1923. From 1924 to 1946 he worked in the Royal Hungarian Institute for Research in Telegraphy, from 1932 serving also on the faculty of the University of Budapest. After a brief period at the Royal Institute of Technology in Stockholm he came to the United States in 1947 and continued his teaching and research at Harvard as a senior fellow at its psycho-acoustic laboratory. His research was concerned almost exclusively with the mechanism of hearing. Over the years, employing techniques and instruments of his own devising, his experiments revealed how sound waves were transformed in the ear into electrical nerve impulses. In particular he showed that the basilar membrane, the site of the nerve-ending receptor cells in the cochlea of the inner ear, was induced by sound energy to set up traveling waves whose points of maximum strength varied with pitch from place to place, thus resolving the long-standing controversy over where and how in the process of hearing frequency analysis is performed. This work made it possible to distinguish between various sorts of deafness and pointed to new methods of treatment for some. In 1961 Békésy was awarded the Nobel Prize for Medicine. His major writings were published in English as *Experiments in Hearing*, 1960, and *Sensory Inhibition*, 1967. He was professor of sensory sciences at the University of Hawaii from 1966 until his death in Honolulu on June 13, 1972.

Belasco, David (1853–1931), producer and playwright. Born on July 25, 1853, in San Francisco, Belasco attracted audiences as a child by reciting ballads in the street. He attended Lincoln College in California and subsequently managed, acted in, and adapted plays for several theaters in San Francisco. He toured in *Hearts of Oak*, which he wrote with James A. Herne in 1879. After 1880 he lived in New York City, where he was stage manager of the Madison Square Theater until 1886, then of the Lyceum. He became an independent producer in 1890 in a theater rented from Oscar Hammerstein. There his most popular productions were his own *The Heart of Maryland*, 1895, and *Madame Butterfly*, 1900, later made into an opera by Giacomo Puccini. He concentrated on plays he had written or adapted himself and later was harshly criticized for ignoring eminent dramatists and actors alike, but by the same token he raised many obscure actors and playwrights to stardom. In 1906 he built the Belasco Theatre in New York City. As a producer he attained unprecedented popularity; he was able to draw crowds on the strength of his name alone. Fanatical about technical precision, he achieved amazingly realistic effects through innovative stage lighting and various mechanical devices. He unfortunately lacked perspective, however, and frequently was criticized for poor taste and sensationalism. As the producer of hundreds of plays and the author of such standards as *The Girl I Left Behind Me* (with Franklin Fyles), *The Charity Ball* and *Lord Chumley* (with H. C. De Mille), *The Darling of the Gods* (with J. L. Long), and *The Girl of the Golden West*, he was dubbed the "bishop of Broadway." Belasco died on May 14, 1931, in New York City.

Belcher, Jonathan (1682–1757), colonial leader. Born in Cambridge, Massachusetts, on January 8, 1682, the son of a prosperous merchant and colonial politician, Belcher graduated from Harvard in 1699 and spent several years in Europe. Upon his return to Boston he set about amassing a fortune as a merchant and from 1718 onward was active in politics. Elected several times to the Massachusetts Council, he was sent by that body to England in 1728 to represent it in a dispute with Governor William Burnet, who died shortly after Belcher's arrival in London. Belcher was able to secure a commission as the new governor of Massachusetts and New Hampshire. He held the post from 1730 until he was dismissed in 1741 after many conflicts with royal authority. In July 1746, having reestablished himself in favor, he was made governor of New Jersey. There his most notable work was his patronage of the College of New Jersey (now Princeton), which he rechartered in 1747. He died in Elizabethtown, New Jersey, on August 31, 1757.

Bel Geddes, Norman, see Geddes, Norman Bel

Bell, Alexander Graham (1847–1922), inventor and educator. Born in Edinburgh, Scotland, on March 3, 1847, Bell was the son of Alexander Melville Bell, a prominent authority on the physiology of speech and like his father before him, a noted teacher of elocution. Young Bell studied at the University of Edinburgh for a year (1864) and, while working as his father's assistant, at University College in London in 1868–1870. As early as 1865 he was conducting research into acoustics and from that time forward was deeply interested in the problem of teaching speech to the deaf. In 1870 Bell and his father sailed to Canada and the following spring he began training teachers at a day school for the deaf in Boston—the first of its kind anywhere—in the use of "visible speech," a system of symbolic representations of the physical process of speech that had been developed by his father and to which he made numerous notational improvements. He introduced the system to other schools in the Boston area as well, including the Clarke Institution for the Deaf, through which he met its founder, Gardiner G. Hubbard. In 1872 Bell opened his own teacher-training school in Boston and the next year was appointed to a professorship in the Boston University School of Oratory. He had for some time been investigating the applications of electricity to the production and analysis of sound, and his work resulted in the invention of a multiplexing telegraph system, patented in 1875, that employed tuned reeds. From this he turned to the possibility of the electrical transmission of voice sounds and by 1874 had a fairly clear notion of the necessary mechanisms. With the advice and encouragement of Joseph Henry and with financial backing from Hubbard and others, he continued experimenting with his harmonic telegraph and on June 3, 1875, was able to transmit barely intelligible speech to his assistant, Thomas A. Watson. He filed for a patent on February 14, 1876, hours before Elisha Gray filed a caveat based on his having developed another telephone, one employing a liquid transmitter. Within a month, and only three days after receiving his patent, Bell was also working with a liquid transmitter when, on March 10, he sent his famous message, "Mr. Watson, come here; I want you," the first complete sentence transmitted by telephone. He demonstrated the device successfully to the American Academy of Arts and Sciences in May and at the Centennial Exposition in Philadelphia in June. After a year of further refinements to the instrument the Bell Telephone Company was formed on July 9, 1877, under the direction of Hubbard, whose daughter Bell married two days later. Litigation over the telephone was instituted by the Western Union Company, holders of Gray's claims, and by others; and it was not until many years later that the suits, some 600 in all, were resolved in Bell's favor by the Supreme Court. Meanwhile the telephone, improved by the addition of Emile Berliner's variable-contact transmitter and induction coil and by other innovations, was introduced by Bell to England and

France in 1877–1878, and the Bell Telephone Company, under Hubbard and Theodore N. Vail, was growing rapidly. His fortune assured, Bell moved to Washington, D.C., in 1879 and turned to other interests; he became a naturalized citizen in 1882. With the money from the Volta Prize awarded him in 1880 by the French government he established the Volta Laboratory (later the Volta Bureau for the Increase and Diffusion of Knowledge Relating to the Deaf), where he carried out experiments leading to the invention of the photophone (which transmitted speech on a beam of light), an audiometer, improvements on Thomas A. Edison's phonograph, and an electrical induction balance for detecting metallic objects in the body. The last, first used in 1881 in an attempt to locate the assassin's bullet in President James A. Garfield, remained a useful medical tool until the advent of X-ray technology. Bell's other interests and activities included studies of eugenics and longevity, the founding with Hubbard of the journal *Science*, later the organ of the American Association for the Advancement of Science in 1883, and of the American Association to Promote the Teaching of Speech to the Deaf in 1890, and contributing heavily to the funding of the Smithsonian Institution's Astrophysical Observatory. He succeeded Hubbard as president of the National Geographic Society in 1896, holding the post until 1904, and from 1898 onward was a regent of the Smithsonian. The great preoccupation of his later years, however, was aviation. He worked with Samuel P. Langley on his early experiments and in 1907 founded and became president of the Aerial Experiment Association, through which the work of Glenn H. Curtiss was financed. One of the most widely honored men of his generation, Bell died at his summer home near Baddeck, Nova Scotia, on August 2, 1922. He was elected to the Hall of Fame in 1950.

Bell, John (1796–1869), public official. Born near Nashville, Tennessee, on February 18, 1796, Bell graduated from Cumberland College (later the University of Nashville) in 1814 and two years later began the practice of law in Franklin, Tennessee. Except for a term in the legislature he devoted himself to his practice until 1827, when he defeated Felix Grundy for a seat in the House of Representatives. In Congress he was generally a supporter of President Andrew Jackson, but broke with him sharply in the controversy over the rechartering of the Bank of the United States and gradually moved into the Whig party. He remained in the House, serving as speaker in 1834–1835, until 1841, when he was appointed secretary of war by President William Henry Harrison. When, after Harrison's death a short time later, John Tyler refused to concede the leadership of the Whigs to Henry Clay, Bell joined in the mass resignation of cabinet members. He resumed his law practice until 1847, when he was elected to the Senate. During two terms in that body, he became a prominent spokesman for moderation; although a Southerner and a slaveholder, he opposed both the abolition and the extension of slavery. He voted against the Compromise of 1850, the Kansas-Nebraska Bill, and the admission of Kansas as a slave state, coming under increasingly heavy criticism from his Southern colleagues. The Whig Party having disintegrated, he formed a passing alliance with the Know-Nothings and considered joining the Republicans. In 1860 he was nominated for president by the hastily organized Constitutional Union party, whose name perfectly described its platform. He carried only Virginia, Kentucky, and Tennessee. Although out of office, he remained in Washington to support President Lincoln's conciliatory policies, but after the firing on Fort Sumter and the call for troops he returned to Tennessee advocating secession. He spent the war years in Georgia; returning to Tennessee in 1865, he lived there in declining health until his death near Dover on September 11, 1869.

Bellamy, Edward (1850–1898), author. Born in Chicopee Falls, Massachusetts, on March 26, 1850, Bellamy studied for a short while at Union College in Schenectady, New York, and, at the age of eighteen, went to Germany for a year of study. While there he developed an interest in the plight of the poor in an urban, industrialized society. For several years after his return he worked with little real enthusiasm as a journalist. He wrote a number of short stories and two novels, one unfinished, and was briefly hailed as a new Hawthorne. In 1888 his concern with social problems found expression in *Looking Backward, 2000–1887*, a utopian novel which pictured the United States in the year 2000 as a happy, peaceful land in which all industry had been nationalized and wealth was equitably distributed among all. An immediate success, the book sold a million copies and Nationalist clubs, devoted to the realization of Bellamy's scheme, sprang up all over the nation. In response he established the *Nationalist* in 1889 and its successor, the *New Nation*, in 1891 to promote the cause. His program influenced the Populist party platform in 1892. A sequel to *Looking Backward*, entitled *Equality*, was published in 1897 but failed to match the earlier book's success. After a long period of poor health, Bellamy died on May 22, 1898, in Chicopee Falls.

Bellow, Saul (1915–   ), author. Born on July 10, 1915, in Lachine, Quebec, Bellow lived in Montreal before moving to Chicago in 1924. He attended the University of Chicago for a time and graduated from Northwestern University in 1937. He became a biographer in a WPA writers' project and taught for nearly four years at Pestalozzi-Froebel Teachers College in Chicago, working also as an editorial researcher. During World War II he served briefly in the merchant marine. His first novel, *Dangling Man*, 1944, concerned the life of a man in Chicago awaiting his call to military duty. His next, *The Victim*, 1947, probed a conflict that figured prominently in his later works—the

self-sacrifice required by society versus the need to be an individual. In *The Adventures of Augie March*, 1953, which won a National Book Award, he treated this problem more deeply and experimented with a rambling literary form. *Henderson the Rain King*, 1959, his next major work, told of a millionaire's adventures in Africa in a symbolic search for meaning. The tragicomic qualities of Henderson were expanded in *Herzog*, 1964, another National Book Award winner. This, Bellow's most nearly autobiographical work, concerned a university professor who comes to grips with his own alienation from society. Through a series of episodes both hilarious and poignant, Herzog arrives at acceptance of his own condition and a consequent relaxation of his need for self-justification. Among Bellow's later works were a play, *The Last Analysis*, 1965; *Mosby's Memoirs and Other Stories*, 1968; *Mr. Sammler's Planet*, 1970, a bestselling novel through which Bellow became the first novelist to win three National Book Awards; and *Humboldt's Gift*, 1975, which won a Pulitzer Prize. In 1976 Bellow was awarded the Nobel Prize for Literature. He was a member of the faculty and of the Committee on Social Thought of the University of Chicago from 1962.

Bellows, George Wesley (1882–1925), painter and lithographer. Born on August 12, 1882, in Columbus, Ohio, Bellows attended Ohio State University, but he was eager to pursue an art career and left school before graduation. He went to New York City in 1904 and studied with Robert Henri, quickly developing a mastery of the palette and a highly individual style and becoming associated with the group of radical young artists known as the Eight. An excellent athlete himself, he was moved by action and tension and transmitted this feeling onto the canvas by using vigorous, thick brush strokes and stark contrasts between light and shadow and solid mass and texture. His first successful painting, "Forty-two Kids," 1907, of urchins tumbling about a dock area, swimming, diving, and playing in groups, was followed by a series that was inspired by Tom Sharkey's famous boxing arena. The series was revolutionary in its bold interpretation of physical conflict. "Stag at Sharkey's," 1907, was the most celebrated of the group. He was active in organizing the Armory Show of 1913 that introduced modern art to the United States. In 1915 he began a series of vigorous war paintings, producing some of the finest American renderings of the subject. He turned to lithography in 1916 and became as skillful and creative in this medium as in paint. An excellent draftsman, he illustrated books and produced memorable drawings. He taught sporadically at the Art Students League in New York and at the Art Institute of Chicago. He died in New York City on January 8, 1925.

Belmont, Alva Ertskin Smith Vanderbilt (1853–1933), socialite and social reformer. Born in Mobile, Alabama, on January 17, 1853, Alva Smith married William K. Vanderbilt in 1875. Although the Vanderbilts were among the very richest people in the world, they were excluded from the "Four Hundred," the cream of New York society, by the arbiters of such matters, Mrs. William B. Astor and Ward McAllister. Mrs. Vanderbilt undertook an aggressive plan to break in: Richard M. Hunt was commissioned to build a $3 million mansion on Fifth Avenue, a gesture which ended McAllister's resistance; then, in 1883, plans were made for an Olympian masquerade ball for 1200 persons—Mrs. Astor not among them—to which, at the last moment, Mrs. Astor asked to be invited. As a final touch Vanderbilt had Hunt build a palace at Newport, Rhode Island, that, with its furnishings, cost $9 million. In 1895 Mrs. Vanderbilt divorced her husband and, a year later, after arranging the marriage of her daughter Consuelo to the Duke of Marlborough, she married Oliver Hazard Perry Belmont. After Belmont died in 1908 she became deeply interested in the cause of women's rights. She brought the English suffragette Christabel Pankhurst to the United States for a speaking tour and opened her houses and her purse to Alice Paul and the militant feminists. With Elsa Maxwell she wrote *Melinda and Her Sisters*, a suffragette operetta, and staged it at the Waldorf-Astoria Hotel. In 1920 she was elected president of the National Woman's party, a post she held for the rest of her life, and she was the founder of the Political Equality League. She is credited with offering the advice "Pray to God. She will help you." In her later years she became a noted architectural designer and was the first woman ever elected to the American Institute of Architects. Mrs. Belmont died in Paris on January 26, 1933.

Belmont, August (1816–1890), financier. Born on December 8, 1816, in Alzey, Germany, Belmont belonged to a wealthy family through whose influence he secured a place in the Rothschild banking firm in Frankfurt am Main in 1831. His remarkable abilities won him a transfer to a more important post in the Naples office three years later. In 1837, while on a mission to Havana, he decided to go to New York City. There he rented a small office on Wall Street and, virtually without capital but retaining an association as agent with the Rothschilds, he began what became August Belmont & Company, which in a startlingly short time was one of the largest banking houses in the country. He became a U.S. citizen in time to vote in the presidential election of 1844. Belmont was active in Democratic politics and from 1853 to 1857 served as U.S. chargé d'affaires at The Hague and then as minister to the Netherlands. He strongly opposed slavery and, although a Douglas Democrat, performed valuable service during the Civil War by soliciting support for President Lincoln and the Union among fellow businessmen and in Europe. In later years he was a noted art collector and sportsman. He died in New York City on November 24, 1890.

Bemis, Samuel Flagg (1891–1973), historian. Born on October 20, 1891, in Worcester, Massachusetts, Bemis graduated from Clark University in 1912, received an M.A. from Clark in 1913, and took a Ph.D. at Harvard in 1916. The following year he joined the faculty at Colorado College and three years later he went to Whitman College in Washington. *Jay's Treaty,* his first book, appeared in 1923 and was extremely well received. After a year with the Carnegie Institution of Washington, Bemis became professor of history at The George Washington University in 1924. Two years later he published *Pinckney's Treaty,* a companion study to the earlier work, which was awarded a Pulitzer Prize. From 1927 to 1929 he edited the ten-volume *American Secretaries of State and Their Diplomacy. The Hussey–Cumberland Mission and American Independence,* 1931, was followed by *The Diplomacy of the American Revolution* in 1935, the same year in which Bemis was appointed Farnam Professor of Diplomatic History at Yale. He remained at Yale, later as Sterling Professor of Diplomatic History and Inter-American Relations, until his retirement in 1960. Others of his books included *A Diplomatic History of the United States,* 1936, an often revised standard text; *The Latin American Policy of the United States,* 1942; *John Quincy Adams and the Foundation of American Foreign Policy,* 1949, which won a Pulitzer Prize; and *John Quincy Adams and the Union,* 1956. In 1961 Bemis, then professor emeritus at Yale and recognized as dean of U.S. diplomatic historians, was named one of three honorary consultants in American history to the Library of Congress. He died in Bridgeport, Connecticut, on September 26, 1973.

Benavides, Alonzo de (1580?– ?), missionary. Born about 1580, probably in the Azores, Benavides had traveled to Mexico by 1603, in which year he entered the Franciscan order there. He was later at the monastery in Puebla and in 1621 became Father Custodian of the Provinces and Conversions of New Mexico. Until 1629 he worked ceaselessly with some 26 companions, converting thousands of Indians of the Apache and Hopi tribes and founding ten missions and convents. In 1630 he journeyed to Spain, where he presented to King Philip IV his famous *Memorial* describing his work in New Mexico, which was to provide historians with an invaluable record of the early Spanish period in that region. The *Memorial* was intended as a plea for more missions to New Mexico and to this same end a revised version was sent to Pope Urban VIII four years later. Benavides returned to Mexico in 1632 and to New Mexico a short time later. He afterward succeeded the archbishop of Goa in Portuguese India. The date and place of his death are not known with any certainty.

Benchley, Robert Charles (1889–1945), humorist and critic. Born on September 15, 1889, in Worcester, Massachusetts, Benchley graduated from Harvard in 1912 and after holding a number of minor journalistic jobs joined the staff of *Life* magazine in 1920 as drama critic. In an amateur revue in 1922 he delivered his classic comedy monologue, "The Treasurer's Report," which launched his career as a humorist. The piece was made in 1930 into one of the first talking movie shorts, the first of more than 40 that he made. Another short, "How to Sleep," won an award in 1935 from the Motion Picture Academy of Arts and Sciences. In 1929 he left *Life* to join the *New Yorker* where, until 1940, he wrote drama criticism and conducted "The Wayward Press," a humorous column published under the pseudonymous byline Guy Fawkes. Benchley's quiet, whimsical humor was directed mainly to depicting the struggles of an ordinary man—himself—who was completely befuddled by the world; often it ascended, or descended, by hardly noticeable steps into pure nonsense. His pieces were collected in several volumes, among them *My Ten Years in a Quandary and How They Grew*, 1936; *After 1903 —What?*, 1938; and *Benchley Beside Himself*, 1943. He appeared in small parts in a large number of feature films, often as a confused, annoyed, and mildly sarcastic drunk. He died in New York City on November 21, 1945.

Bendix, Vincent (1882–1945), inventor and manufacturer. Born in Moline, Illinois, on August 12, 1882, Bendix left home at sixteen and went to New York City. There he studied mechanics and by 1907 had formed the Bendix Company, a pioneer car manufacturing firm. After two years of experimental work he perfected and began production in 1912 of his Bendix starter drive, which led to his automobile self-starter. In the same year he organized the Bendix Brake Company, the first mass producer of four-wheel brakes for automobiles. The Bendix Aviation Corporation, founded in 1929 eventually included his various allied companies engaged in the production of equipment for automobiles, airplanes, radio and radar, and home laundries; Bendix served as board chairman until his retirement in 1942. An enthusiastic promoter of aviation, he endowed the Bendix Transcontinental Air Race in 1931 and later the International Glider Meet. He died in New York City on March 27, 1945.

Benedict, Ruth Fulton (1887–1948), anthropologist. Born on June 5, 1887, in New York City, Ruth Fulton graduated from Vassar College in 1909. She lived in Europe for a year and then settled in California where she taught in a high school. She married S. R. Benedict in 1914; he died in 1936. Beginning in 1919 she studied anthropology under Franz Boas at Columbia University. Taking her doctorate in 1923, she became a Columbia instructor the next year, an associate professor in 1930, and a full professor in 1948, only a few months before her death. Her two-volume *Zuni Mythology*, 1935, was based on 11 years of research into the religion and folklore of American Indians—predominantly the Pueblo, Apache, Blackfoot, and Serrano peoples. *Patterns of Cul-*

ture, 1934, was a major contribution to anthropology. Translated into 14 languages, it brought knowledge of the subject to a wide audience. The book presented a comparison of three primitive societies, suggesting that limitless combinations of human behavior would continually produce new cultures. Five years later, with the publication of *Race: Science and Politics*, she showed that the unity of mankind is a simple fact, despite the arrogance of racists. The phrase "the human race" was given new meaning in her work. During World War II she was a special adviser to the U.S. Office of War Information on dealing with the peoples of occupied territories and enemy lands. A long-standing interest in Japanese culture bore fruit in *The Chrysanthemum and the Sword*, 1946. In the summer of 1948 she began her most comprehensive research undertaking as director of a study of contemporary European and Asian cultures sponsored by the Office of Naval Research and by Columbia. Upon returning from a trip to Europe, she became ill and died in New York City on September 17, 1948.

Benét, Stephen Vincent (1898–1943), author and poet. Born on July 22, 1898, in Bethlehem, Pennsylvania, Benét was the younger brother of William Rose Benét. While a student at Yale he published his first book, a collection of verse entitled *Five Men and Pompey*, 1915, and after graduating in 1919 he devoted himself to a literary career. His first novel, *The Beginning of Wisdom*, 1921, was followed by *Young People's Pride*, 1922, *Jean Huguenot*, 1923, and others; his early verse included *Heavens and Earth*, 1920; *King David*, 1923; *Ballad of William Sycamore, 1790–1880*, 1923; and *Tiger Joy*, 1925. *John Brown's Body*, 1928, a long narrative poem on the Civil War, was written while Benét was living in France on a Guggenheim fellowship; it quickly became one of the most popular and widely read of American poems and was awarded a Pulitzer Prize. Others mong Benét's works were *A Book of Americans*, 1933; *Tales Before Midnight*, 1939, a collection of stories; *Nightmare at Noon*, 1940; and *Western Star*, an epic verse narrative on American history that Benét did not live to complete. Book I of *Western Star* was published posthumously in 1943 and awarded a Pulitzer Prize. Of his short stories the best known was "The Devil and Daniel Webster," published in 1937 in *Thirteen O'Clock*. It was later the basis for a play, an opera for which Benét wrote the libretto in 1939, and a motion picture. Benét died on March 13, 1943, in New York City.

Benét, William Rose (1886–1950), poet, author, and editor. Born in Fort Hamilton, New York, on February 2, 1886, to a family with both military and literary traditions, Benét graduated from Yale in 1907. He then worked for a variety of periodicals, including the *Century* and the *Literary Review* of the *New York Evening Post*, of which he was associate editor from 1920 to 1924. In the latter year he helped found the *Saturday Review* *of Literature* and became its poetry critic. He produced many volumes of poetry himself, including *Merchants from Cathay*, 1913; *The Falconer of God*, 1914; *The Great White Wall*, 1916; *The Burglar of the Zodiac*, 1918; *Moons of Grandeur*, 1920; *Man Possessed*, 1927; *Sagacity*, 1929; *Golden Fleece*, 1935; and *Day of Deliverance*, 1944. His autobiographical poem, *The Dust Which Is God*, 1941, was awarded a Pulitzer Prize. He also wrote novels—among them *First Person Singular*, 1922, and *The Flying King of Kurio*—and a verse novel, *Rip Tide*, 1932. In 1923 he married Elinor Wylie, whose collected poems he edited in 1932. He was also editor of the *Oxford Anthology of American Literature*, 1938, and *The Reader's Encyclopedia*, 1948. He died in New York City on May 4, 1950.

Benjamin, Asher (1773–1845), architect. Born on June 15, 1773, in Greenfield, Massachusetts, Benjamin began the practice of architecture in the 1790s. He worked in various towns in Massachusetts and Connecticut and for a time lived in Windsor, Vermont. About 1803 he settled in Boston. A large number of fine houses and churches have been attributed with more or less certainty to him, among them the Old South Meeting House in Windsor, the Carew and Alexander houses in Springfield, Massachusetts, the First Congregational Church in Bennington, Vermont, and the West Church in Boston. His works were particularly noteworthy for their taste and attention to detail. Benjamin's major contribution to architecture, however, was his series of profusely illustrated guides—*The Country Builder's Assistant*, 1797 and 1798; *The American Builder's Companion*, 1806, several times revised and enlarged; *The Rudiments of Architecture*, 1814; and *The Practical House Carpenter*, 1830. Those books, especially the *Companion*, were of great influence on the day-to-day practice of architecture in America. They presented and explained the best designs available and promoted soundness and refinement in construction. Benjamin's work was a major factor in the spread of the late colonial and Greek Revival styles. He died in Springfield, Massachusetts, on July 26, 1845.

Benjamin, Judah Philip (1811–1884), lawyer and public official. Born on August 6, 1811, on the island of St. Thomas, then in the British West Indies, Benjamin was raised in Charleston, South Carolina, from his early boyhood. He attended Yale in 1825–1827 but did not earn a degree. To prepare for a career in law, he was a clerk in a notary's office in New Orleans. Subsequent work in international law and his compilation of a review of Louisiana law, published in 1834, helped to establish his reputation. He joined the Whig Party and in 1842 was elected to the Louisiana state legislature; in 1852 he was elected to the Senate. One of the first Southerners to advocate secession, he resigned from the Senate in 1861. Three weeks later, Jefferson Davis appointed him attorney general of the Confederacy; shortly

thereafter, he became secretary of war. Although the condition of the Confederate war department was deplorable when he took it over, the shortages of equipment and supplies were blamed on Benjamin. Investigations into his responsibility for severe Confederate losses of men and material at Roanoke Island were being conducted when Davis, presumably as a gesture of confidence, named Benjamin secretary of state. The outcry against him increased, but he ignored it. Eminently rational, he realized earlier than most Southerners that states' rights and slavery could not be maintained. Near the end of 1864, his plan to arm slaves for army service was a source of major alarm. He conceded that the plan would make it possible for slaves to fight for their freedom, and he was censured by the Confederate legislature in 1865. Nevertheless, a bill was passed for enrollment of blacks in the Confederate army. After the fall of Richmond he escaped to the West Indies, whence he sailed to England. There he was admitted to the bar in 1866, and in 1869 became a Queen's Counsel. He was eminently successful in many fields of British law but specialized in appeals, appearing primarily before the House of Lords and the Judicial Committee of the Privy Council. He died in Paris on May 6, 1884.

Bennett, Edward Herbert (1874–1954), architect. Born on May 12, 1874, in Cheltenham, England, Bennett attended Bristol Technical College before emigrating to the United States in 1890. In 1892 he went to work in the office of a San Francisco architect and four years later undertook formal studies of architecture at the Ecole des Beaux-Arts in Paris. Upon taking a diploma in 1902 he worked for a time in New York City, then moved to Chicago and joined Daniel H. Burnham's firm in 1904. He collaborated with Burnham on the landmark Plan for Chicago published in 1909 and for the next 20 years served as consulting architect to the Chicago Plan Commission. In 1919 he organized his own architectural firm and continued to specialize in city planning; among his clients were Minneapolis, Detroit, the borough of Brooklyn, New York, and Portland, Oregon. The firm also designed Grant Park and the Buckingham Memorial Fountain in Chicago, civic centers in Milwaukee, Denver, Pasadena, California, and Buffalo, New York, and portions of the Capitol grounds in Washington, D.C. From 1927 to 1933 Bennett was chairman of the board of architects of the treasury department, and he was a member of the architectural commission and the designer of several buildings for the Century of Progress Exposition in Chicago in 1933. He was also a noted amateur painter. He died on October 14, 1954, in Tryon, North Carolina.

Bennett, Floyd (1890–1928), aviator. Born near Warrensburg, New York, on October 25, 1890, Bennett left school at seventeen and became an automobile mechanic and part owner of a service garage. In 1917 he enlisted in the navy and signed up for aviation training, but although he became a capable pilot he was retained in the service only as an aviation mechanic. His chance came in 1925 when he was assigned to duty with Richard E. Byrd's naval aviation group attached to D. B. MacMillan's expedition to Greenland in that year. Both his character and his ability caught the attention of his commander and he soon became Byrd's close friend and personal pilot. Together they planned a flight over the North Pole; and on a second expedition in the next year they carried out the plan, flying a three-engine monoplane from Spitsbergen to the Pole and back on May 9. Both men were awarded the Congressional Medal of Honor for their feat; Byrd was promoted to commander and Bennett, by special act of Congress, to warrant machinist. Bennett and Byrd then began preparing for an air crossing of the Atlantic in their plane, the *America*. But Bennett suffered serious injuries when the *America* crashed on its first test flight and the attempt was delayed, opening the way for Charles A. Lindbergh to make the first nonstop solo transatlantic flight. Bennett was appointed second in command of Byrd's 1928–1930 expedition to the South Pole, most of the details of which he had planned. He became suddenly ill before the expedition set out and died in Quebec on April 25, 1928. He was mourned throughout the United States as a national hero.

Bennett, James Gordon (1795–1872), editor and publisher. Born in 1795 near Keith, Scotland, Bennett studied for the Roman Catholic priesthood in Aberdeen, but emigrated to Nova Scotia in 1819 and then came to the United States. He worked in Charleston, South Carolina, and in Boston as a teacher, an office clerk, a proofreader, and a translator before settling in New York City in 1823. There he planned a vocational school, which did not open owing to lack of funds, did some newspaper writing, and gave church lectures on political economy. In 1827 he became an editor and Washington correspondent for the *New York Enquirer*, writing bold sketches of national political figures and diverting accounts of social and political activities in the capital and becoming well known as a controversial reporter. He encouraged James Watson Webb, the main proprietor of the *New York Courier*, to effect a merger with the *Enquirer* and became virtual director of the paper in 1829, although he was nominally only associate editor until 1832. Under his leadership the *Courier and Enquirer* gave support to President Andrew Jackson and to Democratic policies until Webb suddenly took control and made the paper a Whig organ. Bennett resigned, founded the short-lived *New York Globe*, and during 1833–1834 was the chief editor and proprietor of the Philadelphia *Pennsylvanian*. Having marked the success of Benjamin H. Day's penny newspaper, the *New York Sun*, he returned to New York and unsuccessfully sought a job with the *Sun*. With $500 in capital he set up editing, reporting, printing, and sales headquarters in a cellar and began issuing his own paper, the *New York Herald*, which had four-column pages and sold for a penny. He declared his political independence and vowed to present "a picture of the world." His paper was unique in printing financial and society news, an account of the New York fire of 1835, and the Helm-Jewett love-nest murder story. Bennett stationed six correspondents in Europe, used the telegraph, hired a police reporter, and during the Civil War had 63 correspondents relaying the news from various battle-fronts. He was frequently censured for sensationalism and the irreverence of his editorials, but the *Herald* was a commercial success. At the time of his retirement in 1866, daily circulation was 90,000. He died in New York City on June 1, 1872.

Bennett, James Gordon (1841–1918), publisher, sportsman, and bon vivant. Born on May 10, 1841, in New York City, the son of James Gordon Bennett (1795–1872), Bennett was educated in Europe and returned to the United States on the outbreak of the Civil War in 1861. He was made managing editor of his father's *New York Herald* in 1866 and became the chief executive officer of the paper when the elder Bennett retired at the end of the year. His early years at the *Herald* were highly successful and marked by many notable journalistic achievements and "scoops." He sponsored Henry Morton Stanley's expedition of 1869–1872 to central Africa to find David Livingstone and financed the *Jeannette* expedition of 1879 to the Arctic. In 1867, with his father's help, he founded the *New York Evening Telegram*, which for many years was unprofitable, although it helped him financially in his last years. He established the Paris edition of the *New York Herald* in 1887; the paper, as Bennett had hoped, helped to cement relations over the next decades between the United States and France. A scandal in his personal life in 1877 drove him from the United States, and thereafter he lived for the most part in France, his outlook becoming more European as the years passed, with a consequent decrease in the popularity of his U.S. newspapers. An avid sportsman, he was an eminent polo player, yachtsman, and coach driver, and he offered cups as prizes in yacht, automobile, balloon, and airplane races. In his later years he was probably the best-known sportsman in France and perhaps in all of Europe. He was at the same time highly erratic and eccentric, and these traits became more marked as he grew older. His style of life was princely—it is estimated that he withdrew and spent some $30 million from the *Herald* during his life—and this, combined with his increasingly unpredictable management of his newspaper empire, led him to the brink of personal and corporate bankruptcy. He was saved by the *Telegram*, which became highly profitable after about 1910, and by the success of the Commercial Cable Company, which he had founded in 1883 with John W. Mackay and which laid a cable across the Atlantic. He died at his estate at Beaulieu, France, on May 14, 1918.

Benny, Jack (1894–1974), comedian. Born Benjamin Kubelsky on February 14, 1894, in Chicago, Benny grew up in nearby Waukegan and as a child studied the violin in hopes of becoming a concert musician. While still in school he began playing in a local theater orchestra and at seventeen went into vaudeville. After service in the navy during World War I he returned to vaudeville with a comedy act, taking first the stage name of Ben K. Benny and then Jack Benny. He toured for several years, gradually rising to star status, and in 1929 appeared in his first movie, *Hollywood Revue of 1929*. In 1931 he was master of ceremonies and star of Earl Carroll's *Vanities*, and the next year he began to star in a network radio program that was broadcast regularly for 23 years. He appeared in several more movies— *Broadway Melody of 1936, Artists and Models, Man About Town, Charley's Aunt, George Washington Slept Here, Hollywood Canteen,* and *Somebody Loves Me* among them—but it was principally through radio (and, later, through television) that he created the image that became an American institution. He used virtually the same comic devices throughout his career—the arched eyebrow, the bemused stare, the shrug, all of which he managed to reflect in his voice on radio, even when not uttering the mildly exasperated exclamation "Well!" To his audiences he was the archetypal miser; he was also vain, sour, an awful violinist, and for several decades remained thirty-nine years of age. His television program employed the same format as the radio show, featuring Eddie "Rochester" Anderson, Dennis Day, Don Wilson, and his real-life wife, Mary Livingston; it continued for more than ten years and in 1959 won an Emmy Award. In 1956 Benny began making seriocomic concert appearances with his violin and raised several million dollars for the support of symphony orchestras. After an absence of 32 years he returned to Broadway in 1963 with his own variety show. He continued to appear on television until shortly before his death in Beverly Hills, California, on December 26, 1974.

Bent, Charles (1799–1847), fur trader. Born on November 11, 1799, in Charleston, Virginia (now in West Virginia), Charles Bent grew up there, in Marietta, Ohio, and in St. Louis, where his brother William was born on May 23, 1809. Charles and William entered the fur trade at an early age and probably worked for a time for John Jacob Astor's American Fur Company. In 1824, with Ceran St. Vrain, they made an independent expedition up the Arkansas River and four years later, organized formally as Bent & St. Vrain, they chose a spot on the Arkansas River near where La Junta, Colorado, now stands and began construction of Bent's Fort. Begun in 1828 and completed in 1832, the fort was soon the most famous of the mountain trading posts; William served as its manager, becoming the first permanent white resident in Colorado, while Charles Bent and St. Vrain directed operations in the field, chiefly in New Mexico. Charles was made civil governor of New Mexico in September 1846, after the province was occupied by U.S. forces in the Mexican War, but was killed in an uprising of Mexicans and Pueblo Indians at Taos a short time later, on January 19, 1847. St. Vrain retired the following year, leaving William in possession of the business. In 1849 he decided to change locations; he attempted to sell Bent's Fort to the government but was offered so low a price that instead he removed everything of value and blew it up. He built Bent's New Fort a short distance down the Arkansas and operated it successfully for ten years, leasing it thereafter to the government, which called it Fort Lyon. From then until his death on May 19, 1869, William ranched in the area.

Bent, William, *see under* Bent, Charles

Benton, Thomas Hart (1782–1858), public official. Born near Hillsborough, North Carolina, on March 14, 1782, Benton moved with his widowed mother to a frontier area south of Nashville, Tennessee, shortly after a brief attendance at the University of North Carolina in 1799. In 1806 he was admitted to the bar, and three years later entered the state senate. After serving as a colonel of volunteers under Gen. Andrew Jackson in the War of 1812, he moved to the frontier town of St. Louis in 1815, where he carried on his law practice and, during 1818–1820, edited the *Missouri Enquirer*. In 1820, mainly as a result of the prominence gained through his editorials in the *Enquirer*, he was elected to the Senate, where he remained for 30 years. As a Westerner, ardent expansionist, Democrat, and hard-money advocate, Benton rose to preeminence in the Senate. Moving easily from his early Jeffersonian ideology into democratic activism, he became a staunch supporter of Jackson after their reconciliation ended an enmity that dated from a shooting brawl in Nashville in 1813. He led the battles against the rechartering of the Bank of the United States and in favor of a separate treasury and was primarily responsible—to the extent of earning the nickname "Old Bullion"—for what monetary stability was achieved in this period. He opposed the annexation of Texas as contrary to treaty, but strongly favored the occupation of the Pacific Coast regions. One of his proposals anticipated the later homestead system of land distribution. A stout believer in the Union and in the primacy of the small freehold farmer, he moderated his early views on slavery when it was clear that the issue was both hindering westward expansion and threatening disunion. His growing dislike of slavery, capped by his opposition to the Compromise of 1850, led to his defeat for reelection in that year. Still popular for his stands on other issues, however, he was elected to the House of Representatives; but his continued apostasy on slavery, in particular his adamant opposition to the Kansas-Nebraska Bill, soon lost him his seat as well as the Missouri governor's race in 1856. During his last years he wrote an important political autobiography, *Thirty Years' View,* 1854–1856, in two volumes. He refused to desert the Democratic party over the slavery issue and opposed the new Republican party even when it nominated John C. Frémont, his son-in-law, for the presidency in 1856. He died on April 10, 1858, in Washington, D.C.

Benton, Thomas Hart (1889–1975), painter. Born on April 15 1889, in Neosho, Missouri, grandnephew of Missouri Senator Thomas Hart Benton, he traveled throughout the Midwest with his father, who was active in politics. Travel aroused his curiosity about the origins of American tradition. He commenced his formal art education at the school of the Art Institute of Chicago in 1906 and, after several years of study in Paris, began a professional career as an artist in 1912. After naval service in World War I, he turned to teaching—at Bryn Mawr, Dartmouth, and the Art Students League of New York. He traveled for ten years during the late 1920s and early 1930s through the southern and western United States and settled finally in Kansas. In 1937 he recorded his travels in *An Artist in America;* a revised edition of the book appeared in 1951. During the 1920s and 1930s increasing attention was given to Benton's style, dubbed Regionalism, which portrayed life in the Midwest and South as he had seen it. His depictions were not always flattering. Nevertheless, Regionalism, with its linear design and flat, cartoonish figures, was welcomed as a truly American style of painting. The colors were appealing and pictures such as "Louisiana Rice Field" and "Threshing Wheat" seemed to strike a peculiarly American note. Other well-known Regionalists included Grant Wood and John Steuart Curry. Benton also exalted American folk themes and legends in works such as "Huck Finn and Nigger Jim" and "The Jealous Lover of Lone Green Valley." Controversial mural paintings of the 1930s earned him the Gold Medal Award of the Architectural League of New York. Later murals were executed for the Missouri state capitol at Jefferson City and for the Truman Library in Independence, Missouri. His paintings are in many major galleries and museums. He died in Kansas City, Missouri, on January 19, 1975.

Benton, William (1900–1973), businessman, publisher, and public official. Born in Minneapolis on April 1, 1900, Benton grew up there and on a ranch in Montana. He attended Carleton College and Yale, from which he graduated in 1921. He entered the advertising business and in 1929, with Chester Bowles, founded the agency of Benton and Bowles, which by 1935 had become a leader in its field. In 1935 he left the firm, having promised himself to do so when he had made a million dollars, and two years later became vice-president of the University of Chicago, of which his Yale classmate Robert M. Hutchins was president. There he led a program of extending and diversifying the activities of the university, organized the "Chicago Round Table," a distinguished and popular radio forum, and moved to acquire the Encyclopaedia Britannica publishing company for the institution. The university accepted the gift, committing the management and the common stock to Benton and retaining the preferred stock and a royalty contract. He became chairman of the board and publisher of Britannica in 1943. In 1945 he resigned from the university to become assistant secretary of state. In that position he began the Voice of America broadcasts, established United States information offices abroad, promoted international exchange visits of professors and students, and led U.S. participation in the United Nations Educational, Scientific, and Cultural Organization (UNESCO). He resigned in 1947 and in 1949 was appointed U.S. senator from Connecticut; in 1950 he was elected to serve two years of an unexpired term. In the Senate he was a champion of freedom and civil rights, and he protested the activities of Sen. Joseph R. McCarthy. After 1952 Benton turned his attention to various public-service and educational pursuits while continuing to oversee the growth of the Britannica Corporation. In 1963 he was appointed U.S. representative to UNESCO by President John F. Kennedy; he retained the post under President Lyndon B. Johnson. He was the author of several books, among them *This Is the Challenge,* 1958, and *The Voice of Latin America,* 1961. He died in New York City on March 18, 1973.

Berenson, Bernard (1865–1959), art critic and art historian. Born on June 26, 1865, in Vilnius, Lithuania, Berenson was brought to the United States at the age of ten. A Boston art collector financed his education at Harvard, from which he graduated in 1887. He then studied at Oxford and the University of Berlin, and in the galleries and museums of Italy trained himself to recognize the works of the Italian masters by their various styles and techniques. Settling in Settignano, near Florence, he acquired I Tatti, an eighteenth-century mansion, which he furnished with Tuscan antiques of the Renaissance, and lived there the rest of his life. By 1910 he had written several major books on Italian art, including *The Venetian Painters of the Renaissance,* 1894; *Drawings of the Florentine Painters,* 1903; and *The Italian Painters of the Renaissance,* 1906, and was considered a leading art historian. He was called upon to authenticate many important paintings purchased by major museums and private collectors during his time. His method of identifying works relied on seeking certain characteristics that appeared in everything produced by an artist and in the works of no other. By this method Berenson "discovered" two unknown Renaissance painters, whom he identified as Alunno di Domenico and Amico di Sandro. During World War II he remained in Tuscany, and after the war he directed the restoration of masterpieces. His autobiographical trilogy, *Sketch for a Self-Portrait,* 1949, *Aesthetics and History,* 1949, and *Rumor and Reflection,* 1952, brought him to the attention of the general public. At his death at I Tatti on

October 6, 1959, his bequest of the villa to Harvard University became known. Still another autobiographical book, *The Passionate Sightseer*, appeared in 1960.

Bergen, Edgar John (1903–1978), entertainer. Born in Chicago on February 16, 1903, Bergren, as his name was originally spelled, early discovered that he had the ability to project his voice from place to place. With help from a professional ventriloquist he developed his talent and by the time he was in high school was entertaining professionally. At about that time he had a professional-quality ventriloquist's dummy made, dubbed him Charlie McCarthy, and with him toured the Chautauqua circuit in summers. In this way Bergen worked his way through a year at Northwestern University in 1924. In 1926 Bergen and McCarthy entered vaudeville and for ten years played in theaters around the country and in Europe. Their success, based on Bergen's flair for writing comedy skits and dialogue and on McCarthy's leering, abrasive, wisecracking personality, led in the early 1930s to appearances in a number of short comedy films. A guest appearance on Rudy Vallee's "Fleischmann Hour" on radio in 1936 was a great hit and led to Bergen's own show, the "Chase and Sanborn Hour," the next year. For more than a decade the program was one of the most popular on radio and for nearly three years of that period it held first place. Guests on the show included many Hollywood stars who traded insults with McCarthy while Bergen attempted to moderate; a long-running comic feud between McCarthy and W.C. Fields was a particular delight to audiences. Bergen and McCarthy appeared in several motion pictures, including *The Goldwyn Follies*, 1938; *A Letter of Introduction*, 1938, for which they received a special wooden Academy Award "Oscar"; *You Can't Cheat an Honest Man*, 1939, with Fields; *Charlie McCarthy, Detective*, 1939; *Look Who's Laughing*, 1941; *Stage Door Canteen*, 1943; *Song of the Open Road*, 1944, also with Fields; and *Fun and Fancy Free*, 1947, a Walt Disney feature. The act was broadened by the addition during the 1940s of Mortimer Snerd, a bumpkin of incredible obtuseness, and Effie Klinker, an irrepressible spinster. For a short time, Bergen and his associates hosted "Do You Trust Your Wife?," a television quiz show, and in later years they continued to appear on television and in nightclubs. Bergen died in Las Vegas on September 30, 1978, just days after announcing his retirement. McCarthy then entered the Smithsonian Institution.

Berger, Victor Louis (1860–1929), Socialist leader and editor. Born in Nieder-Rehbach, Transylvania (now in Romania), on February 28, 1860, Berger grew up in Hungary, where he was educated in private schools. After studying at the universities of Vienna and Budapest, he emigrated to the United States in 1878. In 1881 he became a public-school teacher in Milwaukee. He was active from the start in local politics, and in 1892 he founded the *Wisconsin Vorwärts*. In association with Eugene V. Debs, he helped establish the Social Democratic party, which advocated the national adoption of socialism through orderly means. In March 1900 the group merged with the Socialist Labor party and began a rapid rise in popularity. The following year Berger became editor of the *Social Democratic Herald*, which in 1911 became the *Milwaukee Leader*. He remained at the head of this daily until his death. He continued to write and campaign for the Socialist party and in 1910, when the party captured the mayoralty of Milwaukee, Berger was elected to the House of Representatives, where he served for one term. He thus became the first Socialist ever to sit in the U.S. Congress. His later opposition to U.S. entry into World War I led to sanctions against his newspaper and his own indictment for sedition under the Espionage Act of 1918. In that year he was again elected to the House but was denied his seat because of his antiwar views. In a special election held to fill the seat he was again elected and again was barred. The seat remained vacant for the remainder of the term. He was convicted on the 1918 charge but three years later the decision was reversed by the Supreme Court. In 1923 he was finally admitted to the House, where he served three terms. He died in Milwaukee on August 7, 1929.

Bergh, Henry (1811–1888), reformer. Born in New York City on August 29, 1811, Bergh attended Columbia University for a time, then entered his father's shipbuilding business, succeeding with his brother to the direction of the company in 1837. He later spent many years in travel and served as the secretary of the U.S. legation in St. Petersburg in 1863–1864. He became interested in efforts to preserve the health and safety of animals after seeing frequent abuses of animals in Russia and through contact with the president of the Royal Society for the Prevention of Cruelty to Animals in England. Upon his return to the United States in 1865 Bergh began proselytizing among his friends and others in New York City for action against mistreatment of animals, often using incidents on the street as occasions for impromptu lectures on the subject. He eventually attracted a number of wealthy and influential sympathizers and in April 1866 received from the state legislature a charter for the American Society for the Prevention of Cruelty to Animals (ASPCA). The Society was granted enforcement powers in laws relating to the treatment of animals and it set out vigorously to secure obedience to existing statutes and to win enactment of broader and more stringent measures. Bergh was president of the Society from its inception until his death. In 1875 he took a leading role in organizing the Society for the Prevention of Cruelty to Children. Scores of groups inspired by either or both movements had sprung up across the country by the time he died, on March 12, 1888, in New York City.

Bergren, Edgar, *see* Bergen, Edgar John

Berkeley, Busby (1895–1976), choreographer and film director. Born on November 29, 1895, in Los Angeles, William Berkeley Enos grew up in New York City and graduated from a military academy in 1914. In World War I he served in the army as an entertainment officer. After the war, taking the stage name Busby Berkeley, he made his acting debut with the road company of *The Man Who Came Back*. He played small roles in other Broadway and road productions until 1921, when he turned to directing and worked in various cities in the East. In 1925 he returned to Broadway to stage dance and production numbers for several musicals, including *A Connecticut Yankee*, 1927, *Present Arms*, 1928, and *Street Singer*, 1929. Berkeley began to work in the movies for Samuel Goldwyn in 1930, directing the musical numbers in *Whoopee*; for the next two decades he dominated the world of the Hollywood musical, turning out a succession of lavish, spectacular, and delightful films with which his name was virtually synonymous. His precision-drilled production numbers, created with Ziegfeldian zest and gaiety, were enormously popular, not the least because he abandoned the realistic tradition in favor of a style of fantasy that utilized many pioneering cinematic techniques. Among his films for Goldwyn, Warner Brothers, and Metro-Goldwyn-Mayer (MGM) were *Forty-second Street*, 1933; *Gold Diggers of 1933* and its nearly annual successors; *Footlight Parade*, 1933; *Hollywood Hotel*, 1937; *Stage Struck*, 1937; *Gold Diggers in Paris*, 1938; *Babes in Arms*, 1939; *Strike Up the Band*, 1940; *Lady Be Good*, 1941; *Ziegfeld Girl*, 1941; *For Me and My Gal*, 1942; *Girl Crazy*, 1943; and *Take Me Out to the Ball Game*, 1949. His later films, with few of the grand flourishes of his golden era, included *Easy to Love*, 1953; *Rose Marie*, 1954; and, after a long absence from Hollywood, *Jumbo*, 1962. For several years after 1962 he lived in retirement in California. A retrospective screening of his most famous films at New York's Museum of Modern Art in 1965 marked the beginning of a revival of interest in his and other directors' work of the 1930s, and in 1970 Berkeley came out of retirement to serve as production supervisor for the Broadway hit revival of the 1925 musical *No, No, Nanette*. He died on March 14, 1976, in Palm Springs, California.

Berkeley, Sir William (1606–1677), colonial governor. Born in Bruton, England, in 1606, to a family long prominent in public affairs, Berkeley graduated from Oxford in 1629 and, a popular courtier, was appointed a commissioner of Canadian affairs in the colonial office three years later. He was knighted by Charles I in 1639 and in 1641 was appointed governor of Virginia. For several years after his arrival in the colony in 1642 he conducted a successful administration, encouraging the diversification of crops and in 1644 leading an expedition to the frontier that ended Indian depredations for 30 years. After the execution of Charles I in 1649 Berkeley refused to submit to the government of Oliver Cromwell and offered asylum in Virginia to refugee royalists; he organized a sufficiently strong defense against a fleet sent out by Parliament in 1652 to win concessions from Cromwell's Commonwealth, among them permission to continue to live in Virginia after his removal from office in that year. In 1659, at the request of the colonists, he provisionally resumed the governorship in anticipation of the Restoration and the next year was confirmed in office by Charles II. Berkeley's second administration was markedly different from the first; he curtailed the people's political power, gave undue preference to friends, and generally alienated the populace. His inaction in the face of new Indian uprisings in 1676 led to a number of colonists' taking matters into their own hands. Led by Nathaniel Bacon, they undertook without authority an expedition against the Indians and Bacon was forthwith declared a rebel. The capital, Jamestown, was twice captured by Bacon before his sudden death in October 1676 ended the rebellion. Berkeley ordered the arrest and execution of more thaan a score of Bacon's followers, reputedly moving Charles II to declare that "The old fool has killed more people in that naked country than I have done for the murder of my father." The governor was recalled to account for his actions by royal representatives who had arrived with pardons, which Berkeley ignored, for the rebels. He left Virginia in May 1677, but before he had had an audience with the king he died in Twickenham, on June 9, 1677.

Berle, Adolf Augustus (1895–1971), lawyer, public official, diplomat, and author. Born in Boston on January 29, 1895, Berle graduated from Harvard in 1913 and three years later, after taking a degree from Harvard Law School, began the practice of law in Boston and then in New York City. He served in World War I and was a consultant with the U.S. Peace Commission in Paris in 1918–1919. In 1927 he became a professor of corporation law at Columbia University's law school. In 1932 he published, with Gardiner C. Means, *The Modern Corporation and Private Property*, a pioneer study of the concentration of wealth in industry and the changed meaning of corporate ownership. Largely as a result of this book, which outlined the need for industrial integration and control, Berle was a natural choice by Franklin D. Roosevelt for his "brain trust" advisory staff in the 1932 campaign and the early years of his presidency. Berle was appointed counsel to the Reconstruction Finance Corporation (RFC). From 1938 to 1944 he was assistant secretary of state and during 1945–1946, after representing the United States in a number of conferences of American nations, was ambassador to Brazil. He continued to teach and write on subjects pertaining to Latin America, business organization and law, and the social context and significance of industry. He published, among other books, *New Directions in the New World*, 1940; *The Twentieth Century Capitalist Revolution*, 1954; *Latin America—Diplomacy and Reality*, 1962; *The*

American Economic Republic, 1963; and *Power*, 1969. From 1951 until his death Berle was chairman of the board of the Twentieth Century Fund. He retired from Columbia in 1963, but continued to teach there as professor emeritus until his death in New York City on February 17, 1971.

Berle, Milton (1908–), comedian. Born Milton Berlinger in New York City on July 12, 1908, Berle appeared as a child in several amateur shows, sometimes impersonating Charlie Chaplin, and was signed to tour with a vaudeville company. With his younger sister Rosalind also in the act, and, after a time, with his mother as manager, he was successful enough to win a role in the Broadway musical *Floradora* in 1920. He appeared in a number of silent movies, for the Biograph studios and other companies, that included *Tillie's Punctured Romance*, *The Perils of Pauline*, and *Humoresque*. By 1932, after an engagement at New York's Palace Theater during which a new attendance record was set, he was a national headliner. His unique style of comedy—relying chiefly on energetic delivery, zany antics, a marked proclivity for mugging, and much-publicized belief that all jokes and gags, from whatever source, were in the public domain—won him great popularity in vaudeville and in nightclubs around the country during the 1930s. He starred in the 1936 *Ziegfeld Follies* and appeared in numerous other Broadway productions, including *Life Begins at 8:40* and *See My Lawyer*, and from 1937 was featured in many motion pictures, among them *New Faces of 1937*; *Radio City Revels*, 1938; *Tall, Dark and Handsome*, 1941; *Over My Dead Body*, 1943; and *Always Leave Them Laughing*, 1949. At the same time he was a regular performer on several radio programs. In September 1948 he entered the new field of commercial television as star and master of ceremonies of the "Texaco Star Theater." During the next eight years "Tuesday night with Uncle Miltie" became something of an institution and was such a success that Berle was nicknamed "Mr. Television" for having done more than any other person to establish the popularity of the new medium. He signed a 30-year contract with the National Broadcasting Company in 1951. After a two-year absence he returned to television in 1958–1959 with the "Kraft Music Hall." After that he continued to appear occasionally in movies and as a guest star on television.

Berlin, Irving (1888–), composer. Born on May 11, 1888, in Temoyun, Russia, Israel Baline emigrated with his family to the United States in 1893 and settled in New York City, living in poverty on the Lower East Side. In his youth he began working as a singing waiter in Bowery and Chinatown cafés and cabarets; while in one such job he wrote the lyrics for his first published song, "Marie of Sunny Italy," 1907, and changed his name to Irving Berlin for the occasion. He was soon devoting full time to writing music for clubs and musical revues and quickly became successful. In 1910 he wrote the songs—"Ephraham" and "Goodbye, Becky Cohen"—with which Fanny Brice made her Broadway debut in the *Ziegfeld Follies*, and in 1911 he scored his first great popular hits with "Alexander's Ragtime Band" and "Everybody's Doin' It," which helped popularize, respectively, ragtime music and Vernon and Irene Castle's dance called the "turkey trot." Berlin wrote his first musical comedy, *Watch Your Step* (with "Play a Simple Melody" and starring the Castles) in 1914; in 1919, the year he established his own music publishing company, he wrote "A Pretty Girl Is Like a Melody," the hit of that year's *Ziegfeld Follies* and the theme song of all subsequent editions of the show. Later musical comedies for which he supplied words and music included his own *Music Box Revue* in five editions from 1921 to 1924, which featured such songs as "Say It With Music" and "All Alone;" *Face the Music*, 1932, (with "Let's Have Another Cup o' Coffee"); *As Thousands Cheer*, 1933, ("Heat Wave" and "Easter Parade"); *Annie Get Your Gun*, 1946 ("Anything You Can Do," "Doin' What Comes Natur'lly," "The Girl That I Marry," "Sun in the Mornin'," "They Say It's Wonderful," "There's No Business Like Show Business"); and *Call Me Madam*, 1950 ("It's a Lovely Day Today," "You're Just in Love"). In 1942 he wrote and produced *This Is the Army*, a hugely successful revue with a cast of soldiers that featured "I Left My Heart at the Stage Door Canteen," "This is the Army, Mr. Jones," and a revival of "Oh, How I Hate to Get Up in the Morning," a song which he had first used in a similar World War I show, *Yip-Yip-Yaphank*, in 1918. For the movies Berlin wrote dozens of songs, beginning with "Marie" (for *My Awakening*, 1928), and complete scores, beginning with the Marx Brothers' *Cocoanuts*, 1929 and including many of the great musicals of the 1930s and 1940s, particularly those of Fred Astaire and Bing Crosby: *Top Hat*, 1935 ("Top Hat, White Tie and Tails" and "Cheek to Cheek"); *Follow the Fleet*, 1936 ("Let's Face the Music and Dance"); *Carefree*, 1938 ("Change Partners"); and *Holiday Inn*, 1942 ("Be Careful, It's My Heart," "Happy Holiday"). *Holiday Inn* also included Berlin's greatest single success, "White Christmas," which over the years sold in the millions in sheet music and in tens of millions in various recorded versions, including a record that was Crosby's biggest hit. A close second in popularity among Berlin's songs was "God Bless America," originally written for *Yip-Yip-Yaphank* but laid by for 20 years until it was sung on an Armistice Day radio program in 1938 by Kate Smith, with whom it remained closely identified thereafter; eventually Berlin assigned the royalties from the song to the Boy Scouts and Girl Scouts, and in 1955 he was awarded a special congressional gold medal for composing what had by then become almost a second national anthem. For his contributions to the musical stage Berlin received a special Tony Award in 1963. His marriage in 1926 to Ellin, daughter of the enormously wealthy communications magnate Clarence Hungerford Mackay, created a sensation. The marriage of the diminutive Jewish songwriter to the daughter of a scion of New York society was considered unacceptable by many, including most of her family. Nevertheless, they weathered the storm and lived happily ever after.

Berliner, Emile (1851–1929), inventor. Born on May 20, 1851, in Hannover, Germany, Berliner worked in a printing shop and a dry-goods store after leaving school at the age of fourteen. In 1870 he emigrated to the United States and held a variety of menial jobs, first in Washington, D.C., and later New York City. He found work in a laboratory and there became fascinated by electricity and acoustics; he began studying on his own and was soon carrying out experiments in telephony. His approach was fundamentally different from that of Alexander Graham Bell, who was working on the problem at the same time: where Bell used the mechanical vibrations produced by sound waves to induce magnetically a weak current that yielded poor reproduction over even short distances, Berliner led the vibrations to a variable-pressure contact that impressed the signal as a modulation of a strong, continuous current from a battery, thus making possible clear transmission over much longer distances. The device, invented in 1877 and eventually patented in 1891, became known as a microphone and won Berliner a position with the Bell Telephone Company in Boston in 1878. Five years later he returned to Washington and independent research. Thomas A. Edison's invention of the phonograph inspired Berliner to make several improvements in the mechanical recording of sound. He discarded Edison's cylinder and vertically moving needle and used instead a disc and a needle moving horizontally; by this means the reproduction arm was propelled automatically by the groove on the disc, eliminating the separate drive mechanism of Edison's machine. Calling his invention the gramophone, he patented it in 1887. He went on to work out a method of making many copies of a recording from a metal-plated master disc and to formulate a durable shellac coating for the copies. In later years he was interested in the introduction of pasteurization into milk production and experimented in aeronautics and the development of acoustical building materials, producing important inventions in both fields. Berliner died in Washington, D.C., on August 3, 1929.

Berlinger, Milton, see Berle, Milton

Bernstein, Leonard (1918–   ), conductor and composer. Born in August 25, 1918, in Lawrence, Massachusetts, Bernstein began to take piano lessons as a child and by the age of fourteen had learned all that local instructors could teach him. He went to Boston to study further and graduated from Harvard in 1939. Planning to become a conductor, he entered the Curtis Institute of Music in Philadelphia and in 1940 and 1941 received scholarships in conducting from the Berkshire Music Center in Tanglewood, Massachusetts. By 1942 he was assistant conductor of the Tanglewood orchestra. His first work, the *Sonata for Clarinet and Piano,* received its premiere in 1942. His *Jeremiah* symphony, based on Jewish religious themes, was completed the same year. In 1943 he became assistant conductor of the New York Philharmonic. Substituting for guest conductor Bruno Walter in November of that year he was enthusiastically received, and his career was underway. In 1944 he led the Pittsburgh Symphony in the first performance of his *Jeremiah.* Later that year he conducted the premiere of his first ballet, *Fancy Free,* and its musical-comedy derivative, *On the Town,* which was made into a motion picture in 1949. He conducted the Czech Philharmonic at the Prague International Festival as the representative of the U.S. government in 1946. His second ballet, *Facsimile,* was performed that year. Inspired by the poem of W. H. Auden, in 1949 he completed his second symphony, *The Age of Anxiety.* In 1953 he became the first American composer to conduct at La Scala in Milan. He became permanent conductor of the New York Philharmonic in 1958 but resigned from the post in 1969 to devote his time to composition. Gregarious and personable, he gained national fame as a lecturer on music and as the conductor of a series of concerts for young people on network television. His lectures were compiled in *The Joy of Music,* 1959. His other compositions included the one-act opera *Trouble in Tahiti,* 1952; the scores for the motion picture *On the Waterfront,* 1954; and the musicals *Wonderful Town,* 1953; *Candide,* 1956; and *West Side Story,* 1957; the choral works *Kaddish,* 1963, and *Chichester Psalms,* 1965. In 1971 he was commissioned to write *Mass* for the opening of the John F. Kennedy Center for the Performing Arts in Washington, D.C. In 1973 he delivered a series of lectures at Harvard that were published as *The Unanswered Question,* 1976.

Berra, Lawrence Peter (1925–   ), "Yogi," baseball player. Born on May 12, 1925, in St. Louis, Berra went to work at fourteen and began playing amateur baseball at about that age with an American Legion team. It was while on this team that he acquired the nickname "Yogi." In 1943 he was signed by the New York Yankees and sent to a farm club in Norfolk, Virginia; after a year he enlisted in the navy and served until 1946, when he rejoined the Yankee organization. At the end of the 1946 season he moved up to the parent team as a catcher. In 1947, his first full major-league season, he experienced difficulties and was shifted for a time to the outfield and briefly to the bench, but in 1948 his hitting improved to .305 and in 1949 his fielding average as a catcher was .989. In 1950 he batted .322 and hit 28 home runs, and the next year he was voted the American League's most valuable player, an honor he received again in 1954 and 1955. Valued as much for his cheerfulness and vitality as for his consistently fine play, Berra remained the Yankee's regular catcher until 1963. His genial nature and modesty made him also a great favorite with the fans, as did his well-known penchant for comic books. He held many records including appearing in the most World Series (14) and World Series games (75); most World Series hits (71); most home runs by a catcher (313); and most consecutive errorless games by a catcher (148 in 1957–1959). He played in 14 All-Star games during his career. In 1964 he managed the Yankees' successful drive to a pennant and the next year became a coach of the New York Mets of the National League. Widely considered one of the greatest catchers in the history of the game, Berra was elected to the National Baseball Hall of Fame in 1972. Upon the sudden death of Gil Hodges just before the start of the 1972 season, he was named manager of the Mets.

Berry, Charles Edward Anderson (1926–   ), "Chuck," musician and singer. Born in San Jose, California, on January 15, 1926, Chuck Berry grew up in St. Louis and learned to play the guitar while in high school. After a stint in reform school he began playing at small black clubs around St. Louis and for a time led a blues trio. Although more versatile and showmanlike than many other bluesmen, Berry had little real success until, in 1955, he traveled to Chicago and signed a recording contract with Chess Records, a small company trying to bring black music to a larger audience. The first record he cut, "Maybellene," was played over the air in New York City by disc jockey Alan Freed and was an instant smash hit. Other records followed quickly, including "Roll Over, Beethoven," "School Days," "Rock 'n' Roll Music," "Johnny B. Goode," "Sweet Little Sixteen," and "Memphis," all written by Berry with a driving beat and a sly diffident humor that appealed greatly to the teen-agers of the late 1950s. He was one of the first black musicians to gain a following among white audiences and record buyers and was one of the major shapers of popular music in his day. After about 1960 he lived on an estate near Wentzville, Missouri, and made occasional record albums and live appearances.

Berryman, John (1914–1972), poet. Born in McAlester, Oklahoma, on October 25, 1914, Berryman grew up there and in Florida. After an on-again, off-again college career, he graduated from Columbia University in 1936, studied for two years at Cambridge University, and in 1939 became an instructor in English at Wayne (now Wayne State) University. He moved to Harvard the next year and to Princeton in 1943, remaining there for six years. He had begun contributing poems to various periodicals during the 1930s and was represented in an anthology, *Five Young American Poets*, in 1940. His own first book, *Poems*, appeared in 1942 and was followed by *The Dispossessed* in 1948 and a biography of Stephen Crane in 1950. Although it was some-

what derivative, his early poetry displayed great technical skill and craftsmanship; it was, however, little noticed. During 1951–1952 Berryman was on the faculty of the University of Cincinnati. In 1953 he completed *Homage to Mistress Bradstreet* (it appeared in book form in 1956) and received widespread critical praise. Voiced in a colloquial language that was singularly his own and couched in captivating rhythm, the poem marked Berryman's entrance into the front rank of modern American poets. He further developed the idiom he had created in *77 Dream Songs*, 1964, which was awarded a Pulitzer Prize, and in *His Toy, His Dream, His Rest*, 1968, which won him both a National Book Award and, with Karl Shapiro, the Bollingen Prize. Published together as *The Dream Songs* in 1969, the two volumes constituted the confessional dialogue with himself, by turns anguished and humorous, of a middle-aged man named Henry. After 1955 Berryman taught at the University of Minnesota. On January 7, 1972, he took his own life in Minneapolis. *Delusions, etc.* appeared a short time later.

Bethe, Hans Albrecht (1906–   ), physicist. Born in Strasbourg, then a part of Germany, on July 2, 1906, Bethe studied at the universities of Frankfurt and Munich, taking his Ph.D. in physics at Munich in 1928. He taught in various German universities until he fled the Nazi regime in 1933, going first to England and in 1935 coming to the United States, where he joined the faculty of Cornell University. He had already established a reputation while in Europe with his investigations of particle behavior from a quantum-mechanical standpoint when he turned his attention to the problem of stellar energy. The apparent paradox posed by the extremely long life-spans of stars despite their enormous energy production led him to consider various nuclear reactions as possible sources of stellar energy and by 1939 he had worked out a likely explanation involving the fusion of hydrogen nuclei into helium nuclei by means of a carbon catalyst. This "carbon cycle" has become universally accepted as the primary mechanism of solar and stellar energy production. Bethe became a U.S. citizen in 1941 and was soon involved in wartime research, first at the Massachusetts Institute of Technology, then, from 1943 to 1946, at Los Alamos, New Mexico, where he headed the theoretical physics division of the atomic-bomb project. He was awarded the Presidential Medal of Merit in 1946. The success of the Los Alamos project, together with the continuation of nuclear testing, led him to warn publicly as early as 1947 against the dangers of radioactive fallout. In 1948 he refused to return to Los Alamos to join the hydrogen-bomb project headed by Edward Teller, but by 1951 the Korean War and hints of Soviet progress in the field had induced him to change his mind. He continued, however, to speak and write against nuclear warfare, excessive stockpiling of nuclear weapons, and atmospheric testing. In 1961 he was awarded the Atomic Energy Commission's Fermi Award.

From 1956 to 1964 he served on the President's Science Advisory Committee and in 1958 headed the experts named to make a presidential study of disarmament. From 1953 onward he was an informal adviser to a succession of presidents on nuclear weaponry and disarmament and in 1963 helped negotiate the partial test ban treaty with the Soviet Union. In 1967, in recognition of his contributions to basic nuclear theory and to the understanding of nuclear processes in stars, he was awarded the Nobel Prize for Physics.

Bethune, Mary McLeod (1875–1955), educator. Born on July 10, 1875, in Mayesville, South Carolina, Miss McLeod was the daughter of former slaves. She attended a local school, then traveled to Concord, North Carolina, to enter Scotia Seminary (now Barber-Scotia College), from which she graduated in 1893. After graduating from the Moody Bible Institute in Chicago in 1895 she began a teaching career and until 1903 taught in a succession of small Southern schools; during that time she married A. L. Bethune. In 1904 she moved to the east coast of Florida, where a large black population had grown up at the time of the construction of the Florida East Coast Railway, and in Daytona Beach she opened a school of her own, the Daytona Normal and Industrial Institute for Negro Girls. Having virtually no tangible assets with which to start, she worked tirelessly to build a schoolhouse, solicit help and contributions, and enlist the goodwill of both the black and white communities. In 1923 the school was merged with the Cookman Institute for Men, then in Jacksonville, Florida, to form Bethune-Cookman College in Daytona Beach; Mrs. Bethune remained president of the college until 1942 and resumed the position in 1946–1947 before retiring as president emeritus. Her efforts on behalf of education and of improved racial relations early brought her to national prominence. Awarded the Spingarn Medal of the National Association for the Advancement of Colored People in 1935, she was appointed the next year director of the Division of Negro Affairs of the National Youth Administration (NYA), a post she held until 1944. In 1937 she founded the National Council of Negro Women, of which she remained president, and she was an adviser on minority affairs to President Franklin D. Roosevelt. She also advised the secretary of war on the selection of officer candidates for the Women's Army Auxiliary Corps (WAAC), established in 1942. In 1945 she went as an observer with the U.S. delegation to the organizational conference of the United Nations in San Francisco. Widely honored for her lifelong dedication to her work, she died in Daytona Beach on May 18, 1955.

Bettelheim, Bruno (1903–   ), psychologist and educator. Born on August 28, 1903, in Vienna, Bettelheim graduated in 1921 from the Reform Realgymnasium and took his doctorate from the University of Vienna in 1938. During 1938–1939 he was incarcerated in the Nazi concentration camps at Dachau and Buchenwald; his interviews of other prisoners to determine the effect upon them of the camps and Nazi methods influenced much of his later work. Upon his release, he came to the United States and was associated with the University of Chicago as a researcher in progressive education until 1942, when he went to Rockford College as an associate professor of psychology, remaining until 1944. He first gained international recognition in 1943 with the now classic article "Individual and Mass Behavior in Extreme Situations" in the *Journal of Abnormal and Social Psychology*. Focusing on tyranny and totalitarian terrorism as means of producing complacency or submissiveness, he recounted his experiences and observations in the concentration camps; the article became required reading for all military government officers serving in Europe during World War II and in the subsequent occupation period. Bettelheim returned to the University of Chicago in 1944, becoming a full professor in 1952. At Chicago he accepted the directorship of the Sonia Shankman Orthogenic School, a residential institution for the education and treatment of severely disturbed children who had failed to respond to other therapeutic attempts. He also became known as an adviser to parents, teachers, and social workers on the problems of raising normal children, although he achieved his greatest renown for his remarkable success in treating previously unreachable autistic children. Notable among his books were *Love Is Not Enough*, 1950; *Truants From Life*, 1954; *Symbolic Wounds: Puberty Rites and the Envious Male*, 1954; *The Informed Heart*, 1960; *Children of the Dream*, 1962; and *The Empty Fortress*, 1967. He was also the author of a widely read magazine and newspaper column on child care.

Beveridge Albert Jeremiah (1862–1927), public official and historian. Born in Highland County, Ohio, on October 6, 1862, Beveridge graduated from Asbury College (later DePauw University) in 1885 and two years later was admitted to the bar and began practice in Indianapolis. His considerable reputation as a political orator won him election to the Senate in 1899 as a Republican. One of the original Progressive Republicans, Beveridge supported President Theodore Roosevelt's program of industrial reform and regulation and, like many Progressives, was a proponent of "Anglo-Saxon supremacy." When he was defeated for reelection in 1911 he became active in Roosevelt's Bull Moose Progressive party, but he never again held public office. He had in the meanwhile entered upon a second and highly distinguished career as a writer of history and a commentator on international affairs. His four-volume *Life of John Marshall*, 1916–1919, was widely acclaimed as a major work of historical biography and was awarded a Pulitzer Prize. When he died in Indianapolis on April 27, 1927, he had completed two volumes of a biography of Abraham Lincoln which were published posthumously in 1928.

Biddle, James (1783–1848), naval officer. Born on February 18, 1783, in Philadelphia, Biddle entered the navy as a midshipman in 1800 and was assigned to the *President* under Thomas Truxtun. He was retained in the service despite a reduction of the navy in the following year and served on the *Constellation* in the Mediterranean in 1802. In 1803, during the war against the Barbary states, he was transferred to William Bainbridge's *Philadelphia* and was aboard when the ship was driven aground off Tripoli in October; with Bainbridge and the rest of the crew he was imprisoned for a year and a half. Promoted to lieutenant and given command of a coastal gunboat upon his release, he was on duty against South Atlantic privateers until 1807, when he took a leave of absence and sailed to China on a merchant vessel. Returning to active service, he engaged in enforcement of the 1807 embargo against foreign commerce and then, from 1809 (when the embargo was repealed), served on the *President* and other warships. In 1812 he was appointed first lieutenant of the sloop *Wasp*; after the *Wasp*'s celebrated capture of the more heavily armed British *Frolic* he was detached to bring the prize into port, but both the *Frolic* and the *Wasp* were taken by the 74-gun *Poictiers* and he was imprisoned for a time in Bermuda. Promoted to master-commandant and given the sloop *Hornet*, Biddle engaged and destroyed the *Penguin* and then, in the last naval encounter of the War of 1812, made a skillful escape from a much larger British ship of the line in April 1815. Promoted to captain while at sea, he returned to a hero's welcome in New York City. In 1817, commanding the *Ontario*, he was sent to the Columbia River to lay formal claim to the Oregon Territory; the region actually did not become part of the United States for 30 years. For the next 25 years he saw duty in South American waters, the Caribbean, and the Mediterranean and also served as head of the naval asylum in Philadelphia. In 1846, as commodore of the East India Squadron, he negotiated the first treaty between China and the United States. After commanding Pacific Coast naval forces during the Mexican War he returned to Philadelphia, where he died on October 1, 1848.

Biddle, Nicholas (1786–1844), financier and editor. Born in Philadelphia on January 8, 1786, to a leading Quaker family, Biddle was a precocious youth and entered the University of Pennsylvania at the age of ten. He completed his studies in three years and went on to the College of New Jersey (now Princeton University) for an additional two years of study. After studying law for a time he became, in 1804, secretary to the U.S. minister to France; two years later he moved to London to be secretary to the legation there. He returned to the United States in 1807 and resumed his legal studies and in 1809 was admitted to the bar. From 1806 he had been a regular contributor to *Port Folio*, the first American literary journal, and in 1812 he became its editor. In 1810 he had begun work on the *History of the* *Expedition of Captains Lewis and Clark* at the request of William Clark, whose notes, journals, and oral reports he used; but Biddle's election to the state legislature in 1814 forced him to leave the editing of *Port Folio* and the completion of the *History* to others. He strongly supported the policies of James Madison and James Monroe, wrote Pennsylvania's negative reply to the Hartford Convention's call for extensive constitutional amendments, and compiled *Commercial Regulations*, a digest of international trade laws. In 1819 President Monroe appointed Biddle a director of the Bank of the United States and in 1822 he became its president. Under his scrupulous guidance the bank, a quasi-public institution (the U.S. government owned one-fifth of the stock and could appoint one-fifth of the board of directors), exerted a conservative influence on the economy, maintaining a sound and stable currency, discouraging inflation, and guarding against speculative and unsound financial practices by other banks and institutions. But partly because of his conservatism, and partly because of the bank's very nature as a national institution, both Biddle and the bank acquired many enemies. The entrepreneurs were against the bank because it discouraged speculation. The farmers were against it because it discouraged the giving of long-term mortgages. The workingmen were against it because they distrusted credit in general and wanted their wages in coin instead of paper notes. And the state banks were against it because it exerted national power over their activities. Thus, when the various anti-bank groups rallied behind Andrew Jackson in 1828, Biddle was drawn into politics. With or without his knowledge, bank money was used to finance anti-Jackson campaigns and publications. In 1832 Biddle, perhaps unwisely seeking an early renewal of the bank's charter, pushed the issue into that year's presidential campaign. Jackson's victory doomed the bank. Biddle continued as president through the expiration of the federal charter in 1836 and for several years more under a state charter which he secured from Pennsylvania. He retired to his country estate, Andalusia, in 1839 and remained there until his death in Philadelphia on February 27, 1844.

Bidwell, John (1819–1900), pioneer and public official. Born in Chautauqua County, New York, on August 5, 1819, Bidwell moved later with his family to Pennsylvania and then to Ohio. He was educated in Ashtabula, taught briefly, and in 1839 went to Missouri and took up land near Weston. In May 1841 he joined a California-bound party organized by John Bartleson that, upon its arrival in November, became the first emigrant group to have made the later famous wagon-train journey from Independence, Missouri. Bidwell took a job at John A. Sutter's fort at present-day Sacramento and in 1844 became a Mexican citizen. He did not at first join in the Americans' revolt at Sonoma in June 1846 but he helped draw up the resolution of independence for the short-lived

Bear Flag Republic and served with Colonel John C. Frémont after the latter took command and marched south to Monterey. He was appointed a civil magistrate after the first American capture of Los Angeles in August and later was a major under Commodore Robert F. Stockton in the recapture of the settlement in January 1847. After the end of hostilities he returned to Sutter's Fort and successfully prospected on the Feather River, where he was the first to find gold. In 1849 he bought a huge ranch near Chico and became in time the leading rancher in California. He served a term in the state legislature and was active in Democratic politics. In 1863 he was appointed brigadier general of militia and the next year was elected to the House of Representatives. He ran unsuccessfully for governor in 1867, 1875, and 1890, and in 1892 was the Prohibition party's presidential candidate. Bidwell died at his ranch on April 4, 1900.

Bienville, Jean Baptiste Le Moyne, Sieur de (1680–1768), explorer and colonial administrator. Born in Ville-Marie de Montréal (now Montreal) on February 23, 1680, Jean Baptiste Le Moyne was a younger brother of Pierre Le Moyne, later the Sieur d'Iberville. Upon the death of another older brother in 1691 Jean Le Moyne assumed the title of Sieur de Bienville and the next year he entered the royal French navy and served for five years. When Iberville sailed from France in 1698 with a commission to establish a colony at the mouth of the Mississippi River, Bienville accompanied him and became second in command of the settlement founded at Fort Maurepas, near present-day Biloxi, Mississippi. In 1701, by which time he had done considerable exploring up the Mississippi and Red rivers, he succeeded to the governorship of the colony. In 1702 he built Fort Louis on Mobile Bay, whence Iberville had moved the colony. As Iberville was absent at sea much of the time, Bienville was the virtual governor of the entire Louisiana country and on the death of his brother in 1706 he assumed the position officially. In 1710 he again resettled the colony, founding the town of Mobile. He was replaced as governor in 1713 by Antoine de la Mothe Cadillac, sent by Antoine Crozat, whose company had been granted possession of Louisiana the year before. Bienville proved a valuable deputy to Cadillac, particularly in handling relations with the Indians, several of whose languages he spoke fluently. In 1717 Louisiana passed into the possession of the Compagnie de l'Occident (Company of the West, or Mississippi Company), established in France by the banker John Law. Bienville was restored to the governorship and immediately had to deal with a large influx of new colonists. In 1718 he selected a site for a new settlement, on an elevation on the east bank of the Mississippi, naming it, in honor of the regent of France, La Nouvelle Orléans. Bienville led expeditions which twice captured Pensacola from the Spanish when war broke out in 1719. The failure of Law's company, by then known as the Company of the Indies, in

the bursting of the "Mississippi bubble" of speculative frenzy in 1720 left Louisiana without substantial support from France; nevertheless the colony grew apace. New Orleans became the capital of Louisiana in 1722; in the same year nearly a third of its houses were destroyed by a hurricane. The failure of an expedition against the hostile Natchez Indians in 1723 led to Bienville's recall to France to answer charges of mismanagement, and he remained in Paris from 1724 to 1732, during which time, in 1727, he arranged for the emigration to the principally male colony of a number of *filles à la cassette*, "casket girls," so called from their dowry chests, who under the watchful eyes of the Ursuline nuns of New Orleans became colonists' wives. In 1733 Bienville returned as governor and again was confronted with hostile Indians. In 1736 he ordered a contingent of soldiers at Fort Chartres in the Illinois country to march south against the Natchez and their Chickasaw allies, while he moved to effect a rendezvous; Bienville encountered delays en route and the northern force was decimated. Ceaseless Indian warfare eventually exhausted Bienville. In 1740 he concluded an unsatisfactory treaty with the Indians and in 1743 asked to be relieved of his duties. He returned then to Paris and remained there until his death on March 7, 1768.

Bierce, Ambrose Gwinnett (1842–1914?), journalist, author, and editor. Born on June 24, 1842, in Meigs County, Ohio, Bierce left school early and entered the printer's trade. In 1861 he enlisted in an Indiana volunteer infantry regiment and during the Civil War saw action at Shiloh, Corinth, Chickamauga, and other major battlefields; in 1864 he was seriously wounded at Kennesaw Mountain. On leaving the army in 1866 he journeyed west to San Francisco and while employed at the U.S. mint began to contribute to various periodicals, particularly the *News Letter* and the *Argonaut*. He was editor of the *News Letter* from 1868 until 1872, when he left for a three-year stay in London. While writing for *Fun* and *Figaro* and editing the *Lantern* for the Empress Eugénie of France, he collected much of his earlier work and published it in book form as *The Fiend's Delight*, 1872; *Nuggets and Dust Panned Out in California*, 1872; and *Cobwebs from an Empty Skull*, 1874. Bierce's often vitriolic wit, his fascination with the supernatural, and his precise craftsmanship with language were well exhibited in these books, which also earned him the nickname "Bitter Bierce." Returning to San Francisco, he became associate editor of the *Argonaut* in 1877 and editor of the *Wasp* in 1881. In 1887 he joined William Randolph Heart's *Sunday Examiner* as a columnist. Bierce came to be the acknowledged literary arbiter of the West, holding a position comparable to that of William Dean Howells in the East. In 1891 he published *Tales of Soldiers and Civilians*, based on his Civil War experiences and containing the masterful "Occurrence at Owl Creek Bridge." Two years later appeared *Can Such Things Be?*, a collection of tales of the supernatural. Influenced by Edgar Allan Poe among others, Bierce was in turn a strong influence on O. Henry and Stephen Crane, anticipating in particular the impressionism of the narratives of Crane. After 1897 he was in Washington, D.C., as correspondent for the Hearst newspapers. In 1906 he published the aptly titled *Cynic's Word Book*, later renamed *The Devil's Dictionary*, a collection of ironic and sometimes venomous definitions. In 1913, apparently discontented with American life, Bierce traveled to Mexico, possibly in search of the rebel Pancho Villa; he was last heard from in December of that year and is thought to have died in a battle a month later.

Bierstadt, Albert (1830–1902), painter. Born on January 7, 1830, in Solingen, Germany, Bierstadt was brought by his parents to the United States in 1831 and grew up in New Bedford, Massachusetts. He early became interested in art and from 1853 to 1857 studied in Düsseldorf and Rome. Upon his return he joined an army exploring party and journeyed through Colorado and the Rockies into California, making scores of studies and sketches that he later translated onto canvas. The paintings that resulted from this and subsequent trips—"Laramie Peak," "El Capitan, Merced River," "Valley of the Yosemite," "In the Rocky Mountains," "Great Trees of California," and "Estes Park, Colorado" among them—depicted the magnificent scenery of the West on huge canvases and became immensely popular. He was soon represented in major galleries and private collections throughout the country and abroad. Although striking in their boldness, scale, and subject matter, his works were in a later age judged to be unfortunately literal and passionless. Bierstadt made several visits to Europe, where he was widely honored, and maintained a studio at Irvington, New York, until it burned in 1882. He lived and worked thereafter in New York City. In later years he turned to scenes and historical themes other than those of the West for inspiration for many of his paintings. He executed two works, "The Discovery of the Hudson River" and "The Settlement of California," for the Capitol in Washington, D.C. Bierstadt died in New York City on February 18, 1902. There was a revival of interest in his work, together with that of other painters of the Hudson River School, in the mid-twentieth century.

Bigelow, Erastus Brigham (1814–1879), inventor and manufacturer. Born in West Boylston, Massachusetts, on April 2, 1814, Bigelow was forced by his family's poverty to go to work at the age of ten. Possessing a keen and inventive mind, at the age of twenty-three he devised a loom for making lace and was soon able to machine produce other figured fabrics as well, including silk brocatelle and gingham. In 1843 he and his brother founded the Clinton Company mill for manufacturing ginghams; the town of Clinton, Massachusetts, soon grew up around it. He had begun in 1839 to work on a power loom for weaving ingrain carpeting and by 1851 he had designed machines to produce tapestry, velvet, Wilton, and Brussels carpets. His looms, first used in 1841, revolutionized the industry; they were eagerly adopted in England, and he himself established mills in Lowell, Massachusetts, and in Clinton, which became the home of the major Bigelow carpet works. He was also an economist of note and wrote a number of treatises, particularly on the subject of the tariff. In 1861 he was one of the founders of the Massachusetts Institute of Technology. Bigelow died in Boston on December 6, 1879.

Bigelow, Jacob (1786–1879), botanist and physician. Born in Sudbury, Massachusetts, on February 27, 1786, Bigelow graduated from Harvard in 1806 and four years later received his M.D. from the University of Pennsylvania. From his interest in botany and his work on drug-producing plants came his *Florula Bostoniensis* in 1814; in the enlarged version published in 1824 it remained the standard reference work on New England flora for a quarter of a century. His *American Medical Botany* appeared in three volumes between 1817 and 1820, and in 1820 Bigelow took part in the preparation of the first American pharmacopoeia. In 1815 he became a professor in the Harvard Medical School; the following year he was appointed to the chair of application of science to the useful arts. Other major published works include *Treatise on the Materia Medica*, 1822; *Discourse on Self-limited Diseases*, 1835; and *Brief Expositions of Rational Medicine*, 1858. From 1847 to 1863 he was president of the American Academy of Arts and Sciences. He died in Boston on January 10, 1879.

Bigelow, John (1817–1911), editor, author, and diplomat. Born in Malden, New York, on November 25, 1817, Bigelow was educated at Washington (now Trinity) College in Hartford, Connecticut, and at Union College, Schenectady, New York, graduating from Union in 1835. He was admitted to the bar three years later and began practice in New York City. He served as state prison inspector in 1845–1847, was active in the Free-Soil Democratic party, and contributed articles to numerous periodicals. In 1848 he became, at William Cullen Bryant's invitation, part owner and managing editor of the *New York Evening Post*. During his twelve years with the newspaper he also published a study of Jamaica and a campaign biography of John C. Frémont. In 1861 Bigelow was appointed U.S. consul general in Paris and became minister to France three years later. While in Paris he performed invaluable services to the Union: he discovered and forestalled a plan to deliver ships to the Confederacy, a plan that had the tacit consent of the French government, and wrote *Les États-Unis d'Amérique en 1863* to convince French merchants and officials that their commercial best interests lay with the Union rather than the Confederacy. After the Civil War he handled the negotiations with Napoleon III for the withdrawal of French forces from Mexico. In Paris he discovered the long-lost manuscript of Benjamin Franklin's autobiography and published it in 1868, after his return to the United States; he also wrote a biography of Franklin in 1874 and edited Franklin's works, published in ten volumes in 1887–1888. He served as New York secretary of state in 1875–1877. Several books were the fruit of his experiences in France, most importantly *France and the Confederate Navy, 1862–1868: An International Episode*, 1888, and he wrote a number of works on Swedenborgianism, a biography of his friend Samuel J. Tilden, whose writings he also edited, and many other books. As an executor and trustee of Tilden's estate, he was active in securing the cooperation of the Astor and Lenox libraries with the Tilden Trust in the founding of the New York Public Library. His autobiography, *Retrospections of an Active Life*, appeared in three volumes in 1909 and in two supplemental volumes prepared by his son, Poultney Bigelow, in 1913. Bigelow died in New York City on December 19, 1911.

Bigelow, Poultney (1855–1954), journalist and author. Born in New York City on September 10, 1855, Bigelow was the son of John Bigelow, at that time managing editor of the New York *Evening Post*. He graduated from Yale in 1879 and from the law school of Columbia University in 1882, but never practiced law. Instead he traveled extensively, particularly in Asia and Africa, and made close studies of colonial administration. In 1885 he founded and for two years edited *Outing*, the first American magazine devoted to amateur outdoor sports. Later in his European travels he cultivated his already close friendship with Kaiser Wilhelm II of Germany, which dated back to childhood, and wrote several books on Germany, including *The German Emperor and his Eastern Neighbors*, 1891; *Borderland of Czar and Kaiser*, 1893; and *History of the German Struggle for Liberty*, 1896–1905, in four volumes. He served for a time as London correspondent for *Harper's Weekly* and other American periodicals and during the Spanish-American War was a correspondent for the London *Times*. Others of his writings included *White Man's Africa*, 1898; *Children of the Nations*, 1901; *Prussianism and Pacifism*, 1919; *Japan and Her Colonies*, 1923; and an autobiography, *Seventy Summers*, 1925. Bigelow died on May 28, 1954, in Saugerties, New York.

Biglow, Hosea, *see under* Lowell, James Russell

Bilbo, Theodore Gilmore (1877–1947), public official. Born near Poplarville, Mississippi, on October 13, 1877, Bilbo managed despite poverty to attend Peabody College and the University of Nashville for a time and, after a few years of teaching and working at other jobs, studied law at Vanderbilt University from 1905 to 1907. In 1907 he was elected to the Mississippi state

senate on a platform of Southern populist, anti-railroad sentiment. In 1909 he was censured by his colleagues for announcing that he had sold his vote in the election of a U.S. senator—he claimed to have done so in order to trap the buyer—but he enjoyed a rise in popularity with his rural constituency as a result. In 1912 he was elected lieutenant governor of Mississippi and four years later won the race for governor. His administration was marked by a large state-financed building program and heavy patronage. He ran unsuccessfully for the House of Representatives in 1920 and for governor in 1924, but was returned to the state house in 1928 after again campaigning on an agrarian and racist platform. During his second term he purged the faculties of the state colleges and universities, which subsequently lost accreditation, and brought Mississippi to the verge of bankruptcy. From 1932 to 1934 he worked for the Agricultural Adjustment Administration (AAA) in Washington, D.C., and then, after a campaign in which he made more than a thousand speeches—in a style characterized by biblical phraseology and highly imaginative invective—he was elected to the Senate in 1934. Contrary to expectations, he was at first inconspicuous in that body; as a Democrat he supported, for the most part, President Franklin D. Roosevelt's New Deal, particularly its agricultural policies. After he became Mississippi's senior senator in 1936, however, he gained a reputation as one of the most colorful and tireless speakers in the Senate, and his filibustering tactics became legendary. His addresses to his colleagues were little less demagogic than his stump speeches, especially when he rose to oppose antilynching legislation or to introduce his pet proposal for the deportation of several million Negroes to Africa in the interest of "racial purity." Bilbo remained in the Senate, one of the last voices of Southern populism, until his death in New Orleans on August 21, 1947.

Billings, Frederick (1823–1890), lawyer and businessman. Born on September 27, 1823, in Royalton, Vermont, Billings grew up there and in Woodstock. He graduated from the University of Vermont in 1844, studied law, and in 1849 joined the gold rush to California. Rather than prospecting, however, he opened a law office and soon had a lucrative practice and was head of the leading law firm in San Francisco. He remained there, active in politics and serving for a time as state attorney general, until 1864, when ill health forced his retirement and he returned to Woodstock. Two years later he bought an interest in the Northern Pacific Railway and took charge of its land acquisitions and sales, promoting by his policies the rapid settlement of the farming regions of the Northwest. When the panic of 1873 brought the line to the verge of bankruptcy he devised a plan for its reorganization and in 1879, after the plan's successful adoption, became the line's president. He extended the Northern Pacific's tracks from Bismarck, then Dakota Territory, to the Columbia River and had secured financing for the completion of the line to Portland when Henry Villard of the Oregon Railway and Navigation Company, which then had a monopoly on rail transport to Portland, bought a large interest in the Northern Pacific and after a struggle replaced Billings as president in 1881. Billings continued as a director, and though Villard oversaw completion of the railroad, the plan followed was that of Billings. In his last years Billings devoted much time to philanthropy; among the chief beneficiaries were the University of Vermont, Amherst College, and the towns of Woodstock and of Billings, Montana (named for him). He died in Woodstock, Vermont, on September 30, 1890.

Billings, John Shaw (1838–1913), physician and librarian. Born in Switzerland County, Indiana, on April 12, 1838, Billings graduated from Miami University (Ohio) in 1857 and from the Medical College of Ohio in Cincinnati in 1860. He taught at the Medical College briefly and then entered the army as a surgeon. He performed medical and administrative duties in hospitals and in the field until 1864, when he was attached to the office of the surgeon general in Washington, D.C. There he was given charge of the medical library. Long persuaded of the nation's need for a comprehensive central medical library, he undertook to create one and within ten years had expanded the surgeon general's office collection from a few hundred volumes to more than 50,000. After four years of preparation the first volume of the *Index Catalogue of the Library of the Surgeon General's Office* appeared in 1880 and was followed by a volume each year until Billings's retirement in 1895. The *Index Catalogue*, produced with the help of Dr. Robert Fletcher, was a monumental work of immense value to the medical profession. As a companion guide, Billings and Fletcher also published from 1879 to 1895 a monthly *Index Medicus* covering current medical publications. In 1873 Billings drew up the plans for the physical plant and outlined the operating method and philosophy of the proposed Johns Hopkins Hospital, exerting thereby a powerful influence on future hospital design. He served also as medical adviser to the trustees of the John Hopkins medical school and was instrumental in securing the teaching services of William H. Welch and William Osler. He was active in the American Public Health Association from the time of its founding in 1872, and his interest in preventive medicine led him into the field of vital statistics, of which he was director for the federal censuses of 1880 and 1890. In 1890 was was appointed professor of hygiene and hospital director at the University of Pennsylvania, posts to which he gave full time after his retirement from the army in 1895. In 1896 he became the first director of the New York Public Library, formed jointly by the Astor and Lenox libraries and the Tilden Trust. He designed the central building, supervised the reclassification of the books, organized the system of branch libraries, and secured a $5 million gift from

Andrew Carnegie. From 1902 until his death he devoted most of the time he could spare from the library to organizing the Carnegie Institution of Washington. Billings was one of the most widely honored American physicians of his time, and his achievements were particularly esteemed by his colleagues abroad. He died in New York City on March 11, 1913.

Billings, Josh, *see* Shaw, Henry Wheeler

Billings, William (1746–1800), composer. Born in Boston on October 7, 1746, Billings originally took up the trade of tanner, but his deep love of music led him into choir directing and hymn writing, which occupied an ever-increasing portion of his time. At the Brattle Street and Old South churches in Boston he made marked improvements in the singing of the choirs, introducing the use of the pitch pipe and later the cello for establishing the correct beginning pitch, until then a haphazard enterprise. He also wrote a great many hymns that, though somewhat crude and, because of his lack of formal training in composition, occasionally dissonant, were nonetheless greatly superior to the monotonous church music of the day. His first book of hymns, *The New England Palm Singer: or American Chorister*, was engraved by Paul Revere and published in 1770; it was followed by *The Singing Master's Assistant, or Key to Practical Music*, 1778; *The Psalm Singer's Amusement*, 1781; and *The Continental Harmony*, 1794, all of which reprinted traditional hymns in addition to his own. In 1774 he opened a singing school that in a few years evolved into the Stoughton Musical Society, the oldest such association still in existence in the country. During the Revolution Billings wrote several patriotic songs that gained wide currency. The most popular of these, and the piece for which he is best remembered, was called "Chester" (sometimes known as "Let Tyrants Shake") and began "Let tyrants shake their iron rod, / And Slavery clank her galling chains; / We fear them not, we trust in God; / New England's God forever reigns." Billings's music had great influence in his time but was later largely forgotten. He died in poverty in Boston on September 26, 1800.

Billy the Kid, *see* Bonney, William H.

Bingham, George Caleb (1811–1879), painter. Born on March 20, 1811, in Augusta County, Virginia, Bingham lived in Missouri after 1819. He read law and theology, but as an avocation copied engravings and learned to make his own colors, with encouragement from portraitist Chester Harding. In 1843 he opened his own studio; except for a brief period at the Pennsylvania Academy of the Fine Arts in 1837, he was self-taught. To support himself he painted portraits, his style varying considerably according to his interest in the sitter; but his major paintings depicted river scenes, pioneer life, and political events in the

Missouri River valley. "Jolly Flatboatmen," "Raftsmen Playing Cards," "Canvassing for a Vote," "Emigration of Daniel Boone," and "Verdict of the People," completed between 1840 and 1860, were among the most notable examples of his work. During 1856–1858 he visited Düsseldorf, where his studies of old masters led him to change his style; while he continued to be a popular portraitist, his other work lost much of its interest. He became further involved in politics (he had served in the Missouri legislature in 1848), and was elected state treasurer in 1862 and adjutant general in 1875. He taught art at the University of Missouri for two years before his death in Kansas City on July 7, 1879. His genre paintings slowly came to be recognized as among the best to be produced on the frontier.

Binney, Horace (1780–1875), lawyer. Born in Philadelphia on January 4, 1780, Binney graduated from Harvard in 1797 and was admitted to the bar three years later. He began his practice in his native city, but only after serving a term in the legislature in 1806–1807 did he begin to acquire the clientele and the reputation that his ability warranted. He became particularly expert in marine-insurance and land-title law, and between 1809 and 1815 he published six volumes of *Reports of Cases Adjudged in the Supreme Court of Pennsylvania*. During 1810–1811 he served as president of the common council of Philadelphia and from 1816 to 1819 he was a member of the select council of the city. By the 1820s he was the acknowledged leader of the Pennsylvania bar and was widely recommended for both the state and federal supreme courts, but he declined in 1830 to serve on the state bench. In 1832 he was elected to the House of Representatives as an anti-Jacksonian with no party affiliation; his skill and power in oratory and debate, however, had little effect and he did not seek reelection. From 1837 he confined his legal work to consultations and giving opinions, appearing only once more in court, when he argued brilliantly before the Supreme Court in 1844 the case of *Vidal et al. v. Philadelphia et al.*, in which he successfully opposed Daniel Webster, the counsel for the plaintiffs, and established the legality of the trust created by Stephen Girard for the founding of a school for orphans. In 1850 he gave up legal practice entirely because of ill health and devoted his remaining energies to writing; among his works were *The Leaders of the Old Bar of Philadelphia*, 1859; *An Enquiry into the Formation of Washington's Farewell Address*, 1859; and, during the Civil War, a series of three pamphlets arguing the validity of President Abraham Lincoln's suspension of habeas corpus. Binney died in Philadelphia on August 12, 1875.

Birkhoff, George David (1884–1944), mathematician. Born in Overisel, Michigan, on March 21, 1884, Birkhoff did his undergraduate work at the University of Chicago and at Harvard, from which he graduated in 1905; he received his Ph.D. from Chicago in 1907. He spent most of his teaching career at Harvard, joining its faculty in 1912 and remaining until his death. His mathematical research was mainly in the fields of analysis and analysis applied to dynamics. His dissertation and much of his later work dealt with the solution of ordinary differential equations and with the associated expansions of arbitrary functions. He made basic contributions to the theory of systems of both differential and difference equations. One of his most striking achievements was the proof, in 1913, of a geometric theorem having applications to dynamics that had earlier been merely conjectured by the great French mathematician Henri Poincaré. Perhaps his most important contribution, however, was the so-called ergodic theorem. This theorem transformed the ergodic hypothesis of the kinetic theory of gases, to which vexing exceptions were known, into a rigorous principle; in the process the exceptions were all made intelligible. He developed his own theory of gravitation, subsequent to Einstein; and he also spent several years in the construction of a mathematical theory of aesthetics which he applied to art, music, and poetry. He was dean of the Harvard faculty of arts and sciences from 1935 to 1939 and was extraordinarily stimulating as a lecturer and as a director of research. At the midpoint of the twentieth century, many of the leading U.S. mathematicians had either written dissertations under him or studied with him in postgraduate research. He was president of the American Mathematical Society, 1924–1926, and of the American Association for the Advancement of Science, 1936–1937. He died in Cambridge, Massachusetts, on November 12, 1944.

Birney, James Gillespie (1792–1857), public official and reformer. Born in Danville, Kentucky, on February 4, 1792, Birney was educated at Transylvania University and at the College of New Jersey (now Princeton University), from which he graduated in 1810. He then studied law under Alexander J. Dallas in Philadelphia and, after admission to the bar in 1814, entered practice in Danville. In 1816 he was elected to the legislature. Two years later he moved to a plantation in Alabama and in 1819 was elected to the legislature of that state. He served only a single term and, in financial difficulty, resumed the practice of law in Huntsville in 1823. Never a firm supporter of slavery, though he was himself a slaveholder, he became interested in the work of the American Colonization Society and in 1832 became its agent in the region. Later in the year he returned to Danville. By 1834 he had abandoned belief in colonization and even gradual emancipation as solutions to the slavery question; he freed his own slaves and in 1835 founded the Kentucky Anti-Slavery Society. He planned an abolitionist newspaper, but overwhelming local opposition forced him to move and he went to New Richmond, near Cincinnati, Ohio, to begin publishing the *Philanthropist* in January 1836; even there he met considerable adverse sentiment, but he continued publishing the paper until September 1837, when he turned it over to his assistant, Gamaliel Bailey. He then moved to New York to take office as executive secretary of the American Anti-Slavery Society. He was already at odds with the faction of the society led by William Lloyd Garrison, who disdained legal and political action, and in 1839 he precipitated the inevitable schism by coming out strongly for such action, including the formation of an antislavery party. The Liberty Party was organized the following year and it nominated Birney for the presidency, but he polled only a few thousand votes. Also in 1840 he served as vice-president of the World's Anti-Slavery Convention in London, where he published his *American Churches the Bulwarks of American Slavery*. In 1844 he was again the Liberty party's presidential candidate, and he drew enough support in New York to swing the state from Henry Clay to James A. Polk. The next year a fall from a horse left him partly paralyzed and curtailed all his activities except writing. In 1853 he moved from Bay City, Michigan, where he had lived since 1842, to Eagleswood, near Perth Amboy, New Jersey, where he died on November 25, 1857.

Bissell, George Henry (1821–1884), businessman. Born on November 8, 1821, in Hanover, New Hampshire, Bissell graduated from Dartmouth in 1845 and, after a brief period as a teacher, became a newspaper reporter. He worked for a time in Washington, D.C., and then in New Orleans, where he gave up journalism to become superintendent of schools. He studied law at the same time and in 1853, after moving to New York City, was admitted to the bar. In 1854 he and his law partner became interested in the possibilities of petroleum production. They bought or leased tracts of land around Oil Creek, Pennsylvania, and began collecting surface oil by digging wells and trenches. The work was at first unprofitable, but a report by chemist Benjamin Silliman that outlined some of the commercial possibilities of refined petroleum kept them at work, and Silliman became president of their reorganized Pennsylvania Rock Oil Company. In 1858 Bissell, inspired probably by the salt-water artesian wells in the area, conceived the idea of drilling deep wells in search of oil pools. Edwin L. Drake, a stockholder in Pennsylvania Rock Oil, contracted to do the drilling and in 1859, near Titusville, completed the world's first oil well. Bissell was active in the rapidly growing petroleum industry for the rest of his life. He died an enormously rich man in New York City on November 19, 1884.

Bitter, Karl Theodore Francis (1867–1915), sculptor. Born in Vienna on December 6, 1867, Bitter early became interested in stoneworking and, without finishing his secondary schooling, studied sculpture in the Kunstgewerbeschule and the Kunstakademie until 1887. During his student years he executed a number of decorative pieces for the city. In 1889, after serving one year of a three-year period of required military sevice, he fled from Austria to the United States. In New York City he quickly found work in a firm specializing in architectural decoration; there he attracted the notice of Richard M. Hunt and was encouraged by the architect to launch out on his own. He was immediately successful, executing a commission for interior sculpture for Collis P. Huntington' mansion and in 1891 winning the competition for a bronze gate for Trinity Church in New York City. In 1893 he executed the sculptural decoration for Hunt's Administration Building at the World's Columbian Exposition in Chicago. There followed commissions for large panels in the Pennsylvania Station in Philadelphia, for interior and exterior pieces for the Vanderbilt estate, "Biltmore," in Asheville, North Carolina, and for the representational figures standing before the Metropolitan Museum of Art in New York City. As the volume of his commissions grew, Bitter took on assistants and produced a flood of decorative work, first in New York City and, after 1896, at a large studio in Weehawken, New Jersey. He was named director of sculpture for the Pan-American Exposition in Buffalo in 1901, the Louisiana Purchase Exposition in St. Louis in 1904, and the Panama-Pacific International Exposition in San Francisco in 1915. From about 1900 he began slowly to extricate himself from the production of commercial decorative sculpture and to devote himself to more serious works. He did a number of memorial pieces and busts, his subjects including Thomas Jefferson, James B. Angell, Andrew D. White, and Carl Schurz. His last work was a figure representing "Abundance" for the Grand Army Plaza in New York City; he had just completed the model when he was struck by an automobile and fatally injured. He died in New York City on April 10, 1915.

Black, Greene Vardiman (1836–1915), dentist. Born on August 3, 1836, near Winchester, Illinois, Black grew up on farms, first at Winchester and later near Virginia, Illinois. At seventeen he began the study of medicine in the office of an older brother and three years later switched to dentistry, starting his own practice in 1857. Except for brief infantry service in the Civil War he practiced without interruption until 1870, when he joined the faculty of the Missouri Dental College in St. Louis, an association that lasted for ten years. From 1883 to 1889 he was professor of dental pathology at the Chicago College of Dental Surgery; he subsequently taught at the University of Iowa during 1890–1891. By the latter year he had, through his teaching and his many published articles, achieved an enviable reputation in his field. He was then appointed professor of dental pathology and bacteriology at Northwestern University and in 1897 became dean of the Northwestern dental school, holding both posts until his death. Black made contributions to dentistry on both the practical and theoretical levels; he developed an amalgam alloy for fillings that was the first to win general acceptance among dentists, a method of enlarging the area to be filled beyond the cavity itself in order to prevent further decay, and a wide array of tools and apparatus. On the theoretical side he wrote, in addition to scores of journal articles, a number of textbooks that were long in use, including *Dental Anatomy*, 1891; *Operative Dentistry*, 1908, in two volumes; and *Diseases and Treatment of the Investing Tissues of the Teeth and the Dental Pulp*, 1915. He died on August 31, 1915, in Chicago.

Black, Hugo LaFayette (1886–1971), justice of the Supreme Court. Born on February 27, 1886, in Harlan, Alabama, Black graduated from the University of Alabama with a law degree in 1906 and was admitted to the bar in the same year. He moved his practice to Birmingham in 1907 and was quickly successful. He served as a police judge during 1910–1911 and as prosecuting attorney of Jefferson County in 1915–1917. After serving as an artillery officer during World War I he returned to the practice of law in Birmingham in 1919. In 1926 he was elected to the Senate, where he sat for ten years as a populist-progressive and, for the most part, a staunch supporter of the New Deal, gaining considerable attention particularly with his vigorous investigation of the public utilities lobby in Washington. President Franklin D. Roosevelt appointed Black to the Supreme Court in 1937 and, despite a flurry of controversy over his membership in the Ku Klux Klan in the mid-1920s, he was quickly confirmed. From the outset of his career on the bench he took as his special task the protection of the Bill of Rights, which he held, under the Fourteenth Amendment, to be absolute and superior to any federal or state legislation. The First Amendment rights especially concerned him and in such cases as *Bridges* v. *California*, 1941; *Dennis* v. *U.S.* (dissenting), 1951; *Yates* v. *U.S.* (dissenting), 1957; *Barenblatt* v. *U.S.* (dissenting), 1959; and *Ginzburg* v. *U.S.* (dissenting), 1966, he stood firmly against any restriction of free speech and publication and dismissed the Holmesian "clear and present danger" test as unconstitutional and itself dangerous. His view of the Fourteenth Amendment, early expressed in his dissenting opinion in *Adamson* v. *California*, 1947, gradually became the general view of the Court during the late 1950s and the 1960s as Black emerged as a powerful and persuasive figure. He was ever at pains to hold the authority of the Court and of the executive branch in check; among his most important opinions to that effect were those in *Duncan* v. *Kahanamoku*, 1946, strictly limiting the use of martial law, and *Youngstown Sheet & Tube Co.* v. *Sawyer*, 1952, declaring unconstitutional President Harry S. Truman's seizure of the steel mills during the Korean War. Other notable opinions rendered by Black included those in *Board of Education* v. *Barnette* (concurring), 1943, holding that religious convictions took precedence over a school's patriotic exercises; *Korematsu* v. *U.S.*, 1944, validating Japanese exclusion from the West Coast during World War II; *Engel* v. *Vitale*,

1962, striking down required prayer in New York schools; and *Gideon* v. *Wainwright*, 1963, requiring legal counsel for all those accused of crimes under state laws (a position he had originally taken 21 years earlier in a dissenting opinion in *Betts* v. *Brady*). His dedication to the letter of the Constitution—he usually had a copy of it in his pocket—led him on occasion to take stands that were widely unpopular among liberals, who commonly held him to be one of their own; among his opinions expressing such stands were those in *Korematsu; in Griswold* v. *Connecticut* (dissenting), 1965, in which he could find no constitutional grounds for invalidating a state birth-control law; and in *Berger* v. *New York* (dissenting), 1967, in which he found no prohibition in the Fourth Amendment against electronic eavesdropping. An active member of the Court—and an avid tennis player—into his 80s, Black succumbed at last to illness and resigned in September 1971; eight days later, on September 25, he died in Bethesda, Maryland. His 34 years on the Supreme Court constituted one of the longest terms of service in its history.

Black, Jeremiah Sullivan (1810–1883), lawyer and public official. Born near Stony Creek, Somerset County, Pennsylvania, on January 10, 1810, Black attended several schools at various times but was in the main self-educated. After three years of study in Somerset, Pennsylvania, he was admitted to the bar in 1830 and soon enjoyed a lucrative practice there. He became active in Democratic politics as well; in 1842 he was appointed judge of the district court and in 1851 and 1854 he was elected to the state supreme court. In 1857 he was chosen for the post of attorney general in the cabinet of President James Buchanan. His major achievement in that office was his launching of an investigation, headed by his eventual successor, Edwin M. Stanton, of a fraudulent scheme involving land titles in California. After the election of Abraham Lincoln to the presidency in November 1860 Black urged the outgoing Buchanan to stand firm against secession threats by Southern states and to send troops if necessary to protect federal property there. In a shuffle of cabinet offices in December of that year Black became secretary of state, in which post he continued to advocate a strong unionist position. His nomination to the Supreme Court by Buchanan in February 1861 was rejected by the Senate, and he retired from public service the following month. Returning to Pennsylvania, he resumed the practice of law in York and remained there for the rest of his life, a prominent member of the bar. A friend of President Andrew Johnson, he helped him draft the veto of the first Reconstruction Act in 1867 and was engaged to represent him in his impeachment trial, although he declined to serve after a quarrel with the president's other lawyers. He took part in several other notable legal affairs, including the case *Ex parte Milligan* in 1866, concerning the trial of a civilian by military commission; the Slaughterhouse Cases in 1873, in which the Fourteenth Amendment was first construed by the Supreme Court; and the representation of Samuel J. Tilden before the Electoral Commission in 1877. Black died in Brockie, Pennsylvania, on August 19, 1883.

Black Hawk (1767–1838), Indian leader. Born in 1767 in the Sauk village on the Rock River near the present Rock Island, Illinois, Makataimeshekiakiak, or Black Sparrow Hawk, resented the Americans as dispossessors of the Spanish, with whom his people had traded since 1769. His hatred grew when members of the Sauk and Fox tribes were persuaded by U.S. army officers to sign the treaty of 1804, ceding all of their lands east of the Mississippi River to the United States. In the War of 1812 he aided the British, serving under the command of the Shawnee chief Tecumseh, and then, with encouragement from the British, attempted to rally other tribes against the Americans to halt westward expansion. His rival Sauk chief, Keokuk, had accepted American rule and under the treaty had moved to lands in Iowa. In April 1832 Black Hawk led his tribe back to resettle their disputed homeland in Illinois, hoping to plant crops and avoid the settlers. Alarmed at the "trespass," Gov. John Reynolds summoned federal troops, which arrived at Rock River under the command of Gen. Henry Atkinson. Two Indian envoys were dispatched to confer with Atkinson and were shot by a body of Illinois volunteers; thus began the so-called Black Hawk War. Retreating northward through the Rock River valley, the Indians were slaughtered in the battle at Bad Axe River, in Wisconsin, on August 2, 1832. After aid that had been promised from other tribes never materialized, Black Hawk was captured and imprisoned in the East. He was taken to meet President Andrew Jackson in 1833, and in the same year he dictated an autobiography that is considered to be a classic statement of Indian resentment against white interlopers. In 1834 he was given over to the custody of Keokuk, in whose village near the Des Moines River in Iowa he died, on October 3, 1838.

Blackmun, Harry Andrew (1908–   ), justice of the Supreme Court. Born on November 12, 1908, in Nashville, Illinois, Blackmun grew up there and in the Minneapolis–St. Paul area. He graduated from Harvard in 1929, remained there to take his law degree, in 1932, and after a year as a law clerk entered a Minneapolis firm. While advancing to general partner in the firm he also taught, from 1935 to 1941 at the St. Paul College of Law and from 1945 to 1947 at the University of Minnesota Law School. In 1950 he became resident counsel for the Mayo Clinic in Rochester, Minnesota, a post he held until 1959, when he was appointed judge of the U.S. Court of Appeals for the Eighth Circuit by President Dwight D. Eisenhower. During 11 years on that bench he acquired a reputation for fairness, thoroughness, and judicial caution; he was most often characterized as a moderate who leaned slightly toward

conservatism on some issues. In 1970, after two previous nominees had been rejected by the Senate as unqualified, President Richard M. Nixon named Blackmun to the Supreme Court seat vacated by Abe Fortas; Blackmun was unanimously confirmed and took his seat in June. On the Court he joined Chief Justice Warren E. Burger, a close friend from boyhood.

Blackwell, Antoinette Louisa Brown (1825–1921), social reformer. Born on May 20, 1825, in Henrietta, New York, Miss Brown was a precocious child and at an early age began to speak at meetings of the Congregational church to which she belonged. She attended Oberlin College, graduating from its theological seminary in 1850, after which she was an itinerant preacher until 1852, when she was given a permanent appointment as pastor of the Congregational church in South Butler, New York; she became thereby the first formally appointed woman pastor in the country, although her sex barred her from ordination. She was active in numerous reform movements, particularly those for abolition, temperance, and women's rights. Despite her considerable achievements and the fact that she was an accredited delegate, she was barred from addressing the World's Temperance Convention in New York in 1853 on grounds of her sex. The following year her changing religious convictions led her to resign her pastorate; she became a Unitarian. In 1856 she married Samuel C. Blackwell, a brother of Dr. Elizabeth Blackwell. She remained all her life an ardent supporter of her chosen causes, writing and speaking widely in their behalf. Her last years were spent in Elizabeth, New Jersey, where she died on November 5, 1921.

Blackwell, Elizabeth (1821–1910), physician. Born on February 3, 1821, in Bristol, England, Miss Blackwell came with her family to the United States in 1832, settling in New York City and later in Cincinnati. In 1842 she became a schoolteacher and two years later began reading medical books in her free time. In 1847 she studied with Dr. Samuel H. Dickson of the Charleston Medical College in South Carolina, and later in the year, after being rejected by several other schools, was admitted to the Geneva Medical School of Western New York. She was the object of much ridicule and hostility, both from fellow students and from outsiders, but she nonetheless graduated at the head of her class in 1849, the first woman to receive an M.D. degree in modern times. She then pursued further studies in Paris and London, where she was associated with Florence Nightingale, and returned to practice in New York City in 1850. She opened a private clinic that, over yet more opposition, became in 1857 the New York Infirmary; staffed entirely by women, the hospital grew and offered a full course of medical studies in the Women's Medical College of the New York Infirmary. In 1869 she sailed to England and settled there permanently. She became professor of gynecology at the newly founded London

School of Medicine for Women in 1875 and continued to teach and to write, especially on the subject of public health, until a disabling accident curtailed her activities in 1907. Dr Blackwell died in Hastings on May 31, 1910.

Blaine, James Gillespie (1830–1893), public official and political leader. Born in West Brownsville, Pennsylvania, on January 31, 1830, Blaine graduated from Washington (now Washington and Jefferson) College in 1847 and for the next six years taught school, first in Kentucky and later in Pennsylvania. In 1854 he moved to Augusta, Maine, and edited the *Kennebec Journal,* making it over into a Republican newspaper and helping to establish the new party in that state. From 1858 to 1862 he was in the state legislature and in the latter year was elected to the House of Representatives, where he served until 1876. He was elected speaker of the House in 1869 and was a powerful leader of the Republican ascendancy. His name was proposed to the 1876 Republican national convention by Robert G. Ingersoll, who dubbed him the "Plumed Knight," but the shadow of corruption of President Ulysses S. Grant's administration lost Blaine the nomination for the presidency; immediately afterward, however, he was appointed to fill a Senate vacancy. Failing again to attain the nomination in 1880, he became secretary of state in President James A. Garfield's cabinet. In this post he took the first diplomatic steps toward the securing of U.S. sovereignty over the route of the later Panama Canal by bringing about a modification of the Clayton-Bulwer Treaty of 1850. He also tried to redefine the Monroe Doctrine to make it somewhat less unilateral; but his efforts to organize an inter-American conference on this and other subjects came to an end with his resignation following Garfield's assassination. Blaine finally gained the Republican nomination for the presidency in 1884, only to lose by a narrow margin to Grover Cleveland in a campaign distinguished only by the much-publicized phrase of a New York clergyman and Blaine supporter who characterized the opposition as the party of "Rum, Romanism, and Rebellion;" Blaine's defeat has often been attributed to the subsequent loss of the Irish Catholic and thus the New York City vote. Following Benjamin Harrison's election in 1888, however, Blaine returned to Washington, again as secretary of state. He continued to be concerned with Latin American relations and anticipated in some ways the more famous policies of President Theodore Roosevelt. He was chairman of the first Pan-American Conference, held in 1889. He resigned from the cabinet in June 1892 and died in Washington, D.C., on January 27, 1893.

Blair, Francis Preston (1791–1876), journalist and political leader. Born in Abingdon, Virginia, on April 12, 1791, Blair graduated from Transylvania University in 1811. After brief service in the War of 1812 he studied law but never practiced, instead taking up journalism with Amos Kendall's *Argus of Western America* in Frankfort, Kentucky. He became an ardent supporter of Andrew Jackson, to whose cause he brought such editorial skill that in 1830 he was chosen to go to Washington, D.C., to establish the *Globe* as the official organ of the Democratic party. He conducted the newspaper faithfully, serving also in President Jackson's "kitchen cabinet" of trusted advisers and becoming the most influential political journalist in the nation. He later supported presidents Martin Van Buren and James K. Polk with equal vigor. In addition he published for some time the *Congressional Globe* (predecessor of the *Congressional Record*), which reported the daily proceedings of the Congress. He left the *Globe* in 1845 and retired to his estate at Silver Spring, Maryland, but continued to be an influential commentator on public affairs. A proponent of western expansion without the extension of slavery, in 1848 Blair broke with the Democrats to support Martin Van Buren and the Free-Soil party, and as the slavery issue grew he came more and more to believe that the party to which he had devoted himself was abandoning its principles. He violently denounced the Kansas-Nebraska Bill and in 1856 helped organize the Republican party in hopes of reestablishing the old faith. Active in the election of Abraham Lincoln in 1860, he became a close adviser to the president. He arranged the unofficial (and unsuccessful) peace conference at Hampton Roads, Virginia, in February 1865. He took a moderate stand on Reconstruction, supporting President Andrew Johnson's position against the Radicals, and when the faction he had opposed became dominant he rejoined the Democratic party. He died at Silver Spring on October 18, 1876.

Blair, Francis Preston, Jr. (1821–1875), political leader and public official. Born in Lexington, Kentucky, on February 19, 1821, a son of Francis P. Blair, he graduated from Princeton in 1841, studied law at Transylvania University, and in 1842 joined his brother Montgomery in practice in St. Louis. The Mexican War broke out while he was vacationing in the Southwest and he thereafter served briefly as attorney general of New Mexico. He was among the organizers of the Free-Soil party in Missouri, establishing the *Barnburner* as its official organ, and on that party's ticket was elected to the legislature in 1852 and 1854 and to the House of Representatives in 1856. Defeated for reelection in 1858, he led in the formation of the Republican party in his state and traveled and spoke widely on its behalf. At the Chicago convention in 1860 he at first supported his fellow Missourian Edward Bates for the presidency but later switched to Abraham Lincoln. He was elected to the House again in that year and became chairman of its military affairs committee. Early in 1861 he helped mobilize unionist forces in Missouri and, though he antagonized many by his manner, he was instrumental in keeping the state from joining the Confederacy. In 1862 he recruited seven regiments in Missouri and with the rank of brigadier general and later major general served competently at Vicksburg, in Gen. William T. Sherman's Georgia campaign, and elsewhere. After the war Blair's strong opposition to Negro suffrage and to the Radical Republican's harsh Reconstruction measures moved him back into the Democratic party and in 1868 he was its candidate for vice-president. Under his leadership the Missouri Democrats cooperated closely with Liberal Republicans in winning the state government from the Radicals. He was elected to the legislature, which named him to fill an unexpired term in the Senate in 1870. He failed of reelection in 1872. Blair died in St. Louis on July 9, 1875.

Blair, James (1655–1743), religious leader and educator. Born in Scotland, probably in Edinburgh, in 1655, Blair graduated from the University of Edinburgh with an M.A. in 1673. Ordained in the Church of England in 1679, he served an Edinburgh parish until 1681, when he was suspended by the Scottish parliament for refusing to take a test oath. He then moved to London, where for three years he worked in the office of the Master of Rolls. He attracted the favorable notice of Henry Compton, bishop of London, by whom he was sent to Virginia as rector of Varina parish in 1685. Four years later he was appointed commissary, or ecclesiastical deputy and representative. In 1691, at Blair's urging, the Virginia General Assembly voted to petition the crown for the establishment of a college in the colony. Blair himself drew up the memorial and sailed to England to present it to the king and queen. By the time a charter was granted in 1693 he had also secured funds for the project, and work was begun immediately after his return to Virginia; he became, in accordance with the assembly's wishes and a provision of the charter, the first president of the College of William and Mary in that year. As the college was in Williamsburg, Blair carried out his pastoral duties at the church in nearby Jamestown and then, from 1710, in Williamsburg. Despite numerous obstacles—including the active opposition of three royal governors, whom Blair ultimately succeeded in having removed—he oversaw the steady growth of the college for a half-century, remaining its president until his death. His later years were marked by a series of acrimonious controversies, both political and ecclesiastical, mostly resulting from his position as commissary, an ill-defined office subsisting under the vague authority of the bishop of London. He attempted and failed on occasion to exert authority over the laity and clergy of Virginia and to represent the clergy before the assembly as well as in the ruling council, of which he was a member from 1694 until his death in Williamsburg on April 18, 1743.

Blair, John (1732–1800), justice of the Supreme Court. Born in 1732 in Williamsburg, Virginia, Blair was educated at the College of William and Mary and at the Middle Temple in London. In 1766 he was elected by William and Mary to the Virginia House of Burgesses; he served in that body until 1770 and for five years thereafter was clerk of the governor's council. During the crises that led up to the Revolution he was a loyal and steadfast Virginian and in 1776, having served in the state constitutional convention, he was elected to the Privy Council. In 1778 he was elected a judge of the general court, from which he was elevated two years later to the high court of chancery, and he sat also as a judge of the court of appeals. Blair was a member of the constitutional convention of 1787 and the next year supported the ratification of the Constitution in the Virginia convention called to consider it. In 1789 he was appointed to the Supreme Court by President George Washington. He served faithfully for seven years, resigning in 1796. He retired to Williamsburg, where he died on August 31, 1800.

Blair, Montgomery (1813–1883), public official and political leader. Born in Franklin County, Kentucky, on May 10, 1813, a son of Francis P. Blair, he attended Transylvania University briefly and then won appointment to West Point, from which he graduated in 1835. He served only a short time in the army and in 1837, after studying law at Transylvania, moved to St. Louis to begin practice. There he came under the influence of Sen. Thomas Hart Benton and became active in Democratic politics. He served as U.S. district attorney for Missouri from 1839 to 1841, as mayor of St. Louis in 1842–1843, and as judge of the court of common pleas from 1845 to 1849. In 1853 he moved his practice to Silver Spring, Maryland, where his father lived. He drifted out of the Democratic party to the Free-Soilers and in 1856 joined the Republicans. In 1857 he served as attorney for Dred Scott before the Supreme Court. In 1860 he presided over the state Republican convention and was a delegate to the national convention in Chicago, and the following year he was appointed postmaster general by President Abraham Lincoln. In the cabinet he was among the moderates, supporting Lincoln's policies against the Radical Republicans, while in his department he was an able administrator, introducing free city mail delivery, postal money orders, and the railway post office, among other innovations. The hostility of the Radicals forced his resignation in 1864, but he continued to be a leading spokesman for the moderates. He returned at length to the Democratic party and in 1877 was one of Samuel J. Tilden's counsels before the Electoral Commission. Blair was elected to the Maryland legislature in 1878 and in 1882 ran unsuccessfully for the House of Representatives. He died at Silver Spring on July 27, 1883.

Blakelock, Ralph Albert (1847–1919), painter. Born on October 15, 1847, in New York City, Blakelock studied for a time at Cooper Union and graduated from the College of the City of New York in 1867. He thereafter devoted himself entirely to painting and during his productive years endured complete neglect. His works, at first in the vein of the Hudson River School and later influenced by the haunting impasto paintings of Albert Pinkham Ryder, were nearly all landscapes, often with figures of Indians. Executed in color masses of rich, earthy hues, they aimed at mood rather than representation and were deeply imbued with a sense of dark romanticism and mystery; and he gave them such titles as "Indian Encampment," "Moonlight," "Autumn," "October Sunshine," "Canoe Builders," and "Moonrise." Blakelock's failure to sell his work, and the consequent poverty of his family, led to a mental breakdown in 1899. The remainder of his life, except for a period of two years, was spent in an asylum. Partly because of the circumstances of his life, interest in his paintings grew, and before his death his works were fetching auction prices in five figures. Several were acquired by major galleries and Blakelock was elected to the National Academy of Design in 1913. He died in Elizabethtown, New York, on August 9, 1919.

Blalock, Alfred (1899–1964), surgeon. Born in Culloden, Georgia, on April 5, 1899, Blalock graduated from the University of Georgia in 1918 and after serving in the army in World War I entered the Johns Hopkins Medical School. He took his M.D. in 1922, remained for three years as intern and resident surgeon at Johns Hopkins Hospital, and in 1925 became resident and instructor in surgery at Vanderbilt University Hospital. There he conducted research into the nature of shock and, relating it to loss of blood or blood plasma, showed that large transfusions of blood or plasma relieved the condition; this method became the standard treatment. In 1938 he was named a full professor of surgery. Three years later he returned to Johns Hopkins as chief surgeon of the hospital and chairman of the department of surgery of the medical school. At Hopkins he met Dr. Helen Taussig, head of the children's heart clinic, who had theorized that the cause of cyanosis in infants so afflicted—"blue babies"—was a functional lack of oxygen. She interested Blalock in the idea and in experiments on dogs he demonstrated that such was the case—the anoxemia could be caused experimentally by constriction or blockage of the pulmonary artery. He then developed an operation in which the pulmonary artery and a healthy systemic artery were spliced to bypass the deformation; thus sufficient blood was supplied to the lungs for oxygenation. The operation was first performed in 1944 and was soon refined to a nearly routine procedure that saved thousands of blue babies in subsequent years. The operation marked the beginning of modern heart surgery and remained in use. Blalock later devised, with C. R. Hanlon, a technique, still employed, to correct another congenital defect, the reversal of the major blood vessels of the heart. He retired from Johns Hopkins in 1963 and died in Baltimore on September 15, 1964.

Blanchard, Thomas (1788–1864), inventor. Born in Sutton, Massachusetts, on June 24, 1788, Blanchard displayed considerable mechanical aptitude from an early age. One of his first inventions was an automatic tack-making machine. Later he constructed a lathe that was capable of turning both the regular and irregular portions of gun barrels, and the success of this device won him employment in the U.S. arsenal in Springfield. There he made further improvements in gun-making machinery and about 1818, while puzzling out the problem of turning out gunstocks rapidly and accurately, hit upon his most important idea, that of a lathe for automatically duplicating any given pattern. The mechanism was based on a friction wheel that rolled along a precut pattern and controlled the movement of the cutting tool along the stock. The device, a fundamental contribution to the development of machine tools, made possible the manufacture of large numbers of accurate copies in a short time and thus was the necessary tool that implemented Eli Whitney's earlier notion of interchangeable precision parts as the basis for mass production. Blanchard's invention was held in such high regard that, despite technical errors in his patent and other problems, he was given special consideration by Congress. He built a steam automobile in 1825 but failed to interest anyone in it, and he tried unsuccessfully to promote the construction of a railroad in New York. He later devoted himself to steam navigation, designing and building several types of boats, including stern-wheel shallow-draft vessels of a kind afterward in general use on Western rivers. Blanchard died in Boston on April 16, 1864.

Bland, James A. (1854–1911), musician and composer. Born on October 22, 1854, in Flushing, New York, Bland grew up there and in Washington, D.C., where his father was in government service. During his youth he served for a time as a page in the House of Representatives and in 1873 graduated from Howard University. As a child he had taught himself to play the banjo and had often entertained at private parties; his love of the stage led him in 1875 to join the all-black minstrel troupe headed by Billy Kersands, and for several years he toured the United States with the Kersands troupe, the Original Georgia Minstrels, and other groups. For their performances he wrote a number of songs that attained great popularity, among them "Carry Me Back to Old Virginny," 1878; "Oh, Dem Golden Slippers," 1879; and "In the Evening by the Moonlight," 1879. In 1881 he traveled to England with the Callender-Haverly minstrel show, and the success of his songs there prompted him to remain in that country, where he was soon acclaimed "Prince of the Negro Songwriters." At his peak he gave a command performance for Queen Victoria. After a few years, however, his popularity waned along with that of minstrel music, and in 1901 he returned to the United States. He worked for a time in Washington ·and then moved to Philadelphia, where he died in poverty and obscurity on May 5, 1911. It was not until 1939 that his unmarked grave in Merion, Pennsylvania, was located and a headstone erected by the American Society of Composers, Authors and Publishers (ASCAP), by which he was credited with having written several hundred songs. In 1940 "Carry Me Back to Old Virginny" was adopted as the state song of Virginia.

Blanda, George Frederick (1927–), football player. Born in Youngwood, Pennsylvania, on September 17, 1927, Blanda was an outstanding high-school athlete, starring on the football and basketball teams and constituting his school's entire track and field team. He entered the University of Kentucky in 1945 and there developed into a highly skilled quarterback; on graduating in 1949 he was signed by the Chicago Bears. Though constantly called on for kicking duties he was unable to capture the starting quarterback spot, despite several spectacular performances in relief, until 1952, when he led the National Football League (NFL) in pass attempts and completions. An injury in 1954 sent him back to the sidelines, however, where he remained, except for occasional relief work and for kicking. As a kicker he scored 88 field goals and succeeded in 247 of 250 conversion attempts (including 156 in a row), for a team-record scoring total of 511 points in 10 years with the Bears. After an inactive season in 1959 Blanda was traded in 1960 to the Houston Oilers of the new American Football League (AFL) and there quickly hit his stride as starting quarterback. Three division titles and two league championships followed as Blanda led the AFL in passing in 1961, 1963, 1964, and 1965, played in four AFL all-star games, and continued to score on his kicking. In 1967, at the already remarkable age of forty, he was traded to the Oakand Raiders, where he again became relief quarterback. It was in that capacity that in 1970, the year the NFL and the AFL merged, he came forward in midseason to lead the Raiders from what seemed a certain second-division finish into the conference play-offs; in five consecutive games his touchdown passes and field goals—many late in the fourth quarter and one a 48-yard kick with 3 seconds left to play—earned victories that won the team a divisional championship. He finished the season with 29 pass completions in 55 attempts, including 6 for touchdowns; 36 of 36 conversions; and 16 of 29 field goals. He was widely honored as American Conference player of the year. With the 1971 season, during which he scored on 32 out of 58 passes attempted, 41 of 42 conversions, and 15 of 22 field goals, Blanda became the top scorer in professional football history. He finally retired in 1976 with a record 26 seasons and 342 games to his credit and a career total of 2002 points.

Blanding, Sarah Gibson (1898–), educator. Born on November 22, 1898, near Lexington, Kentucky, Miss Blanding graduated from the New Haven Normal School of Gymnastics (now Southern Connecticut State College) in 1919 and then continued her education part time while teaching physical education at the University of Kentucky. In 1923 she was awarded her B.A. by Kentucky and named acting dean of women, becoming the youngest university dean in the nation. She pursued further studies at Columbia University (M.A., 1926) and at the London School of Economics and in 1929 returned to Kentucky as dean of women and assistant professor of political science; she was promoted to associate professor in 1937. In 1941 she moved to Cornell University to become director of the New York State College of Home Economics and the following year was appointed its dean. During World War II, while overseeing the college's considerable contributions to the home-front war effort, Miss Blanding served also as director of the human nutrition division of the New York State Emergency Food Commission, as the sole woman member of the war department's Joint Army and Navy Committee on Welfare and Recreation, and on several other state and national boards. Her reputation as an administrator of unusually high caliber led to her selection in 1946 as president of Vassar College, the first woman to head the prestigious institution. In the same year she further broke precedent by opening the college to men in order to help accommodate the flood of veterans returning to school. Miss Blanding remained at Vassar until her retirement as president emeritus in 1964. She subsequently served as trustee of and adviser to numerous educational institutions and organizations.

Blatchford, Samuel (1820–1893), justice of the Supreme Court. Born in New York City on March 9, 1820, Blatchford graduated from Columbia College in 1837 and, having served four years as William H. Seward's secretary (1838–1842), was admitted to the bar in 1842. Over the next 25 years he practiced successfully, first with his father, later with Seward, and later still with his own law firm in New York City, and he became a noted authority on maritime law. In 1867 he was appointed a federal district judge for southern New York by President Ulysses S. Grant. In 1872 he became a circuit judge and in 1882 President Chester A. Arthur elevated him to the Supreme Court. In more than 400 opinions from that bench Blatchford built a reputation for great learning and insight and for remarkable clarity of thought. He was particularly expert in matters of patent law and his influence helped shape legislation in that field. He died in Newport, Rhode Island, on July 7, 1893.

Bliss, Tasker Howard (1853–1930), soldier and diplomat. Born on December 31, 1853, in Lewisburg, Pennsylvania, Bliss transferred in his second year from the University of Lewisburg (now Bucknell University) to West Point, from which he graduated in 1875. After a year of service with the artillery he returned to West Point as an instructor, remaining for four years, and then served at various army posts. Fom 1885 to 1888 he taught military science at the Naval War College and in 1888 became aide-de-camp to the commanding general of the army, John M. Schofield, holding the position until the latter's retirement in 1895. Though still only a captain, he then became a special assistant to the secretary of war and in 1897 military attaché at the U.S. legation in Madrid. At the outbreak of the Spanish-American War he was recalled, promoted to major, and appointed chief of staff to Gen. James H. Wilson in the Puerto Rico campaign. Late in 1898 he was placed in charge of the corrupt Cuban customs service and there established high standards of honesty and efficiency. In 1902, by which time Bliss was a brigadier general, he was called to Washington to advise Secretary of War Elihu Root on the establishment of a general staff system. Later in the year he returned to Cuba to negotiate a reciprocity treaty for Secretary of State John M. Hay. He became first commandant of the newly established Army War College in 1903, and two years later he began four years of service in the Philippines. Upon his return to the United States in 1909 he was again briefly commandant of the Army War College and then served as commanding officer of various army departments and as assistant chief of staff, receiving in 1915 promotion to major general. Shortly after the United States entered World War I he became chief of staff and was retained in that post beyond regular retirement age by special order of President Woodrow Wilson. Exercising his great administrative abilities to their utmost, he transformed the army from a small peacetime organization into a huge war machine; in addition he represented the United States on the supreme war council of the Allies, lending strong support there to the unified-command plan, the use of U.S. troops as a separate force, Wilson's Fourteen Points, and the idea of the League of Nations. At the war's end he was a delegate to the Versailles Peace Conference. After his retirement with the brevet rank of general he served as governor of the U.S. Soldiers' Home in Washington from 1920 to 1927. Bliss died in Washington, D.C., on November 9, 1930.

Blitzstein, Marc (1905–1964), composer. Born in Philadelphia on March 2, 1905, Blitzstein early displayed considerable talent as a pianist and had already appeared as a soloist with the Philadelphia Orchestra when he entered the University of Pennsylvania in 1921. He left after two years and devoted himself to studies in music and composition, attending Curtis Institute of Music during 1924–1926 and later studying in Paris and Berlin under Nadia Boulanger ad Arnold Schönberg. His works, which included orchestral, chamber, choral, and stage pieces such as *Jig Saw*, a ballet, 1927; *The Condemned*, 1933; and *Children's Cantata*, 1935, received considerable attention in avant-garde circles and he was particularly applauded for his efforts to create an American form of opera in *Triple Sec*, 1928, *Parabola and Circula*, 1929, and others. Widespread popular success did not come until 1937;

then working with Orson Welles in the Federal Theatre Project of the Works Progress Administration (WPA), he wrote a bluntly proletarian and anticapitalist musical play, *The Cradle Will Rock*. Authorities in the WPA canceled the production, whereupon it was staged by Welles elsewhere, without scenery and almost without cast, but with enthusiastic audiences. He followed with *No for an Answer*, 1939, in much the same vein of populist radicalism. While serving in the Army Air Force during World War II Blitzstein wrote *Freedom Morning*, 1943, a choral work dedicated to Negro troops, and shortly after the war composed his *Airborne Symphony*, 1946. *Regina*, 1949, an opera based on Lillian Hellman's *Little Foxes*, was a popular success, as were *Reuben, Reuben*, 1951, *Juno*, 1959 (from Sean O'Casey's *Juno and the Paycock*), and others, but his greatest triumph was his translation and adaptation of Bertolt Brecht and Kurt Weill's *Die Dreigroschenoper* as *The Threepenny Opera*; after a premier at Brandeis University in 1952 it opened in an off-Broadway theater in 1954 for a record-breaking six-year New York run of 2,611 performances. Blitzstein also wrote a large amount of incidental music for motion pictures and was at work on an opera based on the Sacco-Vanzetti case that had been commissioned by the Metropolitan Opera when he was beaten to death by holdup men in Martinique, in the West Indies, on January 22, 1964.

Bloch, Ernest (1880–1959), composer. Born on July 24, 1880, in Geneva, Switzerland, Bloch began his formal study of music at fourteen with Émile Jacques-Dalcroze; he studied violin for a time under Ernest Reyer and Eugène Ysaÿe, but at length abandoned that instrument to devote himself to the study of composition with François Rasse at the Brussels Conservatory and with Ivan Knorr at Frankfurt. Financial difficulties forced him to return to Geneva in 1904 to work in his father's clock shop, but in his spare time he continued to compose, lectured on metaphysics at the University of Geneva, and in 1909 and 1910 conducted concert series. Despite the excellence of such early pieces as the songs of his *Historiettes au Crépuscule* and *Hiver-Printemps*, a tone poem, Bloch did not come to general notice until the 1910 performance of his opera *Macbeth* at the Opéra-Comique in Paris. With that, and the premiere of his Symphony in C-Sharp Minor (composed in 1902) in the same year, he was able to give full time to music. From 1911 to 1915 he taught composition and aesthetics at the Geneva Conservatory while producing such works as *Two Psalms*, *Trois Poèmes Juifs*, and *Psalm 22*, his earliest effort in what became his major musical field—the embodiment of the ethnic consciousness and spirit of the Jewish people in music. In 1916 he came to the United States as conductor for Maud Allan's dance troupe; the bankruptcy of the troupe left him stranded and he settled in New York City, where during the next year premiere performances of his First String Quartet,

Trois Poèmes Juifs, the *Israel* symphony, and the cello rhapsody *Schelòmo* were given. Bloch taught at the Mannes Music School from 1917 to 1920, was a founder of the Cleveland Institute of Music, which he directed from 1920 to 1925, and directed the San Francisco Conservatory from 1925 to 1930. He became a U.S. citizen in 1924. His symphonic rhapsody *America* won a *Musical America* competition in 1928, and he wrote the *Baal Shem Suite* and several non-Hebraic pieces during the later 1920s as well. A private endowment in 1930 allowed him to return to Switzerland to work there and in Italy on his monumental *Sacred Service,* completed in 1933. After his return to the United States in 1939 he taught at the University of California during the summers and, from 1941 onwards, spent the rest of his time in near-seclusion at his home in Agate Beach, Oregon. Among his later works of particular note were *Symphonic Suite; A Voice in the Wilderness,* for cello; *Rhapsodie Hebraïque;* and *Last Poems,* for flute. Bloch died in Portland, Oregon, on July 15, 1959.

Bloch, Felix (1905–   ), physicist. Born in Zurich, Switzerland, on October 23, 1905, Bloch took his Ph.D. in physics from the University of Leipzig in 1928. During the next several years he worked in a number of major physics laboratories in Europe with such men as Werner Heisenberg, Neils Bohr, and Enrico Fermi, concerning himself with problems in the fields of solid state physics, magnetism, and solid-particle interactions. In 1934 he came to the United States to join the faculty of Stanford University. Since the discovery of the neutron in 1932 he had been interested in the problem of measuring its magnetic moment, and at Stanford, with Luis W. Alvarez of the University of California, Berkeley, he succeeded in 1939 in making the determination, using a method he devised for polarizing a neutron beam. During World War II he worked on the atomic-bomb project at Los Alamos, New Mexico, and in 1944–1945 with a Harvard team investigating countermeasures to radar. Returning to Stanford, he began developing a notion that had first come to him in the radio laboratory at Harvard. He soon found that by imposing two magnetic fields, one strong and constant and one weak and oscillating, on a substance—he used water—he could, through radio-detection techniques, measure the magnetic moment of the atomic nuclei in the substance. This method, nuclear induction, opened up the field of magnetic-resonance spectroscopy that made possible new studies of atomic and molecular binding. For his work Bloch was awarded the 1952 Nobel Prize for Physics jointly with Edward M. Purcell of Harvard, who had independently achieved the same results. During 1954–1955 Bloch served as director of the Conseil Européen de la Recherche Nucléaire, a 12-nation cooperative research project in Geneva, Switzerland. He afterward returned to Stanford to continue his investigations into nuclear and molecular structure.

Bloch, Konrad (1912–   ), biochemist. Born on January 21, 1912, in Neisse, Germany, Bloch graduated from the Technische Hochschule in Munich in 1934 and, having come to the United States in 1936, took his Ph.D. from Columbia University in 1938. He remained at Columbia as an instructor and later associate professor of biochemistry until 1946, becoming a naturalized citizen in 1944 and doing work for the Office of Scientific Research and Development during World War II. From 1946 to 1954 he taught at the University of Chicago and in 1954 became Higgins Professor of Biochemistry at Harvard. Throughout his career Bloch was interested principally in learning the mechanisms by which highly complex molecules, such as the steroids and fatty acids, are synthesized in the body. In particular he investigated the production of cholesterol, a steroid alcohol found in all animal cells. After determining that the liver is the main site of cholesterol synthesis, he used isotopic tracers to show that the acetate ion from acetic acid is the fundamental molecule. Over a period of many years he traced the entire process of synthesis through 36 steps, from acetic acid, $C_2H_4O_2$, through squalene, $C_{30}H_{50}$, a key intermediary, to cholesterol, $C_{27}H_{45}OH$. Bloch's work opened up many new avenues of approach in the investigation of the function of cholesterol and the precise nature of its involvement in atherosclerosis and heart disease. It also had implications for the study of steroid hormones derived from cholesterol. Jointly with Feodor Lynen of Germany, who had made important contributions while working along similar lines, Bloch was awarded the 1964 Nobel Prize for Medicine and Physiology. He continued afterward to pursue studies at Harvard of such topics as peptide bond formation and the biosynthesis of olefinic fatty acids.

Block, Herbert Lawrence (1909–   ), "Herblock," editorial cartoonist. Born on October 13, 1909, in Chicago, Block early displayed sufficient talent at drawing to win a scholarship to the Art Institute of Chicago at the age of twelve. In 1929, after two years at Lake Forest College, he joined the *Chicago Daily News* and, under the pen name of "Herblock," began drawing cartoons for the editorial page. Four years later he moved to Cleveland to work for the Newspaper Enterprise Association. In 1942 he won a Pulitzer Prize for his work in the previous year. From 1943 to 1945 he served in the army's information and education division, and in 1946 he joined the *Washington* (D.C.) *Post.* From that base his cartoons were syndicated to some 200 newspapers around the country. One of the few editorial cartoonists to work from a clear, consistent political philosophy, Herblock won wide praise for his incisive commentaries on governmental bureaucracy, porkbarrel politicking, and illiberal demagoguery. His scathing attacks on Sen. Joseph R. McCarthy's smear campaign against supposed subversives were particularly notable and were made all the more remarkable for the comparative national silence of intimidation in which they appeared. In 1952 a collection of his cartoons was published as *The Herblock Book*. His work was widely exhibited, appearing in the Corcoran Gallery and the National Gallery of Art, both in Washington, D.C., and in the gallery of the Associated American Artists in New York. In 1954 he won a second Pulitzer Prize. Other collections of his cartoons included *Herblock's Here and Now*, 1955; *Herblock's Special for Today*, 1958; *Straight Herblock*, 1964; *The Herblock Gallery*, 1968; and *Herblock's State of the Union*, 1972.

Bloomer, Amelia Jenks (1818–1894), social reformer. Born in Homer, New York, on May 27, 1818, Miss Jenks was educated in a local school and for several years thereafter taught school and tutored pupils privately. In 1840 she married Dexter C. Bloomer, a Quaker newspaper editor of Seneca County, through whom she became interested in public affairs. She began contributing articles to newspapers on various topics. Mrs. Bloomer attended but took no part in the Seneca Falls convention organized by Elizabeth Cady Stanton and Lucretia Mott in 1848; in the following year, however, she began a newspaper for women—probably the first to be edited entirely by a woman—the *Lily*, and opened it to women's-rights advocates as well as temperance reformers. Although she had been rather slow to embrace the cause of women's rights, by 1853 she had become quite active—making speaking appearances in New York City and elsewhere. She became involved in a dress-reform movement as well when she began wearing full-cut trousers under a short skirt in public, attracting considerable ridicule for appearing in the costume, which came to be called "bloomers." The episode had the unfortunate effect of distracting attention from her reform efforts but she continued to publish the *Lily* in Seneca Falls, where she was also deputy postmistress, and later in Mt. Vernon, Ohio. In 1854 she and her husband moved to Council Bluffs, Iowa, and she sold the newspaper. Her interest in reform, expressed in writing and lectures, continued until her death in Council Bluffs on December 30, 1894.

Bloomfield, Leonard (1887–1949), linguist. Born on April 1, 1887, in Chicago, Bloomfield graduated from Harvard in 1906 and did graduate work at the University of Wisconsin and the University of Chicago, taking his Ph.D. from Chicago in 1909. After teaching at the universities of Wisconsin, Cincinnati, and Illinois, he pursued further studies in philology at the universities of Leipzig and Göttingen in 1913–1914. He then taught, in various combinations, courses in German, philology, and linguistics at the University of Illinois until 1921, at Ohio State University from 1921 to 1927, and at the University of Chicago from 1927 to 1940. In 1940 he became Sterling Professor of Linguistics at Yale, a position he held until his death. In developing a theory of and an approach to the general study of language, Bloomfield took inspiration from the work of Franz Boas on the Algonkian Indian language and from John B. Watson's behaviorist psychology. Dismissing explanations of language that depended on the postulation of unobservable mental events, he sought to erect a structural theory that described simply and clearly the actual linguistic data at hand. This scientific rigor proved highly fruitful and his major work, *Language*, 1933, was quickly recognized as perhaps the most important and influential contribution to linguistics since the early nineteenth century. During World War II he helped organize language-instruction schools for the armed services. Basing the schools' method on his belief that the student must learn to speak a language before learning to write it, he developed a system of intensive training that successfully taught thousands of people in a remarkably short time. Bloomfield died in New Haven, Connecticut, on April 18, 1949.

Blount, William (1749–1800), public official. Born in Bertie County, North Carolina, on March 26, 1749, Blount enlisted in the state militia during the Revolution, but little else is known of his early life. After the war, however, he was in the public eye. Between 1780 and 1789 he served a total of six terms in one or the other house of the North Carolina legislature, three times as delegate to Congress under the Articles of Confederation, as a member of the Constitutional Convention of 1787, and as a member of the North Carolina convention that ratified the Constitution. Failing to win election to the Senate in 1789, he sought and won in 1790 appointment by President George Washington as governor of the Southwest Territory, comprising the trans-Allegheny lands ceded by North Carolina to the federal government. He conducted an effective and popular administration and, after presiding over the convention called in 1796 to organize the territory as the state of Tennessee, was elected one of its first two senators. Soon afterward financial problems led him to enter into, or perhaps to instigate, a somewhat obscure conspiracy that was apparently aimed at raising the value of certain Western lands. The idea was to organize an irregular armed force among the frontiersmen and Indians and, with the aid of a British fleet, to drive the Spanish out of Florida and Louisiana. A letter from Blount to a coconspirator among the Cherokees found its way to President John Adams, however, and was forwarded by him to the Senate. By an all but unanimous vote Blount was expelled from that body in July 1797. He returned to Tennessee and the following year was elected to the state legislature, where he became president of the senate. He died in Knoxville a short time later, on March 21, 1800. It is possible that the Blount Conspiracy had some connection with that of Aaron Burr a few years later.

B.L.T., *see* Taylor, Bert Leston

Bly, Nellie, *see* Seaman, Elizabeth Cochrane

Blythe, Herbert see Barrymore, Maurice

Blythe, Vernon, see Castle, Vernon Blythe

Boas, Franz (1858–1942), anthropologist. Born in Minden, Germany, on July 9, 1858, Boas was educated at the universities of Heidelberg, Bonn, and Kiel. In 1883–1884 he was a member of a German expedition to the Arctic; the studies on Eskimo life he made on this journey settled his interests for life. In 1886 he made his first trip to the Pacific Northwest to begin work on his lifelong specialty, the study of the Kwakiutl and other Indian tribes of the region. In 1888 he joined the faculty of Clark University and in 1896 that of Columbia University, where he remained for the rest of his life. He became Columbia's first professor of anthropology and created one of the first and one of the leading anthropology departments in the nation. From 1901 to 1905 he was curator of anthropology at the American Museum of Natural History. Instead of engaging in anthropological theorizing in the fashion of the nineteenth century, Boas carefully accumulated vast amounts of data in the field; on the basis of this information he was able to make valuable and original contributions to linguistics, anthropometry, and cultural anthropology. Probably his greatest achievement was destroying the quasi-scientific justifications for racism which were then subscribed to by a large portion of the world's people. Theories of innate racial differences were exposed as entirely specious by his carefully compiled and documented observations. Among his major written works were *The Mind of Primitive Man*, 1911; *Anthropology and Modern Life*, 1928; and *Race, Language and Culture*, 1940. He died in New York City on December 21, 1942.

Bodenheim, Maxwell (1893–1954), author and poet. Born in Hermanville, Mississippi, on May 26, 1893, Bodenheim received little or no formal schooling. Soon after serving a stint in the army he moved to Chicago and came in contact with the leading literary figures there—among them Carl Sandburg, Ben Hecht, and Harriet Monroe, who published his earliest poems in her *Poetry* magazine in 1914. After a few years he went to New York City and became known as the "Bard of Greenwich Village" and one of the leaders of bohemian society. His first volume of verse, *Minna and Myself*, appeared in 1918 and was followed by *Advice*, 1920; *Introducing Irony*, 1922; *The Sardonic Arm*, 1923; *Against This Age*, 1925; and others. Marked by a conspicuously mannered use of language, his poetry moved from an early imagism to a later involvement in social consciousness. He also wrote a number of plays, among them *The Master-Poisoner*, 1918, with Ben Hecht, volumes of essays, and several novels, including *Blackguard*, 1923; *Crazy Man*, 1924; *Replenishing Jessica*, 1925, which was suppressed for obscenity; *Ninth Avenue*, 1926, in which he supposedly avenged a portrait of himself in Hecht's *Count Bruga*; *Georgie May*, 1927; *Sixty*

Seconds, 1929; *Naked on Roller Skates*, 1931; *Run, Sheep, Run*, 1932; *New York Madness*, 1933; and others. Though he was regarded as something of an enfant terrible during the 1920s, and despite his importance in the literary avant-garde of the day, his work later fell into nearly complete disregard. During 1938–1940 he worked in the Federal Writers' Project, being dismissed finally for allegedly having Communist connections. Bodenheim's last years were spent in abject poverty; he and his wife were found murdered in their shabby, heatless room in New York City on February 6, 1954.

Bogart, Humphrey DeForest (1899–1957), actor. Born in New York City on December 25, 1899, Bogart was the son of socially prominent parents. He attended Phillips Academy in Andover, Massachusetts, for a time and in 1917 joined the navy. After the war he returned to New York, where a job in the office of a theatrical producer led eventually to his appearance on the stage in 1922. For years he played mainly in drawing-room comedies, though during the early 1930s he made a few Westerns for Fox Studios. In 1934, however, he won the role of the sinister Duke Mantee in Robert E. Sherwood's *The Petrified Forest*; the play and Bogart were successful and he was starred in the movie version made two years later. From that time on he was a film star, appearing more often than not in "tough guy" roles, as in *San Quentin*, 1937; *King of the Underworld*, 1939; *High Sierra*, 1941; *The Maltese Falcon*, 1942 (in which he played Dashiell Hammett's Sam Spade); *Casablanca*, 1942; *To Have and Have Not*, 1944, the first of his movies with Lauren Bacall, whom he later married; *The Big Sleep*, 1946; *Key Largo*, 1948; and *The Treasure of the Sierra Madre*, 1948. In many of his later films Bogart was able to break the bonds of type casting and play more sympathetic roles, as in *The African Queen*, 1951, with Katharine Hepburn, for which he won an Academy Award. In 1954 he played the psychopathic Captain Queeg in *The Caine Mutiny*; his final film, *The Harder They Fall*, was released in 1956. He died on January 14, 1957. During his later years and even after his death the audience for his films of the 1940s was undiminished; frequently revived, the films were taken up with renewed interest by succeeding generations of filmgoers, almost to the point of making "Bogey"—or his image—into a major folk figure.

Bok, Edward William (1863–1930), editor and author. Born on October 9, 1863, in Den Helder, the Netherlands, of a distinguished Dutch family, Bok was brought to New York City in 1870. He entered school without knowing a word of English but learned rapidly. Working at various jobs to assist his family, he saved lunch money to purchase an encyclopedia of biography and learned to his satisfaction that many notable men had risen from modest beginnings. In 1882 he began working for publishing companies, first Henry

Holt & Company, then, two years later, Charles Scribner's Sons. At the same time he edited the *Philomathean Review* for Plymouth Church in Brooklyn, of which Henry Ward Beecher was pastor. Writers and politicians with whom he came in contact through his hobby of collecting autographs contributed articles to the *Review*, which became the *Brooklyn Magazine* in 1884. To distribute a weekly column by Beecher, the youthful editor began a newspaper syndicate in 1886. He also put together for his Bok Syndicate a women's page, the famous "Bok page," as well as a column of letters and notes about authors and books, "Bok's Literary Leaves." In 1887 he became advertising manager of *Scribner's Magazine*. Upon the invitation of Cyrus H. K. Curtis he became editor of the *Ladies' Home Journal* in 1889, despite the advice of many of his friends. His subsequent great success was born of industry, intelligence, and creativity. Uncertain of the interests of his female readers, he solicited their ideas for new features, inaugurated personal-advice columns, features on child care, health, and religion, and printed stories and essays by such writers as Mark Twain, Bret Harte, and Rudyard Kipling. He dealt with previously untouchable subjects such as venereal disease, crusaded for wildlife conservation, improvement in Pullman-car facilities, and civic reform, and presented views on woman suffrage. Color reproductions of art masterpieces frequently appeared in the magazine, the circulation of which reached two million before Bok retired in 1919. Thereafter he wrote many books, including his famous autobiography, *The Americanization of Edward Bok*, 1920, which won a Pulitzer Prize. He provided funds for important awards in the fields of public service and citizenship, world peace, and education, and endowed several educational institutions. He died at his home near Lake Wales, Florida, on January 9, 1930, and was buried at the base of the famous "Singing Tower" carillon that he had built there the year before.

Bolden, Buddy (1868?–1931), musician. Born in New Orleans, probably in 1868, Charles Bolden became a barber and for a time published a small newspaper. Few other details of his early life are known, but by 1895 he had become a cornet player and the leader of one of the most popular bands in New Orleans. In constant demand at functions of all kinds, particularly at the regular Sunday gatherings in Lincoln Park, he reputedly had on occasion as many as six or seven groups playing at once in various places in the city, with himself dashing from one to another. Tradition has it that he was a drinker and womanizer of heroic stature and was idolized by virtually the entire black community of the city. It was his music, however, that earned him a place in memory, for he is credited with originating jazz. Almost nothing specific is known of his music beyond the fact that he used blues melodies extensively and that he numbered among his standards "If You Don't Like My Potatoes, Why Do

You Dig So Deep?" "Make Me a Pallet on the Floor," and "Bucket's Got a Hole in It." It is likely that he drew also on the rhythms of ragtime and the harmonies of gospel songs; combining these elements with the instrumentation of a brass band, he produced a musical form that was altogether new and infinitely exciting. The form lived after him through the men he inspired—Bunk Johnson (who for a time played in the Bolden band), Joe "King" Oliver, Louis Armstrong, and others. Bolden never recorded his music; all that remains is legend. After several years of growing mental instability he broke down entirely in 1907. He was committed to the East Louisiana State Hospital in New Orleans in that year and remained there until his death on November 4, 1931.

Bonaparte, Charles Joseph (1851–1921), public official and reformer. Born in Baltimore on June 9, 1851, the grandson of Elizabeth Patterson Bonaparte, he graduated from Harvard in 1872 and from the Harvard Law School in 1874 and entered practice in his native city. Financially independent, he was able to select those cases that particularly appealed to his sense of justice. At the same time he became active in various reform movements, helping found and subsequently serving as chairman of the Baltimore Reform League. For the Maryland Civil Service Reform League he established a periodical, *The Civil Service Reformer*, and in 1881 he joined in organizing the National Civil Service Reform League. His work in this field eventually brought him into association with Theodore Roosevelt, then a member of the U.S. Civil Service Commission. Roosevelt was deeply impressed by Bonaparte's energy, intelligence, and high principles and, upon becoming President, lost little time in enlisting his talents in the service of the federal government. From 1902 to 1904 Bonaparte was a member of the Board of Indian Commissioners; in 1905 he was named secretary of the navy, occasioning considerable and largely droll public comment on his ancestry; and in 1906 he was appointed attorney general. In little more than two years in the latter post he carried through the antitrust suits begun by his predecessor and instituted a great many more, most notably that which resulted in 1911 in the dissolution of the old American Tobacco Company. After leaving the cabinet in 1909 he returned to Baltimore and his law practice; he served for a time as president of the National Municipal League, which he had helped found in 1894 as the mainstay in the fight against corruption in local government, and continued to work for reform at every level of government until his death in Baltimore on June 28, 1921.

Bonaparte, Elizabeth Patterson (1785–1879), socialite. Born on February 6, 1785, in Baltimore, Miss Patterson was the daughter of a wealthy merchant. Early noted for her wit and beauty, she charmed and married Jérôme Bonaparte, brother of France's Emperor Napoleon I, when he visited the United States in 1803. The marriage was immediately disavowed by the emperor. In 1805 the couple sailed for France to attempt to persuade Napoleon to recognize Mrs. Bonaparte. She was denied permission to land anywhere in continental Europe and made her way to England instead, while Jérôme was persuaded by his brother to give her up. Napoleon had the marriage annulled by the council of state after Pope Pius VII refused an annulment and quickly married off Jérôme to Catherine of Württemberg and made him king of Westphalia. Mrs. Bonaparte returned to Baltimore and remained there until 1815, when she secured her own divorce through the Maryland legislature and then again went to Europe. With the handsome pension that had been granted her by Napoleon she became a figure in European society and educated her son, Jerome Napoleon, who was finally acknowledged as legitimate by Napoleon III but excluded from the succession. She returned to Baltimore in 1861 and lived quietly until her death on April 4, 1879.

Bond, George Phillips (1825–1865), astronomer. Born in Dorchester, Massachusetts (now part of Boston), on May 20, 1825, George Bond was the son of William C. Bond. He graduated from Harvard in 1845 and immediately joined the Harvard Observatory in Cambridge, Massachusetts, as assistant to his father. Together the Bonds made numerous contributions to astronomy. In 1848 they discovered Hyperion, the eighth satellite of Saturn, and two years later observed the third and innermost of the planet's rings, the so-called "crape." George Bond led in their pioneering application of the new art of photography to astronomy, particularly for the purpose of mapping, measuring, and determining brightness. They also developed a greatly improved recording chronograph. Other subjects of close study at the observatory included the Orion and Andromeda nebulas and comets, especially the Donati comet of 1858. Upon the death of William Bond in 1859, George succeeded to the directorship of the observatory, retaining the post until his own death just a few years later, on February 17, 1865.

Bond, Julian (1940–   ), civil rights leader and public official. Born in Nashville, Tennessee, on January 14, 1940, Julian Bond grew up there and in Lincoln, Pennsylvania. While attending Morehouse College in Atlanta, Georgia, from 1957 to 1961, he became involved in civil-rights activities, helping to found the Committee on Appeal for Human Rights and a short time later the Student Nonviolent Coordinating Committee (SNCC). Early in 1961 he left college to become communications director for SNCC; he also worked as a reporter and feature writer for the *Atlantic Inquirer*, becoming managing editor in 1963. In 1965 he was elected to the Georgia state legislature from a predominantly black district, but because of his endorsement of a SNCC statement strongly critical of the Vietnam War, he was refused his seat by a vote of 184 to 12. In two special elections in February and in November 1966, he was twice more elected and then was twice more refused the seat. After the Supreme Court declared his exclusion unconstitutional in December 1966, Bond was finally seated in the Georgia house of representatives in January 1967. At the Democratic national convention in Chicago in 1968 he headed an insurgent delegation of Georgia Loyal National Democrats that succeeded in winning half the state's representation from the strongly segregationist regular Democrats. He became the first black man to have his name placed in nomination for the vice-presidential candidacy of a major party, but he was obliged to withdraw his name because of the constitutional age requirement. Having attained a considerable national following, he continued to serve in the state legislature and to speak and write on behalf of civil rights and black participation in politics.

Bond, Thomas (1712–1784), physician. Born in Calvert County, Maryland, in 1712, Bond studied medicine in Annapolis and in Paris, entering practice in Philadelphia in 1734. He soon became one of the city's leading physicians. He devised a plan for a hospital modeled on English voluntary hospitals and for some time sought in vain for financial backing. Finally he secured the support of Benjamin Franklin for the project and with his aid the Pennsylvania Hospital, the first (and now oldest) in the nation, opened in 1752. Bond was a member of the staff for the rest of his life. As an original trustee of the College of Philadelphia (now the University of Pennsylvania), he took part in founding its medical school in 1765 and the next year delivered at the hospital the first course of clinical lectures in America. He was a founding member of the reorganized American Philosophical Society in 1768 and during the Revolution served on the Committee of Safety. Bond died in Philadelphia on March 26, 1784.

Bond, William Cranch (1789–1859), astronomer. Born on September 9, 1789, in Falmouth, Maine (now Portland), Bond grew up there and in Boston. Forced by family circumstances to leave school early and go to work in his father's clockmaking trade, he soon distinguished himself in constructing chronometers of the highest quality. Partly inspired by the solar eclipse of 1806, he took up on his own the study of astronomy and for more than 30 years, with whatever instruments he could make or afford to purchase, carried on constant and precise observations of a variety of celestial phenomena. He discovered in 1811 the first of the many comets credited to his observations. In 1815, while on a trip to Europe, he visited several observatories and made valuable notes for Harvard College, which had tentative plans to build an observatory. After a delay of three decades, Bond took charge of the project in 1839 and upon its completion in 1847, became the first director of the Harvard Observatory. He held the post, ably assisted after 1845 by his son, George Phillips Bond, until his death in Cambridge, Massachusetts, on January 29, 1859.

Bonehill, Capt. Ralph, *see* Stratemeyer, Edward

Bonfils, Frederick Gilmer (1860–1933), publisher. Born near Troy, Missouri, on December 21, 1860, Bonfils attended West Point for three years, worked in a New York City bank, and taught school in Colorado before returning to Missouri and engaging in the real-estate business. He profited handsomely from the opening to settlement of Oklahoma lands in 1889 and increased his fortune by operating the Little Louisiana Lottery in Kansas City, Kansas. In 1895 he traveled to Denver and there met Harry Heye Tammen (1856–1924). Born in Baltimore on March 6, 1856, Tammen had left school at the age of eight and had held various jobs before settling in Denver in 1880. There he worked as a bartender and was the proprietor of a small shop. In 1895 he prevailed upon Bonfils to join him in buying the *Evening Post.* Renaming it the *Denver Post,* they set out to make it one of the most sensational newspapers in the country. They adopted an editorial stance that proclaimed ceaselessly the public good and sought to achieve it by launching vigorous and, as often as not, scandalous attacks on public figures and officials of all kinds. Huge headlines, well-publicized controversies, and a generally theatrical approach to journalism enabled them to multiply the paper's circulation twentyfold in 12 years. Their crusades for or against sundry issues sometimes aroused violent reactions, and in 1900 they were both seriously wounded by an irate lawyer. In 1909 they founded the *Kansas City* (Missouri) *Post* and molded it along the same lines, but finding that city less given to the flamboyant than Denver, they finally sold it in 1922. The motto of the *Denver Post,* inscribed and gilded above the door, was "O Justice, when expelled from other habitations, make this thy dwelling place," a sentiment not infrequently rendered ironic by the methods of Bonfils and Tammen. Prominent among their scrapes with law and ethics was the nationally discussed revelation in 1924 that the *Post's* preliminary investigation into the doubtful dealings concerning Teapot Dome, begun two years earlier, had suddenly been dropped by the paper when an editorial gentlemen's agreement was reached with Harry F. Sinclair, one of those under suspicion in the case. Tammen died on July 19, 1924, after which Bonfils managed the *Post* alone. In his last years he conducted a vicious and protracted battle with Roy W. Howard's rival *Rocky Mountain News.* He died in Denver on February 2, 1933.

Bonner, Robert (1824–1899), publisher. Born on April 28, 1824, near Londonderry, Ireland, Bonner came to the United States in 1839 and learned printing and journalism in the office of the *Hartford Courant.* He moved to New York City in 1844 and opened his own print shop. Seven years later he bought the *New York Merchant's Ledger,* dropped the word *Merchant's* and made it into a family and story newspaper. His management of the *New York Ledger* (later the *Ledger Monthly*) was novel in a number of ways: He accepted no advertising, making his profit solely from circulation, which eventually reached nearly half a million; at the same time he advertised the *Ledger* heavily in other newspapers, often in startling ways, such as printing "Read the *New York Ledger*" over and over again for a full page. He paid high prices to secure the most popular contributors, including Edward Everett and Fanny Fern (Sara Payson Willis Parton). He conducted his personal life as idiosyncratically as he did his newspaper, and he was equally ingenious in publicizing it. He had a passionate interest in horses and racing; his stable was famous for including as many of the fastest horses as he could buy. The *Ledger* ceased publication upon Bonner's death in New York City on July 6, 1899.

Bonneville, Benjamin Louis Eulalie de (1796–1878), soldier. Born in or near Paris on April 14, 1796, Bonneville was the son of a prominent French radical. Among the close friends of the family were the Marquis de Lafayette, the Marquis de Condorcet, and especially Thomas Paine, whom they followed to the United States in 1803. Bonneville graduated from West Point in 1815 and after a few years of routine military assignments was sent to the frontier post of Fort Smith, Arkansas Territory, in 1821. Later transferred to Fort Gibson in what is now Oklahoma, he was put on detached duty in 1825 as aide to the visiting Lafayette; afterwards, promoted to captain, he returned to Fort Gibson and remained there until 1830. After securing financial backing in New York City he took a leave of absence from the army in 1832 for the stated purpose of exploration in the West. With a company of more than a hundred men he established himself on the Green River in Wyoming and attempted to break into the fur trade. Lack of experience was largely responsible for his failure and in 1835 he returned to the East to find that he had been dismissed from the army for overstaying his leave. Over some protest he won reinstatement from President Andrew Jackson in 1836. He later served in the Mexican War, during which he was promoted to lieutenant colonel. He retired in 1861 but soon returned to active duty; given the brevet rank of brigadier general in 1865, he retired permanently in the following year and returned to Fort Smith, where he died on June 12, 1878. Bonneville's fame rested on his journals, edited by an enthusiastic Washington Irving and published in 1837 as *The Adventures of Captain Bonneville, U.S.A., in the Rocky Mountains and the Far West.* Later critics pointed out that, in his assumed role of explorer, Bonneville discovered litle, owing in large part to the fact that his "exploration" expedition was in reality a commercial venture.

Bonney, William H. (1859–1881), "Billy the Kid," outlaw. Born on November 23, 1859, in New York City, Bonney moved with his family to Coffeyville, Kansas, in 1862. After the death of his father he accompanied his mother to Colorado and then to New Mexico, settling in Silver City in 1868. He had little schooling and by the age of twelve commonly passed his time gambling in saloons; he is said to have killed his first man at about that age. In 1876 he and a companion robbed and killed three Indians in Arizona, and for a year he ranged through the Southwest and into Mexico, committing similar crimes. In 1878 he became a leader of one faction in New Mexico's "Lincoln County War," one of the most famous of the Western cattle wars, and added several more names to his toll of slayings, among them that of Sheriff Jim Brady. In August a truce was arranged by the newly appointed governor, Lew Wallace; Wallace was unsuccessful, however, in persuading Billy to lay down his gun. Instead Bonney gathered a band of followers and set out on a spectacular career of killing and cattle rustling. In December 1880 Sheriff Pat F. Garrett fulfilled a campaign promise by capturing Billy. Convicted and sentenced to hang for the murder of Brady, the Kid escaped when under heavy guard, killing two deputies in the process, and remained at large for nearly seven weeks. Finally Garrett discovered him in Fort Sumner, New Mexico, on July 15, 1881, and fatally shot one of the West's most famous desperados, the smiling, cold-blooded, twenty-one-year-old killer of 21 men.

Boone, Daniel (1734–1820), frontiersman. Born on November 2, 1734, near present-day Reading, Pennsylvania, Boone probably had no formal education but did learn to read and write. By the age of twelve he was an expert hunter and trapper. He and his family moved in 1750 to North Carolina, where he worked for his father as a blacksmith. In 1755 he accompanied Gen. Edward Braddock's forces, which included George Washington, on an unsuccessful mission to capture Fort Duquesne from the French and escaped from the bloody ambush that ended the expedition. He first visited the Kentucky wilderness briefly in 1767 and in 1769 returned with his brother and several others for two years of hunting and trapping, during which he explored the region thoroughly. He had twice been captured by Indians but, as an employee of Richard Henderson's Transylvania Company, he brought a party of settlers and later his family to the land in 1775. He blazed an extension of the trail called the Wilderness Road over Cumberland Gap through the Allegheny Mountains; it eventually led to three Kentucky settlements, one of which was called Boonesborough (later Boonesboro). In 1776 Kentucky became a county of Virginia and Boone was named captain of militia. He spent most of his time fighting Indians, trapping, and hunting game for the settlements. He was kidnapped by the Shawnees and adopted by their chief in 1778,

but he escaped in time to warn Boonesborough of an impending attack and aid in its defense. In 1781 and 1787 he served in the Virginia legislature; in 1782 he was sheriff and deputy surveyor of Fayette County. His extensive land claims in Kentucky were never validated and in 1799, following his son Daniel Morgan Boone, he emigrated to Missouri, then Spanish territory. He remained in Missouri until his death in St. Charles County on September 26, 1820. His rank in American frontier history is a high one, for he was greatly influential in extending the new nation beyond the Alleghenies. In frontier legend he has no real rival; the publication by John Filson of *The Discovery, Settlement, and Present State of Kentucke,* 1784, which was claimed to be Boone's work and which contained an "Autobiography," marked the beginning of a continuing celebration of the great frontiersman. He was elected to the Hall of Fame in 1915.

Booth, Edwin Thomas (1833–1893), actor. Born on November 13, 1833, near Bel Air, Maryland, Edwin was the son of Junius Brutus Booth. He traveled with his father during childhood, made his debut in *Richard III* in Boston in 1849, and played minor roles supporting his father, in 1851 standing in for him in the character of Richard III. After the elder Booth's death in 1852, Edwin toured California, Australia, and Hawaii, beginning to win public acclaim in Sacramento in 1856. His style was patterned after his father's, but he had an individual flair for transmitting pathos and suspense. Triumphant appearances in major U.S. cities eventually established him as the foremost American actor of his day and a worthy successor to his father's mantle. After 1863 he co-managed the Winter Garden Theatre in New York, where he staged Shakespearian tragedies including *Hamlet, King Lear, Macbeth,* and *Othello.* The production of *Julius Caesar* starring him and his two brothers, Junius Booth and John Wilkes Booth, as well as his 100-night appearance as Hamlet, were milestones in American theater history. After the assassination of President Abraham Lincoln by his brother John, he retired from the stage until January 1866, when he returned to the Winter Garden as Hamlet. In 1867 the theater burned to the ground. He had built the Booth Theatre by February 1869 and there continued his brilliant career. Owing to poor business advice, the theater went bankrupt in 1874. He performed for nearly 20 years thereafter in the United States, the British Isles, and continental Europe, retaining a firm hold on his reputation and eventually restoring his fortune. In 1888 he founded and became the first president of the Players Club, in New York City. His final performance was as Hamlet in 1891 at the Brooklyn Academy of Music. He died in New York City on June 7, 1893. He was elected to the Hall of Fame in 1925.

Booth, John Wilkes (1838–1865), actor and assassin. Born in 1838 near Bel Air, Maryland, Booth was a son of Junius Brutus Booth and a brother of Edwin Booth. Educated sporadically in private academies, he made his stage debut at seventeen in Baltimore. He developed into a Shakespearian actor, and was given even better reviews than his brother by some critics. From the late 1850s his sympathies in the growing sectional conflict were strongly with the South. In 1859 he was a member of a Virginia militia company that, under the command of Col. Robert E. Lee, seized John Brown at Harpers Ferry, and during the Civil War he planned to kidnap President Abraham Lincoln. He and several conspirators were disappointed in their scheme when Lincoln failed to pass the spot where they expected to seize him on March 20, 1865. After the fall of Richmond and General Lee's surrender at Appomattox, Booth decided on assassination, enlisting one accomplice to murder Vice-President Andrew Johnson and another to kill Secretary of State William H. Seward. On the evening of April 14, 1865, Booth ascended the stairway to the President's box at Ford's Theater and shot Lincoln in the head. He leaped to the stage, crying *"Sic semper tyrannis!* The South is avenged!"* and escaped through the rear of the theater. His accomplices were unsuccessful in their assassination attempt, although Seward was badly beaten. Booth was not located until April 26, when he was found hiding in a barn near Bowling Green, Virginia, and was either killed by his captors or died by his own hand; the facts have never been ascertained. Several of his accomplices were hanged on July 7, 1865. A legend soon arose that Booth somehow miraculously escaped death and was wandering in Mexico, Texas, and Oklahoma. A man named John St. Helene, who committed suicide in Oklahoma in 1903, was believed by many to be Booth, and after his death St. Helene's body was mummified and exhibited in several states. As late as 1924 historians were still writing articles to disprove the myth of Booth's survival.

Booth, Junius Brutus (1796–1852), actor. Born in London on May 1, 1796, Booth early exhibited many remarkable talents and at seventeen chose the theater for a career. Appearances in numerous small theaters in England and on a tour of the Low Countries in 1814 gave him experience and training and he began to advance rapidly in his profession. He made his London debut in 1815 and after 1817, when at the Covent Garden Theatre he played Richard III, he quickly became the object of widespread public adulation, rivaling the reigning Edmund Kean for the title of England's leading tragedian. The debate between their respective followers often erupted into violence and marred more than a few of his and Kean's performances. Booth nonetheless appeared with Kean at the Drury Lane Theatre in several Shakesperian productions. In 1821 he emigrated to the United States and the next year settled on a farm, Tudor Hall, near Bel Air, Maryland. For 30 years thereafter he dominated the American stage, appearing regularly in Boston, New York, Baltimore, New Orleans (where his ability to play in French

made him a particular favorite), and other cities. During 1831 he managed the Adelphi Theatre in Baltimore, and in 1825–1826 and 1836–1837 he made tours of England. An actor of great power and ability, especially effective in portraying violent emotions and villainous characters, Booth remained popular until his death, although in later years his health declined seriously. Early in 1852 he and his son Edwin began a lengthy series of engagements in Sacramento and San Francisco; a brief engagement in New Orleans, undertaken on the return journey, proved too much for him and he died on November 30, 1852, aboard a steamboat en route home from Cincinnati.

Borach, Fannie, *see* Brice, Fannie

Borah, William Edgar (1865–1940), public official and political leader. Born near Fairfield, Illinois, on June 29, 1865, Borah completed less than a year at the University of Kansas. After reading law privately, he was admitted to the bar in Kansas in 1889. Three years later he moved to Boise, Idaho and soon involved himself in politics while becoming a prominent criminal and corporation lawyer. In 1906 he was elected as a Republican to the Senate, where he was to remain for the rest of his life. While Borah was nominally a Progressive Republican, initiating or supporting a great number of reform measures, he was best characterized as a political maverick. He supported President Theodore Roosevelt's industrial policies and led the campaigns for the Sixteenth and Seventeenth amendments; yet he often opposed conservation proposals, was cold to most of President Woodrow Wilson's domestic reform program, and was, before and during World War I, something of a jingoist. From the beginning of his bitter opposition to the League of Nations through the remainder of his career he was a strong isolationist; yet he was largely responsible for the Washington Disarmament Conference of 1921 and for the multilateral Kellogg-Briand Pact of 1928, and he consistently advocated U.S. recognition of the Soviet Union. As chairman of the Senate Foreign Relations Committee from 1924 to 1933 he fought foreign entanglements of all kinds while promoting voluntary cooperation and anticipating much of the later Good Neighbor policy of President Franklin D. Roosevelt. He supported most of the New Deal, although he led Senate opposition to the National Recovery Administration (NRA) and to President Roosevelt's plan to enlarge the Supreme Court. He favored the Neutrality Act of 1935 and remained a leading isolationist until his death in Washington, D.C., on January 19, 1940.

Borden, Gail (1801–1874), inventor. Born in Norwich, New York, on November 9, 1801, Borden moved with his family to Kentucky and later to Indiana Territory during his childhood and received only a little schooling. In his youth he taught school and worked as a surveyor, moving in 1822 to southern Mississippi and there continuing in both occupations. In 1829 he traveled west to join Stephen F. Austin's American colony in Texas, where, after a brief period as a farmer and stockraiser, he became the official surveyor. He was active in the early agitation for Texan independence, attending the San Felipe convention in November 1835 at which a provisional government was established and with his brother founding the *Telegraph and Texas Land Register*, a newspaper that played a vital role in promoting and unifying the revolutionary fervor of the American settlers. After the formation of the Republic of Texas Borden compiled the first topographic map of the territory and in 1838 surveyed and platted the site of the city of Galveston for Michel B. Menard's Galveston City Company. He became an agent for the company soon after the incorporation of Galveston in 1839 and remained in that post for some 12 years. As an early pioneer himself, Borden was familiar with the problems of carrying sufficient quantities of wholesome food while on the move and, with Western emigrants in mind, he set about seeking solutions. By 1851 he had developed a dried-meat biscuit that, although it won a gold medal at the Great Council Exhibition in London that year, was a commercial failure in the face of strong opposition from established army food contractors. He left Texas shortly thereafter and lived for a time with friends in a Shaker community in New Lebanon, New York, where he was inspired by their vacuum-pan method of making maple sugar to use a similar process to condense milk to an easily transportable state. He applied for a patent in 1853, received one, after extensive testing, in 1856, and in 1857 established the New York Condensed Milk Company (later, from 1899, the Borden Company) in Wassaic, New York. Not until the Civil War did he achieve much success, but then the great need for light, nourishing rations for the Union army created a huge demand for his product, and within a short time the general public took to it as well. Further experiments led to a patent in 1862 for a method of condensing fruit juices. Borden returned to Texas, and to the town named for him there, in 1861. In later years he was a leading advocate of sanitary dairying practices. He died in Borden on Janury 11, 1874.

Borden, Lizzie Andrew (1860–1927), accused murderess. Born on July 19, 1860, in Fall River, Massachusetts, Miss Borden was the daughter of a well-to-do businessman who married for a second time in 1865, three years after Lizzie's mother died. Tension grew between the new Mrs. Borden on the one side and Lizzie and her elder sister on the other, much of it seemingly arising from anxiety on the part of the girls as to the eventual disposition of Mr. Borden's wealth. While the problem remained unresolved, Lizzie became active in the affairs of her church and the Woman's Christian Temperance Union. By 1892 the family dissension was approaching a breaking point; on one occasion the elder Bordens suspected they were being poisoned, and at the same time Lizzie

expressed fears for her father's safety. On the morning of August 4, Mr. Borden left the house for a time; upon his return Lizzie told him that Mrs. Borden had gone to visit a friend. He fell asleep and a short time later Lizzie, claiming she had just come in from the barn, awoke the maid and cried that someone had killed her father. Mr. Borden's body was terribly mutilated about the head, apparently with an axe, and a subsequent search of the house revealed the body of Mrs. Borden upstairs, similarly mutilated. Examination showed her to have been killed more than a hour before her husband. Soon afterward Lizzie was found burning a dress in the kitchen stove. She was arrested and charged with both murders, but despite the burden of circumstantial evidence she was acquitted in a sensational trial in June 1893. She was nonetheless ostracized thereafter by the people of Fall River, where she continued to live until her death on June 1, 1927. The grisly murders inspired a great many books, both serious studies and fiction, and one immortal if slightly inaccurate quatrain: "Lizzie Borden took an axe / And gave her mother forty whacks; / And when she saw what she had done / She gave her father forty-one."

Borglum, Gutzon (1867–1941), sculptor. Born on March 25, 1867, near Bear Lake, Idaho Territory, John Gutzon de la Mothe Borglum was the son of Danish immigrant parents. After attending St. Mary's College, Xavier, Kansas, he studied art in San Francisco and then in Paris at the Académie Julien and the École des Beaux-Arts. He exhibited both paintings and sculptures at the Salon and became a close friend of Auguste Rodin. After a brief visit to New York City in 1893–1895 he set up a studio in London and there enjoyed considerable success, winning many commissions for murals and illustrations and holding a command exhibition for Queen Victoria. His work in all mediums was already noted for a distinctly American vitality when, after settling in New York City in 1901, he began to concentrate more and more on sculpture. His "Mares of Diomedes" was the first piece of American sculpture bought for the Metropolitan Museum of Art, and he followed with a rapid succession of works that won him wide admiration—bronze portraits of the Emperor Nero and of John Ruskin, larger figures of Abraham Lincoln, John P. Altgeld, Woodrow Wilson, and Thomas Paine, two equestrian statues of Gen. Philip H. Sheridan, the "Wars of America" group in Newark, New Jersey, the Twelve Apostles for the Cathedral of St. John the Divine in New York City, and the great head of Lincoln in the U.S. Capitol rotunda. The last piece suggested to the Daughters of the Confederacy the idea of a similar memorial to Robert E. Lee to be placed on Stone Mountain, Georgia. Borglum, captivated by the aesthetic effect of sheer volume, saw greater possibilities in the site, however, and soon evolved a design for a huge panoramic relief sculpture across 1300 feet of the mountain's face, showing Lee and other Confederate leaders at the head of some 2000 soldiers in procession. Money was collected and work begun; World War I interrupted the project, but in 1924 the mounted figure of Lee was unveiled. Work stopped the next year when Borglum resigned in a controversy over the handling of funds. He had already toured the Black Hills and selected Mount Rushmore as a site for a proposed South Dakota state memorial when he was officially commissioned by South Dakota to create the work in 1927. Two years later Congress voted to make the project a national memorial and appropriated funds for it. Borglum brought all his engineering genius to the vast work, developing totally new methods of stoneworking to meet the challenge. Conceived as a "shrine of democracy" that would commemorate the founding, expansion, preservation, and unification of the United States, the sculpture consisted of four 60-foot-high heads carved from the living rock— George Washington, unveiled in 1930; Thomas Jefferson, 1936; Abraham Lincoln, 1937; and Theodore Roosevelt, 1939. Borglum died in Chicago on March 6, 1941, leaving completion of the final details of the Mount Rushmore National Memorial to his son, Lincoln Borglum. After 40 years of dormancy, his design for a Confederate memorial at Stone Mountain was revived in the 1960s and work proceeded apace.

Boring, Edwin Garrigues (1886–1968), psychologist. Born in Philadelphia on October 23, 1886, Boring graduated from Cornell University in 1908 and, after periods as an apprentice engineer in a steel mill and as a schoolteacher, returned in 1910 to undertake graduate studies in psychology. Under the influence of Edward B. Titchener he became interested in experimental psychology and he remained throughout his career a champion of that branch over such rivals as the behaviorist and psychoanalytic schools. When he received his Ph.D. from Cornell in 1914 he had already been an instructor there for a year and he remained until 1917, when he entered the Psychological Service of the army. During 1918–1919 he helped edit the monumental *Psychological Examining in the U.S. Army*, 1921, and in 1919 accepted appointment as professor of experimental psychology at Clark University. In 1922 he moved to Harvard as an associate professor, becoming director of the psychology laboratory in 1924 and a full professor in 1928. Boring was more drawn to the professional and academic aspects of his field than to research and early gained wide recognition both as an influential figure in the American Psychological Association, of which he was president in 1928 and in whose growth and later reorganization he played a central role, and as an author and editor. His *History of Experimental Psychology*, 1929, was a major contribution to the field and long a standard text, as was its revised edition of 1950. He wrote also *The Physical Dimensions of Consciousness*, 1933; *Sensation and Perception in the History of Experimental Psychology*, 1942; a series of psychology primers, with M. Van de Water, for men in the armed

forces during World War II; *History, Science and Psychology*, 1966; and others. From 1925 to 1946 he was coeditor of the *American Journal of Psychology* and in 1955 he led in founding *Contemporary Psychology*, which he edited until 1961. In 1956 he was named Edgar Pierce Professor of Psychology at Harvard; the following year he retired. Boring's autobiography, *Psychologist at Large*, appeared in 1961. He died in Cambridge, Massachusetts, on July 1, 1968.

Borlaug, Norman Ernest (1914–   ), agronomist and plant geneticist. Born on March 25, 1914, near Cresco, Iowa, Borlaug graduated from the University of Minnesota with a degree in forestry in 1937 and, also working at various times with the U.S. Forest Service and as an instructor in the university, he took his Ph.D. in plant pathology there in 1941. For three years he engaged in research in plant pathology and pesticides for E.I. du Pont de Nemours & Company and then in 1944 was selected to join a team of agricultural specialists sent by the Rockefeller Foundation to work with the Mexican government in developing new agricultural practices and crops for that nation. Borlaug carried out long and arduous experiments in crop breeding, concentrating on varieties of wheat, in an effort to develop strains that could be grown successfully in the widely varied climates of Mexico. He succeeded in combining many desirable characteristics—high yield, shorter and stronger stalks capable of bearing the heavier heads, climatic adaptability—in hybrids that, with proper cultivation, vastly outproduced native types. His success in Mexico led to his being consulted by numerous other nations and to the rapid spread of the new agricultural technology in which he had pioneered into many parts of the underdeveloped world. Borlaug set up total agricultural programs involving new crop varieties, heavy mechanization, wide use of fertilizers and pesticides, close technical supervision, and the training of local specialists; the result, widely hailed as a "green revolution," opened the possibility of the eradication of endemic hunger in underdeveloped nations and provided hope and, more importantly, time for an eventual solution to the basic problem of population growth. For this work Borlaug was awarded the 1970 Nobel Peace Prize. In 1966 he became head of the International Maize and Wheat Improvement Center in Mexico.

Boucicault, Dion (1820?–1890), playwright and actor. Born in Dublin on December 26, in either 1820 or 1822, Dionysius Lardner Boucicault entered the University of London about 1836, but in 1837 began to act in country playhouses under the name of Lee Moreton. In 1840, again living in London, he offered his first play to the Covent Garden Theatre. It was turned down, but a second play, *London Assurance*, was produced in 1841 and was a great success. Subsequently he wrote *Old Heads and Young Hearts*, 1844, and adapted *Pauline*, in 1851, and *The Corsican Brothers*, in

1852, from Dumas, and *Louis XI* from Delavigne. In 1853 he emigrated to New York City, where his reputation was already established. Of numerous plays that he wrote for the American stage the most notable were *The Young Actress*, 1853, a light musical; *The Poor of New York*, 1857, a surface depiction of the panic of 1837; *Jessie Brown, or the Relief of Lucknow*, 1858, in which he acted; *The Octoroon*, 1859, a milestone in social drama with antislavery implications; and *The Collegians*, 1860. *The Collegians* was the first of several plays written for Laura Keene's theater, among them a number of Irish comedies, including *The Colleen Bawn*, 1860; *Arrah-na-Pogue*, 1864; *The O'Dowd*, 1873; and *The Shaughraun*, 1874. In 1858 Boucicault became part owner of a theater in Washington, D.C., and the next year he managed the Winter Garden Theatre in New York City. From 1862 to 1872 he lived in England, where he revised the script of *Rip Van Winkle* in 1865 for Joseph Jefferson. After 1872 he lived in New York City and at the time of his death on September 18, 1890, was teaching drama. Tremendously influential in the nineteenth-century American theater, he wrote more than 130 plays or adaptations and considerably deepened the treatment of the Irishman as a character. He is also credited with having originated the "long run" by establishing his plays in New York City, then taking them on tour with a different cast.

Bourke-White, Margaret (1906–1971), photographer. Born on June 14, 1906, in New York City, Margaret White studied at Columbia University, the University of Michigan, and Cornell University, graduating from Cornell in 1927. She had already taken up photography, first as a hobby and then on a free-lance professional basis, when on leaving Cornell she moved to New York City; there she quickly established herself as an architectural and industrial photographer. For her professional name she combined her own last name with her mother's maiden name (Bourke) to create the hyphenated form by which she was known thereafter. Her command of the camera brought her increasingly important commissions and from 1929 to 1933 she was an associate editor of *Fortune* magazine, in which many of her pictures were published. Several extensive tours of the Soviet Union resulted in the picture and text books *Eyes on Russia*, 1931; *Red Republic*, 1934; and *U.S.S.R., a Portfolio of Photographs*, 1934. In 1936 she became a member of the original staff of *Life* magazine, of which she remained an editor for 33 years and to which she contributed countless photographs and photo-essays, including the magazine's first cover illustration. With Erskine Caldwell, her husband from 1939 to 1942, she produced *You Have Seen Their Faces*, 1937, a study of the rural South; *North of the Danube*, 1939; and *Say! Is This the U.S.A.?*, 1941. From the outbreak of World War II in 1939 she traveled extensively in Europe, the Near East, and the Soviet Union, covering political and military events, and in 1942 she became the first woman to

be accredited as a war correspondent to the U.S. army. She was at the front in the North African and Italian campaigns and accompanied Gen. George S. Patton's 3rd Army into Germany in 1944, where she recorded on film the opening of Buchenwald and other concentration camps. Later she made photojournalistic studies in India, and in the 1950s was again a war correspondent during the Korean War. Other books of her photographs and text included *Shooting the Russian War*, 1942; *They Called It Purple Heart Valley*, 1944; *Dear Fatherland, Rest Quietly*, 1946; and *Halfway to Freedom: A Study of the New India*, 1949. Her autobiography, *Portrait of Myself*, appeared in 1963. In later years she was rendered inactive by chronic illness. She retired formally from *Life* magazine in 1969, and died in Stamford, Connecticut, on August 27, 1971.

Bourne, Randolph Silliman (1886–1918), critic. Born in Bloomfield, New Jersey, on May 30, 1886, Bourne, who was afflicted with a serious physical deformity, early displayed keen intelligence. Financial difficulties delayed the start of his college education until 1909, when he entered Columbia University. In an intellectual atmosphere dominated by Charles A. Beard, John Dewey, and Franz Boas, he rapidly developed a critical, often iconoclastic, outlook. In 1913, the year of his graduation, a series of articles he had written for the *Atlantic Monthly* was collected and published as *Youth and Life*, an expression of optimism in a coming social and cultural renaissance led by the youth of the country. During a year of travel in Europe he was both heartened by signs of a similar spirit he detected in some groups and dismayed by the growing militarism of others. Upon his return he became a regular contributor to the newly established *New Republic*; for it he wrote wide-ranging critical articles on literature, culture, and education. The approach of war, and the failure of the liberalism of Progressives that it betokened, drove him to a more extreme position. His pacificism estranged him from the editors of the *New Republic* and he began to contribute to the more radical *Masses* and *Seven Arts*. The suppression of dissident journals by war fever cut off Bourne's outlets. While at work on a novel and a major political treatise, he died on December 22, 1918, in New York City. Two volumes of his writings appeared posthumously, *Untimely Papers*, edited by J. Oppenheim, 1919; and *The History of a Literary Radical*, edited by Van Wyck Brooks, 1920.

Boutwell, George Sewall (1818–1905), public official. Born in Brookline, Massachusetts, on January 28, 1818, Boutwell began working as a clerk in Lunenberg, Massachusetts, at thirteen and four years later took a similar job in Groton, at the same time studying law on his own. He became active in Democratic politics and between 1842 and 1850 was seven times elected to the state legislature. His antislavery leanings attracted the support of Free-Soilers, with whose aid he was elected governor in 1851 and 1852. He finally broke with the regular Democratic party on the slavery issue and in 1855 helped organize the Republican party in his state. He also returned to the study of law, gaining admission to the bar in 1862. In that year he was appointed the first U.S. commissioner of internal revenue by President Abraham Lincoln, a post he filled capably during a short tenure. In March 1863 he resigned after his election to the House of Representatives. By that time Boutwell was identified with the Radical wing of the party; he served on the Joint Committee on Reconstruction and in 1867 was one of the floor leaders of the impeachment proceedings against President Andrew Johnson. In 1869 he was named secretary of the treasury by President Ulysses S. Grant, and he again served competently; it was he who on "Black Friday," September 24 of that year, released large amounts of government gold for sale, breaking the attempted cornering of the market by Jay Gould and Jim Fisk. Upon leaving the cabinet in 1873 he entered the Senate for a four-year term, after which he was appointed by President Rutherford B. Hayes to prepare the new edition of the *United States Revised Statutes*, which was issued in 1878. He then returned to the practice of law. Following the Spanish-American War he vigorously opposed annexation of the Philippines; he became the first president of the Anti-Imperialist League in 1898, holding the post until his death, and also returned to the Democratic party because of his views on the issue. In his later years he also published the most notable of his written works, *The Constitution of the United States at the End of the First Century*, 1895; *The Crisis of the Republic*, 1900; and *Reminiscences of Sixty Years in Public Affairs*, 1902. Boutwell died in Groton, Massachusetts, on February 27, 1905.

Bow, Clara (1905–1965), actress. Born on August 6, 1905, in Brooklyn, New York, Miss Bow went to Hollywood by way of a beauty contest while still in high school. A small part in *Down to the Sea in Ships*, 1922, brought her considerable attention and she was soon playing starring roles in such movies as *Mantrap, Kid Boots*, and *Dancing Mothers*, all released in 1926. In 1927 she was a sensation in a film written especially for her by Elinor Glyn and titled, simply and provocatively, *It*. Thereafter known universally as "the It Girl," Miss Bow was the embodiment of beauty, abandon, and sex appeal for the moviegoers of the Jazz Age. Others of the thirty-odd movies in which she starred included *The Plastic Age*, 1927; *Hula*, 1927; *Rough House Rosie*, 1927; *Three Week-Ends*, 1928; *Dangerous Curves*, 1929; and *The Saturday Night Kid*, 1929. Unable to make the transition from silent movies to the talkies, in part because of her strong Brooklyn accent, she retired in 1931. After unsuccessful comeback attempts in *Call Her Savage*, 1932, and *Hoopla*, 1933, she spent most of the rest of her life living quietly on a Nevada cattle ranch owned by her

husband, former cowboy star Rex Bell. Miss Bow died in West Los Angeles, California, on September 26, 1965.

Bowditch, Nathaniel (1773–1838), mathematician and astronomer. Born on March 26, 1773, in Salem, Massachusetts, Bowditch received no formal education after the age of ten. While working, however, first in his father's cooperage and later in a ship chandlery, he continued to read and study on his own. He taught himself algebra, geometry, French, and, in order to read Newton's *Principia*, Latin. At fifteen he compiled an almanac. Between 1795 and 1803 he made several sea voyages, the last as master, and continued his studies. In J. H. Moore's *Practical Navigator*, then the standard work in the field, he discovered a great number of errors; in 1799 he published the first American edition of the book, incorporating his corrections. Further work and revision led to the publication under his own name of the *New American Practical Navigator*, 1802, which, through edition after edition, has been the "seaman's bible" down to the present. For the rest of his life Bowditch was associated as an officer or an actuary with insurance companies in Salem and Boston; he also continued to be interested in scientific subjects and published numerous papers, particularly on comets and meteors. For several years he was engaged in translating the first four volumes of Laplace's *Mécanique céleste*; published 1829–1839 as *Celestial Mechanics*, this massive work, which included extensive commentary and updating by Bowditch, was a landmark in the development of American science. Although he declined several professorships, Bowditch was from 1829 until his death president of the American Academy of Arts and Sciences. He died in Boston on March 16, 1838.

Bowdoin, James (1726–1790), Revolutionary leader. Born on August 7, 1726, to a wealthy Boston family, Bowdoin graduated from Harvard in 1745 and followed the example of his father in becoming a merchant. In 1753 he was elected to the Massachusetts General Court and in 1757 to the ruling Council. There, working closely with John Hancock, James Otis, and Samuel Adams, he spoke and labored for American independence. In 1775–1776 he was a member of the executive council of Massachusetts; ill health forced his resignation and temporary retirement from public life. He had deep scientific and literary interests in addition to his public ones; in 1780 he was a founder and thereafter the first president of the American Academy of Arts and Sciences. During 1779–1780 he served as president of the state's constitutional conventional and in 1785–1787 was the governor of Massachusetts. As governor he worked to stabilize the state's administration and finances and, seeing the great difficulties of conflicting sovereignties under the Articles of Confederation, he urged strongly a more integrated and permanent union of the states. Bowdoin took prompt and strong action in putting down Shays's

Rebellion of disgruntled farmers and debtors in 1787. Shortly thereafter he retired fom the governorship; in the following year he was a member of the convention called to ratify the federal Constitution in Massachusetts. He died in Boston on November 6, 1790. Fours years later the Massachusetts General Court honored his memory by the establishment of Bowdoin College in Brunswick, now part of Maine.

Bowen, Norman Levi (1887–1956), geologist. Born on June 21, 1887, in Kingston, Ontario, Bowen graduated from Queen's University in his native city in 1907. After serving as a field investigator for the Ontario Bureau of Mines he came to the United States in 1909 and three years later took his Ph.D. from the Massachusetts Institute of Technology. He immediately joined the staff of the Carnegie Institution of Washington, with which he was associated for the rest of his career except for periods as professor of mineralogy at Queen's University, 1919–1920, and professor of petrology at the University of Chicago, 1937–1947. After making valuable contributions to the development of an optical-glass industry in the United States during World War I, Bowen devoted his researches principally to the study of the formation of rocks, particularly those produced by heat and pressure. His milestone work, *The Evolution of Igneous Rocks*, 1928, was highly influential in subsequent field investigations. A pioneer in experimental petrology, he also made significant studies of the origin of granite and the metamorphosis of various forms of limestone. He was a codiscoverer of the mineral mullite, a silicate of aluminum that is the basic refractory constituent of fireclay. A member of numerous scientific organizations and widely honored for his work, Bowen retired from the Carnegie Institution in 1952 and died in Washington, D.C., on September 11, 1956.

Bowie, James (1796–1836), Texas revolutionary leader. Born in Logan County, Kentucky, in 1796, Bowie moved with his family to Missouri in 1800 and to Louisiana in 1802. From 1814 he engaged in various enterprises, on his own or with his brothers—lumbering, slave trading, and raising sugarcane—and became something of a figure in New Orleans society. He went to Texas in 1828, possibly after having killed a man in a duel. Settling in San Antonio (then called Bexar), he became a Mexican citizen in 1830 and the following year married the daughter of the vice-governor, acquiring in the meantime extensive land holdings. Despite these attachments to Mexico, he sided with the American colonists as agitation for Texan independence developed. At the beginning of the revolution in 1835 he was a member of the Committee of Safety and became a colonel in the revolutionary army. Early in 1836 he joined the garrison under Col. William B. Travis at the Alamo. He fell ill during the siege and was discovered dead on his cot when General Santa Anna's troops took the stronghold on March 6, 1836. The bowie knife—a stout hunting knife that became widely popular—is believed to have been named after him, although its invention is sometimes credited to his brother Rezin.

Bowker, Richard Rogers (1848–1933), editor, publisher, and author. Born in Salem, Massachusetts, on September 4, 1848, Bowker grew up there and in New York City. He graduated from the College of the City of New York in 1868 and was immediately hired as city editor of the *New York Evening Mail*, becoming literary editor a year later. He moved to the *New York Tribune* in 1875. By that time he had already met bibliographer Frederick Leypoldt and had begun contributing to his *Publishers' Weekly*; the following year the two joined with Melvil Dewey in founding *Library Journal* and organizing the American Library Association (ALA). Bowker was the editor of the *Journal* for more than 50 years. In 1879 he bought *Publishers' Weekly* and also became publisher of the annual *American Catalogue*, a listing of all books in print in the United States. After Leypoldt's death in 1884 he became editor of *Publishers' Weekly* as well, which from 1911 was a publication of the R.R. Bowker Company. He was active in the affairs of numerous libraries and library organizations and in 1899 secured from President William McKinley the appointment of Herbert Putnam as Librarian of Congress. He also contributed to bibliography the first list of publications of American scientific and literary societies, the first organized list of U.S. government publications, and the first list of state documents. In addition he was deeply interested in politics and public affairs and exerted a powerful liberal influence in several directions, working particularly for tariff, postal, civil-service, and copyright reforms. In 1879 he was prominent in the formation of what became the Independent Republican, or "mugwump," movement. He wrote the first national civil-service reform plank for the 1880 Republican national convention and helped organize the Civil Service Reform Association three years later. He was a leading authority on copyright law and helped secure legislation that provided better protection for authors. Bowker's wide range of interests was reflected in his own books, which included *Of Work and Wealth*, 1883; *Copyright: Its Law and Its Literature*, 1886; *Electoral Reform*, 1889; *The Arts of Life*, 1900; *Of Religion*, 1903; *Problems of the Infinitely Little*, 1910; *Economic Peace*, 1923; two volumes of verse; and many others. Bowker had numerous business interests, including a position in the firm headed by his friend Thomas A. Edison. On the fiftieth anniversary of the American Library Association he was elected honorary president. He maintained a keen interest in public affairs to the last, becoming a convert to the New Deal in 1933. He died in Stockbridge, Massachusetts, on November 12, 1933.

Bowles, Samuel (1797–1851), newspaper editor. Born in Hartford, Connecticut, on June 8, 1797,

Bowles was a printer's apprentice at sixteen and advanced to foreman in the printshop of the *New Haven Register*. In 1819 he began publishing the *Hartford Times* in partnership with John Francis, but the venture was unsuccessful and in 1824 Bowles moved to Springfield, Massachusetts, to begin the weekly *Springfield Republican*. This paper was successful, and in 1844, a year after his seventeen-year-old son, Samuel Bowles II, joined the business, the elder Bowles started a daily evening edition. Despite the warnings of business associates, this paper, too, was successful, partly because of the innovation of having a system of local correspondents to provide complete coverage of the upper Connecticut Valley, and partly because of the energy that the younger Bowles brought to the task of editing it, which he was largely doing by the time he was twenty. The *Republican* was already a leading provincial journal when the elder Bowles died, in Springfield, on September 8, 1851.

Bowles, Samuel, II (1826–1878), newspaper editor. Born in Springfield, Massachusetts, on February 9, 1826, the son of Samuel Bowles (1797–1851), the younger Bowles began working in the offices of his father's weekly *Springfield Republican* when he was seventeen. In 1844 his father started a daily evening edition of the paper, and the younger Bowles was largely responsible for it by the time he was twenty. By 1848, through his hard work and competitiveness, he had made the daily edition the leading paper in western Massachusetts. Determined to remain politically independent, he editorially supported the Wilmot Proviso in 1846, denounced the Kansas-Nebraska Bill of 1854, supported the Civil War and Reconstruction policies of President Abraham Lincoln while avoiding the radical views of other Republican newspaper editors, but favored the impeachment of President Andrew Johnson in 1868; he joined the Liberal Republican movement in 1872. His editorials and other writings in the *Republican* were authoritative and won for the paper a national audience and a reputation for independence and integrity. He traveled often for his health after 1862 and published his correspondence from the West in three books, *Across the Continent* and *The Switzerland of America*, both published in 1865, and *Our New West*, 1869. He died in Springfield on January 16, 1878. His son, Samuel Bowles (1851–1915), founded the *Sunday Republican* in the year of his father's death and maintained the high standards of both papers for the rest of his life. He also opened, in the 1880s, one of the first schools for journalists in the country, in the *Republican's* offices in Springfield.

Bowman, Isaiah (1878–1950), geographer and educator. Born on December 26, 1878, in Waterloo, Ontario, Bowman grew up in Michigan and after completing a course at the State Normal College in 1902 and teaching there for a time went to Harvard, from which he graduated in 1905. He then became an instructor in geography at Yale, where he pursued graduate studies, led the 1907 Yale geographical expedition to South America, and took his Ph.D. in 1909. In 1911, by then an assistant professor of geography, he took part in the Yale expedition to Peru, and in 1913 he led the American Geographical Society's expedition to the central Andes. In 1915 he left Yale to become director of the American Geographical Society in New York City. During his 20-year tenure in that office he built the organization into one of worldwide influence, making its *Geographical Review* (previously the *Bulletin*) a major journal and launching the society upon such diverse projects as a comprehensive 1:1,000,000 map of Hispanic America and a program of polar exploration. In 1919 Bowman was chosen by President Woodrow Wilson to serve as chief territorial specialist with the U.S. delegation to the Versailles peace conference. At about that time and later he held several government advisory appointments, including the directorship of the Science Advisory Board and the chairmanship of the National Research Council, both 1933–1935. In 1935 he resigned from his post with the American Geographical Society to accept the presidency of The Johns Hopkins University. There he added greatly to an already strong tradition of high quality in graduate training and research, oversaw the addition of departments of geography, oceanography, and aeronautics, and took a vigorous stand against the overemphasis of athletics. Viewing the science of geography as a grand synthesis of natural history, climatology, demography, and related disciplines, Bowman was the leading force, by both influence and example, in making it a respected field of study at the highest levels. Among his many written contributions were *Forest Physiography*, 1911; *South America*, 1915; *The New World: Problems in Political Geography*, 1921; *Desert Trails of Atacama*, 1923; *The Mohammedan World*, 1924; *International Relations*, 1930; and *Geography in Relation to the Social Sciences*, 1934. Active in many national and international geographical organizations, Bowman continued also to serve in government, holding advisory positions with the Department of State and accompanying the U.S. delegations to the United Nations conferences at Dumbarton Oaks in 1944 and in San Francisco in 1945. He retired from Johns Hopkins in 1948 and died in Baltimore on January 6, 1950.

Boyd, Lynn (1800–1859), public official. Born in Nashville, Tennessee, on November 22, 1800, Boyd grew up there and in Christian County, Kentucky, where he received a little schooling. He took up farming in Calloway County, Kentucky, in 1826 and the following year was elected to the state legislature. Reelected in 1828 and 1829, he moved to Trigg County in 1830 and was again sent to the legislature, in 1831. In 1833 he ran unsuccessfully for the House of Representatives; he was elected in 1835, but lost again in 1837. In 1839 he finally took secure possession of the seat, holding it thereafter through seven reelections, until 1855. A strong Jacksonian Democrat, he became chairman of the military affairs committee during the Mexican War and later chairman of the influential committee on territories. He led the fight for House approval of the Compromise of 1850. During his last two terms, from 1851 to 1855, he was speaker of the House. Returning to Kentucky, he was its favorite-son candidate for the vice-presidency in 1856 and three years later, although he was a candidate for governor, was elected lieutenant governor. Before he could take office he died in Paducah on December 17, 1859.

Boyden, Seth (1788–1870), inventor and manufacturer. Born in Foxboro, Massachusetts, on November 17, 1788, Boyden was the son of a mechanic and occasional inventor and the brother of Uriah A. Boyden. He received only a meager formal education, but early acquired a reputation for mechanical ability and by the time he was twenty-one had devised machines for making nails and files. Four years later he moved to Newark, New Jersey, to go into the leather business, using an improved version of his father's leather-splitting machine. Continued experiments led to his development of a process for manufacturing patent leather in 1819 and the opening of the first U.S. patent-leather factory. Turning his attention to an entirely different problem, he succeeeded in 1826 in duplicating a secret European process for making malleable cast iron. Upon receipt of a patent in 1831 he sold his leather business to open a foundry for producing the malleable iron, only to sell it six years later in order to take up building locomotives and stationary steam engines. He introduced the use of the cutoff governor in steam engines. After a fruitless year in the California gold fields he returned east in 1850 and continued to experiment in several areas; among other things, he developed the Hilton strawberry, invented a hat-forming machine, investigated atmospheric electricity, and is reputed to have made the first daguerreotype in the United States. He died in Hilton, New Jersey, on March 31, 1870.

Boyden, Uriah Atherton (1804–1879), engineer and inventor. Born in Foxboro, Massachusetts, on February 17, 1804, the younger brother of Seth Boyden, Uriah left his father's farm and machine shop in 1825 to go to work for his brother in Newark, New Jersey, returning to Boston later to work as an engineer, although he was not formally trained for the profession. He assisted in the survey for the Boston and Providence Railroad, helped build the Boston and Lowell Railroad, and supervised construction of the Nashua and Lowell Railroad. He was involved in the construction of several textile mills in Lowell and later devoted his energies to hydraulic engineering. In 1844 he designed a type of waterwheel that, incorporating many innovative features, was capable of very high efficiency—upwards of 80 percent—and was soon widely adopted. In his later years he retired from engineering to study various topics in pure physics, among them heat and the velocity of light. He died in Boston on October 17, 1879.

Boylston, Zabdiel (1679–1766), physician. Born on March 9, 1679, in Brookline (then known as Muddy River), Massachusetts, Bolyston followed his father into the medical profession. He was well regarded by his contemporaries but achieved no particular distinction until 1721, when Boston was seized by an epidemic of smallpox. In June of that year Cotton Mather made known to the physicians of Boston the results of experiments with inoculation that had been made a few years before in Constantinople. At Mather's urging, Boylston decided to try the technique. He inoculated his sons and several other persons with satisfactory results. Such an unorthodox and possibly impious practice shocked and angered the community, however; mobs attacked the homes of both Mather and Boylston, and they were greatly abused in print. A pamphlet war ensued, with Mather and Boylston collaborating on *Some account of what is said of Inoculating or Transplanting the Small Pox . . . in Answer to the scruples of many about the Lawfulness of this Method* and a series of other defenses. The debate ran into the following February, by which time Boylston had treated well over 200 persons with great success, considering the fact that he used a virus taken from human smallpox victims which often produced a mild, but contagious, form of the disease. In 1724 he traveled to London to lecture at the Royal College of Physicians and at the Royal Society, to which he was elected in 1726. In that year he published in London the clinical record of his work with inoculation as *An Historical Account of the Small-pox inoculated in New England,* and then returned to America. He remained in active practice, administering occasional inoculations, for some 20 years, retiring at last to his farm in Brookline, where he died on March 1, 1766.

Bozeman, John M. (1835–1867), explorer. Born in Georgia in 1835, Bozeman went west in 1861 to prospect the gold-rich gravel beds of Cripple Creek, Colorado. Tales of even richer strikes in western Montana lured him to the Virginia City region in 1862. At that time Virginia City, Alder Gulch, Bannack, and the other Montana gold towns could be reached from the East only by two circuitous routes: one followed the Missouri River to the head of navigation at Fort Benton and then struck south, the other followed the Platte and the North Platte and then crossed Wyoming through Bridger Pass to Fort Hall and northward. Bozeman decided to seek a more direct route. Setting out from Bannack late in 1862, he traveled east, crossed the Continental Divide at what became known as Bozeman Pass, and eventually turned south through the eastern foothills of the Bighorn Mountains. The area was reserved by treaty to the Indians, however, and Bozeman and his partner were attacked by Sioux. Enduring great hardships, they continued south and east on foot, finally reaching the North Platte and Fort Laramie. In the spring of 1863, despite the dangers with which he was now intimately familiar, Bozeman undertook to lead a caravan of settlers and freighters to Montana. The party turned back after an Indian raid and took the standard southern route through Bridger's Pass to Fort Hall, but Bozeman went on, retracing his own dangerous route and arriving safely in Virginia City. The mounting pressure of migration to the mining regions finally led the army to survey, improve, and guard the Powder River Road along the route of the Bozeman Trail beginning in 1865. Fort Reno was built on the Powder River about halfway from Fort Laramie to the Montana border, Fort Phil Kearny just south of the border, and Fort C. F. Smith at the crossing of the Bighorn River in Montana. The Sioux, angered by the treaty violation and particularly aroused by the prospect of losing the rich hunting grounds of the Bighorn Mountains, were led by Red Cloud in violently opposing the road and, with the Fetterman Massacre near Fort Phil Kearny in December 1866, succeeded in closing the route. Bozeman refused to accept the state of affairs and in April 1867 he set out again from Virginia City; he got as far as the Yellowstone, where he was set upon and killed by Blackfeet on April 20, 1867. A companion was wounded but escaped. Although stubborn and at times injudicious, Bozeman had impressed his name on the history and geography of the West.

Brace, Charles Loring (1826–1890), social reformer. Born in Litchfield, Connecticut, on June 19, 1826, Brace graduated from Yale in 1846 and enrolled in the Yale Divinity School a year later, after teaching school for a time. After an extended visit to Europe he moved to New York City where, in 1853, he helped found the Children's Aid Society. He remained for the rest of his life executive secretary of the organization. Concerned mainly with the growing immigrant population of the city, the society, under Brace's direction, established schools, homes, sanitariums, and camps. The main emphasis of his work was on the encouragement of the greatest possible degree of self-help. In 1872 he published *The Dangerous Classes of New York, and Twenty Years' Work Among Them*, and ten years later *Gesta Christi: A History of Humane Progress Under Christianity*, both of which were major contributions to the literature of philanthropy; he also published during his life a number of travel books and ethnological studies. Brace died in Campfèr, Switzerland on August 11, 1890.

Brackenridge, Hugh Henry (1748–1816), author and judge. Born in Scotland in 1748, Brackenridge and his family came to America in 1753 and settled in York County, Pennsylvania. Gaining his early education by his own efforts, he entered Princeton in 1768. There James Madison and Philip M. Freneau were classmates; he collaborated with Freneau on *The Rising Glory of America*, their 1771 commencement poem. He remained at Princeton for three years more as a divinity student and during the Revolution served as a chaplain, wrote several patriotic verse dramas, and preached in support of independence. He entered the office of Samuel Chase to read law and in 1781 moved to Pittsburgh where, a few years later, he helped to found the *Pittsburgh Gazette*, the town's first newspaper. He served in the state legislature in 1786–1787 and was a strong supporter of the new Constitution in the period leading up to ratification. In 1799, after a short period as editor of the nationalistic *United States Magazine*, he was appointed to the state's supreme court. Between 1792 and 1815 he published in six parts a long, rambling novel, *Modern Chivalry*, a satire on many of the people and institutions of the time. He died in Carlisle, Pennsylvania, on June 25, 1816.

Bradbury, Ray Douglas (1920–   ), author. Born on August 22, 1920, in Waukegan, Illinois, Bradbury grew up there and, from 1934, in Los Angeles. He became interested in writing at an early age and upon graduating from high school took it up seriously while supporting himself with minor jobs. His first published story appeared in 1940 and within two years he was able to devote full time to writing. Nearly all of his early efforts were published in pulp magazines devoted to science fiction and fantasy, but the manifestly high quality of his stories gradually attracted the attention of high-circulation general-interest publications such as the *American Mercury*, the *Saturday Evening Post*, the *New Yorker*, and others. He was represented in the *Best American Short Stories* anthologies for 1946, 1948, and 1952, and in the *O. Henry Prize Stories* of 1947 and 1948. Bradbury's first book, a collection of stories entitled *Dark Carnival*, appeared in 1947. Characterized by a vivid imagination that ranged from the poetic to the grotesque, considerable narrative and descriptive skill, and a constant underlying concern for human values as against the sensational or purely technological elements of most science fiction, his stories were warmly received both popularly and critically. Other collections were published as *The Illustrated Man*, 1951, parts of which were later adapted for the screen; *The Golden Apples of the Sun*, 1953; *The October Country*, 1955; *A Medicine for Melancholy*, 1959; *R Is for Rocket*, 1962; *Twice Twenty-two*, 1966; *I Sing the Body Electric*, 1969; and others. *The Martian Chronicles*, 1950, often accounted his best book, was a collection of pieces dealing with the exploration and colonization of Mars. In 1951 he published a novel, *Fahrenheit 451*, later made into a movie; other novels included *Dandelion Wine*, 1957, a nostalgic tale of childhood, and *Something Wicked This Way Comes*, 1962. Bradbury also wrote a number of plays and many radio scripts and television and movie screenplays, including that for the 1954 motion-picture production of *Moby Dick*.

Bradford, William (1590–1657), colonial leader. Born in Yorkshire, England, probably in March 1590, Bradford began at the age of twelve to read the Bible and soon joined a Separatist congregation. He migrated with the Puritans to Holland in 1609 and for 11 years lived and worked quietly in Leiden. In 1620 he sailed on the *Mayflower*; he was a signer of the Mayflower Compact, helped select the site for the new colony, and in April 1621, with the settlement nearly decimated by the first harsh winter, was chosen governor of Plymouth. Evidently a man of remarkable tact, honesty, and political ability, Bradford was elected governor in 30 of the succeeding 35 years. It seems to have been largely through his efforts that the colony gained a firm footing despite the extreme hardships of the first years; his handling of unruly elements within the colony and of the Indians surrounding Plymouth averted a number of potential disasters. Although he had not received a formal education, Bradford possessed considerable literary ability; his *History of Plimoth Plantation, 1620–1647*, is a vivid account of the early settlement and the major source of information about it. The work was not published in full until 200 years after his death in Plymouth on May 9, 1657.

Bradley, Joseph P. (1813–1892), justice of the Supreme Court. Born in Berne, New York, on March 14, 1813, Bradley possessed an intellectual bent that was frustrated by poverty until 1833, when he entered Rutgers College. He graduated in 1836 and three years later was admitted to the New Jersey bar. An astute student of the law, he specialized in business, patent, and corporation matters and was counsel for several railroad companies. In 1870 President Ulysses S. Grant appointed him to the Supreme Court, where he immediately became involved in the legal problems arising from Reconstruction. In one of his earliest and most controversial opinions, he ruled in *Knox* v. *Lee*, 1871, that the Legal Tender Acts of 1862 and 1863 were constitutional, thus overturning the Court's decision in *Hepburn* v. *Griswold*, 1870, and stirring charges that Grant had appointed him and William Strong specifically to bring about such a reversal. In 1877 he was a member of the electoral commission appointed to decide the Hayes-Tilden election; Bradley's was the deciding vote that gave Rutherford B. Hayes the presidency. He was dedicated to the maintenance of state powers in the federal system; accordingly, he ruled in 1883 in the Civil Rights Cases that in the internal social relations of the states the Fourteenth Amendment had no power. He was also influential in the molding of the modern view of the relationship between federal and state authority over interstate commerce. He died in Washington, D.C., on January 22, 1892.

Bradley, Milton (1836–1911), manufacturer and publisher. Born in Vienna, Maine, on November 8, 1836, Bradley moved with his family to Lowell, Massachusetts, in 1847. He studied for a time at the Lawrence Scientific School at Harvard and in 1856 became a draftsman in a locomotive works. Two years later he went into business for himself as a draftsman and patent agent. In 1860 he took up lithography, opening a shop in Springfield which had the first lithographic press in western Massachusetts. Casting about for a profitable product during the business depression of 1860, he hit upon the idea of a board game which he called "The Checkered Game of Life." The great success of the game led to the formation of Milton Bradley & Company in 1864 (from 1878, when his partners retired, the Milton Bradley Company), one of the earliest game manufacturers in the country. "The Wheel of Life," an optical toy that is said to have been the first moving-picture machine, was also highly popular. The company helped introduce croquet to America and standardized the rules. Bradley became interested in the ideas of German educator Friedrich Froebel and in 1869 published his *Paradise of Childhood*, 1869, the first work on kindergartens to appear in the United States. In promotion of the kindergarten movement Bradley also began manufacturing school materials and children's books and for a time published *Work and Play*, a magazine for children. In 1893 his company took over the *Kindergarten News* and continued it in publication as the *Kindergarten Review*. Bradley himself wrote several books on a color system he had devised and its application to education; they included *Color in the School Room*, 1890; *Color in the Kindergarten*, 1893; and *Water Colors in the School Room*, 1900. He died in Springfield on May 30, 1911.

Bradley, Omar Nelson (1893–1981), soldier. Born on February 12, 1893, in Clark, Missouri, Bradley graduated from West Point in 1915 and was commissioned a second lieutenant of artillery. After serving at various army posts in the West and Midwest he became professor of military science and tactics at South Dakota State College in 1919. A year later he returned to West Point as an instructor in mathematics. In 1925 he graduated from the Army Infantry School, in 1929 from the Command and General Staff School, and in 1934 from the Army War College. From 1934 to 1938 he was again an instructor at West Point, and in 1938 was transferred to duties with the general staff in Washington, D.C. In 1941 he was promoted to brigadier general. His first combat service came in 1943, when he commanded the U.S. 2nd Corps in North Africa under Gen. Dwight D. Eisenhower; later in the year he took part in the invasion of Sicily, and then moved to England to take command of the U.S. 1st Army and participate in the planning for the invasion of Europe. He retained this post until August 1944, two months after his troops had landed in Normandy on D-Day, and then he assumed command of the 12th Army Group, a force of 1.3 million combat troops, the largest ever to serve under a single American field commander. In 1945 he became a full general. From that year until 1947 he was administrator of veterans' affairs, and in 1948 he succeeded Eisenhower as chief of staff of the army. After the unification of the armed services he became in 1949 the first permanent chairman of the joint chiefs of staff, a post he held for four years; during that time, in 1950, he was promoted to general of the army. After retiring from active service in 1953 he pursued business interests. In 1951 he published *A Soldier's Story*, a volume of reminiscences. He died in New York City on April 8, 1981.

Bradstreet, Anne (1612?–1672), poet. Born, probably in 1612, in Northampton, England, Anne Dudley was the daughter of Thomas Dudley. She came to the New World with her parents and her husband, Simon Bradstreet, in 1630; they were members of John Winthrop's party, the first settlers on Massachusetts Bay. At first dismayed by the rude life of the settlement, she soon reconciled herself to it and, in the midst of her husband's public duties—he was twice governor of the colony—and her private ones as mother of eight, she found time to write poetry. Her early work, largely imitative and influenced by that of the sixteenth-century French poet Du Bartas, was conventional, dull, and easily forgotten. It was first published in London in 1650 as *The Tenth Muse Lately Sprung Up in America.* Her later work, unpublished until after her death, became her chief claim to attention; less derivative, it was often, as in "Contemplations," graceful and pleasant. Much of it concerned her deeply personal reflections, and the warmth and frank humanity that pervaded them struck a welcome contrast to the Puritan stereotype. She died on September 16, 1672, in Andover, Massachusetts.

Brady, Alice (1892–1939), actress. Born in New York City on November 2, 1892, Alice Brady was the daughter of theatrical manager William Brady by his first wife. Educated in a convent school and at the New England Conservatory of Music, she abandoned plans for an operatic career and, over her father's objections, entered the theater, making her Broadway debut under an assumed name in a minor role in his 1910 production of *The Mikado.* The next year she appeared under her own name in *The Balkan Princess* and in 1912 won wide acclaim in *Little Women.* After an extensive national tour with DeWolf Hopper's Gilbert and Sullivan opera company in 1914 she moved to Hollywood and made a series of motion pictures, many for her father's company, including *The Gilded Cage,* 1914; *La Boheme,* 1916; *Betsy Ross,* 1917; and *Woman and Wife,* 1918. In 1918 she returned to Broadway in the hit *Forever After* and subsequently enjoyed great successes in *The Bride of the Lamb,* 1926; Eugene O'Neill's *Mourning Becomes Electra,* 1931; *Mademoiselle,* 1932, and many others. During the 1930s she returned to the screen to appear in, among others, *The Gay Divorcee,* 1934; *My Man Godfrey,* 1936; *Three Smart Girls,* 1937; *In Old Chicago,* 1938, for which she won an Academy Award; and *Young Mr. Lincoln,* 1939. Miss Brady died on October 28, 1939, in New York City.

Brady, James Buchanan (1856–1917), "Diamond Jim," financier and bon vivant. Born in New York City on August 12, 1856, Brady worked as a hotel bellboy and as a messenger for the New York Central Railroad before becoming in 1879 a salesman for Manning, Maxwell & Moore, manufacturers of railroad equipment. He soon demonstrated phenomenal selling ability; he became sole U.S. agent for the Fox Pressed Steel Car Truck Company of England in 1888 and amassed a fortune in commissions. A lavishly generous man who loved to eat and dress well, to entertain in royal fashion, and who could tear up an IOU with the easiest grace imaginable, Brady emerged as the king of the Broadway "sports," recognized and admired by all and sundry. His penchant for collecting and wearing diamond jewelry—an estimated $2 million worth—gave him his nickname, and he recognized the value of his reputation, letting on that he had a set of jewelry for every day of the month. He helped organize the Pressed Steel Car Company, becoming its sole sales agent, and later secured the backing of the Mellon banking house for the Standard Steel Car Company, of which he was vice-president in charge of sales. He held vice-presidencies or directorships in several other firms as well, and by 1903 was worth some $12 million. In 1912 he gave to Johns Hopkins Hospital the funds for its Urological Institute, which was named for him, and in his will left a large bequest to New York Hospital for a similar purpose. His last years were plagued by health problems, possibly brought on by his formidable and seldom denied appetite. Brady died in Atlantic City, New Jersey, on April 13, 1917.

Brady, Mathew B. (1823?–1896), photographer. Brady was born about 1823 in Warren County, New York; apart from that little is known of his background except that he was of Irish descent and received little schooling. About 1840 he was introduced to Samuel F. B. Morse, who was conducting experiments with daguerreotypes. Learning the process from Morse, Brady was soon producing plates of his own and by 1844 was sufficiently skilled to establish a commercial studio in New York City. He was rapidly successful, made thousands of portraits, and won awards from the American Institute between 1844 and 1849 that had never been conferred on daguerreotypists before; in 1851 he was awarded a medal at the Crystal Palace exhibition in London. He experimented with tinting and with producing plates on ivory. The ivory plates were in great demand, and with the increase of his fortune his long-cherished plan to make portraits of every distinguished American seemed within the realm of the possible. In 1855 he learned the new wet-plate process of photography from an English expert and, switching to the new medium, used nearly all of his money to train a team of assistants to make a photographic record of the Civil War. They fearlessly tramped through battlegrounds, bivouacs, and officers' quarters, recording every aspect of the conflict; Brady himself was on the scene at Bull Run, Antietam, Fredericksburg, Gettysburg, and Petersburg. Several collections of the photographs were circulated, one in a book, *Brady's National Photographic Collection of War Views and Portraits of Representative Men*, 1870. A set of 2000 photographs was sold to the government, another was sent to a photographic supply house to pay debts, and others went to private collectors. Combined, they formed the basis for all subsequent pictorial records of the war. The great project left Brady in straitened circumstances and the panic of 1873 completed his financial ruin. He maintained a studio in Washington, D.C., for some years but gradually faded in obscurity. Ill and alone in his last years, Brady died in the charity ward of a New York City hospital on January 15, 1896.

Brady, William Aloysius (1863–1950), actor and producer. Born in San Francisco on June 19, 1863, Brady grew up from the age of three in New York City. Left an orphan in his youth, he fended for himself in various odd jobs, then worked his way across the country and, back in San Francisco, began a career on the stage, making his debut in 1882 in *The White Slave*. For the next several years he worked in a succession of West Coast stock and repertory companies and in 1888 formed with a partner the Webster-Brady company, with which he toured for some time and enjoyed considerable success, particularly in Dion Boucicault's *After Dark* and later in *Trilby*. During a tour in the East he saw one of James J. Corbett's boxing exhibitions and promptly became his manager; the association lasted until after Corbett won the world's heavyweight championship in 1892. Brady later also managed James J. Jeffries for a time. With his large income from the stock company and from his pugilistic protégés he moved to New York City, leased the Manhattan Theatre and later built the Playhouse Theatre (1910) and the Forty-eighth Street Theatre (1912), and became one of the leading producers of his day. In all he presented more than 250 plays, including the very successful *Way Down East*, Elmer Rice's *Street Scene*, and a revival of *Uncle Tom's Cabin*. Many of his most popular productions starred his second wife, the much admired Grace George. Brady was also an early producer of motion pictures with his World Film Company and during 1915–1920 was president of the National Assembly of the Motion Picture Industry. He died in New York City on January 6, 1950.

Bragg, Braxton (1817–1876), soldier. Born in Warrenton, North Carolina, on March 22, 1817, Bragg was appointed to West Point and graduated in 1837. He took part in the Seminole Wars of 1837

and 1841 and served with distinction under Gen. Zachary Taylor in the Mexican War. In 1856 he resigned from the army and settled on a plantation in Louisiana, where he also served as commissioner of public works. Five years later he was called to service as a brigadier general in the Confederate army. In 1862, after a qualified success at Shiloh, Bragg was promoted to major general and given command of the Army of Tennessee. Hoping to secure Kentucky for the Confederacy, he moved north; he retired from an indecisive engagement with Gen. D. C. Buell at Perryville in October and from another with Gen. W. S. Rosecrans at Murfreesboro (Stones River) in December. Despite severe criticism of his inability to press his advantages, Bragg retained the favor of Confederate president Jefferson Davis and thereby his command. In the following year he won a notable victory over Rosecrans at Chickamauga but soon thereafter was routed by Gen. Ulysses S. Grant at Chattanooga in November. Bragg surrendered his command to Gen. Joseph E. Johnston and became military adviser to Jefferson Davis. After the war he returned to civil engineering and for four years was commissioner of public works in Alabama. He died in Galveston, Texas, on September 27, 1876.

Brand, Max, *see* Faust, Frederick Schiller

Brandeis, Louis Dembitz (1856–1941), justice of the Supreme Court. Born on November 13, 1856, in Louisville, Kentucky, Brandeis was the son of cultivated Jewish parents who had emigrated from Bohemia (now Czechoslovakia). He was educated in schools in Louisville and in Dresden, Germany, and at eighteen entered Harvard Law School. Graduating at the head of his class in 1877, he remained at Harvard for a year of additional study and, after a few months of practicing law in St. Louis, settled in Boston. From the outset he was guided by an imperious drive to understand all the facts and forces bearing upon the law, and his liberalism drew him immediately to the social and economic issues that underlay much of the legislative activity of the period. Often taking cases without remuneration, Brandeis became widely known as "the people's attorney," for he felt a deep responsibility to aid in making the law responsive to the needs of a rapidly changing society. Typical of his approach was his service as unpaid counsel to the New England Policy-Holders' Protective Committee, formed following revelations in 1905 of scandalous practices by the Equitable Life Assurance Society of New York and the many leading financiers involved in it. Going beyond bare legal maneuvering, he researched the entire subject of life insurance and devised a plan for cheap insurance, within reach of the average working man, sold through and guaranteed by savings banks; his proposal was enacted by the Massachusetts legislature in 1907 and later adopted in several other states. His work in rate-increase hearings before the Interstate Commerce Commission (ICC) in 1911 led him to make an intensive study of the railroad industry and he was later able to detail how, by the application of Frederick W. Taylor's principles of scientific management, the railroads could effect savings of hundreds of millions of dollars annually. Brandeis was particularly interested in labor relations, working on several occasions to settle disputes and serving as counsel to several states that had enacted wages and hours laws and were defending their constitutionality. In the course of these cases he evolved what became known as the "Brandeis brief," in which the legal points were dealt with summarily and then buttressed by a mass of sociological, economic, and historical data in support of the legislation in question; notable among his cases of this kind was *Muller v. Oregon*, 1908. Politically Brandeis was an independent. He supported Theodore Roosevelt in 1904, William Howard Taft in 1908, and first Robert M. La Follette and then Woodrow Wilson in 1912. *Other People's Money*, his analysis of the influence of the moneyed interests, was published in 1914. In 1916 President Wilson named him to the Supreme Court and, despite strong opposition from influential quarters where he was considered a radical, he was confirmed by the Senate after several months of debate, becoming the first Jew to sit on the Court. In 23 years on the bench Brandeis was known chiefly as a dissenter, although he actually broke with the Court majority in fewer than 75 cases. His reputation stemmed, however, from his belief—distinctly a minority one—that political and economic dogmas ought not to serve as grounds for dismissing legislative efforts to meet new challenges; he encouraged an experimental attitude and counseled a presumption of constitutionality in such cases as *Truax* v. *Corrigan* (dissenting), 1921; *American Column and Lumber Co.* v. *U.S.* (dissenting), 1921; and *New State Ice Co.* v. *Liebmann* (dissenting), 1932, in which he warned his colleagues that "we must be ever on our guard, lest we erect our prejudices into legal principles. If we would guide by the light of reason, we must let our minds be bold." He advocated a similar flexibility in interpreting the Constitution to meet new threats to liberty, as in *Pierce* v. *U.S.* (dissenting), 1920, in which he spoke strongly against the invasion of First Amendment rights by the Espionage Act of 1917, and in *Olmstead* v. *U.S.* (dissenting), 1928, in which he viewed the new technique of wiretapping as a violation of the Fourth Amendment. Brandeis was nonetheless convinced that proper judicial procedure was a prime safeguard of the Constitution, outweighing matters of theory or interpretation; in *Whitney* v. *California*, 1927, he ruled against an apellant on procedural grounds while yet deploring the original conviction under a law dealing with criminal syndicalism. In *Ashwander* v. *Tennessee Valley Authority* (concurring), 1936, he propounded the "Ashwander rules" for the proper selection and presentation of Supreme Court cases, his central point being that constitutional issues should be raised only when unavoidable. While on the bench Brandeis scrupulously avoided all extrajudicial activities and involvements except for his support of the Zionist cause, to which he had been devoted since 1912. He retired from the Supreme Court in February 1939 and died in Washington, D.C., on October 5, 1941. Brandeis University, founded in 1947, was named for him.

Brando, Marlon (1924–   ), actor. Born on April 3, 1924, in Omaha, Nebraska, Brando grew up there and in Evanston and Libertyville, Illinois. He left military school in 1943 before graduating and moved to New York City, where he enrolled in drama classes at the New School for Social Research. His work in student productions led to a role in the Broadway production of *I Remember Mama* in 1944 and to subsequent appearances in Maxwell Anderson's *Truckline Cafe*, a revival of G. B. Shaw's *Candida* starring Katherine Cornell, and Ben Hecht's *A Flag Is Born*, all in 1946. The next year he won the male lead in Tennessee Williams's *A Streetcar Named Desire* and received widespread popular and critical acclaim for his powerful portrayal of the primitive, brutal, but nonetheless vulnerably human Stanley Kowalski. Drawing much of his technique from the "Method" school of acting taught at the Actors Studio, Brando often relied on a sullen manner and a slurred, mumbling delivery of lines, a personal style that occasionally overshadowed, for many of his audience, his intense identification with his characters. His first film, *The Men*, 1950, was followed by the movie version of *A Streetcar Named Desire*, 1951; *Viva Zapata!*, 1952; *Julius Caesar*, 1953; *The Wild One*, 1954, in which he set the pattern for motorcycle-riding delinquents for a decade or more; *On the Waterfront*, 1954, for which he won an Academy Award; *Desirée*, 1954; *Guys and Dolls*, 1955; *The Teahouse of the August Moon*, 1956; *Sayonara*, 1957; *The Young Lions*, 1958; *One-eyed Jacks*, 1960, which he also directed; *Mutiny on the Bounty*, 1962; *The Ugly American*, 1963; *Bedtime Story*, 1964; *The Appaloosa*, 1966; *A Countess from Hong Kong*, 1966; *Reflections in a Golden Eye*, 1967; *The Night of the Following Day*, 1968; *The Godfather*, 1972, in which he scored a triumph; and the daring and controversial *Last Tango in Paris*, 1973. Although he was often forced to contend with type casting and with inferior material, Brando never failed to attract large audiences. His insistence on his own privacy, combined with the blaring publicity that attended a number of episodes in his professional career and marital life, distracted many from his work, and it was only gradually that he came to be recognized as one of Hollywood's most serious and capable practitioners of the craft of acting.

Brannan, Samuel (1819–1889), pioneer and public official. Born on March 2, 1819, in Saco, Maine, Brannan moved to Ohio at the age of fourteen.

He learned the printing trade and for a number of years traveled throughout the country as a journeyman printer. In 1842 he became a Mormon and, moving to New York City, began publishing a church newspaper, the *New York Messenger* (later the *New York Prophet*). In 1845 he was chosen leader of a large party of Mormon emigrants bound for California; sailing from New York early in 1846, they were several months on the voyage around the Horn and by the time they arrived in California in July, the formerly Mexican territory had been occupied by U.S. forces. The party settled in Yerba Buena, which the next year was renamed San Francisco. Brannan soon became a leading figure in the new territory, publishing the *California Star*, San Francisco's first newspaper, building a flour mill, and in general keeping abreast of events. From 1847 to 1849 he ran a store at Sutter's Fort at present-day Sacramento, and tradition credits him with bringing the news of James W. Marshall's discovery of gold on the American River in 1848 to San Francisco. He then moved back to San Francisco and, upon its incorporation in 1850, was elected to the city council. He took a major role in many early civic developments, helped organize fire companies and the Society of California Pioneers, and in 1851 promoted the founding of the Committee of Vigilance and became its first president. Always a forceful and direct man, he quickly made the vigilantes a highly effective, if irregular, peacekeeping organization; his zeal was at length judged excessive, however, and he resigned. By that time real-estate ventures had brought him considerable wealth, and he had interests in a wide variety of businesses and utilities as well. His fortune and his reputation suffered badly from the dissipation that marked his later years; he died in poverty and obscurity on May 5, 1889, in Escondido, California.

Brant, Joseph (1742–1807), Indian leader. Born in 1742 on the banks of the Ohio River in what is now Ohio, Brant was the son of a Mohawk chief and was known to the Indians as Thayendanegea. He was educated at Eleazar Wheelock's Indian charity school (which was the forerunner of Dartmouth) in Lebanon, Connecticut. In 1763, soon after leaving school, he served in the French and Indian Wars as one of the Iroquois contingent aiding the British against Chief Pontiac. In 1774 he became secretary to the superintendent of Indian affairs and when the Revolution broke out remained loyal to the British. After a visit to England, during which he was presented at court, he was commissioned a captain by the British and assumed leadership of the Indians in the Mohawk Valley region, directing devastating raids on settlements on the New York–Pennsylvania frontier. He fought ferociously at the head of the Indian forces at the battle of Oriskany in 1777 and at the Cherry Valley Massacre the following year. Although Brant constantly frustrated attempts by other Indian leaders, notably Red Jacket, to secure an early peace with the Americans, at the war's end he took the lead in pacifying the Indian frontier. He devoted himself thereafter to missionary work, translating the Book of Common Prayer and St. Mark's Gospel into Mohawk and attempting to secure the welfare and safety of his people. After failing in efforts to obtain a settlement of the Iroquois Nations' land claims in the United States he turned to the British; on a second visit to England in 1786 he obtained funds to purchase lands in Canada at present-day Brantford, Ontario, and to erect an Episcopal church. He died at his own Ontario estate on November 24, 1807.

Brattain, Walter Houser (1902–   ), physicist. Born on February 10, 1902, in Amoy, China, Brattain grew up in Washington state and graduated from Whitman College in 1924. After taking his M.A. from the University of Oregon in 1926 and a Ph.D. from the University of Minnesota in 1929, he joined the staff of the Bell Telephone Laboratories, Incorporated, with which he remained associated, first in the New York plant and then in New Jersey, until his retirement in 1967. From the beginning he concentrated his researches on the physics of surfaces, a field of study that proved to be highly fruitful. His early investigations concerned thermionic and photoelectric effects on surface layers, and as he experimented with tungsten, cuprous oxide, and then various semiconducting substances such as silicon and germanium, he began looking also into the process of rectification. Semiconductors had long been in use to rectify alternating currents, but Brattain, joined in 1936 by William B. Shockley, sought to employ them as amplifiers as well. The project was interrupted by World War II, during which Brattain worked on magnetic devices for submarine detection for the government, but after the war he and Shockley resumed their researches with John Bardeen added to the team. In December 1947 they succeeded in constructing a solid-state device—a "transfer resistor"—that could rectify and amplify and thus could replace the vacuum tube. By then called a "transistor" the invention of the device, of a type later known as point-contact, was announced in 1948. Perfection of the transistor created a revolution in electronic and communications technology, its tiny size and meager power requirements making possible the design of equipment of previously impossible complexity and compactness. The inventors were widely honored and in 1956 shared the Nobel Prize for Physics. Brattain continued to study and write on the action of semiconductors and the transistor effect; after his retirement from Bell he returned to Whitman College as professor of physics.

Brattle, Thomas (1658–1713), businessman. Born in Boston on June 20, 1658, Brattle was the son of a wealthy merchant and landowner. He graduated from Harvard in 1676, studied and traveled in Europe for a time, and returned to enter a business that, while its precise nature is unknown, was apparently quite prosperous. In 1693 he became treasurer of Harvard College, a position he held for the rest of his life and in which, through both sound practice and personal benefaction, he greatly strengthened the financial standing of the institution. An intelligent man of a liberal persuasion, he strongly denounced the witchcraft trials in Salem in 1692 and, growing restive over the strictly Puritan liturgy of Boston churches, in 1698 organized a new congregation as the Brattle Street Church in Cambridge. There the "relation of experiences" was dropped as a requirement for membership, Bible readings without commentary were used in the services, and the Lord's Prayer was adopted. Such heterodoxy aroused the conservatives led by Cotton and Increase Mather, and the ensuing controversy lasted for several years. Brattle was also an avid amateur scientist with a particular interest in astronomy; he made numerous observations of eclipses and other phenomena, his reports on the comet of 1680 being of value to Isaac Newton in validating Kepler's laws of planetary motion. He died in Boston on May 18, 1713.

Braun, Wernher von (1912–1977), rocket engineer. Born on March 23, 1912, in Wirsitz, Germany (now Wyrzysk, Poland), von Braun as a youth became fascinated with the possibilities of using rockets to explore outer space and in 1930 joined the Verein für Raumschiffahrt, a group of amateur rocket enthusiasts in Berlin. He studied engineering at technological institutes in Zurich and Berlin, took his degree in 1932, and later in the same year became chief of a rocket-research station established by the German army. Two years later he was awarded a Ph.D. by the University of Berlin. In 1936 German Führer Adolf Hitler became interested in rockets as potential weapons and ordered construction of a large research facility at Peenemünde, where von Braun and his group continued their work with greatly improved resources. By 1938 a first model of the liquid-fueled Vergeltungswaffe Zwei (V-2, "revenge weapon two") had been developed. Over the next six years it was enlarged and improved until it was capable of carrying a warhead weighing nearly a ton more than 190 miles in 5 minutes. V-2 launchings against London and Antwerp began in September 1944 and numbered about 3600 before the end of the war. By that time von Braun and a large number of his colleagues had fled before advancing Soviet armies and surrendered to U.S. forces. In 1945 he came to the United States and became technical director of the army's proving grounds for missiles at White Sands, New Mexico. In 1950 he was made director of the missile-research facility at Huntsville, Alabama. Under his supervision the Redstone, Jupiter-C, Jupiter, and other rockets were developed. He continued to press for a program of space exploration and wrote numerous papers, articles, and books on the subject, including *Conquest of the Moon*, 1953, with Fred Whipple and Willy Ley, and *Exploration of Mars*, 1956. He

became a U.S. citizen in 1955. Lack of government support retarded the development of an earth satellite until the launching of *Sputnik I* by the Soviet Union in October 1957 provided the necessary impetus. In January 1958 the Huntsville group orbited *Explorer I*, the first U.S. satellite. Two years later the group became part of the National Aeronautics and Space Administration (NASA); von Braun remained director of the renamed George C. Marshall Space Flight Center at Huntsville and worked on the development of the *Saturn V* rocket for the Project Apollo manned moon landing program. Others among his published works were *First Men to the Moon*, 1960, and *Space Frontier*, 1967. From 1970 to 1972 he served as deputy administrator of NASA; he then retired to enter private industry. He died in Alexandria, Virginia, on June 16, 1977.

Breasted, James Henry (1865–1935), archaeologist and historian. Born on August 27, 1865, in Rockford, Illinois, Breasted entered North-Western (now North Central) College in Naperville, Illinois, at fifteen, but did not receive his B.A. degree until 1890. An interest in botany and chemistry had meanwhile led him to undertake apprenticeships in local pharmacies; during 1882–1886 he attended the Chicago College of Pharmacy, graduating in 1886. Insufficiently stimulated by the work of a pharmacist, however, he began studies at the Congregational Institute (now Chicago Theological Seminary) in 1888, there learning Hebrew and beginning to translate and interpret the Scriptures. He transferred to Yale, studying in 1890–1891 under William Rainey Harper, who suggested that he fit himself for a chair in Egyptology at the new University of Chicago, of which Harper had been named president. Breasted received his M.A. from Yale in 1892, a year after beginning studies in Egyptology at the University of Berlin, where he took his doctorate in 1894. Returning to the United States, he became an assistant in Egyptology (the first such position in the country) and assistant director of the Haskell Oriental Museum at the University of Chicago. In 1896 he became an instructor in Egyptology and Semitic languages at Chicago and in 1905 professor of Egyptology and Oriental history. In the early 1900s he worked primarily in Europe, first for the Prussian Royal Academy of Science to develop with other scholars a dictionary of ancient languages from Egyptian texts, then for the academies of Berlin, Munich, Leipzig, and Göttingen to transcribe and sort systematically Egyptian hieroglyphics from European museums for the *Berlin Egyptian Dictionary*. In the course of that work he collected 10,000 historical documents from which he produced *A History of Egypt*, 1905, and *Ancient Records of Egypt*, 1906–1907, in five volumes. As director of the University of Chicago archaeological expedition to Egypt and the Sudan in 1905–1907 he recorded many inscriptions from deteriorating or formerly inaccessible monuments. During 1908–1919 he lived and taught in Chicago. In 1912 he published *Development of Religion and Thought in Ancient Egypt*, based on his Morse Lectures of that year given at the Union Theological Seminary. He produced with James Harvey Robinson the high-school textbooks *Outlines of European History*, 1914, and *Ancient Times: A History of the Early World*, 1916, the latter reaching a readership beyond the schools and tracing the arts and sciences to pre-Greek origins. In 1919 he delivered the William Ellery Hale Lectures on evolution at the National Academy of Sciences; they were published from October 1919 to March 1920 in the *Scientific Monthly* as "The Origins of Civilization." Shortly thereafter he became the first archaeologist to be elected to the National Academy of Sciences. In 1919 his devotion to uncovering man's earliest history bore fruit in his founding of the Oriental Institute at the University of Chicago, with a grant from John D. Rockefeller, Jr. In its first 40 years the Institute sent 20 expeditions to the Near East and published more than 125 scholarly papers. Breasted was relieved of teaching responsibilities in 1925 to assume full control of the Institute and its research projects. His later writings included *Oriental Forerunners of Byzantine Painting*, 1924; *The Conquest of Civilization*, 1926; the *Edwin Smith Surgical Papyrus*, 1930, two volumes; and *The Dawn of Conscience*, 1933. He died in New York City on December 2, 1935.

Breckinridge, John Cabell (1821–1875), public official and soldier. Born on January 21, 1821, near Lexington, Kentucky, Breckinridge graduated from Centre College of Kentucky in 1839, studied at the College of New Jersey (now Princeton), and then took up law at Transylvania University in Lexington; he was admitted to the Kentucky bar after a year of study. He entered practice in Frankfort, moved to Burlington, Iowa, where he lived for two years, and then returned to Kentucky. In 1847 he was commissioned major of a Kentucky volunteer regiment and served briefly in the Mexican War. In 1849 he was elected to the state legislature as a Democrat and two years later won a seat in the House of Representatives from a normally Whig district. In 1855, despite having established a national reputation and become the leader of the Kentucky Democrats, he returned to his law practice. The next year, however, he was nominated for vice-president as James Buchanan's running mate and was elected with Buchanan. His popularity in his home state was such that in 1859 he was elected to the Senate for the term to begin two years later. In 1860, when Southern Democrats withdrew from the national convention in protest against the nomination of Stephen A. Douglas, a splinter convention was held in Baltimore and Breckinridge was nominated for the presidency. Although reluctant at first, he soon began to campaign vigorously on a moderate Unionist platform. After the election of Abraham Lincoln he continued to preside over the Senate and to work for a compromise solution to the sectional problem until

March 1861. After taking his Senate seat in July in that year's special session, he attempted to maintain the neutrality of Kentucky while voting against Lincoln's war measures. In September military rule was established in Kentucky; Breckinridge fled to the Confederacy and in December was expelled from the Senate. Commissioned a brigadier general in the Confederate army, he commanded the reserves at Shiloh and in 1862 was promoted to major general. He saw action at Vicksburg, Murfreesboro (Stones River), Chickamauga, and elsewhere and was a competent division commander. In 1864 he served with Gen. Robert E. Lee in Virginia and was Gen. Jubal A. Early's second in command in the Shenandoah campaign. In February 1865 he was appointed Confederate secretary of war by Jefferson Davis. After Lee's surrender in April he fled south with other high-ranking Confederate officials. He escaped to Cuba and then to England, where he remained until an amnesty proclamation in 1868 made it possible for him to return to Lexington; he resumed his law practice and was active in railroad development in the state. He died in Lexington on May 17, 1875.

Brennan, William Joseph, Jr. (1906–   ), justice of the Supreme Court. Born on April 25, 1906, in Newark, New Jersey, Brennan graduated from the Wharton School of Finance and Commerce of the University of Pennsylvania in 1928 and then entered Harvard Law School, where he studied under Felix Frankfurter and from which he graduated in 1931. He was admitted to the bar the following year and joined a Newark law firm; specializing in labor law, he remained with the firm for 17 years, except for the period 1942–1945, during which he served in the army. He was appointed to the New Jersey superior court in 1949; the following year he became a judge of the appellate division and in 1952 was elevated to the state supreme court. On both benches he displayed not only high judicial ability but also considerable administrative leadership in devising means to clear the huge backlog of cases from the state court system's calendar and to speed the process of litigation. Brennan, although a Democrat, was named by President Dwight D. Eisenhower to the Supreme Court in 1956; taking his seat in October under a recess appointment, he was confirmed early the next year. Generally considered one of the liberal justices, he often acted as a mediator between liberal and conservative colleagues and on many occasions was able to secure broad agreement by interpreting cases upon narrow constitutional grounds. He was a staunch defender of the Bill of Rights, as evidenced by his opinions in such cases as *Ker* v. *California* (dissenting), 1963, and *Lopez* v. *U.S.* (dissenting), 1963, in both of which he spoke strongly for the right of individual privacy that he saw implied in the Fourth Amendment; in *Katzenbach* v. *Morgan*, 1966, a case involving literacy requirements for the franchise in New York, in which he considerably broadened the standing interpretation of the Fourteenth Amendment; and in *New York Times Co.* v. *Sullivan,* 1966, in which he held that proof of malice was required for conviction under state libel laws. Although he stood for a broad interpretation of the First Amendment he did not take an absolutist position, and in *Ginzburg* v. *U.S.,* 1966, and other cases, he weighed the interests of society against those of the individual. Brennan was also interested in seeing that proper criminal and civil procedures were adhered to by state and federal governments and on several occasions struck down actions by legislative committees that exceeded their constitutional authority. In *Baker* v. *Carr,* 1962 he wrote possibly his most far-reaching opinion, opening the way, under the Fourteenth Amendment, for a virtually complete legislative reapportionment of the country under scrutiny of the federal courts.

Brent, Margaret (1600?–1671?), colonial landowner. Born about 1600 in Gloucester, England, Margaret was the daughter of Richard Brent, Lord of Stoke and Admington. In 1638, with her sister, two brothers, and a number of indentured servants, she sailed for America and settled in St. Marys, Maryland. Her original land grant, the first made to a woman in Maryland, was increased by the proprietor of the colony, Lord Baltimore, and over the next few years was further augmented through family connections, business transactions, and the transportation of more colonists, until she became one of the largest landowners in the colony. She aided the governor, Leonard Calvert, in an armed dispute with William Claiborne of Virginia in 1644–1646, herself raising a troop of soldiers. Calvert, who became her brother-in-law, appointed her executor of his estate. Upon his death in 1647 she took charge of the estate and shortly thereafter received a court appointment as attorney for the proprietor as well. She liquidated some of Lord Baltimore's holdings in order to pay the soldiers who had fought Claiborne, averting thereby a mutiny and possibly a civil war. In 1648 she went before the assembly to request two votes in its proceedings, one for herself as a major landholder and one as attorney for the proprietor. She was refused and Lord Baltimore subsequently condemned her actions. As a result she left Maryland and settled anew in Westmoreland County, Virginia, in 1650 and remained there, living in semifeudal splendor, until her death sometime before May 1671.

Brewer, David Josiah (1837–1910), justice of the Supreme Court. Born of missionary parents at Smyrna (now Izmir), Turkey, on June 20, 1837, Brewer settled with his parents in Connecticut the following year. He attended Wesleyan University and then Yale, graduating in 1856; two years later he was admitted to the bar and traveled west to practice in Leavenworth, Kansas. From 1861 to 1870 he rose through the local judicial ranks and in the latter year was elected to the state's supreme court. In 1884 he was made a

federal circuit judge and five years later President Benjamin Harrison appointed him to the Supreme Court, where he served until his death. Conservatively inclined, Brewer generally expressed in his opinions a strict view of the constitutional limitations on federal power, although he supported such extensions of it as the building of the Panama Canal and the use of labor injunctions. Among his most notable opinions were those in *Reagan* v. *Farmers' Loan and Trust Company,* 1894, in which he ruled that rate fixing under state law was subject to judicial scrutiny; *In re Debs,* 1895, the principal injunction case of the period; *Kansas* v. *Colorado,* 1907, in which he struck down congressional assumption of powers not specifically delegated; and *Muller* v. *Oregon,* 1908, in which he reversed his stand (as in his dissent in *Holden* v. *Hardy,* 1898) and bowed to the force of one of Louis B. Brandeis's most remarkable briefs to uphold a state limitation on working hours for women. From 1895 to 1898 he helped, with Chief Justice Melville W. Fuller, to arbitrate the dispute over the boundary between British Guiana and Venezuela. After the Spanish-American War, in accordance with his views on imperialism and international peace, he advocated independence for the Philippines. Brewer died on March 28, 1910, in Washington, D.C.

Brewster, William (1567–1644), colonial leader. Born in Nottinghamshire, England, in 1567 (the month is unknown and the year was once in dispute), Brewster grew up in or near Scrooby. In 1580 he entered Cambridge University, but remained only a short time. He then became an assistant to William Davison, an important Elizabethan diplomat, and rendered good service until 1589, when Davison fell from favor. Brewster thereupon returned to Scrooby and the following year succeeded his father as bailiff of Scrooby Manor and as postmaster, both high and remunerative positions. He had first been exposed to Separatist religious ideas at Cambridge, and he gradually became the leading member of the little Puritan congregation in Scrooby. As official sanctions against Separatists increased the group adopted the idea of emigration; after a betrayed attempt in 1607 and subsequent imprisonment of several of the congregation, Brewster led and in large part financed an escape to Holland in 1608. The emigrants went first to Amsterdam and in 1609 settled in Leiden. Brewster was by that time nearly penniless, and to support his family first tutored in English and then became a printer, publishing religious books banned in England. In 1617 he began negotiations with the Virginia Company for a grant of land for colonization in America. Three years later, on September 16, 1620, the Leiden group, by then known as Pilgrims, set sail for Plymouth aboard the *Mayflower.* Brewster was from the first the principal member of the congregation of Plymouth Colony; although not an ordained minister nor at any time a holder of public office, he was both the ruling elder and teacher of the church and a valued adviser to Governor William Bradford. He retained his position of eminence until his death in Plymouth in 1644, probably on April 10.

Brice, Fannie (1891–1951), entertainer. Born in New York City on October 29, 1891, Fannie Borach, daughter of a barkeeper on the city's Lower East Side, took "Brice" as a stage name. She appeared first at thirteen in a talent contest at Keeney's Theatre in Brooklyn, singing "When You Know You're Not Forgotten by the Girl You Can't Forget," and won first prize. After that she left school to undertake a theatrical career. She was a pianist, a singer, and an assistant to the projectionist in a movie theater; at sixteen she won a place in the chorus line of the George M. Cohan–Sam Harris production *Talk of New York*, but was dismissed as soon as it became obvious that she could not dance. In one of the many burlesque houses where she sang, Florenz Ziegfeld discovered and hired her for the *Ziegfeld Follies* at $75 a week. She was a *Follies* perennial after 1910, and her comic routines and parodies were highly popular. Already famous as a comedienne, she first attained real stardom in the 1921 edition of the *Follies*, introducing a French torch song, "My Man," which became her trademark. She appeared with such major Broadway performers as W. C. Fields, Eddie Cantor, and Will Rogers in the *Follies* and in such other shows as *Music Box Revue of 1924* and Billy Rose's *Crazy Quilt*, 1930. A role she had played for friends became another *Follies* favorite—Baby Snooks—and in that character she was featured on radio from 1936 until her death. She appeared in one play, David Belasco's *Fannie*, in 1925, and was seen in a few motion pictures, including *My Man*, 1929; *The Great Ziegfeld*, 1936; and *Everybody Sing*, 1938. She died on May 29, 1951, in Hollywood. Her life was the subject of the film *Rose of Washington Square*, 1939, and of *Funny Girl*, a 1964 Broadway musical that was made into a movie in 1968.

Bridger, James (1804–1881), frontiersman, fur trader, and scout. Born in Richmond, Virginia, on March 17, 1804, Bridger moved with his parents to the vicinity of St. Louis about 1812. Both of his parents died during his youth and he was apprenticed to a blacksmith until 1822 when, in response to a newspaper advertisement, he joined William H. Ashley and Andrew Henry on their first fur-trapping expedition from St. Louis to the headwaters of the Missouri River. For the next 20 years he remained in the West as a trapper, gaining an incomparable knowledge of the country and becoming the most famous of the "mountain men." In 1824 he became the first white man to see the Great Salt Lake. In 1830 he formed a partnership with Thomas Fitzpatrick, Milton Sublette, and others, bought out the former Ashley interests that for four years had been held by Jedediah S. Smith, and organized the Rocky Mountain Fur Company; they continued to dominate the Western fur trade until 1834. With the fur trade on the decline, he established Fort Bridger on the Oregon Trail in Wyoming in 1843, and during the following ten years served as scout and guide for a number of exploring and surveying expeditions. About 1849 he discovered the famous Bridger's Pass in southern Wyoming. In 1853 he was driven from the region by the recently arrived Mormons and retired for a time to a farm near Kansas City, Missouri. Four years later he returned to the West as a guide in the army campaign against the Mormons. During 1865–1866 he worked as a guide and explorer in the building of the Powder River army road along the route of the Bozeman Trail. He remained in the West, fabled as the "Old Man of the Mountains," until 1868, when he once again retired to his farm. He died there on July 17, 1881.

Bridges, Harry (1901–   ), labor leader. Born on July 28, 1901, in Melbourne, Australia, Alfred Bryant Renton Bridges completed his schooling in 1917 and, after working for a brief period as a retail clerk, shipped as a merchant seaman. He arrived in the United States in 1920, worked for a time on coastal vessels and as an organizer for the Industrial Workers of the World (IWW), and in 1922, by which time he had acquired the permanent nickname of "Harry," settled in San Francisco as a longshoreman. He immediately began contending with the company union he was forced to join and, after a few earlier failures, in 1933 organized a San Francisco local of the International Longshoremen's Association (ILA). The widespread social and political unrest of the mid-Depression years greatly complicated the issue of unionization and, after attempts at arbitration failed, Bridges called a longshoremen's strike in May 1934 that led quickly to violence, martial law, and a short-lived general strike throughout the city. Arbitration eventually resulted in recognition of the union on the waterfront and settled most of its jurisdictional and working demands. In 1935 Bridges organized seven West Coast locals into the Maritime Federation of the Pacific, which embarked on a vigorous recruitment program as far afield as Hawaii. After a successful five-month strike, unauthorized by the international union, in 1936–1937, he broke with the ineffectual ILA and led the Maritime Federation into the recently organized Congress of Industrial Organizations (CIO). The union was reorganized as the International Longshoremen's and Warehousemen's Union (ILWU) and Bridges became its president; he was also elected to the CIO's executive board and named its Pacific regional director. His activities had already aroused powerful opposition in many quarters, and during the 1930s and 1940s many found cause for suspicion in the often close correspondence of his positions on political issues to the official Communist party line. In 1938 Secretary of Labor Frances Perkins ordered him deported; this opening government move in what turned into a 17-year legal battle was overturned by a hearing officer in 1939. In 1940 the House of

Representatives voted to have him deported. In 1941 a federal judge ruled for deportation as well; the order was reversed and then reinstated in subsequent appeals. Following a favorable Supreme Court decision on the case in 1945 he became a naturalized citizen. The case was reopened in 1949 when he was charged with having falsely denied past membership in the Communist party at his naturalization proceedings; found guilty in 1950, he carried appeals through the courts and was eventually cleared by the Supreme Court in 1953 on the grounds that he was protected by the statute of limitations. The government tried once more to oust him from the country in 1954, but the matter was finally dropped in 1955. During all that time and thereafter Bridges continued to head the ILWU and to mold it into a powerful and tightly organized union. His union was expelled from the CIO in 1950 but nevertheless continued to prosper. He retired after 40 years as president of the ILWU in 1977.

Bridgman, Laura Dewey (1829–1889), first successfully taught blind deaf-mute. Born on December 21, 1829, in Hanover, New Hampshire, Miss Bridgman was struck by scarlet fever at the age of two and left blind and deaf. Her other senses were also affected but she retained the sense of touch, which she developed sufficiently to learn to sew and knit. In 1837 her case came to the attention of Samuel Gridley Howe, director of the Perkins School for the Blind, then in Boston; he brought her to the school and began to teach her by touch. Attaching words made of raised letters to common objects, he was able eventually to convey to her the idea of names; inspired by the sudden revelation of the possibility of communication, she went on to learn the letters and the manual alphabet and with these was able to study a number of advanced subjects, from arithmetic to geography. She was the first blind deaf-mute ever known to have been taught successfully, and Howe's achievement drew much attention, especially after Charles Dickens visited the school in 1842 and enthusiastically described Miss Bridgman's accomplishments in his *American Notes*. She remained at the school for the rest of her life and gradually assumed household duties and helped teach other pupils. In 1887 a jubilee celebration was held to mark the fiftieth anniversary of her coming to the school. She died on May 24, 1889.

Bridgman, Percy Williams (1882–1961), physicist. Born in Cambridge, Massachusetts, on April 21, 1882, Bridgman graduated from Harvard in 1904 and four years later took his Ph.D. in physics there. He immediately joined the faculty of Harvard's physics department, where he remained until his retirement in 1954. In 1919 he became professor of physics and in 1926 he was named Hollis Professor of Mathematics and Natural Philosophy. His field of research through all his active years was the effect of extremely high pressures on materials. Designing equipment capable of producing higher and higher pressures, he tested scores of substances for compressibility, thermal and electrical conductivity, tensile strength, and viscosity. He was eventually able to generate pressures of up to one and a half million pounds per square inch. This work brought him the Nobel Prize for Physics in 1946. In 1939 he startled both academic circles and the general public with the announcement that thenceforward his laboratory would be closed and his hospitality unavailable to visitors representing nations under totalitarian governments. In 1949 he was elected a foreign member of the Royal Society of London, and in 1950 became Higgins University Professor at Harvard. In addition to his extensive laboratory work, he devoted considerable time to philosophical reflection and expressed his views in a number of books, including *The Nature of Physical Theory*, 1936; *The Intelligent Individual and Society*, 1938; *The Logic of Modern Physics*, 1946; and *Reflections of a Physicist*, 1950. Suffering from terminal cancer, Bridgman took his own life on August 20, 1961, in Randolph, New Hampshire.

Brinton, Daniel Garrison (1837–1899), anthropologist. Born in Thornbury, Pennsylvania, on May 13, 1837, Brinton graduated from Yale in 1858 and three years later took his M.D. from Jefferson Medical College. After a year of further study in Heidelberg and Paris he returned to enter practice in West Chester, Pennsylvania, in 1862. Shortly thereafter he was commissioned in the medical service of the army; he saw much action during the Civil War and at the time of his discharge in 1865 had attained the temporary rank of lieutenant colonel. He returned to West Chester, where he practiced until 1867; in that year he moved to Philadelphia and became assistant editor of the *Medical and Surgical Reporter*, of which he advanced to editor in 1874. During this time he devoted much of his energy to the study of anthropology, especially that of the American Indian, as an avocation. He published several papers on aspects of the subject and in 1884 was appointed professor of ethnology and archaeology at the Academy of Natural Sciences in Philadelphia. In 1886 he became professor of American linguistics and archaeology at the University of Pennsylvania and the next year gave up his medical and editorial work entirely. As an anthropologist Brinton was hampered by his total lack of field experience; he nonetheless made important contributions in a number of areas. He was the first to attempt a systematic classification of all Indian languages of North and South America, and in doing so he illuminated many of their interrelationships. Although he went astray in assigning to the Indians a European origin and in ignoring the diffusion theory in accounting for the similarities among myths of different cultures, he was one of the first to present literal rather than literary translations of aboriginal writings, including the vitally important Mayan chronicles. He also demonstrated that the ancient North American mound builders had been merely ancestral Indians rather than people of an altogether different culture. Among his many published works were *Myths of the New World*, 1868; *Aboriginal American Authors and their Productions*, 1882–1890, (also known as the *Library of Aboriginal American Literature*), 8 volumes; *Races and Peoples*, 1890; *The American Race*, 1891; and *Religions of Primitive Peoples*, 1897. Brinton died on July 31, 1899, in Atlantic City, New Jersey.

Brisbane, Albert (1809–1890), social reformer. Born in Batavia, New York, on August 22, 1809, Brisbane received little systematic education; he studied with a number of tutors and spent several restless years in Europe in search of a direction for his reformist inclinations. There he met and for a time studied under Charles Fourier who advocated separate, self-sustaining communities as ideal. In Fourier's works Brisbane discovered a program for the renovation of society that he could fully adopt. In 1834 he returned to the United States and, after a period of ill health, began to introduce the doctrine of Fourierism, which he renamed Associationism. He was encouraged by the apparent early success of the Brook Farm community at West Roxbury, Massachusetts, to which he made numerous visits and which was later (1844) converted into a Fourierist phalanx. His book, *Social Destiny of Man*, 1840, attracted the attention of Horace Greeley, who put the columns of the *New York Tribune* at his disposal. Having expected that a long period of education and preparation would be required for the establishment of Fourierist societies in the United States, Brisbane was overwhelmed when the publicity provided by Greeley prompted the founding of some 30 communities in a very short time. Nearly all were ill-conceived and failed quickly. Brisbane's own North American Phalanx in Red Bank, New Jersey, founded in 1843 and supported by many of the leading reformers of the time, lasted for only 12 years. With the fading of public interest, he gradually abandoned Fourierism and turned his attention to personal affairs. He died in Richmond, Virginia, on May 1, 1890.

Brisbane, Arthur (1864–1936), newspaper editor and journalist. Born on December 12, 1864, in Buffalo, New York, Brisbane was the son of social reformer Albert Brisbane. He was educated in public schools in New Jersey and New York, and later in Europe. At nineteen he became a reporter for Charles A. Dana's *New York Sun* and later was its London correspondent and night editor. In 1887 he became managing editor of the newly established *Evening Sun* and was so successful with it that in 1890 Joseph Pulitzer hired him away to fill a series of editorial and advisory positions with the *New York World*. In 1896 he became editor of the *Sunday World*; his predecessor, who had already established a reputation for sensationalism, had gone over to William Ran-

dolph Hearst's *New York Evening Journal*, and a stiff competition for readership was soon under way. Brisbane indulged in such excesses of sensationalism that Pulitzer became alarmed; he ordered his editor to restore the paper to its previous high standards and to cease featuring his own opinions in print. Instead, Brisbane resigned and in 1897 joined the *Journal*. The battle for circulation continued and within seven weeks Brisbane had increased the *Journal*'s circulation from 40,000 to 325,000. Relying on the spectacular techniques of "yellow journalism," he won readers by a combination of ever-increasing sensationalism and jingoism. The *World* followed suit in spite of Pulitzer; reporting in both papers ran to sheer fiction, and each contributed in major fashion to whipping up the public furor that led to the outbreak of the Spanish–American War in 1898. Brisbane himself was capable of reversing editorial policy on a moment's notice in order to increase circulation. At various times he directed others of Hearst's newspapers and during 1917–1919 owned a number of papers himself. In 1917 he began a daily editorial column, "Today," that was eventually distributed to more than a thousand daily and weekly papers and that was often featured on their front pages. Brisbane invested heavily in real estate in New Jersey and New York City, owned several hotels, and built the Ritz Tower and, with Hearst, the Ziegfeld Theatre. A man of enormous energy, he worked ceaselessly until his death on December 25, 1936, in New York City.

Bristow, Benjamin Helm (1832–1896), lawyer and public official. Born in Elkton, Kentucky, on June 20, 1832, Bristow graduated from Jefferson (now Washington and Jefferson) College in 1851 and two years later was admitted to the bar. He practiced in Elkton and later in Hopkinsville until 1861, when, in accordance with his unionist and antislavery views, he accepted a commission as lieutenant colonel of a Kentucky regiment. He saw action at Fort Henry, Fort Donelson, and at Shiloh, where he was wounded, and by 1863 was colonel of the 8th Kentucky Cavalry. In that year he was elected to the state senate without his knowledge; although reluctant to give up his commission, he understood the need for Union men in the legislature and took his seat in December. He resigned in 1865 and moved to Louisville to resume law practice. Almost immediately he was appointed assistant U.S. attorney and the next year he became U.S. attorney for Kentucky. Faced with widespread civil unrest, he was highly effective in opposing the Ku Klux Klan (KKK) and in protecting the rights of the newly enfranchised blacks; he also made headway against internal revenue frauds and the illicit liquor trade. In 1870 he resigned the post and formed a law partnership with John M. Harlan; his return to practice was brief, however, for in the same year President Ulysses S. Grant named him to the newly created office of solicitor general. He filled the position capably for two years and then again returned to the law, first in a brief association with the Texas & Pacific Railroad and then in private practice. In 1874 Grant called on him once more, this time to take over the scandal-ridden treasury department. As secretary Bristow effected a thorough reorganization, eliminating waste, corruption, and several lower officials. He undertook a secret investigation of the Whisky Ring, a conspiracy of Western distillers and revenue officers to evade payment of the liquor tax. Operatives from outside the department gathered evidence and in 1875 the ring's St. Louis, Chicago, and Milwaukee branches were exposed. Under great pressure from many—including Orville E. Babcock, Grant's private secretary and allegedly a party to the conspiracy—Bristow was forced to resign in June 1876. He had already been mentioned prominently for the Republican presidential nomination and, backed by moderates and others disgusted with Grant's administration, he was among those proposed to the national convention in Cincinnati that year. At length, however, he bowed out of a deadlock and gave his support to Rutherford B. Hayes. Moving to New York City in 1878, he resumed his law practice. In 1879 he was elected the second president of the American Bar Association, and he was also active in the Civil Service Reform Association. Bristow died in New York City on June 22, 1896.

Bromfield, Louis (1896–1956), author. Born on December 27, 1896, in Mansfield, Ohio, Bromfield grew up on a farm and in 1914 entered Cornell University to study agriculture. A year later he transferred to the journalism school of Columbia University. In 1916, during World War I, he sailed to Europe to serve with the American Ambulance Corps in France; he was much decorated and upon his return to New York was awarded an honorary B.A. by Columbia. He took a job with the City News Association, later moved to the Associated Press, and then for several years engaged in a variety of activities, including serving as foreign editor for *Musical America*, as arts critic for the *Bookman*, and as an original staff member of *Time* magazine. He published his first book, *The Green Bay Tree*, in 1924; it was followed quickly by *Possession*, 1925; *Early Autumn*, 1926; and *A Good Woman*, 1927, forming a tetralogy that was highly praised by critics as a penetrating commentary on the American scene. *Early Autumn* was awarded a Pulitzer Prize in 1927. Subsequent books included *The Strange Case of Miss Annie Spragg*, 1928; *Twenty-four Hours*, 1930; *The Farm*, 1933; *The Man Who Had Everything*, 1935; and collections of stories entitled *Awake and Rehearse*, 1929, and *Here Today and Gone Tomorrow*, 1934. In the 1930s Bromfield bought a farm, Malabar, near his boyhood home and built it into a showplace of scientific agriculture. In adition he became deeply interested in politics, supporting the New Deal generally but strongly criticizing its farm policies. He wrote numerous articles on agricul-

ture and economics and continued to produce novels regularly, although with a considerable loss of critical esteem. Compared unfavorably with his early books, although several were bought for the screen, were *The Rains Came*, 1937; *Night in Bombay*, 1939; *Wild Is the River*, 1941; *Until the Day Break*, 1942; *Mrs. Parkington*, 1943; *What Became of Anna Bolton*, 1944; *Kenny*, 1947; and *The Wild Country*, 1948. His farm experiences and reflections on farm life resulted in a number of nonfiction works that were much better received—*Pleasant Valley*, 1945; *Malabar Farm*, 1948; *Out of the Earth*, 1950; *Animals and Other People*, 1955; and others. He died on March 18, 1956, in Columbus, Ohio.

Bronk, Detlev Wulf (1897–1975), physiologist and educator. Born in New York City on August 13, 1897, Bronk interrupted his studies at Swarthmore College to serve in the naval aviation corps during World War I, returning to graduate in 1920. After working for a year he undertook graduate studies briefly at the University of Pennsylvania and from 1921 to 1926 at the University of Michigan, where he was instructor in physics and later in physiology and from which he took his Ph.D. in 1926. For the next three years he taught physiology and biophysics at Swarthmore, serving also as dean of men from 1927. In 1929 he became professor of biophysics and director of the E. R. Johnson Research Foundation at the University of Pennsylvania; in addition he was head of the university's Institute of Neurology, 1936–1940 and 1942–1949, and in 1940–1941 was professor of physiology at Cornell University Medical School. Bronk's researches during this time were concerned primarily with the physiology of the nervous system and the chemical-electrical mechanisms and effects of nerve-impulse transmission. In 1949 he assumed the presidency of The Johns Hopkins University, where he continued in general the policies of his predecessor, Isaiah Bowman. He left in 1953 to become president of the Rockefeller Institute for Medical Research (now Rockefeller University), New York City, where he remained until his retirement in 1968. Also active in government service, he held a great many positions with various advisory boards and became one of the outstanding scientific administrators in the nation. From 1942 to 1946 he was a consultant to the secretary of war and research coordinator for the air surgeon's office, Army Air Forces; from 1946 to 1950 he was chairman of the National Research Council; from 1950 to 1962 president of the National Academy of Sciences; from 1956 to 1963 a member of the President's Science Advisory Committee; and from 1956 to 1964 chairman of the governing board of the National Science Foundation. He served in editorial capacities with a number of professional journals. Among his many honors and awards were the Presidential Medal of Freedom from President Lyndon B. Johnson in 1964 and more than 50 honorary degrees. Bronk died in New York City on November 17, 1975.

Brookings, Robert Somers (1850–1932), businessman, educator, and philanthropist. Born in Cecil County, Maryland, on January 22, 1850, Brookings received little more than an elementary education. At seventeen he joined his brother in working for the St. Louis woodenware firm of Samuel Cupples and four years later the two became partners in the business. After becoming head of the company and developing extensive interests in real estate and other ventures, Robert was a multimillionaire when he decided in 1896 to retire and devote himself to philanthropic enterprises. The next year he became president of the corporation of Washington University. He secured a new site for the institution and, through his own contributions and those he induced other wealthy citizens to make, built up an impressive physical plant and endowment. Inspired by Abraham Flexner's 1910 report, *Medical Education in the United States and Canada*, for the Carnegie Foundation for the Advancement of Teaching, Brookings set about raising the standards of the medical school of the university; within three years he had developed a program that was pronounced unexcelled by the president of the Carnegie Foundation. He was an original trustee ·of the Carnegie Endowment for International Peace and during World War I served as chairman of the price-fixing committee of the War Industries Board. In 1916 he became chairman of the board of the Institute for Government Research in Washington, D.C.; six years later he prevailed upon the Carnegie Corporation of New York to endow the Institute of Economics and in 1924 he himself provided the funds for the Robert Brookings Graduate School of Economics and Government. In 1927 the trustees of the three organizations voted to merge and named the combined research and graduate training center the Brookings Institution. In after years this institution became one of the most prestigious of its kind in the United States, undertaking important research for and about the U.S. government and concerning U.S. economic practices and problems. Brookings relinquished his position with Washington University in the same year and died in Washington, D.C., on November 15, 1932.

Brooks, Gwendolyn (1917–   ), poet. Born on June 7, 1917, in Topeka, Kansas, Miss Brooks grew up in Chicago and graduated from Wilson Junior College in 1936. She had long been fascinated by poetry and had written many poems, one of which was published in *American Childhood* when she was thirteen, and a number of which appeared in the *Chicago Defender* while she was still in her teens. While working at various jobs she attended a poetry workshop of the South Side Community Art Center and began developing a mature technique. She won several local competitions and in 1944 was published in *Poetry* magazine. The following year her first collection, *A Street in Bronzeville*, was warmly received by critics and led to two successive Guggenheim fellowships. *Annie Allen*, her second

volume, appeared in 1949 and was widely praised for its innovative but unstrained use of language and particularly for its elegant lyrical passages. For that book Miss Brooks was awarded the Pulitzer Prize in 1950, becoming the first black woman whose work was so honored. Subsequent writings included a novel, *Maud Martha*, 1953; *Bronzeville Boys and Girls*, 1956; *The Bean Eaters*, 1960; *Selected Poems*, 1963; *In the Mecca*, 1968; and *Riot*, 1970. She taught poetry at various times in several Chicago colleges and in 1968 was named poet laureate of Illinois.

Brooks, Phillips (1835–1893), religious leader. Born on December 13, 1835, in Boston, Brooks graduated from Harvard in 1855, taught briefly at the Boston Latin School, then attended the Episcopal seminary at Alexandria, Virginia, where he was ordained in 1859. From then until 1869 he occupied the pulpits of two Philadelphia churches in turn. He gained a national reputation in 1865 when he delivered a compelling sermon at Independence Hall over the body of President Abraham Lincoln and also offered a stirring prayer at the Harvard commemoration of the Civil War dead. In 1868 his famous Christmas hymn "O Little Town of Bethlehem" was first sung. From 1869 to 1891 he was rector of Trinity Church in Boston. During this period he also served as an overseer of Harvard and the university preacher. He preached to large congregations who appreciated his intelligent, soft-spoken style, and his many volumes of published sermons were popular. His refusal to employ harsh images and thundering oratory, even in response to charges of heresy by contemporary conservatives, won him stature in the eyes of his parishioners. A statue of him by the sculptor Augustus Saint-Gaudens was later erected outside Trinity. His teachings—that man, not the church, was the focus of God's attention, and that the church was established that men might live better lives—profoundly influenced his community. In contrast to the austerity of the Puritan heritage still strong in New England, he preached a Christianity of joy and liberality. Brooks's wide repute was such that in 1880 he was invited to preach in Westminster Abbey; the following Sunday, in the presence of Queen Victoria, he became the first American clergyman to conduct services for the royal family. He was consecrated bishop of Massachusetts in 1891 and died on January 23, 1893, in Boston. He was elected to the Hall of Fame in 1910.

Brooks, Van Wyck (1886–1963), critic and author. Born in Plainfield, New Jersey, on February 16, 1886, Brooks took his B.A. at Harvard in 1907 and began a long career as a distinguished scholar and author. With the exception of a brief period of teaching English at Stanford University during 1911–1913, he devoted his life to writing. His chief interest was in interpreting the cultural, particularly the literary, development of America. His early negative view of the effects of the Puritan heritage, expressed in *The Wine of the Puritans*, 1909; *America's Coming-of-Age*, 1915; *The Ordeal of Mark Twain*, 1920; and *The Pilgrimage of Henry James*, 1925, was exchanged for a more balanced, even appreciative, treatment in his later *The Flowering of New England*, 1936, which won a Pulitzer Prize; *New England: Indian Summer*, 1940; *The World of Washington Irving*, 1944; *The Times of Melville and Whitman*, 1947; and *The Confident Years*, 1952. These last five volumes comprised a series on the history of American literary life entitled *Makers and Finders*. Others of his works included *On Literature Today*, 1941; *The Writer in America*, 1953; and several volumes of memoirs, later collected as *An Autobiography*, 1965. He wrote a number of biographical studies, was an active editor, and translated works by several modern French authors. Brooks died on May 2, 1963, in Bridgewater, Connecticut, where he had lived for many years.

Broun, Heywood, (1888–1939), journalist and critic. Born in Brooklyn, New York, on December 7, 1888, Matthew Heywood Campbell Broun left Harvard without a degree in 1910 and returned to newspaper work with the *New York Morning Telegraph*, for which he had previously worked, beginning in 1908. Moving to the *New York Tribune* in 1912, he developed his unique style as a sports and feature writer and in 1916 became the newspaper's drama critic. He was a correspondent in Europe during the period of U.S. participation in World War I and his dispatches from France, followed after the war by his literary column in the *Tribune*, won him a rapidly growing readership. In 1921 he began his column, "It Seems to Me," in the *New York World*. Eventually syndicated, the column had a huge following; in it, Broun mixed his personal and humorous observations with expressions of his strong awareness of social injustice that, when given such occasion as the Sacco-Vanzetti case, could be roused to a near fury. In 1930 he ran unsuccessfully for the House of Representatives as a Socialist and throughout the Depression he exerted himself on behalf of the unemployed. He was an organizer of the American Newspaper Guild in 1933 and was its first president, remaining in the post until his death. *The Nation* and *The New Republic* printed occasional articles of his, and for a short time he published his own newspaper, *Broun's Nutmeg*. Among his books, most of them collections of his columns, were *Pieces of Hate*, 1922, and *Gandle Follows His Nose*, 1926. He died in New York City on December 18, 1939.

Browder, Earl Russell (1891–1973), political leader. Born on May 20, 1891, in Wichita, Kansas, Browder left school after the third grade in order to help support his family. Under his father's influence he became a Socialist and later, in Kansas City, he met William Z. Foster, with whom he was associated for many years. He helped edit the *Toiler*, a syndicalist journal, and

worked at various jobs until 1919, when he was imprisoned for a year for agitating against military conscription during World War I. In 1921 he moved to New York City and joined the recently organized American Communist party; he was also managing editor of the *Labor Herald* and a close associate of Foster in the Trade Union Educational League. The two remained prominently among the leadership as the Communist party passed through numerous reorganizations. Browder made several trips to the Soviet Union to attend international conferences and in 1927–1928 was director of the Pan-Pacific Trade Union Secretariat in China. In 1930 he became secretary-general of the U.S. Communist party, a post he held for 15 years during the party's period of greatest growth and influence. In 1936 and 1940 he was the party's nominee for the presidency; in both campaigns he urged strong action against the fascist governments of Spain, Italy, Germany, and Japan, and greater cooperation between the United States and the Soviet Union. His 1940 campaign was conducted while he was free on bail, and shortly afterward he served a prison term for irregular use of his passport. In 1944, during World War II, he announced a new policy of reconciliation between socialism and capitalism and the transformation of the party into the Communist Political Association. Also in that year he became editor of the *Daily Worker*, the party's newspaper. The following year he was ousted from the post of secretary-general and in 1946 was expelled from the party for his coexistence policy, which was termed "revisionist" by hard-line Communists. Through the years he published numerous books, among them *Communism in the United States*, 1935; *The People's Front*, 1938; *Our Path in War and Peace*, 1944; *War or Peace with Russia*, 1947; and *Marx and America*, 1958. He died in Princeton, N.J., on June 27, 1973.

Brown, Benjamin Gratz (1826–1885), public official. Born in Lexington, Kentucky, on May 28, 1826, Brown belonged to a politically prominent family. He was educated at Transylvania University and at Yale, from which he graduated in 1847, and after gaining admission to the bar moved to St. Louis in 1849. While conducting his practice he became involved in Democratic politics, strongly supporting Senator Thomas Hart Benton and serving in the legislature from 1852 to 1859. His antislavery leanings led him into the Free-Soil faction and shaped his editorship (1854–1859) of the *Missouri Democrat*. In 1860 he joined in organizing the Republican party in Missouri and attended the national convention in Chicago. He served briefly as a colonel in the Civil War, helping to hold Missouri in the Union, and became a leader of the movement for immediate emancipation. He was elected to fill an unexpired term in the Senate in 1863 and until leaving that body in 1867 was generally aligned with the Radical Republicans. Upon his return to Missouri, however, he stood against the excesses of the Radical regime, becoming prominent in the

Liberal movement that sought amnesty for former rebels, repeal of test-oath requirements, and general reconciliation. He was elected governor in 1870 and in that position was able to lend considerable force to the formation of the Liberal Republican party in 1872, organized nationally to oppose both the Radicals and the administration of Ulysses S. Grant. At the party's convention in Cincinnati that year he ended the debate over a presidential candidate by throwing his support to Horace Greeley, who was thereupon nominated over Charles Francis Adams. Brown accepted the second spot on the ballot; he campaigned vigorously although sometimes imprudently, and went down to defeat with Greeley. He returned to St. Louis and his law practice, specializing in railroad cases, and took little part in politics thereafter beyond publicly returning to the Democratic party and addressing its 1876 convention. Brown died in St. Louis on December 13, 1885.

Brown, Charles Brockden (1771–1810), author. Born of Quaker parents in Philadelphia on January 17, 1771, Brown began to write and to dream of a literary career while yet in school. Set to study law by his parents, he did not give himself entirely to writing until 1793. After publishing a treatise on women's rights, written in dialogue form, he produced, in the space of two years, the four novels that constituted his best work: *Wieland*, 1798; *Ormond* and *Edgar Huntly*, both 1799; and *Arthur Mervyn*, two volumes, 1799–1800. Reflecting the influence of the utopian ideas of William Godwin, the four books were Gothic tales of supernaturalism, horror, and psychological aberration in an American setting. Brown produced a few lesser works during the next years but his dwindling resources, both literary and financial, forced him to seek a more secure livelihood. He became a merchant and, except for some magazine editing and pamphlet writing, never returned to the literary life. His best work had won the admiration of Percy Shelley, however, and he had succeeded in becoming, if only for a time, the country's first professional novelist. He died on February 22, 1810, in Philadelphia.

Brown, Helen Hayes, *see* Hayes, Helen

Brown, Henry Billings (1836–1913), justice of the Supreme Court. Born in South Lee, Massachusetts, on March 2, 1836, Brown graduated from Yale in 1856, spent a year in Europe, and returned to take up the study of law at Yale and at Harvard and on his own in Detroit, where he was admitted to the bar in 1860. The following year he was appointed deputy U.S. marshal and in 1863 assistant U.S. district attorney for eastern Michigan. Upon leaving the latter post in 1868 he served as temporary judge of the circuit court and then returned to private practice. In his public offices he had become intimately familiar with federal law, and in his practice in the busy port of Detroit he

became expert in the field of maritime law; he was thus eminently qualified to sit as U.S. district judge upon his appointment by President Ulysses S. Grant in 1875. He served with great distinction on the district bench for 15 years, publishing a volume of admiralty case reports and achieving recognition as the nation's foremost authority in that field. In 1890 President Benjamin Harrison named him to the Supreme Court. Although he was equal to the challenge of the court and a dedicated laborer under its heavy case load, he delivered few memorable opinions, his chief ones being a dissent in *Pollock* v. *Farmers' Loan and Trust Co.*, 1895, in which the income-tax clauses of the Wilson-Gorman Tariff Act of 1894 were declared unconstitutional, and a controversial concurrence in *Downes* v. *Bidwell*, 1901, one of the Insular Cases, in which he held that none of the constitutionally guaranteed rights and privileges of citizenship extended to the people of annexed territories. Justice Brown retired from the Supreme Court in 1906 and settled in Bronxville, New York, where he lived quietly until his death on September 4, 1913.

Brown, Irving, *see* Adams, William Taylor

Brown, Jacob Jennings (1775–1828), soldier. Born on May 9, 1775, in Bucks County, Pennsylvania, Brown was descended from a line of Quaker farmers. After some years spent teaching school in New Jersey, doing surveying in Ohio, and again teaching, in New York City, he served for a time as secretary to Alexander Hamilton. In 1800 he took up farming on a large estate on the shore of Lake Ontario in western New York. He became active in the state militia and at the outbreak of the War of 1812 was a brigadier general. Placed in command of the New York frontier, he successfully repelled British attacks at Ogdensburg and Sackets Harbor and was consequently appointed brigadier general in the regular army in July 1813. After taking part in the disastrous Montreal Campaign he was promoted to major general and given command at Niagara, replacing Gen. James Wilkinson. With Gen. Winfield Scott leading one of his brigades of regulars, Brown undertook a campaign into Canada in 1814, crossing the Niagara River and taking Fort Erie. Scott won a sharp engagement at Chippawa on July 5 and the army proceeded to Lundy's Lane, where a battle producing heavy casualties on both sides ensued on July 25; although the British position was taken, Brown was forced to retire and to give up his ultimate objective, the capture of York (now Toronto), when expected naval support from Commodore Isaac Chauncey failed to materialize. The battle nonetheless was one of the most famous of the war. After returning to Fort Erie, Brown's forces repulsed a British attack and later, by a highly successful sortie, broke a month-long siege. The northern campaign, the Americans' only really satisfactory one in the war, soon came to an end. Brown became the senior officer of the army in 1815 and six years later was appointed commanding general, a post he held until his death on February 24, 1828, in Washington, D.C.

Brown, James (1933–   ), singer. Born in 1933 in Augusta, Georgia, Brown grew up in the poverty of a Southern black family during the Depression. He received little education and from an early age worked at various jobs, from picking cotton to singing and dancing on street corners for nickels and dimes. After a brief encounter with the juvenile authorities he decided to make his career in music. Forming a trio with which he appeared in small clubs throughout the South, he sang at every opportunity. Combining strains of the blues and gospel traditions with his own highly individual delivery and a marked flair for showmanship, he evolved a style that was both authentic and unique. He gradually enlarged his troupe to a full ensemble that included his band, the Famous Flames, dancing girls, a chorus, and a retinue of retainers. Performances on stage, arranged and rehearsed with military precision, aimed at evoking the maximum emotional response from the audience. Recordings such as "Please, Please, Please" (his frenzied finale in live appearances), "Papa's Got a Brand New Bag," "I Can't Stand Myself," and "It's a Man's World" earned him billing as "Mr. Dynamite" and "Soul Brother Number One" and made his name a guarantee of a sell-out crowd or a record that would sell a million copies. Brown was deeply interested in encouraging young black people to finish their educations ("Don't Be a Dropout" was one of his hits), to develop pride in their heritage ("Say It Loud—I'm Black and I'm Proud!" was another), and to see in his own example the results of devotion to hard work. He was fond of recalling for audiences the radio station in Augusta in front of which he had shined shoes as a child: "I own that station now. That's black power!" Following the assassination of Dr. Martin Luther King, Jr., in April 1968, he made marathon television appearances in Boston and Washington, D.C., urging people to stay off the streets and to mourn in peace; for these and other efforts he was given that year's B'nai B'rith Humanitarian Award.

Brown, John (1800–1859), abolitionist. Born in Torrington, Connecticut, on May 9, 1800, Brown was for most of his life a restless drifter and business failure. By turns a drover, tanner, farmer, and wool dealer, he succeeded only in amassing a burden of debt and a family of 20 children. Although he had felt abolitionist leanings all his life, his first active involvement in the antislavery cause came in 1849 when he settled his family in a Negro community that had been established at North Elba, New York, by Gerrit Smith. Two years later he moved to Ohio and became an agent for the underground railroad. Then in 1855 he followed five of his sons to Kansas to join in the battle between proslavery and antislavery factions for control of the terri-

torial government. He settled near Osawatomie, Kansas, and in after years was often referred to as "Old Brown of Osawatomie." He quickly became a leader of the Free-Soil fighters; his fame became national with the Pottawatomie Massacre of 1856 in which Brown, convinced of a divine call to action, and seven others brutally murdered five settlers suspected of proslavery beliefs, in revenge for previous murders by proslavery men. During the next three years he continued his crusade while seeking financial support for a plan to establish a guerrilla base in the mountains of Maryland and Virginia, from which escaped slaves and their allies could attack slaveholding regions. Elected "commander" of this "free state," he secured backing from a number of prominent Boston abolitionists, including Smith, Theodore Parker, Thomas W. S. Higginson, and Samuel Gridley Howe, and in 1859 organized a headquarters near Harpers Ferry, Virginia (now in West Virginia). On October 16 he and his band of 21 followers entered Harpers Ferry and occupied the federal arsenal; instead of withdrawing to the mountains they remained, holding a number of hostages and exchanging fire with the local militia. Early on the morning of the 18th the arsenal was retaken by a company of U.S. Marines under the command of Col. Robert E. Lee. Of Brown's followers ten had been killed and six more were captured and later hanged. Brown was tried in Charles Town and convicted of murder, promoting slave insurrection, and treason against Virginia. Refusing to plead insanity, for which there was considerable evidence, he maintained a solemn and dignified demeanor throughout the trial. In a remarkable and deeply moving final address to the court Brown explained his course: "I am yet too young to understand that God is any respecter of persons. I believe that to have interfered as I have done—as I have always freely admitted I have done—in behalf of His despised poor, was not wrong but right. Now if it is deemed necessary that I should forfeit my life for the furtherance of the ends of justice and mingle my blood further with the blood of my children and with the blood of millions in this slave country whose rights are disregarded by wicked, cruel, and unjust enactments—I submit; so let it be done!" His execution in Charles Town on December 2, 1859, made him a martyr in the view of many in the North, while it did little to mollify an outraged South, where he was seen virtually as a devil incarnate. "John Brown's Body" became probably the most popular Union song during the Civil War.

Brown, Olympia (1835–1926), religious leader and social reformer. Born in Prairie Ronde, Michigan, on January 5, 1835, Miss Brown was refused admission to the University of Michigan because of her sex and instead attended Antioch College, graduating in 1860. Three years later she graduated from the theological school of St. Lawrence University and entered the ministry of the Universalist church, becoming the first American woman to be ordained by a regularly constituted ecclesiastical organization. She served churches in Weymouth, Massachusetts, Bridgeport, Connecticut, and a number of towns in Wisconsin over the next several years. At the same time her long-latent interest in women's rights was aroused by a meeting with Susan B. Anthony in 1866 and she became one of the cause's leading champions in the West. She campaigned vigorously but unsuccessfully for universal suffrage in Kansas in 1867 and, following her marriage to John H. Willis in 1873, she retained her maiden name. From 1887 to 1917 she was president of the Wisconsin Woman's Suffrage Association and she traveled and spoke widely on its aims. She published *Acquaintances, Old and New, Among Reformers,* in 1911, and managed her husband's newspaper and printing business from his death in 1893 until 1914, when she moved to Baltimore. There she continued an active and independent existence until her death on October 23, 1926.

Browne, Charles Farrar (1834–1867), "Artemus Ward," humorist. Born on April 26, 1834, in Waterford, Maine, Browne was a typesetter and a rewrite man on country newspapers before moving to Boston, where his first literary piece, "The Surrender of Cornwallis," was published in the *Carpet Bag* in 1852. He then traveled west, settling in Cleveland. There, on the staff of the *Cleveland Plain Dealer,* he developed in 1858, the character of "Artemus Ward" or "A. Ward," a traveling showman. With these articles and a series of letters, whose satirical insights into a wide range of subjects were tempered with comic misspellings and verbal puns, he gained a wide reputation. Joining the staff of *Vanity Fair* in New York in 1859, he produced the sketches and burlesque romances that were compiled in *Artemus Ward: His Book,* 1862. In New London, Connecticut, in 1861, he delivered his first "moral" lecture, "Babes in the Wood." It concerned neither babes nor the wood and employed the same droll humor as his writing. He then set out on tour, delivering the lecture to appreciative audiences in many cities. A trip to Washington inspired "Artemus Ward in Washington," concerning an imaginary meeting with President Abraham Lincoln. Browne's admiration for the president and his pro-Union sympathies became apparent during the Civil War, when he wrote such sketches as "High Handed Outrage in Utica" and "The Show is Confiscated." Lincoln greatly admired these works and read "Outrage" to his cabinet in 1862. Traveling to lecture in the Far West during 1863–1864, Browne encountered the Mormons in Salt Lake City, and "Artemus Ward Among the Mormons" became his next platform topic. Delighted audiences in England heard him in 1866; during the tour he became ill, and he died in Southampton on March 6, 1867.

Browning, John Moses (1855–1926), inventor. Born in Ogden, Utah, on January 21, 1855, Browning was the son of a Mormon gunsmith. He early displayed a talent for mechanics and invention, constructing his first gun from scrap at the age of thirteen. In 1879 he patented a breech-loading, single-shot rifle and sold it for a substantial royalty to the Winchester Repeating Arms Company. He went on to design numerous other firearms for various manufacturers; among them were a repeating rifle patented in 1884, a repeating shotgun for Winchester, the Remington automatic-loading shotguns and rifles, the Stevens rifles, and the Colt automatic pistols. His guns were also manufactured by his own company, organized with his brother as the J. M. & M. S. Browning Company. In 1890 the U.S. army adopted his Colt-made machine gun and later, during the Spanish-American War, used his "Peacemaker" machine gun. His Colt automatic pistol was also bought by the army for use during World War I, along with a heavy water-cooled machine gun and an automatic rifle, the famed BAR. The machine gun, in a .50-caliber model firing up to 1250 rounds per minute, was also adapted for use in aircraft. Browning was much honored for his inventions and his weapons were widely used during World War II. While on a business trip, he died near Liège, Belgium, on November 26, 1926.

Brownlow, William Gannaway (1805–1877), religious leader, editor, and public official. Born in Wythe County, Virginia, on August 29, 1805, Brownlow moved with his family to the vicinity of Knoxville, Tennessee, about 1810. He received an adequate education and in 1826 entered the ministry of the Methodist church. For several years he was an itinerant preacher, his fiery style earning him the nickname "the Fighting Parson," but his interest in public affairs led him away from the pulpit and, in 1838, into the editor's chair of the *Tennessee Whig.* From 1839 to 1849 he edited the *Jonesboro Whig and Independent* and then took over the *Knoxville Whig,* making it a strongly influential political journal. A thoroughgoing unionist, Brownlow opposed and ridiculed secession and maintained the *Knoxville Whig* as a champion of the federal government through the outbreak of the Civil War and after all other anti-Confederacy papers in the South had been suppressed. He was finally forced to close down in October 1861. He fled, was captured, imprisoned, and charged with treason to the Confederacy, but in March 1862 was released into Union territory. He spent a time in Ohio writing his *Sketches of the Rise, Progress, and Decline of Secession; with a Narrative of Personal Adventure Among the Rebels,* 1862, and then made a lecture tour of the North. With the occupation of eastern Tennessee by federal forces in 1863 he returned to become active in reorganizing the state government and in 1865 was chosen governor without opposition. He served effectively during a difficult time for two terms, securing the state against further civil disturbances and dealing strongly with the Ku Klux Klan (KKK) and in 1868 was elected to the Senate.

He sold the *Knoxville Whig* in 1869 but upon leaving the Senate in 1875 bought it back and continued as its editor until shortly before his death on April 29, 1877, in Knoxville.

Brownson, Orestes Augustus (1803–1876), religious leader, social reformer, and author. Born in Stockbridge, Vermont, on September 16, 1803, Brownson received no formal education during his youth but was a voracious reader. He joined the Presbyterian church in 1822; two years later he became a Universalist and was ordained in that church in 1826. His ever-growing liberalism soon estranged him from institutional religion, however, and he became an independent preacher. He was involved in the socialist movements of the period and helped to organize the Workingmen's party. He became a Unitarian minister in 1832, but four years later again broke away to establish his own church among the working men of Boston, which he named the Society for Christian Union and Progress. In 1836 he founded the *Boston Quarterly Review*, later merged with the *Democratic Review*, and served as its editor until 1842. He was associated with many of the leading figures of the day, particularly the Transcendentalist group centered around Ralph Waldo Emerson; he shared their enthusiasms but, even more than they, was too intellectually restless to remain long with one idea. Suddenly in 1844 he found an intellectual and religious home in Roman Catholicism, to which he converted rather spectacularly. In the same year he resumed his publishing career, editing *Brownson's Quarterly Review*, a highly personal journal of opinion that appeared from 1844 to 1865 and from 1872 to 1875. He also wrote a number of books, including *New Views of Christianity, Society and the Church*, 1836; *Charles Elwood; or, The Infidel Converted*, 1840, an autobiographical romance; and *The Convert; or, Leaves from My Experience*, 1857. In 1875 he moved to Detroit, where he died on April 17, 1876.

Brubeck, David Warren (1920–   ), pianist and composer. Born in Concord, California, on December 6, 1920, Brubeck grew up on a ranch and began studying piano at an early age with his mother. He graduated from the College (now University) of the Pacific in 1942 and continued his musical studies under composer Darius Milhaud at Mills College until 1949, taking time out to serve in the army as a Special Services entertainer in USOs during World War II. In 1950 he formed a jazz trio that expanded to a quartet the next year. Playing in clubs and on the radio in San Francisco, they built a large local following and began to attract attention elsewhere. They made their New York debut in 1952 and their records were soon much in demand among jazz enthusiasts. With his strong classical background, Brubeck was able to bring to jazz a complexity of rhythm and counterpoint never before attempted. Intended solely for listening, his music made new demands on its audience and rewarded its hearers

with a richness of invention altogether novel in the field. The quartet was soon recognized as the foremost exponent of what came to be called "modern" or "progressive" jazz. The members of the group, hardly changed over a remarkable 17-year association, were perfectly matched in style and taste, and alto saxophonist Paul Desmond shared with Brubeck the burden of the melodic line in an unfailingly creative partnership. Concert tours and record albums—among them *Jazz Goes to College, Jazz: Red Hot and Cool, Time Out*—spread and maintained their popularity throughout the United States and abroad. Brubeck disbanded the quartet at the end of 1967 to devote more time to composition and subsequently joined the Cincinnati Symphony Orchestra in recording his *Light in the Wilderness*, an oratorio.

Bruce, Blanche Kelso (1841–1898), public official. Born a slave in Farmville, Virginia, on March 1, 1841, Bruce received his early education from his owner's son. At the beginning of the Civil War he left his master and opened a school for Negroes in Hannibal, Missouri. After two years of study at Oberlin College, 1866–1868, he moved to Mississippi and became a prosperous planter. He was sergeant at arms of the state senate, assessor and sheriff of Bolivar County, and a member of the Board of Levee Commissioners of the Mississippi. In 1874 he was elected to the Senate, where he was a forceful advocate of civil rights for minority groups—Negroes, Chinese, and Indians alike—and also opposed discrimination against former rebels. The ending of the Reconstruction period prevented Bruce's reelection in 1880; he had been the first Negro to serve a full term in the Senate. He remained in Washington and was appointed register of the treasury in 1881 by President James A. Garfield. President Benjamin Harrison appointed him recorder of deeds for the District of Columbia in 1889, and in 1895 he was returned to the treasury post by President William McKinley. He retained that position until his death on March 17, 1898, in Washington, D.C.

Brulé, Étienne (1592?–1632?), explorer. Born in Champigny-sur-Marne, France, about 1592, Brulé came to America in 1608 with Samuel de Champlain and assisted in the founding of Quebec in that year. Later, at Champlain's behest, he spent a year with the Algonkian Indians, learning their language and the ways of the wilderness. The experience fitted him well for work as an explorer and interpreter and for many years he served Champlain in that double capacity, traveling and living in particular with the Huron. He was the first European to see any of the Great Lakes; he visited Lake Huron about 1612, and after exploring from the head of the Susquehanna River to Chesapeake Bay in 1615 he wandered widely, probably seeing Lakes Ontario, Superior, and Erie as well, and again living with the Huron. In 1629 he turned traitor to the French, selling his services as a guide to English forces pushing north into Canada. The last years of his life were spent in dissipation among the Huron, by whom he was killed in a quarrel in 1632 or 1633.

Brundage, Avery (1887–1975), businessman, sportsman, and sports figure. Born in Detroit on September 28, 1887, Brundage grew up in Chicago and graduated from the University of Illinois in 1909. An outstanding athlete in college, he won a place on the U.S. Olympic team in 1912 and captured the title of amateur all-around champion of America in 1914, 1916, and 1918. He had entered the construction business after graduation and in 1915 became president of the Avery Brundage Company; he amassed a fortune through the company and other enterprises. He maintained his devotion to athletics after his days as a competitor had passed; he was seven times president of the Amateur Athletic Union (AAU) of the United States, vice-president of the International Amateur Athletic Federation from 1930 to 1952, and president of the U.S. Olympic Association from 1929 to 1953. In 1936 he was chosen to serve on the International Olympic Committee (IOC), which exercises total authority over the quadrennial Olympic Games. He became vice-president of the IOC in 1945 and succeeded to the presidency in 1952. As president he became known throughout the world for his dedication to the principle of amateurism and his determination to keep questions of politics and international rivalry out of the Olympics. For his work he was much decorated and honored by nations and organizations; he was also, however, a controversial figure because of the narrowness of his views. Brundage was also noted as a devotee of Oriental art, and in 1966 he gave a huge collection valued at some $30 million to the De Young Memorial Museum in San Francisco. He retired as president of the IOC after the XX Olympiad, held in Munich in 1972. He died in Garmisch-Partenkirchen, Germany, on May 8, 1975.

Bryan, William Jennings (1860–1925), political leader and public official. Born in Salem, Illinois, on March 19, 1860, Bryan graduated from Illinois College in 1881 and from Union College of Law in Chicago in 1883. For four years thereafter he practiced law in Jacksonville, Illinois, then moved to Lincoln, Nebraska, where he continued to practice law and began to speak on political issues. By 1890 he was sufficiently prominent and popular to be elected to the House of Representatives as a Democrat from a normally Republican district. His reelection in 1892 was his last successful bid for office. In Congress he had become known as a free-silver advocate and as generally agrarian in sympathies. After two years of editing a newspaper in Omaha and lecturing, he was sent as a delegate to the Democratic national convention of 1896; there his "Cross of Gold" speech took the meeting by storm and won him the presidential nomination. He campaigned on the free-silver issue and lost; four years later, after the Spanish-

American War, he added antiexpansionism to his platform and lost again to William McKinley, this time by a wider margin. By this time Bryan had become identified, more by association than by intent, with the growing political restlessness among Western and Southern farmers that had given rise to the Populist party; he was also to become a spokesman for the closely related fundamentalist reaction against religious modernism. In 1901 he established a popular political weekly, the *Commoner;* through his writings in that newspaper he remained a potent force in the Democratic party. His association with the paper, combined with his oratorical skill and rapport with the people, led to his nickname, "The Great Commoner." Although the conservative wing of the party captured the presidential nomination in 1904, Bryan controlled the platform. In 1908 he was again nominated and again defeated. In 1912, demonstrating his complete mastery of political management, he secured the nomination for Woodrow Wilson and subsequently the post of secretary of state for himself. Although not qualified by training for the position, Bryan served creditably; his major accomplishment was a series of bilateral treaties providing for the arbitration of international disputes during enforced "cooling-off" periods. His commitment to peace led him to resign in 1915 when, after the sinking of the *Lusitania*, President Wilson protested to Germany in terms that Bryan considered unduly strong and insufficiently expressive of a neutralist policy. He continued to support total neutrality until war actually came; thereafter he counseled loyalty to the president's policies. His remaining years he devoted to his newspaper and to lecturing; he attended every Democratic national convention, although he had lost most of his former influence. In 1921 he moved to Miami, Florida, where, three years later, he drafted for the state legislature a resolution banning the teaching of evolution in the public schools. In July 1925 he was invited to handle the prosecution in Dayton, Tennessee, of John T. Scopes, accused of teaching Darwinian theory in a public school. At the climax of this test of Tennessee's antievolution law, the chief defense attorney, Clarence Darrow, placed the theologically and scientifically naive Bryan on the stand to explain his Fundamentalist views on creation. Bryan died in Dayton on July 26, 1925, shortly after the trial ended.

Bryant, William Cullen (1794–1878), poet and editor. Born of Puritan stock in Cummington, Massachusetts, on November 3, 1794, Bryant turned to the law when his father's financial condition prevented him from continuing his studies at Williams College after only a year there in 1810–1811. He remained an avid reader, however, and was particularly fond of the romantic poets. Already, in 1808, he had written a polemical poem, "The Embargo," later regretted, in which he castigated President Thomas Jefferson. In 1811 he wrote the first draft of what was to be his best-known poem, "Thanatopsis." Admitted to the bar in 1815, Bryant practiced law in Great Barrington, Massachusetts, rather unhappily from 1816 until 1825. In 1817 "Thanatopsis" was published in the *North American Review* and secured immediate recognition for the young poet. He published a small volume of verse in 1821 that contained the final version of "Thanatopsis" along with "To a Waterfowl," "The Yellow Violet," and other lyrics, and within four years was firmly established as the nation's finest poet. In 1825 he went to New York City to work for the *New York Review;* he moved to the *New York Evening Post* in 1827 and two years later became editor and part owner, a position he held for the rest of his long life. His production of verse dropped sharply, and his volume of collected poems in 1832 contained fewer than a hundred pieces. *The Fountain, and Other Poems* and *The White-footed Doe, and Other Poems*, both slim volumes, appeared in 1842 and 1844. He gained prominence as an editor, however; under Bryant's guidance the *Evening Post* became one of the leading Democratic journals in the nation. His liberalism led him to break with the Democrats in 1848 to support the Free-Soilers; he made the breach permanent in 1856 when he became one of the founders of the Republican party. He became a leading abolitionist, even to the extent of finding in John Brown a martyr to the cause. While devoting most of his time to the *Post* he added slowly to his stock of published poems during his later years, though never matching the productivity of the 1820s, and he translated Homer and a number of Spanish poets. In April 1878 he struck his head in a fall and lapsed into a coma; he died on June 12, 1878, in New York City. He was elected to the Hall of Fame in 1910.

Buchanan, Franklin (1800–1874), naval officer. Born in Baltimore on September 17, 1800, Buchanan was commissioned a midshipman in the navy in 1815 and saw his first sea duty under Commodore Oliver Hazard Perry aboard the *Java*. He served mostly in the Mediterranean for five years, sailed on a merchantman to China while on a leave of absence, and was then engaged in antipirate patrol in the West Indies for six years, receiving promotion to lieutenant in 1825. For the next 20 years he served on a series of ships in duty stations around the world and advanced to the rank of commander. In 1845, having submitted a plan of organization for the new U.S. Naval Academy at Annapolis, he was appointed first superintendent of the school by Secretary of the Navy George Bancroft. He spent two years setting the academy upon its course and then petitioned for active duty in the Mexican War, receiving command of the sloop *Germantown*. He returned to shore duty for a time after the war, but in 1852 was given command of the steam frigate *Susquehanna*, Commodore Matthew C. Perry's flagship in the expedition to Japan. Promoted to captain in 1855, Buchanan served in various capacities, including commander of the Washington Navy Yard, until April 1861,

when, in the belief that Maryland would secede from the Union, he resigned. An attempt to retract his resignation a short time later failed and he was dismissed. He then entered the Confederate navy as a captain and took command of the Chesapeake Bay squadron in the ironclad *Virginia* (formerly the *Merrimack*, the name by which it continued to be best known). In March 1862 he attacked the Union squadron that was blockading Hampton Roads, sinking the *Congress*, on which his brother was serving, the *Cumberland*, and other vessels, but sustaining a serious wound that kept him out of the next day's historic engagement with the *Monitor*. In August he was made admiral and thereby became ranking officer of the Confederate navy. Sent to take command at Mobile Bay, he was aboard his flagship, the *Tennessee*, when Adm. David G. Farragut attacked in August 1864; outnumbered and outgunned, the *Tennessee* was taken and Buchanan was wounded and captured. Released from prison in February 1865, he settled in his home in Talbot County, Maryland, and died there on May 11, 1874.

Buchanan, James (1791–1868), fifteenth president of the United States. Born near Mercersburg, Pennsylvania, on April 23, 1791, Buchanan was educated at Dickinson College and, following his graduation in 1809, studied law until his admission to the bar in 1812. He was a highly successful lawyer and moved easily into politics. He served in the Pennsylvania legislature from 1814 to 1816 as a moderate Federalist; in 1820 he was elected to the House of Representatives and as the Federalist party disintegrated, associated himself with the Democrats; he remained in Congress until 1831. In 1832 he began two years' service as minister to Russia and upon his return was elected to represent Pennsylvania in the Senate, where he served until 1845. He was a loyal Democrat and, after slowly defining a conciliatory position on the slavery issue—opposing it in principle while committed to defending it under the Constitution, and at the same time denouncing the abolitionists—he was mentioned for the presidency in 1844. When James K. Polk was nominated, however, Buchanan supported him and was given the post of secretary of state. He held that sensitive position during the annexation of Texas, the Mexican War, and the Oregon boundary negotiations. After a retirement from politics beginning in 1849, he was appointed minister to Great Britain in 1853. In 1854 he joined in the writing of the Ostend Manifesto, which further enhanced his popularity in the South; his absence from the country also prevented his having to take a position in the debates over the Kansas-Nebraska Bill. Upon his return to the United States in 1856 he was nominated for president by the Democrats and duly elected over John C. Frémont and Millard Fillmore, although he did not poll a majority of the popular vote. He constructed a cabinet with balanced North-South representation and continued with little success to try to pacify the South by preventing antislavery agitation and upholding the fugitive slave law. The growing tension was capped by the election of Abraham Lincoln to the presidency in 1860. Buchanan denounced the secession of South Carolina but was essentially helpless; he managed only to forestall hostilities at Fort Sumter until Lincoln took office. During the war he supported the Union. He died on June 1, 1868, at his estate, Wheatland, near Lancaster, Pennsylvania.

Buchman, Frank Nathan Daniel (1878–1961), religious leader, founder of Moral Re-Armament. Born in Pennsburg, Pennsylvania, on June 4, 1878, Buchman studied at Muhlenberg College, receiving his B.A. in 1899 and his M.A. in 1902. He graduated from Mount Airy Lutheran Seminary in Philadelphia in 1902 and was ordained in that year. In the next few years he combined pastoral duties with social work, first in Philadelphia and then at Pennsylvania State College (now University), and at Hartford Theological Foundation in Hartford, Connecticut, where he was a lecturer in personal evangelism. He continued to work among college students in various places, but he always came into conflict with school authorities; he was asked to leave Princeton in 1926. During the early 1920s he had spent some time at Oxford University in England, and there and elsewhere he gathered in the following years a band of faithful adherents, the so-called Oxford Group, which was the core of the later movements known as Buchmanism and Moral Re-Armament (so spelled by its founder), which was also known as MRA. The Oxford Group held conferences called "house parties" during the 1930s in a number of countries, including Great Britain, the Netherlands, the United States, and the Union of South Africa; the campaign for Moral Re-Armament was inaugurated, according to Buchman's own account, in East Ham Town Hall, London, and descrbied by him as "a race with time to re-make men and nations." Up to that time a primarily Protestant Christian organization, Moral Re-Armament during and after World War II became much more ecumenical and its members included adherents of many faiths. After the war the movement had its headquarters in Caux, Switzerland, and also held annual meetings on Mackinac Island, Michigan, where Buchman lived. In his later years he was widely honored for his work, which never ceased to be controversial, some critics viewing Moral Re-Armament as just another anti-Communist and radically conservative protopolitical organization, while others viewed it, more sympathetically, as one of the most vital and vigorous of contemporary evangelical movements. Buchman died in Freudenstadt, Germany, on August 7, 1961, and was buried in Allentown, Pennsylvania.

Buck, Frank (1884–1950), hunter and animal collector. Born on March 17, 1884 in Gainesville, Texas, Buck grew up there and in Dallas. His early fascination with the geography of exotic places found little outlet, but during his childhood he collected and maintained a sizable menagerie of small birds and other animals. In his youth he worked as a cowboy and farmhand, in a carnival, and, after making his way to Chicago, as a hotel bellboy. His marriage in 1904 to a well-known Chicago actress and critic enlarged his opportunities and he became an assistant to the proprietor of the Western Vaudeville Managers Association and a correspondent for the *New York Telegraph*. By 1911 he was financially able to indulge his taste for travel; he pulled up stakes and sailed to South America, bought a number of native birds, and returned to New York City to sell them at a considerable profit. A second trip and even greater profits from selling to dealers in London established him in his new profession. He began traveling farther and farther afield and learned to make his own captures on expeditions through Africa, South America, Asia, Australia, and elsewhere; he maintained headquarters in Singapore. Within a few years he had acquired a fortune and a wide reputation, capturing for zoos and circuses everything from tiny birds to elephants. During 1915 he directed public relations for the Panama-Pacific International Exposition in San Francisco and the next year held a similar position with Mack Sennett's Keystone Company. Buck first came to the attention of the general public in 1930 with the publication of his best-selling first book, *Bring 'Em Back Alive* (with E. Anthony), the title of which was thereafter virtually his second name. That book, as well as *Wild Cargo*, 1931, with Anthony and *Fang and Claw*, 1935, with F. L. Fraser, were subsequently made into successful motion pictures in which Buck himself starred. Others of his books included *Tim Thompson in the Jungle*, 1935, and *On Jungle Trails*, 1937, both with Fraser; *Animals Are Like That!*, 1939, with C. Weld, and an autobiography, *All in a Lifetime* 1941, with Fraser. Other movies in which he appeared include *Jungle Menace*, *Jungle Cavalcade*, and *Jacare*. Buck had his own exhibits at the Century of Progress Exposition in Chicago in 1933 and at the New York World's Fair in 1939, was for a time in 1937–1938 associated with the Ringling Brothers-Barnum and Bailey Circus, and remained a highly popular lecturer and the idol of legions of men and boys until his death in Houston, Texas, on March 25, 1950.

Buck, Pearl S. (1892–1973), author. Born on June 26, 1892, in Hillsboro, West Virginia, Pearl Comfort Sydenstricker was raised in Chen-chiang, China, by her Presbyterian missionary parents. Initially educated by her mother and a Chinese tutor, she was sent at fifteen to a boarding school in Shanghai. Two years later she entered Randolph-Macon Women's College in Virginia, graduating in 1914 and remaining for a semester as an instructor in psychology. In 1917 she married missionary John L. Buck; although later divorced and remarried, she retained the name professionally. She returned to China, and taught English literature in Chinese universities, then resumed studying in the United States at Cornell University, earning her M.A. in 1926. She began contributing articles on Chinese life to American magazines in 1922. Her first published novel, *East Wind, West Wind*, 1930, was written aboard a ship headed for America. *The Good Earth*, 1931, won a Pulitzer Prize and established her as an interpreter of the East to the West. The book was made into a stage play and an Academy Award-winning film. With *Sons*, 1932, and *A House Divided*, 1935, it formed a trilogy, *The House of Earth*. She won the Nobel Prize for Literature in 1938. Subsequently she wrote biographies of her parents, *The Exile* and *Fighting Angel*, both 1936; a long series of novels, including *Dragon Seed*, 1942; *Pavilion of Women*, 1946; *Imperial Woman*, 1956; *Letter from Peking*, 1957; and *The Three Daughters of Madame Liang*, 1969. She also published several novels under the pseudonym John Sedges, including the best-seller, *The Townsman*, 1945. Miss Buck wrote several children's books and two volumes of autobiography, *My Several Worlds*, 1954, and *A Bridge for Passing*, 1962. She died in Danby, Vermont, on March 6, 1973.

Buckley, William Frank, Jr. (1925–   ), editor and author. Born in New York City on November 24, 1925, Buckley grew up and was schooled in France and England as well as the United States. He attended the University of Mexico for a year before serving in the army during 1944–1946. He then entered Yale, graduated in 1950, and the following year published *God and Man at Yale: The Superstitions of Academic Freedom*. In 1952 he joined the staff of the *American Mercury* but resigned a short time later to engage in freelance writing and lecturing. With L. Brent Bozell he wrote *McCarthy and His Enemies*, 1954, which, while conceding certain excesses, was largely a defense of the former senator's anti-Communist crusade. In 1955 Buckley founded the *National Review*, a weekly journal of conservative opinion that grew to enjoy a large circulation, and served thereafter as its editor in chief. He began a syndicated newspaper column, "A Conservative Voice," in 1962 and later produced the column "On the Right" for syndicate distribution to more than 200 newspapers. In addition he was host of a weekly television program, "Firing Line," which featured debates between himself and a variety of opponents. Others among his written works included *Up from Liberalism*, 1959; *The Unmaking of a Mayor*, 1966, written after his unsuccessful campaign for mayor of New York City; *The Jeweler's Eye*, 1968; *Governor Listeth*, 1970; and contributions to many magazines. Noted particularly for his archly patrician manner and dazzling vocabulary in debate, Buckley was held by many to be the principal contemporary intellectual resource of U.S. political conservatism.

Buckner, Simon Bolivar (1823–1914), soldier. Born on April 1, 1823, near Munfordville, Kentucky,

Buckner graduated from West Point in 1844. Assigned first to duty at Sackets Harbor, New York, and then as an instructor at West Point, he sought active duty in the Mexican War and distinguished himself at Churubusco and Molino del Rey, winning promotion to captain. Thereafter he served again at West Point, at New York Harbor, and in the West before resigning from the army in 1855. He lived in Chicago for a time, acquiring and managing large real-estate holdings, and in 1858 moved to Louisville, Kentucky. As the likelihood of civil war grew he became deeply concerned with the effect it would have on the state, which was officially neutral. In 1860 the legislature approved his plan for a large, well-trained militia and appointed him major general. He succeeded in organizing an able home guard to defend Kentucky's neutrality and in June 1861 secured from Gen. George B. McClellan recognition of the state's position. When federal forces invaded the western part of Kentucky he sought their withdrawal from McClellan and then from President Abraham Lincoln; he did not succeed, but Lincoln offered him a brigadier general's commission, which he refused. Soon afterward Confederate forces also entered Kentucky and again he tried in vain to secure their removal and again he refused an offer of a commission. Buckner relinquished command of the militia in July because the state government had become partial to the Union; he was already leaning toward the Confederacy when the legislature officially abandoned neutrality and he forthwith accepted an appointment as brigadier general in the Confederate army and joined the command of Gen. Albert S. Johnston. Early in 1862 he was sent to the relief of Fort Donelson but was soon forced to surrender to his old friend, Gen. Ulysses S. Grant. Imprisoned until August, he returned to duty then and was promoted to major general on the staff of Gen. Braxton Bragg, operating in Tennessee and Kentucky. He later built fortifications at Mobile, rejoined Bragg in time to take part in the battle of Chickamauga, and in 1864 was made lieutenant general in command of the District of Louisiana. At the war's end he entered the newspaper and insurance businesses in New Orleans; in 1868 he returned to Kentucky and became editor of the *Louisville Courier*. The recovery of confiscated properties in Kentucky and Chicago established him as a wealthy man, and he devoted himself to his business interests until 1887, when he was elected governor of Kentucky. Upon leaving office in 1891 and serving in the state constitutional convention that year, he retired to his Munfordville estate. In 1896 he was nominated for vice-president by the Gold Democrats, a splinter party. Buckner died at home on January 8, 1914.

Buckner, Simon Bolivar, Jr. (1886–1945), soldier. Born in Munfordville, Kentucky, on July 18, 1886, the son of Gen. Simon B. Buckner, the younger Buckner graduated from West Point in 1908 and rose in rank through the various grades until

1940, when he was promoted to brigadier general and placed in charge of the Alaska defense command, with headquarters at Fort Richardson, near Anchorage, Alaska. After remaining in this post until June 1944, he was assigned to the central Pacific area and, in September of that year, named commander of the 10th Army. Leading a large combined land and sea force, he invaded the Ryukyu Islands the following spring and fought the last great land campaign of World War II against the deeply entrenched Japanese forces on Okinawa. The fighting continued from the beginning of April to June 21, 1945, and Buckner demonstrated his abilities as a tactician and an aggressive commander. He was killed in action while visiting a forward observation post near the southwest tip of Okinawa on June 18, 1945. Nakagusuka Wan, a naval anchorage on the east coast of Okinawa, was renamed Buckner Bay in his honor.

Budge, Don (1915–   ), tennis player. Born on June 13, 1915, in Oakland, California, John Donald Budge was a talented athlete from childhood. He did not take up tennis seriously until 1930, but after only a few weeks' practice he entered and won the state boys' singles competition that year. In 1933 he won his last junior title and moved into the senior division to win his first title there; he then entered the national junior tournament and won his first U.S. title. He played the tennis circuit in 1934, making his debut on the prestigious Eastern courts, and in 1935 was named to the U.S. Davis Cup team. He won his first national senior title in 1936, taking the doubles at Forest Hills with his partner Gene Mako. He burst into the front ranks of international tennis in 1937 when he won all of his Davis Cup singles and doubles matches, regaining the cup for the United States for the first time in 10 years, and took the singles titles in the U.S., British (Wimbledon), and Australian championships; at Wimbledon he was also on the winning doubles and mixed doubles teams. His five-set victory in the singles finals at Wimbledon that year over Baron Gottfried von Cramm of Germany was one of the most exciting in tennis history. In 1938 Budge performed the unprecedented feat of winning the singles titles in the Australian, French, British, and U.S. championships, the "grand slam" of tennis that not even Bill Tilden had accomplished and that was not to be duplicated for 24 years. That year he also won the Wimbledon doubles and helped retain the Davis Cup for the United States. He turned professional after his victory in the U.S. singles at Forest Hills in September and made his professional debut the following January, winning the U.S. professional title in 1940 and 1942. With his entry into the army in 1943 his serious playing career came to an end, but he returned after World War II to play exhibitions in cities around the world; fans by the thousands came out to see him. His backhand was probably the most graceful and powerful in the history of the game. In 1964 Budge was elected to the National Lawn Tennis Hall of Fame.

Buell, Abel (1742–1822), silversmith, engraver, and inventor. Born in Killingworth, Connecticut, on February 1, 1742, Buell was apprenticed to a silversmith and went into business for himself in his native town when he was about twenty. An attempt to make counterfeit money earned him a prison sentence in 1764. After his release he invented a machine for cutting and polishing precious stones and then became interested in typefounding, producing in 1769 the first American-designed font of type. The Connecticut legislature granted him a sum to establish a foundry in New Haven and his failure to do so, along with an outstanding debt to a New York printer, forced him to flee the colony in 1775. His wife remained behind to manage the business; she paid off his obligations so that he was able to return three years later. He continued to manufacture type and to do copperplate engraving and in 1784 produced the first map of the United States that incorporated the new territorial boundaries described in the Revolutionary peace treaty of 1783. For many years thereafter Buell engaged in a wide variety of activities, including operating a line of packet boats and a marble quarry and manufacturing jewelry. He invented a corn planter and in 1795, after a visit to the textile districts of Great Britain, built a cotton mill in New Haven, one of the first in the country, that, like most of his other enterprises, soon failed. He later did silversmithing in Hartford and later still in Stockbridge, Massachusetts, but returned at last to New Haven and died in the Alms House there on March 10, 1822.

Buell, Don Carlos (1818–1898), soldier. Born on March 23, 1818, near Marietta, Ohio, Buell grew up there and in Lawrenceburg, Indiana. He graduated from West Point in 1841, took part in the Seminole War, and served under generals Zachary Taylor and Winfield Scott in the Mexican War, winning promotions for action at Monterrey, Contreras, and Churubusco. He was later assigned to duty with the adjutant general and at the outbreak of the Civil War was a lieutenant colonel. Promoted to brigadier general, he was sent in November 1861 to take command of the Department of the Ohio in Louisville, Kentucky. He argued against Gen. George B. McClellan's plan to strike into eastern Tennessee, pointing out the lack of available lines of communication, and continued to hesitate until Gen. Henry W. Halleck sent Gen. Ulysses S. Grant up the Tennessee and Cumberland rivers against Fort Henry. In February 1862 Buell moved into Bowling Green and, following Grant's success at Fort Donelson, occupied Nashville later in the month. Placed under the command of Halleck and a short time later promoted to major general of volunteers, Buell was then ordered to join Grant's Army of the Tennessee at Savannah, Tennessee. He arrived there with fresh troops just in time to join battle at Shiloh on April 6; throwing his full force into the fierce contest the next day, he was able to drive Gen. P. G. T. Beauregard from the field. He accompanied Halleck to Corinth, Mississippi, and was then sent to repair the railroad to Chattanooga. During that operation he was much harassed by Confederate raiders, particularly those of John Hunt Morgan. Learning that Chattanooga had been occupied by Gen. Braxton Bragg, he turned north to Murfreesboro. From there he continued north in a race against Bragg to reach Kentucky; arriving in Bowling Green he found Bragg's troops between him and his base in Louisville. He bided his time until Bragg was forced to move off in search of supplies, moved to Louisville to regroup, and then turned back to fight. A small but sharp battle ensued at Perryville on October 8; Bragg withdrew and Buell failed to pursue him promptly. He was abruptly replaced by Gen. William S. Rosecrans and kept inactive for a year and a half while his conduct was investigated. At length he was relieved of the rank of major general of volunteers, and he promptly resigned his regular commission as well in June 1864. He retired to Kentucky and engaged in business until his death in Rockport on November 19, 1898.

Buffalo Bill, *see* Cody, William Frederick

Bulfinch, Charles (1763–1844), architect. Born on August 8, 1763, in Boston, Bulfinch graduated from Harvard in 1781 and from 1785 to 1787 traveled in England and Europe, studying the many architectural works suggested to him by Thomas Jefferson. Soon after his return to Boston he submitted a design for the Massachusetts State House, which was completed in 1798. He followed with plans for various other buildings and monuments, including the Hollis Street Church, the Beacon Hill monument, the Connecticut State House in Hartford, and the Boston Theatre. During the 1790s he devoted much time to domestic architecture, introducing the finely detailed neoclassical Adam style (after Robert Adam) in the Barrell, Derby, and Otis houses and others. He took an active part in civic affairs, serving on Boston's board of selectmen from 1791 to 1795 and as its chairman from 1799 to 1817. He was instrumental in securing street lighting in the city and in opening the common schools to girls. Much of his professional activity was also directed toward civic improvement; he planned the improvement of Boston Common and laid out parks on Boston Neck, in South Boston, and at Mill Pond, and designed India Wharf and a large number of public buildings as well as private houses. Others of his works during the period included the Massachusetts General Hospital, the Cathedral of the Holy Cross, University Hall at Harvard, and New South Church. In 1817 Bulfinch was invited by President James Monroe to succeed Benjamin H. Latrobe as architect of the U.S. Capitol. He followed Latrobe's plans in completing the wings, but added his own details to the west front and redesigned the dome and rotunda. Before the building was completed in 1830, the year of his retirement, he also found time to draw plans for the Unitarian Church in Washington, D.C., the Maine state capital, and many other works. He died in Boston on April 4, 1844.

Bulfinch, Thomas (1796–1867), author. Born in Newton, Massachusetts, on July 15, 1796, Thomas Bulfinch was the son of Charles Bulfinch. He graduated from Harvard in 1814, taught for a year at the Boston Latin School, and then worked for a time in his brother's store. From 1818 to 1825 he lived with his family in Washington, D.C., and after returning to Boston in 1825 engaged in various business pursuits until 1837, when he became a clerk in the Merchants' Bank of Boston. In that position, almost a sinecure, which he held for the rest of his life, he was free to follow his true interests in natural history and literature. The result of his wide reading was a series of books—*Hebrew Lyrical History*, 1853; *The Age of Chivalry*, 1858; *Legends of Charlemagne*, 1863; *Poetry of the Age of Fable*, 1863; *Shakespeare Adapted for Reading Classes*, 1865; and *Oregon and Eldorado*, 1866—that enjoyed a measure of popularity, and one—*The Age of Fable*, 1855—that was a great success. Later known as *Bulfinch's Mythology*, the book was a retelling of the principal myths and an examination of the myth-systems of the world; it became a standard reference work. Bulfinch lived quietly in Boston until his death on May 27, 1867.

Bulkeley, Peter (1583–1659), religious leader. Born on January 31, 1583, in Odell, England, Bulkeley was educated at Cambridge, taking his M.A. in 1608 and remaining there as a fellow for some time. In 1620 he succeeded his father as rector of Odell and came into a sizable inheritance at the same time. He was soon a well-known and highly regarded member of the clergy. His Puritan leanings were initially slight but definite, and as the Church of England during the ascendancy of Bishop Laud became more and more rigorous in its insistence upon absolute orthodoxy, he took thought for America. In 1636 he sailed for the Massachusetts Bay colony with his large family. After a brief stay in Cambridge he moved farther out and founded the town of Concord. There he remained, the town's first minister and one of the most influential figures in the colony, until his death on March 9, 1659.

Bunche, Ralph Johnson (1904–1971), diplomat. Born in Detroit on August 7, 1904, the son of a barber, Bunche graduated from the University of California at Los Angeles in 1927 and received his M.A. (1928) and his Ph.D. (1934) in government from Harvard. After 1928 he taught political science at Howard University; he was chairman of the department from 1929 to 1950. In addition he did post-doctoral work at Northwestern University, the London School of Economics, and at the University of Capetown in Johannesburg, South Africa. Before World War II he did field work with Gunnar Myrdal for

Myrdal's *An American Dilemma,* 1945. In 1941 he joined the U.S. Office of Strategic Services (OSS) and conducted research in French West Africa. By 1946 he was associate chief of the state department's section on dependent areas, but resigned to become director of the division of trusteeship of the United Nations. In 1948 he was deputy to the chief mediator, Count Folke Bernadotte of Sweden, on the UN Palestine Commission. After Bernadotte's assassination, Bunche took up the exceedingly difficult and delicate task upon which he had been engaged and eventually concluded a truce and armistice agreements between the Jews and Arabs. Primarily for that work he won the Nobel Peace Prize in 1950. In 1957 he became UN undersecretary for special political affairs, acting in 1960 as UN special representative in the Congo and in 1963 as head of the UN mission to Yemen. He also carried out difficult assignments in such trouble spots as Suez, Katanga, Kashmir, and Cyprus. From 1967 until his retirement in mid-1971, Bunche was undersecretary-general of the UN; second in official position only to the secretary-general. He was held in respect throughout the world and in his own country he was a figure of considerable moral authority, particularly in matters touching the civil-rights movement. In 1965, with Dr. Martin Luther King, Jr., he led a 50-mile march from Selma to Montgomery, Alabama, on a campaign to gain voting rights for Negroes. He received the Spingarn Medal of the National Association for the Advancement of Colored People (NAACP) in 1949, the Presidential Medal of Freedom in 1963, and was the recipient of numerous other awards and honorary degrees. After a lengthy illness, Bunche died in New York City on December 9, 1971.

Buntline, Ned, *see* Judson, Edward Zane Carroll

Burbank, Luther (1849–1926), horticulturalist. Born on March 7, 1849, in Lancaster, Massachusetts, Burbank was educated in district schools and attended the Lancaster Academy for four years. In 1868 he read Charles Darwin's *Variation of Animals and Plants Under Domestication,* a book that he later credited with having determined him upon his career. In 1870 he acquired a small tract of land near Lunenburg, Massachusetts, and began experimenting with growing improved varieties of vegetables for the market. During five years he spent there he developed the very successful Burbank potato. In 1875 he moved to Santa Rosa, California, and there established nurseries, fields, and orchards that occupied him for the rest of his life. With painstaking care and enormous energy he raised hundreds of thousands of plants representing thousands of different species and varieties, hybridizing some and grafting new stocks to others in order to produce new varieties or to combine the superior characteristics of several varieties in one plant. In addition to 90 varieties of vegetables, he developed 113 new varieties of plums and prunes and

many notable kinds of berries, apples, peaches, quinces, nectarines, and such ornamental plants as callas, lilies, roses, and poppies; his most famous development among ornamentals was the Shasta daisy. Burbank's goal was always the production of improved varieties of cultivated plants rather than scientific experimentation (his record-keeping was sketchy), and it was his special genius to be able to recognize in one of a thousand seedling plants the potentially better specimen. Although many of his much-hailed originations proved to be without value, others have stood the test of time. He published numerous catalogues of his plants and wrote *Luther Burbank, His Methods and Discoveries,* 1914–1915, 12 volumes, and *How Plants Are Trained to Work for Man,* 1921, eight volumes. He died in Santa Rosa on April 11, 1926. His autobiography, *Harvest of the Years,* was published the following year.

Burchfield, Charles Ephraim (1893–1967), painter. Born on April 9, 1893, in Ashtabula, Ohio, Burchfield grew up there and in Salem. He early developed interests in drawing and nature and after finishing high school worked for a time in a local factory to earn tuition for the Cleveland School of Art, from which he graduated in 1916. Following a brief stay in New York City he returned to Salem and his job and devoted his spare time to painting. During World War I he did camouflage work in the army. His early paintings, such as "Church Bells Ringing—Rainy Winter Night," were primarily scenes of nature rendered in a manner that was basically realistic but often imbued with a heavy atmosphere of mystery or even terror. By about 1920, however, Burchfield had begun to find his subjects in the flat, dreary aspects of the towns and small cities of the Midwest. Moving to Buffalo, New York, in 1921 and to nearby Gardenville four years later, he began to produce such works as "Black Iron," "Freight Cars Under a Bridge," "Edge of Town," and "Factory Town." From 1921 to 1929 he worked as a designer in a wallpaper factory in Buffalo, but in the latter year his slowly growing artistic reputation enabled him to begin giving full time to painting. In the late 1930s he was commissioned by *Fortune* magazine to paint several railroad and mining scenes. About 1940 he again radically changed his subject matter, returning to his love of nature for inspiration. "The Coming of Spring," "The Sphinx and the Milky Way," "Three Trees," "An April Mood," and others did not, however, carry the mood of brooding of his earlier paintings, but conveyed instead a more benevolent, romantic sense of the natural world. Burchfield, best known as a watercolorist, enjoyed numerous one-man shows and retrospective exhibitions and was represented in many major galleries and museums; he lectured occasionally at colleges and won many prizes and medals. He died in Gardenville on January 10, 1967.

Burger, Warren Earl (1907–   ), chief justice of the Supreme Court. Born in St. Paul, Minnesota, on September 17, 1907, Burger was prevented by lack of funds from attending college full time. Instead he took a job as an insurance salesman and, after two years of extension courses at the University of Minnesota, studied law at night at St. Paul (now William Mitchell) College of Law. Graduating with high honors in 1931, he joined a prominent St. Paul law firm and became at the same time a member of the law school's faculty, retaining both associations until 1953. He gradually became active in state Republican politics, playing a leading role in the election of Harold Stassen as governor in 1938 and serving as his floor manager at the Republican national convention in 1948 and again in 1952. He was also a member of the Governor's Interracial Commission from 1948 to 1953 and first president of the St. Paul Council on Human Relations. In 1953 President Dwight D. Eisenhower named Burger assistant attorney general. In that post he was responsible for the prosecution of most of the civil actions undertaken by the federal government. One of his most notable projects was the recovery from foreign shipping companies of a number of illegally purchased war surplus vessels; he eventually held some 40 ships in "floating receivership" and won the nickname "Admiral." Eisenhower appointed him to the highly demanding U.S. Court of Appeals for the District of Columbia in 1955 and, after a delay in the confirmation process, he began the next year his 13-year service on the second highest court in the land. In his decisions and in lectures around the country he outlined a judicial philosophy of dedication to the rights of society as well as to individual rights, and on several occasions he criticized Supreme Court rulings in criminal cases that seemed to him insensitive to the former. While opposed to excessively protective and complicated criminal-law procedures, however, he was deeply concerned with improvement of the penal system. Burger's generally conservative approach to law commended itself to President Richard M. Nixon, who in 1969 named him to succeed Earl Warren as chief justice of the Supreme Court. With the approbation of most observers and commentators he was quickly confirmed and in June 1969 sworn in as the fifteenth chief justice.

Burgess, Gelett (1866–1951), humorist. Born in Boston on January 30, 1866, Frank Gelett Burgess graduated from the Massachusetts Institute of Technology in 1887. For three years he worked as a draftsman for the Southern Pacific Railroad and in 1890 became an instructor in topographical drawing at the University of California. In 1894 he made a radical change of profession by becoming associate editor of the *Wave* magazine; the next year, leading a young San Francisco literary group known as Les Jeunes, he became editor of the *Lark,* a witty little magazine in which first appeared his famous quatrain "The Purple Cow": "I never saw a purple cow, / I never hope to see one; / But I can tell you, anyhow, / I'd rather see than be one." The magazine, which lasted only two years, also featured his pen drawings of strange, ill-mannered creatures called "goops," who inspired his book *Goops and How to Be Them,* 1900. In *Are You a Bromide?,* 1907, he invented a new name for a familiar bore—the dullard whose social responses consist of nothing but the blandest of platitudes. Others of his books included *The Heart Line,* 1907, a novel, *Blue Goops and Red,* 1909; *Burgess Unabridged,* 1914; *The Goop Encyclopaedia,* 1915; *Why Men Hate Women,* 1927; *Look Eleven Years Younger,* 1937; *Ladies in Boxes,* 1942; and *New Goops,* 1951. Burgess also originated the term "blurb" to designate a short laudatory comment printed on a book jacket; he defined the word precisely as "self-praise: to make a noise like a publisher." He died in Carmel, California, on September 18, 1951.

Burk, Martha Jane (1852?–1903), "Calamity Jane," frontier figure. Born in Princeton, Missouri, probably in 1852, Martha Jane Canary moved with her parents to Virginia City, Montana, in 1864 or 1865. There she became an expert marksman and rider, dressed habitually as a man, and acquired few of the feminine refinements. By 1867 both of her parents were dead and she roamed at large through the mining districts, reputedly drinking and cussing with the best of them. She wandered into Wyoming in the 1870s and, according to some, scouted for the cavalrymen commanded by G. A. Custer and N. A. Miles; she tagged along with the Newton-Jenney geological expedition into the Black Hills in 1875 and after the gold strike of 1876 became a fixture in Deadwood, South Dakota. She was a companion of "Wild Bill" Hickok, although stories that they were married are most probably untrue. Her nickname is variously explained: one tradition assigns it to her generosity toward the unfortunate, particularly during the smallpox epidemic of 1878, while another holds that it derived from the warning she gave men who seemed about to offend her. She is said to have been a mail carrier in Deadwood for some years. She left after the mining boom ended and in 1891, in El Paso, Texas, married one Clinton Burk, who shortly thereafter deserted her. Her last years were spent in poverty; she died in South Dakota on August 1, 1903, and was buried in Deadwood beside Wild Bill.

Burleigh, Harry Thacker (1866–1949), singer, composer, and arranger. Born in Erie, Pennsylvania, on December 2, 1866, Burleigh worked his way through high school. Afterward, while holding various minor jobs, he devoted much of his time to singing in the choirs of several black churches in Erie. His remarkable voice attracted patrons, and in 1892 he was awarded a scholarship to the National Conservatory of Music in New York City, where he studied voice, piano, and timpani along with music theory and composition. At the Conservatory he formed an association with Czech composer Anton Dvořák, who learned from him of the Negro spiritual song form that deeply influenced Dvořák's symphony *From the New World*, 1893. In 1894, not without giving rise to some controversy, Burleigh was chosen in competition over 60 other men for the post of baritone soloist in the choir of the fashionable St. George's Episcopal Church in New York City, of which J. P. Morgan was an influential lay member. Burleigh remained with the choir until his retirement in 1946. In 1900 he also joined the choir of Temple Emanu-El in New York City, a post he retained for 25 years. He enjoyed a highly successful concert career as well, making numerous European tours and numbering among his triumphs a command performance before Edward VII of England. His concert programs consisted almost entirely of spirituals, a musical form that he was principally responsible for bringing to the attention of the general public. He devoted much effort to preserving this musical heritage of black Americans, setting down many spirituals on paper for the first time and giving them their standard concert arrangements; among the best-known spirituals collected and arranged by Burleigh were "Ain't Goin' to Study War No Mo'," "Balm in Gilead," "By an' By," "De Gospel Train," "Deep River," "Didn't My Lord Deliver Daniel," "Go Down Moses," "Go Tell It on the Mountain," "Joshua Fit de Battle ob Jericho," "My Lord What a Morning," "Nobody Knows the Trouble I've Seen," "Oh Didn't It Rain," "Sometimes I Feel Like a Motherless Child," "Steal Away," "Swing Low, Sweet Chariot," and "Were You There." He also wrote a large number of songs and ballads: he set to music "Little Mother of Mine," a poem by Walter Brown, "Ethiopia Saluting the Colors," Walt Whitman's poem, and "The Young Warrior," a poem by James Weldon Johnson, and he wrote "Down by the Sea" and "Who's Dat Yonder." Burleigh was awarded the Spingarn Medal of the National Association for the Advancement of Colored People (NAACP) in 1917. He died in Stamford, Connecticut, on September 12, 1949.

Burlingame, Anson (1820–1870), public official and diplomat. Born in New Berlin, New York, on November 14, 1820, Burlingame moved with his family to Ohio in 1823 and ten years later to Michigan. He graduated from the Detroit branch of the University of Michigan in 1841 and three years later entered the Harvard Law School, from which he graduated in 1846. Beginning law practice in Boston, he soon became a well-known figure through his brilliant oratorical powers. In 1852 he was elected to the legislature and in 1855 was sent to the House of Representatives, where he served until 1861. In 1856 he made a blistering attack on Preston S. Brooks for his vicious caning of Senator Charles Sumner; Brooks challenged him to a duel and Burlingame accepted, but on terms that forced Brooks to drop the matter. Defeated for reelection in 1860, he was appointed minister to Vienna by President Abraham Lincoln. His record of support for Kossuth and Hun-

garian independence made him unacceptable to Austria, and he was then named minister to China. In Peking he soon emerged as the leader of the Western diplomats and at the same time won the deep trust of the Chinese government by resisting the demands of foreign merchants for greater power in local government and by seeking diplomatic alternatives to provincial wars. While working for the strengthening and modernization of the central government of China, he also promoted goodwill toward it among Americans. In November 1867 he resigned his ministerial post and was immediately appointed by Prince Kung to head a three-man mission to the United States and the European powers, an act that was unprecedented in two ways: Burlingame was the first foreigner to represent the Chinese government, and the mission was China's first diplomatic approach to other nations. Arriving in the United States early in 1868, Burlingame and his party proceeded to Washington, D.C., where he negotiated with Secretary of State William H. Seward the Burlingame Treaty. The treaty, in addition to reaffirming the U.S.–China treaty of 1858, also established the U.S. policy of recognition of Chinese territoriality and provided for unlimited Chinese immigration into the United States, an article that later proved troublesome. He then went on to England, where he secured instead of a treaty a unilateral and rather mild declaration of support and to the Continent, where he was rather less successful in winning the recognition desired by China. On the brink of completing his diplomatic tour de force Burlingame traveled to St. Petersburg, Russia, but died there soon after, on February 23, 1870.

Burnham, Daniel Hudson (1846–1912), architect and city planner. Born in Henderson, New York, on September 4, 1846, Burnham moved with his family to Chicago in 1855. Failing to gain admission to college, he entered business and then found a position in an architectural office. He liked architecture and in 1873, after working for a Chicago firm, formed a partnership with John W. Root that was to be highly influential in the development of American commercial building. Burnham & Root's ten-story Montauk Building was the first to be called a skyscraper, though it was soon surpassed by the Monadnock Building, completed in 1891 and still a Chicago landmark; their Flatiron Building in New York was, in 1902, the world's tallest. Other major commissions included those for Wanamaker's store in New York City, 1903; Union Station in Washington, D.C., 1904; Selfridge's store in London, 1909; and Filene's store in Boston, 1912. The firm's greatest opportunity came with the selection of Chicago as the site of the World's Columbian Exposition, held in 1893. With Frederick Law Olmsted supervising the landscaping, they began the massive task of planning and designing the grounds for the fair. Root's death in 1891 left Burnham in sole command. His remarkable ability to create a workable team from many independent designers, combined with his wide vision as a planner, made the exposition an architectural success. In 1901 he was made chairman of a commission charged with constructing a plan for the development of Washington, D.C. The resulting Burnham Report marked the beginning of real city planning in the United States. He followed with plans for Cleveland, San Francisco, and Manila and other cities in the Philippines. In 1909 he unveiled his monumental plan for Chicago, a long-range proposal for city-wide control of industrial, recreational, residential, and transportation resources, much of which was subsequently put into effect. In 1910 he was appointed chairman of the National Commission of Fine Arts by President William Howard Taft. He died in Heidelberg, Germany, on June 1, 1912.

Burns, Arthur Frank (1904–   ), economist. Born on April 27, 1904, in Stanislau, Austria (now Ivano-Frankovsk, U.S.S.R.), Burns emigrated with his family to the United States in 1913. He graduated from Columbia University in 1925 and while pursuing graduate studies in economics there joined the faculty of Rutgers University as an instructor in 1927, advancing to a full professorship in 1943. He received his Ph.D. in 1934 from Columbia, where he was a visiting professor from 1941 until 1944, when he became a full professor. After 15 years on the staff of the National Bureau of Economic Research he succeeded Wesley C. Mitchell as its director of research in 1945; during that period he served also in a number of advisory posts, notably as chief statistician for the Railway Emergency Board in 1941. From his graduate days onward he specialized in the gathering and analysis of economic statistics and the study of business cycles, publishing a number of widely influential books, including *Production Trends in the United States Since 1870*, 1934; *Measuring Business Cycles*, 1946, with Mitchell; and *Economic Research and the Keynesian Thinking of Our Times*, 1946. In 1953 he was appointed by President Dwight D. Eisenhower to the Council of Economic Advisers, of which he subsequently became chairman. He resigned in 1956 and returned to his duties at the National Bureau of Economic Research, of which he became president in 1957, and at Columbia, where he was named John Bates Clark Professor of Economics in 1959. He continued to serve in numerous governmental advisory capacities and to contribute to the field of economics such works as *The Frontiers of Economic Knowledge*, 1954; *Prosperity Without Inflation*, 1957; *The Management of Prosperity*, 1966; and *The Business Cycle in a Changing World*, 1969. In 1968, after a year as chairman of the National Bureau, he assumed the post of honorary chairman in order to serve as economic adviser to Richard M. Nixon. The following year he became the resident White House economist, enjoying cabinet rank, and in 1970 Nixon appointed him chairman of the autonomous and powerful Federal Reserve Board. He retired from that post in 1978.

Burnside, Ambrose Everett (1824–1881), soldier and public official. Born on May 23, 1824, in Liberty, Indiana, Burnside graduated from West Point in 1847 and was assigned to the artillery, but had entered the army too late to see major action in the Mexican War. He served at various posts until 1853, when he resigned from the army. For a few years he operated a gun factory in Bristol, Rhode Island, turning out a breech-loading carbine of his own invention, but bankruptcy forced him to close it in 1857. Through the influence of Gen. George B. McClellan he was offered a position with the Illinois Central Railroad and continued there until April 1861, when he recruited a Rhode Island regiment and as its colonel took it to Washington. Following the first battle of Bull Run, in which he commanded a brigade, he was commissioned brigadier general of volunteers; in January 1862 he led a seaborne expeditionary force that captured several strongholds, along with ordnance and prisoners, on the North Carolina coast. Promoted to major general, he was then sent to join the Army of the Potomac. In September he took part in the battles of South Mountain and Antietam, his incomplete success at the latter resulting mainly from a confusion of command. In November he was chosen by President Abraham Lincoln to succeed McClellan as commander of the Army of the Potomac. Carrying his plan—to cross the Rappahannock at Fredericksburg in order to approach Richmond—over the objections of Gen. Joseph Hooker and Lincoln, he suffered in December a heavy defeat due to administrative delay, the results of good Confederate intelligence, and his own poor judgment. The next month he was replaced by Hooker and in March 1863 was transferred to command of the Department of the Ohio. There he took strong action against persons and newspapers critical of the government, most notably Clement L. Vallandigham, whom he had imprisoned; but this, like most of his measures of that period, was overruled by Lincoln. In July he stopped Gen. John Hunt Morgan's cavalry raid into Ohio and then marched into eastern Tennessee, successfully clearing it of Confederate forces at Cumberland Gap and holding Knoxville against Gen. James Longstreet. In 1864 he returned to his old corps and with the Army of the Potomac under Gen. Ulysses S. Grant took part in the many battles of the Wilderness Campaign. After several successful showings, however, he again met failure at Petersburg, where his attempt to assault Confederate lines after breaching the fortifications with a mine resulted in a rout. A court of inquiry called by Gen. George G. Meade found him to blame; he left active service as a consequence and eventually resigned. He became an officer of several railroad companies and served three terms, 1866–1869, as governor of Rhode Island. In 1874 Burnside was elected to the Senate, serving until his death in Bristol on September 13, 1881. His name came to be applied to the style of side-whiskers he wore; the term was later anagrammatized to "sideburns."

Burr, Aaron (1756–1836), public official, political leader, and adventurer. Born in Newark, New Jersey, on February 6, 1756, Burr came of a distinguished family. His parents died during his infancy and he grew up in the home of an uncle. He graduated in 1772 from the College of New Jersey (now Princeton), of which his father and grandfather had both been president, and in 1774, having briefly studied and quickly rejected theology, took up the study of law. The next year he enlisted in the Continental army; he served under Col. Benedict Arnold in the Quebec expedition, was for a short time an aide to Gen. George Washington (the two parted on less than cordial terms), and took part with some distinction in the fighting on Long Island and around New York in 1777–1778. Resigning from the army in 1779, Burr resumed his legal studies and in 1782 began to practice. Moving to New York City in 1783, he soon found himself in what was to be a twenty-year personal and political rivalry with Alexander Hamilton. With the aid of the Clinton and Livingston factions of New York Republicans he was elected to the state assembly in 1784, was appointed state attorney general in 1789, and elected to the U.S. Senate in 1790. Defeated for reelection in 1796, he was returned to the assembly. In 1800 he was nominated for vice-president, but confusion arising in the voting for president and vice-president in the electoral college resulted in a tie for the presidency between Burr and Thomas Jefferson and the decision went to the House of Representatives. After 35 ballots Hamilton's adamant opposition to Burr swung Federalist votes reluctantly to Jefferson and Burr became vice-president. By 1804, although he was nominated for governor of New York by his own followers, he had alienated the Clinton and Livingston groups and was replaced on the national ticket by George Clinton. Hamilton again brought about his defeat in the governor's race and in July Burr, having been apprised of several insults that Hamilton had added to the injury, demanded satisfaction. A duel took place on July 11, 1804, at Weehawken, New Jersey, in which Hamilton was fatally wounded. Burr, indicted in both New Jersey and New York, fled to Philadelphia and thence southward. For the next three years he occupied himself with a vague and never fully understood plan to establish an independent nation in the West of that time that would have been comprised of Mexico and several present U.S. states. His coconspirator was Gen. James Wilkinson, secretly in the pay of Spain, who was to secure from that nation the assistance that would be required to make the scheme successful. Burr was indiscreet in his associations, and rumors of many sorts—war with Spain, Western revolution, invasion of Mexico—soon swept the country, ending all chance of secrecy. Wilkinson turned informer and Burr, betrayed in 1806 while leading a troop of colonists down the Mississippi to lands that he had obtained as a base, fled and was arrested in Alabama early in 1807. Tried for treason in the circuit court in Richmond, Virginia, presided over by Chief Justice John Marshall, he was acquitted in September 1807 for lack of evidence of overt treasonable acts. In 1808 he went to Europe and unsuccessfully tried to interest the British and French governments in various schemes of adventurism in Mexico or in the West, most of which would have resulted in war. His request for a passport in order to return to the United States was met with considerable delay but he returned finally to New York City in 1812. He resumed his law practice and remained out of public notice until his death there on September 14, 1836.

Burritt, Elihu (1810–1879), social reformer. Born in New Britain, Connecticut, on December 8, 1810, Burritt received only an elementary schooling and was then apprenticed to a blacksmith. While learning his trade he indulged his passion for study, particularly of languages, and laid the foundation for his later celebrity as the "Learned Blacksmith." In 1837 he moved to Worcester, Massachusetts, where his accomplishments first attracted notice and won from Governor Edward Everett an offer of a Harvard education, which Burritt in embarrassment declined. He began giving public lectures on various topics and soon became deeply interested in the cause of peace. He joined the American Peace Society and in 1844 founded with a partner the weekly *Christian Citizen*; the paper continued to appear until 1851, and meanwhile Burritt edited also the society's *Advocate of Peace and Universal Brotherhood*. He organized a program of correspondence for mutual understanding between U.S. and British citizens during the Oregon dispute and distributed his so-called "Friendly Addresses" on the subject to hundreds of newspapers. In 1846 he went to England and founded the League of Universal Brotherhood, and two years later organized the "Friends of Peace" Congress in Brussels; similar congresses were held in succeeding years in Paris, Frankfurt am Main, London, and other cities. Dedicated to the idea of an international congress and a court of nations by which peace and law could be maintained through debate and arbitration, Burritt sought constantly to avert and seek alternatives to war. In 1852 he again used the means of "Friendly Addresses" to improve Anglo-French relations, and for several years he directed the League's "Olive Leaf Mission," through which pacifist propaganda sheets were distributed with leading European newspapers. In the United States he worked to stave off the Civil War. From 1863 to 1870 he was U.S. consul in Birmingham, England, and thereafter lived on his New Britain farm. Among his many published works were *Sparks from the Anvil*, 1846; *Walk from London to John O'Groat's*, 1864; and *Ten Minute Talks*, 1873. Burritt died on March 6, 1879, in New Britain, Connecticut.

Burroughs, Edgar Rice (1875–1950), author. Born in Chicago on September 1, 1875, Burroughs was educated in private schools, and after leaving a military academy in Michigan enlisted in the army and served with the cavalry until it was discovered that he was underage. Until 1911 he drifted from job to job, working at various times as a cowboy, a miner, and a railroad detective and engaging in a number of unsuccessful business ventures. Finally he decided to try to capitalize on his habitual daydreams of high adventure; the result was a short story, "Under the Moon of Mars," published in 1912 in a pulp science-fiction magazine under the pseudonym "Normal Bean." He continued to sell stories and in 1914 published his first novel, *Tarzan of the Apes*, about the son of an English nobleman who, lost in the jungle in infancy, was raised by apes and grew up to be king of a savage domain. The book enjoyed sufficient success to warrant a sequel, *The Return of Tarzan*, 1915, and then, over a period of 35 years, more than 25 subsequent titles in the Tarzan series. He also wrote a number of science-fiction novels—a long series on Mars, beginning with *A Princess of Mars*, 1917, and many others, including books about Venus and about a mythical land at the earth's core. He was an amazingly prolific writer, regularly producing two and sometimes three novels a year. The Tarzan books sold more than 35 million copies and were translated into 56 languages; the figure of the "Lord of the Jungle" inspired comic strips, movies, and radio and television programs and became the center of a virtual industry. With the earnings from his early books he invested in real estate in California and settled on a ranch near Tarzana, a Los Angeles suburb named for his hero. He interrupted his writing during World War II to serve as a war correspondent in the Pacific. He died in Los Angeles on March 19, 1950, leaving 15 unpublished manuscripts.

Burroughs, John (1837–1921), naturalist and author. Born on April 3, 1837, near Roxbury, New York, Burroughs early grew to know and love the Catskills region. He attended school intermittently and taught for several years after the age of seventeen. His first essays, including "Expression," 1860, and a series published in the *New York Leader*, "From the Back Country," reflected the ideas and literary style of Ralph Waldo Emerson. From 1863 to 1873 Burroughs worked for the treasury department, and in Washington in 1863 he formed a fruitful friendship with Walt Whitman. He wrote *Notes on Walt Whitman as Poet and Person*, 1867, to which Whitman made substantial contributions. A series of nature essays published in the *Atlantic Monthly*, beginning in 1865 ("With the Birds," "In the Hemlocks," and others), became the kernel of his first nature book, published in 1871 and titled, at Whitman's suggestion, *Wake-Robin*. His second book, *Winter Sunshine*, based on observations in England, was published in 1875 and established him in a career which saw the publication of an average of one book every two years for the rest of his life. After 1873 he lived on a farm in Esopus, New York. His reputation as a naturalist developed into that of

a sage, and his isolated cabin, Slabsides, attracted many visitors. He spent considerable time traveling in the United States and abroad and was a friend of other nature enthusiasts, including John Muir and Theodore Roosevelt. His books, recording deep reflections on the conflict between intuitive philosophy and scientific reasoning, included *Locusts and Wild Honey*, 1879, containing keen observation and common-sense deductions; *Whitman, A Study*, 1896, in which he saw scientific achievement as subordinate to the magnitude of vision achieved by Whitman; *The Light of Day*, 1900, celebrating Darwinian theory; *The Summit of the Years*, 1913, calling on "the great thinkers and prophets, poets and mystics" rather than men of science to explain life; and *Under the Apple Trees*, 1916, viewing World War I as a conflict between morality (in the Allies) and science (in the Germans). His greatest contribution, however, was in developing the nature essay into a finely wrought literary form. He died en route from California to New York State on March 25, 1921.

Burroughs, William Seward (1855–1898), inventor. Born in Auburn, New York, on January 28, 1855, Burroughs attended local schools and developed his native mechanical ability in his father's machine shop. He went to work at fifteen, clerking in a bank and later in other businesses, and gradually conceived the idea of a mechanical device that could perform arithmetical calculations. In 1881 he moved to St. Louis and while working in various jobs devoted his spare time to designing a calculator. By 1885 he had a working model on which he filed his first patent application; manufacturing the machine was, however, not commercially feasible. With three partners he organized and sold $100,000 worth of stock in the American Arithmometer Company to finance further experiments. A new model of the machine proved unable to stand heavy use but, with further capitalization, work went on. Finally, in 1891, Burroughs produced a model that printed out each separate entry and the final result of computation and that functioned well under all conditions; two years later he was granted patents covering the first practical adding machine. Production was undertaken almost immediately by American Arithmometer in conjunction with the Boyer Machine Company, and the adding machine quickly proved a great success, being eagerly purchased not only by banks, which Burroughs had considered the only potential market, but by commercial establishments of all kinds. Before the business was firmly established Burroughs died in Citronelle, Alabama, on September 14, 1898. In 1905 American Arithmometer was moved to Detroit and renamed the Burroughs Adding Machine Company (later the Burroughs Corporation) and continued to be a worldwide leader in the field.

Burroughs, William Seward (1914–   ), author. Born on February 5, 1914, in St. Louis, Burroughs was the grandson of William S. Burroughs, inventor of the adding machine. He graduated from Harvard in 1936 and moved to New York City, where for six years he held a variety of minor jobs. From 1944 until 1957 he lived in the grip of heroin addiction. In those years he wandered through Mexico, where he wrote (under the pseudonym "William Lee") his first (and only partially successful) novel, *Junkie*, 1953, then traveled on to South America and to Tangier. Soon after undergoing a successful cure of his addiction in London in 1957 he began a second book, *Naked Lunch*, 1959, which circulated in underground and avant-garde circles for some time before coming to general critical and popular notice following its reissue in 1962. Highly controversial in terms of both content and form, the book projected a horrific vision of the world as a nightmare of degradation, carried forward on a fragmented, collage-like narrative. Elements of the picaresque, of the grotesque, of science fiction, and of the underworldly also entered into subsequent and equally sensational books, including *The Soft Machine*, 1961; *The Ticket That Exploded*, 1962; *Dead Fingers Talk*, 1963; *Nova Express*, 1964; and *Wild Boys*, 1971. Although it was by no means a consensus, there was opinion among many leading critics that Burroughs was to be ranked at the forefront of contemporary American novelists.

Burt, William Austin (1792–1858), surveyor and inventor. Born in Petersham, Massachusetts, on June 13, 1792, Burt grew up there and in New York state. He received little schooling but from an early age studied eagerly on his own and was markedly adept at things mechanical. Broadening his education by whatever means came to hand, he worked as a millwright and surveyor and for a time was also a postmaster and justice of the peace in Erie County, New York. In 1824 he moved his family to a farm near Detroit, where he continued to build mills of various sorts and to do surveying and where he became a member of the Michigan Territorial Council in 1826, Macomb County surveyor in 1831, associate circuit court judge in 1833, and U.S. deputy surveyor, also in 1833. At the same time he applied his inventive mind to a number of problems and in 1829 received a patent for his "Typographer," the first mechanical writing device patented in the United States; a forerunner of the typewriter, it was operated by dialing the desired character and pressing a bar to make the imprint on paper. In 1834 he encountered magnetic interference while surveying in Wisconsin and began to seek an alternative to the magnetic compass; two years later he patented a solar compass, essentially a sundial used in reverse—the angle of the sun and a knowledge of the date and time of day made possible the calculation of the observer's latitude. While surveying the Upper Peninsula of Michigan in 1844 he discovered iron-ore deposits on the site of present-day Negaunee in Marquette County; commercial mining began two years later

and soon Michigan was the leading iron-producing state in the nation. As a member of the state legislature in 1853 he played a leading role in promoting the construction of the Sault Sainte Marie Canal. In 1856 he perfected a third invention of major importance, his equatorial sextant; it was the result of a long interest in astronomy and navigation. Burt died in Detroit on August 18, 1858.

Burton, Harold Hitz (1888–1964), justice of the Supreme Court. Born in Jamaica Plain, Massachusetts, on June 22, 1888, Burton graduated from Bowdoin College in 1909 and from Harvard Law School in 1912. He entered practice in Cleveland and later was employed as an attorney by public-utilities companies in Salt Lake City, Utah, and in Boise, Idaho. After serving in the army in France during World War I he returned to Cleveland and practiced with prominent law firms until 1929. In that year, as a result of his work with a committee formed to plan a regional form of government for Cleveland, he was elected to the legislature. He was also appointed director of law for the city and was acting mayor for some months in 1931. In 1935 he was elected mayor on a reform platform and during three terms made great progress in rooting out the gangster element, in improving public health and safety, and in winning from a recalcitrant state government help in meeting the financial needs of welfare and relief programs. With Works Progress Administration (WPA) aid he carried out numerous civic-improvement projects for the city. Burton was elected as a Republican to the Senate in 1940 and there became prominent for his sponsorship of the "B^2H^2 Bill" (so named for the initials of its four sponsors), which proposed U.S. leadership in establishing an international organization for arbitration and peace-keeping. The main provisions of the bill appeared in the Connally Resolution of 1943 that laid the foundation for the Dumbarton Oaks conference and, ultimately, of the United Nations. In 1945 he was named by President Harry S. Truman to the Supreme Court; the Senate, forgoing the customary hearings, confirmed him immediately and unanimously. During 13 years on the court Burton was known as a generally conservative judge, although he sided with the liberal wing on matters of civil rights. He took a narrow view of the court's power, seeking to decide cases without recourse to expansive philosophical discussion that harbored the possibility of legislation being enacted from the bench. He retired to private life in 1958 and died on October 28, 1964, in Washington, D.C.

Busch, Adolphus (1839–1913), businessman and philanthropist. Born on July 10, 1839, in Mainz, Germany, Busch completed his secondary education there and worked in various jobs until 1857, when he came to the United States and settled in St. Louis. Two years later, with his brother, he opened a brewers' supply store. In 1861 the brothers married the daughters of Eberhard

Anheuser and a short time later Busch became a partner in Anheuser's brewery. He was the firm's secretary until Anheuser's death in 1879, when he became president and changed the company's name to Anheuser-Busch Brewing Association. By that time the brewery had developed, under Busch's direction, a new beer, lighter and drier than most others, which was named Budweiser and which soon became its principal product. Busch pioneered in the pasteurization of beer, making long-distance unrefrigerated shipping (and thus a great expansion of the business) possible; he also acquired a major interest in the St. Louis Refrigerator Car Company and used the newly introduced cars for shipping draught beer. As the brewery grew to huge size he diversified his business investments. He founded the St. Louis Manufacturers' Railway and bought the American rights to the Diesel engine for his Busch-Sulzer Brothers Diesel Engine Company, which produced the first such engine in the country in 1898; these, with numerous other enterprises, contributed to his great wealth. Busch was liberal in his gifts to various causes and institutions, notably to the relief funds for the victims of the San Francisco earthquake (1906), and the Dayton, Ohio, flood of 1913; to Harvard and Washington universities; and to the Louisiana Purchase Exposition in St. Louis in 1904. He died on October 10, 1913, at his hunting lodge near Langenschwalbach, Germany, and was buried in St. Louis.

Bush, George Herbert Walker (1924–   ), vicepresident. Born on June 12, 1924, in Milton, Massachusetts, Bush was the son of Prescott Bush, a successful financier and Republican senator from Connecticut. After graduating from preparatory school, he enlisted in the U.S. Navy Reserve, being for a time the youngest pilot in the navy. After seeing action in World War II, he graduated from Yale University in 1948 with a degree in economics. Settling in Texas, he ventured into the oil and gas business. Eventually he cofounded and became president of the Zapata Offshore Company, which developed offshore drilling equipment. Entering politics, he ran for a seat in the U.S. Senate from Texas in 1964. Although defeated in that election, he was successful in a 1966 race for the U.S. House of Representatives. After two terms in the House and another unsuccessful try at the Senate, Bush was appointed by President Nixon to be the Permanent Representative of the U.S. to the United Nations. Three years later Nixon appointed him chairman of the Republican National Committee. In the aftermath of the Watergate scandal and Nixon's resignation, Bush was chosen by President Ford in 1974 to become chief of the U.S. Liaison Office in the People's Republic of China. A little over a year later, Bush received from Ford yet another appointment, directorship of the Central Intelligence Agency. He held the post until the Democrats won the White House in 1976. In 1980 he ran for the Republican Presidential nomination, making a promising start but ultimately losing to Ronald Reagan. Reagan, however, eventually selected Bush as his running mate. The Reagan and Bush ticket won a decisive victory in the 1980 Presidential election.

Bush, Vannevar (1890–1974), electrical engineer and public offical. Born on March 11, 1890, in Everett, Massachusetts, Bush grew up there and in nearby Chelsea. He graduated from Tufts College in 1913 and, while working first for the General Electric Company, then as a civilian in the inspection department of the navy, and from 1914 as an instructor in mathematics at Tufts, he pursued graduate studies at both Harvard and the Massachusetts Institute of Technology (MIT), receiving a doctorate in engineering from each in 1916. He remained at Tufts as an assistant professor of electrical engineering until 1917, when he undertook antisubmarine research for the navy. In 1919 he was appointed associate professor of electrical power transmission at MIT, where he remained until 1938, from 1923 as full professor and from 1932 as vice-president and dean of the School of Engineering. He had also been from 1917 to 1922 a consulting engineer for the American Radio and Research Corporation and in the latter year had joined in founding the American Appliance Corporation, later the Raytheon Manufacturing Company. In addition to his academic duties at MIT Bush carried on a fertile and highly varied program of research that led to the invention of such disparate devices as improved vacuum tubes, a justifying typewriter, a network analyzer, and, most importantly, a differential analyzer, which was a pioneering form of analog computer built in 1928 and the direct progenitor of later devices in the field. In 1938 Bush was named president of the Carnegie Institution of Washington. In the same year he became a member of the National Advisory Committee for Aeronautics, of which he was chairman from 1939 to 1941. In 1940 he assumed a leading role in mobilizing the U.S. scientific community for the impending war by prevailing upon President Franklin D. Roosevelt to create the National Defense Research Committee (NDRC), of which he was named chairman, and the following year he became chairman of the newly established Office of Scientific Research and Development (OSRD), which absorbed the NDRC. As head of the OSRD until its dissolution in 1946 Bush directed the vast array of research projects undertaken by the government as a vital part of the war effort, including, until its transfer to the Army Corps of Engineers in 1943, the Manhattan Project for the development of the atomic bomb. After the war he served as chairman of the Joint Research and Development Board of the army and navy in 1946–1947 and of its successor body, the Research and Development Board, in 1947–1948. He remained active thereafter as an adviser to many governmental agencies and boards on matters of scientific manpower, organization, and policy. He left the presidency of the Carnegie Institution in 1955, becoming a trustee three years later; he was also a trustee of the Carnegie Corporation of New York from 1939 to 1955, and honorary chairman of the corporation of MIT from 1959. Bush published several nontechnical works, including *Science: The Endless Frontier*, 1945; *Endless Horizons*, 1946; *Modern Arms and Free Men*, 1949; *Science Is Not Enough*, 1967; and *Pieces of the Action*, 1970. He died in Belmont, Massachusetts, on June 28, 1974.

Bushman, Francis Xavier (1883–1966), actor. Born in Baltimore on January 10, 1883, Bushman entered the theater sometime in the early 1900s, acted in a number of stock companies, and in 1907 made his Broadway debut in *The Queen of the Moulin Rouge*. Conflicting publicity stories later obscured many details of his early life, claiming variously that he had run away as a boy to join a circus or that he had been a wrestler or a weight lifter. By 1911 he had come to the attention of the Essanay Studios in Camden, New Jersey (shortly thereafter in Chicago), and in that year he appeared in his first film, a two-reeler entitled *Lost Years*. He was a popular success from the outset, his classic profile and impressive physique, together with his sure command of the histrionic techniques of the silent screen, quickly establishing him as the greatest of the silent era's leading men. Between 1911 and 1918 he made more than 400 films—better than one a week—including *The Magic Wand*, 1912; *The Spy's Defeat*, 1913; *Graustark*, 1915; *Under Royal Patronage*, 1916; *Red, White and Blue Blood*, 1917; and *Social Quicksands*, 1918. Reputedly the highest-paid actor in Hollywood, Bushman lavished his money on estates, servants, and the longest car in the world. Under a clause in his contract the fact that he was married and had several children was kept secret, but when in 1918 he divorced his wife to marry his favorite leading lady, Beverly Bayne, the secret was revealed and his career as the great lover of the screen ended abruptly. He appeared again in *Ben Hur*, 1926, but for the next several decades contented himself with roles in numberless radio dramas and soap operas. He returned on a few later occasions to the movies—*Wilson*, 1943; *David and Bathsheba*, 1951; *Sabrina*, 1954; and *The Ghost in the Invisible Bikini*, 1966, among others. Bushman died in Pacific Palisades, California, on August 23, 1966.

Bushnell, David (1742?–1824), inventor. Born in Saybrook, Connecticut, probably in 1742, Bushnell grew up on a farm and remained there until the death of his father freed him to pursue his education. He entered Yale and graduated in 1775. By that time the idea of an underwater gunpowder mine had occurred to him; returning to Saybrook, he expanded on the notion and soon built a small one-man submarine boat. Powered by two screw propellers cranked from inside, with manually controlled inlet valves and outlet pumps for descending and ascending and equipped with rudimentary phosphorus-lit instruments, the ves-

sel was crude, difficult to operate, and ungainly in appearance, fully warranting its name, *Bushnell's Turtle* (later it was often called the *American Turtle*). The *Turtle* was armed with an ingenious detachable gunpowder mine with an auger bit; operated from inside, the bit allowed the mine to be screwed to the hull of an enemy ship below the waterline. A clock device was intended to delay the explosion while the *Turtle* escaped. Attempts to use the submarine against British ships were made in the harbors of Boston, New York, and Philadelphia in 1776–1777. Problems arose, however, including the difficulty of finding an able and willing operator, and the *Turtle* encountered numerous copper-clad vessels to which the mine could not be attached; as a result, not a single ship was sunk or damaged, although the crew of one was startled. The *Turtle* was nonetheless the first American submarine and probably the first to be used anywhere in warfare. Bushnell finally gave up and joined the Continental army as an engineer; for a few months before his discharge late in 1783 he was in command of the Corps of Engineers at West Point. He then apparently went to France for several years. He turned up in Georgia in 1795 under an assumed name; he taught school for a time and then took up the practice of medicine in Warrenton, where he died in 1824.

Bushnell, Horace (1802–1876), religious leader. Born on April 14, 1802, in Bantam, Connecticut, Bushnell graduated from Yale in 1827, was literary editor of the *New York Journal of Commerce* until 1829, and then studied law for two years while tutoring at Yale. While waiting for admission to the bar, he decided to enter the Yale Divinity School and in 1833 was ordained in the North (Congregational) Church in Hartford, Connecticut. He held the pastorate until 1859, when he resigned because of ill health. He advocated religious instruction for the young, lessened the emphasis on adult conversions, and rejected the doctrine of original sin. Seeing a continuity between the sacred and the profane, the natural and the supernatural, he held that God is present in all His creations and that language is inadequate to express His nature, a belief set forth in his book *God in Christ*, 1849, which led to charges of heresy being brought against him in 1850. The charges were dropped, but criticism by conservatives continued and in 1852 North Church withdrew from the local consociation to avoid a heresy trial. Called the "father of American religious liberalism," Bushnell wrote *Work and Play*, 1864; *The Vicarious Sacrifice*, 1866; *Moral Uses of Dark Things*, 1868; and *Forgiveness and Law*, 1874. He died in Hartford on February 17, 1876.

Butler, Benjamin Franklin (1818–1893), soldier and political leader. Born in Deerfield, New Hampshire, on November 5, 1818, Butler graduated from Waterville (now Colby) College in 1838 and two years later was admitted to the bar. He built up a large practice in Lowell, Massachusetts, and entered politics, serving in the state assembly in 1853 and the state senate in 1859. A Democrat, he was a strong supporter of labor and a defender of immigrants. He was a delegate to the 1860 Democratic national convention and was one of the group that bolted to nominate John C. Breckinridge. When the Civil War began, Butler, called to service as a brigadier general of the Massachusetts militia, strongly supported the Union. In 1861 he occupied Baltimore; in the same year he was promoted to major general and given command of Fort Monroe in Virginia. While in this post he declared escaped slaves to be "contraband" of war, a use of the word which persisted through the war. In 1862 after leading the land forces in support of Adm. David Farragut's naval assault on the city, he became military commander of New Orleans; although he improved the city's sanitation and kept order, he aroused the hatred of the populace. He strained relations with foreign consuls, executed a citizen for lowering the Union flag, and, in his infamous Order No. 28, warned that any disrespect or contempt shown his men by a female would be taken as evidence of moral disrepute and treated accordingly. He was recalled from that post in December 1862. The remainder of Butler's military career was checkered, and he was relieved of command in January 1865. From 1867 to 1875 and from 1877 to 1879 he was a member of the House of Representatives, first as a Radical Republican and then as a Greenbacker. He managed the impeachment trial of President Andrew Johnson and became a strong supporter of President Ulysses S. Grant. He was the Democratic governor of Massachusetts in 1882, and in 1884 was the Greenback and Anti-Monopoly nominee for President. He died on January 11, 1893, in Washington, D.C.

Butler, Nicholas Murray (1862–1947), educator. Born on April 2, 1862, in Elizabeth, New Jersey, Butler specialized in philosophy at Columbia, graduating in 1882 and receiving his doctorate two years later. He studied further at the universities of Berlin and Paris, in Germany meeting Elihu Root, a major influence in his later life. He returned to Columbia in 1885 and became an assistant in philosophy. He delved deeply into the theory of education, its application in teaching, and the organization of schools. To implement his methods of training teachers he helped organize the school that became Teachers College of the University. His teaching methods and curricular innovations were used in a model school. In 1890 he became professor of philosophy and education, a post held for 11 years. He made significant reports on state and local teaching systems and edited a number of educational journals, including *Educational Review*, which he founded. In 1902 he became president of Columbia. Thereafter the school experienced phenomenal growth, expanding its teaching staff, its student body, and its facilities. His major work outside the university was on behalf of peace. In

1907, 1909, and 1910–1912 he directed conferences on international arbitration, and over the signature "Cosmos" contributed a series of articles to the *New York Times*, entitled "The Basis of Durable Peace," that won international recognition. He was a major force in organizing the Carnegie Endowment for International Peace and succeeded Root as its president serving from 1925 to 1945. In behalf of the Kellogg-Briand Pact outlawing war as a tool of national policy, he traveled to Rome in 1930 to secure approval from Pope Pius XI. With Jane Addams he shared the Nobel Peace Prize in 1931. He retired from Columbia in 1945 and died in New York City on December 4, 1947.

Butler, Pierce (1866–1939), justice of the Supreme Court. Born near Northfield, Minnesota, on March 17, 1866, Butler graduated from Carleton College in 1887 and the next year was admitted to the bar in St. Paul. In 1891 he was appointed assistant county attorney and from 1893 to 1897 served two terms as county attorney. He then joined a St. Paul law firm and in 25 years of practice, particularly in the field of railroad law, became one of the most prominent lawyers in the region. He was elected president of the state bar association in 1908. In 1922, at the urging of Chief Justice William Howard Taft, he was appointed to the Supreme Court by President Warren G. Harding. In 16 years on the bench Butler was a powerful presence, an indefatigable arguer for his point of view. During his term the court faced a growing number of cases stemming from the increasing degree of governmental control over business and a great many that concerned generally unpopular manifestations of civil liberties, and he stood foursquare against both trends. A strict constructionist and an economic conservative, he was most often allied with justices Willis Van Devanter, James C. McReynolds, and George Sutherland in the majority during his first years on the court, but was more and more often a dissenter as the tenor of the court slowly liberalized. Butler took a most disapproving view of the New Deal and joined in voting down two of its major instruments, the Agricultural Adjustment Administration (AAA) and the National Recovery Administration (NRA). He died in Washington, D. C., on November 16, 1939.

Butler, Walter C., see Faust, Frederick Schiller

Butterfield, John (1801–1869), businessman. Born on November 18, 1801, in Berne, New York, Butterfield received a scanty education and at an early age went to work for a stagecoach company. Within a few years he worked his way up from driver to partner in the firm. Eventually he had interests in stagecoach, canal-boat, and lake-steamer lines; he founded the streetcar system in Utica, New York, and with others formed the New York, Albany & Buffalo Telegraph Company. In 1849 he added an express business to his enterprises, organizing Butterfield, Wasson & Company, which the next year he merged with two other firms, Wells & Company and Livingston, Fargo & Company, to form the American Express Company, from which in 1852 sprang a sister firm, Wells, Fargo & Company. With the passage of the Overland California Mail Bill in 1857, Butterfield organized the Overland Mail Company and won the contract to carry mail from St. Louis to San Francisco via Little Rock, El Paso, Tucson, Yuma, and Los Angeles. The record run for the original 2800-mile southern Overland Mail route was 22 days; the line was extended to Portland, Oregon, in 1860, making its total length some 3600 miles. The route, later shifted northward because of the Civil War, remained an important link with the West until the completion of the transcontinental railroad in 1869. Butterfield himself continued to live in Utica, of which he was mayor in 1865, and to direct his extensive investments until his death on November 14, 1869.

Button, Richard Totten (1929–   ), figure skater. Born in Englewood, New Jersey, on July 18, 1929, Dick Button asked for and received his first pair of ice skates for Christmas in 1941, when he was twelve years old. Despite early failures and the pessimistic outlook of his teachers he applied himself to learning figure skating with amazing energy and in 1943 placed second in his first competition, the Eastern States Novice meet. The next year he won the Eastern States Junior and U.S. Novice championships. In 1945 he took the Eastern States Senior and the U.S. Junior titles; the following year he became the youngest skater ever to win the U.S. Senior championship. He entered international competition in 1947 with a second place at the world championships in Stockholm, and later in the year retained his U.S. title and brought the North American prize back to the United States for the first time in 24 years. Early in 1948 he became the first and (because U.S. entrants were subsequently barred) the last American to win the European championship. He went on that year to take the Olympic gold medal (with a record point score) and then the world championship. When Button entered Harvard in 1948 he held all five major figure-skating titles, an unparalleled achievement. In all, he was U.S. national champion from 1946 through 1952, world titlist from 1948 through 1952, North American titlist 1947–1952, and again the Olympic gold-medal winner in 1952. After graduating from Harvard in the latter year he began skating professionally in ice shows, a career he continued along with television and movie appearances. Following his graduation from Harvard Law School in 1955, he was admitted to the bar in Washington, D.C. His autobiography, *Dick Button on Skates*, appeared in 1956.

Byrd, Richard Evelyn (1888–1957), naval officer, aviator, and explorer. Born in Winchester, Virginia, on October 25, 1888, Byrd was a direct descendant of William Byrd. After attending Virginia Military Institute and the University of Virginia he entered the U.S. Naval Academy, from which he graduated in 1912. Active service followed for three years; forced to retire for a time because of old leg injuries, Byrd returned to duty and entered the navy's aviation branch in 1917. During World War I he commanded a navy air patrol squadron based in Canada and was active afterward in promoting the development of naval aviation; he was largely responsible for the creation of the navy bureau of aeronautics, and he invented several important aids to aerial navigation. During the early 1920s he helped plan projected transatlantic flights and a dirigible flight over the North Pole. In 1925 he commanded a small naval flying group attached to D. B. MacMillan's Arctic expedition; the next year he went back with a second expedition and on May 9, 1926, with Floyd Bennett as his co-pilot, made the first flight over the North Pole, a round trip from Spitsbergen. The feat won both men the Congressional Medal of Honor and Byrd was awarded the Distinguished Service Medal and promoted to commander. In June of the following year he and three companions piloted a multi-engined aircraft across the Atlantic (he had earlier given special training to Charles A. Lindbergh and, but for equipment difficulties, would probably have beaten him in the race for first crossing). With the status of popular hero combined with considerable skill in public relations, Byrd had little difficulty in securing private sponsors for an expedition to the Antarctic in 1928–1930; vast new land areas were discovered on that trip and, taking off from his base, Little America, he and Bernt Balchen made the first flight over the South Pole on November 29, 1929. Soon afterward he was promoted to rear admiral. From 1933 to 1935 he was in command of a second expedition in Antarctica during which much more unknown territory was mapped; for five months in 1934 he was alone in a weather-observation shack far south of the main base and, nearly dying there of carbon-monoxide poisoning, he suffered from impaired health thereafter. In 1939–1940, under the aegis of the newly established U.S. Antarctic Service, he led another survey expedition. During World War II he was on the staff of the naval chief of operations. In 1946–1947 he was again in Antarctica in command of a huge navy-sponsored expedition called Operation Highjump and made a second flight over the pole. In 1955 he was placed in charge of Operation Deep Freeze, a major scientific and exploratory expedition sent to the Antarctic under navy auspices as part of the program of the International Geophysical Year, 1957–1958. Byrd accompanied the task force to Antarctica, made a last flight over the pole, and returned to the United States. Failing health prevented his rejoining the expedition and he died in Boston on March 11, 1957. Several books by Byrd achieved wide popularity: *Skyward*, 1928; *Little America*, 1930; *Discovery*, 1935; and *Alone*, 1938.

Byrd, William (1674–1744), planter, colonial official, and author. Born on March 28, 1674, on his father's Virginia plantation, Byrd was sent to England to be educated. Admitted to the bar in 1695, he returned to Virginia and, thanks to his wealth, education, and social standing, quickly assumed a position of prominence in the colony. From 1697 to 1705 he was again in England, as the colony's agent; during that time he was made a member of the Royal Society. After his return to his huge plantation he became the colony's receiver-general and colonel of militia, posts his father had held. In 1709 he entered the colony's council, for which he was the spokesman in a struggle for power against Governor Alexander Spotswood, and remained until 1744, serving as its president from 1743. He built a classically beautiful mansion at Westover and there assembled the largest library in the colony. In 1728 he was one of the commissioners appointed to survey the Virginia–North Carolina border; he described the expedition in his witty and satirical *History of the Dividing Line*. In 1737 the future city of Richmond was laid out on his land. Byrd died at Westover on August 26, 1744.

Byrnes, James Francis (1879–1972), public official and justice of the Supreme Court. Born in Charleston, South Carolina, on May 2, 1879, Byrnes was forced by family circumstances to leave school at fourteen and take a job as a clerk in a law office. He continued his education on his own and later, while working as a court stenographer for the state's Second Circuit Court in Aiken, began studying law. He was admitted to the bar in 1903. He continued in his court position until 1908, when he was elected prosecuting attorney for the circuit. In 1910 he was elected as a Democrat to the House of Representatives, where he remained until 1925. In 1925 he had declined renomination in order to run for the Senate; after losing the race he took up law practice in Spartanburg, South Carolina. He was successful in the Senate election in 1930 and again in 1936. During 11 years in the Senate he was a strong supporter of President Franklin D. Roosevelt, and although in later years his enthusiasm for New Deal measures cooled he remained a principal adviser and legislative aide. Although he was hostile to much pro-union legislation, he played a major role in securing for Roosevelt the repeal of the Neutrality Act, 1935, and passage of the Lend-Lease Act, 1941. He was active in Roosevelt's third-term bid in 1940 and the next year was appointed to the Supreme Court. He was on the bench for only a year, resigning to become, at the President's request, director of the Office of Economic Stabilization. In that post, and in the subsequent one of head of the Office of War Mobilization, created in 1943, Byrnes was invested with vast power over the economy and became known as the "assistant president." He was considered a strong possibility for the Democratic vice-presidential nomination in 1944, but the opposition of organized labor ended the idea. In April 1945,

with the end of the war in sight and reconversion of the economy already under way, he resigned to return to South Carolina and the private practice of law. In July, shortly after Roosevelt's death, he was back in Washington as President Harry S. Truman's secretary of state. He immediately embarked on an exhausting series of top-level international conferences—at Potsdam, London, Moscow, Paris, and elsewhere—to bring the diplomatic phase of the war to a close, draw up treaties, and organize the United Nations. His experiences in dealing with the Soviet Union, particularly over the issues of German reunification and the presence of Soviet troops in Iran beyond the agreed withdrawal date, soon converted him from an advocate of friendly cooperation to a hard-line battler in the Cold War. He resigned from the cabinet in 1947 in a disagreement with Truman and after a period of silence began publicly denouncing Truman's Fair Deal programs as socialistic and tending to statism. His popular *Speaking Frankly*, appeared in 1947. In 1950 he was elected governor of South Carolina. During his administration the Ku Klux Klan was effectively suppressed in the state, but Byrnes strongly supported the continuation of racial segregation in the schools. He supported Dwight D. Eisenhower's bid for the presidency on the Republican ticket in 1952. After leaving office in 1955 he lived in retirement in Columbia, South Carolina, where he died on April 9, 1972. An autobiography, *All in One Lifetime*, had appeared in 1958.

Byrns, Joseph Wellington (1869–1936), public official. Born on July 20, 1869, near Cedar Hill, Tennessee, Byrns graduated from Vanderbilt University in 1890 and was immediately admitted to the bar. He began law practice in Nashville the next year and soon became active in politics, winning election to the legislature in 1894 and remaining there, from 1900 in the senate, until 1902. In 1908 he was elected to the House of Representatives and retained his seat until his death; in 13 reelection campaigns he only once had an opponent. Early in his congressional career he was named to the House Committee on Appropriations, and he made economy in government his special cause thereafter. When the Democrats organized the House in 1930 he became chairman of the committee; a conflict of loyalties arose, however, with the coming of the New Deal and his accession to the post of majority leader in 1932, one which he resolved in favor of party regularity. As majority leader he assumed responsibility for steering through the House all the various reform and relief measures of Franklin D. Roosevelt's first administration, despite the fact that their economic and political bases were radically different from his own conservative outlook. In recognition of his work he was elected speaker of the House in 1935, a position he filled with great effectiveness until his death on June 4, 1936, in Washington, D.C.

C

Cabell, James Branch (1879–1958), author. Born on April 14, 1879, in Richmond, Virginia, Cabell began his writing career as a newspaper columnist in Richmond after graduating in 1898 from the College of William and Mary. Then he wrote a series of novels and stories about the "first families of Virginia," among which his own family ranked. *The Cords of Vanity,* 1909, *The Rivet in Grandfather's Neck,* 1915, and *The Cream of the Jest,* 1917, satirized Southern idealism and ancestor worship and, with *Jurgen,* 1919, his best-known book, formed part of the 18-volume Biography of Manuel, a series of romances set in medieval times in the imaginary province of Poictesme. Suppressed at first on charges of obscenity, *Jurgen* won Cabell a wide reputation and, high critical acclaim through the 1920s. Other books of the Poictesme series included *Figures of Earth,* 1921; *The High Place,* 1923; *Something About Eve,* 1927; and *The Way of Ecben,* 1929. He wrote volumes of criticism, among them *Preface to the Past,* 1936, which defended allegory as a literary form, since realism can—perhaps must —distort the spirit of life. Writing after 1930 under the name Branch Cabell, he published *These Restless Heads,* 1932, an autobiographical work; several novels, essays, and stories about Virginia, many of which were published in the *American Mercury* by H. L. Mencken; and a trilogy, *Smirt,* 1934, *Smith,* 1935, and *Smire,* 1937. During 1932–1935 he was, along with George Jean Nathan, Theodore Dreiser, Sherwood Anderson, Eugene O'Neill, and others, active in publishing and editing the sleek, satirical monthly, *American Spectator.* His great popularity of the 1920s faded rapidly and in his later years he was little read or regarded. He died in Richmond on May 5, 1958.

Cable, George Washington (1844–1925), author. Born in New Orleans on October 12, 1844, Cable was forced by the death of his father to end his schooling at fourteen and undertake responsibility for his family's support. Soon after the family was sent out of New Orleans by Union occupation forces in 1863 he joined a Mississippi cavalry regiment and saw considerable action through the remainder of the Civil War, employing what free time he could find to continue his education on his own. Brief employment as a surveyor at the end of the war resulted in a two-year bout with malaria, during which time he began to submit columns of miscellaneous comment and observation to the *New Orleans Picayune.* In 1869, by which time his column was a popular daily feature of the paper, he worked also

for a short time as a reporter. A disagreement with the management of the *Picayune* brought an end to his journalistic career and later in 1869 he entered the office of a firm of cotton factors. Cable had continued to read and study for his own benefit and, having taught himself French, began digging into the old records in the city archives, finding in them a lode of romance and exotic detail that stirred his literary imagination. Encouraged to seek publication of the tales he had begun to write, he sent them to *Scribner's Monthly,* in which six of them appeared during 1873–1876; collected, together with a seventh story, in *Old Creole Days,* 1879, they quickly established Cable's reputation. With *The Grandissimes,* 1880, a novel earlier serialized in *Scribner's,* he became the acknowledged literary voice of old New Orleans and a major figure in what later came to be called the "local color" movement in American fiction. While producing several more books over the next few years, Cable began to concern himself with a variety of reforms, especially with the just and equal treatment of freedmen, and his lectures and essays, some of the latter collected in *The Silent South,* 1885, aroused strong antipathy among his fellow Southerners. For that reason, as well as to place himself closer to the principal literary marketplaces, he left New Orleans in 1885 and settled in Northampton, Massachusetts. He became a popular lecturer, often reading from his own works, and toured widely. He continued to produce books regularly, including such works as *Bonaventure,* 1888; *Strange True Stories of Louisiana,* 1889; *Strong Hearts,* 1899; *Posson Jone and Père Raphael,* 1909; and *Lovers of Louisiana,* 1918, but his later romances lacked the delicate style and charm of the earlier works. Cable died in St. Petersburg, Florida, on January 31, 1925.

Cabot, John (1450?–1499?), explorer. Born probably in Genoa, Italy, about 1450, Giovanni Caboto later became a citizen of the great mercantile city of Venice and there doubtless first conceived the notion of sailing via a westward route to the riches of the Orient. He moved to England about 1484, possibly because of its well-developed commerce and its northerly situation, and Anglicized his name. Not until 1496, however, did contact with Bristol merchants and news of Columbus's success bring him the support he sought; in that year he was granted letters patent by Henry VII and on May 2, 1497, after an abortive attempt the previous year, set sail from Bristol in the tiny *Matthew.* His northern route being much shorter than Columbus's, he reached land after seven weeks at sea, on June 24, and planted English and Venetian flags on what he believed to be the mainland of China. The actual place of his landing is disputed, but it was either in Maine, Newfoundland, Labrador, or Cape Breton Island. Upon his return to England Cabot was widely celebrated for his discovery. He set out again in May 1498 with five ships, determined to find Japan. After exploring the coast of Greenland he crossed Davis Strait and turned southward along the coast of America. Before giving up the search for a route to the Orient he sighted Cape Cod; soon afterward he returned to England. The annuity granted him by Henry VII after the first voyage went unclaimed after 1499 and there are no further records of him. His son, Sebastian Cabot, was later famed as a navigator in the service of England and Spain.

Caboto, Giovanni, *see* Cabot, John

Cabrini, Frances Xavier (1850–1917), saint of the Roman Church. Born in Italy on July 15, 1850, Frances Cabrini was determined from her childhood to make religious work her life's vocation. Delicate health prevented her from becoming a missionary, but her remarkable efforts in an orphanage in Italy, which earned her the name Mother Cabrini, led her bishop to encourage her to take religious vows in 1877; in 1880 she founded the Missionary Sisters of the Sacred Heart of Jesus. Her intention was to extend the order's orphanage and missionary work to China, but she was directed by Pope Leo XIII to utilize her abilities among the Italian poor in the United States. She arrived in New York City in 1889 and from then until her death lived there and in Chicago, traveling extensively throughout the Americas and in Europe founding convents, schools, orphanages, and hospitals. She became a naturalized American citizen in 1909. After her death in Chicago on December 22, 1917, proceedings were instituted that led to her beatification in 1938 and her canonization, announced by Pope Pius XII, on July 7, 1946.

Cadillac, Antoine Laumet de la Mothe (1658–1730), colonial official. Born on March 5, 1658, in Les Laumets, Languedoc, France, Cadillac entered the army and first came to America in 1683, living in Port Royal (now Annapolis Royal, Nova Scotia) and later in Maine. In 1694 he was appointed by the governor of New France, Count Frontenac, commander of the outpost at St. Ignace on the northern shore of the Straits of Mackinac, a vital situation for defense and for the fur trade in the West. The post was ordered abandoned in 1697 and two years later Cadillac returned to France to promote his scheme for a settlement and fort on the Detroit River. He secured a grant and on July 24, 1701, founded Fort Pontchartrain du Détroit, which later, under British rule, was called simply Detroit. Ambitious and not a little avaricious, Cadillac made numerous enemies, particularly among the Jesuit missionaries, whose

position he attempted in many ways to undermine. He was arrested, tried in Quebec, and acquitted in 1704 but at length in 1711 was recalled to France. Appointed governor of Louisiana, he arrived there in 1713 and in three years had again so antagonized the populace and officials there and his superiors in Paris that he was recalled. He may have been imprisoned briefly in the Bastille in 1716–1717. He lived in Gascony for the rest of his life and died at Castelsarrasin on October 15, 1730.

Cage, John Milton, Jr. (1912–   ), composer. Born on September 5, 1912, in Los Angeles, Cage attended Pomona College from 1928 to 1930 and studied music under a number of teachers, including Arnold Schönberg. He taught at various times at the Cornish School in Seattle, Mills College in Oakland, California, the School of Design in Chicago, Black Mountain College in North Carolina, and the New School for Social Research in New York City. He premiered in 1943 in New York City in a concert of his own percussion works. The stage was arrayed with such "non-instruments" as buzzers, pottery, and scrap metal, chosen for their potentiality for making different, not to say startling, sounds. The elements of Cage's music—and controversy over whether his works indeed were music was abundant—were notably silence, sound, and rhythm. No harmony was used. To make a percussion instrument out of such a traditional concert instrument as a piano, he placed nuts, bolts, screws, dolls' arms, and other objects between the strings. For devising the "prepared piano" he won two awards for expanding the horizons of music. He won note as the musical director for Merce Cunningham's ballet ensemble, and his intricate manuscripts written for concert soloists or conductors were shown in museums as examples of superb calligraphy. Since much of his written music was intended to be inspiration for performers rather than compositions to be performed as written, it offered choices of the number and kind of instruments or noninstruments that might be used and of the various sections of the work that might or might not be included in the performance. His many compositions included *Imaginary Landscape No. 4*, 1951, for 12 radios tuned randomly, 24 performers, and conductor; *Water Music*, 1952, for pianist, radio, whistles, water containers, and deck of cards; *4'33"*, 1954, for any instrument or combination of instruments—which are used only as stage props, the work itself consisting only of silence; *Winter Music*, 1957, for one to 20 pianists; *Fontana Mix*, 1958, for magnetic tape; and *Music for Amplified Toy Pianos*, 1960. A performance at New York City's Town Hall in 1958 was recorded as *The Twenty-Five-Year Retrospective Concert of the Music of John Cage*. Many of his lectures and essays on music were collected in *Silence*, 1961, and *A Year from Monday*, 1967.

Cagney, James (1904–   ), actor. Born in New York City on July 17, 1904, Cagney entered the theater after leaving high school. He worked as a dancer in the choruses of a few Broadway shows and for several years toured in the East in vaudeville. His first major acting job came in 1925 in *Outside Looking In*, but he did not score a notable success until 1929, when he starred in *Maggie the Magnificent*. After appearing in *Penny Arcade*, 1930, he was signed by Warner Brothers for its film version, *Sinner's Holiday*, 1930. With *Public Enemy*, 1931, Cagney became a film star virtually overnight and set the pattern for a long series of subsequent movie roles as one or another variation of the "tough guy." The brash, cocky, and pugnacious characters he played in such films as *The Crowd Roars*, 1932; *Mayor of Hell*, 1933; *G-Men*, 1935; *Ceiling Zero*, 1936; *Angels with Dirty Faces*, 1938; *Each Dawn I Die*, 1939; *The Fighting 69th*, 1940; and *Strawberry Blonde*, 1940, ranged from gangsters to unrefined but somehow romantic heroes, and his portrayals never failed to elicit the strong sympathies of the audience by their communication of a sense, even in the most violent hoodlums, of scarred humanity. In 1942 Cagney displayed considerable versatility, along with some of his early vaudeville talents, in *Yankee Doodle Dandy*, a film biography of George M. Cohan, for which he won an Academy Award. Later movies included *Johnny Come Lately*, 1943; *13 Rue Madeleine*, 1946; *The Time of Your Life*, 1948; *West Point Story*, 1950; *What Price Glory?*, 1952; *Mister Roberts*, 1955; *Man of a Thousand Faces*, 1957; *Never Steal Anything Small*, 1959; *Shake Hands with the Devil*, 1959, which he directed; *The Gallant Hours*, 1960, which he also directed; and *One, Two, Three*, 1961.

Cahan, Abraham (1860–1951), journalist, editor, and author. Born on July 7, 1860, in Vilna, Lithuania, then a part of Russia, Cahan studied at the Teachers Institute in his native city and taught in a government school. His revolutionary activities over several years made it necessary for him to flee Russia in 1881. He arrived penniless in New York City and, as with other Jewish immigrants, found a job in a cigar factory. Within a few months he had learned English and met Morris Hillquit, a leading figure in the Socialist movement. Together they founded the *New York Arbeiter Zeitung*, a Yiddish newspaper devoted to Socialism, introducing Jewish immigrants to their new surroundings and to ideas of improving their living and working conditions. He also edited the papers *Neie Zeit* and *Zukunft* and in 1897 was a founder and briefly editor of the *Jewish Daily Forward*, a small paper supported by contributions from Jewish laborers. He soon broke with the radical Socialists and left the *Forward*, turning to journalism on English-language papers—the *New York Sun*, the *New York Evening Post*, and the *Commercial Advertiser*—for five years, becoming well known for his stories of Jewish life. With compassion and literary skill he related the trials of masses of immigrants as he had witnessed them in factories

and ghettoes. In 1896 his first novel, *Yekl, A Tale of the New York Ghetto*, contributed more to increasing others' understanding of his people and their condition than any book that had yet been published. Friends persuaded him to rejoin the *Forward* in 1902. As editor in chief he changed the entire format of the paper; articles on manners and American customs, theater and the arts, politics and economics, written for people whose only education had come from the Torah, won for the *Forward* an eventual circulation of 200,000. He became a powerful spokesman for labor, advocating the formation of unions and the elimination of sweatshops, and remained an influential figure in Socialist circles. His later books included *The Imported Bridegroom and Other Stories*, 1898; *The Rise of David Levinsky*, 1917, his best-known work; and *Blätter von mein Leben*, 1926–1931, a five-volume autobiography in Yiddish. He died in New York City on August 31, 1951.

Calamity Jane, see Burke, Martha Jane

Calder, Alexander (1898–1976), sculptor. Born on July 22, 1898, in Philadelphia, Calder came of a family of sculptors, but he wished to be an engineer and attended the Stevens Institute of Technology in Hoboken, New Jersey, graduating in 1919. Thereafter he worked as an engineer, a seaman, and a lumberjack before deciding to attend the Art Students League in New York City in 1923. To pay his tuition he worked as an illustrator for the *Police Gazette*. On assignment to cover the Ringling Brothers–Barnum and Bailey Circus in 1925, he was fascinated by the sight of performers in motion while maintaining perfect balance. His drawings led to his making small wire sculptures of animals and acrobats in which the surrounding and interior space became part of the design. In 1926 in Paris he first showed *Le Cirque Calder*, whose originality excited such artists as Joan Miró and Jean Cocteau. He added to the miniature circus over many years and filmed it in motion in 1951 in *The Works of Calder*, for which John Cage composed the score. In 1931 he first exhibited the sculptures of wood and metal that Jean Arp dubbed "stabiles." Influenced by Piet Mondrian, the sculptures were nonrepresentational, brightly colored and abstract in form, and suggested motion although they stood in place. In 1932 his first hanging "mobile" (named by Marcel Duchamp) appeared; sections of wire were connected to achieve a delicate balance and from each wire was suspended a sphere or globe or other graceful form. The forms were constantly in motion, initially propelled by motors, but later constructed to move spontaneously at the touch of a fingertip or the slightest breeze. The essential qualities were balance and harmony in every possible configuration that the moving elements would form. Some famous mobiles were used as sets during Martha Graham's dance recitals in the 1930s; and Calder also made a water mobile for the 1939–1940 New York

World's Fair, a 45-foot mobile for Kennedy International Airport in New York City, and the 30-foot motorized *Four Elements* in Stockholm. A stabile in Spoleto, Italy, titled "Teodelapio," is 50 feet high and accommodates passing trucks under its huge spindle legs. Calder also excelled in watercolors, nonrepresentational and vibrantly hued, and in book illustrations, jewelry, tapestries, and wood and bronze figures. He died in New York City on November 11, 1976.

Caldwell, Erskine Preston (1903–   ), author. Born in Coweta County, Georgia, on December 17, 1903, Caldwell was the son of an itinerant preacher and received little formal schooling. At fourteen he struck out on his own, traveled widely, and held a series of highly varied jobs ranging from cabdriver to professional football player. For brief periods between 1920 and 1925 he attended Erskine College in Due West, South Carolina, and the universities of Pennsylvania and Virginia. For several years he lived in seclusion in Maine developing his writing style and in 1932 published a novel, *Tobacco Road*, that won notoriety and huge sales with its searing portrayal of depravity among Southern poor whites. The stage version, dramatized by Jack Kirkland, was on Broadway from 1933 to 1941 in one of the longest runs in history—more than 3000 performances. The novel's title became a common phrase in references to poverty and degeneracy. *God's Little Acre*, 1933; *Journeyman*, 1935; and *Trouble in July*, 1940, followed; all were written with a frankness, bordering sometimes on sensationalism, that led to numerous court battles on charges of obscenity and bolstered sales enormously. Caldwell also published collections of short stories, including *Kneel to the Rising Sun*, 1935, and *Jackpot*, 1940, and wrote several movie scripts. In 1937 he collaborated with photographer Margaret Bourke-White, his wife from 1939 to 1942, in producing *You Have Seen Their Faces*, a word and picture study of the Southern land and people. They also published *North of the Danube*, 1939, a study of Czechoslovakia, and *Say! Is This the U.S.A.?*, 1941. Caldwell continued to write at a prodigious rate, but although his later works enjoyed unabated popularity they were less highly regarded by critics; among them were *All Night Long*, 1942; *Georgia Boy*, 1943; *Tragic Ground*, 1944; *This Very Earth*, 1948; *A Lamp for Nightfall*, 1952; *Love and Money*, 1954; *Claudelle Inglish*, 1959; *Jenny by Nature*, 1961; *In the Shadow of the Steeple*, 1966; and *Summertime Island*, 1968. From 1942 to 1955 he was editor of *American Folkways*.

Calhoun, John Caldwell (1782–1850), public official and political leader. Born on March 18, 1782, in Abbeville District (now County), South Carolina, Calhoun was the son of a slaveholding upcountry farmer and occasional legislator. He received almost no formal education until he was eighteen; two years in a "log college" prepared him to enter the junior class at Yale, from which he graduated in 1804. He then turned to law, studying under Tapping Reeve at his famous school in Litchfield, Connecticut, winning admission to the South Carolina bar in 1807, and establishing his practice in Abbeville. In 1808 and again in 1809 he was elected to the legislature, which during that period was engaged in devising an equitable compromise in the representation of the small farmers of the upcountry and the planters of the coastal districts, a political problem that contributed to Calhoun's development of a sophisticated understanding of the shortcomings of simplistic democratic processes. The year 1811 brought advancement both in society and in politics, as his marriage give him entrée into the planting aristocracy of Charleston and his election to the House of Representatives brought him to the national scene. He quickly allied himself with Speaker of the House Henry Clay and, soon appointed to the influential committee on foreign affairs, became one of the most clamorous of the "War Hawks" eager for war with England. When hostilities began in 1812 he labored mightily to secure all possible legislative support for the military effort and he emerged from the war a thoroughgoing nationalist, advocating a program of military preparedness, internal improvements, and the encouragement of industry by means of modest protective tariffs. Calhoun resigned his seat in Congress to become secretary of war in the cabinet of President James Monroe in 1817; his national stature and his ambition rose together during his years in that post and in 1824 he was able to mount a successful campaign for the vice-presidency. The "era of good feelings" that had succeeded the War of 1812 was by that time yielding to increasing tensions between North and South, and Calhoun and his policies reflected the change; himself a planter faced with falling cotton prices, he began to look askance at the constant pressure by Northern industrialists for higher and higher tariff levels, coming eventually to see such tariffs as constituting government subsidies at the direct expense of agriculture. And, at the same time, events combined to convince him that the South could hope for little protection from prevailing constitutional theory and practice. After four years of patiently presiding over the Senate in the administration of John Quincy Adams, Calhoun found it necessary to postpone his presidential ambitions in the face of the tide of popular enthusiasm for Andrew Jackson in 1828. He was reelected to the vice-presidency and had every hope of enduring to succeed Jackson. A breach between the two soon developed, however: The social ostracism of Peggy O'Neale (Margaret Eaton), who had Jackson's backing, by other cabinet wives was instigated by Mrs. Calhoun and that, together with Jackson's learning that in 1818 Calhoun, as secretary of war, had favored censuring Jackson's conduct in Florida, resulted in the President's settling on Martin Van Buren as his favorite and heir-designate. More important to Calhoun's future was the growing reaction to the "tariff of abominations" (Tariff of 1828), with its high, protectionist duties. Through the South Carolina legislature (his authorship was not revealed until 1831) he issued the "South Carolina Exposition and Protest," in which the tariff was called unconstitutional and the threat of nullification was raised. While attempting in various ways and without success to secure a compromise on the tariff question, he continued to elaborate upon the constitutional theory broached in the "Exposition." His widely circulated 1831 "Fort Hill Letter" outlined his view of sovereignty as originally and still inhering in the several states, whose citizens retained the right to adjudge an act of the federal government as unconstitutional and to prohibit in their states the enforcement of such an act. It was an elaborate and closely reasoned argument, though it proved of little use in affecting the growing conflict. The failure of Congress to meet the objections of the South when it enacted the Tariff of 1832 precipitated a crisis. A South Carolina convention adopted in December an ordinance nullifying the tariffs of 1828 and 1832; while Jackson and the state government rumbled threats, Calhoun resigned the vice-presidency in order to enter the Senate, where the great battle over nullification was to be fought. The result of debate and compromise was the passage of a reduced tariff schedule along with Jackson's Force Bill of 1833, which empowered the president to use armed force against the nullifiers. South Carolina responded to the reduction in tariffs by repealing the first ordinance of nullification and to the Force Bill by adopting another ordinance nullifying it; the crisis was ended, although the problem was not solved. Calhoun remained in the Senate, but his hopes for resolving sectional differences and rebuilding his national following —his former Middle States supporters, especially in Pennsylvania, had been alienated by his antitariff stand—were dashed by the emergence of abolitionism, a maddening and increasingly threatening irritant to the South. He stood therefore as a towering, eloquent, and ever more aggressive champion of his section's interests, almost indifferent to the shifting of party alignments around him; in opposition to Jackson he helped forge the Whig coalition, but he returned to the Democratic fold in the later 1830s. He served briefly as secretary of state in 1844–1845 under President John Tyler and after a short retirement to his South Carolina plantation returned in 1845 to the Senate, where he remained until his death. His last years were devoted to continuing the defense of the South and to refining further his political ideas. He advocated annexation of Texas but also a conciliatory policy toward Mexico, and he was not in favor of war with that nation. As for the territories gained in the Mexican War, he saw them, in light of his political theory, as the joint possession of the states and therefore as open to the lawful institutions—slavery, for pointed example—of any state.

He led, therefore, in the opposition to the Wilmot Proviso proposing the prohibition of slavery in the new Southwestern territories, for he saw the prohibition not only as unconstitutional but also, in view of the geographical and climatic realities, as gratuitous and insulting to the South. *A Disquisition on Government* and *A Discourse on the Constitution and Government of the United States* —the second book unfinished, and both published posthumously—were the last of Calhoun's great achievements and contained the most carefully articulated accounts of his political philosophy; the *Disquisition* worked out his notion of "concurrent majority" as against simple numerical majority in democratic decision making, while the *Discourse* proposed a dual executive at the head of the federal government to represent the divergent interests of the two great sections of the nation. On March 4, 1850, Calhoun made his last appearance in the Senate to hear, in his exhausted and desperately ill condition, his last speech read for him; it was in opposition to Henry Clay's proposed Omnibus Bill, which was nevertheless enacted (the Compromise of 1850). He died in Washington, D.C., on March 31, 1850.

Callas, Maria (1923–1977), singer. Born in New York City on December 3, 1923, Maria Kalogeropoulos was the daughter of Greek immigrant parents. She early developed an interest in singing and at fourteen traveled with her mother to Greece to enter the Royal Conservatory in Athens. Shortly thereafter, in late 1938, she made her operatic debut in Athens in *Cavalleria Rusticana*. Her career began in earnest in 1947, when she appeared in Verona in *La Gioconda*; soon, under the tutoring of conductor Tullio Serafin, she made debuts in Venice, Turin, and Florence; in 1949 she first appeared in Rome, Buenos Aires, and Naples, and in 1950 in Mexico City. Her powerful soprano voice, capable of sustaining both lyric and coloratura roles, was, although not perfect in control, intensely dramatic; combined with her strong sense of theater and her scrupulously high artistic standards, it took her quickly to the forefront of contemporary opera stars. Her talents made possible the revival of nineteenth-century bel canto works, notably those of Bellini and Donizetti, that had long been dropped from standard repertoires. Miss Callas made her debut at the prestigious La Scala in Milan in 1950, singing in *I Vespri Siciliani*; in 1952 she appeared at Covent Garden, London; in 1954–1955 at Chicago's Lyric Opera; and in 1956 at the Metropolitan Opera in New York City, where her opening-night appearance in *Norma* drew a record audience. Her recordings were enthusiastically received, and she was one of the most popular singers of the period. Her much-publicized temperament, which led to several lengthy feuds with rivals and managers, reinforced in the public mind her status as prima donna. Her last operatic performance was in *Tosca* at the Met in 1965; in 1973–1974 she made a final world concert tour. She died in Paris on September 16, 1977.

Calvert, Charles (1637–1715), third Baron Baltimore, colonial governor and proprietor. Born in England on August 27, 1637, Calvert was the son of Cecilius Calvert and grandson of George Calvert. In 1661 he was appointed by his father governor of the colony of Maryland, the proprietary government having been suspended during the English Commonwealth period and resumed with the Restoration. By that time, in the aftermath of the repressions of the Cromwell regime, anti-Catholic feeling was rampant in most of the British American colonies and even in Maryland, where Catholics were a small but visible minority. Such feeling was expressed largely in the form of popular opposition to proprietary government and prerogatives. Calvert responded strongly, restricting suffrage in 1670, vetoing many acts of the assembly, sometimes years after their passage, and using his appointive powers to maintain control of local institutions. Upon the death of his father in 1675 he succeeded to the title of Baron Baltimore and to the proprietorship. A boundary dispute with William Penn and Indian troubles added to his problems, and he sailed to England on several occasions to defend his charter and territory. With the accession of the Protestant monarchs William and Mary in 1689 his position became untenable; the proprietary government in St. Marys was overthrown by Protestant rebels and in 1692 royal rule was instituted. Calvert remained thereafter in England, successfully maintaining his land rights although accused of participating in "popish plots." He died in London on February 21, 1715.

Calvert, George (1579?–1632), first Baron Baltimore, founder of Maryland. Born about 1579 in Kipling, Yorkshire, England, Calvert graduated from Trinity College, Oxford, in 1597 and after a tour of the Continent became in 1606 private secretary to Sir Robert Cecil, a leading diplomat and adviser to the Crown. Calvert soon had the confidence of James I and enjoyed rapid advancement; he became a member of Parliament, undertook a number of missions abroad for the king, was made a clerk of the Privy Council, and in 1617 was knighted. He was appointed a member of the Privy Council and a secretary of state in 1619 and held the latter position until 1625, when he announced his conversion to Roman Catholicism and resigned, leaving the House of Commons as well. He was then created Baron Baltimore of Baltimore. He had long been interested in America and had been a member of the Virginia Company from 1609 to 1620 and in 1622 became a member of the Council for New England. In 1623 he received a charter for a colony in Newfoundland called Avalon. Five years later he took up residence there, but the climate proved too harsh for his wife and in 1629 he moved to Jamestown, Virginia, at the same time petitioning the king for a grant in a more temperate climate. As a Catholic he was not well received in Virginia and soon returned to England. Before the new charter he had requested

was approved he died, on April 15, 1632, in London. The charter was formally granted to his son, Cecilius (1605–1675), second Baron Baltimore, on June 20 of that year, and Cecilius thus became the first proprietor of the colony of Maryland. Cecilius Calvert never visited the colony, however, his presence in England being constantly required to defend the charter against attack.

Calvert, Leonard (1606–1647), colonial governor. Born in England in 1606, Calvert was the son of George Calvert and the younger brother of Cecilius Calvert, who, by then Baron Baltimore and proprietor of the Maryland colony, dispatched him to America with two shiploads of colonists late in 1633. Landing at St. Clements (now Blakiston) Island in March 1634, Calvert established his government at St. Marys (now St. Marys City). Armed with great authority as governor, chief magistrate, chief justice, commander of the armed forces, and personal representative of the proprietor, he began his administration under favorable circumstances but was soon involved in a dispute with several Virginians, particularly William Claiborne, who had earlier established a trading post on Kent Island. Calvert drove Claiborne out and took possession of the island in 1638; in 1644 Claiborne roused anti-Catholic sentiment and at the head of a force of Virginians captured St. Marys. After two years in exile in Virginia Calvert returned, retook St. Marys, and restored order. He died shortly thereafter, on June 9, 1647, leaving his estate to the care of Margaret Brent.

Calvin, Melvin (1911–   ), chemist. Born in St. Paul, Minnesota, on April 8, 1911, Calvin graduated from the Michigan College of Mining and Technology in 1931 and took his Ph.D. from the University of Minnesota in 1935. After two years at the University of Manchester, England, on a Rockefeller Foundation fellowship, he joined the faculty of the University of California at Berkeley. From his graduate-student days until World War II he did research on a number of topics in physical and physical-organic chemistry; during the war he investigated chelate compounds for the National Defense Research Committee and developed a simple means of extracting oxygen from the atmosphere when commercial supplies for welding and other industrial uses were unavailable. In 1946 he became head of the bio-organic chemistry group at the university's Lawrence Radiation Laboratory and the next year was made a full professor. He began looking into photosynthesis in plants, the process whereby chlorophyll, the green pigment in their tissues, uses the energy of sunlight to convert carbon dioxide and water into carbohydrates, fats, proteins, and all the basic substances needed to support life. Using a tracer technique with carbon dioxide formed from radioactive carbon-14, he studied the chemical pathways and many steps involved in photosynthesis. Calvin's researches elucidated in particular the mechanisms of absorption, storage, and transfer of energy by chlorophyll and of the fixation of carbon dioxide from the air. In investigating the fixation process he discovered a chemical cycle involving ribulose diphosphate, which captures carbon dioxide, reacts to transform it into a usable form, and is restored to repeat the process. For this work Calvin was awarded the 1961 Nobel Prize for Chemistry. He continued afterward to investigate photosynthesis and its evolutionary basis and was interested in finding evidence of organic and perhaps life-indicating compounds in meteorites from space. He served as director of the university's Laboratory of Chemical Biodynamics and in 1967 became associate director of the Lawrence laboratory.

Cameron, Simon (1799–1889), public official and political leader. Born on March 8, 1799, in Maytown, Pennsylvania, Cameron was orphaned and left on his own at the age of nine. He received little schooling but apprenticed himself to a printer and for several years followed that trade, advancing to the editorship of the *Bucks County Democrat* in 1821 and to ownership of the *Harrisburg Republican* in 1824. The *Republican* enabled him to gain considerable political influence, and his appointment as state printer in 1826 provided the financial basis for large investments in canal construction, railroad lines, iron manufacture, banking, insurance, and other ventures that made him a wealthy man. In 1845 he began his public career—although he had been involved in politics for a number of years—by assembling a coalition of Whigs, tariff Democrats, and others to back him in a successful campaign for the Senate seat vacated by James Buchanan. He failed to win reelection in 1849 and again in 1855, but in 1857, allying himself with the new Republican party but securing the margin of victory with the votes of three Democratic legislators obtained by questionable means, he was returned to the Senate. By 1860 he had concentrated control of the well-developed state Republican party machinery in his own hands and at the national convention in Chicago appeared as a favorite-son candidate for President. In exchange for a promise of a cabinet post he threw his support to Abraham Lincoln, who, only afterwards informed of the deal, reluctantly named him secretary of war. During ten months in that post Cameron displayed a purely political conception of the office; his favoritism quickly became notorious and in January 1862 Lincoln named him minister to Russia to remove him from Washington. Three months later the House of Representatives approved a resolution censuring Cameron's conduct as secretary of war. The next year Cameron returned to run for the Senate; he lost, but four years later, having reestablished control of the Pennsylvania Republican machine, he was elected. Reelected in 1873, he wielded such power that in 1876 he obtained the appointment of his son, James Donald Cameron, as secretary of war by President Ulysses S. Grant. President Rutherford B. Hayes refused to continue the younger Cameron in office, whereupon the elder resigned from the Senate in 1877 to enable his son to succeed him. He bequeathed him the state Republican machine as well and retired to his farm at Donegal Springs, Pennsylvania, where he died on June 26, 1889.

Camp, Walter Chauncey (1859–1925), football and athletics authority. Born on April 17, 1859, in New Britain, Connecticut, Camp graduated from Yale in 1880 and studied at the Yale Medical School for two years. During his student years he participated in all manner of outdoor sports, but was particularly interested in football. In 1882 he took a job with the Manhattan Watch Company in New York City and the next year joined the New York office of the New Haven Clock Company. In 1888 he moved to New Haven and soon became Yale's athletic director and advisory football coach. The following year he began the practice of selecting an annual All-American football team from among outstanding college players across the nation. From his student days he had devoted considerable attention to the need for formalizing the game and, working as a long-time member of the Intercollegiate Football Rules Committee, he took a major part in transforming the sport from a close copy of British rugby into modern U.S. football. Among his contributions were the set scrimmage, the 11-man team, the quarterback position, the gridiron field, signal calling, and the fourth-down rule. Equally important were his development of strategy and his emphasis on clean, sportsmanlike play. Camp wrote numerous books on sports, among them *Football: How to Coach a Team*, 1886; *American Football*, 1891; and *Walter Camp's Book of College Sports*, 1893. In 1917 he began organizing classes in physical fitness for New Haven residents and was soon called to Washington, D.C., to arrange similar program for senior government officials. Appointed chairman of a commission charged with maintaining physical fitness among naval personnel, Camp developed his famous "Daily Dozen" exercise routine which was widely taken up by civilians. He died on March 14, 1925, in New York City.

Campanius, John (1601–1683), religious leader and missionary. Born in Stockholm, Sweden, on August 15, 1601, Campanius was educated at the University of Uppsala and in 1633 was ordained in the Lutheran church. He taught school for a time and then served as chaplain for an orphans' home. In 1642 he was chosen to accompany the newly appointed governor to the Swedish colony on the Delaware River in America, and early the next year arrived in Fort Christina (now Wilmington). While ministering to the Swedish and German settlers spread across what is now Delaware and southeastern Pennsylvania he undertook missions among the Leni-Lenape (Delaware) Indians. By his kindness and honesty he won their confidence, preparing the ground for William Penn's later dealings with them, and he studied their language and customs carefully. Using a phonetic alphabet of his own devising he translated Martin Luther's *Shorter Catechism* into the Lenapes' language, one of the Algonquian tongues, and appended a vocabulary of what he called "Barbaro-Virgineorum." These labors preceded the more famous work of John Eliot in Massachusetts by some five years. Campanius also made regular meteorological and astronomical observations and studied the flora and fauna of the region. He returned to Sweden in 1648 and ministered to congregations there until his death on September 17, 1683. His translation of the catechism was not published until 1696, but thereafter was used by other missionaries to the Delaware.

Campbell, Alexander, *see under* Campbell, Thomas

Campbell, John Archibald (1811–1889), justice of the Supreme Court. Born in Washington, Georgia, on June 24, 1811, Campbell graduated from Franklin College (now the University of Georgia) in 1825 and entered West Point. Family circumstances forced him to withdraw after three years and he returned home to study law. Not having yet attained his majority, he was admitted to the bar by special act of the legislature in 1829. He soon after moved to Alabama and began practice in Montgomery; there and later in Mobile he was a leading member of his profession, widely respected for his thorough knowledge of law and his skill in argument. He served twice in the legislature and in 1850 was a delegate to the Nashville Convention. In 1853, at the urging of other justices, he was appointed to the Supreme Court by President Franklin Pierce. A strict constructionist, he was eminently dispassionate in his opinions and amid the growing sectional friction of the time found admirers in both the North and the South. He opposed secession on practical grounds, but when it became a fact in 1861 he offered to serve as a mediator between the federal government and Southern commissioners seeking a treaty. Secretary of State William H. Seward, acting without presidential authority, made promises to the commissioners, through Campbell, involving the evacuation of Fort Sumter; when Sumter was instead reinforced, Campbell was accused of treachery by the South and, his position no longer tenable, he resigned from the Court and returned to the South. From 1862 to 1865 he served as assistant secretary of war for the Confederacy and in the latter year was one of its representatives at the unsuccessful Hampton Roads peace conference. Following four months in prison at the end of the war he settled in New Orleans and established a lucrative law practice, soon recapturing his earlier reputation. He appeared in a number of notable cases before the Supreme Court, among them the Slaughterhouse Cases of 1873, in which the Fourteenth Amendment was first construed. Campbell died in Baltimore on March 12, 1889.

Campbell, Thomas (1763–1854), religious leader. Born in Ireland on February 1, 1763, Campbell was of Scottish ancestry and was educated at the University of Glasgow; in 1798 he entered the ministry of the Scottish church. He soon became one of what were called "seceders," independent-minded Presbyterians of strong congregational leanings. In 1807 Thomas sailed to the United States and settled in western Pennsylvania; two years later his son, Alexander, born near Ballymena, Ireland, on September 12, 1788, joined him. Thomas Carey had just organized the Christian Association of Washington (Pennsylvania) and set forth its theological position in a document entitled *Declaration and Address*, urging a primitive Christianity based solely on the Scriptures, with no doctrinal, credal, or hierarchical innovations. Alexander, who had grown up with his father's religious outlook, joined in the association, was licensed to preach, and in 1812 was ordained in the church in Brush Run, Pennsylvania. Determined not to allow the association, known as the Disciples, to become yet another among already too many sects, the Campbells formed an alliance with the Baptists after adopting for themselves the practice of adult baptism by total immersion. In 1823 Alexander began publishing the *Christian Baptist;* seven years later, when the Campbells' steadfast independence and non-Calvinistic theology led to their expulsion by the Baptists, the paper became the *Millennial Harbinger*, which continued to appear for many years. Assisted often by his father, Alexander Campbell also published a hymnal and in 1827 a translation of the Greek Testament. In 1832 the Disciples, commonly called Campbellites, joined with a group of disaffected Methodists, Baptists, and Presbyterians known as "Christians" and led by Barton W. Stone, together they formed a loose association, the Disciples of Christ or Churches of Christ. The Disciples grew in number, aided by Thomas's activities during successive residences in Ohio, Pennsylvania, and Vermont, and by Alexander's travels and public debates, notably those with Bishop John Purcell of Cincinnati and with the Scottish reformer Robert Owen. In 1840 Alexander founded Bethany College in Bethany, Virginia (later West Virginia), and served as its president for the rest of his life. Thomas joined him there and continued to preach until blindness ended his activities; he died in Bethany on January 4, 1854. Alexander preached, taught in the college, and managed a highly successful farm until his death in Bethany on March 4, 1866, by which time the number of Disciples was rapidly approaching half a million.

Campbell, William Wallace (1862–1938), astronomer. Born on April 11, 1862, in Hancock County, Ohio, Campbell graduated from the University of Michigan in 1886 and for two years was professor of mathematics at the University of Colorado. From 1888 to 1890 he was an instructor in astronomy at his alma mater and then joined the staff of the Lick Observatory on Mt. Hamilton, California. Spectrographic analysis was his particular interest, and he applied the technique to the study of a variety of celestial phenomena, including nebulas, novas, and irregular stars. His contributions to both the design and the use of the spectrograph were fundamental to the developing field of astrophysics. In 1901 he became director of the observatory. He began an extensive program of measuring spectrographically the radial velocities of thousands of stars, sending a large telescope and other equipment to Santiago, Chile, to cover the stars of the southern hemisphere as well, and was able to determine from the mass of accumulated data the sun's motion through the galaxy. He published his findings in two classic texts, *Stellar Motions*, 1913, and *Stellar Radial Velocities* (with J. H. Moore), 1928. During his years at Lick he also led seven expeditions to various parts of the world to observe solar eclipses, making significant advances in the study of the solar corona and the flash spectrum and in 1922 recording the bending of stellar light passing near the sun, a phenomenon predicted by Einstein's theory of gravitation. In 1923 Campbell became president of the University of California, holding the post until illness forced his retirement in 1930. From 1931 to 1935 he was president of the National Academy of Sciences. His health having failed seriously, he took his own life in San Francisco on June 14, 1938.

Canary, Martha Jane, *see* Burke, Martha Jane

Candler, Asa Griggs (1851–1929), businessman and philanthropist. Born near Villa Rica, Georgia, on December 30, 1851, Candler grew up on a farm and attended school for only a few years. For a time he studied medicine privately, but then apprenticed himself to a local pharmacist, moving to Atlanta in 1873 to seek advancement in that calling. Within a few years he was able to open his own business, at first in partnership and later on his own, and soon prospered. In 1887 he purchased from an associate, J.S. Pemberton, the formula for a soft drink called Coca-Cola. Introducing improvements into the manufacturing process, he began producing and selling to soda-fountain proprietors small quantities of the syrup base for the drink and, by astute management and advertising, soon made it the most popular of the many soft-drink preparations then available. In 1890 he sold his pharmaceutical business to concentrate his energies on building the Coca-Cola Company; the firm's growth was little less than phenomenal as the popularity of its product spread within a few years to every state in the nation. Production capacity was seldom equal to the booming demand; branch plants were established in several cities around the country, bottling franchises—a notion not originally contemplated by Candler, but one to which he readily agreed—were arranged, and the company grew into one of the South's largest and most successful business firms. Of paramount in-

fluence in the success of the company were Candler's personal concern for his employees (and particularly for the propriety of his salesman's behavior), his faith in his own product, his readiness to protect it against imitations, and his much-publicized care to preserve the secret of the Coca-Cola formula. He retired in 1916 from the presidency of the Coca-Cola Corporation, which three years later, much to his chagrin, was sold to a new corporation organized in Delaware. From his holdings in the company and from other ventures, principally in real estate, he amassed a considerable fortune. He was liberal with his money and was a major force in the modernization of Atlanta, of which he was mayor in 1917–1918. During World War I he advanced millions of dollars in loans to cotton growers faced with disastrously low prices. The Methodist church in particular benefitted from his generosity; he built a church and a church-run hospital in Atlanta and brought nearby Emory College into the city and promoted its growth into a strong university with gifts that eventually totaled some $7 million. Candler died in Atlanta on March 12, 1929.

Caniff, Milton Arthur (1907–   ), cartoonist. Born on February 28, 1907, in Hillsboro, Ohio, Milt Caniff began newspaper cartoon work while still in high school and was on the art staff of the *Columbus Dispatch* while attending Ohio State University. After graduating in 1930 and choosing cartooning over acting as a career—he had appeared in small roles in a few movies during an earlier residence in California—he joined the Associated Press in New York and turned out two minor comic strips for two years. In 1934 he moved to the Chicago Tribune–New York Daily News Syndicate and began an innovative strip, *Terry and the Pirates*, which quickly attracted fans in the tens of thousands. An action-adventure story line set in the mysterious Orient was given strongly adult orientation in *Terry*, the depth of characterization and explicit sexiness of the figures adding to their interest. Terry and dashing Pat Ryan, heroes straight from the movie tradition, faced a succession of bizarre villains, most notably the Dragon Lady, and encountered a series of alluring females of various sorts. When one of the feminine characters, a favorite named Raven Sherman, was allowed to die in an episode in 1941, Caniff and the syndicate were flooded with letters of protest and condolence. Rendered in a dramatic chiaroscuro style with painstaking and thoroughly researched detail and often reflecting current events, such as the Japanese invasion of China, the strip attained a level of sophisticated realism unprecedented in the field. It also inspired a radio program that was popular for many years. During World War II Caniff drew another strip, *Male Call*, for armed services publications and illustrated an official servicemen's handbook on China for the War Department. In 1947 he joined the Publishers-Hall Syndicate, leaving *Terry* to others (the strip continued until 1973) and began *Steve Canyon*, a similar strip featuring a former Air Force officer that became popular. Caniff was the recipient of a great many honors and awards from, among others, the Boy Scouts, the Freedoms Foundation, the armed forces, and various servicemen's organizations.

Cannon, Annie Jump (1863–1941), astronomer. Born on December 11, 1863, in Dover, Delaware, Miss Cannon graduated from Wellesley College in 1884. For several years she pursued studies and researches in astronomy at Radcliffe College and in 1897 was named an assistant in the Harvard Observatory. There she devoted her energies to the ambitious project, begun in 1885 by the observatory's director, Edward C. Pickering, of recording, classifying, and cataloguing the spectra of all stars down to those of the eleventh magnitude. The system of spectral classification used for the project and later universally adopted was largely her work, and she eventually obtained spectra for more than 225,000 stars, publishing them in nine volumes as the *Henry Draper Catalogue*, 1918–1924. In 1911 Miss Cannon became curator of astronomical photographs at the observatory and in 1938 was named William Cranch Bond Professor of Astronomy. After 1924 she continued her work, cataloguing tens of thousands of additional stars for the *Henry Draper Extension*. The work was an invaluable contribution to astronomy, bearing strongly on countless other problems and areas of research and exerting major influence on the evolution of the science from one of mere observation to one of great theoretical and philosophical content. Among the numerous honors and awards accorded her were the first honorary doctorate from Oxford University to be awarded to a woman, 1925, and the Henry Draper Medal of the National Academy of Sciences in 1931. Miss Cannon officially retired from the observatory in 1940 but carried on research until her death in Cambridge, Massachusetts, on April 13, 1941.

Cannon, Joseph Gurney (1836–1926), public official. Born in Guilford County, North Carolina, on May 7, 1836, Cannon grew up there and in Indiana. He studied law privately and attended the Cincinnati Law School for a brief time; in 1858 he was admitted to the Illinois bar. He began practice in Shelbyville and later moved to Danville, which thereafter was his home. From 1861 to 1868 he was a state's attorney, and in 1870 he ran unsuccessfully for the House of Representatives. Elected as a Republican in 1872, he held his seat until 1891 and acquired a reputation for pungent language, rough manners, and markedly illiberal views. During the latter years of his first period in Congress he was closely associated with Thomas B. Reed. After sitting out a term—the Democrats swept Congress in 1890— he was returned to his seat in 1892 and remained in the House until 1913, the last ten years as speaker. His intensely partisan (and occasionally simply arbitrary) use of the powers and prerogatives of the office became notorious as "Cannonism;" at length, in 1910, a coalition of Democrats and rebellious Republicans succeeded in barring the speaker from membership in the Committee on Rules and thereby curtailed his power. Defeated for reelection in 1912, he again returned to the House in 1914 and sat until 1923. In a total of 46 years in the House, Cannon failed to attach his name to a single major legislative measure. He was, however, popular with his colleagues, even after his reign as speaker, and was affectionately referred to as "Uncle Joe." He died in Danville on November 12, 1926.

Cannon, Walter Bradford (1871–1945), physiologist. Born on October 19, 1871, in Prairie du Chien, Wisconsin, Cannon earned his B.A. in 1896, his M.A. in 1897, and his medical degree in 1900 from Harvard. Remaining at the Medical School, he taught zoology during 1899–1900, physiology until 1906, and was thereafter George Higginson Professor of Physiology until his retirement in 1942. He lectured widely and was an exchange professor to France in 1929 and 1930. A pioneer in X-ray observation of the movements of the stomach and intestines, he published the results of his studies in 1911 in *The Mechanical Factors of Digestion*. During 1912 he conducted experiments in hunger perception that led to his theory that peripheral changes such as dryness of the throat or stomach contractions account for the sensation of hunger. He served as head of the American Red Cross medical research program in France in 1917–1918 and in the medical corps of the U.S. army in 1918, doing pioneering research into hemorrhagic and traumatic shock, described in *Traumatic Shock*, 1923. A long series of experiments in emotion perception led to his theory that major emotions are set off by excitation of the sympathetic nervous system. He also showed that administering epinephrine produces the same effects as the stimulation of the sympathetic nervous system—heightened blood pressure, heart rate, and blood flow to the muscles, concentration of the blood sugar, and retarded digestion. In 1929 he published *Bodily Changes in Pain, Hunger, Fear and Rage*. In 1932 he developed the concept of homeostasis, or the constancy of the internal environment of an organism, in *The Wisdom of the Body*. He elucidated the action of chemical medication of nerve impulses in *Autonomic Neuroeffector Systems*, 1937, with A. Rosenblueth, and in *The Supersensitivity of Denervated Structures*, 1949. He also wrote numerous papers and articles on these processes, on medical education, and in defense of medical research. His autobiography, *The Way of an Investigator*, was published in 1945; he died on October 1 of that year in Franklin, New Hampshire.

Cantor, Eddie (1892–1964), entertainer. Born on January 31, 1892, on New York City's Lower East Side, Edward Israel Iskowitz was orphaned at the age of two and was reared by his grandmother.

He attended school only briefly, and when he was old enough to work did so sporadically, preferring to spend his time singing and dancing on street corners. In 1908, under the name Eddie Cantor, he entered and won an amateur-night contest at a Bowery theater and soon afterward got a job as a singing waiter in a Coney Island saloon that also featured the piano playing of Jimmy Durante. Cantor then moved into vaudeville; he worked for the comedy team of Bedini and Arthur, toured for two years in the *Kid Kabaret* show with young George Jessel, and in 1916 attracted much favorable attention with a role on Broadway in *Canary Cottage*. His performances were nearly always in blackface during that period, but what charmed his audiences then and later, when he discarded the device, was his apparently boundless energy; he pranced all over the stage, clapping his hands, goggling his eyes, and singing light-hearted songs with infectious gaiety. He appeared in Florenz Ziegfeld's *Midnight Frolic*, 1917, and in the 1917, 1918, and 1919 editions of Ziegfeld's famed *Follies*. Appearances in a number of Broadway hits followed, notably *Kid Boots* in 1923 and *Whoopee* in 1928. He began appearing in movies as well, beginning with a silent version of *Kid Boots* in 1926 and going on to *Palmy Days*, 1931; *The Kid from Spain*, 1932; *Roman Scandals*, 1933; *Strike Me Pink*, 1936; *Ali Baba Goes to Town*, 1937, and many others; his last film, *If You Knew Susie*, 1948, bore the title of one of his trademark songs. From 1931 to 1939 he was the host of a highly popular weekly radio program, and in 1941 he returned to Broadway with *Banjo Eyes*. Cantor had always been known for his open-handed generosity and his eager willingness to help by appearing at benefit shows—sometimes six performances a night—and during World War II he did yeoman service on behalf of Jewish refugees, the United Service Organizations (USO), and later the relief of Palestinian refugees. He worked for the benefit of the Warm Springs Foundation for the treatment of infantile paralysis and was credited by President Franklin D. Roosevelt with coining the name "March of Dimes" for its fund-raising drives. In 1950 he began a monthly television show that continued, despite his failing health, until 1953. During his career he also wrote a number of books, including two volumes of autobiography, *My Life Is in Your Hands*, 1928 (with D. Freedman) and *Take My Life*, 1957; *Ziegfeld, the Great Glorifier*, 1934; and *As I Remember Them*, 1963. In 1953 *The Eddie Cantor Story*, a film version of his life, was produced, and three years later he was given a special Academy Award for distinguished service to the film industry. One of the most beloved entertainers of his time, he died on October 10, 1964, in Hollywood, California.

Caplin, Alfred Gerald, see Capp, Al

Capone, Alphonse (1899–1947), gangster. Born on January 17, 1899, in Naples, Italy, Al Capone emigrated with his family to the United States,

settling in Brooklyn, New York. There he attended school through the fourth grade and later became a member of the notorious Five Points gang, in which he was associated with Johnny Torrio. At some point in his youth he was slashed across the face with a razor and was afterward known as "Scarface Al." Soon after the beginning of Prohibition in 1920, Torrio, who had moved to Chicago, summoned Capone to that city as his lieutenant in an attempt to corner the local market in bootleg whiskey; Capone, fronting as a used-furniture dealer, organized a gang of "rods" —gunmen—and began a campaign of terrorism to drive out competition. The spectacular series of gang wars that followed was highlighted by the murder of rival leader Dion O'Banion in his flower shop in 1924 and the 1926 daylight machine-gun raid by the remaining O'Banions on Capone's headquarters in the Chicago suburb of Cicero. In 1925 Torrio was shot up and prudently decided to retire, leaving Capone in control of the organization. He soon dominated not only bootlegging but also gambling, prostitution, and dance halls in Chicago. A network of agents smuggled in a constant supply of whiskey from Canada and various Caribbean islands, reaping him a huge fortune. Bribery on a vast scale bought him immunity from police and civic officials; he did not intrude publicly into politics, however, until 1927, when he announced his support for mayoral candidate "Big Bill" Thompson. In a campaign that was dubbed the "pineapple primary" for the use of a novel electioneering device, the hand grenade or "pineapple," Thompson won, further securing Capone's demesne. In 1929 gang warfare reached its peak of brutality with the St. Valentine's Day Massacre of seven members of Bugs Moran's gang. Finally, in 1931, extensive efforts by agents of the U.S. Treasury Department resulted in an indictment being brought against Capone for income-tax evasion. He was convicted, heavily fined, and sentenced to 11 years in prison. By the time of his release from Alcatraz in 1939 he was a helpless paretic; he retired to his Miami Beach estate and died there on January 25, 1947.

Capote, Truman (1924–   ), author. Born on September 30, 1924, in New Orleans, Truman Streckfus Persons was reared by a succession of relatives in the South following his parents divorce. His mother's later remarriage gave him the name Capote and brought him to New York City for his schooling. Intent on a writing career, he set out on it after high school and in 1945 saw his first short stories published in magazines. In 1948 *Other Voices, Other Rooms* appeared and elicited considerable critical notice; a somewhat gothic novel of childhood and Southern decadence, it was particularly admired for its poetic use of language and the rhythmic authenticity of its dialogue. *Tree of Night*, 1949, a collection of stories, and *Local Color*, 1950, various travel pieces, further established Capote as a remarkable stylist. *The Grass Harp*, 1951, a novel, showed to full effect his deep sympathy with children and eccentrics and his ability to capture their worlds in words. Capote tried with limited success to turn to dramatic writing, creating a stage version of *The Grass Harp*, 1952, and a musical, *House of Flowers*, 1954, with music by Harold Arlen. He also wrote a witty screenplay for *Beat the Devil* in the early 1950s. In 1958 he published the collection of stories *Breakfast at Tiffany's*, the title story of which was later made into a movie. In odd contrast to the highly imaginative, slightly other-worldly atmosphere of much of his fiction, he developed an interest in journalism and secured a number of reportorial assignments for the *New Yorker* magazine, among them extended coverage of the tour of a *Porgy and Bess* company in the Soviet Union, which he also described at greater length in *The Muses Are Heard*, 1956. In 1959 he began work on his most ambitious project in reportage, a book-length work dealing with an actual happening, but using many of the techniques of the novel. The story he chose was the mass murder of a farm family in Kansas by a pair of drifters, and he devoted several years to painstaking research and interviews, including a large number with the convicted killers. With considerable advance publicity his "nonfiction novel" *In Cold Blood* appeared in serial form in the *New Yorker* in 1965 and in book form the following year. In the barrage of critical discussion that followed, it became a literary event of major proportions as well as a best seller. *In Cold Blood* was also made into a film. Capote later wrote a number of television plays, including *A Christmas Memory* and *The Thanksgiving Visitor*, both of which subsequently appeared in book form.

Capp, Al (1909–1979), cartoonist. Born on September 28, 1909, in New Haven, Connecticut, Alfred Gerald Caplin grew up there and in nearby Bridgeport. After graduating from high school he studied art at a succession of schools, including the Pennsylvania Academy of Fine Arts, the Philadelphia Museum of Fine Arts, Boston University, and Harvard. In 1932 he took a job as a cartoonist with the Associated Press; his tenure was brief and the next year he was ghost-drawing for other cartoonists. He met Ham Fisher, creator of the comic strip *Joe Palooka*, and was soon working for him. He introduced some hillbilly characters into *Joe Palooka* and by 1934 had worked out the basic theme for his own comic strip, *Li'l Abner*, which began appearing in a few newspapers that year. Set in the fictitious hamlet of Dogpatch, Kentucky, the series depicted the misadventures of Abner Yokum, a hulking, wholesome, and none-too-bright son of the hills, his family, and assorted odd characters. Deftly drawn caricatures of well-known public figures often appeared in the strip, allowing Capp to inject social and political satire into the cultural isolation of Dogpatch. *Li'l Abner* became a huge success, syndicated within a few years to hundreds of papers and reaching an audience of tens of millions daily. It was one of the few examples of

popular art to be studied seriously in academic circles, and it gave rise to at least one minor American institution, "Sadie Hawkins Day," on which unwary males may be captured by predatory females. In 1940 he wrote the script for a movie based on the series; in 1956 the Dogpatch characters appeared in a Broadway musical that, in turn, was made into another movie in 1959. He was also the creator (in 1937) and for some years author of a second successful cartoon strip, *Abbie an' Slats*, drawn by Raeburn Van Buren. Declaring that he had grown tired of the demands of a daily strip, Capp brought *Li'l Abner* to an end with the episode of November 13, 1977. He died on November 5, 1979, in Cambridge, Massachusetts.

Capra, Frank (1897–   ), motion picture director. Born on May 18, 1897, in Palermo, Sicily, Capra was brought by his family to the United States at the age of six and grew up in Los Angeles. He graduated from the California Institute of Technology in 1918 and after brief service in the army spent several years working in a variety of jobs in a number of places. In 1921 he persuaded a minor film entrepreneur in San Francisco to allow him to direct a few short films, and although he had no experience whatever his work attracted the attention of some critics and of Mack Sennett; before long he was with Sennett's Keystone Company, writing comedy material for the *Our Gang* series and for several of Harry Langdon's biggest hits. After a passing association with First National Pictures, for which he directed *For the Love o' Mike*, 1927, Capra joined Columbia Pictures. His reputation grew rapidly with such films as *Ladies of Leisure*, 1930; *Forbidden*, 1930; *Dirigible*, 1931; *Platinum Blonde*, 1931, one of Jean Harlow's first major films; and *The Bitter Tea of General Yen*, 1933; and in 1933 he found what was to be his forte for nearly a decade, the mild social-comment film often featuring naive, idealistic heroes, rich, conniving villains, any number of thoroughly idiosyncratic characters, and a great deal of zany comedy. Huge box-office success attended *Lady for a Day*, 1933; *It Happened One Night*, 1934, for which he won an Academy Award; *Broadway Bill*, 1934; *Mr. Deeds Goes to Town*, 1936, Academy Award; *Lost Horizon*, 1937; *You Can't Take It with You*, 1938, his third Academy Award winner; *Mr. Smith Goes to Washington*, 1939; and *Meet John Doe*, 1941. During World War II he served as chief of the Army Pictorial Service, for which he produced and directed the highly acclaimed film series *Why We Fight*, earning a Distinguished Service Medal and a special award from the New York Film Critics' Circle. Returning to Hollywood, Capra directed *Arsenic and Old Lace*, 1944; *It's a Wonderful Life*, 1947, and *State of the Union*, 1948, both produced by Liberty Films, a short-lived independent company in which he was a partner; *Riding High*, 1950; and *Here Comes the Groom*, 1951. For several years thereafter he worked in television, making a notable series of educational films on science for the Bell Telephone Company;

he later returned to the screen with *A Hole in the Head*, 1959, and *A Pocketful of Miracles*, 1961.

Cardozo, Benjamin Nathan (1870–1938), justice of the Supreme Court. Born in New York City on May 24, 1870, Cardozo attended Columbia College, where he earned his B.A. in 1889 and his M.A. the following year. He studied at Columbia Law School and won admission to the bar in 1891 without taking his law degree. Acting as a counsel to other attorneys, he earned respect and admiration from his peers while remaining unknown to the public. His extensive practice before the Court of Appeals led to *Jurisdiction of the Court of Appeals of the State of New York*, 1903. In 1913 he was elected a justice of the New York supreme court on a fusion ticket in opposition to Tammany Hall. Six weeks later the Court of Appeals selected him as temporary associate justice; the appointment was made final in 1917, and nine years later he became chief judge of that court. Learned in the law and skilled in its complexities, he also brought a flair to common-law litigation, as shown in *MacPherson* v. *Buick Motor Company*, 1916, in which he established the consumer's right of redress against a manufacturer whose defective product caused him injury. His attitudes on the relation of law to life were clearly expressed in the now classic *Nature of the Judicial Process*, 1921; and in *The Growth of the Law*, 1924; *The Paradoxes of Legal Science*, 1928; and *Law and Literature*, 1931. In 1932 he was named to the Supreme Court by President Herbert Hoover, despite opposition on the grounds that there were already two New Yorkers and one Jew on the Court. Cardozo handled an unusually large number of cases in six years on the bench, establishing, like Justices Oliver Wendell Holmes and Louis D. Brandeis, the foundation for a later broad interpretation of federal powers. Cognizant of changing social needs, he exhibited in his decisions an evolutionary application of legal principle and frequently dealt with the confused precedents of many years, thereby eliminating the need for further reference to them. In *Ultramares Corporation* v. *Touche*, 1931, he further clarified the notion of accountability to third parties for negligent misrepresentation. In *Great Northern Railroad Company* v. *Sunburst Oil and Refining Company*, 1932, he affirmed a court's right to use a previous authority and yet to declare that authority invalid in future cases. His opinion in the Social Security cases of 1937 showed the Constitution to be an efficient instrument in meeting critical and broad social needs, and his opinion in *Palko* v. *Connecticut*, 1937, illuminated the role of the Court in executing the due-process clause of the Fourteenth Amendment. His dissent in *Stewart Dry Goods Company* v. *Lewis*, 1935, was a revealing exposition of problems of taxation, and in *Ashton* v. *Cameron County District*, 1936, he argued persuasively that the division of jurisdiction between the federal and state governments did not weaken the structure of either. A polished legal stylist as well as a profound and effective legal philosopher, and a man admired for his personal qualities as well as for his professional excellence, Cardozo ranked as one of the most generally respected men of his time. He died in Port Chester, New York, on July 9, 1938.

Carey, Henry Charles (1793–1879), economist and sociologist. Born in Philadelphia on December 15, 1793, Carey was the son of Mathew Carey. He was educated informally and from an early age was trained in his father's economic thought. He became a partner in Carey, Lea & Carey, his father's publishing house, in 1817 and later was its president. The firm came to be a leader among American publishers, issuing works by such authors as Washington Irving, Sir Walter Scott, and Thomas Carlyle. In 1835 Carey left publishing to devote himself to the study of economics; in that year he published his *Essay on the Rate of Wages*. It was followed by his three-volume *Principles of Political Economy*, 1837–1840. In these and subsequent works he outlined a view of economics whose optimism was in opposition to the dominant tenor of classical English thought, particularly that of David Ricardo and Thomas Malthus. He saw the workings of natural laws as conducive to economic and social progress and the mechanics of a generally laissez-faire economy as productive of wealth throughout society. Like his father, he was an ardent nationalist and an advocate of protectionism. With the publication of later works—*The Past, the Present, and the Future*, 1848; *Harmony of Interests: Manufacturing and Commercial*, 1851; the three-volume *Principles of Social Science*, 1858–1860; and *The Unity of Law*, 1872—he won an international reputation equal to that he enjoyed at home. For several years after 1849 he contributed regularly to Horace Greeley's *New York Tribune*. His home was a center of intellectual life in Philadelphia; he died there on October 13, 1879.

Carey, Mathew (1760–1839), publisher and author. Born in Dublin on January 28, 1760, Carey was partially crippled from infancy and received little formal education, although he studied diligently on his own. He was apprenticed to a printer and began to write occasional articles for publication. In 1779 he published a pamphlet protesting the treatment of Irish Catholics by the government; trouble with the authorities ensued, and he went to Paris where he met and worked for Benjamin Franklin. He returned to Dublin a year later, but his anti-British publications (*Freeman's Journal*, 1780–1783, and *Volunteer's Journal*, 1783–1784) again made it necessary for him to flee and in 1784 he sailed for America. Arriving in Philadelphia with letters of introduction from Franklin, he received an unsolicited loan from the Marquis de Lafayette, whom he had also met in Paris, and became the publisher of a series of journals, including the *Pennsylvania Herald* and the *Columbian Magazine*, of which the *American Museum*, which appeared from 1787 to 1792, was the most notable. These proved unprofitable, however, and he turned to book publishing and selling, reprinting European books and publishing works by American authors (among which was Mason Locke Weem's *Life of George Washington*). Carey was active in civic affairs; his most important contribution was the writing of a number of tracts for the Philadelphia Society for the Promotion of National Industry, of which he was a charter member. In these tracts he revived and popularized Alexander Hamilton's earlier arguments for the encouragement of domestic manufactures through protective tariffs, becoming a leading advocate of the nationalist school of economics. In other works he advocated internal improvements and universal education; his pamphlet *The Olive Branch*, 1814, was an attempt to heal the widening rift between the Federalists and the Republicans during the War of 1812. In 1829 he published a volume of *Autobiographical Sketches*. He died in Philadelphia on September 16, 1839.

Carlisle, John Griffin (1835–1910), public official. Born on September 5, 1835, in what is now Kenton County, Kentucky, Carlisle grew up on a farm, attended local schools, and taught school from the age of fifteen. At twenty he moved to Covington to take up the study of law and in 1858 was admitted to the bar. He soon achieved political recognition, winning election to the legislature in 1859. He opposed secession but remained neutral during the Civil War, continuing to work for the preservation of civil government in Kentucky after leaving the legislature in 1861. In 1865 he was elected to the state senate; he was reelected in 1869 and resigned his seat two years later to become lieutenant governor. In 1876 he ran successfully for the House of Representatives. There he quickly became a leader of the Democrats and their principal spokesman on the subjects of tariff reform and encouragement of shipping. Carlisle was elected speaker of the House in 1883 and during his six years in that position earned the respect of his colleagues by his nonpartisan conduct of the office. In 1890 he was appointed to fill a vacated Senate seat; three years later he resigned it to become President Grover Cleveland's secretary of the treasury. There was a flurry of interest in Carlisle as a presidential candidate in 1896, but he failed to capitalize upon it. During the election he campaigned for the splinter National Democratic party (the Gold Democrats) and their sound-money platform, a step that strongly alienated fellow Kentuckians and led to his settling in New York City after leaving the cabinet in 1897. He resumed private law practice and died there on July 31, 1910.

Carlson, Chester Floyd (1906–1968), inventor. Born on February 8, 1906, in Seattle, Carlson grew up there and in San Bernardino, California. He graduated from the California Institute of Technology in 1930 and eventually found a job in the patent department of a New York City electronics firm. While working there he noted the constant demand for multiple copies of patent specifications and other documents and also the shortcomings of carbon copies—few could be made at a time, and they were often blurred—and of photostats—they were expensive and required much equipment and various materials. He began toying with other means of copying, soon hitting upon the photoelectric effect as the key to a dry process involving no chemicals. By October 1938 he had refined his ideas sufficiently to perform the vital experiment. Taking a sulfur-coated zinc plate, he gave it an electrostatic charge by rubbing it with a handkerchief in the dark and then placed over it a transparent celluloid ruler. He then exposed the plate to light for a few seconds, thus neutralizing the charge except where the markings of the ruler blocked the light. Dusting lycopodium powder over the plate and blowing away the excess, he was left with a perfect image of the ruler. Carlson received his first patent in 1940 for the process that became known as xerography, from the Greek word for "dry." He had in the meantime been studying law at night at the New York Law School, receiving his degree in 1939 and gaining admission to the bar in 1940. In 1944 he made an agreement with the Battelle Memorial Institute, a nonprofit industrial-research organization, for the commercial development of xerography and in 1947 made a second agreement with the Haloid Company. Battelle and Haloid jointly held the first public demonstration of xerography in 1948 and 11 years later, Haloid, by then the Haloid-Xerox Company and later the Xerox Corporation, introduced the Xerox 914, the first commercial xerographic copying machine. Carlson had no corporate connection with Xerox or its dozens of younger competitors, but he amassed a sizable fortune from royalties. Having ushered in a virtual revolution in modern business methods and in the larger field of communications, including printing, he died in New York City on September 19, 1968.

Carmichael, Hoagy (1899–1981), songwriter. Born on November 22, 1899, in Bloomington, Indiana, Hoagland Howard Carmichael was a student at the University of Indiana when he first encountered jazz. An instant enthusiast, he invited Bix Beiderbecke and his Wolverines to play on campus and gave him one of his own songs, "Riverboat Shuffle," which became one of Beiderbecke's best recordings. Carmichael formed a band himself in 1923 and recorded "Washboard Blues," but soon afterward returned to school to take his law degree, in 1926. He practiced law for a time and then joined Jean Goldkette's band. A few months later he again led a band of his own for a short time; finally he moved to New York City and took a job as an arranger in a music-publishing house. In 1929 he wrote what became one of the most popular songs of all time, "Stardust," and thereafter was firmly established as a composer, many of his songs being featured in Broadway and Hollywood musical productions. "Rockin' Chair" and "Georgia on My Mind" were published the next year and in 1931 he assembled for a recording session the most remarkable jazz band ever to play together: it included Tommy and Jimmy Dorsey, Benny Goodman, Bix Beiderbecke, Jack Teagarden, Gene Krupa, Joe Venuti, and Bud Freeman, among others; one of the products of the session was a popular recording of "Lazy River." Others of Carmichael's songs included "Two Sleepy People," "I Get Along Without You Very Well," "Lazybones," and "The Nearness of You." His "Lamplighter's Serenade" was the first song recorded by Frank Sinatra. He appeared in featured roles in a number of motion pictures, including *To Have and Have Not*, 1945, in which he introduced his "How Little We Know"; *The Best Years of Our Lives*, 1946; and *Young Man with a Horn*, 1950. His "In the Cool, Cool, Cool of the Evening" was played in *Here Comes the Groom*, 1951, and won an Academy Award. Carmichael also had a popular radio program during the 1940s and a television show in the 1950s. An autobiography, *The Stardust Road*, appeared in 1946 and with Stephen Longstreet he wrote *Sometimes I Wonder*, 1965. In 1971 he was elected to the Songwriters' Hall of Fame. He died in Rancho Mirage, California, on December 27, 1981.

Carnap, Rudolf (1891–1970), philosopher. Born on May 18, 1891, in Wuppertal, Germany, Carnap attended the universities of Jena and Freiburg between 1910 and 1914 and returned to Jena to take his Ph.D. in 1921. In 1926 he became an instructor in philosophy at the University of Vienna, advancing to professor in 1930, and in 1931 joined the faculty of the German University in Prague, Czechoslovakia. While at Vienna he became a leading member of the famed "Vienna circle," a group of philosophers, mathematicians, and semanticists who developed the doctrine of logical positivism. The doctrine, which came to command one of the major schools of modern philosophy, held that all statements that were not subject to experimental or observational verification were strictly meaningless; the role of philosophy was, as an adjunct to science, to clarify and refine the logical structure of language, rendering it an analogue of mathematics in its formality and its usefulness for rigorous calculation. Metaphysics in all its branches was dismissed utterly by this view. Carnap edited the group's journal, *Erkenntnis*, until 1941; in the meantime he had emigrated to the United States in 1935 and in 1936 had been appointed professor of philosophy at the University of Chicago, where he remained until 1952. After two years at the Institute for Advanced Studies at Princeton University he joined the faculty of the University of California at Los Angeles in 1954, remaining until his retirement in 1962. From 1938 he was associate editor of the *International Encyclopedia of Unified Science*. In later years Carnap somewhat relaxed his severe views of meaning and of the proper scope of linguistics, allowing to the former the inclusion of indirectly verifiable statements and to the latter a study of the relations of linguistic signs to their referent objects. Among

his many publications were *Der logische Aufbau der Welt*, 1928 (translated as *The Logical Structure of the World*, 1967); *The Unity of Science*, 1934; *Logische Syntax der Sprache*, 1934; *Foundations of Logic and Mathematics*, 1939; *Introduction to Semantics*, 1942; *Meaning and Necessity*, 1947; *Logical Foundations of Probability*, 1951; and *Introduction to Symbolic Logic and Its Applications*, 1958. Carnap died in Santa Monica, California, on September 14, 1970.

Carnegie, Andrew (1835–1919), businessman and philanthropist. Born in Dunfermline, Scotland, on November 25, 1835, Carnegie grew up in poverty and received little more than a primary-school education. In 1848 he emigrated to the United States with his family, settling in Allegheny, Pennsylvania (now in Pittsburgh), where he started work in a cotton factory. A year later he became a messenger boy in a Pittsburgh telegraph office and his diligence—he became one of the first persons able to read telegraph messages by ear—led to his promotion to operator and finally to his employment by the Pennsylvania Railroad. In 12 years with that company he introduced the first Pullman sleeping cars and rose to become superintendent of the Pittsburgh division. Convinced by his experience with the railroad and in the Civil War of the coming importance of the iron and steel industries, Carnegie resigned to form his own company, the Keystone Bridge Company, in 1865; for several years he had a number of diverse business interests, but from 1873 onward he concentrated on steel. Gifted with remarkable organizational ability and great business acumen and quick to gauge the value of such associates as Henry Clay Frick and Charles M. Schwab, he built his steel company into a giant that, weathering the depression that followed the Panic of 1893 better than the rest, eventually dominated the industry. In 1889, the year that he consolidated his holdings in the Homestead Steel Works and other plants into the Carnegie Steel Company, he published an article entitled "Wealth"—commonly called "The Gospel of Wealth"—in the *North American Review*; in it he outlined his view that it was the duty of the rich to oversee the distribution of their surplus wealth for the betterment of civilization. It was a novel idea at the time and the article was widely reprinted and discussed. He adhered to his own advice and actively supported a number of philanthropies, among them the building of a great many public libraries, endowing the Carnegie Institute of Technology in 1900 and the Carnegie Institution of Washington in 1902, substantially supporting a great many colleges, establishing Carnegie Hero Funds in the United States and Great Britain in 1904, and financing the construction of the Temple of Peace at The Hague in the Netherlands. Carnegie sold his business to J. P. Morgan's United States Steel Company in 1901 for $250 million, and thenceforth devoted himself entirely to philanthropy and the promotion of peace. The Carnegie Foundation for the Advancement of Teaching was established in 1905 and was followed by the Carnegie Endowment for International Peace in 1910 and the Carnegie Corporation of New York in 1911. In all, his philanthropies totaled some $350 million. He wrote, among other books, *Triumphant Democracy,* 1886; *The Empire of Business,* 1902; and *Problems of Today,* 1908. Carnegie died on August 11, 1919, at his home in Lenox, Massachusetts.

Carnegie, Dale (1888–1955), author and teacher of public speaking. Born in Maryville, Missouri, on November 24, 1888, Carnegie grew up in poverty on a farm. He became interested in public speaking and debating while in high school and, influenced by a Chautauqua lecturer, trained himself to use his voice effectively. After graduating from the state teachers college (now Central Missouri College) at Warrensburg in 1908 he worked as a salesman in the West for International Correspondence Schools and later for Armour and Company. In 1911 he moved to New York City where, following a brief attempt to establish himself in the theater, he became a teacher of public speaking for the Young Men's Christian Association (YMCA) and was soon publishing essays on various topics in periodicals as well. Within a short time he was able to organize several classes of his own in public speaking, hiring teachers and writing a series of pamphlets to serve as texts. After serving in the army during World War I Carnegie was engaged by Lowell Thomas as business manager for a popular lecture tour, and Carnegie later took up a second tour himself. The pamphlets for the speaking courses were collected and published in book form as *Public Speaking: A Practical Course for Business Men,* 1926 (retitled *Public Speaking and Influencing Men in Business,* 1931), and Carnegie followed it with *Lincoln the Unknown,* 1932, and *Little Known Facts about Well Known People,* 1934, the latter leading to a regular radio program of the same title. In 1936 he published *How to Win Friends and Influence People,* a book of common-sense advice, case histories, and optimistic homilies such as "Believe that you will succeed and you will." It was an immediate best seller and brought a great demand for lectures, articles, and a new syndicated newspaper column by Carnegie. He reorganized his classes as the Dale Carnegie Institute for Effective Speaking and Human Relations and branches were opened up in hundreds of cities in North and South America and Europe. In 1948 he wrote another best-selling book of advice, *How to Stop Worrying and Start Living.* He died in New York City on November 1, 1955; by that time his courses were enrolling some 50,000 people a year and *How to Win Friends* had sold nearly 5 mililon copies.

Carothers, Wallace Hume (1896–1937), chemist. Born on April 27, 1896, in Burlington, Iowa, Carothers graduated from Tarkio College in 1920 and pursued graduate studies in chemistry at the University of Illinois. After a year of teaching at the University of South Dakota in 1921–1922 he returned to Illinois to take his Ph.D. in 1924 and remained there to teach organic chemistry. In 1926 he joined the faculty at Harvard and two years later accepted the directorship of a new research laboratory established by E.I. du Pont de Nemours & Company in Wilmington, Delaware. There he organized and oversaw a wide-ranging program of fundamental chemical research, one of the first undertaken by an industrial concern. His own investigations centered on organic substances of very high molecular weight and particularly on those characterized by polymerization, the forming of long chains of repeating molecular units. He made numerous basic contributions to the theory of polymerization and was able to synthesize a great many new compounds. One of these, chloroprene, could be polymerized into a rubberlike material; after it had been commercially developed, the material became widely known as neoprene. In 1935 Carothers brought a long and difficult series of experiments to fruition by combining adipic acid and hexamethylenediamine to form long filaments of what he called "polymer 66." When the filaments were drawn out to a certain length the polymer chains were aligned and pulled to their full extent, making the filaments extremely strong and giving them many of the characteristics of natural fibers such as wool and silk. Having completed the research phase of the work Carothers turned the substance over to other Du Pont staff members for development; a patent was granted in 1937 and in 1938 the company announced the new product, the first usable synthetic fiber, and the next year placed it on the market as nylon. Carothers, however, had in the meantime taken his own life, in Philadelphia on April 29, 1937.

Carpenter, Harlean, *see* Harlow, Jean

Carroll, Charles (1737–1832), Revolutionary leader and public official. Born on September 19, 1737, in Annapolis, Maryland, Carroll was educated in Jesuit schools in France and at the Inner Temple, London. In 1765, upon his return to America, he took possession of Carrollton, a 10,000-acre estate in Maryland, and lived a quiet life as a country gentleman for several years. Although barred from participating in political affairs because he was a Roman Catholic, he took a keen interest in them and in 1773 engaged in a pseudonymous newspaper debate with Daniel Dulany over certain prerogatives asserted by the governor of the colony, aligning himself solidly with the patriot side and gaining considerable prominence. During the next three years he was active in the local non-importation committee and on the committees of correspondence and safety. He served in the first Maryland convention in 1774–1776 and in the latter year was appointed by the Continental Congress to travel with Benjamin Franklin, Samuel Chase, and John Carroll (a cousin) to seek Canadian aid in the Revolution. In July 1776 he was elected to the Second Continental Congress and there signed the Declaration of Independence, using, as he had since 1765, the epithet "of Carrollton" to distinguish himself from relatives of the same surname. In 1777 he was elected to the Maryland senate and later in the year returned to the Continental Congress, where he served on the Board of War and other committees. He continued in the state senate, declined election to the Constitutional Convention in 1787, and in 1789 was elected one of Maryland's first U.S. senators. Upon leaving the Senate in 1792 at the end of its short first term he reentered the state senate and held his seat there until 1801. His prominence during the Revolution and the unstable period that followed had in large measure accounted for the support of the patriot cause by American Catholics. After 1801 he devoted himself to his estate and various business interests; on July 4, 1828, he laid the cornerstone for the Baltimore & Ohio Railroad, of which he was an original director. At his death in Baltimore on November 14, 1832, he was the last surviving signer of the Declaration of Independence.

Carroll, John (1735–1815), Roman Catholic bishop. Born in Upper Marlboro, Maryland, on January 8, 1735, Carroll was sent abroad for his education. He studied in France, entered the novitiate of the Society of Jesus (the Jesuits) in 1753, and on completing his academic studies taught in Catholic academies in Liège and Bruges; in 1769 he was ordained and in 1771 took his vows in the Society of Jesus. The suppression of the Jesuit order in 1773 forced him to England for a time; in 1774 he returned to Maryland. In 1776, at the request of the Continental Congress, he accompanied Benjamin Franklin and his cousin, Charles Carroll of Carrollton, on a fruitless mission to secure Canadian aid in the Revolution. After the war he was active in efforts to prevent foreign domination of the American Catholic clergy; in 1784 Pope Pius VI named him superior of the U.S. Missions. In 1789 Carroll was named bishop of Baltimore, the first bishop of the Roman Catholic Church in the United States. In the same year he established a Catholic college—now Georgetown University—and in 1791 a seminary in Baltimore. He actively promoted missions to the Indians and welcomed a number of religious orders to the United States. In 1806 he laid the cornerstone for the original Baltimore cathedral, for which he had engaged architect Benjamin H. Latrobe, and two years later, with the organization of the church firmly established and, largely through his efforts, expanding rapidly westward, his see became an archdiocese and he became archbishop. He died in Baltimore on December 3, 1815.

Carson, Kit (1809–1868), trapper, guide, Indian agent, and soldier. Born on December 24, 1809, in Madison County, Kentucky, Christopher Carson spent his early childhood in Boone's Lick, on the Missouri frontier. His father was killed by falling timber when he was nine and he received no schooling. In 1825 his mother apprenticed him to a saddlemaker, but he ran away to join an expedition to Santa Fe; he learned to trap for furs and fight Indians, and he established a home base in the region of Taos, New Mexico. He trapped in California and as far north as Montana, associating at various times with Thomas Fitzpatrick, Jim Bridger, and other famous mountain men. He married a woman of the Arapahoe tribe about 1836. On a steamboat from St. Louis, he met John C. Frémont, who subsequently engaged him as a guide on three expeditions during the 1840s. He fought in several battles for the conquest of California and later, visiting Washington, discovered that he was a national hero for his daring in the war. He returned to private life, farming in Taos, driving sheep to Sacramento, and serving as a guide and, from 1853, as U.S. Indian agent to the Ute tribe. He was extremely effective in that position, even though he was illiterate; he dictated his government reports to other people. One of these scribes, an army surgeon, took down his autobiography but embellished it so much that Carson had to admit that it was more fictional than real. He resigned as an Indian agent when the Civil War began, was given the rank of colonel, raised a volunteer regiment, and successfully battled Indian tribes which had terrorized settlers for years. But his final battle in Texas in 1864 was a defeat; 5000 Indians met his poorly armed group of 400 soldiers and retreat was inevitable. Nevertheless, he was made brigadier general of volunteers and in 1866 he was named commander of Fort Garland, Colorado, but had to resign the next year due to ill health. He attended a conference in Washington with the Utes although his health continued to be poor, and made a fruitless trip to the East, hoping to find medical relief. On May 23, 1868, he died at Fort Lyon, Colorado. A temperate, modest, and widely respected man, he holds an important place in American frontier legend.

Carson, Rachel Louise (1907–1964), biologist and author. Born in Springdale, Pennsylvania, on May 27, 1907, Miss Carson early developed a deep interest in the natural world. She entered Pennsylvania College for Women with the intention of becoming a writer, but soon changed her major field of study from English to biology. Graduating in 1929, she went to The Johns Hopkins University for graduate work and in 1931 joined the faculty of the University of Maryland, where she taught for five years; she received her M.A. from Johns Hopkins in 1932. From 1929 to 1936 she also taught in the Johns Hopkins summer school and pursued postgraduate studies at the Marine Biological Laboratory in Woods Hole, Massachusetts. In 1936 she took a position as aquatic biologist with the U.S. Bureau of Fisheries (later the Fish and Wildlife Service), where she remained until 1952. An article in the *Atlantic Monthly* in 1937 served as the basis for her first book, *Under the Sea Wind*, published in 1941; it was widely praised for its combination of scientific accuracy and thoroughness with an elegant and lyrical prose style. *The Sea Around Us*, 1951, became a best seller and was eventually translated into 30 languages. In 1951 a Guggenheim fellowship enabled her to begin her third book, *The Edge of the Sea*, published in 1955. Her final book, *Silent Spring*, 1962, raised a national controversy. In it Carson examined the widespread and rapidly growing use of chemical pesticides and herbicides and charged that indiscriminate use of such substances held great danger of permanently upsetting the natural ecological balance in the world. The book aroused public opinion and prompted numerous governmental inquiries into the problem. She died in Silver Spring, Maryland, on April 14, 1964.

Carter, Henry, *see* Leslie, Frank

Carter, Jimmy (1924–   ), thirty-ninth president of the United States. Born in Plains, Georgia, on October 1, 1924, James Earl Carter graduated from the Naval Academy in 1946. After service on battleships and submarines and in Capt. (later Adm.) Hyman G. Rickover's naval nuclear reactor project he left the navy in 1953 and returned to Plains. He built up the family businesses and gradually involved himself in civic and political affairs. He was elected to the Georgia legislature in 1962 and 1964, and he tried unsuccessfully for the Democratic nomination for governor in 1966. In 1970 he won the nomination and the election. His administration was marked by enlightened racial and social policies and a commitment to careful fiscal management. Limited by satute to a single term as governor, Carter began planning early for an entrance into national politics, and in December 1974 he launched a long and arduous campaign for the 1976 presidential nomination. Carter slowly built a national identity, established an image as a profoundly religious, non-establishment spokesman for the common people, and won 18 state primary elections. He took the Democratic nomination on the first ballot, selected Sen. Walter F. Mondale as his running mate, and in November 1976 narrowly outpolled President Gerald R. Ford. Carter's administration was notable for its campaign for human rights throughout the world, a new Panama Canal Treaty that ceded control of the canal to the Panamanians, and peace accords between Israel and Egypt. A major crisis occurred with the taking of hostages at the American embassy in Iran in 1979, and this crisis eventually became a contributing factor in his defeat by Ronald Reagan in the 1980 presidential election.

Carter, Samuel Powhatan (1819–1891), naval officer and soldier. Born in Elizabethton, Tennessee, on August 6, 1819, Carter was educated at Washington College in Tennessee and at Princeton. In 1840 he entered the navy as a midshipman and after five years of sea duty in the Pacific and on the Great Lakes was transferred to the Naval

Academy to graduate with the class of 1846. Over the next several years he served in the Mexican War, at the Naval Observatory, as assistant professor of mathematics at the Academy, rising in 1855 to the rank of lieutenant. A letter in which he stated that he would remain loyal to the Union should civil war break out came to the attention of Andrew Johnson, then governor of Tennessee, who arranged with the war department to have Carter recruit and train militia in the eastern part of the state. In May 1862 he was commissioned brigadier general of volunteers. He led successful cavalry raids in support of Gen. William S. Rosecrans at Murfreesboro and later he saw action in North Carolina. Made a major general in 1865, Carter was released from the army early in 1866 and returned to the navy, by which he had been promoted to the rank of commander during his army duty. He served again in the Pacific in command of the *Monocacy* and in 1870 was promoted to captain. From that year to 1873 he was commandant of midshipmen at the Naval Academy and then returned to line duty in European waters. In 1878 he became a commodore and in 1882, the year after his retirement, was made rear admiral, retired, thus becoming the only American ever to attain both the rank of rear admiral and that of major general. Carter died in Washington, D.C., on May 26, 1891.

Cartwright, Peter (1785–1872), religious leader. Born on September 1, 1785, in Amherst County, Virginia, Cartwright grew up there and, after 1790, in Logan County, Kentucky, in a frontier atmosphere. Religious instruction from his mother was the bulk of his schooling. At sixteen he was converted at a Methodist revival meeting, and, entering the church, began proselytizing among men in the area, earning an exhorter's license in 1802. The next year he became a traveling preacher, riding a new circuit in parts of Kentucky, Tennessee, Indiana, and Ohio. His physical prowess, courage, and rugged humor gained a ready audience for his message among frontiersmen. Methodism was for him a battle against the devil and against rival sects; he denounced Calvinists, Baptists, Presbyterians, and Shakers alike. His sermons on sin—drinking, gambling, and wearing ruffles but mainly rejecting Methodism—and of redemption—accepting his church —were delivered in such a vehement manner that many listeners experienced spasms, or "the jerks," before they declared themselves converted. He was ordained a deacon in 1806 by Bishop Francis Asbury and an elder in 1808 by Bishop William McKendree. He rode his circuit until 1824, when his hatred of slavery led him to transfer to free territory in Sangamon County, Illinois. His antislavery views won him election twice to the Illinois legislature. In 1846 he lost to Abraham Lincoln in a congressional election. He wrote a colorful *Autobiography*, 1856, and *Fifty Years as a Presiding Elder*, 1871. A major figure in the religious development of the West, he died on September 25, 1872, near Pleasant Plains, Illinois.

Carty, John Joseph (1861–1932), electrical engineer. Born in Cambridge, Massachusetts, on April 14, 1861, Carty joined the Bell Telephone Company in Boston at the age of eighteen. In 1887 he was transferred to the subsidiary Western Electric Company in New York City and two years later became chief engineer of the New York telephone company. He made numerous contributions to the techniques of telephone construction and operation, most notably the invention of a battery that was capable of powering any number of telephones from a central location, the redesigning of the bell-signal circuitry that greatly reduced the overall impedance of a telephone system and thus enabled it to be constructed on a far larger scale than previously, the perfecting of the principles of "phantoming," whereby two pairs of wires can carry three separate telephone circuits, and his discovery of the source and means of suppression of cross-interference between telephone circuits. In 1907 he became chief engineer of the American Telephone and Telegraph Company (AT&T) and quickly moved to consolidate the company's many research establishments into a single large one that later evolved into the world-famous Bell Telephone Laboratories. He directed research into the problems involved in long-distance telephony, both by cable and by radio, and in 1915 achieved both transcontinental and transatlantic voice connections. A member of the Army Signal Corps Reserve, Carty entered active service upon U.S. entry into World War I and, stationed in France, had primary responsibility for maintaining communications between Gen. John J. Pershing and Washington; he eventually attained the rank of brigadier general. He retired as chief engineer of AT&T in 1919 and from that year to 1930 was a vice-president of the company. In 1932 AT&T established the Carty Medal to be awarded by the National Academy of Sciences; he was named as the first recipient but the award was posthumous, Carty having died in Baltimore on December 27, 1932.

Carver, George Washington (1864?–1943), agronomist and agricultural chemist. Born of slave parents on a farm near Diamond Grove, Missouri, about 1864, Carver was left fatherless in his infancy and was stolen and carried into Arkansas with his mother, who was never heard of again. Purchased from his captors for a racehorse worth $300, he was returned to his former home in Missouri. He worked his way through high school in Minneapolis and later through college, taking his bachelor's degree in 1894 and his master's in 1896 from the Iowa State College of Agriculture and Mechanic Arts. In the latter year he accepted an appointment by Booker T. Washington to the faculty of Tuskegee Institute in Alabama, where he remained director of agricultural research until his death. There he conducted experiments in soil management and crop production and directed an experimental farm. He urged Alabama planters to raise peanuts and sweet potatoes, crops that would replenish nutrients in the soil, instead of cotton, which left the land depleted and worthless. In his laboratory he produced hundreds of by-products of the peanut, including milk and coffee substitutes, cheese, flour, ink, dyes, soap, bleach, wood stains, metal polish, shaving cream, linoleum, synthetic rubber, insulating board, and plastics, and of the sweet potato, including flour, vinegar, and molasses. In 1914, at a time when the boll weevil had almost ruined cotton growers, he revealed his experiments and the South began to turn to peanuts, sweet potatoes, and their derivatives for income. Much exhausted land was renewed, and the South became a major supplier of new agricultural products. In 1923 he was awarded the Spingarn medal by the National Association for the Advancement of Colored People (NAACP). In 1940 he donated his savings to the establishment of the Carver Foundation for continuing research in agriculture. He worked during World War II to replace the textile dyes formerly imported from Europe, and in all produced dyes of 500 different shades. He died in Tuskegee, Alabama, on January 5, 1943.

Carver, Jonathan (1710–1780), explorer. Born in Weymouth, Massachusetts, on April 13, 1710, Carver was a sergeant in the British army at the siege of Fort William Henry in 1757. Settling in Massachusetts, he joined a provincial regiment and in 1759 he was promoted to lieutenant; the next year he was made captain. In 1766 he was sent by Maj. Robert Rogers on a journey of exploration westward from Mackinac. He traveled west through the Great Lakes region, via Green Bay and the Fox and Wisconsin rivers, to the Mississippi, and up the river to the region of the Sioux Indians at the Falls of St. Anthony. He remained during the winter of 1766–1767 in a Sioux camp on the Minnesota River. Returning to Mackinac, he met Capt. James Tute at the mouth of the Wisconsin River. Tute was in charge of a party sent by Rogers to seek a route to the Pacific Ocean. Carver joined the party as a draftsman and third in command; they traveled up the Mississippi and reached the shores of Lake Superior by the Chippewa and St. Croix rivers, then proceeded to the Grand Portage. They returned to Mackinac by the north shore of Lake Superior in 1768. Never paid for his services by Rogers, who had hired him without authorization, Carver attempted without success to publish his travel journal, then left for England in 1769 to seek payment and to have the manuscript published. But the project met with many delays and he did not benefit when the journal was finally printed in London two years before his death. Called *Travels Through the Interior Parts of North America in the Years 1766, 1767, 1768*, it became popular at once; through many editions it remained the most widely read account of early American travel and adventure. Although the second part, dealing with Indian manners and customs, was traceable to French authors and brought charges of plagiarism, this detracted little from the book as a whole. Carver's name was later discovered on a *New Universal*

Geography that was published in 1779 and on a discourse on raising tobacco. He died in London on January 31, 1780.

Cary, Alice (1820–1871), author. Born near Cincinnati, on April 26, 1820, Alice, and her sister Phoebe, born on September 4, 1824 grew up on a farm and received little schooling. Nevertheless they were well educated, Alice by their mother and Phoebe by Alice, and they early developed a taste for literature that could not be dampened by their unsympathetic stepmother, whom their father had married in 1837. Alice's first published poem appeared in the *Cincinnati Sentinel* when she was eighteen; for ten years thereafter she continued to contribute poems and prose sketches to various periodicals with no remuneration. Phoebe began to write under Alice's guidance and in 1850 they published *Poems of Alice and Phoebe Cary*, some two-thirds of which was the work of Alice. The book's modest success encouraged them to move to New York City. There they established themselves as regular contributors to *Harper's*, the *Atlantic Monthly*, and other periodicals. Alice, much more prolific than her sister, enjoyed the higher reputation during her lifetime, although Phoebe was later held in greater critical esteem for the wit and feeling of her poems. Their salon became a popular meeting place for the leading literary lights of New York. Alice became the first president of the first U.S. women's club, later called Sorosis. Among Alice's books were two volumes of reminiscent sketches entitled *Clovernook Papers*, 1851 and 1853; *Hagar, A Story of Today*, 1852; *Lyra and Other Poems*, 1852; *The Maiden of Tiascala*, 1855; *Married, Not Mated*, 1856; *Pictures of Country Life*, 1859; *Ballads, Lyrics, and Hymns*, 1866; *Snow-Berries: A Book for Young Folks*, 1867; and *The Lover's Diary*, 1868. Phoebe, much of whose time was devoted to keeping house and, in later years, to caring for Alice, published only *Poems and Parodies*, 1854, and *Poems of Faith, Hope and Love*, 1868, but one of her religious verses, "Nearer Home" (sometimes called from the first line "One Sweetly Solemn Thought") became widely popular as a hymn. After a long illness Alice died in New York City on February 12, 1871; exhausted by grief and stricken with malaria, Phoebe died soon after, on July 31, 1871, in Newport, Rhode Island.

Cary, Phoebe, *see under* Cary, Alice

Cash, Johnny (1932–), singer and songwriter. Born on February 26, 1932, near Kingsland, Arkansas, John Cash grew up learning the hymns, work songs, and country ballads of the rural South and while still in school began writing and playing songs of his own. After a four-year stint in the air force he settled in Memphis, Tennessee, in 1954 and while working at minor jobs continued to develop his musical talents. He formed a trio, Johnny Cash and the Tennessee Two, and performed at county fairs and other local events and in 1955 made his first record, "Hey, Porter." His second, "Folsom Prison Blues," sold well in the country-and-western market and after "I Walk the Line" became a hit in 1956 he began to appear on the "Grand Ole Opry" radio and television show from Nashville. In 1959 his first albums appeared. A short time later, however, exhaustion and illness combined to slow his career and he suffered a decline in popularity that required several years to reverse. In 1963 and 1964 he was awarded gold records for million-copy sales of "Ring of Fire" and "I Walk the Line," and in 1968 his album "Johnny Cash at Folsom Prison," voted best of the year by the Country Music Association, brought him suddenly to the notice of a wider audience. Personal appearances in New York City and London were great successes and in 1969 he began his own national television program. At a time when popular music was adopting many of the sounds of the country-and-western genre, Cash's laconic manner, craggy face, and slightly rough bass voice conveyed a strong impression of authenticity that captured the imagination of millions of listeners who had never before paid attention to his kind of music.

Cass, Lewis (1782–1866), public official. Born in Exeter, New Hampshire, on October 9, 1782, Cass attended Phillips Exeter Academy; upon graduation in 1799, he joined his father in Marietta, Ohio. There he studied law and was admitted to the bar in 1802. In 1806 he became the youngest member of the Ohio legislature. During the War of 1812 he served with distinction under generals William Hull and William Henry Harrison; he rose to brigadier general, and his valuable service won him the governorship of Michigan Territory in 1813. For the next 18 years he effectively oversaw the organization and development of the region and was particularly successful in his relations with the Indians. In 1831 Cass was appointed secretary of war by President Andrew Jackson; he remained in the cabinet for five years, during which time Indian wars largely occupied him. In 1836 he was sent to France as U.S. minister. He remained in the post until 1842, when he resigned because of a dispute with Secretary of State Daniel Webster over the rights of search and seizure on the high seas claimed by Great Britain. Cass represented Michigan in the Senate from 1845 to 1848 and supported the annexation of Texas, the U.S. claim to the entire Oregon region, and the war with Mexico. In 1848 he won the Democratic nomination for president, but the breaking away of the Free-Soilers resulted in his defeat by Zachary Taylor. He returned to the Senate, serving from 1849 to 1857, and was a strong opponent of the Wilmot Proviso and a supporter of the Compromise of 1850. From 1857 to 1860 he was President James Buchanan's secretary of state and in that post secured from Great Britain a relinquishment of its claim to the right of search and seizure. He resigned in protest against Buchanan's weak reaction to South Carolina's secession. Cass later published a number of studies based on his experiences with the Indians and in France. He died in Detroit on June 17, 1866.

Cassatt, Mary (1844–1926), painter. Born on May 22, 1844, in Allegheny (now part of Pittsburgh), Pennsylvania, Mary Cassatt lived in Paris for five years as a young girl and later, as an artist, chose to live and work in that city. She was tutored privately in art in Philadelphia and attended the Pennsylvania Academy of the Fine Arts in 1861–1865, but she preferred learning on her own and traveled to Europe to study. Her first major showing was at the Paris Salon of 1872; four more annual Salon exhibitions followed. In 1874 she chose Paris as her permanent residence and established her studio there. She shared with the Impressionists an interest in experiment and in using bright colors inspired by the out-of-doors. Edgar Degas became her friend; his style and that of Gustave Courbet inspired her own. Degas was known to admire her drawing especially and at his request she exhibited with the Impressionists in 1879 and joined them in shows in 1880, 1881, and 1886. Although she was known to be an American artist, she was generally identified with the French group. Her depictions of mothers and children were celebrated examples of her warm, individual style, which was characterized by the combination of delicate colors and strong line. The etchings she produced were compared in quality to James Whistler's. Equally fine were her color prints and pastels. She had a one-man exhibition in the Gallery of Durand-Ruel in Paris in 1891 and another and larger one in 1893. Her eyesight began to fail about 1900; she ceased work by 1914 and died at her country home north of Paris on June 14, 1926.

Castle, Irene, see under Castle, Vernon Blythe

Castle, Vernon Blythe (1887–1918), dancer and aviator. Born in Norwich, England, on May 2, 1887, Vernon Blythe early intended to pursue a career in engineering but in 1906 came to the United States with his sister, who was an actress. Through her he won a small role in a 1907 Lew Fields production of *The Girl Behind the Counter*, in which he did a brief but fascinating dance routine that caught the audience's attention. Taking the name Castle, he was thereafter often engaged to choreograph dances for other shows. In 1911 he married Irene Foote (1893–1969), who had been born in New Rochelle, New York, on April 7, 1893. They began dancing together at private social functions but had no notable success until 1912, when they went to Paris and were a sensation in café performances. They then returned to New York and were in great demand in cafés and theaters. The Castles introduced a number of new dance steps that were taken up by the public, including the one-step, the turkey trot, and the Castle walk, and Mrs. Castle was also something of a trend-setter in fashion. Their popularity continued unabated until 1916, when Vernon returned to England to enlist in the Royal

Flying Corps. In air combat over France he distinguished himself on a number of occasions and was awarded the Croix de Guerre. He was sent to Fort Worth, Texas, at the beginning of 1918 as a flying instructor and was killed there on February 15, 1918, in a collision of his plane with another aircraft after he had maneuvered to save the other pilot's life. Mrs. Castle, sometimes credited with starting the "bobbed hair" craze of the 1920s, retained her name through subsequent marriages and became known as a devoted protector of animals, founding the Orphans of the Storm shelter in Deerfield, Illnois, in 1928. She died in Eureka Springs, Arkansas, on January 25, 1969.

Cather, Willa Sibert (1873–1947), author. Born on December 7, 1873, in Winchester, Virginia, Miss Cather moved with her family to the frontier village of Red Cloud, Nebraska, when she was nine. In 1895 she graduated from the University of Nebraska; she was a journalist for a few years in Pittsburgh and in 1901 became a schoolteacher. In 1903 she published a book of verse, *April Twilights*, and in 1905 a collection of short stories entitled *The Troll Garden*. The latter won her a position as managing editor of *McClure's Magazine*, where she remained until resigning in 1912 to devote herself entirely to writing. Her first novel, *Alexander's Bridge*, 1912, was a somewhat contrived work, but largely under the influence of the writer Sarah Orne Jewett she found her true literary inspiration in the frontier life of her childhood. *O Pioneers!*, 1913, and *My Antonia*, 1918, set the themes that were to infuse her best work, the heroic spirit of the pioneers and their conquest of hardships. *One of Ours*, 1922, won a Pulitzer Prize; that novel, like *A Lost Lady*, 1923, mourned the passing of the frontier and the virtues associated with it. Miss Cather's disillusionment deepened with the years and was reflected in *The Professor's House*, 1925, and in the essays collected in *Not Under Forty*, 1936. In *Death Comes for the Archbishop*, 1927, and *Shadows on the Rock*, 1931, she turned to an earlier era, that of the French missionaries in America, to recapture a heroism lost to the modern world. In 1940 she published her last novel, *Sapphira and the Slave Girl*. She died in New York City on April 24, 1947.

Catlin, George (1796–1872), painter and author. Born on July 26, 1796, in Wilkes-Barre, Pennsylvania, Catlin studied law in 1817–1818 in Litchfield, Connecticut, and practiced in Pennsylvania for a short time. He gave up that career in 1823 to begin another in portraiture. In this he was successful, although he was self-taught, but he developed a greater interest in the Indian tribes that in the past had battled near his birthplace. When, in 1824, he saw a convention of Indians that had just arrived in Philadelphia from the West, his fascination grew, and after much deliberation and with encouragement from his adventurous wife, he embarked on a journey into the Western wilderness. Catlin met many different tribes of the Great Plains; he found it necessary to gain their complete trust before he could sketch them, since many Indians felt they would surely die if their likenesses were captured. He produced hundreds of sketches, engravings, and paintings, as well as notes on the lives of the Indians. His most famous book, *Letters and Notes on the Manners, Customs, and Conditions of the North American Indians,* two volumes, 1841, was the first of many written studies, all profusely illustrated with his sketches and reflective of his travels throughout the world; they included *Catlin's North American Indian Portfolio: Hunting, Rocky Mountains and Prairies of America,* 1845; *Catlin's Notes of Eight Years' Travel and Residence in Europe,* 1848; *Last Rambles Amongst the Indians of the Rocky Mountains and the Andes,* 1867. While his work is not considered great art, it was spontaneous and knowledgeable, perhaps the most reliable record of Indian life prepared by any scholar. It awakened inhabitants of the eastern United States to the existence and condition of Indian tribes within their own country. Catlin died in Jersey City, New Jersey, on December 23, 1872. Controversy ensued over the disposition of his collection; it was offered for purchase to Congress, but a Southern faction, fearing that the work might arouse compassion for the Indians and hamper the expansion of slavery into the West, prodded Congress into refusal. Subsequently much of the collection was donated to the Smithsonian Institution's National Museum in Washington, D.C.

Catron, John (1786?–1865), justice of the Supreme Court. Born about 1786, probably in Wythe County, Virginia, Catron grew up and received whatever schooling he had in Virginia and Kentucky. In 1812 he moved to Tennessee and after serving under Andrew Jackson in the War of 1812 took up the study of law and was admitted to the bar in 1815. After three years of practice in what was called a "mountain circuit" he moved to Nashville and built a considerable reputation in land law and equity. In 1824 the state supreme court of errors and appeals was enlarged and Catron was elected to it by the legislature; he became chief justice when that position was created in 1831 and continued to serve until the court was abolished by a new state constitution in 1834. During his years on that bench his most notable case was one in 1829 in which he strongly denounced the custom of dueling. Returning to private practice, he took an active role in politics and as a long-time supporter of Jackson used his influence to aid Martin Van Buren's presidential campaign in 1836. In March 1837, after Congress expanded the Supreme Court from seven to nine members, Jackson appointed Catron to one of the new seats in one of his last acts as president. Although he was not a legal scholar, Catron was a capable justice, particularly in equity, and was given to writing vigorous and lengthy opinions. He decided no major cases and most often sided

with his fellow Jacksonian, Chief Justice Roger B. Taney. He strongly opposed secession and in 1861 went to Kentucky and then to Tennessee to hold circuit court sessions and maintain federal authority. Tennessee was by that time virtually committed to the Confederacy and Catron was with difficulty persuaded to leave for his own safety. After presiding over his circuit court in St. Louis he once again attempted to sit in Nashville, Tennessee, and was once again forced to depart. Through the remainder of the war he maintained his Kentucky court in close cooperation with military authorities. Soon after the war ended he died in Nashville, on May 30, 1865.

Catt, Carrie Chapman (1859–1947), reformer. Born on January 9, 1859, in Ripon, Wisconsin, Carrie Lane grew up there and in Charles City, Iowa. She worked her way through Iowa State Agricultural College, graduated first in her class in 1880, and after a short time spent reading law became a high-school principal in Mason City in 1881; two years later she was appointed superintendent of schools, one of the first women to hold such a position. In 1884 she married Leo Chapman, publisher and editor of the *Mason City Republican;* they moved to San Francisco in 1886 and Chapman died soon afterward. Mrs. Chapman worked briefly as a newspaper reporter there and then returned to Iowa in 1887 to become an organizer for the Iowa Woman Suffrage Association. In 1890 she married George W. Catt, a Seattle, Washington, engineer who died in 1905. As an organizer Mrs. Catt was highly successful, and in 1900 she was elected to succeed Susan B. Anthony as president of the National American Woman Suffrage Association. In 1902 she was an organizer of the International Woman Suffrage Alliance, of which she served as president until 1923 and thereafter as honorary chairman. In 1904 she resigned the presidency of the national organization to devote herself to reorganizing it along effective political lines; she was reelected in 1915 and held the office until her death. In 1915 she led a successful woman-suffrage campaign in New York and then opened a massive drive for a constitutional amendment to provide national woman suffrage. Tireless lobbying in Congress and then in state legislatures finally produced a ratified Nineteenth Amendment in 1920. The year before she had prepared for victory by organizing the League of Women Voters to undertake necessary educational work; she was honorary president of the league for the rest of her life. In 1925 Mrs. Catt founded the National Committee on the Cause and Cure of War and served as its chairman until 1932 (thereafter as honorary chairman). She was active also in support of the League of Nations, for relief of Jewish refugees from Germany, and on behalf of a child-labor amendment. She strongly supported the United Nations after World War II. Widely honored as one of the outstanding women of her time, Mrs. Catt died in New Rochelle, New York, on March 9, 1947.

Cattell, James McKeen (1860–1944), psychologist and editor. Born on May 24, 1860, in Easton, Pennsylvania, Cattell graduated from Lafayette College in 1880 and after two years in several European universities and one at Johns Hopkins completed his studies in psychology at the University of Leipzig, taking his Ph.D. in 1886. In 1888 he was appointed the first professor of psychology at the University of Pennsylvania, serving also as head of the department until 1891, when he moved to Columbia University. Cattell conducted pioneering research in psychology, particularly in the areas of mental and psychological testing, the study of individual differences, and the practical applications of psychology. A statistical study of American scientists, stemming in part from his interest in promoting scientific cooperation, led to the compiling of a directory, *American Men of Science*, published first in 1906 and in several more editions through 1939. Cattell left Columbia in 1917 and four years later founded the Psychological Corporation, of which he was for many years president and which was concerned with the practical applications of psychological knowledge and techniques. Cattell was also noted as an editor of scientific journals, including the *Psychological Review* from 1894 to 1904, *Science* from 1894, *Scientific Monthly* from 1900, the *American Naturalist* from 1907 to 1938, and *School and Society* from 1915 to 1939. From 1932 he also edited *Leaders in Education*. He was president of both Science Service and the Science Press and a member and officer of numerous scientific organizations, including the American Psychological Association of which he was president in 1895. Cattell died on January 20, 1944, in Lancaster, Pennsylvania.

Catton, Bruce (1899–1978), historian and journalist. Born on October 9, 1899, in Petoskey, Michigan, Charles Bruce Catton grew up there and in nearby Benzonia. He entered Oberlin College in 1916 but the following year enlisted in the navy, in which he served for the duration of World War I. He returned to Oberlin briefly but in 1920 left to join the staff of the *Cleveland News;* over the next six years he worked successively for the *Boston American* and the *Cleveland Plain Dealer* and from 1926 to 1941 was a Washington correspondent and feature writer for the Newspaper Enterprise Association. In 1942 he became information director for the War Production Board. Three years later he moved to a similar position with the Department of Commerce and from 1950 to 1952 was with the Department of the Interior. He published *War Lords of Washington* in 1948 as a result of his early government service; from 1952 he devoted full time to writing on the Civil War, a subject that had long been a hobby with him. His first undertaking was a three-volume history of the Army of the Potomac, comprising *Mr. Lincoln's Army*, 1951; *Glory Road*, 1952; and *A Stillness at Appomattox*, 1953, the last of which won both a National Book Award and a Pulitzer Prize. Combining thorough

research with a vivid narrative style that brought the figures of history to life and gave human substance to the story, Catton's work was well received by both the public and the critics. *U.S. Grant and the American Military Tradition* appeared in 1954 and was followed by *This Hallowed Ground*, 1956; *America Goes to War*, 1958; and *Grant Moves South*, 1960. He then set to work on his Centennial History of the Civil War and published it in three volumes: *The Coming Fury*, 1961; *Terrible Swift Sword*, 1963; and *Never Call Retreat*, 1965. In 1969 he returned to his biography of Gen. Ulysses S. Grant with *Grant Takes Command*. Catton was editor of *American Heritage* magazine from 1954 to 1959. He died in Frankfort, Michigan, on August 28, 1978.

Cavelier, René Robert, *see* La Salle, *Sieur de*

Cerf, Bennett Alfred (1898–1971), publisher and editor. Born in New York City on May 25, 1898, Cerf graduated from Columbia College in 1919 and after taking a degree from the Columbia School of Journalism became a financial reporter for the *New York Herald Tribune*. He worked also in a stockbrokerage house until 1923, when an investment in the publishing house of Boni and Liveright brought him a vice-presidency in the firm. Two years later he and Donald S. Klopfer bought from Boni and Liveright a reprint series, the Modern Library, and they immediately began to build it into the most popular such series in American publishing history, eventually expanding it to include some 400 titles that sold more than 50 million copies over the next half-century. In 1927 the two formed their own publishing firm, Random House, taking the name from their proposed method of selecting titles for publication. The firm grew rapidly from a limited-editions enterprise into a major house with a list of authors that included such names as Eugene O'Neill, Robinson Jeffers, William Faulkner, Sinclair Lewis, and Robert Penn Warren. Cerf demonstrated a deep concern for freedom of the press in 1933 by engaging in a long and successful legal battle to lift the ban on U.S. publication of James Joyce's *Ulysses*. As Random House grew it acquired several other firms, notably that of Alfred A. Knopf in 1960. Cerf himself edited several anthologies of plays and short stories and more than 20 collections of jokes, puns, and anecdotes; he also conducted a column in the *Saturday Review of Literature* from 1942 to 1957 and wrote two syndicated newspaper columns. From 1952 to 1968, he was a regular panelist on the television program "What's My Line?" He continued as president of Random House until 1965, when he became chairman of the board, a position he held until his retirement in 1970. Cerf died in Mount Kisco, New York, on August 27, 1971.

Chadwick, Henry (1824–1908), journalist and sports figure. Born in Exeter, England, on October 5, 1824, Chadwick came to the United States at the age of thirteen. He began his journalistic career as a contributor to the *Long Island Star* in 1844 and by 1856 was a reporter for the *New York Times*, the *Brooklyn Eagle*, and other newspapers; for three decades he wrote for those and for the *New York Clipper*, a leading sporting paper, as one of the earliest and best sports writers in America. He was a devotee of cricket, which was then still popular in America, but he early saw great possibilities in the new game of baseball. He was a major force in organizing professional baseball and worked ceaselessly to keep it separate from the amateur variety and to keep both free from unsavory associations. Chadwick was chairman of the rules committee of the National Association of Baseball Players, organized in 1858, and in that position exerted considerable influence on the development and codification of the rules of baseball, contributing in particular the scoring system. In 1869 he began publishing an annual handbook on the game that later became *Spalding's Official Baseball Guide*, which was edited by Albert G. Spalding from 1878 to 1880; Chadwick resumed the editorship in 1881 and retained it until his death. In his later year he was known as the "Father of Baseball." He died in New York City on April 20, 1908.

Chafee, Zechariah (1885–1957), lawyer. Born in Providence, Rhode Island, on December 7, 1885, Chafee graduated from Brown University in 1907 and then, after a short time working in his father's business, entered Harvard Law School in 1910. In 1916 he joined the Harvard law faculty, becoming a professor after 1919. The restrictions on freedom of speech that were imposed during World War I roused his concern, and after the publication of his study *Freedom of Speech*, 1920, he very quickly became recognized as a leading thinker on the subject of civil liberties. In 1941 an expanded version of the book was published as *Free Speech in the United States*. From 1929 to 1931 Chafee was a consultant to the National Commission on Law Observance and Enforcement. He was a member of the Freedom of the Press Commission from 1943 to 1947 and, from 1947 onward, of the United Nations Subcommission on Freedom of Information and the Press. Among his other written works were *The Inquiring Mind*, 1928; his notable introduction to the *Records of the Suffolk County Court, 1671–1680*, 1933; *Government and Mass Communications*, two volumes, 1947; and *Blessings of Liberty*, 1956. He died in Boston on February 8, 1957.

Chaffee, Adna Romanza (1842–1914), soldier. Born in Orwell, Ohio, on April 14, 1842, Chaffee set out in July 1861 to enlist in a volunteer Union regiment, and, encountering a recruiting party from the 6th Cavalry en route, promptly joined that unit. He was promoted to sergeant within weeks and, after service in the Peninsular Campaign and at Antietam, became a first sergeant in September 1862. In May 1863 his highly capable service came to the attention of Secretary of War Edwin M. Stanton, who ordered him com-missioned as second lieutenant. Sent with his regiment to join the Army of the Potomac, he saw action at Gettysburg, where he was wounded and narrowly escaped capture, and took part in other major battles; he was advanced to first lieutenant in February 1865. After the war he resigned his commission but within a week was persuaded to seek restoration to rank. Until 1888 he served mainly in the Southwest, fighting in numerous battles with the Indians and rising to the rank of major. Transferred to the 9th Cavalry, he served as an instructor at Fort Leavenworth until 1897, when he was appointed lieutenant colonel of the 3d Cavalry. In May 1898 he was made brigadier general of volunteers for Spanish-American War duty and after his performance in the taking of El Caney in the Santiago Campaign was promoted to major general of volunteers. Following a brief period in the United States he returned to Cuba late in 1898 as chief of staff of the military government, a post he held until 1900. After reverting only briefly to his regular rank of colonel, which he had held since 1899, he was again appointed major general of volunteers in mid-1900 and placed in command of the U.S. contingent in the joint relief expedition sent to China to quell the Boxer Rebellion. After the successful completion of that mission, during which he won the admiration not only of the troops and commanders sent by the other Western powers but also of the Chinese themselves, he was made a major general in the regular army in 1901 and named commander of U.S. forces in the Philippines, where he remained until 1902. Chaffee served as commander of the Department of the East in 1902–1903 and, with the rank of lieutenant general, was chief of staff of the army from 1904 until his retirement in 1906. Settling in Los Angeles, he lived there until his death on November 1, 1914.

Chaffee, Adna Romanza (1884–1941), soldier. Born on September 23, 1884, in Junction City, Kansas, Chaffee accompanied his father, Gen. Adna R. Chaffee, to China in 1900–1901 and then entered West Point, graduating in 1906 and receiving assignment to the cavalry. His horsemanship led to his selection for the Mounted Service School at Fort Leavenworth, from which he graduated in 1908 and, after an advanced course, again in 1912, and he received further training at the cavalry school of the French army. During World War I he served with distinction with the American Expeditionary Force (AEF), seeing action on the St.-Mihiel and Meuse–Argonne fronts and advancing to the rank of colonel. After the war he held numerous troop and staff assignments and graduated from the school of the Line, Fort Leavenworth, in 1921 and from the Army War College, Washington, D.C., in 1925. In 1928 he was appointed to the general staff of the War Department and there worked to promote the development of the mechanized armored striking force, a new kind of army offensive unit based on the tank and other mobile armor. His leadership in the movement for the adoption of such novel weaponry earned him the title of "Father of the Armored Force." In 1934 he was given command of the 1st (mechanized) Cavalry, which eventually comprised 16 armored divisions, and was named a member of the army's Legislative Planning Bureau. In 1938, promoted to brigadier general, he was stationed at Fort Knox in command of the 1st Cavalry of the 7th (mechanized) Cavalry Brigade. Chaffee was promoted to major general in August 1941 and died in Boston less than three weeks later, on August 22, 1941.

Chamberlain, Owen (1920–   ), physicist. Born on July 10, 1920, in San Francisco, Chamberlain grew up there and in Philadelphia. He graduated from Dartmouth College in 1941 and went then to the University of California at Berkeley to pursue graduate studies in physics. The next year he joined the secret Manhattan Engineering District project for the development of the atomic bomb and in 1943 moved to the installation at Los Alamos, New Mexico, where the final work was done and the first bomb detonated in 1945. He later continued his research on slow-neutron diffraction in liquids at the Argonne National Laboratory near Chicago and resumed his studies under Enrico Fermi at the University of Chicago. Upon taking his Ph.D. in 1948 he joined the Berkeley faculty as an instructor. There he undertook a series of studies of the polarization of and interactions between nucleons—neutrons and protons from atomic nuclei—using the cyclotron, a high-energy particle accelerator. He became interested in the antiproton, a particle of mass, size, and spin nearly equal to that of the proton but having an opposite electrical charge. The existence of the antiproton had been suggested as early as 1928, and the possibility had been bolstered by the discovery of the anti-electron, or positron, by Carl D. Anderson in 1932; until the completion in 1954 of the bevatron at Berkeley, however, sufficient energy to conduct the necessary experiments was unavailable. In 1955 Chamberlain, working with Emilio G. Segrè, C. Wiegand, and T. Ypsilantis, obtained evidence for the existence of the antiproton; confirmation followed, and by the end of the year the discovery was considered definite. For this work Chamberlain and Segrè were awarded jointly the 1959 Nobel Prize for Physics. Chamberlain thereafter continued to investigate various aspects of nuclear phenomena at Berkeley, where from 1958 he was a full professor of physics.

Chamberlain, Wilt (1936–   ), basketball player. Born in Philadelphia on August 21, 1936, Wilton Norman Chamberlain began playing basketball in junior high school, and in high school led his team to three consecutive championships. In 1955, having received offers from more than 200 colleges and universities, he entered the University of Kansas, where, in two years of varsity play, he averaged 30 points per game, was twice named an All-American, and led the team to victory in

42 of 50 games. His height—just over seven feet —and his phenomenal ability led to double-, triple-, and even quadruple-teaming by opponents, however, and he left the university after three years to join the Harlem Globetrotters, in whose exhibition games he developed his mastery of the finer points. After a year with the Globetrotters he became eligible for professional basketball and in 1959 signed with the Philadelphia Warriors. In his first professional season he set eight National Basketball Association (NBA) records, including those for average points per game (37.6), rebounds (1941), and total points (2707), and became the first player to be voted top rookie and most valuable player in the same season. In March 1962, in a game against the New York Knickerbockers, he scored a record 100 points. In 1963 he moved with the Warriors to San Francisco; in 1965 he was traded to the Philadelphia Seventy-sixers and in 1968 to the Los Angeles Lakers. After his first few seasons of professional play, and after the initial overreaction to his height (which included hanging the nickname "The Stilt" on him) on the part of commentators, officials, and other players had worn off, Chamberlain was acknowledged to be not merely a big player but a great player. He dominated the career records book, leading in scoring average with over 30 points per game, in field-goal percentage with a mark well in excess of .500, and in total scoring, in 1972 passing the nearly incredible 30,000 mark. He was again voted the league's most valuable player in 1966, 1967, 1968, and 1972. His Philadelphia team won the league championship in the 1966–1967 season, and in the 1971–1972 season he led the Lakers to another championship, setting a record along the way for most consecutive games won. His yearly salary of roughly $500,000 made him one of the highest paid athletes in U.S. history.

Champlain, Samuel de (1567?–1635), explorer and colonial official. Born about 1567 in Brouage (now Hiers-Brouage), France, on the Bay of Biscay, Champlain was bred to the sea from youth. He fought in the French religious wars under Henry of Navarre (Henry IV) from 1589 to 1598; in the latter year he entered the service of Spain and was given command of a ship bound for the West Indies and Central America. He returned to France in 1601 and two years later was appointed by the king to an expedition to New France, in North America, under Aymar de Chatte, lieutenant general of the province. On completing the Atlantic crossing he voyaged up the St. Lawrence River as far as the Lachine Rapids at present-day Montreal and noted the suitability of the region for settlement. Returning to France in 1603, he published a report entitled *Les Sauvages*. With the Sieur de Monts, successor to Chatte, Champlain returned to New France in 1604, founding a colony at Port Royal (later Annapolis Royal), Nova Scotia, in 1605, and exploring the coast as far south as Cape Cod. On this survey voyage he carefully charted the Maine coast, traveled up the

Penobscot River to the present site of Bangor, and named Mount Desert Island. He returned to France in 1607 and, securing permission to found a colony on the St. Lawrence, set out again in 1608. On July 3 of that year he founded Quebec, the first permanent European settlement in Canada (Port Royal was destroyed by the British in 1613). He established close relations with the Algonkians and the Huron and, accompanying a party of Huron across the St. Lawrence in 1609, discovered Lake Champlain. Near there he aided the Huron in a battle with the Iroquois, thus laying the basis of the pattern of Indian alliances with, or hatred toward, the French and British that persisted for a century. After a visit to France in 1610 he founded a trading post and garrison at Mount Royal (now Montreal) in 1611 and the following year was appointed commandant of New France. A report that the Ottawa River led to the "sea of the North" induced him to follow it in 1613 as far as Allumette Island; on the trip he lost his astrolabe, and it lay preserved until a farmer plowed it up more than 250 years after. In 1615 he again followed the Ottawa and by way of Lake Nipissing and the French River reached Georgian Bay and the home of the Huron. He was wounded in another encounter with Iroquois in October; after wintering with the Huron he returned to Quebec in 1616. After four years in France he returned to Canada in 1620. On a visit to France in 1625 he aroused enthusiasm for New France in Cardinal Richelieu and in 1628 was named by him one of the "One Hundred Associates" charged with promoting and governing the province. In 1629 Quebec was captured by a British expedition and Champlain was taken to England. During his exile he published his *Voyages de la Nouvelle France occidentale*, 1632, a successor volume to his earlier *Les Voyages du Sieur de Champlain*, 1613, and *Voyages et découvertes faites en la Nouvelle-France*, 1619. The Quebec settlement was restored to France in 1632 and the next year Champlain returned as governor. He died there on Christmas Day, 1635.

Chandler, Albert Benjamin (1898–   ), public official and sports figure. Born on July 14, 1898, in Corydon, Kentucky, "Happy" Chandler was educated at Transylvania University, from which, after taking time out for service in the army during World War I, he graduated in 1921. He studied law at Harvard and, taking his law degree from the University of Kentucky in 1924, began practice in Versailles, Kentucky, later that year. With his appointment as master commissioner of the county circuit court in 1928 he embarked upon a colorful, if irregular, political career. Running on the Democratic ticket, he was elected to the legislature in 1929 and in 1931 became lieutenant governor. Toward the end of his term in the latter office he took advantage of a temporary absence of the governor to secure passage of a state primary-election law under whose provisions he promptly won the gubernatorial nomination. As governor of Kentucky from 1935

to 1939 he promoted an effective program of tax adjustments and public works. He lost the race for the Democratic senatorial nomination to the incumbent Alben Barkley in 1938, but in 1939, shortly before the end of his term as governor, he resigned from office in order to be appointed by his successor to complete an unexpired term in the Senate. Elected to a full term in 1942, he served only until 1945, when he resigned to become commissioner of professional baseball. After six controversial years in that post, during which he enacted much-needed recruitment reforms but also alienated a number of team owners and managers, he returned in 1951 to Kentucky and his law practice. In 1955 he bucked the regular Democratic establishment of the state, waged a flamboyant primary campaign, and was again elected governor. Chandler again conducted an effective administration, working with particular effect to smooth the process of racial integration in the schools. In 1956 he sought unsuccessfully the Democratic presidential nomination as Kentucky's favorite-son candidate. On leaving office in 1959 he continued his interest in politics, entering gubernatorial primaries in 1963 and 1971, and his connection with sports, serving from 1965 as commissioner of the Continental Football League.

Chandler, Charles Frederick (1836–1925), chemist. Born in Lancaster, Massachusetts, on December 6, 1836, Chandler was educated at the Lawrence Scientific School of Harvard and at the universities of Berlin and Göttingen, taking his Ph.D. from Göttingen in 1856. After working as a janitor while awaiting a faculty opening, he became professor of chemistry at Union College, Schenectady, New York, in 1857 and also taught geology and mineralogy. In 1864 he was invited to join in the organization of the Columbia School of Mines and from that year until 1897 was dean of the school as well as professor of chemistry at Columbia. To these duties he added teaching, at first without remuneration, in the New York College of Pharmacy, of which he was also later president; from 1872 he taught in the College of Physicians and Surgeons as well. He had been a consultant to the New York City Metropolitan Board of Health for seven years when in 1873 he was appointed its president. During 11 years in that position he investigated a wide range of public-health problems and made significant progress in pioneer efforts to allay the dangers arising from milk adulteration, kerosine-lamp explosions, and the operations of gas companies and slaughterhouses. He promoted compulsory vaccination for children and invented the flushing water closet, which, in the public interest, he refused to patent. He was at the same time the leading consultant in the nation to the petroleum industry. In 1897 he served as dean of the faculty of science at Columbia University and continued to head the chemistry department until his retirement in 1910. Chandler died in Hartford, Connecticut, on August 25, 1925.

Chandler, Happy, *see* Chandler, Albert Benjamin

Chandler, Raymond Thornton (1888–1959), author. Born in Chicago on July 23, 1888, Chandler moved to England with his mother when he was nine and was educated there and in France and Germany. For a time he worked as a reporter and later contributed articles and reviews to various British periodicals. During World War I he served in the Canadian army and in 1919 returned to the United States. For several years he engaged in business pursuits and was an executive of several oil companies, but a growing interest in writing and the acceptance of his first story, "Blackmailers Don't Shoot," by *Black Mask* magazine in 1933 led him to turn to letters as a career. In 1939 he published his first book, *The Big Sleep,* and was immediately hailed by critics as a major new talent in the field of mystery writing. Belonging to the "hard-boiled" school of detective fiction, Chandler filled his books with realistic details of depravity and underworld life and carried off the whole enterprise with wit and literary skill. His detective, Philip Marlowe, was a complex, intriguing character, no mere solver of mysteries, who inhabited a world where hard-won victories were likely to turn out to be Pyrrhic. Subsequent books included *Farewell, My Lovely,* 1940; *The High Window,* 1942; *The Lady in the Lake,* 1943; *The Little Sister,* 1949; and three collections of stories—*Five Murderers,* 1944, *Five Sinister Characters,* 1945, and *Red Wind,* 1946. Several of Chandler's novels were made into motion pictures, notably *The Big Sleep,* 1946, starring Humphrey Bogart as Marlowe; and he wrote a number of film scripts and screenplays, including that for *The Blue Dahlia,* 1946. He published *The Long Goodbye* in 1954 and *Playback* in 1958, the latter appearing shortly before his death on March 26, 1959, in La Jolla, California.

Chaney, Lon (1883–1930), actor. Born on April 1, 1883, in Colorado Springs, Colorado, Chaney was the son of deaf-mute parents and thus early acquired ability in pantomime. He attended school for only a few years and then worked at various jobs, including that of a guide at Pike's Peak. He became interested in the theater and after working for a time as a stagehand he joined his older brother, a theater manager, in writing and producing *The Little Tycoon,* in which he also made his first appearance on stage. Chaney performed in vaudeville for some years and eventually began to get jobs as an extra in Hollywood movies. He directed a few Westerns and then won a role in *Hell Morgan's Girl* in 1917. Two years later he appeared in *The Miracle Man* in the first of his characteristic monster roles. Combining with his adept use of pantomime a mastery of the art of makeup, he created a sensational Quasimodo for the 1923 film of *The Hunchback of Notre Dame;* he followed with equally strong appearances in *The Phantom of the Opera,* 1925; *The Road to Mandalay,* 1926; *Mr. Wu,* 1927; *Laugh, Clown,* *Laugh,* 1928; and others. Known as "the man of a thousand faces," he was acknowledged as the leading authority on screen makeup and contributed the article on the subject to the *Encyclopaedia Britannica.* His only speaking role in a film was as a ventriloquist in *The Unholy Three* in 1930. An intensely private man, he never allowed himself to be interviewed or even recognized in public. Chaney died in Los Angeles on August 26, 1930.

Chang and Eng (1811–1874), congenitally united twins. Born in May 1811 in Meklong (now Samut Songkhram), Thailand (Siam), Chang and Eng were of mixed Siamese and Chinese origin. At birth they were found to be joined at the waist by a short cartilaginous tubular structure through which they shared liver tissue and hepatic circulation. They supported themselves in various ways after their father's death and were engaged in a duck and egg business when they were discovered by an Englishman in 1824. In 1829 they were brought to the United States and displayed to the public, ostensibly as an educational exhibit. For the next several years they toured widely in America and Great Britain, creating a sensation wherever they appeared and earning for their owner and later for themselves a considerable income. Their billing as "the Siamese Twins" gave rise to a term that was later used to describe all such unseparated twins. They eventually settled on a farm in North Carolina and became naturalized citizens, adopting the surname Bunker; they married sisters in 1843 and had between them 19 children. In later years they quarreled often and Chang took to drink. The loss of their slaves and much of their property after the Civil War forced them out of retirement for a time. At Mount Airy, North Carolina, during the night of January 16–17, 1874, they died, Chang first and Eng within three or four hours.

Channing, Edward (1856–1931), historian. Born in Dorchester, Massachusetts, on June 15, 1856, Channing was the son of William Ellery Channing. He survived a frail childhood to enter Harvard, where he was strongly influenced by Henry Adams and from which he took his B.A. in 1878 and his Ph.D in 1880. After a year of European travel he returned to Cambridge, Massachusetts, and occupied himself with various writing tasks while he sought a position in the Harvard history department. In 1883 he began teaching occasional classes and holding informal seminars and soon, encouraged and recommended by such professionals as Herbert B. Adams and Justin Winsor, won an assistant professorship. He was promoted to full professor in 1897 and was named McLean Professor of Ancient and Modern History in 1913. He retired in 1929. A caustic and demanding teacher, he nevertheless attracted to his courses large numbers of students, including many who were later famous in historical scholarship and public affairs. Intensely devoted to his work, he had little interest in anything but his projected history of the United States, planned as the product solely of his own labor. Although he did write a number of other books—among them *English History for American Readers*, 1893, with Thomas W. S. Higginson; *The United States of America, 1765–1865*, 1896; and *A Students' History of the United States*, 1898—they were largely by way of preparation for what came to be called among his friends "the Great Work." Backed by a vast amount of original research and imbued with Channing's iconoclastic approach to history, the first volume of his *History of the United States*, entitled *The Planting of a Nation in the New World, 1000–1660*, appeared at last in 1905. By 1925 five more volumes had been published, bringing the *History* up to the Civil War. The sixth volume, *The War for Southern Independence*, was awarded a Pulitzer Prize. Channing tended to emphasize, in contrast to those who held the generally prevailing views of American history, the forces of union and urbanization over those of particularism and the frontier, and he was strongly opinionated in outlook, all of which added to the monumental stature of the *History*. While at work on the seventh volume he died in Cambridge on January 7, 1931.

Channing, William Ellery (1780–1842), religious leader. Born on April 7, 1780, in Newport, Rhode Island, Channing was related to several of New England's leading families. After graduating from Harvard in 1798 he began and quickly abandoned the study of theology and then accepted a position as household tutor to a family in Richmond, Virginia. The experiences of a year and a half in the South proved decisive in many ways: his first-hand observations of slavery confirmed him in his opposition to that institution, which he came to see as detrimental to slave and master alike; at the same time he conceived a firm respect for the integrity of the slaveholder, a view that served to temper his later abolitionist writings. Also during his residence in Virginia he acquired certain ascetic habits that wrought permanent damage to his health. On his return to Newport he resumed his theological studies with new fervor and early in 1802 he returned to Harvard. He had already filled several pulpits around Boston and acquired a reputation as a preacher of remarkable power when, in June 1803, he was installed as minister of the Federal Street (Congregational) Church in Boston; he remained in that position for the rest of his life. The first decade or so of his ministry was a quiet period, marked mainly by his growing popularity as a clergyman of broadly liberal sympathies and deep human understanding. By 1815, however, the quiet was broken by the outbreak of a heated theological controversy between Calvinist conservatives and those whom they viewed as heretics. Because of his large personal following and the fame of his published sermons and lectures, Channing found himself, quite against his will, looked to as the spokesman and champion of the liberal movement. He long resisted the label "Uni-

tarian," fearing its use to erect yet another rigid orthodoxy, but by 1819 he had acquiesced in the name and in the mantle of leadership thrust upon him. In that year he delivered a sermon entitled "Unitarian Christianity" at the ordination of Jared Sparks in Baltimore, and the following year he published in the *Christian Disciple* (later renamed the *Christian Examiner*) an epochal article, "The Moral Argument Against Calvinism," in which he set forth clearly the substance of Unitarianism as "a rational and amiable system, against which no man's understanding, or conscience, or charity, or piety revolts." His faith, which retained the mystical elements of Christianity while insisting on a place for human reason, became to a great extent that of intellectual New England over the next generation; Ralph Waldo Emerson, Henry Wadsworth Longfellow, and Oliver Wendell Holmes, among others, all owed a significant part of their breadth and humaneness to their experience of "Channing Unitarianism." The American Unitarian Association, organized in 1825, was a direct outgrowth of a conference of liberal ministers convened by Channing five years earlier. Much of his limited energy in his last decades he devoted to writing, producing a steady stream of sermons, essays, and reviews for periodicals on a variety of topics—theology, temperance, abolitionism, pacifism—and publishing such books as *Remarks on a National Literature*, 1830; *Slavery*, 1835; *The Abolitionist*, 1836; and *Duty of the Free States*, 1842. Channing died in Bennington, Vermont, on October 2, 1842. He was elected to the Hall of Fame in 1900.

Chanute, Octave (1832–1910), engineer and airman. Born in Paris on February 18, 1832, Chanute emigrated with his parents to the United States in 1838, settling in New York City. After 1853 he gained prominence as a civil engineer and a builder of railroads and railroad bridges. In 1867–1868 he supervised the construction of the first bridge across the Missouri River at Kansas City; he was later a consulting engineer in private practice. In 1886, inspired by the earlier experiments of Otto Lilienthal and others in Europe, Chanute began a rigorous study of aerodynamics; he established a camp on the dunes of the Illinois shore of Lake Michigan near Chicago and, although he was already past sixty, made some 2000 glider flights. Always methodical and scrupulous as to detailed records, he developed a number of improved glider designs as a result of his studies and flights. Wilbur and Orville Wright acknowledged their debt to Chanute's data and designs, and he made several visits to their Kitty Hawk camp prior to their successful powered-aircraft flight of 1903. In 1894 he wrote *Progress in Flying Machines*. He died in Chicago on November 23, 1910.

Chaplin, Charles Spencer (1889–1977), motion-picture actor, director, and producer. Born in London on April 16, 1889, the son of music-hall performers, Charlie Chaplin began his career at the age of seven as a member of a dance troupe. He was soon left on his own and grew up in poverty, shunted from one drab institution to another and sometimes living in the streets. At seventeen he joined the Fred Karno company; playing in New York in 1912, he was discovered by Mack Sennett of the Keystone Company and the next year was signed by that studio for $150 a week. By the time of his second movie, *Kid Auto Races at Venice*, 1914, he had hit upon the costume—baggy trousers borrowed from Fatty Arbuckle, outsized shoes, tight frock coat, derby hat, cane, and false mustache—in which, called variously Charlie the Tramp and the "Little Fellow" he rose to stardom and wealth. A new contract with Essanay Studios in 1915 brought him $1,250 a week; Mutual Pictures gave him $10,000 a week and a $150,000 bonus in 1916; and in 1917 the First National Exhibitors' Circuit paid him a flat million dollars for eight films. *The Tramp* in 1915 was his first experiment in mixing pathos with comedy in the figure of the Little Fellow; as the character developed through *Easy Street*, 1917; *Shoulder Arms*, 1918; *The Kid*, 1921; *The Pilgrim*, 1923; *The Gold Rush*, 1925; and *City Lights*, 1931, he seemed to mellow, losing his early pugnacity and becoming more a representative of the harassed and bewildered victims of circumstance everywhere. These movies enjoyed phenomenal success throughout the world and Chaplin was hailed as a comic genus. In 1918 he began to produce his own films and a year later, with D. W. Griffith, Mary Pickford, and Douglas Fairbanks, he formed the United Artists company to bolster his and their independence. With *Modern Times* in 1936 he extended the scope of the social comment that had been growing in his films; in *The Great Dictator*, 1940, his first talking film, he appeared both as the Tramp and as a caricature of Adolf Hitler. The Little Fellow did not long survive the coming of the talkies, and in the 1940s Chaplin found himself more and more under attack by sundry groups for his presumed personal and political beliefs and for his never having become an American citizen. His personal life—including four marriages, the last to Oona, the daughter of Eugene O'Neill, and a paternity suit in 1944— was exploited in newspaper headlines; *Monsieur Verdoux*, a 1947 version of the Bluebeard story, added fuel to the fire because of its overt attack on the "morality" of the capitalist system, and in 1952 he went into self-imposed exile in Switzerland. The Tramp reappeared for the last time in 1953 in the semiautobiographical *Limelight*. In 1957 Chaplin produced *A King in New York*, a satire on various aspects of American life, and in 1966 produced and directed *A Countess from Hong Kong*. In 1972 he returned triumphantly to the United States to receive a special, if belated, Academy Award for his unique contributions to the cinematic art. Chaplin was knighted by Queen Elizabeth II in 1975. He died at his home in Corsier-sur-Vevey, Switzerland, on December 25, 1977.

Chapman, Frank Michler (1864–1945), ornithologist. Born on June 12, 1864, in Englewood, New Jersey, Chapman did not continue his formal education beyond the secondary level, but his own studies in natural history led to an assistantship at the American Museum of Natural History in New York City in 1887. The following year he became assistant curator of ornithology and mammalogy, advancing to associate curator in 1901. For the museum he developed the exhibits of habitat bird groups and seasonal birds, and he traveled widely throughout the temperate and tropical regions of the Americas, collecting, photographing, and studying birds in their natural surroundings. His *Handbook of Birds of Eastern North America*, 1895, was the first of a series of highly popular books that did much to spread interest in bird study; he published also *Guide to the Study of Our Common Birds*, 1897; *Bird Studies with a Camera*, 1900; *A Color Key to North American Birds*, 1903; *The Warblers of North America*, 1907; and *Our Winter Birds*, 1918. His more technical works, dealing largely with the birds of South America, included *The Travels of Birds*, 1916; *The Distribution of Bird Life in Colombia*, 1917; *Birds of the Urubamba Valley, Peru*, 1921; and *The Distribution of Bird Life in Ecuador*, 1926. Chapman also wrote several books about his adventures in the field, including *Camps and Cruises of an Ornithologist*, 1908; *My Tropical Air Castle*, 1929; and *Autobiography of a Bird-Lover*, 1933. In 1899 he founded *Bird-Lore* magazine (later *Audubon* magazine) and remained its editor until 1935. From 1908 until his retirement in 1942 he was curator of ornithology at the museum. President of the American Ornithologists' Union from 1911 to 1914 and vice-president of the Explorers' Club from 1910 to 1918, Chapman was the recipient of numerous honors and awards. He died in New York City on November 15, 1945.

Chapman, John (1774–1845), "Johnny Appleseed," frontiersman. Born on September 26, 1774, in Leominster, Massachusetts, Chapman left no record of his early life and virtually nothing is known of him before his appearance in Pennsylvania around 1800. From the apple orchards and cider presses of that state he carried seeds into Ohio and, according to legend, planted and tended a trail of seedling orchards along the line of the coming migration of settlers into the western territory. During the years he spent in Ohio and the neighboring regions a great number of stories grew up about him, only a few of them at all verifiable, which were passed on as an oral tradition for decades. He was eccentric in dress, his taste running to a tin plate for a hat, and seems to have been also a religious mystic and a Swedenborgian missionary. Many of the anecdotes concerning him involve acts of extraordinary kindness and generosity to men and animals; in addition he is credited with the more common legendary attributes of great courage and endurance. During the War of 1812 he seems to have set out alone to warn backwoods settlements of the fall of Detroit and the imminence of Indian attacks. By 1828 Chapman had carried his apple orchards as far as Indiana, and he remained there until his death near Fort Wayne in March 1845.

Chapman, John Jay (1862–1933), author. Born in New York City on March 2, 1862, Chapman graduated from Harvard in 1884 and after traveling in Europe entered the Harvard Law School. He had been intensely religious from childhood and was given to extremes in religious practice; in 1887, as penance for having beaten a man for being too attentive to a woman companion, he thrust his left hand into a coal fire and sustained burns that necessitated amputation (he married the woman two years later; their son, Victor Chapman, was the first American aviator killed in World War I). Admitted to the bar in 1888, he practiced for ten years in New York City and was active in reformist political movements; from his experiences he drew two books, *Causes and Consequences*, 1898, and *Practical Agitation*, 1900. In 1900 he suffered a breakdown from which he was two years in recovering and thereafter devoted himself to writing. Much of his large literary output was polemical or crusading in purpose. His interests were wide and his tastes markedly aristocratic, with the result that his writings were fascinating but attracted only a small audience. In 1898 he had published *Emerson and Other Essays*, the first of his characteristic volumes of miscellaneous works; there followed *Learning and Other Essays*, 1910; *Neptune's Isle*, 1912; *William Lloyd Garrison*, 1913, only in part a biography; *Memories and Milestones*, 1915; *Notes on Religion*, 1915; *Greek Genius and Other Essays*, 1915; *A Glance Toward Shakespeare*, 1922; *Letters and Religion*, 1924; *Dante*, 1927; *New Horizons in American Life*, 1932; and others. He also wrote verse—he published *Songs and Other Poems*, 1919—and several verse plays, including the comedy *A Sausage from Bologna*, 1909, and *The Treason and Death of Benedict Arnold*, 1910. Extravagant in expression and gesture, Chapman was something of an anachronism and more than a little eccentric. In 1912, on the anniversary of the lynching of a Negro in Coatesville, Pennsylvania, he traveled there and held a public memorial service, delivering a scathing address to a nearly empty auditorium. He died in Poughkeepsie, New York, on November 4, 1933.

Chase, Philander (1775–1852), religious leader. Born in Cornish, New Hampshire, on December 14, 1775, Chase graduated from Dartmouth College in 1795, by which time he had converted from Congregationalism to Episcopalianism. He studied for the ministry in Albany, New York, where he was ordained a deacon in 1798 and a priest in 1799. From that year until 1805 he was rector of a church in Poughkeepsie; he then transferred to New Orleans, becoming the first resident Protestant minister in that city. In 1811 he was called to a church in Hartford, Connecti-

cut, where he remained for six years. He was moved to take up missionary work in frontier Ohio in 1817 and with great energy but no regular financial support he set about establishing a large number of parishes there; the following year a diocese was organized and Chase was elected bishop, receiving consecration in Philadelphia in 1819. During 1821–1822 he served also as president of Cincinnati College. Becoming convinced that the spiritual needs of the frontier could best be filled by an American clergy, he traveled to England to raise funds for the founding of a seminary in Ohio and returned to establish a college and a town in 1824, naming them for two of his principal benefactors, the college for Lord Kenyon and the town for Lord Gambier. In 1831, following lengthy disagreements with the clergy and the faculty under his jurisdiction, he resigned the bishopric; for a time he remained in Ohio and later moved to Michigan. He was elected bishop of the newly organized diocese of Illinois in 1835 and quickly undertook to repeat his earlier work in Ohio, founding Jubilee College in 1838. He held the bishopric and the presidency of the college for the rest of his life, becoming also in 1843 presiding bishop of the Episcopal church. Chase died on September 20, 1852, at Robin's Nest, Illinois.

Chase, Salmon Portland (1808–1873), chief justice of the Supreme Court and public official. Born on January 13, 1808, in Cornish, New Hampshire, Chase attended Cincinnati College, an Episcopal school run by his uncle, Philander Chase, and graduated from Dartmouth in 1826. He was headmaster of a boys' school in Washington, D.C., having as pupils the sons of most of John Adams's cabinet members, and also read law with Attorney General William Wirt, being admitted to the bar in 1829. Settling in Cincinnati in 1830, he became deeply involved in antislavery activities, writing and lecturing on needed legal reforms. He also edited the three-volume *Statutes of Ohio*, 1833–1835. He subsequently gained prominence as a defense attorney in cases involving runaway slaves and was dubbed "attorney general for runaway Negroes." At first a Whig, he was active in the Liberty party in 1841 and helped organize the Free-Soil party in 1848, elevating the issue of slavery over all political concerns. Recognizing the need for major party support, he enlisted the Democrats as well as the Free-Soilers in the Ohio legislature to win a Senate seat in 1849. There he vigorously opposed the extension of slavery into the territories and unsuccessfully tried to block the Compromise of 1850. Rejecting the Kansas-Nebraska Bill, he wrote the 1854 "Appeal of the Independent Democrats," calling for bans on slavery to be written into federal law; failing in this, he proposed an amendment to the bill that would have allowed residents of a territory to decide whether or not to adopt slavery, but that amendment was also rejected. He joined in the formation of the Republican party in 1854 and was elected the first Republican governor of Ohio in 1855, being reelected in 1859. He failed to win the Republican presidential nomination in 1856 and 1860; but, elected again to the Senate in 1860, he gave up his seat to accept President Abraham Lincoln's appointment as secretary of the treasury in 1861. In that post he undertook the monumental task of administering the country's finances during the Civil War, developing the national banking system in 1863 and reluctantly issuing "greenbacks" as legal tender to help pay for the war. His opinions on the conduct of the war and on reform measures were more aggressive than Lincoln's and led to the formation of an anti-Lincoln faction in the cabinet. He several times presented his resignation to Lincoln; it was finally and abruptly accepted in June 1864. Although put off by Chase's aspirations to the presidency, Lincoln appointed him chief justice of the Supreme Court in October 1864. Chase became an adviser to President Andrew Johnson after Lincoln was assassinated and although he presided over impeachment proceedings against Johnson, he refused to be made a tool of the Radical Republicans. In 1868 and 1872 he was again prominently mentioned for the presidential nomination, but he was at odds with President Ulysses S. Grant and with Congress on problems of Reconstruction and again his ambition was left unfulfilled. In *Ex parte Milligan*, 1866, he ruled that military trials of civilians were illegal unless civil courts were not operative or a region was under martial law. In *Mississippi* v. *Johnson* and *Georgia* v. *Stanton* he avoided political problems by approving the power of the president or of cabinet members to enforce the Reconstruction Acts. In *Cummings* v. *Missouri* and *Ex parte Garland*, both 1867, secession was declared invalid, and devices for preventing former Confederates from holding office were repudiated. In *Texas* v. *White*, 1869, Chase reinforced the view that the Union had never in legal reality been dissolved. In *Hepburn* v. *Griswold*, 1870, he held unconstitutional the Legal Tender Act of 1862 that he had administered while secretary of the treasury. When the Hepburn decision was reversed in 1871 he maintained, in a dissent, his 1870 opinion. In the 1873 Slaughterhouse Cases, in which the Fourteenth Amendment was first construed by the Supreme Court, Chase joined in the dissent from the restrictively narrow interpretation placed on the amendment. He died in New York City on May 7, 1873.

Chase, Samuel (1741–1811), justice of the Supreme Court. Born on April 17, 1741, in Somerset County, Maryland, Chase grew up from the age of two in Baltimore. He began the study of law in 1759 and two years later was admitted to the bar in Annapolis. In 1764 he was elected to the legislature, in which he held a seat for 20 years. An ardent adherent of the patriot cause, Chase was a leader in Maryland of the violent resistance to the Stamp Act by the Sons of Liberty. In 1774 he became a member of the Maryland Committee of Correspondence and was elected to the Continental Congress. He was chosen by that body to accompany Benjamin Franklin, Charles Carroll, and John Carroll to Canada in 1776 to seek a revolutionary alliance; upon the failure of the mission he quickly returned to Maryland to organize support for a political break with Great Britain and then rejoined Congress to sign the Declaration of Independence. Chase continued in Congress, serving on a great many committees, until 1778, when the revelation by Alexander Hamilton of Chase's attempt to corner the flour market forced him to retire for a time. He was returned in 1784 for a year. He attended the conferences that led up to the Constitutional Convention, but not the convention itself, and later voted against ratification of the Constitution by Maryland. In 1788 he became chief judge of the Baltimore criminal court and three years later was named chief judge of the Maryland general court, overriding by force of personality criticisms of his holding both positions simultaneously. President George Washington appointed Chase to the Supreme Court in 1796 and for five years he was the dominant presence on that bench, in particular contributing to the definition of due process in *Calder* v. *Bull* in 1798. Upon the appointment of John Marshall as chief justice in 1801 Chase's prominence was eclipsed. His pugnacious and partisan tendencies were aroused by sundry acts of the administration of Thomas Jefferson and, after a few lesser incidents, in 1803 he made while on his circuit an intemperate charge to a grand jury; Jefferson seized the opportunity and pressured the House of Representatives into voting impeachment in 1804. The charges were heard by the Senate in February 1805 and he was found not guilty. The case turned on the breadth of the phrase "high crimes and misdemeanors," and by construing the expression strictly the Senate upheld judicial independence; this also quite probably saved John Marshall, who as the Court's arch-Federalist would likely have been next in line for attack. Chase, the only Supreme Court justice ever to be impeached, continued on the bench until his death on June 19, 1811, in Baltimore.

Chase, Stuart (1888–), economist. Born on March 8, 1888, in Somersworth, New Hampshire, Chase grew up for the most part in Newton, Massachusetts. He attended the Massachusetts Institute of Technology and graduated from Harvard in 1910. For several years he worked in Boston as an accountant in partnership with his father, but in 1917 he took a staff position with the Federal Trade Commission (FTC) and aided in an investigation of the meat-packing industry. From 1920 to 1922 he was a researcher and writer for the Technical Alliance, a forerunner of the Technocracy movement, and in the latter year joined Labor Bureau, Incorporated, a New York City labor-research group with which he was associated until 1939. Chase's first major book, *The Tragedy of Waste*, appeared in 1925 and set the tone for many that followed in deploring the waste, not only of natural resources, but also of manpower and, under the impact of total mechanization, of the human spirit. Subsequently he published *Your Money's Worth*, 1927, with F. J. Schlink; *Men and Machines*, 1929; *Mexico: A Study of Two Americas*, 1931; *A New Deal*, 1932, the title of which was credited by some with inspiring the Democratic party's election slogan of that year; *The Economy of Abundance*, 1934; *Rich Land, Poor Land*, 1936; *The Tyranny of Words*, 1938; *Idle Money, Idle Men*, 1940; *A Primer of Economics*, 1941; *The Road We Are Traveling*, 1942; *The Proper Study of Mankind*, 1948; *The Power of Words*, 1954; *Guides to Straight Thinking*, 1956; *Some Things Worth Knowing*, 1958; *Live and Let Live*, 1960; *American Credos*, 1962; *Money to Grow On*, 1964; *The Most Probable World*, 1968; and *Danger—Man Talking*, 1969, among others. In his books and his frequent contributions to various periodicals, Chase advocated a tough-minded and scientific approach to such problems as poverty, conservation, and economic organization. During the late 1930s and early 1940s he served as a consultant to several New Deal agencies, and with F. J. Schlink he founded Consumers' Research, a pioneer independent testing bureau.

Chauncy, Charles (1705–1787), religious leader. Born in Boston on January 1, 1705, Chauncy graduated from Harvard in 1721. In 1727 he began his 60 years of service with the First (Congregational) Church in Boston. A man of keen intellect, he soon gained such prominence and influence that he was rivaled only by Jonathan Edwards. He was the recognized leader of theological liberalism in New England and as such came into constant conflict with the conservative Edwards. In a battle of pamphlets they debated the Great Awakening, Chauncy criticizing the emotionalism of the wave of revival in his *Seasonable Thoughts on the State of Religion in New England*, 1743, and other tracts. During the 1760s he devoted his energies to combating the threatened introduction of episcopacy into New England, and he was an ardent supporter of the patriot cause throughout the Revolution. Late in his life he openly embraced Universalism and again engaged in debate with Edwards, issuing in 1782 *Salvation for All Men Illustrated and Vindicated as a Scripture Doctrine* and, two years later, *The Mystery Hid from Ages . . . or the Salvation of All Men*. He died in Boston on February 10, 1787.

Chavez, Cesar Estrada (1927–   ), labor leader. Born on March 31, 1927, near Yuma, Arizona, to a family of Mexican-American migrant farm workers, Chavez went with them in the migration to California during the Depression. He worked in the fields from early childhood, received little formal schooling, and after serving in the navy during 1944–1945 returned to farm work in the region around Delano, California. In 1952 he joined the newly founded Community Service

Organization (CSO), a local grassroots political movement founded by community organizer Saul D. Alinsky; working primarily in voter registration and community relations, Chavez rose to general director of the CSO in 1958. He resigned in 1962 in order to devote his time to organizing the field workers into a union. Earlier efforts at unionization, in some of which he and his family participated, had all failed, leaving the migrant laborers—unprotected by federal law—in poverty and largely at the mercy of labor contractors and their seasonal employers in matters of wages, housing, working conditions, and education. Chavez established the National Farm Workers Association (NFWA) in 1962 and slowly built up a membership among workers in California's Imperial, Coachella, and San Joaquin valleys, all prime agricultural areas. In 1965, although it was still not in a position of strength, he led the NFWA into a strike begun by the parallel Agricultural Workers Organizing Committee of the AFL-CIO against the grape growers around Delano; in 1966 the two groups merged as the United Farm Workers Organizing Committee (UFWOC). With financial support from the AFL-CIO and the United Auto Workers, the UFWOC embarked on a long and difficult strike, employing tactics developed in the civil-rights movement as well as such traditional labor weapons as picketing. The growers of wine grapes soon agreed to union recognition and bargaining, but table-grape growers remained adamant. In 1968 Chavez, who undertook long fasts to dramatize the struggle, promoted the notion of a nationwide boycott of California grapes. The unorthodox and, to many, seemingly impossible idea was a startling success; as the boycott gathered momentum from the support of large segments of the public, sales of California grapes fell off precipitously across the country and "La Causa" (The Cause) assumed the air of an evangelical movement. Finally, in July 1970, the table-grape growers gave in. On the strength of that success, Chavez and the UFWOC moved on to organize workers in the truck-vegetable areas of California, calling for a national lettuce boycott, and later expanded their organizing efforts to include workers in other states as well.

Chayefsky, Paddy (1923–1981), playwright. Born on January 29, 1923, in the Bronx, New York City, Sidney Chayefsky acquired the permanent nickname "Paddy" while serving in the army following his graduation from City College of New York (CCNY) in 1943. He wrote his first theatrical piece, a "GI" musical entitled *No T.O. for Love*, in a hospital while recovering from injuries received in a land-mine explosion in Germany. Returning to New York City after World War II, he worked for a time in a printing shop and continued to write; from radio drama he moved to the new medium of television and in 1952 produced *Holiday Song*, which was sufficiently successful to be rebroadcast. In 1953 *Marty*, a love story of two shy and homely people, elicited a strong audience response as a television play; made into a movie in 1955, it won numerous awards, including three Academy Awards, one for Chayefsky's script. Chayefsky captured and held attention with his treatment both cynical and compassionate, of ordinary persons caught in the little dramas of everyday life; the scenes he created were those of the mass of people and his dialogue was that of the real world. He followed *Marty* with a television drama, *Bachelor Party*, which was made into a film in 1957; a Broadway play, *The Middle of the Night*, 1956, also appeared later in a movie version. For Broadway he wrote *The Tenth Man*, 1959; *Gideon*, 1961; and *The Passion of Josef D.*, 1964; for Hollywood he wrote and co-produced *The Goddess*, 1958, and *The Americanization of Emily*, 1964. He won Academy Awards for his screenplays for *Hospital*, 1971, and *Network*, 1976. He died on August 1, 1981, in New York City.

Chesnutt, Charles Waddell (1858–1932), lawyer and author. Born on June 20, 1858, in Cleveland, Chesnutt was the son of free Negro parents, originally from North Carolina, who took him to North Carolina after the Civil War. He received a sound education and became the principal of a school in Fayetteville, but the continuing lack of improvement in the lot of black people in the South led him in 1883 to move north, first briefly to New York City and then to Cleveland. There he worked as a journalist and a clerk-stenographer and took up the study of law; he was admitted to the bar in 1887 and in the same year a short story of his, "The Goophered Grapevine," was the first piece of writing by a Negro to be accepted for publication by the *Atlantic Monthly*. Chesnutt began a law practice that eventually took him to the front rank of the Cleveland bar and at the same time continued to write, contributing stories to a number of periodicals. In 1899 he published three books, a biography of Frederick Douglass and two collections of stories, *The Conjure Woman* and *The Wife of His Youth and Other Stories of the Color Line*. *The Conjure Woman* portrayed in an objective and realistic manner the lives of various Negro characters in North Carolina; *The Wife* explored with great subtlety the psychological dimensions of color prejudice, not only between black and white but also among blacks of different complexions. Chesnutt also wrote three novels, *The House Behind the Cedars*, 1900, *The Marrow of Tradition*, 1901, and *The Colonel's Dream*, 1905, on similar themes but with somewhat less success. After 1905 he ceased writing, but his stature as the leading black prose writer of the period before the Harlem Renaissance was secure. In 1928 he was awarded the Spingarn Medal. Chesnutt continued to live and practice law in Cleveland until his death there on November 15, 1932.

Chessman, Caryl Whittier (1921–1960), criminal. Born on May 27, 1921, in St. Joseph, Michigan, Chessman was an intelligent but often delinquent child and youth and at sixteen was sent to reform school for auto theft and burglary. A second period in reform school, again for auto theft, was followed by his arrest and conviction in California for robbery and assault. Sentenced to San Quentin prison in 1941, he escaped in 1943, was recaptured the following year, and in 1947 was released on parole. Early in 1948 he was arrested and accused of being the "red-light bandit" who had commited a series of lurid robbery-kidnap-rapes in lovers'-lane areas around Los Angeles. Soon after reentering San Quentin under sentence of death on the kidnaping charges, he began reading books on criminal law and legal procedure and undertook a complex legal defense by himself. In 1954 he published *Cell 2455 Death Row*, an autobiography that was a best seller and that attracted a number of opponents of capital punishment to his side. More appeals—eventually numbering more than 40 at various judicial levels, including the Supreme Court—and a slowly growing sentiment in his favor won him successive stays of execution. A second book, *Trial by Ordeal*, appeared in 1955 after the manuscript was smuggled out of the prison; two other books reached their publishers by similar means. Numerous prominent persons came to Chessman's defense, citing his lengthy residence on Death Row as already sufficient punishment and his books as evidence of rehabilitation; while he denied it constantly, however, there was never an appreciable doubt of his guilt. His became an international cause as well, and his eighth and last stay of execution was secured by the State Department in February 1960, when it was feared that violent demonstrations against his execution might disturb President Dwight D. Eisenhower's scheduled visit to Uruguay. Finally, all avenues of appeal exhausted, Chessman was executed in the San Quentin gas chamber on May 2, 1960, 12 years after his conviction.

Cheves, Langdon (1776–1857), public official and banker. Born in Abbeville District (now County), South Carolina, on September 17, 1776, Cheves moved with his father to Charleston in 1785. While working as a clerk in a mercantile house he acquired an education by his own efforts; he then took up the study of law and in 1797 was admitted to the bar. He quickly rose to the top of his profession in Charleston and from 1802 to 1809 was a member of the legislature. In 1809 he served as state attorney general and in 1810 was elected to the House of Representatives. He was one of the young Southern congressmen—among them Henry Clay and John C. Calhoun—who became known as the "War Hawks" because of their fervent nationalism and eagerness for war with England. In 1814 Cheves succeeded Clay as speaker of the House; at the expiration of his term in 1815 he left Congress and, declining appointment as secretary of the treasury, returned to his law practice in Charleston. In 1816 he was appointed a judge of the South Carolina court of appeals and held the office for three years. In

1819 he was elected to the board of directors of the Second Bank of the United States and two months later was chosen its president. The bank was in straitened circumstances, due largely to a heavy drain of currency to Southern and Western banks, and seemed to many beyond saving. Cheves immediately instituted a rigorous program of halting new loans and calling in old ones, and secured a $2 million loan from Europe; by 1822 the bank was sound and Cheves turned the presidency over to Nicholas Biddle. He was then appointed commissioner of claims arising under the treaty of Ghent. He lived and practiced in Philadelphia until 1826 and in Lancaster, Pennsylvania, until 1829, when he returned permanently to Charleston. There he carried on his practice, engaged in agriculture, and contributed occasionally to periodicals. He was a delegate to the Nashville Convention in 1850 and supported the notion of an independent Southern confederation. Cheves died in Columbia, South Carolina, on June 26, 1857.

Child, Francis James (1825–1896), philologist. Born in Boston on February 1, 1825, Child graduated from Harvard in 1846 and remained at the college as a tutor for three years. His interest in philology led him to undertake further studies at the universities of Berlin and Göttingen during 1849–1851 and in the latter year he was appointed Boylston Professor of Rhetoric, Oratory, and Elocution at Harvard. His first major published work was a five-volume edition of the *Poetical Works of Edmund Spenser*, 1855, which was for some 50 years the standard. In 1863 he wrote a pioneering study of the versification and language of Chaucer for the *Memoirs of the American Academy of Arts and Sciences* and ten years later published a similar piece on the language of John Gower in the same journal. His greatest work, however, began with his eight-volume collection, *English and Scottish Ballads*, 1857–1858, the largest such work to date; from it grew, through years of accumulating manuscripts and painstakingly seeking sources in many other languages, his definitive *English and Scottish Popular Ballads*, 1883–1898, first issued in ten parts and later in five volumes. The collection, monumental both in scope and in depth of research, remains the standard source book in the field. Child became professor of English at Harvard in 1876 and was an influential and admired teacher and scholar until his death in Boston on September 11, 1896.

Child, Lydia Maria (1802–1880), author and social reformer. Born on February 11, 1802, in Medford, Massachusetts, into an abolitionist family, Lydia Maria Francis spent one year in a seminary and was primarily influenced in her education by her brother, a Unitarian clergyman and later a professor at the Harvard Divinity School. Her social position could have sheltered her from social ills, but her keen observation of people and conditions led her into humanitarian work. Her first literary ventures, *Hobomok*, 1824, describing

early Salem and Plymouth life, and *The Rebels*, 1825, describing pre-Revolutionary Boston, were received not for their creativity, but for their interest as re-creations of real life. She also produced several practical volumes, including *The Frugal Housewife*, which went through 21 editions within a decade of its first appearance in 1829, and *The Mother's Book*, 1831. In 1826 she founded the nation's first monthly magazine for children, the *Juvenile Miscellany*. But this venture terminated in 1833, when she and David Lee Child, whom she had recently married, published *An Appeal in Favor of That Class of Americans Called Africans*, which was considered an outrageous abolitionist document because it contained a proposal to educate Negroes. The *Appeal* also won support; it converted some advocates of slavery to abolitionism, and brought about a new awareness of the issue among groups that previously had ignored it. From 1840 to 1844 she and her husband edited the *National Anti-Slavery Standard*, a weekly newspaper published in New York City. In 1852 they settled permanently on a farm in Wayland, Massachusetts, contributing liberally, from a small income, to the abolitionist movement. During this time Mrs. Child wrote books on a number of subjects, including religion, history, and feminism, and spoke out firmly against capital punishment. Having persevered for many years in challenging her contemporaries with difficult questions on social injustice, she died in Wayland on October 20, 1880.

Chisholm, Jesse (1806?–1868?), frontiersman. Born probably about 1806, Chisholm was of mixed Scottish and Cherokee origin. Virtually nothing is known of him except that for some time prior to his death he carried on trading operations from the Mexican border to Abilene, Kansas, following a customary route along which he may have guided an army detachment at one time. By 1868, about the time it is believed he died, Abilene was firmly established as the northern terminus of the great cattle drives coming north from Texas. The trail followed by the herds, known from the beginning of the drives as the Chisholm Trail, closely paralleled the 98th meridian. It became the most famed of the cattle trails, celebrated in Western legend and song. By 1875 the extension of the Atchison, Topeka, and Santa Fe Railroad to Dodge City, Kansas, had shifted the drives westward to the Western Trail; the Chisholm Trail regained importance in 1880 with the building of a new railhead in Caldwell, Kansas, but within a few years the era of the great cattle drives ended and the trail passed into history.

Chisum, John Simpson (1824–1884), frontiersman and cattle rancher. Born in Hardeman County, Tennessee, on August 15, 1824, Chisum moved with his family to Texas in 1837. He worked at various jobs in his youth, including contracting, and for a time was clerk of Lamar County. He began cattle ranching in 1854 in northeastern

Texas, enjoyed considerable success, and began moving his operations progressively westward. In 1866 he drove a herd into New Mexico and sold it to the army. A pioneer in bringing cattle raising to New Mexico, in subsequent years he sold herds to Charles Goodnight, who then drove them up the Goodnight-Loving Trail to the Colorado and Wyoming mining districts. By 1873 Chisum had established himself permanently at South Spring, near Roswell, New Mexico. Five years later one of the most famous of the Western cattle wars erupted in Lincoln County; whether Chisum participated in the "Lincoln County War" is disputed, but most of his associates were prominently involved. According to some sources it was Chisum who hired William H. Bonney as a gunman; it is known that when Bonney went on to infamy as Billy the Kid, Chisum led the drive for restoring law and order to New Mexico and played a major role in 1880 in securing the services of Sheriff Pat F. Garrett, who shortly thereafter killed Billy. At his peak Chisum owned a herd that was estimated to number as many as 100,000 head; it is almost certain that he was the largest cattle owner in the country and therefore probably in the world, and he was widely known as "the cattle king." He died on December 23, 1884, in Eureka Springs, Arkansas. The name of the famous Chisholm Trail has often been incorrectly thought to be derived from his.

Choate, Joseph Hodges (1832–1917), lawyer and diplomat. Born on January 24, 1832, in Salem, Massachusetts, Choate was a cousin of Rufus Choate. Graduating from Harvard in 1852, and from Harvard Law School in 1854, he was admitted to the bar in Massachusetts in 1855 and in New York in 1856. His lifetime association with the New York law firm of Butler, Evarts and Southmayd began in 1856 and three years later he became a partner. He did important legal work on the wills of Cornelius Vanderbilt and Samuel J. Tilden, and in connection with the Standard Oil antitrust case, the Chinese Exclusion acts, admiralty actions such as the *Republic* steamship case, railroad suits, and arguments before the Supreme Court, including the case of *Pollock* v. *Farmers' Loan and Trust Co.,* 1895, in which he established the unconstitutionality of the 1894 income-tax law. A Republican in politics, he delivered major speeches for party candidates. His efforts in forming the Committee of Seventy in 1871 to investigate graft in the city's finances led to the disclosure and destruction of the Tweed Ring. He was a famous after-dinner speaker, his only rival being Chauncey M. Depew. At the age of sixty-seven he was appointed U.S. ambassador to Great Britain, a post in which he served for six years, settling the Alaskan boundary dispute and securing the abrogation of the 1850 Clayton-Bulwer Treaty by means of the 1901 Hay-Pauncefote Treaty, which paved the way for U.S. construction of the Panama Canal. He was head of the U.S. delegation to the Second Hague Conference of 1907. He presided over a number of cultural and humanitarian organizations, including the New York State Charities Aid Association for the Blind, and the American Society for the Judicial Settlement of International Disputes. He died in New York City on May 14, 1917.

Choate, Rufus (1799–1859), lawyer and public official. Born on October 1, 1799, in Essex, Massachusetts, Choate was educated at Dartmouth and graduated at the head of his class in 1819. He studied law and was admitted to the bar in 1822. For the rest of his life his primary interest was the practice of law, particularly trial law, and he became the leading trial advocate of his time. He engaged actively in politics, but with reluctance; he served in the state legislature briefly and in 1830 was elected to the House of Representatives. He resigned from his second term in Congress in order to return to his practice, although he continued to work for the Whig cause in Massachusetts. In 1841 Choate assumed Daniel Webster's vacated seat in the Senate and completed the term. He declined opportunities to sit on both the state and federal supreme courts. In his politics he was a staunch and loyal Whig, and his great oratorical ability did much for the party during his brief periods of service. His last public position was as state attorney general in 1853–1854. Choate was conceded to be the leader of the Massachusetts bar after Webster's death; in criminal law he seems to have had no equal. In what was probably his most famous case, he successfully defended an accused murderer with a plea of somnambulism. He died in Halifax, Nova Scotia, while on his way to Europe, on July 13, 1859. He was elected to the Hall of Fame in 1915.

Chomsky, Noam (1928–   ), linguist. Born in Philadelphia on December 7, 1928, Avram Noam Chomsky graduated from the University of Pennsylvania in 1949, took his M.A. in 1951, and after a period of study at Harvard returned to Pennsylvania to take his Ph.D. in 1955. Later in that year he was appointed assistant professor of modern languages and linguistics at the Massachusetts Institute of Technology. In 1957 he published his first book, a development of his doctoral dissertation, entitled *Syntactic Structures,* in which he outlined a radically new linguistic theory. Against the dominant structuralist view, strongly behaviorist and descriptive in its approach to the phenomenon of language, he proposed that language stemmed from and was governed by certain innate and discoverable proclivities or logical structures in the mind and that a fundamental grammar, consisting of "transformational" rules, could be developed to account for the infinite variety of sentences possible in all languages. Such a "generative" grammar would produce, by means of specified transforms, any number of symbolically expressed sentences that could then be turned into actual language by a simple substitution of basic sounds for symbols. The theory, which Chomsky came to call "Cartesian," was strongly rationalistic and contained profound psychological and philosophical implications; it was also highly controversial and of far-reaching influence in the development of modern linguistics, prompting the formation of a new, major, and vocal school of thought. Chomsky's subsequent works included *Current Issues in Linguistic Theory*, 1964; *Aspects of the Theory of Syntax*, 1965; *Cartesian Linguistics*, 1966; *Language and Mind*, 1967; *Problems of Freedom and Knowledge*, 1971, and others. Chomsky advanced to associate professor at MIT in 1958, to full professor in 1961, and in 1966 was named Ferrari P. Ward Professor of Foreign Literatures and Linguistics. During the mid-1960s he emerged also as a prominent theoretician of the radical politics of the New Left and a leader in the movement against the Vietnam War and in support of draft-resisters; his essays on U.S. foreign, military, and political policies were collected in *American Power and the New Mandarins*, 1969, and *At War with Asia*, 1970.

Chopin, Kate O'Flaherty (1851–1904), author. Born in St. Louis on February 8, 1851, to a prominent family, Kate O'Flaherty received her education in a convent school, supplementing it with her own wide reading. In 1870 she married Oscar Chopin, with whom she lived in his native New Orleans and later on a plantation near Cloutiersville, Louisiana, until his death in 1882. Soon afterward Mrs. Chopin returned to St. Louis. She began writing of her experiences in the South and after an undistinguished first novel, *At Fault*, 1890, her powers developed rapidly. She became a regular contributor of stories to children's magazines and to the leading literary journals of the day and published two collections, *Bayou Folk*, 1894, and *A Night in Acadie*, 1897, which were quickly recognized as major additions to the local-color genre. Her lush descriptions of Louisiana scenes, her sympathetically realistic delineations of Creole and Cajun characters and society, and her finely wrought plots won her a lasting place in American literature. Her second full-length novel, *The Awakening*, 1899, proved too candid about its subject for many critics, however; their attacks on its portrayal of mixed marriage and other commonplaces of bayou life caused her to give up writing. Mrs. Chopin died in St. Louis on August 22, 1904.

Chouteau, Jean Pierre, see *under* Chouteau, René Auguste

Chouteau, Pierre (1789–1865), frontiersman. Born in St. Louis on January 19, 1789, Chouteau was the son of Jean Pierre Chouteau and was known variously as Pierre, Jr., and Cadet (second-born). He began working in his father's store at an early age and in 1809 briefly joined in the St. Louis Missouri Fur Company operations. He later went into business for himself and from 1813 to 1831 engaged in the Indian trade with his brother-in-law. In the latter year he joined Bernard Pratte & Company (later Pratte, Chouteau & Company), which was the Western agent for John Jacob Astor's American Fur Company. Chouteau bought out Astor's interests in 1834 and four years later the firm became Pierre Chouteau, Jr., & Company, which held a virtual monopoly on trade on the upper Missouri for many years thereafter. In 1831 he began operating the *Yellowstone*, the first steamboat on the upper Missouri; he was a passenger on its second voyage upriver from St. Louis the next year, when Fort Pierre, named in his honor, was formally established as a replacement for the earlier and very important Fort Tecumseh. (In 1880 Pierre, also named for him and later the capital of South Dakota, was founded across the river from Fort Pierre.) He gave generously of his services to scientific expeditions, government surveys, missionaries, and artists wishing to explore the West and was also of great help to the Indians of the region. His business interests multiplied to include an iron-mining company in Missouri, a railroad in Illinois, and other ventures, and for a time he directed his empire from New York City. A millionaire several times over, he died in St. Louis on September 6, 1865.

Chouteau, René Auguste (1749–1829), frontiersman and public official. Born in early September 1749 in New Orleans, Auguste Chouteau grew up in the home of Pierre Laclède, with whom his mother formed a liaison in 1757. With his patron he moved to Fort de Chartres in the Illinois country in 1763 and early the next year, on a site chosen by Laclède at the confluence of the Missouri and Mississippi rivers, Chouteau began constructing the trading post that grew to be St. Louis. There he was joined a few months later by Laclède, his mother, and his brother Jean Pierre Chouteau (1758–1849), known as Pierre, who had been born in New Orleans on October 10, 1758. Auguste continued as Laclède's chief lieutenant until Laclède's death in 1778; thereafter he was the principal citizen and businessman of the region. An important trading connection with the Osage Indians was formed and in 1794 the brothers were granted an eight-year monopoly of the trade, Pierre becoming the resident agent with the tribe. The monopoly passed to Manuel Lisa's company in 1802, whereupon Pierre induced the majority of the Osage to migrate to Oklahoma and there continued his trade with them. With the establishment of U.S. government authority in 1804 Lisa's monopoly was terminated and Pierre, appointed by President Thomas Jefferson U.S. agent to all tribes west of the Mississippi, regained his influence among the remaining Missouri Osage. At the same time Auguste was appointed a judge of the court of common pleas; in 1808 in St. Louis he became lieutenant colonel of the St. Louis militia (Pierre became captain, later major, upon organizing the militia's first cavalry troop), and the next year became president of the board of trustees of the newly incorporated town. In later years he served in numerous other public offices, including that of commissioner charged with negotiating treaties with several Indian tribes in 1815 and U.S. pension agent in 1819–1820, but his major importance was as financial backer of much of the expansion of business and trade in St. Louis. He died there on February 24, 1829. In 1809 Pierre and two of his sons had joined Lisa, the Chouteaus' former rival, William Clark, and others in organizing the St. Louis Missouri Fur Company, the first such company to wield great influence in the West; it had a virtual monopoly of the fur trade of the Missouri valley and the upper Missouri region until its dissolution in 1814. The government commissioned the company to return Chief Shahaka to his tribe, the Mandan, in 1809, and Pierre commanded a company of militia on the expedition. During its brief life the company conducted trapping expeditions to and beyond the limits of U.S. influence, to the Columbia River in the Northwest and to the Green River (Utah, Colorado, Wyoming) in Spanish territory. After 1814 Pierre Chouteau continued to operate a number of trading posts in the lower Missouri valley. He established himself on a large estate near St. Louis in 1820 and remained there, the leading citizen of the region, until his death on July 10, 1849. Two of his sons —Auguste Pierre Chouteau (1786–1838) and Pierre Chouteau (1789–1865)—extended the period of the family's preeminence in the development of St. Louis and the West to nearly a century.

Christy, Edwin P. (1815–1862), entertainer. Born in 1815 in Philadelphia, Christy led an obscure life until 1842, when he organized and appeared with a small song-and-dance act called the Virginia Minstrels in a theater in Buffalo, New York. The group soon changed its name to the Christy Minstrels and, while it was not the first minstrel troupe, it introduced new features into the show format that became permanent; among these were the use of variety acts, the semicircle of blackface musicians, and the comedy routines involving the end men, Tambo and Bones, and the whiteface master of ceremonies, Mr. Interlocutor, in the Christy shows invariably played by Christy himself. In 1846 the troupe made their New York City debut and the following year began a highly successful stay of a decade in Mechanics' Hall. Tours of other cities were also very well received and a visit to London established the popularity of the minstrel show there. Many of the songs used by Christry were written by Stephen C. Foster, and in 1851 Christy obtained the right to perform Foster's new songs before their publication; some of Foster's works actually first appeared under Christy's name. The form of the minstrel show changed little after Christy's conception became fixed; other troupes maintained it until minstrelsy declined in popularity in the 1880s. Christy retired a wealthy man in 1854, leaving the Christy Minstrels to carry on under George N. Harrington, who took the name Christy. In his later years he was beset by spells of extreme depression; at one such time he

jumped from a window in New York City and died on May 21, 1862.

Chrysler, Walter Percy (1875–1940), business leader. Born in Wamego, Kansas, on April 2, 1875, Chrysler decided against a college education in favor of an apprenticeship in the machine shops of the Union Pacific Railroad. Becoming an expert machinist, he worked for a succession of railroads in the West and in 1901 became roundhouse foreman for the Denver, Rio Grande & Western in Salt Lake City. Later, with the Chicago Great Western, he advanced to superintendent of motive power and in 1912, after two years with the American Locomotive Company in Pittsburgh, was the company's works manager. In that year, succumbing to both an enthusiasm for automobiles and an intuitive stroke of genius, he took a large cut in salary to become works manager for the Buick Motor Company division of General Motors, in Detroit. He quickly modernized Buick's operations, introduced efficiencies all along the line, and in 1916 became president of the division. Four years later, in a dispute with GM president William' C. Durant, he resigned. He returned to the industry in 1921 to oversee a complete reorganization of the Willys-Overland Company. A short time later he undertook a similar task for the Maxwell Motor Company, became president of the reorganized firm, and set about producing a new and innovative line of cars. In 1924 the new Chrysler car, featuring four-wheel hydraulic brakes, a high-compression engine, and other engineering improvements, was successfully exhibited and the next year the firm became the Chrysler Corporation. In 1928 the company purchased Dodge Brothers and soon began manufacturing De Soto and Plymouth cars as well as Dodge. In 1935 Chrysler retired from the presidency to become chairman of the board of the corporation, having built it into the second largest producer of automobiles in the country. Earlier, as a sideline, he had built the Chrysler Building in New York City, the tallest in the world upon its completion in 1929. In 1937 he published an autobiography, *Life of an American Workman.* He died at his Long Island estate in Great Neck, New York, on August 18, 1940.

Church, Benjamin (1734–1778), physician and Revolutionary spy. Born on August 24, 1734, in Newport, Rhode Island, Church graduated from Harvard in 1754. He took up medicine, studied for a time in London, and settled in Raynham, Massachusetts. A prolific writer, he contributed a number of patriotic essays to newspapers but also replied pseudonymously to them from the Tory side; he may have contributed to the Loyalist journal, the *Censor,* as well. He nonetheless served on Boston's Committee of Correspondence, of which John Adams was also a member. According to Paul Revere, Church was responsible for Governor Thomas Hutchinson's learning the details of a highly secret meeting of Whig leaders in 1774; he continued to hold the confidence of others, however, and was appointed a delegate to the Provincial Congress of Massachusetts in that year. He was present at the battle of Lexington and immediately afterward, on the pretext of seeking medical supplies, hurried to Boston; although he later claimed to have been taken prisoner, he voluntarily visited the British commander, Gen. Thomas Gage. In July 1775 he was named by the Continental Congress director and chief physician of the army hospital in Cambridge. In the same month he sent a coded letter to the commander of a British ship at Newport; the letter was intercepted and deciphered and in October Church was brought before a court-martial presided over by Gen. George Washington. Convicted of "holding criminal correspondence with the enemy," he was expelled by the Provincial Congress and kept under close watch until 1778, when he was allowed to embark on a ship bound for the West Indies. The ship was lost at sea.

Church, Frederick Edwin (1826–1900), painter. Born in Hartford, Connecticut, on May 4, 1826, Church early displayed an artistic bent and studied with a succession of teachers, in 1844 entering the household and studio of Thomas Cole. Thoroughly trained by the founder of the Hudson River School, he continued throughout his career to paint landscapes, although he had no tendency to mysticism or symbolism. He was particularly fascinated by grandeur in nature and after reading Alexander von Humboldt's descriptions of South America he traveled there twice, in 1853 and 1857, for inspiration. "The Falls of Tecemdama," 1954; "The Andes of Ecuador," 1855; the highly popular "Heart of the Andes," 1859; and "Cotopaxi," 1862, were among the paintings that resulted. In 1857 he produced "Niagara Falls," purchased by the Corcoran Gallery in Washington, D.C., and considered by many to be his masterpiece. A trip to Labrador led to "Icebergs," 1863, and "Aurora Borealis," 1865; visits to the West Indies, Europe, and the Middle East followed and moved him to paint "The Vale of St. Thomas," 1867; "The Parthenon," 1871; and "Jerusalem," 1870, among others. Church was extremely adept at rendering striking effects of light—in rainbows, mists, clouds, sunsets—and he had a flair for the dramatic that brought wide attention to his canvases, which commanded high prices. In 1877 an attack of rheumatism left his right arm useless; he carried on with his left until it, too, failed. For the last 20 years of his life he lived in quiet retirement at Olana, his spectacular home on the Hudson above New York City. He died there on April 7, 1900.

Ciardi, John Anthony (1916–   ), poet and critic. Born on June 24, 1916, in Boston, Ciardi grew up there and in nearby Medford. He was educated at Bates College, Tufts College (now University), from which he graduated with high honors in 1938, and the University of Michigan, where he took his M.A. in 1939. A year later

his first volume of poetry, *Homeward to America*, was well received by critics. He became an instructor in English at the University of Kansas City in the same year, remaining until 1942 and returning briefly in 1945 after service in the Army Air Force during World War II. In 1946 he moved to Harvard and the following year published *Other Skies*, which was praised for its clarity and strength. Ciardi was named Briggs Copeland Assistant Professor of English in 1948 and continued in that position until 1953, when he joined the faculty of Rutgers University; there he became professor of English in 1956. In 1955 he was appointed director of Middlebury College's annual Bread Loaf Writers' Conference, with which he had been associated since 1947. He continued to produce books of poems regularly and grew steadily in stature as a major contemporary poet; among them were *Live Another Day*, 1949; *From Time to Time*, 1951; *As If: Poems New and Selected*, 1955; *I Marry You: A Sheaf of Love Poems*, 1958; *In the Stoneworks*, 1961; *In Fact*, 1962; *Person to Person*, 1964; *This Strangest Everything*, 1966; and *The Lives of X*, 1971. He also wrote two widely used introductions to poetry for students, *How Does a Poem Mean?*, 1959, and *Poetry, a Closer Look*, 1963. In 1954 he published a distinguished translation of the *Inferno* of Dante's *Divine Comedy*, in 1961 completed the *Purgatorio*, and in 1971 published the *Paradiso*. *The Reason for the Pelican*, 1959, was his first book of verse for children; it was followed by *Scrappy the Pup*, 1960; *The Man Who Sang the Sillies*, 1961; *The Wish Tree*, 1962; *The King Who Saved Himself from Being Saved*, 1965, and *The Monster Den*, 1966, among others. In 1956 Ciardi became poetry editor for the *Saturday Review* and until 1972 conducted a regular column on various topics in that magazine. In 1961 he resigned his post at Rutgers to devote full time to his literary pursuits.

Clark, Alvan (1804–1887), astronomer and lens maker. Born on March 8, 1804, in Ashfield, Massachusetts, Clark attended a local school and until he was seventeen worked the family farm and mill. He taught himself engraving and followed that trade in various New England towns; later, settling in Boston, he became a successful portrait painter. One of his sons became interested in the making of telescope lenses; his own curiosity aroused, he began experimenting with the techniques involved and soon a new business, Alvan Clark & Sons, was organized in Cambridge. From the start the 6- and 8-inch lenses produced by the Clarks were of the highest optical quality and the resolution of some very close double stars during the testing process attracted the attention and then the patronage of astronomers both at home and abroad. Clark's other son, Alvan Graham Clark (1832–1897), born in Fall River, Massachusetts, on July 10, 1832, entered the firm at the age of twenty. In 1864, while trying out an 18-inch glass made for the Dearborn Observatory in Chicago (now at Northwestern University), he discovered the companion of the white dwarf star Sirius, for which he was honored by the French Academy of Sciences. The company produced the finest and largest telescope lenses of the day, among them the 26-inch lens for the U.S. Naval Observatory, Washington, D.C., in 1873, the 30-inch lens for the Pulkovo Observatory in Russia, and the 36-inch lens for the Lick Observatory, Mt. Hamilton, California, in 1887. Soon after completion of the Lick lens, and before it could be installed, the elder Clark died, on August 19, 1887. His son carried on the business and in 1897 completed construction of the 40-inch lens for the Yerkes Observatory of the University of Chicago, which remains the largest refracting telescope in the world. Just a few days after finishing the nerve-racking task of packing and transporting the great lens to its destination he died, on June 9, 1897, in Cambridge.

Clark, Alvan Graham (1832–1897), see under Clark, Alvan

Clark, Champ (1850–1921), public official and political leader. Born in Anderson County, Kentucky, on March 7, 1850, Clark was christened James Beauchamp but from an early age was known as Champ. He was educated at Kentucky University (now Transylvania College) and Bethany College (West Virginia), graduating from the latter in 1873. For a year he served as president of Marshall College, West Virginia's first normal school, then entered the Cincinnati Law School. In 1875 he moved to Kansas and the next year settled in Missouri, first at Louisiana, where he edited a newspaper and served as city attorney, and in 1880 at Bowling Green, where he thereafter maintained his permanent residence. He was Pike County prosecuting attorney from 1885 to 1889 and in the latter year was elected to the legislature. In 1892 he was elected as a Democrat to the House of Representatives; defeated for reelection in 1894, he was returned in 1896 to the seat that he held for the rest of his life. A noted debater and strongly independent in opinion, Clark was early a prominent member of his party and held memberships on the important and powerful ways and means and rules committees. In 1907 he became minority leader of the House and in that position three years later led the revolt of Democrats and insurgent Republicans against the tyrannical rule of Speaker Joseph G. ("Uncle Joe") Cannon. The next year Clark was elected speaker by the new Democratic majority. At the Democratic national convention in 1912 he was a leading contender for the presidential nomination; he led the field on the first 14 ballots but lost the nomination when William Jennings Bryan switched his support to Woodrow Wilson. He continued in the House as speaker, restoring to that office its lost prestige, until 1919, remaining at the same time a powerful voice in support of progressive causes. In 1919 the Democrats lost the speakership and

Clark became minority leader; the next year he was defeated for reelection. Just before the end of his final term in Congress he died, on March 2, 1921, in Washington, D.C.

Clark, George Rogers (1752–1818), frontier leader and soldier. Born near Charlottesville, Virginia, on November 19, 1752, Clark was an elder brother of William Clark. He received little formal education, but learned surveying from his grandfather and by the time of the Revolution was well known as an explorer in the western frontier region of Virginia, which is now Kentucky. His first military service came during Lord Dunmore's War against the Indians in 1774; soon after the Revolution broke out, he persuaded the Virginia legislature to provide for the protection of the western region and was made commander of frontier militia. With the further approval of the legislature he recruited a force of fewer than 200 men and set out in May 1778 to subdue the Indian allies of the British and to clear the Illinois territory of enemy forces. On July 4 he surprised and captured Kaskaskia; by August he had captured the outposts of Cahokia and Vincennes as well and had won the allegiance of the French settlers in the area. A force from the British stronghold at Detroit recaptured Vincennes in October but failed to maintain the initiative; after a daring and terrible midwinter forced march, he and his men retook the settlement in February 1779. The failure of Virgina to send reinforcements or supplies made his planned march on Detroit an impossibility, and for the rest of 1779 he remained at Fort Nelson, which he had built near what is now Louisville. From 1780, when he was appointed brigadier general, to 1782 he conducted several successful campaigns against the Shawnee and defended St. Louis against a British expedition. The Detroit campaign never materialized for lack of support, but Clark had conquered and held the Old Northwest (the Illinois country), and this was reflected, though not explicitly stated, in the terms of the peace made by the treaty of Paris in 1783. He and his men had received no pay for their services and he himself had advanced considerable sums of money to the cause; although a large tract of land was granted by Virginia to the "Illinois Regiment," Clark never received his due and found himself considerably in debt. He remained in the West as Indian commissioner and led his last military expedition against the Wabash tribes in 1786. In that same year James Wilkinson, secretly a Spanish agent, successfully conducted an intrigue against Clark, who was discredited and relieved of his post. During the next several years he became involved in a number of abortive Western military schemes initiated by the Spanish and French; he accepted commissions freely, apparently reserving his ultimate loyalty to the idea of Western expansion. He took refuge in St. Louis for a time in 1798 rather than surrender his French commission as a general. In 1799 he returned to Louisville and there he lived, except for a few years spent on the Indiana side of the Ohio, until his death on February 13, 1818.

Clark, James Beauchamp, see Clark, Champ

Clark, John Bates (1847–1938), economist. Born in Providence, Rhode Island, on January 26, 1847, Clark graduated from Amherst College in 1872. He did postgraduate work in economics at the universities of Heidelberg and Zurich, where he was strongly influenced by the current German vogue of approaching economics as a form of historical investigation rather than as a field of abstract theorizing. He began to teach economics and history at Carleton College in 1877; four years later he moved to Smith College, and in 1892 returned to Amherst, which had awarded him a Ph.D. two years earlier. In 1885 he helped organize the American Economic Association and in the same year published *The Philosophy of Wealth.* It showed German influence in its insistence on the study of actual economic behavior and its strong Christian Socialist tendencies. In 1895 he joined the faculty of Columbia University, where he remained until his retirement in 1923. His major work, *The Distribution of Wealth,* was published in 1899; it was a detailed logical analysis of economics that had a deep and lasting effect on American economic thought. It was followed by *Essentials of Economic Theory* in 1907 and *The Control of Trusts* in 1912. Clark was an active advocate of peace and from 1910 to 1923 worked with the Carnegie Endowment for International Peace, for which he instituted a comprehensive economic analysis of World War I. He died in New York City on March 21, 1938.

Clark, Kenneth Bancroft (1914–   ), psychologist. Born on July 24, 1914, in the Panama Canal Zone, Clark moved with his mother to New York City when he was five and grew up in Harlem, then in the process of becoming a black ghetto. He graduated from Howard University in 1935, received an M.S. the following year, and after a year of teaching there moved to Columbia University, where he took his Ph.D. in psychology in 1940. While teaching in 1940–1941 at the Hampton Institute he was also associated for two years with Gunnar Myrdal in the research into the role of the Negro in the United States that resulted in Myrdal's monumental study *An American Dilemma.* After a year with the Office of War Information (OWI) Clark joined the faculty of the College of the City of New York (now a part of the City University) in 1942. Four years later, with his wife, also a psychologist, he founded the Northside Testing and Consultation Center, later the Northside Center for Child Development, which offered a treatment program for emotionally disturbed children, especially those troubled by the conditions of ghetto life. In 1950 he published a report on the psychological effects of racial segregation in schools, demonstrating that it was detrimental to the educational and social progress of both black and white children; the report was promi-

nently cited in the 1954 Supreme Court ruling in *Brown* v. *Board of Education* that outlawed such segregation. He continued to concern himself deeply with the problem, working at various times with city and state educational authorities in efforts to improve ghetto schools and publishing *Prejudice and Your Child,* 1955. In 1960 Clark became the first black teacher to be appointed a tenured professor at City College; the next year he was awarded the Spingarn Medal by the National Association for the Advancement of Colored People (NAACP). In 1962 he led in founding Harlem Youth Opportunities Unlimited (HARYOU), a broad, locally administered program designed to supplement the educational facilities of Harlem and to combat the problem of unemployment among the young. HARYOU was later made a major part of the "war on poverty" of the administration of President Lyndon B. Johnson. Clark published *Dark Ghetto* in 1965, continued to serve as a consultant to many private and governmental bodies, and in 1966 became the first black member of the New York State Board of Regents.

Clark, Mark Wayne (1896–   ), soldier. Born on May 1, 1896, at Madison Barracks, New York, Clark was the son of an army officer. He graduated from West Point in 1917 and the following year was sent to France, where he took part in Allied actions in the Vosges Mountains, at St.-Mihiel, and on the Meuse–Argonne front. Promoted to captain in 1919, he returned to the United States and for 20 years served at a succession of posts and attended the Command and General Staff School and the Army War College, where he was also an instructor in 1940. In May 1942 Clark, then a major general, was named chief of staff of the army ground forces and two months later assumed command of all U.S. ground forces in Europe. After overseeing the organization of combat training in England he was assigned to the planning phase of the North African campaign. In negotiations highlighted by a dramatic secret trip to North Africa by submarine he secured the cooperation of the Free French forces in North Africa, a delicate diplomatic task, and served in the campaign itself as deputy to Gen. Dwight D. Eisenhower. In 1943, as a lieutenant general, he was appointed to command the U.S. 5th Army in the invasion of Italy. The Italian campaign involved some of the hardest fighting of the war, with bitter German resistance maintained all the way from the Salerno beachhead through Cassino and Anzio to Rome (taken in June 1944) and north to the Apennines. In December 1944 Clark became commander of the 15th Army Group; the following spring he was promoted to general and in June, after the surrender of Germany, he was appointed high commissioner and commander of U.S. forces in occupied Austria. In 1947 he returned to the United States, commanded the 6th Army and then the Army Field Forces, and in 1952 succeeded Gen. Matthew B. Ridgway as supreme commander of United Nations forces in the Korean War, retaining the post through the long and difficult period of negotiations at the end of the fighting; he signed the armistice for the UN in July 1953. Later that year he retired from the army. From 1954 to 1966 he was president of The Citadel (The Military College of South Carolina). Clark published two volumes of war memoirs, *Calculated Risk*, 1950, and *From the Danube to the Yalu*, 1954.

Clark, Tom Campbell (1899–1977), justice of the Supreme Court. Born in Dallas, Texas, on September 23, 1899, Clark attended the Virginia Military Institute for a year and then served in the army during World War I. He resumed his education at the University of Texas, graduating in 1921 and remaining there to take his law degree the next year. He entered private practice in Dallas and from 1927 to 1932 was civil district attorney for the county; by the latter year he was deeply involved in Democratic politics in Texas. In 1937 he went to work for the Department of Justice as a special assistant. He was particularly active in antitrust and war-fraud prosecutions, rising in 1943 to assistant attorney general in charge of the antitrust division and later in the year moving to the criminal division. In 1945 he was named attorney general by President Harry S. Truman. Clark was a strong supporter of the antisubversive programs undertaken by the government after World War II; he was responsible for the compilation of the attorney general's list of subversive and Communist-front organizations as well as a broadening of the powers of the Federal Bureau of Investigation. In 1949 Truman named him to the Supreme Court; there he joined Chief Justice Frederick M. Vinson in pursuing a course that was mildly liberal in matters of civil rights but strongly favorable to the government's position in most cases, especially where questions of security or subversion were involved. He was often out of sympathy with the liberalized court under Chief Justice Earl M. Warren, although he did join in the unanimous vote to end school segregation in *Brown* v. *Board of Education*, 1954. He dissented in a great many cases in which loyalty oaths for various classes of public employees were held unconstitutional; however, he concurred in the 1962 *Baker* v. *Carr* decision that required equitable legislative apportionment by the states and wrote the majority opinions in *Mapp* v. *Ohio*, 1961, barring the use of illegally obtained evidence in state trials; *School District of Abington* v. *Schempp*, 1963, banning prayers and Bible reading in public schools; and *Heart of Atlanta Motel, Inc.* v. *U.S.*, 1964, upholding the public-accommodations provisions of the 1964 Civil Rights Act. In 1967, upon the appointment of his son, Ramsey, as attorney general, he retired from the court. Justice Clark died in New York City on June 13, 1977.

Clark, William (1770–1838), soldier and explorer. Born in Caroline County, Virginia, on August 1, 1770, William was the younger brother of George Rogers Clark, the conqueror of the old Northwest during the Revolution. In 1785 he moved west with his family and settled near Louisville; four years later he followed his brother into military service and participated in several militia campaigns against hostile Indian tribes. In 1792 he was commissioned a lieutenant in the regular army and served for four years under Gen. "Mad Anthony" Wayne, taking part in 1794 in the battle of Fallen Timbers. Meriwether Lewis, his future partner in exploration, was for a time under his command. He resigned from the army in 1796 and spent several years traveling and attending to his estate in Louisville. In 1803 he was invited by Capt. Lewis to share command of the government-sponsored expedition to the Far West in search of a land route to the Pacific, then being organized at the behest of President Thomas Jefferson. He quickly accepted and devoted the next three years to this project which ended with the explorers' return to St. Louis in 1806. During the journey up the Missouri River, across the Continental Divide, and down the Columbia River to the sea, Clark, although nominally under the command of Lewis, shared equally in the responsibilities of leadership. He devoted particular care to mapmaking and to studying the natural history of the hitherto unexplored region. On his return he began to collect the records, both official and personal, of the expedition, laying the groundwork for Nicholas Biddle's editorial work and the publication of the complete journals in 1814. In 1807, having resigned from the army, Clark was appointed brigadier general of militia and superintendent of Indian affairs for the Louisiana Territory and established his headquarters in St. Louis. In 1813 he became governor of the recently formed Missouri Territory. He led volunteers in several military campaigns during the War of 1812 and established the first U.S. outpost in what is now Wisconsin. For several years after the war he was primarily concerned with establishing treaties with various Indian tribes, often engaging the aid of Auguste Chouteau, and in 1825 he joined the governor of Michigan Territory, Lewis Cass, in the negotiations at Prairie du Chien that attempted to settle permanently all Indian territorial disputes. He took an important part in the suppression of the uprisings of the Winnebago in 1827 and of the Sauk, under the leadership of Black Hawk, in 1832 (the Black Hawk War). Clark was also surveyor general for Illinois, Missouri, and Arkansas during 1824–1825 and in 1828 he platted the site of Paducah, Kentucky. He died in St. Louis on September 1, 1838.

Clarke, James Freeman (1810–1888), religious leader and author. Born in Hanover, New Hampshire, on April 4, 1810, Clarke graduated from Harvard in 1829 and from the Harvard Divinity School in 1833. His first pulpit was that of the Unitarian Church in Louisville, Kentucky, where he remained until 1840. During that time he also edited the *Western Messenger* from 1836 to 1839, printing contributions from his friends (many of them fellow Transcendentalists), including Ralph Waldo Emerson, Orestes A. Brownson, William Ellery Channing, Oliver Wendell Holmes, and Nathaniel Hawthorne. He returned to Boston in 1841 and founded the Church of the Disciples, whose polity was startling to other Boston churches in its freedom and the degree of authority vested in the laity. He remained pastor of that church for the rest of his life, with the exception of the years 1850 to 1854, when ill health forced his temporary retirement to western Pennsylvania. During 1867–1871 Clarke was professor of natural religion and Christian doctrine at the Harvard Divinity School and for 25 years was a member of the Harvard Board of Overseers. A man of wide sympathies and engaging personality, he was a prominent and influential citizen; he opposed slavery and supported reform movements concerned with woman suffrage, temperance, and civil-service reform, and spoke out on politics as well as theology. He promoted Unitarianism in an altogether friendly spirit, taking care to give other denominations and religions, of which he was a close student, due respect for their achievements. Clarke edited the *Christian World* from 1843 to 1848 and the *Monthly Journal of the American Unitarian Association* from 1859 to 1861, the same years he served as secretary of the association, and published more than a thousand articles in various periodicals. He also wrote more than 30 books, among them *The Christian Doctrine of Forgiveness of Sin*, 1852; *The Christian Doctrine of Prayer*, 1854; *Orthodoxy, Its Truths and Errors*, 1866; *Common Sense in Religion*, 1874; *Essentials and Non-Essentials in Religion*, 1878; *Self-Culture*, 1882; *Ten Great Religions*, in two volumes, 1871 and 1883, his best-known work; and *Everyday Religion*, 1886. Clarke died in Jamaica Plain, Massachusetts, on June 8, 1888.

Clarke, John Hessin (1857–1945), justice of the Supreme Court. Born on September 18, 1857, in New Lisbon (now Lisbon), Ohio, Clarke graduated from Western Reserve University in 1877, studied law with his father, and was admitted to the bar in 1878. In 1880 he moved to Youngstown, where he practiced law and also bought an interest in the *Vindicator*, which he molded over the years into an influential newspaper of strong Progressive principles. Clarke achieved considerable prominence at the bar as a railroad counsel, but at the same time he had a deep sympathy for the workingman and for the cause of organized labor; the inevitable conflict was one he never adequately resolved. He declined political office on a number of occasions, although he was a leading Democrat in his state. He broke with the party in 1896 over the silver issue but later returned to the fold, and after moving to Cleveland in 1897 became an associate of such Progressives as Tom L. Johnson and Newton D. Baker. He ran unsuccessfully for the Senate in 1903. In 1914,

probably on Baker's recommendation, he was appointed a federal district judge by President Woodrow Wilson and two years later, upon the retirement of Charles Evans Hughes, was elevated to the Supreme Court. There he most often sided with justices Oliver Wendell Holmes and Louis D. Brandeis on the liberal side of questions, although from time to time he would inexplicably take the opposite view. His opinions ranged from sentimental to reactionary and seemed to some of his colleagues to be based on a higher law known only to himself. Thus, he was a leader in swinging the Court to a strong antitrust position and in promoting, often in dissent, the interests of labor; but he also tended to take a quite narrow view of First Amendment rights, particularly during the "Red Scare" of 1919–1920. In 1922 Clarke resigned from the Court to devote himself to the cause of international peace and arbitration. He had been an ardent supporter of the League of Nations since its formation and from 1922 to 1928 he was president of the League of Nations Non-Partisan Committee (later the League of Nations Non-Partisan Association), a group dedicated to securing U.S. entry into the League. In 1925 he published *America and World Peace*. Conceding defeat in the League campaign, he moved to San Diego, California, where he continued to write and speak on behalf of peace until his death there on March 22, 1945.

Clay, Cassius Marcellus (1810–1903), public official and abolitionist. Born in Madison County, Kentucky, on October 19, 1810, Clay was educated at the College of St. Joseph, Transylvania University, and Yale, graduating from Yale in 1832. While at Yale he heard William Lloyd Garrison speak and, although he was the wealthy son of a slaveholding planter, became an ardent abolitionist. Upon his return to Kentucky he studied law briefly and then entered politics, winning election to the legislature in 1835; defeated for reelection the next year, he was returned in 1837. He moved to Lexington and in 1840 was again sent to the legislature, but in 1841, against the advice of his kinsman, Henry Clay, he introduced abolitionism into his campaign and lost. In 1845 he began an abolitionist newspaper, the *True American*, in Lexington, fitting out his office with cannon and other arms in anticipation of trouble; during an absence the office was captured by his opponents, however, and he was forced to move to Cincinnati. He continued the paper there and later, as the *Examiner*, in Louisville. Clay enlisted for army service in the Mexican War in 1846, distinguished himself in battle, and was for a time a prisoner. Returning to Kentucky, he ran as an antislavery candidate for governor in 1849; five years later he joined the new Republican party. He was close both politically and personally to Abraham Lincoln, and following the election of 1860 he was prominently mentioned for various high positions in the new administration; he was ultimately offered the post of minister to St. Petersburg, Russia, which he accepted. He was recalled later in the year, but after refusing a major general's commission returned to Russia in 1863 and remained for six years, during which time he assisted in the purchase of Alaska. In 1869 he retired to White Hill, his Madison County estate, and took little active part in politics thereafter; he broke with the Republican party in 1872 to support Horace Greeley and in 1876 to support Samuel J. Tilden, but later returned to it. In his last years he was a recluse; he was adjudged insane shortly before his death on July 22, 1903, at White Hill.

Clay, Cassius Marcellus, Jr. (1942–   ), *see* Ali, Muhammad

Clay, Henry (1777–1852), public official. Born on April 12, 1777, in Hanover County, Virginia, Clay received little formal education, but his stepfather's influence and his own industry assisted his study of law, which, for a time, he pursued as clerk to George Wythe. In 1797 he was admitted to the bar; he moved to Lexington, Kentucky, to practice. His reputation grew rapidly and in 1803 he was elected to the state legislature as a Jeffersonian Republican. In 1806, shortly after a brief engagement as defense counsel for Aaron Burr, and again in 1809 the legislature sent him to complete unexpired terms in the Senate, and in 1810 he was elected to the House of Representatives, of which he became speaker almost immediately. He led the "War Hawks" in pressing for war with England in 1812 and served effectively on the peace commission in 1814. He returned to the House in 1815 and was again chosen speaker. His position in his state and region secure, it was with an eye to national leadership that he began developing his earlier advocacy of a protective tariff into his famous "American System" of protected domestic manufactures, internal improvements, and, in a reversal of his previous position, a national bank. The debate over the Missouri Compromise brought Clay to the role of mediator that he played thenceforth; distinctly nationalistic in outlook, he placed primary stress on the preservation of the Union; and his consummate skill in effecting the compromise over the issue of slavery in the Louisiana Purchase states won him wide acclaim. In 1821 he retired to Kentucky briefly, but two years later he returned to the House, where he remained, again as speaker and again as an able proponent of the American System, until becoming President John Quincy Adams's secretary of state in 1825 amid the Jacksonians' charges of corrupt bargaining that, although unsubstantiated, clung to him for the rest of his career (in 1826 he fought a duel with John Randolph over the matter). Clay had made an unsuccessful bid for the presidency in 1824; after again retiring to Kentucky in 1829, he was returned to the Senate in 1831 in preparation for the next year's presidential election. Running as the Whig candidate, he was again defeated, largely on the issue of the Second Bank of the United States, but he remained in the Senate as the leader of the opposition to Andrew Jackson and his political heir, Martin Van Buren. In 1833 he succeeded in effecting a compromise in the controversy over nullification. He was bitterly disappointed when the 1840 Whig nomination that he fully expected went instead to the obscure Gen. William Henry Harrison. He remained loyal, however, until President John Tyler's opposition to Clay's plan to recharter the Second Bank of the United States, an integral part of the American System and an issue over which he had fought with Jackson, caused him to resign his Senate seat in 1842. Two years later he was again nominated for president, but his unfortunate maneuvering on the issue of the annexation of Texas lost him the election to the expansionist James K. Polk. He opposed the coming war with Mexico until the nation was actually committed, whereupon he supported its vigorous prosecution. He was again sent to the Senate in 1849 and there proposed his famous "Omnibus Bill," a measure that led to the Compromise of 1850. Clay, by then widely known as "the Great Compromiser" or "the Great Pacificator," remained in office, in failing health, until his death on June 29, 1852 in Washington, D.C. He was elected to the Hall of Fame in 1900.

Clayton, John Middleton (1796–1856), public official. Born on July 24, 1796, in Dagsboro, Delaware, Clayton graduated from Yale in 1815 and studied law privately at the Litchfield, Connecticut, law school of Tapping Reeve. He was admitted to the bar in 1819 and began practice in Dover, Delaware, soon becoming a leading attorney in the state. He also interested himself in politics, winning election to the legislature in 1824, serving as Delaware's secretary of state in 1826–1828, and in 1828 running successfully as a Whig for the Senate. Reelected in 1835, he was generally an anti-Jacksonian although as a Unionist he did support the president in the nullification crisis in 1832. He resigned his seat in 1836 for personal reasons; in 1837 he was elected chief justice of Delaware and remained on the bench until 1839, when he resigned to campaign for Gen. William Henry Harrison. For a time he devoted himself to scientific farming, but in 1845 he returned to the Senate. He opposed the annexation of Texas and gave his support to war with Mexico only after war was declared. In 1848 he campaigned for Zachary Taylor and was rewarded with the office of secretary of state in March 1849. He conducted himself with vigor in that office, with mixed results. The great achievement of his tenure was the negotiation of the Clayton-Bulwer Treaty, concluded in 1850 with Sir Henry Bulwer, British minister to the United States. The treaty attempted to end years of dissension beween the two nations over Central America; it declared the region neutral, banned the seeking of territorial or military advantages there by either signatory, and arranged for mutual sponsorship of an Atlantic–Pacific canal across the isthmus. The canal was never built under its conditions, nor did the treaty end disputes; instead, it opened new questions of British presence in Central America. The treaty quickly became one of the most controversial in American history, and it was finally abrogated in 1901. Clayton left the cabinet following Taylor's death in 1850 and lived in retirement until 1853, when he returned to the Senate to defend his treaty. He died in Dover on November 9, 1856.

Clemens, Samuel Langhorne (1835–1910), "Mark Twain," humorist and author. Born in Florida, Missouri, on November 30, 1835, Clemens grew up in Hannibal, a village on the Mississippi River that was the setting for many of his later writings. His education was limited and at the age of twelve he was apprenticed to a printer; from 1851 to 1853 he worked on his brother's newspaper and in the latter year set out as an itinerant printer. He had begun already to write occasional short pieces in the current style of journalistic humor, but his best work of this time was a letter to a girl friend on the subject of insects. In 1856 he apprenticed himself to a steamboat pilot and remained happily on the Mississippi until the Civil War put an end to river traffic. In 1861, partly to avoid war service, he set out for Nevada with his brother, who had been appointed to a post in the territorial government. After failures in prospecting and mining had left him in financial distress he took a job with the Virginia City *Territorial Enterprise* as a feature writer. It was while working for the *Enterpise* that he adopted "Mark Twain," a call used on riverboats when sounding water depths, as his nom de plume. In 1864 he moved to San Francisco and continued in journalism, working on the *San Francisco Call* and as correspondent for the *Enterprise;* he contributed also to *The Californian* and the *Golden Era.* The following year he published his first notable piece, "The Celebrated Jumping Frog of Calaveras County," a tall tale, much in the manner of the frontier "Southwestern" humor he had grown up with but with clear evidence of his growing mastery of style. Published first in the New York *Saturday Press* and then reprinted widely, the tale secured him a modest fame. In the next several years he published letters produced during several trips, culminating in *Innocents Abroad,* 1869, a great popular success. In 1870 he settled in Hartford, Connecticut. Then began his most productive period; from that year to 1894 he wrote and published his best-known works: *Roughing It,* 1872; *The Gilded Age,* 1873, with Charles Dudley Warner; *The Adventures of Tom Sawyer,* 1876; *A Tramp Abroad,* 1880; *The Prince and the Pauper,* 1882; *Life on the Mississippi,* 1883; *The Adventures of Huckleberry Finn,* 1884, which, though flawed, remained the masterpiece of his longer writings; *A Connecticut Yankee in King Arthur's Court* 1889; and *Pudd'nhead Wilson,* 1894. The panic of 1893, together with a number of ill-considered investments, brought Clemens into bankruptcy in the early 1890's and there followed a world lecture tour

and the writing of a number of lesser works, including *Following the Equator,* 1897, as he strove to repay his debts. Several deaths in his family, including his wife's, accelerated a tendency in his later years toward a pessimistic and sometimes bitter outlook on humanity; this attitude dominated such writings as "The Man That Corrupted Hadleyburg," 1899, and *The Mysterious Stranger,* published posthumously in 1916. In his last years he began an autobiography and wrote numerous articles, many expressing his growing outrage at the seemingly innate cruelty of mankind. True to his long-standing prediction that as he had come into the world with Halley's Comet, so he would go out with it, Clemens died on April 21, 1910, in Redding, Connecticut. He was elected to the Hall of Fame in 1920.

Cleveland, Grover (1837–1908), twenty-second and twenty-fourth president of the United States. Born in Caldwell, New Jersey, on March 18, 1837, Stephen Grover Cleveland was prevented from attending college by the need to support his widowed mother. After four years of study in a law office in Buffalo, he was admitted to the bar in 1859. He immediately joined the Democratic party. Hiring a substitute for his Civil War service, he entered politics and held a number of local posts, including that of county sheriff in 1870. In 1881 he was the Democratic nominee for mayor of Buffalo; pledged to reform, he was elected and surprised a great many people by actually undertaking to reform the city's government. His record in Buffalo, combined with his lack of identification with political bosses, won him election as governor of New York in 1882. He continued his honest and efficient approach to government and gained a valuable political asset in the open enmity of Tammany Hall. The same qualifications that had made him governor brought him the nomination for president in 1884; in a vicious campaign he defeated the Republican James G. Blaine, whose candidacy, haunted by the shadow of corruption, was hurt by the defection of the "mugwump" faction to Cleveland. In his quiet first term, the first Democratic president since the Civil War devoted himself to promoting honest government by means of civil-service reform and by halting the flow of dubious pension legislation. His advocacy of tariff reduction weakened his political position, however, and he lost the election in 1888 to Benjamin Harrison, although he gained a plurality of the popular vote. He thereupon retired to private law practice. In 1892 he was nominated again and elected to a second term, which proved to be stormy. The panic of 1893 broke soon after his inauguration, and he alienated the pro-silver West by forcing the repeal of the Sherman Silver Purchase Act. The heavy drains on the Treasury forced him to purchase gold from J. P. Morgan and his associates. In response to the Pullman strike of 1894 he sent federal troops into Illinois over the protests of Governor John P. Altgeld. Losing control even of his own party, he was thwarted by Congress in his attempts to lower the tariff. The foreign policy of his second administration was marked by his repudiation of the overthrow of the Hawaiian monarchy by a group of American residents who had had the support of the previous administration, and by his forceful dealing with Great Britain in its border dispute with Venezuela. By 1896 he had lost all influence in his party, and in the Democratic convention of that year the opposition to his fiscal policies resulted in the nomination of William Jennings Bryan. Cleveland retired to live quietly in Princeton, New Jersey, and, his prestige returning with the passage of time, he engaged in private pursuits, including the successful reorganization of the discredited Equitable Life Assurance Society of New York in 1905. He died in Princeton on June 24, 1908. He was elected to the Hall of Fame in 1935.

Clifford, Nathan (1803–1881), justice of the Supreme Court. Born in Rumney, New Hampshire, on August 18, 1803, Clifford worked his way through Haverhill Academy and a year at the New Hampton Literary Institution and then took up the study of law under Josiah Quincy. He was admitted to the bar in 1827 and began practice in Newfield, Maine. He became involved in Democratic politics, serving in the legislature from 1830 to 1834, the last two years as speaker; as state attorney general from 1834 to 1838; and from 1839 to 1843 in the House of Representatives. In 1846 he was appointed attorney general by President James K. Polk. His most important achievement while in that post was serving as special commissioner to Mexico to arrange the treaty of Guadalupe Hidalgo, which ended the Mexican War, in 1848; although he resigned his cabinet post in November 1848, he remained in Mexico for six months more, clearing up the final details of the treaty. He then returned to the private practice of law in Portland, Maine, and twice unsuccessfully sought election to the Senate. In 1858 he was named by President James Buchanan, an old friend of his from Polk's cabinet, to the Supreme Court. In 23 years on the bench Clifford wrote no great opinions; of the nearly 400 cases in which he spoke for the Court, most involved areas—maritime and commercial law, and laws affecting Mexican land grants—in which he was especially competent but which held little public interest. He was unafraid of dissent and wrote dissenting opinions more often than most, on many occasions as the vehicle for his conservative judicial views. In 1877 he presided over the Electoral Commission established to decide the 1876 presidential election, and although he was a devoted Democrat he conducted himself, as on the bench, with utmost impartiality. After his health began to fail, his party loyalty led him to remain on the Supreme Court in the hope that he might last until a Democratic president could appoint his successor. After a year of invalidism, during which he still refused to resign, he died in Cornish, Maine, on July 25, 1881.

Clinton, De Witt (1769–1828), public official. Born in Little Britain, New York, on March 2, 1769, Clinton graduated from Columbia College in 1786 and for three years studied law. In 1790 he began his practice and also became secretary to his uncle, George Clinton, then governor of the state. In 1797 he was elected to the state assembly and from 1798 to 1802 served in the state senate; although he was strongly criticized for his actions as a member of the Council of Appointments—he was charged with introducing the spoils system in New York state—he was appointed to the Senate in 1802. Serving only a few months, during which he introduced the Twelfth Amendment, he resigned in 1803 to become mayor of New York City, an office he held, except for two one-year terms, until 1815; during the same period he was a member of the state senate from 1806 to 1811 and lieutenant governor from 1811 to 1813. He advocated and secured many improvements during those years, including the opening of New York City's first public school and the removal of political restrictions on Roman Catholics. In 1812 the bloc of Northern Republicans, resentful of the "Virginia dynasty" of the party, nominated him to oppose James Madison for the presidency; his campaign was unsuccessful, and his ability to attract Federalist support alienated many in his own party. From 1811 onward Clinton concerned himself primarily with the proposal to construct a canal from Lake Erie to the Hudson River and thus make New York City the seaport for the vast Great Lakes region; he was a member of successive commissions appointed to investigate the project and devoted much effort to enlisting public and legislative support. In 1817 he was elected governor and work began on the canal shortly afterward. The growing opposition of the combined Tammany and Virginia Republican factions led by Martin Van Buren forced him to retire in 1823 after a second term; his removal from the canal commission the next year, however, roused a storm of protest, and he was easily returned to the governor's office. He was thus governor when "Clinton's ditch"—the Erie Canal—was opened in October 1825, and he remained in that office until his death in Albany on February 11, 1828. In addition to his involvement in political affairs, Clinton was known also for his abiding interest in promoting education and scholarship at all levels and for his own not inconsiderable contributions as an amateur naturalist.

Clinton, George (1739–1812), Revolutionary soldier and public official. Born on July 26, 1739, in Little Britain, New York, Clinton went to sea briefly when he was eighteen, served in the French and Indian Wars, and about 1762 took up the practice of law. In 1768 he was elected to the New York Provincial Assembly where he served until 1775, when he was elected to the Continental Congress. In the same year he was appointed brigadier general of the state militia and sent to defend New York City and the Hudson River. Although he was militarily inept and offered to resign his commission, he was retained, given a second commission by Congress, and in 1777 was elected both governor and lieutenant governor of New York. He declined the latter office but remained governor for 18 years. He had a profound distrust of centralized government and strongly opposed New York's ratification of the Constitution in 1788. He was a follower of Thomas Jefferson and was instrumental in promoting Aaron Burr's rise to prominence. He retired from the governorship in 1795 but returned for another term in 1800. In 1804 he was elected vice-president and, after an unsuccessful bid for the presidential nomination in 1808, was reelected to the office for a second term. In 1811, by virtue of his position as president of the Senate, he cast the deciding vote against the rechartering of the First Bank of the United States. He died in Washington, D.C., on April 20, 1812.

Cobb, Howell (1815–1868), public official. Born in Jefferson County, Georgia, on September 7, 1815, to a wealthy and prominent family, Cobb grew up in Athens, Georgia, graduated from the University of Georgia in 1834, and two years later was admitted to the bar. He quickly entered public service, winning election as solicitor general for a district in northeastern Georgia; he held the office for three years and in 1842 was elected to the House of Representatives by the district. Three times returned to his seat, he became a respected figure in Congress and in 1848 was chosen Democratic leader in the House. Although a Southerner and a supporter of the annexation of Texas, the Mexican War, and the extension of slavery, he was markedly independent and in 1849 alienated many of his more extreme colleagues by opposing the notion of a sectional political party for the South. In that year he was elected speaker after one of the bitterest contests the House had ever witnessed. His support of the Compromise of 1850 further angered extremists, and upon his return to Georgia he joined with the Whigs in campaigning for popular approval of the compromise measures. The next year he ran for governor on the Constitutional Union ballot and was elected by a large majority. His efforts to reunite the Georgia Democrats failed, however, and he was ousted from the party. In 1855 he was returned to Congress by his pro-Union district and in 1857 was appointed secretary of the treasury by President James Buchanan. He gave up the Unionist cause following the election of Abraham Lincoln in 1860, however; resigning from the cabinet, he returned to Georgia to urge secession. He presided at the convention held in Montgomery, Alabama, to organize the Confederacy and, until the election of Jefferson Davis, was widely mentioned for the presidency. In mid-1861 he recruited a regiment and led it to the front as its colonel; he was later promoted to major general and commanded the District of Georgia until the end of the Civil War. He then returned to law practice in Macon. Cobb died on October 9, 1868, while visiting New York City.

Cobb, Tyrus Raymond (1886–1961), "Ty," baseball player. Born in Narrows, Banks County, Georgia, on December 18, 1886, Ty Cobb was the son of a noted Georgia educator and political figure. He began playing baseball at the age of nine and by 1905 was appearing regularly with the Augusta team of the South Atlantic League. He had already been nicknamed "the Georgia Peach" by sportswriter Grantland Rice when, in that year, he was signed by the Detroit Tigers. During 22 seasons as an outfielder with the Tigers he established himself as baseball's most aggressive and probably greatest player, certainly its greatest hitter. Other players, umpires, even teammates, were fair game when he lost his temper, and even when he didn't he was a force to be reckoned with. A master of the hook and fallaway slides, he was nearly as well known for spiking basemen as for stealing bases. From 1921 to 1926 he managed the Tigers in addition to playing regularly in the outfield; but after two years with the Philadelphia Athletics under Connie Mack he retired in 1928. By that time he had amassed 58 offensive records—a record in itself—and 12 of them still stand, including highest lifetime batting average (.367), most batting championships won (12), total hits (4191), most runs scored (2244), most games played (3033), most seasons batting .300 or better (23), and, perhaps above all, total bases stolen (829). When the first ballot was taken for the National Baseball Hall of Fame in 1936 Cobb led all other nominees. After his retirement he returned to Atlanta, Georgia, where he lived quietly until his death there, on July 17, 1961.

Cochise (1812?–1874), Indian leader. Born about 1812, probably in present-day Arizona, Cochise was a chief of the Chiricahua band of the Apache. Under Spanish and Mexican rule the Apache had been the particular victims of slave traders and scalp hunters and the Southwest was in constant turmoil. With the coming of U.S. authority in 1850 a brief period of relative peace began. In 1861 the peace was broken when Cochise, falsely accused of having kidnaped a white child, appeared at an army post to deny the charge and was imprisoned. Escaping, he took hostages to exchange for other members of his band still held by the army; the exchange did not take place and both sides executed their hostages. Cochise joined his father-in-law, Mangas Coloradas (or Colorado), chief of the Mimbreño Apaches, in a long series of raids and skirmishes that soon threatened to drive the Americans from Arizona. In 1862, with some 500 warriors, they held Apache Pass against Gen. James Carleton and 3000 California volunteers until forced out by artillery fire. Mangas Coloradas was later captured and killed in prison, leaving Cochise to lead Apache resistance. Gradually driven deeper and deeper into the hidden recesses of the Dragoon Mountains, he nonetheless maintained a reign of terror over white settlers until 1871, when Gen. George Crook assumed command of the army in Arizona.

Using other Apaches as scouts, Crook tracked Cochise down and forced him to surrender. The next year the Chiricahua were ordered transferred to a reservation in New Mexico; refusing to leave the ancestral lands that had been guaranteed them by the Americans, Cochise and a band of followers again took to the mountains and resisted until 1872. In that year a new treaty was negotiated by the Indian commissioner, Gen. Oliver O. Howard, and Cochise retired to an Arizona reservation, where he died on June 9, 1874.

Cochran, Jacqueline (1910?–1980), aviator and business leader. Born in Pensacola, Florida, about 1910, Miss Cochran grew up in poverty in a foster home. At eight she went to work in a cotton mill in Georgia; she later was trained as a beautician and pursued that career in Montgomery, Alabama, in Pensacola, and from about 1931 in New York City. She took her first flying lessons in 1932 and soon mastered the technical aspects of aviation and navigation, later studying privately with a navy pilot friend in San Diego. Meanwhile, in 1934, she had organized a cosmetics firm that grew and prospered under her management. In 1935 Miss Cochran became the first woman to enter the Bendix Transcontinental Air Race; in 1937 she came in third, and in 1938 she won the Bendix Trophy, flying a Seversky pursuit plane. In 1941 she piloted a bomber to England and there, as a flight captain in the British Air Transport Auxiliary, trained a group of woman pilots for war transport service. Upon her return to the United States she undertook a similar program for the Army Air Forces and in 1943 was named director of the Women's Airforce Service Pilots—the WASPs—which supplied more than a thousand auxiliary pilots for the armed forces. At the end of the war she served for a time as a Pacific and European correspondent for *Liberty* magazine. In 1945 she became the first woman civilian to be awarded the Distinguished Service Medal and in 1948 was commissioned a lieutenant colonel in the Air Force Reserve. Eager to make the transition to flying jet aircraft, she became the first woman to break the sound barrier in 1953 and that year set world speed records for 15-, 100- and 500-kilometer courses. She continued to break her old records and set new ones, including an altitude mark of 55,253 feet in 1961, and in 1964 she set the standing women's world speed record of 1429 miles per hour in an F-104G Super Star jet. In 1959 she became the first woman president of the Fédération Aéronautique Internationale. She retired from the Air Force Reserve with the rank of colonel in 1970. She died on August 9, 1980, in Indio, California.

Cody, William Frederick (1846–1917), "Buffalo Bill," frontiersman and entertainer. Born in Scott County, Iowa, on February 26, 1846, Cody had little education and went to work at the age of twelve. By the outbreak of the Civil War he had been by turns a horse wrangler, a mounted messenger for a freight company, an unsuccessful prospector, and a pony-express rider. The family had moved to Kansas some years before the war came; Cody rode with the antislavery guerrillas, the Jayhawkers, for a time before enlisting in 1863 as a scout with the 9th Kansas Cavalry. Later he was a scout with the Union army in operations in Tennessee and Missouri. Soon after the war he took a job as a hunter for a company that had contracted to supply meat for the construction crews of the Kansas Pacific Railroad and during 1867–1868 he killed, by his own count, 4280 buffalo. For the next four years he was again with the army, serving as chief scout of the 5th Cavalry in various Indian campaigns; during this time, in 1869, he met the writer E. Z. C. Judson—"Ned Buntline"—who, seeing in him the makings of a popular hero, dubbed him "Buffalo Bill" and proceeded to feature him in a series of highly fictionalized and sensational dime novels. In 1872 Judson wrote a play, *Scouts of the Plains* (later *Scouts of the Prairies*), which successfully toured Eastern cities with Cody, under his new name, and "Texas Jack" Omohundro, later replaced by "Wild Bill" Hickok, as its stars. In 1876 Cody returned briefly to the 5th Cavalry and in July of that year killed and scalped Yellow Hand, a Cheyenne leader, in a famous duel. He soon returned to the stage and until 1883 divided his time between show business and his Nebraska ranch. In 1883 he organized the highly successful Buffalo Bill's Wild West Show and played to audiences in the East, in Great Britain, and in Continental Europe; the show featured Cody, the famed woman marksman Annie Oakley, and, briefly, Sitting Bull. In the 1890s Cody settled on an extensive tract of land in the Bighorn Basin granted him by the state of Wyoming, and there the city of Cody was built. On January 10, 1917, he died suddenly in Denver; he was buried in a solid rock tomb at the top of nearby Lookout Mountain. His *Life of Hon. Wm. F. Cody, Known as Buffalo Bill*, which first appeared in 1879, went through many editions.

Coffin, Howard Earle (1873–1937), engineer and business leader. Born near West Milton, Ohio, on September 6, 1873, Coffin attended the University of Michigan from 1893 to 1896, when he left to work for the post office. During the next four years he also experimented with internal-combustion engines and in 1898 built a steam-powered automobile. He returned to the university in 1900, but in 1902, before completing his degree requirements, he left to become head of the experimental department of the Olds Motor Works. Three years later he was promoted to chief engineer of the company. In 1906 he left Olds to join in organizing the E. R. Thomas Detroit Company and to become its vice-president and chief engineer. For the company, which in 1908 became the Chalmers-Detroit Motor Company, he designed the Chalmers automobile. In 1909 he and Roy D. Chapin founded the Hudson Motor Car Company, of which he was vice-president until 1930 and for which he designed the Hudson automobile and served as consulting engineer. Coffin was the leader in organizing the cross-licensing system among automobile manufacturers and in formulating a program of industry-wide testing. He was a founder of the Society of Automobile Engineers (later the Society of Automotive Engineers), served as its president in 1910, and promoted the establishment of standard specifications and materials to greatly simplify manufacture and repair and reduce costs. In 1911, in recognition of his contributions to mechanical engineering, the University of Michigan awarded him a B.S. degree as of the class of 1903. In 1915 he was appointed to the Naval Consulting Board, chaired by Thomas A. Edison, and for it conducted a nationwide inventory of war production capability. In 1916 President Woodrow Wilson named him to the Council of National Defense, and as head of its Aircraft Board in 1917–1918 he directed development of the standardized Liberty aircraft engine. He continued to serve as a government consultant on aircraft production and in 1922 led in organizing the National Aeronautical Association to promote progress in the field. In 1925 Coffin founded National Air Transport, Inc., a pioneer commercial aviation company that later became United Air Lines; he was president of National until 1928 and chairman of the board until 1930, when he retired to his home on an island off the coast of Georgia. In his last years he was chairman of the board of Southeastern Cottons, Inc., a major textile firm, and actively promoted the development of the Georgia coast as a resort area. He died on nearby Sea Island on November 21, 1937.

Coffin, Levi (1798–1877), abolitionist. Born on October 28, 1798, near New Garden, North Carolina, Coffin received little formal schooling but managed to acquire enough education to teach school himself on occasion. A devout Quaker, he opened a Sunday school for slaves in 1821 but was soon forced to close it when the owners forbade their slaves to attend. In 1826 he moved to Indiana, settling in Newport (later Fountain City) and becoming a prosperous merchant. He soon discovered that Newport was on an Underground Railroad route for escaping slaves, and he promptly opened his home as a way station. With neighbors contributing clothing and other supplies, Coffin's became one of the most active depots in the country, giving rest and aid to more than 3000 Canada-bound fugitives. In 1847, under the sponsorship of a Quaker convention in Indiana, he moved to Cincinnati and opened a wholesale business that promoted only goods produced by free labor. He continued his abolitionist activities there, becoming widely known as the "president of the Underground Railroad." He and his wife were reputedly the models for Simon and Rachel Halliday in Harriet Beecher Stowe's *Uncle Tom's Cabin,* and the famous episode of Eliza crossing the ice-choked Ohio River was based on the experience of Eliza Harris, one of the escaped slaves whom he had helped. During the Civil War Coffin was active in aiding freed slaves and traveled to England in 1864 to found the Freedmen's Aid Society. In 1867 he was a delegate to the International Anti-Slavery Conference in Paris. He died near Cincinnati on September 16, 1877. Coffin's *Reminiscences of Levi Coffin, Reputed President of the Underground R.R.,* appeared in 1876.

Coffin, Lorenzo S. (1823–1915), reformer and philanthropist. Born near Alton, New Hampshire, on April 9, 1823, Coffin was educated in local schools and attended the preparatory department of Oberlin College for two years. In 1855 he settled on a farm near Fort Dodge, Iowa. He served in an Iowa regiment as quartermaster and then chaplain during the Civil War and soon after his return to Fort Dodge in 1863 was elected superintendent of schools. For many years he was a preacher, and he also devoted himself to the improvement of both education and farming practices in his region. He contributed frequently to agricultural journals and to the *Fort Dodge Messenger.* In 1883 he was appointed state railroad commissioner by the governor. During five years in that office he traveled on freight trains, observed the work of railroad men, and became deeply disturbed by the number of fatal or disabling accidents—from 20,000 to 30,000 annually —suffered by them. Upon investigation he found that a great many accidents occurred during the coupling or hand braking of cars, and he immediately set out to promote the installation of automatic equipment to handle both tasks. Such equipment was already in use on passenger trains and, attracted to the problem by Coffin's barrage of articles and letters to all segments of the press, George Westinghouse developed an improved air brake for long freight trains. Coffin's tireless writing and speaking led at last to an Iowa state law requiring automatic brakes, and within a few years measures requiring automatic brakes and self-couplers were passed by Congress. Fatal accidents on the nation's railroads were cut by some 60 percent as a result of his efforts. In 1893 he organized the "White Button" temperance movement among railroad men; near Chicago he founded the Home for Aged and Disabled Railroad Men, and on his own farm he built Hope Hall, a halfway house for discharged convicts. In 1907 he ran for governor of Iowa on the Prohibition ticket and the next year was the United Christian candidate for vice-president. Coffin died on January 17, 1915.

Cohan, George Michael (1878–1942), composer, playwright, actor, and producer. Born in Providence, Rhode Island, on July 3, 1878 Cohan belonged to a family of vaudevillians and his father providentially changed his birthday to July 4. He began appearing on stage with his parents at an early age, toured with them across the country, and in his teens began writing songs for the act. His first popular success, composed in 1895, was

"Hot Tamale Alley"; "I Guess I'll Have to Telegraph My Baby," 1898, was also a hit. As he moved into comedy and the legitimate stage he reorganized "The Four Cohans" with his wife (replacing his sister), his parents, and himself and in 1901 wrote his first musical comedy, *The Governor's Son*. Three years later he produced *Little Johnny Jones*, which featured such songs as "Give My Regards to Broadway" and the one that gave him his nickname, "Yankee Doodle Boy." His boisterous patriotism became the hallmark of his career; often, in a lagging production, he would rouse the audience to wild enthusiasm simply by dancing across the stage with a flag. Excelling neither in singing, dancing, nor acting, he nonetheless won the hearts of millions by his sheer exuberance on stage. His subsequent musicals and plays, produced mainly by Sam H. Harris (Cohan's partner from 1904 to 1920) or by himself and successes all, included *Forty-five Minutes from Broadway*, 1905 (with "Mary's a Grand Old Name"); *George Washington, Jr.*, 1906 ("You're a Grand Old Flag"); *The Talk of New York*, 1907; *The Man Who Owns Broadway*, 1908 ("There's Something About a Uniform"); *The Yankee Prince*, 1909; *Get-Rich-Quick Wallingford*, 1910; *Broadway Jones*, 1912; *Seven Keys to Baldpate*, 1913; *The Tavern*, 1921; *The Song and Dance Man*, 1923; *American Born*, 1925, and many others. In 1917, on learning of U.S. entry into World War I, he composed a song in honor of the American Expeditionary Force (AEF) and titled it "Over There"; popularized by Nora Bayes, it became virtually the American anthem during the war, and well over a million copies of recordings and sheet music were sold. For "Over There" and "You're a Grand Old Flag" Congress authorized the award of a special Medal of Honor to Cohan in 1940. In 1933 he emerged from semi-retirement to star in Eugene O'Neill's *Ah, Wilderness!* and in 1937 he impersonated Franklin D. Roosevelt in the George S. Kaufman-Moss Hart hit, *I'd Rather Be Right*. Cohan's autobiography, *Twenty Years on Broadway and the Years it Took to Get There*, appeared in 1925; he died in New York City on November 5, 1942, the year in which *Yankee Doodle Dandy*, an Academy Award-winning film based on his life, was released.

Cohen, Morris Raphael (1880–1947), philosopher. Born on July 25, 1880, in Minsk, Russia, Cohen emigrated with his family to the United States in 1892 and settled in New York City. He graduated from the College of the City of New York (CCNY, now a unit of the City University) in 1900 and after a period of teaching in public schools became an instructor in mathematics at CCNY in 1902. During 1904–1906 he pursued graduate studies at Harvard, taking his Ph.D. in 1906, and then returned to City College, becoming professor of philosophy in 1912. As a teacher Cohen was brilliant and extremely popular, his lectures drawing many auditors from the college at large in addition to his own students. As a

philosopher he was radically individual, working out his own synthesis of pragmatism, logical positivism, and linguistic analysis and subscribing to no school of thought. His studies in legal philosophy were particularly penetrating and influential. Among his books were *Reason and Nature*, 1931; *Law and the Social Order*, 1933; *Preface to Logic*, 1944; and *Faith of a Liberal*, 1945. He was also coauthor of the third volume of the *Cambridge History of American Literature*, 1922, and, with E. Nagel, of *An Introduction to Logic and the Scientific Method*, 1934; editor of the Modern Legal Philosophy and the Jewish Social Studies series; and associate editor of the *Journal of the History of Ideas*. Cohen organized the Conference on Legal and Social Philosophy in 1913 and the Conference on Jewish Relations, of which he was president from 1933 to 1941 and thereafter honorary president. He retired from City College in 1938 and for four years thereafter served as professor of philosophy at the University of Chicago. He devoted himself to writing from 1942 until his death in Washington, D.C., on January 28, 1947, leaving the manuscripts for *The Meaning of Human History*, 1948, and the autobiographical *A Dreamer's Journey*, 1949.

Cohn, Edwin Joseph (1892–1953), chemist. Born on December 17, 1892, in New York City, Cohn was educated at Amherst College and at the University of Chicago, from which he graduated in 1914. He pursued graduate work at Harvard and returned to Chicago to take his Ph.D. in 1917. During World War I he served with the Army Sanitation Corps and afterward undertook further studies in Copenhagen and at Cambridge University. In 1922 he joined the Harvard faculty as assistant professor of physical chemistry; in 1935 he became professor of biological chemistry and head of the department of physical chemistry in the medical school, and in 1936 he undertook also the chairmanship of the division of medical sciences. For nearly his entire career Cohn directed his researches to the study of proteins and their components, amino acids and peptides. His early investigations concerned the solubility of proteins and the relation of solubility to their structure. He later became interested in the proteins in blood and for several years worked on the problem of fractionating blood into its various constituents. By the beginning of World War II he had succeeded in separating albumin, globulin, and fibrin fractions from blood plasma, and these, through the organizational work of the navy and the American Red Cross, all proved of incalculable value in treating war casualties; albumin was used to treat shock, globulin to combat various forms of infection, and fibrin to stop hemorrhages. All the fractions were of great usefulness in treating disease and accident victims as well, and serum gamma globulin served later as the basis for mass immunization programs against measles, polio, and other epidemic illnesses. Cohn also developed a concentrated liver extract that was successfully used to treat pernicious anemia. In 1949 he was named Higgins University Professor at Harvard and put in charge of the university laboratory of physical chemistry; the following year he also became chairman of the department of biophysical chemistry. Cohn died in Boston on October 1, 1953.

Colbath, Jeremiah Jones, see Wilson, Henry

Colby, Frank Moore (1865–1925), editor and author. Born in Washington, D.C., on February 10, 1865, Colby graduated from Columbia in 1888 and received an M.A. in political science there the next year. During 1890–1891 he was acting professor of history at Amherst College and from 1892 to 1895 taught at Columbia and at Barnard College. In 1895 he became professor of economics at New York University. Early in his career he had written for encyclopedias to supplement his income and in 1893 he was hired by *Johnson's Encyclopaedia* as history and political science editor. He retained the position for two years and in 1898 became editor of the *International Year Book* (later the *New International Year Book*), which he continued to direct for the rest of his life. In 1899 he published *Outlines of General History,* a popular and long-used textbook, and the following year resigned from New York University to devote full time to his editorial and literary activities. At various times he worked on the *International Encyclopaedia* and *Nelson's Encyclopaedia,* and during 1900–1903 and again for the second edition in 1913–1915 was an editor of the *New International Encyclopaedia.* He wrote informed and widely admired editorials for the *New York Commercial Advertiser* between 1900 and 1902, and many of his later magazine pieces were collected in *Imaginary Obligations,* 1904; *Constrained Attitudes,* 1910; and *The Margin of Hesitation,* 1921. Colby died on March 3, 1925, in New York City.

Colden, Cadwallader (1688–1776), colonial figure, physician, and scientist. Born in Ireland on February 7, 1688, Colden was the son of Scottish parents and was educated at the University of Edinburgh. Upon graduation in 1705 he abandoned plans to enter the ministry in favor of a newly kindled interest in medicine, the study of which he began in London. In 1710 he emigrated to America, settled in Philadelphia, and engaged in medical practice and a mercantile business. Promised the offices of surveyor general and master in chancery by the governor of New York, he moved there in 1718 and two years later received the appointments, in addition becoming a member of the governor's council in 1721. While fulfilling his public duties Colden also vigorously pursued his own interests and proved himself one of the most versatile men of learning in the colonies. He published studies of cancer, smallpox, yellow fever, and the medical implications of climate; he wrote a still authoritative *History of the Five Indian Nations Depending on the Province of New York,* 1727 (later revised); he

collected and classified the flora in the area of his Orange County home and submitted a report to Carolus Linnaeus, who published it approvingly in 1749; and he wrote pamphlets on philosophy, psychology, mathematics, and the natural sciences. Among the last were works on various topics in physics, and his *Explication of the First Causes of Action in Matter, and, of the Cause of Gravitation,* 1745 (later revised as *The Principles of Action in Matter, the Gravitation of Bodies, and the Motion of the Planets explained from those Principles,* 1751), elicited considerable comment from European scientists. In 1760 Colden became acting lieutenant governor of New York and the next year was officially commissioned in the position; from then until 1775 he was, due to the coming and going of governors and to long periods when there was none at all, the abiding governmental authority in the province. He was a strong enforcer of law and a Loyalist, and his popularity, never high, reached its nadir when he was burned in effigy following his refusal to condemn the Stamp Act in 1765. He managed to keep control of the government until after the battle of Lexington in 1775; he then retired to his Long Island estate, where he died on September 28, 1776.

Cole, Thomas (1801–1848), painter and poet. Born on February 1, 1801, in Bolton-le-Moors, England, Cole traveled with his family to the United States settling first in Pennsylvania in 1819, then in Steubenville, Ohio, in 1820. There he worked as a wood-block engraver in his father's wallpaper factory for two years. He met a wandering artist who taught him to paint and, desirous of reproducing the vivid colors of the American autumn and the beauty of its spring, he resolved to devote himself henceforth to painting. He set out on foot at the age of twenty-one, wandering through Ohio and Pennsylvania painting portraits and hoping to make his fortune. In 1823 he settled briefly in Philadelphia, attended the Pennsylvania Academy of the Fine Arts, and wrote in his spare time, contributing poetry and stories to magazines. Business called his family to New York City and he joined them there; he continued to paint and exhibited a few landscapes in a shop window, attracting the attention of John Trumbull, Asher B. Durand, and William Cullen Bryant, among others. Moving to Catskill, New York, Cole began painting scenes of the Hudson River valley; his work grew in popularity and he was joined by Durand and others in the establishment of the Hudson River School, the first native American movement in painting, of which he remained the acknowledged leader. From 1829 to 1832 he traveled and painted in Europe. On his return he spent four years in New York City, during which time he created on commission his great allegorical "Course of Empire," a series of five canvases—"Primeval Nature," "Pastoral Life," "Wealth and Glory," "War," and "Desolation"—now in the New York Historical Society. In 1839 he produced "The Voyage of Life," depicting in four canvases "Childhood," "Youth," "Manhood," and "Old Age." His symbolic work became more religious as he grew older. Of his poems, published principally in periodicals, the best remembered is probably "The Lament of the Forest," which appeared in *The Knickerbocker* magazine in 1841. While working on "The Pilgrim of the Cross," one of a projected series of paintings entitled "The Cross and the World," he became ill and died in Catskill on February 11, 1848.

Colfax, Schuyler (1823–1885), public official. Born in New York City on March 23, 1823, Colfax moved with his family to New Carlisle, Indiana, in 1836. Through the influence of his stepfather he secured his first public office, that of deputy county auditor, in 1841; over the next few years, while nurturing a political career, he was briefly a correspondent for the *Indiana State Journal* and for a short time read law. In 1845 he bought an interest in the *South Bend Free Press* and, changing its name to the *St. Joseph Valley Register*, proceeded to build it into the leading Whig newspaper in the region. He remained editor for 18 years, during which he was very active in politics, although his party affiliation drifted from Whig through Know-Nothing to Republican in 1854. In that year he was elected to the House of Representatives, where he remained until 1869, the last six years as speaker of the House, and became a leading figure in the radical wing of the party. In 1868 he was chosen as Ulysses S. Grant's running mate in the presidential election and in November was elected vice-president. He contributed little while in office and in 1872 was not renominated, in part because of his flirtation with the Liberal Republican party but principally because of his involvement in the Crédit Mobilier scandal. The damage done his career by the revelation of that affair was so great as to render virtually superfluous the subsequent and, at the time, more spectacular discovery that in 1868 he had accepted a sizable campaign contribution from a contractor who had supplied the government with envelopes during the period when Colfax was chairman of the House committee on post offices and post roads. After leaving government in 1873 he engaged in popular lecture tours until his death on January 13, 1885, in Mankato, Minnesota.

Colgate, William (1783–1857), businessman and philanthropist. Born in Hollingbourne, England, on January 25, 1783, Colgate came to the United States with his family in 1795 and settled in Baltimore. He went to work at the age of fifteen and in 1804 moved to New York City, where he found a job with a tallow chandler. Two years later he went into the tallow business for himself and from then to the end of his life enjoyed uninterrupted success. He early began manufacturing soap as his main line, and for a time one of the largest starch plants in the country was operated by his firm. Quick to adopt discoveries and improvements in the soapmaking process, he gradually built his company into a leader in the field. In 1847 he moved the plant to Jersey City, New Jersey, and there, a short time later, began turning out fancy soaps and, later still, a variety of other toiletries. Colgate was liberal with his wealth, devoting a large share of his income to philanthropy. He was a founder of the American Bible Society in 1816 and of the American and Foreign Bible Society in 1836 and was a generous supporter of the Baptist church until 1838, when, in an effort to combat sectarianism, he organized the Tabernacle as a nondoctrinal worship society. Another of his beneficiaries was the Hamilton Literary and Theological Institution in Hamilton, New York, which in 1846 became Madison University and in 1890, in recognition of his many gifts and those of his sons, who continued his business, changed its name to Colgate University. Colgate died in New York City on March 25, 1857.

Collier, John (1884–1968), sociologist and public official. Born on May 4, 1884, in Atlanta, Georgia, Collier was educated at Columbia University. In 1905 he began doing social work among immigrant groups and from 1909 to 1919 was civic secretary of the People's Institute in New York City. In 1910 he joined in organizing the Board of Review of Motion Pictures, of which he was secretary until 1914. From 1915 to 1919 he was also director of the National Training School for Community Workers. In 1919 he moved to California and continued his social and educational work there. He developed an interest in the life, both in the past and the present, of American Indians and in 1923 became executive secretary of the American Indian Defense Association, through which he led in the fight against the infamous Bursum Bill of 1922, which had virtually dispossessed the Pueblo Indians of New Mexico of their treaty-guaranteed lands. From 1926 to 1933 he edited *American Indian Life* and promoted a more liberal government policy toward Indians. In 1933 he was given the opportunity he sought when President Franklin D. Roosevelt appointed him commissioner of Indian affairs. Collier lost no time in giving effect to his ideas and in 1934 obtained from Congress passage of the Indian Reorganization Act. The act marked a radical change in official treatment of Indians: the unfamiliar and impossibly complex practice of individual land allotments was stopped and communal lands were once again allowed to be vested in the tribes (bringing the inevitable charges of Communism and subversion from some congressmen); the tribes were encouraged to organize governments and service agencies; and bans on traditional languages and religions were lifted. Collier continued to use his office in the vigorous defense of Indians against private and public mistreatment until his resignation in 1945 at the end of the longest tenure of any Indian commissioner. From that year until 1950 he was director of the National Indian Institute, from 1947 to 1954 professor of sociology at the College of the City of New York, and from 1947 until his death president of the Institute of Ethnic Affairs. He published *Indians of the Americas*, 1947, and *Patterns and Ceremonials of the Indians of the Southwest*, 1949. Collier died on May 8, 1968, in Taos, New Mexico.

Colón, Cristóbal, *see* Columbus, Christopher

Colt, Samuel (1814–1862), inventor and businessman. Born in Hartford, Connecticut, on July 19, 1814, Colt worked as a youth in his father's textile factory in Ware, Massachusetts, and attended school until he went to sea in 1830. While on a voyage to India he conceived the idea for a repeating firearm that would utilize an automatically revolving set of chambers, each of which would be brought successively into alignment with a single barrel. He made a wooden model for such a revolving-breech pistol and soon after his return to the United States had in hand two working models, one of which exploded. In order to finance improved prototypes he toured for a time as "Dr. Coult," demonstrating "laughing gas" (nitrous oxide) and taking up collections. Finally, with good working models, he secured English and French patents in 1835 and a U.S. patent in 1836. In March of that year he founded the Patent Arms Manufacturing Company, in Paterson, New Jersey, to manufacture his revolvers by the most efficient methods available: mass production of completely interchangeable parts, assembly-line procedure, and inspection of the final product by trained personnel. He also developed a breech-loading revolver rifle. Although popular with individuals, including Andrew Jackson, the Colt revolvers—"six-shooters"—failed to interest the army and the company went out of business in 1842. For the next several years Colt worked on perfecting an underwater mine system for harbor defense; from that he turned to telegraphy and experimented with submarine cable. The outbreak of the Mexican War finally generated a demand for his revolver; many Westerners, particularly Texans, would use no other, and the army, impressed at last, ordered 1000 Colts. He hurriedly subcontracted much of the production to Eli Whitney's factory in Whitneyville, Connecticut, until he began manufacturing in his own factory in Hartford in 1848. Success and fortune secured, he continued to direct the Colt's Patent Fire-Arms Manufacturing Company until his death in Hartford on January 10, 1862. The revolver, the nineteenth century's major development in small-arms weaponry, played a crucial role in the settlement of the West as well as in warfare.

Coltrane, John William (1926–1967), musician. Born on September 23, 1926, in Hamlet, North Carolina, Coltrane took up the saxophone, both alto and tenor, while in high school. He later studied music in Philadelphia, where he made his professional debut, and during 1945–1946 played with the navy band. In 1947 he joined Eddie "Cleanhead" Vinson's group and over the next several years moved from band to band while developing his unique lyrical style. He appeared with Dizzy Gillespie, Earl Bostic, and Johnny Hodges, enjoyed especially fruitful associations with Miles Davis and Thelonius Monk, and near the end of his life formed his own quartet. His playing developed from an early New Orleans sound to a frantic, sometimes cynical-seeming style during the years of the "jump" or "jive" bands of the later 1940s and early 1950s; influenced by Lester Young and later by Charlie Parker, he brought to the somewhat disjointed "bebop" manner a virtuoso mastery of technique and a penchant for long and thoroughly independent solo runs. With Miles Davis he began to mellow, his playing becoming more reflective and more completely expressive of his powers of improvisation. Later still, the music of the East and a deep religious sense affected his style. In 1965 he was voted the top jazz tenorman and "Jazzman of the Year" by *Downbeat* magazine and was accorded similar honors by an international poll of critics in *Jazz* magazine. Coltrane died on July 17, 1967, in Húntington, New York.

Columbus, Christopher (1451–1506), explorer. Born in Genoa, quite possibly of a Spanish-Jewish family, Columbus (Cristóbal Colón) went to sea early in life. In 1476 he was shipwrecked off the coast of Portugal; he made his way to Lisbon, then the center for enterprises of exploration and discovery. During the next several years he made a number of voyages to Iceland, the Madeiras, and elsewhere, and was slowly formulating his ideas on sailing west in order to reach Cathay (China). He was primarily influenced in his ideas about the journey, not by astronomical considerations, but by the books of Esdras in the Apocrypha. His calculations, based on Scripture, placed India just where the Americas lie. He proposed a voyage of exploration, first to the king of Portugal, who rejected it, then to a Spanish nobleman, who could not afford it, and finally to King Ferdinand and Queen Isabella of Spain. From 1486 to 1492 his plan was under consideration; finally, in the latter year, and despite Columbus' extravagant demands for reward for discoveries he might make, permission and money were granted. On August 3 the three-ship fleet—the Niña, the Pinta, and the Santa María—sailed; after a good deal of indecision as to the course and several threats of mutiny, land was sighted in the Bahamas on October 12. Disembarking on the island he named San Salvador, Columbus tarried only briefly and spent the next several weeks sailing in search of gold and the mainland of China. After finding only more islands, including Cuba, and leaving a small colony after the Santa María was wrecked on Hispaniola, he set out for Europe in January. He landed in Portugal, was received with great honor in Spain, and was granted huge privileges in the region he had discovered; he even demanded the reward offered to the first to sight land, to the dismay of the sailor who had actually done so. Later that year he returned to the Caribbean as governor, bringing a large fleet and a company of colonists. He found more islands including Guadeloupe, Puerto Rico, and Jamaica, replaced the Hispaniola colony, which had been wiped out by Indians, and decided that Cuba was the mainland. His administration of the region was tyrannical, and some colonists returned to Spain to lodge complaints. He dispatched a shipload of captive Indians to Spain and in 1496 returned himself. Two years later he set out on his third voyage, landing this time on Trinidad. He apparently spotted but failed to recognize the mainland of South America in the summer of 1498. His governorship meanwhile having resulted in growing hostility among the natives and rebellion among his men, in 1500 he was replaced as governor. He resisted the change, however, and was returned to Spain forcibly. Ferdinand and Isabella were thoroughly disenchanted with Columbus's administrative abilities by this time, but were still indebted to him as an admiral who had made great discoveries for the crown. After toying with the idea of liberating Jerusalem, he decided to return to the New World. In 1502 he made his final voyage; he at last discovered the mainland of Central America, although he apparently did not recognize it as such. He reported that he was quite near to Cathay and that he was being guided by dreams and by voices from on high. Beset by difficulties, his fleet disintegrated and he became seriously ill; in 1504 he returned to Spain and died on May 20, 1506, having been, despite his many shortcomings, unquestionably a man of great vision and courage.

Commager, Henry Steele (1902–   ), historian.
Born in Pittsburgh on October 25, 1902, Commager graduated from the University of Chicago in 1923 and, after doing graduate work there and at the University of Copenhagen, took his Ph.D. at Chicago in 1928. He had already, in 1926, joined the faculty of New York University as an instructor in history; he advanced to assistant professor in 1929 and to full professor in 1931. In 1930, with Samuel Eliot Morison, he published *The Growth of the American Republic*, which then and in later revisions was considered one of the best short histories of the nation. In 1934, he edited *Documents of American History* (revised in numerous subsequent editions) and in 1936 wrote a widely praised biography of Theodore Parker. Commager left New York University in 1938 to become professor of history at Columbia and soon afterward appeared *The Heritage of America*, 1939, another large collection of major documents in American history, which he edited with Allan Nevins. Also with Nevins he wrote *America: The Story of a Free People*, 1942. During World War II he lectured in England and wrote numerous articles for the Office of War Information (OWI) and served on the Committee on the History of World War II of the war de-

partment; in 1945 he published *The Story of the Second World War*. From general history Commager gradually moved into the field of interpretation; through such books as *Majority Rule and Minority Rights*, 1943, *The American Mind*, 1950, and *Freedom, Loyalty, Dissent*, 1954, he emerged as both a major interpreter of the American character and a leading spokesman for liberal Jeffersonian democracy. In 1956 he left his post at Columbia (although he remained adjunct professor) and joined the faculty of Amherst College. He was also much in demand as a lecturer and visiting professor at other colleges and universities throughout the country and abroad. Others among his works were *The Blue and the Gray*, 1950, documents on the Civil War; *The Great Declaration*, 1958, with Richard B. Morris; *The Era of Reform*, 1960; *The Great Proclamation*, 1960; *The Nature and Problems of History*, 1965; *Freedom and Order*, 1966; *The Search for a Usable Past*, 1967; and *Commonwealth of Learning*, 1968. Commager retired from active teaching in 1971.

Commons, John Rogers (1862–1945), economist.
Born on October 13, 1862, in Hollansburg, Ohio, Commons graduated from Oberlin College in 1888 and for two years pursued further studies at The Johns Hopkins University. In 1890 he became an instructor in political economy at Wesleyan University; two years later he returned to Oberlin as professor of sociology. After holding similar positions at Indiana and Syracuse universities, he joined the economics faculty of the University of Wisconsin in 1904. There he devoted himself to the study of American labor and, later, of the role of collective action generally in the development of the American economy. In collaboration with a group of his students he published the ten-volume *Documentary History of American Industrial Society*, 1910–1911, and the four-volume *History of Labor in the United States*, 1918–1935. He was one of a number of professors at the University of Wisconsin who were enlisted by Governor Robert M. La Follette to draft reform legislation for the state; Commons himself was particularly interested in establishing a system of unemployment insurance. From 1913 to 1915 he was a member of the Federal Commission on Industrial Relations, in 1917 he was president of the American Economic Association, and from 1920 to 1928 he was associate director of the National Bureau of Economic Research. His later studies led to the publication of *The Legal Foundations of Capitalism*, 1924, and *Institutional Economics*, 1934, among many other works. He retired from Wisconsin in 1932 and thereafter lived in Fort Lauderdale, Florida, and Raleigh, North Carolina. In 1935 he published *Myself*, an autobiography. He died in Raleigh on May 11, 1945.

Compton, Arthur Holly (1892–1962), physicist.
Born on September 10, 1892, in Wooster, Ohio, Compton came of a family that was renowned

for its educators. He graduated from the College of Wooster, where his father was professor and dean, in 1913 and went on to graduate studies at Princeton, taking his Ph.D. in 1916. After a year teaching physics at the University of Minnesota and a time spent in private industry, he went to Cambridge University for further study. In 1920 he became head of the physics department at Washington University in St. Louis; in 1923 he moved to the University of Chicago and remained there until the end of World War II. In 1923 he published the results of his studies of the scattering of X rays by matter; he observed an increase of wavelength in some of the reflected rays—the Compton effect—and provided an explanation that became a key contribution to the development of the quantum theory of energy. For this work Compton was named winner, with C. T. R. Wilson of Great Britain, of the 1927 Nobel Prize for Physics. He later turned to the study of cosmic rays and in the early 1930s supervised a world-wide cosmic-ray survey. In 1940 he became chairman of the physics department and dean of the physical sciences division at the University of Chicago. In 1941 he was named chairman of a committee of the National Academy of Sciences formed to study the military applications of atomic energy; the next year he became director of the metallurgical laboratory of the Manhattan Engineering District (Manhattan Project), his goal being the synthesis of sufficient plutonium for one or more atomic bombs. From 1945 to 1953 Compton was chancellor of Washington University and from 1953 to 1961 Distinguished Service Professor of Natural Philosophy. A man of broadly humanitarian and deeply religious convictions, he published, in addition to his technical works, *The Freedom of Man*, 1935; *The Religion of a Scientist*, 1938; *The Human Meaning of Science*, 1940; and *Atomic Quest*, 1956, the story of the Manhattan Project. Compton served in many high governmental advisory positions and continued to lecture regularly until his death on March 15, 1962, in Berkeley, California.

Comstock, Anthony (1844–1915), reformer. Born on March 7, 1844, in New Canaan, Connecticut, Comstock lost his mother at the age of ten, whereupon he elevated her image to an ideal in whose honor he fought during his later career. He enlisted in the Union army to replace his younger brother, who had been killed in the battle of Gettysburg, and after his discharge was employed as a shop clerk and a salesman in various towns in Connecticut, Tennessee, and New York. In 1872 he became involved with the Young Men's Christian Association (YMCA) in a crusade against pornographic literature. Such enterprises became his life's work, and he lobbied vigorously and effectively in Washington for laws to prevent obscene literature from being sent through the mails. He became a special inspector for the New York City post office and helped to organize the New York Society for the Suppression of Vice, under whose auspices he worked

indefatigably to prosecute "criminal offenders," a term that encompassed, in his view, many writers and poets as well as painters working from nude models, quack doctors, abortionists, and fraudulent advertisers; he was the society's secretary until his death. His moral judgments were narrow and often arbitrary; he was denounced for censuring valuable works of art, but praised for prosecuting actual frauds. The single-minded vigor with which he conducted his work —through raids, publicity, entrapment, and other means—was reflected in his happy assumption of credit for several suicides among his more vulnerable targets. Among his pamphlets and books for young people were *Frauds Exposed*, 1880; *Traps for the Young*, 1883; *Gambling Outrages*, 1887; and *Morals Versus Art*, 1888. He was responsible for the trial of women's-rights crusader Victoria Claflin Woodhull for the "crime" of exposing a love affair between clergyman Henry Ward Beecher and a parishioner's wife. He instituted legal proceedings against George Bernard Shaw's play *Mrs. Warren's Profession* in 1905; Shaw had by then already coined the term "comstockery" as a disparaging label for puritanical crusading. One of the commissions on which Comstock served was President Woodrow Wilson's International Purity Congress. Comstock died in New York City on September 21, 1915.

Conant, James Bryant (1893–1978), chemist, educator, and diplomat. Born in Dorchester, Massachusetts, on March 26, 1893, Conant was educated at Harvard, graduating in 1913 and receiving his Ph.D. three years later. After duty with the chemical warfare service in World War I, he joined the faculty at Harvard as an instructor in chemistry. His work in the field of organic chemistry won him wide recognition as a brilliant investigator and he advanced rapidly to a full professorship. In 1933 he became president of Harvard, a post he retained until his retirement 20 years later and in which, among other things, he emphasized the idea of general education for undergraduate students. As chairman of the National Defense Research Committee and deputy director of the Office of Scientific Research and Development (OSRD) from 1941 to 1946, he was instrumental in mobilizing scientific manpower and organizing war-related research programs, particularly those leading to the production of the atomic bomb. After the war he was a member of both the Atomic Energy Commission (AEC) and the National Science Foundation. In 1953 he was appointed U.S. high commissioner for West Germany and in 1955 became ambassador to the Federal Republic of Germany, remaining in that post for two years. In addition to publishing such books as *Chemistry of Organic Compounds*, 1933, a widely used text, and the non-technical works *On Understanding Science*, 1947, and *Science and Common Sense*, 1951, Conant wrote extensively on the subject of education, his books including *Education for a Classless Society*, 1940, *Education in a Divided World*, 1948, and *Education and*

Liberty, 1953. On his return to the United States from Germany in 1957 he undertook for the Carnegie Corporation of New York a thorough study of U.S. secondary education that resulted in the highly influential *The American High School Today*, 1959. Subsequently he published *The Child, The Parent and the State*, 1959; *Slums and Suburbs*, 1961, also for the Carnegie Corporation; *The Education of American Teachers*, 1963; *Shaping Educational Policy*, 1964; and *The Comprehensive High School*, 1967. *Two Modes of Thought: My Encounters with Science and Education* appeared in 1964 and *My Several Lives*, an autobiography, in 1970. In 1963 Conant won the Presidential Medal of Freedom. He died on February 11, 1978, in Hanover, New Hampshire.

Condon, Edward Uhler (1902–1974), physicist. Born on March 2, 1902, in Alamogordo, New Mexico, Condon graduated from the University of California at Berkeley in 1924 and took his Ph.D. there two years later. After a year of additional study in Germany at the universities of Göttingen and Munich he lectured at Columbia University and in 1928 joined the faculty of Princeton. A year later he moved to the University of Minnesota and in 1930 returned to Princeton as associate professor, remaining for seven years and conducting researches on atomic and molecular structure and the quantum mechanical interpretation of radiation. In 1937 he became associate director of research for the Westinghouse Electric and Manufacturing Company and there continued to direct basic investigations into a variety of topics in physics and chemistry. During World War II Condon was active in government-sponsored scientific work, helping to organize the radar research laboratories at the Massachusetts Institute of Technology and at Westinghouse and in 1943 joining the University of California branch of the Manhattan Engineering District atomic-bomb project. In 1945 he was appointed director of the National Bureau of Standards by President Harry S. Truman; he served in that position for six years, holding at the same time membership on the National Advisory Committee for Aeronautics. Condon was a leading spokesman for U.S. scientists against the imposition of harsh military-security strictures on scientific research and the free exchange of information, and in 1946 he joined Albert Einstein and others to form the Emergency Committee of Atomic Scientists to urge the rule of reason in nuclear-arms development. In 1951 he became director of research and development for the Corning Glass Works; three years later, retaining a consulting position with that company, he became professor of physics at Washington University in St. Louis. From 1963 he was on the faculty of the University of Colorado. During the 1950s he directed the air force's Project Bluebook, which investigated reports of unidentified flying objects (UFOs). He served also as a government adviser on atomic energy. He died in Boulder, Colorado, on March 26, 1974.

Conkling, Roscoe (1829–1888), lawyer, political leader, and public official. Born on October 30, 1829, in Albany, New York, the son of a New York congressman and federal judge, Conkling studied law in Utica and was admitted to the New York bar in 1850. He made campaign speeches for Zachary Taylor and Millard Fillmore in 1848 and gained recognition for his oratorical and legal skills. In 1850 he became Albany's district attorney. Initially a Whig, he helped form the Republican party and in supporting John C. Frémont, its presidential candidate, won New York state for the party in 1856. In 1858 he was elected mayor of Utica and from 1859 to 1867, except for the years 1863–1865, was in the House of Representatives. An advocate of vigorous prosecution of the Civil War and of repressive measures against the South during Reconstruction, he played a prominent role in bringing impeachment proceedings against President Andrew Johnson. He was elected to the Senate in 1867, 1873, and 1879. As undisputed party leader in his state, he influenced President Ulysses S. Grant's Southern policies and was himself a presidential hopeful in 1876, but lost the nomination to Rutherford B. Hayes, whose bitter enemy he was thereafter. In 1880 he led the move to nominate Grant for a third term, a movement that resulted in splitting the convention. He fought the nomination of James A. Garfield and refused to support his candidacy even after Chester A. Arthur, one of Conkling's chief assistants in the party organization in New York, was selected for the vice-presidency. Continually resisting federal control of jobs in the New York customhouse, he finally resigned his Senate seat in 1881 when Garfield sent federal appointees to fill the posts. Offered a Supreme Court justiceship in 1882 by President Arthur, he declined, but sought reelection to the Senate in 1885 to vindicate himself. Finding himself no longer in a controlling position in the Albany legislature, he returned to a successful legal practice. He died in New York City on April 18, 1888.

Connelly, Cornelia (1809–1879), religious leader. Born in Philadelphia on January 15, 1809, Cornelia Peacock was orphaned at an early age and reared in the strongly Episcopalian household of her half sister. In 1831 she married Pierce Connelly, an Episcopalian clergyman, and moved with him to Natchez, Mississippi, where he was rector of Trinity Church. She became interested in the Catholic church, particularly in convent life, and in 1835 she and her husband became converts to that faith. They spent two years in Rome and then moved to Grand Coteau, Louisiana, where they taught in Catholic schools. In 1840 Connelly announced his intention to enter the priesthood; the only way for him to do so was to obtain from his wife a deed of separation and for her to enter a convent. Although she was the mother of three children, she agreed to the conditions and in 1844 entered a convent in Rome. Connelly was ordained the following year. In 1846 Mrs. Connelly was chosen to establish an order of teaching nuns in England, and a year later she took vows and was made first superior of the Society of the Holy Child Jesus. Her husband subsequently attempted to gain control of the order through her and, failing in that, left the church and instituted civil proceedings for the restitution of his conjugal rights. This action also failed, and for the rest of his life he conducted a public campaign of vilification against her. She bore all such trials with equanimity, devoting her energies to the expansion of her order, which in 1862 established a branch in the United States. She died in England on April 18, 1879, and in 1959 was proposed for beatification.

Connelly, Marc (1890–1980), playwright and author. Born on December 13, 1890, in McKeesport, Pennsylvania, Marcus Cook Connelly was the son of retired vaudevillians who operated a hotel frequented by theatrical people and he early developed a love for the theater. At seventeen he became a reporter for the *Pittsburgh Press* and later the *Gazette Times* and in his spare time directed an amateur theater group. In 1916 his first play, *The Amber Empress*, opened and promptly closed in New York City, and he took a job reporting happenings in the theater district for the *New York Morning Telegraph*. He soon met George S. Kaufman, then a reporter for the *New York Times*, and in 1921 they collaborated on a hit comedy entitled *Dulcy*. They followed with *To the Ladies* in 1922, written for Helen Hayes; *The '49ers*, 1922; *Merton of the Movies*, 1922; *Helen of Troy, New York*, 1923; *Be Yourself*, 1924; and *Beggar on Horseback*, 1924. The two then went their separate ways; Connelly wrote a screenplay in Hollywood, then returned to Broadway with *The Wisdom Tooth*, 1927, which he also directed, and *The Wild Man of Borneo*, 1927. In 1930 *The Green Pastures* opened; based on *Ol' Man Adam an' His Chillun*, 1928, a collection of tales by Roark Bradford, Connelly's play depicted heaven, the angels, and God as envisioned by a black country preacher for his Louisiana plantation congregation. It ran on Broadway for more than 600 performances, toured successfully across the country and abroad, and won the 1930 Pulitzer Prize; in 1936 Connelly codirected the film version. Subsequent plays of his included *The Farmer Takes a Wife*, 1934; *The Flowers of Virtue*, 1942; and *Hunter's Moon*, 1958. He wrote or collaborated on numerous movie scripts, including those for *Cradle Song*, 1933; *I Married a Witch*, 1936; and *Captains Courageous*, 1937. He also had a career as an actor, appearing in a 1944 revival of *Our Town*, in *The Spirit of St. Louis*, 1957, and in both stage and screen versions of *Tall Story*, 1959 and 1960. Connelly won an O. Henry Prize for a short story in 1930, was a regular contributor of articles and humor to the *New Yorker* and other magazines, and in 1965 published a mystery novel, *A Souvenir from Qam*. He taught play-

writing at Yale from 1946 to 1950 and from 1953 to 1956 was president of the National Institute of Arts and Letters. *Voices Offstage*, a volume of memoirs, appeared in 1968. He died on December 21, 1980, in New York City.

Connolly, Maureen Catherine (1934–1969), tennis player. Born in San Diego, California, on September 17, 1934, Miss Connolly began playing tennis at the age of ten. After a few months of training under a professional teacher she entered her first tournament and in 1947 won the girl's fifteen-and-under title in the Southern California Invitational. By the time she was fifteen she had won more than 50 championships and had failed to win only four tournaments. In 1949 she became the youngest girl ever to win the national junior championship, and she successfully defended the title the following year. In 1951, her second year in women's division play, she won eight major tournaments and lost three, and helped the U.S. Wightman Cup team to victory. In September of that year she won the national women's singles championship at Forest Hills and was just a few months short of being the youngest woman ever to hold that title. Dubbed "Little Mo" by an affectionate press, Miss Connolly was deceptively slight and engaging off court, but in action she displayed awesome power in her drives. In 1952 she retained her U.S. title and won the prestigious Wimbledon championship in England. In 1953 she achieved the tennis "grand slam," winning the Australian, French, English, and U.S. championships. In 1954 she won her third Wimbledon title and second French title. From 1951 through 1954 she was a regular Wightman Cup team member and did not lose a single match in four years of cup play. An Associated Press sportswriters' poll named her woman athlete of the year in 1952, 1953, and 1954. In 1954 she suffered a crushed leg in a horseback riding accident and never again entered tournament play. Miss Connolly died in Dallas, Texas, on June 21, 1969.

Conway, Thomas (1735–1800?), soldier. Born in Ireland on February 27, 1735, Conway grew up and was educated in France and there joined the army in 1749. In 1777, then a colonel, he sailed to America to offer his services to the colonists in the Revolution and was appointed brigadier general. He saw action at Brandywine and Germantown and was later proposed for promotion to major general. Gen. George Washington, who held Conway in no high regard either personally or professionally, opposed the idea as unfair to American officers of greater competence and experience. When the promotion failed to materialize, Conway resigned; Congress, which was disturbed by Washington's defeats and some of whose members were already considering his replacement, refused to accept the resignation, promoted Conway to major general, and appointed him inspector general. There followed a very confusing episode. Gen. Horatio Gates, buoyed by his victory at Saratoga, had ambitions to become commander in chief, and some New England members of Congress backed him; some secret correspondence was exchanged on the subject and a letter from Conway to Gates, in which Washington was criticized, was intercepted by Gen. James Wilkinson of Gates's staff. Wilkinson passed along a somewhat dramatized version of Conway's comments to another officer and it came to Washington's attention. Washington wrote to Conway and to Congress on the matter and the whole notion of replacing him immediately dissolved; whether or not an actual conspiracy was afoot, the affair became known as the Conway Cabal, taking its name from the least culpable participant. Conway was subsequently placed third in command under the Marquis de Lafayette (who refused to have him as second) of a proposed Canadian expedition. He was later assigned to a less sensitive post; he again threatened to resign, and in April 1778 Congress accepted the offer. A few months later he was severely wounded in a duel that had arisen because of his criticisms of Washington and, on the point of death, he wrote the commander in chief a letter of full apology. He recovered, however, and returned to France. Again in the French army, he saw duty in Flanders and in India, and in 1787 Conway was appointed governor general of French India. In 1793, once again back in France, he was exiled as a royalist. He died about 1800.

Conwell, Russell Herman (1843–1925), lawyer, lecturer, and clergyman. Born in South Worthington, Massachusetts, on February 15, 1843, Conwell grew up on a farm that served as a station on the Underground Railroad. His education at Yale was interrupted by the Civil War; he raised a company and was eventually promoted to lieutenant colonel. After his admission to the bar in 1865 he moved to Minneapolis to practice; while there he founded the *Minneapolis Daily Chronicle.* Moving to Boston a few years later, he continued to practice law and founded the *Somerville* (Massachusetts) *Journal.* He became interested in a run-down Baptist church in Lexington and having successfully revived it, became its minister in 1879. Three years later he was called to perform the same service for Grace Baptist Church in Philadelphia. He succeeded spectacularly; as a result of his efforts the huge Baptist Temple opened in 1891, three hospitals were established, and a night school he had begun in 1884 became Temple College in 1888; Conwell served as its first president. With his lecture "Acres of Diamonds," first delivered in 1861 but often modified afterward, Conwell achieved widespread fame and became one of the most noted speakers on the Chautauqua circuit. Summarizing the philosophy of industry and stating the idea that opportunity is everywhere, the simple speech was delivered more than 6000 times. It eventually earned its author over $8 million. Conwell died on December 6, 1925, in Philadelphia.

Cooke, Jay (1821–1905), banker. Born near the present site of Sandusky, Ohio, on August 10, 1821, Cooke became a clerk in a local store at the age of fourteen and later held a similar job in St. Louis. In 1837 he went to Philadelphia and after two years working for a canal-boat company entered the banking house of E. W. Clark and Company. By 1842 he was a partner in the firm. He left Clark in 1858 and three years later established his own banking house, Jay Cooke & Company, which almost immediately floated a $3 million Civil War loan for the state of Pennsylvania. The next year Salmon P. Chase, a friend of Cooke's brother Henry, became secretary of the treasury; the government was having great difficulty in selling bonds with which to finance the Civil War, and in October 1862 Chase appointed Cooke special agent to sell the securities. Cooke set up a nationwide syndicate of salesmen as subagents and by January 1864 had exceeded the $500 million authorized by Congress. Meanwhile he had established national banks in Philadelphia and in Washington, D.C. In 1865 Secretary of the Treasury William P. Fessenden prevailed upon Cooke to aid in the sale of a new bond issue; within six months his reorganized distribution system disposed of some $600 million worth. After the war he extended his banking interests, opening branches in New York City and London, and in 1870 plunged most of his available capital into financing the construction of the Northern Pacific Railway, chartered by Congress in 1864 and planned to run from Duluth to Seattle. The speculative bubble in railroad stocks soon burst, however, and in 1873 Jay Cooke & Company failed, precipitating the financial panic of that year. By 1880 he had repaid his creditors, and, through investments in Western mining and other ventures, soon recouped his fortune. He died on February 18, 1905, in Ogontz (Elkins Park), Pennsylvania.

Cooley, Charles Horton (1864–1929), sociologist. Born on August 17, 1864, in Ann Arbor, Michigan, Cooley was the son of Thomas M. Cooley. He graduated from the University of Michigan in 1887, from 1889 to 1891 was engaged in statistical studies for the Interstate Commerce Commission and the Bureau of the Census in Washington, D.C., and then returned to the university as an instructor in political economy. In 1895, having taken his Ph.D. the year before, he became an instructor in the altogether new field of sociology, advancing by 1904 to the rank of professor. He published his first major contribution to sociology in 1902 under the title *Human Nature and the Social Order.* In the book Cooley outlined his fundamental sociopsychological views, particularly that mind is a product of social intercourse and that the self is defined and determined by interaction with others. In *Social Organization,* 1909, he discussed the societal consequences of the psychological processes he had outlined, holding that the public mind that emerges from the socially basic "primary group" of close-knit relationships forms the ground for such moral qualities as loyalty, freedom, and justice; these shared values in turn provide vitality and continuity to the social organization from which they spring. He completed the presentation of his sociological system in *Social Process*, 1918, in which he applied the Darwinian notions of adaptation and natural selection to society. A pioneer in the field, Cooley laid the conceptual foundation for much later work in sociology and, although he eschewed the observational, value-free approach of subsequent scientific studies, his strongly philosophical treatment contained much of continuing value. In 1918 he helped found the American Sociological Society and was chosen its first president. He continued to teach at the University of Michigan until his death in Ann Arbor on May 8, 1929.

Cooley, Thomas McIntyre (1824–1898), educator and judge. Born near Attica, New York, on January 6, 1824, Cooley completed his school and academy education in 1842, took up the study of law, and in 1843 moved to Adrian, Michigan. He was admitted to the bar in 1846 and in ten years of private practice established a reputation for scholarly knowledge of the law and clear, intelligent perceptions of issues. In 1857 he was commissioned by the legislature to compile the state statutes and the next year was chosen reporter for the state supreme court; during the seven years in that position he edited eight volumes of reports. In 1859 he became one of the three professors in the newly organized law school of the University of Michigan. He continued to teach and to serve as secretary and later dean of the department until 1884. At the same time he sat on the state supreme court, first winning election in 1864 and remaining until 1885. Cooley was highly regarded both as a teacher and as a judge, and he brought to both callings a mastery of law and a thorough understanding of its best explication. In 1885 he became professor of history and constitutional law at the university, a position he held for the rest of his life, although in later years he taught little. Over the years he had written extensively on the law, publishing *A Treatise on the Constitutional Limitations Which Rest upon the Legislative Power of the States of the American Union*, 1868; editions of Blackstone's *Commentaries*, 1871, and Story's *Commentaries on the Constitution*, 1873; *The Law of Taxation*, 1876; *The Law of Torts*, 1879; and *The General Principles of Constitutional Law*, 1880. During the mid-1880s Cooley became involved in railroad affairs, several times as an arbitrator and once as a receiver, and in 1887 he was appointed to the new Interstate Commerce Commission by President Grover Cleveland. Elected chairman of the commission, he labored for four years to organize its work and establish its policies. He resigned in 1891 and returned to the university. In 1893 he was elected president of the American Bar Association. He died in Ann Arbor on September 12, 1898.

Coolidge, Calvin (1872–1933), thirtieth president of the United States. Born on July 4, 1872, in Plymouth, Vermont, John Calvin Coolidge graduated from Amherst College in 1895 and two years later began the practice of law in Northampton, Massachusetts. He entered Republican politics and rose steadily; gaining a solid reputation for honesty, party loyalty, and completely unspectacular ability during service in the legislature, as mayor of Northampton, and in the state senate, 1912–1915. After three terms as lieutenant governor of Massachusetts he was elected governor in 1918. His administration would doubtless have passed unnoticed but for the Boston police strike of the following year. In the face of rioting and looting while the police force demanded union recognition, Coolidge delayed action until local authority was clearly paralyzed; he then mobilized the state militia to restore order. In a message to Samuel Gompers, president of the American Federation of Labor (AFL), to which the strikers had appealed, he refused reinstatement to the striking police; one sentence of the message—"There is no right to strike against the public safety by anybody, anywhere, any time"—brought him immediate national fame. He was reelected governor later that year and in 1920, after losing the presidential nomination to Warren G. Harding, easily captured the nomination for vice-president. In his new office he carried on as before, quietly and unremarkably. Harding's death in 1923 made him president; he was sworn in on August 3. For the remainder of the term and after his reelection in 1924, Coolidge maintained his remarkable popularity with his honest, simple, and frugal manner. A strong supporter of business—"The business of America is business," he declared in 1925—he encouraged the stock-market boom of the 1920s, greatly reduced governmental action against trusts, and promptly vetoed bills of a liberal cast. His foreign policy was not so much one of isolationism as of aloofness. With characteristic resolution and brevity, he declined renomination with the statement: "I do not choose to run for President in 1928." He retired to Northampton in 1929 and published an autobiography in that year and occasional articles on public issues. Coolidge died on January 5, 1933, in Northampton.

Cooper, Frank James, *see* Cooper, Gary

Cooper, Gary (1901–1961), actor. Born on May 7, 1901, in Helena, Montana, Frank James Cooper adopted the name "Gary" at the start of his movie career. The son of a Montana supreme-court justice, he went to high school in Bozeman and to a local college in Helena and then attended Grinnell College until 1924, leaving without a degree. He worked as a hand on the family ranch during World War I, tending 450 head of cattle and later commenting that the work had been far from romantic. He moved to Los Angeles after leaving college and worked as a salesman for an advertising firm and a photography studio.

In 1925 he was hired by Western Studios as a rider at $10 a day. Inspired by Tom Mix, he turned to acting. After playing bit parts in several films he received his first major role opposite Vilma Banky in *The Winning of Barbara Worth* in 1926. After that he won successively larger roles, including those in *Wings*, 1927; *The Virginian*, 1928; *Morocco*, 1930; *Lives of a Bengal Lancer*, 1935; *Desire*, 1936; *Mr. Deeds Goes to Town*, 1936; *The Plainsman*, 1937; *The General Died at Dawn*, 1937; *Beau Geste*, 1939; *The Westerner*, 1940; *Meet John Doe*, 1941; *Sergeant York*, 1941; for which he won an Academy Award; *Saratoga Trunk*, 1942; *Pride of the Yankees*, 1942; *For Whom the Bell Tolls*, 1943; *The Fountainhead*, 1949; *Springfield Rifle*, 1952; *High Noon*, 1953, for which he won a second Academy Award; *The Court Martial of Billy Mitchell*, 1955; *Friendly Persuasion*, 1956; *Ten North Frederick*, 1958; and *The Wreck of the Mary Deare*, 1959. So compelling were his heroic roles that he came to personify the "all-American male" for millions. Lanky, and seemingly quite ordinary although good-looking, he personified in his most popular roles the simple, average man who triumphs through courage and goodness of heart. In the homely, laconic Western dialect, often ungrammatical, that he made famous, his most celebrated utterances were "Yup" and "They went that-a-way." Cooper died on May 13, 1961 in Hollywood, California.

Cooper, James Fenimore (1789–1851), author. Born on September 15, 1789, in Burlington, New Jersey, Cooper grew up in Cooperstown, New York, a frontier village on the Susquehanna River founded by his father, who had bought land there in 1785. In 1802 he entered Yale, where he excelled in Latin, but was expelled for a prank in his third year. He became an apprentice seaman in 1806 and in 1808, after a training voyage to Europe, was commissioned a midshipman in the navy, continuing in service for three years. Resigning in 1811, he married a daughter of a wealthy landowning family and settled into the life of a country gentleman. At the age of thirty, in response to certain financial reverses but also, according to legend, to his wife's challenge of his claim that he could write a better novel than the popular English one she was then reading, he began his literary career with *Precaution*, 1820, a conventional effort that, despite its poor reception, encouraged him to continue writing. In 1821 he published *The Spy*, which first featured what became the "Cooper hero"—a solitary man, courageous, straightforward, and a little mysterious—and the innovative device of flight and pursuit. The book quickly became popular, and it was followed by *The Pioneers*, 1823, the first of his *Leatherstocking Tales* and a great success; *The Pilot*, 1823, introducing another innovation, the sea romance; *The Last of the Mohicans*, 1826; and *The Prairie*, 1827. Already the preeminent American literary figure and celebrated around the world, Cooper traveled to Europe in 1826 and

remained for seven years, writing, in addition to two more books of the Leatherstocking saga, a number of other novels—*The Red Rover*, 1827; *The Water-Witch*, 1830; *The Bravo*, 1831; and *The Headsman*, 1833, among them—along with several travel books. Returning to Cooperstown in 1833, he found himself at odds with the mood of the country. He had long considered himself a thorough democrat, and during his seven years' absence had vigorously defended American democracy against European critics; but he found the style of Jacksonian democracy highly distasteful. His own socially and intellectually aristocratic leanings, centered on his notion of the somewhat condescending "democratic" gentleman, found vent in *The American Democrat*, 1838, and two novels, *Homeward Bound* and *Home as Found*, both also 1838. Cooper suddenly was the target of a torrent of public abuse. He responded with a series of libel suits against his least courteous critics that, although he won most of them and in so doing helped establish effective rules of libel in U.S. courts, made him nearly as well known for litigiousness as for literature and did little to endear him to his countrymen. He nonetheless continued writing, publishing books of history, travel, and romance, including *The History of the Navy of the United States of America*, 1839, the final two volumes (in order of writing) of the Leatherstocking series, *The Pathfinder*, 1840, and *The Deerslayer*, 1841, and numerous others such as *The Wing-and-Wing*, 1842; *Afloat and Ashore*, 1844; *Satanstoe*, the first of a trilogy on New York landowners and antirentism, 1845; *The Oak Openings*, 1848; and *The Ways of the Hour*, 1850. By far his best works, and his great contribution to American literature, were those comprising the *Leatherstocking Tales*. In that saga the archetypal noble woodsman, appearing first as Natty Bumppo (Leatherstocking) in *The Deerslayer*, the first of the series in narrative order, progressed through his prime as Hawkeye in *The Last of the Mohicans*, through the French and Indian Wars as the Pathfinder in the novel of that name, to the beginning of a retreat from advancing civilization, again as Bumppo, in *The Pioneers*, and finally, as "the old trapper," to old age and self-imposed exile among the Indians of the Great Plains in *The Prairie*. Employing a "romantic elevation" of such ethical and intellectual seriousness as to be nearly mythopoetic, the books were epic in both intent and effect, and although they often suffered from marked lapses of style—a failing dealt with most severely by Mark Twain in "Fenimore Cooper's Literary Offenses" in 1895—they remained among the most enduring works of American literature. Cooper died in Cooperstown on September 14, 1851. He was elected to the Hall of Fame in 1910.

Cooper, Leon N. (1930–), physicist. Born in New York City on February 28, 1930, Cooper attended the Bronx High School of Science before enrolling at Columbia University, where he received an A.B. in 1951 and took his Ph.D. in 1953.

He subsequently spent a year at the Institute for Advanced Study at Princeton, two years at the University of Illinois, and one year at Ohio State University before joining the Brown University faculty in 1958. During this time Cooper's interest was centered on the phenomenon of superconductivity in metals, the most striking feature of which is the complete disappearance at a temperature—usually in the neighborhood of absolute zero—of the normal resistance to electrical current that is characteristic of the metal or alloy concerned. The understanding of superconductivity, the existence of which had been known since 1911, was greatly advanced by the discovery that the specific temperature at which a metal exhibits this phenomenon is a function of its isotopic mass, a property in turn dependent only on the metallic lattice of the metal. Further intensive study by Cooper and two colleagues at Illinois, John Bardeen and John R. Schrieffer led in 1957 to a theory that explained how the interaction of isotope and lattice produces the energy levels that induce the known characteristics of superconductivity—perfect conductivity and the vanishing of magnetic induction. The theory was hailed as a milestone and Cooper's reputation advanced steadily after this breakthrough; in the late 1950s and in the 1960s he lectured in Italy, Norway, and Paris as well as at a number of American universities. Appointed Henry Ledyard Goddard University Professor at Brown in 1966, he published *Introduction to the Meaning and Structure of Physics* in 1968. He was also noted for his well-received attempts to teach physics to humanities majors. He shared the Comstock Prize of the National Academy of Sciences with Schrieffer in 1968, and in 1972 Cooper, Bardeen, and Schrieffer shared the Nobel Prize for Physics for their theoretical explanation of superconductivity.

Cooper, Peter (1791–1883), businessman, inventor, and philanthropist. Born on February 12, 1791, in New York City, Cooper received little formal education and was apprenticed to a coachmaker at seventeen. He worked in various fields of industry, enjoying particular success in the manufacture of glue, until in 1828 he founded the Canton Iron Works in Baltimore; there, two years later, he built the first American steam locomotive, *Tom Thumb*. Despite its diminutive size and despite also the minor mechanical failure that caused it to lose a well-publicized race with a horse-drawn train over the Baltimore and Ohio tracks on September 18, 1830, the locomotive was instrumental in promoting the rapid growth of railroads in the United States. Cooper's business holdings grew rapidly to include iron mines, foundries, and factories. In 1854 one of his factories produced the first iron structural beams for fire-retardant buildings; two years later he introduced the Bessemer process into American steelmaking. He was a principal financial supporter of Cyrus W. Field and was thus instrumental in the success of the New York, Newfoundland, and London Telegraph Company,

which laid the first transatlantic cable and of which he was president for 20 years. As an inventor he developed such devices as a gravity-driven endless bucket chain in one of his mines and a washing machine, and various ingenious methods for powering watercraft. In 1859 he founded Cooper Union in New York City; that institution devoted to free public education, particularly for adults, in technical and scientific fields and in art, included among its facilities the city's first free public reading room and was long a favorite public forum. Cooper was active also in civic affairs and in 1876 was the presidential nominee of the Greenback party. Cooper died on April 4, 1883, in New York City. He was elected to the Hall of Fame in 1900.

Cooper, Thomas (1759–1839), chemist, educator, and political philosopher. Born in London on October 22, 1759, Cooper was educated at Oxford but took no degree. For ten years or more he dabbled in a variety of pursuits, including medicine, law, the textile business, and chemistry; in the last field he was something more than a talented amateur and attracted the friendship of Joseph Priestley. Politically a radical, he agitated for a number of reforms and in 1792 engaged in a brief public controversy with Edmund Burke. The following year he emigrated to the United States, where he hoped to find greater freedom of thought. Settling in Northumberland, Pennsylvania, he practiced both law and medicine and continued to make experiments in chemistry with Priestley, who had also fled England. In 1800 he served a short prison term following conviction under the Alien and Sedition Acts of 1798, but with the subsequent Republican ascendancy he secured positions as county commissioner in 1801–1804 and as district judge in 1804–1811. From 1811 to 1815 he taught chemistry at Carlisle (now Dickinson) College and from 1816 to 1819 at the University of Pennsylvania. Thomas Jefferson won for him appointment as professor of natural science and law at the University of Virginia, but the heated opposition of the clergy, whom Cooper held in no little contempt, prevented him from assuming the chair. Instead, in 1820 he became professor of chemistry at South Carolina College (now the University of South Carolina) and the next year was elected president. By the breadth of his own learning he brought the college to a position of distinction and inaugurated there an innovative course in political economy. His political views remained strongly libertarian and he was a principal influence on the development of the Southern free-trade, anti-tariff position and a major advocate of nullification and, if necessary, secession, in 1832. His continuing dispute with the clergy led eventually to his resignation as president of the college in 1833 and as professor in 1834. Thereafter he edited, in five volumes, the statutes of South Carolina. Among his writings, many of which were controversial in nature, were *Some Information Respecting America*, 1794; *Political*

Essays, 1800; *Discourses on the Connexion Between Chemistry and Medicine*, 1818; *Lectures on the Elements of Political Economy*, 1826; *On the Constitution*, 1826; and *A Treatise on the Law of Libel and the Liberty of the Press*, 1830. Called by John Adams "a learned, ingenious, scientific, and talented madcap," Cooper died in Columbia, South Carolina, on May 11, 1839.

Coowescoowe, *see* Ross, John

Copland, Aaron (1900–   ), composer. Born on November 14, 1900, in Brooklyn, New York City, Copland studied composition, orchestration, and theory with Rubin Goldmark in New York until 1921; he then moved to Paris and studied with Nadia Boulanger until 1924. While in France, he observed that the native music reflected the character of French life and that no similar relation existed between his own country and its formal music. On his return to the United States, he determined to compose music that Americans would appreciate and that would reflect their environment, culture, history, and legends. Some early work, developing his technique and musicianship and identifying him as a singular composer, included *The Cat and Mouse*, 1919; *Symphony for Organ and Orchestra*, 1924; *Music for Theater*, 1925; *Symphonic Ode*, 1929; *Piano Variations*, 1930; *Short Symphony*, 1933; and *Piano Sonata*, 1941. Prepared to transcribe his ideas into "native" music, he began work that he hoped would relate to and, consequently, please the American audience. His *Lincoln Portrait*, 1942, for orchestra and speaker, and three ballets, *Billy the Kid*, 1938, *Rodeo*, 1942, and *Appalachian Spring*, 1944, used familiar American melodies drawn from popular recordings, folk songs, and cowboy tunes. As a result, he was hailed enthusiastically by modern audiences, which had become accustomed to listening to music with little thought for simple enjoyment. An adventurous composer, he produced other works with jazz rhythms, concurrent themes, wide expanses of tone, and unorthodox instrumental combinations. Later compositions included *Third Symphony*, 1946; *Twelve Poems by Emily Dickinson*, 1950, a song cycle; *The Tender Land*, 1954, an opera; *Piano Fantasy*, 1957; *Nonet*, 1960; *Connotations*, 1962; *Music for a Great City*, 1964; and *Inscape*, 1967. In 1939 he was asked to compose music for the play *Quiet City* and he subsequently wrote scores for several motion pictures, including *Of Mice and Men*, 1939; *Our Town*, 1940; *The Red Pony*, 1948; and *The Heiress*, 1949. He also wrote several books: *What To Listen For in Music*, 1939; *Our New Music*, 1941; *Music and Imagination*, 1952; and *Copland on Music*, 1960. He won the Presidential Medal of Freedom in 1964.

Copley, John Singleton (1738–1815), painter. Born on July 3, 1738, into a Loyalist family in Boston, Copley learned to paint and engrave from his stepfather, Peter Pelham. Pelham died in 1751, leaving his business to Copley, who mastered the engraver's trade and produced mezzotints, at least one of which still survives. His ambition to be a professional painter was realized at the age of eighteen. Conforming to the fashion in colonial portraiture, he soon achieved a reputation and acquired considerable wealth for the time. His portraits, among the subjects of which were Paul Revere, Samuel Adams, and John Hancock, spread his fame through New England. Commissions from Boston, New York, and Philadelphia encouraged him to go farther afield, and in 1766 he sent "The Boy with the Squirrel" to London for exhibition. It earned for him a fellowship in the Society of Artists of Great Britain, as well as an enduring friendship with the prominent artist Benjamin West, who urged Copley to paint in England. During the 1770s Copley's commissions declined, perhaps because of his affiliations with the Loyalists, and he embarked for Europe, vacationing for a year in Italy and in 1775 settling permanently in London. There portrayals of events of historical and biblical significance dominated his work. English art of the time featured idealism, but Copley retained his direct approach, re-creating scenes such as "The Death of Lord Chatham," "The Siege of Gibraltar," "The Arrest of Five Members of the Commons by Charles the First," "Abraham Offering Up Isaac," and "The Victory of Lord Duncan" with a passion that sometimes shocked refined English patrons of art. But Copley's reputation had been established, and in 1783 he became a full member of the Royal Academy. He was visited in London by John Adams and John Quincy Adams, who commissioned portraits. Portraiture failed to bring the degree of financial success he had hoped for, however, while his historical paintings, on which he hoped to found his artistic reputation, went relatively unrecognized. Although he was acknowledged as the first great American painter, he continued to labor in frustration until his death in London on September 9, 1815.

Corbett, James John (1866–1933), boxer. Born in San Francisco on Setpember 1, 1866, Corbett went to work for a bank upon finishing school and advanced to the position of assistant teller, but his love of boxing grew steadily until, in 1886, he began fighting professionally. In 1889, after a string of minor victories, he defeated the well-known heavyweight Joe Choynski in 28 rounds. Having suffered two broken knuckles during the bout, he compensated by using the innovative hook blow. Another victory over Choynski a short time later was followed by Corbett's defeat of Jake Kilrain in New Orleans and Dominick McCaffrey in Brooklyn, New York, in 1890. Established as a leading heavyweight title contender, he became a highly popular figure because of the contrast he struck wtih the common run of boxers, his upright and courteous manner earning him the nickname "Gentleman Jim." In 1891 he was matched with Peter Jackson, a West Indian boxer whom John L. Sullivan, the reigning champion, had refused to fight because of his race; the fight was stopped in the 61st round and declared a draw. It was at about this time that Corbett came under the management of William A. Brady, who in addition to taking over his ring career also found him opportunities on the stage. Finally, on September 7, 1892, in New Orleans, Corbett met Sullivan in the first title match fought with padded gloves and under the Marquis of Queensberry rules. He scored a knockout in the 21st round. An extremely intelligent fighter, Corbett made up for having small hands by developing his agility and great skill in punching and feinting, and is credited with being the first modern "scientific" boxer. He retained the heavyweight crown for just under five years, losing it at last to Robert Fitzsimmons of Great Britain in the 14th round of a match in Carson City, Nevada, on March 17, 1897. He was unsuccessful in two later comeback attempts, losing in 1900 and again in 1903 to James J. Jeffries. Thereafter he appeared on the stage and in vaudeville and made numerous lecture tours; he also had roles in several motion pictures. His autobiography, *The Roar of the Crowd*, appeared in 1925. Corbett died in Bayside, New York City, on February 18, 1933.

Corbin, Margaret (1751–1800), military heroine. Born on November 12, 1751, in what is now Franklin County, then on the western Pennsylvania frontier, Margaret Cochran, having lost both of her parents in an Indian raid when she was five, grew up with relatives. She married John Corbin in 1772, and when he enlisted in the First Company of Pennsylvania Artillery for service in the Revolution she followed him east. On November 16, 1776, Corbin was manning a gun on a ridge near Fort Washington, New York, when he was killed during a Hessian advance. Observing from near by, Margaret immediately leaped to the gun and continued to serve in her husband's stead until she was felled by serious wounds. Upon the surrender of the American position she was not taken among the prisoners. She made her way to Philadelphia and there, completely disabled, came to the attention of the state's Executive Council, by which she was granted temporary relief in June 1779. The next month the Continental Congress approved the granting of a lifetime soldier's pension to her. She was thereafter included on military rolls and in 1783 was formally mustered out of the Continental army. She lived in Westchester County, New York, until her death on January 16, 1800.

Corcoran, William Wilson (1798–1888), banker, art collector, and philanthropist. Born in Baltimore on December 27, 1798, Corcoran attended Georgetown College for a year and then, in 1815, took a job in a dry-goods store operated by his elder brothers. Two years later he opened his own dry-goods firm, W. W. Corcoran & Company. The business prospered for a time and he added a wholesale division, but in 1823 it went bankrupt. For the next several years he engaged in various pursuits and in 1837 opened a brokerage firm in Washington, D.C. Three years later he organized Corcoran & Riggs, bankers, in Washington. In that enterprise he was highly successful, so much so that in 1847 he paid back the creditors of W. W. Corcoran & Company with interest. The next year he was able to assume nearly the whole of the $16 million in bonds issued by the government to finance the Mexican War; he disposed of some $5 million worth in London at an advantageous price, by the entire transaction bolstering the public credit of the United States and, with the subsequent rise in market value of the bonds, reaping at the same time a very respectable profit. In 1854 he retired from active business and devoted himself thereafter to his personal affairs and philanthropies. He began construction of the Corcoran Gallery of Art in Washington in 1859; the Civil War interrupted progress—Corcoran, a Confederate sympathizer, lived abroad during the war—and it was not until 1872 that the gallery opened, with the donor's personal art collection as its nucleus. His gifts to the gallery eventually totaled some $1.6 million. Others among his major beneficiaries were Columbian (now the George Washington) University, the University of Virginia, the College of William and Mary, the Academy of the Visitation in Washington, and other educational and religious institutions, and he founded in Washington in 1869 the Louise Home for "needy gentlewomen." Corcoran died in Washington on February 24, 1888.

Cori, Carl Ferdinand (1896–   ), biochemist. Born in Prague, then in Austria (now in Czechoslovakia), on December 5, 1896, Cori was educated at the German University in Prague, taking his medical degree in 1920. In that year he married Gerty Theresa Radnitz, who was also a native of Prague (born August 15, 1896), and who had also taken her medical degree at the German University in 1920. They moved to Vienna where Carl held positions in the medical clinic of the University of Vienna and in the pharmacology department of the University of Graz, and Gerty was an assistant in the Children's Hospital. In 1922 they came to the United States and became citizens in 1928. They joined the Institute for the Study of Malignant Diseases in Buffalo, New York, Carl as a biochemist and Gerty as an assistant pathologist and from 1925 as assistant biochemist. Carl was also an assistant professor of physiology at the University of Buffalo in 1930–1931. At the institute the Coris became interested in the metabolic processes in tumors, particularly those processes involving carbohydrates. Their studies in the field were basic, leading them to the investigation of sugar metabolism and the action of insulin. They continued their work together at the medical school of Washington University in St. Louis from 1931; there Carl was professor of pharmacology and, from 1942, professor of biochemistry; Gerty was research associate in pharmacology until 1943, then research associate professor of biochemistry, and from 1947 full professor. In 1936, in the course of their research, they isolated a previously unknown form of glucose, glucose-1-phosphate, also known as the Cori ester. They then discovered that this ester is produced from glycogen by the reversible action of the enzyme phosphorylase, and in 1939 they demonstrated the in vitro conversion of the ester to glycogen. Their discovery of the intermediate steps in the glycogen–glucose conversion (afterward known as the Cori cycle) proved to be the opening wedge in the complete elucidation of sugar metabolism and storage in the body and in 1947 they were awarded, with B. A. Houssay of Argentina, the Nobel Prize for Medicine and Physiology. They continued to investigate various aspects of metabolism, including the roles of various hormones in regulating enzyme action, the mechanism of insulin, and other topics. Gerty Cori died in St. Louis on October 26, 1957. Carl Cori continued to teach and carry on research, becoming in 1965 Distinguished Service Professor of Pharmacology and Biochemistry.

Cori, Gerty Theresa, see under Cori, Carl Ferdinand

Corliss, George Henry (1817–1888), inventor and manufacturer. Born on June 2, 1817, in Easton, Washington County, New York, Corliss grew up there and in Greenwich, New York, where he attended school until he was fourteen. He worked for a textile manufacturer for four years and then resumed his education at Castleton Academy in Vermont. Returning to Greenwich, he opened his own boot store and in 1842 patented a boot-stitching machine. Two years later he was hired as a draftsman by the company to which he had taken his device, a machine and steam-engine manufactory in Providence, Rhode Island. His mechanical abilities given free rein, he soon devised major improvements in steam-engine construction and in 1848 organized Corliss, Nightingale & Company to exploit his ideas. Receiving patents in 1849 and 1851, he began building steam engines; in 1856 his large new factory was opened in Providence as the Corliss Steam Engine Company, which thereafter built many of the largest engines in the country. The mechanisms that Corliss had invented consisted of rotary inlet and exhaust valves controlled by a governor of a type known as a drop cutoff; great efficiency and fuel economy resulted in engines so equipped. Corliss continued to improve his machines through the years and also invented a bevel-gear cutter and other devices. For the 1876 Centennial Exposition in Philadelphia the Corliss works built the great 1600-horsepower engine that powered all the exhibits in Machinery Hall. The engine so impressed historian Henry Adams that he called it the symbol of the age. Corliss directed the company for the rest of his life and in 1868 was elected to a term in the Rhode Island legislature. He died in Providence on February 21, 1888.

Cornell, Ezra (1807–1874), businessman and philanthropist. Born on January 11, 1807, in Westchester Landing, New York, Cornell grew up there and in De Ruyter, New York. During his youth he worked at various jobs and exhibited both business ability and a flair for things mechanical. In 1828 he settled in Ithaca, New York, and soon became manager of a flour mill and a plaster mill. Under his direction a larger and mechanically more complex flour mill was built. In 1842 he became associated with Samuel F. B. Morse; developing a method of insulating a telegraph wire and stringing it along a series of poles, he supervised the construction of the first such line from Washington, D.C., to Baltimore in 1844. During the next 11 years he financed and built telegraph lines connecting many major cities in the East and the Midwest and in 1855, when the number of competing telegraph companies had increased to the point that they threatened one another's existence, he was a leader in unifying the major lines in the Western Union Telegraph Company. For some 15 years he was the principal stockholder in the company and he served as a director until his death. The wealth he accumulated was applied to other interests. He established a model farm near Ithaca and in 1863 built a free public library for the city. The passage of the Morrill Act in 1862 inspired him to found an agricultural college; he developed and broadened plans proposed to him by Andrew D. White and in 1865 formally established Cornell University. Three years later the school opened with White as its first president. In addition to receiving outright gifts totaling about $900,000, the school reaped more than $3 million from Cornell's transactions in public lands on its behalf. From 1861 to 1867 he served in the state legislature. He died in Ithaca on December 9, 1874.

Cornell, Katharine (1893–1974), actress and producer. Born on February 16, 1893, in Berlin, Germany, Miss Cornell was the daughter of American parents with whom she returned to Buffalo, New York, later in that year. Her interest in the theater developed in school and in 1916 she joined the Washington Square Players; she later worked with a touring stock company and in 1919 received favorable attention for her portrayal of Jo in a London production of *Little Women*. In 1921 she made her Broadway debut in *Nice People* and later in the year won her first lead in *A Bill of Divorcement*, vaulting into stardom in the role. Subsequently she appeared in *Will Shakespeare*, 1923, *The Way Things Happen* and *Candida*, both 1924, and *The Green Hat*, 1926, among others; the last was directed by Guthrie McClintic, her husband since 1921 and thereafter director of nearly all her plays. After *The Letter*, 1927, *The Age of Innocence*, 1928, and *Dishonored Lady*, 1930, she began managing her own productions and immediately scored a triumph in *The Barretts of Wimpole Street*, 1931, in which she played Elizabeth Barrett Browning;

after a long Broadway run she broke with current theatrical practice by taking the production's first-string cast on an extended and highly successful road tour. Celebrated for their excellence, her later productions included *Lucrece*, 1932; *Alien Corn*, written for her, 1933; *Romeo and Juliet*, 1934; *Saint Joan*, 1936; *The Wingless Victory*, 1937; *No Time for Comedy*, 1939; *The Doctor's Dilemma*, 1941; and *The Three Sisters*, 1942. During World War II she entertained troops in Europe with *The Barretts of Wimpole Street* and in 1943 appeared in a movie, *Stage Door Canteen*. She returned to Broadway in 1946 with *Antigone* and a revival of *Candida* and followed with *Antony and Cleopatra*, 1947; *The Lady*, 1949; and *The Constant Wife*, 1951. During the 1950s she also appeared on television in productions of *The Barretts of Wimpole Street* in 1956 and *There Shall Be No Night* in 1957. With her farewell performance in *Dear Liar*, 1960, Miss Cornell retired from the stage. She died at her home in Vineyard Haven, Massachusetts, on June 9, 1974.

Coronado, Francisco Vásquez de (1510–1554), explorer and colonial figure. Born in Salamanca, Spain, in 1510, Coronado came to America in 1535 in the company of Antonio de Mendoza, first viceroy of New Spain. In 1538 he was appointed to the council of Mexico City and later in the year became governor of Nueva Galicia with his provincial capital in Guadalajara. The next year an exploring party under Fray Marcos de Niza set out to the north, and upon its return Fray Marcos told of hearing of fabulous riches in the Seven Cities of Cíbola. Great excitement ensued and early in 1540 a second expedition was mounted under the command of Coronado. With some 300 Spanish soldiers and nearly 1000 Indians he set out in February and in July reached the Seven Cities, which turned out to be the poor Zuñi pueblos of New Mexico. He conquered them easily and then divided his forces under several lieutenants to explore further. Pedro de Tovar found the Hopi pueblos in Arizona, García López de Cárdenas discovered the Grand Canyon, and Hernando de Alvarado moved east to the Rio Grande, where Coronado joined him and wintered at Tiguex, north of present-day Albuquerque. While there he conquered a few more pueblos and explored the surrounding country; he also heard from a captive Indian of Gran Quivira, to the east, where gold was too plentiful for description. Again dazed by the prospect of riches, he set out in April 1541; by the time he reached Palo Duro Canyon (near Amarillo, Texas) he was nearly overwhelmed by the vastness of the country and sent the bulk of his force back to Tiguex, continuing on with 30 men. He turned north through what is now Oklahoma and in July 1541, near the great bend of the Arkansas River in central Kansas, found Quivira—a settlement of Wichita Indians who had no gold or jewels. Thoroughly disappointed, Coronado returned to Tiguex and in 1542 arrived again in Mexico. An official inquiry into his conduct of the expedition

found him blameless for its failure. In 1544, however, he was fined and removed from the governorship of Nueva Galicia for his cruel treatment of Indians. He moved back to Mexico City, where he retained his council membership until his death on September 22, 1554. Accounted a failure by most, himself included, Coronado nonetheless provided the Southwest with one of the most colorful and remarkable episodes of its early history.

Correll, Charles J., *see under* Gosden, Freeman Fisher

Cortelyou, George Bruce (1862–1940), public official and businessman. Born in New York City on July 26, 1862, Cortelyou graduated from the Massachusetts State Normal School in 1882 and for a year taught school and studied at the New England Conservatory of Music in Boston. He returned to New York in 1883 and became a stenographic reporter. From 1885 to 1889 he was a school principal, but then resumed his stenographic work and began serving as secretary to various public officials in New York City and later in Washington, D.C. In 1895 he became stenographer to President Grover Cleveland and in that year and the next took law degrees from Georgetown and Columbian (now George Washington) universities. In 1900 he became secretary to President William McKinley and held the same post under Theodore Roosevelt until 1903, when, having displayed considerable political and business acumen during the 1902 coal-strike negotiations, he was named the first secretary of commerce and labor by the president. While organizing the work of the new department Cortelyou advised Roosevelt on various issues and in 1904, elected chairman of the Republican National Committee, managed his campaign for reelection. Later in the year he was appointed postmaster general; in less than three years in that office he brought the department to a peak of efficiency through reorganization and an insistence that as many appointments and promotions as possible be based on merit. In March 1907 Cortelyou left the post office to become secretary of the treasury, where again his great administrative abilities proved a valuable asset, particularly in dealing with a financial panic of that year. He also contributed much to the improvement of the Revenue Cutter Service (later part of the Coast Guard). Having served in three cabinet positions in six years, Cortelyou left government service in March 1909 and became president of the New York Consolidated Gas Company, which then and later, as the Consolidated Edison Company, was one of the giants of the utilities industry. His administration was most noteworthy for its liberal policy concerning employee benefits, but he also carried on a major expansion program, acquiring by 1928 control of the power and light services for all of greater New York. He retired in 1935 and died at his estate in Huntington, New York, October 23, 1940.

Corwin, Edward Samuel (1878–1963), political scientist. Born on January 19, 1878, near Plymouth, Michigan, Corwin graduated from the University of Michigan in 1900 and after teaching history for a year at the Brooklyn Polytechnic Institute entered the University of Pennsylvania and took his Ph.D. in 1905. In that year Woodrow Wilson, then president of Princeton University, invited him to become one of the original preceptors there, a new tutorial post established by Wilson in his reorganization of the university. Corwin accepted, serving as preceptor in history, politics, and economics until 1911, as professor of politics from 1911 to 1918, and as McCormick Professor of Jurisprudence from 1918 until his retirement in 1946. During those years he produced a large number of penetrating and widely influential studies of American political institutions and law that established him as a ranking authority; among them were *National Supremacy, Treaty Power versus State Power*, 1913; *The Doctrine of Judicial Review*, 1914; *French Policy and the American Alliance*, 1916; *The President's Control of Foreign Relations*, 1917; *John Marshall and the Constitution*, 1919; *The Constitution and What It Means Today*, 1920; *The President's Removal Power*, 1927; *The Democratic Dogma and Other Essays*, 1930; *The Twilight of the Supreme Court*, 1934; *Court over Constitution*, 1938; *The President: Office and Powers*, 1940; *The Constitution and World Organization*, 1944; and *Liberty Against Government*, 1948. During the mid-1930s he was often consulted by the office of the attorney general and by government agencies on constitutional questions, and he was much in demand throughout his career as a lecturer and visiting professor. From 1949 he was editor of the Library of Congress Legislative Reference Division. Corwin died in Princeton, New Jersey, on April 29, 1963.

Cotton, John (1585–1652), religious leader. Born in Derby, England, on December 4, 1585, Cotton was educated at Cambridge, where he came under the influence of Puritanism. From 1612 to 1633 he was a parish vicar in Boston, Lincolnshire, where his growing adherence to Puritan heterodoxy finally resulted in charges being brought against him in an ecclesiastical court. He fled to London and then, a few months later, emigrated to Massachusetts. In October 1633, shortly after his arrival, he was chosen as teacher of the First Church (Congregational) of Boston, in which position he remained for the rest of his life. Armed with great learning, he quickly became a leading, even dominating, figure in the colony. He staunchly defended established Puritan institutions against both Anne Hutchinson and Roger Williams. His writings were thorough expositions of Congregational theology and polity; *The Way of the Churches of Christ in New England*, 1645, and *The Way of the Congregational Churches Cleared*, 1648, are notable. Like most Puritan leaders, Cotton was politically conservative; he stood for a strong and pervasive civil authority closely linked to the clergy, and while he staunchly supported Congregationalism, he was not led thereby to see any good in political democracy. He also wrote a children's catechism that was long the New England standard, titling it *Milk for Babes, Drawn out of the Breasts of Both Testaments, Chiefly for the Spirituall Nourishment of Boston Babes in either England, but may be of like Use for any Children*; it appeared in 1646. Cotton died on December 23, 1652, in Boston.

Coughlin, Charles Edward (1891–1979), religious and political leader. Born on October 25, 1891, in Hamilton, Ontario, Coughlin was educated at St. Michael's College in Toronto and in 1916 was ordained a priest in the Roman Catholic Church. In 1926 he became pastor of the Shrine of the Little Flower in Royal Oak, Michigan. He soon began making radio broadcasts of sermons and talks to children and in 1930 started using the radio to express his political and economic views as well. In the turmoil of the Depression he gathered a growing audience of followers as he attacked President Herbert Hoover and then supported President Franklin D. Roosevelt and the New Deal. As his influence increased he used donated money to buy time on more and more radio stations; he also published *Christ or the Red Serpent*, 1930; *By the Sweat of Thy Brow*, 1931; and *The New Deal in Money*, 1933. In 1935 he suddenly turned against Roosevelt and began advocating a radical economic policy. In that year he founded the National Union for Social Justice, which in 1936 joined with the late Huey P. Long's Share the Wealth movement, then headed by Gerald L. K. Smith, and with Francis E. Townsend and his followers in supporting the newly formed Union party and its presidential candidate, William Lemke. Coughlin's attacks on Roosevelt grew so violent as to draw a rebuke from the Pope, and the murky finances of the National Union and of the Radio League of the Little Flower were subjected to investigation. Coughlin founded *Social Justice*, a magazine carrying his views on political and international affairs, and counted his followers in the millions. In the later 1930s Coughlin added to his customary expressions of hatred for Communism, attacks on Wall Street and on the Jews, and began making comments that were increasingly favorable to Fascism. He allied himself with the pro-Fascist, anti-Semitic Christian Front, and in his broadcasts grew ever more demagogic. Finally *Social Justice* was barred from the mails under the Espionage Act and ceased publication in 1942; in the same year his church superiors, after bearing years of embarrassment, imposed silence on him. He complied with the order and remained pastor of the Shrine of the Little Flower until his retirement in 1966. He died in Bloomfield Hills, Michigan, on October 27, 1979.

Cournand, André Frédéric (1895–   ), physician and physiologist. Born in Paris on September 24,

1895, Cournand graduated from the University of Paris in 1913, took a certificate in physics, chemistry, and biology the next year, and after service in the French army during World War I returned to the university to study medicine. Soon after taking his medical degree in 1930 he came to the United States and joined the staff of Bellevue Hospital in New York City. While working there in the cardiopulmonary section he also began teaching at the College of Physicians and Surgeons of Columbia University in 1934, becoming full professor in 1951. He became a naturalized citizen in 1941. Shortly after joining Bellevue, Cournand met Dickinson W. Richards, and together they undertook a basic research project on lung and heart physiology and disease that occupied them for 25 years. Seeing great possibilities in a technique first devised by Werner Forssmann of Germany in 1929, in which he had passed a narrow tube through a vein in his arm to his heart, they developed equipment and methods for utilizing such a means of studying conditions in the heart without drugs or surgery. Over a period of several years they found ways to measure blood volume, pressure, and rate of flow in the heart, to determine (by analysis of the oxygen content of extracted blood) the presence of abnormal leakage from chamber to chamber, and to inject radio-opaque substance for close X-ray studies of the active heart. This repertoire of techniques proved a powerful diagnostic tool in cardiac disease and in addition made possible an accurate judgment of the likelihood of success of surgery. For the development of cardiac catheterization, Cournand, Richards, and Forssmann were awarded the 1956 Nobel Prize for Medicine and Physiology. Cournand was on the editorial boards of several medical journals, and he continued to teach at Columbia until his retirement in 1964.

Cousins, Norman (1912–   ), editor and author. Born on June 24, 1912, in Union Hill, New Jersey, Cousins attended Teachers College of Columbia University until 1933. During 1934–1935 he was on the editorial staff of the *New York Evening Post* and in the latter year he moved to *Current History* magazine, of which he was book critic and later managing editor. In 1940 he became executive editor of the *Saturday Review of Literature* (later the *Saturday Review*) and two years later, in a reorganization, became president and editor. Through both his editorial work and his own contributions of essays and reviews he changed a rather staid and lofty literary journal into one of broadly liberal sympathies and at the same time he greatly increased its readership and influence. Feature articles and commentaries on current events were introduced, and Cousins's own liberal-democratic idealism permeated the magazine. During World War II he also edited the magazine *U.S.A.* and served on the overseas editorial board of the Office of War Information (OWI). In later years he was active in promoting the work of the United Nations, in the United

World Federalists, of which he was honorary president, and in many other local, national, and international organizations for peace, cultural exchange, and reform. He served at various times on the boards of the National Educational Television network (NET), *Encyclopaedia Britannica*, and the Samuel H. Kress Foundation, and was widely honored for his involvement and leadership in public affairs. Among his many books were *The Good Inheritance: The Democratic Chance*, 1942; *Modern Man Is Obsolete*, 1945; *Who Speaks for Man?*, 1952; *In God We Trust: The Religious Beliefs of the Founding Fathers*, 1958; *The Last Defense in a Nuclear Age*, 1960; and the autobiographical *Present Tense: An American Editor's Odyssey*, 1968. After 31 years at the helm Cousins resigned as editor of the *Saturday Review* in 1971 and the following year began a new venture, *World* magazine.

Cousy, Robert Joseph (1928–   ), basketball player and coach. Born in New York City on August 9, 1928, Cousy began playing basketball as a child. In high school and college he was a varsity player and in 1950, his last year at the College of the Holy Cross, he was chosen for the All-American team. Following graduation he signed with the Tri-Cities club, was quickly traded to the Chicago Stags, which disbanded before the new season began, and was finally picked up by the Boston Celtics. In his first professional season he scored 1433 points for an average of 21.7 points per game and effectively squelched the idea that at 6'1" he was too small to be anything more than an average player in the professional ranks. Equipped with speed and amazing ability, Cousy created the Celtics' "fast-break" offense and constantly worried opponents—and thrilled fans—with his dazzling passes, fakes, and dribbles. In 1957, the year the Celtics won their first championship, he was voted the National Basketball Association's most valuable player. In all, the Celtics won 7 division titles and 6 championships with Cousy, and he was ranked on the All-Pro first team for 10 of his 13 seasons. When he retired in 1963, "Mr. Basketball," as he was dubbed, had a career total of 16,958 points (18.5 per game) and ranked in the all-time top ten; more importantly, as a playmaker he completed 6949 assists, a figure that put him in the top three in NBA history. In 1963 Cousy became head basketball coach at Boston College, and from 1968 was the coach of the Cincinnati Royals in the NBA, moving with the team (renamed the Kings) to Kansas City and Omaha four years later.

Couzens, James (1872–1936), businessman and public official. Born on August 26, 1872, in Chatham, Ontario, Couzens was named James Joseph Couzens, Jr., but early dropped the Jr. In 1890, after two years of high school and a short time in business college, he moved to Detroit and took a job with the Michigan Central Railroad. Five years later he became a bookkeeper and general assistant in a fuel company. Through his employer he met Henry Ford, and in 1903 he borrowed heavily in order to invest $2500 in the new Ford Motor Company. Later in the year he became general manager of the firm and for the next 12 years played a major role in shaping its practices and policies. Couzens was primarily responsible for the much-heralded $5-a-day wage announced by Ford in 1914 to quiet labor problems, and in all the company's undertakings was second only to Henry Ford in authority. He resigned in 1915 in a disagreement with Ford over military preparedness and turned his attention to public service, selling his Ford stock four years later for just over $29 million. Since 1913 he had been chairman of the Detroit Street Railway Commission and in 1916 he was appointed police commissioner. His forceful, even belligerent, manner and his dedication to equitable enforcement of law offended many of the powerful but so endeared him to the public that in 1918 and again in 1920 he was elected mayor by huge majorities. His years in the office were marked by great progress in municipal affairs. In 1922 he was appointed to a vacant seat in the U.S. Senate and there allied himself with the progressive wing of the Republican party; he was elected to a full term in 1924. A severe critic of the policies of presidents Warren G. Harding and Calvin Coolidge, he advocated high taxes on the rich, opposed Prohibition, fought railroad combinations, and promoted the Muscle Shoals project in Alabama that a decade later became the nucleus of the huge Tennessee Valley Authority (TVA) scheme. At the same time he devoted large portions of his own wealth to philanthropy, giving $2 million to the Children's Hospital of Detroit and in 1929 endowing the Children's Fund of Michigan with nearly $12 million. Reelected to the Senate in 1930, he advocated vigorous action by the federal government to meet the crisis of the Depression and, with the election of Franklin D. Roosevelt in 1932, became an ardent supporter of the New Deal. In 1933 he was a delegate to the World Economic Conference in London. His popularity dimmed in that year when he was unjustifiably blamed for blocking a federal loan to Detroit banks and thus precipitating their closing. In 1936 he declined the Democratic nomination for senator and, because of his New Deal connections, was denied renomination by the Republican party. Couzens died in Detroit on October 22, 1936.

Cowell, Henry Dixon (1897–1965), composer. Born in Menlo Park, California, on March 11, 1897, Cowell was a precocious and entirely self-directed student of music. He began to compose at the age of eleven and at fifteen made his professional debut as a pianist in a recital of his own work in San Francisco. Although he later received some formal training in music theory at the University of California he worked mainly on his own, studying the music of many cultures, both Occidental and Oriental. While still in his teens Cowell was experimenting with new sounds and with new approaches to traditional instruments; he early devised "tone clusters," massive piano chords struck with the fist or even the entire forearm. He made his European concert debut in Germany in 1923 and first performed in New York City in 1924. Thereafter he toured widely, traveling to Europe and to Asia many times to perform and to study and making nearly annual concert and lecture tours of the United States. From 1928 to 1962 he was a lecturer on the faculty of the New School for Social Research in New York City and from 1951 to 1965 was adjunct professor of music at Columbia University. A pioneer in the experimental movement in modern music, an explorer of novel rhythms and tonalities and their relationships, Cowell explained his aim as the discovery of a universal mode of musical expression, one encompassing the musical affinities of all cultures. With Leon Theremin, a Russian electronics engineer, he developed the rhythmicon, a device capable of producing electronically several different but simultaneous rhythms and he composed a concerto for the instrument. He composed a great many works for piano and for orchestra; of his 19 symphonies the most successful were No. 3 (*Gaelic*), 1942; No. 13 (*Madras*), 1956–58; and No. 16 (*Icelandic*), 1964. Other well-received pieces included *Synchrony*, 1930; *Tales from Our Countryside*, 1941; *Persian Set*, 1957; *Ongaku*, 1957; and *Homage to Iran*, 1959. In addition, Cowell was a prolific and influential writer on music. He published *New Musical Resources*, 1919; *The Nature of Melody*, 1938; with his wife, Sidney R. Cowell, *Charles Ives and His Music*, 1955; and edited *American Composers on American Music*, 1933. He also contributed articles and reviews to many periodicals and in 1927 founded the *New Music Quarterly*. Cowell died in Shady, near Woodstock, New York, on December 10, 1965.

Cowles, Gardner (1903–   ), publisher. Born in Algona, Iowa, on January 31, 1903, Cowles graduated from Harvard in 1925 and immediately became city editor of his father's *Des Moines Register and Tribune*. He advanced rapidly through the editorial ranks, becoming executive editor in 1931. By that time the *Register and Tribune* was the leading newspaper in the state and Cowles eagerly sought ways to continue its growth in circulation. He hired George H. Gallup to survey reader reaction to various features—it was Gallup's first public-opinion poll—and discovered the great popularity of pictures. Experiments with rotogravure picture stories were a success and in 1933 a syndicate supplying rotogravure sections was formed. Cowles acquired radio stations in Iowa and South Dakota and in 1935 bought the *Minneapolis Star*. In 1937 he began publication of *Look*, a national weekly pictorial magazine that was immediately successful, its circulation quickly running into the millions. During 1942–1943 he served as deputy director of the Office of War Information (OWI) and then returned to publishing, becoming president of the *Register and Tribune* in 1943. He became chairman of the board and editor in chief of the Cowles Magazines and Broadcasting Company upon its organization, retaining both positions in the successor firm, Cowles Communications, Incorporated, which operated radio and television stations in several states and newspapers as far away as Puerto Rico and Long Island, New York. In the magazine field *Look* was joined by *Venture, Family Circle*, and, briefly, by *Flair*. Cowles Communications grew into one of the largest public media empires in the world. During the late 1960s rising costs forced the liquidation or disposal of a number of the company's publications and in 1971, despite a huge readership, *Look* ceased publication.

Cowles, Henry Chandler (1869–1939), botanist and ecologist. Born on February 27, 1869, in Kensington, Connecticut, Cowles graduated from Oberlin College in 1893 and then went to the University of Chicago to pursue graduate work. His studies in geology that preceded his switch to botany under the influence of John M. Coulter laid the groundwork for his later contributions to the development of plant ecology. Upon taking his Ph.D. in 1898 he joined the faculty of the university, becoming assistant professor in 1907 and professor in 1915. His field studies in the geologically and botanically interesting region around Chicago led to two early and seminal books, *The Ecological Relations of the Vegetation on the Sand Dunes of Lake Michigan*, 1899, and *The Plant Societies of Chicago and Vicinity*, 1901, both originally published in the *Botanical Gazette*. With their emphasis on the interlocking relations of vegetation and geology, the books were major contributions to the infant science of ecology and helped change botany from a merely descriptive study of flora to a study of evolutionary process and development within the larger context of geological change. In 1910–1911 he collaborated with Coulter and C.R. Barnes in writing a two-volume *Textbook of Botany for Colleges and Universities* which was of great influence and long in use. In 1915 he joined in founding the Ecological Society of America, of which he was president in 1918. Cowles became chairman of the department of botany at Chicago in 1925, retaining the position until his retirement in 1934, and during the same period was editor of the *Botanical Gazette*. He died in Chicago on September 12, 1939.

Cowley, Malcolm (1898–   ), author and editor. Born on August 24, 1898, in Belsano, Pennsylvania, Cowley was educated at Harvard, interrupting his studies for brief service in the American Ambulance Corps during World War I, and graduating in 1920. From 1921 to 1923 he pursued further studies at the University of Montpellier in France. After a short time with *Sweet's Architectural Catalogue* he worked as a free-lance writer for several years, contributing book reviews to periodicals and translating a number of works from the French, including Paul Valéry's *Variety*, 1927, and Maurice Barrès's *The Sacred Hill*, 1929. In 1929 he became associate editor of the *New Republic* and oversaw its literary department for 15 years. In the same year his first book of verse, *Blue Juniata*, was published, and five years later appeared *Exile's Return*, a study, partly autobiographical, of post–World War I developments in American literature, particularly in the works of the expatriate generation with whom he had associated in France. *After the Genteel Tradition*, 1937, a study and anthology of twentieth-century writers, began a long series of collections edited by Cowley, including *Books That Changed Our Minds*, 1939, and popular editions of selected works by Ernest Hemingway, William Faulkner, Nathaniel Hawthorne, Walt Whitman, and F. Scott Fitzgerald. He wrote a second volume of poems, *The Dry Season*, 1941, and translated André Gide's *Imaginary Interviews*, 1944. In 1944 he left the *New Republic* and thereafter, although he was a literary adviser to the Viking Press from 1948, he worked independently. His later books included *The Literary Situation*, 1954; *Black Cargoes*, 1962, with D.P. Mannix; *The Faulkner–Cowley File*, 1966; *Think Back on Us*, 1967; and he also edited the collections *Writers at Work*, 1958; *Leaves of Grass: The First Edition*, 1959; and *Fitzgerald and the Jazz Age*, 1966, with his son Robert Cowley. Cowley also contributed to numerous magazines and was widely in demand as a lecturer at colleges and universities. One of the most distinguished critics of modern American literature, he was twice president of the National Institute of Arts and Letters, in 1956–1959 and 1962–1965, and was a chancellor of the American Academy of Arts and Letters.

Cox, Jacob Dolson (1828–1900), soldier, public official, and educator. Born on October 27, 1828, in Montreal, Cox was the son of American parents with whom he returned to New York City shortly thereafter. From 1842 to 1844 he studied in a law office and two years later, having come under the influence of Charles G. Finney, he entered the preparatory department of Oberlin College, from which he graduated in 1851. He had married Finney's daughter Helen in 1849. From 1851 to 1853 he was superintendent of schools in Warren, Ohio, and then, winning admission to the bar, he began the practice of law there. He was active in the organization of the Republican party in the state and in 1859 was elected to the legislature. The following year he was appointed a general in the state militia and in 1861, upon recruiting a large number of men for Civil War service, was commissioned brigadier general of volunteers. Cox saw action in the West Virginia campaign, was in command of the Kanawha Valley region in the summer of 1862, and took part in the battles of South Mountain and Antietam, at Antietam succeeding to temporary command of the 9th Corps. In October 1862 he was promoted to major general, but the promotion was rescinded after the discovery that the quota for the grade had been exceeded. During most of 1863 he commanded the Department of the Ohio and in 1864 participated in the Atlanta Campaign; late in the year he was again promoted to major general. In 1866 he was elected governor of Ohio; and, even though he had supported President Andrew Johnson's Reconstruction policies and had attempted to mediate the dispute between Johnson and the dominant Radicals, he was chosen two years later chairman of the Republican national convention. Upon the election of Ulysses S. Grant, Cox was appointed secretary of the interior; he served only until October 1870, but was effective in opposing patronage and in promoting a merit system. He returned to law practice in Cincinnati and in 1873 became president of the Toledo and Wabash and Western Railroad. He held that position until the beginning of the term in the House of Representatives to which he was elected in 1876. After 1879 Cox took no further part in political affairs. In 1881 he became dean of the Cincinnati Law School, where he remained until 1897, serving also from 1885 to 1889 as president of the University of Cincinnati. He declined a number of positions offered by business and government and during his later years acquired an international reputation as a microscopist. He also wrote several distinguished works on the Civil War, including *Atlanta*, 1882, and *The March to the Sea, Franklin, and Nashville*, 1882, both for the Campaigns of the Civil War series, and *Military Reminiscences of the Civil War*, published posthumously in 1900. Cox died in Magnolia, Massachusetts, on August 8, 1900.

Coxey, Jacob Sechler (1854–1951), businessman and reformer. Born on April 16, 1854, in Selinsgrove, Pennsylvania, Coxey attended public schools in Danville, Pennsylvania, and started work in that city as an engineer in a rolling mill, then entered the scrap-iron business. From 1881 to 1929 he was successful in silica sandstone quarrying in Massillon, Ohio. In the financial panic of 1893 he was forced to discharge about 40 men from his quarries; in protest he organized 100 men to march from Massillon to Washington, to petition Congress for money to create jobs. On March 25, 1894, "Coxey's Army" set out for the capital and arrived 500 strong on May 1. They were arrested for trespassing (Coxey served 20 days in jail after his conviction) and received much adverse publicity. But Coxey managed to appear before a House subcommittee to present his plan for the federal government to purchase $500 million worth of municipal bonds to be liquidated at four percent annually; the money would enable communities to undertake building and improvement projects to provide work for the unemployed. The proposal was pigeonholed. Nicknamed "General Coxey," he was thereafter identified with the "Army." On the fiftieth anniversary of the march he continued the speech

from the Capitol steps that had been interrupted by the police in 1894. His only public office, as mayor of Massillon from 1931 to 1934, allowed him to test his measures on a small scale. He had promised to issue $200,000 in bonds in denominations ranging from 25 cents to $10, bearing interest of one-tenth of one percent, to finance public works projects on which the majority of the city's unemployed would have work. But he failed to raise the money and in 1934 lost his bid for reelection in the primary. He unsuccessfully sought election to the House of Representatives in 1894 as a Populist, in 1916 as an independent, and in 1942 as a Democrat. Nominated for the presidency on the Farmer-Labor ticket in 1932 and again in 1936, he polled only a few thousand votes in the former year and in the latter withdrew to support the Union party candidate, William Lemke. In 1914 he wrote *Coxey's Own Story*. His ideas were never quite understood by the public or the government; he died in Massillon on May 18, 1951.

Cozzens, James Gould (1903–1978), author. Born on August 19, 1903, in Chicago, Cozzens grew up in Staten Island, New York City. He early decided upon writing as a career and demonstrated a remarkable precocity in having a short piece accepted by the *Atlantic Monthly* while he was a student in a private secondary school in Connecticut. He entered Harvard in 1922 and two years later published his first novel, *Confusion*. On the strength of that achievement he left Harvard and began his career in earnest, publishing *Michael Scarlet* in 1925 and, after a year of teaching school in Cuba, *The Cockpit* in 1928. He had by then already begun to attract considerable critical attention and he followed rapidly with *The Son of Perdition*, 1929; *S.S. San Pedro*, 1931; *The Last Adam*, 1933; *The Castaway*, 1934; *Men and Brethren*, 1936; *Ask Me Tomorrow*, 1940; and *The Just and the Unjust*, 1942. His novels were concerned typically with the ethical conflicts experienced by idealistic main characters, often men of the professions, when faced with the necessity of compromise with the practical realities of society, and they exhibited a strong attachment to traditional moral and political values; critics praised his deft storytelling and his meticulous detailing and description. Cozzens' experiences in the army air forces during 1942–1945 furnished material for his Pulitzer Prize winning *Guard of Honor*, 1948, considered by many to be his finest work. *By Love Possessed*, 1957, became a popular success; while the book enjoyed enormous sales, it failed to win the critical esteem of his earlier works. Later books included *Children and Others*, 1964, a collection of stories, and *Morning Noon and Night*, 1968. He died in Stuart, Florida, on August 9, 1978.

Crabtree, Lotta (1847–1924), actress. Born in New York City on November 7, 1847, Charlotte Crabtree grew up in California, where her father went in the Gold Rush of the early 1850s. At the Grass

Valley mining camp she met Lola Montez, who taught her a bit of dancing and stagecraft, and in 1855 she first performed before an audience of miners. Her lively, diminutive figure immediately captivated the audience and, with her mother, she began touring the wild camps of California. In 1859 she began appearing in variety theaters in San Francisco, where her singing, dancing, and melodramatic roles, many written for her, kept her in the limelight. She made her New York debut at Niblo's Garden in 1864 with little success; after three years of touring the country, however, she returned to Wallack's Theatre in *Little Nell and the Marchioness*, adapted for her from Dickens's *The Old Curiosity Shop*, and was a sensation. From then until her retirement she enjoyed huge popularity at home and in England. Her infectious gaiety, perennially winsome, childlike appearance, and occasionally saucy and sweetly risqué manner made her a versatile performer and ranked her in the forefront of the emerging theater of burlesque extravaganza. Among her most popular roles were those she played in *Firefly, Topsy, The Little Detective, Musette, Nitouche,* and *Zip.* Most often known simply as "Lotta," Miss Crabtree left the stage in 1891 and lived in quiet retirement until her death in Boston on September 25, 1924.

Cram, Ralph Adams (1863–1942), architect. Born in Hampton Falls, New Hampshire, on December 16, 1863, Cram moved to Boston in 1889 and, with no formal training in the field, opened an architectural office with C.F. Wentworth. Later he formed the firm of Cram, Goodhue, and Ferguson (Cram and Ferguson after the death of Bertram G. Goodhue in 1924). A thoroughgoing exponent of the Gothic Revival, Cram used that style in designing, among many other such edifices, St. Thomas's Church, New York City, Emmanuel Church, Cleveland, and First Baptist Church, Pittsburgh. The firm drew plans for buildings at West Point and at a number of colleges and universities, including Princeton, Rice Institute, and Williams College. Commissioned to redesign the uncompleted Cathedral of St. John the Divine in New York City, Cram and Ferguson changed the originally Romanesque edifice into a Gothic one. On a few occasions Cram worked in the classic or colonial styles, but his predominant medievalism informed the bulk of his work and pervaded his writings and lectures; in these he called for a return to the values of the Middle Ages—the closeness to the land, the feudal stratification of society, and the autocratic government. He was professor of architecture at the Massachusetts Institute of Technology from 1914 to 1921 and from 1915 to 1922 was chairman of the Boston city planning board. Among his many books were *Church Building,* 1901; *The Gothic Quest,* 1907; *The Ministry of Art,* 1914; *The Substance of Gothic,* 1916; *The Nemesis of Mediocrity,* 1918; *The Great Thousand Years,* 1918; *My Life in Architecture,* 1936; and *The End of Democracy,* 1937. He died in Boston on September 22, 1942.

Crandall, Prudence (1803–1890), educator and social reformer. Born in Hopkinton, Rhode Island, on September 3, 1803, Miss Crandall grew up in a Quaker household and was educated at the Friends' school in Providence. After a brief period of teaching school in Plainfield, Connecticut, she moved to Canterbury, Connecticut, and there in 1831 opened a private girls' academy, which was soon recognized as one of the best of its kind in the state. When early in 1833 she admitted to the school a young Negro girl, she was immediately the focus of heated protest and controversy. In March 1833, on the advice of William Lloyd Garrison and others, she established a new school for "young ladies and little misses of color." The local citizenry were even more outraged and embarked upon a campaign of unremitting persecution and ostracism. In May the Connecticut legislature was prodded into enacting a bill forbidding the establishment of schools for nonresident Negroes without the consent of local authorities. In a case that received wide publicity and enlisted the aid of Arthur Tappan and other prominent abolitionists, Miss Crandall was indicted and convicted under the so-called "Black Law" and imprisoned until July 1834, when the court of appeals reversed her conviction on technical grounds. Local opposition continued and increased, however, and in September 1834 she was forced to give up her school. With her husband, Calvin Philleo, a Baptist minister whom she had married in August, she moved to Illinois; after his death in 1874 she went to live with her brother in southeastern Kansas, dying in Elk Falls on January 28, 1890.

Crane, Hart (1899–1932), poet. Born on July 21, 1899, in Garrettsville, Ohio, Harold Hart Crane had un unhappy childhood during which he witnessed the disintegration of his family. His education ended with high school and thereafter he worked as a salesman, a warehouse manager, and an advertising copywriter. He moved to New York City and in 1926 published his first volume of verse, *White Buildings,* displaying in it considerable technical mastery and a strong tendency toward a mystical perception of experience. Inspired largely by the democratic faith of Walt Whitman, he broke with the fashionable despair of many of his contemporaries and with an almost religious fervor sought a spiritual affirmation of American life and his experience within it. His quest resulted in *The Bridge,* 1930, in which, in rhapsodic fashion, he explored the mystical essence of the American destiny; the many related poems that comprised the book shared the common unifying image of the Brooklyn Bridge as a symbol of the creative power of man. Although the work won considerable critical appreciation—coming eventually to rank with the most important poetic creations of 20th century America—the overall reaction to it at the time was mixed and served to confirm Crane in his growing insecurity. He spent a great deal of time in travel and on April 27, 1932, while aboard ship en route to the United States from Mexico, he jumped or fell overboard and drowned.

Crane, Stephen (1871–1900), author. Born on November 1, 1871, in Newark, New Jersey, Crane was the son of a Methodist minister; his rather indifferent education ended after a year at Lafayette College and another at Syracuse University that was apparently devoted largely to baseball. In 1891 he went to New York City and pursued a bohemian existence, reporting occasionally for the *New York Herald* and the *New York Tribune* and spending a great portion of his time exploring the Bowery slums, from which experience came *Maggie: A Girl of the Streets,* 1893. Published at his own expense, the book was a grimly naturalistic portrayal of slum life and death and was not a success. He was befriended by Hamlin Garland and William Dean Howells, with whose encouragement he produced a powerful novel of the Civil War, *The Red Badge of Courage,* in 1895. The vivid realism and psychological perceptiveness of the book were all the more remarkable for Crane's lack of war experience; the book was an immediate success and became in the course of time an undisputed classic of American literature. In the same year his first volume of poetry, *The Black Riders,* was published; its symbolism, stark imagery, and free form marked an important step from Victorian to modern poetry. Crane's main work in the following years was in short stories, the best of which, including "The Blue Hotel," "The Bride Comes to Yellow Sky," "The Open Boat," and "The Monster," published in several collections during 1896–1900, displayed a complete mastery of the form. He moved to England in 1897 and formed friendships with Henry James, H. G. Wells, and Joseph Conrad. The poverty of his early years in New York, his impulsive stints as war correspondent in Greece and Cuba in 1896 and 1897, and the heedless unconventionality of his life—which was often popularly exaggerated to scandalous proportions—slowly weakened him. He died of tuberculosis at the age of twenty-eight, on June 5, 1900, in Badenweiler, Germany.

Crater, Joseph Force (1889–1937?), judge. Born in 1889 in Easton, Pennsylvania, Crater graduated from Lafayette College in 1910 and entered the law school of Columbia University, taking his degree in 1913. His private practice in New York City was quickly successful and he formed valuable professional and political connections, serving from 1920 to 1926 as secretary to Robert F. Wagner during his service as a justice of the state supreme court and later rising to the presidency of the Cayuga Democratic Club, a branch of the Tammany organization. In April 1930 Governor Franklin D. Roosevelt appointed Crater to fill an unexpired term on the New York supreme court. In August he suddenly interrupted a vacation to return to New York City to attend to some unspecified business. He was in his office on August 5 and again the following morning, when he sent his court attendant to cash two checks amounting to just over $5000—substantially all his cash holdings; it was later learned that he also sold stocks, receiving some $16,000 in cash. That evening, after carrying several portfolios of his files home from the office, he dined with friends in a restaurant on West 45th Street; shortly after 9 P.M. he stepped into a taxi in front of the restaurant and rode off. He was never seen again. A ticket he had ordered earlier for the evening's performance of *Dancing Partner* at the Belasco Theatre was called for by an unidentified person. Judge Crater's wife soon began discreet inquiries, but friends and political associates advised her to avoid publicity. Late in August however, he failed to appear for the opening session of his court and on September 4, the police were officially informed that he was missing. The investigation, which eventually included a grand-jury hearing lasting for months and involving hundreds of witnesses, discovered no evidence as to his whereabouts but came upon hints of political corruption in the Cayuga club that later led to the much-publicized Seabury investigations. The grand-jury investigation ended in January 1931; a few days later Mrs. Crater discovered that someone had entered her apartment and left an envelope containing $6690 in cash, her husband's will, various other papers, and a note listing his debtors and signed "Joe." No other trace of Judge Crater was ever found, although the police investigation eventually spread to Canada, Mexico, and the West Indies, and was complicated by a profusion of impostors. The case, one of the most famous and puzzling of the day, was officially closed in July 1937, when Judge Crater was declared legally dead.

Crawford, Francis Marion (1854–1909), author. Born on August 2, 1854, in Bagni di Lucca, Italy, Crawford was the son of a noted expatriate American sculptor, Thomas Crawford. He received an excellent and cosmopolitan education, at various times attending Cambridge University, a number of institutions in Germany, and the University of Rome. He mastered most European languages, along with Turkish and Russian, and in 1879 left the University of Rome to continue his study of Sanskrit in India. There he edited the *Allahabad Indian Herald* for a time. In 1881 he traveled to the United States to study at Harvard, living in the home of his aunt, Julia Ward Howe. Brilliant, urbane, financially independent, and restless, Crawford was at a loss for a career until 1882 when, at the suggestion of Mrs. Howe's brother, Samuel Ward, he turned happenings of his life in India into a novel, *Mr. Isaacs,* which was an immediate success. Thereafter he devoted himself to writing; his output was prodigious, running to more than 40 books. He had no interest in literary realism or didacticism, remaining content with his great ability as a storyteller; his wealth of experience and knowledge allowed him to construct colorful, romantic settings ranging from India to Italy, from medieval Spain to ancient Persia, and occasionally to contemporary Europe and the United States. Among his novels, all best sellers, were *Dr. Claudius*, 1883; *A Roman Singer*, 1884; *An American Politician*, 1885; *Zoroaster*, 1885; *Saracinesca*, 1887; *With the Immortals*, 1888; *Greifenstein*, 1889; *A Cigarette Maker's Romance*, 1890; *The Witch of Prague*, 1891; *Don Orsino*, 1892; *Katharine Lauderdale*, 1894; *The Ralstons*, 1895; *Taquisara*, 1895; *Via Crucis*, 1898; *In the Palace of the King*, 1900; *The Heart of Rome*, 1903; and *Arethusa*, 1907. He also wrote three historical studies—*Ave Roma Immortalis*, 1898, *Rulers of the South*, 1900, and *Salve Venetia*, 1905—several plays, including *Francesca da Rimini*, produced by Sarah Bernhardt in Paris in 1902; and an exposition of his theory of literature, *The Novel—What It Is*, 1893. Crawford traveled widely and often visited the United States, but he maintained his permanent residence in a villa near Sorrento, Italy. He died there on April 9, 1909.

Crawford, William Harris (1772–1834), public official. Born in Amherst County, Virginia, on February 24, 1772, Crawford moved with his family to South Carolina and then to Georgia. Completing his education at Moses Waddel's Carmel Academy near Appling, Georgia, he taught school in Augusta while reading law and in 1799 began his practice. He coauthored a digest of state statutes and in 1803 was elected to the legislature; four years later he was elected to fill an unexpired term in the Senate and in 1811 was reelected. Although he was a Democratic Republican he supported the First Bank of the United States; he agreed in the main with his Southern colleagues, however, in his nationalism and in his advocacy of war with Great Britain. Upon the death of Vice-President George Clinton in 1812 Crawford was elected president pro tem of the Senate. The next year he was appointed minister to France, in 1815 he became President James Madison's secretary of war, and in 1816 he moved to the treasury, a post for which his interest in and knowledge of public finance better fitted him and which he held until 1825. In the congressional caucus of 1816 Crawford was, through no effort of his own, a leading contender for the presidential nomination, and even though he had clearly deferred to James Monroe, he received only 11 fewer votes. The election of 1820 went to Monroe with virtually no contest, but in 1824 a number of candidates entered the field, with Crawford, John Quincy Adams, Andrew Jackson, and Henry Clay the leaders. Crawford was chosen by the party caucus in Congress, but attendance was so poor as a result of mounting criticism of the caucus as undemocratic, that the event was of little significance beyond marking the end of the caucus system. By that time Crawford was in poor health, having suffered a paralytic attack, and Jackson was busily enlisting support among a variety of disaffected groups. Northern discontent with the South's long hold on the presidency also colored the picture. The election was inde-

cisive—no candidate had a majority of the electoral vote—and Crawford had run third. In the House of Representatives Clay threw his support to Adams, who was subsequently chosen. Adams offered to continue Crawford in the cabinet, but he declined and retired to his plantation near Lexington, Georgia. There he carried on agricultural experiments and served as judge of the state's northern superior circuit court from 1827 until his death in Elberton on September 15, 1834.

Crazy Horse (1849?–1877), Indian leader. Born about 1849 into the Oglala Sioux tribe, Tashunca-Uitco, or Crazy Horse, distinguished himself in battle while yet a youth. Using masterly decoy tactics, he fought in Red Cloud's War over the hated Powder River army road (the Bozeman Trail), playing a leading role in the Fetterman Massacre on December 21, 1866, and the Wagon-Box fight of August 2, 1867, at Fort Phil Kearny. He refused to settle on the Sioux reservations established in 1868. He moved north with a band of 1200 Oglala and Cheyenne (his marriage to a Cheyenne woman had gained him an alliance with the tribe), and joined forces with Sitting Bull. He was the principal leader of the Sioux in the uprising of 1876 and 1877 which broke out, after the invasion of the sacred and treaty-reserved Black Hills country by the army and by gold prospectors, as a protest against the order by the U.S. war department that all Sioux remain on reservations after January 31, 1876. Eight days after Crazy Horse led his warriors to victory over Gen. George Crook at the battle of the Rosebud occurred the most famous battle of the war, fought at the Little Bighorn River in Montana on June 25, 1876. Crazy Horse and his warriors surrounded Col. George A. Custer and his command, assailing them from the north and west, while Gall, war chief of the Hunkpapa Sioux, attacked from the south and west. Custer was killed and his entire immediate command was destroyed. After the battle the Indians dispersed into bands that went separate ways. Crazy Horse led about 800 warriors back to Sioux territory, hoping to gather supplies, but was relentlessly pursued by forces under Col. Nelson A. Miles. He surrendered at the urging of Red Cloud on May 6, 1877, with about 1000 men, women and children, near Camp Robinson, Nebraska. Promised a limited amount of freedom, he was arrested in September on suspicion of agitating for war among the Oglala. He was said to have resisted his captors, and was killed on September 5, 1877.

Creel, George Edward (1876–1953), journalist, editor, and author. Born on December 1, 1876, in Lafayette County, Missouri, Creel attended school in Kansas City and after a year of high school and a time spent in travel took up newspaper work on the *Kansas City World*. During a brief period in New York City in 1898–1900 he worked for the *New York Journal* but in 1900 returned to Kansas City to join a friend in founding the

Kansas City Independent, a literary and public-affairs journal of which Creel became sole owner, editor, and publisher in 1903. His first book, a volume of poems entitled Quatrains of Christ, appeared in 1908. In 1909 he gave up the paper to join Bonfils and Tammen's Denver Post as an editorial writer, but left a year later to do free-lance magazine writing. In 1911 he returned to Denver as editor of the Rocky Mountain News, the Post's rival, a position he held for two years. He became associated with Judge Benjamin B. Lindsey in a number of reform and progressive legislation movements and collaborated with him and Edwin Markham in writing Children in Bondage, 1914. Creel was an enthusiastic supporter of Woodrow Wilson for the presidency in 1912 and 1916, and after leaving the Rocky Mountain News, which he had made into a crusading liberal paper, he contributed numerous articles on reform and on Wilson's "New Freedom" to various periodicals. In 1916 he published Wilson and the Issues. Upon U.S. entry into World War I, Wilson created the Committee on Public Information, consisting of the secretaries of war, state, and the navy, with a civilian head, and named Creel to the chairmanship. For two years Creel directed the government's war-propaganda and information activities, building public enthusiasm for the war effort and promoting the understanding of war aims. News censorship was carried out on a voluntary basis and the committee was highly effective in minimizing the publication of anti-German hate and atrocity literature, encouraging instead an emphasis on Wilsonian idealism and the spirit of Allied cooperation. After the war he devoted himself to writing articles and books, among the latter How We Advertised America, 1920; The War, the World, and Wilson, 1920; The People Next Door, 1926; Sons of the Eagle, 1927; Sam Houston, 1928; Tom Paine—Liberty Bell, 1931; War Criminals and Punishment, 1944; Rebel at Large, 1947; and Russia's Race for Asia, 1949. In 1933 he was appointed chairman of the San Francisco Regional Labor Board and in 1935 chairman of the national advisory committee of the Works Progress Administration (WPA). Creel died in San Francisco on October 2, 1953.

Crehan, Ada, see Rehan, Ada

Crèvecoeur, Michel Guillaume Jean de (1735–1813), author. Born on January 31, 1735, in Caen, France, Crèvecoeur emigrated to Canada and served as a mapmaker during the last phase of the French and Indian Wars. He remained when the conflict ended and explored extensively in the Great Lakes and Ohio Valley regions. In 1765 he became a citizen in New York and settled on a farm in Orange County about 1769. The Revolution put him in a difficult position, for both he and his wife had Loyalist connections, and in 1780 he fled to Europe, leaving behind his wife and two of his children. In London two years later he published a collection of essays, most of them presumably written while working his New

York farm, entitled Letters from an American Farmer and signed "J. Hector St. John," the name he used in America. The essays were vivid, detailed, and optimistic discussions of American life, particularly in the frontier farming regions, and remained a primary source of information about the period. The book was immediately and vastly popular, particularly among European romanticists and revolutionaries, and Crèvecoeur was appointed French consul to three of the new American states. Returning to New York in 1783, he found his house burned, his wife dead, and his children missing, all the result of an Indian raid. He recovered his children and became a popular figure in the new states; he knew both Benjamin Franklin and Thomas Jefferson and corresponded with George Washington. He published numerous articles on medicine and natural history and in 1787 an enlarged edition of the French version of his Letters was issued. Three years later he left the United States to return to France, where he died on November 12, 1813. A second book on America, Voyage dans la Haute Pensylvanie et dans l'État de New York, had appeared in 1801, and a number of previously unknown essays were published in 1925 as Sketches of Eighteenth-Century America, or More Letters from an American Farmer.

Crisp, Charles Frederick (1845–1896), public official. Born on January 29, 1845, in Sheffield, England, Crisp was the son of naturalized American parents who were visiting their native country at the time of his birth. He grew up in Georgia, attended schools in Macon and Savannah, and served for four years in the Confederate army, spending the last year as a prisoner. Returning to Georgia in 1865, he took up the study of law and upon admission to the bar settled in Americus. He was appointed solicitor general of the superior circuit court of his district in 1872 and from 1877 to 1882 was judge of the court. In the latter year he was elected as a Democrat to the House of Representatives and retained the seat for the rest of his life. He became a remarkably skilled parliamentarian and in 1887 saw the Interstate Commerce Act through committee and onto the floor. In 1890 he succeeded to the leadership of his party; the following year, when the Democrats organized the House, he was elected speaker, holding that office through that and the next Congress until 1895. True to the interests of his agricultural constituency, Crisp was a free-silver advocate, and in 1896 he announced his intention to seek a Senate seat on that platform. He did well in a series of debates with his fellow Georgian, Secretary of the Interior Hoke Smith, who was a staunch pro-administration gold-standard man, and was bolstered in his campaign by the election of a pro-silver Georgia legislature. Assured of a Senate seat, Crisp died before the election, in Atlanta, Georgia, on October 23, 1896.

Crittenden, John Jordan (1787–1863), lawyer and public official. Born near Versailles, Kentucky, on September 10, 1787, Crittenden graduated from the College of William and Mary in 1807 and began to practice law in Logan County, Kentucky. In 1809 he was appointed territorial attorney general for Illinois. Returning to Kentucky, he saw military service in the War of 1812 and was at the same time elected to the state legislature. In 1817 he was sent to fulfill an unexpired term in the Senate. From the end of his term in 1819 until 1835 he served in Kentucky in the state legislature, as district attorney, and as secretary of state. In 1835 he was returned to the Senate, and in 1841 President William Henry Harrison named him to the cabinet as attorney general, in which post he remained until joining the mass cabinet resignation a few months later, after John Tyler's succession. He was elected again to the Senate in 1842; he then began to emerge as a prominent national leader with his opposition to the annexation of Texas, to strong action in the Oregon dispute, and to the Mexican War. In 1848 he became governor of Kentucky; in 1850 President Millard Fillmore named him once more attorney general. In 1854 he was once again elected to the Senate where, much disturbed by the slavery issue and the possibility of disunion that it entailed, he opposed the Kansas-Nebraska Bill; when the Whig party disintegrated he joined first the Know-Nothing party and then the Constitutional Union party. Into the sectional crisis occasioned by Abraham Lincoln's election he introduced the Crittenden Compromise in December 1860, proposing constitutional amendments to avert secession and end the threat of civil war. When his proposal was defeated by the congressional Radicals he returned to Kentucky and continued to promote his policy of neutrality for that state. After serving in 1861 as chairman of a convention of border states that requested the seceded states to reconsider their position, he was elected to the House of Representatives, where he continued to oppose the more obnoxious of the Radicals' war measures until his death on July 26, 1863, in Frankfort, Kentucky.

Crocker, Charles (1822–1888), railroad builder and financier. Born in Troy, New York, on September 16, 1822, Crocker moved with his family to Indiana in 1836. He received little schooling and worked at various occupations in his youth. He established a forge near an iron-ore bed of his own discovery in 1845 and operated it until joining the California Gold Rush four years later. After prospecting with no great success for two years, he gave up gold hunting in 1852 to open a store in Sacramento. He prospered rapidly, becoming a leading figure in the community. In 1860 he won election to the legislature. Politics brought him into contact with railroad pioneers Collis P. Huntington, Huntington's partner Mark Hopkins and Leland Stanford, and in 1861 he joined them in forming the Central Pacific Railway Company; while Huntington and Stanford took care of political and financial arrangements, Crocker began organizing the actual work of construction through his Contract and Finance Company, of which he was president until 1869. Under his personal and constant supervision the laying of track began in February 1863, and he drove the work forward at an incredibly rapid pace. When labor shortages developed he recruited Chinese immigrants, an experiment that proved so successful that by 1867 Chinese laborers made up nearly the whole of the work force. The track was completed and joined to the Union Pacific at Promontory Point, Utah, in May 1869, having taken less than half the time allowed for in the government contracts for the western portion of the first transcontinental railroad. Crocker's position as vice-president of the Central Pacific thereafter made few demands on him, but he was active in organizing the Southern Pacific Railroad, was elected its president in 1871, and again supervised track construction in person. In 1884 he effected the merger of the Central Pacific into the Southern Pacific. In addition to his interests in railroads he had extensive investments in real estate and irrigation ventures. Crocker died in Monterey, California, on August 14, 1888, leaving an estate of some $40 million.

Crockett, David (1786–1836), frontiersman and public official. Born near Greeneville, Tennessee, on August 17, 1786, Davy Crockett grew up on the frontier and received virtually no formal education. He served as a scout under Andrew Jackson in the Creek War of 1813–1814, and afterward moved farther west into Tennessee. A poor farmer but an awesome hunter, he was for several years a local magistrate in Giles County and in 1821 and 1823 was elected to the state legislature, building up an enthusiastic local following with his humorous and homely oratorical style. He was elected to the House of Representatives in 1827 and served two terms; defeated in 1831, he returned for a final term in 1833. In 1834 he made a tour of Northern cities in an effort to rouse support for the Whig party, with which he had allied himself; the party's hope was to fashion from Crockett, with his colorful history as a ''b'ar-hunter'' and largely illiterate frontiersman, an answer to the Democrats' Jackson. The determined opposition of the Jackson forces defeated his bid for reelection to the House in 1835. He then left Tennessee to join the war for independence in Texas; he arrived at the Alamo in February 1836 and died in the massacre there on March 6. The growth of Davy Crockett into a legendary figure began before his death, aided by his supposed autobiography, *A Narrative of the Life of David Crockett, of the State of Tennessee*, 1834, and by numerous Whig campaign pieces attributed to him. The mythmaking continued with the publication from 1835 to 1856 of a series of Crockett almanacs, containing numerous accounts, in the best frontier tall-tale tradition, of adventures in which he, Mike Fink, and other frontier heroes had supposedly been involved.

Croghan, George (1720?–1782), frontiersman and colonial figure. Born near Dublin, Ireland, about 1720, Croghan emigrated to America in 1741, landing at Philadelphia. He immediately took up trading with the Indians on the Pennsylvania frontier, learning their languages and building a trade empire sufficiently large to induce the French to take a strong action. By 1754, with the outbreak of the last of the French and Indian Wars, his trade was ruined; he and a few Indians then joined Gen. Edward Braddock's disastrous expedition to capture Fort Duquesne. His ability in negotiating with the Indians led to his appointment in 1756 as deputy superintendent of northern Indian affairs under Sir William Johnson. Through the remainder of the war and afterward he strove to eliminate French influence and to alleviate the hostility to the English, both widespread among the Indians beyond the Appalachian frontier. His greatest achievement was bringing about the treaty that ended Pontiac's Rebellion in 1766. In 1768 Croghan helped to represent the British at the Fort Stanwix treaty negotiations with the Iroquois. Four years later he resigned his post. His early trading and land speculations had suffered badly from the protracted Indian troubles; despite his associations with George Washington, Benjamin Franklin, and other prominent men, his later schemes fared no better, and he was never able to establish his claims to huge tracts in New York, Pennsylvania, and Illinois. In 1778 he finally cleared himself of charges of Tory sympathies arising from some of his speculative ventures, but he died in poverty on August 31, 1782, in Passyunk, Pennsylvania, near Philadelphia.

Croly, Herbert David (1869–1930), editor and author. Born on January 23, 1869, in New York City, Croly completed his studies at Harvard in 1899 after many interruptions. From 1900 to 1906 he edited the *Architectural Record;* he maintained a staff connection with the journal until 1913. In 1909 he published *The Promise of American Life.* Embodying the thesis that democratic institutions are dynamic and need to be flexible and innovative in a changing world, the book had a deep influence on both the New Nationalism of Theodore Roosevelt and the New Freedom of Woodrow Wilson. Five years later he published a sequel, *Progressive Democracy.* In that same year, 1914, he founded the *New Republic,* a "journal of opinion," of which he remained editor until his death. Gathering a brilliant staff, Croly directed the rapid growth of what was often, although incorrectly, thought to be the official organ of the Wilson administration. Although he and his staff supported U.S. participation in World War I, he broke with the government over the Versailles treaty; his denunciation of the vindictive peace terms cost him half his readership. In his later years, with the postwar Republican political ascendancy, he slowly lost interest in public affairs. He died on May 17, 1930, in Santa Barbara, California.

Cronkite, Walter Leland, Jr. (1916–   ), journalist and commentator. Born on November 4, 1916, in St. Joseph, Missouri, Cronkite grew up in Kansas City, Missouri, and in Houston, Texas. While attending the University of Texas in 1933–1935 he worked as a reporter for the *Houston Post* and for the Scripps-Howard syndicate. After a year with the *Houston Press* and another as a radio news editor and broadcaster in Kansas City he joined the United Press (UP) in 1937 and was attached to a succession of news bureaus across the United States and abroad. During World War II he was a correspondent at the front, filing eyewitness stories on the North African campaign, the invasion of Normandy, the Battle of the Bulge, and other headline events. After the war and a period spent in reestablishing UP bureaus in several European capitals, Cronkite covered the Nürnberg trials of Nazi war criminals and then, from 1946 to 1948, was UP bureau chief in Moscow. In 1948 he settled in Washington, D.C., and two years later joined the news staff of the Columbia Broadcasting System (CBS). He quickly became a fixture of CBS news programs, his relaxed manner and broad knowledge of affairs enabling him to deliver lucid extemporaneous summaries of and commentaries on all manner of events. In addition to regular news broadcasting he served as host, moderator, or narrator for a number of CBS television programs concerned with current affairs and news analysis, including "You Are There," "The Morning Show," "The Twentieth Century," and "The Twenty-First Century." As anchorman for the CBS news department Cronkite covered in person many of the most significant events of the 1950s and 1960s and was the world's most widely seen newsman. His regular evening news program won a Peabody public-service award in 1963. In July 1969 he stayed on the air for 24 consecutive hours to cover the landing of *Apollo XI* on the moon, and his technical knowledge of the space program was so extensive that he was voted an honorary astronaut by the astronaut corps.

Crook, George (1829–1890), soldier. Born near Dayton, Ohio, on September 23, 1829, Crook graduated from West Point in 1852 and was assigned to exploration and frontier defense duties in the Northwest. He remained there until 1861, when he was commissioned colonel of volunteers and placed in command of an Ohio infantry regiment. He saw action in West Virginia early in 1862 and, promoted to brigadier general of volunteers, took part in the battles of South Mountain and Antietam. In 1863 he commanded a division of cavalry at Chickamauga and was given the rank of colonel in the regular army. Early in 1864 he conducted successful operations against Confederate railroad traffic in West Virginia and under Gen. Philip H. Sheridan saw action at Winchester, Fisher's Hill, and Cedar Creek in the Shenandoah Campaign, winning promotion to major general. In March 1865, under Sheridan, he led a cavalry division through the battles of the Petersburg Campaign. After the war Crook's rank reverted to lieutenant colonel and he was assigned to Boise, Idaho. There he succeeded in ending an Indian war of several years' duration.

In 1871 he was sent to Arizona to pacify the Apache, who, under Cochise and other leaders, were terrorizing the white settlements then encroaching upon the Indian country. His success in two years was such that he was promoted two grades, to brigadier general, in 1873. In 1875 he took command of the Department of the Platte and, following the discovery of gold in the Black Hills and the consequent invasion of Indian lands by whites, was again heavily engaged in Indian campaigning. He spent all of 1876 in the field against the Sioux and Cheyenne, who defeated him at the battle of the Rosebud, and with his men suffered great hardships. In 1882 he was once more sent to Arizona to put down an uprising of Chiricahua Apache under Geronimo. He pursued the rebels into the Sierra Madre of Mexico and brought them back to the reservation; Geronimo and a small band escaped in 1885, and Crook again tracked them until he was called back to command the Department of the Platte in 1886. Two years later he was promoted to major general and given command of the Division of the Missouri; he moved to his headquarters in Chicago and died there on March 21, 1890.

Crosby, Bing (1904–1977), singer and actor. Born on May 2, 1904, in Tacoma, Washington, Harry Lillis Crosby grew up in Spokane and while attending Gonzaga University there during 1921–1924 joined a local band as drummer and vocalist. In 1925 he formed an act called Two Boys and a Piano with Al Rinker, and together they played vaudeville circuits and Los Angeles theaters until 1927, when they were hired to sing with Paul Whiteman's orchestra. Joined by Harry Barris, they became the Rhythm Boys and were highly successful. The group toured the country with dance bands and made a number of recordings before disbanding in 1930. In 1932 Crosby began broadcasting regularly on radio and in the same year appeared in his first movie, *The Big Broadcast of 1932.* During the 1930s and 1940s he made a series of recordings—"Pennies from Heaven," "Sweet Leilani," "When the Blue of the Night Meets the Gold of the Day" (his theme song), "White Christmas," and others—that made him the most popular of the crooners; dubbed "the Old Groaner," he remained one of the leading American male vocalists for a decade more. He continued his movie career, making a famous series of six *Road* comedies with Bob Hope between 1940 and 1952, beginning with *The Road to Singapore,* 1940; and he starred in *Holiday Inn,* 1942; *Going My Way,* 1944; *The Bells of St. Mary's,* 1945; *Blue Skies,* 1946; *A Connecticut Yankee,* 1949; *White Christmas,* 1954; and many others. For his portrayal of Father O'Malley in *Going My Way* he won an Academy Award. Crosby also engaged in various business pursuits. He continued to appear in movies, on radio, and, rarely, on television, but with diminishing frequency. Following a very successful appearance in London he died in Madrid, Spain, on October 14, 1977, while playing his favorite sport, golf.

Crothers, Rachel (1878–1958), playwright, producer, and director. Born on December 12, 1878, in Bloomington, Illinois, Miss Crothers graduated from the Illinois State Normal University in 1892. She studied dramatics in Boston and New York City and for a time appeared with various theatrical companies, later giving up performing to teach. She wrote her first play, *39 East,* in 1904, but it lay unproduced for 15 years. Her first play produced on Broadway, *The Three of Us,* was a highlight of the 1906 season, and for the next three decades she maintained the extraordinary average of a Broadway play a year, the majority of them popular and critical successes. Her accomplishment was made the more remarkable by the fact that she produced and directed nearly all of her plays herself. Her audiences were particularly delighted by her mastery of dialogue, her characterizations, especially of women, and her deft and often humorous advocacy of established ideals and verities in the face of contemporary social ferment. Among her greatest hits were *A Man's World,* 1910; *Young Wisdom,* 1914; *The Heart of Paddy Whack,* 1914; *Old Lady 31,* 1916; *A Little Journey,* 1918; *Nice People,* 1921; *Mary the Third,* 1923; *Expressing Willie,* 1924; *Let Us Be Gay,* 1929; *As Husbands Go,* 1931; *When Ladies Meet,* 1932; and her last play, *Susan and God,* 1937. During World War I Miss Crothers founded the Stage Women's Relief Fund and in 1932 she helped found the Stage Relief Fund, of which she remained a director until 1951; in 1940 she led in organizing the American Theatre Wing, which operated the famed Stage Door Canteens, and remained its executive director until 1950, when she became president emeritus. Miss Crothers died in Danbury, Connecticut, on July 5, 1958.

Crow, Jim, *see* Rice, Thomas Dartmouth

Culbertson, Ely (1891–1955), bridge player. Born on July 22, 1891, in Poyana de Verbilao, Romania, Culbertson, christened Illya, was the son of an American oil engineer in the Caucasus and a Russian mother. He grew up and was educated principally in Russia, where he formed youthful associations with socialist revolutionaries and enjoyed some rather exciting episodes. He was sent to Yale but remained only briefly, choosing instead to wander about Canada, the United States, and Mexico; he later traveled in Spain and then went to Geneva, where he studied at the university and learned to play auction bridge. In 1917 he returned to the United States, where he was joined by his parents after the Russian Revolution. He had by that time become fanatically devoted to bridge and had developed a system of play that enabled him to gain considerable success. In 1923 he married Josephine Dillon, a wealthy bridge enthusiast, and together they embarked on a program of well-publicized tournament play, later adopting the newly invented game of contract bridge. He founded *Bridge World* magazine in 1929 and the following year published *The Contract Bridge Blue*

Book, which was an immediate best seller. Capitalizing on the rapidly growing popularity of contract bridge and on his own remarkable talent for publicity, Culbertson arranged matches with British teams, which he and his wife won, and in the winter of 1931–1932 they defeated by nearly 9000 points auction bridge's leading team, Sidney S. Lenz and Oswald Jacoby, in a 150-rubber match. The progress of the match was covered as front-page news across the country for more than a month and turned a highly popular game into a temporary craze. Having established himself as the world's top player, he promoted contract bridge through the annual World Bridge Olympics, a newspaper column that was eventually syndicated to some 200 newspapers, books such as *Contract Bridge for Auction Players,* 1932, and *The Gold Book,* 1936, and other enterprises. At the same time Culbertson became deeply interested in movements for peace and world government; in 1942 he founded World Federation, Inc., and in 1946 the Citizens' Committee for United Nations Reform, through the latter advocating a plan for peace by means of armament quotas and an international police force. He contributed articles on peace and mass psychology to various periodicals and published, among other books, *The Strange Lives of One Man,* 1940, an autobiography; *Total Peace,* 1943; *Must We Fight Russia?,* 1946; *Culbertson on Canasta,* 1949; and *Contract Bridge Complete,* 1954. He died in Brattleboro, Vermont, on December 27, 1955.

Cummings, Edward Estlin (1894–1962), poet and painter. Born on October 14, 1894, in Cambridge, Massachusetts, e e cummings, as he styled himself, graduated from Harvard in 1915 and took a master's degree the following year. During World War I he served as an ambulance driver in France, where a misunderstanding with French authorities resulted in his spending six months in a detention camp. The experience was described in his first book, *The Enormous Room,* 1922. In 1923 he published his first book of verse, *Tulips and Chimneys;* it was quickly followed by *XLI Poems,* 1925; *&,* 1826; and *Is 5,* 1926. The poems, characterized by unorthodox typography and a highly experimental approach to style and diction, were, in the main, celebrations of the possibilities of love, life, and joy in the truly alive individual. At the same time Cummings was capable of biting satire in describing the "unman," the soulless creature sunk in the platitudes and conformity of the masses. He exhibited his drawings and paintings and roused the same controversy that attended his poetry. His first play, *Him,* was produced in 1927; among his other works for the stage were *Tom,* 1935, a satirical ballet based on *Uncle Tom's Cabin,* and *Santa Claus: A Morality,* 1946. His later verse was published in, among other volumes, *ViVa,* 1931; *No Thanks,* 1935; *One Times One,* 1944; and *95 Poems,* 1958. His Charles Eliot Norton lectures at Harvard in 1952–1953 were collected and published in 1953 as *i: six nonlectures.* He received the Bollingen Prize

for Poetry in 1957. He died at his farm near North Conway, New Hampshire, on September 3, 1962.

Cummins, Albert Baird (1850–1926), public official. Born in Carmichaels, Pennsylvania, on February 15, 1850, Cummins was educated at nearby Waynesburg College. He held various jobs until 1873, when he began the study of law in Chicago. Admitted to the bar in 1875, he practiced in Chicago for three years and then moved to Des Moines, Iowa, where his firm became within a few years the leading one in the city. He attained a wide reputation in a series of cases, culminating in a Supreme Court action in which, representing the Iowa Grange, he won dissolution of the monopoly in the manufacture of barbed wire. In 1888 he was elected to the legislature and over the next few years came to hold a position of power within the state Republican party. In 1894 and 1900 he ran unsuccessfully for the Senate on a platform calling for the reformation of the party and for breaking the dominance of the railroads over Iowa government and politics. He was elected governor in 1901 and in his first and two succeeding terms secured much Progressive-backed legislation, including provision for senatorial primary elections and the more equitable taxation of railroads. By then a Progressive Republican of national standing, he again sought a Senate seat in 1908, running against the aged William B. Allison. Allison won in the primary but died before the legislature met to elect a senator; after a long fight between the Progressives and the conservative bloc and the holding of a second, special primary, Cummins was elected. In the Senate he and his Iowa colleague, Joseph P. Dolliver, became mainstays of the Progressive bloc. Reelected in 1914 and 1920, Cummins rose to the chairmanship of the Committee on Interstate Commerce and in that position took the lead in 1920 in drafting legislation for the return to private control of the nation's railroads, nationalized during World War I. His proposals for consolidating the roads into a few large and competitive lines and for compulsory labor arbitration were dropped in Senate-House conference, but he did manage to write much Progressive language into the final draft of the Esch-Cummins Act (Transportation Act) of 1920. Early in 1926 he was defeated for renomination and he died in Des Moines soon afterward, on July 30, 1926.

Curley, James Michael (1874–1958), public official and political leader. Born on November 20, 1874, in Boston, Curley grew up in an Irish tenement neighborhood and completed grammar school at the age of sixteen. While working at various jobs he became active in local Democratic politics and rose through the party machinery to his first elective office, a seat on the Boston common council, in 1900. In 1902–1903 he was in the state legislature and from 1904 to 1909 was an alderman. After a year in the Boston city council in 1910–1911 he won election to the House of Representatives, where he remained until resigning in 1914 to take office as mayor of Boston. Defeated for reelection in 1918, he was returned in 1922, defeated in 1926, and again elected in 1930. By that time he was in firm control of the Democratic party in Massachusetts, supplementing the workings of the political machinery with his colorful and engaging personality and his strong appeal to working-class voters. In 1934 he was elected governor; during two years in the statehouse he undertook large and expensive public-works programs and was compared in style to Louisiana's Huey P. Long. Curley's national reputation was by that time well established, although, as a machine politician of the old school, he was something of an embarrassment to his party. In 1932 he had been rebuffed by the group backing Franklin D. Roosevelt for the presidency and, failing to win a place on the Massachusetts delegation to the nominating convention, he had contrived by means he never explained to be elected a delegate from Puerto Rico. Defeated in a Senate race in 1936 and in mayoral elections in 1938 and 1942, he was elected to the House again in 1942, reelected in 1944, and in 1946 returned for a fourth term as mayor, six months of which he spent in federal prison after his conviction for mail fraud; he was released early on the order of President Harry S. Truman, who in 1950 granted him a full pardon. Denied renomination for mayor in 1950 and 1954, he retired from politics after a career spanning half a century. That career inspired Edwin O'Connor's popular novel *The Last Hurrah*, 1956, and the next year Curley published a best-selling autobiography, *I'd Do It Again*. He died in Boston on November 12, 1958.

Currier, Nathaniel (1813–1888), lithographer. Born on March 27, 1813, in Roxbury, Massachusetts, Currier became an apprentice to John B. Pendleton in a pioneer lithographing venture and accompanied him to Philadelphia in 1829 and to New York City in 1833. Upon completing his apprenticeship he set up a lithography house of his own with J. H. Bufford, an artist, and issued "The Ruins of the Merchants' Exchange," 1835, the first of a famous series of prints that was to continue for seventy years. In 1852 he took James Merritt Ives (1824–1895) into the business as a bookkeeper. Born in New York City on March 5, 1824, Ives had improved on his formal education with extensive studies in libraries and art galleries. His abilities as an artist were soon put to use by the firm. He contributed many drawings of his own and directed print production, overseeing the staff of artists employed by Currier. Ives knew the taste of the time, selecting judiciously the subjects for the firm's prints. Many of the prints were hand colored by women who worked in a continuous production line; under Ives's direction, technical perfection was mandatory. In 1857 he became a partner and the firm was thereafter known as Currier & Ives. The prints it produced, all signed "Currier & Ives," were sold both retail and wholesale and some were marketed by mail order. Priced from 15

cents to three dollars, they were highly popular all over the United States; and were distributed abroad through branch offices in European cities. The firm also did considerable advertising work, notably posters and handbills for P .T. Barnum. Currier retired in 1880 and his son Edward West Currier continued the business with Ives. Ives was succeeded by his son Chauncey, who bought out the younger Currier in 1902. Currier died in New York City on November 20, 1888 and Ives in Rye, New York, on January 3, 1895. Between 1840 and 1890 more than 7000 different prints were issued. The firm was dissolved in 1907. More important as manifestations of culture than as art, they became an American institution and by mid-twentieth century were highly prized by collectors.

Curtis, Benjamin Robbins (1809–1874), justice of the Supreme Court. Born in Watertown, Massachusetts, on November 4, 1809, Curtis graduated from Harvard in 1829, studied for two years at the Harvard Law School, and in 1831 began legal practice in Northfield, Massachusetts. In 1834 he moved to Boston and within a few years was recognized as one of the most able members of the city's bar. In 1846 he was elected a member of the Harvard Corporation, succeeding his old teacher, Joseph Story, and in 1851 sat for a term in the state legislature. A Whig and a staunch supporter of Daniel Webster, he was through Webster's influence named to the Supreme Court by President Millard Fillmore later in the same year. In six years on the bench his best-known opinion, also his last, was his dissent in the Dred Scott case in 1857, in which his brother, George Ticknor Curtis, was of counsel for the plaintiff. Justice Curtis, besides disagreeing with the majority decision, objected to the majority opinion written by Chief Justice Roger B. Taney because it first dismissed Scott as having no standing before the Court and then went on to adjudge the case; he let his feelings be known to the newspapers before publication of the opinions, and again objected when Taney subsequently revised his opinion. Curtis thereupon resigned. He returned to Boston and his law practice; as one of the leading attorneys in the nation he argued more than 50 cases before the Supreme Court in his last 17 years. He supported attempts to conciliate the South before the Civil War, and after the war he opposed the radicals' Reconstruction measures. In 1868 he served as President Andrew Johnson's chief defense counsel in his impeachment trial. Curtis continued to practice law until his death, declining several offers of government positons. He died in Newport, Rhode Island, on September 15, 1874.

Curtis, Charles (1860–1936), public official and vice-president of the United States. Born on January 25, 1860, on Indian land that later became part of North Topeka, Kansas, Curtis was of one-quarter Indian descent, a fact later much publicized—and exaggerated—in his political career. In 1879, after three years of high school, he began the study of law and two years later was admitted to the bar. He involved himself in politics as well and in 1885 was elected county attorney for Shawnee County. Elected to the House of Representatives as a Republican in 1892, he retained his seat until 1907, when he entered the Senate. He failed to win reelection in 1912 but two years later was returned to sit for 14 years, during which, although he attached his name to few bills, he acquired a mastery of the art of floor politics that actually powers the legislative process. A conservative and a party regular, Curtis became Republican whip in 1915 and in 1924 succeeded Henry Cabot Lodge as majority leader. At the Republican national convention in 1928 he at first opposed the nomination of Herbert C. Hoover for the presidency, but after his objections were overridden he was chosen as Hoover's running mate. Inaugurated as vice-president in March 1929, he served in an unspectacular fashion; renominated in 1932, he was defeated with Hoover and retired from active politics. Curtis resumed the practice of law in Washington, D.C., and died there on February 8, 1936.

Curtis, Cyrus Herman Kotzschmar (1850–1933), publisher. Born on June 18, 1850, in Portland, Maine, Curtis attended high school until his sophomore year. At thirteen he had started a two-cent weekly called *Young America,* the first of his many publishing ventures. Its headquarters were destroyed, as was the family home, in the Portland fire of 1866 and he moved to Boston; six years later he founded the *People's Ledger.* He moved to Philadelphia in 1876, sold the *Ledger,* and three years later began a magazine called the *Tribune and Farmer,* for which his wife edited a women's page. This became the most popular feature in the magazine, and Curtis built on the idea, starting the *Ladies' Journal,* later the *Ladies' Home Journal,* in 1883. He offered various subscription "specials" to readers, including cash prizes to those who submitted the most names of possible new subscribers. Editors such as Edward W. Bok, hired by Curtis in 1889, made the *Journal* an innovative, pertinent magazine and by 1893 its circulation had reached the million mark. Curtis gave free rein to his staff, which he chose with great care on the basis of their creativity and intelligence. He was one of the first publishers to rely heavily for revenue on the sale of advertising space, and he paid the highest fees then current to obtain contributions from the most popular authors available. In 1890 he formed the Curtis Publishing Company. To its holdings he added the *Saturday Evening Post* in 1897, engaging George H. Lorimer to edit it, building it from a faltering enterprise to one of the most successful magazines in the world; other additions were the *Country Gentleman* in 1911, and newspapers including the *Philadelphia Public Ledger,* the *Philadelphia Evening Telegraph,* the *Philadelphia Press,* the *North American,* the *New York Evening Post,* and the *Philadelphia Inquirer.* Although he stood at the head of a virtual pub-

lishing empire, Curtis remained a private figure; in later years he found much satisfaction in philanthropy, contributing large sums to schools, colleges, and hospitals. He died in Wyncote, Pennsylvania, on June 7, 1933.

Curtis, George Ticknor (1812–1894), lawyer and historian. Born in Watertown, Massachusetts, on November 28, 1812, Curtis graduated from Harvard in 1832, taught for a time, and then went to Harvard Law School. He was admitted to the bar in 1836 and began to practice, first in Worcester and then in Boston. He quickly established a reputation as an able lawyer and was, during his career, patent attorney for such famous inventors as Charles Goodyear, Samuel F. B. Morse, and Cyrus H. McCormick. A Whig and, after the demise of that party, a Democrat, he served in the Massachusetts house of representatives from 1840 to 1843 and later was U.S. commissioner in Massachusetts. As commissioner it was his duty in 1852 to send a Negro named Thomas Sims back to slavery in compliance with the Fugitive Slave Law of 1850, an action that offended his antislavery beliefs. He was thus happier in his role as defending lawyer in the Dred Scott case that reached the Supreme Court in 1857. The loss of this celebrated case helped to precipitate the Civil War. Curtis also appeared before the Supreme Court in the Legal Tender Cases after the end of the war. During the war he moved to New York City, where, although a strong Unionist, he was critical of the administration; a supporter of Gen. George B. McClellan, he later wrote two vindications of him and his career (1886 and 1887). After about 1870 he spent much of his time producing a series of important works in the field of U.S. constitutional history. The best-known of these, written from the Federalist-Whig point of view, went through many editions and revisions, the last published in two volumes in 1889 and 1896 under the title *The Constitutional History of the United States from Their Declaration of Independence to Their Civil War.* His legal treatises included a digest of English and American admiralty cases, 1839; *Treatise on the Rights and Duties of Merchant Seaman,* 1841; *Treatise on the Law of Copyright,* 1847; *Treatise on the Law of Patents,* 1849; and a two-volume commentary on the courts of the United States, 1854–1858. He also wrote biographies of Daniel Webster (1870) and James Buchanan (1883). He died in New York City on March 28, 1894.

Curtis, George William (1824–1892), author, editor, and reformer. Born in Providence, Rhode Island, on February 24, 1824, Curtis was schooled in Massachusetts and at fifteen moved to New York City with his family. He spent two years at the Brook Farm community at West Roxbury, Massachusetts, and was then and afterward strongly influenced by Ralph Waldo Emerson. From 1846 to 1850 he traveled in Europe and the Near East, sending letters back to New York newspapers that were, after his return, collected in *Nile Notes of a Howadji*, 1851, and *The Howadji in Syria*, 1852. In New York City again, he held editorial positions with *Putnam's Magazine*, *Harper's Weekly*, and *Harper's Magazine*, for which he conducted the "Easy Chair" column. His essays were very much in the tradition of Washington Irving—graceful, fanciful, and sentimental—and were collected in *Lotus-Eating*, 1852; *Potiphar Papers*, 1853; and *Prue and I*, 1856. In 1856 he delivered a speech on public issues at Wesleyan University in Connecticut. Titled "The Duty of the American Scholar to Politics and the Times" the speech marked the beginning of Curtis's involvement in public affairs. Through his lectures and, from 1863, his work as political editor of *Harper's Weekly*, he achieved great influence over public opinion. He was a leading Republican from the time of that party's founding, although he refused political office or preferment. He early supported woman suffrage and was a leading advocate of civil-service reform; he was chairman of the National Civil Service Reform League from its founding to his death, and was appointed chairman of a government commission on civil service in 1871 by President Ulysses S. Grant. In 1884, because of his doubts about the political morality of the party's nominee, James G. Blaine, Curtis left the Republican party to become an Independent. In 1890 he became chancellor of the University of the State of New York, a post he held until his death on August 31, 1892, in Staten Island, New York.

Curtiss, Glenn Hammond (1878–1930), aviator and inventor. Born on May 21, 1878, in Hammondsport, New York, Curtiss worked as a telegraph messenger boy and for a time for the Eastman Kodak Company in Rochester before returning home and opening a bicycle shop. He became a highly successful bicycle racer and soon took up the motorcycle, establishing an engine and motorcycle plant in 1902. He continued to race and in 1907 set a land speed record at Ormond Beach, Florida. At the same time he had developed an interest in aeronautics; he produced the engine for the dirigible *California Arrow* that won top prize for airships at the Louisiana Purchase Exposition in St. Louis in 1904 and the next year built Dirigible No. 1 for the army. In 1907 he became director of experimental work of the Aerial Experiment Association founded by Alexander Graham Bell. His first notable airplane, the *June Bug*, was built in 1908 and won the trophy offered by *Scientific American* for the first public flight of more than a kilometer. In 1909 he won the trophy again for a 25-mile flight and as the Aero Club of America's entrant won the James Gordon Bennett Cup and the Prix de la Vitesse at the First International Aviation Meet in France. In 1910 he won his third *Scientific American* trophy and the $10,000 *New York World* prize for a flight from Albany to New York City, and in the same year another pilot in one of his biplanes made the first successful takeoff from a ship. By that time Curtiss had installed pontoon floats on the *June Bug*, renamed it the *Loon*, and experimented with takeoffs from and landings on water; at San Diego, California, in January 1911, he successfully demonstrated the first practical seaplane and was awarded the Collier Trophy. Later in that year, after protracted litigation with the Wright brothers, Curtiss and his associates at the Aerial Experiment Association were awarded a patent for their most important single contribution to aviation, the aileron. He built several seaplanes for the navy and for foreign governments and in 1914 produced a three-engined flying boat for an attempt to cross the Atlantic; the flight never took place because of the outbreak of World War I. During the war the Curtiss Aeroplane & Motor Company produced more than 5000 JN-4 ("*Jenny*") biplanes for use in aviation training at army and navy flight schools, many of which Curtiss himself had established. In 1919 an NC-4 flying boat he had built for the navy made the first transatlantic flight. In his later years Curtiss became interested in other ventures, including Florida real-estate development, and experimented with automobiles and a streamlined automobile trailer. He died in Buffalo, New York, on July 23, 1930. Three years later he was awarded a posthumous Distinguished Flying Cross for his contributions to aviation.

Cushing, Caleb (1800–1879), public official, diplomat, and lawyer. Born on January 17, 1800, in Salisbury, Massachusetts, Cushing grew up there and in nearby Newburyport. He graduated from Harvard in 1817 and after studying law for a year at the Harvard Law School and for three years privately was admitted to the bar in 1821. In 1824 he was elected to the legislature and remained there for several terms. He lost in congressional elections in 1826 and 1831, but in 1835 entered the House of Representatives as a Whig. A conservative and above all a Unionist, he refused to condemn slavery although he disliked it, and he strongly criticized abolitionists for arousing sectional animosity. At the same time he joined John Quincy Adams in fighting the "gag rule" in the House. His Whig regularity was complete in his early years in Congress, as he voted against the Independent Treasury Bill and other Democratic measures, but when John Tyler succeeded William Henry Harrison in 1841 he stood with the new president against the claims to leadership of Henry Clay and, with Tyler, was read out of the party. Cushing left Congress in 1843 firmly identified as a Democrat. His nomination by Tyler as secretary of the treasury was summarily rejected by the Senate, but later in the year he was named minister to China. In that post in 1844 he negotiated brilliantly in obtaining treaties providing for commercial advantages for Americans and establishing the principle of extraterritoriality. In 1845 he was elected again to the Massachusetts legislature and the next year, in keeping with his strongly nationalistic and expansionist views, raised a regiment and as its colonel led it to the Mexican War; he arrived too late to see action, but was promoted to brigadier general before leaving the army. In 1847 and 1848 he was defeated in gubernatorial elections, his support of the Mexican War and of the South making him increasingly unpopular at home. He was nonetheless appointed to the supreme judicial court of Massachusetts in 1852 and in March 1853, having played a leading role in the election of President Franklin Pierce, became attorney general. He conducted that office with skill and high principle, and he was one of Pierce's closest advisers. Upon leaving the cabinet in 1857 he returned to the Massachusetts legislature. In 1860 he served as chairman of the Democratic national convention in Charleston, South Carolina, but despite the fairness with which he presided he could not hold the meeting together. He was still chairman when the party reconvened in Baltimore, and he joined with those opposing Stephen A. Douglas in order to nominate John C. Breckinridge. Although he had long supported the South on constitutional grounds and thus impaired his political prospects in his native state, he was loyal to Abraham Lincoln and the Union during the Civil War and was often consulted by the government on points of law and international relations. From 1864, when he campaigned for Lincoln's reelection, he was a Republican. During the intervals between periods of public service Cushing had maintained a large legal practice, and in 1865 he continued it in Falls Church, Virginia, near Washington. He was recognized as one of the most widely learned men of his generation as well as the possessor of great legal abilities. He undertook various legal and diplomatic tasks for presidents Andrew Johnson and Ulysses S. Grant, most notably serving as chief U.S. counsel at the arbitration of the *Alabama* claims in Geneva in 1871–1872. Late in 1873 Grant appointed him minister to Spain, but before he sailed he was nominated for chief justice of the Supreme Court. Old political enemies rallied to oppose him and he withdrew his name. He remained in Spain from 1874 to 1877, carrying out his diplomatic functions with success. Returning to Newburyport in 1877, Cushing died there on January 2, 1879.

Cushing, Harvey Williams (1869–1939), surgeon. Born in Cleveland on April 8, 1869, Cushing was the fourth generation of his family to enter medicine. He graduated from Yale in 1891 and four years later received his M.D. from the Harvard Medical School. In 1896 he joined the staff of the Johns Hopkins Hospital in Baltimore and during the next four years focused on problems of neurosurgery. During 1900 and 1901 he undertook advanced study with leading surgeons and physiologists in England, Switzerland, and Italy, and then returned to Baltimore to begin a general surgical practice and to serve in various positions with the department of surgery in the Johns Hopkins medical school. He began a thoroughgoing study

of brain tumors, and, although surgical progress in this field was exceedingly slow, in 1910 successfully removed a tumor from Gen. Leonard Wood. He also devoted much attention to the pituitary gland and in 1912 published a landmark monograph on the functions and disorders of the organ. In that year he became surgeon-in-chief of the new Peter Brent Brigham Hospital in Boston, at the same time becoming professor of surgery at Harvard. During World War I he directed a base hospital in France and in 1918 published a classic study of brain injuries from war wounds. In 1925 he published *The Life of Sir William Osler,* a Pulitzer Prize-winning biography of his great former mentor at Johns Hopkins. He continued to produce scientific papers of great value, most of them concerning neurosurgical techniques, and including exhaustive studies and classifications of tumors. In 1932 he retired from Harvard but accepted appointment as Sterling Professor of Neurology at Yale, a post he held from 1933 to 1937. From 1937 until his death he was director of studies in the history of medicine at Yale, and to further that field of research he bequeathed his own extensive library to the school. He died in New Haven, Connecticut, on October 7, 1939.

Cushing, William (1732–1810), justice of the Supreme Court. Born on March 1, 1732, in Scituate, Massachusetts, Cushing graduated from Harvard in 1751. After teaching for a year, he took up the study of law and was admitted to the bar in 1755. From 1760 to 1772 he was a county official in the district of Maine, still at the time part of Massachusetts; in the latter year he returned to succeed his father as judge of the superior court of Massachusetts. In that post he obeyed the state legislature's order to decline the salary offered by the British government. In 1775 he was appointed to the Revolutionary council of state, which after reorganizing kept him as a member of the new supreme judicial court. Two years later, after John Adams resigned as chief justice —a post he had never actually filled—Cushing accepted the position. His most notable act during twelve years on that bench was his ruling in the "Quock Walker case" in 1783 that the Massachusetts Bill of Rights implicitly abolished slavery in the state. In 1779 he was a member of the first Massachusetts constitutional convention and in 1788 was vice-president of the state's committee to ratify the federal Contitution. When the U.S. Supreme Court was organized in September 1789 he was the first associate justice to be appointed to it. He declined the chief justiceship in 1796 because of ill health, but continued as an associate justice until his death on September 13, 1810, in Scituate.

Cushing, William Barker (1842–1874), naval officer. Born on November 4, 1842, in Delafield, Wisconsin, Cushing moved with his family to Chicago, then to Gallipolis, Ohio, and finally in 1847 to Fredonia, New York. He helped support his widowed mother and in 1856 was appointed a page in the House of Representatives. The following year he entered the Naval Academy, but his casual approach to academics and discipline, capped by a prank played on one of his professors, led to his forced resignation in 1861. With the pressing need for sailors for Civil War service, however, he secured a place on the ship *Minnesota* with the rank of acting master's mate. After he had twice successfully sailed captured prize ships into port he was enrolled again in the navy as acting midshipman, receiving promotion to lieutenant before his twentieth birthday. In October 1862, serving as executive officer of the *Commodore Perry*, he acted almost singlehandedly to save the ship from capture when it grounded in the Blackwater River near Franklin, Virginia. With his own command, the *Ellis*, he later captured several prizes, raided Confederate camps along the North Carolina coast, and made a daring escape from near-certain capture. A series of commands on the *Commodore Barney*, the *Shokokon*, and the *Monticello* followed, and Cushing continued to perform brilliant feats in blockade duty and in shore raids. In October 1864 he took a steam launch armed with a bow torpedo up the Roanoke River to Plymouth, North Carolina, and under a hail of fire rammed and sank the last Confederate ironclad, the *Albemarle*, which had of late sunk several Union ships. His launch was blown up and he and one of his crew were the only ones to escape death or capture, swimming down the river to safety. The exploit brought him the thanks of Congress, promotion to lieutenant commander, and other honors. In January 1865 he led a heroic charge over the parapet in the capture of Fort Fisher at Wilmington, North Carolina. Between major adventures he had continued to take, seemingly routinely, one prize ship after another. Although on several occasions he had been long under enemy fire, he received not a scratch through the entire war and many times had, alone among those around him, survived an encounter. Such fortune, together with his courage and daring, fostered among his men an almost superstitious trust in him, and prompted Secretary of the Navy Gideon Welles to refer to him as "*the* hero of the war." After the war he held various commands in the Pacific and Asiatic squadrons and in 1870 became ordnance officer of the Boston Navy Yard. In 1872, at the age of twenty-nine, he was promoted to commander. In 1873, in command of the *Wyoming*, he sailed on his own initiative to Santiago, Cuba, to stop the execution of sailors from the *Virginius*, an American-registered merchantman that had been caught carrying arms to Cuban rebels. The next year he was transferred to the navy yard in Washington, D.C. He died in Washington on December 17, 1874.

Cushman, Charlotte Saunders (1816–1876), actress. Born on July 23, 1816, in Boston, Miss Cushman, encouraged by her musically gifted mother to train for the opera, joined a Boston company, appearing at the age of nineteen as Countess Almaviva in *The Marriage of Figaro*. She was engaged to perform in New Orleans, where, it was said, her instructor attempted to force her natural contralto voice into the soprano range, and her voice failed. She soon met a visiting English actor in New Orleans who offered to give her instruction in dramatics. Under his guidance she appeared as Lady Macbeth in a striking performance. She moved to New York City and secured engagements with several small theaters. In 1837 she appeared as Nancy in *Oliver Twist*, as Meg Merrilies in *Guy Mannering*, and as Romeo, in a predictably controversial production of *Romeo and Juliet*. She was stage manager for the Walnut Street Theater in Philadelphia from 1842 to 1844 and there met William Macready, a formidable English tragedian and manager, who took her as a pupil and encouraged her to perform in London; on his advice, she set sail in 1845. She made her London debut in *Fazio* with Edwin Forrest and subsequently played Queen Katherine in Shakespeare's *Henry VIII*, Lady Macbeth, Romeo (opposite her sister Susan as Juliet), and other popular roles. From 1849 through 1852 she toured the United States, where she was acclaimed as the foremost actress of the day. Her success in such roles as Hamlet and Cardinal Wolsey (in *Henry VIII*) rested on her commanding presence and her mastery of the grand manner. In 1852 she retired, in a fashion, from the stage. She lived in England and continued to make occasional appearances. In 1857 she returned to the United States, giving a series of farewell performances until 1858, when she settled in Rome. Two years later, back in her native land, she gave a farewell to audiences in New Haven, Connecticut. She returned to Rome and remained there until 1870. Criticized for her farewells and reappearances, she was defended on the ground that she suffered from frequent depressions resulting from her enactment of tragic roles. A final series of farewells in 1874–1875, including a public tribute in New York City and her last performance, in Easton, Pennsylvania, ended her long career. She died at her home in Boston on February 17, 1876. In 1915 she became the first member of the theatrical profession to be elected to the Hall of Fame.

Custer, George Armstrong (1839–1876), soldier. Born in New Rumley, Harrison County, Ohio, on December 5, 1839, Custer was appointed to West Point in 1857 and graduated last in his class four years later. His court-martial for a minor dereliction of duty was overlooked in the rush to build up the army rapidly and, commissioned in the cavalry, he joined his regiment on the morning of the battle of Bull Run. He quickly established a reputation for daring and brilliance in battle. He served as an aide to Gen. George B. McClellan during the Peninsular Campaign and in June 1863, at the age of twenty-three, was made a brigadier general. From 1864 to the end of the Civil War he served under Gen. Philip H. Sheridan, who had only the highest praise for the dashing Custer. Made a major general in October 1864, he performed with particular distinction during the final battles around Richmond in April 1865, maintaining a constant pressure on Gen. Robert E. Lee and thus contributing to Lee's decision to surrender. Although a hero of national stature, the disbanding of the volunteer service and the reduction of the standing army forced him to revert to his permanent rank of captain early in 1866. In July of that year the 7th Cavalry was organized and Custer was appointed its lieutenant colonel; he remained, in the absence of a colonel, the regiment's acting commander until his death. The regiment was ordered west to Kansas to take part in what emerged as a rather thoroughly muddled campaign, under Gen. Winfield Scott Hancock, against the Indians of the middle Plains. Suspended from service for a year following a court-martial for absence from duty, Custer was recalled by Hancock's successor, Gen. Philip Sheridan, and was in command at the decisive action of the campaign, the total destruction of a Cheyenne encampment of Black Kettle's people at the Washita River in November 1868. The 7th was disbanded in 1870; Custer remained in the West and resumed command when the regiment was reactivated in 1873. In 1874, the year in which he published *My Life on the Plains*, he led an exploring expedition of 1200 troops and scientists into the Indian reservation lands of the Black Hills. The discovery of gold in the area sparked a massive influx of prospectors and settlers and soon thereafter led to the resumption of skirmishing and, finally, full-scale warfare with the Cheyenne and the Sioux, to whom the Black Hills were reserved by treaty and sacred by tradition. A concentrated offensive against the Indians was mounted in 1876 under the command of Gen. Alfred H. Terry. Approaching the Bighorn Mountains from the east, Terry divided his forces and sent a column under Custer to swing south and come up on the rear of the reported Indian encampment on the Little Bighorn River in present-day southern Montana. Custer drew near the encampment on June 24, 1876, and with characteristic but fatal vainglory decided to ignore Terry's orders to wait for a rendezvous and make a coordinated attack with the rest of the command. Unaware or heedless of the strength of the Indian forces—several thousand warriors under the leadership of Sitting Bull, Crazy Horse, Gall, and other chiefs—"Long Hair" Custer divided his command into three units and launched a surprise attack on the morning of June 25. The battle lasted only a few hours. The central unit, 266 men and officers under Custer, was quickly surrounded on a hill and killed to the last man; the other two units, under Maj. Marcus A. Reno and Capt. Frederick W. Benteen, were able to retreat to defensive positions and were saved from destruction by the arrival of Terry with the main force. "Custer's Last Stand," as the battle soon became known, was the army's worst defeat in the Western campaigns and remained the best-known and most enduringly controversial engagement of the Indian wars.

Cutler, Manasseh (1742–1823), clergyman, scientist, and colonizer. Born in Killingly, Connecticut, on May 13, 1742, Cutler graduated from Yale in 1765 and after a period as a school teacher and then as a merchant and lawyer studied for the ministry and was ordained in the Congregational church in 1771. He was installed as pastor of the church in Ipswich Hamlet (now Hamilton), Massachusetts, and retained the association, despite several long absences, for the rest of his life. During the Revolution he served as a chaplain to units of the Continental army and was cited for heroism. Later he supplemented his pastoral work by studying and then practicing medicine. Possessed of a keen and inquisitive mind, he made extensive investigations and observations in such diverse fields as botany, astronomy, and microscopy. In 1782 he opened a boarding school in his home and continued to operate it for 25 years. In 1786 he joined Rufus Putnam, Winthrop Sargent, and others in organizing in Boston the Ohio Company of Associates with the aim of obtaining from Congress a grant of land in the Ohio country to be settled by Revolutionary veterans. Cutler traveled to New York City to negotiate with Congress. There he may have inspired or hastened passage of the Northwest Ordinance (Ordinance of 1787); he is sometimes credited with authorship of, or a major influence on, the provisions of the ordinance that prohibited slavery and encouraged public education in the Northwest Territory. Three months after passage of the ordinance he concluded his negotiations with the signing of a contract with the Treasury Board providing for the sale of 1.5 million acres on the Ohio River to the company for a price amounting to about 8 cents an acre (66⅔ cents an acre, but payable in government securities worth at the time about 12 cents on the dollar). Cutler also entered into an agreement with William Duer, secretary of the Board, and his group of New York investors—the Scioto Company—for the purchase from the United States of a second grant of 5 million acres west of the Ohio Company's grant. The Scioto Company subsequently became involved in scandal and failed, but the Ohio Company sent out a party of settlers and in April 1788 founded the town of Marietta. Cutler followed and made numerous studies of the country, returning to Ipswich Hamlet in 1789. He served two terms, 1801–1805, in the House of Representatives. He continued his ministerial duties and his various scientific pursuits until his death on July 28, 1823, in Ipswich Hamlet.

D

Daft, Leo (1843–1922), electrical engineer and inventor. Born in Birmingham, England, on November 13, 1843, Daft attended school until he was fifteen and then went to work as a draftsman in his fathers' civil-engineering firm. He became interested in electricity and carried on experiments in the field on his own. In 1866 he moved to the United States; he worked at various jobs until 1871, when he opened a successful photography studio in Troy, New York. Eight years later he gave up photography to devote full time to his electrical experiments and soon joined the New York Electric Light Company, which later became the Daft Electric Company. While concentrating on developing the generators and transmission apparatus for electric-power distribution (as distinct from lighting), and also building several power plants in the East, he investigated the possibilities of electric transportation and in 1883 and 1884 built electric locomotives for railroad lines in Saratoga and Coney Island, New York. In 1884 his company built the machinery for the New York Power Company's first distributing station and, for the Massachusetts Electric Power Company, set up the first complete commercial central power station, with generators and distribution equipment. In 1885 he installed his electric traction system, the first such commercial line, in Baltimore; the system was later adopted by several other cities. The Daft system was powered by double overhead wires from which electricity was drawn by the locomotive through a small carriage called a "troller," from which came the word "trolley." Having pioneered in the field of electric-power distribution, he later turned his attention to other problems and counted among his many patents one for a method of vulcanizing rubber onto metal. Never naturalized, Daft died on March 28, 1922.

Dahlgren, John Adolphus Bernard (1809–1870), naval officer and inventor. Born in Philadelphia on November 13, 1809, Dahlgren received a sound classical education in private schools and at home. At fifteen he was refused enlistment by the navy, but after a short voyage in the merchant service he was appointed acting midshipman in 1826 and assigned to the *Macedonian* under Capt. James Barron. Over the next several years he served in the Mediterranean Squadron, at the Philadelphia Naval Station, and, because of his proficiency in mathematics, from 1834 to 1837 as an assistant to Ferdinand R. Hassler of the Coast Survey. From 1837, when he was promoted to lieutenant, until 1843 he was on leave of absence because of eyesight problems, but he then returned to active service and made an extended Mediterranean cruise on the *Cumberland*. He had already invented a percussion lock when he was assigned to the Washington Navy Yard as ordnance officer in 1847, and there he continued to experiment while promoting the establishment of a full-fledged ordnance department. He succeeded in securing laboratories, a foundry, a test range, and other facilities and began manufacturing cannon of a new type after his own design. A series of tests had shown him that the pressure inside a cannon was greatest at the breech and decreased toward the muzzle; accordingly, he cast cannon thicker at one end, curving smoothly inward to the other in a shape that gave the Dahlgren guns the nickname of "soda-water bottles." The smooth curve further improved the overall strength of the metal by regularizing the pattern of crystallization in cooling. Cast solid and bored smooth, 11-inch Dahlgrens were made in 1851 and installed in shore batteries and after skepticism that ships could support their great weight had been dispelled by a successful voyage of the armed sloop *Plymouth* in 1857, they were mounted on several ships, later including the ironclad *Monitor*. He wrote a number of books on the design and uses of ordnance and in 1855 was promoted to commander. At the outbreak of the Civil War his superior at the Washington Navy Yard, Franklin Buchanan, resigned because of his Confederate sympathies, and although command of the yard was restricted by law to captains, President Abraham Lincoln insisted upon Dahlgren's taking the position. A special act of Congress to make that possible was passed; and in 1862, after being appointed also chief of the Bureau of Ordnance, he was at last promoted to captain. Early in 1863 he was promoted to rear admiral and in July of that year, having requested active duty, he succeeded Samuel F. du Pont as commander of the South Atlantic Blockading Squadron. In combat, his services included the reduction of the defensive batteries around Charleston, South Carolina, and aiding in the capture of Savannah, Georgia. After the war he returned to Washington, served from 1866 to 1868 as commander of the South Pacific Squadron, from 1868 to 1869 again as chief of the Bureau of Ordnance, and from 1869 as commandant of the Washington Navy Yard. Dahlgren died in Washington on July 12, 1870.

Dale, Richard (1756–1826), naval officer. Born in Norfolk County, Virginia, on November 6, 1756, Dale went to sea at the age of twelve and rose to the rating of chief mate in the merchant service by 1775. The next year he became a lieutenant in the Virginia navy. The cruiser on which he was sailing was captured and after a brief confinement on a prison ship he signed as mate on a Tory tender. In July 1776 his vessel was captured by the *Lexington* under Capt. John Barry and Dale immediately entered the Continental navy as a midshipman. He remained on the *Lexington* under succeeding captains and in 1777, when it was taken by the British *Alert* in the English Channel, was imprisoned with the rest of the crew in Mill Prison in Plymouth. After an earlier unsuccessful attempt he escaped in 1779, made his way to France, and was taken on the *Bonhomme Richard* as first lieutenant to Capt. John Paul Jones. In September of that year he took part in the famous battle with the frigate *Serapis*, commanding the gun deck and then, despite a serious wound, leading the boarding party. He remained with Jones on later cruises aboard the *Alliance* and the *Ariel*. In 1781, serving as first lieutenant of the *Trumbull*, he was again wounded in an engagement with the *Iris*. After service on the privateer *Queen of France* he took leave from the navy in 1783 and commanded merchantmen in the East India and China trade until 1801, returning to active service twice for brief periods, in 1794–1795 as fourth-rated captain of the navy and in 1798–1799; in the second term of service he engaged in a dispute over rank with Capt. Thomas Truxtun. In 1801 he was recalled to command an observation squadron in the Mediterranean; with his flagship *President*, Dale carried on a six-month blockade of Tripoli, a move in the war against the Barbary pirates. He then returned to the United States and in December 1802 resigned from the navy, in which he was then the third-ranking officer. He retired to Philadelphia and lived there quietly until his death on February 26, 1826.

Daley, Richard Joseph (1902–1976), public official and political leader. Born in Chicago on May 15, 1902, Daley grew up in a largely Irish neighborhood where local political clubs provided training for potential leaders of the Democratic party. While working in the stockyards he attended law school at night and in 1933 took his degree from De Paul University. In 1936, after several years spent in party organizational work, he was nominated and elected to the legislature, where he remained for ten years, the last five as minority leader of the senate. In 1946, after losing an election for county sheriff—the only such loss of his career—he was appointed deputy comptroller of Cook County (Chicago and the surrounding area). Three years later he was named director of the Illinois department of finance by Governor Adlai E. Stevenson, whom he also served as legislative consultant. In 1950 Daley was chosen Cook County clerk; in 1953 he became chairman of the county Democratic organization, a position of considerable power that he subsequently succeeded in increasing. Finally, in 1955, he was nominated for mayor and, with Chicago a traditionally Democratic city, was elected by a large margin. Inheriting control of an established political machine, Daley consolidated his position as head of both the city government and the party organization; he was reelected by huge majorities in 1959, 1963, 1967, and 1971, and extended his party influence to the state and national levels, becoming known in national election years as one of the Democrats' kingmakers. Under his administration, which was unusual in that it enjoyed the support of business, Chicago in the main prospered and a massive program of public works virtually made over the face of the city. Under the mayor's firm political discipline Chicago's perennial open corruption was brought under a measure of control. With no political ambitions beyond Chicago and little thirst for personal publicity, Daley was not well known nationally until 1968; then, during the Democratic national convention, at which he wielded his customary influence, Chicago was the scene of large and violent clashes between police and crowds of demonstrators protesting the Vietnam War. Public opinion was sharply divided over Daley's stringent police measures, and he became a hotly debated national figure. In 1972 his slate of delegates to the Democratic convention was defeated by a reform group. Elected to an unprecedented sixth term as mayor in 1975, Daley died in Chicago on December 20, 1976.

Dallas, Alexander James (1759–1817), lawyer and public official. Born on June 21, 1759, of Scottish immigrant parents in Jamaica, the West Indies, Dallas was educated in Scotland and England and, after his return to Jamaica in 1780, began the practice of law. On the recommendation of actor Lewis Hallam he emigrated to the United States in 1783. After completing the required two years' residence he was admitted to the Pennsylvania bar in 1785. He devoted time also to other pursuits, attempting, with Hallam, to introduce theater into Philadelphia, contributing essays on political and literary topics to newspapers, and editing for a time the *Columbian Magazine*. From 1791 to 1801 he served as secretary of the Commonwealth of Pennsylvania and became a leading organizer of the Democratic Republican party. In 1801 President Thomas Jefferson appointed him U.S. attorney for the eastern district of Pennsylvania, a post he held for 13 years. In 1814 he was named secretary of the treasury by President James Madison. The War of 1812 had brought the treasury to the brink of bankruptcy, and Dallas immediately set about reestablishing the nation's solvency. His strong message to Congress recommending a greatly increased revenue went far to restore confidence, and Congress responded by levying heavier taxes. For several months during 1815 he served also as acting secretary of war. The bill embodying his plan for rechartering the Bank of the United States was rendered impotent by the Republican opposition in Congress, and on his advice the president vetoed it; however, most of his recommendations were incorporated into John C. Calhoun's Bank Bill in 1816, which established the Second Bank of the United States. The Tariff Act of the same year was also a result of his analysis of the nation's financial requirements and formed the basis of the system of protection that prevailed for 30 years. He retired from the treasury in October 1816 to return to his law practice in Philadelphia, but died soon afterward, on January 16, 1817.

Dallas, George Mifflin (1792–1864), public official, diplomat, and vice-president of the United States. Born in Philadelphia on July 10, 1792, the son of Alexander J. Dallas, the younger Dallas graduated from the College of New Jersey (now Princeton) in 1810. After admission to the bar in 1813 he served as secretary to Albert Gallatin on the latter's diplomatic mission to Russia. Returning in 1814, he joined first the treasury department, then headed by his father, and later, in Philadelphia, the legal staff of the Second Bank of the United States, on which he served in 1815–1817. A staunch Democrat, he rose rapidly through various political offices and in 1831 was appointed to fill an unexpired term in the Senate. In 1833 he became Pennsylvania's attorney general for two years. From 1837 to 1839 he was minister to Russia; after his return to Philadelphia he devoted himself to his law practice, although he maintained a deep interest in politics and continued a long-standing rivalry with James Buchanan. In 1844 he was nominated for vice-president and, with James K. Polk at the head of the ticket, was elected. At the end of his term, during which he was primarily concerned with the tariff problem, he again returned to private life. In 1856, at President Franklin Pierce's request, he succeeded Buchanan as minister to Great Britain; his major accomplishment, a treaty resolving a number of disputes arising from the earlier Clayton–Bulwer Treaty, was nullified by the Senate. He succeeded, however, in obtaining a renunciation of England's claimed right to search vessels on the high seas. He returned to the United States in 1861 and died in Philadelphia on December 31, 1864. The city of Dallas, Texas, was named for him during his vice-presidency.

Dalton, Robert (1867–1892), outlaw. Born in 1867, probably in Cass County, Missouri, Dalton moved with his family to Indian Territory in what is now Oklahoma, then in 1882 to Coffeyville, Kansas. In 1888 he began a brief period as a deputy U.S. marshal in the Indian Territory. The next year, after killing a rival in a love affair, he and his brothers Grattan and Emmet began their criminal careers in earnest (although they may have indulged themselves on a lesser scale from an earlier date) as horse thieves in Kansas. They moved to California late in 1890 and the next year successfully attempted their first train robbery, raiding the Southern Pacific at Alila.

Grattan was captured but later escaped and rejoined his brothers in Oklahoma Territory, where they had returned and recruited other members for the gang. A daring train robbery at Wharton in 1891 brought the serious attention of the authorities and the Daltons lay low for more than a year before robbing in quick succession trains at Red Rock and Adair, Oklahoma Territory. Already a legend and much taken with their own prowess, the gang decided to rob two banks in Coffeyville. Arriving there on the morning of October 5, 1892, they met heavy fire from the aroused townspeople; Robert, Grattan, and two others were killed and Emmet was wounded, captured, and given a long prison sentence. In time the Daltons came to rank almost with the James gang among the desperadoes of Western lore.

Daly, Augustin (1838–1899), playwright, producer, and manager. Born on July 20, 1838, in Plymouth, North Carolina, John Augustin Daly early moved with his widowed mother to New York City where he became deeply interested in the theater. He involved himself in amateur dramatics, finding that he preferred production and direction to acting, and in 1856 produced a small revue in Brooklyn. While working as drama critic for the *Sunday Courier*, with which he was associated for ten years, he began writing for the stage, for the most part making free adaptations of plays in German and French. The first of these to be produced, *Leah the Forsaken*, from S. H. Mosenthal's *Deborah*, opened in Boston in 1862 with Kate Bateman in the leading role and Hezekiah L. Bateman as producer. In 1867 *Under the Gaslight*, an original melodrama that introduced the device of the last-minute rescue of the hero tied to the railroad tracks, opened at the New York Theatre as Daly's first independent production. While it played successfully in London in 1868, he produced in New York's Broadway Theatre *A Flash of Lightning* and a year later *The Red Scarf*, another original that featured the hero tied to a log headed for the buzzsaw. In 1869 he leased the Fifth Avenue Theatre and began assembling a company of players, producing Bronson Howard's *Saratoga* in 1870 and his own *Horizon* and *Divorce*, both markedly realistic for the time, in 1871. Other successes during these years included the adaptations *Hazardous Ground*, 1867, and *Frou Frou*, 1870, and his own *Roughing It*, 1873, and *Pique*, 1875. Daly continued to be successful at the New Fifth Avenue Theatre, opened for him in 1873, until 1877, when the failure of his last original play, *The Dark City*, forced him to give the theater up. Undaunted, he converted the old Broadway Theatre to Daly's Theatre and in 1879 began again. Often transferring the story to an American setting, he produced skillful adaptations as *The Passing Regiment*, 1881; *Seven-Twenty-Eight*, 1883; *A Night Off*, 1885; and *The Lottery of Love*, 1888. With a company that featured such outstanding performers as Ada Rehan, Otis Skinner, and

John Drew, and, at various times, Maurice Barrymore, Joseph Jefferson and Fanny Davenport, he traveled to England in 1884 and to England and continental Europe in 1886, 1888, and 1891, winning admiration for his Shakespearian productions. On the last trip he was selected by Tennyson to adapt and produce his dramatic poem *The Foresters*, which opened at Daly's Theatre in 1892. In 1893 he opened his own theater in London. Having greatly raised the standards of theatrical production in the United States and having given invaluable encouragement to native authors through his more than 90 plays and adaptations, Daly died in Paris while on a business trip, on June 7, 1899.

Daly, Marcus (1841–1900), miner and businessman. Born in Ireland on December 5, 1841, Daly emigrated to the United States in 1857 and remained in New York City for a time before moving to California. There he worked as a miner, became an expert in mining operations, and was eventually employed by large companies as a prospector. In 1876 he was sent to Butte, Montana, to investigate a silver mine. Believing that silver was abundant in that region, he returned to California and persuaded George Hearst, Lloyd Tevis, and James B. A. Haggin to invest $30,000 with him in the Anaconda Silver Mine. A company was formed in 1881 and Daly began working the mine. The silver gave out quickly but a rich vein of copper was revealed; avoiding public notice, Daly bought out neighboring mines and then reopened the Anaconda as a copper mine. A smelter was built in 1884 and the company rapidly expanded its holdings, reorganizing in 1891 as the Anaconda Mining Company with a capitalization of $25 million. Daly quickly became a millionaire several times over and devoted much of his time and money to the development of the area. He founded the city of Anaconda (whose first proposed name was Copperopolis) around the smelter site; built banks, power plants, irrigation projects, the town of Hamilton, and a railroad to Butte; promoted Anaconda for the state capital; and published the *Anaconda Standard*, which, serving a population of 5000, boasted a plant that rivaled in modernity that of any newspaper in the country. He also wielded his wealth and influence in state Democratic politics, although he never ran for office himself, and he contributed heavily to William Jennings Bryan's presidential campaign in 1896. By the end of his life he had succeeded in combining a vast number of mining, processing, and timber holdings into the Amalgamated Copper Company, which was capitalized at $75 million and owned three-fourths of the stock in Anaconda Mining. Daly died in Anaconda on November 12, 1900.

Damrosch, Leopold (1832–1885), musician and conductor. Born on October 22, 1832, in Posen, Prussia (now Poznań, Poland), Damrosch, at his parents' behest, entered the University of Berlin in 1854 to study medicine, but upon taking his degree he turned to music as his true vocation. After studying the violin with a number of teachers and appearing as soloist and conductor in various smaller cities he became in 1857 concertmaster of the Grand Ducal Opera, conducted by Franz Liszt, in Weimar. The following year he was appointed conductor of the Philharmonic Orchestra in Breslau (now Wroclaw), where, after making a few concert tours, he founded in 1862 the Breslau Orchestra Society, of which he remained conductor until 1871, at the same time holding several other musical posts. In that year he accepted an invitation to travel to New York City to become director of the Männergesangverein Arion (the Arion Society), a German choral society. In 1873 he founded the Oratorio Society of New York and five years later the New York Symphony Orchestra, remaining conductor of all three groups for the rest of his life. Beyond instilling technical excellence into his musicians, Damrosch contributed greatly to the increased appreciation of music in the United States; he introduced works—by such moderns as Franz Liszt, Hector Berlioz, Johannes Brahms, and Richard Wagner—that had never before been heard in the country. In 1881 he produced a highly successful music festival in New York City, drawing 10,000 people to each of several concerts to hear the Berlioz *Requiem*, Handel's *Messiah*, Beethoven's *Ninth Symphony*, and other works for orchestra and chorus. In 1883 he took the Symphony on a Western tour and in 1884 was invited to conduct at the Metropolitan Opera in New York City, which for its second season was presenting an all-German program featuring in particular the music of Wagner. Midway through the season the strain proved too much and he died on February 15, 1885.

Damrosch, Walter Johannes (1862–1950), musician and conductor. Born in Breslau, Prussia (now Wroclaw, Poland) on January 30, 1862, Damrosch, the son of Leopold Damrosch, had as a matter of course taken up music early, studying with his father and other teachers. In 1872 he followed his father to New York City, continuing his studies there, singing with the Oratorio Society of New York, and in 1878 touring the South as piano accompanist to violinist August Wilhelmj. In 1880 he arranged the piano score of the Hector Berlioz *Requiem* for his father's great music festival and took part in much of the rehearsal work. Upon the illness and death of the elder Damrosch in 1885 he succeeded to the directorship of the Oratorio Society and the New York Symphony Orchestra and completed the German season at the Metropolitan. Appointed to a permanent position with the Metropolitan as assistant director and second conductor, he continued his father's work of proselytizing for the radical new composers, especially Richard Wagner, the premier American concert performance of whose *Parsifal* he conducted in 1896. He brought Tchaikovsky to America in 1891, introduced new works by Camille Saint-Saëns and Berlioz, and in 1894 produced Wagner's *Die Götterdämmerung* and *Die Walküre*. In 1895 he formed the Damrosch Opera Company, with which he toured successfully until 1900, when he returned to the Metropolitan to conduct Wagner. He reorganized the New York Symphony on a permanent full-time basis in 1903 and for more than 20 years conducted it at home and on numerous tours of the United States, Canada, and, after World War I, Europe. A great many European and American composers owed the first or most important American performance of their music to Damrosch, who with remarkable breadth of vision sometimes introduced works he did not personally care for. In 1925 he conducted the first symphony concert to be broadcast by radio. He resigned from the Symphony in 1927, although he served afterward as guest conductor on occasion, and became musical adviser to the National Broadcasting Company (NBC), for which he pioneered a weekly music-appreciation program for schools in 1928, continuing it until 1942. During his career he composed a number of operas himself, none of great distinction, including *The Scarlet Letter*, 1896; *Cyrano de Bergerac*, 1913; *The Man Without a Country*, 1937; and *The Opera Cloak*, 1942; and in his later years he composed numerous shorter works. His autobiography, *My Musical Life*, appeared in 1923. Damrosch died in New York City on December 22, 1950.

Dana, Charles Anderson (1819–1897), journalist and editor. Born on August 8, 1819, in Hinsdale, New Hampshire, Dana was largely self-taught when he entered Harvard in 1839. He discontinued his studies because of difficulties with his eyesight as well as financial problems, and during 1841–1846 he was a general instructor and managing trustee at the Brook Farm community in West Roxbury, Massachusetts. He contributed essays to the community's paper, the *Harbinger*, and to the *Dial* during this period. After a fire virtually terminated the experiment at the colony, he moved to Boston and became assistant editor of the *Daily Chronotype*. He took advantage of a previous meeting with Horace Greeley to gain employment on the *New York Tribune* and was made city editor in 1847. In his 15-year association with the paper he became nearly as influential as Greeley himself. In 1848–1849 he witnessed revolutionary events in Paris and Berlin that caused him to become disenchanted with his former political ideas. After his return to the *Tribune* in 1849 as managing editor, his writing was notably more concise and reflected a liberal bent, but with a tinge of cynicism. Although he lent valuable support to antislavery forces, he was generally impatient with individual abolitionists and, as was to be his policy in the future, hostile to labor movements; he opposed strikes and advised workers to cooperate with management to correct unfair working conditions. During the Civil War his attitude toward military

and civil policies was notably more aggressive than Greeley's, leading to his resignation in 1862. He was hired by Secretary of War Edwin M. Stanton to observe and report on military operations at the front. Highly impressed with the abilities of Ulysses S. Grant and William Tecumseh Sherman, he wrote glowing reports that reassured President Abraham Lincoln. During 1863–1865 he was an assistant secretary of war; he recorded his impressions of cabinet members and of Lincoln for his *Recollections of the Civil War*, which did not appear until 1898. Having resigned from government service in 1865, he was editor of a short-lived Chicago paper in 1866 and in 1868 was able to purchase the *New York Sun*. There he became the "newspaperman's newspaperman." Although his paper's political coverage was inconsistent and sometimes reactionary, he made the paper famous for its news reporting, which featured the human-interest story and emphasized readability. Dana also edited the *New American Cyclopaedia* (with George Ripley) during 1858–1863 and in 1857 published a highly successful anthology, *The Household Book of Poetry*. He died in Glen Cove, New York, on October 17, 1897.

Dana, James Dwight (1813–1895), geologist and zoologist. Born in Utica, New York, on February 12, 1813, Dana early developed an interest in science and entered Yale in 1830 to study under Benjamin Silliman. He left in 1833 without graduating in order to teach mathematics in the navy, making in 1835 a cruise to the Mediterranean from which he sent back a description of Vesuvius to Silliman's *American Journal of Science*, of which he was subsequently an editor for 49 years. He then returned to Yale briefly as Silliman's assistant and in 1837 published *System of Mineralogy*, long a standard work, great in both scope and detail. From 1838 to 1842 he sailed with the government's exploring expedition to the South Seas and the Antarctic under the command of Lt. Charles Wilkes and upon his return spent 12 years in Washington, D.C., writing the reports of his investigations: *Zoophytes*, 1846; *Geology of the Pacific Area*, 1849; and *Crustacea*, two volumes, 1852–1854. While engaged in this work he married Silliman's daughter Henrietta in 1844, began sharing in the editorship of "Silliman's *Journal*" with Benjamin Silliman, Jr., and in 1849 was appointed to succeed his father-in-law as professor of natural history at Yale, a position he took up actively in 1855. In 1864 his title was changed to professor of geology and mineralogy, and he retained it until retiring 28 years later. While exerting great influence as a teacher, Dana added to his already considerable scientific stature with several more monumental works, publishing *Manual of Mineralogy*, 1848; *Manual of Geology*, 1862; *Textbook of Geology*, 1864; *Corals and Coral Islands*, 1872; and *Characteristics of Volcanoes*, 1890, many of which were long kept in print in revised editions. In declining health in his later years, Dana gradually restricted his activities and was forced to give up his professorship in 1892. His last work was the completion of the fourth revision of *Manual of Geology* early in 1895; he died at his New Haven, Connecticut, home a short time later, on April 14, 1895.

Dana, John Cotton (1856–1929), librarian. Born in Woodstock, Vermont, on August 19, 1856, Dana graduated from Dartmouth College in 1878 and took up the study of law. He moved to Colorado for his health in 1880 and there began practice. Later he was for a time a member of a New York City law firm, but was again forced to seek the dry air of Colorado, where after a stint with a coal and coke company he turned to civil engineering. Finally, in 1889, he was named librarian of the new Denver Public Library and, although he had no training or experience in the field, he soon proved himself a capable and innovative director. He instituted an open-stack system whereby library patrons had free access to the books, thus encouraging browsing and exploration, and in 1894 he organized the first children's department of a public library. In 1898 Dana became librarian of the Springfield, Massachusetts, City Library, and four years later he moved to the Newark, New Jersey, Public Library, with which he remained associated until his death. During 27 years as librarian in Newark the library increased its holdings fivefold while circulation increased even more. He organized branch libraries around the city, including in 1904 a business branch in the downtown district, the first of its kind, that soon became known throughout the country and was widely copied. Dana was a founder of the Newark Museum in 1909 and served thereafter as its director. He was also a founder of the Special Libraries Association, of which in 1909 he was first president. Among his publications were *A Library Primer*, 1896; and *Libraries: Addresses and Essays*, 1916. Dana died in New York City on July 21, 1929.

Dana, Richard Henry (1815–1882), lawyer and author. Born in Cambridge, Massachusetts, on August 1, 1815, the son of a noted poet and essayist of the same name, Dana entered Harvard in 1831. Two years later weakened eyesight forced him to suspend his studies, and he shipped as a common sailor aboard the brig *Pilgrim* from Boston around Cape Horn to California, in the belief that the experience would benefit his eyes. Upon his return to Boston in 1836 he reentered Harvard and graduated in 1837. He taught briefly and then, turning to the law, was admitted to the bar in 1840. In that year he published his account of his voyage, *Two Years Before the Mast*. A vivid, detailed description written from the viewpoint of an ordinary seaman, the book achieved great popularity and has remained a classic; it marked the beginning of a new and vital tradition blending the techniques of literature and journalism. The work contained interesting accounts of the richness of California and is said

to have influenced President James K. Polk in his decision to embark on the Mexican War, one of the results of which was the acquisition of California by the United States. In the book, besides telling a fascinating and exciting story, Dana expressed his desire to better the lot of the sailor, a concern he carried also into his law practice, in which he specialized in maritime cases. In 1841 he published *The Seaman's Friend*, a work on practical seamanship and maritime law. He was an early supporter of the Free-Soil party and later of the Republican party. He gave free legal aid to victims of the Fugitive Slave Law of 1850 and later, during his tenure as U.S. district attorney for Massachusetts, from 1861 to 1866, persuaded the Supreme Court to validate the Union blockade of Confederate ports. He ran unsuccessfully for the House of Representatives in 1868; in 1876 his nomination by President Ulysses S. Grant as minister to Great Britain failed of confirmation by the Senate, partly as a result of the efforts of Simon Cameron, who referred to Dana as "one of those damned literary fellers." In 1878 he traveled to Rome to continue his study of international law; he died there on January 6, 1882.

Daniel, Peter Vivian (1784–1860), justice of the Supreme Court. Born on April 24, 1784, in Stafford County, Virginia, Daniel attended the College of New Jersey (now Princeton) for a time and then took up the study of law in the office of Edmund Jennings Randolph. Admitted to the bar in 1808, he quickly entered into public affairs and the next year was elected to the legislature. From 1812 to 1835 he served as one of the eight (later three) members of the Virginia council of state and for much of the period was also lieutenant governor. In 1834 he declined appointment by President Andrew Jackson as attorney general, but two years later accepted the office of U.S. district judge, succeeding Philip P. Barbour, who had been elevated to the Supreme Court. In 1841, upon the death of Barbour, he was himself named to the Court by President Martin Van Buren. He remained on the bench for the rest of his life, an ardent Jeffersonian and defender of states' rights. Of his opinions, distinguished by clarity and felicitous expression but by no remarkable learning, none was memorable. Daniel died in Richmond, Virginia, on May 31, 1860.

Dannay, Frederic (1905–1982) and **Manfred Bennington Lee** (1905–1971), "Ellery Queen," authors. Born in Brooklyn, New York City, Dannay on January 11, 1905, and Lee on October 20, 1905, the two were cousins who until 1929 pursued separate careers. Dannay had become art director of an advertising agency and Lee, after attending New York University, was a publicity agent for a motion-picture company. In 1929, however, they decided to collaborate on a mystery story to be entered in a magazine contest. Their entry won the contest, but the magazine went out of business; another publisher picked up the manuscript, and it appeared in book form later in the year as *The Roman Hat Mystery* by the pseudonymous "Ellery Queen." *The French Powder Mystery*, 1930, *The Dutch Shoe Mystery*, 1931, and *The Greek Coffin Mystery*, 1932, followed quickly and the two gave up other interests to devote their full time to writing Ellery Queen novels. Queen, the paradigmatic amateur sleuth who is brighter and quicker than anyone else in the plot, soon became one of the most popular detective-fiction characters of all time. Dannay and Lee turned out, over the next 40 years, more than 40 Ellery Queen novels, several others under the name "Barnaby Ross," some 20 juvenile mysteries, more than a dozen short-story collections, and 35 anthologies of mystery stories; and from 1941 they edited *Ellery Queen's Mystery Magazine*. Their Queen books were translated and circulated around the world; sales passed the hundred-million mark in the 1950s and continued unabated. In addition, Ellery Queen was featured as a character in a number of movies and on radio and television. Dannay and Lee often appeared on the lecture platform. Dannay was a visiting professor in 1958–1959 at the University of Texas, to which they later donated their large collection of detective fiction. The long and lucrative partnership was ended by Lee's death in Roxbury, Connecticut, on April 3, 1971. Dannay died on September 3, 1982, in White Plains, New York.

D'Antonguolla, Rodolpho, *see* Valentino, Rudolph

Dare, Virginia (1587–1587?), colonial figure. Born on August 18, 1587, on Roanoke Island, now in North Carolina, Virginia was the first child to be born in America of English parents. Her parents, Eleanor (Ellinor, Elyonor) and Ananias Dare, had been among the more than 100 persons accompanying Governor John White (father of Eleanor Dare) on the second colonizing expedition to Sir Walter Raleigh's Virginia patent. They landed on Roanoke Island, the site of the earlier unsuccessful colony, in July 1587. On August 27, nine days after his granddaughter Virginia's birth, Governor White sailed back to England for supplies; war with Spain delayed his return to Roanoke until 1590, and upon landing he could find no trace of the colonists except for a cryptic inscription hinting that they had gone to seek shelter from hostile Indians among the friendly Croatan tribe. It is believed that what survivors of the "Lost Colony" there may have been were absorbed into the Croatan tribe.

Darrow, Clarence Seward (1857–1938), lawyer. Born on April 18, 1857, near Kinsman, Ohio, Darrow studied for a year at Allegheny College and for an equally short time at the University of Michigan's law school before being admitted to the bar in 1878. After several years of small-town practice in Ohio he moved to Chicago in 1887, where he became a close friend of and later was associated in practice with John P. Altgeld.

He was also for a time in partnership with Edgar Lee Masters. He was active in the Democratic party and in 1890 was appointed city corporation counsel; later he became general counsel for the Chicago and North Western Railway, a position he resigned in 1895 to defend Eugene V. Debs and his associates in the injunction case arising from the Pullman strike. A friend and associate of Henry Demarest Lloyd, Darrow was elected to a term in the legislature in 1902 on the Public Ownership ticket. He gained a national reputation as a labor lawyer and subsequently represented the miners in the arbitration of the anthracite strike of 1902 and in 1907 successfully defended William D. "Big Bill" Haywood and other Western labor leaders on a murder charge. He also defended the conspirators charged with the 1911 bombing of the *Los Angeles Times* and took part in numerous sedition cases. His reputation as a defense attorney soared in 1924 with his efforts for the defense in the kidnapping and murder trial of Nathan Leopold and Richard Loeb, in which he introduced novel forms of evidence based on psychiatric examinations. In 1925 he opposed William Jennings Bryan, whom he subjected to a withering cross-examination on the tenets of Fundamentalism, in the Scopes "Monkey Trial" in Dayton, Tennessee, and the following year conducted the defense in the Sweet case in Detroit, involving violence arising from racial segregation. His cases were almost invariably (and usually intentionally) headline material, as it was his aim to use them to educate and persuade the public to his liberal and civil-libertarian views; but his success at the bar—in more than 50 capital cases he lost not one client to execution—rested on his scrupulous care in preparation and on his masterly summations to juries. His rationalism and ingrained skepticism were also expressed in a number of books, among them *An Eye for an Eye*, 1905; *Crime, Its Cause and Treatment*, 1925; and *The Story of My Life*, 1932. A staunch advocate of Progressive reform, particularly the abolition of capital punishment, Darrow was a popular lecturer and debater. He died in Chicago on March 13, 1938.

Daugherty, Harry Micajah (1860–1941), political manager and public official. Born on January 26, 1860, in Washington Court House, Ohio, Daugherty graduated from the University of Michigan with a law degree in 1881 and immediately began practice in his home town. From 1890 to 1894 he served two terms in the legislature, his only elective office in a long career in politics. Moving to Columbus in 1893, he enjoyed lucrative employment as a corporation counsel and lobbyist until he decided, like Mark Hanna earlier, upon political management as his profession. In 1902 he helped the young Warren G. Harding win election as lieutenant governor; staying with his protégé, he managed Harding's successful Senate campaign in 1914 and in 1919 began planning for the next year's Republican national convention. Although Harding's chances were unpromising, Daugherty conducted a careful preconvention survey of the delegate strength of the leading candidates—Leonard Wood, Frank O. Lowden, and Hiram W. Johnson—and ventured a prediction that not only proved uncannily accurate but also added a phrase to the American political lexicon: "The convention will be deadlocked, and after the other candidates have gone their limit, some twelve or fifteen men, worn out and bleary-eyed for lack of sleep, will sit down, about two o'clock in the morning, around a table in a smoke-filled room in some hotel, and decide the nomination. When that time comes, Harding will be selected." Upon his election the grateful Harding named Daugherty attorney general. Although the appointment dismayed many in the party, the public, and the bar, Harding remained loyal to Daugherty, and to the rest of the "Ohio gang," through the rumors of corruption that soon sprang up. Daugherty, who was already widely unpopular for his strong antilabor actions, was accused of profiting from lax enforcement of Prohibition laws and sundry other forms of malfeasance, and he harbored in the Justice Department a number of unsavory characters, including the notorious Gaston B. Means. After Harding's death in 1923 he refused to open department files to a congressional investigation and in March 1924 was dismissed by President Calvin Coolidge. In 1927 two successive trials for conspiracy to defraud the government ended in hung juries. He was also reputed, but never proven, to have been involved in the Teapot Dome conspiracy. He later attempted to clear his and Harding's names in *The Inside Story of the Harding Tragedy*, 1932, written with Thomas Dixon. Daugherty died in Columbus, Ohio, on October 12, 1941.

Davenport, Thomas (1802–1851), inventor. Born in Williamstown, Vermont, on July 9, 1802, Davenport was apprenticed to a blacksmith at fourteen and seven years later opened his own smithy in Brandon. While prospering in the business, he saw and became fascinated by an electromagnet made by Joseph Henry; he bought the device at some sacrifice and soon constructed a larger one of his own. Observing that the power of the electromagnet was easily controlled by breaking or switching the battery connections, he conceived of a way to turn the electromagnetic force into mechanical power. With four magnets, two fixed as poles and two pivoted to revolve between the others, and all connected to a battery through a crude automatic switching device —a commutator—he had by July 1834 built an electric motor, the first to embody the principles now universal (Henry's motor of a few years earlier had been far less potentially useful, developing an inefficient oscillatory rather than rotational movement). Davenport gave up blacksmithing to develop and promote his invention, meeting with financial and other difficulties at every step. His patent was delayed until 1837, and a number of miniature motor-driven machines he made, including a working model of an elec-

tric trolley car, attracted curious notice but little substantial support. For a time he continued his work in a laboratory in New York City, where he also published a newsletter, *Electro-Magnet and Mechanics Intelligencer*, printed on his electrically powered press, but in 1843 he was forced to return to Brandon. In 1846 he moved to nearby Salisbury, where he remained for the rest of his life. In his last years he invented an electric player piano. Davenport died in Salisbury on July 6, 1851.

Davey, Marie Augusta, *see* Fiske, Minnie Maddern

Davidson, Jo (1883–1952), sculptor. Born in New York City on March 30, 1883, Davidson became interested in drawing and painting as a child and studied for a time at the Art Students League before entering Yale to prepare for a medical career. His discovery of a pronounced talent for sculpture led him to leave Yale after a short time and to devote himself to art; he studied with a number of masters, supporting himself by selling burned-wood portraits, and in 1907 went to Paris to further his training. His early days there were marked by poverty and struggle, but recognition came gradually with shows in Paris and New York in 1909 and the acceptance of one of his pieces by the Salon of 1910. He later moved temporarily to London and there his portrait work brought him sudden and remarkable success; his subjects included Joseph Conrad, Lord Northcliffe, Havelock Ellis, Anatole France, and Sir Rabindranath Tagore. Having received the highest critical acclaim, he undertook to create busts and statues of the world's leading figures, returning to the United States in 1916 to portray Woodrow Wilson and to France in 1919 to execute portraits of the political and military leaders at the Versailles Peace Conference, including Marshal Ferdinand Foch, David Lloyd George, Georges Clemenceau, Bernard Baruch, Gen. John J. Pershing, and others, exhibiting them in a 1920 show entitled "A Plastic History of the War." Davidson remained in France until 1939, although he made trips to the Soviet Union, the United States, and many parts of Europe. In those years he created portraits of Robert M. La Follette, Andrew W. Mellon, George Bernard Shaw, Benito Mussolini, Gertrude Stein, Mme Chiang Kai-shek, James Joyce, H. G. Wells, Mahatma Gandhi, Sir James M. Barrie, and John D. Rockefeller. Soon after returning to the United States in 1939 he made a tour of South America to portray the heads of state of several countries there. During World War II he strongly supported the policies of President Franklin D. Roosevelt and was active in a number of organizations working for refugee relief, support of the war effort, and other causes. Among the subjects of his later sculpture portraits were President Roosevelt, Henry A. Wallace, Gen. Charles de Gaulle, Helen Keller, Ernie Pyle, Will Rogers, and Van Wyck Brooks. Although he enjoyed great financial success and the patronage of a unique assemblage of notables, Davidson was never content to be merely popular; his busts and statues, strong and deeply vital, were through his entire career as greatly admired by critics as by the public. His autobiography, *Between Sittings*, appeared in 1951. Davidson died in Bercheron, France, on January 2, 1952.

Davies, Arthur Bowen (1862–1928), painter and illustrator. Born in Utica, New York, on September 26, 1862, Davies was encouraged by his parents in his early interest in drawing and studied with a private teacher and, after his family moved to that city, at the Art Institute of Chicago. In 1887 he moved to New York City, where, at the Art Students League, he became closely associated with Robert Henri, George Luks, and John Sloan. Of his early works, for the most part small idyllic landscapes such as "Along the Erie Canal" and "Fantasy of the Vine," a few were accepted by the National Academy of Design but none attracted much attention. For a short time between 1888 and 1891 he contributed illustrations to *St. Nicholas* magazine, but success did not begin to come until after 1894, when a studio in New York City and a trip to Europe were given him by patrons—a perceptive art dealer, William Macbeth, and the collector Benjamin Altman. His style thereafter gradually changed to one more abstractly symbolic, his vision growing deeper as his palette narrowed in such works as "Four O'Clock Ladies" and "The Girdle of Ares." Discerning collectors began buying his pictures regularly. In 1908 he helped organize an exhibition of the work of artists, including himself, Henri, Luks, Sloan, and Maurice Prendergast, who came to be known as the Eight, or the Ashcan School. The show was a major event in the revolt of young American artists against the conservatism of the National Academy and of much of the art-buying public, but it was only a prelude to the more important Armory Show of 1913, which was organized largely by Davies as president of the Association of American Painters and Sculptors. The show brought to New York the thitherto unknown works of radical Europeans—the Postimpressionists, the Cubists, and the Futurists. The styles of such modernists somewhat affected Davies' own work in later years. In his last years he experimented successfully with etchings and in color lithography, making signal contributions to those media as well. An intensely private man, he did not seek honors, and other than his work in organizing the two great shows was little involved in public matters. While on one of his many trips to Europe he died in Florence on October 24, 1928.

Davies, Samuel (1723–1761), religious leader and educator. Born in New Castle County, Delaware, on November 3, 1723, Davies was educated at a Presbyterian "log college" in Pennsylvania and in 1747 was ordained a minister. Settling in Hanover County, Virginia, he became almost at once both a leading exponent of the wave of religious revivalism known as the Great Awakening and a principal defender of the liberty of nonconformists in religion against the authority of the established church in Virginia. He traveled constantly through the state and into North Carolina, building up a large membership in the church and winning renown as a preacher unexcelled in America. In 1753 he and Gilbert Tennent were sent by the Synod of New York on a spectacularly successful fund-raising mission to England and Scotland on behalf of the struggling College of New Jersey (now Princeton). In 1755 he led in founding the Presbytery of Hanover, the first in Virginia. Despite his youth he was by that time the most influential clergyman in his region; his championship of religious liberty established an enduring tradition to which was traceable in large part the later success of Thomas Jefferson's efforts to incorporate a provision for such liberty in the Virginia constitution. He was one of the earliest hymnalists in America and his sermons, in nearly a score of editions, continued to be widely read for decades after his death. In 1759 Davies was named to succeed his friend Jonathan Edwards as president of the College of New Jersey and, although his tenure was brief, he introduced a number of major improvements in the college. He died on February 4, 1761, in Princeton, New Jersey.

Davis, Benjamin Oliver (1877–1970), soldier. Born on July 1, 1877, in Washington, D.C., Davis entered Howard University in 1897 and left the following year to serve as a first lieutenant of volunteer troops in the Spanish-American War. Mustered out in 1899, he immediately reenlisted as a private in the 9th Cavalry of the regular army, and during service in the Philippines rose rapidly through the ranks to a commission as second lieutenant in 1901. In 1905, with a promotion to first lieutenant, he was detailed to Wilberforce University as professor of military science and tactics, remaining there for four years. During 1909–1912 he was military attaché in Monrovia, Liberia, and for the next three years was on garrison and border-patrol duty in the West; he returned to Wilberforce in 1915. Another tour of duty in the Philippines in 1917–1920, during which he advanced to lieutenant colonel, was followed by assignment as professor of military science and tactics at Tuskegee Institute, where he remained until 1924. For the next 14 years he alternated between teaching at Tuskegee and Wilberforce, receiving promotion to colonel in 1930. In 1938 he was given his first independent command, that of the 369th New York National Guard infantry regiment. Two years later, in October 1940, he became the first black soldier to hold the rank of general in the U.S. army; his promotion aroused a brief but intense controversy, both on account of his race and because, coming just a month before a presidential election, it was interpreted by some as politically motivated on the part of President Franklin D. Roosevelt. Placed in command of the 2nd Cavalry Brigade at Fort Riley, Kansas, upon his promotion, Davis retired in 1941 but was immediately recalled to active duty and assigned to the office of the inspector general in Washington. During World War II he served in the European theater of operations as an adviser on race relations in the army. Returning to his post as assistant inspector general, Davis retired from the army in 1948 after 50 years of service. He died in North Chicago, Illinois, on November 26, 1970. His son, Benjamin Oliver Davis, Jr. (1912–), also entered military service and became the first black general in the air force.

Davis, Bette (1908–), actress. Born on April 5, 1908, in Lowell, Massachusetts, Miss Davis was christened Ruth Elizabeth but was known from an early age as Bette. After graduating from Cushing Academy in Ashburnham, Massachusetts, in 1925, she decided to seek a career in the theater and for a time studied at the John Murray Anderson Dramatic School in New York City. She made her earliest appearances in small parts with stock companies in Rochester, New York, and Dennis, Massachusetts. A brief stint with the Provincetown Players led to her Broadway debut in *Broken Dishes* in 1929. A subsequent Broadway role in *Solid South* won her a film contract. In Hollywood she again began in small roles in minor productions, including *Bad Sister*, 1930; *Seed*, 1930; and *Waterloo Bridge*, 1931, but in 1932 her performance in *The Man Who Played God* won her considerable attention. She failed, however, to win a part in a substantial production until 1934, when she appeared in *Of Human Bondage*. For *Dangerous*, 1935, she won an Academy Award ("Oscar"), and after roles in *Border Town*, 1935; *Front Page Woman*, 1935; *The Petrified Forest*, 1936; *Marked Woman*, 1937, and other pictures she won a second Oscar for her forceful acting in *Jezebel*, 1938. Often plagued by mediocre scripts, Miss Davis nonetheless turned in a great many performances of the highest caliber, demonstrating endless versatility in such films as *Juarez*, 1939; *Dark Victory*, 1940; *The Little Foxes*, 1941; *The Man Who Came to Dinner*, 1941; *In This Our Life*, 1942; *Watch on the Rhine*, 1943; *The Corn Is Green*, 1945; *June Bride*, 1948; *All About Eve*, 1950; *The Star*, 1953; and *The Virgin Queen*, 1955. She returned to Broadway in a revue, *Two's Company*, in 1952, and later appeared on the stage in *The Night of the Iguana*. Among her later films, in many of which she took to its limit her ability to portray with great depth bizarre or disturbed characters, were *A Pocketful of Miracles*, 1961; *Whatever Happened to Baby Jane?*, 1962; *Hush, Hush, Sweet Charlotte*, 1965; *The Nanny*, 1965; *The Anniversary*, 1968; *Death on the Nile*, 1978; and *Watcher in the Woods*, 1980. For television she made the films *Strangers, The Story of a Mother and Daughter*, 1979 (Emmy Award); and *Family Reunion*, 1981.

Davis, David (1815–1886), justice of the Supreme Court and public official. Born in Cecil County, Maryland, on March 9, 1815, Davis was educated at Kenyon College and, after graduating from Yale Law School in 1835, was admitted to the bar. He moved to Bloomington, Illinois, and in 1844 was elected as a Whig to the state legislature. He was a leading member of the state constitutional convention in 1847 and the following year began 14 years as a circuit-court judge in Illinois. During that time he formed a close friendship with Abraham Lincoln; at the Republican convention of 1860 Davis was the leader of the Lincoln forces and after the successful campaign accompanied the new president to Washington. In 1862 Lincoln appointed him to the Supreme Court. His most important opinion in 15 years on the bench was in *Ex parte Milligan*, 1866, in which, for the Court, he overruled both Congress and President Lincoln in holding that miltiary commissions could not be vested with judicial authority over civilians in regions remote from actual combat. His political leanings had always been rather vague and subject to change; during his tenure on the bench he began to stray from the increasingly radical tenets of the Republican party. In 1872 he was nominated for president by the Labor Reform Convention but, failing to capture the Liberal Republican nomination, which went instead to Horace Greeley, he withdrew from the race. In 1876, while the outcome of the Rutherford B. Hayes–Samuel J. Tilden election awaited decision by the Electoral Commission, it was widely assumed that Davis would sit on the commission and, as the supposedly neutral member of the otherwise evenly split panel, cast the deciding vote. Congressional Democrats, indeed, had counted on his appointment, for he seemed inclined to their side. Suddenly and inexplicably the Democrats in the Illinois legislature elected him to the Senate, disqualifying him for the Commission and clearing the way for another Republican member to decide the presidency. He remained in the Senate until 1883, the last two years as president pro tem. He died in Bloomington on June 26, 1886.

Davis, Elmer Holmes (1890–1958), journalist, broadcaster, and author. Born on January 13, 1890, in Aurora, Indiana, Davis graduated from Franklin College, Indiana, in 1910 and during 1912–1913 pursued further studies as a Rhodes scholar at Oxford University. In 1913 he joined the staff of *Adventure* magazine and the next year became a reporter for the *New York Times*. His historical scholarship and political acumen enabled him to rise to foreign correspondent and, by 1924, to editorial writer for the newspaper. In 1924 he resigned to devote himself to free-lance writing and over the next 15 years he produced a number of novels, including *Friends of Mr. Sweeney*, 1925, *Strange Woman*, 1927, and *Giant Killer*, 1928; a great many short stories, many of them collected in *Morals for Moderns,*

1930, and *Love Among the Ruins,* 1935; and essays on a wide variety of topics, many published in leading journals and later in such collections as *Not to Mention the War,* 1940. In 1939 he was invited to substitute for H. V. Kaltenborn as news broadcaster and commentator on the Columbia Broadcasting System (CBS). In contrast to the prevailing bombastic or suavely ingratiating styles of radio journalists of the day, Davis's manner was calm and straightforward, laced with dry humor and informed comment. He was an immediate success and by 1941 his daily audience was estimated to number more than 12 million. In 1942 he left CBS to become, at the request of President Franklin D. Roosevelt, director of the Office of War Information (OWI), a trying post that he filled with courage and determination until the office was abolished in 1945. He then returned to radio with the American Broadcasting Company (ABC) and remained on the air until his retirement in 1953. In the early 1950s Davis was preeminent among the few public figures and commentators to speak out strongly against the threat to liberty posed by the activities of Senator Joseph R. McCarthy and his ilk; a number of essays on the subject were published in his best-selling *But We Were Born Free,* 1954. *Two Minutes Till Midnight,* on war and peace in the nuclear age, appeared in 1955. Davis appeared for a short time on television in 1954, but ill health limited his work; he died on May 18, 1958, in Washington, D.C.

Davis, Jefferson (1808–1889), president of the Confederate States of America. Born at the present site of Fairview in southwestern Kentucky on June 3, 1808, Davis moved to Mississippi during his childhood; he was educated at Transylvania University and at sixteen was appointed to West Point. After his graduation in 1828 he served in the army for seven years, mainly in Wisconsin. In 1835 he settled on a plantation in Mississippi; his wife Sarah, the daughter of his former commanding officer, Gen. Zachary Taylor, died three months after their marriage, and Davis remained for seven years in semi-isolation on his plantation. In 1845 he was elected to the House of Representatives. The following year he resigned to command a Mississippi volunteer regiment in the Mexican War, and his brilliant action at Buena Vista prevented the defeat of General Taylor. Nationally famous for his exploit, he was sent to the Senate in 1847; he resigned four years later to run unsuccessfully for governor of Mississippi. In 1853 President Franklin Pierce appointed him secretary of war, in which post he notably improved the nation's military capabilities and helped, by advocating a transcontinental rail route across the South, to bring about the Gadsden Purchase. At the end of four years he reentered the Senate. Although he was a determined and eloquent defender of the point of view of the South, he discouraged secessionist activity; because of his moderate views he enjoyed considerable popularity even in the North, and only after the secession of Mississippi in 1861 did he reluctantly acquiesce. He formally withdrew from the Senate in January 1861 and was immediately commissioned major general of Mississippi militia. The convention which met in Montgomery, Alabama, two weeks later named him provisional president of the Confederate States of America, and he was confirmed in the position in the regular election in October. He was inaugurated in Richmond, Virginia, on February 22, 1862. As president of a new and economically disadvantaged nation, and faced with the immediate prospect of war, Davis performed eminently well. While his military judgment was on occasion at fault, he wisely gave Gen. Robert E. Lee wide scope in conducting the war. He was constantly hampered by the opposition of extreme states'-rights advocates, notably Governor Joseph E. Brown of Georgia and Governor Zebulon B. Vance of North Carolina, who objected vigorously to the conscription law urged by Davis in 1862. Throughout the war he labored ceaselessly to increase the South's resources, maintain internal unity, and hold back the growing military power of the Union. In Lee, whom he had originally promoted over the criticism of numerous skeptics, he eventually found not only his most valuable commander but also his most loyal personal supporter. During 1864 Davis was much in the field with Lee. In January 1865 he sent his vice-president, Alexander H. Stephens, and two others to conduct a fruitless peace conference with President Abraham Lincoln at Hampton Roads, Virginia. When, as an inevitable consequence of the economic and manpower superiority of the Union, defeat was imminent, he left Richmond, the Confederate capital, and fled southward with his cabinet; after brief stays in Danville, Virginia, and Greensboro, North Carolina, Davis continued south, planning to cross the Mississippi and continue the struggle if only to obtain more advantageous terms of surrender. On May 10, 1865, he was captured by federal troops near Irwinville, Georgia. For two years he was held prisoner in Fort Monroe, Virginia—at first in shackles, until objecting Northern public opinion was heeded. He was released on bail in 1867 but, because of legal difficulties, was never brought to trial for treason, for which he had been indicted in 1866. In his remaining years he lived on the Mississippi plantation of a friend and traveled occasionally in Europe. In 1881 he published the two-volume *The Rise and Fall of the Confederate Government.* He steadfastly refused to request formal amnesty and never regained his citizenship. He died in New Orleans on December 6, 1889.

Davis, John William (1873–1955), lawyer and public official. Born on April 13, 1873, in Clarksburg, West Virginia, Davis graduated from Washington and Lee University in 1892 and after a year of teaching school returned to the university to take his law degree in 1895. He remained as assistant professor of law until 1897, when he returned to Clarksburg to enter legal practice in partnership with his father. In 1899 he was elected to the legislature as a Democrat from a normally Republican district, and after serving as a delegate to Democratic national conventions in 1904 and 1908 ran successfully for the House of Representatives in 1910. There he played a leading role in preparing the Clayton Antitrust Act for its later passage in 1914. Reelected in 1912, Davis resigned his seat in 1913 to accept appointment by President Woodrow Wilson as solicitor general, a post he held for five years during which he presented the government's side before the Supreme Court in a large number of cases involving progressive legislation. In 1918 he was sent to Bern, Switzerland, to negotiate with German authorities on the treatment and release of prisoners of war, and later in the year was named to succeed Walter Hines Page as ambassador to Great Britain. At the Versailles Peace Conference he was one of Wilson's advisers and helped draft provisions for the government of occupied territories. With the inauguration of President Warren G. Harding in 1921 he resigned his ambassadorship and returned to law practice in New York City, soon becoming a noted corporation counsel. From 1922 to 1924 he was president of the American Bar Association. Davis had already been mentioned occasionally as a presidential possibility when, at the 1924 Democratic national convention, his name appeared late in the voting as an alternative to the deadlocked Alfred E. Smith and William Gibbs McAdoo; on the 103rd ballot (the most ever required in a major party convention) he was nominated, but in November he was badly defeated by the incumbent president, Calvin Coolidge. He then returned to private practice. Although he supported Franklin D. Roosevelt for the presidency in 1932, his Jeffersonian outlook led him to turn elsewhere in 1936 and 1940; during World War II, however, he urged bipartisan support of the President, and he later was a strong advocate of the United Nations. During the 1950s he appeared before the Supreme Court in a number of major cases, many of which he had taken, without fee, in the interest of conservative principles. In 1952 he argued successfully against President Harry S. Truman's seizure of the steel mills and also represented South Carolina in defense of its segregated school system. In all he appeared before the Supreme Court in some 140 cases during his career. His last major legal engagement was his defense of the physicist J. Robert Oppenheimer against charges that he was a security risk. Davis died on March 24, 1955, in Charleston, South Carolina.

Davis, Miles Dewey, Jr. (1926–   ), musician. Born on May 25, 1926, in Alton, Illinois, Davis moved with his family to East St. Louis, Illinois, the next year. He began learning to play the trumpet at thirteen and before he graduated from high school he had sat in with Dizzy Gillespie and Charlie Parker in Billy Eckstine's band. After high school he moved to New York City and for a time studied composition and piano at the Juilliard School of Music. At the same time he began sitting in with various jazz groups in the legendary nightclubs along 52nd Street, absorbing the music of Gillespie, Parker, Lester Young, Coleman Hawkins, and others. After engagements with the Benny Carter and Eckstine bands he organized his own nine-man group in 1948 and, although he won little commercial success, immediately made his mark on music with a series of now-classic recordings that were quickly recognized as a turning point for modern jazz. Featuring such performers as Gerry Mulligan, Kai Winding, John Lewis, Lee Konitz, and Max Roach, and working with arrangements by Gil Evans, the group produced under Davis's leadership a light, controlled sound that ushered in, as the title of a later reissue of the collected recordings claimed, the "birth of the cool." After the dissolution of his group Davis worked with various others while slowly developing his musical ideas, emerging once again as a major creative force in jazz with an appearance at the 1955 Newport Jazz Festival, with such albums as *Miles Ahead* and *Music for Brass*, and with a Carnegie Hall concert in 1957. From that year he worked almost exclusively in a quintet setting; he displayed remarkable perception in choosing his sidemen, a great many of whom later drew on the experience to become leading jazz figures themselves: among them were John Coltrane, Philly Jo Jones, and Herbie Hancock. Over the years his style, always introspective and carefully considered, grew more and more expressive; without the technical brilliance of some of his mentors, Davis surpassed them in depth of feeling, conveying changing moods in a spare but highly lyrical line that moved through the intricate rhythms and chord structures of his compositions. Through concert appearances, several European tours, and such albums as *Milestones, Sketches of Spain, Musings of Miles, Relaxin', Workin', At Carnegie Hall, E.S.P., Miles Smiles, Sorcerer, Bitches' Brew,* and *Live–Evil,* he succeeded in remaining at the forefront of jazz development with a seemingly inexhaustible creative imagination.

Davis, Richard Harding (1864–1916), journalist and author. Born on April 18, 1864, in Philadelphia, Davis was educated at Lehigh and Johns Hopkins universities and in 1886 joined the *Philadelphia Record* as a reporter. He later moved to the *Philadelphia Press* and in 1889 to the *New York Sun.* He had already attracted considerable attention with his colorful and often sensational reporting, and in 1890 he became managing editor of *Harper's Weekly.* During the next several years he undertook extensive travels and his reports to *Harper's* were later collected in a number of volumes: *The West from a Car Window,* 1892; *The Rulers of the Mediterranean,* 1894; *Our English Cousins,* 1894; *About Paris,* 1895; and *Three Gringos in Venezuela and Central America,* 1896. As the country's best-known and most influential reporter he covered every major war in the world from the 1896–1897 Greco-Turkish conflict to World War I, often reporting for papers in London as well as in New York; his dispatches later filled seven volumes. He also published fiction; his collections of short stories included *Gallegher and Other Stories*, 1891; *Van Bibber and Others*, 1892; *The Lion and the Unicorn*, 1899; *Ranson's Folly*, 1902; *The Scarlet Car*, 1907, and *The Man Who Could Not Lose*, 1911; among his novels were *Soldiers of Fortune*, 1897; *The King's Jackal*, 1898; *Captain Macklin*, 1902; *The Bar Sinister*, 1903; and *The White Mice*, 1909. He wrote 25 plays, some of which were successful on Broadway and elsewhere, particularly *Ranson's Folly*, 1904; *The Dictator*, 1904; and *Miss Civilization*, 1906. He died on April 11, 1916, at his home near Mount Kisco, New York.

Davis, Sammy, Jr. (1925–   ), entertainer. Born in New York City on December 8, 1925, Davis was the son of vaudevillians and by the age of four was appearing on stage regularly. He won a role in the Ethel Waters motion picture *Rufus Jones for President* in 1931; a year later he became a member of the Will Mastin Trio, a popular song-and-dance team featuring his father and his adopted uncle. With help from Bill "Bojangles" Robinson the young Davis honed his talents for singing, dancing, and impersonation and soon became the star of the act. During 1943–1945 he served in the army, writing and producing a number of camp shows for the Special Services branch; in 1946 the trio suddenly broke into the circuit of fashionable nightclubs with a smash-hit engagement in Hollywood. Major bookings around the country and later television appearances led to Davis's beginning to work on his own in the early 1950s. He made numerous popular recordings, received top billing at clubs and on television variety shows, and in 1956 made his Broadway debut in the hit musical *Mr. Wonderful*. He starred in a number of motion pictures, including *Anna Lucasta*, 1959, *Porgy and Bess*, 1959, and a series of films featuring as well other members of the much-publicized Frank Sinatra "clan"—*Ocean's Eleven*, 1960; *Sergeants Three*, 1962; and *Robin and the Seven Hoods*, 1964. He returned to Broadway in 1964 in *Golden Boy*, a musical version of the Clifford Odets play. Later movies included *A Man Called Adam*, 1965, and *One More Time*, 1970. Continuing to appear in clubs, concerts, and on television, Davis, who delighted in describing himself as the world's only one-eyed (following an automobile accident in 1954) black (by birth) Jew (following a much-publicized conversion), was widely hailed as one of the greatest entertainers in the world, an opinion based not only on his remarkable talents but also on his boundless energy and sheer exuberance in performance. His autobiography, *Yes I Can*, appeared in 1965, and his contributions to the civil-rights movement won him the 1969 Spingarn Medal of the National Association for the Advancement of Colored People (NAACP).

Davis, Stuart (1894–1964), painter. Born on December 7, 1894, in Philadelphia, Davis grew up in East Orange, New Jersey. Encouraged by his parents in his interest in art, he left school at fifteen to move to New York City and study with Robert Henri. After three years with Henri, a master of the "Ashcan School," he exhibited a number of watercolors at the 1913 Armory Show and there was strongly impressed by the works of the Cubists and other abstract modernists. Also much influenced by the rhythms of jazz, which he tried to convey in the spatial tensions of his paintings, Davis began evolving an abstract mode of expression in which sharply geometric compositions were created from common objects of American life—gas pumps, skyscrapers, cigarette packages, and the like. Davis worked for a short time as a cartographer for army intelligence during World War I, continuing his experiments in painting all the while. During 1927–1928 he painted a remarkable series of geometric and color studies inspired by an eggbeater. After a period in Paris in the late 1920s he returned to New York City and during 1931–1932 taught at the Art Students League. From 1933 to 1939 he executed a number of murals under the auspices of the Federal Arts Project of the Works Progress Administration (WPA), and by 1940 was recognized as a leading American exponent of abstract art. From that year until 1950 he was a member of the faculty of the New School for Social Research. Davis enjoyed a number of exhibitions and retrospectives at major galleries and museums during the 1940s and 1950s and was widely honored, in 1956 winning election to the National Institute of Arts and Letters. In many of his later paintings he inscribed words among the bright color shapes, an innovation that, along with his use of commercial objects and designs, marked him as a precursor of the Pop-art movement of the 1960s. Davis died in New York City on June 24, 1964, a few months before the issue of the first U.S. postage stamp with an abstract design, one executed by Davis.

Davis, William Morris (1850–1934), geographer and geologist. Born in Philadelphia on February 12, 1850, Davis graduated from the Lawrence Scientific School at Harvard in 1869 and the following year received an additional degree in mining engineering. During 1870 he accompanied Raphael Pumpelly and Josiah Dwight Whitney on field explorations in the Great Lakes region and in the Rocky Mountains and then secured a position with the Argentine Meteorological Observatory in Córdoba, where he remained until 1873. After three years spent in business with his father he received in 1876 an appointment from Harvard as assistant in geology to Nathaniel Shaler. He advanced to instructor in 1879, to assistant professor of physical geography in 1885, and to professor in 1890. His observations on numerous field trips, combined with a wide study of geological and geographical literature, early marked him as an outstanding worker in the field.

To descriptive geography he contributed a new precision, coining when necessary new terms such as "peneplain" and "mature," and as a theorist he devoted his energies to the synthesis and rationalization of the huge mass of data and analysis of which he was master. In the process of developing such concepts as that of the cycle of erosion he emerged as a principal founder of the modern science of geomorphology. His skill in constructing maps and diagrams of great clarity added to the value of his teaching and of his published works, which included *The Rivers and Valleys of Pennsylvania*, 1889; *Physical Geography*, 1898; *Geographical Essays*, 1909 (reissued in 1954); *Die erklärende Beschriebung der Landformen*, 1912; *The Coral Reef Problem*, 1928; and *Origin of Limestone Caverns*, 1930–1931. Davis also contributed a great many writings on meteorology, including an authoritative textbook, *Elementary Meteorology*, 1894. In 1898 he became Sturgis-Hooper Professor of Geology, a chair he held until retiring in 1912. During World War I he served with the National Research Council. Widely honored for his work by U.S. and international scientific bodies, he spent most of his last years on the Pacific Coast, carrying on field work and lecturing at various universities. Davis died in Pasadena, California, on February 5, 1934.

Davisson, Clinton Joseph (1881–1958), physicist. Born in Bloomington, Illinois, on October 22, 1881, Davisson graduated from the University of Chicago in 1908 and three years later took his Ph.D. in physics from Princeton. From that year until 1917 he was an instructor at the Carnegie Institute of Technology; he then joined the research staff of the Bell Telephone Laboratories in New York City. At the outset of his work he concerned himself with the problem of secondary emission in vacuum tubes, undertaking a general study of thermionic emission of electrons from metal and metal-oxide surfaces. From there he proceeded to an investigation of electron reflection from such surfaces. Working first with C. H. Kunsman and later with L. H. Germer, he noticed in one experiment involving reflection from a large nickel crystal a remarkable phenomenon: the reflected electrons fell into certain strict patterns in concentric angles, very similar to the crystal diffraction patterns of X rays. The discovery was made soon after the announcement in 1924 of Louis Victor de Broglie's hypothesis that, just as electromagnetic radiation exhibits certain properties that require interpretation as the behavior of particles, so particles, particularly electrons, might under certain circumstances act as waves rather than as material bodies. Davisson's electron diffraction experiments with Germer constituted strong evidence in favor of Broglie's position, and by 1927 he had shown that careful measurements of the diffraction patterns agreed with Broglie's hypothetical equations. For this work Davisson was awarded the 1937 Nobel Prize for Physics jointly with G. P. (later Sir George) Thomson of England, who had published work along similar lines. Davisson later contributed also to the development of electron microscopy. He left Bell Labs in 1946 and from 1947 to 1949 was visiting professor of physics at the University of Virginia. He died on February 1, 1958, in Charlottesville, Virginia.

Dawes, Charles Gates (1865–1951), banker, public official, and vice-president of the United States. Born in Marietta, Ohio, on August 27, 1865, Dawes graduated from Marietta College in 1884 and two years later took a degree from the Cincinnati Law School. Admitted to the bar, he began practice the next year in Lincoln, Nebraska; by 1894 his interests in public-utilities companies were extensive enough to draw him to the Chicago area and he settled in Evanston, Illinois. As a reward for his work in William McKinley's 1896 presidential campaign he was appointed comptroller of the currency in 1898, holding the office until 1902. Upon his return to business in 1902 he organized the Central Trust Company of Illinois, of which he was president until 1921 and chairman and honorary chairman until 1931. In 1917 he was commissioned a major of engineers in the army and by October 1918 had advanced to brigadier general in charge of military procurement for U.S. forces in France. He remained after the war's end to direct the disposal of some $400 million in surplus supplies and equipment and then resigned his commission in 1919, returning to the United States with the reputation of a forceful and effective administrator. In 1921 Dawes was appointed first director of the budget. Early in 1923 Germany, suffering increasing financial difficulties, defaulted on its scheduled reparations payments imposed after the war, a move that threatened to force in turn a halt to Allied repayment of U.S. war loans. Later in 1923 Dawes was named to head a group of financial experts appointed to seek a solution to the serious imbalances in the German economy. A complex plan of industrial and economic reorganization, coupled with U.S. loans and a revised reparations schedule, was submitted to the Allies and to Germany and was approved in August 1924. The Dawes Plan, as it was known, allayed many of the more pressing problems and remained in effect until 1930. For this work Dawes was awarded the 1925 Nobel Peace Prize jointly with British foreign secretary Sir Austen Chamberlain; he used his prize money to endow the Walter Hines Page School of International Relations at the Johns Hopkins University. The success of the Dawes commission had made him a major public figure and in 1924 he was chosen as the Republican candidate for vice-president. Elected by a large majority with Calvin Coolidge, he attempted to make the office of vice-president an active one but enjoyed little success, failing in particular in his efforts to reform and streamline the rules of the Senate. On leaving office in 1929 he served as chairman of a commission sent to reorganize the finances of the Dominican Republic and then was appointed ambassador to Great

Britain by President Herbert C. Hoover. While in that post he was a delegate to the London Naval Conference of 1930. In 1932 he returned to the United States to become president of the Reconstruction Finance Corporation (RFC), organized by the government to supply capital to Depression-hit banks and other institutions. Dawes resigned the position later in the same year and returned to private banking as chairman of the City National Bank and Trust Company of Chicago. He wrote a number of books on banking and several volumes of memoirs, including *A Journal of the Great War*, 1921; *Notes as Vice President*, 1935; and *Journal as Ambassador to Great Britain*, 1939. He died in Evanston on April 23, 1951.

Dawes, Henry Laurens (1816–1903), public official. Born in Cummington, Massachusetts, on October 30, 1816, Dawes graduated from Yale in 1839 and for a time taught school and contributed editorials to local newspapers while preparing himself for the law. He was admitted to the bar in 1842, beginning practice in North Adams, Massachusetts, and later moving to Pittsfield. He soon became involved in political affairs and in 1848 was elected to the state legislature, in which he served also in 1849, 1850, and 1852. After taking part in the state constitutional convention of 1853 he served as U.S. district attorney until 1857, when he was elected as a Republican to the House of Representatives. There he was soon recognized as a legislator of great ability, and he succeeded to the chairmanship of the Committee on Appropriations in 1869 and the Committee on Ways and Means in 1871, the combination endowing him with considerable discretionary power over legislation of all kinds. He was particularly interested in the tariff and stood for the maintenance of protective schedules, especially for the textile industry, which was then centered in his home state. He also supported the plan for the issuance of daily weather bulletins, which led to a national weather service, proposed by Cleveland Abbe in 1869. After 18 years in the House, Dawes was elected to the Senate in 1875. His major accomplishments during three terms in that body were the completion in 1885 of the Washington Monument, which had stood unfinished since 1856, and the writing of the 1887 Dawes General Allotment Act (Dawes Act). An attempt to end the complex of problems surrounding the status of Indian tribes and lands, the act voided the concept of the various tribes' being "domestic nations" and provided for the division of tribal lands into individual holdings, with a view to encouraging the dissolution of the Indians' communal relations and to establishing agriculture along traditional European-American freehold lines. Individual land patents carried with them citizenship and the protections and liabilities of regular civil and criminal law, although outright land ownership was held back for a period of 25 years to guard against sale of the holdings to speculators by Indians unfamiliar with money

values and with the notion of individual ownership of land. Conceived as a great step forward in the cause of "civilizing" the Indian and absorbing him into the mainstream of American life, the Dawes Act was ultimately a failure, both in its attempt to impose an alien culture on the Indian and in the impossible tangle of legalities it generated; it was finally overturned by the Indian Reorganization Act of 1934. Dawes retired from the Senate in 1892. From 1893 to 1903 he headed a commission empowered to negotiate for the abandonment of tribal relations by the Five Civilized Tribes of the Indian Territory, who had been exempted from the act of 1887. He spent his last years in Pittsfield and died there on February 5, 1903.

Day, Benjamin Henry (1810–1889), printer, journalist, and publisher. Born on April 10, 1810, in West Springfield, Massachusetts, Day became a printer's apprentice on the *Springfield Republican* in 1824. He opened his own printing business in 1831, which was closed soon after by a financial panic. In 1833 he began issuing the *New York Sun* in New York City. A four-page, three-column daily, it sold for a penny and catered to the workingman, while most of the papers in the city featured, at six cents, European news and political and financial coverage. The *Sun* covered the proceedings in police court and provided neighborhood news, and reprinted advertisements from other newspapers to make a show of prosperity. It also introduced the institution of newsboys as salesmen. Within three months, through shrewd psychology and his innovative policy of street vending, Day was selling 4000 copies daily; in two years the *Sun's* circulation exceeded that of any paper in the world. The famous "Moon-Hoax," written in 1835 by the *Sun's* chief reporter, was a major factor in boosting circulation. The story told in detail of orange orangutan-like creatures hopping about on the moon, supposedly seen by a British astronomer who was unlikely ever to read the *Sun*. Day took a chance in printing the story, but as it turned out the public was delighted at having been fooled in such an amusing way. In 1838 he sold the paper to Moses Yale Beach, his brother-in-law. He later regretted the move and founded another penny paper, the *True Sun*, in 1840, and in 1842, *Brother Jonathan*, a magazine that reprinted old British novels. In 1862 he retired from business and died in New York City on December 21, 1889.

Day, Clarence Shepard, Jr. (1874–1935), author. Born in New York City on November 18, 1874, the son of a successful Wall Street stockbroker and the grandson of publisher Benjamin H. Day, Clarence graduated from Yale in 1896. Shortly thereafter he became a partner in his father's firm, Clarence S. Day and Company. In 1898 he enlisted in the navy but saw little action in the Spanish-American War and was mustered out in September. Returning to business, he gradually succumbed to a crippling form of arthritis and retired in 1903. He remained in New York City and began contributing prose and drawings to magazines. A collection of this published material, with additions, was published as *This Simian World*, 1920, whch had a measure of success. Its witty, pleasant style set the tone of his later works, most notably the autobiographical *God and My Father*, 1932; *Life with Father*, 1935; *Life with Mother*, 1937; and *Father and I*, 1940, the latter two published after his death. *Life With Father*, as dramatized in 1939 by Howard Lindsay and Russel Crouse, had the longest continuous run of any American play, playing for a decade in New York City and on tour. Day's drawings were humorously distinct caricatures; many of them were compiled in *Thoughts Without Words*, 1928, and *Scenes from the Mesozoic, and Other Drawings*, 1935. He died in New York City on December 28, 1935.

Day, Dorothy (1897–1980), journalist and reformer. Born in New York City on November 8, 1897, Miss Day grew up there, in California, and in Chicago. In 1914, aided by a scholarship, she entered the University of Illinois where she remained for two years. While a student she read widely among socialist authors and soon joined the Socialist party. In 1916 she returned to New York City and joined the staff of the *Call*, a socialist newspaper; she also became a member of the Industrial Workers of the World (IWW). In 1917 she moved from the *Call* to the *Masses*, where she remained until the magazine was suppressed a few months later by the government. After a brief period on the successor journal, the *Liberator*, she spent more than a year in 1918–1919 working as a nurse in Brooklyn. For several years thereafter she continued in journalism in Chicago and New Orleans. In 1927, following years of doubt and indecision, she joined the Roman Catholic church, an act that for some time estranged her from her earlier radical associates. Then in 1932 she met Peter Maurin, a French-born Catholic who had developed a program of social reconstruction—which he called "the green revolution"—based on communal farming and the establishment of houses of hospitality for the urban poor. The program aimed to unite workers and intellectuals in joint activities ranging from farming to educational discussions. In 1933 Miss Day and Maurin founded the *Catholic Worker*, a monthly newspaper, to carry the idea to a wider audience. Within three years the paper's circulation had grown to 150,000, and the original St. Joseph's House of Hospitality in New York City had served as the pattern for houses in a number of cities. The *Catholic Worker* took boldly radical positions on many issues and during World War II was an organ for pacifism and for the support of Catholic conscientious objectors. In later years both Miss Day and the newspaper agitated against nuclear weaponry and preparations for nuclear war; for several years she was jailed repeatedly for refusing to comply with New York City's compulsory civil-

defense drills. The number of settlement houses directly connected with the *Catholic Worker* dwindled in later years, but there remained a significant number taking their inspiration from it. Miss Day lived in the New York house in voluntary poverty; in addition to the establishment in the city, the organization maintained a farm on Staten Island. In 1952 she published an autobiography, *The Long Loneliness*. She died on November 29, 1980, in New York City.

Day, William Rufus (1849–1923), diplomat and justice of the Supreme Court. Born on April 17, 1849, in Ravenna, Ohio, Day graduated from the University of Michigan in 1870 and after two years of studying law, one year privately and one at the university, was admitted to the bar. He began practice in Canton, Ohio, where he became associated with the county prosecuting attorney, William McKinley. The respect he earned in his practice led to his nomination by both major political parties for judge of the court of common pleas in 1886. After three years on that bench he was appointed U.S. district judge by President Benjamin Harrison, but was forced by illness to resign before assuming the post. In 1896 he declined an appointment as attorney general offered to him by McKinley, then president, but in 1897 he was persuaded to become assistant secretary of state. The following year he succeeded the ailing John Sherman as secretary of state. He held the office for a few months only, turning it over to John Hay in September 1898 in order to serve on the commission charged with negotiating the peace treaty ending the Spanish-American War. He was largely responsible for including in the treaty a provision for paying $20 million in compensation to Spain for the U.S. annexation of the Philippines. In 1899 Day was appointed judge of the U.S. circuit court of appeals, joining William Howard Taft, and four years later was named by President Theodore Roosevelt to the Supreme Court. As an effective, learned, and somewhat conservative justice, Day was an active member of the court for nearly 20 years and rendered decisions in a number of areas of the law, chiefly those dealing with commerce, contracts, and finance; his most notable decision was in *Hammer* v. *Dagenhart*, 1918, striking down the Keating-Owen Act of 1916 on the ground that its prohibition of interstate shipment of the products of child labor was not an exercise of the power to regulate commerce but an intrusion into manufacturing regulations, an area of state jurisdiction. Day also spoke for the court in *Dorr* v. *U.S.*, 1903, one of the Insular Cases; *U.S.* v. *Doremus*, 1918; and *Green* v. *Frazier*, 1919; and he concurred in Justice John Marshall Harlan's dissent in *Lochner* v. *New York*, 1905. He resigned in 1922 to serve on a commission adjudicating U.S. claims against Germany. Failing health forced him to resign that office as well in May 1923; he died on July 9, 1923, while vacationing on Mackinac Island, Michigan.

Dayton, Jonathan (1760–1824), Revolutionary soldier and public official. Born on October 16, 1760, in Elizabeth, New Jersey, Dayton graduated from the College of New Jersey (now Princeton) in 1776 and immediately enlisted in the New Jersey militia regiment commanded by his father. Rising eventually to captain, he saw action at most of the major battles of the New Jersey and New York campaigns, was at Yorktown in 1781, and was mustered out in 1783. He then took up the study of law and was admitted to the bar. In 1786 he was elected to the New Jersey assembly and the next year became the youngest delegate to the Constitutional Convention; although he opposed some of its features, he signed the final document. He was elected to but declined to serve in the first U.S. Congress in 1788, but sat in the New Jersey council in 1789 and in the state assembly in 1790. Elected again to the House of Representatives in 1790, he held his seat until 1799 and during his last two terms was speaker of the House. In general a supporter of the administration, he approved the actions of Secretary of the Treasury Alexander Hamilton and of the government during the Whisky Rebellion and as speaker helped reconcile the House to Jay's Treaty. In 1799 he was elevated to the Senate, where he favored the Louisiana Purchase and opposed the Twelfth Amendment and the impeachment of Supreme Court Justice Samuel Chase. After leaving the Senate in 1805 Dayton devoted much of his energy to developing his large holdings in the Ohio country (the Northwest Territory), where the city of Dayton, incorporated in 1805, was named for him. He had some association with Aaron Burr's mysterious conspiracy to establish a new nation in the West and in 1807 was charged with treason, but he was never tried. He lived for the rest of his life in Elizabeth and was once more sent to the legislature in 1814–1815. Dayton died on October 9, 1824, in Elizabeth.

Dean, Dizzy (1911–1974), baseball player. Born in Lucas, Arkansas, on January 16, 1911, Dean (christened Jay Hanna probably, although he sometimes claimed Jerome Herman along with a variety of birth dates and places) grew up in a farm family that lived by sharecropping and migrant work. He received little formal schooling. He loved baseball and, according to one story, for a time played for a high-school team although he was not a student. From 1927 to 1930 Dizzy was in the army and afterwards pitched semipro ball in San Antonio, Texas. There he was spotted by a scout for the St. Louis Cardinals and signed to a farm club in St. Joseph, Missouri. Later sent to the Houston farm club, he was brought up to the Cardinals in September 1930 to pitch a game. Although he won the game he was returned to Houston the next year, supposedly in hopes of deflating some of his brashness; the plan apparently failed, for it was in Houston that he acquired the nickname "Dizzy." In 1932, in his first full season with the Cardinals, he won 18 games and lost 15 and led the National League in strikeouts, shutouts, and innings pitched; his blazing fastball helped him to lead the league in strikeouts for the next three years as well. In 1933 he induced the Cardinals to sign his brother Paul, born in Lucas on August 14, 1913, who, he claimed, was even faster. The two were the inspiration of the team in 1934, Dizzy being named the league's most valuable player that year, a rare honor for a pitcher. After a brief strike for higher pay for Paul they double-handedly put the Cardinals into the 1934 World Series, winning 49 games between them, Dizzy's 30 making it his best season. Twelve of the last 18 Cardinal games that year were won by one or the other of the Dean brothers. Asked how they could hope to defeat the powerful Detroit Tigers in the Series, Dizzy replied: "Me an' Paul'll win two games apiece." They won the first two games, the Tigers took the next three, and then Dizzy and Paul came back to win games six and seven, triumphantly fulfilling the prophecy. Dizzy was the loudest and most devil-may-care of the notably carefree "Gashouse Gang" of the Cardinals; Paul, on whom sportswriters tried in vain to pin the nickname "Daffy," was in fact quiet, retiring, and devoted to his older brother. In 1935 Dizzy won 28 games and lost 12, and Paul's record was 19–12; in 1936 their records were 24–13 and 5–5 respectively, and in 1935 Dizzy struck out a then-record 17 batters in a game against the Chicago Cubs. Dizzy pitched for the National League in the All-Star games from 1934 to 1937, but in the 1937 game he sustained a foot injury that forced him to change his delivery; the resulting arm strain effectively ended his fabulous career. After a final 13–10 season with the Cardinals he was traded to the Cubs, for whom he won a handful of games in 1938 and 1939. He retired in May 1941 with a career total of 150 wins, 83 losses. Paul remained with the Cardinals but had diminishing success; he was traded to the New York Giants in 1940 and in 1943 to the St. Louis Browns; he retired after that season with a career record of 50–34. In 1941 Dizzy had begun a new career as a radio announcer for the home games of the Cardinals and Browns, and he quickly attracted national attention with his unique brand of broadcasting. High spirited and unabashedly partisan on the air, he was an artist in the colorful use of language: "He slud into third," and "I shoulda stood in bed" were among his enduring creations. He was named to the National Baseball Hall of Fame in 1953. After a few more seasons in broadcasting, from 1950 for New York Yankee games, he retired to Dallas, Texas, where he had extensive investments in real estate. He died in Reno, Nevada, on July 17, 1974.

Dean, Man Mountain (1891–1953), wrestler. Born in New York City on June 30, 1891, Frank Simmons Leavitt was unusually large from childhood and at fourteen easily lied his way into the army. He took active interest in sports, particularly football and wrestling, and about 1914 began wrestling professionally as Soldier Leavitt. After border-patrol duty under Gen. John J. Pershing and combat service in France during World War I he continued his sports career, in 1919–1920 playing for the New York Giants football team. Wrestling remained his main interest, however, although he enjoyed only modest financial success. While recuperating from an injury he worked as a traffic policeman in Miami, Florida, and there in 1926 he met and married Doris Dean, who became also his manager. Through her efforts she secured a contract for an exhibition wrestling tour in Germany and at her suggestion changed his name from Leavitt to the more Aryan-sounding Dean; the sobriquet "Stone Mountain," which he had been using for some time, was improved to "Man Mountain." The German tour was a great success, and in England shortly thereafter he was hired as a double for actor Charles Laughton in the filming of *Henry the Eighth*. On his return to the United States Dean continued to work in motion pictures, with eventually more than 30 to his credit, and became in Hollywood a celebrity's celebrity, his wrestling appearances commanding fees as high as $1500. His sheer size—more than 300 pounds—was an attraction in itself, as was his magnificent full beard; his appearance made him one of the first of the showmen wrestlers. In all he appeared in 6783 wrestling matches and achieved worldwide fame before his retirement in 1937 to a farm near Norcross, Georgia. He made occasional public appearances thereafter, engaged briefly in local politics, and studied at the school of journalism of the University of Georgia in Atlanta. Dean died at his Norcross home on May 29, 1953.

Dean, Paul Dee, *see under* Dean, Dizzy

Deane, Silas (1737–1789), colonial figure and diplomat. Born in Groton, Connecticut, on December 24, 1737, Deane graduated from Yale in 1758 and after three years of teaching school and studying law was admitted to the bar. He began practice in Wethersfield, Connecticut, and soon became a prosperous merchant as well. As relations between the American colonies and Great Britain deteriorated, Deane placed himself squarely on the patriot side, leading the opposition to the Townshend Acts in his locality, sitting in the legislature in 1772, and serving as secretary to the Committee of Correspondence in 1773. From 1774 to 1776 he represented Connecticut in the Continental Congress, and early in 1776 was commissioned by that body to sail to France and there obtain supplies and investigate the possibilities that the French might recognize American independence and enter into treaties of commerce and alliance. The first representative of the united colonies to be sent abroad, Deane succeeded in securing the shipment of eight cargoes of arms in 1777, an accomplishment that was of major importance for the American victory at Saratoga that year. He also obtained the

services of a number of European army officers, including the Marquis de Lafayette, Johann Kalb, Kazimierz Pulaski, and Baron von Steuben, and of a great many mercenaries. In Paris he became associated with Edward Bancroft, of whose activities as a British spy he was the unwitting victim. He was joined by Arthur Lee and Benjamin Franklin in negotiating a French alliance and soon after the treaties were signed in February 1778 Deane returned to America to answer charges of disloyalty and embezzlement that had arisen after certain insinuations had been made by Lee. He failed to prove his case and in 1780 returned to France for documentary evidence of his earlier transactions. His inability to quiet the suspicions of Congress led to his renouncing the American cause. He wrote letters to a few old friends, bitterly denouncing the war and the French and advocating reconciliation with Great Britain; these he gave to British authorities, who, pretending to have intercepted them, published them in a Tory newspaper in New York City. He was thereafter an exile, first in Belgium and later in London, where he published *An Address to the Free and Independent Citizens of the United States*, 1784, in defense of his actions. In 1789 he decided to try to reestablish himself in the United States, but soon after boarding a Boston-bound ship in Deal harbor he died, under mysterious circumstances, on September 23, 1789. In 1842 Congress reopened the case; the 1778 audit of his accounts, which had been made under the supervision of Arthur Lee, was found to have been grossly at fault, and consequently a substantial sum was awarded to Deane's heirs as partial restitution.

Dearborn, Henry (1751–1829), soldier and public official. Born on February 23, 1751, in Hampton, New Hampshire, Dearborn took up the study of medicine, beginning practice in 1772 in Nottingham Square, New Hampshire. He organized and commanded a militia company in preparation for war with England and immediately upon hearing of the battle of Lexington marched his men to Cambridge, arriving in time to take part in the battle of Bunker Hill. He then volunteered to join Benedict Arnold's Quebec expedition; he was captured and for more than a year was on parole awaiting exchange. Returning to active service in March 1777, he was promoted to major and saw action at Ticonderoga and Saratoga. After wintering at Valley Forge he distinguished himself at the battle of Monmouth in 1778. In 1779 he accompanied Gen. John Sullivan's expedition against Butler's Rangers and the Indian allies of the British in Pennsylvania and western New York, and in 1781 was on Gen. George Washington's staff at Yorktown. Upon being discharged from the army in 1783 he settled in Kennebec County, Maine (then still a district of Massachusetts), becoming major general of militia and in 1790 being appointed U.S. marshal for the district. Dearborn was elected to the House of Representatives in 1792 and served until 1797.

In 1801 President Thomas Jefferson appointed him secretary of war, in which post he ordered the establishment of a fortification at "Chikago" in 1803; this began the lasting association of his name with the city that was later built around the site of Fort Dearborn. He left the cabinet in 1809 and was collector of the port of Boston until 1812, when President James Madison named him senior major general of the army in command of the northern border in the War of 1812. Marked by delay, miscalculation, and general ineptitude, his campaign of invasion of Canada achieved its closest approach to success in the futile and temporary capture of York (now Toronto) in April 1813. Dearborn's shuffling of troops exposed several important American posts to peril and he won no major gains at all. In July 1813 he was relieved of command in the field. Before retiring in 1815 he presided over the court-martial of Gen. William Hull, whose loss of Detroit to the British had been to a significant degree the result of Dearborn's failure to prepare adequate defenses. He was proposed as secretary of war by Madison in 1815 but a hail of criticism forced the withdrawal of his name. In 1822 President James Monroe appointed him minister to Portugal. After two years in that post Dearborn retired to Roxbury, Massachusetts (now part of Boston), where he died on June 6, 1829.

Death Valley Scotty, see Scott, Walter Edward

De Bow, James Dunwoody Brownson (1820–1867), editor and statistician. Born in Charleston, South Carolina, on July 10, 1820, De Bow was orphaned at an early age and, maintained himself on the edge of subsistence, worked his way through the College of Charleston. After graduating in 1943 he spent a year in the study of law and was admitted to the bar. He quickly left that vocation, however, and began contributing essays on various topics to the *Southern Quarterly Review*. His articles attracted considerable attention and one, on the Oregon question and the relative claims of France, Great Britain, and the United States to the territory, was debated in the French parliament. Convinced of the potential usefulness of a journal devoted to the promotion of economic and social development in the South, De Bow moved to New Orleans, commercial capital of the region, in 1845 and in January 1846 published the first issue of the *Commercial Review of the South and Southwest*. Early financial difficulties, which forced a brief suspension of publication in 1847, were gradually overcome and the journal slowly grew in reputation and circulation until it was acknowledged as the most influential commercial and social periodical in the South, becoming generally known as *De Bow's Review*. In his own contributions De Bow advocated internal improvements for the South, protective tariffs, and, at first, sectional cooperation, although he later moved to a secessionist position. In 1850 he was named to direct the Louisiana Bureau of Statistics and in

1853 was appointed superintendent of the U.S. census by President Franklin Pierce. He oversaw preparation of the reports of the 1850 census and published his own compendium, *Statistical View of the United States*, in 1854. He also lectured widely and contributed articles to the *Encyclopaedia Britannica*. During the Civil War De Bow was the chief government agent for the cotton trade in the Confederacy. Afterward he revived the suspended *Review* and sought to heal the wounds of war. He died on February 27, 1867, in Elizabeth, New Jersey. The *Review* continued to be published until 1880.

Debs, Eugene Victor (1855–1926), labor organizer and political leader. Born in Terre Haute, Indiana, on November 5, 1855, of French immigrant parents, Debs left school at fifteen to work in the shops of the Terre Haute and Indianapolis Railway. He later worked as a locomotive fireman. In 1875 he became secretary of the newly founded lodge of the Brotherhood of Locomotive Firemen in Terre Haute. In 1879 he was elected city clerk, and the following year became national secretary of the union and editor of its magazine. He was elected to the Indiana legislature in 1885. In 1893 he helped found the American Railway Union (ARU) and as its president led the successful strike against the Great Northern Railway the next year. In response to a request from the strikers at the Pullman plant in Illinois later the same year, Debs and the ARU agreed to boycott Pullman cars by refusing to service them. Debs and the other officers were forbidden to obstruct the mails in a federal injunction, and Debs was cited for contempt when he failed to obey the injunction. In the midst of the controversy between President Grover Cleveland and Governor John P. Altgeld over the handling of the strike situation, Debs became a nationally known figure, particularly when he was sentenced to six months in jail on the contempt charge; during his imprisonment, wide reading led him to adopt Socialism as his cause. He supported the Populist movement in 1896 and the following year began to organize, with Victor L. Berger, the Social Democratic party, a forerunner of the Socialist party. Debs was the Socialist presidential candidate four successive times between 1900 and 1912, polling nearly a million votes in 1912. In 1905 he helped to found the Industrial Workers of the World (IWW), although he later disavowed the organization because of its tendency to use violence. He supported himself during those years with article writing, editorial positions, and lecture tours. In 1918 he publicly denounced the wave of sedition prosecutions that was taking place under the 1917 Espionage Act; for this he was himself charged with sedition and, after a widely publicized trial, sentenced to ten years imprisonment. In 1920, while in jail, he was again the Socialist candidate for president and received a larger vote than ever before. As public protest against his harsh treatment mounted, he was released on President Warren

G. Harding's order in 1921. He continued to work for the Socialist cause until his death on October 20, 1926, in Elmhurst, Illinois.

Decatur, Stephen (1779–1820), naval officer. Born on January 5, 1779, in Sinepuxent, Maryland, Decatur grew up in Philadelphia and, after a year of study at the University of Pennsylvania, entered a shipping firm in that city. In April 1798 he was commissioned a midshipman in the navy. He rose quickly and was a lieutenant when, in 1803, he was sent to join the U.S. naval forces in the Mediterranean. In February 1804, during the Tripolitan War, he led a daring raid into the harbor of Tripoli to burn an American frigate, the *Philadelphia*, that had been captured after running aground. He escaped with but one of his crew injured and was promoted to captain. Through 1804 and 1805 he took part in hostilities off Tripoli; in 1805 he negotiated personally with the Bey of Tunis and returned to the United States with a Tunisian ambassador. For several years he held various commands in home waters. Soon after the outbreak of the War of 1812 Decatur sailed in command of the *United States*; in October 1812 he captured the British frigate *Macedonian* in one of the war's great naval victories. The following year he was appointed commodore of a squadron defending New York harbor. In January 1815 he ran the British blockade of the harbor in the *President*; pursued, he disabled the British warship *Endymion* before being forced to surrender to overwhelming numbers. Later in the year he sailed for the Mediterranean in command of a nine-ship squadron sent to deal with new outbreaks by the Barbary pirates (the "Algerine War"). He successfully ended corsair raids from Algiers, Tunis, and Tripoli, ended U.S. payment of tribute to the Barbary states, and secured reparations for damages to U.S. shipping. At a dinner given in his honor shortly after his triumphal return to the United States, he proposed his famous toast: "Our country! In her intercourse with foreign nations may she always be in the right; but our country, right or wrong." From November 1815 until he died he served on the Board of Navy Commissioners. In 1820 he was accused by Capt. James Barron of leading a conspiracy to block Barron's promotion; Barron challenged Decatur to a duel in which, on March 22, 1820, near Bladensburg, Maryland, Decatur was killed.

Decker, Frank, see Duveneck, Frank

Deere, John (1804–1886), blacksmith, inventor, and manufacturer. Born in Rutland, Vermont, on February 7, 1804, Deere was apprenticed to a blacksmith at seventeen. Four years later he established himself in the trade and worked in various towns in Vermont until 1837, when he moved to Grand Detour, Illinois. There he built up a large business as a smith and found, through the frequent repairs he was asked to make, that the wood and iron plows brought by farmers from the East were unsuited to the heavy, fibrous soil of the Plains. He began experimenting with different forms and materials and developed a plow with an iron landside and moldboard and a steel share that he had cut from an old mill-saw disk and bent over a wooden form. This early steel plow—the "Grand Detour plow"—proved highly successful and, in partnership with Leonard Andrus, Deere began a manufacturing business, production increasing rapidly from 10 plows in 1839 to 1000 in 1846. In 1846 he sold out to Andrus and moved to Moline, Illinois, where shipping facilities were better, and opened a new plant. A special arrangement with a mill in Pittsburgh resulted in the first production of plow steel in America in 1847, and by 1857 Deere's factory was turning out some 10,000 plows a year. The business was incorporated in 1868 as Deere & Company; Deere remained its president for the rest of his life. Gradually the company began manufacturing cultivators and other agricultural implements, becoming one of the leading firms in the field. Deere died in Moline on May 17, 1886.

De Forest, Lee (1873–1961), electrical engineer and inventor. Born on August 26, 1873, in Council Bluffs, Iowa, De Forest grew up there and in Talladega, Alabama, where his father was president of the College for the Colored. He graduated from Yale's Sheffield Scientific School in 1896, took his Ph.D. at Yale in 1899, and went to Chicago to work for the Western Electric Company while carrying on research in his spare time. The first of more than 300 patents was granted him for an electrolytic detector that made possible the use of headphones with wireless receivers. In 1906 he invented the three-element or triode electron tube, which he called an audion. The device was quickly recognized as perhaps the single most important development in the field of electronics up to that time; its vast potential as a generator, detector, and amplifier of radio signals was the basis of the rapid growth of the electronics and communications industries. De Forest patented the audion in 1907. In the next few years he was involved in several patent litigations, most notably in a four-way suit involving also Edwin H. Armstrong, Irving Langmuir, and Alexander Meissner of Germany over the right to patent the feedback or regenerative circuit. He made a number of radio broadcasts, including in 1910 the first of live music, featuring Enrico Caruso at the Metropolitan Opera, and in 1916 the first radio news report, but little public note was taken of them. He founded the De Forest Wireless Telegraph Company, the Radio Telephone Company, and the De Forest Radio Company at various times but had little lasting success in those enterprises. By the end of World War I he had sold the rights to the audion and turned to other things. In 1919 he developed a sound system for motion pictures and four years later founded the De Forest Phonofilm Company to produce it. In later years he made important contributions to the electric phonograph, long-distance telephony, facsimile transmission, television, radar, and diathermy. He was an advocate of the educational use of radio and television and decried the commercialization of those media. Essentially a solitary inventor who preferred independent research to business, De Forest made and lost four fortunes in his life. His autobiography, *Father of Radio*, was published in 1950. He died in Hollywood, California, on June 30, 1961.

De Kalb, Baron, *see* Kalb, Johann

De Kooning, Willem (1904–   ), painter. Born on April 24, 1904, in Rotterdam, the Netherlands, De Kooning left school at the age of twelve to be apprenticed to a commercial artist. He arrived in the United States in 1926 as a stowaway on a cattle boat. Supporting himself as a commercial artist and occasionally executing such commissions as that for a series of murals for the 1934 New York World's Fair, he did not exhibit his own work until 1948. Tremendously influenced by the Surrealists, by German Expressionists, and by Arshile Gorky, a leader in the American movement in abstract art, he became a dominant figure in the Abstract Expressionist school after World War II. His work was a furious blend of brushwork and color. The most famous of his paintings, a series on the theme of "Woman," were first shown in New York City in 1953. From the pattern of lines and color in each work emerged the portrait of a woman so grossly distorted as to become almost comical. He claimed to find no peace in art and transmitted none to the canvas. His paintings appeared to be reactions to objects or people rather than representations of them. But in using a kind of representation and design in his art he was said to be unique among Abstract Expressionist painters. De Kooning was elected to the National Institute of Arts and Letters in 1960 and in 1964 was awarded the Presidential Medal of Freedom.

Delamater, Cornelius Henry (1821–1889), engineer, foundryman, and shipbuilder. Born on August 30, 1821, in Rhinebeck, New York, Delamater grew up and was educated in New York City. He went to work at fourteen, first in a hardware store and two years later in the Phoenix Foundry, where his progress was so rapid that by the time he was eighteen he had, in partnership with Peter Hogg, bought out the business. The reputation of the foundry was such that when John Ericsson came to New York to build a propeller-driven ship powered by steam he chose the Phoenix works to construct it. Delamater and Ericsson worked closely together for 20 years in the building of steam power systems for merchant and naval ships, of the ships themselves, and of steam fire engines. The firm also cast the great 36-inch pipes for the Croton Aqueduct, completed in 1842. In 1850 a larger plant was built, and six years later Hogg retired and the firm became the Delamater Iron Works. In 1861

work was begun at the foundry on the engines for Ericsson's ironclad *Monitor*, built for the navy; when it was completed and launched in March 1862 and shortly thereafter engaged the Confederate *Merrimack* the engine-room crew was composed of Delamater employees. After the Civil War the firm continued to construct merchant vessels and warships for the United States and other nations and solidified its position as the leading builder of equipment for the new age of steel and power on the sea. In 1881 John P. Holland chose the Delamater works to build his *Fenian Ram*, the first successful modern submarine. Delamater, widely admired both personally and professionally, continued to direct the operations of the works until his death in New York City on February 7, 1889.

De Lancey, James (1703–1760), colonial official and judge. Born in New York City on November 27, 1703, to a wealthy and aristocratic family, De Lancey was educated in England at Cambridge and the Inner Temple and upon his return to New York City in 1725 was admitted to the bar. Four years later he was appointed to the provincial council, in 1731 was named a judge of the provincial supreme court, and in 1733 was elevated to the position of chief justice of that court. The last promotion came from the hand of Governor William Cosby, who had summarily dismissed the incumbent Lewis Morris; the act was widely unpopular and Morris, James Alexander, and William Smith established an antiadministration newspaper, the *New-York Weekly Journal*, with John Peter Zenger as editor. In 1734 Zenger was arrested on a charge of libel against the governor; at a first hearing the next year he was represented by Alexander and Smith, who challenged the appointment of De Lancey and were promptly disbarred by him. Despite his best efforts, De Lancey failed to secure from the jury the conviction of Zenger, winning only the hearty dislike of much of the populace. In 1744 he was given tenure in office conditioned on good behavior, and with that security began exerting political influence in the council and the assembly. He was already in virtual control of the government when in 1753 he received a commission as lieutenant governor; upon the suicide of the new governor a short time later he became acting governor of New York. He retained his seat on the bench all the while and was the dominant figure in the colony, even during the presence of a regular governor in 1755–1757. The aristocratic and largely Episcopalian faction that he headed became known as the "De Lancey party" in opposition to the more broadly based and Presbyterian "Livingston party," then headed by William Livingston. De Lancey was again acting governor from 1757 until his death in New York City on July 30, 1760.

Delany, Martin Robinson (1812–1885), physician, social reformer, soldier, and journalist. Born on May 6, 1812, in Charles Town, Virginia (now in

West Virginia), the grandson of slaves and the son of free Negroes, Delany attended school in Pittsburgh and New York City. In 1843 he began issuing one of the first Negro weeklies, the *Mystery*, a nationalist paper, which he continued in Pittsburgh for four years. Frederick Douglass joined him briefly in partnership in 1846; Delany then gave up the *Mystery* and from 1847 to 1849 coedited Douglass's *North Star*. In 1849 he entered the medical department of Harvard, having been refused admission to three other medical schools because of his race, and graduated in 1852. He set up practice in Pittsburgh as a surgeon and specialist in women's and children's diseases. In 1852 he wrote *The Condition, Elevation, Emigration and Destiny of the Colored People of the United States*, the first classic statement of American black nationalism. When the book was censured by white and black abolitionists, however, for supporting separatists who saw in colonization a way to avoid racial equality, he attempted to withdraw it from sale. In 1854 he spoke at the first National Emigration Convention, which he had helped to form, proposing resettlement of Negroes in the Caribbean, South or Central America, or eastern Africa. In 1858 the third session of the society commissioned him to head an expedition to Africa's Niger valley. He remained in Africa during 1859, conducting scientific research and signing a treaty with certain chiefs with a view toward imminent colonization. From Africa he went on to a meeting of the International Statistical Congress in London and received wide publicity when his brief comments caused a walkout of almost the entire U.S. delegation. He remained in London, delivered a paper before the Royal Geographical Society, and remained in Europe for nearly seven months lecturing on Africa. In 1861 he returned to Canada, which had been the site of the third Emigration Convention meeting, to an organized community of fugitive slaves and black expatriates. During the first weeks of the Civil War he lectured in the United States and then, his attitude changing with the course of events, he secured permission to recruit free Negroes for an all-black unit of the Union army. Early in 1865 he conferred with President Abraham Lincoln, and shortly thereafter was commissioned major with the 104th Colored troops. He worked for three years after the war with the Freedmen's Bureau to gain voting rights for Negroes. He was a customs inspector in Charleston, South Carolina, and in 1874 ran for lieutenant governor of the state on a Radical Independent Republican ticket, conducting an able campaign and losing by only a narrow margin. In 1876 he switched his support from the radical black Reconstructionist candidate to the moderate white Democratic party nominee for governor, and after the election secured a position as trial justice (justice of the peace). In that post he supported an ill-fated movement for the emigration of 206 blacks from Charleston to Liberia. He published in 1879 *Principia of Ethnology: The Origins of Race and Color*, advocating racial "purity." He briefly resumed his medical practice, moved to Boston, and in January 1885 died in Xenia, Ohio.

Delaware, Lord, *see* De La Warr, Thomas West, *Baron*

De La Warr, Thomas West, *Baron* **(1577–1618),** colonial official. Born on July 9, 1577, in Hampshire, England, the future Lord De La Warr (or Delaware) attended Oxford for a time and in 1597 was elected to Parliament. He later served in wars in the Netherlands and in Ireland under the Earl of Essex. He was knighted during his Irish service and was implicated in Essex's shortlived rebellion of 1601. He was imprisoned only briefly and on the death of his father the next year became twelfth Baron De La Warr and was appointed to the Privy Council. Early involved in the activities of the Virginia Company, in 1609 he was a grantee and member of the council of the company. The following year he was appointed governor and captain general of the company's colony in Virginia and in March of that year sailed for America with three ships laden with settlers and supplies. Arriving at Jamestown in June, he discovered the original colonists and the members of a large expedition sent out the previous year already embarked and on the point of giving up Jamestown completely. De La Warr immediately ordered the colonists back to the settlement, sent lieutenants to Bermuda and England for aid, had fortifications built, and imposed a stern discipline on the colony. In 1611, with Jamestown secure, he returned to England and published his *Relation of the Right Honourable the Lord De-la-Warre, Lord Governour and Captaine Generall of the Colonie, planted in Virginea.* He remained in England working for the interests of the Virginia Company. In 1618 he set out for Virginia again to investigate complaints of tyrannical administration by his deputy, Samuel Argall; while en route he died on June 7, 1618, and was buried at sea. Delaware Bay and the state of Delaware were later named for him.

Delbrück, Max (1906–1981), biologist. Born in Berlin on September 4, 1906, Delbrück took his Ph.D. in physics from the University of Göttingen in 1930, worked for a time as a postdoctoral fellow in the laboratory of Niels Bohr in Copenhagen, and from 1932 to 1937 was an assistant in the Kaiser Wilhelm Institute in Berlin. By 1937, the year in which he emigrated to the United States, he had become fascinated by the possibility of a new approach to biology, particularly in the field of genetics, on the molecular level. For two years he was at the California Institute of Technology studying the mechanism of reproduction in the bacteria-disintegrating viruses known as bacteriophages, or simply "phages." In 1940 he became an instructor in physics at Vanderbilt University, in Nashville, Tennessee, but he continued his work in biology, meeting in that year Salvador E. Luria, with whom he collaborated on studies leading to their confirmation of natural selection in the development of phage-resistant bacterial strains. During that time they became associated also with Alfred D. Hershey and the three worked in close correspondence for the next several years, laying the procedural groundwork for modern molecular genetics. Delbrück became a U.S. citizen in 1945. A year later he and Hershey discovered independently that phage genetic material inside bacteria could undergo random recombination, producing new phage strains. The next year Delbrück, who had advanced to associate professor at Vanderbilt, moved back to the California Institute of Technology, where he remained professor of biology until 1977. The combined efforts of Delbrück, Luria, and Hershey, in which individual contributions were difficult to distinguish, provided a great impetus for the growth of genetic studies and were the inspiration for, among others, James D. Watson, once a student of Luria's, who with Francis Crick later discovered the structure of DNA (deoxyribonucleic acid). During the middle 1950s Delbrück began turning his attention to other problems, especially the physiology of sensory perception. In 1969 the three were jointly awarded the Nobel Prize for Physiology or Medicine for their work in molecular genetics. He died on March 9, 1981, in Pasadena, California.

De Leon, Daniel (1852–1914), political leader. Born on the Caribbean island of Curaçao on December 14, 1852, De Leon studied in Europe before coming to the United States about 1874. While teaching school in New York he sought further education at Columbia University; in 1878 he received his law degree and went to practice for a time in Texas. He soon returned to New York City and in 1883 began teaching Latin-American diplomacy at Columbia, where he remained until 1886. His developing interest in social and political issues led him to support the programs of both Henry George and Edward Bellamy; in 1888 he joined the Knights of Labor and two years later the Socialist Labor party (SLP). He became the party's national lecturer and in 1892 editor of its newspaper, *The People*, and was several times a candidate for public office under its banner. A strictly doctrinaire Marxist, he left the fumbling Knights of Labor in 1895 to found the Socialist Trade and Labor Alliance as a wing of the SLP. A moderate prounion faction within the SLP withdrew four years later to join the Social Democratic party to form the Socialist party. In 1905 De Leon helped organize the Industrial Workers of the World (IWW), with which the STLA was merged. Three years later he was ousted from the IWW when it came under the leadership of antipolitical advocates of direct-action tactics. He formed a smaller organization of his followers shortly thereafter that became known as the Workers' International Industrial Union. He advocated socialism until his death on May 11, 1914, in New York City.

Dell, Floyd (1887–1969), author, editor, and playwright. Born on June 28, 1887, in Barry, Illinois, Dell grew up there and in Davenport, Iowa. On leaving school at seventeen he worked as a reporter in Davenport and later in Chicago, where, as literary editor of the *Evening Post* from 1911 to 1913, he was associated with Carl Sandburg, Ben Hecht, and others of the Chicago literary scene. In 1913 he moved to New York City and soon became a leading figure among the social and literary radicals of Greenwich Village. From 1914 to 1917 he was an editor of the *Masses* and was one of the defendants when the magazine was suspended by the government under the Espionage Act of 1917. He then joined in founding the successor journal, the *Liberator*, of which he was an editor from 1918 to 1924; he was associated as well with the *New Masses* from 1926 to 1929. Early in his Greenwich Village days he had worked with the Provincetown Players and had written a few plays, including *The Angel Intrudes*, 1918. He later turned to the novel, producing *Moon-Calf*, 1920, and its sequel *The Briary-Bush*, 1921, both semiautographical tales in the postwar mode of disillusionment and consciously startling realism. Subsequent novels of Jazz Age youth included *Janet March*, 1923; *Runaway*, 1925; and *This Mad Ideal*, 1925. He turned to more sociological themes in his later novels—*An Unmarried Father*, 1927; *Love Without Money*, 1931; *The Golden Spike*, 1934, and others—and in his nonfiction works, which included *Intellectual Vagabondage—An Apology for the Intelligentsia*, 1926; *The Outline of Marriage*, 1927; and *Love in the Machine Age*, 1930. Among his other plays were *Little Accident*, 1928, a dramatization of *Unmarried Father*, and *Cloudy with Showers*, 1931, both written with actor Thomas Mitchell. In 1929 Dell was more or less officially read out of the radical movement for a list of such offenses as publicly wearing a tuxedo. During the 1930s he moved to Washington, D.C., and worked as an adviser and speech writer for the Works Projects and Public Works administrations. His autobiography, *Homecoming*, appeared in 1933. Having long since disappeared from the public eye, with his once influential writings eclipsed by later developments in realism, Dell died in Bethesda, Maryland, on July 23, 1969.

Dello Joio, Norman (1913–   ), composer. Born on January 24, 1913, in New York City, Dello Joio early began the study of organ and piano with his father, a church organist. He received formal training in theory and composition at the Institute of Musical Art in New York City and from 1939 to 1941 in the graduate division of the Juilliard School of Music. He studied also with Paul Hindemith, with whose aid he was able to blend the liturgical, operatic, and jazz forms that were his principal inspirations into a lyrical neoclassical style of his own. From 1941 to 1943 he was musical director of a ballet company and he wrote during his career a number of ballet scores, including *Prairie*, 1942; *The Duke of Sacramento*, 1942; *On Stage!*, 1944; and *Time of Snow*, 1968. His first compositions to win wide attention were the baroque-influenced *Ricercari* for piano and orchestra, 1945, and *Variations, Chaconne and Finale*, 1948, an orchestral piece reminiscent, like his earlier *Magnificat* 1942, of Gregorian chants. Dello Joio's first opera, *The Triumph of St. Joan*, was premiered in 1950 but subsequently withdrawn from performance; from the score, however, he adapted a symphony, *Triumph of St. Joan*, which at its 1951 premier was coupled with a solo dance by Martha Graham. Other operas included *The Ruby*, 1955, in one act; *The Trial at Rouen*, 1956; and *Blood Moon*, inspired by the life of actress Adah Isaacs Menken, 1961. His orchestral *Meditations on Ecclesiastes* won a Pulitzer Prize for music in 1957; of his many scores for television productions, including "Ballad of the Seven Lively Arts," 1958, that for "The Louvre" in 1965 won an Emmy Award. Dello Joio wrote a great many pieces for chamber ensembles as well as for orchestra and various solo instruments, and also composed a number of choral works, including *Psalm of David*, 1950; *Song of the Open Road*, 1952; *Songs of Walt Whitman*, 1966; and *Days of the Modern*, 1968. From 1944 to 1950 he taught at Sarah Lawrence College and from 1956 at the Mannes College of Music. Widely honored both at home and abroad, Dello Joio was generally acknowledged as the most successful American exponent of the neoclassical manner in contemporary music.

Delmonico, Lorenzo (1813–1881), restaurateur. Born on March 13, 1813, in Marengo, Ticino Canton, Switzerland, Delmonico grew up on a farm and received little schooling. He emigrated to the United States at the age of nineteen and joined two uncles in their wine, confectionery, and catering business in New York City. At his suggestion the firm soon opened a restaurant on William Street and began offering New Yorkers a number of novelties—the restaurant was open through the day, it featured a large and diverse bill of fare, and it made extensive use of salads and vegetables. Using the abundant domestic foodstuffs, Delmonico introduced an array of European dishes never before seen in New York and developed a significant local cuisine as well. The restaurant, which moved to Broad Street after a fire in 1835, was an immediate success and was soon attracting the attention of foreign visitors, accomplished European chefs among them. From 1848 Delmonico was in sole command, his uncles having died, and branch restaurants were opened, including the world-famous establishment at Broadway and 26th Street in 1876. For a number of years the Delmonico organization operated a farm in Brooklyn, and from 1846 to 1856 a hotel was maintained on Broadway. Delmonico's was the forerunner and inspiration of the hundreds of restaurants that followed and helped make New York a culinary center second only to Paris; it was largely responsible also for the acceptance of the restaurant as an American institution. After nearly 50 years at the head of the first and largest business of its kind in the country, Delmonico died in Sharon Springs, New York, on September 3, 1881.

De Mille, Agnes George (1905–   ), choreographer. Born in New York City in 1905, the daughter of a noted American playwright, the niece of Cecil B. deMille, and the granddaughter of Henry George, Agnes de Mille studied ballet and choreography under several famous teachers. She made her dancing debut in 1928, but it was not until after years as a touring dancer and actress in the United States and England and on the Continent, during which she composed dance sequences for a 1936 English film version of *Romeo and Juliet*, that she got her first real chance when she was asked to join the new Ballet Theatre, for which, among other ballets, she choreographed the famous *Rodeo*, 1942. It was her dances for the Broadway musical *Oklahoma!* the next year that not only made her a leading U.S. theatrical artist, but also introduced dance to a wide American public that might never have known much about it without her. *Oklahoma!* was followed by a long series of Broadway shows, among them *Bloomer Girl*, 1944; *Carousel*, 1945; *Brigadoon*, 1947; *Gentlemen Prefer Blondes*, 1949; and *Paint Your Wagon*, 1951. All of these became spectacular movies as well; and for the film versions, too, she created innovative and memorable dance episodes. Perhaps her best-known ballet was *Fall River Legend*, 1948, based on the story of Lizzie Borden. She headed her own company, the Agnes de Mille Dance Theatre, which toured 126 cities in 1953–1954. The recipient of many prizes and awards, she was during the 1940s and 1950s the leading choreographer on Broadway and one of the foremost in the United States. She wrote several books, among them *Dance to the Piper*, 1952; *And Promenade Home*, 1958; *To a Young Dancer*, 1962; and *The Book of the Dance*, 1963.

DeMille, Cecil Blount (1881–1959), motion-picture director and producer. Born on August 12, 1881, in Ashfield, Massachusetts, Cecil B. deMille (thus he spelled his name) was the son of a noted playwright, Henry Churchill De Mille. After attending Pennsylvania Military College and the American Academy of Dramatic Arts he went on the stage at nineteen and later collaborated with his brother, William, and David Belasco in writing several plays. In 1913 he joined Jesse L. Lasky and Samuel Goldwyn in forming the Jesse L. Lasky Feature Play Company (later Famous Players–Lasky) to produce motion pictures in Hollywood. His first film, *The Squaw Man*, was made that year; the first full-length feature made in Hollywood, it contributed to the establishment of film as a serious narrative and dramatic medium. He made several innovations in his early works; perhaps the most consequential was the practice of publicizing the leading players. With *The Ten Commandments*, 1923, he began a series of historical and biblical movies produced on a lavish scale and in the spectacular style that was to become his trademark. In 1924 he formed the DeMille Pictures Corporation; in 1928 he joined Metro-Goldwyn-Mayer, and in 1932 moved to Paramount. In a side venture he organized about 1919 the Mercury Aviation Company, a pioneering air service. Such movies as *The King of Kings*, 1927; *The Sign of the Cross*, 1932; *Cleopatra*, 1934; and *The Crusades*, 1935, all played to huge audiences and laid the basis for a large personal fortune. He turned to American themes for *The Plainsman*, 1936; *The Buccaneer*, 1937; *Union Pacific*, 1938; and *Reap the Wild Wind*, 1941. From 1936 to 1945 he also produced the "Lux Radio Theatre of the Air." *The Greatest Show on Earth* won the Academy Award for the best picture of 1952; in 1956 he brought the cycle of Cecil B. deMille spectaculars to a close with a new and highly successful version of *The Ten Commandments*. In all he produced more than 70 films and was at work on a documentary study of Robert Baden-Powell and the Boy Scout movement when he died in Hollywood on January 21, 1959. His *Autobiography* also appeared in 1959.

Dempsey, Jack (1895–1983), boxer. Born in Manassa, Colorado, on June 24, 1895, William Harrison Dempsey ended his schooling in the eighth grade and later, while working at various jobs, he trained himself rigorously to become a boxer. He fought for the first time in 1914, using the name "Kid Blackie," and the next year adopted the name "Jack." Although he won nearly all of his early fights it was not until 1917, when he met promoter and manager Jack Kearns, that he began his climb to the heavyweight championship. A rather small man for his weight class, he defeated a number of larger fighters, becoming known as "Jack the Giant Killer." In tribute to his ferocity in the ring and his habit of winning by knockouts he was also dubbed the "Manassa Mauler." On July 4, 1919, he met Jess Willard in Toledo and in the fourth round won the championship. He retained the crown for seven years, attracting an unprecedented popular following. In 1923 he defended his title in a savage fight with Luis Firpo. On September 23, 1926, in Philadelphia, he lost by a decision to Gene Tunney before a crowd of 100,000. A year later, after a program of conditioning and a victory over Jack Sharkey, he met Tunney again in Chicago. Drawing a record gate of more than $2.5 million, the fight was to be a subject of controversy for years. In the seventh round Dempsey floored his opponent but, dazed himself, lingered in mid-ring; the referee delayed the count until Dempsey retired to a neutral corner and Tunney was able to regain his feet at the count of nine and go on to win in a ten-round decision. Retiring for a time to refereeing, Dempsey attempted a comeback in 1931 but the next year retired permanently from the ring. During his career he had

lost only 5 of 69 bouts and on five occasions had drawn million-dollar gates. He continued to referee as director of physical fitness for the Coast Guard. He later became a successful New York restaurateur with extensive business interests. He died in New York City on May 31, 1983.

Demuth, Charles (1883–1935), painter. Born in Lancaster, Pennsylvania, on November 8, 1883, Demuth received his early training in art at the Pennsylvania Academy of the Fine Arts in Philadelphia and between 1907 and 1913 made four lengthy visits to Europe for independent study. There he was much influenced by the work of Marcel Duchamp and the Cubists, whose geometric renderings more and more informed his own painting as his career progressed. After returning permanently to the United States he executed several series of illustrations for works that included Henry James's *Turn of the Screw*, Edgar Allan Poe's "Masque of the Red Death," and Émile Zola's *Nana*. He later did a number of portraits of theatrical personalities that displayed a grace and economy reminiscent of the works of Aubrey Beardsley and Toulouse-Lautrec. Demuth's major works, however, were the still-life, landscape, and architectural paintings that occupied his later years. Rendered in a spare manner and employing cool and rather abstract colors befitting their delicately planar construction, the paintings were primarily studies and revealed his somewhat detached intellectual interest in their respective problems. Many of them were exhibited in Alfred Stieglitz's 291 Gallery and, as Demuth came to be recognized as one of the foremost watercolorists of his time, found their way into major private and gallery collections. Long in failing health, he died in Lancaster on October 23, 1935.

Dennie, Joseph (1768–1812), editor and author. Born on August 30, 1768, in Boston, Dennie grew up there and in nearby Lexington and after a number of delays graduated from Harvard in 1790. He spent three years in the study of law, but soon after winning admission to the New Hampshire bar in 1794 decided to devote himself to a life of letters. He began contributing regularly to newspapers and for a time maintained a partnership with Royall Tyler, turning out literary ephemera under the signatures of "Colon & Spondee." A number of essays under the series title "Farrago," written in the Addisonian manner, were published in various New Hampshire periodicals and were reprinted by Dennie in Boston in the short-lived *Tablet* in 1795. His residence in Boston was brief; settling in Walpole, New Hampshire, he gathered a circle of congenial local literati and contributed a series of essays entitled "The Lay Preacher" to the *Farmer's Weekly Museum*. In 1796 he became editor of the paper and made it into a literary periodical of wide circulation; while it enjoyed little financial success, the *Museum* became strongly Federalist under Dennie's guidance and in 1799 he was rewarded by appointment as private secretary to the secretary of state, Timothy Pickering, and by a second appointment as an editor of John Fenno's *Gazette of the United States*. He moved to Philadelphia and held both positions until 1800, when the Federalist era ended. Despite the failure of William Cobbett's plan to publish a deluxe edition of the collected "Lay Preacher" essays (smaller collections appeared in 1796 and 1817), he remained in Philadelphia and in 1801, with Asbury Dickens, founded the *Port Folio*, publishing his own writings, those of local literary lights whom he organized as the Tuesday Club, and those of a number of English authors, all under the editorship of "Oliver Oldschool, Esq." The *Port Folio* soon became the leading literary journal in the United States, a position it held until well after Dennie's death, and established its editor as one of the nation's earliest distinguished men of letters. Dennie died in Philadelphia on January 7, 1812. The *Port Folio* was published until 1827, by which time it had been surpassed by the *North American Review*.

Dennis, Ruth, *see* St. Denis, Ruth

Depew, Chauncey Mitchell (1834–1928), lawyer, businessman, and public official. Born in Peekskill, New York, on April 23, 1834, Depew graduated from Yale in 1856 and two years later was admitted to the bar. While establishing a successful practice in Peekskill he became active in Republican politics and during two terms in the legislature in 1862–1863 impressed party leaders with his considerable abilities. In 1863 he was elected secretary of state of New York, holding the position until 1865. President Andrew Johnson appointed him minister to Japan in 1866, but before undertaking his duties he resigned to accept an offer by Cornelius Vanderbilt to become attorney for the New York & Harlem Railroad. He was highly effective as Vanderbilt's legislative adviser and after helping to lay the legal groundwork for the merger he became in 1869 attorney for the newly consolidated New York Central & Hudson River Railroad; he rose to director in 1874, general counsel in 1875, second vice-president in 1882, and, on W. H. Vanderbilt's death in 1885, to president of the New York Central system. He had all the while retained his involvement in Republican affairs and, despite holding no office, remained a leader of the party. From 1888 to 1924 he attended every national convention, at the first placing Benjamin Harrison's name in nomination and withdrawing his own. He declined nomination to the Senate in 1885 and twice refused posts in Harrison's cabinet. In 1899, however, he accepted nomination to the Senate and after his election resigned the presidency of the New York Central in favor of the chairmanship of the board, a position he held for the rest of his life. Reelected in 1905, he remained in the Senate until 1911. Depew held directorships in a great many major corporations and amassed a sizable fortune, a significant por-

tion of which he gave to Yale. Despite his achievements in both business and politics, his greatest reputation was as an orator and after-dinner speaker, in which field he had no peer save possibly Joseph H. Choate. Depew died in New York City on April 5, 1928, at the age of 94. As he once explained, "I get my exercise acting as pallbearer to my friends who exercise."

De Seversky, Alexander Procofieff (1894–1974), aviator and aeronautical engineer. Born in Tbilisi (Tiflis), Russia, on June 7, 1894, De Seversky was originally named Alexander Nicolaievitch Procofieff-Seversky. He graduated from the Imperial Naval Academy in 1914 and later received aviation training. He was sent to the front soon after Russia entered World War I and became one of that nation's outstanding air aces, credited with 13 German planes downed despite a crash in 1915 that cost him a leg and forced him to learn to fly all over again with an artificial limb. In 1917 he left Russia on a mission to the United States just as the Russian Revolution broke out; en route he acquired a French passport and, through a transcription error, the form of his name that he adopted permanently. He remained in the United States and quickly found employment as a test pilot and consulting engineer for the U.S. Air Service. At the request of Gen. William (Billy) Mitchell he devoted three years to the development of a bombsight for aircraft, a project he completed in 1922. In that year he founded the Seversky Aero Corporation, the first of a series of ventures into the rapidly growing aviation industry. Naturalized in 1927, De Seversky joined the Army Air Corps Reserve and rose to the rank of major while making important contributions to military aviation. In 1936 he developed an all-metal, cantilevered-wing training craft for the army and in 1938 built a turbo-supercharged air-cooled fighter plane that served as the prototype for the P-47. Despite such successes and the development of other aircraft that set numerous speed records and captured no fewer than three Bendix trophies, De Seversky lacked business acumen and in 1939, eight years after founding the new company, was ousted from the presidency of the Seversky Aircraft Corporation, which then became the Republic Aircraft Corporation. He remained nonetheless a major figure in military aviation and in 1942 published the widely read and highly influential *Victory Through Air Power*. During World War II he continued to promote a strong air arm of the armed forces and afterward campaigned for the establishment of an independent air force. In recognition of his contributions to military aviation he was awarded in 1947 the War Department's Medal for Merit and the International Harmon Trophy, the latter presented by President Harry S. Truman. De Seversky continued to promote the cause of aviation, working on defense against nuclear attack, and in later years also developed an interest in solving the problems of air pollution, forming the Seversky Electronatom

Corporation. In 1970 he was elected to the Aviation Hall of Fame in Dayton, Ohio. He died in New York City on August 24, 1974.

De Smet, Pierre Jean (1801–1873), Jesuit missionary. Born in Dendermonde (Termonde), Belgium, on January 30, 1801, De Smet emigrated to the United States in 1821 and entered a Jesuit novitiate near Baltimore. Two years later he was transferred to a new novitiate in Florissant, Missouri, and in 1827 he was ordained. For 11 years he carried out his priestly duties both in the United States and in Europe, where he traveled to enlist support for Jesuit activities in America, and in 1838 began a career as missionary to the Indians of the Plains and Northwest. After two years at the mission of St. Joseph, which he founded near present-day Council Bluffs, Iowa, he set out for Oregon country to make contact with the Indian tribes there and to establish missions; he accompanied the Bartleson-Bidwell wagon train to the West in 1841 and was later guided by Thomas Fitzpatrick. In September 1841 he founded St. Mary's Mission among the Flathead in the Bitterroot Valley south of present-day Missoula, Montana; he later built St. Ignatius's among the Kalispel, St. Paul's near Fort Colville in what is now northeastern Washington state, and the Sacred Heart among the Coeur d'Alene of northern Idaho. De Smet's contacts extended to many other tribes as well, notably the Blackfeet and the Sioux, and by all he was trusted and respected as few other white men had been or were to be. Fearless, indefatigable, and thoroughly straightforward in all his dealings, "Blackrobe," as he was known to many Indians, played an indispensable role in mediating differences among various tribes and between the Indians and white settlers. He rendered particularly valuable service in the treaty council at Fort Laramie in 1851 at which reserved lands were assigned to the Plains tribes, and he helped to bring an end to the "Mormon War" of 1857–1858 and the "Yakima War" in 1858–1859. He also later negotiated a temporary peace with Sitting Bull after having boldly entered the Sioux encampment in the Bighorn valley in 1868. In the intervals between his herculean labors in the West De Smet made a number of visits to the East and to Europe to recruit more missionaries and to seek financial support for his work. He died on May 23, 1873, in St. Louis.

De Soto, Hernando (1496?–1542), explorer. Born about 1496 in Jerez de los Caballeros, Spain, De Soto was of a noble but impoverished family and early came under the patronage of Pedrarias (Pedrarias Dávila or Pedro Arias de Ávila), governor of Panama, whom he accompanied to Central America in 1519. In 1532 he sailed to Peru to join Francisco Pizarro and helped to capture Atahualpa, king of the Incas, and his capital city, Cuzco. He then returned to Spain with a considerable fortune in Inca booty. His valor and moderation in the expedition had attracted the favorable notice of Charles V and in 1536 he was granted the titles of governor of Cuba and *adelantado* (roughly, royally commissioned pioneer) of Florida. He sailed from Sanlúcar de Barrameda in April 1538 and spent a year in Cuba preparing to explore and search for treasure in the region, then known only vaguely, called Florida. In May 1539 he left Havana and after a week landed at Tampa Bay with a party of more than 500 men. He immediately struck north and west, making his way among the Indians by seizing their chiefs and then obtaining food and guidance as ransom, and wintered near Apalachee Bay. From there he sent Francisco Maldonado sailing west along the Gulf coast; Maldonado discovered Pensacola Bay and then turned back to bring more supplies from Cuba. In March 1540 De Soto led his force northeast through Georgia to Cofitachequi, an Indian village in western South Carolina, where a large gift of freshwater pearls from the natives only slightly assuaged his thirst for gold. Moving northwest into what is now North Carolina, he then turned west, following tales of gold into Georgia and southern Tennessee, and finally marched southwest into Alabama, reaching the Coosa Indians in present-day Talladega County. Farther south, near modern Camden, he crossed the Alabama River and at "Mabila," a site that remains unidentified, suffered heavy losses in a battle with Indians. With most of his supplies gone, he ignored the planned rendezvous with Maldonado at Pensacola and instead hurried north between the Alabama and Tombigbee rivers and wintered near the site of Tupelo, Mississippi. Setting out again in the spring of 1541, De Soto continued west and on May 21 discovered the Mississippi River. Crossing into Arkansas, he circled north to near where Memphis, Tennessee, now stands and then turned southwest. Reaching the White River, he followed it down to its junction with the Arkansas, which he then traced upstream to the vicinity of Little Rock. At that point he again headed west and, although some interpretations of the expedition's records place him at some time in Oklahoma and possibly Missouri, he most probably got only as far as the Ouachita River. After wintering near modern Camden, Arkansas, he continued to follow the Ouachita south through Louisiana. Near the site of Ferriday, on the Mississippi, De Soto died on May 21, 1542; his body was sunk in the river. Luis de Moscoso succeeded to command of the expedition, leading it west in search of Mexico. He crossed the Red River near Shreveport and continued possibly as far as the Trinity River in Texas before turning back. At Ferriday Moscoso built crude boats and the 300 or so survivors floated down to the Gulf and then coasted west and south, reaching Tampico in September 1543.

De Vinne, Theodore Low (1828–1914), printer. Born on December 25, 1828, in Stamford, Connecticut, De Vinne entered the office of the *Newburgh* (New York) *Gazette* as an apprentice printer at the age of fourteen. Five years later he moved to New York City and worked in a succession of printing shops, in 1850 taking a job in the establishment of Francis Hart. He rose quickly to foreman and in 1858 to junior partner in the business, and on the death of Hart in 1877 became proprietor of the firm, changing its name to Theo. L. De Vinne & Company. He dedicated himself to producing work of the highest possible quality and in the fulfillment of that aim achieved wide recognition. In addition to books the firm printed a number of periodicals, including *Scribner's Monthly, St. Nicholas,* and the *Century Illustrated Magazine;* the last demanded particularly exacting work in the reproduction of its illustrations and De Vinne raised the art to unprecedented heights. In 1884 he helped found and became president of the Grolier Club, an organization devoted to encouraging high standards in all phases of printing, and himself printed many of the club's publications. Among his own writings were the influential *Practice of Typography,* published in four volumes in 1900–1904, and a number of historical studies of printing, including *The Invention of Printing,* 1876; *Historic Printing Types,* 1886; *Title-Pages as Seen by a Printer,* 1901; and *Notable Printers of Italy During the Fifteenth Century,* 1910. His firm was incorporated as the De Vinne Press in 1908 and he remained president for the rest of his life. Widely honored for his contributions to the art and trade of printing, De Vinne died in New York City on February 16, 1914.

De Voto, Bernard Augustine (1897–1955), author, critic, and historian. Born on January 11, 1897, in Ogden, Utah, De Voto attended the University of Utah for a year and in 1915 transferred to Harvard. His graduation was delayed by World War I, during which he was an army marksmanship instructor, and he finally received his degree in 1920. After two years of teaching school in Utah he became an instructor in English at Northwestern University in 1922. He also began his writing career with a novel, *The Crooked Mile,* in 1924; *The Chariot of Fire,* 1926, and *The House of Sun-Goes-Down,* 1928, followed. In 1927 he moved to Cambridge, Massachusetts, and for two years was a free-lance writer, contributing stories and articles to a number of periodicals. He joined the Harvard faculty in 1929 and three years later published his first major critical work, *Mark Twain's America,* in which, against the grain of prevailing critical practice, he pictured Twain's writings as inextricably embedded in the social and cultural environment of his time. A fourth novel, *We Accept with Pleasure,* appeared in 1934, and *Forays and Rebuttals,* a collection of essays on criticism and other topics, in 1936. In 1935 he took over the "Easy Chair" department of *Harper's Magazine,* continuing to conduct it for the rest of his life, and the next year, resigning from Harvard, became editor of the *Saturday Review of Literature.* After 1938 he devoted full

time to his own writing. The controversies aroused by his often unorthodox views of American literature, to which he took a rather rough, woolly approach, were heightened by the vigorous, even pugnacious, style in which he expressed them. That his scholarship was sound was amply demonstrated in three studies of the exploration and settlement of the West: *The Year of Decision: 1846,* 1943; *Across the Wide Missouri,* which won both the Pulitzer and Bancroft prizes for history, 1947; and *The Course of Empire,* 1952. Others among De Voto's books were *Mark Twain at Work,* 1942; *The Literary Fallacy,* 1944; *Mountain Time,* 1947; *The World of Fiction,* 1950; *The Hour,* 1951; and an edition of *The Journals of Lewis and Clark,* 1953. He also wrote a number of potboiler novels under the pseudonym "John August" to help support his historical researches. One of the most widely read critics and historians of his day, De Voto died in New York City on November 13, 1955.

Dewey, George (1837–1917), naval officer. Born on December 26, 1837, in Montpelier, Vermont, Dewey attended Norwich University and graduated from the U.S. Naval Academy in 1858. He became a lieutenant in 1861 and during the Civil War served under Adm. David G. Farragut in operations on the Mississippi River and against New Orleans and was later on duty with the Atlantic blockade. He rose to commander in 1872, captain in 1884, and commodore in 1896. As chief of the Bureau of Equipment, 1889, and president of the Board of Inspection and Survey, 1895, he became familiar with the modern battleships of the navy. Assigned to sea duty at his own request in 1897, he received word of the outbreak of the Spanish-American War while in Hong Kong. With orders to capture or destroy Spanish vessels in Philippine waters, he entered Manila Bay with his command, the Asiatic squadron, consisting of four cruisers and two gunboats, on May 1, 1898. With the long-remembered words to the captain of his flagship, "You may fire when you are ready, Gridley," he opened fire and sank or destroyed all ten ships of the Spanish fleet, incurring no damage to American vessels and only eight injuries to American seamen. By demonstrating the power of the navy and the superiority of her new ships, the victory earned for the United States the position of the major Pacific power. He was promoted to rear admiral on May 10, 1898, and formally commended by Congress. In August his fleet assisted in the occupation of Manila by land forces under Gen. Wesley Merritt and in September 1899 he returned to the United States, where he was given a hero's welcome. In 1899 he was made admiral of the navy, a rank created especially for him and the highest ever held by an American naval officer. By special provision he was allowed to remain on active duty despite his age, and from 1900 he served as president of the General Board of the navy. He published his autobiography in 1913 and died in Washington, D.C., on January 16, 1917.

Dewey, John (1859–1952), philosopher, psychologist, and educator. Born on October 20, 1859, in Burlington, Vermont, Dewey graduated from the University of Vermont in 1879 and after two years of teaching school continued his studies, receiving his Ph.D. from The Johns Hopkins University in 1884. During the next ten years he taught philosophy at the universities of Minnesota and Michigan, and in 1894 he moved to the University of Chicago as head of the department of philosophy, psychology, and pedagogy. There, two years later, he established the Laboratory School as a testing ground for his educational theories. He remained director of the school until 1904, when he joined the faculty of Columbia University, helping, during the next four decades, to bring its Teachers College to the forefront in American education. His educational thought was widely influential and the principal intellectual resource of the wave of school reform proceeding under the general name of "progressive" education. Based on his development of William James's pragmatism into a scientifically oriented "instrumentalism," Dewey's educational theory pictured the process of education as the accumulation and assimilation of experience, as an acculturation process whereby the child, through experience and activity, develops into a balanced personality of wide awareness. Such a view, expressed in terms of growth, development, and process, was directly opposed to the more traditional educational methodology of lecture, memorization, and mechanical drill. Dewey was an adviser to several countries on the development of national educational systems and remained throughout his life the leading American educational thinker. He was also at various times president of the American Psychological Association, the American Philosophical Society, and the American Association of University Professors, which he had helped found in 1915. He retired from the Columbia faculty in 1930, but continued to add to his long list of books until his death on June 1, 1952, in New York City. Among his works were Psychology, 1887; Critical Theory of Ethics, 1894; The School and Society, 1899; The Child and the Curriculum, 1902; How We Think, 1910; Democracy and Education, 1916; Reconstruction in Philosophy, 1920; Human Nature and Conduct, 1922; Experience and Nature, 1925; The Quest for Certainty, 1929; Art as Experience, 1934; Experience and Education, 1938; Freedom and Culture, 1939; and Problems of Men, 1946. Besides having brought about a revolution in educational practices, he is also generally considered one of the two or three greatest philosophers America has produced.

Dewey, Melvil (1851–1931), librarian. Born in Adams Center, New York, on December 10, 1851, Melville Louis Kossuth Dewey later dropped his two middle names and the final letters of his first name. While attending Amherst College he began working in the library there and continued in the job for two years after his graduation in 1874. In 1876 he published A Classification and Subject Index for Cataloguing and Arranging the Books and Pamphlets of a Library, outlining what became known as the Dewey Decimal System; logical, comprehensive, and simple to apply, the system made provision for indefinite expansion of collections and gradually was adopted by libraries throughout the English-speaking world. In 1876 Dewey left Amherst and traveled to Boston to help organize the founding and first meeting of the American Library Association (ALA), of which he was secretary until 1890 and president in 1890–1891 and 1892–1893. At the same time he joined Richard R. Bowker and Frederick Leypoldt in establishing the Library Journal, working as its editor for a time. In 1883 he was appointed librarian of Columbia College, where four years later he organized the School of Library Economy, the first training institution for librarians in the United States. In 1888 he was named director of the New York State Library and that appointment, together with disagreements with the authorities at Columbia, led him to resign from the college and move to Albany, taking his library school with him. While reorganizing and improving the state library, a task which he carried on until 1906, he served also as secretary and treasurer of the board of regents of the University of the State of New York from 1888 to 1906 and as state director of libraries from 1904 to 1906. The state library became, under his guidance, the most efficient in the nation, and he extended its usefulness with the addition of picture collections and a traveling library system. In 1890 he joined in the founding of the Association of State Librarians. His school, taken into the New York educational system as the State Library School, was highly successful and continued to be one of the most influential in the country. Dewey retired from his various posts in 1906; in later years he was involved in the development of resort properties around Lake Placid, New York, and at Lake Placid, Florida, where he died on December 26, 1931.

Dewey, Thomas Edmund (1902–1971), lawyer and public official. Born on March 24, 1902, in Owosso, Michigan, Dewey graduated from the University of Michigan in 1923 and earned his law degree from Columbia in 1925. Admitted to the bar the following year, he practiced law in New York City until 1931, when he became chief assistant to the U.S. attorney for the southern district of New York. As a special investigator of organized crime in 1935–1937—appointed by Governor Herbert H. Lehman at the insistence of the city's famed "runaway" grand jury—he earned the sobriquet "racket-buster" by obtaining 72 convictions in 73 prosecutions. On an anti-Tammany Hall ticket in 1937 he was elected district attorney of New York County (Manhattan). The next year he ran unsuccessfully for governor on the Republican ticket, but he was victorious in the elections of 1942, 1946, and 1950. As governor he was capable, efficient, and politically moderate. In 1940 he received strong support for the Republican presidential nomination, but lost to Wendell L. Wilkie. That year Dewey's first book, *The Case Against the New Deal*, was published. He won the Republican presidential nomination in 1944 and again in 1948; in the first election he lost, running on a moderate platform, to Franklin D. Roosevelt, who campaigned on his established liberal policies and his position as a wartime incumbent. In 1948 he suffered defeat, widely thought to be an upset, by President Harry S. Truman. He traveled in the Far East during the late 1940s and published *Journey to the Far Pacific* in 1952. That year he helped rally strong party support for Dwight D. Eisenhower, securing the backing of the large New York delegation for Eisenhower's nomination and contributing by his campaigning to Eisenhower's victory. In 1955, when his third term as governor of New York ended, he retired from public office and resumed law practice. Dewey remained a leader of the Republican party, particularly its moderate Eastern wing, until his death in Bal Harbour, Florida, on March 16, 1971.

Dickey, James (1923–   ), poet and author. Born on February 2, 1923, in Atlanta, Georgia, Dickey entered Clemson College in 1942 but left the next year to enlist in the Army Air Forces. After a tour of combat duty in the Pacific theater he returned to the United States and enrolled at Vanderbilt University, from which he graduated in 1949 and took an M.A. the following year. In 1950 he joined the faculty of Rice Institute as an instructor in English, returning in 1952–1954 after a period of service in the Air Force during the Korean War. He began contributing poems to literary journals and in 1954 was awarded a fellowship by the *Sewanee Review*. During 1955–1956 he taught at the University of Florida and then for a period of five years worked as a copywriter for a succession of advertising agencies. His first volume of poetry appeared in 1960 under the title *Into the Stone and Other Poems*. After winning a Guggenheim fellowship in 1961 he occupied residencies in poetry at Reed College, San Fernando Valley State College, and the University of Wisconsin between 1963 and 1966. More volumes of poetry followed rapidly on the first: *Drowning with Others*, 1962; *Helmets*, 1964; *Two Poems of the Air*, 1964; *Buckdancer's Choice*, 1965, which won a National Book Award; *Poems, 1957–1967*, 1967; and *Eye-Beaters, Blood, Victory, Madness, Buckhead and Mercy*, 1970. His reputation grew rapidly; his verse often compared to that of Hart Crane in its vital blend of imagery from the natural and the mechanical realms, was vigorous, blunt, and painstakingly crafted. As an interpreter of contemporary experience Dickey was particularly esteemed for the clarity and diversity of his vision. He published also two collections of critical essays, *The Suspect in Poetry*, 1964, and *Babel to Byzantium: Poets and Poetry Now*, 1968, and in 1970 a much-admired first novel, *Deliverance*, for the motion picture

of which he wrote the screenplay in 1972. Other writings appeared in *Self-Interviews*, 1970, and *Sorties, Journals and New Essays*, 1971. During 1966–1968 Dickey served as consultant in poetry to the Library of Congress and in 1968 he became poet in residence at the University of South Carolina.

Dickinson, Emily Elizabeth (1830–1886), poet. Born on December 10, 1830, in Amherst, Massachusetts, Miss Dickinson was the daughter of a prominent lawyer who was later a congressman and treasurer of Amherst College. She attended Amherst Academy and spent a year at the Mount Holyoke Female Seminary, but her dislike of being away from home led her to return permanently to her father's house in 1848. Her residence there was interrupted only by brief trips to Washington and Philadelphia in 1855 and to Boston and Concord in 1864 and 1865. During her youth she was quite lively and outgoing, but she became progressively more reclusive as the years passed. Although she never married she apparently exeprienced deep, if ambiguous, emotional involvements on two occasions, the second during the 1850s with the Reverend Charles Wadsworth, who may have been the inspiration for the otherwise imaginary lover alluded to in some of her poems. She seems to have written occasional verse from her school days and she continued to write until her death, but the major portion of her work, and the best of it, was produced during the years 1858–1866. Typically short, condensed pieces, her poems combined spare lyricism and metaphysical speculation with highly unorthodox diction and meter; the provinciality and narrowness of her outward life belied both the scope of her thought and the subtlety of her style. She showed her work to only a few persons outside her family circle. In 1862 she sent a few verses to Thomas Wentworth Higginson, who was at once charmed and baffled by them; in a remarkable correspondence that continued for more than 20 years he gently counseled against publication. During her life none of her poems were published with her consent, although several did appear—one was published anonymously in 1878 through the agency of Helen Hunt Jackson, a schoolmate and lifelong friend and the shy poet's leading literary champion. Miss Dickinson's father died in 1874 and the next year her mother became an invalid. She kept more and more to herself until at length she rarely ventured from the house, but she maintained correspondence with a few intimates until her death in Amherst on May 15, 1886. Her sister Lavinia subsequently discovered hundreds of poems neatly tucked away; she prevailed upon a still-dubious Higginson to help prepare a slender volume, *Poems by Emily Dickinson*, 1890. The book met with generally unfavorable critical response, but it was sufficiently well received by the public to warrant the publication of *Poems: Second Series*, 1891, and *Poems: Third Series*, 1896. By 1945 nearly all of Emily Dickinson's poetry had been published and her position as one of America's foremost poets was secure.

Dickinson, John (1732–1808), colonial figure and public official. Born in Talbot County, Maryland, on November 8, 1732, Dickinson moved with his family to Delaware and was educated privately until he took up the study of law in Philadelphia and London. In 1757 he returned from London to begin practice in Philadelphia and, quickly attaining an eminent position at the bar, entered politics, holding a number of public offices in both Pennsylvania and Delaware. In the tense debate that preceded the outbreak of the Revolution he took a conservative, though pro-colonial, position; while he denounced British policies as unjust, he held out hope to the last for reconciliation. As a result of a pamphlet he wrote on the Stamp and Sugar acts he was appointed by the Pennsylvania legislature to the Stamp Act Congress in 1765 and there drafted the resolutions of grievances. In 1767–1768 he published a series called *Letters from a Farmer in Pennsylvania* on the non-importation and non-exportation agreements that had been proposed in the colonies in respose to the Townshend Acts; these won him wide popularity. He drafted a number of petitions to the king on behalf of the Pennsylvania legislature and the first and second Continental Congresses. Although still opposed to precipitate violence and to separation from England, he was largely responsible for the "Declaration . . . Setting Forth the Causes and Necessity of Their Taking Up Arms" issued by the second Continental Congress in 1775. The following year, having aided in the drafting of the Articles of Confederation, he voted against and declined to sign the Declaration of Independence. During the war, however, he served in the militia. He represented Delaware in Congress in 1779; in 1781 he was elected president of the Supreme Executive Council of Delaware and, the next year, of the Pennsylvania council. He was president of the Annapolis Convention in 1786 and the next year was a member of the Constitutional Convention and thereafter supported ratification of the Constitution. His writings through the whole period earned him the title "Penman of the Revolution." He died on February 14, 1808, in Wilmington, Delaware.

Didrikson, Babe, *see* Zaharias, Mildred Ella Didrikson

Dies, Martin (1901–1972), public official. Born on November 5, 1901, in Colorado, Texas, Dies graduated from the University of Texas in 1919 and the following year took a law degree from the National University in Washington, D.C. Admitted to the bar in 1920, he practiced in Marshall, Texas, and later in Orange, while preparing to follow in his father's political footsteps. He was elected in 1931 to the seat in the House of Representatives once held by his father, and despite his youth he quickly won a place on the powerful Rules Committee. Originally a New Deal supporter, he gradually turned against the administration of Franklin D. Roosevelt and by 1937 was one of the leading opposition Democrats in Congress. After several earlier proposals of the kind had failed he won approval in 1938 for the establishment of a Committee to Investigate Un-American Activities, with himself as chairman. The investigations of Nazi activities in the United States which he at first planned soon gave way to inquiries into Communist activities; almost immediately the committee's hearings became the source of sensational stories of infiltration of many aspects of American life by subversives. Wide publicity helped Dies secure the continuation of the committee, which from then on occupied the bulk of his time as a congressman. Although his methods were highly controversial, drawing charges that he was more interested in exposure for its own sake and for its publicity value than in any real legislative purpose, the "Dies committee" was defended with vigor by many who saw just such an undertaking as vital to national security. One of the committee's early reports stated that "While Congress does not have power to deny to citizens the right to believe in, teach, or advocate communism, fascism, and nazism, it does have the right to focus the spotlight of publicity upon their activities," and Dies himself claimed to be more effective in detecting Communist subversion than the Federal Bureau of Investigation (FBI), making the assertion in his book *The Trojan Horse of America*, 1940. His often spectacular revelations of Communist influence in organized labor, Hollywood, consumers' organizations, the Federal Writers' Project, and other groups and movements, and his charges against many prominent persons of being Communists or "Communist dupes," were only occasionally founded in factual evidence; the charges most often were based on hearsay, circumstance, or slander. Dies declined renomination in 1944; in 1945, soon after he left Congress, his committee was given permanent standing as the Committee on Un-American Activities, which continued to lead a checkered and controversial career. Dies served again in the House from 1953 to 1959, but held no important committee posts. In 1941 and again in 1957 he unsuccessfully sought election to uncompleted Senate terms. He retired to his law practice in Texas and in 1963 published *The Martin Dies Story*. He died in Lufkin, Texas, on November 14, 1972.

Dillinger, John (1902–1934), outlaw. Born in Indianapolis on June 28, 1902, Dillinger attended school until he was seventeen and then took a job in a machine shop. In 1920 he moved to Mooresville, Indiana, where he lived for four years, interrupted only by five months in the navy, from which he deserted. In September 1923 he and a partner attempted to rob a grocery store in Mooresville; Dillinger was caught and sent to prison. After twice trying to escape he was transferred to a state prison, but in 1933 he was paroled. Within less than a month he pulled another robbery, this time in Illinois, and then hit the Daleville, Indiana, bank for $3000. By this time he was leading a gang; they successfully robbed two more banks before he was again caught in Dayton, Ohio. With the aid of members of his gang, who in the process killed a sheriff, he soon escaped; after two raids on police stations to acquire weapons they struck the Greencastle, Indiana, bank on October 21 and got away with $75,000; Dillinger was designated "public enemy number one" by the Federal Bureau of Investigation (FBI). Three more bank jobs followed in Wisconsin, Illinois, and Indiana, and in January 1934 he and six companions were arrested in Tucson, Arizona. After a month in jail in Crown Point, Indiana, awaiting trial for the murder of a policeman in East Chicago, he escaped with the aid of a mock pistol he had fashioned from wood. In March he was wounded by police in St. Paul, Minnesota, but remained at large. During April he ranged from Mooresville to Minneapolis. He and his gang retired to a resort in Little Bohemia, Wisconsin; police, informed of his whereabouts, attempted to trap him there, but he successfully fought free, killing two would-be captors. By May a total of $50,000 in rewards was being offered for his capture; a woman friend, the mysterious "Lady in Red," betrayed him and on July 22, 1934, as he left the Biograph Theater in Chicago, he was shot and killed by FBI agents.

Dillingham, William Paul (1843–1923), public official. Born in Waterbury, Vermont, on December 12, 1843, Dillingham was educated in local schools and at Kimball Union Academy in Meriden, New Hampshire. He took up the study of law in the Milwaukee office of a relative and later in that of his father, then governor of Vermont. Admitted to the bar in 1867, he began practice in Waterbury and was elected county prosecuting attorney in 1872, holding the office until 1876. He was elected to four terms in the legislature between 1876 and 1884, was state tax commissioner from 1882 to 1888, and in 1888 was elected governor. Engaging from 1890 in law and banking, he remained active in Republican politics and in 1900 was chosen to fill a vacated Senate seat. He was elected to a full term in 1902 and remained in the Senate until his death. Soon after entering that body he was named to the Committee on Immigration and from 1903 to 1911 was its chairman; he also chaired the U.S. Immigration Commission, which from 1907 to 1910 conducted intensive studies of immigration and filed a 41-volume report, the most thorough survey of the subject ever made. Dillingham's personal conclusions from the study were embodied in a bill he introduced in 1913 providing for the restriction of immigration through a system of quotas; the quotas were to be based on the number of persons from each nation or origin already resident in the United States. The effort to pass

the bill was dropped for the duration of World War I, but in 1920 Dillingham reintroduced his measure; it was passed by Congress but vetoed by President Woodrow Wilson. In May 1921 the third attempt at passage was successful. The traditional policy of open immigration was ended, and each country—except those in Asia, the inhabitants of which were completely excluded—was allotted an annual 3 percent quota, with a ceiling on total yearly immigration of 357,000. The national origins quota system remained, with occasional modifications, in effect until 1968, when it was replaced by a more equitable system through the Immigration and Nationality Amendments of 1965. Dillingham died in Montpelier, Vermont, on July 12, 1923.

DiMaggio, Joseph Paul, Jr. (1914–   ), baseball player. Born on November 25, 1914, in Martinez, California, "Jolting Joe" DiMaggio was the son of immigrant Sicilian parents. He played baseball with a local boys' league in his youth and in 1932 joined an older brother on the San Francisco Seals of the Pacific Coast League. During the 1933 season he hit safely in 61 consecutive games, a league record, and batted .340 overall. The next year, despite a knee injury, he was purchased by the New York Yankees of the American League; after a final year of experience with the Seals he joined the Yankees in 1936 and proceeded to bat .323, to amass an excellent fielding record, and to be chosen for the all-star team of that year. During 13 years with the Yankees (he served in the army during 1943–1945) he was consistently the team's outstanding player; he was on the all-star team every year and, except for 1946, batted over .300 each season, reaching a peak of .381 in 1939 and compiling a career average of .325. He was three times chosen the American League's most valuable player. His greatest achievement at the plate came in 1941, when he batted safely in 56 consecutive games, a major-league record. His fielding was equally remarkable and was all the more impressive for the easy grace of its execution. He was plagued by injuries throughout his career and often played in spite of them; a modest man who declined to play to the stands and whose style of baseball was one of quiet excellence, he was called "the greatest team player of all time" by Connie Mack. His autobiography, published in 1946, bore the characteristically modest title *Lucky to Be a Yankee.* In 1949 his salary was raised to an unprecedented $100,000. In 1951 the "Yankee Clipper" retired, citing an accumulation of injuries and a consequent decline in his ability to live up to the expectations of his teammates and his millions of ardent admirers. In 1954, to the accompaniment of vast publicity, he married movie star Marilyn Monroe, but the marriage was dissolved a year later. In 1955 he was elected to the National Baseball Hall of Fame. After retiring he devoted himself to business pursuits and in 1967 became executive vice president of the Oakland Athletics baseball team.

Dirksen, Everett McKinley (1896–1969), public official. Born on January 4, 1896, in Pekin, Illinois, Dirksen entered the University of Minnesota in 1915 but left two years later to serve in the army during World War I. He returned to Pekin after his discharge in 1919, worked at various jobs, and for a time ran a wholesale bakery with his brothers. From an early interest in amateur dramatics he turned to politics, in 1926 winning election as city finance commissioner. After an unsuccessful campaign for the House of Representatives in 1930 he ran again two years later and won. In the House he hewed closely to the Republican line at first, opposing the New Deal and President Franklin D. Roosevelt's foreign policy; he switched his position on foreign policy in 1941 to advocacy of bipartisan support. He remained in the House until 1948, when ill health forced his retirement to Pekin. Two years later, however, he was fully recovered and successfully ran for the Senate. He quickly established himself as a staunch conservative and came to national attention at the 1952 Republican national convention when, while speaking for the nomination of Senator Robert A. Taft, he turned to Thomas E. Dewey, sitting beside him on the rostrum, shook his finger, and shouted "We followed you before and you took us down the path to defeat." Dirksen's conservatism softened over the years and his positions on foreign aid, civil rights, and other major issues changed often. After his election as Senate Republican leader in 1959 he emerged as a moderate, but his views remained ever unpredictable. Under the Democratic administrations of presidents John F. Kennedy and Lyndon B. Johnson he played an invaluable role in securing Senate approval for many important measures, most notably the Civil Rights Act of 1964, reserving partisan opposition to lesser issues. Dirksen was best known for his oratory and he was the last great practitioner of the nineteenth-century art of magniloquence. He used his mellow bass voice like a musical instrument and relied on poesy rather than power to move his audiences; one of his mottoes was "The oilcan is mightier than the sword." Dubbed "the Wizard of Ooze," among other similar titles, he described himself as "just an old-fashioned garden variety of Republican who believes in the Constitution, the Declaration of Independence, and Abraham Lincoln." Despite the influence he wielded over the legislative process, he was thwarted in a number of pet projects of his later years; among proposals that failed were those for constitutional amendments overturning Supreme Court rulings on legislative reapportionment and religious exercises in public schools, and a bill naming the marigold as the national flower. By the time of his last reelection in 1968 he had attained the status of a venerable figure in the political sphere; he died in Washington, D.C., on September 7, 1969.

Disney, Walt (1901–1966), cartoonist, motion-picture producer, and businessman. Born in Chicago on December 5, 1901, Walter Elias Disney grew up in Marceline and Kansas City, Missouri. After service in World War I—he was too young for the army or navy so he drove a Red Cross ambulance—he began working as a commercial artist and cartoonist in Kansas City. He experimented with animated cartoons and from 1923 to 1926 produced a series of films combining live and animated action called *Alice in Cartoonland.* This and the subsequent *Oswald the Rabbit* series failed to achieve much success. Disney persevered, however, trying a new character named Mickey (originally Mortimer) Mouse; the first two films attracted no attention, but the third, *Steamboat Willie,* the first to employ a sound track, was an immediate and smashing success. More Mickey Mouse shorts followed, gaining a world-wide audience, and Disney soon inaugurated a new series, *Silly Symphonies,* and introduced such new characters as Donald Duck and Pluto. In 1937 he released *Snow White and the Seven Dwarfs,* the first feature-length cartoon movie, which quickly became a classic. There followed a succession of such films, including *Fantasia,* 1940, which combined animation with a sound track by the Philadelphia Orchestra, led by Leopold Stokowski; *Pinocchio,* 1940; *Dumbo,* 1941; *Bambi,* 1942; *Cinderella,* 1950; *Alice in Wonderland,* 1951; *Peter Pan,* 1953; and *Sleeping Beauty,* 1959, all of which have remained favorites through periodic revivals. In 1953 Disney began the *True Adventure* series of nature documentaries with *The Living Desert;* this and the succeeding *Vanishing Prairie,* 1954; *The African Lion,* 1955; and *Secrets of Life,* 1956, won for him the title of Officier d'Académie, France's highest decoration for artists. As dozens of other movies —live-action adventure, comedy, and fantasy— flowed from the Disney studios he began branching out into other areas of entertainment with several television shows—"Disneyland," "The Mickey Mouse Club," "Zorro," and "The Wonderful World of Walt Disney" among them—and built the Disneyland amusement park in southern California; Disneyland achieved such popularity and world renown that Soviet Premier Nikita S. Khrushchev was bitterly disappointed when security considerations prevented him from visiting it during his 1959 tour of the United States. Disney was the recipient of hundreds of honors and awards from around the world; he received a record 29 Academy Awards. He was directing construction of a second Disneyland in Florida, later named Disney World, when he died in Los Angeles on December 15, 1966.

Divine, Father, see Baker, George (1877–1965)

Dix, Dorothea Lynde (1802–1887), teacher, social reformer, and humanitarian. Born on April 4, 1802, in Hampden, Maine, Dorothea Dix left her unhappy home at the age of twelve to live and study in Boston with her grandmother. By the age of fourteen she was teaching in a school for young girls in Worcester, Massachusetts, employing a curriculum of her own devising that stressed the natural sciences and the responsibilities of ethical living. In 1821 she opened her own school in Boston and continued it until 1835, when increasingly serious bouts with tuberculosis forced her to abandon teaching and leave Boston. She lived for a time in England and wrote several books for children. After two years she returned to Boston, still a semi-invalid, and found to her amazement that she had inherited a sum of money sufficient to support her comfortably for life. But her Calvinist beliefs enjoined her from inactivity. Thus in 1841, when a young clergyman asked her to begin a Sunday-school class in the East Cambridge House of Correction, she accepted the offer. In the prison she first observed the treatment of insane and disturbed persons, who were thrown in with criminals, irrespective of age or sex. They were left unclothed, in darkness, without heat or sanitary facilities; some were chained to the walls and flogged. Profoundly shocked, she traveled for nearly two years throughout the state, observed the same conditions in institutions everywhere, and in 1843 submitted to the Massachusetts legislature a detailed report of her thoroughly documented findings. Her dignity, feverish compassion, and determination, as well as the issue itself, moved the legislators, and despite public apathy, disbelief, and occasional active opposition, a bill was passed for enlargement of the Worcester insane asylum. In the next 40 years she inspired legislators of 15 U.S. states as well as legislators in Canada to establish state hospitals for the mentally ill. Her unflagging effort prompted the building of 32 institutions in the United States, several in Europe, and two in Japan, and fostered the reorganization, enlargement, and restaffing, with well-trained, intelligent personnel, of already existing hospitals. She served in the Civil War as superintendent of women nurses. After the war she returned to her work with hospitals; when she died on July 17, 1887, it was in a hospital in Trenton, New Jersey, that she had founded.

Dix, John Adams (1798–1879), soldier and public official. Born in Boscawen, New Hampshire, on July 24, 1798, Dix was well educated at home, at Phillips Exeter Academy, and for a year at the College of Montreal. At the age of fourteen he secured, with his father's aid, an army commission and saw battle at Lundy's Lane in the War of 1812; after the war he remained in the army and rose to the rank of major while studying law and winning admission to the bar in 1824. Resigning his commission, he settled in Cooperstown, New York, in 1828 and began his law practice, becoming at the same time active in Democratic politics. In 1830 he was appointed state adjutant general, a post that made him one of the clique called the "Albany regency." From 1833 to 1839 he was secretary of state of New York and, as ex officio superintendent of public schools, made several notable contributions to

education. In 1841 he served in the legislature and then returned to law; he also published the *Northern Light,* a scientific and literary journal, from 1841 to 1843. In 1845 he was elected to fill an unexpired term in the Senate, where he was a prominent figure in the antislavery wing of the Democratic party. He supported Martin Van Buren on the Free-Soil ticket in 1848 and was himself that party's unsuccessful candidate for governor. Upon leaving the Senate in 1849 he returned to his law practice and during the next several years held positions in a number of railroad companies; during his career he was president of both the Union Pacific and Erie railroads. Attempts to appoint him to high political offices, including a cabinet post, were defeated by Southern Democrats, but in 1860, following a scandal in the office, he was named postmaster of New York City by President James Buchanan. Early the following year the great esteem in which he was held by the Eastern business community was reflected in his appointment as secretary of the treasury. His two months in that position were of great value to the Union; he inspired the confidence of bankers by his efficient organization and personal integrity and of the general public by a famous telegraph message he sent to a treasury officer in New Orleans: "If anyone attempts to haul down the American flag, shoot him on the spot." In March 1861 President Abraham Lincoln commissioned Dix a major general of volunteers. He commanded various rear-area military districts, the last of which was New York, 1863–1865; despite his advancing age he was an effective administrator. From 1866 to 1869 he served as minister to France and in 1872, although still a Democrat, was nominated for governor of New York by the Republicans. Elected by a large majority, he served until 1874, when he was defeated for reelection by Samuel J. Tilden. He then retired to New York City, where he died on April 21, 1879. Fort Dix, in New Jersey, is named for him.

Dixon, Franklin W., *see under* Stratemeyer, Edward

Dixon, Jeremiah, *see under* Mason, Charles

Dobie, James Frank (1888–1964), folklorist and educator. Born on September 26, 1888, in Live Oak County, Texas, Dobie grew up on a ranch and early developed a deep and abiding love for the land and lore of the Southwest. He graduated from Southwestern University in Texas in 1910, was a school principal for a year and an English instructor at Southwestern for two, and in 1914 took an M.A. from Columbia University. He then joined the faculty of the University of Texas, with which he was associated for most of the rest of his teaching career. During World War I he served in the U.S. artillery in France, returning to the university in 1919. In 1920–1921 he took a year off to manage a cattle ranch; from 1921 to 1923 he was at the university, from 1923 to 1925 he was head of the English department of Oklahoma Agricultural and Mechanical College, and in 1925 he returned to the University of Texas as adjunct professor of English. Advancing to full professor in 1933, Dobie remained at the university, except for leaves of absence, until his retirement from teaching in 1947. During the 1920s he had conceived a project of collecting the legends and stories of Texas and the Southwest, and it soon became a lifelong enterprise. Beginning with *A Vaquero of the Brush Country*, 1929, he published over the years more than 30 books chronicling what he saw as the real history of his region; among them were *Coronado's Children*, 1931; *On the Open Range*, 1931; *Tongues of the Monte*, 1935; *Tales of the Mustang*, 1936; *Apache Gold and Yaqui Silver*, 1939; *The Longhorns*, 1941; *The Voice of the Coyote*, 1949; *Up the Trail from Texas*, 1955; and *Cow People*, 1964. During 1943–1944 Dobie was visiting professor of American history at Cambridge University, where his informal and eminently unacademic manner made a considerable impression; he was awarded an honorary M.A. by Cambridge and upon his return described his experiences in *A Texan in England*, 1945. He was secretary and publications editor of the Texas Folklore Society from 1922 to 1942 and was for many years a contributing editor of the *Southwest Review*. He also conducted a weekly column distributed to a number of Texas newspapers and was a leading spokesman for progressivism in the state. His main course at the university, titled "Life and Literature of the Southwest," was widely known both for its unique subject matter and Dobie's own vital and engaging teaching methods. In 1964 he was awarded the Presidential Medal of Freedom by fellow Texan Lyndon B. Johnson; he died a short time later, on September 18, 1964, in Austin, Texas. An autobiographical work, *Some Part of Myself*, appeared in 1967.

Dobnievski, David, see Dubinsky, David

Dobzhansky, Theodosius Grigorievich (1900–1975), geneticist and author. Born in Nemirov, Russia, on January 25, 1900, Dobzhansky graduated from the University of Kiev in 1921. For three years he taught zoology at the Kiev Institute of Agriculture and from 1924 to 1927 was lecturer in genetics at the University of Leningrad. He came to the United States on a fellowship in 1927 to pursue further studies in genetics at Columbia University and the California Institute of Technology. At Caltech he met and worked with Thomas Hunt Morgan, who persuaded him to remain there after the expiration of his fellowship; accordingly in 1929 he was appointed assistant professor of genetics. He rose to full professor in 1936 and the following year became a naturalized citizen. In 1940 he moved to Columbia University as professor of zoology, later becoming Da Costa Professor of Zoology. In his researches Dobzhansky was interested principally in population genetics, the study of

the distribution, interactions, and evolution of the total genetic resources of large, self-contained groups. An anthropological bent, together with his deep convictions about the social responsibilities of the scientist, led him into considerations of the implications for man of recent advances in genetics and to the publication of a number of thoughtful and influential books, including *Genetics and the Origin of Species*, 1937; *Heredity, Race, and Society*, 1946, with L. C. Dunn; *Evolution, Genetics and Man*, 1955; *The Biological Basis of Human Freedom*, 1956; *Radiation, Genes, and Man*, 1959, with Bruce Wallace; *Mankind Evolving*, 1962; *The Biology of Ultimate Concern*, 1967; and *Genetics of the Evolutionary Process*, 1970. From these, particularly *Mankind Evolving*, emerged a view of man as subject to the interacting forces of organic evolution and the cultural environment of his own creation. Dobzhansky advocated the rigorous investigation of all fields of knowledge bearing upon man's self-development, especially those in which incomplete knowledge posed immediate dangers, as in nuclear physics. He saw the belief in genetically based racial differences as a bar to the realization of man's evolutionary potential. He joined the faculty of Rockefeller University in 1962 and moved to the University of California at Davis in 1971. He died in Davis on December 18, 1975.

Dodge, Grenville Mellen (1831–1916), soldier and engineer. Born in Danvers, Massachusetts, on April 12, 1831, Dodge took a degree in civil and military engineering from Norwich University in 1851. He traveled west to Illinois, where after a year of surveying in and around the town of Peru, he secured a position with the Illinois Central Railroad. In 1853 he directed a large portion of a survey across Iowa for the Mississippi & Missouri Railroad; he subsequently settled in Council Bluffs, Iowa, and for the next several years engaged in railroad construction and in business ventures throughout the state. In 1856 he organized a militia company, the Council Bluffs Guards, and five years later volunteered its services for the Civil War. Commissioned a colonel of volunteers, he rose rapidly to major general and, serving at various times in every theater of the war and seeing action in a number of major engagements, he won high praise for his work in bridge and railroad construction and reconstruction for the army. Receiving his discharge in 1866, he entered upon the major phase of his career upon becoming chief engineer of the Union Pacific Railroad. He was elected to Congress in the same year, but after a single term he declined further service in order to devote full time to the Union Pacific. Although some preliminary work on the line running west from Omaha had been done, the bulk of the huge task fell upon Dodge, and he completed it with great success and remarkable speed, the last spike being driven at Promontory Point, Utah, on May 10, 1869. The following year he left the Union Pacific and in 1871 became chief engineer for the Texas & Pacific Railroad. He was associated for many years with that line and several others in the Southwest, supervising construction of many. His last accomplishment was the completion of a trunk line from Santa Clara, Cuba, to Santiago de Cuba in 1903. During his career Dodge oversaw the building of more than 10,000 miles of railroad, and his surveys covered many times that distance. He also headed the Dodge Commission in 1898 to investigate the army's conduct during the Spanish-American War; many changes in army organization resulted from his 1900 report. He retired to Council Bluffs and died there on January 3, 1916.

Dodge, Mary Elizabeth Mapes (1831–1905), author and editor. Born on January 26, 1831, in New York City, Mary Mapes was well educated at home, where her parents frequently entertained such prominent men as William Cullen Bryant and Horace Greeley. In 1851 she married William Dodge, a lawyer whose death seven years later left her with two children to support. She turned to writing and her work quickly found acceptance in juvenile magazines. Her first book for children, *Irvington Stories*, appeared in 1864 and was followed the next year by *Hans Brinker, or The Silver Skates*, a carefully researched story of Dutch youth that came to rank as a classic of children's literature. Combining a wholesome sense of adventure with a simple and cheerful outlook, Mrs. Dodge's work was highly successful in a field where morbid sermonizing and stifling didacticism had often dominated. Subsequent books included *A Few Friends and How They Amused Themselves*, 1869; *Rhymes and Jingles*, 1874; *Theophilus and Others*, 1876; *Donald and Dorothy*, 1883; and *The Land of Pluck*, 1894. Her stories were printed in the leading periodicals of the day and she was acknowledged the preeminent author in the field of U.S. children's literature. In 1870 she became associate editor of *Hearth and Home* and three years later was named the first editor of the newly founded *St. Nicholas Magazine*; she held the position for the rest of her life, building the periodical into the foremost in its field. Her success was aided by the participation of her literary friends—among them Bryant, Henry Wadsworth Longfellow, and John Greenleaf Whittier—some of whom wrote their only juvenile works for her. Two books for young children were compiled from her own contributions to *St. Nicholas*—*Baby Days*, 1876, and *Baby World*, 1884. Mrs. Dodge died on August 21, 1905, at her summer home in Onteora Park, New York.

Doherty, Henry Latham (1870–1939), business leader. Born in Columbus, Ohio, on May 15, 1870, Doherty left school at twelve and went to work as an office boy for the Columbus Gas Company. Possessed of a remarkably quick and penetrating mind, he rapidly absorbed everything about the operations of the company and the latest technological advances in the utilities field and by 1890 had risen to the position of chief engineer. He later became general manager of Emerson McMillin & Company, a banking firm that controlled numerous utilities companies, and was its leading troubleshooter. In 1905 he organized Henry L. Doherty & Company to provide financial and engineering consultation services. In 1910 he formed the Cities Service Company as a holding company controlling a rapidly growing string of utilities. As president he oversaw the extension of Cities Service into natural gas, electricity, and petroleum production; and with a grasp of the potential benefits of rational cooperation among the three fields, built the company into a giant of the industry. His keen appreciation of technology, to which his own contributions were covered in some 140 highly diverse patents, enabled him to keep abreast of all developments relevant to utilities and to lead the way in applying them. The rapid growth of Cities Service, which eventually controlled more than 200 utilities and petroleum operations, was brought about largely by Doherty's financial sleight of hand. His manipulations became almost legendary and played a major role in hastening passage of the Securities Act of 1933 and the Public Utility Holding Company Act of 1935, both designed to end or restrain many of the practices in which Doherty, among others, had freely indulged. After a lengthy illness he died in Philadelphia on December 26, 1939.

Doisy, Edward Adelbert (1893–   ), biochemist. Born on November 13, 1893, in Hume, Illinois, Doisy graduated from the University of Illinois in 1914 and received his master's degree two years later. He was an assistant in biochemistry at the Harvard University Medical School in 1915–1917 and after two years in the army during World War I returned to Harvard to take his Ph.D. in 1920. From 1919 to 1923 he was on the faculty of the Washington University Medical School in St. Louis. In 1923 he became professor of biochemistry at the St. Louis University School of Medicine and in 1924 assumed the additional duties of head of the department. In his researches Doisy attacked a variety of problems concerning the presence, effects, and nature of various chemical substances in the body. He investigated the inorganic constituents of the blood; the chemical action of insulin, particularly of a high-potency form of his own preparation, on the blood; buffer compounds in, and the transportation of carbon dioxide by the blood; and other related topics. A research project on estrogenic compounds resulted in 1929 in the first isolation in pure crystalline form of a female sex hormone, theelin, later known as estrone; he also isolated and investigated theelol (estriol) and dihydrotheelin (estradiol). Synthesized forms of these hormones proved of great value in treating certain endocrinal disturbances, including menopausal symptoms. In 1936 he began a search for a blood factor believed to be responsible for promoting clotting. Vitamin K, as it was named, was isolated and in one of its forms synthesized by its original investigator C. P. Henrik Dam of Denmark; Doisy achieved the same result independently in 1939. Doisy developed methods for producing and handling the delicate compound, which was of great value in treating hemorrhages in the newborn and others lacking natural defenses. For their work Doisy and Dam were awarded jointly the 1943 Nobel Prize for Physiology and Medicine. Remaining at St. Louis University, Doisy was the recipient of many other honors and awards and was president of the American Society of Biological Chemists in 1943–1945 and of the Society for Experimental Biology and Medicine in 1949–1951. He retired from the renamed Edward A. Doisy department of biochemistry in 1965.

Dole, Sanford Ballard (1844–1926), public official and president of the Republic of Hawaii. Born on April 23, 1844, in Honolulu, the son of American missionaries, Dole was educated in missionary schools, and from 1866 to 1868 attended Williams College and studied law. He was admitted to the Massachusetts bar and returned to Honolulu, where he practiced law for 20 years. Sympathetic to the principles of democracy, he nevertheless recognized the suitability of a monarchy for the Hawaiian people; but he was critical of the conduct of the monarchy, and by 1880 had helped to bring about the ousting of its irresponsible ministry. He served in the legislature from 1884 to 1887 and in 1887 played a prominent role in the reform movement that secured a liberal constitution. From 1887 to 1893 he was associate justice of the supreme court of the islands. In the latter year another revolution broke out. Although not one of the original organizers, he soon became a leader of the movement and when Queen Liliuokalani was deposed he became head of the new provisional government. Answering a letter from President Grover Cleveland in which the president opposed the annexation of Hawaii sought by the revolutionists and asked instead that the overthrown regime be restored, Dole emphasized his belief that the two nations would eventually unite, but was firm in criticizing Cleveland for interfering in Hawaiian affairs. In 1894 the Republic of Hawaii was organized with Dole as president. Relations with the United States remained distant until President William McKinley took office. In January 1898 Dole went to Washington and by summer of that year the annexation of the Hawaiian Republic by the United States was complete. When the Territory of Hawaii was organized in 1900, Dole was appointed its first governor. He resigned in 1903 to become U.S. district judge for Hawaii and remained in that post until 1915. He died in Honolulu on June 9, 1926.

Donnelly, Ignatius (1831–1901), reformer, public official, and author. Born in Philadelphia on November 3, 1831, Donnelly early took up the study of law and was admitted to the bar in 1852 but, finding legal practice dull, he set out for Minnesota in 1856. On the banks of the Mississippi near St. Paul he founded Nininger City in the hope of developing a great Western metropolis. He encouraged settlers and saw to it that the town was well supplied with cultural resources. The panic of 1857 destroyed the dream, but Donnelly remained in Nininger City when everyone else left. He entered politics, joined the Republican party, and was elected lieutenant governor of Minnesota in 1859. From 1863 to 1869 he served in the House of Representatives. He became estranged from the Republicans and employed his talents as an orator for a succession of protest-based parties, from the Liberal Republicans to the Grangers and the Greenbackers, in the period of growing Western discontent. From 1874 to 1879 he was in the state senate while editing the weekly *Anti-Monopolist*. Turning for a time to literary pursuits, he wrote in 1882 *Atlantis: The Antediluvian World*, a study in support of the theory of the lost continent; the next year appeared *Ragnarok: The Age of Fire and Gravel*, hypothesizing that ages ago the earth had come into contact with a comet. In 1888 appeared his most famous work, *The Great Cryptogram*, in which, with vast ingenuity, he sought to demonstrate that the works attributed to Shakespeare had actually been written by Francis Bacon, a theory he explored further in *The Cipher in the Plays and on the Tombstone*, 1899. *Caesar's Column*, a utopian novel that for a time rivaled Edward Bellamy's *Looking Backward* in popularity, appeared in 1891. Donnelly had continued all the while his interest in reform politics and took a leading role in the founding of the Populist party, writing most of its Omaha platform in 1892. Known by this time as the "Great Apostle of Protest," Donnelly served again in the state legislature and ran for vice-president on the Anti-Fusion Populist ticket in 1900. He died on January 1, 1901, in Minneapolis.

Donovan, William Joseph (1883–1959), soldier and public official. Born on January 1, 1883, in Buffalo, New York, "Wild Bill" Donovan graduated from Columbia University in 1905 and remained to take a law degree two years later. He began practice in Buffalo and in 1912 also began a military career by organizing a cavalry troop for the New York National Guard. He saw service on the Mexican border with his troop and by the outbreak of World War I held the rank of major. Serving with the 27th ("Rainbow") Division and later as colonel of the 165th Infantry—the former "Fighting 69th" New York regiment—he won numerous decorations, including the Congressional Medal of Honor, and acquired the nickname "Wild Bill." After a time as an unofficial U.S. military observer in Asia he resumed his law practice in 1920; becoming active in Republican politics, he served as U.S. district attorney for western New York from 1922 to 1924, as assistant U.S. attorney general from 1924 to 1925, and as assistant to the attorney general from 1925 to

1929. During that time he was also a member of several international commissions, including the Rio Grande Compact Commission, of which he was chairman, in 1928, and the Colorado River Commission, also as chairman from 1929. In the latter year he declined President Herbert C. Hoover's offer of the governorship of the Philippines. From 1935 to 1941 Donovan made a number of trips as an unofficial observer for the U.S. government to Italy, Spain, England, and the Balkans. He then drew up, at the request of President Franklin D. Roosevelt, comprehensive plans for a military intelligence agency to operate throughout the world. Upon creation of the Office of Strategic Services (OSS) in 1942 Donovan was named to direct its activities. Given the rank of brigadier general in 1943 and promoted to major general in 1944, he oversaw the wide-ranging operations of the OSS, which gathered intelligence and operated clandestinely behind the lines in every theater of World War II, until its dissolution in 1945. After brief service as aide to Justice Robert H. Jackson at the Nuremberg trials of Nazi war criminals he again returned to private practice. On appointment by President Dwight D. Eisenhower he was U.S. ambassador to Thailand from 1953 to 1954. Donovan died on February 8, 1959, in Washington, D.C.

Mr. Dooley, see Dunne, Finley Peter

Dooley, Thomas Anthony (1927–1961), physician. Born in St. Louis on January 17, 1927, Dooley entered the University of Notre Dame in 1944 but left shortly afterward to enlist in the navy. After two years of service in the medical corps he returned to Notre Dame to prepare for medical school. He took his M.D. from the St. Louis University School of Medicine in 1953 and began his internship as a medical officer in the Naval Reserve; he was stationed first at Camp Pendleton, California, and later in Japan. In 1954 he volunteered for service on a ship bearing refugees from North to South Vietnam. The only medical man available for 2000 passengers, he was deeply impressed by the immensity of the medical needs of the people of Southeast Asia. He was then sent to Haiphong to organize and manage camps where refugees could await transportation south; with only minimal facilities, his small medical unit processed and cared for more than 600,000 people in less than a year. Transferred back to the United States in 1955, he described his experiences in Vietnam in Deliver Us from Evil, 1956. Resigning from the navy, he used his income from the book to organize a private medical mission to the village of Nam Tha in northern Laos. Sheer persistence and untiring labor enabled him to overcome the suspicions of the people and to begin attacking the problems of disease among a populace largely deprived of modern medical knowledge. In 1957 he returned briefly to the United States and, with Peter D. Comanduras, founded Medico, an international medical-aid mission sponsored by the International Rescue Committee and supported by voluntary contributions. He then returned to Asia, setting up seven hospitals in Cambodia, Laos, and Vietnam. Dooley wrote two more books, The Edge of Tomorrow, 1958, and The Night They Burned the Mountain, 1960, again using his royalties for medical work. His last years were troubled by a malignant cancer; he visited the United States in 1959 for treatment and then a fund-raising tour, and returned again in late 1960. Hospitalized on the second visit, he died in New York City on January 18, 1961.

Doolittle, Hilda (1886–1961), "H.D.," poet. Born on September 10, 1886, in Bethlehem, Pennsylvania, Miss Doolittle entered Bryn Mawr College in 1904 and while a student there formed friendships with Marianne Moore, a fellow student, and with Ezra Pound and William Carlos Williams, who were at the nearby University of Pennsylvania. Ill health forced her to leave college in 1906; five years later she traveled to Europe for what was to have been a vacation but became a permanent stay, mainly in England and Switzerland. Her first published poems, sent to Poetry magazine by Pound, appeared under the initials H.D., which remained thereafter her nom de plume. Other poems appeared in Pound's anthology Des imagistes, 1914, and her first volume of verse, Sea Garden, 1916, established her as a major voice among the radical young Imagist poets. Subsequent volumes included Hymen, 1921; Heliodora and Other Poems, 1924; Collected Poems, 1925; Hippolytus Temporizes, 1927; Red Roses for Bronze, 1931; a translation of Euripides' Ion, 1937; Collected Poems, 1940; The Walls Do Not Fall, 1944; Tribute to Angels, 1945; and Flowering of the Rod, 1946. Over the years her sharp, spare, and rather passionless manner mellowed and took on rich religious and mystic overtones, becoming in the process less modernist and more open to the wider heritage of tradition. H.D. published also a number of prose works, including four novels—Palimpsest, 1926; Hedylus, 1928; The Hedgehog, 1936; and Bid Me to Live, 1960—and the semiautobiographical Tribute to Freud, 1956. Helen in Egypt, verse, was her last book, appearing shortly after her death in Zurich, Switzerland, on September 27, 1961.

Doolittle, James Harold (1896–), soldier and airman. Born on December 14, 1896, in Alameda, California, Jimmy Doolittle grew up there and in Nome, Alaska. He was educated at Los Angeles Junior College and the University of California and in 1917 enlisted in the army; assigned to the Signal Corps, he served as a flying instructor during World War I, was commissioned first lieutenant in the Army Air Corps in 1920, and became deeply involved in the development of military navigation. In 1922 he was granted a degree as of 1918 by the University of California and then sent by the army to the Massachusetts Institute of Technology (MIT) for advanced engineering studies, taking a Sc.D. degree in 1925.

Assigned to various test-facility stations, he spent five more years in diverse phases of aviation, winning a number of trophy races, demonstrating aircraft in South America, and in 1929 making the first successful test of blind, instrument-controlled landing techniques. In 1930 he resigned his commission, retaining the reserve rank of major, and became manager of the aviation department of the Shell Oil Company, where he helped develop aviation fuel. He continued to race, setting a world speed record in 1932, and to serve on various government and military consultative boards during this period. In 1940, shortly before U.S. entry into World War II, he returned to active duty, and after a tour of industrial plants then converting to war production joined Army Air Forces headquarters for an extended period of planning that bore spectacular results in April 1942. In that month, from the deck of the carrier *Hornet*, Doolittle led a flight of 16 B-25 bombers on a daring raid over Japan, hitting targets in Tokyo, Yokohama, and other cities and scoring a huge victory for U.S. morale at a time when Japan's position in the Pacific seemed impregnable. With the rank of brigadier general (soon after major general), and with a Congressional Medal of Honor for the Japan raid, he was transferred to England, where he organized the 12th Air Force and then commanded it during the invasion of North Africa. In successive command of the Allies' Northwest Africa Strategic Air Force and the U.S. 15th and 8th air forces, Doolittle directed intensive bombing of Germany during 1944–1945, winning promotion to lieutenant general in 1944. In 1945, when air operations ended in the European theater, he moved with the 8th Air Force to Okinawa in the Pacific. In 1946, the war over, he returned to reserve status and rejoined Shell Oil as vice-president and director. He continued to serve on numerous advisory boards concerned with military aviation development, notably the National Advisory Committee for Aeronautics from 1948 to 1958, the last two years as chairman; the Air Force Science Advisory Board as chairman in 1955, and the President's Science Advisory Committee in 1957. Doolittle retired from both the air force and Shell Oil in 1959, but remained active in the aerospace industry.

Dorr, Thomas Wilson (1805–1854), political reformer. Born in Providence, Rhode Island, on November 5, 1805, Dorr was educated at Philips Exeter Academy and graduated from Harvard in 1823. Four years later he was admitted to the bar and began practice in Providence. In 1834 he was elected to the state assembly. Rhode Island was at the time still governed under the colonial charter of 1663; power was in the hands of a proprietary class and suffrage was limited to freeholders and their oldest sons. The privilege of instituting civil suits was similarly restricted. After a long period of occasional attempts at reform, public resentment came to a head in 1841. In that year a "People's party" was organized

and a convention called, all without authority from the legislature; a constitution was adopted and, in a referendum held on the principle of universal manhood suffrage, overwhelmingly ratified. The legislature, in retreat, called a similar convention in 1842 and proposed a "Freeman's" constitution embodying most, but not all, of the reforms demanded by the People's party. This constitution was defeated in a referendum. In April 1842 Dorr was elected governor, at the head of a full ticket, in an election held under the People's constitution; Rhode Island thereupon had two governments as the state supreme court refused to recognize the People's Constitution. The incumbent regime declared martial law; appeals to President John Tyler by both sides resulted in lukewarm support being given to the incumbents. Dorr then decided on rebellion; with a small band of followers he attempted to seize the arsenal in Providence. The revolt was a failure and Dorr escaped to Connecticut. He soon returned, gave himself up, and in 1844 was convicted of treason, for which he received a sentence of life imprisonment at hard labor. His sentence was voided by act of the assembly the following year and in 1851 his civil rights were restored. He died on December 27, 1854, in Providence. In the meantime, a second Freeman's convention late in 1842 had made further concessions to the reformers' demands and a new constitution, although still not providing for universal manhood suffrage, was popularly ratified in November 1842.

Dos Passos, John Roderigo (1896–1970), author. Born on January 14, 1896, in Chicago, Dos Passos graduated from Harvard in 1916 and traveled in Spain, intending to study architecture. When the United States entered World War I he enlisted in the volunteer ambulance corps in the French army, served for a time with the Italian Red Cross, and then became a private in the U.S. army medical corps. His war experiences led to the publication of his first two books, *One Man's Initiation—1917*, 1920, about an ambulance driver, and *Three Soldiers*, 1921, a bitter portrayal of war's effects on the book's three major characters. In *Manhattan Transfer*, 1925, he developed a literary style that was revolutionary in its combination of naturalism and the stream-of-consciousness technique. A portrayal in hundreds of brief episodes of the expansive, many-faceted life of New York City, the book reflected his youthfully radical outlook on life, which found fuller expression in his major work, the trilogy *U.S.A.*, comprising *The 42nd Parallel*, 1930; *1919*, 1932; and *The Big Money*, 1936. Focusing on deterioration, absurdity, and helplessness in the three decades at the beginning of the twentieth century, the trilogy traced the lives of various characters against a fragmented, panoramic background of newspaper headlines and stories, advertisements, and songs of the era. Biographies of notable Americans formed ironic backgrounds for the lives of lesser figures, and

"The Camera Eye" revealed the author's opinions of the action in stream-of-consciousness narrative. With the years his work and thought seemed to grow gradually more conservative. A second trilogy, *District of Columbia*, comprising *Adventures of a Young Man*, 1939, *Number One*, 1943, and *The Grand Design*, 1949, was full of disillusionment with radical and even liberal political movements. It was much less successful than *U.S.A.* Later novels included *Most Likely to Succeed*, 1954; *The Great Days*, 1958; and *Midcentury*, 1961. Dos Passos also wrote a number of travel books, historical and biographical studies, and essays. He died in Baltimore on September 28, 1970.

Doubleday, Abner (1819–1893), soldier and sports figure. Born in Ballston Spa, New York, on June 26, 1819, Doubleday attended schools in Auburn and in Cooperstown, where he became known as an organizer of team ball games. After a time spent working as a surveyor he entered West Point; graduating in 1842, he was assigned to the artillery and during the Mexican War served under Gen. Zachary Taylor at Monterrey and elsewhere. During 1856–1858 he saw action against the Seminoles in Florida and later was stationed at various posts on the Atlantic coast, in 1860 being assigned to Charleston Harbor, where in April 1861 he manned the first of Fort Sumter's guns to respond to the sudden South Carolina bombardment. In May he was promoted to major and for nearly a year served with an infantry regiment in the Shenandoah Valley and around Washington, D.C. Early in 1862 he was made a brigadier general of volunteers and during the year took part in the major battles in Maryland and northern Virginia: the second battle of Bull Run (Manassas), South Mountain, Antietam, and Fredericksburg. As major general he commanded a division at Gettysburg and on the death of Gen. J. F. Reynolds on the first day he succeeded to command of the 1st Corps, holding the field against heavy odds. Despite his performance he was returned to divisional command upon the appointment of a new corps commander; bitterly disappointed, he nonetheless continued to render valuable service through the second and third days of the battle. Doubleday was thereafter on duty in Washington, and in 1866 reverted to the regular-army rank of lieutenant colonel. He advanced to colonel in 1867 and retired from the army in 1873. He settled in Mendham, New Jersey, and died there on January 26, 1893. During the late years of the nineteenth century, as baseball grew into a national sport and pastime, much interest in its origins developed; many who championed the notion of baseball as a native American game nominated Doubleday as its originator, citing his sports activities in Cooperstown and giving the year 1839 for his invention of the game. The story became widespread and in 1907 Albert G. Spalding, baseball player and sporting-goods manufacturer, set up a committee of leading figures in professional baseball to research the history of the game. In its 1908 report the committee ratified the common theory, which subsequently became firmly implanted in American lore. Later investigations showed that a game very similar to baseball, and often called by that name, had been played in America, and even in England, much before Doubleday's time. A variant of the traditional English game of rounders, it had been known in the American colonies as town-ball and by other names and resembled modern baseball much more closely than did the "one-(two, three, or four) old-cat" game cited as baseball's ancestor by the Spalding committee; old cat, a bat-and-ball game, was apparently played when there were too few players for baseball. Doubleday's name remained nonetheless connected with baseball; in 1920 the village of Cooperstown dedicated Doubleday Field as the game's birthplace and in 1939, the supposed centennial of the game's invention, the National Baseball Hall of Fame was established there.

Doubleday, Frank Nelson (1862–1934), publisher. Born on January 8, 1862, in Brooklyn, New York, Doubleday attended the Polytechnic Institute of Brooklyn and at the age of fifteen went to work for the publishing house of Charles Scribner's Sons. He advanced rapidly, in 1884 reviving and editing the *Book Buyer* magazine and becoming business manager of *Scribner's Magazine* on its founding in 1887. In 1897, after 20 years with Scribner's, he joined Samuel S. McClure in organizing Doubleday & McClure; three years later Walter Hines Page joined the firm, which became Doubleday, Page & Company. In addition to a large and important trade-book list the firm published a number of periodicals, including *World's Work*, established in 1900 with Page as editor, *Country Life in America*, and *Garden and Home Builder*. In 1910 Doubleday moved his printing and distributing operations to Garden City, New York, opening there the Country Life Press. He also built a chain of retail book stores, eventually more than 30 in number, and in 1920 bought a half interest in the Heinemann publishing company in England, later acquiring full control. In 1927 the firm absorbed the George H. Doran Company and became Doubleday, Doran & Company, a title retained until 1946, when it was renamed Doubleday & Company. As a publisher Doubleday combined a keen business sense with a warm appreciation for books and writers; among his authors were Frank Norris, Henry George, Hamlin Garland, Gene Stratton Porter, O. Henry, Booth Tarkington, Edna Ferber, Sinclair Lewis, Ellen Glasgow, Joseph Conrad, and Rudyard Kipling. With Kipling he had a particularly close relationship and from him acquired the nickname "Effendi" (Arabic for "chief"), suggested by his initials, by which he was widely known. In 1910 he wrote *A Plain American in England* under the pseudonym "Charles T. Whitefield." Doubleday died on January 30, 1934, in Coconut Grove, Florida.

Dougherty, Walter Hampden, *see* Hampden, Walter

Douglas, Lloyd Cassel (1877–1951), religious teacher and author. Born in Columbia City, Indiana, on August 27, 1877, Douglas graduated from Wittenberg College in 1900 and three years later reecived a degree from Hamma Divinity School. Ordained in the Lutheran church, he assumed a pastorate in North Manchester, Indiana, later moving to ministerial duties elsewhere and from 1911 to 1915 serving as director of religious work at the University of Illinois. He later turned to the Congregational church and held pastorates in Michigan, Ohio, Los Angeles, and Montreal. Although he had written a few religious studies beginning in 1920, he did not begin to write fiction until he was in his fifties; but his first novel, *Magnificent Obsession,* 1929, was a great success and was later made into a motion picture. *Forgive Us Our Trespasses* appeared in 1932, and the following year Douglas retired from active pastoral work to devote full time to writing. Over the next several years he was consistently among the most popular authors in the United States, producing *Precious Jeopardy,* 1933; *Green Light,* 1935; *White Banners,* 1936; *Home for Christmas,* 1937; *Disputed Passage,* 1939; *Dr. Hudson's Secret Journal,* later adapted for a television series, 1939, and *Invitation to Live,* 1940. While the optimistic and direct religious message of his books, combined with a pleasant if undistinguished literary style, attracted a huge readership, the works suffered, in the estimates of most critics, from a strong tendency to sermonize and an overly simplistic view of the world. In 1942 Douglas published his greatest success, *The Robe,* which remained on the bestseller lists for three years and sold in the millions of copies; it was made into the first CinemaScope film in 1953 and was equally successful in that medium. *The Big Fisherman,* another best seller, appeared in 1949, and in 1951 he published an autobiography, *A Time to Remember.* Douglas died in Los Angeles on February 13, 1951.

Douglas, Stephen Arnold (1813–1861), public official and political leader. Born in Brandon, Vermont, on April 23, 1813, Douglas attended schools in his native town and in Canandaigua, New York. He was for a time apprenticed to a cabinetmaker but in 1833, having begun the study of law, he drifted West; settling finally in Jacksonville, Illinois, he won admission to the bar in 1834 and quickly became active in local politics. Rising rapidly to a position of leadership in the Illinois Democratic party, he established effective party organization and discipline and was elected a public prosecutor in 1835 and to the legislature in 1836. In 1837 President Martin Van Buren appointed him federal land registrar in Springfield, which had just become the state capital. For a few months in 1840–1841 he was secretary of state of Illinois and in 1841 was appointed a judge of the state supreme court. Douglas entered upon the national scene with his election to the

House of Representatives in 1843. From the outset he was a prominent and active figure, his political acumen, vast energy, and remarkably short, stout physique combining to earn him the nickname of "the Little Giant." He was an ardent proponent of Western expansion under the banner of Manifest Destiny and strongly supported the U.S. claim to Oregon lands extending to 54° 40′N (he bitterly criticized President James K. Polk's compromise on the 49th parallel); he also supported the annexation of Texas and the Mexican War. In 1847 he was elevated to the Senate, where he was immediately made chairman of the Committee on Territories. The position was, in the aftermath of the Mexican War, one of particular sensitivity, and Douglas was quickly thrust into the thick of the mounting controversy over slavery in the territories. Not a slaveholder (although his wife had inherited slaves), Douglas nonetheless had close ties in both North and South; his own constituency was mixed and he was deeply concerned with maintaining support for the party in all sections of the country. His principal efforts at compromise centered on his own doctrine of "popular sovereignty," (a term he introduced only in 1854 to replace the less dignified phrase "squatter sovereignty"), whereby the issue of slavery would be settled by the people of the several territories themselves. He succeeded in including provision for popular sovereignty in the organizing acts for the territories of Utah and New Mexico and in 1850, the same year in which he secured passage of the Illinois Central Railroad enabling act, he played a major role in effecting the adoption of the measures comprising the great Compromise of 1850. In 1854, however, he submitted to the Senate the Kansas-Nebraska Bill, which in providing for popular sovereignty in those territories explicitly repealed the Missouri Compromise and raised the slavery controversy to fever pitch. While he adroitly maneuvered the bill into law, he lost considerable Northern support. Douglas had, despite his youth, been a serious contender for the Democratic presidential nomination in 1852 and he was again considered in 1856. Returning to Washington in 1857, he supported the administration of James Buchanan until December, when he broke with the president and much of the party to denounce the proslavery Lecompton constitution in Kansas, a courageously independent act that lost him much Southern support without winning a compensating gain in the North. In the same year the Supreme Court's decision in the Dred Scott case dealt a serious blow to his cherished popular-sovereignty doctrine by declaring that the Constitution forbade the regulation of slavery by Congress and therefore, by implication, even by the people of a territory. In his campaign for re-election to the Senate in 1858 he engaged in the series of debates with his Republican opponent, Abraham Lincoln, that brought Lincoln to national attention; Lincoln hammered away, with considerable effect, at Douglas's seeming inconsistency in maintaining his adherence to popular sovereignty while professing approval of the Dred Scott decision. In the debate at Freeport, Illinois, Douglas attempted to reconcile the two in his "Freeport Doctrine," which placed reliance —somewhat dubiously, it seemed to most—on restrictive legislation and the police power for the protection of slavery in a territory; the notion further antagonized proslavery elements, but Douglas was reelected with the aid of a gerrymandered legislature. Afterward, Southern Democrats in the Senate caused him to lose his committee chairmanship. At the 1860 Democratic convention in Charleston, South Carolina, several Southern delegates withdrew in protest against the adoption of a popular-sovereignty plank in the platform. Douglas led the candidates for nomination through 57 ballots but failed to achieve the necessary majority; reconvened in Baltimore two months later, the convention finally nominated him after the withdrawal of more Southern delegates. The bolting states held their own convention, nominated John C. Breckinridge, and hopelessly split the party, opening the way for Lincoln's victory by a narrow popular margin; Douglas ran second in the popular voting and received support from every section of the country. After a vigorous but admittedly useless campaign Douglas threw himself into the work of unifying the country and gave unreserved support to Lincoln. Exhausted by a strenuous speaking tour of the border and Western states, he succumbed to typhoid fever and died in Chicago on June 3, 1861.

Douglas, William Orville (1898–1980), justice of the Supreme Court and author. Born in Maine, Minnesota on October 16, 1898, Douglas was educated at Whitman College, from which he received his B.A. in 1920, and at Columbia Law School, where he gained his law degree in 1925. He was a member of the faculty of the Columbia Law School from 1925 to 1928, and was a professor of law at Yale from 1928 to 1936. He collaborated with the Department of Commerce on studies of bankruptcy from 1929 to 1932 and was named to the Securities and Exchange Commission (SEC) in 1936. He was chairman of the commission from 1937 to 1939, the year that President Franklin D. Roosevelt appointed him to the Supreme Court. Although relatively young, he had been an exceptional law professor and member of the SEC, and his nomination to fill the seat previously occupied by Justice Louis D. Brandeis was widely hailed. He soon established himself as a vigorous though controversial member of the court, generally on its liberal side, wrote many of its opinions in cases involving complicated financial questions, and made numerous pronouncements in behalf of civil liberties. His majority decision in *Terminiello* v. *Chicago*, 1949, declared that free speech must be guaranteed even to a speaker who "stirs the public to anger, invites disputes, brings about . . . unrest, or creates a disturbance." In the course of the opinion he went on to suggest that free speech, in certain circumstances, might serve its fundamental purposes by creating just such conditions. He wrote several notable dissents in antitrust cases, arguing that the Court, and indeed all of American law, tended rather to support monopoly than to oppose it. Apart from his legal work, he was an active outdoorsman, and he wrote a long series of books recounting his experiences in various wilderness and near-wilderness areas of the world; among them were *Of Men and Mountains*, 1950; *Beyond the High Himalayas*, 1952; *North from Malaya*, 1953; *West of the Indus*, 1958; *My Wilderness: East to Katahdin*, 1960; *My Wilderness: The Pacific West*, 1961; *Muir of the Mountains*, 1961, an account of the great naturalist John Muir; and *A Wilderness Bill of Rights*, 1965. He was a strong supporter of conservation measures. A controversial figure all his life, he continued to be an unpredictable and courageous champion of the havenots in society and to befuddle and occasionally outrage the haves. Other books by Justice Douglas were *An Almanac of Liberty*, 1954; *We The Judges*, 1955; *America Challenged*, 1960; *A Living Bill of Rights*, 1961; *Mr. Lincoln and the Negroes*, 1963; *The Bible and the Schools*, 1966; *Points of Rebellion*, 1969; and *Holocaust or Hemispheric Cooperation: Cross Currents in Latin America*, 1971. Douglas retired from the Court in November 1975 and died on January 19, 1980, in Washington, D.C.

Douglass, Frederick (1817–1895), social reformer, journalist, and public official. Born into slavery in Tuckahoe, Maryland, probably in February 1817, Frederick Augustus Washington Bailey was sent to Baltimore as a household servant at the age of nine and there learned to read. In 1833 he was returned to his plantation home as a field hand. An attempted escape in 1836 failed and not long thereafter he was apprenticed to a ship caulker in Baltimore. In 1838, disguised as a sailor, he escaped to New York City; he soon moved to New Bedford, Massachusetts, and adopted the name by which he was afterward known. In 1841 he delivered an extemporaneous speech before a meeting of the Massachusetts Anti-Slavery Society and was immediately hired as an agent of the society. For the next four years he traveled and spoke throughout the North. Disturbed by rumors, based largely on his considerable oratorical ability, that he had not actually been a slave, he published in 1845 his *Narrative of the Life of Frederick Douglass, an American Slave*. Then, to avoid capture, he went to Great Britain, where he continued his anti-slavery efforts for two years. Upon his return his freedom was purchased by public subscription and in Rochester, New York, he founded the *North Star* with Martin R. Delany as joint editor. The newspaper continued publication for 16 years, after 1851 under the name *Frederick Douglass's Paper*. Although at first he followed William Lloyd Garrison, he soon adopted a more conservative approach to abolition; he fled to Canada briefly in 1859 when he was falsely accused of supporting John Brown's raid. He was active in organizing

Negro troops for service in the Civil War. After the war he was assistant secretary to the Santo Domingo Commission, from 1877 to 1881 he was marshal of the District of Columbia, from 1881 to 1886 District recorder of deeds, and from 1889 to 1891 minister to Haiti. Later revisions of his autobiography appeared as *My Bondage and My Freedom*, 1855, and *Life and Times of Frederick Douglass*, 1881. He died on February 20, 1895, in Anacosta Heights, D.C.

Dove, Arthur Garfield (1880–1946), painter. Born in Canandaigua, New York, on August 2, 1880, Dove attended Cornell University and then began working as an illustrator, contributing to various magazines. By 1907 he had decided to turn to serious painting and for a time studied in Paris. One of the most powerful influences on him was photographer Alfred Stieglitz, whom he met in 1910 and in whose 291 Gallery in New York City he exhibited regularly thereafter. Generally held to be the first American abstract artist, Dove nonetheless allowed glimpses of subject matter to appear in many of his works; some paintings, with muted and rolling color masses, suggested landscapes or other natural forms, while others, reminiscent of the work of Albert Pinkham Ryder, were phantasms that bordered on surrealism. Working in many media, he saw his art as an interplay of visual forces; he later created a distinguished body of work in collage form that considerably influenced many younger artists. In later years he was a leader in the movement to win royalty rights for artists for the reproduction of their works. Dove died in Huntington, New York, on November 23, 1946.

Dow, Charles Henry (1851–1902), editor and economist. Born in Sterling, Connecticut, on November 6, 1851, Dow led an obscure early life and in 1872 became a reporter for the nationally known *Springfield Republican*. Three years later he moved to the *Providence Star* for a year and then to the *Providence Journal*, for which he wrote editorials on financial and economic topics and in 1879 a series of vivid reports from Colorado, reporting on the silver-mining boom. In 1880 he moved to New York City and after two years with a financial news service joined Edward D. Jones in organizing Dow Jones & Company to provide news bulletins—"flimsies"—of interest to financial institutions on Wall Street. A year later, in 1883, they began distributing a news summary sheet; this evolved in a few years into a full daily newspaper, the *Wall Street Journal*, first published under that name in July 1889. By that time Dow had already begun compiling, for the subscribers to his bulletin, surveys of stock-price averages, an analysis he is generally credited with originating. Under his editorship the *Journal* grew quickly into the most authoritative and influential publication in the field, and in his own writings for it Dow laid the basis for an increasingly sophisticated method of market-trend analysis that was later elaborated by others into the

"Dow theory." The Dow-Jones averages remained among the most useful and trusted indicators of financial conditions. From 1885 to 1891 he was a member of the New York Stock Exchange and a partner in the brokerage firm of Goodbody, Glyn & Dow, and he remained publisher and editor of the *Wall Street Journal* until 1901, when Clarence Barron succeeded him. Dow died in Brooklyn, New York, on December 4, 1902.

Dow, Herbert Henry (1866–1930), chemist and industrialist. Born on February 26, 1866, in Belleville, Ontario, Dow was the son of American parents with whom he moved first to Connecticut and later to Cleveland. He graduated in 1888 from the Case School of Applied Science (now part of Case Western Reserve University) after writing a thesis on the chemistry of Ohio brines that interested his teachers. With their encouragement he studied the brines of Michigan, Pennsylvania, and West Virginia as well as presented a paper on the subject before the American Association for the Advancement of Science in that year. Continuing his researches, he soon discovered and patented an easy and inexpensive electrolytic method for extracting bromine from brine and in 1889, after a year of teaching at the Homeopathic Hospital College in Cleveland, organized a company in Canton, Ohio, to produce bromine commercially. The company soon failed but his process, with improvements, was successfully applied by the Midland Chemical Company in Midland, Michigan, which in its operations also made the first successful commercial use of the newly developed direct-current generator. Dow moved on to the problem of extracting chlorine from brine and in 1895 organized a company for that purpose in Navarre, Ohio, moving it to Midland the next year; in 1897 he founded the Dow Chemical Company, which absorbed Midland Chemical in 1900. The Dow company produced bromine and chlorine in quantity and soon added bleaching powder, insecticides, and pharmaceuticals to its list of products as Dow continued to find new ways of utilizing various chemically rich brines. Magnesium was extracted beginning in 1918, and various alloys were marketed under the trade name Dowmetal. Solving the problems of continuous espsom salts production led to the development of equipment for the automatic processing of ocean brines. Dow also introduced the first process for making synthetic indigo in the United States, devised means to produce synthetic phenol and aniline, and was the first to extract iodine from brine, using first Louisiana brine and later California petroleum brine. On the strength of his single-minded dedication to the full utilization of brines, Dow was granted more than 100 patents and built up a company that became one of the giants of the chemical industry. He died in Rochester, Minnesota, on October 15, 1930.

Dow, Neal (1804–1897), reformer. Born in Portland, Maine, on March 20, 1804, Dow was the son of Quaker parents. Upon completing a course at the Friends' Academy in New Bedford, Massachusetts, he joined his father's tannery business and rose in time to partner while developing extensive interests in other enterprises and becoming one of the most prominent citizens of Portland. He early enlisted in the temperance movement, his experiences as an employer and as a member of the town fire department having convinced him that strong drink was the principal root of misery and misfortune among the working classes. He was a member of the Maine Charitable Mechanics' Association and in 1834 represented the Portland Young Men's Temperance Society at the state convention that organized the Maine State Temperance Society. In 1838 he led in forming the Maine Temperance Union to promote total abstinence through legislative means. After eight years of intensive public education and lobbying, a law prohibiting the sales of liquor was passed by the legislature. In 1851 Dow was elected mayor of Portland and, with an apparent public mandate, drew up and submitted to the legislature a more stringent bill that strengthened the lax enforcement provisions of the 1846 measure. The bill was passed; known as the "Maine Law," it attracted national, even worldwide, attention to its author. Within a few years several other states had followed Maine's lead in prohibiting liquor. Dow presided over the World's Temperance Convention in New York City in 1853. Soon after his reelection as mayor in 1855 a temporary public reaction led to the repeal of the Maine Law, but in 1858 he secured its reenactment. In 1861 he was appointed colonel of a Maine volunteer regiment for Civil War duty and the following year, while attached to Gen. Benjamin F. Butler's Gulf command, was promoted to brigadier general of volunteers. He was a prisoner of the Confederate army for some months and soon after his release in 1864 resigned his commission. After the Civil War he again traveled widely in the United States and Great Britain lecturing on prohibition and in 1880 was the Prohibition party's presidential candidate. In 1884 he played a major role in winning approval of a prohibition amendment to the Maine constitution. Dow died in Portland on October 2, 1897.

Downing, Andrew Jackson (1815–1852), horticulturist, architect, and landscape designer. Born in Newburgh, New York, on October 30, 1815, Downing completed his formal schooling at the Montgomery Academy at sixteen and joined an elder brother in operating a nursery that had been begun by their father. The many fine country estates near the Downing home provided excclient opportunities to study rural architecture and landscaping. Personable and outgoing, he became friendly with many estate owners, discussing the botany of the area, the construction of their houses, and the maintenance of their gardens, and he wrote essays on these subjects for Boston journals. His work lacked depth and

precision, however, and he returned to nurseries to gather information. *A Treatise on the Theory and Practice of Landscape Gardening*, 1841, established him as an authority on that subject and ran through numerous editions. *Cottage Residences*, 1842, applied the principles of design and function stated in *Landscape Gardening* to modest houses. *The Fruits and Trees of America*, 1845, written with his brother Charles, was the most complete work of its kind, and *Architecture of Country Houses*, 1850, long remained in general use. In 1846 he began to edit a new periodical, the *Horticulturist*, which included a section of correspondence between Downing and his readers. Subsequently, in partnership with Calvert Vaux, he designed estates, both houses and gardens, in the Hudson valley. Of his houses, some were light wooden structures with overhanging rooftops, others were asymmetrically designed cottages with breezy, skeletal porches, and still others were neogothic in style. Recognized as the foremost practitioner of landscaping of the day, he was invited to design the landscaping around the Capitol, the White House, and the Smithsonian Institution in Washington, D.C., but his plans had to be executed by successors, for a fire aboard a steamship on which he was approaching New York harbor led to his death by drowning on July 28, 1852.

Downing, Major Jack, *see* Smith, Seba

Drake, Edwin Laurentine (1819–1880), petroleum entrepreneur. Born on March 29, 1819, in Greenville, New York, Drake grew up there and near Castleton, Vermont. After an elementary education he worked on the family farm until leaving home at nineteen; thereafter he worked in a succession of jobs—hotel clerk in Tecumseh, Michigan; retail clerk in New Haven, Connecticut, and New York City; railway agent in Springfield, Massachusetts; and, from 1850 to 1857, conductor for the New York & New Haven Railroad. At some time toward the end of this period he bought a small amount of stock in George H. Bissell's Pennsylvania Rock Oil Company and late in 1857 made a trip to the site of the company's surface operations near Oil Creek, Pennsylvania. On the way, probably at Bissell's suggestion, he observed the operation of drilling salt-water artesian wells around Syracuse and Pittsburgh and came to share Bissell's belief that drilling would be the best way to obtain petroleum. On his arrival in Titusville, Pennsylvania (with the assumed title of "Colonel"), a new company, Seneca Oil, was organized with Drake as president, and was leased a portion of the Bissell company's land to try the experiment. Drake himself was engaged to supervise the drilling. It took more than a year and a half to work out the many problems involved; the solution to one, the sinking of a retaining pipe liner in the drill hole, was Drake's main technical contribution to the project. Finally, on August 27, 1859, an oil pool was struck at a depth of 69 feet and the world's first oil well was in operation. Drake remained in the oil business for some years, but his poor business sense eventually impoverished him. After a time in New York City he moved to Vermont, then to Long Beach, New Jersey, and in 1870 to Bethlehem, Pennsylvania. In 1873 the citizens of Titusville took up a collection to relieve his poverty and in 1876 he was granted an annuity by the state of Pennsylvania. Drake died in Bethlehem on November 8, 1880.

Draper, Henry (1837–1882), astronomer and physician. Born in Prince Edward County, Virginia, on March 7, 1837, Draper, the son of John W. Draper, was taken by his family to New York City the following year. He graduated from the University of the City of New York (now New York University) with a medical degree in 1857 and after a period of European travel and a year and a half on the staff of Bellevue Hospital was appointed professor of natural science at the university in 1860. He had already developed an interest in astronomy and in that year built an observatory at his father's estate in Hastings-on-Hudson, New York. He constructed a 15½-inch reflecting telescope there that introduced the silver-on-glass mirror to the United States, and made numerous pioneering experiments in celestial photography and spectroscopy. He obtained in 1872 the first spectrogram of a star (Vega) and later made similar studies of the sun, other bright stars, and some of the planets. For his work in organizing the photographic procedures and equipment for an 1874 government expedition to observe the transit of Venus he was honored by a gold medal ordered struck by Congress in 1878. In 1880 he made the first photograph of a nebula, choosing the M42 nebula in Orion, and the next year made the first spectrogram of a comet. Draper had been since 1866 professor of physiology and dean of the medical faculty at the university, and in 1870 he became also professor of analytical chemistry; on the death of his father in 1882 he succeeded to his chair of chemistry, but himself died a short time later, on November 20, 1882, in New York City.

Draper, John William (1811–1882), chemist, physicist, physician, and historian. Born on May 5, 1811, near Liverpool, England, Draper entered London University in 1829 but a short time later emigrated with his family to the United States, settling in Christiansville, Mecklenburg County, Virginia. There he continued the studies and experiments in geology, chemistry, and other fields of science that had occupied him since early youth. He resumed his formal education at the University of Pennsylvania, graduated with a medical degree in 1836, and in the same year was appointed professor of chemistry and of natural philosophy at Hampden-Sydney College. Two years later he became professor of chemistry at the University of the City of New York (now New York University) and in 1839 joined in organizing the university's medical school, in which

he held professorships in chemistry and physiology and of which he became president in 1850. Draper's interests were wide and he made significant contributions in a number of fields. He was excited by the announcement of the daguerreotype process in 1839 and soon developed an improved plate, adding bromine to the silver iodide to produce a coating material of much greater sensitivity than the original. With this plate he was able to greatly reduce the exposure time and consequently to make the first successful portrait daguerreotype in 1840; in the same year he made a daguerreotype of the moon, the first application of a photographic method to astronomy. He had learned the basic daguerreotype process from his friend Samuel F. B. Morse, and he later reciprocated by aiding Morse in the development of long-distance telegraphy. Draper conducted researches into the nature of radiant energy, studying the relations among chemical action, heat, and light, and was an acknowledged forerunner of G. R. Kirchhoff and R. W. Bunsen in developing the notion of spectrum analysis as a powerful tool in chemical research. In 1856 he published *Human Physiology, Statical and Dynamical*, which contained an account of his earlier investigations on the transport of carbon dioxide by the blood, featured the first photomicrographs ever published, and was long a standard text. He delivered a paper before the British Association for the Advancement of Science in 1860 that helped precipitate a famous debate on evolution between Thomas H. Huxley and Bishop Samuel Wilberforce, later expanding it into the highly influential *History of the Intellectual Development of Europe*, 1863. Subsequent books included *Thoughts on the Future Civil Policy of America*, 1865; *History of the American Civil War*, three volumes, 1867–1870; and *History of the Conflict Between Religion and Science*, 1874. A scholar of almost Renaissance breadth, Draper died at his estate in Hastings-on-Hudson, New York, on January 4, 1882.

Dreiser, Theodore (1871–1945), author. Born in Terre Haute, Indiana, on August 27, 1871, Dreiser grew up in a family beset by poverty and not a little religious fanaticism. After a year at the University of Indiana in 1889–1890 he became a newspaper reporter and occasional free-lance writer, working in a number of cities and settling finally in New York City. Under the influence of such writers as Balzac, Dickens, Thomas H. Huxley, and Herbert Spencer, he began to shape his naturalistic view of man as a creature battered by blind forces and his own passions in an amoral, uncaring universe. Translating this attitude into fiction in 1900 with his first novel, *Sister Carrie*, he ran headlong into the first instance of what was to be almost a lifetime of censorship, condemnation, and controversy. The book was for some reason virtually suppressed by its publisher, Frank N. Doubleday, and Dreiser suffered a nervous breakdown as a consequence. He found employment as editor of a series of magazines, including the Butterick chain of romantic pulp magazines, and by 1911 managed to write his second and more successful novel, *Jennie Gerhardt*. He then devoted himself entirely to writing; quickly he produced *The Financier*, 1912, and *The Titan*, 1914, the first two of a trilogy of novels dealing with the world of business and finance. The third volume, *The Stoic*, was published posthumously in 1947. *The Genius*, published in 1915, was violently denounced and suppressed; for a number of years thereafter he wrote mainly minor works—travel books, sketches, essays, short stories. He finally achieved recognition and success with *An American Tragedy*, 1925, a book whose reception benefited much from the changing social mores of the nation and which was later adapted successfully for the stage and the screen. After 1925 Dreiser's output fell off sharply; he ventured into social commentary and into political analysis. Although his plodding, clumsy literary style was more often satirized than imitated, Dreiser was a pioneer in his dispassionately realistic depiction of the new urban America and in his grasp of its peculiar psychology; his work exerted a profound influence on the course of modern American fiction. He died in Hollywood, California, on December 28, 1945.

Dressler, Marie (1869–1934), actress. Born in Cobourg, Ontario, on November 9, 1869, Leila Koerber was the daughter of a poor and sometimes itinerant music teacher and received little schooling while living in a succession of towns in Canada and the United States. At fourteen she left home and joined a touring theatrical company, calling herself "Marie Dressler" after a relative. Periods with other companies, including three years with the George Baker Opera Company, gave her a thorough training in the theater, and after an appearance with Eddie Foy in *Little Robinson Crusoe* in Chicago she made her New York debut in 1892 in Maurice Barrymore's unsuccessful *The Robber of the Rhine*. In 1893 she was in *The Princess Nicotine* with Lillian Russell, and she continued to appear in supporting roles for a number of years, finally winning attention in *The Lady Slavey* in Washington, D.C., in 1896. Other plays followed and in 1906 she toured with Joe Weber, formerly of the great vaudeville team of Weber and Fields. She scored a success at the Palace Theatre in London in 1907 and three years later played her greatest stage role as the lead in *Tillie's Nightmare*, in which, in long runs in New York City and on the road, she sang "Heaven Will Protect the Working Girl." Following an unsuccessful tour in her own show she appeared in a few films made by Mack Sennett, notably *Tillie's Punctured Romance* with Charlie Chaplin in 1914. After World War I, during which she was active in war-bond promotion and in entertaining troops, her stage career suffered a decline, and in 1927 she returned to the movies. In that medium, when she was nearing the age of sixty, she came into her own. Her performance

in *Anna Christie*, 1930, was very well received, and for *Min and Bill* she won an Academy Award in 1931. She appeared also in *One Romantic Night*, *Let Us Be Gay*, *The Late Christopher Bean*, *Prosperity*, *Dinner at Eight*, and other films, but her best-loved and most enduring roles were those she played with robust humor and touching sentiment opposite Wallace Beery—in the unforgettable *Min and Bill*, and in *Tugboat Annie*, 1933. Miss Dressler died on July 28, 1934, in Santa Barbara, California.

Drew, Charles Richard (1904–1950), physician. Born in Washington, D.C. on June 3, 1904, Drew graduated from Amherst College, where he was an outstanding athlete as well as a scholar. He took his medical degree at McGill University in 1933, and taught pathology and surgery at Howard University, subsequently enrolling at Columbia University, where he earned his D.Sc. in 1940. There he conducted research into the properties and preservation of blood plasma. His dissertation outlined an efficient way to store large quantities of blood plasma in "blood banks." As the authority in the field, he organized and directed the blood-plasma programs in the United States and Great Britain during World War II and supervised the American Red Cross blood-donor project; ironically, the Red Cross would not accept donations of his own blood because he was a Negro. As a result of his continued protests and the criticism of others, the Red Cross changed its rule and accepted the blood of Negroes, but kept it in separate banks for black men only. In 1944 he was awarded the Spingarn Medal of the National Association for the Advancement of Colored People (NAACP) for his contributions to science. In 1945 he became professor of surgery at Howard University and chief surgeon at Freedmen's Hospital in Washington, D.C., later becoming chief of staff. Instead of establishing a private practice, he spent his time in teaching and recruiting young Negroes for medical training. On April 1, 1950, he was fatally injured in an automobile accident near Burlington, North Carolina. An untrue story later sprang up that, in need of a blood transfusion, he was turned away from a nearby hospital because of his race, and died on the way to a hospital for Negroes.

Drew, Daniel (1797–1879), financier. Born on July 29, 1797, in Carmel, New York, Drew served briefly in the War of 1812 and then began a livestock business, driving cattle and horses to New York City from upstate and later expanding to the Midwest, bringing in herds from as far as Illinois. He early acquired a reputation for sharp dealing and was known to feed salt to his cattle and then let them drink themselves full in order to increase their weight; the practice was known as "stock watering" and Drew was its master, in that and in the later financial sense of the term. In 1834 he bought an interest in a steamboat line running from Peekskill to New York City; he established the People's Line running to Albany in 1840 and the Stonington Line on Long Island Sound in 1847, competing at every step with Cornelius Vanderbilt's boats. In 1844 he founded the brokerage firm of Drew, Robinson & Company in Wall Street and prospered in the trading of railroad stocks. He invested in the Erie Railroad himself and in 1857 secured election as a director and as treasurer of the line. Placed in a position of control over finances, he was quick to exploit it. Soon after James Fisk and Jay Gould had joined the Erie board of directors the three embarked on a bold scheme to drain the railroad of every possible dollar. Between 1866 and 1868 they fought a spectacularly unscrupulous battle with Vanderbilt over control of the line. Their principal weapon was Drew's issuance of unsecured—"watered"—stock; Vanderbilt won an injunction against the further issue of such stock in 1868, but the three managed to dump 50,000 more shares on the market. Facing arrest in New York, they retreated to Jersey City and barricaded themselves in a hotel; Gould later slipped up to Albany and openly bought legislation legalizing the stock issue. Vanderbilt was forced to compromise. The "Erie War" roused a public outcry but, although it was the most impudent example of the dishonesty rife in high finance at the time, it led to no effective regulation. The three went on to more outrages in bank credit, foreign exchange, and more stock manipulations, reaping huge profits on every hand until 1870, when Fisk and Gould, having lost heavily in their attempt to corner the gold market on "Black Friday" of 1869, turned on Drew and destroyed the value of his Erie holdings. The panic of 1873 wiped out the rest of his fortune and in 1876 he went bankrupt. During his heyday Drew had contributed largely to the Methodist church and had founded the Drew Theological Seminary in Madison, New Jersey, and the Drew Seminary for Young Ladies in his native town. His last years were spent in obscurity in New York City, where he died on September 18, 1879.

Drew, Georgiana Emma, *see under* Barrymore, Maurice

Drew, John (1853–1927), actor. Born in Philadelphia on November 13, 1853, Drew was the son of John and Louisa Lane Drew, both distinguished actors. He himself showed little interest in the theater until he was twenty, when he took a small part in *Cool as a Cucumber* at the Arch Street Theatre, then managed by his mother. After a bit more experience in Philadelphia he made his New York City debut in Augustin Daly's 1875 production of *The Big Bonanza*. He later appeared with Joseph Jefferson in *Rip Van Winkle* and in 1878–1879 toured with his sister Georgiana and her husband, Maurice Barrymore. In 1879 he returned to New York to begin a 14-year association with Daly's company, which he and Ada Rehan led in a long succession of popular comedies; their most successful production of those years was *The Taming of the Shrew*,

which opened in New York in 1887 and was taken to Stratford and London in 1888. In 1892 Drew left Daly for Charles Frohman's young company, drawn both by its contemporary style and by the offer of star billing. In his first Frohman production, *The Masked Ball*, he played opposite Maude Adams and they remained the company's leading couple. An earlier Frohman production, *The Rivals*, 1893, had featured Miss Adams and Drew and the New York debuts of Drew's niece Ethel Barrymore and nephew Lionel Barrymore. Through more than 20 years with the Frohman company Drew rose to a secure position as one of the country's greatest stars, scoring successes in such plays as *The Tyranny of Tears*, *The Will*, *The Duke of Killicrankie*, and *Inconstant George*. After Frohman's death in the sinking of the *Lusitania* in 1915, Drew's career suffered an eclipse. In *The Circle* in 1921 and *The School for Scandal* in 1923 he made something of a comeback and he was enjoying considerable success on the road with *Trelawney of the Wells* in 1927 when he was suddenly taken ill; he died in San Francisco on July 9, 1927. Drew's autobiographical *My Years on the Stage* had appeared in 1922.

Duane, William (1760–1835), journalist. Born near Lake Champlain, New York, on May 17, 1760, Duane was taken to Ireland by his widowed mother in 1765. He took up the printing trade and in 1787 traveled to Calcutta, where he established the *Indian World*. Some time later he was deported for his independent and libertarian views and, after a short and unsatisfactory stay in London, he settled in Philadelphia. He secured an editorial position with Benjamin F. Bache's *Aurora* and from 1798, in sole charge of the paper, made it the leading Jeffersonian journal in the United States. His views led him to agitate against the Alien and Sedition Acts; early in 1799 he was arrested under the Sedition Act but was promptly acquitted. When in the same year he denounced the brutality of an irregular army assembled by Federalists who were hoping for war with France, he was mobbed. A short time later he was again charged with sedition; after several postponements of the trial, the charges were ordered dropped by newly elected President Thomas Jefferson. Duane's steadfast opposition to war with France and to the Alien and Sedition Acts had been instrumental in securing the election of Jefferson in 1800, and consequently the repeal of the acts. Although the removal of the government from Philadelphia to Washington, D.C., lessened his influence, he continued to edit the *Aurora* until 1822 and remained a close friend and valuable supporter of Jefferson, who reciprocated by giving him a lieutenant colonel's commission in 1808. Duane served also as adjutant-general during the War of 1812. After a visit to South America in 1822–1823, he was appointed prothonotary of the Pennsylvania supreme court, a position he retained until his death on November 24, 1835, in Philadelphia.

Dubinsky, David (1892–1982), labor leader. Born on February 22, 1892, in Brest (Brest Litovsk), Russian Poland (now Brest, U.S.S.R.), Dubinsky was originally named Dobnievski. He attended local schools and at the age of ten was apprenticed in his father's bakery in Lodz, where his activities on behalf of a struggling union of bakery workers led to his banishment to Siberia. He escaped and in 1911 emigrated to the United States. In New York City he became a garment worker and joined a cutters' local of the International Ladies Garment Workers Union (ILGWU). He became a naturalized citizen in 1916 and two years later was elected to the local's executive board. Although he was interested in the Socialist party he early denounced Communism and strongly supported U.S. participation in World War I. Dubinsky was elected chairman of his local in 1920, general manager and secretary-treasurer in 1921, and vice-president and board member of the ILGWU in 1922. During the garment workers' strike of 1926 his was the only local to remain out of debt, and in recognition of his astute management he was elected secretary-treasurer of the ILGWU in 1929. Three years later he became president and immediately launched a vigorous membership drive that resulted in a fourfold increase in three years. He joined John L. Lewis in organizing the Committee for Industrial Organization in 1935 to promote industrial unionism over craft unionism, but after the ILGWU was expelled from the American Federation of Labor (AFL) in 1937 he refused to affiliate it with Lewis's new Congress of Industrial Organizations (CIO), leading it instead back into the AFL in 1940. Under his imaginative and dynamic leadership the ILGWU continued to grow, winning greatly increased benefits for workers without resort to crippling strikes and achieving a solvency that allowed it eventually to extend financial aid and, with its own engineering department, technical assistance to manufacturers. The union was among the most successful in the country in combating the infiltration of Communists and racketeers. The ILGWU played an active role in promoting social and political causes, raising money for the campaigns of liberal candidates and reform organizations. Dubinsky himself was a leader in several such movements, joining in the founding of the American Labor party in New York in 1936, the Liberal party of New York in 1944, and Americans for Democratic Action (ADA) in 1947. As a vice-president and board member of the AFL from 1945, he represented it at the International Labor Organization (ILO) in Geneva and in the UN Economic and Social Council. He led in founding the International Federation of Democratic Trade Unions in 1945. In 1955 Dubinsky became a member of the executive council and executive committee of the newly merged AFL–CIO and later was elected a vice-president, holding the post along with the presidency of the ILGWU until his retirement in 1966. He died on September 17, 1982, in New York City.

Du Bois, William Edward Burghardt (1868–1963), historian, educator, author, and reform leader. Born in Great Barrington, Massachusetts, on February 23, 1868, W. E. B. Du Bois was of African, French, and Dutch ancestry. He was educated at Fisk and Harvard universities and soon after obtaining his Ph.D. at Harvard in 1895 joined the faculty of Atlanta University, where he taught economics and history from 1897 to 1910 and edited the *Atlanta University Studies*, 1897–1911. With his *Souls of Black Folk* in 1903 he announced the intellectual revolt against the accommodationist principles of Booker T. Washington that crystalized two years later in the founding, under Du Bois's leadership, of the Niagara Movement. When this group was merged with the newly founded National Association for the Advancement of Colored People (NAACP) in 1909, Du Bois became editor of the association's journal, *Crisis*, holding the post until 1932. In a series of Pan-African Conferences held in 1900, 1919, 1921, 1923, and 1927, he led the call for independence for African colonies, his efforts winning him the 1920 Spingarn Medal of the NAACP. In 1932 he returned to Atlanta University where he was head of the sociology department until 1944, when he rejoined the NAACP as director of research. During 1933–1945 he served as editor in chief of the *Encyclopedia of the Negro*. A thorough scholar and an eloquent public speaker, Du Bois became and remained an influential and profoundly inspiring figure among blacks in the United States and abroad. Others of his books included *The Negro*, 1915; *Darkwater*, 1920; *The Gift of Black Folk*, 1924; *Dark Princess*, 1928; *Black Reconstruction*, 1935; *Dusk of Dawn*, 1940; and *Color and Democracy*, 1945. He was cochairman of the 1945 Pan-African Conference; two years later he published *The World and Africa*. During the 1940s Du Bois began to move from nonideological radicalism toward a Marxist and pro-Soviet viewpoint; this change culminated in his joining the Communist party in 1961. The following year he emigrated to Africa; living in Accra, Ghana, where he became a citizen and was named editor of the proposed *Encyclopedia Africana*. He died in Accra on August 27, 1963; his *Autobiography* appeared five years later.

Dubos, René Jules (1901–1982), bacteriologist. Born on February 20, 1901, in Saint-Brice, France, Dubos graduated from the Institut Nationale Agronomique in Paris in 1921 and from 1922 to 1924 was on the staff of the International Institute of Agriculture in Rome. While there he became interested in soil biology and bacteriology and in 1924 came to the United States to pursue graduate studies at Rutgers University, working at the same time as an instructor and research assistant. Upon taking his Ph.D. in 1927 he joined the Rockefeller Institute for Medical Research, with which, except for a brief period at Harvard in 1942–1944, he was associated until 1957, when he became professor of bacteriology at its successor Rockefeller University. Dubos became a

U.S. citizen in 1938. In his early researches Dubos was a pioneer in the investigation of natural antibiotics. His search for a way to destroy the protective coat surrounding the pneumococcus microbe began with the elegantly simple assumption that a decomposing agent must exist in nature, for otherwise the discarded cases of the microbes would long since have accumulated in huge quantities. In 1929 he found that a certain sample of swamp soil contained such an agent and after ten years' further work succeeded in isolating two, tyrocidine and gramicidin. These proved effective against a broad spectrum of gram-positive bacteria and, although too toxic for internal use, were valuable in treating a variety of external infections. The procedures laid down by Dubos in this work were later adopted by his old teacher, Selman A. Waksman, in the work that led to his discovering streptomycin. Dubos turned to the study of tuberculosis and in 1946 announced his discovery of a method for growing the tubercle bacillus in large quantities in laboratory cultures. His investigation of tuberculosis led him into a broader study of environmental factors in human disease, and he later conducted research into many aspects of man's biological response to his environment, particularly to the polluted urban-industrial environment of his own creation. Voicing concern for the possible long-range effects of many factors introduced by man, from radiation to pesticides, Dubos became a spokesman for a cautious, ecologically sophisticated approach to the control of nature. He wrote a number of widely read and influential books, including *The Bacterial Cell*, 1945; *Louis Pasteur— Free Lance of Science*, 1950; *The White Plague— Tuberculosis, Man and Society*, 1952; *Bacterial and Mycotic Infections of Man*, 1958; *The Mirage of Health*, 1959; *Pasteur and Modern Science*, 1960; *The Dreams of Reason*, 1961; *The Unseen World*, 1962; *The Torch of Life*, 1962; *Health and Disease*, 1965; *Man Adapting*, 1965; *So Human an Animal*, 1968, which was awarded a Pulitzer Prize; and *A God Within*, 1972. With Barbara Ward he wrote the influential United Nations report, *Only One Earth*, in 1972. In 1970 he retired from Rockefeller University to become University Professor and director of environmental studies at the State University of New York. He died on February 20, 1982, in New York City.

Dudley, Thomas (1576–1653), colonial official. Born in Northampton, England, in 1576, to a family of means, Dudley was orphaned early. After commanding a company of troops in an expedition against France in 1597 he became steward to the Earl of Lincoln. At some point he became interested in Puritanism; he was for a time a member of John Cotton's congregation, and he took some part in the formation of the Massachusetts Bay Company. In 1630, along with Governor John Winthrop, he sailed for America as deputy governor of the Massachusetts Bay colony. For the rest of his life he was almost constantly in public office, four times as governor (1634, 1640, 1645, 1650) and 13 times as deputy governor; he also served on numerous public committees. He helped to found New Towne (now Cambridge), Massachusetts, and later lived in Roxbury. He was active in promoting the establishment of a college in Cambridge, was one of Harvard's first overseers, and as governor in 1650 signed the college's charter. In 1643 he was a delegate to the New England Confederation. A harsh and uncompromising Puritan, Dudley was a leading force in the suppression of heresy and dissent in the colony, once even bringing charges against John Cotton. He died on July 31, 1653, in Roxbury.

Duke, James Buchanan (1856–1925), industrialist and philanthropist. Born on December 23, 1856, near Durham, North Carolina, "Buck" Duke experienced poverty during the Civil War. Having served in the Confederate army, his father, Washington B. Duke, arrived home in 1865 and found his farm plundered. The armies had overlooked a planting of leaf tobacco, however, and knowing that a ready market existed in southern North Carolina, Duke made a quick profit. He purchased more tobacco and acquired a large log house in which to process it. The family's subsequent prosperity allowed Buck to attend school in Durham and Eastman Business College in Poughkeepsie, New York. He became an overseer in the tobacco plant and a partner in W. Duke and Sons at eighteen. Besides catering to the vast market for pipe tobacco, cigars, plug, and snuff, the company entered the cigarette business and revolutionized the tobacco industry. All cigarettes had previously been hand-rolled, which satisfied the small demand that then existed. Duke perfected a machine to roll cigarettes faster than the human hand could do it, initiated an international advertising campaign, and reduced the price of his cigarettes, when a government tax was lowered, before other manufacturers did. He established a branch plant in New York City in 1884, capturing the Northern and Western markets. In 1890 the "tobacco war" among five leading cigarette manufacturers led Duke to the American Tobacco Company, with himself as president. The company pursued an aggressive policy and its acquisitions and subsidiaries grew to include the Continental Tobacco Company, the American Snuff Company, the American Cigar Company, the American Stogie Company, and United Cigar Stores Company, formed to provide retail outlets. His invasion of the British market led to the formation of the British-American Tobacco Company. In 1911 the American Tobacco Company was dissolved by the U.S. Supreme Court as being in restraint of trade. Duke was responsible for arranging the reorganization of the components. He helped to found the Southern Power Company; he created a trust fund for his holdings and heavily endowed Trinity College, in Durham, which in 1924 changed its name to Duke University, as well as hospitals, churches, and children's homes in North and South Carolina. He died on October 10, 1925, in New York City, having helped to revolutionize the life style of Americans.

Dukenfield, William Claude, see Fields, W. C.

Dulany, Daniel (1722–1797), colonial figure and lawyer. Born in Annapolis, Maryland, on June 28, 1722, Dulany was educated in England at Eton and Cambridge. Returning to America, he was admitted to the Maryland bar in 1747. From 1751 to 1754 and again in 1756 he was a member of the legislative assembly and, for his support of the proprietary government, was appointed to the ruling council the next year, retaining his seat until the Revolution ended Maryland's colonial status. He served also as commissary general from 1759 to 1761 and for three years thereafter as secretary of the province. He was considered one of the best lawyers in the colonies. Although basically a supporter of the established regime, he vigorously protested what he considered unjust acts of government; it was as a man wishing to be thought of as a loyal British subject rather than as a colonial that he wrote his pamphlet against the Stamp Act of 1765, titling it *Considerations on the Propriety of Imposing Taxes in the British Colonies, for the Purpose of Raising a Revenue, by Act of Parliament.* The popularity he gained with this and other writings was largely lost, however, by his support of other governmental actions. He strongly and consistently opposed the growing radicalism in the colonies, and during the Revolution he remained a Loyalist. In 1781 his property was confiscated; he moved to Baltimore and lived there until his death on March 17, 1797.

Dulles, John Foster (1888–1959), lawyer, public official, and diplomat. Born in Washington, D.C., on February 25, 1888, Dulles graduated from Princeton in 1908 and received his law degree from The George Washington University in 1911. He immediately joined the law firm of Sullivan and Cromwell, with which he was associated during his entire legal career, becoming head of the firm in 1927. In 1917 he served as a special agent for the State Department in Central America; during World War I he was an officer in the army intelligence service, and in 1918–1919 he was counsel to the American Peace Commission at Versailles. Later he helped oversee the payment of war reparations. Dulles figured prominently in the formation of the United Nations (UN); he helped prepare the charter at Dumbarton Oaks, was a member of the U.S. delegation at the San Francisco conference in 1945, and from 1946 to 1949 was the U.S. delegate to the UN General Assembly. In 1949 he served for a brief period in the Senate, filling an unexpired term, and the following year became a consultant for the State Department, in which post he helped win Senate approval of the treaty of peace with Japan. In 1952 President-elect Dwight D. Eisen-

hower appointed him secretary of state. In six years in that position he was the major force in developing U.S. Cold War policy; repudiating President Harry S. Truman's policy of containment of Communist expansion, he advocated active opposition to Soviet policy and the liberation of "captive" nations under Soviet sway. Despite a wealth of knowledge in foreign affairs and vast exertions in behalf of his views, Dulles was often and widely criticized as inflexible and of narrow outlook. He directed the interposition of U.S. naval power between Communist China and the Nationalist-held offshore islands of Quemoy and Matsu; he was the architect of the Eisenhower Doctrine, promulgated in 1957 to meet the threat of Communist aggression and subversion in the Middle East; and he devised the twin strategies of a capability for "massive retaliation" and "brinkmanship." Ill health forced him to resign from the cabinet in April 1959; he died in Washington the next month, on May 24. Among his writings were *War, Peace and Change,* 1939, and *War or Peace,* 1950.

Dunbar, Paul Laurence (1872–1906), poet. Born on June 27, 1872, in Dayton, Ohio, the son of former slaves, Dunbar attended public schools in Dayton, where he was extremely popular with other students, a member of the literary society, editor of the student publication, and composer of the class song at his graduation in 1891. His early ambition to become a lawyer or a minister never materialized; to earn his living he operated an elevator until 1895. Writing poetry consumed his spare hours; his work was published in newspapers, and around Christmas 1893 appeared a collection, *Oak and Ivory,* that was privately printed. He worked in 1893 for Frederick Douglass at the Haitian exhibition at the World's Columbian Exposition in Chicago. Returning to Dayton, he published a second collection of poems, *Majors and Minors,* 1895, which was warmly reviewed by William Dean Howells in *Harper's Magazine* and was subsequently in great demand. *Lyrics of Lowly Life,* 1896, with a sympathetic introduction by Howells, made Dunbar fashionable as a poet and brought him many engagements for readings, one of which took him to England in 1897. Written in dialect, his verse transmitted the nostalgia for old plantation days and the blacks' apprehensive but aggressive and restless feelings about emancipation. A succession of novels, including *The Uncalled,* 1896; *The Love of Landry,* 1900; *The Fanatics,* 1901; and *The Sport of the Gods,* 1902, were, to his regret, not as popular as his poems and short stories. Later volumes of verse included *Lyrics of the Hearthside,* 1899; *Lyrics of Love and Laughter,* 1903; and *Lyrics of Sunshine and Shadow,* 1905. From his return to the United States in 1897 until late 1898 he was an assistant at the Library of Congress. His perseverance and achievement were celebrated among black Americans, and many schools and societies were named for him. He also wrote the Tuskegee Institute school song.

He died in Dayton on February 9, 1906. The collection *Complete Poems* was published posthumously in 1913.

Duncan, Isadora (1878–1927), dancer. Born on May 27, 1878, in San Francisco, the daughter of a poet and a musician, Isadora Duncan was the youngest of four children, all theatrically inclined. Soon after she was born her mother and father were divorced and the family lived in abject poverty. She taught dancing to the children in her neighborhood and with her sister developed a spontaneous style in which they attempted to symbolize music, poetry, and the elements of nature. They won attention in San Francisco and traveled on a spare budget to Chicago and New York City, where Isadora formed an alliance with theatrical manager Augustin Daly. She, her mother, a sister, and a brother embarked on a cattle boat to London. While dancing in a public park, she was discovered by a woman who introduced her through a series of private performances to the elite of London. Similar introductions brought her fame in Paris in 1902. She was hailed in Germany, Austria, and Hungary and after traveling briefly in Greece—she had been profoundly influenced by Greek sculptures she had seen in the British Museum—she returned to Berlin to begin a dancing school for children. Disapproving of what she considered the restrictive bonds of matrimony, she bore two children out of wedlock—a daughter born in 1905 and a son in 1908. At the height of her career, in 1913, they and their nurse were drowned in an accident. She attempted to forget the tragedy through work, but World War I intervened and she was forced to move her school, first to the United States, then to South America, Athens, and Paris in turn. Finally the school disbanded. In 1921 the Soviet government offered her another school in Moscow. There she met and married Sergei Esenin, a wild, dashing poet of the Revolution. On a tour through the United States at the height of the postwar "Red Scare," they were everywhere attacked as Bolshevist spies; as a result she bade a bitter farewell to the United States. Impoverished, they made their way back to the Soviet Union. Their poverty was such that they had to sell her furniture; Esenin went berserk, deserted her, and committed suicide in 1925. The school she had created continued under other management, and she never performed again. Her teaching and dancing had freed ballet from its conservative restrictions and presaged the development of modern expressive dance. Her interpretations of music by Gluck, Brahms, Wagner, and Beethoven were not recorded, but her unrestrained performances in bare feet and loose Grecian-style garb helped to free women's dress and manners. Her last years were spent in France; she died on September 14, 1927, in Nice, strangled when the long scarf she was wearing caught in a wheel of the car in which she was riding. Her autobiography, *My Life*, appeared in 1927.

Dunham, Katherine (1910–   ), dancer, choreographer, and anthropologist. Born in Chicago on June 22, 1910, Miss Dunham grew up there and in nearby Joliet. She early became interested in dance and while a student at the University of Chicago formed a dance group that performed in concert and at the Chicago Civic Opera. On graduating with a degree in anthropology she undertook field studies in the Caribbean area and in Brazil, first with a team from Northwestern University in 1936 and then for nearly two years on a Rosenwald fellowship. By the time she received her M.A. from the University of Chicago she had acquired a vast knowledge of the dances and rituals of the black peoples of tropical America. In 1938 she joined the Federal Theatre Project in Chicago and composed a ballet, *L'Ag'Ya*, based on primitive Caribbean dance; in 1939 she was involved with the cultural studies program of the Federal Writers' Project and in 1940 she moved to New York City, where she choreographed and appeared in the Broadway hit *Cabin in the Sky*. With her own dance troupes— the Tropical Revue and later the Katherine Dunham Dance Company—she performed in concert a number of original dance works, including *Shango, Bahiana, Rites du Passage, Bal Nègre,* and, in forms inspired by the dances of Northern urban blacks, *Flaming Youth 1927, Blues, Burrell House*, and *Ragtime*. She appeared with such major musical organizations as the San Francisco Symphony Orchestra in 1943 and the Los Angeles Symphony in 1945 and later made numerous highly successful tours of the Americas and of Europe. She choreographed and starred in dance sequences in many motion pictures, including *Carnival of Rhythm*, 1941, *Star Spangled Rhythm*, 1942, and *Stormy Weather*, 1943; and in such stage productions as *Carib Song*, 1945, and *Windy City*, 1946. From 1945 she directed the Katherine Dunham School of Cultural Arts in New York City. She was choreographer for the Metropolitan Opera's 1963 production of *Aida* and in 1966 was an adviser to the state department on the World Festival of Negro Arts in Dakar, Senegal. A frequent lecturer in colleges and universities, she was artist in residence at Southern Illinois University in 1967. She wrote numerous articles on dance, often under the pseudonym Kaye Dunn, and two autobiographical books, *Journey to Accompong*, 1946, and *Touch of Innocence*, 1959.

Dunlap, William (1766–1839), playwright, painter, and historian. Born in Perth Amboy, New Jersey, on February 19, 1766, Dunlap lived in New York City from the age of eleven and, his schooling coming to an end a year later, studied drawing and painting. By 1782 he was working as a professional portraitist. Two years later he traveled to England to study further with Benjamin West, but in London he felt the lure of the stage and upon returning to New York in 1787 began writing plays. Commencing with *The Father; or, American Shandyism* (later called *The Father of* *an Only Child*), 1789, many were produced in New York theaters, although with indifferent success. In 1796 he bought an interest in the American Company, in which Lewis Hallam was also a partner; by 1798, when the company moved to the new Park Theatre, Dunlap was in complete charge, Hallam and the other partner having departed. He began producing translations of French and German plays in addition to his own, giving a cosmopolitan tone to the fledgling American theater while encouraging other American authors. His own works, largely imitative, were nonetheless the first significant body of dramatic writing produced in the United States and included the earliest American plays in the Gothic manner: *The Fatal Deception* (published 13 years later as *Leicester*) 1794, *Fontainville Abbey*, 1795, *André*, 1798, and *The Italian Father*, 1799, were among the more notable. In 1805 Dunlap declared bankruptcy and for a year went back to painting for a livelihood but in 1806 he returned to the Park Theatre as assistant to the new manager. He took up painting again in 1811, and from 1814 to 1816 served in the state militia. For several years thereafter he was an itinerant portraitist and miniaturist, also producing a number of large historical canvases which he sent on country tours. He remained, as he had always been, plagued by poverty. Again in New York City, he joined in the founding of the National Academy of Design in 1826 and was active in its affairs thereafter, serving as its vice-president from 1831 to 1838. In his later years he wrote a number of historically valuable studies, including *History of the American Theatre*, 1832; *History of the Rise and Progress of the Arts of Design in the United States*, 1834; and *A History of the New Netherlands, Province of New York, and State of New York, to the Adoption of the Federal Constitution*, 1839–1840. Although great distinction escaped him in all his pursuits, Dunlap managed by dint of energy and versatility to provide great impetus to the progress of the arts in the early years of the United States, an accomplishment recognized by the many leading literary and artistic figures whom he numbered among his friends. He died in New York City on September 28, 1839.

Dunne, Finley Peter (1867–1936), "Mr. Dooley," humorist and journalist. Born in Chicago on July 10, 1867, of Irish immigrant parents, Dunne worked for a number of Chicago newspapers as a reporter and a feature and editorial writer after graduating from high school and by 1897 had become editor in chief of the *Chicago Journal*. In 1892 he wrote his first dialect sketch; the following year he introduced his great literary creation, the worldly philosopher and saloonkeeper Martin Dooley. In a rich Irish brogue Mr. Dooley surveyed the social and political scene about him and, with a singular ability to penetrate sham and a determination to champion the disadvantaged, became a Chicago favorite. In 1898 Mr. Dooley's observations on the victory of "his cousin

George" Dewey at Manila Bay made him nationally famous. In that year the first of a long and popular series of collections of past columns was published as *Mr. Dooley in Peace and in War*. In 1900 Dunne moved to New York City and there contributed articles and Dooley columns to a number of newspapers and magazines including *Collier's*, the *American Magazine*, and *Metropolitan*. He was associated with the leading muckrakers of the period and his approach to the topics of the day offered a welcome contrast to their lack of humor. To his dismay, the articles published under his own name never achieved the popularity of those under Mr. Dooley's, which were devoured by a nation eager to read such pithy comments as (on John D. Rockefeller), "[he is] a kind iv society f'r th' prevention iv croolty to money. If he finds a man misusin' his money he takes it away fr'm him an' adopts it." On the Insular Cases, Mr. Dooley noted, "No matter whether th' Constitution follows th' flag or not, th' Supreme Court follows th' illiction returns;" and on Democratic politics, he recalled, "Man an' boy I've seen the Dimmycratic party hangin' to the ropes a score iv times. . . . I've gone to sleep nights wonderin' where I'd throw away me vote afther this an' whin I woke up there was that crazy-headed, ol' loon iv a party with its hair sthreamin' in its eyes, an' an axe in its hand, chasin' Raypublicans into th' tall grass." He gave up Dooley in 1915; the last volume of the series, *Mr. Dooley on Making a Will and Other Necessary Evils*, appeared in 1919. Dunne continued to write occasionally until his death on April 24, 1936, in New York City.

Dunster, Henry (1609–1659), religious leader and educator. Born in Bury, England, probably in the autumn of 1609, Dunster graduated from Cambridge in 1631 and three years later received his M.A. He taught school and later served as curate of Bury until 1640, when, quite possibly because of Puritan leanings, he emigrated to America. His reputation for learning was such that on August 27, 1640, just three weeks after his arrival in the Massachusetts Bay colony, he was chosen first president of Harvard College. The college, which had begun four years earlier as little more than a school and had since withered to the point of having no physical plant, no finances, no faculty, and no students, was quickly reorganized along the lines of English colleges; Dunster laid down the forms that Harvard was to adhere to for two centuries, raised money, built the president's house himself, and, although he served for little salary and was by no means a wealthy man, contributed a large tract of land to tide the college over a period of straitened circumstances. In 1653 he scandalized the colony by adopting certain Baptist views; the earnest defense offered by his supporters failed to protect him and in October 1654 he was forced to resign. Subsequently tried and convicted for refusing to have his child baptized, he later moved to Scituate, Massachusetts. There, while trying with little success to obtain back salary owed him by Harvard, he served as a minister until his death on February 27, 1659.

Du Pont, Samuel Francis (1803–1865), naval officer. Born on September 27, 1803, in Bergen Point, New Jersey, Du Pont moved with his family to Angelica, New York, and later to Delaware. In 1815 he was offered by President James Madison his choice of appointments to West Point and as a midshipman; he chose the midshipman's berth out of enthusiasm for the navy's exploits in the War of 1812. His first sea duty, a Mediterranean cruise on the *Franklin*, was in 1817; for 30 years he served on a succession of ships in European and South American waters, rising to lieutenant in 1826 and to commander in 1843. In 1846, just returned to San Francisco from Hawaii, he took command of the sloop of war *Cyane*. He transported John C. Frémont's troops to San Diego, then continued south and entered the Gulf of California where, in a series of sea battles and daring landings, he cleared the waters and the coastal area entirely of Mexican forces. On his return to Norfolk, Virginia, in 1848 he was commended officially. For several years he was on shore duty, aiding in organizing the work of the new Naval Academy, promoting the adoption of steam power by the navy, and serving on the Light-House Board. In 1855 he was a member of a board appointed to evaluate all officers of the navy; the board's report, finding 201 officers incompetent, was accepted by the Department of the Navy but aroused a storm of public and congressional criticism, most of which fell on Du Pont personally. He was nonetheless promoted to captain in that year. Following a China cruise in 1857–1859 he was named commandant of the Navy Yard in Philadelphia in 1860 and in 1861 became senior member of the navy's Commission of Conference to plan sea operations and strategy for the Civil War. In September 1861 Du Pont became commander of the South Atlantic Blockading Squadron and was assigned to carry out a planned attack on Port Royal, South Carolina. Despite widespread doubts about the possibility of capturing land fortifications from the sea, he managed the operation brilliantly, taking Port Royal and its two forts with minimal losses on November 7 and providing the Blockading Squadron with an invaluable Southern base. He was rewarded with the thanks of Congress and in 1862 with promotion to rear admiral. Further successes in coastal operations followed and in 1863 he was ordered to attempt the capture of Charleston, South Carolina, a much more heavily defended stronghold than Port Royal. Although he was provided with a number of ironclads and monitors for the mission, he was himself dubious as to their value in such an undertaking. He attacked on April 7, suffered severe damage from the batteries of Fort Sumter, and was forced out to sea. His offer to turn over his command was accepted; in July, after a notable success in the capture of the Con-

federate ironclad *Atlanta*, he was replaced by Adm. John A. B. Dahlgren. He retired to his home near Wilmington, Delaware, and took little part in naval affairs thereafter, although for some time he engaged in a dispute with Secretary of the Navy Gideon Welles over responsibility for the failure of the Charleston attack. Du Pont died in Philadelphia on June 23, 1865. In 1882 Du Pont Circle in Washington, D.C., was named for him, as was the fountain by sculptor Daniel Chester French unveiled there in 1921.

Du Pont de Nemours, Éleuthère Irénée (1771–1834), industrialist. Born on June 24, 1771, in Paris, the son of French economist and statesman Pierre Samuel du Pont de Nemours, Éleuthère learned chemistry under A. L. Lavoisier in the royal French gunpowder factory until the French Revolution closed it down. He then managed his father's printing house, which was also closed in 1797 by the Jacobins for upholding the royalist cause. The family came to America in 1799, intending to found a land and trading company in Virginia. But the son developed an idea for a gunpowder plant after learning of the poor quality and high cost of American powder. He returned to France to purchase machinery and with funds from his fathers' company began construction of a powder mill on an abandoned farm near Wilmington, Delaware, in 1802. He produced a powder far superior to any then available which he sold to the government, to fur companies, and to South America. With the business of the federal government assured by the friendship of President Thomas Jefferson, sales rose meteorically from 1804, the firm's first year of active production, and within a short time Du Pont was firmly established; he amassed a fortune during the War of 1812. Selective in his dealings, he refused large orders from the South Carolina Nullifiers in 1833 rather than offend the federal government. He operated the factory on a semifeudal basis, with workers housed on his property. He died in Philadelphia on October 31, 1834. His descendants, Pierre Samuel, Irénée, Lammot, and others, developed E. I. Du Pont de Nemours and Company into one of the world's foremost chemical and industrial companies.

Durand, Asher Brown (1796–1886), engraver and painter. Born on August 21, 1796, in Jefferson Village, near Newark, New Jersey, the son of an artisan, Durand was educated locally and during his vacations made small engravings with tools he developed himself. His father apprenticed him to a steel engraver, Peter Maverick, in 1812, and he became Maverick's partner after five years. Their most significant commission was an engraving of John Trumbull's "The Signing of the Declaration of Independence"; this was Durand's first major work and won such high praise from Trumbull that he embarked on an independent career in his own studio, engraving portraits, gift books, and banknotes. He turned to painting in the 1830s. Living in New York City, he was a member of a circle that included James Fenimore Cooper, William Cullen Bryant, Samuel F. B. Morse, and other luminaries, many of whom he joined in founding the National Academy of Design in 1826. From 1840 to 1841 he toured Europe, then began to paint landscapes. He is credited, with Thomas Cole, with founding the Hudson River, or American, school of landscape painting, in which romantic scenes were rendered with great attention both to detail and to atmosphere. This style was the first native U.S. movement in art and dominated the country's art scene through the 1870s. Notable among Durand's paintings in this manner were "Summer Woods" and "Kindred Spirits," in the latter of which appear figures of Cole and Bryant. Durand became the first landscape painter to preside over the National Academy of Design, from 1845 to 1861. He died in Jefferson Village on September 17, 1886.

Durant, Thomas Clark (1820–1885), railroad official and financier. Born in Lee, Massachusetts, on February 6, 1820, Durant attended Albany Medical College but upon graduating in 1840 decided against medical practice and took a position in an export house. While managing the firm's New York City office he speculated successfully in the stock market and soon became interested in railroad construction. With a partner, Henry Farnam, he built the Michigan Southern, the Chicago & Rock Island, and the Mississippi & Missouri railroads, on the last employing Grenville M. Dodge as a surveyor. Durant began about 1862 to look into the idea of a railroad to the Pacific; after its chartering by Congress in 1862 he took a leading part in organizing the Union Pacific Railroad, of which, though he was only vice-president, he was the principal source of inspiration. His efforts on behalf of the Union Pacific ranged from lobbying in Washington to actual construction supervision, but centered mainly on the constant problem of securing capital. The line had been organized on something like a shoestring and the New York investors who had supplied the original financing became increasingly cautious. In 1864 he secured a charter for the Crédit Mobilier of America, becoming president, and attracted to it a group of investors headed by Oakes Ames. Crédit Mobilier built the first 247 miles of track and then split into hostile factions. Durant was dropped from the directorate in 1867 but retained his position with the Union Pacific. An agreement was finally reached whereby Ames contracted to build another 667 miles; he then assigned the inflated contracts to seven trustees, including Durant, who turned the profits over to Crédit Mobilier stockholders. The arrangement resulted, as it was designed to, in the nearly total plundering of the Union Pacific of the grants it had received from Congress, and it was complicated by scandals over Ames's peddling of Crédit Mobilier stock at cut-rate prices to prominent public officials, but in the short run it provided the necessary capital and impetus for completing the line, a task to which

Durant applied himself feverishly. On May 10, 1869, he joined Leland Stanford in driving the golden spike linking the Union Pacific and the Central Pacific at Promontory Point, Utah. Two weeks later the Ames faction, completely in the ascendant, ousted him from the Union Pacific. He retired to the Adirondacks and lived there in declining health and falling fortunes until his death on October 5, 1885, in North Creek, New York.

Durant, Will (1885–1981), educator and author. Born on November 5, 1885, in North Adams, Massachusetts, William James Durant grew up there and in Arlington, New Jersey. He graduated from St. Peter's College in 1907 and after brief employment as a reporter for the *New York Evening Journal* entered Seton Hall College (now University), serving as professor of Latin and French while studying for the priesthood. In 1911 he left in disillusionment and moved to New York City, where he moved in radical circles and began teaching in an anarchist school. He became director of the Labor Temple School in 1914 and while teaching adult-education classes there continued his own studies at Columbia University, taking his Ph.D. in 1917. His lectures on philosophy were published in pamphlet form and then as a book, *The Story of Philosophy*, 1926, which became a best seller (well over two million copies were sold during the succeeding decades) and was translated into several languages. On the strength of that success Durant left the Labor Temple School in 1927 to devote himself to writing. Over the next several years he produced *Transition*, 1927, a semiautobiographical novel; *Mansions of Philosophy*, 1929; *Adventures in Genius*, 1931; *On the Meaning of Life*, 1932; and *The Tragedy of Russia*, 1933. He had long been planning a great work, a comprehensive and detailed intellectual history of civilization, and in 1935 the first volume appeared under the title *Our Oriental Heritage*. A rich and lively book, it attempted to weave the many threads of history and culture into a narrative pageant of wide general appeal, and to a large extent the effort succeeded; criticisms of inaccuracies or Durant's interpretations of events were greatly outweighed by appreciations of the breadth of the work and its vivid popularization of solid scholarly material. Durant moved to Los Angeles in 1935 and, except for a brief period of teaching philosophy at the University of California at Los Angeles in that year, thereafter led a secluded life, devoting all his time to researching and writing subsequent volumes in *The Story of Civilization* with his wife, Ada Kaufman Durant, who from 1961 appeared as his coauthor under the name Ariel Durant. A second volume, *The Life of Greece*, appeared in 1939 and was followed by *Caesar and Christ*, 1944; *The Age of Faith*, 1950; *The Renaissance*, 1953; *The Reformation*, 1957; *The Age of Reason Begins*, 1961; *The Age of Louis XIV*, 1963; *The Age of Voltaire*, 1965; and *Rousseau and Revolution*, 1967, for which they won a Pulitzer Prize.

The Story of Civilization series was brought to a close with the appearance of the eleventh volume, The Age of Napoleon, 1975. Durant died in Los Angeles on November 7, 1981.

Durant, William Crapo (1861–1947), industrialist. Born in Boston on December 8, 1861, Durant grew up in Flint, Michigan, and there in 1886 organized the Durant-Dort Carriage Company with a friend, J. Dallas Dort. The first soon grew into the largest buggy manufacturer in the world, with an eventual annual production of 150,000 buggies. In 1904 Durant bought the Flint Wagon Works, which had acquired all rights to an automobile developed by David D. Buick. The company had had little success with the 28-odd cars it had produced, but under Durant's leadership profitable operations were begun and in 1905 he organized the Buick Motor Company. In 1908 he consolidated a number of smaller firms with Buick in forming the General Motors Company, which continued to grow by acquiring during the next two years the Cadillac, Oldsmobile, and Oakland companies. By 1910 General Motors was manufacturing cars and trucks under the emblems of Buick, Cadillac, Elmore, Oakland, Cartercar, Welch, Rapid, and Reliance. Financial reverses in that year, however, led to Durant's being forced out of his controlling position in the company. In 1911 he joined Louis Chevrolet in building a new automobile under the Chevrolet name; Chevrolet lost interest in the business within a few years and in 1915 sold his holdings to Durant, who incorporated the Chevrolet Motor Company and immediately began using his large profits to regain control of General Motors. With the aid of the Du Pont dynasty he gained control and in 1916 became president of General Motors. The Chevrolet company was acquired by General Motors in 1918. Durant again lost control in 1920 as a result of business problems. The next year he founded Durant Motors, which produced the Durant, Star, Locomobile, Flint, and Mason cars and trucks. He sold out and left the automobile industry in 1926 and thereafter engaged in various other business pursuits. The stock-market crash of 1929 wiped out his fortune, which at its peak had been estimated at $120 million. Astute dealings in real estate in and around New York City had enabled him to become moderately wealthy by the time of his death there on March 18, 1947.

Durante, Jimmy (1893–1980), entertainer. Born on February 10, 1893, in New York City, James Francis Durante left school at an early age and within a few years was playing piano in dance halls and saloons on the Bowery and in Coney Island. Later, at the Club Alamo in Harlem, he teamed up with singer Eddie Jackson and dancer Lou Clayton in a raucous nightclub act that was soon drawing mobs of customers. In 1923 they opened their own Club Durant (so named, it was said, because they couldn't afford the final "e" in lights), which, although it lasted for only six months, made Clayton, Jackson, and Durante a headline act in New York. They played the top clubs in the city and in 1929 hit Broadway in Florenz Ziegfeld's Show Girl. After a spot in Cole Porter's The New Yorkers in 1930 Durante accepted a movie offer and the team broke up, although Clayton and Jackson remained his close companions thereafter. Following his first film, Get-Rich-Quick Wallingford, 1932, written by Ben Hecht and Charles MacArthur, he was offered largely forgettable material; his Broadway career blossomed, however, with Strike Me Pink, 1933; Billy Rose's Jumbo, 1935; Red Hot and Blue, 1936, with Ethel Merman; Stars in Your Eyes, 1939; and Keep Off the Grass, 1940. In 1943 he returned to the nightclub circuit and began a regular radio program, finding greater success than ever in both, and he was soon rediscovered by Hollywood, where he starred in a series of top-flight comedies, including Music for Millions, 1944, Two Girls and a Sailor, 1945, and Two Sisters From Boston, 1946. In 1950 he made his debut in—and conquest of—the only remaining medium, television. He had his own show for several years and was thereafter a popular guest on others; a seemingly ageless and tireless entertainer, he also continued to make nightclub appearances as he passed the age of seventy, and he starred in a 1962 film version of Jumbo. Through more than half a century in show business Durante's style remained constant; his magnificent nose (for which he was known as "Da Schnozz" or "Schnozzola" and in regard to which he noted, "Dere's a million good-lookin' guys; I'm a novelty"), his battered hat and piano, and his penchant for mangling or hybridizing most of the longer words in the English language, all were trademarks known around the world. Many of his expressions, such as "Everybody wants to get into da act," "I got a million of 'em," and his puzzling sign-off line of many years, "Goodnight, Mrs. Calabash, wherever you are" (in fact an affectionate greeting to his wife of many years, who died in 1943), were often imitated but never duplicated. He died on January 29, 1980, in Santa Monica, California.

Durocher, Leo Ernest (1906–   ), baseball player and manager. Born in West Springfield, Massachusetts, on July 27, 1906, Durocher played baseball in school and on local church and town teams and at eighteen was signed by a team in Hartford, Connecticut. In 1925 he joined the New York Yankees and after seasons with farm clubs in Atlanta and St. Paul made his first appearance with the home team in 1928. As a major leaguer he quickly acquired a reputation as a cocky, explosive player and the nickname "Lippy." His playing at second base was slower to develop, however, and in 1930 he was sold to Cincinnati, moving from there to the St. Louis Cardinals in 1932. As a member of the rowdy "Gashouse Gang" of the Cardinals, Durocher came into his own; he was the National League's top shortstop in 1933, was a standout player in the 1934

World Series when the Cardinals beat Detroit behind the pitching of Dizzy and Paul Dean, and in 1935 was elected team captain. In 1937 he was traded to Brooklyn for four players, and the next year he became captain and manager of the Dodgers. Managing gradually became his primary role and he stopped playing in 1945. He piloted the Dodgers to a pennant in 1941, their first in 21 years, and kept them in the first division in seven of his nine seasons (he was under suspension in 1947 following one of his more spectacular public outbursts). In 1948 he moved to the New York Giants, where he remained until 1955, taking pennants in 1951 and 1954 and the World Series in 1954. His fame as a tough man on the field and off, and his readiness to argue heatedly and at any length with the umpire, made him one of the most colorful as well as effective managers of his time; he was well known for his dictum: "Nice guys finish last." In 1955 he left the field for the television sports announcer's booth, but in 1961 returned as coach of the Los Angeles Dodgers. In 1965, amid much fanfare, he was named manager of the Chicago Cubs. He remained with that team until 1972, when he was dismissed in midseason.

Duryea, Charles Edgar (1861–1938), inventor and manufacturer. Born on December 15, 1861, near Canton, Illinois, Duryea went into the bicycle business upon finishing school and, with the aid of several improvements of his own devising, prospered. From his original plant in Peoria, Illinois, he later moved the business to Springfield, Massachusetts. From 1886, inspired by a gasoline engine he had seen at the Ohio state fair, he worked on the problem of making an engine small enough to be mounted in a carriage, which it would then power. By 1891 he had working plans and, with his brother, J. Frank Duryea, began construction. A dispute between the two later clouded the question of which was mainly responsible for building the machine—the evidence seemed to favor Frank—but nonetheless the automobile made its first appearance on the streets of Springfield in September 1893. Whether this was the first successful public operation of a gasoline-powered automobile in the United States is also open to question, but theirs was undoubtedly the most advanced machine in the country. In 1895 Frank drove an improved model—with a water-cooled, four-cycle engine and a clutched transmission with three forward speeds and reverse—in a round-trip race between Chicago and Evanston sponsored by the *Chicago Times-Herald;* he covered the 54-mile course in just under eight hours, beating a field that included a German Benz in the first U.S. auto race. The Duryea Motor Wagon Company was organized in 1895 and sold the first American-made commercial car in 1896. The brothers went their separate ways in 1898 and the first company soon went under. Each manufactured his own cars until 1914, Charles with the Duryea Power Company in Reading, Pennsylvania, after 1900. He later devoted much time to writing on the automobile, publishing *The Handbook of the Automobile,* 1906, *The Automobile Book,* 1916, with J. E. Homans; and numerous articles. He died in Philadelphia on September 28, 1938.

Du Sable, Jean Baptiste Pointe (1745?–1818), frontier trader and settler. Born probably in 1745 and almost certainly in Haiti, Du Sable was of French and African parentage. At about the age of twenty he traveled to New Orleans as an agent for a Haitian mercantile firm and later, when the city came under Spanish authority, moved upriver to St. Louis. The continuing retreat of the frontier of French influence drew him farther and farther northward; sometime during the 1770s, living near the present site of Peoria, Illinois, he married a woman of the Potawatomi tribe. His trade with the Indians of the region flourished and he established a post, possibly as early as 1772, on Lake Michigan at the mouth of what is now known as the Chicago River. There in 1779 he was found by Col. Arent Schuyler de Peyster, British commander at Mackinac, who described him, in one of the few reliable reports extant, as "a handsome Negro well educated, and settled at Eschecagou, but much in the French interest." Later in that year Du Sable was arrested by the British for being "much in the French interest" and taken to Mackinac. Because of his established friendship with the Indians he was made superintendent from 1780 to 1784 of Lieutenant Governor Patrick Sinclair's business, the Pinery, on the St. Clair River; he later returned to Eschecagou (an Indian word variously translated as "skunk," "wild onion," and "powerful") and continued to develop his trading establishment, building up also a sizable farm and amassing considerable wealth. He remained there until 1800, when he sold his holdings to Jean Lalime. Some time afterward he moved to St. Charles, Missouri, where he died on August 28, 1818. Du Sable is remembered as the first permanent settler in Eschecagou—later Chicago—his residence there having preceded the building in 1803 of Fort Dearborn by some 20 years.

Duvall, Gabriel (1752–1844), justice of the Supreme Court. Born near Buena Vista, Prince George's County, Maryland, on December 6, 1752, Duvall was a member of a long-established aristocratic family of planters. At the age of twenty-two he was named clerk of the Maryland convention and of the Council of Safety and in 1776 he saw action as a militiaman at Brandywine and Morristown. In 1777 he was appointed clerk of the House of Delegates and the following year was admitted to the bar. From 1782 to 1785 he was a member of the state council; in 1787 he declined to attend the Constitutional Convention, but was a member from 1787 to 1794 of the House of Delegates. He was elected to the House of Representatives in 1794 and served until his appointment to the Maryland supreme court in 1796. Six years later President Thomas Jefferson appointed him first comptroller of the treasury; he held the post until late in 1811, when President James Madison named him to the Supreme Court. From his first term on the bench in 1812 until his retirement 23 years later his contributions to the work of the court were overshadowed by the dominant presence of Chief Justice John Marshall. During his last years on the bench he suffered from an increasingly serious hearing loss and was at length incapable of hearing arguments. He nonetheless held his seat until assured that a worthy successor was available; at last he was informed that Roger B. Taney was President Andrew Jackson's choice for his place on the bench, and he resigned in January 1835, at the age of eighty-two. He retired to his Maryland estate, Marietta, in Prince George's County, and died there on March 6, 1844.

Duveneck, Frank (1848–1919), painter and educator. Born in Covington, Kentucky, on October 9, 1848, Frank Decker early took the name of his stepfather, Duveneck. He spent only a few years in school and upon leaving found work decorating the interiors of churches in Covington and later in Cincinnati. He developed great dexterity in carving and painting and in 1871 traveled to Germany to study painting under Wilhelm Dietz at the Royal Academy in Munich. After his return to the United States in 1873 he again took up decoration and also won a number of portrait commissions. In 1875 he exhibited five paintings at the Boston Art Club that aroused a great deal of interest by their vital and vigorous naturalism. In that year he returned to Munich; in 1877 he went to Venice and the following year, again in Munich, opened a school of his own, attracting a large number of students, many of whom were Americans destined for renown. He moved the school to Italy in 1879, alternating between Florence and Venice, and continued to conduct it until 1888. He tried etching for a time and in 1881 submitted a few prints to the New Society of Painter-Etchers' exhibition in London that attracted considerable notice. He also executed a few sculptures, notably a memorial to his wife in a Florence cemetery. In 1888 Duveneck returned to Cincinnati and continued to teach, now at the Art Academy, which he also served as dean of faculty. While his own paintings were marked by great technical facility and a vision reminiscent at times of Hals, Rembrandt, or Rubens, he was best known and most influential as a teacher and inspirer of others; he numbered among his pupils William Merritt-Chase, John H. Twachtman, and John W. Alexander. In 1915 a number of his works, including "Whistling Boy," "Turkish Page" and "Woman with Forget-me-nots," were exhibited at the Panama-Pacific International Exposition in San Francisco and he was voted a special gold medal by the international jury of critics. Duveneck died in Cincinnati on January 3, 1919.

Du Vigneaud, Vincent (1901–1978), biochemist. Born on May 18, 1901, in Chicago, Du Vigneaud

graduated from the University of Illinois in 1923, and after taking an M.S. degree the following year and working for the E. I. Du Pont de Nemours Company and as an assistant biochemist at the Philadelphia General Hospital, joined the University of Rochester School of Medicine in 1925. There, while conducting research into the structure of insulin, he took his Ph.D. in 1927. He moved to the Johns Hopkins University School of Medicine with a National Research Council fellowship in that year and during 1928–1929 continued his studies at the Kaiser Wilhelm Institute in Dresden, Germany, at the University of Edinburgh, and at University College, London. In 1929 he joined the research staff of the University of Illinois; three years later he was appointed professor and chairman of the department of biochemistry at The George Washington University School of Medicine; in 1938 he accepted similar positions at Cornell University Medical College in New York City. Du Vigneaud's early studies of insulin had centered on the presence of sulfur, which he later showed to be derived from the amino acid crystine, and he then moved on to the investigation of other sulfur-containing organic compounds. In 1940 he found that a substance known then as vitamin H was identical with another present in leguminous plants and known as coenzyme R and was in fact biotin, a rare B-vitamin; he had completely elucidated its structure by 1942. During World War II his laboratory worked in a number of government-sponsored projects and in 1946 achieved the synthesis of penicillin, eliminating the need for its costly and time-consuming manufacture by molds. He then turned to two hormones produced by the posterior lobe of the pituitary gland: oxytocin, involved in control of uterine contractions and lactation; and vasopressin, which plays a major role in controlling blood pressure. He announced the synthesis of oxytocin in 1953 and was quickly honored by a series of major awards, culminating in the 1955 Nobel Prize for Chemistry, which cited his overall work on sulfur compounds of biological importance and his pioneering synthesis of a polypeptide hormone. Du Vigneaud continued to pursue his researches on various organic compounds and their associated metabolic mechanisms at the Cornell Medical College until 1967, when he retired and moved to Cornell University in Ithaca, New York, to become professor of chemistry until 1975. He died in White Plains, New York, on December 11, 1978.

Dwight, John Sullivan (1813–1893), music editor and critic. Born in Boston on May 13, 1813, Dwight graduated from Harvard in 1832 and after four years at the Harvard Divinity School engaged in a variety of activities, contributing essays and reviews to literary periodicals, translating poetry by Goethe and Schiller, serving as a temporary pastor from time to time, and in 1837 leading in the founding of the General Association of the Members of the Pierian Sodality, which later became the Harvard Musical Association. In 1840 he was ordained pastor of the Unitarian church in Northampton, Massachusetts, but the connection lasted only a year and in 1841 he gave up the pulpit and joined the Brook Farm community at West Roxbury. He had been a member of the Transcendentalist Club and a contributer to the *Dial*; at Brook Farm he taught Latin and music and wrote articles on music for the *Harbinger*, with which he remained associated for some time after the dissolution of Brook Farm in 1847. He contributed to several other periodicals as well as organized choral societies in Boston and elsewhere. For a period in 1851 he was music editor of the *Boston Commonwealth* and the following year he began publication of *Dwight's Journal of Music*, which continued to appear regularly under his editorship until 1881; it had a profound influence on the spread of musical education and on the forming of musical taste in America. From 1855 to 1873 he was vice-president of the Harvard Musical Association, through which he led in securing the establishment of a professorship of music at Harvard in 1876; and from 1873 until his death he was the association's president and librarian. He was also active in organizing the Philharmonic Society in Boston in 1865. Dwight died in Boston on September 5, 1893.

Dwight, Timothy (1752–1817), religious leader, educator, and author. Born in Northampton, Massachusetts, on May 14, 1752, Dwight was a grandson of Jonathan Edwards and became the most prominent member of a remarkable family. At an early age he displayed great intellectual ability; he graduated from Yale in 1769, having devoted so much time and effort to his studies that his health was damaged, and, after teaching school for two years, returned to Yale as a tutor. There he became the inspiration of the group of young belles-lettrists known as the Connecticut Wits. In 1777 he resigned to become a chaplain in the Revolutionary army. In 1779 he returned to Northampton, where he established a coeducational school, preached in several churches, and was prominent in local politics. He accepted the pastorate of the Congregational Church in Greenfield Hill, Connecticut, in 1783 and remained for 12 years, founding another coeducational school that achieved considerable success and note. In 1785 he published an epic poem, *The Conquest of Canaan*, written several years earlier during his association with the Connecticut Wits. His other writings, many published posthumously, reflected his strongly Calvinist and Federalist outlook; they included two other lengthy poetical efforts, *The Triumph of Infidelity*, 1788, and *Greenfield Hill*, 1794, along with numerous shorter poems, sermons, addresses, and miscellaneous pieces. In 1795 he was elected president of Yale; he devoted the remainder of his life to the improvement of the college. He maintained a strenuous teaching schedule and preached in the college chapel in addition to carrying out his administrative duties.

Under Dwight's guidance Yale became the standard for colleges springing up in other parts of the country; he himself was the preeminent intellectual figure in New England and possibly in the nation. He died on January 11, 1817, in New Haven. His *Travels in New England and New York*, four volumes, 1821–1822, a vivid and intelligent account of the region, remains his most important book.

Dyer, Mary (?–1660), religious martyr. Born on a date unknown, probably in Somersetshire, England, Mary Dyer came to America with her husband, William Dyer, about 1635 and settled in Boston. She became a subscriber to the antinomian views of Anne Hutchinson and in 1638 followed her into banishment in Rhode Island. Her husband joined in the founding of Portsmouth, Rhode Island, and became a leading figure in the new colony. In 1650 Mary Dyer returned to England and remained for seven years, during which time she became a member of the Society of Friends; on returning to New England in 1657 she took up missionary work on behalf of the Quakers. Severe anti-Quaker laws passed in 1657 and 1658 made her work in Massachusetts extremely perilous; she suffered imprisonment in Boston in 1657 and expulsion from New Haven in 1658 in the course of her missionary travels. In 1659 she was again imprisoned briefly in Boston and then formally banished, a sentence that carried the threat of execution should she return. She nonetheless did return in October to visit and minister to other imprisoned Quakers; arrested and condemned, she was saved by the intercession of her son and again expelled. In May 1660, in obedience to her conscience and in defiance of the law, she returned once more to Boston. An appeal to her to acquiesce in banishment failed and she was hanged publicly on June 1, 1660. Her death came gradually to be considered a martyrdom even in Massachusetts, where it hastened the easing of anti-Quaker statutes.

Dylan, Bob (1941–   ), songwriter and singer. Born on May 24, 1941, in Duluth, Minnesota, Robert Zimmerman was to adopt the surname Dylan from Welsh poet Dylan Thomas. He grew up in Duluth and in Hibbing and at the age of ten began teaching himself to play the guitar and other instruments. He led a rather turbulent youth, running away from home a number of times, and finally, in 1960, after brief attendance at the University of Minnesota, set out on his own. He rode freight trains and hitchhiked around the country, "making my own Depression," worked at odd jobs, and wrote songs inspired by country-and-Western music, the blues, and folk music, particularly that of Woody Guthrie. In 1961 he moved to New York City, where he began to sing occasionally in coffeehouses in Greenwich Village. He was soon attracting considerable attention for both his songs and his highly personal singing style, and in the same year his first record album was released. Melodically simple, his songs were nonetheless often powerful statements of protest, couched in language that ranged from the sardonically humorous to the obscurely allegorical; many were popularized by other performers and some—"Blowin' in the Wind," for example, and particularly "The Times, They Are A-Changin' "—became anthems of the civil-rights and student protest movements of the 1960s. His recordings were without exception best sellers and had a profound influence on popular music, most notably in his blending of traditional forms with the rhythmic and instrumental styles of rock and roll into "folkrock" and his later adoption of country-and-Western arrangements. The lyric of another of his early songs, "A Hard Rain's A-Gonna Fall," marked a trend, later more pronounced, toward a poetic narrative of freely associated images that led some critics to consider Dylan among the serious poets of the day. He himself disclaimed such consideration and remained uninvolved in the protest and reform movements that took up his songs, preferring to retain his privacy.

Dyott, Thomas W. (1771–1861), manufacturer. Born in England in 1771, Dyott came to the United States during the late 1790s. In Philadelphia he opened a shoeshining business, the first of its kind in the city, and prospered. Soon he established a drugstore and began marketing a variety of patent medicines which, with claims that they cured all known human ailments, were distributed throughout the United States and to the farthest Western frontiers. Taking the title "Doctor" about 1812, he was the leading manufacturer of patent medicines in the country. The great demand for glass bottles occasioned by this enterprise and by his sale of bottles in the drugstore led him to begin producing glassware himself; it is uncertain when he began, but in 1833 he bought the Philadelphia and Kensington Glass Works and expanded it into the largest such works in the country. For his more than 400 employees and their families he built the town of Dyottville, sometimes also known as Temperanceville from his refusal to permit any alcohol—a major constituent of his medicines—to be consumed within its boundaries. The organization of the town, disciplined in every detail and heavily paternalistic, he described in his *Exposition of the System of Moral and Mental Labor Established at the Glass Factory of Dyottville*, 1833. The glassworks itself produced a great variety of bottles in assorted grades and with all manner of decoration; many of them were later highly prized by collectors. In 1836 the private, nonchartered bank he had established on his own credit in Dyottville failed and he was forced to close the works. The next year he was convicted as a "fraudulent bankrupt" and briefly imprisoned. He later returned to his drugstore in Philadelphia, where he died on January 17, 1861.

E

Eads, James Buchanan (1820–1887), engineer and inventor. Born on May 23, 1820, in Lawrenceburg, Indiana, Eads lived during his childhood in Cincinnati; Louisville, Kentucky; and St. Louis. He attended school until the age of thirteen, then began working as a Mississippi River steamboat purser to help support his family. He invented a diving bell for salvaging sunken steamers and their cargoes and in 1842 became a partner in a lucrative steamboat-salvaging firm. He left the business three years later to open a glassworks in St. Louis; by 1848 he was heavily in debt, but he returned to the salvage business and within nine years had paid his creditors and made himself a fortune. In 1861, at President Abraham Lincoln's request, he submitted plans to the government for defending the Western rivers. When the Civil War began, he proposed to build a fleet of seven steam-driven, armored artillery ships in two months; the first was ready in 45 days and the others quickly followed. The ships incorporated several improvements of his own devising in armament and armament mounting. His major achievement was the building of the Eads Bridge across the Mississippi at St. Louis; his design solved problems of span and clearance that had been judged insuperable by a team of 27 leading engineers. Work on the bridge began in 1867 and was completed in 1874. He again went against the consensus of less imaginative engineers in proposing to Congress in 1874 to clear a deep-water channel at the mouth of the Mississippi. Work began the following year in the South Pass of the river and by 1879 his ingenious system of jetties, built to control the direction and speed of flow, had forced the river to create its own channel by carrying sediment out into the Gulf of Mexico; the success of the project made New Orleans a major seaport. During his last years he lobbied unsuccessfully on behalf of a proposed alternative to the Panama Canal, a railway that would have transported ships across land by a shorter route. He died in Nassau, the Bahamas, on March 8, 1887. He was elected to the Hall of Fame in 1920.

Eakins, Thomas (1844–1916), painter and sculptor. Born on July 25, 1844, in Philadelphia, Eakins was educated at the Pennsylvania Academy of the Fine Arts and from 1866 to 1869 at the École des Beaux-Arts in Paris, and traveled briefly in Spain, where he was enthralled by the work of Spanish realists, particularly Velázquez and Goya. Returning to Philadelphia in 1870, he studied anatomy at Jefferson Medical College and in 1873 became a lecturer at the Pennsylvania Academy

of the Fine Arts. In teaching he emphasized anatomy and geometrical perspective, believing that technique was as important to a painter as to a draftsman or an engineer. His work was carefully laid out and painted with enormous attention to detail, creating a feeling of stark realism. His portraits and figure studies were true to his sitters, who sometimes found the portrayals too acute. He also made use of photographs and experimented with a rudimentary motion-picture technique in order to study the movement of the human body. In 1886 he was dismissed from his teaching post for introducing a nude model into a coeducational class. Two of his most famous studies were of scenes in clinics, "The Gross Clinic," 1875, and "The Agnew Clinic," 1889. He also painted sports scenes, notably "Max Schmitt in a Single Scull," 1871, and "Between the Rounds," 1899. In sculpture, his works included "The Prophets" for the Witherspoon Building in Philadelphia and figures for the battle monument in Trenton, New Jersey, and for the Soldiers' and Sailors' monument in Brooklyn, New York. He died in Philadelphia on June 25, 1916. After only moderate recognition in his lifetime, he eventually came to be acknowledged one of the greatest of American artists.

Eames, Charles (1907–1978), designer. Born on June 17, 1907, in St. Louis, Eames left school and went to work at an early age. Among his jobs was that of draftsman in a steel mill and, developing there an interest in architecture, he entered Washington University in St. Louis to undertake formal studies. He left after a short time, however, and went into architectural practice, teaching himself fundamentals along the way. His work eventually won him a fellowship from the Cranbrook Academy of Art, then under the direction of Eliel Saarinen; there, with Saarinen's son Eero, he designed a revolutionary chair made of contour-molded plywood on a frame of aluminum tubing. Entered in the Museum of Modern Art's Organic Design Competition in 1940, the chair was awarded top prize in its category and attracted wide attention to the notion of machine-produced furniture of functional and architectural design. During the 1940s, while working as a movie-set designer for Metro-Goldwyn-Mayer, Eames slowly developed a plywood-molding process suitable for use in mass production of furniture; in 1946 his was the first one-man furniture exhibition held in the Museum of Modern Art, marking a major step in the establishment of industrial design as both an important facet of manufacturing enterprise and a legitimate field of creative art. He produced several more designs in a variety of modern materials for "Eames chairs," which were licensed for manufacture and which proved enormously popular. He later branched out into other fields, executing designs for architectural projects and industrial products. With his wife he made a number of documentary films for television and for fairs and exhibitions, including the World's Fair in Brussels in 1958, the American National Exhibition in Moscow in 1959, and the New York World's Fair in 1964. He was a design consultant to a number of leading corporations and in later years devoted considerable time to creating major exposition and museum exhibits, particularly for the International Business Machines Corporation (IBM). His many awards included the first Industrial Designers Institute medal in 1951 and the first Kaufmann International Design Award in 1960. He died in St. Louis on August 21, 1978.

Earhart, Amelia Mary (1897–1937?), aviator. Born on July 24, 1897, in Atchison, Kansas, Amelia Earhart moved often with her family and completed high school in Chicago in 1915. She was an army nurse in Canada during World War I and, after sporadic attendance at Columbia University and the University of Southern California, a social worker at Denison House in Boston before starting her career in aviation. She learned to fly in 1920–1921 despite her family's protests and in 1928, as a passenger, became the first woman to fly the Atlantic; in 1932 she made her own solo crossing, setting a record of just under 15 hours for the flight. Widely hailed both as an aviator and as an inspiring example for the cause of feminism, she became aviation editor for the *Cosmopolitan* magazine in 1928 and published two books, *20 Hours, 40 Minutes,* 1928, and *The Fun of It,* 1932. Married in 1931 to publisher George Palmer Putnam, she continued to use her maiden name. In 1930–1931 she was vice-president of Luddington Airlines, Inc., an early passenger service in the East. In various airplanes and autogiros she set a number of altitude and speed records; in 1935 she made the first solo flight from Honolulu in the Hawaiian Islands to the U.S. mainland and the first nonstop Mexico City–New York flight. In the same year she became a career counselor to women at Purdue University. In 1937 she attempted a round-the-world flight with Frederick J. Noonan as copilot in a twin-engined Lockheed Electra. After a false start that ended with an accident in Honolulu, she set out again from Miami, Florida. On July 2, flying from New Guinea to Howland Island in the central Pacific, trouble developed aboard her plane; radio contact was broken and never resumed. No trace of the plane was ever discovered. Miss Earhart's *Last Flight* appeared in 1938. Despite the extreme unlikelihood of her having survived, speculation as to the nature of her flight and its true outcome—including the notion that hers was a clandestine intelligence mission for the U.S. Navy—continued for decades.

Earle, Ralph (1751–1801), painter. Born in Shrewsbury, Massachusetts, on May 11, 1751, Earle (whose name was sometimes spelled Earl) taught himself to paint and became an itinerant portraitist, traveling throughout Massachusetts and Connecticut in search of commissions. Strongly influenced by the work of John Singleton Copley, he evolved a somewhat erratic but nonetheless vigorous and interesting style that made him a popular portraitist in his day and sustained and increased his reputation in years to come. He remained ·for a time in New Haven in 1774; the next year he was in Lexington, Massachusetts, painting four scenes of the Revolutionary battle there; he returned to New Haven in 1776. In 1778 his Loyalist sympathies forced him to flee to England, where he studied with Benjamin West and enjoyed the patronage of prominent sitters. He returned to the United States in 1785 and for the remaining years of his life continued to wander about New England and New York, executing portraits of well-known personages that were later to win him ranking with the most accomplished American artists of the time; he also led a rather dissolute life that may have contributed to his early death on August 16, 1801, in Bolton, Connecticut.

Early, Jubal Anderson (1816–1894), soldier. Born in Franklin County, Virginia, on November 3, 1816, Early graduated from West Point in 1837 and was immediately sent to take part in the Seminole War in Florida. He resigned his commission the following year and took up the study of law, winning admission to the bar in 1840. Aside from a term in the legislature in 1841–1842 his only public service before the Civil War was as major of a Virginia militia regiment in the Mexican War, during which he saw little but garrison duty in northern Mexico. Early vigorously opposed Virginia's secession, but when war broke out he quickly offered his services and as a colonel took a creditable part in the first battle of Bull Run (Manassas). Promoted to brigadier general and in 1863 to major general, he served with the Army of Northern Virginia throughout the campaigns of 1861–1863. In 1864 he was promoted to lieutenant general and given a large and completely independent command in the Shenandoah Valley, where his assignment was to draw Union forces away from Richmond. Faced with little opposition, he swept down the valley gathering provisions and preparing for an attack on ·Washington itself. He crossed the Potomac and at the Monocacy River engaged and defeated a small force under Gen. Lew Wallace; this delayed him for two days, time enough for Gen. Ulysses S. Grant to dispatch two corps to defend Washington. On July 11 Early's advance troops entered the District of Columbia; within sight of the Capitol, in action viewed by President Abraham Lincoln, he skirmished about Fort Stevens for two days before retiring to the Shenandoah Valley. There he ranged and raided freely until the appearance of Gen. Philip H. Sheridan, by whom he was defeated at Winchester, Fisher's Hill, and, after Sheridan's famous "20-mile ride," at Cedar Creek; finally, in March 1865, his forces were virtually destroyed by Sheridan at Waynesboro. Removed from command, Early set out for the West; following the Confederate surrender in April he continued on to Mexico, later sailing to Canada, where he published his *Memoir of the Last Year of the War for Independence in the Confederate States of America*, 1866. In 1867 he returned to Virginia and soon resumed his law practice in Lynchburg. His widespread unpopularity following Waynesboro gradually gave way to general admiration in the South, largely because he refused to the end of his life to be reconciled to the Confederate defeat. In later years he was for a time president of the Southern Historical Society and was briefly associated in the management of the Louisiana lottery with Gen. P. G. T. Beauregard. Early died in Lynchburg, Virginia, on March 2, 1894.

Earp, Wyatt (1848–1929), frontier figure. Born in Monmouth, Illinois, on March 19, 1848, Wyatt Berry Stapp Earp was of a westering family with whom he early moved to Iowa and by 1864 to California. He became a stagecoach driver and later a buffalo hunter, providing meat at various times for the government and for the railroads and also hunting as a private entrepreneur on Indian lands. He was also a small-time professional gambler by the time he settled in Wichita, Kansas, in 1874. The common notion that he had the previous year been marshal of Ellsworth, another Kansas cattle town, is most probably unfounded; there is also strong evidence that in Wichita he was only a minor peace officer, not deputy marshal as is often claimed, and that after a year or so he was fired following an arrest for brawling. In 1876 he moved to Dodge City, a relatively wide-open cattle town, where he served two terms as assistant marshal, in 1876 and in 1878–1879. He was closely associated with Bat Masterson, another gambler, who was for a time sheriff of Ford County. Earp supplemented his income by dealing faro at the Long Branch Saloon and, (a fact bolstering doubts about his later reputation as the fearless lawman who cleaned up Dodge) was a close friend to such unpleasant companions as Luke Short and "Doc" Holliday, a mean-tempered alcoholic former dentist whose greatest pleasures in life apparently were gambling, killing, and his common-law wife, "Big Nose Kate" Elder (or Fisher). Late in 1878 Earp left Dodge for Tombstone, Arizona, where recent silver strikes promised opportunity. He worked for a time as a Wells Fargo messenger and then as a gambler and guard in the Oriental Saloon, while his brother Virgil became marshal. Tombstone was indeed the wild town that legend suggests—"the town too tough to die"—with a mixed population of miners, cattlemen, cowboys, and various sorts of outlaws. Earp had a falling out with a gang led by Ike Clanton in 1881 and the disagreement soon threatened to erupt into gun-

play. Virgil Earp deputized Wyatt and another brother, Morgan, and the three, together with Doc Holliday, forced a showdown with the Clantons on October 26, 1881, at the O.K. Corral; when the shooting ended, Billy Clanton and Frank and Tom McLowry were dead and Ike Clanton and Billy Claiborne had escaped out of town. Although the gunfight at the O.K. Corral was later often portrayed as a triumph of the law, represented by the Earps, at the time it aroused a considerable portion of the Tombstone citizenry, who strongly suspected it had been little more than murder; Virgil Earp was quickly discharged as marshal. Wyatt wandered north to Colorado in 1882 and traveled widely, later returning to California, where he lived out his last years on the income from mining and real-estate interests. He died in Los Angeles on January 13, 1929. By that time the process of transforming Wyatt Earp into a legendary and heroic figure of the Wild West was already under way, and in succeeding decades it continued as the facts of the case became progressively more difficult to ascertain.

Eastman, George (1854–1932), inventor, industrialist, and philanthropist. Born in Waterville, New York, on July 12, 1854, Eastman moved with his family to Rochester in 1860 and at fourteen went to work in an insurance office. Later, while working as a bookkeeper in a Rochester bank, he became interested in photography and in 1880 perfected a process for making dry plates; he immediately left the bank and with a partner formed the Eastman Dry Plate Company. In 1884 he devised a paper-backed film and, through the reorganized Eastman Dry Plate and Film Company, placed it on the market in roll form the next year. In 1888 he introduced the Kodak, an inexpensive and simple camera ("You push the button; we do the rest," it was advertised) that came already loaded with roll film; the would-be photographer took his pictures, returned his Kodak to the factory, and received back his photos and his reloaded camera. In less than a decade Eastman had transformed photography from a difficult, expensive, and time-consuming art into a hobby accessible to the millions, and the firm's sales reflected its booming popularity. Flexible transparent film was invented in the Eastman laboratory in 1889 and three years later, when the firm was reorganized again as the Eastman Kodak Company, daylight-loading film was perfected. By 1900 the company, relocated to a great new plant known as Eastman Park, employed more than 3000 people and Eastman had introduced a pioneering profit-sharing plan to which he later added a dividend bonus in 1912 and an employee stock-option plan in 1919. Eastman had early begun to keep a wary eye on competition and as his means increased he bought out many rivals, acquired patent rights from others, and blocked most of the rest by making exclusive contracts with his various wholesale and retail outlets. Although an attempt to create an international cartel failed in 1908 and the Eastman Kodak Company of New Jersey, formed as a holding company in 1901, later encountered antitrust difficulties with the government, the firm's dominance of the American market continued to grow, encouraged by Eastman's policy of constant improvement and frequent price reductions; it held a virtual monopoly by 1927. In later years Eastman devoted much of his thought to philanthropy. The Massachusetts Institute of Technology (MIT), the Hampton and Tuskegee institutes, and the University of Rochester were major beneficiaries; to the university he gave the Eastman School of Music and the Eastman School of Medicine and Dentistry in 1919. In all, his philanthropies, including bequests, totaled more than $75 million. Long in ill health, Eastman took his own life on March 14, 1932.

Eastman, Max Forrester (1883–1969), author, editor, and critic. Born on January 4, 1883, in Canandaigua, New York, Eastman graduated from Williams College in 1905 and from 1907 to 1911 was an assistant in philosophy and lecturer in psychology at Columbia University, where he also completed work for a Ph.D. in philosophy but declined to accept the degree. His principal interests at the time were literature and political and cultural radicalism and, as a leader of Greenwich Village bohemian society, he combined his interests in a variety of fruitful ways. In 1913, the year he published his widely influential *Enjoyment of Poetry,* a psychological study of metaphor, he also led in establishing the *Masses,* a magazine dedicated to art, literature, Socialism, and journalistic excellence. He remained its editor until 1918, when it was suppressed under the Espionage Act for its outspoken opposition to U.S. participation in World War I. Along with other staff members, including Floyd Dell and John Reed, Eastman was twice tried for and acquitted of sedition. In 1919 he was a founder of the successor *Liberator* and helped edit it until its suspension in 1924. He had in the meanwhile published two volumes of verse, *Child of the Amazons,* 1913, and *Colors of Life,* 1918, as well as *Journalism Versus Art,* 1916, and *The Sense of Humor,* 1921. During 1923–1924 he made an extended visit to the Soviet Union to observe firsthand the workings of Marxism; his early optimism faded quickly in the face of the fanaticism and the power struggles of the period that resulted in the emergence of Stalin as dictator. On his return to the United States he published a series of penetrating studies of Communism in practice that, while they alienated intellectuals caught in the currently fashionable admiration of the U.S.S.R., were later recognized generally as among the most sober analyses of the day; among them were *Since Lenin Died,* 1925; *Marx and Lenin: The Science of Revolution,* 1926; *Artists in Uniform,* 1934; *Stalin's Russia and the Crisis in Socialism,* 1939; and *Marxism: Is It a Science?,* 1940. He was close to Leon Trotsky during Trotsky's exile in Mexico and translated a

number of his writings. At the same time he remained active in the field of literary criticism and created a major controversy by a series of essays attacking many of the leading novelists and poets of the day for adhering to what he called "the cult of unintelligibility." He put forward a fuller critical theory in *The Literary Mind: Its Place in an Age of Science,* 1931; *Art and the Life of Action,* 1934; and *Enjoyment of Laughter,* 1936, in the last attacking also elements of Freudian theory. Eastman traveled and lectured widely and in 1941 became a roving editor for *Reader's Digest,* a post he retained for the rest of his life. His later writings included *Heroes I Have Known,* 1942; *Reflections on the Failure of Socialism,* 1955; *Great Companions: Critical Memoirs of Some Famous Friends,* 1959; *Seven Kinds of Goodness,* 1967; and two volumes of autobiography, *Enjoyment of Living,* 1948, and *Love and Revolution: My Journey Through an Epoch,* 1965. Eastman died at his winter home in Bridgetown, Barbados, on March 25, 1969.

Eaton, Cyrus Stephen (1883–1979), financier. Born on December 27, 1883, in Pugwash, Nova Scotia, Eaton got his first glimpse of high-level capitalism while working in a clerical position for John D. Rockefeller in Cleveland during a vacation from McMaster University, then in Toronto. Upon graduating in 1905 he returned to Cleveland and, after a period with the East Ohio Gas Company, began investing in gas and electric utilities. He soon effected a consolidation of several Western operations in the Continental Gas and Electric Company. He became a U.S. citizen in 1913. In 1916 he became a partner in the Cleveland banking firm of Otis and Company. His utilities holdings continued to expand and in 1923 he reorganized them as the United Light and Power Company, which three years later was joined with his various investments in rubber and steel under the umbrella of Continental Shares, a stock-issuing holding corporation. His reorganization of the Trumbull Steel Company in 1925 led to other ventures in reorganization and in 1930 to the organization of the Republic Steel Corporation, which grew into the third-largest firm in the industry. In 1929 he joined in founding the Cliffs Iron Corporation, later the Cleveland Cliffs Corporation. Battles with Samuel Insull and the Bethlehem Steel Company over contested holdings weakened his financial empire and the Depression dealt him a severe blow; he was nonetheless able to recoup and regain his position as one of the nation's leading capitalists, holding at various times directorships or chairmanships in Republic Steel, Inland Steel, Youngstown Sheet & Tube, Cleveland Trust, National Acme, Steep Rock Iron Mines (Canada), Chesapeake & Ohio Railway, Baltimore & Ohio Railroad, West Kentucky Coal, Kansas Coal, Kansas City Power and Light, and many other companies. Eaton was also something of a scholar and one of a strikingly independent and liberal bent. Over the years he grew increasingly critical of

American business practices, particularly in regard to organized labor—"The casualness with which we capitalists seem willing, nay, even eager, to invite the collapse of our economic system in almost every industrial dispute for the sole purpose of thwarting labor, is utterly incomprehensible"—and wrote a number of articles and pamphlets and such books as *Financial Democracy*, 1941; *Investment Banking Competition or Decadence?*, 1944; and *The Engineer as Philosopher*, 1961. In the 1950s he began sponsoring an annual "Pugwash Conference" of scholars and scientists from around the world in an effort to strengthen international understanding and further the solution of world problems through the free exchange of ideas. He was particularly concerned with improving U.S. relations with the Soviet Union; he was awarded the 1960 Lenin Peace Prize by the U.S.S.R. He died in Northfield, Ohio, on May 9, 1979.

Eaton, Margaret O'Neale (1799–1879), socialite. Born on December 3, 1799, in Washington, D.C., Peggy O'Neale (or O'Neill) was the daughter of a tavern keeper whose inn was frequented by political figures. At an early age she married John B. Timberlake, a navy purser, and had three children. During his absences at sea Peggy would often act as hostess at her father's tavern and there she met John H. Eaton, a Tennessee senator and close friend of Andrew Jackson. (She met Jackson later, in 1823, when he came to Washington as a senator.) Eaton lodged at the inn and soon rumor connected him with the beautiful and vivacious Mrs. Timberlake. Her husband died while at sea in 1828 and common gossip attributed his death to suicide prompted by jealousy. Later that year Eaton, with the encouragement of Jackson, who had long been fond of Peggy, proposed marriage to her and was accepted, the wedding taking place on January 1, 1829. By that time Jackson had been elected president and a short time later he named Eaton secretary of war. Vice-President John C. Calhoun's wife, Floride, refused to receive Mrs. Eaton and influenced the other cabinet wives to follow suit. Jackson, a widower, was outraged and became the champion of the Eatons; in this he was supported only by Secretary of State Martin Van Buren, a widower of considerable gallantry. The celebrated struggle lasted until Eaton's resignation in 1831, by which time the breach between Jackson and Calhoun was permanently established and Van Buren had become the President's closest political ally. Peggy accompanied her husband to Florida in 1834, where he served as governor, and two years later to Madrid, where he was U.S. minister to Spain, and they both enjoyed a brilliant social life. In 1840 they returned to Washington, where Eaton died in 1856. A few years later Peggy married a dashing young Italian dancing master who soon defrauded her of much of her property and eloped with her granddaughter. She remained in Washington until her death on November 8, 1879.

Eaton, William (1764–1811), soldier. Born in Woodstock, Connecticut, on February 23, 1764, Eaton ran away from home in 1780 to join the Continental army in the last months of the Revolutionary War. Afterward he entered Dartmouth College and, supporting himself by teaching school, graduated finally in 1790. In 1792, while teaching in Windsor, Vermont, he secured a captain's commission in the army and in the years following saw duty against the Indians in Ohio and in Georgia, and as a secret investigator of the Blount Conspiracy in Tennessee in 1797. His performances, particularly in the last assignment, attracted the notice and then the patronage of Secretary of State Timothy Pickering, who in 1798 persuaded President John Adams to appoint Eaton U.S. consul in Tunis. There he renegotiated a treaty that had been rejected by the Senate. In 1801 the neighboring state of Tripoli, under the rule of a usurper, declared war on the United States in an effort to extort larger tributes for the "protection" of Mediterranean shipping from the Barbary pirates. Eaton conceived the idea of helping the dethroned pasha, Hamet Karamanli, to regain control, and in 1803 he returned to the United States to win over President Thomas Jefferson to his plan. In 1804, with official approval, he sailed to Upper Egypt, located the exiled Karamanli, and with him and a handful of U.S. marines set out on a 500-mile trek across the Libyan Desert, gathering a motley army of Greeks, Arabs, and others along the way. In April 1805 he arrived at the city of Derna, which, with the aid of three U.S. warships, he occupied. Before he was able to march on Tripoli, however, he was ordered to abandon his plan and leave the region while a treaty ending the Tripolitan War was negotiated with the usurper. Embittered, he returned to the United States. His last years were marked by almost constant public bickering over what he believed to have been a personal humiliation. In 1807–1808 he served a term in the Massachusetts legislature. Eaton died in Brimfield, Massachusetts, on June 1, 1811.

Eddy, Mary Morse Baker (1821–1910), founder of Christian Science. Born in Bow, New Hampshire, on July 16, 1821, Mary Baker received little formal education but read at home with the aid of her brother. She was from childhood in poor health, subject to seizures and nervous collapse. She married George W. Glover in 1843 and was widowed the following year. She lived then in retirement with her family until 1853, when she married Daniel Patterson, a dentist and homeopath. Her continuing ill health aroused her interest in spiritual healing, and in 1862 she sought help from the notable practitioner Phineas Parkhurst Quimby. She was, she attested, cured immediately; she became a disciple devoted to spreading Quimby's methods and fame. He died in 1866 and the same year, having suffered a relapse, Mrs. Patterson obtained a divorce from her husband, resumed the name Glover, and again retired from the world. Her recovery, against all odds, followed upon her taking up her Bible, and she was later to date her original discovery of Christian Science to 1866. In 1870 she began her own career of healing and teaching; gradually she abandoned Quimby's methods and from her reading of the New Testament evolved her own system, and in 1875 published the first of many versions of *Science and Health*, espousing the doctrine that Mind is the sole reality and that the infirmities of the body, like the body itself, are illusory and susceptible to cure by purely mental effort, as exemplified by her reading of Jesus's words in the New Testament. She gathered a group of followers, one of whom, Asa G. Eddy, she married in 1877. The "Church of Christ, Scientist" was chartered in 1879; in 1881 the Massachusetts Metaphysical College was founded in Boston and continued under her leadership for eight years. In 1883 Mrs. Eddy began to publish the *Christian Science Journal*, which enabled her to extend her influence beyond the immediate New England area. In 1895 she founded what came to be called the "Mother Church" in Boston; the membership rolls grew, and she created an effective and largely autocratic organization to oversee the affairs of the church. The bylaws and edicts promulgated by Mrs. Eddy for the governance of the church and its rapidly multiplying branches were collected in the *Church Manual*, first issued in 1895 and much revised until 1908. The *Journal* was succeeded by the *Christian Science Sentinel* in 1898 and by the *Christian Science Monitor* in 1908. In 1889 she retired from Boston to Concord, New Hampshire, and later to Chestnut Hill, near Boston. She maintained control of the church, despite declining health, until her death on December 3, 1910, in Chestnut Hill.

Edelman, Gerald Maurice (1929–   ), biochemist. Born in New York City on July 1, 1929, Edelman received a B.S. in chemistry from Ursinus College in 1950 and an M.D. from the University of Pennsylvania in 1954. He subsequently served a one-year residency at Massachusetts General Hospital and spent two years as a doctor in the U.S. armed forces. Admitted as a graduate student to Rockefeller University in 1957, he served concurrently as an assistant physician in the university hospital. Upon receiving his Ph.D. in 1960, he joined the Rockefeller faculty; in 1963 he became associate dean of graduate studies, and after 1966 served as a full professor. In 1959 he launched a pioneering program of research in the field of immunology. By the early 1960s his publications on his researches provided a clarification of the chemical structure of antibodies—the blood proteins formed by the human body to fight infection—and established him as the nation's leading molecular biologist. His early papers, along with the reports of independent work on the same problem conducted from a slightly different approach by the English biologist R. R. Porter, sparked a decade of research by many other scientists in the United States and England. By the late 1960s the mass of collected data provided a complete structural knowledge of all the light and heavy chemical chains that compose the antibody molecule. Practical application of this new knowledge was not immediate, but it did give the medical profession new insights into the diagnosis of several diseases, including cancer, and led to improved treatment of certain others. The research also filled an important gap in the growing knowledge of mitosis and the chemistry of human bodily growth and opened a promising approach to solving the problems of immunity involved in organ transplanting. Edelman and Porter shared the 1972 Nobel Prize for Physiology and Medicine for their work. The Nobel Prize committee cited their role in launching worldwide efforts in research as well as the value of their findings to clinical diagnostics and therapy.

Ederle, Gertrude Caroline (1906–   ), swimmer. Born on October 23, 1906, in New York City, Trudy Ederle early became an avid swimmer and between 1921 and 1925 held 29 different national and world amateur records; she broke 7 records in a single afternoon in a meet at Brighton Beach, New York, in 1922. In 1924 she was a member of the U.S. Olympic team and helped win a gold medal in the 400 meter freestyle relay. In 1925 she made an unsuccessful attempt to swim the English Channel, but after setting records in the Battery-to-Sandy Hook swim in that year and the eight-mile swim down the Miami River the next, she returned to France in 1926 to try again. In the face of widespread doubt that a woman could swim the Channel at all, she set out from Cape Gris-Nez near Calais on August 6 and, beating through a heavy sea that forced her to swim 35 miles to cover the 21-mile distance, arrived at Dover after 14 hours 31 minutes, bettering the world record by 1 hour 59 minutes. She was greeted on her return to New York City by a ticker-tape parade and the journalistc and public adulation enjoyed by many overnight heroes during the 1920s. She toured for a time as a professional swimmer, but a series of misfortunes, culminating in a back injury in 1933 that left her in a cast for four years, took her out of the limelight. She made a brave comeback, however, and in 1939 appeared in Billy Rose's Aquacade at the New York World's Fair. Miss Ederle later became a swimming instructor for deaf children and a member of President Dwight D. Eisenhower's Youth Fitness Committee.

Edison, Thomas Alva (1847–1931), inventor. Born in Milan, Ohio, on February 11, 1847, Edison grew up in that town and in Port Huron, Michigan, where, for three months, he received his only formal schooling. For a time he worked as a railroad newsboy and in 1863 became a telegraph operator. He had since childhood experimented constantly with whatever materials lay at hand, and telegraphy turned his mind to electricity. In 1869 he was granted his first patent, for an electrical vote recorder. In that year he moved to New York City and became general manager of a stock-ticker company; he also entered into a partnership in Pope, Edison & Co., an electrical-engineering consulting firm that was bought out for its patents the next year. With his share of the money Edison opened a manufacturing firm—in reality a research and development company—and in the next few years developed, among other things, quadruplex telegraphy and the carbon transmitter that made practical the wide use of the Bell telephone. In 1876 he opened a large new laboratory in Menlo Park, New Jersey; the first major device produced at the new facility was his phonograph for the reproduction of recorded sound, demonstrated in 1877. Unlike most of his inventions, which were typically developments of earlier work by other men, the phonograph was Edison's in both concept and execution. In 1879, after an exhaustive period of trial-and-error experimentation, he demonstrated a practical incandescent illuminating bulb. More important than the bulb itself, however, was his subsequent development of a system of wide and efficient power distribution from central generating stations; in the course of this work, a gigantic engineering undertaking, came improvements in motors and dynamos, the development of a practical electric railway, and many other valuable innovations. During his work on the incandescent bulb Edison had made his only purely scientific discovery, the "Edison effect" of a one-way current between separated electrodes in an evacuated bulb; he paid little attention to the phenomenon, considering it to be of no commercial value, and it was thus left to others to develop the electron tube. The various companies he organized to exploit and develop his inventions were eventually merged into the Edison General Electric Company, which in 1892 joined with one other firm to form the General Electric Company, of which Edison was a major stockholder. In 1887 he moved his laboratory to West Orange, New Jersey. There four years later Edison patented his "kinetograph" camera and his "kinetoscope," a peep-show viewer, that, incorporating his own improvements and those of others, developed eventually into the motion-picture apparatus commonly used today. He returned to work on his phonograph and improved it following the experimental results of Alexander Graham Bell and of Emile Berliner by introducing a wax cylinder to replace his original metal-foil and later a disc for the recording surface. He developed an improved storage battery, a magnetic method for separating iron ore, and improvements in the manufacture of cement, and worked on many other projects. During World War I he served as a consultant to the navy on various problems, particularly chemical production and weapons development. In all his work Edison was dedicated to the practical and useful; commercially unprofitable ventures did not interest him, but a potentially marketable product would elicit from him boundless energy and patience (hence his definition of genius as "one percent inspiration and ninety-nine percent perspiration"). During his life he was granted well over 1000 patents; he came to symbolize for many the archetypal inventor and the practical American genius of technology. He died in West Orange on October 18, 1931. He was elected to the Hall of Fame in 1960.

Edmunds, George Franklin (1828–1919), lawyer and public official. Born in Richmond, Vermont, on February 1, 1828, Edmunds received a rather erratic schooling and was prevented by poor health from attending college, but at seventeen he took up the study of law and in 1849 was admitted to the bar. Two years later he moved his practice from Richmond to Burlington and was soon recognized as a leader of the Vermont bar. He served in the legislature in 1854–1859, the last three years as speaker, and in 1861–1862 as president pro tem of the state senate. In 1866 he was appointed to fill an unexpired term in the U.S. Senate and was thereafter regularly re-elected. He was early associated wtih the Radical Republicans, playing a prominent role in passing the Tenure of Office Act in 1867 and subsequently organizing the rules and procedures for the impeachment trial of President Andrew Johnson, for whose conviction he voted; however, he broke with the party over other matters. He became chairman of the Judiciary Committee in 1872 and held the post until his retirement except for the years 1879–1881, when the Democrats organized the Senate. The Civil Rights Act of 1875, later invalidated by the Supreme Court, was largely drafted by Edmunds, as was the act of 1877 establishing the Electoral Commission to decide the disputed presidential election of 1876; he himself was one of the Senate representatives on the commission. While the only act of Congress to bear his name was the Edmunds Act of 1882, outlawing polygamy in the territories, he contributed in large measure to a number of others, most notably the Sherman Anti-Trust Act of 1890. The high regard in which he was held, based on his legal acumen and unquestioned integrity—the latter quality the more remarkable for the period in which he held power—was demonstrated in the support he received for the Republican presidential nomination in 1880 and 1884 and in his appointment as president pro tem of the Senate (and thereby first in succession to the presidency) following the death of President James A. Garfield in 1881. In his later years he was an imposing, patrician figure in the Senate, respected but also feared for his acerb sarcasm and his intolerance of legislation or legislators he felt to be below his high standards of statesmanship. Edmunds resigned in 1891 and for some years practiced law in Philadelphia, numbering among his many major cases an appearance before the Supreme Court in *Pollock* v. *Farmers' Loan and Trust Co.,* 1895, in which he successfully demonstrated the unconstitutionality of the income-tax provisions of the 1894 Wilson-Gorman Tariff Act. Edmunds later retired to Pasadena, California, where he died on February 27, 1919.

Edwards, Jonathan (1703–1758), religious leader and theologian. Born on October 5, 1703, in East Windsor, Connecticut, Edwards was schooled at home and had already displayed great intellectual ability when, not quite thirteen, he entered Yale. He graduated in 1720 and for two years studied theology. He served briefly as pastor of a church in New York City and then, in 1724, returned to Yale as a tutor. In 1726 he resigned to become the colleague of Solomon Stoddard, his grandfather, in the pulpit of the highly influential Congregational Church in Northampton, Massachusetts; three years later, upon Stoddard's death, he took sole charge. Edwards's preaching was more than effective; his theology, profoundly influenced by Newtonian science and Lockean psychology, evolved into a masterly system of logical analysis that, although stated in terms of contemporary philosophy, contained a great deal of essentially revanchist Calvinism. His developed system was, however, the product of a profound and original philosophical intellect. In 1734–1735 a small wave of revival followed his sermons on "Justification by Faith Alone"; it was the precursor of the much larger wave that occurred in 1740–1742 when George Whitefield's evangelistic tour precipitated the Great Awakening. Although critical of its emotional excesses, Edwards largely approved of the revival and defended it in a number of pamphlets. During this time he delivered his best-known sermon, "Sinners in the Hands of an Angry God," a classically Calvinist exposition of man's natural baseness and God's absolute sovereignty, which described, in vivid detail, the prospects of eternal damnation for the non-elect. His growing insistence on professions by prospective church members not only of faith, but of regenerative experience—a requirement that had been allowed to lapse under the "Half-Way Covenant"—brought him into conflict with his own congregation in the late 1740s. In 1750 he was dismissed from the Northampton church and the following year answered a call to the frontier church in Stockbridge, Massachusetts, where he also served as a missionary to the Indians. In his years there he wrote a series of books and pamphlets, including his *Freedom of the Will*, 1754, refuting the Arminianism that, by way of the Episcopal church, was slowly spreading through New England. In 1757 he was chosen president of the College of New Jersey (now Princeton); he assumed the office in January 1758 but died shortly thereafter, on March 22. He was elected to the Hall of Fame in 1900.

Eggleston, Edward (1837–1902), religious leader, author, and historian. Born on December 10, 1837, in Vevay, Indiana, Eggleston grew up there and in other small Indiana communities on what was then virtually the frontier. He became a Bible agent in 1855 and in 1856 a Methodist circuit rider, but poor health forced him to seek a less strenuous occupation. In 1858 he went to Minnesota in hopes of restoring his health and during the next several years filled a number of pastorates there. He moved to Evanston, Illinois, in 1866, becoming editor of the *Little Corporal*, a Chicago juvenile paper; early in 1867 he began editing the *National Sunday School Teacher* and in the next three years published several children's books. In 1870 he went to New York City and edited the *Independent* until the next year, when he went to *Hearth and Home*, remaining there for a year. In 1871 his first novel, *The Hoosier Schoolmaster*, was serialized in *Hearth and Home*; based on his Indiana boyhood, the book was, despite its sentimentalism, a major contribution to the growth of literary realism. Full of local color, it utilized an authentic vernacular style and depicted a rapidly disappearing backwoods way of life. Other novels followed, including *The End of the World*, 1872; *The Mystery of Metropolisville*, 1873; *The Circuit Rider*, 1874; *Roxy*, 1878; *The Graysons*, 1888; and *The Faith Doctor*, 1891. From 1874 to 1879 he was pastor of the Church of Christian Endeavor in Brooklyn; soon afterward he moved to Joshua's Rock, on Lake George, New York. During the 1890s he became interested in history, and he published a number of articles, biographies, and school texts. He planned a *History of Life in the United States*, but completed only two volumes, *The Beginners of a Nation*, 1896, and *The Transit of Civilization*, 1900. In the latter year he was elected president of the American Historical Association. He died on September 4, 1902, at his home on Lake George, New York.

Eichelbaum, *see* Warner Brothers

Einstein, Albert (1879–1955), physicist. Born in Ulm, Germany, on March 14, 1879, Einstein moved with his family to Munich as a child and received his first schooling there. Formal education failed to excite him, but on his own he developed a deep interest in mathematics. This continued while he completed his schooling in Switzerland and entered the Federal Polytechnic School there to be trained as a teacher of physics and mathematics. He graduated in 1900 and, taking Swiss citizenship, was employed in the patent office in Bern. During the next few years he developed his first major contributions to physics, among them the special theory of relativity, the mass-energy equivalence formula ($E=mc^2$), the foundation of the photon theory of light (an important step toward the quantum theory), and the theory of Brownian motion (the existence of which phenomenon, remarkably, he deduced from theoretical considerations, unaware that it had been observed and studied for decades). The papers announcing these discoveries were all published in 1905; in that year he was awarded a Ph.D. by the University of Zurich, and four years later he became a professor there. A number of teaching positions followed—at the German University in Prague, at the Swiss Federal Polytechnic School, and finally, in 1913, at the University of Berlin, where he also became director of the Kaiser Wilhelm Institute. In 1916 he published the result of his continuing work in the geometrization of physics and the integration of gravitational, accelerational, and magnetic phenomena into his major achievement, the general theory of relativity. His paper on this theory constituted a revolution in physics comparable only to that of the advent of Newtonian mechanics; from then on, while making a number of contributions to statistical and quantum mechanics, he devoted himself primarily to the development of a "unified field theory," uniting magnetic, electromagnetic, and gravitational phenomena into a single set of equations. He was awarded the 1921 Nobel Prize for Physics, largely for his 1905 paper on photons and photoelectricity. In 1932 he made a short visit to the United States; upon his return home he resigned his various positions and the following year left Germany, by then under the Nazi regime, to take up permanent residence in the United States. For the rest of his career he was associated with the Institute for Advanced Study in Princeton, New Jersey. In 1939, at the suggestion of several scientists who, like himself, had become concerned over Germany's apparent efforts to develop a nuclear-fission device, he wrote his famous letter to President Franklin D. Roosevelt that led directly to the establishment of the Manhattan Engineering District project and the development of the atomic bomb. Einstein became a U.S. citizen in 1940. Among his writings were *The Meaning of Relativity*, 1921; *Builders of the Universe*, 1932; *On the Method of Theoretical Physics*, 1933; *Why War?*, with Sigmund Freud, 1933; *The World As I See It*, 1934; and *Out of My Later Years*, 1950. He continued to work in physics as well as for a number of social causes, particularly that of peace, until his death in Princeton, on April 18, 1955.

Eiseley, Loren Corey (1907–1977), anthropologist and author. Born on September 3, 1907, in Lincoln, Nebraska, Eiseley graduated from the University of Nebraska in 1933 and took his M.A. in 1935 and his Ph.D. in 1937 from the University of Pennsylvania. During his student days he had a number of poems and stories published in literary magazines and was active in editing the *Prairie Schooner* review. In 1937 he joined the faculty of the University of Kansas as assistant professor of anthropology and sociology, rising to associate professor in 1942. Two years later he moved to Oberlin College as professor and chairman of the department of sociology and anthropology, and in 1947 he settled finally at the University of Pennsylvania, where he was professor and chairman of the department of anthropology from 1947 to 1959, provost from 1959 to 1961, and University Professor of anthropology and the history of science from 1961; in 1948 he also became curator of early man in the university museum. Throughout his career Eiseley's principal interests were evolution and paleoanthropology, particularly that of North America. During the 1930s he accompanied a number of expeditions to various parts of the West to seek evidences of early human habitation and culture. He wrote numerous articles, both for professional journals and for general-circulation magazines, and in 1957 published his first book, *The Immense Journey*, an evocative narrative of the course of evolution that won high praise from scientists and literary critics alike. *Darwin's Century*, 1958, a review of the development of the theory of evolution, won a Phi Beta Kappa Science Award, and *The Firmament of Time*, 1960, was honored by the John Burroughs Association. Eiseley was especially lucid in expressing the many-faceted and often paradoxical relationship of man to the living world around him. Others of his books included *Francis Bacon and the Modern Dilemma*, 1962; *The Unexpected Universe*, 1969; *The Invisible Pyramid*, 1970; *Night Country*, 1971; and an autobiography entitled *All the Strange Hours*, 1975. Eiseley died in Philadelphia on July 9, 1977.

Eisenhower, Dwight David (1890–1969), thirty-fourth president of the United States. Born on October 14, 1890, in Denison, Texas, "Ike" Eisenhower moved with his family in the following year to Abilene, Kansas, where he grew up in modest circumstances. In 1911 he was appointed to West Point; after his graduation four years later he served at a succession of army installations around the world, rising slowly but steadily in rank and responsibility. In 1926, then a major, he graduated at the top of his class from the Command and General Staff School, and two years later he graduated from the Army War College. From 1933 to 1935 he was in the office of the chief of staff in Washington, D.C., and from 1935 to 1939 in the Philippines, in both assignments serving under Gen. Douglas MacArthur. His performance as chief of staff of the 3rd Army during training maneuvers in 1941 brought him promotion to brigadier general. Soon after the Japanese attack on Pearl Harbor in December 1941 brought the United States into World War II, he was called to the War Plans Division of the army's staff headquarters in Washington. In June 1942 he became commander of U.S. forces in Europe and began the task, both arduous and delicate, of planning the Allies' invasion of the European continent. Promoted to lieutenant general in July, he was named Allied commander in chief for the invasion of North Africa that began in November 1942, and the following year he planned and directed Allied invasions of Sicily and Italy. In November 1943 Eisenhower returned to England to resume personal supervision of the planning of the invasion of France, becoming Allied commander in chief the next month. In that post he oversaw the D-Day landing on June 6, 1944, and the subsequent campaigns leading to the surrender of Germany nearly a year later. He was promoted to the five-star rank of general of the army in December 1944. After briefly commanding U.S. occupation forces in Germany he returned to the United States in November 1945 as army chief of staff. In 1948 he retired to become president of Columbia University; he published in the same year *Crusade in Europe*, his best-selling war memoir. In 1950 President Harry S. Truman recalled him to active duty as commander of the newly organized forces of the North Atlantic Treaty Organization (NATO) in Europe; he served in that post until 1952. Long mentioned by both parties as a potential political candidate, Eisenhower at length abandoned his habitual reticence and consented to be considered for the 1952 Republican presidential nomination. He won the nomination narrowly and the election by an overwhelming margin. Determined to remain above partisanship, and a firm believer in the tradition of separation of powers, Eisenhower viewed the presidency as an office primarily of moral leadership and brought to it a concept of government that he termed, enigmatically, "dynamic conservatism." He was content to leave the practical day-to-day workings of government largely to the direction of his staff and cabinet. His first term was dominated by foreign affairs. Having already fulfilled a campaign promise by traveling personally to Korea, he oversaw the establishment of a truce there in mid-1953. At the same time he took bold initiatives in proposing a new plan for world disarmament and the creation of an international agency to develop peacetime uses for nuclear energy, but this "Atoms for Peace" plan failed to win sufficient world support to become effectual. The disarmament proposal led eventually to a summit conference between Eisenhower and Soviet leader Nikita S. Khrushchev in 1955 in Geneva, at which Eisenhower made his startling "Open Skies" proposal, whereby the United States and the Soviet Union would permit aerial surveillance of each other's territories and military activities. This plan, too, proved too radical. As a counter to Soviet intransigence at the conference table and expansionist moves in many parts of the world, Eisenhower allowed his secretary of State, John Foster Dulles, to construct a network of alliances to meet further Communist expansion with the threat of "massive retaliation." Such hard-line Cold War diplomacy was made credible by vigorous responses to crises, including in 1957 the landing of U.S. troops in Lebanon under the terms of the recently promulgated "Eisenhower doctrine" of military aid to free-world nations. On the domestic front the president, buoyed by his vast popularity, strove to remain above political squabbles, although it was wished by many that he would respond with the force of his prestige to the increasingly violent and scurrilous attacks of Senator Joseph R. McCarthy. Soon after his reelection in 1956—by a margin even greater than that of 1952—he was forced to deal with his first major domestic crisis,

the violent reaction to the court-ordered racial integration of schools in Little Rock, Arkansas. Nationalizing the Arkansas National Guard and sending in additional troops, he restored order in the city and obtained the compliance of local officials with the law; his refusal to exceed his fundamental executive responsibility epitomized his conception of the presidency. That conception changed eventually, however; in 1959, emerging from a long period of illness and stripped by resignation or death of many of his original close advisers, he suddenly undertook an unprecedented campaign of vigorous leadership and personal diplomacy. For the first time he took the initiative with Congress on legislation in various fields and began wielding his veto power with a purpose. More important were his diplomatic moves: after initiating and hosting what proved to be a highly successful visit by Premier Khrushchev, Eisenhower embarked on an 11-nation goodwill tour that showed him to be one of the most widely known and respected figures on the world stage. The high hopes aroused in his last year in office were dashed in May 1960, when the downing of a U.S. U-2 reconnaissance airplane in Soviet territory, coupled with Eisenhower's attempt to dismiss the incident, resulted in the cancellation by Khrushchev of a planned summit conference. After unsuccessfully supporting his two-term vice-president, Richard M. Nixon, in the presidential election of 1960, Eisenhower retired in 1961 to private life. In 1963 he published *Mandate for Change*, a volume of memoirs. Deteriorating health limited his activities and after a lengthy period of hospitalization he died in Washington, D.C., on March 28, 1969.

Eliot, Charles William (1834–1926), educator. Born in Boston on March 20, 1834, Eliot was educated at the Boston Latin School and at Harvard, from which he graduated in 1853, afterward teaching mathematics and chemistry at the college for ten years. After a tour of Europe he became professor of analytical chemistry at the Massachusetts Institute of Technology in 1865. Two years later he made a second visit to Europe, this time devoting close attention to educational practices there; in 1869 he published the results of his study as "The New Education: Its Organization," two articles published in the *Atlantic Monthly*. As one result he was chosen president of Harvard in the same year and began a 40-year career of educational reform and innovation there. Under his leadership the university was completely reorganized: the college, with all undergraduate studies grouped within it, became the nucleus, the entrance and degree requirements and curricula of the professional schools were premised on the college's ability to provide liberal education in both the sciences and the humanities; the graduate school was established (1890); and standards of admission and instruction were raised greatly. He gradually introduced an elective system into the undergraduate college, eliminating the traditional completely prescribed course of study; the professional schools of law and medicine were vastly improved by the raising of standards and by the complete revision of methods of instruction, and the divinity school was made nonsectarian. It was during his tenure that the instruction of women was undertaken by some faculty members in 1879; from that practice evolved the Society for the Collegiate Instruction of Women (or Harvard Annex), which in 1894 was formalized as Radcliffe College. By the end of his tenure in 1909 Eliot had created the modern Harvard University and made it an institution of world renown. His policies spread, affecting not only other colleges and universities, but also the nation's secondary schools, inducing them to raise their own standards. He edited the famous "five-foot shelf of books," the Harvard Classics, which appeared in 1909–1910. In 1909 he retired to private life, although he remained a Harvard overseer and maintained an active interest in educational and public affairs. Among his numerous published works were *The Happy Life*, 1896; *Educational Reform, Essays and Addresses 1869–1897*, 1898; *More Money for the Public Schools*, 1903; *University Administration*, 1908; *The Durable Satisfactions of Life*, 1910; *The Conflict Between Individualism and Collectivism in a Democracy*, 1910; and *A Late Harvest*, 1924. He died two years later, on August 22, 1926, in Northeast Harbor, Maine.

Eliot, John (1604–1690), religious leader and missionary, "the Apostle to the Indians." Born in 1604 in Widford, England, Eliot came from a prosperous family. He graduated from Jesus College, Cambridge, in 1622 and for a time was a teacher. In 1631 a group of Puritan friends persuaded him to emigrate to America with them as their pastor; he settled first in Boston and the next year moved to Roxbury. He joined Richard Mather and others in preparing for publication *The Whole Book of Psalms*, 1640, better known as the *Bay Psalm Book*. He interested himself in the Indians of Massachusetts and in 1646 began preaching to them regularly. By the following year he was preaching in their native Algonkian language. His missionary work was supported by the Massachusetts General Court and, from 1649, by the Society for the Propagation of the Gospel in New England, established in England by act of Parliament. In 1653 he published *A Primer or Catechism, in the Massachusetts Indian Language*, and his translation of the Bible, 1661–1663, was the first Bible in any language to be printed in America. By 1674 he had settled converted Indians—the "praying Indians" —in 14 villages; King Philip's War of the next year scattered them and, because of the treatment that the Christianized Indians received from their fellow tribesmen and from the colonists, set back his work irretrievably. Eliot continued his mission, although now handicapped by the Indians' distrust, until his death on May 21, 1690, in Roxbury.

Eliot, Thomas Stearns (1888–1965), poet and critic. Born on September 26, 1888, in St. Louis, T. S. Eliot, as he signed himself, graduated from Harvard in 1910 and during the next several years pursued further studies at the University of Paris and at Oxford and for a year was an instructor in philosophy at Harvard. From 1914 he lived in London, where he taught school briefly and then took a clerkship in a bank that, from 1917 to 1925, supported him as he established himself as a writer. He was also assistant editor of the *Egoist* from 1917 to 1919. His first book of poems, *Prufrock and Other Observations*, 1917, contained "The Love Song of J. Alfred Prufrock," an expression of profound disenchantment with the impotence of modern life that, together with the contrasts between contemporary and classical times in *Poems*, 1920, prepared the ground for his towering indictment of the twentieth century in *The Waste Land*, 1922. Aided by the advice and editing of Ezra Pound, Eliot brought about in *The Waste Land* a revolution in modern poetry; highly original in metrics and diction, it linked a startling number of allusions (which were explained in lengthy notes) into a closely woven intellectual argument of great power and, in its richly symbolist aspect, of great suggestiveness. Eliot was at the same time elucidating his poetic methods in a series of critical works, including *The Sacred Wood*, 1920, and *Homage to Dryden*, 1924, in which he laid the foundations for a neoclassicism that was particularly indebted to John Dryden, John Donne, and other metaphysical poets of the seventeenth century, since whose time, in his view, English culture had progressively decayed. In 1922 he founded the periodical *Criterion*, which he continued to edit until its last number in 1939. During the later 1920s he was moved to attach himself more firmly to tradition by joining the Church of England (becoming also a British subject in 1927), explaining and defending his acceptance of doctrine and ritual in verse in *Ash Wednesday*, 1930, and in prose in *For Launcelot Andrewes*, 1928; *Thoughts After Lambeth*, 1931; *After Strange Gods*, 1934; and *The Idea of a Christian Society*, 1939. Eliots' championing of religion, like his neoclassicism, seemed reactionary in the predominantly radical intellectual climate of the 1920s and 1930s, but proved to be an anticipation of and an influence upon the return to conservatism that followed World War II. He began experimenting in verse drama with *The Rock*, 1934, *Murder in the Cathedral*, 1935, a modern miracle play on Thomas à Becket, and *The Family Reunion*, 1939; but after 1939 he abandoned dramatic writing for ten years. In 1943 he published *Four Quartets*, poetic meditations on time, history, and eternity that are sometimes held to be his finest work. In 1948, the year his *Notes Towards the Definition of Culture* appeared, he was awarded the Nobel Prize for Literature, a recognition that sealed his rank as one of the leading men of English letters of his time. He later returned to his dramatic experiments in

The Cocktail Party, 1949; The Confidential Clerk, 1953; and The Elder Statesman, 1958, of which only the first achieved any popular success. His reputation continued to rest largely on his poetry, which also included Old Possum's Book of Practical Cats, 1939, and Collected Poems, 1909–62, 1963, and on his critical works, which included The Use of Poetry and the Use of Criticism, 1933, based on lectures given at Harvard, and On Poetry and Poets, 1957. Eliot died in London on January 4, 1965.

Ellery Queen, see Dannay, Frederic

Ellet, Charles, Jr. (1810–1862), engineer. Born in Bucks County, Pennsylvania, on January 1, 1810, Ellet received a rudimentary education and at seventeen began working on a surveying team. In 1828 he took a job with the builders of the Chesapeake and Ohio Canal and, his keen mind rapidly absorbing the principles and techniques of his work, he advanced to assistant engineer within two years. In 1830 he traveled to Paris to study for a time in the École Polytechnique and then returned to do survey work for various railroads, serving later (1836–1839) as chief engineer for the James River and Kanawha Canal. In 1842 he bridged the Schuylkill River at Fairmount, near Philadelphia, with the first important suspension structure in America. After a period as president of the Schuylkill Navigation Company he designed and built a suspension bridge across the Niagara River below the falls in 1847 and two years later built the worlds longest span —more than 1000 feet—in a suspension bridge over the Ohio River at Wheeling, now in West Virginia, for the Baltimore & Ohio Railroad. While serving as an engineer with a succession of railroads in and around Virginia during the 1850s Ellet made notable studies of and recommendations on river improvements, publishing Physical Geography of the Mississippi Valley, 1849, and The Mississippi and Ohio Rivers, 1853; his plans for upland reservoirs and diversion channels for flood control were later revived and put into use. From the time of publication of his Coast and Harbour Defenses, 1855, he devoted much energy to promoting the use of naval rams, taking up residence in Washington, D.C., in 1857 to lobby persistently for the idea. Early in the Civil War he was an outspoken critic of Union military strategy and created a stir with his Army of the Potomac and Its Mismanagement, 1861, and Military Incapacity and What it Costs the Country, 1862. Finally, after the initial successes of the Confederate ironclad Virginia (formerly the Merrimack) in 1862 Ellet was commissioned a colonel and, under War Department orders, sent to build and command a fleet of ram boats on the Mississippi. With nine unarmed rams he joined a squadron under Capt. Charles H. Davis and on June 6, 1862, ran through a Confederate fleet of eight vessels, of which Davis then sank or captured seven, and forced the surrender of Memphis, Tennessee. Ellet sustained a serious wound in the engagement and died on June 21, 1862, at Cairo, Illinois.

Ellington, Duke (1899–1974), composer and bandleader. Born on April 29, 1899, in Washington, D.C., Edward Kennedy Ellington was known from childhood as "Duke." He showed considerable artistic talent during his youth and was offered a scholarship to the Pratt Institute to study art, but, preferring to devote himself to music, he declined it. A largely self-taught pianist, he was much influenced by jazz and ragtime performers. While working as a sign painter he began to play professionally and in 1918 started his own band in Washington. In 1923 he moved to New York City and playing piano at the Kentucky Club, began gathering the musicians who formed the core of his orchestra—Bubber Miley, Sam Nanton, Harry Carney, and Sonny Greer, among others—and made his first recordings. With no formal training in composition, he nonetheless employed daring and innovative musical devices in his works; blending lush melodies with unorthodox and often dissonant harmonies and rhythmic structures based on "jungle" effects, he wrote and arranged songs tailored to his own band and soloists. Radio broadcasts during an engagement at New York City's fashionable Cotton Club from 1927 to 1932 brought him and his group national recognition, and his recordings— particularly "Saddest Tale," "Echoes of Harlem," "Black and Tan Fantasy," and "Mood Indigo"— spread their fame to Europe. Appearances on Broadway and in movies and tours of Europe and the United States further established the orchestra's reputation. Joined by Barney Bigard, Johnny Hodges, and Cootie Williams, the group continued to produce recordings that became jazz classics—"Ko Ko," "Blue Serge," "Bojangles," "Harlem Air Shaft"—and Ellington began to compose longer and more elaborate works. In 1943 Black, Brown, and Beige premiered at Carnegie Hall, in 1947 he wrote Liberian Suite for that country's centennial, and in 1950 he was commissioned by Arturo Toscanini to write Harlem for the NBC Symphony Orchestra. Others among his most famous songs were "Sophisticated Lady,' "In My Solitude," and "Don't Get Around Much Anymore." He composed scores and incidental music for a number of motion-picture and stage productions, including Anatomy of a Murder, Paris Blue, Beggar's Holiday, and Shakespeare's Timon of Athens. In 1965 his first sacred concert, including a musical sermon, which he titled "In the Beginning, God," was performed in New York City; in the next year it was heard in Europe and a second sacred work was premiered at the Cathedral of St. John the Divine in New York City. The Ellington orchestra continued to tour frequently in both the United States and Europe, at times under state departmen auspices. He was recognized as having broken out of the ranks of jazz musicians to become one of the leading American composers of the century; among his many honors and awards were the 1959 Spingarn Medal of the National Association for the Advancement of Colored People (NAACP) and, in 1969, the Presidential Medal of Freedom. In 1971 he was elected to the Songwriters' Hall of Fame. Ellington died in New York City on May 24, 1974.

Ellison, Ralph Waldo (1914–), author. Born in Oklahoma City on March 1, 1914, Ellison played the trumpet from the age of eight and took classical music courses in school. He continued in classical composition under composer William Dawson at the Tuskegee Institute, which he attended from 1933 to 1936. In his junior year he visited New York City and studied sculpture for a time. There he also met Richard Wright, who inspired him to turn to writing. In 1937 he returned to New York City and began contributing essays, short stories, and reviews to various publications, including the *New Masses*, the *Negro Quarterly*, *Cross Roads*, and *Tomorrow*. Although initially attracted to political radicalism, he later focused primarily on his role as an artist. Two of his best short stories, "King of the Bingo Game" and "Flying Home," both published in 1944, concerned the black man's place in white society and his relationship to his own complex heritage. In Ellison's most significant work, *The Invisible Man*, 1953, the theme of identity was again predominant. The winner of the 1953 National Book Award and named by a Book Week poll in 1965 as the "most distinguished single work" published in the previous 20 years, it earned him a place among major contemporary writers. *Shadow and Act*, 1964, a collection of interviews and essays, expressed his abiding confidence that a conscious study and celebration of their own rich culture would release black Americans from the bondage of stereotypes. He lived for two years in Rome and after 1955 taught at Bard College, in Annandale-on-Hudson, New York, lectured at the State University of New York at Stony Brook, Long Island, and was writer in residence at Rutgers University in New Brunswick, New Jersey, and a visiting fellow at Yale. In 1969 Ellison was awarded the Presidential Medal of Freedom, and in 1970 he became Albert Schweitzer Professor in the Humanities in New York University.

Ellsworth, Henry Leavitt (1791–1858), public official and agriculturist. Born in Windsor, Connecticut, on November 10, 1791, Ellsworth was the son of Oliver Ellsworth. He graduated from Yale in 1810, studied law at Tapping Reeve's Litchfield Law School, and began to practice in his native town, moving in 1819 to Hartford. From 1819 to 1821 he was president of the Aetna Insurance Company and was a leading figure in real-estate development and the civic life of the city as well. In 1832 President Andrew Jackson appointed him to supervise the removal and resettlement of Indians from Georgia and Mississippi to lands west of the Mississippi River; on his journey he encountered Washington Irving

and his party, who joined with him for the rest of the trip that Irving described in *A Tour on the Prairies*, 1835. In 1835 Ellsworth was elected mayor of Hartford but resigned within two months to accept from President Jackson the position of first commissioner of patents. Acting on a long-standing interest in farming, he quickly made the Patent Office into a clearinghouse for agricultural information and in 1839 secured from Congress the first appropriation for agriculture—$1000 for research, statistical studies, and the distribution of seed. Subsequent and larger appropriations were soon forthcoming and for his efforts Ellsworth later became known as "the father of the Department of Agriculture," although that department was not created until four years after his death. In 1843 he aided his friend Samuel F. B. Morse in obtaining a $30,000 appropriation for construction of the telegraph line from Baltimore to Washington. He resigned from the Patent Office in 1845 and moved to Lafayette, Indiana, where, while serving as a public-lands agent and becoming himself one of the largest landowners in the region, he also pioneered in promoting the use of agricultural machinery and in the development of farming techniques suited to prairie lands. In 1858 Ellsworth returned to Connecticut and settled in Fair Haven, where he died on December 27, 1858.

Ellsworth, Lincoln (1880–1951), engineer and explorer. Born in Chicago on May 12, 1880, Ellsworth studied at Yale and Columbia universities and in 1902 went to work with the preliminary survey parties for the Canadian Pacific transcontinental railroad. In 1906 he became resident agent at the Pacific terminus at Prince Rupert, British Columbia. Over the next several years he prospected on the Peace River, worked as an engineer for railroads and mining companies, and took part in a U.S. Bureau of Biological Survey expedition to the Rocky Mountains. During World War I he became an aviator. In 1924 he headed a Johns Hopkins University expedition to South America, making a cross-section topographical survey of the Andes region between the Amazon basin and the Peruvian coast. The next year he joined Norwegian explorer Roald Amundsen in an attempt to fly from Spitsbergen, Norway, to the North Pole. The party of six reached nearly 88° N in two aircraft and then was forced to land; the radio being out of commission, they were given up for dead. After a month of working to clear a takeoff strip, however, all six crowded into the remaining plane and returned safely to Spitsbergen. In May 1926 Ellsworth and Amundsen, joined by Umberto Nobile, flew the dirigible *Norge* 3400 miles in the first crossing of the polar basin, from Spitsbergen to Alaska. In 1931 Ellsworth was director of scientific investigation for Sir Hubert Wilkins's submarine expedition to the Arctic, and he represented the American Geographical Society on the flight of the *Graf Zeppelin* over Franz Josef Land and Novaya Zemlya in the same year. He turned his attention to Antarctica in 1933 and after two failures flew across the continent from Dundee Island in the Weddell Sea to the Bay of Whales in the Ross Sea in 1935, discovering the Sentinel and Eternity ranges and claiming for the United States a vast territory, which he named James W. Ellsworth Land (later simply Ellsworth Land) in honor of his father. For this feat, by which he became the first man to accomplish air crossings of both the Arctic and the Antarctic, he was honored with a special congressionial medal. He returned to Antarctica in 1939 and flew over and named the American Highland region, bringing the total territory he had claimed for the United States on the continent to over 380,000 square miles. Two years later, at the age of sixty-one, he led an expedition to Peru to seek the lost tombs of the Inca emperors. Ellsworth described his varied adventures in *The Last Wild Buffalo Hunt*, 1915; *Our Polar Flight*, 1925, with Amundsen; *First Crossings of the Polar Sea*, 1926; *Search*, 1932; and *Beyond Horizons*, 1938. He died in New York City on May 26, 1951.

Ellsworth, Oliver (1745–1807), public official and chief justice of the Supreme Court. Born in Windsor, Connecticut, on April 29, 1745, Ellsworth was educated at Yale and at the College of New Jersey (now Princeton), from which he graduated in 1766. He studied theology briefly, but soon turned to law and was admitted to the bar in 1771. Moving to Hartford in 1775, he quickly rose to prominence and became a political figure; in 1777 he was appointed state's attorney for Hartford County and elected to the Continental Congress, in 1780 he became a member of the Governor's Council of Connecticut, and in 1785 he was named to the state superior court. Little is known of his activities during his six years in the Continental Congress; his national importance dates from the Constitutional Convention in 1787. There he had a major share in developing the Connecticut Compromise, which constructed the bicameral national legislature with representation balanced between states and populations. His "Letters to a Landholder," published in the *Connecticut Courant* and the *American Mercury*, were of great influence in his state's decision on ratification. In 1789 he was elected one of Connecticut's first two U.S. senators; in his seven years in the Senate he became a major force in the new government. He submitted to the floor the first set of Senate rules, presented from conference the final form of amendments to the Constitution that became the Bill of Rights, and contributed to a bill organizing the government of the region south of the Ohio; he drafted bills for the admission of North Carolina to the Union and for the regulation of the consular service. Most important, he was chiefly responsible for the Judiciary Act of 1789, still the basis of the nation's federal judicial structure. In 1796 he was appointed chief justice of the Supreme Court. Three years later he was sent by President John Adams to assist in the negotiation of a new treaty

with France; the resulting treaty of 1800, although not completely satisfactory, succeeded in averting war. In that year, his health badly impaired, Ellsworth resigned from the Supreme Court. Upon his return to the United States he retired to private life in Windsor, Connecticut, where he died on November 26, 1807.

Ely, Richard Theodore (1854–1943), economist. Born on April 13, 1854, in Ripley, New York, Ely graduated from Columbia in 1876 and for four years continued his studies at several European universities, taking his Ph.D. from Heidelberg in 1879. After returning to the United States in 1880 he engaged in journalism until he was invited to become the first professor of political economy at The Johns Hopkins University in 1881. Ely took the lead among younger economists in challenging the naturalistic viewpoints of classical writers on economics and their equally gloomy descendants, the Social Darwinists. He maintained that the economy was susceptible to control and guidance and that purposeful intervention was necessary to achieve economic justice; he was a particularly vocal supporter of the organization of labor and he advocated the public ownership of natural resources and public utilities. For such views he was regularly denounced as a subversive. During 11 years at Johns Hopkins he published several books, among them *French and German Socialism in Modern Times*, 1883, and *Introduction to Political Economy*, 1889. In 1885 he helped found the American Economic Association, of which he served as secretary from that year until 1892 and as president from 1892 to 1901. In 1892 he became head of the economics department at the University of Wisconsin, a position he held for 33 years. His advocacy of progressive economics was widely influential; among his books of the period at Wisconsin were *Monopolies and Trusts*, 1900; *Studies in the Evolution of Industrial Society*, 1903; and *Foundations of National Prosperity*, 1917. He founded and was director and president of the Institute for Research in Land Economics and Public Utilities (later the Institute for Economic Research), and in 1925 moved with it to Northwestern University, where he remained until 1933. Among his later writings were *Elements of Land Economics*, 1926, with E. W. Morehouse; *Hard Times—The Way In and the Way Out*, 1931; and the autobiographical *Ground Under Our Feet*, 1938. The 1937 sixth edition of his *Outlines of Economics*, with R. H. Hess, was for many years the principal textbook in the field. Ely died at his home in Old Lyme, Connecticut, on October 4, 1943.

Emerson, Ralph Waldo (1803–1882), essayist and poet. Born in Boston on May 25, 1803, Emerson came of a long line of New England clergymen. Accordingly, after his graduation from Harvard in 1821 and a few unsatisfactory years spent teaching school to support himself and his widowed mother, he began to study for the ministry at the Harvard Divinity School. He was licensed to preach in 1826 and three years later assumed the pastorate of the Second (Unitarian) Church of Boston. His short time in the pulpit was an unhappy one; his religious doubts and a dislike of being merely the agent of received doctrines and rituals finally culminated in his resignation in 1832. Shortly thereafter he sailed for Europe where he met Samuel Taylor Coleridge, William Wordsworth, and Thomas Carlyle, all of whom, particularly Carlyle, had a profound influence on him. His reading of the English, and through them the German, idealists gave direction to his yet unformed philosophy. Upon his return to the United States he determined upon a literary career; in 1834 he moved to Concord, Massachusetts, his home for the rest of his life. He resumed his preaching, although he was not connected with any church, and began what was to be a life of lecturing. In 1836 Emerson published *Nature*, a small volume that contained the seeds of his later work and was the first coherent expression of the intellectual ferment then simmering throughout New England. The same year saw the first gathering in Concord of what became known as the Transcendental Club—Emerson, Orestes Brownson, Theodore Parker, Margaret Fuller, Bronson Alcott, and others. In 1837 he was invited to deliver the Phi Beta Kappa address at Harvard; his address, "The American Scholar," was heard as a clarion call for intellectual independence—from Europe, from the past, from all obstacles to originality. The following year his address to the graduating class of the Harvard Divinity School roused a storm of denunciation from pulpits, but it established firmly the breadth and vitality of the new Transcendentalist spirit of which Emerson was the central figure. His major work appeared in the next few years, transcribed and expanded from his journals (later published) and his lectures: *Essays, First Series*, 1841; *Essays, Second Series*, 1844; *Representative Men*, 1849; and *The Conduct of Life*, 1860. Together with *Poems*, 1846, and *May-Day and Other Pieces*, 1867, these constituted the expression of his unique, personal relationship to the living, organic universe he felt about him. From 1840 to 1844 the Transcendentalist group published the *Dial*, a journal of literature, philosophy, and social commentary; Emerson was a regular contributor and, for the last two years, editor. In 1847, on a second visit to England, he found himself famous there; he lectured widely, renewed his earlier acquaintances, and made new ones among the leading literary figures. *English Traits*, published in 1856, contained his observations and reflections on this trip. Unlike his Transcendalist friends, he resisted involvement in the reform movements of the time; only on the slavery issue did he assume a consistent and public stand, supporting the antislavery faction in Kansas and championing John Brown. His lecture tours grew both in extent and popularity and, somewhat ironically, he became an institution. After 1860 he added little that was new to his stock of lec-

tures and essays. In 1867, he again delivered the Phi Beta Kappa address at Harvard, ending the 30 years' exile that had followed his Divinity School address. A brief tour of California in 1871 and a last trip to Europe and the Near East in 1872–1873 were the only interruptions of his last quiet years in Concord; he declined slowly into a benign senility and died on April 27, 1882. He was elected to the Hall of Fame in 1900.

Emmett, Daniel Decatur (1815–1904), entertainer and songwriter. Born on October 29, 1815, in Mount Vernon, Ohio, Emmett worked in his father's blacksmith shop until he acquired enough education to become an apprentice printer. He gained an interest in music from his mother and by 1831 had composed "Old Dan Tucker." After working for local newspapers he joined the army at seventeen as a fifer. While stationed at Jefferson Barracks, Missouri, he continued to study music and after his discharge in 1835 toured with a traveling circus. Late in 1842 or early in 1843 he organized the Virginia Minstrels blackface troupe, one of the first of its kind, which first appeared at the Bowery Amphitheatre in New York City in February 1843 and included "Old Dan Tucker" in its first show. The troupe was a great success and subsequently traveled to other cities and to England. The typical minstrel costume of striped shirt and swallowtail coat was Emmett's principal contribution to the form that saw its full development in the shows of Edwin P. Christy, who had formed his Christy Minstrels at almost the same time. The Virginia Minstrels introduced a number of songs by Emmett that quickly became popular standards, including "My Old Aunt Sally," 1843; "Blue-Tail Fly," 1846; and "Jordan Is a Hard Road to Travel," 1853. Emmett eventually disbanded his group and in 1857 joined the Bryant Minstrels, for whom in 1859 he composed a "walkaround" or "hooray" song entitled "Dixie's Land." The line that had inspired him, "I wish I was in Dixie Land," was supposedly a standard lament of showmen stranded in Northern cities in the winter; the term "Dixie Land," for which various origins have been suggested, apparently referred specifically to New Orleans and Louisiana and, by derivation, to the South generally. The song was an immediate and sensational success. In January 1861 it was sung as the curtain piece for a spectacular production in New Orleans and the following month it was played at the inauguration of Jefferson Davis as president of the Confederacy. Thereafter the name "Dixie" was firmly attached to both the South and the song, which became the unofficial anthem of the rebellion. Gen. Albert Pike composed special Confederate lyrics for it and there was at least one Union version as well, but only Emmett's original verses survived the Civil War. Among his other songs were "The Road to Richmond," 1864, and "Here We Are, or Cross Ober Jordan," 1864. In 1865 he organized a new minstrel troupe with which he toured until 1878. He lived in Chicago until

1888 and then returned to Mount Vernon, Ohio, where he died on June 28, 1904.

Endecott, John (1588?–1665), colonial official. Born about 1588, probably in Devonshire, England, Endecott (or Endicott) led an obscure life until 1628, when he was chosen governor for an advance party of Massachusetts colonists sent out by the New England Company, of whose six incorporators and grantees he was one. With some 60 settlers he landed at Naumkeag (later Salem) and quickly established a firm hold there, absorbing the small existing community under Roger Conant and extending the colony's jurisdiction to Merrymount (later Quincy), where he personally led in cutting down Thomas Morton's maypole and otherwise acted to place the region under firm Puritan control. Endecott's role at the time has been interpreted by some as entitling him to rank as the first governor of Massachusetts. He continued as governor for a brief time after the Massachusetts Bay Company took over the patent of the New England Company in 1629; he was officially succeeded by John Winthrop in October of that year, although Winthrop did not arrive in Massachusetts until 1630. Endecott remained nonetheless prominent in the affairs of the colony, working closely with Winthrop as his assistant and his chief military adviser. In 1636 he led an unsuccessful expedition against the Pequot Indians that helped provoke rather than prevent further troubles. He was also active in the early organization of Harvard College. Endecott served as deputy governor in 1641–1644, 1650–1651, and 1654–55, and as governor in 1644–1645, 1649–1650, 1651–1654, and from 1655 until his death. During his last ten-year period of rule, when he was free of the tempering influence of Winthrop, his strong Puritan convictions, combined with his profound lack of tact, humor, and tolerance, resulted in a wave of persecutions and executions of religious dissenters, particularly of Quakers, in Massachusetts. Endecott died in Boston on March 15, 1665.

Enders, John Franklin (1897–   ), bacteriologist. Born on February 10, 1897, in West Hartford, Connecticut, Enders attended Yale and, after service as a navy pilot during World War I, graduated in 1920. Moving to Harvard, he took an M.A. in English literature in 1922 but then turned to an entirely different field, bacteriology, for his Ph.D. in 1930. He became an instructor in bacteriology and immunology in that year, advancing to assistant professor in 1935, associate professor in 1942, and professor in the Children's Hospital of the Harvard Medical School in 1956. After assisting Hans Zinsser in developing the first antityphus vaccine in 1930 Enders undertook a series of studies into bacterial infections and infection resistance. He later became interested in viral diseases such as herpes, influenza, measles, and mumps, and in 1946 established a laboratory at the Children's Hospital to carry on intensive investigations. Soon after becoming chief of the research division of infectious diseases in the hospital in 1947 he was joined in the laboratory by Frederick C. Robbins and Thomas H. Weller. The three began a search for a means of growing the poliomyelitis virus in various cultures and in 1949 announced that their method of inoculating bits of growing monkey or human nonnervous tissue was capable of producing large quantities of the virus for study. For this achievement they were awarded numerous honors, culminating in the joint award of the 1954 Nobel Prize for Physiology and Medicine. While Jonas E. Salk adopted the Enders-Robbins-Weller culture method in the course of developing his antipolio vaccine, Enders applied it to a variety of other viruses, particularly that of measles, for which he had developed an effective vaccine by 1962. In 1962 he became Higgins University Professor at Harvard, and in 1963 he was awarded the Presidential Medal of Freedom by President John F. Kennedy. Enders was editor of the *Journal of Immunology* from 1942 to 1958 and of the *Journal of Bacteriology* from 1964. He retired from his professorship in 1967.

Endicott, John, *see* Endecott, John

England, John (1786–1842), religious leader. Born in Cork, Ireland, on September 23, 1786, England turned from an early interest in the law to study for the Roman Catholic priesthood at the College of St. Patrick and was ordained in 1808. Assigned to a parish in Cork, he quickly became an outspoken champion of Roman Catholicism and Irish nationalism and succeeded in arousing hostility not only among English authorities in Ireland but also among many of the Irish hierarchs who enjoyed power in cooperation with the rulers. He agitated for and won improvements in the conditions on prison ships transporting convicts to Australia and secured permission for Roman Catholic clergy to minister to the penal colonies there. He taught in and for a time was president of St. Mary's Seminary. In 1817 he was transferred to the parish of Bandon, but the move did not stop his active pen and in 1820 he was appointed and consecrated bishop of the newly created diocese of Charleston, South Carolina, a promotion to what was widely viewed as exile. Arriving in Charleston late in that year, he immediately set about organizing the scattered and largely poor Catholic churches of the Carolinas and Georgia, apppointing new priests and in 1822 opening the Philosophical and Classical Seminary to provide educational opportunities otherwise lacking in the region. In the same year he founded the *United States Catholic Miscellany,* the first Catholic newspaper in the country, which was published until 1861. He brought in an Ursuline community to conduct a school for girls and founded the Sisters of Our Lady of Mercy to pursue charitable work and the Brotherhood of San Marino to provide aid to immigrants and laborers. England was as active a democrat and reformer in the United States as he had been in Ireland and attracted the often open opposition of other American prelates, especially those of French origin or training, whom he considered "aristocratic." In 1826, the year he acquired citizenship, he became the first Catholic clergyman to be invited to address Congress. He traveled and spoke widely and, an aggressive controversialist, led in the fight to end discrimination against Roman Catholics in general and against Irish Catholic immigrants in particular. In 1833 he undertook on behalf of the church an unsuccessful diplomatic mission to Haiti. England died in Charleston on April 11, 1842. His writings were collected and published in 1849.

Enos, William Berkeley, see Berkeley, Busby

Ericsson, John (1803–1889), engineer and inventor. Born in Värmland County, Sweden, on July 31, 1803, Ericsson displayed from an early age a fascination with machinery. At thirteen he joined an engineering corps engaged in canal construction and received from his older companions instruction in mathematics, science, and drafting. He later served as a topographer with the Swedish army until 1826, when he went to London. For 13 years he remained there, working as an independent engineer and laying the groundwork for his later achievements. He was particularly interested in developing mechanical sources of motive power; while he made many improvements in steam-engine design and construction, he sought to find a more direct and efficient means of utilizing heat energy and through his life constructed various sorts of "caloric" engines, none of which, however, successfully competed with steam. In 1829 he constructed a locomotive for the competition that was won by George Stephenson's *Rocket.* Later he turned to ship design and propulsion; hitting on the idea of placing the engines below the waterline, he began using a screw propeller instead of the paddlewheel. In 1837 his ship *Francis B. Ogden* was successfully tested, and he followed it with the *Novelty,* the first propeller-driven commercial vessel. Commissioned by Capt. Robert F. Stockton of the U.S. navy to build another such ship, he went to New York City in 1839. His new propulsion system was quickly adopted for a number of commercial steamers, and in 1844 the *Princeton* became the first warship to be so powered. In 1848 Ericsson became a U.S. citizen. In 1861 his proposal for a new type of warship was approved by a government board and in an almost incredibly short time the *Monitor* was built and launched early in 1862. On March 9 it met the Confederate ironclad *Virginia* (formerly the *Merrimack*) in a much-celebrated battle in Hampton Roads. The *Monitor* opened the age of modern warships; powered solely by steam and propeller-driven, constructed entirely of iron and heavily armored, and armed with heavy guns mounted in a revolving turret, it began a revolution in naval warfare. Ericsson was widely hailed for his achievement and continued to design and build

ironclads throughout the Civil War. In 1878 he launched the *Destroyer,* a ship capable of firing underwater torpedoes from its bow. While continuing to work on versions of his "caloric" engine, he also investigated other possible sources of power, particularly solar energy, and made improvements in ordnance. The great number, variety, and importance of his inventions marked him as one of the most creative and far-sighted engineers of his century. He died in New York City on March 8, 1889; the following year, at the request of the Swedish government, his body was returned to his native land.

Ericsson, Leif, see Leif Ericsson

Erikson, Erik Homburger (1902–   ), psychoanalyst and author. Born on June 15, 1902, in Frankfurt, Germany, Erikson was the son of Danish parents. After completing a classical secondary education in Karlsruhe he traveled and pursued artistic interests until 1927, when he settled in Vienna and began teaching in a progressive elementary school. He enrolled in the Vienna Psychoanalytic Institute, where he received his training from Anna Freud and from which he graduated in 1933; during that period he was also certified as a teacher qualified to use Montessori methods. In 1933 he emigrated to the United States and began practice as a children's analyst in Boston, working privately and in association with the Massachusetts General Hospital and with the Harvard Psychological Clinic. In 1936 he joined the Institute of Human Relations at Yale, where he also taught in the medical school. From 1939, the year he became a U.S. citizen, to 1950 he taught and conducted research at the San Francisco Psychoanalytic Institute and at the University of California at Berkeley. Erikson had early begun to take anthropological data into consideration in his psychoanalytic work and his studies of children from various social milieus, including those of Sioux and Yurok Indian tribes, reinforced his conviction of the validity of such a synthesis. His observations led to a theoretical formulation expressed in his first and most widely influential book, *Childhood and Society,* 1950, in which he isolated several stages of development of the psyche, each attended by a crisis of reorientation, and showed how the manifestation of each stage was closely tied to the child's social context. The book greatly broadened the Freudian interpretation of childhood development and introduced the fruitful concept of the adolescent "identity crisis." From 1950 to 1960 Erikson was associated with the Austen Riggs Center in Stockbridge, Massachusetts, and the Western Psychiatric Institute of the University of Pittsburgh School of Medicine. In 1958 he published *Young Man Luther,* a psychohistorical study of Martin Luther in which he applied his analytic theory to the personal and public history of the reformer. Erikson was appointed professor of human development and lecturer in psychiatry at Harvard in 1960, holding the posts until his retirement in 1970. Others of his books included *Insight and Responsibility*, 1964; *Identity: Youth and Crisis*, 1968; and the much-acclaimed *Gandhi's Truth: On the Origin of Militant Nonviolence*, 1969, which won a Pulitzer Prize.

Erlanger, Joseph (1874–1965), physiologist. Born on January 5, 1874, in San Francisco, Erlanger graduated from the University of California in 1895 and took his M.D. from The Johns Hopkins University School of Medicine in 1899. The next year he was appointed an assistant in physiology, and he advanced to instructor in 1901 and to associate professor in 1904. In 1906 he moved to the University of Wisconsin as professor and head of the department of physiology; for a time much of his energy was absorbed in organizational work in the newly opened medical school. At length, however, he was able to return to his researches on the action and nervous stimulation of the heart and on the recording sphygmomanometer he had earlier invented. In 1910 he became professor and chairman of the department of physiology at Washington University in St. Louis and again had to complete the organization of his department before continuing his researches. Erlanger conducted a study of the mechanism whereby the sounds involved in the measurement of blood pressure are produced and then became interested in the electrical properties of the nervous system. He was joined on the Washington faculty by Herbert S. Gasser, a former student of his at Wisconsin, and together they devised a series of experiments with the nervous tissue of frogs that led to vastly increased knowledge of the nature of nerve impulses. They discarded electromechanical recording devices in favor of the new cathode-ray tube, employing it as an oscillograph. They were able thereby to determine the configuration of the impulse, measure its strength and duration accurately, and discover that different sorts of nerve fibers exhibit a wide range of transmission characteristics. Testing of individual fibers revealed the relationship between their thickness and the speed of impulse transmission. Their experiments continued with increasingly sophisticated electronics until Gasser's departure in 1931; they were awarded the 1944 Nobel Prize for Physiology and Medicine. Erlanger's later researches continued along the same lines, shedding light on the mechanism of impulse transmission and on the nature of subthreshold stimuli, and helping to establish the discontinuous nature of such transmission. He retired from Washington University in 1946 and died in St. Louis on December 6, 1965.

Erskine, John (1879–1951), educator, author, and musician. Born in New York City on October 5, 1879, Erskine was drawn to music as a child and studied piano for many years, for a time under composer Edward MacDowell. He graduated from Columbia in 1900, took his Ph.D. in 1903, and for six years thereafter taught English as instructor and then associate professor, at Amherst College. In 1909 he joined the Columbia faculty; he became a full professor of English in 1916. During 28 years there he became a highly popular and influential teacher, numbering among his students Mark Van Doren, Mortimer J. Adler, Clifton Fadiman, and Rexford G. Tugwell. The central thesis of his teaching—that liberal education rested upon the reading and assimilation of the major works of learning and literature of the past—was the primary inspiration for the later "great books" programs instituted at many colleges and universities. Throughout his career he maintained his musical interests; he performed often with private ensembles and occasionally on the concert stage, and was deeply involved with the Juilliard School of Music as trustee from 1927 and as president from 1928 to 1937. He published numerous scholarly works and volumes of poetry, coedited the *Cambridge History of American Literature*, 1917–1919, and in 1925 created something of a sensation with his thoroughly unacademic novel, *The Private Life of Helen of Troy*, a humorous version of the legend set in the contemporary Jazz Age scene. The book was highly successful and was translated into 16 languages. In later books he similarly treated the figures of Sir Galahad, Adam and Eve, François Villon, and others. In 1937 he retired and devoted himself to writing. His other published works included *The Moral Obligation to Be Intelligent*, 1915; *Democracy and Ideals*, 1920; *The Delight of Great Books*, 1928; *The Start of the Road*, 1938, on Walt Whitman; *Give Me Liberty*, 1940, on Patrick Henry; and *What Is Music?*, 1944. *The Memory of Certain Persons*, 1947; *My Life as a Teacher*, 1948; *My Life in Music*, 1950; and *My Life as a Writer*, 1951, were personal reminiscences. Erskine died in New York on June 2, 1951.

Espy, James Pollard (1785–1860), meteorologist. Born on May 9, 1785, in Pennsylvania, Espy grew up there and in Kentucky and in 1808 graduated from Transylvania University. For several years he taught school, first in Xenia, Ohio, then in Cumberland, Maryland, and finally in Philadelphia. He became interested in the mechanics of storms and over a period of time evolved a general convection theory of storms that, while incorrect in many respects, contained the valuable suggestion that the progressive expansion and cooling of upward currents of air was the cause of precipitation. Espy lectured widely in the United States and Europe on his theory, describing it to leading scientific bodies and publishing it in his *Philosophy of Storms*, 1841, all of which won him the popular title of "Storm King." In 1842 he received a congressional appointment as meteorologist to the War Department and six years later was given similar duties with the navy as well. He organized a system for obtaining weather observations, compiled annual reports, and pioneered in the use of the telegraph for collecting current data. In 1852 he transferred his work to the Smithsonian Institution, where

Joseph Henry had begun a major weather service based on the work of a corps of reporting observers. Espy died in Cincinnati on January 24, 1860.

Evans, George Henry (1805–1856), editor and reformer. Born on March 25, 1805, in Bromyard, England, Evans emigrated to the United States with his family in 1820. Apprenticed to a printer in Ithaca, New York, he soon edited his own paper, *The Man;* in 1829, in New York City, he began the *Working Man's Advocate,* the first important U.S. labor paper, which appeared sporadically until 1845; it was dedicated to the support of attempts to organize labor. Evans favored a political approach to the labor problem; his program embraced the natural-rights philosophy of Thomas Jefferson and Thomas Paine and in many ways anticipated that of Henry George. He advocated land reform and a system of free homesteading on public lands as a means of drawing off excess labor from the East and maintaining high wage scales, and to this end he organized the National Reform Association to agitate for political action. His efforts spurred the movement that led eventually to the Homestead Act of 1862. At intervals from 1837 to 1853 he edited also the *Daily Sentinel* and *Young America.* In 1840 he published his *History of the Origin and Progress of the Working Men's Party,* combining an exposition of his plan of reform, opposition to imported reform movements such as Fourierism, and an analysis of the past failures of labor and agrarian organizations. He died on February 2, 1856, in Granville, New Jersey.

Evans, John (1814–1897), physician, businessman, and philanthropist. Born in Waynesville, Ohio, on March 9, 1814, Evans graduated from Lynn Medical College in Cincinnati in 1838 and the next year settled in Attica, Indiana. His successful practice enabled him to begin making profitable real-estate investments and he became active in a number of reform movements; his most notable reform work was helping in the establishment of Indiana's first state hospital for the mentally ill, for which he led in securing legislation and of which he was appointed the first superintendent, moving to Indianapolis in 1845 to fill the post. In 1848 he moved to Chicago to become professor of obstetrics at the Rush Medical College. There he was also publisher and an editor of the *Northwestern Medical and Surgical Journal.* He continued to invest in real estate in the Chicago area and acquired an interest in the Fort Wayne & Chicago Railroad as well. Evans moved to a suburban area north of Chicago and in 1851 was a leader in securing a charter for and in founding Northwestern University there; the town that grew up around the university was named Evanston in his honor and he was active in its early civic affairs. In 1862 Evans was appointed territorial governor of Colorado and quickly became one of the most prominent figures in both the political and the business life of the region. After his

resignation in 1865 he was elected to the Senate, but the failure of Colorado to achieve statehood rendered his election nugatory. As his wealth continued to grow he gave liberally to religious institutions, particularly those of a Methodist persuasion, and in 1864 he founded and thereafter served as president of the board of trustees of Colorado Seminary (later the University of Denver). He actively promoted railroad connections for Denver; the building of the Denver Pacific Railroad & Telegraph Company and the South Park Railroad saved the city from the isolation resulting from its being bypassed by the great transcontinental lines. Mt. Evans, west of Denver, was named for him by an 1895 act of the legislature. He died in Denver on July 3, 1897.

Evans, Oliver (1755–1819), inventor. Born in 1755 near Newport, Delaware, Evans was indentured to a wagon builder at fourteen and continued to study, particularly mechanics and mathematics, on his own time. Throughout his career he suffered from lack of financial support for his inventions and from the failure of the public to understand them. While employed in making card teeth for carding wool, he perfected in 1777 a machine that produced 1500 cards a minute. In 1780 he joined his brothers in a flour-milling venture, and five years later he had ready for use a flour mill with automatic machinery to accomplish every step of the process. The mill was water-powered, used a conveyor system to move the grain and flour through the mill, and required only one operator. Millers refused to adopt the new machinery, fearful of being displaced themselves and reluctant to dismiss their workers. From about 1786 Evans devoted himself largely to experimenting with steam power. He had arrived at the idea of a steam carriage some 13 years previously, but lack of funds prevented him from continuing work on the project. He then turned to the development of a high-pressure stationary steam engine and again proved his detractors wrong by making it practical. By 1802 he had converted the flour mill to steam power, and the next year he started to manufacture steam engines; in 1807 the business became the Mars Iron Works. In one of his most remarkable achievements, he developed in 1804 a steam-powered river dredge, which he steered over land and maneuvered into the water under its own power, thus anticipating both the steamboat and the automobile. In 1817 he planned and built the engines and boilers for the Fairmount Waterworks in Philadelphia. He died in New York City on April 21, 1819.

Evans, Walker (1903–1975), photographer. Born in St. Louis on November 3, 1903, Evans moved with his family successively to Toledo, Ohio; Kenilworth, Illinois; and New York City. He was educated at Phillips Academy, Andover, Massachusetts, and for a year, 1922–1923, at Williams College; in Paris in 1926–1927 he also studied briefly at the Sorbonne. Originally set on a literary career, he turned to photography in about 1928 and then held a series of minor jobs while developing his technique. In one of his jobs he formed a friendship with a co-worker, Hart Crane, in the first edition of whose *The Bridge*, 1930, three of his photographs represented his first published work. Evans had his first gallery show in 1932 and began to receive commissions for illustrative work. From 1935 to 1937 he was employed by the Farm Security Administration, for which he toured the rural countryside recording scenes of poverty and despair in hundreds of photographs. On a leave of absence during this period he joined James Agee in a study of Alabama sharecroppers commissioned by *Fortune* magazine; their work was instead published in book form as *Let Us Now Praise Famous Men*, 1941. Evans's photographs, bleak, devoid of either visual trickery or romanticism, were spare, motionless studies whose impact was heightened by their seeming detachment. A master of photographic naturalism, he seemed to capture rather than create his scenes and moods, imbuing them with a realism of striking force. In 1938 a major exhibition of his works was held at the Museum of Modern Art in New York City; from it were drawn those published in his *American Photographs* in the same year. From 1943 to 1945 he was a contributing editor of *Time* magazine and from 1945 to 1965 an associate editor of *Fortune*, to which he contributed a long series of notable photo-essays. He enjoyed a number of exhibitions and many of his photographs entered the permanent collections of major museums and galleries. Selections of his work were published as *Many Are Called*, 1966, and *Message From the Interior*, 1966. Some 200 of his photographs were featured in a retrospective show at the Museum of Modern Art in 1971. From 1965 until his retirement Evans was professor of graphic design at the Yale School of Art and Architecture. He died in New Haven, Connecticut, on April 10, 1975.

Evarts, William Maxwell (1818–1901), lawyer and public official. Born on February 6, 1818, in Boston, Evarts attended Yale, where he was a founder of the *Yale Literary Magazine*, and upon graduating in 1837 took up the study of law, privately and for a year in the law school at Harvard. Admitted to the bar in 1841, he began practice in New York City and the next year organized a law firm, Butler, Evarts, and Southmayd, that later numbered Joseph H. Choate among its members. Evarts quickly became one of the most prominent lawyers in the city. He handled a number of notable cases and attracted considerable attention in several actions involving the status of slaves in free territory; he was himself opposed to slavery and contributed heavily to the Emigrant Aid Company, but he upheld the constitutional legality of the institution. While pursuing his legal career he became active in Whig politics and, from 1854, in Republican politics. From 1849 to 1853 he served as assistant U.S. attorney for southern New York and in 1860

led the New York delegation to the Republican national convention. During 1863–1864 he twice traveled to England on diplomatic missions, attempting to put an end to the supply of naval matériel to the Confederacy. He appeared for the government in a number of cases, including the 1867 prosecution of Jefferson Davis for treason, and in 1868 was a key member of the defense counsel in the impeachment of President Andrew Johnson. Later in that year Johnson appointed him attorney general; he held the post until March 1869. In 1870 he was a founder and for its first ten years president of the Bar Association of New York City, in which position he led in the fight against the corrupt "Tweed Ring," and also in 1870 he appeared before the Supreme Court in *Hepburn* v. *Griswold*, the first of the Legal Tender Cases. During 1871–1872 he was, with Caleb Cushing and his Yale classmate, Morrison R. Waite, a counsel for the United States in the arbitration in Geneva of the *Alabama* claims, winning the respect of his British opponents for his profound understanding of international law and for his marked courtesy. Evarts was a leading candidate for appointment as chief justice of the Supreme Court in 1873, but the opposition of Senator Roscoe Conkling led to the naming of Waite. In 1875 he defended Henry Ward Beecher in the celebrated adultery case brought against him, and in 1877 was chief counsel for the Republican party in the Electoral Commission's hearings on the disputed presidential election of 1876. In 1877 President Rutherford B. Hayes appointed him secretary of state; on leaving the cabinet in 1881 he resumed his practice until 1885, when he was elected to the Senate. In 1891, after a single term, during which his eyesight began to fail, he retired to New York City. In addition to his legal and political activities, in all of which he earned the highest regard, Evarts was known as an orator and after-dinner speaker; on July 4, 1876, he had given the principal address in Philadelphia on the centennial of the Declaration of Independence. After ten years in retirement he died in New York City on February 28, 1901.

Everett, Edward (1794–1865), clergyman, public official, and orator. Born in Dorchester, Massachusetts, on April 11, 1794, Everett graduated at the head of his Harvard class of 1811 and turned to the study of theology. In 1814 he became pastor of the Brattle Street Church in Boston. A year later, having been appointed professor of Greek literature at Harvard, he began four years of study and travel in Europe by way of preparation for the post; he was awarded a Ph.D. from Göttingen in 1817. In 1819 he entered upon his duties at Harvard and the following year assumed the editorship of the *North American Review*, which he retained until 1823. In 1824 he was elected to the House of Representatives and served there for ten years; although he was already widely noted for his oratory, his politics were vague. From 1835 to 1839 he was governor of Massachusetts, and from 1841 to 1845 U.S. minister to England. Following his election as president of Harvard in 1846, a position he held for three years, he withdrew from politics for a time. He served as secretary of state during the last four months of President Millard Fillmore's administration and immediately thereafter, in 1853, entered the Senate. Adverse reaction among his Abolitionist constituents to his strongly Unionist but otherwise conciliatory and compromising stands, particularly on the Kansas-Nebraska Bill, caused him to resign in 1854. He then devoted himself to lecturing and was eminently successful. In 1860 he accepted the vice-presidential nomination of the Constitutional Union party and, as he expected, lost the election badly. The outbreak of war ended his desire for compromise; throughout the Civil War he traveled and spoke in support of the Union cause. On November 19, 1863, he delivered the principal address, two hours long, at the dedication of the national cemetery at Gettysburg, Pennsylvania; it was the best speech of a great orator, although it is now overshadowed by the short address that followed it. (Everett wrote to President Abraham Lincoln the next day: "I should be glad if I could flatter myself that I came as near the central idea of the occasion in two hours as you did in two minutes.") He had achieved vast popularity in his last years, and partially as a result of the exertions of his many speaking engagements, he died in Boston on January 15, 1865.

Evers, Charles (1923–   ), civil-rights activist. Born in Decatur, Mississippi, on September 11, 1923, James Charles Evers and his brother Medgar Wiley Evers, also born in Decatur, on July 2, 1925, grew up in an atmosphere of racial oppression and both were early impressed by the violence dealt to black men on little or no provocation. They attended high school in nearby Newton and during World War II both served in the army, Medgar in Europe and Charles in the Pacific theater. Afterward both graduated from Alcorn Agricultural and Mechanical College in 1950. They settled in Philadelphia, Mississippi, and engaged in various business pursuits—Medgar was an insurance salesman and Charles operated a restaurant, a gas station, and other enterprises—and at the same time began organizing local affiliates of the National Association for the Advancement of Colored People (NAACP). They worked quietly at first, slowly building a base of support, and in 1954 Medgar moved to Jackson to become the NAACP's first field secretary in Mississippi. He traveled throughout the state recruiting members and organizing voter-registration drives and economic boycotts. Charles remained in Philadelphia, also active in voter registration and other aspects of civil-rights work, until 1957, by which time the mounting hostility of white people in the community had caused his businesses to close. He then moved to Chicago and worked at various jobs, eventually going into business again as operator of a cocktail lounge. During the early 1960s

the increased tempo of civil-rights activities in the South created high and constant tensions and in Mississippi conditions were often at the breaking point. On June 12, 1963, a few hours after President John F. Kennedy had made an extraordinary broadcast to the nation on the subject of civil rights, Medgar Evers was shot and killed from ambush in front of his home. The murder received national attention and made Evers, until then a hard-working and effective but relatively obscure figure outside of Mississippi, a martyr to the cause of civil rights; he was buried with full military honors in Arlington National Cemetery and awarded the 1963 Spingarn Medal of the NAACP. Charles immediately requested and was granted appointment by the NAACP to his brother's position in Mississippi. After several successful campaigns to win employment opportunities for black people he moved his headquarters to Fayette and, under the provisions of the 1965 Voting Rights Act, began intensive registration drives in several southwestern Mississippi counties where blacks had a numerical superiority over whites. By 1966 he had organized a black voting block that was able to elect a county school board member, the first black man to win elective office in the state since Reconstruction. Evers put forward a moderate position on civil rights and was successful in keeping the anxieties of the white community below the threshold of violent reaction. In 1967, 12 black candidates for various offices were elected, along with a number of white moderates, and the traditional white-supremacy style of campaigning began to fade. In 1968, after losing a congressional election, Evers bolted the still predominantly white state Democratic caucus and formed an insurgent delegation that wrested accreditation from the regulars at the party's national convention in Chicago. The next year, following a campaign that was reported throughout the country, Evers was elected mayor of Fayette, becoming the first black mayor of a biracial Mississippi town in a century. In 1971 he was defeated for governor in an election that was, in an unspoken tribute to the work he had already accomplished, remarkably free of open racial appeals.

Evers, Medgar Wiley, see under Evers, Charles

Ewry, Ray C. (1873–1937), athlete. Born in Lafayette, Indiana, on October 14, 1873, Ewry suffered a severe attack of poliomyelitis in childhood and for a time doctors despaired of his life. He recovered gradually, however, and on his doctor's advice began exercising regularly to restore his strength, particularly in his legs. In 1890 he entered Purdue University, where, while studying mechanical engineering, he starred in track and field sports and for a year on the football team. On taking a graduate degree in 1897 he moved to New York City and found employment as a hydraulics engineer with a city department. He continued his interest in sports as a member of the New York Athletic Club (NYAC). In 1900 he won a place on the U.S. team sent to the second modern Olympiad in Paris. Ewry entered three events, the standing high jump, the standing broad jump, and the standing hop, step, and jump, and won all three; his marks in the first, an astounding 5'5", and the third, 34'8½", set Olympic records. At the III Olympiad in 1904 in St. Louis he again won all three of his specialties, setting a record for the standing broad jump at 11'4⅞". An unofficial Olympic meet was held in Athens in 1906 and Ewry continued to dominate his events, although the standing hop, step, and jump had by that time been discontinued. In 1908, at the age of thirty-five, he capped his career with two more wins at the IV Olympiad, held in London, bringing his career total to eight gold medals (ten, counting the 1906 games). His record was eventually largely forgotten, in part because of the general disorganization of the records of the early Olympiads and in part because of the dropping of the two remaining standing events after the 1912 meet; it remained nonetheless secure for 64 years until 1972, when swimmer Mark Spitz won a ninth gold medal at Munich. Ewry died on September 29, 1937.

F

Faber, John Eberhard (1822–1879), manufacturer. Born on December 6, 1822, in Stein, Bavaria (now part of Germany), Faber was of a family of pencil manufacturers; the business had been established by his great-grandfather in 1761 and had been built into a leader among European industries. At his father's wish he studied law at the universities of Erlangen and Heidelberg, but gave more attention to history and classics. Soon after the revolution of 1848 he emigrated to the United States and in New York City in 1849 began to import and market pencils from the Stein factory. The business grew to include a full line of imported stationery as well. Faber later bought tracts of cedar forest in Florida, built a sawmill at Cedar Keys, and began shipping wood back to Bavaria for turning into pencils. At length he decided to eliminate the transportation and tariff costs by manufacturing pencils himself, and in New York City in 1861 he opened the first pencil factory in the United States. Although he had still to import graphite and clay from abroad and the period of the Civil War was an inauspicious time to launch a major enterprise, the business prospered and quickly expanded. Extensive use of machinery in place of manual labor was a large factor in his success. He introduced an innovation in attaching a rubber eraser tip to his pencils and another in his use of metal point protectors. He later built a second factory in Newark, New Jersey, to produce erasers and rubber bands. Faber died at his home in Staten Island, New York, on March 2, 1879.

Fadiman, Clifton Paul (1904–   ), editor and author. Born on May 15, 1904, in Brooklyn, New York, Fadiman graduated in 1925 from Columbia University, where his already marked interest in books was encouraged by John Erskine's lectures on the classics and by Mark Van Doren's English courses. After a time teaching in the Ethical Culture School in New York City he became an editor for the publishing house of Simon & Schuster in 1927. He contributed essays and reviews to a number of periodicals and in 1933 became a regular book reviewer for the *New Yorker,* attracting wide notice with his discriminating independence and his application of common-sensical as well as literary standards. After leaving Simon & Schuster in 1935 he served in advisory capacities with the Limited Editions Club and the Readers' Club, selecting literary works for republication and writing critical introductory essays for a number of them. From 1938 to 1948 he moderated the popular and lively "Information, Please!" radio program. He edited

a number of books, including *I Believe,* 1939, *Reading I've Liked,* 1941, and collections of stories by Henry James, Ambrose Bierce, John P. Marquand, and others, and wrote introductions to editions of works by a wide range of authors. He left the *New Yorker* in 1943 and in 1944 became a member of the editorial board of the Book-of-the-Month Club. He moderated "Conversation" on radio from 1954 to 1957 and on television was master of ceremonies for "This Is Show Business," "What's in a Word?," and "The Name's the Same." From 1951 he contributed a regular column to *Holiday* magazine, publishing a collection of the essays in *Party of One,* 1955. He also wrote or edited *Any Number Can Play,* 1957; *Fantasia Mathematica,* 1958; *The Lifetime Reading Plan,* 1959; *Enter Conversing,* 1962; and *Fifty Years,* 1965. In addition, he edited an anthology of notable quotations from American history and letters, *The American Treasury,* 1955. In 1959 Fadiman became a member of the board of editors of Encyclopaedia Britannica, Inc., for which, with Mortimer J. Adler and Robert M. Hutchins, he edited the ten-volume *Gateway to the Great Books,* 1963, and was a consultant for production of educational films.

Fagan, Eleanora, *see* Holiday, Billie

Fair, A. A., *see* Gardner, Erle Stanley

Fairbanks, Charles Warren (1852–1918), public official and vice-president of the United States. Born near Unionville Center, Ohio, on May 11, 1852, Fairbanks grew up on a farm and supported himself while attending Ohio Wesleyan University, graduating in 1872. While working for the Associated Press in Pittsburgh and Cleveland he studied law and upon his admission to the bar in 1874 established himself in Indianapolis. He soon acquired a wide reputation and a lucrative practice in railroad cases, his influence extending well beyond the borders of Indiana. He also became involved in Republican politics, working as an organizer and manager and eschewing public office until his position within the state party was secure and dominant. In 1896 he was temporary chairman and keynote speaker of the Republican national convention that nominated William McKinley and the next year was elected to the Senate, where he became a prominent member of several important committees and the unofficial spokesman for the McKinley administration; in 1898 he served as chairman of the U.S. members of the U.S.–British joint commission charged with settling the Canada–Alaska boundary dispute. He was reelected easily in 1903 and, following the nomination of Theodore Roosevelt for president in 1904, was named to run for vice-president, a choice that provided conservative balance to the ticket and helped win the doubtful vote of Indiana. Elected with Roosevelt, he served until 1909; he held no other office thereafter, although he was Indiana's favorite-son candidate for the presidential nomination in 1908 and 1916. A thoroughgoing party regular, he supported William Howard Taft over Roosevelt in the Republican split of 1912. In 1916 he was nominated for vice-president on the unsuccessful ticket with Charles Evans Hughes. Fairbanks died in Indianapolis on June 4, 1918.

Fairbanks, Douglas (1883–1939), actor. Born on May 23, 1883, in Denver, Douglas Elton Fairbanks grew up in his native city and eventually attended the Colorado School of Mines. Originally surnamed Ulman, he and his mother adopted the name Fairbanks (from her first husband) upon her divorce from his father in 1900. His dramatic training came at a neighborhood school, where he met actor Frederick Warde, who gave him early encouragement. He and his mother moved to the East in 1900 and he joined one of Warde's repertory theater groups. With them he made his professional debut in Richmond, Virginia, on September 10, 1900, in *The Duke's Jester*. His first major role was the juvenile lead in *A Gentleman from Mississippi*, which played in New York during 1909–1911. In 1915 the lure of Hollywood salaries brought him to the movies. Unlike many former stage actors who could not meet the closeup demands of the cameras, Fairbanks was photogenic and graceful (he was always in prime physical condition), and delighted in acting before the camera; indeed, his broad, athletic stage manner was perfectly suited to the new medium. Like such other stars of the silent film as Charlie Chaplin, Mary Pickford, and William S. Hart, he was admired to the point of worship by a large part of the movie-going public. He portrayed a succession of heroic young American characters in such early movies as *The Americano*, 1916; *He Comes Up Smiling*, 1918; *Knickerbocker Buckaroo*, 1919; and *The Mollycoddle*, 1920. He wrote several books, *Laugh and Live*, 1917, and *Assuming Responsibilities* and *Making Life Worth While*, both in 1918, in which his real-life philosophies seemed as gallant as his film characterizations; as the real-life hero, he married "America's Sweetheart," Mary Pickford, in 1920. In 1919 he had joined with Chaplin and D. W. Griffith to found the United Artists company to produce and distribute films. During the 1920s Fairbanks made the films for which he is best remembered; he played the handsome, swashbuckling hero in such costume spectaculars as *The Mark of Zorro*, 1920; *The Three Musketeers*, 1921; *Robin Hood*, 1922; *The Thief of Bagdad*, 1924; *Don Q, Son of Zorro*, 1925; *The Black Pirate*, 1926; and *The Gaucho*, 1927. When talkies were introduced his popularity gradually de-

clined. In 1935 he and Mary Pickford were divorced and thereafter he spent much of his time in Europe. In 1939 he organized the Fairbanks-International producing company whose first picture, *The Californian*, starred his son, Douglas Fairbanks, Jr. Fairbanks died on December 12, 1939, in Santa Monica, California.

Fairbanks, Douglas, Jr. (1909–   ), actor. Born on December 9, 1909, in New York City, the son of Douglas Fairbanks, he was raised by his mother, Anna Beth Sully, and attended school in California and was tutored privately in London and Paris. At thirteen he made his movie debut in *Stephen Steps Out*, but he was not recognized as a fine actor until 1927, when he appeared in the play *Young Woodley*, in Los Angeles. During the 1930s he became a star in his own right, although in many of his films he continued the line of exuberant heroes begun by his father; his successful movies included *Dawn Patrol*, 1930; *Morning Glory*, 1933; *Catherine the Great*, 1934; *The Prisoner of Zenda*, 1937; and *Gunga Din*, 1939. During World War II he served in the navy with distinction. After the war, he became a successful television producer in England and had extensive business interests there and in the United States.

Fairchild, David Grandison (1869–1954), botanist and agricultural explorer. Born on April 7, 1869, in Lansing, Michigan, Fairchild graduated from the Kansas State College of Agriculture in 1888 and briefly pursued graduate studies at the University of Iowa and at Rutgers University. In 1889 he joined the plant pathology section of the Department of Agriculture. Further studies in Italy and Germany during 1893–1895 prepared him for the first of his many expeditions in search of new and useful plants, a journey to Java and other places in the Dutch East Indies in 1895. After a second expedition in 1896–1897 to the Pacific on which he ranged south to Australia, he returned to Washington, D.C., to assist in organizing the department's section of foreign seed and plant introduction. He continued to serve in that section as an explorer until 1903, as director from 1903 until his retirement in 1928, and thereafter as collaborator and adviser. His explorations took him to every part of the globe and resulted in the introduction into the United States of thousands of new plant species; as late as 1944, at the age of seventy-five, he made a collecting trip through Central America. The Fairchild Tropical Garden near his home in Coconut Grove, Florida, founded in 1938, was named in his honor and was, with the test garden begun there by him 40 years earlier, the recipient over the years of upwards of 200,000 specimens collected on his various journeys. Fairchild published a number of popular books, including *Exploring for Plants*, 1930; *The World Was My Garden*, 1938, his autobiography; *Garden Islands of the Great East*, 1944; and *The World Grows Round My Door*, 1947. He was married in 1905 to

Marian, the daughter of Alexander Graham Bell. Widely honored for his services to American agriculture, Fairchild died in Coconut Grove on August 6, 1954.

Falkner, William Cuthbert, see Faulkner, William Cuthbert

Fargo, William George (1818–1881), businessman. Born in Pompey, in Onondaga County, New York, on May 20, 1818, Fargo early went to work, holding a variety of jobs from grocery clerk to freight agent for the Auburn & Syracuse Railroad. In 1842 he became a messenger for the express firm of Pomeroy & Company, operating between Albany and Buffalo, and the next year was the company's Buffalo agent. He made the acquaintance of a fellow employee, Henry Wells, and in 1844 they formed Wells & Company, later Livingston, Wells & Company, which in 1845 opened the pioneering Western Express from Buffalo to Cincinnati, Chicago, and St. Louis. In 1846 Wells left to form a new Livingston, Wells, & Company in New York City, while the original became Livingston, Fargo & Company. Competition on the Albany–Buffalo run, as well as in the rapidly expanding Western service, became tighter with the appearance of John Butterfield's Butterfield, Wasson & Company in 1849, and in 1850 the three firms merged in a complicated arrangement and organized the American Express Company, of which Fargo was secretary. The discovery of gold in California and the consequent need for express links between East and West led Fargo, Wells, Butterfield, and others to form Wells, Fargo & Company in 1852. At first the company concentrated on transportation from New York to California via Panama, but it soon began running stage lines for gold shipments in California; after the failure of the earlier Adams & Company in 1855, Wells, Fargo & Company was the leading express company in the West. It followed prospectors to new mineral strikes throughout the region and provided transport and banking services to frontier mining communities. By absorbing smaller competitors or driving them out of business it grew constantly; in 1866, with the purchase of the Holladay Overland Mail & Express Company, which earlier had bought out John Butterfield's Overland Mail Company (organized with Fargo's help), the Wells, Fargo Company attained a virtual monopoly on commercial transportation west of the Missouri River. The completion of the transcontinental railroad in 1869 largely curtailed stagecoach operations and the company concentrated on the express and banking businesses thereafter. During these developments Fargo remained largely in Buffalo, of which he was mayor from 1862 to 1866. In 1868 American Express merged with a competitor to become the American Merchants Union Express Company with Fargo as president, a position he retained through the resumption of the American Express name in 1873 and until his death. He was also president of Wells, Fargo in 1870–1872, being succeeded by Lloyd Tevis. Along with the presidency of American Express, Fargo held directorships in the New York Central and Northern Pacific railroads. He died in Buffalo on August 3, 1881.

Farley, James Aloysius (1888–1976), political leader. Born on May 30, 1888, in Grassy Point in Rockland County, New York, Farley worked in the family brick business and in other jobs and played semiprofessional baseball until 1905, when, following graduation from high school, he moved to New York City to study bookkeeping. He joined the Universal Gypsum Company in 1911, rising eventually to salesman. Settling in Stony Point, near his native town, he became interested in local politics and served three terms as town clerk. His marked political abilities, especially in the business of person-to-person campaigning, caused him to rise in the party ranks and in 1918, in reward for campaign services that year, he was appointed by Governor Alfred E. Smith to the post of warden of the port of New York, a job that was abolished the next year. From 1920 to 1923 Farley was supervisor of Rockland County and in 1923 he served a term in the legislature. Smith, whose renomination he had engineered, then appointed him to the state athletic commission, of which he was chairman from 1925 to 1933. In 1926 he resigned from Universal Gypsum and formed James A. Farley & Company, a lime and cement firm that through various mergers became in 1929 the General Builders Supply Corporation, of which he was president until 1933. In 1928 he became secretary of the New York State Democratic Committee and in that year and again in 1930, when he was elected chairman of the committee, played a major role in organizing and conducting the successful gubernatorial campaigns of Franklin D. Roosevelt. Convinced of Roosevelt's great potential, he began in 1931 to round up support for a presidential nomination, traveling throughout the country and exercising his personal charm on party workers and delegates. At the 1932 Democratic national convention Farley headed the Roosevelt forces on the floor and arranged the deal whereby John Nance Garner received the vice-presidential nomination in return for support of Roosevelt by the Texas and California delegations. Assuming then the post of the chairman of the Democratic National Committee, Farley directed the campaign and after the election of Roosevelt was appointed postmaster general. As chief of patronage for the long-out-of-office Democrats, he drew some criticism by his largesse, but in the main conquered all with his geniality and vast popularity (his boast of having "100,000 friends" was but little exaggerated). In 1936 he again directed the Roosevelt campaign and reinforced his reputation as a political wizard, by predicting correctly that Roosevelt would carry all but two states, and as a wit in subsequently explaining that "As Maine goes, so goes Vermont." In 1938 he published *Behind the Ballots*, a volume of memoirs. A rift between Farley and Roosevelt gradually developed, however, and in 1940 he resigned as postmaster general and as chairman of the national committee; because of his opposition to Roosevelt's third-term bid he allowed his own name to go before the convention that year. He later accepted the position of chairman of the board of the Coca-Cola Export Company, later also holding board positions with various foreign subsidiaries of Coca-Cola, and in 1949 he resumed the presidency of General Builders Supply. He retained the chairmanship of the New York State Democratic Committee until 1944, in which year he again openly opposed Roosevelt's renomination. Thereafter he devoted himself to his business interests. He published *Jim Farley's Story* in 1948. He retired from Coca-Cola in 1973 and died in New York City on June 9, 1976.

Farmer, Fannie Merritt (1857–1915), culinary expert. Born in Boston on March 23, 1857, Miss Farmer suffered a paralytic stroke during her high-school years that forced her to end her formal education. She recovered sufficiently to help with household duties and developed such an aptitude and fondness for cooking that her parents enrolled her in the Boston Cooking School. She graduated in 1889 and was asked to remain as assistant director; in 1891 she became head of the school. Although reticent, she nevertheless became much sought after as a lecturer at schools and social gatherings. She left in 1902 to open Miss Farmer's School of Cookery, which was designed to train housewives rather than servants. For a year at Harvard she conducted a course in invalid cooking, and with her sister wrote a regular column for ten years for the *Woman's Home Companion*. Her lasting contribution was twofold: the introduction of standardized level measurements in recipes, and the *Boston Cooking School Cookbook*, published in 1896 and still a best seller in a modernized version, frequently revised, *The Fannie Farmer Cookbook*. Recipes for everyday and classic dishes were accompanied by sections on formal entertaining, proper management of the home and service staff, use of kitchen equipment, and etiquette; revised editions—more than 20 in her lifetime—traced the history of changing food habits. Her largely intuitive knowledge of diet planning predated the modern science of nutrition. She stressed in her cookbook the "knowledge of the principles of diet [as an] essential part of one's education. Mankind will eat to live, will be able to do better mental and physical work, and disease will be less frequent." Her recipes were all personally tested and, thanks to accurate measurements, easy to follow successfully. She died in Boston on January 15, 1915.

Farmer, James Leonard (1920–   ), civil rights activist. Born in Marshall, Texas, on January 12, 1920, Farmer was the son of a classical scholar and teacher at Wiley College who had been the first black Texan to receive a Ph.D. He graduated

from Wiley in 1938 and turned to medicine, only to discover that he could not stand the sight of blood. He then enrolled at Howard University, studied theology, and graduated in 1941; he refused ordination in the Methodist church because it practiced racial segregation. From 1941 to 1945 he was race-relations secretary of the pacifist Fellowship of Reconciliation (FOR). In 1942 he led a group of University of Chicago students in founding the Congress of Racial Equality (CORE), becoming national chairman of the organization. Dedicated to ending racial segregation and discrimination by means of the Gandhian techniques of passive resistance and the sit-in, CORE grew over the years into a national organization with more than 70 chapters. A Chicago restaurant was the target of the first successful desegregation campaign in 1943, and in 1947 CORE sponsored a "Journey of Reconciliation" to test the segregation of interstate buses in the upper South. During the 1950s Farmer and CORE worked steadily though largely unnoticed; but widespread publicity came in 1960 when black college students in Greensboro, North Carolina, staged a sit-in at a local lunch counter and touched off the civil-rights movement of the 1960s. In 1961 CORE mounted the Freedom Rides on interstate buses, the first of which, led by Farmer, met violence and mass arrest in Mississippi. In 1963 he was unable to participate as planned in the March on Washington because he had been jailed for leading a demonstration in Plaquemine, Louisiana, from which he barely escaped with his life. From 1961 to 1966 he was national director of CORE; he was associated with many other civil-rights and reform groups and was a director of the League for Industrial Democracy and of the American Civil Liberties Union (ACLU). In 1965 he became president of the Center for Community Action Education and in 1968, as a Republican, ran unsuccessfully from a New York City district for a congressional seat. He was appointed in 1969 to the post of assistant secretary for administration of the Department of Health, Education, and Welfare; he resigned the following year.

Farmer, Moses Gerrish (1820–1893), inventor. Born on February 9, 1820, in Boscawen, New Hampshire, Farmer attended local schools and after two years at Phillips Academy, Andover, Massachusetts, entered Dartmouth College in 1838. Poor health forced him to withdraw before graduating and he took up teaching in Eliot, Maine, and later in Dover, New Hampshire, where in 1844 he became principal of a girls' school. He had a deep interest in all manner of mechanical and scientific subjects and in about 1844 he invented a machine for printing paper window shades; it quickly led to a profitable business. The work of Samuel F. B. Morse attracted his attention to electricity and in 1847 he built a model electric train with a passenger car and an engine capable of pulling a load of children. He demonstrated the train in various towns but aroused no substantial interest. In the same year he took a position with a telegraph company in South Framingham, Massachusetts, and the next year became a telegrapher in Salem, rising quickly to the superintendency of the Boston–Newburyport line. With W. F. Channing he worked on improving an electric fire-alarm system he had invented earlier and by 1852 had perfected it to the point that it was adopted for installation by the city of Boston. This device, like his train, was the first such in the country. Continuing to investigate the possibilities of the telegraph, he discovered the principle of multiplexing in 1855. The next year he developed a method for electroplating with aluminum and formed an electrotyping firm that prospered until the financial panic of 1857. During 1858–1859 he experimented with incandescent lighting; during 1859 he had two electric lamps illuminating his home. Made with platinum filaments, they preceded Thomas H. Edison's lamps by 20 years. In 1866 he devised a "self-exciting" dynamo that eliminated batteries and thereby made electric illumination practical; two years later he fitted out a house in Cambridge, Massachusetts, with a dynamo and 40 incandescent lamps. As a result of yet another electrical invention, Farmer was appointed electrician to the U.S. Torpedo Station at Newport, Rhode Island, in 1872 and during nine years there made numerous improvements in torpedoes. He resigned in 1881 and, although in poor health, served for some time as consulting electrician to the United States Electric Light Company of New York. A fertile inventor to be ranked with Edison, Farmer failed to achieve the same degree of fame largely because he experimented solely to satisfy his own curiosity and left the commercial development of inventions to others. Working with very limited means, he made nonetheless an amazing number of fundamental discoveries and technological breakthroughs. He spent his last years in Eliot, Maine, and died on May 25, 1893, while arranging a display of his inventions for the World's Columbian Exposition in Chicago.

Farnsworth, Philo Taylor (1906–1971), engineer and inventor. Born in Beaver, Utah, on August 19, 1906, Farnsworth grew up there and on a sheep ranch near Rigby, Idaho. In 1922, while still in high school, he read a popularized account of the pioneer work in transmitting moving pictures by electricity being done in the Soviet Union by Boris Rosing; he soon worked out for himself the basic principles involved and prepared a schematic diagram of the required system. After two years at Brigham Young University (1923–1925) he found financial backers for his proposed television system and began working on its practical development. By 1928 he had demonstrated the basic invention, the "image dissector" camera, which translated a scene into electric currents by electronic rather than mechanical means, making possible an image-scanning speed much greater than had been achieved by Rosing or other workers in the field. The cost of further development mounted and in the early 1930s was as-

sumed by the Philco Corporation. Farnsworth received patents for a wide array of inventions relating to his television system and was soon able to produce clear moving images in a demonstration before the Franklin Institute. In 1938, however, Philco withdrew its support. An attempt by Farnsworth and his remaining backers to begin commercial production of television equipment at a plant in Fort Wayne, Indiana, was ended by World War II; he then turned his attention to radar and other related work. By the end of the war Vladimir K. Zworykin, a former graduate student of Rosing's, had perfected his iconoscope, a television scanner based on a different principle from Farnsworth's, and had won the backing of the Radio Corporation of America (RCA), with whose huge resources the rival system was rapidly pushed into production; a cross-licensing arrangement ironed out patent overlaps with the Farnsworth system. The Farnsworth Television & Radio Corporation became a research division of the International Telephone & Telegraph Company (ITT) in 1949 and Farnsworth thereafter worked as a research consultant on various phases of electronics, later moving into the field of atomic energy and the production of usable power by nuclear fission and fusion. He received in all over 300 domestic and foreign patents and was widely honored as an outstanding engineer and a television pioneer. He died in Salt Lake City on March 11, 1971.

Farragut, David Glasgow (1801–1870), naval officer. Born near Knoxville, Tennessee, on July 5, 1801, Farragut moved with his family to New Orleans in 1807. At the age of nine he was adopted by Capt. David Porter and appointed a midshipman in the navy; apparently in honor of his foster father, he changed his first name from James to David about 1814. From 1811 through the end of the War of 1812 he served under Porter on the *Essex* and, at the age of twelve, was briefly in command of a captured prize ship. For the next several years he served on various ships, principally in the Mediterranean, and for a time studied under the U.S. consul at Tunis. He devoted considerable energy to remedying his neglected education and became fluent in several languages. In 1823–1824 he was again with Porter in a campaign to suppress piracy in Caribbean waters. Farragut was promoted to lieutenant in 1825, to commander in 1841, and to captain in 1855; progress was slow, however, for his duties at sea and ashore during this period, including the Mexican War, had been routine. After the outbreak of the Civil War he was chosen, in December 1861, largely on the recommendation of his foster brother, Cmdr. David Dixon Porter, to command the West Gulf Blockading Squadron; his orders were to capture New Orleans and gain control of the Mississippi. In April 1862, following his instructions, Farragut first attempted to reduce the defending Fort Jackson by mortar fire; this soon proving fruitless, he decided to run past the fort in the dark. Despite heavy fire he passed

Fort Jackson and Fort St. Philip farther upstream, defeated the small Confederate flotilla, and captured New Orleans on April 24. Within days the two forts likewise surrendered and Union troops occupied the city. In July Farragut was promoted to rear admiral. For the next two years he was engaged in the blockade of the Gulf Coast and in controlling traffic on the lower Mississippi and its tributaries, contributing materially to the capture of Vicksburg and the establishment of Union control over the entire river. In 1864 he was given an assignment he had long sought, the capture of the defenses of Mobile Bay. The entrance to the bay was heavily mined except for a narrow channel under the guns of Fort Morgan. On August 5 Farragut began his approach; the ironclads *Tecumseh* and *Brooklyn* led the fleet into the channel and as they came abreast of Fort Morgan the *Tecumseh* struck a mine (or torpedo, as they were then called) and was destroyed. The fleet was thrown into confusion and hesitated; Farragut, on the steam-powered *Hartford*, quickly swung out and headed his ship into the minefield, crying "Damn the torpedoes!" Although several mines were contacted by his ships none exploded, and soon the entire fleet was within the bay; the Confederate ironclad *Tennessee* was captured, along with the rest of the defending flotilla, and by the end of August all the harbor defenses, including Fort Morgan, had surrendered. In December Farragut was appointed to the newly created rank of vice-admiral; however, his active service was virtually at an end, for his health was declining. In 1866 the rank of admiral was created especially for him. He died while visiting the naval yard at Portsmouth, New Hampshire, on August 14, 1870. He was elected to the Hall of Fame in 1900.

Farragut, James, *see* Farragut, David Glasgow

Farrell, Eileen (1920–   ), singer. Born on February 13, 1920, in Willimantic, Connecticut, Miss Farrell was the daughter of former vaudevillians who later became music teachers; with her family she moved to Storrs, Connecticut, and then to Woonsocket, Rhode Island. After graduating from high school in 1939 she traveled to New York City to study singing and in 1940, following a failure to win a place on "Major Bowes' Original Amateur Hour," she auditioned successfully for membership in studio choral and ensemble groups on the CBS radio network. The next year she began her own program, "Eileen Farrell Sings," on which for six years she performed vocal works ranging from operatic arias to popular songs. In 1947 she began making regular concert tours, extending her field to South America two years later, and received wide acclaim for her consistently brilliant performances. An extended engagement with the New York Philharmonic Orchestra in 1950–1951 was the beginning of a long association with that organization, and in 1953 she became a regular performer with the Bach Aria Group as well. A popular guest on television

variety programs, she continued to mix classical and popular music in her repertoire and in 1957 began her formal operatic career with the San Francisco Opera Company. Her mastery of a wide variety of soprano roles steadily raised the critical estimation of her singing and after an appearance in Gian-Carlo Menotti's 1959 Festival of Two Worlds in Spoleto, Italy (the "Spoleto Festival"), where hers was considered by many the outstanding performance, she made her debut with the Metropolitan Opera Company in New York in 1960 in Gluck's *Alcestis*. Firmly established thereafter as one of the best American dramatic sopranos, Miss Farrell continued to win success and the highest critical and popular acclaim for her concert appearances and recordings.

Farrell, James Thomas (1904–1979), author. Born on February 27, 1904, in Chicago, Farrell grew up in an Irish neighborhood on the city's South Side. After attending parochial schools he studied at the University of Chicago for three years, leaving in 1929. During the next several years he worked as an express agent, a cigar-store clerk, a reporter, and in other jobs that contributed to the vast fund of detailed observations that would in part characterize his writing. In 1932 he published *Young Lonigan*, the first volume of a trilogy that, completed by *The Young Manhood of Studs Lonigan*, 1934, and *Judgment Day*, 1935, portrayed the youth, coming-of-age, and defeat of the brash but ultimately aimless Lonigan in his deteriorating section of Chicago. Farrell relied in his novels on the techniques of naturalism earlier developed by Theodore Dreiser and to them wedded the stream-of-consciousness interior narrative of James Joyce to create a full authentic setting and a powerful and convincing characterization of Lonigan. A minor character in the Lonigan trilogy, Danny O'Neill, became the central figure in a series of five novels: *A World I Never Made*, 1936; *No Star Is Lost*, 1938; *Father and Son*, 1940; *My Days of Anger*, 1943; and *The Face of Time*, 1953. Another trilogy comprised *Bernard Clare*, 1946; *The Road Between*, 1949; and *Yet Other Waters*, 1952, while a tetralogy concerned with an exploration of the institution of marriage during the 1920s included *The Silence of History*, 1963; *Lonely for the Future*, 1966; *New Years' Eve / 1929*, 1967; and *A Brand-New Life*, 1968. Others of Farrell's novels included *Gas-House McGinty*, 1933; *Tommy Gallegher's Crusade*, 1939; *Ellen Rogers*, 1941; *This Man and This Woman*, 1951; and *What Time Collects*, 1964. He also published several collections of short stories, among them *Calico Shoes*, 1934; *Can All This Grandeur Perish?*, 1937; *$1,000 a Week*, 1942; *When Boyhood Dreams Come True*, 1946; *An American Dream Girl*, 1950; and *French Girls are Vicious*, 1956. Farrell was a critic of some influence as well as a prolific storyteller, and he published a number of works defending and explaining his naturalistic approach and his concentration on social institutions, particularly those he perceived to be in a state of disintegration:

A Note on Literary Criticism, 1936; *The League of Frightened Philistines,* 1945; and *Literature and Morality,* 1947. He wrote more personally in *Reflections at Fifty,* 1954, and *My Baseball Diary,* 1957. His later books included *Judith and Other Stories,* 1974; *The Dunne Family,* 1976; *The Death of Nora Ryan,* 1978. He died on August 22, 1979, in New York City.

Faulkner, William Cuthbert (1897–1962), author. Born in New Albany, Mississippi, on September 25, 1897, Falkner (who later changed the spelling of his surname) moved as a child to Oxford, Mississippi. After two years of high school he held a number of minor jobs and spent a brief period during World War I with the British Royal Air Force; he saw no combat, however, the war ending before his training was completed. He returned to Oxford and in 1919 published in the *New Republic* his first poem to be printed. He studied at the University of Mississippi for a year and shortly thereafter left for New York City. A year later he was back in Oxford; in 1924 he published *The Marble Faun,* a volume of poetry, on the title page of which, for reasons unknown, he added to his name the "u" that remained for the rest of his life. After brief stays in New Orleans, in Europe, and in Pascagoula, Mississippi, he settled again in Oxford, this time permanently. His first novel, *Soldier's Pay,* appeared in 1926, and his second, *Mosquitoes,* in 1927. Then, under the combined influences of Sherwood Anderson and Balzac, he began to create a special world in the fictional town of Jefferson located in the fictional Yoknapatawpha County. His saga of social change, the decay of the antebellum aristocracy and the rise of the crass and unscrupulous Snopes clan, written in a difficult style and often creating characters of mythic proportions, occupied a long series of books and constituted Faulkner's major achievement: the first book, *Sartoris,* 1929, was followed by *The Sound and the Fury,* 1929; *As I Lay Dying,* 1930; *Sanctuary,* 1931; *Light in August,* 1932; *Absalom, Absalom!,* 1936; *The Unvanquished,* 1938; *The Hamlet,* 1940; *Go Down, Moses,* 1942; *Intruder in the Dust,* 1948; *The Town,* 1957; *The Mansion,* 1959; and *The Reivers,* 1962. He published a number of other novels, short-story collections, and a play, *Requiem for a Nun,* 1951. He won recognition only slowly in the United States; his reputation abroad, however, was sufficient to win him the 1949 Nobel Prize for Literature; belatedly, in 1955, he was also awarded the Pulitzer Prize for *A Fable,* 1954. In his last years he left his customary seclusion to make a number of speaking tours in the United States and abroad, and in 1957 and 1958 he was writer-in-residence at the University of Virginia. Faulkner died at home in Oxford on July 6, 1962. He was awarded a second Pulitzer Prize posthumously, for *The Reivers.*

Faust, Frederick Schiller (1892–1944), "Max Brand," author. Born on May 29, 1892, in Seattle, Faust grew up there and in Modesto, California, and for a time attended the University of California. Discovering that he had a facility for rapid writing and action-filled plotting, he began turning out stories and serials for the popular pulp magazines, principally those devoted to tales of the Wild West. His output was more than prodigious; although it is difficult to ascertain how many stories and novels he published because he employed as many as 20 pseudonyms and because he left at his death a mountain of manuscripts that were released gradually thereafter, estimates of his total work range upward to 530 full-length books and uncounted shorter pieces. Known as the "King of Pulp Writers," he averaged a book (or its wordage equivalent) for about every two weeks of his career. Under his major pseudonym, "Max Brand," he wrote probably a hundred novels with such titles as *The Untamed,* 1918, twice made into a movie; *The Night Horseman,* 1920; *White Wolf,* 1928; *Destry Rides Again,* 1930, his best-known work, of which three film versions were made (with Tom Mix, James Stewart, and Audie Murphy respectively); *Longhorn Feud,* 1933; *Happy Jack,* 1936; *Trouble Trail,* 1937; *Dead or Alive,* 1938; and *The Dude,* 1940. Other books appeared under such pen names as "Evan Evans," "Frank Austin," "George Owen Baxter," and "Walter C. Butler." Faust also wrote a number of film scenarios and scripts, most notably those for the *Dr. Kildare* movie series of the late 1930s; he later used the same characters and plots in *The Secret of Dr. Kildare,* 1940; *Young Dr. Kildare,* 1941; and others. The Westerns that comprised the bulk of his writings were undistinguished but vastly popular; with little knowledge of the history or even the scenery of the West, he used the region as a convenient background for simple characters and plots and held his readers' attention with an unrelenting reliance on the "blazing-guns" mythos. Faust lived in northern Italy until the outbreak of World War II. In 1944, while working as a correspondent for *Harper's* magazine, he joined U.S. troops attacking Santa Maria Infante, Italy, and was killed there by German artillery on or about May 12, 1944.

Fearing, Kenneth Flexner (1902–1961), author. Born in Oak Park, Illinois, on July 28, 1902, Fearing graduated from the University of Wisconsin in 1924 and after a brief period as a journalist in Chicago moved to New York City to work as a free-lance writer. His first book of poetry, *Angel Arms,* appeared in 1929 and won the immediate attention of critics, especially those of a radical or avante-garde persuasion, with its ironic and satiric treatment of many aspects of American life and popular culture. There followed *Poems,* 1935; *Dead Reckoning,* 1938; *Collected Poems,* 1940; and *Afternoon of a Pawnbroker,* 1943, all written in much the same vein, though with increasing sophistication and poetic skill. Fearing's verse, which twice during the 1930s won him Guggenheim fellowships, was loosely constructed and employed a sometimes dazzling array of vernacular phrasings and images from newspapers, movies, or the scenes of everyday city life; in a style that seemed to fall midway between those of W. H. Auden and Ogden Nash, it was both harsh and humorous. In 1939 he published his first novel, *The Hospital*, which drew considerable acclaim; his second, *Dagger of the Mind*, 1941, was a murder mystery, and *Clark Gifford's Body*, 1942, was a modernized version of the story of John Brown. Another mystery novel, *The Big Clock*, 1946, was highly successful and was later made into a motion picture. Subsequent books by Fearing included *Stranger at Coney Island*, 1948, verse; *The Loneliest Girl in the World*, 1951; *The Generous Heart*, 1954; *New and Selected Poems*, 1956; and *The Crozart Story*, 1960. He also wrote a great many stories that were published pseudonymously in various magazines. Fearing died in New York City on June 26, 1961.

Feller, Robert William Andrew (1918–   ), "Bob," baseball player. Born on November 3, 1918, in Van Meter, Iowa, Feller began playing baseball as a child and, encouraged strongly by his father, developed such skill as a pitcher that by 1935 he was playing regularly for a semi-professional team in Des Moines. In 1936, still in high school, he was signed by the Cleveland Indians and in his first appearance on the mound, in an exhibition game against the St. Louis Cardinals, struck out Leo Durocher and six others. He made his first major-league start in August and struck out 15 batters; within a few weeks he had tied the major-league record of 17 strikeouts. Feller played his first full season in 1937, compiling a record of 9 wins and 7 losses as he learned gradually the techniques of big-league pitching. In 1938 he won 17 games and lost 11 and led the league in strikeouts; in one game against the Detroit Tigers he retired a record 18 batters, although he lost the game. In that season he also gave up a record 208 bases on balls. As his control improved his blazing fast ball—once clocked at nearly 100 miles per hour—became a deadly weapon; 1939 was the first of six seasons in which he won 20 games or more (1939, 1940, 1941, 1946, 1947, 1951). In 1940 he won 27, including his first no-hitter, and in 1941 he won 25. From 1942 to 1945 he served in the navy and on his return to baseball in 1946 quickly demonstrated that he had by no means lost his touch; again playing for the Indians, he struck out 348 batters that season, a record that stood for 19 years. Although noted primarily for his fast ball—he was appropriately dubbed "Rapid Robert"—Feller also threw a sharp-breaking and highly effective curve and, in later years, a slider. He continued to play until 1956, compiling a career total of 266 wins against 162 losses; he pitched 3 no-hitters (1940, 1946, 1951), a record that stood for 14 years, and 12 one-hitters; and in 7 seasons (1938, 1939, 1940, 1941, 1946, 1947, 1948) he led the American League in strikeouts. On his leaving the Indians in 1956 his number was retired. He later engaged

in business in Cleveland and in 1962 was elected to the National Baseball Hall of Fame.

Fenollosa, Ernest Francisco (1853–1908), art historian. Born in Salem, Massachusetts, on February 18, 1853, Fenollosa graduated from Harvard at the head of the class of 1874 and for four years pursued further studies at Harvard, in part at the Divinity School, and at the Museum of Fine Arts in Boston. In 1878 he traveled to Japan and became professor of political economy and philosophy at the Imperial University in Tokyo, two years later giving up political economy to concentrate on philosophy and logic. He remained at the university until 1886 and while teaching also studied Japanese art, literature, and culture, becoming a practicing Buddhist along the way. In 1888 he received appointments as manager of both the Academy of Fine Arts in Tokyo and the Imperial Museum. In 1890 he returned to the United States and accepted the position of curator of Oriental art at Boston's Museum of Fine Arts, a position to which he brought a knowledge of the subject probably unmatched by any other American of the day. From 1897 to 1900 he was again in Tokyo as professor of English at the Imperial Normal School, and upon his return to the United States in 1900 he began writing and lecturing extensively on Oriental art and literature. While the extent of his scholarly contributions to the subject is variously judged, Fenollosa holds undisputed rank as a pioneer Orientalist and much subsequent work followed closely on his. Among his publications were *East and West*, 1893, a volume of poems, and *The Masters of Ukioye*, 1896, on Japanese painting. The major written record of his studies appeared only after his death in London on September 21, 1908. *Epochs of Chinese and Japanese Art*, two volumes, 1911, was compiled from his notes by his widow, Mary McNeill Fenollosa; and Ezra Pound, Fenollosa's literary executor, drew heavily on his notes and unpublished writings for *Cathay*, 1915; *Certain Noble Plays of Japan*, 1916; and *Noh, or Accomplishment, a Study of the Classical Stage of Japan*, 1916.

Ferber, Edna (1887–1968), author. Born on August 15, 1887, in Kalamazoo, Michigan, Miss Ferber grew up there and in Appleton, Wisconsin. After graduating from high school in 1905 she worked as a reporter for a local newspaper, moving later to jobs with the *Milwaukee Journal* and then the *Chicago Tribune*. After the publication of her first novel, *Dawn O'Hara*, in 1911, she devoted herself to writing, becoming a prolific producer of magazine stories that were highly popular both at their first publication and in such collections as *Buttered Side Down*, 1912; *Roast Beef Medium*, 1913; *Emma McChesney & Co.*, 1915; *Fanny Herself*, 1917; *Cheerful, by Request*, 1918; *Gigolo*, 1922; and *Mother Knows Best*, 1927. Her novel *So Big*, 1924, placed her in the ranks of the best-selling authors of the day and also was sufficiently esteemed by critics to win a Pulitzer Prize.

Her acute observations of American social life combined with a strong flair for characterization in a series of novels set in picturesque places and times—*Show Boat*, 1926, which Jerome Kern and Oscar Hammerstein II adapted for the great musical of the same name in 1929; *Cimarron*, 1930; *Saratoga Trunk*, 1941; *Giant*, 1952; and *Ice Palace*, 1958, all made into successful motion pictures. Miss Ferber also collaborated with George S. Kaufman on a number of plays, including *Minick*, 1925; *The Royal Family*, 1927, *Dinner at Eight*, 1932; *Stage Door*, 1936; *The Land Is Bright*, 1941; and *Bravo!*, 1949. Several of the plays became movies as well. Although her stories and novels were occasionally dismissed as merely popular romances by some critics, there was in them a constant undercurrent of serious exploration and celebration of the American character and the American land. She published two autobiographical volumes, *A Peculiar Treasure*, 1939, and *A Kind of Magic*, 1963. Miss Ferber died in New York City on April 16, 1968.

Fermi, Enrico (1901–1954), physicist. Born in Rome on September 29, 1901, Fermi studied at the University of Pisa and received his doctorate in 1922. After a period of further study in Germany he became a lecturer in physics at the University of Florence; in 1927 he joined the faculty of the University of Rome and remained there for 11 years. Until 1934 his work was concentrated in the theoretical aspects of atomic physics; he developed a mathematics with which to clarify and apply the Pauli exclusion principle and evolved a theory of beta decay. In 1934 news of the discovery of artificial radioactivity led him to turn to experimental work. He methodically proceeded through the periodic table of elements, bombarding each element with slow neutrons and noting the results; the reaction of uranium, the final natural element, was puzzling and, because of the then-prevalent belief that nuclear fission was well-nigh impossible, he failed to realize that he had achieved it. In the late 1930s he began planning to leave Italy, for life was becoming unpleasant under the Fascist government, especially for his wife, Laura, who was Jewish. In 1938 he was awarded the Nobel Prize for Physics for his work with neutrons; after accepting the award in Stockholm he proceeded to the United States with his family and joined the faculty of Columbia University as a professor of physics. Early in 1939 two German scientists repeated Fermi's experiment with uranium and found that fission had indeed taken place. Fermi, together with several other émigré scientists, sought to interest the U.S. government in the potentials of atomic energy and warned of the danger of its development in Germany; in August they drew up a letter that, signed by Albert Einstein, was sent to President Franklin D. Roosevelt. A small grant to finance work on achieving a sustained nuclear reaction was followed in 1942 by the transfer of Fermi and his team to the Manhattan Engineering District project at the University of Chicago. There on December 2 a controlled chain reaction was achieved, marking the beginning of the "atomic age." Soon thereafter Fermi moved to the new secret installation at Los Alamos, New Mexico, where on July 16, 1945, the first atomic bomb was successfully tested. In 1946 he was awarded the Congressional Medal of Merit for his work; he then returned to the University of Chicago as professor in the Institute for Nuclear Research (later renamed the Enrico Fermi Institute for Nuclear Studies). His work there was concerned mainly with the nature and behavior of mesons. Fermi was a member of the scientific advisory council of the Atomic Energy Commission (AEC) and in 1954 he was the first to receive its $25,000 prize, which subsequently became known as the Fermi Prize. Shortly after, on November 28, 1954, he died in Chicago.

Fern, Fanny, *see* Parton, Sara Payson Willis

Fernow, Bernhard Eduard (1851–1923), forester and educator. Born on January 7, 1851, in Inowroclaw, Germany (now in Poland), Fernow was educated at the University of Königsberg and at the Hannover-Münden Forest Academy. After serving in the Franco-Prussian War in 1870 he joined the Prussian forest service, then a world leader in the field. In 1876 he emigrated to the United States, where he found that no body of thought on or practice in the subject of forestry existed, a situation he immediately set about to amend. While managing a commercial forest tract in Pennsylvania he began publishing articles and in other ways promoting professional forestry as a means for conservation and rational utilization of the timber resources of the country, and in 1882 he played a major role in founding the American Forestry Congress, later the American Forestry Association, of which he was secretary until 1894. His activities marked him as the nation's foremost authority in the field and in 1886 he was appointed chief of the newly organized Division of Forestry in the U.S. Department of Agriculture. In that position he inaugurated a great deal of research work and secured passage of the Forest Reserve Act of 1891, which authorized the president to withdraw publicly owned lands from settlement or commercial exploitation. Fernow resigned in 1898—he was succeeded by Gifford Pinchot—and went to Cornell University to organize the New York State College of Forestry, the first such school in the United States; he remained there as dean until 1903. He later organized similar schools at Pennsylvania State College in 1906 and at the University of Toronto in 1907, remaining at Toronto until his retirement in 1919. In 1902 he had founded the *Forestry Quarterly*, later the *Journal of Forestry*, and he was its editor until 1922. Among his own works were *Economics of Forestry*, 1902; *A Brief History of Forestry in Europe, the United States, and Other Countries*, 1907; and *The Care of Trees in Lawn, Street and Park*, 1910. Fernow died in Toronto on February 6, 1923.

Ferris, George Washington Gale (1859–1896), engineer. Born on February 14, 1859, in Galesburg, Illinois, Ferris grew up there and in Carson City, Nevada. He graduated from Rensselaer Polytechnic Institute in 1881 and during the next four years worked on railroad, bridge, and tunnel construction projects in New York and West Virginia. In 1885 he joined the Kentucky and Indiana Bridge Company, for which he inspected and tested structural steel purchased from mills in Pittsburgh. He eventually formed G. W. G. Ferris & Company to specialize in such work, acting as a consultant to steel users throughout the country. He retained his interest in bridge construction and was involved in a number of projects on the Ohio River. In 1892 Daniel H. Burnham, principal planner of the World's Columbian Exposition in Chicago, announced his desire to present at the fair a great engineering work to match the Eiffel Tower of the Paris Exposition of three years earlier; Ferris responded to the challenge with a design for a great upright wheel to carry passengers up to a lofty vantage point over the exposition grounds. Overcoming considerable skepticism and many financial difficulties, he won approval for the plan and completed the wheel soon after the exposition opened. The Ferris Wheel, 250 feet in height, was capable of carrying 40 people in each of 36 cars; a masterpiece of precision design and construction, it functioned perfectly and in complete safety and was one of the most marveled-over features of the exposition. Ferris died in Pittsburgh on November 22, 1896.

Fessenden, Reginald Aubrey (1866–1932), inventor. Born in East Bolton, Quebec, on October 6, 1866, Fessenden was of New England ancestry. He was educated at Bishop's College (now University) and during 1884–1886 was principal of a school in Bermuda. Moving then to New York City, he took a job with the Edison Machine Works and in 1887 became chief chemist in Thomas A. Edison's laboratory in West Orange, New Jersey. Three years later he became chief electrician for the Westinghouse Electric and Manufacturing Company in Pittsfield, Massachusetts. In 1892 he joined the faculty of Purdue University as professor of electrical engineering and from 1893 to 1900 held a similar chair at the Western University of Pennsylvania (now the University of Pittsburgh). At Western he began seriously investigating the problem of wireless communication and from 1900 to 1902 continued his researches under the auspices of the U.S. Weather Bureau, which hoped to develop wireless as an aid in forecasting. In 1902 he organized the National Electric Signalling Company to sponsor his experiments. In 1901 Fessenden patented his high-frequency alternator, a device that generated a continuous wave instead of the intermittent, damped-spark impulses then used for transmission. The continuous wave promised the broadcast of speech and, after employing Ernst F. W. Alexanderson to build a large 80-kilohertz

alternator, Fessenden established a station at Brant Rock, Massachusetts, from which, on Christmas Eve, 1906, he made the first radio broadcast of voice and music. The transmission was picked up by ships within a radius of several hundred miles. Later that year he made the first transatlantic telegraphic connection between Brant Rock and Scotland. Fessenden's radio equipment also featured another vital invention, a receiver circuit that blended the incoming radio-frequency signal with another, slightly different signal produced locally, yielding a beat-frequency tone in the audible range; the device became known as a heterodyne circuit and was soon generally adopted in radio broadcasting. Among his hundreds of patents most were for inventions relating to radio, such as his radio compass, but many were for such other devices as a sonic fathometer, submarine signaling apparatus, and a turboelectric drive for battleships. In his last years Fessenden lived in North Newton, Massachusetts; he died on July 22, 1932, in Bermuda.

Fessenden, William Pitt (1806–1869), public official and political leader. Born in Boscawen, New Hampshire, on October 16, 1806, Fessenden graduated from Bowdoin College in 1823 and four years later was admitted to the Maine bar. He began practice in Bridgton and in 1829 moved to Portland, where he made his home thereafter. While building a state-wide reputation as an attorney he became involved also in politics; he was elected to the legislature as an anti-Jackson man in 1831, and as the Whig party began to take form he became one of its prominent supporters. After another term in the legislature in 1839 he was elected the following year to the House of Representatives. Two years in Washington left him with a profound distaste for the common run of politicians and saw him move toward an antislavery position, in large part as the result of his admiration for John Quincy Adams. He returned to his law practice in 1843 and again served in the state legislature in 1845 and 1853. In 1854 he was elected to the Senate, where he lost no time in displaying outspoken courage by opposing the Kansas-Nebraska Bill. Fessenden was among the early organizers of the Republican party and, a forceful debater and an unswerving adherent to high principle, was one of the party's leaders in the Senate throughout his career in that body. During the early years of the Civil War he had, as chairman of the Committee on Finance, the principal congressional responsibility for the difficult task of financing the war effort. Upon the resignation of Secretary of the Treasury Salmon P. Chase in June 1864, President Abraham Lincoln appointed Fessenden to the post; he reluctantly accepted and for eight months effectively carried on a policy that was essentially Chase's, although he made it somewhat more conservative and anti-inflationary. Early in 1865 he was reelected to the Senate and in March left the cabinet to resume his seat. Although he irked some colleagues by opposing a few of the more extreme proposals of the Radical Republicans, he became chairman of the Joint Congressional Committee on Reconstruction, of whose influential report of June 1866 he was the main author, and joined with other Radicals in heartily detesting President Andrew Johnson. On the issue of impeaching Johnson, however, he broke with them; considering the charges strictly on their merits, he considered them false and in 1868 voted to acquit Johnson. This action thoroughly alienated his party and much of the general public and might well have resulted in his defeat for reelection; before the question could be put to the test, however, Fessenden died in Portland, Maine, on September 8, 1869.

Fewkes, Jesse Walter (1850–1930), ethnologist and archaeologist. Born on November 14, 1850, in Newton, Massachusetts, Fewkes was educated at Harvard, where he was strongly influenced by Louis Agassiz. After graduating in 1875 and taking his Ph.D. from Harvard in 1877, he pursued further studies at the University of Leipzig and then returned to Harvard in 1881 as an assistant in the Museum of Comparative Zoology. His interests shifted gradually to archaeology, and in 1890 he established the *Journal of American Ethnology and Archaeology*, which continued until 1894. During 1891–1894 he was field director of the Hemenway Southwestern Archaeological Expedition and in 1895 became an ethnologist with the Bureau of American Ethnology of the Smithsonian Institution. Although in the course of his career Fewkes studied Indian ruins in the South, from Tennessee to the Florida Keys, he directed his main efforts to pioneering work in the deserts of the Southwest and of northern Mexico. Fewkes's principal interest was the Hopi Indians, and in studying them he introduced a methodological innovation in relating anthropological studies of the living tribe to the archaeology of their ancestors. He was influential in securing the preservation of the ruins of pueblos and cliff dwellings throughout the Southwest and amassed for the Smithsonian a huge collection of artifacts, many of which were of types first discovered by him. His reports, most of them published by the Bureau of American Ethnology or by the Smithsonian, remain classic works in the field. Fewkes became chief of the bureau in 1918 and retained the position until his retirement in 1928. He died in Forest Glen, Maryland, on May 31, 1930.

Feynman, Richard Phillips (1918–   ), physicist. Born on May 11, 1918, in New York City, Feynman graduated from the Massachusetts Institute of Technology (MIT) in 1939 and three years later took his Ph.D. from Princeton University. His graduate studies in the quantum interpretation of the behavior of subatomic particles led to his appointment in 1942 to the staff of the atomic-bomb project installation at Los Alamos, New Mexico. In 1945 he became associate professor of theoretical physics at Cornell University and

in 1950 moved to the California Institute of Technology as professor of theoretical physics. During the late 1940s Feyman made significant contributions to the refinement of the mathematics of electrodynamics. He devised a computational procedure known as mass and charge renormalization that made mathematically explicable certain puzzling divergences of observed particle behavior from the predictions of accepted electrodynamic theory. For this work he was awarded the 1965 Nobel Prize for Physics jointly with Julian S. Schwinger and Sin-itiro Tomonaga of Japan, both of whom had independently contributed in the same area of research. Feynman's later researches were concerned with the quantum mechanical explanation of the bizarre behavior of liquid helium and, from the late 1950s, with the explanation of the puzzling but crucial phenomenon of weak interactions among certain particles. In the latter work he was associated with Murray Gell-Mann, with whom he also developed the notion of the "quark," a hypothetical particle fundamental to all others.

Fiedler, Arthur (1894–1979), musical conductor. Born in Boston on December 17, 1894, Fiedler came of a musical family with whom he traveled to Vienna in 1910. In 1911 he entered the Royal Academy of Music in Berlin, remaining for four years and studying violin, piano, and conducting. He then returned to Boston and joined the Boston Symphony Orchestra as a violinist, later switching to viola; he remained in the orchestra until 1930. In 1924 he organized the Boston Sinfonietta, a chamber group that he continued to direct and with which he toured successfully for several years. In 1929 he founded the highly popular Esplanade Concerts, a series of free outdoor performances of the Boston Symphony, and in 1930 he became conductor of the Boston Pops Orchestra, formed with members of the Boston Symphony. Under his leadership, the Pops presented annual concert series adroitly blending light classics with works of modern popular composers, folk songs, Broadway show music, marches, and jazz; popular on radio and extremely prolific in the recording studio, the orchestra remained a Boston—indeed a national—institution. Fiedler was active in numerous other musical organizations as well and served on the faculty of Boston University. In 1965 he was, with Richard Rodgers, the first recipient of the Boston Gold Medal for distinguished achievement, and in 1971 he and the Pops earned a Peabody Award for their performances for public television. He died on July 10, 1979, in Brookline, Massachusetts.

Field, Cyrus West (1819–1892), businessman and financier. Born in Stockbridge, Massachusetts, on November 30, 1819, the younger brother of David Dudley and Stephen J. Field, Cyrus W. Field chose not to attend college but instead, at fifteen, took a job in the A. T. Stewart & Company store in New York City. In 1841, after losing heavily in the bankruptcy of a wholesale paper company of which he was a junior partner, he began his own paper business, Cyrus W. Field and Company. Within ten years he had paid his debts and was wealthy enough to retire from business. In 1854 he became interested in the possibility of laying a transatlantic cable. He organized the New York, Newfoundland, and London Telegraph Company and later a similar company in England. With guarantees of business from the U.S. and British governments, the company made its first attempt to lay a cable between Newfoundland and Ireland in 1857; this and two following attempts failed, but the fourth, in 1858 was briefly successful. Queen Victoria sent a message to President James Buchanan over the cable and there was jubilation on both sides of the Atlantic. In the three weeks before this cable failed the value of such a means of rapid communication was amply demonstrated. Field, who had persisted through bankruptcy brought on by the panic of 1857 and through repeated equipment failures and other problems, was widely celebrated until the cable broke; he then found himself once again faced with popular scepticism and the conservatism of investors. In debt again, and with his efforts hampered by the Civil War, Field continued to promote the idea. More failures in 1865 were followed by complete success the next year. Field traveled widely in subsequent years and advocated the laying of submarine cables throughout the world. In 1877 he bought control of the New York Elevated Railway Company and, as its president from 1877 to 1880, was instrumental in bringing a rapid-transit system to New York City. He was later associated with Jay Gould in the development of the Wabash Railroad. His affairs suffered sharply from reverses in later years and his fortune disappeared. He died in New York City on July 12, 1892.

Field, David Dudley (1805–1894), lawyer and legal reformer. Born in Haddam, Connecticut, on February 13, 1805, the elder brother of Stephen J. and Cyrus W. Field, David Dudley Field left Williams College in 1825 to take up the study of law. Admitted to the bar in 1828, he began practice in New York City and was soon a recognized authority on common-law and equity pleading. In 1837 he began working for reform of the New York legal system, calling for complete codification of the state's laws. By means of letters and articles he induced the state constitutional convention of 1846 to report itself in favor of such a reform, and the following year the legislature appointed a commission, with Field the leading member, to carry it out. The result was the Code of Civil Procedure, enacted in New York in 1848 and adopted or used as a model by many states and foreign nations, including Great Britain and Ireland, and a similar code for criminal procedure, adopted in New York several years later. Codes of substantive political, civil, and penal law were created by a subsequent commission under Field's chairmanship between 1860 and 1865, but of these only the penal code was

adopted in New York; like the earlier codes, however, these were widely adopted or copied elsewhere. Encouraged by this success, Field devoted much time from 1866 onward to the elaboration of a code of international law; his *Draft Outline of an International Code*, prepared with the assistance of Frederick A. P. Barnard and others, was published in two volumes in 1872 and issued in an expanded version in 1876. Originally a Democrat, Field supported the Republican party from its founding; he seems to have played a part in Abraham Lincoln's nomination for the presidency in 1860, and he served briefly in the House of Representatives in 1876. In his legal practice he achieved considerable prominence, arguing several major cases on constitutional questions before the Supreme Court, including *Ex parte Milligan*, 1866; *Cummings* v. *Missouri*, 1867; and *U.S.* v. *Cruikshank*, 1876. He also represented Samuel J. Tilden before the Electoral Commission in the dispute following the Hayes-Tilden presidential contest of 1876, and, not without a good deal of controversy, he represented Jay Gould and James Fisk in the Erie Railroad litigations. He died on April 13, 1894, in New York City.

Field, Erastus Salisbury (1805–1900), painter. Born on May 19, 1805, in Leverett, Massachusetts, Field early developed an interest in drawing and painting and for about three months in 1824–1825 studied in the studio of Samuel F. B. Morse in New York City. Living at various times in Hartford, Connecticut, and Monson and Palmer, Massachusetts, Field painted mainly portraits, finding patrons in the small villages and towns of the Connecticut Valley and depicting them in a rather stiff, primitive manner. He also produced a number of scenes from mythology and biblical history, among them a series on the plagues of Egypt and a curious "Garden of Eden" reminiscent of both the work of his near-contemporary, Edward Hicks, and the later tropical landscapes of Henri Rousseau. After 1859 Field was settled in Sunderland, Massachusetts, where he continued to work until his death. A great many of his paintings are lost, but among those that survive is his most remarkable work, "Historical Monument of the American Republic." Painted sometime before the centennial of the Declaration of Independence in 1876, by which it was inspired, it was a huge canvas, 9 feet by 13 feet, and depicted in meticulous and richly ornamented fashion a great, fanciful architectural work of several many-tiered towers, each teeming with symbols and figures representing events and persons of American history. At their tops the seven main towers were connected by steel railroad trestles. The painting, which has since been acquired by the Springfield, Massachusetts, Museum of Fine Art, was utterly unique and sealed Field's later reputation as an outstanding figure among nineteenth-century American folk artists. Field died in Sunderland, Massachusetts, in 1900.

Field, Eugene (1850–1895), journalist, author, and poet. Born in St. Louis on September 2 or 3, 1850, Field lived from the age of six with relatives in Amherst, Massachusetts. Between 1868 and 1871 he attended Williams College, Knox College, and the University of Missouri but took no degree; in 1873, after a European tour that largely exhausted his patrimony, he took an editorial position with the *St. Louis Journal*. He later moved to the *St. Joseph Gazette*, the *Kansas City Times*, and then to the *Denver Tribune*, for which he conducted "Odds and Ends," a daily column of humorous paragraphs and satirical squibs; he published a collection of the columns as *The Tribune Primer* in 1882. In 1883 he joined the *Chicago Morning News* (from 1890 the *Chicago Record*), where his column appeared as "Sharps and Flats." A pioneer in the writing of the featured personal column, Field filled his with a variety of bits and pieces, ranging from satirical attacks on the pretensions of Chicago's meat-packing nouveaux riches (collected in *Culture's Garland*, 1887) to free translations of Horace (collected in *Echoes From the Sabine Farm*, 1892, with his brother Roswell Field), to his own sentimental stories and verse dealing in large part with childhood. Of his verse, his best-remembered pieces were "Little Boy Blue" and "Dutch Lullaby" (also known as "Wynken, Blynken, and Nod"). Although much of his writing was marred by overly broad satire or, in the case of his serious stories and poems, by the use of affected Old English or Dutch dialects, Field nonetheless enjoyed great popularity in his day; a whimsical and charming man to all who knew him, he was also an inveterate practical joker of great ingenuity and wide renown. Others among his books, most of them collections of newspaper writings, were *A Little Book of Western Verse*, 1889; *The Holy Cross and Other Tales*, 1893; *Lullaby Land*, 1894; *The Love Affairs of a Bibliomaniac*, 1896; and the autobiographical *Auto-Analysis*, 1896. Several more collections edited by others appeared in the years following his death in Chicago on November 4, 1895.

Field, Marshall (1834–1906), business leader and philanthropist. Born on August 18, 1834, near Conway, Massachusetts, Field attended school until the age of sixteen, then worked as a shop clerk in Pittsfield. He moved to Chicago in 1856 and worked as a traveling salesman and clerk for a leading wholesale dry-goods house; he became general manager of the business in 1861 and a partner the next year. In 1865 he joined Levi Z. Leiter, another of the partners and Potter Palmer, an established State Street merchant, in forming Field, Palmer, and Leiter. Palmer left in 1867 and the firm became Field, Leiter and Company. The company survived the great Chicago fire of 1871, the financial panic of 1873, and another fire in 1877, largely because of outstanding management and a policy of benefiting the customer in many new ways. Among his important merchandising innovations, Field plainly displayed prices of all merchandise, extended liberal credit, and allowed the return of goods within a reasonable time after purchase. He also was the first to install a restaurant in a department store. In 1881 Leiter sold out his interest and Field and his two brothers were left as the sole owners; the business then became Marshall Field and Company. The firm bought goods on an enormous scale and also began manufacturing items and selling them, at both wholesale and retail, under the company name. Field surpassed his competitors in his ability to anticipate or create consumer demand and to stock for it in advance. By 1895 the store was grossing $40 million a year. He became a noted philanthropist; making large gifts to, among other beneficiaries, the University of Chicago, the World's Columbian Exposition in Chicago in 1893 (for which he built the Columbian Museum, later known as the Field Museum of Natural History and relocated to a new edifice built with a bequest in his will), and his home town of Conway, Massachusetts, where he established a public library. He died on January 16, 1906, in New York City. His descendants were eminent Chicago business leaders: Marshall Field III (1893–1956) established the *Chicago Sun*, which later became the *Sun-Times*; Marshall Field IV (1916–1965) became chairman of the board of Field Enterprises, Inc., and published the *Chicago Daily News* and the *Sun-Times*.

Field, Stephen Johnson (1816–1899), justice of the Supreme Court. Born in Haddam, Connecticut, on November 4, 1816, the brother of David Dudley and Cyrus W. Field, Stephen J. Field spent two years as a youth in the Near East, returning in 1833 to enter Williams College. After graduating first in his class four years later he began the study of law; from his admission to the bar in 1841 until 1848 he practiced law in partnership with his brother David in New York City. In 1849 he journeyed to California; settling in Marysville he engaged in land speculation and law practice in the rough and bustling Mother Lode mining region. In 1850 he was elected to the state legislature, where he took the lead in establishing California's civil and criminal codes. These codes owed much to his brother David's work in New York but in addition contained very liberal provisions for the protection of debtors and gave legal standing to local miners' customs. In 1857 he was appointed to the state supreme court, of which he was chief justice in 1859–1863; there he provided learned leadership in bringing order to a welter of conflicting land and mineral claims. In 1863 he was appointed by President Abraham Lincoln to a newly created tenth seat on the Supreme Court and, although a Democrat, was unanimously confirmed. During his tenure Justice Field was most noted for his dissents, many of which were based on a stern conservatism and a broad view of the Fourteenth Amendment's "privileges and immunities" clause. He opposed the Legal Tender Acts, federal regulation of utilities, the Interstate Commerce Commission (ICC), and the income tax. In 1877 he was a member of the Electoral Commission appointed to decide the disputed Hayes-Tilden presidential contest of 1876. He was mentioned for the Democratic presidential nomination in 1880 and 1884 but was barred by the opposition of California Democrats with whom some of his decisions on the circuit, notably against discriminatory practices toward Chinese immigrants, were highly unpopular. After one of the longest tenures on the Supreme Court, ended only at the urging of his colleagues, he retired in 1897; he died on April 9, 1899, in Washington, D.C.

Fields, W. C. (1880–1946), entertainer and actor. Born in Philadelphia on January 29, 1880, William Claude Dukenfield had a turbulent childhood and at eleven ran away from home. He knocked about aimlessly for a time and then, inspired by an act in a traveling show, began to teach himself juggling. By the time he was fourteen he had begun a professional career; from the Atlantic City boardwalk to touring in vaudeville, he rose by dint of extraordinary ability and determination to star billing as "W. C. Fields, the Tramp Juggler." In 1901, on a European tour, he played a command performance before Edward VII of England. In 1915 he was engaged for the *Ziegfeld Follies*, with which he remained for six years and in which he shared billing with Fanny Brice, Will Rogers, and other stars. His juggling act had long featured a line of comic patter and in 1924 he appeared on Broadway in his first speaking role, that of the preposterously fraudulent Eustace McGargle in *Poppy*. The show was a success and the next year was made into a film by D. W. Griffith. Several more films followed, including *So's Your Old Man*, 1926, and *Running Wild*, 1927, and in 1931, after a few more seasons in New York, where in addition to the *Follies* he had headlined in George White's *Scandals* and Earl Carroll's *Vanities*, he moved to Hollywood permanently. For Mack Sennett he starred in a number of two-reelers, notably *The Chemist*, *The Barbershop*, and *The Fatal Glass of Beer*, and he appeared in numerous Paramount releases, including *Million-Dollar Legs*, 1932; *International House*, 1932; *Tillie and Gus*, 1934; *The Old-Fashioned Way*, 1934; *Mrs. Wiggs of the Cabbage Patch*, 1934; *Mississippi*, 1935; and *The Man on the Flying Trapeze*, 1935. He also gave a critically acclaimed performance as Mr. Micawber in *David Copperfield*, 1935. By that time he was one of Hollywood's leading stars and had firmly established the role that remained essentially unchanged from *Poppy* onward—an often bibulous character notable for bombast, whimsy, broad lasciviousness, chicanery, and an utter disregard for sentimental conventions, particularly those concerning children and dogs. He never failed to delight audiences with his rasping drawl, his bulbous nose, and his slightly befuddled sleight-of-hand. His last four major films, made for Universal, have remained perennially popular classics: *You Can't Cheat an Honest Man*, 1939; *My*

Little Chickadee, 1940, with Mae West; *The Bank Dick*, 1941, for which he wrote the screenplay under the name Mahatma Kane Jeeves; and *Never Give a Sucker an Even Break*, 1941. During the late 1930s Fields was also popular on radio, where he carried on a running battle of wit with Edgar Bergen's Charlie McCarthy. He died in Pasadena, California, on December 25 (a day he pretended to detest), 1946. His lifelong distaste for his natal city outlived him in his self-composed epitaph: "On the whole I'd rather be in Philadelphia."

Fife, Duncan, *see* Phyfe, Duncan

Filene, Edward Albert (1860–1937), business leader and reformer. Born on September 3, 1860, in Salem, Massachusetts, Filene was educated in public schools in Lynn, Massachusetts, and briefly attended a German military academy. About the time he planned to enter Harvard, his father opened a dry-goods and clothing store in Boston but had to abandon its management because of poor health. Edward gave up his college plans to take over the store with his younger brother. Ambitious and competent, he conducted the enterprise energetically; in the rapid expansion of the department store, which in 1891 became William Filene's Sons, he brought several partners into the business by 1911. His innovative ideas included the "Automatic Bargain Basement," which was designed to promote the sale of slow-moving items by featuring low prices that decreased steadily as long as goods remained in stock. Litigation with his conservative partners, stemming from his plan to turn the management of the store over to an employees' cooperative, resulted in his loss of control in 1928, although he remained nominally president of the company. He was active in Boston civic reform. With Lincoln Steffens in 1909 he fostered improvements in municipal educational, public-health, and harbor facilities. He consolidated business groups in forming Boston's first Chamber of Commerce and provided the impetus for similar state, national, and international associations. During World War I he served the government as chairman of the War Shipping Committee. He promoted the American credit-union movement and in 1919 established the Cooperative League (later the Twentieth Century Fund) to do research on the national economy. He was a strong advocate of consumer cooperatives and foresaw an economy of affluence based on high wages and mass distribution of goods. He wrote several books, including *More Profits from Merchandising*, 1925; *Successful Living in This Machine Age*, 1931; and *Next Steps Forward in Retailing*, 1937. Filene died in Paris on September 26, 1937.

Fillmore, Millard (1800–1874), thirteenth president of the United States. Born on January 7, 1800, in Cayuga County, New York, Fillmore received virtually no formal education until he was eighteen. Six months of schooling then were followed by study in a law office while he supported himself by teaching school; he was admitted to the bar in 1823. With the aid of Thurlow Weed, Fillmore entered politics on the Anti-Masonic ticket in 1828, serving three terms in the state assembly, where he successfully sponsored a bill ending imprisonment for debt, and in 1833 was elected as an anti-Jacksonian to the House of Representatives. Sitting out one term, he was elected again in 1836 and remained in Congress until 1843. He had followed Weed out of the Anti-Masonic party and into the Whig coalition in 1834, and in the House he was generally counted in the faction backing Henry Clay. In 1844 he lost both the Whig nomination for vice-president and the gubernatorial contest in New York. In 1848 Clay's support won him the vice-presidential nomination, and he was elected with Zachary Taylor. Taylor's death on July 9, 1850, elevated Fillmore to the presidency. He broke his long association with Weed and allied himself with Daniel Webster, whom he appointed secretary of state, in reversing Taylor's policy of opposition to Clay's "Omnibus Bill." With the preservation of the Union uppermost in his mind, he approved the Compromise of 1850, including the infamous Fugitive Slave Law, his support for which he was at special pains to emphasize. As a direct result both the party and nation were thrown into political tumult and Fillmore failed to be renominated by the fractured Whig party in 1852. In one of the major accomplishments of his administration, in November 1852 he had sent a navy fleet commanded by Commodore Matthew C. Perry to Japan with a request for a treaty; Perry arrived there in July 1853 and the treaty was signed in 1854, opening Japan to Western trade. Fillmore accepted the presidential nomination of the strongly nativist Know-Nothing (American) party in 1856. Basing his campaign on the need for national unity, he was soundly defeated and retired from the political scene. Active thereafter in local affairs, he was a founder of the University of Buffalo, of the Buffalo Fine Arts Academy, and of several other cultural institutions. He died in Buffalo on March 8, 1874.

Filson, John (1747?–1788), frontier explorer and author. Born about 1747 in Chester County, Pennsylvania, Filson led an obscure life until 1783, when he traveled into Kentucky to take up lands there, possibly a reward for service in the Revolution. He acquired extensive holdings in the region and, probably in an effort to attract settlers, published in 1784 his *Discovery, Settlement, and Present State of Kentucke*, a vivid description of the territory combined with the first (though inaccurate) history of the area. Included in the book was the first map of Kentucky, which was later published separately, and appended was a brief autobiographical narrative, "The Adventures of Col. Daniel Boon," which, although written in the first person, was almost certainly composed by Filson himself. The earliest account of the famous frontiersman, the "Adventures" contributed to the wide circulation of Filson's book in America

and in Europe, where several editions were published, and laid the basis for later elaborations on the legend of Boone. After returning from a trip East to secure publication of the book Filson engaged in the fur trade in Louisville, Kentucky. He made a number of expeditions to the Illinois country and in 1788 traveled to Ohio to survey a tract of land he and some associates had bought there and on which they laid out the settlement of Losantiville, which later became Cincinnati. While engaged in that work Filson was killed by an Indian in October 1788.

Fink, Albert (1827–1897), engineer and railroad economist. Born on October 27, 1827, in Lauterbach, Germany, Fink studied architecture and engineering in Darmstadt and soon after taking a degree in 1848 emigrated to the United States. Taking an engineering position with the Baltimore & Ohio Railroad, he quickly won recognition for his abilities and was placed in charge of designing and building bridges, stations, and shops for a section of the line in what is now West Virginia. At Fairmont, on the Monongahela River, he completed in 1852 what was then the longest iron railroad bridge in the United States, employing a new truss design of his own invention that was named for him. In 1857 he joined the Louisville & Nashville Railroad, for which he designed and built over the Green River the largest iron bridge in the country. He became chief engineer of the line in 1860 and was largely responsible for continuing the company's operations and maintaining sound financial practices during and after the Civil War; in 1865 he was promoted to general superintendent. After completing a mile-long truss bridge, the longest of its kind in the world, over the Ohio River at Louisville, Kentucky, he became in 1869 vice-president as well as general superintendent of the line. Vested with wide authority, he began publishing detailed analytical studies of the economics of railroad transportation and financing, work that won him wide acclaim and rank as the principal founder of railroad economics. The soundness of his economic analyses and policies was demonstrated in his successful extension of the Louisville & Nashville line and the company's weathering of the financial panic of 1873. Fink retired in 1875 but soon succumbed to the urgent request of the Southern Railway and Steamship Association that he become its executive director and attempt to quell destructive competition among its 25 member lines. After considerable success in that effort he again retired in 1877, only to be asked to organize and serve as commissioner of the Trunk Line Association of New York City. He held the position effectively until 1889, when failing health, combined with the lessening need for his mediatory role in the wake of the Interstate Commerce Act of 1887, moved him to retire permanently. Fink died on April 3, 1897.

Fink, Mike (1770?–1823), frontier figure. Born about 1770 at Fort Pitt (now Pittsburgh), Pennsylvania, Fink early achieved considerable renown as a scout and particularly as a marksman; his skill with a rifle is said to have earned the admiration of Davy Crockett himself. After ranger service against the Indians in western Pennsylvania he became a keelboatman on the Ohio and Mississippi rivers. Keelboatmen were then generally acknowledged to be the lustiest, most combative, and loudest men alive, and Fink was the uncrowned "king of the keelboatmen." His skill at telling tall tales added to his popularity with his peers and to his own reputation, for his most imaginative narrative efforts were, after the fashion of the time and place, concerned with his own exploits. As a no-holds-barred fighter he was unmatched—he was, by his own admission, "half horse, half alligator." The coming of the steamboat to the Mississippi meant the end of keelboating, and in 1822 Fink joined the first of the W. H. Ashley–Andrew Henry trapping expeditions to the Rocky Mountains. At Fort Henry on the Yellowstone River he died a violent death in 1823, the details of the event quickly becoming lost in the myriad versions that were circulated. Almost immediately the figure of Mike Fink began to grow to legendary proportions as his own tales of prowess were embellished and passed on in both oral and written tradition. He reigned as a folk hero until the Civil War, after which his popularity declined.

Finley, Robert (1772–1817), religious leader and reformer. Born on February 15, 1772, in Princeton, New Jersey, Finley graduated from the College of New Jersey (now Princeton) in 1787; after five years spent teaching school in New Jersey and South Carolina, he returned to college to study for the ministry. He was licensed to preach in 1794 and ordained in the Presbyterian church in Basking Ridge, New Jersey, the following year. During his years here he also conducted a noted school and served as a trustee of the College of New Jersey. His growing concern for the plight of Negroes in America led him to adopt the then-current notion of establishing colonies of free blacks and manumitted slaves in some African territory, and in 1816 he published in Washington, D.C., his *Thoughts on the Colonization of Free Blacks.* While in Washington he discussed his plan with several prominent men, including President James Madison and Henry Clay, and in late December he called a meeting of persons interested in colonization. Presided over by Clay, the meeting resulted in the organization of the American Colonization Society, with Bushrod Washington as president and Finley as a vice-president. Finley then returned to New Jersey and there formed a state affiliate of the society. In 1817 he was appointed president of the University of Georgia; six months after assuming the post he died, in Athens, Georgia, on October 3, 1817. The American Colonization Society was four more years in organizing its work; in 1822 the first group of colonists, eventually numbering more than 10,000, was sent to Liberia.

Finney, Charles Grandison (1792–1875), religious leader and educator. Born in Warren, Connecticut, on August 29, 1792, Finney grew up in Oneida County on the New York frontier. In 1818, after several years of teaching school and studying on his own, he set about preparing for the bar. In 1821 he underwent a rather violent religious conversion and immediately gave up law to devote himself to evangelism. His legal training remained with him, however, and shaped the style and delivery of his sermons. After a year of theological study he was ordained in the Presbyterian church in 1824 and immediately began his revival campaign. Throughout New York and New England and the Middle Atlantic states he preached forcefully, directly, and with great effect; his revivals were widely emotional and were much disparaged by many regular ecclesiastics, who believed that the momentary "conversion experience" that he emphasized was insufficient to promote a deep and lasting Christian consciousness. In 1832 he moved to New York City as minister of the Second Free Presbyterian Church. He chafed at denominational restrictions, however; two years later the Broadway Tabernacle was built for him and in 1836 he led it into the Congregational church. In 1835 he became professor of theology at the newly founded Oberlin College in Ohio and for two years maintained both that position and his pastorate in New York City. In 1837 he resigned from the New York church and became minister of the First Congregational Church in Oberlin. He continued his evangelistic work, devoting a portion of every year to it, and in 1849–1850 and again in 1859–1860 carried his revivals to Great Britain with notable success. Finney's theology, which by and large became the "Oberlin theology," continued to confound conservative clerics and even some New School Calvinists; it and the school long shared a certain stigma of disrepute among some clerics. From 1851 to 1866 he was president of Oberlin College; his pastorate continued until 1872, and he taught theology until shortly before his death in Oberlin on August 16, 1875. Among his writings were *Lectures on Revivals,* 1835; *Lectures on Systematic Theology,* 1847; and *Memoirs,* 1876.

Firestone, Harvey Samuel (1868–1938), industrialist. Born in Columbiana, Ohio, on December 20, 1868, Firestone was educated in local schools and attended a business college in Cleveland for a short time. From 1892 to 1896 he worked as a salesman for an uncle's buggy-manufacturing business; becoming convinced that rubber tires were destined to become standard equipment on vehicles of all sorts, he moved to Chicago in 1896 and formed a company to sell them. Three years later he sold out at a profit and in 1900 moved to Akron, Ohio, where the major rubber manufacturers were located, and organized the Firestone Tire & Rubber Company, with capital consisting of $10,000 in cash and a patent for a method of attaching tires to rims. At first little more than a sales outlet, the company began manufacturing its own tires in 1903 and thereafter quickly prospered. Firestone was quick to adapt to the needs of the automobile and from 1906 was the principal supplier of tires to the company of Henry Ford, whose close friend he became. With the introduction of the "dismountable rim," permitting quick replacement of a tire by a spare, and other innovations, the Firestone company became one of the leaders in the industry within a short span of time. By keeping wages low and by successfully resisting unionization for decades, the company showed sizable profits not only during the expansion years of the 1920s but also into and throughout the Depression. Firestone himself was active in promoting the use of the trucks for freight hauling and the undertaking of huge highway-construction programs. In 1926, in response to rising prices for raw rubber from the British-held monopoly in Southeast Asia, he leased vast African areas in Liberia and established his own plantations there; although he succeeded in securing an independent rubber supply, some of his labor practices and the company's deep involvement in the Liberian economy aroused controversy. Firestone continued as president of the firm until 1932, when he became chairman of the board. By the time of his death the Firestone company had pioneered in low-pressure balloon tires and nonskid treads, had established a number of branch plants that were supplying some 25 percent of the tires used in the United States, and had begun experimenting with synthetic rubber and plastics. Firestone died on February 7, 1938, at his winter home in Miami Beach, Florida.

Fischer, Robert James (1943–   ), chess player. Born in Chicago on March 9, 1943, Bobby Fischer grew up from the age of five in Brooklyn, New York. At six he became interested in chess; by reading and by regular attendance at the Brooklyn Chess Club, he developed rapidly in skill at the game and in 1956, at the age of thirteen, became the youngest player ever to win the U.S. junior chess championship. In January 1958, shortly before he turned fifteen, he capped his meteoric rise to chess fame by winning the U.S. Chess Federation championship. Later that year he was invited to participate in the interzonal chess competition held by the Fédération Internationale des Echecs (FIDE) in Yugoslavia; his tie for fifth place earned him a place among the challengers for the world championship and also ranking by FIDE as an international grand master; he was the youngest player ever to be so rated. Fischer's success hinged on his vast knowledge of the game—he devoured virtually everything in the literature—on his ability to devise innovative strategies, on his brilliant endgame technique, and, to an unknown but much-discussed degree, on his reputation as a temperamental competitor. Known to storm out of major tournaments in protest against ground rules or official rulings, he often delayed play until he was satisfied with every detail of the arrangements. He published his *Games of Chess* in 1959, the year he left high school to devote full time to chess. He retained the U.S. championship in 1959, 1960, and 1961, regained it in 1963, and held it through 1966; he played for the United States in the FIDE international team tournaments in 1960, 1964, 1966, and 1968, and won numerous international titles. In 1971 he won the FIDE challenge tournament and the right to play reigning champion Boris Spassky of the Soviet Union for the world title. Their match in Reykjavíc, Iceland, in the summer of 1972, aroused unprecedented public interest throughout the world and was played, at Fischer's insistence, for a purse of unprecedented size. Fischer established command of the match early on and drove to victory in the 21st game, becoming the first American ever to win the world championship. He was also the first champion to fail to defend the title. After balking at terms for a challenge match with Anatoly Karpov of the USSR, he was stripped of his title in April 1975. He lived thereafter in virtual seclusion.

Fish, Hamilton (1808–1893), public official. Born in New York City on August 3, 1808, Fish graduated from Columbia College in 1827 and three years later was admitted to the bar. In 1842 he was elected lieutenant governor. During his term legislation was passed establishing the state's system of free public schools. In 1851, with the support of William H. Seward and Thurlow Weed, state party leaders, he was elected to the Senate; he served as a loyal Whig until near the end of his term, when the party dissolved and he became a Republican. During the Civil War he served as chairman of the Union Defense Committee and, for the War Department, aided in alleviating the conditions under which Union prisoners of war were held in the South and helped to arrange for prisoner exchanges. After several years devoted to private interests he reluctantly accepted President Ulysses S. Grant's offer of appointment as secretary of state in 1869. Contrary to his original intention, he held the post through the next eight years; he was responsible for the highest achievements of Grant's administration, which was otherwise characterized by mediocrity and corruption. Fish held congressional expansionists in check and achieved the successful arbitration with Great Britain of the *Alabama* claims. He managed to deter Grant from annexing the Dominican Republic and, during the Cuban revolution, resisted great pressure from both Congress and Spain in refusing to allow the United States to adopt a partisan position toward the conflict; to that end he even refused to release a presidential proclamation that he deemed ill advised, later persuading Grant of the wisdom of his action. When the *Virginius*, a ship of U.S. registry belonging to a Cuban revolutionary group in New York City, was captured by Spanish authorities and 53 of its mainly American crew were shot as filibusters, it was only Fish's unruffled diplomacy that ended the threat of imminent war. He was largely responsible for preventing Grant himself from being involved in the corrupt schemes of his associates, and he finally secured the dismissal of some of the more notorious of them. Fish returned to private life in New York City in 1877 and died in Garrison, New York, on September 6, 1893.

Fishbein, Morris (1889–1976), physician, editor, and author. Born in St. Louis on July 22, 1889, Fishbein grew up there and in Indianapolis. He graduated from the University of Chicago in 1910 and took his M.D. from the Rush Medical College two years later. After a year of postgraduate work at Rush he spent a brief period in the Durand Hospital of the McCormick Institute for Infectious Diseases in Chicago, but his practice of medicine ended in 1913 when he became assistant editor of the *Journal of the American Medical Association.* A prolific writer of articles and editorials and a crusading publicist on behalf of the medical profession, Fishbein rose to editor of the *Journal* and of *Hygeia* in 1924 and held the posts for 25 years, during which he wielded great influence. Under his influence the American Medical Association (AMA) evolved into a powerful organization able to affect strongly not only the patterns of U.S. medical practice but also much legislation bearing on medical practice or health matters. He was a staunch opponent of virtually every proposal for government-sponsored or subsidized medicine for the poor or elderly, and he denounced such private enterprises as prepaid group health plans as "socialized medicine" and a threat to the maintenance of high professional standards. Such views, combined with his outspokenness in expressing them, made him a controversial figure. Among his many books were *Medical Follies,* 1925; *An Hour of Health,* 1929; *Shattering Health Superstitions,* 1930; *Fads and Quackery in Healing,* 1933; *Do You Want to Be a Doctor?,* 1939; *Popular Medical Encyclopedia,* 1946; *Joseph Bolivar De Lee: Crusading Obstetrician,* 1949, with S. T. De Lee; and the *Handy Home Medical Adviser,* first published in 1952. He was also editor of a great many books on medical topics and wrote a syndicated medical column. Fishbein left the editorship of the *Journal* and *Hygeia* in 1949; he was for many years a regular contributor to the *Saturday Evening Post* and to *McCall's* and served as medical editor of the *Encyclopaedia Britannica Book of the Year* and editor of *World-Wide Astracts of General Medicine* from 1958 to 1967 and of *Medical World News* from 1960. *Morris Fishbein, M.D.—an Autobiography* appeared in 1969. He died in Chicago on September 27, 1976.

Fisher, Bud, see Fisher, Harry Conway

Fisher, Dorothy Canfield (1879–1958), author. Born Dorothea Frances Canfield on February 17, 1879, in Lawrence, Kansas, Miss Canfield graduated from Ohio State University, of which her father was then president, in 1899 and after further studies at the Sorbonne in Paris entered Columbia University and took her Ph.D. in 1904. She was for a time secretary of the Horace Mann School in New York City, but in 1907, upon her marriage to John R. Fisher, she moved to a farm in Arlington, Vermont, that had been in her family for generations; the farm remained her home for the rest of her life. In 1907 her first novel, *Gunhild,* was published, and she followed it with *Squirrel Cage,* 1912; *The Bent Twig,* 1915; *Hillsboro People,* 1915, a collection of fictional Vermont sketches; and *Understood Betsy,* 1917, a novel that became a minor classic of children's literature. During World War I she and her husband traveled to France to work in a number of relief projects and her experiences there resulted in the stories collected in *Home Fires in France,* 1918; *The Day of Glory,* 1919; and *Basque People,* 1931. Mrs. Fisher was throughout her life deeply interested in education, both of children and adults, and she published a number of works on aspects of the subject, including *The Montessori Mother,* 1913; *Mothers and Children,* 1914; *Why Stop Learning?,* 1927; and *Our Young Folks,* 1943. Her fictional writings—calm, commonsensical appraisals of American life marked by profound concern for the characters—were perenially popular and included also *The Brimming Cup,* 1921; *Rough Hewn,* 1922; *The Home-Maker,* 1924; *Made-to-Order Stories,* 1925; *The Deepening Stream,* 1930; *Seasoned Timber,* 1939; *American Portraits,* 1946; *Four Square,* 1949; and *A Harvest of Stories,* 1956. She wrote several nonfiction works on American history and other topics, most notably *Vermont Tradition: The Biography of an Outlook on Life,* 1953. She was active in numerous educational and charitable organizations, serving as president of the American Association for Adult Education and during World War II providing the principal inspiration for the Children's Crusade for Children. She was also a member of the editorial board of judges of the Book-of-the-Month Club from its inception in 1926 until 1951. Mrs. Fisher died in Arlington, Vermont, on November 9, 1958.

Fisher, Harry Conway (1884–1954), "Bud," cartoonist. Born in Chicago on April 3, 1884, Fisher attended the University of Chicago for a time and in 1905 moved to San Francisco to work as a newspaper artist. He began drawing cartoons and in 1907 created Augustus Mutt, known simply as "A. Mutt," a racetrack tout of diminutive stature but great aplomb, as evidenced by his constant wearing of a top hat. The following year another character appeared, the tall and bemused Jeff, and the *San Francisco Examiner* began printing Fisher's cartoons as a daily comic strip, *Mutt and Jeff,* generally held to be the first strip to appear regularly with the same characters. *Mutt and Jeff* proved highly popular and soon became the first comic strip to be widely syndicated to subscribing newspapers. Fisher, a sports buff who at one time owned a stable of racehorses, employed the humor of the racetrack and the poolroom in the strip; the humor lay principally in the dialogues of his two rather seedy characters, and the draftsmanship was slightly primitive but effective. Collections of *Mutt and Jeff* strips were published in several volumes between 1910 and 1916. Fisher continued to draw the strip until his death in New York City on September 7, 1954; thereafter it was carried on by his assistant, Al Smith.

Fisher, Irving (1867–1947), economist. Born on February 27, 1867, in Saugerties, New York, Fisher graduated from Yale University in 1888 and took his Ph.D. there three years later. He advanced from a tutorial position in mathematics at Yale in 1890 to assistant professor in 1893; two years later, after additional studies in Berlin and Paris, he shifted to economics and in 1898 became a professor of political economy. Applying his mathematical training to his new field, he attempted—with considerable success—to make of economics a more nearly exact science; he found highly original solutions to a number of fundamental problems of economics by mathematical means and, in perhaps his most important contribution, devised the index number as a major tool for the study of price trends. He took as his special province the study of the relation of money supply to prices, a topic he expounded at length in *The Purchasing Power of Money*, 1911. Others of his notable books included *The Nature of Capital and Income*, 1906; *The Rate of Interest*, 1907; *Elementary Principles of Economics*, 1910; *Why Is the Dollar Shrinking?*, 1914; *Stabilizing the Dollar*, 1920; *The Making of Index Numbers*, 1923; *The Money Illusion*, 1928; *The Stock Market Crash*, 1930; *Inflation*, 1933; *After Reflation, What?*, 1933; and *100% Money*, 1935; most of them were widely translated and long in print. By no means confined to the academic world, Fisher was active in numerous reform movements; the range of his interests was suggested by the organizations of which he served as president: American Association for Labor Legislation (1915–1917); National Institute of Social Sciences (1917); American Economic Association (1918); Eugenics Research Association (1920); Pro-League Independents (1920); Econometric Society (1931–1933); and American Statistical Association (1932). He was also a founder of the American Eugenics Society, the Vitality Records Office, the Stable Money Association, and the Index Number Institute. His most strenuous crusading went into his proposal for a "compensated dollar," which would have a constant purchasing power by being defined, not in terms of a specified weight of gold, but in terms of a specified value of gold, that value being determined in turn by reference to the changing index numbers of specified commodities. After retiring from Yale in 1935 Fisher continued to be active in his many business interests and in promoting economic legislation at the state and federal levels until his death in New York City on April 29, 1947.

Fisk, James (1834–1872), financier. Born in Bennington, Vermont, on April 1, 1834, Fisk grew up mainly in Brattleboro; he received little schooling and in his youth held a variety of jobs from waiter to ticket agent for a circus. After a period as a peddler and then as a stock jobber he became a buyer and agent for Jordan, Marsh & Company in Boston, obtaining large Civil War contracts for the firm. After the war he was for a time a cotton buyer in the South and then again a stock jobber. The failure of a short-lived brokerage firm he formed in New York City did nothing to dampen his importuning geniality or his boundless braggadocio, and he soon gained advantage from the acquaintance of Daniel Drew, whose agent he became in a steamboat-line transaction. With Drew's backing Fisk opened the brokerage firm of Fisk & Belden and handled many of Drew's dealings in the stock market. He joined with Drew and Jay Gould in the "Erie War," seeking to wrest control of the Erie Railroad from Cornelius Vanderbilt and smilingly sharing in the public opprobrium heaped on them for their openly corrupt actions. After the conclusion of a compromise with Vanderbilt in 1868 the three went on to other spectacular manipulations of stock, gold prices, foreign credit, and other financial "paper," Fisk earning the title of the "Barnum of Wall Street" for his flamboyant techniques. With the proceeds of the looting of the Erie, of which he was vice-president and comptroller, and of other enterprises, Fisk led the life of a sybarite, developing tastes for French theatricals, Broadway showgirls, expensive horses, and honorary but gaudy military posts. In 1869 he and Gould made their famous attempt to corner the gold market; the scheme was foiled by the government but resulted in a disastrous drop in the market on "Black Friday," September 24, 1869, which ruined hundreds of innocent investors as well as many speculators and had repercussions in the U.S. economy and in Europe as well. To a congressional investigating committee's inquiry regarding the whereabouts of the money involved, Fisk replied that it had "gone where the woodbine twineth," subsequently explaining that he meant simply "up the spout." At the conclusion of the investigation he cheerfully offered the consoling thought that "Nothing is lost save honor." Fisk, who by that time had become almost the epitome of the "robber baron," thereafter continued his career as a voluptuary-about-town until, following a quarrel over certain business matters and a favorite mistress, the actress Josie Mansfield, he was shot by Edward S. Stokes on January 6, 1872; he died the next day in New York City.

Fisk, John, *see* Fiske, John

Fiske, Haley (1852–1929), businessman. Born on March 18, 1852, in New Brunswick, New Jersey, Fiske graduated from Rutgers in 1871. After working for a time as a newspaper reporter he took up the study of law and upon admission to the New York bar was assigned to handle the legal affairs of the Metropolitan Life Insurance Company by the law firm in which he had been studying. While advancing to a full partnership in the firm he acquired a thorough knowledge of the insurance business and in 1891 was elected vice-president of Metropolitan Life. Giving up his law practice to devote full time to the company, he proved to be a fertile source of innovation in the insurance business. It was largely at his suggestion and through his legal work that Metropolitan Life was gradually converted from a stock to a mutual company, voting control being shifted completely from investors to policyholders by 1915. At the same time the company grew rapidly, in large part because of Fiske's greatest contribution, a plan under which Metropolitan undertook in 1909 to organize corps of visiting nurses in major industrial centers to provide otherwise unavailable medical and sanitation services to the families of policyholding workingmen. Originally proposed by Lillian D. Wald, the plan was implemented on a huge scale and was quick to show results, which from the company's point of view were a reduction in annual death claims of some 20 percent and a consequent annual saving of $3.5 million. The idea was subsequently adopted by other insurance companies as well. Fiske became president of Metropolitan Life in 1919 and held the post until his death. Under his direction the company invested considerable sums in improved low-cost housing in New York City and elsewhere. By the time of his death on March 3, 1929, in New York City, it had grown into the largest financial institution in the world.

Fiske, John (1842–1901), philosopher and historian. Born in Hartford, Connecticut, on March 30, 1842, Edmund Fisk Green legally took the name John Fisk when he was thirteen and added the final "e" five years later. He was a gifted child, read widely, and by the time he entered Harvard had already formed a number of heterodox opinions, particularly on the subject of evolution. A follower of Herbert Spencer, he published while still a student two articles on evolution and history in the *North American Review*. He graduated in 1863 and the following year was admitted to the bar. His interest in philosophy and history prevailed over his law practice, however; in 1869 and again in 1871 he was invited to deliver a series of lectures at Harvard and from 1872 to 1879 he was the college's assistant librarian. During a year's leave from that post in 1874 he visited England and wrote his two-volume *The Outlines of Cosmic Philosophy*, in which he attempted to reconcile the new scientific outlook exemplified by the doctrine of evolution with religious tradition. Public lectures in Boston and other places won him wide popularity, and he continued to publish books at an astonishing pace. After about 1885 his written work dealt primarily with American history, particularly the colonial and Revolutionary periods. As with his philosophical works, these did not reflect original scholarship; rather they were lucid syntheses of numerous sources and were widely popular. Notable among his many books were *Myths and Myth-Makers*, 1872; *The Unseen World*, 1876; *Excursions of an Evolutionist*, 1884; *American Political Ideas Viewed from the Standpoint of Universal History*, 1885; *The American Revolution*, 1891; *Through Nature to God*, 1899; and *The Mississippi Valley in the Civil War*, 1901. In 1884 Fiske became professor of American history at Washington University in St. Louis, although he continued to make his home in Massachusetts until his death in Gloucester, Massachusetts, on July 4, 1901. His primary contribution to American thought was popularizing the evolutionary thesis against the adamant opposition in the church.

Fiske, Minnie Maddern (1865–1932), actress. Born in New Orleans on December 19, 1865, Marie Augusta Davey was the daughter of a theatrical manager; she made her stage debut at the age of three under her mother's maiden name as "Little Minnie Maddern." In 1870 she first appeared in New York in *A Sheep in Wolf's Clothing*, later playing Little Eva in *Uncle Tom's Cabin* and supporting Laura Keene in *Hunted Down*. After a decade more of playing child's roles she appeared as an adult in *Fogg's Ferry* at the Park Theatre, New York City, in 1882. She was established as a star by 1890, when she married Harrison Grey Fiske, a playwright and editor of the *New York Dramatic Mirror*, and retired from the stage for a time. She returned in 1893 in her husband's *Hester Crewe* and subsequently appeared in *A Doll's House*, *La Femme du Claude*, and other plays, scoring a great success in *Tess of the D'Urbervilles* in 1897. She was unable to obtain road bookings during the later 1890s because of a dispute between her husband and Charles Frohman's powerful Theatrical Syndicate and so remained in New York. After appearances in *Magda*, *Frou Frou*, and, with Maurice Barrymore, in *Becky Sharp*, she joined her husband in forming their own company and renting the Manhattan Theatre in 1901 in order to be completely independent. Although they lost money in the enterprise, for six years they provided New York with outstanding theater in performances of such modern dramas as *Miranda of the Balcony*, 1901; *Mary of Magdala*, 1902; *Hedda Gabler*, 1903; *Leah Kleschna*, 1904; *The New York Idea*, 1906; and *Rosmersholm*, 1907. The theater closed in 1907 and over the next several years Mrs. Fiske appeared elsewhere in *Salvation Nell*, *Pillars of Society*, *Erstwhile Susan*, *Madame Sand*, and others; she also made numerous successful tours on which she presented her earlier and much-acclaimed interpretations of Ibsen and Shakespeare and a very popular revival of *The Rivals*. A brilliant performer, and a gifted director, and a forceful pioneer in theatrical realism, she gave great encouragement to other actors and to young playwrights and was as popular with her colleagues as with her audiences.

Throughout her career she shunned publicity. The extended tours of her later years were exhausting, and after a brief illness while on the road she died on February 15, 1932, in Hollis, New York.

Fitch, Asa (1809–1879), entomologist. Born on February 24, 1809, in Salem, New York, Fitch was already an eager amateur naturalist when he entered the Rensselaer School (now Rensselaer Polytechnic Institute) in 1826 and took up the study of entomology. On completing the course there he enrolled in the Vermont Academy of Medicine, from which he graduated in 1829, and after further study at the Rutgers Medical College in New York City and a year as assistant professor of natural history at Rensselaer he began medical practice in 1831 in Fort Miller, New York. Seven years later he gave up medicine and returned to Salem to farm and to pursue his entomological studies. Several published papers, many of them dealing in particular with the effect of insects on agriculture, led to a commission from the state to collect and classify the insects of New York and in 1854 to his appointment as state entomologist. From then until his resignation in 1871 he published lucid and instructive annual reports of his valuable and wide-ranging studies that were of great influence both on the practice of agriculture, to which he contributed a great many ideas, and on the growth of professional entomology, especially as a facet of the state's general economic concerns. Several states followed New York in appointing entomologists to official positions, but Fitch remained the leader in the field and his reports remained landmarks. He lived quietly after his retirement until his death on April 8, 1879, in Salem, New York.

Fitch, John (1743–1798), inventor. Born in Hartford County, Connecticut, on January 21, 1743, Fitch received only a few years of schooling and, after a time working on the family farm and brief employment as a sailor, apprenticed himself to a clockmaker. Having learned brass working, he soon opened a brass foundry of his own in East Windsor, Connecticut. He was unsuccessful in this venture and in a brass and silversmith business he later operated in Trenton, New Jersey, largely because of his disregard for economic prudence and efficiency. He served for a short time in the Revolution and then managed a gun factory. From 1780 to 1785 he was engaged in surveying and real-estate speculation in Kentucky and the Northwest Territory. Settling in Bucks County, Pennsylvania, in 1785, he turned his energies to inventing a steam-powered boat. He failed to win financial aid from the Continental Congress and from state legislatures, but from several states he secured 14-year monopolies for steamboat operations on inland waters. With these privileges and his working models Fitch persuaded a group of Philadelphians to finance construction of a 45-foot boat. He successfully demonstrated this first full-scale craft,

which had steam-powered oars for propulsion, on the Delaware River on August 22, 1787, with delegates to the Constitutional Convention looking on. The next year he built a 60-foot paddle-wheeler and in 1790 his third and still larger boat was launched and for a time maintained a regular schedule of trips between Philadelphia and Trenton. In 1791, an earlier dispute over priority having been resolved, he was granted U.S. and French patents. His fourth boat was wrecked in a storm that year and Fitch's financial backers deserted him. He vainly sought aid in France, returned home in poor health, and after more unsuccessful attempts to find financing, moved to Bardstown, Kentucky, where he died on July 2, 1798. It was not until some years later, with the work of Robert Fulton, that steam propulsion became commercially practical.

Fitz, Reginald Heber (1843–1913), pathologist. Born in Chelsea, Massachusetts, on May 5, 1843, Fitz graduated from Harvard in 1864 and remained there to study at the Medical School, taking his M.D. in 1868. After two years of further study in Vienna and in Berlin, where he was in the laboratory of the great pathologist Rudolf Virchow, he returned to Harvard in 1870 as an instructor in pathology. He rose quickly to a full professorship, in 1878. A forceful and effective teacher, he introduced in the United States the concept of disease as an altered state rather than a distinct entity and made clear the need to examine the affected tissues closely in order to understand the disease process; following Virchow, he was a pioneer in the use of the microscope in pathology. In his own researches he demonstrated the efficacy of the methods he taught, publishing in 1886 a report of his scientifically elegant study of a form of acute abdominal pain which he attributed to the inflammation or perforation of the vermiform appendix and for which he outlined a course of radical surgery. This report on the pathology of appendicitis (which he named) remains a classic of medical literature. Three years later he published another major study, this one dealing with acute pancreatitis. Fitz was particularly influential in his continued insistence upon close cooperation between the pathologist and the clinical practitioner, and he contributed greatly to the development of both diagnostic and therapeutic techniques. From 1892 he was Hersey Professor of the Theory and Practice of Physic at Harvard Medical School. He died in Boston on September 30, 1913.

Fitzgerald, Edward, *see* Foy, Eddie

Fitzgerald, Ella (1918–   ), singer. Born on April 25, 1918, in Newport News, Virginia, Miss Fitzgerald was orphaned early in life and was reared in an orphanage in Yonkers, New York. In 1934, at an amateur show at the Apollo Theater in Harlem, she was discovered by bandleader Chick Webb, who immediately hired her and became her musical mentor. With his band she made her first recording, "Love and Kisses," in 1935 and with him she wrote "A-Tisket, A-Tasket," which was released in 1938 and became a nationwide hit. Following Webb's death in 1939 she took over his band for a time and then became a solo performer, successfully touring nightclubs and theaters across the country and abroad. A singer of great flexibility and imagination, she was able to instill life and interest into the poorest of materials and with good songs she created classic renditions. Her repertoire ranged from blues through Dixieland and calypso to popular ballads —among her most popular record albums were those of songs by Irving Berlin, George Gershwin, Cole Porter, and Rodgers and Hart—and she appeared and recorded with such greats as Louis Armstrong, whom she rivaled in scat singing, and Duke Ellington. From 1946 she toured regularly with Norman Granz's Jazz at the Philharmonic group and in 1956 began recording for his Verve label. In 1955 she appeared in the movie *Pete Kelly's Blues*. Known around the world as "the First Lady of Song," Miss Fitzgerald was the acknowledged favorite female vocalist of most top jazzmen and popular musicians and regularly won top honors in polls conducted by such trade magazines as *Metronome* and *Downbeat*; in 1968 she was voted top female singer by the International Jazz Critics' Poll. Others among her most popular single recordings were "That's My Desire," "Oh, Lady Be Good," "Manhattan," and "I'm Thrilled." In 1968 she was elected honorary chairman of the Martin Luther King Foundation. She continued to tour, make records, and appear on television with great success.

Fitzgerald, Francis Scott Key, *see* Fitzgerald, F. Scott

Fitzgerald, F. Scott (1896–1940), author. Born in St. Paul, Minnesota, on September 24, 1896, Francis Scott Key Fitzgerald was educated in elite private schools and thus, despite a middle-class background, was early exposed to the way of life of the wealthy with whom he was to concern himself in his writing. He studied at Princeton but left before graduating; in 1917 he joined the army and during his service began his first novel which, after extensive revision at the urging and with the aid of editor Maxwell Perkins, was published in 1920 as *This Side of Paradise*. The book was successful and Fitzgerald became wealthy himself for a time. With his collections of short stories, *Flappers and Philosophers*, 1920, and *Tales of the Jazz Age*, 1922, he became the recognized spokesman for the youthful rebellion of the 1920s; *Tales of the Jazz Age* contributed a popular name for the era. In 1922 he published his second novel, *The Beautiful and the Damned*. From 1924 to 1930 he lived in Europe where he produced possibly his best single work and his most incisive look at American values, *The Great Gatsby*, 1925, and another collection of stories, *All the Sad Young Men*, 1926. His life during this time, exemplifying in many ways the frenzy

and aimlessness of which he wrote, began to disintegrate; his wife, Zelda Sayre Fitzgerald, became mentally ill, he became progressively dependent on alcohol and had money problems, and his next novel, *Tender is the Night*, was not finished until 1934. The book was a financial failure, and he recorded his subsequent despondency and emotional emptiness in a series of magazine essays entitled "The Crack-Up," published in 1936. A final collection of stories had appeared in 1935 under the title *Taps at Reveille*. The following year he moved to Hollywood to become a screenwriter; in 1940 he rediscovered the talent and the inner drive he had thought lost and began work on a new novel, *The Last Tycoon*. Before it was completed he suffered a fatal heart attack in Hollywood, California, on December 21, 1940.

Fitzhugh, George (1806–1881), author. Born in Prince William County, Virginia, on November 4, 1806, to an aristocratic family, Fitzhugh received only a sketchy early education; he later studied law and in 1829 began practice in Caroline County. During the middle 1850s he was employed for a time in the land-claims department of the attorney general's office. He was throughout his life a staunch defender of slavery as an institution, and he contributed essays on slavery and other Southern topics to various periodicals, notably *De Bow's Review*. In 1854 he published a weighty defense of slavery as *Sociology for the South; or, in the Failure of Free Society*; three years later, after a trip to Boston during which he met Harriet Beecher Stowe and other abolitionists, he published *Cannibals All! or, Slaves Without Masters*. Through these two books he helped to turn the South's position, which had until then been largely defensive, into an aggressive one of positive argument. In surveying social conditions in the North, Fitzhugh pointed to the miserable lot of most of the working class, exploited by capitalists and left to shift as best they might, and offered in contrast the paternalistic vision of institutionalized chattel slavery, in which the master's interest lay in the continuing wellbeing of the workers he owned. The freedom of the Northern laborer was in fact, he claimed, profound insecurity; instead of illusion, slavery offered security and humane treatment. Fitzhugh went on to develop the notion of slavery as the only alternative to Socialism, which he saw as a dire threat in the North. He fully believed the Southern system to be superior, and until the Civil War retained the hope of converting the benighted North. After the war he continued to write for periodicals on the Southern economy and advocated the establishment of industry in the region. Fitzhugh died in Huntsville, Texas, on July 30, 1881.

Fitzpatrick, Thomas (1799?–1854), frontiersman, fur trader, and scout. Born about 1799 in County Cavan, Ireland, Fitzpatrick emigrated to the United States about 1816 and made his way to the frontier. After a time spent trading with the

Indians he joined William H. Ashley and Andrew Henry on their second trapping expedition to the Rocky Mountains in 1823, and he accompanied Jedediah S. Smith in the explorations that led to finding the South Pass through the Rockies in 1824. He remained in the mountains as a trapper for several years and in 1830 joined Jim Bridger, Milton Sublette, and others in organizing the Rocky Mountain Fur Company, which dominated the trade until the appearance of John Jacob Astor's American Fur Company; by 1834 the competition and the dwindling trade forced the partners to disband. Fitzpatrick, by that time reputed by his peers to be the greatest of the "mountain men," thereafter worked for Astor and occasionally as a guide, in 1841 leading the California-bound emigrant wagon train of John Bartleson and John Bidwell as far as Fort Hall and then conducting a part of the group, including Father Pierre Jean De Smet, to the Oregon country. In 1843–1844 he was, with Kit Carson, a guide for one of Capt. John C. Frémont's expeditions and in 1845 he guided Col. Stephen W. Kearny's exploration of South Pass. The next year he led Kearny to Santa Fe and on toward California. In that year he was appointed Indian agent for the Upper Platte region with responsibility for dealing with the Cheyenne, the Arapaho, and some Sioux bands. Long respected and sometimes feared by the Indians of the northern plains, to whom he was known as "Bad Hand" or "Three Fingers" (the result of a rifle accident), Fitzpatrick called a great council of chiefs at Fort Laramie in September 1851 at which, by gifts and argument, he persuaded them to accept the notion of occupying lands reserved for the various tribes, each area clearly demarked and guaranteed. The Sioux, Mandan, Gros Ventre, Assiniboin, Crow, Blackfeet, Cheyenne, and Arapaho were present and all accepted the treaty that, unknown to them, was to make it still easier for the lands of any tribe to be preempted by whites and that would lead directly to the later decades of Indian wars. In 1853 Fitzpatrick negotiated another settlement with the Comanche and Kiowa at Fort Atkinson, near the site of present-day Dodge City, Kansas. He was then called to Washington, D.C., to discuss Indian affairs, but died soon after arriving, on February 7, 1854.

Fitzsimmons, Robert Prometheus (1862–1917), boxer. Born on June 4, 1862, in Helston, England, Fitzsimmons emigrated as a child with his parents to New Zealand, where he grew up working in his father's blacksmith shop and developed, along with great strength, a love of boxing. He had already acquired a considerable reputation as the New Zealand champion when he came to San Francisco in 1890 to try his luck with American fighters. The next year he fought Jack Dempsey the Nonpareil (not to be confused with the later heavyweight champion) in New Orleans and won the middleweight title. After further successes he moved up to heavyweight contention—he weighed only about 160 pounds and with spindly,

awkward legs was virtually all torso—and on March 17, 1897, in Carson City, Nevada, knocked out the champion, James J. Corbett, in the 14th round of a title match; his staggering "solar-plexus punch" had defeated an Irishman on St. Patrick's Day. Fitzsimmons known variously as "the Cornishman," "Fighting Bob," and "Ruby Robert," retained the heavyweight crown for two years, losing it to James J. Jeffries at Coney Island on June 9, 1899. After defeating Tom Sharkey, Gus Ruhlin, and others he attempted to regain the title in 1902 but was again beaten by Jeffries. In November 1903 he won the light-heavyweight title in a 20-round match in San Francisco; he lost it by a knockout two years later. He continued to box until 1914 but advancing age kept him from notable success. In later years he toured in tent shows and in vaudeville and was, in the fashion of fighters of his day, a flamboyant and popular figure. Fitzsimmons died in Chicago on October 22, 1917.

Flagg, James Montgomery (1877–1960), illustrator. Born in June 18, 1877, in Pelham Manor, New York, Flagg early began to draw and at the age of twelve sold some illustrations to *St. Nicholas* magazine. By 1892 he was contributing regularly to *St. Nicholas*, *Life*, *Judge*, and other periodicals, and in 1893 he was commissioned by *St. Nicholas* to cover pictorially the World's Columbian Exposition in Chicago. He studied for a time at the Art Students League in New York City and later under Sir Hubert von Herkomer in England and Victor Marec in Paris. For a number of years he was widely known as a portraitist; his watercolors and oils of well-known sitters attracted attention at the Paris Salon and in shows at the National Academy of Design and elsewhere. He later turned to pen and ink and evolved a vigorous style in the American tradition of Charles Dana Gibson. Declining the title of "artist," Flagg was first and foremost an illustrator and his works, turned out at a prodigious rate, filled the leading magazines of the day, from *Harper's* and *McClure's* to *Cosmopolitan* and *Liberty*. He collected many in humorous books under such titles as *Yankee Girls Abroad*, 1900; *Tomfoolery*, 1904; *If—A Guide to Bad Manners*, 1905; *I Should Say So*, 1914; and *Boulevard All the Way—Maybe*, 1925. A high-living, self-proclaimed bohemian and an enthusiastic celebrant, both in life and in work, of the idealized American girl, Flagg achieved his greatest fame during World War I, when, as official military artist of the state of New York, he created a recruiting poster showing a stern Uncle Sam—modeled on himself—pointing directly at the viewer, with the caption "I Want You." Some four million copies were printed and distributed throughout the country by the U.S. government; the poster was credited with great effectiveness in increasing army enlistments and was reissued during World War II. Flagg was outspokenly critical of modern art—he distinguished between artists and illustrators, holding that illustrators alone could draw—and was a popular lecturer. He also wrote film scripts and musical plays and in 1946 published an autobiography, *Roses and Buckshot*. He died in New York City on May 27, 1960.

Flagler, Henry Morrison (1830–1913), business leader. Born in Hopewell, near Canandaigua, New York, on January 2, 1830, Flagler left home at fourteen and made his way to Ohio, where he held a succession of jobs in various towns. In 1850 he set up as a grain dealer in Bellevue and accumulated from that and other small enterprises a modest fortune; he invested it in a salt-manufacturing venture in Saginaw, Michigan, and ended up deeply in debt. Settling then in Cleveland, he again went into the grain business and renewed an earlier acquaintance with John D. Rockefeller, in whose oil-refining company he invested borrowed money in 1867, the firm becoming Rockefeller, Andrew & Flagler. He remained among the top executives, and Rockefeller's closest colleague, through the organization of the Standard Oil Company in 1870, retaining a vice-presidency until 1908 and a directorship until 1911, and gaining a large fortune. On a trip in 1883 he perceived clearly the vast resort and recreational potential of Florida's east coast and three years later began buying and improving small railroad lines in the region, combining them into the Florida East Coast Railway. He then began extending the line south from Daytona, reaching Palm Beach in 1894 and Miami two years later. Along the route he built a string of palatial hotels—the Ponce de Leon, the Alcazar, the Ormond, the Royal Poinciana, the Breakers, the Royal Palm—and developed the entire coast into a gigantic resort area. The railroad was continued on from Miami through the Everglades and, on a series of remarkable bridges and causeways, to Key West, the work reaching completion in 1912. Flagler made extensive improvements in Miami and established steamship lines to Key West and to Nassau, where he built the Royal Victorian and Colonial hotels. He also encouraged agriculture, especially fruit growing, on the east coast and made gifts for the building of schools, churches, and hospitals. In all he invested some $40 million in his Florida enterprises. Flagler died in West Palm Beach on May 20, 1913.

Flaherty, Robert Joseph (1884–1951), filmmaker and explorer. Born on February 16, 1884, in Iron Mountain, Michigan, Flaherty grew up there and in Ontario. He attended Upper Canada College and the Michigan College of Mines and in 1910 made the first of several exploring and prospecting expeditions to the northern reaches of Canada. Over the next six years he explored the Ungava region, Baffin Island, and the Belcher Islands (one of which was named for him). In 1920 he returned to the Eskimos of the far North whom he had come to admire and for 16 months photographed every aspect of their lives. After editing, the film was released in 1923 as *Nanook of the North* and was quickly recognized as a

major contribution to cinematic art. Sponsored by Jesse L. Lasky, Flaherty went to the South Seas in 1923 and, again with painstaking care, made a film study of Samoan islanders; it was in a review of *Moana*, 1926, that the term "documentary" was first applied to films of its kind. Flaherty cared little for story lines or other artifices; he brought great sympathy to his studies of simple, often harsh ways of life, translated them into powerful and intensely lyrical film sequences, and edited his results into what came to be considered paradigms for documentary filmmakers. He made a number of shorter films, including *The Story of a Potter*, 1925, commissioned by the Metropolitan Museum of Art, and *Industrial Britain*, 1933, but his major achievements were full-length works. *Tabu*, 1932, made with Fred Murnau, was another study of Polynesian life, and his greatest achievement, *Man of Aran*, 1933, was the fruit of 18 months spent on the barren islands off the Irish coast. For Alexander Korda he directed *Elephant Boy* (for which he discovered Sabu, the Indian boy), 1937, and for Pare Lorentz and the U.S. Film Service he made *The Land*, 1941. During World War II he was engaged in the production of educational films for the war department. Flaherty's last film, *The Louisiana Story*, commissioned by the Standard Oil Company, appeared in 1948. He also wrote a number of books, most notably *A Film-Maker's Odyssey*, 1939. Universally hailed as the father of the documentary film, Flaherty died in Dummerston, Vermont, on July 23, 1951.

Flanagan, Edward Joseph (1886–1948), religious leader. Born on July 13, 1886, in Roscommon, Ireland, Flanagan emigrated to the United States in 1904 and two years later graduated from Mount St. Mary's College in Emmitsburg, Maryland. After a year at St. Joseph's Seminary, Dunwoodie, New York, another at the Gregorian University in Rome, and three at the Jesuit University in Innsbruck, Austria, he was ordained a priest in the Roman Catholic church in 1912. Assigned to the archdiocese of Omaha, he served in a parish in O'Neill, Nebraska, for a year and in 1913 became assistant pastor of St. Patrick's parish in Omaha. He became a U.S. citizen in 1919. In 1914 he established a Workingmen's Hotel in Omaha to care for the poor and the derelict, but he soon became convinced that a better approach to such social problems as crime, alcoholism, and unemployability was to attack the root causes in childhood. In 1917 he rented a house and with five young boys, three of them delinquents, began his Home for Homeless Boys. Many more boys came under his care, all in some manner underprivileged and seeming to be destined for aimless lives; although he was operating on a financial shoestring, in 1918 he moved them to a small tract of land outside Omaha, where together they built Father Flanagan's Boys Home. In 1922 the home was incorporated as a municipality, Boys Town, with a town government of boys that was elected by the boys themselves. By 1939 the capacity of Boys Town was 500 and already thousands had passed through and been educated, taught citizenship, and, when necessary, socially rehabilitated under the loving guidance of Father Flanagan, whose deeply held belief, "There is no such thing as a bad boy," was thoroughly vindicated by his spectacular success. The fame of Boys Town was given a great boost by the popular motion picture *Boys Town*, 1938, for his role in which Spencer Tracy won an Academy Award that he subsequently presented to Father Flanagan. Flanagan was for ten years president of the Omaha Welfare Board and a member of numerous other organizations and advisory groups. In 1937 he was designated by Pope Pius XI a domestic prelate and given the title Right Reverend Monsignor. After World War II he served as a consultant to the U.S. government on youth programs in occupied countries; he traveled to Japan and Korea in 1947 to inspect youth facilities there and while on a similar mission to Germany the next year died in Berlin on May 15, 1948.

Flannagan, John Bernard (1895–1942), sculptor. Born on April 7, 1895, in Fargo, North Dakota, Flannagan grew up for the most part in an orphanage. His early love of drawing and wood carving led him to enroll in the Minneapolis Institute of Arts in 1914 and he remained for three years studying painting. From 1917 to 1922 he served in the merchant marine; after his discharge he lived a precarious existence in New York City until he was befriended by painter Arthur B. Davies, who sent him to his farm in Congers, New York, to regain his health. While working as a handyman around the farm he resumed painting, learning a wax technique from Davies and with his encouragement again taking up wood carving. He first exhibited his work in a 1923 show that also featured works by Davies, Maurice Prendergast, and William Glackens. While living in various places in upstate New York he began experimenting in stone sculpture and by 1928 was working almost exclusively in that medium, using, for both financial and philosophical reasons, the native fieldstone of the region. In his carving Flannagan sought to realize the image already hidden in the material; he worked the stone to the minimal degree in producing small animal figures or his many pieces on the theme of birth or rebirth. These, and others such as his mother-and-child pieces, bore titles like "Triumph of the Egg," "Not Yet," "Jonah and the Whale," and "New One," strongly suggestive of his preoccupation with the trauma of coming-into-being. Influenced by none of his predecessors, Flannagan was a uniquely individual and original artist; he neither subscribed to nor was included in any of the contemporary schools or movements of modern art. Aside from two extended visits to Ireland, one on a Guggenheim fellowship in 1932–1933, he remained in rural New York and later Connecticut, traveling to New York City for occasional shows. After

suffering a nervous breakdown in 1934 he began tentative experiments in cast bronze; in the aftermath of an automobile accident and four brain operations in 1939 he was forced to give up his strenuous stoneworking altogether. He cared little for monumental sculpture, but did execute a notable figure, "Gold Miner," for the Samuel Memorial in Philadelphia. Flannagan grew increasingly despondent in his last years and finally, on January 6, 1942, took his own life in New York City.

Flegenheimer, Arthur (1902–1935), "Dutch Schultz," gangster. Born in the Bronx, New York, on August 6, 1902, Flegenheimer grew up in relative poverty and after six years of schooling went to work at a succession of minor jobs. At seventeen he was convicted of burglary and, on emerging from 15 months in a reformatory, he was a minor hero among Bronx gangs, by whom he was nicknamed "Dutch Schultz" after a notorious local bully of an earlier era. Over the next several years he was arrested a great many times on various charges, but never convicted. In 1928 he bought into a Bronx speakeasy and immediately began working into the production and distribution aspects of bootlegging. By the end of Prohibition he had assembled a gang of deadly efficient gunmen, including for a time the maniacal Vincent "Mad Dog" Coll, to protect his iron hold on the liquor traffic in the Bronx and upper Manhattan, and had moved into other enterprises, including the "policy," or "numbers," racket in Harlem, extortion from restaurants, and a window-cleaners' union. The proceeds from his various activities were huge and financed investments in boxers, racehorses, and nightclubs. In 1933 he was suddenly indicted for income-tax evasion. He went into hiding for more than a year while his attorneys won a change of venue, and then emerged at the place of trial, Syracuse, New York, to establish himself as an altogether fine and upstanding character. A hung jury resulted, and for a second trial in Malone, New York, he repeated the ploy and was acquitted. In the meanwhile, however, control of his New York City rackets had passed into other hands. He established himself in Newark, New Jersey, and attempted to regain his influence, but the newly organized crime "syndicate" was wary of the Dutchman's known penchant for solving any given problem by violence. The hostility between Schultz and the syndicate grew and, under the pressure of a grand-jury investigation of the rackets then being conducted by the state's investigator, Thomas E. Dewey, developed into open war. On October 23, 1935, gunmen walked into the saloon that was Schultz's Newark headquarters and shot him and three companions; he died the next day.

Flexner, Abraham (1866–1959), educator. Born in Louisville, Kentucky, on November 13, 1866, Flexner graduated from The Johns Hopkins University in 1886 and for the next 19 years taught school. In 1906 and 1907 he pursued graduate studies at Harvard and the University of Berlin and in 1908 joined the staff of the Carnegie Foundation for the Advancement of Teaching. He was commisioned to study the state of U.S. medical education and, taking the excellent medical school at Johns Hopkins as a model, did so critically and in detail. His report, *Medical Education* in 1910, brought about a revolution in the field; many institutions were forced to close because of the report's criticisms and the publicity that followed, and those that remained raised their standards of admission and instruction and were immeasurably strengthened. Modern medical education dates from the appearance of this report. From 1913 to 1925 Flexner was secretary of the General Education Board, and from 1925 to 1928 director of the board's division of studies and medical education. In 1930 he published *Universities—American, English, German*, a study of the whole spectrum of higher education. In the same year he organized the Institute for Advanced Study at Princeton and served as its director until 1939, when he retired. He published numerous other books, principally on education, and in 1940 *I Remember: An Autobiography*. He died on September 21, 1959, in Falls Church, Virginia.

Flint, Austin (1812–1886), physician and educator. Born in Petersham, Massachusetts, on October 20, 1812, Flint was educated at Amherst and at Harvard, where he took his M.D. in 1833. After three years of practice in Northampton and then Boston he moved to Buffalo, New York, where he remained, with various absences, for 25 years. During 1844–1845 he was professor of the theory and practice of medicine at Rush Medical College in Chicago. In 1847 he led in founding the Buffalo Medical College, in which he held a chair until 1861, although he was actively engaged in teaching there only until 1852, when he joined the faculty of the University of Louisville. He left Louisville in 1856 and from 1859 to 1861 taught at the New Orleans Medical College. He conducted considerable medical research, particularly on the physiology and pathology of the chest, and published his findings in a great number of articles and in several books, including *Physical Exploration and Diagnosis of Diseases Affecting the Respiratory Organs*, 1856, which was published under various titles in revised form many times until 1920; *Diseases of the Heart*, 1859; *A Treatise on the Principles and Practice of Medicine*, 1866, which ran to seven editions, the sixth being prepared with William H. Welch; and *Phthisis*, 1875. A pioneer in the use of the binaural stethoscope, he was the first to describe the heart sound that later came to be known as the Austin Flint murmur. In 1861 he moved to New York City and built a highly successful practice there. In the same year he assumed the professorship of pathology and practical medicine at Long Island College Hospital and joined in organizing the Bellevue Hospital Medical College, at which he became professor

of internal medicine. President of the New York Academy of Medicine in 1873 and of the American Medical Association (AMA) in 1883–1884, Flint was one of the most widely respected physicians of his day and was a teacher of great and lasting influence. He died in New York City on March 13, 1886.

Flint, Timothy (1780–1840), religious leader and author. Born on July 23, 1780, near North Reading, Massachusetts, Flint graduated from Harvard in 1800 and, after a brief period of teaching, entered the ministry. From 1802 to 1814 he was pastor of the Congregational Church in Lunenburg, Massachusetts. In the next year he began a period as a missionary in the Ohio Valley. For a while he tried farming in Missouri and, traveling south to Louisiana, was principal of a seminary in Alexandria. Poor health forced him to return north to Cincinnati. In 1826 he published *Recollections of the Last Ten Years in the Valley of the Mississippi*, an account of the social and economic aspects of the early Western frontier that remains of great value. From 1827 to 1830 he edited the *Western Monthly Review*; in 1828 he published *A Condensed Geography and History of the Western States*, a revised edition of which appeared in 1832. In 1833 he edited briefly the *Knickerbocker Magazine*; in the same year he published *The Biographical Memoir of Daniel Boone, the First Settler of Kentucky*, a book that did much to foster and, through 14 editions, to sustain the Boone legend. Flint published numerous other works, including an edition of James O. Pattie's *Personal Narrative*, 1831, and four romantic novels, *Francis Berrian, or the Mexican Patriot*, 1826; *The Life and Adventures of Arthur Clenning*, 1828; *George Mason, the Young Backwoodsman*, 1829; and *The Shoshonee Valley*, 1830. He died on August 16, 1840, in Salem, Massachusetts.

Fonda, Henry (1905–1982), actor. Born in Grand Island, Nebraska, on May 16, 1905, Henry Jaynes Fonda attended the University of Minnesota from 1923 to 1925 and then, while holding a variety of minor jobs, began working with theater groups in Omaha and Des Moines. In 1928 he moved East and joined the Cape Playhouse and later the University Players Guild in Massachusetts. His first New York City appearance was in a small part in *The Game of Life and Death* in 1929 and he continued in supporting roles until 1934, when he won the lead in *The Farmer Takes a Wife*, for which he received high critical acclaim for his simple, natural style. The following year he went to Hollywood to star in the film version of the play and remained to make a series of movies in which, more often than not, he played ingenuous, straightforward characters that were warmly received by audiences. Among his movies were *Way Down East*, 1935; *The Trail of the Lonesome Pine*, 1936; *Slim*, 1936; *Jezebel*, 1938; *Jesse James*, 1939; *Drums Along the Mohawk*, 1939; *Young Mr. Lincoln*, 1939; *Chad Hanna*, 1940; and

Immortal Sergeant, 1943. Two of his films of this period, *Grapes of Wrath*, 1940, in which he played Tom Joad, and *The Oxbow Incident*, 1943, were especially highly praised. From 1942 to 1945 Fonda served in the navy. After the war he had successes in *My Darling Clementine*, 1946; *Fort Apache*, 1948; and *The Fugitive*, 1947. He returned to Broadway in 1948 in the title role in *Mister Roberts*, widely hailed as his greatest performance; he also starred in the movie version in 1955. He appeared in both the Broadway and Hollywood productions of *The Caine Mutiny Court Martial* in 1954 and 1955; later Broadway roles included those in *Two For the Seesaw*, 1958, and *Critics' Choice*, 1960, and his subsequent movies included *Twelve Angry Men*, 1957; *Advise and Consent*, 1961; *How the West Was Won*, 1963; *The Longest Day*, 1962; *Fail Safe*, 1964; *In Harm's Way*, 1965; *A Big Hand for the Little Lady*, 1966; and *Madigan*, 1968. In 1974 he returned to Broadway in the one-man show *Clarence Darrow*. He finally won an Academy Award for his last film, *On Golden Pond*, 1981. He died on August 12, 1982, in Los Angeles.

Fontanne, Lynn, *see under* Lunt, Alfred

Foot, Andrew Hull, *see* Foote, Andrew Hull

Foote, Andrew Hull (1806–1863), naval officer. Born on September 12, 1806, in New Haven, Connecticut, Foote was the son of a prominent merchant shipper and public official; his name was originally Foot and he himself added the "e" later in life. In 1822 he entered West Point but resigned after six months to accept appointment as a midshipman in the navy. For 20 years he served in the Caribbean, the Mediterranean, and the Pacific, as well as on shore duty at the Philadelphia Navy Yard, and in 1843, as first lieutenant of the *Cumberland* in the Mediterranean, he succeeded in organizing the sailors into a temperance society. His abolition of the traditional grog on the vessel was the beginning of a campaign that resulted eventually in the end of the rum ration for the entire navy in 1862. During 1849–1851 Foote commanded the *Perry* off the coast of Africa and was zealous in putting down the slave trade, a goal he made almost a crusade with subsequent public lectures and his book *Africa and the American Flag*, 1854. From 1851 to 1856 he was again on shore duty, serving on the navy's efficiency board of 1855, and then commanded the sloop *Portsmouth* in the Far East. In late 1856, at the height of hostilities between China and Great Britain, he responded to Chinese shelling by attacking and destroying four barrier forts before Canton. In 1858 he returned to the United States to take command of the Brooklyn Navy Yard. In August 1861 Foote, by then a commodore, was put in charge of naval operations on the vitally important upper Mississippi and its tributaries and in February 1862 his fleet of gunboats provided valuable support to Gen. U. S. Grant in taking Fort Henry and Fort Donelson. Later, in April, he aided Gen. John Pope in capturing the strategic Island No. 10, opening the way to Memphis and the lower Mississippi. Wounds sustained at Fort Donelson forced him to relinquish command in June 1862; he was nonetheless promoted to rear admiral the next month. After a period in charge of the bureau of equipment and recruiting he was named in June 1863 to succeed Samuel F. Du Pont as commander of the South Atlantic Blockading Squadron; before he could assume the command he died in New York City on June 26, 1863.

Force, Peter (1790–1868), printer, archivist, and historian. Born near Paterson, New Jersey, on November 26, 1790, Force moved with his family to Ulster County, New York, and in 1795 to New York City. There he was apprenticed to a printer and by 1813 had achieved sufficient prominence in the trade to be elected president of the New York Typographical Society. After service in the War of 1812 he moved in 1815 to Washington, D.C., where his employer had obtained government printing contracts. He became involved in local politics, winning election to the city council in 1822 and the next year beginning publication of the *National Journal*, a newspaper that favored John Quincy Adams for the presidency and was later a Whig organ; it continued to appear until 1831. He was elected mayor of Washington, running as a Whig, in 1836 and 1838. Force had begun in 1820 to publish annual registers of public officials and the *National Calendar*, an annual compilation of historical and statistical information that appeared in 14 volumes over the years, and his growing interest in collecting old documents and other writings of historical value led to the publication of his four-volume *Tracts and Other Papers Relating Principally to the Origin, Settlement, and Progress of the Colonies in North America*, 1836–1846, which included a great many rare works. He then began a similar project on the documents and written history of the Revolution and under the auspices of the Department of State and with congressional authority published his *American Archives*, which ran, between 1837 and 1853, to nine volumes and covered the years 1774–1776. During the course of his researches he unearthed evidence that the so-called Mecklenburg Declaration of Independence, a set of resolutions supposedly adopted by the people of Mecklenburg County, North Carolina, in 1775, was in fact of doubtful authenticity; subsequent studies by other scholars confirmed Force's evidence. In 1853 Secretary of State William L. Marcy canceled the archive project, which had been planned to include 20 or more volumes, and for several years Force was in straitened financial circumstances because of the large sums he had invested in procuring rare documents. He finally sold his great collection in 1867 to the Library of Congress, where it remains an invaluable resource. He published various other works of historical interest, including *The Declaration of Independence, or Notes on Lord*

Mahon's History of the American Declaration of Independence, 1855. He was a leading member and for a time president of the National Institute for the Promotion of Science. He died in Washington on January 23, 1868.

Ford, Gerald Rudolph, Jr. (1913–   ), thirty-eighth president of the United States. Born in Omaha, Nebraska, on July 14, 1913, Ford grew up in Grand Rapids, Michigan, where he attended the public schools. He received a B.A. from the University of Michigan in 1935 and a law degree from Yale in 1941. He was admitted into the bar in 1941 and began the practice of law in Michigan. During World War II he served in the navy, returning to his law practice in 1946. He won election to the House of Representatives as a Republican in 1948 and was consistently reelected; in 1965 he became House Republican leader. Following the resignation in 1973 of Spiro Agnew, he was President Richard M. Nixon's choice to become vice-president under the twenty-fifth amendment to the Constitution. Ford's nomination won broad congressional support, and he took office in 1974, in the midst of the Watergate scandals surrounding the Nixon administration. When the unfolding of Watergate led finally to Nixon's own resignation on August 9, 1974, Ford succeeded him as President. Nominated for a full term by the Republican party in 1976, he was narrowly defeated by Democrat Jimmy Carter.

Ford, Henry (1863–1947), industrialist. Born on July 30, 1863, near Dearborn, Michigan. Ford attended school until he was fifteen and thereafter worked at a variety of jobs. A natural mechanic, he had been fascinated by machinery from boyhood and while employed as a machinist for the Edison Illuminating Company in Detroit—he rose to chief engineer before leaving the firm in 1899—began experimenting with a self-propelled vehicle. As early as 1892 he had a working "gasoline buggy" and over the next several years continued to improve it, appearing on the streets of Detroit in 1896 in his tiny, tiller-steered Quadricycle. He was briefly associated with the Detroit Automobile Company in 1899, but it was four years later, on the heels of the success of his 999 racing car, that he entered the automobile business seriously. The Ford Motor Company, capitalized in 1903 at a modest $100,000, prospered quickly on the strength of Ford's strategy, learned from the success of Ransom E. Olds, of building more efficiently and selling more cheaply, and on the huge amount of favorable publicity gained from a suit brought against his New York agency by a member of the Association of Licensed Automobile Manufacturers, which represented the patent claims of George B. Selden. The suit dragged on for years and was nearly moot when finally settled in 1911, by which time the Ford firm's annual sales had passed the $10 million mark. Leaving management and sales to James Couzens, Ford concentrated his talents on the manufacturing process, introducing standardiza-

tion and mass-production techniques wherever possible. In 1908 he unveiled his masterpiece, the Model T, the simplicity and economy of which enabled it to capture and hold a huge new market undreamed of by an industry then still strongly oriented to the sporting and luxury appeal of the automobile. By 1913 Ford's constant search for more efficiency had resulted in a revolutionary innovation in manufacturing, the conveyor-belt assembly line; by that means the company was able to surpass all competitors in productivity, and when the Model T series was ended in 1927 more than 15 million of the "Tin Lizzies," or "flivver," had been made, virtually revolutionizing American life in the process. Ford was also an innovator in labor policy, announcing in 1914 a $5 per day minimum wage for employees, considerably above the prevailing industry standard, and a profit-sharing program. At the same time, however, he retained a strongly paternalistic control over workers and working conditions and his was the last major auto firm to accept unionization by the United Automobile Workers (UAW), holding out, through bitter and often violent conflicts, until 1941. The same strain of conservative resistance to change, often following an original innovation, eventually lost Ford his position of leadership in the industry. When he finally gave up the Model T in 1927 to introduce the completely new Model A he was already years behind in adopting hydraulic brakes, six- and eight-cylinder engines, choice of body color (he had stuck stubbornly to standard black), and the now-conventional modern transmission instead of the planetary-gear type. Although the Model A was also a success and Ford at last brought out a V-8 engine in 1932, the company had lost first place to General Motors. Ford's dilatoriness was possible in large part because he had early begun buying out his original partners and other stockholders so that by 1919, when he took over Couzens's shares, he was sole owner. His drive to control every aspect of the company's operations resulted in a remarkable vertical organization, with Ford owning facilities handling every step from the raw-material level through transportation to final processing: the company's holdings included iron and coal mines, a steel plant, rubber plantation, glassmaking plants, a railroad, and a cargo fleet. A man of many and oddly assorted interests, Ford was often in the limelight. In 1915 he chartered the Ford Peace Ship and sailed with a group of pacifists and other reformers to the Scandinavian nations in a futile attempt to bring about an end to World War I. He ran unsuccessfully for the Senate as a Democrat in 1918. He collected Americana, experimented with faddist diets, for a time published a newspaper that printed anti-Semitic articles, and late in life conceived an admiration for Adolf Hitler. In 1919 he turned over the presidency of the Ford Motor Company to his son, Edsel Bryant Ford (1893–1943), whose authority was, however, largely nominal. Edsel Ford devoted himself mainly to such subsidiary enterprises as the acquisition in

1922 of the Lincoln Motor Company, for which he developed the Mercury in 1939 and the Continental in 1941, and the establishment of an aviation division, which produced the highly successful Ford Trimotor (the "Tin Goose") and, during World War II, the B-24 bomber. In 1936 Henry and Edsel Ford together established the Ford Foundation; later, with the acquisition of various family holdings amounting to nearly three-quarters of all Ford stock, the foundation became one of the major philanthropic institutions in the world. On the death of Edsel in 1943 Henry Ford resumed the presidency and held it until 1945, when he turned it over to Edsel's son, Henry Ford II (1917–   ). Among his many other activities the elder Ford had published a number of books, including *My Life and Work*, 1922, and *Today and Tomorrow*, 1926, both with Samuel Crowther. He died in Dearborn, Michigan, on April 7, 1947.

Ford, John (1895–1973), motion-picture director. Born on February 1, 1895, in Cape Elizabeth, Maine, Sean Aloysius O'Feeney was the son of Irish immigrant parents. On graduating from high school in 1913 he followed an older brother to Hollywood, took the name John Ford, and for a time was a stagehand and bit player at Universal Studios. He was soon involved in directing short films and serials, including a few starring Tom Mix, and in 1919 moved to Fox Studios (later Twentieth Century–Fox) as a feature director. His first major film, *Silver Wings*, appeared in 1922 and was followed by *Cameo Kirby*, 1923, and three silent classics, *Iron Horse*, 1924; *Three Bad Men*, 1926; and *Four Sons*, 1928. His reputation grew with *Men Without Women*, 1930; *Up the River*, 1930; *Arrowsmith*, 1931; *Flesh*, 1932; and *The Lost Patrol*, 1934. In 1935 *The Informer* won him his first Academy Award. *Mary of Scotland*, 1936; *The Plough and the Stars*, 1936; *Wee Willie Winkie*, 1937; and *Submarine Patrol*, 1938, followed; *Stagecoach*, 1939, marked the beginning of a long and fruitful association with John Wayne in the making of classic Westerns. The same year saw the release of *Young Mr. Lincoln* and *Drums Along the Mohawk* and in 1940, for *The Grapes of Wrath*, with Henry Fonda, he won a second Academy Award. His third "Oscar" came the next year for *How Green Was My Valley*. During World War II Ford, with the rank of lieutenant commander in the naval reserve, was chief of the Field Photographic Branch of the Office of Strategic Services (OSS). Two documentaries made during this period, *The Battle of Midway*, 1942, and *December 7th*, 1943, won Academy Awards. He returned to Hollywood in 1945 and turned out in quick succession *They Were Expendable*, 1945; *My Darling Clementine*, 1946; and *The Fugitive*, 1947. Thereafter he produced his own films; John Wayne starred in his *Fort Apache*, 1948; *Three Godfathers*, 1948; *She Wore a Yellow Ribbon*, 1949; *Rio Grande*, 1950; and *The Quiet Man*, 1952, which won Ford another Oscar for direction. It was in his Westerns that Ford's characteristic style—his use of simple

but gripping situations, strong characterization, especially in the supporting cast, and striking scenic settings—was most visible. In his direction he employed bold strokes that succeeded in attracting both popular and critical approval. Other later films of note included *What Price Glory?*, 1952; *Mogambo*, 1953; *The Long Gray Line*, 1955; *Mister Roberts*, 1955; *The Searchers*, 1956; *The Wings of Eagles*, 1957; *The Last Hurrah*, 1958; *The Horse Soldiers*, 1959; *Two Rode Together*, 1961; *The Man Who Shot Liberty Valance*, 1962; *Donovan's Reef*, 1963; *Cheyenne Autumn*, 1964; and *Seven Women*, 1966. He died in Palm Desert, California, on August 31, 1973.

Ford, Paul Leicester (1865–1902), historian. Born in Brooklyn, New York, on March 23, 1865, to a wealthy and prominent family, Ford was educated privately and, reared in a home noted for the great library of Americana collected by his father, early displayed a marked interest in books. At the age of eleven he prepared and printed on a small press a genealogy compiled by his great-grandfather, Noah Webster. Drawing upon his father's library, he issued during the next several years a number of bibliographical guides, listing the writings of Webster, 1882; Charles Chauncy, 1884; Alexander Hamilton, 1886; and Benjamin Franklin, 1889. He reprinted much valuable but long-lost historical material in his *Pamphlets on the Constitution of the United States*, 1888, and in 1890 and 1891 issued, with his brother Worthington Chauncey Ford, the 15-volume *Winnowings in American History*. From 1890 to 1893 he served as editor of the *Library Journal*. In 1892–1899 he edited and published his exhaustively researched *Writings of Thomas Jefferson* in ten volumes and in 1895 was chosen by the Pennsylvania Historical Society to edit the works of John Dickinson. In the following year he published *The True George Washington*, an extremely popular biography that went far to correct the prevalent narrow view of Washington for which earlier moralizing writers were responsible. Ford ventured into novel writing with *The Honorable Peter Stirling*, 1894, and although his several works of fiction were more notable for historical richness than literary elegance, he achieved some success with *Janice Meredith*, 1899, which was later dramatized. His scholarly work included a history of the *New England Primer* in 1897 and a biography of Benjamin Franklin in 1899. He was shot and killed in New York City on May 8, 1902, by his despondent brother Malcolm.

Ford, Webster, *see* Masters, Edgar Lee

Forrest, Edwin (1806–1872), actor. Born on March 9, 1806, in Philadelphia, Forrest left school when he was thirteen to help support his family. He began his career as an actor in 1820 as Young Norval in John Home's *Douglas* at Philadelphia's Walnut Street Theatre. He then joined in turn a frontier troupe, an itinerant company in the Midwest, a circus, and a New Orleans theater company. In 1825 he had the good fortune to be engaged to play Iago to the Othello of Edmund Kean, who aided his development as a Shakespearian actor. He triumphed at the fashionable Park Theatre in New York City in 1826 as Othello and was permanently engaged by the less fashionable Bowery Theatre, where audiences responded wildly to the passion of his acting. He returned to the Park in 1829 and offered a series of prizes for plays by native Americans; his power and fortune grew rapidly and by 1834 he had captivated all New York. He was hailed in London in the 1830s but, returning in 1845, at a time when many English actors, including the formidable William C. Macready, were unemployed, he was jeered by some of the audience as he played Macbeth. He believed that Macready had brought about the incident, and retaliated by hissing Macready in an Edinburgh theater where he was starring in *Hamlet*. The feud thus begun reached its peak in 1849: Macready was acting at New York City's Astor Place Opera House, and crowds of Forrest's nativist and unruly fans attacked the theater. Troops were called to quell the mob; the riot resulted in 22 deaths, numerous injuries, and the complete wrecking of the theater. Although Forrest was elsewhere at the time, it was said that he had encouraged the affair, which became known as the Astor Place Riot. Stormy and embittered, he aggravated the feeling against him in 1851 when he brought suit against his wife for divorce and displayed a brutal temper and coarse language during the sensational trial. But his notoriety filled theaters and people came to hear him give speeches vindicating himself between the acts. Although he continued to pack houses through the 1860s, he was by then considered as much a curiosity as a great actor. An injury to his back in 1865 put an end to his career in 1872. He retired to a large house in Philadelphia, which, after his death on December 12, 1872, became a home for aged actors.

Forrest, Nathan Bedford (1821–1877), soldier. Born near Chapel Hill, Tennessee, on July 13, 1821, Forrest received no formal schooling but educated himself to a fair degree. Responsible for the support of his family from the age of sixteen, he worked his way up from farmhand to livestock dealer to trader in slaves in Memphis; he eventually accumulated the money to purchase land in northwestern Mississippi, where cotton planting earned him a moderate fortune. At the outbreak of the Civil War he enlisted in the Confederate army as a private, but four months later, having raised a cavalry troop on his own, was commissioned a lieutenant colonel. Early in 1862 he was in northwestern Tennessee and took part in the defense of Fort Donelson; he refused to surrender with the rest of the garrison and instead escaped with the entire 1500-man mounted force. He was promptly promoted to colonel and, after distinguished service at Shiloh (Pittsburg Landing), where he was badly wounded, to brigadier general. During 1862–1863

he was attached to Gen. Braxton Bragg's command and executed a series of daring raids, harassing Union communications throughout Tennessee and Kentucky; in April 1863 he engaged in a five-day running battle that resulted in the capture of an entire Union cavalry brigade near Rome, Georgia. He played a prominent part at Chickamauga in September and after a violent quarrel with Bragg was transferred to a new command in Mississippi and given the rank of major general. In early 1864 he led raids into Tennessee and in April recaptured Fort Pillow on the Mississippi River; an alleged massacre of the largely Negro garrison there created a major controversy, but the evidence concerning how the men met their deaths remains unclear. Throughout 1864 Forrest displayed his strategic genius in raids in Mississippi, Tenneesee, Alabama, and Georgia, gaining a remarkable victory over a much superior force at Brices Cross Roads, Mississippi, in June and thoroughly exasperating Union leaders. In November he took command of the cavalry of Gen. John B. Hood's Army of the Tennessee and performed gallantly in the disastrous Nashville campaign, achieving particular distinction in valiant rearguard actions. Forrest was promoted to lieutenant general in February 1865. In April he was driven out of Selma, Alabama, by an overwhelming force under Gen. James H. Wilson and on May 9, following news of Gen. Robert E. Lee's surrender at Appomattox, he too surrendered. After the war he lived in Memphis and for several years was president of the Selma, Marion & Memphis Railroad. He was a leading organizer and the first and only Grand Wizard of the short-lived original Ku Klux Klan, which disbanded in 1869. Forrest died in Memphis on October 29, 1877.

Forrestal, James Vincent (1892–1949), public official. Born on February 15, 1892, in Beacon, New York, Forrestal worked for a series of small newspapers in New York state before entering Dartmouth College in 1911. A year later he transferred to Princeton, from which he graduated in 1915. In 1916 he joined a Wall Street firm, later Dillon, Read and Company, as a bond salesman. He returned as head of the bond sales department after serving in World War I as a naval aviator, advancing to a partnership in the firm in 1923 and to its presidency in 1937. In 1940 President Franklin D. Roosevelt, who had been impressed by Forrestal's positive testimony before congressional committees on various New Deal proposals for regulating the securities market, appointed him a presidential administrative assistant. After only a few weeks in that post he was named in August 1940 to the newly created office of undersecretary of the navy. Charged with responsibility for procurement and production, Forrestal played a vital role in building up U.S. naval strength before World War II and in its early phases. He was on several occasions acting secretary of the navy and in May 1944, on the death of Frank Knox, became secretary. Although he had originally opposed the unification of the armed services he threw himself wholeheartedly into the immense task created by the signing of the National Security Act of 1947 by President Harry S. Truman, and in September 1947 he was appointed the first secretary of defense to head the new National Military Establishment, now the Department of Defense. He worked diligently to promote the merger of the Department of the Army, the Department of the Navy, and the new Department of the Air Force and to maintain a high level of preparedness in all three, but came under considerable criticism for his apparent inability to control what many believed to be insubordination on the part of the air force with respect to appropriations and combat strength. He resigned from the cabinet in March 1949 and a few days later entered the naval hospital in Bethesda, Maryland. Diagnosed as suffering from nervous exhaustion and depression, he was thought to be recovering when he jumped from a window to his death on May 22, 1949.

Forrester, Fanny, *see under* Judson, Adoniram

Fortas, Abe (1910–1982), justice of the Supreme Court. Born on June 19, 1919, in Memphis, Tennessee, Fortas graduated from Southwestern College in Memphis in 1930 and then studied at the Yale Law School, where he was editor of the *Yale Law Journal* and from which he graduated at the head of his class in 1933. He remained at Yale as assistant professor of law for four years, during which time he also served as a consultant to the Agricultural Adjustment Administration (AAA) and later to the Securities and Exchange Commission (SEC). In 1937 he began full-time work for the SEC and became assistant director of its public-utilities section the next year. From 1939 to 1941 he was general counsel for the Public Works Administration (PWA); in 1941 he entered the interior department, rising to the post of undersecretary in 1942. Soon after serving as adviser to the U.S. delegation to the United Nations organizational meeting in San Francisco in 1945 and to the first UN General Assembly session in London in 1946 he resigned from Interior and entered private law practice in Washington, D.C., in partnership with Thurman Arnold. The firm, Arnold, Fortas and Porter, was soon one of the most prominent in the city. Fortas became noted not only as a corporation counsel but also as a civil libertarian, defending numbers of government employees and others injured by the Communist-hunting activities of Sen. Joseph R. McCarthy and in 1963 arguing before the Supreme Court the case of *Gideon* v. *Wainwright*, which established the right of indigent defendants to free legal aid in criminal cases. Fortas had long been a close associate and adviser to President Lyndon B. Johnson when Johnson named him to the Supreme Court in 1965, and his acknowledged legal brilliance won nearly universal approbation for the appointment. In 1968, however, when Johnson nominated Fortas to succeed retiring Chief Justice Earl Warren, a massive surge of conservative opposition in the Senate, based on Fortas's advisory service to Johnson, forced the withdrawal of the nomination. The following year revelations of financial arrangements, apparently not illegal but certainly ill advised, between Fortas and a family foundation established by a financier who was subsequently convicted of stock manipulation aroused public and congressional controversy. Fortas resigned from the court, the first justice in history to be forced to do so, and retired to private practice. He died on April 5, 1982, in Washington, D.C.

Forten, James (1766–1842), businessman and social reformer. Born in Philadelphia on September 2, 1766, of free Negro parents, Forten was largely self-educated, although he attended for a short time a school run by the Quaker abolitionist Anthony Benezet. At fourteen he enlisted in the Revolutionary navy as a powder boy and when his ship was captured escaped being sold into slavery through intercession of the son of the British commander. He spent a year in England and became involved with abolitionists there. Upon returning to Philadelphia in 1786 he was apprenticed to a sailmaker, became a foreman at twenty, and 12 years later purchased the business. His zeal for abolitionism grew, especially after 1800, when a petition that he had signed to modify the Fugitive Slave Law of 1793 was flatly rejected by Congress. In 1813, when laws were proposed to compel free Negro residents of Philadelphia to register and to ban any more blacks from entering, he led the opposition in five letters published in pamphlet form, *A Series of Letters by a Man of Color.* In these he anticipated the fundamental tenet of such abolitionists as William Lloyd Garrison and Theodore D. Weld —that Negroes are biologically equal to white men. In 1814 he recruited a force of 2500 Negroes to protect Philadelphia from the threat of a British attack. Approached in 1816 by the American Colonization Society to support the sending of American Negroes to settle in Liberia, he rejected their plans and their implicit offer to make him ruler of the colony, and began a campaign to convince Negroes and white and black abolitionists that the Colonization Society was attempting to avoid the issue of political emancipation and equality. By 1832 he had accumulated a fortune from his sailmaking business, which employed 40 men, both black and white. Second only to the Tappan brothers in making financial contributions to the abolitionist cause, he actively supported William Lloyd Garrison and his antislavery journal, the *Liberator.* The American Anti-Slavery Society frequently met in his home. He died in Philadelphia on March 4, 1842; his eight children continued the fight for reform.

Fosdick, Harry Emerson (1878–1969), religious leader. Born on May 24, 1878, in Buffalo, New York, Fosdick graduated from Colgate University in 1900 and entered Union Theological Seminary, from which he took a degree in 1904; he had been ordained in 1903. While minister of the First Baptist Church of Montclair, New Jersey, he continued his own education, taking an M.A. from Columbia University in 1908, and in that year began teaching at Union. Also in 1908 he published his first book, *The Second Mile*. By 1915, when he became professor of practical theology at Union, he had published *The Manhood of the Master*, 1913; *The Assurance of Immortality*; 1915, and *The Meaning of Prayer*, 1915. In 1919 he accepted appointment as assistant pastor of the First Presbyterian Church of New York City in an experiment in interdenominational ministry. The choice of Fosdick was based on his liberalism and outspoken opposition to credal restrictions, and it was precisely those characteristics of his teaching from the pulpit that aroused controversy in Presbyterian ranks. With his sermon "Shall the Fundamentalists Win?" in 1922 the controversy became a battle; the Presbyterian general assembly split sharply in narrowly resolving to require him to accept traditional doctrine or to resign. He resigned early in 1925. Later in the year, after obtaining explicit agreement on his conditions— that the church would offer interdenominational ministry and open membership—he became pastor of the Park Avenue Baptist Church, which in 1931 became Riverside Church and moved to a great new edifice built largely with funds contributed by John D. Rockefeller. Fosdick retained the Riverside pastorate and his professorship at Union until retiring in 1946. From the time of the battle of 1922 he was the acknowledged leading spokesman for modern liberal Christianity in the country; in books, lectures, and on nationwide radio as well as in his sermons he maintained his view that Christianity consisted of faith in a few fundamental truths that were, however, subject to historical evolution in the terms in which they were expressed; it was the fossilization of mere form that he rejected as impeding the growth of Christianity in the scientific age. Others of his many books were *Christianity and Progress*, 1922; *The Modern Use of the Bible*, 1924; *As I See Religion*, 1932; *The Secret of Victorious Living*, 1934; *A Guide to Understanding the Bible*, 1938; *Living Under Tension*, 1941; *On Being a Real Person*, 1943; *A Great Time to be Alive*, 1944; *The Man From Nazareth*, 1949; *A Faith for Tough Times*, 1952; *Riverside Sermons*, 1957; *Dear Mr. Brown: Letters to a Person Perplexed About Religion*, 1961; and *The Meaning of Being a Christian*, 1964. His autobiography, *The Living of These Days*, appeared in 1956. Fosdick died in Bronxville, New York, on October 5, 1969.

Foster, Stephen Collins (1826–1864), composer. Born on July 4, 1826, in Lawrenceville (later a part of Pittsburgh), Pennsylvania, Foster had from childhood an inclination toward music and began writing songs at an early age. His formal education included little musical instruction and ended with a month at college in 1841. In 1846, by which time he had published a few pieces, he was sent to work as a bookkeeper for his brother in Cincinnati, where he remained for four years. During that time he wrote a number of songs that gained considerable popularity; "O Susannah," virtually the anthem of the California Gold Rush of 1849, "Away Down South," "Uncle Ned," and others were published in *Songs of the Sable Harmonists* in 1848. The following year he published *Foster's Ethiopian Melodies*, including "Nelly Was a Lady," which was popularized by the Christy Minstrels. Returning to his Pennsylvania home in 1849, he continued to write songs in his adopted minstrel mode; he concluded a mutually beneficial agreement with Edwin P. Christy for performance rights, and from then until about 1862 wrote his best songs: "Old Folks at Home" ("Swanee River"), "My Old Kentucky Home," "Massa's in de Cold, Cold Ground," "Camptown Races," "Nelly Bly," "Jeanie With the Light Brown Hair," "Old Black Joe," and "Beautiful Dreamer." In 1860 Foster moved to New York City. Oddly, although his songs drew their inspiration from Southern life and did much to create the popular romantic image of that life, he himself had no firsthand knowledge of the South beyond that gathered on a single brief visit to New Orleans in 1852. His last years were a time of decline and dissolution; with few exceptions his new songs were repetitious, and he went deeper and deeper into debt. He died on January 13, 1864, in New York City. He was elected to the Hall of Fame in 1940.

Foster, William Zebulon (1881–1961), labor organizer and political leader. Born on February 25, 1881, in Taunton, Massachusetts, Foster grew up there and in Philadelphia. He went to work at an early age and soon became a migrant laborer; for many years he worked in industrial jobs, as a merchant seaman, in lumber camps, on railroads, and as a sheepherder. He became interested in labor and political reform and in 1909, after several years' membership in the Socialist party, joined the syndicalist Industrial Workers of the World (IWW) and became a "Wobbly" organizer and pamphleteer throughout the country. After an extended period of study in Europe in 1910–1912 he returned to found the Syndicalist League of North America, a trade-unionist organization that lasted two years. During several more years of labor organizing he achieved prominence for his work with Chicago packinghouse workers in 1917–1918 and particularly for his part in the great steel strike of 1919, in which he was a leader of the American Federation of Labor (AFL). The following year he formed the Trade Union Education League, which in 1921 was designated the U.S. branch of the Red International of Labor Unions, or Profintern. Thereafter, through various reorganizations, Foster was a leading figure in American Communism. He served as secretary-general of the American Communist party until 1930, when ill health forced him to resign in favor of Earl Browder, a longtime associate. He was the

Communist party candidate for president in 1924, 1928, and 1932 and was a regular delegate to international Communist conferences. During the later 1930s and the 1940s Foster became increasingly critical of Browder's leadership and his policy of cooperation with liberal reformists; he kept up an outspokenly extreme position and in 1945, after Browder had come under attack by international leaders, was elected chairman of the U.S. Communist party. In that position he hewed closely to the political line established by the party in the U.S.S.R. Foster was among those indicted in 1948 under the Alien Registration Act of 1940 (Smith Act), but he was excused from trial on charges of advocating the overthrow of the government because of poor health. He remained chairman of the party until 1956, when the sudden repudiation of Stalinism in the Soviet Union and the brutal suppression of the Hungarian revolt precipitated a rift in American Communist ranks; he was delicately removed from power by election as chairman emeritus, a post to which he was reelected in 1959. A prolific pamphleteer and essayist throughout his career, Foster also wrote a number of books, including *The Great Steel Strike and Its Lessons*, 1920; *The Russian Revolution*, 1921; *Misleaders of Labor*, 1927; *Towards Soviet America*, 1932; and two autobiographical volumes, *From Bryan to Stalin*, 1937, and *Pages From a Worker's Life*, 1939. He died on September 1, 1961, soon after arriving in Moscow to seek medical treatment.

Fox, Gustavus Vasa (1821–1883), naval officer and public official. Born in Saugus, Massachusetts, on June 13, 1821, Fox was commissioned a midshipman in the navy about 1841 and for the next 15 years was on active naval service, winning promotion to lieutenant in 1852. After his resignation from the navy in 1856 he became an agent for a textile company in Lawrence, Masschusetts. Early in 1861 he was recommended to Gen. Winfield Scott as a naval consultant on the problem of Fort Sumter at Charleston Harbor, whose surrender had been demanded by South Carolina. His plan for relieving the garrison was tabled by President James Buchanan, but soon after his inauguration President Abraham Lincoln requested Fox to submit a plan for reinforcing Sumter. In April Fox set out for the fort to study conditions and arrived on the 12th, just in time to witness the bombardment by South Carolina forces. Unequipped to aid in the fort's defense, he sailed into the harbor and evacuated Maj. Robert Anderson and his men, who had been allowed to depart by Gen. P. G. T. Beauregard. A few weeks later he was appointed chief clerk of the navy department and in August the post of assistant secretary was created for him. Through the rest of the Civil War he proved an invaluable aid to Secretary Gideon Welles, promoting the construction and deployment of vessels of the *Monitor* class ("monitors") and otherwise employing his extensive knowledge of naval affairs in highly productive ways. It was Fox, for example, who

suggested Capt. David G. Farragut as commander of the naval expedition against New Orleans in 1862. On his resignation in 1866 he undertook, with an impressive naval escort that included the first monitor to cross the Atlantic, a diplomatic mission to Russia. He devoted himself to private business interests thereafter and died in New York City on October 29, 1883.

Fox, Katherine, *see under* Fox, Margaret

Fox, Margaret (1833–1893), spiritualist. Born near Bath, New Brunswick, on October 7, 1833, Margaret Fox moved with her family to a farm near Hydesville, in Wayne County, New York, in 1847. The next year there began to spread through the neighborhood stories about strange sounds—rappings or knockings—in the Fox house. The noises were ascribed to spirits by many, including Margaret and her younger sister Katherine, also born in New Brunswick, in 1839. Margaret and Kate encouraged the belief that spirits were responsible for the noises and an elder sister, Leah Fish of Rochester, quickly began managing regular public demonstrations of her sisters' mediumistic gifts. She took them home with her and soon the "Rochester rappings," in a code whereby "actual communication" could be made with the spirits, were famous throughout the region. In 1850 the three traveled to New York City to begin holding regular, and quite lucrative, seances. Horace Greeley was persuaded of the authenticity of the sessions and in the *New York Tribune* enthusiastically endorsed the Fox sisters' activities. With their subsequent tours of the country, spiritualism became a fad and the subject of major controversy as well; dozens of imitators, including Victoria Claflin Woodhull, began performing as mediums and a great deal of cultist and pseudoreligious crusading sprang up. No body of more or less organized spiritualist thought or technique had previously existed, and modern spiritualism and mediumism dates from the time of the Fox sisters. Margaret attracted the attention of Elisha Kent Kane, who tried to persuade her to give up spiritualism and to seek an education; after his death in 1857 she claimed to have entered into a common-law marriage with him and in 1866 published his letters to her, possibly somewhat altered, as *The Love Life of Dr. Kane*. In the 1870s both sisters traveled to England, where spiritualism attracted a considerable following. Kate married one H. D. Jencken in 1872 and thereafter used the name Fox-Jencken. In 1888 Margaret, who had converted to the Catholic church, appeared at the New York Academy of Music and confessed that the entire matter of spirit rapping had been a hoax. She and Kate had begun it, she said, as a prank on their superstitious mother and had contrived the sounds by various means but principally by movements of their toes. The ranks of confirmed spiritualists, by then legion, condemned her confession as a shabby lie, told probably for money and possibly under the influence of alcohol. Soon thereafter she retracted the confession and returned to spiritualism for her livelihood. She died in Brooklyn, New York, on March 8, 1893; Kate had died a year earlier.

Fox-Jencken, Katherine, *see under* Fox, Margaret

Fox, Richard Kyle (1846–1922), publisher. Born in Belfast, Ireland, on August 12, 1846, Fox early went to work in a newspaper office and was thoroughly trained in journalism by the time he emigrated to the United States in 1874. After a brief period as an advertising salesman for the *Wall Street Journal* he secured the position of business manager for the *National Police Gazette.* Founded in 1845, the *Gazette* was in serious financial straits; Fox was nonetheless able to keep it going and by 1877 had bought out the original proprietors and become sole owner. Under his direction the *Gazette* became far and away the most sensational periodical of the day. Ostensibly devoted simply to reporting crime and police work, it managed to find enough scandalous material, heavily illustrated, to become known as the "barber-shop bible." Fox adopted tinted paper and behind the lurid cover printed on pink stock he filled the pages with breezy accounts of hangings (a column called "Noose Notes"), racy tales of sex and crime, and, in a small way at first but with increasing emphasis, sports news and theatrical reportage. Over a period of years the *Gazette* evolved into essentially a sporting journal, although some of the old spice was retained, especially in the covers and the advertising. As a sports journalist Fox introduced a terse, pithy style and a format that was widely influential; he originated the practice of holding contests, complete with prizes, as a device to build circulation. Competitions in various sports were also sponsored, and he was particularly active in the search for a contender for the heavyweight boxing title held by John L. Sullivan, to whom he presented a lavishly bejeweled belt. At his death in Red Bank, New Jersey, on November 14, 1922, Fox left an estate of some $3 million, including the *Gazette* which passed to his sons and continued in publication until 1932. After a bankruptcy it was reorganized and resumed publication with a virtually unchanged format.

Foxx, James Emory (1907–1967), "Jimmy," baseball player. Born on October 22, 1907, in Sudlersville, Maryland, Foxx grew up on a farm and early began developing the physique that would later earn him the nickname "the Beast." He was signed by Connie Mack's Philadelphia Athletics in 1925 and in that and the next two seasons played mainly with farm clubs, coming up to the home team for a few games each year. Originally a catcher, he soon switched to the infield and played first or third base for most of his career. He joined the Athletics permanently in 1928 and became a mainstay during the team's greatest era. In 1929 he began a string of 13 seasons in which he batted in 100 or more runs; he starred in the World Series in 1929, 1930, and 1931, and in

1932, with 58 home runs, came closer than anyone else ever had (or would again for nearly 30 years) to breaking Babe Ruth's record. He was voted the most valuable player in the American League that year and again in 1933, when he again led the league in home runs with 48 and also won the batting title with a .356 average and the title for runs batted in (163), for the coveted triple crown of baseball. In 1935 he was traded to the Boston Red Sox and that year again led the league with 36 home runs; his 50 homers in 1938 placed him second in that category, but his .349 average, 398 total bases, and 175 runs batted in again earned him an award as the league's most valuable player. He led the league in homers for a fourth time in 1939 with 35. He remained with the Red Sox until 1942, when he moved to the Chicago Cubs of the National League; a final season with the Philadelphia Phillies in 1945 closed out his career. In 20 years in the major leagues he had compiled a .325 batting average; his total of 534 home runs was second to Babe Ruth's record and, although he was later surpassed by a few players (first by Willy Mays in 1966), he remained high in the listings for homers, as he did for runs batted in (1922), total bases (4956), and strikeouts (1311). Double X, as he was called, was elected to the National Baseball Hall of Fame in 1951. He died in Miami, Florida, on July 21, 1967.

Foy, Eddie (1856–1928), entertainer. Born in New York City on March 9, 1856, Edward, or Edwin, Fitzgerald early began singing and dancing on street corners to help support his family, with whom he moved to Chicago in 1865. He continued as a sidewalk entertainer until 1872, when, taking the name Foy, he played a brief engagement in a local concert hall. For several years from about 1878 he toured the mining and cattle towns of the West, finally achieving considerable celebrity in a stock company in San Francisco. His unique comic style and his growing reputation won him major parts in a series of lavish revues in Chicago, beginning with *The Crystal Slipper* in 1888. He was appearing in *Mr. Bluebeard* in 1903 at the Iroquois Theatre there when a fire broke out; despite his heroic efforts to calm the panic-stricken crowd, 602 persons died in the rush to escape from the building. In 1904 he made his New York debut in *Piff! Paff! Pouf!* and he remained a top Broadway musical comedy star for nine years, appearing in such shows as *The Earl and the Girl*, 1905; *Up and Down Broadway*, 1910; and *Over the River*, 1911–1913. In 1913 he went into vaudeville with his children, the Seven Little Foys, in a family act that was a top-billed favorite until his retirement in 1923. Four years later he returned to the vaudeville stage for a farewell tour, in the midst of which he died in Kansas City, Missouri, on February 16, 1928. His autobiography *Clowning Through Life*, with A. F. Harlow, appeared in the same year.

Foyt, Anthony Joseph, Jr. (1935–   ), automobile

racer. Born on January 16, 1935, in Houston, Texas, A. J. Foyt was the son of a midget-car racer and at the age of eleven began driving himself. He left high school in his third year to become a professional racer, moving up from midgets to stock cars and in 1957 to the big open-cockpit cars in national competition. He qualified for (and placed 16th in) the Indianapolis 500 ("Indy") classic in his second year out and two years later, in 1960, amassed enough points to capture his first United States Auto Club (USAC) national championship. In 1961 he won the Indy, retained his USAC title, and set a new record with over $170,000 in winnings. One of the most versatile drivers in professional ranks, Foyt added sports cars to his repertoire in 1963. He was again USAC champion and the winner at Indianapolis in 1964. Mechanical difficulties and injuries plagued him in 1965 and especially in 1966 and kept him out of several events, but in 1967 he resumed his normal grueling schedule and again won the Indy, becoming the fourth man to score three victories in that race; he also teamed with Dan Guerney to capture the first U.S. win in the Twenty-four Hours of Le Mans sports-car classic in France, setting a record pace of 135.48 miles per hour for a total distance of 3251.57 miles, and capped the season with an unprecedented fifth USAC championship. Foyt had continued through the years to race stock cars as well and was consistently among the top drivers on that racing circuit; in 1972 he won the Daytona 500, the richest stock-car race in the country, and earned the only crown he had lacked for a complete sweep in major competition.

F.P.A., *see* Adams, Franklin Pierce

Frank, Glenn (1887–1940), author, editor, and educator. Born in Queen City, Missouri, on October 1, 1887, Frank early intended to make a career in the ministry and in his youth rode a Methodist circuit as a lay preacher. After sporadic attendance at the Missouri State Normal School at Kirksville he entered Northwestern University, supporting himself by touring as a Chautauqua lecturer in the summers. On graduating in 1912 he was appointed executive assistant to the president of the university. Four years later he moved to Boston to work as a research assistant to Edward A. Filene, with whose social and business ideals he was deeply in sympathy. During that period he collaborated with Lothrop Stoddard on *Stakes of the War*, 1918. In 1919 Frank was named associate editor of the *Century* magazine and two years later became editor. In that position and as a regular contributor, as a newspaper columnist and as a lecturer, and in *The Politics of Industry*, 1919, and *An American Looks at His World*, 1923, he gained a wide following as a promoter of liberal reform. His renown was such that in 1925 he was chosen president of the University of Wisconsin. There he made numerous contributions to educational progress, most notably in calling Alexander Meiklejohn to found

and direct the Experimental College from 1927 to 1932. He continued to write as well, publishing *Thunder and Dawn*, 1932, and *America's Hour of Decision*, 1934. During the 1930s he found much to criticize in the New Deal and his reputation as a liberal began to fade. Eventually, having declared himself openly for the Republican party, he alienated the dominant La Follette–Progressive powers in Wisconsin and was dismissed from his university post early in 1937. He then became editor of *Rural Progress*, a farm journal published in Chicago, but continued to live in Wisconsin, becoming active and influential in state and national Republican affairs. In 1940 he was chairman of the platform committee of the Republican national convention and also entered the Wisconsin senatorial race. During the primary campaign he was killed in an automobile accident near Greenleaf, Wisconsin, on September 15, 1940.

Frankfurter, Felix (1882–1965), justice of the Supreme Court. Born in Vienna on November 15, 1882, Frankfurter emigrated with his family to the United States in 1894. He graduated from the College of the City of New York (CCNY) in 1902 and four years later took a law degree with highest honors at Harvard Law School. After a time in private practice he became assistant to Henry Stimson, then U.S. attorney for the southern district of New York. He continued this association when, in 1911, Stimson became secretary of war and placed Frankfurter in a post in the Bureau of Insular Affairs. In 1914 he joined the law faculty at Harvard, where he was professor of administrative law until 1939. During World War I he was legal adviser to the secretary of war, secretary and counsel to the President's Meditation Commission, and, in 1918, chairman of the War Labor Policies Board. After serving as an adviser at the Versailles Peace Conference he returned to Harvard. He participated in the founding in 1920 of the American Civil Liberties Union; in 1927 he became nationally prominent as a liberal with his critique of the Sacco-Vanzetti trial published first in the *Atlantic Monthly* and in book form later that year. Among his other writings of this period were *The Commerce Clause Under Marshall, Taney, and Waite*, 1937; and *Mr. Justice Holmes and the Supreme Court*, 1938. He had been a close adviser to Governor Franklin D. Roosevelt of New York; when Roosevelt was elected president of 1932, Frankfurter declined the office of solicitor general, but in 1939 accepted an appointment to the Supreme Court. During his tenure on the court he became, despite his earlier reputation as a liberal, a strong opponent of the latitudinarian interpretations of First Amendment rights favored by some of his colleagues. He held that individual freedom in a highly complex society required constant redefinition and limitation in the light of experience; he further believed that in cases other than those involving clear-cut violations of established law and precedent, the judicial power must defer to popular prerogative and legislative initiative, and he was notably reluctant to employ the judicial veto to invalidate legislative acts. Notable among his opinions were those in *Minersville School District* v. *Gobitis*, 1940, sustaining a flag-salute law; *Dennis* v. *U.S.* (concurring), 1951, sustaining the conviction of Communist party leaders for conspiracy to teach and to advocate the overthrow of the government; and *Baker* v. *Carr* (dissenting), 1962, in which he decried the Court's becoming involved in what he saw as a political rather than a legal question, to the detriment, he feared, of the Court's moral authority. Forced by ill health to retire from the bench in 1962, Justice Frankfurter was awarded the Presidential Medal of Freedom in 1963; he died on February 22, 1965, in Washington, D.C.

Franklin, Benjamin (1706–1790), printer, author, inventor, scientist, diplomat and public official. Born in Boston on January 17, 1706, Franklin was the tenth and youngest son of a chandler who originally intended him, as a tithe of his sons, for the ministry. Formal education proved too costly, and to the boy less than congenial, and at ten he was taken into the candle and soap business after two years of schooling. Two years later he was apprenticed to his older half-brother James, a Boston printer who in 1721 founded the *New England Courant*. By that time Benjamin was skilled in the printing trade and had begun to read voraciously whatever books he could lay hands upon, paying particular attention to a volume of Addison and Steele's periodical the *Spectator*, the essays in which he greatly admired and strove to emulate. By 1722 he was writing little essays of his own on various topics; of these he quietly slipped a series of 14, signed "Silence Dogood," under the door of the printing shop and delightedly saw them published in the *Courant*. Later in that year James was imprisoned briefly for a barbed newspaper criticism of certain Massachusetts public officials and Benjamin became nominal publisher of the *Courant*, although James forced him to sign new indenture papers secretly. They began to quarrel and in 1723 Benjamin left Boston for New York City and then Philadelphia, where he arrived virtually penniless. He soon found employment in the printing shop of Samuel Keimer. The following year, encouraged by Governor Sir William Keith, who promised him letters of credit, he sailed to England to purchase equipment for a shop of his own. Finding no letters on his arrival—he learned only then that Keith was notoriously unreliable—he took a position in a London printing shop where, in reply to a theological work he set into type, he wrote *A Dissertation on Liberty and Necessity, Pleasure and Pain*, 1725, a deist and necessitarian tract he later regretted. In 1726 he returned to Philadelphia with a Quaker merchant who had befriended him and who gave him employment. Within a few months he was back in Keimer's shop; in 1728 he established his own printing business in partnership with Hugh Meredith and two years later bought out Meredith and became sole proprietor. In September 1730 he took as his common-law wife Deborah Read, daughter of the family with whom he had lodged on his first arrival in the city seven years earlier, and the household was soon enlarged by the addition of Franklin's illegitimate son William (later to be the last royal governor of New Jersey), whose mother has never been certainly identified. During the years following his first visit to England Franklin's boundless energy and enthusiasm for life, learning, and involvement in public affairs blossomed forth. His gregariousness and love of intellectual stimulation were happily served in the Junto, or Leather Apron Club, an informal philosophical and debating society he organized in 1727 and through which he worked to secure the establishment in 1731 of the Library Company of Philadelphia, the first American subscription library, and later of a volunteer fire department and of an organized, paid police force. In 1743 he led in founding the American Philosophical Society, in some respects an outgrowth of the Junto. Franklin's influence in Philadelphia grew to be such that he was usually the first to be approached in regard to a matter of civic improvement, and his involvement virtually guaranteed the success of such a project; it was to him, for example, that Thomas Bond came in 1751 with his idea for the Pennsylvania Hospital, the first in America. That same year saw the founding of the Academy of Philadelphia, largely prompted by Franklin's *Proposals Relating to the Education of Youth in Pennsylvania*, 1749; the academy later became the University of Pennsylvania. His business prospered through the years. Franklin and Meredith had purchased the *Pennsylvania Gazette* from Keimer in 1729 and, as a result of public opinion stimulated by editorials in the paper and by Franklin's *Modest Inquiry into the Nature and Necessity of a Paper Currency*, 1729, had been appointed public printers of Pennsylvania; Franklin later received similar appointments from New Jersey, Delaware, and Maryland. In 1732 he issued the first of a series of almanacs that continued until 1757. From the outset *Poor Richard's Almanack* was a great success and subsequent editions commonly ran to 10,000 copies. Standard almanac material was included, but what made the effort successful and spread Franklin's reputation beyond his own city was the liberal sprinkling of pithy and witty maxims, culled from the aphoristic literature of the world and translated by Franklin into the homespun American vernacular ("There are three faithful friends: an old wife, an old dog, and ready money"; "Experience keeps a dear school, yet fools will learn in no other"; "It is hard for an empty sack to stand upright"; "Never leave that till tomorrow which you can do to-day"; "God helps those who help themselves"). The sayings of the fictional "Richard Saunders" became proverbial wisdom widely repeated throughout the colonies and even in Europe. They epitomized, too, Franklin's character in their homely charm, hard-headed practicality, and emphasis on self-improvement. He himself had set about the personal project of attaining no less a goal than moral perfection by the characteristically direct method of devising a list of useful virtues, 13 in number, and keeping a daily notebook record of his progress in each. During the early 1740s he developed a strong interest in the natural sciences; his invention of the highly efficient Franklin stove in 1740 and its subsequent commercial success (he refused to patent it) encouraged him, and he began reading the works of leading scientists in England and corresponding with their authors. The newly discovered and extremely puzzling phenomenon of static electricity particularly engaged his attention and in 1746 he sent to England for a Leyden jar and other apparatus. In a series of ingenious and elegant experiments he determined the site of a static charge to be the insulating material (glass in this case), elaborated a simple and essentially correct theory of electricity as a single "fluid" composed of "subtle particles," and established such terms as positive and negative (or plus and minus) charges, battery, condenser, conductor, and electric shock. He communicated his discoveries to an English friend in a series of letters, several of which were read before the Royal Society, and in 1751 published a small volume titled *Experiments and Observations on Electricity*. The book was translated into French the next year and overnight established his fame as a scientist. His suggestion in the book for an experiment to demonstrate the electrical nature of lightning was followed by a French scientist in May 1752, repeated several times throughout Europe (and only belatedly in his own famous kite experiment), and, along with his consequent invention of the lightning rod for the protection of buildings, resulted in his being awarded the Royal Society's Copley Medal and honorary degrees from Harvard and Yale in 1753. In order to devote himself to natural science he had retired from the printing business in 1748, leaving it in charge of his foreman David Hall and thereafter deriving an ample income from the flourishing firm of Franklin and Hall. Among his other contributions to science were his observations that storms that appear to originate in the northeast actually move from the southwest, that the boiling point of water depends on the surrounding atmospheric pressure, and that oil is useful for calming waves on bodies of water. Natural science soon gave way, however, to public service. Franklin's long involvement in public affairs had included service as clerk of the Pennsylvania assembly from 1736 and as postmaster of Philadelphia from 1737; in 1751 he became a member of the assembly and two years later was appointed a deputy postmaster general for the colonies. In 1754 he was sent by the assembly to the Albany Congress, called to organize for defense against the French and Indians. His "Plan of Union" was adopted by the Albany meeting but later vetoed by the several colonial legislatures and by the king. In 1757 he was sent to England to represent Pennsylvania in a taxation dispute with the proprietary Penn family; he successfully

negotiated a settlement and took good advantage of his time in England by becoming acquainted with many leading figures and by publishing his influential pamphlet, *The Interest of Great Britain Considered with Regard to Her Colonies, and the Acquisitions of Canada and Guadaloupe*, 1760, to which he appended his *Observations Concerning the Increase of Mankind, Peopling of Countries, etc.*, written nine years earlier and first published in 1755, which anticipated at many points the later and better-known arguments of Thomas Malthus. During his stay he was awarded honorary degrees by Edinburgh and Oxford universities. After two years at home he was again sent to England in 1764 to petition the crown for a royal charter to supersede that of the proprietors. He arrived in time to argue against the recently proposed Stamp Act, but when he failed to persuade Prime Minister George Grenville to abandon the idea he determined to make the best of the situation by buying stamps for Franklin and Hall and nominating a friend as stamp officer for Philadelphia. His failure to foresee the wrathful indignation of his countrymen over the Stamp Act was one of his few political errors. News of his acquiescence led to threats against his home and family and he quickly applied himself to the campaign for repeal of the act. In February 1766 he was called before the House of Commons and interrogated closely on the issue; his lucid and pointed answers to 174 questions not only speeded repeal but outlined clearly for England the American position on numerous points of contention; published shortly thereafter, his replies reestablished his reputation at home on an even higher plane. Pennsylvania retained him as colonial agent in London and he received similar appointments from Georgia in 1768, New Jersey in 1769, and Massachusetts in 1770, making him in effect an ambassador extraordinary for America at large. He remained in England, enjoying close relations with political leaders, scientists, philosophers, and society in general, until 1775. He wrote much on American topics for the newspapers and collaborated with Whig leaders to secure a liberal colonial policy, but by 1772 he was becoming convinced that the differences between the crown and the colonies were irreconcilable. In that year he procured letters written some years earlier to Grenville by Governor Thomas Hutchinson of Massachusetts, urging that a firm policy toward the colonies be followed by the home government. He sent the letters to Boston, where their publication aroused a storm of public outrage against the already unpopular governor. This action, coupled with the publication in England on his own bitterly satirical "Rules by Which a Great Empire May be Reduced to a Small One" and "An Edict by the King of Prussia" in 1773 led to his removal from his postal appointment in January 1774. In March 1775, believing war to be imminent, he sailed for America. On May 6, the day after his arrival in Philadelphia, he was chosen a delegate to the Second Continental Congress, where he helped organize a new postal system, served on the committee for the drafting of the Declaration of Independence, and was a member of a commission sent to induce Canada to support the colonial cause. In September 1776 he was named one of three commissioners to represent the thirteen Colonies in France (the others were Silas Deane, already in Paris, and Arthur Lee, a substitute for Thomas Jefferson, who declined the appointment). Although negotiations for financial and military assistance were delayed by France's reluctance to make a commitment to what might well prove to be a losing cause, the presence of Franklin in Paris brought strong pressure to bear on the government, for from the moment of his arrival he was hailed and welcomed by the entire population, high and low, as the very embodiment of the Enlightenment man, the ideal representative of the natural aristocracy of the New World. His disinterested diplomacy and the simple courtliness of his seventy years further endeared him to the French nation, and the continuing celebration of his presence included the placing of his portrait on art and household objects of every kind imaginable and fostered a brief fad of "lightning-rod hats" to which were attached long, slender chains trailing to the ground. In the midst of vast and intricate intrigue Franklin maintained close contact with the French minister of foreign affairs, the Count Vergennes, and on the heels of the American victory at Saratoga treaties of commerce and defensive alliance were signed in February 1778. Through his influence the colonies obtained large amounts of money and supplies for the war and attracted thousands of Frenchmen to arms in their cause. In 1781 he was joined by John Adams and John Jay and they began preliminary peace negotiations with Great Britain. Despite a promise that Franklin had made to Vergennes, agreement was reached in secret with British representatives (Adams and Jay overruling him in the matter) before France and Spain were consulted. The formal treaty of peace (the Treaty of Paris) was signed on September 3, 1783. Although he requested recall soon thereafter, Franklin was kept in Paris as the representative of Congress until 1785. During his journey homeward he fended off the pains of sundry infirmities by writing two scientific papers, "Maritime Observations" and "The Causes and Cure of Smoky Chimneys." Soon after his arrival in Philadelphia in September he was elected to the executive council of Pennsylvania, by which he was promptly chosen president. His activities thereafter were restricted, although he maintained his connection with the American Philosophical Society and served as first president of the Society for Political Enquiries in 1787. In that year also he was chosen a Pennsylvania delegate to the Constitutional Convention. None of his own proposals—for a unicameral legislature and an executive committee, for example—was adopted by the convention, but toward the end his call for compromise and unanimity prevailed over deep disagreements. His last years were spent quietly, although his mind remained active; at the age of eighty-three he invented bifocal eyeglasses. After being bedridden for a year and in nearly constant pain, he died on April 17, 1790, in Philadelphia. His funeral was the largest ever seen in that city and his death was mourned around the world, most especially in France, where his memory lingered long in the public imagination. In his astounding variety of talents, Franklin was one of the handful of preeminent men of his day, and he was by far the best-known and most admired American then and long after. The French economist Turgot's epigram captured the reverence in which he was almost universally held: "He snatched the lightning from heaven and the sceptre from tyrants." Later generations knew him better perhaps in the more homely light of a greatly successful man of practical affairs, the image conveyed in his *Autobiography*, written piecemeal between 1771 and 1788 for his son William and published posthumously. No simple statement about the man could be more than fractionally satisfactory, but two are profoundly suggestive: Carl Van Doren's description of him as "an harmonious human multitude," and the apocryphal but eminently apt story that although Franklin was an incontestably proper choice for the committee charged with the drafting of the Declaration of Independence, he was not entrusted with the actual writing of the document for fear he might conceal a joke in it. He was one of the original group elected to the Hall of Fame in 1900.

Franklin, John Hope (1915–   ), historian. Born on January 2, 1915, in Rentiesville, Oklahoma, Franklin graduated from Fisk University in 1935, took his M.A. at Harvard in 1936, and after a year of teaching at Fisk returned to graduate studies in history at Harvard, receiving his Ph.D. in 1941. He joined the faculty of St. Augustine's College in 1939 and in 1943 became professor of history at North Carolina College (now North Carolina Central University). In 1947 he moved to Howard University and in the same year published his best-known work, *From Slavery to Freedom: A History of American Negroes*, which quickly became a standard text in the field. Franklin remained at Howard until 1956, when he was appointed professor and chairman of the department of history at Brooklyn College. *The Militant South*, 1956, further enhanced his reputation as a scholar and he later added *Reconstruction After the Civil War*, 1961, *The Emancipation Proclamation*, 1963, and numerous articles and works that appeared under his editorship. Widely in demand as a visiting lecturer, Franklin held Fulbright (1954) and William Pitt (1962) professorships at Cambridge University, was a member and officer of several professional organizations, and a U.S. commissioner for the United Nations Educational, Scientific, and Cultural Organization (UNESCO). He served from 1947 on the editorial board of the *Journal of Negro History* and later on that of the *Journal of American History*. In 1964 he was named professor of American history at the University of Chicago, three years later becoming chairman of the history department and in 1969 being appointed John Matthews Manly Distinguished Service Professor. One of the foremost U.S. historians of his time, Franklin served as chairman of the Board of Foreign Scholarships from 1966 to 1969 and on the board of trustees of Fisk University from 1968. He also held posts with leading U.S. historical associations.

Fraser, James Earle (1876–1953), sculptor. Born on November 4, 1876, in Winona, Minnesota, Fraser grew up in several towns on the northern plains and from 1891 in Chicago. Interested in drawing and sculpture from childhood, he studied at the Art Institute of Chicago in 1894 and later moved to Paris, where he enrolled in the École des Beaux-Arts. By 1896 he had already completed his first major work and the one that remained his best known, "The End of the Trail," for which he drew on his early impressions to depict an exhausted Plains Indian on horseback; the statue won a prize at the Paris Salon of 1898 and brought Fraser to the attention of Augustus Saint-Gaudens, whose pupil and assistant he became for four years, the last two in New York City. In 1902 he established his own studio and was quickly successful, receiving numerous commissions for portrait busts and reliefs, including the bust of Theodore Roosevelt later placed in the Senate chamber. From 1906 to 1911 he taught at the Art Students League. Fraser's early romanticism slowly gave way to a monumental, heroic manner as he began to receive major commissions from the government and private organizations. He executed the statues of Alexander Hamilton and Albert Gallatin for the Treasury Building, the John Ericsson monument in Potomac Park, the massive pediments for the Department of Commerce Building, the allegorical figures "Justice" and "Law" for the Supreme Court Building, and the "Journey Through Life" monument in Rock Creek Cemetery, all in Washington, D.C.; the bust of Saint-Gaudens in the Hall of Fame at New York University, the Theodore Roosevelt equestrian statue for the Museum of Natural History in New York City, and the Benjamin Franklin figure for the Franklin Institute in Philadelphia. He was also a noted designer of medals, including the Edison Medal, the Academy of Arts and Letters Medal, the Navy's Distinguished Service Medal, and the World War I Victory Medal; in 1913 he designed the "buffalo" nickel. "The End of the Trail" was exhibited prominently at the Panama-Pacific International Exposition in San Francisco in 1915, but Fraser did not enjoy a major exhibition of his works until 1951, when a show was held in New York City by the American Academy of Arts and Letters and the National Institute of Arts and Letters (NIAL) in conjunction with his winning of the rarely awarded NIAL Gold Medal for Sculpture. He died in Westport, Connecticut, on October 11, 1953.

Frazier, E. Franklin (1894–1962), sociologist. Born

in Baltimore on September 24, 1894, Edward Franklin Frazier graduated from Howard University in 1916. For the next three years he taught mathematics at Tuskegee Institute, English and history at St. Paul's Normal and Industrial School in Lawrenceville, Virginia, and French in a Baltimore high school. During 1919–1920 he earned his master's degree in sociology at Clark University, and in 1921 conducted research among the longshoremen of New York City as a fellow of the New York School of Social Work. During 1921–1922 he did research among Danish students in Denmark under the auspices of the American-Scandinavian Foundation. Returning to the United States, he was a sociology teacher at Morehouse College in Atlanta and director of the Atlanta School of Social Work. He published an article in 1927 "The Pathology of Race Prejudice," whose treatment of the relation between mental disease and race prejudice precipitated a threat on his life and forced him to leave the city. From 1929 to 1934 he was professor of sociology at Fisk University. He took his doctorate at the University of Chicago in 1931. His dissertation, published as *The Negro Family in Chicago*, and another book, *The Free Negro Family*, appeared in 1932. In 1935 he was appointed to conduct a survey in New York City for Mayor Fiorello H. La Guardia's Commission on Conditions in Harlem, the result of a major racial clash in that year. From 1934 to 1959 he was chairman of the department of sociology at Howard University, and in 1948 he became the first black scholar to head the American Sociological Association. His overall concern was the progress, organization, and function of the Negro family, and his work in this area was recognized as more far-reaching than any done before him. His most important books were *The Negro Family in the United States*, 1939, and *Black Bourgeoisie*, 1957. He studied racial interaction in Africa, the Caribbean, Brazil, and the West Indies, and in 1957 published *Race and Culture Contacts in the Modern World*. He was president of the International Society for the Scientific Study of Race Relations, and chairman of the United Nations Educational, Scientific, and Cultural Organization (UNESCO) committee of experts on race. He died in Washington, D.C., on May 17, 1962. Another major work, *The Negro Church in America*, appeared in 1963.

Freeman, Alice, *see* Palmer, Alice Elvira Freeman

Freeman, Douglas Southall (1886–1953), editor and historian. Born on May 16, 1886, in Lynchburg, Virginia, Freeman graduated from Richmond College (now the University of Richmond) in 1904 and four years later took his Ph.D from the Johns Hopkins University. He entered journalism, first with the *Richmond Times-Dispatch* and later with the *Richmond News Leader*, of which he became editor in 1915. He was also a pioneer in broadcast journalism, conducting a daily newscommentary program on radio from 1925 until his death. He lectured on journalism at several universities, including Columbia in 1934–1935, and later on military history at the Army War College from 1936 to 1940. From 1934 to 1949 he was rector and president of the board of trustees of the University of Richmond. History, particularly military history and that of the South, became a dominant interest and resulted in a number of meticulously researched and carefully written books: *Virginia—A Gentle Dominion*, 1924; *The Last Parade*, 1932; *R. E. Lee*, 1934, a masterly biography in four volumes, which won a Pulitzer Prize; *The South to Posterity*, 1939; and *Lee's Lieutenants*, three volumes, 1942–1944, which he considered his best work. Freeman was chairman of the advisory committee for the Princeton University edition of *The Papers of Thomas Jefferson* and a member of the advisory boards for the *Dictionary of American History* and the *Atlas of American History*. He was an indefatigable worker—in addition to carrying out his journalistic, academic, and literary duties he served at various times as a trustee of the Rockefeller Foundation, the Carnegie Endowment for International Peace, the Woodrow Wilson Foundation, and the General Education Board, was a member of the President's Commission on Higher Education and the Planning Committee of the Library of Congress, and was president of the Southern Historical Society and the Society of American Historians. He retired from the *News Leader* in 1949 to devote more time to a biography of George Washington; two volumes had appeared in 1948, two more were published in 1951, the fifth in 1952, and the sixth posthumously in 1954. Freeman was awarded a second Pulitzer Prize for the six volumes, which were a notable contribution to American biography; the planned seventh volume, completed by J. A. Carroll and M. A. Ashworth, appeared in 1957. Freeman died in Richmond on June 13, 1953.

Freeman, Mary Eleanor Wilkins (1852–1930), author. Born on October 31, 1852, in Randolph, Massachusetts, Miss Wilkins moved with her family to Brattleboro, Vermont, in 1867. She lived at home after studying for a year in 1870–1871 at Mount Holyoke Female Seminary (now Mount Holyoke College), read widely on her own, and began writing children's stories and verse. On the death of her parents about 1883 she returned to Randolph to live with friends and in that year published in a Boston newspaper her first story for adults. She continued to publish in newspapers and magazines, becoming a regular and favorite contributor to *Harper's Magazine*; early collections of her stories included *A Humble Romance*, 1887, and *A New England Nun*, 1891. Narrated in a firm and objective manner with occasional subtle undertones of humor or irony, her stories were deft character studies of somehow exceptional people trapped by poverty or other handicaps in sterile, restrictive situations who consequently underwent deformations of pride. Her use of New England village and countryside settings and dialects placed her stories in the "local-color" school,

and her work thereby enjoyed an added vogue; nevertheless, she avoided the maudlin sentimentality then current in popular literature. Her novels, including *Jane Field*, 1893; *Pembroke*, 1894; *Jerome*, 1897, and *The Heart's Highway*, 1900, were of less interest than her stories, serving mainly to emphasize her mastery of the shorter form. In 1902 she married Dr. Charles M. Freeman of Metuchen, New Jersey, where she lived for the rest of her life. Later collections of her stories included *The Wind in the Rose Bush*, 1903, and *Edgewater People*, 1918. Mrs. Freeman died in Metuchen on March 13, 1930.

Frémont, John Charles (1813–1890), soldier, explorer, and political leader. Born in Savannah, Georgia, on January 21, 1813, Frémont grew up in Charleston, South Carolina, and attended the College of Charleston from 1829 to 1831. He secured a patron in Joel R. Poinsett, a prominent South Carolina politician, and through his efforts was appointed teacher of mathematics aboard the warship *Natchez* on an extended South American cruise. In 1838 Poinsett arranged Frémont's appointment to the army's Topographical Corps; he was a member of J. N. Nicollet's expedition to explore and map the plateau region between the upper Missouri and Mississippi rivers and in 1841 led his own exploratory party along the Des Moines River. Upon his return he married Jessie Benton, daughter of Senator Thomas Hart Benton. In 1842, with Benton's support, he was sent to explore the route of the Oregon Trail and the Wind River Range in order to aid emigration to Oregon; his report, prepared with his wife's help, was widely reprinted. In the next year he set out on a much more extensive expedition. Guided, as he had been the year before, by Kit Carson and also by Thomas Fitzpatrick, he crossed Wyoming and Idaho to Oregon, followed the Columbia River to Fort Vancouver, and turned southeast to Nevada; then, in a move bordering on foolhardiness, he made a winter crossing of the Sierra Nevada westward into the Sacramento Valley of California. He traveled south to Los Angeles, explored parts of Arizona and Utah, and finally returned East in 1844. The journey and the report of it that was subsequently published were sensations and made Frémont a popular hero. While the nature of his sojourns in the West is still a matter of debate—he has been viewed as a true explorer, as a pathfinder, and as a government-sponsored map maker—there is no dispute over the practical significance of his work for settlement and establishment of lines of communication. In 1845, with war with Mexico appearing imminent, he was sent on a third expedition to California with secret orders instructing him, should he find war had begun when he arrived, to convert his party into a military force. Ordered by Mexican authorities to leave shortly after his arrival at Sutter's Fort in December 1845, he refused and briefly raised the American flag over fortifications he built on Gavilan (or Hawk) Peak. After a northward feint toward Oregon, he turned back, possibly in receipt of secret orders, and by a show of force lent his support to the Bear Flag revolt at Sonoma. When news that war had formally been declared reached California, Frémont was appointed major of the "California Battalion," composed of his own men and U.S. volunteers. By January 1847 he had led in the capture of Los Angeles and had secured the entire state. There ensued a conflict of authority over California and Frémont found himself caught between the two feuding principals; after two months as governor upon appointment by Commodore Robert F. Stockton, Frémont was arrested by Gen. Stephen W. Kearny for mutiny, disobedience, and conduct prejudicial to military order. He was found guilty of the last two charges by a court-martial in 1848, and although President James K. Polk suspended his sentence, he resigned from the army. During the next several years he devoted himself to developing his huge estates in California; the discovery of gold made him rich, and he served a brief period as one of California's first senators. In 1856 his wide popularity and his antislavery opinions won him the presidential nomination of the new Republican party. After defeat by James Buchanan he returned to California. During the Civil War he resumed his army commission; with the rank of major general he commanded the Department of the West from headquarters in St. Louis until political enemies and his own recklessness combined to cause his removal. In a subsequent command in Virginia he was ineffectual against Gen. T. J. "Stonewall" Jackson, and in 1862 he again resigned from the army. He was dissuaded from seeking the nomination for the presidency in 1864 and retired to private life. The loss of some of his California holdings was followed by the loss of most of his fortune in the bankruptcy of the Memphis & El Paso Railroad, of which he had become president with the hope of building the line west to San Diego. From 1878 to 1883 he served as territorial governor of Arizona, afterwards returning to California. Early in 1890 he was restored to rank as major general on the retired list, and his pension sustained him until his death on July 13, 1890, while on a visit to New York City. His *Memories of My Life* appeared in 1887.

French, Daniel Chester (1850–1931), sculptor. Born on April 20, 1850, in Exeter, New Hampshire, French was largely self-taught, although he studied briefly with William Morris Hunt, who showed him the significance of color values, and for one year at the Massachusetts Institute of Technology (MIT), where he developed skill in drawing; later studies included lectures in anatomy in Boston from William Rimmer, one month in J. Q. A. Ward's New York City studio, and two years under Thomas Ball in Italy. From 1876 to 1878 he had a studio in Washington, from 1878 to 1887 in Boston and Concord, Massachusetts, and after 1888 he worked in New York City. His first commission, in 1873, was "The Minute Man," commemorating the hundredth anniversary

of the battle of Concord. The monument was unveiled on April 19, 1875, by Ralph Waldo Emerson and placed on the Old North Bridge in Concord. A constant flow of commissions followed. Most famous among his sculptures were busts of Emerson and of Bronson Alcott; the seated bronze figure of John Harvard, outside University Hall in Cambridge, Massachusetts, 1884; "General Lewis Cass" for the state of Michigan, in the statuary hall of the U.S. Capitol, 1888; "Dr. Gallaudet and His First Deaf-Mute Pupil," for the Columbia Institution for the Deaf and Dumb in Washington, D.C.; the 75-foot "Statue of the Republic" at the World's Columbian Exposition in Chicago in 1893; "Death and the Sculptor," a memorial to Martin Milmore, in the Forest Hills Cemetery in Boston, 1893; the memorial group to John Boyle O'Reilly in the Boston Fenway, 1896; the equestrian statues of Gen. Ulysses S. Grant in Fairmount Park, Philadelphia, 1898, and of George Washington, in Paris, 1900, both in collaboration with Edward Potter; the Boston Public Library's low-relief bronze doors, 1902; the "Four Continents" group for the New York customhouse, 1907; the "Standing Lincoln," in Lincoln, Nebraska, 1912; "Alma Mater" for Columbia University, 1915; the fountain at Du Pont Circle in Washington, and the seated marble statue of Abraham Lincoln in the Lincoln Memorial in Washington, dedicated in 1922. The seated Lincoln, probably French's greatest work, offered to hundreds of thousands of visitors every year suggestions of character that each could interpret in his own way. He died in Stockbridge, Massachusetts, on October 7, 1931.

Freneau, Philip Morin (1752–1832), poet and editor. Born in New York City on January 2, 1752, Freneau graduated from the College of New Jersey (now Princeton) in 1771. The commencement poem, "The Rising Glory of America," was a joint effort by him and Hugh Henry Brackenridge and was published the following year. For a few years he taught school; at the outbreak of the Revolution he began issuing satirical pamphlets aimed at the British and the Loyalists. From 1775 to 1778 he was secretary to a wealthy planter in the West Indies, and during that time he wrote some of his best poetry, notably "The Beauties of Santa Cruz," "The Jamaica Funeral," and, particularly, "The House of Night," which in many ways foreshadowed the coming romantic period of English literature. Returning to New Jersey, he served in the militia and later as a privateer; in 1780 his ship was captured and he was imprisoned under brutal conditions that he described the following year in *The British Prison-Ship*. For the next three years he was employed by the Philadelpia post office and contributed poetry to that city's *Freeman's Journal*. His published verse, ranging from patriotic celebrations to vitriolic attacks on the British, earned him the title of "poet of the Revolution." From 1784 to 1790 he was again a sea captain, mainly in West Indian waters. In 1790 he became editor of the *New York Daily Advertiser*;

the following year Secretary of State Thomas Jefferson secured him a translator's post in the State Department and he began publishing the intensely partisan *National Gazette*, an organ of Jeffersonian democracy. The *Gazette* ceased publication in 1793 and Freneau ended his government employment a short time later. For a time he edited the *Jersey Chronicle* and then the *New York Time-Piece;* the remainder of his life was divided between the sea and his Monmouth County, New Jersey, farm, where he died on December 18, 1832. He had continued to write poetry throughout his varied life; such poems as "The Wild Honeysuckle," "The Indian Burying Ground," and "Stanzas Written on the Hills of Neversink" established him as the nation's leading poet in the period before William Cullen Bryant and as an important precursor of the native nature poets.

Frick, Henry Clay (1849–1919), industrialist and philanthropist. Born on December 19, 1849, in West Overton, in Westmoreland County, Pennsylvania, Frick received little more than a rudimentary formal education and from his early youth clerked in stores and worked at various other jobs. In 1871 he organized Frick and Company to construct and operate a number of coke ovens to supply the Pittsburgh steel mills; surviving the panic of 1873, the firm expanded rapidly and by the age of thirty Frick was a millionaire. In 1882 he became associated with Andrew Carnegie, who bought a share in Frick and Company, and seven years later he was invited to become chairman of Carnegie's steel company. He instituted a major reorganization program and greatly improved the firm's financial standing. Overcoming Carnegie's reluctance, he also acquired for the company large holdings in the iron-ore region around Lake Superior, a venture that soon proved highly profitable. In 1892 he faced a bitter strike at the Carnegie Steel Company's plant in Homestead, Pennsylvania, with a degree of adamancy remarkable even in that age of extreme measures in labor relations. He hired a force of 300 Pinkerton guards who attempted unsuccessfully to regain control of the company property occupied by strikers; when they failed to dislodge the strikers in a pitched battle, the Pennsylvania national guard was called in. Frick himself was shot and stabbed by an anarchist, but he recovered and eventually saw the strike broken. After differences with Carnegie he resigned from the steel company in 1900 and the following year played a central role in the negotiations that led to the organization of J. P. Morgan's United States Steel Corporation, of which he became a director. In his later years he continued various business interests while devoting much time to his art collection; he also took up philanthropy, endowing many hospitals and educational institutions and giving a large park and endowment to the city of Pittsburgh. He died in New York City on December 2, 1919. His house, with his art collection, became by bequest a museum and the Frick Collection, though small, remained one of the finest in New York City.

Friedan, Betty Naomi Goldstein (1921–   ), author and social reformer. Born on February 4, 1921, in Peoria, Illinois, Miss Goldstein graduated from Smith College with a degree in psychology in 1942 and after a year of graduate work at the University of California at Berkeley settled in New York City. She worked at various jobs until 1947, when she married Carl Friedan; for ten years thereafter she lived as a housewife and mother in New York suburbs while doing freelance work for a number of magazines. In 1957 a questionnaire that she circulated among her Smith classmates suggested to her that a great many of them were deeply dissatisfied with their lives. She planned and undertook an extensive series of studies on the topic, formulating more detailed questionnaires, conducting interviews, discussing her results with psychologists and other students of behavior, and finally organized her findings, illuminated by her personal experiences, in book form as *The Feminine Mystique*, 1963. The book was an immediate and controversial best seller and was translated into a number of foreign languages. Mrs. Friedan's central thesis was that women as a class suffered a variety of more or less subtle forms of discrimination but that they were in particular the victims of a pervasive system of delusions and false values under which they were urged to find personal fulfillment, even identity, vicariously through the husbands and children to whom they were supposed cheerfully to devote their lives. This restricted role of wife-mother, whose spurious glorification was suggested by the title of the book, led almost inevitably to a sense of unreality or general spiritual malaise in the absence of genuine, creative, self-defining work. The growing public discussion that followed the publication of the book was bolstered by Mrs. Friedan's lectures and radio and television appearances around the country, and in 1966 she founded the National Organization for Women (NOW), a civil-rights group dedicated to equality of opportunity for women. As president of NOW she directed campaigns for the ending of sex-classified employment notices, for greater representation of women in government, for child-care centers for working mothers, for legalized abortion, and other reforms. Although it was later occasionally eclipsed by younger and more radical groups, NOW remained the largest and probably the most effective organization in the women's movement. Mrs. Friedan stepped down from the presidency in 1970 but continued to be active in the work that had sprung largely from her pioneering efforts, helping to organize the Women's Strike for Equality, held on August 26, 1970, the fiftieth anniversary of woman suffrage, and leading in the campaign for ratification of the proposed Equal Rights Amendment to the U.S. constitution.

Friedman, Esther Pauline (1918–   ) and Pau-

line Esther (1918–   ), syndicated columnists. The Misses Friedman, Esther Pauline (Ann Landers) and Pauline, Esther (Abby Van Buren), identical twins, were born on July 4, 1918, in Sioux City, Iowa. They both attended the city's Central High School and its Morningside College and were married, in a double ceremony, on the same day, July 2, 1939—Esther ("Eppie") to Jules W. Lederer and Pauline ("Popo") to Morton Phillips. For the next 16 years their ways parted, Mrs. Lederer having one child and living for the most part in Chicago, Mrs. Phillips having two children and living in Minneapolis, Eau Claire, Wisconsin, and San Francisco. But in 1956 their lives and careers resumed parallel courses. In the fall of the previous year Mrs. Lederer had entered a contest to find a successor to Ruth Crowley, who wrote an advice-to-the-lovelorn column for the *Chicago Sun-Times* under the pen name "Ann Landers." Mrs. Lederer, although she was the only nonprofessional to enter the competition, won it and her first column appeared on October 16, 1955. Its success was rapid, her commonsensical and sometimes astringent replies to questions from readers appealing to thousands and then millions of readers in the United States and abroad. Although Mrs. Phillips insisted that her sister's decision to write a column had no effect on her own course, she did submit in the late fall of 1955 some sample columns to the editor of the *San Francisco Chronicle*; he immediately dropped the paper's regular columnist and substituted Mrs. Phillips, who chose the pen name "Abigail Van Buren." Her column first saw the light in January 1956; like her sister's, it was soon enormously successful, and by the later 1960s the two were far and away the leaders in the field.

Friedman, Milton (1912–   ), economist. Born in Brooklyn, New York, on July 31, 1912, Friedman grew up there and in Rahway, New Jersey. He graduated from Rutgers University in 1932 and the next year received his M.A. from the University of Chicago. He remained at Chicago as a research assistant until 1935, when he moved to Washington, D.C.; there, from 1935 to 1943, he worked as an economist for the National Resources Committee, the National Bureau of Economic Research, and the Department of the Treasury, taking time out in 1940–1941 to serve as visiting professor of economics at the University of Wisconsin. In 1943 he resumed his studies and received his Ph.D. from Columbia University three years later. After a year at the University of Minnesota he joined the faculty of the University of Chicago in 1946 as associate professor of economics, advancing to full professor in 1948. Friedman had begun publishing articles and books while in government service, contributing to *Consumer Expenditures in the United States*, 1939, and publishing *Taxing to Prevent Inflation*, with C. Shoup and R. P. Mack, in 1943. His doctoral thesis was developed into *Income from Independent Professional Practice*, 1946, with Simon Kuznets. Friedman emerged as the leading figure

among conservative economists with his editing of *Studies in the Quantity Theory of Money*, 1956, and a series of books culminating in the monumental *Monetary History of the United States, 1867–1960*, 1963, with A. J. Schwartz. Strongly opposed to the fiscal management approach of the dominant Keynesian school of economics, he was an outspoken champion of the largely discarded quantity theory of money and proposed a return to a laissez-faire economics of the marketplace; he suggested the elimination of governmental regulatory agencies and other devices that, he claimed, had failed in their purpose of stabilizing the economy but had eroded individual liberties. One of his more controversial proposals was for a "negative income tax" to replace the unwieldly welfare system. Friedman was named Paul Snowden Russell Distinguished Service Professor at the University of Chicago in 1962. From 1948 he was on the research staff of the National Bureau of Economic Research, during 1951–1953 on the editorial board of the *American Economic Review* and from 1957 to 1968 on that of *Econometrica*; in 1967 he began a regular column in *Newsweek* magazine. He was an economic adviser to Senator Barry M. Goldwater during the 1964 presidential campaign and later often advised President Richard M. Nixon. Later books included *The Great Contraction*, 1965, with A. J. Schwartz; *The Balance of Payments*, 1967, with R. V. Roosa; *Dollars and Deficits*, 1968; *The Optimum Quantity of Money and Other Essays*, 1969; and *An Economist's Protest*, 1972. In 1976 he was awarded the Nobel Prize for Economics.

Friedman, Pauline Esther, *see* Friedman, Esther Pauline and Pauline Esther

Friml, Rudolf (1879–1972), pianist and composer. Born on December 7, 1879, in Prague, Austria-Hungary, (now in Czechoslovakia), Charles Rudolf Friml studied piano and composition, the latter under Antonin Dvořák, at the Prague Conservatory during 1900–1903. In 1901 he made his first visit to the United States as accompanist to violinist Jan Kubelik; he returned with Kubelik in 1904 and on that tour made his American debut as a composer and pianist, performing his own concerto in New York City. He settled permanently in the United States in 1906, becoming a citizen in 1925. He first wrote for the musical-comedy stage in 1912, when he took over work on the operetta *The Firefly* from Victor Herbert; for it he wrote such songs as "Giannina Mia." Friml followed with a long series of highly successful Broadway operettas, including *High Jinks*, 1913; *The Peasant Girl*, 1914; *You're in Love*, 1916; *Katinka*, 1916; *Sweet Kitty Darling*, 1917; *Gloriana*, 1918; *Sometime* ("Any Kind of Man," sung by Mae West), 1918; *Tumble In*, 1919; *Little Whopper*, 1919; *June Love*, 1920; *Blue Kitten*, 1922; *Cinders*, 1923; *Dew Drop Inn*, 1923; *Rose Marie* ("Indian Love Call"), 1924; *Vagabond King* ("Only a Rose," "Some Day," "Song of the Vagabonds,"), 1925; *The Wild Rose*, 1926; *Palm Beach*

Girl, 1926; No Foolin', 1926; White Eagle, 1927; The Three Musketeers ("March of the Musketeers") 1928; Bird of Paradise, 1930; The Lottery Bride, 1930; and Annina, 1934. Friml also contributed to the Ziegfeld Follies of 1921, 1923, 1924, and 1925. From 1934 he worked in Hollywood on motion-picture scores, his songs including "Donkey Serenade" for the 1937 film version of his own The Firefly. In 1969 his ninetieth birthday was the occasion of gala celebrations sponsored by the American Society of Composers, Authors, and Publishers (ASCAP) and others, at which Friml himself performed. Two years later he was chosen as one of the original members of the new Songwriter's Hall of Fame. Friml died in Hollywood, California, on November 12, 1972.

Frohman, Charles (1860–1915), theatrical manager and producer. Born in Sandusky, Ohio, on June 17, 1860, Frohman was the son of German immigrant parents who were interested in amateur theatricals. He early developed an interest in the theater himself and after moving with his family to New York City in his early youth he began working in various minor capacities in theaters and agencies around the city. After working for a series of newspapers and for a time in a theatrical agency in partnership with his older brothers Daniel and Gustave, he undertook his first independent management job with a road tour of the Wallack's Theatre Company in 1883. On his return to New York he opened a booking office and six years later, in 1889, managed his first great stage success, Bronson Howard's Shenandoah, at the Star Theatre. Three years later he placed John Drew under contract and around him assembled the Empire Theatre Stock Company, which in a long series of brilliant productions developed such unforgettable luminaries of the American stage as Maude Adams, Ethel Barrymore, Julia Marlowe, Billie Burke, William Gillette, and Elsie de Wolfe. Frohman was himself largely responsible for the evolution of the star system and was equally influential in his encouragement of talented young playwrights like Howard, Clyde Fitch, David Belasco, and Augustus Thomas. From the opening of The Little Minister, starring Maude Adams, in 1897 he enjoyed a long and fruitful association with James M. Barrie, whose Peter Pan he introduced, also with Miss Adams, in 1905. Frohman's booking agency later grew into a virtual monopoly as the Theatrical Syndicate, controlling theaters throughout the country and several in London. An ebullient, magnetic personality, Frohman used his vast power to the benefit of the American stage, giving it some of its most memorable performances and one of its grandest and most exciting periods. He died on May 7, 1915, in the sinking of the Lusitania.

Fromm, Erich (1900–1980), psychoanalyst and author. Born on March 23, 1900, in Frankfurt am Main, Germany, Fromm took his Ph.D. from the University of Heidelberg in 1922 and then pursued further studies in psychology and psychoanalysis at the University of Munich and the Psychoanalytic Institute in Berlin. In 1925 he began practice as a psychoanalyst and while achieving considerable prominence undertook studies and researches of his own, gradually moving from a Freudian position to a view of psychoanalysis that gave considerable weight to the shaping forces of culture and society. He lectured at the Psychoanalytic Institute in Frankfurt and at the University of Frankfurt's Institute for Social Research from 1929 to 1932, and, after a visit to America in 1933, emigrated the next year to the United States, lecturing from then until 1939 at the International Institute for Social Research at Columbia University. During 1940–1941 he was a lecturer at the university itself and while serving on the faculty of Bennington College from 1941 to 1950 held lectureships at various times at the American Institute for Psychoanalysis and at Yale. From 1945 to 1951 he was a fellow and from 1947 chairman of the faculty of the William Alanson White Institute of Psychiatry. In 1951 he joined the faculty of the medical school of the National University of Mexico, where he remained, from 1955 as head of the department of psychoanalysis, until 1967; he was at the same time on the faculty of Michigan State University from 1957 to 1961 and from 1962 was an adjunct professor of psychiatry at New York University. Fromm's psychoanalytic theory broadened continually through the years as he turned his attention to general problems of society and the place of the individual within it. He developed a deeply humanistic view, drawing inspiration from fellow neo-Freudians, from the social writings of Marx, and from the humanistic strains in Judeo-Christian tradition. His books, widely influential and remarkably popular, included Escape From Freedom, 1941; Man for Himself, 1947; Psychoanalysis and Religion, 1950; The Forgotten Language, 1951; The Sane Society, 1955, whose title inspired the name of the National Committee for a Sane Nuclear Policy (SANE), which he helped found in 1957; The Art of Loving, 1956; May Man Prevail?, 1961; Beyond the Chains of Illusion: My Encounter with Marx and Freud, 1962; The Dogma of Christ and Essays on Religion, Psychology, and Culture, 1963; The Heart of Man, 1964; You Shall Be as Gods: A Radical Interpretation of the Old Testament and Its Tradition, 1966; and The Revolution of Hope, 1968. In these Fromm emerged as one of the leading psychoanalytic theorists of his time. He retired to Switzerland in 1974 and died in Muralto on March 18, 1980.

Frost, Robert Lee (1874–1963), poet. Born on March 26, 1874, in San Francisco, Frost moved with his family to New England at the age of eleven. Entering Dartmouth in 1892, he remained for less than a term; for the next several years he lived at home, working at various jobs and writing poetry. His first published poem, "My Butterfly: An Elegy," appeared in 1894. In 1897 he entered Harvard, but ill health forced him to withdraw before completing his studies. For a time he farmed in New England and from 1906 to 1912 he taught school, all the while adding to his stock of as yet unrecognized verse. In 1912 he moved his wife and children to England and the next year his first volume of poems, *A Boy's Will*, was accepted for publication there. *North of Boston* followed in 1914. Early in 1915 he returned to New England, where his family had been rooted for generations, to find himself no longer an unknown poet. He held a succession of professorships, fellowships, and residencies at Amherst, the University of Michigan, Harvard, and Dartmouth; his association with Amherst lasted until his death. From his farm in New Hampshire he issued nine more volumes of new poems, including *West-running Brook*, 1928; *A Further Range*, 1936; *A Witness Tree*, 1942; and *In the Clearing*, 1962. He received four Pulitzer Prizes for poetry, in 1924, 1931, 1937, and 1943. His poetry was marked by the use of everyday language and homely images drawn from his rural New England surroundings; it was his unique ability, however, to build from these elements poems that held hints of transcendant symbolic and metaphysical significance. He also developed the art of writing so-called heroic couplets—that is, rhymed iambic pentameter couplets, the favorite verse form of such famous predecessors of Frost as Chaucer, Dryden, and Pope—to an almost unprecedented degree, thus making him one of the great innovators in English prosody. He was among the most honored of poets during his lifetime; he was awarded more than 40 honorary degrees and made a number of goodwill trips abroad for the state department. In 1958 he was consultant in poetry to the Library of Congress and in 1962, on his eighty-eighth birthday, was awarded the Congressional Gold Medal. Late in life he made an impressive appearance at the inauguration of President John F. Kennedy in 1961, reciting his poem "The Gift Outright." He died in Boston on January 29, 1963.

Frothingham, Octavius Brooks (1822–1895), religious leader and author. Born in Boston on November 26, 1822, Frothingham graduated from Harvard in 1843 and during the next three years studied at the Divinity School. He was ordained in the North Church of Salem in 1847, remaining there as minister for eight years until a dispute with the congregation over the issue of slavery led him to move to Jersey City. While ministering to a Unitarian congregation there his reputation grew rapidly and in 1859 a group of followers in New York City organized the Third Congregational Unitarian Society (later the Independent Liberal Church) specifically for him. Theologically he was liberal in the extreme and, finding even the Unitarian church too restrictive, in 1867 he joined in forming in Boston the Free Religious Association, serving as its president for 11 years. Theodore Parker, whose mantle he was generally held to have inherited, was the subject of a distinguished biography published by Frothingham in 1874. Subsequent works, in which he surveyed

and summarized the intellectual life of New England during its finest flowering, included *Transcendentalism in New England*, 1876; *Gerrit Smith*, 1877; *George Ripley*, 1882; and *Memoir of William Henry Channing*, 1886. His own religious thought was best summarized in *The Religion of Humanity*, 1872, and in 1891 he published the autobiographical *Recollections and Impressions, 1822–1890*. He had retired from the active ministry in 1879; in poor health, he lived in Boston from that year until his death on November 27, 1895.

Fry, Franklin Clark (1900–1968), religious leader. Born on August 30, 1900, in Bethlehem, Pennsylvania, Fry graduated from Hamilton College in 1921 and after a year abroad, at the American School for Classical Studies in Athens, entered the Philadelphia Lutheran Seminary. On his ordination in 1925 he began his ministry in Yonkers, New York, moving in 1929 to a pastorate in Akron, Ohio, which he held for 15 years. During that time he was active in the higher administration of the church as a member of its board of American missions and of its executive board. In 1944 he was elected president of the United Lutheran Church in America, one of the largest Lutheran synodic associations in the country, and retained the post until 1962. Following World War II he was a leader in Lutheran-sponsored relief work and church reorganization in Europe, making several trips under the auspices of the Lutheran World Convention and the Federal Council of Churches of Christ in America, and later joining in the founding of Lutheran World Relief, of which he was thereafter president. Dedicated to fostering the growth of ecumenism throughout the world, Fry was also active in the National Council of Churches and in 1954 was elected chairman of the policy-making central and executive committees of the World Council of Churches. From 1957 to 1963 he served as president of the Lutheran World Federation, the first American to hold the position. During his presidency the United Lutheran Church merged in 1962 with several other Lutheran associations to form the Lutheran Church in America, of which he was president from that year until 1968. An acknowledged spokesman and director of Lutheranism in America, Fry was a major force in bringing the church into an active role in contemporary religious affairs and acquired an international reputation as an able administrator in the service of his own church and of the movement for ecumenical union in world Protestantism. He died in New Rochelle, New York, on June 6, 1968.

Fulbright, J. William (1905–   ), educator and public official. Born on April 9, 1905, in Sumner, Missouri, James William Fulbright grew up in Fayetteville, Arkansas. Graduating from the University of Arkansas in 1925, he studied at Oxford on a Rhodes scholarship until 1928 and then took a law degree at The George Washington University in 1934. During 1934–1935 he was a special attorney in the antitrust division of the justice department. In 1935 he joined the George Washington University law faculty and in 1936 moved to the law school of the University of Arkansas; from 1939 to 1941 he was president of the university. In 1942 he was elected as a Democrat to the House of Representatives and two years later was sent to the Senate. Fulbright, repeatedly reelected, became a leading figure in the Senate. In 1946 he sponsored the Fulbright Act, which allotted funds from the sale of surplus war material overseas to finance an educational exchange program between the United States and foreign countries. Regular government support was later established. Under the plan thousands of Fulbright scholarships were awarded. Under other provisions and later additions to the program, including those enacted by the Fulbright-Hays Act of 1961, Fulbright exchange fellowships were available to school teachers, college professors, and research scholars. In 1959 he became chairman of the powerful Foreign Relations Committee of the Senate. During the administrations of presidents Lyndon B. Johnson and Richard M. Nixon he gained national prominence with his outspoken and incisive criticism of the conduct and continuation of the Vietnam War. Among Fulbright's writings were *Prospects for the West*, 1963; *Old Myths and New Realities*, 1964; and *The Arrogance of Power*, 1967. He retired in 1974 after a surprising defeat for renomination by Gov. Dale Bumpers.

Fuller, Alfred Carl (1885–1973), business leader. Born on January 13, 1885, in Kings County, Nova Scotia, Fuller received a grammar-school education and in 1903 left home for Boston. There he worked in various minor jobs and in 1905 became a salesman for a brush company. Struck by the huge sales potential of brushes designed for a variety of specific uses, and with an idea for making twisted-wire brushes by machine, he went into business for himself in 1906 in Hartford, Connecticut. Forming the Capitol Brush Company, he made brushes at night and sold them door-to-door during the day; in 1910 the firm became the Fuller Brush Company and three years later was incorporated, with Fuller as president. From the beginning the company's wares were sold directly to householders through a rapidly growing corps of independent dealers. Within a decade after incorporation sales were approaching $12 million annually and the "Fuller Brush man" was on his way to becoming a fixture of American life. Countless jokes and even a movie (with Red Skelton in 1948) were inspired by (and helped spread the fame of) Fuller's ubiquitous representatives, and one result was that the firm found that it could get by with little formal advertising. The variety of special-purpose brushes grew constantly and an industrial line, featuring brushes widely used in vacuum-cleaner manufacture, was introduced. In 1943 Fuller became chairman of the board of directors, the presidency passing to his son; he became a U.S. citizen in 1948. Cosmetics, toiletries, and other products were later added to the Fuller line and by 1960 the gross revenue of the first effective nationwide direct-sales organization had reached the $100 million level. Fuller's autobiography, *A Foot in the Door*, written with Hartzell Spence, appeared in 1960. Fuller retired in 1968. He died in Hartford on December 4, 1973.

Fuller, Buckminster (1895–1983), inventor and designer. Born on July 12, 1895, in Milton, Massachusetts, to a prominent family, Richard Buckminster Fuller, Jr., was educated at the Milton Academy and attended Harvard during 1913–1915. After a very brief period at the U.S. Naval Academy in 1917 he served apprenticeships with an importer of cotton-mill machinery and at Armour and Company, and was an ensign in the navy during World War I. Upon his discharge he returned to Armour, was a sales manager for a trucking concern for a brief time in 1922, and spent the next five years working for his father-in-law, an architect, in the construction industry. In 1927 he moved to Chicago and began to evolve his unorthodox "comprehensive design" theory, a blend of mathematics, engineering, and philosophy, which materialized in his "Dymaxion" (derived from "dynamic" and "maximum") inventions. His first luxury house, built in 1927, was spacious, comfortable, and portable, supported by one central column, and cost the same amount as a 1927 Ford sedan; the 1933 Dymaxion car could travel 120 miles per hour, cross rough country with ease, park or turn in its own length, and run 30 to 40 miles on a gallon of gasoline. The Dymaxion Corporation, which existed between 1932 and 1935 and again in 1941 but eventually dissolved owing to lack of commercial support, also marketed the Dymaxion steel "igloo" in 1940 and the Dymaxion world map, the first map to receive a U.S. patent, showing the continents "without any visible distortion." The Dymaxion Dwelling Machines Company was established in 1944; it produced the Dymaxion house in Wichita, Kansas, in 1946, a luxurious circular aluminum seven-room structure built with airplane construction methods for $6400. The company was reorganized in 1954 as Geodesics, Inc., and Synergetics, Inc., whose main product was the geodesic dome. Built to provide maximum strength with minimum material, the domes were developed according to Fuller's mathematical principle of "energetic synergetic geometry," devised in 1917, which took into account the paths of force in atoms, molecules, and crystals. The domes were constructed of numerous adjoining tetrahedrons made from alloys with high tensile strength—a design that effectively dispersed any force on the dome's surface. Domes for use in the Distant Early Warning (DEW) lines, defense installations in the Arctic, were easily flown to location, installed in hours, and withstood winds of 125 miles per hour; other domes were used by the air force to house rotating radar antennas and by the marines as front-line shelters. Fuller designed the Union Tank Car Company dome in Baton Rouge, Louisiana; with no interior pillars, it had a diameter of 384 feet and stood as high as a ten-story building. A gold-tinted Fuller dome housed the American National Exhibition in Moscow in 1959 and drew such crowds that the state department erected other exhibition domes in Burma, India, Thailand, Afghanistan, and Japan. Other domes enclosing controlled climates were projected for use in Antarctica, on the ocean floor, and on the moon. Associated at various times with the architecture departments of Yale, Cornell, Princeton, and the Massachusetts Institute of Technology, Fuller lectured on comprehensive design and was appointed to a lifetime professorship in 1959 at Southern Illinois University. He published *Nine Chains to the Moon*, 1938; *No More Second-Hand God*, 1963; *Ideas and Integrities: A Spontaneous Autobiographical Disclosure*, 1963; *Operating Manual for Spaceship Earth*, 1969; *Approaching the Benign Environment*, 1970; *I Seem to Be a Verb*, 1970; *Synergetics*, 1975. From 1972 he was World Fellow in residence at University City Science Center in Philadelphia. He died on July 1, 1983, in Los Angeles.

Fuller, Margaret, Marchioness Ossoli (1810–1850), author, critic, and social reformer. Born in Cambridge, Massachusetts, on May 23, 1810, Sarah Margaret Fuller was an extremely precocious child. Under the severe tutelage of her father she more than compensated for the inaccessibility of formal education to females of the time, but while she acquired wide learning at a very early age, the strain permanently impaired her health. She taught school for a number of years—for two years, 1836–1837, at Bronson Alcott's Temple School in Boston—and wrote occasional critical essays for the *Western Messenger*. In 1839 she began a series of public "conversations" in Boston intended to further the education of women; a brilliant conversationalist, she enjoyed great success and the series was repeated yearly until 1844. In 1840, as a result of her close association with Ralph Waldo Emerson and the Concord circle, she became editor of the Transcendentalist magazine, the *Dial*, to which she contributed a considerable number of essays, reviews, and poems. In 1844 Horace Greeley invited her to become the literary critic for the *New York Tribune*; during the next two years she established herself as the leading American critic of the time. In 1845 she published her pioneering feminist work, *Woman in the Nineteenth Century*. The following year a collection of her essays was published as *Papers on Literature and Art*. Shortly thereafter she sailed for Europe where, her reputation having preceded her, she met and mingled with the leading literary figures. Her letters to the *Tribune*, written by the first American woman to work as a foreign correspondent, were later collected in *At Home and Abroad*, 1856. In Rome, probably in 1847 or 1848, she married the Marchese Angelo Ossoli, an impoverished Italian nobleman and ardent republican. They both became deeply involved in the revolution of 1848–1849 in Italy, led by Giuseppe Mazzini; when the revolutionary Roman republic was crushed, they fled to Florence and she wrote a

history of the episode. In 1850 she sailed with her husband and their child for the United States; on July 19 the ship was wrecked off Fire Island, New York, and all aboard perished. Her memoirs, edited by Emerson and W. H. Channing, were published the following year.

Fuller, Melville Weston (1833–1910), chief justice of the Supreme Court. Born on February 11, 1833, in Augusta, Maine, Fuller graduated from Bowdoin College in 1853 and after studying law at Harvard was admitted to the bar in 1855. The following year he moved to Chicago, where over the next 30 years he built a solid reputation for ability and integrity. He was a member of the Illinois constitutional convention in 1862 and in the same year was elected to a term in the state legislature. Upon the election of Grover Cleveland to the presidency in 1884, Fuller was offered a diplomatic post or appointment as solicitor general but declined both. In 1888, however, Cleveland appointed him chief justice of the Supreme Court, a position he retained until his death. His years on the bench were unspectacular but, as an extremely able administrator, he was acknowledged to be a highly effective chief justice. He took moderate positions on most issues, combining a dedication to the traditional view of the rights of persons and property, a strict-constructionist interpretation of the Constitution, and a broadly humanitarian outlook. Among his most notable opinions were those in *U.S. v. E. C. Knight Co.*, 1895, in which the Sherman Anti-Trust Act was first construed; *Pollock v. Farmers' Loan and Trust Co.*, 1895, in which the income-tax provision of the Wilson-Gorman Tariff Act was invalidated; and *Northern Securities Co. v. U.S.* (dissenting), 1904. He was a member of the arbitration commission in the boundary dispute between Venezuela and Great Britain in 1897–1899 and from 1900 to 1910 was a member of the Permanent Court of Arbitration at The Hague. Fuller died on July 4, 1910, in Sorrento, Maine.

Fuller, Richard Buckminster, Jr., *see* Fuller, Buckminster

Fuller, Sarah Margaret, *see* Fuller, Margaret, Marchioness Ossoli

Fulton, Robert (1765–1815), engineer, inventor, and artist. Born in Little Britain, Pennsylvania, on November 14, 1765, Fulton grew up and attended school in nearby Lancaster. He early exhibited an interest in and a remarkable aptitude for things mechanical; he became an expert gunsmith and as early as 1779 had designed a small paddle-wheel boat. In 1782 he moved to Philadelphia and was financially successful, first as a jeweler's apprentice and later as a painter and miniaturist. In 1786 he went to England to study under the artist Benjamin West; within a few years his interest in painting gave way to his growing interest in engineering. Particularly fascinated by the promise of canal systems for inland transportation, he devised a method for raising and lowering canal boats to integrate them into a surface railroad system. He also secured patents for machines to saw marble, spin flax, and twist hemp rope. In 1796 he published *A Treatise on the Improvement of Canal Navigation*. He submitted a number of proposals for various engineering projects, complete with detailed plans and cost estimates, to the British government. From 1797 he devoted several years to developing a practical submarine; in France in 1800 his *Nautilus* was successfully demonstrated; its naval potential was made clear in a demonstration five years later when, equipped with torpedoes (also of Fulton's invention), it sank a heavy brig. He was unable to secure research funds from either France or Great Britain, however, and dropped the submarine project in favor of the development of a practical steamboat. In partnership with Robert R. Livingston, then U.S. minister to France, he planned a steamboat for service on the Hudson River. Construction of the *Clermont*, with two side paddle wheels, was begun soon after his return to the United States in 1806, and on August 17 of the following year the boat steamed up the river from New York City to Albany, completing the round trip in 62 hours of steaming time. For the remainder of his life, Fulton oversaw the construction of steamboats and the organization of regular freight and passenger lines. His *New Orleans* was in 1811 the first steamboat on the Mississippi. During the War of 1812 he obtained congressional authority to construct a steam-powered warship, virtually a huge mobile floating fort, for the defense of New York harbor; the *Fulton the First*, or *Demologus*, was launched shortly before the end of the war. He died two months later, on February 24, 1815, in New York City. He was elected to the Hall of Fame in 1900.

Funk, Casimir (1884–1967), biochemist. Born in Warsaw, Poland, on February 23, 1884, Funk took his Ph.D. from the University of Bern in 1904 and for two years studied and carried on research in the Pasteur Institute in Paris. From 1906 to 1910 he was an assistant at the University of Berlin and in 1910 joined the Lister Institute of Preventive Medicine in London. His studies in the chemistry of proteins had given him a solid grounding in the status of research on nutritional factors in disease; considerable work had been done by others on elements that, while present in foods in minuscule quantities, were nonetheless apparently vital to health. It remained for Funk, in a series of experiments with diets of brown and polished rice, to ascertain that such a vital substance was indeed present in brown rice and to make the first crude isolation of what came to be called thiamine, (later vitamin B_1), the specific cure for beriberi. In a landmark paper published in 1912 he described his work and suggested that a number of diseases—scurvy, pellagra, rickets—were, like beriberi, deficiency diseases and that their prevention depended on a class of thiamine-like substances that he named vitamines, from *vita*,

Latin for life, and amino, a nitrogen radical found in thiamine. With the later discovery that not all "vitamines" contained the amino group, the "e" was dropped from the word. Funk's work in London had also indicated the existence of a second such substance, nicotinic acid (later called niacin), but he did not pursue it. His 1912 paper, both a summary and a seminal work, marked the beginning of a revolution in biochemistry and nutritional science. In 1913 he was appointed head of the biochemistry department at the Research Institute of the Cancer Hospital in London. Two years later he came to the United States and joined the research staff of the Cornell Medical College. From 1921 to 1923 he was an associate in biochemistry in the College of Physicians and Surgeons of Columbia University, acquiring U.S. citizenship in 1920. He returned to Poland in 1923 as head of the biochemistry department of the State School of Hygiene. There and in a private laboratory in Paris from 1928 to 1935 he carried on research on the chemistry of hormones, and on returning to the United States in 1936 became a consultant to the U.S. Vitamin & Pharmaceutical Corporation, for which he worked to develop synthetic vitamins and commercial vitamin concentrates. He also engaged in research on cancer, seeking chemical approaches to its cause and treatment in the laboratories of his own Funk Foundation for Medical Research, which he founded in 1940. Funk died in Albany, New York, on November 19, 1967.

Funk, Isaac Kauffman (1839–1912), publisher and editor. Born in Clifton, Ohio, on September 10, 1839, Funk graduated from Wittenberg College in 1860 and remained there for an additional year of theological studies. He was ordained a Lutheran minister in 1861 and over the next 11 years held pastorates in Indiana, Ohio, and lastly in Brooklyn, New York. On leaving the pulpit in 1872 he traveled extensively through Europe and the Middle East, later returning to Pittsburgh to join the editorial staff of the *Christian Radical*. In 1876 he moved to New York City and went into business for himself; his idea of circulating books, articles, and other items of use to ministers grew into the *Metropolitan Pulpit*, later known as the *Complete Preacher*, then as the *Preacher and Homiletic Monthly*, and from 1885 as the *Homiletic Review*. In 1877 Funk joined with a former classmate, Adam Willis Wagnalls, in forming I. K. Funk and Company, which undertook the publication of cheap editions of standard works of reference and commentary as well as books of general interest; this "Standard Series" eventually ran to 79 titles. In 1880 Funk began publishing a Prohibition party organ, the *Voice*, which quickly attained a large circulation, and in 1890 he launched one of his most successful ventures, the weekly *Literary Digest*, which reprinted comment and opinion from periodicals around the country. The firm became the Funk & Wagnalls Company in 1891 and two years later completed work on its most important project, the *Standard Dictionary of the English Language*, over which Funk had maintained close supervision. Between 1901 and 1906 the firm also published the 12-volume *Jewish Encyclopedia*. Funk was a strong advocate of spelling reform and in his later years published a number of works on psychic phenomena, including *The Next Step in Evolution*, 1902, and *The Psychic Riddle*, 1907. He died in Montclair, New Jersey, on April 4, 1912. *Literary Digest* continued to appear until 1937, when it failed in the wake of a disastrous attempt to undertake a public-opinion poll to predict the outcome of the 1936 presidential election. The brainchild of Funk's son, Wilfred John Funk, who had only recently become editor, the poll showed Alfred M. Landon a decisive victor over President Franklin D. Roosevelt; in November Landon won only eight electoral votes in a Roosevelt landslide.

Funston, Frederick (1865–1917), soldier. Born in New Carlisle, Ohio, on November 9, 1865, Funston early moved with his family to Iola, Kansas. A restless youth, he worked at various jobs, attended the University of Kansas for a little more than two years, and in the early 1890s found employment as a special agent for the Department of Agriculture, for which he took part in an expedition to Death Valley in 1891 and later made a canoe trip down 1500 perilous miles of the Yukon River. Soon after the outbreak of the Cuban insurrection against Spain in 1895 he offered his services to the Cuban cause and, although he had no qualifications for such a post, was commissioned a captain of artillery. He arrived in Cuba in mid-1896 and for 18 months served creditably in various guerrilla operations, rising to the rank of lieutenant colonel. He returned to the United States in 1898 and upon the U.S. declaration of war against Spain a short time later was given command of the 20th Kansas regiment. Sent to the Philippines, he arrived too late to see action against the Spanish but was quickly thrown into the campaign against the Philippine independence forces led by Emilio Aguinaldo. He distinguished himself at the battle of Calumpit, winning a Medal of Honor and promotion to brigadier general of volunteers, but by early 1901, denied a commission in the regular army, he was scheduled for mustering out along with the rest of the volunteers. Early in March 1901 he learned from captured letters the whereabouts of Aguinaldo's secret headquarters; enlisting a number of pro-U.S. Filipinos disguised as rebel recruits, a defected rebel for a guide, and six U.S. soldiers who posed as prisoners, he led his small raiding party by boat to a beach in northern Luzon and then through thick jungle to the rebel headquarters at Palanan; on March 23 Aguinaldo was taken by surprise and placed under arrest. Funston was promptly transferred to the regular army as a brigadier general. Later placed in command of the Department of California, he was in charge of the early phases of emergency military administration and rescue work following the San Francisco earthquake in 1906. In 1914 he commanded the U.S. forces occupying Veracruz, Mexico, and

served as military governor of the city; later in the year, promoted to major general, he commanded troops on the Mexican border. He was still in that post when, while Gen. John J. Pershing was pursuing Pancho Villa across the border, he died in San Antonio, Texas, on February 19, 1917. His *Memories of Two Wars: Cuban and Philippine Experiences* had appeared in 1911.

Furman, Richard (1755–1825), religious leader and educator. Born in Esopus, New York, on October 9, 1755, Furman grew up near Charleston, South Carolina, and received little if any formal education. In 1770 he underwent a religious conversion and joined the Baptist church; four years later, already an established and popular preacher, he was ordained. He was forced into hiding during the Revolution because of his strong colonial sympathies. After the war he quickly became the leading figure among South Carolina Baptists and in 1787 became pastor of the church in Charleston. Three years later he was a member of the South Carolina constitutional convention. He was long an advocate of the need for a Baptist college in the South. Although he began active efforts in behalf of such a school in 1787, it was not until more than a year after his death that an academy was finally opened, at Edgefield; afterward it became Furman University and moved to Greenville. He was elected first president of the Baptist Triennial Convention organized in Philadelphia in 1814; at the second meeting three years later he was reelected. He met strong opposition to his desire to establish a centralized authority for the Baptist church and his efforts to that end were long thwarted; when, however, the Baptist State Convention in South Carolina was finally formed in 1821 he became its first president. Until his death on August 25, 1825, in Charleston, Furman exercised great influence in both religious and secular matters throughout the South.

Furness, Horace Howard (1833–1912), scholar and editor. Born in Philadelphia on November 2, 1833, Furness graduated from Harvard in 1854 and after a period of travel in Europe and the Middle East returned to Philadelphia and took up the study of law. He was admitted to the bar in 1859; however, he practiced very little, his deafness (which also kept him out of the Civil War) rendering it difficult and his comfortable means making it unnecessary. Through the Civil War he served as an agent of the U.S. Sanitary Commission and from 1866 devoted himself largely to the study of Shakespeare, an enthusiasm that dated from his childhood attendance at Fanny Kemble's public readings and from the influence of Francis J. Child at Harvard. His collection of Shakespeare editions and commentary grew to major proportions and in 1871 he issued his own variorum edition of *Romeo and Juliet*. Encouraged by the reception given the work, he continued his New Variorum editions; *Macbeth* appeared in 1873 and was followed by *Hamlet*, 1877; *King Lear*, 1880; *Othello*, 1886; *The Merchant of Venice*, 1888; *As*

You Like It, 1890; *The Tempest*, 1892; *A Mid-summer Night's Dream*, 1895; *The Winter's Tale*, 1898; *Much Ado About Nothing*, 1899; *Twelfth Night*, 1901; *Love's Labour's Lost*, 1904; *Antony and Cleopatra*, 1907; and *Cymbeline*, 1913. Conservative in his methods—after *King Lear* he used the First Folio text exclusively—Furness assembled the best of the huge body of textual and critical comment and annotations, informed the whole with his own clear, scholarly, and witty judgments, and brought to his self-imposed and formidable task a remarkable dedication. He often gave public readings of Shakespeare, eliciting high praise from such experts as Edwin Booth, and was widely known and loved as a man of great gentleness and generosity; Walt Whitman was among his closest friends, as Ralph Waldo Emerson had been among his father's. His wife, Helen Kate Rogers Furness (1837–1883), compiled *A Concordance to the Poems of Shakespeare*, 1874, and their son, Horace Howard Furness (1865–1930), worked with his father and later carried on the elder man's work. Furness died in Wallingford, near Philadelphia, Pennsylvania, on August 13, 1912.

Furry, Elda, *see* Hopper, Hedda

Furuseth, Andrew (1854–1938), labor leader and reformer. Born on March 12, 1854, near Romsdal, Hedmark, Norway, Anders Andreassen later took his surname from the cottage in which he was born. He left home early and for several years worked as a farmhand and attended school sporadically. About 1870 he made his way to Christiania (now Oslo) and three years later went to sea. Under various flags he sailed all over the world and suffered the abominable food and accommodations, low pay, harsh discipline, and the unjust laws that were the common lot of sailors at the time. In 1880 he began spending long periods ashore on the West Coast; he was an early and active promoter of unionism among seamen and in 1887 was elected secretary of the Sailors' Union of the Pacific. By 1891 he had given up the sea entirely to devote himself to organization, and in 1894 he went to Washington, D.C., to lobby for remedial legislation. During the 1890s he was closely associated with Samuel Gompers and the American Federation of Labor (AFL). Largely as a result of his efforts, laws mitigating some conditions were passed in 1895 and 1898, but it was not until 1915 that real progress was made in the passage of the La Follette Seaman's Act (Furuseth Act), which, among other provisions, abolished prison sentences for desertion of sailors in the merchant marine. From 1908 until his death Furuseth was president of the International Seamen's Union and his efforts on behalf of its members were tireless and ceaseless; he led an almost monastic life and accepted in salary only the union-scale wage for able-bodied seamen. Many of the reforms in legal status, working conditions, and wages that he won profoundly affected not only U.S. seamen but also those of other maritime nations, which were forced to follow suit in order to remain competitive in the market for labor. He contributed to the labor movement in general through his influence in bringing about the passage of the Norris–La Guardia Anti-Injunction Act of 1932. Furuseth died in Washington, D.C., on January 22, 1938; after his body had lain in state at the Department of Labor, the first such honor accorded a labor leader, his ashes were, by his wish, scattered in mid-Atlantic.

G

Gable, Clark (1901–1960), actor. Born on February 1, 1901, in Cadiz, Ohio, William Clark Gable grew up there and in nearby Hopedale. He worked at a variety of jobs in his youth, from oilfield tool dresser to telephone repairman, but from 1918, when he spent a period as a callboy with a stock company in Akron, his ambitions centered on the stage. The next year he worked briefly in a New York City theater, but it was not until 1924, when he married a dramatics teacher in Portland, Oregon, that he began to win small roles in minor productions. In Hollywood that year he also appeared in his first movie, a silent with Pola Negri. He finally made his Broadway debut in *Machinal* in 1928 and received good reviews; two years later, with the help of Lionel Barrymore, he made a screen test that brought him a part in *The Painted Desert*, 1931, his first talkie. At a time when the great romantic heroes of the silent era were disappearing from the screen with the advent of sound, a few producers overlooked doubts about Gable's potential appeal—his outsized ears worried many—and he appeared in a rapid succession of movies, including *Hell Divers*, 1931; *Susan Lennox—Her Fall and Rise*, 1931; *Possessed*, 1931; *Red Dust*, 1932; *No Man of Her Own*, 1932; and *Night Flight*, 1933. His rugged masculinity in roles ranging from that of the redeemable villain to the lighthearted adventurer proved to have great box-office appeal to both men and women, and in 1934, in an unexpected display of versatility, he played the lead in the light comedy *It Happened One Night* and won an Academy Award; he was thereafter firmly established as Hollywood's top romantic star and enjoyed a popularity that grew over the years into something like reverence for the acknowledged "king of the movies." Subsequent major films in which he starred included *Manhattan Melodrama*, 1934; *China Seas*, 1935; *Mutiny on the Bounty*, 1935; *San Francisco*, 1936; *Saratoga*, 1937; *Gone With the Wind*, 1939 (his casting as Rhett Butler was a foregone conclusion; it was clear that the public would accept no substitute); *Boom Town*, 1940; and *They Met in Bombay*, 1941. From 1942 to 1945 Gable served in the Army Air Force, winning a Distinguished Flying Cross and an Air Medal. Among his later movies were *Command Decision*, 1948; *Mogambo*, 1953; *The Tall Men*, 1955; *Run Silent, Run Deep*, 1958; *Teacher's Pet*, 1958; and his last, Arthur Miller's *The Misfits* with Marilyn Monroe, 1961. Gable died in Hollywood on November 16, 1960, shortly after completing the film.

Gadsden, James (1788–1858), soldier, businessman, and diplomat. Born in Charleston, South Carolina, on May 15, 1788, Gadsden graduated from Yale in 1806 and entered business in his native city. Within a few years he joined the army and after serving through the War of 1812 as a lieutenant became an aide to Gen. Andrew Jackson in the first period of the Seminole Wars in Florida. It was Gadsden who discovered the evidence that led to Jackson's executing the British traders Robert Ambrister and Alexander Arbuthnot in 1818. Carrying out fortification and inspection duties throughout the Gulf region, he rose to colonel in 1820 and served briefly as acting adjutant general before resigning in 1822. Having settled in Florida, he was appointed by President James Monroe in 1823 to supervise the relocation of the Seminole to reservations in southern Florida. He remained active in the development of the region for several years, in 1832 negotiating a treaty for the removal of the Seminole to the West and in 1834–1835 serving in the second Seminole War when some of the tribesmen refused to go. In 1839 he gave up his plantation and returned to Charleston and the next year was elected president of the Louisville, Cincinnati & Charleston Railroad, which in 1842 became the South Carolina Railroad Company. He held the position for ten years, during which time he actively but unsuccessfully promoted his idea of uniting small Southern railroads into a great sectional system and linking it with the West by a transcontinental line along a southern route. He continued to advocate the southern route privately from 1850 and finally succeeded in enlisting the support of Jefferson Davis, who as secretary of war secured Gadsden's appointment as minister to Mexico in 1853. In Mexico he immediately began negotiating with President Antonio López de Santa Anna for the purchase of a tract of land south of the Gila River, which had been recognized as Mexican territory in the 1848 Treaty of Guadalupe Hidalgo. Authorized to spend up to $50 million to acquire the land necessary for the southern route to California, Gadsden at last concluded a treaty ceding some 19 million acres to the United States in return for $15 million and the settlement of certain minor claims and disputes. The treaty was hotly debated in the Senate, Northern representatives fearing the possible extension of slavery to the new territory; the much modified version of the treaty finally approved in 1854 provided $10 million for a smaller area—the Gadsden Purchase —of a little less than 30,000 square miles, most of it comprising what is now the southern quarter of Arizona and New Mexico. Gadsden returned to Charleston, South Carolina, in 1856. He died there on December 26, 1858.

Galbraith, John Kenneth (1908–   ), economist. Born in Iona Station, Ontario, on October 15, 1908, Galbraith graduated from the University of Toronto in 1931 and then studied at the University of California, where he took his Ph.D. in 1934. From that year until 1939 he was an instructor and tutor at Harvard and from 1939 to 1941 an assistant professor of economics at Princeton. In 1941 he joined the Office of Price Administration (OPA) as director of price controls and the next year became deputy administrator of the office, serving until 1943. For the next five years he was a member of the editorial board of *Fortune* magazine and in 1945 directed the U.S. Strategic Bombing Survey in Germany and Japan; he also served as director of the state department's Office of Economic Security Policy in 1946 and held numerous advisory posts in government. In 1948 he returned to Harvard as a lecturer and the following year became professor of economics, remaining at Harvard until 1960. In 1952 Galbraith published *American Capitalism: The Concept of Countervailing Power*, in which he analyzed the effects of the creation of huge concentrations of capital and maintained that the principal result was the spontaneous development of opposing groups—labor unions, associations of competing companies, consumer organizations—to wield a "countervailing power" and maintain an economic equilibrium. In *The Great Crash: 1929*, published in 1955, he recounted with characteristic wit the last days of the boom of the 1920s. In *The Affluent Society*, 1958, he decried the American economy's overemphasis on consumer goods, the demand for many of which was artificially created by advertising, and called for greater allocations of wealth to public purposes; it reached a remarkably wide audience for a work of its kind. In 1961 Galbraith was appointed ambassador to India by President John F. Kennedy and he served until 1963, returning then to Harvard, where he became the Paul M. Warburg Professor of Economics. In 1967 he was elected chairman of the Americans for Democratic Action (ADA). In the same year he published *The New Industrial State*, in which he traced the historical shift of economic power from landowners to capitalists to the "technostructure," a managerial and technical elite that he saw as common to all industrial nations East and West. Later books included *The Triumph*, 1968; *How to Control the Military*, 1969; *Ambassador's Journal*, 1969; and *Economics, Peace and Laughter*, 1971.

Gall (1840?–1894), Indian leader. Born about 1840 on the Moreau River in South Dakota, Gall was a Hunkpapa Sioux. His name was originally Pizi and he later acquired his sobriquet when, orphaned and hungry, he attempted to eat the gall of a game animal belonging to another. As he grew into manhood he became noted as a warrior and was informally adopted by Sitting Bull. He was prominent in the battles and skirmishes of Red Cloud's War that accompanied construction of the Powder River Army road and the three forts associated with it along the old Bozeman Trail in 1866–1867, and he spoke out furiously against the treaty negotiated at Fort Laramie in April 1868, which, while conceding the Powder River region to the Indians, provided for tribal reservations for the various Plains tribes. Although he was assigned to the Sioux reservation in Dakota Territory, Gall refused to adopt the government's "civilizing" program of homestead farming and instead accompanied Sitting Bull to the great encampment in Montana on the Little Bighorn River in 1876. By that time he was acknowledged as Sitting Bull's chief lieutenant. When the cavalry force of Col. George A. Custer attacked the camp on June 25, Gall, as war chief, led the counterattack that drove the troops under Maj. Marcus A. Reno back and pinned them down in the hills; then, after joining Crazy Horse in surrounding and annihilating Custer's men, he returned to again attack Reno, who, however, was able to escape the next day on the approach of Gen. Alfred H. Terry's main force. Gall remained with Sitting Bull through the retreat northward into Canada, but in 1880 returned and early the next year surrendered with 300 followers and was placed on the Standing Rock reservation. There he was befriended by James McLaughlin, the resident Indian agent, and gradually reconciled himself to white rule, working thereafter to persuade other Indians to surrender and in 1889 becoming a judge of the Court of Indian Offenses. In opposition to Sitting Bull, he took no part in the final Sioux uprising of 1890. Gall died on December 5, 1894, on Oak Creek, South Dakota.

Gallatin, Albert (1761–1849), public official and diplomat. Born on January 29, 1761, in Geneva, Switzerland, Abraham Alfonse Albert Gallatin grew up with all the advantages of wealth and social position in that city. Resisting the claims of tradition, however, he sailed for America, arriving in Massachusetts in 1780. After a brief and unsuccessful attempt to become a businessman and a short time spent teaching French at Harvard, he acquired land in western Pennsylvania and moved there in 1784. A cultured and well-educated man whose sympathies were nonetheless republican, he became an outstanding figure in the backwoods region; by 1790 he had been elected to the state legislature, where he served for two more terms. He rapidly gained a reputation for integrity and great ability, particularly in the field of government finance. His election to the Senate in 1793 was disallowed because of the length-of-citizenship requirement, but in 1795 he was elected to the House of Representatives, where he remained for six years. In that period he became leader of the House Republicans and maintained a constant pressure on the Federalist administration, especially on Secretary of the Treasury Oliver Wolcott, Jr., from whom he demanded fiscal accountability to the House. He brought about the creation of the Committee on Finance (now the Committee on Ways and Means) and upheld the power of the House to "veto" treaties by withholding appropriations. His constant opposition to naval appropriations which were intended in the main for declared or undeclared war with France, made him a special target for Federalist hatred; he was denounced as a French agent, and the Sedition Act of 1798 was, in the opinion of Thomas Jefferson, aimed in particular at Gallatin. With the election of Jefferson to the presidency, Gallatin became secretary of the treasury; during 13 years in that post he sought constantly to reduce the public debt and, even with the expense of the Louisiana Purchase and of tribute to Barbary pirates, made progress to that end, only to have his efforts nullified by increasing troubles with England that resulted finally in the War of 1812. In 1813 he was sent to arrange for mediation of the dispute by Russia; Great Britain refused to agree to the plan, but offered in the next year to negotiate directly. Gallatin resigned his cabinet post to head the peace commission in the treaty talks. The successful conclusion of the Treaty of Ghent was largely his work. For the next seven years he remained in France as U.S. minister, declining an offer to resume his position in the Treasury. Soon after his return in 1823 he accepted the vice-presidential nomination of the Republicans but was induced to withdraw by Martin Van Buren and retired to his Pennsylvania home. In 1826 President John Quincy Adams appointed him minister to England and he served until the following year. He then concerned himself with private interests; settling in New York City, he became president of the National (later Gallatin) Bank and developed an interest in ethnology. In 1836 he published a treatise on the American Indian tribes and in 1842 founded the American Ethnological Society. He died on August 12, 1849, in Astoria, Long Island, New York.

Gallaudet, Thomas Hopkins (1787–1851), educator. Born in Philadelphia on December 10, 1787, Gallaudet graduated from Yale in 1805 and for a time studied law and literature and was a tutor at Yale. For a few years he engaged in business and then, in 1812, entered Andover Theological Seminary. Although he graduated in 1814, ill health kept him from a career in the ministry. His efforts to teach a few words to a deaf-mute child of his acquaintance led to his being sent by her father and others on a trip to Europe to study formal methods for instructing deaf-mutes. In Paris he studied for several months in the Institut Royal des Sourds-Muets and returned in 1816, bringing with him a brilliant young teacher from the school, Laurent Clerc. After raising money in various quarters he opened a free school for deaf-mutes in Hartford, Connecticut, in 1817; the Connecticut (later American) Asylum was the first such school in the country and probably the first special school to receive state aid. As principal until his retirement in 1830 he gradually enlarged the school, in part with a land grant made by Congress for its support, and trained other teachers who subsequently established schools elewhere in the country. In poor health much of the time, especially after his retirement, he remained none-

theless active in promoting educational opportunities for women and for Negroes and in furthering manual training, the founding of normal schools, and other progressive undertakings. Gallaudet died in Hartford, Connecticut on September 10, 1851. His son, Edward Miner Gallaudet (1837–1917), later established with Amos Kendall the Columbia Institution for the Deaf and Dumb in Washington, D.C., that eventually became Gallaudet College, named for Thomas Gallaudet.

Galloway, Joseph (1731?–1803), lawyer and colonial official. Born in Anne Arundel County, Maryland, about 1731, Galloway studied law in Philadelphia; he began practice in 1747 and before he was twenty was arguing cases before the supreme court of the province. In 1756 he was elected to the Pennsylvania assembly, remaining until 1764, when, along with Benjamin Franklin, he was defeated for reelection because of his stand against a larger Western Pennsylvania representation in the State legislature. Returned to his seat the following year, he was chosen for the powerful office of speaker in 1766 and retained it until 1775. In the years of increasing tension before the Revolution broke out Galloway sought tirelessly for means of reconciling the colonies and Great Britain. While he agreed with the radicals on many points, particularly the illegality of Parliamentary taxation, he upheld the lawful rule of England and refused to consider any but peaceable solutions. Elected a delegate to the First Continental Congress in 1774, he presented to it a "plan of a proposed Union between Great Britain and the Colonies" under which legislative authority over the colonies would be held jointly by Parliament and a colonial legislature of delegates elected by the several assemblies, and in which executive authority would be vested in a Crown-appointed president general. The plan received much favorable comment and was rejected by the Congress by but a single vote; subsequently, however, all references to it were expunged from official records. With the radicals in the ascendant, Galloway refused to attend the Second Continental Congress and outspokenly denounced the move for independence. He fled Philadelphia but returned in September 1777 with Gen. Sir William Howe's army of occupation and served as civil administrator of the city until it was retaken by Continental troops in 1778. He then went to England, where he continued to seek reconciliation and wrote a number of pamphlets criticizing the conduct of the war. On the conclusion of peace his American properties were confiscated and his later requests for permission to return to the United States were denied. Galloway died in England on August 29, 1803.

Gallup, George Horace (1901–   ), statistician and public-opinion analyst. Born on November 18, 1901, in Jefferson, Iowa, Gallup earned his B.A. in 1923, his M.A. in 1925, and his Ph.D. in 1928 from the State University of Iowa. He was head of the department of journalism at Drake University from 1929 to 1931 and professor of advertising and journalism at Northwestern University during 1931–1932; he then became director of research for the Young and Rubicam advertising agency in New York City in 1932. He was made a vice-president of the agency in 1937 and held that position until 1947, also teaching journalism at Columbia University in 1935–1937. He founded the American Institute of Public Opinion in 1935 at Princeton, New Jersey, and originated there the Gallup Polls, statistical surveys of public reactions to nearly every conceivable issue. The polls concentrated mainly on opinions concerning current events and radio and television programming and were published regularly in hundreds of newspapers; they attracted great attention, particularly during presidential elections. (In the 1948 campaign, Gallup polls indicated a victory for Thomas E. Dewey, who lost to Harry S. Truman.) Among other things, the polls seemed to show that the quality of the mass media was held to a low level by business and financial pressures, and, in addition, that educated and uneducated Americans alike seemed to be satisfied with the situation. With a properly educated audience, he felt, the selection of material for mass consumption would ultimately be made by others than profiteers. A British Institute of Public Opinion was founded in 1936 by Gallup and in 1947 he organized and became president of the International Institutes of Public Opinion. Through various other business associations Gallup carried on market research and advertising activities. He wrote, among other books, *Public Opinion in a Democracy*, 1939; *The Pulse of Democracy*, 1940; and *A Guide to Public Opinion Polls*, 1944.

Gamow, George (1904–1968), physicist and author. Born on March 4, 1904, in Odessa, Russia, Gamow took his Ph.D. from the University of Leningrad in 1928 and pursued further studies in nuclear physics at Göttingen, with Niels Bohr at the University of Copenhagen's Institute of Theoretical Physics in 1928–1929 and 1930–1931, and at Cambridge University. In 1931 he was appointed master in research at the Academy of Sciences in Leningrad. He lectured often at other universities in Europe and in 1934, after a summer at the University of Michigan, he established permanent residence in the United States and became a professor of theoretical physics at The George Washington University. He became a U.S. citizen in 1940. Gamow's early researches had contributed greatly to an understanding of the processes of natural radioactivity by means of a quantum-mechanical approach developed about 1928; later he turned his attention to astrophysics, in particular the problems of energy production in stars and of the original creation of the various elements in the universe. To the study of stellar energy he contributed a highly fruitful suggestion, later elaborated by Hans Bethe and by himself in collaboration with Edward Teller and others, that thermonuclear reactions were central to the energy-production processes; in his study of the

creation of elements he worked out in great detail the nuclear processes whereby the heavy elements could have been produced by reactions among the lighter ones following the explosion of a primeval "atom," a conception of cosmic creation commonly termed the "big bang" theory. He also made contributions to other fields, notably his early suggestion of the existence of a genetic code composed of nucleic acid units, but his principal fame rested on a large number of highly popular books in which he explained to his large lay audience, with great wit, charm, and facility, many of the most abstruse concepts of modern science. Among the best-known of his books were *Mr. Tompkins in Wonderland*, 1939, *Mr. Tompkins Explores the Atom*, 1944, and many others concerning the scientific curiosity of that remarkable bank clerk: *The Birth and Death of the Sun*, 1940; *Biography of the Earth*, 1941; *Atomic Energy in Cosmic and Human Life*, 1946; *One, Two, Three . . . Infinity*, 1947; *Creation of the Universe*, 1952; *Matter, Earth, and Sky*, 1958; *Biography of Physics*, 1961; *Gravity*, 1962; *A Planet Called Earth*, 1963; *A Star Called the Sun*, 1964; and *Thirty Years That Shook Physics: The Story of Quantum Theory*, 1966. His books for nontechnical readers won him the 1956 Kalinga Award from the United Nations Educational, Scientific, and Cultural Organization (UNESCO). In that same year he moved to the University of Colorado, where he remained as professor of physics until his death in Boulder, Colorado, on August 19, 1968. *My World Line: An Informal Autobiography* appeared in 1970.

Gannett, Henry (1846–1914), geographer. Born on August 24, 1846, in Bath, Maine, Gannett graduated from the Lawrence Scientific School at Harvard in 1869 and after a brief period with the Harvard Observatory joined the survey staff of Ferdinand V. Hayden as a topographer. On several of Hayden's expeditions to Colorado, Wyoming, and other parts of the West he made the preliminary maps of several previously uncharted areas and contributed a great many place names. In 1882 he was appointed chief geographer of the U.S. Geological Survey, established three years earlier and then under the direction of John Wesley Powell. In that position he organized the various Western field expeditions of the Survey, supervised the preparation of its detailed maps, and served as geographer for the 10th, 11th, and 12th U.S. censuses, to which he contributed much in the way of regional and statistical organization. He also aided in censuses of the Philippines, Cuba, and Puerto Rico. At his urging the U.S. Geographic Board (later the U.S. Board on Geographical Names, then the Board on Geographic Names) was established in 1890 and under his chairmanship until 1910 sought to clarify and regularize place names throughout the country; he himself compiled gazetteers of several states, Puerto Rico, and Cuba. Gannett was a founder of the National Geographic Society in 1888, later serving as its president, and of the Geological

Society of America and of the Association of American Geographers. He was deeply interested in promoting the spread of geographical knowledge and among his writings, most of which were published under the auspices of the Geological Survey, were *Commercial Geography*, 1905, with C. L. Garrison and E. J. Houston, and *Topographic Maps of the United States Showing Physiographic Types*, 1907. Gannett died in Washington, D.C., on November 5, 1914.

Garand, John Cantius (1888–1974), inventor. Born on January 1, 1888, in St. Rémi, Quebec, Garand grew up there and in rural Connecticut. He attended school until he was twelve and then went to work in a textile mill, where he gradually worked his way up to machinist. He later found a position in a tool factory in Providence, Rhode Island, and in his spare time indulged his enthusiasm for guns and target shooting. In 1917, prompted by the reported difficulty the army was experiencing in developing a light machine gun, he took up the problem and on submitting a design to the War Department was given a position in the U.S. Bureau of Standards to perfect it. His first model was built in 1919, too late for use in World War I, but in that year he was appointed a consulting engineer at the U.S. Armory in Springfield, Massachusetts, to work on a semiautomatic infantry rifle. It took 15 years to produce an acceptable model incorporating Garand's basic mechanism, in which a portion of the expanding propellant gas drove a piston that in turn operated the bolt, automatically ejecting the spent shell, cocking the hammer, and reloading the chamber. Weight was the principal problem, but finally in 1934 Garand patented a rifle weighing just over nine pounds that was simply constructed and easy to maintain and fired a clip of eight .276-caliber rounds. Adopted by the army in 1936, modified to use .30-caliber ammunition, and designated the M-1, the Garand rifle was quickly put into mass production to replace the 30-year-old Springfield repeater. The M-1 was highly praised by military commanders, particularly during World War II, when it was credited with giving the U.S. infantry a great advantage. The M-1 remained the basic shoulder weapon of U.S. forces until it was gradually replaced following the appearance of the lighter, fully automatic M-14 in 1957. Garand himself received no royalties from his work, assigning all his patents freely to the government; widely honored, he remained at the Springfield Armory as a consultant until his retirement in 1953. He died in Springfield on February 16, 1974.

Garbo, Greta (1905–   ), actress. Born in Stockholm, Sweden, on September 18, 1905, Greta Lovisa Gustafsson grew up in modest circumstances and on leaving school at fourteen held various jobs. While working as a department-store clerk she met Erik Petschler, a motion-picture director who gave her a small part in *Peter the Tramp* in 1922. From 1922 to 1924 she studied in the Royal Dramatic Theatre School in Stockholm

and in 1924 played a major role in *The Story of Gösta Berling*; the film's director, Mauritz Stiller, gave her the name Garbo and secured for her a contract with Metro-Goldwyn-Mayer in Hollywood in 1925, promising that she would become the world's greatest actress. She remained with MGM for 16 years and made 24 films, beginning with *The Torrent*, 1926; later silent films, including *Flesh and the Devil*, 1927, *Love*, 1927, *Wild Orchids*, 1929, and *The Kiss*, 1929, quickly established her as a star who captivated audiences with her subtle and mysterious allure. Unlike many stars of the silent movies—and unlike her favorite leading man, John Gilbert—she more than successfully made the transition to sound film with *Anna Christie*, 1930, in which her first spoken words on the screen revealed a low, husky voice to match her beauty. Subsequent movies, among them *Susan Lennox—Her Fall and Rise*, 1931; *Mata Hari*, 1931, *Grand Hotel*, 1932, *As You Desire Me*, 1932; *Queen Christina*, 1933; *Anna Karenina*, 1935; *Camille*, 1937; and *Conquest*, 1937, won her a following that was almost a cult, and in *Ninotchka*, 1939, she displayed an unexpected gift for comedy. Her last film, *Two-Faced Woman*, 1941, was less than successful; Garbo retired after its release and became a near-recluse, living mostly in New York City, traveling often under an assumed name, and refusing interviews or publicity of any kind. She became a U.S. citizen in 1951. Her insistence on complete privacy recalled a famous line from one of her films, "I want to be alone," and helped make her literally a legend in her own time. Her films, frequently revived, became classics and she remained for many the epitome of unfathomable glamor.

Garden, Alexander (1730?–1791), physician and naturalist. Born in Aberdeenshire, Scotland, about 1730, Garden graduated with a medical degree from Marischal College, Aberdeen, in 1753 and soon afterward sailed to America, settling in Charleston, South Carolina. There he carried on a large medical practice and continued an early interest in natural history. Encounters with Cadwallader Colden, who introduced him to the work of Carolus Linnaeus, and with John Bartram fired his enthusiasm for field work and led to long and extensive correspondences with them and with other scientists in America and Europe. His travels and collecting expeditions in the South were highly fruitful and he sent to his various correspondents specimens of many new and unusual plants and animals, including salamanders unique to eastern American swamps and the electric eel. He also contributed to the correct classification of a number of American plants. Although many European contemporaries were slow to acknowledge his work, he was elected, at the insistence of Linnaeus, to the Royal Society of Uppsala in 1763 and ten years later became a fellow of the Royal Society of London. Garden was a Loyalist during the Revolution and in 1782 was stripped of his property and banished. He settled in London and traveled extensively in Europe in an effort to restore his health, meanwhile receiving numerous honors. He served as vice-president of the Royal Society of London until his death in London on April 15, 1791. The gardenia was named in his honor by John Ellis, an English botanist and one of Garden's earliest correspondents.

Garden, Mary (1874–1967), singer. Born on February 20, 1874, in Aberdeen, Scotland, Miss Garden came to the United States with her parents when she was six and lived in Chicopee, Massachusetts, and Hartford, Connecticut, before settling in Chicago. She began early studying the violin and the piano and receiving voice lessons, and in 1895 she traveled to Paris to continue her voice training. A soprano, she made her public debut in 1900 in Gustave Charpentier's *Louise* at the Opéra-Comique in Paris and subsequently sang in *La Traviata* and other operas. In 1902 she was chosen by Claude Debussy to sing the female lead in the premiere of his *Pelléas et Mélisande* and her interpretation remained her most famous. Others among her major roles were those in *Le Jongleur de Notre-Dame*, after Jules Massenet had rewritten the tenor part for her; in Massenet's *Thaïs*, in which she made her New York debut in 1907; and in Richard Strauss's *Salomé*. Acclaimed not only for her brilliant and highly individual singing but also for her remarkable dramatic ability in appearances throughout Europe and in London and New York City, she joined the Chicago Civic Opera in 1910 and starred with it until 1931, serving also as general director of the Chicago Opera Association in 1921–1922. She retired from the operatic stage in 1934 but remained active for 20 years in musical circles, making numerous national lectures and recital tours and serving as an audition judge for the National Arts Foundation. Her autobiography, *Mary Garden's Story*, written with Louis Biancolli, appeared in 1951. Miss Garden died in Aberdeen, Scotland, on January 3, 1967.

Gardner, Erle Stanley (1889–1970), lawyer and author. Born on July 17, 1889, in Malden, Massachusetts, Gardner moved with his family to California as a child and, living in one mining town after another, acquired a high-school education. After a short time as a professional boxer he began studying law on his own and in various law offices and in 1911 was admitted to the bar. He practiced in Oxnard and Ventura, California, for several years with considerable courtroom success, becoming known for his quick mind and forensic agility. In the early 1920s he developed an interest in writing and was soon sending mountains of stories to *Black Mask* and other pulp detective-fiction magazines. In 1933 he published his first novel, *The Case of the Velvet Claws*, which featured Perry Mason, a brilliant and unconventional lawyer-detective; stories and Perry Mason books continued to appear at a prodigious rate that increased after 1938, when Gardner gave up regular law practice. The Mason books, suspenseful and fast-paced, were written to

a formula, early established, that involved clashes with police and the district attorney, often the near-disbarment of Mason, and a final courtroom scene in which a dazzling legal maneuver proved the innocence of Mason's client. In the 80 or more Perry Mason novels that Gardner eventually produced, only one legal error was ever detected; many turned on points of law that were highly obscure but astonishingly accurate, and one, *The Case of the Curious Bride*, 1934, helped an Arizona prosecutor out of what had seemed an impasse until he read the book. The character of Perry Mason later inspired several movies and extremely popular radio and television series. Working full time, Gardner dictated his books to a staff of secretaries and turned out well over a million words a year. Several series of mystery stories appeared under pseudonyms, notably "A. A. Fair," and Gardner's lifetime output was in excess of 150 books and uncounted stories. Sales of his books, most of which remained in print for decades, reached 143 million copies in English-language editions by the early 1960s and continued to grow, and he was the most widely translated author in the world. Throughout his career he remained a close student of the law and was a noted authority on criminalistics and penology; in 1948, with *Argosy* magazine, he founded The Court of Last Resort, an organization for the aid of persons believed to have been wrongfully convicted of crimes. Gardner was an active sportsman, explorer, and amateur archaeologist and also wrote a number of travel books. He died in Temecula, California, on March 11, 1970.

Gardner, Isabella Stewart (1840–1924), socialite and art collector. Born in New York City on April 14, 1840, Miss Stewart was educated privately and in a Paris finishing school. In 1860 she married John L. Gardner, a businessman who belonged to a prominent and well-established Boston family, and went to live in his city, which she adopted as her own. Her household was a quiet one until the 1870s, when she began arranging social affairs that soon dazzled and occasionally titillated conservative Boston. A brilliant and unconventional woman, she attracted and was attracted by musicians, artists, actors, and interesting people of all kinds, and she came close to scandalizing Boston society by attending boxing exhibitions by John L. Sullivan and Gentleman Jim Corbett. In music she became known as a patroness of the Boston Symphony and of countless students, for whom she once arranged a private recital by Ignace Paderewski. She also developed a deep interest in art; often advised by her close friend Bernard Berenson, she began collecting paintings and objets d'art and with her husband made numerous trips to Europe and the Orient to add to her collection. After her husband's death in 1898 she continued her interest in art, eventually assembling one of the world's finest collections of Renaissance and Dutch masterpieces, interspersed with major works by such contemporaries as John Singer Sargent and James

A. M. Whistler. In 1899 she began to build on Fenway Court a gallery in the form of an Italian villa; she took an active part in designing and even in the actual construction of the building, arranged her art collection along with personal memorabilia in it, and opened it to the public in 1903. It was a fitting monument to one who was acknowledged to be one of the most remarkable women of her time. Mrs. Gardner died in Boston on July 17, 1924; by her will the Isabella Stewart Gardner Museum was given to Boston as a public institution with the proviso that the collection be maintained precisely as she had arranged it— nothing was to be added, nor was anything to be removed.

Gardner, John William (1912–   ), educator, public official, and reformer. Born in Los Angeles on October 8, 1912, Gardner graduated from Stanford University in 1935 and after receiving his M.A. the following year moved to the University of California to take his Ph.D. in 1938. He was an instructor in psychology at Connecticut College for two years and assistant professor at Mount Holyoke College for two more before being appointed to direct the Latin American section of the Foreign Broadcast Intelligence Service of the Federal Communications Commission (FCC) in 1942. In 1943 he was commissioned a lieutenant in the Marine Corps, was attached to the Office of Strategic Services (OSS) in Europe and the Mediterranean, and served for three years. He joined the staff of the Carnegie Corporation in 1946, rising to the presidency nine years later, at which time he became also president of the Carnegie Foundation for the Advancement of Teaching. During ten years in those positions he became known for innovation in applying foundation funds to the improvement of American education; notable among the many projects he devised were the landmark studies of public schools made by James Bryant Conant. Awarded the Presidential Medal of Freedom in 1964, Gardner was appointed secretary of health, education, and welfare (HEW) by President Lyndon B. Johnson the next year. After three years of directing the various programs of Johnson's "war on poverty" he resigned in 1968 to become chairman of the National Urban Coalition, a privately supported antipoverty organization that, while free of the political pressures that often hampered the work of HEW, had at the same time little effective weight in public affairs. In 1970 Gardner helped organize and became chairman of Common Cause, an association of concerned private citizens that was conceived as a nonpartisan but politically oriented "third force" that would put money and voting power behind favored legislation and candidates and would also function as a "citizens' lobby" counterweighting corporate and partisan political influences in government. Among his writings expressing his educational and social views were *Excellence: Can We Be Equal and Excellent Too?*, 1961; *No Easy Victories*, 1968; and *The Recovery of Confidence*, 1970.

Garfield, James Abram (1831–1881), twentieth president of the United States. Born near Orange, Ohio, on November 19, 1831, Garfield grew up in poverty but, through his own efforts and those of his widowed mother, secured a good education, graduating from Williams College in 1856. For a time he taught school and was a popular lay preacher. He became interested in politics, supported the Republican party, and in 1859 was elected to the Ohio senate. Soon after the outbreak of the Civil War he helped recruit a volunteer regiment and shortly thereafter became its colonel; he saw service at Shiloh, was chief of staff for Gen. William S. Rosecrans's Army of the Cumberland, and performed with such credit, particularly at Chickamauga, that he was promoted to major general of volunteers. In 1863 he resigned from the army to enter Congress as a representative from Ohio; for the next 17 years he was regularly reelected and his seat was in danger only once, in 1874, because of his minor involvement in the Crédit Mobilier scandal. Garfield was a dutifully partisan Republican, voting for the impeachment of President Andrew Johnson, and serving as one of the "visiting statesmen" sent to Louisiana to oversee the election of 1876 and sitting as a member of the Electoral Commission, which awarded the presidency to Rutherford B. Hayes after the disputed election of 1876. His principal legislative interest was in economic policy and he maintained a sound-money position in the face of agitation in Western districts—his own included—for the inflationary issue of greenbacks. In 1880 Garfield was elected to the Senate for the term beginning in March 1881, but he never occupied the seat. At the 1880 Republican national convention he headed the faction favoring John Sherman for the nomination; after Garfield's successful fight against the unit rule proposed by the pro-Grant "Stalwarts" the convention was for 34 ballots in a three-way deadlock between Sherman, Ulysses S. Grant, and James G. Blaine. On the 35th ballot there was a break and on the 36th Garfield was nominated as a compromise candidate. In November he and Chester A. Arthur, the vice-presidential candidate, were elected with a minuscule popular majority. The first months of his administration were taken up by controversy over appointments and by consolidating party leadership; he was adamant in his assertion of presidential appointive power and at length was victorious over the Stalwart leaders, Senator Roscoe Conkling and Senator Thomas C. Platt, in the matter of appointing the collector of customs for the port of New York. On July 2, 1881, while waiting in a Washington railway station, Garfield was shot by Charles J. Guiteau, a disappointed office seeker, probably insane, who shouted that he was a Stalwart and wished to see Arthur become president. For 11 weeks Garfield lingered, incapacitated; the constitutional issue of the conditions of presidential succession was debated publicly and in the cabinet (Congress was in recess); the cabinet split 4–3 over the question of whether Arthur could actually succeed to the presidency or become merely acting president; the matter remained unresolved when Garfield died in Elberon, New Jersey, on September 19, 1881.

Garland, Hamlin (1860–1940), author. Born in West Salem, Wisconsin, on September 14, 1860, the son of a restless farmer who repeatedly moved farther West, Garland grew up in poverty in Wisconsin and later in Iowa and the Dakota Territory. Largely self-educated, he moved to Boston in 1884 to seek a literary career. He was encouraged by William Dean Howells; in 1890 he began to write short stories and sketches, some of which were collected in 1891 as *Main-Travelled Roads*. The starkness of this and subsequent books, including *Prairie Folks*, 1893, and *Wayside Courtships*, 1897, which portrayed in vivid detail the ugliness and despair of Western farm life, failed to find a public. In 1893 Garland moved to Chicago and there published in the following year a set of critical essays entitled *Crumbling Idols*, in which he advocated literary realism, or "veritism," a demand that was relatively advanced for the time. There followed a series of novels, none remarkable, about the Far West In 1917, in something of a reversal, he published the autobiographical and somewhat nostalgic *A Son of the Middle Border;* the book was widely popular and was followed by a series of sequels, including the Pulitzer Prize-winning *A Daughter of the Middle Border* in 1921. In 1923 a number of his magazine stories were collected in *The Book of the American Indian*. In 1929 he moved to Los Angeles, where he lived until his death there on March 4, 1940.

Garland, Judy (1922–1969), actress and singer. Born on June 10, 1922, in Grand Rapids, Minnesota, Frances Gumm was the daughter of former vaudevillians with whom she later moved to Los Angeles. She began appearing on the vaudeville and variety stage at a very early age and for a few years toured with her two older sisters in a singing act. She had already adopted, at George Jessel's suggestion, the name Judy Garland when in 1935 she was signed for motion pictures by Metro-Goldwyn-Mayer (M-G-M). She quickly became Hollywood's top child star, appearing in several of the popular *Andy Hardy* movies with Mickey Rooney, in *Broadway Melody*, 1938, in which she sang "Dear Mr. Gable," and in 1939 in *The Wizard of Oz*, a film that became a perennial favorite and in which she sang what became her lifelong theme, "Somewhere Over the Rainbow;" she won a special Academy Award for her performance. Among her later movies of note were *Strike Up the Band*, 1940; *For Me and My Gal*, 1942; *Presenting Lily Mars*, 1943; *Meet Me in St. Louis*, 1944; *The Harvey Girls*, 1946; *The Pirate*, 1948; *Easter Parade*, 1948; and *In the Good Old Summertime*, 1949. Stardom proved a heavy burden, and she began experiencing personal and health problems that led to the termination of her M-G-M contract in 1950. She toured with great

success as a singer, both in the United States and in Europe, attracting devoted fans in droves and establishing a following that occasionally assumed the dimensions of a cult. In 1954 she returned to the screen in *A Star Is Born* and continued to make concert appearances through the late 1950s and early 1960s despite bouts with illness. During one of her emergent periods she played a supporting dramatic role in *Judgment at Nuremberg*, 1962, that brought her an Academy Award nomination. A short-lived television variety program and personal appearances in London, New York City, and elsewhere marked her last years. Miss Garland, one of the most popular entertainers of her day and the idol of millions around the world, died in London on June 22, 1969. Her daughter, Liza Minnelli (1946–   ), later became a film and musical-comedy star in her own right.

Garner, John Nance (1868–1967), vice-president of the United States. Born in Red River County, Texas, on November 22, 1868, Garner received little schooling and after a brief attendance at Vanderbilt University took up the study of law in a private office. He was admitted to the bar in 1890 and established a practice in Uvalde, Texas, soon becoming involved in local politics and acquiring extensive bank and real-estate holdings. In 1898 he was elected to the state legislature, where he sat for two terms and chaired a redistricting committee that created a new Texas congressional district in 1902. He ran for the new seat and won, beginning 30 years of continuous service in the House of Representatives, during which he held a number of important committee posts and became known as an effective legislator. While he attached his name to no major bills he paved the way for the passage of many and was a master of political maneuver. Widely celebrated as a plain-spoken, poker-playing, and popular politician, he rose to the speakership of the House in 1931 and the next year, at the Democratic national convention, controlled both the Texas and California delegations. For withdrawing his name from presidential contention and releasing his bloc of delegates to vote for Franklin D. Roosevelt he was rewarded with the vice-presidential nomination and in November 1932 was elected along with Roosevelt. During two terms as vice-president, Garner was responsible for maneuvering much New Deal legislation through Congress. He refused to support President Roosevelt's bid for a third term, however, and after a brief campaign to win the nomination himself he retired from politics permanently and settled again in Uvalde. There he remained for the rest of his life, living simply in spite of his considerable wealth and gradually gaining a reputation as a minor political sage. "Cactus Jack" Garner died in Uvalde on November 7, 1967, two weeks before his ninety-ninth birthday.

Garrison, William Lloyd (1805–1879), journalist and reformer. Born on December 12, 1805, in Newburyport, Massachusetts, Garrison received little education and was sent to work at an early age. In 1818 he was apprenticed to a printer; in the office of the *Newburyport Herald* he became an expert compositor while contributing anonymously to its columns. In 1826 he became editor of the local *Free Press*, in which were published John Greenleaf Whittier's earliest poems. Later, in 1828, he edited briefly the temperance journal *National Philanthropist* in Boston; later that year he established the short-lived *Journal of the Times* in Bennington, Vermont. In the next year he joined Benjamin Lundy in publishing the Baltimore monthly *Genius of Universal Emancipation;* a libel suit arising from a statement in that paper landed Garrison in jail for seven weeks in 1830 until Arthur Tappan paid his fine. Determined by then to fight both the institution of slavery and the temporizing American Colonization Society, he issued in Boston the first number of the *Liberator* on January 1, 1831. With the famous statement "I am in earnest—I will not equivocate—I will not excuse—I will not retreat a single inch—*and I will be heard*," he began his battle for complete and immediate emancipation. As much a pacifist as an abolitionist, he relied solely on moral pressure and the mobilization of public opinion to put an end to slavery. Despite persistent financial difficulties he continued to publish the *Liberator* for 35 years. Garrison was also under the constant threat of physical harm and legal action by proslavery elements; the state of Georgia, for example, offered a $5000 reward for his arrest and conviction. He was active in the organization of the New England Anti-Slavery Society in 1832 and of the American Anti-Slavery Society in 1833. In 1835 at a Boston abolitionist meeting at which the English abolitionist George Thompson was scheduled to speak, but which he himself had been warned to avoid, Garrison was attacked by a mob. His single-minded dedication led him occasionally to treat harshly even potential allies in his cause; he alienated most of the Northern clergy and in 1839–1840, largely as a result of his advocacy of women's participation in the antislavery movement and of women's rights in general, the abolitionist movement split into two factions. The exclusion of women caused him to boycott the 1840 World's Anti-Slavery Convention in London; in the next year he was elected president of the American Anti-Slavery Society and held the post for 22 years. By this time favoring peaceful separation of North and South, he made lecture tours around the country and in England. While his increasing distaste for the proslavery clauses of the Constitution led him to burn a copy of the document publicly in 1854, his overriding pacifism aligned him against John Brown and others who advocated violent action. Although he was at first opposed to the idea of forcible reunion, he soon came to support Abraham Lincoln, who openly acknowledged his services. The preliminary Emancipation Proclamation in September 1862 reunited the two abolitionist factions and in January 1865, with the end of the war in sight, Garrison moved the dissolution of the Anti-Slavery Society; similarly, with the ratification of the Thirteenth Amendment, he ended the publication of the *Liberator* During his last years he made two more trips to England and continued to press for prohibition, woman suffrage, better treatment of Indians, and other reforms. He died on May 24, 1879, in New York City.

Garvey, Marcus Moziah (1887–1940), social reformer. Born on August 17, 1887, in St. Ann's Bay, Jamaica, Garvey was largely self-educated and began working as a printer's apprentice at fourteen. He moved to Kingston three years later and became foreman of a large printing company. Blacklisted after leading the employees in a strike for higher wages, he worked briefly for the government printing office, founded two nationalistic publications and a political club, and then sought more lucrative employment in South America. He observed the poor working conditions in many countries and, continuing on to London in 1912, met and assisted an Afro-Egyptian scholar, learning much of Negro history and culture in the course of his work. He returned to Jamaica in 1914 and founded the Universal Negro Improvement Association (UNIA) and the African Communities League. In 1916 he moved to New York City, establishing the headquarters of UNIA there and founding branches during 1919–1920 in nearly every urban area of the country where there was a substantial black population. He also founded the *Negro World*, the weekly UNIA newspaper, which continued from 1919 to 1933. In 1920 he held the first UNIA international convention at Liberty Hall in New York City's Harlem; an estimated 25,000 delegates from 25 nations attended. There he delivered remarkable addresses on Negro rights, urging that black men accept a black Deity, exalting African beauty, expounding on the lives and notable achievements of Negroes throughout history, and projecting plans for Negroes to resettle in Liberia in a "back to Africa" movement. He began several enterprises, including the Black Star Steamship Line and the Negro Factories Corporation, financed by the sale of stock to UNIA members. Much of his traveling became promotional; he declared that black-owned, black-operated ventures would rebuild the confidence of Negroes in their own people and prepare them for economic independence. Throughout this time he was harassed by both white and black members of middle-class society. In 1924, the Liberian government, fearing that his motives were revolutionary, rejected his plans for resettlement. In 1925 he was convicted of fraud in connection with his handling of the funds of the Black Star Line, which had gone bankrupt. He was sentenced to five years' imprisonment, but his sentence was commuted by President Calvin Coolidge and in 1927 he was released and immediately deported to Jamaica. He continued to work actively for his beliefs, making fiery speeches, organizing conventions, writing, and briefly participating in

Jamaican politics, but his influence and prestige were waning. He moved to London in 1935 and died there, obscure and impoverished, on June 10, 1940.

Gary, Elbert Henry (1846–1927), lawyer and businessman. Born near Wheaton, Illinois, on October 8, 1846, Gary studied for a time at the Illinois Institute in Wheaton, read law in the office of an uncle, and in 1867 graduated from the Union College of Law in Chicago. Taking particular interest in corporation law, he soon built up a lucrative practice and served as director of several companies. In 1882 and again in 1886 he was elected judge of Du Page County; although this was his only service on the bench he was ever afterward known as Judge Gary. He took the leading role in the organization of the Federal Steel Company in 1898 and became its president. When J. P. Morgan who had been Federal's principal backer, set out to create the United States Steel Corporation in 1901 he selected Gary to supervise the organization of what was then the largest industrial corporation in the world. Gary became chairman of the executive committee and in 1903 chairman of the board of directors, a position he retained until his death. His standards of business ethics and his attitude toward labor were in some respects remarkably advanced for the time. He saw to it that working conditions at U.S. Steel were conducive to health and safey, introduced a profit-sharing plan for employees, and maintained a high wage scale. In response to public opinion, he abolished the 12-hour day and the 7-day week in U.S. Steel's mills. He was, however, an implacable foe of the closed union shop, and his refusal to negotiate on that issue brought on the steel strike of 1919. Gary died on August 15, 1927, in New York City. The city of Gary, Indiana, begun as a company town in 1906, was named for him.

Gasser, Herbert Spencer (1888–1963), physiologist. Born on July 5, 1888, in Platteville, Wisconsin, Gasser graduated from the University of Wisconsin in 1910, took an M.A. the next year, and began the study of medicine, later transferring to the Johns Hopkins Medical School, from which he received his M.D. in 1915. After a year as a student and instructor in pharmacology at the University of Wisconsin he joined the faculty of Washington University in St. Louis as an instructor in physiology. He carried on various war-related research projects during World War I and in 1920 became an associate professor. After being appointed head of the department of pharmacology in 1921 and subsequently studying for two-years in Europe he began collaborating with Joseph Erlanger, head of Washington's physiology department, in a series of experiments studying the nature of nerve impulses. Discarding mechanical galvanometric detection equipment in favor of the newly developed inertialess electronic device known as the cathode-ray tube, they devised an oscillograph with which they were able not only to detect and measure the tinest nerve impulses but also to distinguish several different strength levels and pulse configurations, which they found to be characteristic of various kinds of nerve fibers. Gasser developed a means of classifying nerve fibers and formulated the relationship between the speed of impulse propagation and fiber diameter. In 1931 he became professor of physiology and head of the physiological laboratory at Cornell Medical College and four years later was chosen director of the Rockefeller Institute for Medical Research (now Rockefeller University), a post he held until his retirement in 1953. For the work with Erlanger the two were awarded jointly the 1944 Nobel Prize for Physiology and Medicine. Gasser's later investigations continued along the same lines and included notable electron-microscope studies of unmyelinated nerve fibers. He died in New York City on May 11, 1963.

Gates, Frederick Taylor (1853–1929), religious leader and philanthropist. Born in Maine, Broome County, New York, on July 2, 1853, Gates graduated from the University of Rochester in 1877 and on completing the course at the Rochester Theological Seminary three years later was ordained in the Baptist church. He assumed a pastorate in Minneapolis and held it until 1888, when he resigned to undertake a fund-raising campaign for a Baptist academy in Minnesota. In that year he was appointed corresponding secretry of the Baptist Education Society and in that position took an active interest in the development of educational facilities throughout the country. He was particularly attracted by the possibility of establishing a major center of higher learning in Chicago and knew of the willingness of John D. Rockefeller to contribute heavily to such an institution; securing the support of the Baptist Education Society and, through extensive publicity, of the general public, he organized the planning of a university that won Rockefeller's approval. He led also in raising funds to supplement Rockefeller's initial gift to the University of Chicago, opened in 1892. Rockefeller subsequently employed him in an advisory capacity in various business matters; Gates eventually became his principal adviser on philanthropy and was instrumental in planning and organizing the Rockefeller Institute for Medical Research, of which he was until his death president of the board of trustees, the General Education Board, of which he was long president, and the Rockefeller Foundation. A man of wide vision, he enjoyed the absolute confidence of Rockefeller and had thereby at his disposal huge sums of money, which he deployed through the various institutions to the general betterment of mankind. He remained active in philanthropic enterprises until his death in Phoenix, Arizona, on February 6, 1929.

Gates, Horatio (1727?–1806), Revolutionary soldier. Born probably in Maldon, England, about

1727, Gates entered the British army at an early age; he served in Nova Scotia in 1749–1750 and later in the middle and northern colonies during the French and Indian War. In 1762 he returned to England, where he remained until 1772 as a civilian. In that year, encouraged by his friend George Washington, he returned to America, settling in Virginia. In 1775 he was commissioned brigadier general by Congress and made adjutant general of the Continental army. Promoted to major general the next year, he commanded the troops retreating from Canada and in 1777 replaced Gen. Philip J. Schuyler in command of the northern department; there, against the invading British army under Gen. John Burgoyne, he won the battle of Saratoga, wth the brilliant assistance of Gen. Benedict Arnold. He was appointed by Congress to the Board of War shortly thereafter. During the next several months there developed the Conway Cabal, a congeries of letters and discussions that gave at least the appearance of an intrigue among a number of officers and members of Congress to have Gates replace Washington as commander in chief. Whether Gates was actually implicated in any plot is not clear; he was at least, however, not unaware of or adverse to its purported purpose. From 1778 to 1780 he resumed command, first in the North and then in the East; he saw little combat and his problems were largely those of supply. After a brief retirement to Virginia he was placed in command in the South in 1780. His disastrous defeat at Camden, South Carolina, in August of that year led Congress to call for an investigation; finally no inquiry was held, but, except for a brief period under Washington's command in 1782, Gates's military service was over. He retired to his Virginia plantation in 1783; in 1790 he freed his slaves and moved to a farm on Manhattan Island, where he died on April 10, 1806.

Gates, John Warne (1855–1911), "Bet-a-million," financier. Born on May 8, 1855, in Turner Junction (now West Chicago), Illinois, Gates was educated in local schools. At nineteen he became a partner in a small hardware store and four years later took a job as a salesman for a barbed-wire company. In a remarkable display of salesmanship he built a corral in San Antonio, Texas, that withstood the assaults of the most recalcitrant longhorns and then, swamped with orders from the ranchers of the area, deserted his employer and established his own company in St. Louis to manufacture barbed wire. Between 1880 and 1898 he negotiated a series of mergers and consolidations among various firms in the field, emerging as president of the American Steel & Wire Company, which held a virtual monopoly in barbed wire, and as the possessor of a huge fortune, gained largely by the liberal "watering" of stock through successive layers of holding companies. He acquired interests in other industries as well, assuming the presidency of the Illinois Steel Company in 1894, trying unsuccessfully to interest other steel magnates in the formation of a

huge combine, and joining with J. P. Morgan in the purchase of the Tennessee Coal & Iron Company in 1906. Although he did not engage in speculation merely for its own sake, the delight he took in it and the daring that he displayed in the stock market earned him the nickname "Bet-a-Million" Gates from the general public and made him something of an anathema to responsible financiers. His exploits in the market were both predatory and legendary; one, however, an attempted bilking of Morgan backfired and he retired from the field to Port Arthur, Texas, where, though on a much smaller scale, he continued to wheel and deal in local real estate and industry. Gates died in Paris on August 9, 1911.

Gatling, Richard Jordan (1818–1903), inventor. Born in Hertford County, North Carolina, on September 12, 1818, Gatling was educated in local schools and in his youth helped his father develop machines for sowing and thinning cotton. For a time he taught school and he later ran a store, continuing meanwhile to exercise his considerable mechanical ability and imagination. He perfected a practical screw propeller in 1839, but the invention was anticipated by just a few months by that of John Ericsson and he received no patent. In 1844 he moved to St. Louis to engage in the manufacture of his sowing machine, which he adapted also to rice and wheat; he later established branch plants in Ohio and Indiana. Following an attack of smallpox, during which he was unable to find medical assistance, he entered the Ohio Medical College in Cincinnati; although he completed the course in 1850 he never practiced, resting content to be able to care for himself and his family. He continued to develop agricultural implements, inventing a hemp-breaking machine and in 1857 a steam plow. Upon the outbreak of the Civil War he turned his attention to military hardware; he succeeded in 1862 in building and patenting a rapid-fire gun that qualified as the first practical machine gun. With further improvements, the gun consisted of ten barrels clustered around a central revolving shaft and an automatic feed and ejection mechanism; crank-driven and making use of newly developed brass cartridge shells, it could fire some 350 rounds per minute. The gun was approved by the War Department too late to be much used in the Civil War, but in 1866 it was officially adopted by the army. In 1870 Gatling moved to Hartford, Conneticut, to supervise manufacture of the Gatling gun at the Colt Patent Fire Arms Manufacturing Company. He made several more improvements in the gun, which eventually attained a rate of fire of 1200 rounds per minute, and then sold his patent rights to the Colt firm. In later years he worked on a new method for casting cannon and built a motorized plow. He died in New York City on February 26, 1903.

Geary, John White (1819–1873), soldier and public official. Born in Westmoreland County, Pennsylvania, on December 30, 1819, Geary attended Jefferson College briefly and then engaged in various pursuits, from school teaching to surveying. He studied law and won admission to the bar, speculated successfully in Kentucky land, and became assistant superintendent and engineer of the Allegheny Portage Railroad. On the outbreak of the Mexican War he returned to Pennsylvania to activate the militia company of which he had long been a member and was chosen lieutenant colonel to the regiment. He was in the forefront of the attack on Chapultepec in 1847 and remained in the city as military commander until the end of the war. Early in 1849 he was appointed by President James K. Polk the first postmaster of San Francisco and postal agent for the entire Pacific Coast; he was succeeded by an appointee of President Zachary Taylor shortly afterward, but almost immediately he was elected alcalde of the city. He was subsequently appointed also to the bench as chief judicial officer of San Francisco under the military government of the state. On the reorganization of the city government the following year Geary was elected the first mayor. In 1852 he returned to Pennsylvania and remained there until 1856, when he was appointed territorial governor of Kansas by President Franklin Pierce. He was able, through vigorous and evenhanded measures, to quiet temporarily the factional warring between proslavery and antislavery forces in Kansas, and his report that "Peace now reigns in Kansas" was widely publicized as part of James Buchanan's presidential campaign that year. Order broke down, however, early in 1857 and the situation became so confused and frustrating that he resigned in March. He again returned to Pennsylvania, where in 1861 he became colonel of a Pennsylvania regiment enlisted for Civil War service. He saw action at Leesburg, which he captured, and also, after promotion to brigadier general, at Cedar Mountain, Chancellorsville, and Gettysburg and in the Chattanooga and Atlanta campaigns. He served as military governor of Savannah until the end of the war and reached the rank of major general. From 1867 to 1873 Geary was governor of Pennsylvania, promoting a somewhat erratic but generally progressive program of legislation. Shortly after completing his second term he died, on February 8, 1873, in Harrisburg, Pennsylvania.

Geddes, Norman Bel (1893–1958), designer. Born on April 27, 1893, in Adrian, Michigan, Geddes very briefly attended the Cleveland Institute of Art and the Art Institute of Chicago. He worked in various jobs in his youth and in 1916 made his way to Los Angeles, where for the Little Theatre he staged six plays, including his own *Nju*. He was also for a short time a movie director. It was at about that time that he adopted the name Bel, his wife's middle name; "Norman-Bel-Geddes" was originally the pseudonym under which they had jointly published articles on art and the theater and in time the hyphens were dropped and he assumed the name himself. In 1918 he se-

cured a personal grant from banker and art patron Otto Kahn and traveled to New York City to present his ideas about stage design. He was commissioned to design several sets for the Metropolitan Opera and his work here soon attracted other producers. Geddes's sets discarded ornamentation in favor of clean, functional, fluid backgrounds that were intended to create an atmospheric space rather than to engage and possibly divert the eye, an approach that proved highly influential in the development of modern theatrical design. The theatrical aspect of his career eventually encompassed the design, direction, or production of some 200 operas, plays, and films. By 1927 Geddes had begun to apply his design concepts to the industrial field, working with projects ranging from automobiles to ocean liners, from radios to refrigerators, and from airplane interiors to skyscrapers. He gradually built up a huge design organization through which his ideas had impact on countless areas of life, and he was the foremost proponent and popularizer of the "streamline" style in the 1930s. For the General Motors Corporation he designed the Futurama exhibit at the 1939–1940 New York World's Fair that drew more interest than any other exhibit, and he continued afterward to advocate the rational traffic system he had worked out for Futurama, publishing *Magic Motorways*, 1940, to develop the idea further. Geddes's design projects of later years were widely diversified; they included theaters in many cities around the world, the Ringling Brothers–Barnum and Bailey circus, camouflage for the armed forces, a plan for downtown Toledo, Ohio, and the main studios of the National Broadcasting Corporation (NBC). He died in New York City on May 8, 1958. His daughter Barbara Bel Geddes (1922–   ) became a noted actress.

Gehrig, Lou (1903–1941), baseball player. Born in New York City on June 19, 1903, Henry Louis Gehrig was a star athlete in several sports in high school and at Columbia University, which he attended from 1921 to 1923. In 1923 he was signed by the New York Yankees and sent to their Hartford, Connecticut, farm club. In 1925 he was brought up to the home team and immediately made a regular player; he played a fine first base while becoming the Yankees' outstanding hitter. He hit .295 in his first season and did not fall below the .300 mark again until his last year in baseball; while compiling a lifetime major-league average of .340 he led the league in 1934 with .363 and had a .361 average for the seven World Series in which he played. He was the American League home-run champion in 1931 (tied with Babe Ruth) with 46, and in 1934 and 1936 with 49; his records of 4 homers in a World Series (1928, a 4-game series) and 4 in a single game (in 1932) are shared by others but unsurpassed, and his career total of 23-grand-slam hits remains unchallenged. He was named the American League's most valuable player in 1927, 1931, 1934, and 1936. Gehrig's most remarkable record was in consecutive games played; he did not miss a single game in 14 seasons, a total of 2130 games, and his stamina earned him the nickname "Iron Horse." The string came to an abrupt end in May 1939, when after a batting slump he voluntarily benched himself. He then traveled to the Mayo Clinic for examination and discovered he was suffering from a rare and fatal form of paralysis. Although his playing days were ended he remained close to the Yankees and later in the year was elected to the National Baseball Hall of Fame, an unprecedented honor for a player so recently retired. Lou Gehrig was appointed a New York City parole commissioner by Mayor Fiorello H. La Guardia late in 1939; he served until his death in New York City on June 2, 1941. The movie *Pride of the Yankees*, his life story, was released in 1942; the role of Gehrig was played by Gary Cooper, who had to learn to throw left-handed in order to undertake the part.

Geisel, Theodor Seuss (1904–   ), "Dr. Seuss," author and illustrator. Born on March 2, 1904, in Springfield, Massachusetts, Geisel graduated from Dartmouth in 1925 and after a few months as a columnist for a home-town newspaper went to Oxford for a year of graduate study in English. Following a period as a successful free-lance cartoonist and illustrator he joined the advertising agency of McCann-Erickson in New York City, where he created the popular "Quick Henry, the Flit!" series of ads in cartoon form. In 1937 he published his first children's book, *And to Think That I Saw It on Mulberry Street*; written and illustrated by Geisel and signed with the pen name "Dr. Seuss," the book won critical acclaim and enough popular success to warrant numerous reprintings. The next year he published *The 500 Hats of Bartholomew Cubbins* and in 1940 *Horton Hatches the Egg*, both likewise successful. From 1940 to 1942 he was a political cartoonist for the New York City newspaper *PM* and from 1943 to 1946 was engaged in making documentary and indoctrination films for the army. One of his films, under the title *Hitler Lives*, won an Academy Award in 1946. *Design for Death*, a feature-length documentary on Japanese history, was written by Geisel and his wife, Helen Palmer Geisel. It also won an Academy Award, in 1947. A film cartoon starring his character Gerald McBoing-Boing won a third Oscar, in 1951. Returning to the field of children's books, he produced *McElligot's Pool*, 1947; *Thidwick the Big-Hearted Moose*, 1948; *Bartholomew and the Oobleck*, 1949; *If I Ran the Zoo*, 1950; *Scrambled Eggs Super!*, 1953; *Horton Hears a Who*, 1954; *On Beyond Zebra*, 1955; *If I Ran the Circus*, 1956; *How the Grinch Stole Christmas*, 1957; *Yertle the Turtle and Other Stories*, 1958; and many others. With *The Cat in the Hat* in 1957, he began a series of primary reading books that, published by Beginner Books, of which he was president, were widely praised by educators. In 1966 *The Grinch* was made into an animated cartoon that became an annual holiday presentation on tele-

vision; *Horton Hears a Who* came to television in 1970. Geisel's books, with their zany creatures and their verse and prose that are often nonsense but always delightful, sold millions of copies.

Gell-Mann, Murray (1929–   ), physicist. Born in New York City on September 15, 1929, Gell-Mann graduated from Yale in 1948 and three years later took his Ph.D. from the Massachusetts Institute of Technology (MIT). After a year of further study and research at the Institute for Advanced Study in Princeton, N.J., he was appointed an instructor in physics at the University of Chicago's Institute for Nuclear Studies. He became an assistant professor in 1953 and in that year published his first major contribution to the study of elementary particles. In an attempt to bring order to the chaotic profusion of new particles that had recently been discovered, he devised a new quantum number to be assigned to the various long-lived particles in integral values; calling the new quantity, with characteristic whimsy, "strangeness," he then postulated a law of conservation of strangeness in particle interactions. By assigning strangeness values to accord with known reactions, he was able to predict previously unobserved reactions while ruling out others as prohibited. This work was assisted by the independent efforts of K. Nishijima of Japan. The predictions were all subsequently confirmed experimentally. Moving to the California Institute of Technology in 1955 and becoming a full professor the next year, Gell-Mann then went on to develop a theoretical schema for all the heavy and intermediate particles, the baryons and mesons. Again, similar work was being done at the same time elsewhere, in this case by Y. Ne'emann of Israel. The theory that resulted was called by Gell-Mann the Eightfold Way, after the eight virtues of Buddhism. In the Eightfold Way, particles were grouped according to various quantum values into sets—supermultiplets—of various sizes and related by formulas describing the possible interactions. The theory early seemed to require the existence of a new particle, the omega minus baryon, and the discovery of such a particle in 1964 was a brilliant success for the Eightfold Way. For his work on the classification of particles and their interactions Gell-Mann was awarded the 1969 Nobel Prize for Physics. His later studies concerned, among other topics, weak interactions among particles; he was associated in that work with Richard P. Feynman, with whom he also hypothesized the existence of the "quark," a particle fundamental to all others.

George, Henry (1839–1897), economist and social reformer. Born in Philadelphia on September 2, 1839, George left school at thirteen and, after two years as a clerk, went to sea in 1855 on a merchant ship. He returned home the next year and went to work in a printing office. In 1857 he worked his way to California aboard a lighthouse tender, but did not succeed in sharing in the gold-mining boom. During the next several years he struggled with poverty, often unable to find work but conscientiously applying himself to self-improvement by reading widely. He wrote unsigned articles for various newspapers during his intermittent periods of employment as a typesetter and, later, as an editor. He became involved also in Democratic politics, though with little success. His intimate knowledge of poverty and a visit to New York City during which he observed the paradox of progress and poverty developing hand-in-hand set him to seeking an explanation of the anomalies of capitalistic economics. In 1871 he published *Our Land and Land Policy*, a pamphlet which anticipated his great and fully articulated work to come. In 1876 he was appointed the state inspector of gas meters; with the security of that job he began work on *Progress and Poverty*. Published in 1879, the book analyzed wealth in terms of land and its value; asserting that to work the land is a natural right and that rent demanded by landlords is a violation of economic law and an obstacle to general prosperity, George proposed a government tax upon land that would be equal to its rent price. Replacing all other forms of taxation, this "single tax" would fund regular government operations and at the same time prevent speculative investment in land, allow economic laws to operate freely, effect a better distribution of wealth, and yield a surplus revenue to be applied to additional public works. In 1880 he moved from California to New York City; on the wave of the popularity that he and his book subsequently enjoyed, he made a number of lecture tours in the United States, Australia, Ireland, and England. Other writings included *The Irish Land Question*, 1881; *Social Problems*, 1883; and *The Science of Political Economy*, 1897. He was defeated for mayor of New York City in 1886 by the Democratic candidate, although he ran well ahead of Republican Theodore Roosevelt. He died in New York City on October 29, 1897.

Gerguson, Harry F., *see* Romanoff, Michael

Gernsback, Hugo (1884–1967), inventor and publisher. Born in Luxembourg on August 16, 1884, Gernsback was educated at the École Industrielle there and at the Technikum in Bingen, Germany. He was an early experimenter in the field of electricity and radio and in 1904 came to the United States to promote an improved dry battery of his own invention. His Electro Importing Company, established the next year, was the world's first radio-supply house. In 1908 he began publishing *Modern Electrics* (later merged into *Popular Science*), the first radio magazine, and later founded *Electrical Experimenter* in 1913 and *Radio News* in 1919. He occasionally published stories on scientific subjects in his magazines and in 1926 he founded *Amazing Stories*, the first magazine devoted exclusively to science fiction, or "scientifiction," as he called it; he later lost control of the magazine but started several others that were combined in 1930 into *Wonder Stories*. His influ-

ence in encouraging the growth and sophistication of the science-fiction genre in its early years was later recognized when the top annual prize for science-fiction novels was named the Hugo Award in his honor. Gernsback Publications issued other periodicals on various special-interest topics, including *Short Wave Craft*, *Everyday Science and Mechanics*, and, from 1933, *Sexology*. He remained an active experimenter in electronics, operating his own radio station in New York City and broadcasting television programs to other amateurs as early as 1928. His inventions, for which he eventually secured more than 80 patents, included numerous radio devices, an early form of bone-conduction hearing aid, and a sleep-learning device he called a "hypnobioscope." In his imaginative writings he anticipated with startling accuracy a number of later inventions such as radar, microfilm, artificial fabrics, and fluorescent lighting. Gernsback died in New York City on August 19, 1967.

Geronimo (1829?–1909), Indian leader. By his own account, Geronimo, a Chiricahua Apache, was born in June 1829 in Arizona and was given the name Goyathlay. He grew up in a period of bloody raiding led by various Chiricahua chiefs, notably Cochise, and after 1858, when his family was killed, he came to be a skillful and courageous leader in raids of revenge against the Mexicans, by whom he was dubbed Geronimo (Jerome). Other raids in Arizona and New Mexico led to his confinement on a reservation in southern Arizona; but when, in 1876, the Chiricahua were moved to another reservation already occupied by Western Apache, serious trouble ensued. Geronimo and his band escaped to Mexico and during the next ten years outbreaks of raiding against American settlers alternated with periodic confinements. The reign of terror in the Southwest finally prompted official action against the wily and daring leader. In 1886 he agreed to surrender to U.S. troops under Gen. George Crook and to be taken to a Florida reservation. Two days later he again escaped. Crook was replaced by Gen. Nelson A. Miles who, with more than 5000 troops, required 18 months to recapture Geronimo and his small band, which included only 35 warriors. Placed under military confinement by order of President Grover Cleveland, Geronimo and his followers were sent to Florida, to Alabama, and finally to Fort Sill, Oklahoma, where they were allowed to remain. Geronimo took up farming and eventually adopted Christianity; his personal appearance was a feature at the Louisiana Purchase Exposition in 1904 in St. Louis and he appeared in Theodore Roosevelt's inaugural procession in 1905. His autobiography, *Geronimo's Story of His Life*, was dictated to S. M. Barrett and published in 1906. He died at Fort Sill on February 17, 1909.

Gerry, Elbridge (1744–1814), vice-president of the United States. Born on July 17, 1744, in Marblehead, Massachusetts, Gerry graduated from Harvard in 1762 and for ten years was employed in his father's mercantile business. From 1772 to 1774 he was a member of the Massachusetts General Court and served on the Committee of Correspondence; during 1774–1775 he was in the provincial congress and a member of the Committee of Safety. Early in 1776 he entered the Continental Congress as a supporter of separation from Great Britain; he was fully in sympathy with the Declaration of Independence, although illness delayed his signing it until September of that year. He remained in Congress until 1781 and, after a time devoted to business interests, returned in 1783 and served for two more years. In the many councils in which he served Gerry impaired his potentially great effectiveness by an inability to maintain settled opinions in practical matters and by a single-minded devotion to a purely theoretical notion of true republicanism. His party affiliations were never clear and always subject to change. In 1787 he was a delegate to the Constitutional Convention, to which he contributed little; his initial opposition to the finished instrument changed later to support, and from 1789 to 1793 he was in Congress as an anti-Federalist who favored Alexander Hamilton's fiscal policies. In 1797 he was appointed by President John Adams to join John Marshall and Charles C. Pinckney in a mission to France to negotiate several outstanding disputes. As the XYZ Affair came to light Marshall and Pinckney left in disgust, but Gerry, believing that he could secure concessions from the French foreign minister, Talleyrand, stayed on for a time and won nothing but criticism at home; the "Affair" was a precipitating cause of the undeclared war with France that began in 1798. Annually from 1800 to 1803 he was the unsuccessful Republican candidate for governor of Massachusetts; in 1810 he ran again and was elected. During his second term a law was enacted redrawing the boundaries of the state's senatorial districts in such a manner as to isolate Federalist strongholds and insure Republican domination of subsequent elections. One of the new districts was thought to resemble a salamander, and the derisive term "gerrymander" was quickly coined to describe this form of redistricting for political advantage. In 1812 Gerry was nominated for vice-president and, with James Madison, was elected; he served until his death in Washington, D.C., on November 23, 1814.

Gershvin, Jacob, *see* Gershwin, George

Gershwin, George (1898–1937), composer. Born on September 26, 1898, in Brooklyn, New York, Jacob Gershvin was the son of Russian Jewish immigrant parents. Known from boyhood as George, he was educated in public schools in New York City and left high school in 1913 to pursue a musical career. He changed his last name to Gershwin soon after joining the Remick music-publishing company as a staff pianist. Before long he was composing songs of his own and in 1919,

the year after he moved to the Harms publishing company, he wrote his first great hit, "Swanee," popularized by Al Jolson. He began contributing music to the Broadway stage, notably for the several editions of *George White's Scandals*, for which he wrote "I'll Build a Stairway to Paradise" in 1922. In 1924 he wrote a complete musical-comedy score in collaboration with his older brother Ira (1896–   ), a highly gifted lyricist and his lifelong partner; *Lady Be Good*, which featured Fred and Adele Astaire, introduced such hits as "Fascinatin' Rhythm" and "The Last Time I Saw Paris." A number of successful Broadway shows followed, including *Tip Toes*, 1925 (with "That Certain Feeling"); *Oh, Kay!*, 1926 ("Do, Do, Do," "Someone to Watch Over Me"); *Funny Face*, 1927, also with the Astaires ('He Loves and She Loves," " 'S Wonderful"); *Treasure Girl*, 1928 ("I've Got a Crush on You"); *Show Girl*, 1929 (with Jimmy Durante singing "I Ups to Him"); *Girl Crazy*, 1930, in which Ethel Merman made her stunning debut ("Bidin' My Time," "But Not For Me," "Embraceable You," "I Got Rhythm"); *Of Thee I Sing*, 1931, a satire by Morris Ryskind and George S. Kaufman for which he wrote "Love is Sweeping the Country" and "Of Thee I Sing" and which was the first musical to win the Pulitzer Prize for drama; and *Pardon My English*, 1933. Gershwin also wrote a great many songs and scores for motion pictures, including several of the Fred Astaire–Ginger Rogers classics; among them and among his miscellaneous pieces were "The Man I Love," "They Can't Take That Away From Me," "Nice Work If You Can Get It," "Our Love Is Here to Stay," "A Foggy Day in London Town," and "Let's Call the Whole Thing Off." Gershwin's musical ambitions went far beyond the popular, however, and in 1924 he appeared as piano soloist with Paul Whiteman's orchestra in the premiere of his *Rhapsody in Blue*; originally commissioned by Whiteman and orchestrated by Ferde Grofé, *Rhapsody in Blue* created a new musical form, symphonic jazz, and its brilliant synthesis of indigenous American rhythms and themes and the classical piano-concerto structure proved a stimulating and seminal influence on both jazz and classical music. The somewhat less successful *Concerto in F*, commissioned by Walter Damrosch, followed in 1925, the delightful *An American in Paris* in 1928, and *Second Rhapsody* in 1932. In 1935 appeared his last major work and his finest, the folk opera *Porgy and Bess*, with libretto by DuBose Heyward and lyrics by Heyward and Ira Gershwin. Although it was slow at first to win audiences, *Porgy and Bess* was eventually recognized as one of the truly great works of the American musical theater; especially memorable were the songs "Summertime," "It Ain't Necessarily So," "I Got Plenty o' Nuttin!," and "I Loves You, Porgy." Gershwin died in Hollywood, California, on July 11, 1937, at the age of thirty-eight.

Gesell, Arnold Lucius (1880–1961), psychologist and physician. Born on June 21, 1880, in Alma,

Wisconsin, Gesell graduated from the University of Wisconsin in 1903 and three years later took his Ph.D. from Clark University. After two years as a teacher of psychology at the Los Angeles State Normal School he joined the faculty of Yale University as assistant professor of education, founding shortly thereafter the Yale Psycho-Clinic (later the Yale Clinic of Child Development). While fulfilling his teaching and administrative duties he undertook to broaden his understanding of the physiological as well as mental parameters of human development by enrolling in the medical course at Yale, and on receiving his M.D. degree in 1915 he was appointed professor of child hygiene in the medical school. His original interest in abnormal child psychology quickly revealed that there was a lack of standards for defining normality, and from about 1919 he concentrated his efforts on a variety of pioneering studies of normal child development. His observations in his clinic of thousands of children at various ages, including his innovative use of motion-picture recordings of behavior, led to a series of books in which he outlined the progressive stages of the child's development from infancy to adolescence; notable among them were *The Normal Child and Primary Education*, 1912, with his wife, B. C. Gesell; *Guidance of Mental Growth in Infant and Child*, 1930; *How a Baby Grows*, 1945; *The Embryology of Behavior*, 1945; *Studies in Child Development*, 1948; *Vision: Its Development in Infant and Child*, 1949, with F. L. Ilg and G. Bullis; and *Infant Development*, 1952. Gesell also produced a number of educational and training films in the clinic. In addition he wrote three best-selling guidebooks that were widely used by parents in the 1940s and 1950s: *Infant and Child in the Culture of Today*, 1943, with Ilg; *The Child from Five to Ten*, 1946, with Ilg; and *Youth: The Years from Ten to Sixteen*, 1956, with Ilg and L. B. Ames. His rigid but for a time influential Gesell Development Schedules, against which children were to be measured for intelligence in terms of a development quotient, or DQ, were later criticized on the ground that they were based on observations of a rather small and strongly homogeneous sample of subject children and therefore failed to consider sufficiently the individual and cultural differences among children. Gesell retired from Yale and from the directorship of the Clinic of Child Development in 1948; for two years he was associated with the child-vision research center of the medical school and from 1950 to 1958 was a consultant to the Gesell Institute of Child Development. He died in New Haven, Connecticut, on May 29, 1961.

Getty, Jean Paul (1892–1976), businessman. Born in Minneapolis on December 15, 1892, Getty was the son of a successful lawyer and oilman. He was educated at the University of Southern California, the University of California at Berkeley, and at Oxford University, from which he took a degree in economics in 1913. He then entered the oil business, speculating with partial backing from his father in oil leases in Oklahoma. By the age of twenty-three he had made his first million dollars. In his will his father left him in 1930 only a moderate fraction of his estate; Getty nonetheless secured the use of some of his mother's larger portion and began buying stock at Depression prices; by 1932 he controlled the Pacific Western Oil Corporation, with whose cash reserves he then went after the Tide Water Associated Oil Company, largely owned by Standard Oil of New Jersey. The stock battle lasted for 19 years and ran an intricate course through diversionary holding companies set up by Standard, principally the Mission Corporation, but by 1951 Getty controlled Mission, the renamed Tidewater Oil Company, and Skelly Oil Company. A vastly complex network of stock ownership linked these and other companies, including Mission Development Company, Spartan Aircraft Company, and eventually real estate, insurance, and marketing firms, but Getty carefully retained control of the entire structure. In order to complete his integrated oil-processing and distributing empire he negotiated in 1949 a lease on oil-rich Saudi Arabian territory and poured development money into the region bordering on Kuwait. Oil production began in 1953 and increased rapidly thereafter. In 1956 Pacific Western became the Getty Oil Company, the master link in Getty's holdings and the world's largest personally controlled oil company. Subsequent reorganizations and mergers of various of his companies, along with heavy investments in transportation and refining facilities, bolstered his position and increased his huge fortune. The most conservative estimates of his total wealth placed it at or above the $1 billion mark, making Getty a prime contender—with Howard R. Hughes and H. L. Hunt his only competition—for the titles of richest American and world's richest private citizen. Although Getty owned an art collection valued at many millions, he indulged in few luxuries and only at an advanced age did he give up living in inexpensive hotel suites. Among his books were *History of the Oil Business of George F. and J. Paul Getty*, 1941; an autobiography, *My Life and Fortunes*, 1963, with Bela Von Block; *How To Be Rich*, 1966; and *As I See It*, an autobiography, 1976. He died at his English mansion, Sutton Place, on June 6, 1976.

Giannini, Amadeo Peter (1870–1949), banker. Born on May 6, 1870, in San Jose, California, Giannini was the son of Italian immigrant parents. At thirteen he left school to go to work in his stepfather's wholesale produce business in San Francisco and in six years was a partner in the firm. He built it into the largest business of its kind in the city and then, in 1901, sold out his share. He became interested in banking and, after unsuccessfully attempting to liberalize the practices of a bank of which he was a director, founded in 1904 the Bank of Italy. From the beginning he was thoroughly unorthodox; he made loans to small farmers and businessmen and, going even more against tradition, actively solicited customers. The bank remained a small one, however, until 1906, when Giannini managed to rescue the gold and securities in the vault from the disastrous fire that followed the great San Francisco earthquake. When the rebuilding of the city began, his was the only bank in a position to make loans. The next year his strong reliance on gold for reserves enabled him to survive the financial panic that closed many larger banks. From that time on the bank grew rapidly and beginning in 1909 Giannini began buying small banks elsewhere in California and converting them into branches of the central institution, creating thereby the first major regional system of branch banking in the country. In 1919 he organized the Bancitaly Corporation to direct the growth of his banking organization and in 1928 the Transamerica Corporation was formed as a holding company for the stock of the Giannini banks. Two years later the Bank of Italy became the Bank of America National Trust and Savings Association. Giannini continued to pursue liberal policies in extending loans to large and small enterprises alike and pioneered in bank financing of the young motion-picture industry. Giannini retired in 1930, but a year later, on learning that his successor had instituted a traditional conservative administration, undertook a successful proxy fight and was reelected chairman of the board of Transamerica. He held the position officially until 1945, when he again retired, but remained thereafter in close touch with the making of corporate policy. By 1948 the Bank of America system had grown to include more than 500 branch banks and, with more than $6 billion in deposits, was the largest bank in the United States and the largest private bank in the world. Giannini died in San Mateo, California, on June 3, 1949.

Giauque, William Francis (1895–1982), chemist. Born on May 12, 1895, in Niagara Falls, Ontario, Giauque was the son of American parents. He graduated from the University of California at Berkeley in 1920 and on taking his Ph.D. two years later was appointed an instructor in chemistry; he rose to professor in 1934. From his graduate days on he devoted his research to the behavior and properties of matter at temperatures approaching absolute zero. In the course of studying the entropy of various gases at extremely low temperatures in order to compare their observed properties with those calculated from theory—a program of research that established quantum statistics and the theory of entropy on a firm experimental basis—he and his co-worker, H. L. Johnston, discovered in 1929 that naturally occurring oxygen contains minute quantities of a second and a third isotope, each heavier than the predominant oxygen isotope. Since the scale of atomic weights then in use employed oxygen as the standard, the discovery forced the development of a second scale to allow for the tiny variation introduced by the heavier isotopes; the separate chemical and physical atomic-weight scales were in use until 1961, when a single scale based on a different standard was adopted. Giauque had in 1926 proposed a means for producing much lower temperatures than were currently possible and by 1933 he was using his "adiabatic demagnetization" method in experiments carried on with D. P. MacDougall. The method became standard for other investigators working in the temperature range of a small fraction of one degree Kelvin, and its invention, together with his preceding studies, brought Giaque honors and awards, culminating in the 1949 Nobel Prize for Chemistry. He continued to teach and do research at the University of California, Berkeley. He died in Oakland, California, on March 28, 1982.

Gibbons, James (1834–1921), religious leader. Born in Baltimore on July 23, 1834, of Irish immigrant parents, Gibbons grew up in Ireland, where his parents had returned in 1837. In 1852 he returned to the United States, settling in New Orleans with his mother. Deciding upon the priesthood as his vocation, he studied at St. Charles College near Baltimore, graduating in 1858, and then at St. Mary's Seminary. He was ordained in 1861. During the Civil War he was pastor of a small parish and chaplain at Fort McHenry and at a number of military hospitals in the Baltimore area; in 1865 he became secretary to the archbishop of Baltimore. His warm personality and remarkable abilities elevated him rapidly in the hierarchy; consecrated titular bishop of Adramyttum and sent to organize the vicariate apostolic of North Carolina in 1868, he became bishop of Richmond four years later and in 1877, after a few months as coadjutor to the then archbishop, was himself made archbishop of Baltimore. In the same year he published *The Faith of Our Fathers*, a clear and eloquent exposition of Roman Catholic doctrine that is still widely popular. Firmly devoted to his native country and to the support of its institutions, he held the U.S. Constitution to be man's greatest achievement in government. Supported by Pope Leo XIII in the belief that the future of the Catholic church lay in the promotion of democratic institutions, he organized the Third Plenary Council of the American hierarchy, which declared its support of American civil institutions. In 1886 he was appointed the second American cardinal by Pope Leo XIII. He was a founder and the first chancellor of the Catholic University, which opened in 1889 in Washington, D.C. His patriotism and tolerance made him widely popular beyond the confines of the Church; his admirers included several presidents. He died in Baltimore on March 24, 1921.

Gibbs, Josiah Willard (1839–1903), mathematical physicist. Born on February 11, 1839, in New Haven, Connecticut, Gibbs graduated from Yale in 1858 and took his Ph.D. there in 1863. For three years he was a tutor at the college. From 1866 to 1869 he studied at the universities of Paris, Berlin, and Heidelberg; two years after his return to New Haven he was appointed professor of mathematical physics at Yale, a position he held for the rest of his life. Devoting himself to work in thermodynamics, he produced in 1876 and 1878 his two great papers titled "On the Equilibrium of Heterogeneous Substances," which greatly extended the field of thermodynamics and laid the theoretical groundwork for the science of physical chemistry. Recognition of the importance of his work was, however, long delayed. In the following years he gave his attention to the calculus of quaternions and to vector analysis; his work on vector analysis was never published by Gibbs, although it was incorporated into a textbook by another that appeared in 1901 and was long in use. Gibbs published a number of papers on the theory of optics during the 1880s. In 1902 came his last great work, *Elementary Principles in Statistical Mechanics*. He died not long afterward, on April 28, 1903 in New Haven. Only very slowly in ensuing decades did he come to be recognized as the greatest American theoretical scientist up to his time. He was elected to the Hall of Fame in 1950.

Gibbs, Oliver Wolcott (1822–1908), chemist. Born in New York City on February 21, 1822, Wolcott Gibbs graduated from Columbia College in 1841 and entered the College of Physicians and Surgeons, taking his M.D. in 1845. After three years of further study in laboratories in France and Germany he returned to become an assistant professor in the College of Physicians and Surgeons and in 1849 joined the faculty of the New York Free Academy, precursor of the College of the City of New York (CCNY). In 1863 he was named Rumford Professor at Harvard, where he taught also in the Lawrence Scientific School. There he created a modern chemistry laboratory, introducing the most advanced techniques and equipment from Europe and, both as a teacher and as a research chemist, laying a firm foundation for the progress of chemistry in the United States. He was a pioneer in spectroscopy and his broad background in physical and medical science enabled him to carry on significant investigations into the physiological actions of various compounds. Other topics to which he contributed were the chemistry of cobalt, platinum, and other rare metals. Gibbs was in 1863 a founder and later, from 1895 to 1900, president of the National Academy of Sciences and a member of many other major organizations; he was president of the American Association for the Advancement of Science in 1897. He was among the first scientists in the world to recognize and publicize the importance of the work of Josiah Willard Gibbs (no relation). Gibbs retired in 1887 and for ten years thereafter continued his researches in his own laboratory. He died in Newport, Rhode Island, on December 9, 1908; four years later the Wolcott Gibbs Memorial Laboratory was completed at Harvard.

Gibson, Althea (1927–   ), tennis player. Born on August 25, 1927, in Silver, South Carolina, Miss Gibson grew up there and in New York City. She began playing tennis at an early age under the auspices of the New York Police Athletic League (PAL) and in 1943 won the state Negro girls' singles championship. Five years later she won the national Negro women's title and held it for ten consecutive years. While attending Florida Agricultural and Mechanical University she continued to play in tournaments around the country and in 1950 became the first black tennis player to enter the national grass-court championship tournament at Forest Hills, Long Island. The next year she entered the prestigious All-England tournament at Wimbledon, again as the first black American ever invited. She graduated from Florida A. & M. in 1953 and was appointed an athletic instructor at Lincoln University, Jefferson City, Missouri. Until 1956 Miss Gibson had only fair success in match tennis play, winning several minor titles but no major ones; in that year she joined a tennis team sent on a world goodwill tour by the state department and on the tour her game suddenly jelled and she won a number of tournaments in Asia and Europe and shared the women's doubles title at Wimbledon. In 1957 she returned to Wimbledon to win the women's singles and doubles titles and, after a ticker-tape reception in New York City, later in the year took the U.S. women's singles championship at Forest Hills. She repeated all three victories in 1958 and in both years was a member of the successful U.S. Wightman Cup team. Having overcome considerable early racial prejudice and having worked her way, on the strength of her smashing serves and deft returns, to top rank in world amateur tennis, she turned professional in 1959 and later took up golf as well. Her autobiography, *I Always Wanted to Be Somebody*, appeared in 1958.

Gibson, Charles Dana (1867–1944), illustrator. Born on September 14, 1867, in Roxbury, Massachusetts, Gibson attended schools in Flushing, New York, and studied at the Art Students League in 1884–1885. His black-and-white illustrations of gay, well-bred people began appearing in *Life*, a humorous weekly, and major publications such as *Scribner's*, *The Century*, and *Harper's*. In much of his work he sought to depict and to glorify the American woman, and he particularly delighted in picturing her in some out-of-doors pastime. His creation of the "Gibson Girl" made him famous and much sought after as an illustrator. *Collier's Weekly* paid him $50,000, the highest fee ever paid an illustrator up to that time, for 52 pen-and-ink sketches. The Gibson Girl enjoyed an enormous vogue and set a fashion in women's clothing and hairstyles—she appeared in soft, wide pompadours, high-collared starched white shirts and dark ascot ties, and dark-colored skirts with hemlines that just skimmed the floor; she wore a sailor hat in the summer, and carried a parasol. The fashion persisted through the 1890s to about 1914. Collections of Gibson's drawings appeared as *Sketches in London*, 1894; *Pictures of People*, 1896; *Sketches in Egypt*, 1899; and *The Social Ladder*, 1902. One series, *The Education of Mr. Pipp*, 1899, inspired a play of the same name.

He illustrated several books, notably *The Prisoner of Zenda*. He died in New York City on December 23, 1944.

Giddings, Joshua Reed (1795–1864), public official. Born on October 6, 1795, in Tioga Point (now Athens), Pennsylvania, Giddings early moved with his family to the Western Reserve, now in Ohio. He received little schooling but educated himself sufficiently so that, after brief service in the War of 1812, he was able to support himself for several years by teaching school. He took up the study of law and was admitted to the bar in 1821, opening a practice in Jefferson, Ohio, that was quickly successful. He served a term in 1826–1828 in the legislature and in 1838 was elected as a Whig to the House of Representatives. There he immediately joined with John Quincy Adams in fighting the "gag rule" designed to suppress debate on antislavery measures, and remained an outspoken critic of slavery and slaveholders throughout 21 years in the House. In 1842 his radical stand on behalf of the slaves of the *Creole*, who had seized the ship and were seeking freedom in a British port, and his opposition to any government action protecting the coastal slave trade, led to his being formally censured by his colleagues; he resigned and appealed to his constituents, by whom he was promptly and overwhelmingly returned to his seat. Giddings was violently opposed to the annexation of Texas and to the Mexican War, viewing both as plots to extend slavery, and in 1848 he joined the Free-Soil party. He was a Republican from the party's founding in 1854, and he in large part set the pattern, in both conviction and manner, for the later Radical Republican faction. Ill health forced him to retire from Congress in 1859, but two years later he was appointed U.S. consul general to Canada by President Abraham Lincoln, whom he had known and influenced through his speeches as early as 1847. Giddings remained in that post until his death in Montreal on May 27, 1864.

Gilbert, Alfred Carlton (1884–1961), business leader. Born on February 15, 1884, in Salem, Oregon, Gilbert was educated at Pacific University and at Yale Medical School, from which he graduated in 1909. He had since childhood been actively interested in athletics and at Yale had starred in track and field sports; at the Olympic tryouts in 1908 he set a world record mark of 12′ 7¾″ in the pole vault and at the Olympic Games in London that year tied with a teammate for the gold medal in the event. He did not begin a medical practice after graduation, but instead established the Mysto Manufacturing Company in New Haven, Connecticut, to produce a variety of apparatus for use by magicians, an outgrowth of another hobby of long standing. In 1912, inspired by the girders and trusses of the suspension towers of a power line, he made a set of miniature cardboard construction pieces and then commissioned a toolmaker to produce a prototype set from steel. Within a short time the Mysto company placed on the market an altogether new sort of toy—the Erector Set, with which budding young engineers could build bridges, derricks, cranes, and all manner of engineering marvels. The Erector kits, in various sizes, proved a commercial success and within three years annual sales were in excess of $750,000. In 1916 the Mysto company became the A. C. Gilbert Company; the toy line was expanded to include chemistry sets, meteorological stations, mineralogy kits, radio kits, tool chests, and other such materials for young scientists and builders, and Gilbert, who remained ever fascinated by such things, himself wrote a series of instructional books on topics ranging from coin tricks to carpentry to acoustics. In 1938 he bought the American Flyer Company of Chicago, then a small firm, and soon made the American Flyer toy electric trains one of the leading lines in the country. In 1956, by which time the company's annual sales were on the order of $20 million, he passed its presidency to his son and assumed the title of chairman of the board. One of his proudest claims for his best-known product was the fact that Sir Donald Bailey, inventor of the panel-truss Bailey bridge of World War II fame, built his first model of the bridge with an Erector Set. Gilbert, who attributed his success to the fact that he remained all his life a boy at heart, died in Boston on January 24, 1961.

Gilbert, Cass (1859–1934), architect. Born on November 24, 1859, in Zanesville, Ohio, Gilbert studied architecture from 1878 to 1879 at the Massachusetts Institute of Technology (MIT) and, afer traveling in Europe, entered the architectural firm of McKim, Mead and White in 1880. Three years later he began private practice in St. Paul, Minnesota. Business came slowly, but in 1896 he was commissioned to design the Minnesota state capitol and that success enabled him to move his office to New York City. He submitted the winning design in a competition for the U.S. customhouse there and followed it with plans for the Union Club. For the 1904 Louisiana Purchase Exposition in St. Louis he designed the Art Building (now the city's art museum) and later designed the St. Louis public library. In 1913 he achieved a national reputation with his Woolworth Building in New York City, long the world's tallest and still considered one of the finest early skyscrapers. He served from 1910 to 1918 on the National Commission of Fine Arts, at the same time executing many commissions in the national capital, including the U.S. Treasury annex, 1919, the Chamber of Commerce, 1924, and the Supreme Court Building, completed in 1935. Among Gilbert's other major works were libraries in New Haven, Connecticut, and in Detroit; the West Virginia state capitol; and the New York Life Insurance Building and the federal court building in New York City. He also drew plans for the state universities of Minnesota and Texas. His design for the George Washington Bridge across the Hudson at New York City was later greatly modified. Gilbert's practice was diverse and the body of his work was remarkably large for one man; thoroughly traditional in taste and having a strong dislike for modern functional design, he was much in demand and often honored for his work. He died on May 17, 1934, in Brockenhurst, England.

Gilbert, Grove Karl (1843–1918), geologist. Born in Rochester, New York, on May 6, 1843, Gilbert graduated from the University of Rochester in 1862 and after a brief period of teaching school became an assistant to a geologist. With five years of such informal training he secured a position with an Ohio state geological survey in 1869 and two years later joined the military survey of the territory west of the 100th meridian under Lt. G. M. Wheeler. During three years with the Wheeler survey he made extensive and remarkable explorations of the Colorado River basin and located and named the bed of ancient Lake Bonneville. From 1874 to 1879 he worked with John Wesley Powell's survey group, and upon the organization of the U.S. Geological Survey in 1879 was appointed a senior geologist. Gilbert was particularly influential in establishing the principles on which the Survey conducted its cartographic work. He was placed in charge of the Appalachian Division in 1884 and from 1889 to 1892 was the Survey's chief geologist; thereafter he relinquished most of his administrative duties to devote more time to research and writing. Most notable among his many publications were *Geology of the Henry Mountains*, 1876, in which he was the first to describe the intrusive igneous structure known as a laccolith; *History of Lake Bonneville, Utah*, 1890, which he and others considered his magnum opus; *History of the Niagara River*, 1890; *Recent Earth Movement in the Great Lakes Region*, 1898; and *Introduction to Physical Geography*, 1902. Generally considered one of the most thoughtful and painstaking geologists of his day, Gilbert was a member of a great many national and international scientific organizations and the recipient of numerous honors and awards. He died in Jackson, Michigan, on May 1, 1918.

Gilbert, Henry Franklin Belknap (1868–1928), composer. Born in Somerville, Massachusetts, on September 26, 1868, Gilbert began studying violin at an early age, later enrolling at the New England Conservatory. While still a youth he organized a musical group that performed in various places in New England. From 1888 to 1892 he studied composition under Edward A. MacDowell and gradually abandoned the violin to devote himself to writing music. To support himself he was forced to work in minor jobs, usually in music-publishing houses, throughout his life and could therefore compose only in his spare time; nonetheless he produced a considerable body of work of consistently high quality. Almost from the start he was attracted by the notion of employing American themes in his music. After early successes, such as his *Celtic Studies*, 1895, by which he attracted the attention of the traditional musical world, he turned to native themes for *Negro*

Episode, 1903, *Comedy Overture*, 1905, originally intended as the overture of an opera based on the Uncle Remus stories; *Dance in Place Congo*, 1906, a ballet inspired by the writings of George Washington Cable and later produced at the Metropolitan Opera House in New York; *Americanesque*," 1909; *Negro Rhapsody*, 1912, written for the 1913 Norfolk, Connecticut, Festival; *Indian Sketches*, 1914; *American Dances in Rag-Time Rhythm*, about 1915; and others. Widely celebrated as the first composer to rely primarily on American folk music, Gilbert was often referred to as "the Mark Twain of music." In his mature period he relied less on specifically Negro or Indian themes; among his later works were the major portion of the music for the Plymouth, Massachusetts, tercentenary celebrations in 1920; *Jazz Study*, 1924; *Symphonic Piece*, 1925; and *Nocturne from Whitman*, 1925, which was accorded a rousing reception at its premier performance by the Philadelphia Symphony Orchestra just two months before Gilbert's death on May 19, 1928, in Cambridge, Massachusetts.

Gilbert, Marie Dolores Eliza Rosanna, *see* Montez, Lola

Gilder, Richard Watson (1844–1909), editor. Born on February 8, 1844, in Bordentown, New Jersey, Gilder grew up there, in Flushing, New York, and elsewhere—wherever his preacher-schoolmaster father moved. He was educated in his father's schools and for a time read law. After brief Civil War service in a Pennsylvania militia unit in 1863 he went to work for the Camden & Amboy Railroad. In 1865 he became a reporter for the *Newark Daily Advertiser*, but a short time later he moved to the newly established *Newark Morning Register*, with which he retained a connection until 1870. He also wrote for and, during 1869–1870, edited *Hours at Home*; when that periodical was merged into *Scribner's Monthly* in 1870 he became assistant editor under Josiah G. Holland. In addition to his editorial duties he conducted a regular column and was responsible for the art features in *Scribner's*. His home in New York City became a favorite gathering place for many of the leading artists and literati of the city and he was host at the meetings that led to the formation of the Society of American Artists in 1877 and the Authors' Club in 1882. In 1881 *Scribner's* was succeeded by the *Century* magazine and Gilder became editor. He shaped the new journal's policies and early developed it into a powerful cultural force, mixing literary coverage and many illustration's with such innovative features as the "Battles and Leaders of the Civil War" series. The series proved highly popular and was later, in 1887, published separately in four volumes. In the magazine and in private life Gilder promoted a wide array of reforms and became a leader of a multitude of civic projects in New York, from the renovation of tenement housing to the erection of the Washington Memorial Arch. His own writings, aside from those as editor of the *Century*, were largely poetic; beginning with *The New Day*, 1876, he published nearly a score of small volumes of verse, much of which was timely and felicitous but undistinguished. Gilder remained an active and influential citizen and cultural arbiter until his death in New York City on November 18, 1909.

Gildersleeve, Basil Lanneau (1831–1924), philologist and educator. Born in Charleston, South Carolina, on October 23, 1831, Gildersleeve received early and thorough training in Latin and Greek from his father. After a single year of regular schooling he entered the College of Charleston in 1845; he later transferred to Jefferson College and thence to Princeton, graduating in 1849. He taught school for a year in Richmond, Virginia, and then traveled to Europe to pursue further studies in the classics at the universities of Berlin, Bonn, and Göttingen, taking his Ph.D. from Göttingen in 1853. For the next three years he worked as a tutor and continued his philological studies and in 1856 was appointed professor of Greek at the University of Virginia. He remained there, teaching also Latin for a time, for 20 years, with the exception of Civil War service in the Confederate cavalry. Although he was recognized from the outset as a teacher of remarkable ability and dedication, he published little until 1867, when his *Latin Grammar* appeared. Widely praised, it remained long in use through subsequent revised editions. Several other Latin textbooks followed, but it was not until after 1876, when he was named the first professor of Greek at the new Johns Hopkins University, that Gildersleeve emerged as the country's foremost classical scholar. His edition of *The Apologies of Justin Martyr*, 1877, was followed by *Pindar: Olympian and Pythian Odes*, 1885; *Essays and Studies, Educational and Literary*, 1890; and, in the province that was particularly his own, *Syntax of Classical Greek from Homer to Demosthenes*, Part I, 1900, and Part II (with C. W. E. Miller), 1911. In addition to those lucid works he published a large number of shorter studies and monographs in the pages of the *American Journal of Philology*, which he founded in 1880 and continued to edit for some 40 years. Gildersleeve's work as an author, editor, and teacher was of very great influence in promoting classical scholarship in the United States, and as an expositor of Greek syntax he was without equal. He retired from Johns Hopkins in 1915 after nearly 60 years of teaching and died in Baltimore on January 9, 1924.

Gill, Theodore Nicholas (1837–1914), zoologist. Born in New York City on March 21, 1837, Gill early developed a deep interest in natural history and after a basic classical education and a brief period of reading law entered the Wagner Free Institute of Science in Philadelphia. His first scientific paper, on the fishes of New York, was published by the Smithsonian Institution in 1856, when he was nineteen. An 1858 expedition to the West Indies, on which he discovered three new species of fish, was virtually the only field experi-

ence of his career and after 1861, when he was appointed to the staff of the Smithsonian in Washington, D.C., he rarely traveled for any purpose. Soon after assuming his position he was placed in charge of the Smithsonian's scientific library and five years later accompanied the collection to the Library of Congress, where he was until 1874 senior assistant librarian. From 1860 he was on the faculty of Columbian College (University from 1873) as adjunct professor of physics and natural history, becoming professor of zoology in 1884 and retiring in 1910, six years after Columbian had become The George Washington University. By far the greater part of his working life, however, he spent in the Smithsonian, organizing and studying the collections made by various expeditions and becoming acknowledged as the world's leading taxonomist. While he specialized in ichthyology, on which topic alone he published nearly 400 papers, his retentive mind commanded a vast amount of information covering the entire field of zoology, and he was a frequent contributor to encyclopedias and other reference works. Among his books were *Arrangement of the Families of Mollusks*, 1871; *Arrangement of the Families of Fishes*, 1872; and *Parental Care Among Fresh-Water Fishes*, 1906. He was president of the American Association for the Advancement of Science in 1897. Gill died in Washington, D.C., on September 25, 1914.

Gillett, Frederick Huntington (1851–1935), public official. Born on October 16, 1851, in Westfield, Massachusetts, Gillett graduated from Amherst College in 1874 and three years later took a degree from the Harvard Law School and was admitted to the bar. He established his practice in Springfield, Massachusetts, and soon became involved in public affairs, serving as assistant attorney general of the state during 1879–1882. In 1890 he was elected to the legislature and after a second term there was sent as a Republican to the House of Representatives in 1892. During long service in that body he held numerous important committee posts and was a powerful voice in support of the merit system in civil service, economy in government, and constructive partisanship. On the election of a Republican majority in 1919 he was chosen speaker; he held the position until 1925 and was conceded even by his Democratic opponents to be thoroughly evenhanded and just in exercising the prerogatives of the office. The major legislative achievement of 32 years in the House was the passage of a bill in 1921 providing for the creation of the Bureau of the Budget and the General Accounting Office (GAO). In 1924, upon the urging of President Calvin Coolidge and other party leaders, Gillett passed up renomination for his House seat in order to run in a crucial senatorial election. He was duly elected, but found the Senate less to his taste and served only one term; in 1931 he retired to Springfield. He published a biography of George F. Hoar in 1934. Gillett died in Springfield on July 31, 1935.

Gillette, King Camp (1855–1932), inventor and business leader. Born in Fond du Lac, Wisconsin, on January 5, 1855, Gillette was educated in Chicago and after working for a time in a hardware store became a traveling salesman for a succession of companies. He had a strong urge to invent something and in 1891 was advised by his employer, William Painter (inventor of the crown bottle cap), to concentrate on developing a disposable product for which demand would be constant. Four years later, faced with a dull straight razor, he suddenly conceived of a razor using a thin, double-edged, and above all disposable steel blade. He soon had a crude model, but it was only after six years of experimentation, with the technical aid of William Nickerson, that he developed a practical blade and razor. In 1901 the Gillette Safety Razor Company was established. Two years later the product was on the market and the sales for 1903 totaled 51 razors and 168 blades. The easy new method of shaving caught on quickly thereafter, however, and as sales soared into the millions annually, beards became steadily less fashionable. Gillette remained president of the company until 1931 and was a director until his death. In his later years he became interested in social and economic reform. In a number of books, including *World Corporation*, 1910, and *The People's Corporation*, 1924, he advocated a reorganization of the economy into a single gigantic trust—an idea similar in many respects to Edward Bellamy's "Nationalist" scheme—a planned utilization of the most advanced technology, the organization of labor into efficient production groups, and the communalization of many domestic functions within huge residential units. A World Corporation to promote these ideas was established briefly in 1910 and Gillette sought unsuccessfully to persuade Theodore Roosevelt to take charge of it. He died in Los Angeles on July 9, 1932.

Gillette, William Hooker (1853–1937), actor and playwright. Born in Hartford, Connecticut, on July 24, 1853, Gillette was educated in local schools and studied at various times at New York University, the Massachusetts Institute of Fine Arts, and Boston University. He had long been interested in dramatics when in 1875 he traveled to New Orleans and joined a stock company there. During the next few years he worked in companies in New York City, Boston, Cincinnati, Louisville, and elsewhere, winning notice particularly in *Faint Heart Ne'er Won Fair Lady* at the Globe Theatre, Boston, in 1875, and in *Broken Hearts*, also at the Globe, in 1876. In 1881 he starred in a production of his own play, *The Professor*, at the Madison Square Theatre in New York City and enjoyed considerable success; later in the year his second play, *Esmeralda*, was a great hit at the same theater, running for a year. *Held by the Enemy*, a spy tale set in the Civil War, was a success in Brooklyn and in New York City in 1886 and in a London production the following year; the hero's role, like all those that he wrote for himself, called for the expression of cool, quiet strength in the midst of confusion and danger. Subsequent plays of his—he did not appear in all of them, nor did he limit his acting to his own vehicle—included *A Legal Wreck*, 1888; *Too Much Johnson*, 1894, and *Secret Service*, 1896, both produced first in New York City and later in London; and *She Loved Him So*, 1899. In 1899, he adopted characters from the writings of Sir Arthur Conan Doyle to produce *Sherlock Holmes*, premiered in Buffalo, New York, and later produced in New York City and London. That play, with himself in the title role, brought him his greatest success both as an actor and as a playwright; he was thereafter firmly identified with the character and played Holmes in frequent revivals of the play and in a 1915 motion picture. Gillette continued to appear in his own plays, new and old, and in those of others, notably in James M. Barrie's *The Admirable Crichton* in 1903, until his retirement from the stage in 1919. He re-emerged in 1929 to tour in *Sherlock Holmes*, last appearing in the role in 1932. He made a second farewell tour in 1935 and retired permanently in 1936. Among the many honors accorded him during his distinguished career was election in 1913 to the American Academy of Arts and Letters. Gillette died in Hartford, Connecticut, on April 29, 1937.

Gilliss, James Melville (1811–1865), naval officer and astronomer. Born on September 6, 1811, in Georgetown (now in Washington), D.C., Gilliss entered the Navy at the age of fifteen. Between 1833 and 1835 he studied for short periods at the University of Virginia and in Paris on leaves of absence and in 1836 was assigned to the Depot of Charts and Instruments in Washington, succeeding Lt. Charles Wilkes as head of the establishment the next year. From 1838 to 1842 he was chiefly engaged in making astronomical observations to correlate with and supplement those being made by Wilkes on his exploratory voyage in the Southern Hemisphere; he found time, however, also to make independent studies of magnetic and meteorological phenomena and, despite the crudity of the instruments at hand, to make corrections in more than a thousand star positions in the standard catalogues. It was largely at Gilliss's prompting that an appropriation was made by Congress in 1842 for the enlargement of the navy's small and inadequate observatory, and he bore the principal responsibility for planning and equipping the new building, traveling to Europe for the purpose and passing the superintendency of the Depot of Charts and Instruments to Lt. Matthew F. Maury. At its opening in 1844 the impressive new Naval Observatory, the first in America designed solely for research, was given into the charge of Maury, much to Gilliss's disappointment. He continued his work, however, and in 1846 published the first volume of astronomical observations issued in the United States. In 1849 he headed an expedition that established a supplementary observatory in Santiago, Chile, and remained there for three years making observations of Mars and Venus and continuing his catalogue work on the stars of the Southern Hemisphere. On his return he published a multivolume report on Chile. Although he was placed on the navy's reserve list in 1855 because of his 20 years' absence from qualifying sea duty, he was retained in his position at the observatory by special order of the secretary of the navy. He directed expeditions to South America in 1858 and to Washington Territory in 1860 to observe solar eclipses and in 1861, on the resignation of Maury, became head of the Naval Observatory. Most of his work during four years in the post concerned organizing and preparing for publication the observatory's masses of raw observational data; he also arranged cooperative research ventures with other observatories. Gilliss died suddenly in Washington, D.C., on February 9, 1865.

Gilman, Daniel Coit (1831–1908), educator. Born in Norwich, Connecticut, on July 6, 1831, Gilman graduated from Yale in 1852, studied briefly at Harvard, and in 1853 was appointed an attaché to the U.S. embassy in St. Petersburg. Before his return to the United States in 1855 he spent some time studying in Berlin. Returning to New Haven, he began an association with Yale that was to last for 17 years. After drawing up a plan of organization for the Yale Scientific School (later the Sheffield Scientific School), he became professor of physical and political geography as well as assistant librarian and secretary to the governing board of the school. He declined offers of university presidencies in 1867 and 1870 but in 1872 accepted a call from the University of California. His three years there were less than successful, largely because of legislative interference in academic matters. In 1875 he was asked to become first president of the new Johns Hopkins University in Baltimore; he accepted gladly and set about gathering a faculty. For a year he traveled over the country and to Europe seeking men who were not only able lecturers but also researchers, the seekers of truth that Gilman believed the true university must have. At Johns Hopkins, free from public pressure, legislative meddling, and theological restriction, emphasis was put on original research and the training of graduate students. In 1889 the Johns Hopkins Hospital, with Gilman as director, was opened; four years later the Medical School opened with admission requirements that, while seeming impossibly high at the time—a college degree was requisite—soon became standard throughout the nation. In a quarter-century at Hopkins, Gilman brought to reality his conception of a great university, and his ideas had tremendous impact on other educators and institutions. In 1901 he retired and for the next three years was the first president of the Carnegie Institution of Washington. He served also at various times on the General Education Board, as president of the National Civil Service Reform League, and with many other educational and humanitarian organizations. He died in Norwich, Connecticut, on October 13, 1908.

Gilmore, Patrick Sarsfield (1829–1892), bandmaster and composer. Born near Dublin on December 25, 1829, Gilmore as a child was fascinated by his town's regimental band, whose conductor admitted him into classes on harmony and counterpoint, taught him to play the cornet, and let him tour with the band in Canada in 1846. Several years later he traveled to Salem, Massachusetts, formed his own military band, and went on to Boston to found Gilmore's Band. He was made bandmaster of the 24th Massachusetts regiment during the Civil War and headed all the army bands in the Department of Louisiana. The first of the huge concerts for which he became known was organized in New Orleans in 1864; in it Gilmore conducted 5000 adults' and children's voices, a 500-piece orchestra, supplementary trumpeters and drummers, and artillery fire. His National Peace Jubilee in Boston in 1869 featured a chorus of 10,000, a 1000-piece orchestra, and Gilmore's characteristic rhythm section; it was followed in 1872 by the World Peace Jubilee, also held in Boston, which included a 20,000-member chorus, 2000 instrumentalists, church bells, cannons fired by electricity and the Boston Fire Department banging out the "Anvil Chorus" on anvils. It was ever Gilmore's conviction that 100 good musicians would produce twice the amount of good music as 50 good musicians. He and his bands played before enthusiastic audiences throughout the United States, Canada, and Europe. He wrote many of the military-band numbers that were played by his and other groups of the time, and composed dance music, popular songs, and, in 1863, the words and music for "When Johnny Comes Marching Home Again," identified with both the Civil and Spanish-American wars. On September 24, 1892, during an exposition in St. Louis, he died suddenly while conducting his band.

Gilpin, Charles Sidney (1878–1930), actor. Born in Richmond, Virginia, on November 20, 1878, Gilpin left school at twelve to be apprenticed in the office of the *Richmond Planet*. For several years, while working as a printer, he took part on occasion in various theatrical productions, appearing in restaurants, at fairs, and on the variety stage as a song-and-dance man. In 1903 he joined the Canadian Jubilee Singers, and for four years with that and other minstrel companies he toured the country. He first played dramatic roles with the Pekin Stock Company in Chicago from 1907, and he continued to tour with repertory and vaudeville companies until 1916, when he moved to New York City and became manager of the Lafayette Theatre Company in Harlem, the earliest black stock company in the city. He remained with the Lafayette until 1919, when, in his Broadway debut, his performance in *Abraham Lincoln* attracted the attention of Eugene O'Neill, who immediately sought him out to take the title role in his new play, *The Emperor Jones*. In the premiere of the play by the Provincetown Players in Greenwich Village Gilpin was a sensation, and he continued in the role through a remarkable three-year run, winning a Drama League Award and, from the National Association for the Advancement of Colored People (NAACP), the Spingarn Medal for 1921. Through the fortune of being cast in a role perfectly suited to his powerful dramatic gifts, Gilpin became one of the first black actors to win a wide following on the American stage. He was forced by ill health to retire in 1926, although he later returned to the stage on occasion. He died in Eldridge Park, near Trenton, New Jersey, on May 6, 1930.

Ginsberg, Allen (1926–   ), poet. Born on June 3, 1926, in Newark, New Jersey, Ginsberg graduated from Columbia in 1948. He lived in New York City until 1953, becoming a close friend of avante-garde writers, including Jack Kerouac and Gregory Corso, and held a variety of jobs until becoming a market-research consultant in 1951. He worked briefly in market research in San Francisco, but soon turned to writing poetry and living in the bohemian style of the "beat generation." He attended graduate school in 1955 at the University of California at Berkeley. That year he gave the first reading of his long, rambling poem "Howl" and became immediately famous in the youth underground, from North Beach in San Francisco to Greenwich Village in New York City. He gave frequent readings thereafter in art galleries, coffeehouses, and universities throughout the country, and in the early 1960s in South America, India, and England. In 1965 he appeared at a gathering of peace marchers in Berkeley and introduced "flower power"—a strategy of friendly confrontation in which flowers were handed to armed policemen, spectators, and the press. He was a Guggenheim fellow in poetry in 1965–1966 and gave readings in Havana, Prague, Moscow, Warsaw, and London. He published *Howl and Other Poems*, 1955; *Empty Mirror*, 1960; *Kaddish and Other Poems*, 1960; *Reality Sandwiches*, 1963; *Ankor-Wat*, 1967; and *Planet News, 1961–1967*, 1969. He appeared in several movies, including *Wholly Communion*, 1965, and *Chappaqua*, 1966, spoke on U.S. military and industrial power on a tour of American colleges in 1968, and was an organizer of the ill-fated Festival of Life in Chicago during the 1968 Democratic national convention. His play, *Kaddish*, opened to good reviews in 1972.

Girard, Stephen (1750–1831), business leader and philanthropist. Born in Bordeaux, France, on May 20, 1750, Girard left home at fourteen to ship as a cabin boy on a merchant vessel. He remained at sea for several years, achieving master's rating; in 1774 he made a voyage to the West Indies as a captain, and then entered the American coastal trade. From that year until 1776 he sailed for a New York mercantile house while carrying on a small trade of his own; then, with the British blockade beginning, he settled in Philadelphia and engaged in a variety of business pursuits. After the Revolution, during which he lived for a time in Mount Holly, New Jersey, to escape the British occupation of Philadelphia, he returned to what was then the principal mercantile city in America and entered foreign trade himself, eventually building a small but highly successful fleet of merchantmen and laying the foundations of a great fortune. During the terrible yellow fever epidemic of 1793 and again in 1797 he remained in the city and worked ceaselessly caring for the victims when much of the population had fled. In 1812, on the expiration of the charter of the Bank of the United States, Girard bought the institution's building and assets and opened the Bank of Stephen Girard, which soon established credit with other American banks and many leading European banks as well. During the War of 1812 Girard joined with John Jacob Astor and other capitalists in expediting the sale of government bonds and in 1814 he himself underwrote nearly the whole of a $3 million stock issue to capitalize the Second Bank of the United States; his bank became known in consequence as the "sheet anchor" of government credit. He spent much of his time from 1826 in planning for the disposition of his estate, carefully constructing an airtight will that provided small bequests for his relatives and retainers, larger ones to the city of Philadelphia and the state of Pennsylvania for various public works, and some $6 million for the founding of Girard College for the education of white male orphan children. Girard died in Philadelphia on December 26, 1831; it was only after his will had withstood several legal challenges that the college was opened in 1848. A Supreme Court decision opened the school to Negro boys in 1968.

Gish, Lillian Diana (1896–   ) and Dorothy (1898–1968), actresses. Born in Ohio, Lillian in Springfield on October 14, 1896, and Dorothy in Massillon on March 11, 1898, the Gish sisters grew up from about 1900 in New York City, although they later moved often as the family's precarious fortunes dictated. In 1902, upon the suggestion of a theatrical acquaintance, both girls were given parts in road-company productions, Dorothy appearing in *East Lynne* and Lillian in *Convict Stripes*. For the next ten years they continued to tour with various companies, often together but occasionally separately; they attended school sporadically, for the most part in Ohio, where their mother returned to live. During their years as child actresses they formed close friendships with Mary Pickford (then still known as Gladys Mary Smith), who in 1912 introduced them to D. W. Griffith. Immediately struck by their beauty and charm, he gave them small parts in a series of silent movies, beginning with *The Unseen Enemy*, 1912, and the next year placed them under contract to his studio. Almost from the start Lillian was the more popular of the two;

an extra measure of winsome appeal won her a large and growing audience of admirers and from her appearance in *Birth of a Nation*, 1915, she was established as one of Hollywood's top stars, soon becoming known as the "First Lady of the Screen." Dorothy, the more vivacious sister, attracted a following of her own in *The Mountain Rat*, 1914, *The Mysterious Shot*, 1914, and others. They appeared together in several of Griffith's greatest films, including *Hearts of the World*, 1918; *Broken Blossoms*, 1919; and *Orphans of the Storm*, 1922. They left Griffith in 1922, Dorothy going to Paramount Studios and Lillian to the Tiffany Company and in 1925 to Metro-Goldwyn-Mayer. Subsequent films of Dorothy's included *Romola*, 1924, in which Lillian also appeared; *Clothes Make the Pirate*, 1925; and two movies made in England, *Nell Gwyn*, 1926, and *Madame Pompadour*, 1927. Lillian's later films included *The White Sister*, 1923; *La Boheme*, 1926; *The Scarlet Letter*, 1926; and *One Romantic Night*, her first sound picture, 1930. With the coming of the talkies they both left the screen for a time and returned to the stage. Dorothy enjoyed a number of Broadway and London successes in *Young Love*, 1928; *The Inspector General*, 1930; *By Your Leave*, 1934; *Missouri Legend*, 1938; and other plays; she continued to appear on the stage and from time to time in films, her last performances being in a 1956 Broadway revival of *Life with Father* and in the film *The Cardinal*, 1963. She died in Rapallo, Italy, on June 4, 1968. Lillian played on the stage in *Uncle Vanya* with great success in 1930 and subsequently appeared in *Camille*, 1932; *Within the Gates*, 1934; *The Star Wagon*, 1937; *Life with Father*, 1941, in which she enjoyed a record run in Chicago while Dorothy was starring with the road company; *Mr. Sycamore*, 1942; *The Magnificent Yankee*, 1945; *Crime and Punishment*, 1948; *The Curious Savage*, 1950; *All the Way Home*, 1960; *I Never Sang for My Father*, 1967; and many others. She continued also to appear occasionally in movies, among them *Miss Susie Slagle's*, 1945, *The Unforgiven*, 1960, and *The Comedians*, 1967; and also appeared on television. Her autobiographical *The Movies, Mr. Griffith and Me* appeared in 1969.

Gist, Christopher (1706?–1759), frontiersman. Born in Maryland, probably near Baltimore, about 1706, Gist led an obscure life until 1750, when, apparently well known as a woodsman and surveyor and at the time living on the Yadkin River in North Carolina, he was engaged by the Ohio Company of Virginia to explore its Western grant. He set out from Maryland, crossed southwestern Pennsylvania, passing the later site of Fort Duquesne, still later Pittsburgh, and entered the Ohio country, traveling down the Ohio River as far as the Miami River, to the west of modern Cincinnati; he then crossed the Ohio into Kentucky—18 years before Daniel Boone—explored nearly as far as present-day Louisville, and returned East in May 1751 with valuable journal descriptions and maps of the Western country.

During 1751–1752 he explored the region between the Monongahela and Little Kanawha rivers and in 1753 returned to establish a small settlement near present-day Brownsville, Pennsylvania. In November 1753, at Cumberland, Maryland, he joined Maj. George Washington as a guide, conducting him, with Governor Robert Dinwiddie's ultimatum, to the French at Fort Le Boeuf; Gist twice saved Washington's life on the perilous winter journey through hostile Indian country. He remained with Washington in 1754 through his second Western expedition, his defeat of a French detachment near Fort Duquesne, and the building and subsequent surrender of Fort Necessity. Gist was again with Washington as a scout in Gen. Edward Braddock's campaign and his disastrous defeat at Fort Duquesne in 1755. In 1756 he journeyed into eastern Tennessee and for some time was an Indian agent there. Gist died either in Georgia or South Carolina sometime in 1759.

Glackens, William James (1870–1938), painter and illustrator. Born on March 13, 1870, in Philadelphia, Glackens early displayed a gift for drawing and after graduating from high school studied at intervals at the Pennsylvania Academy of the Fine Arts. At the age of twenty-one he began working as an artist-reporter for the *Philadelphia Record*, the *Public Ledger*, and the *Press*, coming into contact in the course of his work with such other young painters as John Sloan and George Luks. He was strongly influenced by one of his teachers at the Academy, Robert Henri, and in 1895 accompanied him for a year of travel and study in Europe. On returning to the United States he settled in New York City, continuing to work as an illustrator for newspapers, principally the *New York Herald* and the *New York World*, and for periodicals, notably *McClure's Magazine*, for which he traveled to Cuba during the Spanish-American War, all the while turning more and more attention to his painting. His work as a reporter and illustrator, which he had largely given up by 1905, led him naturally to depict scenes of contemporary life in his serious work and, although he was by no means an artistic radical, he joined with Henri, Sloan, Luks, Arthur B. Davies, Maurice Prendergast, and others in an independent show in 1908 that roused considerable comment in art circles. The group, dubbed "the Eight" and later the "Ashcan School," was in conscious revolt against the conservative dominance of the National Academy of Design, but the mildness of their modernism was revealed at the 1913 Armory Show—for which Glackens headed the American selection committee—that first brought contemporary European painters to attention in the United States. The Eight did not persist as a group; for his part, Glackens soon abandoned his dark palette and street scenes for an impressionistic style modeled closely on the work of Pierre Auguste Renoir. In 1917 he helped organize and was elected the first president of the Society of Independent Artists.

By the time of his death in Westport, Connecticut, on May 22, 1938, Glackens was represented in a great many major museums, galleries, and private collections.

Gladden, Washington (1836–1918), religious leader. Born on February 11, 1836, in Pottsgrove, Pennsylvania, Gladden, who early dropped his given first name Solomon, grew up on the farm of an uncle near Owego, New York. He worked for a local newspaper for a time and in 1856 entered Williams College, graduating three years later. He was licensed to preach soon afterward and was ordained in the Congregational church in 1860. He served several churches in New England during the next several years and from 1871 to 1875 was religious editor for the *Independent*. In 1868 he published *Plain Thoughts on the Art of Living*, the first of 40 books. He was called to the First Congregational Church of Columbus, Ohio, in 1882; there he remained for the rest of his life. An early advocate of what came to be called the "social gospel," Gladden preached a Christianized social order in which enlightenment and religious conscience would eliminate social and economic evils. He opposed Socialism, favoring rather the changing of the unpleasant aspects of the established capitalistic system; he was one of the first clergymen to approve of the labor-union movement, expressing his views in his *Working People and Their Employers*, 1876. He was a widely popular lecturer; he served on the Columbus city council from 1900 to 1902 and was active in the promotion of civic organizations. From 1904 to 1907 he was moderator of the National Council of Congregational Churches and openly condemned the foreign mission board's solicitation of what he considered "tainted" money from John D. Rockefeller. Among his books were *Applied Christianity*, 1887; *Who Wrote the Bible?*, 1891; *Social Salvation*, 1901; *The New Idolatry*, 1905; and his autobiography, *Recollections*, 1909. He died in Columbus, Ohio, on July 2, 1918.

Glaser, Donald Arthur (1926–   ), physicist and biologist. Born on September 21, 1926, in Cleveland, Glaser graduated from Case Institute of Technology in 1946 and undertook graduate work at the California Institute of Technology (Caltech), taking his Ph.D. in physics in 1950. From 1949 he was a member of the faculty of the University of Michigan, advancing from instructor to full professor by 1957. From his early work in cosmic-ray research he was led into a search for a new and improved method of detecting and measuring elementary particles. Working with superheated liquids—liquids heated beyond their boiling points but held by pressure in a delicate equilibrium—he found that with the proper liquid and appropriate equipment he could produce a state of equilibrium that persisted after the release of pressure and that was so sensitive that the passage of a charged particle through the liquid created a local imbalance that revealed itself as a

trail of minute but observable bubbles. His first "bubble chamber" of 1952 was a one-inch container of diethyl ether; later devices were much larger and employed different liquids for various purposes. The bubble chamber held an advantage over the older Wilson cloud chamber in using a much denser medium that vastly increased the chances of occurrence of observable events— collisions and the particles produced from them— in the study of neutral and very high-energy particles; it quickly became standard equipment in nuclear-physics laboratories throughout the world. For his invention and subsequent improvement of the bubble chamber, Glaser was awarded the 1960 Nobel Prize for Physics at the remarkably early age of thirty-four. He had moved to the University of California at Berkeley in 1959 and in 1961 he began a second career, traveling to the University of Copenhagen to study microbiology and then returning to the University of California to conduct research in the field of molecular biology with the aid of his background in nuclear physics and his experience in laboratory instrumentation.

Glasgow Ellen Anderson Gholson (1873–1945), author. Born in Richmond, Virginia, on April 22, 1873, Miss Glasgow was educated privately. In 1897 she published her first novel, *The Descendant*; with *The Voice of the People*, 1900, she began a series of novels depicting the social and political history of Virginia since 1850 that continued in *The Battle-Ground*, 1902; *The Deliverance*, 1904; *The Wheel of Life*, 1906, and others. In *Virginia*, 1913, and *Life and Gabriella*, 1916, she explored the effects of a lingering but long-outmoded Southern code of chivalry. *Barren Ground*, 1925, had a deeply tragic theme set in rural Virginia, as did the later *Vein of Iron*, 1935. With an increasingly ironic approach and a brilliant and satiric treatment she examined the decay of Southern aristocracy and the traumatic encroachment of modern industrial civilization in three novels of manners, *The Romantic Comedians*, 1926; *They Stooped to Folly*, 1929, and *The Sheltered Life*, 1932. Her last novel, *In This Our Life*, 1941, had a similar theme and was awarded a Pulitzer Prize. In 1943 Miss Glasgow published a collection of critical essays entitled *A Certain Measure*. She died in Richmond, Virginia, on November 21, 1945. Her memoirs were published in 1954 as *The Woman Within*.

Glass, Carter (1858–1946), public official. Born on January 4, 1858, in Lynchburg, Virginia, Glass grew up in poverty and received little formal schooling, but while serving an apprenticeship in a newspaper office from the age of fifteen read widely on his own. After several years as a journeyman printer he returned to Lynchburg, became an editor of the *Lynchburg Daily News*, and in 1888 bought the paper, later acquiring and combining with it the *Daily Advance*. Through his strong and widely read editorials and his staunch support of conservative Democratic policies he came gradually to more than local prominence. Elected to the Virginia legislature in 1898, he played a major role in the state constitutional convention that in 1901 severely limited the franchise. Later in that year he was appointed to complete an uncompleted term in the House of Representatives and in 1902 was elected to the seat, holding it from then until 1918. He had little impact in Congress until 1913, when, as chairman of the Committee on Banking and Currency, he drafted, sponsored, and was largely responsible for the passage of the Federal Reserve Act (Glass-Owen Act). Glass was appointed secretary of the treasury by President Woodrow Wilson in 1918 and held the post for two years, resigning in 1920 to fill a vacated Virginia seat in the Senate. In that body, where he remained for the rest of his life, he achieved his greatest renown and power. Opposed to the Republican administrations of the 1920s, he early supported Franklin D. Roosevelt; soon after Roosevelt's election in 1932, however, he let party loyalty go by the board in becoming one of the most outspoken and effective critics of the New Deal, the fiscal policies of which he characterized as outrageous and dishonest; he declined to serve again as secretary of the treasury under Roosevelt. Styling himself a Jeffersonian Democrat, Glass was a tireless advocate of economy in government, the restriction of federal power, strict construction of the Constitution, states' rights, and racial segregation. Perhaps the greatest expert in financial matters ever to serve in Congress, he was the principal author of the 1933 Glass-Steagall Act, which created the Federal Deposit Insurance Corporation (FDIC) and broadened the base and the regulatory authority of the Federal Reserve System. For more than 25 years a leader of the conservative Southern bloc, Glass was a small, feisty man, fearless in debate and as ready to offer his fists as a caustic remark in defense of his principles. From 1942 ill health kept him away from the Senate chamber; he retained his seat, however, until his death in Washington, D.C., on May 28, 1946.

Glass, Hugh (?–1833), frontiersman. Born at a time and place unknown, Glass was reputedly an unwilling member of Jean Laffite's pirate band and later a captive among the Indians of Texas before 1823, the year in which his name is first recorded as a member of William Ashley's second trapping expedition to the upper Missouri country. On the return with Andrew Henry from their encampment to the junction of the Missouri and Yellowstone rivers, he rode, as was apparently his lifelong custom, a little apart from the main body of men and one day was suddenly attacked by a grizzly bear. Glass was mauled so badly that he was expected to die at any moment; Henry therefore took the party on, leaving Glass's burial to two young trappers, one of whom was, according to legend, Jim Bridger. For some reason—one version of the story charitably ascribes it to the approach of a party of Indians—Bridger and the other man, one Fitzgerald, deserted him, taking

his rifle and other equipment. Although left without food or water or means of making fire, Glass very slowly recovered sufficient strength to set out for Fort Kiowa, a hundred miles away. His injuries were such that he could not walk; he therefore crawled the entire distance. He swore vengeance during his long convalescence at Fort Kiowa and the following winter joined another expedition to the Bighorn country to find Bridger and Fitzgerald; however, he ultimately forgave them—Bridger on account of his youth and the other man, some months later at Fort Atkinson, because he returned Glass's rifle. Thereafter Glass engaged in trapping throughout the West, ranging as far south as New Mexico and becoming a favorite subject for tales, many of them quite possibly somewhat tall, told by other mountain men. Glass is thought to have been killed in an encounter with Blackfeet on the Yellowstone River early in 1833; his story was subsequently widely circulated in prose and verse.

Gleason, Herbert John, see Gleason, Jackie

Gleason, Jackie (1916–   ), entertainer. Born on February 26, 1916, in Brooklyn, New York, Herbert John Gleason left high school to enter show business and after several years of working as a master of ceremonies, a carnival barker, a disk jockey, and whenever possible as a nightclub comedian, he won a role in a 1940 Broadway production, *Keep Off the Grass*. His nightclub routine led to a brief motion-picture contract and appearances in *Navy Blues*, 1941, *All Through the Night*, 1942, *Springtime in the Rockies*, 1942, and other films, and in 1944 he scored a hit in the popular Broadway show *Follow the Girls*. He soon added radio broadcasting to his activities and was already rated one of the top comedians in the business when, in 1949, he entered the new medium of television as star of the "Life of Riley" series. The next year he took over as master of ceremonies of the "Cavalcade of Stars," with which he remained until 1952, during the last year appearing also on the "Colgate Comedy Hour." In 1952 he inaugurated his own "Jackie Gleason Show," which ran successfully for three years, establishing him as one of television's highest-paid performers, and was succeeded in 1955 by the even more popular "Honeymooners," a situation-comedy series that was still being enjoyed in syndicated reruns nearly 20 years later. For many of his shows Gleason personally supervised virtually every aspect of production, particularly the musical and dance portions; although he had no musical training whatever, he composed a number of songs by ear, including his own theme, "Melancholy Serenade," and over the years produced nearly 40 albums of recorded music, notably the popular *Music for Lovers Only*. In later years he revealed a considerable dramatic talent; his performance in the 1959 Broadway production of *Take Me Along* earned a Tony award, and his portrayals in such motion pictures as *The Hustler*, 1961, *Requiem for a Heavyweight*, 1962, *Gigot*,

1962, and *Soldier in the Rain*, 1963, won critical as well as popular approval.

Glenn, John Herschel, Jr. (1921–   ), astronaut. Born on July 18, 1921, in Cambridge, Ohio, Glenn grew up in nearby New Concord. He entered Muskingum College in 1939 and in 1942 joined the naval aviation training program. Taking his commission in the Marine Corps, he flew 59 missions in the Pacific theater during 1944–1945, winning two Distinguished Flying Crosses and ten Air Medals. After the war he served at various marine air stations in the United States and abroad and in 1952, by then a major, was sent to Korea, where he flew 90 missions and earned two more Distinguished Flying Crosses and eight Air Medals. Glenn completed test-pilot training in 1954 and was then attached to the Naval Air Test Center and from 1956 to the Fighter Design Branch of the Navy Department's Bureau of Aeronautics in Washington, D.C. While engaged in test-pilot work he made the first transcontinental nonstop supersonic flight in 1957, for which feat he received his fifth DFC. In 1959, shortly after being promoted to lieutenant colonel, he was one of seven men selected for the first astronaut training program of Project Mercury. For nearly three years he trained rigorously with his six fellow astronauts while aiding in the design of the space capsule for the project. Finally, after two of his colleagues had ridden suborbital missions, he was chosen to make the first U.S. flight to orbit the earth; on February 20, 1962, he piloted his *Friendship 7* capsule through 3 orbits of the earth, traveling some 81,000 miles in just under 5 hours and reaching an altitude of more than 185 miles. After splashing down in the Atlantic and undergoing a two-day debriefing session, he returned to Cape Canaveral (Cape Kennedy), starting point of the flight, and was personally greeted by President John F. Kennedy; parades in New York City and Washington and an address to a joint session of Congress followed, firmly establishing Glenn as the popular hero of the day. He remained with the astronaut program until 1964, when he resigned to enter an Ohio senatorial primary election; an injury forced him out of the race. He was again unsuccessful in 1972, but in 1974 he was elected to the Senate. In 1976 he was a keynote speaker at the Democratic national convention.

Glidden, Charles Jasper (1857–1927), businessman and sportsman. Born in Lowell, Massachusetts, on August 29, 1857, Glidden went to work as a telegraph messenger boy at the age of fifteen. He rose quickly to a managerial position with the Franklin Telegraph Company, his office being in Manchester, New Hampshire, and from 1873 to 1877 was a district manager for the Atlantic and Pacific Telegraph Company. He collaborated with Alexander Graham Bell in using the Manchester–Boston telegraph line to test the possibility of long-distance telephony and, convinced of the great potential of the new field, began in 1877 organizing the world's first telephone exchange in

his native town. By 1879 the Lowell District Telephone Company was in operation there and in neighboring towns; Glidden contributed much to the early development of exchange technique, including the use of female operators, whose voices he found were transmitted more clearly than men's. The company, which later became the Erie Telephone & Telegraph Company and part of which later still formed the New England Telephone & Telegraph Company, spread rapidly through Massachusetts, into surrounding states, and as far afield as Minnesota and Texas. Glidden and his associates sold out to the Bell system at a comfortable profit about 1902 and he then turned his attention to the automobile, becoming one of the world's earliest motoring enthusiasts. After organizing a round-the-world motoring tour through 39 countries he undertook in 1904 a tour of the United States that the next year became an official event, with the Glidden Trophy being awarded through the American Automobile Association (AAA). With from 25 to 50 entrants for the tour of more than 1000 miles, the event was the major one of its kind and was held annually, except for 1912, until 1913, after which it was suspended because of its commercial exploitation by manufacturers. Glidden was also deeply interested in aviation; he made a number of balloon ascensions and organized a commercial aviation venture that proved premature. During World War I he served in the aviation section of the Signal Corps reserve and in 1921 became founding president of the World's Board of Aeronautical Commissioners. From 1921 to 1924 he edited the *Aeronautical Digest*. Glidden died on September 11, 1927, in Boston.

Glidden, Joseph Farwell (1813–1906), inventor. Born on January 18, 1813, in Charlestown, New Hampshire, Glidden grew up there and in Orleans County, New York. He received a sound education and for several years taught school, later returning to work the family farm. In 1842 he set out to work his way West with two threshing machines, renting out his services to farmers along the way, and in 1844 he settled near De Kalb, Illinois. He eventually acquired 1500 acres of land and later had extensive interests in local businesses and in a huge Texas ranch. In 1873 he saw at a county fair a sample of a type of barbed wire; various attempts at manufacturing such a fence wire for restraining livestock had been made since 1867, but none had produced a satisfactory material. Improvements soon occurred to Glidden and in 1874 he received a patent for a fence wire consisting of two strands twisted into a cable, a method that prevented the wire from snapping while it kept the barbs securely in place. He subsequently registered other improvements, but rival inventors were close on his heels and patent litigations over the wire lasted for more than 20 years. Glidden nonetheless opened a small factory in De Kalb and in 1875 began manufacturing barbed wire, soon employing power equipment to meet the huge demand for the first practical stock fencing. In 1876 he sold his interest in the Barb Fence Company to the Washburn and Moen Manufacturing Company of Worcester, Massachusetts, for $60,000 and royalties. The De Kalb plant was expanded and further mechanized; by 1880 production had increased more than twentyfold to 80 million pounds a year, while the price had steadily dropped. Barbed wire, more than any other single factor, was the force that tamed the West; it made homestead farming possible in a region where natural fence materials were scarce by protecting crops against the cattle herds of the open range. Cattlemen, although they often fought the fencing of ranges where they were accustomed to grazing their herds at no expense—fence-cutting "wars" and bloodshed were for a time common in Texas and other regions—ultimately also benefited, for fencing led to stock farming and to the development of bigger, stronger breeds than the lanky range cattle. By 1890 the great open range of the West, except for federal lands, was fenced, and the roving herds and cattle drives were things of the past. Glidden took little further part in the wire business after 1876; he lived in De Kalb until his death on October 9, 1906.

Glueck, Sheldon (1896–1980), criminologist. Born on August 15, 1896, in Warsaw, Poland, Sol Sheldon Glueck emigrated with his family to the United States in 1903. In 1913 he went to work for the U.S. Department of Agriculture and remained there, studying part time at Georgetown University, until 1917, when he enlisted in the army for World War I service. On his discharge in 1919 he joined the U.S. Shipping Board and resumed his studies at Georgetown, graduating in 1920 and in the same year becoming a U.S. citizen. He also received a law degree from the National University Law School and then entered Harvard University, from which he received a Ph.D. in 1924. While at Harvard he met and in 1922 married Eleanor Touroff, who had been born in Brooklyn, New York, on April 12, 1898, and graduated from Barnard College in 1919. After taking a diploma in community organization from the New York School of Social Work in 1921 she became head social worker at the Dorchester, Massachusetts, Welfare Center and soon afterward enrolled in the Harvard Graduate School of Education, from which she received a doctorate in 1925. In that year they both joined the Harvard department of social ethics, Sheldon as an instructor and Eleanor as a research criminologist; she became a research assistant for the Harvard Law School Crime Survey in 1928 and in 1930 received a regular appointment in the Law School, advancing to research associate in 1953, while he was appointed assistant professor of criminology in the Law School in 1929, advancing to full professor in 1931, and in 1950 was named Roscoe Pound Professor of Law. Their various titles notwithstanding, they worked from 1925 onward in close collaboration on a long series of pioneering field studies of criminal character and behavior. Their early inter-

est in the effectiveness of various penal and rehabilitative strategies and the phenomenon of recidivism resulted in the heavily documented case studies of *Five Hundred Criminal Careers,* 1930; *Five Hundred Delinquent Women,* 1934; *One Thousand Juvenile Delinquents,* 1934; *Later Criminal Careers,* 1937; *Juvenile Delinquents Grown Up,* 1940; and *Criminal Careers in Retrospect,* 1943. The growing problem of juvenile delinquency led to a closer study of the topic in *Unraveling Juvenile Delinquency,* 1950; *Delinquents in the Making,* 1952; *Physique and Delinquency,* 1956; *Predicting Delinquency and Crime,* 1959; *Family Environment and Delinquency,* 1962; and other works describing investigations in which they sought to detect early signs of potential delinquency (they identified the mesomorphic body type as the most common among criminals) and to point the way to preventive therapy. The Gluecks also published a number of books individually: Eleanor's works included *The Community Use of Schools,* 1927, and *Evaluation Research in Social Work,* 1936, and Sheldon published *Mental Disorder and the Criminal Law,* 1925; *Crime and Justice,* 1936; *War Criminals, Their Prosecution and Punishment,* 1944; and, after serving as consultant to Supreme Court Justice Robert H. Jackson, chief prosecutor at the trials of Nazi war criminals after World War II, *The Nuremberg Trial and Aggressive War,* 1946. Sheldon Glueck later was a member of the advisory committee on criminal procedure of the Supreme Court and also served on committees advising on the Youth Correction Authority Model Bill and the Model Penal Code of the American Law Institute. He retired from the Harvard faculty in 1963 and she followed in 1964, although they continued their researches. Both died in Cambridge, Massachusetts; Eleanor Glueck on September 25, 1972, and Sheldon Glueck on March 10, 1980.

Goddard, Robert Hutchings (1882–1945), physicist and rocketry pioneer. Born in Worcester, Massachusetts, on October 5, 1882, Goddard was from an early age fascinated by rockets and what he envisioned as their potential for flight into space. He graduated from Worcester Polytechnic Institute in 1908 and three years later took his Ph.D. at Clark University, also in Worcester. He was an instructor in physics at Princeton in 1912–1913 and in 1914 joined the Clark faculty where he remained until 1943, after 1919 as a full professor. His work with rockets began, possibly as early as 1908, with static tests and experiments with various fuels, and in 1914 he devised a two-step rocket, the first to employ the staging concept. On the basis of a monograph outlining his researches and ideas for further work, Goddard received in 1916 a grant from the Smithsonian Institution, which in 1919 published the report, the now classic "A Method of Reaching Extreme Altitudes." In that paper he predicted the development of rockets capable of breaking free of earth's gravity and traveling to the moon and beyond.

Goddard's ideas found little public favor, however, and he was often derided as "moon mad;" the weight of popular opinion was against even his clear demonstration that rockets would operate in a vacuum. During the early 1920s he worked on the use of liquid fuels, settling finally on a combination of gasoline and liquid oxygen; the first liquid-fueled rocket was fired in March 1926. In 1929, with the aid of Charles A. Lindbergh, he secured a grant from the Guggenheim Foundation and established a large testing range near Roswell, New Mexico. In that year he fired the first rocket to contain an instrument package; it carried a barometer, a thermometer, and a camera. He began to experiment with gyroscopic guidance systems while improving his fueling apparatus. Goddard's work anticipated much of the progress in rocketry made over the next three decades; he was granted more than 200 patents in the field, some of which, although his work was ignored in the United States, were for developments used by German scientists in producing the V-2 rocket in World War II. During the war Goddard moved to Annapolis, Maryland, and worked on developing rocket motors and jet-assisted takeoff (Jato) units for naval aircraft. He died in Baltimore on August 10, 1945. In 1960 the U.S. government paid $1 million to the Guggenheim Foundation for infringements upon many of Goddard's patents and in 1962 the National Aeronautics and Space Administration's research facility at Greenbelt, Maryland, was named the Goddard Space Flight Center. On July 17, 1969, while the *Apollo XI* astronauts orbited the moon in preparation for their historic landing, the *New York Times* printed a formal retraction of a 1920 editorial comment ridiculing Goddard's claim that rockets could fly through a vacuum to the moon.

Godey, Louis Antoine (1804–1878), publisher. Born in New York City on June 6, 1804, of French immigrant parents, Godey received little schooling and early began working in printing shops. During the 1820s he moved to Philadelphia and secured a position with the *Daily Chronicle*. In 1830, with a partner, he founded the *Lady's Book*, a periodical modeled on a popular British magazine and dependent on material reprinted from foreign sources. In 1837, however, he bought the *Ladies' Magazine* of Boston and induced its editor, Sarah Josepha Hale, to edit *Lady's Book*. The publication soon came to be known as *Godey's Lady's Book* and became the most popular U.S. periodical of its kind, its circulation reaching 150,000 by 1858. In addition to the colored fashion plates and pages of music that were standard fare, the magazine published original stories, essays, and commentaries by American authors, many of them women, and often paid high prices to attract such writers as Nathaniel Hawthorne, Edgar Allan Poe, Henry Wadsworth Longfellow, Ralph Waldo Emerson, and Oliver Wendell Holmes. Perfectly reflecting the intellectual and moral standards, and fashion tastes of the day. *Godey's* was considered by many to be the final word on such matters.

Godey undertook other publishing ventures as well, founding the *Philadelphia Saturday News and Literary Gazette* in 1836 and holding a part interest in a publishing house that issued, among others, the periodical *Lady's Musical Library* in 1842. The *Lady's Book* remained his principal interest, however, and he retained control of it until 1877. In that year he retired and he died in his Philadelphia home on November 29, 1878. *Godey's Lady's Book* was moved to New York City in 1892 and renamed *Godey's Magazine*, under which title it continued to appear until 1898, when it was absorbed by the *Puritan*, one of Frank Munsey's magazines.

Godfrey, Arthur Michael (1903–1983), entertainer. Born on August 31, 1903, in New York City, Godfrey grew up there and in Hasbrouck Heights, New Jersey. At fourteen he left home and for a time drifted around the country, working at various minor jobs. During an enlistment in the navy in 1920–1924 and a later one in the coast guard in 1927–1930 he learned much about the technical aspects of radio and by 1930 had begun to interest himself in broadcasting. In 1930 he took an announcing job with a station in Washington, D.C., and soon attracted considerable notice with his highly unorthodox practice of injecting personal comments—not always altogether flattering to the product—into advertising copy. The station management was unhappy with the idea, but another station perceived the audience appeal in it and encouraged him. By 1934 his popularity was sufficient for him to give up his regular job and become a free-lance broadcaster. Over the next several years he was master of ceremonies or host of a number of programs and in 1941 began a regular morning show. His "Talent Scouts" show began on radio in 1946 and later moved to television, and "Arthur Godfrey Time" was for several years broadcast simultaneously on radio and television. With an easy, chatty manner, a lively sense of humor, and an occasional venture into song—his style was appealing if less than completely musical, and he generally accompanied himself on the ukelele—Godfrey attracted a huge and devoted audience, particularly among housewives; it was once estimated that the total weekly audience for his several concurrent radio and television shows ran to more than 70 million people. Acknowledged in the industry as the master salesman, he was the personality most sought after by potential sponsors, and he let it be known that he chose his patrons carefully, refusing to advertise products in which he did not believe. One of the most appealing personalities produced by the mass media, Godfrey was also a noted horseman, gentleman farmer, aviator, and conservationist. "The man with the barefoot voice," as Fred Allen once described him, retired from radio in 1972. He died on March 16, 1983, in New York City.

Godfrey, Thomas (1704–1749), mathematician and inventor. Born in Philadelphia in 1704, Godfrey received little formal education and at an early age was apprenticed to a glazier. Among the commissions he eventually carried out in his primary vocation was installing the windows in the State House—now Independence Hall—in 1732. He was early befriended by Gov. James Logan, whose great library was opened to him. For a time he lodged in the house of Benjamin Franklin and was an original member of Franklin's Junto club. Godfrey's true interests were astronomy and mathematics, in which he was self-taught, and it was by combining them that he made his great contribution, the invention of the quadrant known as Hadley's quadrant. Godfrey first built such a device in 1730 and was still engaged in testing its usefulness when John Hadley invented a similar one in England in 1731; it is possible that Hadley had heard of Godfrey's work through a relative. Although Godfrey received, at Logan's urging, token and belated recognition from the Royal Society, Hadley's name continued to be associated with the invention. Godfrey's quadrant, actually an octant, represented a great step forward in the art of navigation, making possible the careful determination of the altitude of the sun (and thereby the observer's latitude) without looking directly at it and in spite of the motion of the ship; the modern sextant is its direct descendant. Godfrey died at his home in Philadelphia in December 1749.

Godfrey, Thomas (1736–1763), playwright and poet. Born in Philadelphia on December 4, 1736, Godfrey was the son of Thomas Godfrey (1704–1749). At thirteen, on his father's death, he was apprenticed to a watchmaker. His intelligence attracted the attention of William Smith, provost of the College, Academy, and Charitable School of Philadelphia, who undertook to forward his education and introduced him to other talented young men, including Benjamin West and Francis Hopkinson. After brief service in the militia in 1758 Godfrey moved to Wilmington, North Carolina, to enter business. While there, probably in 1759, he completed a play entitled *The Prince of Parthia*, the first full-length play of any literary merit to be written in America. It also became the first to be produced, at the Southwark Theatre, Philadelphia, in April 1767, four years after Godfrey's death. He also wrote and published a quantity of verse that, while largely imitative, was of remarkably high quality. Godfrey died in Wilmington, North Carolina, on August 3, 1763.

Godkin, Edwin Lawrence (1831–1902), journalist. Born in Moyne, Ireland, on October 2, 1831, Godkin graduated from Queen's University, Belfast, in 1851 and went to London to study law. He held a number of journalistic positions and was correspondent for the *London Daily News* during the Crimean War. Returning to Ireland, he was for a time on the staff of the *Belfast Northern Whig*. In 1856 he traveled to the United States; he studied law and was admitted to the New York bar in 1858, but he apparently practiced little. He continued to write for the *London Daily News*; in 1865, declining a partnership in the *New York Times*, he founded the *Nation* with offices in New York City. This weekly journal quickly became the most informed and intelligent review in the country; in 1881 the *Nation* became the weekly edition of the *New York Evening Post* —an association that lasted until 1918—and Godkin became the *Post*'s associate editor and, two years later, upon the resignation of Carl Schurz, its chief editor. In sixteen years at the head of the paper he made it into one of vast influence; although he was of generally Republican sympathies, he maintained the paper's complete independence, contributing greatly to the "mugwump" (Independent Republican) revolt in 1884. In the *Post*, as he had in the *Nation*, Godkin stood firmly for honest, efficient, and sound government and he conducted a long and fearless campaign against the corruption of New York City's Tammany Hall. He retired from the *Post* in 1899 and died in England on May 21, 1902.

Goeppert, Maria, *see* Mayer, Maria Goeppert

Goethals, George Washington (1858–1928), army officer and engineer. Born on June 29, 1858, in Brooklyn, New York, Goethals attended public schools and the College of the City of New York (CCNY). He had aspired originally to a medical career, but he transferred to West Point and graduated in 1880. As an officer in the army's engineer corps, he was employed on several civil works, including improvements on the Ohio and Cumberland rivers and completion of work on the Muscle Shoals Canal on the Tennessee River. From 1885 to 1889 and again from 1898 to 1900 he taught engineering at West Point. In 1907, with the rank of lieutenant colonel, he was appointed by President Theodore Roosevelt to head the construction of the Panama Canal. In addition to the monumental engineering problems involved, he was charged with supervising 30,000 civilian employees of various nationalities and supplying them with food, shelter, medical care, and recreation. Vested with virtually dictatorial powers, Goethals managed to construct an efficient organization while fostering an esprit de corps among the workers. In 1913 the canal, the greatest ever built, was completed and in 1914, nearly six months ahead of schedule, it was opened to the world, shortening the voyage between the Atlantic and the Pacific by thousands of miles. Goethals was appointed by President Woodrow Wilson the first governor of the Canal Zone; he was promoted to major general and voted the thanks of Congress in 1915. He retired from the army in 1916 and resigned as governor in 1917. He continued to work on both government and private engineering projects until he was recalled to active army duty late in 1917 as acting quartermaster general. He was later also made chief of several supply divisions for the General Staff and a member of the War Industries Board. Retiring again from active duty in

1919, he headed his own engineering firm and was a consultant to many municipalities and particularly to the Port of New York Authority. He died in New York City on January 21, 1928.

Goldberg, Arthur Joseph (1908–   ), public official and justice of the Supreme Court. Born in Chicago on August 8, 1908, Goldberg was the son of Russian immigrant parents. He worked his way through Northwestern University Law School, graduating in 1929, and on being admitted to the bar joined a prominent Chicago law firm. In 1933 he began private practice. From 1936, when he played an active role in President Franklin D. Roosevelt's first reelection campaign, he was closely identified with organized labor; during the late 1930s and early 1940s he represented several major unions in strike negotiations and litigation and continued in that work after World War II service with the Office of Strategic Services (OSS). In 1948 he was appointed general counsel for the Congress of Industrial Organizations (CIO) and for the United Steelworkers of America. In addition to his work on the development and testing in court of labor law he was a leading force in the expulsion of Communists and racketeers from the labor movement. Goldberg was the chief architect of the agreements that resulted in the merger of the CIO with the American Federation of Labor (AFL) in 1955 and served from then until 1961 as special counsel for the AFL–CIO. He was an active supporter of John F. Kennedy in the presidential campaign of 1960 and the next year was appointed secretary of labor, a post in which he pursued an active course in mediating strikes affecting the national interest and in efforts to establish permanently harmonious labor-management relations. Acknowledged as the possessor of one of the best legal minds in America, Goldberg resigned from the cabinet in 1962 to accept appointment to the Supreme Court. His presence shifted the balance of the Court from conservative to liberal, and again he took an activist approach to the work at hand. In 1965, upon the urging of President Lyndon B. Johnson, he resigned from the bench to succeed Adlai E. Stevenson as U.S. representative to the United Nations (UN). There he employed his skill in debate and negotiation to deal with the critical problem of nonpayment of UN dues by many members; he also played a major role in securing a cease-fire agreement between India and Pakistan in September 1965. Goldberg left the UN in 1968 and joined a New York City law firm. In 1970 he was the unsuccessful Democratic candidate for governor of New York and the next year he moved his law practice to Washington, D.C., becoming shortly thereafter also professor of law and diplomacy at American University.

Goldberg, Dora, *see* Bayes, Nora

Goldberg, Rube (1883–1970), cartoonist. Born on July 4, 1883, in San Francisco, Reuben Lucius Goldberg graduated from the University of California with an engineering degree in 1904 and went to work for the engineering department of the city of San Francisco. After a few months, however, he resigned to follow a long-standing love of drawing and became a sports cartoonist for the *San Francisco Chronicle*. A year later he moved to the *San Francisco Bulletin* and in 1907 he traveled to New York City, where he worked for the *New York Evening Journal* and the *New York Evening Mail* until 1926 and for the *New York Journal* from 1926 to 1935. From 1915 his cartoons were syndicated, reaching a large audience that he unfailingly delighted with his zany view of the world. He produced several series of cartoons simultaneously under the titles "Foolish Questions," "Mike and Ike," "The Weekly Meeting of the Tuesday Women's Club," "Boob McNutt," and "Lala Palooza," all of which were highly popular, but his best-remembered efforts concerned the inventions of a certain Professor Lucifer Gorgonzola Butts. In these Goldberg employed his engineering training to devise ridiculously elaborate machines that incorporated such features as moths devouring a sock or a dog wagging its tail into their mechanisms, the whole directed to the accomplishment, in a number of involved steps, of a ludicrously simple task. In lampooning the often needless complications of modern life, his devices attained a unique place in American culture; Rube Goldberg's name eventually entered the vernacular and appeared in *Websters' Third New International Dictionary* as an adjective describing a way of "accomplishing by extremely complex roundabout means what actually or seemingly could be done simply." In 1938, while continuing to draw his syndicated features, he became a political cartoonist for the *New York Sun* and as such won a Pulitzer Prize in 1948. He later moved to the *New York Journal–American*, remaining until his retirement in 1964. He occupied himself thereafter with sculpturing in bronze. The last of the many one-man shows of his works to be held during his lifetime was given in 1970 at the National Museum of History and Technology in Washington, D.C. Goldberg died a short time later, in New York City on December 7, 1970.

Goldberger, Joseph (1874–1929), physician. Born on July 16, 1874, in what was then part of Austria-Hungary (and now part of Czechoslovakia), Goldberger was brought to the United States by his parents at the age of six. He grew up in New York City, attended the College of the City of New York (CCNY) in 1890–1892, and in 1895 graduated from the Bellevue Hospital Medical College. After two more years at Bellevue and two in private medical practice he entered the U.S. Public Health Service in 1899 as an assistant surgeon. He rose to surgeon in 1912. His first assignments were in Cuba and Mexico, where he carried on research into the causes of typhus and yellow fever. Later he pursued simliar studies on dengue and grain (straw-mite) itch. In 1904 he began a lifetime association with the Hygienic Laboratory in Washington, D.C., the major research station of the Public Health Service at that time and forerunner of the National Institute of Health. Goldberger's major work began in 1913, when he was assigned to conduct a major investigation of the cause and possible cure of pellagra, a widespread disease that was endemic in the South, reaching alarming levels of incidence in institutions. He early became convinced that the disease was not an infectious one, but rather one caused by dietary deficiency, and over the next 12 years he conducted innumerable experiments with human and animal subjects, finally proving conclusively by 1925 that pellagra was indeed the result of a deficiency in the diet of a substance he called the pellagra-preventive, or P–P, factor. The factor was shown a decade later to be present in both niacin (nicotinic acid) and niacinamide (nicotinamide), two of the B-complex vitamins. Goldberger's work led to the virtual extinction of the disease through better diet and vitamin therapy. He died in Washington, D.C., on January 17, 1929.

Goldfish, Samuel, *see* Goldwyn, Samuel

Goldman, Edwin Franko (1878–1956), bandmaster and composer. Born on January 1, 1878, in Louisville, Kentucky, Goldman came of a family with a strong musical tradition. He grew up from the age of eight in New York City, and in 1892 he earned a scholarship to the National Conservatory of Music, where he studied under Anton Dvořák and others. Three years later, at the remarkably early age of seventeen, he was engaged as a solo cornetist in the Metropolitan Opera orchestra, where he remained for 10 years. After leaving the orchestra in 1905 he devoted himself to teaching and to organizing a succession of bands and ensembles; in 1911 he formed the New York Military Band with the best musicians available and thereafter bent every effort to making it into an organization equal in quality to the finest symphony orchestras. By 1918 he had raised by subscription sufficient money to sponsor a summer season of free public concerts on the Green at Columbia University. The venture was a great popular success and the Goldman Band, as it soon became known, was launched on a 38-year career of outdoor concert series. Because of new construction at Columbia the concerts were moved to the Central Park Mall in 1922 and two years later the problem of finances was erased by a complete underwriting of the concerts by the Daniel and Florence Guggenheim Foundation. From 1926 concerts were also given in Prospect Park, Brooklyn. Goldman's insistence upon the highest quality of performance, along with his imaginative and broadly appealing repertoire of marches, waltzes, classics, and modern works, won consistently high praise from music critics as well as from the tens of thousands who annually attended the series. He wrote several instructional books that were widely used, notably

The Band Guide and Aid to Leaders, 1916; *Band Betterment,* 1934; and *The Goldman Band System,* 1935. He composed more than a hundred marches and other pieces, including the popular "On the Mall," 1924. The founder and first president of the American Bandmasters' Association, he was elected honorary life president in 1933. The Goldman Band made appearances throughout the country and began broadcasting on radio as early as 1926, but it remained faithful to the summer series in New York City and Goldman himself took great pride in the fact that from 1918 through the 1955 season he never missed a performance. Acknowledged as the true heir to the mantle of John Philip Sousa, Goldman died in New York City on February 21, 1956. The Goldman Band continued its summer concerts under the direction of Goldman's son, Richard Franko Goldman.

Goldman, Emma (1869–1940), anarchist. Born on June 27, 1869, in Kaunas, Lithuania, now in the U.S.S.R., Miss Goldman grew up there, in Königsberg, East Prussia, and in St. Petersburg. Her formal education was limited but she read much on her own and in St. Petersburg associated with a student circle. In 1885 she emigrated to the United States and settled in Rochester, New York. There, and later in New Haven, Connecticut, she worked in clothing factories and came into contact with Socialist and anarchist groups among fellow workers. In 1889 she moved to New York City, determined to join the anarchist cause; she formed a close association with Alexander Berkman who, in 1892, was imprisoned for an attempt to assassinate Henry Clay Frick during the Homestead steel strike. The following year she herself was sent to jail in New York City for inciting a riot by a fiery speech to a group of unemployed workers. Upon her release she embarked on lecture tours of Europe in 1895, of the United States, and again of Europe in 1899. The assassin of President William McKinley claimed to have been inspired by her, although there was no direct connection between them. In 1906 Berkman was freed and he and Miss Goldman resumed their joint activities. In that year she founded *Mother Earth,* a periodical that she edited until its suppression in 1917. In 1910 she published *Anarchism and Other Essays.* She spoke often and widely, not only on anarchism and social problems, but also on current European drama, which she was instrumental in introducing to American audiences. When World War I broke out in Europe she opposed U.S. involvement, and when that nevertheless came about she agitated against military conscription. In July 1917 she was sentenced to two years in prison for these activities. By the time of her release in 1919 the nation was in the throes of hysteria over a largely imaginary subversive network of Communist elements; Miss Goldman was declared an alien and, along with Berkman and more than 200 others, was deported to the Soviet Union. Her stay there was brief; two years after leaving she recounted her experiences in *My Disillusionment in Russia*, 1923. She remained active, living at varous times in Sweden, Germany, England, France, and elsewhere continuing to lecture, and writing her autobiography, *Living My Life*, 1931. She joined the antifascist cause in Spain during the Civil War there and while working in its behalf died in Toronto, Canada, on May 14, 1940.

Goldstein, Betty Naomi, *see* Friedan, Betty Naomi Goldstein

Goldwater, Barry Morris (1909–   ), public official. Born on January 1, 1909, in Phoenix Arizona, Goldwater was educated at Staunton Military Academy and spent a year at the University of Arizona. In 1929 he joined the family department store, Goldwater's, Inc., in Phoenix, becoming president in 1937. During World War II he was a military pilot with the Air Transport Command and afterward he helped organize the Arizona Air National Guard. In 1949 Goldwater was elected to the Phoenix city council; three years later he was elected to the Senate by a narrow margin. He relinquished the presidency of Goldwater's, becoming chairman of the board in 1953 and subsequently devoting himself entirely to politics. As a staunch and articulate conservative, he soon was the acknowledged leader of the conservative wing of the Republican party in its fight against what it perceived to be centralization of government, the creation of a welfare state, and accommodation with Communism abroad. He was reelected to the Senate in 1958 and two years later published his widely read *The Conscience of a Conservative. Why Not Victory?*, a statement of his views on foreign policy, was published in 1962. In 1964 he won the Republican presidential nomination; despite an active and spirited campaign against the incumbent, Lyndon B. Johnson, he was overwhelmingly defeated. He remained active in Arizona politics following his defeat, and in 1968 was again elected to the Senate.

Goldwyn, Samuel (1882–1974), motion-picture producer. Born in Warsaw, Poland, on August 27, 1882, into a poor family, Samuel Goldfish (as his original Polish name was translated) was orphaned at an early age. He ran away to London at eleven and two years later came to the United States. He worked in a glove factory in Gloversville, New York, rose to the position of salesman, and at eighteen was a partner in the firm. In 1902 he became an American citizen. At thirty he owned his own successful wholesale glove business. In 1913 he joined his brother-in-law, vaudeville producer Jesse L. Lasky, and playwright Cecil B. DeMille in founding the pioneer Jesse L. Lasky Feature Play Company. With DeMille, then a novice, as their director, they made the first full-length American film, *The Squaw Man*, which was a great success. They merged with the sole competition, Adolph Zukor's Famous Players, to form Famous Players–Lasky, with Goldwyn becoming

director and chairman of the board, in 1917. In the same year he formed the Goldwyn Pictures Corporation with Broadway producers Edgar and Archibald Selwyn, and in 1918 left the Lasky venture. He changed his name legally to Goldwyn (with Judge Learned Hand commenting, "A self-made man may prefer a self-made name") in 1919. That year he founded Eminent Authors Pictures, Inc., with a view to attracting prominent writers to the industry. Although he soon left that enterprise as well, it began the Hollywood tradition of fierce competition for "name" writers. In 1925 he merged Goldwyn Pictures with Louis B. Mayer's Metro Pictures Corporation to form Metro-Goldwyn-Mayer (M-G-M). Within the year he sold out and organized Samuel Goldwyn, Inc., Ltd., which he controlled. From 1926 to 1941 his independently produced pictures were distributed by United Artists; after that, by RKO. His career was marked by independence and a demand for excellence in artistry and production. Among writers he hired were Ben Hecht and Charles MacArthur, and he introduced some of the greatest stars in the Hollywood film industry, including Pola Negri, Vilma Banky, Will Rogers, and Ronald Colman. The films he produced included *All Quiet on the Western Front*, 1930; *Arrowsmith*, 1931; *Stella Dallas*, 1937; *Wuthering Heights*, 1939; *The Little Foxes*, 1941; *Pride of the Yankees*, 1942; *The North Star*, 1943; *The Best Years of Our Lives*, 1946, for which he won an Academy Award; *The Secret Life of Walter Mitty*, 1947; *Guys and Dolls*, 1955; *Gigi*, 1958; and *Porgy and Bess*, 1959. In 1971 Goldwyn was awarded the Presidential Medal of Freedom. Goldwyn was almost equally well known for his markedly idiosyncratic expressions: "Include me out;" "I'll give you a definite maybe;" "In two words: impossible;" and dozens more such picturesque sayings were attributed to him. He died in Los Angeles on January 31, 1974.

Gompers, Samuel (1850–1924), labor leader. Born in London on January 27, 1850, Gompers grew up in a tenement district and had no formal education after the age of ten. He became, like his father, a cigarmaker. In 1863 the family emigrated to the United States, settling on New York City's Lower East Side; the next year Gompers joined the Cigarmakers' Union and in 1872 became a naturalized citizen. Under the influence of the Socialism then popular among immigrant labor groups as well as the writings of Karl Marx, he developed both a philosophy and a practical plan of labor organization. In 1877 he reorganized the Cigarmakers' Union, introducing high dues and strike and pension funds and establishing the supremacy of the international organization over the locals. He restricted union activities to purely economic ones, seeking higher wages, benefits, and security by the economic leverage of strikes and boycotts and avoiding political action and political affiliations. His formula for success was adopted by a number of other unions; in 1881, in an effort to offset the centralized control of the

Knights of Labor, he helped found the Federation of Organized Trades and Labor Unions of the United States of America and Canada. In 1886 this was reorganized as the American Federation of Labor (AFL) with Gompers as president, a position that, with the exception of one year, 1895, he held until his death. Under his guidance the AFL grew slowly but steadily into the largest labor organization in the country, and it was the alternative represented by the AFL that was in large part responsible for the rapid decline of the Knights of Labor during the 1890s. For the AFL Gompers firmly resisted political alignments or the formation of a labor party; he was equally successful in avoiding all connection with radicalism. Ironically, however, it was the AFL's insistence on trade and craft unionism, with no provision for the inclusion of the unskilled laborer, that provided the main impetus to the formation of the radical Industrial Workers of the World (IWW) in 1905. Viewing the labor union as simply the labor counterpart of the corporation, neither inferior nor superior to it, Gompers early advocated, and in the AFL firmly established, the system of negotiation and written contracts that still prevails in U.S. labor-management relations. During World War I he served on the Council of National Defense formed by President Woodrow Wilson and instituted the War Committee on Labor. He attended the Versailles Peace Conference to advise on international labor legislation. He continued his activities for the AFL until his death on December 13, 1924, in San Antonio, Texas. The following year his *Seventy Years of Life and Labor* was published.

Gonzales, Richard Alonzo (1928–   ), "Pancho," tennis player. Born in Los Angeles on May 9, 1928, Gonzales began playing tennis at the age of twelve and except for a few beginning pointers from a high-school friend, who also gave him the nickname Pancho, he received no instruction in the game at all. Within three years, however, he was the top-ranked player in boys'-division tennis in California. He left high school before graduating and, except for a period in the navy in 1945–1947, devoted himself to tennis thereafter. He made his first tournament tour in 1947 and, although he won no major titles that year, made a strong impression on his opponents and on tour sponsors. In 1948 he set out with a national ranking in 17th place, won a number of regional tournaments, took the national clay-court title, and in September won the lawn-tennis singles championship at Forest Hills. The next year he repeated his championship triumphs on both clay and grass and added the indoor singles and mixed-doubles titles, one of the very few players ever to win such a combination. After playing on the U.S. Davis Cup team that year he turned professional and, in the 12 seasons until his retirement in 1961, held the world championship for a record 8 years. Equipped with a serve of almost overwhelming force, great agility, and a complete arsenal of return shots, Gonzales gained a considerable following not only with his dazzling play but also with his engaging manner; always something of a romantic outsider in the genteel world of tennis, he followed no training regimen at all in rising to the top and to rating by some experts as the greatest player of all time. In 1961 he became coach of the U.S. Davis Cup team and the resident pro at a Nassau resort. With the beginning of open events for both professionals and amateurs in 1968 he returned to the court occasionally and won a number of regional tournaments; in 1969, although he was forty-one years old, he won the longest match ever played at Wimbledon, a 112-game marathon with a much younger player. His autobiographical *Man With a Racket* appeared in 1959.

Goodhue, Bertram Grosvenor (1869–1924), architect. Born in Pomfret, Connecticut, on April 28, 1869, Goodhue received rather little formal education but early developed a marked talent for drawing and a strongly romantic taste. He traveled to New York City in 1884 and secured a position as a draftsman in James Renwick's architectural firm of Renwick, Aspinwall & Russell; there, while learning the fundamental principles of architectural design, he was exposed to the rich Gothic Revival styles of which Renwick was a leading exponent. Gothic, particularly in its medieval versions, appealed strongly to Goodhue and became the basis of his own work for most of his career. During the 1890s he was also much influenced by the arts and crafts movement in England and designed a number of books after the fashion of William Morris. He entered a number of architectural design competitions and on winning one in 1889 for a cathedral in Dallas (never built) he moved to Boston and became head draftsman in Ralph Adams Cram's firm of Cram and Wentworth, which in 1896 became Cram, Goodhue & Ferguson. Specializing in ecclesiastical architecture, the firm designed over the years a great many churches throughout the East. They won the competition for a group of buildings at West Point in 1903 and Goodhue concerned himself especially with the chapel. At that time he opened a branch office of the firm in New York City and remained there, from 1913 working independently. His Gothic designs appeared in St. Thomas's, St. Vincent Ferrer, and St. Bartholomew's churches in New York City, the Cathedral of Maryland in Baltimore, Rockefeller Chapel at the University of Chicago, and in many other massive edifices; his wide-ranging travels led him to occasionally incorporate Byzantine, Romanesque, or Spanish Baroque elements, but the romantic spirit was always dominant. Romanticism dominated and informed also his late attempts to abandon the Gothic in favor of a modern, functional approach, as in the Nebraska state capitol, the National Academy of Sciences building in Washington, D.C., and various unrealized designs for public and monumental structures. Although he was highly successful in his profession, Goodhue was throughout an interpreter of his favored traditions rather than a pioneer. He died in New York City on April 23, 1924.

Goodman, Benny (1909–   ), musician and bandleader. Born in Chicago on May 30, 1909, Benjamin David Goodman began studying the clarinet at the age of ten, first in a local synagogue and later at Hull House. Within a few years he had developed sufficient skill on the instrument to sit in with various jazz bands appearing in the city, which was at the time a center of jazz music, and at fourteen he left school to take a steady job with a dance-hall band. From 1925 to 1929 he traveled with Ben Pollack's band and then free-lanced for a time, working as a popular sideman with various groups, playing college dates with hastily assembled combos, and doing studio work, including Bessie Smith's last recording session. In 1934 he organized his own band; he enjoyed only limited success in New York City and on tour, but the next year at the Palomar Ballroom in Los Angeles the months of disciplined rehearsal and seeking for a workable "big-band" jazz style suddenly bore fruit. With arrangements by Fletcher Henderson, the band introduced a new kind of jazz aptly labeled "swing"—tightly woven, driving ensemble work overlaid with the brilliant improvisations of fine soloists—and Benny Goodman was immediately crowned the "King of Swing." With his "Let's Dance" program on radio his popularity swept the country—fans in the East sat up past midnight to catch the West Coast broadcasts. In 1937 he returned to New York City and a triumphant engagement at the Paramount Theatre, where droves of jitterbuggers jammed the aisles. In addition to the big-band music, Goodman developed also a form of chamber jazz in which two, three, or as many as five of his leading sidemen, notably Teddy Wilson, Gene Krupa, and Lionel Hampton, would join him in lyrical small-combo renditions of jazz and popular songs. In 1938 the band introduced jazz to Carnegie Hall in a wildly successful concert, recordings of which later became jazz classics. Goodman's own clarinet playing combined virtuoso technique with a master's depth of improvisation and was not limited to jazz; he had an abiding interest in classical clarinet music and from 1938 worked also in that field, performing with major symphony orchestras, making recordings, and commissioning works by Béla Bartók, Paul Hindemith, and Aaron Copland. After World War II the popularity of big bands declined, but Goodman organized a new one in 1955 and demonstrated that his own following was still strong. He made numerous successful tours, notably to the Far East in 1956–1957, to the World's Fair in Brussels in 1958, and to the Soviet Union in 1962, where his was the first U.S. jazz band to be allowed to play. He later appeared occasionally on television and his recordings continued to sell steadily.

Goodman, Theodosia, *see* Bara, Theda

Goodnight, Charles (1836–1929), cattleman. Born in Macoupin County, Illinois, on March 5, 1836, Goodnight moved with his family to Milam County, Texas, in 1846. At the age of twenty he went into cattle ranching and for several years was also an active vigilante and involved with Texas Ranger operations against the Indians on the Texas frontier. In 1866 he pioneered in what soon became a general movement of cattle ranching into New Mexico, establishing a great range on the Pecos River; the trail he established from Belknap, Texas, to Fort Sumner, New Mexico, became known as the Goodnight Trail and, with Oliver Loving, he continued it north into Wyoming, that section becoming the famed Goodnight-Loving Trail. He established another ranch near Granada, Colorado, to which he laid out the New Goodnight Trail. In 1876, after fighting and settling one of the early sheepherder-cattlemen wars in the West, he returned his cattle operations to Texas, settling in the Palo Duro Canyon area, and the next year entered into partnership with John G. Adair, an Irish investor, and began developing the JA Ranch, which eventually ran almost 100,000 cattle on nearly a million acres of range. A huge, powerful man, an expert horseman and thoroughly knowledgeable on the trail, Goodnight was the paradigm cattle baron of the Old West; he ruled his demesne firmly, pacifying Indians, rooting out outlawry, and in 1880 organizing a stockmen's association to govern the affairs of the Panhandle region and to set up cooperative and systematic range work and patrols. On his ranch he developed a superior breed of beef animal from longhorn, shorthorn, and Hereford stock, and he built up and preserved a large herd of buffalo, which had been threatened with extinction on the southern Plains. From a cross of Angus cattle and buffalo he produced the cattalo. Goodnight remained active and continued to be the dominant figure in West Texas until his death on December 12, 1929.

Goodrich, Samuel Griswold (1793–1860), "Peter Parley," author and publisher. Born on August 19, 1793, in Ridgefield, Connecticut, Goodrich received only an elementary education before going to work as a clerk in Danbury and later in Hartford. He served in the Connecticut militia in the War of 1812 and, after a brief and unsuccessful manufacturing venture, opened a publishing house in 1816. He issued textbooks and juveniles, writing some of them himself, and continued the enterprise after moving to Boston in 1826. Two years later he published the first issue of the *Token*, an annual giftbook that, during its 15 years of existence, printed early works of Nathaniel Hawthorne, Henry Wadsworth Longfellow, and Lydia Maria Child. In 1827 he published *The Tales of Peter Parley About America*, the first of what became over the years a series of more than a hundred books (not counting the many imitations) bearing the "Peter Parley" name. Treating such subjects as history, geography, science, biography, and morals, the books were easily digestible instruction for children and were highly popular; in 1856 he claimed sales of some 7 million copies of the series over the years. Although he wrote a few of the Peter Parley books himself, most were produced under his supervision by others, including on one occasion Nathaniel Hawthorne. From

1832 to 1834 he edited *Parley's Magazine* and in 1841 established *Merry's Museum*, another children's periodical with which he was connected until 1854. Goodrich also took an interest in public affairs, winning election to the Massachusetts house of representatives in 1836 and to the state senate the following year. From 1851 to 1853 he was U.S. consul in Paris. After his return in 1855 he lived in New York City until his death on May 9, 1860.

Goodspeed, Edgar Johnson (1871–1962), biblical scholar and educator. Born in Quincy, Illinois, on October 23, 1871, Goodspeed graduated from Denison University in 1890 and pursued further studies at Yale, the University of Chicago, from which he received his Ph.D. in 1898, and the University of Berlin. In 1902 he joined the faculty of the University of Chicago as an instructor in biblical and patristic Greek; he advanced to professor in 1915, was chairman of the New Testament department from 1923, and was Ernest DeWitt Burton Distinguished Service Professor from 1933 until his retirement in 1937. Goodspeed early acquired an interest in Greek papyrology and in 1902 his first published work appeared under the title *Greek Papyri from the Cairo Museum*. He collaborated with Bernard P. Grenfell and Arthur S. Hunt in translating newly found papyri from Egypt published in the important work *Tebtunis Papyri*, 1907. By means of these and subsequent works, including *Index Patristicus*, 1907; *The Conflict of Severus*, 1908; *Index Apologeticus*, 1912; *Die altesten Apologeten*, 1915; *The Story of the New Testament*, 1916; *Harmony of the Synoptic Gospels*, 1917, with Ernest DeWitt Burton; and others, he prepared himself for his major work, a completely original *New Testament: An American Translation*, 1923, which rendered the vernacular Greek in equally vernacular American English. Later he published similar treatments of *The Apocrypha*, 1938, and *The Apostolic Fathers*, 1950. The *Complete Bible: An American Translation*, done in collaboration with J.M.P. Smith, appeared in 1939. He served from 1930 as a member of the committee established by the International Council of Religious Education to prepare the Revised Standard Version of the New Testament, published in 1946. A leading figure in the field of biblical exegesis, he pursued his preference for grammatical and historical approaches to biblical literature in such books as *The Formation of the New Testament*, 1926; *The Meaning of Ephesians*, 1933; *An Introduction to the New Testament*, 1937; and *Problems of New Testament Translation*, 1945. Other notable books included *History of Early Christian Literature*, 1942; *How to Read the Bible*, 1946; *Paul*, 1947; and *A Life of Jesus*, 1950. He also wrote a number of guides for students of biblical literature; a well-received mystery novel, *The Curse in the Colophon*, 1935; and an autobiography, *As I Remember*, 1953. After his retirement from the University of Chicago in 1937 he lived in California, and from 1938 to 1942 he was a lecturer at the University of California at Los Angeles. Goodspeed died in Los Angeles on January 13, 1962.

Goodyear, Charles (1800–1860), inventor. Born on December 29, 1800, in New Haven, Connecticut, Goodyear received a public-school education and then took a job with a hardware firm in Philadelphia. In 1821 he returned to Connecticut and became a business partner of his father, a hardware manufacturer and inventor of farm implements. Four years later he opened his own store in Philadelphia as a retail outlet for his father's products; but by 1830 both father and son were bankrupt. It was in that year that the India-rubber industry came into being; although it enjoyed considerable growth for a short time, it soon began to suffer because of the poor quality of goods made with raw rubber—the substance was sticky and could not withstand heat or cold. Goodyear determined to find a method of treating rubber that would make it a practical material for manufactured items. For ten years he worked on the problem in both Philadelphia and then in New York, going deeper and deeper into debt and on at least one occasion pursuing his experiments in debtors' prison. In 1836 he had some slight success with a process of treatment with nitric acid, but rubber so treated still melted in the summer. About 1838 he met Nathaniel M. Hayward, a fellow experimenter who had discovered that sulfur could eliminate the stickiness of rubber; Goodyear acquired Hayward's patent and continued to work with the new process. One day in 1839 in Woburn, Massachusetts, where he was then living, he accidentally dropped some rubber mixed with sulfur on a hot stove; the rubber did not melt and seemed greatly improved. By 1844 he had perfected and patented this "vulcanization" process, which has remained basic in the rubber industry. Soon a number of companies were licensed to use the process and Goodyear exhibited rubber goods at expositions in London and Paris in the 1850s; he failed to secure a patent in England, however, because of legal technicalities, and in the United States his patent was widely infringed upon. He finally established his rights in 1852 but his lawyer, Daniel Webster, received more in fees than Goodyear ever reaped from his discovery. He died in New York City on July 1, 1860, leaving his family some $200,000 in debt.

Goren, Charles Henry (1901–), bridge player. Born on March 4, 1901, in Philadelphia, Goren graduated with a law degree from McGill University, Montreal, in 1922, studied for an additional year there, and in 1923 entered law practice in his native city. By that time an avid though still an amateur bridge player, he began concentrating as much on the game as on his legal career and gradually acquired a considerable local reputation. After a period of serious study of the game, in particular of the various methods of estimating the worth of hands and calculating appropriate bids, he evolved his own point-count system and outlined it in a book, *Winning Bridge Made Easy*,

1936. He gave up his law practice in that year and thereafter devoted himself entirely to bridge. Further refining his system, which broke radically from the then-dominant "honor-trick" method of Ely Culbertson, he published several more books, among them *Contract Bridge in a Nutshell*, 1946; *Point Count Bidding at a Glance*, 1950; and most notably *Contract Bridge Complete*, 1951, whose huge sales in this and a new edition of 1957 were bolstered by Goren's own tournament successes. In 1944 he succeeded Culbertson as bridge columnist for the *Chicago Tribune*, by which his column was syndicated to more than 200 newspapers, and in 1957 he began a regular column on bridge for *Sports Illustrated*. Goren's method came eventually to be the most widely used in the game, spreading to other bridge-playing nations after sweeping the United States; employing it, Goren himself accumulated more tournament master points than any other player in the world, winning in 1958 the Life Masters Pairs championship with his favorite partner, Helen Sobel. Among his later books were *Goren's Bridge Complete*, 1963, and *Bridge Is My Game*, 1965.

Gorgas, Josiah (1818–1883), soldier. Born in Dauphin County, Pennsylvania, on July 1, 1818, Gorgas left school early to help support his family, but he nonetheless won appointment to West Point and graduated in 1841. Attached to the ordnance service, he spent six years at the Watervliet Arsenal, New York, except for a period in 1845 when he made an inspection tour of European arsenals. In 1847–1848 he served in the Mexican War, taking part in the siege of Veracruz and then commanding the ordnance depot there. Thereafter he served in arsenals in various places, rising to the rank of captain in 1855. In 1861, influenced by his wife's Southern connections, he resigned his commission and entered the Confederate service as a major. Appointed chief of ordnance for the entire Confederate army, he immediately faced the seemingly impossible task of supplying it with arms and ammunition. Little federal ordnance had been captured and most of it was obsolete, and manufacturing facilities in the South were virtually nonexistent. While the army fought with the arms at hand and supplemented them with captured material, Gorgas quickly surveyed the available raw materials and began establishing mines, mills, factories, and foundries to produce bullets, powder, small arms, and cannon. Imports from Europe, run through the Union blockade, helped tide the army over until his necessarily rather crude and highly decentralized manufacturing and distribution system went into operation. Despite the heavy handicaps under which he was forced to work—political and financial problems were at times added to the physical difficulties—he succeeded in providing a steady flow of arms and ammunition throughout the war; he was promoted to brigadier general in 1864. From the end of the war until 1869 he managed an iron works in Alabama, then joined the University of the South as headmaster of the

junior department, later becoming professor of engineering and in 1872 vice-chancellor. In 1878 he was named president of the University of Alabama, but ill health forced him to resign a year later; he remained as librarian until his death in Tuscaloosa, Alabama, on May 15, 1883.

Gorgas, William Crawford (1854–1920), army officer and physician. Born on October 3, 1854, in Mobile, Alabama, Gorgas was the son of Josiah Gorgas. He received an irregular education, but graduated from the University of the South in 1875. He wanted to follow a military career, but could not gain admission to West Point; instead, he entered Bellevue Medical College in New York City, graduated in 1879, served an internship at Bellevue Hospital, and was appointed in 1880 a surgeon in the Army Medical Corps. He survived an attack of yellow fever while serving in Texas and, thereafter immune to the disease, was often stationed at posts where it was particularly prevalent. He became head of sanitation at Havana in 1898 after it was occupied by U.S. forces in the Spanish-American War. He succeeded in greatly improving sanitary conditions in the city, but not until Walter Reed, also working in Cuba, had demonstrated that yellow fever was transmitted by a species of mosquito was Gorgas able to make headway in eliminating the disease. He immediately began to scour Havana for the mosquito's breeding places and to destroy them. The city was quickly rid of mosquitoes and disease disappeared. For this work he won international fame and in 1903 was made a colonel by a special act of Congress. In March 1904 he became chief sanitary officer for the Panama Canal project. Initiating measures against yellow fever, he was opposed by the Canal Commission, who thought the plans were extravagant. When an outbreak occurred in November 1904 funds were allotted and efforts against the mosquito proceeded. By 1905 yellow fever had been eliminated from the Canal Zone and sanitary conditions had been vastly improved. In 1914 Gorgas was promoted to brigadier general and made surgeon general of the U.S. army. During World War I he supervised the army medical service, retiring in 1918 with the rank of major general. For the International Health Board of the Rockefeller Foundation he was asked to investigate the control of pneumonia among miners in South Africa and also fought yellow fever in South and Central America and in West Africa. He died in London on July 3, 1920. He was elected to the Hall of Fame in 1950.

Gorgeous George (1915?–1963), wrestler. Born in Seward, Nebraska, about 1915, George Raymond Wagner grew up there and in Houston, Texas. To help support his family he quit school at fourteen and went to work. For five years he held a variety of jobs, including gas-station attendant, auto wrecker, and typewriter repairman. As a youth he had shown himself a fairly adept wrestler against friends and schoolmates, and at nineteen he accepted an offer to go into professional wrestling. For several years he knocked about the country appearing in small-time, low-paying bouts. Then, after winning a state light-heavyweight championship in Portland, Oregon, he decided the time had come to push his career and at the same time add some appeal to wrestling. The sport itself was not well off; in New York state it could not even be classed as a sporting event, only as an "exhibition;" moreover, wrestling crowds were so small that there was little money to be made in it. Billing himself as Gorgeous George and taking his cue from the success of Man Mountain Dean a decade and more before, Wagner began to leaven wrestling with showmanship; he wore flashy, expensive robes, hired a valet and bodyguard to accompany him to the ring, and had his long hair bleached blond and waved. He became a feature attraction at wrestling arenas around the country, and in the early days of television, from 1947 to 1952, proved to be one of the most popular stars on television. His earnings rose accordingly, and by 1950 he was making more than $70,000 a year. He was a more than fair wrestler and won most of his matches, especially in the first few years. In 1947 he settled in California, where he was extremely popular on television, and bought himself a turkey ranch as a hedge against the inevitable day of retirement. In the mid-1950s, as more serious wrestlers came along and as he approached forty, Gorgeous George retired. In his later years he owned and operated a bar in the San Fernando Valley. He died on December 26, 1963, in Hollywood, California.

Gorham, Nathaniel (1738–1796), merchant and public official. Born in Charlestown, Massachusetts, on May 27, 1738, Gorham was apprenticed at fifteen to a New London, Connecticut, merchant, with whom he remained until 1759, when he went into business on his own in his native town. He early took an interest in civic and political affairs and from 1771 to 1775 was a member of the Massachusetts legislature. During 1774–1775 he was a delegate to the Provincial Congress and from 1778 to 1781 he sat on the Board of War. After serving in the Massachusetts constitutional convention in 1779–1780 he was elected to the state senate in 1780 and to the house in 1781, where he served for six years, three of them as speaker. In 1782, 1783, and during 1785–1787 he was a delegate to the Continental Congress, serving from June 1786 as president of that body. He represented Massachusetts in the Constitutional Convention in 1787 and, as chairman of the committee of the whole, was presiding officer of the convention when it met in that capacity. He was active in debate at the convention and advocated the provision of a strong central government. He signed the final version of the Constitution and the next year was a member of the Massachusetts ratifying convention. In state politics he remained prominent as judge of the Middlesex court of common pleas

from 1785 and as a member of the governing council in 1788–1789. In 1788 he formed a partnership with Oliver Phelps of Connecticut and purchased a huge tract of land, more than 6 million acres, that had been ceded by New York to Massachusetts after the Revolution. The massive speculation proved a disaster to Gorham, however, and by 1790 he was bankrupt, sales of land to settlers having been insufficient to enable him to meet the payments due the state. He died in Charlestown, Massachusetts, on June 11, 1796.

Gorky, Arshile (1904–1948), painter. Born on October 25, 1904, in Khorkom Vari, Turkish Armenia, Gorky was originally named Vosdanig Manoog Adoian. After a period of study at the Polytechnic Institute in Tblisi (now in the U.S.S.R.), he emigrated to the United States in 1920 and settled first in Providence, Rhode Island. He continued his studies at the Rhode Island School of Design, at the New School of Design in Boston, and briefly in 1925 at the National Academy of Design in New York City; from 1926 to 1931 he taught at the Grand Central School of Art, New York City. From the time of his first one-man gallery show in 1932 he was marked as one of the leading Abstract Expressionists in America. The early Cubist influences in his work fell away during the later 1930s and he adopted a more fluid, organic manner, occasionally suggesting a Surrealist vision in his late paintings. During the 1940s he was much influenced by Vasili Kandinsky and by Willem de Kooning, with whom he shared a studio for a time. During 1935–1938 he was enrolled in the Federal Arts Project, for which he executed a mural for the Newark (New Jersey) Airport, and in 1939 he was commissioned to do a mural for the Aviation Building at the New York World's Fair. Gorky enjoyed a number of exhibitions in his lifetime and in 1946 was represented in the "Fourteen Americans" show at the Museum of Modern Art. In that year a number of his canvases were destroyed in a fire in his studio in Sherman, Connecticut. Following an automobile accident in which he was seriously injured he took his own life on July 21, 1948. His works were acquired by several major museums and galleries and included in many group exhibitions and several one-man retrospectives, notably at the Museum of Modern Art in 1963.

Gorrie, John (1803–1855), physician and inventor. Born in Charleston, South Carolina, on October 3, 1803, Gorrie graduated from the College of Physicians and Surgeons, New York City, in 1833 and later in that year established his practice in Apalachicola, Florida. While becoming prominent as a physician he also took an active part in civic affairs for a few years, serving as postmaster from 1834 to 1838, as city treasurer and a councilor from 1835 to 1837, and as mayor from 1837 to 1839. In his medical work he conceived a plan for treating victims of malaria and other fevers in rooms kept at a low temperature and began experimenting with means to achieve cooling. Using the common expansion method and employing ordinary air as the coolant, he eventually —possibly as early as 1842—produced a machine that successfully cooled a room. Gorrie gradually became interested in the problem of mechanical refrigeration for its own sake and by 1845 had given up his medical practice. Continuing his experiments, he developed machinery for producing ice about 1849 and in 1851 received what was probably the first U.S. patent for a refrigerating device. After giving public demonstrations of his invention he spent a considerable amount of time and energy in an unsuccessful search for financial backing to build a large commercial ice plant. Exhausted, he died in Apalachicola on June 16, 1855. Gorrie was later chosen as one of Florida's two representatives to be portrayed in sculpture for Statuary Hall in the U.S. Capitol.

Gosden, Freeman Fisher (1899–   ) and Charles J. Correll (1890–1972), "Amos" and "Andy," actors. Born in Peoria, Illinois, on February 2, 1890, Correll worked as a stenographer and later as a stonemason following graduation from high school and in his spare time took part in amateur theatrical productions. In 1918 he was hired by the Joe Bren Company, which supplied scripts, props, and direction to local theater groups around the country, and the next year he was sent to Durham, North Carolina, to train Gosden, who had just joined the company, in his duties in connection with a production. Gosden had been born in Richmond, Virginia, on May 5, 1899, and had worked as a salesman and served in the navy during World War I before his work with small-town variety shows had won him a position in the Bren Company. After producing the show in Durham the two went their separate ways for five years; in 1924 they met again in Chicago, to which each had been called to become managers for the company, Correll taking charge of the show division and Gosden of the new circus division. They began appearing occasionally on radio in music and comedy skits early in 1925 and within a few months left the Bren Company to join the staff of station WGN. In 1926 they began a regular comedy program that featured their impersonations of two stock Negro characters named Sam and Henry; the program proved highly successful, but the two decided to move to another station that would allow them to syndicate their show to stations outside the Chicago area. In March 1928 they joined WMAQ and made the first broadcast of their new show, "Amos 'n' Andy," featuring the slow, amiable Amos (Gosden) and the shrewd, glib Andy (Correll) as co-owners of the "Fresh-Air Taxicab Company of America." The popularity of the show on 45 subscribing stations soon attracted the attention of the National Broadcasting Corporation (NBC), which in 1929 began broadcasting the show nationwide. The misadventures of the two characters and their motley assortment of acquaintances, including the Kingfish, Light-

nin', and Madame Queen—Gosden and Correll themselves played nearly all of the roles—quickly entranced the radio public. Through the 1930s "Amos 'n' Andy" was the most popular show on the air and the daily 15-minute broadcast had, at its peak, some 40 million listeners, about two-thirds of the available audience; telephone companies noted sharp drops in calls during the broadcasts and many movie theaters regularly interrupted films to play the show over the house speakers. The show also inspired a number of books and a comic strip. In 1943 it became a weekly half-hour program and it continued in that form until 1958, when Gosden and Correll retired to Beverly Hills, California; in 1949 "Amos 'n' Andy" came to television with black actors in the well-established roles. It was finally withdrawn from syndication in 1965 under mounting criticism of the stereotyped images of black people it projected. Correll died while visiting Chicago on September 26, 1972.

Gosnold, Bartholomew (?–1607), explorer and colonizer. Born probably in Sussex, England, at a date unknown but before 1572, Gosnold entered Jesus College, Cambridge, in 1587 and remained for a time. He later became interested in the possibilities for colonization and commercial exploitation of the New World and in 1602 sailed on the *Concord* from Falmouth to the Azores and thence on a more northerly course than was at the time customary, one which proved also significantly shorter. He struck land on the southern Maine coast and continued southward, naming Cape Cod, where he landed, and giving the name Martha's Vineyard, in honor of his daughter, to a small island nearby (the name was later transferred to a larger island and the original became known as No Man's Land). On another island, which he called Elizabeth (now Cuttyhunk), he landed, built a small fort, and planted a crop. After exploring the coast down to Narragansett Bay he returned to England with a cargo of furs, cedar, and sassafras, the last believed to be a cure for syphilis. After some years of trying to interest English merchants in a colonization scheme he was appointed commander of the *God Speed* and vice-admiral of the fleet sent out in 1606 by the London Company. On their arrival in America he opposed the selection of the swampy site of Jamestown, Virginia, for settlement, but was overruled. As one of seven governing councilors of the colony, Gosnold supported the efforts of John Smith to instill and maintain discipline. Along with many others he died of swamp fever (malaria) within a few months of landing, on August 22, 1607.

Gottschalk, Louis Moreau (1829–1869), pianist and composer. Born in New Orleans on May 8, 1829, Gottschalk began studying both the piano and the violin at the age of four and later took up the organ as well. At thirteen he traveled to Paris to continue his studies in composition and there numbered Hector Berlioz among his teachers. Soon after his first Paris performance in 1845, a recital that made a considerable impression upon Frédéric Chopin, he set out on a concert tour that took him to Italy, Spain, Switzerland, and elsewhere in Europe; he delighted audiences everywhere and was decorated by the queen of Spain. Concluding his tour with a final triumphal concert in Paris in 1853, he then returned to the United States and appeared at Niblo's Garden in New York City. He declined an offer of management from P. T. Barnum, who was eager to repeat his recent success in tour management with Jenny Lind, and undertook a heavy schedule of concerts in New York and other Eastern cities, achieving a popularity (except in Boston, where he was not well received) unmatched by any other American concert performer of the day. Along with the works of the European masters he played also his own compositions, which were extremely well received and which included, in addition to such piano pieces as "Tremolo Étude," "Morte," and "Bamboula," several symphonies and two operas. From 1856 to 1862 he lived in the West Indies; he returned to New York City 1862 and began touring in the United States, Canada, and South America, again with huge success. While on tour in Brazil Gottschalk died in Tijucas on December 18, 1869.

Goudy, Frederic William (1865–1947), type designer and printer. Born on March 8, 1865, in Bloomington, Illinois. Goudy grew up there and in Shelbyville, Illinois. After graduating from high school in 1883 he worked at a variety of jobs, from janitor to bookkeeper, and in a number of small printing shops learned the rudiments of that trade. A job as an accountant in a Chicago bookstore led to an interest in typography and in 1895, soon after establishing the short-lived Camelot Press, he designed his first typeface, Camelot. The press printed the *Chap-Book,* a small literary magazine, which, like the press, failed in 1898; Goudy then worked as a freelance graphic designer. In 1905 he founded the Village Press in nearby Park Ridge, Illinois, later moving it to New York City and then to Marlboro in upstate New York; he specialized in printing limited editions, he and his wife, Bertha Sprinks Goudy, personally engaging in every phase of production. A fire destroyed his shop in 1908 and for ten years or so he was again a free-lance designer, producing during that period the Kennerley typeface. Reestablishing the Village Press after World War I, he worked almost exclusively as a typographer and also designed a great many typefaces of exceptional beauty, including Goudy, Goudy Old Style, Village, Hadriano, Garamond, Deepdene, and Forum; noted for their simplicity and sturdy strength many of his faces are still widely used. Goudy also published a number of books, including *The Alphabet,* 1918; *Elements of Lettering,* 1921; *Typologia,* 1940; and the autobiographical *Half-Century of Type Design and Typography, 1895–1945,* 1946. Another fire in 1939 had destroyed the old mill

that housed his shop and with it a great many of his original designs; again he rebuilt and continued to work until his death in Marlboro on May 11, 1947.

Gould, Chester (1900–   ), cartoonist. Born on November 20, 1900, in Pawnee, Oklahoma, Gould attended Oklahoma Agricultural and Mechanical University and graduated from Northwestern University in 1923. From 1924 he worked for various Chicago newspapers, becoming a regular cartoonist for the Hearst syndicate. In 1931 he joined the *Chicago Tribune,* which that year accepted a new cartoon strip created by Gould and originally entitled *Plainclothes Tracy;* published under the title *Dick Tracy,* the strip was an immediate success and was soon widely distributed through the *Tribune* syndicate. Featuring the stubborn-jawed and perennially behatted detective Tracy and his friends Tess Trueheart (later Mrs. Tracy) and Sam Catchem, the strip profited early by the widespread public interest in crime-fighting heroes during the 1930s and closely followed actual police methods, both in the story and in its attached "Crimestoppers Notebook" of tips on self-protection. As a balance to the realism of method and the violence that were novel elements for a comic strip, Gould introduced an occasional bit of science fiction—sometimes, as with Tracy's famous two-way wrist radio, an anticipation of actual technological developments—and a good measure of whimsy, particularly in the criminal characters whom Tracy fought—Mole, Pruneface, Flat Top, B-B Eyes, Mumbles, and other such bizarre figures. The stories were simple, the conflicts clear-cut, the characters one-dimensional, and the drawing only adequate; yet the strip achieved enormous popularity and retained it for more than four decades, eventually reaching nearly 100 million daily readers through 600 newspapers in the United States and hundreds more in other countries.

Gould, Jason, *see* Gould, Jay

Gould, Jay (1836–1892), financier. Born on May 27, 1836, in Roxbury, New York, Gould was christened Jason but was known throughout his life as Jay. He grew up in relative poverty and received little formal education; nonetheless, possessed of a quick mind and native shrewdness and untroubled by scruples, he soon began finding opportunities for money making. His earnings from three years as a surveyor and from the publication of his *History of Delaware County, and Border Wars of New York* in 1856 enabled him to open a tannery in Pennsylvania the next year. By 1860 he had begun speculating in railroad securities; after taking profits from the Rutland and Washington and the Rensselaer and Saratoga railroads and serving as manager of the latter, he became a director of the Erie Railroad in 1867. Gould, with codirectors James Fisk and Daniel Drew, engineered the sale of watered stock by means of which they held off Cornelius

Vanderbilt's attempted takeover and reaped huge personal gains in the "Erie War." By admitting New York City's "Boss" William M. Tweed to their councils and judiciously spreading bribes among state legislators, Gould and Fish continued to profit by stripping the Erie. In 1869 the two plotted to corner the market in gold and to induce President Ulysses S. Grant to go along with the scheme; Grant seemed to acquiesce until he finally understood what was afoot, whereupon he ordered a massive sale of government gold that broke the "corner" at the expense of a disastrous fall in the price of gold in the panic on Black Friday, September 24, 1869. Grant's reputation suffered from his seeming early complicity in the plot. In 1872 Gould was deposed from control of the Erie, whereupon he turned to Western railroads. Beginning with holdings in the Union Pacific and the Kansas Pacific, in which he later sold stock at a huge profit, he began assembling an empire that included the Missouri Pacific, the Texas & Pacific, and others, and accounted for half the track mileage in the Southwest. He also branched into other fields; from 1879 to 1883 he owned the *New York World*, by 1886 he was in virtual control of the New York City elevated railways, and at the same time he was in control of the Western Union Telegraph Company. A prototype of the "robber baron" capitalist, Gould remained ruthless, unscrupulous, and friendless to the end. He died on December 2, 1892, in New York City, and his business interests were taken over by his eldest son, George Jay Gould (1864–1923).

Goyathlay, *see* Geronimo

Grace, William Russell (1832–1904), businessman and financier. Born in Queenstown, Ireland, on May 10, 1832, Grace went to sea at fourteen and two years later took a position in a firm of ship chandlers in Liverpool. In 1850 he made his way to Callao, Peru joined a chandlery there, and within a few years had with his brother taken over the business, which became Grace Brothers & Company. Between 1860 and 1865 he spent much time in world travel, but in the latter year he settled in New York City and formed W. R. Grace & Company as an agency of the Peruvian firm. With his extensive contacts and influence in Peru he was able to secure virtually monopolistic contracts to supply materials to Henry Meiggs for the building of railroads there in the 1870s; he also supplied arms and equipment to the Peruvian army and navy. The huge debts left by the Meiggs operations and by Peru's war with Chile in 1879 eventually put the country in a desperate position as foreign holders of government bonds began to apply pressure; in 1890 Grace stepped in and, in return for concessions that amounted to control of nearly the whole of Peru's developed and undeveloped resources, assumed the debt of two bond issues. The concessions, nominally controlled by the largely British Peruvian Corporation but actually under the firm hand of the Grace company, included the rich

Cerro de Pasco silver mines, originally a Meiggs holding, all the nation's guano resources, five million acres of oil and mineral lands, and several railroad leases. Nicknamed the "Pirate of Peru," Grace organized the New York & Pacific Steamship Company in 1891, later adding the Grace Steamship Company, and four years later combined his New York and Peruvian firms as William R. Grace & Company. The company proceeded to open mercantile and banking offices, acquire mineral and agricultural holdings, and make extensive industrial- and utility-development investments in Chile and other Latin American nations. Meanwhile, in New York City, Grace served two terms, 1880–1882 and 1884–1886, as reform, anti-Tammany mayor—he was the first Roman Catholic to occupy the office—and in 1897 founded the Grace Institute for commercial and domestic education for girls. He died in New York City on March 21, 1904.

Grady, Henry Woodfin (1850–1889), journalist and orator. Born in Athens, Georgia, on May 24, 1850, Grady graduated from the University of Georgia in 1868 and during the next year studied law at the University of Virginia. During his years as a student he had contributed occasionally to the *Atlanta Constitution;* determining upon a journalistic career, he wrote for and edited a number of Georgia newspapers during the next several years. In 1876–1877 he was the Georgia correspondent for the *New York Herald.* In 1880, with a loan from Cyrus W. Field, he bought a one-fourth interest in the *Atlanta Constitution* and from then until his death was editor of the paper. He attracted wide attention wih his cogent analysis of the South's situation in the post–Civil War era and his realistic program for revitalization, including industrialization, crop diversification, and, not the least, a reasonable accommodation on the race issue. In December 1886 he addressed the New England Club of New York City, summing up his viewpoint in the title of his speech, "The New South." The speech was very well received and soon became a standard oratorical piece; Grady subsequently delivered a number of addresses throughout the country on this and related subjects. He died in Atlanta on December 23, 1889, soon after returning from a speaking engagement in Boston.

Graham, Billy (1918–   ), evangelist. Born on November 7, 1918, on a farm near Charlotte, North Carolina, William Franklin Graham was converted at a revival meeting at sixteen, after which his ambitions turned from baseball to preaching. He studied for six months at Bob Jones University, a Fundamentalist college, and in 1937 resumed studying at the Florida Bible Seminary (now Trinity College) in St. Petersburg. He had led one gospel meeting and secured 12 conversions before being ordained a Southern Baptist minister in 1939. He earned his B.A. degree in 1943 at Wheaton College in Illinois and briefly was minister of the First Baptist Church in Western Springs, Illinois, before commencing his nationwide evangelistic campaign. In 1949 he became the first vice-president of Youth for Christ Internationai, and in the same year he held an eight-week series of tent meetings in Los Angeles, preaching to 350,000 people, among whom he won 6000 conversions. In Boston, in South Carolina, and in Portland, Oregon, during the first six months of 1950, he won more than 22,000 "declarations for Christ." In 1957 he held a 16-week campaign at Madison Square Garden in New York City, part of which was televised, and won more than 50,000 conversions from among the almost 2 million people who attended, and another 30,000 conversions from among television viewers. In 1958 he was similarly successful in San Francisco at the Cow Palace. His first trip outside the United States was to England and Europe in 1954–1955; subsequently he toured the Far East (1956), Australia and New Zealand (1959), and Africa and the Holy Land (1960). Compared with John Wesley in winning conversions and with Billy Sunday in his vigorous, magnetic preaching, he used modern communications to reach vast audiences. His Oregon revival was made into a 45-minute film, and a Sunday radio program, "Hour of Decision," was broadcast nationally and internationally. Using modern business methods to handle arrangements for his appearances and to communicate with his followers, he established the Billy Graham Evangelistic Association, Inc. From 1949 to 1951 he was president of Northwestern Schools, a Fundamentalist institution in Minneapolis. He produced religious films, wrote a daily newspaper column, and published books including *Revival in Our Times*, 1950; *Peace with God*, 1953; *The Secret of Happiness*, 1955; *My Answer*, 1960; and *World Aflame*, 1965.

Graham, Florence Nightingale, see Arden, Elizabeth

Graham, George Rex (1813–1894), editor and publisher. Born in Philadelphia on January 18, 1813, Graham apprenticed himself to a cabinetmaker at the age of nineteen and while learning his trade also undertook the study of law. In 1839, after seven years of work and study, he was admitted to the bar. Within only two months, however, he changed careers entirely by accepting a position as assistant editor of the *Saturday Evening Post*. At the same time he bought the *Casket*, a minor periodical, and the next year *Burton's Gentleman's Magazine*; combining the two, he began publishing *Graham's Magazine* in 1841. From the first he followed an enlightened editorial policy, filling the pages of the magazine with work of the highest quality by offering unusually large payments to the leading authors of the day, and using excellent and expensive illustrations in a way that was lavish for the times. On his editorial staff at various times he employed Edgar Allan Poe, Rufus W. Griswold, Bayard Taylor, and other literary luminaries. His investment paid huge dividends as the subscription list grew nearly eightfold in the first year alone, and other publications began to copy his policies. Graham had interests in the *North American and United States Gazette*, whose organization by merger he helped accomplish, the *Philadelphia Evening Bulletin*, and various mining and real-estate ventures. Financial problems forced him to mortgage *Graham's Magazine* in 1848; he regained control in 1850, but three years later was bankrupt and sold it; the magazine continued to appear until 1858. After 1853, in declining physical and mental health, Graham drifted to New York City, briefly held a position on the *Newark Daily Journal*, and was supported by various friends and relatives until 1887, when he was committed to the Orange Memorial Hospital in Orange, New Jersey; there he remained until his death on July 13, 1894.

Graham, Martha (1894?–), dancer and choreographer. Born in Pittsburgh, probably in 1894, Martha Graham lived in Santa Barbara, California, after she was eight, and after completing her formal education in California schools devoted herself to dancing. She studied with Ruth St. Denis and Ted Shawn in Los Angeles at their influential Denishawn school and toured in the United States with the Denishawn company. Her first professional appearance was in 1920 with Shawn; later that year she first performed as a lead dancer, in *Xochitl*, a modern ballet derived from Aztec legend. In 1923 she joined the Greenwich Village Follies, remaining for two seasons and afterward worked to develop her own dancing style, which relied heavily on improvisation, highly individual choreography, and on new ways of developing a libretto. She taught at the Eastman School of the Theatre in Rochester and experimented with group arrangements. In 1926 she premiered as a solo dancer in New York City, introducing works of her own creation, and began to acquire an audience of discriminating and enthusiastic admirers. Interpretations of Ernest Bloch's *Baal Shem Suite* and of Claude Debussy's *Nuages et Fêtes*, and her own *Désir, Tanagar,* and *Revolt,* were several works in her early repertoire. In the 1930s, with her own dance company, she introduced *Primitive Canticles, Incantation,* and *Dolorosa,* dances that reflected her fascination with Mexican Indians and their religious rituals. She studied in Mexico in 1932 as the first dancer to receive a Guggenheim fellowship. Later she introduced *Letter to the World,* inspired by the life and poetry of Emily Dickinson, *Deaths and Entrances,* inspired by Emily Brontë, and numerous works based on Greek legends and characters: *Cave of the Heart* (Medea); *Errand into the Maze* (Minotaur); *Night Journey* (Jocasta); and *Clytemnestra*. Many of her sets were designed by such modern abstract artists as Alexander Calder and Isamu Noguchi, her costumes were of unconventional materials and designs that heightened the abstract mood of her performance, and her scores were commissioned from such composers as Aaron Copland, Norman Dello Joio, and William Schuman. Universally renowned as the foremost native

American exponent of her art, she performed in major cities of the United States and made numerous foreign tours. Miss Graham retired from active performing in 1970, continuing thereafter as choreographer of her troupe and as director of the Martha Graham Center of Contemporary Dance.

Graham, Sylvester (1794–1851), reformer. Born on July 5, 1794, in West Suffield, Connecticut, Graham grew up in the homes of various relatives and was from early childhood in delicate health. Intending to enter the ministry, he studied briefly at Amherst Academy in 1823; after a prolonged illness he became a lay preacher in New Jersey. In 1830 he became an agent for the Pennsylvania Temperance Society; his reading and thinking on the subject of temperance led him to speculation on the general topic of diet and health and he began adding his thoughts to his temperance lectures. Lecture series in Philadelphia and New York City in 1830 and 1831 were followed by tours throughout the East that occupied him for many years. His prescriptions for healthful living, although often distorted by devoted followers, were not essentially radical and contained much that later seemed merely commonsensical; he advocated the avoidance of alcohol and other stimulants and of meat, eating fresh fruits and vegetables, cold shower baths, fresh air and hard mattresses for sleeping, loose, light clothing, and regular exercise. He also promoted the use of coarsely ground, unsifted, whole-grain wheat flour rather than the white—and often adulterated—flour used by many bakers; such whole-wheat flour became known as graham flour and from it he developed the graham cracker. His followers grew in numbers and soon included scores of prominent faddists, among them Horace Greeley, while at the same time he and his fellow health evangelists were widely ridiculed and lampooned, especially by bakers, butchers, and distillers. Graham lectured and wrote on other aspects of health, anatomy, and child rearing as well, occasionally speaking too frankly for the sensibilities of many. Among his many writings were *The Young Man's Guide to Chastity*, 1834; *Treatise on Bread and Bread-Making*, 1837; and *Lectures on the Science of Human Life*, two volumes, 1839. His last years, marked by declining health and popularity, were largely devoted to lectures and writings on biblical subjects. Graham died in Northampton, Massachusetts, on September 11, 1851.

Graham, William Franklin, *see* Graham, Billy

Grange, Harold Edward (1903–   ), "Red," football player. Born on June 13, 1903, in Forksville, Pennsylvania, Grange grew up there and in Wheaton, Illinois, where through high school he starred in several sports, particularly track—in which he won several state championships—and football. In 1922 he entered the University of Illinois. The next year, in his first season of varsity football, he scored 12 touchdowns from his halfback position and was named to Walter Camp's All-American team; he was again an All-American in the two following years. In 1924 he became a national idol in leading Illinois against a series of football giants; on October 18, against the reigning Big Ten champions from the University of Michigan, he opened the game with a 100–yard kickoff return, scored 3 more times in the next 10 minutes, added his fifth touchdown in the second half, and passed for another, making the final tally 39–14. It was that day that Red Grange's speed, agility, and phenomenal field sense earned him the nickname "Galloping Ghost" from Grantland Rice. The 1925 season was something of a disappointment as Illinois fielded a weak team; by that time, however, Grange's name was magic and the fans came out in droves. Against Pennsylvania that year he ran for 363 yards and 3 touchdowns in a 24–2 victory over the Eastern powerhouse. When the season ended he left college, amid a storm of controversy and criticism, to join the Chicago Bears, making his professional debut on Thanksgiving Day against the Chicago Cardinals. On a grueling barnstorming tour arranged for the Bears by his agent, Charles C. "Cash and Carry" Pyle, Grange got considerable battering and few points in the 1925 season, but his name drew unprecedented crowds—73,000 for a game with the New York Giants—and gave an invaluable boost to the fledgling National Football League (NFL), then only four years old, widely considered less than fully respectable, and until then subsisting on audiences that sometimes only slightly outnumbered the players. In 1926 Grange played for the New York Yankees, a team that was organized by Pyle and a year later admitted to the NFL. He was badly injured during the 1927 season and sat out the next year entirely; in 1929 he rejoined the Bears and remained until 1935, when age and injuries, both of which had affected his speed and reflexes, forced him to retire. The earnings of his professional years, along with those from movie and vaudeville appearances and commercial endorsements, assured him a comfortable income; he opened an insurance agency in Chicago and later occasionally appeared as a commentator for televised professional football games. He was one of the first players to be elected to the Football Hall of Fame in 1963.

Grant, Cary (1904–   ), actor. Born in Bristol, England, on January 18, 1904, Archibald Alexander Leach became interested in the theater while still in school and at fifteen joined a troupe of comic acrobats with whom he toured for a year. After a New York City engagement in 1920 he left the troupe and for several years held a variety of jobs, including that of Coney Island barker, while gaining a place in the American theater. Experience in vaudeville and road companies led to a Broadway role in the Shubert brothers' production of *Boom, Boom* in 1929 and for three years he appeared regularly in musical comedies. In 1932 he traveled to Hollywood and was signed by Paramount Studios, taking the name Cary Grant for his new career; his first movie, *This Is the Night*, 1932, was followed by such films as *Blonde Venus*, 1932; *She Done Him Wrong*, 1933 (in which Mae West addressed to him her famous line, "Come up and see me sometime"); *I'm No Angel*, 1933; *Thirty-Day Princess*, 1934; *Born to Be Bad*, 1934; *Last Outpost*, 1935; *Big Brown Eyes*, 1936; *Suzy*, 1936, and many others. By then firmly established as a romantic lead, he displayed a mastery of sophisticated comedy in a series of classic movies during the 1930s and 1940s, including *Topper*, 1937; *The Toast of New York*, 1937; *Bringing Up Baby*, 1938; *Holiday*, 1938; *His Girl Friday*, 1940; *The Philadelphia Story*, 1940; *Talk of the Town*, 1942; *Arsenic and Old Lace*, 1944; *The Bishop's Wife*, 1947; *Mr. Blandings Builds His Dream House*, 1948; and *I Was a Male War Bride*, 1949. His notable dramatic roles, played with his inimitable light touch, included those in *In Name Only*, 1939; *Suspicion*, 1941; *Mr. Lucky*, 1943; *Destination Tokyo*, 1943; *None But the Lonely Heart*, 1944; *Night and Day*, 1946; *Notorious*, 1946; *Crisis*, 1950; *To Catch a Thief*, 1955; *The Pride and the Passion*, 1957; *An Affair to Remember*, 1957; *Indiscreet*, 1958; *North by Northwest*, 1959; *Charade*, 1963; and *Father Goose*, 1964. In his later films Grant lost none of his romantic appeal and he likewise retained the sure command of gesture and expression that was his hallmark. Although many of his films through the years won various Academy Awards, he himself had not received an Oscar—although he had been nominated for *None But the Lonely Heart*—until 1970, when he was presented with a special Academy Award for his total contribution to films and in recognition of his having been for more than three decades one of the most popular stars in Hollywood.

Grant, Hiram Ulysses, *see* Grant, Ulysses S.

Grant, Ulysses S. (1822–1885), eighteenth president of the United States. Born in Point Pleasant, Ohio, on April 27, 1822, Grant worked on the family farm and attended local schools and in 1839 was appointed to West Point. He had already decided to reverse his given names, Hiram Ulysses, when on his arrival at West Point he discovered that he was recorded as Ulysses S., most likely on his congressman's mistaken assumption that he bore his mother's maiden name, Simpson. He acquiesced in the change, although he later maintained that the middle initial did not stand for anything. He graduated in 1843, having distinguished himself in horsemanship and little else, and was assigned to the infantry. In 1845 his regiment joined the U.S. forces under Gen. Zachary Taylor in Texas. Although he was not in sympathy with the Mexican War, Grant served well in Palo Alto, Resaca de la Palma, Monterrey, and, under Gen. Winfield Scott, in the Mexico City campaign, being distinguished for bravery in the battles of Molino del Rey and San Cosme Garita in September 1847. From 1848 to 1854 he was stationed at posts in New York, Michigan, the Oregon Territory, and California; in 1854, frustrated by lack of advancement, financial difficulties, and separation from his family, he resigned his captaincy and rejoined his family in Missouri. For six years he farmed and undertook various business ventures without success in either field and in 1860 he moved to Galena, Illinois, to become a clerk in a leather-goods store operated by his father and brothers. Shortly after the outbreak of the Civil War the following year he aided in organizing a Galena militia company, and while waiting in vain for a reply from Washington to his application for an army commission he served as an aide to the state adjutant general. In June the governor of Illinois appointed him colonel of a militia regiment and two months later, on post in Missouri, he was promoted to brigadier general. Placed in command of the District of Southeast Missouri, with headquarters in Cairo, Illinois, he saw little action, save for a brief and inconclusive engagement at Belmont, Missouri, until January 1862, when Gen. Henry W. Halleck approved his plan to move on forts Henry and Donelson in Tennessee. Aided by a flotilla of gunboats under Commodore Andrew H. Foote, Grant quickly forced the abandonment of Fort Henry, on the Tennessee River, and then vigorously beseiged Fort Donelson, on the Cumberland. On February 16 he informed the fort's commander, Gen. Simon B. Buckner, that "No terms except an unconditional and immediate surrender can be accepted." Buckner and some 15,000 troops, hopelessly surrounded, gave up their arms. The victory, not only Grant's but also the Union's first great success, aroused public enthusiasm in the North and brought Grant promotion to major general of volunteers. His popularity sagged in April, when he failed to anticipate and was slow to react to a powerful attack on his forces at Shiloh, near Pittsburg Landing, Tennessee, by Gen. Albert S. Johnston (killed on April 6, he was succeeded by Gen. P. G. T. Beauregard). The arrival of reinforcements under Gen. D. C. Buell and Gen. Lew Wallace enabled Grant to clear the field on the second day of battle, but Union casualties were extremely high and brought forth a storm of public protest. After several months of planning Grant set out in November to take Vicksburg, the last major Confederate stronghold on the Mississippi River. The campaign was slow to develop and was further delayed by a series of minor Confederate victories, but in April 1863, encouraged by the success of Adm. David D. Porter's fleet in running past the Vicksburg batteries, Grant boldly cast loose from his communications and supply lines and landed his 20,000 men south of the city. Vicksburg was soon isolated and under siege and on July 4 the garrison surrendered; the Mississippi was under complete Union control when near-by Port Hudson fell a few days later, and the Confederacy was cut in half. Grant was made a major general in the regular army and in October was placed in command of the Military Division of the Mississippi; in November he moved to bring the war in the West to a virtual conclusion. Relieving Gen. William S. Rosecrans, who had allowed himself to be trapped at Chattanooga by Gen. Braxton Bragg, he directed a carefully coordinated attack on Bragg's strong points on Lookout Mountain and Missionary Ridge and drove him from the field, November 24 and 25. He was then promoted to lieutenant general and named commander of the Union armies. Making his headquarters with Gen. George G. Meade's Army of the Potomac, he brought his considerable strategic talents to bear on the unsolved problem of evolving an overall plan of war; his cardinal strengths—dogged determination, patience, and a clear understanding of the situation—proved the key. In May 1864 he began the final campaign, sending Gen. William T. Sherman against Gen. Joseph E. Johnston and toward Atlanta (the Atlanta Campaign) and at the same time pitting the Army of the Potomac against Gen. Robert E. Lee's Army of Northern Virginia with the object of taking Richmond. The brutal, costly war of attrition that moved slowly through the Wilderness Campaign (May–June) and the battles of Spotsylvania and Cold Harbor took an enormous toll but had precisely the desired effect of wearing down Lee's resources. In June Lee entrenched at Petersburg, before Richmond, and settled in for the months-long siege of the Petersburg Campaign. In what has been called the first example of modern warfare, Grant pitted the total resources of the Union against the Confederacy and made the outcome almost inevitable. Ignoring public protests against heavy casualties and the seemingly interminable seige—"I propose to fight it out on this line if it takes all summer," he had earlier said—he forced Lee to withdraw from his position to seek supplies. The desperate move ended a week later, on April 9, 1865, when Lee surrendered to Grant at Appomattox Courthouse, Grant offering magnificently generous terms. The war ended with Johnston's surrender on April 26. Grant moved then to Washington, D.C., where he oversaw the demobilization of the army and the military administration of Reconstruction. In 1866 he was appointed to the newly revived rank (created in 1799 for George Washington and never since used) of general of the army. He served as interim secretary of war for several months in 1867–1868 during the dispute over the Tenure of Office Act between Congress and President Andrew Johnson and became permanently estranged from Johnson over the issue. He had long been courted by Republicans as a potential presidential candidate and the break with Johnson strengthened his position with the dominant Radical Republicans. Nominated in 1868, he was elected by a small popular majority but a large electoral vote and quickly demonstrated his complete lack of political sophistication by assembling an unwieldy cabinet of friends, former associates, and assorted others. Only the Department of State, under Hamilton Fish, was in fully capable hands; Fish oversaw negotiation of the Treaty of Washington (1871), laying the foundation for the amicable

arbitration of U.S.–British disputes, including the *Alabama* claims, and he managed to blunt Grant's persistent efforts to secure the annexation of Santo Domingo as a naval base. The Crédit Mobilier scandal tarnished the Republicans' reelection campaign of 1872, but Grant's popular majority in his defeat of Horace Greeley was nonetheless larger than before. Soon, however, revelations of widespread corruption in the government, involving Grant's private secretary in the Whisky Ring, the secretary of war in corruption in the conduct of Indian affairs, and other high officials, soured the tone of the administration; Grant, scrupulously honest himself, became the target of reformers and critics of every stripe. Outside the field of foreign policy, only the fiscal measures of his administration were particularly creditable; a notable achievement was the passage of the Specie Resumption Act of 1875 and other sound, hard-money bills. On retiring from office in 1877 he made a world tour on which he was hailed as a hero, and then returned to Galena. The old-guard faction of the Republican party, then known as the Stalwarts, pushed hard to nominate him again in 1880, but the two-term tradition defeated the attempt. In 1881 he moved to New York City, where, with characteristic credulity, he invested nearly all of his money in a banking firm that three years later was discovered to have defrauded him. To pay his debts he wrote an article on the battle of Shiloh for the *Century* magazine and then, with the encouragement of his friend Mark Twain, began preparing his memoirs. *The Personal Memoirs of U.S. Grant* were completed just a few days before his death on July 23, 1885, at his Adirondack retreat at Mount McGregor; the two volumes, published in 1885–1886 by Twain, restored the Grant family to solvency and were hailed as a major work of autobiography. Grant was elected to the Hall of Fame in 1900.

Graupner, Gottlieb (1767–1836), musician. Born in Verden, Prussia (now in West Germany), on October 6, 1767, Johann Christian Gottlieb Graupner came of a musical family and early became proficient on several instruments. For a time until 1788 he was an oboist in a regimental band; in that year he went to London, where during 1791–1792 he was first oboist in the orchestra organized and conducted by Franz Joseph Haydn. In 1793 he sailed to America, stopping briefly in Prince Edward Island and in 1795 moving to Charleston, South Carolina, where he performed in the City Theatre orchestra; in 1796 he settled in Boston. There he made concert appearances, played in the Federal Street Theatre orchestra, and in 1800 opened a music store and publishing house. He became a naturalized citizen in 1807. In addition to his other activities he gave private instruction in several instruments. About 1810 he realized a long-standing dream in organizing what was originally called the Phil-harmonic Society, of which he remained thereafter president. The first regular concert orchestra in the country, the Philharmonic became, under Graupner's direction, the finest musical organization of any kind, drawing heavily on immigrant European musicians; it continued to perform until 1824. In 1815 Graupner joined in forming a choral society that soon evolved into the Handel and Haydn Society, one of the earliest choral groups, and by far the most accomplished, in the country. During all that time he continued his own concert work and his business and composed numerous works, most of which were later lost. Often referred to as the father of American orchestral music, Graupner died in Boston on April 16, 1836.

Graves, Morris Cole (1910–   ), painter. Born on August 28, 1910, in Fox Valley, Oregon, Graves grew up there and in Seattle. Before completing high school he shipped as a merchant sailor and in 1929 and 1930 visited Japan, where he quickly succumbed to the influence of nature in Japanese art and thought. In 1932, while visiting relatives in Beaumont, Texas, he finished high school and after a brief period in Los Angeles he returned to Seattle, in 1936 enrolling in the Federal Arts Project there. Later that year he held his first one-man show at the Seattle Art Museum. Living in virtual isolation on the shore of Puget Sound for many years, Graves read deeply in Oriental philosophy and was influenced also by Mark Tobey, who shared his interest in Oriental culture. His paintings, first in heavy oil impasto and later in watercolors and gouache, worked toward a spare simplicity of manner and a mysterious, sometimes almost metaphysical symbolism very often employing birds or other small animals. He occasionally included suggestions of Oriental calligraphy in his rather impressionistic inks done on delicate paper. His work was first seen in New York City in 1939 and several of his pieces were included in the "Americans, 1942" show at the Museum of Modern Art. A number of other solo and group exhibitions followed and in 1946 Graves was awarded a Guggenheim fellowship. Major retrospective exhibitions of his work were held in Oslo, Norway, in 1955 and at the Whitney Museum of American Art in 1956, the latter show subsequently traveling from New York to several other cities. He was represented in a great many museum and private collections. During the later 1950s and the 1960s he began working in a more abstract manner than previously and the Oriental influences in his paintings became less apparent. He was engaged for a time by the National Aeronautics and Space Administration (NASA) to execute a series of paintings on space-flight subjects.

Gray, Asa (1810–1888), botanist. Born on November 18, 1810, in Sauquoit, New York, Gray was educated at the Fairfield Academy in Herkimer County, New York. By the time he graduated from the Fairfield Medical School in 1831 his interest had turned to botany and he never practiced medicine. For the next eleven years he lectured at various schools, made numerous field trips to study the flora of New York, New Jersey,

and other areas, and became associated with John Torrey, also a botanist, under whose tutelage he continued his rapid development to scientific maturity. Gray's first publication, *North American Gramineae and Cyperaceae,* 1834–1835, was widely praised and was followed a year later by his first textbook, *Elements of Botany.* With Torrey he published the two-volume *Flora of North America* between 1838 and 1843, and in 1842 appeared his *Botanical Text-Book* (after 1879 called *Structural Botany*), long a standard work. By 1842 Gray was acknowledged to be the foremost botanist in the United States, and in that year he became Fisher Professor of Natural History at Harvard, a chair he held until his death. At Harvard he assembled a large botanical library, developed an extensive herbarium, trained a distinguished new generation of botanists, and continued to publish a steady stream of articles, monographs, reviews, and books that placed him among the world's leading naturalists. In 1848 he issued his *Manual of the Botany of the Northern United States,* which has remained the primary work in the field ever since. A pioneer in plant geography, he published in 1859 a study of the botany of Japan and its relation to that of North America, a work that was hailed by scientists around the world as a truly great piece of scientific research. Gray had long been in correspondence with Charles Darwin when Darwin sent him an advance copy of *The Origin of Species;* from that time forward he was the chief American defender, and most perceptive critic, of Darwin's theory of evolution; he succeeded in perplexing a number of opponents by subscribing to both Darwinian theory and the Christian religion. He published many popular texts on botany— *First Lessons in Botany and Vegetable Physiology,* 1857; *How Plants Grow,* 1858; *Field, Forest, and Garden Botany,* 1869; and *How Plants Behave,* 1872, among them—and in 1878 issued his last great work, the *Synoptical Flora of North America.* Gray was a founder in 1863 of the National Academy of Sciences, for 10 years president of the American Academy of Arts and Sciences, for 14 years a regent of the Smithsonian Institution, and the recipient of a great many honors from universities and societies throughout the world. He died at home in Cambridge, Massachusetts, on January 30, 1888. He was elected to the Hall of Fame in 1900.

Gray, Elisha (1835–1901), inventor. Born in Barnesville, Ohio, on August 2, 1835, Gray left school at an early age to help support his family and while working as a carpenter and later in a machine shop studied for five years, 1857–1862, in the preparatory and college divisions of Oberlin College. He concentrated on the physical sciences, particularly the study of electricity, and despite poor health invented in the span of a few years a great many useful devices for improving and extending the flexibility of the telegraph. In 1872 in Chicago he formed the Gray & Barton Company, with which he was associated for about two years and which later evolved into the Western Electric Company. His interest in telegraphy led him to seek a means of transmitting various tones electrically as a way of carrying several simultaneous messages on the same wire; after obtaining patents for such a system in 1875 he went on to the problem of transmitting voice messages. He conceived of a telephone employing a liquid transmitter and an electromagnetic metal diaphragm receiver and filed for a caveat on February 14, 1876, just a few hours after Alexander Graham Bell had applied for a patent on his telephone. Bell's application rested on experiments he had carried on since the previous year and contained only a passing reference to the possibility of employing the liquid transmitter he used a month later in his famous message to Mr. Watson. Gray sold his claims to the Western Union Telegraph Company, which engaged in long and bitter infringement litigation with the Bell Telephone Company; the result was a legal victory for Bell but only an unclear picture of the actual priorities of the case. Although disappointed by the outcome of the controversy, Gray continued to experiment with various electrical devices, being granted some 70 patents, including two in 1888 and 1891 for his telautograph for the electrical transmission of handwriting or drawings, which he demonstrated at the World's Columbian Exposition in Chicago in 1893. In that year he organized the first International Electrical Congress. From 1880 until his death he was professor of dynamic electricity at Oberlin. Gray died in Newtonville, Massachusetts, near Boston, on January 21, 1901, in the midst of a series of experiments with an undersea signaling device.

Gray, Harold Lincoln (1894–1968), cartoonist. Born on January 20, 1894, in Kankakee, Illinois, Gray graduated from Purdue University in 1917 and after serving an enlistment in the army during World War I joined the staff of the *Chicago Tribune.* For several years he was a reporter and then an assistant draftsman for the *Andy Gump* cartoon strip; he then created a strip of his own that began appearing in 1924 as *Little Orphan Annie.* The strip featured twelve-year-old Annie, whom Gray described as having "a heart of gold, but a wicked left," her faithful dog Sandy, whose contribution was an occasional "Arf," and her guardian and mentor, Oliver "Daddy" Warbucks, a billionaire capitalist and defender of free enterprise, rugged individualism, the Puritan ethic, and the Gospel of Wealth. In no sense comic, *Little Orphan Annie* was a deadly serious and often didactic work on the constant threats to the American way of life posed by a panoply of subversive elements ranging from simple crooks to blind liberals to wily Communists. Annie's was a picaresque life of adventure and intrigue in which virtue fought evil at every turn, and each quality was manifested in the simplest of characterizations. One of the most controversial of comic strips, sharing a political outspokenness, if not a philosophy, with Al Capp's *Li'l Abner, Little*

Orphan Annie was also one of the most popular and long-lived, eventually reaching more than 400 newspapers through syndication. Gray continued to produce daily installments of the strip until his death in La Jolla, California, on May 9, 1968; it was continued thereafter by a successor.

Gray, Horace (1828–1902), justice of the Supreme Court. Born in Boston on March 24, 1828, Gray graduated from Harvard in 1845 and after a period of travel in Europe entered the Harvard Law School. Following further study in a private law office he was admitted to the Massachusetts bar in 1851. He soon enjoyed a successful practice and in 1854 was appointed reporter of the state supreme court, a post he held until 1861. In addition to his court duties and his extensive practice he was also active in politics, being among the early organizers of the Free-Soil party and later the Republican party in Massachusetts. In 1864 Governor John A. Andrew, to whom he had been a close adviser, named him to the state supreme court. He remained on that bench for 17 years, from 1873 as chief justice. Gray was appointed to the Supreme Court by President Chester A. Arthur in 1881, was confirmed in 1882, and held his seat for the rest of his life. Although he was often overshadowed by some of his better-known colleagues, he brought to the Court considerable judicial experience and wide legal learning, particularly in the area of the common law and in his command of precedent, which formed the basis of his methodology. The most notable case in which Gray delivered the opinion of the Court was *Juilliard* v. *Greenman,* 1884, one of the Legal Tender Cases, validating the continued circulation of Civil War legal tender notes. Gray died on September 15, 1902, in Washington, D.C.

Gray, Robert (1755–1806), sailor and explorer. Born in Tiverton, Rhode Island, on May 10, 1755, Gray early went to sea and during the Revolution served the patriot cause. He continued in the merchant service afterward and in 1787, for a Boston mercantile combine, set out in command of the sloop *Lady Washington* and in company with the sloop *Columbia* on a voyage to the Northwest. There he gathered a cargo of sea otter skins and, transferring his command to the *Columbia,* sailed to China and thence to Boston, establishing the three-cornered China trade that was followed for decades and becoming, on his return in 1790, the first American sailor to carry the flag around the world. Later in that year he sailed again in the *Columbia* and during a successful hunting season in 1791–1792 made extensive explorations in the region from Vancouver Island and Juan de Fuca Strait south along the coast, discovering in 1792 the harbor that became known as Grays Harbor and on May 12 entering the rumored great river of the Northwest, which he named Columbia after his ship. He then returned to Boston, again circumnavigating the globe by way of China, arriving in July 1793. Gray engaged in the Eastern coastal trade thereafter and in the summer of

1806 died en route to Charleston, South Carolina; he was apparently buried at sea. His explorations of the Northwest coast and in particular his discovery of the Columbia River were later the basis of the successful U.S. claim to the Oregon country over the rival claim of Great Britain.

Grayson, David, see Baker, Ray Stannard

Greeley, Horace (1811–1872), editor, reformer, and political leader. Born near Amherst, New Hampshire, on February 3, 1811, Greeley ended his schooling, which had been irregular, in 1826 when he became an apprentice printer. Five years later, at the age of twenty, he made his way to New York City and worked for a time as a journeyman printer. Founding a small printing office of his own with a partner, he began, in 1834, to issue the New Yorker, a magazine of good quality that was published, with persistent financial difficulties, until 1841. He contributed to other papers during those years, notably to the Daily Whig, and in 1838 he was offered the editorship of the Jeffersonian, a Whig campaign sheet. In 1840 he edited the similar Log Cabin; the following year he established the New York Tribune, a daily Whig newspaper, which came to exemplify the highest standards of journalism and which grew rapidly, along with Greeley's influence. A zealous reformer, although by no means a radical one, he was also something of a faddist, and his enthusiasms found expression in his paper; notable among them were his support of Albert Brisbane and the Fourierist doctrine, of the spiritualist seances of the Fox sisters, and of the health and diet prescriptions of Sylvester Graham. He opposed slavery vehemently, supported free homesteading as a cure for the industrial ills of the East—"Go West, young man," he was popularly quoted as advising, "and grow up with the country"—and advocated the organization of labor. The Tribune attracted some of the foremost journalists of the day, including Charles A. Dana and Margaret Fuller; by the outbreak of the Civil War it was the leading newspaper in the country outside the South, where it and Greeley were anathema. In his editorials he opposed the Mexican War and the Kansas-Nebraska Act; he favored the Free-Soil movement and in 1854 finally broke with the Whigs to join the newly founded Republican party. In 1860, however, he supported Abraham Lincoln only reluctantly and in 1864, after a futile singlehanded attempt to arrange a peace conference in Canada, did so only at the last minute; his various stands during the Civil War epitomized his sometimes poor judgment and his tendency to vacillate on issues that were not morally clear-cut. After the war he advocated total amnesty for former rebels, hoping to heal the wounds of sectional strife; he was among the group that in May 1867 signed a bail bond for Jefferson Davis, an act that ruined the sale of his theretofore popular history of the Civil War, The American Conflict, two volumes, 1866. On the other hand he generally supported the Radicals' program of Reconstruction, particularly the Fourteenth and Fifteenth amendments. In 1868 he published a volume of memoirs, Recollections of a Busy Life. As the Tribune grew and control passed to others, Greeley found himself with less and less power; his long-standing political ambitions had also been thwarted, largely through the efforts of his earlier Whig ally, Thurlow Weed. In 1872 he made a final bid for office; joining the Liberal Republican group that was dissatisfied with Ulysses S. Grant, he became its presidential nominee and later that also of the Democratic party. The choice was a poor one, for Greeley was too easily lampooned to be taken seriously. He was defeated overwhelmingly and, utterly exhausted, died shortly thereafter, on November 29, 1872, in Pleasantville, New York.

Greely, Adolphus Washington (1844–1935), soldier and explorer. Born on March 27, 1844, in Newburyport, Massachusetts, Greely enlisted in a militia regiment in 1861 and served throughout the Civil War, seeing action in several major battles, sustaining serious wounds on three occasions and rising in rank from private to the temporary rank of major. At the end of the war he entered the regular army as a second lieutenant. In 1881, then a first lieutenant, he volunteered for a scientific expedition to the Arctic being planned by the army according to the recommendations of the 1879 International Polar Geographical Conference, which had designated 1882–1883 as the first International Polar Year. Placed in command of a 25-man party sent to establish a meteorological station, Greely sailed in July 1881 from Newfoundland aboard the Proteus and in August landed at Lady Franklin Bay on the eastern shore of Ellesmere Island. There he established his base camp, Fort Conger, where detailed meteorological, oceanographic, and geophysical observations were carried out and from which exploratory expeditions set out for the interior, discovering Lake Hazen and, on the western coast, Greely Fjord, and in May 1882 reaching their farthest north, 83° 24'. Supply and relief ships sent out in 1882 and 1883 failed to reach Fort Conger and in August of 1883, by prearrangement, Greely and his men broke camp and made their way south by boat to Cape Sabine, beyond which they could not go. With dwindling provisions they wintered there and by the time relief arrived in June 1884 there were left only Greely and six others, one of whom died shortly thereafter. Although he was publicly much criticized at first, it eventually became clear that, given his explicit orders and sheer physical necessity, he had performed correctly and courageously throughout the ordeal. Promoted to captain in 1886, he became by order of President Grover Cleveland brigadier general and chief of the signal service the following year. In that post he was responsible over the next 20 years for the construction of tens of thousands of miles of telegraph lines and submarine cables in Puerto Rico, Cuba, the Philippines, Alaska, and elsewhere, and for the army's earliest adoption of wireless telegraphy; he was also head of the U.S. Weather Service until it was transferred to the Department of Agriculture in 1891. In 1906 he was promoted to major general and placed in command of the Northern Military Division; later transferred to the Pacific Military Division, he oversaw army relief operations following the San Francisco earthquake in that year. Greely retired in 1908. In addition to his work on the official and scientific reports of the Lady Franklin Bay Expedition he wrote several other books, including *Three Years of Arctic Service*, 1886; *American Weather*, 1888; *American Explorers*, 1894; *Handbook of Arctic Discoveries*, 1896; *True Tales of Arctic Heroism*, 1912; and *Reminiscences of Adventure and Service*, 1927. He was widely honored for his scientific work and in 1935 was belatedly awarded the Congressional Medal of Honor. Greely died later that year, on October 20, 1935, in Washington, D.C.

Green, Duff (1791–1875), journalist, public official, and businessman. Born in Woodford County, Kentucky, on August 15, 1791, Green was educated in a local academy and for a time taught school while studying medicine. He served in the War of 1812, rising from private to captain, and in 1816 moved to Missouri, where he worked as a government surveyor, speculated in land, established a large mercantile business, and secured mail contracts. He also studied law, building up a successful practice soon after his admission to the Kentucky bar, and became involved in politics, serving in the state constitutional convention in 1819 and later in the legislature. In 1823 he bought the *St. Louis Enquirer*, in which he actively supported the presidential candidacy of Andrew Jackson in 1824. In 1825 he moved to Washington, D.C., and began the *United States Telegraph*, soon the official organ of the Jacksonian Democrats; in reward for his support he was appointed printer to Congress in 1829 and he was one of the most influential members of Jackson's "kitchen cabinet" of advisers. Green broke with Jackson over several issues in 1831 and enlisted in the forces backing John C. Calhoun. He continued to edit the *Telegraph* until 1836 and then in Baltimore published the *Reformer* in 1837–1838 and founded the *Pilot* in 1840. His support of the William Henry Harrison–John Tyler ticket in the election of 1840 led to his appointment in 1841 as President Tyler's unofficial representative in England, where his advocacy of free trade won him a warm reception by many political leaders and his published articles on economic topics and Anglo-American relations were widely read. Green returned to the United States in 1844 and in New York City established the *Republic*, in which he promoted free trade, internal improvements, civil-service and postal reform, and Western expansion. Many of these projects were aimed at bolstering the development of the South, to whose cause Green was devoted, and to establishing firm commercial and political ties between that section and the West. Later in 1844 he was sent by Tyler to Galveston, Texas, as U.S. consul; he made an unsuccessful attempt to negotiate the transfer of Southwestern territory from Mexico to the United States and after helping generate public clamor for the annexation of Texas strongly supported the Mexican War. Green acquired extensive business interests throughout the South and the Southwest; he organized a number of railroads, built portions of the East Tennessee & Georgia Railroad and the Chesapeake and Ohio Canal, invested in coal and iron lands, and secured charters from several states for a railroad connecting the South with the Pacific Coast. To finance the last project he organized the Pennsylvania Fiscal Agency in 1859 and was about to begin construction when the Civil War broke out. Through the war he supported the Confederacy, turning over his Jonesboro Iron Works in Tennessee to ordnance production. He lost control of the Pennsylvania Fiscal Agency; in 1864 it was rechartered as the Crédit Mobilier of America for the purpose of building the Union Pacific Railroad. After the war Green lived in Dalton, Georgia, and devoted much of his time to writing on economic and political topics. He died in Dalton on June 10, 1875.

Green, Edmund Fisk, *see* Fiske, John

Green, Hetty (1835–1916), financier. Born in New Bedford, Massachusetts, on November 21, 1835, Henrietta Howland Robinson came of a wealthy family; she was connected on the maternal Howland side to one of the great mercantile families of New England. In 1865 both her father and a maternal aunt died, leaving her in their wills a total of about $10 million. Two years later she married Edward H. Green, but by mutual consent their finances were kept separate and she managed hers with single-minded dedication both before and after his death in 1902. She became a major and feared operator on Wall Street, where in addition to extensive holdings in railroad and other stocks and in government bonds she maintained a considerable liquid fund for lending purposes. She also invested heavily in mortgages and real estate, particularly in Chicago. As her fortune grew Hetty Green, sometimes called the "witch of Wall Street," lived with her son and daughter in inexpensive lodgings, avoiding all display of wealth and virtually all society. Her eccentricities made her a favorite subject for newspaper gossip and all manner of stories were circulated concerning her miserliness; the most widely repeated was perhaps that of her supposed refusal to hire a doctor to treat her son's injured leg, resulting eventually in a forced amputation. Reputed, probably correctly, to be the richest woman in America, she lived for much of her later life in a small apartment in Hoboken, New Jersey. On her death in New York City on July 3, 1916, she left an estate of more than $100 million.

Green, Paul Eliot (1894–1981), playwright. Born near Lillington, North Carolina, on March 17, 1894, Green interrupted his studies at the University of North Carolina to serve in the army in World War I, returning to the University to graduate in 1921. He pursued further studies there and at Cornell, devoting much of his time to the writing of short plays based on the lives and folkways of the North Carolinians among whom he had grown up. Strongly influenced by Frederick H. Koch and his Carolina Playmakers, Green published such plays as *The No 'Count Boy*, 1924; *The Lord's Will*, 1925, a collection; *In Abraham's Bosom*, 1926, which won a Pulitzer Prize the next year; *Lonesome Road*, 1926; *The Field God*, 1927; *In the Valley*, 1928, another collection; *Potter's Field*, 1929; *The House of Connelly*, 1931, which was chosen as the first production of the Group Theatre in New York City; *Hymn to the Rising Sun*, 1936; *Johnny Johnson*, 1936, with music by Kurt Weill; and *Native Son*, 1941, in collaboration with Richard Wright. Many of his plays of the 1930s aimed toward what Green termed a symphonic form of drama in which music, mime, dance, and other elements blended into a single imaginative statement on a historical theme. He first attempted a full-scale symphonic treatment in *The Lost Colony*, 1937; other symphonic dramas included *The Highland Call*, 1941; *The Common Glory*, 1948; *Faith of Our Fathers*, 1950; *Wilderness Road*, 1956; *The Founders*, 1957; *The Confederacy*, 1958; *Cross and Sword*, 1964; *Texas*, 1966; and *Trumpet in the Land*, 1970. Many became annual presentations. Green also wrote a number of novels, short stories, and essays and several scripts for motion pictures—*Cabin in the Cotton*, 1932; *State Fair*, 1932; *David Harum*, 1934; *Black Like Me*, 1963; and others—and for radio, many of the latter collected in *The Free Company Present*, 1941; and *Wings for to Fly*, 1959. He was an instructor and associate professor of philosophy at the University of North Carolina from 1923 to 1939 and professor of dramatic art from 1939 to 1944, and served as president of the American Folk Festival from 1934 to 1945. He died on May 4, 1981, in Chapel Hill, North Carolina.

Green, William (1873–1952), labor leader. Born on March 3, 1873, in Coshocton, Ohio, Green was the son of a coal miner and himself entered the mines at the age of sixteen. He soon became active in the Progressive Miners Union and from 1890 in the successor United Mine Workers of America (UMW). Elected subdistrict president in 1900, he rose to Ohio district president for the UMW in 1906, but only two years later did he give up working in the mines to devote full time to union business. He remained district president until 1910, when, after an unsuccessful campaign for the union presidency, he was elected to the Ohio legislature; during two terms there he wrote and secured passage of a state workmen's-compensation law. In 1912 Green became secretary-treasurer of the UMW and the next year assumed a seat on the executive council of the American Federation of Labor (AFL) as fourth vice-president. He retained both offices, serving also as a member of the AFL's advisory committee at the 1919 Versailles Peace Conference, until 1924, when, through the influence of UMW president John L. Lewis, who was his close associate, he was chosen over several senior officials to succeed Samuel Gompers as president of the AFL. Through a period of declining union membership that lasted into the depression, Green sought mainly to give to the labor movement a sense of solid respectability and to eradicate—or at least to disavow—all traces of radicalism. A staunch advocate of peaceful coexistence with management, he was vociferously anti-Communist and was widely admired, particularly among businessmen, as a responsible leader of organized labor. He served on the President's Commission on Economic Security in 1934, on the Labor Advisory Council of the National Recovery Administration (NRA), on the original National Labor Board (NLB) in 1935, and from 1935 to 1937 on the governing council of the International Labor Organization (ILO). Although he had earlier favored the idea of industrial unionism, he strongly opposed the formation of the Committee for Industrial Organization (CIO) in 1935 by several AFL unions, breaking with the CIO leader, Lewis, over the issue, and worked hard to defend the craft tradition of the AFL against the increasingly militant demands of unskilled workers. He led in expelling the CIO unions, of which the UMW was the largest, from the AFL in 1936 and two years later, under pressure from Lewis, resigned his membership in the UMW. The AFL and the newly independent and renamed (1938) Congress of Industrial Organizations kept up a struggle over jurisdictions and for the support of public and business opinion until World War II, when they agreed to an uneasy truce; Green took the lead in pledging the support of labor for the war effort, calling for a no-strike, no-lockout policy for labor and management. The rivalry resumed after the war and was again submerged for a time only by the vital necessity of concerted opposition to the Taft-Hartley Act of 1947, against which Green strove mightily but in vain. He retained the presidency of the AFL until his death in Coshocton, Ohio, on November 21, 1952.

Greene, Nathanael (1742–1786), Revolutionary soldier. Born on August 7, 1742, in Warwick, then a township, Rhode Island, Greene spent the years before the outbreak of the Revolution helping to manage his father's iron foundry and served for a short time in the colonial legislature. Although raised a Quaker, he was expelled from the Society of Friends for his unseemly interest in military matters. In 1774 he helped organize a company of militia that was kept from going to the scene of conflict in Massachusetts in April 1775 by Rhode Island's Loyalist governor. The legislature, however, authorized the raising of three regiments and appointed Greene brigadier in command. Soon given a similar commission in the Continental army, he served through the siege of Boston and after briefly commanding the army of occupation there early in 1776, he set out to aid in the defense of New York City. He was promoted to major general in August; after his loss of Fort Washington in November he joined Gen. George Washington in New Jersey and during the next year rendered valuable service at Trenton, Brandywine, Germantown, and, in 1778, at Monmouth. In March 1778 he assumed, in addition to his field command, the office of quartermaster general and, in the light of congressional and state recalcitrance in matters of finance and supply, discharged his duties more than creditably until relinquishing the office in August 1780. The next month, with Washington temporarily absent, Greene was in command of the entire army, and it was during this period that Benedict Arnold's plottings came to light. In October Greene was sent to South Carolina to replace Gen. Horatio Gates as commander of the army in the South; he arranged an efficient and dependable supply system and soon had the army, demoralized earlier at Camden, again in fighting trim. Facing Gen. Cornwallis, he shrewdly divided his army, sending a force under Gen. Daniel Morgan to the victory at Cowpens in January 1781; he then regrouped and allowed the British a Pyrrhic victory at Guilford Courthouse in March. Greene continued to hound the British, who had another expensive win at Hobkirk's Hill in April. By this time the movements and battles forced by Greene had exhausted the British and induced Cornwallis to give up his plans for conquest in the South and to retire with the bulk of his army northward to Yorktown, Virginia. In September, after a prolonged rest, Greene's forces won a major victory at Eutaw Springs, South Carolina, and by December they had laid seige to the last British stronghold in the South, Charleston, upon which the regulars defeated in September had fallen back. Although the earlier surrender of Cornwallis at Yorktown had effectively ended the war, Greene found it necessary to maintain the seige for a full year before the British withdrawal was complete. After the war Greene experienced financial difficulties resulting from the mismanagement of funds and supplies by subordinate officers and government contractors and from the reluctance of the government to reimburse him for his heavy personal expenditures in supporting his army. He retired to an estate near Savannah, Georgia, and died there on June 19, 1786.

Greenhow, Rose O'Neal (?–1864), Confederate spy. Born on an unknown date in Washington, D.C., and reared in the elegance of prewar Southern society, Rose O'Neal was the widow of prominent physician and historian Robert Greenhow and was living in Washington when the Civil War began. A staunch Southerner, she remained in Washington during the first year of the war, and was suspected then of spying; She was later tried for treason, on March 25, 1862, but the evidence supporting the charge was vague and her methods remained unknown. She remained self-confident and polite throughout the trial and her judges decided to impose exile—she was to remain in the South, or at least stay away from Washington. Mrs. Greenhow had already amassed large amounts of information on Union battle strategy, which she had passed to Confederate generals, several of whose victories were apparently due to her counsel. She went to England, where, in two years' time, she stockpiled a huge amount of gold for the Confederacy, planning to smuggle it through the Union naval blockade of the North Carolina coast; but before reaching her destination, she was shipwrecked and drowned.

Greenough, Horatio (1805–1852), sculptor. Born on September 6, 1805, in Boston, the son of a prosperous merchant, Greenough began at the age of twelve to make miniature figures from chalk and plaster. Throughout his school career he studied drawing, painting, clay modeling, and stonecutting with local teachers and early attracted a patron and mentor in Washington Allston. He graduated from Harvard in 1825, then traveled to Italy, becoming the first American to study sculpture there. He worked diligently, but contracted malaria in 1827 and had to return to Boston. Regaining his strength, he modeled John Quincy Adams from life and did several portrait busts, including one of Chief Justice John Marshall. In 1828 he returned to Italy and established a studio in Florence, fulfilling commissions for portraits, busts, and sculptured groups. Requested by James Fenimore Cooper to model a group based on a painting by Raphael, he completed "Chanting Cherubs," which prompted much criticism when seen in the United States, for the display of naked infants horrified many. But Greenough successfully defended his work and a similar piece, "The Child and the Angel," was subsequently exhibited without protest. In 1833, largely through Cooper's influence, he was commissioned by the U.S. government to create a statue of George Washington to be placed in the Capitol rotunda. All of his patriotism and republican feeling converged in this statue, on which he worked for eight years in Italy and which evolved into a colossal, half-draped marble figure, more reminiscent of a Roman senator than of an American president. When placed in the Capitol the statue shook the floor and was immediately removed to the grounds outside, to the regret of almost no one but Greenough at the time. It was later moved to the Smithsonian Institution. In 1851 he completed a group called "The Rescue," which depicted a pioneer family under attack by Indians, and which was placed on the portico of the Capitol. In the same year he returned home and established himself in Newport, Rhode Island. His *Aesthetics in Washington*, 1851, and *Travels, Observations and Experiences of a Yankee Stonecutter*, 1852, in which he propounded a theory of functionalism in which he was ahead of his time, have come to be considered, more than his sculpture, his major contributions to the development of American art. He died in Somerville, Massachusetts, on December 18, 1852.

Gregg, Josiah (1806–1850), frontier trader and author. Born on July 19, 1806, in Overton County, Tennessee, Gregg moved with his family to Illinois in 1809 and to Missouri in 1812. Little is known of his early life, but he apparently acquired a sound education and possibly studied medicine. In 1831 he set out for the Southwest in a successful effort to improve his health and remained there as a trader. He became interested in the history of the region and particularly in that of the Santa Fe trade, and after what must have been considerable research in Mexican archives he produced a book, *Commerce of the Prairies*, which was published soon after he took the manuscript to New York City in 1844. Several editions quickly followed, along with translations, and the book remained thereafter the single most authoritative and complete study in its field for the pre-Mexican War period. Gregg was attached as an agent and translator to various army units in the Southwest during the Mexican War and in 1849 traveled to California. There he engaged in exploration and surveying; during an exhausting crossing of the Coast Range in the northern part of the state he died near Clear Lake on February 25, 1850.

Gregg, William (1800–1867), pioneer industrialist. Born on February 2, 1800, near Carmichaels, Monongalia County, in what is now West Virginia, Gregg apparently received no schooling. He was apprenticed to a watchmaking uncle with whom he also operated a small cotton factory during the War of 1812. By 1824 he had completed his training and begun his own watchmaking business in Columbia, South Carolina. Within ten years ill health forced his retirement, but he had amassed a modest fortune and was free to follow his growing interest in manufacturing. He acquired an interest in a small cotton factory and quickly reorganized it into a profitable enterprise. In 1838 he moved to Charleston, then in many respects the capital city of the South, and began to develop his ideas on the need for industrialization in the one-crop "Cotton Kingdom." In 1844, as a result of a tour of the textile-manufacturing areas in New England and the Middle States, he published a series of articles on industrialization in the *Charleston Courier*; they appeared as a pamphlet, *Essays on Domestic Industry*, in the following year. The effect was immediate. A factory was begun in Charleston and in 1846, after obtaining with great difficulty a charter of incorporation from the reluctant South Carolina legislature, Gregg began erecting a factory and a town for workers near Aiken. Opened two years later, the enterprise was highly successful; landless whites, having no place in the predominantly agricultural economy, eagerly took up

factory work and Graniteville quickly reached a population of 900. With this example, similar factories were built throughout the South; Graniteville's success was such that in 1858 Gregg could, in South Carolina, openly advocate a protective tariff. In 1856 and 1857 he served in the state assembly, but apart from that interruption he devoted himself to his mill and his mill town. He supported secession in 1860 and during the Civil War was able to maintain the factory's production. In 1867 a flood seriously damaged the factory, and the exhaustion and exposure that he suffered in his efforts to save or repair as much of the plant as possible led to his death on September 13, 1867.

Grew, Joseph Clark (1880–1965), diplomat. Born in Boston on May 27, 1880, Grew came of a patrician banking family. He was educated at Groton and at Harvard, where he took his degree in 1902. He then embarked on a world tour, spending most of his time in the Far East. An incident involving a tiger described in his published account of his travels, *Sport and Travel in the Far East*, attracted the attention of President Theodore Roosevelt; as a result, in 1904 Grew obtained a clerk's position at the U.S. consulate in Cairo and soon afterward became deputy consul general. During the next several years he served in a number of consulates in Mexico and also in St. Petersburg, Vienna, and Berlin. In 1918 he returned to Washington as chief of the state department's Division of Western European Affairs, and the following year he was in attendance at the Versailles Peace Conference. After a series of diplomatic assignments of increasing responsibility he became in 1924 undersecretary of state and oversaw the transition of the foreign service from a basis of political patronage to one of professional career preparation. In 1927 he was named ambassador to Turkey; four years later President Herbert C. Hoover appointed him ambassador to Japan. During ten years there he struggled constantly to stem the growing conflict between Japanese and U.S. claims in the Far East. Early in 1941 he warned the U.S. government of the possibility of a Japanese attack on Pearl Harbor; when the coming of war late in that year proved him to have been prescient, he returned to the state department. For eight months in 1944–1945 he was again undersecretary of state, then retired to private life. He published his two-volume autobiographical work, *Turbulent Era: A Diplomatic Record of Forty Years*, in 1952. He died on May 25, 1965, in Manchester, Massachusetts.

Grey, Pearl, *see* Grey, Zane

Grey, Zane (1875–1939), author. Born in Zanesville, Ohio, on January 31, 1875, Grey was given the name Pearl but later adopted the family name of his mother, who was descended from Ebenezer Zane, founder of Zanesville. Largely in order to play varsity baseball he attended the University of Pennsylvania, taking a degree in dentistry in 1896. He began practice in New York City but was more interested in writing and in 1904, upon publishing at his own expense a historical novel based on the early records of the Zane family, he gave up dentistry entirely. He drew upon the same source for *Spirit of the Border*, 1905, which enjoyed considerable success, but after two more novels he turned to the Wild West for his material. *The Heritage of the Desert*, 1910, proved highly popular and *Riders of the Purple Sage*, 1912, was a huge best seller, firmly establishing Grey as an author. Once having discovered his forte, he produced a flood of Westerns, including *Desert Gold*, 1913; *The Lone Star Ranger*, 1915; *Wildfire*, 1917; *The U.P. Trail*, 1918; *To the Last Man*, 1922; *The Call of the Canyon*, 1924; *Wild Horse Mesa*, 1928; *West of the Pecos*, 1937; and *Western Union*, 1939. From 1917 to 1926 he had a top best seller every year and most of his 54 adult novels long remained in print, sales in the United States alone passing the 30 million mark in the 1960s. Grey also wrote a number of boys' books, many about baseball, and several volumes of outdoor adventure, often drawing on his expert's knowledge of fishing. It was his Westerns, however, that brought him fame as one of the most popular authors of the twentieth century; packed with action, adventure, and many of the elements—in particular the figure of the lone-wolf gunfighter—that soon became standard features of the genre, they were of profound influence on subsequent popular treatments of the West in literature and movies and on television. Grey died at his home in Altadena, California, on October 23, 1939, leaving twenty or more manuscripts to be published over the next several years.

Grier, Robert Cooper (1794–1870), justice of the Supreme Court. Born on March 5, 1794, in Cumberland County, Pennsylvania, Grier was educated by his father, a Presbyterian minister and schoolteacher, and at Dickinson College, from which he graduated in 1812. He then assisted his father in an academy in Northumberland, Pennsylvania, becoming its principal upon his father's death in 1815. At the same time he studied law and was admitted to the bar in 1817, moving to Bloomsburg and later to Danville to practice. He enjoyed marked success in law and in 1833 was appointed president judge of the district court of Allegheny County. After 13 years on that bench he was appointed to the Supreme Court by President James K. Polk. Although a Democrat, Grier was even more a Unionist and through the critical times before and during the Civil War he staunchly upheld the power of the federal government and the authority of the president. He concurred in the Dred Scott decision in 1857 and, in his most important opinion, spoke for the Court in the 1863 Prize Cases, validating President Abraham Lincoln's proclamation of a blockade of Confederate ports and the subsequent seizure of neutral shipping. From 1867 he suffered

a sharp decline in health and was finally prevailed upon to resign in February 1870. Grier died a short time later, on September 25, 1870, in Philadelphia.

Griffith, D. W. (1875–1948), motion-picture director and producer. Born in Oldham County, Kentucky, on January 22, 1875, David Lewelyn Wark Griffith was the son of an aristocratic but Civil War–impoverished Southern family. At sixteen he took a job in a Louisville newspaper office; in 1897 he won a small part in a production by the Mefert stock company, and for several years toured with that and other theater groups, also working at odd jobs at the same time. In 1907 a play he had written was staged unsuccessfully; a scenario for a movie version of the opera *Tosca* was rejected but gained him a job as a movie actor. After a brief time at Thomas A. Edison's studio in West Orange, New Jersey, he moved to the Biograph company; he advanced quickly and directed his first film in 1908. During the next 23 years he directed or produced nearly 500 films and was the single most important figure in establishing the basic techniques of cinematic art. On the technical side his innovations and improvements, all soon part of the cinematographer's essential repertoire, included the close-up, the fade-in and fade-out, high- and low-angle shots, the pan, the flashback, soft focus, the use of a moving camera, and others. At the same time he gave serious attention to content and opened the film to history, philosophy, and social comment. *The Birth of a Nation*, his first great film, opened in 1915 and was a sensation, both for its obvious artistic merit and its technical innovations and for its controversial element of racism. It was followed by the epic *Intolerance* in 1916, *Broken Blossoms* in 1919, *Way Down East* in 1920, *Orphans of the Storm* in 1922, *America* in 1924, and *Abraham Lincoln* in 1931. Griffith also had a keen eye for potential talent and the list of stars he introduced to motion-picture audiences included Mary Pickford ("America's Sweetheart"), Dorothy and Lillian Gish, Lionel Barrymore, Joseph Schildkraut, Harry Carey, Mack Sennett, and Donald Crisp. In 1919 he had formed the United Artists Company with Mary Pickford, Douglas Fairbanks, and Charlie Chaplin. He made no more films after 1931; he retired to private life and sold his interest in UA in 1933. In 1935 the Academy of Motion Picture Arts and Sciences honored Griffith with a special award for his many contributions to the industry. He died in Hollywood, California, on July 23, 1948.

Griffiths, John Willis (1809–1882), naval architect. Born in New York City on October 6, 1809, Griffiths was apprenticed to his father, a shipwright, and early learned the fundamentals of shipbuilding and design. By the age of nineteen he had already designed a major vessel, the frigate *Macedonia*. Working for the Navy Yard in Portsmouth, Virginia, and later for a New York shipbuilding firm, he began proposing numerous innovations in ship design, including the use of the ram on warships, and in 1836 published a remarkable series of articles in the *Portsmouth Advocate* outlining his ideas. In 1842 he delivered in New York City the first formal lectures on naval architecture ever given in America and opened a free school in shipbuilding. After several years devoted to refining his ideas and two years of actual construction he saw launched in 1845 his *Rainbow*, a vessel built for the China trade and the first of the famous "extreme" clippers, the fastest ships afloat. While Donald McKay was working with the same basic approach to clipper design, Griffiths took it farther, producing ships with an extremely narrow bow, high stern, and aft-displaced beam. Primarily a theoretician rather than a shipbuilder, he advocated pure functionalism of design, claiming that beauty would flow naturally from it. The *Sea Witch*, another extreme clipper, was launched in 1846. In 1848 he invented an iron keelson for strengthening wooden ships and during the early 1850s he desiged a number of steamships that proved to be the finest of their time, showing a model of one at the Crystal Palace exhibition in London in 1851. He was coeditor and part owner of the *Nautical Magazine and Naval Journal* from 1856 to 1858, when he was appointed a special naval constructor for the U.S. government; in that capacity he designed the *Pawnee*, a gunboat that featured twin screws, a drop bilge, and a remarkably shallow draft. Later inventions of his included the bilge keel to prevent rolling, triple screws, an improved rivet, and a timber-bending machine which he used in building the *New Era* in 1870 and the *Enterprise* in 1872. From 1879 Griffiths was editor of the *American Ship* in New York City. His published works included *A Treatise on Marine and Naval Architecture*, 1850; *The Ship-builder's Manual and Nautical Referee*, 1853; and *The Progressive Shipbuilder*, 1874–1875. He died in Brooklyn, New York, on March 30, 1882.

Grimké, Sarah Moore (1792–1873) and **Angelina Emily (1805–1879)**, social reformers. Born in Charleston, South Carolina, Sarah on November 26, 1792, and Angelina on February 20, 1805, the Grimké sisters came of a wealthy and aristocratic family. They early developed an antipathy toward both slavery and the limitations on the rights of women. Sarah made a number of visits to Philadelphia, where she became acquainted with the Society of Friends; at length, in 1821, she became a member and left her Southern home permanently. Angelina followed and in 1829 also became a Quaker. In 1835 Angelina wrote a letter of approval to William Lloyd Garrison that was subsequently published in the *Liberator*; from that time on, the sisters were deeply involved in the abolitionist movement, Angelina always taking the lead. In 1836 she wrote a pamphlet, *An Appeal to the Christian Women of the South*, in which she urged those addressed

to use their moral force against slavery; the institution, she argued was harmful not only to Negroes but to women. Sarah followed with *An Epistle to the Clergy of the Southern States*. Under the auspices of the American Anti-Slavery Society, they began to address small groups of women in private homes; this practice grew naturally into the first appearances of women speaking publicly before large mixed audiences on the issue. The General Association of Congregational Ministers of Massachusetts issued a pastoral letter strongly denouncing women preachers and reformers, and the sisters thereafter found it necessary to crusade equally for women's rights. There followed Angelina's *Appeal to the Women of the Nominally Free States*, 1837, and Sarah's *Letters on the Equality of the Sexes and the Condition of Woman*, 1838. In 1838 Angelina married the abolitionist Theodore Dwight Weld, and both sisters soon afterward retired from public activity. They assisted in Weld's school in New Jersey for a time; later all three moved to Hyde Park, now in Boston, Massachusetts. There the sisters died, Sarah on December 23, 1873, an Angelina on October 26, 1879.

Grinnell, George Bird (1849–1938), naturalist and author. Born in Brooklyn, New York, on September 20, 1849, Grinnell graduated from Yale in 1870 and in that year made his first trip to the West as a member of a paleontological expedition headed by Othniel C. Marsh. For four years thereafter he worked in his father's banking office in New York City but in 1874 he returned to Yale to study under O. C. Marsh in the Peabody Museum. During that period he served as naturalist with the Black Hills expedition led by Col. George A. Custer in 1874 and with an expedition to the Yellowstone country in 1875. In 1876 he became natural-history editor of *Forest and Stream* magazine; on taking his Ph.D. in 1880 he became editor in chief, a post he held until 1911 and in which he made the magazine into a leading journal of natural history and conservation. During his many sojourns in the West for scientific, hunting, exploring, or official purposes he developed deep and abiding interests in the history and welfare of the Plains Indians—with many of whom he formed close friendships and with whom he negotiated a number of treaties for the government—and also in the preservation of wilderness regions and wildlife. In 1886 he helped found the Audubon Society for the protection of birds and the next year joined with Theodore Roosevelt and other conservation-minded sportsmen in organizing the Boone and Crockett Club, of which he was president from 1918 to 1927. A leader of the New York Zoological Society, he helped plan the New York Zoological Park in the Bronx. He was active in the promotion of the idea of national parks and wildlife preserves and was largely responsible for the establishment of Glacier National Park in 1910. He joined in the formation of the American Game Association in 1911 and in 1925 served as president of the National Parks Association. Among his many books were *Pawnee Hero Stories and Folk Tales*, 1889; *Blackfoot Lodge Tales*, 1892; *Trails of the Pathfinders*, 1911; *Indians of Today*, 1911; *When Buffalo Ran*, 1920; *The Cheyenne Indians*, 1923; *Two Great Scouts*, 1929; and a series of outdoors books for boys. He edited or coedited *American Big-Game Hunting*, 1893; *Trail and Campfire*, 1897; *Hunting and Conservation*, 1925; and other books. Grinnell died in New York City on April 11, 1938.

Griswold, Rufus Wilmot (1815–1857), critic and editor. Born on February 15, 1815, in Benson, Vermont, Griswold went to work in a newspaper office in Albany, New York, at the age of fifteen and for some years was a journeyman printer. About 1837 he was licensed to preach by the Baptist church but he probably never held a pastorate. For a little more than a year from early 1838 he edited the *Vergennes Vermonter* and then spent periods writing for various journals in New York City and Philadelphia. He came suddenly to notice in 1842 with the appearance of an anthology edited by him, *The Poets and Poetry of America*, which remained long in print through several editions. In the same year he succeeded his friend Edgar Allan Poe as literary editor of *Graham's Magazine*, holding the post for a year and a half during which he emerged as one of the most influential literary arbiters in the country. Among the great many books that he produced over the next few years were *The Poets and Poetry of England in the Nineteenth Century*, 1844; the first American edition of *The Prose Works of John Milton*, 1845–1847; *The Prose Writers of America*, 1847; and *The Female Poets of America*, 1848, the past two of which were also long in print and established Griswold as an outspoken literary nationalist. His last years were marked by serious personal and health problems and by public controversy, particularly following a strange, severely candid obituary he published in 1849 on the death of Poe, who had, ironically, named Griswold his literary executor. *The Works of the Late Edgar Allan Poe*, in four volumes, 1850–1856, was competently edited by Griswold but included a biographical memoir that was in part maliciously false and letters into which passages complimentary to himself were inserted. He edited the *International Monthly Magazine* from 1850 to 1852 and Phineas T. Barnum's *Illustrated News* during 1852–1853, and in 1855 he published his most important written work, *The Republican Court, or American Society in the Days of Washington*. Griswold died in New York City on August 27, 1857.

Grofé, Ferde (1892–1972), composer and arranger. Born on March 27, 1892, in New York City, Grofé, originally named Ferdinand Rudolf von Grofé, grew up there and in Los Angeles. He came of a family of concert musicians and studied the piano, the violin, and the rudiments of composition. At fourteen he left home and held a series of jobs, including playing piano in dance halls where he was exposed to the raw vitality of early jazz. In 1909 he joined the Los Angeles Symphony Orchestra as a violinist and remained with it for ten years; after a short period conducting a dance-hall band he joined Paul Whiteman's orchestra as a pianist and arranger and began creating the soft, sweet, and slightly jazzy arrangements of dance music for which Whiteman became famous. Grofé's first renown came in 1924, when he orchestrated George Gershwin's *Rhapsody in Blue* for its premiere by the Whiteman group. Thereafter he devoted more and more time to composition and later in 1924 produced his *Mississippi Suite*, premiered with considerable success by Whiteman at Carnegie Hall the next year. There followed *Metropolis*, inspired by the sights and sounds of New York City, in 1927, *Three Shades of Blue* in 1928, and his best-known work, the *Grand Canyon Suite*, which was first performed in Chicago, again by Whiteman, in 1931. Like most of his works the *Grand Canyon Suite* was program music and it utilized to the full Grofé's remarkable talent for creating beautiful and quite unusual sounds. Subsequent compositions, inspired by various aspects of American life and many commissioned by major corporations, included *Symphony in Steel*, 1935; *Hollywood Suite*, 1937; *Café Society*, 1938, a ballet; *Wheels*, 1939; and works "on" such topics as the Hudson River, San Francisco, New England, aviation, Knute Rockne, Niagara Falls, and the 1964 New York World's Fair. Grofé appeared often as conductor of concert programs of his own music and as a pianist and wrote frequently for films. He died in Santa Monica, California, on April 3, 1972.

Gronlund, Laurence (1846–1899), political reformer and author. Born in Copenhagen, Denmark on July 13, 1846, Gronlund received his M.A. from the University of Copenhagen in 1865 and began to study law. Two years later he emigrated to the United States and became a teacher of German in Milwaukee. He continued to study law and was admitted to the bar in Chicago in 1869. He apparently did not find legal practice agreeable and as he became increasingly interested in Socialism, a development which he obscurely attributed to his reading of Blaise Pascal's *Pensées*, he gradually gave it up entirely. In 1878 he published *The Coming Revolution: Its Principles*, which was followed in 1884 by his major work, *The Cooperative Commonwealth*. In that book he presented, in a form somewhat modified to fit particular American circumstances, essentially a Marxist prescription for Socialist revolution against a rigid and moribund capitalistic system. The book was the first satisfactory exposition in English of the principles of Socialist and Marxist economics. During his remaining years he traveled widely lecturing on Socialism and he continued to write. He consistently opposed half-way measures such as the single tax, although he supported Henry George's campaign for mayor of New York in 1886. In 1888 he became a member of the executive committee of the Socialist Labor party. His views slowly mellowed as events such as the passage of the Interstate Commerce Act, 1887, and the Sherman Anti-Trust Act, 1890, indicated that U.S. capitalism had a reserve of adaptability and might after all be viable. He gradually abandoned revolution in favor of government leadership in the evolution of a Socialist state, an idea he developed in *New Economy: A Peaceable Solution of the Social Problem*, 1898. Shortly after joining the staff of the *New York Evening Journal*, he died in New York City on October 15, 1899.

Gropius, Walter Adolf (1883–1969), architect. Born in Berlin on May 18, 1883, Gropius attended German technical institutes, in Munich in 1903 and in Berlin from 1905 to 1907. He was head assistant to Peter Behrens in his architectural practice in Berlin until 1910, when he founded his own architectural firm. His prewar designs included factories and residences as well as furniture, interior designs, and a benzene-powered locomotive; they were notable for their functional, sparse lines and innovative use of materials. In designing the Fagus factory at Alfeld, built in 1911, he employed a steel skeleton as the entire support of the structure; the only walls were "curtain walls" of glass. At the Werkbund Exhibition at Cologne in 1914 he created a stir with his model factory and its adjacent headquarters building, introducing a transparent staircase, glass-enclosed office units, and a roof garden. In 1918 he combined two art schools at Weimar under the name Staatliches Bauhaus and became director of the revolutionary architecture center, where art, science, technology, and humanism were considered to be partners. Students working with talented painters, typographers, weavers, furniture designers, and other practitioners of the fine and applied arts learned skills in production as well as design. In 1925 the Bauhaus, which developed a reputation for teaching "architectural socialism," was moved to Dessau, where it was housed in a new building, one of the finest designed by Gropius, 1925–1926. Gropius resigned from the directorship in 1928 and maintained a private practice in Berlin from 1928 to 1934. In 1933 the school closed with the advent of the Nazi regime. Gropius remained in self-imposed exile in England from 1934 to 1937, working in 1936–1937 with London architect Maxwell Fry, with whom he designed the Village College residence in Cambridgeshire. In 1937 he was called to Harvard as professor of architecture and remained in the United States thereafter. He continued Bauhaus methods at Harvard, where he was made chairman of the department of architecture in 1938, and at the New Bauhaus in Chicago, later called the Institute of Design, founded with László Moholy-Nagy in 1937. He collaborated with Marcel Breuer on many projects, including a 250-unit defense housing project called Aluminum City in New Kensington, Penn-

sylvania, in 1941. In 1946 he established the Architects' Collaborative in Cambridge, Massachusetts, and with his colleagues completed the Container Corporation of America plant in Greensboro, North Carolina, the U.S. embassy in Athens, 1957, and the famous Harvard graduate center in 1949–1950 comprising seven dormitory buildings and a community center. Among Gropius's many books were *The New Architecture and the Bauhaus*, 1935; *The Bauhaus, 1919–1928*, 1938; *Rebuilding Our Communities*, 1946; and *Scope of Architecture*, 1955. He died in Boston on July 5, 1969.

Gropper, William (1897–1977), painter and illustrator. Born in New York City on December 3, 1897, Gropper early left school to work in various jobs in the garment and sweatshop district. His love of drawing, however, led him to study with Robert Henri and George Bellows in 1912–1913, at the National Academy of Design in 1913–1914, and at the New York School of Fine and Applied Art from 1915 to 1918. In 1920 he joined the staff of the *New York Herald Tribune* as a cartoonist, but his leftist political sympathies and particularly his support of the Industrial Workers of the World (IWW) soon led to his dismissal. He then worked as a free-lance cartoonist, contributing not only to radical publications such as the *New Masses* and the *Sunday Worker* but also to such fashionable periodicals as *Smart Set*, *Vanity Fair*, and *Spur*. The publication of a collection of his cartoons, *The Golden Land*, in 1927 brought him to public notice and in 1928 he published *Fifty-Six Drawings of the U.S.S.R.*, the result of a lengthy visit the previous year, during which he had worked for *Pravda*. Gropper was also interested in painting and finally, in 1936, he held a one-man show at the ACA Gallery in New York City; several other solo and group exhibitions followed and he received a Guggenheim fellowship in 1937. His paintings were closely related to his cartoons, both in manner and in subject; whether satirical or sentimental, they expressed a strong commentary on society in their sympathetic views of the downtrodden and their biting caricatures of businessmen, bosses, and especially senators, his favorite targets. In addition to works on canvas and paper Gropper executed a number of murals, notably for the Department of the Interior Building in Washington, D.C., and the post offices in Freeport, New York, and Detroit. The recipient of numerous prizes for his work, Gropper was represented in a number of major gallery, museum, and private collections. He died in Manhasset, New York, on January 6, 1977.

Gross, Samuel David (1805–1884), surgeon. Born near Easton, Pennsylvania, on July 8, 1805, Gross began the study of medicine with a local practitioner but, deciding that he required a better basic education, he attended schools in Wilkes-Barre and Lawrenceville, New Jersey, and then entered Jefferson Medical College, graduating in

1828. For two years he practiced in Philadelphia and during that time published translations of several French and German medical books and in 1830 his own *Treatise on the Anatomy, Physiology and Diseases and Injuries of the Bones and Joints*. After three years in Easton he joined the faculty of the Medical College of Ohio and in 1835 became the first professor of pathological anatomy in the newly opened Cincinnati Medical College. In 1839 he published his *Elements of Pathological Anatomy*, the first systematic treatment of the topic in the English language; the book secured his reputation and long remained a standard work. Gross moved to the medical school of the University of Louisville as professor of surgery in 1840, remaining until 1856, except for the year 1850–1851, which he spent at the University of the City of New York (now New York University); in 1856 he became professor of surgery at Jefferson Medical College. In 1847 he joined in the founding of the American Medical Association (AMA) in Philadelphia. A teacher of power and influence, Gross was recognized also as a surgeon of surpassing skill; he passed on to his students his passion for detail and for the utmost care at every step. His major reputation, which became worldwide, rested on his writings. *A Practical Treatise on the Diseases and Injuries of the Urinary Bladder, the Prostate Gland, and the Urethra*, 1851, was a standard text for more than 30 years; *A Practical Treatise on Foreign Bodies in the Air-Passages*, 1854, was long held to be the definitive discussion; and his monumental *System of Surgery, Pathological, Diagnostic, Therapeutic, and Operative*, two volumes, 1859, was as admired for its literary qualities as for its comprehensive scholarship. Gross also wrote *A Manual of Military Surgery*, 1861, for the army, and he edited and contributed to *The Lives of Eminent American Physicians and Surgeons of the Nineteenth Century*, 1861. He received numerous honorary degrees and was a leading member of many medical organizations. He continued to teach until 1882 and to practice until his death in Philadelphia on May 6, 1884. His *Autobiography*, edited by his sons, appeared three years later.

Grosvenor, Gilbert Hovey (1875–1966), editor. Born on October 28, 1875, in Constantinople (now Istanbul), Turkey, Grosvenor was the son of American parents. He remained in Turkey, where his father was a professor in the American-sponsored Robert College, until 1890, with the exception of the years of the Russo-Turkish War, which he spent in Massachusetts. In 1890 the family returned permanently to the United States and Grosvenor soon entered Amherst College, graduating in 1897. For two years he taught at the Englewood (New Jersey) Academy and in 1899 was invited by Alexander Graham Bell to edit the *National Geographic Magazine*, then a small and irregularly published technical bulletin of the National Geographic Society in Washington, D.C. His salary was paid personally by

Bell, whose elder daughter, Elsie, Grosvenor married in 1900. His title was changed to managing editor in 1900 and to editor in chief in 1903. From the outset it was his idea to build the magazine into a large-circulation publication aimed at a lay audience; the introduction of an unprecedented amount of photographic illustration and, as early as 1910, of color photography greatly increased the appeal of the magazine, and the publication of nontechnical and noncontroversial articles on a wide variety of topics—travels to exotic places, wildlife, explorations—led within six years to a tenfold increase over the 1899 circulation of about a thousand. By selling memberships in the society instead of subscriptions and making the magazine a free service to members he was able to secure tax-exempt status as a nonprofit educational organization; revenues, including income from advertising, were then devoted to sponsoring over the years a great many scientific research projects, including polar expeditions, archaeological digs in many parts of the world, undersea and atmospheric research, and the Mt. Palomar Sky Survey (1949–1956). The society also published technical monographs for specialists and a distinguished series of maps, and its photographic library grew to be one of the largest and most valuable in the world. By 1905 the society was financially independent; another tenfold increase by 1912 brought membership to 100,000 and by the 1960s more than 4 million people were enrolled. Grosvenor had been director of the society since 1899 and in 1920 had become president; he retained that office and the editorship of the magazine until 1954, when he was elected chairman of the board of trustees. Noted also as an author and frequent contributor to the *National Geographic Magazine* and as a conservationist, he died on February 4, 1966, at his estate, formerly that of his father-in-law, at Baddeck, Nova Scotia.

Grow, Galusha Aaron (1822–1907), public official. Born in Ashford, Connecticut, on August 31, 1822, Grow moved with his family to a large farm in Susquehanna County, Pennsylvania in 1834. He graduated from Amherst College in 1844 and three years later was admitted to the bar. He began practice in Towanda, Pennsylvania, in partnership with David Wilmot and in 1850, as the compromise candidate of the pro- and anti-Wilmot Democratic factions, was elected to the House of Representatives. There, while gradually aligning himself with the antislavery forces, he stood from the outset as a leading advocate of reform in the system of disposing of public lands and of the development of a homestead law. He was active in the organization of the Republican party as a coalition of free-soil and antislavery groups in 1854 and was thereafter one of its most prominent and effective spokesmen in Congress. On the organization of the special war session of Congress in 1861 he was elected speaker of the House; he retained the post, in which he oversaw the passage of the Homestead Act in 1862, until 1863, when, as a result of a Democrat-inspired redistricting in Pennsylvania, he was defeated for reelection. He remained active in Republican politics while engaging in various business pursuits that included a period, 1871–1875, as president of the International & Great Northern Railroad in Texas. Finally, in 1894, he eluded the hostile Pennsylvania Republican machine dominated by Matthew S. Quay and won election to a vacated seat in the House. He was reelected three times, served as chairman of the education committee, and retired in 1903 at the age of eighty. He died in Susquehanna County, Pennsylvania, on March 31, 1907.

Guess, George, see Sequoya

Guest, Edgar Albert (1881–1959), journalist. Born on August 20, 1881, in Birmingham, England, Guest emigrated to the United States with his parents in 1891 and settled in Detroit. He left school at thirteen and in 1895 took a job with the *Detroit Free Press*, advancing in a few years from copyboy to police reporter to exchange editor. He became a naturalized citizen in 1902. About 1900 he began writing verses for a weekly column entitled "Chaff;" the feature proved highly popular and soon became the daily "Breakfast Table Chat," which he conducted for the rest of his life. His rhymes—he never claimed for them the status of poetry—were of the simplest sort, full of folksy vernacular and expressing quietly optimistic thoughts on such topics as the home, motherhood, friendship, and all the common virtues and verities. Guest was thoroughly realistic about his work, knowing it for doggerel and sentimental jingle; but it was, he explained, precisely what he liked and what, moreover, millions of other ordinary people liked, and the ridicule of unkind critics and intellectuals left him unscathed. After printing privately a few small collections of his verses he published in 1916 *A Heap o' Livin'*, which eventually sold more than a million copies. Nearly a score of subsequent collections, all highly successful, followed over the years, bearing such titles as *Just Folks*, 1917; *When Day Is Done*, 1921; *Harbor Lights of Home*, 1928; and *Mother*, 1948. He also wrote a few inspirational prose works, including *Making a House a Home*, 1922, and *Between You and Me*, 1938. From 1931 to 1942 he conducted a regular radio program and later appeared occasionally on television. Guest's column was syndicated at its peak of popularity to some 300 newspapers across the country and he was often commissioned to write verses for greeting cards. He died in Detroit on August 5, 1959.

Guggenheim, Daniel (1856–1930), see under Guggenheim, Meyer

Guggenheim, Meyer (1828–1905), industrialist. Born on February 1, 1828, in Langnau, Switzerland, Guggenheim emigrated to the United States at the age of nineteen, settled in Philadelphia, and for many years engaged in various mercantile

pursuits, including peddling. In 1872 he founded with a partner the firm of Guggenheim and Pulaski, importers of Swiss embroidery. In 1881 the business was reorganized as M. Guggenheim's Sons with his four oldest sons as partners. A venture in copper-mine stock in 1887 led him to leave the lace business and to form the Philadelphia Smelting and Refining Company in 1888. A second smelter was established in Mexico in 1891 and a third, also in Mexico, in 1894; as the company's installations multiplied, Guggenheim was able to rely heavily on his seven sons, principally the oldest, Daniel, born in Philadelphia on July 9, 1856, to manage operations in the field. In 1899, the American Smelting and Refining Company was formed to consolidate the leading companies in the field; Guggenheim, however, refused to join and instead decided to compete with the trust for business. He outbid American Smelting at the mine, formed alliances with and rendered financial aid to mine owners, and established the Guggenheim Exploration Company to seek new ore deposits throughout the world. Within two years he had demonstrated the superiority of his methods and in 1901 merged with American Smelting, taking control of the entire combine. Daniel Guggenheim became chairman of the executive committee and four of the sons were on the board of directors. Meyer Guggenheim died in Palm Beach, Florida, on March 15, 1905. His policies were continued by Daniel, who extended the company's holdings and processing operations into copper and nitrate in Chile, tin in Bolivia, gold in Alaska, and diamonds and rubber in the Belgian Congo (now Zaire). His administration of the company was marked by his insistence upon employing the most modern and efficient techniques available and by his enlightened, although paternalistic, views on labor. He continued at the head of the company, as chairman or president, until 1919. He founded the philanthropic Daniel and Florence Guggenheim Foundation and in 1926 the Daniel Guggenheim Fund for the Promotion of Aeronautics. He died at his Long Island home in Port Washington, New York, on September 28, 1930. Another Guggenheim son, Simon, born in Philadelphia on December 30, 1867, played a prominent role in the growth of the family holdings. He was a U.S. senator from Colorado from 1907 to 1913 and from 1919 until his death in New York City on November 2, 1941 was president of the American Smelting and Refining Company. In 1925 he established the John Simon Guggenheim Memorial Foundation, named for his son and often called simply "The Guggenheim Foundation," to provide financial support through fellowships to scholars and artists pursuing advanced study abroad.

Guggenheim, Simon (1867–1941), see under Guggenheim, Meyer

Gulick, Luther Halsey (1865–1918), educator. Born in Honolulu on December 4, 1865, Gulick came of a family of Congregationalist missionaries. He studied briefly in the preparatory department of Oberlin College in 1880 and then, after recuperating from the first of the many bouts of illness that would plague him through life, at the Sargent School of Physical Training (now Sargent College of Boston University) in 1885; in 1889 he received his M.D. from the Medical College of the University of the City of New York (now New York University). From 1886 he had been associated with the Young Men's Christian Association (YMCA) Training School in Springfield, Massachusetts, as organizer and then director of an instructional course in physical training, and while there he aided James Naismith, one of his students, in developing the game of basketball. He retained his post there until 1903, serving also from 1887 to 1903 as secretary of the physical training department of the YMCA International Committee. Gulick was the designer of the YMCA's triangle emblem, representing the three aspects—physical, spiritual, social—of the whole man. From 1900 to 1903 he was principal of the Pratt Institute High School in Brooklyn, New York, and in 1903 he became director of physical education for the New York City public school system, for which he organized the Public School Athletic League. He held the position until 1906, and the following year he became the first director of the Russell Sage Foundation's child hygiene department, with which he remained associated until 1913. In 1910, with his wife Charlotte Vetter Gulick, he founded the Camp Fire Girls, a recreational, educational, and service organization for young girls. Gulick's health declined seriously in his last years and he was largely inactive. Among his written works were *The Efficient Life*, 1907; *Mind and Work*, 1908; *The Heathful Art of Dancing*, 1910; *The Dynamics of Manhood*, 1917; and *Morals and Morale*, published posthumously in 1919. He also edited at various times a number of journals devoted to physical education and his own "Gulick Health Series" pamphlets. He died on August 13, 1918, in South Casco, Maine.

Gumm, Frances, *see* Garland, Judy

Gunther, John (1901–1970), journalist and author. Born in Chicago on August 30, 1901, Gunther graduated from the University of Chicago in 1922 and, after a brief period as a reporter for the *Chicago Daily News*, traveled to Europe. He worked for a time for the United Press and in 1924 rejoined the *Daily News* as a roving correspondent, touring, interviewing leading political figures, and gathering background information all over Europe and the Middle East. During this period he also wrote several novels, including *The Red Pavilion*, 1926, and *The Bright Nemesis*, 1932, which had only small success. He left the *Daily News* to become a free-lance journalist and writer in 1936, the year in which he published *Inside Europe*, the first of his massive informal studies of the major sociopolitical regions of the world. A synthesis of a vast amount of fac-

tual material, personal impressions, biographical studies of outstanding persons, and analyses of current affairs, the book was a critical and popular success and was revised several times in the next few years. *Inside Asia* appeared in 1939 and was followed by *Inside Latin America*, 1941; *Inside USA*, 1947; *Inside Africa*, 1955; *Inside Russia Today*, 1958; *Inside Europe Today*, 1961; and *Inside South America*, 1968; each involved months or years of travel, interviews, and research in the preparation, and all were received with equal acclaim. Other journalistic and biographical studies published by Gunther included *The High Cost of Hitler*, 1939; *D Day*, 1944, drawn from his experiences as a war correspondent in Europe; *Behind the Curtain*, 1949; *Roosevelt in Retrospect*, 1950; *The Riddle of MacArthur*, 1951; *Eisenhower, the Man and the Symbol*, 1952; *Taken at the Flood*, 1960, a biography of Albert Lasker; *Meet Soviet Russia*, 1962; *Chicago Revisited*, 1968; and *Twelve Cities*, 1969. Gunther was at various times a radio and television commentator, contributed often to various periodicals, and was the host of the "John Gunther's High Road" travel program on television for several years. His *Fragment of Autobiography* appeared in 1962; he died in New York City on May 29, 1970.

Gustafsson, Greta Lovisa, *see* Garbo, Greta

Guthrie, Woody (1912–1967), folk singer and composer. Born on July 14, 1912, in Okemah, Oklahoma, Woodrow Wilson Guthrie was one of five children reared in an atmosphere of guitar playing, ballad singing, prizefighting, Indian square dancing, and the singing of Negro blues. His formal schooling ended in the tenth grade. Subsequently the family suffered a series of tragedies: his father went bankrupt, their house burned down, his sister died, and his mother developed Huntington's chorea, a fatal and hereditary degenerative disease. Thus, at the age of fifteen, Guthrie got the urge to travel. He left for Houston, played the harmonica there in barbershops and poolhalls, then went back to Okemah and learned to play the guitar. The Depression and the devastating dust storms hit the Southwest soon after, and he left for California by freight train, singing in saloons for his dinner, observing people and situations wherever he stopped off. He allied himself firmly with the labor union movement, having witnessed mistreatment of migrant workers throughout the land. He began writing songs, such as "So Long (It's Been Good To Know Yuh)," "Hard Traveling," "Blowing Down This Old Dusty Road," "Union Maid," and "Tom Joad" (from a character in John Steinbeck's *Grapes of Wrath*), expressing both his understanding of and his impatience with social ills. He traveled to New York, sang first in hobo camps, then in waterfront taverns to meetings of workingmen in Madison Square Garden, and, eventually, to concert audiences in Town Hall. He joined folk singers Pete Seeger, Lee Hays, and Millard Lampell in the Almanac Singers, entertaining primarily union groups and audiences of farm and factory workers. He joined the merchant marine in 1943, served through three invasions, and sailed on two ships that were torpedoed. In 1944 he rejoined the Almanac Singers briefly and wrote *American Folksongs*, a collection of 30 songs and sketches. He wrote more than 1000 songs that spoke as fervently of the goodness of the American people and the beauty of the American land as of the imperfections of the American system. One of his last songs, and probably his most famous, "This Land Is Your Land," was taken up as an anthem by many civil-rights and other reform movements of the 1950s and 1960s. Guthrie's final years were spent fighting Huntington's chorea and he died, almost a legend, on October 4, 1967, in New York City.

Gwinnett, Button (1735?–1777), public official. Born in Gloucestershire, England, probably in the early part of 1735, Gwinnett became a merchant and for several years was engaged principally in trade with the American colonies. He emigrated to America before 1765 and settled in Georgia, first in Savannah and later on a large plantation on St. Catherines Island. He became involved in local politics, served a term in 1769 in the assembly, and in 1776 was chosen by the Georgia Council of Safety as a delegate to the Continental Congress. During his brief attendance in Philadelphia he signed the Declaration of Independence. Later in that year he was elected speaker of the Georgia assembly, and he took a leading role in the convention called to draft a state constitution. Early in 1777, upon the death of the governor, he was named president of the state of Georgia, a position that included civil command of the militia. A dispute with the military commander over responsibility for the failure of an expedition against British posts in Florida led to a duel; both were wounded, Gwinnett mortally. He died at his home in Savannah on May 19, 1777. He is remembered chiefly for the extreme rarity of his autographs; sought after because of his having been one of the signers of the Declaration of Independence, they have been forced by collectors to exceedingly high values, one having sold at auction in 1927 for $51,000.

H

Haaglund, Joel Emmanuel, *see* Hill, Joe

Hadley, Arthur Twining (1856–1930), economist and educator. Born in New Haven, Connecticut, on April 23, 1856, Hadley was an exceptional student and graduated first in his Yale class of 1876. He remained at Yale for a year of additional study and then spent two years at the University of Berlin. Upon his return in 1879 he became a tutor at Yale and four years later an instructor in political science. In 1885 he published his first book, *Railroad Transportation, Its History and Its Laws;* in it he demonstrated the fallacy of the Ricardian theory of free competition as applied to industries having relatively large permanent investments, and he pinpointed precisely this high proportion of fixed to variable costs as a source of instability and tendency toward combination. Also in 1885 he was called to testify before a Senate committee then drafting the Interstate Commerce Act and shortly thereafter was appointed commissioner of labor statistics for Connecticut. He continued teaching at Yale while contributing articles on economics and railroads to various publications. From 1886 to 1891 he was professor of political science in the graduate school, during 1890–1891, acting professor of political economy in the Sheffield Scientific School, from 1891 to 1899, professor of political economy in the college, and during 1892–1895, dean of the graduate school. In 1896 he published *Economics: An Account of the Relations Between Private Property and Public Welfare*, his most influential work, in which he argued that to expand governmental powers would not answer the challenge of concentrated private economic power, and that only a morally enlightened public could solve the problem. Three years later Hadley was elected president of Yale. During his long tenure in that position he relinquished his teaching, but traveled and spoke widely while overseeing an unprecedented growth of the university. He retired in 1921 but continued as a director of several railroads. In 1925 he published *The Conflict Between Liberty and Equality*. While on a world tour he died in Kobe, Japan, on March 6, 1930.

Hagen, Walter Charles (1892–1969), golfer. Born in Rochester, New York, on December 21, 1892, Hagen began playing golf at a very early age. He burst onto the national scene in 1914, while still only twenty-one, when he won the U.S. Open championship. Again Open champion in 1919, he embarked on a remarkable series of victories in 1921, when he won the Professional Golfers' Association (PGA) title; he won that

same title each year from 1924 to 1927. He won the British Open for the first time in 1922, first American to win "the second oldest cup in sports," and won it again in 1924, 1928, and 1929. In the same period he took assorted other titles, including the Canadian Open and the French Open. Between 1927 and 1935 he played on each of the first five U.S. teams in the biennial Ryder Cup competition, in 1927 as captain of the team. He was acknowledged as the best golfer of his day—at least until Bobby Jones came along—and was voted one of the three best players (with Jones and Ben Hogan) of the first half of the twentieth century in a sportswriters' poll in 1950. He combined superb golfing skill with a genial flair for playing to the gallery that made him enormously popular and helped to establish the game in the United States; but his real forte was match play, and there was probably no one who could beat him man to man over 18 holes. He retired from professional play in 1929 (except for subsequent Ryder Cup play) with accumulated golf earnings of more than a million dollars. His autobiography, *The Walter Hagen Story*, appeared in 1956. He died in Traverse City, Michigan, on October 5, 1969.

Haggin, James Ben Ali (1827–1914), lawyer and businessman. Born in Harrodsburg, Kentucky, on December 9, 1827, Haggin studied law in his father's office and was admitted to the bar in 1845. After brief periods spent in Missouri, Mississippi, and New Orleans, he journeyed West in 1850 and shortly thereafter opened a law office in Sacramento in partnership with Lloyd Tevis. Their association, which endured and prospered until Tevis's death in 1899 and which was sealed by their marrying sisters, grew gradually in scope from a successful law practice until they were numbered among the major financial powers of the West. Their various enterprises, some separately and some jointly undertaken, were central to much of the mining, transportation, and agricultural development of the region, particularly that of California. Haggin was especially active in mining investments, eventually acquiring major interests in more than a hundred gold, silver, and copper mines from Alaska to South America; with Tevis and George Hearst he invested heavily in Marcus Daly's Anaconda Copper Company in Montana. He bought up land and built huge irrigation systems on vast acreages in the San Joaquin and Sacramento valleys and Kern County in California that, after lengthy litigation of the novel legal issues involved in such extensive diversion of waters, formed the basis of the later intensive agriculture of those areas. He was also interested in horse breeding and the farm he established near Lexington, Kentucky, produced many of the finest racers of the 1880s. Haggin died at his summer home in Newport, Rhode Island, on September 12, 1914, leaving an estate of some $15 million.

Hagglund, Joel Emmanuel, see Hill, Joe

Haionhwat'ha, see Hiawatha

Halas, George Stanley (1895–1983), football player and coach. Born in Chicago on February 2, 1895, Halas graduated from the University of Illinois, where he had been a star end on the football team, in 1918. After a year of World War I service in the navy he played baseball briefly with the New York Yankees and with a club in St. Paul, Minnesota, but football remained his primary interest and in 1920 he joined in founding the American Professional Football Association (APFA), buying one of the original $100 franchises on behalf of the Staley Starch Company of Decatur, Illinois. In 1922 he moved his team to Chicago and renamed it the Bears; in that year, too, the APFA changed its name, becoming the National Football League (NFL). Professional football remained a commercially marginal venture until 1925, when Halas hired Harold "Red" Grange, the spectacular "Galloping Ghost" from the University of Illinois, who drew unprecedented crowds to the Bears' games. Halas relinquished the coaching position in 1929 but resumed it in 1933 and within a few years revolutionized football by introducing—or reviving, for it had been discarded some 30 years earlier—the T-formation, which, as perfected in Chicago, made the game one of speed, deception, and more than ever before, forward passing. In 1942 he entered the naval reserve on active duty, serving until 1946, when he again became coach of the Bears. He stepped down again in 1955, only to return three years later, and continued to coach until his final retirement in 1967. He drove his team to NFL championships in 1933, 1940, 1941, 1946, and 1963, in the last year winning wide acclaim as the coach of the year; his career record was 320 wins, 147 losses, and 31 ties. He remained one of the mainstays of the league, the last of its original franchise holders, and probably its most active team owner. In 1963 he was chosen a charter member of the Football Hall of Fame and the next year he handed on the presidency of the Bears to his son. He died on October 31, 1983, in Chicago.

Haldeman-Julius, Emanuel (1889–1951), author and publisher. Born in Philadelphia on July 30, 1889, Emanuel Julius later, on his marriage in 1916, prefixed the surname of his wife, Marcet Haldeman, to his own. He was active in various political and reform movements and by 1919 was publishing a Socialist newspaper in Girard, Kansas. In that year he experimentally printed two slim pamphlets, one containing Oscar Wilde's *Ballad of Reading Gaol* and the other *The Rubaiyat of Omar Khayym,* and offered them for sale at the nominal price of ten cents. Public response was such that he quickly added dozens, then scores of titles to his Little Blue Books series, scouring the world's literature and philosophical writings for material. At their peak of popularity the Little Blue Books blanketed the country at the rate of half a million annually, and by 1949 total sales had passed three million. The catholicity of his tastes and interests was reflected also in his own writings, among which were *The Color of Life,* 1920; *The Art of Reading,* 1922; *Studies in Rationalism,* 1924; *Iconoclastic Literary Reactions,* 1925; *An Agnostic Looks at Life,* 1926; *Free Speech and Free Thought in America,* 1926; *Myths and Myth-Makers,* 1927; *The First Hundred Million,* 1928; *The Outline of Bunk,* 1929; and *The Big American Parade,* 1929. He published also a number of novels including *Dust,* 1921, and *Violence,* 1929, both written with his wife, and *The Hawk and the Sparrow,* 1950; several volumes of short stories; books devoted to self-education, including the remarkable "How To" series of 1942–1943, to which H. G. Wells and Bertrand Russell also contributed; biographies of notable world leaders; and two volumes of autobiography, *My First Twenty-five Years,* 1949, and *My Second Twenty-five Years,* 1950. Haldeman-Julius also published at various times such periodicals as the *American Freeman,* the *Agnostic,* and the *Critic and Guide.* He died in Girard, Kansas, on July 31, 1951.

Hale, Edward Everett (1822–1909), religious leader and author. Born in Boston on April 3, 1822, Hale was educated at the Boston Latin School and at Harvard, from which he graduated in 1839. For two years he taught school and studied for the ministry; he began to preach in 1842 and four years later was ordained minister of the Church of the Unity in Worcester, Massachusetts. In 1856 he became pastor of the South Congregational (Unitarian) Church in Boston. He was a prolific writer, producing some 150 books and pamphlets during his lifetime; he readily lent his pen to a wide spectrum of popular causes and reforms. In 1863 he published in the *Atlantic Monthly* his most famous tale, "The Man Without a Country," which proved to have a marked effect in arousing patriotic fervor during the Civil War. This and other stories were collected in *If, Yes, and Perhaps* in 1868. There followed a steady stream of collections and novels, including *Four Possibilities and Six Exaggerations, with Some Bits of Fact,* 1868; *The Ingham Papers,* 1869; *Ten Times One Is Ten,* 1871, and *In His Name,* 1873. In his writings as in his preaching he was a powerful advocate of the renovation of society through the influence of a liberal Christianity; he was thus an early apostle of the Social Gospel movement that developed in the last decades of the nineteenth century. From 1870 to 1875 he edited the Unitarian journal *Old and New.* Notable among his later works were *Franklin in France*, two volumes, 1887–1888; *A New England Boyhood*, 1893; *James Russell Lowell and his Friends*, 1899; and *Memories of a Hundred Years*, 1902. In 1903 he was elected chaplain of the United States Senate; he held that position until his death on June 10, 1909, in Roxbury, Massachusetts.

Hale, George Ellery (1868–1938), astronomer. Born in Chicago on June 29, 1868, Hale was interested in the natural sciences, particularly astronomy, from his early youth and while attending the Massachusetts Institute of Technology (MIT) spent his summers carrying out original research in his own "Kenwood Observatory" next to his Chicago home on Kenwood Avenue. There he invented in 1891 the spectroheliograph, a device by which the sun may be photographed in selected monochromatic light, thus revealing the distribution of elemental gases in the outer regions. He graduated from MIT in 1890 and two years later was appointed associate professor of astrophysics at the newly opened University of Chicago, where he remained, from 1897 as full professor, until 1904. In 1895 he founded the *Astrophysical Journal*, which became the leading publication in its field in the world, and in the same year persuaded Charles T. Yerkes to donate funds for the construction of an observatory for the university; Yerkes Observatory, equipped with Alvan G. Clark's great 40-inch lens, opened in 1897 at Williams Bay, Wisconsin, and Hale remained its director until 1904. In the latter year he moved to Pasadena, California, to begin planning and building the Mt. Wilson Observatory on a nearby peak with funds he had secured from the Carnegie Institution of Washington. The observatory was not associated with any university and was devoted purely to research; its 60-inch reflecting telescope went into operation in 1908 and its 100-inch instrument, for more than 30 years the world's largest, was completed in 1917. Hale was director at Mt. Wilson until 1923 and in that period carried on pioneering solar research, numbering among his discoveries the magnetic fields associated with sunspots and, with Walter S. Adams, the 23-year cycle of polarity reversal in those fields. He was active in the work of the National Academy of Sciences and led in organizing both the National Research Council in 1916 and the International Astronomical Union in 1919; the California Institute of Technology (Caltech) and the Henry E. Huntington Library and Art Gallery owed much to his great organizational abilities. Failing health forced him to resign as director of Mt. Wilson in 1923, but five years later he succeeded in securing a grant from the Rockefeller Foundation for the construction of an even greater observatory for Caltech on Mt. Palomar in Southern California, a project that engaged his energies for the rest of his life. Among his nontechnical writings were *Ten Years' Work of a Mountain Observatory*, 1915; *The New Heavens*, 1922; *The Depths of the Universe*, 1924; *Beyond the Milky Way*, 1926; and *Signals from the Stars*, 1931. He received numerous honorary degrees and awards for his invaluable contributions to astronomy and was a member of a great many national and international scientific organizations. Hale died in Pasadena, California, on February 21, 1938; ten years later the huge 200-inch Hale telescope, named for him, was installed at Mt. Palomar.

Hale, John Parker (1806–1873), public official. Born in Rochester, New Hampshire, on March 31, 1806, Hale graduated from Bowdoin College in 1827 and three years later was admitted to the bar, beginning practice in Dover, New Hampshire. He early became active in politics, serving a term in the state legislature in 1832 and as U.S. attorney from 1834 to 1841. In 1842 he was elected as a Democrat to the House of Representatives, but his speeches against the annexation of Texas and the consequent extension of slavery led to his break with the party in 1845 and he was not renominated. He then began organizing a new political coalition of Whigs and independents in New Hampshire around the slavery issue and in 1846 was elected to the Senate, where he was the first of the great antislavery spokesmen of the period before the Civil War. During his term he also wrote and saw passed a bill abolishing flogging in the navy. In 1847 he was nominated for the presidency by the Liberty party, but he withdrew his name the next year in favor of the candidate of the larger Free-Soil party, Martin Van Buren. He was the Free-Soil nominee in 1852. In 1853 he left the Senate, resumed his law practice, and involved himself in organizing the Republican party in his state; he was appointed to an unexpired term in the Senate in 1855, was then elected to a full term, and served until 1865. Hale served during the Civil War as chairman of the Committee on Naval Affairs and in that positon entered into relations with navy contractors that, while legal, were ethically dubious; a controversy with Secretary of the Navy Gideon Welles ensued and Hale failed to be renominated in 1864. On leaving the Senate in 1865 he was appointed U.S. minister to Spain by President Abraham Lincoln; again his actions in certain matters were questionable and he was recalled in 1869. He retired to Dover, New Hampshire, and suffered declining health until his death there on November 19, 1873.

Hale, Lucretia Peabody (1820–1900), author. Born in Boston on September 2, 1820, Miss Hale was a sister of Edward Everett Hale and with him grew up in a cultivated family much involved with literature. She was educated privately and through much of her life was in delicate health. She began publishing stories in the leading periodicals in about 1858; over the next 30 years she produced a large number of books, many of them on religious subjects or on the art of needlework. She collaborated with her brother Edward and others on *Six of One by Half a Dozen of the Other*, 1872, a novel, and in 1888 published a book of games as *Fagots for the Fireside*, but her major reputation was gained by a series of whimsical sketches, many first published in magazines, that filled two books, *The Peterkin Papers*, 1880, and *The Last of the Peterkins*, 1886. The Peterkins, a family of quite Bostonian and quite ingenuous folk devoted to self-improvement and lofty notions, encountered in the sketches a variety of difficulties arising from their naïveté and were rescued from disaster in each case by the commonsensical Lady from Philadelphia. The little tales were engagingly humorous and immensely popular, attaining over the years the status of classics of children's literature. In addition to writing, Miss Hale was interested in education, serving for a time on the Boston School Committee and occasionally teaching students in her home or through a correspondence school. Her last years were marked by failing health and she died in Boston on June 12, 1900.

Hale, Nathan (1755–1776), Revolutionary soldier. Born on June 6, 1755, in Coventry, Connecticut, Hale graduated from Yale in 1773. He taught school from then until July 1775, when, war having broken out, he was commissioned a lieutenant in the Connecticut militia. He soon joined the Continental army, served at the siege of Boston, and on January 1, 1776, was promoted to captain and after March of that year served in the defense of New York City. According to legend, in May 1776 Hale led a small band of men in seizing a provision sloop from under the guns of a British man-of-war. In September he volunteered to undertake a reconnaissance mission on Long Island, behind enemy lines. Disguised as a Dutch schoolmaster, he gathered the required intelligence and was returning to his regiment on Manhattan Island when he was captured by the British on September 21. Brought before Gen. Sir William Howe, he was ordered hanged the next day. On the gallows he made a brief speech, ending, again according to tradition, with the words, "I only regret that I have but one life to lose for my country." Since that time he has been revered as a martyr to American independence and as a model for American youth.

Hale, Sarah Josepha Buell (1788–1879), editor and author. Born on October 24, 1788, in Newport, New Hampshire, Sarah Josepha Buell was educated by her mother and an older brother and, later, by her husband, David Hale, a lawyer, whom she married in 1813. She submitted some articles to newspapers but was basically a housewife, raising five children, until her husband died in 1822. In financial straits, she then embarked on a literary career. Her poems, written over the signature "Cornelia," were printed in local journals and gathered in *The Genius of Oblivion*, 1823. A novel, *Northwood, a Tale of New England*, 1827, brought her an offer to go to Boston as editor of a new publication, the *Ladies' Magazine*, which she accepted in 1828. As editor she wrote most of the material for each issue herself —literary criticsm, sketches of Amercan life, essays, and poetry. She supported patriotic and humanitarian organizations and staunchly advocated education for women and opportunities for women to teach; however, she always remained apart from formal feminist movements. She also published during this period *Poems for Our Children*, 1830, containing "Mary Had a Little Lamb." In 1837 Louis A. Godey purchased the *Ladies' Magazine* and established Mrs. Hale as editor of his *Lady's Book*, soon known as *Godey's Lady's Book*, which he published in Philadelphia; with Godey she made the *Lady's Book* into the most influential and widely circulated women's magazine published in the country up to that time. She continued to call for female education in the liberal arts and in medicine, and for women teachers (her articles aided the founding of Vassar College), and wrote of women as America's cultural and moral cornerstone, always advocating that their influence be wielded in the home and in schools and not through political power. She was also active in promoting child welfare and published a number of books, including cookbooks, poetry, and prose. Her major achievement was the *Woman's Record, or Sketches of Distinguished Women*, 1853, 1869, 1876; in the course of this ambitious project she completed some 36 volumes of profiles of women, tracing their influence through history on social organization and literature. She retired from *Godey's* two years before her death in Philadelphia on April 30, 1879.

Hall, Abraham Oakey (1826–1898), public official. Born on July 26, 1826, in Albany, New York, Hall graduated from the University of the City of New York (now New York University) in 1847 and turned to the study of law, for a year at Harvard Law School and later privately in New York City and in New Orleans. He was admitted to the Louisiana bar in 1849 and in 1851 returned to New York City, where his practice grew into a partnership and ultimately into the firm of Brown, Hall & Vanderpoel. Politically ambitious, he was appointed assistant district attorney in 1851 and served as district attorney in 1855–1858 and again in 1862–1868. During his second term he switched his political affiliation from the Republican party to the powerful Tammany organization of the Democratic party and with the aid of the Tammany machine was elected mayor in 1868. The dapper and jovial Hall, widely known as "Elegant Oakey" or simply "the Elegant One," was perfectly suited to the job at hand: glossing over, diverting attention from, and otherwise covering up for the huge frauds on the city treasury being perpetrated by his friends and associates in the Tweed Ring. When the activities of "Boss" William Marcy Tweed and the Ring were revealed in 1871, Hall disclaimed all knowledge of them and refused to resign, and when he was tried in 1872 for complicity in the looting he successfully defended himself. He devoted himself thereafter to literary and journalistic work, publishing a large number of books and plays, none memorable, and serving as city editor of the *New York World* from 1879 to 1882 and as London correspondent for the *New York Herald* from 1882 to 1887 and for the *New York Journal* in 1890–1891. He also secured admission to the bar while in England and carried on a practice there. Hall died in New York City on October 7, 1898.

Hall, Asaph (1829–1907), astronomer. Born in Goshen, Connecticut, on October 15, 1829, Hall was educated in local schools and read widely on his own, a habit he continued through his apprenticeship to a carpenter and a period of working as a journeyman. By 1854 he had saved enough money to enter college. He remained only briefly, but long enough to learn the rudiments of astronomy and of observational techniques. After a time spent teaching school in Ohio and working again as a carpenter, he took a position in 1858 in the Harvard Observatory and began supplementing his meager income by making astronomical observations for surveyors and almanac compilers. The publication in professional journals of several papers of his on the orbits of comets and asteroids led to his being offered a post in the Naval Observatory in Washington, D.C., in 1862. The following year he became professor of mathematics there. Working with the observatory's 26-inch telescope, Hall carried on systematic and meticulous observations for nearly three decades, concentrating his efforts on the problems of solar parallax, double stars, and in particular planetary motion. It was in the last field that he made his greatest discovery; in August 1877 he sighted the two satellites of Mars, named by him Phobos and Deimos, and carefully determined their orbits. Hall retired from the observatory in 1891 and returned to Goshen, Connecticut. From 1895 to 1901 he lectured on astronomy and mathematics at Harvard and he continued to publish reports on his observations until a short time before his death in Annapolis, Maryland, on November 22, 1907.

Hall, Charles Martin (1863–1914), chemist and manufacturer. Born on December 6, 1863, in Thompson, in Geauga County, Ohio, Hall was educated at Oberlin College and even before his graduation in 1885 had become interested in the problem of producing pure aluminum in sufficient quantities and with sufficient ease to make its commercial use feasible. In the more than 40 years since the isolation of slightly impure aluminum the problem had defied experienced chemists, but after a few months of experimenting Hall succeeded in February 1886 in separating a pure sample from a batch of alumina (aluminum oxide). His process was an electrolytic rather than a thermal one but it required relatively little expenditure of power and no complex apparatus; it was patented in 1889. It took him two years to find financial backing for a commercial aluminum plant, but in 1888 his Pittsburgh Reduction Company, sponsored by Andrew Mellon and others, began production in Kensington, Pennsylvania.

In 1890 Hall became a vice-president of the company, which later became the Aluminum Company of America (Alcoa); with further refinements in the reduction process, aluminum came to be one of the most versatile and widely used of all the metals. The electrolytic process had been developed independently by P. L. T. Héroult in France at almost the same time, but a lengthy litigation over patent priority was resolved in Hall's favor in 1893. Eventually Hall and Héroult became close friends and together developed the Hall-Héroult process now generally used in the industry. A devoted alumnus of Oberlin, Hall left the college more than $3 million. He died in Daytona Beach, Florida, on December 27, 1914.

Hall, Granville Stanley (1844–1924), psychologist and educator. Born on February 1, 1844, in Ashfield, Massachusetts, G. Stanley Hall graduated from Williams College in 1867 and studied for a year at the Union Theological Seminary before going to Germany, where he remained until 1872, to study experimental psychology. Returning to the United States, he was professor of psychology at Antioch College for four years, and in 1876–1877 taught English at Harvard, where he completed his doctoral studies in 1878 under William James. He continued his studies in Germany before becoming a lecturer in the new field of educational psychology at Harvard in 1880–1881. For seven years thereafter he was a lecturer and professor of psychology and pedagogics at The Johns Hopkins University, where he established in 1883 one of the first psychological laboratories in the country. In studies there he applied the ideas of Charles Darwin, Wilhelm Wundt, and Sigmund Freud, among others, to strengthen and enlarge the base of psychology. His many outstanding students and followers included John Dewey. In 1891 his efforts bore fruit in the founding of the American Psychological Association, of which he was first president. At various periods he edited journals that he also established, among them the *American Journal of Psychology*, founded in 1887, the *Pedagogical Seminary*, 1891, the *Journal of Religious Psychology and Education*, 1902, and the *Journal of Applied Psychology*, 1915. He published almost 500 works, which touched on every significant branch of psychology. *The Contents of Children's Minds on Entering School*, 1883, launched the new field of child psychology. Other major works were *Adolescence*, 1904; *Youth*, 1906; *Educational Problems*, 1911; *Founders of Modern Psychology*, 1912; and *Senescence, the Last Half of Life*, 1922. Recognized as the leading authority on educational standards in the country, he was chosen, in 1888, as the first president of Clark University, Worcester, Massachusetts. There he founded the first institute of child psychology in the country and established a curriculum of graduate studies in the fields of education and psychology. He resigned in 1920. In 1923 his autobiography, *Life and Confessions of a Psychologist*, appeared. He died on April 24, 1924, in Worcester, Massachusetts.

Hall, James (1793–1868), lawyer and author. Born in Philadelphia on August 19, 1793, to a family of a literary bent, Hall was educated largely at home. He began to study law but broke off to serve in the War of 1812; he saw considerable action and performed commendably, but in 1817, after some difficulty with his commander, he was court-martialed and dismissed from the service. Although he was restored to rank by presidential order, he resigned from the army the following year, after his admission to the bar. In 1820 he traveled West. Settling in Shawneetown, Illinois, he quickly attained local prominence and was elected circuit prosecuting attorney; four years later he became circuit judge and in 1828 state treasurer. In 1828 he compiled the *Western Souvenir* and published *Letters from the West.* From 1829 to 1832 he edited the *Illinois Intelligencer* and in 1830 began editing the *Illinois Monthly Magazine,* the first literary magazine to originate west of the Ohio country, which became, upon Hall's removal to Cincinnati in 1832, the *Western Monthly Magazine,* published until 1836. In 1832 he published *Legends of the West* and afterward produced valuable factual works about the region, among them *Sketches of History, Life, and Manners in the West,* 1834–1835; *Statistics of the West at the Close of the Year 1836;* and *The Romance of Western History,* 1857. In addition he produced a considerable amount of fiction, including *Harpe's Head,* 1833, and *Tales of the Border,* 1835. In all his writings he drew an accurate and vivid picture of the early Western frontier and much of his work is invaluable in this respect; at the same time he did much, through his editorial activities, to hasten the process of civilizing that same frontier. He died in Cincinnati on July 5, 1868.

Hall, James (1811–1898), geologist. Born in Hingham, Massachusetts, on September 12, 1811, Hall attended the Rennselaer School (later the Rennselaer Polytechnic Institute) in Troy, New York, and in his spare time and summers devoted all his resources to studying the geology and natural history of various regions in New York and Pennsylvania. Soon after graduation in 1832 he became librarian at Rennselaer and later in the year was appointed assistant professor of chemistry, natural science, and geology there; he was later promoted to full professor. Through the patronage of Stephen Van Rennselaer he made a geological expedition to the St. Lawrence Valley and in 1836 was appointed one of four geologists commissioned to make comprehensive geological surveys of New York State. Although the area to which he was assigned was considered the least interesting geologically of the four, his report, *Geology of New York: Part IV,* 1843, vastly outshone the other three to become a classic work in the field. Hall devoted the rest of his life to stratigraphic geology and the study of invertebrate paleontology, largely in New York but also as far west as California and Oregon; he was state geologist of Iowa in 1855–1858 and of Wisconsin in 1857–1860. His work in New York was aided by his appointment as director of the state's Museum of Natural History in Albany in 1866, but even during periods when no state funds were forthcoming he continued his researches at his own expense. His position was finally made official with the creation specifically for him of the office of state geologist in 1893. The many volumes of *The Paleontology of New York,* published between 1847 and 1894, contained the bulk of his work in paleontology, and his other writings ran to more than 30 books and more than 250 papers. Hall was a charter member of the National Academy of Sciences from its founding in 1863 and of many other scientific organizations, was the recipient of numerous honors and awards, and enjoyed a worldwide reputation. At the age of eighty-five he traveled to St. Petersburg, Russia, to attend the International Geological Congress and he also took part in its expedition to the Ural Mountains. Hall died two years later, on August 7, 1898, in Bethlehem, New Hampshire.

Hall, Joyce Clyde (1891–1982), businessman. Born on December 29, 1891, in David City, Nebraska, Hall began selling postcards while still in high school and on graduating in 1910 moved to Kansas City, Missouri, and in partnership with a brother opened a wholesale jobbing business in cards. Within a short time they had begun to deal in greeting cards as well and in 1916 Hall Brothers bought an engraving plant to produce their own Hallmark brand cards. From then on the company grew steadily, taking advantage both of the booming popularity of greeting cards themselves and of Hall's flair for developing attractive marketing devices, such as the independent display rack, and especially the special-occasion card, a notion eventually refined by Hallmark into a system of several thousand potential "sending situations" with an appropriate card—or many—for each situation. By 1968 Hallmark was by far the largest manufacturer of greeting cards in the world, producing annually more than a billion Christmas cards alone. Hallmark was the first line of greeting cards to use the works of well-known artists, ranging from Norman Rockwell and Walt Disney to Grandma Moses and, in a most surprising innovation in 1950, including Sir Winston Churchill; popular authors, notably Edgar A. Guest, were commissioned from time to time to supply verses. The company sponsored a number of international competitions for artists, both as a means of discovering usable art and artists and as an effective public-relations device, and it advertised on radio and television; the "Hallmark Hall of Fame" dramatic series was long one of the most admired programs on television. Hall, who was throughout his career active in civic affairs in Kansas City, retired from the presidency of Hallmark in 1966, retaining thereafter his position as chairman of the board. He died in Leaward, Kentucky, on October 29, 1982.

Hallam, Lewis (1740–1808), actor and theatrical manager. Born in England in 1740, Hallam was the son of theatrical parents whom he accompanied when they were sent to America in 1752 as part of a troupe dispatched by his uncle, a theater manager in London. In Williamsburg, Virginia, they presented on September 15, 1752, *The Merchant of Venice*, the first professional theatrical production in the colonies and the true beginning of regular theater in America. The company subsequently appeared in Philadelphia, in New York, where in 1753 they built the first theater in the city, and elsewhere; except for a period, 1754–1758, in Jamaica, in the West Indies, during which Hallam's father, manager of the troupe, died and the company came under control of his stepfather, they continued to tour the colonies as the American Company until 1775, when they again removed to Jamaica for the duration of the Revolution. By the time the company returned to the new United States in 1784 Hallam had succeeded to the management, a position he held with various partners, including William Dunlap, until 1797; he remained the company's leading man for nine years thereafter before being forced out by younger actors. Although he was in no sense a great actor, Hallam was versatile and in his way competent on the stage, and while in his role as manager he was often quarrelsome and inept, his dedication to the company kept it alive through a variety of hazards and contributed immensely to the firm establishment of the American theater, particularly in New York City. He died in Philadelphia on November 1, 1808.

Halleck, Henry Wager (1815–1872), soldier. Born in Westernville, in Oneida County, New York, on January 16, 1815, Halleck graduated from West Point in 1839 and was commissioned a second lieutenant of engineers. After a period of work on the fortification of New York Harbor he made an inspection tour of European fortifications in 1844 and a short time later delivered a course of lectures at the Lowell Institute of Boston that was published in 1846 as *Elements of Military Art and Science*, long a popular text and reference work, particularly among volunteer officers in the Civil War. On the outbreak of the Mexican War in 1846 he sailed to California and over the next eight years served in various capacities, including that of secretary of state in the military government, and in 1849 helped draft the state constitution. He was promoted to captain in 1853. During the latter part of his service in California he studied law and soon after his resignation from the army in 1854 he began practice in San Francisco, forming the firm of Halleck, Peachy & Billings, which became one of the most prominent in the state. Halleck acquired extensive and diverse business interests, was president of the Pacific & Atlantic Railroad, and served as a major general of the California militia. His *International Law*, 1861, was widely admired and in a condensed version was used in many schools,

and he published several studies and translations in the field of mining law. In August 1861, on the recommendation of Gen. Winfield Scott, President Abraham Lincoln commissioned Halleck a major general in the regular army and in November appointed him to command the Department of Missouri (after 1862, and the inclusion of Kansas and Ohio, the Department of the Mississippi). From his headquarters in St. Louis he quickly instilled stern discipline and established efficiency throughout the previously lax command and during 1862 enjoyed the reflected glory of the successes of his subordinate commanders, Ulysses S. Grant, D. C. Buell, and John Pope. In his one excursion into the field, at Corinth, Mississippi, in May 1862, he showed himself, however, to be an overly cautious and ineffective warrior. In July 1862 he was called to Washington D.C., as general in chief of the armies and principal military adviser to the President. Again he demonstrated great administrative abilities in recruiting, training, and organizing vast numbers of troops—services direly needed at the time—but his grasp of military affairs in the field was poor and his advice to his generals was often useless or worse. In March 1864 Grant was placed in supreme command and Halleck was moved to the new office of chief of staff, an administrative post more suited to his talents and one that, although representing a technical demotion, he accepted with grace. During the last weeks of the war he commanded the Military District of the James; from 1865 to 1869 he commanded the Division of the Pacific and in the later years was transferred to the Division of the South. He died in Louisville, Kentucky, on January 9, 1872.

Halsey, William Frederick (1882–1959), naval officer. Born on October 30, 1882, in Elizabeth, New Jersey, Halsey was the son of a navy captain. He graduated from the Naval Academy in 1904 and after service on the *Missouri* and the *Don Juan de Austria* was commissioned ensign in 1906. After various assignments he was placed in command of the First Group, Torpedo Flotilla, in the Atlantic in 1913. From 1915 to 1917 he was an executive officer on the staff of the Naval Academy, and during World War I he commanded a number of destroyers assigned to patrol and escort duty, for which he won the Navy Cross. From 1918 to 1921 he held several Destroyer Division commands and then spent a year with the Office of Naval Intelligence. After nearly two years duty as a naval attaché in Germany, Denmark, Norway, and Sweden, he returned to the line and held a succession of commands. From 1932 to 1934 he studied at the Naval and Army War colleges and then took naval flight training at Pensacola, Florida, qualifying as an aviator in 1935 at the age of fifty-two. The next five years were spent with the carriers *Yorktown* and *Saratoga* and for a time as commander of the Pensacola air station. In 1938 Halsey was promoted to rear admiral and in 1940 to vice-admiral. When the Japanese attacked Pearl Harbor with devastating effect on December 7, 1941, he was commanding a force of ships returning from Wake Island, and his was virtually the only operational U.S. battle force left in the Pacific. In February 1942 he led the first U.S. offensive in the Pacific, a strike of carrier-based aircraft at the Gilbert and Marshall islands. He was placed in command of the South Pacific fleet and the South Pacific area in October; by then an admiral, in that month he defeated the Japanese in the battle of Santa Cruz and in November beat them again at Guadalcanal in a battle crucial to the entire campaign to capture the Solomon archipelago. In June 1944 he became commander of the Third Fleet and engaged in operations throughout the western Pacific. Living up to his motto "Hit hard, hit fast, hit often," he was noted for his daring and imaginative tactics and made brilliant use of air power in delivering crushing blows to Japanese forces. "Bull" Halsey, as he was known, helped turn the battle of Leyte Gulf into the most overwhelming victory in naval history and then, during 1945, carried the war to the Japanese homeland with naval and air strikes at Tokyo and other cities. On September 2 the surrender terms were signed aboard his flagship, the *Missouri*. In December 1945 he was promoted to the five-star rank of fleet admiral. After his retirement in 1947 he served on the boards of several major corporations. He died on August 16, 1959, on Fishers Island, New York.

Halsted, William Stewart (1852–1922), surgeon. Born in New York City on September 23, 1852, Halsted was educated at Andover and at Yale, from which he graduated in 1874. He then entered the College of Physicians and Surgeons in New York City and received his medical degree in 1877. After interning at Bellevue Hospital and aiding in the organization of New York Hospital he traveled to Europe to pursue further studies, chiefly in Vienna under A. C. T. Billroth and in Würzburg under Ernst von Bergmann. On his return to New York City in 1880 he quickly became one of the outstanding surgeons in the city, serving Bellevue, New York, Presbyterian, and Roosevelt hospitals. During the next year, 1881, he achieved probably the first successful blood transfusion in the United States, giving his own blood to his sister, who was hemorrhaging after childbirth. During his almost ceaseless practice he began evolving a philosophy of surgery that proved to be of wide and permanent influence; emphasizing the body's natural powers of resistance and recuperation, he employed (and trained his many students in) asepsis, complete hemostasis, and great care in the handling of tissues. In 1884 he discovered the anesthetic properties of cocaine when injected into a nerve, although his experiments in making the discovery resulted in his becoming addicted to the drug; two years were required for his recovery. In 1886 he moved to Baltimore and carried on research in the laboratory of William H. Welch until the opening of the Johns Hopkins Hospital three

years later; appointed acting surgeon and head of the outpatient department in the hospital, he became professor of surgery in 1890 and established a residency program and the first school of surgery in the country. While training a great number of young surgeons in his operative techniques, which included from 1890 the wearing of rubber gloves by all operating-room personnel, he made major contributions to many types of surgery, particularly those dealing with hernia, breast cancer, the gall bladder and duct, arteries and aneurysms, and the thyroid gland. Halsted remained active in teaching, research, and surgical practice at Johns Hopkins until his death in Baltimore on September 7, 1922. His collected papers, edited by W. C. Burket, were published two years later.

Hamilton, Alexander (1755–1804), political leader and public official. Born on Nevis in the Leeward Islands on January 11, 1755 (probably; he himself claimed 1757), Hamilton experienced much irregularity in his home life and education. Deserted by his father, his mother died when he was thirteen and he spent the next four years working in a general store. His obviously remarkable abilities induced his relatives and friends to further his education; in 1772 he was sent to school in New Jersey and the following year he entered King's College (now Columbia) in New York City. He interrupted his studies to join in the public debate on revolution. Three pamphlets written by him in 1774–1775 in defense of the patriot cause were highly effective; at least one, written before he was twenty, was widely assumed to be the work of John Jay and John Adams. When the Revolution began he organized a company and served with distinction in New York and New Jersey. In 1777 Gen. George Washington made him his aide-de-camp and personal secretary; four years later, hopeful of military glory, Hamilton impetuously resigned from Washington's personal staff and performed creditably in command of a battalion at Yorktown. In 1781 he moved to Albany, New York, to study law, and the next year he was admitted to the bar. He had published a number of newspaper essays advocating the formation of a strong federal government and as a member of Congress in 1782–1783 he worked for this same cause. In 1783 he moved to New York City, where in the courts as well as in the press he effectively defended Loyalists against discrimination. In 1786 he was a delegate to the Annapolis Convention and introduced there a resolution to hold what came to be the Constitutional Convention in the following year. He was also a delegate to that convention, although he contributed little to the final document. On his return to New York he began a campaign to secure New York's ratification of the Constitution; after publishing a series of ineffectual letters to that end, he joined with James Madison and John Jay in writing the 85 essays and newspaper articles that were collected in two volumes as *The Federalist* in 1788;

the papers succeeded in winning over a majority in New York. Hamilton was author of at least two-thirds of the *Federalist* papers, and at the New York ratifying convention in 1788 he led and won the fight for approval of the Constitution. In 1789, as the new government was organized, President Washington appointed him secretary of the treasury. He immediately set about stabilizing the nation's finances; by insisting upon full payment of the national debt, the assumption by the federal government of state war debts, and a system of taxation to pay for it all, he intended firmly to establish the nation's credit while increasing the power of the central government over that of the states. In his reports to Congress he also proposed the creation of the Bank of the United States and suggested a system of protective tariffs to encourage the growth of domesic industry. The Whisky Rebellion of 1794 in western Pennsylvania, brought on by his excise tax on distilled liquor, provided him with an opportunity to strengthen further the supremacy of the federal government and to satisfy his taste for military action, and he accompanied the militia force sent by Washington to suppress the outburst. As factionalism developed within the government, giving rise to the Federalist and Republican parties, Hamilton emerged as the leader of the Federalists; his main opponent was Secretary of State Thomas Jefferson, and friction between the two men increased to feud proportions. A strong nationalist, staunch defender of the rights of property, and fearful of democracy ("Your people, Sir, is a great beast"), Hamilton was, in his grasp of political reality, a worthy adversary to Jefferson and a voice for conservatism in the government. He thought of himself more or less as Washington's prime minister and constantly interfered in the affairs of other departments, particularly Jefferson's. The discord between them reached its highest pitch during the war between England and France that began in 1793. Jefferson had long advocated close ties with France, Hamilton with England; Hamilton persuaded Washington to issue a proclamation of neutrality that was generally interpreted as pro-British and he usurped Jefferson's functions by arranging for John Jay to be sent to England to negotiate a treaty. Jay's Treaty of 1794 was unpopular, but Hamilton managed to secure its ratification. In 1795 he left the cabinet but retained considerable influence in the government while gaining a reputation as the leading member of the New York bar. He wrote most of Washington's Farewell Address of the next year and in 1798 he secured, through Washington's influence, an appointment as inspector general of the army. With the rank of major general, he organized the army to resist a threatened French invasion. Nothing came of the situation; war was averted by diplomacy and in 1800 he resigned his commission. In that year, in an attempt to prevent the reelection of President John Adams, his rival for leadership of the Federalists, he wrote an intemperate attack on Adams; a copy of the privately circulated letter was obtained by Aaron Burr and published. Adams was defeated, but following the tie vote in the Electoral College that resulted, Hamilton broke with most Federalists by supporting Jefferson against Burr, who became vice-president as a result of the tie-breaking vote in the House. In 1804, when Burr was a candidate for governor of New York, Hamilton again opposed him; after his defeat Burr demanded a duel of honor because of some derogatory remarks attributed to his enemy. Hamilton reluctantly agreed and was mortally wounded at their meeting in Weehauken, New Jersey; he died the next day, July 12, 1804. He was elected to the Hall of Fame in 1915.

Hamilton, Edith (1867–1963), educator and author. Born on August 12, 1867, in Dresden, Germany, of American parents, Miss Hamilton grew up in Fort Wayne, Indiana. From a very early age she was an eager student of Greek and Roman literature and following her graduation from Bryn Mawr College with an M.A. degree in 1894 she spent a year in 1895–1896 in Europe at the universities of Leipzig and Munich, becoming the first woman to attend classes at Munich. In 1896 she returned to the United States and helped organize and was appointed headmistress of the Bryn Mawr School in Baltimore, a preparatory institution. She remained headmistress for 26 years, retiring in 1922 to devote herself to her classical studies and writing. She published a number of articles on aspects of Greek life and art, and in 1930 her first book, *The Greek Way*, appeared. Vivid and engaging as well as thoroughly scholarly, the book was a critical and popular success; it was followed by *The Roman Way*, 1932, which was equally well received. Miss Hamilton turned to other sources of tradition in *The Prophets of Israel*, 1936, and later in *Witness to the Truth: Christ and His Interpreters*, 1949. Others of her books included *Three Greek Plays*, 1937, translations; *Mythology*, 1942; *The Great Age of Greek Literature*, 1943, an expansion of *The Greek Way*; *Spokesmen for God*, 1949, an expansion of *The Prophets of Israel*; and *The Echo of Greece*, 1957. While visiting Greece in 1957 at the age of ninety she was made an honorary citizen of Athens in recognition of her devotion to the ancient ideals of that city. Miss Hamilton died in Washington, D.C., on May 31, 1963.

Hamlin, Hannibal (1809–1891), vice-president of the United States. Born in Paris Hill, Maine, on August 27, 1809, Hamlin was educated in a local school and a nearby academy and after brief periods as a surveyor, newspaper printer, and schoolteacher, took up the study of law in a Portland office. On winning admission to the bar in 1833 he began practice in Hampden, Maine, and soon became active in politics, serving in the legislature from 1836 to 1841. In 1842 he was elected as a Democrat to the House of Representatives, where he remained until 1847; after another term in the legislature in that year he was elected to complete an unexpired term in the Senate in 1848, returning to the seat for a full term in 1851. He became gradually more and more outspoken in his dislike of slavery and he opposed in particular the Kansas-Nebraska Bill of 1854; finally, two years later, he broke with the Democrats and joined the Republican party. In that year he was elected governor of Maine, the first Republican to hold the office; early in 1857 he left the Senate to assume the governorship, but a few weeks later he resigned to return to the Senate. His position as an Easterner and a former Democrat made Hamlin a strategic choice for the Republican vice-presidential nomination in 1860 on the ticket headed by Abraham Lincoln. Although he sided more often than not with the Radical wing of the party, he remained throughout his term in office on close terms with President Lincoln. Failing of renomination in 1864, in 1865 he was appointed collector of the port of Boston, but he gave up the post a year later in protest against President Andrew Johnson's Reconstruction policies. After two years as president of a small Maine railroad he ran successfully for the Senate in 1868 and remained there for two terms, supporting Radical Reconstruction and serving for a time as chairman of the Committee on Foreign Relations. On leaving the Senate he was for a year, 1881–1882, U.S. minister to Spain. Hamlin then retired to Bangor, Maine, where he lived, still an influential figure in state Republican affairs, until his death on July 4, 1891.

Hammerstein, Oscar, II (1895–1960), lyricist. Born on July 12, 1895, in New York City, Hammerstein was the grandson and namesake of a noted composer and operatic impresario. He graduated from Columbia in 1916 and studied law for a time before turning to a career in the musical theater. Among his earliest major efforts was the Vincent Youmans musical *The Wildflower*, 1923, for which, with Otto Harbach, he wrote the lyrics. Subsequently he wrote lyrics for Rudolf Friml's *Rose Marie*, 1924; Jerome Kern's *Sunny*, 1925 ("Sunny," "Who?"); Sigmund Romberg's *Desert Song*, 1926 ("Blue Heaven," with Harbach); Kern's *Show Boat*, 1927, from Edna Ferber's novel ("Bill," "Can't Help Lovin' That Man," "Why Do I Love You?," "Only Make Believe," "You Are Love," "Ol' Man River"); Romberg's *New Moon*, 1928 ("Lover Come Back to Me," "Stout-Hearted Men," "One Kiss," "Wanting You"); Kern's *Sweet Adeline*, 1929 ("Don't Ever Leave Me"); Kern's *Music In the Air*, 1932 ("The Song Is You," "I've Told Ev'ry Little Star"); Romberg's *May Wine*, 1936; and Kern's *Very Warm for May*, 1939 ("All the Things You Are"). He also wrote lyrics for a number of other songs during this period, including "I Won't Dance," 1935, with Harbach and Kern; "When I Grow Too Old to Dream," 1935, with Romberg; and "The Last Time I Saw Paris," 1940, with Kern; the last song, when interpolated in the 1941 film

Lady, Be Good!, won an Academy Award. In 1943 he formed a highly successful partnership with composer Richard Rodgers and for more than 15 years they created some of the finest and most influential musicals ever to appear on the American stage. They set sophisticated and often strikingly realistic stories to bright and eminently memorable music in a remarkable series of productions: *Oklahoma!*, 1943, which featured also the innovative choreography of Agnes de Mille and which ran for more than 2200 performances on Broadway and was awarded a special Pulitzer Prize ("The Surrey with the Fringe on Top," "People Will Say We're in Love," "Oklahoma," "Oh, What a Beautiful Mornin'"); *Carousel*, 1945 ("June Is Bustin' Out All Over," "You'll Never Walk Alone," "If I Loved You"); *South Pacific*, 1949, which ran for nearly 1700 performances and won a Pulitzer Prize for drama ("Younger Than Springtime," "There Is Nothin' Like a Dame," "Bali Ha'i," "Happy Talk," "Some Enchanted Evening"); *The King and I*, 1951 ("I Whistle a Happy Tune," "Shall We Dance?," "Getting to Know You," "Hello, Young Lovers"); *Me and Juliet*, 1953 ("No Other Love"); *Flower Drum Song*, 1958 ("I Enjoy Being a Girl"); and *The Sound of Music*, 1959 ("My Favorite Things," "The Sound of Music," "Climb Every Mountain"). After 1949 Rodgers and Hammerstein served as their own producers. They also wrote for motion pictures, notably *State Fair*, 1945 ("It Might As Well Be Spring," winner of that year's Academy Award, "It's a Grand Night for Singing"), and for television. Hammerstein died in Doylestown, Pennsylvania, on August 23, 1960.

Hammett, Dashiell (1894–1961), author. Born on May 27, 1894, in St. Marys County, Maryland, Samuel Dashiell Hammett left school at thirteen and for years worked at a succession of jobs, including newsboy, freight clerk, and railroad laborer. For eight years he was a detective for the Pinkerton agency. During World War I he served overseas in the Motor Ambulance Corps and soon after his discharge began writing detective stories, a great number of which were published in *Black Mask* magazine. In 1929 appeared his first two novels, *Red Harvest* and *The Dain Curse*, both drawing on his Pinkerton experiences. The next year he published *The Maltese Falcon*, probably his finest work, in which, through his protagonist, Sam Spade, he brought a new style of hard-bitten realism to the genre of detective fiction. His characterization and dialogue were esteemed highly by many critics and compared to those of Ernest Hemingway by some. After *The Glass Key*, 1931, and *The Thin Man*, 1934, he wrote no more novels. *The Thin Man* introduced a new hero, Nick Charles, who combined the toughness of Sam Spade with wit and urbanity and who became the subject of a number of movies and of a radio series written by Hammett. In 1942 *The Maltese Falcon* was made into a perennially popular movie starring Humphrey Bogart. During World War II Hammett, then forty-eight, enlisted in the army and served for two years in the Aleutian Islands. Long a supporter of left-wing political causes, he encountered considerable harassment in the early 1950s because of his associations; his refusal in 1951 to divulge the names of members of an allegedly subversive organization brought him a contempt citation by Congress and six months in prison, and in 1953 his books were for a time removed from U.S. Information Service libraries overseas. He died in New York City on January 10, 1961.

Hampden, Walter (1879–1955), actor. Born in Brooklyn, New York, on June 30, 1879, Walter Hampden Dougherty spent a year at Harvard and then attended the Brooklyn Polytechnic Institute, from which he graduated in 1900. He went abroad immediately thereafter and in 1901, in England, joined a touring repertory troupe with which he remained for three years, gaining much valuable experience in stage techniques and in the production of Shakespearian plays. He graduated to the London stage and won a considerable following with his forceful characterizations, attracting particular attention in replacing the younger Henry Irving in a production of *Hamlet* in 1905. In 1907, by which time he had dropped his last name, he returned to the United States. He was soon engaged to star opposite the great Russian actress Alla Nazimova in several Broadway productions and for many years he continued to appear in various new plays and revivals while taking every opportunity to encourage Shakespearian productions on Broadway. In 1918 he organized and starred in a regular series of Shakespearian matinees and the following year he formed his own touring company, with *Hamlet* as the mainstay of its repertory. For the 1923–1924 Broadway season he leased the National Theatre and produced a revival of Edmond Rostand's *Cyrano de Bergerac* that proved immensely popular; the title role remained thereafter identified with Hampden and he performed it more than a thousand times during his career. In 1925 he leased the Colonial Theatre in New York City, renamed it Hampden's Theatre, and produced and starred in a highly successful series of Shakespearian plays and other dramas with Ethel Barrymore as his leading lady. That venture lasted for five years and in 1931, at the Amsterdam Theatre, he first appeared in yet another role that became a favorite, *The Admirable Crichton.* For another 22 years he continued to reign as one of the most popular figures of the U.S. stage and as perhaps its outstanding exponent of the grand romantic style of acting. He toured frequently, often in *Cyrano,* appeared on radio and, from his 1939 role in *The Hunchback of Notre Dame,* in movies, and in 1949 he starred in a highly acclaimed television production of *Macbeth.* His last Broadway appearance was in Arthur Miller's *The Crucible* in 1953. Hampden's eminence in the American theater was signalized in 1927 by his election as president of the Players'

Club, the fourth man, after Edwin Booth, Joseph Jefferson, and John Drew, to receive the honor; he retired from the position in 1954. Hampden died in Los Angeles on June 11, 1955.

Hampton, Wade (1818–1902), public official and soldier. Born in Charleston, South Carolina, on March 28, 1818, Hampton came of a wealthy planting family with traditions of public and military service. He graduated from South Carolina College (now the University of South Carolina) in 1836 and began assuming duties in connection with the family's vast plantation holdings, which he inherited on the death of his father in 1858. From 1852 to 1861 he served in the state legislature. When the question of secession arose he was opposed as he considered the time inopportune; but when the Civil War began he raised "Hampton's Legion" and as its colonel saw action as early as the first battle of Bull Run (Manassas), receiving there the first of many wounds. Promoted to brigadier general in 1862, he was wounded at Fair Oaks (Seven Pines) and in July was assigned to the cavalry of the Army of Northern Virginia, becoming in September Gen. J. E. B. Stuart's second in command. Hampton fought at Antietam, Gettysburg, in the Wilderness, and in the Shenandoah Valley; he was promoted to major general in 1863 and in May 1864, on the death of Stuart, became commander of the cavalry corps. By that time he was reduced to largely defensive activities, which he nonetheless carried out with remarkable success in light of the shortages of mounts and supplies. He aided Gen. Robert E. Lee in the defense of Petersburg and early in 1865 joined Gen. Joseph E. Johnston in harrying the Union troops advancing through the Carolinas under Gen. William T. Sherman. He became a lieutenant general in February. After an abortive attempt to aid Jefferson Davis in escaping to Texas at the war's end he returned to South Carolina and set about supporting the moderate Reconstruction policies of President Andrew Johnson. While working for reconciliation he opposed Radical rule, and in 1876 led the Democratic party back to power in South Carolina as its successful candidate for governor. Reelected in 1878, he resigned in 1879 to enter the Senate, where he remained until 1891. From 1893 to 1897 he served as U.S. commissioner of Pacific railways. Hampton died in Columbia, South Carolina, on April 11, 1902.

Hancock, John (1737–1793), merchant and public official. Born in Braintree, Massachusetts, on January 12, 1737, Hancock was raised by a wealthy uncle in Boston. He graduated from Harvard in 1754, entered his uncle's mercantile business, and ten years later inherited it along with a large estate. His identification with the patriot cause dated from the Stamp Act of 1765, which, as a leading merchant, he both protested and evaded by smuggling. In 1769, soon after the British seized one of his ships, he was elected to the Massachusetts General Court, remaining a member until 1774. In 1770 he was made chairman of the Boston town committee formed as a result of the Boston Massacre. He was elected president of the first and second provincial congresses in 1774–1775 and in 1775 was forced to flee to Lexington and then to Philadelphia as one (with Samuel Adams) of the rebels specifically excepted from the pardon offered by Gen. Thomas Gage. From 1775 to 1780 Hancock was a delegate to the Continental Congress, serving as president for his first two years, and on July 4, 1776, he was the first to sign the Declaration of Independence. (His comment on the bold flourish with which he signed his name in large letters was "There, I guess King George will be able to read that.") Although wealthy and popular, he was a man of limited ability and was sorely disappointed when denied command of the Continental army, a position he had eagerly sought. In 1780 he served in the convention to frame the Massachusetts constitution and under it was elected the state's first governor; he served until 1785 and was then elected to Congress. In 1787 he returned to the governorship and the next year presided over the Massachusetts convention for the ratification of the Constitution. Regularly reelected as governor, Hancock was in his ninth term when he died in Quincy, Massachusetts, on October 8, 1793.

Hancock, Winfield Scott (1824–1886), soldier. Born on February 14, 1824, in Montgomery County, Pennsylvania, Hancock graduated from West Point in 1844 and was ordered to duty in Texas. During the Mexican War he served under Gen. Winfield Scott, for whom he had been named, and saw considerable action, rendering distinguished service at Contreras and Churubusco. From 1848 to 1861 he served in the Seminole War, in Kansas, and in the West, demonstrating in every assignment a gift for organization and command. In September 1861 he was appointed a brigadier general of volunteers; he earned high praise for his part in the Peninsular Campaign, led a division at Antietam, and in November 1862 was promoted to major general of volunteers. In July 1863, by then commander (by virtue of his performance at Chancellorsville) of the 2nd Corps of the Army of the Potomac, he was conspicuous in the battle of Gettysburg; he established defenses on Cemetery Ridge and absorbed Gen. Robert E. Lee's unsuccessful flanking attempt and Pickett's Charge, in which he sustained a serious wound. In 1864 he led his corps through the fighting in the Wilderness, but he was often in Washington during the last months of the war. Rated as the most capable of the Union generals not exercising an independent command, Hancock had been promoted to the regular rank of brigadier general in 1864 and in 1866 became a major general. During 1866–1867 he was engaged in operations against the Indians, principally the Cheyenne, in Kansas, and was then transferred to command of the Department of Louisiana and Texas, where his refusal to usurp

totally the functions of civil government roused the ire of Radical Republicans. He commanded the Department of Dakota from 1870 to 1872 and the Division of the Atlantic and the Department of the East from 1872 to 1886. His anti-Radical stand had led to interest in him on the part of the Democratic party as early as 1868, and in 1880 he was nominated for the presidency; politically naïve, he lost the election by a narrow margin to James A. Garfield and then returned to his military duties. Hancock died at his headquarters on Governor's Island, New York, on February 9, 1886.

Hand, Learned (1872–1961), jurist. Born on January 27, 1872, in Albany, New York, Billings Learned Hand was the son and grandson of noted New York judges. He graduated from Harvard in 1893 and received his law degree there three years later. He practiced law in Albany and New York City until his appointment as U.S. judge for the Southern District of New York in 1909. He held the post until 1924, when he was appointed to the Federal Court of Appeals for the Second Circuit, of which in 1939 he became chief judge. He retired from that bench in 1951, but continued to sit on special cases. During his long service in the federal judiciary he rendered verdicts in nearly every field of law; most notable were those in an antitrust suit against the Aluminum Company of America in 1945, later upheld by the Supreme Court, and in the prosecution of 11 Communist party members under the Smith Act in 1950, upheld by the Supreme Court in *Dennis v. U.S.,* 1951, but later reversed. Although he never served on the U.S. Supreme Court, he was sometimes referred to, because of the respect in which his opinions were held, as the "tenth man" on that court. In 1958 Hand delivered the Holmes addresses at Harvard; in those lectures he cautioned judges against the temptation to go beyond their constitutionally limited function and legislate from the bench. He did not support, however, a congressional attempt to place severe limits on judicial discretion. The lectures were published as *The Bill of Rights* in 1958. He also published *The Spirit of Liberty,* 1952 (revised edition, 1960). On April 10, 1959, he was honored by the national bench and bar for his 50 years of service. Considered one of the greatest jurists of his day, Hand died on August 18, 1961, in New York City.

Handlin, Oscar (1915–   ), historian. Born on September 29, 1915, in Brooklyn, New York, Handlin graduated from Brooklyn College in 1934 and pursued further studies in history at Harvard and in Europe. He taught at Brooklyn College during 1937–1939 and in 1939 returned to Harvard as an instructor in history, receiving his Ph.D. there the following year. *Boston's Immigrants, 1790–1865,* developed from his doctoral dissertation, was published in 1941 and won wide acclaim from critics and scholars. Promoted to assistant professor of history in 1944 and, after a year in the social-science department, to associate professor in 1948, Handlin soon gained a reputation as an imaginative and original historian and one with a flair for attracting a popular as well as a professional audience. *Commonweatlh*, 1947, written with his wife, Mary F. Handlin, was well received and was followed by, among others, *This Was America* 1949, a widely read anthology of the writings of foreign visitors to America; *The Uprooted*, 1951, a study of the personal aspects of nineteenth-century immigration that won a Pulitzer Prize; *The American People in the Twentieth Century*, 1954; *Chance or Destiny*, 1955; *Race and Nationality in American Life*, 1957; *Al Smith and His America*, 1958; *The Newcomers*, 1959; *The Americans*, 1963; *Fire-Bell in the Night*, 1964; and *History of the United States*, two volumes, 1967–1968. Books edited by Handlin included *Immigration as a Factor in American History*, 1959, with J. Burchard; *The Historian and the City*, 1963; *The Children of the Uprooted*, 1966; and, with Arthur M. Schlesinger, Arthur M. Schlesinger, Jr., Samuel Eliot Morison, and others, the distinguished *Harvard Guide to American History*, 1954. Handlin became a full professor of history in 1954 and held the Winthrop chair from 1962 to 1965, when he was named to the Charles Warren professorship. From 1958 to 1966 he was director of the Center for the Study of the History of Liberty in America and in 1966 became director of the Charles Warren Center for Studies in American History. One of the leading historians of U.S. society, he exerted a marked influence not only on the process but also on the style of historical scholarship.

Handy, William Christopher (1873–1958), musician and composer. Born in Florence, Alabama, on November 16, 1873, W. C. Handy was the son of former slaves. His deeply religious family intended him for the ministry and strongly disapproved of his interest in secular music; after finishing his schooling he left home to continue the study of music and of his chosen instrument, the cornet. He walked to Birmingham, taught school for a time, and worked in a steel mill. In 1893, in the midst of that year's business depression, he organized a quartet to perform at the World's Columbian Exposition in Chicago; for several years thereafter he drifted and worked at numerous jobs, only some of them connected with music. Finally he settled in Memphis, Tennessee, and began to work seriously on developing the musical form that came to be called "blues." He had assimilated the music he had grown up with —spirituals, work songs, rambling folk ballads, and particularly the little-known music then called "jass"—and he produced, in written form, a type of song that combined elements of all—basically ragtime, with melody lines modified by a strongly nostalgic or melancholy feeling achieved principally by the use of "blue notes"—largely flatted thirds and sevenths. For a candidate in the Memphis mayoralty election of 1909 he wrote a campaign song, "Mr. Crump"; in 1911, somewhat

altered, it was published as "Memphis Blues." There followed in the next few years a flood of songs in the new mode: the immortal "St. Louis Blues" in 1914, "Beale Street Blues," "Yellow Dog Blues," and some 60 others, which he published in his several anthologies of Negro music. In 1941 his autobiography appeared under the title that had long been acknowledged to be his, *Father of the Blues*. Although blind and in poor health in his later years, he continued to direct his own music-publishing company in New York City until his death there on March 28, 1958.

Hanna, Mark (1837–1904), businessman, public official, and political leader. Born in New Lisbon (now Lisbon), Ohio, on September 24, 1837, Marcus Alonzo Hanna moved with his family to Cleveland in 1852 and attended Western Reserve College for only a few months before joining his father's wholesale grocery business. In 1864 he served briefly in the Union army and three years later became a partner in his father-in-law's coal and iron business. During the next several years he devoted himself to business, with great success; he helped organize the Union National Bank and bought the *Cleveland Herald*, the city's opera house, and a good deal of the street-railway system. In 1885 the coal and iron company was reorganized as M. A. Hanna & Company. As his business connections widened and his fortune increased, Hanna became interested in politics; he saw that the continued growth of industry necessitated an acknowledged interdependence between business and government, and he became convinced that government could safely be entrusted only to the Republican party. Accordingly in 1880 he contributed heavily to James A. Garfield's presidential campaign and actively organized the businessmen of Cleveland in his support; in 1888 he promoted, though unsuccessfully, Ohio Senator John Sherman for the nomination. He then took another Ohio politician, Congressman William McKinley, under his wing. McKinley was defeated for reelection to the House in 1890, largely because of his sponsorship of the tariff bill of that year, but in 1891 won the governorship of Ohio; two years later Hanna managed his reelection to that office and, retiring from business, began planning for the presidential election of 1896. With a large staff whose salaries were paid out of his own pocket he set about convincing party leaders of McKinley's suitability; he succeeded so well that the governor was nominated on the first ballot. Named chairman of the Republican National Committee, Hanna raised a campaign fund of unprecedented size by adding to the normal solicitation of contributions a regular system of assessments on large businesses. After McKinley's election Hanna declined the office of postmaster general, and accepted appointment to John Sherman's vacated seat in the Senate in 1897; he was elected to the seat the following year and quickly became a leader in the Republican inner circle as well as McKinley's closest adviser. He directed the campaign of 1900 and was again eminently successful in raising large sums of money from the business community. By nature and interest strongly pro-business, Hanna saw also, as many of his colleagues did not, that the organization of labor was a natural and necessary response to the concentration of industry. He remained a major power in the Republican party until his death on February 15, 1904, in Washington, D.C.

Hansen, Alvin Harvey (1887–1975), economist. Born on August 23, 1887, in Viborg, South Dakota, Hansen graduated from Yankton College in 1910 and after three years as a school principal and superintendent in South Dakota entered the University of Wisconsin. He received his M.A. in 1915, served as an instructor in economics for a year at Wisconsin and from 1916 to 1919 at Brown University, and received his Ph.D. from Wisconsin in 1918. In 1919 he moved to the University of Minnesota as associate professor of economics, remaining there, after 1923 as full professor, until 1937. Hansen's early writings, including *Economic Stabilization in an Unbalanced World*, 1932, and *A New Plan for Unemployment Reserves*, 1933, marked him as a leading exponent of the Keynesian approach to government fiscal policy and in 1933 he began a career as an influential government adviser upon his appointment as research director and secretary of the Commission of Inquiry on National Policy in Economic Relations. The next year he became an economist for the Department of State and he later served on the Advisory Council on Social Security (1937–1938), as chairman of the economic advisory council of the National Industrial Conference Board (1938–1939), and as special economic adviser to the Federal Reserve Board (1940–1945). In those and other posts he was an effective advocate of the "compensated economy," in which government spending, borrowing, and taxation are keyed to changing levels of private investment in order to maintain a steadily growing economy and constant employment. Acknowledged as the chief theoretician of the New Economics and its view of government as an active factor in a stable and developing economy, Hansen was also sensitive to the practical necessities of government policy and attracted wide attention with such books as *Full Recovery or Stagnation?*, 1938; *Fiscal Policy and Business Cycles*, 1941; *Economic Policy and Full Employment*, 1947; *Economic Analysis of Guaranteed Wages*, 1947, with Paul A. Samuelson; *A Guide to Keynes*, 1953; *The American Economy*, 1957; *Economic Issues of the 1960s*, 1960; and *The Dollar and the International Monetary System*, 1965. From 1937 until his retirement Hansen was Lucius N. Littauer Professor of Political Economy at Harvard. He served at various times on the staffs of *Econometrica*, *Quarterly Journal of Economics*, *Review of Economic Statistics*, and other journals. He died in Alexandria, Virginia, on June 6, 1975.

Hansen, Marcus Lee (1892–1938), historian. Born in Neenah, Wisconsin, on December 8, 1892, Hansen grew up there and in Michigan, Minnesota, and Iowa where his father, a Baptist minister, served various churches. From 1912 to 1914 he attended Central College (now University), Pella, Iowa, and in 1916 graduated from the State University of Iowa. After earning an M.A. there in 1917 he enrolled at Harvard to work on his doctorate in history under Frederick Jackson Turner. His studies were briefly interrupted by service in World War I, and before earning his Ph.D. he studied in Europe in 1922 and taught for two years at Smith College. Hansen's area of specialization was the history of immigration, a field in which he became the country's first serious and comprehensive scholar. By the time he received his doctorate in 1924 he was convinced that an adequate history of immigration could not be written from the sources then available. During 1925–1927 he toured Europe on a research grant, searching archives and old newspaper files. What he uncovered led him to project a need for twenty more years of such research before he could write definitively on the mass movement of millions of immigrants to the United States, on why they had left Europe, and what impact their emigration had on American sociey and vice versa. In 1927–1928 Hansen researched the ethnic composition of the United States in 1790 for the American Council of Learned Societies (ACLS). In 1928 he joined the history faculty at the University of Illinois, becoming a full professor two years later. Before he was able to consider his work complete, he died on May 11, 1938, in Redlands, California, while on leave of absence from the university. During his lifetime various articles and lectures of Hansen's were published, notably his May 1937 lecture "The Problem of the Third Generation Immigrant," but his other and major works were published posthumously. *Mingling of the Canadian and American Peoples*, edited by J. B. Brebner, and *The Atlantic Migration, 1607–1860*, edited by Arthur M. Schlesinger, appeared in 1940, and the latter received the Pulitzer Prize for history. *The Immigrant in American History*, also edited by Schlesinger, composed primarily of lectures given in 1935 at the University of London, was published in 1940.

Hanson, Howard Harold (1896–1981), composer, conductor, and educator. Born on October 28, 1896, in Wahoo, Nebraska, Hanson received his musical education at Luther College in Wahoo, the University of Nebraska, the Institute of Musical Art (later the Juilliard School) in New York City, and Northwestern University, from which he graduated in 1916. In that year he was appointed professor of musical theory and composition at the Conservatory of Fine Arts of the College of the Pacific and three years later he became dean of the conservatory. Two early compositions, his incidental music for the *California Forest Play of 1920* and his symphonic poem *Before the Dawn*, 1920, earned him the Prix de Rome in 1921 and a three-year period of advanced study at the American Academy in Rome. During that time he produced his first mature works, including *North and West*, 1923; *Lux Aeterna*, 1923; and his Symphony No. 1, the *Nordic*, 1923. Hanson returned to the United States in 1924 and was appointed director of the newly organized Eastman School of Music at the University of Rochester, in New York. There he early established a vigorous tradition of encouragement for native American composers by providing a regular program of public performances of their works, the biannual American Composers' Concerts, later known as the American Music Festivals. He organized the Eastman-Rochester Symphony Orchestra, which introduced, usually with Hanson as conductor, more than a thousand works by contemporary American composers. Hanson's own compositions achieved considerable popularity, particularly his Symphony No. 2, the *Romantic*, 1930, which was also perhaps his most characteristic work. Others included the choral *Lament for Beowulf*, 1925; the opera *Merry Mount*, on a New England historical theme, commissioned and premiered in 1934 by the Metropolitan Opera; *Songs from "Drum Taps,"* after Walt Whitman, 1935; the Symphony No. 4, the *Requiem*, which won a Pulitzer Prize in 1944; the Symphony No. 5, the *Sinfonia Sacra*, 1955; the choral *Song of Democracy*, 1957; the *Bold Island Suite*, 1962; and the choral *Song of Human Rights*, 1963. Hanson's music was boldly and imaginatively rhythmical, romantic in an austere manner reminiscent of the works of Jean Sibelius, and masterfully, sometimes brilliantly, orchestrated. Although he was one of the most popular of modern American composers of serious music, he occasionally fell in the estimation of some critics, by whom he was thought to be repetitive and uninventive. In 1958 he founded the Eastman Philharmonia, a student orchestra that became, three years later, the first such organization to undertake a State Department–sponsored goodwill tour of the Soviet Union; the orchestra also toured successfully in other parts of Europe and in the Middle East. Hanson served as an adviser on musical and cultural affairs to the State Department and to the New York State Council of the Arts and was a member of the International Music Council of the United Nations Educational, Scientific, and Cultural Organization (UNESCO). He retired from the directorship of the Eastman School in 1964. His *Harmonic Materials of Modern Music*, a textbook, appeared in 1960. He died on February 26, 1981, in Rochester, New York.

Hanson, John (1721–1783), public official. Born in Charles County, Maryland, on April 13, 1721, Hanson first came to public notice outside his own district in 1757 with his election to the Maryland assembly. He remained in that body almost continuously for 22 years, the last six as representative of Frederick County. He was active in the agitation against repressive parliamentary government, signing the Maryland non-importation agreement in 1769 and, as a member of the Maryland convention of 1775, the "Association of Freemen." He played a leading role in preparing the state's defenses in anticipation of war and was an early advocate of independence. In December 1779 the assembly elected him to the Continental Congress, where, upon taking his seat the next year, he labored successfully to resolve the dispute over Western lands between Maryland, Virginia, and other states and thus smoothed the way for ratification of the Articles of Confederation in 1781. On November 5, 1781, Hanson was elected "President of the United States in Congress Assembled"; although the post was in fact merely that of presiding officer of Congress under the Articles of Confederation and he had little executive authority, he has nonetheless occasionally been referred to as the "first President of the United States." On the completion of his one-year term he retired and died at Oxon Hill, Prince Georges County, Maryland, on November 22, 1783.

Harding, Chester (1792–1866), painter. Born in Conway, Massachusetts, on September 1, 1792, Harding moved with his family to Madison County on the New York frontier in 1806 and, having received little or no formal schooling, became a chairmaker. After serving as a drummer in the New York militia expedition to the St. Lawrence in the War of 1812 he worked as a cabinetmaker, a tavern keeper, and, in Pittsburgh, as a house and sign painter. On trying his hand at portraiture he discovered a native talent for such work and went on the road, stopping for periods in Paris, Kentucky, and in St. Louis. Returning East, he enjoyed increasing success and became a society favorite in Boston, where in a six-month period he received and executed 80 portrait commissions. In 1823 he sailed to England and despite his backwoods origins was lionized by society and the nobility for three lucrative years. He returned to Boston in 1826 and in 1830 settled in Springfield, Massachusetts, continuing to paint many of the noted personages of the day. Among Harding's most celebrated sitters were Daniel Boone, whom he had visited during his stay in St. Louis, Robert Owen in England, Timothy Pickering, John Marshall, John C. Calhoun, Daniel Webster, and Gen. William T. Sherman. Many of his canvases were eventually acquired by major galleries and museums in the United States. Harding died in Boston on April 1, 1866.

Harding, Warren Gamaliel (1865–1923), twenty-ninth president of the United States. Born on November 2, 1865, in Blooming Grove, Ohio, Harding completed his schooling with three years of study at Ohio Central College, a nearby academy. In 1882 he moved with his family to Marion, Ohio, and there, after a short and unsatisfactory period studying law, he took a position with the *Marion Democratic Mirror*. In 1884 he and a partner bought the *Marion Star* and for the next several years as its editor he devoted himself to making it a success; as Marion's population grew the newspaper prospered, and Harding's interests and influence gradually expanded. He became involved in local Republican politics and with impressive oratorical abilities soon gained a measure of prominence. In 1898 he was elected to the state senate; after a second term he was elected lieutenant governor in 1902, but two years later he declined renomination and returned to his newspaper. In 1910 he ran for governor and was severely defeated. Although he thought his political career ended, his reputation as a public speaker led to his being chosen to present William Howard Taft's name to the Republican national convention of 1912; two years later he was elected to the Senate by a huge majority and in 1916 gave the keynote address at the Republican national convention. His Senate career, like his earlier political life, was undistinguished by any quality other than party regularity. This very quality, however, combined with his geniality and lack of pretension, enabled him to emerge as a dark-horse compromise candidate from the 1920 Republican convention despite the brilliance of the leading contenders, Leonard Wood, Hiram Johnson, and Frank Lowden, and the fact that a campaign begun for him the preceding year by his old Ohio political manager, Harry M. Daugherty, had revealed an almost total absence of popular support. Conducting a colorless, inactive, and confusing campaign—he was endorsed by various Republican factions as both an opponent (which he actually was) and as a supporter of the League of Nations—he won the election over James M. Cox by a large margin, primarily because of national ennui following World War I and his own call for a "return to normalcy." His administration proceeded much as had that of Ulysses S. Grant after the Civil War: he made a large number of ill-advised appointments and was unknowingly surrounded by corruption. With the president devoted mainly to gatherings of his "Ohio gang" cronies around the White House poker table, leadership was left to the ruling party clique in the Senate, and the high point of Harding's term, the Washington Disarmament Conference of 1921–1922 and the subsequent naval arms-limitation treaty, came through the initiative of others. By 1923 Washington was rife with rumors of widespread corruption in various government departments, and a Senate investigation into the Teapot Dome oil-lease transfers was begun. In June Harding set out on a transcontinental tour; while in Alaska he received a long cipher message from Washington, apparently informing him of the extent of the corruption that was about to be exposed. Deeply shaken, he traveled south toward San Francisco and was soon reported to be suffering from food poisoning and other ills; he died in that city on August 2, 1923, under circumstances that are still not completely clear. In the investigations of corruption that followed, many of Harding's friends and appointees were forced out of office, including Attorney General Daugherty, Secretary of the Interior Albert B. Fall, who served a jail term, Secretary of the Navy Edwin N. Denby, and others.

Hardy, Oliver, see under Laurel, Stan

Harlan, John Marshall (1833–1911), justice of the Supreme Court. Born in Boyle County, Kentucky, on June 1, 1833, Harlan was educated at Centre College of Kentucky. After graduation in 1850 he entered Transylvania University to study law and was admitted to the bar three years later. Taking up practice in Frankfort, he was elected county judge in 1858; on completing his term the next year he ran unsuccessfully for the House of Representatives and in 1860, not yet reconciled to the policies of the Republicans, he was a presidential elector for the Constitutional Union party. During the Civil War he commanded a volunteer Union infantry regiment until resigning his commission in 1863; in the same year he was elected state attorney general. In 1864 he opposed President Abraham Lincoln's bid for reelection and supported Gen. George B. McClellan. The next year he won a second term as attorney general, upon the completion of which, in 1867, he retired to private law practice in Louisville. He moved slowly from the conservative to the radical wing of the Republican party and was the unsuccessful candidate for governor of Kentucky in 1871 and 1875. As head of the Kentucky delegation to the Republican national convention in 1876 he was instrumental in securing the nomination of Rutherford B. Hayes; in gratitude Harlan was offered a diplomatic post but declined it. In 1877 President Hayes appointed him to a commission sent to resolve the conflict between two rival state governments in Louisiana, and later in the year he was named to the Supreme Court. During nearly 34 years on the bench he was a powerful advocate of a balanced view of national sovereignty and states' rights. He was never the least inclined to muffle a dissent; most of his notable opinions were outspoken dissents and verged occasionally on bitterness, as Harlan seemed to flourish in the heat of controversy. In the Civil Rights Cases of 1883 he dissented from the Court majority in upholding a broad interpretation of the Thirteenth and Fourteenth amendments. He was also in the minority in upholding in 1895 the right of the federal government to tax personal income; in declaring, as the lone dissenter, in *Plessy* v. *Ferguson* in 1896, that segregated schools did not constitute equal treatment under law and that the Constitution is "color-blind"; and in holding, in *Hawaii* v. *Mankichi*, 1903, and in *Dorr* v. *U.S.*, 1904, two of the Insular Cases, that the Constitution "follows the flag." He vigorously opposed judicial legislation, particularly when the Court read the word "unreasonable" into the Sherman Anti-Trust Act's prohibition of practices resulting in "restraint of trade." In 1892 he was called upon by President Benjamin Harrison to aid in the arbitration of the Bering Sea seal-hunting dispute with Great Britain. He continued on the bench until his death on October 14, 1911, in Washington, D.C.

Harlan, John Marshall (1899–1971), justice of the Supreme Court. Born in Chicago on May 20, 1899, Harlan was the grandson and namesake of Justice

John M. Harlan (1833–1911). He was educated in private schools and at Princeton and after graduating in 1920 entered Oxford University as a Rhodes scholar, taking a degree in jurisprudence in 1923. Returning to the United States, he took a position with a prominent Wall Street law firm and enrolled in the New York Law School, from which he graduated in 1924. Soon after his admission to the bar in 1925 he left the firm for a time to serve as chief of the prohibition section of the office of the U.S. attorney for the Southern District of New York. From 1928 to 1930 he was special assistant state attorney general; returning to the law firm, he was named a partner in 1932. During World War II he served in the Army Air Forces, afterward returning to his lucrative and prestigious practice, in the course of which he was engaged in such major cases as the Du Pont–General Motors antitrust suit in 1953. He served also as chief counsel of the New York State Crime Commission from 1951 to 1953. In early 1954 Harlan was appointed judge of the U.S. Court of Appeals, Second District, by President Dwight D. Eisenhower; just a few months later Eisenhower named him to succeed Robert H. Jackson of the Supreme Court. Taking his seat in March 1955, Harlan soon proved himself a conscientious and firmly independent member of the Court. His opinions, lucid, closely reasoned, and often lengthy, were widely admired among lawyers and fellow judges. Harlan hewed closely to precedent and was decidedly opposed to the notion of an activist Court, a position that placed him often in disagreement with Chief Justice Earl Warren and the Court's majority. His strict-constructionist reading of the Constitution led him more often than not into alliance with Justice Felix Frankfurter, whose philosophical heir he was sometimes held to be. Notable among his opinions were those in *Yates* v. *U.S.*, 1957, setting limits on the government's freedom to prosecute alleged Communists under the 1940 Smith Act; *Barenblatt* v. *U.S.*, 1959, upholding the investigative power of the House Committee on Un-American Activities; *Baker* v. *Carr*, 1962, in which he dissented from the decision that federal courts can review legislative districting; and *Miranda* v. *Arizona*, 1966, in which he dissented from the majority opinion securing the privilege against self-incrimination. In general he stood strongly for the tradtional federal division of powers between state and national governments, for the power of government to protect itself and its citizens against subversion, criminality, and obscenity, and against the tendency of the Court to intrude into matters not under its strictly construed constitutional purview. Harlan resigned his seat for reasons of health in September 1971 and died a short time later, on December 29, 1971, in Washington, D.C.

Harlow, Jean (1911–1937), actress. Born in Kansas City, Missouri, on March 3, 1911, Harlean Carpenter grew up from the age of ten in the California home of her maternal grandfather. She left private school in Lake Forest, Illinois, at sixteen to be married and settled in Beverly Hills, California. In 1928 she was persuaded to register with the Central Casting Bureau in Hollywood and soon, under the name Jean Harlow (Harlow was her mother's maiden name), she was playing small parts in short films, many of them silent comedies directed by Hal Roach. After a small role in *The Saturday Night Kid*, 1929, she was chosen by Howard Hughes to star in his *Hell's Angels*, 1930, in which she was an immediate sensation. A rapid succession of movies followed —among them *Platinum Blonde*, 1931; *The Secret Six*, 1931; *Public Enemy*, 1931; *The Beast of the City*, 1932; and *Red Dust*, 1932—all designed to exploit her worldly-wise manner and her striking, frankly sensual beauty. The design was enormously successful and despite her obvious lack of dramatic ability Miss Harlow became, virtually overnight, one of Hollywood's top box-office attractions. Her wardrobe, her enticing languor, and her platinum-blonde hair were all, with varying degrees of success, widely copied. In *Red-Headed Woman*, 1932, she displayed a certain knack for light comedy and thereafter she concentrated on such roles, notably in *Dinner at Eight*, 1933, and *Bombshell*, 1933. Her last years were marked by unhappy marriages and serious bouts of illness; she died in Los Angeles on June 7, 1937, at the age of twenty-six. Her last film, *Saratoga*, was released a month later.

Harnett, William Michael (1848–1892), painter. Born on August 10, 1848, in County Cork, Ireland, Harnett was brought by his parents to the United States at an early age and with them settled in Phildelphia. He took up the trade of silver engraving and in 1867 began studying painting in his spare time at the Pennsylvania Academy of the Fine Arts. In 1869 he moved to New York City and studied at the National Academy of Design and at Cooper Union while working as an engraver for a jewelry firm. By 1875 he was ready to abandon his trade and devote full time to painting, and in that year his work was first exhibited at the National Academy of Design. Harnett's best works, and those for which he is remembered, were painstakingly exact still lifes in the tradition of the seventeenth-century Dutch realist *trompe l'oeil* painters and their American disciple of the preceding century, Raphael Peale. In such paintings as "Emblems of Peace," "After the Hunt," and "The Old Violin," he grouped guns, pipes, books, musical instruments and sheet music, busts, candles, scraps of newspaper, and other common objects around a common theme and rendered them in meticulous detail; into a realism that surpassed the photographic he also occasionally injected a suggestion of whimsical, if tenuous, intent. From 1880 to 1886 he traveled and studied in Europe, visiting there again briefly in 1889; otherwise he lived and worked in New York City. His early reputation, which attracted a number of followers and imitators, faded soon after his death in New York City, on October 29, 1892, and his paintings came to be looked upon by most critics as mere exercises in visual trickery. Interest in his work revived about 1939, however, and while his first modern admirers were the Surrealists, who fancied in his paintings a foreshadowing of their own aesthetics, he was thenceforth firmly established among the leading American artists of the nineteenth century.

Harper Brothers, printers and publishers. Born in Newtown, Long Island, New York, James on April 13, 1795, John on January 22, 1797, Wesley (as Joseph Wesley was known) on December 25, 1801, and Fletcher on January 31, 1806, the Harper brothers grew up in an atmosphere of Methodist piety and respect for books and learning. James and John were both early apprenticed to New York City printers and in 1817 they went into business for themselves as J. & J. Harper. They soon acquired a reputation as efficient and highly capable printers and enjoyed success from the outset. In 1818, largely to take up the slack between jobs, they printed and issued under their own imprint an edition of John Locke's *Essay Concerning Human Understanding* and thus launched themselves as publishers. Wesley joined the firm in 1823 and Fletcher, who had served an apprenticeship under his older brothers, became a partner in 1825; in 1833 the firm's name was changed to Harper & Brothers, and it was a token of the close cooperation and understanding that existed among the four that James once claimed that any one of them might at any time be *the* Harper. As their list of titles grew and the business expanded an informal division of labor became established. James attended to the mechanical aspects in the pressroom, where he introduced some of the earliest steam-powered presses and large-scale electrotyping equipment; John concerned himself principally with business and the technical matters of production, from typesetting to proofreading; Wesley was the firm's chief editor and critic; and Fletcher, an energetic and enterprising businessman, was active in every facet of the business and contributed greatly to its continued success by securing in 1839 a contract to supply books to the New York state school system. Harper & Brothers ventured into the periodical field in 1850 with *Harper's New Monthly Magazine*, created by James and thereafter managed by Fletcher. Fletcher added *Harper's Weekly* in 1857 and *Harper's Bazar* (later Bazaar) in 1867. *Harper's New Monthly Magazine* built its success on the serialization of popular novels, largely from England, and both its editorial staff and its famous "Editor's Easy Chair" department featured through the years some of the brightest names in American letters. In 1900 the name of the magazine was changed to *Harper's Monthly Magazine* and in 1925 it became simply *Harper's Magazine. Harper's Weekly* quickly became widely known and admired for its wealth of high-quality illustration and for the increasingly political and crusading tone of much of its content. In its pages Thomas Nast carried

on his cartoon battle against the Tweed Ring; the battle, maintained despite Tammany Hall's retaliations on the Harper schoolbook trade, was strongly encouraged and supported by Fletcher, whose deep interest in civic affairs reflected that of James, reform mayor of New York City in 1844. The *Weekly* was bought out by the *Independent* in 1916. *Harper's Bazar*, a magazine designed for women and as a complement to the *Weekly*, was purchased by William Randolph Hearst in 1913 and in 1929 the name was altered to *Harper's Bazaar*. The four Harper brothers continued to direct their publishing firm throughout their lives; they died in New York City, James on March 27, 1869, Wesley on February 14, 1870, John on April 22, 1875, and Fletcher on May 29, 1877. The business remained in family hands until 1900; it is now known as Harper & Row.

Harper, Fletcher, *see under* Harper Brothers

Harper, James, *see under* Harper Brothers

Harper, John, *see under* Harper Brothers

Harper, Joseph Wesley, *see under* Harper Brothers

Harper, Robert Goodloe (1765–1825), lawyer and public official. Born sometime in January 1765 near Fredericksburg, Virginia, Harper grew up there and in Granville County, North Carolina. He served briefly under Gen. Nathanael Greene in the Revolution and in 1785 graduated from the College of New Jersey (now Princeton). Moving to Charleston, South Carolina, he taught school for a time while studying law and on winning admission to the bar in 1786 he began practice in Ninety Six, South Carolina. He served in the state legislature in 1789 and in 1794, after a three-year business sojourn in Philadelphia, he returned to South Carolina and was elected to the House of Representatives. Within a short time after taking his seat he came under the influence of he powerful Federalists and began to give up his earlier and almost fanatically pro-French views. He supported Jay's Treaty in 1794, John Adam's presidential candidacy in 1796, and the Alien and Sedition Acts in 1798. His pugnacity brought him to a position of leadership among Federalists, and his *Observations on the Dispute Between the United States and France,* 1797, established his reputation at home and abroad. In June 1798, at a Philadelphia dinner honoring John Marshall on his return from France and the diplomatic debacle of the XYZ Affair, Harper proposed a toast that became famous: "Millions for defense, but not a cent for tribute." Leaving Congress in 1801, he settled first in Baltimore and later on a nearby estate and resumed his law practice, achieving considerable prominence at the bar in Maryland and Pennsylvania. He was appointed major general of the Maryland militia during the War of 1812 and in 1816 was elected to the Senate, resigning later in the year under the pressure of his law practice and business interests. He was also the Federalist candidate for the vice-presidency in that year. Harper was a founding member of the American Colonization Society in 1817 and, after being influential in the choice of Africa as the site of the proposed colony, suggested the names Liberia for the colony and Monrovia for its capital. He died in Baltimore on January 14, 1825.

Harper, Wesley, *see under* Harper Brothers

Harper, William Rainey (1856–1906), scholar and educator. Born on July 26, 1856, in New Concord, Ohio, Harper graduated from Muskingum College at the age of fourteen. After a few years spent working in his father's dry-goods store and studying languages on his own, he began graduate work at Yale and was awarded a Ph.D. in 1875, shortly before his nineteenth birthday. Thereafter he taught briefly at each of several small colleges and in 1879 was called to the Baptist Union Theological Seminary in Chicago, where he had his first opportunity to teach in his field of primary interest, the Hebrew language. In Chicago he founded two journals, the *Hebrew Student* (later the *Old and New Testament Student,* later still *Biblical World*) and *Hebraica* (later the *American Journal of Semitic Languages and Literature*) and developed a correspondence course in Hebrew. He published a number of textbooks and study aids and established the American Institute of Hebrew. From 1885 he was active in the Chautauqua movement, offering summer courses himself and serving for many years as president of its college of liberal arts. In 1886 he became professor of Semitic languages at Yale; during his tenure there he achieved national recognition as an educator. Particularly effective as a teacher and organizer, he was selected as the first president of the new University of Chicago in 1891. Determined from the outset to create a major educational and research institution, Harper insisted upon complete academic freedom for the brilliant faculty he soon gathered. While he was seldom innovative in his plans, his ability to form and execute a comprehensive program of development for the university rendered his services invaluable. While carrying on extensive duties as president he continued to teach full time and was head of the department of Semitic languages. Among his writings, his most important works appeared near the end of his life: *A Critical and Exegetical Commentary on Amos and Hosea* and *The Trend in Higher Education,* both 1905. He died in Chicago on January 10, 1906.

Harriman, Averell (1891–   ), businessman, public official, and diplomat. Born in New York City on November 15, 1891, William Averell Harriman was the son of E. H. Harriman. He graduated from Yale in 1913 and two years later became a vice-president of the Union Pacific Railroad and a director of the Illinois Central Railroad. In 1917

he became chairman of the board of the Merchant Shipbuilding Corporation, a post he held for eight years. He held high positions in many other firms and from 1932 to 1946 returned to the Union Pacific as chairman of the board. At the request of President Franklin D. Roosevelt he entered the government service in 1934 as a divisonal administrator for the National Recovery Administration (NRA). He remained with the NRA for a year; in 1941, after three months in the Office of Production Management, he was sent to Great Britain and then to the Soviet Union as special representive of the president. During 1942 he continued to represent the United States on a number of joint boards in London and in 1943 was appointed ambassador to the U.S.S.R. Three years later he became ambassador to Great Britain, a position he had held only six months when he was named secretary of commerce by President Harry S. Truman. From 1948 to 1951 he represented the United States in various diplomatic capacities in Europe and for two years thereafter was director of the Mutual Security Agency. In 1954 he was elected governor of New York; he ran again in 1958 but was defeated. In 1961 President John F. Kennedy appointed Harriman assistant secretary of state for Far Eastern affairs, and two years later he became undersecretary of state for political affairs. In 1965 he was named ambassador-at-large by President Lyndon B. Johnson and undertook a number of assignments, notably, from 1968 to 1969, as chief U.S. negotiator at the peace talks in Paris seeking an end to the Vietnam War. In 1969 he was awarded the Presidential Medal of Freedom.

Harriman, Edward Henry (1848–1909), financier and railroad executive. Born February 25, 1848, in Hempstead, New York, Harriman left school at fourteen to become a broker's clerk in Wall Street. By 1870 he was in a position to buy a seat on the New York Stock Exchange. He first became interested in railroads in 1881; in that year he acquired the Lake Ontario Southern, reorganized it, and reaped a large profit from its sale. Two years later he became a director of the Illinois Central and in 1887 vice-president. In 1897 he allied himself with the banking firm of Kuhn, Loeb & Company, which was reorganizing the bankrupt Union Pacific Railroad; the next year he became chairman of the line and the dominant figure in its administration. Displaying a broad, detailed knowledge of railroading as well as great financial acumen, he directed the revitalization of the company and the rehabilitation of its track and equipment with such skill and energy that within three years it was showing a profit and expanding its facilities. Early in 1901 he acquired control of the Southern Pacific and of its subsidiary, the Central Pacific, setting up a highly efficient central administration for the entire system and restoring its physical equipment. Later in the year, seeking control of the Chicago, Burlington & Quincy Railroad in order to have rail access to Chicago, he entered upon a titanic struggle with James J. Hill of the Northern Pacific; the contest triggered a panic on Wall Street in May 1901. A settlement was reached in the forming of the Northern Securities Company to hold the contested property in trust, but in 1904 the holding company was ordered dissolved by the Supreme Court and Harriman was left in a minority position; however, he was able to convert his holdings into a huge cash profit. President of the Union Pacific from 1903, he began buying stock in other lines, extending his influence eventually over some 60,000 miles of track. Prompted by President Theodore Roosevelt, the Interstate Commerce Commission (ICC) launched an investigation into the Harriman holdings in 1906; revelations of ruthless business methods made in that and other inquiries aroused a storm of public opprobrium. The popular image of Harriman as a ruthless, heartless, financier was somewhat tempered by his involvement in a boys' club, perhaps the first of its kind in America, for the sons of immigrants on New York City's East Side, by his sponsorship of a fruitful scientific expedition to Alaska in 1899, and by his gift of a parcel of wilderness parkland to New York State. He died at Arden, his estate in Orange County, New York, on September 9, 1909.

Harriman, William Averell, see Harriman, Averell

Harris, Benjamin (fl. 1673–1716), publisher. Born in England at a date unknown, Harris first came to public notice in 1673 when he published from his London bookshop a small religious book entitled *War with the Devil*. His career was a checkered one; he was deeply involved with the Earl of Shaftesbury in anti-Catholic activities, was associated in some way with the infamous Titus Oates in the disclosure of the supposed "Popish Plot," and was on several occasions warned, fined, or imprisoned for publishing seditious or merely scurrilous newspapers and pamphlets. His position became perilous when the Catholic James II came to the English throne in 1685 and the next year Harris sailed to America, settling in Boston and opening a bookshop there that was quickly successful. He published an almanac in 1687 and soon became the leading publisher in the colonies, numbering among his titles *The New England Primer* which, with its crude woodcuts, simple rhymes (including the well-known children's prayer, "Now I lay me down to sleep"), and Calvinist theology, sold more than 5 million copies in its century of importance as a schoolbook; he also issued several works by the Mathers. The bookshop served also as a coffeehouse and became a social and literary gathering place for Bostonians. On September 25, 1690, Harris issued the first—and last—number of *Publick Occurrences Both Forreign and Domestick*, which, although it was promptly suppressed by the authorities, was the first newspaper published in America. Harris was the government's official printer in 1692–1693; in 1695, after a final edition of his almanac, he returned to London. There he

published a series of newspapers, the most successful being *the London Post* from 1700 to 1706. He continued as a publisher and seller of books at least until 1716. The date and place of his death are unknown.

Harris, Chapin Aaron (1806–1860), dentist. Born in Pompey, Onondaga County, New York, on May 6, 1806, Harris was educated in local schools and in 1824 began the study of medicine in the Ohio office of an older brother. He began practice in Greenfield, Ohio, in 1826 and two years later turned to dentistry. After three years of practice in Greenfield and eight in various Southern cities he established himself in Baltimore in 1839. In that year he published *The Dental Art, a Practical Treatise on Dental Surgery*, later revised and retitled *Principles and Practice of Dental Surgery*, which remained in print for nearly 60 years. Also in 1839 he led in founding the *American Journal of Dental Science*, the first such journal in the world. After a year of planning and lobbying the legislature for a school charter, he helped open and became first dean and professor of operative dentistry and dental prosthesis in the Baltimore College of Dental Surgery, the first such institution in the world, opened in 1840 (and now part of the University of Maryland). In 1844 Harris became president of the college and of the American Society of Dental Surgeons, of which he had been a founder in 1840. He joined in organizing the American Dental Convention in 1855 and was its president in 1856–1857. A serious student of dentistry, he published a great many articles, translations of European texts, and *A Dictionary of Dental Science, Biography, Bibliography and Medical Terminology*, 1849, and was a preeminent figure in the establishment of dentistry on a firm professional basis. Harris died in Baltimore on September 29, 1860.

Harris, Joel Chandler (1848–1908), journalist and author. Born on December 9, 1848, in Eatonton, Georgia, Harris ended his schooling in 1862 when he became an apprentice on a local newspaper, the *Countryman*. In that job and on a succession of other Southern newspapers he gradually established a reputation as a humorist. In 1876 he joined the *Atlanta Constitution*, with which he was associated for the next 24 years. With painstaking care he perfected a written transcription of plantation Negro speech with which he was intimately familiar and in 1879 published "The Tar-Baby Story," the first of the Uncle Remus series. The fidelity of the dialect and the warmth and humor of this and subsequent tales made them immediately and widely popular; a collection entitled *Uncle Remus: His Songs and His Sayings* was published in 1880 and followed by a number of sequels, including *Nights with Uncle Remus*, 1883; *Daddy Jake, the Runaway*, 1889; *Uncle Remus and His Friends*, 1892; *The Tar Baby*, 1904; and *Uncle Remus and Br'er Rabbit*, 1906. As the foremost writer of the local-color school in the 1870s and 1880s, Harris wrote in addition to the animal fables of Uncle Remus a number of books reflecting the Georgia scene; most notable of these were *Mingo, and Other Sketches in Black and White*, 1884; *Free Joe and Other Georgia Sketches*, 1887; and *Gabriel Tolliver*, 1902. *On the Plantation*, 1892, was autobiographical. In 1907 he established *Uncle Remus's Magazine* and continued to edit it until his death in Atlanta, Georgia, on July 3, 1908.

Harris, Louis (1921–   ), public-opinion analyst. Born on January 6, 1921, in New Haven, Connecticut, Harris graduated from the University of North Carolina in 1942 and then served for three years in the navy. In 1946 he joined the American Veterans' Committee (AVC), where his work in the area of public opinion led in 1947 to his taking a position with the polling organization headed by Elmo Roper. He was at first involved in the communications-media aspects of Roper's work, later moving into political affairs and research and in 1954 becoming a partner in the firm. He left the Roper organization in 1956 to establish Louis Harris and Associates, Inc., in New York, an opinion-polling firm that soon had commissions and workers across the country. Much of his work in the first years of the company was market research for private industry, but he gradually came to be consulted by public officials and candidates for office who were seeking accurate reports on the state of opinion among their current or prospective constituents. Harris developed a method of polling that was more complex and potentially more revealing than most, going beyond simple percentage breakdowns of "yes" and "no" answers to find the reasons, attitudes, and biases behind first responses. The Harris organization came to national prominence in the 1960 presidential campaign, when it was consulted by John F. Kennedy for reports and advice on key primaries and on the general election; Harris himself became a close personal adviser to Kennedy. Firmly established as a political pollster and manager, Harris became in 1962 public-opinion analyst for the Columbia Broadcasting System (CBS); in six years with CBS he worked to develop and refine sophisticated computerized techniques for analysis and prediction. In 1963 he began writing weekly columns for *Newsweek* magazine and for the *Washingcon Post* and its syndicate of more than 100 newspapers across the nation. He moved his columns in 1969 to *Time* magazine and to the *Chicago Tribune* and its national syndicate.

Harris, Roy Ellsworth (1898-1979), composer. Born on February 12, 1898, in Lincoln County, Oklahoma, Harris grew up there and in Southern California. After serving in the army in World War I he attended the University of California at Berkeley in 1919–1920 and then, while working as a truck driver, began studying music. The success of an early orchestral work, *Andante*, won him a Guggenheim Fellowship in 1926 and

he traveled to Paris to study with Nadia Boulanger; during 1930–1933 he held a fellowship from the Pasadena (California), Music and Art Association. His first major composition, a 1927 concerto for clarinet, piano, and string quartet, was followed by his *First Symphony* in 1933 and by *When Johnny Comes Marching Home*, 1935, a symphonic overture based on the Civil War song of that title. The best known of his symphonies, the *Third*, was well received in 1939 and marked Harris as one of the leading American composers of the day. His music, while cast for the most part in classical forms, drew inspiration for its broad melodic strokes and rhythmic asymmetries from a visionary and romantic attachment to the American land and tradition and was often compared in feeling to the poetry of Walt Whitman and Carl Sandburg. Harris was appointed composer in residence at Cornell University in 1941 and the next year moved to Colorado College; from 1948 to 1967 he was on the faculty of the Utah State Agricultural College and from 1967 was associated with the University of California at Los Angeles (UCLA). Other major works included *Challenge*, 1940; the choral *Folksong Symphony*, 1940; the *Sixth Symphony*, subtitled *Gettysburg Address*, 1944; *Kentucky Spring*, 1949; the *Seventh Symphony*, 1952; *Festival Folk Fantasy*, 1956; *San Francisco Symphony*, 1962; and the *Eleventh Symphony*, 1968. He also wrote many works for string and keyboard chamber ensembles. Although occasionally criticized as uneven or awkward, his music was original. From 1974 he was composer in residence at California State University at Los Angeles. He died in Santa Monica, California, on October 1, 1979.

Harris, Townsend (1804–1878), businessman and diplomat. Born in Sandy Hill (now Hudson Falls), New York, on October 3, 1804, Harris received little schooling and at thirteen traveled to New York City to take a job in a dry-goods store. Joined later by his father and brother, he became a partner in their successful importing firm and while building up the business devoted much of his free time to wide reading, acquiring in the course of his self-education a command of several languages. He was active also in local Democratic politics; as a member and later president of the city Board of Education he led in planning and founding the Free Academy (later the College of the City of New York, CCNY) in 1847. In 1849, after the dissolution of his partnership with his brother, he left New York on a merchant vessel of which he was a part owner; on arriving in California he became sole owner of the ship and set out to trade in the Orient. In Shanghai in 1853 he encountered Commodore Matthew C. Perry, then en route to Japan, and tried unsuccessfully to join the expedition. The rebuff turned his thoughts to consular service, however, and he applied for a consular appointment. Although he hoped for appointment to Canton or Hong Kong, both major centers of the China trade, he was named in 1854 to the poorly paid post at Ningpo, a Chinese port of lesser importance. Instead of accepting the post, he returned to the United Sates and through the influence of Secretary of State William L. Marcy, in 1855 was named he first U.S. consul general to Japan, which had been opened to the United States under the terms of a treaty negotiated by Perry. On his way to Japan he stopped in Siam (Thailand) to negotiate a new commercial treaty, and in August 1856 arrived in the Japanese port of Shimoda. For more than a year he faced discouragement by Japanese officials, but he gradually overcame their reluctance to treat with him (and thus open Japan to Westerners). By pointing out the fate suffered by China at the hands of imperialistic European nations and by demonstrating to Japanese satisfaction that a treaty with the United States not only could be had on favorable terms but also would serve as a buffer against other Western powers and their unbridled rapacity, Harris won a preliminary agreement in December 1857. Seven months later a full treaty was signed, providing for exchange of diplomatic representatives and also covering trade, tariffs, and extraterritoriality. From then until his return to the United States late in 1860 Harris was resident consul in Edo (now Tokyo) and enjoyed the confidence of the Japanese government, serving even as a confidential adviser in Japan's subsequent negotiations with other Western nations. He became almost a legendary figure in Japan in the decades following his departure. On his return to the United States he settled in New York City; he was a prominent War Democrat and Union League Club member and devoted much of his time and money to supporting temperance, foreign missions, and his church. Harris died in New York City on February 25, 1878.

Harris, William Torrey (1835–1909), philosopher and educator. Born near Killingly, Connecticut, on September 10, 1835, Harris studied for a little more than two years at Yale, then began to teach school in St. Louis in 1857. He was notably successful as a teacher and rose rapidly in the city's public-school system, becoming its superintendent in 1868. At the same time, under the influence of Bronson Alcott and Theodore Parker, he began reading deeply in the German idealistic philosophers, particularly G. W. F. Hegel. In 1867 he founded the *Journal of Speculative Philosophy*, which, continuing until 1893, published original translations of Hegel, F. W. J. von Schelling, and on J. G. Fichte; it also published the early writings of the American philosophers Charles S. Peirce, Josiah Royce, William James, and John Dewey. As an educator Harris was highly effective; although not primarily an innovator, he was receptive to ideas and was a leader in developing a broad curriculum for the schools; his annual reports were widely used as models. In 1880 he resigned his position and moved to Concord, Massachusetts, to help Alcott establish the Concord School of Philosophy. The school endured for several years but had little effect on the course of American philosophy; the vitality of Transcendentalism

was long gone, and idealism in all its forms was in general retreat from naturalism. In 1889 he was appointed U.S. commissioner of education, a position he held until 1906. During his years in that post he published the most important of his nearly 500 titled works: *Introduction to the Study of Philosophy*, 1889; *The Spiritual Sense of Dante's Divina Commedia*, 1889; *Hegel's Logic*, 1890; and *The Psychologic Foundations of Education*, 1898. He also held a number of editorial positions, including that of editor in chief of the first edition of *Webster's New International Dictionary*, 1909. He died on November 5, 1909, in Providence, Rhode Island.

Harrison, Benjamin (1833–1901), twenty-third president of the United States. Born in North Bend, Ohio, on August 20, 1833, of a line of political figures, including his grandfather, President William Henry Harrison, Benjamin was educated at nearby Farmers' College and at Miami University in Ohio, from which he graduated in 1852. He was admitted to the bar two years later and moved to Indianapolis to begin practice. As he advanced in his profession he developed an interest in politics, becoming an ardent Republican and holding some minor party and public offices. At the outbreak of the Civil War he raised the 70th Indiana infantry regiment and, with the rank of colonel, commanded it for three years, first in relatively quiet duties in Kentucky and Tennessee and from 1864 as part of Gen. William T. Sherman's forces in Georgia. In March 1865 he received temporary promotion to brigadier general. Returning to Indiana after the war, he continued to gain in prominence in both law and politics. He supported the Radical Republican program, opposing both the Liberal Republican and Greenback parties. He failed to win the nomination for governor in 1872; four years later he was nominated but lost the election. The campaign of that year, however, brought him national attention. In 1880 he was chairman of the Indiana delegation to the Republican national convention and was instrumental in securing James A. Garfield's nomination; shortly thereafter he declined the offer of a cabinet post, accepting instead nomination to the Senate, to which he was duly elected. There he was a strong supporter of civil-service reform, the Interstate Commerce Act of 1887, and the tariff, and took great interest in Indian and territorial affairs. He failed to be reelected in 1887 but the next year was Indiana's favorite-son candidate at the Republican national convention. He was nominated and, although he polled a smaller popular vote than President Grover Cleveland, won the presidency in the electoral college. Most of the notable achievements of his administration were in the field of foreign affairs; an active foreign policy resulted in a number of international conferences, including the first International Conference of American States (Pan American Conference), in 1889, and treaties overseen by Harrison and his capable secretary of state, James G. Blaine, that marked something of a departure in U.S. relations with the rest of the world. On the domestic side, Harrison's four years were less successful. Although the Sherman Anti-Trust Act was passed in 1890, the same year saw the passage of the highly unpopular McKinley Tariff and the politically motivated Sherman Silver Purchase Act. The Veterans Bureau, released from Cleveland's strict scrutiny, embarked on a program of extravagance that became sufficiently notorious to force the resignation of the pension commissioner. Largely because of the tariff, Congress came under Democratic control after 1890. Growing popular discontent, primarily over financial and labor issues, led to Harrison's defeat by Cleveland in his bid for reelection in 1892. He returned to Indianapolis and resumed his legal practice. He published a number of articles and speeches in various periodicals, many of which were collected in *This Country of Ours*, 1897, and *Views of an Ex-President*, 1901. His legal reputation was such that he was chosen by Venezuela as its chief counsel in the arbitration of its boundary dispute with Great Britain in 1898–1899. Harrison died in Indianapolis on March 13, 1901.

Harrison, Peter (1716–1775), architect and merchant. Born in York, England, on June 14, 1716, Harrison emigrated to America in 1740 and settled in Newport, Rhode Island, where he farmed and carried on a prosperous mercantile business in partnership with his brother. There exist varying accounts of his early exposure to and interest in architecture, but it is unlikely that he received formal training at any time. He was nonetheless conversant with the published works of eminent English architects and had sufficient ability to adapt their designs to American settings and materials with marked success, and he introduced to America the Neo-Palladian style that had been established in England. Harrison designed a number of striking buildings, including the Redwood Library, 1750, the Brick Market, 1761, and the Congregation Jeshuat Israel synagogue, 1761, all in Newport; King's Chapel, Boston, 1754, possibly his finest work; and Christ Church, Cambridge, Massachusetts, 1761. Like most men in his calling then and for some decades afterward he was a talented amateur rather than a professional; but the number and distinction of his works were exceptional for the time, and he is often held to have been the first real architect in America. In 1761 he moved to New Haven, Connecticut, continuing there in practice and becoming customs collector in 1768. He died in New Haven on April 30, 1775.

Harrison, Ross Granville (1870–1959), biologist. Born on January 13, 1870, in Germantown, Pennsylvania, Harrison graduated from the Johns Hopkins University in 1889 and took his Ph.D. there five years later. In 1894 he joined the faculty of Bryn Mawr College and after a year of study in Germany in 1895–1896 returned to Johns Hopkins to teach anatomy in the medical school.

He traveled to Germany again and in 1899 received an M.D. from the University of Bonn; after eight more years at Johns Hopkins he was appointed Bronson Professor of Comparative Anatomy and head of the new department of zoology at Yale. In that year, 1907, he perfected a method of culturing animal tissue in a liquid medium, thereby making it possible to study tissues in an environment free of the incalculable variables and mechanical difficulties of *in vivo* examinations. The method was itself a contribution of vast importance to biology and with it he made another, the discovery that embryonic nerve fibers develop outward toward the body's periphery from cells of the central nervous structures rather than differentiating from other cell types at predetermined sites. Harrison later turned his attention to the study of embryonic development. He was able to demonstrate that the three axes of developing limbs become fixed at different times and thus that proto-limb tissues are, if taken early enough, reversible; thus, tissue taken at the proper moment from a developing left limb could be transplanted upside down and made to develop into a right limb. From many such experiments he was eventually able to formulate general laws of asymmetry for all vertebrate forms. In addition to his research work he was an influential teacher and was largely responsible for the emergence into the first rank of the biological science departments at Yale. From 1927 he was Sterling Professor of Biology, and on his retirement from Yale in 1938 he became chairman of the National Research Council, a post he held through World War II until 1946. In it he was highly effective in organizing, in cooperation with the National Academy of Sciences, the war effort of the scientific establishment of the nation. He was also managing editor of the *Journal of Experimental Zoology* from 1903 to 1946. Harrison died in New Haven, Connecticut, on September 30, 1959.

Harrison, William Henry (1773–1841), ninth president of the United States. Born at Berkeley, his family's plantation in Charles City County, Virginia, on February 9, 1773, Harrison was the son of a wealthy and politically prominent father. He studied for three years at Hampden-Sydney College and then, in 1790, moved to Philadelphia, where he attended the College of Physicians and Surgeons and worked under Dr. Benjamin Rush. In 1791 he joined the army and was sent to the Northwest Territory; there, as aide-de-camp to Gen. Anthony Wayne, he campaigned against the Indians and fought in the decisive battle of Fallen Timbers in 1794. In 1798 he resigned his captaincy and was appointed secretary of the Northwest Territory; the following year he was sent by the Territory to the House of Representatives. In 1800 he was appointed governor of Indiana Territory, a position he held until 1812. He negotiated a number of land-cession treaties with the Indians, including the 1809 Treaty of Fort Wayne, by which the Delaware, the Miami, the Potawatomie, and several other tribes ceded more than 2½ million acres on the upper Wabash River. Following the conclusion of the treaty growing dissatisfaction among the tribes caused them to form a confederacy under the Shawnee chief Tecumseh and his brother the Prophet, with the aim of ending encroachment by whites. Harrison led a successful military campaign against an Indian encampment at the Tippecanoe River in November 1811. Although the battle was actually inconclusive, Harrison won an immediate military reputation. His plans for a further Indian campaign were interrupted by the outbreak of the War of 1812, and he became major general of Kentucky militia and later brigadier general in command of the regular army in the Northwest. Harrison's forces reoccupied Detroit in 1813, following Perry's victory on Lake Erie. Under his leadership the decisive victory over the British and Indians at the Thames River in Ontario, in which Tecumseh was killed, was won in October 1813, permanently securing the frontier of U.S. territory against the British. He resigned from the army in 1814 and in the same year oversaw the negotiations for a final peace treaty with the Indians. Settling at North Bend, Ohio, he served in the House again from 1816 to 1819, in the Ohio legislature from 1819 to 1821, and in the Senate from 1825 to 1828. For a little more than eight months in 1829 he was U.S. minister to Colombia and in that time provoked considerable controversy by his connection with revolutionaries in that country. For the next several years he remained largely out of the public eye; then in 1835, on the strength of his military record, his lack of political commitment, and his availability, he was chosen by dissident Whigs to head a presidential ticket against Martin Van Buren in the next year's election. Although he lost, plans were immediately laid for 1840; in that year he won the regular Whig nomination and John Tyler was named his running mate in a move to placate Southerners offended by the party's refusal to nominate the too-outspoken Henry Clay. He waged a remarkable campaign, employing campaign songs, the "log cabin and hard cider" symbols of his frontier days, and the slogan "Tippecanoe and Tyler Too!" and was overwhelmingly elected. Left in a state of exhaustion by the campaign and by the importunities of the hordes of office seekers who immediately appeared, he contracted pneumonia and died in Washington, D.C., on April 4, 1841, one month after his inauguration, the first president to die in office.

Hart, Albert Bushnell (1854–1943), historian and political scientist. Born on July 1, 1854, in Clarksville, Pennsylvania, Hart graduated from Harvard in 1880 and three years later, after advanced study in France and Germany, took his Ph.D. from the University of Freiburg. He then joined the Harvard faculty as an instructor, rising to full professor of history in 1897 and to Eaton Professor of the Science of Government in 1910. An indefatigable researcher and writer, he was the author, coauthor, or editor of more than 100 volumes during his career, nearly all of them on topics in American history and most in his special fields of government and foreign policy. Among his works were *Introduction to the Study of Federal Government,* 1891; *Formation of the Union, 1750–1829,* 1892; *Guide to the Study of American History,* 1896, with Edward Channing, revised with Frederick Jackson Turner in 1912; *Foundations of American Foreign Policy,* 1901; *Manual of American History, Diplomacy and Government,* 1908; *The Monroe Doctrine: An Interpretation,* 1917; and *We and Our History,* 1932. He edited, among other books, *American History Told by Contemporaries,* five volumes, 1897–1929; *Source Book of American History,* 1899; *American Patriots and Statesmen,* five volumes, 1916; and the 28 volumes of the American Nation series, 1904–1918, to which he contributed *Slavery and Abolition,* 1906, and *National Ideals Historically Traced,* 1907. Hart edited the *American Historical Review* from 1895 to 1909 and also wrote several distinguished biographies, notably *Salmon Portland Chase,* 1899, *Abraham Lincoln,* 1914, and *George Washington,* 1927. An expert on the subject of George Washington, he served during 1926–1932 as historian of the U.S. Commission for the Celebration of the 200th Anniversary of the Birth of George Washington. He was president of the American Historical Association in 1909 and of the American Political Science Association in 1912; active also in numerous committees on governmental reform, he was a prominent Republican and Progressive and was a close friend, admirer, and adviser of Theodore Roosevelt. Following his retirement from Harvard in 1926 he continued to work and write with undiminished energy. Hart died in Boston on June 16, 1943.

Hart, Moss (1904–1961), playwright and director. Born on October 24, 1904, in New York City, Hart left school at fifteen and after two years in various minor jobs took a position as an office boy for a theatrical producer. At eighteen he was moved to write and submit anonymously to his employer a play entitled *The Hold-up Man;* produced in Chicago, it betrayed the inexperience of its author and was a resounding failure. For several years thereafter Hart worked with little-theater groups and as entertainment director for a number of the Catskill Mountain resorts of the "borscht circuit." After writing a few plays that were neither published nor produced, he wrote in 1929 the first draft of *Once in a Lifetime,* a satire on Hollywood. Conditionally accepted for Broadway and then revised in collaboration with George S. Kaufman, the play opened in 1930 and enjoyed a run of two years, appearing in 1932 in a film version. Hart wrote the books for several musicals, including *Face the Music,* 1932, and *As Thousands Cheer,* 1933, both with Irving Berlin, and *Jubilee,* 1935, with Cole Porter, but his greatest successes were written with Kaufman: *Merrily We Roll Along* 1934; *You Can't Take It with You,* 1936, which won a Pulitzer Prize and was later a popular movie; *I'd Rather Be Right*, 1937, a spoof on President Franklin D. Roosevelt, with music and lyrics by Richard Rodgers and Lorenz Hart and starring George M. Cohan; *The Man Who Came to Dinner*, 1939, inspired by and, for a time, starring Alexander Woollcott; and *George Washington Slept Here*, 1940. Hart also wrote, among others, *Lady in the Dark*, 1941, with music by Kurt Weill and lyrics by Ira Gershwin; *Winged Victory*, 1943; *Christopher Blake*, 1946, a serious drama; and *Light Up the Sky*, 1948. Among the movie scripts he wrote were those for *Flesh*, 1932; *Broadway Melody of 1936*, 1935; *Gentlemen's Agreement*, 1947, which won an Academy Award; *Hans Christian Andersen*, 1952; and *A Star Is Born*, 1954. He enjoyed also a distinguished career as director of several of his own plays and such others as *Dear Ruth*, 1944; *Miss Liberty*, 1949; *Anniversary Waltz*, 1954; *My Fair Lady*, 1956, for which he won a Tony Award; and *Camelot*, 1960. His autobiographical account of his early years in the theater, *Act One*, appeared in 1959. Hart died in Palm Springs, California, on December 20, 1961.

Hart, William Surrey (1870–1946), actor. Born in Newburgh, New York, on December 6, 1870, William S. Hart grew up in the Midwest, principally in South Dakota, where he came into contact with Indians and cowboys and observed the last vestiges of the Old West. At nineteen he went on the stage in New York City and after ten years of moderate success attracted considerable attention in an 1899 production of *Ben Hur*. Subsequent stage roles in *The Squaw Man*, *Dead or Alive*, *The Virginian*, and *Trail of the Lonesome Pine* established him as a popular actor and as one particularly adept at portraying Westerners. In 1914 he went to Hollywood to appear in a short Western film, *The Bargain*; the two-reeler was a surprising success and several more followed, bearing such titles as *On the Night Stage*, *His Hour of Manhood*, and *The Passing of Two-Gun Hicks*. Hart quickly became the leading cowboy star of the day, eclipsing earlier heroes with his stern, forceful portrayals of taciturn gunmen who, seeming to be seeking redemption for former evil ways, displayed impersonal, detached nobility in the face of great dangers, stark Western landscapes, and the blandishments of sundry feminine characters. Moving from Mutual Film Studios to Triangle Films to Artcraft to Famous Players–Lasky (later Paramount), he gradually took over the direction and nearly complete control of the production of his films in order to assure the greatest possible realism and authenticity, a goal to which he was thoroughly dedicated and which accounted both for his early great success and for his later decline in the face of younger, more romantic stars. Other notable films of Hart's were *Mr. Silent Haskins*, *Darkening Trail*, *The Dawnmaker*, *The Disciple*, *Hell's Hinges*, *The Aryan*, *Truthful Tulliver*, *The Gunfighter*, *The Square Deal Man*, *The Last Card*, *Silent Man*, *Blue Blazes*

Rawden, *Breed of Men*, *Wagon Tracks*, *Sand*, *Desert Dust*, *Travelin' On*, and *Wild Bill Hickok*; after *Tumbleweeds* in 1925 he retired from the movies, no longer able to command the autonomy he required. Hart later wrote an autobiography, *My Life East and West*, 1929, and several Western books, including *Hoofbeats*, 1933; *The Law on Horseback*, 1935; and *All Points West*, 1940. His last years were spent on his Horseshoe Ranch near Newhall, California; he died there on June 23, 1946.

Harte, Bret (1836–1902), author. Born in Albany, New York, on August 25, 1836, Francis Bret Harte, familiarly known as Frank, spent an unsettled childhood, moving often until alighting in New York City following his father's death in 1845. At thirteen he ended his irregular schooling and went to work and in 1854 traveled to California. For the next several years his situation was precarious; he taught for a while, worked for Wells Fargo, and made a short visit to a mining district. For two years he worked on the *Northern Californian* in Union (now Arcata) until his editorial denunciation of the massacre of some 60 peaceful Indians forced him to leave town in 1860. During those years he wrote constantly, both poetry and prose sketches; some of his writings were published but few showed much promise. Moving to San Francisco, he took a printer's job on the *Golden Era* and published a number of pieces in that newspaper during the next several years. In 1864 he began to contribute to the newly established *Californian* and occasionally served as its editor. Four years later he became the first editor of the *Overland Monthly* and, assigned to produce some sketches of local life, soon published under his pen name, Bret Harte, "The Luck of Roaring Camp" and, six months later, "The Outcasts of Poker Flat." The stories were a sensation in the East; after the further success of his comic poem *Plain Language from Truthful James* (commonly known as *The Heathen Chinee*) and his collection *The Luck of Roaring Camp and Other Sketches*, 1870, he left California for Boston in 1871. He was accepted in the highest literary circles and was offered an extremely lucrative contract for contributions by the *Atlantic Monthly*; however, he fulfilled the contract only with difficulty and it was not renewed. Within a short time his success had come virtually to an end. Through his use of scenes and dialect from the exotic California mining regions, his colorful characters, and his attention to detail, he had produced novelties that were technically skillful but superficial, and as his limited stock of experience became exhausted, his work became repetitive. Harte's example and many of his techniques provided impetus for the growth of what came to be known as the local-color school; it was left to such authors as Mark Twain—one of Harte's circle in San Francisco—to realize the potential for literature in the movement. After *Tales of the Argonauts* in 1875 little inspiration was left; in financial difficulty, he accepted a consulship in Germany in 1878 and in Glasgow, Scotland, two years later. His popularity in England had not waned and at the end of his appointment in 1885 he moved to London, where he remained for the rest of his life. There he continued to write, reworking his worn material, until his death in London on May 5, 1902.

Hartline, Haldan Keffer (1903–1983), biophysicist. Born on December 22, 1903, in Bloomsburg, Pennsylvania, Hartline graduated from Lafayette College in 1923 and four years later took an M.D. degree from The Johns Hopkins University Medical School. He remained at Hopkins as a research fellow until 1929 and in 1931 moved to the University of Pennsylvania, becoming assistant professor of biophysics in 1936 and, after spending a year at Cornell University as associate professor of physiology, returning to Pennsylvania in 1941. He advanced to associate professor of biophysics in 1943 and to full professor in 1948. In 1949 he was appointed professor and chairman of the department of biophysics at Johns Hopkins, where he remained until 1953; in that year he became professor of biophysics at the Rockefeller Institute (now Rockefeller University) in New York City. From the early 1930s Hartline's researches centered on the neurophysiology of vision. Working primarily with the horseshoe crab and the frog, he was able to isolate single nerve fibers in the optic nerve and to record the patterns of their electrical responses to light. He found in various experiments that the frequency of electrical nerve impulses varies directly with the intensity of the light stimulus and that different receptor cells respond to a stimulus in different ways, some generating bursts of impulses only at the onset of stimulation, some only at its cessation, and some at both times with occasional impulses in between. Most importantly, he discovered that photoreceptivity is not a passive response but a dynamic balance of excitatory and inhibitory mechanisms organized in small areas of the retina, and that the phenomenon of lateral inhibition, in which the response of a receptor cell is inhibited by the stimulation of those surrounding it, apparently increases visual acuity by magnifying light-and-dark contrasts. For his work Hartline was awarded the 1967 Nobel Prize for Physiology or Medicine jointly with George Wald and with R. A. Granit of Sweden. He died on March 17, 1983, in Fallston, Maryland.

Harvard, John (1607–1638), philanthropist. Born in London in November 1607, Harvard came of a well-to-do family. He graduated from Emmanuel College, in 1632 and three years later was awarded a master's degree. Very little is known of the circumstances of his life beyond the fact that by 1635 he had inherited a considerable estate; it is possible that he entered the clergy. In 1637 he sailed to America and settled in Charlestown in the Massachusetts Bay colony. There he was quickly accepted as a leading member of the community, becoming a teaching elder in the church. He died on September 14, 1638, "of a consumption," and in his will left half of his estate—an amount estimated variously at from £400 to £800—and his extensive library of some 400 volumes of classics and theology to the college that had been given a grant by the General Court in 1636. Classes had begun in the summer of 1638 in New Towne and the institution rested on a rather precarious financial basis until Harvard's great bequest more than doubled its resources. The name of New Towne was changed in 1638 to Cambridge in honor of the alma mater of many of the Massachusetts clergy, and in March 1639 the General Court voted to call the first college in America Harvard.

Harvey, Coin, *see* Harvey, William Hope

Harvey, Frederick Henry (1835–1901), restaurateur. Born in London in 1835, Harvey emigrated to the United States about 1850 and found a job working in a New York City restaurant. Within a few years he was able to open his own restaurant in St. Louis, but the outbreak of the Civil War in 1861 brought an end to the business and for several years thereafter he worked in various capacities for railroad lines. While working as a freight agent for the Chicago, Burlington & Quincy Railroad, he was struck by the exceedingly poor eating and refreshment facilities available to passengers, and it occurred to him that a clean, well-run restaurant close to a major station—perhaps in it—would be both a boon to passengers and a lucrative business. He approached the Burlington management with the idea and was rebuffed with the joking suggestion that he try the struggling new Atchison, Topeka, & Santa Fe. The Santa Fe bought the idea and in 1876 the first Fred Harvey restaurant opened in the depot in Topeka, Kansas. The response of passengers was spectacular, for Harvey was careful to provide excellent food, courteous service, and a handsome setting for his patrons. He was soon able to open several more restaurants along the Santa Fe line and at several other major depots and junctions. He also began operating clean, efficient hotels in conjunction with his restaurants, and the Harvey House accomodations quickly became famous throughout the Southwest. The restaurants all held to the first Harvey standards: fine food, set off by Irish linen and Sheffield silverware, and served by the attractive, polite, and well-trained "Harvey Girls," whom he hired and sent West by the hundreds; later Will Rogers was to observe that Harvey "kept the West in food and wives." The restaurants continued to multiply as the Santa Fe extended its routes west to Los Angeles and east to Chicago, and with the coming of the great through trains in 1890, Harvey began operating a fleet of dining cars in his accustomed lavish and gracious style. By the time of his death on February 9, 1901, in Leavenworth, Kansas, the list of Harvey enterprises included 47 restaurants, 30 dining cars, and 15 hotels.

Harvey, William Hope (1851–1936), "Coin," monetary reformer. Born on August 16, 1851, in Buffalo, Virginia (now West Virginia), Harvey attended local schools and, briefly, Marshall College. He studied law privately and was admitted to the bar in 1870, practicing in Barboursville, West Virginia, until 1874, when he moved to Huntington. After subsequent moves to Cleveland in 1876, to Chicago in 1879, and to Gallipolis, Ohio, in 1881, he abandoned the law to manage his large interests in Western real estate and mining properties and was for a time superintendent of a large silver mine in Colorado. With the panic of 1893, brought on in large part by the heavy outflow of gold from the Treasury to European investors, Harvey returned to Chicago and, through the Coin Publishing Company, began agitating for the free and unlimited coinage of silver to inflate the currency. He published the weekly *Coin* and Coin's Financial Series, booklets on the monetary crisis and his solution to it. The third in the series, *Coin's Financial School*, 1894, was cast in the form of a symposium of leading bankers, financiers, public officials, and others, led by one "Coin," a silver advocate who, in the course of the book, brought the great men around to his point of view. The use of actual names lent credence to the book and many among the more than a million people who read it and accepted its rather glib reasoning believed also that the discussions in the booklet had actually taken place. Newspaper debates and subsequent pamphlets such as *A Tale of Two Nations*, 1894, and *Coin's Financial School Up to Date*, 1895, kept Coin Harvey in the forefront of the fight for silver coinage and prepared the way for the presidential campaign of William Jennings Bryan in 1896. After the failure of the silver cause in that year Harvey broadened his attack on the structure and institutions of finance in such pamphlets as *Coin on Money, Trusts, and Imperialism*, 1899. In 1900 he retired to an estate in Monte Ne, near Fayetteville, Arkansas, and, while investing in local resort property and contributing to public improvements, continued to publicize his ideas, publishing *The Remedy*, 1915; *Common Sense, or the Clot on the Brain of the Body Politic*, 1920, *The Book*, 1930, and many other works. In 1932 he was the presidential candidate of the Prosperity party and of a wing of the Liberty party. He died in Monte Ne on February 11, 1936.

Hassam, Childe (1859–1935), painter. Born in Dorchester (now part of Boston) on October 17, 1859, Frederick Childe Hassam, who was known throughout life as Childe, began developing his talent for drawing while in school and later, employed as a wood engraver and illustrator, studied at the Boston Art Club. Following a brief trip to Europe in 1883 he returned to Paris in 1885 for nearly four years of further study, during which he exhibited successfully at the Salon of 1887 and at the Paris Exposition in 1889. On his return to the United States in 1889 he established himself in New York City and was soon prominent in artistic circles as the leading American exponent of Impressionism. The foremost member of the group of Impressionists known as the Ten American Painters, Hassam outshone his peers, combining a brilliant palette with vigorous brushwork to produce vibrantly colorful studies of New York street scenes often made gay by flags, New England seascapes, and rural landscapes. He was elected to the National Academy of Design in 1906 and in 1913 he exhibited his work at the great Armory Show in New York City. The recipient of numerous medals and awards, Hassam died at his home in East Hampton, Long Island, New York, on August 27, 1935. A member of both the National Institute and the American Academy of Arts and Letters, Hassam in his will bequeathed all of his paintings still in his possession to the Academy, with the direction that the income from their sale, if such there was, be used to establish a fund for the encouragement of American art. In fact, the income was great enough so that the Academy was able largely to subsist on it.

Hasseltine, Ann, see under Judson, Adoniram

Hassler, Ferdinand Rudolph (1770–1843), geodesist. Born in Aarau, Switzerland, on October 7, 1770, Hassler was educated at the University of Bern and occupied himself in geodetic field work and surveying until 1805, when he emigrated to the United States. The failure of a land company in which he had invested left him stranded in Philadelphia for a time, but in 1807 he was appointed acting professor of mathematics at West Point. In that year his plan of organization for a comprehensive survey of the coastline of the United States was adopted as the most likely to fulfill the purposes of Congress, which had authorized such a survey. The turbulent political situation at the time, verging on war now with France and now with Great Britain, prevented the start of actual field work, however. In 1811 he was commissioned to travel to England to secure instruments for the still-pending survey. Soon after his arrival there the War of 1812 began and Hassler was unable to return to the United States until 1815. The next year the U.S. Coast Survey, established in 1807, was formally organized with Hassler as superintendent. After two years of work establishing base lines and a preliminary network of triangulation around New York Bay from Long Island to New Jersey, the work of the Survey was transferred to the navy; Hassler spent the next 12 years in survey work on the northeastern border and in teaching and farming in New York state. In 1830 he was appointed superintendent of weights and measures by President Andrew Jackson and two years later, with the reactivation of the Coast Survey under the auspices of the Treasury, he was again put in charge. The work of the Survey occupied him for the rest of his life; operations were extended as far south as Florida, and early in 1843 he developed a master plan for a regional organization of further work. He died later that year, on November 20, 1843, in Philadelphia, and was succeeded by Alexander D. Bache, who carried on the work of the Survey along the lines laid down by Hassler.

Hastie, William Henry (1904–1976), public official and judge. Born on November 17, 1904, in Knoxville, Tennessee, Hastie graduated from Amherst College in 1925 and after two years of teaching school in Bordentown, New Jersey, entered Harvard Law School, taking his degree in 1930. After a brief period on the faculty of Howard University he began private practice in the District of Columbia in 1931. From 1933 to 1937 he held a position in the Department of the Interior and in 1937 was appointed judge of the District Court of the Virgin Islands. In 1939 he returned to Howard as dean of the law school, and during seven years in that post also served, in 1940–1943, as a consultant to the secretary of war on matters of race relations and racial policy in the armed services. He resigned from his consultant's position in 1943 in protest over his continuing discrimination against black servicemen and later in that year was awarded the Spingarn Medal by the National Association for the Advancement of Colored People (NAACP). In 1946 he was appointed the first black governor of the largely black territory of the Virgin Islands by President Harry S. Truman. In 1949 Hastie was named judge of the U.S. Third Circuit Court of Appeals in Philadelphia, again becoming the first black to hold such a post. He was later promoted to chief judge of the court. Hastie retired from the bench in 1971. He died in East Norriton, Pennsylvania, on April 14, 1976.

Hatch, William Henry (1833–1896), public official. Born on September 11, 1833, near Georgetown, Kentucky, Hatch attended school in Lexington and studied law in Richmond, winning admission to the bar in 1854. He began practice in Hannibal, Missouri, and soon became active in Democratic politics, serving two terms, 1858–1862, as district circuit attorney. From 1862 to 1865 he held a commission in the Confederate army; on returning to Hannibal and his law practice at the end of the war he resumed also his political connections, but was barred from active participation in public affairs until the Democratic resurgence in Missouri in 1871. Defeated for the gubernatorial nomination in 1872, he was elected in 1878 to the House of Representatives, where he remained, through seven subsequent reelections, until 1894. He was closely associated in the Democratic leadership of the House with John G. Carlisle and Charles F. Crisp and served for several sessions as chairman of the Committee on Agriculture. Most of his legislative efforts were directed to the betterment of agriculture, and he numbered among his achievements the creation of the Bureau of Animal Industry in 1884, a meat-inspection act in 1890, and the Hatch Act of 1887, which provided for federal support for agricultural research. Such research was already being carried on by agricultural experiment stations supported by 15 states and by numerous other establishments under college, university, and private auspices; the Hatch Act secured direct federal funding for those stations and encouraged the creation of stations in states where they were lacking, laying a firm foundation for agricultural research that proved over the years to be of great value. Hatch was also active in winning the elevation of the Department of Agriculture to cabinet status in 1889. In his last years in Congress he supported a number of Populist causes. Defeated for reelection in 1894, he retired to his farm in Hannibal, Missouri, and died there on December 23, 1896.

Hathorne, Nathaniel, *see* Hawthorne, Nathaniel

Hawkins, Benjamin (1754–1816), public official and Indian agent. Born in Warren County, North Carolina, on August 15, 1754, Hawkins attended the College of New Jersey (now Princeton), leaving in his last year to join Gen. George Washington's personal staff as an interpreter of French. He returned to North Carolina in 1779 and served in the Congress of the Confederation in 1781–1784 and 1786–1787. In 1789 he was elected one of the state's first two senators. He had already had experience in negotiating with Indians—he had been largely responsible for a treaty with the Cherokee in 1785 and later for treaties with other Southern tribes—when, on his being defeated for reelection to the Senate in 1795, he was named a commissioner to negotiate land cessions and permanent boundaries with the Creek Confederacy by President Washington. On his successful conclusion of the Treaty of Coleraine in 1796 Hawkins was appointed U.S. agent to the Creek and general superintendent for all the Southern tribes. He left his prosperous plantation in North Carolina to establish his agency in Macon, Georgia, later moving it west to the "Old Agency" on the Flint River in Crawford County; there he built a model farm to teach and encourage the Creek in the practice of agriculture. He had enjoyed the respect and confidence of the Creek since his earliest dealings with them, and for 16 years peace reigned in the territory of what were becoming known as the Five Civilized Tribes. However, the gradual encroachment of illegal white settlement on Indian lands, combined with the work of British agitators and the growing idea of Indian solidarity that was brought to the Creek by Tecumseh in 1812, finally resulted in the outbreak of the Creek War. Numbers of Creek joined Tecumseh and began raiding white settlements, while others tried vainly to stop the marauders by enlisting in a regiment organized by Hawkins. Andrew Jackson and his Tennessee volunteers settled the matter by crushing the entire Creek nation at the battle of Horseshoe Bend (Tohopeka) in 1814 and forcing them to cede much of their land to the U.S. Hawkins, his life's work with the peaceful Creek destroyed, died at his Crawford County, Georgia, agency soon afterward, on June 6, 1816.

Hawks, Howard Winchester (1896–1977), motion-picture director. Born on May 30, 1896, in Goshen, Indiana, Hawks was educated at Phillips Exeter Academy and at Cornell University. He had already enjoyed a certain renown as a champion junior-division tennis player and a professional race driver when in 1922 he joined the Famous Players–Lasky motion-picture company as a prop man. He graduated quickly to script writing and in 1926 directed his first film, *The Road to Glory*. His career as a director thereafter encompassed all the major genres of film, from Westerns to war movies and from screwball comedies to science fiction, and he displayed a remarkable talent for infusing his films with his own personal style. The consistent strength of his direction, together with his mastery of action scenes and understated dialogue and his ability to work equally well with actors as diverse as John Wayne and Cary Grant, made him one of the most successful directors in Hollywood and one of the heroes of the French "auteur" school of film criticism. Among his many notable movies were *A Girl in Every Port*, 1928; *The Dawn Patrol*, 1930; *Scarface*, 1932; *Twentieth Century*, 1934; *Barbary Coast*, 1935; *Ceiling Zero*, 1936; *Bringing Up Baby*, 1938; *Only Angels Have Wings*, 1939; *His Girl Friday*, 1940; *Sergeant York*, 1941; *To Have and Have Not*, 1944; *The Big Sleep*, 1946; *Red River*, 1948; *I Was a Male War Bride*, 1949; *The Big Sky*, 1952; *Gentlemen Prefer Blondes*, 1953; *Rio Bravo*, 1959; *Hatari*, 1962; *Red Line 7000*, 1965; *El Dorado*, 1967; and *Rio Lobo*, 1971. He died in Palm Springs, California, on December 26, 1977.

Hawthorne, Nathaniel (1804–1864), author. Born in Salem, Massachusetts on July 4, 1804, Hawthorne (whose name was spelled Hathorne until he changed it while in college) came from a long Puritan line that included one of the judges in the Salem witchcraft trials. When he was four years old his father died and his mother became a virtual recluse; thus he early formed the habits of solitude and self-sufficiency that he retained throughout life. In 1825, after he graduated from Bowdoin College, where he was a classmate of Henry Wadsworth Longfellow and a close friend of Franklin Pierce, he returned to Salem and devoted himself to writing. He burned a good deal of his work, but numerous sketches and stories appeared in various periodicals. Apart from the forgettable *Fanshawe*, published anonymously in 1828 and later regretted by its author, his first volume was a collection of stories under the title *Twice-Told Tales*, published in 1837. Hawthorne's finances were perennially precarious and he did considerable literary hackwork, including the job of compiling *Peter Parley's Universal History*, 1837, for Samuel G. Goodrich. In addition, in 1839–1840 he held a political patronage job in the Boston customhouse and when the Whig victory of 1840 deprived him of the security of that posi-

tion, he joined the Brook Farm association in West Roxbury, Massachusetts, for a brief time. In 1842 he moved with his new wife, Sophia Peabody, sister of Elizabeth Peabody, to Concord and became a somewhat reserved member of the famous circle of notables there, which included Ralph Waldo Emerson, Henry David Thoreau, and Bronson Alcott. Also in 1842 appeared the second series of *Twice-Told Tales;* four years later the results of his happy life in Concord were contained in another collection, *Mosses from an Old Manse*. In 1846, having returned to Salem, he received another customhouse appointment and remained in the position for three years. Shortly afterward, in 1850, he published *The Scarlet Letter*. He then moved to Lenox, Massachusetts, became a close friend of Herman Melville, and in the next two years produced *The House of the Seven Gables* and *The Blithedale Romance*. He also produced two delightful children's books in that period: *A Wonder-Book for Girls and Boys*, 1852, and *Tanglewood Tales for Girls and Boys*, 1853. In 1852 he returned to Concord, and the following year, after having written a campaign biography for President Franklin Pierce, he was appointed to the U.S. consulate in Liverpool. Four years in that post were followed by two in Italy and another in England; early in 1860 appeared *The Marble Faun*, and later in 1860 Hawthorne returned again, and finally, to Concord. His last major work, *Our Old Home*, based on his experiences in England, was published in 1863. On May 19, 1864, he died in Plymouth, New Hampshire, after a long illness. He left a legacy of writings that are among the best of American literature. His dark and brooding preoccupation with evil was always in sharp contrast with the prevailing optimism of the Concord circle, just as he himself always stood somewhat apart; in coming to terms with his Puritan heritage while surrounded by the Transcendentalists' rebellion, he achieved a breadth of view and a depth of analysis that far surpassed that of his Concord contemporaries. In expressing these emotional and intellectual tensions in clear and precise prose and, most importantly, in dealing with them in richly symbolic terms, he created works of art at once American and universal. His masterwork, *The Scarlet Letter*, must stand as one of the few great American novels. He was elected to the Hall of Fame in 1900.

Hay, John Milton (1838–1905), diplomat and author. Born in Salem, Indiana, on October 8, 1838, John Hay graduated from Brown University in 1858 and, after studying law in Springfield, Illinois, in an office next door to that of Abraham Lincoln, was admitted to the bar in 1861. Immediately afterward he accompanied President-elect Lincoln to Washington as assistant private secretary and served him until his assassination. In March 1865 Hay was appointed secretary to the legation in Paris; he remained there until 1867 and from 1867 to 1870 was attached successively to the U.S. legations in Vienna and Madrid. In 1870 he returned to the United States and for the next five years was an editorial writer for the *New York Tribune*. He published a notable volume of poetry in 1871, *Pike County Ballads and Other Pieces*; later in the same year appeared *Castilian Days*, a record of travel and impressions in Spain. In 1875 he moved to Cleveland, where he remained until his appointment as assistant secretary of state in 1879; he stayed in Washington after resigning his office in 1881, continuing to write, associating on close terms with Henry Adams and Clarence King, and becoming a fixture of the city's social scene. In 1883 he published anonymously a novel, *The Bread-Winners*; in 1890, with John G. Nicolay as coauthor, he published the ten-volume *Abraham Lincoln: A History*, earlier serialized in the *Century* and long the standard Lincoln biography. In 1897 President William McKinley continued the tradition of choosing literary figures as ambassadors to Great Britain by appointing Hay. After successfully maintaining England's goodwill during the Spanish-American War, Hay was named secretary of state the following year. His first task in the post was to oversee the peace negotiations with Spain, in which he fully supported the decision to retain the Philippines. He was a determined although not an aggressive protector of U.S. interests throughout the world, his most notable contribution to foreign affairs being the Open-Door Policy in China, promulgated in 1899–1900. In two notes circulated among the European powers with interests in that country, the second coming at the height of the nationalistic Boxer rebellion, he proposed a policy of freedom of trade with China by Western nations and a cooperative effort to guarantee Chinese territorial and administrative integrity. The actual policy was not Hay's, but the skill with which it was made public was completely his and was primarily responsible for the general acceptance of the Open-Door principle. In 1901 he negotiated the Hay-Pauncefote Treaty with Great Britain, abrogating the 1850 Clayton-Bulwer Treaty and opening the way for the negotiations and other treaties leading to the eventual construction of the Panama Canal. By 1903 and the outbreak of the Colombian revolution, President Theodore Roosevelt had taken over direction of a great deal of U.S. foreign policy and Hay's role is unclear. In 1903, however, he won a diplomatic victory in the settlement of the Alaskan boundary dispute with Canada. He was increasingly beset by ill health and died on July 1, 1905, in Newburg, New Hampshire.

Hayakawa, Samuel Ichiye (1906–), semanticist and educator. Born on July 18, 1906, in Vancouver, British Columbia, Hayakawa graduated from the University of Manitoba in 1927 and took his M.A. from McGill University in 1928 and his Ph.D. from the University of Wisconsin in 1935. He remained at Wisconsin as an instructor in English in the university extension division until 1939, moving that year to Chicago to join the Armour Institute of Technology, which in 1940 became the Illinois Institute of Technology (IIT).

His studies in philology and linguistics led to an interest in the phenomenon of language itself and after a meeting with Alfred Korzybski he devoted himself to the new field of general semantics, publishing in 1941 *Language in Action*, a popular account of Korzybski's ideas. In 1943 he founded the magazine *ETC: Review of General Semantics*, of which he remained thereafter editor. After five years as associate professor of English he left IIT in 1947. Two years later he published a much-revised edition of *Language in Action* under the title *Language in Thought and Action*, which became a standard text for courses in general semantics. From 1950 to 1955 Hayakawa lectured at the University of Chicago and in the latter year was appointed professor of English at San Francisco State College. Subsequent books on aspects of general semantics included *Language, Meaning, and Maturity*, 1954, and *Our Language and Our World*, 1959, both collections of articles previously published in *ETC*, and *Symbol, Status, and Personality*, 1963. Hayakawa also contributed frequently to periodicals and was supervisor of the editorial board of Funk & Wagnalls Standard Dictionaries. He came to national prominence in 1968 when, in the midst of a student strike led by militant black students, he was named acting president of San Francisco State College, an appointment later made permanent. He took an inflexible stand against negotiation and the suspension or disruption of the college schedule and quickly called in police to clear the campus; his actions made him a controversial figure. He resigned the presidency in 1973 and served as a Republican in the Senate from 1979 to 1983.

Hayden, Ferdinand Vandeveer (1829–1887), geologist. Born on September 7, 1829, in Westfield, Massachusetts, Hayden graduated from Oberlin College in 1850 and three years later was awarded an M.D. from Albany Medical College. Under the influence of James Hall, the geologist and paleontologist, he deferred medical practice, however, and made a collecting trip to the South Dakota Badlands in 1853; his enthusiasm for geology and exploration dated from this trip, and during the next six years he made numerous expeditions into the West and Northwest, often under army auspices. He joined the army as a surgeon when the Civil War broke out and by June 1865 had reached the temporary rank of lieutenant colonel. In 1865 he was appointed professor of geology at the University of Pennsylvania, retaining the position until 1872. During this period he began in 1867 a 12-year series of explorations and scientific investigations of the Western territories, primarily in the Rocky Mountain region. His work was celebrated throughout the world and played an important part in laying the foundations for the U.S. Geological Survey, organized in 1879, and in bringing about the establishment in 1872 of Yellowstone National Park. He remained with the Geological Survey as a geologist until his retirement in 1886. He died in Philadelphia on December 22, 1887.

Hayes, Helen (1900–   ), actress. Born on October 10, 1900, in Washington, D.C., Helen Hayes Brown made her professional debut with a Washington, D.C., company, the Columbia Players, at the age of five as Prince Charles in *The Royal Family*. She went to New York City in 1909 and performed in *Old Dutch* and other plays, returning to Washington after two years to resume acting with the Columbia Players and to study at the Sacred Heart Convent, from which she graduated in 1917. That year she appeared again on Broadway in *Pollyanna*, beginning a long and distinguished career paralleled only by that of Ethel Barrymore. She was hailed for her performances in *Penrod*, 1918; in *Dear Brutus*, 1918; as Cleopatra in George Bernard Shaw's *Caesar and Cleopatra*, 1925; as Maggie Wylie in James M. Barrie's *What Every Woman Knows*, 1926; in *Coquette*, 1927; in *Mr. Gilhooley* and *Petticoat Influence*, 1930; in Maxwell Anderson's *Mary of Scotland*, written for her, 1933–1934; in Laurence Housman's *Victoria Regina*, generally regarded as her most brilliant role, 1935–1939; in *Ladies and Gentlemen*, 1937; as Viola in Shakespeare's *Twelfth Night*, 1940; in Anderson's *Candle in the Wind*, 1941–1942; as Harriet Beecher Stowe in *Harriet*, 1944; in Barrie's *Alice-Sit-by-the-Fire*, 1946; as Addie in Anita Loos's *Happy Birthday*, 1946–1947; as Amanda Wingfield in Tennessee Williams's *The Glass Menagerie* in London in 1948; again on Broadway in Joshua Logan's *The Wisteria Trees*, 1950; and as Mrs. Howard V. LaRue 2nd in Mary Chase's *Mrs. McThing* in 1952; and in Paris as Mrs. Antrobus in a revival of Thornton Wilder's *The Skin of Our Teeth* in 1955. Her movie career included warmly received roles in *The Sin of Madelon Claudet*, 1931, for which she won an Academy Award; *Arrowsmith* and *A Farewell to Arms*, both in 1932, *The White Sister, Another Language,* and *Night Flight*, 1933; *What Every Woman Knows*, 1934; *Vanessa—Her Love Story*, 1935; *My Son John*, 1952; and *Anastasia*, 1956. In radio she starred in 1935 in the "New Penny" series, in 1936 in the "Bambi" series, in 1940 and 1941 in the "Helen Hayes Theatre," in 1945 in "This Is Helen Hayes," in 1948–1949 in "Electric Theatre," and in 1956 in "Weekday." She also acted in television productions of *Dear Brutus* and other plays. In 1955, in recognition of her 50 years on the stage, New York's Fulton Theatre was renamed the Helen Hayes Theatre in her honor. Miss Hayes continued to be active in the theater and in repertory companies, and from time to time appeared on television and in motion pictures. She served on the National Arts Council from 1966 to 1970 and again from 1971. Her performance in *Airport*, 1970, won her an Academy Award for supporting actress. Her autobiography, *A Gift of Joy*, with L. Funke, appeared in 1965.

Hayes, Roland (1887–1977), singer. Born on June 3, 1887, in Curryville, near Rome, Georgia, Hayes was the son of former slaves. He grew up in great poverty on a tenant farm and later in Chat-tanooga, Tennessee, and received little schooling until, at twenty, he entered the preparatory department of Fisk University. Supporting himself with a variety of menial jobs, he developed a deep and intensely spiritual interest in music and occasionally made his way by singing. He did not attract any particular notice, however, until 1911, when he went to Boston with the Fisk Jubilee Singers for a concert. He remained in that city and under the tutelage of a succession of teachers trained his remarkable tenor voice and developed a repertoire of operatic arias, European folk and art songs, and the spirituals of his own Afro-American heritage. His career began in earnest in 1917; already thirty years old, he boldly hired Symphony Hall in Boston and gave a solo concert performance that was a great popular success. He traveled to London in 1921 and gave a series of concerts, including a command performance before George V. A European tour followed, during which he studied further with a number of European teachers, and in 1922 he returned to the United States a celebrity. Thereafter widely in demand, he continued to tour at home and abroad, appearing with many of the world's leading orchestras. As one of the first black Americans to win an international reputation on the serious concert stage—he was credited by many with paving the way for the later success of such black performers as Paul Robeson and Marian Anderson—he was awarded the 1925 Spingarn Medal by the National Association for the Advancement of Colored People (NAACP). Hayes retired from the stage in the 1950s, returning in 1962 for a formal farewell concert in Carnegie Hall. He died in Boston on January 1, 1977.

Hayes, Rutherford Birchard (1822–1893), nineteenth president of the United States. Born in Delaware, Ohio, on October 4, 1822, Hayes graduated from Kenyon College in 1842. He studied law privately and then at Harvard Law School and took his degree in 1845. For the next few years he practiced in Lower Sandusky (now Fremont), Ohio, but was not notably successful until he moved to Cincinnati in 1849. There he became socially prominent and involved himself in politics, first with the Whigs and later with the Republican party. In 1861 he was commissioned a major in an Ohio volunteer regiment; he served capably in a number of capacities through the Civil War, and by the time of his resignation in June 1865 was a major general of volunteers. In 1864 he had been nominated and, with no campaigning on his part, elected to the House of Representatives. He generally supported the Republican leadership in Congress, although he shied away from the extreme Radicals. He was reelected in 1866 but resigned the following year to run for governor of Ohio. He was successful in that campaign and was reelected in 1869; after four years of competent and mildly reformist administration he stood by precedent and declined renomination. Heavy Democratic gains in Ohio, together with his own presidential ambitions, induced him to stand again, however, in 1875, and he was duly elected after a campaign that attracted national attention. The next year he defeated James G. Blaine for the Republican presidential nomination and managed to unify the old guard and reformist wings of the party for the election. In that famous election the Democrat Samuel J. Tilden appeared at first to have won; Republicans, however, challenged the returns from four states—South Carolina, Louisiana, Florida, and Oregon—which had a total of 22 electoral votes. A 15-member Electoral Commission, five from each house of Congress and five from the Supreme Court was created by Congress, with the candidates' consent, to examine the contested votes and decide the dispute. The Republicans had an 8 to 7 majority on the commission and the contested electoral votes were awarded to Hayes by a one-vote margin, precisely along party lines. Meanwhile a bargain had been struck whereby the Southern Democrats agreed to accept the verdict in return for the withdrawal of all remaining federal troops from South Carolina and Louisiana. After a private ceremony on March 3, Hayes was publicly inaugurated on March 5, 1877, and the troop withdrawal was completed by May, ending Reconstruction and returning the South to white rule. The new president soon alienated much of his own party by insisting on merit-based appointments and thoroughgoing reforms in a number of government departments. In one such dispute he secured, against the opposition of Senator Roscoe Conkling of New York, the dismissal of Chester A. Arthur as collector of customs for the port of New York. He followed a sound fiscal policy under which specie payments were resumed and the coinage of silver begun only over his veto of the Bland-Allison Silver Act, 1878. Despite his sympathy for labor he took a firm stand in the railroad strike of 1877; he vetoed a bill to exclude Chinese immigrants because it violated a treaty; and during 1879 he defeated a sustained attempt by Congress to usurp presidential power by attaching to appropriations bills riders nullifying federal election laws. Hayes adhered to an earlier pledge not to seek reelection in 1880; he returned to Ohio and busied himself in various humanitarian and reform causes. He was active in promoting education, was from 1883 president of the National Prison Association, and, as he became increasingly disturbed by the concentration of wealth and power in a few hands, evinced some agreement with Socialist ideas. He died on January 17, 1893, in Fremont, Ohio.

Hayne, Robert Young (1791–1839), public official. Born in St. Paul's Parish, Colleton District (now County), South Carolina, on November 10, 1791, Hayne attended school in Charleston and studied law in the office of Langdon Cheves. He was admitted to the bar in 1812 and after brief service in the militia during the War of 1812 was elected to the state legislature in 1814, remaining there for four years. From 1818 to 1822 he was state attorney general and in 1822 was elected to the Senate. In that body he quickly attained prominence as an eloquent defender of states' rights and he showed himself to be an equally ardent and effective opponent of the protective tariff in the debates of 1824 and 1828 on that topic. Unopposed for reelection in 1828, he came to the peak of his renown two years later in a great debate with Daniel Webster. With an eye to forging closer ties between the South and the West, Hayne had seconded Thomas Hart Benton of Missouri in denouncing a Connecticut resolution for a restriction on the sale of public lands; Webster replied for the East, and for nearly two weeks the debate ranged over states' rights, the Constitution, nullification, and other related issues, calling forth some of the finest oratory ever delivered in the Senate, including Webster's famed "Liberty and Union, now and forever, one and inseparable!" speech. Hayne was aided in constructing his arguments by Vice-President John C. Calhoun, in whose favor Hayne resigned his seat in 1832 to become governor of South Carolina during the nullification crisis. While Calhoun defended South Carolina's course in the Senate, Hayne, who had been prominent in the South Carolina nullification convention, prepared the state for resistance to the tariff and to the Force Bill of President Andrew Jackson. After the compromise arranged by Henry Clay he remained governor until 1835 and was then mayor of Charleston until 1837. Hayne was president of the Louisville, Cincinnati & Charleston Railroad from its organization in 1836 and spent his last years attempting to create a railway link between Charleston and the Ohio Valley shipping route to the West; the reluctance of potential investors, capped by the depression that followed the panic of 1837, rendered his exhausting efforts useless. He died in Asheville, North Carolina, on September 24, 1839.

Hays, Arthur Garfield (1881–1954), lawyer. Born on December 12, 1881, in Rochester, New York, Hays was educated at the College of the City of New York (CCNY) and at Columbia, from which he graduated in 1902. He took his law degree from Columbia in 1905 and was admitted to the bar in the same year. He soon established a highly lucrative practice, representing many Wall Street and corporate institutions as well as public figures and wealthy individuals. During the early years of World War I he lived in London as a representative of U.S. shipping interests. At the same time, however, he took a passionate interest in the cause of civil liberties; from 1912 he was general counsel for the American Civil Liberties Union (ACLU), with which he remained associated for the rest of his life, later as national director. Hays took part in many of the most important and celebrated civil-liberties cases of his time: those arising from the coal miners' unionization struggles in Pennsylvania in the 1920s; the 1925 Scopes "Monkey Trial" in Tennessee and the 1926 Sweet case, involving racial discrimination in Detroit housing, in both cases being associated with Clarence Darrow; the defense of H. L. Mencken and the *American Mercury* against obscenity charges in Boston in 1926; the Sacco-Vanzetti case in 1927; the defense of the Communists accused of burning the Reichstag in Berlin in 1933; the trials of the "Scottsboro boys" in Alabama; and several cases arising from the coal miners' war of the 1930s in Harlan County, Kentucky. Hays was also active in politics, early as a supporter of Theodore Roosevelt and later as a founder of the Farmer-Labor party in 1919 and as a La Follette Progressive in 1924. He contributed to numerous liberal periodicals and published several books, including *Let Freedom Ring*, 1928; *Trial by Prejudice*, 1933; *Democracy Works*, 1939; and the autobiographical *City Lawyer*, 1942. Hays died in New York City on December 14, 1954.

Hays, John Coffee (1817–1883), "Jack," frontiersman and soldier. Born in Wilson County, Tennessee, on January 28, 1817, Hays became a surveyor in his youth and after several years in Mississippi moved to Texas, arriving in 1836 shortly after the battle of San Jacinto. After four years of scout service with the Texas army in the border regions he was appointed a captain of the Texas Rangers, which was then a somewhat irregular collection of partisan bands only occasionally supported by the Texas government. Jack Hays's detachment, more disciplined and notably more effective than most, traced its success to the respect commanded by its leader; his calm assurance, democratic leadership, and martial skills soon came to be the ideal of the Rangers and remained so throughout their subsequent history. Hays was reputedly the first to introduce Samuel Colt's new revolving pistol—the "six-shooter"—to the West and to prove its value in a number of engagements with Comanche marauders. His Rangers became a powerful light cavalry force, able to hold their own against superior numbers and admired by both the Indians and the Mexican border garrisons. He served in the army through the Mexican War, for the most part as colonel of a volunteer Texas cavalry regiment attached to the command of Gen. Zachary Taylor, and he proved an invaluable asset to Taylor as a scout, advance-force commander, guerrilla fighter, and utterly fearless leader in battle, winning particular distinction at Monterrey. Discharged in 1848, he made his way to California the next year and from 1850 to 1853 was sheriff of San Francisco County. After a term as state surveyor general he left public service and devoted himself to extensive business and real-estate interests. Hays died at his home near Piedmont, California, on April 28, 1883.

Haywood, William Dudley (1869–1928), "Big Bill," labor leader. Born in Salt Lake City on February 4, 1869, Haywood was christened William Richard, but later changed his middle name to that of his father. He got his first taste of mining at the age of nine. Several odd jobs followed in the next few years, along with a little rudimentary schooling, and at fifteen he was again working as a miner in Nevada. For a time he tried being a cowboy and a homesteader, but he soon returned to the mines. In 1896 he became a charter member of the Silver City, Idaho, local of the Western Federation of Miners (WFM); three years later he was a member of the national executive board and in 1900 was named secretary-treasurer of the WFM, with headquarters in Denver. Closely attuned to the mood of the rank-and-file membership and a highly aggressive advocate of industrial unionism, Haywood soon became the WFM's principal leader and spokesman, a position he retained through the violent period between 1900 and 1905, when the Western mining regions were torn by warfare between labor and mine owners. He presided over the founding of the Industrial Workers of the World (IWW) in Chicago in June 1905. Later that year Frank R. Steunenberg, the anti-union former governor of Idaho, was murdered, and a WFM member arrested for the crime implicated Haywood and others, all of whom were promptly jailed in Boise. Labor rallies around the country raised enough money to engage Clarence S. Darrow for the defense and, with William E. Borah leading the prosecution, the trial, which took place in 1907, received wide publicity The acquittal that followed the disclosure of perjury on the part of the accuser made Big Bill something of a popular hero. In that year the WFM withdrew from the IWW, objecting to the predilection of the "Wobblies" for violent direct-action tactics, and in 1908 Haywood was dismissed from WFM leadership. At the head of the IWW, however, he continued to organize, write, and speak in behalf of the idea of "one big union" encompassing all workers, and he continued to advocate the destruction of the class of idle capitalists. The IWW was strong among its original miner and lumberjack constituents and in spreading east, attempted the organization of other workers, including harvest workers and, in strike actions that attracted worldwide attention to Lawrence, Massachusetts, in 1912 and Paterson, New Jersey, in 1913, the largely immigrant labor in the textile industry. From 1901 to 1912 Haywood was a member of the Socialist party, although he was finally dismissed from inner party councils because of his advocacy of violence. In 1917 he was one of the large number of IWW leaders and members arrested for sedition—they denounced World War I as a capitalist attack on the worldwide working class—and the next year he was convicted and sentenced to 20 years in prison. While free on bond in 1921 he escaped to the Soviet Union, where he remained until his death on May 18, 1928. His autobiography, *Bill Haywood's Book*, appeared in 1929.

H. D., see Doolittle, Hilda

Hearn, Lafcadio (1850–1904), author, translator, and critic. Born on June 27, 1850, on Leukas (Santa Maura) in the Ionian Islands of Greece, Hearn was of British and Greek parentage and was given the names Patricio Lafcadio Tessima Carlos. From the age of six he was reared by a great-aunt in Dublin, who sent him to schools in England and France. In 1869 he came to the United States; after a time in New York City he moved to Cincinnati and barely supported himself with menial jobs until he met Henry Watkin, a printer who took him under his wing and taught him typesetting and proofreading. Hearn soon found a job on a newspaper; during the next several years he reported for a succession of Cincinnati newspapers, wrote feature articles that won considerable attention, and did translations from French literature. In 1877 he went to New Orleans, where for four years he led a marginal existence that was little mitigated by his salary on the *Item*. Finally, in 1881, he joined the *New Orleans Times-Democrat* and conducted a column of translations from French and Spanish that led to the publication of his first book, *One of Cleopatra's Nights*, 1882. It was followed by *Stray Leaves from Strange Literatures*, 1884; *Gombo Zhèbes*, 1885; *Some Chinese Ghosts*, 1887; and his first novel, *Chita*, 1889. During this period he contributed to the *Century* magazine, *Harper's Weekly*, and *Harper's Bazar*, writing articles on folklore, legend, and, after leaving New Orleans in 1887, on the West Indies. In 1890 he was commissioned by *Harper's New Monthly Magazine* to write articles on Japan, but soon after arriving in that country he broke with the magazine. He obtained a teaching position and the next year married a Japanese woman of a samurai family. In 1893 he began teaching at the government college in Kumamoto. He published *Glimpses of Unfamiliar Japan* in 1894, the first of a series of brilliant books that gave Western readers their first studied, sympathetic view of Japanese culture. In 1895 he became a Japanese citizen with the name Koizumi Yakumo and the following year went to teach at the Imperial University in Tokyo, remaining until 1903. In rapid succession he published, among other books, *Gleanings in Buddha-Fields*, 1897; *Exotics and Retrospectives*, 1898; *In Ghostly Japan*, 1899; *Shadowings*, 1900; and *A Japanese Miscellany*, 1901. In 1903 he was invited to lecture at Cornell University; the invitation was later withdrawn, but Hearn published his prepared lectures as *Japan: An Attempt at an Interpretation*, 1904, and the book became his best-known work. He died on September 26, 1904, in Okubo, now part of Tokyo, Japan.

Hearst, George (1820–1891), businessman and public official. Born near Sullivan, Missouri, on September 3, 1820, Hearst lived on the family farm until 1850, when he joined the tide of emigration to California. Several years of prospecting brought him little financial return but great expertise in the practical geology of mining, and in 1859 he began a rapid rise to wealth with a successful speculation in Nevada mining property. Over the next decades his holdings grew as, in partnership at various times with James B. A. Haggin, Lloyd Tevis, and Marcus Daly, he invested in such rich properties as the Ophir silver mine in the famed Comstock lode in Nevada, the Homestake gold mine in the Black Hills of South Dakota, and the Anaconda copper mine in Montana. His vast fortune, which he and his wife, Phoebe Apperson Hearst, dispensed liberally in philanthropy, brought him commensurate influence in San Francisco and in California generally, but, except for a term in the legislature in 1865–1866, he resisted the temptation to enter politics until 1882, when, with the backing of his *San Francisco Examiner* (acquired in payment of a debt in 1880), he sought the Democratic nomination for governor. He failed to obtain it and three years later, in a senatorial election, was defeated by Leland Stanford. Finally, in 1886, he was appointed to an unexpired term in the Senate. Elected to a full term in 1888, he served until his death in Washington, D.C., on February 28, 1891. William Randolph Hearst, the publisher, was his son.

Hearst, William Randolph (1863–1951), publisher. Born in San Francisco on April 29, 1863, Hearst was the son of George Hearst. He studied at Harvard, leaving in 1885 without a degree. Having become interested in journalism, in 1887 he persuaded his father to let him take over the *San Francisco Examiner*, which he was successful in making into a paying venture, and in 1895 he invaded the domain of Joseph Pulitzer by buying the foundering *New York Morning Journal*. Lowering the newspaper's price to a penny, he introduced a number of circulation-building features—colored comic strips, a color magazine section, sensational crime reporting, society gossip, and a jingoistic approach to foreign affairs—and soon attained record sales. Under his editorial control the *Journal* and the *New York Evening Journal*, introduced the next year, carried a strong anti-British bias and were generally Populist in outlook. Hearst supported the candidacy of William Jennings Bryan in 1896 and the following year published a spectacular and largely falsified series of articles and editorials that did much to arouse public clamor for the war with Spain that began in 1898. The competition between the *Journal* and Pulitzer's *New York World*, included staff raids—Hearst hired away Richard F. Outcault, among others—and the battle of headlines that gave rise to the term "yellow journalism." The struggle for circulation continued to produce journalistic excesses until Pulitzer reined in Arthur Brisbane, his editor and Hearst's equal in flamboyance. As he began to assemble a publishing empire by acquiring or establishing newspapers across the country, including the *Chicago American*, the *Chicago Examiner*, and the *Boston American*, his growing political ambition was rewarded by his election to the House of Representatives from a New York district in 1902; during two terms in Congress he generally supported liberal and progressive programs but won little attention. In 1904 he was considered for the Democratic presidential nomination; the following year he narrowly missed election as mayor of New York City, in 1906 he lost the governor's race, and in 1909 he was again defeated for mayor. He continued to add to his publishing holdings by purchasing several magazines, including *Cosmopolitan* and *Harper's Bazaar*. He also became interested in the young movie industry and in 1913 one of his companies produced *The Perils of Pauline*. His isolationism and dislike of England led him to oppose the entry of the United States into World War I; when peace came he campaigned vociferously against the League of Nations while demanding full repayment of war loans made to allied nations. In 1922 he tried again for political office by seeking the Democratic nomination for senator. He failed when the nominee for governor of New York, Alfred E. Smith, refused to run on the same ticket with Hearst; in an earlier series of articles and cartoons in the Hearst papers, Smith had been linked with the milk trust. In that year Hearst's holdings consisted of 20 major newspapers, 2 news services, a feature syndicate, and 5 leading magazines, the whole constituting a communications empire that he ruled with an iron hand. In 1927 he moved permanently to his 240,000-acre ranch at San Simeon, California, where he had built an enormous castle housing a fortune in works of art. Although untutored, he was long an avid collector. His huge miscellany of art and architectural treasures and curios filled several warehouses in addition to his home and included Etruscan tombs, Egyptian mummies, a Spanish monastery, entire rooms from other buildings disassembled and shipped to the United States at enormous cost, and large collections of paintings, furniture, silver, and armor. At the peak of his fortunes, in 1935, he had added to his holdings 8 more newspapers, 13 magazines, 8 radio stations, 2 movie companies, a castle in Wales, and extensive real estate in New York City, California, and Mexico. But within two years the Depression had made such inroads on his empire that reorganization was necessary. In 1937 most of his art collection was dispersed, much of it being sold in department stores during the next several years. By 1940 the Hearst enterprises were stabilized, but he had lost all but nominal control. World War II brought prosperity back to his publishing companies and other enterprises, but he himself was largely out of public notice. His last years were spent in virtual seclusion and he died on August 14, 1951, in Beverly Hills, California.

Heatter, Gabriel (1890–1972), journalist and radio commentator. Born in New York City in 1890, Heatter grew up in Brooklyn, New York; and attended school there. While in high school in 1905 he worked as a warm-up speaker in William Randolph Hearst's mayoral campaign. For several years thereafter he worked on the *Brooklyn Times* and other newspapers, including the *New York Evening Journal* and the *New York Herald*. He then worked as staff writer for *Forest and Stream* magazine, as a free-lance writer, and for a period as editor of a steel company's house organ. In 1932 he wrote an open letter to Socialist leader Norman Thomas that was published in the *Nation;* subsequently invited to discuss the letter, which was highly critical of Socialism, on a local radio station, WMCA, he was discovered to have a rich, mellifluous voice that carried great emotion and conviction over the air. As a result, Heatter was hired as a news broadcaster. He attained considerable national attention with his on-the-air coverage for the Mutual Broadcasting System of the 1935 trial of Bruno Richard Hauptmann, kidnapper of Charles A. Lindbergh's infant son, of Hauptmann's execution in 1936, when he was forced to cover a delay in the schedule by ad-libbing for more than 40 minutes. His handling of what in radio broadcasting constituted a crisis brought him powerful sponsorship and a regular nationwide news program. Heatter's delivery on the air, his deep, oratorical manner with broad ministerial flourishes, attracted a huge audience —at one time some 120 million listeners nightly —and earned him such nicknames as "the Crier" and "the Voice of Doom," although his manner was often in odd contrast to his unshakeably optimistic viewpoint. Until 1941 he also conducted a second program, "We, the People," featuring interviews with ordinary citizens from various places and disparate walks of life. His news broadcasts, later supplemented by his "A Brighter Tomorrow" commentaries, continued regularly on radio and then on television until 1965, and his daily opening words, "Ah—there's good news tonight," became a national catch phrase and provided the title for his autobiography, published in 1960. Heatter died in Miami Beach, Florida, on March 30, 1972.

Hecht, Ben (1894–1964), journalist and author. Born in New York City on February 28, 1894, Hecht grew up in Racine, Wisconsin. In 1910, on finishing high school, he went to Chicago and became a reporter for the *Chicago Journal*, moving four years later to the *Chicago Daily News*, for which he was a correspondent in Germany and Russia in 1918–1920. In Chicago he became closely associated with many of the figures of the city's flourishing literary movement, including Sherwood Anderson, Maxwell Bodenheim, and Margaret Anderson, and he began writing stories for such publications as the *Little Review* and *Smart Set*. In 1921 his first novel, *Erik Dorn*, was published and was well received by critics; he followed with *Gargoyles*, 1922; *Fantaszius Mallare*, 1922; *The Florentine Dagger*, 1923; *Humpty Dumpty*, 1924; *The Kingdom of Evil*, 1924; *Count Bruga*, 1926; and others. His *1001 Nights in Chicago*, a collection of his much-admired newspaper human-interest stories appeared in 1922. He founded the Chicago *Literary Times* in 1923 and continued to publish it for two years. In his early attempts at writing for the stage, Hecht was largely unsuccessful, but in 1928 he collaborated with Charles MacArthur, another Chicago newspaperman, to write the raucously comic play *The*

Front Page, which was a great hit on Broadway that year and in later film versions. The two succeeded again with *Twentieth Century* in 1933. Hecht continued to publish fiction, including *A Jew in Love,* 1930, and *A Champion from Far Away* and *Actors' Blood,* both collections of stories and both issued in 1932, earning recognition for his powerful, vital, and occasionally cynical style along with criticisms of his flirtations with obscenity. He also became a prolific producer of motion-picture scenarios and scripts, numbering among his credits *Underworld, Scarface, Viva Villa, Nothing Sacred, Design for Living, Notorious, Gunga Din,* and, with MacArthur, *Crime Without Passion, Wuthering Heights,* and *The Scoundrel,* the last of which won an Academy Award for best screenplay in 1935. During the 1940s Hecht became active in various efforts on behalf of Jewish refugees and later supported the struggle for the creation of an independent Israel; his books *Guide for the Bedeviled,* 1944, and *Perfidy,* 1961, and the play *A Flag Is Born,* 1946, were expositions of his thoughts on those subjects. Others of his books included *1001 Nights in New York,* 1941; *Collected Stories,* 1945; *The Sensualists,* 1959; *Child of the Century,* 1954, an autobiography; and *Gaily, Gaily,* 1963, and *Letters from Bohemia,* 1964, volumes of reminiscences. Hecht died in New York City on April 18, 1964.

Hecker, Isaac Thomas (1819–1888), religious leader. Born in New York City on December 18, 1819, Isaac Hecker was the son of German immigrant parents. He left school at eleven to work in the family bakery, but continued to study on his own and soon came under the influence of Orestes A. Brownson, who in 1843 prompted him to join the Transcendentalist community at Brook Farm. He found the six-month experience, and a subsequent brief stay at Bronson Alcott's Fruitlands colony, unsatisfactory to his rapidly developing but as yet inchoate religious bent. He returned home, but in 1844 he traveled to Concord, Massachusetts, where he boarded with Henry David Thoreau and his family and continued his studies in philosophy and theology. In that year, again with the assistance of Brownson, his way became clear to him and he was baptized in the Roman Catholic church. Entering the Redemptorist order and taking his middle name from St. Thomas Aquinas, he studied and completed his novitiate in Belgium and Holland, was ordained a priest in England in 1849, and in 1851 returned to New York City as a Redemptorist missionary. Gradually growing dissatisfied with the largely German hierarchy of the order, he developed with four fellow priests a plan for an English-speaking missionary order to minister to the rapidly Americanizing immigrant population. In 1857 he was chosen to travel to Rome to present the plan. On his arrival there he was expelled from the Redemptorist order for having made the journey without permission, but Pope Pius IX approved his plan and released him and his colleagues from their vows. In New York City in July 1858 the

new order of Missionary Priests of St. Paul the Apostle, or the Paulist Fathers, was formally organized with Hecker as superior; he remained in that office until his death. In addition to tireless work on behalf of his order, Hecker dedicated much of his time to the cause of a Catholic press; in 1865 he founded the *Catholic World,* the next year he formed the Catholic Publication Society, and in 1870 he began the *Young Catholic.* His own writings included *Questions of the Soul,* 1855, *Aspirations of Nature,* 1857, and *The Church and the Age,* 1887. He died in New York City on December 22, 1888. A few years later the publication in France of a biography of Hecker created a controversy over his asserted efforts to create a separate American Catholic church; the charge was dismissed and the discussion was ended in 1899 by the encyclical *Testem Benevolentiae* of Pope Leo XIII.

Heffelfinger, William Walter (1867–1954), "Pudge," football player. Born in Minneapolis on December 20, 1867, Heffelfinger developed in his youth a strong interest in the still novel game of football. That interest dictated his choice of college and in 1888 he entered Yale, where football was rapidly developing under the leadership of Walter C. Camp. He quickly became a regular member of the squad and from his position at guard led the Yale team through a season in which it scored a total of 698 points to none for its opponents. The largest man on the team, although he weighed less than 190 pounds, "Pudge" (as he was known to all but his teammates) had remarkable agility and crushing power. As a defensive player he was able to defeat the popular flying-wedge offense by the simple expedient of leaping up and into the oncoming rush and bringing it and the ball carrier down in a heap. He helped develop and then perfected the tactic of pulling out of the line of scrimmage to barrel around end and run interference for the backfield. He was named to Camp's first All-American team in 1889 and again in 1890 and 1891. His reputation as the greatest blocker of all time was reinforced in 1916, when, at the age of forty-eight, he returned to Yale at the request of coach Tad Jones to help prepare the football team for its upcoming season; suiting up with men 25 years and more his junior, he joined in the scrimmage and within minutes knocked out five varsity players, including two All-Americans. He continued to play football on occasion in All-Star and old-timers' games, his last at the age of sixty-five. Heffelfinger died on April 2, 1954, in Blessing, Matagorda County, Texas.

Hefner, Hugh Marston (1926–   ), editor and publisher. Born in Chicago on April 9, 1926, of strict Methodist parents, Hefner was forbidden to smoke, drink, or attend movies on Sundays as he grew up. He enrolled at the University of Illinois after two years of service in the army and graduated in three years, in 1949. He did one semester of postgraduate work in psychology at Northwestern University and worked as a personnel manager, a department-store advertising copywriter, and a subscriptions writer for *Esquire* magazine until 1952, when he resigned, having made plans for a new magazine. With about $10,000 in capital he put together the first issue of *Playboy* magazine, which appeared on the newsstands in December 1953, featuring a nude calendar photograph, later much celebrated, of Marilyn Monroe. Regular articles on dining, drinking, men's fashions, and personal problem-solving, in addition to a large photograph of the girl chosen as each month's "playmate," put forth the image of the modern "playboy," which Hefner himself sought to personify. The literary quality of the magazine—which published fiction as well as articles and interviews with notable figures in the arts, politics, and sports—was consistently high. He purchased in 1965 what had been the Palmolive Building, long a Chicago landmark, and not without attendant controversy renamed it the Playboy Building. It housed the editorial employees of the magazine and those of its subsidiary Playboy Clubs International, Inc., Playboy Products, and the Playboy Press. The Playboy Clubs, private key clubs luxuriously appointed and staffed by "bunny" hostesses and providing nightclub and resort facilities to their members, spread across the United States, to the Caribbean, and to Europe, where the magazine also achieved popularity. In 1968 the magazine ranked 12th in the nation, with a circulation of more than 5 million.

Heifetz, Jascha (1901–   ), violinist. Born on February 2, 1901, in Vilna, then part of Russia (now capital of the Lithuanian S.S.R.), Heifetz was the son of a violinist and was introduced to the instrument at the age of three. At four he had already demonstrated such natural talent that he was admitted to the Royal School of Music in Vilna. His first public appearance came in 1908 and in 1910 he began studies under Leopold Auer at the St. Petersburg Conservatory. His official debut was made in St. Petersburg on April 30, 1911. By 1914, when he made his first European tour, his mastery of technique was so absolute that he was able to devote his energy and thought to interpretation with great critical success. Overcoming the doubts concerning prodigies that were widespread in the music world, he was hailed as the greatest violinist of the day, a judgment that was confirmed in his triumphal American debut at Carnegie Hall in October 1917. Heifetz subsequently settled in the United States, becoming a citizen in 1925 and acquiring homes in Connecticut and California. He continued to tour widely and often, attracting capacity audiences around the world and becoming a much-sought-after recording artist. During World War II he gave concerts for servicemen in North Africa and the Mediterranean theater. In 1947, having spent an estimated 100,000 hours playing the violin, he began a sabbatical of a year and a half which he devoted to rest and a reassessment of his reper-

toire and technique; he returned to the public and won his accustomed acclaim in 1949. During the 1950s and 1960s he continued to appear in concert, although less often, made more recordings and several instructional films for educational television, and in 1960 began teaching master classes at the Institute for Special Musical Studies of the University of Southern California (USC). Despite increasingly infrequent performances he remained one of the acknowledged reigning masters of the violin.

Heinlein, Robert Anson (1907–   ), author. Born in Butler, Missouri, on July 7, 1907, Heinlein grew up there and in Kansas City, Missouri. He won appointment to the U.S. Naval Academy and following graduation in 1929 served as a line officer until receiving a discharge for a physical disability in 1934. He entered the University of California at Los Angeles (UCLA) to pursue graduate studies in mathematics and physics, but ill health forced him to withdraw after a short time. For four years he held various jobs and in 1939 he published his first magazine story, launching a writing career in science fiction that, except for service as a mechanical engineer at the Naval Air Material Center in Philadelphia during World War II, was thereafter uninterrupted. His first book, *Rocket Ship Galileo*, 1947, was the basis of his scenario for the 1950 movie *Destination Moon*. While producing a steady stream of stories for magazines, he published several more books— *Beyond This Horizon*, 1948; *Red Planet*, 1949; *Sixth Column*, 1949; *The Man Who Sold the Moon*, 1950; *Waldo; and Magic, Inc.*, 1950 (from which came the term "waldo," referring to the pantograph gauntlets used to handle radioactive materials); *The Green Hills of Earth*, 1951; *The Puppet Masters*, 1951; *Revolt in 2100*, 1953; *Starman Jones*, 1953; *Tunnel in the Sky*, 1955; *The Door into Summer*, 1956; and others, establishing himself as the foremost American science-fiction writer. His books drew heavily on his background in science and engineering and proceeded carefully from the known to the speculatively reasonable. Utilizing a vivid narrative style, a wide range of characters, and a coherent and generally optimistic view of man in the universe, Heinlein went far to raise the level of science fiction above that of the "bug-eyed monster" school. Other books were *The Menace from Earth*, 1959; *Starship Troopers*, 1959; *Stranger in a Strange Land*, 1961; *Farnham's Freehold*, 1964; *The Moon is a Harsh Mistress*, 1966; *I Will Fear No Evil*, 1970; and *Time Enough for Love*, 1974.

Heinz, Henry John (1844–1919), businessman. Born on October 11, 1844, in Pittsburgh, Heinz grew up there and in nearby Sharpsburg, where he attended a business college and then entered his father's brick-manufacturing business. While rising to a partnership in the firm and contributing much to its efficiency and growth he carried on a second business in fresh produce, which he raised on his own land and sold wholesale in

Pittsburgh. In 1869 he entered into a partnership to produce grated horseradish. That venture failed in 1875, but in 1876, with a brother and a cousin, he formed the F. & J. Heinz Company to make and market pickles and other such prepared food products; tomato ketchup was among his first, and was followed by other sauces, soups, condiments, and, of course, baked beans. The company grew rapidly. Reorganized in 1888 as the H. J. Heinz Company, it had already surpassed the figure Heinz publicized when, in 1896, he first used the famous "57 Varieties" slogan. In 1905 the firm was incorporated and Heinz served thereafter as its president. In addition to being an astute businessman he was also a conscientious employer and citizen; he pursued an enlightened policy with regard to his workers, was an industry leader in the movement for sanitary and healthful food preparations, lobbying effectively in support of the 1906 Pure Food and Drug Act, and devoted much time and money to Sunday-school work and to the Sarah Heinz settlement house in Pittsburgh, founded in 1894 and named for his wife. By the time of his death in Pittsburgh on May 14, 1919, his company had grown to include seed farms and several container factories in addition to more than a score of food-processing plants.

Held, John, Jr. (1889–1958), illustrator and author. Born on January 10, 1889, in Salt Lake City, Utah, Held began working as a cartoonist in 1907 and three years later moved to New York City, where, after serving in the navy during World War I, he became a fixture of the cosmopolitan circles of the 1920s. His contributions to the humorous weekly *Life* and to *Judge, College Humor*, and other such periodicals brought him fame as the leading graphic interpreter—and in part creator—of the Jazz Age. He supplied the illustrations for F. Scott Fitzgerald's *Tales of the Jazz Age*, 1922, and Anita Loos's *Gentlemen Prefer Blondes*, 1925, among other books of the times, and in his line drawings captured both the appearance and the spirit of "flaming youth"; his representations of "flappers" (a word he was sometimes credited with inventing) with their bobbed hair, beads, short skirts, rolled stockings, and cigarette holders, and young men with raccoon coats, hip flasks, and pennants, were at once pictures, ideals, and satires of the period. In woodcuts for the *New Yorker* and other sophisticated magazines he portrayed the more languid cosmopolitan scene. During the 1920s and early 1930s he also produced a comic strip, *Margie*, featuring a typical flapper and her contemporaries. Held wrote short stories as well and published several books: *Grim Youth*, 1930; *Women Are Necessary*, 1931; *The Saga of Frankie and Johnny*, 1931; *The Flesh Is Weak*, 1932; *A Bowl of Cherries*, 1933; *Crosstown*, 1934; *The Gods Were Promiscuous*, 1937; and *Held's Angels* 1952, with Frank B. Gilbreth, Jr. He was artist in residence at Harvard in 1940 and at the University of Georgia in 1941. During World War II he served with the Army Signal Corps. He died on March 2, 1958, in Belmar, New Jersey.

Hellman, Lillian (1905–   ), playwright. Born in New Orleans on June 20, 1905, Miss Hellman was educated at New York and Columbia universities. After a year working in a New York publishing house she began reviewing books for the *New York Herald Tribune* in 1925, and from 1927 to 1930 she was employed as a play reader. At the same time she began devoting more and more time to her own writing. Her first major success came with her play *The Children's Hour*, 1934, which enjoyed great popularity on the stage and in later film versions; after *Days to Come*, 1936, she again scored a hit with *The Little Foxes*, 1939, also later made into a movie. Subsequent plays, in which she continued to draw powerful and bitter pictures of intolerance and exploitation, included *Watch on the Rhine*, 1941, which won a New York Drama Critics' Circle Award and was also later adapted for the screen; *The Searching Wind*, 1944; *Another Part of the Forest*, 1946; *The Autumn Garden*, 1951; *Toys in the Attic*, which won her a second Critics' Circle Award, and others. From 1935 she wrote often for the movies, both original scenarios and adaptations of some of her own plays; among her film scripts were those for *The Dark Angel*, 1935; *Dead End*, 1937; *The Little Foxes*, 1940; *The North Star*, 1943; and *The Searching Wind*, 1945. Miss Hellman also adapted a number of works for the stage, including Jean Anouilh's *The Lark*, 1955; and *My Mother, My Father, and Me*, 1963, from Burt Blechman's novel *How Much?* She wrote the book for *Candide*, 1956, a musical based on Voltaire's story, with Richard Wilbur, who wrote the lyrics and Leonard Bernstein, who composed the score. In 1964 she was awarded the gold medal for drama by the National Institute of Arts and Letters and the American Academy of Arts and Letters. She also published several books: *An Unfinished Woman*, 1969; *Pentimento: A Book of Portraits*, 1973; and *Scoundrel Time*, 1976.

Helper, Hinton Rowan (1829–1909), author. Born in Davie County, North Carolina, on December 27, 1829, Helper graduated from a local academy and clerked in a store until, in 1850, he traveled to New York City and then by sea to California. In 1853 he returned to North Carolina and wrote *The Land of Gold*, published in 1855. Two years later he published *The Impending Crisis of the South: How to Meet It*, in which he attacked slavery as the cause of the South's economic weakness. Marshaling statistics to support his thesis, he demonstrated that the free labor of slaves was responsible for the depressed condition of non-slaveholding whites and of the South generally; he waxed vehement in his denunciation of slavery and soon found it expedient to leave the South for New York City. The book was a sensation: the reaction in the South was so extreme that it could hardly be read with safety, even for the purpose of refutation; it was banned by several state legislatures and, as was not even the case with *Uncle Tom's Cabin*, a number of men were lynched for possessing it. In the North its already wide circulation was increased during the Republican presidential campaign of 1860. Largely overlooked at the time was the fact that Helper's attack on the institution of slavery included no expression of sympathy for the slaves themselves. After serving as U.S. consul in Buenos Aires from 1861 to 1866 he clarified his point of view in three more books, *Nojoque*, 1867; *Negroes in Negroland*, 1868; and *Noonday Exigencies*, 1871; all three were explicitly racist and advocated the deportation of all Negroes from the United States. He maintained a deep interest in South America, particularly in the development of its commerce and transportation; a plan he had conceived for a railroad from Hudson Bay to the Strait of Magellan grew into an obsession, and he spent his last years in fruitless lobbying, letterwriting and publishing in an effort to achieve this dream. He committed suicide in Washington, D.C., on March 9, 1909.

Hemingway, Ernest Miller (1899–1961), author. Born on July 21, 1899, in Oak Park, Illinois, Hemingway went to work as a reporter for the *Kansas City Star* instead of attending college. He served with a volunteer ambulance unit in Italy in World War I until he was seriously wounded. Recovering in Milan from his wounds, he became a European correspondent for the *Toronto Star*. He settled in France, where he mingled with a group of expatriate artists and writers and was especially influenced by Gertrude Stein and Ezra Pound. His early short stories, compiled in *Three Stories and Ten Poems*, 1923, *In Our Time*, 1925, and *Men Without Women*, 1927, shared with his novels, *The Torrents of Spring*, 1926, and *The Sun Also Rises*, 1926, the theme of shattered individuals seeking refuge from the demands of a world they had never made. *A Farewell to Arms*, 1929, which firmly established his reputation, portrayed an English nurse and an American ambulance-service officer whose intense relationship was in stark contrast to the background of war. In 1933 another collection of stories appeared as *Winner Take Nothing*, and in 1938 he published *The Fifth Column and the First Forty-nine Stories*. *Death in the Afternoon*, 1932, concerning one of his consuming interests, bullfighting, and *The Green Hills of Africa*, 1935, concerned with another, big-game hunting, focused on the corruption of individual goodness by mass culture. He acknowledged the possibility of men triumphing over social problems in *To Have and Have Not*, 1937, and attempted to show that the bondage of one people leads to the bondage of all in his novel of the Spanish Civil War, *For Whom the Bell Tolls*, 1940. A foreign correspondent during World War II, he was involved in most of the major European campaigns and was present at many battles, and he was one of the first Americans to return to Paris after it was retaken by Allied forces in 1944. His sardonic, not to say bitter, view of war and especially of World War II was reflected in *Across the River and into the Trees*, 1950. This novel was not a success, and unfriendly

critics exulted that he had lost whatever greatness he had possessed. But *The Old Man and the Sea*, a short novel about an aged Cuban fisherman's lonely expedition to catch a great fish, appeared in 1952, won a Pulitzer Prize, and in 1954 Hemingway was awarded the Nobel Prize for Literature. His exceptionally terse, journalistic style had great emotional impact and influenced a generation of American writers. He died at his home in Ketchum, Idaho, by suicide, on July 2, 1961. Sketches of his life in Paris in the early 1920s appeared posthumously as *A Moveable Feast*, 1964.

Hench, Philip Showalter (1896–1965), physician. Born on February 28, 1896, in Pittsburgh, Hench graduated from Lafayette College in 1916 and took his M.D. from the University of Pittsburgh School of Medicine in 1920. In 1921 he became a fellow of the Mayo Foundation at the University of Minnesota and two years later joined the Mayo Clinic as first assistant in medicine. In 1925 he was made an associate in the division of medicine and in 1926 became staff consultant and head of the department of rheumatic diseases. Hench pursued further studies in Germany at the University of Freiburg and the Von Mueller Clinic in Munich during 1928–1929 and received the M.S. degree from the University of Minnesota in 1931. He began a teaching career at the Mayo Foundation and rose to a full professorship by 1947. His major work, in the field of rheumatoid arthritis, began when he noticed that jaundice, pregnancy, and starvation diets all had the effect of remitting its painful symptoms. Working in close association with the noted steroid chemist Edward C. Kendall, he investigated and by 1941 had decided to try cortisone, (then known as compound E), a secretion of the adrenal cortex on arthritic patients. Problems with the synthesis of compound E delayed the experiment, as did World War II, during which Hench served in the Army Medical Corps. After his discharge from the army with the rank of colonel in 1946 he returned to Mayo and two years later the compound E experimental treatments began. By early 1949 Hench and Kendall were able to show motion pictures of running patients who had formerly been bedridden. For his work with cortisone and other hormones, Hench, along with Kendall and another worker in the field, Dr. Tadeus Reichstein of Switzerland, were awarded the 1950 Nobel Prize for Physiology and Medicine. Hench was a member of numerous national and international medical associations and was civilian consultant to the surgeon general of the army. He contributed articles to medical periodicals and served as chief editor of the *Annual Rheumatism Review* and as associate editor of the *Annals of Rheumatic Diseases*. He retired from the Mayo Clinic in 1957 and died on March 30, 1965, in Ocho Rios, Jamaica.

Henderson, David Bremner (1840–1906), public official. Born in Old Deer, Scotland, on March 14, 1840, Henderson emigrated with his family to the

United States in 1846, settling first in Winnebago County, Illinois, and three years later moving to Fayette County, Iowa. After brief attendance at Upper Iowa University he enlisted in the Union army for service in the Civil War. He sustained wounds at Fort Donelson and at Corinth and in 1863 returned to Iowa to serve as commissioner of the board of enrollment, but in 1864 he accepted a commission as colonel of an Iowa volunteer regiment. On receiving his discharge in 1865 he studied law, won admission to the bar, and began practice in Dubuque. Over the next several years he held various local offices, including those of collector of internal revenue in 1865–1869 and as assistant U.S. attorney in 1869–1871. In 1882 he was elected as a Republican to the House of Representatives and retained the seat for ten terms, serving on the committees on appropriations, rules, and the judiciary and becoming a strong and influential advocate of a liberal pension policy for Civil War veterans and their families. He was a party regular and introduced no major legislation during his congressional career. In 1899 he was elected speaker of the House, and he held the post through a second term to 1903. His easy, relaxed conduct of the office stood in sharp contrast to the methods of his immediate predecessor, Thomas B. Reed. Declining renomination in 1902, Henderson practiced law for a short time in New York City and then retired to Dubuque, Iowa, where he died on February 25, 1906.

Henderson, Richard (1735–1785), public official and colonizer. Born on April 20, 1735, in Hanover County, Virginia, Henderson moved with his family in 1742 to Bute (later Granville) County, in the frontier region of North Carolina. He studied with tutors and later in a law office, was admitted to the bar, and while engaging in practice served as county deputy sheriff under his father. In 1768 he was appointed an associate judge of the state superior court, and in that capacity was in the midst of the civil disturbances brought on by the Regulators, vigilante bands of settlers on the frontier who objected violently to what they believed to be malfeasance and extortion on the part of state officials; in September 1770 he was forced to flee his courtroom in Hillsboro and two months later his farm in Granville County was burned. He resigned from the bench in 1773. Meanwhile he had become actively interested in Western settlement and in 1769 had engaged his neighbor, Daniel Boone, to cross through the Cumberland Gap into the wilderness beyond and to explore the territory. In 1774 he organized the Louisa Land Company, which early the next year was renamed the Transylvania Company, and in March 1775 he traveled to the Western country to meet Chief Attakullakulla of the Overhill Cherokee tribe at the Watauga River. There he negotiated the treaty of Sycamore Shoals, by which the Indians sold to the company all the land between the Kentucky and Cumberland rivers, an area comprising much of present-

day Kentucky and Tennessee. Shortly thereafter Henderson followed Boone to the site the latter had chosen and built Boonesborough (later Boonesboro), one of the first two relatively permanent settlements in the Kentucky country. With the outbreak of the Revolution he became entangled in the conflicting claims of North Carolina and Virginia to the region; the Transylvania colony, refused recognition by the Continental congress, failed and Henderson returned to North Carolina; the company ultimately was reimbursed with sizable land grants for its pioneering efforts. In 1779–1780 he was a member of the joint North Carolina–Virginia boundary commission and at that time took part in a colonization scheme in what is now Tennessee, establishing the settlement that later became Nashville. In 1781 he was elected to the North Carolina legislature and the next year to the council of state. He died on January 30, 1785, in Hillsboro, North Carolina.

Hendricks, Thomas Andrews (1819–1885), vice-president of the United States. Born near Zanesville, Ohio, on September 7, 1819, Hendricks early moved with his family to Indiana, settling in Shelby County. He graduated from Hanover College in 1841 and two years later was admitted to the bar, beginning practice in Shelbyville. In 1848 he was elected as a Democrat to the legislature, and in 1850–1851 he played a prominent role in the Indiana constitutional convention. Elected to the House of Representatives in 1851, he remained there until 1855, when he was defeated by a coalition of Know-Nothings, Whigs, and other anti-Democrats. He was appointed commissioner of the U.S. General Land Office by President Franklin Pierce in 1855; after his resignation in 1859 and an unsuccessful gubernatorial campaign in 1860 he moved his law practice to Indianapolis. In 1863, in a wave of popular reaction against the Civil War, he was elected to the Senate, where he vigorously opposed the draft, emancipation, the issuance of greenbacks, Radical Reconstruction measures, and the Thirteenth, Fourteenth, and Fifteenth amendments to the Constitution. In 1868 he was among the contestants for the Democratic presidential nomination. He left the Senate in 1869; in 1872 he was elected governor of Indiana, one of the first Democrats to be elected to a governor's chair in a Northern state after the Civil War. In 1876 he won the vice-presidential nomination and with Samuel J. Tilden went down to defeat with the rendering of the decision of the Electoral Commission appointed to decide the disputed election. He was again prominently mentioned for the presidential nomination in 1880 and in 1884, and in 1884, was again awarded second place on the Democratic ticket. Elected along with Grover Cleveland in that year, he was inaugurated in March 1885, and died a few months later, on November 25, 1885, in Indianapolis.

Hennepin, Louis (1626–1701?), Franciscan missionary and explorer. Born in Ath, Hainaut (now part of Belgium), on May 12, 1626, Jean Louis Hennepin entered the Recollect order of the Franciscans. In 1675 he sailed to Canada on a ship bearing also René Robert Cavelier, Sieur de la Salle, who was returning to Canada with supplies. La Salle secured the services of Hennepin as chaplain at Fort Frontenac on Lake Ontario in 1678 and the next year included him in his party journeying across the Great Lakes to the Illinois country. Hennepin accompanied La Salle's expedition as far as the Mississippi River, where, on the site of present-day Peoria, they built Fort Crève Coeur. From there La Salle turned back to Fort Frontenac for more supplies, sending Hennepin and two others north to explore the upper Mississippi. The three were captured by Sioux Indians, whom they accompanied on various hunting expeditions. During this period of wandering in the Minnesota country, Hennepin discovered and named the Falls of St. Anthony on the Mississippi at the site of present-day Minneapolis. In July 1680 the three men were rescued by Daniel Greysolon, Sieur Duluth (or du Lhut or Dulhut), for whom the city in Minnesota is named), and returned to Quebec. In 1682 Hennepin sailed back to France and the next year published his *Description de la Louisiane*, which first revealed to Europe many of the wonders of the upper Mississippi country and which was extremely popular. In 1697, a safe ten years after La Salle's death, he published *Nouvelle découverte d'un très grand pays situé dans l'Amérique*, in which he pirated writings by other missionary explorers and claimed to have followed the Mississippi to its mouth. The revelation of the falseness of that claim cast doubt on many other statements in his books, but he nevertheless remained valuable for their descriptive material and for their excellent maps. He was later expelled from France for seeking favors from the king of England and fell into disfavor with the superiors of his order. He then passed into obscurity. He made his way to Rome and was last heard of there in March 1701, although there is some evidence that he may have survived until 1705 and died in Utrecht.

Henri, Robert (1865–1929), painter and art teacher. Born in Cincinnati on June 25, 1865, Henri began formal art studies at the Pennsylvania Academy of the Fine Arts in 1886. Two years later he traveled to Paris, studying at the Académie Julien and later briefly at the École des Beaux-Arts. He returned to the United States in 1891, settling in Philadelphia and beginning a distinguished career as a teacher at the Women's School of Design. Around him gradually gathered an informal group of like-minded young artists, including John Sloan, William Glackens, George Luks, and others, all of whom were in good-natured revolt against the academic strictures of the established schools of painting and were interested in the portrayal of the city scenes around them. In 1896 Henri went again to Paris, where he taught for a time and exhibited successfully at the Salon; upon his return he moved his home and studio to New York City. Over the next several years he taught in a succession of small art schools, and his influence on the course of American art came to be recognized as a major one; notable among his many later famous students were George Bellows, Edward Hopper, and Rockwell Kent. In 1908 he joined with Sloan, Glackens, Luks, Arthur B. Davies, Maurice Prendergast, and others in organizing an exhibition of works in the new realist manner; a loosely knit group known as the Eight, they were also derisively referred to by later artistic conservatives as the "Ashcan School." A second exhibition in 1910 of the group, known as Independent Artists, was also influential. From 1915 to 1923 Henri taught at the Art Students League in New York City and in 1923 published a volume of essays, notes, and other pieces on life and art as *The Art Spirit*, which was well received by critics and students. The sense of freedom and vitality that pervaded the book and the paintings by which he was represented in a great many galleries and museums assured the continuance of his influence beyond his death in New York City on July 12, 1929.

Henry, Andrew (1775?–1833), explorer and fur trader. Born in York County, Pennsylvania, about 1775, Henry traveled west to Missouri about 1800, settling first in Ste. Genevieve and later in the lead-mining district of what is now Washington County. He engaged for several years in mining there. Early in 1809 he joined in the organization of the St. Louis Missouri Fur Company, which included among its partners Manuel Lisa, Auguste and Pierre Chouteau, and William Clark. In the spring of that year he set out with the company's first expedition to the upper Missouri River country. After passing the winter of 1809–1810 at Fort Manuel, near the confluence of the Bighorn and Yellowstone rivers, he led a smaller party to the Three Forks of the Missouri and there erected a fort. Harassment by Blackfoot Indians drove most of the party back to Fort Manuel in July 1810, but Henry and a few others went on, crossed the Continental Divide to the Snake River, and near the mouth of what became known as Henry's Fork built a small outpost, Henry's Post, as the first tangible evidence of the existence of the American fur trade west of the Rockies. The fur catch was small, however, and early the next year Henry and the rest of the party returned to St. Louis. He resumed his mining interests and in 1814, in connection with his duties as a major of militia, he met William H. Ashley. In 1822 the two organized another attempt to establish a permanent fur trade in the Far West, enlisting a large company of men that included Jim Bridger, Jedediah Strong Smith, Joseph R. Walker, Mike Fink, William L. Sublette, and, later, Thomas Fitzpatrick. The first expedition set out in April 1822 with Henry as second in command; when they reached the mouth of the Yellowstone, Ashley returned to St. Louis, leaving Henry to erect a fort and begin sending out trapping parties. Violent encounters with Blackfoot Indians hampered Henry's efforts and in 1823, after a defeat at their hands on the upper Missouri, he was forced to hurry back to the Mandan villages in the Dakota country to assist Ashley, who was returning with their second expedition, against the Arikara. The rest of the year and the winter were spent on the Yellowstone and the Bighorn and early in 1824 Henry followed the Jed Smith–Thomas Fitzpatrick party over South Pass, which they had discovered, to the Green River valley. Collecting the furs of the various trapping parties, he returned to St. Louis later that year. He took no further part in the business, retiring to his home, where he died on June 10, 1833.

Henry, Joseph (1797–1878), physicist. Born on December 17, 1797, in Albany, New York, Henry displayed little interest in his schooling and after a brief apprenticeship to a watchmaker became involved with an amateur theatrical group. By the age of sixteen, however, he had become fascinated by natural science and entered Albany Academy, supporting himself by teaching in country schools and later in the academy itself. His intention was to study medicine after graduation, but his future was altered by his appointment in 1825 to a state surveying party. His interest switched to engineering, and the following year he became professor of mathematics and natural philosophy at Albany Academy. There, in his spare time, he embarked on a series of investigations into electrical phenomena, particularly those related to magnetism. His first major achievement was building a powerful electromagnet, for which he developed insulated wire in order to make a closely wound coil of several layers; electromagnets of the same type are still generally employed. He discovered and formulated the basic principles governing the behavior of various sorts of coils and by 1829 had constructed primitive versions of the telegraph and the electric motor. In 1832 he was appointed professor of natural philosophy at the College of New Jersey (now Princeton) and there continued his research. In 1832 he read Michael Faraday's announcement of the discovery of the self-inductance of current in a coil; he promptly resumed his own earlier investigations of this phenomenon and, although he never attempted to claim credit, clearly established that he had independently observed it, possibly as early as 1830. In recognition of his work his name was given to the henry, the unit of electrical inductance, by international agreement in 1893. Continuing the same line of research, Henry discovered the induction of a current in one coil by that in another, showed how the induced current could be varied by different coil arrangements, and thus laid the groundwork for the development of the transformer. He found that an induced current could also be generated by an electrical discharge, or spark; in one experiment, in which a current was set up in a coil by a lightning flash miles away, he appears to have been the first to record the action of electromagnetic waves, although he himself was unaware of their existence. Subsequently, in 1842, he correctly concluded that such discharges are oscillatory in nature. He collaborated with his brother Stephen in work on solar radiation and determined that sunspots are cooler than the surrounding areas of the sun's surface. In 1846 he was chosen first secretary and director of the new Smithsonian Institution in Washington, D.C. In that position, determined to prevent the institution from becoming merely a repository of knowledge, he developed a program of active support for basic scientific research, organized a corps of volunteer weather observers whose work led eventually to the creation of the U.S. Weather Bureau, and began a program of publication and distribution of scientific papers. From 1852 he was a member of the federal Light-House Board and was its chairman after 1871. He participated in the organization of the American Association for the Advancement of Science (AAAS) and the National Academy of Sciences, serving as president of the Academy from 1868. He died in Washington, D.C., on May 13, 1878. He was elected to the Hall of Fame in 1915.

Henry, O., *see* Porter, William Sidney

Henry, Patrick (1736–1799), political leader and public official. Born in Hanover County, Virginia, on May 29, 1736, Henry showed little promise for the future in his early years; after a sketchy education he proceeded to fail as a farmer and twice as a storekeeper and by 1759 was deeply in debt. He turned at last to law, was admitted to the bar in 1760, and within a short time had achieved great success and a wide reputation. In a case in 1763 known as the Parson's Cause, in which a minister of the established church challenged the authority of the colonial legislature to pay clerical salaries in money when tobacco, the usual medium, was scarce, a crown veto of the legislature's act roused much public anger. At a hearing to determine the plaintiff's due, Henry appeared for the defense and by invoking the doctrine of natural rights managed to win a virtual victory in holding the award to the amount of one penny. In 1765 he entered the House of Burgesses and quickly became a leader of the growing opposition to the dominant tidewater aristocrats. With the announcement of the Stamp Act in that year he introduced a number of radical resolutions against it and succeeded in carrying several of them with his first great speech, which concluded with the famous observation "Caesar had his Brutus, Charles the First his Cromwell, and George the Third—may profit by their example." Through the next several years he was the recognized leader of the radical faction in Virginia and was increasingly prominent throughout the colonies. He was a member of Virginia's first Committee of Correspondence and a delegate to the first and second Continental Congresses. In 1775, at the Virginia convention that met in place of the legislature dissolved by the governor, he introduced a number of revolutionary resolutions, including one for the arming and training of the militia, and carried the convention with the speech containing the words "I know not what course others may take, but as for me, give me liberty or give me death." He became commander of the Virginia militia, but resigned in 1776 because of the opposition of political enemies. In that year he helped draft the state's constitution and under it was elected governor. He was reelected in the two succeeding years; an effective wartime governor, he authorized George Rogers Clark's 1778 military exedition that conquered the Old Northwest. After a brief retirement he served in the legislature from 1780 to 1784, during which time, after the peace treaty in 1783, he surprised his followers, and alienated some, by advocating equitable treatment for former Loyalists. From 1784 to 1786 he was again governor, and from 1787 to 1790 again in the legislature. He opposed the Constitutional Convention in 1787 and refused to be a delegate to it; when the Constitution was being considered in Virginia, he led the opposition to ratification. He acquiesced in its adoption but immediately began a campaign that resulted in the adoption of the ten amendments comprising the Bill of Rights. In 1788 he retired to his legal practice and private life; through the succeeding years he became gradually estranged from the Republican leaders, Thomas Jefferson and James Madison, as he reconciled himself to the new federal government. He declined several high government offices but finally, in 1799, he was prevailed upon by George Washington to seek another term in the state legislature as a Federalist in order to oppose the Kentucky and Virginia Resolves. He was elected, but before taking his seat he died on June 6, 1799, at his estate in Charlotte County, Virginia. He was elected to the Hall of Fame in 1920.

Hepburn, Katharine (1909–   ), actress. Born in Hartford, Connecticut, on November 8, 1909, Miss Hepburn graduated from Bryn Mawr College in 1928 and immediately sought a theatrical career. After a period of study and working in summer stock she made her Broadway debut in a small role in *Night Hostess* in 1928. After other parts in *These Days*, 1929, *A Month in the Country*, 1930, and *Art and Mrs. Bottle*, 1930, she drew considerable attention with her performance in *The Warrior's Husband*, 1932, and was given a film contract by RKO Studios. In Hollywood she appeared in a rapid succession of movies, including *Bill of Divorcement*, 1932; *Christopher Strong*, 1933; *Morning Glory*, 1933, for which she won an Academy Award; *Little Women*, 1933; *Spitfire*, 1934; *The Little Minister*, 1934; *Alice Adams*, 1935; *Mary of Scotland*, 1936; *A Woman Rebels*, 1936; *Quality Street*, 1937; *Stage Door*, 1937; *Bringing Up Baby*, 1938; and *Holiday*, 1938, the last for Columbia. She returned to the stage, touring in *Jane Eyre*, and to Broadway in *The Philadelphia Story*, 1939, which had been rewritten with her own sharp, aristocratic manner in mind. The 1940 M-G-M film version with Cary Grant brought her a New York Film Critics' Circle Award. In 1942 she made *Woman of the Year*,

the first of a series of highly popular movies with her long-time friend, Spencer Tracy; with Tracy she also appeared in *Keeper of the Flame*, 1943; *Without Love*, 1945; *Sea of Grass*, 1947; *State of the Union*, 1948; *Adam's Rib*, 1949; *Pat and Mike*, 1952; and *Desk Set*, 1957. Others of her films of that period included *Dragon Seed*, 1944; *The African Queen*, 1951; *Summertime*, 1955; *The Rainmaker*, 1956; and *Suddenly Last Summer*, 1959, and she continued also to appear occasionally on the stage, for a time especially in Shakespearian roles. For *Long Day's Journey into Night*, 1962, she won a Cannes Film Festival award and for *Guess Who's Coming to Dinner*, 1967, which was Tracy's last film, she won another Academy Award. With *The Lion in Winter*, 1968, she became the only woman ever to win three Oscars for best actress. Subsequently Miss Hepburn appeared in *The Mad Woman of Chaillot*, 1969, and in the 1969 Broadway production of *Coco*. A decided individualist in private life, she brought to all her roles a sinewy strength and an aura of confidence that could range from frank cheerfulness to roaring zeal to hauteur. Her later films included: *The Trojan Women*, 1971; *Rooster Cogburn*, 1975; *On Golden Pond*, 1981, for which she again won an Oscar.

Herbert, Victor (1859–1924), composer and conductor. Born in Dublin on February 1, 1859, Herbert was sent to Germany at the age of seven to study music. After a period under various masters he toured Europe as a solo cellist and in 1882 held the first chair in the orchestra conducted by the younger Johann Strauss in Vienna. Later he studied composition at the Stuttgart Conservatory. In 1886 he emigrated to the United States and was engaged as first cellist for the New York Metropolitan Opera House orchestra; he appeared also with Theodore Thomas's orchestra and with the New York Philharmonic, with which he gave the premiere performances of his *Concerto and Suite for Cello* in 1887 and his better-known *Second Cello Concerto* in 1894. In 1893 he succeeded Patrick S. Gilmore as leader of the famed 22nd New York Regiment Band and during five years in that position began composing light operettas for the New York stage. Beginning with *Prince Ananias*, 1894, he produced a series of brilliant, sophisticated, and enormously popular operettas, including *The Wizard of the Nile*, 1895; *The Serenade*, 1897; *The Fortune Teller*, 1898; *Babes in Toyland*, 1903; *Mlle. Modiste*, 1905; *The Red Mill*, 1906; *Little Nemo*, 1908; *Naughty Marietta*, 1910; *Sweethearts*, 1913; *The Only Girl*, 1914; *Hearts of Erin* (later called *Eileen*), 1917; and *Her Regiment*, 1917. From 1898 to 1904 Herbert was conductor of the Pittsburgh Symphony Orchestra; he then returned to New York City and organized his own orchestra, with which he appeared regularly thereafter. He also wrote two grand operas, *Natoma*, on an Indian theme, premiered in Philadelphia in 1911, and *Madeleine*, performed at the Metropolitan Opera House in 1914, and numerous shorter pieces. He was active in the campaign for effective copyright protection for musical works in 1909 and in 1914 led in founding the American Society of Composers, Authors, and Publishers (ASCAP) to oppose the practice of broadcasting copyrighted music without payment of royalties. He composed the score for *The Fall of a Nation*, 1916, probably the first original musical score for a film, and he wrote the music for the *Ziegfeld Follies* editions of 1919, 1921, and 1924. Herbert died in New York City on May 26, 1924.

Herblock, *see* Block, Herbert Lawrence

Herne, James A. (1839–1901), actor and playwright. Born in Cohoes, New York, on February 1, 1839, James Ahern left school to go to work at thirteen. He developed theatrical ambitions on seeing a play in Albany and in 1859, changing his name to James A. Herne, made his stage debut with a small touring company. Within a few years he had worked his way through repertory companies in Troy and Albany to a position in the supporting cast for Junius Brutus Booth and Edwin Booth. Later he returned to touring, briefly managed a theater in New York City, and in the 1870s achieved considerable prominence on the stage in San Francisco. There he collaborated with David Belasco in writing *Chums*, later retitled *Hearts of Oak* and first acted in 1879, which proved to be a great success; Herne toured with it for several years and earned a small fortune. Three subsequent plays written by Herne, *The Minute Men*, 1886, *Drifting Apart*, 1888, and *Margaret Fleming*, 1890, departed from the kindly sentimentality of *Hearts of Oak* for a realism that was, for the time, remarkably sharp and direct. These were pioneering efforts at realism and all, but especially *Margaret Fleming*, anticipated a major trend in twentieth-century drama, despite the poor reception of their original productions. *Shore Acres*, premiered in Chicago in 1892, combined realism with sentiment and became Herne's most popular work. *The Reverend Griffith Davenport*, 1899, met a mixed reception, but *Sag Harbor*, 1899, his last play and an adaptation of earlier themes, was another great success. Particularly adept at homely detail and the creation of strong characters, Herne employed, even in his sentimental plays, simple, informal dialogue; similarly, his acting and his direction of other players aimed at a naturalness far in advance of the posturing and emotional excesses of the commonly accepted "grand manner." He died in New York City on June 2, 1901.

Herrick, Myron Timothy (1854–1929), businessman, public official, and diplomat. Born in Huntington, Lorain County, Ohio, on October 9, 1854, Herrick attended Oberlin Academy for a year and a half and Ohio Wesleyan University for two years. In 1875 he took up the study of law in Cleveland and three years later was admitted to the bar. While carrying on a successful practice in Cleveland he gradually acquired extensive business interests, particularly in banking, and became deeply involved in Republican politics. He served two terms, 1885–1887, on the Cleveland city council and formed close alliances with Mark Hanna and William McKinley. His active participation in McKinley's presidential campaigns in 1896 and 1900 brought him offers of cabinet and diplomatic posts, all of which he declined because of the burden of his business affairs in banking and railroad management. In 1901 he was elected president of the American Bankers Association. At Hanna's urging he accepted nomination for governor of Ohio in 1903; although he was elected by a huge margin, the conservative course he pursued in office, and particularly controversial vetoes of a number of bills, led to his defeat for reelection in 1905. Herrick then returned to his business interests until 1912, when President William Howard Taft appointed him ambassador to France. He was continued in that post by President Woodrow Wilson until December 1914, and in his last months in France he performed signal service on behalf of Americans and nationals of other neutral countries who had been caught in the outbreak of World War I and also organized relief services for war refugees and victims. He assumed charge of the Paris embassies of several other nations and was alone among foreign diplomats in remaining in the city after the French government had fled to Bordeaux in September. At nearby Neuilly he established an American ambulance hospital. Shortly after his departure for the United States he was awarded the Grand Cross of the Legion of Honor for his services to France. Herrick continued to be active in the organization of war-relief efforts in the United States and in 1916 ran unsuccessfully for the Senate. In 1921 he was again named ambassador to France by President Warren G. Harding; warmly received by the government and people of France, he served ably in the post until his death in Paris on March 31, 1929.

Herriman, George Joseph (1880–1944), cartoonist. Born in New Orleans on August 22, 1880, Herriman was apparently of partly black ancestry, but he and his family may have taken on white identities after moving to Los Angeles during his childhood. He worked at various jobs before joining the *Los Angeles Herald* in 1897, and by 1901 he was publishing color cartoons regularly in the Sunday edition. Two years later he created his first comic strip, *Lariat Pete*, for the *San Francisco Chronicle*. Later he moved to New York, where he painted billboards at Coney Island and held other jobs until he found a position on the *New York World*. By about 1908, when he joined the *New York Evening Journal*, flagship of the Hearst chain, he had devised several strips, including *Major Ozone, the Fresh Air Fiend*, *The Family Upstairs*, *Professor Otto and his Auto*, and *The Dingbat Family*. In an episode of *Dingbat* in 1910 he introduced in a sort of subplot carried on below the regular action two new characters, a cat and a mouse. Their non sequitur adventures soon attracted attention, and in 1911 they were formally introduced as *Krazy*

Kat and Ignatz. By 1913 *Krazy Kat* had displaced all of Herriman's other work, and with superb draftsmanship and a sharp, whimsical imagination, he carried on the strip until his death. The strip was avidly followed not only by the mass audience but also by a devoted coterie of artists and avant-gardists. Krazy Kat, wistful, sentimental, and blindly devoted to the cynical Ignatz Mouse, was the perennial dupe, the target of a steady stream of epithets and bricks from Ignatz as Offissa Bull Pupp tried vainly to mediate. The world of *Krazy Kat*, a surrealistic desert landscape, was also inhabited by such characters as Mrs. Quakk Wakk, Mock Duck, Don Koyote, and other mildly improbable creatures. *Krazy Kat* was the first comic strip drawn and written (in an odd and oddly poetic vernacular) for adult appreciation, and it retained its popularity long after Herriman's death in Hollywood, California, on April 25, 1944.

Hersey, John Richard (1914–   ), author. Born on June 17, 1914, in Tientsin, China, of American missionary parents, Hersey was fluent in Chinese before he learned English and attended the Chinese and American grade schools in Tientsin. At ten, moving to the United States, he entered the Hotchkiss School; he graduated from Yale in 1936 and took a year of postgraduate work at Clare College, Cambridge University. In the summer of 1937 he became personal secretary to Sinclair Lewis. That autumn he was employed as a writer by *Time* magazine, of which he later became an editor; he was also later a senior editor of *Life* magazine and a correspondent for major periodicals, including the *New Yorker*. His first overseas assignment for *Time* in 1939 was in the Far East, where he interviewed Chiang Kai-shek, and other prominent figures. He compiled *Men on Bataan*, 1942, from information gathered in the Far East, from statements by friends of Gen. Douglas MacArthur and families of soldiers, and with the aid of *Time's* vast library of news dispatches and clippings. The book was the first of a series of extremely popular documentary and fictional accounts of war dealing with the human aspects of major news stories; they included *Into the Valley*, 1943, based on Hersey's experiences with a company of marines on Guadalcanal; *A Bell for Adano*, 1944, awarded a Pulitzer Prize and made into a motion picture, a radio drama, and a Broadway play; *Hiroshima*, 1946, a powerful account of the atom-bombing of the city and the aftermath of nuclear holocaust; and *The Wall*, 1950, describing the doomed rebellion against the Germans of the Jews of Warsaw's ghetto. He wrote, among other books, *The Marmot Drive*, 1953; *A Single Pebble*, 1956; *The War Lover*, 1959; *The Child Buyer*, 1960; *White Lotus*, 1965; *Under the Eye of the Storm*, 1967; *The Algiers Motel Incident*, 1968; and *The Conspiracy*, 1972.

Hershey, Alfred Day (1908–   ), bacteriologist and geneticist. Born on December 4, 1908, in Owosso, Michigan, Hershey graduated from Michigan State in 1930 and received his Ph.D.

there four years later. He joined the faculty of the Washington University medical school in St. Louis in 1934 as an assistant in bacteriology, advancing by 1942 to the rank of associate professor. In that year he met and formed informal but close working relationships with Max Delbrück and Salvador E. Luria; the three corresponded, confirmed each others' experimental work and drew inspiration from it, and together laid much of the foundation of modern molecular genetics. Hershey was particularly interested in bacteriophages, or simply "phages," viruses that attack and disintegrate bacteria. In 1945 he and Luria discovered independently that phages were subject to spontaneous mutations, and in 1946 he found—and Delbrück independently confirmed—that different strains of phages were capable of combining or exchanging genetic material and of acting as carriers of genes from one strain of bacteria to another. In 1950 Hershey joined the genetics research laboratory of the Carnegie Institution of Washington in Cold Spring Harbor, New York. Two years later he employed radioisotope tracers to locate the site of mutations of genetic characteristics of phages in the DNA molecules of the nucleus, finding also that in the process of invasion, only the nuclear genetic material of the phage enters the bacterial cell, the outer coat being left outside. He continued his work at the laboratory, becoming director of the facility in 1962, and with his two colleagues was widely recognized as having made invaluable contributions not only to the field of molecular biology but also to the development by others of practical vaccines for polio, German measles, mumps, and other viral infections. In 1969 the work of the three men was recognized formally with the joint award of the Nobel Prize for Physiology and Medicine.

Hershey, Milton Snavely (1857–1945), businessman and philanthropist. Born on September 13, 1857, in Dauphin County, Pennsylvania, Hershey was educated in rural schools and then apprenticed to a confectioner in nearby Lancaster. An attempt to go into business for himself in Philadelphia in 1876 failed, as did a later venture in New York City, but about 1888 he returned to Lancaster and began the Lancaster Caramel Company, which prospered. In 1900 he sold the firm for $1 million and three years later, after considerable experimentation, formed a new company to manufacture chocolate bars. Around his factory the town of Hershey grew up and his personal fortune increased enormously as the Hershey Chocolate Company developed rapidly into the world's largest manufacturer of chocolate products. In 1909 he founded a home and school, later known as the Hershey Industrial School, for orphan boys and in 1918 endowed it with a gift of $18 million. The M. S. Hershey Foundation contributed to the maintenance of public schools in the Hershey district and established the Hershey Junior College on a tuition-free basis in 1938. Hershey died in Hershey on October 13, 1945.

Herskovits, Melville Jean (1895–1963), anthropologist. Born on September 10, 1895, in Bellefontaine, Ohio, Herskovits grew up there, in El Paso, Texas, and in Erie, Pennsylvania. He entered both Hebrew Union College and the University of Cincinnati in 1915 and after service in the army during World War I transferred to the University of Chicago, graduating in 1920. He pursued graduate studies in anthropology under Franz Boas at Columbia University, taking his Ph.D. in 1923 and then lecturing at Columbia and at Howard University while, with a National Research Council fellowship, he carried on a four-year program of research on the anthropometry of the American Negro. In 1927 he became assistant professor of anthropology at Northwestern University; he advanced to full professor in 1935 and became chairman of the department of anthropology in 1938. In 1928 his *American Negro: A Study in Racial Crossing* appeared with its thesis that black Americans constituted a homogeneous and culturally definable population group. After publishing *Anthropometry of the American Negro*, 1930, he began a series of field trips to South America, the West Indies, and Africa to study Negro groups and tribes, discussing his findings in *Outline of Dahomean Religious Belief*, 1933; *Rebel Destiny and Among the Bush Negroes of Dutch Guiana*, 1934, both with his wife, Frances S. Herskovits; *Life in a Haitian Valley*, 1937; *Dahomey*, 1938; *The Economic Life of Primitive Peoples*, 1940; and, after working with Gunnar Myrdal's massive research project on American Negroes, *The Myth of the Negro Past*, 1941, in which he outlined the cultural heritage of black Americans. During World War II he served in various consultant capacities to the government; from 1939 to 1950 he was chairman of the Commission on Negro Studies of the American Council of Learned Societies (ACLU) and in 1957–1958 of the African Studies Association. From 1949 to 1952 he edited the *American Anthropologist*, and in 1951 he organized at Northwestern a pioneering program of African studies, which he directed thereafter, becoming professor of African affairs in 1960. Other published works included *Trinidad Village* 1947, with his wife; *Man and His Works*, 1948; *Economic Anthropology*, 1952; *Franz Boas, the Science of Man in the Making*, 1953; *Cultural Anthropology*, 1955; *Dahomean Narrative, a Cross-Cultural Analysis*, 1958, with his wife; *The Human Factor in Changing Africa*, 1962; and *Cultural Dynamics*, 1964. Herskovits died in Evanston, Illinois, on February 25, 1963.

Hewitt, Abram Stevens (1822–1903), businessman, philanthropist, public official, and political leader. Born in Haverstraw, New York, on July 31, 1822, Hewitt graduated from Columbia College in 1842 and remained there as an instructor in mathematics while studying law. Although he was admitted to the bar in 1845, he never practiced; instead he formed a close association with his father-in-law, Peter Cooper, and Cooper's son Edward and with Edward organized the firm of Cooper, Hewitt and Company to pioneer in the manufacture of iron girders and beams. Following a visit to England, Hewitt built the first open-hearth smelting furnace in America at the firm's works in Trenton, New Jersey, and began producing iron for gun barrels for the government's Civil War requirements, refusing to take a profit on the contract. The firm continued to prosper with the introduction of the first American commercial-grade steel in 1870 and the construction of several branch works; during the five-year depression that followed the panic of 1873 Hewitt and Cooper maintained production at full capacity, operating at a loss in order to keep their workers employed. Hewitt had meanwhile become active in philanthropy and public service. He aided Peter Cooper in planning and organizing Cooper Union, serving from its founding in 1859 as secretary of the board of trustees. In 1867 he was appointed U.S. commissioner to the International Exhibition in Paris by President Andrew Johnson. In 1871 he and Edward Cooper joined with Samuel J. Tilden in a campaign to oust the Tweed Ring from New York City government and from the Tammany Hall Democratic organization; the success of the campaign brought him prominence in the party and he was elected to the House of Representatives in 1874, serving until 1886 with the exception of the 1879–1881 term. He was chairman of the Democratic National Committee in 1876 and played a central role in the resolution of the dispute over the outcome of the Hayes-Tilden election. In 1886 he was elected mayor of New York City, defeating both Henry George and Theodore Roosevelt, and subsequently conducted an effective reform administration; his policies alienated the old guard of Tammany, however, and after being refused renomination he ran as an independent and was defeated. His later years were devoted to philanthropy. He gave a substantial endowment to Cooper Union in 1902 and in the same year became the first chairman of the board of trustees of the Carnegie Institution of Washington. Hewitt died in Ringwood, New Jersey, on January 18, 1903.

Heyward, DuBose (1885–1940), author. Born on August 31, 1885, into an aristocratic but impoverished family in Charleston, South Carolina, Edwin DuBose Heyward was selling newspapers at nine and at fourteen left public school and worked as a clerk in a hardware store. An attack of infantile paralysis at seventeen left him an invalid for three years. Later he engaged in the insurance business and was a partner in Heyward and O'Neill until 1924. His earliest literary efforts were in verse; with Hervey Allen he published *Carolina Chansons* in 1922 and *Skylines and Horizons* in 1924; *Jasbo Brown* followed in 1931. In 1923 he married Dorothy Kuhns, whom he had met at the MacDowell Colony in New Hampshire and who was later to collaborate with him on the dramatizations of two of his novels, *Porgy* and *Mamba's Daughters*. Largely through her influence, Heyward left the insurance business in 1924 and began his first novel, *Porgy*, 1925. Set in Charleston's Catfish Row waterfront district, the book was a great success and the stage version of 1927 formed the basis of George Gershwin's opera *Porgy and Bess*, 1935, for which Heyward wrote the libretto and collaborated with Ira Gershwin on the lyrics. Heyward wrote five other novels —*Angel*, 1926; *Mamba's Daughters*, 1929, dramatized in 1939; *Peter Ashley*, 1932; *Lost Morning*, 1936; and *Star Spangled Virgin*, 1939, as well as a play, *Brass Ankle*, 1931. The Gullah-speaking Negroes of South Carolina and the Sea Islands chain provided much material for his work, as did Southern mountaineers and his own native Charleston. The recipient of several honorary degrees, he was among the founders in 1920 of the Poetry Society of South Carolina. Heyward died in Tryon, North Carolina, near his Hendersonville home, on June 16, 1940.

H. H., *see* Jackson, Helen Hunt

Hiawatha (fl. 1570), Indian leader. Hiawatha, or Haionhwat'ha, has survived in historical tradition and legend as one of the founders of the League of the Five Nations of the Iroquois. His is the hereditary name and title of the chieftain of the Turtle clan of the Mohawk Indians, although he himself is sometimes said to have been an Onondaga because he lived with that tribe. The earliest record of the name dates from 1570, the same year usually given for the founding, through the influence of the prophet Dekanawidah and Hiawatha, of the federal union of the Mohawk, Oneida, Onondaga, Cayuga, and Seneca tribes into the League of the Five Nations, or the Iroquois Confederacy. Hiawatha's goal was to establish a universal and lasting peace by uniting the often antagonistic tribes, but the result was a warlike and formidable empire. The confederacy attained a relatively high form of governmental organization. Hiawatha is also associated with a great many legends; he is known as a sorcerer, as the incarnation of human progress and civilization, and as a teacher. Henry Wadsworth Longfellow's poem *The Song of Hiawatha*, 1855, based on earlier writings by Henry Rowe Schoolcraft, is largely romantic and has little basis in historical fact.

Hickok, James Butler (1837–1876), "Wild Bill," frontier figure. Born in Troy Grove, Illinois, on May 27, 1837, Hickok early acquired a reputation as a crack shot with pistol and rifle. He left the family farm in 1855 and made his way west to Leavenworth, Kansas. After holding various farm jobs and serving briefly in Gen. James H. Lane's Free-State irregulars he became a stagecoach driver on the Santa Fe Trail and later the Oregon Trail. During this period there were said to have taken place two of his later much-publicized exploits, an encounter with a cinnamon bear at Raton Pass in which, armed only with bowie knife, he killed the bear while sustaining a terrible mauling, and a shoot-out with the infamous

McCanles gang at Rock Creek Station, in Jefferson County, Nebraska, in which he killed the leader and two others. Hickok served as a spy and scout for the Union army in Missouri during the Civil War and, again later, was credited with numerous wartime adventures. In 1866 it is probable that he became a deputy U.S. marshal in Fort Riley, Kansas, in the midst of a rough frontier territory infested with horse thieves and cattle rustlers. Later, as marshal of Hays City in 1869 and of Abilene in 1871, both notoriously violent cattle towns, and as an Indian fighter with Gen. Winfield Scott Hancock, Gen. Philip H. Sheridan, and Col. George A. Custer, he became widely known as a ready killer and a dedicated gambler. His reputation reached the East, where it was blown up to legendary proportions by sensational magazine articles and dime novels, and he quickly took advantage of his new fame by starring as "Wild Bill," with Buffalo Bill Cody, in the tour of the play *Scouts of the Prairies* by Ned Buntline (E. Z. C. Judson). He then joined Buffalo Bill's touring Wild West Show in 1872–1873. His career in show business was brief, however, and by 1876 he was reduced to gambling again. He moved to Deadwood, Dakota Territory, in that year and on August 2, 1876, while engaged in a poker game in Saloon No. 10, he was shot dead from behind by Jack McCall; the cards he held at the time—two pairs, aces and eights—became known as the "Dead Man's Hand." As was the case with most Western characters, Hickok's fame grew with the passage of time and he became in the hands of later writers the classic frontier hero—upright, fearless, and almost superhuman in his ability to outfight and outshoot desperadoes of all sorts in any numbers. Estimates of the number of men he killed ranged from two or three dozen, exclusive of Confederates and Indians, up to more than a hundred. His relationship with Calamity Jane (Martha Jane Burke) almost certainly did not extend to the often-claimed marriage.

Hickok, "Wild Bill," *see* Hickok, James Butler

Hicks, Edward (1780–1849), painter. Born on April 4, 1780, in Attleboro (now Langhorne), Pennsylvania, Hicks spent most of his life in nearby Newtown. Originally a coach, sign, and ornamental painter, he became an itinerant Quaker preacher and was involved in the schism usually attributed to the activities of his distant cousin, Elias Hicks. True to the Quaker spirit, he withdrew from preaching when he decided that his ability to draw large audiences was making him vain. He took up easel painting and became a self-taught painter of landscapes and religious and historical subjects. His works, all on wood panels, were largely copies of those of well-known artists, yet they were stamped with his own individual touch. His moral allegory "The Peaceable Kingdom," based on a Biblical passage in *Isaiah* (11:6–9), of which he painted as many as 100 versions between 1830 and 1840, was simple in technique but conveyed strongly the artist's fascination with the idea and the details of the animals. This best-known of his works earned him a place among American primitive painters of the early 1800s. Hicks died on August 23, 1849, in Newtown, Pennsylvania.

Hicks, Elias (1748–1830), religious leader. Born in Hempstead township, Long Island, New York, on March 19, 1748, Hicks grew up in a Quaker family. For a time he was apprenticed to a carpenter, but after his marriage in 1771 he settled on the farm of his wife's family in Jericho, Long Island, where he lived for the rest of his life. During the 1770s he began preaching locally, attracting much attention by his impassioned, forceful, and effective manner, which Walt Whitman later commended highly. He gradually began traveling farther and farther afield to preach, crossing repeatedly through the opposing lines during the Revolution and later extending his range north to Canada, south to North Carolina, and west to Indiana. He was particularly interested in education, helping to establish many local Quaker schools, and in the abolition of slavery. He was influential in bringing about the formal renunciation of slavery by the Society of Friends and in the adoption of antislavery legislation by New York State, and in 1811 he published the widely read and influential *Observations on the Slavery of the Africans and Their Descendants*, in which he advocated a boycott of the products of slave labor. In his theology Hicks was a spokesman for the quietist and individualist strain of Quakerism that saw salvation as the result of each believer's following his own "inner light" through which the ongoing revelation of God was achieved; he was strongly opposed to evangelicalism and at the 1817 yearly meeting in Baltimore successfully resisted the adoption of a creed. The rising tide of evangelicalism among segments of the Society, together with the growing influence, both theological and personal, that Hicks exerted on others, led inevitably to a schism in 1827–1828. Hicks himself did not advocate and took no part in the splits that occurred in Pennsylvania, New York, Ohio, Maryland, and elsewhere, but the Liberal branch was unanimously dubbed the Hicksites by the conservative (and at first outnumbered) Orthodox branch. Hicks continued to travel and preach until his death in Jericho, Long Island, New York, on February 27, 1830.

Higginson, Thomas Wentworth Storrow (1823–1911), social reformer, soldier, and author. Born on December 22, 1823, in Cambridge, Massachusetts, Higginson graduated from Harvard in 1841 and after two years of teaching returned to the college to pursue a rather aimless course of study. Finally in 1846 he enrolled in the divinity school at Harvard and graduated the following year. He became the pastor of the First Religious Society of Newburyport, Massachusetts, and immediately launched into a number of reform activities. He founded an evening school for workers, frequently wrote editorials for newspapers, ran for the House of Representatives on the Free-Soil ticket in 1848, and so often infused his sermons with radical declarations on women's rights, abolitionism, and other causes that after two years he was at odds even with his liberal Unitarian congregation and was relieved of his duties. He had for some years been advocating extreme action against slavery, and in 1851 he joined the Boston Vigilance Committee organized to oppose enforcement of the Fugitive Slave Law of 1850. In 1852 he became pastor of the Free Church in Worcester, Massachusetts, a position he retained until 1861. In 1854, when Anthony Burns, an escaped slave, was being held in Boston for forcible return to the South, Higginson purchased axes and led in breaking down the courthouse door and liberating Burns. He aided in sending antislavery settlers and supplies to Kansas and in 1856 made a visit to the state and met John Brown. A series of letters to the *New York Tribune* on the trip were collected in *A Ride Through Kansas*, 1856. In 1861 he helped raise a company of Massachusetts troops and headed it as captain; the next year he resigned to accept a commission as colonel of the 1st South Carolina Volunteers, the first Negro regiment in the Union army. He continued to serve until 1864 and recorded his experiences in *Army Life in a Black Regiment*, 1870. From the end of the war until 1878 he lived in Newport, Rhode Island; there he became a regular contributor to the leading magazines—*Scribner's, Harper's, Atlantic Monthly, North American Review*—and wrote his only novel, *Malbone*, 1869. In 1875 he published his popular *Young Folks' History of the United States* and ten years later a *Larger History of the United States*. From 1878 until his death he lived again in Cambridge. He continued to produce a steady stream of magazine articles and essays on a wide range of subjects, many of which were collected into books, and he wrote a number of biographies, notably of Henry Wadsworth Longfellow, John Greenleaf Whittier, and Margaret Fuller. He was, in a remarkable correspondence that spanned more than 20 years, one of the very few people to whom Emily Dickinson revealed herself as a poet, and although he was often baffled by her unorthodox poetics and had serious doubts about publishing her work, after Emily's death he joined her sister in editing *Poems by Emily Dickinson*, 1890, and *Poems: Second Series*, 1891. He died in Cambridge, Massachusetts, on May 9, 1911.

Hilgard, Ferdinand Heinrich Gustav, *see* Villard, Henry

Hill, Ambrose Powell (1825–1865), soldier. Born on November 9, 1825, in Culpeper, Virginia, Hill graduated from West Point in 1847 and went immediately into service in the Mexican War. He was later stationed at Fort McHenry, in Florida, and in Texas, and he saw action in the Seminole Wars between 1849 and 1855. From 1855 until 1860 he was attached to the U.S. Coast Survey in Washington, D.C. Hill resigned his commission in 1861 with the beginning of the Civil War and was given command of a Virginia regiment that was in reserve at the first battle of Bull Run (Manassas). He was promoted to brigadier general in February 1862 and, after performing well at Williamsburg and Fair Oaks (Seven Pines) in the Peninsular Campaign, was made major general in May of the same year. He instituted an effective system of command and discipline and developed his division into one of the best in the Confederate army; for the speed with which it marched it was dubbed the "Light Division." He was in the thick of the Seven Days' Battle in June 1862, gave invaluable support to Gen. Thomas J. "Stonewall" Jackson at Cedar Mountain (Cedar Run) and the second battle of Bull Run at the end of August, and aided in the capture of Harpers Ferry in September. His timely arrival at Antietam (Sharpsburg) helped prevent the battle from becoming a decisive Union victory. Following the death of Jackson after the battle of Chancellorsville in May 1863, where Hill too was wounded, he was promoted to lieutenant general in command of the 3rd Corps of the Army of Northern Virginia. On July 1, 1863, for a time in command of all Confederate troops in the locality, he encountered a Union force at Gettysburg, Pennsylvania, and launched an immediate attack that, while resulting in heavy casualties, was for the day successful; in the next two days of fighting, however, he was unable to make further gains. Hill took a prominent part in the various battles of the Wilderness Campaign and was entrenched before Petersburg when he was killed by Union fire on April 2, 1865.

Hill, George Washington (1884–1946), businessman. Born on October 22, 1884, in Philadelphia, Hill attended Williams College for two years and then, in 1904, entered the employ of the American Tobacco Company, of which his father was a vice-president. After three years of training at the field and factory levels he was placed in charge of sales for the newly acquired Pall Mall division in 1907 and soon made the brand the national best seller among higher-priced cigarettes. In 1911, after the Supreme Court–ordered breakup of the huge company into smaller, competitive units, Hill became vice-president of what remained the American Tobacco Company. Six years later, in a move designed to meet the challenge of the rival Camels brand in the popular market, he and his father, then president, introduced Lucky Strikes; from then on, the promotion of Luckies was Hill's personal crusade and, as American Tobacco president from 1925, he closely directed the advertising campaign that went into making the new brand a success, writing much of the copy himself. From the original slogan "It's toasted," he went on to devise such famous phrases as "Reach for a Lucky instead of a sweet," which caused trouble with the sugar industry and the Federal Trade Commission (FTC) in 1927; "Lucky Strike Green has gone to war," when the color of the package was changed to white during World War II; "LS / MFT—Lucky Strike means fine tobacco."

The campaign of 1927, which included endorsements by famous women, was influential in making public cigarette smoking by women socially acceptable, and by 1930 Luckies had captured the national sales lead from Camels. Again with Hill maintaining close personal control over production, Lucky Strike sponsored the popular and long-lived "Your Hit Parade" radio program, first broadcast in April 1935, and later sponsored Jack Benny's radio show. Frequently engaged in litigation with stockholders or the government over various business practices, Hill enjoyed one of the largest salaries in the country—approaching half a million dollars annually—in return for which he was an ardent, ceaseless, and successful proselytizer for his product. He died on September 13, 1946, in Matapedia, Quebec.

Hill, James Jerome (1838–1916), financier and railroad magnate. Born near Guelph, Ontario, on September 16, 1838, Hill ended his schooling at fourteen and thereafter clerked in a store until setting out, four years later, to seek his fortune in the Orient. Finding no opportunity to travel to the Far East, he settled instead in St. Paul, Minnesota, in 1856. He obtained a position with a trading company that operated a number of steamboats and gradually took on more and more responsibility; by 1865 he was venturing into business on his own. His interests grew to include railroad transportation and in 1878, with three Canadian partners, he bought the bankrupt St. Paul & Pacific Railroad. With Hill as general manager the company was reorganized the next year as the St. Paul, Minneapolis & Manitoba Railway and a vigorous building program was undertaken; the line was thoroughly renovated and extended north and west. In 1882 he became president; eight years later the Great Northern Railway Company was organized to unify the St. Paul line and a number of smaller lines into one system and in 1893 the railroad was extended to Seattle. He oversaw directly the siting and building of the line and did much to encourage homesteading in the regions opened up by it. Hill's foresighted and close personal supervision of the company's activities and finances made it highly profitable and the most successful of the transcontinental systems. With his associates, including the powerful J. P. Morgan, he acquired a large interest in the Northern Pacific Railway, and Hill and the Morgan interests obtained joint control of the Chicago, Burlington & Quincy in 1901. His holdings in the Burlington line came under strong attack by Edward H. Harriman and the Union Pacific, then seeking access to Chicago. The stock war, which precipitated a financial panic in 1901, was finally settled by the establishment of the Northern Securities Company, which assumed control of the Great Northern, the Northern Pacific, and the Burlington, and in which the Hill-Morgan faction held the controlling interest. In one of the landmark cases of the era, the Supreme Court declared in 1904 that the arrangement was in violation of the Sherman Anti-Trust Act and the holding company was dissolved. Hill also had extensive investments in banks and played an important role in the development of the Mesabi iron-ore range in Minnesota. He retired as president of the Great Northern in 1907, serving as chairman of the board from then until 1912. He died on May 29, 1916, in St. Paul, Minnesota.

Hill, Joe (1879–1915), labor organizer and songwriter. Born in Sweden in 1879, Joe Hill was originally named Joel Emmanuel Haaglund or Hagglund, although some sources give his name as Joseph Hillstrom. He worked as a seaman and came to the United States about 1901. Virtually nothing is known of him—he was reticent about biographical details—until 1910, by which time he had joined the Industrial Workers of the World, (IWW), a radical labor organization founded five years earlier. He took part in organizing and strike activities among dock workers in San Pedro, California, and in a short-lived communalist revolution in Tijuana, Mexico, and late in 1913 appeared in Utah. During those years of hobo life he was one of the IWW's staunchest supporters and became well known to its growing membership—the "Wobblies"—through the pages of the *Industrial Worker* and *Solidarity*, both of which printed his essays, letters, and songs. It was the songs that won the greatest attention; the most famous, "The Preacher and the Slave," contained the phrase "pie in the sky" that became a part of the American lexicon. Others of his best songs were "Casey Jones—the Union Scab," "Coffee An'," "There Is Power in a Union," "Nearer My Job to Thee," and "The Rebel Girl." Hill's works were the mainstay of a movement that had a remarkable penchant for singing. In January 1914 he was arrested in Salt Lake City, Utah, on a murder charge; tried in June, he was quickly convicted on circumstantial evidence that left, for many, considerable doubt of his guilt. Hill and the IWW claimed that the charge had been trumped up simply to eliminate him. He remained in prison for 22 months while various appeals were entered and denied. By October 1915 the Swedish government, Samuel Gompers of the AFL, and President Woodrow Wilson had tried without success to secure a new trial. Utah officials remained adamant and on November 19 Hill was executed by a firing squad. The night before his death he had wired to the head of the IWW, William "Big Bill" Haywood: "Don't waste any time in mourning. Organize." The message, and massive funeral observances in Salt Lake City and Chicago, confirmed his martyrdom, and his reputation grew in time to legendary proportions.

Hillkowitz, Morris, *see* Hillquit, Morris

Hillman, Sidney (1887–1946), labor leader. Born on March 23, 1887, in Zagare, Lithuania, then part of Russia (now the Lithuanian S.S.R.), Hillman studied to be a rabbi but participation in the abortive Russian revolution of 1905 led to his imprisonment for several months. After his release he went to England and in 1907 came to the United States. In Chicago he found a job with Sears, Roebuck & Company; in 1909 he became an apprentice cutter in the clothing factory of Hart, Schaffner, & Marx and was soon deeply involved in union activities. He led a strike against the company in 1910–1911 and was the labor spokesman when negotiations were finally begun. The resulting contract, largely his work, soon came to be considered a model for labor-management agreement; it clearly defined the interests of the contracting parties and established a mechanism for discussion and arbitration of disputes. In 1914 Hillman went to New York City to become chief clerk for the Cloakmakers Joint Board and later in the year became the first president of the Amalgamated Clothing Workers of America, a position he held for the rest of his life. Through his strenuous efforts the 40-hour week became nearly universal in the men's clothing industry by the end of World War I; by 1940 the union had enrolled 350,000 members and had contracts with 96 percent of the country's manufacturers of men's clothing. He secured contracts providing for uniform wage scales across the nation, thus ending the threat of the "runaway shop," the moving of a factory to an area where low wages prevailed. Services to members that were provided by the union included banking, unemployment insurance, and housing, in a cooperative housing development. Consonant with Hillman's insistence on cooperation as the cornerstone of industrial relations, union funds were occasionally loaned to companies in temporarily straitened circumstances and the union's research staff offered suggestions for improving manufacturing efficiency. In 1935 Hillman joined John L. Lewis and others in forming the Committee for (later Congress of) Industrial Organizations (CIO). President Franklin D. Roosevelt appointed him to the Advisory Commission to the Council of National Defense; in 1941 he became codirector of the Office of Production Management and the next year was named director of the labor division of the War Production Board. In 1943 Hillman left government service to become chairman of the CIO's Political Action Committee, playing a major role in Roosevelt's reelection campaign of 1944. He was also a vice-chairman of the World Federation of Trade Unions from its organization in 1945. He died at his home on Long Island, New York, on July 10, 1946.

Hillquit, Morris (1869–1933), lawyer, reformer, and author. Born in Riga, Latvia, then part of Russia (now in the Latvian S.S.R.), on August 1, 1869, Hillquit (or Hillkowitz, his original name) emigrated to the United States in 1886; for a brief time he attended high school in his adopted city of New York, but soon was forced to go to work. Like many other young immigrants he joined the Socialist Labor party; he also became involved in labor-union organization and in 1888 helped found the United Hebrew Trades. He helped Abraham

Cahan found the *New York Arbeiter Zeitung*, the first Yiddish newspaper in America, and in 1891 entered the law school of the University of the City of New York (now New York University), graduating two years later. Devoting himself thereafter to the Socialist cause, he soon became a prominent leader and unofficial spokesman for the Socialist Labor party and later for the coalition Social Democratic party of Eugene V. Debs and still later for the Socialist party, its direct outgrowth. He spoke before innumerable audiences and engaged in a number of debates, including one with Samuel Gompers before a congressional committee in 1909. The party's policy on peace, announced soon after the outbreak of World War I, was largely Hillquit's work, as was its later condemnation of U.S. participation in the war, which was deemed the immoral and inevitable outcome of capitalist imperialism. The Espionage Act of 1917 greatly increased demands for Hillquit's legal services as numbers of Socialists and others were prosecuted, generally on dubious charges. He had already been three times a candidate for the House of Representatives when in the same year, 1917, he ran unsuccessfully for mayor of New York City; despite the prevalent anti-Socialist mood that often approached hysteria, he won a remarkably large portion of the vote. Tuberculosis interfered with his activities after 1917, but he managed to be twice more a candidate for the House and in 1932 ran again for mayor. He continued to work, speak, and write on behalf of Socialism until his death in New York City on October 7, 1933. Among his published works were *History of Socialism in the United States*, 1903, revised in 1910; *Socialism in Theory and Practice*, 1909; and *Socialism Summed Up*, 1912.

Hillstrom, Joseph, *see* Hill, Joe

Hilton, Conrad Nicholson, **(1887–1979)**, hotel owner. Born on December 25, 1887, in San Antonio, New Mexico, Hilton, during his youth, assisted in his father's many businesses, which included renting lodgings to transients and after periods at St. Michael's College and in 1907–1909 at the New Mexico School of Mines he joined his father in full-time partnership. He was elected as a Republican to New Mexico's first state legislature in 1912. At the end of his term in 1913 he became cashier in the New Mexico State Bank of San Antonio and two years later rose to the presidency. After service in World War I he attempted to expand his banking business. The failure of negotiations to purchase an interest in a small Texas bank led to his investing instead in a hotel; several other such purchases followed in Texas cities, and by 1925 he was in a position to build a new hotel in Dallas. He had already assembled a sizable chain of hotels when the Depression of the 1930s forced him to reduce his operations, but profits from oil leases enabled him to remain in business and by 1939 he was building again. He began acquiring large, established hotels in major

cities across the country, including the Town House in Los Angeles in 1942, the Roosevelt and the Plaza in New York City in 1943, the Palmer House in Chicago in 1945, and in 1949 the most prestigious hotel in the nation, the Waldorf-Astoria in New York City. His chain was organized as the Hilton Hotel Corporation in 1946, and it prospered on the strength of Hilton's mastery of financing and his ability to turn to profitable use every bit of space in his hotels. Luxurious resort hotels were bought or built in cities around the world under the aegis of the Hilton International Company, and in 1954 the firm acquired a controlling interest in the rival Statler hotel chain. In 1966, by which time the Hilton group included more than 60 hotels in the United States alone, Hilton turned over active management to his son Barron Hilton. His autobiographical *Be My Guest* appeared in 1957. He died on January 3, 1979, in Santa Monica, California.

Hine, Lewis Wickes **(1874–1940)**, photographer. Born in Oshkosh, Wisconsin, on September 26, 1874, Hine left school to go to work at fifteen, but he continued his education on his own and in 1900 entered the University of Chicago. The next year he moved to New York City to accept a teaching position at the Ethical Culture School and continued his own education at Columbia and at New York University, from which he took a degree in 1905. He became interested in photography and particularly in the potential of the camera for recording social conditions and making them known to a wide audience. He made an extensive photographic study of immigrants arriving at Ellis Island and of their subsequent lives in the tenements and sweatshops of New York. In 1907 he began working for the National Child Labor Committee, for which he traveled widely to factories, mills, and mines where children worked long hours under deplorable health and safety conditions; his stark, eloquent pictures of such children, coupled with their own comments, repeatedly shocked the nation. In 1909 he joined the staff of *Charities and Commons* (later *Survey*) magazine as a photographer. His photographs were acknowledged at the time to be immensely powerful as reform propaganda; later they came to be valued as social history and admired as masterpieces of photographic art. After World War I Hine was commissioned to record the European relief work of the American Red Cross and he later worked as an industrial photographer; in 1931 he made a remarkable study of the construction of the Empire State Building, and in 1932 he published a collection of photographs as *Men at Work*. Hine died on November 3, 1940, in Hastings-on-Hudson, New York.

Hines, Duncan **(1880–1959)**, author and publisher. Born in Bowling Green, Kentucky, on March 26, 1880, Hines attended a local business college for two years and in 1898 went to work for the Wells, Fargo express company. That job and later ones for various mining companies in the West and in Mexico accustomed him to travel and it became almost a way of life for him when, in 1905, he moved to Chicago and became a sales and promotion representative for advertising and printing companies. On his trips around the country Hines, who since childhood had possessed a keen appreciation of good food, was ever eager to discover and try new restaurants in search of the elusive satisfying meal, and over the years he compiled a large notebook on worthy dining establishments. His advice was often sought by friends and acquaintances who were planning trips, and gradually his informal consultations as an expert in the field grew to unmanageable proportions. Finally, in 1936, he published his collected reports on restaurants across the nation as *Adventures in Good Eating*, issuing it at his own expense. Word-of-mouth advertising increased its sales constantly and in 1938, the first year the book showed a profit, he issued his *Lodging for a Night*, a guide to inns and hotels. In 1939 he returned to Bowling Green with his suddenly large publishing business and that year published *Adventures in Good Cooking and The Art of Carving in the Home*, which contained favorite recipes from recommended restaurants. The *Duncan Hines Vacation Guide* appeared in 1948. *Adventures in Good Eating* remained the staple of his business, however, and for the rest of his life he traveled almost constantly, seeking new restaurants, following up tips on out-of-the-way places, rechecking already recommended establishments, and continually revising the book with his latest evaluations; eventually he acquired a volunteer staff of hundreds of assistant itinerant gourmets, many of them well-known personalities. The book, which held uncompromisingly to Hines's standards and included no advertising, sold in the hundreds of thousands of copies to formerly defenseless travelers, and it was credited with having exerted vast influence on the culinary and sanitary practices of the American restaurant. In later years Hines lent his name to a line of packaged food products. He died in Bowling Green, Kentucky, on March 15, 1959.

Hinmatonyalakit, *see* Joseph

Hires, Charles Elmer (1851–1937), businessman. Born near Roadstown, near Bridgeton, New Jersey, on August 19, 1851, Hires went to work at the age of twelve in a drugstore and in 1867 moved to Philadelphia where he found similar employment. He acquired some professional training in night classes at the Philadelphia College of Pharmacy and the Jefferson Medical College. After a brief venture as a partner in a drugstore in Bridgeton, New Jersey, he returned to Philadelphia and in 1869 opened his own store. He noted at a nearby excavation site a clayish soil that he identified as fuller's earth. Arranging to have the excavated earth dumped in his cellar, he pressed it into cakes labeled "Hires' Special Cleaner" and reaped a handsome profit by selling it to wholesale drug houses. In 1875, while honeymooning at a New

Jersey boarding farm, he was served by the landlady a remarkably tasty and refreshing decoction of sassafras bark, sarsaparilla root, juniper berries, pipsissewa, and other herbs. He returned home with the recipe and after considerable experimentation developed a packageable, water-soluble concentrate from which the drink could be made. On the suggestion of his friend Russell H. Conwell he named the preparation "root beer" and introduced it with great success at the Centennial Exposition in Philadelphia in 1876. Hires's root-beer concentrate was soon available in 25-cent packages (enough to mix 5 gallons) at soda fountains, and by the early 1880s was also sold as a liquid, in 3-ounce bottles. Heavy advertising in the *Philadelphia Public Ledger* and later in such national publications as the *Ladies' Home Journal* opened a booming market, although it also attracted the attention and ire of the Woman's Christian Temperance Union (WCTU), which, especially after the introduction of ready-to-drink bottled root beer in 1893, was slow to accept that the word "beer" was being used loosely. From the incorporation of the Charles E. Hires Company in 1890 Hires served as president of the rapidly growing concern, and between 1896 and 1918 he also organized a number of companies to manufacture condensed milk. The Hires Company, although later surpassed in sales by Asa G. Candler's Coca-Cola Company and others, long remained the world's leading producer of root beer. Hires died in Haverford, Pennsylvania, on July 31, 1937.

Hiss, Alger (1904–   ), public official and diplomat. Born in Baltimore on November 11, 1904, Hiss graduated from The Johns Hopkins University in 1926 and from Harvard Law School in 1929. After a year as secretary to Supreme Court Justice Oliver Wendell Holmes he began a private law practice in Boston in 1930, moving to New York City in 1932. In 1933 he was appointed assistant to the general counsel of the Agricultural Adjustment Administration (AAA), and he rose quickly through the ranks of government officials of the New Deal period, moving to the Department of Justice as a special attorney in 1935 and to the Department of State as assistant to the assistant secretary of state in 1936. After a period in the office of Far Eastern political relations in the department he joined the new office of special political affairs in 1944, quickly rising to deputy director and in 1945 to director of the office. In those posts he was deeply involved in developing plans for and organizing meetings on the projected United Nations (UN); he attended the Dumbarton Oaks Conference, was an adviser to President Franklin D. Roosevelt at the Yalta Conference in February 1945, and was temporary secretary general of the embryonic United Nations organized in San Francisco in April 1945. After serving as chief government adviser to the U.S. delegation to the first UN General Assembly in London early in 1946, Hiss was chosen to succeed Nicholas Murray Butler as president of the Carnegie Endowment for International Peace in December of that year; he held the post until May 1949. In August 1948, at the height of the controversy over whether loyalty oaths should be required of government employees and in the midst of a wave of charges that Communists and Communist sympathizers had infested the government, and particularly the State Department, since the 1930s, the House Committee on Un-American Activities held hearings at which Whittaker Chambers, a senior editor of *Time* magazine, admitted that he had served as a courier for the Communist party and thus for the Soviet Union and named Hiss as one of his principal contacts in the government. Hiss denied the charge and filed a slander suit against Chambers. Chambers then produced a cache of microfilms (the "pumpkin papers," named for their hiding place) containing copies of secret State Department documents typed on what the FBI claimed to have been Hiss's typewriter. The statute of limitations prevented prosecution of Hiss for the alleged espionage, but late in 1948 he was indicted for perjury for having denied Chambers's allegations. At both the first trial, which ended in a hung jury, and the second, both in New York City, Chambers's sanity figured prominently among the issues. In January 1950 Hiss was convicted of perjury; sentenced to five years in prison, he served until November 1954. The Hiss case, an explosive national issue from the start and one that provoked an endless round of public charges and countercharges from every conceivable quarter, was the most famous and controversial of the postwar period of Communist scares; because of its lack of clear resolution it remained a topic of debate thereafter. Following his release Hiss lived quietly in New York City; his *In the Court of Public Opinion*, 1957, reiterated his assertion of innocence, but otherwise, except when he delivered occasional lectures on the New Deal, he remained largely out of public notice.

Hitchcock, Alfred Joseph (1899–1980), motion-picture director and producer. Born in London on August 13, 1899, Hitchcock studied at St. Ignatius College and London University before going to work as an electrical engineer for a cable firm. In 1920 his growing interest in the young motion-picture industry led to a position with the British studios of Famous Players–Lasky as a title artist. Three years later he joined Gainsborough Pictures as a scenario writer and over the next few years worked also as a set designer, art director, and assistant director. In 1925 he directed his first film, *The Pleasure Garden*. *The Lodger*, 1925, a silent melodrama about Jack the Ripper, attracted considerable attention and was followed by such films as *Blackmail*, 1929; *The Skin Game*, 1932; and *The 39 Steps*, 1935, in which Hitchcock used an innovative and highly effective sound-montage technique; the last established for him a wide reputation as an adept handler of tense, dramatic, and delightfully involuted plot lines. His *The Lady Vanishes*, 1938, won the New York Film

Critics' Circle Award for direction and brought Hitchcock a permanent place in Hollywood, to which he moved in 1939. He followed with a rapid succession of enormously popular movies in which, over the years, he further honed his deft touch until he was acknowledged to be the master of the suspense-film genre. Among his most successful films were *Rebecca*, 1940, which won the Academy Award for best picture of the year; *Suspicion*, 1941; *Shadow of a Doubt*, 1943; *Spellbound*, 1945; *Notorious*, 1946; *Under Capricorn*, 1949; *Stage Fright*, 1950; *I Confess*, 1952; *Dial M for Murder*, 1954; *Rear Window*, 1954; *To Catch a Thief*, 1955; *The Trouble with Harry*, 1955; *The Man Who Knew Too Much*, 1955; *Vertigo*, 1958; *North by Northwest*, 1959; *Psycho*, 1960; *The Birds*, 1963; *Marnie*, 1964; *Torn Curtain*, 1966; *Topaz*, 1969; *Frenzy*, 1972; and *Family Plot*, 1976. In 1968 he was awarded a special Academy Award for his contributions to the industry. Hitchcock was admired critically for the adroit manipulation of suspense that attracted huge audiences and especially for the economy with which he employed quick-cut montages to build his films. From 1955 to 1965 he hosted a highly popular television mystery program and from the late 1950's he edited and published a number of collections of mystery stories. He received a knighthood in January 1980, and shortly after, on April 29, he died in Los Angeles.

Hitchcock, Thomas, Jr. (1900–1944), "Tommy," polo player. Born on February 11, 1900, in Aiken, South Carolina, Hitchcock was the son of a 10-goal polo player and early took up the game himself. By the age of sixteen he was a member of the Meadow Brook Club team, then the leading team in the country. In 1917 he left St. Paul's School to enlist in the army aviation corps for service in World War I; rejected because of his age, he sailed to France, joined the French aviation service, and was assigned to the famed Lafayette Escadrille. He shot down several German aircraft in combat and in March 1918 was captured when his plane was forced down behind enemy lines. He escaped a few months later and rejoined his squadron, which later was transferred to the U.S. army as the 103rd Pursuit Squadron. After the war he resumed his polo playing and his position on the Meadow Brook team and after graduating from Harvard entered banking. In 1922 he achieved the 10-goal rating, the highest possible handicap, and retained it for 13 consecutive years; in 1935 he dropped to a 9-goal rating, although he was still the top-ranked American player, and from 1936 to 1940 was again a 10-goal man. He captained the U.S. team in victories over Great Britain in Westchester Cup competition in 1921, 1924, 1927, 1930, and 1939, compiling a remarkable record by losing no games to the British team. He also led the U.S. team against Argentina for the Copa de las Americas in 1928. In dominating the game for nearly 20 years, Hitchcock earned the generally acknowledged title of greatest American player of all time; many thought him the game's greatest player. He retired from international competition after the 1939 Westchester Cup match. In 1942 he obtained a commission as lieutenant colonel in the Army Air Corps; sent to England as an air attaché, he secured, despite his age, appointment as commander of a P-51 fighter group. He died in a plane crash in England on April 19, 1944.

Hoar, Ebenezer Rockwood (1816–1895), judge and public official. Born in Concord, Massachusetts, on February 21, 1816, Hoar was a son of Samuel Hoar and a grandson of Roger Sherman. He graduated from Harvard in 1835, studied law in his father's office and at Harvard Law School, from which he took a degree in 1839, and entered practice in Concord in 1840. He quickly attained prominence as an attorney and was associated with Daniel Webster and Rufus Choate in several cases. Like his father he was active politically, at first as an antislavery Whig; while a member of the state legislature in 1846 he made the remark that he would rather be a "Conscience Whig" than a "Cotton Whig" and thus gave the former name to his wing of the party. He anticipated even his father in protesting the Whigs' nomination of Zachary Taylor in 1848 and in agitating for a new party. From 1849 to 1855 he was a judge of the court of common pleas, and in 1859 he was appointed to the Massachusetts supreme court. He remained on the bench until 1869, when President Ulysses S. Grant named him attorney general. In that post he served ably, but he alienated political leaders by his refusal to bow to the wishes of certain senators to use nine newly created federal judgeships for patronage purposes. His nomination to the Supreme Court was consequently rejected out of hand by the Senate, and in 1870 he was dismissed from the cabinet to make way for a successor chosen to please the Southern bloc in the Senate. In 1871 Grant nonetheless appointed Hoar to the joint commission that negotiated the treaty arranging for the arbitration of the *Alabama* claims. He served a single term in the House of Representatives in 1873–1875, where his brother, George Frisbie Hoar, was one of his colleagues; he ran again, unsuccessfully, against Benjamin F. Butler in 1876. He remained active in Republican affairs and at Republican national conventions thereafter, although he refused to reenter public service, and he devoted much time to Harvard. He died in Concord, Massachusetts on January 31, 1895.

Hoar, George Frisbie (1826–1904), public official. Born in Concord, Massachusetts, on August 29, 1826, Hoar was a son of Samuel Hoar and a grandson of Roger Sherman. He graduated from Harvard in 1846 and from the Harvard Law School in 1849, beginning practice in Worcester, Massachusetts. He served terms in both houses of the state legislature and in 1854, with his father and brother was deeply involved in organizing the Republican party in Massachusetts. He was elected to the House of Representatives in 1869 and

remained there until elevated to the Senate in 1877. He was a member of the electoral commission appointed to resolve the disputed Tilden-Hayes presidential election of 1876, and in the Senate, where he sat for the rest of his life, he was a prominent member of several important committees. He was author of the Presidential Succession Act of 1886, which placed the members of the cabinet in line of succession after the vice-president; of the 1887 bill that repealed the vestiges of the Tenure of Office Act; and of much of the Sherman Anti-Trust Act of 1890. A fervent crusader for civil-service reform and honesty in government, he became after the Spanish-American War a leading opponent of imperialism. Possessed of an abiding interest in education and scholarship, Hoar served for many years as an overseer of Harvard, as a regent of the Smithsonian Institution in 1880, and at various times as president of the American Antiquarian Society and the American Historical Association; he was also a founder and lifelong sustainer of the Worcester Polytechnic Institute, founded in 1865, and of Clark University, founded in 1887. Hoar's *Autobiography of Seventy Years* appeared in 1903; he died in Worcester, Massachusetts, on September 30, 1904.

Hoar, Samuel (1778–1856), lawyer and public official. Born in Lincoln, Massachusetts, on May 18, 1778, Hoar graduated from Harvard in 1802 and after a period as a private tutor in Virginia took up the study of law and was admitted to the bar in 1805. He began practice in Concord, Massachusetts, and achieved considerable prominence, ranking with Daniel Webster and Rufus Choate as a leader of the state bar. He served in the state constitutional convention of 1820 and in 1825 was elected to the state legislature, where he remained for eight years. From 1835 to 1837 he served a term in the House of Representatives and was an outspoken opponent of slavery and an advocate of its abolition in the District of Columbia. In 1844 he was sent by the governor of Massachusetts to seek a court test of certain South Carolina laws that bore heavily on free black citizens, particularly sailors, visiting in that state from Massachusetts; his expulsion from Charleston at the hands of a mob aroused a furor in the North. A Federalist until the dissolution of that party after the War of 1812, Hoar was later a Whig, becoming prominent in the antislavery "Conscience Whig" wing of the party. On the nomination of Zachary Taylor for president in 1848—an apparent ratification by the Whigs of expansionism and the extension of slavery—he became a leader in the organization of the Free-Soil party in Massachusetts. After another term in the state legislature in 1850, during which he was responsible for the defeat of a proposal to place Harvard under state control, he became active in founding the Republican party in Massachusetts in 1854–1855, chairing the committee that issued the call for an organizing convention. Hoar died in Concord on November 2, 1856.

Hoard, William Dempster (1836–1918), publisher, agriculturist, and public official. Born on October 10, 1836, in Munnsville, New York, Hoard spent much of his youth on dairy farms and acquired a sound knowledge of their management. In 1857 he traveled west to Wisconsin, where he farmed, taught music, and rode circuit as a Methodist exhorter, all with little success. After serving in the Union army in the Civil War he undertook in 1865 a short-lived venture into the nursery business in Columbus, Wisconsin. In 1870 he founded the *Jefferson County Union* in Lake Mills, Wisconsin, moving it three years later to Fort Atkinson. In that paper he urged strongly the general adoption of dairying as more suited to Wisconsin's resources than other agricultural pursuits, and in furtherance of this aim he helped to organize the Jefferson County Dairyman's Association in 1871 and the Wisconsin State Dairyman's Association and the Northwestern Dairyman's Association in 1872. In 1873 he lobbied successfully for advantageous rates for the use of railroad refrigerator cars to carry Wisconsin's dairy products to the huge Eastern market, and he was an influential proponent of scientific dairy-farming methods. His advocacy influenced the introduction into Wisconsin of tuberculin tests for cattle, the use of silos, and the planting of alfalfa as a feed crop, and he played a major role in securing legislation establishing county normal and agricultural schools and farmers' institutes. In 1885 he founded *Hoard's Dairyman*, which was soon recognized as one of the foremost agricultural journals and enjoyed an international circulation. As the "Jersey Cow candidate" he was elected governor of Wisconsin in 1888; his championship of a law requiring the teaching of English in all schools in a state with a large foreign-born population aroused much opposition and that, combined with the Democratic sweep of 1890, prevented his reelection. From 1907 to 1911 he was a member, and after 1908 president, of the board of regents of the University of Wisconsin, and he exerted his influence to establish the state soil survey. He continued to publish and edit the *Union* and *Hoard's Dairyman* until his death in Fort Atkinson, Wisconsin, on November 22, 1918.

Hoban, James (1762?–1831), architect. Born in County Kilkenny, Ireland, about 1762, Hoban studied architectural drawing in the school of the Dublin Society during his youth. He was involved in the design and construction of several Dublin buildings before he emigrated to the United States after the American Revolution and established himself as an architect in Philadelphia. Later he lived in South Carolina, where he designed the state capitol, and in 1792 he moved to the District of Columbia to seek opportunities in the new city to be built there. He submitted entries in the design competitions for the U.S. Capitol and the president's mansion and won the latter; from 1793 to 1800 he oversaw the construction of what within a few years began to be called the White House, from the Virginia freestone used on its front. Hoban also built two hotels in the city, served for a time as superintendent of the work progressing on the Capitol, and acquired extensive real-estate holdings in the District. From 1802 until his death he was a member of the city council of Washington, D.C. Following the War of 1812 he rebuilt the burned White House and designed and built the offices of both the state and war departments. Hoban died in Washington on December 8, 1831.

Hobart, Garret Augustus (1844–1899), vice-president of the United States. Born in Long Branch, New Jersey, on June 3, 1844, Hobart graduated from Rutgers in 1863 and after a brief period teaching school took up the study of law. Admitted to the bar in 1869, he began practice in Paterson, New Jersey, and quickly became active in business and politics as well. He served in the state legislature in 1873–1875, the last year as speaker of the assembly, and again in 1877–1882, the last two years as president of the senate. From 1880 to 1891 he was chairman of the state Republican committee and in 1884 became a member of the Republican National Committee. His interests in railroad, utilities, and banking enterprises brought him wealth and additional influence in political affairs. Although he had never served in Congress, having lost a senatorial election in 1884, his position as the leading Republican in an important and traditionally Democratic state and his strong conservative stand on the gold issue made him a popular choice for the Republican vice-presidential nomination in 1896. He was elected as William McKinley's running mate and inaugurated with McKinley in March 1897. He enjoyed general respect and goodwill as presiding officer of the Senate and was a close adviser and effective supporter of the President. Early in 1899 his health began to fail and he died at his home in Paterson, New Jersey, on November 21, 1899.

Hocking, William Ernest (1873–1966), philosopher. Born in Cleveland on August 10, 1873, Hocking grew up there and in Maryland, Michigan, and Illinois. After graduating from high school in Joliet, Illinois, he became a surveyor. He attended Iowa State College for two years and in 1895, upon reading William James's *Principles of Psychology*, determined to attend Harvard. After four years of teaching school in Davenport, Iowa, he enrolled at Harvard and pursued studies in psychology and philosophy under James, Josiah Royce, George Santayana, and George Palmer. Graduating in 1901, he remained to take his M.A. the next year and, after a year of study in several German universities, returned to Harvard for his Ph.D. in 1904. From that year to 1906 he was an instructor at both Harvard and at Andover Theological Seminary. From 1906 to 1908 he taught at the University of California (Berkeley) and then joined the faculty at Yale. In 1912 he published his first major work, *The Meaning of God in Human Experience*, outlining a philosophical view that reflected the influence of both Royce and James in modifying the absolute idealism of the one with the pragmatism of the other. In 1914 he became professor of philosophy, at Harvard, where he remained, after 1920 as Alford Professor and after 1937 as chairman of the philosophy department, until his retirement in 1943. In 1917, at the request of the British government, he undertook a study of the psychology of morale; the results of his investigations among British and French combat troops were published as *Morale and Its Enemies*, 1918. During 1931–1932 he headed the Laymen's Foreign Missions Inquiry Commission in the Far East and was coauthor and editor of its report, *Re-Thinking Missions*, 1932. In his writings Hocking continually expressed his belief that a philosophy, even though idealistic, should have real implications for the common man, and he applied his own system to concrete problems in such works as *Human Nature and Its Remaking*, 1918; *Man and the State*, 1926; *The Spirit of World Politics*, 1932; *Lasting Elements of Individualism*, 1937; *Freedom of the Press*, 1947; *The Coming World Civilization*, 1956; *The Meaning of Immortality in Human Experience*, 1957; and *Strength of Men and Nations*, 1958. Hocking died in the stone house he had built himself in Madison, New Hampshire, on June 12, 1966.

Hoe, Richard March (1812–1886), inventor. Born on September 12, 1812, in New York City, Hoe left school at fifteen to go to work in his father's firm, R. Hoe & Company, manufacturers of printing presses and related equipment. In 1830 he assumed virtual charge of the business and on the death of his father three years later became the senior partner. From 1829 he had, with his father, experimented with and made various improvements on the Napier flatbed and cylinder press and had sold a version of the machine; Hoe devised several variants, employing large or small and single or double cylinder arrangements, which were widely used in book and woodcut printing. In 1846 he patented a new press in which the flatbed was discarded and the type form was attached instead to a central cylinder, about which revolved from four to ten impression cylinders. This was the first rotary press, soon known the world over as Hoe's "lightning" press, and its introduction into newspaper printing, beginning with Arunah S. Abell's *Philadelphia Public Ledger* in 1847, revolutionized that business by printing 8000 papers per hour and thus making possible huge daily editions. Hoe added further improvements and increased the speed of the press over the years, building in 1871 a rotary web perfecting press that, incorporating advances patented six years earlier by William A. Bullock, was fed by webs, or continuous rolls of paper, and printed both sides in a single operation; the first such press was installed in the pressroom of the *New York Tribune*. Hoe's subsequent addition of high-speed folding apparatus in 1875 essentially completed the modern newspaper press. Branch plants

were opened in Boston and London to manufacture the Hoe press for newspapers around the world, and in New York City Hoe developed an apprentice school in the home plant for the training of press operators. The firm also introduced other types of specialized presses, including the stop-cylinder press in 1853 and the steam-powered lithography press about 1868. Hoe died on June 7, 1886, while vacationing in Florence, Italy.

Hoffa, James Riddle (1913–1975?), labor leader. Born on February 14, 1913, in Brazil, Indiana, Hoffa grew up there and from 1925 in Detroit. He left school at fourteen to help support his family. At seventeen, working for the Kroger Grocery Company, he organized the warehousemen into a union, won a brief and well-timed strike, and the next year secured a union charter from the American Federation of Labor (AFL). In 1932 he led his local into the International Brotherhood of Teamsters and three years later was elected president of Detroit Local 299 of the Teamsters. A fearless, aggressive, and wily master of union politics, he extended his influence by various means into other locals, proving himself both a gifted organizer and a ruthlessly ambitious power broker. By the 1940s he was in virtually absolute control of the Central States Council of the union and in 1952, in return for throwing his support to the campaign of Dave Beck for the Teamsters' presidency, he was named a vice-president of the international union. It took him only five years to consolidate his power—dealing, allegedly, on several occasions with underworld figures through whom "paper" locals were established and rivals intimidated—to the point where he was able to succeed the beleaguered Beck as president of the Teamsters. With the same drive that had marked his rapid rise, Hoffa pushed a major membership expansion campaign, absorbed other unions or formed alliances with them, and, particularly after the ouster of the Teamsters from the AFL–CIO on charges of corruption late in 1957, molded the Teamsters into possibly the most powerful single union in the nation. Persistent attempts by the federal government to curb his influence and to prove him guilty of corrupt practices failed; with his success in 1964 in bringing all the country's truckers under a single contract—a step feared by some as posing a threat of a paralyzing nationwide strike—and his vigorous efforts to unite all other transport workers—railway, airline, and waterborne shipping—into a federation with the Teamsters, he loomed as a potential czar of American commerce. The government's legal battles against Hoffa were led by Robert F. Kennedy, who, first as counsel to the McClellan investigating committee of the U.S. Senate and from 1961 as attorney general, publicly declared Hoffa his principal target. Finally, in 1964, Hoffa was found guilty of having tampered with the jury in a trial two years earlier; a series of appeals that finally reached the Supreme Court kept him out of prison until 1967, but in March of that year he began an eight-year sentence, to which a five-year sentence for mail fraud and mis-handling of the union's welfare fund had been added after a conviction of those charges in the meantime. He retained the presidency of the union and of his Detroit local until 1971, when he resigned in an attempt to speed his release on parole. In December, after four years and nine months in prison, he was released with a commuted sentence on the order of President Richard M. Nixon with the condition that he take no part in union affairs for eight years. He disappeared from a suburban Detroit restaurant on July 30, 1975, and was presumed kidnapped and murdered.

Hoffer, Eric (1902–1983), philosopher. Born in New York City on July 25, 1902, Hoffer early exhibited a precocious intelligence, but as a result of an accident he was blind for several years and consequently received no formal schooling. On regaining his sight at fifteen he began what became a lifelong habit of wide and voracious reading. At eighteen he left home and made his way to California, where for more than 20 years he worked as a migrant farmhand, lumberjack, railroad laborer, and in other such jobs; in 1943 he settled in San Francisco and began working as a longshoreman on the docks. He had by this time already begun to translate his reading and his experiences into writing occasional articles, published in journals and magazines, and in 1951 he published his first book, *The True Believer,* a study of fanaticism and mass movements that was well received by critics. *The Passionate State of Mind,* 1955, a collection of epigrammatic observations on politics and other aspects of the human condition, further demonstrated Hoffer's keen perceptions and mastery of generalization. After the appearance of two other books—*The Ordeal of Change,* 1963, and *The Temper of Our Time,* 1967—he retired from his dockworker's job in 1967. He continued thereafter to read, observe, and write, publishing magazine articles and *Writing and Thinking on the Waterfront,* 1969; *In Our Time,* 1976; and *Before the Sabbath,* 1979. Hoffer was widely celebrated as an inspiring example of self-education and by many as the paradigm worker-intellectual; the reception accorded his books was occasionally colored by awareness of his unique background. He died on May 21, 1983, in San Francisco.

Hofmann, Hans (1880–1966), painter and art teacher. Born in Weissenburg, Germany, on March 21, 1880, Hofmann grew up in Munich, where after two years in an architect's office he began the study of painting in 1898. From 1904 to 1914, with the patronage of a Berlin businessman, he lived and studied in Paris. From an early leaning toward Impressionism he moved on, bolstered by his association with Henri Matisse in Paris, to Fauvist and Cubist experiments in still-life and landscape painting and then to still more abstract works. In 1915 he opened his own painting school in Munich, continuing to direct it for 16 years and eventually attracting students from all over Europe and from the United States. After two summers spent teaching at the University of California at Berkeley, Hofmann joined the faculty of the Art Students League in New York City in 1931. The next year he founded his Hans Hofmann School of Fine Arts there, and from 1934 he also directed a summer school in Provincetown, Massachusetts. He became a U.S. citizen in 1941. Although he had exhibited often in Europe and on a few occasions in the United States, his first major U.S. show did not come until 1944, at the Art of This Century gallery in New York City, and even afterward he continued for many years to be primarily known as a teacher. Hofmann was acknowledged to be one of the principal inspirations for the style of painting that came to be known as Abstract Expressionism, a style that for decades remained dominant in American art and of which his own works were excellent representatives—bright, bold, spontaneous improvisations in color and form. In 1957 a major retrospective of his paintings was held in New York City at the Whitney Museum of American Art, subsequently traveling to other cities. Several other such shows followed, notably at New York's Museum of Modern Art in 1963, and late in his life he became as widely celebrated as a painter as he had been as a teacher. He gave up his school in 1958 to devote full time to painting and was the recipient of a number of honors and awards. Hofmann died on February 17, 1966, in New York City.

Hofstadter, Richard (1916–1970), historian. Born on August 6, 1916, in Buffalo, New York, Hofstadter graduated from the University of Buffalo in 1937 and pursued graduate studies in history at Columbia University. He was an instructor at Brooklyn College and at the College of the City of New York (CCNY) in 1940–1941 and in 1942, on receiving his Ph.D. from Columbia, became assistant professor of history at the University of Maryland. In 1944 his Ph.D. thesis was published, as the winner of the American Historical Association's Albert J. Beveridge Memorial Prize, under the title *Social Darwinism in American Thought, 1860–1915;* acclaimed by critics, it was the work in which Hofstadter first revealed his unorthodox approach to historiography. He moved to Columbia University in 1946 as assistant professor of history, advancing to a full professorship in 1952 and in 1959 becoming DeWitt Clinton Professor of American History. In *The American Political Tradition and the Men Who Made It,* 1948; *The Development and Scope of Higher Education in the United States,* 1952, with C. DeWitt Hardy; *The Age of Reform,* 1955, a study of the Populist, Progressive, and New Deal eras that won a Pulitzer Prize; and *The Development of Academic Freedom in the United States,* 1955, with Walter P. Metzger, he continued to cut across lines of specialization to investigate broadly conceived aspects of American history, aiming particularly at the areas where politics and ideas meet and conflict. Calling himself a historian of "political culture," Hofstadter expressed his novel and influential interpretations in a literary style that was admired on its own account and that helped attract readers from outside the ranks of professionals. Others of his books included *Anti-Intellectualism in American Life*, 1963, which won another Pulitzer Prize; *The Paranoid Style in American Politics*, 1965; *The Progressive Historians: Turner, Beard, Parrington*, 1968; *The Idea of a Party System*, 1969; and *American Violence, A Documentary History*, 1970, with Michael Wallace. He was possessed of an abiding interest in contemporary affairs, with the result that much of his work in the field of history had marked relevance to the present age. Regarded as one of the most distinguished historians of his day, Hofstadter died in New York City on October 24, 1970.

Hofstadter, Robert (1915–   ), physicist. Born in New York City on February 5, 1915, Hofstadter graduated from the College of the City of New York (CCNY) in 1935 and three years later took his Ph.D. at Princeton University. After a year as an instructor in physics at City College he joined the ordnance research laboratory of the U.S. Bureau of Standards in 1942, where his work included development of the proximity fuse. From 1943 to 1946 he was employed in similar work by the Norden Corporation; in 1946 he returned to teaching and research at Princeton. In 1950 he became associate professor of physics at Stanford University, advancing to full professor in 1954. Hofstadter's researches at Princeton were largely in the fields of infrared spectroscopy, photoconductivity, and the development of crystal and scintillation counters. After moving to Stanford he began working with a high-energy linear electron accelerator to study the structure of atomic nuclei. He then undertook a closer study of the constituent particles of nuclei and was able to announce precise determinations of the size and shape of the proton and the neutron in 1956 and 1957. He was awarded the 1961 Nobel Prize for Physics jointly with Rudolf Mössbauer of Germany. He continued his researches at Stanford thereafter, becoming director of the high-energy physics laboratory in 1967. Hofstadter was at various times editor of several scientific journals and was a prolific writer of reviews and papers.

Hogan, William Benjamin (1912–   ), "Ben," golfer. Born near Stephenville, Texas, on August 13, 1912, Ben Hogan grew up in Fort Worth and began working as a golf caddie at the age of eleven. By 1932 he had a job as resident pro at the Oakhurst, Texas, country club and had begun trying his skill on the professional tour. He enjoyed little success in his first few tours, but he won many friends and admirers by the determination and courage that were to be the hallmarks of his career. By 1940 he was beginning to win or place high in tournaments; he was the pro tour's leading money winner in 1940, 1941, and 1942, but captured no major titles in those years. After service in the Army Air Corps in 1943–1945 he returned to the tour and in 1946 suddenly took the golf world by storm, winning the Western Open, the North and South Open, the Professional Golfers' Association (PGA) tournament, and several others, also taking first place among money winners. After an off year in 1947 he came back in 1948 to repeat his victories in the PGA and the Western Open and take his first U.S. Open title. In 1949 an automobile accident nearly cost him his life, and it was generally assumed that his playing days were at an end. He fought back grimly against incapacity, however, although he could never thereafter play without pain, and in 1950 recaptured the U.S. Open title. In 1951 he won the U.S. Open and the Masters Tournament and in 1953 he again captured those titles—breaking the Masters record by five strokes—and added a victory in his first British Open. He lost the 1954 Masters in a playoff with Sam Snead and placed second in the Masters and the U.S. Open in 1955 and the Open in 1956. His subsequent attempts to win a record fifth U.S. Open were unsuccessful. For a number of years he was associated with the Hershey, Pennsylvania, Country Club, and he wrote several books and articles on golf, notably *Power Golf*, 1948. He was named one of the three greatest golfers of the first half of the twentieth century—with Walter Hagen and Bobby Jones—by a commission of sportswriters in 1950.

Hokinson, Helen (1893–1949), cartoonist. Born in Mendota, Illinois, on June 29, 1893, Miss Hokinson traveled to New York City in 1920 to study at the Academy of Fine Arts. Although she specialized in fashion art during her five years of formal training, she had a keen interest in cartooning and the acceptance of one of her early efforts by the newly founded *New Yorker* magazine in 1925 decided her career. Over the next two dozen years she drew more than 1700 cartoons, published principally in the *New Yorker* and nearly all of them detailing the life of the middle-aged American matron. Her characters, slightly overweight, behatted, and ranging in mental state from outright addled to merely puzzled, populated garden clubs, literary societies, civic meetings, and luncheons, and they entertained numberless notions and aspirations that were at once ridiculous and engagingly innocent. Miss Hokinson's cartoons lampooned with a gentle touch that won her great popularity, not only among the satirically inclined but also among the very ranks of those she chided. She continued to publish her cartoons regularly until her death in an airplane accident near Washington, D.C., on November 1, 1949.

Holabird, William (1854–1923), architect. Born on September 11, 1854, in Amenia Union, Dutchess County, New York, Holabird attended West Point for two years and on resigning in 1875 moved to Chicago and secured a position as draftsman in the architectural office of William Le Baron Jenney. Five years later he opened his own office as senior partner of a firm that became Holabird & Roche in 1883. The firm's first major commission came in 1886 and called for the design of a commercially profitable building on a small downtown lot. Holabird had noted the success of Jenney's Home Insurance Building, completed the year before, which utilized an iron and steel skeleton, and for his Tacoma Building he extended and improved the technique, using load-bearing metal throughout the structure. It was the Tacoma Building, completed in 1888, that firmly established the skeleton method of construction for tall buildings, and from that date Holabird & Roche were the major developers of Jenney's original idea into the modern urban office building. Subsequent important works of the firm, all in Chicago, included the Caxton Building, 1890; the Pontiac, 1891; the Marquette, 1894; the Tribune Building, 1901, in which was first tried the construction of multiple basements, thereafter a standard feature of large commercial buildings; the Cook County Building, 1906; the Congress Hotel, 1907; the LaSalle Hotel, 1909; Chicago City Hall, 1910; the Sherman Hotel, 1912; and the John Crerar Library, 1919. Holabird died in Evanston, Illinois, on July 19, 1923.

Holbrook, Josiah (1788–1854), educator. Born in Derby, Connecticut, in 1788, Holbrook graduated from Yale in 1810 and returned to his native town to open a school. He failed with an experimental industrial school established in 1819 and an agricultural school started in 1824, but while working as an itinerant lecturer he continued to ponder the question of educational opportunities for adults in the rural sections of the country, and in 1826 he published an article, "Associations of Adults for Mutual Education," in the *American Journal of Education*, in which he outlined a scheme for the organization in small towns and villages throughout the nation of voluntary associations to serve as meeting places for adults interested in self-improvement and the promotion of schools and other educational institutions. In that year he founded such a group in Millbury, Massachusetts, calling it a "lyceum" after the ancient school of Aristotle in Athens. The idea caught on quickly and similar groups sprang up across New England and New York and in the Middle West; by 1834 there were some 3000 local lyceums loosely organized into the American Lyceum Association. Holbrook was engaged for a time in manufacturing scientific and mathematical apparatus for use in lyceums; for two years, 1830–1832, he published a series of *Scientific Tracts Designed for Instruction and Entertainment and Adapted to Schools, Lyceums and Families*, and during 1832 he published the weekly *Family Lyceum*. During the late 1830s and early 1840s he established a short-lived central "Lyceum Village," first in Ohio and then in New York, and in New York City he worked from 1842 to 1849 as secretary of a bureau through which regular courses of study were supplied to local lyceums and by which lecture tours were arranged. The lyceum circuit

attracted many of the outstanding lecturers and public figures of the day, including Ralph Waldo Emerson, Henry David Thoreau, Daniel Webster, Nathaniel Hawthorne, Henry Ward Beecher, and others, and remained until the Civil War one of the most potent forums in the country for public debate and the spread of ideas. Holbrook continued to promote the lyceum movement for the rest of his life, living after 1849 in Washington, D.C. He died near Lynchburg, Virginia, on June 17, 1854.

Holiday, Billie (1915–1959), "Lady Day," singer. Born on April 7, 1915, in Baltimore, Eleanora Fagan was the daughter of a professional musician who for a time played guitar with the great Fletcher Henderson band. She later adopted the name Billie from a favorite movie actress, Billie Dove; Holiday was her father's name. She grew up in poverty in a ghetto area of Baltimore; as a child, in return for running errands for a local brothel keeper, she was allowed to linger and listen to recordings by singer Bessie Smith and trumpeter Louis Armstrong. In 1928 she moved with her mother to New York City and after three years of subsisting by various means she found a job singing in a Harlem nightclub. She had had no formal musical training, but with an almost instinctive sense of musical structure and with a wealth of experience gathered at the root level of jazz and blues she developed a singing style that was deeply moving, individual, and inimitable. In 1933 she made her first recordings, with Benny Goodman and others; two years later a series of recordings with Teddy Wilson and members of Count Basie's band brought her wider recognition and launched her career as the leading jazz singer of her time. She toured with Basie and with Artie Shaw in 1937 and 1938 and in the latter year opened at the plush Café Society in New York City. From about 1940 she performed exclusively in cabarets and in concert. Her recordings between 1936 and 1942 marked her peak years; during that period she was often associated with saxophonist Lester Young, who gave her the nickname "Lady Day" (it was she, in turn, who dubbed him "Pres"). In 1947 she was arrested for a narcotics violation and spent a year in a rehabilitation center; no longer able to obtain a cabaret license to work in New York City, she nonetheless packed New York's Carnegie Hall ten days after her release. She continued to perform in concert and in clubs outside of New York and she made several tours during her later years. The constant struggle with heroin addiction more and more affected her voice, although not her style. In 1956 she wrote an autobiography, *Lady Sings the Blues* (with William Dufty). She died in New York City on July 17, 1959.

Holladay, Ben (1819–1887), businessman and financier. Born in Carlisle County, Kentucky, in October 1819, Holladay received little formal schooling and early moved with his family to Missouri. In his youth he engaged in various mercantile activities, including the Indian trade, and during the Mexican War he secured a contract to supply Gen. Stephen W. Kearny's Army of the West. At the end of the war he was able to purchase enough surplus wagons and oxen from the army to undertake major freighting operations and began hauling goods from Missouri to the Mormon country in Utah, driving cattle to California mining districts, and engaging in other such ventures. In March 1862 he bought at public auction the holdings of the bankrupt freighting firm of Russell, Majors and Waddell, which had gone broke financing the Pony Express. The Central Overland, California and Pikes Peak Express thus acquired, brought with it the government contract for the overland mail between Missouri and the Far West, a contract that was soon to be worth more than a million dollars in annual subsidies. Holladay quickly put the stagecoach runs on schedule, built new way stations, improved equipment, personnel, and passenger accommodations, and extended his lines into the Colorado, Montana, and Idaho mining districts. Controlling the entire network of thousands of miles of routes with an iron hand, he reaped huge profits and earned the nickname "Napoleon of the Plains." In 1866, foreseeing the effects the approaching transcontinental railroad would have on the overland freight and mail business, he sold out to Wells, Fargo & Company. The next year he organized the Northern Pacific Transportation Company, which absorbed the California, Oregon, and Mexican Steamship Company he had formed in 1863, and soon he was operating steamers along the Pacific coast from Mexico to Alaska. In 1868 he bought a controlling interest in the Oregon Central Railroad and launched a vigorous program of construction, selling his steamship interests in the course of financing the project. The panic of 1873 dealt a severe blow to the line and three years later he was forced out of the company by its German bondholders, an action that ruined him financially. Holladay died in Portland, Oregon, on July 8, 1887.

Holland, John Philip (1840–1914), inventor. Born on February 29, 1840, in Liscannor, County Clare, Ireland, Holland was educated in Limerick and from 1858 worked as a schoolteacher in various towns. He had long been interested in ships and by 1870 had read the literature on early experiments with submarine boats and had drawn plans for one of his own. In 1873 he emigrated to the United States and the next year settled and resumed teaching in Paterson, New Jersey. His submarine plans were rejected by the navy in 1875, but the Fenian Society of expatriate Irish nationalists, who saw in the submarine a potent weapon for Irish independence from Great Britain, supplied capital for construction of a model. Preliminary success in tests in the Passaic River in 1877 brought funds for building the full-scale *Fenian Ram*, which Holland tested successfully in New York Harbor in 1881–1883. It featured an internal-combustion engine and advanced control

and balance mechanisms. From 1879, when he gave up teaching, Holland devoted all his time to improving the submarine and on several occasions after the success of the *Fenian Ram* managed to arouse the technical, but not financial, interest of the navy. In 1895 his J. P. Holland Torpedo Boat Company was at last awarded a navy contract to build a submarine. The resulting *Plunger* was built in Baltimore under the supervision of Adm. George W. Melville and largely without Holland's advice, and it was as a consequence thoroughly unsatisfactory. With what money he had left Holland built and in 1898 launched the *Holland*, incorporating for the first time a combination of internal-combustion power for propulsion on the surface with electric power from storage batteries for running submerged and, as in the *Fenian Ram*, rudder planes that enabled the craft to dive rather than passively sink to a desired depth. Fitted also with a torpedo tube and a dynamite gun in the bow, the 53-foot *Holland* was tested rigorously and in April 1900 was finally accepted as the navy's first submarine. Holland subsequently built several more submarines for the navy and filled orders from Great Britain, Russia, and Japan as well. He was later troubled by difficulties with the financiers who controlled his company and in his last years abandoned submarines to carry on experiments in aviation. Holland died in Newark, New Jersey, on August 12, 1914.

Holland, Josiah Gilbert (1819–1881), author and editor. Born in Belchertown, Massachusetts, on July 24, 1819, Holland grew up in straitened circumstances and fragile health. After leaving school he held various jobs, including that of schoolteacher, until 1840, when he entered the Berkshire Medical College. Although he completed the course in 1844 he had little liking for the medical profession and soon abandoned it. In 1848, after publishing the *Bay State Weekly Courier* for a time, he returned to teaching in Richmond, Virginia, becoming a few months later superintendent of schools in Vicksburg, Mississippi. He returned to Massachusetts the next year and became assistant editor of the *Springfield Republican* under Samuel Bowles. His varied contributions to the newspaper helped greatly in establishing its popularity and he collected them in several books, including a *History of Western Massachusetts*, 1855; *The Bay-Path: A Tale of New England Colonial Life*, 1857; *Timothy Titcomb's Letters to Young People, Single and Married*, 1858, written as "Timothy Titcomb;" and *Bitter Sweet, a Poem in Dramatic Form*, 1858. In 1857 Holland sold the financial interest he had acquired in the *Republican* and gave up his regular position, although he continued to contribute to the paper for the rest of his life and served as its editor on occasion during Bowles's absence. His popularity as an author grew rapidly and he published a great many books of moral essays, poetry, and fiction; among them *Gold Foil Hammered from Popular Proverbs*, 1859; *Lessons in Life*, 1861; *Letters to the Joneses*, 1863; *Plain*

Talks on Familiar Subjects, 1865; and two series of *Every-Day Topics*, 1876 and 1882. All of these were in the popular mold of didactic writing and led to a great demand for his services as a lecturer, and his verses and novels—such as *Miss Gilbert's Career*, 1860; *Katrina, Her Life and Mine in a Poem*, 1867; *The Marble Prophecy and Other Poems*, 1872; *Arthur Bonnicastle*, 1873; *The Mistress of the Manse*, 1874; *Sevenoaks*, 1875; *Nicholas Minturn*, 1877; and *The Puritan's Guest and Other Poems*, 1881, combined didacticism with melodrama and sentimentality in a manner perfectly suited to the taste of the day. In 1870 Holland helped found and became first editor of *Scribner's Monthly*, which was renamed the *Century Illustrated Magazine* ("the *Century*") in 1881. At the time of his death in New York City on October 12, 1881, he was among the best established of popular authors, but within a short time his works ceased almost entirely to be read.

Hollerith, Herman (1860–1929), inventor. Born in Buffalo, New York, on February 29, 1860, Hollerith graduated from the Columbia University School of Mines in 1879. He was employed as a statistician on the U.S. census of 1880 and in that connection met John S. Billings, director of vital statistics for the census, who suggested to him the possibility of using mechanical means of tabulating the vast quantities of raw data involved in their work. After a year, 1882–1883, as an instructor in mechanical engineering at the Massachusetts Institute of Technology (MIT) and another in St. Louis, during which he experimented with railroad braking systems, Hollerith returned to Washington, D.C., in 1884 and secured a position in the Patent Office. He began working seriously on Billings's suggestion, at first trying a method of recording data on perforated tape and then adopting the more flexible medium of punched cards. The heart of his system was an electric sensing device in which counts were recorded when a hole or pattern of holes at preselected sites allowed the passage of current between contacts on either side of the card; by this means the encoded raw data could be tabulated for any combination of categories with great speed. After successful preliminary trials the system was adopted for the census of 1890 and subsequently for census counts in Canada, Norway, and Austria in 1891 and in Great Britain in 1911. The punched-card tabulating system, the direct ancestor of modern data-processing systems, completely revolutionized the work of statisticians and made possible vastly more sophisticated analyses of data. In the U.S. census of 1900, with a decade of improvement behind, Hollerith's system made possible the completion of the population volume in 19 months, as compared to the estimated 8 years that would have been required for a force of 100 clerks to deal with merely the data on sex, birthplace, and occupation. Hollerith left the Patent Office in 1890 and in 1896 organized the Tabulating Machine Company, which in 1911 merged with two other firms to become the Computing-Tabulating-Recording Company, which in 1924 became International Business Machines (IBM). Hollerith remained with C-T-R as a consulting engineer until 1921; he died in Washington, D.C., on November 17, 1929.

Holley, Alexander Lyman (1832–1882), engineer and editor. Born in Lakeville, Connecticut, on July 20, 1832, Holley graduated from Brown University in 1853. While in college he received his first patent, for a steam engine cutoff. Between 1853 and 1855 he worked for companies engaged in the manufacture of railroad locomotives and then, from 1855 to 1857, published *Holley's Railroad Advocate*. In 1857 he and an associate traveled to Europe under the auspices of several railroad companies to inspect European railroads and study their practices, publishing a comprehensive report upon their return the next year. In 1858 he began an association with the *New York Times* that lasted for nearly 20 years; he was technical editor for the *American Railway Review* and in 1860 published *American and European Railway Practice*. He engaged in a number of engineering projects until 1862 when, while on business in England, he became acquainted with the new Bessemer process for making steel. The following year he bought the rights to the use of the process in the United States and, effecting a pooling of potentially conflicting patents with the holders of William Kelly's patent, within two years had a steel plant in operation in Troy, New York. By 1867 the experimental stage was completed and the first steel rails had been produced. For the rest of his life Holley designed and built steel plants all over the country and patented a number of improvements on the Bessemer process. He was foremost in his field and largely responsible for laying the foundations of the steel industry in the United States. He died on January 29, 1882, in Brooklyn, New York.

Holley, Robert William (1922–   ), biochemist. Born on January 28, 1922, in Urbana, Illinois, Holley graduated from the University of Illinois in 1942 and then entered Cornell University, from which he took his Ph.D. in 1947. After a year of further study and research at Washington State College he returned to Cornell in 1948 as assistant professor of organic chemistry at the New York State Agricultural Experiment Station, advancing to associate professor two years later. From 1957 to 1964 he was associated with the U.S. Department of Agriculture's Plant, Soil and Nutrition Laboratory in Ithaca, New York, and in 1964 he was appointed professor of biochemistry at Cornell, where he remained until becoming a resident fellow of the Salk Institute in La Jolla, California, in 1968. From 1947 Holley's researches concentrated on the analysis of cellular proteins and the nucleic acids involved in their synthesis. Of the latter he paid particular attention to ribonucleic acid (RNA) and found that, while it was concentrated principally in the ribosomes of the cell, a small quantity of a considerably less complex sort of RNA was diffused through the cell sap. These smaller molecules functioned as transporters of amino acids to the ribosomes, where protein molecules were then built up from them by the larger RNA particles. Working with yeasts, he was able to isolate a quantity of pure transfer RNA (tRNA) of a type specific to the amino acid alanine and then, by a painstaking process of applying to it various enzymes known to be specific to particular nucleotide units (constituents of nucleic acids), he broke down the tRNA molecules into short segments and gradually built up a picture of the entire 77-unit molecule. In 1965 he announced the complete determination of the structure of the alanine tRNA molecule, the first such complete analysis of a nucleic acid in terms of the actual sequence of nucleotides in the chain-like molecule. For this achievement, one of far-reaching consequence for the study of genetic mechanisms, Holley was awarded the 1968 Nobel Prize for Physiology and Medicine, jointly with Har Gobind Khorana and Marshall W. Nirenberg.

Holm, Saxe, see Jackson, Helen Hunt

Holmes, Oliver Wendell (1809–1894), physician, educator, and author. Born in Cambridge, Massachusetts, on August 29, 1809, Holmes graduated from Harvard in 1829. Although tempted by a life of letters, he chose to enter a more secure profession and enrolled in the Harvard Law School; the following year, finding law a dull study, he transferred to a private medical school. In that same year, 1830, he achieved his first recognition as an author when his poem "Old Ironsides" appeared in the *Boston Daily Advertiser*; a year later he published an article in the *New England Magazine* entitled "The Autocrat of the Breakfast-Table," which was followed by another of the same name in 1832. In 1833 he sailed to France for two more years of medical study; upon his return he completed his studies at Harvard Medical School and in 1836 was granted an M.D. In the same year he published his first book of verse, entitled *Poems*. During the next several years his literary activities were greatly diminished as he devoted himself to practice, to research—which Harvard recognized with three Boylston prizes—and teaching, first at the Tremont Medical School, which he helped to found, then at Dartmouth as a professor of anatomy, and finally, from 1847, at Harvard Medical School. Although little of his medical research was truly original, he did provoke heated controversy with his 1843 essay on "The Contagiousness of Puerperal Fever," in which he blamed unsanitary obstetricians for the spread of the disease. Along with his popularity at Harvard there developed a demand for Holmes as a lyceum lecturer and occasional poet; by 1857 his reputation was such that when James Russell Lowell was asked to be the first editor of the *Atlantic Monthly*—the name of the magazine was Holmes's suggestion—he accepted only on condition that the doctor be secured as a contributor. In the first issue that year appeared the first of a series of articles under the revived title of 25 years earlier, "The Autocrat of the Breakfast-Table." Beginning "I was just going to say when I was interrupted," the piece and the ones that followed were widely read and appreciated; the series, which also contained two of his most famous poems, "The Chambered Nautilus" and "The Deacon's Masterpiece; or, The Wonderful One-Hoss Shay," was collected in book form and published the next year. There followed three similar series of witty, conversational pieces, all later published as separate volumes: *The Professor at the Breakfast-Table*, 1860; *The Poet at the Breakfast-Table*, 1872; and *Over the Teacups*, 1891. Holmes also wrote three novels in the 1860s, all first serialized in the *Atlantic*, and based on his preference for a psychological rather than religious interpretation of morality and behavior; of them only *Elsie Venner*, 1861, is memorable. In 1882 he retired from the Harvard medical faculty, where he had also been dean of the medical school from 1847 to 1853. The best-known and best-loved American man of letters of his day, Holmes enjoyed a worldwide reputation as a witty, urbane, and warmly humane commentator on matters and events. He was Boston's unofficial laureate and one of the moving spirits of that city's literary golden age. He was a mainstay of the Saturday Club and an indispensable figure at every public occasion. He continued to write, publishing several volumes of verse, some collections culled from his earlier work, and biographies of John Lothrop Motley and Ralph Waldo Emerson, among others. He died in Boston on October 7, 1894, having outlived the rest of the generation of great New England literary figures who had been his contemporaries and companions. He was elected to the Hall of Fame in 1910.

Holmes, Oliver Wendell (1841–1935), justice of the Supreme Court. Born in Boston on March 8, 1841, Holmes was the son of Oliver Wendell Holmes (1809–1894) and grew up on familiar terms with the literary and intellectual eminences who made up his father's circle of friends. He entered Harvard in 1857 and although his undergraduate career was marked by a somewhat rebellious attitude toward intellectual orthodoxy—a frame of mind for which he was indebted to his father and to Ralph Waldo Emerson—he graduated as class poet in 1861. Shortly before graduation he had enlisted in the Massachusetts militia, and the following September, by then a lieutenant, he marched with the 20th Massachusetts Volunteers to the Civil War. He saw much action, was three times seriously wounded (at Ball's Bluff, Antietam, and Fredericksburg), each time returning to the front, and although he was later to describe war as an "organized bore" he was profoundly affected by his three years' exposure to its stark realities. He was mustered out in 1864 as a captain. Entering Harvard Law School that year, he took his degree in 1866 and after a visit to Europe, where he formed a number of lasting friendships with prominent figures, was admitted to the bar in 1867. First in the office of Chandler, Shattuck & Thayer and later as a partner in Shattuck, Holmes & Munroe, he carried on a practice while devoting his major energies to legal scholarship, and in that enterprise his penchant for philosophy, which had once almost seduced him from the law, found suitable expression. From 1870 to 1873 he served as coeditor of the *American Law Review*, to which he contributed as well, and in 1873 he capped four years of arduous labor with the publication of the 12th edition of James Kent's *Commentaries on American Law*. An invitation to deliver a series of lectures at the Lowell Institute of Boston in 1881 gave Holmes opportunity to collect and systematize his thoughts on law, which had thus far been the subject only of his fugitive essays; the book that resulted, *The Common Law*, 1881, was a deceptively slim volume that represented a revolution in legal philosophy. The opening sentence set the theme: "The life of the law has not been logic; it has been experience." He went on to examine the history of the common law and to find it to be not a system of logical deductions from axioms arrived at by metaphysical intuition, but an evolving patchwork of pragmatic responses to changing situations. This thoroughly skeptical yet rational approach to law was incomprehensible to some, but among others it established immediately Holmes's reputation both at home and abroad. He was named to the new Weld chair of law at Harvard in January 1882 but remained there only until the end of the year, when he was appointed to the Massachusetts supreme court. During 19 years on that bench, the last three as chief justice, he wrote some 1300 opinions on all phases of the law and in doing so found his true calling—"to think under fire—to think for action upon which great interests depend"—but nonetheless found insufficient scope for the full elaboration of his ideas. That scope came in 1902, when President Theodore Roosevelt, in the mistaken belief that Holmes was an activist liberal of his own stripe, named him to the Supreme Court. Holmes was not long in disabusing Roosevelt of his opinion; in 1904 he wrote a notable dissent in *Northern Securities Co.* v. *U.S.*, one of the government's prime antitrust cases, and noted in passing that "great cases like hard cases make bad law." Although he spoke for the Court in such major cases as *Swift & Co.* v. *U.S.*, 1905, another antitrust suit; *Schenck* v. *U.S.*, 1919, in which he formulated his "clear and present danger" test in defining conditions under which the right of free speech could be interfered with and upheld an application of the 1917 Espionage Act; and *Missouri* v. *Holland*, 1920, which affirmed the power of Congress to act through its treaty power in areas normally closed to it, it was in his dissents that he best elucidated his constitutional theory. In *Lochner* v. *New York*, 1905, he clearly stated his view that the Court was bound to give legislative acts all benefit of doubt: "The 14th Amendment does not enact Mr. Herbert Spencer's *Social Statics*. . . . A Constitution is not intended to

embody a particular economic theory, whether of paternalism and the organic relation of the citizen to the state or of laissez faire. It is made for people of fundamentally differing views, and the accident of our finding certain opinions natural and familiar, or novel, and even shocking, ought not to conclude our judgment upon the question whether statutes embodying them conflict with the Constitution of the United States." In *Adair* v. *U.S.*, 1908, he supported an act outlawing "yellow-dog" labor contracts. In *Hammer* v. *Dagenhart*, 1918, he upheld the power of Congress to restrict from interstate commerce the products of child labor. In *Abrams* v. *U.S.*, 1919, he declared "that the ultimate good desired is better reached by free trade in ideas—that the best test of truth is the power of the thought to get itself accepted in the competition of the market, and that truth is the only ground upon which [men's] wishes safely can be carried out. That at any rate is the theory of our Constitution. It is an experiment, as all life is an experiment." In *Adkins* v. *Children's Hospital*, 1923, he put his view succinctly: "The criterion of constitutionality is not whether we view the law to be for the public good." Holmes's intense concentration on legal issues often confused many, for it led him with apparent inconsistency to come down on first one and then the other side of the vaguer but more publicly attractive social and economic issues of his day. His conception of the freedom due men to work out, through legislative experiment, new solutions to new problems and of the consequent responsibility for restraint on the part of the judiciary, combined with a finely honed literary style, made him one of the towering figures in the Court's history, rivaled only by John Marshall in the extent of his influence. Holmes remained active into his tenth decade, but finally, in January 1932, he resigned from the Supreme Court. He died in Washington, D.C., on March 6, 1935, just two days before his ninety-fourth birthday. His sizable estate he left without restriction to the United States; it was eventually used to finance a history of the Supreme Court. He was elected to the Hall of Fame in 1965.

Holt, Luther Emmett (1855–1924), physician and educator. Born on March 4, 1855, in Webster, New York, Holt graduated from the University of Rochester in 1875 and studied medicine at the University of Buffalo and at the College of Physicians and Surgeons in New York City, from which he took his M.D. in 1880. While conducting a private practice he developed a deep interest in pediatrics and at various times served in positions in the New York Infant Asylum, the New York Foundling Hospital, and other such institutions. In 1888 he was appointed director of the Babies Hospital of New York and two years later became also professor of the diseases of children at New York Polyclinic Hospital. His course for pediatric nurses evolved into a small booklet, *The Care and Feeding of Children*, 1894, that enjoyed such huge sales as to require more than 75 additional printings. *The Diseases of Infancy and Childhood,* 1896, immediately became and for decades remained the standard English-language text in the field. Holt led in founding and was elected president of the American Pediatric Society in 1898 and later served as editor of the *American Journal of Diseases of Children.* In 1901 he became professor of pediatrics at the College of Physicians and Surgeons, and in 20 years in that post exerted a profound influence on the development and recognition of pediatrics as a fully articulated field of medicine; his work as a teacher was widely celebrated and was of a value to medicine equal to that of his research and writings. Holt was a member of numerous medical and reform organizations concerned with the health of children and was one of the early advisers on and an original director of the Rockefeller Institute for Medical Research, founded in 1901. He retired from the College of Physicians and Surgeons in 1921 and two years later was again elected president of the American Pediatric Society. In the same year he accepted an invitation to serve as visiting professor of pediatrics at the Union Medical College in Peking, China, where he died a few months later, on January 14, 1924.

Homer, Winslow (1836–1910), painter. Born on February 24, 1836, in Boston, Homer was apprenticed to a lithographer in 1855. Two years later he opened his own studio and began a career as an illustrator, working for *Ballou's Pictorial* and *Harper's Weekly. Harper's* sent him to Washington to sketch Lincoln's inauguration. Later he drew camp scenes, episodes from army life, and battle scenes from Virginia; the emotion and intensity of this Civil War experience affected much of his later work. After returning to his studio he continued to paint war subjects, producing, among others, "Sharpshooter on Picket Duty" and "Prisoners from the Front," and exhibited at the National Academy of Design and elsewhere. After a trip to France he turned to landscape painting. He continued to contribute to *Harper's* and other periodicals and traveled extensively in search of subject material for his paintings. He produced "Snap the Whip" in 1872 and showed it at the Centennial Exposition in Philadelphia four years later. A trip to England in 1881–1882 reawakened his boyhood love of the sea. He turned away from city life to settle at Prouts Neck, near Scarboro, Maine, in 1883, whence he ventured forth on painting trips to Florida and the Caribbean. His watercolors and oils portraying the drama of the sea made him famous as both critical and popular acceptance came to him during the 1880s. Outstanding among them were "The Fog Warning," "Banks Fisherman," "Eight Bells," "Gulf Stream," "Rum Cay," "Mending the Nets," and "Searchlight, Harbor Entrance, Santiago de Cuba." Although his style was realistic, it was never merely pictorial, instead conveying the dignity and vitality of its subject matter. He died at Prouts Neck, Maine, on September 29, 1910. His paintings, and in particular his watercolors, were already in great demand during his lifetime and they continued to command rapidly mounting prices as collectors and the nation's leading museums vied for his best works.

Hone, Philip (1780–1851), businessman and diarist. Born in New York City on October 25, 1780, Hone grew up in modest circumstances and in 1797 went to work as an assistant in his elder brother's auction business. Within three years he was a partner in the growing concern, and he soon emerged as one of the most prosperous citizens of the city. In 1821, having decided that he had amassed a sufficient fortune, he retired from business to devote himself to civic affairs and the cultivation of the arts. He added to his large library and art collection on visits to Europe, and he numbered among his intimates many of the leading figures of the day—Washington Irving, Junius Brutus Booth, James Fenimore Cooper, and Samuel F. B. Morse among them. He was an eminent figure among New York Whigs and was on close terms with many of the party's national leaders; his influence did not lead him to become politically ambitious, however, for his only public office was that of mayor of New York City in 1825, in which year he presided in genial style over the sumptuous ceremonies at the opening of the Erie Canal and the city's reception of the Marquis de Lafayette. During the later 1820s he acquired interests in the coal fields of eastern Pennsylvania and became a chief proponent of the Delaware & Hudson Canal, whose western terminus was named Honesdale in his honor in 1827. In 1829, having dispatched Horatio Allen to England to make the necessary inspections and arrangements, he imported the *Stourbridge Lion,* the first locomotive to run on an American railroad. Financial reverses following the panic of 1837 led him to seek appointment as postmaster of New York City; disappointed in that effort, he served for a time as president of the American Mutual Insurance Company and later was appointed by President Zachary Taylor to a lucrative post in the port of New York. Despite all his varied activities, however, Hone is chiefly remembered for the detailed and illuminating diary that he kept faithfully from 1828 to 1851; his position as a friend or associate, host or guest, of nearly all the public figures of the day afforded him a unique opportunity, and the 28 volumes of his diary, published in part in 1889, represent the best single source of information on the social and political life of New York City for the period. Hone died at his home in New York City on May 5, 1851.

Hood, John Bell (1831–1879), soldier. Born in Owingsville, Kentucky, on June 1, 1831, Hood graduated from West Point in 1853 and for eight years served at posts in New York and California and then in Texas in a cavalry regiment whose lieutenant colonel was Robert E. Lee. He resigned from the army in 1861 and accepted a Confederate commission; he rose quickly through the ranks and by March 1862 was a brigadier general. He established a reputation as a "fighting general" at Gaines' Mill, the second battle of Bull Run (Manassas), and at Antietam, (Sharpsburg) and in October 1862 was promoted to major general. Attached to Gen. James Longstreet's corps, his division was at Gettysburg in July 1863 and on the second day of the battle he led the assault on Round Top and was seriously wounded. In September he accompanied Longstreet to Tennessee to reinforce Gen. Braxton Bragg and was prominent on the field at Chickamauga, where he sustained a wound that necessitated the amputation of a leg. Promoted to lieutenant general in February 1864, he was sent to assist Gen. Joseph E. Johnston in opposing Gen. William T. Sherman's advance through Georgia. Johnston's continual retreat in the face of Sherman's overwhelming superiority in numbers was a succession of depressing but unavoidable defeats and in July he was removed, Hood then succeeding to command of the Army of Tennessee with the temporary rank of full general. Faced with an impossible task, Hood, too, slowly gave way before Sherman; two attempted counterattacks failed and he found himself besieged in Atlanta. After five weeks he was forced to abandon the city before being completely encircled. He attempted to resume the offensive by circling rapidly west and north to strike behind Sherman's lines, but at Franklin and at Nashville in November–December 1864 he was repulsed with heavy losses by detached units of Sherman's forces. At his own request he was relieved of his command in January 1865. Sent west on a recruiting mission, Hood heard of the Confederate surrender at Appomattox in April and himself surrendered in Natchez, Mississippi, in May. Afterward he established himself in a mercantile business in New Orleans; his last years were passed there in poverty and he died on August 30, 1879.

Hooker, Joseph (1814–1879), soldier. Born on November 13, 1814, in Hadley, Massachusetts, Hooker graduated from West Point in 1837 and was assigned to the artillery. He saw action in the Seminole Wars, served for a time as adjutant at West Point, and, although a staff officer, was three times distinguished for his conduct during the Mexican War—at Monterrey, National Bridge, and Chapultepec—from which he emerged with the temporary rank of lieutenant colonel. In the reduction of the army that followed the war, opportunities narrowed and Hooker resigned in 1853. For several years he operated a large farm near Sonoma, California, later serving in 1858–1859 as superintendent of military roads in Oregon and in 1859–1861 as a colonel in the California militia. In 1861 he sought a Union commission and was appointed brigadier general of volunteers. He first came to prominence in the Peninsular Campaign of 1862, serving through the siege of Yorktown and bearing with his division the full force of the Confederate rearguard attack at Williamsburg, for which action he was pro-

moted to major general of volunteers. Placed in command of the 1st Corps of the Army of the Potomac, he was on the field at South Mountain and at Antietam (Sharpsburg), where he was wounded; his vigorous execution of battle plans, which had already earned him the nickname "Fighting Joe," now brought him appointment as brigadier general in the regular army. Following the Union defeat at Fredericksburg in December, Gen. Ambrose E. Burnside was relieved and President Abraham Lincoln, despite serious reservations caused by Hooker's penchant for expressing insubordinate opinions, appointed Hooker to command the Army of the Potomac. He instituted an effective reorganization of his command, but in spite of excellent planning and a huge superiority in numbers he failed to achieve the expected defeat of Gen. Robert E. Lee's forces at Chancellorsville in May 1863, remaining in a defensive position while Lee outmaneuvered him and struck north into Pennsylvania. Hooker foresaw that the climactic battle would likely be at Gettysburg, but just days before it began he concluded that he no longer commanded the confidence of the government and was at his own request replaced by Gen. George G. Meade. In September he assumed command of the 11th and 12th Corps (later consolidated as the 20th Corps), which were bound for the Department of the Cumberland to reinforce Gen. William S. Rosecrans at Chattanooga. His success in the Battle Above the Clouds at Lookout Mountain, Tennessee, in November 1863 won him promotion to major general. When Gen. Ulysses S. Grant, who had replaced Rosecrans, was in turn succeeded by Gen. William T. Sherman, Hooker's corps became part of the vast army invading Georgia in 1864. During the Atlanta Campaign Sherman showed his distrust of Hooker by passing over him to appoint Gen. Oliver O. Howard to the command of the Army of the Tennessee, and Hooker promptly requested and was granted relief from duty. From then until 1865 he commanded the Northern Department, from 1865 to 1866 the Department of the East, and from 1866 until his retirement as major general in 1868 the Department of the Lakes. Hooker died in Garden City, New York, on October 31, 1879.

Hooker, Thomas (1586–1647), religious leader. Born in Marfield, Leicestershire, England, probably on July 7, 1586, Hooker was educated at strongly Puritan Emmanuel College, Cambridge, and after taking his A.B. in 1608 and his A.M. in 1611 remained at the college as a fellow for several years. Appointed to the parish of Esher, Surrey, about 1620 and then to St. Mary's Church, Chelmsford, Essex, in 1626 he developed into a popular and influential exponent of Puritan piety and zeal and attracted the unfavorable attention of Archbishop William Laud. After a form of clerical exile to Little Baddow in 1629 he was ultimately placed under bond and ordered to appear before the ecclesiastical Court of High Commission. Instead he fled to Holland in 1630 and three years later, on the ship that also bore John Cotton, he sailed for the Massachusetts Bay Colony, settling among several former parishioners in New Towne (later Cambridge). His pastorship there brought him both popularity and influence, but he fell out with the leaders of the colony over the issues of limited suffrage and the extent of magisterial authority. In 1636 he led a group of his parishioners to Connecticut and there joined an earlier group in the establishment of a settlement that became Hartford. Hooker's political notions, while not fully democratic in the later sense nor in any way antitheocratic, were much in advance of general Puritan thought and were in large part embodied in the Fundamental Orders promulgated by the Connecticut General Court in 1639, often regarded as the first written constitution in America. Hooker remained generally on good terms with the Massachusetts leaders, joining them in defending Congregationalism against the threat of Presbyterianism and other heresies and working with them to form what became the New England Confederation, the first such union of American colonies. He remained pastor of the Hartford church until his death there on July 7, 1647. His most important work, *A Survey of the Summe of Church-discipline*, appeared the next year.

Hooton, Earnest Albert (1887–1954), anthropologist. Born on November 20, 1887, in Clemansville, Wisconsin, Hooton graduated from Lawrence University in 1907 and entered the University of Wisconsin, from which he received his Ph.D. in 1911 while studying on a Rhodes scholarship at Oxford University. At Oxford his interest turned from the classics to anthropology, and on taking a research degree in 1913 he joined the faculty of Harvard as an instructor in anthropology, advancing to a full professorship in 1930. Hooton was particularly interested in physical anthropology, an undeveloped field in which he steered an independent course and to which he made great contributions both as a researcher and as a teacher. From his early studies of the ancient inhabitants of the pueblo near Pecos, New Mexico, he evolved a scheme of physical types by which he sought to identify Mediterranean and African antecedents of American Indian stock. Other studies of the Guanches, the aboriginal people of the Canary Islands, and of Irish males, of criminals in Massachusetts, and of successive generations of Harvard students, led him to develop a general theory of somatotypes, by which he hoped to relate various emotional and intellectual characteristics and complexes to types of physique. The emphasis on the biological determination of behavior that was a consequence of this view was a matter of some controversy, particularly with regard to Hooton's notions of criminality. In addition to many scientific papers Hooton published a number of popular books that were noted for their wit and graceful style, among them *Up From the Ape*, 1931; *Apes, Men, and Morons*, 1937; *Crime and the Man*, 1939; *Why Men Behave Like Apes and*

Vice Versa, 1940; and *Man's Poor Relations*, 1942. He was curator of Harvard's Peabody Museum from 1914, editor of the Harvard African Studies series from 1918 to 1933, and an active teacher until his death in Cambridge, Massachusetts, on May 3, 1954.

Hoover, Herbert Clark (1874–1964), thirty-first president of the United States. Born on August 10, 1874, in West Branch, Iowa, of Quaker parents who died during his childhood, Hoover grew up in the home of an uncle in Oregon. His early education was irregular, but chance and determination brought him to the newly opened Stanford University in 1891. He worked his way through Stanford, studying mining engineering, and graduated in 1895; his first job out of college was pushing a mine cart for two dollars a day. His professional rise was rapid, however; in 1897 he joined Bewick, Moreing & Company, an international mining concern, and was sent to oversee operations in Australia and later in China, where he witnessed the Boxer Rebellion. In 1908 he organized his own firm, which was highly successful. In 1914, in London, the U.S. ambassador called on him to organize the evacuation of the more than 100,000 Americans trapped by the outbreak of World War I in Europe; later in the same year he became chairman of the volunteer Committee for Relief in Belgium devoted to obtaining money and food for the relief of war-devastated Belgium, and in the course of three years he directed the expenditure of $1 billion. With U.S. entry into World War I in 1917 Hoover was appointed by President Woodrow Wilson as U.S. Food Administrator, and his effective supervision of voluntary rationing and conservation of food throughout the nation added the verb "hooverize" to the American vocabulary of the time. As the war drew to a close he was given responsibility for general civilian relief in Europe; 23 million tons of food were distributed to more than 30 nations, and when the signing of the peace treaty ended his official duties he organized a volunteer agency to continue the work. He returned to the United States in 1919 and in 1921 President Warren G. Harding named him secretary of commerce, a position he retained, under President Calvin Coolidge, until 1928. As secretary, Hoover took the initial steps leading to government supervision of radio broadcasting and commercial aviation and promoted studies that led to the construction of the Hoover (originally Boulder) Dam and the St. Lawrence Seaway. He worked constantly through numerous committees to establish regular methods of voluntary cooperation among the nation's many economic interest groups. His insistence on voluntary action as opposed to government regulation was characteristic, and in 1922 he explained his views in *American Individualism*. In 1927 he again showed his skill in directing relief operations during the disastrous Mississippi flood of that year. With the retirement of Coolidge from politics in 1928, Hoover became a prominent presidential possibility; at the Republican national convention he was nominated on the second ballot and in the election easily defeated Alfred E. Smith. The prospect of a successful administration led by a moderate Republican deeply interested in governmental efficiency and economy was ruined within a few months after Hoover's inauguration when the nation's financial structure, weakened by the frenzy of speculation that rested largely on unsecured credit, crumbled suddenly in the stock-market crash that began in October 1929; warning signs had been disregarded by previous administrations, and Hoover had had no time to stem the speculative boom on Wall Street. Democratic gains in the congressional elections of 1930 severely limited his scope of remedial action in the depression that followed the crash. Despite such efforts as a tax cut and the creation of the Reconstruction Finance Corporation (RFC)—later a mainstay of the New Deal program—the Republican party, and Hoover in particular, bore the onus of the Depression, and Hoover was rejected in favor of Franklin D. Roosevelt in the 1932 presidential election. He retired to private life until the end of World War II, when he returned to public service to organize civilian relief operations in Europe. In 1947 he was named chairman of a commission—popularly known as the Hoover Commission—a term since used to designate any such body—created by Congress to examine and make recommendations on the organization of the executive branch of government. The suggestions of this and a second commission he headed, appointed in 1953 by President Dwight D. Eisenhower, were largely adopted. Among his published works were *Addresses Upon the American Road, 1938–1955*; *Memoirs*, three volumes, 1951–1952; *The Ordeal of Woodrow Wilson*, 1958; and *An American Epic*, four volumes, 1959–1964, a record of relief work since World War I. He died in New York City on October 20, 1964.

Hoover, John Edgar (1895–1972), law enforcement official. Born in Washington, D.C., on January 1, 1895, J. Edgar Hoover was intended by his parents for the ministry, but following his graduation from high school he became a messenger in the Library of Congress while studying law at night at George Washington University. He took his degree in 1916, added a master of laws the next year, and found employment as a file reviewer for the Department of Justice. In 1919 he became special assistant to Attorney General A. Mitchell Palmer and was assigned to oversee the large number of deportation cases then arising from the "Red Scare" hysteria of the post–World War I years. Two years later he became assistant director of the department's Bureau of Investigation; the bureau had been touched by the scandal and disrepute of the Harding era, and in 1924, when Hoover became director, he immediately set about reorganizing it on a fully professional basis. As the scope of the bureau's jurisdiction was increased, its standards were correspondingly raised; by 1935, when its name was changed to the Federal Bureau of Investigation (FBI), he had

established a vast fingerprint file, a crime laboratory, and a training academy. During the 1930s he mounted a campaign to offset the glamorous publicity that often attended crime and criminals and, for a time at least, "G-men" were included among the heroes of American children, as the bureau's list of "ten most wanted criminals" provided a continuing scoreboard of its successes against bank robbers, gangsters, and other lawbreakers. He wrote *Persons in Hiding*, 1938, and as part of his remarkably tenacious campaign against Communism in later years, *Masters of Deceit*, 1958, and *A Study of Communism*, 1962. He was the recipient of numerous honors and awards and active in many organizations, among them the Boys' Clubs and the Boy and Girl scouts. In later years his administration of the FBI was often criticized as autocratic and narrow and he himself had become the focus of what often appeared to be a cult of personality; but despite occasional rumors that his dismissal was being considered he continued in office, by special presidential dispensation, far beyond the normal retirement age and remained for many an indomitable symbol of fearless law enforcement. Hoover died in Washington, D.C., on May 2, 1972, after 48 years at the helm of the FBI; before burial his body lay in state in the Capitol rotunda.

Hope, Bob (1903–   ), entertainer. Born on May 29, 1903, in Eltham, Kent, England, Leslie Townes Hope came with his family to the United States when he was four and grew up in Cleveland. He took singing and dancing lessons while in school, and after graduation from high school and a brief period as an amateur boxer he entered show business, slowly working his way up from local theaters to vaudeville tours and musical comedy. He made his Broadway debut in *The Sidewalks of New York* in 1927 and the next year began developing a comedy monologue routine, taking at the same time the name Bob Hope. Vaudeville appearances led eventually to star billing on the RKO circuit and in 1932 he made his first major Broadway hit in *Ballyhoo*. By that time he had perfected his remarkable timing in his comic delivery; combining an encyclopedic command of gags and one-liners with a nimble and topical wit, he became renowned as a master of the ad lib and of rapid-fire patter. Featured roles in *Roberta*, 1933; *Say When*, 1934; the *Ziegfeld Follies* of 1935; and *Red Hot and Blue*, 1936, made him one of Broadway's top attractions and in 1935 he began a career in radio, starting his own show three years later. His motion-picture debut in *The Big Broadcast of 1938*, released in 1937, featured his rendition of "Thanks for the Memory," which was thereafter his theme song; it was a best-selling recording the next year as well as the title of his second movie. Subsequent films included *College Swing*, 1939; *The Road to Singapore*, 1940, the first of a series of six highly successful *Road* comedies with Bing Crosby which took the two to Zanzibar in 1941, Morocco in 1942, Utopia in 1946, Rio in 1948, and Bali in 1953; *My Favorite*

Blonde, 1942; Let's Face It, 1943; Monsieur Beaucaire, 1946; Paleface, 1948; and Fancy Pants, 1950. During World War II Hope assembled a troupe of entertainers and toured tirelessly in every theater of the war entertaining U.S. and Allied troops, often in combat zones. He continued in such efforts after the end of the war, taking shows to virtually every U.S. outpost and in due course to Korea and to Vietnam; some of his later annual Christmas tours were recorded for subsequent television broadcast at home. His television career began in 1950 and over the years he appeared in TV shows of his own and frequently as a guest star; in 1968 he was given a special Peabody Award for his three decades of broadcasting. Later films included The Lemon Drop Kid, 1951; Son of Paleface, 1952; Casanova, 1953; Seven Little Foys, 1955; Beau James, 1957; and A Global Affair, 1964. He also wrote a number of books, among them I Never Left Home, 1944; So This Is Peace, 1946; and I Owe Russia $1200, 1963. His numerous and diverse business interests made him one of the wealthiest of the stars and his troop tours and other charitable activities brought him countless honors and awards, including in 1969 the Presidential Medal of Freedom.

Hope, John (1868–1936), educator. Born in Augusta, Georgia, on June 2, 1868, Hope was the son of a Scottish immigrant father and a black mother. With friends and relations on both sides of the color line, and possessed himself of blond hair, blue eyes, and a fair complexion, he could easily have lived as a white, but he preferred, particularly as segregationist and white-supremacist attitudes hardened after the ending of Reconstruction in 1876 to identify himself with black people. Despite narrowed circumstances after the death of his father he secured an education at Worcester Academy in Massachusetts and at Brown University, from which he graduated in 1894. For four years he taught at Roger Williams University in Nashville, Tennessee, and in 1898 he was appointed professor of classics at Atlanta Baptist College. In 1906, by which time the school had been renamed Morehouse College, he was chosen president, the first black man to hold the post. In the same year he was the only college president to attend the second meeting of the Niagara Movement, of which he was a founder and which within a few years merged with the new National Association for the Advancement of Colored People (NAACP). Hope had long been a forceful proponent of social and political equality for black Americans and had publicly opposed Booker T. Washington on the issue, especially following Washington's "Atlanta Compromise" address of 1895; holding that Washington's emphasis on technical skills for blacks was an empty concept in the absence of the freedom to exercise them, Hope strove to promote both equality and intellectual excellence. During World War I he served as a YMCA secretary with black U.S. troops in France and afterward, as a result of his experiences with racial discrimination in the army

and of the wave of race riots that swept the country in 1919–1920, he led in founding the Commission on Interracial Cooperation and became its first president. In 1929 Morehouse College, Spelman College (for women), and Atlanta University merged into the Atlanta University System, and Atlanta became the first U.S. graduate school for Negroes. Hope was the unanimous choice as president. He continued in that position, directing the fortunes of the university with clear-sighted and firm authority, until his death in Atlanta, Georgia, on February 20, 1936.

Hope, Laura Lee, see Stratemeyer, Edward

Hope, Leslie Townes, see Hope, Bob

Hopkins, Esek (1718–1802), naval officer. Born in what is now Scituate, Rhode Island, on April 26, 1718, Hopkins went to sea at the age of twenty and, by dint of ability and his marriage three years later into a wealthy merchant family, rose quickly to command of a large merchant fleet. During the French and Indian War he engaged in some highly profitable privateering and became a figure of considerable consequence in Rhode Island, serving at various times in the colonial legislature. He retired to his farm in North Providence in 1772, but in 1775 he was appointed brigadier general in command of the colony's military forces and charged with preparing defenses for the war that appeared imminent. Two months later, in December, the Continental Congress decided to organize a naval fleet and, partly through the influence of Hopkins's elder brother, who was chairman of the naval committee, he was named commodore of the fleet. Early in 1776 he joined the new navy of eight small converted merchant ships in Philadelphia and was ordered to sail to Chesapeake Bay and attack the British fleet there. After some delay Hopkins set forth but, choosing to view his orders as discretionary, he avoided the strong British force in the Chesapeake and sailed to the Bahamas, where he attacked the British post on New Providence and captured much valuable war matériel. On his return in April 1776 he fought an inconclusive battle with the British ship Glasgow in Long Island Sound. Later in the year a congressional investigation of his conduct resulted from growing dissatisfaction with his lack of accomplishment, his disobedience of orders, and the long idleness of the fleet following the Bahamas venture. Despite a spirited defense by John Adams he was formally censured. Problems of recruitment and increasing hostility toward him on the part of his officers served to keep the fleet idle in Narragansett Bay, where in December it was finally bottled up by British ships. Formal charges were brought against Hopkins before Congress in March 1777; he was suspended from command at that time and dismissed from the naval service in January 1778. Hopkins remained an influential figure in Rhode Island, serving in the legislature from 1777 to 1786 and as a trustee of Rhode Island College (now Brown University) from 1782. He died in Providence, Rhode Island, on February 26, 1802.

Hopkins, Harry Lloyd (1890–1946), public official. Born in Sioux City, Iowa, on August 17, 1890, Hopkins graduated from Grinnell College in 1912 and immediately entered the social-work field, becoming director of a boys' camp in New York. During the next several years he was connected at various times with the Association for Improving the Condition of the Poor, the New York City Board of Civil Welfare, the American Red Cross, and the New York Tuberculosis and Health Association. In 1931 Governor Franklin D. Roosevelt of New York called on him to head the state's Temporary Emergency Relief Administration. Two years later, with Roosevelt in the White House, Hopkins became administrator of the new Federal Emergency Relief Administration. In a little more than five years some eight to ten billion dollars passed through his hands and he was dubbed "the world's greatest spender." He was active in organizing the Works Progress Administration (WPA), later the Work Projects Administration, and was one of its staunchest defenders. In 1938 he became secretary of commerce. A close and trusted adviser and confidant whom Roosevelt found increasingly valuable, he directed the Roosevelt forces at the 1940 Democratic national convention; ill health, however, forced him to resign from the cabinet later that year. In 1941 he began a long series of missions concerned with foreign affairs when he went to England as Roosevelt's personal representative to discuss U.S. assistance for Britain's war effort. After discussions with the British government and King George VI, and later with Joseph Stalin in Moscow, he returned to the United States to direct the operation of the Lend-Lease Administration and to serve on a number of advisory and directory boards, becoming thereby a member of the so-called "Little War Cabinet." As a special assistant to Roosevelt from 1942, he attended every major Allied "summit conference" during the war except for the last one, at Potsdam, which, however, he had arranged for during another trip to Moscow in early 1945. He retired in 1945 because of the ill health that had long plagued him and died on January 29, 1946, in New York City.

Hopkins, Mark (1802–1887), educator and philosopher. Born in Stockbridge, Massachusetts, on February 4, 1802, Hopkins graduated from Williams College in 1824. He turned to the study of medicine, which he interrupted for two years to serve as a tutor at Williams; he was granted his M.D. by the Berkshire Medical College in 1829 and moved to New York City, but practiced for only a short time. In 1830 he returned to Williams as professor of moral philosophy and rhetoric; from that year until his death he was in charge of instruction for the senior class. In 1836, although he had had no training in theology, he was ordained in the Congregational church and became in the same year president of the college, a post

he held until 1872. From 1857 to 1887 he was also president of the American Board of Commissioners for Foreign Missions. Not preeminently a scholar or a creative thinker, he was greatly effective as a teacher; his teachings, both in the classroom and in the pulpit, embodied the secularized Puritanism that marked much of the theology of the nineteenth century. Often called the "gospel of wealth," it stressed individualism, the pursuit of wealth and progress, and the idea that possession is a form of stewardship; property as a mark of personal worth is to be held and administered as a trust for the benefit of society. Hopkins delivered a number of lecture courses at the Lowell Institute in Boston and these were published in books that enjoyed great popularity: *Lectures on the Evidences of Christianity,* 1846; *Lectures on Moral Science,* 1862; *The Law of Love and Love as a Law,* 1869; and *An Outline Study of Man,* 1873. At a dinner meeting of Williams alumni in New York City in 1871, President James A. Garfield, class of 1856, declared, "Give me a log hut with only a simple bench, Mark Hopkins on one end and I on the other, and you may have all the buildings, apparatus, and libraries without him." Hopkins continued to teach and to deeply influence the students in his charge until his death in Williamstown, Massachusetts, on June 17, 1887. He was elected to the Hall of Fame in 1915.

Hopkins, Samuel (1721–1803), religious leader and theologian. Born on September 17, 1721, in Waterbury, Connecticut, Hopkins graduated from Yale in 1741 and the following year was licensed to preach by the Congregational church. After studying theology privately under Jonathan Edwards he was ordained minister of the Congregational Church in Great Barrington, Massachusetts, in 1743. His association with Edwards resumed in 1751 when Edwards took charge of the church in nearby Stockbridge and continued until 1758, when Edwards became president of the College of New Jersey, now Princeton. Not merely a disciple, Hopkins modified the theology of Edwards and presented it in a form that, while as logically rigorous as the work of his master, was more palatable and more suited to the age; Hopkinsianism was long a major school of Congregational theology. The titles of some of his published works indicate the trend of his thought: *Sin, thro' Divine Interposition, an Advantage to the Universe,* 1759; *An Enquiry Concerning the Promises of the Gospel, Whether Any of Them Are Made to the Exercises and Doings of Persons in an Unregenerate State,* 1765 (answered, of course, in the negative); and *The True State and Character of the Unregenerate, Stripped of All Misrepresentation and Disguise,* 1769. In 1769, having alienated a number of his parishioners with his stern, unemotional, and demanding sermons, he was dismissed from his church. The following year he assumed the pastorate of the First Church in Newport, Rhode Island, where, with the exception of the years 1776–1780, when the town was under British occupation, he remained for the rest of his life. During the early 1770s he began to speak out against slavery, becoming one of the first Congregationalists to do so, and worked to establish missions to Africa. In 1776 he published *A Dialogue Concerning the Slavery of the Africans; Shewing It to Be the Duty and Interest of the American States to Emancipate All Their African Slaves.* His theological summa appeared in 1793 as *A System of Doctrines Contained in Divine Revelation.* Hopkins died in Newport on December 20, 1803.

Hopkinson, Francis (1737–1791), public official, author, and judge. Born in Philadelphia on September 21, 1737, Hopkinson studied at the College of Philadelphia (now the University of Pennsylvania) and was granted that institution's first degree in 1757. He was awarded an M.A. three years later and in 1761 was admitted to the bar. A man of wide interests and talents, he published poems in various periodicals, was an accomplished harpsichordist, and composed several songs and hymns, later claiming, perhaps justly, to be the first native-born American to have done so. His professional life was unsettled; he gave up law for a time, holding some minor government posts and operating a dry-goods store. In 1773 he moved to Bordentown, New Jersey, and resumed his law practice; he was successful and by 1776 had achieved sufficient prominence to be elected to the Continental Congress. He was a signer of the Declaration of Independence. His career as a political satirist and pamphleteer had begun two years earlier with *A Pretty Story;* during the Revolution, while serving in a number of government positions, he kept up a steady barrage of anti-British writings, among them *A Letter to Lord Howe, A Letter Written by a Foreigner,* and *An Answer to General Burgoyne's Proclamation,* all in 1777, and *A Letter to Joseph Galloway* and the popular poem *The Battle of the Kegs* in 1778. In 1777 he helped design the first national flag authorized by Congress. He was judge of the Pennsylvania admiralty court from 1779 to 1789 and from the latter year until his death was U.S. district judge for eastern Pennsylvania. He strongly supported the adoption of the Constitution and wrote several articles favoring it. In his later years he maintained his wide interests and wrote prolifically; in 1788 he published *Seven Songs for the Harpsichord or Forte-Piano.* He died in Philadelphia on May 9, 1791.

Hoppe, William Frederick (1887–1959), billiard player. Born on October 11, 1887, in Cornwall on the Hudson, New York, Willie Hoppe began learning to play pool as a child, using an old table in his father's hotel. By the time he was eight his skill was such that he went on a barnstorming tour of the country with his father and older brother, giving exhibitions while standing on a box that boosted him to table height. Already widely known as the "Boy Wonder," he took up billiards as well and in 1903 won the Young Masters 18.2 balkline championship. Three years

later, in Paris, he won the world's 18.1 title, which he held in 1906–1907, 1909–1911, and 1914–1927. In 1907 he won the world's 18.2 championship, later holding it in 1910–1920, 1923, 1924, and 1927. With the rise in popularity of three-cushion billiards he quickly rose to a position of nearly total dominance of that game, holding the world's title in 1936, 1940–1943, 1945, and 1947–1952. In addition to his total of more than 50 world championships, Hoppe held high-run records in nearly every variant form of billiards. By the time of his retirement from championship play in 1952 he was acknowledged to be the greatest player in the history of the game. He wrote a number of articles on billiards and published *Thirty Years of Billiards*, 1925, and *Billiards as It Should Be Played*, 1941. Hoppe died in Miami, Florida, on February 1, 1959.

Hopper, DeWolf (1858–1935), actor. Born in New York City on March 30, 1858, William D'Wolf Hopper later dropped his first name and modified the spelling of his second. For a time in his youth he studied law in the office of Joseph H. Choate, but a successful performance in an amateur theatrical production at the age of twenty turned him to a career on the stage. After his professional debut in New Haven, Connecticut, in 1878 he used money supplied by his family to form his own road company, with which he toured for a few years. Among his most notable performances were those in *Hazel Kirke*, 1883; *Castles in the Air*, 1890; *Wang*, 1891, which he produced himself; and John Philip Sousa's *El Capitan*, 1896. During 1900–1901 he starred at the Weber and Fields Music Hall, but his real love continued to be light opera, for which, with his commanding presence and rich bass voice, he was eminently suited. From 1911 he appeared principally in productions of Gilbert and Sullivan works, touring the country with great success. He appeared in two minor motion pictures in 1915 and later was popular on radio. From 1888 until the end of his life he was renowned for his recitations of Ernest Thayer's "Casey at the Bat," which he declaimed with such force and drama that audiences demanded it of him at virtually every performance; the ballad achieved its place in American folklore almost entirely because of him. Hopper was noted also for the number of his marriages; of his six wives the best known was actress and later columnist Hedda Hopper. A volume of reminiscences, *Once a Clown, Always a Clown*, written with W. W. Stout, appeared in 1927. Hopper died in Kansas City, Missouri, on September 23, 1935.

Hopper, Edward (1882–1967), painter. Born on July 22, 1882, in Nyack, New York, Hopper moved to New York City in 1899 to study commercial illustration and entered the New York School of Fine and Applied Art in 1900, studying under Robert Henri. Except for brief periods in Europe and summers in New England, he lived and worked in New York City for the rest of his life. Throughout his career, despite changing fashions in art, he continued to paint starkly realistic scenes of contemporary life that were somber despite their bright colors. His subjects included city streets, New England cottages, finely detailed Victorian houses, roadside lunch counters, theater interiors, and barren apartments, all depicted with a pervading calm, devoid of urban hubbub. He was known as the "painter of loneliness," and his most famous paintings were "Early Sunday Morning" and "Nighthawks." He exhibited at the Armory Show in 1913 and had his first one-man show in 1920; later he enjoyed major retrospective shows at the Museum of Modern Art and the Whitney Museum of American Art in New York City. He produced but a few paintings each year. He died in New York City on May 15, 1967.

Hopper, Hedda (1890–1966), actress and columnist. Born on June 2, 1890, in Hollidaysburg, Pennsylvania, Elda Furry early developed a love for the stage and at eighteen ran away from her sternly Quaker family to seek her fortune in the theater. After a period in the chorus of an opera company she made her Broadway debut in *The Motor Girl*, 1909; while playing a role in *A Matinee Idol* a short time later she met DeWolf Hopper, whom she married in 1913. It was at his suggestion—reportedly to end the confusion arising from the similarity of her first name with those of his four earlier wives—that she changed her name to Hedda. After a brief retirement she returned to the stage and in 1915 made her film debut in Louis B. Mayer's *Virtuous Wives*. She subsequently appeared in scores of movies, but failed to attain stardom and eventually found her career fading. For a few years she worked at other jobs, including real-estate sales and fashion commentary. In 1936 she began broadcasting regularly on radio, reporting from Hollywood on the latest gossip about the stars and moguls of the movies. Two years later she began writing a Hollywood gossip column for the Esquire Syndicate, later moving it to the syndicate of the *Des Moines Register and Tribune* and in 1942 to the *Chicago Tribune–New York Daily News* syndicate. Miss Hopper's detailed knowledge of the faces and foibles of the film colony served her as a reservoir of valuable information and gave her a ready entrée into the most private affairs of the leading characters, and her large readership and the publicity outlets she commanded made her a powerful arbiter of the morals and mores of the industry. Her rivalry with the earlier-established Louella Parsons grew into a celebrated feud, to which she added others no less publicized over the years. Generally considered to be more friendly and tolerant than her arch-rival, she remained for the rest of her life a popular, if somewhat feared, figure in Hollywood, noted for her lively and often ungrammatical language, her numberless exotic hats, and later her markedly right-wing political views. She died in Hollywood on February 1, 1966.

Hopper, William D'Wolf, *see* Hopper, DeWolf

Hornsby, Rogers (1896–1963), baseball player. Born on April 27, 1896, in Winters, Texas, Hornsby grew up in North Fort Worth and by the age of fifteen was playing local semiprofessional baseball. After four years with various minor-league teams around the state he was signed by the St. Louis Cardinals in 1915 and made his major-league debut late that year. In 1916, his first full season, he hit .313, and over the next four years his average rose steadily while he was also becoming a crack second baseman. In 1920 he led the National League with a .370 average and held the batting crown for six consecutive seasons, a league record; his .424 in 1924 remained the highest season average in modern (since 1900) baseball. "The Rajah," as he became known, won the triple crown—leading the league in batting, home runs, and runs batted in—in 1922 and 1925, in 1922 leading also in fielding for second basemen. During the 1925 season Hornsby was named manager of the Cardinals and with his league-leading performance was named the National League's most valuable player. As player-manager he led the Cardinals to a World Series victory in 1926, but after a salary dispute he was traded to the New York Giants at the season's end. After a single season and a .361 average with the Giants he moved to the Boston Braves as player-manager, but remained again for only one year, during which he hit a league-leading .387. In 1929 he joined the Chicago Cubs, in that season hitting .380 and winning the award for the most valuable player for the second time. During the 1930 season he became player-manager for the Cubs, continuing so until mid-1932, when he briefly rejoined the Cardinals. His full-time playing career ended that year, although as manager of the St. Louis Browns from 1933 to 1937 he did take the field occasionally; by the end of 1937 Hornsby had compiled a lifetime batting average of .358, second only to Ty Cobb's .367. Over the next 15 years he managed a succession of minor- and major-league teams, the majors including the Baltimore Orioles, the St. Louis Browns for the second time, and the Cincinnati Reds; he was at the helm of the Fort Worth team of the Texas League when he was elected to the National Baseball Hall of Fame in 1942 and in later years was a scout or coach for the Cleveland Indians, the Chicago Cubs, and the New York Mets. His autobiographical *My War with Baseball* appeared in 1962. Hornsby died in Chicago on January 5, 1963.

Houdini, Harry (1874–1926), magician. Born on March 24, 1874, in Budapest, Hungary, Houdini, originally named Ehrich Weiss, emigrated with his parents a few weeks later to the United States and settled in Appleton, Wisconsin. He became an avid follower of circus and sideshow performers and early took up magic himself. In 1882 he was a trapeze artist in New York City, where he had moved to earn money for his family. When the family joined him he developed a magic act with his brother, called "Hardeen," as his assistant; in 1894 he married and his wife became his assistant, performing under the name Beatrice Houdini. They made appearances in circuses, in 1895 at Tony Pastor's theater, and then in a chain of vaudeville houses, but remained relatively unknown, despite Houdini's remarkable skill. Although he was adept at many forms of magic, his forte was escape acts in which he extricated himself from ropes, shackles, and various locked containers. He went abroad in 1900 and executed an escape from Scotland Yard, gaining wide publicity and becoming a main attraction at the Alhambra Theatre in London. He successfully toured the Continent for four years. Returning to the United States, he received international news coverage for his escapes, which completely baffled audiences. In one feat, he was shackled with irons and locked into a roped, weighted box that was dropped from a boat into water; in another, he was suspended upside down 75 feet in the air and in his position freed himself from a straitjacket. If success depended on muscular power or adroitness, he would perform his escape in front of spectators; but frequently his acts depended on his extensive knowledge of lock mechanisms, and his more complicated feats were done in enclosures. He occasionally used an unseen tool or assistant, but he stressed that supernatural forces did not aid him. He undertook a study of Robert-Houdin (Jean Eugene Robert Houdin), the French magician from whom he had adopted his name, and discovered that Houdin's dexterity had been exaggerated and wrote, instead of the planned tribute, *The Unmasking of Robert-Houdin*, 1908. He also published *Miracle Mongers and Their Methods*, 1920, and *A Magician Among the Spirits*, 1924, to discredit mind readers and mediums; he had discovered their tricks in the course of several attempts to contact his dead mother. Nevertheless, he planned with his wife an experiment in supernaturalism—the one who died first would attempt to contact the other through a medium. He died in Detroit on October 31, 1926, after a stomach injury led to peritonitis; his wife revealed the failure of the experiment before her death in 1943. Houdini also edited and was the major contributor to *Conjurers' Monthly* during 1906–1908. He established the London Magicians' Club and the Society of American Magicians. His books and papers on spiritualism and magic were bequeathed to the Library of Congress.

Hough, Emerson (1857–1923), author. Born in Newton, Iowa, on June 28, 1857, Hough graduated from Iowa State University in 1880. He took up the study of law and on winning admission to the bar he moved to the frontier town of Whiteoaks in south-central New Mexico, to begin practice. His deep interest in the outdoors distracted him from law and soon he abandoned practice to write essays and sketches on the life of cowboys and miners. After brief stints with newspapers in Iowa and Ohio he joined the staff of *Forest and Stream* magazine in 1889. He continued to write, contributing to other periodicals as well, and became a leading advocate of conservation and the national-parks movement; his reports on an extensive tour of exploration of Yellowstone National Park were instrumental in prompting the passage of legislation protecting the few remaining buffalo in the park. His first book, *The Singing Mouse Stories*, appeared in 1895 and was followed by *The Story of the Cowboy*, 1897; *The Girl at the Half-way House*, 1900; *The Mississippi Bubble*, 1902; *The Way to the West*, 1903; *The Law of the Land*, 1904; *The Story of the Outlaw*, 1907; *54–40 or Fight!*, 1909; *The Sowing*, 1909; *John Rawn*, 1912; *The Lady and the Pirate*, 1913; *The Passing of the Frontier*, 1918; *The Sagebrusher*, 1919; *The Covered Wagon*, 1922, which was made into an enormously successful motion picture for Paramount the next year; *Mother of Gold*, 1924; and others. Hough also wrote a series of juvenile novels of outdoor adventure, including *The Young Alaskans*, 1910; *The Young Alaskans in the Rockies*, 1913; and *The Young Alaskans on the Trail*, 1914. For several years he conducted a regular "Out of Doors" column in the *Saturday Evening Post*. He died on April 30, 1923, in Evanston, Illinois.

Houghston, Walter, see Huston, Walter

House, Edward Mandell (1858–1938), political leader and diplomat. Born in Houston, Texas, on July 26, 1858, House was the son of a wealthy planter and merchant. He was educated in private schools in England and Connecticut and attended Cornell University for a year, leaving on the death of his father in 1880 to return to Texas to manage the family plantations. Ten years later he sold out, securing his financial future. He became interested in Democratic politics and from 1892 to 1904 was chief adviser and campaign manager to a succession of Texas governors; he consistently refused appointment to public office, but was given the honorary Texas title of colonel, by which he was thereafter known. House began to look to the national scene about 1910 and in 1912 was active in securing the Democratic presidential nomination for Woodrow Wilson, lining up support in Texas and, most importantly, negotiating for support from William Jennings Bryan. A close bond quickly developed between House and Wilson, and although House refused a cabinet appointment he became the President's most trusted adviser and lieutenant and was often referred to as the "silent partner" in executive matters. His influence with other leaders in the administration and in Congress made him an invaluable channel of communication for the President and went far to win passage of many of Wilson's legislative proposals. His presence was felt most strongly in the realm of foreign affairs, however; he maintained wide contacts with leaders abroad, particularly in Great Britain, and labored long to reduce Anglo-American and European tensions. After seeking unsuccessfully to head off the threat of a general European war, he bacame Wilson's chief liaison with Allied leaders in World War I. His discussions with British foreign secretary Sir Edward Grey in 1916 led to a proposal for U.S. mediation of the war and an offer of U.S. assistance should Germany decline to negotiate. Although Britain failed to act upon the idea, House continued to work closely with Allied leaders at conferences in 1916 and 1917, arranging for U.S. aid and, after U.S. entry into the war, for the coordination of U.S. and Allied efforts. He drafted the preliminary versions of Wilson's Fourteen Points and the Covenant of the League of Nations, and in the pre-armistice conference of the Allies in October 1918 he gained a major diplomatic victory in persuading the European Allies to accept the Fourteen Points as the basis for peace negotiations with Germany. At the Versailles Peace Conference Wilson himself was the principal U.S. delegate, House serving as his general assistant and factotum. The close relationship between the two was strained by the demands of the conference; House's practical and realistic openness to compromise irritated Wilson, who was determined to see the letter of the Fourteen Points and the Covenant carried into practice. After the signing of the Treaty of Versailles on June 28, 1919, Wilson returned to the United States, leaving House to help organize the League's mandate system. By the time House also had returned and had recovered from an illness, Wilson was in extremely poor health and in the care of associates who had no liking for House; no invitation to him from the White House was forthcoming, his letters to the President were ignored, and the long and fruitful friendship was undramatically dissolved. House thereafter retained both his contacts with European political and intellectual leaders and his association with the Democrat party, although in domestic politics he chose to exercise little active influence except for serving as an occasional adviser to Franklin D. Roosevelt in 1932. House died in New York City on March 28, 1938.

House, Royal Earl (1814–1895), inventor. Born in Rockland, Vermont, on September 9, 1814, House grew up in Susquehanna County, Pennsylvania, and received no formal schooling. At home, however, he acquired a sound basic education and early revealed a marked bent for mechanics. He had already devised an improved waterwheel and patented a machine for sawing barrel staves when, in 1840, after a quickly abandoned attempt to study law in Buffalo, New York, he became interested in electricity and the idea of the telegraph. After four years of work he had designed and built a printing telegraph that wrote out messages in the common alphabet. A successful demonstration of his device won him financial backing to perfect it and in 1846 he received a patent for a printing telegraph capable of printing more than 50 words per minute. Over the next few years a number of successful printing telegraph

lines were built on the Eastern Seaboard and as far west as Ohio and to their construction House contributed such innovations as the use of stranded wire, far more efficient than single wire, and a glass screw insulator of his own design and manufacture. Although his system was in many respects superior to that of Samuel F. B. Morse and his associates and although he successfully defended it in patent litigation in 1849–1850, his printing telegraph was gradually superseded by the improved Morse system in the 1850s. House continued to experiment with various electrical devices, patenting many, until his death in Bridgeport, Connecticut, on February 25, 1895.

Houston, Samuel (1793–1863), soldier and public official. Born on March 2, 1793, near Lexington, Virginia, Houston grew up there and, after his father's death, in the frontier region of Tennessee. He received little schooling and at the age of fifteen, rather than take a clerkship in a local store, he moved into the woods and for three years lived among the Cherokee Indians. He served in the War of 1812 under Andrew Jackson and took part in the battle of Horseshoe Bend against the Creek. Remaining in the army after the war, he became an Indian agent and helped oversee the removal of the Cherokee from Tennessee to Arkansas. The next year he resigned and took up the study of law; he was soon led into politics and in 1823 was elected to the House of Representatives, remaining there for two terms. Returning to Tennessee in 1827 he was elected governor; soon after he won reelection in 1829, however, his wife of three months deserted him and he resigned and returned to the Cherokee. Houston was formally adopted into the Cherokee nation and for a few years operated a trading post in their territory. He made several trips to Washington, D.C., to plead for equitable treatment of the Indians and in 1832 was sent by President Andrew Jackson to negotiate with several tribes in Texas. He was caught up in the growing agitation for Texas independence and in 1833 attended the San Felipe convention that drew up a petition to the Mexican government requesting statehood and wrote a constitution. By 1835 he had settled permanently in Texas and was appointed commander of the small army then being organized. In April 1836 he engaged the Mexican army under Gen. Santa Anna and, although outnumbered by more than two to one, dealt it a smashing defeat at San Jacinto, capturing Santa Anna. In September 1836 Houston was elected president of the Republic of Texas and served until 1838. From 1838 to 1840 he was in the Texas legislature and from 1841 to 1844 was again president. The next year, with the admission of Texas to the Union, he was sent to the Senate, where he remained for nearly 14 years. He spoke and voted always as a Union Democrat rather than as a Southerner, and he strongly opposed the Kansas-Nebraska Bill of 1854. In 1859, his pro-Union stand having become unpopular, he was defeated for the Senate but was again elected governor. He vigorously opposed secession but finally acquiesced; refusing to swear allegiance to the Confederacy, however, he was deposed in March 1861. He retired to Huntsville, Texas, where he died on July 26, 1863.

Hovick, Rose Louise, *see* Lee, Gypsy Rose

Howard, Oliver Otis (1830–1909), soldier. Born in Leeds, Maine, on November 8, 1830, Howard graduated from Bowdoin College in 1850 and entered West Point, from which he graduated four years later. After serving as an ordnance officer at various posts he returned to West Point in 1855 as an instructor in mathematics and remained there until 1861, when he resigned his commission to become colonel of a Maine militia regiment. He rose quickly to brigadier general of volunteers and saw action at the first battle of Bull Run (Manassas) and in the Peninsular Campaign, during which, at Fair Oaks (Seven Pines) he lost his right arm, and at South Mountain, Antietam, and Fredericksburg. Promoted to major general of volunteers in March 1863, he committed blunders at Chancellorsville, where his 11th Corps was routed by Gen. T. J. "Stonewall" Jackson, and on the first day of fighting at Gettysburg, where his subsequent performance nonetheless won the thanks of Congress. In the fall of 1863 he was transferred to Tennessee, and in 1864 he took part in Gen. William T. Sherman's campaign in Georgia, in July winning promotion (over Gen. Joseph Hooker) to command of the Army of the Tennessee, with the regular rank of brigadier general. In May 1865 he was appointed by President Andrew Johnson commissioner of the Bureau of Refugees, Freedmen and Abandoned Lands—known generally as the Freedmen's Bureau—and to the immense task he brought honesty, enthusiasm, deeply felt religious and humanitarian convictions, and virtually no administrative abilities; the result was rampant corruption in the Bureau, which he stoutly refused to recognize. Under his administration, however, a number of schools and other institutions were established, including in 1867 Howard University in Washington, D.C., named in his honor. He continued with the Freedmen's Bureau until 1872 and was president of Howard University from 1869 to 1873. In 1872 he was sent by President Ulysses S. Grant to Arizona country to negotiate with Cochise, whom he persuaded to accept reservation life for his Chiricahua Apache. In 1874, having returned to active military duty, he was made commander of the Department of the Columbia; in that post he fought in 1877 the memorable war with the Nez Percé under Chief Joseph and was nearly beaten. From 1880 to 1882 Howard was superintendent of West Point, from 1882 to 1886 commander of the Department of the Platte, and commander of the Division of the East from 1886, when he was promoted to major general, until 1894, when he retired from active service. In 1893 he was awarded the Congressional Medal of Honor for his action at Fair Oaks 31 years earlier. Passing his last years in Burlington, Ver-

mont, Howard wrote a number of books on military history and other topics including *Nez Percé Joseph,* 1881; *Fighting for Humanity,* 1898; *My Life and Experiences Among Our Hostile Indians,* 1907; and an *Autobiography,* 1907. He died in Burlington on October 26, 1909.

Howard, Roy Wilson (1883–1964), editor and publisher. Born on January 1, 1883, in Gano, Butler County, Ohio, Howard grew up there and in Indianapolis, where upon graduating from high school in 1902 he went to work as a reporter for the *Indianapolis News.* After brief stints with the *Indianapolis Star,* the *St. Louis Post–Dispatch,* and the *Cincinnati Post,* he moved to New York City in 1906 to become a correspondent for the Scripps-McRae newspaper chain. The following year he was named the first general news manager for the chain and was placed in charge of the New York office of the Scripps-McRae Press Association, a wire service that was then in the process of becoming the United Press (UP) of which Howard became president in 1912 at the age of twenty-nine. For the relatively new and aspiring UP he set a personal example of aggressiveness, going himself to Europe during World War I to interview the crown prince of Germany and David Lloyd George of Great Britain and, on a tip, breaking the news of the armistice four days early. The UP was firmly established as a major wire service by 1921, when Howard left the presidency. In that year he became chairman of the board and business director for the Scripps-McRae chain; in 1925 he succeeded to the editorial codirectorship (with Robert P. Scripps) and the chain became Scripps-Howard, which grew over the years to control many major metropolitan dailies. Howard brought into the chain the *New York Telegram* in 1927 and four years later merged it with another purchase to create the *World-Telegram;* in 1950 he added yet another paper to make the *World-Telegram and The Sun,* of which he remained editor until 1960 and president until 1962. In 1936 he gave up the chairmanship of the Scripps-Howard chain, taking the title of president; in 1953 he passed the presidency to his son and became chairman of the executive committee and a director. Throughout his career, during which he exercised major influence at various times over some 30 leading newspapers across the country, Howard was an outspoken, powerful, and somewhat unpredictable figure. Politically he was, more often than not, characterized as a liberal, yet his ardent support of Franklin D. Roosevelt in 1932 soon turned to equally ardent opposition. The breadth of his views was reflected in the variety of popular columnists he employed for his newspapers, from Heywood Broun to Westbrook Pegler, and from Hugh S. Johnson to Eleanor Roosevelt. Howard died in New York City on November 20, 1964.

Howard, Sidney Coe (1891–1939), playwright. Born in Oakland, California, on June 26, 1891,

Howard graduated from the University of California at Berkeley in 1915 and after an extended stay in Switzerland he entered Harvard to study under George Pierce Baker in his famed 47 Workshop. During World War I he served in the U.S. ambulance corps and later as an officer in the U.S. aviation service. In 1919 he joined the staff of the humorous weekly *Life*, becoming literary editor in 1922, and in 1923 he became a feature writer for William Randolph Hearst's *International Magazine*; he frequently contributed articles on social and political issues to other periodicals as well. Howard had experimented with the writing of drama since his undergraduate days and he later wrote *Swords*, which was produced in 1921 by the Provincetown Players and on Broadway, and *Casanova*, produced in 1923, but his first real success came in 1924 with *They Knew What They Wanted*, which won a Pulitzer Prize. Dealing with a variety of social and psychological topics and executed with great dramatic skill, particularly in characterization, Howard's subsequent plays included *Lucky Sam McCarver*, 1925; *Ned McCobb's Daughter*, 1926; *The Silver Cord*, 1926; *Salvation*, with Charles MacArthur, 1928; *The Late Christopher Bean*, 1932, adaptation of a French work; *Alien Corn*, 1933; *Yellowjack*, with Paul de Kruif, 1934; *Dodsworth*, from Sinclair Lewis' novel, 1934; *Paths of Glory*, from a novel by Humphrey Cobb, 1935; *The Ghost of Yankee Doodle*, 1937; and *Madam, Will You Walk?*, 1939 (first produced 1953). In addition he published a collection of stories, *Three Flights Up*, 1924, and wrote a number of screenplays, including those for *Arrowsmith*, 1932, *Dodsworth*, 1936, and *Gone With the Wind*, 1939, for which he won an Academy Award. In 1938 he joined Maxwell Anderson, Robert Sherwood, and others in organizing the Playwrights Company. Howard was at work on a dramatization of Carl Van Doren's *Benjamin Franklin* when he died in a tractor accident on his farm near Tyringham, Massachusetts, on August 23, 1939.

Howe, Edgar Watson (1853–1937), editor and author. Born in Wabash County, Indiana, on May 3, 1853, Howe moved with his family to Harrison County, Missouri, in 1856. He received little schooling and by the age of twelve was an apprentice printer in his father's newspaper office. Later, as a journeyman printer, he worked for newspapers in Missouri, Iowa, Nebraska, Wyoming, and Utah, and in 1872 tried his luck at publishing with his own short-lived *Golden Globe* in Golden, Colorado. In 1877, with an older half-brother, he founded the *Atchison* (Kansas) *Daily Globe* and enjoyed from the start remarkable success. The *Globe* was popular and influential as a small-town local, but it gradually attained a national reputation from Howe's pithy aphorisms and paragraphs crackling with pungent wit disguised in a homely manner. Quoted and reprinted in newspapers cross the country, Howe's comments on all things within his purview earned him the nickname of "the Sage of Potato Hill,"

the latter being the name of his Atchison farm. In 1883, with a critical boost from William Dean Howells, his first book was published as *The Story of a Country Town*, a hugely popular novel that anticipated much of the realism of such later authors as Sinclair Lewis and Sherwood Anderson. He retired from the editorship of the *Globe* in 1911 and began *E. W. Howe's Monthly*, which, consisting of little else than his own caustic observations on things in general, continued to appear until 1933. Others of Howe's books included *The Confession of John Whitlock*, 1891; *Country Town Sayings*, 1911; *Ventures in Common Sense*, 1919; and *The Indignation of E. W. Howe*, 1933. His autobiography, *Plain People*, appeared in 1929. Howe died in Atchison, Kansas, on October 3, 1937.

Howe, Elias (1819–1867), inventor. Born on July 9, 1819, in Spencer, Massachusetts, Howe was raised on a farm and received only sketchy formal schooling. Interested in machinery and tools, he worked in his father's gristmill and sawmill and later was an apprentice in several machine-tool shops between 1835 and 1837. Traveling then to Boston, he went to work for a watchmaker and one day overheard a conversation in which the idea of a sewing machine was discussed. He at once began to try to construct such a device and by 1845 had created one that featured an eyed needle to carry the upper thread and a shuttle-like holder for the lower thread; these worked together to fasten stitches at regular intervals in fabric. He secured patent rights in 1846 but could not sell the machine. He sold one machine and British patent rights to a British corset maker and went to England to develop it further, returning to Boston in 1849. He discovered that other inventors, notably Isaac M. Singer, had developed sewing machines based on his invention and were violating his patent. Litigation that extended through 1854 finally secured his claim and he was awarded royalties on all sewing machines sold in the United States until the expiration of his patent in 1867. After the Civil War, during which Howe raised and served in a Connecticut regiment, he established a factory in Bridgeport to manufacture sewing machines. Having created a manufacturing revolution with a machine that made possible the mass production of clothing, he died in Brooklyn, New York, on October 3, 1867. He was elected to the Hall of Fame in 1915.

Howe, Julia Ward (1819–1910), author and social reformer. Born in New York City on May 27, 1819, Miss Ward came of a wealthy family. In 1843 she married Samuel Gridley Howe and took up residence in Boston. Always of a literary bent, she published her first volume of poetry, *Passion Flowers*, in 1854; this and subsequent works had little success. For a while she and her husband published the *Commonwealth*, an abolitionist newspaper. In February 1862 the *Atlantic Monthly* published her poem "Battle Hymn of the Republic," to be set to an old folk tune also used for "John Brown's Body." The song became the semi-official Civil War song of the Union army and Mrs. Howe became famous. After the war she involved herself in the woman-suffrage movement, was the first president of the New England Woman Suffrage Association, and from 1869 took a leading role in the American Woman Suffrage Association. She also took up the cause of peace and in 1870 published her "Appeal to Womanhood Throughout the World," a call for an international conference of women on the subject of peace. In 1871 she became first president of the American branch of the Woman's International Peace Association. She continued to write throughout her life, her publications including travel books, poetry, collections of essays, and biographies, notably that of Margaret Fuller. She died on October 17, 1910, in Newport, Rhode Island. Of her children the best known was Laura Elizabeth Howe Richards (1850–1943), author of the classic children's tale *Captain January*, 1910.

Howe, Samuel Gridley (1801–1876), educator and social reformer. Born in Boston on November 10, 1801, Howe graduated from Brown University in 1821 and then entered Harvard Medical School, taking his M.D. in 1824. Soon thereafter he sailed to Greece to aid in that country's war for independence from Turkey; for six years he fought, was a surgeon for the fleet, and helped in the reconstruction that followed. In 1831, having returned to Boston, he accepted an offer to direct a newly founded school for the blind. During an inspection tour of such schools in Europe he was imprisoned for aiding a revolt in Poland; he returned the following year and in August opened a new school in his father's house in Boston. He was eminently successful in educating blind children; his triumph was in the case of Laura Dewey Bridgman, a blind deaf-mute child who entered the school (by then the Perkins School for the Blind) in 1837. His success in communicating with and then educating Miss Bridgman aroused the enthusiasm of Charles Dickens during his visit to the United States in 1842. In 1843 Howe married Julia Ward, who was later to write "The Battle Hymn of the Republic." He worked for a great number of causes: he supported Horace Mann in the crusade for common and normal schools; pioneered in the education of mentally retarded children; worked for prison reform; and aided Dorothea Lynde Dix in improving the care accorded the mentally ill. With his wife he published for a time the *Commonwealth*, an abolitionist newspaper. In 1846 he ran unsuccessfully for the House of Representatives as a Conscience Whig and he was a secret supporter of the activities of John Brown. He was chairman of the Massachusetts Board of State Charities from 1865 to 1874. He died in Boston on January 9, 1876.

Howells, William Dean (1837–1920), author, critic, and editor. Born in Martins Ferry, Ohio, on March 1, 1837, Howells was the son of an itin-erant printer and was taken into the trade himself at the age of nine. He spent his early years in a succession of small Ohio towns and received little formal education; his determination to become a writer, however, led him to study on his own. After four years as an editorial writer for the *Ohio State Journal* in Columbus, he published in 1860 his first book of verse—*Poems of Two Friends*, with John J. Piatt—and his first book of prose, a campaign biography of Abraham Lincoln. As a consequence of writing the biography he visited New England and met James Russell Lowell and was introduced to the Boston circle; he also was given the post of consul in Venice, which he held from 1861 to 1865. Upon his return to the United States he was briefly on the staff of the *Nation* and then in 1866 began a long association with the *Atlantic Monthly*, beginning as assistant editor. In the same year he published his observations of four years in Italy as *Venetian Life*. He quickly made himself a part of the social and intellectual life of Cambridge and Boston and in 1871 became editor in chief of the *Atlantic*; in the next ten years he made the magazine into one of national importance and a champion of young and unorthodox writers. In particular he encouraged two men who were perhaps polar opposites in literature, Henry James and Samuel Clemens (Mark Twain), and in doing so demonstrated a truly remarkable breadth of appreciation. At the same time he was developing his own literary career by publishing a number of novels, including *Their Wedding Journey*, 1872, *A Foregone Conclusion*, 1875, and *The Lady of the Aroostook*, 1879. In 1881 he severed his connection with the *Atlantic* and for several years his novels were serialized in the *Century* magazine. These years saw the growth of Howells's awareness of the need for a realistic portrayal of (and even involvement in) the society surrounding the writer; his realism, although later often dismissed as meek and compromising, showed a steady development of this understanding, while it was always restrained from belonging in the naturalistic school by a certain moral optimism. *The Undiscovered Country*, 1880, was followed by *Dr. Breen's Practice*, 1881; *A Modern Instance*, 1882, one of his very best; and *The Rise of Silas Lapham*, 1885, probably his best-known novel. He became an editor of *Harper's Magazine* and from 1886 to 1892 wrote a long series of critical articles for the "Editor's Study" in *Harper's*, many of which were collected as *Criticism and Fiction*, 1891. He again demonstrated his catholic yet discriminating taste in approving of such diverse writers as Emily Dickinson, Hamlin Garland, Stephen Crane, Frank Norris, and Thorstein Veblen. His move to New York City in 1888 marked something of a turning point in his outlook; a starker vision of life appeared in his work and he began to express a view of society much like that of Tolstoi. In *Annie Kilburn*, 1889, he took up the cause of labor; there followed *A Hazard of New Fortunes*, 1890; *The Quality of Mercy*, 1892; and *The World of*

Chance, 1893. Finally, in 1894, he published *A Traveler from Altruria*, an explicitly utopian novel that pictured a genial socialist commonwealth that was more clearly delineated in *Through the Eye of the Needle*, 1907. His last major novel, *The Landlord at Lion's Head*, appeared in 1897. From 1900 until his death Howells conducted the "Easy Chair" column in *Harper's* and continued to add to his voluminous bibliography with travel sketches, biographies, dramas, and reminiscences, being acknowledged as the "dean of American letters." His long and productive life ended on May 10, 1920, in New York City.

Hrdlička, Aleš (1869–1943), anthropologist. Born on March 29, 1869, in Humpolec, Bohemia (now Czechoslovakia), Hrdlička emigrated to the United States in 1882. He graduated from the New York Eclectic Medical College in 1892 and took a second degree from the Homeopathic and Allopathic Medical College two years later. From 1894 to 1898 he was associated with the state hospital system, from 1896 as an associate in anthropology with the Institute of New York State Hospitals. He traveled to Europe in 1896 for further study in what were rapidly becoming his specialties, physical anthropology and anthropometry, and at home he continued his studies of bodily and skeletal measurements of various classes of mentally and physically abnormal patients. Between 1898 and 1902 he accompanied a number of expeditions to the Southwest and Mexico under the sponsorship of the American Museum of Natural History, compiling anthropometric data on American Indian groups. In 1903 he was appointed assistant curator of the National Museum of the Smithsonian Institution and charged with principal responsibility for organizing its physical anthropology division. He advanced to curator in 1910 and retained that post until his retirement in 1942, during this span building up one of the world's largest collection of skeletal remains. His field studies continued until 1910 and thereafter he organized regular expeditions to all parts of the Americas and the world. The early history of man in America remained his principal interest and he was, as a result of his anthropometric studies, an early proponent of the later generally accepted theory that the American Indian had Asian origins, although his dating of the ancestral migration via Siberia—some 10,000 years ago—has subsequently been pushed back. In 1918 he founded and served as first editor of the *American Journal of Physical Anthropology*, and in 1929 he helped found and became first president of the American Association of Physical Anthropologists. Among his many books were *Ancient Man in North America*, 1907; *Ancient Man in South America*, 1912; *Physical Anthropology*, 1919; *Old Americans*, 1925; *Anthropology of the American Indian*, 1927; *The Skeletal Remains of Early Man*, 1930; *Children Who Run on All Fours*, 1931; and *Practical Anthropometry*, 1939. Hrdlička was an associate in anthropology at the Smithsonian Institution from 1942 until his death on September 5, 1943, in Washington, D.C.

Hubbard, Elbert Green (1856–1915), author and publisher. Born in Bloomington, Illinois, on June 19, 1856, Hubbard traveled to Chicago at sixteen and for four years worked for various newspapers there. In 1880 he moved to Buffalo, New York, where for 12 years he was employed as a sales and promotion manager for a manufacturing firm. In 1892 he decided to follow his interest in learning and his desire to write, and on a visit to England that year he met William Morris, whose Kelmscott Press and other efforts to revive pre-industrial handicrafts deeply impressed him. On his return he published three rapidly produced novels, *One Day: A Tale of the Prairies*, 1893, *Forbes of Harvard*, 1894, and *No Enemy (But Himself)*, 1894, and in 1895 founded in the Buffalo suburb of East Aurora the Roycroft Press, modeled closely on Morris's establishment. There he published a series of monthly booklets called *Little Journeys*, biographies interlarded with his own wide-ranging comments, and the *Philistine*, an experimental and controversial literary magazine begun in 1895 that quickly attracted an unexpectedly large number of subscribers. Continuing in print until Hubbard's death, the *Philistine* contained at first contributions from other authors, but from 1899 it was written entirely by Hubbard himself. One of the issues of 1899 contained his most famous story, "A Message to Garcia," which drew from an incident of the Spanish-American War a moral of self-reliance and perseverance; it was widely reprinted and circulated in millions of copies. The conservatism and business-oriented ethics of the story and of much of his other writings was in sharp contrast to his appearance and manner and the activities in the several craft shops at Roycroft, which seemed to many wildly radical. The Roycroft Shops eventually became widely renowned for their high quality work in leather, metal, and wood. In 1908 he founded another monthly, *The Fra*, which, less intensely personal than the *Philistine*, continued until 1917. Other books of Hubbard's included *Time and Chance*, 1899; *So Here Cometh White Hyacinths*, 1907; *The Man of Sorrows*, 1908, all of which exhibited an informal, epigrammatic, and occasionally avantgarde style. Hubbard was much in demand as a lecturer and the Roycroft establishment, where as many as 500 craftsmen and students were occupied, attracted large numbers of visitors. Hubbard died in the sinking of the *Lusitania* on May 7, 1915.

Hubbard, Frank McKinney (1868–1930), "Kin," humorist. Born on September 1, 1868, in Bellefontaine, Ohio, Kin Hubbard was the grandson of Capt. John B. Miller, who acted in a wagon-theater that traveled through the Midwest, and the son of the publisher of the *Bellefontaine Examiner*. From childhood he had a love of circuses and theaters and in his youth produced his own blackface minstrel shows. He taught himself to sketch, went to local schools, and learned the printer's trade from his father. In 1891 he became a police reporter and artist on the *Indianapolis News*, and about 1894 returned to Bellefontaine to work in the post office for his father, who had become postmaster. He was subsequently employed on the *Cincinnati Commercial Tribune* and the *Mansfield* (Ohio) *News*. In 1901 he rejoined the *Indianapolis News* and remained there for the rest of his life. In 1904, while riding on a political-campaign train, he made sketches of several Hoosier characters and printed them in the *News* with succinct captions; a typical example was "Ther's some folks standin' behind th' President that ought t' git around where he kin watch 'em." The feature appealed to the editor, who encouraged him to do a series; and thus "Abe Martin," a farmer from Brown County, Indiana, was born. Since the caricatures were merely signed "Hub," it was Abe Martin, the character, who became identified with the "home-cured philosophy" that accompanied them—"Very often the quiet feller has said all he knows," or "If capital an' labor ever do git t'gether it's good night fer th' rest of us," or "Ther ought t' be some way t' eat celery so it wouldn' sound like you wuz steppin' on a basket." Soon syndicated (as were his weekly essays "Short Furrows"), the sketches and sayings were collected and published at least once a year from 1906 to 1929. Hubbard made an international tour as Abe Martin in 1924 but usually declined radio and stage appearances, preferring to remain at home ("Of all th' home remedies a good wife is th' best") and cultivate his garden. He died on December 26, 1930, in Indianapolis.

Hubbard, Gardiner Greene (1822–1897), lawyer and civic leader. Born in Boston on August 25, 1822, Hubbard graduated from Dartmouth College in 1841 and studied law at Harvard and in the office of Benjamin R. Curtis. He entered practice in Cambridge, Massachusetts, where he also took a leading role in such civic improvements as the construction of an illuminating gas system, an improved water supply, and a streetcar line to Boston. Prompted by his daughter's deafness, he led in founding the Clarke Institution for the Deaf in 1867 and served as its president for the first ten years. He was also a member of both the Massachusetts and the Boston school boards. Interested in the efficient organization of telegraph and postal systems, he served as chairman of a presidential commission appointed in 1876 to study and make recommendations for the U.S. Post Office Department. In 1871 he met Alexander Graham Bell, then a teacher in the Horace Mann School for the Deaf; attracted by Bell's electrical experiments, Hubbard became his principal backer and, upon the patenting of the telephone in 1876, the principal organizer of its commercial exploitation. In 1877 Bell married Hubbard's daughter, Mabel, and two years later Hubbard followed the two to Washington, D.C., where he lived for the rest of his life. While working to promote the adoption of the telephone in other countries he was active also in local public affairs; for 12 years he was a trustee of Columbian (now George Washington) University, from 1895 a regent of the Smithsonian Institution, and he was long interested in the activities of the Columbia Historical Society. In 1883 he joined Bell in founding the journal *Science*, which later became the organ of the American Association for the Advancement of Science (AAAS), in 1888 he founded and became first president of the National Geographic Society, and in 1890, again with Bell, he was a founder of the American Association to Promote the Teaching of Speech to the Deaf, of which he was thereafter a vice-president. Hubbard died in Washington, D.C., on December 11, 1897.

Hubbard, Kin, *see* Hubbard, Frank McKinney

Hubble, Edwin Powell (1889–1953), astronomer. Born in Marshfield, Missouri, on November 20, 1889, Hubble graduated from the University of Chicago in 1910 and subsequently studied at Oxford on a Rhodes scholarship. Taking a B.A. in jurisprudence, he returned to the United States and for a year practiced law in Kentucky, but his interest in science drew him back to the University of Chicago, where he received a Ph.D. in 1917, having meanwhile begun astronomical researches at the university's Yerkes Observatory. During World War I he served in France as chief ballistician for the ordnance service. In 1919 he joined the staff of the Mt. Wilson Observatory in California, with which he was associated for the rest of his life. His primary interest was the study of nebulas, huge agglomerations of stars about which little was then known. With his discovery in 1923 of a Cepheid variable star—a pulsating star whose period of variation in brightness is directly related to its actual luminosity and whose distance can therefore be accurately determined—in the Andromeda nebula, he succeeded in demonstrating that Andromeda and other nebulas like it were independent galaxies and lay at vast distances from our own. He undertook a sky survey of the density and distribution of these extragalactic nebulas; on the basis of the survey he developed a classification scheme for the various forms of nebulas based on a suggested evolutionary pattern. In 1929 he announced the results of his investigations concerning the spectral red shifts displayed by these nebulas, a phenomenon interpreted as an instance of the Doppler effect whereby the frequency of wave radiation—in this case light—is changed by the speed of approach or recession of the radiating object relative to the observer. A shift toward the red end of the spectrum had been observed in the light from distant galaxies and this was taken to indicate that they were all receding from ours, that the universe was in fact expanding. Hubble's research demonstrated a simple relation between a galaxy's distance and its speed of recession, and further assigned a numerical value to the still-accepted "Hubble's constant." This discovery had a profound effect on cosmology and stimulated the formulation of numerous cosmological models. His work strained the capabilities of the 100-inch Mt. Wilson telescope and provided a strong impetus for the building of the great 200-inch instrument at Mt. Palomar, opened in 1948. Hubble continued his investigations into the nature of extragalactic nebulas until his death on September 28, 1953, in San Marino, California.

Hudson, Henry (?–1611), explorer. Born presumably in England at a date unknown, Hudson left no trace of his life before 1607, although it may be assumed that he had by that time acquired considerable experience at sea. In the spring of that year he was engaged by the Muscovy Company, a joint-stock mercantile enterprise that had for more than 50 years dominated English trade with Russia and was constantly searching for new trade routes to the East. Sent to discover a northeast passage to Japan and China, Hudson sailed the *Hopewell* to the Shetland Islands, thence to the east coast of Greenland, and then traced the edge of the polar ice pack east to Spitsbergen (Norway) at about 80°N; on the return voyage he discovered an island in the Greenland Sea that he named Hudson's Tutchers (now Jan Mayen Island), and on arriving in England in September he sparked a new industry by reporting on the possibilities of whaling off Spitsbergen. In 1608 he made a second voyage for the Muscovy Company, seeking a passage between Spitsbergen and Novaya Zemlya (Russia) and again finding it impossible to skirt the ice pack. In 1609 he was hired by the Dutch East India Company for the same task; leaving Amsterdam in April with the *Half Moon* and a Dutch and English crew, he entered the Barents Sea bound for Novaya Zemlya but was turned back by ice and foul weather. To head off an impending mutiny he offered to sail west to America and search for a northwest passage to the Orient—either to the north via Davis Strait or in the latitude of Virginia. The crew choosing the latter, the *Half Moon* set sail in May and by July was off the coast of Newfoundland. Hudson coasted south as far as Chesapeake Bay and then turned north again, pausing to enter Delaware Bay, and on September 3 entered the present-day New York harbor. He ascended the great river that was to be named for him, sailing as far as the site of Albany before concluding that the waterway would not lead him on to China, and after a month of exploration and trading with the Indians he sailed down the Hudson and departed from New York harbor, arriving in Dartmouth, England, in November. He was thereupon forbidden by the British to sail in the service of any other country. In 1610 a group of promoters in England formed a new company to sponsor a search for the Northwest Passage, and Hudson was again chosen to command the expedition. In April he set sail in the *Discovery* and in June or July passed to the south of Greenland and entered the great strait that thereafter bore his name. On

August 3 he sighted the present Hudson Bay, which he described as a "Sea to the Westward" and which he spent three months exploring. On November 1 the *Discovery* moored for the winter in the southwest corner of the present James Bay and within days was frozen in. By the end of the winter rations were extremely short and the crew mutinous. After an unsuccessful foraging expedition by boat, Hudson took the *Discovery* out of its anchorage on June 12, 1611. Mutiny broke out ten days later and on the morning of June 22 Hudson, his son, and seven others were set adrift with no provisions in a small boat. No trace of any of them was ever found. The remainder of the crew, choosing Robert Bylot captain, began the return voyage immediately. Several were killed in an encounter with Eskimos, and of those who arrived safely in England in September, four were tried and acquitted of mutiny in 1618. In modern histories, Hudson is often referred to as "Hendryk," "Hendrick," or "Henryk." There seems to be no contemporary account of his adventures that employs any of these names; but the fact that he later acquired a Dutch-sounding name suggests a good deal about the international character of the explorations of the New World that he forwarded so valiantly. His various employments also laid the foundation for rival and occasionally conflicting claims, by the Dutch to the Hudson River region and by the British to Hudson Bay.

Hudson, Manley Ottmer (1886–1960), lawyer, educator, and judge. Born in St. Peters, Missouri, on May 19, 1886, Hudson graduated from William Jewell College in 1906, took an M.A. the following year, and then entered Harvard Law School, receiving his degree in 1910. From that year until 1919 he was a professor of law at the University of Missouri, serving also during 1912–1919 as secretary of the Missouri Peace Society and in 1917 receiving an S.J.D. degree from Harvard. In 1919 he was an adviser on international law to the U.S. delegation to the Versailles Peace Conference. Later in 1919 he joined the Harvard Law School faculty and in 1923 he was named Bemis Professor of International Law, a post he held until his retirement in 1954. In the period immediately following World War I Hudson involved himself deeply in the work of the League of Nations, serving for several years on the legal staff of the secretariat. Recognized not only as a scholar and expert, but also as a leading advocate of the application of international law, he published two influential works during the 1920s, *The Permanent Court of International Justice*, 1925, and a handbook, *The World Court*, 1928. In 1933 he was appointed by President Franklin D. Roosevelt to the Permanent Court of Arbitration (the Hague Tribunal) and in 1936, on the resignation of Frank B. Kellogg, to the Permanent Court of International Justice (the World Court). He retained his seats on both until 1945. His series of *World Court Reports*, four volumes appearing between 1935 and 1943, supplemented the series that he began earlier on *International Legislation*, nine volumes, 1919–1945. Other books of his included *Progress in International Organization*, 1932, and *International Tribunals, Past and Present*, 1944; from 1924 he was editor of the *American Journal of International Law*. After World War II Hudson worked with the United Nations, as he had done with the League of Nations some 25 years before, and from 1949 he served as chairman of its International Law Commission. He died in Cambridge, Massachusetts, on April 13, 1960.

Huggins, Charles Brenton (1901–   ), surgeon. Born on September 22, 1901, in Halifax, Nova Scotia, Huggins graduated from Acadia University in 1920 and four years later received his M.D. from the Harvard Medical School. After a two-year internship at the University of Michigan Medical School hospital he was appointed an instructor in surgery there, moving in 1927 to a similar position on the faculty of the University of Chicago Medical School. He advanced to a full professorship in 1936. His general field was surgery of the genitourinary system and he specialized in the treatment of cancer of the prostate and mammary glands. In the course of his research he discovered that both forms of cancer were linked to the levels of certain hormones in the bloodstream; from this discovery he developed a set of radical procedures for treating cancers that were unresponsive to other approaches; his measures include surgical castration and the administration of female hormones for the control of prostate cancer and, as a last resort, adrenalectomy coupled with sustaining administration of cortisone for control of highly recalcitrant prostate and breast cancers. Working with various chemicals known to have powerful carcinogenic properties, he found many of them to possess structures analogous to the structures of certain hormones, and derived from that knowledge a method of using large doses of hormones to control certain forms of cancer in rats, a step preliminary to human therapeutic application. Huggins was named director of the Ben May Laboratory for Cancer Research of the University of Chicago in 1951 and in 1962 became William B. Ogden Distinguished Service Professor at Chicago. His many honors and awards for his pioneering investigations of the relation of endocrine hormones to cancer culminated in the award of the 1966 Nobel Prize for Physiology and Medicine jointly with Francis P. Rous.

Hughes, Charles Evans (1862–1948), chief justice of the Supreme Court. Born on April 11, 1862, in Glens Falls, New York, Hughes was educated at Madison (now Colgate University) and at Brown University, from which he graduated in 1881. After a period of teaching and private law study he entered the law school of Columbia University and was granted a degree in 1884; he began practice and for three years was a tutor at Columbia. He taught in the law school at Cornell University from 1891 to 1893 and then returned to his practice in New York City. His public career began in 1905 when he served as counsel to a legislative committee investigating the gas and electric lighting industries; as a result of this work he was considered for mayor of New York City, but he declined nomination in order to aid in an investigation of the practices of insurance companies. In 1906, however, he was nominated for governor and defeated William Randolph Hearst. He served two terms, 1906–1910, which were marked by extensive reform of the state's government. In 1910 he was appointed to the Supreme Court by President William Howard Taft. He had been prominently mentioned for the presidency since 1908 but had consistently refused to be considered; finally, in 1916, he accepted a Republican draft and resigned from the Supreme Court to campaign. After being narrowly defeated by the incumbent Woodrow Wilson he returned to his law practice, serving also as chairman of New York City's World War I draft appeals board and in an investigation of the aircraft industry. With the election of Warren G. Harding to the presidency in 1920, Hughes became secretary of state. He was unsuccessful in his advocacy of U.S. membership in the League of Nations and was forced therefore to negotiate a separate U.S. peace treaty with Germany. He was the chief organizer of the Washington Disarmament Conference in 1921–1922 that produced an arms-limitation treaty, and he succeeded in maintaining the Open Door policy in China and in supporting U.S. interests in the Pacific. At the Pan-American Conference in Santiago in 1923 he negotiated a 15-nation treaty arranging for the arbitration of disputes. After leaving the cabinet in 1925 he aided in the reorganization of the state government in New York, represented the U.S. at two further Pan-American conferences, was a member of the Permanent Court of Arbitration (Hague Tribunal), and in 1929 served as a judge on the Permanent Court of International Justice (World Court) at The Hague. In 1930 President Herbert Hoover appointed him chief justice of the Supreme Court. He generally took a liberal stand, particularly in civil-rights cases, and preferred a loose-constructionist interpretation of the Constitution. As the Supreme Court began to invalidate early New Deal legislation in the 1930s, Hughes occupied a middle ground, often dissenting from the Court's conservatism but writing its decision against the National Industrial Recovery Act in *Schechter* v. *U.S.*, 1935. When President Franklin D. Roosevelt proposed his "court-packing" plan in 1937, Hughes denounced it and was instrumental in its defeat; he later denied that the approval by the court of several major New Deal acts at about the same time was an accommodation to the President. He retired in 1941 and died on August 27, 1948, in Osterville, Cape Cod, Massachusetts.

Hughes, Howard Robard (1905–1976), industrialist, aviator, and motion-picture producer. Born in Houston, Texas, on December 24, 1905, Hughes was the son of a developer and manufacturer of oil-well drilling equipment, the owner of Hughes

Tool Company in Houston. He was educated at the Rice Institute in Houston and the California Institute of Technology (Caltech). While he was still in his teens his father died, and he assumed control of the tool business shortly thereafter. With an estimated yearly income of $2 million at the age of twenty he went to Hollywood to produce motion pictures. Among his box-office hits were *Two Arabian Nights*, winner of the Academy Award in 1928; *Hell's Angels*, starring the almost unknown starlet Jean Harlow, which won an Academy Award in 1930; *The Front Page*, 1931; *Scarface*, 1932, which introduced Paul Muni and began a trend in gangster movies; *The Sky Devils*, 1932; and, after his purchase of the RKO film company in 1939 (an unsuccessful venture), *The Outlaw*, 1941. He organized and became president of an experimental aircraft enterprise, Hughes Aircraft Company. In a plane of his own design he set the world's air speed record, 352 miles per hour, in September 1935. In January 1937 he broke his own transcontinental flying record made a year earlier with a new time of 7 hours, 28 minutes, 25 seconds. In July 1938, in a twin-engine Lockheed, he set an around-the-world flight record of 3 days, 19 hours, 8 minutes, 10 seconds. He designed, built, and flew a 220-ton plywood flying boat—then the world's largest plane—on November 2, 1947. In 1939 he had, through Hughes Tool, begun buying stock in the company that later became Trans World Airlines (TWA), and by 1959 he held three-fourths of the common stock of the company; his control met with considerable opposition and litigation, however, and in 1966 he sold out in one of the largest stock transactions in history, amounting to more than a half billion dollars. Hughes Tool was also the major stockholder in Northeast Airlines from 1962 to 1964. In the late 1960s he purchased huge tracts of land in and near Las Vegas, Nevada, becoming virtual owner of the famous Las Vegas "strip" of hotels and gambling casinos and buying up at the same time a controlling interest in Air West, an airline serving Las Vegas. He took up residence in the top floors of one of his hotels and continued to live, as he had for years, in utter seclusion. He later transferred his headquarters, under extraordinary security, to the Bahamas, to Nicaragua, and then to London. He apparently broke silence, however, with a telephone call to newspaper reporters in 1972 to scotch the imminent publication of an "autobiography" that was subsequently revealed as a major literary hoax. A recluse beset by phobias and increasingly enfeebled and unbalanced, Hughes died on April 6, 1976, aboard a plane flying him from Acapulco to Houston for medical treatment.

Hughes, James Mercer Langston, *see* Hughes, Langston

Hughes, John (1797–1864), religious leader. Born on June 24, 1797, in County Tyrone, Ireland, Hughes emigrated to the United States in 1817. In 1820 he began religious training at Mount St. Mary's College in Emmitsburg, Maryland, and in 1826 was ordained a Roman Catholic priest. He became prominent as a "fighting Irish priest" while at the head of two Philadelphia parishes, during which time he debated with Protestant clergymen over issues of the day. In 1838 he was made bishop coadjutor of New York City and was immediately identified as a champion of the interests of the growing Eastern population of Irish and German Catholic immigrants. Succeeding to the bishopric of the see in 1842, he saw an end to the lay trustee system in New York, securing state legislation removing the control of church property from secular administrators and instead giving title to the bishop (later the archbishop), or his designates, on behalf of the Roman Catholic Church. His proposal to establish properly equipped and well-staffed parochial schools for all Catholics led to a fierce battle in which the Protestant-dominated public schools were finally secularized in 1841, and his people were pledged to the development of a parochial school system. He founded in 1841 St. John's College, which eventually grew into Fordham University. Threats and abuse from the Nativist and Know-Nothing parties, reaching heights in 1844 and 1854, prompted him to threaten to use force if necessary to defend Catholic institutions. In 1850, when the see of New York was elevated to an archbishopric, he became its first archbishop, and thereafter made frequent trips to Europe and to the Vatican, becoming the foremost spokesman for American Catholics. In 1854 he battled the radical Irish press set up in New York City by political exiles. During the Civil War he was an active pro-Unionist and, as a special representative of President Abraham Lincoln, promoted the Union cause in Europe. His personal appeal was a major factor in bringing the draft rioting of 1863 to an end. In 25 years as bishop, he built more than 100 new churches and helped found St. Joseph's Provincial Seminary in Troy, New York, and the North American College in Rome. In 1858 he began construction of St. Patrick's Cathedral in New York City. He died in New York City on January 3, 1864.

Hughes, Langston (1902–1967), author. Born in Joplin, Missouri, on February 1, 1902, James Mercer Langston Hughes moved often as a child until his family settled in Cleveland when he was fourteen. In 1921, shortly after he graduated from high school, his first poem, and one that remains perhaps his best-loved, "The Negro Speaks of Rivers," was published in the *Crisis*. After an extended visit to Mexico he entered Columbia University in 1921 but left the following year. For several years he drifted, working his way to Africa on a freighter and living for periods in Paris and Rome. While working as a busboy in a Washington, D.C., hotel in 1925, he showed some of his work to Vachel Lindsay, who immediately arranged for its publication. Hughes was awarded a scholarship to Lincoln University in Pennsylvania. His first volume of poetry, *The Weary*

Blues, appeared in 1926 and was followed the next year by *Fine Clothes to the Jew*. In 1926 he received the Witter Bynner Undergraduate Poetry Award; he graduated from Lincoln in 1929 and the next year published his first prose work, *Not Without Laughter*. Poetry continued to be his primary interest and he came to be called the "Poet Laureate of Harlem." His collections included *The Dream Keeper*, 1932; *Scottsboro Limited*, 1932; *Shakespeare in Harlem*, 1942; and *Fields of Wonder*, 1947. He also wrote dramas, including *Mulatto* and *Simply Heavenly*; song-plays like *Black Nativity* and *Jerico Jim Crow*; a collection of stories under the title *The Ways of White Folks*, 1934; and newspaper columns in the *New York Post* and the *Chicago Defender*. In his columns he chronicled the adventures and set forth the philosophy of his fictional character Jesse B. Semple, usually known as Simple, and many of them were collected in book form as *Simple Speaks His Mind*, 1950, *Simple Stakes a Claim*, 1957, and others. In later years Hughes edited a number of anthologies of the work of black authors and wrote several books and articles on outstanding black figures. He died in New York City on May 22, 1967. His autobiography, *The Big Sea*, had appeared in 1940.

Hull, Cordell (1871–1955), public official. Born on October 2, 1871, in Overton County, Tennessee, Hull was educated at Montvale College in Celina, Tennessee. An ardent Democrat before he was twenty, he entered National Normal University at Lebanon, Connecticut, in 1889, transferred to Cumberland University Law School the following year, and graduated and was admitted to the bar in 1891. He practiced law briefly in Celina before winning election to the state legislature in 1893. In 1897 he left the legislature to recruit a volunteer company for the Spanish-American War; they went to Cuba as part of the 4th Tennessee regiment but saw little action. In 1903 he was elected a Tennessee circuit-court judge and from 1907 to 1931, except for one term, served in the House of Representatives, where his concerns focused on tax and tariff problems. He prepared the first federal income-tax bill in 1913 and the later revised act, and the federal inheritance-tax law in 1916. An advocate of President Woodrow Wilson's economic program and of the League of Nations, he was convinced by 1919 that low tariffs and the removal of other trade barriers would promote if not secure world peace. In 1931 he was elected to the Senate and in 1933 became secretary of state under Franklin D. Roosevelt. He was successful at a number of Pan-American conferences —at Montevideo in 1933, at Buenos Aires in 1936, at Lima in 1938, and at Havana in 1940—in formulating the Good Neighbor policy and establishing a united hemispheric front against aggression in case of war with any European nation. In 1934 he won passage of the Trade Agreements Act, designed to stimulate trade with Latin America by giving the president the power to adjust tariffs within established limits. As neutrality

became impossible in 1940 after the outbreak of World War II, he supported President Roosevelt in drawing the United States closer to the Allies. Despite steadily weakening health, he led a U.S. delegation to a foreign ministers' conference in Moscow in 1943. He also played a major role at the Dumbarton Oaks Conference in Washington that laid the groundwork for the founding of the United Nations at the San Francisco conference in 1945. He was called by President Roosevelt the "father of the United Nations," and he was awarded the Nobel Peace Prize in 1945. He resigned from the cabinet after the 1944 presidential election, owing to his health, and died on July 23, 1955, at Bethesda, Maryland.

Hull, Isaac (1773–1843), naval officer. Born in Derby, Connecticut, on March 9, 1773, Hull grew up in Newton, Massachusetts, in the home of his uncle William Hull. He went to sea as a cabin boy at fourteen and within six years was master of an oceangoing merchantman. In 1798 he was given a commission in the navy and assigned to the frigate *Constitution*. During the undeclared naval war with France he distinguished himself by sailing into the harbor of Puerto Plata, Santo Domingo (now the Dominican Republic) and cutting out the French privateer *Sandwich*. Ranked second on the lieutenant's list at the end of the war, he was given command of the brig *Argus* in 1803 and assigned to Commodore Edward Preble's squadron for service in the Tripolitan War; promoted to commander in 1804, he provided the naval support for William Eaton's capture of Derna the next year. Hull's promotion to captain in 1806 was followed by four years of shore duty, but in 1810 he returned to the line as commander of the *Constitution*. After a mission to Europe bearing Joel Barlow, U.S. minister to France, and a payment on Dutch loans, he returned to the United States in time to refit his ship before the outbreak of the War of 1812. In July 1812, while en route to New York harbor, he encountered five British warships off Egg Harbor, New Jersey, and with brilliant seamanship confounded them, despite the dead-calm sea, by escaping after a three-day chase. Putting out in August from Boston, where he had taken refuge, he met the British *Guerrière* off Barnegat Bay, New Jersey, on August 19 and, after holding his fire to gain position, so disabled the enemy vessel in a half-hour battle that it could not be brought to port. This first U.S. naval victory of the war rallied the country, destroyed the myth of British naval invincibility, and earned for the *Constitution* the nickname "Old Ironsides." Requesting relief from his command, Hull was briefly commandant of the Boston Navy Yard, then transferred to the yard in Portsmouth, New Hampshire; in 1815 he again took charge of the Boston yard. He returned to sea duty in 1824 with the rank of commodore, sailing the *United States* to take command of the Pacific squadron. After a leave of absence following his return to the United States in 1827 he became in 1829 commander of the Washington, D.C., Navy Yard, holding the post until 1835. In 1838 he was appointed commander of the Mediterranean squadron; on his return from that post in 1841 he took an extended leave and the next year settled in Philadelphia. Hull died there on February 13, 1843, his last words being "I strike my flag."

Hull, William (1753–1825), Revolutionary soldier. Born in Derby, Connecticut, on June 24, 1753, Hull graduated from Yale in 1772 and, after studying at the Litchfield Law School, was admitted to the bar in 1775. Commissioned a captain in his town militia in July of that year, he served through the Revolution, seeing action at Boston, White Plains, Trenton, Princeton, Saratoga, Monmouth, and elsewhere, rising to the rank of lieutenant colonel, and winning the praise of Gen. George Washington. After the war he established a law practice in Newton, Massachusetts, and became active in local civic and political affairs and also helped to suppress Shays's Rebellion. A prominent Jeffersonian, he was appointed governor of the newly created Michigan Territory in 1805. In 1812 he was commissioned brigadier general and given a force of some 2000 men in anticipation of war with England. He helped devise a disastrous strategy of complete reliance on his land forces to hold the Great Lakes region and even to capture large portions of Canada; this course seriously retarded the development of a U.S. naval presence on the lakes. Upon launching his men in their assigned invasion of Canada from Detroit in July 1812 he pursued an extremely cautious and time-consuming policy that, combined with Gen. Henry Dearborn's failure to advance on Niagara, enabled the British to reinforce their positions in the West. British troops under Gen. Isaac Brock forced Hull back to Detroit; fearing both the British and warring Indians, he surrendered the post without a fight on August 16. Promptly court-martialed, he was convicted of cowardice and neglect of duty, but in recognition of his Revolutionary service President James Madison stayed his death sentence. Hull returned to Newton, Massachusetts, and died there on November 29, 1825.

Humphrey, Hubert Horatio (1911–1978), vice-president of the United States. Born in Wallace, South Dakota, on May 27, 1911, Humphrey attended the public schools of Doland, South Dakota, where his family had moved. He studied at the Denver College of Pharmacy in 1932–1933 and, after working as a pharmacist for several years, received his B.A. from the University of Minnesota in 1939 and his M.A. from Louisiana State University in 1940. While at L.S.U. he also taught political science and, after receiving his degree, went back for a year of teaching at Minnesota. From 1942 to 1945 he served in several federal posts in Minnesota, was an instructor with the Army Air Forces, worked as a radio news commentator, and acted as the state campaign director for Franklin D. Roosevelt during the 1944 presidential campaign. During this period he helped to merge the Democratic and Farmer-Labor parties in the state and in 1945 he was elected mayor of Minneapolis on a fusion ticket. He was elected to the Senate in 1948 and re-elected in 1954 and 1960; in 1956 he served as U.S. delegate to the United Nations (UN) General Assembly. In 1960 he made an unsuccessful bid for the Democratic presidential nomination. Known as a liberal, he was elected by his fellow senators as assistant majority leader in 1961 and was chosen to manage the 1964 civil-rights bill in the Senate. With strong bipartisan support, and despite a three-month filibuster by the opponents of the bill, he was able to marshal enough votes for passage. At the 1964 Democratic national convention President Lyndon B. Johnson announced that he had chosen Humphrey as his running mate, and Humphrey campaigned ably for the national ticket and shared Johnson's landslide victory that year. He announced his intention to seek the Democratic presidential nomination in 1968 shortly after Johnson withdrew from consideration and he emerged as the front-running candidate after the murder of Robert F. Kennedy in June. Humphrey was nominated by the Democrats at a chaotic convention in Chicago in August but lost by a narrow margin to Richard M. Nixon in November. After the election he accepted a position as a professor of political science at the University of Minnesota. He was reelected to the Senate in 1970 and 1976. In these years he was acknowledged the elder statesman of liberalism. He died in Waverly, Minnesota, on January 13, 1978.

Humphreys, Joshua (1751–1838), shipbuilder. Born in Delaware County, Pennsylvania, on June 17, 1751, Humphreys was early apprenticed to a Philadelphia ship carpenter. Rising quickly to charge of the shipyard where he was employed, he then opened his own yard and by the age of twenty-five was the foremost marine architect in America. He was called upon by Congress in 1776 to refit eight small merchant vessels as a naval fleet for Revolutionary War service under the command of Esek Hopkins. During the war, and particularly afterward, during the organization of the United States, he devoted much thought to the problem of American naval inferiority. When Congress provided for the creation of a navy in 1794 Humphreys submitted his ideas on ship design to Secretary of War Henry Knox and in June of that year was appointed naval constructor to the government and directed to prepare detailed models for the six frigates authorized by Congress. His plans accepted, Humphreys proceeded with actual construction, himself supervising the building of the *United States* in Philadelphia, while the *Constitution, Chesapeake, Constellation, President,* and *Congress* were built elsewhere, all of them except for some modifications on the *Chesapeake,* to his specifications. These first ships of the line of the U.S. navy incorporated numerous design innovations; longer, broader, and lower in the water than European warships carrying comparable armament, they presented a more difficult target and were faster and more maneuverable, while the concentration of guns on one deck made for more efficient fire control. The six made the navy, despite its smallness, a more than adequate force, and among them they accounted for some of the most celebrated battles in U.S. naval annals. Humphreys completed his work as naval constructor in 1801; in 1806 he was commissioned to build a major naval yard in Philadelphia. While he rejected numerous offers of employment from foreign nations, his design ideas came to be widely adopted by other navies of the world. He died on January 12, 1838, in Haverford, Pennsylvania.

Huneker, James Gibbons (1860–1921), musician, critic, and author. Born in Philadelphia on January 31, 1860, Huneker was educated in a military academy in his native city and then studied law until about 1878. He also studied the piano and went to Paris for further music studies, later continuing his musical training at the National Conservatory of Music in New York City, where he was also a teaching assistant from 1886 to 1898. He began contributing a weekly column on music and musical affairs to the *Musical Courier* in 1887, maintaining the association until 1902; in 1891 he became music critic for the newly established *New York Evening Recorder*, for which he ventured some drama criticism as well. From 1895 to 1897 he filled similar positions on the *New York Morning Advertiser*. From his earliest days as a newspaper columnist he was recognized as a man of wide and sensitive sympathies, interested in all the arts and capable of capturing the spirit of a work or an occasion in rich, witty prose. With the publication of his first book, *Mezzotints in Modern Music*, 1899, he emerged as a critic of major importance, and his *Chopin: The Man and His Music*, 1900, established his reputation at home and abroad. As music and, later, drama critic for the *New York Sun* (1900–1912), music critic for the *Philadelphia Press* (1917), for the *New York Times* (1918), and for the *New York World* from 1919 until his death, and as a frequent contributor to periodicals, Huneker let his sensibilities range over music, art, drama, literature, and personalities and acquired a devoted following in the United States and Europe by the sheer brilliance of his style. Among his other books were *Overtones: A Book of Temperaments*, 1904; *Iconoclasts: A Book of Dramatists*, 1905; *Egoists: A Book of Supermen*, 1909; *Promenades of an Impressionist*, 1910; *Franz Liszt*, 1911; *New Cosmopolis*, 1915; *Ivory, Apes and Peacocks*, 1915; *Unicorns*, 1917; *Bedouins*, 1920; and *Variations*, 1921. *Old Fogy*, 1913, and *Steeplejack*, 1920, were autobiographical. Huneker died in Brooklyn, New York, on February 9, 1921.

Hunsaker, Jerome Clarke (1886–   ), aeronautical engineer. Born in Creston, Iowa, on August 26, 1886, Hunsaker graduated from the U.S. Naval Academy in 1908 and was posted to the navy's construction corps. He was sent to the Massachu-

setts Institute of Technology (MIT) in 1912 for graduate study in engineering and was awarded an M.S. degree and given an instructorship there. During 1913–1914 he studied abroad, at the National Physical Laboratories in London and at the Eiffel Observatory in Paris. He returned to MIT in 1914 and there organized the nation's first college course in aeronautics and aircraft design. Awarded a D.Sc. degree in 1916, he gave up academic work that year to take charge of the Aircraft Division of the navy's Bureau of Construction and Repair. In that post he greatly advanced the science of aircraft design and pushed the navy to the forefront in the development of air power. Hunsaker designed the NC–4 flying boat that, built by Glenn H. Curtiss, became in May 1919 the first heavier-than-air craft to cross the Atlantic Ocean. For that and other achievements he was awarded the Navy Cross in 1920. He also designed the huge airship *Shenandoah*, built in 1923 and in service until it crashed in a storm in 1925. In 1923 Hunsaker was named assistant naval attaché at the U.S. embassy in London, and he filled similar posts in Paris, Berlin, and Rome before retiring from the navy in 1926 with the rank of commander. From 1926 to 1928 he was with the Bell Telephone Laboratories, working on problems of radio communication for aircraft, and from 1928 to 1933 he was with the Goodyear-Zeppelin Corporation. In 1933 he returned to MIT to head the department of mechanical engineering, later becoming chairman also of the department of aeronautical engineering, posts he held until his retirement in 1951. He continued to serve as an adviser to the navy and to the government on aviation matters and from 1941 to 1956 was chairman of the National Advisory Committee for Aeronautics.

Hunt, Haroldson Lafayette (1889–1974), businessman. Born on February 17, 1889, near Vandalia, Illinois, H. L. Hunt grew up on a farm and received only a few years of schooling. At sixteen he left home and for five years worked his way around the West and Southwest, settling in the Delta region of Arkansas in 1911 to invest a small inheritance in cotton lands. Acquiring over the next several years some 15,000 acres in Arkansas and Louisiana, he turned to other interests when the cotton market fell in 1920. He began trading in oil leases in the new Arkansas fields to build the capital necessary to drill his own wells, and within four years had made his first million dollars. Extending his operations into Oklahoma and Louisiana and then into the great East Texas field in the early 1930s, he organized his holdings into the Hunt Oil Company in 1936, establishing his headquarters in Dallas the next year. The company and its subsidiaries soon came to be the largest independent producers of oil and natural gas in the country and Hunt's fortune grew to fabulous proportions. He remained personally obscure, however, until 1951, when he founded Facts Forum, a nonprofit educational foundation through which he promoted highly conservative political views by means of radio and television programs and the publication of right-wing political tracts. Facts Forum was dissolved in 1956, but in 1958 he founded Life Line, which continued the work of its predecessor. Hunt's own commentaries for Life Line were distributed to hundreds of radio stations throughout the country, and from 1964 his newspaper column was widely reprinted. Probably his best-known contribution to political thought was his idea that the voting power of citizens should be weighted in proportion to their wealth. He was also a noted admirer of Calvin Coolidge. With business interests including real estate, livestock, and food processing in addition to oil, Hunt enjoyed an income roughly estimated at $1 million per week; reports of his remarkably frugal way of life contrasted sharply with educated guesses that his total fortune might run as high as two to three billion dollars, making him, with J. Paul Getty and Howard Hughes, one of the three richest Americans. He died in Dallas on November 29, 1974.

Hunt, Richard Morris (1827–1895), architect. Born in Brattleboro, Vermont, on October 31, 1827, Hunt grew up in an artistically inclined family; his elder brother was William Morris Hunt. After graduating from the Boston Latin School in 1843 he continued his education in Geneva, Switzerland, and then in Paris, where in 1846 he entered the École des Beaux-Arts. He studied painting, sculpture, and architecture, the last becoming his major interest. In 1854 he was appointed inspector of works on the construction of additions to the Louvre and the Tuileries, in Paris, and he also took an important part in designing the Pavillon de la Bibliothèque. On returning to the United States in 1855 he was first employed on the additions to the U.S. Capitol in Washington, D.C.; settling then in New York City, he opened a studio in 1858. After a second extended visit to Europe in the 1860s Hunt began to win commissions for major works. He designed, among other structures, the Lenox Library and the Tribune Building in New York City, the Theological Library and Marquand Chapel at Princeton, the Divinity School and the Scroll and Key Building at Yale, the Yorktown (Virginia) Monument, the base of the Statue of Liberty and portions of the Metropolitan Museum of Art in New York City, and the National Observatory in Washington, D.C. His best-known achievements, however, and those in which his advocacy of the eclectic traditions of the Beaux-Arts school was most evident and effective, were the many mansions and country houses he built for the wealthy. Hunt numbered several Vanderbilts, Astors, and Belmonts among his clients and for them designed such famous residences as Marble House and The Breakers in Newport and, for George W. Vanderbilt, the fabulous Biltmore estate near Asheville, North Carolina. A gold medal from the Royal Institute of British Architects for his Administration Building for the World's Columbian Exposition in Chicago in 1893 was but one of a great many American and European honors and awards accorded him for his work as an architect and also for his dedication to high standards and to the professional training of students, many of whom he took into his own office. He had in 1857 joined in the founding in New York City of the American Institute of Architects, which now has chapters throughout the United States, and he remained thereafter one of its most influential members, serving as president in 1888–1891. Hunt died on July 31, 1895, in Newport, Rhode Island.

Hunt, Walter (1796–1859), inventor. Born on July 29, 1796, in Martinsburg, Lewis County, New York, Hunt early displayed a remarkable talent for mechanics. Before he was twenty he had invented a machine for spinning flax and, receiving a patent in 1826, he moved to New York City to open a plant to manufacture the device. The firm failed to prosper, however, and he turned to real estate as a means of subsistence while continuing to bend his fertile imagination to other tasks. In 1827 he invented an iron alarm gong for use on streetcars and in firehouses and police stations. Other inventions followed quickly: a restaurant steam table, a knife sharpener, the Globe stove, and in 1834 a sewing machine utilizing the all-important lock stitch. He failed to patent the sewing machine, however, selling it instead to a blacksmith who, after making a few improvements, also abandoned it. When Elias Howe applied for a patent on a machine of the same kind in 1846, Hunt sued; his priority in invention was acknowledged but his claim was disallowed because of his failure to apply for a patent. Hunt went on to devise an icebreaker boat, a nail-making machine, a self-closing inkwell later widely used in post offices, a "fountain pen" that was a commercial failure but that fixed forever the name of such an instrument, and the Antipodean Performers—suction shoes with which acrobats could walk on ceilings. One morning early in 1849, while worrying about a debt owed a draftsman, he toyed with a short piece of wire, bending it into various shapes until he suddenly invented the safety pin; he sold the idea for $400 to pay the debt. Hunt made numerous improvements on the breech-loading rifle and its cartridges that were later bought by Oliver F. Winchester; other ideas for the improvement of firearms were adopted by manufacturers of repeating pistols and the Springfield rifle. In 1854 he invented a disposable paper collar and took care to patent and secure a royalty agreement on it; unfortunately the paper collar became immensely popular only after his death. In 1858 Isaac M. Singer, seeking to clear up the extremely complicated patent status of the sewing machine, offered him $50,000 for his possible interest and claims. Before the first of the five annual payments fell due, Hunt died in New York City on June 8, 1859. In the decades after his death the paper collar, the fountain pen, and the Globe stove, on which he held patents, became as ubiquitous as the sewing machine and the safety pin.

Hunt, Ward (1810–1886), justice of the Supreme Court. Born in Utica, New York, on June 14, 1810, Hunt was educated at Hamilton College, Schenectady, and at Union College from which he graduated in 1828. He studied law at the Litchfield Law School in Connecticut and in a private office in Utica and was admitted to the bar in 1831. His practice was quickly successful and he became interested in Democratic politics, winning election to the state legislature in 1838 and becoming mayor of Utica in 1844. An opponent of the extension of slavery, he broke with the Democrats to support the Free-Soil party in 1848 and eight years later helped organize the Republican party in New York state. After two earlier defeats in elections for the state supreme court Hunt was elected as a Republican to the court of appeals in 1865. During 1868–1869 he served as chief judge of the court and in 1869 became commissioner of appeals. In December 1872 he was appointed by President Ulysses S. Grant to the Supreme Court. He served from January 1873 until overcome by invalidism six years later; he declined to offer his resignation, however, until a special act of Congress in 1882 granted him the full retirement pay that was normally predicated on ten years' service. Hunt died in Washington, D.C., on March 24, 1886.

Hunt, William Morris (1824–1879), painter. Born in Brattleboro, Vermont, on March 31, 1824, Hunt came of an artistic family that produced also Richard Morris Hunt, his younger brother. He attended Harvard for three years and then traveled to Europe, where he studied briefly in the academy of art in Düsseldorf before taking up painting under Thomas Couture in Paris. His strong native talent soon revealed itself and, under the influence of Jean François Millet, whose close friend he became, gained great vitality and maturity. Hunt absorbed deeply the work and thought of Millet and the other painters of the Barbizon School and returned to the United States in 1856 as both a practitioner and a proselytizer. In Newport, Rhode Island, in Brattleboro, in the Azores, and finally, from 1862, in Boston, he continued to refine his art acquiring a great reputation, a large and wealthy clientele, and a devoted following of students. He bowed to the pressures of success to the extent of allowing himself to become a highly fashionable portraitist, numbering among his sitters Massachusetts Chief Justice Lemuel Shaw, Mrs. Charles Francis Adams, William M. Evarts, James Freeman Clarke, and others, but he was nevertheless strongly influential in molding cultivated taste to value the works of Millet, Théodore Rousseau, Diaz de La Peña, Camille Corot, and himself; it was Hunt who, more than any other, turned the eyes of American artists and art lovers to France. Many of his paintings, along with a number by his Barbizon friends, were burned in the great Boston fire of 1872. In 1875 he was commissioned to execute two vast murals for the senate chamber of the New York state capitol in Albany; the allegorical "Discoverer" and "The Flight of Night" were later destroyed by the dampness of the stone panels on which they were painted. Hunt drowned while visiting the Isles of Shoals, off the New Hampshire coast, on September 8, 1879.

Hunter, Clingham, M. D., *see* Adams, William Taylor

Hunter, Robert Mercer Taliaferro (1809–1887), public official. Born in Essex County, Virginia, on April 21, 1809, Hunter graduated from the University of Virginia in 1828 and two years later was admitted to the bar. Elected to the legislature in 1834, he remained there as an independent for three years, but in 1837 he declared himself a Whig and won election to the House of Representatives, where he served three terms; during his second term, 1839–1841, he was speaker. During that same period he came under the influence of John C. Calhoun and his extreme doctrine of states' rights, with the result that he lost the support of Northern Whigs and the speakership in 1841 and also, on becoming formally a Democrat, failed to be reelected from his recently gerrymandered district in 1843. Hunter became one of the leading strategists in the campaign to win the presidency for Calhoun in 1844 and again in 1848. He returned to the House in 1845 and in 1847 was elevated to the Senate, where he remained, an effective and widely respected champion of states' rights, until 1861. He was prominently mentioned as a presidential possibility in 1860 and received much convention support until, after the party split irreconcilably, he led the Southern move to unity behind John Breckinridge. Although he did not openly counsel secession, he abandoned hope of compromise and left the Senate in March 1861 to urge it quietly in Virginia. In July he was appointed secretary of state for the newly formed Confederacy; he resigned early in 1862 to enter the Confederate senate, holding his seat until 1865. Toward the end of the war, more and more a critic of the government of Jefferson Davis, he gave thought to compromise and in February 1865 joined Alexander Stephens and John A. Campbell in an unsuccessful peace conference with President Abraham Lincoln at Hampton Roads, Virginia. After several months of imprisonment following the war, he returned to his ruined estate and was active in efforts to hasten the restoration of Virginia to the Union and to protect the state from the excesses of Reconstruction. From 1874 to 1880 he was treasurer of Virginia, and he served as collector of the port of Tappahannock from 1885 until his death near Lloyds, Virginia, on July 18, 1887.

Huntington, Collis Potter (1821–1900), railroad builder. Born on October 22, 1821, in Harwinton, Connecticut, Huntington left school and went to work at fourteen. From 1836 to 1842 he was an itinerant peddler, then he opened a store in Oneonta, New York. After seven successful years he joined the Gold Rush to California in 1849, taking a load of merchandise to Sacramento.

There he established a new store; he later took in Mark Hopkins as a partner and Huntington & Hopkins became a prosperous mercantile company. In 1860, with Hopkins, Leland Stanford, and Charles Crocker, he financed a survey seeking a possible railroad route eastward from Sacramento across the Sierra Nevada; he went to Washington, D.C., to assist in securing government grants to underwrite construction costs and remained in the East as agent for the company. The line, the Central Pacific Railroad of California, was completed in a remarkable feat of engineering and joined to the Union Pacific at Promontory Point, Utah, in May 1869. Work was begun on another transcontinental route leading south through California and across the southern tier of states, and in 1884 the new line and the Central Pacific were merged into the Southern Pacific Company, with Stanford as president and Huntington as vice-president and chief executive. He spent most of his time in the East, managing the company's finances and lobbying in Washington. On his own he invested in several other railroads, particularly the Chesapeake & Ohio, which he improved and extended, establishing its eastern terminus at Newport News, Virginia. He also had interests in a number of steamship companies. In 1890 he succeeded Stanford as president of the Southern Pacific system, which by then encompassed more than 9600 miles of track. He died near Raquette Lake, New York, on August 13, 1900.

Huntington, Ellsworth (1876–1947), geographer and explorer. Born in Galesburg, Illinois, on September 16, 1876, Huntington received his B.A. from Beloit College in 1897, his M.A. from Harvard in 1902, and his Ph.D. from Yale in 1909. He taught geography from 1897 to 1901 at Euphrates College in Harput, Turkey, and in 1907 at Yale, and was assistant professor of geography at Yale from 1910 until he was promoted to research associate in 1917, with the rank of professor. His researches dealt primarily with the effects of climate on land structure, population, and social organization. In 1901 he explored the canyons of the Euphrates River, winning the Gill Memorial prize of the Royal Geographical Society. During 1903–1904 he participated in Raphael Pumpelly's expeditions in central Asia, remaining there and in Persia (Iran) until 1905, and from that year to 1906 he was with an expedition in India, China, and Siberia. He published *Explorations in Turkestan*, 1905, and *The Pulse of Asia*, 1907. In 1909 he led an eight-month Yale expedition to Palestine, the Syrian desert, and Asia Minor, and was special correspondent on the mission for *Harper's*. *Palestine and Its Transformation* appeared in 1911. During 1910–1913 he conducted investigations of climate in Mexico, Central America, and the United States as a research associate of the Carnegie Institution of Washington. He published in 1914 *The Climatic Factor*, in 1915 *Civilization and Climate*, and in 1922, with S. S. Visher, *Climatic Changes*. During 1918–1919 he was a captain in U.S. military intel-

ligence. His *World Power and Evolution* appeared in 1919. Others of his many publications included *Earth and Sun*, 1923; *The Character of Races*, 1924; *The Pulse of Progress*, 1926; and *Tomorrow's Children—The Goal of Eugenics*, 1935. *Mainsprings of Civilization*, 1945, was the fruition of all his research. The recipient of numerous awards, he retired from Yale in 1945 and died in New Haven, Connecticut, on October 17, 1947.

Huntington, Henry Edwards (1850–1927), railroad builder, art collector, and philanthropist. Born in Oneonta, New York, on February 27, 1850, Huntington was a nephew of Collis P. Huntington. After working in hardware stores in his home town and in New York City he became in 1871 superintendent of a sawmill in St. Albans, West Virginia, owned by his uncle. Ten years later he assumed charge of construction of a section of railroad line that was later incorporated into the Chesapeake, Ohio & Southwestern Railroad. From 1884 to 1890 he was associated with the Kentucky Central, first as construction superintendent, later as receiver, and finally as vice-president and general manager. His connection with these and other lines in which his uncle held an interest led to his appointment as assistant to the president of the Southern Pacific Railroad in 1892. While advancing to the post of first vice-president he began investing heavily in San Francisco street railways, building up a large and efficient system that he sold in 1898. Transferring his operations to Los Angeles, he bought, built, and consolidated a major urban transit system that served as a starting point for the construction of an interurban eleric railway network throughout Southern California. On the death of Collis P. Huntington in 1900, Huntington sold the controlling interest in the Southern Pacific to E. H. Harriman; in 1910 he sold his transit holdings to the Southern Pacific and turned his attention to real estate, of which he was already one of the state's largest owners, and to the development of electric power. At his estate in San Marino he built a mansion and stocked it with an art collection and a library that was a rich repository of rare early English editions and Americana. When he died in Philadelphia on May 23, 1927, Huntington left the art collection and library, together valued at $30 million, along with the mansion and an $8-million endowment, to the public as the Henry E. Huntington Library and Art Gallery, which remained thereafter a major center of scholarly research.

Hurok, Solomon (1888–1974), impresario. Born on April 9, 1888, in Pogar, Russia, Sol Hurok emigrated to the United States in 1906 and for a year lived in Philadelphia, where he worked at various jobs. Moving to New York City, he continued to support himself in a variety of ways while following his interest in music into the work of arranging musical programs for local labor organizations and clubs. He quickly demonstated considerable administrative ability, a cultivated taste, financial acumen, and a flair for dealing with artistic temperaments. He became a U.S. citizen in 1914. By 1915 he was presenting weekly popular concerts at the New York Hippodrome, featuring such luminaries of the music and dance worlds as Mischa Elman, Alma Gluck, and Anna Pavlova. Success bred more success, and Hurok broadened his field to present major productions throughout the country, taking under his management the foremost soloists and ensembles in the world; among those who first appeared in the United States under his aegis were the Habima Players, the Russian Grand Opera with Feodor Chaliapin, and the Comédie Française; he also presented Isadora Duncan, Richard Strauss, the Moscow Art Players, Artur Schnabel, Marian Anderson, Jan Peerce, the Ballet Russe de Monte Carlo, Emlyn Williams, the Sadler's Wells Ballet with Margot Fonteyn, the Azuma Kabuki Dancers, Arthur Rubinstein, Isaac Stern, Alicia Markova, the Royal Ballet, the Moiseyev Folk Ballet, and the Bolshoi Ballet. Renowned for the unfailing taste and quality of his presentations, Hurok was also noted for his remarkable diplomatic talents, revealed particularly in his negotiations with the Soviet Union on cultural exchanges. From 1955 he served as a consultant to the National Broadcasting Corporation (NBC), for which he arranged many musical and ballet productions for television. In his influence on the development of a knowledge and appreciation of music and dance in the United States, he was often compared to the phonograph. His autobiographical *Impresario* was published in 1946, and more memoirs appeared in 1953 as *S. Hurok Presents*. He died in New York City on March 5, 1974.

Hussey, Obed (1792–1860), inventor. Born in Maine sometime in 1792, Hussey grew up on the island of Nantucket, Massachusetts. Little is known of his early life; he may have been a sailor for a time. By 1830 he had already invented a number of industrial and agricultural machines and was at work on another in Cincinnati when it was suggested to him that he devise a machine for harvesting grain. He devoted some two years to the project while living mainly in Baltimore, and in July 1833 he successfully demonstrated his reaper near Carthage, Ohio. Patented in December of that year, Hussey's reaper was horse drawn and featured a sawtoothed cutting bar driven reciprocally by a crankshaft geared to the main wheels; the cut stalks fell onto a platform from which they were raked by hand for binding. He began manufacturing reapers in 1834 and sold many in New York, Pennsylvania, Maryland, and Illinois. With the patenting of a rival reaper by Cyrus H. McCormick in 1834 a stiff competition developed and in 1838 Hussey opened a large factory in Baltimore. Both Hussey and McCormick exhibited their machines successfully at the Crystal Palace Exhibition in 1851 in London; however, Hussey gradually lost ground to his rival as he stubbornly refused to adopt improvements or modifications developed by others, (although he did add his own open top and slotted finger bar

in 1847), while McCormick was quick to make improvements. Hussey sold the business in 1858 and turned his attention to a steam plow; he was still at work on that invention when, on August 4, 1860, he fell under a train in New England and was killed.

Huston, John (1906–   ), motion-picture director. Born on August 5, 1906, in Nevada, Missouri, Huston was the son of actor Walter Huston, and he grew up in a succession of towns as his father traveled as an engineer and later as a vaudevillian. He left high school in Los Angeles without graduating and after a period as a professional boxer moved to New York City and dabbled in the theater. Over the next several years he served with the Mexican cavalry, worked as a reporter, published a number of short stories, was employed briefly as a screenwriter in Hollywood, and studied art in Paris. He settled in Hollywood in 1938 and became a writer for Warner Brothers, producing scripts for such movies as *Jezebel*, 1938; *The Amazing Dr. Clitterhouse*, 1938; *Juarez*, 1939; *High Sierra*, 1941; and *Sergeant York*, 1941, and in 1941 made his debut as a director with the highly successful *Maltese Falcon*. A few less well-received films followed before Huston entered the army in 1942. For three years he made widely admired documentary records of World War II, including *The Battle of San Pietro*, 1944, and after his discharge a year later and an engagement in New York City directing a Broadway production of Jean-Paul Sartre's *No Exit* in 1946 he returned to Hollywood. *Three Strangers*, 1947, based on one of his own stories, was followed by *The Treasure of the Sierra Madre*, 1948, for which he wrote the screenplay and which won him an Academy Award and a New York Film Critics' Circle Award for direction. Subsequent movies for which he wrote the screenplay as well as directed included *Key Largo*, 1948; *The Asphalt Jungle*, 1950; *The Red Badge of Courage*, 1951; *Beat the Devil*, 1954; *Moby Dick*, 1956 for which he won another New York Film Critics' Circle Award; and *The Night of the Iguana*, 1964. He directed a number of other films, including *The African Queen*, 1951; *The Misfits*, 1961; *Freud*, 1962; *The Bible*, 1966, in which he also appeared as Noah; *Casino Royale*, 1967; *Reflections in a Golden Eye*, 1967; *Fat City*, 1972; *The Man Who Would Be King*, 1975; *Wise Blood*, 1979; and *Annie*, 1982. Huston was admired in particular for the economy and taut strength of his direction and his ability to draw from his actors outstanding and often unexpected performances.

Huston, Walter (1884–1950), actor. Born on April 6, 1884, in Toronto, Huston (originally Houghston) studied both dramatics and engineering in school. At eighteen he made his stage debut in Toronto and for three years thereafter traveled with a road company and in vaudeville and won a few small roles in New York City. In 1905 he gave up the stage and for four years was employed as an engineer in various utilities plants in Montana, Texas, and Missouri. He returned to vaudeville in 1909 and for the next 15 years was half of a successful song-and-dance team. Huston's career as an actor finally began in earnest in 1924, when he made his real New York City debut in *Mr. Pitt*, winning general critical acclaim. Performances in *Desire Under the Elms*, 1924; *The Fountain*, 1925; *Elmer the Great*, 1928; and *The Commodore Marries*, 1929, established him as an actor of great sensibility and versatility. He then turned to motion pictures for a time, beginning with *Gentlemen of the Press*, 1929, and *Abraham Lincoln*, 1930; in 1934 he returned to Broadway in *Dodsworth* in which he was warmly received; his performance in the film version of *Dodsworth* two years later won him the New York Film Critics' Circle Award. He was a great hit in the Broadway production of *Knickerbocker Holiday*, 1938. He continued to appear in motion pictures, including *All That Money Can Buy*, a 1941 film version of Stephen Vincent Benet's story "The Devil and Daniel Webster" in which Huston gave one of his best performances as Mr. Scratch (the Devil); *Yankee Doodle Dandy*, 1942; and most of the early films directed by his son John; in these he often took tiny roles (he was on screen just long enough to die in *The Maltese Falcon*), but in *The Treasure of the Sierra Madre*, 1948, he played with Humphrey Bogart and won an Academy Award for best supporting actor. Huston died on April 7, 1950, in Beverly Hills, California.

Hutchins, Robert Maynard (1899–1977), educator. Born in Brooklyn, New York, on January 17, 1899, Hutchins was the son of a Presbyterian minister who became president of Berea College in Kentucky. After two years of study at Oberlin College, he served in the ambulance services of both the U.S. and the Italian armies during World War I, then entered Yale, from which he graduated in 1921. He received his LL.B. from the Yale Law School in 1925 and immediately began to teach there; he was named dean in 1927. In 1929, at the age of thirty, he was elected president of the University of Chicago, where he remained until 1951, for the last six years as chancellor. At Chicago he was an effective administrator who made a number of highly controversial innovations, some of which brought savage attacks on him. Among them were the abolition of big-time football, the introduction of a "Great Books" program, the reorganization of the graduate school, and the institution of the so-called Chicago Plan —a four-year liberal-arts program starting after the sophomore year in high school. Early educational specialization was discouraged, and students were required to take courses in mathematics and in the physical, biological, and social sciences and in the humanities. At the same time he wrote a number of books that argued eloquently for his ideas, among them *The Higher Learning in America*, 1936. He left Chicago in 1951 to become associate director of the Ford Foundation and in 1954 president of its Fund for the Republic, which soon split off from the parent organization; the Fund then founded the Center for the Study of Democratic Institutions, first in Pasadena and then in Santa Barbara, California, of which Hutchins became president and in 1969 chairman of the board. He continued also as president of the Fund. The Center, by means of publications and convocations of scholars and politicians, was principally "directed at discovering," as he said, "whether and how a free and just society may be maintained under the strikingly new . . . conditions of the second half of the 20th century." His later books, in which, among other things, he defended nonconformity and protest, included *The Conflict in Education*, 1953; *University of Utopia*, 1953; *Some Observations on American Education*, 1956; *Education for Freedom*, 1963; and *Education: The Learning Society*, 1968. Chairman of the board of editors of *Encyclopaedia Britannica* from 1943, he was editor in chief of *Great Books of the Western World*, 1952. He died in Santa Barbara, California, on May 14, 1977.

Hutchins, Thomas (1730–1789), surveyor and geographer. Born in 1730 in Monmouth County, New Jersey, Hutchins was orphaned in his youth. He grew up in the frontier region of Pennsylvania, serving in the colonial militia during the French and Indian Wars and then entering the regular British army. An accomplished surveyor and military engineer, he planned posts and fortifications at Fort Pitt, at present-day Pittsburgh, and at Pensacola, Florida, and he published several topographical and historical works on the Middle Atlantic and Gulf regions. He was in London when the Revolution began and, on declining to serve against his countrymen, was briefly imprisoned in 1779. Released the following year, he resigned his captain's commission and made his way back to America by way of France, where he secured a recommendation from Benjamin Franklin. Soon after landing in Charleston, South Carolina, he joined the staff of Gen. Nathanael Greene; in May 1781 he was named by Congress geographer of the army in the South and in July became geographer of the United States. He retained the title after the end of the war, and he was employed also by various states for official surveying work, including running the western portion of the Pennsylvania–Virginia boundary in 1783. With the passage of the Ordinance of 1785 Hutchins became responsible for beginning the immense task of surveying and platting the public lands of what soon became known as the Northwest Territory. Beginning at the intersection of the Ohio River with the Pennsylvania border, he ran the Geographer's Line due west along 40°38'2" N latitude in six-mile lengths; for the first four of those lengths and a part of the fifth he completed laying out the six-mile-square townships south of the line that, with the two lengths later surveyed by his successors, formed the Seven Ranges, the basis for the land survey of nearly all the country lying to the west of the original 13 states. He made three expeditions west—in 1785, 1786–

1787 and 1788–1789—in the course of the work, pausing in 1787 to run the New York–Massachusetts boundary. On the third trip to the scene of the survey he fell ill and died in Pittsburgh on April 28, 1789.

Hutchinson, Anne (1591–1643), religious leader. Born in Lincolnshire, England, in 1591, Anne Marbury was the daughter of a clergyman and grew up in an atmosphere of learning. In 1612 she married William Hutchinson. She became a follower of John Cotton and in 1634, a year after Cotton had gone to Massachusetts Bay, she sailed for Boston with her husband and family. Her kindliness and intellect soon won her a position of influence in the community and when she organized regular religious meetings in her home she attracted large numbers of people, including many ministers. At first concerned only with discussion of recent sermons she gradually began to use the meetings to expound her own theological views; in opposition to the orthodox "covenant of works" she set forth a "covenant of grace," holding that faith alone was necessary or sufficient for salvation. Her teachings were viewed by conservatives as a veiled attack on the theocratic polity of the Puritan settlements and factions quickly formed in what came to be known as the Antinomian Controversy. Principal among her supporters were her brother-in-law, the Reverend John Wheelwright, John Cotton, and the governor, Sir Henry Vane; ranged against them were the deputy governor, John Winthrop, and the Reverend John Wilson. In 1637 Winthrop won the governorship from Vane, who returned to England, and a synod of churches was called at which Mrs. Hutchinson and her adherents were denounced. Cotton recanted and became one of her severest critics; Wheelwright was banished. After being convicted by the General Court of "traducing the ministers," Mrs. Hutchinson was also banished from Massachusetts Bay and a short time later was formally excommunicated. Early in 1638 she moved with her family and others to the island of Aquidneck, now called Rhode Island. Following the death of her husband in 1642 she resettled at Pelham Bay, Long Island, where in August 1643 she was killed by Indians in what was considered by many to be an act of divine judgment.

Hutchinson, Thomas (1711–1780), colonial official. Born in Boston on September 9, 1711, Hutchinson came of a wealthy family and on graduating from Harvard in 1727 entered his father's mercantile house, soon amassing a fortune of his own. In 1737 he was chosen to serve on the board of selectmen of Boston and later in the year was elected to the General Court of Massachusetts Bay, where he remained, except for the year 1739, until 1749; as a member of that body he represented Massachusetts in England in 1740 in a boundary dispute with New Hampshire, and he served as speaker in 1746–1749. In 1749, an established public figure and a leading advocate of

sound, conservative fiscal practices, he was made a member of the Massachusetts council, on which he continued to sit until 1766. He was a representative at the Albany Congress in 1754 and there supported Benjamin Franklin's Plan of Union for the American colonies. In 1758 he became lieutenant governor and two years later was given the additional duties of chief justice of the superior court; these offices, together with his position as a council member and, from 1752, judge of probate for Suffolk County, resulted in the spread of the not entirely just opinion that he was interested principally in his own advancement. Conscientious on the bench, he upheld the legality of such unpopular measures as the Stamp Act of 1765 while privately viewing them as unjust and ill conceived. Hostility to him increased rapidly and in August 1765 his Boston home was sacked by a mob. He continued to serve as chief justice until 1769, when he became acting governor, and he was in that position during the Boston Massacre of 1770, after which he removed British troops from the city. In 1771 he was commissioned governor and by that time, in reaction to constant agitation by Samuel Adams and others of the patriot party, he had hardened his position on the authority of Parliament to the point where he encouraged the passage of laws designed to emphasize that authority. The publication in 1773 of the "Hutchinson letters," in which he had earlier expressed such sentiments to friends in England and which had come into the hands of Benjamin Franklin and then been sent to Whig leaders in Boston, aroused a storm of controversy. Later in the year he demonstrated his complete failure to understand the depth of public resentment over the tax issue and the influence of such popular leaders as Adams by adamantly insisting on the unloading of tea cargoes from Dutch East India Company ships; the result was the Boston Tea Party, in which a mob boarded the ships and dumped the tax-bearing tea into the harbor. In 1774 Gen. Thomas Gage was appointed governor of Massachusetts and Hutchinson sailed to England to serve as an adviser to George III and his ministry on American affairs and to complete his valuable *History of the Colony and Province of Massachusetts Bay*, three volumes, 1764–1828. He lived comfortably but unhappily in England thereafter, fully expecting to return to his native America when the popular unrest had at last been quelled by the loyal element. He died in Brompton, later part of London, on June 3, 1780.

Hyatt, Alpheus (1838–1902), zoologist and paleontologist. Born in Washington, D.C., on April 5, 1838, Hyatt entered Yale in 1856 but after a year there and another in Rome transferred to the Lawrence Scientific School at Harvard, from which he graduated in 1862. For three years he served with a Massachusetts regiment in the Civil War and then returned to Cambridge, Massachusetts, to continue the studies in natural history that he had begun under the influence of Louis

Agassiz. He was placed in charge of the fossil cephalopod section of Harvard's Museum of Comparative Zoology, a responsibility he retained for the rest of his life. In 1867 he was appointed curator of the Essex Institute in Salem and in the same year joined in founding there the Peabody Academy of Sciences and the *American Naturalist*, of which he was an editor for four years. He moved to Boston in 1870, becoming custodian of the Boston Society of Natural History, under the auspices of which he conducted the Teachers School of Science for the rest of his life, and also professor of zoology and paleontology at the Massachusetts Institute of Technology (MIT), a post he held until 1888; from 1877 until his death he held a similar post at Boston University, and from 1881 he was curator and ex-officio scientific director of the Boston Society of Natural History. In addition Hyatt was named paleontologist to the U.S. Geological Survey in 1889. He played a major role in the establishment of the marine biological laboratory now located at Woods Hole, Massachusetts, and served as its first president. Hyatt's own researches concentrated on the paleontology of various invertebrate groups and with his numerous publications he became recognized as the foremost worker in the field of invertebrate paleontology in the country. Among his major scientific works were *Observations on Fresh Water Polyzoa*, 1866; *Fossil Cephalopods of the Museum of Comparative Anatomy*, 1867; *Revision of North American Porifera*, 1875–1877; "The Genesis of the Tertiary Species of Planobis at Steinheim," in *Memoirs* of the Boston Society of Natural History, 1880; *Genera of Fossil Cephalopoda*, 1883; *Larval Theory of the Origin of Cellular Tissue*, 1884; *Genesis of the Arietidae*, 1889; *and Phylogeny of an Acquired Characteristic*, 1894. Hyatt died in Cambridge, Massachusetts, on January 15, 1902.

I

Iberville, Pierre Le Moyne, Sieur d' (1661–1706), naval officer and colonizer. Born in Ville-Marie de Montréal (now Montreal) on July 16, 1661, Pierre Le Moyne came of a prominent French-Canadian family that produced a number of military and political leaders. At fourteen he was appointed a midshipman in the French navy, and after several years in France and at sea he returned to Canada to join in the effort to expel the British from the region. In 1686 he performed brilliantly in a long, arduous, and successful expedition from Montreal against the Hudson Bay Company's trading outposts on Hudson Bay. Over the next several years he undertook a number of other expeditions against the British into the northern country and elsewhere, in 1690 capturing and destroying the town of Schenectady, in 1696 capturing Fort Pemaquid, Maine, and St. John's, Newfoundland, and mounting a serious threat to the city of New York, and in 1697, with one small vessel, sinking or capturing, three British warships and capturing Fort Nelson, on Hudson Bay. With the end of Anglo-French hostilities following the Treaty of Rijswijk in 1697 he looked to other exploits. Called to France, he was commissioned to establish a colony at the mouth of the Mississippi River. He set sail from Brest late in 1698 with his brother, the Sieur de Bienville, and 200 colonists aboard four ships and reached Mobile Bay in January 1699. Leaving the colonists there, he sought the Mississippi River and explored it, possibly traveling as far upstream as the confluence of the Red River, discovering along the way the great lake near present-day New Orleans that he named for his patron, the Comte de Pontchartrain, France's minister of marine. Finding no suitable place for a settlement, he returned to Mobile Bay and thence transported the colonists westward to a spot near the site of present-day Biloxi, Mississippi, where he built Fort Maurepas, the first permanent colony in the Louisiana Territory. Returning with supplies in 1700, he also built a fort near the present site of New Orleans and made further explorations; on a second return, in 1701, finding the settlement at Fort Maurepas decimated by disease, he transferred the survivors back to a site on the Mobile River. The outbreak of war between France and England prevented him from returning with more colonists. Made commander of the French fleet in the West Indies, Iberville spent his last years in naval service. He died in Havana, Cuba, on July 9, 1706, while preparing for an expedition against British posts in the Carolinas.

Ickes, Harold LeClair (1874–1952), public official. Born in Blair County, Pennsylvania, on March 15, 1874, Ickes moved during his youth to Chicago and graduated from the University of Chicago in 1897. While working as a reporter for various Chicago newspapers he studied law at the university, taking his degree and winning admission to the bar in 1907. His practice, which included a large number of civil-liberties cases, gradually dwindled as he became increasingly active in municipal and national reform and political movements. Although nominally a Republican, he often broke with the party to support progressive candidates and organizations, enlisting in Theodore Roosevelt's Bull Moose Progressive party in 1912 and later working with Robert M. La Follette and the Progressive party. During World War I he took part in administering the relief and recreational activities of the Young Men's Christian Association (YMCA) among U.S. soldiers in France. In 1924 he directed the Illinois operations of Hiram W. Johnson's presidential campaign. Despite his wide-ranging activities Ickes remained little known to the general public until 1933, when, in an effort to broaden support for his administration by the addition of a Republican to his cabinet, President Franklin D. Roosevelt named Ickes, who had supported his candidacy vigorously, to the post of secretary of the interior. Ickes quickly emerged as a dedicated protector of natural resources, much in the conservationist tradition of Theodore Roosevelt and Gifford Pinchot. With the passage of the National Industrial Recovery Act in June 1933 Ickes became administrator of the petroleum industry, a post in which he continued through World War II, and head of the Public Works Administration (PWA). Through the PWA he controlled the spending of more than $5 billion for federal and nonfederal public works ranging from great hydroelectric and flood-control dams in the West to small-town post offices; while he kept PWA's enterprises free, so far as was possible, of politics and graft, earning the nickname "Honest Harold" in so doing, his care resulted in delays that sometimes defeated much of the pump-priming intent of the agency. A colorful and peppery figure, Ickes engaged in numerous controversies and feuds, not only with Republicans on the campaign trail but also with Democrats. In a dispute with President Harry S. Truman he resigned from the cabinet in February 1946; thereafter he lived in retirement on his Maryland farm, contributing articles to periodicals and, until 1949, writing a syndicated newspaper column, "Man to Man." Notable among his books were *The New Democracy*, 1934; *Back to Work*, 1935; *Autobiography of a Curmudgeon*, 1943; *My Twelve Years with F. D. R.*, 1948; and *The Secret*

Diary of Harold L. Ickes, three volumes, published posthumously in 1953–1954. Ickes died in Washington, D.C., on February 3, 1952.

Ingersoll, Robert Green (1833–1899), lawyer and orator. Born in Dresden, New York, on August 11, 1833, Ingersoll was the son of a stern Congregational minister. He received little formal education as the family moved to Ohio, to Wisconsin, and finally to Illinois; his efforts at self-education, however, enabled him to be admitted to the Illinois bar in 1854. Three years later he established himself in Peoria and soon became locally prominent. During the Civil War he commanded a volunteer cavalry regiment; in late 1862 he was captured by Confederate forces and by June 1863 had been paroled and discharged from the army. He had been in 1860 an unsuccessful Democratic candidate for the House of Representatives; in 1867, having converted to Republicanism, he was elected attorney general of Illinois, serving for two years, and this was to be his only public office in more than 30 years of political activity. As the spread of Darwinism provoked wide and violent controversy, Ingersoll took to the lecture platform as a powerful advocate of scientific and humanistic rationalism and propounded the view called by T. H. Huxley "agnosticism." In a time when Darwinians and agnostics were generally shunned, Ingersoll was widely in demand as a speaker, his personality and integrity clearly giving the lie to the charges of immorality and manifest wickedness commonly lodged against men of his persuasion. Among his famous addresses, which were widely reprinted, were "The Gods," "Some Mistakes of Moses," "Why I Am an Agnostic," and "Superstition." He was an active campaigner for the Republican party as well; at the 1876 national convention he presented the name of James G. Blaine for the nomination, dubbing him "the Plumed Knight" in one of his oratorical flights. He moved to Washington, D.C., in 1879 and continued both his lecturing and his law practice. He was chief counsel for the defense in the trials resulting from the "star route" frauds of 1882. Three years later he moved to New York City and continued to work as a lawyer, lecturer, and political orator until his death there on July 21, 1899.

Ingersoll, Robert Hawley (1859–1928), businessman. Born in Delta, Eaton County, Michigan, on December 26, 1859, Ingersoll received little schooling and until he was twenty remained on the family farm. He then traveled east to seek his fortune, farming for a time in Connecticut and then moving to New York City. Within a year there he had accumulated sufficient capital to start a small business of his own, manufacturing and selling rubber stamps. Joined by a younger brother, he established the firm of Robert H. Ingersoll & Brother, soon added other items, and developed a large line of wholesale notions and novelties, including a toy typewriter, a patent pencil, a patent key ring, bicycles, and a cheap sewing machine. As sales strained the capacity of

their Brooklyn factory they added products from other manufacturers to the line, gradually building up a considerable mail-order business and eventually opening a chain of retail outlets. In search of a cheap and large-volume item on which to anchor the enterprise, Ingersoll bought a quantity of watches from the Waterbury Clock Company in 1892; selling quickly at a dollar each, the watches proved to be precisely the reliable item he was looking for and he contracted for a steady supply of watches, made to his specifications under the name "Universal." The name was soon changed to "Ingersoll" to combat competition and the watch quickly caught on with the public, selling more than 70 million by 1919 and truly earning the reputation of "the watch that made the dollar famous." Despite the success of the watch, however, the firm went into receivership in 1921 and the next year was sold to the Waterbury Clock Company. In 1924 Ingersoll reentered business with the New Era Manufacturing Company, which produced the Ingersoll Dollar Razor Strop; the new enterprise enjoyed only limited success and Ingersoll had been retired for some time when he died in Denver on September 4, 1928.

Ingraham, Joseph Holt (1809–1860), author and religious leader. Born in Portland, Maine, on January 25 or 26, 1809, Ingraham may have attended Bowdoin College, although official records do not confirm his later claim to have done so. At some point, however, he secured appointment as professor of languages at Jefferson College in Washington, Mississippi. The college figures in his early book, *The South-West, by a Yankee*, 1835, but the next year, with the publication of *The Pirate of the Gulf*, an elaborately fictionalized tale of Jean Laffite that remained in print for more than 60 years, he began a career as a vastly prolific author of sensational and gory adventure books. Often styling himself "Professor Ingraham" and employing a large variety of settings, an almost ludicrous romanticism, and a forthright blood-and-thunder sense of story he enjoyed immense success with such novels as *Burton, or the Sieges*, 1838; *The Quadroone, or St. Michael's Day*, 1841; *Jemmy Daly, or the Little News Vendor*, 1843; *Rafael, or the Twice Condemned*, 1845; *Scarlet Feather, or the Young Chief of the Abenaquies*, 1845; *Ringold Griffitt, or the Raftsman of the Susquehannah*, 1847; and *The Beautiful Cigar Girl, or the Mysteries of Broadway*, 1856. By 1846 he claimed to have written 80 novels; his total production, including novels serialized in periodicals, is impossible to determine. About 1849 he established a school for girls in Nashville, Tennessee. In 1851, by which time he had returned to Mississippi and undergone a thorough religious conversion, he became a deacon of the Episcopal church in Natchez and the following year was ordained a priest. His clerical duties slowed but did not stop his pen and he managed to produce three novels set in biblical times—*The Prince of the House of David*, 1855;

The Pillar of Fire, 1859; and *The Throne of David*, 1860—each of which equalled or exceeded the popularity of his earlier works. He used a portion of his royalties from the three to buy up and destroy copies of some of his youthful thrillers, which had proved an embarrassment in his new life. Ingraham served parishes in Aberdeen, Mississippi; Mobile, Alabama; Riverside, Tennessee; and, from 1859, in Holly Springs, Mississippi, where he died on December 18, 1860.

Ingraham, Prentiss (1843–1904), author. Born in Adams County, Mississippi, on December 22, 1843, Ingraham was the son of Joseph H. Ingraham. He attended Jefferson College, in Mississippi, and Mobile Medical College. He left school in 1861 to enlist in the Confederate army. He eventually became a commander of scouts in Texas and, apparently, acquired a taste for war and adventure. After the Civil War ended he traveled to Mexico to fight under Benito Juarez and later took part in the Austro-Prussian War and performed martial exploits in Crete, in Africa, and in the Cuban revolution beginning in 1868, in which he held the ranks of naval captain and cavalry colonel. In 1870 he settled in London and began mining his experiences and his vivid imagination for material for a veritable flood of sensational novels of romance and adventure. More prolific even than his father, he produced nearly 700 novels, most of them for Erastus F. Beadle's Dime Library and Half Dime Library. Living later in New York City and Chicago, he became a close friend of Buffalo Bill Cody, about whom he wrote more than 200 of his books. Among his titles were *The Beautiful Rivals, or Life at Long Branch*, 1884; *Buck Taylor, King of the Cowboys, or Raiders and Rangers*, 1887, about one of the stars of Buffalo Bill's Wild West Show; *Darkie Dan*, 1888; *Cadet Carey of West Point*, 1890; *Red Rovers on Blue Waters*, 1890; *An American Monte Cristo*, 1891; *The Wandering Jew of the Sea*, 1891; *Trailing with Buffalo Bill*, 1899; *Land of Legendary Lore*, 1899; and *The Girl Rough Riders*, 1903. These and others virtually poured from his pen, along with a number of successful plays and countless short stories and poems. "Colonel" Ingraham, as he often styled himself, died at the Beauvoir Confederate Home in Beauvoir, Mississippi, on August 16, 1904.

Inman, Henry (1801–1846), painter. Born on October 28, 1801, in Utica, New York, Inman received some elementary instruction in drawing in his boyhood but after the family moved to New York City in 1812 he made preparations to enter West Point. In 1814 he visited the studio of the celebrated painter John Wesley Jarvis. His intelligent comments on a painting Jarvis was exhibiting, together with proofs of his skill in drawing, led Jarvis to take him on as an apprentice for a period of seven years, during which he received an excellent training in art. He accompanied his master on his travels and soon was painting in the background and drapery of portraits. In 1822, his apprenticeship completed, he opened his own studio in New York City. His early years were successful and prosperous and many eminent sitters came to him, although he often decried the fact that only portraits sold, forcing him to paint landscapes and genre works only in his spare time. As early as 1826 he had helped to found the National Academy of Design, of which he served as vice-president from 1826 to 1830 and from 1838 to 1844. In 1832 he moved to Philadelphia, where he was associated in a lithography business; he is said to have introduced lithography to the United States in about 1828. About 1840, by which time he was back in New York City, affairs began to go badly for him. He had been drawn into speculations which led him to the verge of bankruptcy; he found it harder than before to attract wealthy subjects; and the asthma from which he had long suffered became more severe. At this juncture, three generous friends arranged to send him to England, where he painted portraits of the poet William Wordsworth, Thomas Babington Macaulay, and Dr. Thomas Chalmers. He was received with acclaim—Wordsworth said he was the first American of genius he had ever met—and was urged to stay on in London, but family problems and declining health forced him to return to New York in 1845. He embarked on an ambitious series of paintings for the U.S. Capitol in Washington, but while at work on the first of them he died, in New York City, on January 17, 1846. Among his American portraits were those of Chief Justice John Marshall, President Martin Van Buren, William H. Seward, De Witt Clinton, John James Audubon, Nathaniel Hawthorne, Peggy O'Neale Eaton, and Clara Barton. His genre paintings, however, such as "Picnic in the Catskills," "The Young Fisherman," "Rip Van Winkle's Awakening," and "An October Afternoon," have proved of more enduring interest.

Inness, George (1825–1894), painter. Born on May 1, 1825, on a farm near Newburgh, New York, Inness was frail as a child but possessed a strong temperament and was both obstinate and ambitious. In school at Newark, New Jersey, he frequently missed classes because of poor health; but he was generally indifferent to lessons even when attending. With the consent of his father, he left school to study art with a local teacher who soon taught him as much as he knew. He went on to New York City in the 1840s and worked for a firm of map engravers for a year. He painted country landscapes and studied art briefly, then set up a studio in 1845. His art was immensely serious to him, and the result was a period of strained, technical painting. Within a few years after 1847 he married twice, made several brief trips to Europe, and came under the influence of the Barbizon School, which emphasized spontaneity and suggestion in landscape painting, with the result that his work became more individual and less reminiscent of the Hudson River School, with which he had been identified. He moved to

Boston in 1859 and lived in Medfield, Massachusetts, in the 1860s; there he concentrated on tonal variations, intensities of light, and contrasts between the earth, air, and sky. During the 1870s, while living in New York City, his initial preoccupation with structure and technique gave way to mystical, extremely personal visions of landscapes that were characterized by glistening colors and vagueness of form. His conversion to Swedenborgianism about that time may have prompted the change; whatever its springs, his final period saw the creation of many of his finest and most compelling works, including "Evening at Medfield" and "Autumn Oaks." He argued hotly over social issues, espousing the single tax and abolitionism. During his last years he had several generous patrons, and although he was the most prosperous landscape painter of his time he remained indifferent to money. After 1878 Inness lived and worked in Montclair, New Jersey. Traveling in Scotland, he died at Bridge of Allan on August 3, 1894.

Insull, Samuel (1859–1938), utilities executive. Born in London on November 11, 1859, Insull studied bookkeeping as a youth and went to work as an assistant bookkeeper for one of Thomas A. Edison's representatives in England. Highly recommended, he came to the United States in 1881 to become Edison's private secretary, a post that led to his being made vice-president of the Edison General Electric Company when it was formed in Schenectady, New York, in 1889. The company was in process of establishing branch utility companies in major U.S. cities, and Insull was named president of the Chicago Edison Company in 1892. In 1896 he became a U.S. citizen. Within ten years after that date he had managed to garner all of Chicago's electricity-supply business for his company, which in the meantime, upon consolidation with Commonwealth Electric, of which he was also president, had been renamed the Commonwealth Edison Company. He advocated centralization of the industry and by 1917 was supplying most of Illinois and communities in neighboring states from the central Chicago electrical station. During the 1920s his electricity production and distribution systems showed phenomenal growth, based in part on the use of huge central stations and in part through the establishment of holding companies, the first of which Insull had founded in 1912 as Middle West Utilities. He also promoted the sale of utility-company stock to a great number of investors during the period. After the stock-market collapse that began in 1929 his pyramid of holding companies also collapsed, and in 1932 he fled to Europe to escape prosecution. Extradition proceedings were instituted and he was forced to return to Chicago in 1934; there he was tried three times, on charges of fraud, violation of federal bankruptcy laws, and embezzlement. Many felt that he was being treated as a scapegoat for the entire stock-market crash, but he had carried many investors down with him in his fall and he was the subject of intense contro-

versy for several years, although he won acquittal in each of his three trials. He died in Paris on July 16, 1938.

Iredell, James (1751–1799), justice of the Supreme Court. Born in Lewes, England, on October 5, 1751, Iredell secured at the age of seventeen appointment as comptroller of customs at Edenton, North Carolina, where he also served as agent for a family mercantile business. He was licensed to practice law in 1771. After serving as collector of the port from 1774 to 1776 he became active in the patriot cause and, following independence, in organizing the laws and government of North Carolina. For a time in 1777–1778 he was a judge of the state superior court and from 1779 to 1781 was state attorney general. While a member of the council of state in 1787 he was charged with codifying and revising the statutes of North Carolina; the resulting "Iredell's Revisal" was published in 1791. He was a staunch supporter of the Constitutional Convention in 1787 and the next year led his state's Federalists in the movement for ratification. In 1790 he was named by President George Washington to the Supreme Court; at thirty-eight he was the youngest among the original justices. His most notable opinions in nine years on the Court were those in *Chisholm* v. *Georgia* (dissenting), 1793, in which he argued strongly that, in his opinion, only a constitutional provision that did not exist could, if it did, supersede the common-law principle that a state is immune to suit by citizens of another state, an argument that lent the weight of legal opinion to the subsequent campaign for adoption of the Eleventh Amendment; *Ware* v. *Hylton* (dissenting), 1796, which he first confronted on his circuit and in which it was held that a provision for the free recovery of debts owed to British subjects written into the peace treaty of 1783 was paramount over a Virginia statute restricting that freedom; and *Calder* v. *Bull*, 1798, in which, five years before an actual test in *Marbury* v. *Madison*, he elucidated the principle of judicial review. Largely as a result of the strain of the long and arduous travels required to cover his circuit in the South, Iredell's health failed within a few years of his appointment and he died in Edenton, North Carolina, on October 20, 1799.

Ireland, John (1838–1918), religious leader. Born in County Kilkenny, Ireland, on September 11, 1838, Ireland was brought to America in 1849 by his parents, who settled in St. Paul, Minnesota Territory, in 1853. He was educated in the cathedral school and there came to the notice of Bishop Joseph Crétin, who sent him to France for theological studies. Returning to St. Paul for his ordination in the Roman Catholic priesthood in December 1861, he enlisted the following May as a chaplain in the Union army and was assigned to the 5th Minnesota Volunteers. He served with distinction until ill health forced his resignation from the service in April 1863; he was nationally prominent in the Grand Army of the Republic (GAR) in later years. He was named pastor of the St. Paul cathedral in 1867, in which post he was a leader of the fight, both in and out of the Roman Catholic Church, against political corruption and particularly against the evils of liquor and the liquor interests. These activities led to his being dubbed the "Father Mathew of the West" after the famed Irish temperance leader, Theobald Mathew. He represented Bishop Thomas L. Grace in Rome at Vatican Council I in 1870–1871 and there met many ecclesiastical authorities; he was consecrated bishop and made vicar apostolic of Nebraska five years later. Bishop Grace interceded with the Vatican, however, and arranged to have him appointed his bishop coadjutor, with right of succession, in December 1875. Grace resigned because of ill health in 1884 and Ireland became bishop of St. Paul on July 31 of that year. In the meantime he had devoted much of his energy to attempts to ameliorate the miserable condition of Catholic immigrants, mainly Irish, in the cities of the East. He acquired tracts of railroad land in 1879, for which he held himself responsible, and arranged for the sale of plots to Catholics. More than 4000 families thus took up settlement on more than 400,000 acres of land in western Minnesota under the auspices of his Catholic Colonization Bureau, and "Ireland's towns" became thriving rural centers. When St. Paul became an archdiocese he was made archbishop, on May 15, 1888. By that time he was one of the best-known and most highly respected Roman Catholic churchmen in the country, but he was also a center of controversy, owing to his outspoken views on such matters as race, education, labor, and the relations of church and state. He refused to accept a color line and always insisted that nothing less than complete equality for blacks was required—"equal rights and equal privileges, political, civil, and social." He founded several colleges and seminaries, including the St. Paul Seminary, was an important influence in the establishment of Catholic University in Washington, D.C., and was the father of the so-called Faribault Plan, whereby parochial schools were rented to the state during school hours and used for religious and moral instruction in the early morning and late afternoon. The plan, similar to modern "shared-time" programs, provoked criticism from many ecclesiastics and he had to go to Rome to defend it, which he did successfully. His views about the relation of church and state in a democracy were progressive and indeed ahead of his time, and he was charged with being too "American" by clerics both in Europe and in the United States. A Republican—still another mark against him in the eyes of many U.S. Catholics—he attempted, in negotiations with President William McKinley, to ward off the Spanish-American War; later, he was a trusted adviser of President Theodore Roosevelt. Held by Europeans to be the intellectual leader of U.S. Catholicism and the most important American Catholic after James Cardinal Gibbons, he was many times rumored to

be about to receive a cardinal's hat, but this never occurred. He devoted his last years to overseeing the construction of St. Paul Cathedral, for which he laid the cornerstone in 1907, and to the building of the Basilica of St. Mary's in Minneapolis. He died in St. Paul on September 25, 1918. He had outlived most of his enemies and was hailed in obituaries throughout the nation and the world as perhaps the greatest American churchman of his time.

Irving, Washington (1783–1859), author. Born in New York City on April 3, 1783, Irving grew up in an atmosphere of learning and refinement but cared little for school and not at all for college. In 1798, however, he undertook to fit himself for the law. His period of desultory study stretched over six years, during which he found entertainment in travel, in the gay life of cosmopolitan New York City, and in writing a series of lightly satirical "Letters of Jonathan Oldstyle, Gent." for his brother's *Morning Chronicle*. During 1804–1806 he toured Europe for his health and then returned to New York and was admitted to the bar. He found writing more to his liking, however, and in 1807–1808, with several associates including his brother and James Kirke Paulding, he published a series of papers entitled *Salmagundi: Or, the Whim-Whams and Opinions of Launcelot Langstaff, Esq. and Others*. These, like his earlier letters, were largely genteel satires on fashionable society. In 1809 he published *A History of New York*, by "Diedrich Knickerbocker," which had grown from a parody of a pretentious guidebook into a richly comic history of Dutch New York. During the next six years he wrote little; he published an American edition of Thomas Campbell's poetry and edited the *Analectic Magazine* in 1813–1814, but was mainly occupied with lobbying efforts on behalf of his family's importing firm and with a position on the governor's military staff during the War of 1812. In 1815 he sailed to England on behalf of the family business, but meetings with Sir Walter Scott and other literary figures, together with the failure of the family firm, turned him back to writing. A number of occasional essays, tales, and travel pieces were collected in 1819–1820 as *The Sketch Book of Geoffrey Crayon, Gent.*, published in London and an immediate success there and in the United States. Among the contents were "Rip Van Winkle," "The Legend of Sleepy Hollow," and "The Spectre Bridegroom," which have been called the first modern short stories. The voluminous travel notes that Irving had accumulated enabled him to issue a sequel, *Bracebridge Hall*, 1822, that, while not of the quality of *The Sketch Book*, was equally popular and firmly established him as the nation's leading man of letters. He remained in Europe, traveling on the Continent and gathering notes; *Tales of a Traveller*, 1824, the result of a visit to Germany, was a weak effort and was poorly received. Early in 1826, at the invitation of Alexander H. Everett of the U.S. legation in Madrid, he journeyed to Spain to produce a translation of a recent scholarly biography of Christopher Columbus. He quickly decided to write an original work instead and in 1828 appeared *History of the Life and Voyages of Christopher Columbus*, which was followed three years later by *The Companions of Columbus*. His sojourn in Spain awakened a deep interest in Spanish history and folklore and resulted in *A Chronicle of the Conquest of Granada*, 1829, and, in *Sketch Book* style, *The Alhambra*, 1832. From 1829 to 1832 he was secretary of the U.S. legation in London. In 1832 he returned at last to the United States, where he was received as a hero, and settled at Sunnyside, his house on the Hudson near Tarrytown. A trip to the West inspired him to write *A Tour on the Prairies*, 1835, *Astoria*, 1836, and *The Adventures of Captain Bonneville U.S.A.*, 1837. From 1842 to 1846 he served as U.S. minister to Spain, afterward returning to Sunnyside permanently. Like his books on the West, his later works were competent but not memorable; they were principally biographical and included *Oliver Goldsmith*, 1849; *Mahomet and his Successors*, 1849–1850; and a five-volume *George Washington*, 1855–1859. He died at Sunnyside on November 28, 1859. The size of Irving's literary output, as well as its position in the early history of the republic, led many critics to rank him as the first American man of letters or as one of the foremost American authors; the unevenness of his work, however, has gradually produced a more temperate evaluation of him as a writer of some innovativeness, occasional brilliance, and considerable historical significance. He was elected to the Hall of Fame in 1900.

Iskowitz, Edward Israel, *see* Cantor, Eddie

Ives, Charles Edward (1874–1954), composer. Born in Danbury, Connecticut, on October 20, 1874, Ives was the son of a military bandmaster who encouraged his early interest in music and gave him his first instruction. He later studied music at Yale, but composition was to be an avocation; upon graduation from Yale in 1898 he entered the insurance business, in which he remained until 1930. By far the greatest portion of his major work was done in the eighteen years after leaving Yale, although his music was little known for many years thereafter. He received the Pulitzer Prize in 1947 for his *Third Symphony*, composed 36 years earlier. The *Second Symphony* was first performed in 1952, the *Fourth* in 1965. Exceedingly complex, his work combines polytonal and polyrhythmic structures with vernacular elements, such as popular melodies, march music, and hymns, drawn primarily from his native New England. Concerned with the evocation of whole scenes of life, the music is often dissonant and occasionally seems disjointed or amorphous. As the titles of some of his works imply—"Harvest Festival," 1898; "Thanksgiving," 1904; "Washing-

ton's Birthday," 1909; "Decoration Day," 1912; "The Indians," 1912; "Lincoln, the Great Commoner," 1912; "Fourth of July," 1913; "Three Places in New England," 1903–1914; and "Concord, Mass., 1840–60" for example—his music was by intent distinctly and distinctively American. He also wrote piano and violin sonatas, chamber music, and numbers of songs, many to his own texts. Ives died in New York City on May 19, 1954.

Ives, Frederic Eugene (1856–1937), inventor. Born on February 17, 1856, near Litchfield, Connecticut, Ives grew up on a farm there and later in Norfolk. After a three-year apprenticeship in the office of the *Litchfield Enquirer* he took a job in 1873 in an Ithaca, New York, printing shop, but within a short time he left to devote himself to a long-standing hobby by opening a photographic studio. His skill in photography soon developed to such a degree that in 1875 he was placed in charge of the Cornell University photographic laboratory, where he had a free hand in conducting experiments along various lines. His first major accomplishment there was the perfection of a "swelled gelatin" process for making line photoengravings; it was used with great success by the college newspaper. More years of work led finally in 1878 to the development of a process whereby continuous-tone subjects, such as photographs, could be translated into a dot pattern in which the sizes of the dots varied with the tone; the pattern could then be used to make a printing plate that would reproduce with considerable accuracy the tonal range of the original. Ives moved to Philadelphia in 1879 to work with a printing-plate manufacturer and by 1881 was making commercial printing plates by his mechanical "halftone" process. Further experiments resulted in 1885 in an improved, optical method of creating the dot pattern by means of a screen consisting of two plates, each covered with finely ruled lines, sandwiched at right angles to each other to make a crossline screen. The subject, when photographed through the screen, was optically translated into the required dot pattern. The halftone process as devised by Ives remained essentially unchanged thereafter. In 1885 he also introduced a color-printing process utilizing three halftone color-separating screens. Among his later inventions were the photochromoscope, a color-photography process employing three negatives; the halftone photogravure printing process; the modern short-tube single-objective binocular microscope; the parallax stereogram; and a colorimeter and tint photometer. He also made numerous contributions to the development of color cinematography. His *Autobiography of an Amateur Inventor* appeared in 1928. He died in Philadelphia on May 27, 1937.

Ives, James Merritt, *see under* Currier, Nathaniel

J

Jackson, Andrew (1767–1845), seventh president of the United States. Born on March 15, 1767 to Irish immigrant parents in the Waxhaw settlement on the Carolina frontier—probably in what is now South Carolina—Jackson received little formal schooling. The back-country warfare during the Revolution, in which he took part, left him without a family at fourteen. In 1784 he began the study of law in Salisbury, North Carolina, was admitted to the bar in 1787, and the next year traveled across the Appalachians to the region that was to become Tennessee. He soon gained appointment as prosecuting attorney for the district, then part of North Carolina, and, with the collection of debts as his principal duty in that unsettled area, he became allied with the comparatively wealthy class. In 1791 he married Mrs. Rachel Robards, whose first, unhappy marriage they both mistakenly believed had been dissolved. A divorce on grounds of desertion and adultery was won by her first husband in 1793, whereupon she and Jackson were quietly remarried; the episode was a source of gossip and innuendo throughout Jackson's career. He engaged in land speculation, trade, and planting, and in 1795 established his home at The Hermitage, a plantation near Nashville. The following year he helped draft the constitution of the new state of Tennessee and was immediately elected to its one seat in the House of Representatives. In 1797 he was elected to the Senate but was forced by financial reverses at home to resign a year later; he was soon appointed to the state supreme court and served there until 1804, when he resigned, again for financial reasons. In 1802 he had been elected major general of the state militia and from 1804 to 1812 this post was his only connection with public life; in 1812, with the outbreak of war with England, it ceased to be a largely honorary position. The next year he set out in command of a militia force to subdue the Creek Indians, allies of the British, who had perpetrated a massacre at Fort Mims in Mississippi, and at the battle of Horseshoe Bend (Tohopeka) in March 1814, he succeeded in wresting from the Indians a vast region in the Mississippi Territory and thus ended the Creek War. He proceeded to Pensacola, Florida, capturing it in November, and then hurried to New Orleans where he repulsed an attempted British invasion on January 8, 1815. News of his victory reached Washington shortly ahead of news that the war had been ended before the battle by the signing of the treaty of Ghent. Jackson—nicknamed "Old Hickory"—was by then a national figure and already was considered by many a potential president. He retained the major general's commission in the regular army that had been given him after his victory over the Creek, and he was made commander of the Southern district. In 1818 he was sent to put down the latest in a series of outbreaks (the Seminole Wars) by the Seminole Indians and in doing so invaded Spanish Florida; in capturing Spanish territory and in executing two British subjects, Alexander Arbuthnot and Robert Ambrister, for stirring up further Indian toubles, he raised a diplomatic and political storm in which John Quincy Adams was his staunchest supporter. By virtue of his frontier origins, his philosophy of expansionism, his exploits against the Indians and the British, and his obvious independence, Jackson was by now the hero of the West and South and, by association at least, was the representative of the growing democratic spirit in those sections. Although for a time he disavowed presidential aspirations, friends and supporters began preparing for the campaign of 1824; after a brief period as territorial governor of Florida in 1821 he retired to The Hermitage until he was elected to the Senate in 1823. At the end of the electoral balloting in the next year's presidential election he led three other candidates; the contest went to the House for decision and Adams was chosen. When Henry Clay, who had controlled the deciding votes, became secretary of state in Adams's cabinet the Jackson group raised the cry of "corrupt bargain." Organizing and campaigning began immediately for 1828, however, and that year Jackson defeated Adams decisively. Almost from the beginning his administration was beset by controversy; objections to his application of the spoils system were followed closely by the social ostracism of the wife of the secretary of war, who had Jackson's social backing, by other cabinet wives, an affair which began the split between Jackson and Vice-President John C. Calhoun, whose wife led in the ostracizing of Peggy O'Neale Eaton. Other problems followed from a continuing rivalry between officials of the executive branch and Jackson's personal advisers, who formed the "kitchen cabinet." The protective Tariff of 1828 became a crucial issue in the growing area of disagreement between the North and the South and Jackson and Calhoun had adopted clear and completely opposed positions by 1830; in 1832 South Carolina, with Calhoun's support, nullified the tariffs of 1828 and 1832. Jackson immediately and vehemently denounced the move and in March 1833 secured from Congress both the authority to use federal troops to insure the state's compliance with federal law and a reduction of the objectionable rates. South Carolina then withdrew its earlier nullification proclamation but saved face by nullifying Jackson's Force Bill of 1833; the clash over the states'-rights issue was thus postponed. Meanwhile Jackson had been reelected over Henry Clay—and Calhoun had been replaced by Martin Van Buren—in a campaign based primarily on the issue of the Second Bank of the United States. Jackson had vetoed a bill rechartering the bank earlier in the year and thereby reinforced his popularity; he was vindicated in the election and thereafter continued his campaign against the bank by withdrawing from it all deposits of federal money. By the time the bank's charter expired in 1836 the government's money had been distributed among several state banks; this action, combined with the policy begun the same year of accepting only gold or silver in payment for public land, led directly to a financial panic in 1837, after Jackson had been succeeded as president by Van Buren. When Jackson left office in March 1837, the general but disorganized movement of voters, largely Westerners and Southerners, that had originally elected him had been transformed into the Democratic party; despite the fact that he had often had little sympathy for the movement and had in fact often allied himself with opposing interests, his name became firmly attached to it. He was in many ways more the accepted symbol than the living representative of "Jacksonian democracy." His rise from humble frontier origins to national eminence, his success in dealing with the established political powers, and his concept of a vigorous president all appealed to the restless, optimistic young nation. His policies were those of the democratic frontier: monetary inflation; expansionism—he attempted but failed to arrange for the annexation of Texas after its revolution; Indian removal—he refused to move to enforce a Supreme Court ruling in 1832 that voided a Georgia attempt to annex Cherokee land and thus set the stage for the Indians' relocation across the Mississippi; and energetic nationalism. Even more popular on leaving the presidency than he had been on entering it, he retired to his home and remained there in declining health until his death on June 8, 1845 at The Hermitage, where he was buried. He was elected to the Hall of Fame in 1910.

Jackson, Charles Thomas (1805–1880), chemist and geologist. Born in Plymouth, Massachusetts, on June 21, 1805, Jackson studied medicine privately, then at Harvard from which he graduated in 1829, and for three years in Europe, during which time he also pursued strong interests in geology and other scientific fields. On his return voyage to the United States in 1832 he conversed at length with a fellow passenger, Samuel F. B. Morse, on the possibilities of an electric telegraph and on his own experiments along that line. He practiced medicine in Boston from 1832 to 1836, when he gave it up in favor of chemistry and mineralogy, opening a laboratory and in 1837 receiving commissions from the states of Massa-

chusetts and Maine to survey public lands. He was appointed the first state geologist of Maine in the same year and later held similar posts in Rhode Island, 1840, and New Hampshire, 1841–1844; his annual reports were competent, but his field studies revealed little that was new or significant. Except for a brief association with a federal survey of the Lake Superior region in 1847 Jackson remained thereafter mainly in Boston, teaching and working in his laboratory. When Morse patented his telegraph Jackson publicly claimed credit for the invention; while there was some basis for his claim it is clear that, in characteristically erratic fashion, he had failed to foresee the potential of the telegraph and to pursue his early experiments. Similarly, in 1846, after suggesting to William T. G. Morton the use of ether as an anesthetic during tooth extractions, he attempted to claim priority in the development of anesthesia and embarked on a long and bitter public controversy despite the fact that again he had himself made no effort actually to apply principles that were not at all unknown to science. Through an accident of publication, however, he was for a time widely honored in Europe for the discovery of the medical use of ether. He later also claimed credit for the invention of guncotton. Continual public dispute marked his later years; his mental condition worsened and he died on August 28, 1880, in the McLean Asylum in Somerville, Massachusetts.

Jackson, Helen Hunt (1830–1885), author. Born in Amherst, Massachusetts, on October 15, 1830, Helen Maria Fiske was the daughter of a professor of classics at Amherst College and from an early age was a close friend of Emily Dickinson. She married Edward B. Hunt, an army officer, in 1852, and his death in 1863 and that of her son in 1865 left her alone and without resources. She moved to Newport, Rhode Island, and with the encouragement of Thomas W. S. Higginson began contributing poems and prose sketches to various periodicals, principally the *New York Independent* and *Hearth and Home*. As an author she was successful from the outset, although throughout much of her career she signed little of her work, using instead of her own name such pseudonyms as "Saxe Holm" and "H. H." Her first book, a volume entitled *Verses*, appeared in 1870 and was followed by such popular but minor efforts as *Bits of Travel*, 1872; *Bits of Talk About Home Matters*, 1873; *Mercy Philbrick's Choice*, 1876; *Hetty's Strange History*, 1877; and *Nelly's Silver Mine*, 1878. From 1875, when she married William S. Jackson, she lived in Colorado Springs, Colorado, and her life in the West generated in her a deep sympathy for American Indians. She described the consistently shoddy and cruel treatment of Indians by the government in *A Century of Dishonor*, 1881, the considerable impact of which was greatly surpassed by that of her subsequent novel *Ramona*, 1884. While *Ramona* aroused something of a public outcry on behalf of the Indians, its great and lasting popularity was due in large part to its picturesque and romantic setting in old California. As a result of the publication of *A Century of Dishonor* she had been appointed in 1882 by the federal government to investigate the condition of the Mission Indians of California. Mrs. Jackson died in San Francisco on August 12, 1885.

Jackson, Howell Edmunds (1832–1895), justice of the Supreme Court. Born in Paris, Tennessee, on April 8, 1832, Jackson was the son of distinguished Virginians who had moved to Tennessee in 1830. He was educated in private schools and at West Tennessee College, from which he graduated in 1849. He studied at the University of Virginia for two years, then read law in Jackson, Tennessee, for three more, and finally graduated first in his class from the law school of Cumberland University in 1856. He practiced law in Jackson and in Memphis until the Civil War broke out. He opposed secession, but when Tennessee left the Union he followed the fortunes of his state and was made receiver of sequestered property, a post he held throughout the war. After the war he returned to the practice of law and earned a reputation for great learning and integrity. In 1880 he was nominated for the state legislature without his knowledge, but he accepted the challenge, waged a spirited campaign, and was elected. Upon his taking his seat a bitter struggle ensued over the election of a U.S. senator by the legislature. Factional disputes made the election of any of the established Democratic candidates impossible, and Jackson's name was proposed by a Republican member of the legislature and he was chosen on the first ballot. His qualities of quiet competence were exhibited in the Senate as well, and in 1886 President Grover Cleveland appointed him to the federal bench, Sixth Circuit. He served with great distinction as presiding judge of the Cincinnati circuit court of appeal from 1891, among other achievements construing the Interstate Commerce Act of 1887 and the Sherman Anti-Trust Act of 1890 with such elaborate care that, on appeal, the Supreme Court accepted his views in their entirety. Early in 1893, when a vacancy occurred on the Supreme Court, President Benjamin Harrison, a Republican, nominated him to the seat, partly because he knew that no Republican would be confirmed by the incoming Democratic Senate and partly because of Jackson's national reputation as a jurist of complete probity. His career on the Court began auspiciously, but within a matter of months after his appointment he developed tuberculosis and was soon unable to continue his work. In March 1895, however, the famous income tax-case of *Pollock* v. *Farmers' Loan & Trust Company* came before the Court. The other eight justices were divided four and four and Jackson summoned the last of his strength to take his place on the bench to hear the rearguments. He expected to cast the deciding vote in favor of the constitutionality of the act providing for an income tax, but one of the other justices changed his mind, whereupon the act was declared unconstitutional by a vote of five to four. Jackson died at his home near Nashville, Tennessee, on August 8, 1895.

Jackson, Jesse Louis (1941–   ), civil-rights leader. Born on October 8, 1941, in Greenville, North Carolina, Jackson was brought up in the poor black section of that city. He took the name of his stepfather after his mother married Charles H. Jackson while Jesse was still a child. At all-black Sterling High School he starred on the football, basketball, and baseball teams; upon his graduation he was offered a contract by the Chicago White Sox baseball team but turned it down because the offer was much smaller than one made to a white star player. He thereupon accepted an athletic scholarship at the University of Illinois, but on being told that blacks could not play quarterback he transferred to the predominantly black Agricultural and Technical College of North Carolina at Greensboro, where he starred at quarterback on the football team, was an honor student, and was elected president of the student body. While still a student he became involved in civil-rights activities, in 1963 leading the student sit-down campaign in downtown Greensboro that eventually led to the integration of the city's restaurants and theaters. He graduated in 1964 and in 1965 entered Chicago Theological Seminary. In the same year he went to Selma, Alabama, to join Dr. Martin Luther King, Jr., in the civil-rights marches and protests he was leading in that city. Jackson soon became a close associate of King and was named by him head of the Chicago branch of Operation Breadbasket when the program was instituted by the Southern Christian Leadership Conference (SCLC). Jackson was named national director of Operation Breadbasket in August 1967 and was singularly successful in the ensuing years in forcing manufacturing and merchandising firms to hire more black workers by threatening a black boycott of their products. His greatest success came in 1968, when the A&P supermarket chain agreed to employ hundreds of additional black workers and utilize black-run service organizations in areas where store customers were predominantly black. After the assassination of Dr. King on April 4, 1968, the charismatic Jackson was often mentioned as the heir to his power and influence in the black community, but it was said that he refused to wear King's mantle on the grounds that black leaders tend ultimately to be corrupted by the white "power structure." Ordained a Baptist minister on June 30, 1968, he continued as a potent force in the political affairs of Chicago. He was removed as head of Operation Breadbasket in 1971 after a dispute with SCLC leaders, and he then founded a similar but more broadly oriented organization, Operation Push (People United to Save Humanity).

Jackson, Mahalia (1911–1972), gospel singer. Born in New Orleans on October 26, 1911,

Mahalia Jackson was the third of six children of a longshoreman and barber who preached on Sundays in a neighborhood church. She attended public schools in New Orleans and was brought up in a strict religious atmosphere involving, among other things, disapproval of all kinds of secular music. Her father's family included several entertainers, but she was forced to confine her own musical activities to singing in his choir and listening—although surreptitiously—to recordings of Bessie Smith and Ida Cox as well as of Enrico Caruso. When she was sixteen she went to Chicago and joined the Greater Salem Baptist Church choir, where her remarkable contralto voice soon led to her selection as a soloist. She was popular in storefront and tent churches but for a long time was not accepted by the larger, more formal black congregations because of the syncopated rhythms of her songs. But her fame grew and in 1934 her first recording, "God Gonna Separate the Wheat from the Tares," became very popular and led to a series of other recordings. Her first great hit (altogether, eight of her records sold more than a million copies each) was "Move on Up a Little Higher," which appeared in 1945. It, and indeed all of her other famous songs, including "I Believe," "He's Got the Whole World in His Hands," "I Can Put My Trust in Jesus," "Just Over the Hill," "When I Wake Up in Glory," and "Just a Little While to Stay Here," were gospel songs—songs with texts drawn from biblical themes and strongly influenced by the harmonies, rhythms, and emotional force of blues. Despite her admiration for Bessie Smith, and despite the fact that she is said to have possessed the greatest potential blues voice and style since the death of Miss Smith, Miss Jackson resolutely refused to sing anything but religious songs, or indeed to sing at all in surroundings that she considered inappropriate. Thus she would never sing in a nightclub or in any place where liquor was served. But she sang on the radio and on television and, starting in 1950, performed to overflow audiences in annual concerts at Carnegie Hall in New York City. She was enormously popular abroad; her version of "Silent Night," for example, was one of the all-time best-selling records in Denmark. She made a notable appearance at the Newport Jazz Festival in 1957—in a program devoted entirely, at her request, to gospel songs—and she sang at the inauguration of President John F. Kennedy in January 1961. She sang in churches and in prisons and hospitals as well as in concert halls and in command performances before heads of state. In her later years she was closely associated with the civil-rights movement, but she also suffered from ill health, and although advised by her doctors to curtail her demanding schedule, she refused to do less than all she could to help heal the divisions, as she said, between black and white people in the United States and elsewhere. She died in Evergreen Park, Illinois, on January 27, 1972, after a lifetime devoted to making "a joyful noise unto the Lord."

Jackson, Robert Houghwout (1892–1954), justice of the Supreme Court. Born on February 13, 1892, in Spring Creek, Warren County, Pennsylvania, Jackson grew up there and in Jamestown, New York. He entered Albany Law School, New York (now part of Union University) while in his teens and completed the two-year course in a single year. Returning to Jamestown to practice law, he was admitted to the bar in 1913, when he became twenty-one; he had still been a minor when, with the court's permission, he pleaded his first case. He continued his studies, earning a B.A. from the Chautauqua Institution toward the end of World War I, and entered city politics in Jamestown, serving as counsel for various municipal agencies. After the 1929 financial crash he helped merge the three Jamestown banks and became a director of the consolidated institution. His service on a New York state judicial commission brought him to the attention of Governor Franklin D. Roosevelt, who, after his election to the presidency, appointed Jackson general counsel for the Bureau of Internal Revenue in 1934. He served with distinction in that post and as special counsel for the Securities and Exchange Commission (SEC), conducting a series of investigations of large corporations accused of infringing the antitrust laws. He moved to the Department of Justice in 1936, where he served as assistant attorney general of the Antitrust Division, solicitor general (1938–1939), and attorney general (1940–1941). In all of those posts he was the chief legal defender of New Deal legislation. He was named by Roosevelt an associate justice of the Supreme Court in June 1941, and he became noted for his dissents, opposing the "legalistic" opinions of some of his colleagues and insisting that the Court take account of "contract and custom" and adhere to the spirit of the country's history. He disapproved of too-broad interpretations of the Bill of Rights, asserting in one dissent that "the choice is . . . between liberty with order and anarchy without either." He supported the Court's findings against the Communist party, although he disagreed with some of the more extreme legal measures taken against it. He was appointed in May 1945 to the International Military Tribunal by President Harry S. Truman and served as chief U.S. prosecutor in the Nuremberg trials of former German Nazi leaders from November 1945 to September 1946. He conducted the prosecution of such figures as Hermann Göring, Joachim von Ribbentrop, Franz von Papen, Wilhelm Keitel, Julius Streicher, and Alfred Jodl, presenting the core of the indictment charging them, as individuals, with conspiring to wage aggressive war. He returned to the Supreme Court at the end of 1946. He was the author of several books, including *The Struggle for Judicial Supremacy,* 1941, about his New Deal legal activities, and two volumes dealing with his work with the International Military Tribunal—*The Case Against the Nazi War Criminals,* 1946, and *The Nürnberg Case,* 1947. Jackson died on October 9, 1954, in Washington, D.C.

Jackson, Sheldon (1834–1909), missionary and educator. Born in Minaville, New York, on May 18, 1834, Jackson graduated in 1855 from Union College, Schenectady, New York. He pursued theological studies at Princeton Theological Seminary and was ordained by the Albany presbytery of the Presbyterian church on his graduation in 1858. He immediately took up missionary duties among the Choctaw Indians in the Indian Territory, where he spent a year. He was then made a missionary superintendent, in which post between 1859 and 1883 he founded more than 100 churches in Minnesota, Wisconsin, Iowa, Nebraska, Wyoming, Montana, Colorado, Utah, Idaho, and Nevada, and also opened schools in New Mexico and Arizona. In 1884 he went to the Territory of Alaska as chief Presbyterian missionary, and continued his work by establishing and organizing churches and schools there. He made a lasting contribution to the Alaskan economy by introducing reindeer from Siberia in 1891; the animals served as an important and much-needed food resource. As the U.S. superintendent of public instruction in Alaska from 1885 to 1908 he worked unceasingly to bring about the admission of the Territory to the Union as a state, but he did not live to see this dream realized. From 1887 to 1897 he edited the *Sitka North Star* and also published a number of books on Alaska. He was honored by being elected moderator of the general assembly of the Presbyterian church in 1897. He died on May 2, 1909, in Asheville, North Carolina.

Jackson, Thomas Jonathan (1824–1863), "Stonewall," soldier. Born on January 21, 1824, in Clarksburg, Virginia (now in West Virginia), Jackson was orphaned early in life and was brought up by relatives. Despite limited schooling he received an appointment to West Point in 1842 and graduated four years later. Commissioned a second lieutenant of artillery, he was immediately sent to join the army in Mexico, where he distinguished himself at the battles of Veracruz, Cerro Gordo, and Chapultepec. For three years after returning to the United States in 1848 he served at various posts, but in 1851 he accepted an appointment as a professor at the Virginia Military Institute (VMI) and resigned his commission, living quietly for the next ten years in Lexington, Virginia. With the outbreak of the Civil War in 1861 he was ordered to move his cadet corps to Richmond; he was commissioned a colonel in the Confederate army and sent to Harpers Ferry. In July, by then a brigadier general, he was ordered to the field at the first battle of Bull Run (Manassas), and there his stout resistance to the Union advance earned him the nickname "Stonewall" from Gen. Barnard E. Bee. In October Jackson was promoted to major general and a month later assumed command of the forces in the Shenandoah Valley; there, early in 1862, he began his famous Valley Campaign in which, by rapid movements of his forces, he tied up much greater numbers of Union troops, pre-

vented reinforcements from being sent to join Gen. George B. McClellan's campaign against Richmond, and threatened Washington. In June he won successive victories at Cross Keys and Port Republic and the Union invasion of the Confederacy was checked. By this time Jackson was working closely with Gen. Robert E. Lee and the two formed an apparently invincible team. In June Jackson's forces hurried by train to Richmond to help expel McClellan from Virginia. In the Seven Days' Battles he fought to exhaustion and, after failing to pursue the enemy through White Oak Swamp, he retired from the line before the battle of Malvern Hill on July 1. In August Stonewall Jackson and his famed "foot-cavalry" executed an encircling movement and at the second battle of Bull Run again drove the Union forces back to the Potomac. In September he took conspicuous part in the action at Antietam (Sharpsburg). In October he was made a lieutenant general and placed in command of one of Lee's two corps and in December he led his troops at Fredericksburg. In early May 1863 Jackson performed his last great service. Outnumbered by more than two to one, Lee's forces were threatened at Chancellorsville; Jackson was sent in another encircling movement and took the enemy completely by surprise, rolling up the right flank of Gen. Joseph Hooker and forcing him to retreat. In the confusion of this twilight attack, however, Jackson was caught in the rifle fire of his own men. Lee wrote to him two days later: "You are better off than I am, for while you have lost your *left*, I have lost my *right* arm." A stern and respected leader of men and a master tactician, Jackson had been indeed Lee's right arm, and he was, in fact, lost to Lee and the South. He contracted pneumonia in his weakened state and died on May 10, 1863, at Guinea Station (now Guinea), south of Fredericksburg, Virginia. He was elected to the Hall of Fame in 1955.

Jacobi, Abraham (1830–1919), physician. Born in Westphalia (Germany), on May 6, 1830, Jacobi was educated at the universities of Greifswald, Göttingen, and Bonn, receiving an M.D. from Bonn in 1851. His participation in the Revolution of 1848 led eventually to his imprisonment; he escaped in 1853 and after a brief stay in London emigrated to the United States. He established a practice in New York City, devoting care to the poor and in particular to children. Within a few years he was a recognized authority on the diseases of infants and children, and in 1857 he was appointed a lecturer in that field at the College of Physicians and Surgeons. In 1860 he was named professor of children's diseases at the New York Medical College, the first physician in the United States to hold such a chair. From 1865 to 1870 he held a similar post at the University of the City of New York (now New York University) and in 1870 assumed the professorship of pediatrics at the College of Physicians and Surgeons, with which he was associated until his retirement in 1902. In addition to his teaching duties he maintained a full practice and published a number of important books, including *Contributions to Midwifery, and Diseases of Women and Children*, with E. Noeggerath, 1859; *Dentition and Its Derangements*, 1862; *The Intestinal Diseases of Infancy and Childhood*, 1887; and *Therapeutics of Infancy and Childhood*, 1896. He also published a notable series of annual reports on his free pediatric clinic, the first of its kind in the country, and in 1862, with Noeggerath, founded the *American Journal of Obstetrics*. Widely acknowledged to be the founder of pediatrics in the United States, Jacobi remained active after his retirement from teaching, serving as president of numerous professional societies, including in 1912–1913 the American Medical Association (AMA). He died on July 10, 1919, in Bolton Landing, New York. His wife, Mary Corinna Putnam Jacobi (1842–1906), was also an outstanding physician and a pioneer in the movement to open medical schools to women.

James, Henry (1811–1882), author and philosopher. Born in Albany, New York, on June 3, 1811, James was the son of a successful merchant who left him a comfortable fortune which he was able to pass on in turn to his children. He graduated from Union College, Schenectady, in 1830 and five years later entered Princeton Theological Seminary, but he soon realized that he could not accept his father's rigidly orthodox Presbyterianism. He did not arrive at any resolution of his spiritual difficulties until 1844, when, in England, he came under the influence of the writings of Emanuel Swedenborg. The main source of his social and political views was the French socialist Charles Fourier, and his own synthesis of the thought of Swedenborg and Fourier was expounded in lectures, articles, and books, his best-known work being *Society the Redeemed Form of Man, and the Earnest of God's Omnipotence in Human Nature*, 1879. He was closely associated with Ralph Waldo Emerson and many of the Brook Farm circle and contributed frequently to the *Harbinger* and to Horace Greeley's *New York Tribune*. In the mid-1850s he began to devote himself primarily to the education of his sons, William the philosopher, Henry the novelist, Wilkinson, and Robertson and his daughter Alice. He spent the years 1855–1858 in Europe with the two older boys and returned there with them in 1859–1860; he settled at Newport, Rhode Island, in 1860, and then moved to Boston in 1864 to be near William, who was completing his education at Harvard. From 1866 the James family lived and participated actively in the intellectual life of the academic community; the elder Henry James enjoying a reputation not only as a thinker on religious and social topics but also as a brilliant conversationalist. Remaining a dogged fighter for his ideals until the end, he died in Cambridge on December 18, 1882.

James, Henry (1843–1916), author and critic. Born in New York City on April 15, 1843, James was named for his father (1811–1882), and was the younger brother of William James. His early life and education were unconventional; his father determined that the children should be given as wide a view of the world as possible and moved the family back and forth across the Atlantic while engaging a succession of tutors to provide formal education. In 1860 the family settled, more or less, in Newport, Rhode Island; two years later Henry began a brief period of study at the Harvard Law School, but literature soon claimed him and his first story was published anonymously in 1864. James continued to live in Cambridge, whither his family followed him in 1866. While writing criticism regularly for the *Nation* from 1865 to 1869, he was encouraged to continue the writing of fiction by William Dean Howells, who published his stories in the *Atlantic Monthly*. Until 1875 he alternated between living in the United States and Europe, accumulating the experiences that found expression in his early stories and novels with international settings; in 1871 he published the first of them, "A Passionate Pilgrim." In 1875 he chose Europe as his permanent home; at first he lived in Paris, where he was close to Ivan Turgenev and was a member of Gustave Flaubert's circle, but the following year he moved to London. During the next several years he concentrated in his writing on the contrast and conflict of America and Europe, the one young, rude, brash, naïve, the other old, civilized, corrupt, yet wise. The first novel of the period was *Roderick Hudson*, 1875; there followed among others, *The American*, 1877; *The Europeans*, 1878; *Daisy Miller*, 1879; and perhaps the masterwork of the genre, *The Portrait of a Lady*, 1881. In 1881 he also published one of his few novels with an exclusively American scene and cast of characters, *Washington Square*. The next two decades were an extended transitional period for James, during which the conflict between national traditions ceased to be central in his work and he concentrated, with vast sensitivity and perception, on people as they developed morally and intellectually and as they formed relationships of various sorts with others. This period saw the publication of *The Siege of London*, 1883; *The Author of Beltraffio*, 1885; *The Bostonians*, 1886; *The Princess Casamassima*, 1886; *The Aspern Papers*, 1887; *The Real Thing and Other Tales*, 1893; *The Spoils of Poynton*, 1897; *What Maisie Knew*, 1897; "The Turn of the Screw," 1898; *The Awkward Age*, 1899; and *The Sacred Fount*, 1901, among many others. During the early 1890s he wrote unsuccessfully for the theater, and despite his disappointment with failure, his subsequent work showed increasingly a concern for the dramatic, while he decreased the number of his characters in order to portray more vividly and analyze more deeply the tensions and forces of relationships. In addition to his fiction, James maintained all the while a steady flow of criticism, essays, and travel books, notable among which were *French Poets and Novelists*, 1878; *Hawthorne*, 1879; *A Little Tour in France*, 1885;

Partial Portraits, which included his essay "The Art of Fiction," 1888; and *Essays in London*, 1893. With the turn of the century he began his final period of fiction writing, represented by three large novels in which, through diverse characters and situations, he delved into the relation of the individual to society and developed an ethical framework upon which, in his view, depended both the rational growth of the individual and the maintenance of civilized society. The first of the three to be written was *The Ambassadors*, published in 1903; it was preceded in publication by *The Wings of the Dove*, 1902, and followed by *The Golden Bowl*, 1904, his last completed novel. In his remaining years he continued to write in his favorite nonfiction modes, publishing *English Hours*, 1905, and *Italian Hours*, 1909, along with several other books of criticism and essays; he returned briefly to the drama and late in life produced several autobiographical works. A trip to the United States in 1904–1905, during which for the first time he traveled the length and breadth of the country, resulted in the penetrating analysis published as *The American Scene*, 1907. James's reputation was somewhat slow to become established, but by mid-20th century he was acknowledged as a master of modern literature, a unique creative force whose works claimed attention as among the most expressive of their time. As an explorer of the imagination and the sensibilities of man in modern culture and as a pioneer of impressionism in literature he remained without peer. In 1915, prompted by his sympathy for England and its allies in World War I and much dismayed by the determined isolationism of the United States, he became a British subject, after 40 years' residence in England, and the following year he was awarded the Order of Merit by King George V. He died soon afterward in London, on February 28, 1916.

James, Jesse Woodson (1847–1882), outlaw. Born near Centerville (now Kearney), Missouri, on September 5, 1847, Jesse grew up on a farm and had little schooling. His father died when he was four, and his mother twice remarried. The family, like many of the people of the region, was openly sympathetic to the Confederacy, and during the Civil War their home was raided twice by Northern militiamen. At fifteen, Jesse joined the pro-Confederate guerrilla raiders led by William C. Quantrill. At the end of the war he surrendered with the others in the band but while doing so was shot. He turned fugitive and after recovering he took to crime, forming a gang with his brother Frank, the Younger brothers (Cole, James, and Robert), and a few others, and embarked on a career of robbery that lasted for 15 years. The most famous of their exploits, and possibly the least successful, was an attempt to rob a bank in Northfield, Minnesota, in September 1876; all of the band except Jesse and Frank James were killed or captured. The brothers lay low until 1879, when they resumed their activi-

ties with a new gang. Until 1880 they enjoyed the sympathy and protection of a great number of people in their native region; in that year public sentiment shifted against them, however, and concerted efforts began for their capture. Jesse had been living quietly in St. Joseph, Missouri, under the name Thomas Howard when a large price was put on his head by the governor; prompted by the reward, Robert Ford, a member of his outlaw band, shot him in the back of the head on April 3, 1882. The legend of Jesse James, already begun during his lifetime, grew steadily after his death until he became one of the country's folk heroes, celebrated in ballads, stories, and dime novels. Later in 1882 Frank surrendered, was tried twice and acquitted, and retired to obscurity on his farm near Excelsior Springs, Missouri, where he died in 1915.

James, William (1842–1910), psychologist and philosopher. Born in New York City on January 11, 1842, William was the son of Henry James the elder and was the elder brother of the novelist Henry James. Prompted by the father's determination that the children develop as broadly cosmopolitan an outlook as possible, the family was almost constantly on the move between New York, New England, and various places in Europe, and the children were educated by private tutors and in private schools as occasion allowed. By 1860 James had acquired a basic liberal education and began to study art under William Morris Hunt; within a year he changed his mind and in 1861 entered the Lawrence Scientific School at Harvard. Three years later he enrolled in the Harvard Medical School. He interrupted his studies in 1865 to accompany Louis Agassiz on an exploring and collecting expedition to the Amazon; he returned in poor health and after a brief resumption of his studies sailed to Europe, where he remained seeking in vain to restore his health. He returned to Harvard late in 1868 and took his medical degree the following year. The next three years, during which he was virtually an invalid, were a crucial period; he continued to read widely and in the writings of Charles Renouvier, a French philosopher and psychologist, he apparently found the intellectual strength to overcome his chronic morbidity and depression and to adopt free will as an active, operative principle. In 1872 he was appointed instructor in physiology at Harvard; by 1880 he had shifted to the field of psychology, created the country's first experimental laboratory for psychological research, and been transferred to the department of philosophy. On an extended European visit in 1882–1883 James formed close associations with a number of leading psychologists and philosophers and began active research into parapsychological phenomena. During the 1880s his teaching at Harvard came more and more to be concerned with ethical and religious problems, and his work in pure psychology ended with the publication of his monumental work of 12 years, *The Principles of Psychology*, in 1890.

Both definitive and seminal, the book gained wide acceptance not only in scientific circles but, with its clear and vivid prose, was also well received by the general public. In his subsequent teaching, lecturing, and writing, James went beyond his radically empiricist psychology, using it as a tool to explore philosophical questions. Nearly all of his books were collections of earlier articles or of lectures; thus, for example, *The Will to Believe and Other Essays in Popular Philosophy*, published in 1897, was actually begun in 1879. Similarly, his Gifford Lectures at the University of Edinburgh in 1901 and 1902 were published as *The Varieties of Religious Experience*, 1902. In that book James achieved a reconciliation of sorts between science and religion by investigating the claims of religion from a standpoint of thoroughgoing empiricism and concluding that the weight of evidence lay in favor of the existence of dimensions of consciousness beyond the realm of everyday experience. The work remains a classic in its field. His Lowell Lectures in Boston in 1906 were collected and published the next year as *Pragmatism: A New Name for Some Old Ways of Thinking*; the term he had borrowed from Charles S. Peirce was thereafter firmly attached to his own philosophy. James's later works, many of which were directed to the controversy raised by *Pragmatism*, included *A Pluralistic Universe* and *The Meaning of Truth*, both 1909, and, posthumously, *Some Problems of Philosophy*, 1911, and *Essays in Radical Empiricism*, 1912. His teaching career at Harvard ended in 1907; he was increasingly beset by ill health, and he died in Chocorua, New Hampshire, on August 26, 1910.

Jameson, John Franklin (1859–1937), historian. Born near Boston on September 19, 1859, J. Franklin Jameson was a scholar from his youth. Graduating from Amherst College in 1879, he was named a graduate fellow at Johns Hopkins in 1881 and received his Ph.D. there a year later. He was an assistant and associate in history at Johns Hopkins from 1882 to 1888, professor of history at Brown University from 1888 to 1901, professor and head of the department of history at the University of Chicago from 1901 to 1905, director of the department of historical research at the Carnegie Institution of Washington from 1905 to 1928, and chief of the manuscript division of the Library of Congress from 1928 until his death. It was in the last two posts that he made his greatest mark on American historiography. The last three decades of his working life were devoted to the collation, expansion, and systematic publication of historical documents held in various government and private collections. Vast new resources were made accessible by his work. Jameson served as managing editor of the *American Historical Review* from 1895 to 1901 and from 1905 to 1928 and was chairman of the Historical Manuscripts Commission from 1895 to 1899 and from 1905 to 1908. He was a founder of the American Historical Association in 1884 and served as its president in 1906–1907. He was the author of many scholarly books and articles, including *A History of Historical Writing in America*, 1891; *Dictionary of United States History*, 1894; and *The American Revolution Considered as a Social Movement*, 1926. He edited the *Correspondence of John C. Calhoun*, 1900; *Original Narratives of Early American History*, 19 volumes, 1906–1917; and *Privateering and Piracy*, 1923. He served as chairman of the committee on management of the *Dictionary of American Biography* in his later years. He died in Washington, D.C., on September 28, 1937.

Jansky, Karl Guthe (1905–1950), engineer. Born on October 22, 1905, in Norman, Oklahoma, Jansky was educated in local schools and upon receiving his B.S. from the University of Wisconsin in 1928 went to work for the Bell Telephone Laboratories. In the summer of 1931 he began a series of studies of atmospheric static with the aim of finding means of decreasing the interference of static with transoceanic telephone calls. Using a primitive rotating antenna, he recorded the arrival and the intensity of static at a wave length of 14.6 meters. He was able to correlate two types of static with local and distant thunderstorms, but a third type remained mysterious. After working for more than a year and after allowing for the earth's rotation and its revolution about the sun, he concluded that the radiation causing this third type of static must originate outside the solar system, probably from a fixed source in the direction of the constellation Sagittarius, either in the Milky Way or in the center of the galaxy. The publication of his results—the first intimations that radio waves were produced by celestial objects—led to further researches by Grote Reber and others, and eventually to the enormously fruitful development of radio astronomy. During World War II Jansky was engaged in research on radio direction finders; for his efforts he received an Army-Navy certificate of appreciation. He died at Little Silver, New Jersey, on February 14, 1950.

Jarrell, Randall (1914–1965), poet. Born in Nashville, Tennessee, on May 6, 1914, Jarrell received his B.A. in 1935 and his M.A. in 1938 from Vanderbilt University. He taught English at Kenyon College from 1937 to 1939 and at the University of Texas from 1939 to 1942, whereupon he joined the Army Air Corps and served through World War II, until 1946. He then continued to follow an academic career, serving as professor of English or poet in residence at a number of institutions, including Sarah Lawrence College in 1946–1947, Woman's College of the University of North Carolina in 1947–1951 and 1953–1954, and the University of North Carolina at Greensboro in 1961–1965. His first book of poems, *Blood for a Stranger*, appeared in 1942; it was followed by *Little Friend, Little Friend*, 1945; *Losses*, 1948; *Seven-League Crutches*, 1951; *Selected Poems*, 1955; *The Woman at the Washington Zoo*, 1960; and *The Lost World*, 1965. He also published critical essays in *Poetry and the Age*, 1953, and *Sad Heart at the Supermarket*, 1962; a novel, *Pictures from an Institution*, 1954; and three popular children's books—*The Gingerbread Rabbit*, 1963; *The Bat Poet*, 1964; and *The Animal Family*, 1965. He received two National Book Awards, the first, for poetry, in 1960, and the second, for fiction, in 1962. He was consultant in poetry to the Library of Congress from 1956 to 1958. On October 14, 1965, he was struck by a car and killed near Chapel Hill, North Carolina.

Jarves, James Jackson (1818–1888), art critic and collector. Born in Boston on August 20, 1818, Jarves received his formal schooling in Boston at Chauncey Hall, but acquired the better part of his education by reading and by collecting and observing natural objects. He planned to attend Harvard, but impairment of his vision forced him to abandon formal studies. He began traveling, first to California, then to Mexico and Central America, noting for future books the things he saw. He settled in Honolulu in 1838 and founded there in 1840 the first newspaper in the Hawaiian (then the Sandwich) Islands, the *Polynesian*. Appointed in 1848 as special commissioner for the Hawaiian monarchy to make commercial treaties with the United States, France, and Great Britain, he traveled to Europe and found the atmosphere there so pleasant, especially in Italy, that he established a permanent residence in Florence. He began to purchase paintings by early Italian masters and eventually developed a collection that in quantity and quality surpassed any in the United States. But it was not received warmly when shown in the United States in 1860 and there were even ill informed questions as to its authenticity; there were no offers to purchase the collection, and although Jarves probably could have sold items individually, he was reluctant to do so, since he recognized the value of the collection as a whole for the study of early religious art. Finally, in 1871, the paintings were sold at auction to Yale University, the only bidder; the Jarves Collection is today considered priceless. In 1881 he donated his collection of Venetian glass to the Metropolitan Museum of Art in New York City, and in 1887 he sold his collection of rare Venetian laces and costumes and Renaissance fabrics. Although his personal fortune was spent on his collections, he accomplished his main purpose— to bring European art to his native country, even though the value of his efforts was not recognized for a generation. Among his writings were *Scenes and Scenery in the Sandwich Islands*, 1843; *Scenes and Scenery in California*, 1844; *Parisian Sights*, 1852; *Italian Sights*, 1856; *Art Hints*, 1855; *Art Studies*, 1861; and *The Art Idea*, 1864. He died in Switzerland on June 28, 1888, and was buried in the English cemetery in Rome.

Jay, John (1745–1829), public official, diplomat, and chief justice of the Supreme Court. Born in New York City on December 12, 1745, Jay came of a wealthy family. After graduation from King's College (now Columbia) in 1764, he began the study of law; he was awarded an M.A. by King's in 1767 and the next year was admitted to the bar. For six years he practiced law and prospered; then, in 1774, he was elected to the First Continental Congress. There, a staunch conservative and opposed to independence for the colonies, he drafted the *Address to the People of Great Britain*. In May 1776, still a delegate to Congress, he began serving also in the New York provincial congress and thus was absent from the signing of the Declaration of Independence; nonetheless, and despite his earlier opposition to the declaring of independence, he supported it after the fact and drafted the resolutions whereby New York ratified the Declaration. In 1777 he wrote the state's first constitution and shortly thereafter was elected its first chief justice, a position he held until December 1778. He returned then to Congress and was elected its president. In September 1779 he was appointed by Congress minister plenipotentiary to Spain and sent to Madrid to secure Spanish recognition and aid; recognition of U.S. independence was refused flatly, and the request for a loan met with minimal response even after Congress, against Jay's own judgment, offered to withdraw all claims to navigation rights on the Mississippi River. In 1782 Jay joined the joint peace commission in Paris, where his insistence on a point of protocol delayed treaty negotiations for a year; meanwhile, he helped John Adams persuade Benjamin Franklin that they should violate their instructions from Congress by entering into a preliminary agreement with Great Britain without informing France. Soon after the complicated maneuverings among the United States, Great Britain, France, and Spain were completed and the Treaty of Paris signed in 1783, Jay returned to New York, intending to resume his law practice. Instead, he learned that Congress had appointed him secretary for foreign affairs and for six years he struggled against the narrow confines of the office and the limits of national power generally. He strongly supported the Constitution and in New York contributed five essays to the *Federalist* papers, 1787–1788, as part of the campaign for ratification. When the new government was organized he was appointed in 1789 the first chief justice of the Supreme Court, turning over his duties in foreign affairs to Secretary of State Thomas Jefferson. In five years on the bench he was primarily responsible for organizing the Court and establishing its procedures. His most significant decision was in *Chisholm v. Georgia*, in which he ruled that a citizen of one state could sue another state in federal court; this opinion was almost immediately nullified by the passage of the Eleventh Amendment. In 1794, largely at Alexander Hamilton's behest, Jay was sent to England as minister extraordinary to arrange a treaty of commerce and to seek settlement of a number of U.S.–British disputes; the resulting Jay's Treaty was denounced at home and became a bitter partisan issue, for while it provided for British evacuation of the Northwest—

an unfulfilled provision of the Treaty of Paris—and set up mixed claims commissions to settle other matters, it made no mention of England's violations of maritime law, particularly the impressment of U.S. sailors. By averting possible war with England with such concessions, moreover, the treaty brought on a crisis in relations with France, particularly in its failure to deal with the problem of British seizure of French property from American ships. The Federalists, swallowing their own dissatisfaction with the treaty, managed to win ratification of Jay's Treaty in the Senate by the barest possible margins over the vehement opposition of the Anglophobe Democratic-Republicans. Returning to the United States in 1795, Jay found that he had been elected governor of New York; he resigned from the Supreme Court and served as governor for two terms. In 1801 he retired to his farm near Bedford, New York, and lived there until his death on May 17, 1829.

Jeffers, Robinson (1887–1962), poet. Born in Pittsburgh on January 10, 1887, John Robinson Jeffers was educated by his father, a classical scholar, and in a number of private schools. He studied for a year at the University of Western Pennsylvania (now the University of Pittsburgh) and then, his family having moved to California, at Occidental College, graduating in 1905. Unsure of his vocation, he pursued graduate studies at the University of Southern California, at the University of Zürich, and at the University of Washington as his interests shifted from English literature to medicine to forestry. A bequest from a relative in 1912 gave him financial security and he was able to devote himself to writing; after the outbreak of World War I had disrupted plans to live in Europe, he and his wife settled amid the magnificent scenery of the California coast near Carmel. There he built with his own hands Tor House, a dwelling and tower of native granite, and there he lived for the rest of his life. His first important volume of verse, *Tamar and Other Poems*, 1924 established his reputation as an original and deeply disturbing poet. In this and subsequent books—*The Roan Stallion*, 1925; *The Woman at Point Sur*, 1927; *Cawdor*, 1928; *Thurso's Landing*, 1932; *Give Your Heart to the Hawks*, 1933; *Solstice*, 1935; *Be Angry at the Sun*, 1941, and others—he developed a view of humanity that was profoundly pessimistic. He constructed a cosmic scheme in which the smallness, transience, and meanness of humanity contrasted unfavorably with the brooding sea and mountains that surrounded him, and even those passed into insignificance before the eternal night and a strangely dark and impersonal pantheism. In 1946 his adaptation of Euripedes' *Medea* was successfully produced in New York City; other plays, *The Cretan Woman* and *The Tower Beyond Tragedy*, were also staged with some success. Later volumes included *The Double Axe*, 1948; *Hungerfield*, 1954; and *The Beginning and the End*, 1963. He remained at Tor House, something of a recluse, until his death on January 20, 1962.

Jefferson, Joseph (1829–1905), actor. Born on February 20, 1829, in Philadelphia, the son and grandson of actors, Jefferson made his debut at the age of three in August von Kotzebue's *Pizarro*, and the following year supported Thomas Dartmouth Rice as a miniature "Jim Crow." His education came from travel and experience with troupes throughout the country. After his father's death he acted and managed theaters in the South. Arriving in New York City in 1849, already a seasoned performer at the age of twenty, he organized his own troupe but enjoyed only minor success. He toured Europe in 1856. With Laura Keene's celebrated company in New York City after 1856, he was acclaimed in roles including Dr. Pangloss in *The Heir at Law*, Asa Trenchard in *Our American Cousin*, and Bob Acres in *The Rivals*. The years 1861–1864 were spent touring Australia. In 1859 he had adapted Washington Irving's story "Rip Van Winkle" for the stage and played the title role, but he did not achieve great success in it until Irish playwright and actor Dion Boucicault revised the script. Jefferson's appearance in the new version in 1865 at the Adelphi Theatre in London was a triumph. He became identified with the role, and it was conceded that no other actor could approach him in it. From then until the end of his 72-year career, the role of Rip was the mainstay of his repertoire, as the play was of the U.S. theater. He succeeded Edwin Booth as president of the Players' Club in 1893, delivered vivid lectures on acting, and wrote a perceptive and witty *Autobiography*, 1889. He died in Palm Beach, Florida, on April 23, 1905.

Jefferson, Thomas (1743–1826), third president of the United States. Born on April 13, 1743, on his father's plantation, Shadwell, in Goochland (now in Albemarle) County on the western fringe of settlement in Virginia, Jefferson graduated from the College of William and Mary in 1762 and, after an unusually diligent and comprehensive study of law under George Wythe, was admitted to the bar five years later. He entered politics as a matter of course, advancing from county positions to Virginia's House of Burgesses in 1769. He served in that body until its dissolution in 1775; he early identified himself with the more radical faction, was a member of the Virginia Committee of Correspondence, and in 1774 wrote the officially rejected but nonetheless widely circulated and highly influential *Summary View of the Rights of British America*. In 1775 he was sent as a delegate to the Continental Congress. He was not an orator and confined his work to committees; his ability and literary gifts were acknowledged in his selection as a member of the committee charged to draft the Declaration of Independence and in the deference shown by the other committee members, who chose him to do the actual writing, to his powers of composition; his draft, with a few changes, became the text adopted on July 4, 1776. He was a signer of the completed document later that year. In October 1776 he returned to the Virginia legislature, by now the House of Delegates, and set about re-organizing the government and laws of the state on republican principles under its new constitution. Within ten years his proposals for the abolition of the slave trade and for the adoption of complete freedom of religion, had been adopted. In 1779 he was elected governor, but this first and a subsequent term were not notably successful; as a result of his own unwillingness to sacrifice principle to expediency even under emergency conditions, he had to bear responsibility for the events of the British invasion in 1781. By his narrow interpretation of his term of office he effectually resigned the governorship before a successor could be elected; retiring to Monticello, he was there with several legislators when a British force raided the estate and Jefferson barely escaped capture himself. In 1783 he was returned to Congress and there, again in committee work, he made important contributions: he advocated a decimal monetary system and submitted a series of reports on the organization of government in the Western territory, the proposals contained in which were almost without exception included in the later Ordinance of 1787, which organized the Northwest Territory. In 1784 he was sent to France to aid in the negotiation of commercial treaties, and the following year he succeeded Benjamin Franklin as U.S. minister to France. The publication in France in 1785 of his *Notes on State of Virginia* greatly enhanced his already high reputation and extended it into the fields of science and general scholarship. During his years in Europe he traveled widely, gathering impressions and knowledge that were later useful in the United States. He kept in close touch with developments at home and generally favored the adoption of the Constitution, although he was critical of its failure to include a Bill of Rights. He returned to Monticello late in 1789 but his stay was brief; in March 1790 he became the first U.S. secretary of state. The next three years were a period of difficulty and disappointment for him. Strongly opposed to factionalism, he came reluctantly but necessarily to the leadership of a faction; convinced of the danger of monarchism in the opposing faction, led by the Federalist Alexander Hamilton, secretary of the treasury, he fought constantly but with little success against Hamilton's influence and interference. The philosophies of the two men, and of the parties of which they were the acknowledged leaders, were best expressed in 1791 in their written opinions on the constitutionality of a national bank, in which they exemplified the strict- and loose-constructionist approaches to the Constitution. Jefferson resigned from the cabinet at the end of 1793 but remained the leader of the Democratic Republican party. His retirement to Monticello ended with the presidential election of 1796, in which he ran second to John Adams, a Federalist, and thus became vice-president. He played little part in the administration headed by a leader of the opposition party, but when the Federalists forced the passage of the Alien and Sedition Acts in 1798,

he drafted the Kentucky Resolves of 1798—the similar Virginia Resolves were the work of his close colleague James Madison—in which he developed the states'-rights theory that the sovereignty delegated by the states to the federal government can be withdrawn when the federal government oversteps its authority; that is, an act of the federal government may be nullified by a state on grounds of unconstitutionality. In the election of 1800 the Republican candidates for president, Jefferson and Aaron Burr, defeated the Federalists but were themselves tied for the presidency in the electoral college; after the choice went to the House of Representatives Jefferson was chosen. He was the first president to be inaugurated in Washington, D.C. There soon followed a controversy over federal appointments, as (although his actions were greatly exaggerated by the Federalists) Jefferson first introduced something like a spoils system. His first administration was signalized, however, by the Louisiana Purchase, an action that, in the irony of practical affairs, violated Jefferson's political principles in having no constitutional authority behind it. Nonetheless, he demonstrated his freedom from doctrinaire policy by seizing the opportunity to capitalize on France's financial difficulties and to acquire a vast new territory for the expansion of the United States. The expedition he authorized Meriwether Lewis and William Clark to undertake into the new country bore his characteristic marks of scientific curiosity and systematic investigation. From 1801 to 1805 he faced the problem of the piratical Barbary states; vigorous naval action, however, eventually resulted in the submission of Tripoli, with the other states following suit soon thereafter. The Barbary Wars, desultory though they were, proved invaluable in bringing the tiny U.S. Navy to a high level of proficiency. Soon after his reelection in 1804 he was faced with the almost impossible problem of maintaining neutrality in the face of war between England and France; determined to avoid U.S. involvement, he resorted finally to the Embargo Act of 1807, which, although based on firm constitutional grounds, was again a great extension of federal power and was widely criticized. In 1809 he retired permanently to Monticello and remained there for the rest of his life. He continued active in his many fields of interest, however, particularly in the establishment of state-supported education in Virginia; after long and arduous efforts he brought about the chartering of the University of Virginia in 1819. The organization, the design and architecture of the campus, and the curriculum of the university were all his work, and he supervised them closely. He was also the university's first rector. An accomplished architect, he had earlier designed his own house at Monticello and he now designed the state capitol in addition to the buildings of the university and a number of residences, and was instrumental in bringing about the Classic Revival in America. He continued his scholarly pursuits and was from 1797 to 1815 president of the American Philosophical

Society. In 1813 he and John Adams, who was also in retirement, became reconciled and began a voluminous correspondence between Monticello and Quincy, Massachusetts; the experience and perspective that the two elder statesmen brought to bear on the problems and future of their country were unmatched, and the result was one of the most remarkable and extensive exchanges of view ever recorded. On July 4, 1826, the fiftieth anniversary of the adoption of the Declaration of Independence, both men died. At his own direction, Jefferson's tombstone recorded the three achievements that he himself valued most highly: ". . . author of the Declaration of American Independence, of the statute of Virginia for religious freedom, and father of the University of Virginia." To his contemporaries in Europe he was regarded as second among Americans only to Benjamin Franklin in breadth of intellect and weight of achievement; more a philosopher than the ever practical Franklin, Jefferson approached closely the ideal of the universal, Renaissance man. He was elected to the Hall of Fame in 1900.

Jeffries, John (1745–1819), physician and balloonist. Born in Boston on February 5, 1745, Jeffries graduated from Harvard in 1763 and received his medical degree seven years later from Marischal College, Aberdeen, Scotland. After practicing in Boston for a short time he became a surgeon on a British naval vessel in 1771 and later worked in British military hospitals. Barred from America because of his Loyalist sympathies, he began to practice medicine in England and soon became interested in balloon flights. He made two notable flights in the company of the French aeronautical pioneer Jean Pierre (or François) Blanchard. During the first, on November 30, 1784, he made a number of careful observations with scientific instruments that he had procured at his own expense; they constitute the first scientific data obtained in the free air, to a height of more than 9000 feet, and accord well with modern observations. The second flight was the first aerial crossing of the English Channel. Jeffries and Blanchard set out from Dover on January 7, 1785. Halfway across, the balloon began to descend, and it was necessary to jettison all of the scientific instruments except the barometer; shortly thereafter even the outer clothes of the aeronauts and all of their food had to be thrown overboard. An updraft caught them near the French coast and they were carried safely inland to the forest of Guînes, near Ardres, after about three hours aloft. They were received with jubilation by the people and dignitaries of Calais and Paris, and Jeffries was complimented by Louis XVI and dined with Benjamin Franklin, the U.S. minister to France. Jeffries returned to his native Boston about 1790 and established a flourishing practice, dying there on September 16, 1819.

Jenney, William Le Baron (1832–1907), architect. Born on September 25, 1832, in Fairhaven, Massachusetts, Jenney attended Phillips Academy, Andover, then Harvard's Lawrence Scientific School and the École Centrale des Arts et Manufactures in Paris, graduating in 1856. Settling in New Orleans, he became for a time an engineer with the Tehuantepec Railroad Company, then returned to Paris to further his studies in architecture, remaining from 1859 to 1861. Returning to the United States, he enlisted in the Union army and served capably as an engineer, having earned the rank of major by 1866, when he resigned. He worked in Pennsylvania as an engineer until 1868. Then he established an architectural and engineering firm in Chicago, Jenney, Mundie, and Jensen. In his early buildings, mainly office structures, he strove to get maximum light and to make hallways and entrances as spacious and attractive as possible. His concepts were developed in *Principles and Practice of Architecture*, 1869. With the Home Insurance Building, his major contribution, built in 1884–1885, he inaugurated skeletal construction, an internal framework of iron and steel beams that supported the walls and roof of the building and determined its outer form. The forerunner of the skyscraper, it was the first structure of its kind to use steel as a building material and also introduced the best plumbing system yet developed in an office building of its size. He went on to design the Leiter Building in 1889–1890, the Fair store in 1890–1891, and other structures in Chicago, further developing steel skeletal construction. He was later honored by the Bessemer Steamship Company of New York, which recognized his service to the steel industry by naming one of their ships after him. In 1905 he retired and moved to Los Angeles, where he died on June 15, 1907.

Jessel, George Albert (1898–1981), entertainer. Born in New York City on April 3, 1898, Georgie Jessel was the son of a poor playwright. He left school after only six months to help support the family; his grandfather was a tailor, and the boy sang for the customers while they were waiting to have their pants pressed. He prevailed on his mother to arrange an audition at the theater in Harlem where she sold tickets, and he was engaged as a member of a trio of boys, all under ten, who sang in the theater pit because the law prohibited the appearance on the stage of performers under sixteen. Another member of the trio was Walter Winchell. Gus Edwards put Jessel in an act with Eddie Cantor when he was ten, and he toured for years, but by the time he was sixteen he was no longer a cute child and the act broke up. He went to England, but when he returned from London in 1917, he could not find work. Sitting around with "the boys" one afternoon, he called his mother on the telephone and proceeded to tell her funny stories about the day's happenings. His friends recognized this as the basis of an act, and he developed and used it for more than 40 years; he published an autobiography in 1946 under the title *Hello Momma*. He had his first big success in 1925, when he left vaudeville to play the straight lead in *The Jazz*

Singer, which endured for more than 1000 performances. He moved back and forth between the stage and Hollywood during the later 1920s and the 1930s and made some ventures into radio which were not particularly successful. A close friend of Mayor James J. "Jimmy" Walker, he was New York City's unofficial toastmaster for many years; indeed, he was perhaps best known as a master of ceremonies, a role in which he performed thousands of times, often for no fee (he celebrated his 1250th benefit appearance in New York City in 1943). He retired from the stage in 1943 and signed a contract with Twentieth Century–Fox as a producer and writer of musicals. Among his pictures were *The Dolly Sisters*, 1945; *Nightmare Alley*, 1947; *Dancing in the Dark*, 1949; *Golden Girl*, 1951; and *Wait 'Til the Sun Shines, Nellie*, 1952. He wrote a number of popular songs, published collections of after-dinner speeches, and learned to speak four languages. In later years he ceased to work in the theater but continued to serve as the country's "toastmaster general." He was given the Jean Hersholt Humanitarian Award of the Academy of Motion Picture Arts and Sciences in 1970. He died on May 24, 1981, in Los Angeles.

Jessup, Philip Caryl (1897–   ), lawyer, educator, and judge. Born on January 5, 1897, in New York City, Jessup graduated from Hamilton College in 1919 after an interruption of his studies for military service during World War I and went on to do graduate work at Yale and Columbia, receiving his Ll.B. degree from Yale in 1924, his Ph.D. from Columbia in 1927. He joined a New York City law firm in 1927, remaining with it until 1943. He had begun teaching at Columbia in 1925 as a lecturer on international law. He became a full professor in 1935 and was named Hamilton Fish Professor of International Law and Diplomacy in 1946. He served in the first of many posts as an adviser to the federal government on various matters of international law in 1924, when he was named an assistant solicitor in the Department of State; among his other important posts were those of assistant to Elihu Root at the Conference of Jurists on the Permanent Court of International Justice (the World Court) at The Hague, 1929; legal adviser to the American ambassador to Cuba, 1930–1931; assistant secretary-general of the United Nations Relief and Rehabilitation Administration (UNRRA), 1943; assistant secretary-general of the United Nations (UN) Monetary and Finance Conference at Bretton Woods, 1944; U.S. representative to the UN Committee on the Progressive Development of International Law and Its Codification, 1947; deputy U.S. representative to the United Nations, 1948–1952; and chairman of the Chile–Norway Permanent Conciliation Commission during the same period. He was named U.S. ambassador-at-large in 1949, a position from which he resigned in 1953. During the 1950s he suffered attacks by Senator Joseph R. McCarthy, but in 1961 he was appointed a judge of the International Court of Justice, one of the most prestigious juridical positions in the world. He resigned his Columbia professorship at that time. The recipient of many awards, honors, and decorations, both from U.S. institutions and from foreign governments, he was also the author of several influential books, including a two-volume biography of Elihu Root, 1938; *A Modern Law of Nations*, 1948; *Transnational Law*, 1956; *The Use of International Law*, 1959; and, with H. J. Taubenfeld, *Controls for Outer Space and the Antarctic Analogy*, 1959. He was in addition the author of a number of important articles in his field, and he served on the editorial boards of several law publications.

Jewett, Sarah Orne (1849–1909), author. Born on September 3, 1849, in South Berwick, Maine, Miss Jewett was often taken by her father, a physician, on visits to the fishermen and farmers of the area and developed an appreciation of their way of life and of the sights and sounds of her surroundings. These experiences, and reading in her family's ample library, formed the bulk of her education; although she also attended the Berwick Academy, she considered her schooling insignificant compared to the learning she gained on her own. During her childhood she began to write of the perishing farms and neglected, shipless harbors around her. She published her first story, "The Shipwrecked Buttons," in a children's magazine in 1869. Numerous later sketches of a New England town, "Deephaven," that resembled South Berwick, were published in the *Atlantic Monthly* and were collected in *Deephaven*, 1877, her first major book. There followed *A Country Doctor*, 1884; *A Marsh Island*, 1885; *A White Heron*, 1886; *A Native of Winby*, 1893, and other novels and collections of stories, children's books, and vignettes published in the *Century* and *Harper's* as well as in the *Atlantic*. Her best novel, *The Country of the Pointed Firs*, 1896, portrayed, like *Deephaven*, the isolation and loneliness of a declining seaport town and the unique humor of its people. The portrayal of this provincial and rapidly disappearing society made her an important local-color novelist, and in this she was a profound influence on Willa Cather. The best of her writing resembled nineteenth-century French fiction, especially that of Gustave Flaubert, whom she greatly admired, in its naturalism, precision, and compactness. She frequently visited Boston and other large cities, but lived and wrote in the same house in which she was born. Her writing career ended after a disabling accident in 1902. She died in South Berwick on June 24, 1909. Her collected poems were published posthumously as *Verses*, 1916.

Johns, Foster, *see* Seldes, Gilbert Vivian

Johnson, Albert Mussey, *see under* Scott, Walter Edward

Johnson, Alvin Saunders (1874–1971), economist, educator, and editor. Born on a farm near Homer,

Nebraska, on December 18, 1874, Johnson was descended on his mother's side from a long line of distinguished scholars that included the astronomer Tycho Brahe. He received his B.A. from the University of Nebraska in 1897 and his M.A. in 1898. After military service during the Spanish-American War he went to New York City to continue his study of economics at Columbia University, from which he received his Ph.D. in 1902. He taught at Bryn Mawr College in 1901–1902, at Columbia from 1902 to 1906, and at the universities of Nebraska, Texas, and Chicago and at Stanford and Cornell universities during the next 10 years. He returned to New York City in 1917 to become editor of the *New Republic*, of which he had been one of the founders, and during the next six years himself wrote much of the material published in the magazine. From 1919 he was associated with Thorstein Veblen, John Dewey, James Harvey Robinson, and Charles A. Beard, first as a cofounder and then as a teacher, in their work at the New School for Social Research, the youthful institution that they all thought could change the world by providing a solid education in politics and economics for adults. When it appeared that the work of the school would not be revolutionary in impact, many of his colleagues gradually lost interest, but Johnson, more pragmatic, agreed to become director of the school in 1923 and during the next 22 years helped it to develop into one of the most successful and influential institutions of adult education in the United States. He was instrumental in building its new and architecturally controversial building on West 12th Street in New York City in 1930 and defended the school ably against attacks from more traditional educators. Concerned from 1933 with the plight of refugee scholars from Hitler's Europe, Johnson in 1933 established the Graduate Faculty of Political and Social Science, a "university in exile" that served as a haven for many noted scholars and thinkers and eventually became a distinguished institution of graduate study in its own right. He retired from the New School in 1945, in his seventy-first year, but continued during the remaining 26 years of his long life to be intellectually active in many enterprises. He died on June 7, 1971, in Upper Nyack, New York. He published a number of books, among them an economics textbook in 1909; two novels, *The Professor and the Petticoat*, 1914, and *Spring Storm*, 1936; and a work about adult education, *The Public Library—a People's University*, 1938, as well as a large number of articles. *Progress: An Autobiography* appeared in 1952.

Johnson, Andrew (1808–1875), seventeenth president of the United States. Born in Raleigh, North Carolina, on December 29, 1808, Johnson received no formal education as a child and was early apprenticed to a tailor. In 1826 he moved with his mother and stepfather to Tennessee and settled at length in Greeneville, opening his own tailor shop. He had by that time taught himself to read;

his wife, Eliza McCardle, whom he married the following year, helped him to further his education. He became interested in politics and the cause of workingmen, was elected to local office, and served in the legislature in 1835-37, 1839-41, and 1841-43. In 1843, as a Jackson Democrat, he was elected to the House of Representatives, where he remained for ten years. In 1853, gerrymandered out of his district by Tennessee's Whig legislature, he ran successfully for governor and was reelected in 1855. During all those years he supported a number of democratic reforms, governmental economy, education, and, breaking with his party, a homestead program for settling Western lands. While he was no great friend of slavery, he supported it and denounced Abolitionists in deference to the interests of his constituents and as a matter of political regularity. In 1857 he was elected to the Senate, where he voted and spoke as an orthodox Southern Democrat until his sectional feelings were overridden by his devotion to the Union; he opposed secession and campaigned against it in his own state, and when Tennessee finally seceded in June 1861 he alone among Southern senators remained in his seat and refused to join the Confederacy. This action was hailed throughout the North and made Johnson a major political figure. In 1862 President Abraham Lincoln appointed him military governor of Tennessee with the rank of brigadier general, and in the face of strong opposition he managed to restore civil government to the state before the Civil War ended. In 1864 he was the obvious choice for the vice-presidential nomination on Lincoln's coalition Union (Republican) ticket; he was duly elected and on April 15, 1865, succeeded the assassinated Lincoln as president. The task before him was that of reconstructing the defeated Confederate states, and in this he wished to follow the policy of moderation that had been outlined by Lincoln and that he himself had applied in Tennessee. The Radical Republicans in Congress, released from the restraint of Lincoln's power and prestige, began formulating their own program. During 1865 Johnson oversaw the reestablishment of civil government in the South; ordinances of secession were formally repealed, and the Thirteenth Amendment was ratified in all but one of the former Confederate states. The issue of suffrage he left to state determination. In December Congress met and, under Radical leadership, began dismantling Johnson's program and substituting its own ideas of Negro suffrage and disenfranchisement of former Confederate soldiers. The Radical strength in both houses, enough to override any presidential veto, had, by late 1866 and in spite of Johnson's plea for moderation during that year's congressional elections, completely eclipsed executive authority. Radical Reconstruction began early in 1867; Johnson was faithful in administering laws that he was powerless to keep from the books, although he employed the narrowest possible interpretation of them in doing so. On March 2, 1867, the date of the first Reconstruction Act, Congress also passed the Tenure of Office Act, forbidding the president to dismiss any office-holder who had been appointed with the Senate's approval without obtaining senatorial concurrence in the dismissal. Passage of the act was a conscious effort by Congress to usurp presidential power. Convinced of the act's unconstitutionality and seeking to test it in the courts, Johnson asked for the resignation of Secretary of War Edwin M. Stanton, long a secret collaborator with congressional Radicals; Stanton refused to resign and Johnson suspended him, appointing Gen. Ulysses S. Grant to serve in his place. In January 1868, Congress restored Stanton, and in February Johnson dismissed him; on February 25 the president was formally impeached for "high crimes and misdemeanors." Johnson was defended by Benjamin R. Curtis, William M. Evarts, and others, while his accusers were represented by, among others, Thaddeus Stevens, George S. Boutwell, and Benjamin F. Butler. The trial, held in the Senate with Chief Justice Salmon P. Chase presiding, began on March 5, and although the eleven articles of impeachment dealt almost exclusively with the Tenure of Office Act, masses of irrelevant and even fraudulent charges and testimony turned the trial into a mockery—some of Johnson's enemies even wished to implicate him in the murder of Lincoln. Finally, on May 16 and May 26, votes were taken on three of the articles of impeachment, and seven Republicans joined the pro-Johnson men in acquitting the president; the vote was one short of the two-thirds majority needed for conviction. The other charges were then dropped. Other notable events of his administration were the purchase of Alaska from Russia in 1867 and the departure, under U.S. pressure, of French forces from Mexico in the same year. Johnson was an embittered, man when he left office in March 1869 and returned to Tennessee. As passions cooled, the impeachment came to be viewed generally as a mistake and an injustice. After several unsuccessful attempts, he was elected to the Senate in 1875; but less than five months after taking his seat he died, on July 31, 1875, near Carter Station, Tennessee.

Johnson, Eastman (1824–1906), painter. Born in Lovell, Maine, on July 29, 1824, Jonathan Eastman Johnson (he did not use his first name) began to attract notice with his crayon portraits at an early age. At sixteen he went to Boston and worked in a lithography shop and later drew crayon portraits in a number of cities, notably in Washington, D.C., where he set up an impromptu studio in one of the Senate committee rooms. He went abroad in 1849, studying first in Düsseldorf, where he was associated with Emanuel Leutze, then traveling in France and Italy and settling for four years at The Hague, where he became so accomplished that he was asked to become court painter. He returned to New York City in 1858, opened a studio, and soon gained a high reputation, winning election to the National Academy of Design within two years. He traveled in the South both before and after the Civil War in order to study Negro life and painted a series of genre pictures of great popularity, the best known of which was "Old Kentucky Home." Others included "Husking Bee," "Old Stage-Coach," and "Cranberry Pickers." He numbered among his sitters for portraits John Quincy Adams, Daniel Webster, Henry Wadsworth Longfellow, Ralph Waldo Emerson, William H. Vanderbilt, Edwin Booth, and presidents Chester A. Arthur, Grover Cleveland, and Benjamin Harrison. He never ceased to study and learn throughout his long life, and a self-portrait painted in 1899 was said to be technically superior to anything he had produced earlier. He died in New York City on April 5, 1906.

Johnson, Hiram Warren (1866–1945), public official. Born in Sacramento, California, on September 2, 1866, Johnson attended the University of California through the junior year, until he was twenty. In 1888 he was admitted to the California bar and began to practice law in Sacramento with his father, Grove Johnson, and his brother. He began a campaign of opposition to the political machine over which his father presided by working vigorously in behalf of a reform candidate for mayor. In 1902 he and his brother moved their practice to San Francisco, but he soon dissolved the partnership and became a prominent trial attorney. In 1906 he joined the successful prosecution in bribery cases connecting major city officials with the city's politically powerful public-utility corporations. In 1910, on a reform program, he was elected governor of California and won reelection in 1914. His administration was one of the most progressive in the nation and was successful in ending the domination of the state government by the Southern Pacific Railroad, for which his father was an attorney. In 1912 he ran for the vice-presidency on the ticket of the Bull Moose Progressive party, which with presidential candidate Theodore Roosevelt he had helped to organize, calling for a change in party machinery and for aggressive social legislation. Elected to the Senate in 1917, he earned a reputation for implacable isolationism. He was a leading contender for the 1920 Republican presidential nomination, which eventually went to Warren G. Harding. He opposed U.S. entry into World War I as well as the League of Nations and the World Court; he supported the neutrality acts of the 1930s, and later advocated a federal ban on loans to governments in default of their war debts. He was an opponent of such preparedness measures as conscription and Lend-Lease, and he also resisted the formation of the United Nations. Elected to a fifth Senate term in 1940, he died in Bethesda, Maryland, on August 6, 1945.

Johnson, Howard Deering (1896?–1972), businessman. Born in Boston, probably in 1896, Johnson left elementary school to aid in his father's failing cigar-importing business. He covered his sales route in a Stutz Bearcat automobile, carrying all sales information in his head at his father's insistence that he make no notes and remember customers' names. (Even when he headed a $100 million-a-year company, he still had no office or secretary.) He entered the food business in 1924 when he agreed to take over a run-down and debt-encumbered drugstore and soda fountain in Wollaston, Massachusetts. He concentrated first on selling newspapers there and soon had 75 boys delivering papers each morning, and then he turned to ice cream, investing $300 in the recipe of an elderly German immigrant whose product was highly regarded. (The secret, as he later divulged, was in doubling the customary butterfat content and using natural rather than artificial flavors.) He continued to expand his ice-cream business until he arrived at the magic figure of 28 flavors, which became a trademark of the restaurants that carry his name. The first of these was established in 1929 in southern Massachusetts. It was owned by a man named Reginald Sprague, who called it "Howard Johnson's" to capitalize on the fame of the ice cream and who signed a contract to buy food products supplied by Johnson exclusively. Johnson's foods set a high standard for the time, and the familiar white clapboard restaurants, trimmed with orange and blue and topped by a cupola, soon began to spring up along the major highways of the East Coast. Johnson insisted on cleanliness and, to insure a family trade, required that every franchisee have high chairs available for infants. By 1940 he had some 135 restaurants in operation in the New England states, New York, New Jersey, and Florida and was a millionaire. The gasoline rationing of the World War II years forced most of them to close. He survived by supplying food for workers in defense plants and by making candy and marmalade for the armed forces. After the war the chain of restaurants resumed growth at the rate of more than 25 a year, and motor lodges and a higher-priced chain of Red Coach Grills were added. The winning of exclusive food-service contracts for a great many turnpikes and other limited-access highways was a major factor in the firm's spectacular expansion. By the time he had retired in favor of his son, in 1964, the Howard Johnson chain was the third largest distributor of food in the United States, after the army and the navy. He died in New York City on June 20, 1972.

Johnson, Hugh Samuel (1882–1942), soldier, public official, and journalist. Born in Fort Scott, Kansas, on August 5, 1882, Johnson was brought up to the music of bugle calls and ran away from home at fifteen to join the Rough Riders. His father caught him on the railway platform and mollified him by promising that he could go to West Point. He graduated in 1903, the youngest in his class, and was commissioned a second lieutenant of cavalry. After years of routine military service, during which he published two books of boys' adventure stories, he was sent by the army to the University of California, where he earned a B.A. in 1915 and a doctor of jurisprudence degree the next year. In 1916 he was a member of

Gen. John J. Pershing's command during the Mexican Border Campaign but was soon transferred to Washington, where, as deputy provost marshal general, he devised and directed the conscription program during World War I. He also served on the War Industries Board, with Bernard Baruch, and headed the Purchase, Storage, and Traffic Division of the general staff. He resigned from the service in 1919, after having attained the rank of brigadier general, and entered business; among his activities was serving as an industrial and economic adviser to Baruch, who brought him to the notice of Governor Franklin D. Roosevelt of New York. Roosevelt appointed him director of the National Recovery Administration (NRA) in June 1933. Johnson struck Washington like a cyclone and became, with his gruff and forcefully direct manner, a particular favorite of the press, but he was not a good administrator, and he resigned from the NRA in 1934. His experiences were recounted, pithily, in *The Blue Eagle from Egg to Earth*, 1935. In that year, after a widely noted attack on Father Charles E. Coughlin and Senator Huey P. Long in a dinner speech, he was immediately signed to write a daily newspaper column for the Scripps-Howard syndicate. He accepted the job of director of the New York City branch of the Works Progress Administration (WPA) shortly thereafter, but he was unhappy with both the philosophy and the technicalities of the WPA, and he resigned after a few months. He turned against Roosevelt after the "courtpacking" incident of 1937 and continued in his column for the rest of his life to excoriate Roosevelt and the New Deal, charging that the United States was unprepared for war and urging national rearmament. In 1940 he violently opposed Roosevelt's attempt to win a third term in the White House, while he painted alarming pictures of the threat of a Fascist invasion of the United States. Johnson was also a popular lecturer and radio commentator. He died in Washington, D.C., on April 15, 1942.

Johnson, Jack (1878–1946), boxer. Born in Galveston, Texas, on March 31, 1878, John Arthur Johnson learned to box at the Galveston Athletic Club. In 1901 he was jailed for a time for fighting Joe Choynski—prize fighting being at that time illegal—and in his cell learned from Choynski much of the skill that would later make him the craftiest boxer of his time. From 1902 to 1908 he fought all over the country, losing only three bouts. After two years of trying he finally broke the color line in boxing by persuading world heavyweight champion Tommy Burns to accept his challenge. On December 26, 1908, in Sydney, Australia, Johnson knocked out Burns, becoming the first black boxer to win the title. The public outcry that followed became a call for a "white hope" to retrieve the title; James J. Jeffries, who had earlier quit boxing with an undefeated record, was coaxed out of retirement to meet Johnson. On July 4, 1910, in Reno, Nevada, the "Galveston Giant" ended all dispute with a decisive victory. His record purse of $120,000 was the beginning of the small fortune that he amassed in the next few years and that he almost as quickly spent in lavish living. The already shaken white boxing public was further alienated by his marriage to a white woman. In 1912 he was convicted of violating the Mann Act and, while free on bond, he fled to Canada and then to Europe. There he continued to fight and to live in kingly fashion. In 1915 he traveled to Havana, Cuba, to meet Jess Willard; in the twenty-sixth round of their title bout he lost the heavyweight crown; he later claimed to have thrown the fight. His wealth dissipated, he returned to the United States in 1920, surrendered himself on the 1912 conviction, and served a one-year sentence. After his release he fought a few more bouts and made numerous personal appearances at carnivals and in vaudeville theaters. He died in Raleigh, North Carolina, on June 10, 1946, following an automobile accident.

Johnson, James Weldon (1871–1938), author, social reformer, and editor. Born in Jacksonville, Florida, on June 17, 1871, Johnson attended Atlanta University for both his secondary and college education, there being no high school for Negroes in Jacksonville. He took his B.A. in 1894 and returned to his home city; he became principal of a Negro school there and organized a program of secondary education. At the same time he studied law and in 1897 was the first Negro to be admitted to the Florida bar. With his brother John Rosamond Johnson, a talented composer, he began to write songs and soon produced "Lift Every Voice and Sing," often called the Negro national anthem. In 1901 the brothers moved to New York City and for several years were successful songwriters for Broadway. Johnson continued his studies during this time and in 1904 was awarded an M.A. by Atlanta University; he later studied also at Columbia University. As a result of his efforts in the Republican presidential campaign of 1904, he was appointed by President Theodore Roosevelt U.S. consul in Puerto Cabello, Venezuela, in 1906; in 1909 he took charge of the consulate in Corinto, Nicaragua, and served there until 1912. In 1912 he published anonymously a novel, *Autobiography of an Ex-Colored Man*, reissued under his name in 1927. With the end of his diplomatic career he became editor of the *New York Age* and during a ten-year association with that newspaper continued his writing, publishing *Fifty Years and Other Poems* in 1917. In 1916 he joined the National Association for the Advancement of Colored People (NAACP) as a field secretary and he was highly effective in organizing new branches of the association throughout the country; from 1920, when he investigated charges of brutality by U.S. Marines in Haiti, until his resignation in 1930 he was its executive secretary. He was also active in agitating for anti-lynching legislation. In 1925 he was awarded the NAACP's Spingarn Medal. He was one of the leading spokesmen and interpreters of the cultural movement of the 1920s known as the Harlem Renaissance. In 1922 he published his *Book of American Negro Poetry*, an anthology, and in 1925 and 1926 two collections with the same title, *Book of American Negro Spirituals*; his prefatory and critical essays in these volumes were intelligent and influential appraisals of Negro contributions to American culture. In 1927 he published *God's Trombones*, a book of seven Negro folk sermons in verse. Johnson's later works include *Black Manhattan*, 1930, an informal history; *Saint Peter Relates an Incident of the Resurrection Day*, 1930, a verse satire on racial prejudice; and *Along This Way*, 1933, his distinguished and valuable autobiography. From 1930 until his death he was professor of creative literature at Fisk University and from 1934 was a regular visiting professor at New York University. He died in an automobile accident in Wiscasset, Maine, on June 26, 1938.

Johnson, John Arthur, *see* Johnson, Jack

Johnson, John Harold (1918–   ), publisher. Born in Arkansas City, Arkansas, on January 19, 1918, Johnson was educated in a segregated elementary school for Negroes there and in Chicago, where his mother took him in 1933—they were visiting the Century of Progress exposition and decided to stay. An honor student at Du Sable High School on the city's South Side, he worked on the school paper and as a consequence decided on journalism for a career. A speech before an Urban League convocation in 1936 led to his being asked by the president of the Supreme Liberty Life Insurance Company to join the firm as an office boy; Johnson worked his way up in the organization while studying at the University of Chicago and at Northwestern and began buying stock in it. By 1964 he was the principal stockholder and later became chairman of the board of what was reputed to be the largest black-owned business in the North. One of his first duties at Supreme Liberty Life had been to prepare a digest of news concerning American blacks for the company newspaper, an activity that led in 1942 to his independent founding of *Negro Digest*. The first issue of this black-oriented monthly sold some 3000 copies, but when Eleanor Roosevelt wrote for one of the regular features, titled "If I Were a Negro," circulation soared above 100,000, inspiring Johnson to consider another magazine. The first issue of *Ebony* appeared on the newsstands in November 1945, selling out its press run of 25,000 copies; the magazine passed the million mark in circulation in 1967. The Johnson Publishing Company also published two other magazines, *Tan*, from 1950, and *Jet*, from 1951, as well as books, and in the late 1960s was grossing more than $12 million a year. Johnson was especially successful in attracting advertisers to his periodicals; general consumer products were advertised in addition to ethnically oriented products, his magazines being the first in the country in which this occurred. Although some black militants were critical of *Ebony's* slowness to join the civil-rights movement of the 1950s and 1960s, others felt that the mere presence of the magazine on the newsstands should be considered a source of black pride, and Johnson was personally a strong supporter of the movement, giving liberally of time and money to various causes. Elected to the board of trustees of Tuskegee Institute in 1954, he was on the board of the Urban League from 1958 and received a number of honors from the black and white communities, including the Spingarn Medal of the National Association for the Advancement of Colored People (NAACP) in 1966.

Johnson, Jonathan Eastman, *see* Johnson, Eastman

Johnson, Lyndon Baines (1908–1973), thirty-sixth president of the United States. Born on a farm near Stonewall, Texas, on August 27, 1908, Johnson grew up there and in Johnson City, named for his grandfather. For three years after graduating from high school he worked at odd jobs at home and for a time in California; in 1927 he entered Southwest Texas State Teachers College and graduated in 1930. He taught high school in Houston for a year and then accepted an invitation to accompany a Texas congressman to Washington as a staff member. In 1934 he married Claudia Alta Taylor, who was known by her nickname Lady Bird and who proved a valuable companion throughout Johnson's career. In 1935 he was appointed Texas director of the National Youth Administration (NYA), a New Deal agency, and two years later, running as a New Deal Democrat, he was elected to the House of Representatives. For 11 years he represented his district, remaining relatively obscure but gaining valuable experience and guidance from his fellow Texan, Sam Rayburn. Early in World War II he served with the navy in the Pacific but returned to Washington when President Franklin D. Roosevelt recalled all legislators from the armed forces. In 1948, after a Democratic primary runoff election which he won by only 87 out of nearly a million votes, Johnson was elected to the Senate. His progress in that body was rapid; he became Democratic whip in 1951 and the Senate minority leader in 1953. Then and as majority leader after 1955—during which year he suffered a serious heart attack from which he recovered remarkably quickly—he demonstrated a mastery of the legislative process and of the problems of party discipline; although his policies of constructive cooperation with the Republican administration of President Dwight D. Eisenhower were debated within the party, the technical brilliance of his leadership was universally conceded. He was primarily responsible for securing passage of the Civil-Rights acts of 1957 and 1960 and supported extensions of social-welfare programs. In 1960 he mounted a strong campaign to win the Democratic presidential nomination; when John F. Kennedy was chosen instead, the nation was astonished by the choice of Johnson as Kennedy's running mate. Johnson was later credited with attracting enough Southern and Western support to Kennedy to enable the ticket to win over Republican Richard M. Nixon by a narrow margin. For the next two and a half years Johnson dutifully filled the often frustrating office of vice-president, serving at times as a U.S. emissary to other nations. Then, on November 22, 1963, Kennedy was assassinated in Dallas, Texas, and Johnson, who was accompanying him, was promptly sworn in as president. He quickly took the initiative and secured from Congress passage of legislation, notably measures dealing with civil rights, the schools, and the economically disadvantaged, earlier proposed by Kennedy. In August 1964, on the basis of a report, later shown to be highly dubious, of an attack by North Vietnamese forces on U.S. navy ships in the Gulf of Tonkin he ordered retaliatory air and sea action against the country and obtained from Congress the "Gulf of Tonkin resolution" giving him discretionary powers to respond with force to further provocations. Soon after his reelection in 1964, when he defeated Senator Barry M. Goldwater by the largest popular margin recorded, international affairs began to monopolize the attention of the administration and to divert both time and money from Johnson's proposals to create the "Great Society" at home. In April 1965 several thousand troops were dispatched to the Dominican Republic to meet the supposed danger of a Communist takeover in that country. Soon thereafter, with the Tonkin Gulf resolution as authority, the president ordered the beginning of a rapid buildup of U.S. forces in South Vietnam to prevent the defeat of the pro-Western regime there by the North Vietnamese and their Communist allies in the South, the Viet Cong guerrillas. Intensive bombing of the North was continued while hopes for a quick victory dimmed as the war dragged on through 1966 and 1967, and in the United States opposition to the administration's policy grew apace. Demonstrations against the war grew to unprecedented size and frequency and displayed increasing bitterness. Violent outbreaks became almost common and across the country there were numerous confrontations between antiwar activists and police. As a consequence, Johnson's popularity ebbed to such a degree that in March 1968, in the New Hampshire Democratic presidential primary, he outpolled his challenger, Senator Eugene J. McCarthy, by a margin so slim as to constitute a defeat for an incumbent. On March 31 he addressed the nation, announcing a reduction of the highly controversial bombing of North Vietnam and, in a move that stunned the nation, declaring that he would neither seek nor accept renomination, but utilize the remainder of his term in a nonpartisan search for peace. He did not, however, remain aloof from politics during his remaining time in the White House; his influence brought the Democratic nomination to his vice-president, Hubert H. Humphrey, at the tragically strife-ridden Democratic national convention in Chicago in August. In January 1969 he retired to his LBJ Ranch near Johnson City, Texas, to work on his memoirs and to aid in assembling the documents of his administration for the new Johnson library at the University of Texas. His *Vantage Point: Perspectives of the Presidency* was published in 1971. Johnson died at his ranch on January 22, 1973.

Johnson, Philip Cortelyou (1906–   ), architect. Born in Cleveland on July 8, 1906, Johnson grew up in New London, Ohio, and after attending Eastern preparatory schools graduated from Harvard in 1927. On a post-graduation trip to Europe he met the German architect Ludwig Mies Van Der Rohe and consequently determined to follow architecture as a profession. He became interested in a new and distinctive style in modern architecture, which he named and in the course of the next three decades promoted as the International Style, and he returned to the United States as an apostle of Mies. He studied and wrote articles about architecture, and in 1932 he was appointed chairman of the department of architecture of the Museum of Modern Art, in New York City, for which he planned a series of striking exhibits in which architectural and industrial arts were combined. He entered the Graduate School of Design at Harvard in 1940, where he studied under Marcel Breuer and, after building a controversial house in Cambridge, graduated in 1943. After service with the army engineers during World War II he returned to the Museum of Modern Art to merge its departments of architecture and industrial design and in 1953 he established design offices in New York City and New Canaan, Connecticut. He designed, among other structures, his own residence, the famous Glass House in New Canaan (1949); the Rockefeller Town House, New York (1950); the Museum of Modern Art Annex, together with its sculpture garden (1950–1954); the Oneto House, on the Hudson River (1952); the Hodgson House in New Canaan (1952); and the Port Chester (New York) Synagogue (1954). For most of these designs he won awards and prizes. Perhaps his most remarkable design was that of the Seagram Building in New York City (1956), a bronze skyscraper that rises 38 stories above a half-acre plaza with trees and pools; his collaborator in its design was Mies, who in the interim had moved to the United States. Johnson was associated with the planning of Lincoln Center for the Performing Arts in New York City, for which he designed the New York State Theater (1964), and, from 1958, was a trustee of the Museum of Modern Art. Among Johnson's writings on architecture were *The International Style* with H. R. Hitchcock, Jr., 1932; *Machine Art*, 1934; and *Mies van de Rohe*, 1947.

Johnson, Reverdy (1796–1876), lawyer and public official. Born on May 21, 1796, in Annapolis, Maryland, Johnson graduated from St. John's College in 1811 and five years later was admitted to the bar. Beginning his practice in Upper Marlboro in 1816, he served that year and the next as

deputy attorney general of Maryland; in 1817 he moved to Baltimore and in 1821 was elected as a Whig to the state senate. He was reelected in 1826 but resigned two years later to devote more time to his law practice. As a lawyer, Johnson became nationally prominent; he was a leading expert on constitutional law and appeared in a number of important cases before the Supreme Court, including *Brown* v. *Maryland*, 1827; the Wheeling Bridge cases, 1852 and 1856; *Seymour* v. *McCormick*, 1854, in which he and his colleague Thaddeus Stevens won firm confirmation of Cyrus McCormick's reaper patent; and, for the defense, *Dred Scott* v. *Sanford*, 1857, in which he was credited with major influence in securing a decision against the slave Scott on grounds that as a non-citizen he had no legal standing. In 1845 he was elected to the Senate, where he was a generally regular Whig; he served until 1849 when President Zachary Taylor appointed him attorney general. He joined in the mass resignation of the cabinet following Taylor's death in 1850. He soon allied himself with the Democratic party and in 1860 and 1861 was again in the Maryland legislature, where he led the fight to keep Maryland in the Union. In 1862 he was sent by President Abraham Lincoln to investigate complaints against the military governor of New Orleans and in 1863, upon his return, he again entered the Senate. During five years in that body he exhibited so mediatory an approach to vital issues that he was known as "the Trimmer." He was by turns moderate and radical on Reconstruction; he opposed Negro suffrage but voted for the Fourteenth Amendment; he sought a quick end to military occupation of the South but later voted for the bill that organized military government by district there. He voted for acquittal in the impeachment trial of President Andrew Johnson. He was chief defense counsel in the trial of Mary Surratt and others for complicity in the assassination of President Lincoln. In 1868 he resigned from the Senate to succeed Charles Francis Adams as U.S. minister to Great Britain and in a year of service in that post performed creditably, although the agreements he negotiated for the settlement of various disputes were not ratified. In 1869 he returned to his Maryland practice; he pleaded for the defense in a number of loyalty cases and won an acquittal in *U.S.* v. *Cruikshank*, 1876, a landmark case that established a narrow construction of an 1870 civil rights enforcement act. He died on February 10, 1876, in Annapolis, Maryland.

Johnson, Richard Mentor (1780–1850), vice-president of the United States. Born in Beargrass, an early settlement on the site of present-day Louisville, Kentucky, in 1780, Johnson received little formal education, but he studied law under professors at Transylvania University and was admitted to the bar in 1802. In 1804 he was elected to the state legislature and served there until 1807, when he entered the House of Representatives, to which he was reelected as a Democrat five successive times. With the outbreak of the War of 1812 he became the colonel of a Kentucky regiment of mounted riflemen; serving under Gen. William Henry Harrison, he performed gallantly at the battle of the Thames in 1813, sustaining serious wounds and reputedly killing Tecumseh. He returned to his seat in the House as soon as he recovered and in 1818 was honored by a congressional resolution and the presentation of a ceremonial sword. The following year he retired from the House and was elected to the Kentucky legislature and subsequently by that body to the Senate, where he served for ten years. He was a leading advocate of the abolition of imprisonment for debt, and he kept up a campaign to that end until the Senate approved his bill in 1832. He also added to his national reputation by his authorship in 1829 of a committee report on religious freedom occasioned by a heated public controversy over the propriety of operating post offices on Sunday. He was defeated for reelection in 1829 but was elected instead to the House of Representatives. He was a thoroughly regular Democrat and an even more regular supporter of President Andrew Jackson; he was a close and trusted assistant to the President and in 1836 was hand-picked by him to be Martin Van Buren's running mate. His selection for the vice-presidential nomination was ratified by the party, but in the election none of the four candidates for vice-president received a majority of the electoral vote. In the only such occasion in U.S. history, Johnson was chosen for the post by the Senate. His four-year term was uneventful, but he became estranged from party leaders and in 1840 the party refused to make a nomination for vice-president. He returned to Kentucky, served again for a brief time in the legislature, and died in Frankfort on November 19, 1850.

Johnson, Thomas (1732–1819), justice of the Supreme Court. Born in Calvert County, Maryland, on November 4, 1732, Johnson came of a family long prominent in England and in Maryland. Educated at home, he was sent by his family to Annapolis to study law and was elected a delegate to the provincial assembly in 1762. He early opposed the colonial policies of the British Parliament and was appointed to several committees of remonstrance against them. A delegate to the Maryland convention in Annapolis in 1774, he was chosen as one of the members charged with organizing a colonial congress, and he represented Maryland when the First Continental Congress met in Philadelphia in September 1774. A member of the Second Continental Congress as well, he was chosen to nominate George Washington as commander in chief of the Continental army; this was but the first of many occasions on which he indicated his deep loyalty to and enormous respect for Washington. He supported reconciliation with Great Britain as long as that seemed possible, but, although he was not in Philadelphia on the day the Declaration of Independence was adopted, he voted for the declaration in Maryland on July 6, 1776. He was a member of the convention of 1776 that framed the first constitution of the state of Maryland and was chosen as first brigadier general of the state militia. He raised and equipped recruits and led a contingent from Frederick, Maryland, to Washington's New Jersey headquarters in 1777. He was elected first governor of Maryland in February 1777 and was reelected in November 1777 and again in 1778. After serving in the Maryland legislature until the end of the war, he joined with Washington in a project to extend the navigation of the Potomac River. Again in the legislature in 1786–1787, he was in 1788 a strong supporter of the new Constitution and worked for its ratification in Maryland. In 1790–1791 he served as chief judge of the General Court of Maryland; nominated by President Washington to the Supreme Court in 1791, he took the oath of office a year later. He had also in 1791 been named to the board of commissioners of the Federal City, and it was largely his decision to name it Washington. He resigned from the Supreme Court in 1793 and from the commission the following year, owing to failing health, a condition that also forced him in 1795 to decline Washington's request that he become secretary of state. He died at his home, Rose Hill, near Frederick, Maryland, on October 26, 1819, convinced that he would rejoin his idol beyond the grave.

Johnson, Tom Loftin (1854–1911), inventor, businessman, public official, and social reformer. Born near Georgetown, Kentucky, on July 18, 1854, Johnson came of a family impoverished by the Civil War. Moving from place to place, they settled for a time in Staunton, Virginia, where young Tom helped to recoup the family fortunes by establishing a newspaper-selling monopoly on the only train that stopped there. The family moved to Louisville, Kentucky, where he was employed in 1869 by the Louisville Street Railroad, for which he produced his first invention, a farebox for coins. The railroad was partly owned by the Du Pont family, with whose backing he later bought and rehabilitated the Indianapolis Street Railroad. From Indianapolis he moved to Cleveland, where he bought and operated another street railway and became involved in the establishment of several steel works. He produced important inventions for use in the railroad and steel industries and carried on a brisk competition with Mark Hanna in Cleveland until he sold out his interests in order to enter politics. He had earlier read Henry George's *Progress and Poverty* and had become a dedicated single-taxer and free-trader, and he proclaimed this faith even as he was elected to the House of Representatives as a Democrat in 1890 and 1892. He joined with other single-taxers to build a home for George in Brooklyn, New York, supported the great reformer in his two New York City mayoral campaigns, and continued to aid liberal economic and social causes for the rest of his life, including woman suffrage. He was elected mayor of Cleveland in 1901 and reelected three times. During eight years in office he virtually revolutionized the city government and is held to have been the outstanding mayor produced in the country up to that time. He conceived his task as primarily one of educating the electorate and to that end held meetings in an enormous circus tent during which public affairs were discussed by, and in the presence of, audiences numbering several thousand people. His slogan was "Home rule; three-cent fare; and just taxation," and he devoted himself especially to securing municipal ownership of the street-railway system. He was defeated for reelection in 1909 and died in Cleveland two years later, on April 10, 1911; in the same year his autobiography, *My Story*, with E. J. Hauser, was published. During his mayoralty Johnson became perhaps the best known urban populist-reformer in the nation and, at a time when muckrakers were exposing corruption virtually everywhere, Cleveland was considered to be the best-governed city in the United States.

Johnson, Walter Perry (1887–1946), baseball player and manager. Born on November 6, 1887, in Humboldt, Kansas, Johnson drifted to the West Coast when he was eighteen and was soon offered a contract to play baseball with a team in Tacoma, Washington. He did not accept, but in 1907 he signed with the Washington Senators of the American League. During the next 21 years, a record length of service with a single major-league team, he pitched 802 games, won 414, and set more than 40 other records; he recorded 113 shutouts (in 1908 pitching 3 in 4 days) and 3497 strikeouts, and pitched a total of 5923 innings. In one period in 1913 he pitched 56 consecutive scoreless innings, a record that stood for 55 years; in 1913 he won 36 games while losing only 7. His 414 victories—the second-highest total ever achieved by a pitcher and the highest of any pitcher in the twentieth century—were the more remarkable for having been gained for a perennial second-division team. His fast ball was the principal weapon in his arsenal and it was considered to be the fastest of all time, earning him the nickname "Big Train." In 1924 he was voted the American League's most valuable player. After his retirement from playing in 1927 he managed the Senators from 1929 to 1932 and the Cleveland Indians from 1933 to 1935. In 1936 he was one of the first five men chosen for membership in the National Baseball Hall of Fame. Johnson served for a time as president of the Association of Professional Baseball Players and appeared on radio as a sports broadcaster. He later became prominent in Republican politics in Maryland and in 1940 ran unsuccessfully for the House of Representatives. He died in Washington, D.C., on December 10, 1946.

Johnson, Sir William (1715–1774), colonial official. Born in County Meath, Ireland, in 1715, Johnson had come to America by early 1738, in which year he was managing an estate in the Mohawk Valley of New York that belonged to his uncle, Sir Peter Warren. In 1739 he purchased a tract of land of his own, the first in a series of acquisitions that continued throughout his life and finally resulted in his possessing one of the largest landed estates in the colonies. He set about developing his properties with great energy, engaged successfully in the fur trade, and made it his business to cultivate the friendship of the Indians of the Six Nations, particularly the Mohawk, who were his neighbors. In 1745 he was able to restrain the Six Nations from allying with the French in King George's War; in consequence he was appointed colonel of the Six Nations and given responsibility for their affairs by Gov. George Clinton in 1746. His affairs prospered in the later 1740s, and he was appointed a member of the Council of New York in 1750, a post he held for the rest of his life. In spite of the protests of the Indians, he resigned as manager of the affairs of the Six Nations following a dispute with the New York assembly, but he continued as an unofficial adviser both to the tribes and to the colonial government. He was persuaded to take up duties with the Indians again by Gen. Edward Braddock in 1755, a year that saw the resumption of the French and Indian Wars, and he was at the same time commissioned a major general and placed in command of the British force sent against Crown Point. At Lake George, on September 8, 1755, he was attacked by a force of French and Indians under Baron Ludwig August Dieskau. Johnson soundly defeated the force led by Dieskau, but he failed to capture Crown Point. His victory over Dieskau made him a hero, however. George II made him a baronet in November 1755, and the next year he was named sole agent and superintendent of the affairs of the Six Nations, a superintendent also being appointed for the tribes south of the Ohio River. He devoted himself in the years that followed to protecting the northern frontiers; he was in charge of the force that finally took Niagara on July 25, 1759, and he joined Gen. Jeffery Amherst in his successful attack on Montreal the next year. The fall of Canada brought a vast new territory and many strange tribes under his jurisdiction, and even with the able assistance of his deputy, George Croghan, he was often overwhelmed by the difficulty of his task. He favored a centralized and independent Indian department as well as centralized control of the fur trade, and he attempted to restrain settlement by whites in Indian hunting grounds and even advocated the drawing of an Indian boundary beyond which whites were not to pass, although he found an attempt to do so in the Proclamation of 1763 unworkable, and in 1768 negotiated the treaty of Fort Stanwix, which pushed the settlement line west to the Tennessee River. His many friendly negotiations with Indian leaders resulted in vast increases in his own estates, but he nevertheless respected the Indians and worked for a resolution of differences advantageous to both sides. He supported education for

Indians and missionary activities among them, and he never ceased to be held by the Indians themselves in high esteem, in part because of the genuine interest manifested in his command of their language and adoption of their clothing and customs. After the death of his first wife he took an Indian woman named Caroline, who was the niece of a Mohawk chief, as his housekeeper, and by her had three children; she was succeeded by Molly Brant, sister of Joseph Brant, by whom he had eight children. When Lord Dunmore's War broke out in Virginia in 1774, he was called upon again to try to keep the Six Nations from becoming involved. On July 11, 1774, at his home, Johnson Hall, shortly after giving a long speech to the Indians in reply to their complaints about white encroachments and the Indian trade, he was taken ill and died.

Johnson, William (1771–1834), justice of the Supreme Court. Born in Charleston, South Carolina, on December 27, 1771, Johnson graduated from Princeton in 1790 and, after reading law with Charles Cotesworth Pinckney, was admitted to the bar in 1793. Departing politically from his Federalist mentor, he aligned himself with the new Jeffersonian Republican (Democratic Republican) party and was elected three times to the South Carolina legislature between 1794 and 1798, in his last term serving as speaker. In December 1798 he was elected to the state's highest court, where he remained until his appointment to the U.S. Supreme Court in 1804 by President Thomas Jefferson, who hoped to counter the control of the Court by Chief Justice John Marshall, a Federalist. Johnson's 30 years on the Court were marked by a protracted struggle with Marshall, who, in trying to make the Court the acknowledged spokesman of the law and the Constitution, not only wrote the opinions in important cases but also sought the unanimous support of his colleagues for them. After 1811, although only two Federalists remained on the seven-man bench, Marshall continued to dominate the Court's decisions in most major cases. Nevertheless, Johnson managed to create a tradition of dissent, partly at Jefferson's insistence; he wrote to Jefferson in 1822 that, despite many difficulties, he had finally managed to prevail upon the justices "to adopt the course they now pursue which is to appoint someone to deliver the opinion of the majority, and leave it to the discretion of the rest to record their opinions or not *ad libitum*." After Marshall's opinions, those of Johnson were the most numerous in the early years of the Court, and his emphasis on the government's power to control economic affairs anticipated later developments. As was then the custom, Johnson continued to hold circuit court in Charleston while serving on the Supreme Court, and his judicial independence was shown in decisions in which he declared illegal several federal and state measures. Although he was deeply concerned for individual rights, his impetuous manner nevertheless often involved him in controversy. He moved from South Carolina to Pennsylvania in 1833, partly because of his opposition to nullification, and died, following surgery, in Brooklyn, New York, on August 4, 1834.

Johnson, William Samuel (1727–1819), public official and educator. Born in Stratford, Connecticut, on October 7, 1727, Johnson was the son of Samuel Johnson (1696–1772), Anglican clergyman and first president of King's College in New York City. He graduated from Yale in 1744 and in 1747 received an A.M. from Harvard; he then read law and within a short time became a leading member of the Connecticut bar. He was elected to the lower house of the Connecticut colonial assembly in 1761 and 1765 and sat in the upper house from 1766 until the Revolution. Although he joined in opposing some of the more flagrantly ill-conceived acts of Parliament, attending the Stamp Act Congress in 1765 and later supporting the non-importation movement, he was by temperament and conviction a conservative and during his term as Connecticut's colonial agent in London in 1767–1771 he formed even closer ties with the mother country, along with friendships with Dr. Samuel Johnson and other prominent figures. In 1771 he returned to his seat in the Connecticut assembly and was also named a judge of the superior court, but his lack of sympathy with the more radical Whigs, culminating in his refusal to serve as a delegate to the Continental Congress when elected in 1774, led to his retirement from public life. During the Revolution he was widely thought to entertain Loyalist leanings and in 1779 he was briefly detained on suspicion of corresponding with the British, but his stolid integrity continued nonetheless to command respect. In 1784 he was elected to the Congress under Articles of Confederation, where he remained until 1787, when he was chosen a Connecticut delegate to the Constitutional Convention. There his tact, moderation, and eloquence had considerable effect, particularly in the debate between the large and small states over representation. After signing the Constitution he returned to Connecticut to work for its ratification and in 1789 was elected one of the state's first senators. He had also been chosen in 1787 the first president of Columbia College, successor to the King's College of his father's day. In 1791, after the federal government moved from New York City to Philadelphia, he resigned from the Senate in order to continue to devote his efforts to the college, which flourished under his guidance. He resigned the presidency for reasons of health in 1800 and retired to Stratford, Connecticut, where he died on November 14, 1819.

Johnston, Albert Sidney (1803–1862), soldier Born in Washington, Kentucky, on February 2, 1803, Johnston was appointed to West Point in 1822 and on graduating four years later was commissioned in the infantry. After a series of posts —including service as a regimental adjutant in the Black Hawk War—he resigned his commission in 1834 because of the illness of his wife.

After her death the next year he tried farming near St. Louis but soon gave it up and went to Texas, where he enlisted as a private in the Texas army. His progress upward was swift. Within a year he had been appointed adjutant general and, as senior brigadier general, he assumed command of the army in 1837. His rapid rise aroused the jealousy of a rival who challenged him to a duel in which he was seriously wounded. He was well again by the end of 1838, when he was appointed secretary of war of the Republic of Texas. However, he fell out with Gen. Sam Houston and resigned in 1840, taking up farming at China Grove, in Brazoria County, where he suffered financial difficulties. Upon the outbreak of the Mexican War he offered his services, was commissioned a colonel in the Texas Volunteers and in 1849 a major in the U.S. army, and in 1855 assumed command of a cavalry regiment whose lieutenant colonel was Robert E. Lee. He was appointed commandant of the Department of Texas in 1856 and in the next year conducted a successful and bloodless campaign against the Mormons in Utah. He sailed to San Francisco at the end of 1860 to take command of the Department of the Pacific, but when Texas seceded from the Union a few months later he resigned his commission, although he continued to serve until relieved. Offered the position of second in command of the Union army under Gen. Winfield Scott, he refused and returned to the South. Jefferson Davis appointed him the second-ranking general in the Confederate army and placed him in command of the Western Department. He set about creating an army in Kentucky to defend the Confederacy's vulnerable flank there, but he was hindered by his inability to obtain enough troops or supplies. At the hands of Gen. Ulysses S. Grant and other Union commanders he suffered a series of reverses in engagements—Fort Henry, Fort Donelson, Nashville, Murfreesboro—in which his men were usually heavily outnumbered. He finally gained a celebrated victory over Grant at the battle of Shiloh (Pittsburg Landing) in Tennessee, where, on April 6, 1862, he struck a surprise blow at a strong Union position and rolled back Grant's men until they broke in rout and withdrew to the Tennessee River. He was mortally wounded, however, and died that day on the field. Bereft of his leadership and facing freshly reinforced Union troops, the Confederate forces were compelled to retire on the second day of the battle.

Johnston, Joseph Eggleston (1807–1891), soldier. Born near Farmville, Virginia, on February 3, 1807, Johnston graduated from West Point in 1829. For eight years he served as an artillery officer, seeing action in the Seminole War, and then resigned in 1837 to become a civil engineer. A year later renewed Indian troubles in Florida brought him back into the army as a lieutenant in the topographical engineers. He performed with distinction under Gen. Winfield Scott during the Mexican War and by 1860 he had attained the rank of brigadier general and was quartermaster general

of the army. He resigned his commission when Virginia seceded from the Union and offered his services to his native state. He was named brigadier general of the Confederate forces and placed in command of the Army of the Shenandoah. In July 1861 he evaded the Union force that was intended to tie him down at Harpers Ferry and joined Gen. P. G. T. Beauregard at the first battle of Bull Run (Manassas); he was the ranking officer at this first major Confederate victory and was subsequently promoted to general and placed in command of the Army of Northern Virginia. The next spring he was charged with opposing Gen. George B. McClellan's drive on Richmond in the Peninsular Campaign. Johnston withdrew toward Richmond, fighting a rearguard action at Williamsburg and then making a poorly coordinated attack at Fair Oaks (Seven Pines), during which he was badly wounded. Upon his recovery in November 1862 he was placed in command of the Department of the West. In May 1863 he took personal command as Gen. Ulysses S. Grant threatened Vicksburg; his evacuation order to Gen. J. C. Pemberton at Vicksburg was countermanded by Jefferson Davis, and Johnston, cut off from the city, could only watch as Vicksburg surrendered in July. In December he took command of the Army of Tennessee; his force, too weak to move northward, entrenched itself near Dalton, Georgia, awaiting attack by Gen. William T. Sherman's forces from the north. Sherman preferred to maneuver and Johnston, outnumbered and outflanked, found himself forced to retreat slowly toward Atlanta. Only one battle stood out from the constant skirmishing and in that, at Kennesaw Mountain, Johnston was victorious for the moment. In July 1864, with his back to Atlanta, he was replaced in command by Gen. John B. Hood. In February 1865 Gen. Robert E. Lee restored him, with orders to oppose Sherman's march northward through the Carolinas. After two months of maneuvers and minor engagements he was forced to surrender to Sherman on April 26 at Durham Station, North Carolina. In the years following the war he engaged in the insurance business in Savannah, Georgia, and in 1878 was elected to a term in the House of Representatives from Richmond, Virginia. He remained in Washington, D.C., thereafter and in 1885 was appointed U.S. railroad commissioner by President Grover Cleveland. Johnston died on March 21, 1891, in Washington, D.C.

Jolliet, Louis (1645–1700), explorer. Jolliet (or, less commonly, Joliet) was baptized in or near Quebec City, Canada, on September 21, 1645, but little is known about his early years. In 1669 the French intendant, Jean Talon, dispatched Jolliet on a supplying expedition to Lake Superior; on that journey he first met Father Jacques Marquette and on the return he made the first traverse from the upper Great Lakes into Lake Erie by way of the Detroit River. In the fall of 1672 he was chosen by Talon to investigate the Indians' accounts of a great river, called by the Indians the

Mississippi, which the French—although probably not the Indians—thought emptied into the "South Sea" (the Pacific). In the spring of 1673 Jolliet embarked at Sault Ste. Marie and went to Michilimackinac (now St. Ignace, Michigan), where he was joined by Father Jacques Marquette. With five companions they left St. Ignace on May 17 and, in two birchbark canoes, coasted around Lake Michigan to Green Bay, and then, guided by Indians, followed the Fox River into central Wisconsin. They made a portage (at Portage, Wisconsin) to the Wisconsin River and then followed it downstream until it joined the Mississippi, which they reached on June 17, 1673. They descended the Mississippi to the mouth of the Arkansas River, where they turned back, in part because they feared that they would meet opposition from Spanish settlers on the lower river but also because they had come to the conclusion, from their observations and from information supplied by friendly Indians, that the Mississippi must flow not into the Pacific but into the Gulf of Mexico. Starting their return journey on July 17, they proceeded to the Illinois River, which they ascended, visiting the Illinois Indians and portaging at the site of present-day Chicago in order to reach Lake Michigan. In the Lachine Rapids near Montreal Jolliet's canoe overturned and his journal and papers were lost. He later made a map from memory that agrees well with a map made by Father Marquette. Jolliet explored Hudson Bay in later years and also charted the Labrador coast. He was rewarded for his achievements by the gift of Anticosti Island, in the Gulf of St. Lawrence, on which he built a fort that was destroyed by the British in 1691. An excellent mapmaker, he was appointed royal hydrographer of New France, probably in 1697. He died in 1700 on one of the islands (possibly Anticosti) in the St. Lawrence. The city of Joliet, Illinois, is named after him. Because of the loss of his papers, Marquette's report, rather than Jolliet's, became the official account of the Mississippi expedition, and as a result Marquette has gained a disproportionate share of the credit for the first exploration by white men of "the Father of Waters," as the Indians called the Mississippi.

Jolson, Al (1886–1950), entertainer. Born on May 26, 1886, in or near St. Petersburg (now Leningrad), Russia, Asa Yoelson was the son of a Jewish cantor. He arrived in the United States at seven and grew up in Washington, D.C., where he made his stage debut. He appeared in *The Children of the Ghetto* in New York's Herald Square Theatre in 1899, and traveled in vaudeville and circus acts, performing for a time with Jolson, Palmer, and Jolson, composed of himself, a friend, and his brother. In Brooklyn, New York, about 1909, he first sang in blackface, thereafter his trademark. In that year he signed with Lew Dockstader's minstrel company and, moving rapidly to phenomenal success as a singer and entertainer, he appeared in the Broadway musical comedies *La Belle Paree*, 1911, and *Honeymoon*

Express, 1913. Some of his greatest performing triumphs were scored with songs introduced in Lee Shubert's Winter Garden shows in New York City, among them *Sinbad*, 1918; *Bombo*, 1921; *Big Boy*, 1925; and *Artists and Models*, 1926. By 1921 he was considered the country's top entertainer and was one of the few stars to have had a theater named in his honor. His motion-picture debut was in *The Jazz Singer*, 1927, the first feature length talking picture. He also appeared in *The Singing Fool*, 1928, *Say It With Songs*, 1929, and other movies, and sang the sound tracks for two screen accounts of his life, *The Jolson Story*, 1946, and *Jolson Sings Again*, 1949. In these were featured his standards, including "You Made Me Love You," "Waiting for the Robert E. Lee," "I Want a Girl Just Like the Girl That Married Dear Old Dad," "April Showers," "Rock-a-Bye Your Baby with a Dixie Melody," "Swanee," and "My Mammy." He collaborated on writing many of his hits, including "Back in Your Own Back Yard," "California, Here I Come," "Me and My Shadow," "Sonny Boy," "There's a Rainbow 'Round My Shoulder," and "You Ain't Heard Nothin' Yet," the last inspired by his favorite remark to his audiences. He was on radio at various times, including a stint in 1934 as the original host of the Kraft Music Hall. He sang on virtually every war front during World War II and had just returned to San Francisco after visiting U.S. toops in the Korean War when he died, on October 23, 1950.

Jones, Bobby (1902–1971), golfer. Born in Atlanta, Georgia, on March 17, 1902, Robert Tyre Jones, Jr. began to play golf in his childhood. He won a junior tournament when he was only nine, and at fourteen he advanced as far as the third round of the 1916 U.S. National Amateur tournament. While pursuing his education—he graduated from the Georgia School (now Institute) of Technology in 1922, took a second degree in English literature from Harvard in 1924, and studied law at Emory University in 1926–1927—he became one of the most idolized sports heroes of the 1920s, in so doing also firmly establishing the popularity of golf in the United States. The U.S. Open of 1923 was the first major tournament he won; he subsequently won the Open in 1926, 1929, and 1930, the U.S. Amateur in 1924, 1925, 1927, 1928, and 1930, and the British Open in 1926, 1927, and 1930. His feat in 1930 of winning the "Grand Slam" of golf, the Open and Amateur tournaments in both the United States and Great Britain, has never been duplicated. He won in all a record total of 13 major championships. In 1922, 1924, 1926, 1928, and 1930 he was a member of the U.S. Walker Cup team. Following the 1930 season he made a series of golf instructional films, thus relinquishing his amateur standing, and with no further heights to reach he retired from the game. Having been admitted to the Georgia bar in 1928, he opened a law practice in Atlanta and also helped establish the Augusta National Golf Club. In 1934 he founded the annual Masters Tournament at Augusta; it became one of the most prestigious in the country. Confined to a wheel chair after suffering a spinal injury in 1948, he continued to manage various business interests from his Atlanta home. In 1958 he became the first American since Benjamin Franklin to be honored with the freedom of the burgh of St. Andrews, Scotland, site of the world's most famous golf course. *Golf Is My Game* appeared in 1960. Jones died in Atlanta, Georgia, on December 18, 1971.

Jones, Casey (1864–1900), railroad engineer. Born on March 14, 1864, near Cayce, Kentucky, John Luther Jones was known throughout life as "Casey," after his hometown. At sixteen he went to work for the railroad and by 1890 had become an engineer for the Illinois Central. On the night of April 29, 1900, according to the story later generally accepted, although never fully authenticated, he pulled into Memphis, Tennessee, on the "Cannonball Express" and learned that the engineer scheduled for the return run was ill. He immediately volunteered to replace him and at about 11 P.M. pulled out of Memphis. Highballing along to make up for lost time, he was near Vaughan, Mississippi, when, at about 4 o'clock on the morning of April 30, he spied a freight train stopped on the tracks ahead. He shouted to his fireman "Jump, Sim, and save yourself," and rode the engine into the collision. His body was found in the wreckage, one hand on the whistle cord and the other on the brake. Casey's name was immortalized by a friend, a black roundhouse worker named Wallace Saunders, who wrote a ballad memorializing his deed. By means of the song, later embellished by others and eventually sung in many variant versions, Casey Jones became the hero of railroad men and of portions of the labor movement in the early twentieth century. In 1938 a bronze tablet was dedicated to his memory in Cayce.

Jones, Charles Jesse (1844–1918), "Buffalo," buffalo hunter and game warden. Born in Illinois in 1844, Buffalo Jones received an education in the frontier country of Illinois and Kansas that was as rough as it was scanty. By the 1860s he had become a renowned buffalo hunter, "slaying his thousands," as a nineteenth-century report put it, for their hides. It was in the summer of 1872 that the thought first occurred to him that the buffalo might have some other use than providing rugs, and that same year he captured some 12 to 15 bison. In 1886, when buffalo had become extremely scarce, "Colonel" Jones (as he was also called) was crossing the plains from Kansas to Texas and saw how thousands of domesticated cattle had dropped dead in their tracks in the face of a recent blizzard; but on his reaching an area frequented by buffalo, "every animal," he wrote, "was as well and wiry as a fox." He determined to capture bison calves and cross them with cattle to produce a hardier breed. During the next several years he managed to round up several dozen calves and by the end of the century

appeared to have established the new breed; which he named "cattalo," and by 1898 there were in existence more than 500 head whose lineage was traceable to the efforts of Buffalo Jones. In 1897 a similar project planned for Alaskan musk oxen was thwarted when the Eskimos refused to allow him to take live animals out of their territory. Known to every big-game hunter from one end of the country to the other and a personal friend of President Theodore Roosevelt, he was named game warden of Yellowstone National Park in 1902 and was the most notable figure at the Madison Square Garden Sportsmens' Show in New York City in 1904. He died in 1918.

Jones, John Luther, *see* Jones, Casey

Jones, John Paul (1747–1792), sea captain and naval officer. Born in Kirkcudbrightshire, Scotland, on July 6, 1747, John Paul (who later changed his name) received little schooling and at the age of twelve was apprenticed to a merchant shipper. He sailed as a cabin boy to Fredericksburg, Virginia, and there visited his elder brother, a tailor. In 1766 his apprenticeship ended when his master's business failed and for two years he shipped in the slave trade. By 1769 he had his own command, the merchant ship *John;* the following year he flogged the ship's carpenter, who then shipped on another vessel and soon died, and in Scotland Paul was arrested for murder. He was cleared, but in 1773, again commanding a ship in the West Indian trade, he killed the leader of a mutiny. Advised to flee, he returned to Fredericksburg and added "Jones" to his name. With the outbreak of hostilities between Great Britain and the American colonies he traveled to Philadelphia and in December 1775 was commissioned senior lieutenant of the Continental navy. Assigned to the *Alfred,* the first naval vessel on which the Grand Union flag was flown, he sailed with the small fleet under the command of Esek Hopkins to the Bahamas early in 1776; his knowledge of the islands aided greatly in the capture of a large quantity of war matériel at New Providence and he soon was given command of the sloop *Providence.* He was commissioned a captain in August 1776 and in a six-week cruise captured eight vessels and destroyed eight more. In October he took over the *Alfred* and returned from another highly successful cruise in December. He found himself barred from promotion, largely because of intraservice politics; he was promised command of a frigate, however, and in November 1777 he sailed the *Ranger* to France to receive the frigate *Indien* from its French builders, only to have politics interfere again when the *Indien* was sold to France. From February to May 1778 he sailed the *Ranger* around the British Isles, made two shore raids, and captured a British naval sloop, the first enemy warship to surrender to an American vessel. He saw no further action until August 1779, when he set sail with a squadron of five ships, with his command aboard a refitted merchant ship that he renamed *Bonhomme Richard* in honor of

Benjamin Franklin, creator of *Poor Richard*. Again he sailed around the British Isles, capturing a number of prizes; in September he came upon the Baltic trading fleet and its naval escorts, *Countess of Scarborough* and *Serapis*. Jones engaged the *Serapis*, although he was heavily outgunned and outmanned. He maneuvered in close, lashed the vessels together, and in three and a half hours of one of the fiercest and bloodiest naval battles on record simply wore down the enemy with his blank refusal to give up (it was in this battle that he is supposed to have replied to a suggestion that he surrender: "I have not yet begun to fight!"; at length the *Serapis* surrendered and Jones transferred his crew to the British ship, the heavily damaged *Bonhomme Richard* sinking two days later. From October 1779 to April 1780 he cruised about the *Alliance*; he then returned to Paris, where he was lionized. Louis XVI presented him with a sword and made him, with the permission of Congress, a chevalier of France. In December he borrowed the French ship *Ariel* and returned to the United States. In 1781, by way of thanks for his services, Congress appointed him to command of the huge 74-gun *America*; delays in construction were followed by the decision to give the ship to the French government instead, and Jones's services to the Revolution were over. In 1783 he was sent to France to negotiate payment for captured U.S. prize ships held by France, and in 1788 he performed a similar service in Denmark. On his last visit to the United States, in 1787, Congress honored him with the only gold medal given to a Continental naval officer. In 1788 he accepted a commission from Empress Catherine as a rear admiral in the Russian navy; his services were valuable in the war against Turkey, but he was the victim of intrigues and was dismissed in 1789. He retired to Paris and remained there in declining health until his death on July 18, 1792. His unmarked grave lay undiscovered for more than a century, but in 1905 what were believed to be his remains were returned to the United States under escort of U.S. naval vessels and placed in a crypt in the chapel of the U.S. Naval Academy in Annapolis, Maryland. He was elected to the Hall of Fame in 1925.

Jones, John Winston (1791–1848), public official. Born near Amelia Courthouse, Virginia, on November 22, 1791, Jones was educated privately and graduated from the law school of the College of William and Mary in 1813. He was admitted to the bar in the same year and began practice in Chesterfield County, Virginia, serving as prosecuting attorney for the state's fifth circuit in 1818 and as a member of the state constitutional convention in 1829 and 1830. He was elected to the House of Representatives as a Democrat in 1834 and was reelected to the four succeeding congresses but declined to be renominated in the fall of 1844; he was speaker of the House in his last term. After retiring from the House as Virginia's long-time Congressman, he resumed the practice

of law, served as speaker of the Virginia house of delegates, and engaged in farming at his family's estate, Bellwood, near Petersburg, Virginia, where he died, on January 29, 1848.

Jones, LeRoi, *see* Baraka, Imamu Amiri

Jones, Mary Harris (1830–1930), "Mother Jones," labor leader. Born in Cork, Ireland, on May 1, 1830, Mary Harris was brought to the United States in 1835. She worked as a schoolteacher until, in 1861, she married a certain Jones, a member of the Iron Molders' Union, in Memphis, Tennessee. In 1867 her husband and her four children died in a yellow-fever epidemic in Memphis, and four years later she lost all her possessions in the Chicago fire. She began to attend meetings of the newly formed Knights of Labor and from that time devoted her life to speaking and organizing efforts in the cause of workingmen. For more than half a century Mother Jones appeared wherever there were labor troubles, in Pittsburgh during the great railroad strike in 1877, in Chicago at the time of the Haymarket riot of 1886, in Birmingham in 1894, among the coal miners of Pennsylvania in 1900–1902, in the Colorado coalfields in 1903–1906, in Idaho in 1906, where she was involved in a copper-mine strike, in Colorado again in 1913 and 1914, in New York City in 1915–1916, where she was active in the garment- and streetcar-workers' strikes, and throughout the country in 1919 in the nationwide steel strike of that year. In 1923, at the age of ninety-three, she was still working among striking coal miners in West Virginia. A little old woman in a black bonnet, she was a compelling speaker and a fierce adversary of capitalists and industrialists everywhere. On her hundredth birthday she was honored by a reception at her home in Silver Spring, Maryland, during which she read a congratulatory telegram (one of many) from one of her old enemies, John D. Rockefeller, Jr., and made a fiery speech for the motion-picture cameras. She died in Silver Spring six months later, on November 30, 1930.

Jones, Mother, *see* Jones, Mary Harris

Jones, Robert Tyre, Jr., *see* Jones, Bobby

Jones, Rufus Matthew (1863–1948), religious leader and educator. Born into a pious Quaker family in South China, Maine, on January 25, 1863, Jones was educated in Quaker schools and at Haverford College, from which he graduated in 1885. He received an M.A. from Haverford a year later and was offered the opportunity to pursue further graduate studies at the University of Pennsylvania, but his undergraduate research on mysticism and its role in Quaker history had convinced him that his vocation was for a life of teaching and spreading the gospel of Quakerism. After several years of teaching in Quaker preparatory schools he joined the Haverford faculty, where he remained for more than 40 years, from

1904 to 1934 as professor of philosophy and ethics and thereafter as professor emeritus. A minister of the Society of Friends from 1890, he preached widely in colleges, churches, and meetings, although he never wrote a sermon, always speaking extemporaneously. From 1905 to 1921 he worked on his major published work, four volumes of a six-volume history (the other two by W. C. Braithwaite) of Quakerism and other forms of spiritual and mystical religion; Jones's contributions appeared as *Studies in Mystical Religion*, 1909; *The Quakers in the American Colonies* (with others), 1911; *Spiritual Reformers in the 16th and 17th Centuries*, 1914; and *The Later Periods of Quakerism*, 1921. Others of his books included *Practical Christianity*, 1899; *Social Law in the Spiritual World*, 1904; *Quakerism, a Religion of Life*, 1908; *The Story of George Fox*, 1919; *A Service of Love in War Time*, 1920; *A Preface to Christian Faith in a New Age*, 1932; *The Testimony of the Soul*, 1936; *Spirit in Man*, 1941; and *The Radiant Life*, 1944. During various periods he was editor of several Quaker newspapers. A militant pacifist, he helped to found in 1917 the American Friends Service Committee and fought successfully to have service with the Committee's overseas units accepted as an alternative for conscientious objectors to service in the armed forces. The Committee, under his direction, helped to rebuild destroyed French villages, fed the children of German prisoners, rehabilitated Polish refugees, and provided help for victims of famine in the Soviet Union. Later, during the Spanish Civil War, it fed the starving of both sides, and it was one of the few non-Jewish organizations in the United States to attempt to provide assistance to the Jewish victims of German Nazi tyranny; Jones himself journeyed to Germany with two companions in 1938 and persuaded the head of the Gestapo to allow the Committee to help. Later, during World War II, he led the Committee's activities in aiding Polish, French, and other refugees, both in Europe and in the United States, and he joined with other religious leaders in 1948 to plead for peace between Jews and Muslims in Palestine during the struggle for the establishment of the state of Israel. For its work during the war the American Friends Service Committee was awarded, jointly with the Friends Service Council of Great Britain, the Nobel Peace Prize in 1947. During his later years probably the best-known Quaker in the world, Jones wrote several volumes of autobiography, among them *Small-Town Boy*, 1941, about his childhood in Maine, where he also spent his summers as an adult. He died in Haverford, Pennsylvania, on June 16, 1948.

Jones, Samuel Milton (1846–1904), manufacturer, public official, and social reformer. Born in the small village of Ty Mawr, in Caernarvonshire, Wales, on August 3, 1846, Jones was brought to the United States by his parents at the age of three and the family settled in Lewis County, New York. Owing to the poverty of his family, he worked for most of his childhood, managing to acquire only about 30 months of schooling. In 1864, when he was eighteen, he went to Titusville, Pennsylvania, and found work in the oil fields. He soon rose to prominence in the new industry, eventually engaging in the oil business in Pennsylvania, West Virginia, and especially in Ohio and Indiana. He invented a sucker rod that greatly improved the method of extracting oil from the earth, and in 1893 he founded a firm in Toledo, Ohio, to manufacture it. His direction of the Acme Sucker-Rod Company was both efficient and benevolent, and he instituted many reforms in relations with his employees that were called "socialistic" by his political enemies, including an eight-hour day, paid vacations, the elimination of child labor and piece-work, and a minimum wage. Each year at Christmas he gave his workers a bonus of 5 percent of their annual wages, and he concluded, after a four-year test of this and other measures, that "the Golden Rule works. It is perfectly practicable and is worthy of a trial." Known thereafter as "Golden Rule" Jones, he was nominated by the Republicans for the mayoralty of Toledo in 1897 and was elected, but he soon fell out with his political sponsors, his reforms both of the municipal government, in which he fought corruption, and of industrial conditions in the city being disliked by such magnates as Mark Hanna. He was repudiated by the Republicans in 1899 but ran as an independent and was reelected by a landslide; he was reelected in 1901 and again in 1903. He instituted an eight-hour day and a minimum wage for city employees; advocated municipal ownership of services and utilities; the direct popular nomination of candidates for public office by petition, without the intervention of caucuses, primaries, delegates, or political parties; and he promoted municipal civil service and such public amenities as parks and kindergartens. He died in Toledo, still in office, on July 12, 1904. His campaign for reform in the city was carried on by his successor, Brand Whitlock.

Joplin, Scott (1868–1917), pianist and composer. Born in Texarkana, Arkansas, on November 24, 1868, Joplin spent his youth travelling about the Mississippi valley, doing odd jobs and playing the piano. After a time in St. Louis, playing in various honky-tonks, and a stint as a band leader at the World's Columbian Exposition in Chicago in 1893, he arrived in Sedalia, Missouri, in 1896, where he attended George Smith College for Negroes, taking courses in harmony and composition. A devoted and serious musician, he attracted companions of a like temperament and began to develop a style of ragtime that brought customers to such bistros as the Maple Leaf Club in the "sporting district" of Sedalia. There, in 1899, he met music publisher John Stark, who published his "Original Rag," the first ragtime piece to appear in sheet-music form, and "Maple Leaf Rag," one of the most famous of American jazz compositions. The next year Stark and Joplin moved to St. Louis, where Joplin was frustrated by the exploitation of ragtime then being undertaken by "commercial" pianists of the time. He nevertheless stuck to his personal style and continued to work in the ragtime manner, a lively and danceable although rather formal musical mode that, while allowing a certain scope for improvisation and embellishment, more importantly gave the evolving school of jazz music a necessary structural underpinning on which to build. Besides "Maple Leaf Rag," he wrote such pieces as "Sugar Cane Rag," "Wall Street Rag," and "Gladiolus Rag." Joplin wrote two ambitious compositions, *A Guest of Honor*, a ragtime opera that was produced in St. Louis in 1903, and *Tremonisha*, another ragtime opera that he produced at his own expense and that played a single performance in New York City's Harlem in 1911. He died in New York City on April 11, 1917, leaving many published works and some mechanical piano rolls of his music, but no recordings.

Jordan, David Starr (1851–1931), biologist, educator, and philosopher. Born near Gainesville, New York, on January 19, 1851, Jordan early developed a deep interest in botany. In 1869 he entered Cornell University; his knowledge in his chosen field was already so extensive that in his junior year he was appointed to an instructorship. He graduated with an M.S. in 1872 and in the next two years taught at small colleges in Illinois and Wisconsin; in 1874 he began a year of teaching high school in Indianapolis during which he also earned an M.D. from the Indiana Medical College. The next year he joined the faculty of Northwestern Christian University (now Butler University), where he remained for four years. In 1876 he published the first of many editions of his influential *Manual of the Vertebrates of the Northern United States*. He became head of the department of natural sciences and professor of zoology at Indiana University in 1879 and six years later was the president of the institution. To his well-established reputation as a biologist was now added an increasing respect for his administrative talents, and the result was a call to become the first president of Stanford University in 1891. He held the post, guiding the university through the financial and organizational crises of its early years, until 1913, becoming in that year chancellor of the university and in 1916 chancellor emeritus. Despite the burdens of the presidency of the institution, Jordan maintained the intellectual pursuits that were gradually leading him into more philosophical questions. He made invaluable studies of the fisheries of many regions, served on various international fisheries commissions, and published the widely adopted *Fishes of North and Middle America* (with B. W. Evermann), 4 volumes, 1896–1900, and *Guide to the Study of Fishes*, 1905. While he remained one of the nation's leading biologists and perhaps the world's outstanding ichthyologist, he began also to speak out against war, which, in his view, violated the process of natural selection by killing off precisely the strongest and most capable members of the human species. He became a champion of international arbitration of disputes and of progressive reform and world federalism. He wrote constantly to promote these causes; among his books were *The Care and Culture of Men*, 1896; *Imperial Democracy*, 1899; *The Human Harvest*, 1907; *War and Waste*, 1914; and *Democracy and World Relations*, 1918. From 1910 to 1914 he was chief director of the World Peace Foundation and in 1915 served as president of the World Peace Congress. He opposed U.S. entry into World War I, although he supported the "democratic crusade" after U.S. participation became fact; in his concern with human heredity and his advocacy of eugenic practices he joined also in the period's wave of theorizing on the "racial" superiority of Nordic peoples. In 1922 he published his autobiographical *The Days of a Man*, and in 1924 his *Plan of Education to Develop International Justice and Friendship* won a $25,000 prize. He died on September 19, 1931, in Stanford, California.

Joseph (1840?–1904), Indian leader. Born about 1840, probably in Oregon's Wallowa Valley, which had been long inhabited by the Nez Percé, Joseph was given the name Hinmatonyalatkit, meaning "thunder coming up over the land from the water." His father, also known as Joseph, was leader of one of the major Nez Percé bands; in 1863, the year gold was discovered on their lands, this band refused to participate in a renegotiation of the land-cession treaty of 1855. Other bands did renegotiate, however, and government authorities held the new treaty ceding the disputed lands to be binding on all Nez Percé. Upon the death of his father in 1873, Joseph succeeded him as leader of the resisting Nez Percé and, as Chief Joseph, continued his father's policies of passive noncompliance with the 1863 treaty. After years of delay the government finally took action in 1877; through Gen. Oliver O. Howard an ultimatum was issued, ordering Joseph and his people to leave the lands coveted by the whites or be removed forcibly. Joseph was troubled, but decided to leave: "I would give up everything rather than have the blood of my people on my hands. . . . I love that land more than all the world. A man who would not love his father's grave is worse than a wild animal." In his absence, however, Nez Percé braves killed several whites; on hearing of this Howard dispatched troops to capture the band. In the ensuing battle of White Bird Canyon the soldiers were nearly annihilated by the Nez Percé, led by chiefs other than Joseph. During this and 18 subsequent conflicts he guided his warriors' decisions, counseled his people, and cared for the women, children, aged, and wounded. The army assumed that he was the war chief or battle leader, however, and his reputation grew to legendary proportions. After two days' fighting near Kamiah, Idaho, Howard and 600 soldiers finally succeeded in weakening the tribe's fighting power. Joseph, rather than surrender, executed a masterly retreat. Heading for the Canadian border and the huge nation of Sitting Bull, he led 750 people through four states, twice over the Rockies, across what is now Yellowstone National Park, and across the Missouri River, a distance of more than 1500 miles. They outfought pursuing troops and were in Montana, within 30 miles of the Canadian border when fresh troops under Gen. Nelson A. Miles surrounded them, on October 5, 1877. Joseph surrendered with dignity: "I am tired of fighting. Our chiefs are killed. . . . It is cold and we have no blankets. The little children are freezing to death. My people, some of them, have run away to the hills, and have no blankets, no food; no one knows where they are—perhaps freezing to death. I want to have time to look for my children and see how many of them I can find. Maybe I shall find them among the dead. Hear me, my chiefs! I am tired; my heart is sick and sad. From where the sun now stands I will fight no more forever." He devoted himself thereafter to the tribe's welfare. He and his band were sent to Indian Territory (Oklahoma) and in 1885 they were moved to the Colville Reservation in Washington. There Chief Joseph died, on September 21, 1904.

Joy, James Frederick (1810–1896), railroad magnate. Born in Durham, New Hampshire, on December 2, 1810, Joy graduated from Dartmouth College at the head of his class in 1833 and then entered the Harvard Law School, receiving his law degree in 1836. He was admitted to the bar that year and also moved to Detroit, where he began the practice of law. He soon became interested in railroad building and finance, and the next year, one of general financial panic throughout the country, he began to help arrange the sale of the Michigan Central Railroad to a group of private investors, an enterprise that was not successfully completed until 1846. The further extension of this railroad to Chicago involved legal problems with the state of Illinois that were solved by Joy with the help of Abraham Lincoln, then a Springfield lawyer; turn about being fair play, Joy later gave able assistance to Lincoln in his bid for the presidency and supported his policies throughout the Civil War. From 1850 Joy was deeply involved in the effort to extend the U.S. railroad network westward from Chicago, and at one time or another he owned many lines; his first combine he named the Chicago, Burlington & Quincy, and it remained for the rest of his career the foundation of his considerable power and fortune. Several of the lines that he bought included large federal grants of land among their assets, and Joy traded and parlayed his acquisitions into the creation of the "Joy system," the first important railroad combination in the West. He began to sell off his railroad properties in 1870 and from that time ceased to be the dominant figure in Western railroading, although he continued to exert a powerful influence on the transportation industry. From 1881 to 1884 he was president of the *Detroit Post and Tribune* and for many years was a director of the Detroit National Bank. He died at his home in Detroit on September 24, 1896.

Judd, Charles Hubbard (1873–1946), psychologist and educator. Born in Bareilly, India, on February 20, 1873, Judd was brought to the United States in 1879. He graduated from Wesleyan University in 1894 and then went to Germany to do graduate work, obtaining his Ph.D. from the University of Leipzig in 1896. He taught philosophy and psychology at several U.S. universities during the next ten years and, having joined the faculty in 1902, held the rank of professor and served as director of the psychological laboratory at Yale from 1907 to 1909. In the meantime he had published *Genetic Psychology for Teachers*, 1903, and a widely used textbook, *Psychology: General Introduction*, 1907. He left Yale in 1909 to become head of the department of education at the University of Chicago, a post in which he remained until 1938; he also was a professor of education and for part of the time chairman of the department of psychology. He based a number of works on his research and experience at Chicago, including *Psychology of High School Subjects*, 1915; *Introduction to the Scientific Study of Education*, 1918; *Psychology of Social Institutions*, 1926; *Psychology of Secondary Education*, 1927; *Education and Social Progress*, 1934; *Education as Cultivation of the Higher Mental Processes*, 1936; and *Educational Psychology*, 1939. He made a number of school surveys, directed many research studies, and edited various journals and monographs, but it was mainly through his writings, which became standard works in most U.S. schools of education, that he exerted his enormous influence on education and the training of educators in the early twentieth century. He died in Santa Barbara, California, on July 18, 1946.

Judson, Adoniram (1788–1850), missionary. Born in Malden, Massachusetts, on August 9, 1788, Judson graduated from Brown University in 1807 and spent the next year teaching school and writing two textbooks for young ladies. He then entered Andover Theological Seminary and determined to become a foreign missionary. He led in founding the movement that became the American Board of Commissioners for Foreign Missions, under whose auspices he sailed to England in 1811 to obtain financial aid, a mission that was delayed when his ship was captured by a French privateer and he was imprisoned in France. Upon his release he returned to the United States, and soon after his ordination in February 1812 he set off for Burma, where he spent most of the rest of his life. Reaching Calcutta, India, in June 1812, he found himself at odds with his Congregationalist sponsors, was baptized by immersion, and, as a Baptist, set about the evangelization of Asia. Arriving at Rangoon in July 1813, he threw himself into the study of the Burmese language and eventually was able to translate the entire Bible into Burmese. He was in Ava in 1824 when war broke out between England and Burma and he was imprisoned for two years as a spy, his life being saved by the heroic efforts of his first wife. In 1829 he moved to Moulmein, which became the chief seat of the Baptist mission in Burma, and during the next 25 years converted many thousands of Burmese to Christianity and also began work on a Burmese dictionary. He was able to complete the English-Burmese part, published in 1849 as *Dictionary, English and Burmese*, and it is still a standard work, but he was unable to finish the Burmese-English vocabulary before his death, which occurred on April 12, 1850, three days out from Burma on a voyage for his health. He was buried at sea. He married three remarkable women, all missionaries. His first wife, Ann Hasseltine Judson (1789–1826), met Judson while both were studying at Andover Theological Seminary and, after their marriage, accompanied him to India, the first woman to go to foreign lands as a missionary. During his two-year imprisonment at the time of the Anglo-Burmese War she followed her husband from prison to prison, her baby in her arms, and managed to supply him with food, as well as interceding with the governor to save his life on several occasions when he had been marked for execution. Worn out by her now almost legendary exertions in his behalf, she died on October 24, 1826, the child dying soon afterward. Judson's second wife was Sarah Hall Boardman (1803–1845), the widow of a missionary who had preceded Judson to Moulmein. Mrs. Boardman worked with Judson both before and after their marriage, but her health failed in 1845 and she died in the course of the journey back to the United States. The next year he took as his third wife the missionary and author Emily Chubbock (1817–1854), who wrote many novels for children and young people under the pen name of "Fanny Forrester." She survived him, dying in 1854 in Hamilton, New York.

Judson, Ann Hasseltine, *see under* Judson, Adoniram.

Judson, Edward Zane Carroll (1823–1886), "Ned Buntline," author and adventurer. Born in Stamford, New York, on March 20, 1823, Judson ran away to sea as a youngster; after serving as a cabin boy he became an apprentice in the navy and by 1838 had earned a midshipman's commission. He left the navy in 1842 and served, he later claimed, in the last Seminole War. In 1844 he was in Cincinnati and founded two successive and equally short-lived newspapers; he had already begun to write stories in the action-and-violence mode, some of which were published in the *Knickerbocker Magazine*, and the pseudonym he used for these efforts was given also to the first of his Cincinnati ventures, *Ned Buntline's Magazine*. In Kentucky in 1845 he successfully tracked down and captured two fugitive murderers and then established the sensational *Ned Buntline's Own* in Nashville, Tennessee. The following year he shot and killed the husband of his alleged mistress and was arrested; he somehow survived an actual lynching and left for New York City. He reestablished *Ned Buntline's Own* there and made it a jingoist, nativist, unruly, and highly popular

sheet. There developed a heated public controversy in 1849 over the respective merits of Edwin Forrest, a popular American actor, and William Charles Macready, his English counterpart, then appearing in New York City, with whom Forrest had been feuding; the culmination was a riot at the Astor Place Opera House in May, led by Judson, in which more than a score were killed and the theater was wrecked. He was fined and jailed for a year for his part in the Astor Place Riot. Three years later, in St. Louis, he was involved in another riot, this one precipitated by an election. He was a leading organizer in the 1850s of the American party and was said to be the source of its alternate and better-known name, the Know-Nothing party. He had been continuing his literary career all the while, publishing his stories in cheap pamphlet form and thus becoming one of the chief creators of the "dime novel" genre, to which he contributed some 400 examples. In 1856 he moved to a farm in New York state; he joined the Union army during the Civil War and was dishonorably discharged in 1864. On a trip to Nebraska in 1869 he met William F. Cody, whom he immediately dubbed "Buffalo Bill" and cast as the hero of a long series of dime novels. In 1872 he wrote and produced a play, *Scouts of the Plains*—later *Scouts of the Prairies*—which starred Cody and J. B. "Texas Jack" Omohundro, also a dime-novel hero, who was later replaced by James B. "Wild Bill" Hickok. The play was highly successful in Chicago, St. Louis, and New York City. Cody soon found another and more generous manager and Judson retired to Stamford, New York, where he died on July 16, 1886.

Judson, Emily Chubbock, *see under* Judson, Adoniram

Judson, Sarah Hall Boardman, *see under* Judson, Adoniram

Julian, Percy Lavon (1899–1975), chemist. Born in Montgomery, Alabama, on April 11, 1899, Julian graduated from DePauw University at the head of his class in 1920 and then taught chemistry for two years at Fisk. In 1922 he was awarded an Austin fellowship by Harvard and he continued graduate studies there until 1926, receiving his master's degree in 1923 and holding a series of minor fellowships instead of a teaching appointment because he was black. During 1926–1927 he taught chemistry at West Virginia State College and from 1927 to 1929 was an associate professor of chemistry at Howard University. In 1929 he traveled to Europe on a General Education Board fellowship and received a Ph.D. from the University of Vienna two years later. He then returned to Howard as a full professor and head of the department of chemistry. In 1932 Julian moved to DePauw as a research fellow and teacher. Julian's synthesis in 1935 of the drug physostigmine, used in the treatment of glaucoma, attracted considerable attention in scientific circles and the following year he accepted the post of director of research of the soya-products division of the Glidden Company in Chicago. At Glidden he developed a soya protein similar to but cheaper than milk casein that later found application in the treatment of paper and in fire extinguishers. Over the next several years Julian and his associates developed scores of soya derivatives, indoles, sterols, steroids, and phosphatides. Of particular importance were the steroids, many of which, once derived or synthesized by Julian from a soya base, greatly reduced the cost of therapy for many diseases, most notably arthritis. In 1945 Julian became director of research and manager of fine chemicals development at Glidden. In 1953 he left the company to establish his own firm, Julian Laboratories, Inc., and a sister company, Laboratorios Julian de Mexico; he remained president of both companies until 1964. From 1964 he served as president of Julian Associates and director of the Julian Research Institute. He was a special consultant to the National Institute of Arthritis and Metabolic Diseases and the recipient of numerous professional and civic awards, including the 1947 Spingarn Medal of the National Association for the Advancement of Colored People (NAACP). Julian died in Waukegan, Illinois, on April 19, 1975.

Julius, Emanuel, see Haldeman-Julius, Emanuel

Juneau, Solomon Laurent (1793–1856), fur trader and settler. Born in L'Assomption, Quebec, on August 9, 1793, Juneau entered the employ of a Mackinac fur trader in 1816 and two years later settled at the mouth of the Milwaukee River on the shore of Lake Michigan. Becoming an agent for the American Fur Company, he enjoyed considerable success in trading, remaining on excellent terms with the Indians of the area, and in 1831 became a citizen of the United States. In 1833 he formed a partnership with Morgan L. Martin of Green Bay for the purpose of founding a town around his post; the site was platted in 1835 and lots were offered for sale in Milwaukee East Side, generally known as Juneautown. Four years later the village was merged with Milwaukee West Side (Kilbourntown), built on the opposite bank by rival speculators, to create the town of Milwaukee. Juneau had served as his village's first president and postmaster and on the incorporation

of the city of Milwaukee in 1846 was elected its first mayor. He donated a large part of his own land holdings in the city for such public purposes as the Milwaukee Female College and the Roman Catholic cathedral and remained the leading citizen until 1852, when he moved some 40 miles to the northwest and founded the village of Theresa. He died on November 14, 1856, on the Menomini Indian reservation near Theresa.

Just, Ernest Everett (1883–1941), biologist. Born in Charleston, South Carolina, on August 14, 1883, Just graduated from Dartmouth College with high honors in 1907 and was immediately named to the faculty of Howard University. While advancing from instructor to full professor and head of the department of zoology in 1912 he pursued further studies at the Marine Biological Laboratory at Woods Hole, Massachusetts, and at the University of Chicago. In 1912 he was also appointed professor of physiology in the medical school of Howard University, a post he held for eight years and in which he made signal contributions to the improvement of medical education for black students. In 1915 he was chosen to receive the first Spingarn Medal awarded by the National Association for the Advancement of Colored People (NAACP). In 1916 he received his Ph.D. from the University of Chicago. Just's researches centered on the cellular processes of marine organisms, the mechanisms of fertilization, cell division, and water transport. In his major published work, *Biology of the Cell Surface*, 1939, he advanced the theory, which proved to be highly fruitful, that in the egg cell the ectoplasm, the outer boundary layer of the cytoplasm, plays a vital role in initiating fertilization and through constant interaction with the rest of the cytoplasm is central to the process of cell differentiation. In 1939 he also published his other principal work, *Basic Methods for Experiments on Eggs of Marine Animals*. For several years in the 1930s Just carried on his work at various laboratories in Europe, having tired of the treatment so often accorded him in the United States, even by professional colleagues, because of his race. He returned to the United States in 1941 and died that year, on October 27, in Washington, D.C.

K

Kahn, Otto Herman (1867–1934), banker, art collector, and philanthropist. Born in Mannheim, Germany, on February 21, 1867, Kahn came of a wealthy and cultured family and was early directed to a career in banking. After an apprenticeship in a small bank in Karlsruhe and a year of military service he entered the employ of the Deutsche Bank in Berlin in 1888. Soon transferred to the bank's London office, he remained there for five years, during which he became a naturalized British subject. In 1893 he accepted the offer of a position in a New York City banking firm and four years later became a member of Kuhn, Loeb & Company in New York City, with which he remained thereafter associated and of which he soon became the principal figure. In business affairs he was associated particularly with Edward H. Harriman, whom he rendered great assistance in the reorganization and financing of such major components of the Harriman railroad system as the Missouri, Pacific, the Union Pacific, and the Baltimore & Ohio. Kahn became a U.S. citizen in 1917. With the means to indulge a deep interest in the arts that dated from childhood, he began assembling what was to become one of the outstanding private art collections in the world. He bought an interest in the Metropolitan Opera Company in 1903 and four years later, to save the company from financial collapse, joined William K. Vanderbilt in taking over complete ownership; he later bought out Vanderbilt's share and at his death still owned nearly all of the stock in the company. Besides contributing heavily to the support of the opera he brought Arturo Toscanini from Milan's La Scala in 1908 to conduct the Met's orchestra, and also brought La Scala's director, Giulio Gatti-Casazza, to fill the same post at the Met. Kahn was chairman of the Met from 1911 until 1918 and then president until 1931. He contributed also to the support of opera companies in Boston and Chicago and gave generously to countless museums, theaters, schools, orchestras, and other cultural and educational institutions throughout the country. His benefactions also included a large gift for the restoration of the Parthenon of Athens, sponsorship of a tour of the United States by the Russian ballet, and the donation of a number of prizes for black artists. Probably the greatest patron the arts in the United States ever enjoyed, Kahn died in New York City on March 29, 1934.

Kaiser, Henry John (1882–1967), industrialist. Born near Canajoharie, New York, on May 9, 1882, Kaiser left school at the age of thirteen to go to work for a dry-goods firm in Utica. By the time he was twenty he had become sole owner of a photography business. He sold the business in 1906 to go to Spokane, Washington, where he first entered the hardware business and then, in 1912, became a road builder. Soon his energy and ingenuity brought him to the fore and by 1930 he had to his credit many miles of highway in California and up the West Coast into British Columbia and even in Cuba. In connection with his road-building activities, he built a number of sand, gravel, and cement plants, which he employed to good effect in his next "career," that of dam construction. In 1931 he organized the Six Companies, a group of contractors, and built Boulder (now Hoover) Dam—finishing the project in 1936, two years ahead of schedule—and subsequently, as president of Bridge Builders, Inc., was involved in the construction of the San Francisco–Oakland Bay Bridge (1936), one of the world's largest suspension bridges; the Grand Coulee Dam (1942), one of the world's largest concrete structures; and the Bonneville Dam (1943). In 1939 he formed the Permanente Cement Company to supply materials for Shasta Dam (1945). At the outbreak of World War II in 1941 he became one of the most prominent, colorful, and successful figures in industry. He began by building ships, establishing a chain of seven shipyards on the Pacific Coast north of Richmond, California, in which vessels were constructed, thanks to prefabrication and advanced assembly methods, with a speed and in a volume never before approached. The record was set by the construction of the *Robert E. Peary*, which was launched four and a half days after keel-laying and delivered three days later, on November 12, 1942. The Kaiser yards built some 1460 ships during the war, most of them the famed Liberty-class cargo vessels. Finding it difficult to obtain enough steel for his ships, Kaiser built the Pacific Coast's first steel plant in 1942, and he constructed a magnesium plant that met a substantial portion of the wartime need for this metal. He also acquired other plants manufacturing airplanes, jeeps, and other vehicles. Most of his services to the war effort were provided without profit. Also in 1942 he established the Permanente Foundation (later the Kaiser Foundation), a pioneer nonprofit health-maintenance organization providing hospital and medical facilities to Kaiser workers. After the war the Permanente program was opened to public enrollment and by the 1960s it had more than 1,250,000 members. At the war's end Kaiser continued to expand his activities, building from 1945, through Kaiser Industries, a giant industrial empire that included steel, cement, aluminum, and automobile plants. The automobiles—Kaiser ("Henry J.") and Frazer cars—were built by the Kaiser-Frazer Corporation, which he founded in partnership with Joseph W. Frazer. The business was ultimately a failure, owing, Kaiser said, to its being undercapitalized; the Kaiser and Frazer cars ceased production in 1954, except for an Argentinian subsidiary, but Kaiser continued to manufacture Jeeps until his death. His first aluminum facility, built in 1946, showed sales in its first year of $41 million and earnings of more than $5 million and he continued to expand the operation until Kaiser Alumium became one of the largest aluminum-processing organizations in the world. At his death the Kaiser companies were turning out some 300 products at 180 plants in 32 states and 40 foreign countries and they employed more than 90,000 people. In 1965 he received the Murray-Green Award from the AFL–CIO Executive Council for outstanding service to the labor movement; he was the first industrialist to receive this highest award bestowed by organized labor. He died in Honolulu on August 24, 1967.

Kalb, Johann (1721–1780), soldier of fortune. Born in Germany, on June 29, 1721, Kalb was of peasant birth, but by the time he was twenty-two and serving as a lieutenant in a French infantry regiment he was styling himself Jean de Kalb; he was later often called "Baron de Kalb." Unremittingly ambitious for glory, he served with distinction as a major in the Seven Years' War; after the war his marriage to an heiress gave him an independence he had theretofore lacked. He went to America on a secret mission for the French government in 1768, remained for four months, and had to return to France when his dispatches were intercepted, but he retained a desire to fight in the New World. He got his wish in 1777, when, with a promise from Silas Deane of a major general's commission, he arrived in America with his young friend, the Marquis de Lafayette, but Kalb was again disappointed when Lafayette was made a major general and he himself was left without a command. Late in the year, on the point of returning to France, he also was made a major general and was assigned to serve under Lafayette. He spent the winter of 1777–1778 with Gen. George Washington at Valley Forge and was with the Continental army until 1780, although he had no opportunity to distinguish himself. In April of that year he was ordered to South Carolina, where he served under Gen. Horatio Gates in the Carolina Campaign. Gates wanted, against Kalb's advice, to attack the British after Charleston had fallen to Gen. Sir Henry Clinton, and they encountered Lord Cornwallis's army near Camden, South Carolina, on August 16, 1780. Gates's troops fled the enemy three times and, when his position was seen to be hopeless, led his few remaining men forward in a last desperate attack. Kalb fell seriously wounded and he died three days later at Camden.

Kalish, Sophie, see Tucker, Sophie

Kalogeropoulos, Maria, see Callas, Maria

Kaltenborn, Hans von (1878–1965), news commentator. Born in Milwaukee on July 9, 1878, H. V. Kaltenborn got his first job as a newpaperman with the *Merrill* (Wisconsin) *News* when he was fifteen years old. Serving as a sergeant during the Spanish-American War, he worked as a war correspondent for several Wisconsin newspapers, and after the war went to Europe on a cattle boat to begin a long career as a foreign correspondent. Deciding that he needed a college education, he entered Harvard in 1905 and graduated cum laude in 1909. He joined the *Brooklyn Eagle* in 1910 and remained with it for 20 years, working his way up from reporter to associate editor. His career as a radio commentator began in 1922 when, under the sponsorship of the *Eagle*, he began to discuss current events over the air on local stations. In 1929 he joined the Columbia Broadcasting System (CBS) as chief news commentator and switched to the National Broadcasting Company (NBC) in the same capacity in 1940. He scored many notable firsts in radio and television news broadcasting, but his most famous feat may have been his series of almost nonstop broadcasts during the Munich crisis, in 1938, when he went on the air 102 times in 18 days, living in the studio and subsisting on soup supplied by his wife in order to be on hand to relay the latest news of the negotiations between Adolf Hitler and British Prime Minister Neville Chamberlain. In 1936 he concealed himself in a haystack during an engagement in the Spanish Civil War and gave his listeners a taste of the actual sounds of battle. He broadcast reports during World War II from virtually every major front in Europe and the Pacific. He retired from NBC in 1955 but in 1956, as he had done in every presidential campaign since 1932, he covered the events leading up to the reelection of President Dwight D. Eisenhower, and thereafter carried out occasional special assignments. He wrote several books, among them an autobiography, *Fifty Fabulous Years*, 1956. He died in Brooklyn, New York, on June 14, 1965.

Kane, Elisha Kent (1820–1857), physician and Arctic explorer. Born in Philadelphia on February 3, 1820, Kane entered the University of Virginia in 1838 with the intention of becoming an engineer, but an attack of rheumatic fever left his heart permanently damaged and he transferred to the University of Pennsylvania, from which he received a medical degree in 1842. Determined not to be hindered by ill health in his search for experience and adventure, he joined the navy as a surgeon, visited India, China, and Ceylon, traveled in the Philippine Islands (where he descended into a volcanic crater), and served as a surgeon in Africa, where he contracted a lingering fever that further weakened his health.

He returned to the United States in time to serve with distinction in the Mexican War and in 1850, assigned to the U.S. Coast Survey, joined the first Grinnell expedition under Lt. E. J. De Haven of the navy, organized to seek traces of Sir John Franklin, the British Arctic explorer who had disappeared in the Lancaster Sound region in 1845 while searching for the Northwest Passage. The two ships provided to the navy by Henry Grinnell did not find Franklin or his party, but Kane had seen and learned enough so that his book *The U.S. Grinnell Expedition in Search of Sir John Franklin*, 1853, became a best seller; it was reissued in 1915 as *Adrift in the Arctic Ice Pack*. Kane set to work with characteristic energy and enthusiasm to organize a second expedition, which departed under his command from New York harbor, in the brig *Advance*, in May 1853. Kane and his men passed through Smith Sound into previously unknown waters that are now named Kane Basin, spent the ensuing winter on the west coast of Greenland, where they suffered greatly from severe hardships, and the next summer explored farther north than any previous expedition, passing 80°N and finding what is now Kennedy Channel, connecting the Kane and Hall basins. The party's careful observation and recording of scientific data laid the foundation for subsequent rigorous Arctic studies. The *Advance* was frozen in for still another winter and was finally abandoned by Kane and the surviving members of his party in May 1855. Traveling 1200 miles through open water and broken ice, they finally arrived in August 1855 at Sanderson's Hope, near Upernavik, Greenland, after 83 terrible days, having accomplished one of the great feats in the annals of Arctic exploration. Kane's *Arctic Explorations: The Second Grinnell Expedition in Search of Sir John Franklin, in the Years 1853, '54, '55*, published in two volumes in 1856, became one of the country's most widely read books of the nineteenth century. By this time Kane's health, never strong, was ruined, but he continued to travel, going first to England and then to Havana, where he died on February 16, 1857. A national hero, he was mourned widely, his body lying in state in New Orleans, then in Louisville, Kentucky, Columbus, Ohio, and Baltimore and finally in Independence Hall in Philadelphia. He had been a close friend of spiritualist Margaret Fox and in 1866 she published a crudely edited book, *The Love Life of Dr. Kane*, printing what purported to be their correspondence and containing the claim that they had shared a common-law marriage.

Kangaroo, Captain, *see* Keeshan, Robert James

Kaplan, Mordecai Menahem (1881–   ), religious leader and educator. Born on June 11, 1881, in Swenziany, Lithuania (now in the U.S.S.R.), Kaplan was brought to the United States at the age of eight. He graduated from the College of the City of New York (CCNY) in 1900 and two years later took an M.A. degree from Columbia University and completed the course of study at the Jewish Theological Seminary of America in New York City. From 1902 to 1909 he was rabbi of a New York congregation; in 1909 he was named principal of the Teachers Institute of the seminary and held the post until 1931; from 1931 until 1946 he served as dean. He served also as professor of homiletics in the seminary's Rabbinical School from 1910 to 1947 and thereafter as professor of the philosophies of religion. In 1916 Kaplan founded the Jewish Center in New York City, the first synagogue center in the United States, and continued as its rabbi until 1922, when he organized the Society for the Advancement of Judaism, of which he remained leader until 1944. With the publication of *Judaism as a Civilization* in 1934 Kaplan emerged as a controversial interpreter of Jewish tradition and the founder of the Reconstructionist movement within Judaism. His view that Judaism is a full-flowered though transnational civilization of which the Jewish religion is but the ancient cultural core found continuing expression in the biweekly *Reconstructionist*, which he began in 1935 and edited thereafter, and in subsequent books, including *Judaism in Transition*, 1936; *The Future of the American Jew*, 1948; *A New Zionism*, 1955; and *Judaism Without Supernaturalism*, 1958. The *New Haggadah for the Pesar Seder*, 1941; the *Sabbath Prayer Book*, 1945, which aroused a storm of controversy by denying that the Jews are a chosen people and that the Torah is divinely inspired, a controversy that led the Union of Orthodox Rabbis to the unprecedented step of excommunicating him; the *High Holiday Prayer Book*, 1948; and the *Festival Prayer Book*, 1958.

Karloff, Boris (1887–1969), actor. Born in London on November 23, 1887, the son of a British civil servant, William Henry Pratt adopted the stage name "Boris Karloff" in Canada in 1911, where he had gone to escape his family's urging that he join the consular service. His first stage role, as a member of a touring company, was as the villain, at $30 a week. He toured with that troupe and subsequently in a road company of *The Virginian* throughout most of western Canada and the United States, winding up broke in Los Angeles in 1917. Hearing that Universal Pictures was seeking extras, he applied successfully, but his movie career did not amount to much until he was cast in the part of the Monster in *Frankenstein*, released in 1931. "The appalling creature called to life by Frankenstein" was of course the hit of that movie, and Karloff played in a large number of sequels, notably *The Bride of Frankenstein*, 1935; *Son of Frankenstein*, 1938; and *The House of Frankenstein*, 1944. He also scored in the title role of *The Mummy*, 1932, and played in such other famous horror movies of the 1930s as *The Mask of Fu Manchu*, 1932; *The Black Cat*, 1934; *The Raven*, 1935; *The Invisible Menace*, 1938; and *Black Friday*, 1940. He was so successful as a movie monster that it was not until 1941 that he made his Broadway debut, as the villainous brother in *Arsenic and Old Lace*, which played 1444 performances at the Fulton Theatre and in which he played on the road as late as 1961, appearing also in the film version in 1944. He was the host for a series of television thrillers and edited two anthologies of horror tales. Without his monster makeup a man of great gentleness and charm, he died in Middleton, Sussex, England, on February 2, 1969 having long since given up regretting the typecasting that both made and limited his acting career.

Kármán, Theodore von (1881–1963), aeronautical engineer and physicist. Born in Budapest on May 11, 1881, von Kármán graduated from the Budapest Royal Technical University in 1902. He taught for a year at the university and for two years held a position in mechanical engineering before enrolling at the University of Göttingen in 1906 to work for his doctorate. He received his Ph.D. degree two years later and remained at the university as a faculty member until 1912. At that time he was offered the directorship of the new Aeronautical Institute at the University of Aachen. Except for military service in the Austrian air force during World War I, he remained at Aachen until coming to the United States in 1930 to teach at the California Institute of Technology (Caltech) and to serve as head of the Guggenheim Aeronautical (from 1942 the Jet Propulsion) Laboratory there. Von Kármán became a U.S. citizen in 1936. He became professor emeritus at Caltech in 1949 and in 1951 helped found and was chosen chairman of the advisory group for aeronautical research and development for the North Atlantic Treaty Organization (NATO), a post he retained for the rest of his life. During the years he held teaching and research posts in Germany and the United States, von Kármán also served as engineering consultant to several airplane-manufacturing corporations in Europe, Japan, and the United States. He was one of the leading theoreticians of aerodynamics in the twentieth century, and his research made possible the development of supersonic aircraft rocket flights and of guided missiles. In 1935, at the Fifth Volta Congress in Italy, he announced his theory of air resistance to bodies moving with supersonic speed, leading to the concept known as the Kármán vortex trail. During World War II he cooperated with the air force on its first jet-propulsion program and began research on the Bell X-1 plane, the first aircraft to break the sound barrier. He also developed a supersonic wind tunnel at Caltech to aid in ballistic-missile research. In 1942 he formed the Aerojet Engineering Corporation, which became, under the later name of Aerojet-General, one of the leading manufacturers of rockets and missiles. In 1944 he became chairman of the scientific advisory board for the air force, a post he held until 1955 when the General Dynamics Corporation hired him as a consultant on guided missiles and nuclear research. He was the author of many books and articles in the fields of aeronautical engineering and physics, including *Aerodynamics*, 1954. He died in Aachen, Germany on May 7, 1963.

Kaufman, George Simon (1889–1961), playwright and director. Born in Pittsburgh on November 16, 1889, Kaufman attended public schools in Pittsburgh and in Paterson, New Jersey, studied law for three months, and became a salesman. He contributed humorous quips and verse regularly to Franklin P. Adams's satirical column in the *New York Evening Mail* and in 1912, through F.P.A.'s influence, began to write his own humor column for the *Washington (D.C.) Times*. In 1914 he took over Adams's column in the *Evening Mail* and the next year became a writer in the drama department of the *New York Tribune*, working under Heywood Broun. He became a writer in the drama department of the *New York Times* in 1917 and remained with the paper, later as drama editor, until 1930. His first successful play was based on Dulcinea, a character created by F.P.A. *Dulcy*, written with Marc Connelly, was the hit of the 1921–1922 Broadway season. He wrote seven other plays with Connelly, the most famous of which were *Merton of the Movies* and *To the Ladies*, both 1922, and *Beggar on Horseback*, 1924. In that year he wrote *The Butter and Egg Man*, with no collaborator, and in 1925 he completed the book for a Marx Brothers musical, *The Coconuts*. With Edna Ferber he wrote a number of plays, among them *The Royal Family*, 1927; *Dinner at Eight*, 1932; *Stage Door*, 1936; *The Land Is Bright*, 1941, and *Bravo!*, 1949. With Ring Lardner he wrote *June Moon*, 1929. He shared Pulitzer Prizes in drama for *Of Thee I Sing*, 1931, written with Morris Ryskind and Ira Gershwin, with a score by George Gershwin, and for *You Can't Take It with You*, 1936, written with Moss Hart. He also collaborated with Hart on *Once in a Lifetime*, 1930, *The Man Who Came to Dinner*, 1939, and *I'd Rather Be Right*, 1937, which starred George M. Cohan as Franklin D. Roosevelt. He wrote *The Solid Gold Cadillac* with Howard Teichmann in 1953 and *Silk Stockings* with Abe Burrows in 1955, and through the years directed Broadway productions of the plays *June Moon, Let 'Em Eat Cake, Bring on the Girls, Of Mice and Men, My Sister Eileen, Guys and Dolls, Romanoff and Juliet,* and *The American Way*. He wrote or directed at least one hit on Broadway every year from 1921 to 1941. He died in New York City on June 2, 1961.

Kay, Ulysses Simpson (1917–   ), composer. Born in Tucson, Arizona, on January 7, 1917, Kay was the nephew of the New Orleans jazz cornetist Joe "King" Oliver, who encouraged the boy in music. Turning from jazz to serious music, he graduated from the University of Arizona in 1938 and received a master of music degree from the Eastman School of Music in 1940. Further musical studies at the Berkshire Music Center under Paul Hindemith and at Yale were interrupted by naval service during World War II, after which he studied at Columbia, in 1946–

1949. A ballet, *Dame Calinda*, had been completed in 1941, together with several choral compositions; his significant work of the later 1940s included *Suite for Strings*, 1947, *Concerto for Orchestra*, 1948, and music for the film *The Quiet One*, 1948. He lived in Italy from 1949 to 1952, having won a Prix de Rome and a Fulbright fellowship. Other awards and fellowships followed, and in 1958 he was a member of the first group of U.S. composers to participate in a cultural-exchange mission to the Soviet Union. A prolific composer for films and television, he produced a notable *Essay on Death*, 1964, in tribute to President John F. Kennedy, and he also wrote a number of orchestral pieces, among them *Markings*, 1966, a tribute to Dag Hammarskjöld. He also composed chamber music, choral works, organ and piano music, short band pieces, and two operas, *The Boor*, 1955, and *The Juggler of Our Lady*, 1956. In 1968 he was named professor of music at Herbert H. Lehman College of the City University of New York.

Kaye, Danny (1913–   ), comedian and actor. Born in Brooklyn, New York, on January 18, 1913, David Daniel Kominsky adopted "Danny Kaye" as his stage name in 1933 while playing in a review in Utica, New York. Earlier, he had left high school and run away from home to Florida with $1.50 in his pocket, a sum that was increased by earnings as a soda jerk. After years as a "toomler"—a creator of tumult or all-around entertainment on the "borscht circuit" of resorts in the Catskill Mountains of New York—he got his first real break in 1939 when, at Camp Tamiment in Pennsylvania, he met Sylvia Fine, whom he married the next year and whose witty songs for him were one of the bases of his success. The year 1941 marked his first great Broadway success, in a part written especially for him by Moss Hart in *Lady in the Dark*. This engaging musical, starring Gertrude Lawrence, was followed by Cole Porter's *Let's Face It*, in which Kaye again performed in a role written for him. His first film was *Up in Arms*, 1944, but his first great movie success was in *The Secret Life of Walter Mitty*, 1947, in which he played seven different roles. Other films in which he appeared included *The Inspector-General*, 1949; *White Christmas*, 1954; *The Court Jester*, 1955; and *The Five Pennies*, 1959, but it was probably in the title role of *Hans Christian Andersen*, 1952, that he made his most enduring and endearing success. After this movie, life imitated art when Kaye, becoming a kind of living symbol of the charm and joyousness of the tales of the Danish writer, entertained children throughout the world on tours as ambassador-at-large of the United Nations Children's Emergency Fund (UNICEF). The star of his own television show from 1963 to 1967, he returned to Broadway in 1971 as Noah in the musical *Two by Two*.

Kazan, Elia (1909–   ), stage and film director and author. Born in Constantinople (now Istan-

bul), Turkey, on September 7, 1909, Elia Kazanjoglous, who shortened the family name while a young man, was brought to the United States by his Greek parents in 1913. Growing up in New York City and in New Rochelle, New York, he graduated from Williams College in 1930 and, after a short stay at the Yale Drama School, joined the Group Theatre in New York City. There he met Clifford Odets, who was also an unknown at the time, and acted in a number of his plays and also in several movies, including *Blues in the Night*, 1941. He had dabbled in stage directing for several years, as with *Casey Jones*, 1938, when he scored his first directorial hit with Thornton Wilder's *The Skin of Our Teeth*, 1942, which, besides delighting audiences with its frantic pace, won him the New York Drama Critics' Circle Award for the best directing of the year. Further directorial successes followed in short order, including *Harriet*, with Helen Hayes, 1942; *One Touch of Venus*, 1943; *Jacobowsky and the Colonel*, 1944; and *Deep Are the Roots*, 1946. His association with the work of playwright Arthur Miller began with his direction of Miller's *All My Sons* in 1947; he also directed Miller's *Death of a Salesman*, 1949, and his *After the Fall*, 1964. Probably his greatest Broadway fame, however, came with his direction of a series of plays by Tennessee Williams starting with *A Streetcar Named Desire*, 1947, and including *Cat on a Hot Tin Roof*, 1954, and the less successful *Camino Real* and *Sweet Bird of Youth*. Kazan also directed Robert Anderson's *Tea and Sympathy*, 1953, and Archibald MacLeish's *JB*, 1958, for which he won the Antoinette Perry (Tony) Award for direction. Kazan was a founder of the Actors Studio, a major training ground for actors. From 1944 he was also a distinguished film director, his first film, *A Tree Grows in Brooklyn*, 1945, being also his first success; it was followed by a number of films, some of which attained almost legendary fame in the history of the medium in the post-World War II period, including *Gentleman's Agreement*, 1947, for which he won an Academy Award; *Boomerang*, 1947; *Pinky*, 1949; *Panic in the Streets*, 1950; a version of *Streetcar*, 1951; *Viva Zapata*, 1952; *On the Waterfront*, 1954, for which he won a second Academy Award; *East of Eden*, 1955; *A Face in the Crowd*, 1957; *Splendor in the Grass*, 1961; and *America, America*, 1963, which he adapted from his first novel, *America, America*, a best seller published in 1962. Another novel, *The Arrangement*, appeared in 1967 and was also a best seller.

Kazanjoglous, Elia, *see* Kazan, Elia

Kearny, Philip (1814–1862), soldier. Born in New York City on June 1, 1814, Kearny early determined upon a military career. Family pressure sent him to Columbia College, from which he graduated with a law degree in 1833, but in 1837, soon after the death of his grandfather and guardian and his inheriting of a substantial fortune, he secured a commission as second lieutenant of cavalry and was attached to the 1st Dragoons, on duty on the Western frontier under the command of his uncle, Col. Stephen W. Kearny. In 1839 he was sent to France to study cavalry tactics and training, serving with the French cavalry in Algeria in 1840 and preparing a manual for the U.S. army on his return. After further service on the frontier and as aide to Gen. Alexander Macomb and to Gen. Winfield Scott he resigned his commission early in 1846, only to return to duty a month later for service in the Mexican War. Recruiting and equipping his own cavalry company, he performed with distinction in battle, losing an arm at Churubusco. Promoted to major, he remained in the army until 1851, when he retired for several years to his New Jersey estate. The prospect of adventure and glory lured him to France in 1859, where he served with the Imperial Guard of Napoleon III in Italy and became the first American to earn the cross of the French Legion of Honor. On the outbreak of the Civil War he returned to the United States and was appointed a brigadier general of the New Jersey militia. During the Peninsular Campaign he played a conspicuous role at the battles of Williamsburg and Fair Oaks (Seven Pines) and was promoted to major general. His fearlessness and dash made him a highly popular as well as valuable commander; his leadership in a dozen cavalry engagements won the respect of his superiors and the enemy alike. While on a reconnoitering mission near Chantilly, Virginia, Kearny unwittingly crossed Confederate lines and was killed on September 1, 1862.

Kearny, Stephen Watts (1794–1848), soldier. Born in Newark, New Jersey, on August 30, 1794, Kearny left Columbia College, which he had entered in 1811, to serve in the War of 1812, during which he exhibited conspicuous bravery and was promoted to captain. He occupied various posts on the Western frontier and fought in numerous Indian wars and skirmishes during the subsequent decades, serving with Gen. Henry Atkinson and aiding in the establishment of several army outposts. In May 1846 he was named commander of the Army of the West and shortly thereafter given the rank of brigadier general. The Mexican War having broken out, he entered Santa Fe, New Mexico, with some 1700 troops on August 18, 1846, and for the next month was military governor of the territory, organizing in short order a civil government. He set out with just over 100 men for California on September 25 and, after heavy losses at San Pasqual on December 6, joined with forces already there under Commodore Robert F. Stockton and took San Diego in December and San Gabriel and Los Angeles in January 1847. The defeated Californians, however, surrendered (on January 13) not to Kearny or Stockton but to Lt. Col. John C. Frémont, a fact that fed a bitter quarrel that had already begun between Kearny and Stockton as to who was to exercise final authority. Kearny's authority was supported by Washington, and

Kearny removed Frémont, who had been appointed governor by Stockton, from his command and arrested him; a court-martial later convicted Frémont of insubordination and conduct prejudicial to military order, whereupon he resigned from the army. After completing the pacification of California as military governor until August 1847 and waiting for a time at Fort Leavenworth, Kansas, Kearny proceeded to Mexico, where for a time in 1848 he was governor-general of Veracruz and later of Mexico City. In September 1848 he was promoted to major general despite the heated opposition of Sen. Thomas Hart Benton, Frémont's father-in-law, but while at Veracruz he had contracted a tropical disease from which he died in St. Louis, Missouri, on October 31, 1848.

Keaton, Buster (1895–1966), comedian. Born on October 4, 1895, in Piqua, Woodson County, Kansas, while his parents were touring in a tent show with the magician Harry Houdini, Joseph Frank Keaton is said to have received his nickname when Houdini remarked "What a buster!" when the six-month-old boy fell downstairs! He performed in the family variety act, the Three Keatons, from an early age, being tossed about the stage with reckless abandon and learning to fall without hurting himself, a skill that later came in handy in his movies, where he never used a double. He also perfected his famous deadpan stare during those early years. The Keaton family did their last variety turn at the Palace Theater in New York City in 1917, whereupon Buster was signed by Fatty Arbuckle to appear in a film, *The Butcher Boy.* A practically endless series of successful slapstick and knockabout comedies followed, most of them filmed without a script, and Keaton emerged as one of the great clowns of the silent screen, rivaled only by Charlie Chaplin and Harold Lloyd. But, although like them he was a master mime, unlike them he did not survive the transition to talking pictures, and his career went into a sharp decline after 1930. In about 1950 he achieved a new success on British television, and at about the same time his old silent movies began to be revived and he was featured in a side-splitting scene in *Limelight,* 1952, with his old friend Chaplin. His 1927 film *The General* was reissued to universal acclaim in 1962. The new interest in his old films led to television work and then to roles in several comedies including *A Funny Thing Happened on the Way to the Forum,* 1966. He died in Hollywood on February 1, 1966.

Keene, Carolyn, see Stratemeyer, Edward

Keene, Laura (1820?–1873), actress and theatrical producer. Born in London about 1820, Mary Moss grew up in obscurity and little is known of her life before she joined the theatrical company of Madame Vestris, with whom she soon gained, as Laura Keene, a wide reputation in the comedies and extravaganzas produced at the Olympic Theatre in London. In 1852 she traveled to the United States to appear with the New York City company of James W. Wallack; her U.S. debut was a great success, but she soon left Wallack to appear in Baltimore and then, in 1854, in San Francisco, where she was the principal attraction at the Metropolitan Theatre. After an unsuccessful Australian tour she was again in San Francisco, reigning supreme in the theater and trying her hand also at management and production with the staging of a number of popular and tastefully conceived extravaganzas. In 1855 she returned to New York City to open the Metropolitan Theatre as Laura Keene's Varieties Theatre, the next year moving to the new Laura Keene's Theatre; for eight years she was a major theatrical producer, the first woman in the United States to achieve that status, and her company included such eminent figures as Joseph Jefferson, Dion Boucicault, and Edward H. Sothern. One of her greatest successes was the production of *Our American Cousin*, and it was during her appearance in her revival of that play at Ford's Theater, Washington, D.C., in April 1865 that President Abraham Lincoln was assassinated. After giving up her theater in 1863 her career gradually declined. She continued to act, touring with various companies throughout the country, to write and to lecture, and in 1869 attempted a comeback as manager of a Philadelphia theater, but lacking fresh material and caught by changing tastes in entertainment, she faded from public notice. In 1872 she helped found and edit *The Fine Arts*, a short-lived magazine. Miss Keene died in Montclair, New Jersey, on November 4, 1873.

Keeshan, Robert James (1927–   ), "Captain Kangaroo," television actor. Born in Lynbrook, Long Island, New York, on June 27, 1927, Bob Keeshan began working as a page boy at the National Broadcasting Company (NBC) when he was sixteen. After service in the Marine Corps during World War II he returned to NBC, where his first television job was as a stagehand on the enormously popular children's show "Howdy Doody" in 1947. He was soon promoted to appearing on camera as the voiceless, horn-honking, seltzer-squirting clown, Clarabell; he played the character until he left Howdy Doody and NBC in 1952. Interim employment in television on WABC–TV's "Time for Fun" and "Tinker's Workshop" led to the acceptance by the Columbia Broadcasting System (CBS) of a Keeshan idea for a new network show, which premiered as "Captain Kangaroo" on the morning of October 3, 1955. Keeshan played the title role of Kangaroo, so called because of the enormous pockets of his costume, all of which contained "surprises." Believing that "we aren't playing to small animals, but to young humans of potentially great taste," Keeshan insisted that the show be nonviolent and that it have significant educational content; his success was reflected in the citation of the Peabody Award that "Captain Kangaroo" won as the best children's program on television in 1958: the show was described as "certainly the only one which puts the welfare of the children ahead of that of

the sponsor . . . which instructs them in safety, ethics and health without interrupting the serious business of entertaining them at the same time." Keeshan also appeared on several other children's programs and was the author of books and articles for children.

Kefauver, Carey Estes (1903–1963), public official. Born on a farm near Madisonville, Tennessee, on July 26, 1903, Estes Kefauver graduated from the University of Tennessee, where he had been a football star, in 1924 and received his law degree from Yale three years later. Admitted to the Tennessee bar in 1926, he practiced law in Chattanooga until 1939, when he accepted the post of state commissioner of finance and taxation. He resigned soon afterward to run as a Democrat for a vacated seat in the House of Representatives, and was elected in September 1939. He was reelected to the next four congresses, distinguishing himself by his support of New Deal and Fair Deal measures and by his opposition to big-business mergers that fostered monopoly. He announced his intention to run for the Democratic nomination for a Senate seat in November 1947 and waged a spirited campaign against the state Democratic machine, headed by the notorious "boss" of Memphis, Edward H. Crump. Crump ran a newspaper advertisement referring to Kefauver as a "pet coon," whereupon Kefauver countered by appearing in a coonskin cap and declaring in a speech: "I may be a pet coon, but I'll never be Mr. Crump's pet coon." He was elected to the Senate in 1948 and reelected in 1954 and 1960. He gained national attention when, as chairman of a Senate Judiciary subcommittee, he conducted a televised Senate investigation of organized crime in 1950–1951—the first such use of the new medium—and published *Crime in America*, 1951, a book based on the results of the hearings. He campaigned vigorously for the Democratic presidential nomination in 1952 but was defeated by Adlai E. Stevenson on the third ballot; again in 1956 he sought the nomination and won several primaries, but he withdrew shortly before the convention and accepted the second spot on the unsuccessful Democratic ticket. His investigations of professional sports and of the pharmaceutical industry in 1959 again reflected his dislike and distrust of monopolies wherever found, but the image of the man in the coonskin cap continued to haunt him, and he was probably never taken as seriously as he wished or deserved. His popularity with his constituency was nonetheless remarkable; a strong supporter of civil-rights legislation, he won his 1960 reelection against a segregationist opponent. He died in Bethesda, Maryland, on August 10, 1963.

Keifer, Joseph Warren (1836–1932), soldier and public official. Born near Springfield, Ohio, on January 30, 1836, Keifer attended Antioch College briefly and, after studying law, began to practice in Springfield in 1858. He was commissioned a major in the Ohio militia in April 1861 and served throughout the Civil War, being seriously wounded at Wilderness. He became a brigadier general in 1864 and was mustered out in June 1865 as a major general of volunteers. A member of the Ohio state senate in 1868–1869 and a delegate to the Republican national convention in 1876, he was elected to the House of Representatives in the latter year and was reelected three times, serving from March 1881 to March 1883 as speaker. Failing in his campaign for renomination in the fall of 1884, he returned to his successful law practice. He was a major general of volunteers again during the Spanish-American War and then was elected again to the House, where he remained for three terms, 1905 to 1911. An advocate of world peace, he was on his way to Stockholm to address a peace conference when war broke out in Europe in 1914. Keifer was the president of a bank in Springfield, Ohio, for more than 50 years, and he died there on April 22, 1932.

Keller, Helen Adams (1880–1968), author and lecturer. Born on June 27, 1880, near Tuscumbia, Alabama, Helen Keller was afflicted at the age of 19 months with an illness that left her blind, deaf, and mute. She was examined by Alexander Graham Bell at about the age of six; as a result he sent to her a twenty-year-old teacher, Anne Mansfield Sullivan, from the Perkins Institution, which Bell's son-in-law directed. Miss Sullivan (later Mrs. John A. Macy), a remarkable teacher, remained with Helen from March 2, 1887, until her death in 1936. Within months Helen had learned to feel objects and associate them with words spelled out by finger signals on her palm, to read sentences by feeling raised words on cardboard, and to make her own sentences by arranging words in a frame. During 1888–1890 she spent winters in Boston at the Perkins Institution learning Braille. Then she began a slow process of learning to speak—feeling the position of the tongue and lips, making sounds, and imitating the lip and tongue motions—at Boston's Horace Mann School for the Deaf. She also learned to lip-read by placing her fingers on the lips and throat of the speaker while the words were simultaneously spelled out for her. At fourteen she enrolled in the Wright-Humason School for the Deaf in New York City, and at sixteen entered the Cambridge School for Young Ladies in Massachusetts. She won admission to Radcliffe College, entering in 1900, and graduated cum laude in 1904. Having developed skills never approached by any person so handicapped, she began to write of blindness, a subject then taboo in women's magazines because of the relationship of many cases to venereal disease. The pioneering editor Edward W. Bok accepted her articles for the *Ladies' Home Journal,* and other major magazines—*The Century, McClure's,* and the *Atlantic Monthly*—followed suit. She wrote of her life in several books, including *The Story of My Life,* 1902; *Optimism,* 1903; *The World I Live In,* 1908; *Song of the Stone Wall,*

1910; *Out of the Dark,* 1913; *My Religion,* 1927; *Midstream,* 1929; *Peace at Eventide,* 1932; *Helen Keller's Journal,* 1938; *Let Us Have Faith,* 1940; and *The Open Door,* 1957. In 1913 she began lecturing, primarily on behalf of the American Foundation for the Blind, for which she established a $2-million endowment fund, and her lecture tours took her around the world. Her efforts to improve treatment of the deaf and the blind were influential in removing the handicapped from asylums. She also prompted the organization of commissions for the blind in 30 states by 1937. Awarded the Presidential Medal of Freedom in 1963, she died in Westport, Connecticut, on June 1, 1968, universally acknowledged as one of the great women of the world.

Kelley, Oliver Hudson (1826–1913), agriculturalist and reformer. Born in Boston on January 7, 1826, Kelley worked at odd jobs after leaving school and gradually made his way west, settling finally in 1849 in Minnesota, where he took up land and began farming. He immediately became an enthusiastic promoter of Minnesota, contributing letters and articles to Eastern publications to attract settlers to the region. He went to Washington, D.C., in 1864 as a clerk in the U.S. Bureau of Agriculture, under whose auspices he then undertook several inspection tours to gather information on farming conditions in the South and the Middle West. It was in the course of such a tour that he conceived the idea of a fraternal organization through which farmers might work for their mutual benefit, and on February 19, 1868, he and six associates met at his home in Georgetown, D.C., to organize the National Grange of the Patrons of Husbandry, best known as "the Grange." The progress of the Grange was slow at first, but Kelley was indefatigable—some said fanatical—in his efforts on its behalf, and by 1875, when he published his *Origin and Progress of the Patrons of Husbandry,* the number of local Granges throughout the country had passed 20,000, a spectacular growth attributable in large part to the general economic depression following the panic of 1873. The success of the organization was aided also by the fact that it accepted women as members—indeed, Kelley's original notion was of a social and educational organization for farming families—and that it was viewed as a counterforce to the industrial and transportation monopolies of the era. It was particularly strong in the South and in the Middle West, where in addition to sponsoring various cooperative enterprises for farmers it turned to political action in pressing for state regulation of rates charged by businesses involved with the public interest, with special attention to railroad freight and grain-storage rates. Joined by other like-minded groups in what came to be known as the Granger movement, it found its greatest success in the so-called "Granger laws" enacted in several states and validated in a series of "Granger cases," culminating before the Supreme Court in *Munn v. Illinois,* 1877. Despite such success, the Grange lost membership between 1875 and 1880 owing to the failure of many of its cooperative enterprises. A slow rebuilding, along with a rapidly changing political atmosphere, turned the later Grange from political activism. Kelley resigned from the post of secretary of the National Grange after serving for ten years. He later engaged with little success in land speculation in Florida. With a pension from the National Grange from 1905, he spent his last years in Washington, D.C., where he died on January 20, 1913.

Kellogg, Frank Billings (1856–1937), lawyer, public official, and diplomat. Born in Potsdam, New York, on December 22, 1856, Kellogg moved to a farm in Minnesota in 1865. He studied law in Rochester, Minnesota, and was admitted to the bar in 1877. He moved to St. Paul in 1887 to continue his law career and soon became counsel for a number of large industrial and financial organizations. He agreed to serve the Theodore Roosevelt administration as a special prosecutor of those accused of monopoly in restraint of trade, and he brought suit against the Standard Oil Company in 1906 and against the Union Pacific Railroad the next year, winning both cases for the government. With his success in the Standard Oil case before the Supreme Court in 1911 he became nationally known as the "trust buster." He was the Republican national committeeman for Minnesota from 1904 to 1912, and in 1916 he was elected to the Senate. He continued to be known as an antimonopolist during his career in the Senate, and, a rarity among Republicans, he supported the principle of the League of Nations, although he came to share Republican reservations in regard to the Treaty of Versailles; but he quarreled publicly with Sen. Robert La Follette of Wisconsin and, owing to the resurgence of the Farmer-Labor party in his own state, failed to win reelection in 1922. He was appointed by President Calvin Coolidge as ambassador to Great Britain in December 1923 and was influential in bringing about acceptance of the Dawes plan for the payment of reparations by Germany. In January 1925 he became secretary of state in the Coolidge cabinet, succeeding Charles Evans Hughes, and served until 1929. He engaged skillfully in a number of complicated diplomatic negotiations with South American countries, with Mexico, and with the European powers in China, but his major achievement was the Kellogg-Briand Pact, formulated in 1928 with French foreign minister Aristide Briand, the signatories of which solemnly renounced war as an instrument of national policy and pledged themselves to settle all disputes by peaceful means. The pact, also called the Pact of Paris, was ratified by the Senate early in 1929 and on July 24 of that year was declared by President Herbert C. Hoover to be in full force and effect; it was eventually signed by 62 nations, most of which were later involved in World War II. For his efforts in behalf of it Kellogg received the Nobel Peace Prize in 1929. Upon retiring from the State Department he resumed the practice of law

and from 1930 to 1935 sat on the Permanent Court of International Justice (the World Court) at the Hague. He died on December 21, 1937, in St. Paul, Minnesota.

Kellogg, Will Keith (1860–1951), businessman. Born in Battle Creek, Michigan, on April 7, 1860, Kellogg left school at fourteen to work as a traveling salesman for his father, a manufacturer of brooms. Four years later he took a position in the Battle Creek Sanitarium, operated by his brother, Dr. John H. Kellogg, who was something of a pioneer in the theory and practice of sound nutrition. During the early 1890s the brothers carried on numerous experiments in preparing cereal grains in various ways, hitting at length on a method of rolling cooked wheat mush into flakes; oven toasting of the flakes yielded a tasty and pleasantly crunchy breakfast food of high nutritional value, which they introduced into the menus of Dr. Kellogg's establishment and then began selling by mail order to other users of health foods. The mail-order business grew and in 1900 it became the Sanitas Food Company. After further experiments and the development of a new flaked product made from corn, a less easily worked grain, Will Kellogg organized in 1906 the Battle Creek Toasted Corn Flake Company, which shortly thereafter became the W. K. Kellogg Company, and launched an ambitious national advertising campaign to promote cornflakes, not merely as a health food but as a healthful, enjoyable, and above all convenient breakfast food for everyone. In succeeding—and in overcoming the problems of a rapidly growing business, including a disastrous fire that destroyed his plant in 1907, and the many competitors that sprang up around him—Kellogg worked a minor revolution in American life, largely displacing with his cornflakes and other cold cereals the traditional heavy, hot breakfast. Large-scale advertising continued to play a vital role in the growth of the firm. Kellogg retired as president in 1929 and the next year established the W. K. Kellogg Foundation in Battle Creek, which, after taking over most of his fortune, became one of the nation's major philanthropic institutions. Kellogg remained chairman of the board of the company until 1946; he died in Battle Creek on October 6, 1951.

Kelly, Alvin A. (1893–1952), "Shipwreck," flagpole sitter. Born on May 13, 1893, Shipwreck Kelly worked in shipyards, on the construction of skyscrapers, and served in the navy in World War I, but his real career began in the 1920s, when he became the champion flagpole sitter of all time. His feats aloft attracted the wide publicity and enthusiasm accorded all manner of performers during that less than entirely sane and sober decade. Altogether, he said, he had spent a total of 20,613 hours sitting on the tops of flagpoles and on other high perches, including 47 hours in snow, 1400 hours in rain and sleet, and 210 hours in below-freezing temperatures. His greatest feat was accomplished in the summer of

1930 when he remained atop a flagpole on the Steel Pier at Atlantic City for 1177 hours (more than 49 days). When he slept he placed his thumbs in holes drilled in the flagpole shaft; any movement would cause a twinge of pain, and he would right himself without waking up. He claimed to have survived five sea disasters (hence his nickname), two airplane accidents, three automobile accidents, and a train wreck without receiving a scratch. He served in the merchant marine during World War II and died in New York City on October 11, 1952.

Kelly, Ellsworth (1923–   ), painter and sculptor. Born in Newburgh, New York, on May 31, 1923, Kelly served in the army engineers in World War II and then studied at the Museum of Fine Arts in Boston and at the École des Beaux-Arts in Paris. He completed his studies in 1950 but remained in Paris for another four years. His early paintings were figurative, and his first one-man show was held at the Galerie Arnaud in 1951. In 1950 he began to make abstract collages and in the early 1950s turned to Mondrian-like grid paintings based on random combinations of colors and shapes. In 1954 he returned to the United States and produced the first of his curvilinear, biomorphic compositions, the paintings of 1954–1955 being almost entirely in black and white. He had his first U.S. one-man show in 1956 in New York City; others followed at frequent intervals. Also during the mid–1950s he created his first architectural sculptures, including a massive work for the Philadelphia Transportation Center. In 1959 his work was included in the "Sixteen Americans Show" of the Museum of Modern Art in New York City, and in 1963, when that museum purchased one of his paintings, he became one of the youngest American artists to be included in its permanent collection. He was one of the four artists chosen to represent the United States at the Venice Biennale in 1966 and he was massively represented at the prestigious "New York Painting and Sculpture 1940–1970" exhibition at New York City's Metropolitan Museum of Art, more than 10 percent of the show being given over to his work. He exhibited regularly in New York City after 1965 and his work was represented in the permanent collections of many major museums.

Kelly, Emmett (1898–1979), clown. Born in Sedan, Kansas, on December 9, 1898, Kelly, unlike many circus performers, did not come from a circus background but was the son of a railroad worker. In his youth he exhibited a talent for drawing, and he left home for Kansas City in 1917 to try to become a professional cartoonist. He was unsuccessful in this career but he did create one memorable cartoon character, "Weary Willie," a sad-faced hobo with a bright pink, bulbous nose who always got the short end of the stick and never had any luck at all (as Kelly himself later described him in his autobiography, *Clown,* 1954).

Willie as a character was not brought to life by Kelly, however, for many years; from 1920 to the early 1930s he worked at odd jobs and in various circuses, usually as a trapeze artist. It was while working as a clown for the Hagenbeck-Wallace Circus in about 1931 that he created the makeup for, and began to appear regularly as, Weary Willie, a role that he continued to play for the remainder of his life. After tours with several circuses in the 1930s and a stint in nightclubs during World War II, he joined the Ringling Brothers–Barnum and Bailey Circus in 1942, remaining with that circus off and on, for the next 15 years, during which he became a star attraction. In 1957, after a labor dispute, he left Ringling and was signed by the Brooklyn Dodgers baseball team to entertain before the games at Ebbets Field. Perhaps his most memorable achievement as a Dodger came in his last game at Ebbets Field when he gave Casey Stengel a hotfoot. He appeared in several films, including *The Greatest Show on Earth,* and was often seen on television. The country's best known clown, he died in Sarasota, Florida, on March 28, 1979.

Kelly, Grace Patricia (1929–1982), actress and princess of Monaco. Born in Philadelphia on November 12, 1929, the daughter of a wealthy contractor and former Olympic oarsman and the sister of an Olympic oarsman, Grace Kelly was educated in convent and private schools and then attended the American Academy of Dramatic Arts in New York City, working as a photographer's model to pay her own tuition. After several seasons of summer stock she made her Broadway debut in 1949 in August Strindberg's *The Father.* Her first film part, a small one, was in *Fourteen Hours,* 1951, but the next year she appeared as Gary Cooper's Quaker wife in *High Noon* and her career began to blossom. She was signed to a seven-year contract by Metro-Goldwyn-Mayer (MGM), was featured in *Mogambo,* 1953, and starred in *Dial M for Murder* and *Rear Window,* both in 1954. In December of that year *The Country Girl,* a screen version of the play by Clifford Odets, in which she starred opposite Bing Crosby, was released, and she won an Academy Award for her performance. Other pictures followed, including *High Society,* 1956, but her movie career was cut short, to the mixed distress and delight of her fans, when on April 19, 1956, she married Prince Rainier III, ruler of Monaco, and retired from the screen. Princess Grace died on September 14, 1982, in Monte Carlo as a result of an automobile accident.

Kelly, Shipwreck, see Kelly, Alvin A.

Kelly, Walter Crawford (1913–1973), cartoonist and illustrator. Born in Philadelphia on August 25, 1913, the son of a theatrical scene painter who taught him to draw, Walt Kelly was brought up in Bridgeport, Connecticut, where he was cartoonist for the high-school paper. He went to Hollywood in 1935 and worked for six years as an animator of Walt Disney films; he moved to New York City in 1941 to illustrate children's books. His famous comic strip, *Pogo*, featuring an opossum named Pogo, who lived in the Okefenokee Swamp in Georgia, began to appear in the *New York Star* in 1948 and shifted to the *New York Post* upon the demise of the *Star* in 1949. By 1952 it was syndicated in some 225 newspapers in the United States, Canada, Mexico, Japan, and other countries and had some 37 million readers. By the later 1960s these figures had swelled to more than 450 newspapers and more than 50 million readers. Pogo was described by Kelly as "the reasonable, patient, softhearted, naïve, friendly little person we all think we are," and the comic strip described Pogo's adventures with other denizens of the swamp, including the cigar-smoking alligator Albert; the turtle Churchy LaFemme; Dr. Howland Owl, a nearsighted scientist; Porkypine; Deacon Mushrat and P. T. Bridgeport, whose respective speeches appeared in Old English and circus-poster script; Seminole Sam, a shrewd fox; and other characters, some of whom bore more than passing resemblances to public figures. Kelly published a number of Pogo books and also illustrated several volumes of children's stories, including *The Glob*, 1952, and *I'd Rather Be President*, 1956. He and his cartoon characters appeared often on television and in 1952 Pogo, under the banner "I Go Pogo," challenged Dwight D. Eisenhower and Adlai E. Stevenson for the presidency. The language of Pogo and his friends was an amalgam of Elizabethan English, French, and Negro dialects, heavily interspersed with puns and Freudian allusions, with which Kelly commented on subjects of current interest. Most famous of these comments was Pogo's remark concerning the ecological crisis: "We have met the enemy and he is us." Kelly died in Hollywood on October 18, 1973.

Kelly, William (1811–1888), inventor. Born in Pittsburgh on August 21, 1811, Kelly was educated in public schools and until 1846 engaged in the dry-goods business in Philadelphia. Moving to Eddyville, Kentucky, in that year, he operated the Suwanee Iron Works & Union Forge, manufacturing kettles. As charcoal became scarce he began casting about for an alternate method of heating pig iron; observation and experiment led to the development of a process whereby a blast of air was shot through the molten iron, causing combustion of the carbon dissolved in it and greatly increasing its temperature. The impurities were thus eliminated and a low grade of steel was obtained. Kelly built several furnaces employing this "pneumatic process" for converting iron to steel but kept his discovery secret. When Bessemer in England announced his independent discovery of the same process and applied for a U.S. patent in 1857, Kelly revealed his work and established his priority, receiving his own patent the same year. In 1862 he built a converter for the Cambria Iron Works in Johnstown, Pennsylvania;

before it was completed, however, Kelly-process steel had been poured at the Wyandotte Iron Works in Michigan in 1864. Kelly's patent came under the control of the Kelly Pneumatic Process Company, with which he had nothing to do and which later merged with the company of Alexander L. Holley, Bessemer's sole U.S. licensee. The Bessemer name came into exclusive use for the Kelly-Bessemer steelmaking process and Kelly remained in relative obscurity, receiving for his discovery less than a twentieth of the royalties paid to his more fortunate counterpart. After 1861 he operated an axe factory in Louisville, Kentucky, where he died on February 11, 1888.

Kelsen, Hans (1881–   ), legal philosopher. Born in Prague, Czechoslovakia, then in Austria-Hungary, on October 11, 1881, Kelsen was educated at the universities of Heidelberg, Berlin, and Vienna, receiving his Ll.D. from Vienna in 1906. He taught public law and jurisprudence at Vienna from 1911 until 1930, when he was named professor of international law and jurisprudence at the University of Cologne, where he was dean of the faculty of law in 1932–1933. Unwilling to live under the Nazi regime in Germany, he left for Switzerland in 1933, teaching at the Graduate Institute of International Studies of the University of Geneva until 1940; during 1936–1938 he taught at the German University of Prague. In 1940 he came to the United States at the invitation of Harvard University, and he was naturalized in 1945. After two years in Cambridge, Massachusetts, he went to the University of California at Berkeley to teach international law and jurisprudence, remaining there until his retirement in 1952. He was the author of many books, both in German and English, several of which were translated into a number of other languages. He made a major contribution to the theory of jurisprudence as early as 1911, when he introduced the concept known as the "pure theory of law," a formal-logical analysis of the law considered as a system of norms; it was a normative and positive doctrine, opposed both to sociologism (law as fact) and to natural law. Among his important books were *General Theory of Law and State*, 1945; *The Law of the United Nations*, 1950–1951, in which he criticized the UN charter; *Principles of International Law*, 1952; *Théorie pure de droit*, 1953, a volume that included a complete bibliography of his writings to that date; and *What Is Justice?*, 1957. He visited Vienna in 1965, at the age of eighty-four, to take part in the celebration of the 600th anniversary of the University of Vienna, and was at that time honored for his role in the writing of the Austrian constitution in 1920.

Kemble, Fanny (1809–1893), actress and author. Born in London on November 27, 1809, Frances Anne Kemble was the daughter of the actors Charles Kemble and Maria Theresa De Camp and the niece of the two most distinguished English actors of the later eighteenth century, John Philip

Kemble and his sister Sarah Siddons. She was educated mainly in France and made her debut in her father's company at Covent Garden in London in October 1829, playing Juliet. Her success was instant and she was able to recoup the family's and indeed the theater's fortunes, which had declined. In 1832 she came with her father to the United States and enjoyed the same immediate success, playing, among other parts, that of Juliet to her father's Romeo, he being then fifty-seven. She toured for two years, winning acclaim everywhere, particularly in *The Hunchback*, written especially for her by James Sheridan Knowles. In June 1834 she married Pierce Butler, a Philadelphian who was also a Georgia planter, and retired from the stage. But she was shocked and disturbed to see at first hand the plantation that was the source of her husband's wealth, and as she learned more about the institution of slavery she drew away from her husband, from the South, and finally from the United States, which she left in 1846 to return to the London stage. Her husband divorced her for abandonment in a famous case in 1848, but in the meantime she had returned to the United States for a series of enormously successful readings from Shakespeare, which continued into the 1860s. The earnings from the readings made it possible for her to purchase a cottage in Lenox, Massachusetts. In her later years she traveled much between England and the United States. She wrote several plays, a volume of poems, and several volumes of reminiscence, but her most lasting writings were a series of journals, notably *Journal of a Residence on a Georgian Plantation*, 1863, which was adapted from her diary of 1838–1839 and issued during the Civil War to influence British opinion against slavery. She returned to England in 1877 and lived in London until her death there on January 15, 1893.

Kemble, Gouverneur (1786–1875), manufacturer. Born in New York City on January 25, 1786, Kemble graduated from Columbia College in 1803 and devoted the next few years to literary pursuits. He was a close friend of Washington Irving and a member of Irving's coterie, which often assembled at the Kemble home in Passaic, New Jersey, dubbed "Cockloft" in Irving's *Salmagundi* papers. Kemble's interest in business emerged when, while serving as U.S. consul in Cadiz during the War of 1812, he studied Spanish methods of casting cannon. Returning to the United States after notable service securing supplies for the U.S. navy in the Tripolitan War, he "turned Vulcan and began forging thunderbolts," as Irving expressed it, at the West Point Foundry, which he established in 1818 at Cold Spring, New York, across the Hudson River from West Point. He produced the best cannon cast in America up to his time, continuously improving them and becoming the chief supplier of the Union armies during the Civil War. Beginning by making smoothbore, low-trajectory "Columbiads," the West Point Foundry later turned to producing

Dahlgren cannon, named after their inventor, J. A. B. Dahlgren. The Dahlgren smoothbores were followed by the giant Parrott rifles developed by Robert Parker Parrott, who had become Kemble's successor at the foundry and his brother-in-law in 1839. All told, the foundry produced more than 3000 cannon and 1.6 million projectiles. Kemble served in the House of Representatives from 1837 to 1841 and was a delegate to Democratic national conventions in 1844 and 1860, but in his later years he devoted himself mainly to hospitality, holding open house for the professors and principal officers of the U.S. Military Academy at West Point every Saturday evening until the end of his life. He died at Cold Spring, New York, on September 16, 1875.

Kendall, Amos (1789–1869), journalist and public official. Born in Dunstable, Massachusetts, on August 16, 1789, Kendall was brought up on a farm; he had little formal schooling, but he nevertheless managed to enter Dartmouth College, from which he graduated at the head of his class in 1811. He studied law for a time but in 1814 went to Kentucky, where for a year he was a tutor in the household of Henry Clay. In 1816 he took charge in Frankfort of the influential newspaper *Argus of Western America*. Giving his political support first to Clay, he shifted it in 1826 to Andrew Jackson, with whom he was associated closely throughout Jackson's career. After Jackson won the presidency in 1828—with Kendall's help in Kentucky—Kendall went to Washington, where he served for six years as fourth auditor of the treasury and, from 1835 to 1840, as postmaster general under Jackson and his successor, Martin Van Buren. He performed capably in those posts, ending abuses and administering with marked skill, but it was as a member of the group closest to Jackson, the so-called "kitchen cabinet," that he exerted his major influence on government policy. Probably the most important and powerful adviser to both Jackson and Van Buren, he wrote many of Jackson's major speeches, including the veto in July 1832 of the bill to recharter the Bank of the United States. He played a major role in bringing Francis P. Blair to Washington to found and edit the pro-administration *Globe* and he himself contributed often to its pages. Van Buren failed to win reelection, and in 1840 Kendall returned to journalism, at first without much success. In 1843 he became an agent for claims against the government, bought a farm near Washington on which he worked to regain his failing health, and defended himself against unjust charges growing out of his management of the post-office department. In 1845 he was employed by Samuel F. B. Morse as his business agent on a percentage basis. Kendall handled the sale or letting out of patents on Morse's telegraph, organized several companies, and consolidated many small telegraph firms into a few large ones, and by 1859 he was wealthy. He performed his last significant public service in the winter of 1860–1861, when he lobbied actively against the secession of the Southern states. A noted philanthropist in his later years, particularly on behalf of the Columbia Institution for the Deaf and Dumb (later Gallaudet College) in Washington, D.C., of which he was a founder, he died on November 12, 1869.

Kendall, Edward Calvin (1886–1972), biochemist. Born in South Norwalk, Connecticut, on March 8, 1886, Kendall graduated from Columbia University in 1908 and received his Ph.D. in 1910, whereupon he spent four years at St. Luke's Hospital, New York City, spending much time studying the thyroid gland. In 1914 he joined the staff of the Mayo Clinic in Rochester, Minnesota, as head of the biochemistry section, and he remained in that post until his retirement in 1951, serving also during his last six years at the clinic as head of the laboratory of biochemistry and from 1921 to 1951 as professor of physiological chemistry at the Mayo Foundation, an affiliate of the University of Minnesota. During many years on the Mayo staff he continued his studies of the thyroid, first isolating the active constituent—thyroxine—of the gland and then crystallizing glutathione and establishing its chemical nature. He next turned his attention to the adrenal cortex and, in 1948, managed partially to synthesize the adrenal hormone cortisone, following this achievement by synthesizing hydrocortisone, also found in the adrenal cortex. For his work in isolating cortisone and applying it clinically in the treatment of rheumatoid arthritis, which had been done in association with Philip S. Hench, he received the 1950 Nobel Prize for Physiology and Medicine jointly with Hench and a Swiss researcher, Tadeus Reichstein. After 1951 Kendall became a visiting professor of biochemistry at Princeton University, where he continued his researches. He was the recipient of many awards and honors in addition to the Nobel Prize and was the author of *Thyroxin*, 1929. He died in Princeton, New Jersey, on May 4, 1972.

Kennan, George Frost (1904–   ), diplomat and historian. Born in Milwaukee on February 16, 1904, Kennan graduated from Princeton in 1925 and a year later entered the U.S. Foreign Service, serving during the next few years in Geneva, Hamburg, Berlin, Tallinn, Riga, Kaunas and other "listening posts" around the Soviet Union, with which the United States had no diplomatic relations at the time. From 1929 to 1931 he studied Russian language, history, and political theory in Berlin, under the auspices of the State Department, and he accompanied Ambassador William C. Bullitt to Moscow when the U.S. embassy was opened there in 1933. Filling other diplomatic posts during the 1930s, Kennan was named first secretary of the U.S. legation in Berlin in 1940, served in diplomatic posts in Lisbon and Moscow during World War II, and in 1946 was appointed deputy for foreign affairs at the National War College in Washington, D.C. In 1947 Secretary of State George C. Marshall named Kennan di-

rector of the policy-planning staff of the Department of State, charged with responsibility for long-range planning, particularly with regard to the Soviet Union. Kennan's views were later expressed in a famous and highly influential article, signed "X," that appeared in *Foreign Affairs* for July 1947 and that analyzed in detail the structure and psychology of Soviet diplomacy. In the article he advanced the principal arguments for a policy of "containment" of the Soviet Union, a policy that was in its essentials adopted under Secretary of State Dean Acheson and his successor, John Foster Dulles. He was chosen as a principal adviser to Secretary of State Dean Acheson in 1949 and returned to Moscow as U.S. ambassador in 1952 but was declared persona non grata by the Soviet government in 1953. Meanwhile he had joined the Institute for Advanced Study in Princeton, New Jersey, where, from 1956 as permanent professor in the school of historical studies, he spent much of his time during the next 15 years, interrupting his studies and his writing to serve as ambassador to Yugoslavia, 1961–1963. Despite his earlier identification with the principle of containment, Kennan revised his view of U.S.–Soviet relations in the late 1950s, advocating then a program of U.S. "disengagement" from Europe and other potential crisis areas, a demilitarization and neutralization that, he believed, would allow political differences to be worked out without the constant threat of war. He was the author of many books, among them *American Diplomacy 1900–1950*, 1951; *Realities of American Foreign Policy*, 1954; the two volume *Soviet-American Relations, 1917–1920, 1956–1958* (*Russia Leaves the War*, the first volume, won a Pulitzer Prize, a National Book Award, and the Bancroft and Parkman prizes for history); *Russia and the West Under Lenin and Stalin*, 1961; and *Memoirs, 1925–1950*, 1967, which won a Pulitzer Prize and a National Book Award. *Memoirs, 1950–1963*, appeared in 1972.

Kennedy, Edward Moore (1932–   ), public official. Born in Brookline, Massachusetts, on February 22, 1932, the youngest of nine children of Joseph P. and Rose Kennedy, and their fourth son, Kennedy (who was called Ted or Teddy from childhood) was educated at secondary schools in the United States and then in England during the period when his father was U.S. ambassador to Great Britain, and entered Harvard in 1950. A youthful escapade in his freshman year led to his suspension, whereupon he spent two years in military service in Europe and then returned to Harvard, graduating in 1956. He entered the University of Virginia Law School the following fall and received his Ll.B. degree in 1959. The previous year he had had his first taste of active politics when he served as manager of his brother John's campaign for reelection to the Senate from Massachusetts; John's landslide victory helped to establish Ted's reputation as a capable politician. He was engaged in further political work in 1960, as John F. Kennedy first obtained the Democratic nomination for the presidency and then the presidency itself. In 1962 Ted Kennedy sought his own first political office, running for the two unexpired years of John's Senate term. He won by a huge majority in Massachusetts, and when his brother Robert won a Senate seat from New York in 1964 and Ted was reelected from Massachusetts, they became the first pair of brothers to serve in the Senate at the same time since the first years of the nineteenth century. By that time John was dead of an assassin's bullet, and Ted aided Robert's bid for the Democratic presidential nomination in 1968; but in June of that year Robert, too, was assassinated, and Ted became a leading candidate for the nomination. He refused to allow his name to be considered that year but, with the election of Richard M. Nixon to the presidency in 1968, he was mentioned more and more often for the nomination in 1972. His political career suffered a setback, however, in the summer of 1969, when an automobile accident on Chappaquiddick Island, off Martha's Vineyard, led to the drowning of a young woman, and his behavior at the time was questioned by many; partly as a result, Ted, although he was reelected handily to the Senate in 1970, refused to be a presidential candidate in 1972, and turned down the offer of the vice-presidential nomination proffered by Senator George S. McGovern, the Democratic nominee. (His brother-in-law, Sargent Shriver, ultimately joined McGovern on the ticket.) But Kennedy had placed McGovern's name in nomination at the 1972 convention and campaigned vigorously for him in the race, and his future prospects continued to seem bright, especially after his state of Massachusetts was the only one whose electoral vote was captured by McGovern in the November presidential election.

Kennedy, John Fitzgerald (1917–1963), thirty-fifth president of the United States. Born on May 29, 1917, in the Boston suburb of Brookline, Kennedy was the son of Joseph P. Kennedy, a prominent businessman and financier, and an elder brother of Robert F. and Edward M. (Ted) Kennedy. Educated in private schools, he entered Princeton at eighteen, but, after a short illness, transferred to Harvard; he graduated in 1940 and his senior thesis, a study of England's reaction to the rise of European fascism, that he had undertaken while serving as secretary to his father, then U.S. ambassador in London, was published the same year as *Why England Slept* and became a best seller at the time. After brief graduate study in business at Stanford University he enlisted in the navy in 1941; during World War II he served as commander of a PT boat in the Pacific theater and in 1943 his craft was sunk and its crew rescued in an episode later much publicized. In 1945 he received his discharge from the navy and the next year entered politics. With the unusually vigorous campaigning that came to be characteristic he won election to the House of Representatives from a Boston district, and his support of the New Deal legacy in domestic af-

fairs and his close attention to the needs of his constituents helped win him reelection in 1948 and 1950. In 1952 he demonstrated his effectiveness as a campaigner by defeating the incumbent Henry Cabot Lodge for a U.S. Senate seat from Massachusetts. While convalescing from two major spinal operations in 1954 he wrote *Profiles in Courage*, published in 1956 and awarded a Pulitzer Prize. Kennedy became more involved with international affairs during his Senate years, and by 1956 was able to wage a vigorous battle for the Democratic vice-presidential nomination. He lost, but he began almost immediately to lay the groundwork for a presidential campaign in 1960; he traveled and spoke widely, wrote numerous articles, was reelected to the Senate in 1958 by a record margin, and by 1960, when he won seven state primaries, was far and away the leading candidate. The Democratic national convention nominated him on the first ballot and in November he won the election, defeating the Republican Richard M. Nixon with only a minuscule plurality in the popular vote. Kennedy was the youngest man inaugurated and first Catholic ever elected to the presidency and in his inaugural address laid down the famous challenge: "Ask not what your country can do for you—ask what you can do for your country." The image of youth and vigor constantly projected by Kennedy and his family made him immensely popular at home and abroad; however, his legislative program, the "New Frontier," emphasizing domestic social programs, including federal aid to education, medical care for the elderly, stepped-up space research, and measures in the areas of civil rights and urban ills, as well as increased foreign aid, met with mixed reactions in Congress and was only in part effected. In April 1961, with the failure of the ill-conceived invasion of Cuba at the Bay of Pigs by Cuban anti-Communist refugees supported, trained, and equipped under U.S. auspices, the prestige of the United States and of the president was dealt a severe blow. Kennedy was forced to deal with a series of challenges in foreign affairs, including the building by East Germany of the Berlin Wall, the Cuban missile crisis in October 1962, occasioned by the installation there of Soviet Union–supplied long-range missiles, which were removed at Kennedy's insistence in the world's closest approach yet to nuclear war, and intensifying conflicts in Laos and Vietnam. More positive steps were taken in the establishment of the Alliance for Progress, aimed to aid Latin America, and of the Peace Corps, a program of technical and educational aid to underdeveloped nations by U.S. volunteers. At home the scene was dominated by the civil-rights movement; Kennedy sent federal troops to open the University of Mississippi to a black student who had been denied admission on the basis of race, and maintained a liberal position favoring integration and then efforts of such black leaders as Martin Luther King, Jr. A significant step toward eventual disarmament was taken in September 1963 with the signing by the United States and the

Soviet Union of a treaty banning all but underground tests of explosive nuclear devices. On a visit to Dallas, Texas, on November 22, 1963, Kennedy was shot by a sniper while riding in a motorcade through the city, dying almost immediately. The suspected killer, apprehended almost immediately, was himself shot two days later by an onlooker while in police custody, but despite the researches of a presidential commission headed by Chief Justice Earl Warren, certain of the facts surrounding the assassination remained in question in many minds, although the commission did come to the unanimous conclusion that the assassination had been accomplished by Lee Harvey Oswald, "acting alone." Although brief, the Kennedy administration left a deep mark on the nation; providing an example of youth, vigor, confidence, and political pragmatism of a particularly intellectual sort, he created an almost euphoric aura among his followers, especially the young. Hindsight in later years dimmed somewhat the glow of the era, but for many it remained an American Camelot.

Kennedy, Robert Francis (1925–1968), public official. Born in Brookline, Massachusetts, on November 20, 1925, Robert F. Kennedy was a son of Joseph P. Kennedy and the younger brother of John F. Kennedy. He graduated from Harvard in 1948 and from the Law School of the University of Virginia in 1951, and almost immediately entered public service as an attorney for the criminal division of the Department of Justice. He resigned that post to manage John Kennedy's 1952 campaign for a U.S. Senate seat from Massachusetts but returned to Washington shortly thereafter, serving on the staffs of several Senate committees and, from 1957 to 1960, as chief counsel of the Select Committee on Improper Activities in the Labor or Management Field. In that post he devoted much of his energy to the government's attack on James R. Hoffa, president of the International Brotherhood of Teamsters, who was finally jailed after prosecutions by Kennedy's department. In 1960 he managed his brother's campaign for the Democratic presidential nomination and then for the presidency. He was appointed attorney general after the Kennedy electoral victory, one of the youngest men ever to hold the post, and served with distinction as the administration's chief strategist in promoting civil rights and in litigation concerning trusts and rackets. After the president's assassination in November 1963, he stayed on as attorney general under President Lyndon B. Johnson, but he resigned the post in 1964 to run for the Senate from New York and was elected in November of that year. He soon emerged as a national leader and as a spokesman for the liberal wing of the Democratic party, inheriting much of his brother's constituency of the young, the poor, and the black, and in March 1968 he announced his candidacy for the Democratic presidential nomination. When Johnson withdrew from consideration for reelection later in the

month Kennedy appeared to have a good chance to win the nomination, but his fortunes in various state primaries were mixed—he won in Indiana and Nebraska but lost in Oregon, the first time a member of the Kennedy family had ever lost a public election. It appeared that the California primary, early in June, might be decisive, and he won it; but while celebrating his victory at a gathering of supporters in Los Angeles on June 5, he was shot and fatally wounded by Sirhan Sirhan, a Jordanian-born resident of California. Senator Kennedy died on the morning of June 6, 1968. Among his books were *The Enemy Within*, 1960, and *Pursuit of Justice*, 1964.

Kennedy, Ted, *see* Kennedy, Edward Moore

Kent, James (1763–1847), lawyer and judge. Born in Fredericksburgh (now Southeast), Putnam County, New York, on July 31, 1763, Kent was schooled privately and graduated from Yale in 1781. He took up the study of law, was admitted to the bar in 1785, and began practice in Poughkeepsie, New York. In 1793 he moved to New York City and, through the influence of his Federalist friends John Jay and Alexander Hamilton, was appointed the first professor of law at Columbia College; his lectures were not particularly successful and in 1798 he resigned. In 1798 he was appointed to the state supreme court, where he remained until 1814, after 1804 as chief justice, and in 1814 he became chancellor of the New York court of chancery, remaining there until his compulsory retirement (at age sixty) nine years later. His decisions while on the bench were recorded by the law reporter William Johnson in a long series of *Reports for New York*, and these were widely circulated and influential in other states. In 1824 and 1825 he resumed his professorship at Columbia and in 1825 set about revising and expanding his lectures for publication. The result was *Commentaries on American Law*, in four volumes, 1826–1830. Relying, as he had on the bench, on English common law whenever possible and otherwise on Roman law, Kent produced the first major systematic work on Anglo-American law; his discussion of international law in particular was widely admired and his treatment of constitutional law was long the standard Federalist interpretation. The *Commentaries* appeared in five subsequent editions during his lifetime and under his editorship, and numerous translations were made of various portions of the work. Kent died in New York City on December 12, 1847. He was elected to the Hall of Fame in 1900.

Kent, Rockwell (1882–1971), painter, illustrator, and author. Born in Tarrytown Heights, New York, on June 21, 1882, Kent studied architecture at Columbia University but did not complete the course, dropping out in his junior year to seek a career in art. He worked as a lobsterman and a carpenter and in other casual jobs and partly supported himself by doing architectural renderings during the following decade, earning little or nothing as a painter. Finally, in 1917, he incorporated himself as "Artist Kent, Inc.," sold shares in himself, and went to Alaska to paint and make woodcuts. Published in a book, *Wilderness: A Journal of Quiet Adventure in Alaska*, in 1920, the paintings and prints resulting from his stay in the North soon became collectors' items; Kent thereupon bought up all outstanding shares in Artist Kent and disincorporated himself. *Wilderness* was followed by *Voyaging: Southward from the Strait of Magellan*, 1924, a record, in words and pictures, of a cruise in a small boat in the waters off Cape Horn, and by *N by E*, 1930, an account of a sojourn in Greenland. By that time he was one of the most successful American artists and illustrators, and in due course was represented in the permanent collections of many major museums in the United States and abroad. In 1938 he included a "radical" message, written in an obscure Eskimo dialect, in a mural he was painting for the Post Office Building in Washington, D.C., which led to trouble with various patriotic organizations. A founder or member of many organizations later deemed to be Communist or "fronts" for Communist organizations, he was dogged by various congressional investigating committees and government bureaus throughout the 1940s and 1950s. He was chairman of the National Council for American-Soviet Friendship and received the International Lenin Peace Prize from the Soviet government in 1967; he contributed the money portion of the award to the people of North Vietnam. Apart from his paintings and books, he was probably best known as an illustrator, and his illustrations for special editions of Shakespeare's plays, Melville's *Moby Dick*, Voltaire's *Candide*, Chaucer's *Canterbury Tales*, and Whitman's *Leaves of Grass*, among others, continued to be highly regarded. He worked successfully in lithography and woodcut, finding both techniques perfectly suited to his hard, stark style of sharp contrasts and angular construction. A globe-trotter who had traveled everywhere and lived in many places, he spent most of his later years on a farm in Au Sable Forks, New York. Among his other books were *Rockwellkentiana*, with C. Zigrosser, 1933; *This Is My Own*, 1940; the autobiographical *It's Me O Lord*, 1955; and *Greenland Journal*, 1963. Kent died in Plattsburgh, New York, on March 13, 1971.

Keokuk (1788?–1848?), Indian leader. Born about 1788 in the Sauk village on the Rock River, near the site of present-day Rock Island, Illinois, Keokuk (or Keokuck), whose name meant "the watchful" or "he who moves alertly," was partly of French descent. He grew up in the Fox clan of the Sauk tribe and early distinguished himself as a horseman and warrior. As a war chief, he worked with considerable success to displace a rival chief of the Sauk, Black Hawk of the Thunder clan, relying for much of his growing influence in the tribe on the support of U.S. authorities, whose side, whether for personal advantage or in recognition of the futility of resistance, he took in numerous disputes, beginning with his refusal to join the British cause in the War of 1812. By 1832 he was seriously challenging Black Hawk for leadership of the tribe and when Black Hawk led a portion of the Sauk in taking up arms to defend hereditary hunting grounds in Illinois against white encroachment, fighting the valiant but hopeless Black Hawk War of that year, Keokuk remained at peace, agreeing to cede the tribe's lands and to be moved west to a reservation in Iowa. He took charge of the defeated Black Hawk after the U.S. army's victory at Bad Axe River in Wisconsin in August 1832 and in 1833 went with him on a tour of several Eastern cities. The two returned to the East in 1837 and Keokuk made in Washington, D.C., a stirring speech in defense of certain Sauk claims against the Sioux. Made chief of the united Sauk clans by order of President Andrew Jackson, Keokuk continued to accommodate the wishes of the U.S. government, giving up the Iowa reservation in 1845 for one yet farther west in Kansas. During his last years he was out of favor with whites and Indians alike, and he died, probably early in 1848, at the Sauk Agency in Franklin County, Kansas.

Kern, Jerome David (1885–1945), composer. Born in New York City on January 27, 1885, Kern began writing songs while still in high school in Newark, New Jersey, where his family had moved in 1895. After a period at the New York College of Music he spent the years 1903–1905 in further musical studies in England and Germany, supporting himself while in London by writing for various musical shows. It was not until 1910 that he wrote his first complete show, *Mr. Wix of Wickham*; he followed with almost a show a year and achieved success with *The Red Petticoat*, 1912, and especially with *The Girl from Utah*, 1914, written with Herbert Reynolds (Michael E. Rourke) and featuring Kern's first great song-hit, "They Didn't Believe Me," and *Have a Heart*, produced in 1916 in collaboration with P. G. Wodehouse, the title song of which was adopted for that year's edition of the *Ziegfeld Follies*. With Wodehouse he proceeded to turn out *Leave It to Jane*, 1917; *Oh, Boy!*, 1917 (with "Till the Clouds Roll By," later the title of a 1946 film biography of Kern); *Oh, Lady, Lady!*, 1918; and others. In 1920 he contributed the music for the hit show *Sally* ("Look for the Silver Lining"), and in 1925 collaborated for the first time with Oscar Hammerstein II on *Sunny* ("Who?"). In 1927 Kern and Hammerstein again joined their talents to create a stage classic, *Show Boat*, from Edna Ferber's novel ("Can't Help Lovin' That Man," "Why Do I Love You," "Only Make Believe," "Bill," "You Are Love," "Ol' Man River"), and they followed with *Sweet Adeline*, 1929 ("Don't Ever Leave Me"); *Music in the Air*, 1932 ("The Song Is You," "I've Told Ev'ry Little Star"); and *Very Warm for*

May, 1939, ("All the Things You Are"). Kern worked also with Otto Harbach on *The Cat and the Fiddle*, 1931 ("She Didn't Say Yes"), and *Roberta*, 1933 ("Smoke Gets in Your Eyes"). Kern began writing music for motion pictures with *Men of the Sky*, 1931, and followed with a film version of *Roberta*, 1935, for which he added "Lovely to Look At" to the score; *Swing Time*, 1936 ("A Fine Romance," "The Way You Look Tonight"); and *You Were Never Lovelier*, 1942 ("Dearly Beloved"). In 1940 he collaborated with Hammerstein on the popular "The Last Time I Saw Paris," which, when interpolated the next year into the otherwise all-Gershwin score for the film *Lady, Be Good*, won an Academy Award. The composer of nearly 50 musical-comedy scores, Kern was widely acknowledged as the dean of American show-music composers when he died in New York City on November 11, 1945.

Kerouac, Jack (1922–1969), author. Born in Lowell, Massachusetts, on March 12, 1922, John Kerouac entered Columbia College in New York in 1940 on an academic and athletic scholarship but soon dropped out. After two months of service in the navy and a variety of casual jobs he returned to Columbia in 1942 but left again to take up residence in an apartment near the campus that became a meeting place for the university's young intellectuals, including Allen Ginsberg and Neal Cassady. From 1943 to 1950 Kerouac roamed through the United States and Mexico, publishing in 1950 his first novel, *The Town and the City*, a book that was highly regarded by critics and that showed little relationship to his later work. He had spent three years on *The Town*, but he wrote his most famous novel, *On the Road*, during a frantic three weeks in 1951 typing continuously on 20-foot strips of art paper, the ends of which he pasted together. The novel was published in segments in literary magazines over the next few years and did not appear in its entirety until 1957, whereupon it amassed sales of 500,000 copies in paperback. By then the apostle of the "beat generation," Kerouac followed *On the Road* with other novels published in quick succession: *The Dharma Bums*, 1958; *The Subterraneans*, written in three days, also 1958; *Doctor Sax*, 1959, and its sequel, *Maggie Cassidy*, which appeared the same year; *Big Sur*, 1962; and *Desolation Angels*, 1965. *On the Road* contained a famous description of people "who never yawn or say a commonplace thing, but burn, burn, burn like fabulous yellow roman candles exploding like spiders across the stars and in the middle you see the blue centerlight pop and everybody goes 'Awww!'" The figure seemed to fit Kerouac himself, for after 1959 his appeal to the reading public faded. He died in St. Petersburg, Florida, on October 21, 1969. Despite the shortness of his success, it nevertheless outlasted the beatnik subculture of which he was the acknowledged spokesman in prose, as Allen Ginsberg was its spokesman in verse.

Kerr, Michael Crawford (1827–1876), public official. Born in Titusville, Pennsylvania, on March 15, 1827, Kerr graduated from the law department of the University of Louisville in 1851, and, after being admitted to the bar in Kentucky, began the practice of law in New Albany, Indiana, the next year. He became prosecuting attorney for Floyd County, Indiana, in 1855 and served as reporter of the Indiana Supreme Court from 1862 to 1864, when he was elected to the House of Representatives as a Democrat. His congressional career was notable for his aggressive stands against the tariff and every form of monopoly and his insistence on the equality of all citizens; at the same time he bitterly opposed the Radical Republicans' Reconstruction program. Defeated by a handful of votes in 1872, he was returned to the House in 1874 and was chosen speaker of the House on December 6, 1875. But his health had already begun to fail and he died at his home in Rockbridge County, Virginia, on August 19, 1876.

Kettering, Charles Franklin (1876–1958), engineer and inventor. Born on August 29, 1876, near Loudonville, Ohio, Kettering received mechanical and electrical engineering degrees from Ohio State University in 1904. Employed by the National Cash Register Company of Dayton, he devised in the course of his duties an electric motor for cash registers. After becoming head of the inventions department, he left in 1909 and, with the company's former works manager, Edward A. Deeds, formed the Dayton Engineering Laboratories (later called Delco) to develop improved electrical equipment for automobiles. In the first two years of his work in the new company he developed and produced an improved ignition and lighting system and the first self-starter for automobiles; both were used to equip Cadillacs and made him famous as an inventor. In 1914 he established the Dayton Metal Products Company and the Dayton-Wright Airplane Company. Two years later Dayton Engineering was purchased by the United Motors Corporation, which in 1918 joined the General Motors Corporation (GM). In 1925 Delco's independent research facilities were moved to Detroit and merged with GM's laboratories to form the General Motors Research Corporation, of which Kettering, who had been a vice president of GM since 1920, became president and general manager. In that position he led investigations into ways of achieving maximum engine performance and into the nature of friction and combustion and also contributed to the development of such products and improvements as leaded (ethyl) gasoline and high-octane fuels, fast-drying lacquer, chromium plating, crankcase ventilators, balancing machines, engine-oil coolers, two-way shock absorbers variable-speed transmissions, the high-speed diesel engine for trains, and the high-compression automobile engine. He established at Antioch College the Charles Franklin Kettering Foundation for the Study of Chlorophyll and Photosynthesis, cofounded the Sloan-Kettering

Institute for Cancer Research in New York City, and sponsored the Fever Therapy Research Project at Miami Valley Hospital in Dayton, Ohio, which developed the Hypertherm, or artificial-fever machine, for use in the treatment of diseases. In June 1947 he resigned from General Motors. He died in Dayton on November 25, 1958.

Key, Francis Scott (1779–1843), lawyer and poet. Born in the present Carroll County, Maryland, on August 1, 1779, Key graduated from St. John's College in 1796 and began the study of law. He began to practice in 1801 and the next year moved to Georgetown, near Washington, D.C., becoming there a moderately successful attorney. In September 1814 he was sent to secure the release of a Maryland physician, Dr. William Beanes, who had been taken prisoner by British troops retiring from the burning of Washington and was being held aboard a British ship. Key was successful in his mission; his return to the District was delayed, however, by the British attack on Baltimore during the night of September 13–14. His ship lay off the besieged Fort McHenry and when morning revealed the U.S. flag still flying over the fort, Key exultantly dashed off some descriptive verses that were circulated as a broadside in Baltimore the next day under the title "Defense of Fort M'-Henry." Within a few days the poem had been published in a newspaper and had also been linked to the tune of a popular English drinking song, "To Anacreon in Heaven;" soon the new patriotic song was being sung throughout the nation. Key's few other verse works were of little note; he remained in Georgetown and Washington for most of the rest of his life and from 1833 to 1841 was U.S. attorney for the District of Columbia. He died in Baltimore on January 11, 1843. The song, known from about 1815 as "The Star-spangled Banner," grew in popularity and became something of an unofficial national anthem; this status was bolstered when it was adopted by the navy in 1889 and by the army in 1903. Finally the objections that had been voiced to the song—among them its musical difficulty—were overridden and it was officially adopted by Congress as the national anthem in 1931.

Khorana, Har Gobind (1922–   ), biochemist. Recorded as having been born on January 9, 1922 (there is doubt about the correct date), in the tiny Indian village of Raipur, Punjab, now in Pakistan, Khorana received his first education under a tree, where the local teacher held classes. He received his B.S. from the University of the Punjab in Lahore in 1943 and his M.Sc. two years later. A scholarship from the government of India made possible further study at the University of Liverpool, from which he received his doctorate in organic chemistry in 1948. A Nuffield fellow at Cambridge from 1940 to 1952, he went in 1952 to the University of British Columbia, from which he moved, with four of his assistants, to the University of Wisconsin in 1960. He became a U.S.

citizen in 1966 and in 1970 moved again, with most of his research team, to the Massachusetts Institute of Technology (MIT) as professor of biology and chemistry. His work on the synthesis of enzymes was begun at Liverpool and continued for some years, and he first achieved international eminence in 1959 with the announcement that he had synthesized coenzyme A. He then turned his attention to the genetic code, studying intensively the nucleotides that determine heredity. He was able to synthesize all of the 64 trinucleotide combinations in the ribonucleic acid (RNA) messenger polymer of yeast, and by 1966, building on the work of Marshall W. Nirenberg of the National Institutes of Health and taking account of independent researches by Robert W. Holley of Cornell University, he was able to announce that the genetic code was completely deciphered in terms of the three-nucleotide "codon" groups and the amino acids to whose synthesis they were specific. For their researches Khorana, Nirenberg, and Holley shared the 1968 Nobel Prize for Physiology and Medicine, the citation stating that they had "written the most exciting chapter in modern biology."

Kidd, William (1645?–1701), pirate. The somewhat unfairly notorious Captain Kidd was born in Greenock, Scotland, in about 1645, the son, tradition says, of a Calvinist minister. During most of his adult life he was a successful sea captain in legitimate commerce. By 1690 he was established as a shipowner and sea captain in New York City. When war broke out between France and England following the accession to the throne of William III of England, Kidd was engaged to fight the French as a privateer in British service and did so successfully. In 1695 he was commissioned to root out the many pirates that infested the waters around the island of Madagascar, preying on the ships of the East India Company. He was named commander of an expedition to that purpose which was financed by a group of noble lords, and he sailed from New York harbor on September 6, 1696, with a crew of desperadoes. After a year at sea, at the end of which they reached Madagascar, they had taken no prizes; a third of the crew was dead of cholera; tempers were short, and Kidd struck and killed one of his gunners in the course of a mutinous uprising. This occurrence seems to have tipped the scales in favor of a life of crime for Kidd, and shortly afterward, on January 30, 1698, Kidd captured a rich Armenian merchantman. The booty was divided among the crew, which was transferred to the captured ship and Kidd took other prizes. News of this reached England and a fleet was dispatched to capture Kidd and his pirates. On learning that he had been declared a pirate, Kidd sailed from the West Indies to New England to protest his innocence. Tricked by a promise of pardon into coming ashore in Boston, Kidd was taken to England as a prisoner. He was privately examined by the Board of Admiralty, who feared that the lords behind the Madagascar venture, who by this time had come in for public obloquy, would defend him in any public trial. He remained in Newgate Prison until March 27, 1701, when he was brought before the House of Commons for examination. If he had been willing to accuse his backers he might have escaped blame, but he protested his innocence. He was tried for the murder of his gunner on May 8, 1701, and convicted, and also convicted of three charges of piracy. He was hanged in London on May 23, 1701. Legends of hidden treasure began to circulate almost immediately after his death, and Captain Kidd's buried caches are still occasionally sought, although no treasure attributed to him has been found.

Kilmer, Joyce (1886–1918), poet and author. Born in New Brunswick, New Jersey, on December 6, 1886, Alfred Joyce Kilmer attended Rutgers College and graduated from Columbia College in 1908. After a year spent teaching Latin in a New Jersey high school he moved with his new wife, Aline Murray Kilmer, to New York City to seek a literary career. He worked for a dictionary publisher and wrote for magazines and in 1913 obtained a position with the *New York Times* book review. He was poetry editor of the *Literary Digest* and of *Current Literature*, wrote introductions to books, and lectured widely on current literary subjects. His first book of poems, *Summer of Love*, appeared in 1911; *Trees and Other Poems* was published in 1914, the title poem, which achieved world-wide fame, having appeared in *Poetry* magazine in August 1913. He enlisted in the army when the United States joined the Allies in World War I and sailed for France early in 1918. At the end of July 1918 his regiment, the 165th, attacked on the front along the Ourcq River in the Aisne, and on July 30 Kilmer was found among the dead. Although he was only a sergeant in rank, he was buried with the officers at the spot, was mentioned in dispatches, and was awarded the Croix de Guerre by the French army. Among his other books were *Main Street and Other Poems*, 1917; *The Circus, and Other Essays*, 1916; and *Literature in the Making*, 1917, a series of interviews with writers.

King, Clarence (1842–1901), geologist. Born on January 6, 1842, in Newport, Rhode Island, King graduated from the Sheffield Scientific School at Yale in 1862. The following year he and a companion set out to cross the continent on horseback; upon reaching California he joined the state geological survey under Josiah D. Whitney, and for nearly three years did much exploring, particularly in the desert and mountain regions of the South. In 1866 he returned to the East and secured congressional approval for his plan for a government-sponsored survey along the 40th parallel from eastern Colorado to California. With King in charge, the survey was a masterful work of scientific exploration; the field and laboratory work occupied some ten years and King's con-

tribution to the seven-volume *Report of the Geological Explanation of the Fortieth Parallel*, 1870–1880, was *Systematic Geology*, 1878, which combined scientific and literary excellence. King introduced the method of indicating the topography of a mapped region by means of contour lines. Upon his urging, Congress unified the many government surveys into the single U.S. Geological Survey in 1879, and he served as its director for two years, assembling the staff and organizing its activities with great administrative skill. After 1881 he devoted his time primarily to geological research, also serving frequently as a consulting mining engineer. A series of his articles in the *Atlantic Monthly* were collected and published in 1872 as *Mountaineering in the Sierra Nevada*, his only other major written work. In poor health during his last years, King died on December 24, 1901, in Phoenix, Arizona.

King, Ernest Joseph (1878–1956), naval officer. Born in Lorain, Ohio, on November 23, 1878, King is said to have tried to run away to sea at the age of seven, only to be turned back by the tempting smell of some freshly baked cookies at the house of a neighbor. As a plebe at the U.S. Naval Academy he had his baptism of fire during the last days of the Spanish-American War and, after graduating in 1901, was commissioned an ensign in the navy in 1903. He saw staff duty with the Atlantic Fleet during World War I and served in various naval assignments during the 1920s, including command of the New London, Connecticut, submarine base. In 1928, at the age of 49, he took aviation training and the next year became assistant chief of the Bureau of Aeronautics. In 1930 he was named captain of the aircraft carrier *Lexington* and he held the post until named chief of the Navy Bureau of Aeronautics by President Franklin D. Roosevelt in 1933. It was customary to name an admiral to the post, but Roosevelt, finding that no admiral could fly a plane, chose King, who was shortly promoted to rear admiral. Made vice-admiral and commander of the five-carrier Aircraft Battle Force in 1938, he was appointed chief of the Atlantic Fleet in 1940 and, a few days after Pearl Harbor, became commander in chief of the combined fleet with the rank of full admiral. By executive order of the president in March 1942 he became the first man to combine this post (COMINCH) with the position of chief of naval operations (CNO); in his dual capacity he commanded the greatest aggregation of fighting ships, planes, and men in the history of naval warfare. Known as a rigid disciplinarian, he was raised to the five-star rank of fleet admiral in 1944; the same year saw him present at the landing of U.S. forces on Utah Beach, Normandy, on D-Day. In addition to his heavy responsibilities for the conduct of a naval war around the globe, King was also President Roosevelt's chief naval advisor and in that capacity was involved in high-level diplomacy at conferences of Allied leaders at Casablanca, Teheran,

Cairo, and Yalta. He resigned his posts in 1945—a five-star admiral need not retire—but returned to limited duty in 1950, after an extended illness, as an adviser to the secretary of the navy, the Department of Defense, and the president. A determined foe of the unification of the armed services, he died on June 25, 1956, at Portsmouth, New Hampshire.

King, Frank (1883–1969), cartoonist. Born in Cashon, Wisconsin, on April 9, 1883, King grew up in nearby Tomah. He early displayed a talent for drawing and was employed as a cartoonist by the *Minneapolis Times* from 1901 to 1905, when he interrupted his career to study at the Chicago Academy of Fine Arts for a year. He spent a few months in 1906 working for an advertising agency and then joined the staff of the *Chicago Examiner*, from which he moved in 1909 to the *Chicago Tribune*, were he drew a regular Sunday cartoon. In 1919 he began a series of cartoons dealing with automobiles with the title *Gasoline Alley*. The strip greatly increased its appeal in 1921 when the main character, Walt, adopted a foundling, Skeezix. Concentrating on ordinary events, devoid both of sentimentality and sensationalism, King was the first America cartoonist to allow his characters to grow and age. Millions of readers obtained quiet satisfaction from the adventures of Walt, Skeezix, and their friends, and Walt's marriage and the births and marriages of his children and grandchildren, as affectionately described in words and pictures by their creator, were featured in hundreds of daily and Sunday papers around the country. King died in Winter Park, Florida, on June 24, 1969; *Gasoline Alley*, which had thrived for half a century, continued to appear at the hands of a successor.

King, Martin Luther, Jr. (1929–1968), religious leader and social reformer. Born on January 15, 1929, in Atlanta, King was christened Michael Luther by his father, a minister, who later changed both their names in honor of the great Protestant reformer. He entered Morehouse College at fifteen; in 1947 he was ordained to the ministry in his father's Ebenezer Baptist Church in Atlanta, and the next year took his B.A. from Morehouse. He pursued his studies at Crozer Theological Seminary, where he was awarded a B.D. in 1951, and at Boston University, where he took his Ph.D. four years later. He had been installed as pastor of the Dexter Avenue Baptist Church in Montgomery, Alabama, and was still new and relatively unknown in the city's black community when, in December 1955, Mrs. Rosa Parks was arrested for refusing to give up her bus seat to a white man and a boycott by the black community of Montgomery's segregated buses began. King was placed in charge of the boycott and after more than a year of pressure and agitation on both sides the Supreme Court ruled against racial discrimination in intrastate as well as interstate transportation. Early in 1957 the Southern Christian Leadership Conference (SCLC) was formed with King as its president; through this organization he was able to broaden his civil-rights activities to affect the entire South. He developed a Gandhian strategy of nonviolent but active and massive confrontation with injustice and the unresponsive institutions of white society; his insistence on nonviolence, later rejected by more militant black activists, was in this early period often overlooked in the widespread criticism of his use of confrontation in his effort to secure implementation of federal equal-rights laws. In 1959 he moved to Atlanta, becoming co-pastor of his father's church. During the early 1960s he continued active in the civil-rights movement and became the major figure in the struggle on behalf of blacks through his leadership in antidiscrimination demonstrations and voter registration drives at Selma and Birmingham, Alabama, and Albany, Georgia. He played a central role in organizing the assembly climaxing the massive March on Washington in 1963, where he delivered his famed sermon-speech, "I Have a Dream." In December 1964 King was awarded the Nobel Peace Prize. By 1966 he had begun to bring his campaign to Northern cities where de facto segregation was subtle and all-pervading. He was in great demand as a speaker, and he found time to publish several books about his work, including *Stride Toward Freedom*, 1958; *Why We Can't Wait*, 1964; and *Where Do We Go From Here: Chaos or Community?*, 1967. During this last period he also denounced U.S. participation in the war in Vietnam, declaring that it was an immoral adventure that was draining away resources needed to eliminate poverty and hunger in the United States. Throughout 12 years of active involvement in the civil-rights movement he had met with strong and often violent opposition; he had been jailed, stoned, and beaten, his house had been bombed, and many threats had been made against his life. In the spring of 1968 he was in Memphis, Tennessee, to help the struggle of city workers, largely black, to improve the conditions of their employment; on April 4 he was shot to death by a sniper as he emerged from his room at a motel. The following year James Earl Ray pleaded guilty to the murder and received a prison sentence of 99 years.

King, Richard (1825–1885), steamboater and rancher. Born in Orange County, New York, on July 10, 1825, King was apprenticed to a jeweler at the age of eight, but he soon escaped from his uncongenial master, made his way to Mobile, Alabama, and became a steamboat cabin boy. Except for one eight-month period, during which the generosity of one of his employers enabled him to acquire his only formal schooling, and for brief service in the Seminole Wars, he worked as a steamboatman for nearly 20 years, serving as a pilot on a government vessel on the Rio Grande during the Mexican War and afterward operating his own steamboat on that river. He formed a partnership with a former commander in 1850 and

Kenedy & Company operated more than a score of vessels on the Rio Grande for many years, during the Civil War greatly facilitating the cotton trade between Mexico and the Confederacy. From 1852, however, King's principal interest was in ranching. In that year he purchased for less than two cents per acre a 15,500–acre tract of grazing land on Santa Gertrudis Creek southwest of Corpus Christi, Texas; subsequent additions to the ranch, acquired, it was said, often by ruthless means, increased his holdings enormously and by the time of his death he controlled more than 600,000 prime acres. The nation's largest ranch featured also probably its largest cattle herd, numbering at one time upwards of 100,000 head. King was interested also in breeding and imported a number of improved strains of cattle for experimental purposes. Ruling his demesne with a firm, even harsh, hand, he was nonetheless widely noted for his hospitality. He died on April 14, 1885. His heirs continued to expand the family holdings and eventually the King Ranch encompassed nearly a million acres, an area larger than that of Rhode Island; the family developed properties in other states and foreign countries, established breeding programs that produced the Santa Gertrudis breed of cattle, a Brahman-Shorthorn cross, as well as championship quarter horses and thoroughbreds, and in 1903 saw the city of Kingsville, Texas, laid out on former King Ranch land.

King, Rufus (1755–1827), public official and diplomat. Born in Scarboro, Maine, then a part of Massachusetts, on March 24, 1755, King graduated from Harvard in 1777 and three years later was admitted to the bar. He served in the Massachusetts General Court (legislature) from 1783 to 1785 and in the Continental Congress from 1784 to 1787. In the latter year he helped draft the Ordinance of 1787, which through his influence contained a prohibition of slavery and involuntary servitude in the Northwest Territory, and he introduced the resolution that sanctioned a call for what became the Constitutional Convention. He was a member of the Constitutional Convention of 1787, and there favored a strong central government; he was later instrumental in securing ratification of the Constitution by Massachusetts. In 1788 he moved to New York City and the next year was elected to the New York state legislature, which in turn elected him one of New York's first two U.S. senators. In the Senate he was a leading Federalist and strongly supported Alexander Hamilton's programs; soon after reelection in 1795 he resigned to accept President George Washington's offer of the U.S. ministry in London. He performed creditably during his tenure, 1796–1803, and on his return to the United States began a period of semiretirement on his Long Island estate while the Republican party was in its ascendancy. He was the unsuccessful Federalist candidate for vice-president in 1804 and 1808, but in 1813 was elected again to the Senate. In 1816 he was a candidate for the presidency and was again

defeated. During his last term in the Senate, beginning in 1819, he became a strong opponent of slavery, denouncing the Missouri Compromise of 1820 for delaying an inevitable showdown between North and South on the issue. He favored orderly abolition of slavery, the proceeds of the sale of public lands to be used to compensate slaveholders. He declined reelection in 1825 and was appointed minister to Great Britain by President John Quincy Adams. Plagued by ill health, he returned in the summer of 1826 to Jamaica, Long Island, where he died on April 29, 1827.

King, William Rufus de Vane (1786–1853), vice-president of the United States. Born in Sampson County, North Carolina, on April 7, 1786, King graduated from the University of North Carolina in 1803 and thereafter studied law, being admitted to the bar in 1806. After service in the North Carolina legislature he was elected to the House of Representatives in 1810, resigning in 1816 to accompany U.S. Minister William Pinkney to St. Petersburg, Russia, as secretary of the legation. He moved to Alabama on his return in 1818 and became one of that new state's first U.S. senators. A strong supporter of Andrew Jackson and president pro tempore of the Senate from 1836 to 1841, he remained in that body until April 1844, when he was appointed by President John Tyler as U.S. minister to France. He was charged with trying to persuade the French not to object to the U.S. annexation of Texas; they did not protest the annexation, although it is not clear that this was owing to King's efforts. He returned to the United States in 1846 to seek reelection to the Senate; although not successful, he was named to complete an unexpired term in 1848 and was later elected to the seat. On the death of President Zachary Taylor in 1850 and the succession of Millard Fillmore to the presidency, King was elected president of the Senate. At the Democratic national convention of 1852 he supported the candidacy of James Buchanan, and when Franklin Pierce was nominated instead, King was given the second place on the ticket partly to placate Buchanan's followers. Pierce and King were elected, but King was already in the last stages of tuberculosis, and he went to Cuba to try to find a cure; he was allowed to take the oath of office there, on March 4, 1853. Returning home shortly thereafter, he died the day after he reached his plantation, King's Bend, near Cahaba, Alabama, on April 18, 1853; he thus never actually served as vice-president.

Kino, Eusebio Francisco (1644?–1711), missionary and explorer. Born probably in 1644 in the Alpine Tirol region—villages in both Italy and Austria have been cited as the exact place—Kino was the son of Italian parents and early determined upon a career as a missionary. In 1665 he entered the Jesuit order; he excelled in mathematics and on completing his studies taught that subject at the University of Ingolstadt while awaiting assignment to a foreign mission. Assignment came finally in 1678, although it was not to China, as he had hoped, but to New Spain. After two more years of waiting in Cadiz he sailed for America late in 1680, arriving in Mexico City the following spring. Father Kino accompanied a colonizing expedition to Lower California in 1683, remaining there until drought forced the abandonment of the enterprise two years later. In 1687 he was assigned to the Pimería Alta district in present-day northern Sonora and southern Arizona, where for the rest of his life he ministered to the various Indian tribes of the region, made extensive explorations, and founded a large number of missions, including the famed San Xavier del Bac, near present-day Tucson, Arizona, in 1700. He made several journeys from his headquarters at Mission Dolores to the Colorado and Gila rivers, establishing the Camino del Diablo district route north from Sonora and in 1701 proving definitely that Lower California is a peninsula, not an island as had been generally believed. He was the first to describe the ruins of the Casa Grande pueblo and was also influential in encouraging agriculture and establishing the breeding of cattle and horses in his large district. Kino died at Mission Magdalena, Sonora, which he had founded, on March 15, 1711. Kino's autobiographical *Favores Celestiales* was first published in 1919 as *Historical Memoir of Pimería Alta*.

Kinsey, Alfred Charles (1894–1956), zoologist and student of human sexual behavior. Born in Hoboken, New Jersey, on June 23, 1894, Kinsey was educated at Bowdoin College and at Harvard, from which he earned his D.Sc. degree in 1920. He joined the faculty of Indiana University that year, becoming in 1929 professor of zoology. His rapid academic rise was partly the result of the fact that he had become by the late 1920s the world's leading expert on the gall wasp. He also published several high-school biology textbooks. His interest in human sexual behavior began in the 1930s. Concerned about the scarcity of scientific research into the subject, he initiated a program of studies on his own and founded the Institute for Sex Research at Indiana University in 1942, incorporating it five years later. With grants from the National Research Council and the Rockefeller Foundation he conducted an extensive statistical survey of the sexual activity of American men and women, he and his aides interviewing personally some 18,500 subjects all over the country, keeping their names scrupulously secret. The appearance of *Sexual Behavior in the Human Male* in 1948 created a sensation, and its staid medical-book publisher was hardly able to keep up with the demand for copies. The book shattered many myths about human sexual practices, showing, among other things, that several of the so-called "perversions" are so common as almost to be considered normal. The "Kinsey Report" became the subject of heated discussion throughout the country and its compiler was praised and

vilified, in about equal measure, by millions of persons, most of whom never read the book. (Those who did were struck by its almost total lack of eroticism.) Despite the care with which the interviews had been conducted, some sociologists criticized the work on methodological grounds. Kinsey himself was staggered by the response. He continued the Institute's program of interviews, however, and in 1953 brought out *Sexual Behavior in the Human Female*, which, although it revealed many hitherto unsuspected facets of feminine sexuality, did not stir up nearly so much interest as the earlier volume. Kinsey planned to follow these two books with reports on the sexual behavior of men in prison, of Europeans, and of animals, but he died, his work unfinished, on August 25, 1956, in Bloomington, Indiana. Many of the obituary notices suggested that he had helped to inaugurate, although probably not intentionally, a revolution in individual and social awareness.

Kiskadden, Maude, *see* Adams, Maude

Kissinger, Henry Alfred (1923–   ), political scientist and public official. Born in Fürth, Germany, on May 27, 1923, Kissinger was brought to the United States in 1938 and, after service in U.S. military intelligence in World War II, entered Harvard, where he majored in government. Graduating from Harvard summa cum laude in 1950, he received his M.A. there in 1952 and his Ph.D. two years later. Named a lecturer in the Harvard department of government in 1957, he became a full professor in 1962. He began to serve the federal government as a consultant in the 1950s after the publication of two notable books, *Nuclear Weapons and Foreign Policy*, 1957, and *A World Restored: Metternich, Castlereagh and the Problems of Peace*, also 1957. He was a consultant to the National Security Council in 1961 and 1962, to the Arms Control and Disarmament Agency, 1961–1969, and to the Department of State, 1965–1969. He published *The Necessity for Choice: Prospects of American Foreign Policy* in 1961, and *The Troubled Partnership: A Reappraisal of the Atlantic Alliance* followed in 1965. In December 1968 he was named by the incoming president, Richard M. Nixon, as Presidential Assistant for National Security Affairs. It was a title that could have meant little or much, but in fact Kissinger soon emerged as the President's principal adviser on foreign policy. Playing a vital role in achieving a U.S. shift from the goal of maintaining "superiority" in nuclear weapons to that of nuclear "sufficiency," he was also a central figure in attempts to reach a negotiated settlement of the Vietnam War and indeed in all of the Nixon administration's defense and foreign-policy decisions. He participated in secret talks with the leaders of the People's Republic of China in 1971, leading to the admission of Communist China to the United Nations in that year, and arranged the visit of Nixon to China the next year. He also was instrumental in arranging the president's visit to the Soviet Union in May 1972 and was extremely active in the fall of 1972 in trips to Paris, Hanoi, and Saigon to try to bring about a settlement of the Vietnam War. An agreement, with provisions for exchange of prisoners of war and international supervision of a cease-fire, was finally concluded early in 1973. In 1973 Nixon named him secretary of state; soon after he was awarded the Nobel Peace Prize together with the North Vietnamese negotiator, Le Duc Tho, who declined it. Kissinger, retained in his post by President Gerald Ford, retired to private life in 1977.

Kittredge, George Lyman (1860–1941), educator and Shakespeare scholar. Born in Boston on February 28, 1860, Kittredge was educated at the Roxbury Latin School and at Harvard, from which he graduated with honors in 1882. After a five-year stint teaching Latin at the Phillips Exeter Academy in New Hampshire, he became an instructor in English at Harvard in 1888, and after rapid promotions was made a full professor in 1894. Although he never received a Ph.D.— "Who would examine me?" he once quipped—he soon gained a reputation as a brilliant scholar and teacher. His Shakespeare classes were especially notable, but he also studied and taught the works of Chaucer and other medieval writers as well as the Latin classics. He was particularly interested in linguistics and in the history of English, and *Words and Their Ways in English Speech*, written by him in association with J. B. Greenough, appeared in 1901 and was long a standard work. He published, among others, *The Old Farmer and His Almanack*, 1904, *Chaucer and His Poetry* in 1915, *Shakespeare*, 1916, and *Witchcraft in Old and New England* in 1929, all to wide acclaim; but his one-volume *Complete Works of Shakespeare*, which appeared in 1936, was probably his best-known book, remaining the leading U.S. edition of Shakespeare for a generation and selling in the hundreds of thousands of copies. Books edited by him included *English and Scottish Popular Ballads* (with H. C. Sargent), 1904, *Gawain and the Green Knight*, 1916, and *Ballads and Songs*, 1917. Kittredge retired from teaching in 1936 but continued to give public lectures and issued annotated editions of several of Shakespeare's plays in the last years of his life. Universally acknowledged as the leading American scholar of early English literature, he died on July 23, 1941, in Barnstable, Massachusetts.

Kline, Franz Joseph (1919–1962), painter. Born in Wilkes-Barre, Pennsylvania, on May 23, 1919, Kline was educated at Girard College and the School of Fine and Applied Art of Boston University, 1931–1935, and continued his studies in London in 1937–1938. He taught at Black Mountain College in 1952, at the Pratt Institute in Brooklyn, New York, in 1953, and at the Philadelphia Museum Art School the next year. His first one-man exhibition was at the Charles Egan

Gallery in New York City in 1950, and this was followed by many other one-man and group exhibitions in cities in the United States and abroad. His work was included in the collections of the Museum of Modern Art, the Guggenheim Museum, the Whitney Museum of American Art, and the Metropolitan Museum of Art, all in New York City, as well as in many other museums and galleries. Beginning his career as a realist, he turned to a nonrepresentational style of painting, becoming in due time one of the leading members of the movement known as "action painting," a branch of Abstract Expressionism. Typically, his early abstractions were black on white or black on gray, the canvases usually large and sometimes huge, and the slashes and streaks of paint bold and dynamic. He began to add color to his compositions toward the end of his life. He died in New York City on May 13, 1962, at the height of his powers.

Knopf, Alfred Abraham (1892–   ), publisher. Born in New York City on September 12, 1892, Knopf graduated from Columbia College in 1912. He had intended to become a lawyer, but his interests turned to literature in his college years and he journeyed to England after graduation to meet John Galsworthy, from whom he gained an enthusiasm for the work of Joseph Conrad and W. H. Hudson. On returning to the United States he went to work as a clerk for Doubleday, Page & Company and was soon promoted to the editorial department, but by 1915 he was ready to go into business for himself. He launched his firm with only $5000 in capital, but he possessed great energy and many novel ideas, and he was fortunate in hiring as an assistant Blanche Wolf (1894–1966), whom he married in 1916. Together they chose the borzoi, or Russian wolfhound, as the colophon of their publishing house, and in time the imprint became probably the most distinguished in U.S. publishing in the twentieth century. The Knopfs' first successful book was Hudson's *Green Mansions*, but the firm soon acquired a list of what were or, under their aegis, came to be standard works and authors, among them Thomas Mann, Max Beerbohm, T. S. Eliot, D. H. Lawrence, E. M. Forster, Jean-Paul Sartre, Albert Camus, Sigmund Freud, Franz Kafka, and Mikhail A. Sholokhov, and—among its American authors—Clarence Day, Willa Cather, John Hersey, John Updike, Conrad Aiken, Theodore Roethke, Samuel Eliot Morison, and Oscar Handlin. The Knopfs were noted for their almost uncanny ability to discover authors of great potential and a dozen Knopf authors were Nobel prize winners in literature, among them Sigrid Undset, Mann, Ivan Bunin, André Gide, Camus, and Knut Hamsun. The all-time best-selling Knopf book was Khalil Gibran's *The Prophet*, with well over 2 million copies in print. Knopf books were distinguished as well in design and set ambitious standards for U.S. publishing. Knopf published the original *American Mercury* for 11 years after founding the magazine with H. L. Mencken and

George Jean Nathan in 1924, and he issued most of Mencken's books in later years. The firm was acquired by Random House in 1960, but Knopf retained the autonomy of his imprint. Blanche W. Knopf, who became president of the firm in 1957 when Alfred Knopf became chairman of the board, died on June 4, 1966; Alfred Knopf became chairman emeritus in 1972.

Knox, Henry (1750–1806), soldier. Born in Boston on July 25, 1750, Knox became the sole support of his mother at the age of twelve, when his father died, and he left school to go to work for a bookseller. When he was twenty-one he established his own bookshop in Boston; the business throve, but he gave it up for a military career when the Revolutionary War broke out. He had joined the Boston Grenadier Corps in 1772 and he became an avid student of tactics, particularly of artillery; parading in uniform, he attracted the attention of the daughter of the royal secretary of the province, whom he married in 1774 against her family's wishes. He and his wife left Boston a year later, despite lucrative offers made to induce him to support the Loyalist cause. Commissioned a colonel and given command of the Continental army artillery in November 1775, he overcame enormous difficulties in conveying 55 artillery pieces that had been captured by Ethan Allen at Fort Ticonderoga back to Boston, where they were used to take the city; the British evacuated Boston in March 1776, Mrs. Knox's parents departing with them. Knox remained throughout the war a trusted adviser to Gen. George Washington, with whom he had formed a close friendship; indeed, he was probably closer to Washington during the years of the war than any other man and was present at almost every important engagement in the northern campaigns as well as at Yorktown. He participated in the fighting around New York City in 1776, and when Washington crossed the Delaware River on Christmas night of that year to march on and take Trenton, New Jersey, it was Knox who organized the movements of the troops, his stentorian voice carrying over the gale as he relayed the orders of his chief. He was promoted to brigadier general after the battle of Trenton. He was with Washington at the winter quarters at Valley Forge during 1777–1778, and in 1779 he was the founder of a military academy in Morristown, Pennsylvania, that was the progenitor of West Point. After sitting on the court-martial that tried British Major John André as a spy in 1780, he was promoted to major general on November 15, 1781, shortly after the siege of Yorktown, where he had directed the artillery to good effect, "the resources of his genius," as Washington said, supplying "the deficit of means." The chief organizer of the Society of the Cincinnati in 1783 and its secretary for many years, he was the first to shake Washington's hand in Fraunces Tavern in New York City on December 4, 1783, when Washington bade farewell to his officers. From 1782 he commanded the

fort at West Point and after resigning from the service in 1784, Knox returned to Boston to reenter business. He was elected secretary of war by Congress, operating under the Articles of Confederation, on March 8, 1785; he was retained in the post by President Washington in the new government organized in 1789 under the Constitution. His career in the cabinet was darkened by disputes with Alexander Hamilton and he resigned on December 28, 1794, to return to private life, after having helped lay the groundwork for the reestablishment of the U.S. navy. He lived during his last years on a large estate near Thomaston, Maine. A large man—during his heyday he is said to have weighed at least 300 pounds, his wife being hardly smaller, so that they were known in New York as "the largest couple in the city"—he was a tremendous eater, and he died suddenly and unexpectedly on October 25, 1806, as a consequence of having swallowed a chicken bone.

Knox, Philander Chase (1853–1921), lawyer and public official. Born in Brownsville, Pennsylvania, on May 6, 1853, Knox graduated in 1872 from Mount Union College, where, as a student, he became friendly with William McKinley, then a county district attorney. Admitted to the bar of Allegheny County, Pennsylvania, in 1875, he formed a law partnership in 1877 in Pittsburgh and for the next 20 years devoted himself to his practice, attaining recognition as one of the ablest corporation lawyers in the nation. In 1899 his old friend McKinley, by then president, offered him the post of attorney general; he declined because he was at the time deeply involved in the reorganization of the Carnegie Steel Company (a merger of Carnegie and Henry C. Frick interests), which was later sold to United States Steel; when McKinley renewed the offer in 1901 Knox accepted. His first significant action was the initiation of a suit against the Northern Securities Company under the Sherman Anti-Trust Act of 1890, and he directed the litigation through the courts, arguing the case before the Supreme Court and winning it in 1904. He was sent to Paris to investigate the offer of the New Panama Canal Company to sell its holdings in the Isthmus of Panama to the U.S. government for $40 million, and upon his certification of clear title the offer was accepted and President Theodore Roosevelt went on to begin construction of the Panama Canal. In the meantime, in June 1904, Knox had been appointed to fill the Senate seat vacated by the death of Matthew S. Quay of Pennsylvania, and, after being elected to the seat in the fall of that year, entered upon a full six-year term. He resigned from the Senate in March 1909 to become secretary of state under President William Howard Taft, with whom he had formed a close friendship. He was the most powerful figure in Taft's cabinet, which he had helped him to select, and he reorganized the Department of State, instituting far-reaching reforms. His most notable actions were in support of U.S. capital investments—the so-called "dollar diplomacy"—in the Far East in 1909–1910 and in Nicaragua and Honduras in 1911; he was indefatigable in his efforts to protect U.S. commercial interests abroad, although he insisted that the government's policy should not be construed as imperialist. Under his guidance the application of the Monroe Doctrine was broadened to include Asian as well as European nations in its prohibition of aggressive activities in the Western Hemisphere. Returning to Pittsburgh and to his law practice in 1913, he was elected once more to the Senate in 1916 and there took a leading part in the fight against the ratification of the Treaty of Versailles and against U.S. membership in the League of Nations. Although Senator Henry Cabot Lodge was the spokesman for the Republican opposition to the treaty and the League, it was Knox who did most of the important and ultimately successful work behind the scenes. After the defeat of the treaty he introduced a resolution for a separate peace with Germany and this was passed on July 2, 1921, and signed by President Warren G. Harding. Knox died suddenly in Washington, D.C., shortly after leaving the Senate chamber, on October 12, 1921.

Koch, Frederick Henry (1877–1944), educator and founder of theater groups. Born on September 12, 1877, in Covington, Kentucky, Koch graduated from Ohio Wesleyan University in 1900 and received an M.A. degree from Harvard in 1909. In 1905 he had become an instructor in English at the University of North Dakota and established there the Sock and Buskin Society, which was more formally organized in 1910 as the Dakota Playmakers, with Maxwell Anderson as a charter member. Koch was professor of dramatic literature at North Dakota from 1917 to 1918 and from 1918 at the University of North Carolina. From 1931 he was Kenan Professor of Dramatic Literature and from 1936 head of the department of dramatic art at North Carolina. He was regarded as a central figure in American folk playwriting and as a pioneer in promoting rural community drama groups. He founded, and often directed, numerous theater groups, including the Carolina Playmakers at the university in Chapel Hill, North Carolina, the North Carolina Bureau of Community Drama, and the Forest Theatre. The Carolina Playmakers secured for their work the first state-subsidized playhouse in the nation, and their popular tours through the South encouraged the spread of the little theater movement into rural areas. To make better known the folk-play movement, Koch lectured and gave summer playwriting courses at several universities. He edited folk-play collections, among them *American Folk Plays*, 1939, and *Alabama Folk Plays*, 1943, and he wrote plays for community theater groups, at times with collaborators. He was editor of the *Little Theatre Monthly* and the *Carolina Play-Book* and dramatic editor of the *Southern Literary Messenger*. He died while visiting Miami, Florida, on August 16, 1944.

Koerber, Leila, see Dressler, Marie

Kominsky, David Daniel, see Kaye, Danny

Kooweskoowe, see Ross, John

Kornberg, Arthur (1918–   ), biochemist. Born in Brooklyn, New York, on March 3, 1918, Kornberg graduated from high school at fifteen and received his B.S. from the College of the City of New York (CCNY) in 1937. He first became interested in enzymes while doing graduate work at the University of Rochester School of Medicine, from which he received his M.D. in 1941, and he proceeded with his enzyme researches when, after a year of residency at the Strong Memorial Hospital in Rochester and brief military service as a medical officer in the Coast Guard, he was in 1942 made an officer of the U.S. Public Health Service and assigned to the National Institutes of Health in Bethesda, Maryland. He advanced to medical director of the Public Health Service in 1951 and remained at Bethesda until 1952, first in the nutrition section and then as head of the enzymes and metabolism section; he then left to become head of the department of microbiology at the Washington University School of Medicine in St. Louis. From 1959 he was head of the department of biochemistry at the Stanford University School of Medicine. While at Bethesda and at Washington University, Kornberg and his group set themselves the task of ascertaining just how the genetic material works in cells, and, building on earlier work by other investigators, tried from about 1952 on to synthesize DNA (deoxyribonucleic acid), which had been identified as the substance in the cell that carries the genetic code. Success came in 1957, when he produced artificial DNA, the chemical and physical structure of which was exact but which was biologically inert. For these efforts Kornberg was awarded the 1959 Nobel Prize for Physiology and Medicine jointly with Severo Ochoa, who had synthesized RNA (ribonucleic acid), which translates the directions given by the DNA into the production of protein. At Stanford Kornberg then led his group in further researches, with the ultimate aim of synthesizing biologically active DNA. In 1967 he was able to announce that the DNA of a virus, Phi X174, had been synthesized in a test tube and that, when the DNA was added to a culture of *Escherichia coli* cells, it produced exactly the same effects as natural DNA. The author of *Enzymatic Synthesis of DNA*, 1962, as well as many technical papers in his field, Kornberg was a member of a number of scientific associations and the recipient of several prizes and awards in additon to the Nobel Prize.

Korzybski, Alfred (1879–1950), semanticist. Born in Warsaw on July 3, 1879, Alfred Habdank Skarbek Korzybski was educated as an engineer at the Warsaw Polytechnic Institute and taught mathematics, physics, and languages in Warsaw prior to World War I. After war broke out he saw service with the imperial Russian general staff and in 1915 went on a military mission to Canada and the United States. When the czarist regime collapsed in 1917 he remained in the United States as secretary of the French-Polish military mission; in 1920 he was a member of the Polish commission to the League of Nations. He became a U.S. citizen in 1940. His first book, *Manhood of Humanity: The Science and Art of Human Engineering*, appeared in 1921. It analyzed human history and culture in terms of man's "time-binding capacity"—the ability to transmit ideas from generation to generation—and proposed a new ethics based on time-binding as a central value. Human time-binding capacities are seen at their most effective, Korzybski asserted, in the sciences, where progress is steady and cumulative. Having described human intellect at its best, he then undertook to study it at its worst, and in his second and only other book, *Science and Sanity: An Introduction to Non-Aristotelian Systems and General Semantics*, published in 1933, he expressed his insights into language usage, including those gained during two years of study of psychiatric patients at St. Elizabeth's Hospital in Washington, D.C.; the book offered a critique of traditional assumptions about language in the context of a comparison of sane and unsane ways of using and reacting to it. It contrasted the rigid and almost subconscious assumptions implicit in everyday speech, derived mainly from Aristotelian two-valued logic, with the multivalued and thereby vastly more precise usages common in the sciences. The result was a system of linguistic retraining that he called general semantics, which would, he thought, release and develop men's time-binding capacities and thus produce immense intellectual progress. In 1938 he founded and became director of the Institute of General Semantics in Chicago; he moved it to Lakeville, Connecticut, in 1946. He died in Sharon, a neighboring town, on March 1, 1950.

Kościusko, Thaddeus (1746–1817), soldier. Born in Belorussia, then under the control of the union of Poland and Lithuania, and now part of the Soviet Union, Tadeusz Andrzej Bonawentura Kościuszko received a meager education from an aged uncle but on his own read Plutarch, who inspired him with a thirst for military glory. Graduating from the Royal School at Warsaw in 1769, he was commissioned a captain in the Polish army, but he found little to do in that role and went to Paris, where he studied military engineering and painting. News of the American Revolution stirred him to apply to Benjamin Franklin for a recommendation to the Continental Congress that his services be accepted. Arriving in Philadelphia in August 1776, he was commissioned a colonel of engineers in the Continental army on October 18 of that year. He distinguished himself at Ticonderoga and made an important contribution to the brilliant victory over Gen. John Burgoyne at Saratoga, on September 17, 1777, and the next year was placed in charge of building the fortifications at West Point. From 1780 to the end of the war he served meritoriously under generals Horatio Gates and Nathanael Greene in the Carolina Campaign. In 1783 he received the thanks of Congress and was made a brigadier general. Finding himself once again with no duties to perform, he left New York City for Paris in July 1784 and thence went to Poland, where he languished in rural retirement. He reemerged as major general of the Polish army in 1789 and led pathetically inadequate forces against the Russians in the spring of 1792. Upon the defeat of the Poles and the second partition of his country in 1793 he retired to France, but he returned to Poland in 1794 to lead an uprising in that year. He was chosen dictator and instituted liberal reforms, but he was defeated by a vastly superior Russian force in October 1794 and taken prisoner. Released by Czar Paul I on his promise that he would not again take up arms against Russia, he revisited the United States in 1797. Congress appropriated more than $18,000 in pay that was due him and made him a grant of 500 acres of land in Ohio. He returned to France in 1798 to live in retirement near Fontainebleau, refusing in 1806 to aid Napoleon in his invasion of Russia because of his previous promise to the czar. He moved to Switzerland in 1816 and died in Solothurn on October 15, 1817. His remains were carried to Kraków (Cracow) and interred in the cathedral, while the people of Poland mourned him as a national hero. He had freed the serfs on his Polish estate earlier the same year, and his will directed that the funds derived from the sale of his Ohio lands be used to free as many slaves as possible. The money was employed to found the Colored School at Newark, New Jersey, one of the first educational institutions for black students to be established in the United States.

Koufax, Sanford (1935–   ), "Sandy," baseball player. Born in Brooklyn, New York, on December 30, 1935, Sandy Koufax was raised there and in Rockville Centre on Long Island, and played baseball and basketball for Lafayette High School in Brooklyn, from which he graduated in 1953. He entered the University of Cincinnati that year on an athletic scholarship, but his feat of striking out 34 batters in his first two games as a pitcher the following spring led to a contract with the Brooklyn Dodgers in December 1954. Required because of the bonus rule to remain with the parent club for two years, he lacked the opportunity to gain valuable minor-league experience; as a result, during his first few years in the big leagues, he was a promising but unsuccessful pitcher, with a blazing fast ball over which he had little control. Thus, between 1955 and 1960 he enjoyed only two winning seasons, 1957 and 1959 —and even then his records were only 5 wins to 4 losses and 8–6, respectively—and after six years in the major leagues he had won only 36 games while losing 40. His strikeout record, however, had been considerably more impressive, as in most of the 1955–1960 seasons he had struck out more than one batter per inning pitched. In 1959 he had seemed for the first time to come into his own, striking out 16 batters in one game and 18 in another—thereby tying the major-league record—and had pitched in his first World Series, losing a 1–0 game to the Chicago White Sox. But in 1960 he was again relatively ineffective, winning 8 games while losing 13, although he struck out 197 batters in 175 innings. The next year, however—1961—he was on his way. He won 18 games while losing 13, struck out 269 batters (leading the National League) in 256 innings, and, perhaps more important, walked only 96 men. He pitched only five more years, retiring after the 1966 World Series because of soreness in his arm that was apparently incurable and that, he was warned, could lead to permanent disability; as he retired the claim was widely advanced that he was the greatest pitcher of all time. In those five seasons, 1962–1966, he won 111 games and lost only 34, led the league every year in lowest earned-run average and three times in strikeouts (his total of 382 strikeouts in 1965 established a new record), pitched four no-hitters (more than any other man), the last of them, in 1965, being a perfect game, and won four out of the six World Series games that he pitched. He also won the Cy Young Award three times during this period (in 1963, 1965, and 1966), a record unequaled by any other pitcher. After his retirement he lived in California and worked as a commentator on radio and television broadcasts of sporting events, usually baseball games. He was elected to the National Baseball Hall of Fame in 1972.

Koussevitsky, Serge (1874–1951), conductor. Born in Vyshni Volochek, Russia, on July 26, 1874, Sergei Alexandrovitch Kussevitsky employed the French form of his name—Serge Koussevitsky—during most of his life as a professional musician. As a youngster he studied the double bass in Moscow and became a virtuoso on the instrument—he was perhaps the greatest of all double bass players—and gave concerts in Russia, Germany, and England before 1900; he often played his own compositions for the instrument, and his concerto for double bass, 1905, became a standard in the repertory. He also studied conducting in Moscow and made his first appearance as a conductor in Berlin in 1908. In 1909 he founded his own orchestra in Moscow and also, in the same year, established a music-publishing firm that, in the years before World War I, published works by Sergei Rachmaninoff, Igor Stravinsky, Sergei Prokofiev, and others. Between 1910 and 1914 he made frequent tours with his orchestra to towns along the Volga River that had never heard such music before. After the Russian Revolution he was made director of the State Symphony Orchestra in Petrograd (later Leningrad), but he left Russia in 1920 and the next year organized annual concerts in Paris, in which he conducted new works by Russian and French composers. He came to the United States to lead the Boston Symphony Orchestra in 1924, remaining its conductor and director until his retirement in 1949; he became a U.S. citizen in 1941. During 25 years in Boston he gave the premiere performances of many works of American composers, including Aaron Copland, Roy Harris, and Walter Piston; and he often commissioned new works, the fiftieth anniversary of the Boston Symphony, in 1931, being marked by newly commissioned works by Prokofiev and Maurice Ravel, among others. Perhaps his most memorable achievement was the founding in 1934 of the annual summer Berkshire Symphonic Festivals (now the Berkshire Festival), outdoor performances by the Boston Symphony; from 1938 held at Tanglewood, an estate in Lenox, Massachusetts. The series was an innovation that led to similar concerts in many other parts of the United States. In 1940 he founded, also at Tanglewood, the Berkshire Music Center, a summer school at which students worked under the direction of outstanding musicians. In 1942 he established the Koussevitsky Foundation to commission and perform new orchestral works. A highly romantic, not to say rhapsodic conductor, he was greatly beloved by audiences not only in Boston but wherever he conducted, in the United States and abroad. He died in Boston on June 4, 1951.

Krehbiel, Henry Edward (1854–1923), music critic. Born in Ann Arbor, Michigan, on March 10, 1854, Krehbiel was brought up and educated in Cincinnati. He manifested musical talent at an early age, playing the violin and leading the choir of his father's church. He studied law for a while but soon gave it up for journalism, becoming a reporter for the *Cincinnati Gazette*. His spare time was spent in studying music, and he was the *Gazette*'s music critic from 1874 to 1880. In the latter year he was invited by Whitelaw Reid to join the *New York Tribune* as music critic, in which position he remained for 43 years. Although his tastes leaned to the classical, he was sympathetic to many younger composers, especially Richard Wagner, and he appreciated folk music, making a special study of Negro spirituals. He published a number of books on music, his most famous work being a three-volume *Life of Ludwig van Beethoven*, 1921, which he edited from the biography in German by A. W. Thayer, adding much material of his own. Other works by Krehbiel included *Studies in the Wagnerian Drama*, 1891; *A Book of Operas*, 1909; *Afro-American Folk-Songs*, 1914; and an English version of Wagner's *Parsifal*, 1919. He died on March 20, 1923, in New York City.

Kreisler, Fritz (1875–1962), musician and composer. Born in Vienna on February 2, 1875, Kreisler early took to the violin and at the age of seven was admitted to the Vienna Conservatory of Music. After studying there for three years under

Joseph Hellmesberger and Leopold Auer he was awarded a gold medal for his violin playing. He then entered the Conservatoire in Paris to study violin under Joseph Massart and composition under Léo Delibes. In 1887 he was awarded the Premier Grand Prix de Rome by the Conservatoire. The next year he undertook a concert tour of the United States with the pianist Moriz Rosenthal, making his American debut at Steinway Hall, New York City, on November 10. After the tour he returned to Austria and, on being refused a second-violin chair in the Vienna Philharmonic Orchestra, abandoned the violin to study medicine for a time. Later he studied art in Paris and at twenty was called for service in the Austrian army, becoming a captain. In 1899 he resumed playing, made a second and highly acclaimed debut in Berlin, and thenceforth was regarded as one of the premier musicians of the day. A tour of the United States during 1901–1903 was a great success and for the next decade Kreisler was hailed there and in Europe for his superb technique, lush tone, and profound interpretations of the works of the masters. In 1914 he reentered the Austrian army for service in World War I, but a wound sustained later that year resulted in his dischage. He returned to the United States in 1915, but many of his concert engagements were canceled because of war hysteria. In 1915 he published *Four Weeks in the Trenches: The War Story of a Violinist*. After the war he resumed his career as a successful and popular concert violinist. He composed two operettas, *Apple Blossoms*, performed in New York City in 1919, and *Sissy*, performed in Vienna in 1932, and a great many short violin pieces that were widely admired. He was the center of a musical controversy in 1935 when he revealed that a number of pieces that he had been including in his programs for many years, and which he attributed to such masters as Antonio Vivaldi, François Couperin, Gaetano Pugnani, and Niccolo Porpora, were in reality his own compositions. Kreisler became a U.S. citizen in 1943. He continued to perform in concert in Europe and the United States and on the radio— he was a pioneer in the broadcasting of classical music—until his retirement in 1950. In 1952 the Library of Congress presented him with a virtually priceless Guarnieri (Guarnerius) del Gesú violin made in 1737. Kreisler died in New York City on January 29, 1962.

Kress, Samuel Henry (1863–1955), businessman, art collector, and philanthropist. Born on July 23, 1863, in Cherryville, Pennsylvania, Kress attended public schools in nearby Slatington and taught school from 1880 to 1887. He began his business career by buying a small store in Nanticoke in 1887 and another in Wilkes-Barre in 1890. F. W. Woolworth's success with his five-and-ten-cent stores in Pennsylvania suggested to Kress the idea of starting the same kind of chain-store business in the South. The result was the opening of the S. H. Kress & Company "5, 10, and 25 cent store" in Memphis in 1896. It proved an immediate success and was soon followed by similar stores in other Southern cities. By 1900 Kress had moved his headquarters to New York City; in 1907, with 51 stores in operation, S. H. Kress & Company became a corporation and at the time of Kress's death there were 264 stores in the chain. During a 1921 visit to Italy he began a massive art collection which grew to include more than 2000 items, many of them masterpieces of medieval and Renaissance Italian painting and sculpture. Through the Samuel H. Kress Foundation, established in 1929, he donated to various museums the major part of his collection, which was valued at over $75 million. The largest single beneficiary of his generosity was the National Gallery of Art in Washington, D.C., of which he was elected president in 1945. He served as a trustee of both the National Gallery and of the Metropolitan Museum of Art in New York City. For his 1929 contribution of money for the restoration of the Gonzaga Palace in Mantua and other historic landmarks throughout Italy, Kress was awarded the Grand Cross of the Order of the Crown of Italy. A paralytic stroke in 1945 left him bedridden and a younger brother took over distribution of his collection to more than 40 American museums, many in the South and West. The foundation also made financial grants to numerous medical and research institutions. Kress died in New York City on September 22, 1955.

Kroeber, Alfred Louis (1876–1960), anthropologist. Born in Hoboken, New Jersey, on June 11, 1876, Kroeber took his B.A. from Columbia in 1896 and remained to take his M.A. in 1897, and his Ph.D., under Franz Boas, in 1901. That year he established a department of anthropology at the University of California at Berkeley and was attached to it, as a professor of anthropology after 1919, until 1946. From 1925 to 1946 he was also director of the university's anthropology museum. His major anthropological expeditions were to New Mexico in 1915–1920, to Mexico in 1924 and 1930, and to Peru in 1925, 1926, and 1942. His research focused on the Indians of California, but also encompassed the Zuñi, the Plains tribes, and the Indians of Mexico and South America; he extended the domain of archaeology —especially that of California, Mexico, and Peru —to include linguistics, folk culture, family structure, religion, and social organization. He analyzed such cultural manifestations as art, fashion, and language for their repetitive features among civilizations. His textbook, *Anthropology*, 1923, revised in 1948, was long regarded as the most authoritative in the field. Among numerous other publications were *Handbook of the Indians of California*, 1925; *Three Centuries of Women's Dress Fashions*, with Jane Richardson, 1940; *Peruvian Archeology in 1942*, 1944; *Configurations of Culture Growth*, 1944; *A Mohave Historical Epic*, 1951; *Style and Civilizations*, 1957; *Sparkman Grammar of Luiseño*, with G. Grace,

1960; and *A Roster of Civilizations and Culture*, 1962. He was a founder of the American Anthropological Association and its president in 1917, a member of numerous other scientific organizations, and winner of many honorary degrees and awards, including the Huxley and Viking medals. He died in Paris on October 5, 1960.

Krutch, Joseph Wood (1893–1970), author, critic, editor, and naturalist. Born in Knoxville, Tennessee, on November 25, 1893, Krutch grew up there and received a B.S. from the University of Tennessee in 1915. He went to New York City to study English at Columbia University, where he received his M.A. in 1916 and his Ph.D. in 1923. An instructor in English at Columbia in 1917–1918, he also taught at the Brooklyn Polytechnic Institute, Vassar College, Columbia's School of Journalism, and at the New School for Social Research. He returned to Columbia's English department in 1937, remaining until 1952, the last nine years as Brander Matthews Professor of Dramatic Literature. His doctoral dissertation, published in 1924 as *Comedy and Conscience After the Restoration*, had indicated what was to be his lifelong interest in the theater, and he was drama critic and an editor of the *Nation* from 1924 to 1952 and served in 1940–1941 as president of the New York Drama Critics' Circle. He also wrote a series of scholarly books; a study of Edgar Allan Poe appeared in 1926; *Five Masters*, treating the lives and works of Boccaccio, Cervantes, Richardson, Stendhal, and Proust, in 1930; and a biography of Dr. Samuel Johnson, published in 1944. When Krutch left his Columbia post in 1952 his achievements as a drama and literary critic, as an inspiring teacher, and as a raconteur already constituted a full career. Yet he set out upon another, in the course of which he gained his greatest fame. In the later 1940s he had begun to travel in the Southwest, partly for his health, and he developed a passion for the desert and the mountains. His superb biography of Henry David Thoreau had appeared in 1948, and now, partly in emulation of Thoreau, he retired to the Tucson area to live in an adobe house in the desert. Books flowed from his desert study. *The Twelve Seasons*, a dozen essays, each focused on a month, had appeared in 1949; 1952 saw the publication of *The Desert Year*, a lyrical study of his new environs. There followed *The Best of Two Worlds*, 1953; *The Voice of the Desert*, 1955; *The Great Chain of Life*, 1957; *Grand Canyon: To-day and All Its Yesterdays*, 1958; *The Gardener's World*, 1959; *The Forgotten Peninsula* (about Baja California), 1961; *The World of Animals*, 1961; and *Herbal*, 1965, all expressing his deep concern with and affection for the natural world. He wrote and narrated three television specials—on the Sonora Desert in 1963, on the Grand Canyon in 1965, and on Baja California in 1968. He also continued to contribute articles and essays to many publications, to edit collections of these and of the works of others, and to write occasional drama criticism.

He produced in 1954 *The Measure of Man*, a study of humanity that won a National Book Award and that was in some degree an updating of an early, famous book, *The Modern Temper*, whose pessimism had shocked readers when it first came out in 1929; *Human Nature and the Human Condition* followed in 1959, and an autobiography, *More Lives Than One*, was published in 1962; it drew together all the strains of his thought and experience in an eloquent plea for a sane relationship between man and nature. He died in Tucson on May 22, 1970.

Kubelsky, Benjamin, *see* Benny, Jack

Kubrick, Stanley (1928–   ), motion-picture director. Born in the Bronx, New York, on July 26, 1928, Kubrick had a generally sketchy education owing to his penchant for spending hours on end in movie houses. He began to take photographs as a child and by the time he was seventeen was a member of the photographic staff of *Look* magazine, but he soon decided that still pictures were "too passive" and he bought a second-hand movie camera. His first film, a 15-minute documentary called *The Day of the Fight*, was made in 1949; it cost him $3800 and when he sold it to RKO-Pathé News for $4000 and saw it screened at New York City's Paramount Theatre, he decided to devote his life to making movies. His progress was amazingly rapid, for he managed to teach himself almost everything he needed to know and thus avoided the time-consuming apprenticeship usual for directors. Among his early films were *Fear and Desire*, 1953, *The Killing*, 1956, and *Paths of Glory*, 1957, which led to Marlon Brando's asking Kubrick to direct him in *One-eyed Jacks*. The arrangement did not work out and Kubrick resigned from the film although he and Brando remained friendly. In 1960 he directed *Spartacus*. Kubrick's next production was a film version of Vladimir Nabokov's novel *Lolita*, released in 1962, which was notable mainly for the fact that the producers were able to obtain a seal of approval (for adults only) from the Legion of Decency for the film, whose subject matter was considered extremely daring for the time. Kubrick's career then took off as he produced three extraordinary films during the next nine years. The first, *Dr. Strangelove, or How to Stop Worrying and Love the Bomb*, 1964, was a madcap vision of life under the shadow of nuclear annihilation. The second, *2001: A Space Odyssey*, 1968, was a collaborative effort of Kubrick and science-fiction writer Arthur C. Clarke. An enigma to most viewers, the visually dazzling film was endlessly discussed and interpreted, and Clarke himself wrote a book about what it meant. The third, *A Clockwork Orange*, 1971, adapted from a novel by Anthony Burgess, was attacked by many critics for its violence, but it too helped fortify Kubrick's reputation as one of the most innovative of U.S. film directors. He later directed *Barry Lyndon*, 1975, based on the William Thackeray novel, and *The Shining*, 1980.

Kusch, Polykarp (1911–   ), physicist. Born at Blankenburg, Germany, on January 26, 1911, Kusch was brought to the United States in 1912, the family eventually settling in Cleveland. He became a U.S. citizen in 1922. He received his B.S. from the Case School of Applied Science (now Case Western Reserve University) in 1931 and his M.Sc. and Ph.D. from the University of Illinois in 1933 and 1936, respectively. In 1937 he became an instructor in physics at Columbia University but his academic career was interrupted during the next few years as he spent a year working as a development engineer in the Westinghouse laboratory at Bloomfield, Pennsylvania, in 1941–1942, and another year toward the end of World War II with the Bell Telephone Laboratories in New York City. Returning to Columbia in 1946 as an associate professor of physics, he was promoted to full professor in 1949. His work after the war centered on some of the problems of quantum mechanics, and he was able to provide evidence as early as 1947 that called into question earlier calculations of the magnetic moment of the electron. Further experiments involving extremely delicate measurements of magnetic moments in an electron beam confirmed the anomalous values earlier suggested and also anomalous values for the hyperfine interactions of hydrogen. This work touched off a revolution in nuclear physics and led, within a few years, to the evolution of a new set of scientific principles for quantum mechanics, particularly by Julian S. Schwinger. For these researches he was awarded the Nobel Prize for physics in 1955, sharing the honor with Willis E. Lamb, Jr., of Stanford University. Kusch afterward continued his research and teaching at Columbia, and he served as dean of faculties from 1969 to 1971.

Kussevitsky, Sergei Alexandrovitch, *see* Koussevitsky, Serge

Kuznets, Simon (1901–   ), economist. Born in Kharkov, Russia, on April 30, 1901, Kuznets was six when his father emigrated to the United States in 1907, but 15 years passed before he was able to join him. He had studied economics in Russia, and upon his arrival in New York City he was accepted at Columbia University, from which he received his B.A. in 1923 and his Ph.D. in 1926. The next year he was asked by Wesley C. Mitchell to join the National Bureau of Economic Research, which Mitchell had founded. Kuznets accepted and was associated with the Bureau throughout his career. He began to teach economic statistics at the University of Pennsylvania in 1930 and at the same time initiated a series of studies of national earnings, income levels, and productivity that eventually culminated in his formulation of the concept of gross national product, or GNP, the now universally accepted measure of the wealth of nations. John Kenneth Galbraith called the GNP "one of the greatest discoveries of all time," and for it Kuznets received the Swedish National Bank's Nobel Memorial Prize for Economics for 1971. He studied the concept in all of its ramifications for many years, publishing a number of significant works on the subject that included *National Income and Its Composition, 1919–38,* 1941; *National Product Since 1869,* 1947; and *Economic Growth of Nations: Total Output and Production Structure,* 1971. The first two were published by, and the research for them was done under the auspices of, the National Bureau of Economic Research. The last book, which was highly controversial, attacked the critics of economic growth and showed that some costs of growth could be paid for out of national income. Kuznets became a professor of economics at The John Hopkins University in 1954; in 1960 he moved to Harvard. He retired from Harvard in 1971 but continued his research and writing.

L

Lachaise, Gaston (1882–1935), sculptor. Born in Paris on March 19, 1882, Lachaise, whose father was a cabinetmaker, entered a craft and trade school at thirteen. Aspiring to the finer arts, he left the school and entered the École des Beaux-Arts in 1898; there he showed much promise but little interest in the French styles of the day in art. In 1905 he worked briefly in the shop of René Lalique, famed maker of art-nouveau glass objects, and then embarked for the United States, settling in Boston in 1906. Six years as an assistant to an academic monument sculptor culminated in his going to New York City and opening his own studio in 1912. He was naturalized in 1916. At thirty he launched his true career as an artist who celebrated the voluptuous female figure with "Standing Woman," a proud figure, massive yet buoyant, and his most famous bronze. Many American museums eventually acquired copies of this statue, which was finally cast in 1927. His first years in New York City were marked by an association with sculptor Paul Manship, but he later worked independently. Lachaise was represented in the Armory Show in 1913 and during the following years enjoyed several one-man shows and appreciative patrons. He was also highly respected for his portrait sculptures, his subjects including John Marin, Marianne Moore, and E. E. Cummings. He died in New York City unexpectedly on October 18, 1935, the year of a retrospective show at the Museum of Modern Art.

Laclède, Pierre (1724?–1778), fur trader and founder of St. Louis. Born about 1724 in the Pyrenean village of Bedous, France, Pierre Laclède Liguest came of a prominent family and retained the surname Liguest legally, although preferring Laclède. His training appears to have been for a commercial life, and shortly after he arrived in New Orleans in 1755 he became active in a fur-trading company which bore his name and which, in 1762, obtained the exclusive although limited right to trade with the Indians of the Missouri valley. Although the territory in which he flourished was ceded to Spain in that same year and the British became sovereign of all the land east of the Mississippi in 1763, Laclède proceeded with his plans for a trading post west of the great river. In February 1764 he sent the fourteen-year-old René Auguste Choteau, son of his close friend Marie Thérèse Choteau, to clear a site Laclède had selected near the junction of the Missouri with the Mississippi. Frenchmen leaving British rule farther east quickly followed the original party of 30 to the settlement that Laclède later

named after Saint Louis, Louis IX of France, and in April Laclède himself undertook to head the community, continuing to do so until civil government was established some 18 months later. Trade increased and a small garrison of French troops accepted Laclède's invitation to settle in St. Louis; although his own finances finally suffered reverses, Laclède's hopes for a thriving metropolis were eventually fulfilled. Laclède died on June 20, 1778, on his return from a two-year stay in New Orleans, at the confluence of the Missouri and Arkansas rivers. He was buried in an unmarked grave.

Ladd, William (1778–1841), pacifist. Born on May 10, 1778, in Exeter, New Hampshire, Ladd was a descendant of a family that first settled in New England in 1634. He graduated from Harvard in 1798 and married a year later; he then followed in his father's footsteps, becoming the captain of a large brig out of Portsmouth, New Hampshire. He interrupted his career at sea, which lasted until 1812, to experiment with a plan of labor reform in Florida that he hoped would eventually abolish slavery. At thirty-four he took up farming, settling in Minot, Maine, and devoting himself to new methods of cultivation until 1819, when his interests became focused on world peace. He then became increasingly active as a lecturer and propagandist and as an organizer of local peace societies. In 1828 he founded the American Peace Society, which endured until the formation of the United Nations (1945); under Ladd's leadership it effectively exploited the techniques of petition and pressure-group tactics in influencing both state and national legislatures. His *A Brief Illustration of the Principles of War and Peace, by Philanthropos* appeared in 1831, and thereafter he was a central figure in the often bitter disputes about the peace question that afflicted the growing movement. Ladd's views, cogently argued, usually prevailed in the Society, especially his insistence on the abolition of both offensive and defensive wars. His opposition on a point of principle to William Lloyd Garrison prompted Garrison to lead a splinter group out of the Society in 1838. In 1837 Ladd was ordained in the Congregationalist ministry, gaining an additional audience for his incessant efforts in behalf of the peace movement. His *Essay on a Congress of Nations,* 1840, outlined his most important contribution. He urged the formation of two institutions, in form not unlike those fostered by the American political experiment: a congress of nations that would establish the principles of international law, and an international court to arbitrate disputes. Elihu Burritt became an able advocate of these ideas both at home and in Europe as Ladd's health failed. Despite partial paralysis Ladd continued to speak in public until just before his death on April 9, 1841, in Portsmouth, New Hampshire. The "Apostle of Peace" was one of the few American thinkers of his time to grapple with the problems of international organization that would become even more pressing in the next century.

Laemmle, Carl (1867–1939), motion-picture producer. Born on January 17, 1867, in Laupheim, Germany, into a poor family, Laemmle received little schooling and at thirteen was apprenticed to a stationery dealer. At seventeen, on the death of his mother, he joined an elder brother in Chicago, where he held clerical jobs until moving, in 1894, to Oshkosh, Wisconsin, to take a bookkeeping position in a clothing firm. Four years later he married the niece of the owner of the firm. A quarrel with his employer in 1906 encouraged him to strike out on his own. While looking for a suitable business opportunity in Chicago he spotted a nickelodeon whose potential for profit he thought interesting, and within a year he had opened two prospering movie houses, acquired a partner, and begun distributing films to other local theaters. Laemmle and other independents faced the prospect of a short supply of films in their competition with the General Film Company, a coalition with a virtual monopoly in film-making. In order to service other small distributors resisting the giant film trust, he began making his own films in New York City, where, in the year 1910 alone, he produced 100 short movies. It was Laemmle who first conceived the notion of "selling" the personalities of movie actors. His first star, lured from the powerful Biograph Studios, was the popular but until then anonymous Florence Lawrence—known to audiences only as "the Biograph girl"—whom he publicized in ways later common in Hollywood. Laemmle soon scored an even greater coup in hiring away Biograph's "Little Mary"—Mary Pickford. In 1912, his business now located in Hollywood, California, he merged with other producers to form Universal Pictures Corporation. He thus rode the rising tide of a new industry that during his lifetime became the principal provider of entertainment for the world's most prosperous country. Universal thrived under his direction and in both the silent and talkie eras he launched the careers of many actors, including Lon Chaney, directors, including Erich von Stroheim, and at least one other producer, Irving Thalberg. Perhaps his most memorable film was *All Quiet on the Western Front,* 1930. Laemmle held sole control of Universal from 1920 until 1936, when he sold the business, reportedly for some $5.5 million. He died in Hollywood on September 24, 1939.

La Farge, John (1835–1910), artist. Born in New York City on March 31, 1835, of French parentage,

La Farge was reared in an atmosphere of culture and learning. When he was six he asked his grandfather, a miniaturist, to teach him to paint, and his interest in art persisted throughout his formal schooling. After he graduated from Mount St. Mary's College, Maryland, in 1853, he studied law briefly and without enthusiasm, then went to Paris in 1856. For a short time he joined classes taught by the painter Thomas Couture, but he gained his training primarily in galleries and museums; he traveled through Europe to study the old masters. He returned to the United States in 1858, briefly resumed reading law, and then returned to his painting with William Morris Hunt in Rhode Island. He concentrated on the relationships of light and color, executing a work, "Paradise Valley," in 1866–1868 that anticipated French impressionism. He painted flowers and landscapes in which the delicacy of flowers was contrasted to solid objects. Invited by the architect Henry H. Richardson to decorate the interior of Trinity Church in Boston in 1876, he produced a series of murals that led to other church commissions, including one for "The Ascension," in the Church of the Ascension in New York City; his church murals have remained unrivaled in the United States. He became fascinated by medieval stained glass and invented an opalescent glass that he used in windows of his own design; his work began a revival of the craft and contributed to his worldwide fame. Travels with Henry Adams through the South Seas and to Japan were recorded in a series of watercolors and two books, *An Artist's Letters from Japan,* 1897, and *Reminiscences of the South Seas,* 1912. His other books, examining artists and art movements with depth and precision, included *Considerations on Painting,* 1895, *Great Masters,* 1903, and *The Higher Life in Art,* 1908. He died in Providence, Rhode Island, on November 14, 1910.

Lafayette, Marquis de (1757–1834), soldier. Born on September 6, 1757, at Chavaniac in Auvergne of an aristocratic French family, Marie Joseph Paul Yves Roch Gilbert du Motier, the Marquis de Lafayette, lost his father, killed fighting the British at Minden, when he was two. Upon the death of his mother and grandfather in 1770 he inherited the family fortune. His formal schooling, begun when he was eleven, ended when he was fifteen. He enlisted in a company of musketeers and two years later transferred to a regiment of dragoons. Bent on the glory of a military career, he acquired a captaincy of dragoons, but dissatisfied with the court life at Versailles and with his imagination fired by an account of the American Revolution, he arranged through Silas Deane in Paris for a commission in the Continental Army. He left for America in April 1777 despite opposition from king and family and in July met with the Continental Congress. He agreed to serve without pay and without a specific command and was commissioned a major general; in August he conferred with Gen. George Washington in a meeting that proved to be the beginning of a long and warm friendship. Whatever reservations the army or Congress might have had about the youthful foreign adventurer were erased at the battle of Brandywine, September 11, 1777, where he fought well and was wounded. Recovering in a month's time, he rejoined Washington and again distinguished himself in a skirmish with German mercenaries. In December he was given his own command and after spending the winter with Washington at Valley Forge was appointed to lead an expedition into Canada. The invasion proved abortive owing both to lack of supplies and, as Lafayette thought, to the Conway Cabal; but in May 1778 his strategy of retreat from Barren Hill was highly praised and a month later at the battle of Monmouth his participation as a division commander stood out in the defeat. In the succeeding months Lafayette played an increasingly important role both in the field and as an instrument of the growing alliance with France, which by May had become a reality. A French fleet under Count d'Estaing reached Rhode Island in July 1778 and Lafayette served as liaison during and after an unsuccessful attack on Newport. In early January 1779 he went to France a popular hero, staying there for some time in order to obtain substantial French help for the American cause. In April 1780 he returned to the United States with news of the forthcoming dispatch of a French expeditionary force under Count de Rochambeau and was restored to command of the Virginia light troops. In March 1781 he participated in the unsuccessful attempt to capture Benedict Arnold and beginning in April held a major command in the campaign in Virginia against Gen. Charles Cornwallis, who, hemmed in on the south by Lafayette and cut off from his own navy by the French West Indies fleet barring the entrance to Chesapeake Bay, finally capitulated at Yorktown on October 19, 1781, virtually bringing the Revolution to a close. Lafayette's spirited generalship and his role in securing French assistance had played a large part in the American victory. He returned to France in 1782 "the hero of two worlds," universally hailed as "America's Marquis." His reception by his friends in the United States during a six-month visit in 1784 was equally warm; he was made a citizen of several states and he departed again filled with enthusiasm for republicanism and ready to launch a new career in his native land. In 1787 he was chosen to the first assembly of notables and early in 1789 sat in the estates-general. There he presented the first draft of the Declaration of the Rights of Man and the Citizen. He played a prominent part in the French Revolution and shortly after the capture of the Bastille in 1789 was placed in command of the new Paris militia. By 1790 he and the king were the two most powerful figures in France. In 1791, however, he resigned his command and accepted the rank of lieutenant general for the impending war with Austria. For five years, 1792–1797, after his suspension by the antimonarchical Assembly and his attempted flight to America, he was a captive of the Prussians and Austrians; returning to France in 1799 he was not active in public life again until 1815, when he briefly entered the Chamber of Deputies, where he again served in 1818–1824. In 1824, at the invitation of President James Monroe, he made a triumphant return to the United States. Touring for more than a year, he became the idol of a new generation of Americans, "the doyen," as Thomas Jefferson put it, "of the soldiers of liberty of the world." Congress voted him land and money, a timely act for he had lost most of his fortune in the turmoils in France. On returning to France, once again to another enthusiastic reception, he reentered politics. In 1827 he was again seated in the Chamber of Deputies and during the revolution of July 1830 again took command of the national guard. At first supporting Louis Philippe but later attacking him for unkept promises, Lafayette continued to espouse liberal causes in the Chamber of Deputies until his death in Paris on May 20, 1834.

Laffite, Jean (1780?–1825?), privateer. Little is known of Laffite's origins; he was probably born in France about 1780 and doubtless spent his youth at sea. In 1809 he and his brother Pierre ran a blacksmith shop in New Orleans that served as a front for smuggled goods. He soon became chief of the band of smugglers and established his headquarters on the islands of Barataria Bay. Between 1810 and 1814 he operated perhaps a dozen ships under privateering commission from Cartagena (in present-day Colombia), preying on Spanish vessels in the Gulf of Mexico and selling the booty in Louisiana. When the British courted his assistance during the War of 1812 Laffite warned Louisiana officials about what he had discovered about English plans. The Americans responded by raiding Laffite's colony on Barataria Bay, Louisiana, and bringing his ships to New Orleans. Laffite was finally able to convince Gen. Andrew Jackson of his loyalty and he and his men did valiant service manning the artillery during the battle of New Orleans in January 1815. In February President James Madison honored a promise made by Jackson and granted pardons to Laffite and the men from his Barataria colony. In 1817 he and nearly a thousand of his followers went to the island that was later the site of Galveston, Texas, founded the settlement of Campeche, and reverted to privateering against the Spanish. Laffite continued to respect American shipping but eventually some of the Campeche pirates escaped his control and in 1819 several were hanged in New Orleans for piracy. In 1821, following the capture and scuttling of an American merchantman by some of Laffite's men, U.S. naval forces dispersed the Galveston colony. Laffite himself picked a crew and sailed away in his favorite ship, the *Pride*. Until about 1825 there were stories of his activities on the Spanish Main, but after that, stories of his exploits were only legendary.

La Follette, Robert Marion (1855–1925), public official and political leader. Born in Primrose, near Madison, Wisconsin, on June 14, 1855, La Follette worked his way through the University of Wisconsin, graduated in 1879, and the following year was admitted to the bar. At the same time he began his practice he also entered politics and was elected district attorney; characteristically he had campaigned by himself, ignoring the Republican party organization. He was reelected in 1882 and then from 1885 to 1891 served in the House of Representatives. He was, in outlook and voting record, a reasonably regular Republican at this time, in his last term helping to draft the McKinley tariff legislation. He lost his seat in the popular reaction against the tariff in 1890 and returned to his law practice in Madison; the next year, however, he began a campaign against the established party leadership in Wisconsin with charges of corruption and bribery and for ten years, while evolving a legislative reform program and gaining his own strong constituency, maintained his war against the Republican bosses. In 1900 he won the governorship but was prevented from realizing any of his legislative proposals by a legislature dominated by Republican stalwarts; in 1902 he was reelected and given a friendly legislature that proceeded to institute his program of direct primaries for nominating candidates, state civil service, and state regulation and equitable taxation of the railroads as well as equitable taxation of other corporate property. These reforms, which he had first proposed during the 1890s, became the goals of progressives across the nation under the name of the "Wisconsin Idea." Another of La Follette's innovations was his recruitment of expert advisers from the faculty of the University of Wisconsin. In 1906 he resigned as governor to enter the Senate, to which he was twice returned. In the Senate his independence and progressive views estranged him from party leaders; his name was placed in nomination for the presidency at the 1908 Republican national convention but the dominant conservatives easily secured the victory for William Howard Taft. To broaden the movement for reform he founded *La Follette's Weekly Magazine* (later the *Progressive*) in 1909 and two years later organized the National Progressive Republican League; as the League's revolt against Taft gained momentum Theodore Roosevelt became interested and, when La Follette's health failed temporarily in 1912, he incorporated it into his own Bull Moose Progressive campaign. La Follette rejected Roosevelt's pragmatic politics and after 1912 cooperated with the reform program of Woodrow Wilson, on several occasions crossing the party line to join Senate Democrats in support of progressive legislation. He in turn was able to enlist Democratic support for passage of his Seaman's Act of 1915. He broke with Wilson over U.S. policy in World War I and later over the League of Nations and the World Court. He voted against U.S. entry into the war and lost thereby some of his supporters. He suffered more seriously when a false newspaper report in 1917 seemed to show him as imperfectly patriotic and led to his censure by the Wisconsin legislature and talk of expelling him from the Senate, but the national reaction that followed the war restored him to public favor. He continued to steer a course independent of the Repubican party. It was he who introduced a resolution calling for a Senate investigation of the Teapot Dome scandal. In 1924 a coalition of liberal and reformist groups, as the Progressive party, nominated him for president and he and his running mate, Senator Burton K. Wheeler, polled nearly 5 million votes, one-sixth of the total, but gained only the electoral votes of Wisconsin. He died in Washington, D.C., on June 18, 1925. His *Autobiography, a Personal Narrative of Political Experiences*, had appeared in 1913.

La Guardia, Fiorello Henry (1882–1947), public official. Born in New York City on December 11, 1882, La Guardia attended high school in Prescott, Arizona, and was for a time employed as a reporter for the *St. Louis Dispatch*. At sixteen he went to Budapest and worked at the U.S. consulate. After working at the consulates at Trieste and Fiume (Rijeka) he returned to the United States and became an interpreter at Ellis Island. He graduated from New York University law school in 1910 and was admitted to the bar. Having established a legal-aid bureau to represent poor people in court for no fee, he became well known to immigrants in the fourteenth congressional district, who elected him to the House of Representatives on the Republican ticket in 1916. He allied himself with progressive forces and voted to liberalize House rules. When the United States entered World War I he resigned to command U.S. bombing squadrons on the Italian-Austrian front. He returned to Congress in 1918 and after serving as president of the New York City board of aldermen in 1920–1921 was reelected to the House in 1922. Called a "chronic dissenter," he fought for child-labor laws and woman suffrage, vigorously opposed Prohibition and pork-barrel legislation, and prompted resignations by Federal judges whom he exposed for graft. He was co-sponsor of the 1932 Norris-La Guardia Anti-Injunction Act that restricted the use of injunctions and helped establish labor's right to strike, picket, and conduct boycotts. In 1933, on a reform-fusion ticket, he unseated Tammany Hall in New York City's mayoral election. Twice reelected, in his 12 years as mayor he began slum-clearance and low-cost-housing projects, improved the operations of the police and fire departments, battled gangsters, gamblers, slot machines, and official corruption, and built recreational facilities, health clinics, roads and bridges, and La Guardia Airport. A colorful campaigner and redoubtable political battler, La Guardia was held in great affection by the legions of people whose welfare he advanced and by whom he was known as the "Little Flower." In 1941 he was named director of the U.S. Office of Civilan Defense and he became director general of the United Nations Relief and Rehabilitation Agency (UNRRA) in March 1946, but resigned in December. He died in New York City on September 20, 1947, perhaps the city's most controversial and certainly its most beloved mayor.

Lahr, Bert (1895–1967), entertainer. Born in New York City on August 13, 1895, Irving Lahrheim left school at fifteen and toured the country with a vaudeville troupe for three years. An additional seven years with the Columbia Burlesque Circuit established him as a top performer. His experience in vaudeville was invaluable in creating the character of the "Dutch cop," a role that fascinated him from childhood and which he perfected in an act with his future wife, Mercedes Delpino. *Delmar's Revels* (a flop in 1927) marked his first appearance in a Broadway musical, but the following year his role in *Hold Everything* launched a successful career as one of the leading comedians of his time. He appeared regularly on Broadway thereafter, in, among other shows, *The George White Scandals* of 1935 and was seen with Ethel Merman in *Du Barry Was a Lady*, 1939. His first dramatic role was in *Burlesque*, 1946, which ran for more than a year. Lahr also made numerous Hollywood films, some of them remakes of successful stage plays; perhaps his most memorable movie role was as the Cowardly Lion in *The Wizard of Oz*, 1939, a role for which his drooping features and his unique combination of wit and gentle humor ideally suited him. In later years he occasionally was seen on television. He played Estragon in *Waiting for Godot* on Broadway in 1956 and also appeared in Broadway productions of Aristophanes and Shakespeare. He died on December 4, 1967, in New York City.

Lahrheim, Irving, *see* Lahr, Bert

Lake, Mother, *see* Barry, Leonora Marie Kearney

Lake, Simon (1866–1945), engineer and inventor. Born in Pleasantville, New Jersey, on September 4, 1866, Lake included in his schooling instruction at the Franklin Institute in Philadelphia. At twenty-three he began manufacturing in Baltimore several machines useful in ship construction and design. Shortly thereafter he began experimenting with designs for underwater vessels; his first experimental submersible was completed in 1894 and in 1897 he built the gasoline engine powered *Argonaut*, which operated successfully in the open sea in 1898, the first submarine to do so. The design was rejected by the U.S. navy in favor of one by John P. Holland, but Lake found buyers in Europe. He spent several years as a consultant to the Russians, who in 1906 bought his *Protector* and were interested in submarines for clearing ice-bound ports, and to the British and the Germans, who later used one of his models when constructing their U-boats. His expertise was utilized during World War I by the

U.S. navy, which adopted his torpedo-boat design, but his main interest was always in peaceful uses of the submarine and in 1932 he designed another submersible for use in underwater salvage operations. In his later years he devoted much of his time to looking for sunken gold in New York harbor. He died on June 23, 1945, in Bridgeport, Connecticut.

Lamar, Joseph Rucker (1857–1916), justice of the Supreme Court. Born on October 14, 1857, in Elbert County, Georgia, Lamar grew up at Cedar Grove, his mother's family home, and, after his mother died in 1864, in Augusta with his father. After attending private schools he went to the University of Georgia. He graduated from Bethany College, West Virginia, in 1877 and studied law at Washington and Lee University, being admitted to the Georgia bar in 1878. He began practicing law in 1880 in Augusta and, quickly rising to prominence, was elected to the state legislature for two terms, 1886–1889. His publication, with two fellow commissioners, of *The Code of the State of Georgia*, 1896, a recodification of civil law, established him as one of the leading members of the legal profession and led to his appointment to the state supreme court in 1904. He stepped down from that bench for reasons of health after two years, returning to what proved to be an illustrious career as a trial lawyer until his appointment by President William Howard Taft to the U.S. Supreme Court in 1911. His five years on the Court were marked by two important decisions: *Gompers* v. *Bucks Stove and Range Co.*, 1911, which upheld the right of the courts to punish violations of injunctions while at the same time setting aside Gompers's conviction on procedural grounds; and *United States* v. *Midwest Oil Co.*, 1914, which upheld the president's right to withhold public oil lands from private exploitation. In 1914 Lamar represented President Woodrow Wilson at a conference called to settle differences with Mexico, but later had to refuse an appointment to a Pan-American Conference because of his failing health. He died on January 2, 1916, in Washington, D.C.

Lamar, Lucius Quintus Cincinnatus (1825–1893), justice of the Supreme Court. Born in Putnam County, Georgia, on September 17, 1825, Lamar graduated from Emory College (now University) in 1845 and two years later was admitted to the bar. In 1849 he moved to Oxford, Mississippi, and served as adjunct professor of mathematics at the University of Mississippi there while practicing law. He went back to Georgia in 1852, served a year in the state legislature, and in 1855 returned permanently to Mississippi. In 1857 he was elected to the House of Representatives; reelected in 1859, he served until the eve of the Civil War and then, in December 1860, resigned, returned to Mississippi, and drafted the state's ordinance of secession. He served in the Confederate army for more than a year until ill health forced his resignation, whereupon in November 1862 he was appointed special commissioner to Russia by Confederate President Jefferson Davis. After several months in Paris vainly waiting for the Confederate legislature's confirmation of his mission he returned to the Confederacy early in 1864. He continued to work in support of the South and the Davis administration until the war ended, when he resumed his law practice and taught metaphysics and law at the University of Mississippi. In 1872, as the grip of Reconstruction began to relax, Lamar was elected Mississippi's first postwar Democrat in the House. He quickly became a leader among Southern political figures and prominent nationally as he fought the vestiges of radical Reconstruction and, more importantly, acted for reconciliation. He supported the ultimate resolution by the Electoral Commission of the disputed presidential election of 1876 and was that year elected to the Senate, where he became the leading spokesman for the "new South." In 1885 President Grover Cleveland offered him the post of secretary of the interior; primarily to further the reunion of North and South, he accepted and served ably for more than two years. Then, in 1887, the President appointed him to the U.S. Supreme Court. In his short tenure on the bench he delivered few opinions, but the learning, intelligence, and judgment he brought to the Court were later attested to by his colleagues. Lamar died in Macon, Georgia, on January 23, 1893.

Lamar, Mirabeau Buonaparte (1798–1859), soldier and public official. Born on August 16, 1798, in Louisville, Georgia, Lamar first planned upon a career as a merchant but in 1823 accepted a position as secretary to Governor George M. Troup of Georgia. Three years later he became the editor of the *Columbus* (Georgia) *Enquirer*. After an unsuccessful bid for a seat in the House of Representatives and the death of his wife in 1833 he traveled to Texas in 1835 and the following year returned to serve as commander of the Texas cavalry, under Sam Houston, at the battle of San Jacinto. His bravery in the field earned him a place in the provisional government headed by D. G. Burnet and brought about his election as vice-president of Texas in 1836. In 1838, succeeding Houston, he became the second president of the Republic of Texas. During his three-year term he founded a new capital at Austin in 1840 and promoted measures to assure continued Texan independence and to extend the sovereignty of the Republic west to the Rio Grande (taking in much of New Mexico), goals that he felt required the expulsion of the Comanche and Cherokee Indians. Later, his sympathy with the Southern position on slavery led him, after 1844, to support statehood for Texas. After the admission of Texas as a state in 1845 and after the Mexican War, in which Lamar participated, he retired to his plantation at Richmond, Texas. A brief term as U.S. minister to Nicaragua and Costa Rica in 1857–1859 and the appearance of a book of poems, *Verse Memorials*, 1857, followed. He died in Richmond, Texas, on December 19, 1859.

Lamb, Willis Eugene, Jr. (1913–   ), physicist. Born in Los Angeles on July 12, 1913, Lamb graduated from the University of California (Berkeley) in 1934 and four years later took his Ph.D. there. He joined the physics faculty of Columbia University in 1938, advancing to full professor in 1948 and remaining until 1951, when he moved to Stanford. From 1956 to 1962 he served as Wykeham Professor of Physics at Oxford University and from 1962 as Ford Professor of Physics at Yale. While still at Columbia, Lamb, aided by R. C. Retherford, carried out a series of experiments utilizing an electron beam to raise atomic hydrogen to various states of excitation in order to make precise studies of energy levels. He found that two states, previously believed to be of equal energy on the basis of the prevailing quantum theory of P. A. M. Dirac, actually differed by a significant measure. This difference, subsequently known as the "Lamb shift," led to refinements in quantum theory that yielded results in very close agreement with the shift as measured by Lamb by radio-frequency resonance. His work then and later on the fine structure of hydrogen and helium atoms meshed with that of Polycarp Kusch on the magnetic moment of the electron to prompt a host of new discoveries in the field of particle interactions and radiation, and Lamb and Kusch were awarded jointly the 1955 Nobel Prize for Physics.

Lamy, Jean Baptiste (1814–1888), religious leader. Born on October 14, 1814, at Lempdes in the province of Auvergne, France, Lamy attended the seminary of Montferrand and was ordained a priest in 1838. The following year he volunteered to undertake missionary work in the lower Ohio valley frontier country in the United States. His first posts were at Danville and Wooster, Ohio, but he was later transferred to Covington, Kentucky, across the river from Cincinnati. When the United States took control of New Mexico at the time of the Mexican War, 1846–1848, Roman Catholic authorities at Baltimore petitioned Rome for an American prelate to be sent to Santa Fe, New Mexico. Lamy was named vicar apostolic and on reaching Santa Fe in 1851 he found only 14 priests in the whole territory, which embraced all of New Mexico, most of Arizona, and parts of Colorado, Utah, and Nevada. Lamy and his vicar-general, the Reverend Joseph Machebeuf, journeyed throughout the area preaching, teaching, and trying to restore church discipline. Major efforts were devoted to the building of missions and hospitals and especially schools, which were particularly important because there was no system of public education in New Mexico at the time. Lamy's work aroused a great deal of opposition from local clerics and parish leaders in the early years, for they regarded him as a foreigner come to disturb their way of life. He reinforced this attitude somewhat by surrounding himself with French-born and French-trained clergy and nuns, and he did not hesitate to depose the most obstreperous (but often influential) Spanish-speaking priests. To ratify his authority, he traveled to Durango, in Mexico, to obtain credentials from the Mexican bishop, and was himself consecrated bishop of Santa Fe in 1853 and archbishop in 1875. Fifteen years after his arrival there were in the territory 48 priests and 135 missions with schools attached. He also succeeded in raising enough money to build a French-style cathedral in Santa Fe. On July 18, 1885, Archbishop Lamy resigned his office, and on February 13, 1888, he died in Santa Fe. His life and work were commemorated in Willa Cather's novel *Death Comes for the Archbishop*, 1927.

Land, Edwin Herbert (1909–   ), inventor. Born in Bridgeport, Connecticut, on May 7, 1909, Land attended Harvard and while still a student made discoveries in the field of polarized light. After developing a plastic film, which he called Polaroid, that was capable of polarizing light passed through it, he left school in 1932 and, with a former Harvard physics instructor, George Wheelright, opened the Land-Wheelright Laboratories in Boston. In 1935 they began manufacturing polarizing filters for cameras and the next year introduced sunglasses employing Polaroid lenses. In 1937 Land organized the Polaroid Corporation and served thereafter as its president, chairman of the board, and director of research. In 1941 he developed a technique for producing three-dimensional photographs by means of differently polarized double exposures. During World War II he performed research for the army, developing many optical devices for night reconnaissance, range-finding, and weapon-sighting, and was a consultant on guided missiles. In 1947 he announced his invention of a one-step photographic process whereby a finished picture was produced inside the camera within a minute after the exposure. The Polaroid Land camera was a huge commercial success—sales passed the million mark by 1956—and certain of the several later models delivered color prints. Further improvements and refinements followed at a rapid pace. Land applied underlying principles of the camera in developing a dosimeter, a device used to monitor the exposure to radiation of persons working with radioactive materials. In 1948 he developed a color-translation technique that made possible full-color still and motion pictures of living cells. He was the recipient of numerous honors from scientific organizations and served as president of the American Academy of Arts and Sciences.

Landers, Ann, *see* Friedman, Esther Pauline

Landis, Kenesaw Mountain (1866–1944), judge and baseball official. Born at Millville, Ohio, on November 20, 1866, Landis graduated from Chicago's Union College of Law in 1891 and, until his appointment in 1905 as a federal district judge, was a practicing lawyer in Chicago. His career on the bench was noted for a judgment (later reversed) against the Standard Oil Company of Indiana in 1907 that imposed a fine in excess of $29 million. He also presided over the trials in which William D. Haywood and Victor L. Berger were convicted of violating the Espionage Act of 1917. In September 1920 eight members of the great 1919 Chicago White Sox baseball team were indicted for fraud in connection with the 1919 World Series by a grand jury presided over by Judge Landis. The "Black Sox" bribery scandal, which for a while threatened to undermine the prestige of the game, marked the beginning of a new career for Landis, who was chosen as the first commissioner of professional baseball in January 1921. In one of his first rulings he banned the eight Chicago players from organized baseball for life, even though they had been acquitted of the charges. His tenure as commissioner, which inaugurated a new era of peace and prosperity for major-league baseball, was marked by the absolute finality of his decisions, which were never reversed. He served as commissioner until his death in Chicago on November 25, 1944, having worked relentlessly to keep baseball an honest game, worthy of its reputation as the national pastime.

Landon, Alfred Mossman (1887–   ), public official and businessman. Born on September 9, 1887, in West Middlesex, Pennsylvania, the son of a oil promoter, Landon accompanied his family to Independence, Kansas, at the age of seventeen. He received a law degree from the University of Kansas in 1908 and by 1912 had formed his own oil-producing company. His association with the progressive faction of the Republican party began in 1912 when he went to the Bull Moose party's convention in Chicago with his father. He proved to be a good campaign organizer and after World War I became prominent among Kansas Republicans. He served briefly as secretary to Governor Henry J. Allen of Kansas in 1922 and in 1928 was elected chairman of the state's Republican central committee. Financially secure, he decided to try for the governorship and in 1932 was elected to his first term despite the national Democratic sweep of that year. He did even better in the nonpresidential year of 1934, becoming the sole Republican gubernatorial incumbent to be reelected. The victory made him a leading contender to challenge the incumbent Franklin D. Roosevelt for the presidency in 1936 and he won the Republican nomination by a landslide. Unwilling to oppose Roosevelt's New Deal policies directly—Landon himself, as a progressive Republican, had endorsed many of them—he promised more efficient and frugal relief from the burdens of the Depression. Despite a vigorous campaign that included four national tours, he experienced a crushing defeat, winning only two states—Maine and Vermont—and eight electoral votes. The loss ended his national career, although he remained active in Kansas politics as well as in the oil business. In 1938 he was chosen by President Roosevelt to represent the United States at the Pan-American Conference in Lima, Peru.

Landsteiner, Karl (1868–1943), physiologist. Born in Vienna on June 14, 1868, Landsteiner received his M.D. degree from the University of Vienna in 1891 and later served as an instructor in pathology there from 1909 to 1919. His early researches concentrated on the composition of the blood, and as early as 1901 he was able to show that human blood is of several types, which he classified on the basis of blood antigens he labeled A, B, and O. This discovery led to the use of only matching or similar blood types in transfusions, which eliminated much of the danger of the procedures. In the course of his work on blood, which also took him into the field of other antigens, he discovered the mechanism that causes paroxysmal hemoglobinuria, a condition in which hemoglobin appears in the urine. A medical research worker for nearly 50 years, he made investigations ranging over many areas, but his principal concerns were in immunology, bacteriology, and pathology. His later work centered on viral diseases, and he studied especially poliomyelitis; his achievement in transmitting the disease to monkeys led, some years later, to the development by others of a vaccine and eventually to the almost complete control of the disease by immunization. In 1940, with Alexander S. Wiener, he discovered a further blood factor of great importance, the Rh (for Rhesus monkeys used in the research) factor. Landsteiner moved from Vienna to the Netherlands after World War I, and, after a short stay there (1919–1922), came to the United States to join the Rockefeller Institute for Medical Research (now Rockefeller University) in New York City; he was a member of the Institute from 1922 to 1939 and thereafter a member emeritus. He became a naturalized U.S. citizen. He was widely honored for his work, receiving the 1930 Nobel Prize for Physiology and Medicine for his discovery of blood groups. He died in New York City on June 26, 1943.

Lane, James Henry (1814–1866), soldier and public official. Born in Indiana, probably in Lawrenceburg, on June 22, 1814, Lane grew up on the frontier and studied law with his father before being admitted to the bar. Exemplary service in command of a regiment in the Mexican War opened a political future that began notably with a term as lieutenant governor of Indiana, 1849–1853; this was followed by a term in the House of Representatives. In 1855 he emigrated to Kansas Territory, which, after the Kansas-Nebraska Act of 1854 that repealed the Missouri Compromise of 1820, became a bloody jousting ground for proslavery and antislavery forces until it was finally admitted to the Union as a free state on the eve of the Civil War. Throughout the period of the Border War, Lane was prominent among the Free-State forces, organizing a militia to defend Lawrence against the "Border Ruffians" in the "Wakarusa War" of December 1855, and, as a senator-elect under the Topeka constitution, journeying to Washington the following spring to advance the Free-Soil movement and to secure the admission of Kansas to the Union as a free state. In that effort he failed, Senator Stephen A. Douglas taking the lead in persuading the Senate to refuse to recognize Lane's credentials. In August 1856 he made his way back to the territory with an "army" of irregulars he had collected during a tour of the Old Northwest and began ravaging proslavery settlements. Hostilities subsided late in 1856 after intervention of federal troops and, when proslavery forces later lost control of the legislature, the Free-State party never thereafter relinquished its dominance. Kansas became a state in January 1861, and Lane was sent by the legislature to the Senate as a Republican. In Washington he gained the favor of President Abraham Lincoln, who commissioned him brigadier general of volunteers in June 1861 and enlisted his support in several military ventures in the Civil War. In July 1862 he became the Kansas recruiting commissioner and was instrumental in organizing a brigade of black troops for the Union forces. He was not without enemies in Kansas, but an attempt to thwart his reelection to the Senate failed as Lane's effective stump oratory secured a friendly state legislature. He finally lost favor at home by adhering to Lincoln's conservative Reconstruction policy, and after being implicated in a scandal over Indian contracts he became sufficiently depressed to commit suicide. He died on July 11, 1866, near Fort Leavenworth, Kansas.

Langdell, Christopher Columbus (1826–1906), lawyer and educator. Born in New Boston, New Hampshire, on May 22, 1826, Langdell was educated at Harvard, graduating from the law school in 1854 after several years spent teaching school. He practiced as a lawyer in New York City until 1870, when Harvard's president, Charles W. Eliot, who had known Langdell when both were students in the early 1850s, called him back as a professor in the law school, where he shortly became dean. Langdell's influence on the future course of legal education was great. His first innovation was simple enough: there were no examinations at Harvard Law at the time, and a student merely resided at the school for three years and then received his Ll.B. Langdell instituted a final examination as a requirement for the degree, at one stroke raising the quality of legal training, first at Harvard and then at other schools, which soon adopted the procedure. His second innovation was more controversial. Believing that the number of basic legal principles was very small and that the student would learn more by deriving principles from the study of actual cases, he originated the case-study method of teaching law and published three casebooks, *A Selection of Cases on the Law of Contracts*, 1871; *A Selection of Cases on Sales of Personal Property*, 1872; and

Cases of Equity Pleading, 1875. He also published *A Summary of Equity Pleading*, 1877; *A Summary of the Law of Contracts*, 1879; and *A Brief Survey of Equity Jurisdiction*, 1905. At first, other legal scholars were sharply opposed to this method, preferring the older one of having the teacher elucidate principles in lectures; but in 1890, by which time some of Langdell's students had proved their competency as lawyers, the Columbia Law School adopted the procedure and it soon became common throughout the United States. Langdell retired as dean in 1895 but continued to teach until 1900; he died in Cambridge, Massachusetts, on July 6, 1906.

Lange, Dorothea (1895–1965), photographer. Born in Hoboken, New Jersey, in 1895, Miss Lange studied at the New York Training School for Teachers and then, pursuing an early interest in photography, with photographer Clarence White at Columbia University. She opened a studio in San Francisco and her reputation as an innovator grew rapidly. In the 1930s she was selected by the Farm Security Administration (FSA) to record the migration of farm people from the Dust Bowl of the Great Plains region, especially Oklahoma. She lived for some time with the migratory workers—the "Okies"—and the undertaking resulted, with the help of her husband, Paul S. Taylor, in *An American Exodus: A Record of Human Erosion*, 1939. Her first exhibition was held in 1934, and thereafter her skill as a documentary photographer was firmly established. Her most famous portrait, "Migrant Mother," which hangs in the Library of Congress, was selected by a University of Missouri panel in 1960 as one of the 50 best photographs of the preceding half-century. She died on October 11, 1965, in San Francisco and was honored the next year by a retrospective show at the Museum of Modern Art in New York City.

Langer, Susanne (1895–   ), philosopher. Born in New York City on December 20, 1895, Susanne Katherina Knauth graduated from Radcliffe College in 1920 and, after graduate study at Harvard and at the University of Vienna, received her M.A. from Radcliffe in 1924 and her Ph.D. in 1926. She joined the Radcliffe faculty the next year as a tutor in philosophy and remained until 1942, the year of her divorce from the historian William L. Langer, whom she had married in 1921. She became an assistant professor of philosophy at the University of Delaware in 1943 and from 1945 to 1950 was a lecturer in philosophy at Columbia; during the next few years she was a visiting professor at a number of institutions and joined the faculty of Connecticut College in 1954, remaining there until 1962, when she became professor emeritus and resident research scholar. She published over the years a series of important work in philosophy that led to her being considered among the leading American philosophers of the twentieth century. The first, *The Practice of Philosophy*, 1930, was followed

in 1942 by *Philosophy in a New Key: A Study in the Symbolism of Reason, Rite, and Art*, which reached its third edition in 1957, in which she applied some of the ideas of Ernst Cassirer to various art forms, especially music, and suggested that music is a language capable of expressing and conveying emotional states—and as such is perhaps more communicative than conventional language. *Feeling and Form*, 1953, extended the analysis to other arts. Also in 1953 she published *An Introduction to Symbolic Logic*; her *Problems of Art* appeared in 1957, *Philosophical Sketches* in 1962, and *Mind: An Essay on Human Feeling*, two volumes, 1967–1973. She also edited *Reflections on Art*, 1958.

Langer, William Leonard (1896–1977), historian. Born in Boston on March 16, 1896, Langer graduated from Harvard in 1915 and, after teaching school from 1915 to 1917 and World War I service in Europe, returned to Harvard to take his M.A. in 1920 and his Ph.D. in 1923. He spent a year at the University of Vienna in 1921–1922 and in 1921 married Susanne Knauth, who, as Susanne K. Langer, became a distinguished philosopher; they were divorced in 1942. Langer joined the faculty of Clark University in 1923, returning to Harvard in 1927. He was named Coolidge Professor of History in 1936 and he retired in 1964. During World War II he served in Washington, D.C., as an analyst for the Coordinator of Information, 1941–1942, and as chief of the research and analysis branch in the Office of Strategic Services (OSS), 1942–1945; for his work in the OSS he received the Presidential Medal of Merit in 1946. After the war he continued to serve the federal government in an advisory capacity, holding many posts over the years as a consultant to the Department of State, the Army War College, the Central Intelligence Agency (CIA), and the President's Commission on National Goals; from 1961 he was a member of the President's Foreign Intelligence Advisory Board. The author of many books on military history and U.S. foreign policy in the twentieth century, he first published an account of his experiences with a poison-gas unit in World War I; it was reissued as *Gas and Flame in World War I* in 1965. *The Franco-Russian Alliance 1890–1894*, 1929, was the first in a series of monographs on diplomatic history; it was followed by *European Alliances and Alignments 1871–1890*, 1931, and *Diplomacy of Imperialism 1890–1902*, 1935. *Our Vichy Gamble*, defending the U.S. decision to deal with the French Vichy government from June 1940 to December 1942, appeared in 1947. Continuing his studies among previously inaccessible government papers on the background of U.S. participation in World War II, he published in 1952 *The Challenge to Isolation 1937–1940* and in 1953 *The Undeclared War 1940–1941*, both with S. Everett Gleason. Langer was also editor of *An Encyclopedia of World History*, 1940 (fifth edition, 1972), and of the series of books that began to appear in 1932 under the general title of *The Rise of Modern Europe*. Langer was a member of professional organizations and was president of the American Historical Association in 1957. He died in Boston on December 26, 1977.

Langford, Nathaniel Pitt (1832–1911), explorer and conservationist. Born on August 9, 1832, in Westmoreland, near Utica, New York, Langford went west to St. Paul, Minnesota, in 1854, where for eight years he worked, as had his father, as a bank cashier. In 1862 he joined an expedition to Montana where gold had been discovered the previous year. Leaving the main party, he and some companions made their way to Bannack, where a great influx of prospectors had swelled the mining town beyond its ability to cope with thieves and others willing to kill for gold. Langford was instrumental in organizing a volunteer committee of vigilantes to enforce the law and punish offenders. His *Vigilante Days and Ways*, 1890, remains one of the best accounts of such informal frontier justice. He remained a prominent figure in Montana, serving as U.S. collector of revenue after it became a territory in 1864; in 1868 he was appointed territorial governor by President Andrew Johnson, although the Senate failed to confirm the appointment. In 1870 he helped organize and took part in an expedition into the region that is now Yellowstone National Park. Struck by its beauty, he kept a journal later published as *Diary of the Washburn Expedition of the Yellowstone and Fire Hole Rivers in the Year 1870*, 1905. In 1872 Congress, partly as a result of his efforts, created the national park at Yellowstone and Langford served, without compensation, as its first superintendent and protector until 1877. After 1876, although he remained active in Montana politics for another decade, he lived in St. Paul, where he died on October 18, 1911, having spent many of his later years in historical study of the areas he knew and loved best.

Langley, Samuel Pierpont (1834–1906), astronomer and aviation pioneer. Born on August 22, 1834, in Roxbury, Massachusetts, Langley early developed a deep interest in astronomy and as a boy built his own telescopes. His formal education ended with graduation from high school in 1851 and thereafter he was self-taught for the most part. For the next 14 years he was occupied mainly in civil engineering and architecture in the Midwest. In 1865 he was granted an assistantship in the Harvard Observatory; after a year there and another as assistant professor of mathematics and director of the observatory at the Naval Academy, he joined the faculty of Western University of Pennsylvania, now the University of Pittsburgh, in 1867, taking charge also of the Allegheny Observatory. During 20 years in those two posts Langley pursued a line of research into solar phenomena that, in addition to being a highly valuable pioneering study in itself, contributed significantly to the reorientation of astronomy from a geometrical to a physical basis. In 1878 he invented the bolometer, a device with which he was able to measure the sun's energy output at chosen points along its radiation spectrum; for the first time solar radiation in the infrared region was investigated, and in 1881 he set up his equipment on. Mt. Whitney, in California, in order to determine the constant of solar radiation and the transmission characteristics of the atmosphere. Through lectures, magazine articles, and his widely read *The New Astronomy*, 1888, Langley contributed greatly to popular interest in astronomy. In 1887 Langley was appointed assistant secretary and, later in the year, secretary of the Smithsonian Institution; he remained in the post until 1906. Under his administration of the Smithsonian, the National Zoological Park and the Astrophysical Observatory were founded. At the Astrophysical Observatory he continued his researches, constructing a map of the solar spectrum including the Fraunhofer absorption lines in the infrared region, and making the first energy measurement of the sun's corona. At the same time, at first with moral and financial support from Alexander Graham Bell, he was investigating the possibilities of flight in aircraft that were heavier than air; in 1893 he offered the first fully reasonable explanation of the flying ability of birds and began experimenting with various wing shapes for a powered aircraft. By 1896 he had twice flown steam-powered pilotless planes, once for a distance of 4200 feet; his were the first heavier-than-air, powered craft to fly successfully. With a grant from the War Department he began constructing a larger machine, powered by a gasoline engine and capable of carrying and being controlled by man. It seems likely that with continued work Langley would have achieved powered, controlled, heavier-than-air flight before the Wright brothers, but unfortunate accidents exhausted his funds before he could complete his work. He died on February 27, 1906, in Aiken, South Carolina.

Langmuir, Irving (1881–1957), chemist. Born on January 31, 1881, in Brooklyn, New York, Langmuir early developed a strong interest in scientific subjects and during his school years carried on independent studies in a home laboratory. In 1903 he graduated from the Columbia School of Mines and three years later took his Ph.D. from the University of Göttingen. From 1906 to 1909 he taught chemistry at the Stevens Institute of Technology in Hoboken, New Jersey, and in 1909 joined the research staff of the General Electric Company's research laboratory in Schenectady, New York, where he remained for more than 40 years. His first major accomplishment came in 1912, when he discovered that filling incandescent light bulbs with inert gases greatly increased the illuminating life of the tungsten filaments. Later work led to the development of atomic-hydrogen welding in 1927 and of the mercury-condensation vacuum pump in 1930 as well as to subsequent progress in high-vacuum electron tubes. On the theoretical side, he had by 1916 worked out a thorough and mathematically elegant account of the phenomenon of adsorption, and conducted pioneering studies into thermionic emissions and electron plasmas (the last a term he first applied). One of his best known experiments was a characteristically simple one in which a carefully weighed amount of oil was dropped on a pan of water and allowed to spread to a moveable barrier; by moving the barrier until the oil film was spread to the breaking point, it was a simple matter to calculate the dimensions of the oil molecule. In 1932 his investigations into the nature of molecular films and the chemistry of surfaces, which opened an entirely new field of study, were recognized with the award of the Nobel Prize for Chemistry. Also in that year he became associate director of the General Electric laboratory. During World War II he did research for the U.S. army, developing a smoke generator for use as camouflage and working on the problem of ice formation on aircraft wings. The research into aircraft icing led to his development in 1946 of a method of artificially producing rain by seeding clouds with Dry Ice (solidified carbon dioxide) and silver iodide. In 1950 Langmuir retired from General Electric, continuing, however, to serve as a consultant to the company and to the army's Project Cirrus, begun in 1947 to develop his cloud-seeding technique. He died on August 16, 1957, in Falmouth, Massachusetts.

Langston, John Mercer (1829–1897), public official and educator. Born on December 14, 1829, in Louisa County, Virginia, Langston was one of three sons born to Ralph Quarles, a wealthy planter, and Lucy Langston, a woman of African and Indian descent whom Quarles had emancipated 23 years earlier. At his father's death in 1834 the boy was entrusted to a friend of Quarles's in Chillicothe, Ohio, along with sufficient funds to provide for his upbringing. He attended Oberlin College, graduating in 1849 and taking a degree in theology in 1853, and after an additional year spent reading law was admitted to the Ohio bar. His career in politics began in 1855 when he was elected clerk of Brownhelm township; ten years later he served on the town council of Oberlin, a principal Northern terminus of the Underground Railroad. During the Civil War he was active in recruiting black troops for the Union army and in the Reconstruction period he was called to Washington to serve briefly in 1868 as inspector general of the Freedmen's Bureau. In 1869, shortly after Howard University was opened by the Bureau, he became its dean, and during the next seven years he also served as the university's vice-president and organized its law school. His tact and administrative ability were well recognized, and in 1877 he was named U.S. minister to Haiti and chargé d'affaires for Santo Domingo; he remained in the diplomatic service until 1885. After returning to the United States he accepted the presidency of Virginia Normal and Collegiate Institute and in 1888 successfully ran for the House of Representatives as a Republican, although it required two years for him to contest the results of the election and unseat his Democratic opponent. He retired in Washington, D.C., after his bid for a second term failed. Before his death in Washington, D.C., on November 15, 1897, he published *From the Virginia Plantation to the National Capitol*, 1894.

Lanier, Sidney (1842–1881), poet and critic. Born in Macon, Georgia, on February 3, 1842, Lanier early developed deep interests in music and literature but did not give them full expression for many years. He graduated from Oglethorpe University in 1860 and after a brief period as a tutor joined a volunteer regiment to fight for the Confederacy in the Civil War. After more than three years of service he was captured in November 1864 and imprisoned in Maryland; while in prison he contracted tuberculosis. He was released early in 1865 and returned to Macon, where he worked in his father's law office while writing his first book, a novel entitled *Tiger-Lilies*, 1867. With his health slowly deteriorating, he decided to devote himself to his chosen arts; in 1873 he moved to Baltimore and became first flutist with the Peabody Orchestra; and, giving more time to poetry, he published in 1875 two of his finest pieces, "Corn" and "The Symphony," and gained immediate national attention. His "Centennial Meditation" for the 1876 expositon in Philadelphia was less well received, but it led him to begin a series of studies of versification that resulted in *The Science of English Verse*, 1880. This book and *The English Novel*, 1883, also reflected the research done for his post as lecturer in English literature at The Johns Hopkins University, to which he was appointed in 1879. He wrote also a number of lesser books—"potboilers"—for immediate income; but his poetry, at its best as in "The Marshes of Glynn," remains his primary contribution to American literature. A small collection of his poems had appeared in 1876 (dated 1877), but his complete *Poems* were not published until 1884. He died on September 7, 1881, in Lynn, North Carolina. He was elected to the Hall of Fame in 1945.

Lansing, Robert (1864–1928), lawyer and public official. Born in Watertown, New York, on October 17, 1864, Lansing graduated from Amherst College in 1886 and practiced law in his father's firm in Watertown until 1892. His marriage in 1890 to Eleanor Foster, whose father became secretary of state under President Benjamin Harrison two years later, opened up a new career for him. Between 1892 and his appointment by President Woodrow Wilson as counselor to the Department of State in 1914 he became one of the leading American experts on international law, serving as U.S. counsel in the arbitration of the Bering Sea fur-seal controversy, 1892, and in the Alaskan boundary dispute, 1903, and also serving as U.S. agent before other international tribunals. One of the principal organizers of the American Society of International Law, he also helped found in 1907 and thereafter edited the *American Journal of International Law*. His experience and reputation made him a logical choice for secretary of state in June 1915, after the resignation of William Jennings Bryan. In the succeeding years he worked harmoniously with President Wilson, although at times his office was bypassed on important matters. He foresaw the entry of the United States into World War I and viewed the event in the same light as did the President. He also sought, as did Wilson, an end to the Mexican Border Campaign, hoping to preclude, in view of the crisis in Europe, a U.S. commitment on two fronts; and he arranged for the purchase from Denmark in 1917 of certain of the Virgin Islands, as protection in the Caribbean. In November 1917 he concluded the Lansing-Ishii agreement with Japan, in which, in order to secure Japanese support for the Allies, the United States acknowledged Japan's special interest in China, a partial abrogation of the Open Door policy. A rift in his relationship with Wilson, centering primarily on the League of Nations, began after the armistice. Lansing was willing to postpone the formation of such an organization as being secondary in importance to a treaty of peace. His role at the Versailles Peace Conference, which Wilson attended against the advice of Lansing, was minimal. Despite his reservations about the Treaty of Versailles, Lansing worked for its approval by the Senate and, until Wilson forced his resignation in February 1920, took the responsibility for foreign policy during the President's long illness. Lansing returned to private practice in Washington and, in 1921, published two books about the Versailles conference and his role in it; *The Big Four and Others at the Peace Conference* and *The Peace Negotiations: A Personal Narrative* were followed by a third volume in the same year, *Notes on Sovereignty from the Standpoint of the State and of the World*. He died in Washington on October 30, 1928.

Lardner, Ring (1885–1933), journalist and author. Born on March 6, 1885, in Niles, Michigan, Ringgold Wilmer Lardner attended public high school and the Armour Institute of Technology for one term. In 1905 he turned to a career in journalism, worked for two years as a sportswriter on the *South Bend* (Indiana) *Times*, then for various papers in Chicago, Boston, and St. Louis, and returned to the *Chicago Tribune* from 1913 to 1919 to write a feature sports column, "In the Wake of the News." In 1919 the Bell Syndicate began to distribute his work widely and his popularity increased greatly. From journalism he graduated to fiction writing. He published a series of letters from "Jack Keefe" in the *Saturday Evening Post;* they were compiled in *You Know Me, Al*, 1916, a title that became a catch phrase for admissions of personal stupidity. Keefe was a fictitious baseball player with a mind as small as his ego was large. Lardner's disdain for the hero status accorded sports figures by the public was well expressed by these letters and by books that followed—*Treat 'Em Rough*, 1918, and *The Real Dope*, 1919—in which Keefe was the major char-

acter. With a complete mastery of the American vernacular and a sardonic twist to his humor, Lardner wrote *Gullible's Travels*, 1917, *Own Your Own Home*, 1919, *The Big Town*, 1921, *How to Write Short Stories (with Samples)*, 1924, and *The Love Nest*, 1926. *Round Up*, 1929, contained "Hair Cut," his supremely ironic portrayal of the life of a small Midwestern town. His deft and often wildly funny stories were simulated reportage of living characters, generally either stupid or despicable, and showed him to be a master of the form. He also wrote for the theater, collaborating with George M. Cohan on *Elmer the Great*, 1928, and with George S. Kaufman on *June Moon*, 1929. He died in East Hampton, Long Island, New York, on September 25, 1933.

La Salle, Sieur de (1643–1687), explorer and colonial leader. Born probably in Rouen, France, where he was baptized on November 22, 1643, René Robert Cavelier, the Sieur de La Salle, was educated by Jesuits and took his first vows in the order. He left the novitiate, however, in 1666 and later in that year left France for Canada. He received a grant of land near Montreal and there established himself. By 1669 the urge to explore led him to join an expedition bound for the western country to found missions. On that journey La Salle followed the St. Lawrence into Lake Ontario and explored some of the country on the south shore, making the acquaintance of Louis Jolliet during his travels. It was later often claimed that on this or a subsequent visit to the Ontario country in 1670 or 1671 La Salle traveled far enough to have been the first European to sight the Ohio River, but such claims are largely discounted. His abilities and his enthusiasm for the expansion of French influence in North America commended him to the Count de Frontenac, who arrived in New France as governor in 1672 and the next year built Fort Frontenac on Lake Ontario (on the site of present-day Kingston, Ontario) to serve as a base for westward exploration. In 1674 La Salle sailed to France to defend Frontenac's actions and secured for himself the command of the outpost and trapping privileges in the western country. A second visit to France three years later won him further privileges and a patent of nobility, and he returned to Fort Frontenac in 1678 with a newly acquired lieutenant, Henri de Tonty. In that year also he obtained the services of Father Louis Hennepin as chaplain of Fort Frontenac. Plans for a major expedition into the West ripened quickly and in 1679 a shipyard was established on the Niagara River above the falls where the *Griffon*, the first commercial sailing vessel on Lake Erie, was built and launched. La Salle and his party, including Hennepin, navigated Lake Erie and at the Detroit River met Tonty, who had been sent ahead to arrange for the collection of furs. The combined party then sailed northward on Lake Huron, through the straits of Michilimackinac, and southwest to Green Bay on Lake Michigan. From there La Salle sent the *Griffon* back bearing a great load of furs to pay his creditors in

Montreal; the ship was never heard of again. The explorers moved by land to the site of St. Joseph, Michigan, and there built Fort Miami. They proceeded thence to the Kankakee River and canoed down it and the Illinois to Lake Peoria, where Fort Creve Coeur was erected in January 1680. From there a small party including Hennepin was dispatched to explore the upper Mississippi while La Salle, leaving Tonty in command, undertook a hazardous journey by land back to Fort Frontenac to secure supplies being held up by his creditors. On his return west in the fall he found Fort Creve Coeur abandoned; he sought Tonty to the west along the Illinois as far as the Mississippi, but turned back finally to Fort Miami and then again to Fort Frontenac. By mid–1681 he was back in the Illinois country with new supplies; on this trip he was reunited with Tonty, who had wintered at Green Bay and found his way to Michilimackinac. A new fort was established on the Illinois River near present-day Ottawa, Illinois, and from there La Salle led a party of some 50 men early in 1682 to the Mississippi River and down to its mouth on the Gulf of Mexico. There on April 9 he formally took possession of the entire watershed of the Mississippi and its tributaries for Louis XIV of France and in his honor named the huge domain Louisiana. Filled with dreams of a vast and rich realm, separate from Canada and under his own command, he began his return journey, pausing to build a permanent settlement, Fort St. Louis, on the Illinois and sending a party to establish another at the mouth of the Chicago River. At that moment his loyal supporter Frontenac was recalled to France and was succeeded by a new governor of a rival party. La Salle carried his report of the western country and his arguments for its development directly to France, where he was received with high honors. Appointed governor of Louisiana, he set sail from France in 1684 with four ships and 400 men, bound for the mouth of the Mississippi to establish a colony. He fell ill en route and after a stop in the West Indies fewer than half his men continued with him. The expedition then missed the mouth of the Mississippi and landed in Matagorda Bay in present-day Texas. Realizing the error, La Salle tried in vain to locate the Mississippi. When the expedition's numbers were reduced to 45 he made a futile attempt to reach Canada; on a second attempt in January 1687 he fell foul of a mutiny and was killed by one of his companions. Of the remaining colonists, a handful survived to reach Fort St. Louis.

Lashley, Karl Spencer (1890–1958), psychologist. Born in Davis, West Virginia, on June 7, 1890, Lashley was educated at the University of West Virginia (B.A., zoology, 1910), at the University of Pittsburgh (M.S., bacteriology, 1911), and at The Johns Hopkins University (Ph.D., genetics, 1914). He taught psychology and neuropsychology at a number of universities, including Johns Hopkins when he was a student there, Minnesota from 1917 to 1926, the University of Chicago,

1929–1935, and Harvard, 1935–1955. From 1942 to 1955, while continuing to teach neuropsychology at Harvard, he was also director of the Yerkes Laboratory of Primate Biology at Orange Park, Florida. During his long and fruitful career he made contributions to a number of areas in psychology; he is best known, perhaps, for his work on the relationship between brain mass and learning ability. This work led to, among other things, intense efforts in the post–World War II period to teach such animals as chimpanzees and dolphins to communicate in language—for his research suggested that these animals' relatively high ratio of brain mass to total weight made them prime prospects for success in the endeavor. He also demonstrated that much brain tissue has an equal potential for learning, which led to the conclusion that every psychological function does not necessarily have a specific localization in the cortex. Lashley did important work on the physical connections between the brain and the senses, making careful measurements and observations of the effects of brain damage in white rats. His *Brain Mechanisms and Intelligence* appeared in 1929 and throughout his career he wrote more than 100 papers, many of them influential, on subjects in his field. He retired to Florida in 1955 and died in Poitiers, France, on August 7, 1958.

Lasker, Albert Davis (1880–1952), businessman, public official, and philanthropist. Lasker was born to American parents in Freiburg, Germany, on May 1, 1880, and grew up in Galveston, Texas. He served a brief stint as a reporter before joining, at eighteen, the advertising firm of Lord and Thomas. He rose quickly in the firm owing to his introduction of techniques that were later adopted throughout the industry; by 1908 he was sole owner of Lord and Thomas. In 1917 he accepted appointment by President Woodrow Wilson as special assistant to the secretary of agriculture and the following year became assistant chairman of the Republican National Committee. Lasker served under President Warren G. Harding from 1921 to 1923 as chairman of the United States Shipping Board, which in 1922 undertook to reduce U.S. naval strengths as required by treaty. Lasker was also instrumental, after the "Black Sox" baseball scandal of 1919—he was a part owner of the Chicago Cubs—in the reorganization of major-league baseball under a single commissioner, Judge Kenesaw Mountain Landis. Before retiring from business in 1942 to devote his time to philanthropy, he liquidated his advertising firm. For a decade before his death in New York City on May 30, 1952, he dispensed considerable sums of money through the Albert and Mary Lasker Foundation, was a prominent donor to Jewish charities, and gave more than $4 million to the University of Chicago, of which he had served as a trustee from 1937 to 1942. The Albert and Mary Lasker Foundation, over which his wife, Mary Woodard Reinhardt Lasker, presided after his death, became a major source of funds for medical research and public health projects, and it awarded annually the highly regarded Lasker Award to medical scientists of outstanding accomplishment.

Lasky, Jesse Louis (1880–1958), motion-picture producer. Born on September 13, 1880, in San Jose, California, Lasky attended public high school, worked as a reporter for a while, played cornet in a San Francisco theater orchestra before going to Nome, Alaska, in 1900 in search of gold. He lost the family stake of $3000, made his way home and went back to the cornet, landing a job in Honolulu. In 1902 he became associated with the magician Herrmann the Great, and in the next decade made his first fortune producing vaudeville acts. He lost everything in 1911 in an ambitious and costly venture with a music hall called the Folies-Bergère in New York City. He started over again, venturing into the motion-picture business with Cecil B. DeMille and his brother-in-law Samuel Goldwyn. Their Jesse L. Lasky Feature Play Company, which produced *The Squaw Man*, the first American feature-length film in 1914 (and the first to be made at a site selected by DeMille as perfect for movie-making—Hollywood, California) merged with Adolph Zukor's Famous Players to form first Famous Players–Lasky, and then the Paramount–Famous Players–Lasky Corporation in 1916. The new coalition was one of the leading studios in Hollywood until it went bankrupt in 1932. Lasky made another comeback, however, this time as an independent producer for other Hollywood studios, including Twentieth Century–Fox and RKO Radio Pictures. In 1935 he formed the short-lived Pickford–Lasky Productions with Mary Pickford. In 1940 he went to Warner Brothers, where he began making a series of film biographies (Lasky by now had produced more than a thousand pictures), the most notable of which was *Sergeant York*, 1941, starring Gary Cooper. Other films in this genre were *The Adventures of Mark Twain*, 1942, and *Rhapsody in Blue*, 1945, based on the life of George Gershwin. In 1945 he once again formed his own company and continued with his biographies (for example, *The Great Caruso*, 1951) as well as with comedies. Lasky's autobiography, *I Blow My Own Horn*, appeared in 1957, shortly before his death in Beverly Hills, California, on January 13, 1958.

Lasswell, Harold Dwight (1902–1978), political scientist. Born in Donnellson, Illinois, on February 13, 1902, Lasswell graduated from the University of Chicago in 1922 and, after graduate study there and at the universities of London, Geneva, Paris, and Berlin, received his Ph.D. from Chicago in 1926. He had begun to teach in the political science department of the university in 1922; he was made assistant professor in 1927 and associate professor in 1932. In 1938 he spent a year at the Washington (D.C.) School of Psychiatry and then, during World War II, he served with the Library of Congress as director of war communications research. He also lectured at the New School for Social Research in New York City and

at the Yale Law School, and after the war he joined the Yale law faculty full time, becoming eventually Edward J. Phelps Professor of Law and Political Science. He was also from time to time a visiting professor at numerous institutions in the United States and abroad. The recipient of a number of academic prizes and awards and a member of many professional organizations, Lasswell wrote over the years a large number of influential works on a wide range of subjects in his field; among them were *Propaganda Technique in the World War*, 1927; *Psychopathology and Politics*, 1930; *Politics: Who Gets What, When, How*, 1936; *Democracy Through Public Opinion*, 1941; *Politics Faces Economics*, 1946; *Power and Society: A Framework for Political Inquiry*, with A. Kaplan, 1950; *The World Revolution of Our Time*, 1951; *Policy Sciences: Recent Developments in Scope and Method*, with D. Lerner, 1951; *The Future of Political Science*, 1963; and *Policy Sciences*, 1971; he also wrote a number of important papers. Perhaps his most notable contribution was his development, in association with others, of the notion of "policy sciences," an amalgam of law, political science, sociology, and psychology into one discipline. From 1976 he was associated with Policy Sciences Center, a research center. He died on December 18, 1978, in New York City.

Latrobe, Benjamin Henry (1764–1820), architect and engineer. Born in Fulneck, near Leeds, England, on May 1, 1764, Latrobe was educated in England and Germany and in 1786 began to study engineering and architecture. In 1796 he sailed to the United States, landing in Virginia; the next year he designed and supervised the construction of a penitentiary in Richmond and completed, with modifications, the Virginia state capitol designed by Thomas Jefferson. In December 1798 he moved to Philadelphia in order to oversee the execution of his design for the Bank of Pennsylvania, the beginning of Greek Revival architecture in the United States. By 1801 he had constructed a water-supply system for the city, the first in the country; he received numerous private commissions as well and built several distinguished residences that were long Philadelphia landmarks. In 1803 he was appointed by President Jefferson to the newly created post of surveyor of public buildings; moving to Washington, D.C., he immediately set about the redesign and completion of the south wing of the Capitol. During his government service which lasted until 1817, he designed, built, or remodeled a great number of public structures. His private practice flourished at the same time; he built many private homes, performed engineering tasks for canal companies, and donated designs for buildings to several educational institutions. From 1805 to 1818 he was engaged in the design and construction of Baltimore's Roman Catholic Cathedral, for which work, like that for schools and colleges, he accepted no pay. In 1813 he retired briefly from government service and moved to Pittsburgh, where he was involved with Robert Fulton in a steamboat-building scheme that ultimately bankrupted him. The burning of many buildings in Washington by the British in 1814 necessitated his return there to rebuild the Capitol. Some years later he designed terrace and portico additions for the President's house. He designed the edifice of the Second Bank of the United States in Philadelphia—completed after his death—and in 1820 journeyed to New Orleans to complete work on a water-supply system that had been begun by his son Henry, who had died of yellow fever. Latrobe also succumbed to fever, dying on September 3, 1820. Latrobe is credited, above and beyond his specific works, with having professionalized both architecture and engineering in the United States and with establishing high standards of integrity in both design and performance that were carried on by his many able students.

Laurel, Stan (1890–1965) and **Oliver Hardy (1892–1957)**, comedians. Arthur Stanley Jefferson Laurel was born in Ulverston, England, on June 16, 1890, into a theatrical family, and grew up in show business. He came to the United States in 1910 with a vaudeville troupe that included Charlie Chaplin, whom he greatly admired. He eventually made his way to Hollywood, where he joined the Hal Roach studio in 1917 as a writer and director. Oliver Nowell Hardy was born in Atlanta, Georgia, on January 18, 1892, and studied law at the University of Georgia, but gave up law for an acting career. He made his first film in 1913, and also tried his hand at directing short comic films before going to Hollywood at about the same time as Laurel. Laurel and Hardy did not work together until 1926, when they made *Putting Pants on Philip* for Hal Roach. After that film they made none apart. Their partnership survived the transition to the talkies, and during the 25 years after their first joint effort they made about 200 films, captivating audiences around the world although not ever quite reaching the heights of popularity achieved by Chaplin, W. C. Fields, and the Marx Brothers. They relied very little on scripts, working out their material as the shooting progressed and leaving the unusable footage on the editing-room floor—Laurel himself did most of the editing. Their format was developed early: skinny Laurel was the naïve sidekick of a fat and irritable Hardy and he inevitably involved them in what Hardy usually referred to as "a fine mess." Through sundry forms of mayhem—they raised chaotic action on the screen to a choreographic art—they bumbled their way out again. The formula was simplicity itself and it never failed. Among their most popular films were *From Soup to Nuts*, 1928; *Two Tars*, 1928; *Double Whoopee*, 1929; *Big Business*, 1929; *The Music Box*, 1932 (all short subjects); *Pack Up Your Troubles*, 1932; *Babes in Toyland*, 1934; *Our Relations*, 1936; *Way Out West*, 1937; *Swiss Miss*, 1938; and *A Chump at Oxford*, 1940. Hardy died in Hollywood on August 7, 1957, and Laurel rarely appeared in public after that. The Laurel and Hardy films enjoyed a comeback on television during the 1960s, bringing substantial new income to Laurel before he died in Santa Monica, California, on February 23, 1965.

Laurens, Henry (1724–1792), merchant, planter, and political leader. Born in Charleston, South Carolina, on March 6, 1724, Laurens received his education in the colonies and then spent three years, until the death of his father in 1747, as a clerk in England. Returning to Charleston to settle the estate, he remained and became active as an importer-exporter. His business thrived and he became one of the wealthiest men in Charleston, later acquiring considerable land as well. As his interest in business lessened he became more active politically. He served in the state assembly continuously, except for 1764–1765, from 1757 until 1774. In the growing disputes between England and her American colonies he sided with the colonies. In 1771 he took his sons to London and remained to look after their education. After three years spent in influential British circles he despaired of a diplomatic reconciliation of the mother country with the colonies and returned to South Carolina in December 1774. He served on the Council of Safety in 1775 and, after helping to draft a state constitution, as vice-president of the state in 1776. In January of the following year he became a delegate to the Continental Congress and in November succeeded John Hancock to become the second president of the Congress. Laurens resigned the presidency in December 1778 in the controversy over the actions in France of U.S. representative Silas Deane. He remained in Congress until November 1779, when he undertook a mission to the Netherlands to gain financial support for the colonies. His departure was delayed until August 1780, and he was captured by the British off Newfoundland and imprisoned in the Tower of London despite his insistence on diplomatic immunity; in addition, the discovery among his papers of the outline of a treaty between the United States and the Netherlands led to a British declaration of war against the Dutch. He remained confined for more than a year (October 1780 to December 1781) and was finally exchanged for Gen. Charles Cornwallis in April 1782. Laurens was the subject of considerable criticism after his release for sending what were felt to be submissive petitions to British authorities during his imprisonment, but his diplomatic status was confirmed by Congress in September 1782 and in November he joined John Adams, Benjamin Franklin, and John Jay at the peace conference that produced the Treaty of Paris in 1783. He returned to the United States late in 1784 and retired to his plantation near Charleston the next year; ill health kept him inactive thereafter, and he died at his plantation on December 8, 1792.

Lawes, Lewis Edward (1883–1947), penologist. Born in Elmira, New York, on September 13, 1883, Lawes was the son of a prison guard at the nearby New York State Reformatory. He attended Elmira Free Academy and served a three-year enlistment in the army before taking his first job in 1905 as a guard at Clinton prison in Dannemora, New York. He spent seven years as a guard before attending the New York School of Social Work in 1912. He then advanced rapidly through several posts and in 1915 became superintendent of the New York City Reformatory. His reputation as a realistic reformer grew and in 1919 Governor Alfred E. Smith asked him to take on the difficult post of warden of Sing Sing state prison at Ossining, New York. During 21 years in the position Lawes became perhaps the best-known prison warden in the United States, rarely refusing an opportunity to publicize his ideas. A strong supporter of the idea that prisons should try to rehabilitate inmates, he was also throughout his career an opponent of capital punishment. He was the author of several books on prison life and penology, the most notable being *Twenty Thousand Years in Sing Sing*, 1932, which became a Book-of-the-Month Club selection as well as the basis for a film. He retired in 1941, and he died in Garrison, New York, on April 23, 1947.

Lawrence, Abbott (1792–1855), merchant, manufacturer, public official, and philanthropist. Born in Groton, Massachusetts, on December 16, 1792, Lawrence attended Groton Academy of which his father had been one of the founders. In 1808 he joined his brother, Amos (1786–1852), in Boston where in 1814 they formed the firm of A. & A. Lawrence, one of the first to resume trade with Great Britain after the War of 1812, importing large quantities of English goods. By 1830 they were perhaps the most prominent merchants in Boston and they were also instrumental, first as distributors and soon as manufacturers, in the development of the rising New England textile industry. Amos, who was an invalid after 1831, left the business entirely to his brother and devoted himself to philanthropy. Abbott's early recognition of the necessity for an expanded transportation system to supply domestic markets led him to promote many New England railroads, notably the Boston and Albany. Between 1835 and 1840 he twice served in the House of Representatives, representing a Boston district. During the next decade he was the principal promoter of a booming industrial site northwest of Boston where the Lawrence textile mills were established; at the incorporation of the community in 1853, the new town was given the family name. Lawrence remained active in politics and in 1848 conducted an unsuccessful campaign for the vice-presidency; he served as U.S. minister to Great Britain from 1849 to 1852. Like his brother Amos, he was a generous philanthropist. Their contributions to Groton Academy, along with those of a third brother, William (1783–1848), led to its changing its name to Lawrence Academy in 1846. His greatest memorial is the Lawrence Scientific School, established in 1847 at Harvard University, for which he contributed a large sum. His death on

August 18, 1855, was marked by speeches given by Edward Everett and Robert Winthrop at a public memorial in Boston.

Lawrence, Amos Adams (1814–1886), merchant and philanthropist. Born on July 31, 1814, in Boston, in the same year that his father, Amos, and his uncle, Abbott, established the firm of A. & A. Lawrence in Boston, Lawrence graduated from Harvard in 1835. By 1843, when he became a partner in the firm of Mason and Lawrence, his family were the leading textile merchants in Boston. Very soon, Lawrence became the principal partner and Mason and Lawrence was highly successful, becoming the selling agent for several large textile mills. Like his uncle he eventually went into manufacturing, acquiring the Ipswich Mills in 1860. The venture eventually proved profitable and the mills grew to become the largest of their kind (cotton knit goods) in the country. Interested in education and philanthropic activities, he was the benefactor of Lawrence University, which was established in Appleton, Wisconsin, in 1847, and of another college at Lawrence, Kansas (also named after him) that later became the state university. He also devoted time and money to Harvard, to Massachusetts General Hospital, and to other institutions. He was deeply concerned lest Kansas become a slave state, and to avert this he actively promoted in the 1850s the Emigrant Aid Company, which sent antislavery settlers to Kansas. He was also an admirer of John Brown, to whom he gave money as well as assistance to his family after Brown's capture following the raid at Harpers Ferry, which, however, he condemned. In 1858 and again in 1860 he ran unsuccessfully for the governorship of Massachusetts. During the Civil War he supported the policies of President Abraham Lincoln and raised a force that became the 2nd Massachusetts cavalry regiment, although poor health kept him from active military service. He died in Nahant, Massachusetts on August 22, 1886.

Lawrence, Ernest Orlando (1901–1958), physicist. Born in Canton, South Dakota, on August 8, 1901, Lawrence attended St. Olaf College and graduated from the University of South Dakota in 1922. After further study at the University of Minnesota and the University of Chicago he went to Yale in 1925 as a National Research fellow in physics. Taking his Ph.D. in 1925, he remained at Yale until moving to the University of California at Berkeley in 1928 as an associate professor of physics. He became a full professor two years later. In the same year he demonstrated his first model of the cyclotron, popularly called the "atom smasher," a device in which, by means of an alternating electrical field within a permanent magnetic field, atomic particles can be accelerated to extremely high speeds and energy levels. In 1933 the first large-scale cyclotron was completed, employing an 80-ton magnet. With this machine and larger ones built under his direction in 1938 and 1942 he was able to convert stable forms of many elements into radioactive isotopes, some of which were subsequently employed as tracers in biological and medical research and in the treatment of cancer, and he was also able to conduct researches into atomic structure and prepare new grounds in the field of high-energy physics. In 1936 he became director of the University of California's Radiation Laboratory at Berkeley, and three years later was awarded the Nobel Prize for Physics for his invention of the cyclotron. During World War II he was associated with Arthur H. Compton and Harold C. Urey in the production of plutonium for the first atomic bombs, and in 1957 he was named recipient of the Fermi Award by the Atomic Energy Commission (AEC). He died in Palo Alto, California, on August 27, 1958.

Lawrence, James (1781–1813), naval officer. Born in Burlington, New Jersey, on October 1, 1781, Lawrence decided against a career in the law to become a midshipman in the navy when he was about to become seventeen. By 1802 he had risen to first lieutenant and during the Tripolitan War served with a gallantry—he was second in command to Stephen Decatur on the daring raid into Tripoli harbor to burn the captured *Philadelphia* —that was commended by his superiors and received the recognition of Congress. By the time war broke out with England in 1812 he had commanded several ships, achieving the rank of master-commandant in December 1811. As commander of the *Hornet* early in the war his most notable encounter occurred off the coast of South America near present-day Georgetown, Guyana, on February 24, 1813, when the *Peacock*, a brig having slightly less firepower than the *Hornet*, succumbed to Lawrence's superior tactics in a short but hot exchange that sent her to the bottom. On June 1, 1813, with the rank of captain, he went to sea again as commander of the *Chesapeake*. In what was later claimed to be a pointless sea fight, he took on the frigate *Shannon* off Boston harbor and, although the ships were about evenly matched, was decisively beaten and his ship captured. Lawrence died a hero on shipboard, however, and his famous appeal, "Don't give up the ship," spoken after he was wounded, is cherished by the U.S. navy and has served to rally succeeding generations of its fighting men.

Laws, Samuel Spahr (1824–1921), educator. Born on March 23, 1824 in Ohio County, Virginia (now a part of West Virginia), Laws graduated from Miami University (Ohio) in 1848 and from the Princeton Theological Seminary three years later. After a brief term as a pastor in St. Louis, he became associated in 1854 with Westminster College in Fulton, Missouri, teaching physics for a year and then serving as its president from 1855 to 1861. The Civil War interrupted his career briefly. His support of the Confederacy forced his resignation at Westminster and he was imprisoned by Union forces. Paroled, he spent some time in Paris and, toward the end of the war, went to New York City, where he became vice-president of the New York Gold Exchange; he later invented the stock ticker, which printed out price quotations received by telegraph. His versatility and wide range of interests led him to study both law and medicine; he took an Ll.B. from Columbia in 1870 and an M.D. degree from Bellevue Hospital Medical College in 1875. In 1876 he accepted the presidency of the University of Missouri; the position, which he retained until 1889, included a professorship of mental and moral philosophy. During 13 years at Missouri, his longest stay in any position, he insisted on rigid student discipline and administered his responsibilities with a fierce efficiency. In 1893 he went to the Presbyterian Theological Seminary in Columbia, South Carolina, as Perkins Professor of Natural Science in Connection with Revelation and Christian Apologetics. He retired in 1898, thereafter engaging primarily in research on various theological and scientific subjects. His published works included *Metaphysics: A Lecture*, 1879; *Christianity: Its Nature*, 1903; *Polygamy and Citizenship in Church and State*, 1906; and *The At-onement by the Christian Trinity*, 1919. He died on January 9, 1921, at Asheville, North Carolina, in his ninety-seventh year.

Lazarus, Emma (1849–1887), poet and essayist. Born in New York City on July 22, 1849, Emma Lazarus came of a wealthy family and was educated privately. She early displayed a talent for poetry and her first book, *Poems and Translations*, 1867, was praised by Ralph Waldo Emerson, to whom her next, *Admetus and Other Poems*, 1871, was dedicated. These and subsequent volumes—the prose work *Alide: An Episode of Goethe's Life*, 1874; a verse tragedy, *The Spagnoletto*, 1876; and a fine translation, *Poems and Ballads of Heinrich Heine*, 1881—were pleasant, cosmopolitan in flavor, sometimes excellent, but lacking in real distinction. About 1881, however, with the wave of immigration to the United States from European and Russian ghettoes, she took up the defense of persecuted Jews and of Judaism and worked for the relief of immigrants. She published numerous essays in behalf of this minority and in 1882 produced *Songs of a Semite*, which included such powerful pieces as "The Dance to Death," "The Banner of the Jew," and "The Crowing of the Red Cock." Her sonnet on the Statue of Liberty, "The New Colossus," was chosen to be inscribed on the base of the monument; it remains a most moving and eloquent expression of an American ideal since lost: "Give me your tired, your poor," the sonnet concludes, "Your huddled masses yearning to breathe free, / The wretched refuse of your teeming shore. / Send these, the homeless, tempest-tossed to me; / I lift my lamp beside the golden door." Her last book, a series of prose poems published under the title *By the Waters of Babylon*, appeared in 1887; Miss Lazarus died in New York City on November 19 of that year.

Lea, Homer (1876–1912), soldier. Born in Denver on November 17, 1876, Lea was educated at Occidental College and at Stanford University, which he attended from 1897 to 1899 ostensibly to study law; but his obsession as a student was with military history, and he often predicted that he would become one of the great military commanders of history. These boasts were scoffed at by his friends and schoolmates, since he was a frail hunchback who was rebuffed when he tried to enlist in the U.S. army. He left Stanford in 1899 to go to China, arriving in time to join in the cooperative expedition mounted by the United States and several European powers for the relief of Peking during the Boxer Rebellion. He experienced many adventures and narrowly escaped death a number of times as he gained the esteem of the Chinese for his courage and military knowledge. Within a few months of his arrival in China he had met and become associated with the reformer K'ang Yu-wei, the leader of a movement attempting to overthrow the Manchu rulers of China; Lea was soon put in command of a group of volunteers in this effort. The plot being discovered, he fled to Hong Kong and there met Sun Yat-sen, with whom he later went to Japan, becoming, incredibly, his chief of staff before he had reached the age of twenty-five. He returned to the United States in 1901 but in 1904 was back in China with Sun Yat-sen; he continued to serve as Sun's confidential adviser even after his return to California during his last years. He is probably best known for his authorship of two books, the first, *The Vermillion Pencil*, 1908, being a novel of the Manchu regime, and the second, *The Valor of Ignorance*, 1909, containing astute predictions of the course of military history in the twentieth century, particularly with regard to war between an aggressive Japan and the United States that would begin with a Japanese attack on Hawaii. His last book, *The Day of the Saxon*, 1912, predicted Japanese attacks on the British empire in the Far East. He died on November 1, 1912, near Los Angeles. He is remembered as one of the most brilliant, as well as one of the most enigmatic, figures in U.S. military history.

Leach, Archibald Alexander, *see* Grant, Cary

Leadbelly, *see* Ledbetter, Huddie

Leahy, William Daniel (1875–1959), naval officer and public official. Born on May 6, 1875, in Hampton, Iowa, Leahy graduated from the U.S. Naval Academy in 1897. His career in the navy spanned both world wars as well as the Spanish-American War and the subsequent insurrection in the Philippines, where he saw action as an ensign. It was as a commander during World War I that he became a close friend of the assistant secretary of the navy, Franklin D. Roosevelt. He reached the rank of admiral in 1930 and in 1939 he retired as chief of naval operations, was awarded the Distinguished Service Medal, and was appointed governor of Puerto Rico.

Throughout World War II, President Roosevelt relied heavily on his administrative ability and military advice. Between December 1940 and April 1942 he served as U.S. ambassador to the Vichy government in France; he was then recalled to fill the newly created position of chief of staff to Roosevelt. He remained at the President's side throughout the war and, after Roosevelt's death in April 1945, continued in the same position of trust under President Harry S. Truman until March 1949, when he retired for a second time, with the rank, held since December 1944, of admiral of the fleet, being the first naval officer to achieve that five-star rank since Adm. George Dewey in 1899. His war memoirs, *I Was There*, appeared in 1950. Leahy died on July 20, 1959, in the Bethesda, (Maryland) Naval Hospital.

Lear, William Powell (1902–1978), electronic engineer and manufacturer. Born in Hannibal, Missouri, on June 26, 1902, Lear attended public school in Chicago through the eighth grade and at sixteen joined the navy, where he received his first exposure to radio electronics. After World War I he took up flying and began to experiment with radio receivers. One of his early designs (for an automobile radio) was sold to the Motorola Corporation in 1924, but it was not until ten years later that his inventions produced sufficient capital to permit him to establish a company of his own. In 1934 he sold a design for an amplifier to the Radio Corporation of America (RCA) for a large sum and founded the Lear Avia Corporation. The company manufactured and supplied several navigational aids developed by him to the growing aircraft industry. A second company, Lear, Inc., founded in 1939, thrived during World War II, filling more than $100 million worth of defense contracts. He met with equal success after the war with a lightweight automatic pilot that could be used in jet aircraft. By 1962 Lear was ready for a new venture. He sold his interest in Lear, Inc., to begin manufacturing small jet aircraft for private use. Incorporating many of his own designs in these planes, he was able to compete with the larger companies that had moved into the field. Within five years Lear Jet Corporation was the leading manufacturer of private jet aircraft. The Lear Motors Corporation, formed in 1967, proposed ambitious plans to develop a practical steam-powered automobile. Lear died in Reno, Nevada, on May 14, 1978.

Lease, Mary Elizabeth Clyens (1853–1933), lecturer and political reformer. Born on September 11, 1853, in Ridgway, Elk County, Pennsylvania, Mary Elizabeth Clyens grew up on a farm in McKean County, and, after 1860, in Kansas. She was educated in Roman Catholic schools and before her marriage to Charles Lease in 1873 taught briefly in a parochial school. She moved to Texas with her husband, where she raised three of her four children, but she returned to Kansas (where women had the vote) about 1885, at which time she was admitted to the Kansas bar. Her career as a public speaker dates from that year, when she began speaking on behalf of Irish home rule and raising funds for the Irish National League. Her considerable ability as a speaker fired her ambition for political office and in 1888 she was one of the speakers before the Union Labor party's state convention in Wichita, and she also ran for county office. Thereafter she was prominent in the Populist (People's party) movement in Kansas, stumping the state in 1890 (she delivered about 160 speeches) and in 1893, after the People's party victory, she received an appointment as president of the State Board of Charity. She was the orator of choice on Kansas Day at the World's Columbian Exposition in Chicago in 1893, where she also attended the World Peace Congress and was elected national vice-president. Her bid that year for the U.S. Senate, however, failed, despite a growing number of supporters. Her forte was political agitation rather than administration, and her popularity derived mainly from her powerful and colorful speaking; she was perhaps best known for her advice to Kansas farmers to "raise less corn and more Hell." The fact that she was occasionally known as Mary Ellen led opponents to dub her Mary Yellin. After 1896 her influence in Kansas waned and she decided to go east, joining the *New York World* as a political writer. She remained active as a speaker in New York for numerous reform causes—including prohibition, woman suffrage, and birth control—and later joined forces with the Theodore Roosevelt Progressives in the Bull Moose campaign. She never returned to Kansas except for a short period in 1902 in order to obtain a divorce. From 1908 until her retirement from public life in 1918 she was a lecturer for the New York City Board of Education. Her major written work, *The Problem of Civilization Solved*, 1895, proposed to end militarism, poverty, and business monopoly by a complex scheme of colonization of tropical regions. She died on October 29, 1933, at Callicoon, New York.

Leavenworth, Henry (1783–1834), soldier. Born on December 10, 1783, in New Haven, Connecticut, Leavenworth grew up in Vermont and in Delhi, New York, where he was admitted to the bar in 1804. He began his military career as a captain in the infantry at the beginning of the War of 1812 and in 1813 was promoted to major. He distinguished himself at the brief but hard-fought battle of Chippewa, July 5, 1814, which restored waning American military prestige, and was promoted to the temporary rank of lieutenant colonel. Later that month, after the battle of Lundy's Lane at Niagara, he was made a temporary full colonel. After the war he served a term in the New York state legislature, but in 1818 he returned to the military as a regimental commander. The next 16 years were spent in exemplary service on the frontier, at first in the Old Northwest and later in the Southwest. In 1819 he established Fort Snelling in what is now

Minnesota; in 1821 he was named commandant at Fort Atkinson, built two years earlier opposite Council Bluffs, in what later became Nebraska, and in 1823 he led a controversial punitive expedition against the Arikara Indians following their attack on a fur trapping party led by William H. Ashley. He became a temporary brigadier general in July 1824. He served at Green Bay, Wisconsin, as colonel of the 3rd Infantry before going, in 1826, to Jefferson Barracks, near St. Louis, of which he became commander in 1829. Shortly before his death on July 21, 1834, near the junction of the Washita and Red rivers, at the border of present day Texas and Oklahoma, he was named commander of the entire southwestern frontier, as he was considered the man most likely to achieve a stable peace with the Indians. A cantonment (later fort) that he had built in the summer of 1827 in present-day Kansas bears his name as does the city later established nearby. He was reburied at Fort Leavenworth in 1902.

Leavitt, Frank Simmons, *see* Dean, Man Mountain

Ledbetter, Huddie (1888?–1949), "Leadbelly," folk singer and composer. Born about 1888 in Mooringsport, near Shreveport, Louisiana, Leadbelly, as he came to be known, was of Negro and Cherokee descent and was raised on a farm near the state's western border. From childhood his main interest was music; he was given a small accordion, then a guitar, and he finally acquired the 12-string guitar that he made famous. Until 1934, when he was forty-five, he lived a roaming life centered around music, liquor, and women, and he often was in trouble with the law, being sent to prison repeatedly. In 1934 he met John and Alan Lomax, who recognized his great talent. The three men toured the country intermittently over a period of some 15 years, with Leadbelly helping them to gather songs from prisons and in small towns in the South and with the Lomaxes sponsoring him in the professional folk-singing world. Finally reaching New York City, he gave concerts in Town Hall, appeared on national radio and television programs, and won worldwide fame. He toured college campuses, performed in nightclubs, in Hollywood, and gave a notable concert in Paris. He was a true artist of the folk tradition; he could transform a simple tune into a strange and beautiful composition, but he also composed original songs, among them his well-known theme song, "Good Night, Irene." Despite the fact that he occasionally found it expedient to dilute some of his material for urban folk, he entranced audiences by his presence and delivery; frequently he introduced a song by telling a little story in order to get the audience, as he said, into his mood. His style was individual and spontaneous and seemed to have sprung from a world other than the impersonal, fast-paced one that heard and applauded him. He recorded many of the blues and work songs gathered by him and the Lomaxes for the Library of Congress, together with monologues on his early life and times. He died on December 6, 1949, soon after returning to New York City from a concert tour in France.

Lederberg, Joshua (1925–   ), geneticist. Born in Montclair, New Jersey, on May 23, 1925, he grew up in New York City, graduating from Stuyvesant High School in 1941 and Columbia College in 1944. He interrupted his studies at Columbia University Medical School to work at Yale with Edward L. Tatum, whose pioneering biochemical research had attracted his interest. The success of their experiments, which demonstrated that, contrary to traditional theory, sexual reproduction occurs in bacteria, opened up a whole new area of study and laid the groundwork for all subsequent work in bacterial genetics. Lederberg never returned to Columbia, receiving his Ph.D. in microbiology from Yale in 1948 and then accepting a post in genetics at the University of Wisconsin. He soon became the leading expert in his field and by 1957 had organized a department of medical genetics at Wisconsin. In 1958, for work that he had essentially completed as a graduate student, he shared the Nobel Prize for Physiology and Medicine with Tatum and George W. Beadle. In 1959 he became chairman of a new department of genetics at Stanford and after 1962 directed Stanford's Kennedy Laboratories for Molecular Medicine. Lederberg later made significant discoveries about the effect of viruses on bacteria and about the breeding of viruses which may eventually shed light on means of controlling them. An adherent of the biochemical theory of the origin of life—the view that life originated by the action of natural energy sources on hydrocarbons and oxygen—he was active in the search for evidence of life on other planets. In 1978 he was named president of Rockefeller University.

Ledyard, John (1751–1789), explorer and adventurer. Born in 1751 in Groton, Connecticut, Ledyard grew up in Hartford and was sent to Dartmouth College to prepare to be a missionary; however, he found himself uninterested in making Christians of the Indians and left the school after a year. In 1774 he shipped as an ordinary seaman on a voyage to the Mediterranean. Two years later he sailed from London as a corporal of marines with Capt. James Cook's third voyage around the Cape of Good Hope, about which he later published *A Journal of Captain Cook's Last Voyage to the Pacific*, 1783, which drew heavily upon an account by a shipmate. It was during this voyage that he first conceived of plans for what he felt would be a prosperous fur trade with China. He was unable to pursue this scheme until after the American Revolution, the latter part of which he spent confined to barracks because he refused to fight the Americans; he deserted from the British marines at Long Island in 1782. His efforts to raise capital in the United States, however, proved futile, although he did stimulate American interest in the profitable possibilities of the North Pacific sea otter. In 1784

he went to France to attempt to interest the U.S. minister, Thomas Jefferson, and the naval hero John Paul Jones in his project. Jefferson was unable to help him raise money and Ledyard undertook a new project aimed at opening up the Pacific Northwest and attracting attention to its commercial potential, namely, to walk across Siberia, take a boat across Bering Strait, and continue on foot across North America to Virginia. Although Jefferson supported the idea and attempted to help set it afoot, the empress Catherine of Russia disapproved of the plan from the beginning, and when Ledyard arrived at Irkutsk in early 1788, having left St. Petersburg the previous September, he was arrested and forced to abandon the journey. Subsequently he planned what proved to be his final adventure, an exploration of the African interior in search of the source of the Niger River. He died on January 10, 1789, as he was about to leave Cairo with a caravan. His dreams of African exploration, as well as of the establishment of a fur trade with China, his most consuming passion, were later realized by others.

Lee, Ann (1736–1784), religious leader and founder of the American Shakers. Born on February 29, 1736, in Manchester, England, Ann Lee was the unlettered daughter of a blacksmith who was probably named Lees. At the age of twenty-two she joined a sect known as the Shaking Quakers, or Shakers, because of a ritualized dance which had originated among a sect known as the Prophets in France in 1688, many of whose adherents later fled to England to avoid persecution. She married at twenty-six but lost all four of her children in infancy. In the following years she agonized over her conviction of sinfulness, suffering great remorse about her marriage. After a prolonged period of penance in 1770, during which she apparently experienced a divine illumination, she began to preach a new gospel, opposing marriage and sexual relationships and affirming the dual nature of God—the incarnation of the masculine in Christ to be followed during the present millennium by a feminine incarnation in the person, she concluded, of Ann Lee. Regarded thereafter as such by her followers, she was referred to as Ann the Word or Mother Ann and was celebrated as the leader of the Shakers. Prompted by a vision in 1774, she came to the New World with eight disciples. A successful colony was established near Albany (subsequently at Watervliet), New York, which Mother Ann joined in 1776, having spent the previous months in New York City. Necessarily dependent upon converts because of its ban on marriage, the group met with great success. Whole congregations of Baptists joined the Shakers and, despite occasional persecution (owing, in part, to the group's pacifism), their numbers swelled to several thousand during the next five years. Led by Mother Ann's visions, the Shakers at Watervliet evolved beginnings of the communal life which later became the distinctive pattern of Shaker social organization. For two years, 1781–1783, she toured New England preaching her gospel of celibacy, frugality, and industry. She died at Watervliet on September 8, 1784. After her death her followers organized the United Society of Believers in Christ's Second Appearing, which was also known as the Millennial Church and, most commonly, as the Shakers, and which by 1826 had grown to encompass 18 Shaker villages in eight states. The intensive communal life of the Shaker settlements was of a remarkably stable nature. Within it developed styles of work that resulted particularly in furniture-making and other crafts. The Shakers gradually disappeared as an active religious sect, but their influence on American crafts and design proved permanent.

Lee, Arthur (1740–1792), diplomat. Born on December 21, 1740, at Stratford, his family's estate in Westmoreland County, Virginia, Lee, a younger brother of Richard Henry Lee, was educated in England and at the University of Edinburgh, where in 1764 he received the degree of doctor of medicine. He returned to Williamsburg, Virginia, in 1766 to practice medicine but before long found himself taking an active part in the growing political controversy with England. His series of ten "Monitor Letters" first appeared in the *Virginia Gazette* during the first quarter of 1768, shortly before he returned to England to study law. His reputation, which was further enhanced by the subsequent "Junius Americanus Letters," inspired by the "Junius Letters" of 1769 and like them addressed to a British public, made him a logical choice in 1770 for the post of colonial agent of Massachusetts in London. During the next five years he published a series of appeals concerning American affairs while becoming active in British political circles. His diplomatic career, which was destined to be surrounded by controversy, began shortly after he was admitted to the British bar in 1775. In November of that year the Continental Congress asked him to act as its London agent and in October 1776 asked him to join Benjamin Franklin and Silas Deane as commissioners to negotiate alliances with or seek aid from France and other European nations. Lee joined Franklin and Deane in Paris in December, but he soon began to quarrel with Deane, against whom he made charges of disloyalty and embezzlement that were never substantiated. The tension was relieved somewhat when Lee went to seek aid in Spain in February 1777, where he had minimal success, and then to Berlin, from May to July, where he met with no success at all. When he returned to Paris he resumed his invective against Deane, extending the charges to include Franklin, of whom he was possibly jealous. Despite their strained relations, all three commissioners concluded and signed important treaties of commerce and alliance with France on February 6, 1778; Deane had been officially recalled in December 1777 and he departed soon after the treaties were signed. In his defense to Congress Deane made countercharges that finally brought

about Lee's recall in September 1779; Lee, however, did not return home for another year. In 1781 he was elected to the Virginia House of Delegates and from 1782 to 1784 served in the Continental Congress, where he remained a controversial figure. His last polemics were against the adoption of the federal Constitution, the ratification of which in 1789 essentially dictated his retirement after he had served, from 1785, on the U.S. Treasury Board. He died on December 12, 1792, at his estate in Middlesex County, Virginia.

Lee, Charles (1731–1782), soldier. Born at Dernhall, Cheshire, England, in 1731, Lee early decided on a military career. At twenty he was commissioned a lieutenant in the 44th Regiment and during the French and Indian War participated in several battles in North America. His regiment was part of Gen. Edward Braddock's contingent at the British defeat at Fort Dusquesne, Pennsylvania, in July 1755, and Lee was wounded in July 1758 during the ill-fated attack on Fort Ticonderoga by Gen. Sir James Abercromby. He also took part in the British success at Fort Niagara in 1759 and at Montreal in September 1760. Returning to England, he was promoted to major in 1761 and within another year to lieutenant colonel. He fought in Portugal with much distinction under Gen. John Burgoyne in 1762 but the following year his regiment was disbanded. Between 1765 and 1770 he twice went to Poland. During the civil war there in 1769–1770 his friendship with the king brought him a general's commission, and he participated in the campaign against the Turks. Illness forced him to retire and he returned to England and, in 1773, came back to America and acquired land in Virginia. When the Revolution broke out Lee resigned from the British army and sided with the colonies. His apparent usefulness and his not inconsiderable ability to promote his talents led to his appointment as major general in the Continental army. Second only to Artemas Ward, he became the ranking major general after Ward's retirement in March 1776. His record of service, however, did not live up to expectations and is still shrouded in controversy. His dislike of Gen. George Washington made him slow to obey orders, and his belief that the Americans could not stand up to the British regulars in head-on combat more than once put him at odds with his commander in chief. This belief led him to refuse to join the main army in Washington's retreat from White Plains in October 1776 and resulted in his being captured in December by a small party of British dragoons. He was imprisoned in New York City until April 1778, when he was exchanged. He rejoined the army just before the battle on Monmouth in June 1778 and, after agreeing rather unwillingly to lead the attack, he began a retreat in the heat of the battle; had Washington not intervened, the Continental troops might well have lost the day. A subsequent court-martial suspended Lee from command for 12 months. He passed the time by addressing letters abusive of Washington and other leaders to Congress, one of which resulted in his being challenged and wounded in a duel by John Laurens. In January 1780 Lee was dismissed from the service after writing an insulting letter to Congress. He died in Philadelphia on October 2, 1782. The discovery in 1868, among the papers of the British Gen. Sir William Howe, of a document in Lee's hand outlining a plan for defeating the colonies, led to serious questions about whether his conduct at Monmouth had been treasonable. The document had apparently been prepared by Lee while he was confined by the British in New York City, although it is not clear to what use, if any, it was put.

Lee, Fitzhugh (1835–1905), soldier. Born at Clermont, his family estate in Fairfax County, Virginia, on November 19, 1835, Lee was the grandson of Henry "Light-Horse Harry" Lee and the nephew of Robert E. Lee. He graduated from West Point in 1856, joined the cavalry, and after being wounded fighting Indians in Texas was assigned to the faculty of West Point in 1860. Upon the outbreak of the Civil War he joined the Confederate army, following the example of his uncle. He was on the staff of Gen. Joseph E. Johnston at the first battle of Bull Run (Manassas) and in August 1861 was commissioned lieutenant colonel of the 1st Virginia Cavalry. He saw action in the Peninsular campaign at Antietam (Sharpsburg), and Chancellorsville, and was of invaluable service in reconnaissance for the Army of Northern Virginia. He commanded cavalry divisions under J. E. B. Stuart, Wade Hampton, and Robert E. Lee, and was promoted to brigadier general in 1862 and to major general in 1863. In 1864 he was with Gen. Jubal A. Early in the Shenandoah Valley and was severely wounded at Winchester. In March 1865 he became senior cavalry officer in the Army of Northern Virginia. He led the last charge of the Confederates at Farmville, Virginia, on April 9, 1865, the same day that his uncle Robert surrendered the Army of Northern Virginia to Gen. Ulysses S. Grant at Appomattox. After the end of the war he made many and notable attempts to reconcile the South to the consequences of defeat, and when the Democratic party was returned to power in the South he entered politics, being elected governor of Virginia in 1886 and serving until 1890. Appointed by President Grover Cleveland consul general in Havana in 1896, he was retained in the post by President William McKinley and found himself at the center of a storm of intrigue and revolution. Remaining in Havana as consul general until the sinking of the *Maine* and the subsequent U.S. declaration of war on Spain, he thereupon rejoined the U.S. army as major general of volunteers, becoming one of three former Confederate generals to hold that rank during the Spanish-American War. He was made military governor of Havana and of Pinar del Río province in 1899, served briefly as commander of the Department of the Missouri, and retired as a brigadier general in the regular army in 1901. He died in Washington on April 28, 1905. His biography of Gen. Robert E. Lee had appeared in 1894, and he also wrote *Cuba's Struggle Against Spain*, 1899.

Lee, Gypsy Rose (1914–1970), entertainer and author. Rose Louise Hovick was born in Seattle, Washington, on January 9, 1914, and escaped a formal education almost completely, since she made her stage debut at about the age of four with her sister June Havoc, later well known as an actress; the place was a Knights of Pythias hall in Seattle. June and Rose—who took the name Gypsy Rose Lee some years later—toured as child actors until the late 1920s, when their careers parted, although at the height of their success they were making $1250 a week. At the age of about fifteen Miss Lee took striptease lessons from a lady known as Tessie the Tassel-Twirler and by the year 1931 was in New York City, where, besides practicing her specialty at Minsky's and other palaces of burlesque, she was introduced to the writers and intellectuals of the town by Damon Runyon. It was about this time that H. L. Mencken coined the word "ecdysiast" for her, in an attempt to make respectable the skill that she had perfected far beyond most of her competitors. While stripping in a show at the New York World's Fair in 1940 she began to write a murder mystery, completing the first draft while touring, writing in crowded dressing rooms, in planes and trains, and in the bathtub. *The G-String Murders* was published in 1941 and became a best seller; it was followed the next year by another successful whodunit, *Mother Finds the Body*. When New York's burlesque theaters were closed in 1942 she improved the occasion by appearing in a Broadway show, *Star and Garter*, to rave reviews. She was featured in several films, including *Stage Door Canteen*, in which she performed a satire on the striptease, and was the star of her own television talk show for several years in the later 1960s. Her autobiographical *Gypsy: A Memoir*, 1957, became the basis for a hit Broadway musical and a motion picture. She died on April 26, 1970, in Los Angeles.

Lee, Henry (1756–1818), "Light-Horse Harry," soldier and public official. Born at Leesylvania, his family's estate in Prince William County, Virginia, on January 29, 1756, Lee graduated from the College of New Jersey (now Princeton) in 1773. His plans for a career in the law were abandoned with the outbreak of the Revolution. In 1776 he became a captain in the cavalry and in 1778 was made a major and given a command consisting of three troops of cavalry and three companies of infantry that soon came to be called "Lee's Legion." "Light-Horse Harry," as he came to be known, and his Legion won one of the most dramatic victories of the war in storming and capturing the fort at Paulus Hook, New Jersey (now Jersey City), on August 19, 1779. His reputation as a brilliant cavalry officer was enhanced in the Southern theater after he was sent to aid Gen. Nathanael Greene in the Carolina Campaign; he fought with distinction at Guilford Courthouse, Eutaw Springs, and Augusta. Lee, by then a lieutenant colonel, participated in the victorious siege of Yorktown that essentially ended the Revolution. A hero at war's end, and a comrade and confidant of Gen. George Washington, he became active in Virginia politics. He served concurrently, from 1785 to 1788, in the state legislature and in the Continental Congress, and he voted for ratification of the new federal Constitution in 1788. He later served three terms, from 1792 to 1795, as governor of Virginia. When Washington asked his aid in suppressing the Whisky Rebellion of 1794 he complied. After one term in the House of Representatives, 1799–1801, he retired from politics. At the death of Washington he wrote a congressional resolution containing the words he spoke in an address in Philadelphia a short time later, perhaps the most famous eulogy in American history: "First in war, first in peace, and first in the hearts of his countrymen." After 1800 he became involved in land speculation that ruined him financially. In 1808–1809 he was confined to debtors' prison, where he wrote his memoirs. In July 1812 he was injured in a Baltimore riot while defending the editor of an antiwar newspaper. His health deteriorated after that and during his last years he left his family in Virginia and lived in the West Indies, hoping for a recovery. He died at Cumberland Island, Georgia, on March 25, 1818, while attempting to return home before expiring. He was the father, by his second wife, of Robert E. Lee.

Lee, Ivy Ledbetter (1877–1934), public-relations consultant. Born on July 16, 1877, in Cedartown, Georgia, the son of a Methodist minister, Lee graduated from Princeton in 1898. After graduation he went to New York City, where he worked as a reporter at various times for New York papers, the *Journal, Sun, Times*, and *World*, while studying political science at Columbia University in the evening. In 1903 he managed a mayoral campaign for a citizens' committee backing the candidacy of Seth Low and the following year was hired as a press agent for the Democratic National Committee. He admired businessmen and was fascinated by the operations of industry; he formed friendships easily and was thus able to learn the workings of many major corporations. In 1906–1907 he acquired two accounts, one the Pennsylvania Railroad and the other a group of mine owners in Pennsylvania whose employees were on strike and who were being severely criticized in the press. Lee's public-relations philosophy was tested when a train crash threatened the reputation of the Pennsylvania Railroad; instead of following the usual practice of distorting or suppressing information, he provided transportation for newsmen to the scene of the accident and answered their questions honestly. To his shocked client he pointed out that a company would al-

ways receive bad publicity if the situation warranted it, but that a frank admission of the facts would promote respect for the company's integrity and possibly arouse public sympathy. In 1910 he went to Europe to organize offices for a London banking firm, and during 1911 and 1912 he lectured at the London School of Economics. In 1912 he returned to New York and met John D. Rockefeller, Jr. Two years later, following the Ludlow Massacre, in which striking workers at the Rockefeller-owned Colorado Fuel and Iron works at Ludlow, Colorado, had been fired upon by troops using machine guns and a number of women and children had been killed, Lee persuaded Rockefeller to travel to Colorado and talk to the miners personally, and this simple act soon improved relations between the wealthy Rockefellers and the outraged public. The Rockefeller family retained his services and soon John D. Rockefeller, Sr., was attracting unusually favorable publicity by handing out dimes to children. Lee represented numerous and varied organizations, including the Portland Cement Company, Harvard, the Red Cross, Bethlehem Steel, the Guggenheim interests, the Republic of Poland, and the Episcopal diocese of New York. He expressed his opinions of their enterprises honestly to his employers, urging improvements so that there would be no need to withhold information from the public; he became known as the "physician to corporate bodies." He died in New York City on November 9, 1934, having almost singlehandedly made of public relations a respectable profession.

Lee, Jason (1803–1845), missionary and pioneer. Born on June 23, 1803, on a farm near Stanstead, Quebec, in an area then considered to be part of Vermont, Lee joined the Methodists after a religious conversion at the age of twenty-three and attended Wilbraham Academy in Massachusetts. For two years he served as a minister in Stanstead before accepting, in 1833, a commission from the New England conference of the Methodist Episcopal church to establish a mission to the Flathead Indians in the Oregon country. Although the Flathead project was abandoned after the party reached Fort Vancouver in September 1834, by which time Lee and his three assistants had been joined by Nathaniel J. Wyeth's second expedition, they were able to establish a successful settlement in the Willamette Valley near the present Salem, Oregon. Other missions were founded in the valley and in 1838 Lee returned east with a petition, which he presented to Congress in October, for territorial status for Oregon. He returned to Oregon by sea in the summer of 1840 with a party of 50 —"the Great Reinforcement." During the next few years Lee drifted away from his first concern with missions to the Indians and toward the idea of establishing a permanent white settlement. He continued to take the initiative for territorial organization, presiding over a meeting held at Champoeg in 1841 to organize a government and remaining in a position of leadership through the actual establishment of territorial government in 1843. Lee was instrumental in the founding in 1842 of the Oregon Institute, later Willamette University, the first institution of higher education in the Far West. A second journey east in 1844 ended in disappointment and death. Learning en route that he had been removed from his missionary posts, he defended himself before a mission board that, although exonerating him of all charges, refused to reappoint him. He returned to Stanstead, Quebec, in ill health and died shortly afterward, on March 12, 1845. His remains were transported to Salem, Oregon, and reburied there in 1906.

Lee, Light-Horse Harry, *see* Lee, Henry

Lee, Manfred Bennington, *see under* Dannay, Frederic

Lee, Richard Henry (1732–1794), public official. Born on January 20, 1732, at his family's estate, Stratford, in Westmoreland County, Virginia, Lee began his education with private tutoring and completed his studies in England; he returned to Virginia about 1752. In 1757, following a family tradition of public service, he became a justice of the peace, and the next year entered the House of Burgesses, beginning 17 years of continual service in that body. He quickly established himself as an advocate of liberal policies and, as friction between Great Britain and the colonies increased during the period of the Stamp Act and the Townshend Acts, he was firmly on the American side. In 1766 he organized a local non-importation association, the first such group in the colonies; he drafted a number of petitions and protests for the House of Burgesses and became closely associated with Patrick Henry and Thomas Jefferson. In 1773 he proposed the system of intercolonial committees of correspondence to coordinate the efforts of the several colonies, and the following year he was chosen one of Virginia's delegates to the First Continental Congress. He remained in Congress for five years. In June 1776 he introduced a resolution that led directly to the writing of the Declaration of Independence, adopted on July 4; another of his resolutions called for a confederation among the colonies and, in order to achieve this end, he later worked to induce Virginia to relinquish its claims to Western lands. He retired from Congress in 1779 because of ill health, but the next year was elected to the Virginia legislature, remaining there until being returned in 1784 to Congress, where he served for three years, the first as president. He refused to be a delegate to the Constitutional Convention in 1787 because of his membership in Congress, and he opposed ratification of the Constitution because of its provision for a strong central government and its lack of a bill of rights, publishing his arguments in a series of "Letters of the Federal Farmer to the Republican." After losing the battle over ratification in Virginia, Lee

was chosen one of that state's first senators in the new government. In the Senate he proposed a number of resolutions to correct the oversights in the Constitution and several of these were adopted as part of the Bill of Rights, the first ten amendments, ratified in 1791. He continued in the Senate until ill health again forced his resignation in 1792; he retired to his Virginia estate, Chantilly, near Stratford, and died on June 19, 1794.

Lee, Robert Edward (1807–1870), soldier. Born at Stratford, his family's estate in Westmoreland County, Virginia, on January 19, 1807, Lee was the son of Henry (Light-Horse Harry) Lee, a famed Revolutionary War cavalry officer, and a member of a family long distinguished in public and military service. He grew up and was schooled in Alexandria and in 1825 won appointment to West Point. He graduated second in his class four years later and until 1846 was with the army engineers, acquiring a reputation as a highly competent engineer in work on Mississippi River flood control and Atlantic coastal defenses. In 1846 he was ordered to Texas and the next year joined the command of Gen. Winfield Scott in Mexico; he distinguished himself at Veracruz, Cerro Gordo, Mexico City, Churubusco, and Chapultepec, and when the Mexican War ended in 1848, Lee had been made a colonel. For four years he was again with the army engineers and then in 1852 was appointed superintendent at West Point. Three years later he was sent to command a frontier cavalry regiment in Texas, but he found himself dealing mainly with court-martial duties and this, combined with his father-in-law's death and his wife's chronic illness, led him to consider resigning from the army. He was on leave at his estate, Arlington House, on the Potomac opposite Washington, when, in October 1859, he was ordered to Harpers Ferry to dislodge John Brown and his raiders from the federal arsenal there. As sectional strife gave way to secession, Lee maintained a devotion to the Union and an antipathy to slavery, but as his own state of Virginia began to talk of breaking away he wavered; he declined an offer of the command of all federal forces because he would not fight his own people; hoping to stay out of the hostilities, he resigned his commission in April 1861 and retired to his home. Within three days, however, he had accepted appointment as commander of Virginia's forces, with the rank of general. For several months he was concerned solely with preparing defenses for the anticipated invasion of Virginia and in serving informally as military adviser to Confederate President Jefferson Davis and did not assume field command until the campaign in which western Virginia, soon to be admitted to the Union as West Virginia, was lost by the Confederacy. His prestige shaken by his failure, he was nonetheless retained by President Davis and sent to fortify the southern Atlantic coastal region. In March 1862 he became military adviser to Davis and, despite his lack of direct authority, managed to work through and around Davis and the Confederate commander, Gen. Joseph E. Johnston, to send Gen. T. J. "Stonewall" Jackson on his spectacular Valley Campaign. When Johnston was incapacitated by a wound at Fair Oaks (Seven Pines) in the Peninsular Campaign, Lee assumed command of the Army of Northern Virginia on June 1, 1862. Already a masterly strategist, he soon gained, under the pressure of dealing with often incompetent or recalcitrant subordinates, considerable tactical skill as well. In the Seven Days' Battles (June 26–July 2) he forced Gen. George B. McClellan to retreat from his position threatening Richmond, ending the Union's Peninsular Campaign. Lee then, in a brilliantly conceived and executed maneuver, and relying on Jackson as his most able lieutenant, defeated Gen. John Pope at the second battle of Bull Run (Manassas). An attempt to carry the war to the North by invading Maryland was stymied by the interception of Lee's general orders by the Union forces and by his subsequent near-defeat by McClellan at Antietam (Sharpsburg). Three months later, in December 1862, he dealt heavy casualties to the Union army in repulsing Gen. Ambrose E. Burnside's attack at Fredericksburg. After a long hard winter, action resumed in May 1863 when Gen. Joseph Hooker, Burnside's successor at the head of the Army of the Potomac, attempted to move south to Richmond; daring strategy gave Lee a major victory at Chancellorsville, but cost him the invaluable Jackson. He struck north again, this time into Pennsylvania, in the summer of 1863; the lack of cooperation from various subordinates in the fighting of July 1–3 culminated in disastrous defeat at Gettysburg in the greatest battle, and the turning point, of the war. There was little significant action then until May 1864, when Gen. Ulysses S. Grant headed for Richmond with a force outnumbering Lee's nearly two to one. The chronic shortages of men and equipment that Lee had so far overcome now became decisive; limited to a defensive role in the Wilderness Campaign, Lee slowly retreated through Spotsylvania and Cold Harbor, sending Grant's casualty list up to 50,000 in a month. Finally and hopelessly entrenched in Petersburg, Lee could only watch as Grant developed his siege lines during the winter of 1864–1865. In February 1865 he was named general-in-chief of all the armies of the failing Confederacy, but the action had little practical consequence. With retreat impossible, Lee saw the coming end of the bloody Petersburg Campaign after his defeat at Five Forks in early April; Petersburg also fell, Richmond was taken, and Lee surrendered to Grant at Appomattox Courthouse on April 9, 1865. Lee was released immediately on parole; in September he accepted appointment as president of Washington College in Lexington, Virginia, and he held that post until his death. He counseled acceptance of the defeat and hard work to restore the Union; his own application for amnesty and pardon was unanswered. He died on October 12, 1870, in Lexington, Virginia, and subsequently the college changed its name to Washington and Lee University. As a military leader Lee commanded the respect of his colleagues, friend, foe, and foreign observer alike. His weakness, if he had one, was a tendency to trust too much in subordinates. From even his political and military enemies he won admiration for his valor and true gallantry, and the quiet dignity of his demeanor at Appomattox placed him firmly in the affections of his fellow Southerners and eventually of all Americans. He was elected to the Hall of Fame in 1900.

Lee, Tsung-Dao (1926–   ), physicist. Born in Shanghai on November 24, 1926, Lee was largely educated in China, attending the National Chekiang University and the Southwest Associated University in K'un-ming. In 1946 he received a fellowship to study physics at the University of Chicago, from which he received his Ph.D. in 1950. His career as a theoretical physicist developed at some of the leading U.S. centers of research. After a year at the University of California at Berkeley, he joined the Institute for Advanced Study in Princeton, New Jersey, where he continued some speculations begun as early as 1945 in collaboration with his countryman, Chen Ning Yang. Their work involved the principle of conservation of parity, or the principle that elementary events in space and their reflections are symmetrical and possess equal probability of real existence. The principle had previously been considered to be generally valid, but Lee and Yang showed that for certain processes—slow decays of certain elementary particles—it had not been established, and they described a number of experiments that should be performed to test it. The experiments, undertaken by C. S. Wu and others, proved that their guess about the invalidity of the parity principle was correct. For this work Lee and Yang were awarded jointly in 1957 the Albert Einstein Commemorative Award in science and the Nobel Prize for Physics, Lee being, at thirty-one, the second youngest Nobel laureate in history (Yang was thirty-five). Lee had left the Institute for Advanced Study for Columbia University in 1953, where, in 1956, he became the youngest full professor on the faculty. In 1964, after three years as professor of physics at the Institute, he was named Enrico Fermi Professor of Physics at Columbia. His and Yang's overthrow of the parity principle quickly led to many substantial advances in the field of elementary particles, and Lee himself made important contributions to statistical mechanics, field theory, astrophysics, and turbulence theory.

Lee, William, *see* Burroughs, William Seward (1914–   )

Le Gallienne, Eva (1899–   ), actress and director. Born in London on January 11, 1899, Miss Le Gallienne, daughter of poet Richard Le Gallienne, was brought up there and in Paris. She was educated at the Collège Sévigné and during World War I, unable to return to Paris, studied at Tree's Academy in London (later the Royal Academy of Dramatic Art). She made her debut in *The Laughter of Fools* at London's Prince of Wales Theatre in 1915, but although she received excellent notices it was a number of years before she could gain any but small parts in plays, either in Britain or in the United States, where she made her debut in New York City in *The Melody of Youth*, 1916. Her first big successes came in 1920 when she portrayed Elsie Dover in *Not So Long Ago*, and in 1921, when she starred in *Liliom*, but afterward she still found it difficult to get satisfactory parts and she spent the long periods between engagements reading such authors as Chekhov and Ibsen, whose plays she later not only starred in but also directed. The theatrical work for which she was best known began in 1926 when her Civic Repertory Theatre presented its first production on 14th Street in New York City; over the next six years, until the project was ended because of the Depression, the Civic Repertory presented some 34 different plays and provided New York audiences with a kind of theatrical experience then almost unique, and always rare, in the United States, although relatively common in England and France. From 1932 to 1946 Miss Le Gallienne starred in many plays, and in 1946 she was able once again to realize her dream of a repertory theater when the American Repertory Theatre, headed by her in association with Margaret Webster and Cheryl Crawford, opened with a production of Shakespeare's *Henry VIII*. The experiment ended after one season. Miss Le Gallienne herself, however, continued to be a mainstay of the American theater. The autobiographical *At 33* appeared in 1934 and was followed in 1953 by another autobiographical work, *With a Quiet Heart*; she also wrote a children's book, *Flossie and Bossie*, 1949, and a biography of Eleanora Duse, 1966, and translated a number of Ibsen's plays, which she published at various times with prefaces written from the actor's point of view.

Legaré, Hugh Swinton (1797–1843), lawyer and public official. Born in Charleston, South Carolina, on January 2, 1797, Legaré remained permanently crippled after a bout with smallpox contracted from inoculation at the age of five. He was an exceptional student at Moses Waddel's Carmel Academy in Georgia (his first schooling was received from his mother) and graduated first in his class from South Carolina College (now the University of South Carolina) at the age of seventeen. He concentrated on studying law for three years and spent two additional years in Europe, studying Roman law, the sciences, and languages. He returned to South Carolina in 1820, where he served as representative from Charleston in the state legislature in 1820–1822 and again from 1824 to 1830. Although a conservative, he opposed John C. Calhoun and nullification in 1828. Between 1828 and 1832 Legaré collaborated with Stephen Elliot and others on the *Southern Review.*

Of this, one of the best literary journals of its time, he was a founder, a principal contributor, and, at times the editor. In 1830 he became attorney general of South Carolina and in 1832 accepted appointment as U.S. chargé d'affaires in Belgium. On his return in 1836 he served one term in the House of Representatives. His support of William Henry Harrison and John Tyler (a close friend) in the campaign of 1840 earned him the post of U.S. attorney general after Harrison's death and Tyler's succession to the presidency in 1841. Eminently qualified for the post, he presented briefs before the Supreme Court that were widely admired. An able and influential cabinet member, he was appointed interim secretary of state when Daniel Webster resigned in May 1843, but died soon afterward, in Boston, on June 20, 1843.

Lehman, Herbert Henry (1878–1963), banker, public official, and philanthropist. Born in New York City on March 28, 1878, Lehman came of a wealthy banking family. He attended private schools and graduated from Williams College in 1899; after working for a textile concern, of which he became a vice-president, he joined the family investment house, Lehman Brothers, in 1908. In 1914 he was a cofounder of what became the American Joint Distribution Committee, an international relief fund for Jews in distress. Too old for combat duty in World War I, he served for a time in the office of Assistant Secretary of the Navy Franklin D. Roosevelt and then received a captain's commission in the army; he was concerned with procurement and expediting war material and for his services was promoted to colonel and awarded in 1919 the Distinguished Service Medal. During the 1920s he became interested in politics; he was a close friend of Al Smith and managed his New York gubernatorial campaign in 1926. In 1928 he was nominated by the Democratic party for lieutenant governor on a ticket with Roosevelt and both were elected; reelected in 1930, he became the successful candidate for governor in 1932 when Roosevelt left New York for the presidency. Lehman's ten years as governor were marked by unquestioned integrity in his administration and by dedication to liberal principles. His legislative program was dubbed the "Little New Deal" in recognition of both its similarity to Roosevelt's national program and his own close association with the President. In 1935, in a move that demonstrated his remarkable sincerity in promoting honest government, he appointed Thomas E. Dewey, a Republican, as special prosecutor assigned to clean up the corruption in the Democratic-ruled borough of Manhattan; three years later he was reelected over Dewey, the beginning of whose political career dated from his 1935 investigations. Upon leaving the state house in 1942 Lehman was appointed by Roosevelt director of the Office of Foreign Relief and Rehabilitation and remained in charge when the agency was merged into the United Nations Relief and Rehabilitation Agency (UNRRA) the next year; he served in that post without salary until 1946. In that year he ran unsuccessfully for the Senate; three years later he was elected to fill an unexpired Senate term, and retained his seat in the 1950 election. He quickly became the chief spokesman for liberals in the Senate and was one of the few who dared to oppose openly Senator Joseph R. McCarthy's in famous campaign of accusations of disloyalty. Lehman came during these years to be called "the conscience of the Senate." In 1956 he retired from national public life but retained his interest in state and city politics, leading a reform movement that broke the hold of Tammany Hall on the Democratic Party. He continued his lifelong program of philanthropy; the number and size of his gifts he never revealed, but he was conceded to be, if anything, even more liberal in this respect than in politics. He died in New York City on December 5, 1963, the day before he was to receive the Presidential Medal of Freedom from President Lyndon B. Johnson.

Leidy, Joseph (1823–1891), anatomist and paleontologist. Born in Philadelphia on September 9, 1823, Leidy graduated with a medical degree from the University of Pennsylvania in 1844. His scientific interests extended much beyond medicine, however, and after only two years of medical practice he became a lecturer in anatomy at Franklin Medical College and began devoting much time to independent studies in paleontology and anatomy, fields that in his work became complementary to a highly fruitful degree. Papers on fossil shells and horses and on other topics led to his appointment as librarian and curator of the Academy of Natural Sciences in Philadelphia, and in 1847 he became chairman of the board of curators, a post he held for the rest of his life. His discovery of the *Trichinella spiralis,* a pork parasite, in 1846 and his *Researches into the Comparative Anatomy of the Liver,* 1848, established him as an outstanding anatomist and in 1853, the year he published the pioneering *Flora and Fauna Within Living Animals,* he was named professor of anatomy at the University of Pennsylvania, again a post he retained for life, becoming also chairman of the department of biology in 1884. His *Ancient Fauna of Nebraska* appeared in 1854 and laid much of the foundation of American vertebrate paleontology; Leidy was the principal paleontological consultant for Ferdinand U. Hayden's surveys, 1867–1879, his studies of the collected fossils resulting in such major works as "On the Extinct Mammalia of Dakota and Nebraska," 1869, and *Fresh Water Rhizopods of North America,* 1879. His *Elementary Treatise on Human Anatomy,* 1861, long remained a standard text and the complete bibliography of his works, attesting to his enormous energy and the scope of his interests, ran to more than 600 titles. In addition to his duties at the University of Pennsylvania he served also as professor of natural history at Swarthmore College from 1870 to 1885; in 1863 he was a founding member of the National Academy of Sciences and from 1881 was president of the Academy of Natural Sciences in Philadelphia. Leidy died in Philadelphia on April 30, 1891.

Leif Ericsson (fl. 1000), explorer. Born the third son of Eric Thorvaldsson, or Eric the Red, Norse colonizer of Greenland, Leif Ericsson, or Eiriksson, was apparently the first European to set foot on North American soil. Two principal sources for the story of his voyage differ markedly, the weight of evidence leaning to the version related in the *Saga of the Greenlanders.* In that version, one Bjarni Herjolfsson had sighted a new island in 986 after being blown off course during a voyage from Iceland to Greenland. About 1000 Leif set out to find Bjarni's island and struck land at a point not identified. He coasted south, giving the names Helluland, Markland, and Vinland to coastal regions sighted by his 35-man crew, and wintered at Vinland, which was described as a land of meadows and woods with many grapevines. The identification of the region is not settled, but it is generally held to have been in Labrador or Newfoundland; remains of a Norse-style settlement found at L'Anse aux Meadows, Newfoundland, may be those of the short-lived colony established in Vinland by Thorfinn Karlsefni some 20 years after Leif's voyage. Knowledge of Vinland reached Iceland and Norway, but the name appeared less and less frequently in manuscript sagas as time passed and relations between Norway and its Atlantic island outposts were broken off. Some hint of Vinland's existence may nonetheless have penetrated to western Europe before the great explorations of the fifteenth century.

Leisler, Jacob (1640–1691), colonial figure. Born in Frankfurt am Main, Germany, sometime in early 1640, Leisler arrived in New Amsterdam (subsequently New York City) in 1660 as a soldier in the service of the Dutch West India Company. He married well in 1663 and soon became one of the leading merchants of the colony, which passed to England in 1664. In the aftermath of the Glorious Revolution, which brought William and Mary to the English throne in 1689, Governor Sir Edmund Andros of the New England Dominion, which included New York, was deposed. The political instability of the succeeding months brought a number of factions to the fore in the already troubled political affairs of New York, where Andros's lieutenant governor, Francis Nicholson, remained precariously in control. In May 1689, Leisler, a captain in the militia, figured prominently in an attack on the fort at New York. After Nicholson fled to England in June the faction proclaiming the sovereignty of William and Mary, which included Leisler, named him commander in chief. With popular support in several counties, he proclaimed himself lieutenant governor in December, after seizing correspondence from England addressed to Nicholson or, in his absence, to "such as for the time being take care for preserving the peace and administering the laws . . . of New York." Leisler thus became the chief executive of the entire province of New York, whose principal problem during his brief tenure was defense against the French and the Indians. He summoned, for this purpose, the first intercolonial congress in America in May 1690. In January 1691 English troops arrived to challenge him, but it was not until March that he relinquished his authority and, command of the fort to the newly appointed governor, Henry Sloughter, without the open fight that had been threatening since January. Leisler was thereupon tried for treason and convicted, and on May 16, 1691, he and his son-in-law, Jacob Milborne, were hanged. The question of the legality of his governorship remains controversial, although Parliament reversed the attainder, whereby their civil and legal rights had been extinguished, in 1695 and restored the confiscated estates to the heirs of both. In 1702 the New York assembly also voted them a large indemnity.

LeMay, Curtis Emerson (1906–), air-force officer. Born in Columbus, Ohio, on November 15, 1906, LeMay attended Ohio State University after trying unsuccessfully for an appointment to West Point. Although he did not complete the requirements for an engineering degree until 1932, he received a second lieutenant's commission upon completing the Reserve Officers Training Corps (ROTC) program and went on active duty in the army in 1928. In September of that year he became a cadet in the Army Air Corps flying school and received a regular commission in January 1930. Although he did not become a captain until 1940, his abilities as a pilot, navigator, and bombadier had been recognized. After the United States entered World War II in 1941 LeMay rose quickly in rank. In March 1942 he was promoted to full colonel and made commander of a bombardment group that was stationed in England with the 8th Air Force. Highly decorated for his combat service, he was made a brigadier general in September 1943 and advanced to major general six months later. As a division commander he became known as an innovator in tactics for bomber formations. LeMay also served in the China theater and in 1945, as the commander of the 21st bomber command based in the Marianas, sent numerous B-29 raids over Japanese cities. In 1947 he was made European commander of the air force (by then an independent service) and in that capacity directed the airlift of supplies to Berlin, under blockade by Soviet forces in Germany, in 1948. His reputation made him a logical choice, immediately thereafter, for chief of the Strategic Air Command (SAC), the planes of which, prior to the development of guided missiles, were the only carriers for the U.S. atomic weapons that were rapidly accumulating during the Cold War period. Under his command SAC developed a policy of constant alert, with aircraft aloft at all times and ready to respond instantly to the threat of attack. He was promoted to full general in 1951 and in 1961 became chief of staff of the Air Force. He retired in 1965. Partly as a result of his strong support of the U.S. military role in the Vietnam war, in 1968 he was a more or less reluctant vice-presidential candidate on the American Independent party ticket headed by Alabama Governor George C. Wallace; after their defeat LeMay again retired to private life.

Le Moyne, Jean Baptiste, *see* Bienville, Jean Baptiste Le Moyne, Sieur de

Le Moyne, Pierre, *see* Iberville, Pierre Le Moyne, Sieur d'

L'Enfant, Pierre Charles (1754–1825), architect. Born in Paris on August 2, 1754, L'Enfant studied for a time under his father, a painter, but in 1776 enthusiastically joined the American Revolutionary army as a private. He was commissioned lieutenant of engineers and two years later promoted to captain; after much disappointingly dull service in the North he transferred to the Southern theater of war, was wounded at Savannah, and captured at Charleston in May 1780. Finally released in 1782, he was soon honored by Congress with a promotion to major. In 1783 his designs for the medal and diploma of the Society of the Cincinnati, a fraternal organization of Revolutionary officers of which he was a member, were accepted and he was sent to Paris to have them executed and to organize the French branch of the Society. Returning the next year, he settled in New York City and began a career in architecture. In 1787 he planned and oversaw the conversion of the old city hall into Federal Hall, the temporary seat of the new national government. Four years later he was engaged by President George Washington to survey the site chosen for the new capital city and to create an over-all plan for it. L'Enfant threw himself into the task with vast energy and, assuming an imperious and proprietary attitude toward the entire federal project, soon antagonized nearly everyone with whom he was associated, including Congress. His basic plan for radial boulevards, formal parks, and an imposing, monumental atmosphere not unlike that of Versailles was widely approved; he ordered work begun on a large scale even before the plans were complete, however, and sought constantly to override the authority of the commissioners of the federal district and even that of the President. His immediate undertakings far exceeded his budget; at one point he discovered that the home of a prominent citizen lay in the path of a projected street and, with no authority whatever, had it torn down. Finally he was dismissed in February 1792. He continued to practice privately and was associated with Alexander Hamilton and Robert Morris in planning an industrial city in New Jersey, but he soon was at odds with the directors of the enterprise and was relieved of his position. Morris engaged him to design and build a house in Philadelphia; the grandiose plans that L'Enfant carried over Morris's objections were never completely carried out, but the expense contributed to the latter's bankruptcy in 1798. L'Enfant obtained a number of small commissions from the government in later years, but his claim of $95,000 for his services in the planning of Washington was rejected and Congress awarded him $3800 instead. In 1812 he declined a professorship of engineering at West Point. His last years were spent at the estate of a friend in Maryland, where he died penniless on June 14, 1825. L'Enfant's great plan was largely forgotten during the 19th century and the city's growth became haphazard. During the 1890's, however, interest in an orderly rebuilding of the central region grew and in 1901 a Senate-appointed commission, consisting of Daniel H. Burnham, Charles F. McKim, Augustus Saint-Gaudens, and Frederick Law Olmsted, Jr., recommended the revival of L'Enfant's original scheme for a central system of parks and malls. In 1909 L'Enfant's remains were moved to the Arlington National Cemetery.

Leonard, Helen Louise, see Russell, Lillian

Leontief, Wassily W. (1906–   ), economist. Born on August 5, 1906, in St. Petersburg (now Leningrad), Russia, Leontief graduated from the University of Leningrad in 1925 and took his Ph.D. from the University of Berlin in 1928. In 1931 he moved to the United States and soon after was appointed an instructor in economics at Harvard; in 1946 he became Henry Lee Professor of Economics. In 1948 Leontief organized the Harvard Economic Research Project on the Structure of the American Economy. Instead of merely compiling statistics to reflect the gross productivity of the economy, Leontief conceived a means of analyzing and graphically displaying the dynamic interplay of the various major sectors of the economy. The graph models he developed showed sales and purchases among various industries as well as sales to ultimate consumers; expanded to cover several hundred separate categories, they gave an integrated view of the entire economy from which could be calculated the effects on the whole economy of changed conditions in any one category. This "input-output" system was adopted by scores of nations for their economic planning, and for its development Leontief was awarded the 1973 Nobel Memorial Prize for Economics.

Leopold, Aldo (1886–1948), forester and conservationist. Born in Burlington, Iowa, on January 11, 1886, Leopold grew up an avid sportsman and amateur naturalist. He graduated from Yale in 1908 and remained there to study for a year in the school of forestry. In 1909 he joined the U.S. Forest Service and was assigned to the district comprising what were then the territories of Arizona and New Mexico. In 15 years he spent in field work he advanced from forest assistant to chief of operations for his district. His principal interest was wildlife preservation and by 1921 he had begun to campaign actively within the Forest Service for a new concept in conservation, that of preserving wilderness areas for their value as wilderness—large, ecologically sound regions undisturbed by man. He was persuasive in his

arguments and in 1924 the first such area was created in the Gila National Forest in New Mexico. In that year Leopold ended his field career and became associate director of the Forest Products Laboratory in Madison, Wisconsin. Three years later he retired from the Forest Service and after a few years as a private consultant on forestry and game mangement he was appointed in 1933 professor of wildlife management at the University of Wisconsin, a position he held for the rest of his life. He was a prominent member of many conservationist organizations, among them the Audubon Society, of which he was a director from 1935, the Ecological Society of America, and the Wilderness Society, of which he was a founder in 1935. In 1934 he was named to President Franklin D. Roosevelt's Special Committee on Wild Life Restoration. While teaching in Madison he bought an abandoned farm in the Wisconsin Dells region and there spent much of his time observing and reflecting on the impact of man on the delicately woven web of nature. Combining his talents as a highly competent and sensitive naturalist and as a graceful, gifted writer, he recorded his thoughts in *A Sand County Almanac*, published posthumously in 1949. The book introduced a new term for an old but sadly ignored concept; Leopold spoke of developing a "land ethic," whereby man would engage nature on an ethical rather than on a materialistic plane and would view nature, not as a mere repository of exploitable resources, but as the living basis of his own being. Leopold died on April 21, 1948, of a heart attack suffered while helping to fight a brush fire on a neighboring farm near Baraboo, Wisconsin. *A Sand County Almanac* remained little known for many years, but gradually came to be recognized as a classic of nature writing and a landmark statement of the ecological point of view.

Leopold, Isaiah Edwin, see Wynn, Ed

Leslie, Frank (1821–1880), engraver and publisher. Born in Ipswich, England, on March 29, 1821, Henry Carter concealed his early talent for engraving from his family by using the pseudonym Frank Leslie. In 1842 he was working as an engraver for the *Illustrated London News*, and six years later decided to seek his fortune in the United States. Retaining his pseudonym (he changed his name legally in 1857) he worked in Boston and New York City. In 1853, while with the *Illustrated News* in New York, he developed a technique for dividing illustrations and assigning the work to several men that reduced from weeks to days the time needed to produce an engraving. The perfecting of the technique enabled him, after he went into the publishing business for himself in 1853, to accompany reports of current news events with illustrations. His *Frank Leslie's Ladies' Gazette of Paris, London, and New York Fashions* first appeared in January 1854. In 1855 he ventured into what was to become his most celebrated publication, *Frank Les-*

lie's *Illustrated Newspaper*, whose first issue on December 15 proclaimed his intention of "seizing promptly and illustrating the passing events of the day." Sending his artists on to battlefields to depict the fighting, he was highly successfully during the Civil War. In the decade after the war his list of publications, to which, with the exception of *Day's Doings*, he always affixed his name, appealed to numerous markets—fashion, gossip, scandal, humor—and he also published weekly illustrated magazines for children. Among the most successful were *Frank Leslie's Lady's Journal*, first issued in 1871, and *Frank Leslie's Popular Monthly*, which he began in 1876 and which became, thirty years later, *The American Magazine*. In 1867 he was appointed a U.S. commissioner to the International Exposition in Paris, at which he was decorated by Napoleon III. His *Frank Leslie's Historical Register of the United States Centennial Exposition, 1776, 1877*, of which he was justly proud, nevertheless lost money, and in the panic of that year his business was forced into receivership. At his death in New York City on January 10, 1880, there still remained more than a quarter of a million dollars in outstanding debts. The business was revived, however, by his second wife, Miriam Florence Folline Leslie (1836?–1914), who in 1882 had her name legally changed to Frank Leslie and continued to use it on publications. Miriam Leslie, who was born in New Orleans about 1836 and had been married twice before, was an able writer and an experienced editor. She had worked for Leslie in the 1860s and in 1871 became the editor of *Frank Leslie's Lady's Journal*; she married Leslie in 1874. She managed the business successfully, rescuing it from the financial straits into which it had fallen, and remained at its head for 15 years before leasing it to a syndicate in 1895. Business problems forced her to return to active management in 1898 and assume the editorship of the *Popular Monthly*. She was also the author of a number of popular books, including *California: A Pleasure Trip From Gotham to the Golden Gate*, 1877; *Rents in Our Robes*, 1888; *Are Men Gay Deceivers*, 1893; and *A Social Mirage*, 1899. Her fourth marriage, in 1891, to William C. Kingsbury Wilde, an English critic and brother of Oscar Wilde, ended in divorce two years later. She retired with a considerable fortune in 1901 and at her death on September 18, 1914, willed a large part of it to promote the cause of woman suffrage.

Leslie, Miriam Florence Folline, *see under* Leslie, Frank

Leutze, Emanuel Gottlieb (1816–1868), painter. Born in Schwäbisch-Gmünd, Württemburg (now in Germany) on May 24, 1816, Leutze was brought in infancy to the United States, his family settling first in Fredericksburg, Virginia, and later in Philadelphia. He displayed artistic talent from an early age and attracted considerable attention with his early portraits. In 1841 he traveled to Germany to pursue formal art studies, enrolling in the Royal Academy in Düsseldorf and remaining to live and work in Germany until 1859. He returned to the United States in that year and on the strength of his already considerable reputation as a painter of historical subjects was in 1860 commissioned to execute a large mural for the House of Representatives' wing of the U.S. Capitol. The finished work, entitled "Westward the Course of Empire Takes Its Way" (occasionally known as "Westward Ho"), combined realistic Western landscape with a complex allegorical representation of the process of settlement on the frontier. Leutze's other major works included "The Landing of the Norsemen," "The Settlement of Maryland," "Cromwell and Milton," and "Washington at Monmouth," but by far his best-known painting, widely reproduced and, despite its somewhat overly dramatic composition, of enduring popularity, was "Washington Crossing the Delaware," ultimately acquired by the Metropolitan Museum of Art in New York City. Leutze died in Washington, D.C., on July 18, 1868.

Levine, Jack (1915–), painter. Born on January 3, 1915, in Boston, the son of a Lithuanian immigrant shoemaker, Levine received his first art training at the Jewish Welfare Center. Later, while studying at the Museum of Fine Arts in Boston, devoting his attention to the drawing techniques of the old Italian masters, he won the patronage of Denman Ross, a lecturer in design theory at Harvard, who was his teacher from 1929 to 1931. In 1935 he began working for the artists' project of the Works Progress Administration (WPA) in a studio in a poor section of Boston, and began painting scenes that reflected his sensitivity to social and political ills; these eventually made him famous and ranked him with such protest painters as Ben Shahn. His style was expressionistic and combined tense brushwork, strong colors, and dramatic exaggerations. In this period he completed "Brain Trust," "The Feast of Pure Reason," "The Street," "String Quartet," and other works. In 1945, having spent three years in the army, he received a Guggenheim fellowship and in 1946 was given a grant by the American Academy of Arts and Letters and, continuing in the genre of social commentary, produced "Welcome Home," "Apteka," "The Tombstone Cutter," "Every Inch a Ruler," "The Royal Family," "Pawnshop," "Gangster Funeral," and "The Trial." His paintings were featured in many important exhibitions and won several awards; in 1955 he was given a retrospective show at the Whitney Museum of American Art in New York City. His work has been collected by major museums throughout the country.

Levy, Uriah Phillips (1792–1862), naval officer. Born in Philadelphia on April 22, 1792, Levy went to sea against his family's wishes when he was ten, serving as a cabin boy on several coastal vessels. Before he was twenty he was master of the schooner *George Washington*, of which he was also part owner. The ship was lost in the course of a mutiny in January 1812 and in October of that year he applied for a commission in the navy. Commissioned a sailing master, he was aboard the *Argus* as acting lieutenant in 1813 and was given command of a prize; when the British later retook it he spent 16 months as a prisoner of war. After the war he was promoted to lieutenant and during the next quarter-century rose steadily in rank despite frequent bitter altercations in which he became involved: he was court-martialed six times during this period, cashiered twice from the service and then reinstated, and involved in at least one duel, which resulted in the death of his opponent. Most of these conflicts were brought about by the contempt in which he was held by many of his associates in the navy —for not only had he risen to command from the ranks, but he was also a Jew, one of the very few Jewish officers in the service. He was promoted to captain in 1844 but for the next decade, despite frequent petitions, was unable to obtain a command; in 1855, as a consequence, he was dropped from the official captains' list. A successful appeal before a congressional board of inquiry in 1857 restored him to rank and resulted in his being given command of a ship; he was shortly promoted to commodore and by 1860 was commander of the Mediterranean Squadron. He retired at the onset of the Civil War but, an ardent patriot, offered his personal fortune to President Abraham Lincoln for the defense of the Union. Before his death in New York City on March 22, 1862, he had, because of his intense admiration for Thomas Jefferson, purchased Monticello, Jefferson's home near Charlottesville, Virginia. The property had fallen into disrepair, and Levy evidently hoped to restore it and offer it to the nation as a public shrine. He willed Monticello to the United States at his death, but litigation among his heirs kept the estate in private hands until 1923, when it was bought by subscription and opened to the public after restoration had been completed.

Lewis, Gilbert Newton (1875–1946), chemist. Born in Weymouth, Massachusetts, on October 23, 1875, Lewis was educated at the University of Nebraska, at Harvard University, from which he received his B.A. in 1896, his M.A. in 1898, and his Ph.D. in 1899, and at the universities of Leipzig and Göttingen. He joined the research laboratory of physical chemistry at the Massachusetts Institute of Technology (MIT) in 1905 and was made professor of chemistry at MIT in 1911; in 1912 he became professor of physical Chemistry and dean of the college of chemistry at the University of California at Berkeley, with which he was associated for the remainder of his career. His major researches were in the field of molecular structure, and he was probably the first investigator to realize the importance of the electron pair in valence theory. In the course of this work he was able to further the understanding of acids, bases, and free radicals, and he de-

vised new and more inclusive definitions for each on the basis of the electron-sharing behavior of various atoms and ions. Lewis was the first to isolate in pure form the isotope of hydrogen known as heavy hydrogen, or deuterium. He also made contributions to the understanding of the phenomena of fluorescence and phosphorescence. He collaborated at Berkeley with Ernest O. Lawrence in the construction of the cyclotron and was coauthor with Irving Langmuir of the Lewis-Langmuir theory of atomic structure. He was the recipient of numerous scientific honors, including awards from England, Sweden, and Russia, and wrote a number of influential papers and several books, among them *Valence and the Structure of Atoms and Molecules*, 1923, and *Thermodynamics and the Free Energy of Chemical Substances*, with Merle Randall, also 1923. He died in Berkeley, California, on March 23, 1946.

Lewis, John Llewellyn (1880–1969), labor leader. Born near Lucas, Iowa on February 12, 1880, of Welsh immigrant parents, Lewis grew up in a coal-mining district surrounded by the turmoil of the early period of U.S. labor organization; his father was blacklisted for several years for union activities. John left school after the seventh grade and at fifteen entered the mines; possessed of a strong drive for self-improvement, he read widely and deeply and was in later years recognized as something of an expert on English literature, American history, and the Bible. He wandered about the West for a few years in his early twenties, then returned to the mines and joined the United Mine Workers of America (UMW). In Lucas and later in Panama, Illinois, he advanced to president of the UMW local, to Illinois lobbyist for the union, and in 1911 to general field agent of the American Federation of Labor (AFL), with which the miners' union was affiliated. Finally, in 1920, he was elected president of the UMW, a position he held for 40 years. Closely associated with him in the UMW leadership was William Green, who in 1924 was elected president of the AFL. The two did not long remain allies, however, as Lewis, far less conservative than Green, looked to new fields for organized labor. Although Lewis held extensive control over a major union, his period of great national prominence and influence did not begin until 1935; in that year he joined with several other labor leaders to form the Committee for Industrial Organization (CIO), a group within the AFL intended to promote industrial unionism as a necessary complement to the AFL's traditional devotion to trade and craft unionism. Green and other leaders of the AFL, however, refused to accept the new move and, after an order to disband had been ignored, expelled ten unions involved in the CIO, including the UMW. The Committee then reorganized itself as the independent Congress of Industrial Organizations (also CIO) and elected Lewis its first president. In the next few years he presided over the often violent struggle to introduce unionism into previously unorganized industries, particularly steel and automobiles; these were the years of the Little Steel strike, the Republic Steel Massacre in Chicago, and the great sitdown strike against General Motors. In 1940 he reversed his earlier support of President Franklin D. Roosevelt and attempted to rally labor against the president's third-term bid; taking Roosevelt's reelection as a repudiation, he resigned as president of the CIO, being succeeded by his long-time lieutenant, Phillip Murray. In 1942 he withdrew the UMW from the CIO; in 1946 he led the mine union back into the AFL, only to withdraw it the next year. A series of miner's strikes during World War II won wage increases but alienated large segments of the public and the strikes were responsible in part for the passage of the Smith-Connally Antistrike Act and the Taft-Hartley Act, both of which placed new restrictions on labor unions. In 1946 Lewis called for a strike of bituminous coal miners; President Harry S. Truman countered by ordering government seizure of the mines, and the strike ended immediately with some concessions to the soft-coal miners that were soon extended to anthracite miners as well. Within a few months, however, Lewis called for another strike and ignored a federal court injunction against it; early in 1947 he was found guilty of contempt of court and both he and the union were fined heavily. In 1948 he was again convicted of contempt and fined for ignoring another injunction against a strike called over a pension dispute. In 1952, with the extra impetus provided by an Illinois mine disaster of the previous year in which 119 men were killed, he succeeded in persuading Congress to set federal safety standards for mines. He remained president of the UMW until his retirement in 1960, after which time, as president emeritus, he served as chairman of the board of trustees of the union's welfare and retirement fund until his death on June 11, 1969, in Washington, D.C.

Lewis, Meriwether (1774–1809), soldier, explorer, and public official. Born in Albemarle County, Virginia, on August 18, 1774, Lewis grew up there, and in Georgia, where his family moved when he was ten. He returned alone to Virginia three years later to be educated by private tutors and was still there when, as a member of the local militia, he was sent to take part in the suppression of the Whisky Rebellion in 1794. A year later he enlisted in the regular army and served for several years, including a brief period under the command of his future companion in exploration, William Clark. In 1801 President Thomas Jefferson offered him the position of private secretary and he immediately accepted; for two years thereafter he lived in the executive mansion in Washington, D.C., while Jefferson laid plans for an exploring journey to seek a land route across the continent and prepared Lewis to lead it. He was sent to Philadelphia to learn mapmaking and other needed scientific skills. Finally, in 1803, with a $2500 appropriation from Congress and detailed

instructions from Jefferson, Lewis set out for Illinois to recruit and train an exploring party. At his request, a share of the command had been offered to William Clark, and the names of the two men were thenceforth linked. Training and equipping some 40-odd men occupied the winter and early spring of 1803–1804; in May 1804 they set out "under a jentle brease up the Missourie" in three well-stocked boats and by November had reached the villages of the Mandan, where they built Fort Mandan and wintered near what is now Bismarck, North Dakota. The next April, 16 men were sent back to St. Louis to report on the expedition's progress, and the rest, having built canoes, continued up the Missouri to the three forks, which they named the Jefferson, the Madison, and the Gallatin rivers. They were accompanied now by a French-Canadian, Toussaint Charbonneau, and his Shoshone wife, Sacagawea, whom they had engaged as interpreters and guides. Procuring horses from the Shoshone, they crossed the Continental Divide and then made their way by canoe down the Clearwater, Snake, and Columbia rivers, reaching the Pacific Coast in November 1805. They wintered near present-day Astoria, Oregon, and in March 1806 began the return journey. Just beyond the Great Falls of the Missouri the party split, Lewis exploring northward along the Marias River and Clark striking south to the Yellowstone. They reunited the parties at the Missouri-Yellowstone confluence and continued eastward. Their arrival in St. Louis in September 1806 was cause for national celebration, not the least because in their overlong absence they had been given up as lost. The maps, notes, and mineral and botanical specimens they brought back were invaluable to scientists, and their journey to the West had greatly reinforced U.S. claims to the Oregon country; and among the remarkable accomplishments of the entire project was the fact that in more than two years of exploring unknown territory, traveling 4000 miles and dealing with sometimes hostile Indians, only one man had died. In November Lewis was appointed governor of the Louisiana Territory and for nearly two years he carried out his duties with great skill from headquarters in St. Louis. In 1809, finding that some of his drafts on the government had not been honored, he set out for Washington to clear up the matter; he was near Nashville, Tennessee, when, under mysterious circumstances, he died on October 11, 1809. The journals of the Lewis and Clark expedition were finally published in 1814 under the editorship of Nicholas Biddle.

Lewis, Sinclair (1885–1951), author. Born on February 7, 1885, in Sauk Centre, Minnesota, Harry Sinclair Lewis entered Yale in 1903. In his senior year he left college to join Upton Sinclair's socialist community in New Jersey, but he returned to Yale to graduate in 1908. For several years he was a reporter and editorial writer for various newspapers and magazines, and he worked for a number of publishing companies. His first novel, a book for juveniles, was published in 1912; a series of minor novels followed, and from about 1915 his short stories were appearing regularly in popular magazines. In 1920 his first major work, *Main Street*, was published; a satirical, iconoclastic, and markedly sociological treatment of the American myth of the Small Town, the book won Lewis immediate fame and recognition as a serious author and began a controversy that his work was to continue to feed throughout his life. Two years later he published *Babbitt*, a study of the typically complacent, conservative, conformist American businessman that added "Babbitt" and "Babbittry," both pejorative terms, to the vocabulary of popular sociology. *Arrowsmith*, about the frustrations of a man of science, appeared in 1925 and the next year was awarded a Pulitzer Prize, which Lewis declined. *Elmer Gantry*, 1927, was concerned with a revivalist, a religious charlatan; *Dodsworth*, 1929, portrayed a retired industrialist touring in Europe. In 1930 Lewis became the first American to win the Nobel Prize for Literature. He was the most popular and most effective of the debunking writers between the World Wars; unlike the expatriates, however, he remained in the United States and founded his incisive criticisms and satirical characterizations on an underlying optimism and a profound sense of humor. Most notable among his later works were *It Can't Happen Here*, 1935, a description of a future Fascist takeover in the United States, *Cass Timberlane*, 1945, and *Kingsblood Royal*, 1947. In all he produced 22 novels, together with three plays, *Jayhawker* and *Dodsworth*, 1934, and *It Can't Happen Here*, 1936. Between 1928 and 1942 he was married to journalist Dorothy Thompson. He died in Rome on January 10, 1951.

Leypoldt, Frederick (1835–1884), publisher and bibliographer. Born in Stuttgart, Germany, on November 17, 1835, Leypoldt emigrated to the United States in 1854 and later became a naturalized U.S. citizen. He got his first job in a bookstore in New York City that specialized in foreign works, and in 1859 he founded his own foreign bookstore in Philadelphia, which flourished during the Civil War. The dearth of imported books during the war led him to publish some himself, his first work being a translation by Fanny Fuller of *The Ice-Maiden*, by Hans Christian Andersen. Soon convinced that he was more interested in publishing than in bookselling, with Henry Holt he founded Leypoldt and Holt in New York in 1866. Within two years, however, he gave up book publishing, too, leaving the business to Holt (who by 1873 had made it Henry Holt and Co.) and began the career that made him famous by taking over direction of the firm's *Literary Bulletin*, which, after five years of varied titles and several acquisitions, became *Publishers' Weekly*. Of this influential publication Leypoldt was owner and editor until 1879, when he sold it to Richard R. Bowker; Leypoldt remained its editor, except for a six-month period in 1879, until his death. *Publishers' Weekly* at-

tempted to keep up to date on publishing offerings, but the results were not satisfactory to Leypoldt, who had for many years felt the need of a trade catalogue of current publications. He launched several attempts after 1869 to serve this need, finally succeeding in 1873 with *The Uniform Trade List Annual*, later known as the *Publishers' Trade List Annual*, which continued after his death under the sponsorship of Bowker. The *American Catalogue*, a list of all books in print in the United States, was begun by Leypoldt in 1876; this, too, passed to the Bowker firm upon his death. The third Bowker-Leypoldt collaboration of note was in the founding of *Library Journal*, also in 1876, in which venture they were joined by Melvil Dewey; he aided the other two as well in the founding that year of the American Library Association (ALA). Leypoldt also established other literary and library reference aids, including the *Index Medicus* (from 1927 the *Quarterly Cumulative Index Medicus*), which he began in 1879 and, although it ran at a loss, continued because of its great value to medicine. He died on March 31, 1884, in New York City.

Libby, Willard Frank (1908–1980), chemist. Born in Grand Valley, Colorado, on December 17, 1908, Libby moved with his family to California about 1913. He graduated from the University of California at Berkeley in 1931 and remained to take his Ph.D. in 1933. Appointed an instructor in that year, he did research on, among other topics, radioactive materials, the gaseous state, and the behavior of neutrons. This work led in 1941 to his involvement with the Columbia University division of the Manhattan Engineering District project, to which his principal contribution was the development of a gaseous-diffusion method for separating the various isotopes of uranium. With the successful completion of the project's atomic-bomb program he moved in 1945 to the University of Chicago, becoming professor of chemistry and a member of the Institute for Nuclear Research. On the basis of reports by other investigators that cosmic-ray bombardment of the earth's upper atmosphere produced free neutrons and that neutrons could react with nitrogen to produce radioactive carbon 14, Libby hypothesized that such a transmutation process did in fact take place, that it had been going on long enough to establish an equilibrium in the amount of carbon 14 present in the biosphere, and that minute quantities of carbon 14 were therefore present in all living things. Careful experiments confirmed this idea. He then went on to show that since the proportion of carbon 14 in organic matter was kept constant by life processes but at death began to diminish at a known rate, (the half-life of the isotope), sensitive measurements of the amount of carbon 14 in material of organic origin —wood, charcoal, or bone, for example—could be used to ascertain with considerable precision the age of a specimen. Announced in 1949, the radiocarbon dating technique provided a powerful and even revolutionary tool to archaeologists, geologists, and other scientists, although in the late 1960s research on tree rings led to significant revision of its time scale. From 1955 to 1959 Libby was a member of the Atomic Energy Commission (AEC) and in 1959 he became professor of chemistry and director of the Institute of Geophysics and Planetary Physics at the University of California at Los Angeles. In 1960 he was awarded the Nobel Prize for Chemistry for his work with radiocarbon. He died on September 8, 1980, in Los Angeles.

Lichtenstein, Roy (1923–), painter. Born in New York City on October 27, 1923, Lichtenstein graduated from Benjamin Franklin High School in 1940. He served in the army during World War II and later attended Ohio State University, from which he received a master of fine arts degree in 1949. He remained at Ohio State as an instructor until 1951, after which he lived in Cleveland, supporting himself by free-lance work. His main preoccupation, however, was his paintings of American cowboys and Indians. In 1957 he moved to Oswego to teach at the college of the State University of New York there, remaining until 1960. From 1960 to 1963 he taught at Douglass College of Rutgers University. His work, which at first had showed Cubist influence and, after 1957, evidences of Abstract Expressionism, now became innovative in his choice of subject matter. His treatments of the cartoon characters Popeye, Mickey Mouse, and Donald Duck in the late 1950s and early 1960s were tentative at first, but reinforced by his colleagues, he became convinced he could make a significant contribution in the cartoon format. The comic-strip canvases imitated the popular art form down to the flat, hard-edged color regions filled by a half-tone dot pattern, and they presented single forceful images susceptible of immediate apprehension—a dramatic bit of dialogue in a strained romance, perhaps, or a scene of combat action, complete with representations of the sounds of weaponry. His "comic-strip" paintings were given two showings in New York City in 1962. The first, his initial one-man show, created a sensation and earned him much critical acclaim as well as many detractors. The second was in a group show labeled "The New Realists." In 1963 he was commissioned to contribute to the pavilion of the New York World's Fair of the next year, and in 1964 another New York City show brought national recognition; his "Pop" style, was by then extended to include landscapes. His work also attracted attention in Europe; he was represented in the Venice Biennale 1966, and in January 1968, a one-man show of 80 works at the Tate Gallery was held in London. A retrospective show of more than 100 works was held at the Guggenheim Museum in New York City in 1969.

Lieber, Francis (1800–1872), editor and political scientist. Born in Berlin on March 18, 1800, Lieber studied at the universities of Jena, Halle, and Dresden, interrupting his studies in 1815 to serve in the last campaign of the Napoleonic Wars at Waterloo, and was awarded a Ph.D. from Jena in 1820. In 1819 he had been imprisoned briefly for harboring too-liberal political views. In 1822 he joined the large number of liberal young Germans who enlisted in the Greek war of liberation from Turkish rule; he found the experience disillusioning and soon went to Rome, where he met and was profoundly influenced by the German diplomat-historian B. G. Niebuhr. In 1823 he returned to Berlin and continued studying mathematics until he was imprisoned again in 1824 for his liberal views. In 1826 he went to England, was employed for a time as a tutor, and the next year emigrated to the United States. He soon embarked upon his first major scholarly enterprise, founding and editing the *Encyclopaedia Americana*, which appeared in 13 volumes from 1829 to 1833. In 1835 he accepted a professorship of history and political economy at South Carolina College (now the University of South Carolina), where he remained for 21 years. During this time he established a reputation as the nation's leading political theorist and was the first to construct a rigorous and systematic philosophy of political science. His major writings, *Manual of Political Ethics*, 2 volumes, 1838–1839, *Legal and Political Hermeneutics*, 1839, and *On Civil Liberty and Self-Government*, 2 volumes, 1853, were widely read and highly praised. Lieber was a strong advocate of nationalism, although he opposed the centralization of political power. Among his many shrewd insights into the political functioning of a modern state was his crediting of the vast complex of voluntary and nonpolitical associations in society with the maintenance of civil liberty. In 1857 he was invited to occupy the chair of history and political science at Columbia, and he retained this post until transferring to the Columbia Law School in 1865, where he remained for the rest of his life. During the Civil War he devised for the War Department *Instructions for the Government of the Armies of the United States in the Field*; this work, the first such code of military law and procedure in the world, was adopted as General Orders No. 100 in 1863. It was later adopted by the armed forces of several nations and was also embodied in international law. Lieber died in New York City on October 2, 1872.

Liguest, Pierre Laclède, see Laclède, Pierre

Lilienthal, David Eli (1899–1981), lawyer and public administrator. Born on July 8, 1899, in Morton, Illinois, Lilienthal graduated from DePauw University in 1920 and from the Harvard Law School in 1923. He was admitted to the Illinois bar and practiced law in Chicago from 1923 to 1931. Specializing in labor law, he also edited, from 1926 to 1931, the *Public Utilities Carriers Service* for the Commerce Clearing House of Chicago. In 1931 he accepted an appointment to the Wisconsin Public Service Commission to revamp the public utilities of that state. His specialized knowledge as well as his liberal politics brought him to the attention of President Franklin D. Roosevelt and in 1933 he became one of the early New Deal appointees to the three-member board of the controversial Tennessee Valley Authority; he remained on the board, after 1941 as chairman, until 1946. The first corporation ever created by act of Congress, the TVA implemented a recovery and development program for an area of 40,000 square miles that supported 3 million people in parts of seven states. The undertaking was opposed by private power companies and by strong political factions, especially in Tennessee. Lilienthal, an able speaker, often defended TVA publicly, and his policies, even before he became chairman, had generally been implemented since its inception. An able writer, he published the popular *TVA: Democracy on the March*, 1944, in defense of his accomplishments when the autonomy of TVA was threatened. Fearing that the project could become a patronage plum, he never allowed any of its employees to engage in politics; "A river," he was quoted as saying, "has no politics." An ardent conservationist, he proposed in 1944 a 30-year program for the preservation and restoration of the nation's soil. In 1946 he was appointed by President Harry S. Truman chairman of the Atomic Energy Commission (AEC), an appointment that was confirmed after stormy Senate hearings in which foes of the TVA vented their complaints. Lilienthal remained with the AEC for four years, during which time he helped formulate the nation's basic policies on nuclear research and atomic weapons, including the controversial Baruch Plan presented to the United Nations. Throughout his career a prominent figure in the field of agricultural and industrial planning, he was chief executive of the Development and Resources Corporation from 1953 to 1979. During 1967–1969 he served as cochairman of a group studying the problem of postwar development in Vietnam. Among his other books were *This I Do Believe*, 1949, written as a defense of his public career; *Big Business in a New Era*, 1953; *The Multinational Corporation*, 1960; *Change, Hope, and the Bomb*, 1963; and *Atomic Energy, a New Start*, 1980. Five volumes of his *Journals* appeared from 1964 to 1971. He died on January 15, 1981, in New York City.

Lincoln, Abraham (1809–1865), sixteenth president of the United States. Born in a log cabin near Hodgenville, Kentucky, on February 12, 1809, Lincoln grew up in the poverty of a frontier farming family. At the age of seven he moved with his family to present-day Spencer County, Indiana, and two years later his mother died; his father remarried in 1819 and Lincoln long retained fond memories of his stepmother, Sarah Bush Johnston. He received little formal education and what schooling he had was sporadic, but he early showed a desire for learning and his endeavors to educate himself—reading by firelight, walking miles to borrow books—have become legendary. He seems not to have been particularly happy with life on his father's farm; he did odd jobs on

his own when possible, among them splitting rails, and in 1828 he made a flatboat voyage downriver to New Orleans. Two years later the family moved to Illinois; Lincoln was now of age and ready to strike out on his own, and after a second trip to New Orleans he settled at New Salem, near Springfield, Illinois, in 1831. For five years he worked at various jobs, including an unsuccessful stint as a storekeeper, and also served as a captain of militia in the Black Hawk War of 1832; in his spare time he studied law and a year after his admission to the bar in 1836 he moved to the state capital, Springfield, to further his practice. His first political involvement had been as a member of the state legislature, from 1834 to 1841; although he was deeply democratic in spirit, his views on national policy, especially on economics, led him into the Whig party. His later career was foreshadowed only by his reaction to the Alton riot of 1837, in which abolitionist Elijah P. Lovejoy was killed, and the legislature's subsequent resolutions against antislavery agitation; in his protest against the resolutions he expressed his disapproval of both slavery and abolitionists. His law practice in Springfield and on circuit was successful, and in addition to handling criminal and civil cases he was an effective lobbyist and counsel for the Illinois Central Railroad. In his most notable case he saved the first bridge across the Mississippi from being torn down by shipping interests. During the Springfield years he made only a brief return to politics, serving for one term as Illinois' only Whig in the House of Representatives in 1847–1849; there he was a party regular, opposing the Mexican War and stumping for Zachary Taylor for the presidency in 1848. His party efforts were unrewarded, his positions were unpopular at home, and his political career seemed at an end; but the Kansas-Nebraska Bill introduced in the Senate in 1854 by his Illinois rival Stephen A. Douglas brought Lincoln back into the public eye and launched the great phase of his life. Speaking widely against the measure, which proposed to repeal the Missouri Compromise and allow the two territories to settle the question of slavery within their borders, he regained and surpassed his earlier prominence in Illinois politics, although he was unsuccessful in a bid for the Senate in 1855. The next year, however, he joined the migration of disorganized Whigs to the new Republican party and soon was its recognized leader in the state, receiving considerable support for the vice-presidential nomination on the ballot with John C. Frémont in that year. In 1858 he challenged Douglas directly in the campaign for Douglas's Senate seat and in a series of famous joint debates hammered away at the incumbent's avoidance of the moral aspect of the slavery issue and his paradoxical advocacy of the "popular sovereignty" doctrine of the Kansas-Nebraska Act, on the one hand, and of certain implications of the Dred Scott case, on the other. The tactic was effective; although Lincoln lost the election, he gained a national reputation that continued to grow, reaching sufficient proportions on the strength of such adroit performances as his famed speech at Cooper Union, in New York City, in February 1860 to win him the presidential nomination at the Republican national convention in Chicago in May 1860. While taking no active part in the campaign, he maintained close control over it from Springfield; the vote split on sectional lines and the Democratic party itself was similarly split, with the result that, although he failed to gain a majority of the popular vote, Lincoln was elected to the presidency by the Electoral College. From 1854, through the Douglas debates, in the campaign of 1860, and at his inauguration in March 1861, he had maintained a moderate position on slavery; he was willing to allow it to remain, with full federal sanction, in the South, but he was adamantly opposed to its extension into the territories. He summed up his view of the sectional dispute and of his responsibility in one brief passage of his inaugural address: "In *your* hands, my dissatisfied fellow countrymen, and not in *mine* is the momentous issue of civil war. The government will not assail *you*. You can have no conflict without being yourselves the aggressors. *You* have no oath registered in heaven to destroy the government, while *I* shall have the most solemn one to 'preserve, protect, and defend' it." Among the councils of the slave states, however, little faith was placed in Northern moderation on the issue, and upon taking office Lincoln was already faced with a hostile Confederacy of seven former, now seceded, states. Further, Fort Sumter, in Charleston harbor, was being threatened by South Carolina forces. After considerable hesitation, the president tried a characteristically conciliatory approach: apprising the governor of South Carolina of his intentions, he dispatched a relief expedition to deliver needed supplies to the fort but sent no arms or reinforcements, thus demonstrating both a dedication to peace and a determination to maintain the federal presence despite South Carolina's secession. The plan did not conciliate the South Carolina authorities; on April 12, 1861, Charleston harbor batteries fired on Fort Sumter and opened four years of bloody conflict. With Congress in recess, Lincoln quickly assumed broad executive powers, proclaiming a blockade of Southern ports, issuing calls to the states for troops, suspending habeas corpus, and initiating expenditures without appropriations. His acts were ratified and his assumed powers confirmed when Congress assembled in July, but by then he was faced with the tangled problems of military organization and strategy. Lacking a fully competent commander for the Union forces and himself without military knowledge, he suffered through the disastrous Union defeat at the first battle of Bull Run (Manassas) and several subsequent setbacks. The search for a sound system of command and for a man equal to the task was long and frustrating; not until he brought Gen. Ulysses S. Grant from the Western theater of war in 1864 did the Union army begin to function efficiently and with an integrated over-all strategy. Meanwhile, domestic political problems diverted much of the President's

energy from the prosecution of the war. In forming his cabinet he had created a somewhat unstable coalition of conservative and radical advisers, and this was a source of constant and increasing friction; and as the war dragged on, popular sentiment in the North began to shift against him, particularly after war requisitions, conscription, and high casualty rates began to place a heavy burden on the public. In contrast to popular feeling, Congress was coming more into the hands of Radical Republicans, and Lincoln, always an astute politician, found it expedient to accommodate the Radicals to a degree, and this, in addition to the humanitarian impulse, was a significant force behind his issuance of the preliminary and final emancipation proclamations of September 1862 and January 1863. Although the final Emancipation Proclamation was largely symbolic—it applied only to areas not under federal control—and, Lincoln believed, probably unconstitutional, it cast a new light on the war to preserve the Union, won additional and needed liberal support abroad, and forestalled a schism between Radical and moderate Republicans. The establishment of a new rationale for the war was furthered in November 1863 when he spoke at the dedication of a national cemetery on the site of the battle of Gettysburg, fought the preceding July; the emphasis was now placed on the preservation of popular government rather than simply the Union. Lincoln's Gettysburg Address remains, in its brevity and utter simplicity, the most eloquent expression, not merely of the administration's war aims, but also of a large part of the American faith. As the election of 1864 approached, Lincoln's prospects for reelection appeared dim. His policies were under intense criticism and military failures had given rise to a widespread desire for peace, and the nomination by the Democrats of a former Union commander, Gen. George B. McClellan, on a peace platform seemed ominous. In the few months before the election, however, Union military fortunes rose as Gen. Philip H. Sheridan routed Confederate forces in the Shenandoah Valley and Gen. William T. Sherman captured Atlanta and planned his "march to the sea." Lincoln was reelected by a large electoral vote, although his popular majority was small; by the inauguration in March 1865, victory was in sight and the President was already calling for patience and moderation in the reorganizing of the South: "With malice toward none, with charity for all, with firmness in the right as God gives us to see the right, let us strive on to finish the work we are in, to bind up the nation's wounds, to care for him who shall have borne the battle and for his widow and his orphan—to do all which may achieve and cherish a just and lasting peace among ourselves and with all nations," were the moving concluding words of his brief second inaugural address. While he pushed the Thirteenth Amendment through Congress and submitted it to the states, he was slowly developing the Reconstruction policy whose outlines he had described as early as 1863; but he had vetoed the Radical-sponsored punitive Wade-Davis Bill the summer before and was now faced with increasing hostility from Congress, which wished to set the policies of Reconstruction. The reestablished governments of Louisiana, Arkansas, Tennessee, and Virginia failed to receive congressional recognition, and it seems certain that, had Lincoln lived out his term, he would have met the same rancorous opposition from the Radicals that wrecked his successor's administration. On April 11, 1865, two days after Gen. Robert E. Lee's surrender to Grant at Appomattox, Lincoln made what was to be his final public address; he again called for the swift readmission to the Union of the Confederate states, a general policy of leniency and forgiveness, and a rededication to harmonious union. Three days later, on the evening of April 14, he was shot by actor John Wilkes Booth while attending a performance at Ford's Theatre. He died the next morning and was buried amid deep national mourning in Springfield, Illinois. In the years and decades that followed the figure of Abraham Lincoln gathered about itself the trappings of a towering legend, until he became in every sense a mythic hero. His rise from poor frontier farmer to great national leader, his ingrained democracy and humanity, and perhaps most of all his image as one more saddened than angered by treachery and treason, touched a deep chord in the American imagination as it had never before, nor has it since, been touched. He was elected to the Hall of Fame in 1900.

Lincoln, Benjamin (1733–1810), soldier and public official. Born in Hingham, Massachusetts, on January 24, 1733, Lincoln was educated in the common schools there before taking up farming. He was not prominent in Massachusetts politics until shortly before the Revolution; he then served in the legislature in 1772–1773 and in the provincial congress in 1774–1775. Having been a member of the militia since 1755, he was, when the Revolutionary War broke out, a brigadier general. In May 1776 he was promoted to major general, and in the Northern campaigns of the war he commanded troops at New York in 1776 and earned laurels in Vermont. At the battle of Saratoga in 1777 he was instrumental in the defeat of Gen. John Burgoyne; he was wounded in the campaign and forced to remain inactive for about ten months. After his recovery he was placed in command of the Continental army in the Southern department. He did not fare as well in the unfamiliar terrain of the South; after a success at Charleston in 1779 he blundered at Savannah and in May 1780 surrendered his army to Gen. Sir Henry Clinton at the end of the British siege of Charleston. He was exchanged in time, however, to take part in the final campaign of the Revolution, ending with Gen. Charles Cornwallis's surrender at Yorktown, where he accepted the ceremonial sword. In 1781 the Continental Congress appointed him secretary of war. He resigned the post in 1783 and returned to private life. In 1787 he took part in suppressing Shays's Rebellion in

Massachusetts, and in 1788 ran successfully for lieutenant governor of his native state. He was a member of the Massachusetts convention called to consider the proposed federal Constitution in 1788 and worked hard for ratification. In his later years he received a federal appointment as collector of the port of Boston, in which post he served from 1789 to 1809. He was also, in 1789 and again in 1793, appointed to treat on behalf of the federal government with various Indian tribes. He retired a year before his death at Hingham, Massachusetts, on May 9, 1810.

Lindbergh, Charles Augustus (1902–1974), aviator. Born in Detroit on February 4, 1902, Lindbergh entered the University of Wisconsin in 1920 but left in 1922 to enroll in the flying school in Lincoln, Nebraska, run by the Nebraska Aircraft Corporation. In 1923 he bought a World War I surplus Curtiss "Jenny" and made his first solo flight, subsequently making barnstorming trips through the Southern and Midwestern states. He entered the army flying school at Brooks Field, Texas, in 1924, completed his training in a year, and was commissioned a captain in the U.S. Air Service. In 1926 he became an airmail pilot on the St. Louis–Chicago route. Drawn by a $25,000 prize offered several years before by Raymond Orteig for the first nonstop flight from New York to Paris, in 1927, with several St. Louis businessmen as his backers, he purchased a Ryan monoplane with a single radial air-cooled engine, which he christened *The Spirit of St. Louis*. On May 10 he flew the plane from the factory in San Diego to Curtiss Field on Long Island, New York, making one stop in St. Louis and setting a transcontinental record of 21 hours and 20 minutes. After being delayed by bad weather, he embarked on May 20 from Long Island's Roosevelt Field, crossed the Atlantic, and 33½ hours later arrived at Le Bourget airfield near Paris, having flown 3600 miles. He was met by a tumultuous crowd which was only with difficulty restrained from wrecking the *Spirit* for souvenirs. After a reception given by the French government, he returned to the United States to be greeted with New York City's greatest ticker-tape parade. Dubbed "Lucky Lindy" and the "Lone Eagle," he was received as the supreme hero of the adulatory decade of the 1920s and was voted the Congressional Medal of Honor. In December he arrived at Mexico City from Washington after a 27-hour 10-minute flight and at a reception held there in his honor he met Anne Spencer Morrow, daughter of U.S. ambassador Dwight W. Morrow. They were married in 1929 and during the first years of their marriage they made numerous flights together to various parts of the world. In 1932 their two-year-old son was kidnapped and later found murdered; the publicity attendant upon the search for the child and, later, for his kidnapper made it the most sensational crime of the 1930s. A carpenter, Bruno Richard Hauptmann, was convicted of the crime and executed in 1936. From 1935 until 1939 the family lived in Europe, during which time Lindbergh was able to survey German air power and make significant reports to the U.S. government. In 1936 he worked with Dr. Alexis Carrel in experiments that led the latter to develop an artificial heart. In the United States during 1940–1941 he was a leading member of the isolationist America First Committee and made speeches across the nation urging that the United States remain out of the European war. For these activities he was criticized by President Franklin D. Roosevelt, and in April 1941 he resigned his colonel's commission in the Army Air Corps. After the United States entered the war he was employed in a civilian capacity as consultant to the Ford Motor Company and the United Aircraft Company, for which he accompanied 50 combat missions in the Pacific Theater. After the war he went to Germany with a naval commission to survey the development of German jet aircraft, rockets, and guided missiles. He then settled in Darien, Connecticut. He was named brigadier general in the Air Force Reserve by President Dwight D. Eisenhower in 1954 and was a consultant to the Department of Defense and to Pan American World Airways. For his story of the flight to Paris, *The Spirit of St. Louis*, 1953, he won a Pulitzer Prize. He also wrote the autobiographical *We*, in 1927, and *Of Flight and Life*, 1948. His wife was a writer of note, her books including *Listen, the Wind*, 1938; *Gift from the Sea*, 1955; and *Bring Me a Unicorn*, 1972. He died at his home in Kipahulu, Maui, Hawaii, on August 26, 1974.

Lindgren, Waldemar (1860–1939), geologist. Born near Kalmar, Sweden, on February 14, 1860, Lindgren became interested in geology at an early age and chose to attend Europe's leading mining school; he graduated from the Royal Academy of Mines at Freiberg, Germany, as a mining engineer in 1882, remaining an additional year for graduate study. Beckoned by stimulating career opportunities in the American West, he emigrated to the United States in 1883. For a year he worked on a railroad survey under Raphael Pumpelly, and in 1884 he joined the staff of the United States Geological Survey, with which he was associated until 1915. He lectured for a year, 1897–1898, at Stanford University and in 1908 began lecturing at the Massachusetts Institute of Technology (MIT). Lindgren was appointed chief geologist of the Geological Survey in 1911 and in 1912 became head of the geology department at MIT. His *Mineral Deposits*, 1913 (fourth edition, 1933), the fruit of many years of field work, marshaled strong evidence and forceful reasoning behind a controversial theory of the manner in which ores were deposited and opened up the possibility of a classification of ores on genetic lines. If, as he proposed, ores were formed in ascending (and hence cooling) volcanic materials or in solutions rising from magmatic regions, the presence of any given mineral in an ore became an index to the temperature and pressure at deposition. He further stressed a parallel process whereby minerals were laid down gradually by being replaced by others in moving solution. The clarity provided by, as well

as the fruitfulness of this "hydrothermal" view, eventually led to its general acceptance over such rival schemes as that of "lateral secretion." When Lindgren retired from his position in the geology department at MIT in 1933 his singular contributions were honored by the Penrose Medal of the Geological Society of America and in addition he became the president of the International Geological Congress. He died in Brookline, Massachusetts, on November 3, 1939.

Lindsay, Vachel (1879–1931), poet. Born on November 10, 1879, in Springfield, Illinois, Nicholas Vachel Lindsay studied for three years at Hiram College and in 1900 moved to Chicago. He attended night classes at the Art Institute from then until 1903 and later, in 1904–1905, continued his art studies at the New York School of Art. Devoutly religious, he also lectured on behalf of the Young Men's Christian Association (YMCA) and the Anti-Saloon League. In 1906 he set out on foot to wander through the South, trading poems for food and lodging. He spent a few years in Illinois, again lecturing, and in 1912 walked west to New Mexico. During these years he was writing and polishing his early poems and in 1913 *Poetry* magazine published his "General William Booth Enters into Heaven," an elegy on the founder of the Salvation Army that was also the title piece in his first volume of verse, published also in 1913. Highly original in all respects, the work was particularly remarkable for its rhythmic qualities. During the next several years he published a number of volumes of verse containing his best pieces—"The Congo," title piece of his second volume in 1914, "Bryan, Bryan, Bryan, Bryan," "Abraham Lincoln Walks at Midnight," "The Santa Fe Trail," "The Eagle That Is Forgotten." In addition to the compelling rhythms of the poems, which combined elements of ragtime, evangelical exhortation, and even band music (often calling, in marginal glosses, for particular chanting styles or instrumental accompaniments), he worked with a seemingly intuitive understanding of the appeal of popular and cult heroes and made them the subjects of many of his finest compositions. As his poetry grew rapidly in popularity he toured the country giving recitals. His chanting of his works attracted large audiences, and his success was crowned in 1920 when he became the first American poet to be invited to recite at Oxford. His early prose works such as *Adventures While Preaching The Gospel of Beauty*, 1914, and *A Handy Guide for Beggars*, 1916, were of value for the autobiographical information they contained, but his later writings were almost uniformly without interest except as eccentricities; they included *The Golden Whales of California*, 1920, *Going-to-the-Sun*, 1923, and the more worthy of this later group *The Candle in the Cabin*, 1926, written in verse; and, in prose, *The Art of the Moving Picture*, 1915, *The Golden Book of Springfield*, 1920, and *The Litany of Washington Street*, 1929. He died in Springfield, Illinois, on December 5, 1931.

Lindsey, Benjamin Barr (1869–1943), judge. Born on November 25, 1869, in Jackson, Tennessee, Lindsey moved to Denver at the age of sixteen and was admitted to the Colorado bar in 1894. He secured legislation to establish the first juvenile court in the United States in 1899 and as its presiding judge from 1900 to 1927 made it the model for others that were subsequently established throughout the country. On the basis of his philosophy that juvenile delinquency was not an isolated problem but one that related to many other social factors, he introduced reforms that protected juvenile offenders and made them wards of the court. He felt that juveniles should be treated rather than punished. He moved to California in 1928; as judge of the superior court from 1934, "Judge Ben" Lindsey became known as a reformer, contending vigorously against the outmoded political system that made individualized legal treatment impossible. In Los Angeles in 1939 he helped establish and presided over a new conciliation court, which dealt specifically with divorce cases that might be susceptible to reconciliation. He proposed a family court that would deal simultaneously with cases involving both divorce and delinquency. He also advocated "companionate marriage," in which couples would practice birth control and, if childless and if their marriage proved unsound, could separate at any time by mutual consent without legal proceedings. He was throughout his career a leading and highly controversial reformer. Among his written works were *Problems of the Children*, 1903; *Children in Bondage*, with Edwin Markham and George E. Creel, 1914; *Childhood, Crime, and the Movies*, 1926; and *The Companionate Marriage*, with Wainwright Evans, 1927. *The Dangerous Life*, with Rube Borough, 1931, was an autobiography. He died in Los Angeles on March 26, 1943.

Linton, Ralph (1893–1953), anthropologist. Born in Philadelphia on February 27, 1893, Linton graduated from Swarthmore College in 1915, having already taken part in archaeological expeditions to New Mexico, Guatemala, and Colorado, and in 1916 took an M.A. from the University of Pennsylvania. After more field work and service in World War I he resumed his academic studies at Columbia and Harvard, taking his Ph.D. from the latter in 1925, and also resumed field work, traveling to the Marquesas, Polynesia, Madagascar, and South Africa during the 1920s, from 1922 to 1928 as assistant curator for ethnology of the Field (now Chicago) Museum of Natural History in Chicago. His early publications included *The Material Culture of the Marquesas Islands*, 1924, and *Guide to the Polynesian and Micronesian Collections, Field Museum*, 1925, and culminated in a classic of ethnography, *The Tanala, a Hill Tribe of Madagascar*, 1932. In 1928 he became professor of anthropology at the University of Wisconsin; nine years later he moved to Columbia University, where from 1939 he was also chairman of the department of anthropology. In 1946 he was named Sterling Professor of Anthropology at Yale. *The Study of Man*, a highly influential work of synthesis which attempted, through the use not only of anthropology but also of sociology and psychology, a thoroughgoing definition of human culture, appeared in 1936 and was followed by, among others, *The Cultural Background of Personality*, 1945, and *The Tree of Culture*, 1955. Linton was a member of numerous scientific organizations and bodies, including in 1931–1932 and again in 1940–1945 the National Research Council, and in 1946 he served as president of the American Anthropological Association. Widely honored for his contributions to the development of cultural anthropology, he died in New Haven, Connecticut, on December 24, 1953.

Lipmann, Fritz Albert (1899–   ), biochemist. Born in Königsberg, Germany (now Kaliningrad, U.S.S.R.), on June 12, 1899, Lipmann studied medicine at the universities of Königsberg, Munich, and Berlin. He received an M.D. from Berlin in 1922 and, in 1927, a Ph.D. in chemistry. He initiated his laboratory research with work on cellular metabolism, cooperating with Otto F. Meyerhof (a Nobel Prize winner in 1922) from 1927 to 1930, and then assisting Albert Fischer. After a year, 1931–1932, with the Rockefeller Institute (now Rockefeller University) in New York City, he joined Fischer, who fled Nazi Germany in 1932, at the Biological Institute of the Carlsberg Foundation in Copenhagen. When the rising tide of Nazism threatened Denmark, Lipmann came to the United States in 1939. He joined the Cornell University medical laboratories in that year and immediately applied for U.S. citizenship; he was naturalized in 1944. In 1941 he became associated with Massachusetts General Hospital as head of the biochemical research department and, after 1946, held a concurrent appointment at Harvard, where he became a professor of biological chemistry in the Medical School in 1949. He left both posts in 1957 to rejoin the Rockefeller Institute. Throughout his career he was motivated by the hope of demonstrating the source of metabolic energy, and he made significant contributions to the understanding of the chemistry of bodily processes. In the late 1940s his achievements began to be recognized with an increasing number of honors. In 1953 he shared the Nobel Prize for Physiology and Medicine with H. A. Krebs of Great Britain for his discovery of coenzyme A, a vital catalyst in cellular metabolism. His work in isolating and later demonstrating the structure of the enzyme became a model for many experimenters in the field, many of whom he had trained.

Lippmann, Walter (1889–1974), journalist, editor, and author. Born in New York City on September 23, 1889, Lippmann graduated from Harvard in 1910. He joined Lincoln Steffens briefly on *Everybody's Magazine*, and in 1913 published his first book, *A Preface to Politics*, containing penetrating criticism of popular prejudices. In 1914 he was a founder of the *New Republic*, a liberal weekly, and became its associate editor. In numerous contributions to that magazine his praise of the Progressive party principles of 1912 influenced President Woodrow Wilson, who conferred personally with Lippmann and selected him to assist in formulating the Fourteen Points and in developing the concept of the League of Nations. In 1917 he was an assistant secretary of war and an aide to Secretary of War Newton D. Baker, and during World War I he was a captain in U.S. military intelligence. He attended the Versailles Peace Conference and returned to the United States in 1919, rejoining the *New Republic*. In 1921 he joined the staff and eight years later became editor of the *New York World*. Two thousand or more of his editorials were printed in that paper before he left it in 1931 and began to produce a column, "Today and Tomorrow," for the *New York Herald Tribune*. Syndicated internationally in at least 200 newspapers, the column won Pulitzer prizes in 1958 and 1962, earned him a wide following, and established him as the nation's foremost analyst of social, political, and ethical problems, as well as of U.S. foreign policy. An acute and highly individual commentator on the contemporary scene, he sought a "liberal democracy" and warned against the forces in modern society that led away from that goal. He contributed articles to more than 50 magazines, wrote a large number of books on famous men and events, and ten books of political philosophy, including *Public Opinion*, 1922; *A Preface to Morals*, 1929; *The Good Society*, 1937; and *Essays in the Public Philosophy*, 1955. *The Essential Lippmann*, an anthology of his writings, was published in 1963. He died in New York City on December 14, 1974.

Lipset, Seymour Martin (1922–   ), sociologist. Born in New York City on March 18, 1922, Lipset graduated from the College of the City of New York (CCNY) in 1943 and received his Ph.D. from Columbia in 1949. In the interim he had served as a lecturer at the University of Toronto, 1946–1948, and was from 1948 to 1950 an assistant professor at the University of California at Berkeley. In 1950 he returned to Columbia, becoming an associate professor within a year and remaining until 1956; from 1954 to 1956 he was also assistant director of the Bureau of Applied Social Research, where he worked with such colleagues as Robert Staughton Lynd, Robert K. Merton, and Paul Lazarsfeld. He was professor of sociology at Berkeley from 1956 to 1966, during his last four years there serving also as director of the Institute of International Studies; but he spent the academic year 1965–1966 as a visiting professor at Harvard, and upon the completion of this appointment he became professor of government and social relations at Harvard. An influential writer as well as teacher in his field, he published several books; including *Agrarian Socialism*, 1950; *Social Mobility in Industrial Society*, with R. Bendix, 1959; *Political Man*, 1960, which won the MacIver Award of the American Sociological Society; and *The First New Nation*, 1963, a study

of the first years of the United States against the background of the emergence nearly two centuries later of many other new nations onto the world scene. He also edited or coedited a large number of important works in his field, among them *Class, Status and Power*, 1953; *Culture and Social Character*, 1961; and *Party Systems and Voter Alignments*, 1967, as well as three books on the student political agitation of the 1960s, *The Berkeley Student Revolt*, 1965; *Students and Politics*, 1967; and *Students in Revolt*, 1969.

Lisa, Manuel (1772–1820), fur trader. Born in New Orleans on September 8, 1772, Lisa went to St. Louis, probably before he was twenty, and became active in the fur trade. One of the leading traders by the turn of the century, in 1802 he was granted a monopoly by the Spanish government for trade with the Osage Indians. After the Louisiana Purchase of 1803 and the success of the Lewis and Clark Expedition, St. Louis became the crossroads of westward expansion as well as the starting point of many exploring and trading parties. After 1807 Lisa himself averaged about one expedition a year. His first, in 1807, established a trading post at the mouth of the Bighorn River in what is now Montana. In the spring of 1808 he built a fort there which he named after his son Raymond (subsequently Fort Manuel), the first such outpost in the upper Missouri River country. In 1809 he became associated with William Clark of exploring fame, Jean Pierre Chouteau, Andrew Henry, and others in the St. Louis Missouri Fur Company, which sent out its first expedition of 350 men in 1809 and continued to flourish until 1814. Perhaps the most famous of his 12 or 13 expeditions up the Missouri was in 1811; in a race that was legendary among rivermen, the river barge of a search party led by Lisa overtook, near the confluence of the Niobrara River with the Missouri, boats sent out by the John Jacob Astor interests three weeks earlier. In 1812 he built Fort Lisa, for a decade the most important post on the upper Missouri, near the site of present-day Omaha. In 1814 Lisa married a woman of the Omaha tribe (his second of three marriages), and in the same year was appointed subagent for the Indian tribes on the Missouri above the mouth of the Kansas River by William Clark, by then governor of Missouri Territory. He spent his last winter at Fort Lisa with his third wife and died in St. Louis on August 12, 1820.

Little, Malcolm, *see* Malcolm X

Livermore, Mary Ashton Rice (1820–1905), suffragette and social reformer. Born on December 19, 1820, in Boston, Mary Rice grew up and was educated in public schools there before attending the Female Seminary in Charlestown, where she remained to teach after graduation. In 1845, while teaching in Duxbury, Massachusetts, she married Daniel P. Livermore, a Universalist minister and ardent temperance advocate. Livermore served several New England parishes in the next ten years. They decided to emigrate to Kansas in 1857 but ended their journey at Chicago, where for 12 years they edited the *New Covenant*, a Unitarian periodical. Through her Civil War work with the U.S. Sanitary Commission Mrs. Livermore became convinced that extending the vote to women was the key to many social reforms, including temperance, and she began to devote an increasing amount of energy to the woman-suffrage movement. Elected president of the Illinois Woman's Suffrage Association, she launched, in 1869, the *Agitator*, a suffragist paper. She moved back east to Melrose, Massachusetts, in that year to become editor of the *Woman's Journal*, a new Boston periodical, with which the *Agitator* merged. The years after 1872 were devoted to lecturing. An accomplished public speaker, she never tired in her efforts to arouse public opinion on the need for educating women and for changing the liquor laws. She remained active in the suffrage movement in Massachusetts, serving for ten years as president of that state's woman-suffrage association; for an equal period of time she was president of the Massachusetts branch of the Woman's Christian Temperance Union (WCTU). *My Story of the War: A Woman's Narrative of Four Years Personal Experience* appeared in 1888 and was followed in 1897 by *The Story of My Life, or, The Sunshine and Shadow of Seventy Years*. She was joint editor, with Frances E. Willard, of *A Woman of the Century*, a highly successful compilation of biographies that first appeared in 1893. She died in Melrose, Massachusetts, on May 23, 1905.

Livingston, Edward (1764–1836), lawyer, public official, and diplomat. Born at Clermont, the family manor in Columbia County, New York, on May 28, 1764, the younger brother of Robert R. Livingston, Edward Livingston graduated from the College of New Jersey (now Princeton) in 1781. An additional year of study under private tutors was followed by his entering an Albany law office where, together with Alexander Hamilton, Aaron Burr, and James Kent, he studied until his admission to the bar in 1785. He began practice in New York City and attained considerable prominence. In 1794 he was elected as a Democratic Republican to the House of Representatives; there he led the continuing opposition of Jay's Treaty through the withholding of appropriations. He was continued in office until 1801 and in that year, when the House was called upon to decide the presidency, he supported Thomas Jefferson over Burr. In that year also he was appointed U.S. attorney for the state of New York and elected mayor of the city; two years later, recovering from yellow fever, he discovered that a confidential clerk had absconded with a large amount of government money and, taking responsibility upon himself, he resigned both his offices, relinquished his property, and shortly thereafter left for New Orleans. The sale of his property and his earnings from the large law practice he

soon established in his new home enabled him to repay the Treasury for the loss and also pay his private debts by 1826. In 1806 he was falsely accused by Gen. James Wilkinson of complicity in Aaron Burr's conspiracy for Western revolt. A series of court cases involving Livingston's possession of a valuable parcel of riverfront property eventually involved the federal government and further strained his relations with Jefferson. During the War of 1812 Livingston was active in organizing the defense of Louisiana against the British and served as an adviser to Gen. Andrew Jackson in New Orleans. In 1820 he was elected to the Louisiana legislature and the next year was appointed by that body to prepare a code of criminal and penal law; completed in 1824, the code was accidentally burned but was rewritten and finally presented the next year. Although not adopted in Louisiana, the code was widely praised and gained him fame throughout the world. In 1822, running as a Democrat, he was again elected to the House; he remained until 1829, when he entered the Senate. To that body he submitted his proposed *System of Penal Law for the United States of America*, but no action was taken. In 1831 President Jackson appointed him secretary of state, and as one of the President's closest advisers he drafted the 1832 proclamation on nullification and also drew up other state papers. In 1833 he became U.S. minister to France, where he attempted to secure reparations for maritime spoliation suffered during the Napoleonic period; after two years of diplomatic muddle, he resigned and returned to his recently inherited New York estate in Dutchess County, where he died on May 23, 1836.

Livingston, Henry Brockholst (1757–1823), justice of the Supreme Court. Born in New York City on November 25, 1757, the only son of William Livingston, Henry graduated in the class of 1774 from the College of New Jersey (now Princeton) and the following year obtained a captaincy in the Continental army. He received two promotions, reaching the rank of lieutenant colonel, during the campaign in the North. He was with Benedict Arnold's command during Gen. Horatio Gates's successful conduct of the Saratoga Campaign in 1777 and also served as aide to generals Philip J. Schuyler and Arthur St. Clair. When John Jay (who had married Livingston's sister Sarah in 1774) sailed to solicit aid from Spain in 1779, he accompanied him to Madrid as private secretary. When Jay was sent on to Paris in 1782 Livingston set out for home, only to be captured by the British. He took advantage of his parole to study law at Albany, New York, and was admitted to the bar in 1783. His subsequent practice in New York City was very successful. In 1802 he received an appointment to the state supreme court, where James Kent was one of his colleagues, and was considered by President Thomas Jefferson for the Supreme Court two years later; Jefferson appointed William Johnson on that occasion but named Livingston to the next vacant seat, his appointment as associate justice being confirmed in December 1806. His 17 years on the Court—he served until his death in Washington, D.C., on March 18, 1823—were spent under the shadow of Chief Justice John Marshall, whose policy it was to write most of the Court's decisions, and all of the important ones, himself. Livingston was the author of some 38 majority decisions, all on cases involving no constitutional questions, and he wrote a few minor dissenting opinions. His keen and independent legal mind was revealed, however, in some noteworthy decisions written when sitting as judge of the circuit court. In 1808, for example, he held that treason could not be proved if the motive were primarily private gain, a conclusion of political importance in later years. He upheld in 1810 the constitutionality of the Embargo Acts, a matter that the Supreme Court itself never ruled on, and in 1817 he upheld the right of the states to enact bankruptcy laws in opposition to the federal government.

Livingston, Robert R. (1746–1813), lawyer, public official, and diplomat. Born on November 27, 1746, in New York City, Livingston was the elder brother of Edward Livingston and a member of a long-prominent New York family. He graduated from King's College (now Columbia) in 1765 and in 1770 was admitted to the bar, practicing for a time in partnership with John Jay. He was appointed New York City recorder in 1773, but two years later his sympathies for the colonial cause led to his dismissal from that post and his election to the Continental Congress. In this and subsequent periods of service in Congress, he was especially noted for his wide-ranging activity and influence in committee, although his membership on the committee charged with drafting the Declaration of Independence bore little result and he was absent from the signing. Having returned to New York in 1776, he aided in the drafting of the state's first constitution and under it became the first chancellor of New York in 1777; he held the position until 1801. From 1779 to 1781 he was again in Congress and was again one of its busiest members; in 1781 he was appointed secretary of the newly created U.S. department of foreign affairs and in that position supervised the instructing of the peace negotiators in Paris and made considerable progress in securing recognition of U.S. diplomatic representatives in world capitals. In June 1783 he returned to New York and, in addition to serving another term in the House of Representatives in 1784–1785, was active in state affairs. In 1788 he was a leading advocate of ratifying the Constitution and the following year he administered the presidential oath to George Washington in New York City. Receiving what he considered insufficient recognition for his efforts on behalf of the ratification of the Constitution, he became an anti-Federalist, opposing Jay's Treaty and, in a gubernatorial election, opposing Jay himself. Soon after Thomas Jefferson's presidential victory of 1800, however, came appointment as U.S. minister to France; he sailed for France in October 1801. There, after some preliminary diplomacy concerning the possible purchase of New Orleans from the French, he was joined by James Monroe in April 1803, and the two proceeded, without authorization, to purchase the entire Louisiana Territory. While in France he met Robert Fulton and provided him with technical and financial assistance in developing a steamboat. Livingston had long been interested in the possibilites of steam navigation and had secured from New York a monopoly on steamboating on the state's rivers in 1798; he now renewed the monopoly with Fulton and, resigning his office, returned to New York in 1804 to continue working with Fulton. The first commercially successful boat, demonstrated in 1807, was named for Livingston's estate, Clermont. Livingston thereafter maintained his interest in steam navigation, scientific farming, and other practical pursuits and remained out of public life. He died at Clermont, Columbia County, New York, on February 26, 1813.

Livingston, William (1723–1790), public official. Born in Albany, New York on November 30, 1723, Livingston grew up there and attended Yale, from which he graduated with the class of 1741. Deciding on a career in the law, he became associated with James Alexander, who had been the first counsel of John Peter Zenger in the famous seditious-libel case in New York City in 1735. Livingston was admitted to the bar in 1748. In 1751 he took a prominent part in the controversy over the establishment of King's College (subsequently Columbia), being opposed to its proposed governance by trustees associated with the Anglican church. A severe critic of the conservative establishment, he rose to prominence in New York provincial politics as a champion of the liberal cause that opposed Parliamentary interference in colonial rule. An able writer, he contributed articles to the *Independent Reflector*, 1752–1753, and the "Watch Tower" section of the *New York Mercury*, 1754–1755, that confirmed his reputation as a biting satirist. In 1758 his faction was successful at the polls, and Livingston himself served in the New York legislature in 1759–1760. His political influence, like that of the Whig party, waned and he retired from New York politics to the New Jersey countryside in 1772. A short, unhappy life as a gentleman farmer proved only an interlude and he soon took up the patriot cause in launching a second career. He represented New Jersey in the first and second Continental Congresses, and in June 1776 took command of the New Jersey troops. He was chosen, after the Declaration of Independence, to be the first governor of the state of New Jersey. As a delegate to the Constitutional Convention in 1787 he supported the New Jersey plan that opened the deliberations. He was largely responsible for his state's unanimous ratification of the new Constitution on December 18, 1787 and signed the document on behalf of New Jersey.

Livingston died at Elizabethtown, New Jersey, on July 25, 1790.

Lloyd, Harold Clayton (1894–1971), actor and motion-picture producer. Born on April 20, 1894, in Burchard, Nebraska, Lloyd was dazzled by the theater at an early age and appeared, at eleven, in a production of *Tess of the D'Urbervilles* in Omaha. An accomplished actor by the age of eighteen, he joined a stock company after graduating from high school. His career in the silent movies began in 1912 in San Diego, California; the following year he moved to Los Angeles and played character parts for the Universal studios. In 1914 he became associated with the producer Hal Roach, for whom during the next ten years he blossomed as a comedian in numerous short films. The scenarios of these early ten-minute comedies were inprovised during the shooting, a practice not uncommon in the early days of the film industry; the technique called for Lloyd to merge the role of writer, director, and actor. The productions became longer after 1919 and in 1922 he graduated to feature-length comedies. In 1924, already commanding a high salary, he also became his own producer, establishing the Harold Lloyd Corporation. The typical Lloyd film portrayed him as a shy, bespectacled, and bumbling youth whose misadventures included some of the most hair-raising, not to say foolhardy, stunts ever filmed, all of which were genuinely enacted by Lloyd himself, without tricks or stand-ins. Among his most popular films were *Be My Wife*, 1919; *Now or Never*, 1921; *I Do*, 1921; *Doctor Jack*, 1922; *Safety Last*, 1923; *Why Worry?*, 1923; *Girl Shy*, 1924; *For Heaven's Sake*, 1926; *The Kid Brother*, 1927; and *Speedy*, 1928. *The Freshman*, 1925, perhaps his most memorable silent film, was also a huge financial success; its gross of about $3 million established a record for the time. *Welcome Danger*, 1929, was his talking-picture debut, and until his retirement as an actor in 1938, his reputation as a comedian and stunt man remained undiminished. By 1940 he had appeared in some 500 films and was with, Buster Keaton and Charlie Chaplin, accounted one of the three great clowns of the motion pictures. During the 1940s he worked primarily as a producer and remained content to reissue some of his earlier classics. *Harold Lloyd's World of Comedy*, a compilation of his best scenes from earlier films, was released in 1962. He died on March 8, 1971, in Hollywood, California, where in his later years he was active in the business community.

Lloyd, Henry Demarest (1847–1903), journalist, author, and social reformer. Born in New York City on May 1, 1847, Lloyd graduated from Columbia College (1867) and the Columbia Law School, was admitted to the bar, and engaged for a time in reform activities in New York City, including campaigning against Tammany Hall. In 1872 he joined the staff of the *Chicago Tribune* as financial and literary editor and editorial writer; during 13 years on the paper his continuing interest in reform led him to conduct numerous investigations into abuses affecting the public interest, particularly those perpetrated by corporations and trusts; he published his findings in articles that, by their thorough documentation and crusading tone, became sensations. Such articles as "The Story of a Great Monopoly," published in the *Atlantic Monthly* in 1881, made Lloyd the first of the great journalistic muckrakers. In 1885 he left the *Tribune* and devoted himself to the cause of progressive reform. He wrote a number of books on problems of labor and monopoly, his most famous being his study of the Standard Oil Company, *Wealth Against Commonwealth*, 1894. In the same year he defended Eugene V. Debs in the legal battles growing out of the Pullman strike of 1894 and accepted the nomination of the National People's party for the House of Representatives. During his last years he traveled extensively, particularly in England and New Zealand, where he studied new methods of dealing with the problems of labor; his observations and his advocacy of similar reforms in the United States were contained in several books, among them *Labour Copartnership*, 1898, and *A Country Without Strikes*, 1900. He was one of the principal spokesmen for the anthracite miners in the negotiations that followed the great coal strike of 1902. He died while engaged in a campaign for public ownership of street railways in Chicago, on September 28, 1903.

Locke, Alain LeRoy (1886–1954), teacher and critic. Born in Philadelphia on September 13, 1886, Locke graduated from Harvard in 1907 and subsequently became the first Negro to be awarded a Rhodes scholarship, studying at Oxford during 1907–1910 and for an additional year at the University of Berlin. In 1912 he joined the philosophy department of Howard University, where, on receiving his doctorate from Harvard in 1918, he became department chairman and, in time, one of the most respected members of the faculty. An inspiring teacher, he continued to attract students to the university until his retirement in 1953. Locke first gained national prominence as a chronicler of the Harlem Renaissance that flourished after World War I. He was asked by the *Survey Graphic* to prepare a special Harlem issue; it appeared in March 1925, and that same year was expanded into *The New Negro: An Interpretation*, a collection of works by the best talents that had led to the revival. The title essay by Locke was marked by its sensitivity to the deep feeling of race that was becoming the "mainspring of Negro life." *The New Negro* embodied his belief that the artist, as the most conspicuous member of W. E. B. Du Bois "talented tenth," was the key to improving race relations in the American community. Locke's subsequent efforts as teacher and writer were devoted to displaying the compatibility of black nationalism with the true realization of the American ideal. He was perhaps the leading critic of black culture in the interval between the world wars. His many works included *Four Negro Poets*, 1927; *Plays of Negro Life*, edited with Montgomery Gregory, 1927; *The Negro in America*, a social study, 1933; *The Negro and His Music*, 1936; and *Negro Art: Past and Present*, 1936. An able student of African culture, Locke published *The Negro in Art*, 1941; it was highly praised for its appreciation of the influence of African art on modern painting and sculpture. He also urged black American artists to make use of their ancestral heritage in their own work. His *Le Rôle du Nègre dans la Culture Américaine*, 1943, was written while he was in Haiti as Inter-American Exchange Professor. He died in New York City, after a long illness on June 9, 1954, leaving unfinished a study that became the basis of M. J. Butcher's *The Negro in American Culture*, 1956. A revival of interest in Locke's work occurred in the late 1960s and early 1970s.

Locke, David Ross (1833–1888), "Petroleum V. Nasby," journalist. Born in Vestal, New York, on September 20, 1833, Locke began at the age of ten a seven years' apprenticeship on the *Democrat*, a political journal published in nearby Cortland. For two years thereafter he was an itinerant printer, and in 1852 he settled in Plymouth, Ohio, long enough to help found the *Plymouth Advertiser*. He soon resumed wandering from town to town and was editor of the *Findlay* (Ohio) *Jeffersonian* when, in March 1861, he published his first "letter" over the signature Petroleum Vesuvius Nasby. The character Nasby—later depicted in illustrations by cartoonist Thomas Nast—was the embodiment of everything Locke detested: Nasby was dissolute, intemperate, illiterate, dishonest, cowardly, and hypocritical. Through the ironic manipulation of this "late pastor uv the Church uv the New Dispensation, Chaplain to his excellency the President, and p.m. at Confederate x roads, kentucky," Locke maintained a running attack on slavery, Copperheads, and the Democratic party. Nasby wrote, as the humorous fashion of the day required, with unorthodox spelling and tortured grammar, and his logical processes were absurd. The Nasby letters were a great success, enjoyed even by President Abraham Lincoln, who was known to read them to his cabinet on occasion. A collection in book form, *The Nasby Papers*, appeared in 1864 and the next year Locke became editor of the *Toledo* (Ohio) *Blade*, soon acquiring a controlling interest in it. He refused offers of government employment from both Lincoln and President Ulysses S. Grant; in 1871 he went to New York City to join the *Evening Mail*, but before long had returned to Ohio. He became a highly popular lecturer on the lyceum circuit; the Nasby letters continued to appear in collections, and others of Locke's publications included *The Morals of Abou Ben Adhem*, 1875, and *The Demagogue*, 1881. Later Locke crusaded for prohibition. The final Nasby letter was published in 1887 and Locke died in Toledo on February 15, 1888.

Lockwood, Belva Ann Bennett (1830–1917), lawyer and social reformer. Born at Royalton, Niagara County, New York, on October 24, 1830, Miss Bennett was married at 18 and widowed six years later. She graduated from Genesee College in 1857. She had previously taught school, and after college she continued as a teacher in various towns in upper New York state until 1868, when she moved to Washington, D.C., to study law. The same year, she married Ezekiel Lockwood. Because the faculty of the National University Law School refused to allow her in their classes, she was privately tutored, and after graduating in 1873 was admitted to the bar. Offended by the legal and economic discrimination against women in American society, Mrs. Lockwood became one of the most effective advocates of women's rights of her time. Her law practice dealt primarily with claims against the government, and her work in Washington gave her the opportunity to lobby on behalf of legislation favorable to women. She drafted a bill for equal pay for equal work by women in the civil service, and the bill was enacted into law. In 1879 she helped secure passage of a law admitting women to practice before the Supreme Court and was herself the first to be so admitted. She gained some national prominence as a lecturer on women's rights, and in 1884 and 1888 was nominated to run for the presidency on the ticket of the National Equal Rights party. Active in a wide range of reform movements, she was chosen by the Department of State to be a delegate to the International Congress of Charities, Correction, and Philanthropy at Geneva in 1896, and to peace congresses in Europe in 1906, 1908, and 1911. As a lawyer in the District of Columbia she aided the women of the district in securing equal property rights and equal guardianship of children. When the statehood bills for Oklahoma, New Mexico, and Arizona came before Congress, she prepared amendments granting suffrage to women in the proposed new states. She held office in several reform organizations, including the International Peace Bureau, the Nobel Peace Prize nominating committee, the League of Women Voters, and the National and American Woman Suffrage associations. Mrs. Lockwood died on May 19, 1917, in Washington, D.C.

Lodge, Henry Cabot (1850–1924), author and public official. Born in Boston on May 12, 1850, Lodge graduated from Harvard in 1871 and entered the Law School, taking his law degree in 1875. He had been assisting Henry Adams in editing the *North American Review* from 1873 to 1876, and in the latter year was awarded his Ph.D. in political science by Harvard and was admitted to the bar. From 1876 to 1879 he lectured on American history at Harvard. In 1880–1881 he was a member of the Massachusetts legislature and after suffering defeat in the Mugwump revolt in 1884 was elected as a Republican to the House of Representatives in 1886. In three terms in the House he increased his reputation for party regularity while championing the protection of voting rights and civil-service reform; in the course of his efforts in the latter field, he recommended young Theodore Roosevelt for a seat on the Civil Service Commission. Lodge also contributed to the drafting of the Sherman Anti-Trust Act of 1890. He had continued his scholarly career during these years as well, publishing several distinguished biographies—*Alexander Hamilton*, 1882; *Daniel Webster*, 1883; and *George Washington*, 1889—and a number of historical studies, and editing the nine-volume *Works of Alexander Hamilton*, 1885–1886, and *The Federalist*, 1891. In 1893 he was elected to the Senate and remained in that body for the rest of his life. He rose steadily in prominence both within his party and nationally; he was a member of the Alaskan Boundary Commission in 1903 and of the U.S. Immigration Commission from 1907 to 1910. Staunchly Republican and conservative, he was a leading opponent of the Populist free-silver campaign and an equally strong supporter of the imperialist policies that stemmed from the Spanish-American War. He supported President Theodore Roosevelt's maneuvers to gain control of the Panama Canal Zone, was a vigorous advocate of naval strength, and opposed woman suffrage, compulsory international arbitration, the direct election of senators, and prohibition. With little sympathy for progressive reform legislation and far from an idealist in practical affairs, he became soon after the election of 1912 the principal critic of the Woodrow Wilson administration. He called for U.S. entry into World War I after the sinking of the *Lusitania*, supported vigorous action when war did finally come, and advocated harsh peace terms. He had long arrogated to himself the Senate's leadership in the field of foreign affairs when, in 1918, he became both Republican floor leader and chairman of the foreign relations committee. Utilizing the powers of both positions, he organized Senate opposition to the League of Nations. When the Versailles peace treaty, which included, against his wishes, the Covenant of the League of Nations, was submitted to the Senate for ratification, he reported it out of committee with a number of amending reservations; these, intended to retain what he considered an essential degree of national sovereignty, were unacceptable to the President. The amendments were approved by the Senate, whereupon Wilson directed Democratic senators to vote against the treaty, which was duly defeated. Lodge's prestige rose greatly as a result of this victory. He viewed the 1920 presidential election as a national plebiscite on the issue of the League and played a major role in securing the Republican nomination for Warren G. Harding. In 1921 he was a delegate to the Washington conference on arms limitation and later led the opposition to Harding's proposal that the United States join the World Court (Permanent Court of International Justice). Lodge died in Boston on November 9, 1924.

Lodge, Henry Cabot (1902–   ), public official and diplomat. Born in Nahant, Massachusetts, on July 5, 1902, into a family prominent in his state's politics, he was the grandson of Henry Cabot Lodge. After attending Middlesex School in Concord, he completed his studies at Harvard in three years and graduated with the class of 1924 after already having begun a career in journalism with the *Boston Transcript*. Later he was an editorial writer for the *New York Herald Tribune*. It was no surprise when he entered Massachusetts politics in 1932, serving four years in the legislature. In 1936 he opposed a national Democratic tide to win a Senate seat as a Republican from Massachusetts and was reelected six years later. He served with the army during World War II, leaving the Senate to go on active duty (he had been a reserve officer since 1924) before Pearl Harbor and serving in combat with British forces in North Africa. In 1944 he resigned his Senate seat to return to combat; serving in the European and Mediterranean theaters he attained the rank of lieutenant colonel. Lodge was again successful at the polls in 1946. On his return to the Senate he became a member of the influential foreign relations committee, where he abandoned his family's traditional and his own earlier isolationism, advocated military preparedness, and supported the United Nations (UN). In 1952 he devoted much of his time to promoting the candidacy and the election campaign of Dwight D. Eisenhower, while losing his Senate seat to the ambitious and hard-working John F. Kennedy. The following year he was appointed by President Eisenhower as chief of the U.S. mission to the UN with ambassadorial rank and cabinet membership, a position that made him influential in the formulation of foreign policy. During the next seven years his frequent exposure during nationally televised UN debates contributed to his prominence, and he was chosen as his vice-presidential running mate by Richard M. Nixon for the election of 1960. Their loss in the close race temporarily eclipsed both men's careers. Shortly before his assassination in 1963, however, President Kennedy appointed Lodge U.S. ambassador to South Vietnam, whose survival as a republic in Southeast Asia had become a primary concern of U.S. foreign policy. Still hopeful of becoming a Republican president, he resigned his post during the 1964 primaries but failed, after showing early strength, to win the nomination. He returned to South Vietnam in 1965 as ambassador, remaining until 1967. In 1968 he accepted the U.S. ambassadorship to the Federal Republic of Germany, relinquishing the position to become chief U.S. negotiator at the Paris peace talks on Vietnam that began in January 1969. After almost a year of fruitless negotiations with the North Vietnamese representatives, he resigned in December 1969.

Loeb, Jacques (1859–1924), physiologist. Born on April 7, 1859, in Mayen, Germany, Loeb was educated at the universities of Berlin, Munich, and Strasbourg taking his M.D. from Strasbourg in 1884. He began research work at the University of Würzburg in 1886 and two years later moved to Strasbourg; from 1889 to 1891 he was at Anton

Dohrn's famed biological station in Naples. In his early work he was primarily concerned with investigating the so-called instinctual behavior of animals and plants, and was able to demonstrate that many "instinctual" responses were actually explainable in relatively simple chemical terms and were evoked automatically by specific stimuli. His observations led him to formulate his famous theory of tropisms: the tropisms, like the hypothetical instincts, were inherited, but unlike instincts, they were demonstrably determined mechanically by the subject's physiology. In 1891 he traveled to the United States and joined the faculty of Bryn Mawr College; the next year he moved to the University of Chicago and in 1902 went to the University of California at Berkeley. His work with tropisms led him to investigate, from a mechanist viewpoint, sexual attraction and reproduction in lower animals. By introducing controlled variations in the chemical and physical environment he was able to induce parthenogenetic reproduction in the eggs of sea urchins and frogs. He also demonstrated that the phenomenon of regeneration, the replacement of lost tissues or members, was also chemically determined and therefore subject both to error and to the control of the experimenter. All of Loeb's researches were dominated by his desire to substitute rigorous scientific explanations for superstitious, mystical, or otherwise baseless explanations of the life process. In 1910 he joined the Rockefeller Institute for Medical Research (now Rockefeller University) in New York City; there he continued his experimental work and in his last years made valuable contributions to the chemistry of colloids. He died while vacationing in Bermuda on February 11, 1924. Among his publications were *The Dynamics of Living Matter*, 1906; *The Mechanistic Conception of Life*, 1912; *The Organism as a Whole*, 1916; and *Forced Movements, Tropism, and Animal Conduct*, 1918; he also was a founder of the *Journal of General Physiology*.

Loeb, James Morris (1867–1933), banker, philanthropist, and classicist. Born in New York City on August 6, 1867, Loeb graduated in 1888 from Harvard, where he studied under and formed a close friendship with Charles Eliot Norton. In deference to his father's wishes, he joined the family banking firm, Kuhn, Loeb & Company, and remained with the firm until his father died in 1901. During that period he contributed substantial amounts to further education and civil and political reform. He made numerous gifts to Harvard, in 1902 establishing the Charles Eliot Norton traveling fellowship to enable Radcliffe and Harvard students to attend the American School for Classical Studies in Athens. In 1905, as a memorial to his mother, he endowed the Institute of Musical Art in New York City, which later was combined with the Juilliard Musical Foundation to become the Juilliard School of Music. After 1905 he lived in Europe, first in Munich and after 1913 in Murnau, Germany, and devoted himself to collecting ancient art objects, playing the cello and piano, and

to various literary endeavors. He translated many important works on Greek drama and poetry by French scholars, among them Paul Delcharme's *Euripides and the Spirit of His Dreams* in 1906, and Maurice Croiset's *Aristophanes and the Political Parties at Athens* in 1909. In 1910 he founded the Loeb Classical Library, which eventually comprised 360 volumes of Greek and Latin literature; in each book a complete edited original text appeared opposite its English translation. The translating and editing was done by outstanding American and British scholars. Loeb was active in societies to further studies of ancient Greece and Rome, in the Archaeological Institute of America, and humanistic organizations in Germany. He died in Murnau on May 28, 1933. In his will he left large endowments to Harvard's department of classics, to the American School for Classical Studies in Athens, Columbia University, the Murnau town council, and the German Institute for Psychiatric Research in Munich, which he had founded and maintained. His collections of ancient pottery, bronzes, vases, gold ornaments, and engraved gems were left to the Museum der Antiker Kleinkunst in Munich.

Loesser, Frank Henry (1910–1969), composer and lyricist. Born in New York City on June 29, 1910, Loesser took little advantage either of his family's musical heritage or of his own schooling. He attended the College of the City of New York (CCNY) very briefly and then spent several years in various pursuits, from editing a newspaper in suburban New Rochelle to spot-checking for a New York restaurant chain. During the early 1930s he began writing songs, often in collaboration with William Schuman, and enjoyed some success in getting them into musical revues and clubs. One of his earliest hits, "I Wish I Were Twins," was popularized by Fats Waller. In 1936 he was hired to compose film scores and songs for the Universal studios and the next year he moved to Paramount, where over the next decade he wrote music for an enormous number of movies; among his best-known compositions were "Two Sleepy People," introduced in the 1938 Bob Hope vehicle *Thanks for the Memory;* "Spring Will Be a Little Late This Year," 1944; "On a Slow Boat to China," a great hit in 1948; and "Baby, It's Cold Outside," which won an Academy Award as part of the sound track for *Neptune's Daughter*, 1948. During 1942–1945 he served in the army, carrying on the morale-building work he had begun early in 1942 when, inspired by a remark attributed to a navy chaplain during the Japanese attack on Pearl Harbor, he wrote "Praise the Lord and Pass the Ammunition," the first song hit of World War II and one that eventually sold more than 2 million recordings. Subsequent war songs included the moving folk-style ballad "Rodger Young," 1945. In 1948 Loesser wrote his first Broadway show, *Where's Charley?*, featuring "Once in Love with Amy," "My Darling, My Darling," and "The New Ashmolean Marching Society and Students' Conservatory Band"; later shows, all great successes, included *Guys and Dolls*, 1950 ("Luck Be a Lady," "I've Never Been in Love Before"); *Most Happy Fella*, 1956 ("Standin' on the Corner," "Joey, Joey"); and *How to Succeed in Business Without Really Trying*, 1961 ("I Believe in You"). Others of his songs included "Hoop-Dee-Doo," (with M. DeLugg, 1950, and those for the 1953 film *Hans Christian Andersen*, starring Danny Kaye ("Wonderful Copenhagen," "Thumbelina"). Loesser died in New York City on July 28, 1969.

Loewy, Raymond Fernand (1893–   ), industrial designer. Born on November 5, 1893, in Paris, Loewy grew up there and attended the University of Paris, graduating as an electrical engineer in 1910. After advanced engineering studies at the École de Laneau and military service during World War I he came to the United States in 1919 (he was naturalized in 1938). For eight years he worked as a fashion illustrator for a number of leading periodicals, including *Vogue* magazine, and was also a display designer for fashionable department stores in New York City. In 1927 he launched a new career as a designer of industrial products. Organizing his own firm, he also became, in 1929, art director of Westinghouse Electric Company. The search for new products during the Depression of the 1930s provided a strong impetus for the infant field of industrial design. The ancient principle that form should follow function dictated, Loewy felt, a renaissance in design when applied to modern materials and methods of manufacture. The logic of this new functionalism, as it came to be known, freed the designer from preconceived notions of style or form and, when successful, reestablished a relationship between a manufacturer and his customer that had been lost when craft-based industries declined with the industrial revolution. Loewy's design of a refrigerator for Sears, Roebuck and Company in 1934 established the economic success of this approach. Awarded first prize for the refrigerator at the International Exposition in Paris, 1937, he thereafter was eagerly sought as a consultant by scores of American and European companies. Raymond Loewy Associates, formed with five partners in 1945, grew in the postwar economic boom to become the largest firm of industrial designers in the world. In addition to designing numerous electrical appliances, the firm became one of the leading interior designers of buildings, including department stores (Gimbels, Lord and Taylor), and, notably, the celebrated steel and glass Lever Brothers building in New York. Loewy's youthful interest in locomotives and automobiles led him to accept commissions for railroad cars, buses, trucks, and airplane and boat interiors. Perhaps his most memorable accomplishment in transportation was the 1952 Studebaker automobile. Other successful projects included designs for low-priced dishes and furniture. Early in the space-exploration program President John F. Kennedy called upon Loewy to help design interiors for human comfort in orbiting space stations, and for Project Apollo Loewy contributed appreciably to the habitability of the *Saturn I* and *Saturn V* spacecraft.

Logan, George (1753–1821), public official. Born on the family estate, Stenton, near Germantown, Pennsylvania, (now in Philadelphia), on September 9, 1753, Logan was the grandson of the James Logan who had come to Pennsylvania with William Penn in 1699. He studied in England and at the University of Edinburgh, from which he received a medical degree in 1779. Upon his return to the United States in 1780 he devoted himself to scientific farming at Stenton, which he inherited upon the death of his father. A founder of the Philadelphia Society for the Promotion of Agriculture, he produced several pamphlets on agriculture. He served in the Pennsylvania assembly in 1785–1787 and as a Democratic Republican supporter of Thomas Jefferson in the state house of representatives in 1795–1796 and 1799. A Quaker and an ardent peace advocate, he undertook a private mission to France at his own expense in 1798 in the hope of averting a threatened war. Although he was hardly responsible for warding off the war, which did not materialize, his mission, which was the butt of considerable criticism at home, was cordially received in France and produced significant results, including the release of American navy men being held prisoner. His action was subsequently responsible for the passage in 1799 of the so-called Logan Act, which prohibited meddling in affairs of state by private citizens. In 1801 he was appointed, and later elected, to the Senate on the resignation of Peter Muhlenberg. He served the full six-year term to which he was elected but declined to run again. Undaunted by the Logan Act, he again undertook a private mission when war was threatening with England in 1810. He met with no success on this occasion. Retiring to Stenton, he spent his remaining years quietly and died there on April 9, 1821; later he was interred in the Logan graveyard in Stenton Park, Philadelphia.

Logan, James (1674–1751), colonial official, judge, and scholar. Born on October 20, 1674, in Lurgan, Ireland, where his Scottish father was a schoolmaster, Logan was tutored in the classical languages by his father. Completing his studies in 1697, he began his career as a merchant in Bristol, England. He came to the American colonies in 1699 in the company of William Penn, whom he first served as private secretary. His appointment by Penn as provincial secretary in 1701 was the beginning of a long career of public service in Pennsylvania. One of the few of Penn's lieutenants who remained loyal, Logan served as commissioner of property and, after 1703, was a member of the governing council, of which he remained secretary until 1717. Charges brought against him in 1706 by the democratic faction which he opposed came to naught, and as champion of the proprietary cause (Logan himself had made a fortune in land speculation and in trading with the Indians) he subsequently became the council's president. His first judicial appointment came in 1726, and in rapid succession he advanced to the common pleas court, 1727, and then to chief justice of the supreme court, 1731–1739. When the governor stepped down in 1736, Logan's seniority on the council made him acting governor of the province until 1738. He retired from the council in 1747 to devote himself entirely to the scholarly pursuits that even during his public career he never neglected. A friend of John Bartram, his contributions as a botanist were recognized by Carolus Linnaeus, who named a large order of more than 30 genera of plants in his honor, and his English version of Cicero's *On Old Age* was printed by Benjamin Franklin in 1744; it was the first translation of a classical author by an American. His major scientific work, *Experimenta et Meletemata de Plantarum Generatione*, 1739, was translated from the original Latin and published in London in 1747. A successful businessman, an able scientific investigator, an accomplished classical scholar, an honorable public official, a loyal friend, and the founder of a family that remained prominent in Pennsylvania, he was one of the best representatives of the Quaker aristocracy that settled in the colony. He died at Stenton, his estate near Germantown (now in Philadelphia), on October 31, 1751. His collection of books, about 3000 volumes, remains a special collection in the Philadelphia library.

Logan, James (1725?–1780), Indian leader. Born about 1725 in the Delaware Indian village of Shamokin (subsequently Sunbury, Pennsylvania), Logan, whose Indian name was Tah-gah-jute, was the son of a Cayuga woman and of Chief Shikellamy, believed to have been a Frenchman raised by the Oneida Indians. Sometimes confused with his elder brother John Shikellamy, who also became a chief and succeeded his father as Iroquois representative at Shamokin, Logan, who never became a chief, was supposedly named for the Quaker James Logan, member of the council and chief justice of Pennsylvania, who for years had successfully traded with the Indians and who numbered the elder Chief Shikellamy among his friends. Logan himself was an outspoken friend of the whites, both in Pennsylvania and later, until the events of 1774 in Ohio, where he was prominent among the Mingo bands. Logan's friendship turned to bitter hatred after his Shawnee wife and some other relatives were killed at the Yellow Creek massacre that precipitated Lord Dunmore's War in 1774. Although he always accused a certain Capt. Michael Cresap of his family's slaughter, it later appeared to have been committed by other whites. Logan spent the rest of his life seeking vengeance. At the war's end in November 1774, although he reputedly had scalped some 30 white men, which might have seemed ample revenge, he did not accept the invitation to attend the peace-treaty meeting. His refusal was conveyed and translated at the conference by John Gibson in the form of a short oration, the eloquence of which caused it to be re-

printed in many colonial newspapers, and even in European journals, at the time. Although its authenticity has been challenged, the statement became a permanent part of American Indian lore after Thomas Jefferson made use of it in Query VI of *Notes on the State of Virginia* as evidence against the allegedly degrading effects of living in the New World. "I appeal to any white man to say, if ever he entered Logan's cabin hungry, and he gave him not meat; if ever he came cold and naked, and he clothed him not," he is reputed to have said; "During the course of the last long and bloody war, Logan remained idle in his cabin, an advocate for peace. [But] Colonel Cresap, the last spring, in cold blood and unprovoked, murdered all the relations of Logan, not even sparing my women and children. There runs not a drop of my blood in the veins of any living creature. This called on me for revenge. I have sought it; I have killed many; I have glutted my vengeance. For my country, I rejoice at the beams of peace. But do not harbor a thought that this is the joy of fear. Logan never felt fear. He will not turn on his heel to save his life. Who is there to mourn for Logan? Not one!" Logan continued to ravage white settlements until his death in 1780. He died at the hands of a relative near Lake Erie while aiding the British at Detroit during the Revolution.

Logan, John Alexander (1826–1886), soldier and public official. Born on February 9, 1826, near what is now Murphysboro, Illinois, Logan had scant schooling; he received only some instruction in law before taking part in the Mexican War as a lieutenant of volunteers. He held local offices after he graduated from the law department of Louisville University and began to practice law in his native town in 1851 and was elected to the House of Representatives as a Democrat in 1858 and again in 1860. He had an excellent combat record in the Civil War. He saw action as a private soldier in a Michigan regiment at the first battle of Bull Run and then returned to Illinois, where, organizing the 31st Illinois regiment, he was made its colonel; he later advanced to brigadier general and then to major general after the Union capture of Vicksburg in 1863. He commanded a corps of the Army of the Tennessee in the Atlanta Campaign and was briefly commander of the entire army at the battle of Atlanta after the death of Gen. J. B. McPherson on July 22, 1864. However, Gen. William T. Sherman, although acknowledging his courage in combat, claimed that he neglected logistics and had him returned to his corps command. Declining to remain in the regular army, Logan resumed his political career as a Republican, serving in the House of Representatives in 1867–1871 and, after that, except for an interval in 1878, in the Senate until his death. A Radical Republican after the war, he was instrumental in the formation of the Grand Army of the Republic, (GAR) and served three times as its president; GAR support contributed to his selection as the vice-presidential candidate on the ticket with James G. Blaine in 1884. It was as commander of the GAR that he successfully urged the observance of Memorial Day, a practice inaugurated in 1868. He died in Washington, D.C., on December 26, 1886.

Lomax, Alan, *see under* Lomax, John Avery

Lomax, John Avery (1867–1948), folklorist. Born on September 23, 1867, in Goodman, Mississippi, Lomax went to Texas at an early age. Graduating from the University of Texas in 1897, he stayed on as registrar until 1903, when he moved to Texas Agricultural and Mechanical College to teach English. He remained there until 1910, taking time out to earn an M.A. from Harvard in 1907. He served an additional seven years (until 1917) as secretary of the University of Texas, but in the early 1900s he had begun his life's work, the collecting of folk songs that he had heard in his youth. Convinced that folk songs and ballads, up to that time considered not quite respectable music, revealed a history of the people who sang them that was otherwise undocumentable, he published *Cowboy Songs and Other Frontier Ballads* in 1910; the book included "Home on the Range" and other songs that have since earned permanent popularity. Similar volumes, including *Plantation Songs of the Negro*, 1916, and *Songs of Cattle Trail and Cow Camp, 1918.* His autobiography, *Adventures of a Ballad Hunter,* appeared in 1947. After 1917, supporting himself by selling books, he traveled extensively throughout the country collecting and recording folk ballads. During the Depression he was made the first curator of the Archives of American Folk Song in the Library of Congress and, after 1932, he devoted all of his time and the remainder of his life (he died in Greenville, Mississippi, on January 26, 1948) to recording, editing, and publicizing folk songs. Of the estimated 60,000 songs in the Library of Congress collection he is responsible for about one-third. Carried out while traveling more than a quarter of a million miles, mostly by car and often with his son Alan Lomax, his work did much to set the tone of the modern study of American song. Alan Lomax was born in Austin, Texas, on January 15, 1915, attended various preparatory schools, and received a B.A. in philosophy in 1936 from the University of Texas. Prior to graduation he had already interrupted his studies in 1933 for a recording trip with his father and had then collaborated with him in the preparation of *American Ballads and Folk Songs,* 1934, and *Negro Folk Songs As Sung by Lead Belly,* 1936, the latter book first bringing the great black singer Huddie Ledbetter to public attention. After a trip to collect songs in Haiti, Alan Lomax was made assistant to his father at the Archives, 1937–1942. He helped to prepare a new edition of his father's *Cowboy Songs and Other Frontier Ballads* that appeared in 1938 and, also, with his father, edited *Cowboys Songs,* 1937, and *Our Singing Country,* 1939. With the growth of awareness of and interest in folk music he easily made the transition to commercial broadcasting and later recording. He produced programs and also frequently sang for

the Columbia Broadcasting System (CBS) from 1939 to 1944, and he was in charge of folk music for Decca Records in 1947–1949. In the 1950s he edited a series of recordings of songs of the American South as well as songs of Spain for Columbia Records. He also wrote and produced in the same decade a series of 30 folk-music documentaries for the British Broadcasting Corporation (BBC). A frequent lecturer on college campuses, he was made in 1961 a research associate in the anthropology department of Columbia University, where he had studied briefly in 1938. His last book with his father was *Folk Song: USA,* 1947. Among his other publications were *Mr. Jelly Roll,* 1949; *Folk Songs of North America,* 1960; *Penguin Book of American Folk Songs,* 1961; and *Folk Song Style and Culture,* 1968. Pioneering with his father in the documentary approach—recording unknown singers in their native settings—he helped launch several careers and contributed greatly to the systematic and scholarly study of folk song.

Lombardi, Vincent Thomas (1913–1970), football coach. Born in Brooklyn, New York, on June 11, 1913, Lombardi attended Catholic schools there and planned to enter the priesthood. He won four letters in athletics in high school, and at Fordham University, from which he graduated in 1937 after majoring in business, he was an outstanding guard on a football team with a national reputation. He began his long coaching career in 1939 at St. Cecelia High School in Englewood, New Jersey, and by 1947 the school's exceptional football team had won six state championships. His ambition to coach a college football team was then nurtured by a post at Fordham for two years, 1947–1948. In 1949 he went to West Point as assistant coach to Colonel "Red" Blaik and remained for five years. Still hoping to lead a college team, he nonetheless signed a contract in 1954 with the New York Giants professional football team as offensive coach. When the team's record improved the following year and then, in 1956, the Giants won their first National Football League championship in 18 years, his reputation as a coach was well established. In 1959 he became head coach and general manager of the Green Bay Packers, then at the bottom of the National Football League. In his first season they achieved a respectable standing and in the next eight seasons won five league championships and six titles in their Western division as well as Super Bowls I and II against the American Football League champions in 1967 and 1968. His record for nine years at Green Bay was 141 wins, 39 losses, 4 ties. In 1969 Lombardi left the Packers and it appeared that he was about to repeat the performance with the Washington Redskins. He died, however, on September 4, 1970, in Washington, D.C., after one winning season with the Redskins, the team's first in 14 years. A dedicated football man and a relentless taskmaster, he always had the respect of his players, who often played better for him than they had for anyone else. This was especially true of the feared Green Bay Packers, whose championship team was essentially composed of the same individuals who had played so poorly before the renaissance inspired by Lombardi.

Lombardo, Guy Albert (1902–1977), bandleader. Born on June 19, 1902, in London, Ontario, Lombardo was encouraged in a musical career at an early age and was playing the violin in a trio by the age of twelve. After completing high school in 1920 he formed a band of nine (including two of his brothers), and they met with success playing at resorts. Hoping to take advantage of opportunities in the growing U.S. broadcasting industry, he brought the band to the Midwest in 1924. By 1927, success in Cleveland had brought engagements in Chicago, where he changed the band's name to the Royal Canadians, and in 1928 he signed his first radio contract. The following year the band found what proved to be a permanent winter home in New York City's Roosevelt Hotel, and their broadcast appearances at the Waldorf-Astoria Hotel on New Year's Eve soon became a national tradition. In the heyday of the big bands in the 1930s and 1940s the Royal Canadians' popularity as a dance band was probably exceeded by none, despite the unfavorable opinion of many music critics of Lombardo's style. The band's staying power on radio, and later on television, as well as success in several films and with numerous recordings, brought the Royal Canadians huge earnings and enabled Lombardo to extend his business interests to include producing musicals in summer stock and music publishing. His appearance at the New York World's Fair in 1964–1965 marked 40 years of uninterrupted success at playing the "sweetest music this side of heaven." He died in Houston, Texas, on November 5, 1977.

London, Jack (1876–1916), author. Born on January 12, 1876, in San Francisco, John Griffith London grew up in poverty and at fourteen left school to lead a wandering and adventurous life. Although he was employed briefly by the fish patrol in San Francisco Bay, he spent more time on the other side of the law as an oyster pirate. His passionate interest in the sea led to little more than waterfront loafing until 1893, when he shipped as a common sailor aboard a sealing vessel that ventured as far as Japan. Upon his return he drifted from job to job and finally in 1894 he traveled east; he wandered for a time, was jailed for a month for vagrancy in New York City, and then, determined to make something of himself, returned to California and to school. He completed high school in a year and entered the University of California in 1896. His experiences as a hobo and an occasional worker, and his wide reading, particularly of Herbert Spencer, had made him by this time a Marxian Socialist. He left college after a few months, and, failing to find a market for his writing, in mid-1897 joined the Klondike gold rush; ill health forced him to return the next year and he turned again to writing. His stories finally began to be accepted by magazines and many of them were collected for his first book, *The Son of the Wolf,* 1900. In these stories, as in most of his writings, he drew on his personal experiences: from the far North came *The Call of the Wild,* 1903, and *White Fang,* 1906; his earlier sea voyage was reflected in *The Sea Wolf,* 1904. and a period in 1903 spent in the slums of London furnished him with the material for *The People of the Abyss,* 1903. In 1904 he spent six months as a correspondent during the Russo-Japanese War, and the following year he settled permanently in Glen Ellen, Sonoma County, California. In 1907 he sailed to the South Pacific in his ketch and four years later recounted his experiences in *The Cruise of the Snark.* In much of his writing London displayed a fascination with strength, violence, and the primitive; his popularity rested on the action and adventure described in his tales and owed little to the constant tension between his Nietzschean predilections and his Socialistic convictions, a conflict he made explicit in *The Iron Heel,* 1907. His later writings included the novels *Martin Eden,* 1909, *Burning Daylight,* 1910, and *The Valley of the Moon,* 1913; three autobiographical books, *Tales of the Fish Patrol,* 1905, *The Road,* 1907, and *John Barleycorn,* 1913; and numerous essays and stories. In 1914 he sailed to Veracruz, Mexico, as a war correspondent. Beset by alcoholism, London took his own life at his ranch in Glen Ellen on November 22, 1916.

London, Meyer (1871–1926), lawyer, political leader, and public official. Born on December 29, 1871, in Suwalki, Poland (then a part of Russia), London joined his family in New York City in 1891, where he worked during the day and studied law at night. Admitted to the bar in 1898, he specialized in labor law and became prominent as a union organizer, especially among Jewish garment-trade workers. Politically active as a Socialist on New York's Lower East Side, he was one of the founders, at the turn of the century, of the Socialist party of America. In 1914 he became the second Socialist in the nation to win a seat in the House of Representatives, where he served three terms (1915–1919 and 1921–1923), despite the fusion candidates run against him by the Republicans and Democrats after 1916. While in Congress he urged labor reforms and worker's benefits and was noted for his opposition to U.S. participation in World War I. London retained his interest in Russian politics and, although he opposed the Czar, he did not support the Bolsheviks. His criticism of Allied policy toward the Russian Revolution in 1917 (which he felt aided the Bolshevist coup in October of that year) as well as his stand on the war brought him under sharp attack both outside and inside the U.S. Socialist camp. His death in an automobile accident in New York City on June 6, 1926, was mourned by thousands of workers.

Long, Crawford Williamson (1815–1878), surgeon. Born in Danielsville, Georgia, on November 1,

1815, Long graduated from Franklin College (subsequently part of the University of Georgia) in 1835, and after reading medicine at Transylvania University received a degree in medicine from the University of Pennsylvania in 1839. A brief but successful career as a surgeon in New York City was cut short in 1841 by his return, owing to family difficulties, to Jackson County, Georgia. His practice there was uneventful until he began experimenting, in March 1842, with the suitability of sulphuric ether as an anesthetic during surgery. He had noticed the pain-killing effect of the gas when, earlier that year, he had administered it to a group of friends for other purposes. By September 1846 (the period of William T. G. Morton's first use of ether during a tooth extraction), Long had completed eight successful operations with the anesthetic without, however, publishing his results. He put forth his claim to have made the first surgical use of sulphuric ether in a paper published in December 1849, at a time when Morton, Charles T. Jackson, and Horace Wells were all claiming credit for the discovery. Long's reticence, while not depriving him of the honor of priority, and indeed redounding to his credit as an indication of his careful, scientific approach to his discovery, nonetheless removed him from the general development of general anesthesia, which, by the time of his publication in 1849, had become accepted practice. By the time of his death on June 16, 1878, Long's claim to have been the first user of ether during surgery was generally recognized. He died in Athens, Georgia, where, after 1850, he had established himself and become a prominent surgeon.

Long, Huey Pierce (1893–1935), public official. Born near Winnfield, Louisiana, on August 30, 1893, Long, a farmer's son, did not graduate from high school, but in brief periods of study at the law schools of the University of Oklahoma and Tulane University, interspersed with stints as a traveling salesman, acquired enough legal knowledge to be admitted to the bar in 1915. Three years later, after practicing law in Winnfield, he was elected to the Louisiana Railroad Commission and in ten years in the post (the board's name later was changed to the Public Service Commission) he made valuable contributions to the equitable regulation of public utilities, and this performance gave substance to his claim to represent the poor, dispossessed, rural folk of the state. Long's flamboyant and unconventional campaign style was perfectly attuned to the mounting grievances and long-suppressed agrarian populism of the majority outside the cities, and his attacks on the practices of the Standard Oil Company and on the governor, for which he was convicted of libel, served only to broaden his popularity. After an initial defeat for the governorship in 1924, he captured the governor's chair and great political power in 1928. Although he managed to carry out most of his promised public-works program—a vast and useful one including roads, bridges, and a major expansion of Louisiana State

University—he was hampered for a time in his quest for power by the opposition of the New Orleans–based Democratic party machine; he forced the "old regulars" of that faction into his camp in 1930 by being elected to the Senate by a huge margin while retaining the governor's seat, which he kept until he could hand it over to a trusted lieutenant. With the forced cooperation of the regular party structure, he centered virtually all political power in the state in his own hands, retaining it by graft, blackmail, patronage, and a continuous barrage of populist, even demagogic appeals to the mass of rural voters who felt they were for the first time exercising their own power over their traditional enemies, the rich and the urban business establishment. The failure of an attempt to impeach him in 1929 on a variety of charges involving corruption served to consolidate his position. In January 1932 he formally entered the Senate. "The Kingfish," as he was called, appeared to most of the nation to be merely a backwoods buffoon; nevertheless, while retaining his nearly complete control of state affairs, he embarked in 1933 on a campaign to gain national power. Reversing his earlier support of the New Deal, he formulated his own "Share the Wealth" program, which, although economically unsound, appealed strongly to great numbers of people. He explained the program in his book *Every Man a King*, 1933. In 1934 a challenge to his control in Louisiana called him home from Washington, and by means of a number of new laws that he put through a legislature completely under his control he abolished local government in the state and became a virtual dictator who held power over offices and jobs on every level and in all branches of the government. In August 1935 he announced his intention to run for president, a move that was seen as a real threat to President Franklin D. Roosevelt in its potential for uniting the supporters of such disparate movements as those of Francis E. Townsend, Charles E. Coughlin, the Technocrats, and others into a single, sizeable bloc. A month later he was shot while at the state capitol in Baton Rouge; he died in Baton Rouge two days later, on September 10, 1935. The remnants of the "Share-the-Wealth" movement, under the lead of Gerald L. K. Smith, merged the next year with Coughlin's National Union for Social Justice.

Longfellow, Henry Wadsworth (1807–1882), poet. Born in Portland, Maine (then a part of Massachusetts), on February 27, 1807, Longfellow was educated in private schools and at Bowdoin College, from which he graduated in 1825, having been a classmate of Nathaniel Hawthorne. Determined from an early age upon a literary career, he resisted pressure to go into the practice of law and accepted an extraordinary offer to return to Bowdoin as professor of modern languages made with the proviso that he first pursue further study in Europe. He remained in Europe until 1829, studying assiduously, although informally, in France, Spain, Italy, and Germany. In 1835, after six years at Bowdoin, he received a similar offer from Harvard, and following an additional year in Europe, he became professor of modern languages there, a demanding position that he held for 18 years. He had had poems published in periodicals from time to time since his youth—"The Village Blacksmith" appeared in 1840—and while at Bowdoin he had become a noted translator and critic of European literature; his trips to Europe exposed him to German romanticism, a major influence on his writing, and soon after taking up residence in Cambridge, Massachusetts, to enter upon his Harvard duties he published his first book of verse, *Voices of the Night*, 1839, which contained "Psalm of Life" and "The Light of the Stars." In the same year he published *Hyperion*, a romance based on his European experiences. He continued to publish poetry regularly and it enjoyed an increasing popularity; *Ballads and Other Poems*, 1841, containing "The Wreck of the Hesperus," was followed by *Poems on Slavery*, 1842; *Poems*, 1845; *The Belfry of Bruges and Other Poems*, 1846, including "The Arsenal at Springfield"; the widely celebrated *Evangeline*, 1847; *The Seaside and the Fireside*, 1850, containing "The Building of the Ship"; and *The Golden Legend*, 1851. In 1854 he gave up teaching and soon produced *The Song of Hiawatha*, 1855; *The Courtship of Miles Standish, and Other Poems*, 1858 which contained also "My Lost Youth"; and *Tales of a Wayside Inn* (which began with "Paul Revere's Ride"), 1863. The death of his second wife in 1861 had a profound and lasting effect on Longfellow; for solace he turned to Dante's *Divine Comedy* and his distinguished translation appeared in three volumes in 1865–1867. By that time he was the best-known and best-loved American poet and his fame was worldwide; he received honorary degrees from Oxford and Cambridge in 1868 and his home, long a center of Boston intellectual life in its greatest period, attracted the outstanding men of the world. Sweetness, gentleness, romantic vision shaded by melancholy, were the characteristic features of both his poetry and himself; universally venerated in old age, he continued to live quietly in Cambridge and to write. Among others, his later works included *The Divine Tragedy*, 1871; *Christus, a Mystery*, which he intended as his masterwork, 1872; *The Hanging of the Crane*, 1874; *Ultima Thule*, 1880; and, published posthumously, *Michael Angelo*, 1883. Longfellow died in Cambridge on March 24, 1882, and two years later was honored by the placing of a memorial bust in Poets' Corner of Westminster Abbey; he was the first American to be so recognized. He was elected to the Hall of Fame in 1900.

Longstreet, Augustus Baldwin (1790–1870), lawyer, author, clergyman, and educator. Born in Augusta, Georgia, on July 9, 1790, Longstreet attended preparatory school in the South before going to Yale University in 1811, and, after graduating in 1813, attended the Litchfield Law School in Connecticut. Admitted to the Georgia bar in 1815, he proved himself a capable lawyer in prac-

tice in Greensboro before serving in the state legislature in 1821. The following year he became a judge of the superior court; he held the post for three years before retiring from public office and, in 1827, returning to Augusta. *Georgia Scenes*, which appeared anonymously in 1835 and for which he is chiefly remembered, was first serialized as a series of sketches in the *Southern Recorder*, published in Milledgeville, Georgia. Although somewhat crude, the sketches were at the time very popular and were important as an early manifestation of local-color writing and of what came to be known as frontier humor. The book appeared with his name in an 1840 edition. In 1834 he launched the *Augusta State Rights Sentinel* in support of nullification, editing it until 1836. Increasingly of a religious bent after leaving the bench, he became in 1838 a Methodist minister. From 1839 he pursued a successful career as a college president. He served as the president of Emory College, in Georgia, from 1839 to 1848, and after a brief tenure in 1849 at Centenary College in Louisiana, headed the University of Mississippi until 1856. The following year he accepted the presidency of the University of South Carolina. An ardent advocate of secession, he was also prominent in the controversy within his church in the 1840s over the compatibility of slavery and Christianity. He was deeply affected by the Civil War and expended much labor in vain to find a way to avoid the terrible destruction it threatened. In 1865 he returned to Mississippi and he continued to write vindications of the South after the war. He died in Oxford, Mississippi, on July 9, 1870.

Longstreet, James (1821–1904), soldier. Born on January 8, 1821, in Edgefield District, South Carolina, Longstreet attended West Point with William T. Sherman and Ulysses S. Grant. Graduating in 1842, he was wounded and decorated during the Mexican War and had advanced to the rank of major before resigning his army commission at the outbreak of the Civil War. Commissioned a brigadier general in the Confederate army in June 1861, he won distinction in the first battle of Bull Run (Manassas) and was made a major general. His performance at Williamsburg in May 1862 and in the Seven Days' Battles in the Peninsular Campaign won the praise of Gen. Robert E. Lee, and he fought well at Antietam and Fredericksburg. A cautious general, he also tended to be tardy in execution when he privately opposed the general strategy, a recalcitrance that proved of little consequence at the second battle of Bull Run in August 1862 but that would later sometimes lose the day for Lee. The most celebrated instance of this was at the battle of Gettysburg in July 1863, where, a lieutenant general, he was in command of the 1st Corps, on the right wing, and second in command to Lee. Owing partly to a misunderstanding about the battle plans and partly to a lack of confidence in Lee's decision to take the offensive, he was slow to follow Lee's orders to attack at Gettysburg on July 2 and 3.

The Confederate failure there is often attributed to his delay in attacking, but it remains open to question whether the blame should be shouldered by Lee, whose inability to cope with unwilling officers was, perhaps, his single failing as a general. Longstreet's service in the remainder of the war reinforced his reputation as a good tactician and a less than able strategist. He was at Chickamauga, failed in an attack on Knoxville in November, and in the spring of 1864 was called back to Virginia; he served capably through the Wilderness Campaign and was with Lee at the surrender at Appomattox in 1865. After the war his Republicanism made him an unpopular figure in the South and probably contributed to his continuing disparagement as a general. His loyalty to the Republicans was rewarded by several federal appointments, among them that of U.S. minister to Turkey by President Grant and later that of commissioner of Pacific railways. His war memoirs, *From Manassas to Appomattox*, 1896, proved valuable to historians. He died at Gainesville, Georgia, on January 2, 1904.

Longworth, Nicholas (1869–1931), public official. Born on November 5, 1869, into a prominent family in Cincinnati, Ohio, Longworth graduated from Harvard in 1891 and studied for an additional year at Harvard Law School. In 1894 he received a law degree from the Cincinnati Law School and was admitted to the bar. He began his political career in 1898 as a member of the Cincinnati Board of Education, and after one term in the lower house of the state legislature (1899–1901) and one term in the state senate (1901–1903), was elected as a Republican to the House of Representatives. In 1905 he accompanied Secretary of War William Howard Taft on a tour of the Philippines with a party that included the daughter of President Theodore Roosevelt, Alice Lee Roosevelt. They were married in the following year at a memorable White House ceremony. Longworth supported Taft in the presidential election of 1912, in opposition to his father-in-law and his wife; it probably accounted for his single political defeat. Reelected to the House in 1915, he held his seat until his death. A hard worker with a reputation for fairness, he rose in time to become Republican floor leader, 1923, and, after 1925, served as speaker of the House. After his death in Washington on April 9, 1931, Alice Longworth continued to hold a leading position in Washington's social life.

Lorimer, George Horace (1867–1937), editor. Born on October 6, 1867, in Louisville, Kentucky, Lorimer completed high school in Chicago, where his father was a popular Baptist minister. He left Yale without graduating to work for Armour and Company in Chicago. His success prompted him to go into business for himself, but a venture as a wholesale grocer failed. He next tried reporting for Boston papers, and after some study at Colby College he landed a job in 1898 as literary editor of the *Saturday Evening Post*, recently purchased by Cyrus H. K. Curtis in the hope of reviving it. Within a year Lorimer, who had been filling the post all along on an acting basis, was made editor in chief, and under his guidance the *Post* became one of the leading periodicals of its day. In his efforts to portray the contemporary scene in business and the arts he showed a keen appreciation of public taste. Young writers were pleased with his quick decisions and early payment on acceptance of their work. Lorimer himself set the tone of the magazine with his *Letters From a Self-made Merchant to His Son*, which first appeared in the *Post* in 1901–1902 and later achieved great popularity as a book. Two other books were less successful, *Old Gorgon Graham*, 1904, and *Jack Spurlock—Prodigal*, 1907; the former was a further exposition of his philosophy of getting on in the world of free enterprise. The list of contributors to the *Post* attracted by his policy of prompt acceptance and payment grew to include Mary Roberts Rinehart, Willa Cather, and Ring Lardner; others drawn to the magazine were Sinclair Lewis, Joseph Conrad, Stephen Crane, Theodore Dreiser, F. Scott Fitzgerald, John Galsworthy, O. Henry, Booth Tarkington, Emerson Hough, Frank Norris, Jack London, Stephen Vincent Benét, and John P. Marquand. Under his guidance the *Post's* circulation grew from about 1800 in 1898 to 1 million in 1908 to more than 3 million by the time he retired. Lorimer also took an active interest in politics and his aggressive editorial support was sought by more than one president. In 1912 he supported the "Bull Moose" Progressive party and reform and then championed Woodrow Wilson, but by 1920 his conservatism asserted itself and he allied himself and the *Post* firmly with the Republican party. He was a champion of Herbert Hoover, and one of his bitterest political disappointments was the reelection of President Franklin D. Roosevelt in 1936. Lorimer served as president of the Curtis Publishing Company in 1932–1934 and was thereafter chairman; he retired from the *Post* in January 1937 and died in Wyncote, Pennsylvania, on October 22, 1937.

Louis, Joe (1914–1981), boxer. Born on May 13, 1914, in a sharecropper's shack in Lexington, Alabama, Joseph Louis Barrow grew up in Detroit. He sold newspapers, shined shoes, and drove an ice wagon until he became a sparring partner for boxers in a local gym at the age of sixteen. In his first fight he was floored six times in three rounds. Rapidly improving his style, he won 50 of 59 amateur bouts, 43 by knockouts, and he was a Golden Gloves light-heavyweight champion. He won the light-heavyweight title in the National Amateur Athletic Union tournament in 1934 and turned professional in Chicago on July 4, 1934, knocking out Jack Cracken in the first round. In his first year of professional boxing he won 10 out of 12 fights with knockouts, establishing a reputation in the Midwest for his paralyzing punches. He went East to fight former heavyweight champion Primo Carnera, scored a sixth-round knockout, and was called thereafter the "Brown Bomber." On June 22, 1937, he knocked out James J. Braddock in the eighth round for the heavyweight championship of the world, the youngest fighter ever to win the crown. He defended it 25 times, more than the eight preceding champions combined, scored knockouts against 21 of his challengers, and won four bouts by decisions. In his professional career he knocked out six world champions—Carnera, Jack Sharkey, Braddock, Max Baer, Max Schmeling, and "Jersey Joe" Walcott. In the army during World War II he fought exhibition matches for the troops and won two title fights, donating his share of the purse to army and navy relief. He retired undefeated in 1949, one of the most beloved, sportsmanly figures in boxing. He grossed an estimated $4,225,000 and drew three million-dollar gates, but because of huge tax liabilities was never a millionaire. He made unsuccessful comeback attempts against Ezzard Charles and Rocky Marciano to try to pay the taxes owed the government. Thereafter he was an executive of the International Boxing Club. In 71 professional bouts he was defeated only three times, and only once by a knockout, by Max Schmeling in 1936. In 1954 he was elected to boxing's Hall of Fame. He died in Las Vegas, Nevada, on April 12, 1981.

Louis, M., Father, see Merton, Thomas

Lovecraft, Howard Phillips (1890–1937), author. Born in Providence, Rhode Island, on August 20, 1890, H. P. Lovecraft was a precocious but sickly child. Unwilling to go on to college because of his health, he was largely self-taught, studying several languages and science, which attracted him at an early age. Except for about two years during his middle thirties, when he became involved in an unsuccessful marriage in Brooklyn, New York, he spent his life as a recluse in Providence, writing at night or with the shades drawn during the day, and carrying on a voluminous correspondence. Although he was virtually unknown except to a close circle of friends during his lifetime, his reputation as a master of horror stories grew after his death. He was often compared with Edgar Allan Poe, in part because of his unique blend of terror with dark fantasy. "All of my stories," he wrote of his work, "unconnected as they may be, are based on the fundamental lore or legend that this world was inhabited at one time by another race who, in practising black magic, lost their foothold and were expelled, yet lived on outside ever ready to take possession of this earth again." His first story, completed in 1908, was not published until 1916. Some 50 others appeared over the next 20 years, mostly in the magazine *Weird Tales*. *The Shunned House* appeared in 1928 and, shortly before his death, *The Shadow over Innsmouth*, 1936. He died in Providence, Rhode Island, on March 15, 1937. His writings were collected posthumously in *The Outsider and Others*, 1939, *Beyond the Wall of Sleep*, 1943; and *Marginalia*, 1944. His *Selected Letters* appeared in 1948 and *Something About Cats and Other Pieces* in 1949.

Lovejoy, Arthur Oncken (1873–1963), philosopher. Born in Berlin on October 10, 1873, he attended the University of California and received an M.A. from Harvard before studying at the University of Paris. His teaching career, which spanned 39 years, began at Stanford University in 1899–1900. He was at Washington University, St. Louis, from 1901 to 1909 and then at the University of Missouri for a year. From 1910 until his retirement in 1938 he taught philosophy at The Johns Hopkins University. Relatively unknown to the general public, he was highly respected by his peers in the field of philosophy. Convinced that the number of distinct philosophical ideas in the Western tradition was limited, he abandoned the traditional categories of philosophic inquiry to concentrate on the simple unitary notions which were the notions that all philosophers relied upon; his method of study thus became essentially historical in tracing the evolution of the basic ideas of Western thought. His chief work was *The Great Chain of Being*, 1936, based on his William James Lectures delivered at Harvard in 1933. His other works included *The Revolt Against Dualism*, 1930, and, with George Boas, *Primitivism and Related Ideas in Antiquity*, 1935. *Essays in the History of Ideas*, 1948, which has been described as tracing the unit ideas of philosophies through intellectual history, has had many imitators and has inspired more than one literary critic. Lovejoy died in Baltimore on December 30, 1963.

Lovejoy, Elijah Parish (1802–1837), reformer and editor. Born on November 9, 1802, in Albion, Maine, Lovejoy graduated from Waterville (now Colby) College in 1826. He taught school in Maine and from 1827 in St. Louis. He studied for the ministry at Princeton, was licensed as a Presbyterian minister in 1833, and returned to St. Louis to edit a Presbyterian newspaper, the *St. Louis Observer*. He used the weekly to support movements for temperance and for the gradual emancipation of slaves. He incurred the wrath of the St. Louis citizenry but refused to alter the paper's content, and in 1836 moved to Alton, Illinois, where he anticipated support from the sizable New England immigrant population of the region. He was not welcomed, however. His press arrived from St. Louis on a Sunday while he was observing the Sabbath and was pushed into the river. He was assured of funds for a new press by the townsfolk, who politely voiced their hope that he would temper his treatment of the slavery issue; but to their dismay, the *Alton Observer* covered activities of many anti-slavery groups as Lovejoy himself came to embrace abolitionism. Time and time again the paper's press was smashed, but each time the Ohio Anti-Slavery Society sent him a new one. On November 7, 1837, soon after another new press had been delivered, a group of abolitionists determined to defend it stood guard as an armed band of citizens approached the warehouse where the press was being stored. Lovejoy dashed into the street as he saw one of the citizens attempt to set fire to the warehouse and was shot. News of his death stunned the nation. He became the "martyr abolitionist," and his compatriots used the circumstances of his death—the "Alton riot" —to illustrate the incongruity of the existence of slavery in a democracy where the freedom of the press and of speech were supposedly guaranteed.

Low, Juliette Gordon (1860–1927), founder of the Girl Scouts. Born on October 31, 1860, into a prominent Savannah, Georgia, family, Juliette Magill Kinzie Gordon was educated at private schools in Virginia and New York City. She married a fellow Savannahan residing in England, William M. Low, at the age of twenty-six. Her interest in the Scout movement stemmed from her friendship with Robert and Agnes Baden-Powell, who in 1908–1910 organized the Boy Scouts and their sister organization, the Girl Guides, in England. She formed a small troop in Scotland on a visit there and then returned to the United States, where she formed the first troop of Girl Guides in the United States with 16 girls in Savannah in March 1912. In 1913 she established a national headquarters in Washington, D.C., (later moved to New York City) and during 1914 she traveled through New England and to Chicago organizing troops. In 1915, by which time the name had been changed to the Girl Scouts, the movement was formally organized and Mrs. Low was elected president, a post she retained until 1920, at which time she was honored with the title of founder, and her birthday was set aside as Scouts Founder's Day. Her devotion to the movement, which continued unabated after her retirement, was largely responsible for its national growth. At the time of her death in 1927, Girl Scout troops were thriving in every state of the Union and by midcentury the organization had grown to include more than 2 million members. Mrs. Low died in Savannah on January 18, 1927.

Low, Seth (1850–1916), merchant, political reformer, public official, and educator. Born in Brooklyn, New York, on January 18, 1850, into a prominent merchant family, Low attended Brooklyn Polytechnic Institute and graduated from Columbia College as valedictorian of the class of 1870. He then joined his father's importing firm, with which he remained associated until it was liquidated in 1887. A founder of the Brooklyn Bureau of Charities, he became politically active as a Republican because of his interest in civic reform. When he became mayor of Brooklyn in 1882 he reorganized the public-school system, instituted civil-service reform, and rid the city of debt. Reelected for a second two-year term, he later lost party support by his insistence on the independence of local politics from the politics of the national scene. His 12-year tenure, 1890–1901, as president of Columbia was equally impressive.

He transformed the small college into a large institution on a new campus in Morningside Heights and himself contributed a library building. Under Low's guidance Barnard College (for women), Teachers College, and the College of Physicians and Surgeons became associated with Columbia, which officially became a university during his tenure, and the graduate program was totally reorganized. He was one of the drafters of New York City's new charter in 1897, but his hope of becoming the first mayor of Greater New York was thwarted by Tammany Hall. Campaigning as a reformer, he was elected mayor in 1901, and his administration was marked by his commitment to displace patronage with civil service and by a vigorous program of modernization and expansion of public utilities and transit facilities. He failed of reelection in 1903, but his commitment to public service was not blunted. A frequent arbitrator in labor disputes, he served on the Colorado Coal Commission in 1914 and in the same year was elected president of the New York Chamber of Commerce. Appointed to the board of directors of Tuskegee Institute in 1905, he served as chairman of that board from 1907 until his death at Bedford Hills, New York, on September 17, 1916. His ideas on municipal government became well known when at the invitation of James Bryce he contributed the chapter on city government for the first edition of Bryce's *The American Commonwealth*, 1888.

Lowden, Frank Orren (1861–1943), lawyer and public official. Born at Sunrise City, Minnesota, on January 26, 1861, Lowden grew up in Iowa, where he worked as a farmhand and schoolteacher before graduating from the state university in 1885. He graduated from the Union College of Law in Chicago in 1887. An already successful law practice was further enhanced by his marriage in 1896 to Florence, the daughter of George M. Pullman. A prominent corporation lawyer, he never lost his interest in farming, and at his estate, Sinnissippi, near Oregon, Illinois, he experimented with field crops, livestock, and forestry. In 1904 he made an unsuccessful bid for the Republican gubernatorial nomination. Elected to the House of Representatives in 1906, he held his seat until 1911, sponsoring several measures in his quest to assist agriculture. Lowden became nationally prominent as governor of Illinois in 1917–1921. He toppled the existing budgetary and administrative structure in his efforts to centralize the government under the governor's control, initiated an extensive road and waterway program, and took decisive action in the Chicago race riots in 1919. His political career peaked out at the 1920 Republican National Convention, where he was a contender for his party's presidential nomination. Lowden was deadlocked with Leonard Wood through eight ballots; on the ninth, both were forced to give way to Warren G. Harding. In 1924 he refused the vice-presidential nomination on the Republican ticket, and although he still had presidential aspirations in 1928, his campaign for the nomination lacked luster. His principal concern after 1920 was farmers' welfare; during the Depression he supported federal aid to farmers. The Domestic Allotment Act of 1936, which coupled government aid with soil restoration, was modeled on his proposal of 1929. He died at Tucson, Arizona, on March 20, 1943.

Lowe, Thaddeus Sobieski Coulincourt (1832–1913), aeronaut and inventor. Born at Jefferson Mills (later Riverton), New Hampshire, on August 20, 1832, Lowe was one of the early users of the free balloon for meteorological purposes. Interested in verifying his conjectures about the direction and intensity of currents in the upper atmosphere, he made his first ascent in 1858. In April 1861, two years after John Wise's spectacular flight from St. Louis to Henderson, New York (800 miles in 20 hours), Lowe flew from Cincinnati, Ohio, to Pea Ridge, South Carolina, in record time and although his interests were purely meteorological, he became a prisoner of the Confederacy until his innocent intentions were proved. Lowe later offered his services to the Union army. Made chief of the aeronautic section of the army, he performed valuable service as a balloonist-observer during the war, making the first airborne use of both the recently invented telegraph and the camera, just coming into widespread use. Lowe turned his ingenuity to other areas after the war. His ice-making machine invented in 1865 was incorporated into the design of a refrigerated boat, but a business venture in transporting perishable foods failed. His work on the design of regenerative metallurgical furnaces (1869–1872) resulted in a practical alternative for producing fuel gas. His New Lowe Coke Oven (1897) marked a notable improvement in the manufacture of high-grade coke. In the early 1890s he achieved some celebrity by constructing an inclined railway up a peak in the San Gabriel Mountains in Southern California. The peak, at whose summit he established an observatory, is near Mt. Wilson and is named in his honor. He died in Pasadena, California, on January 16, 1913.

Lowell, Abbott Lawrence (1856–1943), educator and political scientist. Born in Boston, Massachusetts, on December 13, 1856, A. Lawrence Lowell was the brother of Amy and Percival Lowell. Upon graduating from Harvard in the class of 1877 he enrolled in the Harvard Law School and received an Ll.B. in 1880. He was a practicing lawyer in Boston until 1897, when he returned to Harvard as a lecturer. Made a full professor of the science of government in 1900, he was elected to succeed Charles W. Eliot as president of the university in 1909. Under Lowell's guidance Harvard reorganized its undergraduate curriculum by introducing a tutorial system and instituted general examinations that could replace course requirements. Attracted by the British system of colleges, he introduced the residential house system that distributed the undergraduate student body into seven groups. He launched new professional

schools of architecture, business administration, education, and public health. He also originated and endowed the Harvard Society of Fellows, which provided an opportunity for talented graduate students to pursue independent research without the need of meeting formal requirements for higher degrees. An authority on European government, he published *Essays in Government*, 1889, and *Government and Parties in Continental Europe*, 1896, before he began teaching; his *Government of England* appeared in 1908. His principal writings on education, *Conflict of Principle*, 1932, revised edition 1956, and *At War with Academic Tradition in America*, 1934, were published shortly before and shortly after he retired from the presidency of Harvard in 1933. Other writings, including a biography of his brother Percival and an autobiography, *What a College President Has Learned*, 1938, appeared before his death in Boston on January 6, 1943.

Lowell, Amy (1874–1925), poet and critic. Born on February 9, 1874, in Brookline, Massachusetts, Amy Lowell came of a long-prominent Massachusetts family and was the sister of Abbott Lawrence Lowell and Percival Lowell. She was educated in private schools and by her mother and until she was twenty-eight did little but alternately live at home and travel abroad. About 1902 she decided to devote her energies to poetry, although it was eight years before her first piece was published and two more before her first volume, *A Dome of Many-Coloured Glass*, appeared. On a visit to England in 1913 she met Ezra Pound and discovered his circle, the Imagists, and the following year her second book, *Sword Blades and Poppy Seed*, included her first experimental work with free verse and "polyphonic prose." She edited the three numbers of *Some Imagist Poets*, 1915–1917, and subsequent volumes of her own work included *Men, Women, and Ghosts*, 1916, which contained her well-known "Patterns;" *Can Grande's Castle*, 1918, with "The Bronze Horses;" *Pictures of the Floating World*, 1919; *Fir-Flower Tablets*, 1921, a collection of translations from the Chinese, with Florence Ayscough; and, posthumously, *What's o'Clock*, 1925, including "Lilacs;" *East Wind*, 1926; and *Ballads for Sale*, 1927. Her critical work included *Six French Poets*, 1915; *Tendencies in Modern American Poetry*, 1917; and a two-volume biography of John Keats, 1925, undertaken after delivering at Yale an address commemorating the centennial of his death. Miss Lowell became the leading exponent of the modernist movement in poetry in the United States and succeeded Ezra Pound as the guiding spirit of Imagism. She was a brilliant and popular conversationalist and lecturer; unconventional in her life as in her poetry, she enjoyed a fame that edged into notoriety. In 1922 she published *A Critical Fable*, a playful verse treatment of several contemporary poets patterned on the *Fable for Critics* of her collateral ancestor, James Russell Lowell. She died suddenly on May 12, 1925, in Brookline, Massachusetts.

Lowell, Francis Cabot (1775–1817), industrialist. Born in Newburyport, Massachusetts, on April 7, 1775, Lowell grew up in Boston where, at fourteen, he entered Harvard University. Graduating with the class of 1793, he subsequently went into the importing and exporting business with an uncle, William Cabot. In 1810 he went to England for a rest cure but spent much of his two-year stay there in a careful study of the power looms that sustained the great textile mills of Lancashire. After returning home, in a move that was to have a profound effect on U.S. manufacturing and society, he undertook to establish a cotton factory during the War of 1812. Arguing that the lack of English imports at the time provided an excellent opportunity for the venture, he was able to attract sufficient investors to form the Boston Manufacturing Company and to purchase land at Waltham, Massachusetts. Enlisting the aid of the talented mechanical designer Paul Moody, he undertook during the years 1812–1814 to construct the necessary spinning and weaving machinery to equip a complete factory. Relying on some drawings but also to a large extent on Lowell's recollections, they produced a power loom that in weaving speed exceeded their English model and also made notable improvements in other machines. The factory was in successful operation at the end of the war when reestablishment of trade threatened its share of the domestic market, as it was unable to compete with the plethora of cheap English cotton goods. However, Lowell and his associates met with success in their Washington lobbying and the 1816 tariff supplied the needed protection. His mill, the first in the world to process raw cotton into finished cloth under one roof, provided an impetus for a number of other Boston merchants to make the transition to manufacturing. Lowell, who died prematurely in Boston on August 10, 1817, did not live to see the transformation of New England into an industrial society, but his innovations in machinery and his paternal concern for his employees both became key aspects in the later building of the great "textile city" of Lowell, Massachusetts, which was named for him.

Lowell, James Russell (1819–1891), author, editor, educator, and diplomat. Born in Cambridge, Massachusetts, on February 22, 1819, Lowell graduated from Harvard in 1938 and two years later took his Ll.B. from the Harvard Law School. In 1841 his first volume of poetry appeared, entitled *A Year's Life;* a second, *Poems,* followed three years later. In 1843 he began another facet of his career by editing the short-lived *Pioneer* and publishing in it works by Edgar Allan Poe, Nathaniel Hawthorne, and John Greenleaf Whittier; and in 1845 he published his first critical work, *Conversations on Some of the Old Poets.* Under the influence of his wife, Maria White Lowell, a reformer and poet in her own right, he took up the cause of abolition and contributed a great number of articles on the subject to various periodicals; in 1846 he began to publish a series of "letters" in dialect in which "Hosea Biglow," a shrewd Yankee character, commented satirically upon the Mexican War and the prospect of the extension of slavery. The collected *Biglow Papers* appeared in 1848, along with the *Fable for Critics,* a broadly humorous survey of the contemporary literary scene, and *The Vision of Sir Launfal.* After a period of writing and traveling he succeeded Henry Wadsworth Longfellow in 1855 as professor of modern languages at Harvard, a position he held for some 20 years. In 1857 he helped found and began a four-year period as editor of the *Atlantic Monthly* during which the magazine became the focus of the New England renaissance. During the Civil War the second series of *Biglow Papers* was published in the *Atlantic* and appeared in book form in 1867. From 1864 to 1872 Lowell and Charles Eliot Norton jointly edited the *North American Review,* and Lowell published in its pages a number of critical and biographical articles. He produced numerous books of essays, including *Fireside Travels,* 1864; *Among My Books,* 1870, and *My Study Windows,* 1871; his volumes of poetry included *Under the Willows,* 1869, *Three Memorial Poems,* 1877, and *Heartsease and Rue,* 1888. In 1876 Lowell contributed his services to the presidential campaign of Rutherford B. Hayes, and the following year was rewarded by being appointed U.S. minister to Spain; three years later he was appointed minister to Great Britain, a post he conducted with grace and skill for five years, 1880–1885. In the six remaining years of his life he lived in Cambridge, Massachusetts, making several more visits to England. He continued to produce poetry, criticism, and political essays as the United States' acknowledged leading man of letters. He died in Cambridge on August 12, 1891. He was elected to the Hall of Fame in 1905.

Lowell, Percival (1855–1916), astronomer and author. Born in Boston on March 13, 1855, Lowell was a member of a distinguished family and the brother of Amy Lowell and Abbott Laurence Lowell. He graduated from Harvard in 1876, traveled for a year, and then devoted himself to diverse business interests until 1883; for the next decade he traveled in Asia and published his experiences and reflections in a series of books: *Chōson—The Land of the Morning Calm,* 1885; *The Soul of the Far East,* 1888; *Noto,* 1891; and *Occult Japan,* 1895. He had maintained all the while an interest in astronomy, and at the end of his travels he decided to devote himself to it. After careful consideration he selected a mesa near Flagstaff, Arizona, as the site for his observatory, and in 1894 began making observations on a regular basis. His primary interest was the planet Mars; having confirmed G. V. Schiaparelli's earlier reports of fine markings, or "canals," on the surface, Lowell elaborated a theory of intelligent life fighting the slow disappearance of water from the planet. His and the staff's observations of Mars and other planets were among the most advanced being carried on at the time. He described his work and his theory in several books, including *Mars*, 1895; *Mars and Its Canals*, 1906; *Mars as the Abode of Life*, 1908; and *The Genesis of the Planets*, 1916. From 1902 he was a non-resident professor of astronomy at the Massachusetts Institute of Technology (MIT). Mathematical investigations of anomalies in the orbit of Uranus led him in 1905 to postulate the existence of an undiscovered planet beyond Neptune; a systematic search was begun that culminated in the discovery of Pluto in 1930, 14 years after Lowell's death on November 12, 1916, in Flagstaff. The Lowell Observatory continued to grow and carry on significant astronomical research with a permanent endowment fund.

Lowell, Robert Traill Spence, Jr. (1917–1977), poet. Born in Boston on March 1, 1917, Robert Lowell, of a family long prominent in the political, commercial, and intellectual life of New England and indeed of the United States, graduated summa cum laude from Kenyon College in 1940 after having been a student at Harvard during 1935–1937. He was an editorial assistant in the New York City publishing house of Sheed and Ward in 1941–1942 and was a conscientious objector during World War II. His first book of poems, *Land of Unlikeness*, appeared in 1944, by which time he had already determined on a literary career. *Lord Weary's Castle* was published in 1946 and received a Pulitzer Prize the next year. He received a Guggenheim fellowship for 1947–1948 and during the same years also served as a consultant in poetry to the Library of Congress. Later books were *The Mills of the Kavanaughs*, 1951; *Life Studies*, 1959, for which he received a National Book Award; *Phaedra* and *Imitations*, 1961, for the second of which he received a Bollingen Prize for translations; *For the Union Dead*, 1964; *Near the Ocean: Poems*, 1967; *Notebook of a Year*, 1969; *History*, 1973; and *Day by Day*, 1977. He also published distinguished translations of works by, among others, Aeschylus and Baudelaire, as well as essays and reviews. He died on September 12, 1977, in New York City.

Lowie, Robert Harry (1883–1957), anthropologist. Born in Vienna on June 12, 1883, Robert Heinrich Lowie came to New York City in 1893 and was educated at the College of the City of New York (CCNY), from which he graduated in 1901 at the age of eighteen, and at Columbia University. His mentor at Columbia, where he received a Ph.D. in anthropology in 1908, was Franz Boas. In 1908 he accepted a position with the American Museum of Natural History in New York City, under whose auspices he did pioneering field work among the Plains Indians, including the Northern Shoshoni, Assiniboin, Blackfeet, and Crow. In 1921 he left the Museum to become associate professor of anthropology at the University of California at Berkeley; he became a full professor in 1925 and served as department chairman for fourteen years, retiring in 1950. A prolific writer, he made his principal contribution to the ethnology of the American Indian; most notable among his many studies are his monographs on the Crow. In his later years he became interested in South American and German culture. He also contributed original ideas to the study of folklore, family structure, and primitive religion. His books included *The Assiniboine*, 1909; *The Sun Dance of the Crow Indians*, 1915; *Culture and Ethnology*, 1917; *Primitive Society* 1920; *Primitive Religion*, 1924; *Origin of the State*, 1927; *Crow Indians*, 1935; *The History of Ethnological Theory*, 1937; *Social Organization*, 1948; and *Toward Understanding Germany*, 1934. Two volumes of his collected papers and his autobiography appeared posthumously. From 1924 to 1933 he was editor of the *American Anthropologist*. Honored by election to the National Academy of Sciences in 1931, he also served as president of the American Ethnological Society in 1920–1921 and of the American Anthropological Association in 1935. He died at Berkeley, California, on September 21, 1957.

Luce, Clare Boothe (1903–   ), author and public official. Born in New York City on April 10, 1903, and educated in private schools, Miss Boothe was employed by the Condé Nast publications from 1930; she was associate editor of *Vogue* in 1930 and edited *Vanity Fair* in 1930–1934. After the dissolution of her first marriage in 1929 and her marriage to Henry R. Luce in 1935 she wrote several plays, including *The Women*, 1936, revived on Broadway in 1973; *Kiss the Boys Goodbye*, 1938; and *Margin for Error*, 1939. She also wrote books, including *Stuffed Shirts*, 1931, and *Europe in the Spring*, 1940. During 1943–1947 she was a member of the U.S. House of Representatives from Connecticut and was U.S. ambassador to Italy from 1953 until her retirement in 1956. In 1959 President Dwight D. Eisenhower appointed her ambassador to Brazil, but she resigned a month later after winning a bitter fight for confirmation in the U.S. Senate.

Luce, Henry Robinson (1898–1967), editor and publisher. Born on April 3, 1898, in Tengchow (now P'eng-lai), China, the son of a Presbyterian missionary, Luce came to the United States at fifteen to study at the Hotchkiss School in Connecticut. There he met Briton Hadden. Together they attended Yale from 1916 to 1920, and served in World War I in 1918. Luce went to Oxford for a year after graduation and, following a stint as a reporter on the *Chicago Daily News*, joined Hadden on the *Baltimore News*. They resigned in 1922 and by rewriting articles from such papers as the *New York Times*, put together the first issue of *Time*, a weekly news magazine they had been planning since college, and published it on March 3, 1923. Successful at once, *Time* quickly acquired an aggressive newsgathering staff and doubled its initial circulation of 12,000 within a year. Hadden established its nimble style with word inventions (like "GOPolitics," "cinemaddict," "socialite," and "tycoon"), inverted sentence structure, and in innovative format, and these were carried on after his death in 1929 by Luce, who projected his personal philosophy into the magazine's editorial stance. Credited with developing the collective, collaborative style of group journalism and creating the modern news magazine, Luce treated news coverage as a continuing story. A staunch Republican, he defended big business and free enterprise and advocated aggressive opposition to world Communism. In 1930 he began *Fortune,* a monthly business magazine; in 1936 *Life,* a weekly pictorial journal that was discontinued in 1972; and in 1954 *Sports Illustrated.* He purchased *Architectural Forum* in 1932, spun off from it *House and Home* in 1952, and consolidated it under *Fortune* in 1964. In 1967 *Time* had a weekly circulation of 3.5 million and *Time* and *Life* together had some 2 million subscribers to their 4 foreign editions apiece. Luce retired as editor in chief of Time Inc. in 1964 and became editorial chairman of the publications. He also produced television programs, operated radio and television stations, and sponsored the *March of Time* radio broadcasts and movie shorts from 1928 to 1943. From 1935 he was married to Clare Boothe Luce. He died in Phoenix, Arizona, on February 28, 1967.

Ludwick, Christopher (1720–1801), Revolutionary patriot and philanthropist. Born on October 17, 1720, in Giessen, Germany, Ludwick was taught to bake by his father. His adventurous early years included military service (1737–1741), more than three years as a baker in India, and seven years at sea as a common sailor. Quitting the sea in 1753, he settled in 1754 in Philadelphia, where, with equipment bought in London, he opened a bakery shop. During the next 20 years he married, his business prospered, and he became a respected landowner and member of the community. A champion and financial supporter of the Revolution, he achieved distinction upon volunteering in 1776 for a dangerous mission to a camp of German troops on Staten Island; disguised as a deserter, he induced hundreds of the mercenaries to join the patriot cause. In May 1777 Congress appointed him superintendent of bakers and director of baking for the Continental army. Admired for his honesty by Gen. George Washington, he was known as the Baker General and remained a popular figure in the army throughout the conflict. After the war he found himself in financial difficulties. Most of his possessions had been plundered by the British, and he had little capital to work with. Although he never reestablished his prewar prosperity, he nevertheless was generous in philanthropy with his remaining fortune. A regular contributor to churches and charities, he left what remained of his estate for the support of free schools for the poor. He died in Philadelphia on June 17, 1801.

Lugosi, Bela (1884–1956), actor. Born in Lugos, Hungary (now Lugoj, Romania), on October 29, 1884, Lugosi became a student at the Academy of Theatrical Art in Budapest. His first acting appearances were in Budapest, where he made his debut in 1900. Within a decade he had become one of the principal actors of that city and in 1913 was playing leading roles at the Royal Hungarian National Theater in a repertoire that included Shakespeare and Ibsen. After World War I, during which he was an officer in the Hungarian army, he fled the political turmoil of his native land. Arriving in New York City in 1921, he organized a company of Hungarian actors and soon began to accept English-speaking parts. A number of important roles preceded his appearance as the vampire in *Dracula* in 1927, a role that was to have a profound effect on his career. After a successful season on Broadway the play toured for two years. In 1930, with the advent of sound films, Lugosi launched a new career as a screen star in *Renegades.* During the next 20 years he made more than 60 films, working with every major Hollywood studio and with some of the minor ones. His re-creation of *Dracula* for the screen in 1931 was a huge success, and in most of his roles thereafter, with the notable exception of that of a Russian in *Ninotchka,* 1939, he portrayed sinister characters and fanciful monsters designed to curdle the blood of his large following. Among his memorable films were *Fifty Million Frenchman,* 1931; *Murders in the Rue Morgue,* 1932; *Chandu the Magician,* 1932; *International House,* 1933; *The Black Cat,* 1934, remade in 1941; *Murder by Television,* 1935; *Mark of the Vampire,* 1935; *The Raven,* 1935; *The Invisible Ray,* 1936; *Black Friday,* 1940; *The Wolf Man,* 1941; and *Night Monster,* 1942. In 1944 he returned to the New York stage after a long absence for the role of Jonathan Brewster in *Arsenic and Old Lace.* In his later years Lugosi was afflicted with a drug addiction that hampered his career and consumed much of his large fortune. He committed himself for a cure, which he claimed was a success, shortly before his death in Hollywood on August 16, 1956. He was buried, at his request, in the cape that ever since his creation of the role had remained the mark of Dracula.

Lundy, Benjamin (1789–1839), abolitionist. Born to a Quaker family on January 4, 1789, in Hardwick, Sussex County, New Jersey, Lundy received meager schooling before going, in 1808, to Wheeling, Virginia (subsequently in West Virginia), to become an apprentice to a saddlemaker. The evils of the slave trade, which was much in evidence there, made a lasting impression on him during four years in the town. In 1816 he began to urge the creation of a central organization for the increasing number of antislavery societies—such as the Union Humane Society that he himself had founded at St. Clairsville, Ohio, the previous year—that were making their appearance in the border states. Lundy then spent about two years in St. Louis, where he had gone to liquidate his saddle business, agitating for the antislavery cause. In 1821 he launched at Mt. Pleasant, Ohio, the

Genius of Universal Emancipation, an antislavery paper that shortly was moved to Greenville, Tennessee, and after 1824 to Baltimore. In 1827 he was assaulted and severely injured by an enraged slave-trader. In 1828 he was successful in enlisting the aid of William Lloyd Garrison, who from September 1829 until March 1830 served as associate editor of the paper. Lundy then was forced to move on to Washington, D.C., and between 1830 and 1835 the paper appeared irregularly from various places. In the decade between 1825 and 1835 he traveled extensively in his efforts to find a suitable location for settling black freedmen. Convinced, as were most of the advocates of colonization, that former slaves could not live with their former masters, he traveled twice to Haiti (1825 and 1829), visited the Wilberforce colony of freedmen and refugee slaves in Canada in 1832, and between 1830 and 1835 made three trips to Texas, at that time not part of the Union. He opposed the annexation of Texas as a subterfuge to extend the domain of slavery, and his *The War in Texas*, 1836, was a spirited contribution to the controversy over the matter. In 1836 he launched in Philadelphia the *National Enquirer and Constitutional Advocate of Universal Liberty* to combat annexation, and was of considerable assistance to John Quincy Adams, who was one of the leaders in Congress of the effort to prevent Texas from becoming a state. In 1838 Lundy was succeeded as editor of the *Enquirer* by John Greenleaf Whittier and the paper became known as the *Pennsylvania Freeman*. Lundy died on August 22, 1839, in Illinois, where he had spent his last year with his family and had once again published the *Genius*.

Lunt, Alfred (1893–1977) and **Lynn Fontanne (1887?–1983)**, actors. Born in Milwaukee, Wisconsin, on August 19, 1893, Lunt regularly spent his summer vacations from school in Finland with his stepfather. Initially intent on becoming an architect, he attended Carroll College in Waukesha, Wisconsin, and Harvard briefly before accepting a $5-per-week salary with the Castle Square Theatre in Boston. His stage debut there in *The Gingerbread Man* in 1913 was followed by a few years on the road, including vaudeville engagements, before he had the opportunity to play the important lead in *Romance and Arabella* in New York City in 1917. He first saw Lynn Fontanne in 1917 in New York City, where she was appearing in the *Wooing of Eve*. Two years later they played together in summer stock, after which their careers parted briefly. Lunt was a huge success in *Clarence*, which opened in 1919 and continued with a road tour through 1921, while Miss Fontanne went to England and then returned for the lead in *Dulcy*, 1921, a role that brought her acclaim for both her beauty and ability. The theatrical career of Miss Fontanne, who was born in London about 1887, began in her early teens in *Alice-Sit-by-the-Fire*, 1905, when she was being coached by Ellen Terry. By 1909 she was appearing regularly in London and in 1910 had a short unsuccessful season in New York City. An important part came her way in *Gertrude* (London, 1914) and she joined the Laurette Taylor repertory company when they came to New York in 1916. Her work that year in a number of small parts stood out, and she won notice in *The Wooing of Eve* and *Harp of Life* before her hit in *Dulcy*. When Lunt married the star of *Dulcy* in May 1922 they had both won recognition as New York actors. After their marriage they became the most celebrated couple in the history of the American stage. Their first appearance together on Broadway was in *Sweet Nell of Old Drury*, 1923, and in 1924 they opened in *The Guardsmen* to rave notices. "They have youth and great gifts and unmistakable attitude of ascent," wrote Alexander Woollcott on opening night, "and those who saw them last night bowing hand in hand may well have been witnessing a moment in theatre history." They were rarely seen on stage apart after that, and their partnership was accepted as a matter of course by themselves and their public. They starred together in *Arms and the Man*, 1925; *The Goat Song*, 1926; *Pygmalion*, 1926; *The Brothers Karamazov*, 1927; and *The Doctor's Dilemma*, 1927. *Caprice*, in 1929, was Lunt's first appearance in London. *Design for Living*, which opened in New York in 1933, marked the first of their several successful appearances in plays by Noël Coward. Other memorable Lunt-Fontanne collaborations included *Reunion in Vienna* (London 1934); *The Taming of the Shrew*, 1935 and again in 1940; *Idiot's Delight*, 1936; *The Sea Gull*, 1938; and *Amphitryon 38*, London, 1938, and United States, 1938–1939. *There Shall Be No Night*, a play set in Finland, opened in New York in May 1940 and was in the middle of a successful road tour before it was recalled by its author, Robert Sherwood, in December 1941. The Lunts continued their success after World War II in *O Mistress Mine*, 1945; *I Know My Love*, 1950; *Quadrille* (London, New York, and many other cities, 1952–1955); and *The Great Sebastian*, 1956. They officially retired from the stage after *The Visit*, 1958–1960. Lunt also tried his hand at directing as early as 1941. He directed Helen Hayes in *Candle in the Wind* that year and the Broadway production of *First Love* in 1961. In 1965 he directed *Così fan tutte* at New York City's Metropolitan Opera and in 1966 did *La Traviata*. In 1965 the Lunts came out of retirement to tape a performance of *Magnificent Yankee* for television's "Hallmark Hall of Fame" program, for which they both received Emmy awards from the Academy of Television Arts and Sciences. In 1967 Miss Fontanne made her first appearance without her husband in almost 40 years in a television production of *Anastasia*. The Lunts received numerous honors for their contributions to the theater, including in 1964 the Presidential Medal of Freedom. The Lunts celebrated their fiftieth wedding anniversary in 1972, and when once asked if she had ever contemplated divorce, Miss Fontanne replied: "Murder yes, but divorce, no." Alfred Lunt died in Chicago on August 3, 1977. Lynn Fontanne died in Genesee Depot, Wisconsin, on July 30, 1983.

Luria, Salvador Edward (1912–), microbiologist. Born on August 13, 1912, in Turin, Italy, Luria received an M.D. degree from the University of Turin in 1935 and later studied at the University of Rome. He became interested in the study of viruses in Rome, in 1938, and he continued his research at Columbia University from 1940 to 1942. At Vanderbilt University in 1942 he began a collaboration with Max Delbrück and Alfred D. Hershey that over the next ten years resulted in discoveries for which all three were jointly awarded the Nobel Prize for Physiology and Medicine in 1969. They complemented each other superbly in their work, which took on significance for genetics when they discovered that the bacteria they were studying reproduced sexually and that the spread of the bacteriophage virus was essentially owing to reproduction that passed on hereditary characteristics. Their pioneering work shed much light on the attempt to control viruses and opened up new areas of research in genetics. Luria left Vanderbilt in 1943 for Indiana University, where he remained until 1950. He was at the University of Illinois until 1959, when he was appointed Sedgwick Professor of Biology at the Massachusetts Institute of Technology (MIT). An outspoken critic of the war in Vietnam, he donated a substantial portion of his third of the Nobel Prize (about $25,000) to antiwar groups.

Lurton, Horace Harmon (1844–1914), justice of the Supreme Court. Born in Newport, Kentucky, on February 26, 1844, Lurton was educated privately until the age of fifteen and spent two years at the old University of Chicago before enlisting in the Confederate army in 1861. He was taken prisoner twice during the Civil War, at Fort Donelson and during a cavalry raid into Ohio, but survived to enroll in the Cumberland University law school, from which he graduated in the class of 1867. He became a successful lawyer in Clarksville, Tennessee, where he practiced until elected to serve on the supreme court of Tennessee in 1886. In 1898–1910 he also held an appointment as professor of law at Vanderbilt University, the last five years as dean. Lurton had just been made chief justice of the Tennessee supreme court when he received an appointment from President Grover Cleveland to the 6th U.S. circuit court of appeals in 1893. His learning and adherence to principles of strict interpretation of the Constitution impressed William Howard Taft, presiding judge of the 6th circuit, whom Lurton succeeded when Taft became president of the Philippine Commission in 1900. When Taft became president, he took the first opportunity to appoint Lurton to the U.S. Supreme Court. Confirmed in 1910, he served as an associate justice until his death in April, 1914, in Atlantic City, New Jersey. His career on the Court had been marked above all by conservatism and by his devotion to constitutional principles, and he was adamant in insisting on the separation of governmental powers and in resisting the temptation to legislate by means of judicial interpretation of the Constitution.

Luther, Seth (1790?–1850?), labor reformer. Born about 1790, probably in Providence, Rhode Island, Luther had early schooling that he himself termed meager. Three pamphlets that he published in the early 1830s give some account of his career: They reveal that in 1817 he made an extensive tour of what was then the frontier and later returned East. He worked in the New England cotton mills that at that time were revolutionizing U.S. industry and as a carpenter, probably in Providence or near Boston. His experience made him a champion of labor reform, and he apparently spoke in many mill towns about the exploitation of child labor. His *Address to the Working-men of New England* attacking the factory system appeared in 1832 and was in a third edition by 1836; *An Address on the Right of Free Suffrage* was published in 1833; and the following year he wrote *An Address on the Origin and Progress of Avarice,* which advocated comprehensive reforms, including free labor schools and the abolition of monopolies, capital punishment, debtors' prisons, and the militia system. He was made a secretary at the General Trades Convention held in Boston in 1834 and was one of the drafters of the Boston circular advocating a ten-hour work day that was of some influence in the general strike at Philadelphia in 1835. He was one of the speakers at the National Trades Union convention in 1835. Eleven years later his presence was recorded in Manchester, New Hampshire, a textile-mill town. His forceful critique of the factory system may well have contributed to the growing social consciousness that led Massachusetts to pass a child-labor law in 1842, the first such legislation in the United States. He is believed to have died about 1850.

Lynch, Charles (1736–1796), planter, soldier, and justice of the peace. Born in 1736 at the family estate, Chestnut Hill, near the present site of Lynchburg, Virginia, which was named after his younger brother, Lynch was a prosperous and prominent landowner in Bedford County by the 1750s and became a justice of the peace there in 1766. Three years later he was a member of the House of Burgesses, where he championed the movement toward independence and later took a leading part in the preparations for the coming war. Serving in the Revolutionary army as colonel of militia from 1778, he commanded a force of volunteers at Guilford Courthouse, North Carolina, under Gen. Nathanael Greene in 1781, and remained with Greene until the surrender of Gen. Charles Cornwallis at Yorktown later that year. After the war he served from 1784 to 1789 in the Virginia senate. He is chiefly remembered for his administration of summary justice to thieves, outlaws, and Tories in his capacity of justice of the peace; the dispatch with which he handled cases is said to have led to the term "lynch law." Actually, his adoption of extralegal procedures occurred only during the early years of the Revolution, when the Bedford County courts were in disarray, and his main intent—for example, in imprisoning Tories after the Loyalist conspiracy in the county in 1780—was to support the Revolution. Thus, although his conduct was investigated by the legislature in 1782, he was exonerated on the grounds of military expediency. Lynch died at his Staunton River estate on October 29, 1796.

Lynd, Robert Staughton (1892–1970), sociologist. Born in New Albany, Indiana, on September 26, 1892, Lynd graduated from Princeton in 1914 and spent the next few years as managing editor of *Publishers' Weekly* in New York. After World War I he entered Union Theological Seminary, from which he obtained a B.D. degree in 1923; meanwhile he had begun to be deeply interested in sociology and anthropology and in 1921 had married Helen Merrell, with whom he did much of his most important work in later years. Their first joint publication appeared in 1929. Titled *Middletown: A Study in Contemporary American Culture*, it was not only a considerable popular success but also, by its application of methods and approaches derived from the study of "primitive" peoples to an ordinary Midwestern American city—Muncie, Indiana—it ushered in a new era in American sociology. Henceforth, sociologists saw themselves, to some extent at least, as anthropologists; and anthropologists recognized that, in order to do their work well, they would have to become sociologists, too. The Lynds' famous book was followed in 1937 by a sequel, *Middletown in Transition: A Study in Cultural Conflicts*, which carried the story of Muncie farther, examined such questions as the effect on Midwestern life of the automobile, and showed how Indianans were reacting to the Depression of the 1930s. Lynd worked in various research organizations in and around New York City during the 1920s, and in 1931 he joined the faculty of Columbia University as a professor of sociology, in the same year receiving his Ph.D. there. He retired from Columbia in 1960. Besides the two Middletown books Lynd also published, in addition to articles in social-science publications, *Knowledge for What?*, 1939, in which he expressed his concern about the responsibility of social science. Mrs. Lynd, who later became a professor of social philosophy at Sarah Lawrence College, published *England in the 1880's* in 1945. Lynd died in Warren, Connecticut, on November 1, 1970.

Lyon, Mary Mason (1797–1849), educator. Born on February 28, 1797, near Buckland, Massachusetts, Miss Lyon was an exceptional student at Sanderson Academy at Ashfield and later at Amherst Academy and the seminary at Byfield. Supporting herself by teaching from the age of seventeen, she became at twenty-five the associate principal at Amherst, where she also taught for three years. The next ten years were spent teaching at the Adams Female Academy in Londonderry, New Hampshire, and at the seminary at Ipswich, Massachusetts. During these years of teaching she nursed a growing conviction that the education of women, which during the early years of the nineteenth century was supported largely by individual male champions, should be institutionalized. Her success as a teacher and administrator led her in 1834 to undertake the raising of funds for a school devoted to the liberal education of women. Her aim was to make such an education available to students of moderate means, and to make it of such a caliber, too, that even the wealthy should not find better. With enthusiasm and an indomitable spirit as well as considerable tact and diplomacy she secured the necessary financial support for her plan. Mount Holyoke Female Seminary opened for classes at South Hadley, Massachusetts, on November 8, 1837, with about 80 students. It was an immediate success, and some 400 women were turned away in 1838 for lack of space. The cause of female education had entered a new era. Mary Lyon served as the principal of Mount Holyoke for 12 years, during which time the curriculum was expanded and new buildings added. She died in South Hadley on March 5, 1849, having to a notable extent changed the character of women's education during her lifetime; in after years Mount Holyoke College became one of the leading institutions of higher learning for women in the United States. Mary Lyon was elected to the Hall of Fame in 1905.

M

McAdoo, William Gibbs (1863–1941), railroad executive and public official. Born near Marietta, Georgia, on October 31, 1863, McAdoo attended the University of Tennessee for a brief period and then, in 1882, became a deputy clerk in the U.S. circuit court at Chattanooga, where he read law in his spare time. He was admitted to the bar in 1885, but his practice disappointed him and he lost money in an attempt to reorganize the street-railway system in Knoxville. He went to New York City in 1892, where he practiced law and during the next few years organized and headed two companies, later consolidated as the Hudson Manhattan Railway Company, that dug the first tunnels (the "Hudson tubes") under the Hudson River and ran trains to New Jersey. He met Woodrow Wilson about 1910 and was an early supporter of the campaign to make him president. After his election in 1912 following a campaign managed by McAdoo, Wilson appointed him secretary of the treasury, a post he held until 1918, and he was one of the leading figures in the administration, serving also as the first chairman of the new Federal Reserve Board and as director general of the U.S. railroads from 1917 to 1919, when they were being run by the government during World War I. He also successfully directed four Liberty Bond sales drives during the war. In 1914, his wife having died two years earlier, he married Wilson's daughter Eleanor in a White House ceremony. He left the cabinet in 1919 and resumed his law practice. After 1920 he was the acknowledged leader of one branch of the Democratic party, and he came close to gaining the presidential nomination at the national convention in San Francisco in that year. In 1924 he came even closer; the convention was deadlocked between McAdoo and Alfred E. Smith, and only on the 103rd ballot was John W. Davis finally nominated as a compromise candidate. Living in California, McAdoo was active in local politics and was elected to the U.S. Senate in 1932. He resigned in 1938 and died in Washington, D.C., on February 1, 1941. An autobiography, *Crowded Years*, appeared in 1931.

McAllister, Ward (1827–1895), socialite. Born in Savannah, Georgia, sometime in December 1827, Samuel Ward McAllister was the son of a prominent Georgia lawyer and bon vivant. After passing his bar examinations he went with his father to join his brother, Hall McAllister, in a law firm in San Francisco in the short space of the two years between 1850 and 1852 the firm provided Ward with enough money so that he was thereafter comfortably off. He supplemented his fortune the next year by marrying the daughter of a Georgia millionaire, whereupon he determined to devote himself to society. He bought an estate, Bayside Farm, near Newport, Rhode Island, and then spent several years in Europe practicing the social arts. He returned to the United States intent on converting Newport into the social capital of the country and making himself the arbiter of society, efforts in which he was largely successful—he gave exquisite dinners, arranged balls, and organized fêtes champêtres complete with music and dancing. By the early 1870s he was already the acknowledged arbiter of New York City society, and in 1872 he organized the Patriarchs, a group of the heads of the oldest families in the city, whose approval or disapproval of social aspirants was considered final. His most enduring creation, however, was the notion of "the Four Hundred"—the number of persons in New York society whose opinion could be said to count. There are several versions of the origin of the concept. According to one, Mrs. William B. Astor, a protégée of McAllister's in social matters, was planning a ball for February 1, 1892, and found that her ballroom would not accommodate everyone she wanted to invite. McAllister volunteered to cut the list down to the 400 that would fit into the room. According to another version, he remarked to Charles Crandall of the *New York Tribune* in 1888 that "there are only about four hundred people in fashionable New York Society. If you go outside that number you strike people who are either not at ease in a ballroom or else make other people not at ease." In 1890 he published a fascinating book, *Society As I Have Found It*, which combined reminiscences with rules for entertaining and advice on handling servants. He died in New York City on January 31, 1895.

MacArthur, Arthur (1845–1912), soldier. Born in Chicopee Falls, Massachusetts, on June 2, 1845, MacArthur went with his family to Milwaukee as a boy and was educated there. He joined the Union army shortly after the outbreak of the Civil War, becoming a second lieutenant in the 24th Wisconsin volunteers at the age of seventeen and serving with distinction throughout the war. He was promoted to major in 1864 and to lieutenant colonel and colonel the next year; his regiment gained fame in Gen. Philip H. Sheridan's division of the Army of the Cumberland and he himself was known as the "Boy Colonel of the West." Wounded three times, he was cited for gallant and meritorious service at many battles, from Perryville and Murfreesboro (Stones River) to Atlanta and Franklin (November 1864). He won the Congressional Medal of Honor (awarded in 1890) for seizing his regimental colors at a critical moment during the battle of Missionary Ridge, November 25, 1863, and planting them on the captured enemy works at the crest of the ridge. He was mustered out at the end of 1865 but reentered the regular army the next year, returning to the rank of second lieutenant, and served from 1866 to 1886 in various Indian campaigns in the Southwest. At the beginning of the Spanish-American War in 1898 he was made a brigadier general and assigned to the Philippines; his brigade paved the way for the taking of Manila shortly after. Cited again for gallantry, he was promoted to major general and placed in charge of the main body of U.S. troops opposing the insurrectionary forces of Emilio Aguinaldo, whom he defeated in 1899. In 1900–1901 he was commander of the 8th Corps of the army of the Philippines and was military governor of the islands, in that position instituting many democratic reforms. During the Russo-Japanese War of 1904–1905 he was a special observer with the Japanese army; upon his return home in 1906 he received a promotion to lieutenant general and became the ranking officer of the army. He retired in 1909 and died in Milwaukee on September 5, 1912. Douglas MacArthur was his son.

MacArthur, Douglas (1880–1964), soldier. Born on an army post near Little Rock, Arkansas, on January 26, 1880, MacArthur was the son of Arthur MacArthur, a distinguished soldier, and grew up on military posts. He gained appointment to West Point and graduated first in his class of 1903; choosing to join the Corps of Engineers, he was sent to survey and study the Philippines, where his father had been military governor a few years earlier, and other Far Eastern nations. With the U.S. entry into World War I, he helped organize the 42nd ("Rainbow") Division and, with the temporary rank of brigadier general, was its commander. He soon displayed the independence and preference for his own judgments that marked his entire career; he won the Distinguished Service Cross and Distinguished Service Medal, and at the end of the war was placed in command of the U.S. occupation zone. From 1919 to 1922 he was superintendent of West Point, from 1928 to 1930 commander of the Philippines Department, and from 1930 to 1935, a longer period than any of his predecessors, army chief of staff. In this last post he was called upon by President Herbert Hoover in the summer of 1932 to rout the Bonus Army of unemployed veterans from Washington in a much-criticized action that came to be known sarcastically as the "battle of Anacostia Flats." In 1935 he was sent to organize the defense forces of the Philippines in anticipation of the islands' independence; he was appointed field marshal of the Philippines and in 1937, rather than be transferred to other duties before his task was complete, he resigned

from the U.S. army. He was still in the islands in command of the Philippine military establishment when, in response to increasing tension in the Far East, the Philippine army was merged with the U.S. forces still remaining there in July 1941; MacArthur was recalled to active duty and placed in command of the combined U.S. Army Forces in the Far East (USAFFE) with the rank of lieutenant general. On the same day that Pearl Harbor was raided by Japanese aircraft—December 7, 1941—Japanese forces invaded the Philippines; overwhelmed, MacArthur and his men retreated into the Bataan peninsula at the entrance to Manila Bay and finally to the fortified island of Corregidor. In February 1942, two months before the garrison finally surrendered, he was ordered to leave the Philippines for Australia. Awarded the Medal of Honor and appointed supreme commander of the Allied forces in the Southwest Pacific area, he began his counter-offensive in the fall of that year and oversaw the "island-hopping" strategy that led the Allied forces slowly through New Guinea and the smaller islands toward Japan. In October 1944 he fulfilled his famous promise "I shall return"—of more than two years earlier by landing in the Philippines; two months later he was promoted to the rank of general of the army. The Philippines were finally secured in July 1945 and on September 2 of that year MacArthur accepted the surrender of Japan aboard the battleship *Missouri*. Appointed commander of the Allied occupation forces in Japan, he spent the next six years overseeing the reorganization of the government and the economy of the nation. When in June 1950 North Korea launched the invasion of South Korea that began the Korean War, MacArthur was ordered to provide assistance to South Korea. Following United Nations (UN) resolutions that provided for concerted military assistance to South Korea under unified command, he was made supreme commander of UN forces in Korea; the suddenness of the initial attack, the weakness of the South Korean army, and delay in dispatching U.S. forces allowed the North Koreans to overrun almost the entire peninsula and to bottle up the UN forces in a small area around Pusan. Carrying his plan over the objections of the joint chiefs of staff and others, MacArthur launched a daring amphibious counterinvasion of the North at Inchon in September 1950 and a few days later recaptured Seoul, the South Korean capital. The forces hemmed in at Pusan broke out and swept northward. By October they had reached the 38th parallel, the border between North and South Korea; following President Harry S. Truman's instructions, which were only later ratified by the UN, MacArthur ordered the troops to cross the demarcation line and invade the North, and by late November some units of the UN forces had reached the Yalu River, the North Korean border with Communist China. Faced with conflicting intelligence reports concerning the massing of Chinese forces just north of the Yalu and the substantial numbers of

Chinese troops already in Korea, MacArthur chose to discount the likelihood of Chinese intervention and to press on to the river in force. In late November, as the last advance was begun, the Chinese poured vast numbers of troops across the Yalu, driving the UN forces back south of the 38th parallel. MacArthur, convinced that the entry of China into the fighting meant a "new war" and that war should be carried by air directly to the new enemy, publicly disagreed with U.S. policy on war aims; ordered to refrain from public disputation by President Truman, he persisted in calling for action against China, thus risking warfare with China, and on April 11, 1951, he was relieved of his command by the president. His return to the United States was that of a hero; immense crowds greeted him in city after city, and this, combined with a stirring address to a joint session of Congress, made him a potential political figure. He retired to private life, however, retaining his five-star rank as general of the army and active status and becoming in 1959 the senior officer of the army. He died in Washington, D.C., on April 5, 1964.

McAuliffe, Anthony Clement (1898–1975), soldier. Born on July 2, 1898, in Washington, D.C., McAuliffe attended West Virginia University in 1916–1917 before entering West Point, graduating in the class of 1919. Commissioned a second lieutenant of artillery, he did tours of duty at several bases in the United States and in Hawaii. Promoted to captain in 1935, he became a major in 1940 and was promoted to lieutenant colonel shortly before the Japanese attack on Pearl Harbor in 1941 and to full colonel shortly afterward. McAuliffe was many times decorated for his bravery during World War II. As a temporary brigadier general with the 101st Airborne Division he was among the first troops that parachuted into Normandy in the Allied invasion of France in early June 1944. He immediately replaced Brig. Gen. D. F. Pratt, who was killed in the drop, as deputy division commander under Maj. Gen. Maxwell D. Taylor. He distinguished himself at Carentan and later, after the airborne invasion of the Netherlands in September, at Veghel. His greatest moment came during the Battle of the Bulge, when in command of the 101st Airborne he held the strategic Bastogne salient until Gen. George S. Patton, Jr., joined him from the south. His command was completely surrounded by the advancing German army in the Ardennes forest when his response to the enemy's surrender demand—"Nuts!"—inspired his troops to a last-ditch stand that helped turn the tide in what proved to be the last major counteroffensive in the battle of Europe. The entire division received a Presidential Citation (the first such award), and McAuliffe himself (whose reply to the Germans became celebrated) was decorated as well by the Belgian government. He later commanded the 103rd Infantry Division, whose breakthrough in Alsace and final drive for Berlin were highly acclaimed. After the war he held a number of administrative posts in the army, including deputy director of research and development, and in 1949, after a tour of duty in Japan, was promoted to major general in command of the chemical corps. He later returned to the European theater as commander of the 7th Army and was promoted to the rank of general shortly before becoming commander in chief of the U.S. army in Europe (1955–1956). He then retired to accept a post in business. He died in Washington, D.C., on August 11, 1975.

McCarthy, Eugene Joseph (1916–   ), public official. Born on March 29, 1916, in Watkins, Minnesota, McCarthy received a B.A. from St. John's University, Minnesota, with the class of 1935. He taught high school while working for a master's degree at the University of Minnesota (he received his M.A. in 1939) and between 1940 and 1943 returned to St. John's to teach economics and education. He was a civilian with military intelligence in 1944 before teaching again in high school (1945) and at the college of St. Thomas in St. Paul, Minnesota, where he was appointed acting chairman of the sociology department in 1946. He launched his political career as a member of the Democratic–Farmer–Labor party, running successfully for the House of Representatives in 1948. He left the House for a seat in the Senate in 1958, to which he was reelected in 1964. In the Senate he became a respected member of the Finance and Foreign Relations committees. A soft-spoken opponent of the intrusion of the state into the private lives of citizens, he was known for his scholarly manner, trenchant wit, and independence of mind. His opposition to the war in Vietnam as well as his concern over the growing power of the presidency led him to enter the Democratic race for the 1968 presidential nomination. His candidacy, which came as a surprise in 1967, was not taken seriously until after a strong showing in the New Hampshire primary in March 1968. The campaign that year proved to be one of the most dramatic in recent history. At the end of March, President Lyndon B. Johnson announced he would not accept his party's nomination. McCarthy's success (42 percent of the popular vote) in the New Hampshire primary may well have prompted the action of Robert F. Kennedy, also a critic of the war, who then entered the race. McCarthy lost ground to Kennedy in later primaries and, despite Kennedy's assassination in Los Angeles after his victory in California, ultimately was defeated by Hubert H. Humphrey at the strife-torn Democratic national convention in Chicago in August. McCarthy returned to the Senate, where he announced that he would not seek reelection to his seat in 1970. His seat was won by Humphrey, who had lost the presidential election to Richard M. Nixon in 1968. An occasional lecturer on college campuses who sometimes gave readings of his poems, McCarthy ran a lackluster campaign for the 1972 presidential nomination, which was won by Senator George S. McGovern.

McCarthy, Joseph Raymond (1908–1957), public official. Born in Grand Chute, near Appleton, Wisconsin, on November 14, 1908, McCarthy left school at fourteen, worked for a time, and then completed high school in a single year. In 1930 he entered Marquette University to study engineering but soon switched to law; he graduated and was admitted to the bar in 1935. He quickly became interested in politics and was at that time a Democrat but in his first successful bid for office, in which he was elected a state circuit judge in 1939, he ran as a Republican and was thenceforth identified with that party. In 1942, retaining his judgeship, he was commissioned a lieutenant in the Marine Corps and served in the Pacific theater and in the United States, reaching the rank of captain. In 1944, a year before his discharge, he campaigned unsuccessfully for the Senate; two years later he sought the Senate seat then held by Robert M. La Follette, Jr., and won a surprising victory, despite widespread rumors that he was being supported by Wisconsin Communists. McCarthy's career in the Senate was quiet and undistinguished until 1950 when, in a speech to a Republican women's club in Wheeling West Virginia, he created a furor by claiming to have a list of some large number (the figure was later disputed) of "known Communists" currently employed by the Department of State. The sensation caused by this and subsequent anti-Communist speeches of a similar tenor led to his being called to testify before a subcommittee of the Senate Committee on Foreign Relations; unable to produce proof or even real evidence of Communist affiliation or subversive actions on the part of any government employee, he was excoriated for having perpetrated "a fraud and a hoax" by the committee chairman, Senator Millard Tydings, a Democrat from Maryland. In the fall elections McCarthy and several aides carried on a secret smear campaign, later revealed, that succeeded in defeating Tydings. Despite the low esteem of the Senate, however, he won an increasing amount of popular support for his campaign of accusations by capitalizing on the postwar fears and frustrations of the nation; his position was secure enough by 1951 to enable him to attack, among others, Gen. George C. Marshall, formerly chief of staff and secretary of state. In 1952 he was reelected, although he ran behind the Republican ticket in Wisconsin, and in the reorganization of Congress he acquired the chairmanship of the Permanent Subcommittee on Investigations. For the next two years he was constantly in the public eye, investigating the State Department, the Voice of America, and innumerable individuals; although he failed to present an actionable or even plausible case against anyone, a number of persons lost their jobs or were brought into public disrepute through his efforts. He charged that the country had seen "twenty years of treason" under the administrations of Franklin D. Roosevelt and Harry S. Truman, and he finally broke with leaders of his own party to include President Dwight D. Eisenhower in his list of "traitors." His slanderous attacks on persons who were not only innocent but defenseless gave rise to the term "McCarthyism" referring to such tactics. The climax of his anti-Communist crusade came in 1954, when his committee's investigations of the army and the Department of Defense were broadcast on nationwide television. The detailed exposure of his interrogative tactics dismayed many supporters and vindicated those who earlier had spoken out against them; in August a Senate committee was appointed to investigate his activities and make recommendations, and on December 2, 1954, having lost his committee chairmanship after the fall elections, he was formally condemned by the Senate on two counts: his refusal to explain a financial transaction of several years before, and his abuse of fellow senators. His popularity and power dropped sharply and were never regained; he died on May 2, 1957, in Bethesda, Maryland.

McCarthy, Mary Therese (1912–   ), author. Born on June 21, 1912, in Seattle, Washington, Miss McCarthy was left an orphan at the age of six. Raised in Minneapolis until the age of eleven by paternal grandparents, about whose harsh treatment she later recalled nothing sympthetic, she then joined her maternal grandparents in Seattle. She was educated at private schools and at Vassar College, from which she graduated in 1933. She then began a career as a critic for the *New Republic* and the *Nation*. From 1937 to 1948 she was a drama critic for the *Partisan Review*. She was encouraged to undertake fiction by her second husband, Edmund Wilson (married in 1938, divorced 1946); her first story, "Cruel and Barbarous Treatment," was published in the *Southern Review* for Spring 1939. It later became the opening chapter of *The Company She Keeps*, 1942, a loosely connected series of stories that showed the promise that justified the encouragement of her distinguished husband-critic. She dealt with politics and utopia in *The Oasis*, 1949, and *Cast a Cold Eye*, 1950, was another series of stories. *The Groves of Academe*, 1952, which displayed her talent for satire, was followed by *A Charmed Life*, 1955. In 1956 and 1959 she experimented with lavishly photographed travelogues of Venice and Florence. *Memories of a Catholic Girlhood*, 1957, which was autobiographical, was praised over her fiction, which at its best seemed to be straining to meet her own critical standards. Her theater criticism was collected from time to time and her diverse interests were represented in *On the Contrary; Articles of Belief: 1946–1961*, a collection of 21 essays. *The Group*, 1966, which followed seven Vassar girls from 1933 through their subsequent careers, became the most popular of all her works and was made into a film. The most controversial of her writings was a series of essays on the Vietnam War which first appeared in the *New York Review of Books* and were later collected in *Vietnam*, 1967, and *Hanoi*, 1968. Her confession that she went to Southeast Asia "looking for material damaging to American interests" infuriated some critics, but others emphasized the sensitivity with which she treated the suffering of the Vietnamese and the ironies of the war. *Birds of America*, a novel about Americans in Europe, appeared in 1970.

McCauley, Mary Ludwig Hays (1754–1832), "Molly Pitcher," Revolutionary heroine. Born of German stock in Trenton, New Jersey, on October 13, 1754, Molly Ludwig lived on a small dairy farm until her father arranged for her employment as a servant to a doctor in Carlisle, Pennsylvania. She was married shortly thereafter to a John Hays who, during the Revolution, was present as a member of the 7th Pennsylvania regiment at the battle of Monmouth, on June 28, 1778. The day was a hot one and Molly, who was with her husband, assisted the artillerymen in the battle by bringing drinking water in a pitcher, earning thereby the nickname "Molly Pitcher." After her husband collapsed from the heat she took his place at his gun and served heroically for the remainder of the battle. Thereafter she led an uneventful life at Carlisle with her husband after the war. Hays died in 1789 and Molly's second marriage, to George McCauley, brought her no respite from her work as a servant. During the last ten years of her life she received a pension of $40 a year that was authorized by an act of the Pennsylvania assembly in 1822 in commemoration of her heroism at Monmouth. She died in Carlisle on January 22, 1832.

McClellan, George Brinton (1826–1885), soldier. Born in Philadelphia on December 3, 1826, McClellan won appointment to West Point at fifteen, and graduated second in his class in 1846. He was assigned to Gen. Winfield Scott's command in the Mexican War and, distinguishing himself in several actions, emerged from the war a captain. From 1848 to 1851 he was an instructor in military engineering at West Point, and from 1851 he engaged in a number of army projects, including river and harbor work and railroad surveys. In 1855 he submitted a new design for cavalry saddles that was adopted and retained for many years as the "McClellan saddle." In 1857 he resigned his commission to become chief engineer for the Illinois Central Railroad; he became vice president of the line the next year and in 1860 president of the Ohio and Mississippi Railroad. At the outbreak of the Civil War he was commissioned a major general of Ohio volunteers and a month later, upon being commissioned in the regular army, he assumed command of the Department of the Ohio. By July 1861 he had secured for the Union the territory that later became West Virginia; in that month he went to Washington to take command of the Department of the Potomac, then in great confusion since the Union defeat at the first battle of Bull Run (Manassas), and by November, when he succeeded Winfield Scott as general-in-chief of the Union armies, he had effectively organized, equipped, and trained the troops, restored morale, and made

them into a capable and eager fighting force. He hesitated, however, to undertake offensive operations, and his hesitation lasted so long that President Abraham Lincoln, losing patience, finally issued his General War Order No. 1 in January 1862, decreeing a general Union advance. McClellan delayed while obtaining permission to substitute his own plan for an approach to Richmond along the Yorktown peninsula; in March the campaign was begun with McClellan, who had relinquished his supreme command, in command of the new Army of the Potomac. He was overly cautious, consistently overestimating Confederate strength, and as the Peninsular Campaign dragged on no decisive victories were won by either side; after the Seven Days' Battles in July, in which he repulsed Gen. Robert E. Lee's all-out attack designed to be decisive for the Confederacy, he failed to press his advantage after Malvern Hill and withdrew his army from Virginia at the end of a failed campaign. Returning to Washington, he again exercised his great organizational talents in preparing for the defense of the capital, threatened as a result of the defeat of Gen. John Pope in the second battle of Bull Run. As Lee invaded Maryland, McClellan moved to meet him, but even with the advantage of having come into possession of a copy of the Confederate general's orders, he moved too slowly; instead of the overwhelming victory that was within reach, there came only the check at Antietam, after which McClellan failed to pursue the retreating Lee. In November 1862 he was finally removed from command. In 1864 the Democratic party nominated him for president on a peace platform; he had been and still was an advocate of vigorous prosecution of the war, but he nonetheless accepted the nomination and tried with little success to reconcile his views with the platform. The Democrats were soundly defeated in the election and McClellan resigned his commission and sailed to Europe for a three-year visit. Upon his return he served as chief engineer for New York City's Department of Docks, and was from 1878 to 1881 governor of New Jersey. He died on October 29, 1885, in Orange, New Jersey. *McClellan's Own Story*, an autobiographical work, appeared two years later, in 1887.

McCloskey, John (1810–1885), religious leader. Born in Brooklyn, New York, on March 10, 1810, McCloskey was the son of Irish immigrants. He attended Thomas Brady's classical school in New York City before entering Mount St. Mary's College (Emmitsburg, Maryland) in 1821, where he graduated in 1828 and continued his studies until his ordination in 1834. He went to Rome in 1835, where he studied at the Gregorian University for two years, and returned to New York City in 1837 as rector of St. Joseph's church. In 1841 he became the first rector of St. John's College, subsequently Fordham University. His diplomatic skill in ironing out difficulties at St. Joseph's earned him the confidence of Bishop John Hughes of New York, who in 1843 asked that he be made his coadjutor.

In 1844 McCloskey was consecrated bishop with the right of succession to New York. He ably assisted Bishop Hughes for three years before becoming the first bishop of the newly created diocese of Albany, New York. Although he went out of his way to discourage the appointment, he was named to succeed Bishop Hughes as archbishop of New York in 1864. His installation was marked by general approval, and without any noticeable change in the old heirarchy he was successful in quieting the competing claims of the several religious orders active in the archdiocese. A forceful administrator, he was adept in raising money for charities as well as for the renewed construction of St. Patrick's Cathedral, work on which had been suspended during the Civil War; it was finally dedicated in May 1879. He was made a cardinal in 1875, the first American to become a prince of the Roman Catholic church, an achievement that was hailed by non-Catholics as well as his coreligionists. Active until 1884, he died in New York City on October 10, 1885.

McClure, Samuel Sidney (1857–1949), editor and publisher. Born on February 17, 1857, in County Antrim, Ireland, McClure was brought to the United States at the age of nine. He worked his way through Knox College, earning his B.A. degree in 1882 and his M.A. degree in 1887. He was editor and manager of the *Wheelman*, a small publication for bicyclists, in 1882, and an employee of the De Vinne Press in New York City during 1883–1884. In 1884 he founded the McClure Syndicate, the first newspaper syndicate in the country. At first he offered reprints of previously published stories to newspapers across the country; as the syndicate became more prosperous he purchased novels from such writers as Rudyard Kipling, Thomas Hardy, and Robert Louis Stevenson and distributed them for simultaneous serialization in the newspapers subscribing to his service. He founded *McClure's Magazine* in 1893. Initially he planned to publish in it contemporary American and English literature and news of scientific discoveries and world events. Having hired Ida M. Tarbell in the late 1890s, he assigned her to write a story on the Standard Oil Company, anticipating an account of the trust's services to the public, but was shocked to receive her carefully documented exposé of the bribery, coercion, and violence used by the company to gain and hold power. He nevertheless published the story and thus launched the age of the great journalistic muckrakers. Hiring other noted journalists—including Ray Stannard Baker, William Allen White, and Lincoln Steffens—he financed their research into and reporting on nearly every aspect of American life. Subsequent articles created public enthusiasm for reform and brought about unprecedented legislative action. Advertisers, rather surprisingly, were anxious to be represented in *McClure's*, since this was considered a mark of integrity, and the magazine became far more potent in shaping public opinion than the daily newspapers. In 1906 McClure disclosed plans for a model community where he would apply his theories on social organization; this led to discontent among the staff, and Miss Tarbell, Steffens, and Baker resigned to found another muckraking journal, the *American Magazine*, in 1906. *McClure's* was sold and he relinquished his business ties. He began a scholarly retirement, writing *My Autobiography*, 1914; *Obstacles to Peace*, 1917; *The Science of Political and Historical Self-Organization, and the Influence of Human Organization on History*, 1934; *The Achievements of Liberty*, 1935; and *What Freedom Means to Man*, 1938. He died on March 21, 1949, in New York City.

McCormack, John William (1891–1980), public official. Born on December 21, 1891, into reputedly the "poorest family in South Boston," McCormack had to leave school just before completing the primary grades to help support the family. He worked as a newsboy and later as an errand boy in a law firm where he was encouraged to read for the law. Admitted to the bar in 1913, he became in time a prosperous trial lawyer and a partner in the firm of McCormack and Hardy. He began his political apprenticeship in the Massachusetts legislature, serving in the lower house from 1920 to 1922 and in the state senate from 1923 to 1926. In 1928 he was elected to the House of Representatives. He became noted for his expertise in tax matters as well as for his wit. A supporter of the New Deal, he was instrumental in the election in 1936 of Sam Rayburn as Democratic majority leader of the House. In 1940 he succeeded Rayburn in that post and at Rayburn's death in 1961, McCormack became the 45th speaker of the House of Representatives, a post that, for one year after the assassination of President John F. Kennedy in November 1963, placed him next in line of succession to the presidency. Like his predecessor, McCormack proved an able compromiser between the Northern and Southern factions of the Democratic party. He retired from his seat and the speakership in 1970. He died in Dedham, Massachusetts, on November 22, 1980.

McCormick, Cyrus Hall (1809–1884), inventor and industrialist. Born on February 15, 1809, in Rockbridge County, Virginia, McCormick received little formal education but was strongly influenced by his father, Robert McCormick, an inventor of agricultural implements who had long sought to perfect a mechanical reaper. In 1831 the son succeeded where the father had not; the principles and basic construction of this first McCormick reaper have remained virtually unchanged down to the present. Not until 1834, faced with the threat of competing inventors, notably Obed Hussey, did McCormick obtain a patent, and he kept his reaper from the market for several years more as he continued to make improvements in the mechanism. In 1844 he attempted to gain a national market by licensing manufacturers in a number of cities, but quality suffered and from 1847 he concentrated production in one plant in

Chicago. The expiration of his basic patent in 1848 signaled a burst of competition from many rivals. In the complex and protracted patent litigaions that ensued, such legal luminaries as Edwin M. Stanton, William H. Seward, and Abraham Lincoln took part. McCormick's market position was protected in part by the many improvements he had made in the reaper, which remained under patent, and the vigor with which he promoted his product, traveling the world over to demonstrate it. His showing at the Crystal Palace exhibition in London in 1851 was particularly useful. In later years he became interested in the Presbyterian church and made generous contributions to what became, after his death, McCormick Theological Seminary in Chicago. He was also active in the Democratic party in Illinois, and had diverse business interests throughout the country. He died in Chicago on May 13, 1884, and the McCormick Harvesting Machine Company enjoyed the benefits of the considerable business acumen of McCormick's wife, Nancy (Nettie) Fowler McCormick, who took charge of the firm after his death. In 1902 the firm merged with the Deering Harvester Company to form the International Harvester Company, with Cyrus McCormick, Jr., as its president.

McCormick, Robert Rutherford (1880–1955), editor and publisher. Born in Chicago on July 30, 1880, McCormick was the grandson of Joseph Medill and a nephew of Cyrus H. McCormick. He graduated from Yale in 1903 and entered Northwestern University's law school, winning admission to the bar in 1908. He was the Republican alderman from Chicago's 21st ward from 1904 to 1906 and from 1905 to 1910 was president of the board of trustees of the city's Sanitary District. With the death of Robert W. Patterson in 1910 he became editor of the *Chicago Tribune*, jointly with his cousin Joseph Medill Patterson. In 1911 he became president of the Tribune company and from 1914 he and Patterson were also the paper's publishers. He was a war correspondent in Europe in 1915, and in 1917 and 1918 was an artillery officer with the American Expeditionary Force (AEF) in France. In 1925 he became sole editor and publisher of the *Tribune*, while Patterson became editor of the *New York Daily News*, which the two had founded in 1919. A staunch and unwavering Republican, he espoused a variety of causes, including freedom of the press, big business, and nationalism; he denounced labor unions, Jane Addams and the Chicago school board, the Russian Bolsheviks, the New Deal, and the Fair Deal; and invariably he adhered to extreme isolationism, opposing U.S. entry into both World Wars, although he supported the war efforts after the country had become involved. He gave frequent public and radio addresses to bolster his aggressive newspaper campaigns. When he first joined the *Tribune*, daily circulation was 200,000; at his death it had grown to 892,058, the largest in the Midwest; Sunday circulation was 1,392,384, and the paper was the world leader in advertising

revenue. He enlarged the *Tribune's* business empire to include paper mills and forest lands in Canada, hydroelectric installations, shipping companies, radio and television stations, and publishing houses. Colonel McCormick, as he was generally known, died in Wheaton, Illinois, on April 1, 1955.

McCoy, Joseph Geating (1837–1915), cattleman. Born in Sangamon County, Illinois, on December 21, 1837, McCoy grew up in various Western towns and on the open range and may have served in the Civil War; in fact, very little is known about his early years. At the end of the Civil War, Texas had about 5 million head of cattle, most running free and many unclaimed, because their worth, in the absence of a ready market, was nil. No way of getting them to market existed until 1866, when a few cattlemen rounded up small herds and drove them overland to the Missouri-Pacific railhead at Sedalia, Missouri. The route, however, was so hazardous—with Indians, irate Missouri farmers afraid of diseased cattle infecting their own, and woodlands that drove longhorns into a frenzy—that few cared to make the drive, even for the enormous profits available. A number of cattlemen sought other markets, but McCoy was the first and most successful when in 1866 he settled on the little village of Abilene, Kansas, on the Kansas Pacific Railroad, as a new shipping point for cattle driven from the Texas range. He worked out an advantageous deal with the Hannibal & St. Joseph Railroad under which he would earn royalties based on the number of head shipped East; he bought most of Abilene and constructed stockyards and loading chutes and announced that the new market existed. By the end of 1867 some 35,000 cattle had passed through Abilene; the next year Abilene saw 75,000 longhorns shipped from Abilene, and between then and 1871 some million-and-a-half made the journey. The Long Drive over the Chisholm Trail to Abilene had many advantages for Texas drovers: it passed through open, unsettled country, and there was abundant grass and water along the way. But after 1871 the increasing settlement of eastern Kansas led to the progressive shifting westward of the terminus from Abilene to Ellsworth and then, at the head of the new Western Trail, to Dodge City. After about 1875 the obstacles in the way of the Long Drive became insuperable, and the problem was eventually solved as the cattle industry became established near the railheads in Kansas and the railroads were extended into Texas. McCoy later established cattle drives to other towns in Kansas. He served for a time as an agent for the Cherokee Nation, and he contributed to the livestock report included in the 11th Census. His *Historic Sketches of the Cattle Trade of the West and Southwest* appeared in 1874. He died in Kansas City, Missouri, on October 19, 1915.

McCullers, Carson Smith (1917–1967), author. Carson Smith was born on February 19, 1917, in

Columbus, Georgia, in a region that provided the setting for all of her later fiction. At seventeen she went to New York City to study at Columbia and New York universities and at twenty was married to Reeves McCullers. Her life after that was clouded by illness and tragedy. Repeated strokes incapacitated her for long periods and partial paralysis confined her to a wheelchair in her later years. She was left a widow in 1953. Her achievement as a writer, a career that was successfully launched by her first novel, *The Heart Is a Lonely Hunter*, 1940, was the outgrowth of her own sensitive character and, doubtless, of her own loneliness. Her fictional characters suffered from various physical and psychological handicaps that complicated their natural but often bizarre search for compassion. *Reflections in a Golden Eye*, 1941, a shorter work set in a Southern army post that chronicled the unhappy life of a captain (a latent homosexual) and his wife (a nymphomaniac), confirmed her earlier success; it was made into a film released in 1967. *The Member of the Wedding*, 1946, proved her most popular work. The sensitive portrayal of Frankie, a lonely adolescent whose attachment to her brother precipitates a crisis at his wedding, was equally successful in a dramatic version, 1950, which she herself wrote and for which she won a New York Drama Critics Circle award. Her other works included *The Ballad of the Sad Café*, 1951, a collection from which the title story was dramatized for Broadway by Edward Albee in 1963; *The Square Root of Wonderful*, 1958, another play; and *Clock Without Hands*, 1961. Mrs. McCullers died in Nyack, New York, on September 29, 1967.

McCutcheon, John Tinney (1870–1949), cartoonist. Born near South Raub, Tippecanoe County, Indiana, on May 6, 1870, McCutcheon spent his early years on the family farm and then moved to Lafayette, Indiana, when he was six; he graduated from Purdue University in 1889. In that year he went to Chicago and began to work as a newspaper cartoonist; he was with the *Chicago Record* from 1889 to 1901, the *Chicago Record-Herald* from 1901 to 1903, and after 1903 with the *Chicago Tribune* as the paper's chief cartoonist. He did his first political cartoons for the *Record* during the 1896 presidential campaign. He sailed around the world on the *McCulloch* in 1898 and was at Manila Bay during the famous Spanish-American War battle of that year, and during 1899 he toured Southeast Asia and China and Japan, returning to the Philippines at the end of the year. He went to South Africa in 1900 to cover the Boer War, hunted big game in Africa in 1909–1910, covered the Mexican Revolution in 1914, and was a war correspondent in Europe in 1915–1916. He explored Asia's Gobi region in 1925, went down the Amazon River after crossing the Andes in 1929, and crossed the Atlantic on the *Graf Zeppelin* in 1935. His cartoons, many of them political, which helped to establish the *Tribune's* editorial policy in the eyes of readers and also aided greatly in the success of the paper, were collected in a number of volumes over the years: *Cartoons by McCutcheon*, 1903; *Bird Center Cartoons*, 1904; *The Mysterious Stranger and Other Cartoons*, 1905; *Congressman Pumphrey, the People's Friend*, 1907; *In Africa*, 1910; *T.R. in Cartoons*, 1910; *and Dawson '11—Fortune Hunter*, 1912. He won a Pulitzer Prize for his cartoons in 1931. He retired in 1945 and died in Lake Forest, Illinois, on June 10, 1949. The *Tribune* continued to publish one of his cartoons on its front page every year around Hallowe'en; titled "Indian Summer," it showed shocks of corn with ghostly Indians lurking among them, and was felt by many Midwesterners to somehow typify the best and the most sentimental in their region.

Macdonough, Thomas (1783–1825), naval officer. Born on December 31, 1783, at The Trap (subsequently Macdonough), New Castle County, Delaware, Macdonough entered the U.S. navy in 1800 as a midshipman. For creditable service during the Tripolitan War he was made second officer on a Moorish prize vessel, and later served under Stephen Decatur, whom he accompanied in the daring raid to burn the captured *Philadelphia*. Promoted to lieutenant in 1807, he left the service in 1810 to engage in a private trading venture. The War of 1812 brought him back to active duty and in October of that year he was placed in command of a small fleet on Lake Champlain with orders to keep the English navy at bay. Both sides avoided a contest when they lacked the advantage, and no decisive battle was fought until September 1814. By that time Macdonough, holding the rank of master-commandant, had nursed his fleet to 14 vessels with 86 guns, while the British had 2 more vessels and a 6-gun advantage. Having lost their entire squadron on Lake Erie to Commodore Oliver Hazard Perry in September of the previous year, the British needed a victory on Lake Champlain to insure the chances of their planned invasion of the Hudson valley. On September 11, 1814, Macdonough deployed his forces at Plattsburgh Bay and in the ensuing battle there skillfully outmaneuvered and ultimately captured the British fleet for a brilliant victory that saved New York state and Vermont from occupation by British troops. The victory earned him the thanks of Congress and a captaincy. After the war his career was uneventful. While in command of a squadron in the Mediterranean he became ill and before he could reach home, died at sea on the merchantman *Edwin* on November 10, 1825.

McDougall, William (1871–1938), psychologist. Born on June 22, 1871, in Chadderton, England, McDougall received his B.A. degree in 1894 from St. John's College, Cambridge. He completed medical studies at London's St. Thomas Hospital in 1897, taking an M.A. degree in the same year, and in 1898 he became a fellow of St. John's. His interest shifting from medicine to psychology, he left his internship to participate in a Cambridge anthropological expedition to the Torres Strait, his function being to use modern scientific methods to ascertain the sensory capacity of the natives. During the expedition he also aided Charles Hose in his study of headhunters in Borneo; together they produced *The Pagan Tribes of Borneo*, two volumes, 1912. On his return to Cambridge he heard lectures by Henry Sidgwick and James Ward, and in 1900 studied the techniques of experimental psychology under G. E. Müller in Göttingen. Of prime influence on his thinking were the theories of William James, which appealed to his interest in the broad theoretical and humanistic implications of psychology rather than the precise methodology favored by the Germans. He returned to England late in 1900 as a reader at University College, London, and assistant to James Sully in the school's new experimental laboratory. For four years he conducted research in the psychophysics of vision, publishing the results of a series of experiments designed to confirm Thomas Young's three-color hypothesis of vision. Other research in mental concentration (which he identified with conscious perception) and its relation to neurological processes led to his theory that the foundation of intellectual operations is a hierarchical system of neural circuits. He argued for the merit of this physiological view over the traditional philosophical view in *Physiological Psychology*, 1905, and *Psychology the Study of Behavior*, 1912. In 1904 he became a reader in mental philosophy at Oxford, where he propounded Sir Francis Galton's methods for statistical measurement of personality traits. In 1908 his major work, *An Introduction to Social Psychology*, in which he outlined his view of human psychology as derived from the animal instincts of an earlier evolutionary epoch and as directed and modified by conscious purpose. This "hormic" (from Greek *horme*, "purposeful activity") view, though grounded in his physiological approach, conflicted sharply with the mechanistic and behavioristic theories rapidly gaining favor. In 1920 he came to the United States as professor of psychology at Harvard. In his Lowell lectures of that year, published in 1921 under the title *Is America Safe for Democracy?*, he declared the supremacy of the Nordic "race" on the basis of army mental tests and also noted class differences according to mental ability. His views were decried by the press and by many of his peers; the hostility of his opponents to both his views on eugenics and his basic anti-behaviorist theoretical bias never entirely subsided and overshadowed his significant contributions to scientific psychology. While at Harvard he also published *Outline of Psychology*, 1923, exploring the role of purpose in action, and *Outline of Abnormal Psychology*, 1926, further developing the "hormic" psychology. In 1927 he moved to Duke University as professor of psychology, furthering his investigations of whether acquired behavior characteristics can be inherited and publishing among other works *Modern Materialism and Emergent Evolution*, 1929; *The Energies of Men*, 1932; *Psycho-Analysis and Social Psychology*, 1936; and *The Riddle of Life*, 1938, on his theory of interaction between the body and soul. At Duke he strongly supported the work of Joseph B. Rhine on extrasensory perception (ESP), a topic that had long fascinated him. He died in Durham, North Carolina, on November 28, 1938.

MacDowell, Edward Alexander (1861–1908), pianist and composer. Born on December 18, 1861, in New York City, MacDowell was an ambitious, precocious child. He began music studies at an early age and after studying for several years with Teresa Carreño in New York City, he went to Paris in 1876 to enroll in the Conservatoire. He was not comfortable with French music, however, and went to Germany in 1878, where he studied at the Frankfurt Conservatory. There he found his métier, and three years later he was made head piano instructor at the Darmstadt Conservatory and began to compose with fervor. Encouraged by fellow musicians and composers, he took his A-minor concerto to Franz Liszt, who was sufficiently impressed to arrange to have MacDowell's *First Modern Suite* accepted for the Allgemeiner Deutscher Musik-Verein held in Zürich in 1882; MacDowell himself performed. The reception of this composition stimulated him to spend the next several years composing songs, piano sonatas, and symphonic poems, many inspired by the German landscape, others by legend and literature, among them *Hamlet and Ophelia*, 1885, and *Lancelot and Elaine*, 1888. In 1884 he returned to the United States, where he married Marian Nevins, who had been his pupil in Germany. He took his bride back to Germany, and they lived in Wiesbaden until 1888, when they returned to Boston. There he took private pupils, performed publicly his own works and those of others with various orchestras and ensembles, and continued to compose. Even though he had not lived in his native country for many years, he drew on American historic themes and settings for some of his finest works, including *Indian Suite*, 1892; *Woodland Sketches*, 1896; *Sea Pieces*, 1898 and *New England Idylls*, 1902. He accepted an invitation from Columbia University to head a new department of music in 1896. He formed an orchestra and chorus and attempted to integrate the musical arts with the academic curriculum, but was faced with strong opposition from conservative academicians and with the argument that talented pupils did not study in American universities but went to European conservatories for musical training. He resigned in bitterness in 1904 and retreated to his farm in Peterborough, New Hampshire. He continued to compose but made only rare public appearances before he died in New York City on January 23, 1908. After his death, his wife organized the MacDowell Colony at their New Hampshire farm for American composers, writers, and artists to use as a summer residence. MacDowell was the first American composer to gain serious attention in Europe and, although not a composer of the first rank, he left behind works of genuine merit. He was elected to the Hall of Fame in 1960.

McDowell, Ephraim (1771–1830), surgeon. Born on November 11, 1771, in Rockbridge County, Virginia, McDowell moved with his family to Danville, Kentucky, in 1784. His early education was at the seminaries at Georgetown and Bardstown before he undertook the study of medicine with a private physician in Staunton, Virginia. He attended the University of Edinburgh medical school (1793–1794) without receiving a degree and before returning to Danville in 1795 also received private instruction from a noted Scottish physician, John Bell. His skill as a surgeon became renowned in his part of the country and he regularly attracted students to his office. Although he was lax as a keeper of case histories, the revolutionary character of his surgery no doubt led him to publish, in 1817, a report of three successful ovariotomies. The first operation was consented to by a Mrs. Jane Crawford. Aware that she might not survive it, she allowed the operation to be done without anesthetics on Christmas Day in 1809—McDowell removed an ovarian tumor that weighed more than 20 pounds. Mrs. Crawford survived the ordeal and lived for more than 30 years after. Although his breakthrough in abdominal surgery was not generally recognized until much later—his own scanty reports were published in obscure journals and his letters to colleagues evoked no response—he performed at least 13 such operations, 12 of them successful, as well as 32 successful bladder operations. He also devised a radical surgical treatment for hernia; one of his patients for a hernia as well as for a bladder operation was James K. Polk. In 1819 McDowell helped found Centre College in Danville. He died in Danville on June 25, 1830.

McDuffie, George (1790?–1851), public official. Born near Augusta, Georgia, on August 10, 1790 (some authorities give 1788), McDuffie had virtually no schooling until, while working as a clerk in a general store in Augusta, he was taken under wing by the brother of his employer at about the age of twelve and sent to Moses Waddel's school in Willington, South Carolina. He later went to the University of South Carolina, graduating in the class of 1813. Admitted to the bar in 1814, he practiced law for a year in Pendleton, South Carolina, before joining Eldred Simkins in a law partnership in Edgefield. In 1814 he was elected to the South Carolina legislature and in 1821 succeeded his law partner in the U.S. House of Representatives. A noted and fiery orator, he quickly became one of the most radical advocates of states' rights. He was the principal proponent of the charge of "corrupt bargain" between John Quincy Adams and Henry Clay after the election of 1824. In debate he verged often on the violent, and he issued or received on several occasions challenges of honor, one of which resulted in a duel in which he suffered permanent injury. Vigorously opposed to the protective tariff, he later became a prominent advocate of nullification, pushing the logic of his position to embrace secession and war if necessary. The eloquence of his speech at Charleston on May 19, 1831, is often claimed to have swayed Calhoun (then vice-president under Andrew Jackson) to adopt his open advocacy of nullification. The following year he was a delegate to the nullification convention, and he was somewhat disgusted by the compromise tariff of 1833 that ended the crisis without speaking to the issue of states' rights. As chairman of the House Ways and Means Committee, McDuffie also opposed President Jackson over the issue of renewing the charter of the Second Bank of the United States. He retired from Congress to become governor of South Carolina in 1834, serving until 1836. Although his influence in the state waned after his governorship, he was elected to the U.S. Senate in 1842 but did not complete the term. In 1846 McDuffie returned, in poor health, to his home, Cherry Hill, in the Sumter District of South Carolina. His illness, stemming in part from the wound sustained in a duel during his freshman term in Congress, made his last years wretched. He died on March 11, 1851, at Cherry Hill.

Macfadden, Bernarr (1868–1955), physical culturist and publisher. Born on August 16, 1868, in Wayne County, Missouri, Macfadden, who was originally known as Bernard Adolphus McFadden, was left an orphan at eleven. His rise to prominence began in 1898, when he began publishing *Physical Culture* magazine and introduced in New York City a method of healing by physical culture that he called "Physcultopathy," the public promotion of which was later, from 1931, carried on by the Macfadden Institute of Physical Culture. Emphasizing health foods and fasting, this cult of the body had considerable success over a period of some 20 years. During the 1920s Macfadden founded or bought several pulp periodicals. The first and perhaps most successful was *True Story*, established in 1919; a popular purveyor of sex to the general public, it had a circulation of more than a million at its peak. Others included *True Romances*, established 1923; *Dream World*, 1924; *True Detective Mystery Magazine*, 1925; and *Master Detective* magazine, 1929. As president of Macfadden Publications he also brought out *Photoplay*, *Movie Mirror*, and *True Detective*, and from 1931, when he bought it from the *Chicago Tribune-New York Daily News* syndicate, until 1942, when he was forced to sell it, he was publisher of the enormously popular *Liberty* magazine. At his peak he published more than a dozen magazines and had daily newspapers in ten cities, including the New York *Evening Graphic* in 1924–1930. Never tiring in his devotion to the gospel of health, he inaugurated "Cosmotorianism," known as "the happiness religion," in 1947. Macfadden devoted a large part of his fortune to charity, including schools for poor children. In later years he was much given to stunts to demonstrate the effect of his physical culture practices; on his eighty-fourth birthday, for example, he parachuted into Paris. He died in Jersey City, New Jersey, on October 12, 1955.

McGillicuddy, Cornelius, see Mack, Connie

McGillivray, Alexander (1759?–1793), Indian leader. Born in what is now the state of Alabama in the late 1750s, McGillivray was the son of a Scottish merchant and, reputedly, a French-Creek princess (Sehoy Marchand) of the Wind Clan. Little is known of his early life. He grew up among Indians and at about the age of fourteen left his father's trading post for Charleston, South Carolina, and later Savannah, Georgia, where arrangements had been made for his education and introduction to white society. He reportedly received some training for business in a counting house and, on his own time, taught himself history. His father's pro-British sentiments at the outbreak of the Revolution led to the confiscation of his property and his subsequent return to Scotland, while McGillivray returned to his mother's tribe, among whom his education as well as his descent (which was traced through the female among the Creek) assured him a position of leadership. In 1778 he was given the rank of colonel by the British, for whom he exerted his influence as chief of the Creek to promote attacks on the frontier settlements. After the Revolutionary War he devoted his efforts to the attempt to present a united Indian front against the westward push of the white Americans that threatened both the interests of his people and his own interests as a trader. After the British retired he sought to exploit the aid of the Spaniards who, having reacquired the Floridas by treaty in 1783, wanted to establish a trading empire in the old Southwest. In 1784 he concluded a treaty with Spain on behalf of the Creek confederacy that also assured him a monthly salary for his services in assuring a Spanish monopoly of Creek trade. Throughout 1785 and 1786 Creek warriors conducted a war of attrition against settlements in Georgia and along the Cumberland in an effort to restore the Indian line of 1773 and to discourage American traders. McGillivray met with some measure of success so long as he was supplied with Spanish arms and the Americans were preoccupied with their own national problems. Repeatedly courted by the Americans, he was finally induced by the new government to come to New York City to conclude a peace treaty in 1790. The terms included a tribute of $1200 annually and the rank of brigadier general for McGillivray and the loss of some disputed lands for the Indians. This treaty was subsequently repudiated by him in an agreement with Spain in 1792, which, although it provided for a stipend triple that paid by the Americans, was motivated by other reasons as well. He died at Pensacola on February 17, 1793, before concluding the terms of an alliance of all Southern Indians with Spain against the United States.

McGovern, George Stanley (1922–   ), public official. Born in Avon, South Dakota, on July 19, 1922, McGovern grew up there and in Mitchell, South Dakota, and originally contemplated a career as a minister. His attendance at Dakota Wesleyan University was interrupted by World War II, during which he served in the Army Air Force, flew about 35 combat missions, and won the Distinguished Flying Cross. He graduated from Dakota Wesleyan in 1945 and then began graduate study in history at Northwestern University, from which he received his M.A. in 1949 and his Ph.D. in 1953; during the years 1949–1953 he taught history and political science at Dakota Wesleyan. By this time he had determined on a political career, and he left teaching in 1953 to become executive secretary of the South Dakota Democratic party, a position he retained until 1965. He was first elected to the House of Representatives in 1956 and reelected in 1958; defeated for reelection in 1960, he was named special assistant to President John F. Kennedy the next spring and made director of the Food for Peace program, a post from which he resigned in 1962 to run for the Senate from South Dakota. Elected in that year, he was reelected in 1968. He first came to national prominence in 1968, when, after the assassination of Robert F. Kennedy in June, he attempted to secure the backing of the Democratic coalition of the liberals and opponents of the Vietnam War that had supported Kennedy's run for the nomination. Failing in this—Hubert H. Humphrey was the Democratic standard-bearer that year, having won the nomination at the strife-torn national convention in Chicago in August—McGovern campaigned loyally for Humphrey but let it be known privately that he would seek the Democratic nomination in 1972. He announced his candidacy in January 1971, 18 months before the convention, and after winning more delegates than any other candidate in the various presidential preference primaries was chosen by the national convention in Miami Beach in July. The polls showed all through the campaign that McGovern was far behind President Richard M. Nixon, but he campaigned vigorously nevertheless; on Election Day, however, the polls turned out to be right, as McGovern won only 17 electoral votes to Nixon's 521, in one of the worst defeats in U.S. political history. McGovern thereupon returned to his seat in the Senate.

McGraw, John Joseph (1873–1934), baseball player and manager. Born on April 7, 1873, in Truxton, New York, McGraw began his baseball career as a pitcher on sandlot teams in his home town. After some minor-league experience he joined the old Baltimore Orioles of the American Association in 1891, staying with them when they became one of the 12 clubs in the merged National League the next year. He starred at third base all during the 1890s, when the Orioles won the league championship three times, and managed the team during part of the 1899 season. After a brief association with the St. Louis club and a largely unsuccessful season as manager of a new American League franchise in Baltimore, he emerged from the "baseball war" between the two rival leagues as manager of the New York

Giants of the National League, a position to which he was appointed in July 1902. He was a player-manager for four seasons after that, and when he retired as a player with a lifetime batting average of .334 the Giants had already won two league pennants, in 1904 and 1905, and the 1905 World Series, the first conducted under regular league supervision. Under his guidance the Giants went on to win pennants in 1911–1913, 1917, and a record four in a row from 1921 to 1924, crowning the 1921 and 1922 seasons by winning their second and third World Series. A rigid disciplinarian, McGraw earned the sobriquet "Little Napoleon." He developed a great many stars of the playing field and, through international tours of the Giants in 1914 and 1924, helped spread the game around the world. A shrewd strategist and a devoted student of the game, when he retired from his post as manager of the Giants in June 1932, his accomplishments had been rivaled only by those of Connie Mack of the Philadelphia Athletics. McGraw wrote a number of books on baseball, including *Scientific Baseball*, 1906; *How to Play Baseball*, 1914; and *My Thirty Years in Baseball*, 1923. He died in New Rochelle, New York, on February 25, 1934, and was named to baseball's National Hall of Fame in 1937.

McGuffey, William Holmes (1800–1873), educator. Born near Claysville, Pennsylvania, on September 23, 1800, McGuffey moved with his parents to the Western Reserve region of Ohio two years later. He received little formal schooling but, possessed of a prodigious memory, worked diligently to educate himself; he began to teach in a rural school at the age of thirteen and, while continuing to teach in Ohio and Kentucky, supplemented his independent studies with occasional periods under private tutors and later at an academy in Pennsylvania. Finally, he entered Washington (now Washington and Jefferson) College and graduated in 1826. The previous year he had been appointed instructor in ancient languages at Miami University in Oxford, Ohio; the awarding of his A.B. degree was followed by a promotion to professor at the university. In 1829 he was ordained in the Presbyterian church; although he never had a congregation of his own, he was a frequent and popular guest preacher. He became head of the department of mental philosophy and philology at Miami in 1832; in addition to his own teaching duties he took a great interest in improving the standards of teaching in elementary schools. In 1836 he accepted the presidency of Cincinnati College. In the same year appeared the first and second *Eclectic Readers*, the first two in a series destined to make his name famous, which McGuffey had prepared at the request of a Cincinnati publishing house; the third and fourth *Readers* were issued in the next year. During his years in Cincinnati he was instrumental in founding the common school system in Ohio. In 1839 he became president of Ohio University in Athens and remained there for four years. During 1843–

1845 he taught at Woodward College in Cincinnati, and in 1845 he was appointed professor of moral philosophy at the University of Virginia, a post he held until his death on May 4, 1873, in Charlottesville, Virginia. The *Reader* series, popularly called "McGuffey's Readers," was extended to a fifth in 1844 and a sixth in 1857 and was supplemented by a spelling book prepared by McGuffey's brother, Alexander Hamilton McGuffey, in 1846. The *Readers*, anthologies of selections from English and American literature, represented a great improvement over the textbooks then generally available to small schools; they were immediately and vastly popular, running through many editions as they were employed as standard texts for nearly a century in the Middle West. The eventual sales reached an estimated 122 million. In addition to the high intellectual level of much of the material, the *Readers* were characterized by an all-pervading emphasis on morality, although it was often the morality in which virtue and vice are immediately and materialistically rewarded and punished. *McGuffey's Eclectic Readers* exerted a profound influence on generations of Americans.

Machen, John Gresham (1881–1937), theologian. Born on July 28, 1881, in Baltimore, Machen was educated at Johns Hopkins, from which he graduated in 1901, and Princeton (M.A., 1904), Princeton Theological Seminary (B.D., 1905), and the universities of Marburg and Göttingen in Germany. In 1906 he returned to the Princeton Seminary, where he gave instruction in the New Testament. He was ordained in the Presbyterian ministry in 1914. After World War I, during which he served overseas for a year with the Young Men's Christian Association (YMCA), he became one of the leading spokesmen for the conservatives in the controversy between Fundamentalists and the Modernists that dominated Presbyterian theology during the 1920s and 1930s. A learned Christian apologist, he made his most eloquent contribution to the cause of the Fundamentalist faction in *Christianity and Liberalism*, 1923, which argued that the theological liberalism was incompatible with the historical Christian faith. His views forced his resignation from the Princeton Seminary when the school was reorganized along liberal lines in 1929. He then withdrew to Philadelphia, where he joined other Fundamentalists in founding Westminster Theological Seminary, where he became professor of New Testament. Later, his move to counter liberal tendencies by organizing, in 1933, the Independent Board for Presbyterian Foreign Missions led to his being suspended from the ministry as a schismatic in 1935. He spent his last months in organizing the Presbyterian Church of America, subsequently known as the Orthodox Presbyterian church. Machen died in Bismark, North Dakota, on January 1, 1937. His chief work and most scholarly book after leaving Princeton Seminary was *The Virgin Birth of Christ*, 1930, a second edition of which appeared in 1932.

McIntire, Samuel (1757–1811), architect, woodcarver, and furniture maker. Born in Salem, Massachusetts, sometime in January 1757, McIntire was the gifted son of a housewright. His early work in the designing of a house in Salem for Jerathmeel Peirce attracted the attention of Elias H. Derby, the most prominent of Salem merchants. Derby and his descendants remained the chief patrons of McIntire, who never strayed far from his native town. The Peirce house, completed in 1779, featured detail exquisitely copied from Batty Langley's *Treasury of Designs,* 1740, and was a modification of earlier New England houses. Massive, but balanced in scale, it stood out from its predecessors and many of its features were often copied in the vicinity. His earliest public building was the Salem Assembly House. Completed about 1782, it was replaced ten years later by his Washington Hall. The design of the Salem Court House, built in 1785 and demolished in 1839, was a good example of his early work, which culminated in a competitive design submitted in 1792 for the U.S. Capitol in Washington, D.C. After that he adopted the neoclassicism of Robert Adam that had been introduced into New England by Charles Bulfinch. The Theodore Lyman house in Waltham, begun in 1793, exemplified his new elegance. The most ambitious of his commissions for Elias Derby was a great house, known locally in Salem as the "Mansion," begun in 1794. Bulfinch made the first designs and McIntire the final ones; he also executed lavish carvings of great delicacy for the house. The mansion was demolished in 1815 to make room for other buildings, but three of the main rooms of Oak Hill, built in Peabody from McIntire's design by Elizabeth Derby West about 1801, survive in the Museum of Fine Arts in Boston. For other clients, including other Derby heirs, he produced magnificent carved mantels and other decorations. Other fine McIntire houses include those of Samuel Cook, 1804, and John Gardner, 1805. Notable among his later public buildings were the South Church, begun in 1804 and destroyed by fire in 1903, and Hamilton Hall, built around 1806. Later houses and buildings, done in brick, were not as successful. Of his carvings, including medallions, busts, and furniture in the Sheraton manner unsurpassed in their reliefs of eagles, baskets of fruit, and pendants, more than 100 pieces survive, constituting some of the finest examples of American furniture of the Sheraton style. Known in his later years as the "architect of Salem," McIntire died on February 6, 1811, having to a notable extent changed the face of his native town.

MacIver, Robert Morrison (1882–1970), sociologist. Born in Stornoway, in the Outer Hebrides of Scotland, on April 17, 1882, MacIver was educated at Edinburgh and Oxford universities, graduating from Oxford in 1907, and was a lecturer on political science, 1907–1911, and on sociology, 1911–1915, at the University of Aberdeen. In 1915 he went to Canada as professor of political science at the University of Toronto and served on the Canadian War Labor Board during World War I. From 1922 to 1927 he was head of the department of political science at Toronto and in 1927 moved to New York City to become professor of social science at Barnard College of Columbia University; he was made Lieber Professor of Political Philosophy and Sociology at Columbia in 1929. His *Community: A Sociological Study* was published in 1917 and was followed by, among many books, *The Modern State,* 1926; *Society: Its Structure and Changes,* 1931; *Social Causation,* 1942; *The Web of Government,* 1947, perhaps his most important book; *Academic Freedom in Our Time,* 1955, on a subject of continuing concern to him; and *The Prevention and Control of Delinquency,* 1966, based on his work as director from 1956 to 1961 of New York City's Juvenile Delinquency Evaluation Project. He also wrote two textbooks, *Elements of Social Science,* 1921, and *Society—A Textbook of Sociology,* 1937, and published his autobiography, *As a Tale That Is Told,* in 1968. He retired from Columbia in 1950 and from 1963 to 1965 was president, and from 1965 to 1966 chancellor, of the New School for Social Research in New York City, where he died on June 15, 1970.

Mack, Connie, (1862–1956), baseball player and manager. Born on December 23, 1862, in East Brookfield, Massachusetts, Cornelius McGillicuddy began his baseball career while working in a shoe factory. The limited space on the scoreboards that were then in use led him to shorten his name to Connie Mack, and he was thus universally known for the rest of his life. The East Brookfield team won the central Massachusetts championship in 1883 and Mack, a catcher, was signed by a professional team in Meriden, Connecticut. Through the next several years he played for teams in Washington, Buffalo, Pittsburgh, and Milwaukee. His career as a manager began with the Pittsburgh Pirates in 1894, and he continued to double as a catcher until 1901, when, under the auspices of the newly formed American League, he became manager and part owner of the Philadelphia Athletics. Mack's managing technique, based on infinite patience and respectful treatment of his players, was unique in a day when physical punishment for mistakes on or off the playing field was not uncommon. The Athletics won their first league pennant in 1902; they won again in 1905 and that year played and lost to John J. McGraw's Giants in the first official World Series. League champions in 1910, 1911, 1913, 1914, 1929, 1930, and 1931, the Athletics were also world champions in 1910, 1911, 1913, 1929, and 1930. In 1914 and again in 1933 Mack startled the baseball world by disassembling star player combinations and undertaking slow rebuilding programs for the Athletics; he became known as a discoverer and mentor of young players and numbered among his protégés Chief Bender, Rube Waddell, Lefty Grove, and Jimmy Foxx. When, during the "centennial" of baseball in 1939, a number of old-timers were installed in the new

National Baseball Hall of Fame in Cooperstown, New York, Mack was the only living one among them. His bust in the Hall of Fame was inscribed with the title that was his by acclamation, "Mr. Baseball." He retired from active management in 1951 and in 1955 sold his controlling interest in the Athletics. He died in Philadelphia on February 8, 1956, at the age of ninety-three.

Mackay, Clarence Hungerford (1874–1938), businessman and philanthropist. Born on April 17, 1874, in San Francisco, Mackay was the son of John William Mackay (1831–1902), one of the "silver kings," miners who exploited the Big Bonanza of the previously worked and abandoned Comstock Lode that between 1873 and 1878 yielded approximately $150 million worth of silver. He was educated by Jesuits in Paris and graduated from Beaumont College in England in 1892. He went to work in 1894 for his father who by that time had successfully established the Commercial Cable Company (with the younger James Gordon Bennett) and the Postal Telegraph Cable Company in competition with the Western Union Telegraph Company directed by Jay Gould. In 1884, the elder Mackay and Bennett had laid cables to Europe but the dream of a Pacific cable remained to be fulfilled by Clarence Mackay, who inherited the Commercial Cable–Postal Telegraph empire at his father's death in 1902. The transpacific cable was completed in 1903. Clarence Mackay placed a cable in service between New York and Cuba in 1907 and from Miami to Cuba in 1920. Other cables established wire communications with southern Europe via the Azores in 1905 and with northern Europe through Ireland in 1923. In 1928, he merged his communication companies, which by now included radio interests, with the International Telephone and Telegraph Corporation (ITT), thus creating the first company to combine radio, cable, and telegraph services under one management. The Mackay interests suffered severe reverses during the Depression of the 1930s. In 1935 Postal Telegraph went into receivership, although Mackay remained its head until his death, and associated companies followed suit in 1938. ITT survived the crash. Mackay, who died in New York City on November 12, 1938, had been a noted sportsman and leader of New York society during his lifetime. Harbor Hill, his Long Island estate (designed by Stanford White and now demolished) was the scene of many a fashionable party, including a legendary dinner for the Prince of Wales in 1924. A generous patron of the arts, he served as chairman of the board of the Philharmonic Society of New York, as a trustee of the Metropolitan Museum of Art, and as a director of the Metropolitan Opera Company. Beginning in 1908, he gave a total of $2 million in memory of his father to the University of Nevada to establish the Mackay School of Mines.

McKay, Claude (1889–1948), poet. Born on September 15, 1889, near Clarendon Hills, Jamaica, in the West Indies, McKay lived with his parents until he was six. Then an older brother, a schoolteacher and a lay preacher in the Anglican church, became his guardian. His brother exposed him to such writers as Huxley and Gibbons and introduced him to an English squire, an authority on Jamaican dialect and folklore, who taught him to write poetry and to incorporate dialect into it. McKay wrote two books of verse in dialect, *Songs of Jamaica*, 1911, and *Constab Ballads*, 1912, and emigrated to the United States that year. He entered the Tuskegee Institute but transferred to Kansas State College where he majored in agriculture. After two years of study he left and attempted to work as a free-lance writer. He was offered menial jobs instead. His poems, contributed to the *Liberator*, became intense and angry as he grew more aware of the inferior status allotted him as a black in his new homeland. In 1919, a year marked by race riots throughout the country, he wrote "If We Must Die." This poem, and two volumes of verse, *Spring in New Hampshire*, 1920, and *Harlem Shadows*, 1922, marked the beginning of the Negro civil-rights movement of the 1920s, and of a development in the arts known variously as the Harlem Renaissance and the New Negro Movement. One of the movement's most militant spokesmen, he encouraged his people to fight for their honor and freedom. From 1922 to 1934 he lived in Russia and Europe. His subsequent writings emphasized the distinction between blacks and whites; he sought to discover and encourage the wellsprings of a black culture and in doing so moved away from the integrationists toward a mild form of black nationalism. He became a U.S. citizen in 1940, a convert to Roman Catholicism in 1944, and worked with youth in Chicago ghettos with Bishop Bernard J. Sheil. Others among his works were three novels, *Home to Harlem*, 1928, *Banjo*, 1929, and *Banana Bottom*, 1933; a short-story collection *Gingertown*, 1932; and the autobiographical *A Long Way from Home*, 1937. He died in Chicago on May 22, 1948.

McKay, Donald (1810–1880), shipbuilder. Born in Nova Scotia on September 4, 1810, McKay moved to New York City in 1827 and became an apprentice ship carpenter. For several years after the completion of his indenture he was a journeyman shipwright, and he established a firm reputation with the building of a number of fine vessels. In 1845 he opened his own shipyard in East Boston, Massachusetts; for five years he concentrated on building packet boats, but in 1850 launched his first clipper, the *Stag Hound*. The clipper, a product of long experimentation in developing fast sailing ships and the triumph of art in marine architecture, was brought to its highest development by McKay during the next five years, where there was demand for rapid transportation to California. His *Flying Cloud* set a record for the New-York-to-San Francisco run around Cape Horn of 89 days in 1851. Ignoring widespread skepticism, he built the huge *Sovereign of the Seas*, registered at 2421 tons, in 1852 and won worldwide fame when it proved practical. The next year he began work on the largest clipper ever attempted, the *Great Republic*, of 4555 tons; although it burned before launching, it was rebuilt and became the pride of the U.S. merchant fleet. His *James Baines* set standing records for the Boston–Liverpool and around-the-world passages, and the *Lightning* once covered 436 nautical miles in 24 hours, also a standing record for sail. By 1855 the era of the extreme clipper was at an end and economic depression forced him to close his yard two years later. A trip to England convinced him of the superiority of ironclad, steam-powered vessels for naval use, but he was unable to convince the U.S. government that it should order them. In 1863 he reopened his yard to build iron ships and produced several vessels for the navy, among them the monitor *Nausett*. He was financially unsuccessful, however, and in 1869, shortly after launching his last sailing ship, the *Glory of the Seas* (which survived until 1923), he sold the yard. He died at his farm near Hamilton, Massachusetts, on September 20, 1880.

MacKaye, Benton (1879–1975), forester and regional planner. Born in Stamford, Connecticut, on March 6, 1879, MacKaye was a son of Steele MacKaye. He received a B.A. from Harvard in 1900 and a master's degree from the Harvard School of Forestry in 1905. For the next 13 years he did research with the U.S. Forest Service and between 1918 and 1922 was associated with the Labor Department in an effort to reclaim the stump lands left by the logging industry. In 1921 he proposed establishment of the Appalachian Trail, extending from Maine to Georgia. Later in the 1920s he worked with the U.S. Indian Service and with the Regional Planning Association of America, which was working upon the problem of maintaining rural regions. A prolific writer of articles for magazines and for the newspapers, he published perhaps his most influential book, *The New Exploration, a Philosophy of Regional Planning*, in 1928. Concerned with the conflict between urban industrial society and rural communal life, he urged that country life be preserved both for its own sake and as a refuge for the urbanized man seeking escape from the confusion of the city. During the 1930s and early 1940s he devoted his efforts to the overall regional planning aspects of the Tennessee Valley Authority (TVA) project. From 1942 to 1945 he worked with the Rural Electrification Administraton (REA). He was a lifelong champion of a balanced environment and of the possibility of the coexistence of both urban and rural life, and his *From Geography to Geotechnics*, 1968, explored a half-century of government land policies. He died on December 11, 1975, in Shirley, Massachusetts.

MacKaye, James Morrison Steele, *see* MacKaye, Steele

MacKaye, Steele (1842–1894), actor, inventor, theater manager, and playwright. Born on June 6, 1842, in Buffalo, New York, James Morrison Steele MacKaye was indulged as a youth by wealthy parents, educated in Paris at the Ecole des Beaux-Arts, and permitted to tinker with painting, acting, or anything that struck his fancy. He joined the 7th Regiment in the Civil War and in the regimental theater made his stage debut as Hamlet. After the war he painted, purchased and managed an art gallery, and invented "photosculpture," (a process by which relief sculpture is produced photographically) and tried to market it through a company he formed. In 1869 his father denied him further financial support. He sailed to France to study acting with Francois Delsarte, whose method involved the study of gymnastics to achieve coordination of body and voice; he returned to the United States to introduce the system, lecturing on it at Harvard and elsewhere. In New York City he acted in 1872 in *Monaldi* in a theater he had reconstructed. In 1873 he appeared in London as Hamlet, the first American to play the role in England. He returned to the United States and opened a "school of expression" for student actors. Two of his plays, *Rose Michel*, 1875, an adaptation from a French original, and *Won at Last*, 1877, were produced with enough success to finance his rebuilding of a playhouse which he renamed the Madison Square Theater. There he introduced such innovations of his own invention as artificial ventilation, overhead and indirect lighting, and the elevator stage, creating the first of the modern "intimate" theaters. In 1880, *Hazel Kirke*, the play for which he is best known as a playwright, opened at his theater and played for more than a year, a phenomenal success for the time. These profitable productions could have reaped him a fortune, but his inexperience with money matters left him often short of funds. He lost the controlling interest in his theater, but built another, the Lyceum, where he established the nation's first professional acting school, now the American Academy of Dramatic Arts. An accomplished teacher, he also wrote nearly 30 plays—others included *Marriage*, 1872, *Paul Kauvar*, 1887, and *Money Mad*, 1889—and lectured on the social aspects of the theater and the educational value of dramatic study. He received more than 100 patents for inventions in theatrical fittings, of which the best known and most ubiquitous was the folding seat. For the World's Columbian Exposition in Chicago in 1893 he proposed a fantastic auditorium, the massive "Spectatorium," seating 12,000 and containing 25 moving stages on which *The World Finder*, his epic drama of Columbus' discovery of America, would be enacted. For the production Anton Dvorák composed his symphony *From the New World*. Completion of the project was prevented by dwindling funds, and only a working model resulted. En route to California, MacKaye died in Timpas, Otero County, Colorado, on February 25, 1894.

McKean, Thomas (1734–1817), public official. Born in New London, Chester County, Pennsylvania, on March 19, 1734, McKean studied law in New Castle, Delaware, and after his admission to the bar in 1754 established a flourishing legal practice there and in Pennsylvania and New Jersey. He held minor political offices in Delaware before serving in the Delaware assembly from 1762 to 1779. He helped in the compilation in 1762 of the provincial laws (a task he was to repeat for Pennsylvania 20 years later), and in 1765 he served as a member of the Stamp Act Congress. A vigorous opponent of the Act, he used his prerogative as justice of the court of common pleas to authorize the transaction of business on unstamped paper. He eventually became speaker of the Delaware assembly in 1772–1773, exerting the influence of that office to promote support for a colonial assembly. Although he lived in Philadelphia after 1774, he represented Delaware in the Continental Congress in 1774–1776 and 1778–1783. One of the most active members of the Congress, he was instrumental in breaking a tie vote in favor of independence and was a signer of the Declaration of Independence, probably (although the date is disputed) after his return to the Congress in January 1778. He served five months as president of Congress in 1781. One of the chief framers of the Delaware constitution in 1776, he served briefly as acting president of Delaware the following year. In July 1777 he accepted the office of chief justice of Pennsylvania, a post that he retained until he became governor of Pennsylvania in 1800 and that, until he relinquished his seat in Congress in 1783, made him an officeholder in two states. His speeches in support of the U.S. Constitution in the Pennsylvania Convention of 1787 were published in *Commentaries on the Constitution of the United States of America*, 1792. In the convention of 1789–1790 he was a conservative influence in the forming of a new state constitution for Pennsylvania. During three terms as governor of Pennsylvania his administration was never free of controversy. Accused of introducing the spoils system in that state's politics, he made no secret of preferring his political friends while in office. His last gubernatorial victory in 1805 was won with support from the many factions who opposed radical democratic innovations that were being forwarded, sometimes violently, by the extremists among Republicans led by William Duane. He retired in 1808 and died in Philadelphia on June 24, 1817.

McKenna, Joseph (1843–1926), justice of the Supreme Court. Born on August 10, 1843, in Philadelphia, McKenna moved with his family to Benicia, California, at the age of eleven. He graduated from the law department of Benicia Collegiate Institute in 1865 and was admitted to the bar that same year. He served as district attorney of Solano County in 1866–1870 and later left his law office in Fairfield to serve a term in the state house of representatives as a Republican (1875–1876). His ambition for a congressional seat was thwarted three times before his election to the U.S. House of Representatives in 1884. Reelected four times, he served under William McKinley on the House's Committee on Way and Means in 1889–1890. He resigned in 1892 without complet-

ing his fourth term when he was appointed a judge by President Benjamin Harrison for the ninth (West Coast) U.S. circuit court. President McKinley brought him back to Washington as attorney general in 1897 and later that year proposed his name for associate justice of the U.S. Supreme Court. McKenna's record on the circuit, undistinguished by most standards, contributed to the controversy over his appointment, but he was confirmed in January 1898. His performance improved on the Supreme Court, although his critics continued to make the most of what was apparently a naturally slow pace in his work. Clearheaded and interested particularly in the practical implications of cases, McKenna left no opinions of enduring importance. He retired in 1925 after 27 years on the bench and died in Washington, D.C., on November 21, 1926.

Mackenzie, Ranald Slidell (1840–1889), soldier. Born on July 27, 1840, in New York City, Mackenzie attended Williams College before entering West Point. He graduated first in his class in 1862, the second year of the Civil War, and received his baptism of fire almost at once. A model officer, he distinguished himself at the second battle of Bull Run (Manassas), at Fredericksburg and Gettysburg, and was promoted to colonel of the 2nd Connecticut Heavy Artillery Volunteers after the seige of Petersburg. Wounded three times (one wound left him without some fingers) and ranking as a major general before his twenty-fifth birthday, he was a cavalry corps commander during the closing days of the war, from Five Forks to Appomattox. Praised by Gen. Ulysses S. Grant "as the most promising young officer in the army," he remained in the military after the war as a colonel. During the next two decades Mackenzie acquired a reputation as a master tactician in the field and as one of the most formidable Indian fighters in the Southwest. His success against the Indians with the 4th Cavalry in West Texas in the early 1870s opened the way to the pacification of the whole state and led to his appointment as commander of Fort Sill in the Indian Territory. In 1876 he served with Gen. Philip H. Sheridan in his campaign against the Sioux and Cheyenne Indians. Called "Bad Hand" (because of his earlier wound) by the Indians, he routed the bands of Red Cloud and Red Leaf in Nebraska, and his victory over Dull Knife in November 1876 in the Bighorn Mountains was instrumental in the final defeat of Crazy Horse. He later took part in Indian-fighting expeditions into Colorado and Utah as well as Arizona and New Mexico. More of a fighter than an administrator, he was at his best in the field. Strong-willed and courageous, he was forced by ill health to retire at forty-three. He was a brigadier general at the time of his death on Staten Island, New York, on January 19, 1889.

McKim, Charles Follen (1847–1909), architect. Born on August 24, 1847, in Isabella Furnace, Chester County, Pennsylvania, McKim, the son of a noted abolitionist, was educated at Theodore

Dwight Weld's school, in public school in Philadelphia, and for a year in 1866–1867 at Harvard's Lawrence Scientific School. From 1867 to 1870 he studied architecture at the École des Beau-Arts in Paris, and in 1870 returned to the United States and entered the office of Henry H. Richardson, then busy with the construction of Trinity Church in Boston. In 1878 he formed a partnership with two other young architects and the following year the company became McKim, Mead, and White, for many decades the nation's leading architectural firm. For several years the company subsisted on private commissions for city residences and summer homes as McKim developed his ideas on the necessity of basing sound design on classical and Renaissance precedents, a view strongly opposed to that of his early mentor, Richardson. His first monumental work, the Boston Public Library, was begun in 1887; engaging the services of John Singer Sargent and Augustus Saint-Gaudens, among others, McKim produced a model of functional planning within a thoroughly classical architectural contex. With this and his later designs, he became the leading exponent of the neoclassical revival in American architecture. In 1891 he designed the old Madison Square Garden in New York City and in 1892 the Rhode Island state capitol. In 1893 the World's Columbian Exposition in Chicago featured McKim's Agricultural Building and New York State Building, and in 1899 he designed the University Club in New York City. In 1901 he joined Daniel H. Burnham, Saint-Gaudens, and Frederick Law Olmsted in a group commissioned by the Senate to study and make recommendations for the development of Washington, D.C. He was primarily responsible for the central area around the Capitol and made the preliminary sketches for the Lincoln Memorial, which were elaborated later by one of his associates. During 1902–1903 he supervised the faithful restoration of the White House. In subsequent years his outstanding works included several buildings on the Morningside Heights campus of Columbia University, the Pierpont Morgan Library, and Pennsylvania Station, all in New York City. Throughout his life he was deeply interested in improving the training available to young artists in several fields; his own office was an excellent school for those whose field was architecture, and from 1894 onward he supported and supervised his major contribution to the future of American art, the American Academy in Rome. McKim retired in 1908 and died a year later, on September 14, 1909, at St. James, Long Island, New York.

McKinley, John (1780–1852), justice of the Supreme Court. Born on May 1, 1780, in Culpeper County, Virginia, McKinley grew up in Kentucky, where he later became a practicing lawyer in Frankfort and in Louisville. He began his political career in Alabama, having moved to Huntsville about 1818, as a member of the state legislature in 1820. He lost an extremely close race for a vacant Senate seat in 1822 but succeeded four years later, as a Jacksonian Democrat, in winning a Senate seat. He made an unsuccessful bid for reelection in 1830 and then entered the state legislature in 1831. Elected to the U.S. House of Representatives in 1832, he declined to run for a second term and in 1836 won a virtually uncontested election for the Senate. McKinley, who had been a loyal supporter of Andrew Jackson since 1824 and of Jackson's choice of Martin Van Buren to head the Democratic ticket in 1836, was rewarded, when Van Buren proved victorious, with an appointment to the Supreme Court; he was confirmed as an associate justice of the Supreme Court in April 1837. He served until his death in Louisville, Kentucky, on July 19, 1852.

McKinley, William (1843–1901), twenty-fifth president of the United States. Born in Niles, Ohio, on January 29, 1843, McKinley studied for a year at Allegheny College before illness and his family's limited means curtailed his formal education. For a time he taught school and in 1861 he enlisted in an Ohio volunteer regiment of the Union army. He served with distinction, performing notably at Antietam and seeing action also at South Mountain, Fisher's Hill, and Cedar Creek; became an aide to Col. Rutherford B. Hayes; and at the time of his discharge in 1865 held the rank of major. He took up the study of law, first privately in Youngstown, Ohio, and then for a year at the Albany (New York) Law School, and began practice in 1867 in Canton, Ohio. He was soon involved in politics and in 1876 was elected as a Republican to the House of Representatives, where, except for one term, he remained until 1891. An ardent advocate of the protective tariff, he employed his position as chairman of the Committee on Ways and Means during his final term to secure passage in 1890 of what soon became known as the McKinley Tariff Act; popular reaction against this measure led to a sweeping victory for the Democratic party in the 1890 election and McKinley was one of many Republican victims. His reputation was nonetheless secure in Ohio and was growing steadily on the national scene. With the aid of Mark Hanna, a Cleveland businessman who was rich, Republican, and an incomparable political manager, he was elected governor of Ohio in 1891 and again in 1893. In 1896 he was chosen by the Republicans to oppose William Jennings Bryan in a presidential campaign fought mainly over the issue of free silver. He remained relatively passive while Hanna, as chairman of the Republican National Committee, organized the nation's business interests; representing the conservative, pro-tariff, antisilver position, McKinley was elected by a substantial margin. The record-high Dingley Tariff passed by Congress early in 1897 marked the beginning of what might have been a quiet Republican administration; the following year, however, the continuing insurrection against the Spanish colonial government in Cuba began to capture public attention, and a series of incidents culminating in the sinking of the U.S. battleship *Maine* in Havana harbor on February 15 with a loss of 260 lives, along with a great deal of sensational journalism in the "yellow press," created a wave of war hysteria. McKinley attempted to soothe a rankled public and Congress with diplomacy, securing several concessions from Spain that, a few weeks earlier, might well have satisfied the pro-Cuban faction, but finally he gave Congress its head; war was effectively declared on April 20 when a joint congressional resolution called for U.S. intervention to secure Cuban independence. This limited aim was quickly forgotten as the first victory of the war that had been formally declared by the U.S. on April 25 came with the destruction of the Spanish fleet at Manila Bay on May 1, and the subsequent capture of the Philippine Islands by the Pacific fleet commanded by Com. George Dewey. Santiago, Cuba, was taken in July, after the destruction of the Spanish home fleet, and in August hostilities ceased. With the signing of the peace treaty in December 1898 and its ratification in February 1899, the United States was suddenly in possession of an empire—Cuba, Puerto Rico, Guam, and the Philippines—and McKinley faced unforeseen problems, not the least of which was a continuing struggle for independence in the Philippines, requiring the use of U.S. armed forces there until 1901. The annexation of Hawaii in 1898 and of Wake Island and American Samoa in 1899 made the United States a full-fledged Pacific power. Thus McKinley's secretary of state, John Hay, could take the initiative in issuing his Open Door policy toward China and thus it was too that U.S. troops played a major role in putting down the Boxer Rebellion in China in 1900. As the details of colonial administration were slowly being worked out, imperialism was becoming a partisan issue. In the election of 1900 the Democrats, while retaining their free-silver plank and the candidacy of Bryan, gave priority to the issue; McKinley, his campaign again directed by Hanna, was reelected despite a considerable amount of anti-imperialist disaffection within his own party. Garret Hobart, his first-term vice-president, had died in 1899, and into the vacancy came Theodore Roosevelt, nominated largely at the behest of New York Republicans who hoped thereby to sidetrack a rising political figure with disturbingly reformist ideas. Soon after beginning his second term, McKinley found confirmation for his colonial policies when the Supreme Court decided in the first of the Insular Cases that the Constitution did not necessarily follow the flag: Guam, Puerto Rico, and the Philippines were declared to be not within the area of free trade. There is reason to suspect that before his death the president was moving away from his firm belief in protection toward a position favoring freer, if not free, trade. Before he was able to elaborate any new views to the nation, however, he was shot by Leon Czolgosz, an anarchist, while visiting the Pan-American Exposition in Buffalo, New York. He died in Buffalo eight days later, on September 14, 1901.

McKuen, Rod Marvin (1933–   ), singer, composer, and poet. Born in Oakland, California, on April 29, 1933, McKuen never knew his father, received very little schooling, and worked at odd jobs in several Western states after leaving home at about the age of eleven. At sixteen he went to work as a disc jockey for an Oakland radio station. His late-night program addressed to teenagers, "Rendezvous with Rod," became popular in the San Francisco Bay area; its success for more than three years was largely owing to his practice of also giving advice to the lovelorn. Serving in the army from 1953 to 1955, he worked for the Special Services branch in Tokyo before serving in Korea. His experience in Korea led to his *Elephants in the Rice Paddies*, 1954, a book whose disparagement of the army made it unavailable in the United States. He also launched his career as a poet that year with *And Autumn Came*. Returning to the San Francisco Bay area after his discharge in 1955, he sang in a night club in San Francisco (the first songs of his composing date from this period) before landing a two-year contract with the Universal studios in Hollywood. In 1959 he went to New York City, where he worked as a composer for television and began to attract attention as a singer. His first song hit, "Mister Oliver Twist," with lyrics by Gladys Shelly, was promoted by a nationwide singing tour at bowling alleys in 1961. McKuen first attracted a large following in France in the early 1960s, where he perfected his singing style under the influence of several French singers, including Jacques Brel, and where one of his later record albums, in English, won the Grand Prix du Disque in 1966. In the United States he captured the popular imagination following the release of a musical version of some of his poems ("The Lonely Things") recorded by Glen Yarbrough. In the late 1960s and early 1970s McKuen enjoyed a huge success as a popular poet and *chansonnier*. His book *Stanyon Street and Other Sorrows*, 1966, sold well, as did *Listen to the Warm*, 1967, and *Lonesome Cities*, 1968. Other collections followed and together his books had sold more than 2 million copies by the early 1970s in a country not noted for its purchase of books of poetry. Some 50 records had equal success. McKuen continued to write film scores—*Joanna*, 1968, and *The Prime of Miss Jean Brodie*, 1969— and other works, including a concerto for four harpsichords.

McLaren, Daniel, *see* Rice, Dan

McLean, John (1785–1861), justice of the Supreme Court. Born on March 11, 1785, in Morris County, New Jersey, McLean had little early schooling because of frequent moves by his family to frontier farmlands. The family eventually settled near Lebanon, Ohio, and at the age of eighteen he went to Cincinnati as an indentured court clerk and read law in the office of an attorney there. Returning to Lebanon after being admitted to the bar in 1807, he ran a successful law practice and launched the *Western Star*, a weekly, before his election to the House of Representatives in 1812 as a Democrat. Reelected in 1814, he resigned in

1816 to accept a post as a judge of the Ohio supreme court. In 1822 he left the Ohio bench to become commissioner of the U.S. General Land Office under President James Monroe. When Monroe appointed him postmaster general in 1823 he began reforms that during a five-year administration changed the postal system from a disorderly haven for incompetent officials to an efficient operation based on merit appointments and economy. McLean's policy of nonpartisan appointments led to a conflict of views with President Andrew Jackson, whose open advocacy of the spoils system threatened McLean's recent reorganization. Unwilling to make political appointments, he resigned in 1829 to accept an appointment to the Supreme Court, where he served as associate justice for 31 years. Noted, when on circuit, for his charges to grand juries, he was an effective jurist, seldom reversed, forceful, and devoted to duty. His most celebrated opinion while on the court was his dissent in the Dred Scott case in 1857, in which he contended that the "peculiar institution" of slavery had no abstract legal sanction and was rooted in force and upheld only by local law. Mentioned as a presidential candidate as early as 1831, he was prominent at the Free-Soil party's convention in Buffalo in 1848 and at the first Republican national convention in 1856 he was the principal opponent of John C. Frémont, garnering 196 votes to Frémont's 259. He died in Cincinnati on April 4, 1861.

MacLeish, Archibald (1892–1982), poet and public official. Born in Glencoe, Illinois, on May 7, 1892, a member of a wealthy Midwestern mercantile family, MacLeish was educated at private schools, at Yale, from which he graduated in 1915, and at the Harvard Law School, from which he received his Ll.B. in 1919. After World War I army service overseas in 1917–1918, he practiced law for three years, from 1920 to 1923, but then turned to poetry full time. During the 1920s an expatriate, living in Paris and other European cities and moving in a literary circle that included Ernest Hemingway, F. Scott Fitzgerald, Gertrude Stein, and others, he published several books of poetry, among them *The Happy Marriage*, 1924; *Streets in the Moon*, 1926; and *The Hamlet of A. MacLeish*, 1928, that showed the influence, then extremely fashionable, of Ezra Pound and T. S. Eliot. In 1928 he returned to the United States, became a writer for *Fortune* magazine in 1930, and published another book, *New Found Land*, 1930, whose simple lyric eloquence and deep patriotism sounded a note that came to be typical of him thereafter. In the 1930s he became deeply concerned about the threats to American society and to world democracy posed particularly by Fascism. *Conquistador*, 1932, dealing with the Spanish conquest of Mexico, was the first of his "public" poems and won him the first of three Pulitzer Prizes. Other works from these years during which he protested against what he considered the country's blindness to its real peril, were *Frescoes for Mr. Rockefeller's City*, 1933; *The Fall of the City*, 1937; *Public Speech*, 1936, *Air Raid*, 1938;

America Was Promises, 1939 (the use of the past tense in the title was intended to shock readers into an awareness of their condition); and *The Irresponsibles*, 1940. In 1939 he was named Librarian of Congress, serving until 1944; he also performed other public duties during the World War II years, and was assistant secretary of state in 1944–1945. He aided in the foundation of the United Nations Educational, Scientific, and Cultural Organization (UNESCO) and, in the years after World War II, continued to speak out in defense of American democracy. Among his most notable works of the postwar years were *Act Five and Other Poems*, 1948, and *Collected Poems 1917–1952*, 1952, which won both a Pulitzer Prize and a National Book Award. *J. B.*, 1958, a biblical allegory in verse, not only won a Pulitzer Prize for drama but also enjoyed a triumphant production on Broadway. He taught at Harvard from 1949 to 1962 and at Amherst from 1964 to 1967. His book of poems, *The Wild Old Wicked Man*, appeared in 1968 and his play, *Scratch*, in 1971. He died in Boston on April 20, 1982.

McLoughlin, John (1784–1857), fur trader. Born in Rivière du Loup, Quebec, in 1784, McLoughlin studied medicine in Scotland and returned to Canada to enter the service of the North West Company, of which he became a partner in 1814. Following a merger with the Hudson's Bay Company in 1821 he was placed in charge of that company's fur trade in the Columbia River department, a region that included what are now the states of Washington and Oregon and that had been abandoned by John Jacob Astor's American Fur Company since the War of 1812. Under "Dr. McLoughlin" as chief factor, the Hudson's Bay Company erected, in 1825, Fort Vancouver at present-day Vancouver, Washington; the fort became the wilderness metropolis of the vast Oregon country and for all practical purposes constituted the only white settlement of the region until 1834. Despite agreement between England and the United States that their nationals could engage in commerce in the disputed Oregon country without prejudice to either nation's land claims, McLoughlin's control of the Indian trade thwarted the efforts of U.S. traders to break the British monopoly. On the other hand he was constantly under criticism from his company for providing material assistance to U.S. settlers, who began arriving in increasing numbers after 1840; his cordial reception and initial aid to the first group of missionaries to Oregon led by Jason Lee in 1834 had helped sustain that venture, and his extension of credit to other settlers who survived the ordeal of the Oregon Trail gained him a number of friends who later proved valuable. He did, however, strongly discourage U.S. settlement north of the Columbia River. The Hudson's Bay Company's hope that the Columbia River would eventually become the national boundary between Canada and the United States was thwarted by the agreement of 1846 that established the boundary at the 49th parallel. His efforts had not served to quiet the criticism of his superiors, and he retired from the company in 1846. The company was then forced to move its headquarters to Vancouver Island, by then British, McLoughlin remaining to develop a town at the falls of the Willamette River on land that originally had been staked out under the auspices of the Hudson's Bay Company but that he now claimed as his own. The venture involved him in a controversy with Americans who felt he was still pursuing British interests. Although supported by American friends (Oregon became a territory in 1848), his claim to the land filed with the provisional government of Oregon was denied under the Donation Land Act of 1850. McLoughlin accommodated himself reasonably well under the circumstances, but the land ownership remained an issue until after his death on September 3, 1857. Rights to the land were restored to his heirs for a nominal fee by the state government in 1862, Oregon having been admitted to the Union in February 1859.

McMaster, John Bach (1852–1932), historian. Born on June 29, 1852, in Brooklyn, New York, McMaster graduated from the College of the City of New York (CCNY) in 1872. He taught English there for a year, worked at mapmaking for another year, and from 1874 to 1877 was a practicing engineer, publishing during that period works on bridge and dam construction. In 1877 he accepted a post as instructor in engineering at the College of New Jersey (now Princeton). While still at Princeton he began to carry out an earlier resolve to write a history of the United States. The first volume was completed in 1881; its publication two years later brought him immediate recognition as an innovator in historical writing and an offer to continue the work while teaching at the University of Pennsylvania. Appointed professor of American history at Pennsylvania in 1883, he remained with that institution until his retirement in 1920. *Volumes of The History of the People of the United States from the Revolution to the Civil War*, to be his principal work, continued to appear, the second of eight volumes in 1885 and the last in 1913. A pioneer in placing emphasis on the social and economic forces that influenced the course of events, he originated a genre of historical writing that is still practiced. His ingenuity in interpreting contemporary sources as well as his talent for narrative made his textbooks widely popular in primary and secondary schools throughout the United States. Among his other works were *Benjamin Franklin as a Man of Letters*, 1887; *With the Fathers*, 1896; *The Struggle for Social, Political and Industrial Rights of Man*, 1903; and *The United States in the World War*, two volumes, 1918–1920. After his retirement he supplemented his magnum opus by *A History of the People of the United States During Lincoln's Administration*, 1927. MacMaster died in Darien, Connecticut, on May 24, 1932, having made a notable impact on historical studies during his lifetime.

McMillan, Edwin Mattison (1907–   ), physicist. Born in Redondo Beach, California, on September 18, 1907, McMillan earned a B.A. in 1928 and M.A. in 1929 at the California Institute of Technology (Caltech), and three years later took a doctorate in physics from Princeton University. From 1932, with the exception of the World War II years, he was associated with the University of California at Berkeley, where he became preeminent in the field of high-energy physics. From 1934 he was a member of the staff of the radiation laboratory at Berkeley, of which he became associate director in 1954 and director in 1958. The years 1932–1935 were devoted wholly to research. He joined the Berkeley faculty as an instructor in 1935 and a year later advanced to associate professor. In the spring of 1940 his research led him to the discovery that uranium, when bombarded by neutrons, could be transformed into neptunium (element 93), and the following year, with the help of Glenn T. Seaborg, he succeeded in isolating plutonium (element 94). This work was interrupted by the urgent need to develop effective radars and sonars for World War II, and in 1942 he assisted in establishing the atomic-energy laboratory at Los Alamos, New Mexico, that produced the first atomic bombs. In 1946 he returned to Berkeley as a full professor. In 1951 he shared the Nobel Prize for Chemistry with Seaborg for his work on the discovery of the first transuranium elements. After the war his conception of the synchroton, a machine for accelerating electrons to very high energies, developed independently and nearly simultaneously by Russian physicist Vladimir I. Veksler, represented a great improvement over the cyclotron and made possible notable advances in the study of fundamental particles. In 1963 he shared the Atoms for Peace award with Veksler. The recipient of numerous other awards, he also served as chairman in 1966 of the 13th international conference on high-energy physics.

Macon, Nathaniel (1758–1837), public official. Born on December 17, 1758, at Macon Manor in what is now Warren County, North Carolina, Macon attended the College of New Jersey (now Princeton) for two years 1774–1776, and then studied law in North Carolina. During 1776–1777 he served with the New Jersey militia. Enlisting again in 1780, he served as a private during the Revolution and then reluctantly began a political career in the North Carolina senate, where he remained until 1785. Unwilling to serve in the Continental Congress in 1786, he later opposed the calling of the Federal Constitutional Convention and the proposed Constitution, but nonetheless accepted his election to the House of Representatives in 1791, where, in time, he became speaker, 1801–1807. He remained in the House as an important leader of the Democratic Republican forces until elected in 1815 to the Senate, where he served for two terms, the last two years of service as that body's president pro tempore. From the beginning of his career in the House he opposed the Federalists and later remained on close terms with Thomas Jefferson, whose presidential term coincided with Macon's as House speaker. Despite an exaggerated fear of extending the powers of the central government and an equal reluctance to spend government money, he supported Jefferson in carrying out the Louisiana Purchase. In 1810 the House committee on foreign relations, of which Macon was then chairman, reported a bill, subsequently passed, that empowered the president to revive the nonintercourse policy against either Britain or France should the other nation cease its interference with U.S. shipping. The bill became known as "Macon's Bill No. 2," although he himself opposed it. Although he was opposed to building a navy as well as to conscription and the taxes needed to wage war, he voted for the declaration of war against England in 1812. After the war his parochialism became even more marked; he opposed building roads and canals, the rechartering of the Bank of the United States, and the protective tariff. Outspoken in the defense of slavery, he voted against the Missouri Compromise in 1820 and was loath to see Andrew Jackson, although a friend, become president in 1828. In 1824 he received the electoral vote of Virginia for the vice-presidency and in 1828 he retired from the Senate, noted for integrity and hard work, and with a reputation for opposition to a host of measures that subsequent events proved to be with the tide of the nation's development. In 1835 he voted against his state's revised constitution after serving as president of the convention that drafted it. He died at Buck Spring, his home in Warren County, North Carolina, on June 29, 1837.

McParlan, James (1844–1919), detective. Born in Ulster in northern Ireland in 1844, McParlan emigrated to the United States in 1863. He made his way to Chicago, where he drove a wagon team for a coal company. In the early 1870s he joined the Pinkerton National Detective Agency, whose headquarters were in Chicago. When Franklin Gowen, president of the Philadelphia and Reading Railroad and of its coal and iron subsidiary, went to the agency for help in crushing the secret society known as the Molly Maguires, violent labor agitators who had adopted the label "Molly Maguires" from an Irish land-reform group of 20 years before and who, since about 1862, had enforced a reign of terror in the anthracite-mining region of eastern Pennsylvania, Allan Pinkerton sent McParlan. Working among the Irish Catholics of the area in 1873, he gained admission to the fraternal Ancient Order of Hibernians, some of whose lodges were under the control of the Mollies. Gaining the confidence of the local Molly leaders, he made daily reports of their activities, which included sabotage against coal operators and, occasionally, murder. A series of sensational trials followed in 1876–1877, and McParlan's testimony was instrumental in gaining more than 60 convictions, including those of 11 of 19 men who were eventually hanged. Pinkerton's account of the matter appeared in *The Molly Maguires and the Detectives*, 1877, and Sir Arthur Conan Doyle contributed to McParlan's legendary status as a detective by making his exploit the

subject of a melodramatic story, *The Valley of Fear*, 1915. McParlan later became head of the Denver branch of the Pinkerton agency, which at the turn of the century was involved in the suppression of the Western Federation of Miners (WFM) in Idaho. In 1905, one of the disaffected miners assassinated a former governer of Idaho, Frank Steunenberg. McParlan added to his fame by obtaining the confession of Harry Orchard, who falsely implicated several prominent members of the WFM and of the Industrial Workers of America (IWW) including Big Bill Haywood. McParlan died in Denver on May 19, 1919.

McPherson, Aimee Semple (1890–1944), evangelist. Born on October 9, 1890, near Ingersoll, Ontario, Sister Aimee, as she was called by her followers, was married first to a Pentecostal evangelist, Robert Semple, with whom she did missionary work in China. After his death she returned to the United States and later married Harold McPherson. Her marriage ended when she decided to devote her life to preaching and healing. She traveled through the United States, England, Canada, Australia, and other countries, finally settling in 1918 in Los Angeles, penniless but with a large following. She founded a religious movement that she called the International Church of the Four-Square Gospel, a name derived from her vision of heaven with four walls. Based on tenets of hope and salvation for the needy, it especially appealed to migrant Southerners and Midwesterners who found themselves frustrated by the complexities of life in Southern California. Her adherents provided the funds to build the huge Angelus Temple in Los Angeles, where her sermons were heard and broadcast simultaneously over the radio station she had also purchased. Sunday services at the temple were attended by thousands of worshipers, who sat spellbound throughout extravaganzas that included patriotic and quasi-religious music played by a 50-piece band, the breathtaking entrance of Sister Aimee, prayers, and singing, all climaxed by a dramatic sermon. Theologically a Fundamentalist, she based much of the appeal of her movement on faith healing, adult baptism by immersion, and a pervading aura of optimism and spectacle. She compiled a book of sermons, *This Is That*, 1923, and wrote *In the Service of the King*, 1927, and *Give Me My Own God*, 1936. She frequently made newspaper headlines, most notably in 1926, when she disappeared for a time (she claimed to have been kidnapped), and she was accused of a number of improprieties, but none was proved and none detracted from her following. She died on September 27, 1944, in Oakland, California, from an overdose of sleeping powders. Her son Rolf McPherson continued the movement.

McReynolds, James Clark (1862–1946), justice of the Supreme Court. Born on February 3, 1862, in Elkton, Kentucky, McReynolds was valedictorian of the class of 1882 at Vanderbilt University in Nashville, Tennessee. After a year of graduate study at Vanderbilt he obtained a law degree from the University of Virginia in 1884. He began law practice that same year in Nashville after a short interval in Washington as secretary to Senator Howell E. Jackson of Tennessee. Recognized locally as an able lawyer, he became known as an expert in corporation law and in 1900 returned to Vanderbilt as professor of law, insurance, and corporations. He began his political career with an unsuccessful bid for the House of Representatives as a "Gold Democrat" in 1896. In 1903 he went to Washington, D.C., as an assistant attorney general, serving in that post until 1907, when he was named a special counsel to act as chief prosecutor of the government's case against the tobacco trust. He won a notable victory and emerged with a reputation as a trustbuster. A nonsmoker, he regarded the American Tobacco Company as a gang of "commercial wolves and highwaymen." He resigned as special counsel early in 1912 but in 1913 was appointed attorney general by President Woodrow Wilson; in that post he continued to invoke the Sherman Antitrust Act, proceeding against the railroads, the American Telegraph and Telephone Company (AT&T), and the National Wholesale Jewelers' Association among others. He proved, however, a controversial member of the cabinet and Wilson named him to the Supreme Court in 1914. His long career on that bench marked him as a strict constructionist of the powers of the government under the Constitution, an advocate of laissez-faire economics, and a tenacious dissenter against virtually all the innovations of the New Deal, concerning which his comments grew increasingly bitter. His dislike of President Franklin D. Roosevelt led him to boycott receptions at the White House after 1933, and he was the central target of Roosevelt's "court-packing" scheme of 1937. Known as the "Lone Dissenter" during his last years on the Court, he retired in 1941, having opposed going off the gold standard (his eloquent but violent dissent in 1935 was toned down in the official reports) and social-security measures, and was the only dissenter against the constitutionality of the Tennessee Valley Authority (TVA). He died in Washington, D.C., on August 24, 1946.

McTammany, John (1845–1915), inventor. Born near Glasgow, Scotland, on June 26, 1845, Mc-Tammany early had an ambition to become a pianist but was thwarted by his parents' poverty. He received little schooling and worked at odd jobs before joining his father in Uniontown, Ohio, in 1862. Seriously wounded while fighting in the Civil War, he conceived the idea of a mechanical player piano while repairing a music box during his convalescence. His facility with machines led him to master his conception quickly after the war, but he spent a great deal of time on the construction of three protopyes before his first public exhibition of the instrument in St. Louis in 1876. Much of the rest of his life was devoted to attempts to market his invention and to costly litigation to defend his rights against

pirates. More than once reduced to poverty, he finally obtained a patent in 1881, but eventually lost control of his manufacturing company. A voting machine, also employing a perforated roll, on which he received a patent in 1892, was the first such equipment ever employed in an election, but once again he was unable to translate his ingenuity into a commercial success. He died a pauper and a broken man at the Stamford, Connecticut, military hospital on March 26, 1915. He was honored by a public funeral, the accompanying music for which was performed by a grand player piano.

Macy, Anne Mansfield Sullivan, see under Keller, Helen Adams

Madison, James (1751–1836), fourth president of the United States. Born in Port Conway, Virginia, on March 16, 1751, Madison came of a moderately wealthy family of Virginia planters. He was educated at the College of New Jersey (now Princeton) and continued his studies for a year beyond his graduation in 1771. He returned home in 1772 and two years later began his long political career by being chosen a member of his county's Committee of Safety. In 1776 he was elected to the Virginia constitutional convention and became ex officio a member of the first state legislature the following year. His prominence in the convention, where he fought for the establishment of complete freedom of religion, secured him a place on the governor's council early in 1778 and he remained in that body until his election nearly two years later to Congress under the Articles of Confederation. During his single term, 1780–1783, he became an outspoken advocate of revision of the Confederation in order to strengthen the central government. During 1784–1786 he was a member of the Virginia House of Delegates, where again he spoke for the establishment of complete religious freedom, introducing and securing passage of Thomas Jefferson's bill to that end. Beginning in 1785 he proposed a series of interstate conferences that led to the Annapolis Convention of 1786 and culminated in the Federal Constitutional Convention the next year. At the Convention he was a dominant figure; a number of proposals for an effective central government, outlined by him in a letter to George Washington in April 1787, became the basis of the "Virginia Plan" introduced by Edmund Jennings Randolph. Madison managed the Convention with great skill, was responsible for many of the crucial compromises, and all the while diligently kept the only nearly complete record of the proceedings and deliberations. As a consequence of his efforts, he is often called the "father of the Constitution." During the campaign for ratification of the Constitution he joined with Alexander Hamilton and John Jay in writing the *Federalist* papers; 29 of the 85 essays appeared over his pseudonym, "Publius." He also led the proratification forces in the Virginia ratifying convention. Elected a representative to the first

Congress, he took the lead in organizing the new government and in adding to the Constitution the amendments comprising the Bill of Rights. Although strongly identified up to this time with the nationalist view, Madison slowly shifted his position during his years in Congress; he opposed Hamilton's financial policies vigorously and as party alignments developed he emerged as the congressional leader of the Jeffersonian Republicans (Democratic Republicans). He shared Jefferson's preference for close relations with France rather than with England, and he denounced President George Washington's seemingly pro-British Neutrality Proclamation of 1793 as well as Jay's Treaty in 1795. He remained in Congress until 1797; then, from his home, Montpelier, in Orange County, Virginia, he kept close watch on public affairs and in 1798, when Federalist hysteria produced the Alien and Sedition Acts, he and Jefferson wrote, respectively, the Virginia and Kentucky Resolves, protesting the unconstitutionality of the measures and raising—although this interpretation was later denied by Madison—the specter of nullification. When Jefferson was elected to the presidency in 1800, Madison was his immediate choice for secretary of state; during the next eight years the two men worked in perfect harmony through a succession of crises occasioned by war between Britain and France and the constant harassment of U.S. neutral shipping that was, for the United States, its central feature. In 1808 he was the clear successor to the presidency; he won a strong victory over his Federalist opponent and continued the policies of Jefferson unaltered. The difficulties with Britain and France continued and worsened, particularly with Britain; Madison was apparently deceived by Napoleon I of France into issuing a nonintercourse proclamation against Great Britain in November 1810, making war with that country virtually inevitable. War was also vigorously urged by the "War Hawk" faction in Congress, largely composed of younger men from frontier districts. In June 1812 war was formally declared, beginning a painful and dangerous period for the nation, which was totally unprepared and part of which, New England, was totally unsympathetic. Military disasters fostered the growth of popular discontent; New England, through the activities and correspondence of the Essex Junto, which eventually led to the secret Hartford Convention late in 1814, seriously considered secession, or at least extensive revision of the Constitution; great areas of the Northwest were lost to British forces from Canada; and Washington, D.C., was burned by invading British forces. Nevertheless, Madison managed to win reelection in 1812. The war was ended by the treaty of Ghent in December 1814, with the United States having failed to gain a single one of its war aims and having had to bargain from weakness simply to regain its territory. But the mere fact that the war was over, coupled with a few spectacular though belated victories—notably that of Gen. Andrew Jackson at New Orleans—restored to the president much popular

favor. The remainder of his administration was marked most prominently by his brief backing away from Jeffersonian principles in approving both the charter of the Second Bank of the United States and the nation's first system of protective tariffs. Madison retired to Montpelier in 1817; his public service after that time was limited to participation in the Virginia constitutional convention of 1829 and, upon the death of Jefferson in 1826, acting as rector of the University of Virginia until his own death at Montpelier on June 28, 1836. Madison's wife, Dolley (or Dolly) Payne Todd, whom he married in 1794, was noted for her open and occasionally brilliant hospitality. She served as hostess of the President's House during the administration of widower Thomas Jefferson and during her husband's administration was the brightest social figure Washington had yet known. In fleeing the city in 1814 she saved many state documents and a portrait of Washington from the President's House. Madison was elected to the Hall of Fame in 1905.

Magnes, Judah Leon (1877–1948), religious leader and educator. Born in San Francisco on July 5, 1877, Magnes graduated from the University of Cincinnati in 1898 and studied for the rabbinate at Hebrew Union College, also in Cincinnati. Ordained a rabbi in 1900, he went to Berlin for further graduate studies and received his Ph.D. from the University of Heidelberg in 1902. After a year, 1903–1904, as librarian at Hebrew Union he went to New York City to serve as rabbi at a Reform temple in Brooklyn, 1904–1906, and then at Temple Emanu-El, in Manhattan, which he left in 1910 after a conflict with the trustees. He served as rabbi of Congregation B'nai Jeshurun in New York City in 1911–1912, but from this time on he was deeply involved in Jewish ecumenical and relief activities, and from 1912 to 1920 he was the leader of the Society for the Advancement of Judaism. He left the United States for Palestine in 1922 and spent most of the rest of his life there. He founded Hebrew University in Jerusalem in 1925, serving as its first chancellor, 1925–1935, and thereafter as president. He supported the Allied cause during World War II, despite his intense pacifism which produced in him an internal struggle. An ardent Zionist, he founded Ihud ("Unity"), a society devoted to the formation of a united Palestine and to the resolution of Jewish-Arab differences. Magnes died in New York City on October 27, 1948.

Mahan, Alfred Thayer (1840–1914), naval officer and historian. Born on September 27, 1840, in West Point, New York, Mahan was the son of a professor of military engineering at the U.S. Military Academy. After two years at Columbia College he entered the U.S. Naval Academy, from which he graduated in 1859. During nearly 40 years of active duty in the navy he served in numerous capacities at sea and ashore. He saw blockade duty during the Civil War and later served on the staff of Adm. J. A. B. Dahlgren. He progressed steadily in rank and responsibility; in 1885 he was promoted to captain and the following year, in recognition of his abilities and his reputation for scholarship, he received a call to lecture on naval history and strategy at the Naval War College in Newport, Rhode Island. He soon became the institution's president and held the post until 1889. The next year his lectures were published under the title *The Influence of Sea Power upon History, 1660–1783*; a thoroughgoing analysis of sea power in its broadest manifestations, the book broke new ground in the examination of international affairs and won immediate recognition abroad. In 1892 Mahan's second major work appeared, entitled *The Influence of Sea Power upon the French Revolution and Empire, 1793–1812*, and, like the first, it became a classic. Assiduously studied in translation, the two books greatly influenced the worldwide buildup of naval forces in the period prior to World War I. In 1892–1893 he was again president of the Naval War College, and in 1893, on a cruise in European waters, in command of the cruiser *Chicago*, he was publicly honored by the British government and awarded honorary degrees by both Oxford and Cambridge universities. He retired from the navy in 1896 but was recalled to service on the naval strategy board during the Spanish-American War. He was a member of the U.S. delegation to the peace conference at The Hague in 1899, and in 1902 was elected president of the American Historical Association. Notable among Mahan's many other works were *The Life of Nelson*, 1897; *The Interest of America in Sea Power, Present and Future*, 1897; and *The Major Operations of the Navies in the War of American Independence*, 1913. He died in Washington, D.C., on December 1, 1914.

Mahpiua Luta, *see* Red Cloud

Mailer, Norman (1923–   ), author. Born on January 31, 1923, in Long Branch, New Jersey, Mailer grew up in Brooklyn, New York, and graduated from Harvard in 1943 with a degree in engineering. He had begun to write short stories in college and won *Story* magazine's college competition in 1941 with "The Greatest Thing in the World." Drafted into the army in 1943, he was an infantryman in the Philippines during World War II and afterward served with the U.S. occupation forces in Japan. He returned to New York City in 1946 and in 1948 published a searing novel of the war, *The Naked and the Dead*, which brought him immediate fame and critical praise and was compared in its expression of bitterness toward war to Ernest Hemingway's *A Farewell to Arms*. In the late 1940s he went through a period of political search that left him hostile to both Communism, as reflected in his book *Barbary Shore*, 1951, and to the authoritarianism he saw in the United States. After a brief time as a script writer in Hollywood, he completed *The Deer Park*, 1955, a picture of a psychopathic Hollywood personality, which he adapted for off-

Broadway stage production in 1967. He settled in New York City's Greenwich Village in late 1951 and aided in organizing the *Village Voice*, becoming a frequent contributor to the newspaper. His pithy essays also appeared in *Partisan Review*, *Commentary*, *Esquire*, and *Dissent*, the last of which introduced his definitive treatise on "hipsterism," "The White Negro," in 1957. Numerous works followed: *Advertisements for Myself*, 1959, autobiographical-confessional essays; *The Presidential Papers*, 1963, a collection of his magazine essays on President John F. Kennedy; *Deaths for the Ladies, and Other Disasters*, 1962, a book of verse; *Cannibals and Christians*, 1966, a miscellaneous collection of writings and two allegorical novels, *An American Dream*, 1965, and *Why Are We in Vietnam?*, 1967. He won the National Book Award and shared a Pulitzer Prize in nonfiction for *The Armies of the Night*, 1967, a report on the 1967 march on the Pentagon by anti-Vietnam War demonstrators in which he participated prominently. The next year he wrote *Miami and the Siege of Chicago*, on the two presidential nominating conventions of 1968. *Of a Fire on the Moon*, about the U.S. moon-exploration program, appeared in 1971, as did *Prisoner of Sex*, a searing attack on the women's liberation movement. He ran unsuccessfully for mayor of New York City in 1969 on a secessionist platform calling for the city to become the 51st state. A restless, unruly personality, he was recognized as a driving force in modern American literature.

Main, John, *see* Parsons, Elsie Worthington Clews

Makataimeshekiakiak *see* Black Hawk

Makemie, Francis (1658?–1708?), religious leader. Born in County Donegal, Ireland, about 1658, Makemie went to Scotland to attend the University of Glasgow in 1675. His ordination by the Presbytery of Laggan, Ireland, in 1682 followed a request from the Maryland colonial council for ministers to be sent to the New World. Shortly after his arrival in Somerset County, Maryland, sometime in 1683, he founded the first Presbyterian church in America at Snow Hill. Supporting himself by trading, he met with success as an evangelist in the Southern colonies. He traveled to North Carolina in 1683–1684; two of his four extant letters to Increase Mather from the Elizabeth River region of Virginia are dated 1684 and 1685. He preached on the Eastern Shore of Maryland and Virginia in 1690–1691 and then went to London to seek aid for his work. He returned in 1692 to face growing opposition from the Anglican church, which, in the person of George Keith, a former Quaker zealot, attacked his published catechism. He defended his faith in *An Answer to George Keith's Libel*. In 1696–1698 he also preached in Barbados, in the West Indies, where he had for some time been engaged in trade. In 1698 he inherited his father-in-law's estate (Makemie had married the daughter of a Virginia merchant sometime in the 1690s) and the following year established a residence on the Eastern Shore of Virginia. On a trip to Ireland and Scotland in 1704–1705 he enlisted two colleagues and with their help succeeded, in 1706, in uniting parishes in Maryland, Pennsylvania, New Jersey, and Virginia (Makemie was licensed there under the Toleration Act in 1699) into the first American presbytery. As organizer and first moderator of the presbytery Makemie earned recognition as the founder of Presbyterianism in America. In January 1707 he was imprisoned by Lord Cornbury, governor of New York, for preaching in that colony without a license. His acquittal, which was shortly followed by the recall of Cornbury, marked a notable victory for the dissenting churches in the colonies. Makemie died at his home in Accomack, Virginia, in late 1707 or early 1708.

Malamud, Bernard (1914–   ), author. Born in Brooklyn, New York, on April 26, 1914, Malamud showed an early interest in writing fiction. Educated at the College of the City of New York (CCNY), (B.A., 1936), and at Columbia University (M.A., 1942), he taught English in evening high schools during the 1940s. He then left New York City for a post at Oregon State College, where he became a professor of English. *The Natural,* 1952, an allegorical novel about a baseball player, remained relatively unnoticed until *The Assistant* brought him to the attention of the public and the critics in 1957. Malamud, financed by a *Partisan Review* fellowship, had spent the previous year writing in Italy and in 1958 he published *The Magic Barrel,* a collection of stories. He won a Rosenthal Prize that year and a National Book Award for fiction in 1959; and his subsequent rise to prominence coincided with a growing interest during the 1960s in writers dealing with Jewish tradition and experience in the United States. *A New Life, 1961,* about a writer's soul searching, and *Idiots First,* 1963, more stories, received mixed reviews, but *The Fixer* brought him a second National Book Award and a Pulitzer Prize in 1967 and also became the basis of a successful film. Along with Saul Bellow and Philip Roth, Malamud remained in the vanguard of writers who made use of Jewish protagonists to unfold their personal moral vision. He returned East in 1961 to teach literature at Bennington College, and during 1966–1968 was a visiting lecturer at Harvard University. In 1964 he was elected to the National Institute of Arts and Letters. Later works included *Pictures of Fidelman,* 1969, and *The Tenants,* 1971.

Malbone, Edward Greene (1777–1807), miniaturist. Born in Newport, Rhode Island, sometime in August 1777, Malbone was largely self-taught as a painter and began his professional career in 1794 in Providence. He soon developed a remarkably fine technique as a miniaturist, possessing the "happy talent," as the painter and critic Washington Allston put it, "of elevating the character without impairing the likeness." His skill at such "elevation," as well as the extraordinary beauty of his miniature portraits, the result of techniques he devised himself, soon brought him national fame, and during his career he was the most sought-after miniaturist in the country. In 1796 he moved to Boston after which he spent much time in Philadelphia and New York City. In 1801 he moved again, this time to Charleston, South Carolina, where he remained for the rest of his life except for a visit in that year to England, where he met and won the praise of Benjamin West, and another brief period in Boston in 1804–1805. He died while visiting Savannah, Georgia, on May 7, 1807. Many of his miniatures survive and are highly valued by collectors. Generally regarded as the greatest of American miniaturists, Malbone took no pupils, but his informal advice to younger artists led to the creation of a flourishing American school of this rare art in the early years of the nineteenth century.

Malcolm X (1925–1965), religious leader and reformer. Malcolm Little was born on May 19, 1925, in Omaha, Nebraska. His father, a Baptist preacher and follower of Marcus M. Garvey, soon moved his family to Lansing, Michigan; his death in 1931 led to Malcolm's separation from his family, first to a foster home, and finally, in 1938, to a reform home in Mason, Michigan. He completed the eighth grade there, and from 1941 to 1946 lived in Boston and in New York City's Harlem. Known as "Detroit Red," he was involved in a number of petty criminal activities and in 1946 was convicted on several counts of robbery and sentenced to seven years in prison. While in prison he became acquainted with the teachings of Elijah Muhammad, leader of the "Nation of Islam," the Black Muslims. Adopting this faith, he set about educating himself and, upon his release in 1952, changed his name to Malcolm X and devoted himself to religious and social work. A remarkable orator and an assiduous follower of Elijah Muhammad, Malcolm rose quickly in the organization, becoming the sect's first "national minister" in 1963. The Black Muslims enjoyed great gains in membership and publicity as a result of the increasing national attention given Negro rights, status, and culture; however, the sect's insistence on black separatism and avoidance of active participation in the civil-rights struggle gradually alienated Malcolm. Finally, in March 1964, he broke publicly with Elijah Muhammad, forming his own Muslim group. Following visits to Mecca and several new African nations, he formed the Organization of Afro-American Unity in New York City later in 1964. Malcolm's speeches, often brilliantly eloquent, were militant, even strident, calls for conscious black identity and pride. In his last months, as a result of his African experiences, he began to approach in his thinking a socialistic alternative to American capitalism. On Februry 21, 1965, Malcolm X was fatally shot while preparing to speak in a Harlem auditorium. In the wake of his death, his often radical disagreements with other black leaders were largely forgotten, and he quickly achieved the status of a cultural hero for a new and activist generation of black Americans.

Mallon, Mary (1870?–1938), "Typhoid Mary," typhoid carrier. Believed to have been born in the United States in about 1870, Mary Mallon gave rise to the most famous outbreaks of carrier-borne disease in medical history. She was first recognized as a carrier of the typhoid bacteria during an epidemic of typhoid fever in 1904 that spread through Oyster Bay, New York, where she worked as a cook. By the time the disease had been traced to its source in a household where she had recently been employed, she had already left. She continued to work as a cook, moving from household to household until 1907, when she was found working in a Park Avenue home. Between 1907 and 1910 she was institutionalized at Riverside Hospital on North Brother Island, in New York City, the authorities of which finally released her on the promise that she would seek employment other than a cook. Four years later, after another outbreak of typhoid fever, she was found to be working as a cook in a sanatorium in New Jersey, and after that she remained in detention on North Brother Island until her death in New York City on November 11, 1938. Her history as a carrier implicated her in three deaths from typhoid and more than 50 other cases, while, as is not uncommon, she herself remained immune.

Mann, Horace (1796–1859), educator and public official. Born on May 4, 1796, in Franklin, Massachusetts, Mann experienced an unhappy childhood marked by poverty and hard work. His education was sporadic and of inferior quality until, in 1816, he studied with an itinerant teacher who in six months prepared him for college. He entered the sophomore class at Brown University and graduated in 1819. After a brief time in a law office he became a tutor at Brown; in 1821 he entered the Litchfield Law School in Connecticut, and two years later was admitted to the bar. For ten years he practiced in Dedham, Massachusetts, and in 1833 moved to Boston. In 1827 he was elected to the state house of representatives and served there for six years; in 1835 he was elected to the Massachusetts senate, where he remained for two years, the second year as president. In 1837 a bill was enacted creating a state board of education to supervise the common-school system. He relinquished his law practice and a promising political future to accept the post of secretary to the board, a position of little power but of potentially great influence. The school system of Massachusetts, which dated back to the early colonial period, had deteriorated seriously in the preceding 40 or 50 years, largely because of decentralized control and dwindling financial support. Wielding little more than moral suasion, Mann worked a virtual revolution during 12 years as secretary. He organized county educational conferences, promoted the establishment of the

nation's first normal schools, founded the *Common School Journal* in 1838, secured enlarged appropriations for salaries, new schools, and facilities, and a minimum school-year law, and issued 12 annual reports in which he argued powerfully for free, public-supported common education that would be nonsectarian, professionally conducted, and dedicated to training citizens for a democracy. The annual reports and the reforms they outlined traveled beyond Massachusetts and profoundly affected educational practices throughout the nation. In 1848 Mann resigned the secretaryship to succeed, after election as an Antislavery Whig, to John Quincy Adams's seat in the House of Representatives. In 1852 he ran unsuccessfully for governor of Massachusetts as a Free-Soiler. The next year he accepted the presidency of Antioch College in Yellow Springs, Ohio, where he remained, teaching as well as administering the school, until his death in Yellow Springs on August 2, 1859. He was elected to the Hall of Fame in 1900.

Mansfield, Richard (1854?–1907), actor. Born on May 24, 1854, or 1857, in Berlin, where his mother, a singer, was on tour, Mansfield spent his youth, after his father's death in 1859, accompanying his mother on concert tours of England and the Continent. In 1872 they settled in Boston, where as early as 1876 he appeared in an amateur production of *School.* He also tried singing and painting without attracting much attention. Dissatisfied, he went to London in 1877, and during the next five years had a most encouraging reception as a singer in Gilbert and Sullivan operettas. Mansfield returned to the United States after his mother died in 1882 and that same year opened in New York City in the operetta *Les Manteaux Noirs.* Determined to become a star in the legitimate theater, he finally managed to obtain an important role, as Baron Chevrial in *A Parisian Romance,* in 1882. He created an immediate sensation. A premature attempt to form his own acting company in 1884 ended in failure, but he became a star in *Prince Karl* in 1886, and from that year he was his own producer. His portrayal of Dr. Jekyll and Mr. Hyde in 1887 established him as unquestionably brilliant and remained among his chief roles. His Shakespearian debut was as Richard III in London in 1889, and he added Shylock in 1893 and Julius Caesar in 1902. *Beau Brummell,* 1890, was almost always performed on his frequent road tours, and his *Cyrano de Bergerac,* 1898, was in such demand that he uncharacteristically devoted a whole year to its performance. His staging of *Arms and the Man,* 1895, and *The Devil's Disciple,* 1897, were the first productions of plays by George Bernard Shaw in the United States. In 1906 his *Peer Gynt,* the first American production of Ibsen's play, was a success in its Chicago opening, but, after moving it to New York City and acting Peer and Baron Chevrial on the same day, Mansfield collapsed from exhaustion. After a year's struggle to regain his health he died in New London,

Connecticut, on August 30, 1907. Mansfield's ambition soared with his popularity and he worked with a feverish intensity throughout his career, frequently playing different roles on successive nights and not uncommonly displaying his versatility in several acts from different plays in a single night. Although he was a master of the grand romantic manner, his imagination and grasp of human psychology gave him a breadth uncommon in nineteenth century acting, a breadth that enabled him to appreciate and successfully produce the works of such modern playwrights as Shaw and Ibsen.

Mantle, Mickey Charles (1931–   ), baseball player. Born on October 20, 1931, in Spavinaw, Oklahoma, Mantle was groomed for a baseball career by his father, who named him for Mickey Cochrane, a great catcher for the Detroit Tigers. He played baseball in high school, where he also excelled in football and basketball. An injury received during football practice when he was fifteen aggravated an osteomyelitic condition that plagued him for the rest of his baseball career. A switch hitter, he played shortstop in the minor leagues after signing a contract with the New York Yankees of the American League on completing high school. When the 1951 season opened he was moved from the minors to a regular center-field position with the Yankees, a team that had dominated major-league baseball since 1921 and still had Joe DiMaggio in left field. He set a team record for strikeouts (111) while playing only 96 games in 1951, but was an impressive long-ball hitter and participated in the World Series, which was won by the Yankees. He again injured his ankle in the second game of that series and rarely went through another season without an injury. He batted over .300 in 1952 and in 1956, 1957, and 1962 was named the American League's most valuable player. In 1956 he led the league in home runs (52), runs batted in (130), and hitting (.353). Although he was known primarily as a home-run hitter (he hit one 565 feet in 1953), he hit over .300 during 10 of the 14 seasons that constituted the peak of his career. His highest average was .365 in 1957 and he had a career average (18 seasons) of .298; his best year for home runs was 1961, when he hit 54 while losing to teammate Roger Maris in a race to beat Babe Ruth's season record. He played in 12 World Series, contributing greatly to the Yankee's continuing dominance (until 1964), and established a number of Series records, including that of 18 home runs. During 1967 and 1968 he played at first base in an effort to prolong his career. His batting average dropped to .237 in 1968 and he retired after spring training in 1969, having compiled a career total of 536 home runs and a major league record of 1710 strikeouts.

March, Francis Andrew (1825–1911), philologist and lexicographer. Born in Millbury, Massachusetts, on October 25, 1825, March graduated from Amherst College in 1845, having studied Anglo-

Saxon there under the direction of Noah Webster. Following graduation he taught for ten years in various secondary schools and at Amherst and then, in 1855, joined the faculty of Lafayette College. In 1857 he was named professor of English language and comparative philology at Lafayette, occupying the first chair of this kind in the United States; he became professor emeritus at Lafayette in 1907. He published his *Method of Philological Study of the English Language* in 1865 and five years later issued the monumental *Comparative Grammar of the Anglo-Saxon Language,* a work that remained standard for two generations. Also in 1870 appeared his *Anglo-Saxon Reader,* a collection for beginning students that was long in use in U.S. colleges. He edited a volume of *Latin Hymns,* 1874, and wrote an article, "Recent Discussions of Grimm's Law," 1873, that prefigured the later discovery of Verner's Law of linguistic development. From 1879 to 1882 he was director of American readers for the *New English Dictionary* (now known as the *Oxford English Dictionary*). With his son Francis Andrew March, Jr. (1863–1928), who was also a noted lexicographer and a professor at Lafayette, he contributed greatly to the completion of the *Standard Dictionary,* 1893–1895, and edited *A Thesaurus Dictionary of the English Language,* published in 1903. The elder March died in Easton, Pennsylvania, on September 9, 1911.

Marchegiano, Rocco Francis, *see* Marciano, Rocky

Marciano, Rocky (1923–1969), boxer. Born in Brockton, Massachusetts, on September 1, 1923, Rocco Francis Marchegiano left school and what appeared to be a promising future as a football player during his sophomore year of high school to help support his family. Although he received some coaching in the art of self-defense from an uncle as early as the age of twelve and was not unknown for his prowess in early neighborhood scraps, Marciano's interest in boxing was not stimulated until after he was inducted into the army in 1943. He progressed through supervised recreational matches (rewarded by additional leave time), unofficial bouts aimed at the defense of U.S. prestige and at silencing his company's bully, to several fights as a junior amateur shortly before his discharge in 1947. The future champion attracted the attention of New York City boxing promoters by winning 27 of 30 amateur fights before turning professional in 1947. He won his first bout with a first-round knockout, and during 1948 scored 12 more KO's. Brought along slowly by his trainer, he responded to coaching extremely well and by mid-1951 was an established contender for the heavyweight crown. In October of that year he won his thirty-eighth professional fight (consecutive victories, and all but five by knockouts) in a poignant match with the aging former heavyweight champion, Joe Louis. The victory came by a knockout in the eighth round—he was only the second opponent ever to knock Louis out—and assured him a crack at the coveted title. He eliminated three other contenders before meeting Jersey Joe Walcott in Philadelphia on September 23, 1952, for the heavyweight championship. The fight ended, again by a knockout, in the thirteenth round and Marciano became world champion. He successfully defended his title six times before retiring undefeated in 1956. His record brought him quick election to boxing's Hall of Fame (1959). He died in a plane crash ten years later, on August 31, 1969, leaving an unblemished record in the professional ring: 49 consecutive victories, all but 6 by knockouts.

Marcuse, Herbert (1898–1979), philosopher. Born in Berlin on July 19, 1898, Marcuse attended the University of Berlin and received a doctorate in philosophy from the University of Freiburg in 1922. During the 1920s his thinking was influenced by the psychoanalytic theories of Wilhelm Reich as well as the post-Marxian sociology that was current in Germany. His first book, published in 1932, was on the philosophy of G.W.F. Hegel. He was one of the founders of the Institute of Social Research at Frankfurt, whose unpopularity with the Nazis forced him to flee Germany when Hitler came to power in 1933. He spent a year in Switzerland before coming to the United States, where he subsequently lectured at Columbia University. Marcuse became an American citizen in 1940, and during and after World War II his aid was enlisted as an intelligence analyst, both for the Office of Strategic Services (OSS) and for the Department of State's Office of Intelligence Research. An expert on Soviet affairs, he accepted a post with the Russian Institute at Columbia in 1951 and later lectured at the Russian Research Center at Harvard. In 1954 Marcuse went to Brandeis University, where he gained considerable popularity with the students and was honored by a specially endowed chair. His *Eros and Civilization*, 1955, a neo-Freudian account of the origin of political power, and *One-Dimensional Man*, 1964, an attempt to explain the repressive nature and totalitarian potential of American society, became uncommonly popular for philosophical works, especially among those students who saw in his work a justification for the radical politics that espoused the abandonment of democratic processes in order to achieve the goals of a revolutionary cause. Marcuse made some enemies at Brandeis, and when he reached retirement age in 1965 he moved to the University of California campus at San Diego. His lectures were immensely popular with students at San Diego, and during the widespread disorders on university campuses in the United States and Europe in 1968 his name was prominent among those mentioned as prophets of the New Left. Marcuse did not applaud the campus demonstrations, and a movement to terminate his contract for the 1968–1969 academic year was thwarted by the university administration. Several of his early essays were collected and published as *Negations: Essays in Critical Theory*, 1968. He died on July 29, 1979, in Starnberg, West Germany.

Marcy, William Learned (1786–1857), public official. Born on December 12, 1786, in Southbridge, Massachusetts, Marcy graduated from Brown University in the class of 1808 and moved to Troy, New York, where he shortly began a law practice. He saw military service and reached the rank of captain during the War of 1812. He began his political career as recorder of Troy in 1816, supported Martin Van Buren (then in the state senate) while editor of the *Troy Budget* after his removal from the recorder's office in 1818, and in 1821 was rewarded with the post of adjutant general of the New York militia. One of the leading figures in the powerful Democratic political alliance known as the Albany Regency, he served as state comptroller from 1823 to 1829 and in the latter year was appointed to the New York supreme court by Van Buren, then governor. He served as an associate justice until 1831. A short career in the U.S. Senate (December 1831–December 1832) was remarkable only for a speech in defense of Van Buren's ministry to England, in which his remark that "To the victor belong the spoils of the enemy" sufficiently caught the public imagination to give rise to the term "spoils system." He resigned from the Senate in January 1833 after being elected governor of New York. He served three consecutive two-year terms during which he commissioned the first geological survey of the state, and, although defeated in his bid for a fourth term, remained a powerful figure in New York with ambitions for national office. Van Buren, by then president, appointed him a commissioner of Mexican claims in 1839, and for his part in throwing New York's support behind James K. Polk (and against Van Buren) in the presidential election of 1844 he became secretary of war in Polk's cabinet. He proved an able minister during the Mexican War and managed to emerge unscathed and even victorious after squabbles with both Gen. Winfield Scott and Gen. Zachary Taylor. He was then out of office for about three years but returned to Washington as secretary of state, serving with distinction from 1853 to 1857 in the cabinet of President Franklin Pierce. His chief accomplishments in the office were the settlement of the boundary dispute with Mexico (culminating in the Gadsden Purchase); his handling of the *Black Warrior* affair—the seizure of a U.S. ship by Spanish authorities—and the subsequent Ostend Manifesto on the advisability of seizing Cuba, which he and the government disavowed; and the dispatch of Townsend Harris as consul general to Japan. He retired from office having negotiated a record number of treaties, including the 1854 Reciprocity Treaty with Canada. He died at Ballston Spa, New York, on July 4, 1857.

Margulois, David, *see* Merrick, David

Marin, John Cheri (1872–1953), painter. Born on December 23, 1872, in Rutherford, New Jersey, Marin studied architecture at the Stevens Institute of Technology and, after working for several years as a draftsman, turned to the study of art at the Pennsylvania Academy of the Fine Arts in 1899–1901 and the Art Students League in New York City in 1901–1903. In Europe during 1905–1911, he was deeply influenced by the individuality of James McNeill Whistler's watercolors and etchings. His own style was technically experimental, using short, blunt brush strokes and bold contrasts that imparted a vigorous, dynamic quality. Famous by 1920 for his watercolors (including "Sunset, Casco Bay" and "Lower Manhattan from the River"), he also later achieved great success in oils. His paintings of the Maine seacoast, completed in the later part of his career, reflected the influence of Cubism. He was among the American modern artists to be introduced and promoted by Alfred Stieglitz in his 291 Gallery in New York City, and in 1936 was honored by a retrospective show at the Museum of Modern Art, New York City. He received the Fine Arts Medal of the American Institute of Architects in 1948. By the time of his death in Addison, Maine, on October 1, 1953, Marin was represented in major museums and private collections throughout the United States.

Marion, Francis (1732?–1795), "the Swamp Fox," Revolutionary soldier. Born in Berkeley County, South Carolina, probably in 1732, Marion first saw military service against the Cherokee in 1759 and again in 1761. The first provincial congress, to which he was elected in 1775, elected him a captain in the second of two regiments then being raised, and he served under Gen. William Moultrie when the British were repulsed at Sullivans Island in June 1776. The following September his regiment was taken over by the Continental Congress and he was promoted to lieutenant colonel. He fought at Savannah in the fall of 1779 but escaped capture when Charleston fell to the British in May 1780. After the disastrous defeat of Gen. Horatio Gates at Camden in August, he gathered around himself a band of intrepid guerrillas whom he trained to fight while living off the land. For the next few months Marion operated in the enemy's territory. The only Continental force worth mentioning in South Carolina, "Marion's brigade" harassed the British by cutting communications, successfully engaging Loyalist strongholds, and sometimes risking an attack on larger bodies of British regulars. At home in the supposedly impassable swamps, he surprised the enemy in swift attacks and then dispersed his men to avoid capture. Even the dreaded Col. Banastre Tarleton could not find Marion, saying: "As for this damned old fox, the devil himself could not catch him." The remark earned Marion, who was promoted to brigadier general in 1781, the sobriquet "Swamp Fox." He made two unsuccessful attempts to capture Georgetown, but a third attempt, in concert now with Gen. Nathanael Greene's forces, recaptured the town in April 1781. He was in command of the militia at the major victory at Eutaw Springs on September 6, 1781, for which he received the thanks of Con-

gress. He continued to serve ably under Greene until the end of the war. After the war he served several terms in the South Carolina senate and from 1784 to 1790 was commander of Fort Johnson, on Charleston harbor, a post that was essentially a sinecure in reward for his labors. He died at his plantation home in Berkeley County on February 27, 1795.

Markham, Edwin (1852–1940), poet. Born in Oregon City, Oregon, on April 23, 1852. Charles Edward Anson Markham was raised by his mother on a ranch in central California. He spent an unhappy childhood. Often desperately lonely when put to work tending sheep, he was discouraged by his mother from pursuing his early interest in reading. His hopes of achieving a good education were only partially fulfilled by attending the California State Normal school at San Jose, but he managed to work his way through a classics program at Christian College in Santa Rosa by 1873. He subsequently taught in county high schools, became a county superintendent of schools in 1879, and eventually, after he had succeeded in publishing some of his early poems, was appointed headmaster of the Tompkins Observation School in Oakland in 1890. An obscure poet, unhappy in his personal life (two marriages had already failed), he began to enjoy a more settled existence after the death of his mother in 1891. About 1895 he adopted the name Edwin, and he entered into what proved to be a successful third marriage in 1898, but he might well have remained permanently unnoticed but for the publication, in the *San Francisco Examiner* in January 1899, of "The Man with the Hoe," inspired by Jean François Millet's painting of the same title. The French peasant of the poem and the painting was immediately seized upon as a symbol of exploited workers throughout the world, and Markham achieved instant fame when the poem was reprinted in newspapers across the nation. It was eventually translated into 40 languages. *The Man with the Hoe and Other Poems,* 1899, became a best seller and Markham left school administration and moved to Staten Island, New York, in 1901. His second volume, *Lincoln and Other Poems,* 1901, was also successful, largely because of the competence displayed in the title piece, "Lincoln, the Man of the People." Markham thereafter devoted himself to writing and, after financial reverses, increasingly to lecturing after 1910. A number of articles he had written on the subject of child labor were incorporated into the volume *Children in Bondage,* 1914, compiled by George Creel, Benjamin B. Lindsey, and Markham. With the exception of a few memorable poems, his later work was undistinguished. His volumes of verse appeared periodically until 1937, and he continued to command respect as a lecturer until his health failed in 1935. He died on Staten Island on March 7, 1940.

Marquand, John Phillips (1893–1960), author. Born in Wilmington, Delaware, on November 10, 1893,

Marquand graduated from Harvard with the class of 1915, saw battle with the American Expeditionary Force in France during World War I, and began his writing career with the *New York Herald Tribune* in 1919. He quit the paper a year later for a stint in advertising before undertaking to write a novel. *The Unspeakable Gentlemen* was an immediate success in the *Ladies' Home Journal* in 1922 and launched J. P. Marquand on a successful career as a writer of popular fiction. For the next 15 years his stories appeared regularly, often in the *Saturday Evening Post*, and his skill as a writer increased. The most celebrated of his stories of this period recounted the adventures of a soft-spoken Japanese detective, Mr. Moto. The good-natured satire on the aspirations of a vanishing class of New England gentry for which Marquand was chiefly known began with *The Late George Apley*, 1937, which won a Pulitzer Prize in 1938. A dramatization by Marquand and George S. Kaufman was produced in 1944, and later the tale was also made into a motion picture. This was followed by *Wickford Point*, 1939, and *H. M. Pulham, Esquire*, 1941, the latter reinforcing his reputation as a satirist. "A very sad book," Marquand said of it, "about a completely frustrated individual." Other works on which his reputation as a serious writer rests include *B. F.'s Daughter*, 1946; *Point of No Return*, 1949; *Melville Goodwin, U.S.A.*, 1951; and *Sincerely, Willis Wayde*, 1955. At his best, critics agreed, he was a shrewd reporter of shifting American social patterns and a superb chronicler of the endless search for status among the ranks of the would-be upper class. Marquand died at his home in Newburyport, Massachusetts, on July 16, 1960, having achieved the rare distinction of writing readable books for a mass audience without losing the respect of the critics.

Marquette, Jacques (1637–1675), Jesuit missionary and explorer. Born in Laon, France, into a prominent family, on June 1, 1637, Marquette became a Jesuit novice at seventeen. Ten years passed before his ambition to become a missionary in the New World was given the blessing of his superiors. Ordained a priest shortly before he left for New France, he arrived in Quebec on September 20, 1666. The next six years were spent learning Indian languages and establishing frontier missions. He first met Louis Jolliet at the mission he established at Sault Ste. Marie in 1668–1669. Père Marquette spent 18 months on the southern shore of Lake Superior at a spot that subsequently became Ashland, Wisconsin, during 1669–1671, establishing a relationship of mutual trust and admiration with the Illinois Indians. A conflict with the local Sioux Indians precipitated a move eastward, and at Michilimackinac he founded another mission (now St. Ignace, Michigan) on the Straits of Mackinac. When Jolliet was commissioned by Governor Frontenac in late 1672 to explore the mighty river renowned among the Indians—the Mississippi—he sought out Marquette at St. Ignace to inform him that he had been chosen by Claude Dablon, superior general of the Jesuit mission in America, to join the expedition. They left St. Ignace in the spring of 1673 in two canoes along with five other Frenchmen. They headed westward to Green Bay and then followed the Fox River. With assistance from Indians they portaged to the Wisconsin River at present-day Portage, Wisconsin, and followed it to the Mississippi. They then followed the great river south for a month to where it is joined by the Arkansas, at which point they turned northward again from fear of capture by the Spanish, who had settled on the lower river. They returned to the north by the Illinois River route and visited the Illinois Indians before portaging to Lake Michigan at the site of Chicago. Marquette completed his journal while trying to regain his failing health during the winter of 1673–1674. He felt sufficiently strong by October of that year to undertake another trip down Lake Michigan to found a mission among the Indians. Caught by the onset of winter, he and two French companions built a cabin on the site of Chicago, thus becoming the first white men to live there (December 4, 1674–March 30, 1675). He proceeded to what is now Utica, Illinois, in April and spent Easter with the Illinois Indians, founding his third mission, Immaculate Conception, there. His strength declining rapidly, he abandoned the mission in an attempt to reach St. Ignace. He died en route, near present-day Ludington, Michigan, at a river that now bears his name, on May 18, 1675. His journal of that first trip by white men down the Mississippi, for which he is justly famous, was first published in 1681.

Marquis, Donald Robert Perry (1878–1937), author. Born in Walnut, Illinois, on July 29, 1878, Don Marquis tried his hand at verse before he was twenty, and worked on newspapers in Washington, D.C., and Atlanta before he became associated with Joel Chandler Harris on *Uncle Remus's Magazine*. In New York City after 1909, he eventually joined the *New York Evening Sun*, writing a daily column "The Sun Dial," for ten years, from 1913 to 1922; it established him as a humorist and a satirist with few peers in the world of journalism. Two of his most inspired inventions first appeared there, Archy the cockroach (the reincarnation of a poet) and Mehitabel the alley cat. Archy's sardonic philosophical and poetical reflections were supposedly written, as were his accounts of Mehitabel's rowdy misadventures, in lower-case letters on Marquis's office typewriter by Archy's headlong plunges onto the keys; they attracted a large following and survived to appear in three "archy and mehitabel" books in the late 1920s and early 1930s. Understandably uneven at times, the column at its best was whimsical, satirically iconoclastic, and often bitter. A subsequent column, "The Lantern," was written for the *New York Tribune* after 1922. Marquis also carried out numerous other literary projects during his newspaper career. Among his principal works, which included light and serious poetry, comic and dramatic plays, as well as novels and essays, were *Donny's Own Story*, 1912; *Dreams and Dust*, 1915; *Hermione*, 1916; *The Old Soak*, 1921 and 1922, which was very well received on the Broadway stage; *Noah an' Jonah an' Cap'n John Smith*, 1921; *Sonnets to a Red-Haired Lady*, 1922; *The Almost Perfect State*, 1927; and *Out of the Sea*, 1927. Marquis's health was never good in his adult life and he died in Forest Hills, New York, on December 29, 1937, after a long illness. *Sons of the Puritans*, an unfinished autobiographical novel, was published posthumously in 1939.

Marsh, George Perkins (1801–1882), diplomat and linguist. Born in Woodstock, Vermont, on March 15, 1801, Marsh entered Dartmouth with very little formal preparation at the age of fifteen and graduated in 1820 with a reputation for brilliance and a mastery of the principal Romance languages and of German. He quickly gave up teaching for law, was admitted to the bar in 1825, and shortly had a flourishing practice in Burlington, Vermont. It was not long before he entered politics and in 1835 he was appointed to the supreme executive council (forerunner of the state senate) of Vermont. At about this time he undertook a study of the languages of Northern Europe; he published a compendium of the Icelandic language in 1838, and *The Goths in New England* appeared in 1843. He went to the House of Representatives as a Whig in 1843, but resigned six years later to accept President Zachary Taylor's appointment as U.S. minister to Turkey. He was noted at Constantinople for his ability to converse with the Norwegian, Swedish, Danish, French, Spanish, and Italian ministers in their own languages as well as for acquiring fluency in Turkish and a familiarity with Persian and Arabic. Instrumental in arranging for the exiled Lajos Kossuth and his Hungarian compatriots to go to the United States in 1851, he was sent to Greece the following summer, where his ability in Greek facilitated his handling the case of an illegally imprisoned American clergyman. He lost his post in Turkey in 1854 under Franklin Pierce's administration and did not receive another appointment until Abraham Lincoln took office. In the interval he was busy in Vermont making a study for the government of the feasibility of artificially propagating fish and as state railroad commissioner, 1857–1859. A book on introducing the camel to the United States appeared in 1856 and his reputation as a linguist became established after lectures at Columbia, 1855, and at the Lowell Institute in Boston, 1860–1861. These were published as *Lectures on the English Language*, 1860, and *The Origin and History of the English Language*, 1862. He was an early American contributor to the *Oxford English Dictionary*. In 1861 he became minister to the newly established kingdom of Italy. His prestige during 21 years of service in Italy was singular and Italian confidence in his integrity so great that he was once asked to arbitrate a boundary dispute with Switzerland. His last major work, *Man and Nature: Or, Physical Geography as Modified by Human Action*, was first published in 1864 and issued in Florence in an Italian translation in 1870. Rewritten and republished in 1874 under the title *The Earth as Modified by Human Action*, the book was highly praised by conservationists of a later day. Marsh died in Vallombrosa, Italy, on July 23, 1882.

Marsh, Othniel Charles (1831–1899), paleontologist. Born in Lockport, New York, on October 29, 1831, Marsh studied the classics at Yale (B.A., 1860), despite a growing interest in fossils, before continuing with graduate work in science there and in Germany at the universities of Berlin, Breslau, and Heidelberg. He returned to Yale in 1866 with an appointment as professor of vertebrate paleontology, the first such chair established in the United States. He had already made his first important discovery in 1855, a fossil reptile that he found in Nova Scotia. Aided by his uncle, George Peabody, who gave him $150,000 to establish a natural-history museum at Yale, he made his first trip to the American West in 1868. He inherited a large share of Peabody's fortune at the latter's death in 1869 and in 1870 he financed the first of what subsequently became almost annual expeditions to Wyoming and other Western states. These trips continued to be made at his own expense until 1882, after which, as vertebrate paleontologist for the U.S. Geological Survey, he received liberal government support. Marsh's chief rival for this newly created post was Edward D. Cope, and after Marsh's appointment their rivalry led to bitter feuding that clouded both their reputations. Marsh collected a wealth of material and never succeeded in publishing the results of all his finds, but a host of short papers appeared in the *American Journal of Science* and he published two major works, *Odontornithes*, 1880, on extinct toothed birds (he was their discoverer), and *Dinocerata*, 1884, on archaic horned mammals. In his publications on fossil finds he utilized studies of such scientists as Samuel W. Williston, Oscar Harger, Max Schlosser, and George Baur, who were his associates or in his employ. Highly possessive of his sites and his finds in later years, he was criticized for not turning over fossils collected under government auspices to the National Museum of Natural History. He eventually donated most of his finds to Yale's Peabody Museum. Marsh's unsurpassed collections in almost every area of paleontology earned him an international reputation. They were examined by T. H. Huxley in 1876 and won great praise from him, and they even came close to tempting Charles Darwin to visit America; although he did not make the trip, Darwin acknowledged that Marsh's work was a singular contribution in support of evolutionary theory. Marsh received numerous awards, presented many papers before academic audiences, and served as president of the National Academy of Sciences for 12 years. His last years were shadowed by financial worries and by loss of government support for his work. He died in New Haven, Connecticut, on March 18, 1899.

Marsh, Reginald (1898–1954), painter. Born to American parents in Paris on March 14, 1898, Marsh graduated from Yale in 1920 and began a career as a magazine illustrator in New York City. He worked for several "slick" magazines as well as the *Daily News* and soon began to study painting at the Art Students League under John Sloan. He continued his apprenticeship by copying old masters in Europe in 1925, remained active as an illustrator (chiefly for the *New Yorker*) after his return, and subsequently came under the influence of Kenneth H. Miller, again at the Art Students League. The year 1928 found him in Europe once more; on returning to New York City he opened a studio on Union Square. Within a year he had enough paintings for a first show, which was held in 1930. Consisting primarily of depictions of less than elegant people and life in New York, the show received a mixed reception, owing in part to critics' inability to conceive of Marsh as other than a magazine illustrator. During the 1930s he continued to have frequent shows and despite some adverse criticism earned a reputation as a serious artist and began to teach at the Art Students League. By 1940 he was being honored with an increasing number of prizes, had achieved considerable success with his frescoes in the New York custom house and the Post Office in Washington, D.C., and was represented in the Metropolitan Museum of Art as well as other museums throughout the United States. Working most often in watercolor and then tempera and making etchings as well, he made periodic attempts with oils that slowed the rapid pace of his work. "The Bowery" and "High Yaller" (both in the Metropolitan) are perhaps his best-known works. Poignant and often humorous, his work was never without sympathy for his subjects despite a tendency for caricature. He was commissioned by *Life* magazine in 1943 to complete a series of paintings depicting World War II, and until the end of his career he continued to illustrate editions of such books as Theodore Dreiser's *An American Tragedy* and *Sister Carrie* and John Dos Passos's *U.S.A.* Marsh continued to teach at the Art Students League until his death on July 3, 1954, in Bennington, Vermont.

Marshall, George Catlett (1880–1959), soldier and public official. Born in Uniontown, Pennsylvania, on December 31, 1880, Marshall graduated from Virginia Military Institute (VMI) in 1901 and a year later received a commission as second lieutenant in the army. After service in the Philippines he attended the army's School of the Line, graduating in 1907, and in 1908 graduated from the Command and General Staff School. During World War I he served in high planning and administrative posts with the American Expeditionary Force (AEF) in Europe; his great abilities as a staff officer were soon recognized and his request for a combat command was refused. From 1919 to 1924 he was an aide to Gen. John J. Pershing, and after three years in China he became assistant commandant of instruction at the

army's infantry school at Fort Benning, Georgia. In 1933 he seemed for a time to have been consigned to obscurity when he was assigned as senior instructor for the Illinois National Guard, but in 1939 he was chosen over the heads of several senior officers to become the army's chief of staff. He served in this position until 1945, carrying the major responsibility for organizing, training, supplying, and deploying U.S. troops in World War II. He was also a principal adviser to President Franklin D. Roosevelt on strategy and attended the major Allied planning conferences from Casablanca to Potsdam. From December 1944 he held the five-star rank of general of the army. Soon after resigning as chief of staff in November 1945 Marshall was sent by President Harry S. Truman to attempt—unsuccessfully—a mediation of the civil war in China. In 1947 he was appointed secretary of state by Truman; in June of that year, in a speech at Harvard, he proposed the European Recovery Program, a massive program of aid to the devastated nations of Europe that was undertaken the following year and became known universally as the Marshall Plan. In January 1949 he resigned from the cabinet, but returned in September 1950 as secretary of defense, a post he held for a year during the early phase of the Korean War. He retired permanently from public service in 1951. During 1949–1950 he served as president of the American Red Cross. In 1953 he was awarded the Nobel Peace Prize, primarily for his plan for European recovery. He died on October 16, 1959, in Washington, D.C.

Marshall, James Wilson (1810–1885), California pioneer. Born in Hope, New Jersey, on October 8, 1810, Marshall was trained by his father as a wheelwright. He left home in the early 1830s and headed West. He lingered for a while in Indiana and Illinois before settling on a farm near Fort Leavenworth, Kansas. His health eventually forced him to seek a more suitable climate and in the spring of 1844 he set out for California. The trip was by wagon train along the Oregon Trail and took more than a year. He spent the winter in Oregon and in the spring joined James Clyman's party for the last leg over the mountains to California. In July 1845 they arrived at the settlement of New Helvetia shortly after Fort Sutter had been completed on the present site of Sacramento, and were greeted with the enthusiastic hospitality that John A. Sutter customarily extended to all Americans who found their way there. Marshall was one of about 150 Americans who arrived that year, making a total probably not exceeding 700 in the Sacramento Valley. He bought land in the valley and began to raise livestock. When the American settlers seized Sonoma and set up the Bear Flag Republic in June 1846, Marshall joined them. In 1847 he joined with Sutter to build and operate a sawmill on the American River near present-day Coloma, 35 miles northeast of the fort. Marshall supervised the construction, the last stage of which involved freeing the wheel in the millrace by blasting the river bed upstream and digging a deeper channel under the wheel. As the water rushed through on the morning of January 24, 1848, Marshall spotted what he thought was gold; Sutter, on being shown the find, confirmed it. The two men tried to keep the secret, but this soon proved impossible. The subsequent events belong to the story of California, which soon became the scene of the most dramatic gold rush in world history. For Marshall, as for Sutter, the discovery proved unfortunate. Their land claims were never recognized by the government or by the flood of prospectors, and running the mill under gold-rush conditions was hopeless. Marshall eventually was driven from the property and at times wandered in the hills around Coloma, disgruntled and occasionally subject to delusions. From 1872 to 1878 the state granted him a small pension. He died in the vicinity of Coloma on August 10, 1885. In 1890 he was honored with a bronze statue near the site of his discovery.

Marshall, John (1755–1835), chief justice of the Supreme Court. Born on September 24, 1755, near Germantown in present-day Fauquier County, Virginia, to well-connected parents who were also well educated for a frontier region, Marshall grew to manhood with little formal schooling and little exposure to the world beyond the backwoods. In 1775 he joined a regiment of Virginia minutemen and the next year enlisted in the Continental army; he served through Brandywine, Germantown, Monmouth, and Valley Forge and in 1779 returned home. After a brief period studying law, including a month at the College of William and Mary, he began practice and from 1780 onward was increasingly involved in state politics. Several terms in the legislature and on the Virginia executive council were followed by election to the state's consitutional ratifying convention in 1788, where he supported ratification. This support, along with his rising prominence at the bar, led President George Washington to offer him the post of U.S. attorney for Virginia; Marshall declined, remaining in Richmond to become the leader of the Federalist party there. In 1797–1798 he was one of the commissioners sent to France, in connection with Jay's Treaty, who became embroiled in the XYZ Affair. He gained from that post both popularity and financial solvency. In 1799 he finally entered federal service by successfully running as a Federalist for the House of Representatives; the next year he declined the post of secretary of war offered by President John Adams but was persuaded to become secretary of state. In January 1801, before the administration's term had expired, Adams nominated him chief justice of the Supreme Court; Marshall was confirmed by the Senate on January 27, but he did not occupy the post until the State Department could be turned over to a successor in March 1801. In that month Marshall began 34 years service as the nation's highest magistrate, taking as his primary task the elaboration of a set of principles

and policies aimed at creating a strong and effective national government. He immediately ended the Court's practice of producing separate opinions from each judge on each case and substituted a single majority opinion that during his tenure was usually written by himself. His first major policy-making opinion, and his most famous, came in 1803 in the case of *Marbury* v. *Madison*. William Marbury, one of President Adams's "midnight appointments" to the office of justice of the peace for the District of Columbia just before the end of his term, was suing for delivery of his duly signed and sealed commission by the reluctant administration of Thomas Jefferson; Marshall's opinion held that Marbury's claim was valid but that Section 13 of the 1789 Judiciary Act, under which the suit was brought, conflicted with the constitutional limitations on the Supreme Court's area of original jurisdiction and was therefore invalid. Although judicial review was not unknown at the time, and although many had assumed it would be practiced under the new government, this was the first instance of its use and Marshall established it firmly in his rendering of the Court's unanimous decision. Thus the most important, and often controversial, of the Court's powers, that of expounding the Constitution and striking down statutes not compatible with it, was early settled by Marshall. He further strengthened the standing of the Court by allowing the writing of only a single opinion in each case, which was then delivered by himself. Judicial dissent was kept in chambers, even in instances when Marshall found himself in the minority. The force of his intellect and of his determination to stamp his federalist views firmly on the Court served to keep such instances rare. In subsequent cases—for example, *U.S.* v. *Peters*, 1809, *Cohens* v. *Virginia*, 1821, and *Gibbons* v. *Ogden*, 1824—he established the unity of the federal court system and its authority over state actions where federal law was concerned. In *McCulloch* v. *Maryland*, 1819, he upheld Congress's power to create the Bank of the United States on essentially the same grounds that Alexander Hamilton had argued in 1790, that of powers implied though not enumerated in the Constitution. *Fletcher* v. *Peck*, 1810, anticipated the Fourteenth Amendment in holding states responsible for due process in their internal affairs, and the celebrated *Trustees of Dartmouth College* v. *Woodward*, 1819, upheld the inviolability of contracts with states. In these and many other decisions, Marshall exerted a profound influence on the legal and judicial history of the United States and in this field he remains the preeminent figure; more effectively perhaps than any other man he oversaw the transition of the country from a confederation to a nation. He was a controversial figure, the center of political debate for decades, not the least in 1807 when, on circuit in Richmond, Virginia, he presided over the treason trial of Aaron Burr. Marshall died in Philadelphia on July 6, 1835. He was elected to the Hall of Fame in 1900.

Marshall, Louis (1856–1929), lawyer and civic leader. Born on December 14, 1856, in Syracuse, New York, Marshall attended public schools and studied law in a private office before graduating from Columbia Law School in 1877. After practicing for 16 years in Syracuse, he became a partner in the firm of Guggenheimer, Untermyer & Marshall in New York City in 1894, an association that lasted until his death. He is chiefly remembered for his defense of minorities in issues involving their constitutional rights. Instrumental in bringing about many constitutional reforms, he took a special interest in immigration cases and was often successful in keeping restrictions against aliens to a minimum. He often appeared in defense of blacks, his most noted case being *Nixon v. Herndon*, which began the long struggle to eliminate voting restrictions in primary elections. Often involved in labor disputes, he mediated the New York cloakmakers' strike in 1910 in proceedings that became a model for later arbitration. He became prominent in Jewish affairs after the turn of the century. His work as a director of the Educational Alliance and as chairman of a commission appointed by New York City's Mayor Seth Low in 1902 resulted in better housing opportunities for Jews and less harassment of them by city officials. One of the founders of the American Jewish Committee in 1906, he served as its president after 1912. He was also a founder of the Jewish Welfare Board and long served as chairman of the board of the reorganized Jewish Theological Seminary. In 1911 he was largely responsible for the abrogation of the Russian-American treaty of 1832, which he attacked because of the Russians' reluctance to admit Jews with U.S. passports. During and after World War I he used his position of leadership in one of the largest Jewish communities in the world to aid the plight of Jews internationally. He helped form and became chairman of the American Jewish Relief Committee that gave substantial aid to refugees in Palestine. At the Versailles Peace Conference of 1919 he successfully advocated treaties, supported by the United States and signed by a number of European countries, intended to protect minority rights. Although Marshall was not initially a Zionist, he hoped that Palestine might become a permanent refuge for persecuted Jews. In 1929 he attended a meeting of Zionists and non-Zionists that was called in Switzerland. The subsequent constitution of the United Jewish Agency was largely drafted by Marshall, and he was elected chairman of its council. His efforts were cut short by his death on September 11, 1929, in Zurich.

Marshall, Thomas Riley (1854–1925), vice-president of the United States. Born in North Manchester, Indiana, on March 14, 1854, Marshall lived in Illinois, Kansas, and Missouri before attending public schools in Indiana. He graduated from Wabash College in 1873 and then studied law in the office of Judge Walter Olds, in Fort Wayne. Admitted to the bar on his twenty-

first birthday, he became a popular and successful lawyer in Columbia City, where he practiced from 1875 until 1909. A loyal Democrat like his father, he only once, in 1880, sought public office, running for county prosecutor. He emerged as a candidate for governor when the state convention became deadlocked in 1908. He served one term and succeeded in achieving a number of reforms, including a child-labor law, but failed in his attempt to bring about the adoption of a new state constitution. He was entered as a favorite-son candidate for the presidency at the Democratic national convention of 1912, which finally nominated Woodrow Wilson to head the ticket and chose Marshall as his running mate. He served under Wilson for two terms, the first vice-president to succeed himself in almost a century. As presiding officer of the Senate he earned a reputation for fairness, tact, and poise and exerted his influence for administration measures without alienating their opponents. Initially opposed to U.S. participation in World War I, he later supported Wilson and the League of Nations idea. After the war he opposed woman suffrage and prohibition. He was noted for his whimsical wit; his casual remark during a tedious Senate debate on the needs of the nation that "What this country needs is a really good five-cent cigar," remains a part of the nation's folk wisdom. His memoirs, *Recollections of Thomas R. Marshall: A Hoosier Salad*, 1925, did nothing to alter his reputation as a popular vice-president. On that office he offered perhaps the final word: "Once there were two brothers. One ran away to sea, the other was elected vice-president, and nothing was ever heard of either of them again." He retired from office in 1921 to practice law in Indianapolis; in 1922–1923 he served on the U.S. Coal Commission. Marshall died in Washington, D.C., on June 1, 1925.

Marshall, Thurgood (1908–   ), justice of the Supreme Court. Born in Baltimore on July 2, 1908, Marshall was the great-grandson of a slave "of independent spirit," and the son of a steward in a country club. He worked as a grocery clerk, waiter, and baker to earn his tuition at Lincoln University in Pennsylvania, graduating cum laude in 1930, and took his law degree magna cum laude from Howard University in 1933, being admitted to the bar that year. Beginning private practice in Baltimore, he concentrated on the field of civil rights and argued a number of cases for the local branch of the National Association for the Advancement of Colored People (NAACP). In 1938 he was named special counsel for the NAACP and two years later became head of its legal services division. Serving with the organization for 23 years, he undertook 32 major cases and won 29 of them. He established major constitutional precedents in *Smith v. Allwright*, 1944, securing Negro voting rights in Texas primary elections; *Morgan v. Virginia*, 1946, declaring unconstitutional segregated seating on interstate buses; *Sweatt v. Painter*, 1950, winning admission of a qualified black student to the University of Texas law school; and *Shelley* v. *Kraemer*, 1948, declaring state implementation of segregated housing agreements to be a violation of the Fourteenth Amendment. He won a reversal of the 1896 *Plessy* v. *Ferguson* "separate but equal" ruling on accommodations in the historic *Brown* v. *Board of Education* case in 1954, in which the Supreme Court held unanimously that racial segregation in public schools was a denial to Negro pupils of their rights under the Fourteenth Amendment. In 1961 he was nominated to the U.S. Court of Appeals by President John F. Kennedy. The Senate failed to consider the nomination before recessing, but he was renominated in 1962 and was approved on a floor vote, over the bitter protests of Southern senators. In 1965 President Lyndon B. Johnson appointed him U.S. solicitor general, the first Negro to hold this position, and in 1967, nominated by President Johnson, he became the first black member of the Supreme Court.

Martin, Abe, *see under* Hubbard, Frank McKinney

Martin, Glenn Luther (1886–1955), aircraft manufacturer. Born in Macksburg, Iowa, on January 17, 1886, Martin grew up in Liberal, Kansas, where his success in designing and marketing a kite at the age of eight was prophetic of his aerodynamical abilities and talent for business. After attending Kansas Wesleyan University for a short time, he accompanied his family to Santa Ana, California, in 1905, and worked there as an automobile mechanic. Encouraged by the success of the Wright brothers, he leased an abandoned church to use as a factory and built his first airplane in 1909. Powered by a Ford Model V motor, the craft flew about 100 feet at an altitude of 2 feet. In the years prior to World War I, Martin achieved notoriety as a barnstorming pilot and attracted considerable attention for an overwater flight, the first in aviation history, from Los Angeles to Catalina Island in one of his airplanes in 1912. He incorporated his aircraft business in 1911 and the next year moved to a factory in Los Angeles. One of the first to realize the military potential of aircraft, he built in his Los Angeles factory a trainer and other aircraft for the U.S. army in 1914. In 1917 he merged his firm briefly with the Wright Company, but withdrew later in the same year to conduct business independently. His first bomber, manufactured by the Glenn L. Martin Company in Cleveland in 1918–1919, appeared too late for service in World War I but established him as one of the leading airplane manufacturers in the United States. The plane, slightly modified in design, was used by Col. Billy Mitchell in 1921 to successfully demonstrate the strategic capability of an air force. Martin flying boats, which were eventually, as the first of the "clippers," to make possible transoceanic commercial air service, began to appear in the late 1920s, an undertaking that led him to move his

manufacturing facilities to Middle River, Maryland, near Baltimore. In 1932 the Martin enterprises produced the B-10, a twin-engine craft that greatly increased the speed and range of heavy bombers; the company later also produced the B-26 Marauder, the navy's PBM Marina flying boat. A number of Martin aircraft played important roles during World War II, most notably the Martin Marauder. Among the honors he received for his leadership in the aircraft industry were the 1933 Collier Trophy and the 1944 Guggenheim Medal of the Institute of Aeronautical Sciences. Toward the end of his life he took a great interest in civic affairs, education (he gave large sums to support the engineering schools at the University of Maryland), and wildlife conservation. He retired from active control of his company in 1953 and died in Baltimore on December 4, 1955.

Martin, Homer Dodge (1836–1897), painter. Born on October 28, 1836, in Albany, New York, Martin studied painting briefly with James M. Hart but taught himself the rudiments of his profession while wandering about the mountains of New York and New England. He sold an occasional landscape and managed to have two accepted for exhibition by the National Academy of Design when he was twenty-one. Moving to New York City in 1865, he did better but his wife, whom he married in 1861, had to continue to work as a journalist. He was made an associate of the National Academy in 1868 and was granted full membership in 1874, but his unwillingness to mix with the circles that might have bought his paintings, as well as the sombreness of his pictures, kept him from financial success. Forced to turn to magazine illustration for support, he met with some success; in 1881 the *Century* magazine sent him to England to sketch. In 1882 he settled down for a four-year stay in the French countryside, where his early Hudson River School style matured into one less imbued with the terrible grandeur of his previous work and more marked with a sense of contemplation amid natural beauty. At this time he began at least one of the works ("Ontario Sand Dunes") which later brought him fame. He completed the painting on his return to New York and, despite steadily failing sight during his last years as well as financial worries, he found himself for the first time the complete master of his talent. "The Sun Worshippers" and "Westchester Hills," perhaps his most melancholy works, were completed in the late 1880s. The year 1892 found him in St. Paul, Minnesota, still struggling to get out of debt and enjoying only an occasional sale. Several of his last canvases, among his noblest work, were Normandy scenes painted from memory. "Adirondack Scenery," sometimes considered his best painting and also from this period, revived the scenes of his youth. Martin died in St. Paul on February 12, 1897, after a long bout with cancer. Within a decade his works were commanding high prices and he has since earned a place among the best American landscape painters of the nineteenth century, his canvases finding places in many major galleries and museums.

Martin, Joseph William, Jr. (1884–1968), public official. Born in North Attleboro, Massachusetts, on November 3, 1884, Martin delivered newspapers as a youth, and during high school held part-time jobs in local newspaper shops. He decided against college to become a reporter, working on two papers. At the age of twenty-four he joined several others in the purchase of the *Evening Chronicle* in North Attleboro and in time gained complete control of the paper. He began his political career as a Republican campaign manager, served in the Massachusetts legislature from 1912 to 1917, and remained active in state politics until he was elected to the House of Representatives in 1924. He survived the lean Republican years of the 1930s despite his opposition to the New Deal, and his organizational talents were rewarded with the post of party whip in the House in 1933. Under Martin's guidance, in the Congressional campaign in 1938 the Republicans made a noticeable dent in the overwhelming majority held by Democrats in the House of Representatives. He was elected in 1939 to the post of minority leader, which he held for 20 years. The Republicans were not in a majority in the House during this period except in 1947–1949 and 1953–1955, periods when Martin served as speaker. As a result he never achieved the prominence of Sam Rayburn, his Democrat counterpart. His role in the House remained that of a self-effacing coordinator of the opposition party, in which he proved eminently capable. A tireless party worker, he served on the Republican National Committee from 1936 to 1942, the last two years as chairman. He also served as permanent chairman of every Republican national convention from 1940 to 1956. He was replaced as Republican floor leader by a slim margin in January 1959 at the age of seventy-four. He remained in the House for 42 years, until he lost a primary election in 1966. He died in Fort Lauderdale, Florida, on March 6, 1968.

Martin, Luther (1748?–1826), lawyer and public official. Born near New Brunswick, New Jersey, either on February 9, 1744 or, more likely, 1748, Martin graduated from the College of New Jersey (now Princeton) in 1766 and, after teaching school at various places, was admitted to the Virginia bar in 1771. He began his practice in that state but soon moved to Somerset County, Maryland, where he had established a lucrative practice by the outbreak of the Revolution. A prominent patriot, he was appointed in February 1778 the first attorney general of Maryland, a position he retained until 1805. During the Revolution he prosecuted Loyalists severely and was sent to Congress in 1785. He was also a delegate to the Federal Constitutional Convention of 1787, but he disapproved of the plan to establish a strong central government, walked out of the convention without signing the Constitution, and fought vainly against its ratification in Maryland the next year. He had in 1783 married the daughter of Capt. Michael Cresap, who was accused of having killed the family of the Indian leader James Logan; when Thomas Jefferson reprinted Logan's famous and touching speech about the murders in his *Notes on the State of Virginia*, 1787, Martin reacted violently, publishing angry letters in the Baltimore newspapers and conceiving a hatred for Jefferson that led him into the Federalist party. In 1805 he successfully defended Associate Justice Samuel Chase of the Supreme Court in his impeachment trial in the U.S. Senate and in 1807 was one of the lawyers who defended Aaron Burr in his treason trial, in the process attacking Jefferson's administration with great bitterness. He became a judge in Baltimore in 1813; in 1818, 40 years after his first appointment to the post, he was again named attorney general of Maryland, in which capacity he represented the losing side in *McCulloch* v. *Maryland* (1819) before the Supreme Court. Opposing him in this celebrated case upholding the constitutionality of the Bank of the United States were Daniel Webster, William Pinkney, and William Wirt. In his later years Martin subsisted almost entirely on brandy, and the incapacitation produced by this, combined with stroke suffered in 1820, forced him to resign from the bench in 1822. Destitute thereafter and broken in health, he was supported by an extraordinary tax levied by the Maryland legislature on all lawyers practicing in the state. On the withdrawal of this subsidy in 1823 he was allowed to spend his last years in Burr's home in New York City, where he died on July 10, 1826. A brilliant although irascible lawyer, he was often referred to in later years as "the Thersites of the law," and Henry Adams called him "the notorious reprobate genius."

Marx, Groucho (1895–1977), humorist. Born in New York City on October 2, 1895, Julius Henry Marx made his stage debut in 1906 as a soprano in *The Messenger Boys*. Two years later he went on tour with the LeRoy Trio, who mimicked female singers, but his voice changed and he returned to New York City. He next performed about 1911 in a group called the Three Nightingales, organized by his mother, the daughter of a German ventriloquist and herself a yodeling harpist and the sister of Al Shean of the comedy team of Gallagher and Shean. The group was reorganized first as the Four Nightingales and then as the Six Mascots before finally becoming the Four Marx Brothers—Adolph (1893–1964), who took the name Arthur ("Harpo"), Milton ("Gummo," 1894–1977), and Leonard ("Chico," 1891–1961). After World War I Milton went into the raincoat business and was replaced by the youngest brother, Herbert ("Zeppo," 1901–1979). Their nicknames were created by monologist Art Fischer, and over their vaudeville years the brothers evolved their stage personalities: Groucho, the crack-shot wit; Harpo, the idiot, a mute kleptomaniacal harpist who frequently communicated by pantomime or by horn; Chico, a pianist, soliloquist, confidence man, and Harpo's "interpreter," who spoke incorrigibly broken English; and Zeppo, the straight man of the group. One of their most memorable early vaudeville shows was *On the Mezzanine*. In 1924 they conquered the musical stage with *I'll Say She Is*, followed by *Coconuts*, 1926, and *Animal Crackers*, 1928, the last two of which were made into movies in 1929. Their one silent film was *Humor Risk*, 1919, a travesty on *Humoresque*. Their talking films included *Monkey Business*, 1931; *Horsefeathers*, 1932; and *Duck Soup*, 1933. Zeppo, who had always seemed aloof from the comic mayhem of the other three, left the group after *Duck Soup* to open a theatrical agency, and the remaining trio was then seen in *A Night at the Opera*, 1935; *A Day at the Races*, 1936; *Room Service*, 1938; *A Day at the Circus*, 1938; *Go West*, 1940; *The Big Store*, 1941; *A Night in Casablanca*, 1946 (for which Harpo refused a large sum of money to speak one word); and *Love Happy*, 1948, the brothers' last film together. Groucho, the group's mainstay, wrote many of the zany routines (other screenplays and stage scripts were provided by such notables as George S. Kaufman, S. J. Perelman, and Ben Hecht), and also contributed to the screen play for *The King and the Chorus Girl*, 1937, and the play *Time for Elizabeth*, 1948. He appeared in *Copacabana*, 1947; *It's Only Money*, 1951; and *A Girl in Every Port*, 1951; moderated the quiz show "You Bet Your Life" on radio and television, and wrote *Beds*, 1930; *Many Happy Returns*, 1940 (about income tax problems); and the autobiographical *Groucho and Me*, 1959. Fascinated by words, he uttered devastating and atrocious puns that made mincemeat of logic, or of notable personalities, or of guests on "You Bet Your Life." As much a part of his humor as verbal twists were his leer, wagging eyebrows, bent-over gait, frock coat, mustache, and cigar. He was the last Marx brother to remain prominent in show business, though the trio's popularity remained high through frequent revivals of their films. He died in Los Angeles on August 19, 1977.

Mason, Charles (1728?–1786), and **Jeremiah Dixon** (? –1777), surveyors and astronomers. Mason was born in England about 1728 and between 1756 and 1760 was associated with the Greenwich Observatory as an astronomer. In 1761 he and Jeremiah Dixon, about whom almost nothing is known except that he was English and worked with Mason for the next few years, were commissioned by the Royal Society to make observations of the transit of Venus; they were required by this work to go to Sumatra, but their journey was interrupted by a hostile encounter with a French vessel and ultimately they were obliged to make their observations at the Cape of Good Hope. Mason and Dixon earned their place in American history when they were employed by the colonial proprietors of Pennsylvania and Maryland to establish the boundary between the

two colonies. The preceding boundary dispute, which went back nearly a century, arose from incompatible and even impossible grants embodied in the Maryland charter granted to Cecilius Calvert, Baron Baltimore, in 1632 and the subsequent grant to William Penn 50 years later. An initial attempt at settlement was made in 1685, when the Crown ordered the disputed territory to be divided equally. But the vagueness of the original delineations, made in ignorance of New World geography, prolonged the dispute until it grew to encompass competing claims for the cities of Baltimore and Philadelphia. The solution agreed upon by the parties in 1750 involved drawing an arc of 12 miles' radius around the city of New Castle, Delaware, a line first struck in 1682 by the Duke of York as a boundary between Delaware and Pennsylvania, and then running a line westward from the point where the line dividing the Delaware peninsula was tangential to this arc— as it turned out, at approximately 39° 43' N. Beginning in 1763, Mason and Dixon resurveyed the Delaware tangent line and the New Castle arc and by 1768, at a cost of $75,000, had located and extended the Pennsylvania–Maryland boundary line west for 244 miles, setting milestones brought from England along the way, every fifth one of which bore the arms of Penn on one side and of Calvert on the other. Mason and Dixon's Line was ratified by the crown in 1769; it was later extended farther west to settle a boundary dispute between Pennsylvania and Virginia. Running between free states on the north and slave states to the south, it eventually became a highly emotional symbol in the sectional dispute over slavery and is still popularly regarded as the dividing line between North and South, although it ends at the Ohio River. Mason and Dixon returned to England in 1768 and for several years thereafter Mason was engaged in various astronomical projects, including observations in Ireland and Scotland and compiling of a catalogue of stars. Eventually he returned to the United States and died in Philadelphia on October 25, 1786. About the later career of Dixon nothing is known; he died in Durham, England, in 1777.

Mason, George (1725–1792), planter and public official. Born in 1725 in Fairfax County, Virginia, to a long-established Virginia family, Mason received little formal education, but through his own efforts and those of his guardian, an uncle, he read much and gained a wide knowledge of law. He was much interested in western settlement and from 1752 until 1773 was a member and treasurer of the Ohio Company. Throughout his life he considered himself a private citizen and his periods of public service were undertaken with reluctance and sometimes, because of his low esteem for the common run of politicians, with outright distaste. Nonetheless, as a large landowner he naturally became involved in public affairs, first locally and by 1759 in the Virginia House of Burgesses. After a single term in this body he withdrew to private life, but during the mounting conflict between the colonies and Great Britain in the 1760s and 1770s he wrote numerous tracts defending the colonial position, including the resolutions that became the basis of the Virginia non-importation association in the dispute over the Townshend duties, and the Fairfax Resolves, which were adopted eventually by the Continental Congress. In 1775 he was a member of the July Convention and the next year of the state's Committee of Safety; in May of 1776 he drafted Virginia's first constitution, including a Declaration of Rights that, with its doctrine of inalienable rights, was drawn upon by Thomas Jefferson in writing the Declaration of Independence. The constitution itself served as a model for those of several other states. A member of the Virginia House of Delegates from 1776 to 1788, Mason was active in supervising the organization of the new state government and was instrumental in arranging George Rogers Clark's expedition to secure the Northwest country. In 1787 he was a delegate to the Federal Constitutional Convention in Philadelphia and was one of its most active members. As a lifelong opponent of slavery, he objected to the compromise that allowed continuation of the slave trade until 1808. Although he had favored replacing the Articles of Confederation with a stronger instrument, he decided at length that the proposed Constitution went too far in the direction of centralization of government and he left the convention early, returning to Virginia to oppose ratification. His objections, clearly and forcefully maintained, were in large part responsible for the adoption of the first ten amendments—the Bill of Rights—to the Constitution, which again were influenced greatly by his earlier Declaration of Rights. Mason declined public office thereafter, including appointment as one of Virginia's first two senators, and retired to his plantation home, Gunston Hall, which he had completed in 1758. He died on October 7, 1792.

Mason, James Murray (1798–1871), public official and Confederate diplomat. Born on November 3, 1798, in Fairfax County, Virginia, the grandson of George Mason, Mason graduated from the University of Virginia in 1818, studied law at the College of William and Mary, and was admitted to the bar and began practice in Winchester, Virginia, in 1820. He was elected to the Virginia house of delegates in 1826, representing his "back country" district until 1832 (except for the year 1827) and serving in the Virginia constitutional convention in 1829. He supported the reelection of President Andrew Jackson in 1832, served one term in the House of Representatives, from 1837 to 1839, and was appointed in 1847 to fill a vacant seat in the Senate, where he became a close associate of John C. Calhoun. A staunch advocate of the Southern system, Mason was the author of the Fugitive Slave Law of 1850. He eventually became chairman of the Senate Foreign Relations Committee before resigning from the Senate in 1861 to take part in the Virginia convention that

voted secession from the Union. He served briefly as a Virginia delegate to the provisional Confederate Congress. After the outbreak of the Civil War he was appointed by Jefferson Davis, in August 1861, as the Confederate States' commissioner to Great Britain. He left for England accompanied by John Slidell, commissioner to France, aboard the British mail ship *Trent*. The two emissaries were intercepted at sea by Capt. Charles Wilkes of the U.S. navy and imprisoned in Boston for two months; they were released on January 1, 1862, by order of President Abraham Lincoln, who had been urged to this action by Senator Charles Sumner, Mason's successor as chairman of the Foreign Relations Committee. The *Trent* Affair almost led to a diplomatic break with England and to a British declaration of war against the United States. Arriving in England, Mason made many efforts, all ineffectual, to get the British government to recognize the Confederacy as an independent nation, if not to wage war on the states of the North; there was much British sympathy for the Southern cause, strengthened by a British need for Southern cotton, but the British could afford to wait and see. After the Confederate defeats at Antietam and Gettysburg, and the first Emancipation Proclamation that followed Antietam, there was no longer any possibility of gaining British recognition. Mason established a newspaper, the *Index*, in Britain and courted Confederate sympathizers there, but he was never able to secure an official audience. His commission was withdrawn in late 1863 but he did not return to Virginia until after the second proclamation of amnesty in 1868. He died near Alexandria, Virginia, on April 28, 1871.

Mason, Lowell (1792–1872), musician, composer, and educator. Born in Medfield, Massachusetts, on January 8, 1792, Mason was a musical prodigy, playing several instruments during his youth, and was active as a church choir leader before undertaking similar employment in Savannah, Georgia, in 1812. He also taught singing, but was reticent about attaching his name to a collection of church hymns he compiled with the aid of F. C. Abel. It appeared as *The Boston Handel and Haydn Society's Collection of Church Music* in 1822 and was a success. He returned to Massachusetts in 1827 to become director of music for a succession of churches and president of the Handel and Haydn Society in Boston, a post he held until 1832. He continued to collect sacred tunes; *The Juvenile Psalmist*, 1829, *The Juvenile Lyre*, 1830, and *Lyra Sacra*, 1832, were among several of his books that had appeared by 1832. His list of titles eventually exceeded 50. Mason is chiefly remembered for his part in introducing musical education into the public schools and to a lesser extent, for his attempt to provide musical instruction for adults. In 1833 he founded the Boston Academy of Music and for several years worked out there a system of musical instruction for children based on that of the Swiss educator J. H. Pestalozzi, which emphasized learning singing before making any attempt to master musical notation. His *Manual of Instruction* appeared in 1834. By 1837 he had succeeded in introducing his methods in the Boston public schools and from 1838 to 1841 he was placed in charge of all music instruction. His subsequent success in organizing conventions for training instructors in his methods extended his influence throughout New England and even to the frontier. Mason was also a popular composer of hymns, of which he wrote more than 1200; among those still well known are "From Greenland's Icy Mountain," "My Faith Looks Up to Thee," and "Nearer, My God, to Thee." He moved to New York City in 1851 and two years later founded the New York Normal Institute there. He died on August 11, 1872, in Orange, New Jersey, where he had lived since 1854. His extensive musical library, comprising some 8000 volumes as well as manuscripts that dated to the sixteenth century, was willed to Yale.

Massasoit (1590?–1661), Indian leader. Massasoit, also known as Ousamequin (Yellow Feather), who was described as "in his best years" when he and a group of other chiefs took the initiative in making friendly overtures to the Pilgrims at Plymouth in March 1621, was chief of the Wampanoag Indians. Earlier references to a "king of the country" by John Smith may have been to Massasoit, whose domain extended over the present Massachusetts and Rhode Island and who made his home near what is now Bristol, Rhode Island. He was noted for his lifelong efforts to maintain peace with the white men. A treaty of friendship he made with the Pilgrims in 1621 inaugurated 40 years of peace between his tribe and the colonists, and in 1623 he was instrumental in warding off an attack aimed at destroying Thomas Weston's plantation. During this period many of his tribesmen succumbed to an unknown illness and Massasoit himself apparently escaped death only after he was ministered to by the men at Plymouth in 1623. In 1632 Edward Winslow sheltered him from a conspiracy of the Narragansett Indians. In 1638 he inexplicably appeared in Boston with a peace offering and again, four years later, was cordially received by Governor John Winthrop. A letter of Roger Williams (with whom he was also friendly), written in December 1661, mentions his death. His son Metacomet, known as King Philip, proved more hostile toward the whites.

Masters, Edgar Lee (1869–1950), poet and biographer. Born on August 23, 1869, in Garnett, Kansas, Masters moved during his childhood to Lewistown, Illinois. He attended Knox College for a year, was admitted to the bar in 1891, and moved to Chicago. His law practice was slow to develop —he was for a brief time in practice with Clarence Darrow—and he found ample time to write; he published a volume of poetry in 1898 and several other books afterwards, none of which was successful or significant. He hovered on the periphery of the great Chicago group of young writers, how-

ever, and during 1914, under the pseudonym of Webster Ford, he published a number of poems in *Reedy's Mirror*, a St. Louis literary paper; the series, consisting of free-verse monologues by persons who spoke from the graveyard where they lay buried in Spoon River, a fictitious Illinois town, attracted attention and was published in book form as *Spoon River Anthology* in 1915. The book was a sensation on the American literary scene and remained high in the esteem of critics by dint of its direct, sombre view of human nature and its spare, simple verses. By 1940 it had gone through 70 editions and had been translated into several foreign languages; the success had ruined Masters's legal practice, however, and, moving to New York City, he devoted himself to writing thereafter. Although he was immensely prolific, none of his later works was equal to the quality of the *Anthology*, or gained as much attention. *Domesday Book*, 1920, was accounted by many critics and by Masters himself the best of his later verse, but *The New Spoon River*, 1924, was not successful. His biography *Vachel Lindsay: A Poet in America*, 1935, was awarded the Mark Twain Medal. His biography of Abraham Lincoln in 1931 took a harshly debunking approach to an American mythic hero and aroused a storm of controversy; he also wrote biographies of Walt Whitman and Mark Twain. In 1936 he published *Across Spoon River*, his autobiography. He died in Philadelphia on March 5, 1950.

Masterson, William Barclay (1853–1921), "Bat," frontier peace officer. Born on November 24, 1853, in Iroquois County, Illinois, Bat Masterson moved to Kansas with his family at the age of seventeen. During his twenties he hunted buffalo, established a reputation as an Indian fighter, served as an army scout, and at twenty-three became a deputy marshal at Dodge City, Kansas. The following year, after a brief sojourn in the gold-rush town of Deadwood, South Dakota, he served as sheriff of Ford County. Early in 1878 he joined the ranks of the fearless frontier marshals after his deft capture of the notorious Dave Rudabaugh. Later that year he brought quick retribution to the killers of his brother Edward, who was gunned down by two men while acting as the marshal of Dodge City. In 1880 Bat was associated with Wyatt Earp in and around the infamous Tombstone, Arizona. Noted also as a gambler and something of a dandy, Masterson achieved a national reputation as a defender of order in lawless Kansas. He was also active in Colorado and in 1891 he was married in Denver. A boxing enthusiast, he went to New York City in 1902 to become a sports writer on the *New York Morning Telegraph*. From 1905 to 1907 he served as a federal deputy marshal (appointed by his admirer, President Theodore Roosevelt) but resigned because it interfered with his newspaper work. In time he became sports editor of the *Telegraph* and an officer of the company that published it. He died in New York City on October 25, 1921, a minor hero. His name, along with a small number of others, has become a permanent part of the legend that surrounds American westward expansion.

Mather, Cotton (1663–1728), clergyman, author, and scholar. Born in Boston on February 12, 1663, Cotton Mather was the eldest son of Increase Mather and grandson of Richard Mather and of John Cotton, for whom he was named. He graduated from Harvard in 1678 and, sharing his father's interest in science, studied medicine for a time. He took an M.A. in 1681. He turned to the ministry, however, and in 1685 was ordained, joining his father in the pulpit of Boston's Second Church, where he remained for the rest of his life. He worked closely with his father, and during the latter's absence in England, where he sought the restoration of the colonial charter revoked by Charles II, Cotton promoted by his writings the revolt against the Stuart-appointed royal governor, Sir Edmund Andros. On his father's return with a new charter and a new governor, Sir William Phips, he plied his pen in the service of both. His scientific curiosity, combined with a marked proclivity for mysticism, led him into the study of spiritualism and possession; his *Memorable Providences Relating to Witchcrafts and Possessions,* 1689, made a public issue of the subject and contributed to the hysteria that resulted in the Salem witchcraft trials of 1692. Mather did not participate in the trials, and disapproved of the excesses and lapses of reason displayed by the judges. *Wonders of the Invisible World,* 1693, was a narrative of some of the trials. After this time his political influence, which through his association with his father in the charter dispute had been considerable, began to wane as the new charter of 1691 proved less than unanimously popular and as colonial politics became increasingly secular. His devotion to the church was undiminished, however, and through his tireless efforts in the cause of orthodox Congregationalism and his vast body of written work—some 450 separate titles—his fame continued to grow. His books ranged in subject matter from natural history, as in his *Curiosa Americana,* 1712–1724, to church music, in *The Accomplished Singer,* 1721, and from church polity in *Ratio Disciplinae,* 1726, to moral essays such as those in *Bonifacius,* 1710, later known to and loved by Benjamin Franklin as *Essays to do Good.* His most famous work, *Magnalia Christi Americana,* was published in 1702 and remained the most complete history of New England for many years. His struggle against heterodoxy was unavailing. Dissenting churches, such as the Brattle Street Church founded in 1698, flourished, and Harvard became less and less strictly Congregationalist in policy; in 1703, by which time it was clear that his hopes for the presidency of Harvard were in vain, he resigned his fellowship in the college after 13 years and promoted the founding of Yale as a new bastion of the faith. He took great interest in the proper training of children, organized a school for the education of Negroes, and concerned himself with ministering personally to his parishioners. In 1713 he was elected to the Royal Society; in 1721 he joined his father in the often unpopular campaign of encouraging Zabdiel Boylston to experiment with inoculation against smallpox. In 1723 Mather succeeded his father as pastor of the Second Church. At the time of his death in Boston on February 13, 1728, Cotton Mather was probably the best known of Americans; he remains the most famous of the Puritan divines.

Mather, Increase (1639–1723), religious leader, educator, and political leader. Born in Dorchester, Massachusetts, on June 21, 1639, Increase was the son of Richard Mather. He graduated from Harvard in 1656 and the next year sailed to Britain; in 1658 he took an M.A. from Trinity College, Dublin, and remained in the British Isles, serving in various clerical posts, until the restoration of the Stuarts in 1660 made Puritanism again uncomfortable in England. Returning to Massachusetts in 1661, he joined his father at the church in Dorchester and remained there until he became teacher of Boston's Second Church in 1664; he occupied the pulpit there for the rest of his life. His strong personality, forceful preaching, and broad scholarship won him increasing prominence; in 1674 he was appointed licenser of the press, in 1675 a fellow of Harvard, and ten years later president of the college. He was a prolific writer, and though most of his works were theological in nature, he wrote also on history, science, and politics. Prominent among his more than 150 books were *The Life and Death of that Reverend Man of God, Mr. Richard Mather,* 1670; *A Brief History of the Warr with the Indians,* 1676; *A Relation of the Troubles Which Have Hapned in New-England by Reason of the Indians There,* 1677; and *Essay for the Recording of Illustrious Providences,* 1684. Although always first and foremost devoted to his ministry, he was drawn into political affairs by the dispute over the Massachusetts charter during the 1680s. He led the protest against revocation of the charter and in 1688 sailed to England in an attempt to have it restored. Negotiations with powerful politicians of the Stuart court and with James II himself came to naught; but in 1690 he was appointed an official agent of the colony and managed to win some concessions from William III in the new charter of 1691, which joined the Massachusetts Bay and Plymouth colonies. He returned to Boston the next year with Sir William Phips, the new royal governor, whom the king had allowed him to nominate. Mather was identified strongly with both the governor and the charter and when they proved unpopular with a large number of the colonists, he found himself embroiled in a political controversy that eventually, in 1701, cost him the presidency of Harvard. During the Salem witchcraft trials in 1692 he expressed private disapproval of the proceedings but publicly held his peace until October, when he wrote *Cases of Conscience Concerning Evil Spirits,* a work that was circulated widely and played a vital role in ending the period of hysteria. After leaving Harvard he largely forsook politics but remained a leader of New England Congregationalism. He died on August 23, 1723, in Boston. His eldest son, Cotton Mather, became the most famous of Puritan clergymen.

Mather, Richard (1596–1669), religious leader. Born in 1596 in Lowton, England, Mather taught school for several years before spending a few months in 1618 studying at Brasenose College, Oxford. In November of that year he was called to the pulpit at Toxteth Park, now part of Liverpool, and a short time later was ordained. During the course of his ministry there he displayed an increasing tendency toward Puritanism, with the result that in 1633 and again in 1634 he was suspended by ecclesiastical authorities. In 1635 he decided to emigrate to America; he set sail with his family in May and on August 17 landed in Boston. Immediately offered several pulpits, he chose that of Dorchester, where he remained as teacher for the rest of his life. He quickly became a leader of New England Congregationalism and a central figure in the elaboration of both doctrine and polity. One of his earliest written works, done in collaboration with the Reverend John Eliot and another minister, was *The Whole Booke of Psalms*, 1640, better known as *The Bay Psalm Book*. Other major works by Mather were *Church-Government and Church-Covenant Discussed*, 1643, and particularly *A Platform of Church Discipline*, 1649, which under the common title of the Cambridge Platform served for many years as the basic document of New England Congregationalism. He was a chief proponent of the Half-Way Covenant, of 1662, which broadened church membership and helped maintain ecclesiastical power in the colony. Of his six children, four became ministers; the youngest, Increase Mather, became one of the most prominent and influential of all New England clergymen. Richard Mather died on April 22, 1669, in Dorchester, Massachusetts.

Mather, Stephen Tyng (1867–1930), conservationist. Born in San Francisco on July 4, 1867, Mather was a descendent of Richard, Increase, and Cotton Mather of Massachusetts. He graduated from the University of California at Berkeley in 1887 and subsequently worked as a reporter for the *New York Sun*. In 1893 he became associated with the Pacific Coast Borax Company and the following year organized and became manager of its Chicago branch. After the turn of the century he joined others in forming his own company, Thorkildsen-Mather Borax and eventually became president of the Sterling Borax Company. Mather's chief accomplishment was preserving and extending the system of national parks, an effort to which he devoted his last 15 years. In 1915 he became assistant to Secretary of the Interior Franklin Lane and two years later organized and became director of the Interior Department's National Park Service. Under his auspices the national parks estab-lished by Congress grew from 14 to 21; he was directly responsible for the establishment of more than half of these, although a number of areas that did not meet his high standards of excellence were dropped from the system; among those added were the Grand Canyon, Rocky Mountain, Bryce Canyon, Grand Teton, Hawaii, Zion, and Great Smoky Mountains parks. Integral to his accomplishment was the establishment of the criteria as to what indeed constituted a national park as well as the principle that excluded indusrial users from these scenic areas, during a period in which the automobile and the accompanying highways were first beginning to contribute to the destruction of the nation's open lands. Mather died in Brookline, Massachusetts, on January 22, 1930.

Mathewson, Christopher (1880–1925), "Christy," baseball player. Born on August 12, 1880, in Factoryville, Pennsylvania, Christy Mathewson, who was also known as "Matty" and as "Big Six" (after a famous fire engine), left Bucknell University, where he had starred in both baseball and football, in 1900 to join the Norfolk team of the Virginia baseball league. After a dazzling season in which he won 22 of 24 games pitched, he was bought by the New York Giants of the National League. A disappointing start in major league ball led to his being sent down to a farm club. The Cincinnati team picked him up, and promptly traded him back to the Giants again, where his career began in earnest. One of the first college men to play in the major leagues, he won 20 games (including a no-hitter against St. Louis) in his first full season, 1901, despite having a weak team behind him. He won 30 games in 1903, his first full season with a stronger Giant team under John J. McGraw, while establishing a record of 267 strikeouts that endured for more than 50 years. Mathewson won 33 and lost 12 the following year and in 1905 won 31 games while losing 9. In the World Series that year he accomplished his most famous feat, shutting out the powerful Philadelphia Athletics three times in five days, allowing them a total of only 14 hits in the 27 innings he pitched. He enjoyed a fourth 30-victory season in 1908, winning the astonishing total of 37 games while losing only 11, and was a 20-game winner in eight other seasons. A right-handed pitcher, he was equally effective against right- and left-handed batters owing to his perfecting of the fadeaway pitch (later known as the screwball), which broke away from left-handers. He pitched for the Giants until 1916, when he joined the Cincinnati Reds as player-manager. When he retired as a player at the end of the 1916 season he had amassed a record of 372 wins and 187 losses and had struck out a total of 2499 batters. He managed the Reds during the 1917 season and part of the 1918 season and then enlisted in the army, returning to become a coach with the Giants after World War I. Failing health, probably the result of having been gassed during the war, virtually ended his career in 1920. His last five years were devoted to a losing battle against tuberculosis, and although he served as president of the Boston Braves from 1923 to 1925 he spent much of his time at a tuberculosis sanatorium in Saranac Lake, New York, where he died on October 7, 1925, in the midst of the World Series of that year. He was one of the first five players to be named to the National Baseball Hall of Fame in 1936; his bust bears the statement, never since disputed: "Matty was master of them all."

Mathias, Robert Bruce (1930–), decathlon champion. Born in Tulare, California, on November 17, 1930, Bob Mathias exhibited athletic promise at baseball as early as the age of six. At Tulare high school he played football and basketball in addition to starring in track and field events. During his junior year in 1947 he won state high school competitions in the discus and the shot put and also did well in the high jump. His coach, Virgil Jackson, then began to groom him for the first post–World War II Olympic Games that were to be held at London in the summer of 1948. When Mathias began training for the decathlon he had never attempted pole vaulting or throwing the javelin, but in the early summer of 1948 he did well in those events at the annual Pacific Coast games at Pasadena, California. He beat the national decathlon champion at the Olympic tryouts and went on to a dazzling victory in London, beating 19 competitors while still only seventeen in a grueling event that takes two days and includes the 100-meter dash, broad jump, shot put, high jump, 400-meter run, 110-meter hurdles, discus throw, pole vault, javelin throw, and 1500-meter run. The immediate comparison to Jim Thorpe who won the decathlon in Stockholm in 1912 (but was later disqualified) was inevitable. Mathias afterward remained active in decathlon competition, winning a record four national championships before competing again in the 1952 Olympic games at Helsinki. There he won the gold medal for an unprecedented second time, scoring 7887 points to break his own previous record. He enrolled in 1949 at Stanford University, where he also played football. After graduation he served in the Marine Corps from 1954 to 1956 and from 1956 to 1963 was a goodwill ambassador for the Department of State. He was elected to the House of Representatives from the 18th district of California in 1966 and was reelected in 1968 and 1970.

Matoaka, see Pocahontas

Matthes, François Émile (1874–1948), geologist and geographer. Born in Amsterdam on March 16, 1874, Matthes came to the United States in 1891 and four years later graduated from the Massachusetts Institute of Technology (MIT). He was naturalized in 1896 and in that year joined the topographic section of the U.S. Geological Survey, under whose auspices he spent the next 17 years mapping various trackless wilderness regions in the West, including the Bighorn Mountains,

Glacier and Grand Canyon national parks, Yosemite Valley, Mount Rainier, and the Sierra Nevada. His travels resulted not only in maps distinguished by his excellent and beautiful sketches of outstanding national features, but also in an abiding interest in problems of geomorphology, particularly the effects of glaciation. A gifted writer he published the popular *Glacial Sculpture of the Bighorn Mountains,* 1900, and *Mt. Rainier and Its Glaciers,* 1914, in addition to more technical papers, articles, and books, including the classic *Geologic History of the Yosemite Valley,* 1930, and *Geologic History of Mt. Whitney,* 1937. Matthes was also interested in glaciers as indicators of climatic change. He died in Berkeley, California, on June 21, 1948.

Matthews, Stanley (1824–1889), justice of the Supreme Court. Born in Cincinnati on July 21, 1824, Matthews graduated from Kenyon College in 1840 and was admitted to the bar in Tennessee and practiced law in Columbia before returning to Cincinnati in 1844. He achieved some distinction as an assistant prosecuting attorney there and, through his editorship of the *Cincinnati Morning Herald,* as an antislavery agitator. His first service on the bench came under Ohio's new constitution in 1851. He served briefly on the court of common pleas for Hamilton County before returning to private practice. In 1858 he was appointed by President James Buchanan as U.S. attorney for Ohio's southern district and attracted attention in this post as the unpopular prosecutor of W. B. Connelly under the Fugitive Slave laws, despite the fact that the action went against his own private convictions. He served as a colonel in the Union army during the Civil War, but resigned after being elected to the Cincinnati superior court in 1863. He returned to private practice again after the war. Matthews supported the reelection of President Abraham Lincoln in 1864 and first achieved national prominence as counsel before the Electoral Commission appointed in 1877 to decide the Hayes-Tilden dispute over the electoral vote for the presidency. Rutherford B. Hayes was duly elected despite Samuel J. Tilden's majority of the popular vote, and when Hayes appointed John Sherman of Ohio secretary of the treasury in March 1877, Matthews was elected to the Senate to fill the vacancy. He served two years. Hayes, who had known Matthews since their days at Kenyon, nominated him early in 1881 to succeed Noah H. Swayne on the Supreme Court. The appointment was not confirmed by the Senate, which dragged up the Connelly affair and had by no means forgotten Hayes's partisan capture of the White House. Renominated by President James A. Garfield, after the change of administration in March, to the same vacancy, Matthews was again opposed by the Senate Judiciary Committee but in May was confirmed by the full Senate by a margin of one vote. Despite the widespread doubts of his independence, he proved to be a capable associate justice. He wrote a number of the Court's opinions on complex financial cases, but possibly his most important opinion was in the case of *Yick Wo* v. *Hopkins*, 1886, in which he held for the Court that a law was unconstitutional, even if fair and impartial on its face, if it was administered in such a way as to deprive citizens of the equal protection of the laws as required by the Fourteenth Amendment. He died in Washington, D.C., on March 22, 1889.

Matzeliger, Jan Ernest (1852–1889), inventor. Born in Surinam (Dutch Guiana) in 1852, Matzeliger was the son of a Dutch colonial engineer and a black mother. At the age of ten he was apprenticed in the government machine shop, where he developed an interest in machines of all sorts; at about the age of twenty he emigrated to the United States and for the next five years worked in machine shops in various places. In 1877 he was in Lynn, Massachusetts, working in a shoe factory, when he began to work out ideas for improving the machinery then available for making shoes; he had been challenged by a conversation that he overheard among some workmen, to the effect that no machine would ever replace hand lasting of shoes, and he set about immediately to prove them wrong. Working alone and at night, he experimented with various designs and by September 1880 was sure enough that he was on the right track to seek financing. With backing, he worked on a second model machine and then a third, which he patented in 1883, and finally a fourth, which could make an entire shoe in one minute. Having succeeded on the mechanical side, he was full of plans to develop the idea commercially and to make a fortune for himself. The Consolidated Hand Method Lasting Machine Company, formed with his backers in 1883, languished after he developed tuberculosis and could work no longer. Matzeliger died in Lynn, Massachusetts, in 1889. His patent and stock were acquired by the United Shoe Machinery Company and, once put into general use as the final machine necessary to fully automate shoemaking, the lasting machine brought about a huge increase in production and decrease in price.

Mauldin, William Henry (1921–   ) "Bill," cartoonist. Born on October 29, 1921, in Mountain Park, New Mexico, Mauldin studied at the Chicago Academy of Fine Arts in 1939 and began to train with the 45th Infantry Division of the U.S. army in 1940. He became a staff cartoonist for the *45th Division News* and, going overseas in 1943, joined the Mediterranean staff of the army newspaper *Stars and Stripes*, covering campaigns in Italy, France, and Germany. He developed the cartoon soldiers named Willie and Joe, whose progressively deteriorating appearance and disenchanted attitudes reflected those of many U.S. soldiers overseas. The cartoons were featured in 100 newspapers in the United States, as well as in *Stars and Stripes*, collected in several volumes, including *Up Front*, 1945, and made Mauldin famous. He won a Pulitzer Prize in 1945 for a cartoon captioned "Fresh American troops, flushed

with victory," which showed grimy soldiers plodding through a storm in the mud. His postwar depictions of Willie and Joe trying to adjust to civilian life (collected in *Back Home*, 1947) and a new series of cartoons mocking racists, overzealous patriots, and stereotyped liberals were distributed to as many as 180 newspapers by the United Features Syndicate. During 1950–1951 he worked in Hollywood as a technical consultant and an actor in the war film *Teresa* and as co-star with Audie Murphy in *The Red Badge of Courage*, both released in 1951. Also released that year was *Up Front*, a movie based on the Willie and Joe cartoons. *Bill Mauldin in Korea*, 1952, was published after he visited the Korean zone. In 1956 he ran unsuccessfully as a Democrat for a seat in the House of Representatives from New York. Two years later he became editorial cartoonist for the *St. Louis Post-Dispatch*, his work for that paper being syndicated eventually to some 140 newspapers. Finding his métier in satirical social and political commentary, he became the first formidable rival to Herblock of the *Washington Post*. In 1958 he won a second Pulitzer Prize for his cartooned impression of Soviet novelist Boris Pasternak's fate: "I won the Nobel Prize for Literature. What was your crime?" In 1962 he joined the *Chicago Sun-Times*, which distributed his editorial cartoons to more than 200 newspapers. He wrote and illustrated numerous articles for popular magazines and published other collections, including *Sort of a Saga*, 1949; *What's Got Your Back Up*, 1961; *I've Decided I Want My Seat Back*, 1965; and *The Brass Ring*, 1972.

Maury, Matthew Fontaine (1806–1873), naval officer and oceanographer. Born near Fredericksburg, Virginia, on January 14, 1806, Maury grew up there and, from the age of five, on a farm near Franklin, Tennessee. In 1825 he entered the navy as a midshipman and in the following nine years made three lengthy cruises, the first of which was the return voyage of Lafayette to France after his visit in 1825 and the second of which was a circumnavigation of the globe on the *Vincennes*. Under various pseudonyms, he published a number of articles criticizing the administration of the navy and suggesting reforms. In 1836 he published his first major work, *A New Theoretical and Practical Treatise on Navigation*. An accident in 1839 rendered him permanently lame and unfit for sea duty, but three years later, with the rank of lieutenant, he was appointed superintendent of the navy's Depot of Charts and Instruments, including from 1844 the new Naval Observatory (later united as the U.S. Naval Observatory and Hydrographic Office but again separate from 1866). He launched an intensive program of research into winds and currents and in 1847 published his *Wind and Current Chart of the North Atlantic*; this work, with later sailing directions, proved highly valuable in reducing sailing times. It produced worldwide interest in his work, which culminated in 1853 in an international conference in Brussels, where his navigational system was universally adopted. He represented the United States at the meeting and secured the adoption of a plan for international cooperation in the gathering and collating of oceanographic data. With new sources of information available, he revised his earlier work and compiled charts for other ocean areas. In 1855 he published *The Physical Geography of the Sea and Its Meteorology*, considered the first work of modern oceanography. He later encouraged the idea of an Atlantic telegraph cable, preparing charts of optimum locations, and was often consulted by Cyrus Field when the latter undertook the project. In 1855 a naval board convened to review the officer list placed him on leave of absence; in 1858 President James Buchanan restored him to active service with the rank of commander, retroactive to 1855. In 1861, shortly after the secession of Virginia from the Union, he resigned from the U.S. navy and was promptly commissioned a commander in the Confederate navy. Placed in charge of coast, harbor, and river defenses, he conducted experiments with an electric torpedo, continuing the work in England, where he was sent in 1862 as a special agent of the Confederacy. His reputation gained him considerable influence there, and he secured a number of warships for the Confederate fleet. While returning home in 1865 he learned of the fall of the Confederacy and went instead to Mexico. He was appointed imperial commissioner of immigration by Emperor Maximilian and attempted unsuccessfully to establish a colony of Virginians in that country. From 1866 to 1868 he was again in England, but in the latter year he returned to the United States to become professor of meteorology at the Virginia Military Institute (VMI). Others of his books were *Physical Geography*, 1864; *The World We Live In*, 1868; and *Manual of Geography*, 1871. During his later years he was much honored. He died in Lexington, Virginia, on February 1, 1873. He was elected to the Hall of Fame in 1930.

Maverick, Samuel Augustus (1803–1870), cattle rancher and public official. Born in South Carolina in 1803, Maverick went to Texas in 1835 and immediately became involved in the agitation by settlers that led to Texas's independence from Mexico. He was a member of the convention that established the Republic of Texas in 1836, was mayor of San Antonio in 1839, and served in the Texas congress in 1845 and in the first legislature of the state after it was admitted to the Union. He owned a ranch of some 385,000 acres in south Texas, and in 1845 accepted as payment for a debt about 400 head of cattle that he neglected to brand before putting them in the care of one of his men. The cattle were allowed to run wild and were caught and branded by others. At the time this appropriation of unbranded stock was reasonably legal, as ownership was determined by the brand, but it was not considered honest on the range. When Maverick objected to the practice as applied to his own herd, the term "maverick" came to be used for an unbranded yearling found

wandering and unattended; and eventually it was used as a verb to describe the taking of such animals as well as various kinds of dishonesty, and as a noun to describe individuals pursuing their own course in defiance of orthodoxy, custom (though not necessarily of right), or law (though not necessarily of justice). Maverick died in Texas in 1870.

Maxim, Hiram Percy, *see under* Maxim, Hiram Stevens

Maxim, Hiram Stevens (1840–1916), inventor. Born on February 5, 1840, near Sangerville, Maine, Maxim was a mechanically precocious child and learned several trades, including that of carriage maker, before he was twenty. During the Civil War he worked at various jobs in Canada and upstate New York, then settled down in the engineering firm of an uncle in Fitchburg, Massachusetts. His mechanical ingenuity led to a number of inventions and his first patent, granted in 1866, was for a hair-curling iron. In the 1870s he was in New York City, and his success with illuminating gas equipment led to a post as chief engineer of the United States Electric Light Company in 1878. His improvements in the incandescent carbon lamp proved a major advance in the design of light bulbs, but Maxim never was able to profit from it. At the Paris Exposition in 1881 he was decorated for his design of an electric pressure regulator. He subsequently opened a laboratory in London and shortly began working on a fully automatic machine gun, an idea that he first heard from his father; its success was to secure for him an international reputation. By June 1884 he had progressed to the point where he had a workable design, using the principle of short recoil for generating a complete cycle, including reloading, in a single barrel. The gun fired 660 rounds per minute, and subsequent improvement and the introduction of smokeless powder assured the success of the Maxim gun. The Maxim was manufactured by the Maxim Gun Company, organized in 1884; four years later the firm was merged with the makers of the Nordenfeldt, an earlier rapid-fire gun, and in 1896 with Vickers Sons as Vickers Sons and Maxim, which, on Maxim's retirement 15 years later, became Vickers, Ltd. His machine gun was quickly adopted by every major power including the United States. It was used with devastating effect during World War I and permanently changed modern warfare. Maxim became a British subject in 1900 and was knighted by Queen Victoria in 1901. Although he was known primarily for his machine gun, Maxim obtained more than 250 patents in Britain and the United States during his career. In the early 1890s he designed a steam-powered flying machine that was aerodynamically sound, but was unable to lift the necessary weight of water and fuel. He retired in 1911 and died at Streatham, England, on November 24, 1916. The Maxim gun reached its full potential only after the development of suitable explosives, the chief credit for which is due his brother, Hudson Maxim. Hiram Maxim's son, Hiram Percy Maxim (1869–1936), was also an inventor of note, patenting the Maxim silencer of firearms and an automobile muffler.

Maxim, Hudson (1853–1927), inventor. Born on February 3, 1853, in Orneville, Piscataquis County, Maine, Hudson at 18 changed his given name Isaac. For a while he studied chemistry at Wesleyan Seminary at Kents Hill, Maine. About 1871 he was associated with Hiram in New York City, but he achieved his first success as a publisher (along with Alden Knowles) with their book on penmanship. In the mid-1880s he joined his brother at his gun factory in England but returned to Massachusetts after the merger with Nordenfeldt as American representative of the company in 1888. He immediately began to experiment with high explosives and within a year had secured his first patent. A conflict with Hiram led to their estrangement and the termination of his contract with Maxim-Nordenfeldt in 1891, but his success in perfecting a practical dynamite led to the establishment of his own Maxim Powder Company in New Jersey in 1893. During the next two years he devoted himself to improving smokeless explosive powder, first introduced by the French in 1885, whose progressive burning qualities were ideally suited to the requirements of a rapid-fire gun. The controlled rapid burning of Maxim's improved powder stabilized and extended the range of the gun's projectile, while providing a consistent pressure for activating the recoil of the gun. Obtaining patent protection by 1895, he was unable to interest his brother in purchasing his patent and in 1897 he sold factory and patents to E. I. du Pont de Nemours & Company, remaining with them as consulting engineer. By 1900 he had perfected maximite, a powerful explosive of such stability that it remained undetonated even as the shell penetrated heavy armor, then to be exploded by a delayed-action fuse, also of his design. A more stable version of his smokeless powder was marketed as stabillite, and his motorite came into extensive use as a torpedo propellant. During World War I Maxim served as chairman of the committee on ordinance and explosives of the U.S. Naval Consulting Board. He died at Lake Hopatcong, New Jersey, on May 6, 1927.

Maxwell, Elsa (1883–1963), columnist, songwriter, and professional party-giver. Born in Keokuk, Iowa, on May 24, 1883, Miss Maxwell was raised in California and attended Miss West's Private School in San Francisco. She left school at the age of fourteen but later claimed to have continued her education at the University of California and the Sorbonne. Although she never had a music lesson in her life, she began to earn a living from music in her early teens. She left San Francisco in 1905 as an odd-jobs girl in a Shakespearean troupe and thereafter was a pianist in a New York City nickelodeon, an accompanist to vaudeville performer Dorothy Toye, and a performer in South African music halls. In 1907 she began a songwriting career that resulted in some 80 published compositions. At about the same time she started meeting socially important people, showing up at soirées in the United States and in Europe and working her way up the social ladder. By the end of World War I, she was giving parties for royalty and high society throughout Europe. During 1925–1926 she organized the International Motor Boat Races at the Lido in Venice and in 1926, under the auspices of the Prince of Monaco, she planned the Monte Carlo Beach Club, the Casino Hotel, and the Piscine Restaurants of Monte Carlo. Miss Maxwell returned to New York City in the early 1930s; but New York during the Depression was not her cup of tea, and she went to Hollywood in 1938, where she appeared in several not very successful movie shorts, including *Elsa Maxwell's Hotel for Women,* 1939, and *The Lady and the Lug,* 1940. Her radio program, "Elsa Maxwell's Party Line," began in 1942; she also wrote a syndicated gossip column. All the while she continued to organize parties for prominent social figures. In 1936 her *I Live by My Wits* was published serially in *Harper's Bazaar;* in 1938, her *Life of Barbara Hutton* was serialized in *Cosmopolitan.* Her autobiography, *My Last Fifty Years,* appeared in 1943, followed by *R.S.V.P.* in 1957; in 1957 she also published *How to Do It; the Lively Art of Entertaining* and she began weekly television appearances on the Jack Paar show. Miss Maxwell died in New York City on November 1, 1963.

Mayer, Joseph, see under Mayer, Maria Goeppert

Mayer, Louis Burt (1885–1957), motion-picture producer. Born in Minsk, Russia, on July 4, 1885, Mayer came with his parents at the age of three to St. John, New Brunswick, where he attended public schools and later worked with his father in the ship salvaging business. Attracted to a career in show business during business trips to the United States, he purchased a burlesque house in Haverhill, Massachusetts, in 1907, converted it to a successful nickelodeon, and before long acquired the remaining theaters in Haverhill. He subsequently formed a partnership with Nat Gordon, and the Gordon-Mayer chain soon became the leading movie house circuit in New England. Mayer became a U.S. citizen in 1912. He began distributing films under his own name in 1914. After D. W. Griffith's *Birth of a Nation* opened in New York City in 1915 he purchased the New England rights for $25,000, an unprecedented price for a single film. The success of the film established motion pictures as popular entertainment and founded Mayer's private fortune. In 1918 he moved to Los Angeles and founded the Louis B. Mayer Pictures Corporation and later the production company known as Metro Pictures Corporation. Both firms were eventually absorbed by Marcus Loew, who in 1924 also purchased the Goldwyn Pictures Corporation, from which Samuel Goldwyn had resigned. The new firm became known as Metro-Goldwyn-Mayer (M-G-M), and Mayer was retained as vice-president in charge of production; the ultimate control of distribution remained with Loew's Inc. Under Mayer's auspices the roaring lion (the M-G-M trademark introduced by Mayer) became familiar to every moviegoing American. His most memorable productions included *Ben Hur, The Merry Widow, The Good Earth, Captains Courageous, Dinner at Eight, Treasure Island, Grand Hotel,* and *The Barretts of Wimpole Street.* He was instrumental in the development of a number of stars, including Greta Garbo, Joan Crawford, Clark Gable, and Spencer Tracy. During the late 1930s and early 1940s his annual salary approached a million dollars. In the late 1920 and early 1930s he was also active in California Republican politics. In 1929 he declined an offer made by President Herbert Hoover, a personal friend, to become ambassador to Turkey, and in 1934 he released fabricated newsreels about the activities of Upton Sinclair that contributed to Sinclair's defeat in the California gubernatorial election that year. Mayer resigned from M-G-M in 1951 after three years in which he was no longer the chief of production. The following year he became board chairman of Cinerama Productions but met with little success and soon relinquished his control to Stanley Warner Corporation. His last years were devoted to an unsuccessful attempt to gain control of Loew's, Inc. He died in Santa Monica, California, on October 29, 1957.

Mayer, Maria Goeppert (1906–1972), physicist. Born on June 28, 1906, at Kattowitz, Germany (now Katowice, Poland), Miss Goeppert earned a doctorate in physics at the University of Göttingen under a committee of three Nobel Prize winners, including Max Born, in 1930. That same year she married the American physical chemist Joseph Mayer and accompanied him to The Johns Hopkins University in Baltimore. During the next nine years she was associated with Johns Hopkins while raising two children and collaborating with Karl Herzfeld and her husband in the study of organic molecules. In 1939 she and her husband both received appointments in chemistry at Columlumbia University; their *Statistical Mechanics* appeared in 1940. Although they remained at Columbia throughout World War II, Mrs. Mayer also lectured at Sarah Lawrence College and conducted research on isotopes for the atomic-bomb project during the war. After the war her interests centered increasingly in nuclear physics, and in 1946 she became a senior physicist at the Argonne National Laboratory in addition to serving as a volunteer professor of physics at the University of Chicago, where she received a regular appointment as full professor in 1959. In 1948–1949 she published several papers concerning the stability and configuration of protons and neutrons that orbit in an atomic nucleus. Working independently of the German physicist J. H. D. Jensen, she nevertheless arrived at theories similar to his about the structure of the nucleus. This led to a collaboration and the joint publication of *Elementary Theory of Nuclear Shell Structure,* 1955. The work established her as a leading authority in the field and in 1963 she and Jensen and E. P. Wigner of Princeton shared the Nobel Prize for Physics for their theoretical contributions. Also noted for her work in quantum electrodynamics and spectroscopy, Mrs. Mayer accepted an appointment at the University of California at San Diego in 1960, as did her husband. She died in San Diego on February 20, 1972.

Mayhew, Jonathan (1720–1766), religious leader. Born on October 8, 1720 in Chilmark, Martha's Vineyard, Massachusetts, Mayhew was a descendant of the island's first governor, Thomas Mayhew (1593–1682), the son of a noted minister and preacher to the Indians. Jonathan graduated from Harvard in 1744 and three years later became pastor of West Church, Boston, where he preached until his death 19 years later. He quickly showed evidence of moving away from the older Puritan beliefs and toward a less rigid religious position. His *Discourse Concerning Unlimited Submission and Non-Resistance to the Higher Powers,* delivered as a sermon on January 30, 1750, the centenary of the execution of Charles I of England, was an attack on the divine right of kings and ecclesiastical absolutism and heralded the first signs of discontent with unpopular laws imposed by Britain. The sermon, John Adams wrote to Hezekiah Niles in 1818, "was read by everybody; celebrated by friends, and abused by enemies." It was Adams, too, who called Mayhew a "transcendent genius." His sermons had a profound effect on the life of Boston and he is generally considered the first to have abandoned traditional Trinitarian doctrine (1755) and to have begun the movement toward Unitarian congregationalism. This movement did not culminate until after the Revolution, but in this as well as in his political sentiments he was ahead of his time. He defended free will against the Calvinist belief in predestination, opposed both religious and political arbitrary rule, and, at a sermon delivered at Harvard in 1765, preached against popish idolatry. The following year a sermon on the Stamp Act considered the possibility that "certain extraordinary conjunctures" could justify private citizens who might "take the administration of government in some respects into their own hands." His sermons were supplemented by letters to newspapers and by pamphlets, which together made him one of the most influential men in Massachusetts. Mayhew died in Boston on July 9, 1766, having to a notable extent provided divine sanction for the movement toward independence.

Mayo, William James (1861–1939), and Charles Horace Mayo (1865–1939), physicians. Born in Minnesota, William in Le Sueur on June 29, 1861, and Charles in Rochester on July 19, 1865, the Mayo brothers were sons of William Worrall Mayo (1819–1911), who had emigrated from England in 1845, studied medicine in Indiana and at the University of Missouri, and settled in Minnesota in 1855 to become the region's most prominent physician. Both sons aided their father in his medical practice from early youth and in due time studied medicine formally. William took his medical degree from the University of Michigan in 1883 and Charles graduated from the Chicago Medical College (now part of Northwestern University) in 1888. In the aftermath of a disastrous tornado that struck Rochester in 1883, the Sisters of St. Francis began erecting a permanent hospital in the town; it opened in 1889 with the Mayos as its sole staff. St. Mary's Hospital had the only adequate surgical facilities accessible to much of Minnesota and Iowa and all of the Dakotas, and consequently the three doctors enjoyed a huge practice. The brothers traveled regularly to other medical centers to keep abreast of progress in medical and surgical techniques; as their proficiency increased, so did their practice and reputation. Gradually other doctors were attracted to Rochester for advanced study in surgery, and as the staff of St. Mary's multiplied a form of group practice was evolved, the first such system to be applied in private practice in America. The cooperative clinic that took form and that came to be known as the Mayo Clinic was broadened to include specialists in various medical fields and was able to attract highly skilled practitioners. The Mayos, who until 1915 had performed all the surgery at St. Mary's, were able to specialize as well, William in surgery of the abdomen and Charles in surgery of the thyroid and the nervous system and in ophthalmology. In 1907 William became a member of the board of regents of the University of Minnesota, a position he held until his death, and from 1915 to 1936 Charles held positions on the university's surgical faculty. In 1915 they established the Mayo Foundation for Medical Education and Research, and two years later the foundation was transferred to the University of Minnesota as part of its graduate school. In 1919 the bulk of the rest of their holdings was vested in the Mayo Properties Association, a perpetual charitable and educational organization. With the clinic reorganized from a partnership into a voluntary association, the brothers retired from medical practice, William in 1928 and Charles in 1930. Both died in 1939, Charles in Chicago on May 26 and William in Rochester on July 28. The Mayo Clinic continued to grow in both size and reputation. It eventually commanded the services of over 300 physicians and attracted more than 150,000 patients a year from all over the world.

Mays, Willie Howard, Jr. (1931–   ), baseball player. Born on May 6, 1931, in Fairfield, Alabama, Mays, whose autobiography *Born to Play Ball* was published in 1955, played semiprofessional baseball at the age of fourteen. He began playing professional ball with the Birmingham Black Barons of the Negro National League, a team on which his father had also starred, in 1948, two years before he completed high school.

The New York Giants of the National League bought his contract in 1950, and after a short stay in the minor leagues, he began playing center field for the Giants in May 1951. Noted for his unorthodox "bread basket" catches that created an instant of suspense before he trapped the ball, he quickly became popular with the fans and earned the rookie of the year award after his first season. His career was interrupted by army service in 1952–1953, but he had a spectacular first full season in 1954. The Giants won the World Series after a long drought, while Mays won the National League's batting championship with a .345 average and its most valuable player award as well. A popular song, "Say Hey Willie," memoralized his favorite saying and attested to his large following. The following year he led both leagues with 51 home runs, becoming one of only a few major-league players ever to hit more than 50 home runs in one season. He moved to San Francisco with the Giants in 1957 and remained their most feared batsman. He hit 49 home runs when San Francisco won the National League pennant in 1962 and in 1965 he hit 52, missing by four the National League record of 56, achieved by Hack Wilson of Chicago in 1930. Mays again was named his league's most valuable player in 1965 after an interval of 11 years. At one time second among the major-league home-run hitters, in the early 1970s he ranked third behind Babe Ruth and Hank Aaron. Mays was traded to the New York Mets after the season started in 1972, and in his first home appearance in New York City since 1956 pleased everyone by hitting a home run. He announced his retirement in 1973.

Mazzei, Philip (1730–1816), physician and colonial agent. Born on Christmas Day of 1730 at Poggio a Caiano, Italy, Mazzei studied medicine in Florence and during 1752–1755 practiced in Turkey. He subseqently became a wine merchant in London and in 1773 came to Virginia with the intention of introducing the culture of two Italian staples, olives and grapes, to the New World. During the Revolution he became an ardent patriot and his farm, adjacent to Thomas Jefferson's Monticello, languished. In 1779 he was commissioned by the then governor of Virginia, Patrick Henry, to proceed to Tuscany to obtain a loan for the Commonwealth of Virginia, but he arrived in Europe without any official papers, having destroyed them to avoid incrimination while briefly in the hands of the British. Mazzei's efforts in Italy were opposed at every turn by Benjamin Franklin, the chief European emissary of the Continental Congress, because his was not a federal commission. He remained on the payroll of Virginia, of which he was a naturalized citizen, during Jefferson's term as governor, maintaining with Jefferson an official and politically important correspondence. He returned to America in late 1783 but, failing in his efforts to obtain a consular post, went back to Europe for good in June 1785. However he continued to correspond with

Jefferson and other Virginians long after that date. One letter from Jefferson to him found its way into a Florentine newspaper, was translated with some distortion of meaning, and was reprinted in the United States in 1797, causing a minor scandal and much embarrassment to Jefferson as some of its heatedly anti-Federalist passages seemed aimed at George Washington. His useful *Récherches historiques et politiques sur les États-Unis de l'Amérique septentrionale* appeared in four volumes in 1788 without attracting much attention. He later became a Polish citizen, serving as an adviser to Stanislas II. He retired with a pension, later paid by the Russians, until his death in Pisa, Italy, on March 9, 1816. An account of his life and travels was published in Italian in 1813.

Mead, George Herbert (1863–1931), philosopher and social psychologist. Born in South Hadley, Massachusetts, on February 27, 1863, Mead graduated from Oberlin College in 1883 and received a second B.A. degree from Harvard University, where he studied with Josiah Royce, in 1888. He subsequently studied in Germany, where he felt the influence of Wilhelm Wundt, before accepting a post in philosophy at the University of Michigan in 1891. He went, along with John Dewey, to the newly organized University of Chicago in 1894 and in time became one of the most illustrious members of the faculty. His influence extended to many students and colleagues, who after his death edited the several books, composed of lecture notes and unpublished manuscripts, that thereafter brought his thinking to the attention of a wider audience. Known primarily as a teacher, he gained his reputation chiefly by his famous course in social psychology, which after 1900 was presented annually for 30 years. The substance of these lectures was published posthumously as *Mind, Self and Society,* 1934, his most influential book. A behaviorist, or better, social behaviorist, in his viewpoint, he developed a theory of the self which described it as a function of man's linguistic ability, an emergent product of the mastery of imaginative role-playing that is an inseparable part of a child's developing the use of language. The use of symbolic language, he held, first involves the calling-up of internal hypothetical reactions—role-playing—and, after selection among alternatives on the basis of likely responses, the public communication of thought. Philosophically he was a pragmatist who, along with Dewey, made a notable contribution to the development of that theory in the United States. The notion of emergence also characterized his cosmological views, which were an attempt to picture the processes of nature as dynamic, and nature itself as having room for the evolution of new forms that would be inexplicable in purely mechanistic terms. Relativism, which presented problems similar to that of behaviorism in his psychology, did not, in his view, bar belief in an objective reality, despite the fact that reality was changing and susceptible to several points of view. Shortly before his death in Chicago on April 26, 1931, Mead delivered the Paul Carus lectures in Berkeley, California; supplemented by other material, they were published as *The Philosophy of the Present,* 1932. Two subsequent volumes appeared as *Movements of Thought in the Nineteenth Century,* 1936, and *The Philosophy of the Act,* 1938.

Mead, Margaret (1901–1978), anthropologist. Born on December 16, 1901, in Philadelphia, Margaret Mead was the daughter of an economics professor and a sociologist. The teaching of Franz Boas and Ruth Benedict at Columbia, where she received her B.A. (from Barnard College) in 1923 and her M.A. in psychology in 1924, led her to choose anthropology as her field. She took her doctorate at Columbia in 1929. In 1925–1926 she made the first of many field trips to the South Seas, to the island of Tau in Samoa, where she observed the development of native children through adolescence (*Coming of Age in Samoa,* 1928). On the second trip, during 1928–1929, she investigated the development of social behavior in children of Manus, in the Admiralty Islands in the western Pacific (*Growing Up in New Guinea,* 1930). Her expedition of 1931–1933 was also to the New Guinea area, where she studied three primitive tribes, the Arapesh, Mundugumor, and Tchambuli (*Sex and Temperament,* 1935). The three books appeared together as *From the South Seas* in 1939. Using a method frequently used in subsequent works—contrasting the values of two or more cultures—she prompted significant questioning of rigid social standards. Like Ruth Benedict, she stressed the impermanence of human values and their independence on time and environment. She was one of few anthropologists to reach popular as well as professional audiences. In 1932 she published the results of her study of an unnamed American Indian tribe ("the Antlers") in *The Changing Culture of an Indian Tribe.* In 1935 she edited 13 papers of Columbia graduate students, publishing them as *Cooperation and Competition Among Primitive Peoples* in 1937, to refute the notion of primitive society as a Darwinian jungle. During 1936–1939 she did field work in Bali and New Guinea, producing *Balinese Character: A Photographic Analysis,* 1941, with Gregory Bateson, and *Growth and Culture: A Photographic Study of Balinese Childhood,* 1951, with Frances MacGregor. Using her knowledge of primitive cultures, she explored American cultural standards in *And Keep Your Powder Dry,* 1942. During World War II she wrote pamphlets for the Office of War Information (OWI) to aid communication between British and American troops. One of her most important books appeared in 1949, *Male and Female: A Study of the Sexes in a Changing World.* It examined traditional male-female relationships, using observations in the Pacific and the East Indies for reference in discussing such topics as the mother's influence in perpetuating male and female roles and the different concepts of marriage held by various cultures. She also published *Soviet Attitudes Toward Authority*, 1951; *Childhood in Contemporary Cultures*, 1955, with Martha Wolfenstein; *New Lives for Old*, 1956; *An Anthropologist at Work*, 1958, about Ruth Benedict; *Continuities in Cultural Evolution*, 1964; and numerous papers. She became assistant curator of ethnology at the American Museum of Natural History in New York City in 1926, associate curator in 1942, and curator in 1964, remaining in that post until 1969. From 1954 she was an adjunct professor of anthropology at Columbia University and from 1968 to 1971 she was also chairman of the social sciences division at Fordham University. She served on national public-health and mental-health councils and was a frequent visiting lecturer at universities. *Blackberry Winter*, a volume of autobiography, appeared in 1972. She died on November 15, 1978, in New York City.

Meade, George Gordon (1815–1872), soldier. Born of American parents in Cadiz, Spain, on December 31, 1815, Meade graduated from West Point in 1835, was commissioned in the artillery, and was immediately ordered to Florida for service in the Seminole Wars. In 1836 he resigned from the army and for six years engaged in engineering work for the Alabama, Florida & Georgia Railroad and in surveying the boundaries of Texas and Maine. In 1842 he reentered the army as a second lieutenant in the Topographical Engineers. He remained with the Maine survey work for a year and then was transferred to Philadelphia to work on lighthouse construction. After service in the Mexican War, during which he saw action at Palo Alto and Resaca de la Palma and was given temporary rank as first lieutenant for gallantry at Monterrey, he again engaged in engineering and survey duties in Philadelphia, Florida, and the Great Lakes region. In 1861, with the beginning of the Civil War, he was appointed brigadier general of volunteers in Pennsylvania. He took part in Gen. George B. McClellan's Peninsular Campaign in 1862 and later in the year was seriously wounded at Frayser's Farm (Glendale); he recovered sufficiently to command his brigade at the second battle of Bull Run (Manassas) in August and a month later, at Antietam, he temporarily took command of the 1st Corps when Gen. Joseph Hooker was wounded. In November he was promoted to major general of volunteers and in December, following the Union defeat at Fredericksburg, he was given command of the 5th Corps. On June 28, 1863, after the battle of Chancellorsville, President Abraham Lincoln named Meade to succeed Hooker as commander of the Army of the Potomac. He reluctantly accepted; just three days later his army made contact with Gen. Robert E. Lee's army at Gettysburg and Meade displayed great tactical skill in repulsing the Confederate forces, although, like many of his predecessors, he failed to press his advantage; nevertheless, Gettysburg proved to be a decisive battle. He was made brigadier general in the regular army and in January 1864 was voted the thanks of Congress. He retained command of the Army of the Potomac, but when Gen. Ulysses S. Grant was placed in command of all Union forces in March 1864 and made his headquarters with the Army of the Potomac in the field, Meade's independence was greatly reduced. He gave complete loyalty to Grant, however, and in August 1864 was promoted to major general in the regular army. After the war he commanded the Military Division of the Atlantic and later the Department of the East. From 1868 to 1869 he was commander of Georgia, Alabama, and Florida in the Department of the South, and then returned to his earlier post with the Military Division of the Atlantic. He died in Philadelphia on November 6, 1872.

Means, Gaston Bullock (1879–1938), espionage agent, swindler, and detective. Born on July 11, 1879, in Blackwelder's Spring, near Concord, North Carolina, Means completed three years at the University of North Carolina in 1901. Until 1914 he worked as a cotton salesman for Concord Mills. During the early part of World War I he earned a small fortune by supplying, to a naval attaché of the German embassy, data on Allied shipping to which his business gave him access. Late in 1914 he joined the William J. Burns International Detective Agency and managed to convince his first client, a wealthy Chicago widow, Maude King, of his interest in her welfare sufficiently to enable him to make use of her funds for speculating in cotton futures. By 1917 he had run through most of her money. In August of that year she visited him at Concord and shortly was found dead, having been shot from behind with a weapon that a subsequent trial established had been recently purchased by Means. He remained cool and confident and was acquitted of a charge of murder in December 1917 despite the evidence of his debt and expert ballistic testimony. The King murder trial received national attention, but Means remained with the Burns agency. His cleverness and extraordinary ability to maintain others' confidence in his character led Burns, the head of the agency and director of the Federal Bureau of Investigation under President Warren G. Harding, to appoint him as a special agent of the FBI in 1921, despite public knowledge of then pending charges of fraud. He was retained as a paid informer even after public pressure forced his dismissal by Attorney General Harry M. Daugherty after five months. By 1925 Means was under several indictments for extortion and forgery, and he was convicted on two of them, receiving a four-year prison sentence. While in prison he enlisted the aid of a minister's wife, May Thacker, in writing *The Strange Death of President Harding*, 1930, a book that was a popular success, primarily because of the sensationalism of its suggestion that Harding had been poisoned by his wife. Mrs. Thacker repudiated her part in the venture when Means disappeared after his release without documenting his charges.

Perhaps his boldest exploit was a scheme to capitalize on the kidnapping of the infant son of Col. Charles A. Lindbergh in 1932. He persuaded the socially prominent Evalyn Walsh McLean that he could recover the child if she gave him $104,000 to pass on to the kidnappers. She raised the money and gave it to Means but became suspicious after his alleged second meeting with the kidnappers produced only more demands. After Mrs. McLean went to the police, Means was convicted of grand larceny and was sentenced to 15 years in prison. He died of complications following an operation at the Medical Center for Federal Prisoners at Springfield, Missouri, on September 12, 1938. He had spent his last years in vain attempts to obtain his release from prison, his usual argument, to the FBI, being that he could succeed in solving certain notorious crimes where they had failed.

Meany, George (1894–1980), labor-union official. Born on August 16, 1894, in New York City, Meany attended public schools before becoming a plumber's apprentice at sixteen. He joined the local plumbers' union after he became a journeyman plumber in 1915, and in 1922 became the union's business agent, a post he held for 12 years. In 1934 he was chosen president of his New York Local 463 but, more importantly, he also served as president of the New York State Federation of Labor from 1934–1939. He became secretary-treasurer of the American Federation of Labor (AFL) in January 1940 and subsequently was appointed to the National Defense Mediation Board, a body comprised of representatives of labor, industry, and the public, created by President Franklin D. Roosevelt in March 1941 to prevent production losses caused by strikes. Known as the National War Labor Board after the Japanese attack on Pearl Harbor, it was empowered to resolve any dispute that might interrupt work that contributed to the war effort. One of the leaders in the postwar fight against Communist influence in American unions, Meany backed President Harry S. Truman's efforts to encourage an international federation of unions that were free of such influence and in 1951 was chosen a member of the executive board of the International Confederation of Free Trade Unions, formed in 1949. After the passage of the Taft-Hartley Act in 1947 Meany led the way in the abandonment of the AFL's traditional nonpartisan political policy and in 1948 became the first head of its League for Political Education, a group that formed close ties with the liberal wing of the Democratic party. In 1952 he became president of the AFL and embarked on a program to end the breach with the Congress of Industrial Organizations (CIO), which had been the chief rival of the AFL since the internal labor-movement conflict of the mid-1930s and an independent federation since 1938. In 1955, after prolonged negotiations, the AFL and CIO merged into a new federation, with Meany at its head. Under Meany's guidance a number of reforms and financial codes were instituted to regulate the sometimes corrupt practices of member unions of the AFL-CIO, and in 1957 financial irregularities in the operations of the powerful International Brotherhood of Teamsters led to their expulsion. That same year Meany was elected vice-president of the International Confederation of Free Trade Unions and also was appointed a U.S. delegate to the United Nations General Assembly. The AFL-CIO continued to be plagued by jurisdictional disputes even after 1955, and satisfactory working relations were never achieved between Meany and Walter Reuther, who had headed the CIO before the merger and subsequently was head of the industrial union division of the AFL-CIO and president of the United Auto Workers. The UAW withdrew from the AFL-CIO in 1968 and, with the expelled Teamsters, formed the Alliance for Labor Action. They were joined in 1969 by the International Chemical Workers' Union, which then was expelled from the AFL-CIO. Meany retired as president of the AFL-CIO in 1979 and died on January 10, 1980, in Washington, D.C.

Medill, Joseph (1823–1899), editor and publisher. Born on April 6, 1823, near St. John, New Brunswick, to a family of shipbuilders of Irish descent, Medill studied law in Massillon, Ohio, and was admitted to the bar in 1846. He opened a practice but soon turned to journalism and joined three younger brothers in purchasing the *Coshocton (Ohio) Whig*, which he renamed the *Republican*. Moving to Cleveland in 1851, he founded the *Daily Forest City*, combined it with a Free-Soil journal, and renamed it the *Cleveland Leader*. Having been active in Whig politics, he could foresee the demise of the party after the election of 1852 and therefore he began to help in organizing a new antislavery party, which he suggested be named "Republican." The party was founded in 1854. In 1855 he bought a share in the *Chicago Tribune*, becoming business manager and managing editor of the paper, and, using its resources and his own influence, succeeded in uniting disgruntled factions under the Republican banner. He firmly advocated the nomination of Abraham Lincoln for president in 1860 and supported Republican Civil War policies, advocating even harsher moves against the Confederacy than were being taken with regard to property confiscation and emancipation. He conducted effective editorial campaigns for the adoption of laws to provide soldiers in battle with the opportunity to vote in elections, and for the eradication of political corruption in Chicago. He also advocated the harsh Reconstruction policies of the Radical Republicans after the coming of peace. He was elected to the Illinois constitutional convention in 1869 and was elected mayor of Chicago shortly after the great fire of 1871. He oversaw the reorganization of the government and the rebuilding of the city, and projected the building of the Chicago Public Library. Also in 1871 he was appointed one of the first members of the U.S. Civil Service Commission. In 1874 he resigned as mayor and acquired the controlling interest in the *Chicago Tribune*. As its editor in chief he guided the paper's conservative, pro-business, anti-labor union, and sometimes (as during the events leading to the Spanish-American War) jingoistic editorial position until his death in San Antonio, Texas, on March 16, 1899. He had founded a journalistic dynasty: his son-in-law, Robert W. Patterson, became editor in chief of the *Tribune*; in 1900 a grandson, Joseph M. McCormick, became manager of the paper, and later another grandson, Robert R. McCormick, gained control. Still another grandson, Joseph M. Patterson, became publisher of the *New York Daily News*; and Eleanor M. Patterson, a granddaughter, founded and edited the *Washington Times-Herald*. The family established in 1921 the Medill School of Journalism at Northwestern University in Evanston, Illinois, and dedicated it to the memory of Joseph Medill.

Meeker, Nathan Cook (1817–1879), journalist and social reformer. Born on July 12, 1817, in Euclid, Ohio, Meeker matriculated at Oberlin College but ended his education at seventeen. He led an unsettled existence in several states for most of his adult life, despite his marriage at the age of twenty-four. He flirted with Fourierism after his marriage and for three or four years was a member of the Trumbull phalanx of Fourierists in Braceville, Trumbull County, Ohio. He was associated with Campbellites in Hiram, Ohio, in the 1850s, and also tried his hand at writing a novel, which was never published. Meeker then went to Illinois, where he worked as a newspaper correspondent. After the Civil War he found employment as the agricultural editor of Horace Greeley's *New York Tribune*. He achieved some prominence for his articles on the Oneida Community and published a collection of stories, *Life in the West*, in 1868. Meeker is primarily remembered for his subsequent founding of the Union Colony, a cooperative agricultural settlement near Denver, Colorado, at Greeley, named after the publisher, with whose active support the community was organized in New York as a joint stock venture. Under Meeker's guidance in 1870 the colony selected a site, purchased land, recruited colonists, and transported them to the new settlement. The company wrote into the charter and the land deeds (which, unlike those at Oneida, recognized private ownership) a prohibition against intoxicants and poolrooms. By the end of the year Meeker had launched the *Greeley Tribune*, in which for eight years his editorials were a source of encouragement to the settlers. On September 29, 1879, Meeker was murdered, along with other whites, by Ute Indians at the White River Reservation, where for the previous year Meeker, who had been named Indian agent, had been engaged in an attempt to convert the Indians to the landowning domestic virtues of the white man.

Meiggs, Henry (1811–1877), entrepreneur and railroad builder. Born in Catskill, New York, on July 7, 1811, Meiggs went into the lumber business as a young man and by the time he was twenty-six had his own lumberyard in Williamsburg, New York (now part of the borough of Brooklyn, New York City), and within a year or so was president of the village board of trustees. He lost this first prosperity very quickly, however, being bankrupt by the year 1842, and spending most of the 1840s in various attempts, largely vain, to recoup his finances. The discovery of gold in California provided an opportunity and he hired a ship, loaded it with lumber, and set off for San Francisco via Cape Horn. People would pay almost anything for finished lumber in San Francisco at the time, and he sold his cargo at a huge profit and invested the money in lumbering operations in the region, at the same time learning Spanish and becoming once again involved in civic activities. He gave the city a music hall and was elected to the board of aldermen of San Francisco; but this good fortune did not last, either, and in October 1854 he fled with his family to Chile, leaving debts of $800,000 behind him. It is not known exactly how he accomplished his next rise, except that he was always able to inspire confidence and knew Spanish, but within a few short years he was superintending the construction of the Santiago al Sur Railroad, and in 1861 won from the Chilean government a contract to complete the line between Valparaiso and Santiago for $12 million within four years. This task had already bankrupted several other contractors, but Meiggs got the job done within less than two years and earned a profit of nearly $1.5 million. He immediately built himself a magnificent house in Santiago—it cost half a million dollars—and set about other business ventures, most notably the building of railroads for the Peruvian government. During the next 15 years he constructed railroads up and down the Peruvian coast and also into the Andes—to Lake Titicaca and to Cuzco, the ancient Inca capital—securing in the process some $120 million worth of government contracts and building more than 1000 miles of standard-gauge road; he outdistanced all competitors by bribing government officials with a generosity not before known. His Callao, Lima & Oroya Railroad was the highest in the world when it was completed about 1880; the line tunneled under Mount Meiggs at 15,658 feet and remained one of the world's engineering wonders. But the enormous cost of building it bankrupted the Peruvian government, and Meiggs was ruined once again. Desperate measures—which included his winning from the Peruvian government a short-lived concession to operate the Cerro de Pasco silver mines—were not this time availing, and a series of paralytic strokes led to his death on September 29, 1877, in Lima.

Meigs, Josiah (1757–1822), lawyer, educator, and public official. Born on August 21, 1757, in Middletown, Connecticut, Meigs graduated from Yale College in the class of 1778 and taught at Claverack, New York, before returning to Yale as a tutor, serving from 1781 to 1784. Admitted to the bar in 1783, he was elected the first city clerk of New Haven, Connecticut, thé following year, holding the post until 1789. A supporter of the Revolution, he launched, with others, the *New Haven Gazette* (later the *New Haven Gazette and Connecticut Magazine*) in 1784 in support of a stronger central government. The paper, which published writings of the noted Connecticut Wits, ceased publication after 11 states had ratified the Constitution in 1788. In 1789 his law practice carried him to St. George, Bermuda, where he remained for five years. He left there with a reputation as an able lawyer, but also as an unpopular figure. In October 1794 Meigs received an appointment from his friend Ezra Stiles as professor of mathematics and natural philosophy at Yale. His politics (now ardent Jeffersonianism), as well as the death of President Stiles, left him a controversial figure on the Yale faculty and he resigned in 1800 for a position with the newly founded University of Georgia. Chartered in 1785, the university did not open at Athens until 1801 and for about the next five years conducted classes in the open air and in various temporary quarters. Meigs became the second president of the institution shortly after his arrival and the university thrived under his administration, the first permanent building being completed in 1804. But he was plagued by his wife's dislike of the frontier, and his ill-concealed contempt for the people of the region again created enemies. In 1810 he resigned as president and the following year was dismissed by the trustees. President James Madison appointed him surveyor general of the United States in 1812 and subsequently he received an appointment as commissioner of the U.S. General Land Office, a post for which his earlier law practice had made him well suited. In his last years he became president of the Columbian Institute and one of the founders of Columbian College (subsequently The George Washington University). He died in Washington, D.C., on September 4, 1822.

Meiklejohn, Alexander (1872–1964), educator. Born on February 3, 1872, in Rochdale, England, Meiklejohn was brought to the United States in 1880. He graduated from Brown University in 1893, received an M.A. there in 1895, and a Ph.D. from Cornell in 1897. He taught philosophy at Brown from 1897 to 1912, the last six years as professor of logic and metaphysics, and was dean from 1901 to 1912. He was named president of Amherst College in 1912, holding the post until 1924. In 1926 he became a professor of philosophy at the University of Wisconsin and was director of the Experimental College there from 1927 to 1932. Until his retirement in 1938 he oversaw many educational innovations and gave strong support to the Great Books programs established during those years at the University of Chicago and at St. John's College. In the course of his work at Wisconsin he found time to serve as the chairman of the School for Social Studies in San Francisco, 1933–1936, and after his retirement he continued to be active in education, serving as a visiting professor at Dartmouth in 1938 and at St. John's in 1940. He was the author of a number of books, among them *The Liberal College*, 1920; *The Experimental College*, 1932; *What Does American Mean?*, 1935; *Education Between Two Worlds*, 1942, probably his best-known book; and *Free Speech and Its Relationship to Government*, 1948. He received the Presidential Medal of Freedom in 1963 and died in Berkeley, California, on December 16, 1964, at the age of ninety-two.

Mellon, Andrew William (1855–1937), financier, public official, and art collector. Born in Pittsburgh on March 24, 1855, Mellon was educated in the city's public schools and at Western University of Pennsylvania (now the University of Pittsburgh), which he left shortly before the graduation of his class of 1872. He opened a successful lumber company and two years later, having demonstrated considerable business ability, entered T. Mellon & Sons, the banking house that had been a established by his father. Within ten years ownership of the business was in his hands. Thoroughly grounded in sound business and financial practices, possessed of great acumen, and particularly able to judge accurately the potential in a prospective venture, he quickly expanded his interests; he backed the founding and growth of a number of companies that became industrial giants, among them the Aluminum Company of America, the Gulf Oil Corporation, Union Steel Company (later merged with United States Steel), and many others. In 1902 the banking house at the center of his financial empire became the Mellon National Bank. While becoming one of the major figures in American capitalism and one of its richest men, Mellon nevertheless remained largely unknown to the public. Although he had long been a major financial contributor to the Republican organization in Pennsylvania, not until 1921 did he achieve national prominence; in that year he was chosen by President Warren G. Harding to serve as secretary of the treasury. For the next 11 years he presided over the greatest business boom, and the beginning of the worst depression, in the nation's history. A staunch conservative, he urged constantly upon Congress schedules of taxation that rested as slightly as possible upon the wealthy and upon business; his program embodied the view that the nation's greatest interest was business, that in order to aid business government should allow enterprises to retain a maximum of profit for reinvestment and expansion, and that wealth retained or created at the top of the capitalist system would filter down to the lower levels. Despite considerable congressional opposition from progressives of both parties, this program was widely popular, although somewhat less so after 1929. Before the Depression reversed the trend he had reduced the national debt from $24 billion to $16 billion in eight years. In handling the repayment of World War I loans made to the nation's European allies, he followed currently popular opinion and resisted a realistic view of European finance; the result was a system whereby huge amounts of capital were lent to Germany, used by that country to cover its reparaions payments to other nations, and then returned to the United States as repayment by those nations of yet other loans. Mellon's popularity—he was generally considered the greatest secretary of the treasury since Alexander Hamilton—declined after the stock-market crash in October 1929. The onset of the Great Depression took Mellon, as it did most men of finance, by surprise and to the end of his tenure in office he underestimated its seriousness. Various stopgap fiscal maneuvers to shore up the economy proved futile. In 1932 President Herbert Hoover replaced him and he became U.S. ambassador to Great Britain, a position he held for just over a year. He returned to his private business interests in 1933. In 1937 he donated his large art collection—assembled over many years—to the federal government, along with sufficient funds to construct and endow the National Gallery of Art in Washington, D.C. While work was in progress on this great project, he died on August 26, 1937, in Southampton, Long Island, New York.

Melville, George Wallace (1841–1912), naval engineer and explorer. Born on January 10, 1841, in New York City, Melville early exhibited mechanical ability and eventually attended the Brooklyn Polytechnic Institute. He joined the navy as a third assistant engineer in 1861 and served throughout the Civil War. His career progressed routinely until 1873, when he volunteered to go to the Arctic as chief engineer of the *Tigress* on a mission to rescue the men of the *Polaris*, which had set out for the North Pole under Charles F. Hall two years earlier. In 1879 he volunteered to accompany the expedition led by George W. De Long as chief engineer aboard the *Jeannette.* They sailed through the Bering Strait but were caught in the Arctic ice pack near Herald Island and drifted west for 22 months, keeping afloat largely through Melville's efforts. After the *Jeannette* sank near the New Siberian Islands, Melville took charge of one of three small boats, only two of which made it to the delta of the Lena River in Siberia. Many of the crew, including De Long, perished. Melville, the sole surviving boat commander, then led a 500-mile expedition in the Arctic night along the Siberian shore to recover the bodies of De Long and his boat crew as well as the ship's records. His *In the Lena Delta*, 1884, is an account of the hardships suffered on the journey. Melville returned to the Arctic once again in 1884, aboard the flagship *Thetis* under Winfield Scott Schley, who rescued seven of the 25 members of the A. W. Greely expedition of 1881. Melville's sustained bravery and technical skill received the recognition of Congress and in 1887 he was selected over other ranking officers to become chief of the navy's Bureau of Steam Engineering. Under his auspices the bureau led the way in the conversion to more modern equipment. He designed the machinery of 120 navy ships; three of them, the *San Francisco, Columbia,* and *Minneapolis,* were for a time the world's fastest warships. He introduced the watertube boiler and the triple-screw system, and significantly increased efficiency by setting the boilers vertically. He also made an important contribution to the administrative reforms that streamlined the entire navy as well as the naval engineering department. Melville retired as a rear admiral in 1903. He died in Philadelphia on March 17, 1912.

Melville, Herman (1819–1891), author. Born on August 1, 1819, in New York City, Melville came of a family long distinguished on both sides but which was left virtually destitute at his father's death in 1832. At fifteen he ended his formal schooling and at nineteen, after holding a series of minor jobs, signed as a cabin boy aboard a New York–Liverpool packet. The experiences of the four-month round trip were the core of his largely autobiographical work, *Redburn,* 1849. In January 1841 he set sail again aboard a whaler bound for the South Seas, but after 18 months on the whaler he jumped ship and escaped with a companion into an island jungle. His subsequent four weeks in benevolent captivity among the Taipi tribe on Nuku Hiva, one of the Marquesas Islands, became *Typee,* his first book; his life on Tahiti and the nearby island of Mooréa (Eimeo) was described in *Omoo;* and his service as a seaman aboard a navy frigate returning to the United States furnished him with the background for *White-Jacket.* In October 1844 he returned to his mother's home near Troy, New York, and began to write of his experiences. *Typee* appeared in 1846 and was followed a year later by *Omoo;* the two books, full of high adventure and romantic visions of South Seas life, secured him considerable fame, although his harsh depiction of hypocrisy and venality among Christian missionaries in the islands aroused a storm of controversy. In 1847 he moved to New York City and produced *Mardi,* 1849, another sea story that was, however, more allegorical and less successful than its predecessors; he followed with *Redburn* in the same year and *White-Jacket* in 1850. Also in 1850 he purchased a farm near Pittsfield, Massachusetts, and began work on his greatest book, *Moby Dick,* completed and published the next year. At Pittsfield he formed a close friendship with his near neighbor, Nathaniel Hawthorne, to whose influence much of the power and insight of *Moby Dick* are probably due. The book, although a critical and popular failure at the time, has come to be recognized as one, perhaps the best, of the very few truly great American novels and a masterpiece of world literature. The visions of evil in the white whale and in the growing and corrupting monomania of Ahab, the pervading mystical atmosphere, and the richly and subtly symbolic narrative show Melville at the height of his powers. In 1852 appeared *Pierre,* a book that was to a large degree autobiographical and that was also a psychological study that anticipated much later literature. After this time his work suffered a decline. A few short stories, published in magazines and collected in 1856 as *The Piazza Tales*, remain noteworthy, particularly "The Encantadas," "Bartleby," and "Benito Cereno;" with the exception of *The Confidence-Man*, 1857, a dense allegory of American materialism, he wrote little prose thereafter, and his poetry, except for a few of his *Battle-Pieces*, 1866, was undistinguished. He journeyed to the Holy Land and to Europe in 1856–1857 and briefly visited Hawthorne, then U.S. consul in Liverpool; in 1863 he left his farm to return to New York City. In 1866 he obtained a long-sought government position as a customs inspector, in New York City, a post he held until 1885. In these last years he lived in utter obscurity. *Clarel*, a long, somewhat obscure narrative poem, appeared in 1876. He regained his former literary powers in his last complete work, *Billy Budd, Foretopman*, completed in 1891 but not published until 1924. He died in New York City on September 28, 1891. His work remained largely forgotten in the United States until the beginning of the 1920s, when a revival of interest in American literature brought about a critical and public rediscovery of him and of many similarly neglected authors.

Menard, Michel Branamour (1805–1856), Texas pioneer. Born at Laprairie, Quebec, on December 5, 1805, Menard left home before he was fifteen and learned the rudiments of fur trading with the Indians in the vicinity of Detroit. He joined his uncle, Pierre Menard, an established trader in Kaskaskia, Illinois, in 1823, who sent him to trade with the Shawnee and Delaware Indians. Menard earned the respect and confidence of the Shawnee and eventually decided to live with them. Long since dispersed from their original tribal home in Ohio, the Shawnee were scattered in villages in various parts of Missouri and Arkansas. Often forced to move, Menard followed the Shawnee southward and they manifested their trust in him by adopting him and making him a chief. From the Arkansas Territory he went with the Shawnee to the vicinity of Shreveport and subsequently got Mexican approval to settle in Nacogdoches, Texas. He prospered in Texas, traded with the Mexicans, and shortly began to speculate in land. Immediately after Texan independence from Mexico, he purchased for $50,0000 about six square miles of land, which he had earlier claimed, on the east end of Galveston Island. Within two years he had platted a town site (laid out by Gail Borden) whose lots were first sold in 1838 by the Galveston City Company, which he also organized. Galveston grew steadily as did his investment and other business ventures. In 1840–1842 he served in the Texas congress. He died on September 2, 1856, in Galveston. Menard County, Texas, was named for him in 1858.

Menard, Pierre (1766–1844), fur trader and public official. Born on October 7, 1766, in St. Antoine,

Quebec, Menard moved to Vincennes, in present-day Indiana, when he came of age and began trading with the Indians. By 1789 he had established a store at Kaskaskia in the Northwest Territory, (now in Illinois) and as he prospered he began to take an interest in local politics. When the territory began to be broken up into counties he became a major in the Randolph County militia (1795). After William Henry Harrison became the governor of the newly designated Indiana Territory in 1800, he appointed Menard judge of the county court of common pleas in 1801, and in 1803 he was elected to the territorial legislature. Menard thus held three public posts, and in 1806 he was placed in command of the county militia with the rank of lieutenant colonel. The Illinois Territory, which included Kaskaskia, was set off from Indiana in 1809 and Menard relinquished his seat in the Indiana legislature but retained his judgeship until 1811. In 1809 he joined Jean Pierre Chouteau, his brother-in-law, and others in the St. Louis Missouri Fur Company and took part in the company's first expedition that year, which returned the Chief Shahaka of the Mandan to his village. The following year he led company trappers as far as the Columbia River. Menard returned to Kaskaskia and again became active in Illinois politics. He was elected to the legislative council in 1812 and served as its first president until statehood was achieved for Illinois in 1818, upon which he was elected by acclamation as the state's first lieutenant governor. He retired after one term. Menard, like many of the pioneer traders, was later called upon to act as an Indian commissioner; he served under two presidents, John Quincy Adams and Andrew Jackson. He died on June 13, 1844, at his home in Kaskaskia, a place long famous for hospitality throughout the frontier.

Mencken, Henry Louis (1880–1956), journalist, editor, and critic. Born in Baltimore on September 12, 1880, H. L. Mencken graduated from the Baltimore Polytechnic Institute, a high school, and in 1899 joined the staff of the *Baltimore Morning Herald* as a police reporter. Four years later he was city editor and in 1906 switched to the *Baltimore Sun*, with which, together with the *Evening Sun*, he was associated at intervals throughout his career. In 1908 he was hired to review books for the *Smart Set*, a witty, urbane periodical that also featured the drama reviews and criticism of George Jean Nathan; in 1914 the two assumed coeditorship of the magazine. In 1924, while Mencken was also a contributing editor of the *Nation* (1921–1932), they left *Smart Set* to found the *American Mercury*, and for ten years Mencken, both as an editor and as a writer, continued to dominate American criticism in its pages. After Nathan's departure in 1930, Mencken edited the magazine alone. A vigorous and colorful writer, he consistently and gleefully attacked every sacred cow within reach; in his omnivorous iconoclasm he was particularly caustic toward sham, prudery, Prohibition, the middle class (or "booboisie") and, later, the New Deal. While belittling the excesses and deficiencies of currently popular sentimental literature, he promoted such younger writers as Theodore Dreiser, Sherwood Anderson, and Sinclair Lewis. The Scopes "Monkey Trial" in Dayton, Tennessee, in 1925, which he reported from the scene, provided a golden opportunity for Mencken to exercise his acerbic wit. Many of his reviews and essays were collected in the six-volume series of *Prejudices*, 1919–1927. His most lasting work came in a surprisingly uncharacteristic form: *The American Language*, 1919, a solid, thorough, and scholarly treatment of the subject that, together with two supplements issued in 1945 and 1948, constituted an effort of primary value and established him as the leading authority on American English. The radical change in the temper of the country brought on by the Depression of the 1930s lessened the popular appeal of a perennial cynic; he continued to report on the American scene after 1933, but with diminished influence. He published numerous books of essays and criticism, including *Damn! A Book of Calumny*, 1947, which was composed largely of those enraged denunciations of him that had delighted him most; *Notes on Democracy*, 1926; *Treatise on the Gods*, 1930; *Making a President*, 1932; and *Minority Report*, 1956, and three autobiographical works, *Happy Days*, 1940; *Newspaper Days*, 1941; and *Heathen Days*, 1943. In 1948 he suffered a stroke from which he never fully recovered; he died in Baltimore on January 29, 1956.

Menéndez de Avilés, Pedro (1519–1574), colonizer. Born on February 15, 1519, at Avilés, Spain, Menéndez went to sea at fourteen. His early service in the Spanish navy was under Charles V, who in 1549 recognized his abilities with a commission to rid the Spanish coast of pirates. Five years later, at the age of thirty-five, he was made captain-general of the Indies fleet. Philip II, who succeeded to the Spanish throne in 1556 and whose zeal to extend Spanish influence equaled that of Charles, granted Menéndez the right to explore and to establish and govern a colony in Florida. He left Cadiz with 11 ships and 1500 men in June 1565, about a year after French Huguenots had established Fort Caroline at the mouth of the St. John's River. In late August he entered and named the Bay of St. Augustine, where he built a fort for Spain, the nucleus of the oldest surviving settlement on the continent. Twice challenged by a French fleet under Jean Ribaut, he succeeded in holding them off, and in September ravaged the French outpost. Menéndez refused to take prisoners and killed many Frenchmen, including Ribaut (whose fleet had been wrecked), after they surrendered, justifying his actions on the grounds that his victims were Protestants, that is heretics. He subsequently established other posts in Florida and at Port Royal on Chesapeake Bay, first colonized in 1562 by Ribaut, all the while making efforts to convert the Indians to Roman Catholicism, but without much success. He returned to Spain for supplies in 1567, and during his absence

the French got some measure of revenge by attacking Fort San Mateo, formerly Fort Caroline, in the spring of 1568. According to a widely accepted story, the French commander, Dominique de Gourgues, hanged his Spanish prisoners on the spot where the Huguenots of Fort Caroline had been executed by Menéndez, inscribing on a tablet: "I do this not unto Spaniards but as to traitors, robbers, and murderers." It was a reply to Menéndez's earlier inscribed claim that he had killed the French force "not as Frenchmen but as Lutherans." De Gourgues felt unequal to an attack on St. Augustine and returned to France. Menéndez returned to Florida in 1571 to find that his settlements were suffering badly. He went back to Spain in 1572, planning to return with more settlers. He died in Santander on September 17, 1574, having established Spanish sovereignty over Florida.

Menken, Adah Isaacs (1835?–1868), actress and poet. Born into a Jewish family, probably in a suburb of New Orleans, about 1835, the later Miss Menken apparently was given the names Adah Bertha, but other facts concerning her early life, including her father's name, are obscured by later and confused publicity stories. Her father, who was probably a Spanish Jew, died before she was two, and her mother was left a widow and without means. Adah became fluent in several languages, including Hebrew, German, Spanish, and French, and displayed a talent for singing and dancing as well. She married Alexander Isaacs Menken in Livingston, Texas, on April 3, 1856, and thereafter retained his name on the stage through several marriages, all of them short-lived. She appeared on the stage at Shreveport, Louisiana, as early as 1857 and made her debut in New Orleans the same year. She began to publish verse at about that time; several poems appeared in the *Cincinnati Israelite* during 1857–1859 and in the *New York Sunday Mercury* in 1860–1861. She first appeared on the stage in New York City in 1859, but it was not until she opened in Albany, New York, in an adaptation of Lord Byron's *Mazeppa*, in 1861, that she achieved lasting recognition. Appearing in the play's climactic scene almost nude and strapped to a running horse, she created a sensation in several cities, including Albany, Baltimore, and San Francisco. Strikingly beautiful, the central figure in a scandalous divorce case as well as in rumored infidelities, and a talented poet who received encouragement from Walt Whitman, she numbered Mark Twain and Henry Wadsworth Longfellow among her friends and admirers. Her fame preceded her to London, where she opened in *Mazeppa* in 1864; her literary entourage there soon included Charles Dickens, A. C. Swinburne, and D. G. Rossetti. In 1865 she had a run in New York City and the following year another, and made a successful U.S. tour before returning to Europe in August 1866; everywhere she played before record audiences. About six weeks after the birth of her second son (the first had died in infancy) she opened in late December 1866 in *Les Pirates de la Savane* in Paris. She received acclaim unprecedented for an American actress, and added Théophile Gautier and Dumas *père* to her train. The Paris engagement was interrupted by performances in Vienna and in the fall of 1867 she returned to Astley's Theatre in London. She gave what proved to be her last performance at the Sadler's Wells Theatre on May 30, 1868. She died in Paris at the age of thirty-three, on August 10, 1868, a month after she had collasped during a rehearsal for a revised version of *Les Pirates*. Eight days later her *Infelicia*, a collection of poems that was dedicated to Dickens, appeared in London.

Menninger, Karl Augustus (1893–   ), psychiatrist. Born on July 22, 1893, in Topeka, Kansas, the son of psychiatrist Charles Frederick Menninger (1862–1953), Karl graduated from the University of Wisconsin in 1914 and received his medical degree from Harvard in 1917. He interned in the Kansas City General Hospital during 1918–1919 and was an assistant physician in the Boston Psychopathic Hospital in 1920. That year he founded the Menninger Clinic for psychiatric research and therapy in Topeka with his father. They were later joined by his brother, William Claire Menninger (1899–1966), also a psychiatrist; the brothers established the Menninger Foundation in 1941 to provide clinics for research, professional education, and diagnosis and treatment, and programs on the relation of psychiatry to law, religion, industry, and education. He made the community in Topeka aware of the aims of the clinic through various public appearances, working on the principle that knowledge of psychiatry's basic concepts would overcome prejudice. Kansas revamped its entire mental-health program under his guidance and became a model for the nation. The Menninger Clinic remained a major national center for psychiatric training, treatment, and research. After World War II he helped establish the Winter Veterans' Administration Hospital in Topeka, and remained there as director until 1948. During 1946–1962 he was clinical professor of psychiatry at the University of Kansas. State and national organizations enlisted his services as mental-health adviser, among them the Illinois State Department of Welfare, the Office of Vocational Rehabilitation of the Department of Health, Education and Welfare, and the prison bureau of the Department of Justice. He edited the *Bulletin* of the Menninger Foundation and wrote, among other works, *The Human Mind*, 1930; *Man Against Himself*, 1938; *Manual for Psychiatric Case Study*, 1952; *Theory of Psychoanalytic Technique*, 1958; *The Vital Balance*, 1963; and *The Crime of Punishment*, 1968. He was one of the most admired and widely honored psychiatrists in the United States in the twentieth century.

Menotti, Gian-Carlo (1911–   ), composer. Born on July 7, 1911, in Cadegliano, near Lugano, Italy, Menotti was composing by the age of six, completed an opera at eleven, and enrolled in the Milan Conservatory of Music soon thereafter. He came to the United States with his mother in 1927 and enrolled in the Curtis Institute of Music in Philadelphia, where he studied for five years under Rosario Scalero. He first attracted national attention with his opera *Amelia Goes to the Ball*, which was first performed in Philadelphia in 1937 and later by the Metropolitan Opera Company in New York City. *The Old Maid and the Thief*, initially given in a radio performance in 1939, and *The Island God*, performed by the Metropolitan Opera in 1942, were less favorably received. The ballet *Sebastian*, 1944, and a piano concerto, 1945, preceded *The Medium*, 1946, a melodrama on spiritualism that had a long run on Broadway and later was frequently performed along with the short, dramatic *The Telephone*, 1947. *The Consul*, first performed in New York City in 1950, won a Pulitzer Prize. His opera *Amahl and the Night Visitors*, written for television, was given its premier broadcast on December 24, 1951, and came to be presented annually on Christmas Eve. Menotti's special genre, often called chamber opera, and for which he wrote his own librettos, was as much dramatic as it was musical. The striking libretto of *The Saint of Bleecker Street* won the New York Drama Critics' Circle award in 1954 and earned him a second Pulitzer Prize in music as well. The more traditional opera *Maria Golovin*, 1958, was produced in Brussels and by David Merrick on Broadway without much success. Menotti also wrote the libretto for Samuel Barber's Pulitzer Prize-winning opera *Vanessa*, 1958, and also his *A Hand of Bridge*, 1960; the opera *Labyrinth*, television premiere 1963; the comic opera *The Last Savage*, Paris, 1963; and *Martin's Lie*, 1964. Menotti's dramatically effective stage music presented a striking contrast to the richer and relatively more melodious music of pieces like *Sebastian*. His other instrumental works included the symphonic poem *Apocalypse*, 1951, and a violin concerto, 1953. He began teaching at the Curtis Institute of Music in 1941 and in 1958 established in Spoleto, Italy, and became director of the annual Festival of Two Worlds ("the Spoleto Festival"), presenting music, opera, and dramatic works.

Menuhin, Yehudi (1916–   ), violinist. Born on April 22, 1916, in New York City, Menuhin grew up in San Francisco, where at the age of four he began taking violin lessons. At seven he made an appearance as soloist with the city's symphony orchestra, and the next year, 1925, he appeared at the Manhattan Opera House in New York City. After initial study in San Francisco with Louis Persinger it was decided he should continue his training in Europe. Accompanied by his mother, who with the aid of tutors undertook his education, Menuhin gave his first European concert at the Paris Opera House in 1927, playing both Beethoven and the Brahms concertos in addition to one of Bach's. The triumph was repeated later that year in New York City's Carnegie Hall. He shortly began to study with the celebrated Georges Enesco, whose interest in and influence on the child prodigy continued for the next quarter of a century. He made his first appearance in London at Albert Hall in 1929. His reputation grew with each concert. In England he came under the influence of Sir Edward Elgar, whose violin concerto became a permanent part of his repertoire. Menuhin also studied with Adolph Busch. At nineteen he began a world tour that took him to 63 cities and then announced his retirement. He returned to the concert stage when he came of age in 1937 and thereafter remained in the ranks of the world's leading violin virtuosos. During World War II he toured the major Allied war zones and subsequently gave numerous benefit concerts to aid European refugees. By the end of the war he was a popular musical idol and in 1945 he performed in the Soviet Union, the birthplace of his parents. In the early 1950s he toured Japan and India, where he became fascinated with the sitar music of Ravi Shankar, whose virtuosity he later introduced to the United States. Noted for his interest in contemporary music, Menuhin commissioned works from Béla Bartók, William Walton, and Ernest Bloch. Although he was sometimes criticized for a lack of profundity in his interpretations of the great standard violin works, Menuhin's later career established him as a modern master of Bach, and he was generally regarded as at his best in the performance of chamber music, where his charm, reticence, and studied dedication captivated thousands of music lovers. His early recordings of the sonatas of Mozart and Beethoven, with his sister Hephzibah, four years his junior, accompanying him on the piano, are now eagerly sought by collectors.

Meredith, James Howard (1933–   ), civil rights advocate. Born in Kosciusko, Mississippi, on June 25, 1933, Meredith served nine years in the air force before attending Jackson State College, a Negro institution, where he received better than average grades. Early in 1961, seven years after the celebrated Supreme Court decision in *Brown v. Board of Education* that heralded the racial desegregation of the nation's schools and two years after the court ruling had become binding, he applied for admission to the University of Mississippi and was rejected. The University of Mississippi had a 114-year history of unbroken segregation. Meredith then enlisted the aid of the National Association for the Advancement of Colored People (NAACP) and filed suit in federal district court. After prolonged appeals, the Supreme Court upheld an appellate court order that he be admitted in the coming term. The ensuing events precipitated a crisis in the recurring struggle between federal and state authority. Governor Ross R. Barnett of Mississippi invoked the old doctrine of interposition, declared himself school registrar, and succeeded in barring Meredith's admission on four successive occasions when he attempted to register in late September. Rioting on the campus threatened for several days and

finally broke out on September 30, despite a nationally televised address by President John F. Kennedy urging peaceful desegregation. The Mississippi national guard, already federalized, was sent in to quell the disturbance, which had attracted others besides students. Sporadic gunfire killed two people, one a French newspaper correspondent, whose death highlighted the extensive coverage given the matter in the foreign press. Meredith, who was protected from the violence by a federal guard, was enrolled the following day despite the threat of continued rioting. The events added new urgency to the national issue of desegregation. Meredith completed ten strenuous months at the university, living on campus without his family and constantly under federal guard, despite serious misgivings he had felt about enrolling for the second semester. He graduated in August 1963 and three years later published his account: *Three Years in Mississippi.* After graduation he spent some time in Africa and attended the Columbia University Law School, receiving a law degree in 1968. In June 1966 Meredith, accompanied only by a few friends, started to walk the 220 miles from Memphis, Tennessee, to Jackson, Mississippi in an effort to encourage Negroes to overcome their fears and register to vote. Shortly after he crossed the Mississippi border he was wounded by blasts from a shotgun. The incident provoked a strong reaction as nationally prominent figures of the civil-rights movement, with whom Meredith had heretofore shunned association, came to his bedside and then completed his planned three-week walk. Meredith, who had always viewed his efforts as a personal mission, remained suspicious of their motives but returned to lead the march at its close on June 26, when 12,000 persons came to Jackson for a final rally. After his graduation from Columbia, Meredith pursued private business interests.

Mergenthaler, Ottmar (1854–1899), inventor. Born on May 11, 1854, in Hachtel, near Würzburg, Germany, Mergenthaler wanted to be an engineer but at fourteen became an apprentice to a watchmaker. He developed, in the course of four-years training, a keen ability in precision instrument making. Emigrating to the United States in 1872 (he was naturalized in 1878), he joined the business of August Hahl, his former master's son, a manufacturer of scientific equipment in Washington, D.C., and after 1876 in Baltimore. The firm was commissioned to construct a patent model of a typewriting device, which used rudimentary papier-mâché molds for typecasting. Although the device proved unworkable, its intent—to eliminate the laborious task of composing type by hand—stimulated Mergenthaler to produce an efficient mechanical typesetter. In developing his final model, he passed through various stages—attempting to avoid metal type completely by directly making an inked transfer for lithographic reproduction, and also using the basics of stereotyping to punch letters into papier-mâché molds for casting in metal. Finally he employed sturdy individual copper molds, or matrices, for each character; the matrices, selected by the operation of a keyboard, were used to cast the line of words in a molten but fast-cooling alloy, rapidly producing lines of type of column width. The machine was named the Linotype when Whitelaw Reid of the *New York Tribune* (the first publishing enterprise to use the machine, which it adopted in 1886), examined a line-long "slug" and cried, "It's a line of type!" The first patent was obtained by Mergenthaler in 1884. He had begun his own instrument manufacturing business the year before, and later secured patents on other successful inventions, but the Linotype remained his major concern. He constantly made and patented improvements and was widely honored for his invention. At the time of his death in Baltimore, on October 28, 1899, three Mergenthaler Linotype factories, in New York, England, and Germany, were in full operation and more than 3000 Linotypes were in use. More than any other invention of its time, the Linotype brought about a dramatic upsurge in publishing.

Merman, Ethel (1909–   ), musical-comedy actress. Born on January 16, 1909, in Astoria, New York, Ethel Zimmerman went to public school in Long Island City. She worked as a secretary and sang in nightclubs before opening in George Gershwin's musical *Girl Crazy* in 1930, billed as "Ethel Merman." Without any formal musical training, she became an immediate sensation and launched a new hit song, "I've Got Rhythm." Virtually everything she appeared in after that was a success and she soon was recognized as the large-voiced, bouncy queen of a new era of musical comedy. Her triumphant debut was followed by an appearance in George White's *Scandals* of 1931, in which her rendition of "Life is Just a Bowl of Cherries" became another hit. "Eadie Was a Lady," from *Take a Chance*, 1932, was so popular that the lyrics appeared in the *New York Times* after the Broadway opening. The success of Cole Porter's *Anything Goes*, 1934, was repeated in the movie version, 1936, in which she starred with Bing Crosby. Other memorable shows included *Du Barry Was a Lady*, 1939, *Panama Hattie*, 1940, and *Annie Get Your Gun*, 1946, which was probably her biggest success and was revived for her 20 years later at Lincoln Center in New York City. After *Call Me Madam* closed its run (1950–1952) she announced it would be her last Broadway show, but she returned to do *Happy Hunting*, 1956, and to another huge success in *Gypsy*, 1959. The apparently ageless first lady of the American musical comedy stage, Miss Merman was noted for her unflagging humor only slightly less than for her "wake 'em up in the last row" voice. During the 1960s she made numerous appearances on television as well as in nightclubs.

Merriam, Charles (1806–1887), publisher. Born on November 21, 1806, in West Brookfield, Massachusetts, Merriam was of a family engaged in newspaper and book publishing. He received his early education in a local school before becoming an apprentice printer in Hartford, Connecticut, at fourteen. Between 1823, when his father died, and 1831 he acquired some additional schooling, taught school and worked as a printer in Boston. In 1831 he went to Springfield with the intention of launching a newspaper with his brother George (1803–1880) but they soon abandoned that prospect for book selling and publishing, opening a small shop in that year. The G. & C. Merriam Company was formed in Springfield in 1832 and quickly became known as a publisher of textbooks, law books, and Bibles, in addition to operating a bookstore which was initially under Charles's direction. At the death of Noah Webster in 1843 the firm acquired the rights to his two-volume *American Dictionary of the English Language*, and in 1847 brought out an edition in one volume, the first of the Merriam-Webster dictionaries, under the editorship of Webster's son-in-law, Chauncey A. Goodrich. Reissued with illustrations in 1859, the dictionary became the firm's mainstay and the printing and bookstore portions of the business were eventually dropped. Charles, whose literary abilities exceeded George's (they were joined in the firm by a third brother, Homer, in 1856), took an active part in overseeing publication of the dictionary and often read proof. The first of the editions popularly known as the *Unabridged*, the result of an extensive revision under Noah Porter (later president of Yale), came out in 1864. Charles Merriam retired from active participation in the firm in 1876. He also had banking and insurance interests, but his fortune came mainly from the success of the dictionary. In his later years he actively promoted the library at Springfield and completely financed the library in his native West Brookfield. He died in Springfield on July 9, 1887. Three years after his death G. & C. Merriam published *Webster's International Dictionary* and subsequent abridged and unabridged versions remained the leading dictionaries in the United States.

Merrick, David (1912–   ), theatrical producer. Born in St. Louis on November 27, 1912, Merrick (who changed his name from Margulois in 1939) became interested in the theater at an early age, but despite this graduated from Washington Universiy in St. Louis and continued on for a law degree from St. Louis University. He subsequently practiced law in St. Louis and New York City until 1949, gravitating more and more toward the theater after about 1945. He received a sizable return for a $5000 investment in Herman Shumlin's production of *The Male Animal*, 1940, and later was associated with Shumlin as a general manager. Merrick launched his own career as a producer with *Clutterbuck* in 1949. In 1954 he was represented on Broadway with *Fanny* and the following year with *The Matchmaker*. In 1957 he began what became a regular policy of presenting several attractions at a time: *Jamaica*, *Look Back in Anger*, and *Romanoff and Juliet* established him in that season as the most successful producer on Broadway. Noted for his unorthodox publicity stunts, especially feuding with critics (his antics probably kept *Fanny* going for its 888 performances), he was referred to as "the Barnum of Broadway producers." Among his other productions were *The World of Suzie Wong, The Entertainer,* and *La Plume de Ma Tante,* in 1958; *Destry Rides Again* and *Gypsy* in 1959; *Irma la Douce* and *Becket* in 1960; and *Stop the World —I Want to Get Off* and *Oliver* in 1962. *Hello, Dolly* won a Tony Award in 1963. The success of *Oh, What a Lovely War,* 1964, prompted a subsequent movie version, and his production of *Rosencrantz and Guildenstern Are Dead* brought him another Tony Award in 1967. Merrick continued his unprecedented success with *Promises, Promises* and *Forty Carats* in 1968.

Merton, Robert King (1910–   ), sociologist. Born in Philadelphia on July 5, 1910, of immigrant parents, Merton grew up in the slums of South Philadelphia but managed to win a scholarship to Temple University, where he majored in sociology and from which he graduated in 1931. He did graduate work at Harvard, from which he received an M.A. in 1932 and a Ph.D. in 1936. He was a junior faculty member at Harvard from 1934 to 1939, then went to Tulane University. In 1941 he accepted a position as assistant professor of sociology at Columbia, becoming associate professor in 1944, professor in 1947, and Giddings Professor of Sociology in 1963. His work ranged over many areas of his field, from sociological aspects of scientific development in seventeenth-century England (the subject of his doctoral dissertation) to the sociology of deviant behavior, the sociological background of the U.S. war-bond drives in the early 1940s, the character of medical students and the reasons for their choosing a medical career, the "professionalization" of nursing, and the subsequent careers of Nobel laureates after their winning of the prize. He wrote a number of scholarly papers that contributed to his high reputation in his field and was the author, coauthor, or coeditor of several influential books: *Mass Persuasion,* 1946; *Social Theory and Social Structure,* 1949; *Continuities in Social Research,* 1950, with Paul F. Lazarsfeld; *Freedom to Read: Perspective and Program,* 1957, with Richard P. McKeon and Walter Gellhorn; *Sociology Today,* 1959, with Leonard Broom and Leonard S. Cottrell, Jr.; and *Contemporary Social Problems,* 1961, with Robert A. Nisbet. Associate director of Columbia's Bureau of Applied Social Research from 1942, Merton was a member of many professional groups and was president of the American Sociological Society in 1956–1957.

Merton, Thomas (1915–1968), poet and author. Born at Prades in the French Pyrenees on January 31, 1915, Merton was the son of a landscape painter, an Anglican originally from New Zealand, and an American Quaker mother. The family came to the United States in 1916, but at eleven Thomas returned with his father to France

and was educated there and in England, briefly at Cambridge, until, his father having died, he returned to the home of his maternal grandparents in New York City in 1933. He entered Columbia University in 1935, graduating in 1938 and receiving his M.A. in 1939. After teaching English briefly at Columbia and flirting with the Communist party, he became a convert to Roman Catholicism in late 1938. He had been writing since he was about ten, and by his graduation from Columbia had produced several unpublished manuscripts; in 1940 he wrote the posthumously published *My Argument with the Gestapo,* 1969. In 1941 he was teaching at St. Bonaventure College and writing poetry. That same year he became a novice at the Abbey of Our Lady of Gethsemane in Kentucky, the largest monastery of the Trappist order. Although the order was originally one of the most austere in Catholicism, its seventeenth-century founder, Rance, eschewing all intellectual work, the modern Trappists encouraged scholarship, especially in history and theology. Merton's first book, *Thirty Poems,* published in 1944, celebrated his conversion; later collections of poetry included *Man in the Divided Sea,* 1946, and *Figures for an Apocalypse,* 1948. These works won him critical respect, but his autobiography, *The Seven Storey Mountain,* 1948, created a sensation, bringing not only him but also the Trappists in Kentucky much attention. Merton was ordained a priest in 1949 and thereafter was known within his order as Father M. Louis. His later works, none of them as popular as his autobiography but all influential within a circle of admirers, included *Seeds of Contemplation,* 1949; *The Ascent to Truth,* 1951; *The Sign of Jonas,* 1953; *No Man Is an Island,* 1955; *Thoughts in Solitude,* 1958; *The Secular Journals,* 1959; *The New Man,* 1962; *Life and Holiness,* 1963; *Mystics and Zen Masters,* 1967; and *Faith and Violence: Christian Teaching and Christian Practice,* 1968. As a Trappist monk he lived an eremitical existence—the Trappists are sworn to silence except during prayer—but he continued to be interested in various secular activities, including the civil-rights movement. He died on December 10, 1968, while attending a congress of monks in Bangkok, Thailand.

Metacomet, *see* Philip

Metz, Christian (1794–1867), religious leader. Born at Neuwied, Prussia (now Germany), on December 30, 1794, Metz came of a family with long-standing connections with the Community of True Inspiration, a Protestant sect that originated in Germany early in the eighteenth century. Its doctrine, set forth by one of the founders, Eberhard Gruber, held that divine inspiration did not cease with the prophets and apostles but continued to be experienced from time to time through new prophets. The community was in a state of decline in 1817 when Metz, who was a carpenter, and two others were recognized by its members as prophets. His gift of inspiration proved the most lasting of the three and he subsequently presided over a revival of the community. In 1842, on the basis of new revelations, he led 800 members in a migration to the United States. They settled on a 5000-acre site near Buffalo, New York, purchased from the Seneca Indians, which they named Ebenezer. They remained there, living a communal life, until 1854, when the need for additional land prompted a move to the Iowa frontier. Under Metz's auspices the community's holdings at Amana, as the new settlement was named, eventually grew to 25,000 acres and seven villages, all held in common. Incorporated in Iowa as the Amana Society in 1859, the community wrote a constitution, built schools and churches, and became successful in its agricultural and business enterprises. Metz's capable administrative and spiritual leadership continued until his death there on July 27, 1867. After the Civil War, the Amana community began to experience some difficulty in retaining its younger members, but it remained the most successful experiment in Christian communism in the United States. Under the strain of the Great Depression of the 1930s, all property was divided and private enterprise restored in the form of a joint stock company in 1932. The civil and religious functions of the Amana community were also separated at that time.

Michelson, Albert Abraham (1852–1931), physicist. Born on December 19, 1852, in Strelno, Prussia (now Strzelno, Poland), Michelson came to the United States with his parents in 1854 and grew up in Virginia City, Nevada, and in San Francisco. He won appointment to the U.S. Naval Academy, graduated in 1873, and after two years of regular navy duty returned there as an instructor in chemistry and physics. After four years of teaching he returned to his own studies, in Germany and France, resigning from the navy in 1881. In 1883 he became professor of physics at the Case School of Applied Science (now Case Western Reserve University) and in 1889 moved to the newly established Clark University; finally, in 1892, he was appointed head of the physics department of the new University of Chicago and there remained until his retirement. Throughout his life his main interest was the study of light. His first published paper in 1878 concerned the measurement of the speed of light; this problem and that of optical interference were the subjects of the bulk of his researches and writings. His major work in optical interference began in 1881 with his invention of the interferometer, a device for studying the nature and behavior of light on the nearly infinitesimal scale of the single wavelength. At the time it was generally believed that electromagnetic phenomena—light, for example—occurred in and were transmitted by a universal substrate or medium called the ether. The ether was presumed to be uniform, and it was therefore predicted that the earth, moving at high speed in a constantly changing direction along its curved orbit, ought to show a changing velocity with respect to it. This change would appear as a slight difference in the speed of light rays traveling in different directions. After some preliminary experiments in 1881 Michelson collaborated with Edward W. Morley in conducting the famous Michelson-Morley experiment in 1887 that demonstrated the absence of the "ether wind." This result, confirmed many times, was a major foundation for Albert Einstein's development of his theory of relativity. In later work Michelson continued to refine the determination of the speed of light, established the exact length of the meter measure, using the wavelength of cadmium light, and in 1920 used his stellar interferometer to make the first reliable measurement of the diameter of a star. In 1907 he was the first American to be awarded the Nobel Prize for Physics, being honored for his optical measuring instruments and his work in meteorology and spectroscopy. During World War I he was called to service in the naval reserve and did much valuable work, particularly the development of a rangefinder. He was the recipient of a large number of honors and awards in addition to the Nobel Prize and was a member of the world's leading scientific societies. In 1925 he became the first Distinguished Service Professor at the University of Chicago. He retired in 1931 and died shortly thereafter, on May 9, 1931, in Pasadena, California. Among his published works were *Velocity of Light*, 1902; *Light Waves and Their Uses*, 1903; and *Studies in Optics*, 1927. He was elected to the Hall of Fame in 1970.

Michener, James Albert (1907–   ), author. Born on February 3, 1907, in New York City, Michener grew up in Doylestown, Pennsylvania. He traveled extensively throughout the United States during vacations from high school and continued his education at Swarthmore College, earning a B.A. in 1929, before studying at several European universities in 1931–1933. He taught English in Pennsylvania for about three years and then went to Colorado State College, where he received an M.A. in 1936 and taught history until 1939. He spent two years as a visiting professor at Harvard before becoming an editor for the Macmillan Company in 1941. He remained with Macmillan until 1949 except for the period 1944–1945, which he spent on active duty in the Pacific theater with the navy. A frequent contributor to professional education journals before the war, he wrote two books, one with H. M. Long, and became recognized as an expert in the teaching of social studies. While in the Solomon Islands with the navy he began writing a series of short pieces that were published as *Tales of the South Pacific*, 1947. An immediate popular success, the book won a Pulitzer Prize in 1948 and was successfully adapted by Richard Rodgers and Oscar Hammerstein II for the Broadway musical *South Pacific*, 1949. Michener's talent for blending fact and fiction also marked such later popular successes as *Return to Paradise*, 1951, and *Hawaii* 1959. The Korean War provided the setting for *The*

Bridges at Toko-ri, 1953, and *Sayonara*, 1954. *The Voice of Asia*, 1951, and *Japanese Prints*, 1959, reflected his continuing interest in Asia. *The Source*, 1965, a novel about the ancient and modern Jew, exploited the device of an archaeological dig in Palestine. *The Bridge at Andau*, 1957, documented the anti-Communist uprising in Hungary during 1956. Other works of nonfiction included *Report of the County Chairman*, 1961, based on his experience with the Bucks County, Pennsylvania, Citizens for Kennedy in the 1960 election; *Iberia*, 1968, based on his travels in Spain; and *Presidential Lottery*, 1969. During 1967–1968 Michener served as secretary of the Pennsylvania Constitutional Convention. His later books included *Kent State*, 1971; *Centennial*, 1974; *Chesapeake*, 1978; *The Covenant*, 1980; *Space*, 1982; and *Poland*, 1983.

Mies Van Der Rohe, Ludwig (1886–1969), architect. Born on March 27, 1886, in Aachen, Germany, Ludwig Mies (he added Van Der Rohe later in life) learned the fundamentals of architecture from his father, a mason and stonecutter. He attended a trade school at Aachen and became a draftsman's apprentice. From 1905 to 1907 he worked with furniture designer Bruno Paul in Berlin, and from 1908 to 1911 he studied under Peter Behrens, who also influenced the architects Le Corbusier and Walter Gropius. He opened an office in Berlin in 1913, then served in the German army as a bridge and road builder during World War I. In 1919 and 1921 he planned the first steel and glass skyscrapers, which became his trademark. He introduced "ribbon windows," rows of glass evenly divided by vertical concrete slabs, in a plan for an office building drawn up in 1922. International recognition came from his Weissenhof multiple-dwelling exhibit at the Deutscher Werkbund exposition in Stuttgart in 1927, his German Pavilion at the Barcelona International Exhibition in 1929, and his contemporary Tugendhat House in Brno, Czechoslovakia, completed in 1930. Between 1926 and 1932 he led a group of German architects whose purpose was to adapt art to the technological age. In 1930 he became head of the Bauhaus school at Dessau, which was closed in 1933 by the Nazi regime for being "un-German." He came to the United States in 1938 to direct the school of architecture at the Armour (now Illinois) Institute of Technology, a post he held until 1958. He became a U.S. citizen in 1944. During the rapid increase in building after World War II, his designs materialized in cities across the United States. Based on his concepts of order, logic, and clarity, they used minimal ornamentation to achieve striking effects. Among the most famous were the Seagram Building in New York City, 1956, bronze and tinted-glass tower in a spacious concrete plaza, designed in collaboration with Philip C. Johnson; Crown Hall at the Illinois Institute of Technology, a "glass house" with mobile space dividers, one of 20 buildings he planned for the campus; the Chicago Federal Center, a symmetrical group of high-

and low-rise structures; and twin glass apartment towers in Chicago overlooking Lake Michigan. His chairs became as famous as his buildings, among them the MR of cane and tubular steel; the steel-framed, leather-upholstered Tugendhat, whose design forms a square S; the Brno, which forms a curved S; and the Barcelona, whose legs form an X. An acknowledged master of twentieth-century architecture, he died in Chicago on August 18, 1969.

Mifflin, Thomas (1744–1800), soldier and public official. Born on January 10, 1744, in Philadelphia, Mifflin attended Quaker schools and graduated from the College of Philadelphia (subsequently the University of Pennsylvania) at the age of sixteen. When he came of age he formed a partnership with his brother and soon was established as a prominent merchant in Philadelphia. His identification with the patriot cause was marked by his opposition to the Stamp Act in 1765, and thereafter his political fortunes rode the rising tide of sentiment for independence. While in the Pennsylvania assembly, 1772–1775, he championed a colonial congress and was elected to the first and second Continental Congresses. In May 1775 he received a major's commission in the Continental army, but he saw limited front-line duty after his appointment as quartermaster general of the army in August 1775. He rose in rank steadily and was made brigadier general in May 1776 and major general nine months later, but he was unhappy with his role and proved increasingly lax in carrying out his responsibilities, eventually pleading ill health and resigning the post of quartermaster in October 1777. Mifflin's part in the cabal against Gen. George Washington that bears Thomas Conway's name was brief but central, hinging on his membership, from November 1777, on the Board of War. Like Gen. Horatio Gates, whom he successfully promoted as president of the Board of War, Mifflin doubtless expected his own advancement through the alleged plan to make Gates commander in chief. He made enemies as the plot became public and when Washington put an end to it his influence waned, although he disavowed complicity. Accused of embezzlement while serving as quartermaster, he blamed his subordinates; his resignation from the army, offered in August 1778, was accepted the following February without investigation of his handling of funds. He remained influential in Pennsylvania politics and in 1782 was elected to Congress under the Articles of Confederation, serving as its president from November 1783 to June 1784. He was a member of the Constitutional Convention of 1787, speaker of the Pennsylvania general assembly, 1785–1788, president of the state supreme executive council, 1788–1790, and the overwhelming choice for the office of governor under Pennsylvania's new constitution in 1790. He served three successive terms, until 1799, but he lost control of his personal finances and of the governor's office during his last term. Incurably extravagant and by then habitually careless, he was forced by his creditors to leave Philadelphia in 1799. He died a pauper at Lancaster, Pennsylvania, on January 20, 1800, and his funeral was paid for by the state.

Miles, Nelson Appleton (1839–1925), soldier. Born on August 8, 1839, near Westminster, Massachusetts, Miles was commissioned captain of volunteers in the 22nd Massachusetts regiment at the outbreak of the Civil War. His baptism of fire came at Fair Oaks (Seven Pines) in June 1862, after which his bravery earned him a promotion to lieutenant colonel. He was promoted to colonel after Antietam, distinguished himself at Fredericksburg and again at Chancellorsville, and for his actions at the latter, where he was seriously wounded, was given the temporary rank of brigadier general and later, in 1892, the Congressional Medal of Honor. He was present at almost every major engagement of the Army of the Potomac and in 1865, at the age of 26, he was named major general of volunteers in command of the 2nd Army Corps. As commandant at Fort Monroe, Virginia, after the Confederate surrender, he became custodian of Jefferson Davis after he was captured in May 1865 and, for keeping Davis shackled in his cell, he was the target of severe public criticism, even in the North. Nevertheless he was made a colonel in the regular army and, in 1869, commander of the 5th Infantry. His subsequent service on the Western frontier was dedicated and courageous during recurring hostilities with the Indians. He achieved victories against the Cheyenne and Comanche in 1875 and later was instrumental in pacifying the Sioux under Crazy Horse. He captured Chief Joseph in 1877 after the Indian's incredible march toward sanctuary in Canada, and the following year neutralized Chief Elk Horn near Yellowstone. In 1886 he came to the aid of Gen. George Crook, finally capturing the elusive Apache leader Geronimo after an 18-month pursuit through the Southwest and into Mexico. In the last uprising of the Sioux in South Dakota in late 1890, during which Sitting Bull was killed, Miles restored U.S. control over the Indians; but his reputation was permanently tarnished by the massacre of some 200 Sioux, including women and children, at Wounded Knee, South Dakota, on December 29, 1890. Miles was placed in command of the Department of the East, with headquarters at Governor's Island, New York, in 1894 and in September 1895 became the army's commander in chief. His role during the Spanish-American War was mostly administrative, although he did take troops to Puerto Rico to occupy the island. Late in that year he was reprimanded for having commented publicly on Adm. George Dewey's report on charges against Adm. Winfield S. Schley; in 1902, on his return from an inspection tour of the Philippines, he aroused a controversy with his criticisms of the conduct of certain U.S. officers there. Miles retired from the army in August 1903. He spent his remaining years in Washington, D.C., where he died on May 15, 1925. He published two vol-

umes of autobiography, *Personal Recollections and Observations of General Nelson A. Miles*, 1896, and *Serving the Republic*, 1911.

Millay, Edna St. Vincent (1892–1950), poet. Born on February 22, 1892, in Rockland, Maine, Miss Millay was raised with two younger sisters by their widowed mother, who recognized and encouraged her talent in writing poetry. At nineteen she entered "Renascence," a poem of about 200 lines, in an anthology contest, and although she did not win a prize, she attracted critical recognition and a patron who sent her to Vassar. She enrolled at twenty-one and graduated in 1917, in that year publishing *Renascence and Other Poems* and moving to Greenwich Village in New York City. There she submitted verse and short stories under the pseudonym "Nancy Boyd" to magazines, and to augment her modest income wrote skits for the Provincetown Players and joined them briefly as an actress. In 1920 she published *A Few Figs from Thistles*, her second book of verse, and in 1921 *Second April*. In the latter year she also published three plays, *Aria da Capo, Two Slatterns and a King*, and *The Lamp and the Bell*. She won a Pulitzer Prize in 1923 for *The Harp-Weaver and Other Poems*. Also in 1923 she married Eugen Jan Boissevain, and lived thereafter in a large, isolated house in the Berkshire foothills near Austerlitz, New York. In 1925 the Metropolitan Opera Company commissioned her to write an opera with Deems Taylor; the resulting work, *The King's Henchman*, first produced in 1927, became the most popular American opera up to its time and, published in book form, sold out four printings in 20 days. Her youthful appearance, the independent, almost petulant tone of her poetry, and her political and social ideals made her a symbol of the youth of her time. In 1927 she donated the proceeds from "Justice Denied in Massachusetts" to the defense of Sacco and Vanzetti and personally appealed to the governor of the state for their lives. The night of their execution she was arrested in the death watch outside the Boston Court House. Three later books, *There Are No Islands Any More*, 1940; *Make Bright the Arrows*, 1940; and *The Murder of Lidice*, 1942, expressed her continuing concern with contemporary affairs. She also published *The Buck in the Snow and Other Poems*, 1928; *Fatal Interview*, 1931; *Wine from These Grapes*, 1934; *Conversation at Midnight*, 1937; and *Huntsman, What Quarry?*, 1939. The flippant and stylish cynicism of much of her early work gave way in later years to more personal and mature writing, and although she continued to fall occasionally into inflated rhetoric she produced, particularly in her sonnets and other short poems, a considerable body of intensely lyrical verse. She died in Austerlitz in Columbia County, New York, on October 19, 1950.

Miller, Arthur (1915–   ), playwright and author. Born on October 17, 1915, in New York City, Miller was raised in modest circumstances, attending local public schools. Combining studies with full-time jobs, he completed a four-year course at the University of Michigan in six years and graduated in 1938. He began writing in college and won a measure of fame when his first novel *Focus*, about anti-Semitism, was published in 1945. He had written an earlier play, *The Man Who Had All the Luck*, 1944, and a book about life in the army, *Situation Normal*, also 1944. His first successful play was *All My Sons*, 1947, presented in New York City, which explored the guilt of a manufacturer of inferior war equipment and the effect of his crime on his family; it won the New York Drama Critics' Circle Award. *Death of a Salesman*, 1949, won a Pulitzer Prize. Generally considered Miller's best play, it pictured a salesman's struggle to maintain his life on illusion. In *The Crucible*, 1953, Miller's account of the Salem witch trials closely paralleled political events of recent times in the United States. His other plays typically placed characters in rigid social structures, the drama being produced by the character's attempt to overcome the system and achieve self-determination. He became known as an intellectual, and his marriage to movie actress Marilyn Monroe in 1956 was regarded by some as bridging a culture gap; they were divorced in 1960. Other plays included *A View from the Bridge*, 1955; *After the Fall*, 1964; *Incident at Vichy*, 1964; and *The Price*, 1968. His play *The Creation of the World and Other Business* was staged on Broadway during the 1972–1973 season. Adapted for the screen were *Death of a Salesman* in 1951, *The Crucible* in 1958, and *A View from the Bridge* in 1962. In 1961 he wrote the screenplay for *The Misfits*, Miss Monroe's last movie. His other published works included a collection of stories, *I Don't Need You Any More*, 1967, and stories and essays for *Harper's*, *Life*, *Esquire*, *Holiday*, the *Nation*, and other magazines.

Miller, Cincinnatus Hiner, see Miller, Joaquin

Miller, Glenn (1904–1944), bandleader and arranger. Born in Clarinda, Iowa, on March 1, 1904, Miller acquired his first trombone at thirteen, reportedly paying for it by milking cows. He spent his youth in Nebraska and Oklahoma and attended high school in Colorado. He began playing in dance bands as early as 1920, when he was only sixteen, and continued to do so while attending the University of Colorado during 1924–1926. After a year on the West Coast he joined Ben Pollack's band in 1927 and came with it to New York City. He began arranging music about this time, often for groups other than the one with which he was playing, and within a few years had established a reputation as a talented arranger. In 1934 he was playing and arranging music for Tommy and Jimmy Dorsey's orchestra and the following year his services were sought by Ray Noble for his first American band. He launched his own career as a band leader in 1937 but the first attempt proved abortive. The Glenn Miller Orchestra was reorganized with fresh

young talent in 1938 and began to tour, soon riding the crest of the "big band" craze. Miller's first successful recording as a bandleader was "In the Mood," 1939; the orchestra swiftly became known nationally after that. Other highly successful recordings followed: "Sunrise Serenade," 1939, sold more than a million copies, as did "Moonlight Serenade," the orchestra's theme song and Miller's best-known composition; "Tuxedo Junction," 1940, became popular only after the Miller recording. In 1940 Miller's band performed regularly on network radio, and the following year the orchestra was featured in the film *Sun Valley Serenade*, in which they introduced one of their most enduring hits, "Chattanooga Choo-Choo." At the peak of its popularity in late 1942, Miller announced that he was disbanding the orchestra and that he would enter military service. He was commissioned a captain in the army and later became a major in the Army Air Force. He organized a large orchestra that regularly made broadcasts to troops in every theater of war and in 1944 he took a band to England. He was reported missing after a flight that departed from England for Paris on December 15, 1944. After his disappearance the band came under the direction of Ray McKinley, who continued to tour with it under the Miller name; Buddy De Franco took over after McKinley. The distinctive "Glenn Miller sound" was widely imitated by other bands after the war. A biographical film, *The Glenn Miller Story*, was released in 1953.

Miller, Henry John (1860–1926), actor director, and producer. Born on February 1, 1860, in London, Miller emigrated to Canada with his family in the early 1870s, settling in Toronto. He decided to become an actor after seeing a production of *Romeo and Juliet* at the age of fifteen. His ambition brought him to the United States, where by 1890 he was an established leading man, having played opposite Helena Modjeska and Clara Morris, who was also a Canadian pursuing her career in the United States. By his own account the most important influence on his career was that of Dion Boucicault, the Irish-born actor and playwright who was one of the leading figures in the American theater after the Civil War. After Boucicault's death in 1890, Miller became the principal male actor of the Empire Theatre Stock Company in New York, where he acquired a national reputation while appearing in such popular plays as *The Younger Son*, *Sowing the Wind*, and *The Importance of Being Earnest*. In 1899 he opened at the Herald Square Theater in *The Only Way*, a play based on Dickens's *A Tale of Two Cities*, which had a successful run in New York City and did not close on the road until 1901. Miller is chiefly remembered for his efforts in bringing William Vaughn Moody's prose play *The Great Divide*, 1906, to the American stage. It was Moody's greatest success, and launched Miller's new career as a producer-director as well as actor. He scored another triumph with Charles

R. Kennedy's *The Servant in the House*, 1908, and in 1909 he took both plays to London. By 1918 he had built his own theater, where he directed and starred in a number of successful productions, including *Daddy Longlegs* and *The Changelings*, but his best-known production remained the Moody play. He died in New York City on the eve of a new opening on April 9, 1926.

Miller, Henry Valentine (1891–1980), author. Born in New York City on December 26, 1891, Miller grew up in Brooklyn, where his father was a tailor. As a youth he read widely and also learned to play the piano, but he was restless and uncertain about a career. Matriculating in New York University, he left after only two months and went to work in Manhattan. In 1911 he used money intended for college to pay for a tour of the Southwest. He showed up in San Diego in 1913, returned to New York City in 1914 to help his father until 1917, and then went to Washington, D.C. In about 1920 he went to work for the Western Union telegraph company in New York City. By 1923 he had written his first book and although he had been unable to find a publisher, he nevertheless left his job the following year to devote himself to writing. He tried working for pulp magazines without success and then left for Europe with his wife, remaining there during 1928–1929. He returned to France alone in 1930, taking with him the outlines of two books that he was later to complete as *Tropic of Capricorn* and *The Rosy Crucifixion*. The next decade proved decisive in Miller's career. Still in France, he began work as an editor and published a story, "Mademoiselle Claude," in 1931. He had completed *Tropic of Cancer* by the end of 1932; reputedly delivered to Obelisk Press by Ezra Pound with the comment, "Here's a dirty book that's worth reading," it was nevertheless not published until 1934, in Paris. It was banned in the United States, but copies soon made their way across the Atlantic, beginning Miller's career as an underground writer. Largely an autobiographical account of his life in Paris, *Cancer* combined an almost surrealistic celebration of sex with a lyrical exuberance that remained one of his best qualities as a writer. His *Tropic of Capricorn* (Paris, 1939), which drew on an earlier phase of his life, also was banned. Except within literary circles, Miller was known only by reputation when he returned to the United States in 1940. He went to California, where he continued to write. *The Colossus of Maroussi*, 1941, a travel book inspired by a trip to Greece in 1939, was received favorably; and his *Air-conditioned Nightmare*, 1945, dealing caustically with the United States, kept him in the public eye. After settling at Big Sur in 1944 he continued his autobiographical opus with the *Rosy Crucifixion* trilogy: *Sexus*, 1949; *Plexus*, 1953; and *Nexus*, 1959, all three published in Paris. The publication of the *Tropic* books in the United States (*Cancer* in 1961, *Capricorn* in 1962) provoked a series of obscenity trials that culminated in a 1964 Supreme Court decision affirm-

ing their right to publication. An American edition of *The Rosy Crucifixion* was quickly brought out, appearing in 1965 and Miller became wealthy for the first time in his life. He lived at Big Sur, where he painted and attracted a colony of followers, until 1964. *Big Sur and the Oranges of Hieronymus Bosch*, 1956, was an account of the life there. Elected to the American Institute of Arts and Letters in 1958, Miller enjoyed a reputation as something more than a writer of "dirty books," perhaps as an American Rabelais. He moved to Pacific Palisades, California, and died there on June 7, 1980.

Miller, Joaquin (1837–1913), poet. Born near Liberty, Indiana, on September 8, 1837, Cincinnatus Hiner (later Heine) Miller migrated westward with his family, which eventually settled on the frontier, near Eugene, Oregon, about 1852. The events of his early life are often exaggerated, but his reputation extended to gambling, horse stealing, mining for gold, and fighting Indians. He went to Columbia College in Eugene, Oregon, for about a year (1858–1859), studied law briefly before being admitted to the bar in Portland, Oregon, and made some money operating a pony express (1862). In 1863 he acquired the *Eugene Democratic Register*, in which he published his first article, a defense of the legendary California brigand Joaquín Murieta. Thereafter nicknamed "Joaquin," he later adopted this as a pen name. His success as an Indian fighter led to his election as county judge in Canyon City, Oregon, in 1866. His first volumes of verse, *Specimens*, 1868, and *Joaquin et al.*, 1869, attracted little attention but sufficed as an introduction to the literary circles of San Francisco. In 1870 he embarked for England. *Pacific Poems*, 1871, printed privately there, attracted the attention of the critics. Introduced in London by William Rossetti, he created a sensation with his frontier manners and flamboyant Western costumes, and *Songs of the Sierras*, 1871, quickly found a publisher. Widely acclaimed by the British, he became known as the "Byron of Oregon." American critics found *Songs*, on which his reputation chiefly rests, excessively romantic. Largely ignored after his return to the United States, he set out for South America and Europe and may also have journeyed to the Near East. He continued to publish poetry, his books including *Songs of the Sunlands*, 1843; *The Ship in the Desert*, 1875; *The Baroness of New York*, 1877; and *Songs of Italy*, 1878. He also tried his hand at plays, of which *The Danites in the Sierras*, 1877, was the most popular. In 1886 he settled near Oakland, California, where he remained an eccentric figure. His *Complete Poetical Works* appeared in 1897. He died at his home on February 17, 1913, having made a significant early attempt to celebrate the West.

Miller, Perry Gilbert Eddy (1905–1963), historian and critic. Born on February 25, 1905, in Chicago, Miller attended the University of Chicago, receiving his B.A. in 1928 and his Ph.D. in 1931. He subsequently went as an instructor to Harvard, where in 1946 he became a full professor of American literature, and in 1960 Powell M. Cabot Professor of American Literature. His first book, *Orthodoxy in Massachusetts*, 1933, established him in a field where he remained preeminent among scholars. *The Puritans*, 1938, edited with T. H. Johnson, and *The New England Mind*, 1939 and 1953, toppled many conventional notions about the Puritans, and the latter book soon became the standard work in its field. His academic career was interrupted by service in the army during 1942–1945. Long-expected works on Jonathan Edwards were published in 1948 and 1949 and did much to confirm Edwards's reputation as a seminal American thinker. Miller lectured in Europe and Japan in the early 1950s and spent 1953–1954 at the Institute for Advanced Study at Princeton, returning there once again in 1962–1963. *Roger Williams*, 1953, was his last major work on the Puritan intellectuals. In his later years he focused his attention on the great American writers of the nineteenth century. His last works included *The Raven and the Whale*, 1956; *Consciousness in Concord*, 1958; and *The Golden Age of American Literature*, 1959. He died in Cambridge, Massachusetts, on December 9, 1963, having notably contributed to the reawakening of interest in the Puritan tradition. A historian of ideas as much as a literary critic, Miller described his personal intellectual quest in *Life of the Mind in America*, a volume that was published in 1965, two years after his death.

Miller, Samuel Freeman (1816–1890), justice of the Supreme Court. Born on April 5, 1816, in Richmond, Kentucky, Miller studied medicine at Transylvania University and received his M.D. degree in 1838. While carrying on his medical practice in Barbourville, Kentucky, he read law and in 1847 was admitted to the bar. The Kentucky constitutional convention of 1849 reaffirmed the legality of slavery in the state and Miller, mildly abolitionist in sentiment, decided to leave; in 1850 he settled in Keokuk, Iowa, and opened a law office. He became prominent at the bar and increasingly involved in organizing and supporting the Republican party. In 1862 his name was put forward by the Iowa delegation in Congress for appointment to the Supreme Court; President Abraham Lincoln nominated him and he was confirmed by the Senate on July 16. Although he had had little formal preparation for the post, he was throughout 28 years on the bench particularly sensitive to the main issues of justice that often tended to be obscured by the technicalities of particular cases. He was, moreover, acutely aware of larger constitutional implications in the cases he heard. He dissented when, in 1870, the Court ruled against the applicability of wartime paper currency to previously incurred debts, and he was with the majority when the Court reversed itself on this point in the Legal Tender Cases the following year. His most important contribution came in 1873, when he wrote the opinion of the

conservative majority in the Slaughterhouse Cases, the first occasion on which the Court was called upon to construe the Fourteenth Amendment; pointing out the violence any other view would do to the federal system, he held that the "privileges and immunities" clause applied to federal rather than to state citizenship and that the Supreme Court was charged with passing upon the constitutional validity of only that legislation which impinged upon rights stemming from federal citizenship. Despite the nationalizing intentions of the authors of the amendment, he thus effectively precluded the possibility of the Court's interposing itself between a state and its citizens; while this decision preserved the federal system, it had as an unfortunate byproduct a virtual validation of discriminatory state legislation in the area of intrastate jurisdiction, which remained in effect for the next six or seven decades. Miller continued to serve on the Court until his death on October 13, 1890, in Washington, D.C.

Miller, William (1782–1849), religious leader. Born on February 15, 1782, in Pittsfield, Massachusetts, Miller grew up in Low Hampton, Washington County, New York and moved to Poultney, Vermont, after his marriage in 1803. A respected farmer, he held minor political offices and later served with the rank of captain during the War of 1812. A serious student of the Bible on his own after a religious conversion about 1816, his reading of the Scriptures (especially of Daniel 8:13–14) convinced him of the imminence of Jesus's reappearance on earth. He did not begin public preaching until 1831, but he soon proved to be a master of his apocalyptic theme, and in 1833 he became a licensed Baptist preacher. In 1836 he published *Evidence from Scripture and History of the Second Coming of Christ, About the Year 1843*, the first of many publications. The Millerite, or Adventist, movement began to rise to national prominence about 1839. Millerite publications were established in Boston (*Signs of the Times*) and New York City (*Midnight Cry*) and Miller himself took to the road, preaching in tents. At his peak during the summers of 1842 and 1843 (Miller had settled on March 1843–March 1844 as the time period for the Second Coming) he estimated that he had made between 50,000 and 100,000 sincere converts to his views. In anticipation of the Coming, thousands left their homes, farms, and jobs to prepare for judgment. When 1843 came to an end, some of his associates—Miller himself was hesitant about a date—set October 22, 1844, as the final date by which Jesus would return. When he did not, this second, or "Great Disappointment," brought the movement to an end. Miller and others persevered in their beliefs but no longer insisted on a definite date. On April 29, 1845, a representative company of Millerites met in Albany, New York, in what was announced as a "mutual conference of Adventists," but the cohesion provided by a spectacular crusade was difficult to translate into an organized church. The Millerite movement as such ended there, although Adventism was far from crushed, enjoying its next revival around the time of the Civil War. The present Seventh-Day Adventists (originally Sabbath-keeping Adventists), probably an outgrowth of the Millerites, were active by 1849; the Advent Christian Church was organized in 1861, and other smaller sects also seemed traceable to Millerism. Miller himself continued to preach on occasion before his death at Low Hampton, New York, on December 20, 1849.

Millikan, Robert Andrews (1868–1953), physicist. Born on March 22, 1868, in Morrison, Illinois, Millikan grew up there and in Maquoketa, Iowa. He graduated from Oberlin College in 1891; after taking his Ph.D. at Columbia University in 1895 he spent two years in further study at the universities of Berlin and Göttingen. Upon his return to the United States in 1896 he was appointed an instructor at the University of Chicago; he became a full professor of physics in 1910. His earliest major researches concerned the electron and particularly the determination of its electrical charge. By improving upon the techniques of his predecessors he was able to arrive at an accurate determination of the charge and then, by isolating the electron, to show that the charge was a discrete constant rather than a statistical average. In 1913 this work brought him the Comstock Prize of the National Academy of Sciences. Turning to an examination of the photoelectric effect, he was able to obtain experimental confirmation of Albert Einstein's photoelectric equation and to make a most accurate evaluation of the Planck constant. During World War I he served as chief of the science and research division of the Army Signal Corps with a lieutenant colonel's commission. In 1921 he left the University of Chicago to become director of the Norman Bridge Laboratory of the California Institute of Technology (Caltech) in Pasadena, and become also chairman of the Caltech executive council. From 1922 to 1932, he represented the United States on the League of Nations committee for intellectual cooperation. In 1923 he was awarded the Nobel Prize for Physics for his work on electrons and photoelectricity. During the 1920s he devoted much of his time to an attempt to discover the cause of a long-noted and puzzling phenomenon, the apparently spontaneous gradual discharge of a charged electroscope. Examining the rates of discharge under various conditions, from balloons ten miles in the air to the bottoms of mountain lakes, he finally evolved the theory, later fully confirmed, that the cause of the discharge was radiation coming to the earth from outer space. These "cosmic rays," as he called them, he thought to be the "birth cries" of new atoms. Millikan also pursued research into X rays and ultraviolet radiation. During World War II he worked on developing jet and rocket propulsion systems for military use. Among his many publications, in addition to technical papers and textbooks, were *Evolution in Science and Religion,* 1927; *Science and the New Civilization,* 1930; and

Autobiography, 1950. He died at his home in San Marino, California, on December 19, 1953.

Mills, Robert (1781–1855), architect and engineer. Born on August 12, 1781, in Charleston, South Carolina, Mills was educated at the College of Charleston and then, determining to prepare himself for a career in architecture, moved to Washington, D.C., in 1800 to study under the Irish-born architect James Hoban. Three years later he took up residence at Monticello as he continued his training under the guidance of Thomas Jefferson; at Jefferson's suggestion he entered the office of Benjamin H. Latrobe and remained there until 1808, absorbing the principles of Greek Revival design and gradually taking on work of his own. Thus thoroughly prepared, he entered upon an independent career as an architect, the first native American to follow this profession and one destined to be a major influence in the revival of the classical style. From 1808 to 1817 he practiced in Philadelphia designing residences, churches, and the State House in Harrisburg and supervising the rebuilding of Independence Hall. In 1814 the city of Baltimore held a competition for designs for a proposed monument to George Washington and his design was adopted; begun in 1815, the structure was completed 14 years later. In 1817 he moved to Baltimore, but in 1820 he returned to Charleston, where he remained for ten years, carrying on his private practice while serving as chief engineer for the state board of public works. In this capacity he oversaw an ambitious program of improvements, including many roads and canals, while designing a number of public buildings; particularly notable was his State Hospital for the Insane, remarkable for being precisely that rather than, as was the nearly universal practice, a prison. In 1830 he moved to Washington, D.C., and his work on federal buildings led to his appointment by President Andrew Jackson six years later as architect of public buildings. His major works there were the Treasury, 1836–1842, the Post Office, begun in 1839, and the Patent Office, 1839. In 1836 a competition was held to select a design for a monument to George Washington in the capital and again his entry was successful. Work was begun on the Washington Monument in 1848, but lack of funds delayed its completion until 1884. In 1851 he retired from his public post and thereafter undertook little work. He died in Washington on March 3, 1855.

Minnewit, Peter, *see* Minuit, Peter

Minot, George Richards (1885–1950), physician. Born on December 2, 1885, in Boston, Minot graduated from Harvard in the class of 1908 and received an M.D. in 1912. Subsequently he was associated with the Massachusetts General Hospital (1912–1913) and the Johns Hopkins Medical School and hospital (1913–1915), returning to Massachusetts General to implement his researches on transfusion and diseases of the blood. In 1923 he accepted concurrent appointments at

Huntington Memorial and Peter Bent Brigham hospitals in Boston. In the early 1920s Minot became interested in the work of George H. Whipple on the effectiveness of raw beef liver in treating experimentally induced anemia in dogs. With William P. Murphy he decided to investigate the effect of raw liver in patients with pernicious anemia, and in 1926 they announced their successful therapy—the ingestion of liver—for a disease which had previously been invariably fatal. In 1928 he returned to Harvard as professor of medicine while at the same time becoming director of the Thorndike Memorial Laboratory at Boston City Hospital. He held both posts until 1948. Minot, Murphy, and Whipple shared the Nobel Prize for Physiology and Medicine in 1934 for their work on anemia. He continued his research on anemia and nutritional disturbances at Thorndike, where before his retirement the active principle in liver therapy was isolated. Known as Vitamin B_{12} or cyanocobalamin, it became the standard medication for pernicious anemia after 1948. Minot was also noted for his work with chemist Edwin J. Cohn in preparing efficient liver extracts. The recipient of numerous medals and awards, he published some 160 papers, chiefly on the blood, concerning which he was an internationally recognized authority. Minot died in Brookline, Massachusetts, on February 25, 1950.

Minton, Sherman (1890–1965), justice of the Supreme Court. Born on October 20, 1890, near Georgetown, Indiana, Minton worked his way through Indiana University, graduating in 1915. He spent the following year at Yale Law School where, before receiving an Ll.M. degree, he helped organize the Yale University Legal Aid Society for the Poor. His law practice, begun in New Albany, Indiana, in 1916, was interrupted by World War I, during which he served as a captain in the infantry. He returned to New Albany in 1919 and joined a law firm, becoming a partner in 1922. From 1925–1929 he practiced in Miami, Florida, but returned once again to New Albany. He began his political career by accepting appointment as the first public counselor of the Indiana Public Service Commission, a post in which, during 1933–1934, he substantially lowered the state's public-utility rates. In 1935 he won election as a Democrat to the Senate, where he proved an able champion of the New Deal and soon became assistant majority whip and chairman of the Senate's Lobby Investigating Committee. He was also a strong supporter of President Franklin D. Roosevelt's 1937 bill for the reorganization of the Supreme Court. He failed in his bid for a second term in the Senate, but Roosevelt retained his services as an administrative assistant in January 1941, and in May of that same year, the Senate approved his appointment to the 7th U.S. Circuit Court of Appeals. President Harry S. Truman called on him in 1948 to serve on a three-man board that investigated a coal strike called by John L. Lewis over an injunction; Lewis was subsequently convicted of contempt and fined for ignoring the injunction. In October 1949 Minton was elevated to the Supreme Court. His record on the bench was conservative, although he supported Chief Justice Earl Warren's efforts in the unanimous *Brown* v. *Board of Education* school-desegregation decision of 1954. He retired from the Court for reasons of health in October 1956 and lived quietly in New Albany, Indiana, until his death there on April 9, 1965.

Minuit, Peter (1580?–1638), founder of New Amsterdam. Born in Wesel, Rhenish Prussia (now in Germany), about 1580, Minuit (sometimes Minnewit) was probably of Dutch ancestry; little is known of his early life. He was in Holland in the early 1620s and apparently (his name appears as a council member) made the trip to New Netherland with the group of colonists that arrived in 1625. If so, he returned to Holland that same year and embarked again for the New World in January 1626. He arrived with additional colonists at Manhattan Island, now in New York City, on May 4, 1626. The Dutch West India Company's settlement was then under the leadership of Willem Verhulst, who had recently replaced the first director, Cornelius May. When Verhulst was recalled in September, Minuit was named the first director general of the colony. His reputation largely rests on his subsequent acquisition for the company of the entire island of Manhattan. Calling the local Algonquian Indian chiefs into council, he purchased the island from them for merchandise valued at 60 guilders (about $24). He then proceeded to erect Fort Amsterdam at the lower end of the island, to change the name of the island from the Indians' Manhattan to New Amsterdam, and to make it the seat of the New Netherlands government. In a short time he became involved in a controversy with Dutch Reformed ministers and the company secretary that led to his recall in 1631. Never reinstated, he later invested in a joint Swedish and Dutch venture to establish a colony in Delaware. He was given command of two shiploads of Swedish and Finnish colonists who in March 1638 established themselves along the Delaware River on land Minuit purchased from the Indians; there they erected Fort Christina, named in honor of the child queen of Sweden, on the site of the present Wilmington, Delaware. Governor Minuit called the territory—which extended indefinitely westward from the Delaware River between Bombay Hook Island and the mouth of the Schuylkill River—New Sweden. In June 1638 he set out on a trading expedition to the West Indies and perished during a storm that destroyed his ship.

Mitchell, John (?–1768), physician, botanist, and cartographer. The date of Mitchell's birth is unknown and his place of birth is disputed, although it was probably somewhere in the British Isles. He studied botany at the University of Edinburgh and may have received a medical degree there. Emigrating to Virginia sometime in the 1720s, he is known to have practiced medicine in and around Urbanna between 1735 and 1746, administering to the poor and in 1738 serving as justice of the peace. During the same period, the late 1730s and early 1740s, he developed a treatment for victims of yellow fever in Virginia. His methods became known to Benjamin Rush, who used them to save many lives during the yellow-fever epidemic in Philadelphia in 1793. Mitchell was known to many prominent men of the time. He corresponded with Cadwallader Colden, the British horticulturist Peter Collinson, and Benjamin Franklin, among others; his letters to Franklin and Colden described his experiences with yellow fever. A collector of plants, he was one of the first to adopt the classification system of Carolus Linnaeus, with whom he also corresponded, and is credited with the discovery of some 25 plant genera. He returned to England because of poor health in 1746 and spent the rest of his life in and around London. A man of varied interests and a respected scientist, he wrote, among other papers, *An Essay upon the Causes of the Different Colours of People in Different Climates* (a matter that had begun to vex Virginians about that time), published by the Royal Society in about 1747. He was elected a fellow of the Society the following year. Mitchell is chiefly remembered for a map he undertook in 1750: published in February 1755 in London by the Board of Trade, to whose archives he had access, it was entitled *Map of the British and French Dominions in North America with the Roads, Distances, Limits, and Extent of the Settlements.* Engraved on copper, the map was large in scale (1:2,000,000) and measured 52¾ × 76¼ inches; the reference to France was eliminated in the title in the 4th edition (London, 1775). Known throughout Europe and freely plagiarized, official editions numbered at least 20 by 1792. It was the map of choice at the peace negotiations in Paris in 1783 after the Revolution, and its authority was relied upon for so many land grants and treaties that by 1829 it was given official status by Great Britain and the United States. Some of its unavoidable errors gave rise to numerous boundary disputes, especially the Maine boundary controversy, and the map figured in litigation over boundaries as late as 1932. Its reputation as "the most important map in American history" remained unquestioned. Mitchell died in London in 1768.

Mitchell, Margaret (1900–1949), novelist. Born in Atlanta, Georgia, in 1900, Miss Mitchell attended Washington Seminary in Atlanta before enrolling at Smith College. When her mother died she left college and returned home. Between 1922 and 1926 she was a writer and reporter for the *Atlanta Journals;* in 1925 she married John R. Marsh. After an ankle injury in 1926 she left the paper and, for the next ten years, worked on a romantic novel about the Civil War and Reconstruction era from a Southern point of view. Entitled *Gone with the Wind,* it was published in 1936 and, an unprecedented success, it was awarded a Pulitzer

Prize the next year. Within six months after publication a million copies had been sold; once it was reported that 50,000 copies were sold in one day. It went on to become the largest-selling novel in U.S. publishing history and within five years had been translated into 18 languages. It eventually sold in 40 foreign countries, most notably in Germany. Miss Mitchell sold the motion-picture rights to Metro-Goldwyn-Mayer (M-G-M) for $50,000; the subsequent film, 1939, which starred Vivian Leigh as Scarlett O'Hara and Clark Gable as Rhett Butler, won several Academy Awards in 1940 and became the largest moneymaker ever produced by M-G-M. Miss Mitchell died following an automobile accident in Atlanta on August 16, 1949, her only novel having exceeded eight million copies in worldwide sales.

Mitchell, Maria (1818–1889), astronomer. Born on August 1, 1818, on the island of Nantucket, Massachusetts, Miss Mitchell was educated in the island schools, but her mathematical ability, which outstripped that of her teachers, and her interest in science led her to pursue those studies on her own. Her interest in astronomy was stimulated by her father, who let her assist in his own work of rating chronometers and encouraged her independent use of his telescope. She worked as a librarian during the day (often acting as an informal teacher) and became a regular observer of the skies at night. In October 1847 she succeeded in establishing the orbit of a new comet. The discovery gained her immediate recognition in scientific circles; the following year brought her a gold medal from King Christian VIII of Denmark and election to the American Academy of Arts and Sciences, the first woman to achieve this honor. A gift of a large, equatorial telescope was arranged by a group of prominent American women and her accomplishments were subsequently kept in the public eye by feminists. She traveled to Europe in 1857–1858 and in 1861 moved with her father to Lynn, Massachusetts. Reluctantly, but encouraged by her father, she accepted in 1865 an appointment at the newly opened Vassar Female College, which had been founded at Poughkeepsie, New York, four years before. As director of the observatory and professor of astronomy there she was, in those early days, the most prominent member of the faculty; several of her students later testified to the great influence she had as a teacher. Elected to the American Philosophical Society in 1869, she was increasingly honored in her later years. She died in Lynn, Massachusetts on June 28, 1889. She was elected to the Hall of Fame in 1905.

Mitchell, Silas Weir (1829–1914), physician and author. Born in Philadelphia on February 15, 1829, Mitchell was educated at the University of Pennsylvania and at Jefferson Medical College, from which he received his M.D. in 1850. Subsequently he studied abroad under Claude Bernard and Charles Robin. During the 1850s he became established as a physician in Philadelphia, publishing his first medical paper in 1852. As an army surgeon during the Civil War, he became interested in nervous diseases and first received wide recognition for his collaboration with G. R. Moorehouse and William W. Keen on *Gunshot Wounds and Other Injuries of Nerves*, 1864. His research after the Civil War produced important contributions to the physiology of the cerebellum and numerous articles on toxicology. In all he published some 170 papers (119 on neurological subjects) on a wide variety of topics, including snake venom, knee jerks, and opium, and he did pioneering work in several fields. In the 1870s he achieved renown for his advocacy of the "rest cure," a pioneering application of psychology to medicine, and his *Fat and Blood*, 1877, a popular account of his treatment for functional nervous disorders, became a best seller in Europe and the United States. His association with the Philadelphia Orthopaedic Hospital lasted 40 years, during which time the hospital became the nation's principal institution for the study and treatment of nervous disorders. Toward the end of the Civil War Mitchell had begun to write fiction; his first story, "The Case of George Dedlow," was notable for its psychological insight and its portrayal of a soldier about to go into combat. It was published in the *Atlantic Monthly* in July 1866. His first poems appeared in 1882 and were published periodically thereafter; *The Complete Poems* eventually were included in his collected works, published in 16 volumes in 1913–1914. He is chiefly remembered for his historical romances, the first of which, *Roland Blake*, 1886, depicted a woman obsessed with power. It was *Hugh Wynne, Free Quaker*, 1897, however, that Mitchell recognized as his best book; that book was followed by *The Adventures of François*, 1899, about the French Revolution; *Constance Trescot*, 1905; and *The Red City*, 1907, a story set in post-Revolutionary Philadelphia. In his last book, *Westways*, 1913, he returned to the Civil War. Highly honored during his later years, Mitchell died in Philadelphia on January 4, 1914.

Mitchell, Wesley Clair (1874–1948), economist. Born in Rushville, Illinois, on August 5, 1874, Mitchell graduated from the University of Chicago in 1896 and, after further study there and at the universities of Vienna and Halle, received his Ph.D. from Chicago in 1899. After a year in the Bureau of the Census as a statistician, 1899–1900, he returned to the University of Chicago to become an instructor and then, from 1902, assistant professor of economics. From 1909 to 1912 he was professor of political economy at the University of California. He then went to Columbia as a visiting professor in 1913, was made professor of economics the next year, and, after a year serving on the War Industries Board during World War I and two years teaching at the New School for Social Research, 1919–1921, he began an association with Columbia that lasted the rest of his academic career; he retired from the university in 1944. His best-known activities, how-

ever, developed out of his long tenure as director of research for the National Bureau of Economic Research, of which he was one of the founders in 1920; he remained in his post there until 1945. Many of his books were published under the Bureau's auspices and reflected work done by him and his associates in the organization, his position in this quasi-governmental body led to his service as a consultant and adviser to various federal agencies and to several presidents. He wrote many books, among them *A History of the Greenbacks*, 1903, an adaptation of his doctoral dissertation; *Business Cycles*, 1913; *Business Cycles, the Problem and Its Setting*, 1927; and *The Backward Art of Spending Money*, 1937. Mitchell died in New York City on October 29, 1948.

Mitchell, William (1879–1936), "Billy," soldier and aviator. Born of American parents in Nice, France, on December 29, 1879, Billy Mitchell, as he was called throughout his life, grew up in Milwaukee. He was educated at Racine College and at Columbian (now George Washington) University; he left Columbian in 1898 before graduating to enlist for service in the Spanish-American War. He served in Cuba and the Philippines and in 1901 was commissioned in the regular army and attached to the Signal Corps. After a number of assignments around the world he attended the Army Staff College and in 1912 became the youngest member of the General Staff. In 1915 he was assigned to the aviation section of the Signal Corps; he learned to fly the following year and began his twenty-years' advocacy of the use of military air power. He was already in Europe as an observer when the United States entered World War I, and as the war progressed he advanced rapidly in rank and responsibility as he proved a highly effective air commander. In September 1918 he successfully attempted a mass bombing attack with nearly 1500 planes, and in October he led a large bombing force in a behind-the-lines air strike; in that month he was promoted to brigadier general. His plans for strategic bombing of the German homeland and for massive parachute invasions were cut short by the armistice and he returned home as assistant chief of the army's Air Service. He outspokenly advocated the creation of a separate air force and continued working on improvements in aircraft and their use. He claimed that the airplane had rendered the battleship obsolete and, over the vociferous protests of the Navy Department, proved his point in 1921 and 1923 by sinking several captured and overage battleships from the air. He was persistently critical of the low state of preparedness of the tiny Air Service and of the poor quality of its equipment; but his harrying of the upper military echelons won him only a transfer to an obscure post in Texas and demotion to the rank of colonel. When, in September 1925, the navy's dirigible *Shenandoah* was lost in a storm, he made a statement to the press charging "incompetency, criminal negligence, and almost treasonable administration of the national defense by the

War and Navy Departments." He was, as he expected, immediately court-martialed and, after he had made the trial a platform for his views, was convicted of insubordination and sentenced to five years' suspension from rank and pay. On February 1, 1926, he resigned from the army. He continued to promote air power and to warn against the danger of being outstripped by other nations, particularly Japan. He hypothesized a possible attack by Japanese aircraft launched from great ships and directed at the Hawaiian Islands. He died in New York City on February 19, 1936. Subsequent events, including the Japanese air attack on Pearl Harbor in December 1941, proved the validity of many of his prophesies. In 1946 Congress authorized a special medal in his honor that was presented to his son two years later by Gen. Carl Spaatz, chief of staff of the newly established independent air force. Among Mitchell's published works were *Our Air Force, the Keystone of National Defense*, 1921; *Winged Defense*, 1925; and *Skyways, a Book on Modern Aeronautics*, 1930.

Mix, Tom (1880–1940), motion-picture actor. Born on January 6, 1880, in Mix Run, Cameron County, Pennsylvania, Thomas Edwin Mix learned to handle horses from his father while growing up in Iowa. Between 1898 and about 1904 he was in the army, serving during the Spanish-American War and also, reportedly, in China. In 1906 he went to work as a cowboy in Oklahoma and shortly thereafter began to appear in Wild West shows as a rider and a roping specialist, thus attracting the attention of the Selig Company when they came to make Western movies in Oklahoma in 1910. A short time later he was appearing in their silent films. His public appeal led to a movie contract with William Fox in 1918, and he enjoyed spectacular popularity and received a huge annual salary during the 1920s. Immaculately dressed in a white suit, black boots, and ten-gallon hat, he was the leading box-office attraction of the decade, sharing his fame with his horse Tony. He lived lavishly and soon became known in Europe as an unofficial ambassador of Hollywood. He had starred in about 100 feature films, all Westerns, before he retired in 1928 with the advent of talking pictures. During the next decade his own Wild West show and circus toured nationally. An attempt at a comeback in sound films during the 1930s was unsuccessful. He died after an automobile accident near Florence, Arizona, on October 12, 1940.

Mizner, Addison (1872–1933) architect and real-estate entrepreneur. Born in Benicia, California, in 1872, Mizner was educated in San Francisco and Guatemala, where he learned to love and understand Spanish culture and tradition. In the mid-1890s Addison studied for a time at the University of Salamanca, in Spain, returned in 1897 to San Francisco to work in an architectural office, and then joined a younger brother, Wilson, born in Benicia in 1876, in the Yukon. Addison went to New York City in 1904 and Wilson followed him in 1906 to manage the Hotel Rand, for which Addison designed the most ornate bar in the city. It was during this period that Wilson's reputation as a wit and bon vivant became established: his famous sign in the hotel, "Carry out your own dead," attested to his sense of humor. In 1918 Addison went to Palm Beach, Florida, to rest in the sun. There he met Paris Singer, a son of the sewing-machine magnate, who was seeking to construct a resort complex on the as yet unspoiled Florida east coast. Their first effort was a convalescent hospital in medieval Spanish style that, after World War I, became the famous and exclusive Everglades Club. Commissions to build other structures in this remarkable combination of traditional Spanish and cheap American architecture flowed thick and fast. The next building to be completed was Mr. and Mrs. Edward T. Stotesbury's house, El Mirasol, and that was followed by ever larger, more expensive, and more ornately "antique" resort palaces for Harold S. Vanderbilt, Rodman Wanamaker, A. J. Drexel Biddle, Jr., John S. Phipps, and others. Altogether, Addison built more than $50 million worth of mansions in a half-decade. Having exhausted the best possibilities of Palm Beach, he turned in 1925 to nearby Boca Raton. He organized the Mizner Development Corporation, with himself as president and Wilson as vice-president and treasurer, and in a period of six months sold more than $30 million worth of lots—a record even for that flamboyant time. But in the spring of 1926 the Florida land-speculation bubble burst and the Mizners went bankrupt. Wilson became a Hollywood screenwriter; Addison remained in Palm Beach, executing a few relatively minor architectural commissions and writing his memoirs, only the first volume of which, *The Many Mizners*, was completed. The book was published in 1932 and Addison died shortly afterward, in Palm Beach, on February 5, 1933. Wilson died in Hollywood on April 3 of the same year.

Mizner, Wilson, *see under* Mizner, Addison

Moholy-Nagy, László (1895–1946), painter, designer, and photographer. Born in Bacsbarsod, near Baja, Hungary, on July 20, 1895, Moholy-Nagy studied law in Budapest before turning to stage designing, painting, and experimenting with woodcuts and other techniques. An abstract painter initially identified with the Constructivists in his native Hungary, he went to Berlin in 1921 and in 1923 joined the Bauhaus, the famous experimental art school at Weimar (later at Dessau) as head of the metal workshop. There he also edited the *Bauhausbook* series. In a Bauhaus class in experimental photography which he directed, he developed a technique for which he later became famous. He delighted in the new forms created by the distortions produced by lenses of abnormally short or long focal length. He eventually made complex abstract compositions by placing objects directly on sensitized paper, which was then exposed to light. The results were especially striking with translucent objects, which left profiles modulated by gradations of light. These "photograms" were the photographic equivalents of abstract paintings of the time. He achieved similar effects with oil paintings on transparent or polished surfaces. He left the Bauhaus in 1929 and moved to Berlin, where for a number of years he designed sets for the State Opera. In 1935 he joined the trek of German artists fleeing the Nazi regime; he went to London, where he designed the sets for H. G. Wells's film *The Shape of Things to Come*, then he traveled to the United States. In 1937, with Walter Gropius as his adviser, he organized in Chicago the New Bauhaus, the first American school of design based on the Bauhaus program of a curriculum that developed the talents presumably possessed by everyone. Reorganized as the Institute of Design in 1939, ten years later it merged with the Illinois Institute of Technology. Moholy-Nagy died in Chicago on November 24, 1946. His *Vision in Motion* appeared the next year.

Mondale, Walter Frederick (1928–   ), public official. Born on January 5, 1928, in Ceylon, Minnesota, Mondale was educated at Macalester College and the University of Minnesota, graduating from the latter in 1951. After army service he entered the University of Minnesota Law School, from which he graduated in 1956. For four years he worked in a Minneapolis law firm, and during 1958–1960 he was also a special assistant to the state attorney general. Active in the Democratic-Farmer-Labor party of Minnesota since college, Mondale was appointed to an unexpired term as attorney general in 1960 and later in that year elected to a regular term. Reelected in 1962, he attracted national attention in 1963 with his amicus curiae brief supporting the cause of free legal counsel for indigent defendants in a Florida case, *Gideon* v. *Wainwright*. In 1964 he was appointed to the Senate seat vacated by his long-time political mentor, Hubert H. Humphrey, and in 1966 he was elected to a full term. He was a prominent and effective promoter of liberal legislation in the Senate. He was reelected in 1972. In 1976 he was chosen to run for vice-president on the Democratic ticket headed by Jimmy Carter, and in November he shared Carter's narrow victory. Four years later the Carter-Mondale ticket lost the presidency to the Republican ticket headed by Ronald Reagan with George Bush.

Monroe, Harriet (1860–1936), editor and poet. Born in Chicago on December 23, 1860, Miss Monroe was educated at the Dearborn Seminary in Chicago and graduated from the Convent of the Visitation in Georgetown, D.C., in 1879. During the next decade her ambition to become a dramatist and a poet was encouraged by such literary figures as Robert Louis Stevenson and William Dean Howells, and in 1892 she published *Valeria and Other Poems*. That same year she received a $1000 commission for *The Columbian Ode*, which celebrated the opening of the World's Columbian Exposition in Chicago. Thereafter a recognized poet, she continued to publish verse in national magazines while also serving as art and drama critic for Chicago newspapers. *The Passing Show: Five Modern Plays in Verse* was published in 1903, but none of the plays were performed. Miss Monroe would have remained only a minor figure but for her ambitious project to establish a forum for contemporary poets. She found backers and solicited work from more than 50 poets, with the result that *Poetry: A Magazine of Verse* was launched in October 1912 and it thrived for 24 years. Young new writers were drawn to the magazine and it quickly became the leading poetry journal in the English-speaking world. A list of its contributors, beginning with Ezra Pound (he served as London editor for the magazine's first six years) and including W. B. Yeats, Robert Frost, T. S. Eliot, Wallace Stevens, Vachel Lindsay, Edgar Lee Masters, and Carl Sandburg, became an index of major contemporary poets. Although Miss Monroe was a champion of the Imagists, the magazine did not confine itself to any school; rather her passion for innovation succeeded in toppling many conventional poetical forms and the magazine did not settle into any literary groove. Her own verse over this period included two volumes of verse, *You and I*, 1914, and *The Difference*, 1924. *Poets and Their Art*, 1926, contained essays and a selection of her editorials. In 1917 she edited with Alice Henderson (the magazine's assistant editor) the influential *The New Poetry: An Anthology of Twentieth-Century Verse in English*. It was revised and reissued in 1923 and 1932. She died while attending a poetry conference in Arequipa, Peru, on September 26, 1936.

Monroe, James (1758–1831), fifth president of the United States. Born in Westmoreland County, Virginia, on April 28, 1758, Monroe studied for two years at the College of William and Mary, cutting his education short to take part in the Revolution. He saw action in several battles, was wounded at Trenton, and rose to the rank of major; but in 1780 he left the army and took up the study of law under the tutelage of Thomas Jefferson, then governor of Virginia. In 1782 he was elected to the Virginia legislature and from 1783 to 1786 served in Congress under the Articles of Confederation. He was a delegate to the 1786 Annapolis Convention that led to the calling of the Constitutional Convention the next year, but he did not attend the latter. In 1787 he was in the Virginia House of Delegates and the following year was a member of the state's ratifying convention for the federal Constitution, where he was among the opposition. Beaten by James Madison for election to the House of Representatives that year, he succeeded in winning a Senate seat in 1790 and, as befitted a long-time friend of Jefferson, aligned himself firmly with the Democratic Republicans. Despite their political differences, President George Washington appointed him U.S. minister to France in 1794. His two years in that position were less than successful; in particular he was unable to justify to the French government the apparently pro-British Jay's Treaty. Monroe was recalled in 1797 and from 1799 to 1802 was governor of Virginia. In 1803 he was sent by President Jefferson to aid Robert Livingston in the negotiations with the French government that resulted in the Louisiana Purchase. Shortly before the purchase treaty was concluded he was appointed minister to Great Britain; he undertook the duties of that post in July 1803 and, with the exception of a few months spent in Madrid in 1804–1805 in an unsuccessful attempt to purchase the Floridas from Spain, he remained in London until December 1807. While there he was joined by William Pinkney, with whose aid he negotiated a commercial treaty that was originally intended to rectify the omissions and unfortunate provisions of Jay's Treaty; the resulting agreement was, if anything, worse, and Jefferson refused to accept it. His friends and supporters in Virginia, including John Taylor of Caroline, promoted him for the presidency in 1808, but he was defeated by James Madison. In 1810 Monroe was again in the Virginia legislature, and he served as governor again during 1811. In November 1811 President Madison appointed him secretary of state and in September 1814, after the disastrous defeat of U.S. forces at Bladensburg, he took on for six months the additional duties of secretary of war. The subsequent improvement in U.S. military fortunes redounded to his credit and solidified his position as heir apparent to Madison. He won the nomination narrowly, but the election was heavily his and in March 1817 he was inaugurated as president. Reelected in 1820 by all but one vote of the electoral college, he presided over eight years of calm prosperity that have come to be known as "the era of good feeling." Monroe showed considerable political sagacity in assembling a brilliant Cabinet headed by John Quincy Adams, John C. Calhoun, William H. Crawford, and William Wirt, all of whose services he retained through two terms. The principal events of the period were the settlement of disputed fishing rights in Labrador and Newfoundland waters in 1818; the acquisition of the Floridas from Spain in 1819–1821; the Missouri Compromise of 1820, which he signed despite doubts about its constitutionality; the veto of the Cumberland Road Bill on constitutional grounds in 1822; the recognition as independent nations of former Spanish colonies in Latin America; and, partly as a result of that step, the formal announcement of U.S. foreign policy with regard to relations between the hemispheres. In this message, delivered in December 1823, Monroe concisely enunciated policies that had actually been followed, though unstated, for some time; their formulation owed as much to Secretary of State John Quincy Adams as to Monroe, but the decision to publish was the president's. Referred to at the time as "the principles of President Monroe," the policy statement came eventually to be called the Monroe Doctrine and to be accepted as an axiom of U.S. foreign policy. In essence, the message declared the age of European colonization in the New World at an end and established two complementary dicta, the noninterference of European governments in the affairs of American nations and of the United States in those of Europe. In 1825 he retired to his home near Leesburg, Virginia; his public service after that time was limited to acting as regent of the University of Virginia from 1826 and presiding over the state constitutional convention in 1829. He died while on a visit to New York City on July 4, 1831, the third of the first five U.S. presidents to die on an anniversary of the Declaration of Independence (John Adams and Thomas Jefferson both died on July 4, 1826). He was elected to the Hall of Fame in 1930.

Monroe, Marilyn (1926–1962), motion-picture actress. Born in Los Angeles on June 1, 1926, Norma Jean Mortenson later took her mother's name, Baker. Her mother was frequently confined in an asylum, and she was reared by 12 successive sets of foster parents, and for a time she lived in an ophanage. In 1942 she married a fellow worker in an aircraft factory. She was divorced soon after World War II, became a popular model, and in 1946 signed a short-term contract with Twentieth Century-Fox, taking as her screen name Marilyn Monroe. After a few brief appearances in movies made by the Fox and Columbia studios she found herself jobless and thence supported herself by modeling for photographers. One of the photographs, taken of her in the nude and used as a calendar illustration, later became a national sensation. In 1950 she played a small uncredited role in *The Asphalt Jungle* that reaped a mountain of fan mail; another appearance, in *All About Eve,* 1950, won her another contract from Fox and an intense publicity campaign that soon made her name a household word. In a succession of movies, including *Let's Make It Legal,* 1951, *Don't Bother to Knock,* 1952, and *Monkey Business,* 1952, she advanced to star billing on the strength of her studio-fostered image as a "love goddess." In 1953 she starred in *Gentlemen Prefer Blondes* and *How to Marry a Millionaire.* Her fame grew steadily and became international; she became the object of unprecedented popular adulation. In 1954 she married baseball hero Joe DiMaggio and the attendant publicity was enormous. With the end of their marriage less than a year later she began to grow discontented with her career. She studied for a time with Lee Strasberg at the Actors' Studio in New York City, and in *There's No Business Like Show Business,* 1954, *The Seven-Year Itch,* 1955, and *Bus Stop,* 1956, she began to emerge as a talented comedienne. In 1956 she married playwright Arthur Miller and retired for a time from Hollywood, although she costarred with Sir Laurence Oliver in *The Prince and the Show Girl,* 1957. In 1959 she won critical acclaim for *Some Like It Hot,* in 1960 she appeared in *Let's Make Love,* and in 1961 was seen in her last role, in *The Misfits,* written by Arthur Miller, whom she had divorced the year before (the movie also featured Clark Gable's final performance). Her 23 movies grossed for their first runs a total of more than $200 million, and her fame surpassed that of any other entertainer of her time. After several months as a virtual recluse, Miss Monroe died in her Hollywood, California home, on August 5, 1962, having taken an overdose of sleeping pills.

Montagu, Ashley (1905–   ), anthropologist. Born on June 28, 1905, in London, Montague Francis Ashley Montagu studied at the University of London from 1922 to 1925. He was associated with the British Museum in 1926, subsequently pursued graduate studies at Columbia University, and also worked with the department of vertebrate paleontology at the American Museum of Natural History in 1927. He spent 1928–1929 at the University of Florence, and in 1929 and 1930 was curator of physical anthropology at the Wellcome Historical Medical Museum in London. He returned to the United States in 1930. From 1931 to 1938 he was assistant professor of anatomy at New York University, but during the year 1931–1932 he also taught child development at the New School for Social Research; he taught other courses there in 1938 and from 1948 to 1959. Returning to Columbia in 1934, he studied anthropology under Franz Boas and received his Ph.D. in 1937. He then joined the Hahnemann Medical College and Hospital in Philadelphia, remaining there until 1949. During this period, in 1940, he became a U.S. citizen. His first book was *Coming into Being Among the Australian Aborigines*, 1937. From the 1930s Montagu was keenly interested in problems relating to race, a subject that first brought him public notice; in 1942 he published *Man's Most Dangerous Myth: The Fallacy of Race*, which was subsequently several times reissued. In 1946 he wrote, directed, produced, and financed a film called *One World or None*. Chosen by the United Nations Educational, Scientific, and Cultural Organization (UNESCO) in 1949 as a member of the group of authorities meeting to consider the main aspects of the race problem, he drew up the basic draft of UNESCO's "Statement of Race," July 1950. To explain and amplify the statement, Montagu published a book, *Statement on Race*, in 1951. In 1949 he became chairman of the anthropolgy department at Rutgers University. Public response to his article in the *Saturday Review* of March 1, 1952, entitled "The Natural Superiority of Women," prompted a book of the same title in 1953. By 1955 he was able to resign his academic post at Rutgers to devote himself to his own projects. From that time he wrote many books: his technical works included *The Reproductive Development of the Female*, 1957, and, with C. Loring Bruce, *Man's Evolution*, 1965; among his books for a more popular audience were *The Cultured Man*, 1958; *The Humanization of Man*, 1962; *The American Way of Life*, 1967; and *Sex, Man, and Society*, 1969. A prolific writer of articles for scientific journals and popular magazines, he at various times held visiting professorships at several universities, including Harvard (1945), Delaware (1955), and the University of California at Santa Barbara (1962).

Montez, Lola (1818–1861), adventuress and dancer. Born in Limerick, Ireland, in 1818, Marie Dolores Eliza Rosanna Gilbert, the daughter of a British army officer, spent much of her girlhood in India but was educated in England. At nineteen she eloped with Capt. Thomas James and returned to India. Her first marriage ended in divorce in 1842 and the following year she launched a career as a dancer. Her disastrous debut (she appeared as "Lola Montez, the Spanish dancer") in London in 1843 would probably have ended the career of anyone less beautiful, but she danced again at the Paris Opéra in 1844, before an equally unimpressed audience. Her receptions in Berlin, Warsaw, and St. Petersburg were somewhat better; then in late 1846 she danced in Munich. Louis I of Bavaria was so struck by her beauty that he offered to make her a countess and to provide her with a castle. She accepted, became Countess of Lansfeld, and remained as his mistress; under her influence (Louis's cabinet became known as the "Lolaministerium"), he inaugurated liberal governmental policies, but his infatuation with her helped to bring about the collapse of his regime in the revolutions of 1848; in March of that year Louis abdicated in favor of his son. Lola fled and soon was married to Lt. George Heald, another British officer. The years 1851–1853 found her in the United States, touring in *Lola Montez in Bavaria*. Her third marriage, to Patrick P. Hull of San Francisco, terminated in divorce, the second union reportedly having ended with Heald's death. She settled in New York City after a tour in Australia in 1855–1856 and gathered a following as a lecturer on such topics as fashion, gallantry, and beautiful women, as well as earning a reputation for aiding women in distress. Her *Art of Beauty* appeared in 1858 and she died in Astoria, New York, on January 17, 1861.

Moody, Dwight Lyman (1837–1899), evangelist. Born on February 5, 1837, in East Northfield, Massachusetts, Moody attended school until he was thirteen and moved to Boston at seventeen to work in his uncle's shoe store. Although he had been baptized by a Unitarian minister, he attended a Congregational church in Boston and received full membership in 1856. He moved to Chicago in that year and worked as a shoe salesman. His interest in religion grew and he formed a church school for slum children in 1858. Two years later, he decided on evangelism as his life's work, intending to devote himself to the underprivileged. He became president of the Chicago branch of the Young Men's Christian Association (YMCA) in 1866, after organizing and leading volunteers from the association to the aid of soldiers on the battle fronts of the Civil War. During 1873–1875 he conducted evangelistic tours through Scotland, Ireland, and England in association with Ira D.

Sankey, organist and composer; the tour was highly successful and upon returning to the United States Moody found himself in great demand. He established his headquarters in Northfield, Massachusetts, and soon set out on the first of a series of evangelistic tours that eventually encompassed the whole country. His great success was due mainly to his manner in preaching; he spoke directly to the common man with a sincere, friendly approach that inspired religious renewal in thousands. Another successful tour of Great Britain occupied the years 1881–1883 and a final visit there was made in 1891–1892. Never ordained himself, he was careful to seek cooperation from established religious leaders; his background attracted support from businessmen, and his businesslike administration of his tours presaged the methods of twentieth-century evangelists. He preached a simple, conservative, personal Christianity sharply in contrast with the Social Gospel movement of the same period. His visits to universities inspired the formation of YMCA branches on campuses as well as student volunteer associations to send missionaries abroad. Contributions maintained these ventures and supported his Northfield Seminary (now School) for girls, founded in 1879, and Mount Hermon School for boys, founded in 1881, both in Northfield, and the Chicago (later Moody) Bible Institute in 1889, for men and women who desired training as lay church workers or missionaries. Considerable income was also earned by the hymn collections he published with Sankey—*Sacred Songs and Solos*, 1873, and *Gospel Hymns*, 1875. He died in Northfield on December 22, 1899.

Moody, Helen Wills, *see* Wills, Helen Newington

Moody, William Henry (1853–1917), justice of the Supreme Court. Born in Newbury, Massachusetts, on December 23, 1853, Moody graduated from Harvard in 1876 and subsequently studied law at Harvard Law School and in the office of the younger Richard Henry Dana. Admitted to the bar, in 1878 he began his practice in Haverhill. He soon gained prominence and began to hold minor political office. His reputation as a trial lawyer was established during his service as district attorney of the eastern district of Massachusetts beginning in 1890, and he first received wide recognition while acting as special prosecutor during the famous Lizzie Borden murder trial. In 1895 he was elected as a Republican to the House of Representatives and was soon on the important Appropriations Committee. His quick rise to national prominence occurred during Theodore Roosevelt's administration; impressed with his abilities, the president appointed him secretary of the navy in 1902. In 1904 Moody succeeded Philander C. Knox as attorney general and vigorously pursued the administration's policy of trust-busting, acting most notably against the "beef trust" (*Swift and Co. v. U.S.*). In late 1906 his nomination to the Supreme Court was confirmed despite rumblings from business interests who feared the reputation he had made while serving as the nation's prosecutor. He served as an associate justice until November 1910, when ill health forced his retirement. He died in Haverhill, Massachusetts, on July 2, 1917. During his very short stay on the bench—he sat on the Court for only four years—he produced a remarkable body of work, writing 67 opinions, five of them dissents. Probably his most important dissent was in the Employers' Liability Cases, 1908, when he disagreed with the Court's view that the 1906 Employers' Liability Act was unconstitutional; his dissent anticipated later Supreme Court decisions. His opinion for the majority in *Twining* v. *New Jersey*, 1908, sharply limiting the privilege of immunity from self-incrimination in state cases, was also influential, although the tenor of the Court's decisions later changed on this point.

Moody, William Vaughn (1869–1910), poet, playwright, and educator. Born in Spencer, Indiana, on July 8, 1869, Moody entered Harvard in 1889, completed four years' work in three, then spent his final year touring Europe and tutoring. He graduated in 1893 and stayed on at Harvard for two years, the first to obtain his M.A. degree and the second as an instructor in English literature. In 1895 he joined the faculty of the University of Chicago where, except for the academic year 1899–1900, he remained until 1907. Long interested in literature as a vocation as well as a field of study, Moody had contributed substantially to and helped edit the *Harvard Monthly* in his undergraduate days; throughout his teaching career he continued to write, and when he resigned his professorship it was to devote full time to writing. His first major published work appeared in 1900; it was a verse drama, *The Masque of Judgment*, the first part of a projected trilogy concerned with the innate rebelliousness of man, his alienation from God, and a final reconciliation achieved through the mediation of woman. The trilogy was continued in *The Fire-Bringer*, 1904, and *The Death of Eve*, not yet completed when he died. In 1901 appeared *Poems*, which included his "Ode in Time of Hesitation," first published in the *Atlantic Monthly* the previous year, in which he expressed his reaction to the problems of contemporary civilization, particularly that presented by U.S. imperialism in the Philippines. In 1905, with Robert Morss Lovett, he published a successful textbook, *A First View of English Literature*, the proceeds of which gave him the leisure to devote himself to his best work, a prose drama, *The Great Divide* (originally *A Sabine Woman*), 1906, in which he portrayed opposing strains in the American character, the inhibited Puritan heritage and the open, wide-ranging Western outlook. This alone among his plays enjoyed great success on the stage and was the leading contribution to American drama in the first decade of the twentieth century. Another play, *The Faith Healer*, 1909, was well received critically but was not successful. Moody died in Colorado Springs, Colorado, on October 17, 1910.

Mooney, James (1861–1921), ethnologist. Born on February 10, 1861, in Richmond, Indiana, Mooney was educated in public schools and taught briefly before joining, in 1879, the *Richmond Palladium*, a daily newspaper for which he wrote editorials. He had already begun the studies of the American Indian that became his life work but several years passed before he found financial support for them. In 1885 he went to Washington, D.C., where he met John Wesley Powell, the director of the U.S. Geological Survey and chief of the Smithsonian Institution's Bureau of American Ethnology. Powell, who was noted for his encouragement of promising field workers, got him a post with the Bureau, with which he stayed for the rest of his life, making notable contributions to the study of the American Indian. He also published some early papers on Irish customs, but he is chiefly remembered for studies of the Cherokee, the Kiowa, and the Sioux. His monographs, published in various volumes of annual reports of the Bureau, include studies of Cherokee mythology, 1900, and of their sacred rituals, 1891. He also tramped the Western frontier on several extended field trips. He became an expert on the Ghost Dance religion that precipitated the final Sioux uprising of 1890 in South Dakota, and contributed greatly to knowledge of the earlier westward Sioux migration. A good deal of Mooney's early work in listing tribes was reflected in the *Handbook of American Indians*, edited by F. W. Hodge and published in two volumes, 1907–1910, to the preparation of which he contributed much. His "Calendar History of the Kiowa Indians" was published in 1898. Mooney also took time out from his field work to prepare the government's Indian exhibits for the great expositions at Chicago (1893), Omaha (1898), and St. Louis (1904). He was engaged on a major work on Kiowa heraldry at the time of his death on December 22, 1921.

Moore, Alfred (1755–1810), justice of the Supreme Court. Born in New Hanover County, North Carolina, on May 21, 1755, Moore studied law and was admitted to practice in 1775. The onset of the Revolution caused him to spend the next six years as a military officer, first in the North Carolina Continental regiment, with which he took part in the defense of Charleston, South Carolina, in June 1776, and then, from 1777 to 1781, as a colonel in his state's militia. Following the war he combined a political career with the running of his family's sizable plantation. From 1782 to 1791, as attorney general for North Carolina, he attained prominence as one of the ablest lawyers in the state. After a term in the state legislature in 1792 he practiced law until 1798, when he was elected a judge of the state superior court. Late in 1799 President John Adams appointed Moore to the U.S. Supreme Court, where he served as an associate justice until 1804, when ill health forced him to give up his seat on the bench. He died six years later, on October 5, 1810, in Bladen County, North Carolina.

Moore, Clement Clarke (1779–1863), lexicographer and poet. Born on July 15, 1779, in New York City, Moore attended Columbia College, of which his father, Benjamin Moore (1748–1816), after a long association had eventually become president. Benjamin Moore, also the second Protestant Episcopal Bishop of New York, wanted his son to become a priest but Clement's scholarly interests prevailed after he graduated from Columbia in 1798. His *A Compendious Lexicon of the Hebrew Language in Two Volumes* appeared in 1809 with the expressed hope that it might aid others to acquire a knowledge of Hebrew. His donation in 1819 of 60 lots in New York City facilitated the erection of the General Theological Seminary, an institution that he served as professor of Oriental and Greek literature from 1823 to 1850. Moore is principally remembered for a ballad, perhaps written for his children and first published anonymously in the *Troy* (New York) *Sentinel* on December 23, 1823, entitled "A Visit from St. Nicholas." Popularly known by its opening lines, " 'Twas the night before Christmas, when all through the house," long before it appeared in the author's *Poems*, 1844, it has since earned a permanent place in Christmas literature. Moore died on July 10, 1863, in Newport, Rhode Island.

Moore, Marianne Craig (1887–1972), poet. Born on November 15, 1887, in St. Louis, Miss Moore graduated from Bryn Mawr in 1909, attended Carlisle Commercial College in Pennsylvania, and subsequently gave vocational training to students at the Indian School. She was later an assistant librarian in the New York Public Library and acting editor of the *Dial* from 1925 to 1929. She lived most of her life in New York City, in her later years in Brooklyn. Her verse and literary criticism appeared in many journals and periodicals in England and the United States. *Poems*, 1921, published by friends in London, was followed by publication in the United States of *Observations*, 1924; *Selected Poems*, 1935; *The Pangolin and Other Verse*, 1936; *What Are Years*, 1941; *Nevertheless*, 1944; and her Pulitzer Prize–winning *Collected Poems*, 1951. From the start of her writing career she used highly personal metrical forms, consistent in themselves but inimitable. Her verse was marked by wit and irony, deep moral concern and carefully considered feeling. She often employed imagery from the natural world, but her concerns never strayed far from human responsibility. Among her other writings were a translation, *The Fables of La Fontaine*, 1954, and *Predilections*, 1955, a collection of essays on her favorite authors. Other books included *Like a Bulwark* 1956; *O To Be a Dragon*, 1959; *The Arctic Ox*, 1964; and *Tell Me, Tell Me*, 1966. She won many honors, among them the Dial Award for *Observations*, and in addition to the Pulitzer, the Bollingen Prize, the National Book Award, and the Gold Medal of the American Institute of Arts and Letters for *Collected Poems*. Miss Moore died at her New York City home on February 5, 1972.

Moore, Stanford (1913–1982), biochemist. Born in Chicago on September 4, 1913, Moore attended Vanderbilt University before receiving a Ph.D. in organic chemistry from the University of Wisconsin in 1938. He subsequently joined the Rockefeller Institute for Medical Research (now Rockefeller University), where in time he became a full professor. The author of numerous papers on proteins, he served as chairman of the panel on proteins of the committee on growth of the National Research Council of the National Academy of Sciences during 1947–1949. One of the principal contributors to the rapidly increasing knowledge of cellular protein synthesis that was gained after World War II, Moore concentrated his research on enzymes, the specific catalysts that direct the chemical processes of metabolism. The importance of his work for the description of life processes at the molecular level, as well as his elucidation of the biological activity of the enzyme ribonuclease, were specifically cited when Moore was awarded the Nobel Prize for Chemistry in 1972. He shared the prize with William H. Stein, a colleague at Rockefeller, and Christian B. Anfinsen, both of whom also worked with the same enzyme. Moore served as a member of the editorial board of the *Journal of Biological Chemistry* from 1950 to 1960. In 1963 he received the Chromatography Award of the American Chemical Society. He died on August 23, 1982, in New York City.

Moore, William Henry (1848–1923), lawyer and financier. Born on October 25, 1848, in Utica, New York, Moore attended Amherst College from 1867 to 1870 and leaving without taking a degree, proceeded to study law. He was admitted to the bar in 1872 and began practice in Chicago, where he shortly became a partner in the firm of Small, Burke, and Moore. His brother, James H. Moore (1852–1916), eventually joined the firm, which until the late 1880s specialized in corporation law. The brothers then branched out into the field of industrial mergers, an area of finance then dominated by J. P. Morgan, with whom they alternately feuded and collaborated over the next two decades. Their first major venture involved the reorganization and recapitalization of the Diamond Match Company. Promoting its stock on rumors of foreign contracts, they forced the price to artificial levels in 1896; but some of the original insiders then began to unload, the rapid decline of the Diamond Match boom closed the Chicago Stock Exchange for three months in August 1896, and the Moores lost $4 million. But William Moore retrieved his losses by confidently going ahead with plans for another merger, already in the works. Having formed the New York Biscuit Company by consolidating other firms in 1890, he and his brother and two other associates —variously known as the "Moore gang" or the "Big Four from the Prairies"—forced a price war on their sole remaining competitor, the American Biscuit and Manufacturing Company, that resulted in 1898 in the formation of the National Biscuit

Company. The enormous success of this company, which enjoyed a virtual monopoly, propelled the Moore group into their next venture, in the steel business. By early 1899 Moore had gained control of three steel companies, National Steel, American Steel Hoop, and American Tin Plate, with a total capitalization of $142 million. In May, Moore and his syndicate offered $320 million for the steel holdings of Andrew Carnegie and Henry Clay Frick. Moore paid $1 million for a three-month option; but, unable to raise the money in time, he lost his option. In 1900 they organized the American Sheet Steel Company and in 1901 the American Can Company, both of which they sold on very favorable terms to Morgan, who had seized the opportunity to become chief founder of the United States Steel Corporation, the largest of U.S. corporations, in 1901. Moore was involved with Morgan in the venture and made a great deal of money out of it; but from that time on he was more interested in railroads than in steel. He acquired the Chicago, Rock Island & Pacific line in 1901 and used it as the basis of a structure that continued to grow until about 1910. The Rock Island was greatly expanded and to it were added the St. Louis & San Francisco, the Chicago & Alton, and the Lehigh Valley. Inroads were soon made into other major lines as well, but by that time all of his properties were so heavily overcapitalized— the Rock Island's capitalization was nearly tripled in a single stroke of promotion in 1902—that the entire house of cards suddenly came tumbling down. Moore was forced into receivership in 1914 and was finally ousted from his railroad holdings by the Interstate Commerce Commission (ICC) in 1917. The entire episode was described as probably the most blatant and thorough piece of manipulation and looting in the history of the railroad industry. He spent his last years breeding and racing horses and died in New York City on January 11, 1923.

More, Paul Elmer (1864–1937), philosopher, editor, and critic. Born on December 12, 1864, in St. Louis, More attended Washington University there, receiving his B.A. in 1887 and his M.A. in 1892. He took a second M.A. at Harvard in 1893, where he met Irving Babbitt, and taught Sanskrit there during 1894–1895. He then taught Sanskrit and classical literature at Bryn Mawr from 1895 to 1897. After a two-year retreat to Shelburne, New Hampshire, he returned to the world of affairs and began a career in literary criticism in 1901 as literary editor of the *Independent*; moving to the *New York Evening Post* in 1903, he remained until 1909, when he became editor of the *Nation* for the next five years. At the *Nation* he was responsible for developing an outstanding corps of reviewers and for raising the quality of literary comment to unprecedented levels. In 1914 he returned to studies and lecturing at Princeton, and retired in 1934. The 11-volume *Shelburne Essays*, 1904–1921, reflected the scope of his literary interests, which were based on his thorough training in the classics. His other books of criticism included *Life of Benjamin Franklin*, 1900; *Nietzsche*, 1912; *Platonism*, 1917; *The Religion of Plato*, 1921; *Hellenistic Philosophies*, 1923; and *New Shelburne Essays*, 1928–1936. His judgments followed the standards of reserve and rationalism of the classics. He shunned the idealistic concepts of humanitarianism and equality, attacked liberal politics, and mistrusted the romantic movement in all its manifestations. During the 1920s he joined Babbitt in the movement for a new humanism, an attempt to revive the classical virtues and values. He was often rebuked for his patricianism, especially during the Depression of the 1930s, but was nonetheless held in high esteem for the enduring worth of his work. He died in Princeton, New Jersey, on March 9, 1937.

Morgan, Daniel (1736–1802), soldier. Born in Hunterdon County, New Jersey, in 1736, Morgan moved to Virginia while still a youth. He served as a civilian wagoner with Gen. Edward Braddock's expedition in 1755 and as a lieutenant in opposing Pontiac's Rebellion in 1763–1764, and in 1775, with the outbreak of the Revolution, received a commission as a captain of Virginia riflemen. He was with Col. Benedict Arnold during his assault on Quebec in December 1775 and, assuming command after Arnold was wounded, he and his men penetrated well into the city before being forced to surrender. He was commissioned colonel shortly after his exchange by the British in late 1776. Placed in command of a corps of 500 men, he joined Gen. Horatio Gates in September 1777 and took a leading part in the victorious Saratoga Campaign against Gen. John Burgoyne. He then joined Gen. George Washington for the campaign around Philadelphia but, dissatisfied with his rank and not in the best of health, he resigned from the army in July 1779 and retired to Virginia. He returned to active service in 1780, and again joined Gates after the latter's defeat at Camden, South Carolina. After Gen. Nathanael Greene succeeded Gates in command in the South, Morgan was given command of a corps in North Carolina and promoted to brigadier general. He is chiefly remembered for his brilliant victory over Col. Banastre Tarleton, January 17, 1781. Retreating before the British advance from Charleston, he took a stand with his outnumbered force at Cowpens, routed Tarleton decisively, and then escaped from the pursuing Gen. Charles Cornwallis into North Carolina. It was an important victory in the Southern department and he was decorated by Congress in recognition of it. He again retired to Virginia and prospered after the war. In November 1794 he commanded the Virginia militia, which was sent to suppress the Whisky Rebellion in western Pennsylvania. He served one term in the House of Representatives (1797–1799) as a Federalist and died in Winchester, Virginia, on July 6, 1802.

Morgan, John (1735–1789), physician. Born in Philadelphia on June 10, 1735, Morgan graduated in 1757 from the College of Philadelphia (later the University of Pennsylvania) in its first graduating class. He served a six-year medical apprenticeship, from 1750 to 1756, and was a surgeon in the French and Indian War. He continued his medical studies from 1760 to 1765 in London, at the University of Edinburgh (M.D., 1763), in Paris, and in Italy. He had an established reputation as a physician (his dissertation on the formation of pus had achieved favorable notice) and had been elected to the Royal Society when he returned home to become the College of Philadelphia's professor of the theory and practice of medicine in 1765. The chair had been established at his recommendation that the college open a medical school, the first in the American colonies. His *A Discourse upon the Institution of Medical Schools in America* was the first American writing on the subject and proposed two reforms: The separation of drug selling from the practice of medicine and the separation of both from surgery, and the establishment of liberal studies for medical students. Both were ahead of their time and met strong opposition. Initially hopeful of a perpetual union with Great Britain, he eventually supported the patriot cause. In October 1775 he received an appointment as director general of hospitals and physician-in-chief of the Continental army. He launched a program of reform in the medical department whose exacting requirements made enemies among his subordinates, and he never received the full cooperation of Congress. Within a year his authority was reduced and in early 1777 he was summarily dismissed. His defense, in *A Vindication of His Public Character . . .*, 1777, was later publicly acknowledged by Congress as justified, and Gen. George Washington personally exonerated him. Morgan thereafter devoted himself to his considerable practice and to teaching. He was one of the founders of the Philadelphia College of Surgeons and a member of the American Philosophical Society. He also wrote *Recommendation of Inoculation . . .*, 1776. He died in Philadelphia on October 15, 1789. A journal of Morgan's European travels was published in 1907.

Morgan, John Hunt (1825–1864), soldier. Born in Huntsville, Alabama, on June 1, 1825, Morgan grew up near Lexington, Kentucky. He saw action in 1847 at Buena Vista during the Mexican War and in 1857 organized the Lexington Rifles. He joined the Confederate army in 1861 and shortly became a captain of cavalry. Early in 1862 he began the dashing raids for which he became famous. Striking quickly and avoiding direct combat he interrupted telegraph communications, destroyed railroad lines and equipment, and burned Union supplies, in addition to taking prisoners. He operated very effectively, mostly in Tennessee and his native Kentucky, throughout 1862 and early 1863, and by the end of 1862 had been promoted to brigadier general. His best-known and most daring exploit was conducted in June and July of 1863. With more than 2000 men under his command, he led an unauthorized raid into Indiana and eventually was pursued into Ohio. Although penetrating farther north than any other Confederate force during the war, he inflicted relatively little damage and accomplished little. Most of his force finally surrendered and Morgan himself was captured and confined at the state prison in Columbus, Ohio. Nevertheless, he escaped before the end of the year and early in 1864 assumed command of the Department of Southwestern Virginia. Morgan was soon raiding in Kentucky again, but some of his men now began pillaging nonmilitary establishments in eastern Kentucky. Unwilling, perhaps unable, to restore discipline and now suffering heavier losses than before, he began to be thought of less value to the Confederacy in this stage of the war. Under investigation and about to be relieved of his command, he decided to lead one more raid, aiming at Knoxville, Tennessee, but was surprised and killed by Federal troops at Greeneville on September 4, 1864.

Morgan, John Pierpont (1837–1913), financier. Born on April 17, 1837, in Hartford, Connecticut, J. P. Morgan graduated from English High School in Boston in 1854 and studied for two years at the University of Göttingen. His banking career began in 1857 when he joined the New York City firm of Duncan, Sherman & Company, U.S. agents of George Peabody and Company of London, of which his father, Junius Spencer Morgan (1813–1890), was a partner. In 1860 he became special agent in the United States for George Peabody and Company (later J. S. Morgan & Company). From 1864 to 1871 he was a member of Dabney, Morgan & Company, and in 1871 he joined with Anthony J. Drexel in forming Drexel, Morgan & Company, which thrived through his ability and leadership and upon Drexel's death became J. P. Morgan & Company in 1895. The firm's move into major financial circles came in 1873, when Morgan was able to break Jay Cooke's monopoly on government bond sales; Cooke's bankruptcy in that year firmly established Morgan's position. The most prosperous private banking house in the country and one of the world's most powerful, it was able to replenish the federal reserve with $62 million in gold during the depression of 1895 thus preserving the redeemability of Treasury notes. Having obtained control of the Albany and Susquehanna Railroad in 1869, Morgan became active in railroad development and by 1890 owned a controlling interest in many of the country's major lines. More important than his ownership, however, was his great ability as an organizer; in contrast to the financial raiders of the day—Jim Fisk, Jay Gould, William H. Moore, and the like —Morgan was a rationalizing and stabilizing influence. He was quick to eliminate inefficiency, costly competition, and instability, and, as his reputation grew, he was much sought after for the performance of such services. Such railroads as the Chesapeake & Ohio, the Southern, the Erie, and the Northern Pacific were at one time or an-

other in his hands and he was particularly allied with James J. Hill in such enterprises. In 1901 he purchased the steel interests of Andrew Carnegie, merging them with his own and others' steel holdings to form the world's largest corporation, the United States Steel Corporation. He was also active in the formation of the General Electric and International Harvester corporations, as well as the unsuccessful International Mercantile Marine and the short-lived Northern Securities Company, dissolved by the Supreme Court in 1904. In 1907 he headed a group of bankers who preserved the solvency of major U.S. banks and corporations to halt an impending financial panic. By this time he was the preeminent figure in U.S. finance, the symbol of concentrated economic power. The living embodiment of what was often called the "money trust," he vigorously denied the existence of such a trust as well as the possession by himself or anyone of great power. His intensely private nature and aristocratic manner, on the other hand, fostered suspicions of sinister manipulation and disregard of laws and justice. In 1912 Congress formed the Pujo Committee, largely to investigate the extent of his holdings, and found, among other things, that 11 House of Morgan partners held 72 directorships in 47 major corporations. This corporate domination was widely criticized, although Morgan himself was little affected, feeling as he did morally bound to protect the interests of stockholders in his organizations, and, indeed, his prestige was such that the criticism was of little impact. He made large contributions to schools, hospitals, libraries, churches, and museums, although his philanthropies, unlike those of John D. Rockefeller, were unsystematic. He acquired an enormous personal art collection, much of which, after his death, was given to the Metropolitan Museum of Art in New York City. His great book collection, housed in a magnificent marble building, also in New York, became a public institution in 1924. An avid yachtsman, he built the *Columbia*, which won prizes in several international competitions. He died on March 31, 1913, in Rome, leaving a vast estate that has been greatly increased by successive generations of Morgans, notably John Pierpont Morgan, Jr. (1867–1943), and his sons, Junius Spencer Morgan (1892–1960) and Henry Sturgis Morgan (1900–   ).

Morgan, Lewis Henry (1818–1881), anthropologist. Born on November 21, 1818, near Aurora, New York, Morgan graduated from Union College in Schenectady in 1840. He went to Rochester about 1844 and there practiced law for many years. Long interested in Indian life and lore and a champion of Indian welfare—as a result of his efforts to defeat a bill in Congress unfavorable to the Seneca he was adopted by that tribe in 1847—in the 1840s he began to make intensive studies of the social organization and material culture of the Iroquois Indians, which led to the publication in 1851 of his first book, *The League of the Ho-dé-no-sau-nee, or Iroquois.* He thereupon undertook field trips to the West and Southwest and to the Hudson Bay area and began work on his monumental study, *Systems of Consanguinity and Affinity of the Human Family*, 1871, in which he founded the scientific study of kinship. *Ancient Society, or Researches in the Line of Human Progress from Savagery Through Barbarism to Civilization* appeared in 1877, with a revised edition the next year. The work was taken up by the Marxists and its theory of cultural evolution was reflected in Friedrich Engels's *The Origin of the Family, Private Property, and the State*. Morgan's theory of the evolution of the family through mankinds' progress from promiscuity to monogamy has long been considered obsolete, but many of his theses remain valid, notably the concept of the importance of technology in cultural evolution. Among his other books were *The American Beaver and His Works*, 1868, a delightful account of this remarkable animal, and *Houses and House-Life of the American Aborigines*, 1881. His *Indian Journals, 1859–1862* were reissued in 1959. He was a member of the National Academy of Sciences and was president of the American Association for the Advancement of Science in 1880. He served as a New York state assemblyman from 1861 to 1868 and as a state senator in 1868–1869. He died in Rochester, New York, on December 17, 1881. He is often called the "Father of American anthropology."

Morgan, Thomas Hunt (1866–1945), biologist. Born on September 25, 1866, in Lexington, Kentucky, Morgan attended the State College of Kentucky, graduating in 1886 and taking his M.S. in 1888. In 1890 he received his doctorate from The Johns Hopkins University and the next year joined the faculty of Bryn Mawr. In 1904 he moved to Columbia University as professor of experimental zoology. His early work was principally concerned with embryology, but about 1909 he turned his attention to the study of the mechanism of heredity. Doubtful himself, Morgan set out to seek evidence of the existence of physical units of heredity, the genes whose existence was then only postulated. Working closely with a number of students, including Hermann J. Muller, he undertook a series of experiments in breeding varieties of *Drosophila*, the common fruit fly. In *Mechanism of Mendelian Heredity*, 1915, they described their findings: Genes did indeed exist as discrete entities and were found at specific locations along the chromosomes of cell nuclei. In this work and the subsequent *Theory of the Gene*, 1926, Morgan and his associates laid the foundation of the science of genetics. In 1928 he became director of the newly established Kerckhoff Laboratories of Biological Sciences at the California Institute of Technology (Caltech) in Pasadena, where he remained for the rest of his life. From 1927 to 1931 he served as president of the National Academy of Sciences and in 1929–1930 was president of the American Association for the Advancement of Science. In 1933 he was awarded the Nobel Prize for Physiology

and Medicine for his pioneer work in genetics; he was the first native-born American and the first non-physician to receive the award. In his later work he returned to embryology; his publications included *Heredity and Sex*, 1913; *The Physical Basis of Heredity*, 1919; *Evolution and Genetics*, 1925; *Experimental Embryology*, 1927; *The Scientific Basis of Evolution*, 1932; and *Embryology and Genetics*, 1933. He died in Pasadena, California, on December 4, 1945.

Morgan, William (1774?–1826), Freemason. Born probably in Virginia, possibly on August 7, 1774, Morgan was a stonemason and a wanderer and apparently a man of not much standing in the communities where he resided. Very little of what is known of his early life has remained unquestioned, but he appeared in Rochester, New York, in the early 1820s, and in May 1825, on the strength of his claim of previous membership, was admitted to the Masonic lodge in Le Roy, New York. In 1826 he was working in nearby Batavia, where, in one account, he joined an effort to establish a Masonic lodge there. Whether because of an attempt to ostracize him or not, he in any case decided, with the help of a local printer named David Miller, to publish a volume on the secrets of the order. As rumors of his plan circulated that summer, various efforts at intimidation were made, including an attempt to burn Miller's printshop. Charged with theft and indebtedness, apparently as a pretext for seizing and arraigning him, Morgan was committed to the Canandaigua jail in September 1826 and from there was kidnapped. His ultimate fate was never known, but the opinion was widely held that he had been murdered. A subsequent search unearthed a body that was thought to be Morgan's; it was later convincingly shown to have been that of one Timothy Monroe. For a long time after his disappearance rumors placed him in Canada and as far away as Turkey. The planned book, *Illustrations of Masonry*, which appeared in late 1826, added to the excitement and Governor De Witt Clinton, himself a Freemason, offered a reward of $1000 for information concerning Morgan's whereabouts and double that amount for proof of his murder. Much attention was focused on the trials the following January of four men connected with his abduction. It was proved that they were Freemasons and that Morgan had been spirited off to Canada, but all other facts remained obscure. They received light sentences and the furor continued. Masonic leaders, who had in general been uncooperative in the search for clues and culprits, were now accused of obstructing justice. Anti-Masonic elements in the press, churches, and temperance and antislavery movements joined in condemning all Freemasonry as responsible for the "murder." The political potential of the spirit uniting these elements was not invisible to the leaders of the declining National Republican party in New York. Thurlow Weed, publisher of the *Rochester Telegraph* and subsequently of the *Anti-Masonic Enquirer*, led the press assault on Freemasonry, refusing support to candidates for state office who were members of the order. The Anti-Masons in New York polled 30,000 votes and elected 15 members of the state assembly that fall (1827), and the Anti-Masonic party was safely launched. Its influence soon spread to Pennsylvania and into New England, especially Vermont, and launched several careers, most notably those of William H. Seward and Thaddeus Stevens. The Anti-Masons met in national convention in 1831 and in the presidential election won seven electoral votes for its candidate, William Wirt. The party, unorganized at best and with no basic political philosophy on which to build, dwindled as a political force until it merged with the Whigs in 1835.

Morgenthau, Henry (1856–1946), lawyer, businessman, and diplomat. Born in Mannheim, Germany, on April 26, 1856, Morgenthau came to the United States with his family after the Civil War. He received a law degree from Columbia in 1877 and shortly became a partner in the New York City firm of Lachman, Morgenthau and Goldsmith. They specialized in real-estate law and often were involved in highly profitable land transactions. He left the firm in 1899 to form his own company, Central Realty Bond and Trust Company, which, in 1905, he merged with the Lawyer's Title and Insurance Company. Between 1905 and 1913 he was president of the Henry Morgenthau Company in addition to organizing several other real-estate companies. After 1912 Morgenthau devoted virtually all of his time to public service. He served as chairman of the finance committee of the Democratic National Committee during both of Woodrow Wilson's campaigns (1912 and 1916), and during 1913–1916 was U.S. ambassador to Turkey. After World War I broke out (Turkey eventually sided against the Allies) he also looked after the interests in Turkey of Britain, France, Russia, and six other nations. As an incorporator of the American National Red Cross, he attended the 1919 Geneva convention at which the League of Red Cross Societies was founded. During 1919 he also investigated anti-Jewish pogroms in Poland, and was appointed vice-chairman of Near East Relief, Inc. After the treaty of Lausanne (1923), which provided for an exchange of populations between Greece and Turkey, he took charge of the Greek migration from western Anatolia. His last public service was for President Franklin D. Roosevelt at the Geneva conference called to stabilize the world price of wheat, and as a technical expert at the World Monetary and Economic Conference in London, both in 1933. He published several books about his relief work and his diplomatic experiences, the most popular being *Ambassador Morgenthau's Story*, 1918, which also appeared in England as *Secrets of the Bosphorus* and was translated into French and other languages. He was active in several Jewish philanthropic agencies but until his death in New York City on November 25, 1946, he remained an outspoken opponent of Zionism.

Morgenthau, Henry, Jr. (1891–1967), public official. Born in New York City on May 11, 1891, Morgenthau was the son of Henry Morgenthau (1856–1946). He attended Cornell University but never took a degree, and in 1913 acquired a dairy and fruit farm in Dutchess County, New York, about 15 miles from the Hyde Park home of Franklin Delano Roosevelt. Common interests in farming and conservation drew the two men together, and their friendship lasted until Roosevelt's death. Morgenthau's public career reflected Roosevelt's rising political fortunes. He was given an appointment in the Navy Department when Roosevelt was assistant secretary and was New York state conservation commissioner and chairman of the agricultural advisory committee during Roosevelt's governorship, 1928–1932. From 1922 until 1933 he was publisher of the *American Agriculturist*. In Washington, D.C., after 1933, he served successfully as chairman of the Federal Farm Board, governor of the Farm Credit Administration, and undersecretary of the treasury, all upon President Roosevelt's appointment. The latter assignment was his only training for his appointment as secretary of the treasury in 1934, a post he filled ably until July 1945; he was second in length of service only to Albert Gallatin, who served from 1801 to 1813. His conservative economic views, especially his desire to maintain a balanced budget, often led to conflicts with Roosevelt, but in the end he supported the financing of the New Deal programs and the unprecedented expansion of the nation's budget during World War II. Under his auspices the Treasury Department was totally reorganized into an efficient fiscal operation, overseeing some $370 billion in expenditures. He resigned from the Treasury after Roosevelt's death, unable to agree with President Harry S. Truman on a policy for the postwar reconstruction of Germany; his "Morgenthau Plan," calling for a permanent partition of Germany and the dismantling of all its heavy industries to "repastoralize" the nation, had earlier been opposed by other Cabinet officials and by Roosevelt as well. His later years were devoted mainly to his farm and to continuing the philanthropic work of his father. He was chairman of the United Jewish Appeal, 1947–1950, and director of the American Financial and Development Corporation, 1951–1954, which issued $500 million in bonds for the new nation of Israel. He died in Poughkeepsie, New York, on February 6, 1967. *From the Morgenthau Diaries*, 1959, drew on his more than 800 bound volumes of official and personal records that were turned over to the Franklin D. Roosevelt Memorial Library in Hyde Park, New York.

Morison, Samuel Eliot (1887–1976), historian. Born in Boston on July 9, 1887, Morison entered Harvard in 1904; he graduated in the class of 1908 and studied for a year in France before returning to Harvard for an M.A., 1909, and a Ph.D., 1913. He subsequently traveled to Europe again and taught briefly at the University of California before accepting a post on the Harvard faculty in

1915. In 1918 he enlisted in the army, serving as a private, and stayed in Paris after the armistice while attached to the Russian division of the American Commission to Negotiate Peace and as a delegate to the Baltic Commission of the Peace Conference. He returned to Harvard and to teaching in 1919, and published his second book (his dissertation on Harrison Gray Otis, one of his ancestors, had appeared in 1913), *Maritime History of Massachusetts 1783–1860*, 1921, before going to Oxford University in 1922 as the first Harmsworth professor of American history. He returned to Harvard again as a full professor in 1925 and remained there, except for service during World War II, and from 1941 as Jonathan Trumbull professor of American history, until his retirement in 1955. His two-volume *Oxford History of the United States* appeared in 1927. Morison remained a prolific and sometimes popular writer without abandoning the scholarship that lay behind his authoritative publications. Two of his more than 25 books won Pulitzer prizes: *Admiral of the Ocean Sea: A Life of Christopher Columbus*, 1942, and *John Paul Jones*, 1959. He prepared for the Columbus biography by making several voyages over the routes that Columbus traveled. Appointed historian of naval operations with the rank of lieutenant commander in 1942, prior to commencing his 15-volume *History of U.S. Naval Operations in World War II*, 1947–1962, he spent three years, 1942–1945, primarily in the Pacific theater, taking notes during most of the major naval campaigns. He retired from the Navy in 1951 with the rank of rear admiral. In addition to his five-volume tercentennial history of Harvard, 1929–1936, his other major works included the widely used textbook *Growth of the American Republic*, 1930, and several later revised editions, written with Henry Steele Commager; *Portuguese Voyages to America*, 1940; *The Intellectual Life of Colonial New England*, 1956; *The Story of Mount Desert Island*, 1960; *One Boy's Boston*, 1962, an account of his youth; and *Two-Ocean War*, 1963, a shorter history of naval operations in World War II. His *Oxford History of the American People*, 1965, became a standard work in the field, although it was admittedly often personal in its judgments. *The European Discovery of America: The Northern Voyages* appeared in 1971; it was the first of two volumes on the subject, the second devoted to the southern (and more famous) voyages of such explorers as Columbus. His research for these books involved not only poring over old manuscripts in libraries but also travel by airplane and boat and on foot through Canada, New England, and the Caribbean, activities that he pursued enthusiastically despite advancing years. Morison received many honorary degrees and awards and was a recipient of the Presidential Medal of Freedom in 1964. He died in Boston on May 15, 1976.

Morley, Edward Williams (1838–1923), chemist and physicist. Born on January 29, 1838, in Newark, New Jersey, Morley grew up in New England.

Largely educated in his early years by his father, he graduated from Williams College in 1860 and remained there for another year to study astronomy. He studied at Andover Theological Seminary from 1861 to 1864 with the intention of entering the ministry, but changed his plans for reasons of health after graduation. He taught at a private school briefly before accepting a post at Western Reserve College in Hudson, Ohio (subsequently Western Reserve University in Cleveland), in 1869. He remained there as professor of natural history and chemistry until his retirement in 1906. He gained recognition for his contribution to the Loomis-Morley hypothesis, 1880, correlating the amount of oxygen in the atmosphere at sea level with atmospheric pressure, and in 1895 he published the results of more than ten years of experiments on the densities of hydrogen and oxygen and on the ratio of their combination to form water. He contributed more than 50 scientific papers on various subjects, virtually all of them presenting the results of precise measurements accomplished by instruments of his own design. Morley is principally remembered for the celebrated experiment he conducted in 1887 with Albert A. Michelson, who at the time was at nearby Case School of Applied Science. Using Michelson's newly invented interferometer, they attempted to measure the velocity of the earth through a postulated substance, the "ether" (conceived of as a universal space-filling medium through which all electromagnetic radiation, such as light, is propagated), by the effect earth's velocity might be expected to have on the velocity of light. Michelson and Morley failed to detect anything of the order of magnitude to be expected on the hypothesis of. a fixed "ether," a result that astounded the world of physics and that was not satisfactorily explained until the acceptance of Einstein's theory of relativity. The experiment is of such fundamental importance to physical theory that it has often been repeated. In 1904, a year before Einstein put forward his theory, Morley and Dayton C. Miller carried out new measurements to test the hypothesis that the earlier results were owing to differential contraction of the materials used in the measuring apparatus; and they did additional experiments, to test atmospheric variables, in 1905 and 1906. Later, again with Miller, he made precise determinations of the velocity of light in a magnetic field and of the thermal expansion of various gases. Morley's accomplishments were increasingly honored during his later years. He served as president of the American Association for the Advancement of Science in 1895 and as president of the American Chemical Society in 1899. Morley died in West Hartford, Connecticut, on February 24, 1923.

Morphy, Paul Charles (1837–1884), chess player. Born in New Orleans on June 22, 1837, Morphy was taught to play chess by his father and grandfather at the age of ten and progressed rapidly within two years. When not quite thirteen he played three games with J. Löwenthal, a Hungarian master visiting New Orleans, winning two and drawing one. He attended Spring Hill College from 1850 to 1854 and received a law degree from the University of Louisiana in 1857 before pursuing the game further. He accepted an invitation to compete at the New York City Chess Congress in the fall of 1857 and attracted much attention by winning first prize. In 1858–1859 he was in Europe and created a sensation in the chess world by trouncing all the masters who would meet him. In England his challenge was not accepted by the celebrated Howard Staunton, but Staunton's powers had in any event declined after his defeat by Adolph Anderssen in 1851 and Morphy was satisfied to beat J. Löwenthal, who had recently defeated Staunton. He went on to successfully meet half a dozen good English players (England dominated the game in that decade) and later won a match with D. Harrwitz in Paris. His most celebrated victory followed over Anderssen, the strongest player of the time, and thus Morphy succeeded to the unofficial world title. His effectiveness was largely owing to his departure from the then current fashion of attacking prematurely. Although second to none in combination play, Morphy delayed attacking until he had completed his development. By simply bringing out knights and bishops, posting the queen safe from harassment, and castling, he repeatedly achieved a won game after a dozen or so moves. On two or three occasions he played blindfolded against eight strong players simultaneously, each time with great success. Morphy's success was brilliant but brief. On his return to the United States in April 1859 he vacillated between pursuing a career in chess (not highly rewarding in the nineteenth century) or in law. He was unsuccessful in law practice and apparently gave in to pressures not to pursue the former. He played sporadically until about 1869 and twice visited Paris before his death, but without competing publicly. He died in New Orleans on July 10, 1884, and is still recognized as one of the modern masters of chess.

Morrill, Justin Smith (1810–1898), public official. Born in Strafford, Vermont, on April 14, 1810, Morrill attended the common schools and two local academies but left school when he was fifteen to go to work in a general store. He became a partner in 1831 when he turned twenty-one, and amassed a sufficient fortune to be able to retire at thirty-eight, when he went to live on a country estate near Strafford. A long congressional career—nearly 44 years of service in the House and Senate—began in 1854 when he was elected as a Whig to the 34th Congress, taking his seat in March 1854. The next year he played a leading role in organizing the Republican party in Vermont. He served in the House until 1867, as chairman of the Ways and Means Committee after 1865, whereupon he entered the Senate as a Republican, to remain through repeated reelections until his death. A financial conservative, he sponsored the Morrill Tariff Act of 1861 that inaugurated the era of protectionism, and thereafter was a potent foe of free-traders. Also a champion of sound money, he opposed all of the schemes to adopt paper currency during and after the Civil War and disapproved of silver as a monetary standard. For special needs, and to supplement tariff revenues, he favored internal-revenue measures. In his long career he made many contributions to the appearance of the national capital, being influential in the landscaping of the Capitol grounds, the building of the Washington Monument and the Library of Congress, and other projects. But his most enduring achievement is doubtless the Morrill Land Grant Act of 1862, which provided grants of land to states for the endowment of colleges in which the leading object was to be the teaching of subjects "related to agriculture and the mechanic arts," without, however, excluding the general sciences and classical studies. He first proposed such a measure in 1857, but President James Buchanan vetoed it; President Abraham Lincoln signed it into law five years later. From the "land-grant colleges" grew the present system of state universities. The first Morrill Act was supplemented in 1890 by a second Morrill Act, which provided monetary grants to the colleges and universities, thus establishing the principle of federal aid to education. Morrill died in Washington, D. C., on December 28, 1898.

Morris, Gouverneur (1752–1816), public official and diplomat. Born in the family manor house in Morrisania, now part of New York City, on January 31, 1752, Morris graduated from King's College (now Columbia) in 1768 and was admitted to the bar three years later. A political conservative, he at first opposed the separation of the colonies from Great Britain, but he soon adopted a middle position between the democratic radicals and the Loyalists; he acted as something of a mediator in the New York provincial congress that succeeded the colonial legislature and in the New York constitutional convention of 1776, where he was successful in securing a provision for religious freedom, although not one for the abolition of slavery. From 1777 to 1779 he was in the Continental Congress where, in 1778, in response to Lord North's offer of conciliation, he drafted the report that declared independence to be a prerequisite of peace. The report was included in his *Observations on the American Revolution*, 1779. Shortly after his failure to be reelected to Congress in 1779 he moved to Philadelphia. A series of articles on finance that appeared in the *Pennsylvania Packet* in 1780 led to his appointment as assistant to the superintendent of finance, Robert Morris (no relation). During his tenure in that office, 1781–1785, he submitted a proposal that, modified by Jefferson, became the basis for the national currency. A delegate to the Constitutional Convention in 1787, he seems to have spoken more often than anybody; he was an advocate of a strong central government that would include such features as a president with life tenure and senators appointed by the president, also for life, and he strongly opposed the concessions made to the slaveholding states. A member of the committee on style and arrangement, he was principally responsible for the final literary form of the Constitution. Shortly after the convention adjourned he returned to New York; his pronounced antidemocratic sympathies kept him from public office, and in 1789 he sailed to Europe on business and remained for nearly a decade. In Paris he watched and recorded in his diary the progress of the French Revolution and carried on a mild intrigue with members of the royalist party; he was appointed U.S. minister to France in 1792, but his often and publicly stated antipathy to the later radical developments of the Revolution led to a request by the French for his recall in 1794. Business interests and travel delayed his return to the United States until 1798. He served briefly in the Senate as a Federalist from 1800 to 1803, occupying his last political office. From 1810 he served for a time as chairman of the Erie Canal Commission. In private life he continued to align himself with the extreme Federalists and even supported the idea of New England secession during the War of 1812. He died in Morrisania on November 6, 1816.

Morris, Robert (1734–1806), merchant, financier, and public official. Born on January 31, 1734, in Liverpool, England, Morris came to America in 1747, joining his father in Maryland. After only a little schooling he entered a large mercantile house in Philadelphia, and such were his talents in business that at the age of twenty he became a member of the firm. His sympathies lay with the colonies at the outbreak of the Revolution, although he took a conservative position and was slow to accept the idea of separation from Britain; he served as vice-president of the Pennsylvania Committee of Safety in 1775–1776 and as a delegate to the Continental Congress from 1775 to 1778. He opposed the Declaration of Independence and after its adoption delayed signing it for some weeks. In Congress he served on several committees, particularly those concerned with finance and trade. Upon leaving Congress he was immediately elected to the Pennsylvania Assembly, where he remained until 1779. In that year charges were brought that he had taken personal advantage of his central role in congressional finance; but although he had never failed to direct public business to his own firm when possible and to collect a regular profit, several investigations cleared him of profiteering. In 1780–1781 he was again in the assembly and in the latter year accepted the urgent call of Congress to become superintendent of finance under a newly unified system. One of his first acts was to establish the Bank of North America in Philadelphia. Only Morris's great organizational ability and his own personal credit prevented the government's bankruptcy; he was able to secure the money needed to transport Gen. George Washington's army from New York to Yorktown, Virginia, in order to force the surrender of Gen. Charles Cornwallis in 1781, and yet the future of the nation appeared so doubtful to one even of his great resourcefulness that in 1783 he was only with difficulty persuaded to retain his post. In 1784 he resigned and from 1785 to 1787 was again in the Pennsylvania assembly; he was a delegate to the Annapolis Convention in 1786 and to the federal Constitutional Convention the next year. He was elected one of Pennsylvania's first senators, serving from 1789 to 1795 as a Federalist and supporter of Alexander Hamilton's financial policies. He had liquidated his mercantile interests and invested heavily in Western lands; when this speculative venture failed to yield returns, he found himself bankrupt and from 1798 to 1801 was held in debtor's prison in Philadelphia. His last years were spent in declining health in Philadelphia, where he died on May 7, 1806.

Morrow, Dwight Whitney (1873–1931), lawyer, banker, and diplomat. Born on January 11, 1873, in Huntington, West Virginia, Morrow attended Amherst College, where he was a classmate of Calvin Coolidge, graduating in 1895. The next year he entered the law school of Columbia University and upon graduating in 1899 joined the law firm of Reed, Simpson, Thacher and Barnum. He became a partner in 1905 and attained a reputation in the field of corporation law. In 1911 he drafted a workmen's compensation law for New Jersey and in 1917 was chairman of a commission called to investigate the state's prison system. In 1914 he became a partner in the banking house of J. P. Morgan & Company, where, in addition to his regular business activities, which included the organization of the Kennecott Copper Corporation, he was involved in arranging for financial and material aid to the Allied powers in Europe. Soon after the United States entered World War I, he became an adviser to the Allied Maritime Transport Council; he was also an adviser on transportation problems to Gen. John J. Pershing, commander of U.S. forces in Europe, and for his work was awarded the Distinguished Service Medal. After the war he served as a consultant to the government of Cuba and succeeded in restoring that country's finances. In 1925 he was chairman of the President's Aircraft Board, which helped formulate national policy on civil and military aviation. He was appointed ambassador to Mexico by President Coolidge in 1927 and during three years in the post reestablished cordial relations between that nation and the United States, settled or arranged for future settlement of outstanding disputes between them, and helped restore harmony between the Mexican government and the Roman Catholic church. In 1930 President Herbert Hoover named him a delegate to the London Naval Conference. Later in the same year, running as a Republican, he was elected to the Senate from New Jersey; he died at his home in Englewood, New Jersey, a short time later, however, on October 5, 1931. His daughter Anne Spencer Morrow married aviator Charles A. Lindbergh in 1929.

Morse, Carlton Errol (1901–   ), radio dramatist. Born in Jennings, Louisiana, on June 4, 1901, Morse attended high school in Ashland, Oregon, and Sacramento, California, before graduating from the University of California in 1922. He worked for several newspapers in Sacramento, Seattle, and San Francisco between 1922 and 1929 before joining the production staff of the National Broadcasting Company (NBC) in 1930. He went on to become the most successful dramatist of radio's golden age, 1930 to 1950, as the creator and writer of two exceptional radio programs. "I Love a Mystery," a mystery-adventure series, had its debut in 1939 and remained popular until 1944. A half-hour weekly program after 1940, it followed the adventures of cool, analytical Jack Packard and two associates, Doc and Reggie, who ran the A-1 Detective Agency. Their secretary, Gerry Booker, provided the love interest. In such productions as "Blood on the Cat" and "No Ring, No Ring Finger, No Husband," Morse's plots emphasized the "tough" of the agency's motto: "No job too tough, no mystery too baffling." His greatest success, however, was the serial drama "One Man's Family." It was launched on April 29, 1932, as a half-hour weekly program on the West Coast, but soon was being broadcast nationally. After 1950 the program ran 15 minutes a day, Monday through Friday. It followed the experiences of three generations of the Barbour family of San Francisco in plots and characterizations that were generally superior to most soap-opera fare. "One Man's Family," the announcer introduced each program, "is dedicated to the mothers and fathers of the younger generation and to their bewildering offspring." Then followed the identification of book and chapter, which by the last broadcast (May 8, 1959) was Chapter 30 of Book 134, totaling 3256 episodes. The series was noted for its realism (most characters had their flaws) and its success was testified to by its large and faithful following. Morse lived in retirement after 1959.

Morse, Charles Wyman (1856–1933), speculator and promoter. Born on October 21, 1856, in Bath, Maine, Morse was already deeply involved in the shipping business before graduating from Bowdoin College in 1877. He remained in New England in the family firm, C. W. Morse and Company, for the next 20 years, but in 1897 he descended on Wall Street, having outgrown local speculative opportunities. He gained his first notoriety in 1899 when he engineered a merger of several New York City ice firms into the American Ice Company, a sensational achievement that earned him the sobriquet "Ice King." Doubling the price of ice the next year aroused the public, and a subsequent investigation revealed that he had used company funds to corrupt public officials; but he was able to unload his stock in the firm before the price fell and he withdrew with a reported $12 million. He next attacked banking and shipping, proceeding always with a piratical fury that was remarkable even for this time. Employing a bewildering array of manipulative techniques, propping up one syndicate or pool or holding company with another, and creating an enormous financial pyramid, he succeeded in consolidating coastal shipping from Maine to Texas—thus earning a second sobriquet, "Admiral of the Atlantic Coast"—but failed in his effort to obtain an absolute monopoly because of the personal intervention of President Theodore Roosevelt. His banking ventures, entered into with Frederick Augustus Heinze and others and extending to 12 banks, were adversely affected by Morse's secret (according to Heinze) unloading of h s copper holdings during the panic of 1907, which in itself was largely centered on their banks; at the end of that year they were summarily drummed out of the banking business by a committee of fellow Wall Streeters. The Bank of North America, their principal bank, was subsequently investigated by District Attorney Henry L. Stimson, and Morse received a 15-year prison sentence for criminal irregularities. He bought his way out of prison with the help of the notorious Harry M. Daugherty (whose fee Morse never paid), later attorney general under President Warren G. Harding. Convinced that there was no real need to abandon his methods as long as everyone else practiced them, Morse was soon back to promotions, this time in shipping. A golden opportunity came with World War I, when he organized a holding company, United States Shipping, to consolidate the assets of 16 subsidiary steamship companies. With U.S. entry into the war he obtained numerous government contracts for building ships. He used his government loans to build shipyards instead of ships (although he did construct some vessels) as well as to speculate in other fruitful fields. Finally indicted on many counts in the early 1920s, he was eventually acquitted on criminal charges, but the government won a civil judgment of some $11.5 million in 1925 against one of his shipbuilding subsidiaries. He was declared legally incompetent the next year and spent his last years in Bath, Maine, where he died on January 12, 1933.

Morse, Jedidiah (1761–1826), religious leader and geographer. Born in Woodstock, Connecticut, on August 23, 1761, Morse received his B.A. from Yale in 1783 and studied theology there until 1785. Licensed to preach in that year, he subsequently taught school before being ordained in 1786. In April 1789 he was installed as minister of the First Congregational Church of Charlestown, Massachusetts, where he remained until 1819. He was prominent among the defenders of orthodoxy during the rise of Unitarianism among the Congregationalists early in the nineteenth century and to this end in 1805 he founded the *Panoplist*, serving as its editor for five years. He also labored at organizing Andover Theological

Seminary, founded in 1808, but his efforts in combating "liberal views" had only negative results. The Unitarians left the fold to form their own churches and the controversy in his own parish eventually forced his resignation. His conservative views were equally apparent in politics, where he remained an uncompromising Federalist. Morse is chiefly remembered as the "Father of American geography." His interest in the subject went back to his early experience in teaching, when he first felt the need for an adequate textbook. His *Geography Made Easy*, 1784, was the first American book on the subject and went through 25 editions during his lifetime. *The American Geography*, 1789, a more ambitious work, was later reissued as *The American Universal Geography*. *Elements of Geography*, 1795, intended for children, was followed by the *American Gazetteer*, 1797. Seeking far and wide for geographical information, he collaborated with Elijah Parish on *A New Gazetteer of the Eastern Continent*, 1802. Enjoying a virtual monopoly in the field, his books were in constant demand. He also collaborated with Parish on *A Compendious History of New England*, 1804, published on commission of the federal government a report on the conditions of a number of Indian tribes in 1822, and succeeded in completing *Annals of the American Revolution*, 1824, before his death in New Haven, Connecticut, on June 9, 1826. His son Sidney Edwards Morse (1794–1871) carried on his geographical work and another son, Samuel F. B. Morse, achieved even greater distinction as an inventor.

Morse, Samuel Finley Breese (1791–1872), painter and inventor. Born on April 27, 1791, in Charlestown, Massachusetts, Morse was the eldest son of Jedidiah Morse. He graduated in 1810 from Yale, where he had developed a strong interest and considerable facility in painting; overcoming his parents' objections, he sailed to England in 1811 in company with Washington Allston to study art under Allston and Benjamin West. On his return in 1815 he opened a studio in Boston, but his high ambitions were shattered by the discovery that the American public had little taste for any save portrait art, and little money for that. Although he soon attained a reputation as a portraitist and eventually took students into his studio, his earnings were meager and irregular and did not improve significantly after he moved to New York City in 1823. His social and intellectual life was altogether satisfactory, however, and his devotion to art led him to be the principal founder of the National Academy of Design in 1826 and to serve as its first president from that year until 1845. A few historical canvases, executed for the purpose of sending them on tour, were coolly received and only much later appreciated. In 1829 he left New York for a three-year period of study and travel in Europe; on the return voyage in 1832 a chance conversation on recent discoveries in electromagnetism sparked in him the idea for an electrical device for the transmission of information. He drafted preliminary sketches of a telegraph while still on board ship, but for several years made little progress on the idea. For a few years he was caught up in the wave of nativist agitation and in 1836 ran unsuccessfully for mayor of New York City on the Native-American ticket. He continued to paint and taught art at the University of the City of New York (now New York University). In 1837 he was introduced to the work of the physicist Joseph Henry, who had published a detailed proposal for a telegraph six years earlier; the two corresponded on the idea and by 1838 Morse had both a working model and a usable code, still in use and bearing his name, for translating letters and numbers into dots and dashes. His major innovation in developing practical telegraphy was a relay device that, placed at intervals along the wire, enabled messages to be sent over great distances. Public interest was difficult to arouse, but with the aid of Alfred Vail, who foresaw clearly the potential for the device, Congress was persuaded finally in 1843 to appropriate $30,000 to construct a telegraph line from Washington, D.C., to Baltimore. The line was built, largely by Ezra Cornell, and on May 24, 1844, Morse tapped out the first message—"What hath God wrought!"—from the Supreme Court chamber in the Capitol. Congress failed to take advantage of an offer by Morse and Vail to sell all rights to the telegraph for $100,000 and the two partners, joined by Amos Kendall and others, proceeded to develop it privately. For the next several years he was caught up in a storm of litigation over patent rights—one of his rivals was Charles T. Jackson, a fellow passenger on the fateful 1832 voyage—and with a few unfortunately chosen partners. His patent claim was finally validated by the Supreme Court in 1854. Morse was also a pioneer daguerreotypist and had numerous other scientific interests; in 1857–1858 he was associated with Cyrus Field in laying a transatlantic telegraph cable; and in 1858 he was honored by a number of European nations. In 1861 he was again president of the National Academy of Design; in the same year he helped found Vassar College. Throughout his later years he was a prominent philantropist. He died in New York City on April 2, 1872. He was elected to the Hall of Fame in 1900.

Mortenson, Norma Jean, *see* Monroe, Marilyn

Morton, Jelly Roll (1885–1941), jazz musician and composer. Born in New Orleans on September 20, 1885, Ferdinand Joseph La Menthe Morton launched his career as a piano player about 1902 while attending St. Joseph's Catholic College. One of the pioneer ragtime piano players, he later often invited scorn by claiming that he "invented jazz in 1901." Morton was nevertheless one of the important innovators in the transition from early jazz to orchestral jazz that took place in the Storyville sporting district of New Orleans at the turn of the century. Shortly before the end of that era (Storyville was officially closed by the U.S.

navy in 1917) he moved west to California, where he lived from 1917 to 1922. The popularity of New Orleans jazz spread rapidly to the North and West during the 1920s. Morton preserved much of this music on records after he organized Jelly Roll Morton's Red Hot Peppers in 1926. Recording in Chicago until 1930, he made a series of records that brought him a national reputation. Morton's music was more formal than the early Dixieland jazz, although his arrangements only sketched parts and allowed for improvisation. By the time he was recording such orchestral jazz, however, a revolution was being staged, primarily by Louis Armstrong and other instrumentalists of his calibre. The emergence of jazz as a soloist's art in the 1930s eclipsed Morton's fame. By 1937 he was in Washington, D.C., managing an obscure nightclub. The following year Alan Lomax prevailed upon him to make a series of recordings for the Archives of American Folk Song of the Library of Congress, and he played and sang his compositions, and narrated his life story, in more than 100 recordings, which once again brought him public attention. As a jazz composer he is best known for such pieces as "King Porter Stomp," "London Rag," "Bert Williams," and "The Jelly Roll Blues." He died in Los Angeles on July 11, 1941.

Morton, Julius Sterling (1832–1902), public official and agriculturist. Born in Adams, New York, on April 22, 1832, Morton moved westward with his family, first to eastern Michigan and then to Detroit. He was educated at Union College in Schenectady, New York (B.A. 1856) and at the University of Michigan (B.A. 1858). He had married and moved with his bride to Nebraska Territory in 1854, settling in Nebraska City, where he lived throughout most of the rest of his life. He founded and for many years edited the *Nebraska City News* and was soon involved in territorial politics, serving in the legislature in 1855–1856 and in 1857–1858; he was appointed territorial secretary by President James Buchanan in 1858 and during three years in the post was for a time acting governor. A Democrat, he held no public offices after the Civil War, but eventually, in 1893, he was appointed secretary of agriculture by President Grover Cleveland and he served throughout Cleveland's term of office. For many years he had employed his quarter-section of land outside Nebraska City as an agricultural showplace; there he experimented with various crops and indulged his passion for planting trees. As early as 1868 he called for the observance of a special day devoted to the planting of trees, and as a result the first Arbor Day was celebrated in April, 1872; from the year 1885, Morton's birthday, April 22, was designated as Arbor Day in Nebraska; the date was soon to be celebrated in other Western states and in several foreign countries. His four sons, all of whom enjoyed extraordinary financial success in various fields, shared his love of trees, and Joy (1855–1934) established the Morton Arboretum in Lisle, Illinois, which received its endowment from the enormous profits of his Morton Salt Company. Julius Sterling Morton died in Lake Forest, Illinois, on April 27, 1902. His Nebraska City estate, Arbor Lodge, became a state park.

Morton, Levi Parsons (1824–1920), vice-president of the United States. Born on May 16, 1824, in Shoreham, Vermont, Morton undertook a career in business at an early age in Hanover, New Hampshire, in Boston in the early 1850s, and in New York City in 1855. His New York business failed through no fault of his own but his Wall Street banking firm, established as L. P. Morton and Company in 1863, emerged as one of the nation's most prominent after the Civil War. By 1869 there was a London agent, Morton, Rose and Company, and in the 1870s the American firm, now named Morton, Bliss and Company, helped fund the national debt during the resumption of specie payments. A political career opened up after the London house became the U.S. government's fiscal agent (1873–1884) for the $15.5 million paid to the United States by Great Britain for the losses inflicted by the British-built Confederate cruiser *Alabama* during the Civil War. Morton failed in a bid for the House of Representatives in 1876, but he was elected as a Republican from New York to the House in 1878. He gave up his seat to serve as U.S. minister to France from 1881 to 1885. His ambition to sit in the Senate was thwarted after his return to the United States; he accepted instead nomination for the office of vice-president under Benjamin Harrison and was duly elected with Harrison, serving from 1889 to 1893. He was a faithful, though not slavish, partisan, mildly conservative and an advocate of civil service reform and other good-government measures. He firmly resisted untoward pressures from party bosses, particularly Thomas C. Platt. His last political office was as governor of New York, a post in which he served in 1895 and 1896. Although he went as a favorite son to the Republican national convention in 1896, he was never seriously in the running for the presidency. At the age of seventy-five Morton's political career was over, and in 1899 he launched the Morton Trust Company. He retired after its merger with Guaranty Trust Company in 1909 but lived 11 years longer. He died in Rhinebeck, New York, on May 16, 1920, his ninety-sixth birthday.

Morton, Oliver Perry (1823–1877), public official. Born in Salisbury, Wayne County, Indiana, on August 4, 1823. Oliver Hazard Perry Throck Morton spent part of his youth in Ohio and later, from 1843 to 1845, attended Miami University in Ohio. He subsequently opened a law office in Centerville, Indiana, and began a political career as early as 1848, but he returned to what proved to be a flourishing law practice after a brief attendance at the Cincinnati College Law School. Originally a Democrat, he broke with the party over the Kansas-Nebraska Act. His political fortunes rose with the Republican tide; he helped bring the new party to national prominence and in 1856 ran unsuccessfully on its ticket for governor of Indiana. He was on the winning Republican ticket as lieutenant governor in 1860 and succeeded to the governorship in 1861 when, by pre-arrangement, Governor Henry S. Lane resigned to enter the Senate. Morton achieved a national reputation as Indiana's "war governor." Faced with numerous factions sympathetic to the Confederacy and with an increasingly hostile legislature after 1862, he successfully promoted enlistments in the Union forces and thwarted attempts to curtail his own executive power. Refusing to call the legislature in 1863, he ruled for two years virtually by fiat, while meeting government expenses primarily through private appeals and assistance from Washington. Reelected in 1864, he resigned in 1867 to enter the Senate. Initially sharing President Andrew Johnson's moderate attitude toward Reconstruction, he soon emerged as a leader of the Radical Republicans. Finally, uncompromisingly opposed to Johnson, he voted for his impeachment. He is generally given a large measure of the credit for the ultimate ratification of the Fifteenth Amendment to the Constitution, 1870, which enfranchised the Negro. A prominent but unsuccessful candidate for the Republican nomination for the presidency in 1876, he was hampered by his physical condition (a stroke in 1865 had left him paralyzed below the waist) as well as by his partisanship. He opposed the bill establishing an Electoral Commission to settle the disputed results of the presidential election of 1876, but he later served with customary partisanship on the commission. He died in Indianapolis on November 1, 1877, shortly after another stroke.

Morton, Thomas (1590?–?1647), anti-Puritan colonist. Little is known of Morton's early life, but it is recorded that he was in Massachusetts in 1622 and returned in 1624 as one of the owners of the Wollaston Company, which established a settlement within the limits of modern Quincy. Morton took charge of the colony after most of the settlers moved on to Virginia in 1626. Merrymount, as he named it, was anathema to the strict Pilgrim settlements. "Having more craft than honesty," as William Bradford later described him, Morton was a source of firearms and supplies to the Indians, and thus he gained a virtual monopoly of the local beaver-fur trade. The Pilgrims despised him not only for this trade advantage but also for the conviviality and wild festivities he encouraged. He was also an Anglican who mounted vitriolic attacks (often in bawdy verse) on the solemn Pilgrim way of life. The Pilgrims cut down the maypole he had erected in 1627 and the following year dispatched Miles Standish to subdue the settlement. Morton was arrested and sent to England, but he returned within two years and his troubles resumed, this time with John Endecott and Bradford. The Puritans did not tolerate him long. Morton was taken into custody again in 1630 and his property confiscated. Exiled to England, he remained briefly in prison there before joining forces with the enemies of Massachusetts in an attempt to get the charter of the Puritans revoked. His *New English Canaan*, a compendium of observations of and satires upon New England and its people published in 1637, caused much consternation among the colonists. He returned to Plymouth in 1643, but was quickly driven into Maine where, except for an unwise venture into Massachusetts that once again put him in prison, he remained and died about 1647. This raucous Englishman later became the subject of a short story by Nathaniel Hawthorne, "The Maypole of Merrymount;" two novels by John L. Motley, *Morton's Hope*, 1839, and *Merry Mount*, 1849; and Howard Hanson's opera, *Merry Mount*, 1934.

Morton, William Thomas Green (1819–1868), dentist and pioneer anesthetist. Born on August 9, 1819, in Charlton, Massachusetts, Morton attended the common schools until he was seventeen, then studied dentistry in 1840 at the Baltimore College of Dental Surgery. He practiced in Farmington, Connecticut, for two years, then moved to Boston, hoping to further his education at Harvard, but was deterred by financial problems. For a time he practiced in partnership with Horace Wells, who experimented in using nitrous oxide (laughing gas) as an anesthetic. Later, learning through Charles T. Jackson that inhalation of sulphuric ether created total loss of consciousness, Morton experimented with the chemical for use in oral surgery. By experimenting with it himself and administering it to various animals, he determined that the recipient would always return to normal consciousness. On September 30, 1846, he used ether on a patient and quickly completed a painless tooth extraction. On October 16 he successfully administered ether to a patient at the Massachusetts General Hospital in preparation for removal of a neck tumor. Several other publicized anesthetizations followed. Controversy over his lay status and his refusal to disclose the components of the anesthetic was laid to rest, announcement of his discovery was made in a medical journal, and he received a patent (he called the drug "letheon") and prepared to license its use by hospitals and doctors. He sought additional financial rewards from Congress and various petitions to that end were introduced and debated until the Civil War. Wells, Jackson, and Crawford W. Long, who, it was discovered, had used ether during an operation in 1842 challenged Morton's claims to sole credit for the discovery. Litigation and controversy dragged on until, totally impoverished, Morton died in New York City on July 15, 1868. Despite the justifiable claims of others, it was he who brought ether into common use. His published writings included *Remarks on the Proper Mode of Administering Sulphuric Ether by Inhalation*, 1847; *On the Physiological Effects of Sulphuric Ether*, 1850; and *Comparative Value of Ether and Chloroform, with Hints upon Natural and Artificial Teeth*, 1850. He was elected to the Hall of Fame in 1920.

Mosby, John Singleton (1833–1916), soldier. Born in Edgemont, Powhatan County, Virginia, on December 6, 1833, Mosby entered the University of Virginia at fifteen. While there he shot and wounded a fellow student in a quarrel; a subsequent six-month jail sentence was annulled and he was fined $1000. He graduated in 1852, was admitted to the bar in 1855, and practiced law in Bristol, Virginia, until the outbreak of the Civil War. Enlisting in the Confederate cavalry in 1861, he was present at the first battle of Bull Run (Manassas) and later was attached as a scout to Gen. J.E.B. Stuart's cavalry during its famous ride around Gen. George McClellan's army in June 1862 during the Peninsular Campaign. Mosby is remembered for his activities as a ranger, which he began early in 1863. Operating initially with nine men in Union-occupied northern Virginia, he attacked isolated Union outposts and cut communications and supply lines. The band avoided capture by dispersing immediately after an attack and regrouping at a prearranged location. Mosby steadily attracted recruits who preferred the undisciplined life of his rangers to that of the regular army. Self-supplied, audacious, and resourceful, his men followed the practice (legitimate under the law applying to partisans) of dividing among themselves the property they captured. "Mosby's Rangers" made one of their most spectacular raids when they slipped through Union lines at Fairfax Court House on March 9, 1863, and captured Gen. Edwin H. Stoughton and about a hundred of his men. Mosby was promoted to captain for this exploit and not long after, to major. By June 1863 his irregular forces were designated Company A, 43rd Battalion Partisan Rangers. Impossible to hunt down systematically, the Rangers were declared outlaws (because they confiscated private property as well as Union supplies) by the Union forces. Eventually, in 1864, several of them were captured and, under Gen. Ulysses S. Grant's orders, were hanged without trial. Mosby retaliated by hanging an equal number of Union cavalrymen and the executions of Rangers ended. In December 1864, when he was promoted to colonel, his force numbered eight companies. He conducted his final raid the day following Gen. Robert E. Lee's surrender at Appomattox on April 9, 1865; 11 days later he disbanded his troops after a final review at Salem (now Marshall), Virginia. He returned, a popular hero, to law practice in Warrenton, Virginia, but soon made enemies in the South by entering politics as a Republican. An admirer of Grant, he supported him for the presidency in 1872. He held minor political offices after that: he was U.S. consul at Hong Kong, 1878–1885, and assistant attorney for the department of justice, 1904–1910. He published two books on his war experiences, *Mosby's War Reminiscences*, which appeared in 1887, and *Stuart's Cavalry in the Gettysburg Campaign*, 1908. He died in Washington, D.C., on May 30, 1916.

Moses, Anna Mary Robertson (1860–1961), "Grandma Moses," painter. Born on September 7, 1860, on a farm in Greenwich, New York, Anna Robertson had only a few month's education during the summers of her childhood. At about the age of thirteen she left home to earn her living as a hired girl. After her marriage to Thomas Moses in 1887 the couple lived near Staunton, Virginia, until, in 1905, they settled on a farm near Eagle Bridge, Rensselaer County, New York, where she lived the rest of her life. She had drawn as a child and painted her first large picture in 1918, but it was not until her late seventies that she turned to oil paints to occupy her time. At first she copied illustrated postcards and Currier & Ives prints, but gradually she began to draw on experiences from her childhood, as in "Apple Pickers" and "Sugaring Off." Her early paintings were given away or sold for small sums. In 1939, several of her paintings that were hanging in a drugstore window in Hoosick Falls, New York, impressed Louis Caldor, an engineer and art collector who then drove to her farm and bought her remaining stock of 15 paintings. That same year, three of those paintings were exhibited at the Museum of Modern Art in New York City in a show entitled "Contemporary Unknown Painters." From the beginning her work received favorable criticism. In October 1940 a one-man show of 35 paintings was held at Galerie St. Etienne in New York City; in November of that year Gimbel's department store brought "Grandma" Moses to New York City on the opening day of a Thanksgiving exhibition of her works. Thereafter, her paintings were shown throughout the United States and in Europe. Grandma Moses produced some 2000 paintings; her innocent style (labeled American primitive) was acclaimed for its purity of color and its attention to detail, and she was praised for the depth and scope of her landscapes. Two fine examples of her work are the 1941 "Black Horses" and the 1946 "From My Window." From 1946, her paintings were often reproduced in prints and on Christmas cards. Her autobiography, *My Life's History*, was published in 1952. She died on December 13, 1961, at the age of a hundred and one in Hoosick Falls, New York.

Moses, Robert (1888–1981), public official. Born in New Haven, Connecticut, on December 18, 1888, Moses grew up in New York City. He graduated from Yale in 1909 and then studied in England, taking a B.A. at Oxford in 1911 and an M.A. in 1913; he received a Ph.D. from Columbia in 1914. He began a long career of public service for the state and especially the city of New York in 1913, when he joined the city's bureau of municipal research. His experience there led to an appointment in 1919 by Governor Alfred E. Smith as chief of staff of the New York state reconstruction commission, which sought administrative reforms in the state government. Moses served as New York's secretary of state in 1927–1928; he declined nomination for mayor of the New York City in 1933 and the next year was the unsuccessful Republican candidate for governor. His real career, however, had already begun a decade earlier. In 1924 Smith had named him head of both the New York and Long Island state park commissions, and for the next 40 years, more or less, through various state administrations at Albany and under various titles, he was virtual czar of the state's park system. From 1934 to 1960 he was also park commissioner of New York City. He had a hand in the development of almost every park in the state, but he is probably best known for his efforts to create and develop Jones Beach and Bethpage state parks on Long Island. He felt strongly that there was no sense in creating a park unless people could get to it and use it, and he was therefore also one of the most powerful advocates in New York and, indeed, in the nation, of parkways and limited-access roadways. New York City residents faced special problems in reaching the parks, since the city's central borough is an island; Moses therefore found himself involved in bridge as well as highway construction. He was largely responsible for the building of the Henry Hudson Parkway and other parkway routes, and he was called the "Father of the Triborough Bridge." From 1946 to 1968, in addition to his many other titles, he was chairman of the consolidated Triborough Bridge and City Tunnel authorities. In the later 1950s he became deeply interested in the development of the St. Lawrence Seaway and Power Project, and in 1964–1965 was president of the New York World's Fair. Always a controversial figure, he was attacked during the earlier part of his career by business interests who asserted that his building of parks and parkways was a waste of government funds; later, with the growing consciousness of ecology in the 1950s and 1960s he became the bane of conservationists, who bitterly fought and defeated some of his projects in those years. He wrote many articles and several books, including *Theory and Practice in Politics*, 1939. In an important sense, he was responsible more than any other man for the look of New York City and its environs at mid-twentieth century. He died on July 29, 1981, in West Islip, New York.

Moss, Mary, *see* Keene, Laura

Motley, John Lothrop (1814–1877), historian and diplomat. Born in Dorchester, now a district of Boston, on April 15, 1814, Motley spent two years at the experimental Round Hill School in Northampton, Massachusetts, run by George Bancroft and Joseph Cogswell and then went to Harvard, from which he graduated in 1831. He studied for two years in Germany, ostensibly reading law but in reality living the easy life of a wealthy Bostonian abroad and making the acquaintance of young German scholars and nobles, among them Otto von Bismarck, and then spent two years traveling in Britain and on the Continent. He returned to Boston in 1835, determined to devote his life to literature. He married and took up residence in a house built for him by his father on his Boston estate. His first productions were two novels based on Thomas Morton and his settlement at Merrymount; their lack of great success seems to have turned his ambitions to a

diplomatic career, and he spent a few months in 1841 as secretary to the U.S. legation in St. Petersburg, Russia. But he did not like the climate and found living expensive, and he returned to Boston. The study of history began to claim his attention and his first essay, on Peter the Great, appeared in the *North American Review* in 1845. About 1847 he decided upon the subject matter of his life's work—the history of the Netherlands in the sixteenth and seventeenth centuries. He threw himself into his researches, discussed his discoveries with his wide circle of distinguished friends—among them Oliver Wendell Holmes, William H. Prescott, Henry Wadsworth Longfellow, Ralph Waldo Emerson, Nathaniel Hawthorne, James Russell Lowell, Louis Agassiz, Richard Henry Dana, and Charles Sumner—and finally, in 1856, brought out in London and New York the work by which he is best known, *The Rise of the Dutch Republic*. No longer considered to be historically valid, and even at the time sharply criticized by Dutch historians, the book was nevertheless tremendously popular and influential. Written in a brilliant style, it emphasized the drama of the exciting events of which it told, and was imbued throughout with its author's strong feeling for liberty and democracy and his prejudice against Spanish Roman Catholic absolutism. Indeed, Motley once said that his prime motive in writing it had been to point out the parallels between the Dutch struggle for independence from Spain and the American colonies' struggle with Great Britain. He served as U.S. minister to Austria from 1861 to 1867 and as minister to Britain in 1869–1870 and at the same time continued his researches. *The History of the United Netherlands, 1584–1609* appeared in four volumes from 1860 to 1867, and *The Life and Death of John of Barneveld* in two volumes in 1874, but neither of these works achieved the popularity of his earlier book. He planned to carry his history down to 1648, but he died in England on May 29, 1877, before he could complete it. He was elected to the Hall of Fame in 1910.

Mott, John Raleigh (1865–1955), religious leader. Born in Livingston Manor, Sullivan County, New York, on May 25, 1865, Mott grew up in Iowa, where he attended Upper Iowa University. He transferred to Cornell in 1885 and before graduating in 1888 became active in the Young Men's Christian Association (YMCA). In 1888 he became student secretary of the International Committee of the YMCA, and after 1898 he also served as the organization's foreign secretary. On relinquishing those posts in 1915 he became general secretary of the YMCA, serving until 1931. He also served as head of the national council of YMCAs in the United States and as president of the world Alliance of YMCAs from 1926 to 1937. Mott served the organization well during a period of great international expansion. During World War I he was the moving force behind the YMCA's welfare program for Allied troops and for prisoner of war camps on both sides of the conflict. Mott was also a pioneer in—and perhaps made an even greater contribution to—the world ecumenical movement that grew out of the widespread missionary work of the late nineteenth and early twentieth centuries. His missionary work began with the Student Volunteer Movement for Foreign Missions, which was in a state of decline when he became chairman of its executive committee in 1888. In 1893 he organized the Foreign Missions Conference of North America and in 1895 the World's Student Christian Federation, for which, as its general secretary, he undertook a world tour, 1895–1897, to promote its activities. He subsequently served as general chairman of the federation from 1920 to 1928. This pioneer work led to the first World Missionary Conference at Edinburgh in 1910, where the modern ecumenical movement had its beginnings. Mott presided over the conference and once again undertook a world tour, working on behalf of its program and to bring national ecumenical conferences into being. Out of this grew, after a delay caused by World War I, the International Missionary Council. Mott became its first chairman in 1921, contributing greatly to the development of ecumenical confidence and mutual trust, particularly in the formation of national Christian councils in many parts of Asia and Africa. He retired from that post in 1942, and was then made honorary chairman of the conference. When the International Missionary Council joined other ecumenical groups to form the World Council of Churches in 1948 he became honorary president of that body. Mott was also a prolific writer, publishing some 15 volumes during his lifetime. His last book, *The Larger Evangelism*, appeared in 1944. The recipient of numerous awards, he received in 1946, for his international church and missionary work, the Nobel Peace Prize, which he shared with Emily Greene Balch. He died in Orlando, Florida, on January 31, 1955.

Mott, Lucretia Coffin (1793–1880), social reformer. Born on January 3, 1793, in Nantucket, Massachusetts, Lucretia Coffin attended public school for two years in Boston in accordance with her father's wish that she become familiar with the workings of democratic principles. Later she was enrolled in a boarding school of the Society of Friends (Quakers) near Poughkeepsie, New York, and studied and taught there until she moved back to her father's home, by then in Philadelphia. In 1811 she married James Mott, a fellow teacher from the school. About 1818 she began to speak at religious meetings with such fervor that she was accepted as a minister of the Friends. She joined the Hicksite (Liberal) branch of the Society when a rift occurred in the 1820s and traveled across the country lecturing on religion and social reform, including temperance, the abolition of slavery, and peace. In 1833 she joined in the founding of the American Anti-Slavery Society and immediately thereafter she led in organizing the Philadelphia Anti-Slavery Society, of which

she was chosen president. But she met opposition within the Society of Friends when she spoke of abolition, and attempts were made to strip her of her ministry and membership. Rebuffed as a delegate because she was a woman at the World's Anti-Slavery Convention in London in 1840, she still managed to make her views known. With Elizabeth Cady Stanton, she helped found the women's-rights movement at the Seneca Falls, New York, convention of 1848. She and her husband opened their home to runaway slaves escaping via the Underground Railroad after the Fugitive Slave Law was adopted in 1850. A fluent, moving speaker, she retained her poise and femininity before the most hostile audiences. Her last address was given to the Friends' annual meeting in 1880. She died that year on November 11, in her home outside Philadelphia.

Moultrie, William (1730–1805), soldier and public official. Born in Charlestown (now Charleston), Carolina, on December 4, 1730, Moultrie was already a prominent landowner at an early age and was first elected to the provincial assembly in 1752; he served in that body, except for short intervals, until 1771. After fighting against the Cherokee in 1761 as a company commander with the rank of captain, he became strongly interested in military affairs. He championed the patriot cause in the provincial congress in 1775, and he was shortly elected colonel of South Carolina's 2nd regiment. In March 1776 he took command of a fort he had built of sand and palmetto logs on Sullivan's island in Charleston harbor. It was named Fort Moultrie in his honor after he successfully beat off a heavy bombardment by the British on June 28, 1776. For the victory, which delayed British plans to establish a foothold in the southern colonies for about two years, he received the thanks of Congress, and three months later was made a brigadier general in the Continental army. He subsequently served under Gen. Benjamin Lincoln in Georgia, 1778–1779, and again delayed British success in South Carolina by dislodging them from Beaufort in February 1779. He surrendered after the successful British siege of Charleston, March 12–May 12, 1780, and remained a prisoner on parole until exchanged in February 1782. He ended his war service with the rank of major general. His war record made him even more prominent in South Carolina politics, and after serving as lieutenant governor he became governor of the state, serving from 1785 to 1787 and again from 1792 to 1794; he served in the state senate between terms. He retired from public life after his second term as governor. Two volumes of his war memoirs appeared in 1802; he died in Charleston on September 27, 1805.

Mount, William Sidney (1807–1868), painter. Born on November 26, 1807 at Setauket, Long Island, New York, Mount grew up on a Long Island farm near Stony Brook. At seventeen he joined an older brother, already established as a sign painter, in New York City. He studied during the year 1826 at the National Academy of Design, before returning to Setauket to paint. He soon began to exhibit his works and in 1832 was admitted to the Academy, becoming a full member the following year. By 1833 he had achieved widespread recognition as a painter of portraits; among his many subjects were Bishop Henry U. Onderdonk, Daniel Webster, and Zachariah Green. Mount was one of the first American painters to venture into the commercially untried field of landscape painting and soon was painting the popular genre pictures on which his reputation rests. His genial portrayals of country life include "Dancing on the Barn Floor," "Eel Spearing at Setauket," "Long Island Farmhouse," "Raffling for the Goose," and "Bargaining for a Horse." These were popular among his contemporaries and he is still considered one of the best American anecdotal painters. Mount spent most of his life at Setauket and died there after a long period of inactivity, on November 19, 1868.

Mowatt, Anna Cora Ogden (1819–1870), author and actress. Born on March 5, 1819, to American parents in Bordeaux, France, Miss Ogden came to New York City with her family when she was seven. As a child she exhibited a talent for acting and a precocious interest in Shakespeare, whose plays she devoured before she was ten. She was married early, at fifteen, to James Mowatt, and under the pseudonym "Isabel" published her first book, a verse romance titled *Pelayo; or, The Cavern of Covadonga,* at seventeen; she defended it against critical attacks in *Reviewers Reviewed* the next year. Her husband suffered financial reverses during the next few years, and in 1841 she determined to pursue a career as an author and actress. She gave poetry readings and, under the pseudonym "Helen Berkley," wrote for the fashionable magazines. Her first successful play, *Fashion; or, Life in New York,* a social satire written at the suggestion of Epes Sargent and for which she is chiefly remembered, opened in March 1845. She made her acting debut later that year in another of her popular plays, *The Lady of Lyons.* Another play, *Armand, the Child of the People,* was also well received in New York City in 1847, and she took both plays to England and acted in them there, also taking several Shakespearian roles, for the next four years. She returned for an American tour after the death of Mowatt in 1851, but recurring illness forced her from the stage, and she wrote *Autobiography of an Actress,* published in 1854. She married William F. Ritchie in that year, which also marked her permanent retirement from the stage. She continued to write, producing several novels both before and after her departure for Europe following the outbreak of the Civil War. She lived mostly in Florence during her last years but died in Twickenham, England, on July 21, 1870. *Italian Life and Legends,* 1870, appeared posthumously.

Mozee, Phoebe Anne Oakley, see Oakley, Annie

Muggeridge, Edward James, see Muybridge, Eadweard

Muhammad Ali, see Ali, Muhammad

Muhammad, Elijah (1897–1975), religious leader. Elijah Muhammad was born Elijah Poole on a tenant farm near Sandersville, Georgia, on October 10, 1897. The son of former slaves (his father became a Baptist minister), he attended school through the fifth grade and left home at sixteen. He lived for a time in Atlanta, married in 1919, and moved with his family to Detroit in 1923. He held a variety of jobs, encountering racial discrimination and later the effects of the Depression of the 1930s, living from 1929 to 1931 on relief. For a brief period he was a Baptist preacher. In 1931 he met and became an assistant to Wali Farad, who founded the Nation of Islam, a Muslim sect later known widely as the "Black Muslims." Farad's doctrines included a denunciation of Christianity as a deceptive tool of white men to keep blacks in a state of servility. In what came to be a tradition of the Nation of Islam, Elijah was relieved of his "slave" name and given an Islamic surname, Karriem; later he was renamed Muhammad to indicate his position of leadership in the movement. In 1934, under Farad's direction, he established Muhammad's Temple of Islam No. 2 in Chicago; Farad had established the original mosque in Detroit in 1931. Shortly thereafter, in a way that baffled police and FBI investigators, Farad disappeared, and Elijah was named the Messenger of Allah and head of the growing organization. In *The Supreme Wisdom: Solution to the So-called Negroes' Problem,* which came to be a basic text of the movement, Elijah perpetuated the status of Farad as a deity, the incarnation of Allah, and spread the conviction that blacks would one day rule the world. His nationalist philosophies, which paralleled in some respects those of Marcus M. Garvey in the 1920s, helped foster the intricately structured, prosperous Black Muslim movement. He advocated strict personal morals and economic prudence, thus aiding the welfare of tens of thousands of blacks. He organized temple-sponsored business enterprises in Chicago and Detroit, as well as parochial schools. In 1934 he was arrested and paroled on charges of contributing to the delinquency of a minor, after refusing to withdraw his son from a Black Muslim school and enter him in a public school in Detroit. He lived in Washington, D.C., from 1935 to 1941 and spent the next six years in prison for violating selective-service laws by speaking at a military induction center on the similarity of prejudice against Japanese and black Americans. He directed the Black Muslim movement from jail, and the size of his following continued to increase. On his release, he moved to Chicago, supervised the business of Temple No. 2, and formulated and administered his national policies through his own fiery preaching and through the work of his ministers, most notably his principal disciple, Malcolm X. By 1962 there were at least 49 Temples of Islam in areas of large black population in the United States and an estimated quarter of a million Black Muslims. He was allowed to make the traditional Muslim pilgrimage to Mecca during a tour of Africa and the Middle East during 1959–1960. He made numerous radio broadcasts, wrote special publications, and contributed articles to newspapers and to journals of the movement. The movement gained considerable publicity and prestige with the conversion of heavyweight champion boxer Cassius Clay, who took the name Muhammad Ali, in 1964. The following year, however, a serious schism developed as Malcolm X broke away to attempt to form a broader movement. The assassination of Malcolm, allegedly by Black Muslims loyal to Elijah Muhammad, marked the beginning of sporadic violence that dogged the movement for several years. The Black Muslims continued to grow and prosper, nonetheless, and undertook numerous business enterprises. Elijah Muhammad died in Chicago on February 25, 1975.

Muhlenberg, Frederick Augustus (1750–1801), religious leader and public official. Born on January 1, 1750, at Trappe, Pennsylvania, Frederick Augustus Conrad, a son of Henry Melchior Mühlenberg and brother of John Peter Gabriel Mühlenberg, was educated at the University of Halle in Germany (1763–1770) and returned to Philadelphia in 1770 to accept ordination in the Lutheran church. He performed ministerial duties in a number of places for the next several years and from 1773 to 1776 was pastor of Christ Church (Lutheran) in New York City, leaving the city upon its occupation by the British. His espousal of the patriot cause curtailed his ministry, and he abandoned the pulpit altogether for a political career in 1779, serving twice as a delegate to the Continental Congress, in 1779 and 1780. He served in the Pennsylvania assembly from 1780 to 1783, as speaker much of the time, and was president of the Council of Censors in 1783–1784. He held minor political posts until 1787, when he was elected president of the Pennsylvania convention that ratified the new U.S. Constitution on December 12, (Pennsylvania was the second state to ratify). Elected in the fall of 1788 as a Democratic Republican to the 1st Congress, 1789–1791, he was elected first speaker of the House of Representatives on April 1, 1789; reelected three times to the House, he again served as speaker from 1793 to 1795. Beginning with his second term in the House he was nominally a Federalist, but his allegiance to that party was never strong and he was badly defeated as Federalist candidate for governor of Pennsylvania in 1793 and 1796; his defeat in the second effort was largely owing to his having courageously cast earlier in the year the deciding vote in the House calling for approval of appropriations necessary for the unpopular Jay's Treaty, an action that effectively ended his political career. At Muhlenberg's death in Lancaster, Pennsylvania, on June 4, 1801, he was receiver general of the Pennsylvania land office.

Mühlenberg, Henry Melchior (1711–1787), religious leader. Born in Einbeck, Germany, on September 6, 1711, Mühlenberg studied theology at the University of Göttingen and in 1738–1739 was a teacher in the Waisenhaus, an orphans' school in Halle. In 1739 he was ordained a Lutheran minister in Leipzig, and in 1741 he accepted a call from the United Congregations, the Lutheran churches in Philadelphia, New Providence (now Trappe), and New Hanover, Pennsylvania. His position, although his ministry was technically limited to the three congregations, made him virtual leader of all American Lutherans. Soon after his arrival in 1742 he managed to head off an incipient schism in the church. He traveled throughout the colonies, particularly in New Jersey, Maryland, and New York, and in 1748 organized the first Lutheran synod in America, the Evangelical Lutheran Ministerium of Pennsylvania. He made his home, when not on one of his many journeys to other Lutheran settlements, in New Providence until 1761. From that year until 1776 he lived in Philadelphia, but with the outbreak of the Revolution he returned to New Providence, where he stayed for the rest of his life. After 1779 his activities were restricted, and his last appearance before the synod was in 1781. In 1784 he was awarded the degree of doctor of divinity by the University of Pennsylvania. Three years later, on October 7, 1787, he died at his home in New Providence.

Muhlenberg, John Peter Gabriel (1746–1807), religious leader, soldier, and public official. Born in Trappe, Pennsylvania, on October 1, 1746, John Peter was the eldest child of Henry Melchior Mühlenberg and a brother of Frederick Augustus Muhlenberg. He went with two of his brothers to study at the University of Halle, Germany, in 1763, but was back in Philadelphia by 1767. He subsequently studied privately for the ministry, and assisted his father before going to England for ordination (apparently as an Episcopalian) in early 1772. Later that year he became pastor of a Lutheran church in Woodstock, Virginia, where he soon gained favor in the pulpit and as an enthusiast for the Revolution. His patriotic fervor eventually gained the upper hand; organizing a militia company in Virginia, composed mostly of Germans, he was made colonel and fought under Col. William Moultrie at the important defeat of the British at Sullivans Island, South Carolina, in June 1776. Commissioned brigadier general in the Continental army in early 1777, he took part in a number of battles including Brandywine, Germantown, Monmouth Court House, and Stony Point, and at Yorktown commanded the first brigade of light infantry. After the war, at the close of which he was serving as a major general, he moved to Philadelphia. His war record now opened a political career that he was quick to pursue. Elected to the Supreme Executive Council of Pennsylvania in 1784, he became vice-president of the state under Benjamin Franklin, 1785–1788, exerted his considerable influence in favor of ratification of the Constitution, and along with his brother Frederick Augustus became a member of the House in the first U.S. Congress, convened in 1789. He was reelected, again as a Democratic Republican, in 1793 and served a third term during 1799–1801. He worked harmoniously with the supporters of Thomas Jefferson, whom he supported for president in 1796 and in 1801, and in 1801 he won a Senate seat. He resigned from the Senate almost immediately and returned to Philadelphia, where, after 1802, he served as a collector of the port of Philadelphia. He died at his home near the city on October 1, 1807.

Muir, John (1838–1914), naturalist. Born on April 21, 1838, in Dunbar, Scotland, Muir emigrated with his family to a homestead near Portage, Wisconsin, in 1849. His early education was obtained largely by his own efforts, but from 1859 to 1863 he studied at the University of Wisconsin, taking no degree, however, because of his refusal to follow a curriculum of required courses. He made extensive journeys on foot through the Midwest and into Canada. He had a remarkable aptitude for mechanical invention that he pursued until an accident in 1867 damaged an eye and he turned to the study of nature, from the outset keeping voluminous daily journals of his travels, his observations, and his reflections. In 1867 he walked from Indianapolis to the Gulf of Mexico, publishing his journal of the trip in 1916 as *A Thousand-Mile Walk to the Gulf*. In 1868 he went to California and for several years devoted himself to nature study, giving particular attention to trees, forests, and glaciers, and ranging into Utah, Nevada, the Northwest, and Alaska where he discovered Glacier Bay and the great glacier later named for him, and, to study other species of forest trees, to South America, Africa, and Australia. The center of his interest, however, was the Yosemite Valley. For 11 years after 1880 he engaged in horticulture with sufficient success to enable him to retire in 1891 and devote the rest of his life to his studies. In 1890 a decade of effort, recorded primarily in several brilliant articles in *Scribner's Monthly* and *Century* magazines, culminated in the passage by Congress of the bill establishing Yosemite National Park; the next year Congress passed a bill empowering the president to create forest preserves from the public domain. Muir was appointed an adviser to the National Forestry Commission in 1896; when the forest preserves established as a result of the commission's work were threatened by commercial interests, he wrote articles for *Harper's Weekly* and the *Atlantic Monthly* that succeeded in arousing public concern and saving the preserves. He later influenced President Theodore Roosevelt's decision to increase greatly the amount of protected public land. Among Muir's other books were *The Mountains of California*, 1894; *Our National Parks*, 1901; *Stickeen*, 1909; *My First Summer in the Sierra*, 1911; and *The Yosemite*, 1912. *Travels in Alaska*, 1915; *The Cruise of the Corwin*, 1917; and *Steep Trails*, 1918, appeared posthumously. He died in Los Angeles on December 24, 1914. Muir Woods, a

500 acre stand of sequoia near San Francisco, was given to the United States in 1907 by William Kent, California congressman, who suggested the name; the following year the tract was named a national monument.

Muller, Hermann Joseph (1890–1967), geneticist. Born on December 21, 1890, in New York City, Muller studied at Columbia University; he graduated in 1910, took his M.A. in 1911, and, after a time at the medical school of Cornell University, returned to Columbia, taking his doctorate in 1916. He worked closely during that time with Thomas Hunt Morgan in the experiments that revealed the existence of genes as carriers of heredity and was a coauthor of *The Mechanism of Mendelian Heredity*, 1915. From 1915 to 1918 he was an instructor in biology at Rice Institute in Houston, Texas, then after two years on the Columbia faculty, went to the University of Texas in 1920. Muller continued his research into heredity and was able to explain the various modes of arrangement and combination of genes and to clarify the manner in which mutations occur. During the 1920s he began to use X-ray bombardment on *Drosophila*, the common fruit fly, and in 1927 successfully produced artificial mutations. From 1933 to 1937 he was senior geneticist at the Institute of Genetics in Moscow; but he became disillusioned with Soviet policy, especially the attempt to force scientific fact to fit Soviet ideology. He lectured at the University of Edinburgh from 1937 to 1940, from 1940 to 1945 was at Amherst College, and from 1945 until his death was professor of zoology at the University of Indiana. In 1946 he was awarded the Nobel Prize for Physiology and Medicine for his pioneering work on mutations. In his later years he was a controversial figure among scientists; he proposed the establishment of a sperm bank to preserve the genetic characteristics of outstanding men, and warned against the use of nuclear weapons because of their potential for creating harmful mutations in human genes. In 1953 he became Distinguished Service Professor of Zoology at the University of Indiana. Others of his writings included *Out of the Night*, 1935, on eugenics; and *Genetics, Medicine, and Man*, 1947, with Clarence C. Little and Laurence N. Snyder. He died in Indianapolis on April 5, 1967.

Mulliken, Robert Sanderson (1896–   ), chemist and physicist. Born in Newburyport, Massachusetts, on June 7, 1896, Mulliken studied chemistry at the Massachusetts Institute of Technology (MIT), where he took a B.S. in 1917, and was with the army's Chemical Warfare Service during World War I. He pursued further studies at the University of Chicago during 1919–1921, earning a Ph.D. in 1921, and remained there for another two years on a National Research Council fellowship. He then did research on molecular spectra at Harvard from 1923 to 1925. He subsequently taught physics at New York University before returning to the University of Chicago in 1928, where in 1931 he became a full professor of physics and in 1956 Ernest DeWitt Burton Distinguished Service Professor. He remained as Distinguished Service Professor of Physics and Chemistry after he reached the mandatory retirement age of sixty-five in 1961, and from 1965 was also associated with Florida State University at its Institute for Molecular Biophysics. Influenced by Friedrich Hund during a visit to Europe in 1927, he made one of the pioneer applications of quantum mechanics to molecular chemistry, proposing a theory that expressed electron orbits as a wave function. This novel conception required thinking of electrons as forming a "cloud" and orbiting around the molecule as a whole rather than around the nuclei of the separate atoms. His molecular-orbital theory, as it became known, thus was wedded to the statisical wave mechanics of the Schrödinger equation, yielding, analogously to the new quantum physics, only probabilistic descriptions of molecular properties. The advent of computerized molecular research eased the acceptance of the theory, which, in practice, became the basis of polymer chemistry and led to the development of many synthetic materials. A prolific writer on his findings, Mulliken published theoretical papers throughout the 1930s, and after World War II, during which he engaged in war-related research, he extended his work to include a statistical conception of the nature of chemical bonds—a logical next question that bore upon the chief weakness of his theory. Increasingly honored for his work during his later years, Mulliken was awarded the Nobel Prize for Chemistry in 1966 for "his fundamental work concerning chemical bonds and the electronic structure of molecules by the molecular-orbital method."

Mumford, Lewis (1895–), author and social critic. Born in Flushing, New York (now part of New York City) on October 19, 1895, Mumford was educated in the public schools and attended Columbia and New York universities, the College of the City of New York (CCNY), and the New School for Social Research. He did not graduate from any of them, although he later received several honorary degrees. He had determined on a literary career early in life and supported himself and his family by writing a long series of articles and books. He served from 1919 as an editor of the *Dial*. Apart from his periodical articles on topics in art, architecture, urban planning, conservation, social criticism, and related fields, some of them of profound influence on his contemporaries, his books included *The Story of Utopias*, 1922; *Sticks and Stones*, 1924; *The Golden Day*, 1926; *Herman Melville*, 1929; *The Brown Decades*, 1931; *Technics and Civilization*, 1934; *The Culture of Cities*, 1938; *The Condition of Man*, 1944; *The Conduct of Life*, 1951; *Art and Technics*, 1952; *The Human Prospect*, 1955; *The Transformations of Man*, 1956; *The City in History*, 1961, for which he won a National Book Award; *The Highway and the City*, 1963; *The Myth of the Machine: Technics and Human Development*, vol. 1, 1967; *The Urban Prospect*, 1968; *The Culture of Cities*, 1970; and *The Myth of the Machine: The Pentagon of Power*, vol. 2, 1970. These books ranged from architecture, of which he was accepted as perhaps the leading American critic of the twentieth century, to literature and literary history, the effects of technology on human life, and speculations on human progress. He was professor of humanities at Stanford University from 1942 to 1944, professor of city and regional planning at the University of Pennsylvania from 1951 to 1959, research professor at that institution from 1959 to 1961, and visiting professor at the Massachusetts Institute of Technology (MIT) from 1957 to 1960. The recipient of many medals and awards, he was president of the American Academy of Arts and letters from 1962 to 1965.

Muñoz Marín, Luis (1898–1980), public official. Born in San Juan, Puerto Rico, on February 18, 1898, Muñoz was the son of the island's renowned patriot, Luis Muñoz Rivera, who had led the autonomist forces in achieving a measure of independence from Spain before the United States' takeover of Puerto Rico. Muñoz grew up in San Juan and in Washington, D.C., where his father served as the island's resident commissioner until his death in 1916. The son continued to live in the capital, attending Georgetown University and Georgetown Law School and starting a career as a free-lance writer. In 1919 he moved to New York City and wrote articles on Latin American culture that appeared frequently in such journals as the *Nation*, *Smart Set* and the *American Mercury*. In his early political views he espoused Socialism and the cause of Puerto Rican independence from the United States. After living in New York City for more than a decade, he returned to San Juan in 1926 and became editor of his father's newspaper, *La Democracia* (later *Diario de Puerto Rico*); he left the post in 1928 but resumed it in 1932, the year in which he was elected on the Liberal party ticket to the Puerto Rican senate for one term. He soon became one of the most popular politicians on the island, for in the depths of the Depression of the 1930s he was able, through contacts with the administration of President Franklin D. Roosevelt in Washington, to channel government spending to Puerto Rico. He also favored breaking up large land holdings to distribute land among poorer farmers. He lost his seat in the 1936 election because of rifts within the Liberal party and returned to Washington for a time. In 1937 he broke with the party for its failure to support the poor. On July 22, 1938, at the inland town of Barranquitas, his father's birthplace, Muñoz founded the Popular Democratic party. He temporarily shelved the issue of Puerto Rico's political status vis-à-vis the United States and for the next decade concentrated on economic and social problems. The Popular Democratic party won a notable victory in 1940 and Muñoz was returned to the senate. The next year President Roosevelt named Rexford G. Tugwell governor of Puerto Rico. Tugwell and Muñoz worked well together to promote the island's economy, alleviating food shortages and planning for industrial and agricultural development. In the years after World War II the island's development was aided by Operation Bootstrap, which fostered industrial growth by encouraging investment through favorable tax exemptions. The island's income tripled in the decade 1940–1950 and unemployment dropped. In 1947 President Harry S. Truman appointed him the island's first native-born governor, and the following year Muñoz became the island's first elected governor. His Popular Democratic party took a stand on the island's status by proposing autonomous self-government and the retention of economic ties with the United States. On October 30, 1950, Truman signed the Puerto Rico Commonwealth Bill, and in a referendum on June 4, 1951, the island's residents accepted it by an overwhelming majority. On July 25, 1952, the new Commonwealth Constitution went into effect. As the island's economy improved and tourism grew, Muñoz's popularity was strengthened. He won the governorship again in 1952, 1956, and 1960. By 1964, when he decided to step down, he had become, like his father before him, an acknowledged leader of his country and a politician of great power and prestige. His handpicked successor won the 1964 election, but in 1968 Muñoz's Popular Democratic party was turned out of office for the first time. Muñoz maintained an active interest in politics, combating a new push for statehood urged by the right and a resurgent independence movement identified to a degree with the left. In 1968 he stepped aside as Popular Democratic party leader. He died in San Juan on April 30, 1980.

Munro, George (1825–1896), publisher. Born on November 12, 1825, at West River, Pictou County, Nova Scotia, Munro worked as a printer, attended Pictou Academy, and was the headmaster of Free Church Academy in Halifax before emigrating to New York City in 1856. He gained familiarity with publishing in the United States, a considerable portion of which was devoted to issuing dime novels, while working for the American News Company and at other jobs. He joined the firm of Beadle & Adams as a clerk shortly after they became established in the pulp field in the early 1860s and about 1863 entered the fierce competition among often short-lived companies by organizing his own firm. Within a short time Munro's Ten Cent Novels, indistinguishable from the Beadle product, had gained a foothold and during the next 30 years Munro's company became one of the five that dominated the field. About 1866 he also introduced a family paper, the *Fireside Companion*, which appeared weekly until 1907. Success in the dime-novel industry, which operated with inexpensive raw materials (provided by hack writers), a low markup, and large sales, required shrewd reckoning and a keen sense of the expectations of the audience. The predictable plots and characteriza-

tion of the Westerns that initially dominated the field were, in fact, essential to their success. "The game," as one pulp magazine editor put it, "is to give the ordinary guy what he wants." In a field where innovation was risky, Munro launched the Old Sleuth detective series, which opened up new vistas of escape, action, and excitement for the public. Written for a time after its beginning in 1885 by Harlan Halsey, the series eventually included more than 600 titles. Munro carried the production formula to its logical conclusion by eliminating the expense of paying the writer. His Seaside Library series, which presented works by Charles Dickens, Sir Walter Scott, the Brontës, and others (without author's compensation) in a ten-cent format, was distributed by mail in an arrangement with the American News Company. He made a fortune before such use of literary works was forbidden by international copyright regulations. In his later years Munro made generous charitable contributions to educational institutions in Canada and in New York City, where he died on April 23, 1896, as the dime-novel industry itself began to decline.

Munsey, Frank Andrew (1854–1925), publisher. Born in Mercer, Maine, on August 21, 1854, Munsey worked as a telegraph operator for Western Union before coming to New York City at the age of twenty-eight. He ventured into magazine publishing with a capital of about $300 (mostly borrowed), launching the *Golden Argosy* for children in 1882. He struggled for ten years before achieving a successful format. His magazines adapted the proven methods of the dime-novel publishers and soon supplanted them. *Argosy*, the first successful pulp magazine, grew out of *Golden Argosy* and appeared in 1896, specializing in adventure stories. It was selling 500,000 copies per issue from the newsstands at its peak in 1910. *All-Story*, another Munsey success, added love stories (virtuous courtships that culminated in marriage) to its contents, and in 1912 it serialized *Tarzan of the Apes* by Edgar Rice Burroughs, two years later issued in book form as the first of a famous series. Munsey thrived in a highly competitive field by quickly ending unsuccessful ventures and gaining control of his competitors, often buying their publications in order to merge or kill them. Indifferent to the success of any given magazine under his control, he nevertheless took pride in the fact that *Munsey's Magazine* (begun in 1889 as *Munsey's Weekly*), which survived until his death, led the world in circulation in 1907. Immensely wealthy by 1910, he began acquiring newspapers. With the singular devotion to work for which he was known, he set about buying, merging, and consolidating New York dailies. His list of papers included at one time the *New York Star*, the *New York Press*, the *New York Sun*, the *New York Herald*, the *Daily Continent*, the *Globe*, the *Mail and Express*, and also extended to the *Baltimore Star*, the *Philadelphia Times*, the *Boston Morning Journal*, and the *Washington Times*. The *New*

York Evening Sun was the most prominent of all his papers, and the *New York Evening Telegram* also proved lasting. He later speculated heavily in the stock market and at one point owned a chain of grocery stores. Munsey died in New York City on December 22, 1925, having succeeded in adapting mass-production methods to the publishing of popular magazines and newspapers at a time when consolidation was a marked feature of many industries. A bachelor, he left most of his fortune of nearly $20 million to the Metropolitan Museum of Art in New York City.

Münsterberg, Hugo (1863–1916), psychologist. Born in Danzig, Prussia (now Gdańsk, Poland), on June 1, 1863, Münsterberg attended the Danzig gymnasium, studied with Wilhelm Wundt at the University of Leipzig, where he received his Ph.D. in 1885, and then went to the University of Heidelberg where he took his M.D. in 1887. He accepted a position in psychology at the University of Freiburg in 1887 and immediately began important pioneer researches in experimental psychology. His work was first published in 1888 as *Die Willenshandlung*, quickly followed by *Beiträge zur experimentellen Psychologie*, two volumes, 1889–1892. In 1889 he was in Paris for the First International Congress of Psychology and met William James, then completing his own masterpiece, *The Principles of Psychology*, 1890. James had already read *Die Willenshandlung* and was so impressed that he insisted on immediate copies of Münsterberg's work in progress; James's enthusiasm for Münsterberg is revealed in the favorable references to him in the *Psychology*. On completing *Beiträge*, Münsterberg accepted an invitation to come to Harvard as professor of psychology and to continue his work. Taking a leave from Freiburg, he stayed for three years, 1892–1895, and in 1897 returned permanently, unable to resist the urging of James and Harvard's President Charles W. Eliot. He thrived in the genial atmosphere of Harvard, which was experiencing one of its great periods in psychology and philosophy. By 1905 he had a permanent laboratory in experimental psychology, of which he was thereafter director, and soon led the way in showing the application of psychology to other fields. An able lecturer, Münsterberg often left the campus to lecture in other cities. He enjoyed a wide range of interests, including among them, like James and many other prominent thinkers of the day, the field of psychic research. He worked rapidly, often impulsively, and was eager to attempt a more popular exposition of his ideas. A prolific writer, he produced many published works, including *Psychology and Life*, 1899; *Grundzüge der Psychologie*, 1900; *The Principles of Art Education*, 1905; *On the Witness Stand*, 1908; *Psychology and the Teacher*, 1909; *Psychology and Industrial Efficiency*, 1913; *Psychology and Social Sanity*, 1914; and *Grundzüge der Psychotechnik*, 1914. He made three trips to Berlin in his later years—in 1910, when he

became one of the founders of the Amerika-Institut, and twice in 1912. His last years at Harvard were spent in the shadow of the anti-German feeling caused by World War I. He died suddenly, while lecturing to a class at Radcliffe College, on December 16, 1916.

Murel, John A., *see* Murrell, John A.

Murieta, Joaquín (? –1853?), bandit. No one knows when or where Murieta (or Murrietta) was born, and the difficulty is compounded by the fact that "he" was certainly not one man but several, perhaps as many as five Mexican outlaw leaders of roving bands that preyed on U.S. settlers in central and southern California in the early 1850s. The grievance of such bands was real enough: their country, they maintained, had been stolen from them, and they were not permitted, as aliens, to look for gold on their own territory, gold that the Americans had found; in addition, there were many stories about the hanging of the half-brother of the outlaw leader, the murder of his beautiful mistress, and so forth. Many times two or more "Joaquíns" were known to be in daring raids at the same time but in different places. In the spring of 1853 the California legislature commissioned a Texan named Harry Love to equip 20 men and lead them in a search for any or all of the Joaquíns who had so far been dimly identified. Love set out on May 11 and found not a single Joaquín until July 25, when they came upon a party of Mexicans in the region of Tulare Lake. In the course of a gun fight, several of them were killed. One was Manuel García, alias Three-Fingered Jack; they cut off his hand for identification purposes, pickled it in alcohol, and later exhibited it around the state. Another victim, nameless, may have admitted to being the leader of the gang; they decapitated him and used his head for similar purposes. Both the hand and the head were also employed to claim a large reward promised by the legislature, which Love shared with his men. Californians were aware that they had been swindled to some degree, but, for reasons not known, the banditry died down in the following years; and in 1854 appeared *The Life and Adventures of Joaquín Murieta*, by a Cherokee half-caste named Yellow Bird, who was also known as John Rollin Ridge. The blood-and-thunder story was so popular that the question of Murieta's true fate faded into legend.

Murphy, Audie (1924–1971), soldier and actor. Born on a farm near Kingston, Hunt County, Texas, on June 20, 1924, Murphy grew up in poverty. His father, a sharecropper, abandoned the large family during the Depression of the 1930s and his mother died shortly before he enlisted in the army in June 1942, just before his eighteenth birthday. During 30 months of combat service he rose from private to lieutenant, serving with the 7th Army in the campaigns in Tunisia, Sicily, Italy, France, and Germany. Wounded three times, he was repeatedly decorated for gallantry in action, earning the Distinguished Service Cross, the Legion of Merit, the Silver Star with Oak Leaf Cluster, the Bronze Star, and, from the French, the Croix de Guerre with palm. Toward the end of war in Europe, on January 26, 1945, Murphy single-handedly held off a German force of six tanks and some 250 men, earning the Congressional Medal of Honor (his 24th medal) for bravery. On his return to the United States he was celebrated as the most highly decorated hero of the war. Overwhelmed by newspaper and magazine publicity, he was induced to embark on a Hollywood film career. His first film, *Beyond Glory*, was released in 1948. Although he was never much of an actor, his appearances in films were well bolstered by publicity and he continued to make money, mostly in Westerns. His biggest success was *To Hell and Back*, 1955, a film version of his autobiography in which he played himself in the leading role. His films, which eventually numbered about 40, continued to appear in the 1960s but his popularity faded. He turned to business ventures (he had reportedly earned more than $2 million as an actor) but without success; hounded by creditors, he declared bankruptcy in 1968. He died in a plane crash near Roanoke, Virginia, while en route to Atlanta, Georgia, on a business trip. The wreckage of the light plane, which was reported missing on May 28, was discovered on June 1, 1971.

Murphy, Frank (1890–1949), justice of the Supreme Court. Born on April 13, 1890, in Harbor Beach, Michigan, Murphy received a law degree from the University of Michigan in 1914. After World War I, in which he served as a captain in the U.S. forces in Germany, he studied law in England and at Trinity College, Dublin, before beginning private practice in Detroit. He launched his political career as chief assistant U.S. attorney for eastern Michigan in 1919–1920; he served as judge of the recorder's court, 1923–1930, and then successfully ran for mayor. Detroit was badly hit by the Depression of the 1930s and Murphy attracted national attention for his relief efforts. He resigned in 1933 to accept President Franklin D. Roosevelt's appointment as governor-general of the Philippines; he also served as the first U.S. high commissioner, 1935–1936, to the Islands after they achieved commonwealth status. He won the governorship of Michigan in the Democratic sweep of 1936 and again came into national prominence during subsequent labor disputes in the state's auto industry. His refusal to employ troops to break the sit-down strikes earned him the support of organized labor but probably cost him reelection in 1938. As U.S. attorney general in 1939 he was noted for establishing a civil-liberties unit in the criminal division of the Justice Department and, indeed, he had a record of militant defense of civil rights when he was named to the Supreme Court by President Roosevelt in January 1940. Except for brief military service as a lieutenant colonel in World War II,

he served for almost a decade on the bench, continuing to exert himself on behalf of civil rights; almost invariably he was to be found on the side of racial and religious minorities. He upheld the separation of church and state against attempts by the Roman Catholic church to bridge the separation in matters of education, despite the fact that he himself was a Catholic. His most memorable dissent was in the case of *Korematsu* v. *U.S.*, 1944, in which he denounced the decision to intern the Japanese-Americans of the West Coast in guarded camps after the outbreak of World War II. The internees received sizable reparations for their treatment in a vindication of Murphy by the Supreme Court, 20 years after his death. He also strongly defended the rights of labor, notably in *Thornhill* v. *Alabama*, 1940, a case in which he wrote the majority opinion extending constitutional protection, under the First Amendment, to picketing. He died in Detroit, on July 19, 1949.

Murphy, Michael Charles (1861–1913), athletic trainer and coach. Born on February 28, 1861, in Westborough, Massachusetts, Murphy devoted much of his early life to sports at a time when they were just beginning to be accepted as a regular extracurricular activity in schools. As much a student of athletic technique as a participant, he achieved marked success as a sprinter before opening an athletic training camp near Westborough in the 1880s. His success in preparing athletes for competition brought him an offer of employment at Yale. He served as trainer there from 1887 to 1889, spent three years with the Detroit Athletic Club, then went back to Yale as track coach and football trainer from 1892 to 1896. From 1896 to 1900 he coached at the University of Pennsylvania, but he returned to Yale for a final stint, which lasted from 1900 to 1905. From 1905 until his death he again coached at Pennsylvania, where his track and field teams enjoyed an enviable record. His success at Yale had been no less remarkable. He was responsible for a number of innovations in technique in several sports, most notably the crouching start in sprint races. Noted for his ability to inspire confidence and for his skill in keying up his athletes to compete, he became a logical choice for coach of the U.S. Olympic team in 1908. The games, held in London, were dominated by the United States. He coached the U.S. Olympic team again for the 1912 games at Stockholm, where U.S. athletes won many medals despite the disqualification of their greatest competitor, Jim Thorpe. The VI Olympiad, scheduled for Berlin in 1916, for which Murphy was again selected as U.S. coach, was prevented by World War I. Murphy died in Philadelphia on June 4, 1913.

Murphy, William Parry (1892–   ), physician. Born in Stoughton, Wisconsin, on February 6, 1892, Murphy earned a B.A. from the University of Oregon in 1914 and then taught high-school physics and mathematics until 1916. His studies at Harvard Medical School were interrupted by World War I, during which he served in the army medical corps. After obtaining his M.D. degree in 1920 he interned at Rhode Island Hospital in Providence, then began private practice in Brookline, Massachusetts, in 1923. At the same time he entered upon a lifelong association with Peter Bent Brigham Hospital in Boston, first as an associate in medicine and later as a consultant in hematology. Shortly after his appointment at the hospital, he began experimenting on the effects of insulin on a colleague, Dr. George R. Minot. Also a Harvard graduate and newly appointed to the hospital staff, Minot had recently developed diabetes and was among the first patients in Boston to receive insulin. In addition to their work with insulin, Murphy and Minot, by systematically employing a liver diet, achieved the first successful treatment of pernicious anemia in 1926. This followed earlier experiments of George H. Whipple, who had fed raw beef liver to dogs with experimentally induced anemia, and in 1934 all three shared the Nobel Prize for Physiology and Medicine for their work. Murphy was soon made an associate in medicine at Harvard Medical School, where he had been an instructor since 1923. In 1948 he was appointed lecturer in medicine and ten years later he retired. He published numerous research papers, notably on leukemia, and a textbook, *Anemia in Practice: Pernicious Anemia,* 1939. In 1965 he received the Distinguished Achievement Award of the City of Boston.

Murray, John Courtney (1904–1967), theologian. Born in New York City on September 12, 1904, Murray entered the Society of Jesus (the Jesuits) in 1920 at the age of fifteen, after graduating from St. Francis Xavier High School. He attended Boston College, where he took his B.A. in 1926 and his M.A. in 1927, interrupting his schooling to teach in the Philippines for three years. He continued his studies at Woodstock College, Maryland, being ordained a priest a year before receiving the S.T.L. degree in 1934, and at the Gregorian University in Rome, where he completed a doctorate in theology in 1937. Murray immediately began to teach at Woodstock, where he was professor of theology for 20 years. In 1941 he became editor of *Theological Studies,* published at Woodstock, in whose pages he began to explore the problems of religious pluralism that soon were to bring him widespread attention outside Roman Catholic circles. A frequent contributor to lay journals, he also appeared as a lecturer at several universities. He was visiting professor at Yale, 1951–1952, and was active in the discussions held at the Center for the Study of Democratic Institutions in Santa Barbara, California, during the 1950s. His celebrated book *We Hold These Truths,* 1960, presented a forceful argument for religious liberty and established him as one of the leading Roman Catholic ecumenicists. A firm believer in the power of dialogue in social discourse, he came increasingly

under attack by more conservative elements in his church for his liberal views, and he eventually had to bear an order of silence imposed by his religious superiors. His views were vindicated, however, at the Second Vatican Council (Vatican II), 1962–1965, in which he played a prominent part, notably as the principal architect of the council's Declaration on Religious Liberty. During his last years he was director of the John La Farge Institute, where he was active in promoting dialogue between blacks and whites, Roman Catholics and Protestants, Marxists and Christians. His *The Problem of God* appeared in 1964, but he never wrote a book on the theology of the Trinity, a subject on which he had long been recognized as an expert. He died in New York City on August 16, 1967.

Murray, Lindley (1745–1826), grammarian. Born at Sevatra Creek (subsequently part of Dauphin County), Pennsylvania, on June 7, 1745, Murray attended a school in Burlington, New Jersey, after leaving home because of differences with his father. He eventually studied law and prospered first as a lawyer and later (1779–1783) as a merchant in New York City. Wealthy but in poor health, he left permanently for England in 1784. He settled at Holgate, near York, where for more than 40 years he occupied his time with gardening and producing the English grammars for which he became famous. Murray wrote at a time of growing interest in correct English usage. He clung tenaciously to the convictions that Latin was a superior language to English, or to any other "modern" language, and that somehow Latin grammar embodied universally valid canons of logic and thus of usage. His *English Grammar,* 1795, which maintained this view, became immensely popular despite its many errors. In its complete and abridged forms it appeared in at least 16 editions before 1801; the 62nd edition of the full work came out in London in 1864, and the 133rd edition of the abridged version in the same year. In all, upwards of 2 million copies were sold. *English Exercises* and a separate *Key* to them appeared in 1797. He followed these with an *English Reader,* 1800, and *An English Spelling Book,* 1804, long favorite textbooks in both Great Britain and New England. His books were dominant in their field for a generation after his death. A pious Quaker and for many years a minister, he also wrote religious tracts, of which *The Power of Religion on the Mind in Retirement, Sickness, and Death,* 1787, was the most celebrated. Often known as the "father of English grammar," Murray died at York, England, after many years of illness, on January 16, 1826.

Murray, Philip (1886–1952), labor leader. Born on May 25, 1886, in Blantyre, Lanarkshire, Scotland, Murray received only elementary schooling before entering the coal mines at the age of ten. In 1902 he emigrated with his father to the United States, settling in Pittsburgh and finding employment again as a coal miner. He became a citizen in

1911. He joined the United Mine Workers of America (UMW) and soon was elected president of his local. By the age of twenty-six he was on the international executive board of the UMW and at thirty-four was vice-president, a post he held until 1942. When his superior, John L. Lewis, helped form the Committee for Industrial Organization (CIO) in 1935 to promote the growth of mass industrial unions, Murray was charged with the important and difficult task of organizing the steel industry. As head of the Steel Workers' Organizing Committee from 1936 he successfully directed the campaigns against both the Big Steel and Little Steel companies and became president of the United Steel Workers of America (USWA). In 1938 he was elected vice-president of the independent Congress of Industrial Organizations (CIO), successor to the earlier committee, and two years later became president, succeeding John L. Lewis, a position he held, along with his USWA post, until his death. He broke with his old ally, Lewis, however; Murray supported Franklin D. Roosevelt's reelection in 1940, while Lewis favored Republican Wendell Willkie, and as a result Lewis took the UMW out of the CIO. During both World War II and the Korean War Murray exercised his leadership to elicit full labor support for the nation's wartime economic policies, but in peacetime he fought hard and successfully for an increased standard of living, for pensions and other benefits, and for fair treatment for the workers to whom he was responsible; he also led the campaign to expel from the CIO Communist-dominated unions. He died suddenly in San Francisco on November 9, 1952.

Murrell, John A. (1804?–1850?), outlaw. According to his own statement, as recorded by his captor, Virgil A. Stewart, in 1834, Murrell (or Murrel, or Murel) was born in Tennessee in 1804, but there is doubt about the place, the date, and indeed, about all the facts of his life. He came to public notice in 1823 when he was fined in a court in Williamson County, Tennessee, for "riot;" he appeared before the same court in 1825 for "gaming" and was sent to prison for a year in 1826 after a conviction for horse stealing. Upon his release he began to organize a gang of thieves, fences, and murderers that reputedly swelled to a total of more than 1000 members and that operated in the South and Southwest for the next decade. Initially the gang specialized in highway robberies, being able to dispose of the spoils quickly through organizational channels, but soon Murrell realized that greater profits were to be made in Negro-stealing, and he made that into a fine art. He would convince a dissatisfied Negro slave, on the promise of freedom and a trip north via the Underground Railroad, to run away from his master, and would then sell him to another slave owner several counties away. This could be repeated several times before the slave would become too "hot" to sell, at which point he was murdered and his body disposed of. In 1834 Stewart managed to gain Murrell's confidence by, among other things, swearing allegiance to the gang. He then, in July of the same year, brought Murrell to trial in Jackson, Tennessee. Found guilty of Negro-stealing, Murrell was sentenced to ten years in prison, a fate that proved fortunate for him; for in the summer of 1835, after Stewart had testified that Murrell had been trying to instigate a slave rebellion, more than 20 members of the gang were lynched while Murrell was safe in his prison cell. He was released from the Nashville penitentiary in April 1844 and died a few years later of tuberculosis in Pikeville, Tennessee.

Murrietta, Joaquín, see Murieta, Joaquín

Murrow, Edward Roscoe (1908–1965), journalist. Born on April 25, 1908, in Greensboro, North Carolina, Murrow moved to Blanchard, near Bellingham, Washington, when he was four years old. He was a compassman and topographer for timber cruisers in Washington for two years before entering college. In his sophomore year he changed his first name from Egbert to Edward. He attended Stanford University and the University of Washington and graduated from Washington State College in 1930, after which he traveled for two years to American and European colleges arranging for debates and travel as president of the National Student Federation. From 1932 to 1935 he was assistant director of the Institute of International Education. In 1935 he began working for the Columbia Broadcasting System (CBS) as director of talks and education. Summoned to London in 1937, he became director of the CBS European bureau, hiring William L. Shirer to aid him in reporting events on the Continent as war approached. During World War II he hired and trained a corps of war correspondents which included Eric Sevareid, Charles Collingwood, Howard K. Smith, and Richard C. Hottelet. His own broadcasts, beginning "This. . . . is London," which were also later made from North Africa and the Continent, familiarized millions of Americans with his terse, authoritative, and highly descriptive reportorial style. In 1941 selections from his London broadcasts were published as *So This Is London.* In 1946, returning to the United States, he became a CBS vice-president and director of pubic affairs. He resigned in 1947 to return to radio news broadcasting, and from 1950 to 1951 narrated and produced the "Hear It Now" series, presenting weekly news summaries through recordings made at the scenes of events. The series provided the format for the 1951–1958 television series, "See It Now," re-creations of events which he narrated and coproduced. The series was distinguished principally by Murrow's own incisive analyses of current affairs, and he achieved particular renown for his strong stand against the activities of Sen. Joseph R. McCarthy. From 1958 to 1960 he moderated and produced "Small World" telecast discussions among world figures who spoke from various points on the globe. The informal "Person to Person," which he began in 1953, a series of interviews in the subjects' home settings, became his most popular program. In 1961 he was appointed by President John F. Kennedy to head the U.S. Information Agency (USIA), remaining in the post through 1964. He died on April 27, 1965, in Pawling, New York.

Musial, Stanley Frank (1920–   ), baseball player. Born on November 21, 1920, in Donora, Pennsylvania, Stan Musial excelled at basketball as well as baseball during high school. He chose baseball as a career instead of accepting an athletic scholarship to the University of Pittsburgh after graduation in 1938, signing a contract with the organization of the St. Louis Cardinals of the National League, the team with which he was associated thereafter. He began his career as a pitcher in the Mountain State League, but made a successful transition to the outfield after a shoulder injury. He was called up from the minor leagues at the end of the 1941 season and made an impressive debut, hitting .426 in 12 games. The years 1942–1944 were banner ones for St. Louis, which won three straight National League pennants and, in 1942 and 1944, the World Series as well. Musial made a great contribution to this effort, posting batting averages of .315, .357, and .347. His batting average in 1943 led the league, a feat he repeated six times, in 1946, 1948, 1950–1952, and 1957. He was also chosen the National League's most valuable player in 1943, earning that honor again in 1946 and a record third time in 1948. He missed the 1945 season while serving in the navy, but came back stronger than ever. His best year at the plate was 1948, when he hit .376, led the league in most other batting statistics, and smashed 39 home runs. "Stan the Man," batting left handed and alternating at two positions (first base and left field), had a lifetime batting average of .331 in 22 seasons; he had established numerous records by the time he retired from active play after the 1963 season. His career total of 3630 hits was a league mark and for both leagues stood second only to Ty Cobb's record; he was third behind Cobb and Babe Ruth in total runs with 1949. He held a major league record for total bases (6134), and league records for consecutive games played (895) and years batting in more than 100 runs (10). He hit a career total of 475 home runs. Perennially on the All-Star team after 1943, Musial was elected to the National Baseball Hall of Fame in 1969. From 1963 he was a vice-president of the St. Louis Cardinals.

Muybridge, Eadweard (1830–1904), photographer. Born at Kingston upon Thames, England, on April 9, 1830, Edward James Muggeridge changed his name shortly before he came to the United States in his early twenties. Soon established as a photographer he accepted a commission from the U.S. Coast and Geodetic Survey to direct photo-graphic surveys of the Pacific Coast. His views of the Yosemite region and of Alaska, which were widely exhibited in the late 1860s, brought him to the attention of Leland Stanford, former governor of California and a sportsman who wished to investigate the gaits of horses. In 1872 Muybridge, along with John Isaacs, a railroad engineer on the Central Pacific (which was owned by Stanford), used a series of single cameras which took pictures in sequence as a moving horse broke threads attached to their shutters. Having established that a horse during part of his stride was completely off the ground (the query that had led to the project), Muybridge became interested in continuing to work with this technique with other animals and with human athletes. The project was interrupted in 1874 when he was accused and tried for the murder of his wife's lover. Acquitted, he left for Central America on a photographic expedition financed by Stanford. In 1877 he returned to Stanford's stud farm in Palo Alto, California, and continued his work on rapid sequence photography. Making improvements in the shutter mechanisms and employing photographic materials of increased speed, he achieved exposures of up to 1/2000 of a second, thus making possible the first photographs of objects in rapid motion. By 1878 he had devised a means of projecting transparencies cinematically. His zoopraxiscope, a refinement of earlier projectors, showed an object moving in a single spot while the scenery ran past (owing, of course, to his still primitive use of multiple cameras). He now began to publish his work: *Panoramic San Francisco* and *The Pacific Coast of Central America* appeared in 1877. His *The Attitudes of Animals*, 1881, and *The Horse in Motion*, 1881–1882, attracted international attention. Jean Meissonier, a French painter engaged in a controversy over the positions of horses in his pictures, used Muybridge's photographs and the zoopraxiscope to silence his opponents. In 1881, Étienne Marey, a physiologist interested in animal motion (and the developer, in 1882, of the "photographic gun," a camera equipped with a magazine of plates that could be exposed to rapid succession), invited Muybridge to Europe, where he lectured and demonstrated to enthusiastic audiences. He returned to lecture in the United States in 1883. Supplied with funds by the University of Pennsylvania, he produced a vast atlas of consecutive-series photographs of humans, animals, and birds. He exposed 100,000 plates, some at shutter speeds of 1/6000 second, of which approximately one-fifth comprised his major work, *Animal Locomotion*, 1887. The years after 1887 were spent principally in England, although he continued to lecture in Europe and he mounted an exhibit at the World's Columbian Exposition in Chicago in 1893. He died at Kingston upon Thames, England, on May 8, 1904.

N

Nabokov, Vladimir Vladimirovich (1899–1977),
author. Born in St. Petersburg, Russia (now Leningrad), on April 23, 1899, into a family belonging to the Russian nobility, Nabokov attended Prince Tenishev Gymnasium in St. Petersburg. He left Russia with his family in 1919 and entered Cambridge University, earning his B.A. from Trinity College in 1922. For the next 18 years he lived in Germany and France. His poetry, plays, short stories, and novels of the period, written in Russian under the pseudonym V. Sirin and translated into many languages, established him as the major post-1917 Russian-émigré writer. Among his early novels, later translated into English, were *The Defense*, 1930 (English, 1964); *Kamera Obskura*, 1932 (published in the United States in an altered version as *Laughter in the Dark*, 1938); *Despair*, 1934 (1966); *Invitation to a Beheading*, 1935 (1959); and *The Gift*, 1937 (1963), which introduced parody as a major device in his work. In 1940 he came to the United States and taught literature for a year at Stanford University. He was naturalized in 1945. From 1941 to 1948 he taught at Wellesley College and from 1948 to 1959 was professor of Russian literature at Cornell University. After 1959 he devoted himself to writing. His works written in English included the novels *The Real Life of Sebastian Knight*, 1941, and *Bend Sinister*, 1947; *Nikolai Gogol*, 1944, an important critical work; *Nine Stories*, 1947; *Conclusive Evidence: A Memoir*, 1950, an account of his life in prerevolutionary Russia; *Pnin*, 1957, a short satirical work; *Nabokov's Dozen*, 1958, a collection of 13 stories; *Poems*, 1959; *Speak, Memory!*, 1967, an autobiographical work; *Ada*, 1969; *Glory: A Novel*, 1971; *Transparent Things*, 1972; *A Russian Beauty*, 1973, stories; *Look at the Harlequins*, 1974, a novel; and the short story collections *Tyrants Destroyed*, 1975, and *Details of a Sunset*, 1976. With the controversial, best-selling *Lolita*, 1955, he gained a popular audience and some notoriety. A satirical tale reversing the cliché contrast of European worldliness and American innocence, the book told of the love of a middle-aged European man for a passionate twelve-year-old American nymphet; the plot was tempered for a popular 1962 motion-picture version. His major English work was considered to be *Pale Fire*, 1962, which displayed the heights of his verbal skill and intricate structural effects. He published English translations of the works of Aleksander Pushkin and Mikhail Lermontov and also contributed essays and short stories to such magazines as the *New Yorker*, *Atlantic Monthly*, *Harper's*, and *Esquire*. Also a noted lepidopterist, he was a research fellow in entomology from 1942 to 1948 at Harvard's Museum of Comparative Zoology and published in its journal, "Nearctic Members of the Genus *Lycaeides* Hübner," 1949. He died on July 2, 1977, in Montreux, Switzerland, at the resort hotel he had lived in since 1966.

Nader, Ralph (1934–   ), reformer. Born on February 27, 1934, in Winsted, Connecticut, the son of Lebanese immigrants, Nader was educated at Princeton's Woodrow Wilson School of Public and International Affairs, graduating magna cum laude in 1955, and at the Harvard Law School, from which he graduated with distinction three years later. While at Harvard he edited the *Harvard Law Record* and also became interested in the problem of automobile safety; his first article on the subject, "American Cars: Designed for Death," was published in the *Record* during his senior year. He settled in Hartford, Connecticut, and opened a law office, but most of his time was spent studying auto accident cases, writing magazine articles, and testifying before local government committees. By 1964 he had become convinced that he could not win his fight if he continued to work at the local level; he therefore prevailed upon a friend, Assistant Secretary of Labor Daniel P. Moynihan, to engage him as a consultant and began to work on a study that called upon the federal government to take responsibility for auto safety. He also worked closely at that time with Senator Abraham A. Ribicoff of Connecticut. Nader left the Labor Department in 1965 to devote himself to finishing his book, *Unsafe at Any Speed: The Designed-in Dangers of the American Automobile*, which was published later in the year and became a highly controversial best seller. The book was especially critical of General Motors' Corvair, which Nader criticized further in testimony before a Senate subcommittee under Ribicoff's chairmanship in February 1966. Federal legislation might have passed Congress that year in any event, but in March 1966 Nader announced publicly that for at least a month he had been the subject of a harassing investigation by the auto industry. Denials were immediately forthcoming, but a few days later General Motors' president, James M. Roche, admitted that his company had "investigated" Nader, that there had been "some harassment," and that the inquiry had been "most unworthy of American business." Nader later sued General Motors for invasion of privacy, claiming $26 million in damages. The suit was settled out of court. The National Traffic and Motor Vehicle Safety Act was passed by the Senate on June 24, 1966, and by the House six weeks later, but within less than a year Nader was charging that it was not being enforced owing to "intimidation" by the auto industry. He continued his campaign, at first virtually a one-man operation, in behalf of the American public and against the industrial giants of the country; later he was joined by a group of young lawyers and consumer advocates, many of whom worked for no pay, and who were collectively known as "Nader's Raiders." The Corvair was withdrawn from production in 1969, after sales had fallen by 93 percent, and Nader was also given credit for the passage of federal laws regulating gas pipelines, radiation dangers, food packaging, coal-mine safety, and the use of cyclamates in diet foods and of DDT in the control of insect pests. The consumer revolution that he had initiated in the United States in the 1960s spread gradually to other countries as well, and "consumerism" became a potent political, as well as economic, factor in public affairs.

Nagurski, Bronco (1908–   ), football player. Born in the Rainy River district of Ontario on November 3, 1908, Bronislaw Nagurski was brought up in International Falls, Minnesota. He played every position for his high-school football team, but coaches paid little attention to high-school fooball in those days and he arrived completely unheralded at the University of Minnesota in 1926. On the first day of practice he caught the attention of the freshman coach by knocking the tackling dummy from its moorings, and he was soon the star of the freshman team, playing tackle on both defense and offense. He starred for Minnesota for three years on the varsity, playing tackle almost exclusively the first two years and in his senior year playing tackle on defense and fullback on offense. In his senior year he was named to every All-American team; one newspaper chose only ten All-American players that year—1930—naming Nagurski both as tackle and fullback. Grantland Rice declared at that time that he thought Nagurski was probably the finest player the college game had ever seen, an opinion that Rice did not have to change when Nagurski joined the Chicago Bears that year and turned the team overnight from an also-ran to a contender. Again he played both tackle and fullback; in the latter position he not only ran with the ball but also passed it, often to his teammate Red Grange. As a runner he was unparalleled and was said to have been the only man in the history of the National Football League who could run his own interference. He starred for the Bears until 1937, when he retired owing to arthritis, having gained more than 4000 yards running in the 872 times he carried the ball as a professional fullback. Since 1933 he had also been wrestling, and his arthritis apparently did not affect him in the ring as it did on the field. He won more than 300 professional wrestling matches. He came out of retirement in 1943 to play one more year of football with the Bears, performing with his old strength and skill. He refused to play fullback until the last game, saying he was

rusty and at thirty-five too old to run with the ball. But in that last game, which the Bears needed to win for the conference championship, he agreed to take the ball during the last quarter, and his running set up the points that won the game. Probably the strongest man ever to play the game, he was small compared to many later players; he was a little over six feet tall and never weighed more than about 235 pounds. After 1943 he retired permanently to farming and business interests in International Falls.

Naismith, James (1861–1939), originator of basketball. Born in Almonte, Ontario, on November 6, 1861, Naismith graduated from McGill University in 1887 and spent the next three years at Presbyterian College in Montreal while at the same time serving as director of physical education at McGill. After graduating from Presbyterian in 1890 he enrolled at the Young Men's Christian Association (YMCA) Training School in Springfield, Massachusetts, for its recently established course in physical education. During his first winter his class was assigned by the school's director, Luther H. Gulick, the task of inventing a game that would hold the attention of students in the winter months—between the football and baseball seasons. Early in 1891 Naismith tacked up two peach baskets at either end of the running track in the gymnasium and made up a set of simple rules for "basketball." His fellow students and Gulick liked the game, and in fact its rules never changed a great deal from the ones that Naismith laid down that winter. He devised other games during his later career as a member of the physical-education department of the University of Kansas from 1898 to 1937 (he had obtained an M.D. degree from the University of Colorado in 1898), but none of them took hold as basketball had, and Naismith was virtually forgotten as the inventor of perhaps the only major modern game that owes its origin to a single man. In 1936, however, when basketball was introduced as an Olympic sport, Naismith was sent to the games in Berlin with funds raised by the National Association of Basketball Coaches to witness the occasion. He wrote a number of articles on physical education and two books, *The Basis of Clean Living*, 1918, and *Basketball, Its Origin and Development*, 1941. He died in Lawrence, Kansas, on November 28, 1939.

Namath, Joseph William (1943–   ), football player. Born in Beaver Falls, Pennsylvania, on May 31, 1943, Joe Namath was a natural athlete from childhood. He starred in football, basketball, and baseball while in high school and upon graduation received numerous scholarship offers from colleges around the country, as well as offers from six major-league baseball teams. He chose the University of Alabama and helped to make its football team one of the nation's dominant aggregations throughout his varsity career, from 1962 to 1965. Despite the fact that he suffered a serious injury to his knee during his senior year, he was the player most sought after by professional teams that year and signed a contract for a bonus of several hundred thousand dollars with the New York Jets of the budding American Football League (AFL) the day after the Orange Bowl game, in which he had starred. David "Sonny" Werblin, owner of the Jets, previously one of the country's leading show-business managers, knew that all his team needed was a real star, and Namath filled that description. As one result, the National (NFL) and American football leagues merged in 1967 to avoid further suicidal bidding conflicts for star college players. Namath performed up to expectations, turning the Jets from a mediocre team into an exciting and successful enterprise. His greatest moment came in the 1969 Super Bowl game in Miami. The NFL had won the previous two interleague games easily, and now the Jets had to face the great Baltimore Colts. In that game, Namath completed 17 of 28 passes, read the Colt defenses superbly, and led his team to a stunning 16–7 upset victory. In later years Namath repeatedly suffered further knee injuries and never reached the same heights again, although he remained perhaps the greatest drawing card in football. Often in trouble with various football authorities, while in college and with the Jets, because of his easygoing attitudes toward training, he was nevertheless—as "Broadway Joe"—one of the toasts of New York.

Nasby, Petroleum Vesuvius, see Locke, David Ross

Nash, Ogden (1902–1971), poet. Born on August 19, 1902, in Rye, New York, to a family which had given its name to Nashville, Tennessee, Nash grew up in various cities along the East Coast, from Georgia to New England. He attended Harvard during 1920–1921, and taught at St. George's School in Newport, Rhode Island, where he had formerly been a student, but left after one year because of harassment by his fourteen-year-old pupils. During the late 1920s he worked in New York City as a bond salesman, an advertising copywriter, and a manuscript reader and began contributing his verse—a unique and eccentric meeting of words and rhyme—to numerous magazines, including the New Yorker, whose editorial staff he joined. He published numerous books of his verse reflections on little boys, women's hats, salads, parsley, diets, bankers, debt, animals, literature, and other such phenomena. They included Hard Lines, 1931; Bad Parents' Garden of Verse, 1936; The Face Is Familiar, 1941; Musical Zoo, 1947; Versus, 1949; Parents Keep Out, 1951; and You Can't Get There From Here, 1957. Nash's verse was unmistakable and inimitable; his outrageous rhymes and manic scansions gave rise to such poems as his classic "Reflections on Ice-Breaking;" "Candy Is / dandy / But liquor / Is quicker." He wrote librettos in 1943 for the Broadway musical One Touch of Venus, with S. J. Perelman, and in 1958 for the television special "Art Carney Meets Peter and the Wolf."

He appeared occasionally on radio and television and gave lectures and poetry readings throughout the country. Nash died in Baltimore on May 19, 1971.

Nast, Thomas (1840–1902), cartoonist and illustrator. Born in Landau, Germany on September 27, 1840, Nast came to the United States with his mother in 1846. An early love of drawing led him to study art at the National Academy of Design in his adopted home, New York City. At fifteen he was hired as a draftsman for Frank Leslie's Illustrated Newspaper; in 1859 his work first appeared in Harper's Weekly. He joined the newly established New York Illustrated News the same year, covering the funeral of John Brown and, in England, covering the first international heavyweight boxing title match between the British and American champions. He went from England to Italy to cover Garibaldi's revolt in 1860. In 1862 he became a regular staff artist for Harper's Weekly, a position he held until 1886. His work during the Civil War earned him the great influence he was to retain for the remainder of his career; his support of a vigorous prosecution of the war was acknowledged even by President Abraham Lincoln, who called him "our best recruiting sergeant." His most famous work was done in his campaign against New York City's Tammany Hall "Tweed Ring" in 1869–1872; his efforts were triumphantly climaxed when one of his caricatures led to the arrest in Spain of William Marcy ("Boss") Tweed. The Democratic party's donkey symbol and the Republican elephant were both invented by Nast and were firmly established by 1874; he also invented the Tammany tiger and contributed much to the development of the common American image of Santa Claus. Nast's technical contribution to the craft of political cartooning consisted mainly in his simplification of both the illustrative technique and the caption, thus making the effect more immediate and forceful. Beset by financial difficulties, he did little work of note after leaving Harper's Weekly. In 1902 he was appointed consul general at Guayaquil, Ecuador, by President Theodore Roosevelt. He died there on December 7, 1902.

Nathan, George Jean (1882–1958), editor and drama critic. Born in Fort Wayne, Indiana, on February 14, 1882, Nathan grew up in Cleveland, to which his family had moved when he was four. He graduated from Cornell University in 1904 and, after a year of additional study at the University of Bologna, Italy, became a reporter for the New York Herald. In 1906 he became associate editor and drama critic for the Outing and Bohemian magazines and began a half-century as the nation's most influential observer of the theater. From 1914 to 1923 he was, with H. L. Mencken, coeditor of Smart Set, and in 1924 the two—the "critical Katzenjammer Kids"—founded the American Mercury. By 1925 Nathan was one of the most widely read as well as the highest-paid drama critic in the world. He severed his connection with the *Mercury* about 1930 and two years later joined Theodore Dreiser, Eugene O'Neill, Sherwood Anderson, and others in founding the *American Spectator*, which, like *Smart Set* and the *Mercury* before it, was a magazine of literature and the arts, much given to a satirical view of American life and culture. Such was Nathan's influence that in 1932 he was threatened with investigation by a congressional subcommittee on the ludicrous grounds that criticism such as his had destroyed native theater; in a more realistic view, he was acknowledged by the end of his career to have done more than any other person to elevate the standards of the stage and of audiences in the United States. During his career he was associated with more than 30 periodicals. He published more than a score of books of criticism, including an annual *Theatre Book of the Year* from 1943 to 1951, and such volumes as *The Eternal Mystery*, 1913; *The Popular Theatre*, 1918; *The Theatre, The Drama, The Girls*, 1921; *Materia Critica*, 1924; *Art of the Night*, 1928; *Testament of a Critic*, 1931; *The Bachelor Life*, 1941; and *The Entertainment of a Nation*, 1942. He was critic for the *New York Journal–American* when illness forced his retirement in 1956. He died in New York City on April 8, 1958.

Nation, Carry Amelia Moore (1846–1911), social reformer. Born on November 25, 1846, in Garrard County, Kentucky, Carry Moore attended school sporadically as her family moved back and forth between Kentucky, Missouri, and Texas. She secured a teaching certificate from the Missouri State Normal School and taught school for a brief period. Her mother suffered from delusions; her father, a prosperous land owner before the Civil War, was ruined by the war and moved to Belton, Missouri. There Carry met her first husband, Dr. Charles Gloyd, an alcoholic who resisted her efforts at reform and died, leaving her with a hatred for liquor and saloons. Her second husband, David Nation, a lawyer and minister, divorced her for desertion in 1901. By that time she had become deeply involved with her own branch of the temperance movement, proclaiming that any property connected with liquor as well as liquor itself was doomed to destruction. Since 1880 Kansas had been a "dry" state, but prohibition was openly flouted. In 1890 antiprohibitionists began to agitate for repeal of the law. Carry Nation conceived the theory that since establishments selling liquor were in violation of the law, they were outside the law's protection as well. Thus she began in the 1890s a series of hatchet-swinging "missions" through saloons in towns and cities in Kansas and later moved on to large cities across the country. Alone or with a few hymn-singing supporters, she invaded "joints," castigated the "rummies" present, and concluded with a highly destructive "hatchetation" of the property. Frequently arrested for disturbing the peace, she paid her fines by selling souvenir hatchets. She published newsletters called the *Smasher's Mail*, the

Hatchet, and the *Home Defender*, and an autobiography in 1904. She was for a time much in demand as a temperance lecturer and she appeared in her customary deaconess's garb, holding a hatchet. Poor health finally forced her to retire to the Ozark Mountains in Arkansas. She died after a period of hospitalization in Leavenworth, Kansas, on June 9, 1911. Despite her spectacular campaign, the later enactment of national prohibition was largely the result of the efforts of more sedate reformers, who had been reluctant to support her.

Neal, John (1793–1876), author. Born in Falmouth (now Portland), Maine, on August 25, 1793, Neal was orphaned by the death of his father when he was one month old. He grew up in and around Portland but found himself stranded in Baltimore in 1815 after a business venture failed. He thereupon threw himself into writing, during the next eight years composing two narrative poems, a tragedy in verse, and five novels, *Keep Cool*, 1817; *Logan, a Family History*, 1822, a romanticization of the story of the Indian chieftain; *Errata, or the Works of Will Adams*, two volumes, 1823; *Seventy-Six*, 1823, a historical romance; and *Randolph*, also 1823. In addition, during this period he studied history, literature, languages, and the law and edited several periodicals. When he went to England in December 1823 he was probably the closest rival to James Fenimore Cooper among American fiction writers. He remained in England, supporting himself mainly by writing for periodicals, until 1827. A notable incident of his stay in England was his publication of an anonymous review of American writers in *Blackwood's* magazine, in the course of which he devoted ten pages to Washington Irving, eight to himself—and half a page to Cooper. He praised himself highly though offering sensible criticism of his own faults. He returned to New York City in 1827 but shortly afterward settled in Portland, intending to practice law; he made astute investments in Maine granite quarries and soon had a comfortable fortune. He continued to write, producing in the next few years half a dozen more novels and many stories and articles, and he edited several periodicals for short periods. In the 1860s he wrote three dime novels and a children's book, *Great Mysteries and Little Plagues*, 1870. His autobiography, *Wandering Recollections of a Somewhat Busy Life*, appeared in 1869, having been three times rewritten. He died in Portland, Maine, on June 20, 1876.

Neihardt, John Gneisenau (1881–1973), author and poet. Born on January 8, 1881, near Sharpsburg, in Christian County, Illinois, Neihardt grew up there, in Kansas City, in northwestern Kansas, and in Wayne, Nebraska, where he attended Nebraska Normal (now Wayne State) College and graduated in 1897. For several years thereafter he worked at various jobs, from farmhand to newspaper reporter, and continued to read widely on his own, particularly the Greek poets and dramatists. He had begun to write verse at the age of twelve and in 1900 he published his first book, *The Divine Enchantment*. Between 1901 and 1907 he lived and worked among the Omaha Indians of Nebraska, penetrating deeply, as few white men had ever done, into their language, customs, religion, and philosophy; he later extended his studies to the Oglala Sioux as well. After a collection of short stories, *The Lonesome Trail*, was published in 1907, several volumes of verse appeared, including *A Bundle of Myrrh*, 1908; *Man Song*, 1909; *The River and I*, 1910; and *The Stranger at the Gate*, 1912. In 1915 he published the first part of a projected epic of the early Western pioneers and their conflicts with the Indians, *The Song of Hugh Glass*; a second book, *The Song of Three Friends*, appeared four years later and won a prize from the Poetry Society of America. In 1921 Neihardt was named poet laureate of Nebraska by special act of the state legislature. He served as literary critic for the *Minneapolis Journal* from 1912 until 1923, when he was appointed professor of poetry at the University of Nebraska, and he was literary editor of the *St. Louis Post–Dispatch* from 1926 to 1938. During 1944–1948 he served in various capacities with the Office of Indian Affairs and in 1948 became poet in residence and lecturer in English at the University of Missouri, where he remained until his retirement in 1966. *The Song of the Indian Wars*, 1925, continued his Western epic, and following publication of *The Song of the Messiah*, 1935, Neihardt was honored by the National Poetry Center as the foremost poet of the nation; with *The Song of Jed Smith*, 1941, the epic was completed and the five "Songs" were collected and published as *A Cycle of the West*, 1949. Others of his works included *The Splendid Wayfaring*, 1920; *Two Mothers*, 1921; *Collected Poems*, 1926; *Poetic Values*, 1926; *Black Elk Speaks*, 1932, his most widely read book; *When the Tree Flowered*, 1951; *Eagle Voice*, 1953; *Lyric and Dramatic Poems*, 1965; and the autobiographical *All Is But a Beginning*, 1972. He died in Columbia, Missouri, on November 3, 1973.

Nelson, Samuel (1792–1873), justice of the Supreme Court. Born in Hebron, in Washington County, New York, on November 10, 1792, Nelson's parents intended him to study for the ministry but, after graduating from Middlebury College in 1813, he chose to enter the practice of law. He was admitted to the bar in 1817 and opened an office in Cortland, New York, where he soon became a successful attorney. Postmaster of Cortland from 1820 to 1823, he was also, in 1821, a delegate to the New York constitutional convention, being one of those who supported the abolition of the property qualification for suffrage. He was appointed a circuit-court judge in 1823 and in 1831 was named an associate justice of the supreme court of the state of New York; he became chief justice of this court in 1837 and

remained in the post until 1845. In 1845 he was nominated by President John Tyler to the U.S. Supreme Court and was quickly confirmed by the Senate, taking his seat on March 5. During nearly 28 years on the Court—he resigned owing to poor health on November 28, 1872—he established a reputation as a capable, conservative jurist and as an expert in the fields of admiralty and maritime law, international law, and patent law. Concentrating on the technical questions raised by cases in those areas, he avoided whenever possible taking part in the disputes about constitutional matters that occupied his more famous colleagues. For example, his was the only opinion in the Dred Scott case that did not enter into discussion of political and constitutional questions; he asserted that Scott was not a citizen of Missouri and that he therefore could not sue in a federal court. Nelson thus avoided making a determination of the constitutionality of the Missouri Compromise of 1820. His essential conservatism was also manifested during the Civil War; loyal to the Union, he nevertheless urged a policy of conciliation toward the Confederacy and opposed the expansion of federal power. He was named in 1871 by President Ulysses S. Grant as a member of the Joint High Commission that met in Geneva to settle the *Alabama* claims, his technical knowledge giving him a dominant position on the commission. After his retirement from the Supreme Court he returned to his home in Cooperstown, New York, where he had maintained a close friendship with James Fenimore Cooper. He died there on December 13, 1873.

Neumann, John Nepomucene (1811–1860), religious leader. Born in Prachatice, Bohemia (now in Czechoslovakia), on March 28, 1811, Neumann was educated at the diocesan seminary at Česke Budějovice (Budweis) and the University of Prague, where, besides receiving his religious training, he learned English, as he was eager to become a missionary in the United States. Failing to be accepted by several American congregations to which he applied, he nevertheless arrived in 1836 in New York City, where he was ordained on June 25. After several years of work among the missions of New York state, he joined the Redemptorist Fathers and took full vows in the order in Baltimore on January 16, 1842. Continuing to preach and to do mission work, he was chosen vice-provincial of the order in 1847 and became pastor of a Baltimore church in 1851. He wished to remain in a subsidiary position, but when he was appointed by Archbishop Francis P. Kenrick as bishop of Philadelphia in 1852 he accepted the consecration. Among his more notable achievements were the establishment of some 100 parochial schools and a model seminary, the writing of several doctrinal aids for children in both English and German, and the founding of U.S. branches of several orders of nuns; but he was best known for the purity of his life and for his deep personal love of God. He died on January 5, 1860, in Philadelphia. Miracles were said to have occurred at his tomb, and a church commission was instituted to inquire into the question of his ultimate beatification in 1886. On December 11, 1921, he was declared venerable; he was beatified on October 13, 1963, and on June 19, 1977, he was canonized by Pope Paul VI.

Neumann, John von (1903–1957), mathematician. Born in Budapest on December 28, 1903, and christened Janos, von Neumann was a scientific prodigy, receiving simultaneously in 1926 a Ph.D. in mathematics from the University of Budapest and a degree in chemical engineering from the Federal Institute of Technology in Zurich. He was a lecturer at the University of Berlin from 1926 to 1929, when he became an assistant professor at the University of Hamburg. He was a visiting lecturer at Princeton the next year, and soon came to the United States to stay, becoming a citizen in 1937. He was named professor of mathematics at the Institute for Advanced Study when it was opened at Princeton in 1933, and he remained associated with that institution until his death. His scientific interests were extraordinarily wide and he made many contributions to mathematical and physical theory. His best-known early work was his invention of the theory of rings of operators—the so-called Von Neumann algebras —begun in the late 1920s; his *Mathematical Foundations of Quantum Mechanics*, published in German in 1926 and in an English translation in 1955; and his elaborate theory of numbers as sets, published as early as 1923. His most famous achievement, *The Theory of Games and Economic Behavior*, was written with Oskar Morgenstern and published in 1944; a revised edition appeared in 1953. He also did immensely important work in pure mathematics during his first years at Princeton—for example, on continuous groups— which showed that the branch of mathematics known as analysis had interesting and hitherto unsuspected connections with geometry and algebra, the other two classical divisions of the subject. He thus was a leading figure in the twentieth-century movement toward the unification and integration of all mathematics. In the later 1930s he began to serve as a consultant to the government and the army and navy. He was instrumental in speeding up research on aspects of physics that led to the development of the atomic bomb and from 1945 to 1954, as director of the Institute's electronic computer project, his efforts in the building of the mathematical analyzer, numerical integrator, and computer (MANIAC) speeded development of the hydrogen bomb. He was named to the Atomic Energy Commission (AEC) in 1954 and in 1956 won the AEC's Fermi Award for his work on computer development. He contracted cancer in 1956 but continued to work for the commission from his bed at Walter Reed Hospital in Washington, D.C. He died there on February 8, 1957. His *Theory of Self-reproducing Automata* appeared in 1966, edited by A. W. Burks. This astounding work was an attempt to produce a general cybernetic theory for the generation of increasingly sophisticated computers and, eventually, robots that could reproduce their kind. Von Neumann's pioneering work in cybernetics was in part a result of his earlier ground-breaking treatment of game theory, which had led also to new approaches to such diverse fields as economics and military strategy.

Neutra, Richard Josef (1892–1970), architect. Born in Vienna on April 8, 1892, Neutra made an early choice of a career in architecture. His education at the Technische Hochschule in Vienna was interrupted by World War I, but it was his presence in the Balkans in 1915 that brought him his first commission, a tea house at Trebinje in Herzegovina, Yugoslavia. On completing his studies at the University of Vienna in 1917 he spent a year at the University of Zurich. Immediately thereafter he began work as an architect in Switzerland and in 1921 collaborated on the Berliner Tageblatt building, at the time the tallest in Berlin. Prize money from a project in Haifa, Palestine (now in Israel), financed his emigration to the United States in 1923 and after working briefly in New York City he moved to Chicago. He continued his apprenticeship with an architectural firm there and formed an association with Frank Lloyd Wright before establishing his own practice in Los Angeles in 1925. His subsequent rise to prominence was rapid. Lovell Health House, one of many houses undertaken in the Los Angeles and San Francisco areas in the late 1920s and early 1930s, brought him widespread attention, and the design for his "ring-plan" school was exhibited at New York City's Museum of Modern Art in 1929, the year in which he became a U.S. citizen. Noted for his willingness to explore the use of new materials in construction, he received numerous commissions for apartments, office buildings, and schools. His growing list of prizes were followed by commissions for extended federal-government projects, which contributed to his international reputation as one of the leading architects concerned with urban planning. His work for the U.S. government in 1939–1941 included the residential centers of the National Youth Administration (NYA) and several large public housing developments projected for Texas and California. He was the architect of Channel Heights in San Pedro, California, a 160-acre development designed in 1943 and noted for its segregation of automobile traffic. After World War II he launched an extensive building program for the government of Puerto Rico and was commissioned to supervise a ten-year development plan for Guam. Other commissions included Elysian Park Heights in Los Angeles; the Museum of Natural History in Dayton, Ohio; the Mathematics Park in Princeton, New Jersey; the graduate student housing at the University of Pennsylvania; the Roberson Memorial Cultural Center in Binghamton, New York; and various projects throughout the world. He advocated, like Frank Lloyd Wright, integrating his buildings with the natural site, but Neutra characterized his own architectural approach as "biorealism," a philosophy presented in his *Mystery and Realities of the Site*, 1951. *Survival Through Design*, 1954, *Life and Human Habitat*, 1956, and *Therapy by Design*, 1965, presented his views on the influence of architecture on mental health. He died on April 16, 1970, in Wuppertal, Germany.

Nevins, Allan (1890–1971), historian and editor. Born in Camp Point, in Adams County, Illinois, on May 20, 1890, Nevins was brought up on his family's western Illinois farm and entered the University of Illinois in 1908, graduating in 1912. He remained at the university for another year to write his master's thesis, published in 1914 as a *Life of Robert Rogers*. He had been editor of the *Daily Illini* while in college, and for many years after graduation he continued to forge a distinguished career as a journalist. He went to New York City where he spent ten years on the *New York Evening Post*, serving at the same time as literary editor of the *Nation*; from 1923 to 1935 he was literary editor of the *New York Sun*; and for some years thereafter he was an editorial staff writer on the *New York World*. Meanwhile, he had edited *American Social History as Recorded by British Travelers*, 1923; written *The American States During and After the Revolution, 1775–1789*, 1924, and *The Emeregnce of Modern America, 1865–1878*, 1927; and had also served as a professor of history at Cornell during 1927–1928 and become an associate professor of history at Columbia Univesity in 1928. He was named De-Witt Clinton professor of American history at Columbia in 1931 and remained in that chair until 1958, when he became professor emeritus. At Columbia he was instrumental in establishing the unprecedented oral history project. During the eight years between 1928 and 1936 he produced three distinguished biographies, one of John Charles Frémont in 1928, one of Grover Cleveland in 1932, and one of Hamilton Fish in 1936. The latter two works won Pulitzer prizes in Biography in 1933 and 1937. The year 1935 saw the publication of a volume on Abram S. Hewitt and the year 1940, one on John D. Rockefeller. These studies of aspects of American industrial history were followed by *Study in Power*, an expanded version of the Rockefeller book, in 1953, and by a three-volume study of Henry E. Hill, between 1954 and 1963. In the late 1940s Nevins turned to Civil War history, producing the two-volume *Ordeal of the Union*, 1947, which won the Bancroft Prize; under the same general title he continued the work in subsequent volumes including *The Emergence of Lincoln*, 1950; *The War for the Union: The Improvised War, 1861–1862*, 1959; and *The War for the Union: War Becomes Revolution*, 1960. Later, from 1961 to 1966, upon appointment by President John F. Kennedy, he served as chairman of the Civil War Centennial Commission. Nevins wrote and edited many books—his total output exceeded 60—including among them *The Heritage of America*, 1939, and *America: the Story of a Free People*, 1942, both with Henry Steele Commager. From his royalties he endowed a chair of American history at Columbia with a gift of half a million dollars. After his retirement from the Columbia faculty in 1958 he was named senior research associate at the Henry E. Huntington Library in San Marino, California, where he continued his research and writing. He died in Menlo Park, California, on March 5, 1971, and in that year *The Organized War, 1863–1864* and *The Organized War to Victory, 1864–1865*, the seventh and eighth volumes of his Civil War history appeared.

Newcomb, Simon (1835–1909), astronomer and mathematician. Born on March 12, 1835, in Wallace, Nova Scotia, the son of an itinerant schoolteacher, Newcomb received little or no formal schooling. He early developed an avidity for study, however, and was particularly fascinated by mathematics. At the age of eighteen, after about two years as an apprentice to an herb doctor, he traveled to Maryland, and for several years taught in country schools while spending his spare time in Washington, D.C., studying under the occasional guidance of Joseph Henry. On Henry's recommendation he was taken into the office of the *American Ephemeris and Nautical Almanac* in Cambridge, Massachusetts, in 1857. While working as a computer for the *Nautical Almanac* he enrolled in Harvard's Lawrence Scientific School and graduated in 1858. In 1861 he was named professor of mathematics by the navy and assigned to the U.S. Naval Observatory in Washington, D.C. His work there was an extension of that done for the *Nautical Almanac*; he set about finding and correcting errors in published values for the positions and motions of various celestial objects, including a large number of reference stars, the moon, several planets, and the sun. His work on the orbits of Neptune and Uranus and on the solar parallax was particularly valuable and widely hailed. In 1877 he became superintendent of the *Nautical Almanac* office and commenced the moumental task of thoroughly revising the motion theories and position tables for all the major celestial reference objects. Assisted by George W. Hill, he carried on the vastly complex computations required to construct new tables of values that came into standard use throughout the world, and some of which yet remain in use. In 1879 he inaugurated a series, *Astronomical Papers Prepared for the Use of the American Ephemeris and Nautical Almanac*, in which the results of these researches were published. From 1874 he served as editor of the *American Journal of Mathematics*. He also found time to lecture at various colleges and in 1884 was appointed professor of mathematics and astronomy at The Johns Hopkins University, remaining there until 1894. In 1896 he attended an international conference in Paris, held largely at his instigation, at which it was decided to adopt for worldwide use a common system of astronomical constants; the system was largely his, and a similar conference in 1950 reaffirmed that decision. In 1897 he reached the compulsory retirement age for navy captains; he continued his work thereafter under grants from the Carnegie Institution of Washington. In 1899 he helped found and for the next six years was the first president of the American Astronomical Society; he was a member of the world's leading scientific societies, and to his many honors was added in 1906 promotion to the rank of rear admiral (retired). Among his books were *Popular Astronomy*, 1878; *The Stars*, 1901; *Astronomy for Everybody*, 1902; and *Compendium of Spherical Astronomy*, 1906. His autobiography, *Reminiscences of an Astronomer*, appeared in 1903. He died in Washington, D.C., on July 11, 1909. He was elected to the Hall of Fame in 1935.

Nichols, Mike (1931–   ), comedian and director. Born Michael Igor Peschowsky in Berlin on November 6, 1931, Nichols got his name when his father, a Jewish doctor who fled the Nazi regime and established a medical practice in New York City, himself took a new name. He was educated at private schools in the East and at the University of Chicago, which he left after two years of premedical work to study acting. After attending the Actors' Studio in New York City he returned to Chicago to become one of a six-member group of performers at the Compass nightclub, where he worked for three years. The group, which also included Elaine May, staged ad-lib comic playlets on themes suggested by the audience and was enormously successful. In 1957 Nichols and May struck off on their own, going to New York City, where they quickly established themselves as a popular nightclub team. Appearances on various television shows that same year and the next helped them to win a national reputation. They played to a capacity audience in New York City's Town Hall on May 1, 1959, and they opened on Broadway on October 8, 1960, in *An Evening with Mike Nichols and Elaine May*, to enthusiastic reviews. The show ran until July 1, 1961. Nichols's independent career as a stage and film director began in the early 1960s. He staged Neil Simon's *Barefoot in the Park* in 1963, winning a Tony Award, and followed it with *The Knack* and *The Odd Couple*, both 1964; *The Apple Tree*, 1965; *Luv*, 1966; *The Little Foxes*, 1967; *Plaza Suite*, 1968; and Simon's annual hit for 1971–1972, *The Prisoner of Second Avenue*. He won additional Tony awards for *The Odd Couple* and *Luv*. He was equally successful as a film director; among his most notable films were *Who's Afraid of Virginia Woolf*, 1965, with Elizabeth Taylor and Richard Burton; *The Graduate* 1967, up to that time the highest-grossing film in history; *Catch-22*, 1969; and *Carnal Knowledge*, 1971. For his direction of *The Graduate* Nichols won an Academy Award.

Nicklaus, Jack William (1940–   ), golfer. Born in Columbus, Ohio, on January 21, 1940, Nicklaus was introduced to golf by his father at the age of ten, when, in his first round, he shot a 51 for 9 holes. By the time he was twelve he was outdriving his father. Jack eventually became one of the hardest and most accurate hitters in golf, consistently using shorter irons and lighter woods than his competitors. His putting was the weakest part of his game, but since he was usually on the green under par, he often holed out under par nonetheless. He won the Ohio Open while still in high school and after entering Ohio State University in 1957 continued to improve his game. He won the U.S. Amateur championship in 1959, while still only nineteen, and the next year he led the U.S. team to victory in the World Amateur team championship, shooting a 269 for four rounds at the famous Merion Golf Club in Philadelphia—18 strokes lower than Ben Hogan's total when he won the U.S. Open at Merion in 1950. Nicklaus regained the U.S. Amateur title in 1961 and in December of that year turned professional. He won no tournaments on the professional tour during the spring of 1962, but in the U.S. Open in June he tied Arnold Palmer over 72 holes and beat him in the playoff to become the youngest U.S. champion in nearly 40 years. He then took the Masters and the Professional Golfers' Association (PGA) titles in 1963; became the first to win two Masters tournaments in a row, in 1965 and 1966; captured the British Open in 1966 and 1970; and was U.S. Open champion again in 1967, when he was named golfer of the year. In his first 10 years on the tour he won more than $1 million in prizes and was on his way to becoming the greatest money winner in the history of golf. In 1972, determined to be the first golfer ever to win the professional "grand slam"—the Masters, the U.S. Open, the PGA, and the British Open—he won the Masters and the U.S. Open but was beaten in the last round of the British Open by his old nemesis, Lee Trevino. Later he lost the PGA as well. In 1973, however, his decisive win in the PGA gave him a record total of 14 major tournament victories, surpassing the mark set by Bobby Jones.

Nicolet, Jean (1598–1642), explorer. Born in Cherbourg, France, in 1598, Nicolet accompanied Samuel de Champlain to New France (Canada) in 1618, when he was twenty years old. After two years spent living among the Indians on Allumette Island, in the Ottawa River, he was sent from the colony by Champlain to live among the Nipissing; he became their official interpreter in 1624. Returning to New France in 1633, he set out again on an exploring and mapping expedition westward in 1634. Arriving at Huronia on the east of Lake Huron, he embarked in a large canoe with seven Huron Indian paddlers and traveled northward into Lake Huron. He passed through the Straits of Mackinac, entered Lake Michigan, and reached Green Bay, where he made contact with the Winnebago Indians of whom he had been told and who he had hoped would prove to be Asians. He was thus evidently the first European to see Lake Michigan and Green Bay and to set foot in what is now Wisconsin. Disappointed that he had not found a passage to the Orient, he returned to Three Rivers, Quebec, and remained there until his death, brought about by a storm on the St. Lawrence River during which he drowned, on November 1, 1642.

Nicollet, Joseph Nicolas (1786–1843), mathematician and explorer. Born in Cluses, France, on July 24, 1786, the young Nicollet was quickly recognized as a mathematical prodigy and was teaching mathematics at the age of nineteen. By 1817 he was in Paris, working with the great scientist Pierre Simon Laplace; in the 1820s he was a professor of mathematics at the Collège Louis-le-Grand in Paris. He emigrated to the United States in 1832, landing at New Orleans but soon moving to St. Louis, where he met the famous Chouteau family of fur traders and explorers. He set out on his first exploratory expedition in 1836, ascending the Mississippi in search of its source. He arrived at Fort Snelling in present-day Minnesota on July 26 and then spent two months striving to reach the headwaters of the river, getting as far as Leech Lake, where he had many adventures among the Chippewa Indians of the region. Accompanied by Lt. John C. Frémont, he headed an official expedition to survey the region between the upper Missouri and Mississippi rivers sent out in 1838. In 1839 he made a second survey by steamboat. From Fort Pierre in present South Dakota he rode northward across the plains to the sources of the Red River of the North, reaching Devils Lake in North Dakota. He prepared a detailed map of the region on his return to Washington and wrote a *Report Intended to Illustrate a Map of the Hydrographical Basin of the Upper Mississippi*, which was published by the government in 1843, shortly after Nicollet's death in Washington on September 11 of that year.

Niebuhr, Reinhold (1892–1971), theologian. Born on June 21, 1892, in Wright City, Missouri, the son of a clergyman, Niebuhr attended Elmhurst College, Eden Theological Seminary, and Yale Divinity School, where he earned his B.D. in 1914 and his M.A. in 1915. Ordained to the ministry of the Evangelical Synod of North America in 1915, he was pastor at Detroit's Bethel Evangelical Church until 1928, when he joined the staff of the Union Theological Seminary in New York City as associate professor of the philosophy of religion. He became professor of applied Christianity in 1930 and retired in 1960. Initially a religious liberal and social idealist, he came into increasing contact with the realities of mundane life, notably during his pastorate in Detroit, and gave deep consideration to the nature of international conflicts, with the result that a stern and realistic shift took place in his theological outlook. His book *Moral Man and Immoral Society*, 1932, marked the beginning of the neo-orthodox movement in the United States. It attacked the form of Christianity whose focus on a "gospel of love" rendered it inadequate to deal with such real and active problems as political coercion. He aimed for and achieved a reinterpretation of the teachings of Christianity that took into account the social and political problems of modern times. In defiance of optimism, idealism, and the like, he argued that the true character of nations and people made essential the doctrines of sin and repentance. His concept of "human nature and destiny" was based on Augustinian theology and emphasized that at the root of mankind's highest achievements was the taint of ambition and self-love. Although he had earlier embraced radical Socialism, after World War II he turned against totalitarian Communism, as well as doctrinaire Socialism, although without losing his deep social concern. His developed theological position—which placed the Augustinian-Reformation view of man in an existentially interpreted environment—was stated more completely in his Gifford Lectures, published as *The Nature and Destiny of Man*, two volumes, 1941–1943. He paid greater attention to history and man's fundamental historicity in his later writings, including *Faith and History*, 1949; *The Irony of American History*, 1952; *The Self and the Dramas of History*, 1955; *The Structure of Nations and Empires*, 1959; *Beyond Tragedy: Essays on the Christian Interpretation of History*, 1961; *The Structure of Nations and Empires*, 1963; and *Man's Nature and His Communities*, 1965. Niebuhr died in Stockbridge, Massachusetts, on June 1, 1971.

Niles, Hezekiah (1777–1839), editor. Born in Jefferis's Ford in Chester County, Pennsylvania, on October 10, 1777, Niles was brought up as a Quaker and attended the Friends' School in Wilmington, Delaware, and was apprenticed to a printer in Philadelphia when he was seventeen. In 1797, upon release from the apprenticeship, he returned to Philadelphia where he entered into a small publishing business that soon failed and for a time edited an unsuccessful literary magazine, the *Apollo*. In 1805 he went to Baltimore as editor of the *Evening Post* and continued in that position until the paper was sold in 1811, whereupon he issued the prospectus for his *Weekly Register*. He edited his paper, later called *Niles' Weekly Register*, until 1836, making it one of the most influential of its time. A supporter of Henry Clay and of the "American System," he was a prime mover in the protectionist conventions at Harrisburg, Pennsylvania, in 1827 and at New York City in 1831. He opposed the rechartering of the Bank of the United States in 1811 but supported the incorporation of the Second Bank during Andrew Jackson's administration; this brought him into sharp conflict with Jackson, whom he refused to support, and he left the Democratic party in 1829 for the Whigs. An opponent of slavery, he wrote many editorials calling for its abolition. Besides his writings in periodicals, he published *Principles and Acts of the Revolution in America* in 1822. He died in Wilmington, Delaware, on April 2, 1839.

Nimitz, Chester William (1885–1966), naval officer. Born on February 24, 1885, in Fredericksburg, Texas, Nimitz entered the U.S. Naval Academy at the age of fifteen and graduated in 1905. After serving a sea tour on the China Station and later gaining experience as a submarine commander, he became a lieutenant and received command of the Atlantic Submarine Flotilla. He went to Germany in 1913 to study advances in diesel engines in that country and in Belgium; returning to the United States, he was able to supervise the construction of the first diesel ship's engine for the navy. In 1916 he was promoted to lieutenant commander, and during World War I he was chief of staff to the commander of the submarine division of the Atlantic Fleet. After attending the Naval War College in 1922–1923, Nimitz was assigned to the staff of the commander in chief of the U.S. fleet. From 1926 to 1929 he was at the University of California, where he organized the first training division for officers in the naval reserve. Before World War II he furthered his education at advanced naval schools and had reached the rank of rear admiral by 1938. The next year he was made chief of the Bureau of Navigation and immediately after the Japanese attack on Pearl Harbor on December 7, 1941, he was named commander in chief of the Pacific Fleet. With both fighting ships and Marine Corps forces under his command, he directed a series of sea battles and island landings—Midway, 1942; the Solomon Islands, 1942–1943; the Gilbert Islands, 1943; the Marshalls, Marianas, Palaus, and the Philippines, 1944; and Iwo Jima and Okinawa, 1945—which, combined with the island-hopping operations under Gen. Douglas MacArthur, won victory over Japan for the United States. In 1944 he was promoted to the newly created rank of admiral of the fleet. On September 2, 1945, the surrender of Japan was received aboard his flagship, the battleship *Missouri*. During 1945–1947 he was chief of naval operations and afterward served as special assistant to the secretary of the Navy. He coedited with E. B. Potter *Sea Power, a Naval History*, 1960. He died near San Francisco on February 20, 1966.

Nirenberg, Marshall Warren (1927–   ), biochemist. Born in New York City on April 10, 1927, Nirenberg moved with his family to Orlando, Florida, when he was ten. He graduated from the University of Florida in 1948 and received an M.Sc. in biology from that institution in 1952. He had worked in the university's nutrition laboratory while taking graduate courses in the early 1950s, but in 1952 he moved to the University of Michigan to do graduate work in biochemistry, and he received his doctorate from Michigan in 1957. A postgraduate fellowship from the American Cancer Society allowed him further study at the National Institutes of Health in Bethesda, Maryland, and from 1960 he was a research fellow in the metabolic enzymes section. His first important paper on the genetic code was delivered at the International Congress of Biochemistry in Moscow, in 1961. It described how he and his associate, J. H. Matthaei, had employed radioactive tracers of carbon 14 to unravel the chemical "language" of the nucleic acids, including DNA (deoxyribonucleic acid) and RNA (ribonucleic acid). In April 1962, at Atlantic City, an audience of 3000 chemists and biologists gathered to hear the results of Nirenberg's further researches. He was able to report that he and his associates had converted "brainless" bacteria into tobacco virus proteins—perhaps a step toward the creation of life in the laboratory. For this and other work on the mechanism of protein synthesis, on nucleic acids, and on the regulatory mechanisms involved in the synthesis of macromolecules, he received the 1968 Nobel Prize for Physiology and Medicine jointly with Robert W. Holley and Har Gobind Khorana. The recipient of many other awards as well and editor of *Biopolymers*, published in 1963, Nirenberg was head of the section on biochemistry and genetics of the National Heart and Lung Institute from 1962.

Nixon, Richard Milhous (1913–   ), thirty-seventh president of the United States. Born in Yorba Linda, California, on January 9, 1913, the child of Quaker parents, Nixon graduated in 1934 from Whittier College and then went to Duke University law school, where he received his Ll.B. in 1937. After five years of law practice in Whittier, California, he joined the navy, being discharged in 1946 as a lieutenant commander. In the fall of 1946, running on the Republican ticket, he challenged the veteran Democratic representative of California's 12th congressional district, H. Jerry Voorhis, and after a series of platform debates in which he suggested that Voorhis had the support of Communist elements, defeated him in the November election. He was unopposed for reelection in 1948. While in the House he helped write the Taft-Hartley Act and, as a member of the House Un-American Activities Committee, played a large part in preparing the congressional investigation of Alger Hiss. On the strength of the reputation gained in this affair, and after a campaign marked by innuendos about the loyalty of his opponent, Helen Gahagan Douglas, he defeated her in the senatorial race in California in 1950. He continued to speak often around the country on various issues, particularly the dangers of Communism, and was nominated for vice-president by the Republicans at their convention in 1952 as Gen. Dwight D. Eisenhower's running mate. The campaign opened with charges that he had benefited illegally from a fund raised by his supporters, and he was asked, although not by Eisenhower, to withdraw. Instead, he made a dramatic defense of his actions in a nationwide television broadcast, was retained on the ticket, and was elected with Eisenhower. As vice-president he was a leading spokesman of the administration, particularly during the periods when Eisenhower was incapacitated by illness. He presided over meetings of the cabinet and the National

Security Council in the President's absence and represented the government on several trips throughout the world, on most of which he was well received, although he encountered hostile crowds in Venezuela in 1958. In 1959, at the opening of the American National Exposition in Moscow, he met Premier Nikita S. Khrushchev of the Soviet Union in the course of touring the exhibition and engaged him in a much-publicized "kitchen debate," (so called because of its setting at the exhibition), from which Nixon was felt by U.S. observers to have emerged victorious. With Eisenhower's blessing he was nominated by the Republicans as their presidential candidate in 1960, but although he campaigned vigorously he was defeated by John F. Kennedy in an extremely close race. The turning point in the campaign was a series of television debates of which it was generally agreed that Nixon had been the loser. He returned to California and ran for governor against incumbent Democrat Edmund G. "Pat" Brown in 1962. He lost, whereupon, in an emotional speech to newspapermen, he announced his intention to retire from politics. In *Six Crises*, published that year, he told the story of the turning points of his career. He went to New York City in 1963 and joined a prominent law firm. In 1966 he actively campaigned for Republican congressional candidates, and it became obvious that he did not mean his retirement to be permanent. In 1968 he was nominated for president at the Republican national convention in Miami Beach on the first ballot. Nixon's campaign was aided by wide dissatisfaction with his opponent, Vice-President Hubert H. Humphrey, who, in the wake of President Lyndon B. Johnson's withdrawal, was trying vainly to unify the Democrats. Declaring that his primary intention was to unify the country, and that, to that end, he had a "secret plan" to end the war in Vietnam, Nixon conducted a relatively muted campaign, particularly after the Democrats had shown the rifts within their party at their convention in Chicago in August. Nixon won the election and was inaugurated on January 20, 1969. Nixon's first administration concerned itself primarily with the closely related problems of the war in Vietnam and domestic economic problems; "Vietnamization" and the withdrawal of U.S. ground forces from Vietnam were undertaken, and price and wage controls were imposed. There were also major events in other areas. During 1969-1970 two Nixon nominees to the Supreme Court, both Southerners and conservatives, were rejected by the Senate. Nixon made a round-the-world goodwill tour in 1969 and late in that year the Strategic Arms Limitation Talks (SALT) with the Soviet Union began, resulting finally in an arms-limitation treaty of considerable potential, signed during a Nixon visit to the Soviet Union in May 1972. In a notable reversal of long-standing U.S. policy, Nixon supported the admission of the People's Republic of China (Communist China) to the United Nations in 1971, then sped the arrangements for an epochal and widely televised visit to China early in 1972, the first made by a U.S. pres-

ident to that nation. The trip raised hopes for an eventual settlement of the Vietnam question, which had remained the subject of widespread dissent, particularly in the wake of a U.S. incursion into Cambodia in 1970. Bombing of North Vietnam intensified and its harbors were mined in 1972. In 1972 Nixon was renominated by the Republican national convention in Miami Beach, and in November he was, with Vice-President Spiro T. Agnew, reelected by one of the largest margins in history—520 of the 538 electoral votes —over Senator George S. McGovern. During the unorthodox campaign, Nixon had for the most part refused to appear before the public to debate partisan issues, but he had clearly descried the mood of the people. In January 1973, after months of negotiations conducted by Nixon's principal adviser on foreign affairs, Henry Kissinger, American involvement in the war in Vietnam came to an apparent end. U.S. forces were withdrawn and U.S. troops held prisoner were released. Fighting continued, however, in Vietnam and in Laos and Cambodia, where, over mounting public and Congressional pressure, the air force continued to lend heavy air support to anti-Communist forces. At home Nixon steadily lost popularity as the economy failed to respond to his anti-inflation moves, as Vice-President Agnew was forced to resign in a bribery scandal, and, more importantly, as a series of spectacular revelations about the "Watergate bugging" of Democratic party headquarters in Washington during the 1972 campaign implicated high campaign, Cabinet, and White House officials in a series of criminal misdeeds. The Watergate affair escalated into a contest over executive privilege and separation of powers, Nixon refusing to yield to various investigators White House documents or the tape recordings of private conversations which it was discovered he had made and kept. His public support melted further when, to relieve pressure on himself and his White House aides, he fired the special prosecutor of the case over the resignations of the attorney general and his assistant (an affair called "the Saturday Night Massacre"). By July 1974 impeachment proceedings were under way. Bowing to a Supreme Court order, Nixon at last released a tape that showed him to have been deeply implicated in the cover-up conspiracy. Amid a storm of public denunciation, he resigned from office on August 9, 1974, the first President ever to do so. Nixon retired to the seclusion of his San Clemente, California, estate.

Nizer, Louis (1902–   ), lawyer. Born in London on February 6, 1902, Nizer was brought to the United States in 1905, his family settling in Brooklyn, New York. He graduated from Columbia College in 1922 and from the Columbia Law School two years later, being admitted to the bar in 1924. He was a founding member of the law firm of Phillips, Nizer, Benjamin & Krim in 1926 and later became the senior partner of the firm, which specialized in cases in the entertainment field. Nizer's clients included many famous show-business personalities, ranging from Charles Chaplin to Mae West. In what was probably his most famous case, he handled a libel suit brought by author Quentin Reynolds against columnist Westbrook Pegler and his publishers. When the trial ended on June 29, 1954, Reynolds was awarded nearly $200,000 in punitive damages against Pegler, the Hearst Corporation, and the *New York Journal–American*. A noted orator while in college, Nizer became much sought after as a toastmaster and after dinner speaker, and in 1940 he published an account of his experiences in this area, *Thinking on Your Feet: Adventures in Speaking*. Another book, *What to Do with Germany*, 1944, was widely read; Gen. Dwight D. Eisenhower ordered that all of his staff officers read and report on the book. Accounts of some of Nizer's most interesting and celebrated cases were included in later books, many of which were best sellers: *Between You and Me* was published in 1948, *My Life in Court*, in 1962, and *The Jury Returns*, in 1966.

Nock, Albert Jay (1870–1945), author. Born in Brooklyn, New York, on October 13, 1870, Nock grew up there and, from the age of nine, in Alpena, Michigan, where his father was a clergyman. He went to boarding school when he was fourteen and later attended St. Stephen's (now Bard) College. When he was a young man he played semiprofessional baseball, then taught classics at various schools, and was eventually ordained an Episcopalian minister. In 1910, dissatisfied with his life he established himself in New York City in hopes of launching himself in a literary career. He started with the *American Mercury* and during the next ten years wrote astute and entertaining articles for most of the leading magazines of the day. From 1920 to 1924 he was editor of the *Freeman*, which during its brief life was a vehicle for his personal philosophy. From 1925 to 1940 he lived much of the time abroad, chiefly in Belgium. When World War II began he returned to the United States, spending his declining years in the hills of Connecticut and Vermont. Most of his books were written in the last 20 years of his life; among them were *Jefferson*, 1926; *On Doing the Right Thing, and Other Essays*, 1928; *The Theory of Education in the United States*, 1932; *Our Enemy, the State*, 1935; and *Henry George: An Essay*, 1939. None of these books was especially popular, but in them he developed his political and social theories, which were antidemocratic in the extreme and verged on a kind of gentlemanly anarchism. His ideas bore their richest fruit in his informal autobiography, *Memoirs of a Superfluous Man*, 1943, in which he expressed his dislike of practically everything that was happening not only in the United States but also in the Soviet Union and the rest of the world. Written in an engagingly personal style, it was a best seller and became a minor classic. Several books, including a collection of his letters, were published after his death, which occurred in New Canaan, Connecticut, on August 19, 1945.

Noguchi, Hideyo (1876–1928), bacteriologist and immunologist. Born in Inawashiro, Japan, on November 24, 1876, Noguchi graduated from Tokyo Medical College in 1897. The next year he became a special assistant at Tokyo General Hospital and a lecturer in general pathology and oral surgery at Tokyo Dental College. He served at the Government Institute for Infectious Diseases in 1898–1899 and was sent to Ying-k'ou (Newchwang), China, as physician in charge of the Central Hospital and bacteriological laboratory during an outbreak of bubonic plague. Returning to Tokyo at the outbreak of the Boxer Rebellion, he completed several texts on bacteriology, pathology, and dentistry. He came to the University of Pennsylvania in 1899 to work in Simon Flexner's pathology laboratory. There he assisted in Silas Weir Mitchell's research on snake venoms, showing himself to be a dedicated, industrious, and adroit experimenter. In 1904 he published *The Action of Snake Venom upon Cold-blooded Animals*, which secured his reputation. Also in 1904 he began an association with the Rockefeller Institute for Medical Research (now Rockefeller University) in New York City, under whose auspices he worked for the rest of his career. Immediately he turned to clarification of August von Wassermann's principles and method for diagnosing syphilis, and, using a variation of Theobald Smith's method of obtaining pure cultures of spiral organisms, he isolated the spirochetes of syphilis (*Treponema pallidum*) and grew them free of contaminating bacteria, making possible the preparation of extract luetin. He devised the luetin reaction, or skin test for syphilis. In 1913, with J. W. Moore, he observed the presence of *Treponema pallidum* in the brains of patients dead of paresis. He also demonstrated the presence of the organism in the central nervous systems of patients dying of general paresis and of tabes dorsalis, thus establishing syphilis as the cause of both disorders. The first to produce cultures of numerous pathogenic spiral organisms and saprophytic forms, he grew the globoid bodies of poliomyelitis, but erroneously identified them as causative agents. (A virus was later shown to cause poliomyelitis.) He was successful in demonstrating that two clinically different diseases, Oroya fever and verruga peruana, were produced by the same agent, *Bartonella bacilliformis*. He made several trips to South America to conduct these and other investigations into yellow fever. He also did research on rabies and trachoma. In 1927 he joined other scientists in British West Africa, after it was learned that the causative agent in yellow fever was a virus. In the course of his work there he contracted yellow fever and subsequently died in Accra (now Ghana), on May 21, 1928.

Noguchi, Isamu (1904–   ), sculptor. Born in Los Angeles on November 7, 1904, Noguchi was the son of a Japanese poet and an American writer. He was brought up in Japan from the age of two until he returned to the United States at thirteen to attend high school in Indiana. After graduation he studied sculpture with Gutzon Borglum, creator of the great monuments at Mt. Rushmore, South Dakota, and at Stone Mountain, Georgia, who discouraged him from further training. He entered Columbia University as a premedical student, completing the two-year course. He returned to his art and in 1926 won a Guggenheim fellowship to go to Paris and study sculpture under Constantin Brancusi. In 1927 and 1928 he studied in Europe, again as a Guggenheim fellow, but several unsuccessful showings prompted him to do a series of realistic heads in bronze, which he exhibited with great success in New York City in 1930–1931. He was able to travel around the world on the proceeds of his sales, studying primitive art in the Orient and working in London in 1933 and in Mexico in 1936, where he completed a relief sculpture of colored cement 65 feet long. Returning to the United States, he submitted the award-winning design for a plaque to decorate the entrance of the Associated Press building in New York City's Rockefeller Center. Cast in stainless steel, the sweeping, rhythmical design was enthusiastically received at its unveiling in 1941. Thereafter he completed many works, including the "Kuros," 1945, and his work was exhibited in museums in New York City and in Japan. In 1958 he designed a garden for the UNESCO building in Paris. His art naturally extended into the environment, using such materials as stone, terra-cotta, and plastic and the shapes of plants, animals, and geological formations. His designs for objects and environments—including chairs, lamps, tables, playground equipment, a fountain at the 1939–1940 New York World's Fair, backdrops for Martha Graham's dance recitals, and a bridge at Hiroshima, Japan—contributed immensely to the extension of the modern abstract art movement.

Nordica, Lillian (1857–1914), opera singer. Born in Farmington, Maine, on December 12, 1857, Lillian Norton received her stage name from Italian singing master Antonio San Giovanni when she was studying with him during 1878–1879. She had earlier studied music at the New England Conservatory of Music, making her concert debut about 1876 at Madison Square Garden in New York City as soloist with Patrick Gilmore's famous band. After touring with Gilmore's band in the United States and Europe she traveled to Italy to study opera with San Giovanni and made her operatic debut as Brescia in *La Traviata*, on April 30, 1879, in Milan. Her debut as prima donna at the Paris Opéra occurred on July 21, 1882, when she sang the part of Marguerite in Gounod's *Faust* to great acclaim. Having become the first American operatic singer to win acclaim in the critical houses of Europe, she returned home. She then sang Marguerite in her American operatic debut at the New York Academy of Music on November 26, 1883. Thereafter she was one of the most sought-after sopranos in America, in England, and on the Continent, the prima

donna of London's Covent Garden Theatre and of New York City's Metropolitan Opera. Her preeminence was well known in the French and Italian roles and in 1893 she left the stage for several months to study Wagnerian opera. Her appearance at Bayreuth in 1894 was a success and her Isolde to Jean de Reszke's Tristan at the Metropolitan on November 27, 1895, was a triumph; her great successes in subsequent years were usually in Wagnerian roles, notably those of Elsa, Isolde, and Brunnhilde. After 1908 her appearances were only occasional, but she set out on a concert tour that was to take her around the world. Her ship was grounded in the Gulf of Papua in December 1913, and she contracted pneumonia and died of complications of the disease in Batavia, Java, on May 10, 1914. *Lillian Nordica's Hints to Singers*, which included many of her letters, was published in 1923.

Norris, Benjamin Franklin, *see* Norris, Frank

Norris, Frank (1870–1902), author. Born in Chicago on March 5, 1870, Benjamin Franklin Norris moved with his family to San Francisco in 1884. In 1887, having demonstrated considerable artistic ability, he was enrolled in the Académie Julien in Paris; two years later, having decided that literature was his true vocation, he withdrew, returned to the United States, and entered the University of California in 1890. He remained there for four years and, although he did not graduate, continued his studies for another year at Harvard. During 1895–1896 he was in South Africa as a correspondent for the *San Francisco Chronicle;* he returned in 1896 to San Francisco and joined the *Wave*, a literary journal. In 1898 he moved to New York City, joined the staff of *McClure's Magazine*, and went to Cuba as a correspondent during the Spanish-American War. In 1898 he published his first book, *Moran of the Lady Letty*, a sea adventure and love story that had been serialized in the *Wave*. In 1899 he returned to New York City, where he joined the publishing firm of Doubleday, Page, and Company, and published *Blix*, a partially autobiographical novel, and *McTeague*, a story of greed and violence and the first of his novels in the naturalistic vein inspired by Emile Zola. With this book and those that followed, he joined Theodore Dreiser in the front rank of American writers. In 1901 appeared *The Octopus*, the first book of a projected trilogy entitled *The Epic of the Wheat*. The first volume concerned California wheat growers and their struggle against the railroad trust; the second volume, *The Pit*, 1903, was a tale of the Chicago Board of Trade, where the wheat passed from speculator to speculator; the final volume, to have been entitled *The Wolf*, never written, was to have shown the wheat, as bread, feeding a famine-stricken village in the Old World. Another novel, *Vandover and the Brute*, was published in 1914, long after Norris's death. In 1902 he returned to California; on October 25 of that year he died, in San Francisco.

Norris, George William (1861–1944), public official. Born in Sandusky County, Ohio, on July 11, 1861, Norris early in life became his family's main support. Unable to attend school regularly, he gained his early education by his own efforts. He obtained a law degree from Northern Indiana Normal School and Business Institute (now Valparaiso University) in 1882 and moved to Beaver City, Nebraska, in 1885. He soon entered local politics, serving as county prosecuting attorney for three terms and, from 1895 to 1902, as district judge. In 1902 he successfully campaigned for the House of Representatives as a Republican and continued to represent his district until 1912, during which time he led the House progressives in their struggle to reform the rules in order to strip the speaker, then "Uncle Joe" Cannon, of his autocratic prerogatives. In 1912 he began a 30-year career as senator from Nebraska. Staunchly independent, he opposed U.S. entry into World War I and proposals for U.S. participation in the League of Nations and denounced the treaty of Versailles. He fought for a number of political reforms and for farm relief, sponsored the Norris–La Guardia Anti-Injunction Act in 1932, and wrote the Twentieth Amendment to the Constitution in 1933. His major efforts were directed to securing public ownership and operation of hydroelectric resources; although he was twice stymied by presidential vetoes, his work finally resulted in the creation of the Tennessee Valley Authority (TVA). The first dam, in Tennessee, completed in the program was named in his honor. Nominally a Republican, he was far from a strict partisan; he supported Theodore Roosevelt's Bull Moose Progressive candidacy in 1912, Progressive candidate Robert M. La Follette in 1924, and Democrat Franklin D. Roosevelt in his four campaigns. He ran for the Senate as an Independent Republican in 1936. Defeated for reelection in 1942, he retired from public life and died on September 2, 1944, in McCook, Nebraska. His autobiography, *Fighting Liberal*, appeared the next year.

North, Frank Joshua (1840–1885), soldier and frontier figure. Born in Ludlowville, Tompkins County, New York, in 1840, North grew up in Ohio and moved with his family to Nebraska Territory in 1856, where he came into close contact with the Pawnee Indians, learning their language and also Indian sign language. In 1861 he became a clerk-interpreter at the Pawnee reservation near the confluence of the Loup and the Platte rivers in Nebraska. Three years later he served as lieutenant of a force of Pawnee volunteers in actions against hostile Indians around Fort Riley, Kansas. Later in 1864 he was authorized by Gen. S. R. Curtis to enlist a company of Pawnee scouts to participate in a number of engagements with warring tribes in 1865. He was discharged in 1866. The next year he was asked to organize and command a battalion of four companies of Pawnee and was charged with protecting the work gangs on the Union Pacific Railroad against attacks by hostile Indians, mostly Cheyenne. From then until 1877 he led this and other companies of Pawnee against their traditional enemies, the Cheyenne and the Sioux. These skirmishes culminated in the campaign of 1876 under Gen. George Crook, in the course of which Crazy Horse was pursued throughout Wyoming. Mustered out in April 1877, North engaged for five years thereafter in a ranching operation in Nebraska with William F. "Buffalo Bill" Cody and later joined Buffalo Bill's Wild West Show, leading his Pawnee in exhibitions of Indian warfare. He was probably the best revolver shot of his time on the plains, having beaten "Wild Bill" Hickok and others in competition in 1873; and he was an extraordinary leader of Indians in warfare, only one of his men being killed and a handful wounded in six extensive campaigns. In 1884 while appearing in one of the Wild West shows in Hartford, Connecticut, he was severely injured. He died as a result of these injuries on March 14, 1885, in Columbus, Nebraska, his home for many years.

Northrop, John Howard (1891–   ), biochemist. Born in Yonkers, New York, on July 5, 1891, Northrop became interested in science at an early age, both of his parents being scientists. He studied chemistry and biology at Columbia, graduating in 1912, and receiving his M.A. in 1913 and his Ph.D. two years later. He studied for a year in 1915–1916 under Jacques Loeb at the Rockefeller Institute for Medical Research and in 1916 was appointed to an assistantship there; he became an associate in 1917, an associate member in 1920, and a member in 1924. He retired from the institute, which in the interim had become Rockefeller University, in 1962. He was also at various times a visiting professor and a professor of bacteriology at the University of California at Berkeley, and a lecturer at Columbia and Johns Hopkins universities. His early work at the Rockefeller Institute and for the army's Chemical Warfare Service during World War I involved fermentation to produce acetone and ethyl alcohol, and this led in 1920 to the beginning of his lifelong studies of enzymes, about which almost nothing was known when he began his work. He showed that enzymes obey chemical laws and are essentially protein in character; he obtained pepsin in crystalline form in 1930, crystallized, with Moses Kunitz, trypsin and chymotripsin and their precursors trypsinogen and chymotrypsinogen, and isolated, with Robert M. Herriott, crystalline pepsinogen. For his work on enzymes he shared the 1946 Nobel Prize for Chemistry with Wendell M. Stanley and an associate at the Rockefeller Institute, James B. Sumner. Northrop also did important work on starch, bacteriophages, the agglutination of bacteria, and the effects of temperature on insects, and in 1941 he produced a crystalline form of purified diphtheria antitoxin. His book *Crystalline Enzymes* appeared in 1939. For many years he edited the Rockefeller Institute publication, *Journal of General Physiology*.

Norton, Charles Eliot (1827–1908), author, editor, and educator. Born in Cambridge, Massachusetts, on November 16, 1827, Norton graduated from Harvard in 1846 and entered a mercantile house. After three years as a businessman he spent two years traveling and studying in Europe and the Orient. From 1851 to 1855 he managed his own importing firm and then spent another two years in Europe. For several years he wrote articles and reviews for the *Atlantic Monthly*, edited by James Russell Lowell, and in 1864–1868 he was coeditor with Lowell of the *North American Review*. In 1865 he was one of the founders of the *Nation*. He was a central figure in the Boston-Cambridge-Concord intellectual circle and was a close friend of many European notables, particularly Thomas Carlyle and John Ruskin; much of his contribution to literature consisted of volumes of letters to and from the great men who were his friends. In 1873 he began to lecture at Harvard on the history of art, a new course introduced by his cousin Charles W. Eliot, the innovative president of the college. The chair was the first such in the United States; Norton gave the course until 1897 and his skill, scholarship, and lasting influence were widely acknowledged. Among his books were *Considerations on Some Recent Social Theories*, 1853; *Notes of Travel and Study in Italy*, 1860; *Historical Studies of Church Building in the Middle Ages*, 1880; and *History of Ancient Art*, 1891, a collection of his lectures edited by H. F. Brown and W. H. Wiggin. In 1891–1892 he published his prose translation of Dante's *Divine Comedy;* notable among works he edited were *The Poems of John Donne*, 1895; *The Poems of Mrs. Anne Bradstreet*, 1897; and *The Love Poems of John Donne*, 1905. He died on October 21, 1908, in Cambridge, Massachusetts.

Norton, Lillian, *see* Nordica, Lillian

Noyes, Arthur Amos (1866–1936), chemist and educator. Born in Newburyport, Massachusetts, on September 13, 1866, Noyes became interested in chemistry while in high school. Eager to go to the Massachusetts Institute of Technology (MIT), but lacking funds, he studied the institute's first-year subjects on his own and was admitted into the sophomore class on a scholarship, graduating in 1886. He received his M.A. in organic chemistry the next year. He spent the academic year 1887–1888 as a teaching assistant in chemistry at MIT, forming during this period a close friendship with one of his students, George Ellery Hale. He then went to the University of Leipzig, Germany, to study under the noted physical chemist ·Wilhelm Ostwald. Returning to MIT in 1890 after gaining his doctorate from Leipzig, Noyes began a 19-year association with the institution that included two years, 1907–1909, as its acting president and also as the first director of its research Laboratory of Physical Chemistry (which he had founded) from 1903 to 1917. During that time he taught analytical, organic, and physical chemistry and wrote two important text-

books in chemistry that revolutionized the study of the subject. The first was a book on qualitative analysis that appeared in 1894 and was re-issued many times in subsequent years under various titles; the other was *General Principles of Physical Science*, which appeared in 1902 and was expanded, with the collaboration of M. S. Sherrill, in 1922 under the title *A Course of Study in Chemical Principles*. An important later work, the result of some 25 years of study of the chemical properties of the rarer elements, was *A System of Qualitative Analysis for the Rare Elements*, written with W. C. Bray and published in 1927. Another research topic of major interest to Noyes was the study of electrolyte solutions. In 1913 he became associated on a part-time basis with his former student Hale at the Throop College of Technology in Pasadena, California (later the California Institute of Technology—Caltech), and in 1919 he moved to the school on a full-time basis. Working together with Hale and the physicist Robert A. Millikan, he led the institution to preeminence in the field of physics and chemistry. Founder in 1895 of *Review of American Chemical Research*, which later became *Chemical Abstracts*, Noyes served as president of the American Chemical Society in 1904 and as president of the American Association for the Advancement of Science in 1927. He died in Pasadena, California, on June 3, 1936, leaving his estate to Caltech for the support of research in chemistry.

Noyes, John Humphrey (1811–1886), social reformer. Born on September 3, 1811, in Brattleboro, Vermont, Noyes graduated from Dartmouth College in 1830 and then studied law. Having attended a meeting of the great revivalist, Charles Grandison Finney, he was converted and shortly thereafter entered Andover Theological Seminary, later transferring to Yale. He proclaimed to his teachers that total release from sin could be attained by any individual by will and self-determination. In 1834 he announced that he had attained perfection and his license to preach was promptly revoked. He traveled about the country, becoming convinced of the evils existing in the secular world. Under his leadership a Bible group that he had formed at his home in Putney, Vermont, became a community in 1836; based on his doctrine of Perfectionism, it was an association of "Bible communists" who hoped to revive the communal living of early Christianity. In 1837 Noyes proclaimed the doctrine of free love. Noyes and several of his followers were arrested for adultery, but escaped and fled to Oneida, in central New York, to found the similar but larger and more elaborately structured Oneida Community. Also devoted to perfection and communal living, the community practiced "complex marriage," in which each woman in the group was considered each man's wife, and each man, each woman's husband. Male continence was stressed, mutual consent to sexual activities made mandatory, and childbearing was founded on a program of eugenics. Noyes's control over the group continued undisputed for 30 years and the community was the most successful of the many utopian experiments of the period. A branch community flourished in Wallingford, Connecticut, from 1850 to 1880. But by 1879 tension within and around the community prompted him to end Oneida's practice of complex marriage and to move to Canada, where he was safe from legal proceedings. Noyes had published a number of tracts setting forth his views, including *Bible Communism*, 1848; *History of American Socialisms*, 1870; *Scientific Propagation*, 1873; and *Home Talks*, 1875. He died in Niagara Falls, Ontario, on April 13, 1886. Before that time, the Oneida Community had reorganized as a joint-stock company in 1881 and become a cooperative community. As such, it achieved wide recognition for the manufacture of silver flatware.

O

Oakley, Annie (1860–1926), markswoman. Born on August 13, 1860, on a farm in Darke County, Ohio, Phoebe Anne Oakley Mozee, who came to be known as Annie Oakley, early developed an amazing proficiency with firearms. As a child she hunted game with such success that, by selling it in Cincinnati, she was able to pay off the mortgage on the family farm. When she was about fifteen she won a shooting match in Cincinnati with Frank E. Butler, a vaudeville marksman; some years later they were married, and until 1885 they played vaudeville circuits and circuses as a team. In that year they joined "Buffalo Bill" Cody's Wild West Show and "Little Missy," billed as "Miss Annie Oakley, the Peerless Lady Wing-Shot," was one of its star attractions for 17 years. She never failed to delight her audiences, and her feats of marksmanship were truly incredible. At 30 paces she could split a playing card held edge-on; she hit dimes tossed into the air; she shot cigarettes from her husband's lips; and, a playing card being thrown into the air, she riddled it before it touched the ground (thus giving rise to the custom of referring to punched complimentary tickets as "Annie Oakleys"). She was equally successful touring Europe, and in Berlin performed her cigarette trick with, at his insistence, Crown Prince Wilhelm (later Kaiser Wilhelm II) holding the cigarette. A train wreck in 1901 left her partially paralyzed for a time, but she recovered and returned to the stage to amaze audiences for many more years. She died on November 2, 1926, in Greenville Ohio.

Ochoa, Severo (1905–   ), biochemist. Born in Luarca, Spain, on September 24, 1905, Ochoa was educated at Málaga College, from which he graduated in 1921, and at the University of Madrid, from which he received his M.D. with honors in 1929. From 1929 to 1931 he was a student and research associate at the Kaiser Wilhelm Institute for Biology in Berlin and then at the Kaiser Wilhelm Institute for Medical Research in Heidelberg, where he studied with Otto Meyerhof, 1922 Nobel laureate in physiology and medicine. He taught physiology and biochemistry at the University of Madrid from 1934, but left Spain in 1936 because of the outbreak of the Civil war, going first to Heidelberg, then, in 1938, to Oxford, and finally traveling to the United States in 1940. He spent a year at the medical school of Washington University in St. Louis and then joined the faculty of the New York University College of Medicine in 1941, becoming chairman of the department of pharmacology in 1946 and of the department of biochemistry in 1954. He became a U.S. citizen in

1956. His work on enzymes and the intermediary metabolism of the cell began while he was still in Europe, but it was not until the early 1950s that he made the key breakthroughs that were to change the course of future work in biochemistry. His first achievement was the discovery and isolation of triphosphopyridine nucleotide (TPN), a vital agent in both plant photosynthesis and animal metabolism. This led to his announcement in 1955 of the enzymatic synthesis of ribonucleic acid (RNA), a basic constituent of all living tissue. Ochoa was able to obtain RNA artificially in a test tube and, using RNA, to create an artificial virus —an important step toward the ultimate goal of creating life in the laboratory out of inert materials. For his work on RNA he shared the 1959 Nobel Prize for Physiology and Medicine with Arthur Kornberg.

Ochs, Adolph Simon (1858–1935), newspaper publisher. Born in Cincinnati on March 12, 1858, of German immigrant parents, Ochs moved with them to Knoxville, Tennessee, in 1865. He received fairly regular schooling until he was eleven, when he became an office boy for the *Knoxville Chronicle.* With but a few interruptions he remained in the newspaper business for the rest of his life. At fourteen he was a printer's devil; he moved to Chattanooga and worked on the *Dispatch* there until it failed, whereupon, at the age of twenty, he borrowed some money and bought control of the faltering *Chattanooga Times.* Within a short time he had brought the paper to a position of financial and journalistic soundness from which it progressed to become one of the leading journals in the South. In 1891 he helped found the Southern Associated Press and was its chairman for its first three years. In 1896 he gained control of the *New York Times;* once powerful, the *Times* was considered moribund by many in the business. Explaining his philosophy of journalism in the simple masthead slogan he introduced—"All the News That's Fit to Print"—Ochs set about rebuilding the *Times* in competition with the much more popular exponents of "yellow journalism." Eschewing sensationalism and subordinating editorial opinion to unbiased news reporting, he insisted upon an accurate, complete coverage of the news directed to the intelligent reader. In 1898 he reduced the cost of the *Times* to one cent, a price then considered the emblem of the yellow sheets, and within a year circulation tripled. While setting high and influential standards for integrity—he refused to follow the then-common practice of allowing major advertising clients to dictate editorial policy—the *Times* achieved financial security and grew to be one of the world's leading newspapers. He introduced many new features including rotogravure illustration and the book review supplement. Retaining ownership of the *Chattanooga Times*, he also published the *Philadelphia Public Ledger* (merged with the *Philadelphia Times*) from 1901 to 1912. From 1900 to his death he was a director of the Associated Press. In 1913 he began to publish the *New York Times Index*, the only such service in the United States, and he was the principal financial backer for the compilation and publication of the *Dictionary of American Biography*. He died in Chattanooga, Tennessee, on April 8, 1935.

O'Connor, Sandra Day (1930–   ), justice of the Supreme Court. Born in El Paso, Texas, on March 26, 1930, Sandra Day graduated from Stanford University in 1950 with a degree in economics. Two years later she was awarded the LL.B. degree from that institution. Admitted to the California bar in 1952 (the year in which she married John Jay O'Connor) and the Arizona bar in 1957, she engaged in private practice in the latter state for several years. From 1965 to 1969 she served as assistant attorney general for Arizona. In 1969 she accepted a gubernatorial appointment to fill a vacancy in the Arizona state senate; she won that seat in her own right in the 1970 and 1972 elections. She was elected majority leader of the state senate in 1972, becoming the first woman to hold that office in any state senate in the country. Switching from the legislative to the judiciary branch of government, she ran successfully for a judgeship on the Maricopa County Superior Court in 1974. Five years later she was chosen by Arizona governor Bruce Babbitt as his first appointee to the Arizona Court of Appeals. As an appellate judge, she was concerned with such matters as workmen's compensation, divorces, bankruptcies, tenant-landlord disputes, and appeals from criminal convictions. She was nominated by President Reagan on July 7, 1981, to fill a vacancy on the U. S. Supreme Court. Easily winning confirmation by the U.S. Senate, she was sworn in on September 26. She became the first woman to serve on the Supreme Court in its 191-year history.

Odets, Clifford (1906–1963), playwright. Born on July 18, 1906, in Philadelphia, the son of a printer, Odets was raised in the Bronx, New York. He left high school to become a poet, then turned to acting in repertory theater. He was associated with the Theatre Guild and in 1931 helped to found the Group Theatre with Lee Strasberg and others. In 1935 he began to write plays himself and won immediate success with *Waiting for Lefty* and *Awake and Sing*, both performed by the Group Theatre in 1935. The two plays soon established him as the leading proletarian playwright in the United States and, in the turmoil of the Depression of the 1930s, he enjoyed a great vogue. He began writing movie scripts, beginning with *The General Died at Dawn*, in 1936. His great success, *Golden Boy*, was pre-

sented, again by the Group Theatre, on the stage in 1937. He directed the film *None But the Lonely Heart*, selected best movie of the year by the National Board of Review in 1949. His play, *The Big Knife*, was also produced in 1949, followed by *The Country Girl*, 1950, and his last play, *The Flowering Peach*, 1954. In 1960 he again took up film directing with *The Story on Page One* and later directed *Wild in the Country*, 1961. He died in Los Angeles on August 15, 1963.

O'Fearna, Sean Aloysius, *see* Ford, John

O'Feeney, Sean Aloysius, *see* Ford, John

Ogden, William Butler (1805–1877), railroad executive and public official. Born in Walton, New York, on June 15, 1805, Ogden planned to study law, but, his father dying when he was fifteen, he was forced to take over the family estate, which he administered with characteristic decisiveness. In 1834 he was elected to the New York legislature, but the next year, at the urging of his brother-in-law, he moved to Chicago to take charge of family real-estate interests there. He sold one-third of the property for a sum equal to the original cost of the whole, and thereafter began to buy and sell real estate on his own account, becoming in time one of the richest men in the city. For a period in the 1830s and 1840s his holdings were said to have doubled in value every year. When Chicago was incorporated in 1837, Ogden, who was one of its most enthusiastic boosters, was elected its first mayor, and he threw himself into the task of improving the streets and building bridges to connect the city's three parts, divided by branches of the Chicago River; Ogden Avenue was named after him. After his term as mayor he devoted himself to the building of railroads east and west from Chicago. He was president of the Chicago & North Western Railway from 1859 to 1868 and was elected the first president of the Union Pacific in 1862. Ogden was elected as a Republican to the Illinois senate in 1860 (he had been a Democrat when mayor of Chicago), but he split with the party in 1862 because of President Abraham Lincoln's preliminary Emancipation Proclamation and retired from politics. He bought an estate in Fordham Heights, outside New York City, in 1866 and lived there until his death on August 3, 1877.

Oglethorpe, James Edward (1696–1785), soldier and colonist. Born in London on December 22, 1696, Oglethorpe was educated at Eton and at Corpus Christi College, Oxford, and entered the army in 1712. He served under Prince Eugene of Savoy against the Turks in 1717 and he was present at the siege of Belgrade, but in 1719 he returned to England to succeed his brother as master of the family estate and to live a quiet life in the country. He entered the House of Commons in 1722. A resolute humanitarian, in 1728 he wrote a pamphlet, *The Sailor's Advocate*, exposing the evils of the system of impressing seamen. His membership on a Parliamentary committee investigating penal conditions led him to the idea of founding a colony in America for newly freed and unemployed debtors. He secured a charter for the colony of Georgia in 1732 and the next year accompanied the first party of 120 settlers, who founded Savannah. Oglethorpe returned to England in 1734, by which time Georgia was attracting other immigrant groups, including German Lutherans, Scottish Presbyterians, and German Moravians. Late in 1735 he made a second journey to Georgia, bringing with him the brothers John and Charles Wesley; Charles soon returned to England, but John remained for nearly two years, and he later credited his Georgia mission with having had a profound influence on the evolution of Methodism. In 1736 Oglethorpe built Fort Frederica on St. Simons Island as a defense against the Spanish in Florida to the south. The protests of the Spanish were added to those of settlers in the Carolinas, whom he had offended by attempting to regulate their trade with the Indians, and those of the London trustees of the Georgia colony, who suspected him of mismanaging their affairs. After another trip to England to settle satisfactorily the domestic questions, he returned to Georgia in 1738 with a British regiment. War broke out between England and Spain in 1739, and Oglethorpe set about defending Georgia against the Spanish. He failed in an attempt to capture St. Augustine during the war of Jenkins' Ear, but he repelled a Spanish attack on Fort Frederica in 1742, thereby gaining great popularity both with his soldiers and with the colonists. After another unsuccessful attempt on St. Augustine, he returned to England in 1743. He was promoted to major general two years later, and promoted to general in 1765, although he had seen no military service for some 20 years Oglethorpe and the other trustees surrendered their charter in 1752 and Georgia became a royal province. He died at Cranham Hall, Essex, on June 30, 1785.

O'Hara, John Henry (1905–1970), author. Born on January 31, 1905, in Pottsville, Pennsylvania, O'Hara came of a well-to-do family and was educated in several preparatory schools. His first published short story appeared in the *New Yorker* magazine in 1928 and he quickly became a regular contributor of smart, slick fiction. In 1934 he published *Appointment in Samarra*, his first novel and a great success. The appearance of *Butterfield 8* in 1935 firmly established him as a major writer of popular fiction, and to some critics his hard-boiled realism and sharp eye and ear for description and dialogue ranked him high among the outstanding American authors of the day. Through most of his career, however, critical appreciation of his work lagged behind popular acceptance, and at his death he was said by some to be the most underrated of contemporary literary figures. In 1940 he collected a number of his *New Yorker* sketches about a street-wise nightclub singer into a book, *Pal Joey*, that was another great success and that he turned into the book for a smash-hit Broadway musical, with music and lyrics by Richard Rodgers and Lorenz Hart, in the same year. Some other early books of his included *The Doctor's Son and Other Stories*, 1935; *Hope of Heaven*, 1938; and *Files on Parade*, 1939. For a time during World War II O'Hara was a correspondent in the Pacific. After the war he gradually abandoned the night life and the occasionally legendary alcoholic escapades of his youth for serious concentration on writing. For a time he lived in Hollywood and wrote motion picture scenarios and scripts, and his many books appeared regularly and in rapid succession: *Pipe Night*, 1945, and *Hellbox*, 1947, were collections of stories; his later novels included *Rage to Live*, 1949; *The Farmers' Hotel*, 1951; *Ten North Frederick*, 1955, which won a National Book Award; *A Family Party*, 1956; *From the Terrace*, 1958; *Ourselves to Know*, 1960; *The Big Laugh*, 1962; *Elizabeth Appleton*, 1963; and *The Instrument*, 1967. Other story collections included *Selected Short Stories*, 1956; *Assembly*, 1961; *The Cape Cod Lighter*, 1962; *The Hat on the Bed*, 1963; *49 Stories*, 1963; *The Horse Knows the Way*, 1964; and *Waiting for Winter*, 1967. O'Hara died in Princeton, New Jersey, on April 11, 1970.

O'Keeffe, Georgia (1887–   ), painter. Born in Sun Prairie, Wisconsin, on November 15, 1887, Miss O'Keeffe studied at the Art Institute of Chicago in 1904–1905, at the Art Students League in New York City in 1907–1908, and subsequently under other painters. Beginning as an advertising illustrator, she supported herself until 1918 by teaching art at various schools and colleges around the country, but after that date she devoted herself entirely to painting. She sent some drawings to a friend in New York City in 1916, who showed them to Alfred Stieglitz, the photographer and founder of the famous 291 Gallery. Stieglitz exhibited the drawings and, when Miss O'Keeffe moved to New York in 1918, introduced her to such painters as John Marin, Marsden Hartley, Arthur Dove, and Charles Demuth, all of whom showed at "291." Stieglitz and Miss O'Keeffe were married in 1924. Her early paintings were abstract, but in the 1920s she produced a series of lyrical depictions of flowers, intermixing these with careful, precise paintings of New York City and the East River. She found what became her characteristic style during a visit to New Mexico in 1929, when she became enchanted by the bleak landscape under the broad desert skies, and she thereafter often painted desert scenes, sometimes with a blanched skull of a longhorn in the foreground. She settled permanently in New Mexico after Stieglitz's death in 1946. She became in her later years the dean of Southwestern painters.

Oldenburg, Claes Thure (1929–   ), sculptor. Born in Stockholm on January 28, 1929, Oldenburg was the son of a Swedish diplomat whose career took him and his family first to Norway, during 1933–1937, and then to Chicago, where the elder Oldenburg was consul general. Claes was educated at Chicago's Latin School and at Yale, from which he graduated in 1950, whereupon he returned to Chicago to study at the Art Institute, supporting himself by working as a police reporter and in odd jobs. He moved to New York City in 1956 and rented an apartment in the East Village, at that time just coming into its own as a center of avant-garde artistic activity. Influenced by the French novelist Louis-Ferdinand Céline and by the artists Jean Dubuffet, Marcel Duchamp, and Jim Dine, Oldenburg produced works for his first one-man show, held at the Judson Gallery in Greenwich Village in May 1959, that consisted mostly of bundle-like "sculptures" made of paper, wood, and string, the inspiration for which, the artist said, had been the heaps of rubbish that he had seen as he walked the streets of his run-down neighborhood. Building on what he called the "ray gun" concept, Oldenburg expanded his works of this period into a total "scene" that he dubbed "The Street," exhibited at the Martha Jackson Gallery in the fall of 1960, and then moved the next year to another scene, "The Store," that eventually became a complex "metaphor" for color, as "The Street" had been a "metaphor" for line. During the 1960s he moved on again, creating a total "Home" environment that was, he said, a "metaphor" for volume, the works of this period being executed and shown in California. Earlier, he had opened an actual store on East Second Street in New York City that was variously called the Ray Gun Manufacturing Company and the Ray Gun Theatre, where he conducted artistic "happenings," and that resulted in two books, *Store Days: Documents from The Store*, 1961, and *Ray Gun Theatre*, 1962. It was at about this time that Oldenburg began to produce his characteristic "soft sculptures," made at different times of cloth, plastic, foam rubber, and other materials and representing ordinary objects but in gigantic size—a ten-foot ice-cream cone, a five-by-seven-foot hamburger, a nine-foot-high slice of cake, a six-foot tube of toothpaste, a folded shirt the size of a double bed. A soft bathroom and a soft car followed in due course in his effort to create what he called monuments of ordinary useful things. Toward the end of the 1960s Oldenburg began to propose a series of real monuments having symbolic significance for various cities—a huge banana for Times Square, an electric fan for the Statue of Liberty, a windshield wiper for Grant Park in Chicago—but the only one of his proposals to be realized was a gigantic lipstick erected on the Yale campus as a gift from the artist to his alma mater. Oldenburg had a retrospective show at the Museum of Modern Art in New York City in 1969 and, as it became evident that he had far transcended the Pop-art movement in which he had his start, his works began to appear in the permanent collections of museums both in the United States and abroad. By the 1970s he was one of the most successful and spectacular of American artists.

Oldfield, Barney (1878–1946), automobile racer. Born on January 29, 1878, in Wauseon, Ohio, Berna Eli Oldfield was a bicycle racer in his youth. About 1900 he became acquainted with the bicycle racer Tom Cooper, who introduced him in 1902 to Henry Ford, who was looking for a fearless driver for his racing car, the 999. The first time Oldfield drove the 999 he covered 5 miles in 5 minutes and 28 seconds, and on June 15, 1903, at Indianapolis, he became the first man to travel at the speed of a mile a minute. For the next 15 years he was a familiar figure at American automobile racetracks, winning many races and surviving many crackups. In 1910 he set a speed record of 131.724 miles per hour that endured until after World War I. For a number of years he annually drove a car—usually a Ford—across the continent from east to west, his time for the journey being about equal to that considered normal for ordinary drivers a decade later. Because of his well-publicized achievements his name became synonymous with speed, and any daredevil driver was called a "Barney Oldfield." After his retirement from racing in 1918 he continued to be involved in tire manufacturing and auto safety engineering (the 999 had had no safety devices whatsoever). He died in Beverly Hills, California, on October 4, 1946.

Olds, Ransom Eli (1864–1950), automobile manufacturer. Born in Geneva, Ohio, on June 3, 1864, Olds attended schools in Cleveland and in Lansing, Michigan, and studied briefly at a small business college in Lansing. In 1885 he bought an interest in his father's machine shop and the next year, after much experimentation, he produced his first "horseless carriage," a three-wheeled, steam-powered vehicle whose first, pre-dawn, test drive roused a terrible commotion in the neighborhood. By 1893 Olds had devised a more practical four-wheeled vehicle, and in 1895 he built his first gasoline-powered automobile. In 1896 he organized the Olds Motor Vehicle Company, capitalized at $50,000, and built six autos in the first year. In 1899 the firm was reorganized as the Olds Motor Works in Detroit and began producing the quickly popular Oldsmobile passenger cars in quantity. The Olds firm pioneered in large-scale production and established the basic pattern for the Detroit automobile industry. In 1902 fire destroyed the factory and the new plant built immediately afterward in Lansing incorporated many automatic features that would later, in the hands of Henry Ford, become the full-scale assembly line. Between 1902, when the famed "curved-dash" Oldsmobile was introduced, and 1904, when Olds sold the firm (it was eventually acquired by General Motors), some 4000 cars a year were turned out. A daring transcontinental journey undertaken by two Oldsmobile drivers in 1904—a 44-day trek from Detroit to Portland, Oregon—inspired the popular song "In My Merry Oldsmobile." In 1904 Olds organized the Reo Motor Car Company, of which he was president until 1924 and chairman of the board from then until his retirement in 1936. He was a benefactor of many colleges, notably Michigan State College (now University) and Kalamazoo College. He died in Lansing on August 26, 1950.

Oldschool, Oliver, Esq., *see* Dennie, Joseph

Old Stager, *see* Adams, William Taylor

Oliver, Joseph (1885?–1938), "King," musician and songwriter. Born probably in 1885 and probably in New Orleans, Oliver grew up with his prospects circumscribed by poverty, meager education, and his race. For a time in his youth he worked as a domestic servant, but from an early age his great interest was music. He played cornet with various marching and club bands in New Orleans, gradually gaining a reputation as a virtuoso and by 1918 becoming known as "King." In 1917 he moved to Chicago and continued to work as a journeyman cornetist until 1920, when he organized his own band. The style of music that had only lately become widely known as "jazz" and that was rapidly catching on with audiences beyond the black communities of New Orleans, St. Louis, and Chicago, found in Oliver one of its most important and energetic early exponents. His band toured California in 1921–1922 and in 1922 was reorganized as King Oliver's Creole Jazz Band, featuring, among others, young Louis Armstrong on second horn, Johnny Dodds backing and filling with clarinet figures, and Lillian Hardin (Armstrong's first wife) on piano. Oliver's arrangements rested on the persistent beat of syncopated march music and involved a blend of orchestrated harmony and free-flowing polyphony, the musicians—all first-rate—weaving their own musical line in and around the melody and each other's instruments; the strong blues feeling of the ensemble and solo playing combined with a pervasive sense of gaiety, constituted much of the essence of jazz and much of its appeal. Oliver composed a large number of songs, many becoming jazz standards: "Doctor Jazz," "West End Blues," "Dixieland Blues," "Dippermouth," and "High Society" were among them. The Creole Jazz Band endured only until 1924, but it made a number of recordings that soon came to be prized by collectors. After that time Oliver's career, fortunes, and health began a slow decline. A stint in New York City in the late 1920s was only partially successful; in 1937 he settled in Savannah, Georgia, where he died on April 8, 1938.

Olmsted, Frederick Law (1822–1903), landscape architect. Born on April 27, 1822, in Hartford, Connecticut, Olmsted was prevented by weak eyesight from entering Yale in 1837, as he had planned. Instead he studied engineering for a time, worked for two years in a New York City mercantile house, attended lectures at Yale for a year, and sailed to the Orient aboard a trading vessel. In 1844 he embarked on a farming career; he studied scientific methods of agriculture, served virtual apprenticeships on prize farms, and in 1847 began his own operations, which included a small nursery business. His observations during an extended visit to England and Europe were published in 1852 as *Walks and Talks of an American Farmer in England*. In 1852, on commission from the *New York Times*, he traveled down the Atlantic coast into the South and later wrote a clear, unbiased report of his findings, *A Journey in the Seaboard Slave States*, 1856. Subsequent trips resulted in *A Journey Through Texas*, 1857, and *A Journey in the Back Country*, 1860, and in 1861 the three books were condensed into one, *Journey and Explorations in the Cotton Kingdom*, which was particularly influential in England during the Civil War. In 1857 he was appointed superintendent of New York City's Central Park, then in process of construction. A competition was held to select a new plan for the park, and Olmsted collaborated with Calvert Vaux in developing the successful design. In 1858 he became chief architect of the park and from then until 1861 worked assiduously to create a park that would be both a work of art and a functional part of the city. From 1861 to 1863 he was secretary of the U.S. Sanitary Commission, the forerunner, in providing comforts and care for soldiers, of the Red Cross. From 1863 to 1865 he was in California, where he secured the establishment of the magnificent Yosemite Valley as a state park and served as the first president of the park's commission. In 1865 he returned to New York City to continue work on Central Park. Thereafter, for several decades, he created parks and landscaped settings all over the country: Brooklyn's Prospect Park, Philadelphia's Fairmount Park, Riverside and Morningside parks in New York City, the grounds of Stanford University, those of the Capitol in Washington, D.C., Mt. Royal Park in Montreal, the park system of Boston, and many others. He was the outstanding landscape architect of his time and his works stand yet unequaled. In 1892–1893 he helped to design and supervised the execution of the plans for the grounds for the World's Columbian Exposition in Chicago, now Jackson Park, and during the last year of his career he devoted much time to the landscaping of Biltmore, the famed Vanderbilt estate near Asheville, North Carolina. He retired in 1895 and lived quietly until his death on August 28, 1903, in Brookline, Massachusetts.

Olney, Richard (1835–1917), lawyer and public official. Born on September 15, 1835, in Oxford, Massachusetts, Olney was educated at Brown University and the Harvard Law School, from which he graduated in 1858. Admitted to the bar the next year, he entered the office of a noted Boston lawyer who, in quick succession, conferred on Olney his daughter in marriage and his law practice. Olney confined himself mainly during the next 30 years to corporation law, since his abrasive personality did not promise success in court trials; and as a Democrat in Massachusetts, he saw little possibility of realizing his political ambitions, which were nevertheless strong. He was elected to the state legislature in 1873 but other attempts to win public office failed. In 1892, with the election of Grover Cleveland, a Democrat, to the presidency, his chance came, and he was named attorney general, although he was little known outside a narrow circle of influential businessmen and Democratic leaders. He entered the office in 1893, but the year before he had written a secret communication that, when it was later discovered, became symbolic of the attitude of business toward government interference with commerce in this period. Railroad men, on the whole, hated the Interstate Commerce Commission (ICC), and they entertained some hope, upon Cleveland's election, that it could be got rid of. But Olney, then serving as counsel to the Chicago, Burlington & Quincy Railroad, wrote its president, with remarkable frankness, that in his opinion "it would not be a wise thing to abolish the Commission," which could be expected, as it grew older, to support rather than oppose the railroads in their aims. "The part of wisdom," Olney said in a statement that later became famous, "is not to destroy the Commission but to utilize it." The attitude thus expressed was soon manifested in other ways. In the summer of 1894 there occurred in Illinois the great Pullman strike, which pitted Eugene V. Debs and his American Railway Union against one of the most powerful railroad corporations. Olney supported the Pullman Company to the hilt, obtaining an injunction against the strikers, sending troops to the scene, arresting Debs and his associates, and arguing before the Supreme Court the next year against the unsuccessful appeal of their conviction for disobeying the injunction. In 1895, on the death of Cleveland's secretary of state, Olney was named to that position, and soon found himself deeply involved in the Venezuela Boundary Dispute, a controversy between Great Britain and Venezuela. He managed U.S. interests aggressively and finally forced the British to give way and accept arbitration. Olney's dispatch of July 1895 to the U.S. minister in London declared that "the United States is practically sovereign on this continent, and its fiat is law upon the subjects to which it confines its interposition," a policy sometimes referred to as the Olney Corollary to the Monroe Doctrine. Olney thereafter worked hard to bring about a comprehensive settlement of outstanding Anglo-American disputes, but his efforts were frustrated by the Senate, which refused to ratify an arbitration treaty he had prepared. He was also concerned throughout his time in the cabinet with problems connected with Cuba and China. He retired when William McKinley was inaugurated in 1897 and refused all further offers of public office, although he remained an influential figure in the Democratic party. He continued to practice law in Boston until his death there on April 8, 1917.

Oñate, Juan de (1550?–1625?), colonial governor. Born in New Spain, in what is now Mexico, although the exact place is not known, about 1550, Oñate was the son of a governor of Nueva Galicia and one of the richest men in America; he himself married a descendant of both Hernando Cortés and Montezuma. After a spirited competition for the place, he was appointed by the viceroy the first governor of New Mexico in 1595, which meant in effect that he had the right to conquer and settle the area, although at his own expense. After equipping an expedition, he led his force across the Rio Grande in 1598 and took formal possession, in a ceremony at a site near the present El Paso, Texas, "of all the kingdoms and provinces of New Mexico." Establishing headquarters at San Juan at the mouth of the Rio Chama near present-day Los Alamos, he explored a wide region over the next several years, pushing as far as Kansas in one direction and the Gulf of California in another, and put down Indian uprisings. Partly because of interference from Mexico City, in 1607 he resigned his position. In resigning he may have been bluffing, but the viceroy called his bluff, accepted his resignation, and ordered Oñate back to Mexico, where he was charged with immorality, cruelty toward the Indians, and misrepresenting the value of the colony to Spain. He was convicted of some of the charges in 1614, heavily fined, and deprived of his titles. He spent much of the rest of his life trying to reverse the verdict, and in 1624 he appears to have succeeded with respect to the sentence but not with respect to the restoration of his titles. In that year he is known to have been in Spain, but thereafter he disappears from history.

O'Neale, Peggy, *see* Eaton, Margaret O'Neale

O'Neill, Eugene Gladstone (1888–1953), playwright. Born on October 16, 1888, in a Broadway hotel in New York City, O'Neill was the son of James O'Neill, an actor, and grew up on the road. His family life was highly unstable; he was educated at boarding schools and during 1906–1907 attended Princeton. For the next six years he sailed as a seaman, worked on the waterfront and as a reporter, and suffered through bouts of alcoholism; the period climaxed in a suicide attempt. In 1912 he entered a tuberculosis sanatorium, where he spent several months. While there he began to experiment with drama and during 1914–1915 he studied at George Pierce Baker's 47 Workshop at Harvard. In 1916 the Provincetown (Massachusetts) Players produced his *Bound East for Cardiff*, a one-act play that was also staged later in the year by the Playwrights Theater in New York City. Several more short works followed, including *The Long Voyage Home*, 1917, and *The Hairy Ape*, 1922, and in 1920 his first full-length drama, *Beyond the Horizon*, opened on Broadway and won the first of his four Pulitzer prizes. During the next 23 years he completed more than a score of plays and rose to the forefront of the American theater. His major works included *The Emperor Jones*, 1920, about a moral disintegration of a black Pullman porter turned dictator of a tropical island; *Anna Christie*, 1922 (Pulitzer Prize) about a prostitute's struggle for redemption; *Desire Under the Elms*, 1924, about a father-and-son conflict; *The Great God Brown*, 1925, a symbolic, formalized struggle between idealism and materialism; *Strange Interlude*, 1928 (Pulitzer Prize), a Freudian examination of woman that employed Elizabethan monologistic asides; The trilogy *Mourning Becomes Electra*, 1931, based on a Greek tragedy; *Ah, Wilderness!*, 1933, his only comedy; *The Iceman*

Cometh, a complex symbolic drama written in 1939 but produced and published in 1946; and the semi-autobiographical *Long Day's Journey into Night*, written by 1941 but not produced until 1956 (Pulitzer Prize). In treating the drama as literature and in utilizing characters—drug addicts, prostitutes, derelicts of all sorts—previously confined to the novel, O'Neill set a new high standard for American drama and became, both at home and abroad, the best known and most widely admired American dramatist. In 1936 he became the first U.S. playwright to be awarded the Nobel Prize for Literature. After 1943 a crippling disease ended his writing. He died in Boston on November 27, 1953.

O'Neill, Peggy, *see* Eaton, Margaret O'Neale

O'Neill, Rose Cecil (1874–1944), illustrator, doll designer, and author. Born in Wilkes-Barre, Pennsylvania, on June 25, 1874, Miss O'Neill was educated in convents in Omaha, Nebraska, and in New York City, where at the age of fifteen she sought work as an illustrator. She left the New York convent in 1892 and rejoined her family. She returned to New York City in 1896 to marry Gray Latham, whom she divorced in 1901. She had begun to earn a considerable income with illustrations for such magazines as *Harper's*, *Good Housekeeping*, and *Puck*. In 1902 she married the editor of *Puck*, Harry Leon Wilson, and illustrated several of his books; but this marriage soon ended and Miss O'Neill was on her own. She did some painting and illustrating and wrote several books, including *The Loves of Edwy*, 1904, and *The Lady in the White Veil*, 1909, but it was not until 1910 that she began to enjoy major commercial success with her famous "Kewpies," to which the *Ladies' Home Journal*, under Edward Bok, devoted a full page in December 1909. She soon began marketing Kewpie dolls, patented in 1913; these modernized American Cupids swept the country for the next three decades and their sales allowed Miss O'Neill all the leisure she required to paint in Washington Square and Capri and to entertain flamboyantly at her home in Westport, Connecticut, and to write such extremely Gothic romances as *Garda*, 1929, and *The Goblin Woman*, 1930, and a sonnet cycle based on Shakespeare's sonnets, *The Master-Mistress*, 1922. But all of these were of relatively little account compared to the popularity of the Kewpie dolls, which resulted in four books written and illustrated by her: *Kewpies and Dottie Darling*, 1913; *Kewpies: Their Book, Verse, and Poetry*, 1913; *Kewpie Kutouts*, 1914; and *Kewpies and the Runaway Baby*, 1928. Miss O'Neill died on April 6, 1944, in Springfield, Missouri.

O'Neill, Thomas Philip, Jr. (1912–   ), public official. Born on December 9, 1912, in Cambridge, Massachusetts, O'Neill graduated from Boston College in 1936 and, already a veteran of city politics, was elected to the state legislature in the same year. Regularly reelected, he became Democratic floor leader in 1947 and majority leader in 1948. In 1952 he ran successfully for the congres-sional seat vacated by John F. Kennedy, and in the House, under the sponsorship of John W. McCormack, he quickly became part of the inner circle of Democratic regulars around Sam Rayburn and Lyndon Johnson. Generally liberal in his views, particularly on matters of education and civil rights, he was an effective member of the House Rules Committee from 1955. Early in the Vietnam war he became an opponent of further U.S. involvement, and in 1968 he supported the presidential primary campaign of Sen. Eugene J. McCarthy. In 1971 O'Neill was elected Democratic whip, and in 1972 he became majority leader. In December 1976 he was chosen speaker of the House for the 95th Congress, succeeding the retiring Carl Albert.

Onsager, Lars (1903–1976), physical chemist. Born in Oslo, Norway, on November 27, 1903, Onsager studied in Trondheim, Norway, and at the Swiss Federal Institute of Technology in Zurich before coming to the United States in 1928 as an associate in chemistry at Johns Hopkins. After teaching also at Brown, he went to Yale in 1933 as a Sterling fellow and received his Ph.D. from Yale two years later. An assistant professor at Yale from 1934 to 1940 and an associate professor from 1940 to 1945, he was named J. Willard Gibbs Professor of Theoretical Chemistry in 1945, the year in which he became a U.S. citizen. His early work in statistical mechanics had attracted the attention of Peter Debye, under whose supervision he carried out his researches in Switzerland; but he was eventually to supersede Debye's analysis of electrolytic processes. He continued to work on electrolytes after he came to the United States, and he published a number of papers during the next 20 years that greatly influenced the course of research in physical chemistry. As early as 1931 he had become aware, and had shown both mathematically and by experiment, that the rate of entropy increase in interacting irreversible processes may be assumed to be a minimum, and his further work with regard to this principle led to its acceptance as the fourth law of thermodynamics. For these researches he was awarded the 1968 Nobel Prize for Chemistry. He also carried out many other important investigations and published influential papers concerning the theory of thermal diffusion, orientational order in bacterial communities, quantum mechanics, and order-disorder and many-body problems. He was the recipient of the Rumford Medal, 1953, the Lorentz Medal, 1958, the Debye Award, 1965, and the National Science Medal, 1968. He died on October 5, 1976, in Coral Gables, Florida.

Oppenheimer, J. Robert (1904–1967), physicist. Born in New York City on April 22, 1904, Oppenheimer was educated at the Ethical Culture School and at Harvard, from which he graduated in 1925 after three years' study. He continued his studies at Cambridge University and from there, at the invitation of Max Born, went to Göttingen, where he received his doctorate in 1927. After two more years at the universities of Leiden and Zurich, he returned to the United States and joined the faculties of the California Institute of Technology (Caltech) and the University of California at Berkeley, becoming full professor at both in 1936. He was a remarkable teacher and inspired great devotion in his students; he was especially noted for his broad grasp of the entire range of quantum and nuclear physics. In 1941 he became associated informally with the atomic-bomb project, codenamed the Manhattan Engineering District; by the next year, on leave from Caltech, he was in a position of great authority, helping to select and then taking charge of the huge staff—which included Enrico Fermi and Niels Bohr—of the government atomic-energy laboratory at Los Alamos, New Mexico. His leadership and administrative ability contributed so much to the success of the project that afterward he was publicly hailed, more so than any of the purely scientific staff, as the father of the atomic bomb. In 1946 he was awarded the Presidential Medal of Merit. He served as a top government adviser on atomic policy; from 1946 to 1952 he was chairman of the general advisory committee of the Atomic Energy Commission (AEC) and as the leading scientific consultant to the U.S. delegation to the United Nations Atomic Energy Commission was the principal author of the preliminary reports on the subject as well as of the subsequent Baruch Plan for United Nations control of atomic energy. A consistent advocate of civilian and international control of atomic energy, he opposed the building of the hydrogen bomb but was overruled by President Harry S. Truman in 1949. In 1947 he became director of the Institute for Advanced Study in Princeton, New Jersey. In December 1953 charges were lodged against him accusing him of disloyalty, Communist sympathies, and possible treason. His security clearance was revoked by the AEC and then by President Dwight D. Eisenhower, cutting him off from government research. An investigative board appointed by the AEC in 1954 cleared him of the serious charges of disloyalty but maintained that he was a security risk. The AEC itself reached a similar conclusion; it held him to have been imprudent in his associations and upheld the revocation of his security clearance. The decision, not unanimous, was protested by scores of his fellow scientists, who saw the action as a manifestation of repression inspired by the "anti-Communist" hysteria created by Senator Joseph R. McCarthy. The official proscription of Oppenheimer eased in later years and seemed to come to a symbolic end in 1963 when he was awarded the AEC's highest honor, the Fermi Award, by President Lyndon B. Johnson. Oppenheimer retired from the Institute for Advanced Study in 1966 and died in Princeton, New Jersey, on February 18, 1967. A man of wide cultural interests, he concerned himself with the role of science and the scientist in the world; his writings included *Science and the Common Understanding*, 1954, *The Open Mind*, 1955, and *Some Reflections on Science and Culture*, 1960.

Optic, Oliver, see Adams, William Taylor

O'Reilly, John Boyle (1844–1890), author, editor, and Irish patriot. Born in Castle Dowth, near Drogheda, Ireland, on June 28, 1844, O'Reilly spent several years during his youth as a printer's apprentice on Irish and English newspapers but returned from England to Ireland in 1863 to enlist in the British army. Joining the secret Fenian organization of Irish patriots, he was recruited by Fenian leader John Devoy to enroll other Irish soldiers. His activities, considered traitorous by the British, were discovered in 1866 and on July 9 of that year he was sentenced to be shot, the sentence being commuted the same day to life imprisonment and later to 23 years at hard labor. Deported with other political prisoners to Australia in January 1868, he never ceased his efforts to escape and, aided by a Roman Catholic priest and the officers of several U.S. whaling vessels, made his way to Philadelphia, where he arrived on November 23, 1869, taking out his first naturalization papers the same day. The story of his escape had preceded him, and he arrived in Boston a minor hero. Obtaining a job on the *Pilot*, a weekly read by many Irish-Americans, he was soon the paper's editor; in 1876 he and the archbishop of Boston bought the paper. In association with his friend Devoy he supported the worldwide activities of the Irish Republicans, among other things planning the successful rescue in 1876 of the remaining Irish prisoners in Western Australia. An ardent Fenian throughout his life—although he deplored the disputes among Fenian leaders—he made the *Pilot* the most important Irish-oriented paper in the country. He himself became a national figure, partly because of the aura surrounding his early imprisonment and escape and partly because of his writings, which were mostly sentimental, though capable, ballads and songs. He published *Songs from Southern Seas*, 1873; *Songs, Legends and Ballads*, 1878; *The Statues in the Block*, 1881; and *In Bohemia*, 1886, all collections of poems; *Moondyne*, 1879, a novel of convict life in Australia; and *Ethics of Boxing and Manly Sport*, 1888. Although an inveterate Irish patriot and the leader of Irish-Americans in New England, he always emphasized the responsibilities of American citizenship and retained a sense of Ireland's debt to the United States. He died in Hull, Massachusetts, on August 10, 1890; a memorial to him in the Fenway in Boston was erected by popular subscription.

Ormandy, Eugene (1899–   ), musician and conductor. Born in Budapest on November 18, 1899, Ormandy was a musical prodigy who began playing the violin before he was four. The youngest student at Hungary's Royal State Academy of Music at five, he received the academy's degree at fourteen and its artist's diploma at sixteen. Meanwhile he had won acceptance as a concert violinist. An able student of the composer Zoltán Kodály, he also studied with Béla Bartók. He was awarded a state diploma as professor of music at the age of seventeen, and by 1919 he was teaching master classes at the State Conservatory. In 1921 Ormandy journeyed to the United States and in 1927 he became a U.S. citizen. He remained at first in unaccustomed obscurity as a violinist in the orchestra at the Capitol Theater in New York City, but he rose in time to become the theater's principal conductor and in the late 1920s was quick to realize the potentialities of radio for reaching a wider musical audience, becoming a regular conductor of musical broadcasts. His rise to prominence in the United States began after an appearance as guest conductor of the New York Philharmonic in 1930. Invited to return for a short engagement the following season, he also made a notable appearance with the Philadelphia Orchestra in 1931 as a last-minute substitute for the great Arturo Toscanini. From 1931 to 1936 he was a regular guest conductor at Philadelphia while devoting his principal efforts to rejuvenating the Minneapolis Symphony Orchestra. He subsequently shared the podium at the Philadelphia Orchestra with Leopold Stokowski for two years and in 1938 succeeded Stokowski as musical director. Under Ormandy's direction the orchestra remained one of the nation's foremost, and after 1949 it was annually greeted with enthusiasm by European audiences. The recipient of numerous honorary degrees and foreign decorations, Ormandy was the last of the great European-born conductors who exercised such an imposing influence on American symphony orchestras during the first half of the twentieth century.

Orr, James Lawrence (1822–1873), public official. Born in Craytonville, in Anderson County, South Carolina, on May 12, 1822, Orr began the study of law at the University of Virginia in 1839 but returned home to complete his studies in a law office and was admitted to the bar when he became twenty-one, in 1843. For a short time he supplemented his income from the law by working as a journalist, but in 1844 he entered politics, becoming a member of the state legislature, in which he distinguished himself. He was elected as a Democrat to the House of Representatives in 1848 and held his seat until 1859. He voted against the Compromise of 1850 but at the same time led the movement in his state against immediate secession, which, combined with his later opposition to Know-Nothingism and his support of Senator Stephen A. Douglas, made him popular in the North. As a result he was elected speaker of the House for the 1857–1859 session. But as the country headed toward civil war, his opposition to secession, which endeared him to Northerners, offended his constituents and he was defeated in a bid for the Senate in 1858. Failing to obtain the Democratic nomination for president at the national convention in 1860, he thereupon joined the other South Carolina delegates in withdrawing from the convention and advocated the state's secession from the Union. After a short period of military service during which he raised and commanded Orr's Regiment of Rifles in South Carolina, he was elected a senator of the Confederate States of America in 1861. Recognizing the inevita-

bility of the defeat of the Confederacy earlier than most, he again changed his views, quarreled with President Jefferson Davis, and from 1864 advocated a negotiated peace. The small majority that agreed with his position was able to elect him governor of South Carolina in 1865, in which post he shrewdly compromised with the Reconstructionist officers of the federal government in his state. Once more, however, he lost the support of his constituents, whereupon he joined the Radical Republicans, was elected to the U.S. circuit-court bench in 1868, and, after supporting President Ulysses S. Grant's opposition to the Ku Klux Klan at the Republican national convention of 1872, was appointed by Grant U.S. minister to Russia. He died in St. Petersburg, on May 5, 1873.

Osborn, Fairfield (1887–1969), conservationist. Born in Princeton, New Jersey, on January 15, 1887, Osborn was christened Henry Fairfield but dropped his first name at an early age. He graduated from Princeton in 1909, spending the next year in England for further study at Cambridge University. After several years of minor jobs in various parts of the country and army service as a captain of artillery in France in World War I, he returned to enter the investment business in New York City, but his main interest continued to lie in the natural sciences. From 1922 a trustee of the New York Zoological Society, of which his father was president, he retired from business in 1935 to become secretary of that organization and become president in 1940, in which position he remained until 1968. With characteristic energy and success, Osborn threw himself into all of the activities of the society—maintenance of the New York Zoological Park, the Bronx Zoo, in New York City; the publication of a bimonthly magazine; the sponsorship of research; and support of the Conservation Foundation. He also wrote articles and two popular and influential books, *Our Plundered Planet*, 1948, and *The Limits of Our Earth*, 1953. The former was one of the first works to sound the clarion call for action to stop mankind from destroying the natural environment upon which human life depends. The second book contained further comment on his theme of cooperation with nature and argued that the collapse of ancient civilizations was at least partly owing to the misuse of available natural resources. It also strongly urged population control, a crusade that much occupied Osborn during his last years. He died in New York City on September 16, 1969.

Osborn, Henry Fairfield (1857–1935), paleontologist and museum administrator. Born in the town of Fairfield, Connecticut, after which he was named, on August 8, 1857, Osborn spent most of his boyhood in New York City, studying in New York schools, and then at Princeton, from which he graduated in 1877. In that year he and two other students made a fossil-collecting trip to Colorado and Wyoming, but, although the experience was repeated twice more in the next few years, Osborn decided that he was not a natural field collector and subsequently concentrated on theoretical research, leaving the field work to assistants. Further studies under William Henry Welch at the Bellevue Hospital Medical College were followed by a trip to Europe in 1879, during which he met the great English biologists of the time, including Charles Darwin. Returning to Princeton as a student and teacher, he became professor of natural science in 1881 and professor of comparative anatomy two years later; he joined the faculty of Columbia University in 1891 as a professor of biology and then of zoology and remained associated with Columbia until his death; during 1892–1895 he was also dean of the faculty of pure science. But his interest in academic work slackened as the great work of his life at the American Museum of Natural History in New York City came to occupy more and more of his time and effort. He had been named curator of vertebrate paleontology at the museum in 1891, at the time of his move to Columbia, and he continued to build up that department of the museum until, in addition to being a research center of great influence, it contained the world's largest and most important collection of vertebrate fossils. At the same time he became deeply interested in museum administration and was from 1908 until 1933 president and thereafter honorary president, of the museum, his long tenure being marked by extraordinary advances in almost every area—buildings, city appropriations and endowment, scientific staff, and membership. From 1900 he was also associated with the U.S. Geological Survey, as vertebrate paleontologist until 1924 and thereafter as senior geologist. An ambitious and untiring worker, he wrote an enormous number of books, articles, and monographs, his published output running to nearly 1000 items comprising more than 12,000 pages. Among his more important and influential scientific works were *The Age of Mammals in Europe, Asia and North America*, 1910; *Equidae of the Oligocene, Miocene, and Pliocene of North America*, 1918, on fossil horses; *The Titanotheres of Ancient Wyoming, Dakota, and Nebraska*, two volumes, 1929, on a family of large extinct mammals; and the posthumous *Proboscidea, A Monograph of the Discovery, Evolution, Migration, and Extinction of the Mastodonts and Elephants of the World*, also in two volumes, 1936–1942. He also wrote popular books for the laymen, including *Men of the Old Stone Age*, 1915 (revised edition 1925), which stirred a whole generation of would-be paleontologists and fossil hunters. Through his educational work at the museum he also helped to create public interest in and understanding of paleontology and can be said to have made "dinosaur" a household word. He received almost every honor open to a man of his professions anywhere in the world, including membership in some 61 learned societies and the national academies of some 15 countries. His autobiographical *Fifty-two Years of Research, Observation and Publication* appeared in 1930; he died five years later, on November 6, 1935, in Garrison, New York.

Osceola (1804?–1838), Indian leader. Born probably among the Creek Indians on the Tallapoosa River in Georgia about 1804, Osceola was also known as Powell, suggesting that his father (or grandfather) was English or Scottish; but according to another view he was of pure Indian stock. He moved to Florida Territory with his mother and is believed to have fought with the Indians against Gen. Andrew Jackson in the first phase of the Seminole wars while still in his teens. His opposition to efforts to remove the Seminole westward under treaty is recorded as early as 1832, when he opposed the treaty of Paynes Landing, and on April 22, 1835, when the Seminole chiefs silently refused to acknowledge the treaty, Osceola is said to have angrily thrust his knife through the document in protest. He was thereupon arrested and imprisoned, but he escaped by feigning a change of heart and led a band of young braves in the murder of a Seminole chief who had agreed to the arrangement and in the killing of the U.S. Indian agent at Fort King, near present-day Ocala. This event precipitated the second period of the Seminole Wars, in the course of which Osceola, although not a chief, established himself as probably the dominant military leader of the Seminole. Hiding the women and children of the tribe deep in the Everglades, he harassed the U.S. troops for two years with brilliant guerilla tactics, with the result that the U.S. officer in command, Gen. Thomas S. Jesup, was severely criticized for his ineffectiveness. Jesup, enraged, tricked Osceola and several of his followers into coming out of the Everglades into St. Augustine in October 1837 under a flag of truce; when the Indians entered the compound they were arrested and imprisoned despite public protests. Osceola was later removed to Fort Moultrie near Charleston, South Carolina, where he died, possibly from poison or mistreatment, on January 30, 1838. The Second Seminole War continued in a desultory fashion for several more years and resulted in the extermination of most of the tribe.

Osler, Sir William (1849–1919), physician and educator. Born at Bond Head, near Windsor, Ontario, on July 12, 1849, Osler was educated at Toronto and McGill universities, taking his M.D. from McGill in 1872. Even before that, at the age of twenty, he had begun to publish the graceful sketches that he was to collect in later books and that went far to establish his reputation as one of the most humorous and human, as well as one of the most learned, doctors of his time. After two years of postgraduate study in various European and British hospitals, he returned to Canada in 1874 to become professor of medicine at McGill, moving from there to the University of Pennsylvania in 1884—the offer being tendered to him while he was in Europe during the summer of 1884 and the difficult decision to leave Canada being made on the basis of a flip of a coin. In 1889 he was appointed physician-in-chief of the new Johns Hopkins Hospital in Baltimore, and was chosen by William Henry Welch, chief of pathology at The Johns Hopkins University medical school (at that time not yet open), as professor of medicine in the new school. For the next 16 years —until 1905, when he accepted the Regius professorship of medicine at Oxford—Osler taught medicine at Hopkins with enormous skill and gathered around him a distinguished group of associates and students, many of whom went on to become leading medical practitioners of the early twentieth century; it was largely owing to Osler, who established both clinical and tutorial practice on the best European models, and Welch that Hopkins gained its reputation as the premier medical school of the United States. Osler did considerable research on cardiovascular diseases and anatomy, on blood platelets, and on other topics, and his textbook *The Principles and Practice of Medicine* was published in 1892 and for the next 30 years dominated the field, reaching its 11th edition in 1930; it was translated into many other languages. The book is credited with influencing the founding of the Rockefeller Institute for Medical Research and the Rockefeller Foundation, for it was read by one of John D. Rockefeller's advisers, who urged him to support work in medical research and education. Among Osler's other books were *Aequanimitas*, 1889; *The Master Word in Medicine*, 1903; *Science and Immortality*, 1904; and *The Student Life*, 1905, addresses or collections of addresses given on various occasions. At Oxford he continued to teach and to gather around him young men of extraordinary promise, was a curator of the Bodleian Library, and was the recipient of many honors and awards, including a baronetcy conferred on him at the coronation of George V in 1911. He was among the founders of the Royal Society of Medicine in 1907 and he was widely renowned as a medical historian, his great library of medical books going after his death to Johns Hopkins and to McGill. At his death in Oxford on December 29, 1919, Osler was eulogized by Dr. Welch as "probably the greatest figure in the medical world; the best known, the most influential, the most beloved." *The Life of Sir William Osler*, by the surgeon Harvey W. Cushing, one of his most brilliant associates at Hopkins, appeared in 1925 and won a Pulitzer Prize.

Ossoli, Marchioness, *see* Fuller, Margaret

O'Sullivan, Timothy H. (1840–1882), photographer. Born in New York City in 1840, O'Sullivan was the son of Irish immigrants. They settled in Staten Island, New York, where the boy grew up and where he came to know the great pioneering photographer Mathew Brady. He became an apprentice to Brady around 1855 and went with Brady's associate, Alexander Gardner, to Washington in 1856 to open a studio there. He assisted Brady in photographing Abraham Lincoln's inauguration in 1861 and also accompanied him to the battlefield of Bull Run in July of that year. Later in 1861, when Brady and Gardner ended their association, O'Sullivan went with Gardner rather than Brady and served with him throughout the war, although during the years 1864–1865 he worked independently on many occasions. He was present at most of the major battlefields of the war, from the second battle of Bull Run to Petersburg, and just missed photographing the surrender of Gen. Robert E. Lee to Gen. Ulysses S. Grant at Appomattox, Virginia, in April 1865. After the war he joined the expedition led by Clarence King to survey along the 40th parallel between eastern Colorado and the California coast. Leaving San Francisco in July 1867, the group spent two seasons exploring an area of some 5000 square miles. O'Sullivan took the first photographs of many places of great interest and natural beauty, including the Truckee River, the Shoshone Falls of the Snake River, the valley of the Provo River, and Great Salt Lake itself. In 1870 he was official photographer to the expedition exploring the Isthmus of Panama, but he confined his pictures to the coastal and open-country areas, finding that his primitive equipment could not endure the heat and humidity of the jungle. The next year found him photographing Death Valley and a long stretch of the Colorado River, and in 1873 and 1875 he took many photographs in the Southwest. By that time his photographs were being published and attracting wide attention. In 1880 he was named chief photographer to the U.S. Treasury, but because of ill health he resigned the post soon afterward and died of tuberculosis at his father's home in Staten Island, New York, on January 14, 1882.

Otetiani, *see* Red Jacket

Otis, Elisha Graves (1811–1861), inventor and manufacturer. Born on August 3, 1811, in Halifax, Vermont, Otis was educated in public schools and worked variously in the construction and trucking business and in a grist mill, a carriage shop, a machine shop, a saw mill, and a bedstead factory. In the last enterprise he became in 1852 supervisor of construction of a new plant in Yonkers, New York; there, for working convenience, he developed a mechanical elevator with an innovative safety device to prevent it from falling even if the lifting chain broke. In 1853 he planned to leave the firm and join the Gold Rush to California, but two New York City firms whose representatives had seen the safety elevator requested replicas of it. He purchased space in the Yonkers plant and began manufacturing elevators. Demand for the device was small, however, until he publicly demonstrated its safety at the American Institute Fair in New York City in 1854, standing in an elevator and ordering the rope cut. With the effectiveness of the safety device proven, orders from industry for freight elevators gradually increased. In 1857 he installed the nation's first safe passenger elevator, in the Haughwout store in New York City. It was immediately popular and caused a revolution in the construction industry and in architecture. Providing a safe, efficient means of vertical transportation, it helped make practical the skyscraper, which soon followed. He patented numerous other devices, but his patent for a steam elevator in 1861 firmly established the Otis Elevator Company. Otis died in Yonkers on April 8, 1861, leaving the business to his sons.

Otis, Harrison Gray (1837–1917), soldier, editor, and publisher. Born in Marietta, Ohio, on February 10, 1837, Otis received little formal education; he served as a printer's apprentice in his teens and took a commercial course at a college in Columbus, Ohio. He moved to Kentucky before the Civil War, became a Republican, and served as a delegate to the Republican Party's national convention of 1860. When the Civil War broke out he enlisted as a private in the Union Army and served with distinction throughout the conflict, seeing action in 15 engagements, including the first battle of Bull Run (Manassas) and Antietam (Sharpsburg), and being twice wounded; at war's end he held the rank of lieutenant colonel. He worked in a succession of jobs after the war—as a legislative reporter in Ohio, as foreman in the government printing office in Washington, D.C., as chief of a division in the U.S. patent office, and from time to time as a Washington reporter for Ohio newspapers—but his great career in journalism did not begin until he moved to California in 1876. Settling first in Santa Barbara, he edited the *Santa Barbara Press* for several years and then moved to Los Angeles, where in 1882 he acquired an interest in the *Los Angeles Times*, which by that time had absorbed the *Weekly Mirror*. Within four years he had gained full control of the Times-Mirror Company, and for the next three decades he was one of the most powerful editors in California and, indeed, in the nation. Closely identified with Los Angeles, he helped to organize its chamber of commerce in 1888 and engaged in many civic activities. He served as a brigadier general of volunteers during the Spanish-American War and reached the rank of major general, but the war was only a brief interruption in his long, sometimes bitter, and always forceful editorship and ownership of the *Times*, which he used to espouse his conservative Republicanism and his unrelenting opposition to labor unions. On October 1, 1910, the offices of the paper were bombed by union men and 21 employees were killed; the trial of the McNamara brothers, James B. and John J., the next year ended when they confessed to having committed the crime, all of the lurid details of which had been endlessly reported in the *Times*. Otis retained complete control of every department of the paper until 1914, when he transferred his controlling interest to his daughter and son-in-law, Mr. and Mrs. Harry Chandler, but even after that he continued to direct its day-to-day operations until his death in Hollywood, California, on July 30, 1917. Besides profiting from his Times-Mirror holdings he made a fortune in California real estate, and he gave his Los Angeles home to the city as a public art gallery.

Otis, James (1725–1783), lawyer and public official. Born on February 5, 1725, in West Barnstable, Massachusetts, Otis graduated from Harvard in

1743, was admitted to the bar in 1748, and then settled in Boston. In the next ten years he established himself as a leader of the bar and served for a time as king's advocate general of the vice-admiralty court. In 1760 the long-disregarded provisions of the 1733 Sugar Act were revived by the British government and royal officials in Massachusetts sought to renew their writs of assistance, general search warrants earlier issued to customs officers. When the case came to court in February 1761 Otis was the chief spokesman for the opposition; he raised the doctrine of natural law underlying the rights of citizens and declared that even if affirmed by Parliament, such writs would be void. He lost the case, but the writs were destined to be a continuing issue contributing to the outbreak of the Revolution. Otis was elected almost immediately to the Massachusetts General Court where, with his father, who was speaker of the house, he led the opposition to the royal governor. In September 1762 he published the first of his many political pamphlets, *A Vindication of the Conduct of the House of Representatives of the Province of Massachusetts Bay*. He continued on the General Court, becoming equally well known for his fiery oratory and for his pamphleteering, and until 1769 was the major political leader in the province, as his writings were the basic and most prominent documents in the early part of the revolutionary struggle. In 1764, the year he was chosen to chair the committee of correspondence established by the General Court, he wrote *The Rights of the British Colonies Asserted and Proved* and in 1765 instigated, organized, and served in the intercolonial Stamp Act Congress. In that year also he wrote several powerful pamphlets, notably *Considerations on Behalf of the Colonists, in a Letter to a Noble Land* and *A Vindication of the British Colonies Against the Aspersions of the Halifax Gentleman*. Although he was a stout defender of the rights of the colonists, Otis opposed throughout his career the use of violence, and considered separation from Great Britain unthinkable. He was instrumental in organizing the non-importation movement that followed the Townshend Acts in 1767, but exerted himself equally in preventing active opposition to British occupation of Boston. Despite such scruples, he was branded by royal officials as an incendiary and threatened with trial for treason. On September 5, 1769, in a scuffle with a Crown officer, Otis was struck a severe blow to the head; he had for some time been exhibiting signs of instability and from that time on he was clearly unbalanced. Although he was reelected to the General Court during a lucid period in 1771, his public career was, to all intents and purposes, over. He was struck and killed by lightning in Andover, Massachusetts, on May 23, 1783.

Ousamequin, *see* Massasoit

Outcault, Richard Felton (1863–1928), cartoonist. Born in Lancaster, Ohio, on January 14, 1863, Outcault was educated at McMicken College (later a part of the University of Cincinnati) and studied art in Paris. He moved to New York City in the early 1890s, but the careful, precise drawings required of him in his work for the *Electrical World* and the *Street Railway Journal* cramped his style, and he sought other outlets for his talents, which were comic as well as graphic. His chance came with the development by the *New York World* of a process for printing color pictures, and Outcault was asked by the *World's* Sunday editor, Morril Goddard, to submit some drawings. Thus was the colored comic, or "funny paper," born. Outcault's first color drawing, entitled "The Origin of a New Species," appeared on Sunday, November 18, 1894, and was shortly followed by a series—the first regular newspaper cartoon feature—called *Hogan's Alley* with a rambunctious, urchinesque central character whose smart-alecky comments on the passing scene were written across his outlandish nightshirt. Through a printing-room error the nightshirt appeared in a brilliant canary shade and its wearer was promptly dubbed the "Yellow Kid." From 1896 the *New York Journal* also printed color comic pages, and the subsequent competition, which raged for two decades, led to the term "Yellow Kid journals," soon shortened to "Yellow journals," and, by a natural conversion, to "yellow journalism." Outcault's famous *Buster Brown* comic strip began in the *New York Herald* in 1902, and Buster and his dog Tige brought their creator fame and fortune. He continued the series until the end of World War I, publishing several books of Buster Brown and Tige cartoon strips, and co-authoring a dramatic version of their adventures. Outcault died on September 25, 1928, in Flushing, New York.

Owen, Robert Dale (1801–1877), social reformer, author and public official. Born in Glasgow, Scotland, on November 8, 1801, Owen was the son of the great English reformer Robert Owen and of Ann Dale, whose father, David Dale, was the proprietor of the cotton mills at New Lanark, Scotland, where Robert Owen put into effect his theories of social and industrial reform. Robert Dale Owen attended the New Lanark school and studied under private tutors and, for several years, in Switzerland. He came to the United States with his father in 1825 and went early the next year to the community at New Harmony, Indiana, which was ever after to be associated with his and his father's names. But New Harmony soon failed as a self-sufficient socialist community, and the younger Owen accompanied Frances Wright, whom he had met at New Harmony, first to her own community, Nashoba, near Memphis, Tennessee, and then to Europe, where he met the Marquis de Lafayette, William Godwin, Jeremy Bentham, and Mary Wollstonecraft Shelley, all of whom increased his already great determination to realize the social ideals of his father. He returned to New Harmony in 1828 but left it again the next year to go to New York City, where he edited the *Free Enquirer*, founded with Miss Wright as the successor to the *New Harmony Gazette*, which he had edited in Indiana. Owen and a group of like-minded reformers worked for two years in New York to alter the course of the New York Working Men's Party, substituting a program of public education for the party's original utopian hope for the equal division of property. But after a six-month sojourn with his father in England, Owen returned once more to New Harmony to undertake the most important activities of his career. He served three terms in the Indiana legislature, 1836–1838, during which time he succeeded in securing funds for the public schools, and two terms in the House of Representatives as a Democrat, 1843–1847, during which time he introduced the bill organizing the Smithsonian Institution and saw to it that the organization became a teaching as well as a research center. He was also chairman of the House's Building Committee, and out of his experiences there wrote *Hints on Public Architecture*, 1849. Back in Indiana after 1847, he lobbied successfully for property rights for married women and for liberalized divorce laws and engaged in a debate with Horace Greeley on the subject of divorce in the *New York Tribune* that was distributed in pamphlet form. He was named U.S. chargé d'affaires at Naples in 1853 and minister to the kingdom of the Two Sicilies two years later. At this time he came under the influence of spiritualism, about which he wrote two books, *Footfalls on the Boundary of Another World*, 1860, and *The Debatable Land between This World and the Next*, 1872; both revealed his interest in but his skepticism about the subject. Back in the United States in 1858, he became an ardent supporter of emancipation, and he wrote a letter to President Abraham Lincoln in September 1862 that is said to have influenced Lincoln more than any other document that reached him on the subject. During the first two years of the Civil War Owen was again in Europe as an agent of the state of Indiana, empowered to purchase arms to equip the troops raised by the states. In 1863 the War Department appointed him chairman of a committee to investigate the condition of freedmen, out of which grew his book *The Wrong of Slavery*, 1864. He was, however, an opponent of immediate Negro suffrage, urging instead that the right to vote be withheld from freedmen for ten years. After the war he devoted most of his time to writing pamphlets on social and political questions, *Beyond the Breakers*, 1870, a novel, and a series of autobiographical articles that appeared in the *Atlantic Monthly* during 1873 and in book form under the title *Threading My Way* in 1874. He died at his home on Lake George, New York, on June 24, 1877.

Owens, James Cleveland, *see* Owens, Jesse

Owens, Jesse (1913–1980), athlete. Born on September 12, 1913, in Danville, in Morgan County, Alabama, James Cleveland Owens, known as J.C. and then as Jesse, set his first track record while attending Fairview Junior High School in Cleveland, running the 100-yard dash in 10 seconds flat. In 1932, while attending East Technical High

School in Cleveland, he won national attention by running the 100-yard dash in 10.3 seconds and, the next year, as a triple winner in the National Interscholastic Championships held at the University of Chicago. In 1934 he enrolled in Ohio State University, where his career in track and field events was little short of phenomenal. In one day—May 25, 1935—at the Big Ten (Western Conference) track and field championships, he broke world records in the 220-yard dash (20.3 seconds), the 220-yard low hurdles (22.6 seconds), and the running broad jump (26'8¼"—a record that was not broken for 25 years), and tied a fourth world record for the 100-yard dash (9.4 seconds). He went on to win four gold medals in the 1936 Olympic Games in Berlin, tying the Olympic record in the 100-meter sprint (10.3 seconds), setting the Olympic and world records in the 200-meter sprints (20.7 seconds), setting the Olympic and world records for the running broad jump (26'5 5/16"—his jump in 1935 had not yet been officially accepted), and running anchor on the world-record-breaking 400-meter relay team (39.8 seconds). Rather than present Owens, a Negro, with the victory medals, German dictator Adolf Hitler left the stadium, his theory of an Aryan "master race" seriously embarrassed. The attendant publicity brought even wider fame to Owens, who nevertheless chose to leave sports after the 1936 Olympics. He graduated from Ohio State in 1937 and ventured into business, eventually becoming secretary of the Illinois Athletic Commission, a post he left in 1955 to embark on a goodwill tour of India for the U.S. Department of State. Thereafter he established the "junior sized Olympic games" and a sports clinic for boys under the aegis of the Illinois Youth Commission. Owens died on March 31, 1980, in Tucson, Arizona.

Oxnam, Garfield Bromley (1891–1963), religious leader and author. Born in Sonora, California, on August 14, 1891, G. Bromley Oxnam graduated from the University of Southern California in 1913 and two years later took his S.T.B. degree from Boston University. He pursued studies also at Harvard and at the Massachusetts Institute of Technology (MIT) and abroad in England, China, Japan, and India. In 1916 he was ordained in the Methodist Episcopal church, taking his first pastorate in Poplar, Tulare County, California. He soon moved to the Church of All Nations in Los Angeles, where he remained until 1927. During that period he taught social ethics at the University of Southern California (1919–1923), was active in missionary and extension work of the church, and published his first books, including *The Mexican in Los Angeles*, 1920; *Social Principles of Jesus*, 1923; and, following a visit to the Soviet Union, *Russian Impressions*, 1927. In 1927 he was appointed professor of practical theology at Boston University, and the next year he became president of DePauw University, a post he held until 1936. Elected a bishop of the Methodist church in 1936, he served as resident bishop of the Omaha area from 1936 to 1939, of the Boston area from 1939 to 1944, of the New York area from 1944 to 1952, and of the Washington, D.C., area from 1952 until 1960, when he retired. Early in his career Oxnam earned a reputation as a liberal and a champion of social justice by his outspoken support of the rights of labor and of ethnic minorities; to these concerns he later added a vigorous and courageous defense of democratic freedom against Fascist, Communist, and reactionary movements. His defense of religious liberty before the House of Representatives' Committee to Investigate Un-American Activities in 1953, at the height of the anti-Communist hysteria spurred by Senator Joseph R. McCarthy, won applause around the world. Oxnam was president in 1944–1946 of the Federal Council of the Churches of Christ in America and in 1950 helped organize its successor, the National Council of the Churches of Christ in the United States of America. From 1948 to 1954 he was president of the World Council of Churches. Others among his books were *Youth and the New America*, 1928; *The Ethical Ideals of Jesus in a Changing World*, 1941; *Facing the Future Unafraid*, 1944; *Labor and Tomorrow's World*, 1945; *The Church and Contemporary Change*, 1950; *The Christian's Vocation*, 1950; *On This Rock*, 1951; *I Protest*, 1954; and *A Testament of Faith*, 1958. He died in White Plains, New York, on March 12, 1963.

P

Page, Walter Hines (1855–1918), author, editor, and diplomat. Born on August 15, 1855, in Cary, North Carolina, Page was educated at Trinity College (now Duke University), Randolph-Macon College (where he obtained a degree), and The Johns Hopkins University. After a few months spent teaching school he found a position as reporter for the *St. Joseph* ("Missouri") *Gazette* in 1880 and in a short time was its editor. In the summer of 1881 he toured the South, recording his observations and recommendations in a series of articles that he successfully offered for syndicated newspaper publication. Later that year he was commissioned by the *New York World* to make a similar tour of the West. By 1882 he was literary editor and regular literary critic of the *World*. From 1883 to 1885 he was in Raleigh, North Carolina, directing and editing the *State Chronicle*, a newspaper that distinguished itself by its outspoken and unconventional editorial opinions. In it Page advocated strongly a "New South" program of primary education for both races, scientific agriculture, industrialization, and, above all, a long-overdue deemphasis of the Civil War. In 1887, back in New York City, he joined the staff of *Forum*, a monthly review then in financial straits; within four years he had assumed control and by the time he resigned as editor in 1895, *Forum* was one of the country's leading periodicals. In 1895 he accepted an offer to become literary adviser and associate editor of the *Atlantic Monthly* and three years later became the magazine's editor. In 1900, by now a partner of Frank N. Doubleday in the publishing house of Doubleday, Page, & Company, he became editor of *World's Work*, a magazine of politics and public affairs, remaining in the post until 1913. He wrote two books embodying his views on the revitalization of the South, *The Rebuilding of Old Commonwealths*, 1902, and *The Southerner*, 1909, a semiautobiographical novel published under the pseudonym "Nicholas Worth." He was active in many public and philanthropic activities, including the Southern Education Board, the General Education Board, the program to eradicate the hookworm, and President Theodore Roosevelt's Commission on Country Life. A lifelong Democrat, he was an early supporter of Woodrow Wilson for the presidency in 1912; after the election he was appointed U.S. ambassador to Great Britain. For the first year, Page and Wilson were in complete harmony as the ambassador strove to eliminate frictions in Anglo-American relations; after the outbreak of World War I in 1914, however, the two drifted apart as Page ardently supported the

Allied cause while Wilson insisted upon U.S. neutrality. Never in open opposition to the president, Page nonetheless kept up a barrage of pro-Allied notes and memoranda to him and, after the sinking of the *Lusitania*, he called for a declaration of war on Germany. When Wilson at length did request a declaration of war from Congress, he did so in terms and with arguments directly from Page's communications over a period of nearly three years. In declining health, Page was finally forced to resign his post in August 1918; he returned to North Carolina and died on December 21, 1918, in Cary, near Raleigh.

Paige, Leroy Robert (1906–1982), "Satchel," baseball player. Born sometime in 1906 in Mobile, Alabama, Paige started pitching professional baseball in the all-Negro Southern Association in the mid-1920s with such teams as the Birmingham Black Barons, the Nashville Elite Giants, the New Orleans Black Pelicans, and the Black Lookouts of Chattanooga; in this period he was given his nickname because of his "satchel-sized" feet. He played winter ball during the 1930s in South and Central America and the Caribbean, and summer ball in the Northwest, playing at one time or another with teams in Mexico, Puerto Rico, Venezuela, Cuba, the Dominican Republic, and, in the United States, in Denver, Colorado, and Bismarck, South Dakota. He built an extraordinary record and in his heyday charged $500 to $2000 to pitch a game, frequently traveling some 30,000 miles in a season. In 1933 he pitched 31 games and lost 4. In 1934 he started 29 games in 29 days with the Bismarck team, which reportedly won 104 of 105 games. In the Negro National League he pitched for the Crawford Giants of Pittsburgh, the Homestead Grays of Baltimore, and the Kansas City Monarchs—clinching the Monarch's victory in the Negro World Series in 1942 and pitching 64 scoreless innings in 1946 in another winning pennant drive. He encountered top major-league players—including Rogers Hornsby (whom he struck out 5 times in one game), Jimmy Foxx, and Charley Gehringer—in exhibition games. In 1934 he broke Dizzy Dean's 30-game winning streak with the St. Louis Cardinals in a Hollywood All-Stars game by striking out 17 men and allowing no runs, while Dean struck out 15 and let one run in. Although past his prime at forty-two, Paige finally broke the baseball color bar in 1948 and was signed by Bill Veeck of the Cleveland Indians. The team won the American League pennant and the World Series. His drawing power undiminished, he attracted 200,000 fans in three games. In 1950 he moved to the St. Louis Browns and was their most valuable relief pitcher in 1951, 1952, and 1953. He continued to play in exhibition games. Called by Joe DiMaggio in 1937 "the best pitcher I have ever faced," he was one of the all-time great American baseball players. In 1971 Paige was enshrined in the National Baseball Hall of Fame after it opened to stars of the Negro league. He died in Kansas City, Missouri, on June 5, 1982.

Paine, Robert Treat (1731–1814), public official and judge. Born in Boston on March 11, 1731, Paine came of a noted Massachusetts family and was educated at the Boston Latin School and at Harvard, from which he graduated in 1749. Although he was first destined for the ministry and served as chaplain to the New England troops on the Crown Point expedition of 1755, he soon adopted the law as his calling and was admitted to the bar in 1757, moving his practice from Portland, Maine, to Taunton, Massachusetts, in 1761. A member of the provincial assembly several times during the 1770s, he was chosen one of the five Massachusetts delegates to the First Continental Congress, which met in Philadelphia in 1774. He had earlier been one of the prosecuting attorneys in the murder trial of British soldiers following the Boston Massacre, and his spirited argument to the effect that Parliament had no right to quarter troops in a town against its consent had made his name known throughout the colonies. He also served in the Second Continental Congress, voted for the selection of George Washington as commander in chief, and signed John Dickinson's Olive Branch Petition of July 1775, the final appeal by Congress to the Crown to settle colonial differences short of war; when he later also signed the Declaration of Independence he became one of the very few men to have signed both documents. Although he was elected to Congress in 1777 he did not go to Philadelphia but remained in Massachusetts, in that year being elected the state's first attorney general, a post he retained until 1790, when he was appointed by Governor John Hancock to the state supreme court. He served on the court until 1804, when he retired because of increasing deafness. In 1779–1780 he had participated in the drafting of the Massachusetts state constitution, and he was active in the suppression of Shays's Rebellion. In 1780, reflecting his lifelong interest in astronomy, he was one of the founders of the American Academy of Arts and Sciences. He died in Boston on May 11, 1814.

Paine, Robert Treat (1773–1811), poet and editor. Born in Taunton, Massachusetts, on December 9, 1773, Paine was the son of Robert Treat Paine (1731–1814). He was christened Thomas but took his oldest brother's name after the latter died of yellow fever in 1789. Paine was educated at the Boston Latin School and at Harvard, from which he graduated in 1792. His first poems were written during his college years and he read one of them, a poem on liberty, at his commencement. He made some attempt at a business career for a few

years after graduation, but he was not happy as a clerk and by 1794 he had determined on a literary and theatrical career. In October of that year he founded the *Federal Orrery*, but the magazine's satirical contents belied its name; his father and his father's conservative Federalist friends dropped him as he became more and more Jacobin and republican in his sentiments. Not at all disconcerted by these social rebuffs, which led him to sell the *Orrery* in 1796, he wrote a series of poems and songs that were successful enough financially to support him, and one of which, "Adams and Liberty," composed in June 1798, was the equivalent of a national best seller. In that year he was reconciled with his father and agreed to study law, but his conversion was short-lived, and by 1804 he was once again deeply involved in his old habits, although he was never able to regain his youthful verve. He was very ill in 1804 and almost died; after several years of dismal poverty he did die, in the attic of his father's house in Boston, on November 13, 1811.

Paine, Thomas (1737–1809), author, political theorist, and humanitarian. Born in Thetford, England, on January 29, 1737, Paine received little formal education and spent the first 37 years of his life in poverty, wandering from job to job with few prospects for the future. He served an apprenticeship under his father, a corset maker, served briefly on a privateer in 1756, and was twice dismissed from a post as exciseman, apparently as a result of agitating for higher wages. A fortuitous meeting with Benjamin Franklin in London encouraged him to seek his fortune in America and in November 1774 he arrived in Philadelphia with introductions from Franklin, and worked for a time as editor for the *Pennsylvania Magazine.* In January 1776 he published the pamphlet *Common Sense;* in powerful and stirring language he called for independence from England and marshaled a number of supporting arguments for his thesis. The pamphlet was a huge success and may have sold as many as half a million copies; it was issued in Europe as well as in the colonies. Paine soon enlisted in the Continental Army, became an aide to Gen. Nathanael Greene, and began a series of 16 pamphlets entitled *The Crisis* that appeared over some seven years; the first of these appeared in December 1776 and began with the memorable line, "These are the times that try men's souls." The pamphlet had an electrifying effect on the dispirited Continental Army and on the country at large. In April 1777 he was appointed secretary of the congressional committee on foreign affairs, a post he held until forced to resign two years later for his indiscreet publication of certain secret papers. In November 1779 he became clerk of the Pennsylvania assembly and in 1781 he accompanied John Laurens to France to seek money and supplies for the Continental forces. He continued writing effectively in support of the Revolution and of the government's policies and as a result he was given a Loyalist's confiscated farm by New

York and a sum of money by Pennsylvania at the war's end. Until 1787 he lived rather quietly, working on a design for a pierless iron bridge he was trying to perfect. In 1787 he went to England to market his bridge, but again was caught up in politics; in answer to Edmund Burke's highly critical view of the French Revolution he issued in 1791 the first part of his *Rights of Man*, to which a second part was added the next year. The U.S. publication of the work was arranged for by Thomas Jefferson as a means of combating the "Federalist heresy." The book, an extended and detailed piece of republican and constitutional propaganda, sold so well in England that the government indicted Paine for treason and outlawed him; he escaped to Paris and, having been made an honorary French citizen, was then elected to the Revolutionary Convention in September 1792. When the Revolutionary moderates fell from favor and the Terror ensued, Paine, who had advocated exile rather than execution for the king, was imprisoned for a year during 1793–1794, by Robespierre. After Robespierre's fall he was released at the request of James Madison, then minister to France, who claimed Paine as an American citizen. On his release he was readmitted to the Convention. In 1794 and 1796 appeared the first and second parts of *The Age of Reason*, a long work of deistic and humanistic apologetics that won its author the unwarranted reputation of an atheist because of his attack upon sectarianism. The imputation of atheism weighed more heavily with many people than did Paine's undeniable and invaluable services to the American Revolution; when he returned to New York City in 1802 he found no welcome, and he lived in a virtual state of ostracism until his death in New York City, on June 8, 1809. In 1819 his remains were taken to England by William Cobbett and eventually knowledge of his resting place was lost. He was elected to the Hall of Fame in 1945.

Palmer, Alexander Mitchell (1872–1936), lawyer and public official. Born in Moosehead, Pennsylvania, on May 4, 1872, A. Mitchell Palmer, as he styled himself, was an ardent Quaker all of his life, although his reputation for combativeness later led to his acquiring the contradictory nickname "the Fighting Quaker." A dedicated student, he graduated from Swarthmore College summa cum laude at the age of nineteen, in 1891, and after studying law with a Pennsylvania judge he was admitted to the bar in 1893. While building a successful practice in Stroudsburg, Pennsylvania, he became interested in Democratic politics and was elected to the House of Representatives on a reform ticket in 1908 and reelected in 1910 and 1912. His legislative career was distinguished, and in 1912 he moved onto the national scene when he managed Woodrow Wilson's successful campaign for the Democratic presidential nomination. He declined Wilson's offer of appointment as secretary of war because of his Quaker beliefs but, after an unsuccessful campaign for the Senate in 1914, accepted an appointment as Alien Property

Custodian when World War I began. During less than 18 months between October 1917 and March 1919 he sequestered some $600 million worth of property and funds owned by or owed to enemy aliens and in the process became a highly controversial figure. Named attorney general on the retirement of Thomas W. Gregory in March 1919, he conducted the office vigorously and became even more controversial as he led the government's attack on supposed radicals. The preeminent figure in the "Red Scare" of 1919–1920, Palmer himself participated in raids on private homes and the premises of suspect organizations and mercilessly pressed for the deportation of aliens and agitators, among them Emma Goldman and Alexander Berkman. During the last months of his tenure in office he was faced by a number of congressional investigations of his actions, which were notorious as the "Palmer raids," but he managed to sail through unscathed. A candidate for the Democratic presidential nomination in 1920, he lost out to James M. Cox, and retired from office in 1921. But he continued to be a leading Democrat throughout the 1920s, campaigning vigorously for John W. Davis in 1924 and for Alfred E. Smith in 1928, and he supported Franklin D. Roosevelt in 1932 and wrote most of the party's platform that year. He died in Washington, D.C., on May 11, 1936. His name and fame were recalled during the McCarthy years of the early 1950s, when another "Red Scare" swept the country under the impetus of charges made by Senator Joseph R. McCarthy.

Palmer, Alice Elvira Freeman (1855–1902), educator. Born in Colesville, near Binghampton, New York, on February 21, 1855, Alice Freeman taught herself to read at the age of three and, on the family's moving later to the nearby town of Windsor, entered Windsor Academy, where she became engaged to a young teacher at the age of fourteen. When her fiance left to enter Yale Divinity School in 1870 she decided that she would rather have a college education than be married, and she determined to get one even if, as she said, it took her 50 years to do it. In fact, it took her nearly seven years, for she faced many obstacles, not only those hindering all American women seeking an education at the time but also family financial difficulties. She received her B.A. from the University of Michigan in 1876 and a Ph.D. from the same institution in 1882—but by 1882 she had received a success of which she could never have dreamed and was president of Wellesley College. She had been first invited to Wellesley in 1877, on the recommendation of President James B. Angell of Michigan, but she declined the offer of an instructorship in mathematics on the grounds that she did not yet know enough. A second invitation came in 1878, this time to teach Greek, but again she declined, on the grounds that her sister was ill and the family needed her. On the death of her sister the next year Henry Fowle Durant, Wellesley's founder, asked her again, and this time she accepted the position of head of the department of history, although she was only twenty-four. Durant died in 1881 and, Wellesley's president resigning soon after, Miss Freeman was appointed vice-president and acting president, and she became president the next year, at the age of twenty-seven. Her youth, however, was no obstacle, either in her own eyes or in those of others, and during six years in the presidency she brought about striking changes in the institution, transforming it from a glorified boarding school into a distinguished college. She retired from the presidency of Wellesley in 1888, shortly after her marriage to George Herbert Palmer, professor of philosophy at Harvard, but she continued to be active in various fields of education until her death. In 1882, she helped found the Association of Collegiate Alumnae (later the American Association of University Women), and twice served as president, 1885–1886 and 1889–1890. From 1888 she was a Wellesley trustee and from 1889, a member of the Massachusetts board of education; she served on a number of educational committees and commissions and from 1892 to 1895 was dean of women at the new University of Chicago. Not wishing to leave Boston and her husband for extended periods of time, she arranged to be in Chicago for only 12 weeks each year, at her own convenience, and was provided with a sub-dean of her own choosing who would manage the office in her absence. She resigned the post when she decided that a full-time dean was required, but she had nevertheless accomplished much during her short tenure. In the meantime, she had worked in Boston to bring about the formal attachment of Radcliffe College to Harvard University. She died in Paris while on a trip to Europe with her husband on December 6, 1902. She was elected to the Hall of Fame in 1920.

Palmer, Arnold (1929–   ), golfer. Born in Youngstown, Pennsylvania, on September 10, 1929, Palmer was the son of the golf professional at the Latrobe Country Club. He received his first golf club at the age of three and by the time he was nine, after careful tutoring by his father, was able to play nine holes in 45. He played golf on the Latrobe High School team and received a golfing scholarship at Wake Forest College (now University), which he attended intermittently from 1947 to 1954, with three years out for service in the coast guard. After leaving college without a degree he took a job as salesman for a painting-supply company, but he was frustrated by his inability to play as much golf as he wanted, and after winning the U.S. amateur title in 1954 he turned professional. The next year he won his first important championship, the Canadian Open, but the first prize was only $2400 and this early period was, in fact, hard financially for the man who later became the first golfing millionaire. His first big year came in 1958, when he won the Masters title at Augusta, Georgia, and two other championships, and garnered some $42,000, a dazzling sum for a golfer in those days. He did not do so

well the next year, but in 1960 he came into his own, winning both the Masters and the U.S. Open; in both those tournaments he was trailing at the beginning of the last day but put together amazing strings of birdies on the last few holes to overtake his opponents. These characteristic final "charges" endeared him to the galleries, and it was soon apparent that he was becoming the most popular golfer since Bobby Jones. Accompanied everywhere on the courses by hordes of fans, who were dubbed "Arnie's Army," he was cheered for every accomplishment and his opponents were booed when, as sometimes happened, they beat him. He won the British Open in 1961 and 1962 and took the Masters again in 1962 and 1964, thus becoming the first golfer to win that coveted title four times. He won the Vardon Trophy for the lowest average scores on the tour in 1961, 1962, 1964, and 1967; in 1967 his total winnings passed $1 million, and in 1968 his official winnings were even higher. During the first part of the 1960s, at least, he was "Mr. Golf" in the minds of countless Americans, and his preeminence was acknowledged on July 21, 1970, when, at a dinner in Pittsburgh, he was named athlete of the decade. His actual tournament winnings were eventually only a small part of his income, which was greatly increased by endorsements and various business ventures, and he lived as spectacularly as he played, flying to tournaments in his own plane from his palatial home in Latrobe. By the end of the decade, however, it was apparent that he was no longer the premier golfer in America, Jack Nicklaus having wrenched the crown from him. Palmer continued to play in most tournaments, winning some of them, but his struggles to manage his errant putter and his fight with physical pain caused by an old hip injury only endeared him all the more to his countless followers.

Palmer, Bertha Honoré, *see under* Palmer, Potter

Palmer, Daniel David (1845–1913), founder of chiropractic. Palmer was born on a farm near Toronto on March 7, 1845, but little is known of his early years; he was apparently almost entirely self-educated. He was a small businessman in What Cheer, Iowa, during the 1880s; his son Bartlett Joshua Palmer was born there in 1881, and after his wife's death in 1883 he took up "magnetic healing" and moved to Burlington, Iowa, and then, in 1895, to Davenport, Iowa. It was at about this time that he became interested in osteopathy, and he made his first attempt to cure by means of "spinal adjustments" in September 1895, when he adjusted the spine of his janitor, who complained of difficulty in hearing. The janitor's deafness was not much improved, but Palmer, undaunted, continued to treat patients, apparently with some success. Gradually he evolved a theory of disease as resulting from the impinging of misaligned skeletal structures, particularly vertebrae, on nerves, especially those of the spinal cord, with a consequent lowering of resistance to infection or simple mechanical distress. Treatment consisted of mechanical adjustment of the skeleton, again particularly the vertebrae, using various manipulations to force them into proper position to relieve pressure on nerves. The body's own healing process would then be sufficient to cure diseases or other maladies. The name of the new discipline was supplied by a learned patient, who combined the Greek words *cheir*, hand, and *praktikos*, into chiropractic; Palmer himself translated the Greek words as "done by hand." He started the Palmer School of Chiropractic in Davenport in 1898 but at first had few students, although his son graduated in 1902. He went to Portland, Oregon, in 1903 to start another school, but this was an outright failure and he soon returned to Davenport, where his son had begun to make a success of the first school. He was arrested in 1906 for practicing medicine without a license and spent six months in jail; after his release he went to Oklahoma City and then returned to Portland, but his efforts to make a living by teaching foundered, and he retired to private practice. With Bartlett he published *The Science of Chiropractic*, 1906; his *Textbook of the Science, Art and Philosophy of Chiropractic*, published in 1910, was especially notable for its virulent attacks on all other practitioners of medicine, including other chiropractors and including especially his son. In 1913 he returned to his son's flourishing school in Davenport as an uninvited guest at a gala homecoming of former students and was struck by a car while leading a parade through town. He died of his injuries two months later, in Los Angeles, on October 20, 1913. Under the leadership of Bartlett and his son, David Daniel, chiropractic grew, against opposition from the medical establishment, to number its practitioners in the tens of thousands and to be licensed in most states.

Palmer, George Herbert (1842–1933), educator and philosopher. Born in Boston on March 19, 1842, Palmer was named after the English poet George Herbert, a fact that, he felt, placed him under an obligation that he discharged in 1905, when his monumental three-volume edition of Herbert's English works appeared. Palmer was educated at Phillips Academy at Andover and at Harvard, from which he graduated in 1864, and undertook further philosophical studies at the University of Tübingen during a European tour in 1867–1869, at Andover Theological Seminary, from which he received a B.D. in 1870, and at the University of Glasgow, where he studied Hegel under Edward Caird. He joined the Harvard faculty in 1870 as a tutor in Greek and, although he moved to the philosophy department two years later, continued to conduct Greek readings and published a long-admired translation of the *Odyssey* in 1884. He became a full professor of philosophy in 1883 and was named Alford Professor of Natural Religion, Moral Philosophy and Civil Polity in 1889; he became professor emeritus in 1913. Harvard's philosophy department during his years there was a distinguished one, numbering among its members William James, Josiah Royce—who succeeded to Palmer's chair—and George Santayana, but Palmer was by no means the least important in this extraordinary group of men, and his favorite and best-known course, in the field of ethics, was highly regarded by students and professional philosophers alike. On the basis of his lectures in that course he wrote a number of books, notably *The Field of Ethics*, 1901; *The Nature of Goodness*, 1903; *The Problem of Freedom*, 1911; and *Altruism: Its Nature and Varieties*, 1919. He wrote many other books as well, including scholarly studies of Sophocles's *Antigone*, Shakespeare's sonnets, and Vergil's *Georgics* and *Eclogues*; works in the field of pedagogy; and treatises on the Lord's Prayer and other subjects. One of his most charming books was the biography of his wife, Alice Elvira Freeman Palmer, which he published in 1908; although he outlived her by more than 30 years, he never ceased to revere her memory. In 1915 he collected and published a volume of her verses as *A Marriage Cycle*. He lived in Harvard Yard until his death in Cambridge, Massachusetts, at the age of ninety-one, on May 7, 1933. His *The Autobiography of a Philosopher* had appeared three years before.

Palmer, Potter (1826–1902), merchant and real-estate entrepreneur. Born in Albany County, New York, on May 20, 1826, Palmer was largely self-educated and at the age of eighteen obtained a job in a general store in Durham, New York. In 1847 he opened his own dry-goods store in nearby Oneida, moving it shortly afterward to Lockport; but these small New York towns did not give him the opportunity he sought and in 1852 he opened a dry-goods store on Lake Street in Chicago. Within the next 15 years he managed to make a fortune for himself and to revolutionize merchandising in Chicago and indeed throughout the country. He made many innovations, including allowing customers to examine merchandise in their homes before buying it and to exchange it, after it was bought, for other items; these, combined with his heavy use of advertising and his insistence on the attractive display of items in his store, added up to what was called the "Palmer system," which was adopted by his competitors. Exhausted and ill, he retired in 1867, leaving the business to his partners, Marshall Field and Levi Z. Leiter (the firm later became Marshall Field and Co.), and spent three years in Europe recuperating. Returning in 1870, he set about building up State Street, then a country road, constructing the first Palmer House hotel there, together with some 32 other buildings. The great fire of 1871 destroyed most of them, but he rebuilt with all the more energy in the fire's wake and constructed, at the corner of State and Monroe streets, a new Palmer House that figured thereafter in the history of Chicago. Having practically created State Street he then turned to the North Shore, constructing roads and houses on swamplands and erecting a magnificent home for himself on Lake Shore Drive. Palmer died in Chicago on May 4, 1902. He had been assisted in many of his later enterprises by his wife, the former Bertha Honoré, the daughter of a prominent Chicago real-estate tycoon. He had married her shortly before the fire in 1871 and she outlived him by many years. Mrs. Palmer, who had served in 1891–1893 as president of the Board of Lady Managers of the World's Columbian Exposition and in 1900, at the appointment of President William McKinley, as a delegate to the Paris Exposition, continued to be prominent in cultural and philanthropic affairs, becoming in time the grande dame of Chicago society. She also devoted considerable attention to the management of her husband's estate, which under her astute care doubled in value by the time of her death in 1918.

Panofsky, Erwin (1892–1968), art historian. Born in Hanover, Germany, on March 30, 1892, Panofsky was destined for scholarship both by his parents' cultured background and by his own brilliant, inquiring mind. He was brought up in Berlin and attended the universities of Freiburg, Berlin, and Munich, receiving his Ph.D. from Freiburg in 1914. After service in World War I he taught at the University of Hamburg until 1934, when he fled Hitler's regime in Germany to come to the United States. He was a visiting professor at New York University for a year and at the same time gave lectures at Princeton, but the next year, 1935, he was made a professor at the Institute for Advanced Study in Princeton, with which he was associated for the rest of his life. He was Charles Eliot Norton Professor of Poetry at Harvard in 1947–1948, succeeding Igor Stravinsky and Robert Frost in the chair. He wrote a large number of articles and books in the field of art history, composing them in English after he came to the United States. His writings covered an enormous range; they included *Style and Medium in the Motion Picture*, 1934, still considered a classic early work on film; *Studies in Iconology*, a report of researches in the backgrounds of Renaissance literature, 1939; *The Codex Huygens and Leonardo da Vinci's Art Theory*, 1940; *Gothic Architecture and Scholasticism*, 1951; *Early Netherlandish Painting*, 1953; *The Life and Art of Albrecht Dürer*, 1955; and *Pandora's Box: The Changing Aspects of a Mystical Symbol*, 1956, a fascinating account of the transformations of a single myth through 2500 years of art and literary history. *Meaning in the Visual Arts*, a collection of papers in and on art history, appeared in 1955 and became a best seller in a paperback version. Probably the leading art historian in the world during his career, Panofsky was also noted for his interest in a wide array of other subjects as well; he was an expert on such things as old movies, the history of the detective story, and the works of Mozart. The recipient of many awards and honors, he died in Princeton, New Jersey, on March 15, 1968.

Park, Robert Ezra (1864–1944), sociologist. Born in Luzerne County, Pennsylvania, on February 14, 1864, Park graduated from the University of Michigan in 1887 and thereupon embarked on a career as a newspaperman, first in Minneapolis, then in Chicago, then in Detroit. About 1898, in Ann Arbor, Michigan, he was introduced by John Dewey to Franklin Ford. Ford, an ex-newspaperman, confirmed Park's growing suspicion that he should not remain a journalist, and he decided to to go Harvard to study in greater depth some of the problems he had seen in his work. After a year at Harvard, where he met and was strongly influenced by William James, he went to Europe to study under Georg Simmel and Wilhelm Windelband at the University of Heidelberg, from which he received his Ph.D. in 1904. Returning to Harvard in that year, he became an assistant in philosophy, but he was as uneasy in the academic world as in the journalistic one; while journalism necessarily was concerned with mere surface events and not the "Big News," as he called it, academics, he felt, were superficial in another way, lacking in experience of the real life that lay behind and beneath their studies. Invited to become secretary of the Congo Reform Association, he went to Africa and in a series of articles published in *Everybody's Magazine* in 1906–1907 revealed the vicious exploitation of African workers by Belgian authorities in the Congo. In the course of this work he met Booker T. Washington and was persuaded by him to study the Negro in the South, and Park therewith began to arrive at the insight and understanding about race relations and problems that later led to his gaining a reputation as one of the world's leading experts on the subject. He spent seven winters in the South working with and under the direction of Washington; many of the papers and essays later collected in *Race and Culture*, 1950, grew out of his experience at this time. From 1913 to 1933 he was a member of the sociology staff at the University of Chicago; he was considered by his students a wonderful teacher because he always seemed to want to learn from them more than to teach them. It was during this period that he did his major work on urban sociological problems, or "human ecology," as he called it, publishing *The Immigrant Press and Its Control*, 1922, and *The City, Suggestions for the Study of the Urban Environment*, 1925, and writing the papers that were later collected in *Human Communities*, 1952. In 1921 appeared his influential textbook, *Introduction to the Science of Sociology*, written with W. E. Burgess; in it he insisted, as he did in all of his works, on the importance of empirical research and did much to promote such research among sociologists of the next generation. His theoretical papers in sociology were collected in *Society*, 1955. After leaving Chicago he went to Fisk University, where he taught and did research until 1943; he died the next year, on February 7, 1944, in Nashville, Tennessee. Others of his phrases besides "human ecology" seemed likely to survive in sociological lore, among them "the man farthest down" (the title of a book he wrote with Booker T. Washington and published in 1912) and "the marginal man" (which appeared in the titles of several articles). Both, of course, were central to his understanding of sociological problems and conflicts.

Parker, Charlie (1920–1955), "Bird," jazz musician. and composer. Born in Kansas City, Kansas, on August 29, 1920, Charles Christopher Parker, Jr., was a professional on the alto saxophone at seventeen. He played with the best bands in Kansas City before moving to New York City's Harlem in 1939. There, in the early 1940s, he at various times played with the bands of Noble Sissle, Earl "Fatha" Hines, Cootie Williams, and Andy Kirk, as well as with the first Billy Eckstine group. He joined the jam sessions at Minton's Play House, where trumpeter Dizzy Gillespie, drummer Kenny Clarke, and pianist Thelonius Monk were the other participants in the founding of "bop" or "bebop," a progressive form of jazz that emphasized listening over dancing. Known as "Yardbird" or simply "Bird," Parker made records in 1944 with Lloyd "Tiny" Grimes and in 1945 with Gillespie—notably "Hot House" and "Salt Peanuts"—that made him the leading exponent of bop and the idol of young musicians. His extemporaneous style was endlessly creative, an amazing synthesis of rhythm, tone, melody, harmony, and form. Bebop (named for a rhythmic device) featured the soloist, who improvised on chords rather than themes, effecting continually new melodies and rhythms. Parker formed a quintet in 1947 with Max Roach, Miles Davis, and others; their recordings were especially acclaimed and reissued many times after Parker's death. While his last years were marked by physical decline, his music was constantly played and his style influenced a generation of jazz musicians. In 1955 he made his last appearance at Birdland in New York City, a Broadway jazz hall named in his honor. He died on March 12, 1955, in New York City.

Parker, Dorothy (1893–1967), author. Born in West End, near Long Branch, New Jersey, on August 22, 1893, Dorothy Rothschild was educated at a finishing school and in a New York City convent —both of them a far cry from the ambiance of her later life. She joined the editorial staff of *Vogue* in 1916 and the next year moved to *Vanity Fair*; also in 1917 she married Edwin Pond Parker II, whom she divorced in 1928 but whose surname she retained in her professional career, being known usually as "Miss Parker" thenceforth. She left *Vanity Fair* in 1920 to try her hand at freelance writing and was soon successful; her first book of light, witty, and sometimes cynical verse, *Enough Rope*, was published in 1926 and became a best seller. In 1927 she also became book reviewer for the *New Yorker* and was associated with that magazine for much of the rest of her career. Earlier in the 1920s she had been one of the founders of the famous "Algonquin Round Table" at the Algonquin Hotel in Manhattan, and was by no means the least of a group of dazzling

wits that included Robert Benchley, Robert E. Sherwood, James Thurber, George S. Kaufman, F.P.A., and others—although the number of people who later claimed to be members far exceeded the 10 or so that were usually at lunch at a special table in the Algonquin provided for them by its manager, Frank Case. It was there, in conversations that spilled over first from the offices of *Vanity Fair* and later from those of the *New Yorker*, that Miss Parker established her reputation as one of the most brilliant conversationalists in New York; her off-the-cuff comments could slice an individual's head off without his ever knowing he had been touched. The theme of the bright but heartbroken girl-about-New York was important in many of her later poems, collected in *Not So Deep as a Well*, 1936, and in her fine, moving short stories, collected in *Here Lies*, 1939; the best known of them was "Big Blonde." In 1933 she married Alan Campbell and thereafter collaborated with him on a number of film scenarios; she lived with him in Hollywood, California, until his death in 1963, when she returned to New York City. She had collaborated with Arnaud d'Usseau on a play, *Ladies of the Corridor*, that was produced on Broadway in 1953. She died in New York City on June 7, 1967.

Parker, Francis Wayland (1837–1902), educator. Born on October 9, 1837, in Bedford, New Hampshire, Parker was orphaned in his early childhood and raised by a farmer who permitted him to go to school for only eight weeks each winter. When he was thirteen he enrolled in a school in Mount Vernon, New Hampshire, and left his guardian. He excelled in his studies, and at sixteen began to teach. When he was twenty-one he was invited to become principal of a school in Carrolton, Illinois. He filled this post until the Civil War, in which he served for nearly four years, and afterward he returned to teaching, working in Dayton, Ohio. Fascinated with the ideas for liberal teaching propounded by E. A. Sheldon in *Object Lessons*, he attempted to put them to use in his own classes, with encouraging results. He traveled to Germany in 1872 to observe the teaching methods and liberal school environment pioneered by Friedrich Froebel, J. N. Pestalozzi, and others, and, much impressed, returned to the United States in 1875 to become, at the instance of Charles Francis Adams, Jr., superintendent of schools in Quincy, Massachusetts. There and, from 1880 to 1883 in Boston, he inaugurated his program of progressive education sometimes called the "Quincy movement." His liberal system stressed the development of both teacher and student as individuals on different levels. It encouraged activity and self-expression for students and allowed teachers to practice instruction as an art. Called to Chicago as principal of the Cook County Normal School in 1883, he revamped the entire curriculum and instituted his own pedagogic creed. In 1899 he received a large endowment to found the Chicago Institute, incorporated in 1901 into the University of Chicago as the School of Education with Parker as its first director. The move to introduce education as a discipline into the university curriculum was an innovation that Parker and the university welcomed, and during his brief tenure there he was associated with John Dewey. Among his writings, his *Talks on Pedagogics*, 1894, and *Talks on Teaching*, 1896, expressed views that generally were warmly received by communities that had grown tired of the stern, repressive methods of traditional schoolteachers. He died in Chicago on March 2, 1902.

Parker, John (1729–1775), Revolutionary soldier. Born in Lexington, Massachusetts, on July 13, 1729, Parker had his first combat experience during the French and Indian War, seeing action at Louisburg and Quebec; it is probable that he later saw service as a member of Rogers' Rangers. In peacetime a farmer and mechanic, he was a captain of minutemen by 1775. On the night of April 18, 1775—a date immortalized by Henry Wadsworth Longfellow's poetic account of Paul Revere's ride—Parker placed a guard of his minutemen around the house in Lexington where John Hancock and Samuel Adams were hiding to protect them from an approaching British contingent under Maj. John Pitcairn. His force numbered about 130 men, but when reports indicated that the British were not coming after all, he dismissed them. Early the next morning, April 19, it was evident that the British were indeed coming, and he tried to reassemble his men, but found only from 40 to 70 of them. The British appeared, and Parker is supposed to have declared: "Stand your ground. Don't fire unless fired upon. But if they mean to have a war, let it begin here." There is considerable doubt that he actually spoke the words, but they are engraved on a stone on the Lexington green and on the memories of students of American history. In any event, someone did fire—although it is not certain whether the first shot left a British or an American musket—and in the skirmish that followed eight Americans were killed. Parker then assembled the rest of his company of irregulars and marched toward Concord, harassing the British as they retreated back to Boston. Soon afterward, however, he became very ill, and he died on September 17, 1775.

Parker, Quanah, *see* Quanah

Parker, Theodore (1810–1860), religious leader and social reformer. Born in Lexington, Massachusetts, on August 24, 1810, Parker received little schooling but was an intellectually and spiritually precocious child. Admitted to Harvard in 1830, he was prevented from attending by lack of funds; in 1834, however, he entered the Harvard Divinity School and graduated two years later. By this time he was conversant with 20 languages. In June 1837 he began his ministry at the Unitarian Church in West Roxbury. He was closely associated with the progressive spirits of the time and place— William Ellery Channing, Wendell Phillips, Ralph Waldo Emerson, Bronson Alcott, and other members of the Transcendentalist circle—and became himself a leader, never a disciple, in liberal thought. A growing tendency toward a rational approach to religion and a scientifically critical appraisal of the Bible became gradually apparent in Parker's sermons; in May 1841 he delivered one entitled "The Transient and Permanent in Christianity" that provoked nearly as hostile a reaction as had Emerson's famed address at the Divinity School three years earlier. A series of lectures published as *A Discourse of Matters Pertaining to Religion*, 1842, followed the next year by his translation of one of the pioneer works of German "higher criticism," Welhelm M. L. De Wette's *Beiträge zür Einleitung in das Alte Testament*, widened the schism between Parker and the orthodox clergy. He returned from a year in Europe in September 1844 and the following January resigned from the West Roxbury pulpit to take charge of the newly organized Twenty-eighth Congregational Society of Boston. There he drew huge congregations, necessitating a move to the more spacious Music Hall in 1852. He became a leader in movements of all sorts for social reform—especially for education, prison reform, temperance, and most particularly for the abolition of slavery. He was prominent in the resistance to the Fugitive Slave Law of 1850 and a strong supporter of John Brown's plans for war not because they might suceed but because they would precipitate the civil war that Parker saw as inevitable. He lectured widely, carried on voluminous correspondence with public leaders, and is thought to be the source of the phrase "government of the people, by the people, for the people" later utilized by Abraham Lincoln in the Gettysburg Address. His health began to fail in 1857; two years later he withdrew completely from public affairs and, seeking a restoration of his health in European travel, died in Florence, Italy, on May 10, 1860.

Parkman, Francis (1823–1893), historian. Born in Boston on September 16, 1823, Parkman came of an old Puritan family and was heir to a mercantile fortune. He graduated from Harvard in 1844, having spent several months in 1843–1844 in European travel, entered the Harvard Law School, and took his degree in 1846. As he had been primarily interested in the rigor of legal training, he did not seek admission to the bar but instead traveled west to Independence, Missouri, the jumping-off point for Western emigrants, and thence to Westport, Kansas. He set out on the Oregon Trail; in the months that followed he observed Indians of several tribes, lived with the Sioux, traveled and talked with frontiersmen of all sorts, and absorbed the sights and sounds and feel of unsettled, almost unexplored territory. In October 1846 he returned to Boston; his health, always marginal, had worsened during the trip and was to continue to decline. He described his journey in a series of articles in the *Knickerbocker Magazine* that appeared in book form in 1849 as *The California and Oregon Trail* (now known simply as *The Oregon Trail*, the serial title). He then undertook a long-contemplated massive work of history, *France and England in North America*. From 1848 to 1851, hampered by a nervous disability and eyesight that rendered reading impossible, he worked on the first volume, *History of the Conspiracy of Pontiac*. For several years thereafter he was unable to continue and contrived to pass the time by writing a novel, *Vassall Morton*, 1856, and by developing an interest in horticulture that led eventually to his *Book of Roses*, 1866, and a professorship of horticulture at Harvard in 1871. Meanwhile his health had improved sufficiently for him to continue work on his magnum opus. He employed copyists to research European archives, and his extensive and critical use of documentation was one of his major contributions to historiography. Subsequent volumes of his history were *Pioneers of France in the New World*, 1865; *The Jesuits in North America*, 1867; *The Discovery of the Great West* (later *La Salle and the Discovery of the Great West*), 1869; *The Old Régime in Canada*, 1874; *Count Frontenac and New France Under Louis XIV*, 1877; *Montcalm and Wolfe*, 1884; and *A Half-Century of Conflict*, 1892. Long before the series had been completed, Parkman was established as America's foremost historian, and the breadth of his research, the deep understanding he displayed of men and nature alike, and the high literary skill he possessed have kept his works at the forefront of American historiography. He died on November 8, 1893, in Jamaica Plain, Massachusetts. He was elected to the Hall of Fame in 1915.

Parley, Peter, *see* Goodrich, Samuel Griswold

Parrington, Vernon Louis (1871–1929), educator and literary historian. Born in Aurora, Illinois, on August 3, 1871, the son of a public-school principal, Parrington grew up in the Midwest (for which he retained a bias throughout his life), attended the College of Emporia (Kansas) for several years, and graduated from Harvard in 1893. He began to teach at the College of Emporia, moved four years later to the University of Oklahoma, where he taught until 1908, and then went to the University of Washington, where he was successively assistant professor and professor of English until his death. At Washington he was an effective teacher, much beloved by his students, and he developed a notable series of courses in American literature; but his failure for a time to produce published works was an obstacle to administrative and public recognition. However, the publication in 1927 of the first two volumes of *Main Currents in American Thought: An Interpretation of American Literature from the Beginning to 1920* changed all that. That work, besides winning a Pulitzer Prize in 1928, was immediately recognized as a classic in its field and its author was lionized both in the United States and in England. Happy in his new fame, he continued to work on the third volume, *The Beginnings of Critical Realism in America*, which he did not have time to finish before his sudden death in England on June 16, 1929;

it appeared in the form in which he left it in 1930. Among his other books were *The Connecticut Wits*, 1926, and *Sinclair Lewis, Our Own Diogenes*, 1927, but it is on *Main Currents* that his reputation continues to rest. Influenced by William Morris, John Ruskin, Hippolyte Taine, and the political program of the Populists, the work was not so much a history of American literature as an interpretation of the development of American thought in terms of the concept of democratic idealism, which he saw as the characteristic American idea.

Parrish, Maxfield Frederick (1870–1966), painter and illustrator. Born in Philadelphia on July 25, 1870, Parrish was the son of a landscape painter and etcher who encouraged the boy in his artistic ambitions. He studied at Haverford College and at the Pennsylvania Academy of the Fine Arts, and after completing his formal schooling undertook further training in painting and illustration with the distinguished illustrator Howard Pyle. Before he was thirty he was already well known as an illustrator and mural painter, and his posters and magazine covers were admired by a wide public. His colors were flat and stark, but his designs were intricate, carefully executed, and decorative; his backgrounds were especially full of detail, so that viewers could spend long periods of time discovering all of the various elements in his pictures. He illustrated many beautiful books and rare editions, including *The Arabian Nights*, *Mother Goose*, Washington Irving's *Knickerbocker's History of New York*, Eugene Field's *Poems of Childhood*, and Kenneth Grahame's *Dream Days* and *The Golden Age*; the last two were especially suited to his talent, for all of his pictures were marked by sentimentality and a hazy, almost dreamlike unreality. Perhaps his best-known mural was painted for the King Cole Bar of the St. Regis Hotel in New York City; covering a wall at least 50 feet wide, it depicted the legendary Old King Cole surrounded by his court and was a favorite of New Yorkers for five decades. After the 1920s Parrish's style of illustration went out of fashion, but he continued to paint until his death at the age of ninety-five in Plainfield, New Hampshire, on March 30, 1966.

Parrott, Robert Parker (1804–1877), inventor and manufacturer. Born in Lee, New Hampshire, on October 5, 1804, the son of a New Hampshire shipowner who served a term in the U.S. Senate, Parrott graduated from West Point in 1824. He spent the next five years at West Point as an instructor in natural philosophy, after which he served at various army posts. His career may be said to have begun in 1834, when he was assigned by the army to ordnance duty; he was promoted to captain in 1836 and sent to Washington, D.C., as assistant to the chief of the Bureau of Ordnance. He set himself to study the subject in all of its aspects, and when he was appointed the Army's inspector of ordnance at the West Point Foundry, at Cold Spring, New York, in 1836, he soon came to the attention of Gouverneur Kemble, president of the foundry, who prevailed upon him to resign his commission and take over management of the foundry. One of his first actions was to purchase 7000 acres of woodland in New York to provide a dependable source of charcoal, and he also bought an iron furnace to provide a supply of pig iron. For the next four decades he managed the entire enterprise while he continued his study of ordnance. He learned in 1849 of the secret production of a rifled cannon by the Krupp factory in Germany, and he immediately set to work to produce such a weapon. After more than ten years of experimentation he patented the design for the famous Parrott rifle, which was a cast-iron rifled cannon whose breech was strengthened by a wrought-iron hoop; the rifle was cheap and easy to produce and allowed for the use of a larger explosive charge than other guns could accommodate. In the same year, 1861, he patented an explosive shell with a ring of brass around it that expanded when the weapon was fired, filling the grooves inside the rifle and thus attaining significantly greater accuracy than was previously possible. These developments came just before the Civil War, and Parrott offered his guns to the Union army at cost. Thousands of cannon, of various calibers, were made, and they were used in every important engagement of the war, from the first battle of Bull Run in July 1861 to the siege of Richmond near the war's end; they were accounted the most effective ordnance in the world at the time. After the war Parrott ceased the manufacture of guns at the West Point Foundry but continued to operate, with his brother Peter, his charcoal and pig-iron supply operations; he sold the business to his brother in 1877 and retired. He died in Cold Spring, New York, on December 24, 1877.

Parsons, Elsie Worthington Clews (1875–1941), "John Main," anthropologist. Born in New York City on November 27, 1875, into a socially prominent family, Elsie Clews graduated from Barnard College in 1896 and then studied sociology under Franklin H. Giddings at Columbia, receiving her M.A. in 1897 and her Ph.D. in 1899. She began to teach sociology at Barnard in 1899, but in 1900 she married Herbert Parsons, a prominent lawyer and U.S. congressman, and began to produce a family that eventually included six children; she retired from teaching in 1905 to devote herself to her family and to her work. Her first book, *The Family,* was published in 1906; a textbook, it contained a lengthy discussion of trial marriage, which helped it to enjoy a large sale. She published her next few books, including *Religious Chastity,* 1911, *The Old Fashioned Woman,* 1913, and *Fear and Conventionality,* 1915, which dealt with relatively daring subjects for the time and ardently championed women's rights, under the name "John Main" to avoid embarrassing her husband in his political career. She went on a trip to the Southwest in 1915 and there met the anthropologists Franz Boas and P. E. Goddard, who in-

terested her in their work among the American Indians of the region, and she spent the rest of her life studying these and other tribes herself. After further studies under Boas at Columbia, she embarked on a 25-year career of field research and writing that established her as perhaps the leading authority on the Pueblo Indians and on other tribes in North America, Mexico, and South America. *Mitla: Town of the Souls,* 1936, was a highly regarded product of her study of a community in the state of Oaxaca, Mexico, and her most important book, the two-volume *Pueblo Indian Religion,* appeared in 1939. She also published a number of works on West Indian and American Negro folklore. During the last 25 years of her life she undertook at least one field trip a year; she died in New York City on December 19, 1941, a month after returning from one such trip, during which she studied the Peguchi Indians of Ecuador. She served as president of the American Ethnological Society from 1923 to 1925 and at the time of her death was president of the American Anthropological Association.

Parsons, Louella (1893–1972), newspaper columnist. Born in Freeport, Illinois, on August 6, 1893, Louella Oettinger obtained her first newspaper job while she was still in high school, as dramatic editor for the *Dixon* (Illinois) *Morning Star.* Her starting salary was $5 a week, a sum that was multiplied by several hundred times before she was through. She married John Parsons in 1910, when she was seventeen. When he died four years later she went to Chicago and became a reporter on the *Chicago Tribune.* In 1912 she had had her first contact with the movie industry, selling a script to the Essanay company for $25, and she soon began the first movie column in the country, in the *Chicago Record-Herald* in 1914. When the paper was bought by William Randolph Hearst in 1918 she was out of a job, for Hearst had not yet discovered that movies were news; but she moved to New York City and started a similar column in the *New York Morning Telegraph* that caught Hearst's attention, and after some shrewd bargaining on both sides he obtained her services. She was associated with various Hearst enterprises for the rest of her career. She underwent a crisis in 1925 when she contracted tuberculosis and was told she had only six months to live. She decided to spend her last days in California, but the disease waned and she emerged as the Hearst syndicate's Hollywood columnist. She made several attempts to start a radio program in the late 1920s and early 1930s, but it was not until 1934 that she found a successful formula: an interview program, "Hollywood Hotel," on which stars appeared gratis to publicize their films. The Radio Guild put a stop to all such free appearances in 1938, but by that time Louella —as she was always called—had established herself as the arbiter of the actions of the Hollywood colony, her judgments being considered as final in most cases, and her disfavor being feared more than that of any film critic. Her daily gossip column eventually appeared in some 400 news-papers in the United States, and other countries, and although its items were often inaccurate, it was accorded the devotion traditionally reserved for the Bible by millions of readers. Volumes of memoirs appeared as *The Gay Illiterate*, 1944, and *Tell It to Louella*, 1961. With the decline of Hollywood as the center of the moving-picture industry after World War II her influence also declined, but she continued to write the column until December 1, 1965, when it was taken over by her assistant, Dorothy Manners, who had in fact written it for more than a year. Miss Parsons died in Santa Monica, California, on December 9, 1972.

Parsons, Talcott (1902–1979), sociologist. Born on December 13, 1902, in Colorado Springs, Colorado, Parsons graduated from the Horace Mann School in New York City in 1920 and four years later from Amherst College. He spent the next year at the London School of Economics, where he studied under L. T. Hobhouse, Morris Ginsberg, and the anthropologist Bronislaw Malinowski, who deeply influenced his later thought. He then went to the University of Heidelberg, from which he received his Ph.D. in 1927 and where he came under the influence of the work of Max Weber, several of whose books he later translated into English. He went to Harvard in 1927 and for four years taught economics, shifting to the sociology department in 1931; he was an assistant professor from 1936 to 1939, was promoted to associate professor in 1939, and to professor in 1944. In 1946 he helped to found and became first chairman of the depart-ment of social relations at Harvard, remaining chairman until 1956. In a series of books, begin-ning with the *Structure of Social Action*, 1937, and including *Toward a General Theory of Action*, 1951, *Structure and Process in Modern Societies*, 1959, *Social Structure and Personality*, 1964, and *Sociological Theory and Modern Society*, 1968, he proposed and argued strongly for an eclectic and systematic approach to social science that would take into account findings from economics and anthropology as well as sociology. The recipient of many honors in his field, Parsons served as president of the American Sociological Society in 1949 and as president of the American Academy of Arts and Sciences in 1967. He retired from Harvard in 1973 and died in Munich, West Ger-many, on May 8, 1979.

Parsons, Theophilus (1750–1813), judge. Born in Byfield, Massachusetts, on February 24, 1750, Parsons was an indefatigable student, excelling in his work at Dummer Academy and at Harvard, from which he graduated in 1769. He read law at Falmouth (now Portland), Maine, and began his practice there in 1774, but a year later was forced to flee when the town was destroyed by a British fleet. He returned to his father's house in Byfield and found there Judge Edward Trowbridge, a Loyalist who had retired from Cambridge, Massa-chusetts. Trowbridge sent for his law library, then by far the largest in New England, and Parsons was able to obtain a more extensive knowledge of English law than was available to almost any other lawyer in the colonies. He studied so hard, in fact, that he fell victim to consumption, but he soon recovered and resumed his practice in New-buryport, Massachusetts. By this time—1777—he had become deeply concerned with the future form of government in Massachusetts—he assumed that the Revolution would succeed—and he became the leading member of the Essex County convention that opposed the Massachusetts constitution of 1778 and he wrote the convention report, called *The Essex Result*, that later became the founding document of the Federalists in Massachusetts. The Massachusetts constitution of 1780, a much more Federalist document than the previous one, was written by John Adams largely on the basis of Parsons's advice. By this time he and his asso-ciates in opposition to the 1778 constitution had become known as the Essex Junto, a name given them by John Hancock; but although Parsons and Hancock disagreed on many matters, Parsons wrote the address that Hancock gave to the state convention that ratified the federal Constitution in 1788, mainly as a result of the address. By 1800, when he moved from Newburyport to Boston, Par-sons had a very large law practice; from then until his death he was accounted the leading lawyer in the United States. In 1806 he was named chief justice of the supreme judicial court of Massa-chusetts, and in that post his influence was exerted not only throughout his state but also throughout the entire country. At the time there were few reports of court decisions in the United States, and there was in addition a strong prejudice against British and in favor of French precedents among many lawyers and judges. But partly because of his previous study of Judge Trowbridge's law library, and partly because of his assiduous read-ing of English reports since the 1770s, Parsons was able to provide in his lengthy decisions a rich background of English law that ultimately led to the adoption, in all of the states of the Union except Louisiana, of the English common-law tradition instead of the French one. Parsons may thus be said to have in large part created the sub-sequent law of the United States, and there is no doubt that he created the law of Massachusetts. He was throughout his life an inveterate reader of books on almost every subject, and his ex-periments in many scientific fields were said to have frightened his servants. He wrote an unpub-lished Greek grammar—in fact, he published almost nothing in his life, and never spoke in public unless it was required by his legal duties—was a founder of the Boston Athenaeum and of the Social Law Library, and was known through-out New England as a generous and delightful host. Although he paid attention to everything else, he paid almost no attention whatsoever to his dress, and his wife traveled with him on the cir-cuit to insure that he would be presentable when he appeared on the bench. He died in Boston on October 30, 1813.

Parsons, Theophilus (1797–1882), lawyer and educator. Born in Newburyport, Massachusetts, on May 17, 1797, Parsons, son of Theophilus Parsons (1750–1813), moved with his family to Boston three years later. He graduated from Harvard in 1815, and after reading law with William Prescott, father of the historian William H. Prescott, and making a trip to Europe in 1817, took up the practice of law, first in Taunton, Massachusetts, from 1822 to 1827, and then in Boston. He became a professor at the Harvard Law School in 1848 and remained in the post for 21 years. His courses were popular with students and he was renowned throughout New England for his wide learning. He wrote many influential treatises on the law: *The Law of Contracts*, two volumes, 1853–1855; *The Elements of Mercantile Law*, 1856 and 1862; *The Laws of Business*, 1857; *A Treatise on Maritime Law*, two volumes, 1859; *A Treatise on the Law of Promissory Notes and Bills of Exchange*, two volumes, 1863 and 1876; *A Treatise on the Law of Partnership*, 1867; *A Treatise on the Law of Marine Insurance and General Average*, two volumes, 1868; and *A Treatise on the Law of Shipping*, two volumes, 1869. He also wrote *The Constitution*, 1861, *The Political, Personal, and Property Rights of a Citizen*, 1874, and works on Swedenborgianism (which he had espoused since the 1820s). His treatise on contracts went through nine editions and was enormously influential; it had been written with the salaried assistance of a student, Christopher Columbus Langdell, who thus paid his way through the Harvard Law School. Langdell succeeded to Parson's chair at Harvard in 1870. Parsons died in Cambridge, Massachusetts, on January 26, 1882.

Parton, James (1822–1891), author. Born in Canterbury, England, on February 9, 1822, Parton emigrated to the United States with his widowed mother in 1827. Growing up in White Plains, New York, he attended an academy there and after graduation stayed on as a teacher; a trip abroad in 1842 was followed by four more years of teaching in a school in Philadelphia. In 1848 he sent an essay to Nathaniel Parker Willis's *New York Home Journal*; Willis liked it and hired him as an editor, in which position he remained until 1854. But his salary was small and the work was hard, and he was ever afterward grateful for the chance that led him to a New York restaurant in 1854, where in the course of a conversation with the proprietors of the Mason Brothers publishing firm he suggested that a biography of Horace Greeley would be as popular as Benjamin Franklin's *Autobiography*, which had recently appeared. The Mason brothers took him up on it, advancing $1000 to cover the year of work that he estimated the book would require. *The Life of Horace Greeley*, published in 1855, was a best seller and moreover was a new departure in American biography, being unique in its time for the realism and skill with which it presented its subject to the public. For the next 35 years Parton continued to write, mostly biographies that usually were great successes both with readers and critics. His best biographies—all still readable and valuable—were *The Life and Times of Aaron Burr*, 1857, revised in two volumes, 1864; *Life of Andrew Jackson*, three volumes, 1859–1860; *Life and Times of Benjamin Franklin*, two volumes, 1864; *Life of Thomas Jefferson*, 1874; and *Life of Voltaire*, two volumes, 1881. He also produced biographies of John Jacob Astor, 1865; George Washington, 1872; and Fanny Fern (his wife, Sara Payson Willis Parton), 1873, as well as many biographical sketches in such works as *General Butler in New Orleans*, 1863; *Famous Americans of Recent Times*, 1867; *People's Book of Biography*, 1868; *Triumphs of Enterprise, Ingenuity, and Public Spirit*, 1871; *Le Parnasse Français*, 1877, *Noted Women of Europe and America*, 1883; *Captains of Industry*, in two series, 1884 and 1891; and *Some Noted Princes, Authors, and Statesmen of Our Time*, 1885. He also wrote a number of topical works on political issues and controversies and was a steady contributor to periodicals. His wife died in 1872 and four years later, despite legal difficulties, he married her daughter by a previous marriage, Ellen Willis Ethredge, whom he had earlier adopted. He had moved to Newburyport, Massachusetts, in 1875, where he lived for most of the rest of his life; he died there on October 17, 1891.

Parton, Sara Payson Willis (1811–1872), "Fanny Fern," author. Born in Portland, Maine, on July 9, 1811, Sarah Payson Willis, sister of Nathaniel P. Willis, grew up there and in Boston. She was three times married, the last time to James Parton, the biographer. She began her writing, mostly essays, in the late 1830s, following the death of her first husband, and her articles were published in local newspapers. In 1853 she published a collection of essays, *Fern Leaves from Fanny's Portfolio*, which made her an established author. In 1856, after marrying Parton and moving to New York City, she began writing for the *New York Ledger* and remained associated with the paper until her death. At the same time she published additional books of essays, and several short stories. She also tried her hand at the novel: her first, *Ruth Hall*, 1855, satirized her brother Nathaniel and his social life. Other works included *The Play-Day Book: New Stories for Little Folks*, 1857; *Folly as It Flies*, 1858; and *Ginger Snaps*, 1870. She died in New York City on October 10, 1872.

Pastor, Tony (1837–1908), actor and theater manager. Antonio Pastor was born in New York City on May 28, 1837. His father was a violinist in an opera-house orchestra, his brothers were circus performers, and he himself made his performing debut at the age of six, singing comedy duets at a temperance meeting. He made his first stage appearance at the age of nine, at Barnum's American Museum, and the next year toured with Raymond & Waring's Menagerie; during his teens he worked mostly in circuses, as a ringmaster and as a singing clown. About 1862 he opened his own music hall on lower Broadway in New York City; his speciality was singing original songs about events in the Civil War. He opened Tony Pastor's Opera House on the Bowery in partnership with Sam Sharpley in 1865, and during the next ten years devoted himself to creating vaudeville entertainment that the whole family could attend, a rare phenomenon for the time. He moved to another Broadway theater in 1875 and in 1881 acquired a theater on Fourteenth Street, which, as Tony Pastor's, prospered until his death. He wrote more than 2000 songs and was an accomplished comic singer and actor, but his real talent lay in producing and directing, and he worked to good effect with most of the leading American actors and entertainers of the last decades of the nineteenth century. Probably the greatest serious vaudevillian of his time, he died in Elmhurst, New York, on August 26, 1908.

Pastorius, Francis Daniel (1651–1720?), lawyer and colonizer. Born in Sommerhausen, Germany, on September 26, 1651, Pastorius studied at the universities of Altdorf, Strasbourg, Basel, and Jena, and received a doctorate in law from Altdorf in 1676. He began the practice of law at Windsheim but moved in 1679 to Frankfurt am Main, where he soon met some friends of William Penn and for the first time became interested in America. In April 1683 a group of Quakers appointed him as their agent to buy land in Penn's domain; he arrived in Philadelphia in August of that year, arranged to purchase 15,000 acres from Penn, and in October laid out near Philadelphia the settlement that he called Germantown. He was the town's chief citizen for the rest of his life, serving as its first mayor and continuously as mayor, clerk, or keeper of records until 1707. He also served in the provincial assembly in 1687 and 1691, and was a teacher in the Friends' school in Philadelphia from 1698 to 1700 and the master of a school in Germantown from 1702 until 1719. In 1688 he and others signed a protest against slave-keeping, the first such document in the English colonies, but to no immediate effect. One of the most learned men in Pennsylvania in his time, he wrote a number of works in German, Latin, and English, and published, among others, *A New Primmer or Methodical Direction to Attain the True Spelling, Reading & Writing of English,* possibly the first schoolbook written in Pennsylvania. Its date of publication is not known. He died, probably in Germantown, sometime between December 26, 1719, and January 13, 1720.

Patch, Sam (1807?–1829), stunt diver. Born in Rhode Island about 1807, Patch went to sea at an early age and about 1825 became a cotton-spinner in Paterson, New Jersey, to support his widowed mother. In 1827 he declared that he was going to dive into the Passaic River from a bridge which was then being built. The police stopped him, but he managed to dive from a nearby precipice 75 feet into the stream, and, after later diving

from the bridge itself, determined on a stunt-diving career. Accompanied by a fox and a small bear, he wandered from town to town, diving from cliffs, bridges, and the masts of ships; sometimes the bear was forced to dive with him. He had become a national celebrity by the time he arrived at Niagara Falls, New York, in October 1829 and dived into the Niagara River from a cliff on Goat Island. He then announced that his next feat would be a dive from a scaffold over the falls of the Genesee River at Rochester, New York. He took soundings of the water at the bottom of the falls and even made a successful practice dive, but on the announced day, November 13, 1829, something went amiss; his body turned in the air as he fell, and he hit the water sideways 125 feet below his starting point. He did not surface, but his reputation was such that for months the newspapers carried stories rumoring his reappearance; however, on the following March 17 his body was found frozen in the ice at the river's mouth on Lake Ontario. He was for many years after a figure of popular legend, and a great horse, the pacer Sam Patch, was named for him.

Paterson, William (1745–1806), justice of the Supreme Court. Born in County Antrim, Ireland, on December 24, 1745, Paterson emigrated to America with his family in 1747, settling in Princeton, New Jersey. He graduated from the College of New Jersey (now Princeton) in 1763 and began the study of law the next year; he was admitted to practice in 1769. He lived for a while in New Bromley, in Hunterdon County, New Jersey, moved back to Princeton in 1772, and in 1779 purchased a farm on the north bank of the Raritan River near New Brunswick, New Jersey. It remained his home for the rest of his life. A deputy to the provincial congress in 1775 and 1776, he was in 1776 also a member of the convention that drew up the state constitution, and in the same year was named attorney general of New Jersey, a position he retained until 1783. The work was onerous, especially the long rides on horseback from one court session to another, and he declined to serve in the Continental Congress after his election in 1780. He accepted election, however, as a delegate to the federal Constitutional Convention of 1787, where he played a significant part. As a representative of one of the smaller states, he objected to the Virginia ("large-state") Plan, which called for representation according to population, and proposed in its place the New Jersey (or "small-state") Plan, also called the Paterson Plan, which was "federal" in the sense that it called for the states to have equal votes in the legislature. The final Constitution, which he helped to have ratified in New Jersey, embodied a compromise between these two positions, all of the states being represented equally in the Senate, and the House of Representatives being organized on the basis of population. One of New Jersey's first two U.S. senators, Paterson helped to write the Judiciary Act of 1789 but in 1790 resigned from the Senate to become governor of New Jersey. In 1792 he was chosen to codify the laws of his state and in 1800 published the *Laws of the State of New Jersey*, a work of wide influence during the following century. Meanwhile, in 1793, he had been named to the U.S. Supreme Court, for which he wrote a number of important opinions. He presided over the trials of several of the persons indicted for treason following the Whisky Rebellion and also over that of Matthew Lyon, accused of violating the Sedition Act of 1798. He last appeared on the Court bench in the summer of 1806; in September he set out for Ballston Spa, New York, to seek respite from failing health, but died along the way, at Albany, on September 9, 1806. Paterson, New Jersey, founded in the 1790s, was named for him.

Patten, Gilbert (1866–1945), "Burt L. Standish," author. Born in Corinna, Maine, on October 25, 1866, Patten was kept at home by his parents against his will until he was eighteen; he then ran away and took a job in a machine shop. His decision to flee had been helped by the sale the year before of his first story to a pulp magazine; he continued to write steadily until his death. He spent a month in Omaha, Nebraska, in 1889, which qualified him, he believed, as a literary expert on the West, and for the next few years many of his stories were published under the pseudonyms "William West" and "Wyoming Will." The year 1896 saw the first use of his favorite nom de plume, "Burt L. Standish," and the creation of his famous fictional character Frank Merriwell, of Fardale Academy and, later, of Yale. Patten wrote some 209 books about the virtuous Yale athletic hero and his younger, equally upright, brother Dick, although, as he later said, he had probably forgotten some of the titles so the number may have been larger; of the 209, 208 were juveniles, and one, published in 1941 after a long hiatus, was about the hero grown up. Approximately 125 million copies of the Merriwell books were sold during a quarter-century or so of popularity, and the character, so brilliant and physically capable that he was once called a combination of Tarzan and Einstein, was an inspiration to two generations of American boys. But even though, in the early part of the century, Patten was selling as many as 135,000 copies of his Merriwell books a week, he never made a sizable fortune. He worked for the Street and Smith company, a pulp factory of fabulous productivity, at a small salary ($50 a week for a while) with no royalties. Frank Merriwell began to appear in a comic strip in 1931 and in a radio program, for which Patten wrote scripts, in 1934. The author of some 40 to 50 other books, Patten, an ardent Socialist, died in poverty in Vista, California, on January 16, 1945.

Patterson, Eleanor Medill (1881–1948), newspaper publisher. Born in Chicago on November 7, 1881, "Cissy" Patterson, as she was called, came of one of the great American newspaper families, her grandfather, Joseph Medill, having been editor in chief of the *Chicago Tribune*, her father, Robert W. Patterson, and her cousin, Robert R. McCormick, being in turn editors and publishers of it, and her brother, Joseph Medill Patterson, being the publisher of the *New York Daily News*. Miss Patterson, however, was slated for a career in society by her ambitious mother; she took the first appropriate step in this direction when she was nineteen, marrying an impecunious Polish nobleman, Count Joseph Gizycki. But the count had other interests besides his wife, and Cissy left him after three years. The count followed her, abducted their baby daughter, and initiated an international episode of the greatest interest to readers of society pages on both sides of the Atlantic. It took a year to get the baby back, with the help of the enormous Patterson and McCormick fortune, and another 15 years or so for Cissy to get a divorce, which cost, it was rumored, some half a million dollars. As Eleanor M. Gizycka she published two novels, *Glass Houses*, 1926, and *Fall Flight*, 1928. Another marriage ended in 1929, and Cissy, at forty-five, was left with her social career a disaster. Undaunted, she decided that she, too, would try her hand at the newspaper business— she had inherited an interest in the *Tribune*, but beyond membership on its board of directors played no part in it—and persuaded her old friend William Randolph Hearst to let her edit the *Washington Herald*. He agreed in 1930, the same year that she changed her name legally to Mrs. Eleanor Patterson, and she went to work to try to revive the floundering daily. She was an eccentric editor in chief, often arriving at the office in riding costume or in evening clothes; she feuded with a series of city editors, but she was also courageous, going out on many important stories herself, usually in disguise. In addition, she had the family genius for circulation-building publicity. Within a few years the paper's circulation had more than doubled and soon it was in the black. In 1937 she leased the *Herald* from Hearst, together with his evening paper, the *Washington Times*. When the publisher of the *Washington Post*, Eugene Meyer, moved to buy the *Herald* from Hearst, Mrs. Patterson bought it herself and combined it with the *Times*, which she also bought, into the *Washington Times-Herald*. Like the rest of her family she was a bitter opponent of President Franklin D. Roosevelt and an inveterate opponent of the New Deal. Her paper thrived during World War II, but it became less prosperous afterward. She died near Marlboro, Maryland, on July 24, 1948.

Patterson, John Henry (1844–1922), manufacturer. Born into a prosperous family on a farm near Dayton, Ohio, on December 13, 1844, Patterson attended local schools and went for a year to Miami University, in Ohio, leaving in 1864 to enlist in the Union army. After the war, having seen no action, he entered Dartmouth College, from which he graduated in 1867 with a lasting prejudice against college men and college education in general. Returning to Dayton, he found himself with nothing to do. He stayed on the family farm for a while, then became a tollgate keeper on a canal, then went into the coal business with his brothers. In 1884, at forty, he bought the National Manufacturing Company in Dayton, which made cash registers, at the time a generally ignored device. The firm occupied a small factory in the worst slum district of Dayton and employed only 13 persons, and Patterson was so strongly ridiculed for putting his money into it that the day after the sale was consummated, he offered the previous owner $2000 to let him out of the deal. The seller refused, whereupon Patterson set to work to try to revive the business, making a number of improvements in the cash register and even taking out several patents in his own name. But his real genius lay in merchandising and sales, and he revolutionized these vital aspects of business life in subsequent decades. He changed the firm's name to the National Cash Register Company, afterward known throughout the world as NCR, promoted sales conventions, founded sales schools, invented the idea of the exclusive sales territory, paid large commissions to salesmen, and organized a force of well-trained service men to maintain equipment after its sale. A physical-culture enthusiast, he insisted that his executives report at five in the morning for calisthenics; but he also made many innovations in employee benefits, justifying his generous treatment with the terse remark, "It pays." By the time he died, while on a trip to Atlantic City, New Jersey, on May 7, 1922, he had transformed the unpromising Dayton firm into one of the world's leading manufacturing companies.

Pattie, James Ohio (1804–1850?), frontiersman. Born in Bracken County, Kentucky, in 1804, Pattie moved, according to his own somewhat dubious account, with his family to Missouri in 1812. In 1824 he and his father joined an expedition to Santa Fe, arriving there on November 5 of that year. During the next three years he engaged in a number of exploratory and trapping expeditions, moving ever westward, and in early 1828 he and his father and six companions reached Santa Catalina Mission in Lower California (Baja California). Their presence, however, was not welcomed by the Mexican authorities, and the party was arrested and imprisoned and, again according to Pattie, subjected to brutal treatment. His father died in prison on April 24, 1828. Pattie and his companions were released in 1829 when, during a smallpox epidemic, he used the vaccine his father had brought to vaccinate some 20,000 people in California. He made his way via Mexico City to Cincinnatti, where he arrived in August 1830. His *Personal Narrative* appeared the following year, edited and perhaps largely written by Timothy Flint, author also of a famous biography of Daniel Boone that, like the Pattie book, helped to make its subject a legend. Although the *Personal Narrative* contained many errors and was, according to one of Pattie's companions on the trip to California, mostly false, it became immediately popular and acquired a lasting place in the lore of

the American frontier. Little is known of Pattie's life after 1831; he joined the Gold Rush to California in 1849 and probably visited San Diego. During the winter of 1850 he spent some time at a camp in the Sierra Nevada; he left camp one day as bad weather was setting in and was never heard of again.

Patton, George Smith, Jr. (1885–1945), soldier. Born on November 11, 1885, in San Gabriel, California, Patton studied for a year at the Virginia Military Institute (VMI) and in 1904 won appointment to West Point, from which he graduated in 1909. Commissioned a second lieutenant and assigned to the cavalry, he served at a number of army posts, quickly gaining a reputation for ability and driving energy. After taking part in Gen. John J. Pershing's expedition into Mexico in pursuit of Pancho Villa in 1916 he was assigned to Pershing's staff at the head of the American Expeditionary Force (AEF) sent to France in 1917. He received training in the use of tanks, then a new weapon, and commanded a tank brigade at St.-Mihiel and in the Meuse-Argonne offensive. He was wounded and later received the Distinguished Service Cross, the Distinguished Service Medal, and the temporary rank of colonel. After the war he returned to the United States and during the next 20 years was stationed principally at Fort Myer, Virginia, where in 1938 he assumed command of the 3rd Cavalry. In 1940, with war appearing imminent, he was assigned to the 2nd Armored Division at Fort Benning, Georgia, and the following year became divisional commander with the rank of major general. There and later in the California desert he molded the 2nd, and then the larger 1st Armored Corps, into a highly efficient force. He was sent with his men to take part in the North African campaign in November 1942; he occupied Morocco and early in 1943 took charge of the 2nd Corps in Tunisia. In July he commanded the 7th Army in the invasion and rapid capture of Sicily. It was during this campaign that, in an incident later much publicized, he slapped a hospitalized soldier whom he suspected of malingering; he was sharply reprimanded by Gen. Dwight D. Eisenhower and was widely criticized in the press. In the invasion of France that began in Normandy on June 6, 1944, Patton, then a lieutenant general, commanded the 3rd Army, which, in a series of rapid and unconventional armored sweeps, advanced to the Rhine by March 1945 and then sped across Germany cutting the country in half. Throughout this final campaign of the war, "Old Blood and Guts," as he was known, displayed great courage, daring, and ruthlessness, wearing all the while his matched ivory-handled revolvers. In April 1945 he was promoted temporarily to four-star general. His public criticisms of the postwar denazification program of Germany led to his removal in October as commander of the 3rd Army; he was transferred to the 15th Army. He died in a car accident in Germany on December 21, 1945. An autobiography, *War as I Knew It*, appeared in 1947.

Paul, Alice (1885–1977), social reformer. Born in Moorestown, New Jersey, on January 11, 1885, Miss Paul graduated from Swarthmore College in 1905 and during the following year did graduate work at the New York School of Social Work. In 1906 she went to England for three years to do settlement work and during her stay was jailed three times for suffragist agitation. She also continued to do graduate work at the universities of Birmingham and London, and received an M.A. degree in absentia from the University of Pennsylvania in 1907 and her Ph.D. from the same institution in 1912. In 1912 she became chairman of the congressional committee of the National American Woman Suffrage Association, but she soon differed with what she considered its timid policies and in 1913 she and a group of other militants withdrew to found the Congressional Union for Woman Suffrage, which in 1917 merged with the Woman's party to form the National Woman's party, in which she was a dominant figure during the next three decades. She devoted herself after the successful conclusion of the campaign for ratification of the Nineteenth Amendment, which enfranchised women, in 1920 to the study of law, but she also found time to continue her activities on behalf of equal rights for the women of the United States and of the world. She managed to have introduced into Congress in 1923 the first equal-rights amendment in behalf of women; when it failed of passage, she turned her attention to the international field, concentrating, with considerable success, on obtaining support for her crusade from the League of Nations. She always insisted that many of the troubles of the world had their basis in the fact that women were not allowed to exert their potential political power, and she reiterated this view when World War II broke out; it need not have occurred, she declared, and probably would not have if women had had their say at the Versailles Peace Conference at the end of World War I. Elected chairman of the National Woman's party in 1942, Miss Paul continued thereafter to work for women's rights in general and for an equal-rights amendment to the Constitution in particular, a dream that was partly realized in 1970, when such an amendment passed the Congress and was referred to the states for ratification. In the interim she was able to have included in the preamble to the charter of the United Nations an affirmation of the equal rights of women and men. She died in Moorestown, New Jersey, on July 9, 1977.

Paul, John, see Jones, John Paul

Paulding, Hiram (1797–1878), naval officer. Born on December 11, 1797, on a farm in Westchester County, New York, Paulding was a son of one of the captors of Major John André during the Revolution. Appointed a midshipman in 1811, when he was thirteen, he was soon ordered to the Champlain Squadron and, for his gallant services as an acting officer of the *Ticonderoga* at the battle of Lake Champlain (Plattsburgh), September 11,

1814—he was still only sixteen—was awarded $1500 in prize money and a sword by Congress. After the War of 1812 he studied at Norwich Military Academy in Vermont, graduating in 1823. The next year he accomplished another remarkable feat. On duty in the Pacific aboard the *United States,* he volunteered to carry Commodore Isaac Hull's dispatches from the Peruvian port of Callao to Simon Bolivar's headquarters deep in the Andes. The journey involved a 1500–mile trek through the mountains on horseback and was completed in record time. In 1825 he volunteered for a cruise in the South Seas, as first lieutenant of the *Dolphin,* in pursuit of mutineers from the whaleship *Globe.* He came upon the mutineers on a small island, where they had ensconced themselves among several hundred native allies. Paulding seized one of the men and, using his captive's body as a shield, marched him away to one of his ship's boats, through a crowd of angry islanders. He described this and other events in his *Journal of a Cruise of the U.S. Schooner Dolphin,* 1831, and published an account of his Andean adventure in *Bolivar in His Camp,* 1834; both were popular in their time. He cruised in the Mediterranean in 1830–1832 and 1834–1837 and was promoted to captain in 1844, whereupon he took the *Vincennes* on a three-year cruise to China. He returned to be given command of the new frigate *St. Lawrence* and sailed her to Bremen, the first U.S. warship to visit that German port; he was consulted on the creation of a German navy and was offered a high command in it, which he declined. He was commander of the Washington Navy Yard from 1851 to 1855 and during the next three years commanded the navy's home squadron, operating mostly in the Caribbean; late in 1857 he took into custody William Walker and 150 filibusters at San Juan del Norte, Nicaragua, and sent them home. Sentiment in the Northern states as well as in the Nicaraguan government generally approved this action, but President James Buchanan freed Walker, whose regime in Nicaragua had been recognized by the U.S., and relieved Commodore Paulding of his command. Appointed head of the Bureau of Detail in March 1861, he had the unpleasant task of overseeing the evacuation of the Norfolk, Virginia, Navy Yard; the job was well done under the difficult circumstances of those early days of the Civil War, but some 3000 cannon had to be left for the Confederate Army, and Pauling was severely criticized. He was one of the strongest advocates of the revolutionary design of the *Monitor* and was credited with helping to win its adoption. Later in the war he commanded the New York Navy Yard, in which position he oversaw the supplying and servicing of the Union's blockading fleet. He had been promoted to rear admiral (retired) in 1861 and after the war served as governor of the Naval Asylum at Philadelphia and as port admiral of Boston. He finally retired in 1870 and died at his farm near Huntington, New York, on Long Island Sound, on October 20, 1878. At his death he was the last surviving officer of the battle of Lake Champlain.

Paulding, James Kirke (1778–1860), author and public official. Born in Putnam County, New York, on August 22, 1778, Paulding was the son of a merchant and patriot whose generous actions in behalf of the Revolutionary army later involved him in bankruptcy. His mother, however, in the face of financial reverses, managed to support the family by taking in sewing, and thus James and his brother and sister were well educated. Brought up in Tarrytown, New York, James left for New York City to live with his brother, later a congressman and mayor of New York City, and to work in public office. There he met the young Washington Irving, with whom he collaborated in 1807–1808 in the humorous papers entitled *Salmagundi*, the success of which confirmed his choice of a literary career. His next book was *The Diverting History of John Bull and Brother Jonathan*, 1812, a humorous account of the relations between England and America during the two preceding centuries and an effort quite in the manner of the "Knickerbocker group" of which he was reckoned a member. He followed this with several poetic parodies of English writers, but when these were angrily reviewed in England he countered with *The United States and England*, 1815, which brought him to the attention of President James Madison, who named him secretary of the Board of Navy Commissioners. This post required his presence in Washington, D.C., where he lived until 1823; in 1818 he married Gertrude, the sister of Gouverneur Kemble. But even though his official duties required much of his time, he continued to write, producing several more notable contributions to the "literary war" with English writers that took place in the first decades of the nation's life: *Letters from the South*, 1817; *A Sketch of Old England*, 1822; and *John Bull in America*, 1825. All of these were popular, and he was able to devote himself mostly to writing for the next two decades, publishing a series of novels and short stories, many of them dealing with the Dutch colonists of New York. *Koningsmarke*, 1823; *The Dutchman's Fireside*, 1831; *Westward Ho!*, 1832; *The Old Continental*, 1846; and *The Puritan and His Daughter*, 1849, were all novels that enjoyed a considerable vogue during Paulding's lifetime. Free of romanticism and of extravagances of imagination, emotion, or language, Paulding's works embodied a sense of realism that was marred only by the occasional evidences of haste in composition. He also wrote a *Life of Washington*, 1835, and a book about slavery that appeared in 1836, as well as many articles in periodicals. From 1824 to 1837 he served as U.S. navy agent for New York. One of the best-known men in New York, he was asked by another New Yorker, newly-elected President Martin Van Buren, to serve in his cabinet as secretary of the navy, and he filled the office with distinction from 1837 to 1841. In 1842 he traveled through the West with Van Buren and four years later retired to his estate near Hyde Park, New York, where he lived happily for the rest of his life, dying there on April 6, 1860.

Pauling, Linus Carl (1901–   ), chemist. Born in Portland, Oregon, on February 28, 1901, Pauling attended Oregon State College and after graduating in 1922 went to the California Institute of Technology (Caltech), where he took his Ph.D. in 1925. His primary interest was in the field of physical chemistry, and during 1926–1927, aided by a Guggenheim fellowship, he studied atomic and quantum physics with leading European scientists in Munich, Zurich, and Copenhagen. In 1927 he returned to Caltech as assistant professor of chemistry, becoming a full professor four years later. His early investigations into the structure of crystals led him to consider the nature of chemical bonds and the structure of molecules, a line of research that was to prove the most fruitful in modern chemistry. Applying quantum mechanics to the problem, he developed his resonance theory of chemical valence by means of which he was able to construct models for a number of anomalous molecules, most notably for the benzene molecule, which had been inexplicable in conventional chemical terms. He published the results of these early researches in *The Nature of the Chemical Bond and the Structure of Molecules and Crystals*, 1939. In 1937 he became chairman of the division of chemistry and chemical engineering and director of the Gates and Crelin laboratories at Caltech. He began to turn his attention to more complex chemical structures, particularly the amino acids and peptide chains that constitute proteins. His researches were interrupted during World War II by service on a number of government scientific boards, for which he was awarded the Presidential Medal of Merit in 1948. His work on protein structure was announced shortly before his winning of the Nobel Prize for Chemistry in 1954 for his work on chemical bonds and molecular structure. During his investigations of organic proteins he discovered a structural fault in blood hemoglobin that was responsible for hereditary sickle-cell anemia; and as he continued to look into hereditary defects and diseases that might be traceable to structural errors on the molecular level, he became increasingly concerned over the threat to humanity posed by radioactive fallout from the testing of nuclear weapons. He spoke and wrote in favor of a cessation of such testing, publishing *No More War!* in 1958. The same year he presented to the United Nations a petition signed by more than 11,000 scientists calling for a halt to nuclear testing. On October 10, 1963, the effective date for the provisions of the U.S.–Soviet treaty partially banning such testing, Pauling was awarded the 1962 Nobel Peace Prize, becoming the first person to win two unshared Nobel prizes. (Marie Curie was also twice a Nobel laureate, but one award was for joint work with two other physicists.) In 1964 he resigned his professorship at Caltech, having given up his administrative posts six years earlier; from 1963 until 1969 he was associated with the Center for the Study of Democratic Institutions at Santa Barbara, California; from 1967 to 1969 he was a member of the faculty of the University of

California at San Diego. In 1969 he joined the faculty of Stanford University as a professor of chemistry.

Payne, John Howard (1791–1852), actor and playwright. Born in New York City on June 9, 1791, Payne early determined to pursue a stage career, although for a time his family strongly objected. Thus, for six months, while he was still only fourteen, he published an anonymous eight-page critical review of the New York theater; that same year, in February 1806, his first play, *Julia, or The Wanderer*, was produced. Such precocious achievements brought him little financial success but they opened the doors of New York literary society to him, and he met at this time and later became a close friend of most of the city's writers, notably Washington Irving. He attended Union College, Schenectady, New York, for two years, but his father's bankruptcy gave him his chance to drop out and go on the stage as an actor. He made his debut in February 1809, in John Home's *Douglas*, and was an instant success, soon taking both New York City and Boston by storm not only in contemporary dramas but also in Shakespeare's *Romeo and Juliet*, *Hamlet*, and *Lear*. His lack of dramatic training soon caught up with him, however, and by 1810 he was without theatrical work. Other ventures also failed, but he sailed for London in January 1813, ever hopeful and with his passage paid by loving friends, in the expectation of recouping his fortunes in the theater there. He was disappointed, however, and 20 years in Europe were marked by increasing debts. He was, in fact, briefly in debtor's prison after the failure of an attempt to produce his own works at the Sadler's Wells Theatre, which he leased in 1820. He did some acting, but without great success, and wrote or adapted a number of plays for the London and New York stage, a few of which, including *Brutus, or the Fall of Tarquin*, 1818, and *Charles the Second; or, The Merry Monarch*, 1824, on which he collaborated with his old friend Irving, were highly regarded. The previous year, however, he had adapted *Clari, or, The Maid of Milan* into an opera for Charles Kemble and had written for it the song "Home, Sweet Home!" (music by Henry Rowley Bishop), which was to give him a sort of immortality, though little financial return, as it became enormously popular throughout the world. He returned to New York City in 1832, still hopeful but besieged by creditors, enjoyed a benefit given in his honor, the proceeds of which went to pay some of his debts, and hovered on the outskirts of the theatrical world for the next ten years. In all he wrote or adapted some 60 plays during his career, ten or so with Irving, and these were presented with many of the greatest English and American actors of the day. In 1842, through the good offices of friends, he was named U.S. consul in Tunis; retaining the post until recalled by President Polk in 1845, he was reappointed to it in 1851. But his health had already begun to fail, and he died in Tunis on April 9, 1852.

Payson, Lt. Howard, *see* Stratemeyer, Edward

Peabody, Elizabeth Palmer (1804–1894), educator. Born in Billerica, Massachusetts, on May 16, 1804, Miss Peabody opened a school in Lancaster, Massachusetts, at the age of sixteen. She began another school in Boston two years later, at the same time attending a class in Greek conducted by the young Ralph Waldo Emerson. Another school begun in Boston in 1825 led to a friendship with the William Ellery Channing family; she served as Channing's private secretary for the next nine years, eventually writing a book of reminiscences of him that appeared in 1880. In 1834 she moved to the Temple School in Boston as assistant to its director, Bronson Alcott, whose unconventional educational methods she described anonymously in *Record of a School*, 1835. She returned to her parents' Salem, Massachusetts, home in 1836, occupying her time by attending meetings of the new Transcendental Club in Emerson's home. The next year she discovered that her girlhood friend Nathaniel Hawthorne was the author of some stories she had read in the *New England Magazine*, and she thereupon introduced Hawthorne to her Transcendentalist friends and to her sister, Sophia, whom he married in 1842; another of her sisters, Mary, married Horace Mann in 1843. In 1839 she had opened a bookshop in Boston that soon became the center of Transcendentalist activities in the city. The shop had a back room, and there she set up a press on which were printed three of Hawthorne's books, some works of Margaret Fuller, who also held her famous "conversations" there, the Transcendentalist organ, the *Dial*, published from premises in 1842–1843, and various pamphlets of the Anti-Slavery Society. From about 1845 she devoted herself to education, publishing in 1856 a useful text, *Chronological History of the United States*, establishing in Boston in 1860 one of the first U.S. kindergartens, and issuing from 1873 to 1875 the magazine *Kindergarten Messenger*. Gaining her living primarily by lecturing, she gave most of the proceeds to further the education of Indians. She lectured on history at Alcott's Concord School of Philosophy from 1879 to 1884 and published her last book, *A Last Evening with Allston*, in 1886. She died after a long and full life at Jamaica Plain, Massachusetts, on January 3, 1894.

Peabody, George (1795–1869), merchant, financier, and philanthropist. Born in South Danvers (now Peabody), Massachusetts, on February 18, 1795, Peabody was apprenticed to a grocer at the age of eleven. Moving to Georgetown, D.C., he became in 1814 manager of Elisha Riggs's dry-goods warehouse and soon was a partner in the firm. Riggs & Peabody moved to Baltimore in 1815 and when Riggs retired in 1829 Peabody became senior partner. As president of the Eastern Railroad in 1836, he accumulated a sizable fortune; he thereupon decided to move to England to arrange, as a broker, for the importation of capital into the

United States for various enterprises. He settled in London in 1837 and remained there, except for frequent trips to the United States, for the rest of his life. Already a powerful international financier, he grew in wealth and influence over the years; by 1854 he took Junius Spencer Morgan into partnership in George Peabody and Company. The possessor of an enormous fortune for his day, he gave most of it away during his lifetime, a fact which startled his contemporaries. He did what he could as an individual during the years preceding the Civil War to shore up U.S. credit abroad, provided the money to exhibit American products at the Crystal Palace exhibition in London in 1851, backed Elisha Kent Kane's search for the lost Arctic explorer Sir John Franklin in 1853, and was the host at elaborate Fourth of July dinners that were a feature of the London social season. His benefactions totaled nearly $10 million and included making the founding endowments of the Peabody Institute in Baltimore, the Peabody Institute in Peabody, Massachusetts, the Peabody Museum at Yale, the Peabody Museum at Harvard, and the Peabody Academy of Sciences in Salem, Massachusetts; he also created the Peabody Education Fund, for institutions in the South, and gave $2.5 million to the city of London to build workers' houses. Oxford awarded him an honorary degree in 1867 and he received the freedom of the City of London in 1869; Queen Victoria wanted to make him a baronet but, as a good American, he declined, whereupon she sent him a letter and her picture. In 1868 the name of his native town was changed in his honor. He died in London on November 4, 1869; after a state funeral in Westminster Abbey his body was brought home on the British warship *Monarch*, escorted by a French and an American naval vessel, and buried in Peabody. He was elected to the Hall of Fame in 1900.

Peale, Charles Willson (1741–1827), painter and naturalist. Born on April 15, 1741, in Queen Annes County, Maryland, Peale was apprenticed to a saddler at thirteen. He opened his own saddlery in 1762 but the business was closed down by Loyalist creditors when he joined the Sons of Freedom. He developed an interest in portraiture, seeking instruction from John Hesselius and advice from John Singleton Copley, and received funds from several patrons for study with Benjamin West in London, where he went in 1767. He returned to live in Annapolis, Maryland, in 1769, and his work was warmly received. In 1776 he moved to Philadelphia and painted government officials and important visitors to the country, becoming one of the foremost portraitists in America. He helped to recruit soldiers for the Continental army and was made a captain after fighting at Trenton and Princeton in 1777. During the war he made numerous miniature portraits of Continental officers, later enlarging them into a noted collection of mezzotints. He was elected to the Pennsylvania General Assembly in 1779 but returned to painting and engraving after 1780. Most famous for his portraits of George Washing-

ton, he completed nearly 60 based on seven he had actually painted from life; the one completed in 1772 was the first painting of Washington ever done. Conservative rather than romanticized depictions, his portraits were probably accurate portrayals of the first president. Other sitters included John Hancock, Benjamin Franklin, John Quincy Adams, Nathanael Greene, James Monroe, Thomas Jefferson, and Alexander Hamilton. Peale founded a museum (later the Philadelphia Museum and later still the Peale Museum) and supplied it with paintings and collections of natural objects, including the bones of a mastodon unearthed in 1801 in the course of the first American scientific expedition, which he had organized. He helped establish the Pennsylvania Academy of the Fine Arts in 1805. He also wrote several books, including *An Essay on Building Wooden Bridges*, 1797; *Introduction to a Course of Lectures on Natural History*, 1800; and *An Epistle to a Friend on the Means of Preserving Health*, 1803. He was accomplished also in the fields of taxidermy, shoemaking, carpentry, dentistry, and optometry. He taught all of his children to paint; several—notably Raphaelle, Rembrandt, and Titian Ramsay Peale—became noted artists, and Titian was a naturalist as well. Peale died in Philadelphia on February 22, 1827.

Peale, Norman Vincent (1898–   ), religious leader and author. Born in Bowersville, Ohio, on May 31, 1898, Peale was graduated from Ohio Wesleyan University in 1920 and ordained in the Methodist Episcopal church in 1922. Pastor in Berkeley, Rhode Island, from 1922 to 1924, he found time to do further graduate work in theology at Boston University, receiving his M.A. and his S.T.B. degrees in 1924. An appointment, from 1924 to 1927, as pastor of the Kings Highway Church in Brooklyn, New York, during which time he increased the size of the congregation from 40 to 900, was followed by a pastorate in Syracuse, New York, where he remained until 1932; he moved in that year to the Marble Collegiate Church in New York City, where he remained pastor thereafter. In 1937, with Dr. Smiley Blanton, a psychiatrist, he founded the Religio-Psychiatric Clinic, the nation's first service combining religion and psychiatry for the sake of mental health; the organization became the American Foundation for Religion and Psychiatry in 1951. Peale's first well-known book, *The Art of Living*, based on his network radio program of the same name, appeared in 1948; it was followed by other works, most of them best sellers, including *The Power of Positive Thinking*, 1952; *The Amazing Results of Positive Thinking*, 1959; *The Tough-minded Optimist*, 1962; *Sin, Sex and Self-Control*, 1965; and *Enthusiasm Makes the Difference*, 1967. Host of a popular television program, "What's Your Problem?" and author of a syndicated column, "Confident Living," Peale was the recipient of many awards and honors, and in 1969 became president of the Reformed Church in America. He directed his many religious, social, and literary activities that, together, had made him one of the best-known clergymen in America, from his Foundation for Christian Living in Pawling, New York.

Pearl, Raymond (1879–1940), biologist. Born in Farmington, New Hampshire, on June 3, 1879, Pearl graduated from Dartmouth College in 1899 and pursued graduate studies in zoology at the University of Michigan, taking his Ph.D. in 1902 and remaining there as an instructor for three years more. After a year at University College in London, where he studied under the noted statistician Karl Pearson, he became associated with the University of Pennsylvania, moving in 1907 to the University of Maine as head of the department of biology of the Maine agricultural experiment station. During these early years, in the course of investigating such topics as morphological variation in mankind and other species and the physiology of reproduction in domestic fowl, Pearl made extensive application to biology of the methods of statistical analysis, demonstrating clearly the usefulness of such an approach and in so doing laying the foundation of what became known as biometrics (or biometry). In 1918 he moved to The Johns Hopkins University, where he helped organize the School of Hygiene and Public Health and served as professor of biometry, statistician of the John Hopkins Hospital, and from 1925 as director of the Institute of Biological Research. In 1923 he became professor of biology in the medical school and in 1930 in the school of hygiene. While continuing to advance the techniques of biometrics he conducted significant research on fertility, population dynamics, longevity, and other topics. Among the more than 700 titles in his bibliography the most notable included *Diseases of Poultry*, 1915; *The Nation's Food*, published in 1920 after his service in 1917–1919 as chief of the statistical division of the U.S. Food Administration; *The Biology of Death*, 1922; *Introduction to Medical Biometry and Statistics*, 1923, long a standard text; *Studies in Human Biology*, 1924; *The Biology of Population Growth*, 1925; *Alcohol and Longevity*, 1926; and *The Natural History of Population*, 1939. Pearl also founded two influential journals, the *Quarterly Review of Biology* in 1926 and *Human Biology* in 1929. He remained associated with Johns Hopkins until his death in Hershey, Pennsylvania, on November 17, 1940.

Pearson, Drew (1897–1969), newspaper columnist. Born in Evanston, Illinois, on December 13, 1897, Andrew Russell Pearson was educated at Phillips Exeter Academy and at Swarthmore College, from which he graduated in 1919. He went to Europe to seek a diplomatic career but soon found himself deeply involved in U.S. relief activities abroad after World War I; he served with the American Friends Service Committee in the Balkans until 1921 and also worked for the British Red Cross. After a year of teaching in the United States he set out for Asia and Australia, lecturing on the Chautauqua circuits and reporting for various newspapers. Primarily a foreign correspondent until 1929, he joined in that year the staff of the *Baltimore Sun*, moving within a few months to the capital as the paper's Washington bureau head. There he met Robert Allen, chief of the Washington bureau of the *Christian Science Monitor*, and together they wrote *The Washington Merry-Go-Round*, an exposé which appeared anonymously in 1931. The book was an instant success and was followed in 1932 by *More Merry-Go-Round*, but when their identities were discovered they were both fired from their jobs. In December 1932 they began to write a daily column, "Washington Merry-Go-Round," which was published at first in only 12 papers, but by 1942, when Allen left it to go into the army, in more than 350 papers in the United States and abroad, and by 1969, at Pearson's death, in more than 650 papers. The column was known for its merciless muckraking, and although the accuracy of the reporting was often challenged, the column did result in the retirement from public life of a long list of corrupt political figures and in the jailing of some of them. Sardonically proud of his reputation for being unpredictable, Pearson was not above marketing packaged fertilizer under the name "Drew Pearson's Best Manure" and advertising it as "better than in the column." He died in Washington, D.C., on September 1, 1969. The column was continued by Pearson's associate of ten years, Jack Anderson.

Peary, Robert Edwin (1856–1920), explorer. Born in Cresson, Pennsylvania, on May 6, 1856, Peary graduated from Bowdoin College in 1877 and two years later joined the U.S. Coast and Geodetic Survey. In 1881 he was commissioned a lieutenant in the navy's civil engineering corps. From 1884 to 1888 his official duties were involved with the surveying of a proposed Atlantic–Pacific canal route through Nicaragua, but during a six-month leave in 1886 he began his real career with an exploratory journey into the interior of Greenland. In 1891, while on an 18-month leave, he returned to Greenland, wintered there, and the following spring sledged northward far enough to gain substantial evidence of the insularity of Greenland. The daring and difficult journey into the region later called Peary Land, during which valuable scientific observations were made, won Peary a considerable reputation which eased the problem of financing his subsequent explorations. He made more trips to Greenland in 1893–1895, 1896, and 1897, and transported two huge meteorites from the ice fields to the United States. In 1898 he published a record of his Arctic experiences in *Northward over the "Great Ice"* and announced his intention of reaching the North Pole. Securing a five-year leave from the navy, he surveyed northern routes and passages from 1898 to 1902, failing, however, to reach the Pole, although he attained the latitude 84° 17' N. In 1905–1906, with the ice-breaking ship *Roosevelt*, built to his specifications and underwritten by the Peary Arctic Club, he steamed and sledged to within 175 miles of the Pole, reaching 87° 6' N. After publishing *Nearest the Pole* in 1907 he set out in 1908 on his final Arctic journey; accompanied only by his personal aide, Matthew A. Henson, and four Eskimos, he reached the North Pole on April 6, 1909. On his return to the United States he learned that Dr. Frederick A. Cook, a surgeon who had been with him in 1891, had claimed to have reached the Pole a year earlier, and a long and unpleasant controversy ensued. Cook's claim was eventually shown to be spurious, and even at the time was taken seriously by few experts, being largely a matter of publicity and newspaper controversy. Therefore, after publishing *The North Pole* in 1910, Peary was voted the thanks of Congress and given the naval rank of rear admiral (retired) in 1911. In his later years he was much interested in aviation and during World War I organized the National Aerial Coast Patrol Commission and served as chairman of the National Committee on Coast Defense by Air. He died in Washington, D.C., on February 20, 1920.

Peckham, Rufus Wheeler (1838–1909), justice of the Supreme Court. Born in Albany, New York, on November 8, 1838, Peckham was educated in Albany and Philadelphia and, after traveling in Europe with his brother, Wheeler Hazard Peckham, took up the study of law. He was admitted to the bar in 1859 and began practice in Albany, filling the vacancy caused in his father's law firm by the latter's elevation to the supreme court of the state of New York in the same year. During the next two decades he gained a solid reputation as a lawyer, served as district attorney of Albany County from 1869 to 1872, and in 1881 became corporation counsel for the city of Albany. Two years later he too was elected to the state supreme court and in 1886, to the court of appeals. His brother Wheeler was nominated for a seat on the U.S. Supreme Court in 1895 by President Grover Cleveland but failed to be confirmed by the Senate, whereupon Cleveland nominated Rufus, who was quickly confirmed. His service on the highest U.S. court was distinguished both by scholarship and conservatism. He wrote a number of careful opinions, but the best known was rendered for the majority in a case made famous by the dissent of Oliver Wendell Holmes. A certain Lochner, a baker, had contracted with his employees for a longer than ten-hour working day, and in the court's decision in *Lochner* v. *New York*, 1905, Peckham declared that the Fourteenth Amendment prohibited the states from curtailing a man's right to make his own economic arrangements with his employees. Holmes's sharp dissent declared that "the Fourteenth Amendment did not enact Mr. Herbert Spencer's *Social Statics* [advocating extreme individualism]" and later, under President Franklin D. Roosevelt's New Deal, Holmes's view became the prevailing interpretation of the Fourteenth Amendment. Peckham died at Altamont, near Albany, New York, on October 24, 1909.

Pegler, Westbrook (1894–1969), newspaper columnist. Born in Minneapolis on August 2, 1894, the son of a journalist, James Westbrook Pegler began working for the United Press (UP) in Chicago in 1910. He spent two years in high school and resumed work with UP, going to London as a foreign correspondent in 1916. During World War I he served in the navy. Returning to the United States, he turned to the lucrative field of sports writing. On the advice of a colleague, he changed his byline from J. W. Pegler to Westbrook Pegler. He was so successful with his brawny, rough reporting style and his choice of amusing or unexpected events to enliven the column that he was hired in 1925 to write a nationally syndicated sports feature for the *Chicago Tribune*. On days when there was little news in sports, he turned to the world of international events, the subject of much of his later controversial reportage. He was hired by the *New York World–Telegram* in 1933 to write a nationally syndicated column of general commentary, called "Fair Enough." In it he vented what he called the opinions of the "average man." He attacked the Supreme Court, the Newspaper Guild, wealthy people, the income tax, other journalists (including Heywood Broun and Walter Winchell), Upton Sinclair, and national figures ranging from Elsa Maxwell to Franklin D. Roosevelt. He moved to the Hearst-owned King Features Syndicate in 1944, changing his column's name to "As Pegler Sees It." In 1954 the author Quentin Reynolds became the first to challenge his published abuse; in a libel suit against Pegler and the Hearst interests Reynolds was awarded almost $200,000, a record amount in punitive damages for libel decreed by a U.S. court. In 1962, after his column had been edited frequently over his protests, Pegler broke with the Hearst enterprises, and for two years wrote for *American Opinion*, the organ of the John Birch Society. He died in Tucson, Arizona, on June 24, 1969.

Peirce, Benjamin (1809–1880), mathematician and astronomer. Born in Salem, Massachusetts, on April 4, 1809, Peirce was the son of a noted scholar who later served as librarian of Harvard. Educated in Salem, where as a youth he came under the influence of the scientist Nathaniel Bowditch, and at Harvard, from which he graduated in 1829, he taught at George Bancroft's Round Hill School in Northampton, Massachusetts, for two years after leaving college and then joined the Harvard faculty. Until 1833 he was tutor in mathematics at the college, from 1833 to 1842 was university professor of astronomy and mathematics, and from 1842 until his death was Perkins Professor of Mathematics and Astronomy. His first mathematical works were published in the *Mathematical Diary* in the later 1820s; for the next 10 or 15 years he devoted himself mainly to writing textbooks, two of which—one on algebra and one on geometry—went through numerous editions. The first two volumes of a projected four-volume treatise "on curves, functions, and forces" appeared in the 1840s: the first dealt with analytical geometry and differential calculus, and was published in 1841; the second dealt with integral calculus and associated topics and was issued in 1846. What was originally intended as the third volume appeared in 1855 under the title *A System of Analytic Mechanics*; his most distinguished work in mathematics, it was dedicated to his old mentor, Bowditch. The fourth volume never appeared. The great comet of 1843 provided the impetus for the foundation of the Harvard Observatory, in which he took a leading part, and he made many notable astronomical observations there and elsewhere. He was also a leader in the founding of the Dudley Observatory at Albany, New York, in 1855. One of a committee of five charged with drawing up the plan of organization of the Smithsonian Institution in 1847, he was director of the longitude determinations of the U.S. Coast Survey from 1852 to 1867 and from 1867 to 1874 was superintendent of the Survey, showing himself to be an able administrator in the post. He secured greater appropriations from Congress for the work of the Survey and expanded its efforts from coastal survey alone to the geodetic survey of the entire country. From 1849 to 1867 he was consulting astronomer for the *American Ephemeris and Nautical Almanac*. His most original mathematical work was done at a remarkably late age (creative work in mathematics characteristically is done at an early age) and the results of it were published in *Linear Associative Algebra*, 1870; the book was memorable not only for, in effect, inaugurating a new branch of mathematics, but also for its famous first sentence: "Mathematics is the science which draws necessary conclusions." The author of many papers on mathematical and astronomical subjects, Peirce was one of the country's outstanding mathematicians of his time. In 1863 he helped found the National Academy of Sciences. He died in Cambridge, Massachusetts, on October 6, 1880.

Peirce, Charles Sanders (1839–1914), mathematician, logician, and philosopher. Born in Cambridge, Massachusetts, on September 10, 1839, Peirce was a son of Benjamin Peirce. Educated largely by his father, Charles entered Harvard in 1855 and graduated in 1859 with a less than mediocre record. However, his interests were broad, ranging from physics to logic and philosophy, and for most of his life he pursued them concurrently. In 1861 he joined the U.S. Coast Survey and during 30 years' association with it performed research on gravity, helped compile a nautical almanac, and represented the Survey at international conferences. He was awarded an M.A. by Harvard in 1862 and an Sc.B., the first such degree, the next year. He lectured at Harvard on the philosophy of science in 1864–1865, later lectured on logic, and carried on research at the Harvard Observatory. In 1867 he read a paper to the American Academy of Arts and Sciences in which he discussed the symbolic logic of George Boole, until then virtually unknown in the United States, and from then until the end of his life he

was probably the world's leading logician. Much work fundamental to modern symbolic logic, the logic of classes, and the logical foundations of mathematics, was done by Peirce over the next two decades. However, little of his work was published, and an appreciation of his originality and brilliance in the field was long delayed. During 1869–1870 he delivered the university lectures on philosophy at Harvard, and from 1879 to 1884 he lectured on logic at Johns Hopkins. As his work in logic had grown out of his concern with the foundations of science and mathematics, so he was led at the same time into a study yet more basic, an inquiry into ontology and epistemology. Departing from the realism of the medieval philosopher Duns Scotus, he gradually developed his own philosophical system, which he called pragmatism. He first clearly expounded this idea in 1878 in an article in *Popular Science Monthly*; he continued to develop his philosophy in considerable detail throughout his life, but his work was considered so recondite by publishers that little of it came to public notice. In 1887 he retired to a remote house near Milford, Pennsylvania, and spent the rest of his life there in research and writing. Apart from payment for the few articles he managed to have published in periodicals he had little income and was at times forced to accept financial aid from William James—in whose honor he adopted the middle name "Santiago," or Saint James—and others. His "pragmatism" became, in the hands of James and John Dewey, the distinctive American philosophy, although Peirce rejected much of James's interpretation and modification and eventually applied the term "pragmaticism" to his own work in order to preserve its identity. Nonetheless, the central principle of pragmatism—that the practical effects of ideas or beliefs, their real consequences, are the measure of their very being—remains Peirce's. He died in Milford, Pennsylvania, on April 19, 1914; his reputation grew apace as his many papers and assorted manuscripts were found, assembled, and published.

Pendleton, Edmund (1721–1803), Revolutionary patriot and public official. Pendleton was born in Caroline County, Virginia, on September 9, 1721, to a distinguished family. But both his father and grandfather died the year he was born, and his mother remarried, and he was carelessly brought up. He was apprenticed at fourteen to the clerk of the county court and this gave him the opportunity not only to study law but also to come into contact with many influential Virginians. He was admitted to the bar in 1742, became a justice of the peace of Caroline County in 1751, and in 1752 was elected to the House of Burgesses, remaining in that body for much of the rest of his life. He first came into conflict with Patrick Henry in 1765 on the Stamp Act issue, when he found himself the leader of the "Conservatives" in the House of Burgesses. He opposed Henry on almost every question thereafter. He nevertheless opposed the act in principle and was chosen a member of the colony's Committee of Correspondence in 1773 and was a delegate to the First Continental Congress in 1774–1775. President of Virginia's Committee of Safety in 1775–1776, and thereby head of Virginia's Revolutionary government, he again came into conflict with Henry, disapproving of what he considered Henry's hotheaded insistence on armed rebellion. He nevertheless served ably in seeing to it that Virginia troops were armed and supplied and he drafted the instructions to Virginia's representatives in Congress to move for independence. Working with Thomas Jefferson and George Wythe, Pendleton thoroughly revised the laws of Virginia and was the first speaker of the House of Delegates under the new state's first government. He was named first president of the supreme court of appeals in 1779 and retained that post until his death, exerting his influence on national politics mainly through a series of letters to his friends in Congress, notably James Madison. He was president of the Virginia convention that voted to ratify the new Constitution in 1788 and strongly supported the adoption of the new framework of government. He believed the interests of his state were of foremost importance, and he declined several federal offices offered by his friend President George Washington, of whose administration, in fact, he came to disapprove; to the end of his life, therefore, he was a Republican supporter of Jefferson, with whom he had earlier differed on basic questions of political principle. One of the greatest of the Revolutionary patriots in Virginia, Pendleton was relatively little known outside his state when he died on October 26, 1803, at his estate, Edmundsbury, in Caroline County.

Penn, William (1644–1718), religious reformer and founder of Pennsylvania. Born in London on October 14, 1644, the son of Adm. Sir William Penn, the younger Penn studied for a time at Oxford, was dismissed for Puritan leanings in religion, continued his education during an extended European tour, and finally spent a year in law study at Lincoln's Inn in 1665. The next year he went to Ireland to oversee his father's estates and soon came under the influence of Thomas Loe, a powerful Quaker preacher. In 1667 he was briefly imprisoned for attending a Quaker meeting and in 1669, back in London, he was incarcerated in the Tower for writing heterodox theological texts, especially *The Sandy Foundation Shaken,* 1668. While in prison he composed *No Cross, No Crown,* an exposition of Quaker-Puritan morality. In 1670 he was again arrested for street preaching; he pleaded his own case and, contrary to the judge's direction, was acquitted, whereupon the jury was arrested. The eventual vindication of the jurymen in this matter, termed "Bushell's Case," was a landmark in English law. In that same year he wrote his lucid and thorough work on religious toleration, *The Great Case of Liberty of Conscience.* Upon the death of his father, also in 1670, Penn inherited a moderate fortune and a large claim upon the King for loans the admiral had

made to the Crown. For several years he concerned himself with writing religious tracts and with missionary travels through Europe. He became a trustee of the West Jersey province in America and played a considerable role in establishing in 1677 the "Concessions and Agreements" for its government; this document was a remarkable outline of libertarian and democratic principles and was unique in its provisions for the fair treatment of Indians. Four years later, with 11 other Quakers, he bought the proprietary rights to East Jersey. Later in 1681, in order to create a commonwealth of toleration for Quakers and other dissenters, he pressed his claim against the King and was granted a charter giving him proprietary rights over the huge tract of land in America that he named, at the King's urging, Pennsylvania, in his father's honor. The following year he secured the "three lower counties" (now Delaware) from the Duke of York; at first part of Pennsylvania, the territory later became a separate province. The Frame of Government that he drew up to guide what he called his "holy experiment" in Pennsylvania was not so radical a departure as the Concessions for West Jersey had been, but it provided for complete religious liberty and contained an innovation that made it a workable and self-adjusting constitution—an explicit clause permitting amendments. He laid out the city of Philadelphia—a name signifying brotherly love and taken from an ancient Lydian city, seat of one of the original seven Christian churches—on the then-new grid plan and took care to establish and preserve friendly and honorable relations with the Indians. From late 1682 until mid-1684 Penn was in America, inspecting his province, which had soon attracted some 3000 settlers, and visiting other colonies; but a boundary dispute with Charles Calvert, the third Lord Baltimore, proprietor of Maryland, called him back to England, where, in the court of James II—formerly the Duke of York—he enjoyed considerable influence and prestige. Soon after the accession of William and Mary, however, he fell under suspicion and during 1692–1694 he was deprived of the governorship of Pennsylvania. During several years of virtual retirement he wrote a number of important works, including *An Essay Towards the Present and Future Peace of Europe,* 1693, in which he proposed a system of arbitration among disputing nations, and, for the Board of Trade in London, a plan of union for the American colonies. At last, his troubles at home somewhat cleared and new ones developing in Pennsylvania, he returned there in December 1699; he successfully solved many of the province's problems but new difficulties with his affairs in England prevented his remaining in America and he left late in 1701. His last years were difficult; his deputy governors for Pennsylvania were ill chosen, his oldest son was a disappointing prodigal, and he spent several months in debtors' prison for the malfeasance of his steward. He was at the point of selling Pennsylvania to the Crown in 1712 when a stroke rendered him virtually helpless; he died on July 30, 1718, in Ruscombe, Berkshire. Penn was elected to the Hall of Fame in 1935. From 1712 until her death in 1727 Penn's wife Hannah acted as proprietor of Pennsylvania; she was succeeded by the oldest son John, who died in 1746, and then by Thomas Penn, who remained chief proprietor until 1775.

Pennell, Joseph (1857–1926), graphic artist, illustrator, and author. Born in Philadelphia on July 4, 1857, Pennell was descended from a long line of Quakers, the first of whom had come to America in the seventeenth century. Educated at Friends' schools in Philadelphia and Germantown, Pennsylvania, he early showed a talent for drawing that was refined at the Pennsylvania Academy of the Fine Arts. His first published drawings appeared in *Scribner's Monthly* in 1881, and hardly a month went by for the next 45 years in which Pennell's drawings and illustrations of landscapes, buildings, cities—particularly New Orleans, which he visited in 1882—did not appear in some U.S. or English periodical. His first collaboration with Elizabeth Robins, whom he married in 1884, had occurred three years earlier, when he illustrated an article she wrote for the *Century;* after their marriage they toured Europe on bicycles each summer for many years and published a series of books on the cities and countryside of England, France, and Italy. The Pennells moved to London in the year of their marriage and lived there until returning to the United States for good at the end of World War I. While in London in the 1880s and 1890s Pennell taught, and they met and became intimate with most of the literary and artistic lights of the day, including James McNeill Whistler, whose *Life* they published in 1908 and whose works they collected assiduously for years, giving the collection finally to the Library of Congress. Pennell produced in all more than 900 plates, for etchings and mezzotints, more than 600 lithographs, and an enormous number of drawings and watercolors; he was the foremost graphic artist of his time and did more than any other to raise the art of illustration in America to a high level. Teacher of etching at the Art Students League in New York City from 1922 and for many years and at various times a newspaper art critic, Pennell published a number of books on art, including *Pen Drawing and Pen Draughtsmen,* 1889; *Lithography and Lithographers,* 1898; and *Etchers and Etching,* 1919. His autobiography, *The Adventures of an Illustrator,* appeared in 1925. He died in Brooklyn, New York, on April 23, 1926.

Penney, James Cash (1875–1971), businessman. Born in Hamilton, Missouri, on September 16, 1875, Penney came from a long line of fundamentalist Baptist preachers. He graduated from Hamilton High School in 1893 and in 1895 got his first job, as a clerk in a dry-goods store in Hamilton, at a salary of $2.27 a month. After moving to Colorado in 1897 he met T. M. Callahan, a merchant who engaged him to manage a store in Evanston, Wyoming. In 1902 he was sent by Callahan to Kemmerer, Wyoming, to open another store, and was given the opportunity to purchase one-third of the business for $2000. This generosity on the part of his employer deeply affected him, and later, in the early days of his J. C. Penney Company, he adopted the same principle, allowing each store manager to share in the profits of the store; later, store managers were given or were permitted to purchase stock in the company, and finally all employees shared in the profits of the organization. Penney's first wholly owned store was opened in 1904; in 1908 he bought out Callahan's interest in two stores in the West and had the beginnings of a chain; by 1911 there were 22 J. C. Penney stores; in 1913, when the headquarters of the J. C. Penney Company were moved from Salt Lake City to New York City, there were 48; by 1916 there were 127; and the 500th store opened in Hamilton, Missouri, on the premises where Penney had first worked, in 1924. Operated as a partnership until 1927, the company sold stock publicly in that year and continued to grow at a breathtaking rate; at Penney's death in 1971 there were 1660 stores, with annual sales of more than $4 billion, making J. C. Penney the second largest nonfood retailer in the country, after Sears, Roebuck and Company; all 50,000 employees shared in the profits. Penney was chairman of the board of directors from 1916 to 1946 and then became honorary chairman, remaining in that position until 1958; but he continued active in the firm's affairs until his death in New York City, at the age of ninety-five, on February 12, 1971. During the last several decades of his life he had founded a number of charitable organizations and had deeply interested himself in the breeding of Guernsey cattle. A devout Christian throughout his life, he published *50 Years with the Golden Rule,* 1950, and *View from the Ninth Decade,* 1960.

Pennington, William (1796–1862), public official. Born in Newark, New Jersey, on May 4, 1796, Pennington graduated from the College of New Jersey (now Princeton) in 1813 and was admitted to the practice of law in 1817. His father was a federal district judge, and he himself served from 1817 to 1826 as clerk of the district and circuit courts. His geniality made him many friends in politics and helped him to build a lucrative law practice. Despite his boast that he knew nothing of importance about the law he was elected governor of New Jersey in 1837 and reelected to five one-year terms. His tenure was marked by the "Broad Seal War," a controversy in 1838 over the election of five Democratic Congressmen; Pennington, a Whig, certified the election of five Whigs, and it was only after the House of Representatives intervened that the duly elected Democrats were able to take their seats. He was apparently not corrupt; he was merely easygoing and willing to follow the fortunes of his party wherever they led. Elected to the House of Representatives in 1858, he found himself at the center of another battle, this time over the organization of Congress; he was finally elected speaker of the House after eight weeks of balloting. However, his ignorance of the procedures of the House, which gave rise to many contemporary stories, was the only notable thing about his tenure in the office. He died in Newark, New Jersey, on February 16, 1862.

Penrose, Boies (1860–1921), political leader and public official. Born in Philadelphia on November 1, 1860, Penrose was educated at Harvard, from which he graduated in 1881, and was admitted to the Pennsylvania bar in 1883. Of a reforming bent as a young man—his study of *The City Government of Philadelphia*, with Edward P. Allinson, was published by The Johns Hopkins University in 1887—he soon began to cultivate the acquaintance of influential politicians, at the same time building up his law practice, and was elected to the state legislature in 1884. He advanced to the state senate in 1887. He served there for ten years, whereupon, in 1896, he was elected to the U.S. Senate, in which body he remained until his death. His main interest was high protective tariffs, and he was chairman of the Senate Finance Committee from 1911. An opponent of most measures backed by Progressives, notably prohibition and woman suffrage, he was a prominent figure at the Republican national conventions of 1900, 1904, 1908, and 1916. In 1912 he became involved in a controversy over political contributions and was attacked by Theodore Roosevelt and other Progressives as a cynical political boss, which considerably lessened his influence in that year. In fact, although he was certainly one of the great bosses of the time, possessed of the necessary craft, ruthlessness, and grasp of organizational detail, his interest was in power only, and, the possessor of a comfortable fortune, he was said never to have made a dollar through politics. He devoted himself from 1904, when he succeeded Matthew S. Quay as head of the state party, to running the enormous Republican organization in Pennsylvania, covering some 5000 election districts and utilizing up to 25,000 political workers, and thus had little time or inclination for national policy and lawmaking. He was a vigorous sportsman, tall and massively built, who took special pleasure in big-game hunting. But even this common interest did not endear him to Roosevelt, who disapproved of his refusal to use his excellent abilities in behalf of the public. He died in Washington, D.C., on December 31, 1921.

Pepper, William (1843–1898), physician and educator. Born in Philadelphia on August 21, 1843, Pepper was educated at the University of Pennsylvania, from which he graduated in 1862, and the university's medical school. His father, a distinguished physician and member of the faculty of the medical school, died in 1864, the year that Pepper completed his studies and received his M.D. degree. Pepper spent several months after graduation caring for the dying man

and then took up his duties as resident physician at the Pennsylvania Hospital. His long association with the medical school of the University of Pennsylvania began in 1868, when he was appointed lecturer on morbid anatomy; two years later he was made a lecturer on clinical medicine, in 1876 he became the school's first professor of clinical medicine, and in 1884 was appointed to the professorship of the theory and practice of medicine, a chair that his father had occupied some 20 years before. Meanwhile he had gone to Europe in 1871 to study methods of medical education on the Continent and had returned full of zeal for the founding of a teaching hospital in association with the medical school. It was largely as a result of his efforts and enthusiasm that this institution came into being in 1874, the first of its kind in the country. The demands of his large practice, combined with his teaching and his activities in such posts as medical director of the Centennial Exposition at Philadelphia in 1876, were extremely heavy; but in 1880 he was also named provost of the University of Pennsylvania, a position equivalent to that of president. During the next 14 years he had a profound influence on the rise of the university to the status as one of the great academic centers of the country. He established a nursing school, established and endowed the William Pepper Laboratory of Clinical Medicine, reorganized the college, the dental and law schools, and the Towne Scientific School, and was involved in the founding of the Wharton School of Finance and Commerce and the Veterinary School. In addition, he was instrumental in inaugurating one of the most distinguished and successful programs of university extension courses in the United States. Numerous other schools and departments were either established or expanded during his tenure, and the entire university was placed, for the first time, on a sound financial footing. But he did not confine himself even to these many activities on behalf of the university. He was also deeply concerned with the intellectual life of the community at large, and when his uncle, George S. Pepper, died in 1890, leaving a bequest of $250,000 to found a public library, he himself added funds of his own and oversaw the creation of the great institution that ultimately became the Philadelphia Free Library. He also aided in the development of the University Museum, supporting the expeditions that helped to make the university famous for archaeological studies, and providing funds from his own fortune and collecting money from his friends to make the museum's collection one of the nation's finest. In addition, he was a distinguished medical researcher and did pioneering work on malaria, pernicious anemia, tuberculosis, and the diseases of children; he wrote one or more books on each of these subjects as well as on others. His published works included the five-volume *A System of Practical Medicine*, 1885–1886, which he edited, and two major addresses collected as *Higher Medical Education, the True Interest of the Public and the Profession*, 1894.

Pepper retired from his teaching duties in 1894. Exhausted by the extraordinary variety and extent of his many projects, he died in Pleasanton, California, on July 28, 1898, at the age of fifty-four.

Pepperrell, Sir William (1696–1759), colonial merchant, soldier, and public official. Born in Kittery, Maine (then a part of Massachusetts), on June 27, 1696, Pepperrell (or Pepperell) was the son of a penniless Englishman who had come to America about 1690 and prospered as a merchant in lumber and fish. Indifferently educated, the younger Pepperrell joined his father's shipbuilding and mercantile business and by the time he was thirty-three had acquired on his own account most of the present townships of Saco and Scarboro, Maine. Earlier, in 1723, he had married the daughter of a wealthy merchant and three years later was elected for the first time to the Massachusetts General Court; in the same year he became colonel in command of the Maine militia and in 1727 he was named to the colony's council, on which he remained until his death, serving as acting governor in 1756. In 1730 his friend Jonathan Belcher, governor of Massachusetts and New Hampshire, removed all of the incumbent justices and appointed Pepperrell chief justice; Pepperrell thereupon hurriedly began to study law and in time became a capable judge. With the death of his father in 1734, he inherited a fortune that made him one of the richest and most powerful men in New England. Ten years later, when King George's War broke out between England and France, he was appointed commander of the land forces in the Louisbourg expedition by Governor William Shirley. The siege of the French fortress on Cape Breton Island began on April 30, 1745, with support from a small fleet. Pepperrell knew little about military maneuvers, but his ignorance served him well, for when the defenders saw American troops moving unpredictably in what was described as a rather boisterous enterprise, they panicked and surrendered on June 17. As a reward Pepperrell was created a baronet in 1746, the first native of the American colonies to be so honored. He also served in the last of the French and Indian wars, being promoted to major general in 1755 and to lieutenant general four years later, but he died in the same year, on July 6, 1759, in Kittery. His holdings in lumber, fishing, and real estate had continued to grow and upon his death he left everything to his grandson, who, however, was a Loyalist in the Revolution; he fled to England whereupon all the Pepperrell properties were confiscated.

Peralta, Pedro de (1585?–1666), colonial official. Born probably in Navarre, Spain, about 1585, Peralta may have been trained at the university and seen military service before he arrived in Mexico City during the winter of 1608–1609. On March 5, 1609, he was named the third governor of New Mexico, succeeding Juan de Oñate and his son Cristóbal, with instructions to found a new capital city. He spent most of the year 1609 at Zacatecas, assembling supplies, set out for San Gabriel, near the mouth of the Chamas River, and reached there about March 1610. Sometime during the next few months he founded the city of Santa Fe, giving it the official name of Villa Real de la Santa Fé de San Francisco de Asis ("royal city of the holy faith of St. Francis of Assisi"). The conflict suggested in this name between the royal and the church authorities came to the surface in 1612 when the chief Franciscan missionary in the colony, Fray Isidro de Ordóñez, put forth the claim that he had been appointed comisario of the Holy Inquisition; Peralta demanded his credentials, whereupon Ordóñez excommunicated him and, when this was disregarded, captured the governor and held him prisoner for a year in the Sandia pueblo. Peralta escaped to Santa Fe in December 1612 and before he was recaptured managed to send a message that ultimately resulted in his release. His defense of royal authority was later rewarded by appointments as lieutenant commander of the port of Acapulco, alcalde of the royal warehouse in Mexico City, and royal treasurer in Caracas, Venezuela; but in the last post, which he held in 1651–1652, he again came into conflict with enemies, with the result that he had to resign. He arrived in Madrid in 1652 and remained there until his death in 1666.

Perelman, Sidney Joseph (1904–1979), humorist. Born in Brooklyn, New York, on February 1, 1904, S. J. Perelman grew up in Providence, Rhode Island, and attended Brown University, from which he graduated in 1925. While in college he had been editor of the humor magazine, *Brown Jug*. After graduating he contributed humorous articles to *Judge*, moved to *College Humor* in 1929, and, from 1931, published many of his best pieces in the *New Yorker*. During the 1950s, his work also appeared in *Holiday* magazine. While at Brown he had become a good friend of Nathanael West, and he married West's sister Laura in 1929; in 1932 the three bought a farm at Erwinna, Bucks County, Pennsylvania, which was for some years Perelman's headquarters. Since he was already well known as a humorous writer with a wildly original way with words, he was recruited by the Marx Brothers to help out on the film scripts of *Monkey Business*, 1931, and *Horsefeathers*, 1932; these endeavors, which pleased him, were followed by work on many other motion pictures, which did not. After a long hiatus he returned to Hollywood in 1956 to write the script for the film *Around the World in Eighty Days*, for which he won an Academy Award. Meanwhile he had contributed skits to Broadway shows; written (with his wife) two comedies, *All Good Americans*, 1934, and *Night Before Christmas*, 1941; produced the book for *One Touch of Venus*, 1943, with Ogden Nash; and engaged in various other theatrical activities. His first collection of magazine pieces, *Dawn Ginsbergh's Revenge*, appeared in 1929, and was followed by *Parlor, Bedlam, and Bath* in 1930. A long list of books followed, including *Strictly from*

Hunger, 1937; *Crazy Like a Fox*, 1944; *The Best of S. J. Perelman*, 1947; *Westward Ha!, or, Around the World in Eighty Clichés*, 1948; *The Swiss Family Perelman*, 1950; *The Ill-tempered Clavichord*, 1953; *The Road to Miltown, or, Under the Spreading Atrophy*, 1957; *The Most of S. J. Perelman*, 1958; *The Rising Gorge*, 1961; and *Baby, It's Cold Inside*, 1970. *The Beauty Part*, a play about American cultural affectation that opened on Broadway in December 1962, expressed his long-standing ire, increasing with the years, at the ridiculousness of life in the United States. After his wife died in 1970 Perelman sold his farm and moved to London as a "resident alien." But his preference for English civility and good manners did not endure, and within less than two years he was back in the United States, continuing to be repelled by it but also, like his mentor H. L. Mencken, continuing to write about it in his uniquely sidesplitting fashion. Perhaps his favorite target, as manifesting everything that he disliked about his native country, was Hollywood; in 1959 he produced an hour-long television show on Hollywood, "Malice in Wonderland." He died on October 17, 1979, in New York City.

Perkins, Frances (1882–1965), public official. Born in Boston on April 10, 1882, Miss Perkins graduated from Mount Holyoke College in 1902 and for some years taught school and served as a social worker for the Episcopal church. She worked for a time with Jane Addams at Hull House in Chicago and then resumed her studies at the Wharton School of Finance and Commerce at the University of Pennsylvania, then at Columbia University, where she took an M.A. in social economics in 1910. From that year until 1912 she was executive secretary of the Consumers' League of New York, directing studies of working conditions and hours and of female and child labor. She led the lobbying efforts that resulted in state legislation on factory safety standards in 1911 and on hours and wages in 1913. From 1912 to 1917 she was executive secretary of the New York Committee on Safety, and from 1917 to 1919 executive director of the New York Council of Organization for War Service. She was appointed in 1919 to New York's State Industrial Commission by Governor Alfred E. Smith and in 1923 was named to the State Industrial board, of which she became chairman in 1926, by his successor, Franklin D. Roosevelt, who in 1929 appointed her state industrial commissioner. She was, both before and after the onset of the Great Depression of the 1930s, a strong advocate of unemployment insurance and close government supervision of fiscal policy. When Roosevelt assumed the presidency in 1933 he named Miss Perkins secretary of labor, making her the first woman to serve in a cabinet position. For twelve years she oversaw an unprecedented program of government interest in labor, during a period when labor itself was experiencing great problems in the areas of organization, of government supervision, and of political activism. She was directly responsible for supervising New Deal

labor legislation, particularly the Fair Labor Standards Act. During her tenure the department's activities were greatly extended, and much of the controversy surrounding the New Deal devolved upon her. She left the cabinet in June 1945; from 1946 to 1953 she was a member of the U.S. Civil-Service Commission, and in subsequent years was a much-sought-after lecturer on labor and industrial problems. *The Roosevelt I Knew*, a record of her association with the late president, was published in 1946. She died in New York City on May 14, 1965.

Perkins, George Walbridge (1862–1920), business executive and financier. Born in Chicago on January 31, 1862, Perkins went to school for only a few years and at fifteen became an office boy at the New York Life Insurance Company. During the next 25 years, as he advanced rapidly up the corporate ladder to first vice-president, in addition to extending the company's business in Europe he made many basic changes in the insurance industry that were later adopted by almost all the company's competitors. Perhaps his most important reform involved the agency system. Until his time, insurance companies farmed out territories to general agents who in turn hired their own soliciting agents, usually underpaid and often irresponsible men who also tended to shift their allegiance from company to company to coincide with that of the general agents. Beginning in 1892, Perkins dispensed with general agents and instead hired local solicitors directly from company headquarters, eventually creating a force of well-trained and loyal salesmen. He increased field commissions but, more importantly, he introduced, in 1896, a system of benefits and in addition saw to it that agents received retirement pensions and shared in company profits. These innovations revolutionized the insurance business and, even more, deeply influenced the course of all businesses depending on direct sales by agents to consumers. In 1901 Perkins left New York Life and joined the banking house of J. P. Morgan & Company as a specialist in the organization of large corporations. A believer in cooperation rather than competition who also maintained that large corporations were more efficient than small ones, he played an important part in the organization of the International Harvester Corporation, the International Mercantile Marine Company, the Northern Securities Company, and the United States Steel Corporation. He had made a fortune in his business activities, and he retired from the House of Morgan in 1910 to devote himself to politics and to writing. He was a prominent figure in the Progressive party from 1912; he rendered important services during World War I, among them the raising of some $200 million for welfare work among U.S. soldiers abroad as chairman of a finance committee of the Young Men's Christian Association (YMCA); and he published a number of articles and books, including "The Modern Corporation" in *The Currency Problem . . . Addresses Delivered at Columbia University*, 1908;

National Action and Industrial Growth, 1914; *The Sherman Law*, 1915; and *Profit Sharing*, 1919. From 1900 he had served as chairman of the Palisades Interstate Park Commission, which developed a 50-square-mile park along the west bank of the Hudson River in New York and New Jersey. He died in Stamford, Connecticut, on June 18, 1920.

Perkins, Marlin (1905–), zoo director. Born on March 28, 1905, in Carthage, Missouri, and brought up there and in Pittsburg, Kansas, Richard Marlin Perkins early evinced a love for animals and created a tumult at a military academy he attended by keeping some snakes in a closet. He attended the University of Missouri from 1924 to 1926, majoring in zoology, but left without a degree to take a job at the St. Louis zoo; within two weeks he was put in charge of its reptiles. He greatly increased the snake collection and in addition interested many St. Louisans in snakes, and by 1938, when he became head of the Buffalo, New York, zoo, had acquired a solid reputation not only as a herpetologist but also as a zoo showman. After seven years at the Buffalo institution, years that were marked by many improvements in the zoo and by innovations in displaying the animals to visitors, Perkins moved to Chicago as director of the Lincoln Park Zoo. There he enjoyed a dazzling success, turning the zoo from a pedestrian place into an exciting magnet to visitors on Sunday outings; the zoo was finally attracting millions of visitors a year. The Children's Zoo, an assemblage of baby animals and winning creatures loved by children, was especially popular; the children were able to pet the rabbits and monkeys and feed the llama, which ran among them in a large building, on occasion nibbling at their hair. As early as 1945 Perkins became convinced that television was an ideal medium for the exhibition of zoo animals, and after numerous disappointments he started his celebrated TV program "Zoo Parade" in 1949. Broadcast from Lincoln Park in Chicago, it won several awards and continued on the air until 1957; its successor, "Wild Kingdom," which was filmed in the field all over the world and which won two Emmy awards, had its debut in 1962, the year that Perkins moved from Chicago to St. Louis as director of the municipal zoo there. The author of several books about animals, including *Animal Faces*, 1944, and *Zoo Parade*, 1954, he was several times close to death as a result of snake bites, one of which occurred on camera while he was exhibiting a large rattlesnake.

Perkins, Maxwell Evarts (1884–1947), editor. Born in New York City on September 20, 1884, Perkins attended St. Paul's School and graduated from Harvard in 1907. After a stint as a reporter on the *New York Times* he joined the publishing house of Charles Scribner's Sons as an editor in 1910, becoming head of the editorial department, then secretary and later vice-president of the firm. When he arrived at Scribner's the firm was known as one of the old-guard publishing houses, with a lucra-tive backlist of titles by such standard but staid authors as Edith Wharton, Henry van Dyke, Gertrude Atherton, and John Galsworthy. But none of these was young, and Galsworthy was not an American; and Perkins set out to try to persuade the conservative Scribner brothers that the publishing house should concentrate on younger American authors who wrote with a specifically American slant. He was triumphantly successful in this aim, during the next 35 years developing as major Scribner authors such giants of American letters as F. Scott Fitzgerald, Ernest Hemingway, and Thomas Wolfe, to say nothing of such commercial and sometimes also critical successes as James Boyd, J. P. Marquand, Arthur Train, S. S. Van Dine, and Christine Weston. As a commercial editor—that is, one who was able to identify and publish books that would be best sellers—he had hardly a peer in his time; but as a creative editor he was even more preeminent, being almost universally regarded as the dean of his profession. His relationship with authors was complex and often profound, the one between him and Thomas Wolfe establishing a now almost mythical standard of literary symbiosis. The manuscripts of Wolfe's major novels, such as *Look Homeward, Angel* and *Of Time and the River*, arrived on Perkins' desk as inchoate masses of typescript, much too long, much too wordy, and almost completely disorganized. In long, agonizing conferences and exhaustive correspondence, Perkins and Wolfe together created the great Wolfe novels out of these materials. Perkins appeared as a character in Wolfe's *You Can't Go Home Again*, under the name of "Foxhall Edwards." Perkins was not always successful in persuading the Scribners to publish books by authors of whom, for one reason or another, they did not approve. They thought Ring Lardner was "only a sportswriter," for example, but Perkins won out in that case; but he was not able to sign Erskine Caldwell after one of the Scribner brothers read *Tobacco Road* and decided that he did not want to publish its sequel, *God's Little Acre*, one of the great best sellers of the twentieth century. Perkins never published anything himself, being content to bask in the reflected glory of his authors. However, a book of his letters, entitled *Editor to Author*, was published by Scribner's in 1950. He died in Stamford, Connecticut, on June 17, 1947.

Perkins, Richard Marlin, *see* Perkins, Marlin

Perrot, Nicolas (1644–1717), explorer and fur trader. Born in France in 1644, Perrot emigrated to New France (Canada) while he was still in his teens and quickly set about learning the languages and ways of the Indian tribes. He may have gone to Lake Superior with a trading expedition in 1663; in 1668 he was in Green Bay, where he and Toussaint Baudry were the first French traders to deal with the Algonquian tribes, who regarded him highly and called him "Father" because he brought them weapons. Returning to Montreal in 1670, he was engaged as interpreter by the governor, Count Frontenac, to join the expedition sent to take formal possession for France of "the West," the region of the Great Lakes, and he was present at the ceremony that occurred at Sault Ste. Marie on June 14, 1671. He spent most of the next 15 years as a fur trader and came to be regarded as one of the most knowledgeable Frenchmen concerning the Indians. He built Fort St. Nicolas at the confluence of the Wisconsin and Mississippi rivers to guard against Iroquois raids in 1685 and a year later built Fort St. Antoine on Lake Pepin; from there he carried on the first trade with the Sioux and there, on May 8, 1689, he took formal possession for France of the upper Mississippi region. During King William's War in 1689–1697 he worked to retain the loyalty of the Indians of the Wisconsin region to France. In his later years his trading operations failed, he was heavily in debt, and although in 1701 the Indians asked him to become their ruler the request was turned down by the governor. He spent much of his time after 1700 in writing about his experiences, but only one volume survives; it was published in Paris in 1864, edited by R. J. P. Tailhan. One of the greatest envoys to the Indians of the seventeenth century, Perrot was largely responsible for maintaining the Western tribes' friendship for France. He died in Lower Canada on August 13, 1717. Perrot State Park in Minnesota is named after him.

Perry, Matthew Calbraith (1794–1858), naval officer. Born on April 10, 1794, in South Kingstown, Rhode Island, Matthew was the younger brother of Oliver Hazard Perry. He joined the navy as a midshipman in 1809 and saw his first service aboard the *Revenge,* commanded by his brother. His duties on various ships, including the *President* and the *United States* during the War of 1812, took him to the Mediterranean and Africa, to the West Indies to suppress piracy, and to Russia, where the Czar offered him a post in his naval service. From 1833 to 1837 he was second officer of the New York Navy Yard. Perry took a deep interest in naval education; he successfully advocated an apprentice system for the training of seamen and helped establish the course of instruction at the U.S. Naval Academy. He was likewise a strong proponent of modernization of the navy and in 1837, promoted to captain and taking command of the country's first steam warship, the *Fulton,* he organized the first corps of naval engineers. On the *Fulton* off Sandy Hook, a peninsula in New Jersey, he conducted during 1839–1840 the navy's first gunnery school. From 1841, the year in which he was given the honorary title of commodore, to 1843 he was chief of the New York Navy Yard and in the latter year assumed command of the African Squadron, which was sent, pursuant to provisions of the Webster-Ashburton Treaty, to suppress the slave trade. During the Mexican War he commanded the expedition that captured Frontera, Tabasco, and Laguna in 1846 and the following year was in command of naval supporting forces at the siege and capture of

Veracruz. In November 1852 he sailed in command of a squadron, on his recommendation much strengthened, to attempt to secure a treaty with Japan, whose rulers were then pursuing a policy of isolation from the West. Determined "to demand as a right, and not to solicit as a favor, those acts of courtesy which are due from one civilized country to another," he arrived in the bay of Edo (now Tokyo), the capital, in July 1853, and demanded, with considerable pomp, an interview with the highest possible official in order to deliver President Millard Fillmore's letter, threatening to land a force if necessary. The Japanese government acceded to his demand and Perry soon left, promising to return to receive a reply. He returned in February 1854, distributed gifts, and accepted a treaty, signed on March 31, 1854, providing for hospitable treatment of shipwrecked sailors and for fueling and supply privileges at two Japanese ports. Perry returned to the United States in 1855; the next year his report of his mission was published in three volumes as *Narrative of the Expedition of an American Squadron to the China Seas and Japan.* He died in New York City on March 4, 1858.

Perry, Oliver Hazard (1785–1819), naval officer. Born in South Kingstown, Rhode Island, on August 23, 1785, Perry, the older brother of Matthew C. Perry, entered the navy as a midshipman in 1799. He served in the West Indies and in the Mediterranean during the Tripolitan War and from 1807 to 1809 was engaged in building and commanding coastal gunboats to enforce the Embargo Act of 1807. In 1812 he was promoted to master commandant. After the outbreak of the War of 1812, he was ordered to Erie, Pennsylvania, in February 1813, to direct the construction of a naval fleet—consisting of ten small ships—for service on the Great Lakes. The work occupied most of the summer; in May Perry participated in the capture of Fort George on Lake Ontario and in August the fleet at Erie was ready for action. He moved his base of operations to Put-in-Bay, north of Sandusky, Ohio, and awaited the appearance of the British fleet of six ships under Capt. Robert Barclay. Early on September 10 Perry sighted the enemy; the battle was joined shortly before noon, the main burden being borne by Perry's flagship, the *Lawrence,* which, despite the U.S. superiority in firepower, was virtually destroyed. Perry transferred to the *Niagara,* continued the fight, and soon forced the British to surrender. Lake Erie was securely under U.S. control and Perry sent to Gen. William Henry Harrison his famous message: "We have met the enemy and they are ours." Shortly after the battle of Lake Erie he joined Harrison in the battle of the Thames, in Ontario, and in October returned to the East. President James Madison ordered his promotion to captain and in January 1814 he was voted a gold medal and the thanks of Congress and was everywhere received as a great hero. After the war he saw further service in the Mediterranean and in 1819 was given command of a fleet sent on a mission to Venezuela. He contracted yellow fever while on the Orinoco River and died a few days later, on August 23, 1819. He was buried in Trinidad, but in 1826 his remains were reinterred in Newport, Rhode Island.

Pershing, John Joseph (1860–1948), soldier. Born on September 13, 1860, in Laclede, Missouri, Pershing worked on his father's farm and taught school during his youth. He graduated from the Kirksville (Missouri) Normal School in 1880 and, although not planning an army career, entered West Point, from which he graduated as senior cadet captain in 1886. Assigned to the 6th Cavalry, he participated in several Indian campaigns, including one against Geronimo, and the fighting against the Sioux that ended at Wounded Knee. He was an instructor in military tactics at the University of Nebraska from 1891 to 1895 and there took a law degree in 1893. After further service in the West he was sent to West Point as an instructor in tactics, 1897–1898. In 1898, by then a captain, he served in Cuba during the Spanish-American War and shortly thereafter, having organized the Insular Bureau to administer Puerto Rico and the Philippines, was sent to the Philippine Islands as adjutant general of Mindanao Department. He led his troops successfully against Muslim (Moro) insurgents there in 1903, for which he was congratulated by President Theodore Roosevelt. In 1906, having fulfilled assignments with the General Staff in Washington and as U.S. military attaché in Tokyo during the Russo-Japanese War, he was promoted from captain to brigadier general —over the heads of 862 more senior officers —by Roosevelt. After three further periods of service in the Philippines—where he finally put down the Muslim rebels in 1913—and assignments as an observer in the Balkans and as commander of the 8th Brigade in San Francisco, he was sent to patrol the troubled Mexican border in 1915. The following March, after Francisco "Pancho" Villa's bloody raid on Columbus, New Mexico, Pershing led a large force into Mexico in pursuit of Villa (the Mexican Border Campaign), but a year later the search ended without success. In 1917, now a major general, he was named to command the World War I American Expeditionary Force (AEF) to be sent to France; he arrived there ahead of his troops and set about planning for their deployment. In October 1917 he assumed the rank of general on an emergency basis. Determined, with the support of the U.S. government, to preserve the identity and integrity of the AEF, Pershing was constantly at loggerheads with the Allied high command and, except for a time of crisis early in 1918, adamantly refused to split his forces into replacement units for the French and British armies. Finally in September 1918, the Allied commander-in-chief, Marshal Ferdinand Foch, gave Pershing and the independent AEF a combat assignment, the assault on the St.-Mihiel salient. Success there was followed by the Meuse-Argonne offensive that wound up the war and led to the armistice. Per-

shing returned to the United States in September 1919, was greeted as a hero, and by special act of Congress was made general of the armies, a rank never held before (although it had been created by Congress in 1799 for George Washington). From July 1921 to September 1924 he was army chief of staff; after his retirement from that post he remained, according to the terms of his rank, nominally on active duty as the senior officer of the army. He maintained an office in the War Department that was later transferred to the Pentagon. In 1931 he published his widely read memoirs, *My Experiences in the World War* for which he won a Pulitzer Prize. From 1941 he made his permanent residence in a special wing of the army's Walter Reed Hospital in Washington, D.C., where he died on July 15, 1948.

Persons, Truman Streckfus, *see* Capote, Truman

Peschowsky, Michael Igor, *see* Nichols, Mike

Peters, Curtis Arnoux, *see* Arno, Peter

Peterson, Roger Tory (1908–   ), ornithologist and naturalist. Born on August 28, 1908, in Jamestown, New York, the young Peterson first became interested in birds in the seventh grade. He enjoyed not only observing them but also drawing them, and his artistic talents were improved by study at the Art Students League, 1927–1928, and the National Academy of Design, 1929–1931, both in New York City; but the exigencies of the Depression of the 1930s put an end to his formal education, and for several years he taught school on the secondary level in Massachusetts. His first and in many ways his most successful and famous book, *Field Guide to the Birds, Giving Field Marks of All Species Found in Eastern North America,* which he both wrote and illustrated, was published in 1934 and in turn put an end to his schoolteaching career. A great commercial success—it was selling in its second half million by 1970— it won him also the Brewster Medal of the American Ornithologists' Union and a job with the Audubon Society as director of education; in addition its ingenious methods for indentifying birds were adapted by the air force in World War II for airplane spotting. Beginning with the publication of his first book Peterson thereafter lived mainly by the sale of his books and magazine articles, but he never ceased to retain his enthusiasm for bird watching and for the observation and recording in pictures of other natural creatures and objects. Among his many later books, besides the series of Field Guides by other authors that he edited from 1946, were *Field Guide to Western Birds,* 1941; *Birds over America,* 1948; *How to Know the Birds,* 1949; *Wildlife in Color,* 1951; and *A Bird-Watcher's Anthology,* 1957. He also wrote an account, in collaboration with James Fisher, of a tour by the two men from Maine down the East Coast and across the Gulf states to Mexico and up the Pacific Coast to Alaska, which was published in 1955 under the title *Wild America.* The recipient in 1952 of the John Burroughs Medal and of many other awards and honors, Peterson, not only through his many publications and paintings but also through his almost incredible skill in identifying birds, achieved a reputation as the most highly regarded American ornithologist since John James Audubon.

Petigru, James Louis (1789–1863), lawyer and political leader. Born in Abbeville District, South Carolina, on May 10, 1789, the son of William Pettigrew, James changed the spelling of his name to Petigru in about 1809, the year that he graduated from South Carolina College (later the University of South Carolina): He supported himself by teaching both while in college and after graduation, while he was studying law. He was admitted to the bar in 1812. Settling first in Coosawhatchie, in Jasper County, he moved to Charleston in 1819, where he established a successful practice and in time became the undisputed leader of the South Carolina bar, a position he retained until his death. Elected attorney general in 1822, he resigned the position reluctantly in 1830 to run as a Unionist for the state legislature; defeated for the South Carolina senate, he was elected shortly afterward to the lower house, where he remained until 1833. A firm opponent of nullification, he waged a valiant fight during the next few years against what he considered the wrongness, if not the insanity, of many of his friends' and colleagues' views on the subject. After the nullification controversy died down he held no political office except that of U.S. attorney during part of President Millard Fillmore's administration, but he continued to exert an influence on the affairs of his state despite his disapproval of many of its official policies. He strongly opposed secession but was highly emotional in his support of the Confederate cause during the Civil War; nevertheless, he disliked almost everything about the Confederate government. Although he was an unwavering supporter of the Union cause until the end of his days, Petigru never lost the love and respect of his fellow South Carolinians. He died in Charleston on March 9, 1863.

Pettigrew, James Louis, see Petigru, James Louis

Philip (1639?–1676), Indian leader. Born about 1639 in the region of the Wampanoag Indians (part of what is now Massachusetts and Rhode Island), Metacomet, who was called Philip by the English and who became known as King Philip, was the son of Massasoit, chief of the Wampanoag. When his older brother, Wamsutta, or Alexander, died in 1662, Philip succeeded him as chief and promised to honor the peace treaty and generous land grants that their father had arranged with the *Mayflower* colonists. But conflict over interpretation of the land treaties created tension. The Indians were willing to let the settlers use the land, but, lacking any notion of "ownership," had not conceived of being barred from it for hunting and fishing, while the English had definite concepts of

"boundary" and "trespass." Despite Philip's promise, he was suspected as early as 1671 of planning revolt, and in that year was fined and his people were partially disarmed. In 1675 an Indian informer called John Sassamon revealed Philip's plans for revolt and was murdered, purportedly by three Indians whom the colonists identified as the culprits and executed. Furious at this violation of their jurisdiction, the Indians began war before strategy was even decided upon. Philip's role as a war chief was not clear, but he is not now regarded as the principal leader that the colonists thought him to be; indeed, he may have tried unsuccessfully to restrain the younger braves from going on the warpath. Called "King Philip's War," the fighting began around Narragansett Bay, raged through the Plymouth and Massachusetts Bay colonies, and extended as far west as the Connecticut River. The Wampanoag were aided by the Narragansett, Nipmuck, Sakonnet, and Pocasset tribes, and were completely victorious until the colonists began destroying their corn crops, capturing their women and children, and offering amnesty to those who would disavow Philip's rule. Twelve towns were completely destroyed and thousands of settlers killed. In the final battle, on August 12, 1676, at Kingstown (now Kingston), Rhode Island, the Indians were overwhelmed by colonists aided by Mohegans. Philip sought refuge in a swamp near Mt. Hope, in what is now Bristol, Rhode Island, but was found and killed by an Indian aiding the English. King Philip's War was extremely costly to the colonists, both in lives and money, but its successful conclusion effectively destroyed the tribal and intertribal structures of southern New England and ended resistance to further white settlement.

Phillips, Wendell (1811–1884), social reformer. Born on November 29, 1811, in Boston to a wealthy and influential family, Phillips was educated at the Boston Latin School, at Harvard College, from which he graduated in 1831, and at the Harvard Law School. Admitted to the bar in 1834, he practiced briefly in Boston, but gave up the law to embrace the cause of abolitionism. In 1837, after the murder of Elijah P. Lovejoy in the anti-abolitionist riot in Alton, Illinois, he responded passionately at a public gathering and delivered an address that drew cheers. After that he traveled across the nation, using his oratorical skills to gain support for abolitionism, prohibition, woman suffrage, penal reform, better treatment for Indians, regulation of corporations, and the labor-union movement. He was a forceful and uncompromising speaker and on several occasions was nearly mobbed. He allied himself with William Lloyd Garrison on the slavery issue and contributed frequently to Garrison's newspaper, the *Liberator*. He was a delegate to the 1840 World's Anti-Slavery Convention in London, where he supported Garrison's proposal that women be allowed to address the convention. They agreed that the Constitution compromised weakly on the issue of slavery, that the North should separate from the

South, and that the movement for abolition should continue to have no ties to political parties, although Phillips did not follow Garrison in insisting upon nonviolence. Phillips opposed the annexation of Texas and the war with Mexico, and during the Civil War he often criticized President Abraham Lincoln's conduct of the war and the government, although he applauded the Emancipation Proclamation. It was over the issue of disbanding the American Anti-Slavery Society that the two broke apart in 1865; Phillips succeeded Garrison as president of the society until it was finally dissolved in 1870. That year he was nominated by both the Labor Reform and Prohibition parties for the governorship of Massachusetts. Unsuccessful in his campaign, he resumed his speaking tours. Widely in demand as an orator, he had a large repertoire of both controversial and noncontroversial addresses; a collection was published in 1863 as *Speeches, Lectures, and Letters*. He increased his championships of labor, being far advanced of his time in this regard. Vigorously railing at academic conservatives at the age of seventy, he espoused youth and progress. He always retained the prestige of his New England heritage, was impervious to criticism, and spoke to hostile and friendly audiences alike. He died in Boston on February 2, 1884.

Phips, Sir William (1651–1695), colonial governor. Born in Maine, then a part of Massachusetts, on February 2, 1651, Phips (or Phipps) was apprenticed to a ship's carpenter by his impecunious parents and practiced his trade for many years in Boston, where he married a wealthy widow. In the early 1680s he became interested in the possibility of finding sunken Spanish treasure ships, and he gained the backing of Charles II for one such venture in 1683. It failed, but another, financed by the Duke of Albemarle, succeeded when Phips found an enormously valuable sunken treasure off the coast of Haiti in 1686. For his feat he was knighted the next year and was also made provost marshal-general of Boston by James II. In 1684 the old charter government of Massachusetts had been replaced by dominion rule, and Phips, in London in 1687, came into contact with Increase Mather and worked with him, after the ascension to the throne of William III, to reinstate the old system. Again in Boston in 1690, Phips was a close associate of the Mather faction and was chosen to command the expedition of Massachusetts troops against Nova Scotia in King William's War; he was triumphantly successful, winning a victory over the French at Port Royal (now Annapolis Royal) and returning to Boston to find himself a hero. This was the high point of his career. Another military expedition into Canada failed, and although he was shortly afterward named the first royal governor of Massachusetts at Mather's suggestion, the political situation deteriorated around him from the time he arrived in Boston in May 1692 until his death three years later, the new charter of 1691 proving unpopular, and he was never able to cope with it. His first governmental action was perhaps his best: Arriving in the midst of the witchcraft persecutions at Salem, he at first appointed a special court to try all cases of alleged witchcraft. After some months during which many were executed, scores were jailed awaiting trial, and the frenzy worsened, Phips took the advice of Cotton Mather and ruled out the use of unsubstantiated "spectral" evidence; the cases were then promptly disposed of and the reign of terror ended. But he came into conflict with various religious groups, annoyed the merchants by adhering to a free-trade policy, failed to aid the customs officers in their efforts to collect taxes for the Crown, gave at least tacit support to pirates, and by his pompous nouveau-riche manners he offended both rich and poor. In 1694 he was ordered to England and he died in London on February 18, 1695.

Phyfe, Duncan (1768?–1854), cabinetmaker. Born about 1768 near Inverness, Scotland, of a family named Fife, Duncan came to the United States in 1784 and settled with his family in Albany, New York, where he was apprenticed to a cabinetmaker. In 1792 he moved to New York City and opened a joiner's shop, which came eventually to employ more than 100 workmen—carvers and cabinetmakers—and made furniture for the wealthy families of the city. The finest American furniture maker of his day, Duncan Phyfe (he changed the spelling of his name about 1793) was unsurpassed in using mahogany and in achieving perfect proportion, line, and detail. Precision in design, in wood carving, and in final construction made his pieces—notably settees, sofas, chairs, and tables—as sturdy as they were beautiful. His earlier designs were drawn from the Adam, Hepplewhite, and Sheraton traditions in English furniture, but his mature work possessed a style of its own, one which endured and retained his name. His decorations typically were such ornaments as harps, lyres, bowknots, and acanthus leaves. After 1825 his designs reflected the popular taste for heavier furniture, the so-called American Empire style derived from French Directoire and Consulate designs. His "butcher's furniture," as he himself called it, of the period 1830–1847, although characteristically well made, was a bow to popular taste and inferior to his earlier work. In 1837 his sons joined the firm, which became Duncan Phyfe and Sons. Ten years later he sold the business and retired. He died in New York City on August 16, 1854.

Piccard, Jean Félix (1884–1963), chemist and aeronautical engineer. Born in Basel, Switzerland, on January 28, 1884, Jean was the twin brother of Auguste Piccard, who later gained fame for his bathyscaphe. He attended the Swiss Federal Institute of Technology in Zurich, from which he received a degree in chemical engineering in 1907 and a doctorate in organic chemistry in 1909. He subsequently held academic posts in Europe and at the University of Chicago, where he taught from 1916 to 1919. He returned to the University of Lausanne as a full professor, serving from

1919 to 1926, but in 1926 came again to the United States, accepting a post at the Massachusetts Institute of Technology (MIT). He became a U.S. citizen in 1931. After 1929 he held research positions in private industry but in 1936 he became a lecturer in aeronautics and in 1937 a full professor at the University of Minnesota. Piccard's importance stems from his mature career in balloon aeronautics. Prompted doubtless by the success of Auguste, who in 1931 had designed and made use of the first pressurized cabin for manned balloon flight, reaching an altitude of over 55,000 feet in 1932, Jean and his wife Jeannette made a notable flight on October 23, 1934. Making use of Auguste's gondola, which Jean modified, the Piccards executed a fully controlled flight from Michigan to Ohio, climbing to an altitude of over 57,500 feet to gather data. In 1935, while with the Bartol Research Foundation, Piccard began experimenting with cellophane, then a new material, for the construction of sounding balloons. A new design was evolved, half spherical, half conical, and successfully flown. In June 1936 he launched another plastic-film balloon, the first to level off and carry instruments over a constant course for a prolonged period. The following year he proposed replacing the single-bag balloon with a number of smaller bags of the same total volume in an effort to reduce the weight of the aircraft and thus achieve higher altitudes. He flew the first multiple balloon aerostat (the *Pleiades*), using 98 latex balloons, on July 18, 1937, but the craft's poor maneuverability remained a serious practical difficulty. After World War II the availability of new plastics led to further experimentation with his 1936 design. In 1946 he undertook his project Helios, which called for 80 giant plastic balloons. Although the project was aborted in 1947, Piccard designed an improved structure for the pressurized cabin and launched a 250,000–cubic-foot balloon that became the prototype of the polyethylene Skyhook series of balloons with which the U.S. air force sent manned flights to altitudes of over 100,000 feet and, in the late 1950s, unmanned flights to a height of 150,000 feet. Piccard died in Minneapolis on January 28, 1963.

Pickering, Edward Charles (1846–1919), astronomer. Born in Boston on July 19, 1846, Pickering was the great-grandson of Timothy Pickering. Educated at the Boston Latin School and at Harvard, he graduated from Harvard's Lawrence Scientific School in 1865. After a year of teaching there he joined the faculty of the Massachusetts Institute of Technology (MIT), rising within a short time to a chair in physics and introducing the laboratory method of instruction. Shortly after marrying Elizabeth, the daughter of Jared Sparks, he was named in 1877 director of the Harvard Observatory. There, during the next 42 years, he guided the transformation of the institution from a bastion of the old astronomy of description to eminence in the new astronomy of stellar structure and evolution. The observatory possessed two large telescopes, both of which he immediately utilized for photometric observations, a field hitherto little explored. At the time there was no universally accepted scale of stellar magnitudes, but Pickering devised one, constructed the first meridian photometer, and catalogued the magnitudes of some 80,000 stars, in the process personally making more than a million photometric settings. He also made a "photographic library," as he called it, a vast collection of photographs, made over a period of many years, of all of the 300,000 stars down to the 11th magnitude, that provided a history of the universe during that period. Perhaps his greatest work, however, done in association with his young assistant, Annie Jump Cannon, was the creation of the Henry Draper Catalogue of the spectra of some 225,000 stars. This established the spectral classification now universally accepted and led to the solution of many problems in astronomy. He founded Harvard's observatory at Arequipa, Peru, to study the stars of the Southern Hemisphere, and did important work on variable stars, discovering and cataloguing thousands of these cosmic curiosities that later yielded astounding discoveries about the universe. Widely honored, he twice received the gold medal of the Royal Astronomical Society and in 1906 was president of the American Astronomical Society, of which he had been a founder a few years before. He published little under his own name, but the record of his work appears in more than 60 volumes of the *Annals of the Astronomical Observatory of Harvard College*, 1875–1919. He died in Cambridge, Massachusetts, on February 3, 1919. His brother William Henry Pickering (1858–1938) was also a distinguished astronomer. He helped plan and construct the Lowell Observatory in Flagstaff, Arizona, and in 1899 discovered the ninth satellite of Saturn (Phoebe); in 1905 he discovered Saturn's tenth satellite (not fully confirmed until 1967). In 1919 he predicted the existence and location of a ninth planet, actually discovered more than a decade later and named Pluto.

Pickering, Timothy (1745–1829), soldier, public official, and political leader. Born in Salem, Massachusetts, on July 17, 1745, Pickering graduated from Harvard in 1763, returned to Salem, and was there admitted to the bar five years later. He held numerous local offices and from 1766 was a member of the militia. In 1775 he published a manual of drill and discipline that was widely adopted by state militias and by the Continental army. In the same year he became colonel of his regiment, and valuable services in the early phase of the Revolution led to his appointment by Gen. George Washington to the post of adjutant general in 1777. He became a member of the Board of War and from 1780 to 1785 was quartermaster general. In 1786 he moved to Pennsylvania and in 1787 to the Wyoming Valley, bringing with him a commission from the Pennsylvania government to organize the new Luzerne County and settle land-claim disputes with Connecticut settlers in the region. He spent three difficult but fruitful years there; he helped found the town of Wilkes-Barre and was elected to both the Constitutional ratifying convention of 1788 and the Pennsylvania constitutional convention of 1788–1789. In 1790 he applied to President Washington for the office of postmaster general; he received instead a commission to treat with the Seneca Indians. He was offered the postmastership in 1791 and held it for four years while continuing as an Indian commissioner. In 1795 he became secretary of war and later that year, following the resignation of Edmund Randolph, he took what was intended to be temporary charge of the State Department as well. He resigned his war portfolio in 1796 but was retained as secretary of state by President John Adams; a Federalist of Alexander Hamilton's faction, he was eager for war with France and schemed constantly with Hamilton to defeat various of Adams's policies. Pickering came at length into open conflict with Adams and was dismissed in 1800. Moving back to Massachusetts, he remained an influential Federalist leader and was in the U.S. Senate from 1803 to 1811. There and in the House of Representatives, from 1813 to 1817, he opposed the policies of Thomas Jefferson and of James Madison, most particularly the Embargo Act of 1807 and the War of 1812. He seriously considered secession on the part of New England and conducted private discussions and even agitated to that end. After 1817 he devoted himself to farming, in which he was a noted experimenter and advocate of scientific practices and education. He died in Salem, Massachusetts, on January 29, 1829.

Pickering, William Henry, see under Pickering, Edward Charles

Pickett, George Edward (1825–1875), soldier. Born in Richmond, Virginia, on January 25, 1825, Pickett studied law as a youth but in 1842 he entered West Point, from which he graduated last in his class in 1846. Commissioned a second lieutenant of infantry, he went immediately to serve in the Mexican War, seeing action from the siege of Veracruz to the surrender of Mexico City. He was distinguished for his gallantry at Contreras and Churubusco in August 1847. In September of that year he was first over the parapet at Chapultepec, where he tore down the enemy's flag and hoisted his regiment's in its stead. Garrison duty in Texas from 1849 to 1855, during which he was promoted to captain, was followed by service in the Northwest. There he became involved in a potentially dangerous dispute between U.S. settlers and British forces at San Juan Island. He remained in command of a force occupying the island until 1861, when he returned to Richmond, resigned from the U.S. army, and was commissioned a colonel in the Confederate infantry. Made a brigadier general in February 1862 and a major general six months later, he distinguished himself at Williamsburg, Fair Oaks (Seven Pines), and Gaines' Mill, but was severely wounded in the last engagement and did not return to action until the battle of Fredericksburg in December, where he commanded Gen.

Robert E. Lee's center. At Gettysburg his division, part of Gen. James Longstreet's corps, survived the first two days of battle relatively unscathed, and waited for orders all through the morning of July 3, 1863. A Confederate artillery barrage against the Union position began shortly after noon and at about two o'clock in the afternoon Pickett and his 4500 muskets and some 10,000 men from Gen. A. P. Hill's command, were given the order to charge by Longstreet, who in turn had been ordered to advance by Lee. They descended into a valley between two ridges over half a mile of broken ground in the face of terrible musket and artillery fire and ascended the other side toward the well entrenched Union position on Cemetery Ridge, but their line was broken after a few men had actually reached the Union lines and the assault was driven back. Less than a fourth of the gallant troops returned from the charge. This repulse determined the battle and more. Pickett himself, who is said to have blamed Lee for the disaster, realized at the time that it meant the end of "our cause," as he wrote his fiancée, La Salle Corbel, three days after the battle. He continued to serve with devotion throughout 1864 and 1865, gaining a notable victory over Gen. Benjamin F. Butler at City Point in April 1864 and, in the greatest engagement of his career, bearing the brunt of the Union attack at Five Forks on April 1, 1865; he was present shortly afterward at Lee's surrender at Appomattox. After the war Pickett declined a brigadier general's commission offered by the Khedive of Egypt and an appointment by President Ulysses S. Grant as marshal of Virginia, and instead worked as an agent of the Washington Life Insurance Company (a New York company) in Virginia. He died in Norfolk, Virginia, on October 25, 1875, and was buried in Richmond. After his death his fame continued steadily to rise, and "Pickett's Charge" remained one of the most celebrated actions in U.S. military history.

Pickford, Mary (1893–1979), actress. Born on April 8, 1893, in Toronto, Gladys Mary Smith began acting at five. She went on tour at the age of eight and four years later received a part in a play in which her mother was also appearing. At thirteen she was brought to New York City by producer David Belasco. She adopted the name Mary Pickford and starred in *The Warrens of Virginia,* for which she created the role of Betty Warren. At fifteen she began working in the movies as an extra for D. W. Griffith, but returned to Belasco and played the ingénue lead of Juliet in *A Good Little Devil. Hearts Adrift* was a screen hit and in 1913 she turned entirely to movie acting. Within two years her salary rose from $40 a week to $10,000 a week plus a share of the profits. She organized the Mary Pickford Corporation in 1916 to produce her films, among them *Daddy Long Legs.* Then, in 1919, she joined Charlie Chaplin, D. W. Griffith, and Douglas Fairbanks in establishing the United Artists Company. Her innocent gestures and facial expressions in ingénue roles won for her the title "America's Sweetheart." The public responded with enthusiasm to her marriage in 1920 to Douglas Fairbanks; during 16 years of marriage they were Hollywood's leading couple. Her other famous films included *Tess of the Storm Country, Stella Maris, Pollyanna, Rebecca of Sunnybrook Farm, Poor Little Rich Girl, Little Lord Fauntleroy,* and *Coquette,* for which she won an Academy Award in 1929. She retired from the screen in 1932, returned to the stage briefly in *Coquette,* 1935, and thereafter devoted herself to business and to civic and charitable activities. She married Buddy Rogers in 1937 and published an autobiography, *Sunshine and Shadow,* in 1955. She died in Santa Monica, California, on May 29, 1979.

Pierce, Franklin (1804–1869), fourteenth president of the United States. Born on November 23, 1804, in Hillsborough, New Hampshire, Pierce was the son of Benjamin Pierce, a prominent Democratic politician. He graduated from Bowdoin College in 1824, was admitted to the bar in 1827, and two years later was elected to the New Hampshire legislature as his father began a second term as governor. He remained in the state legislature for four years, the last two as speaker, and in 1833 was elected to the House of Representatives. In two terms in the House and from 1837 until his resignation in 1842 in the Senate he was a quietly regular Democrat. From 1842 he served as U.S. attorney for New Hampshire and practiced law in Concord; he declined appointments to the Senate and to the post of U.S. attorney general, but remained active in local Democratic politics. He served in the Mexican War as a colonel, then as a brigadier general, of volunteers under Gen. Winfield Scott and saw limited action at Contreras, Churubusco, and Mexico City. As the Democratic national convention of 1852 approached, friends of Pierce prepared to nominate him for the presidency in the event of an expected deadlock among the leading candidates, Lewis Cass, James Buchanan, and Stephen A. Douglas. All went as anticipated and the compromise candidate Pierce, virtually unknown, was elected president by a large margin over General Scott, the Whig candidate. A nationalist before all, the new President tried to promote sectional unity in the composition of his cabinet; his choices included Jefferson Davis to head the War Department and William L. Marcy as secretary of state. Taking his election as an expression of popular approval of the Compromise of 1850, he made every attempt to end the sectional controversy over slavery, but without success. In other respects, his domestic policy was marked by encouragement of transcontinental railroads; for one possible southern route a tract of land, the Gadsden Purchase, was acquired from Mexico in 1853, completing the outline of the United States that would remain unchanged for more than 100 years, until the admission to statehood of Alaska and Hawaii. In 1854 he approved the Kansas-Nebraska Act that, while establishing two new territories and encouraging railroads and settlement, abolished the Missouri Compromise; because of his power to appoint territorial officials, Pierce stood responsible for the preservation of peace in an area that in a very short time was the scene of a miniature civil war over the question of slavery. Later in 1854 a communication arrived at the Department of State from Pierre Soulé, U.S. minister to Spain, whom Pierce had directed to meet with the ministers to Great Britain and France, James Buchanan and John Mason, to discuss the possible acquisition of Cuba; intended to be secret, the message leaked to the public and the Ostend Manifesto, as it came to be known, caused widespread concern, for it advocated forcible seizure of the island should Spain continue to refuse to sell it. Although the idea was popular in the South, the publicity effectively ended the possibility of such action. In 1856 the administration extended recognition to the dictatorship established in Nicaragua by William Walker, U.S. adventurer who had led an armed party into that country and established his own government, and who sought to introduce slavery there, with an eye to annexation of the country by the United States. At the Democratic national convention of 1856 Pierce was repudiated by being ignored; his party considered that his ineptness rendered a second term out of the question and it turned instead to a safe, conservative choice, James Buchanan. Pierce retired to Concord, New Hampshire, and remained there in obscurity; during the Civil War he strongly opposed President Abraham Lincoln's policies and made himself unpopular at home. He died in Concord on October 8, 1869.

Pike, Albert (1809–1891), lawyer, soldier, and Freemason. Born in Boston on December 29, 1809, Pike was brought up in Byfield and Newburyport, Massachusetts. He attended schools in Newburyport and in Framingham, Massachusetts, but at the age of fifteen he apparently took over his own education, studying privately and writing poetry until 1831, when he left New England for the West. He went to St. Louis and on to Independence, Missouri, where he joined an expedition to Santa Fe, New Mexico, and ended up in 1833 in Arkansas, where he taught school. Under the pen name of "Casca" he wrote a series of articles for the Little Rock *Arkansas Advocate* that resulted in his being asked to join the staff. He soon purchased an interest in the paper and by 1835 was its sole owner. By that time he had begun to study law seriously, and he was admitted to practice in 1837, the year he sold the *Advocate.* He was a capable lawyer, serving as first reporter of the Arkansas supreme court and publishing in 1842 *The Arkansas Form Book,* a useful compilation of information for lawyers. He served in the Mexican War as commander of a cavalry troop, but his criticisms of his commander led to a duel with another officer in which several shots were fired, but no one was hurt. During the period between the Mexican and Civil wars he continued to practice law, becoming a figure of some prominence in Arkansas, where he shed the principles of his Massachusetts background sufficiently to support slavery in the state. He was a Whig in a predominantly Democratic area and later promoted the Know-Nothing party. An opponent of secession, too, he nevertheless threw in his lot with the Confederacy when the Civil War began, and was appointed a brigadier general in command of the Indian Territory. His Indian troops were unpredictable, however, and once more he came into conflict with his superiors, criticizing his commander in an open letter to President Jefferson Davis that subjected him to much obloquy. During 1862 he was involved in a complicated series of moves that included his resignation from the army, an attempt to resume his command, his arrest for insubordination and treason, and his final retirement for the rest of the war. Regarded with suspicion by officials on both sides of the conflict, he was finally pardoned by President Andrew Johnson in 1865 and regained his civil rights; thereupon, he once again took up the practice of law. From 1867 to 1868 he practiced in Memphis and thereafter in Washington, D.C. Meanwhile he had become a Freemason; in 1859 he had been elected Sovereign Grand Commander of the Supreme Grand Council, Southern Jurisdiction of the United States, of the Scottish Rite Masons. He held that position for the next 32 years during which time he performed with dedication. He spent years rewriting the rituals of the order and published *Morals and Dogma of the Ancient and Accepted Scottish Rite of Freemasonry* in 1872; revised editions appeared in 1878, 1881, and 1905. He wrote capably on legal subjects and also produced many poems that were highly regarded in their time but are now largely forgotten. They were published in book form in a few private printings, in *Nugae*, 1854, and posthumously in three volumes —*Gen. Albert Pike's Poems*, 1900; *Hymns to the Gods and Other Poems*, 1916; and *Lyrics and Love Songs*, 1916—by his daughter; but only his Confederate version of "Dixie" is read today. He died in Washington, D.C., on April 2, 1891.

Pike, Zebulon Montgomery (1779–1813), soldier and explorer. Born on January 5, 1779, in Lamberton, now part of Trenton, New Jersey, the son of an army officer, Pike attended school until entering his father's unit as a cadet at the age of fifteen. In five years he reached the rank of lieutenant. He served mainly on the frontier, and in 1805 was sent by Gen. James Wilkinson, recently appointed governor of the Louisiana Territory, to lead a party of 20 men from St. Louis to the source of the Mississippi River and to assert the U.S. claim to the region. He returned in eight months, mistakenly reporting Leech Lake, in Minnesota, as the source of the Mississippi, but he had informed Indians in the region that they must accede to U.S. rule and warned British officers and subjects that they were violating U.S. territorial rights by remaining there. In July 1806 he was ordered by Wilkinson to travel southwest from St. Louis to the Arkansas River country and gain information about the Spanish territories. Passing through Colorado, he attempted to scale the peak now named after him, but failed. On entering Spanish

territory he built a small log fort on the Conejos River. The Spanish learned of his presence, and he was taken without resistance to Santa Fe by New Mexican troops. Tried by authorities in Chihuahua, Mexico, he was released in July 1807, but deprived of his notes and maps. His *Account of the Expeditions to the Sources of the Mississippi and Through the Western Parts of Louisiana*, three volumes, 1810, contained the first reliable account of the southwestern region to appear in English and encouraged U.S. expansionism. Upon his return from Mexico, he was questioned concerning his possible connection with the conspiracy of Aaron Burr and Wilkinson to build an empire in the Southwest. He was cleared of all charges by Henry Dearborn, the secretary of war. In 1812 he advanced to the rank of colonel. A brigadier general in the War of 1812, he was killed on April 27, 1813, while leading a victorious attack on York (now Toronto), Canada.

Pillsbury, Charles Alfred (1842–1899), businessman. Born in Warner, New Hampshire, on December 3, 1842, Pillsbury graduated from Dartmouth College in 1863, whereupon he went to Montreal to work in a store. But after a few years he went to Minneapolis, where his uncle, John S. Pillsbury, a state senator and later governor for three terms, was already engaged in various businesses. Arriving in 1869, he bought a share in a small flour mill. He knew almost nothing about milling, but he set himself to study the business with great energy. He soon realized that some new machinery recently invented by Edmond La Croix and George T. Smith, which made possible the use of Northwestern spring wheat for high quality bread flour and was called "new process" milling, was the wave of the future. He prevailed upon Smith to become head miller of the Pillsbury Mill and to install the new machines. Adapting new devices and methods as they became available, Pillsbury saw his business grow rapidly over the next two decades, until by 1889 his three principal mills could produce 10,000 barrels of flour a day and C. A. Pillsbury & Company was the largest flour miller in the world. Much of this success was attributable to Pillsbury's use of advertising and his promotion of brand-name flour. An organizer of the grain trade of the Northwest and a supporter of railroads and of low freight rates that he hoped would give Minneapolis independence from Chicago transportation interests, he was also a daredevil speculator in the wheat market, and only his very large income kept him solvent and saved him from paying the price of indiscreet ventures. The Pillsbury mills were sold in 1889 to an English syndicate, becoming Pillsbury-Washburn Flour Mills Company, Ltd., and although Pillsbury stayed on as managing director, he was not as successful in this position as he had earlier been as a lone entrepreneur. He nevertheless maintained the company's position of preeminence in the industry, adopted generous policies toward the firm's employees, and gave liberally to charity. He died in Minneapolis on September 17, 1899.

Pinchot, Gifford (1865–1946), forester and public official. Born on August 11, 1865, in Simsbury, Connecticut, Pinchot graduated from Yale in 1889 and for a time studied in Europe, primarily at the École Nationale Forestière in France. In 1892, in the forest at the Vanderbilt estate, Biltmore, in North Carolina, he undertook one of the earliest programs of systematic forestry work done in the United States. Four years later he became a member of the National Forest Commission created to draw up a plan for government forest reserves. In 1897 he became an adviser to the secretary of the interior on these reserves and the next year was named chief of the Division of Forestry in the Department of Agriculture (later the Bureau of Forestry and later still the Forest Service), a post he held until 1910. Under his guidance the service was greatly extended and a heightened awareness of conservation problems was brought home to the American public. In 1902 he traveled to the Philippines and made recommendations on the management of the forests there. The following year he became a professor at the Yale School of Forestry, of which he had been a founder, and held the position until retiring in 1936. He served on a large number of governmental bodies, including the Committee on Public Lands in 1903, the Inland Waterways Commission in 1907, and as chairman of President Theodore Roosevelt's Comission on Country Life in 1908. Also in 1908 he became chairman of the National Conservation Commission and from 1910 to 1925 was president of the National Conservation Association. His dismissal as head of the Forest Service in 1910 by President William H. Taft was the result of a much publicized controversy involving the secretary of the interior, Richard A. Ballinger, and charges of conflict of interest brought by, among others, Pinchot. He actively supported Theodore Roosevelt in the formation of the Bull Moose Progressive party in 1912 and two years later ran unsuccessfully for the U.S. Senate in Pennsylvania on the party's ticket. From 1920 to 1922 he was commissioner of forestry in Pennsylvania and in the latter year, successfully bucking the regular Republican organization, was elected governor. His administration was marked by governmental and financial reform; he served another term from 1931 to 1935. He died in New York City on October 4, 1946. Among his many published works were *A Primer of Forestry*, 1899; *The Fight for Conservation*, 1909; *The Training of a Forester*, 1917; and his autobiography, *Breaking New Ground*, 1947.

Pinckney, Charles (1757–1824), diplomat and public official. Born in Charleston, South Carolina, on October 26, 1757, Charles Pinckney was a second cousin of the brothers Thomas and Charles Cotesworth Pinckney. Educated in his native city, he was admitted to the bar in 1779, the same year that he enlisted for military service in the Revolution. He saw action at Savannah and was captured by the British when Charleston surrendered in 1780; he was a prisoner until 1781. In 1779 and 1780 he had served in the state legislature and was a delegate to Congress under the Articles of Confederation from 1784 to 1787. As early as February 1786 he was convinced that a stronger federal government than that provided by the Articles was required for the new country, and he was one of the prime movers in the events that led up to the federal Constitutional Convention in Philadelphia in 1787. A delegate, he was a member of the committee on rules of procedures and participated effectively in the debates, but his most signal contribution was a draft of a new constitution that he submitted at the beginning of the deliberations. No copy of the "Pinckney Draught" survives, and he could not himself later remember all the details of the document, but subsequent research has established that it contained some 31 or 32 provisions that were incorporated into the constitution that was finally adopted. This made him one of the most important individual contributors to the U.S. Constitution, although his later claim that he had almost single-handedly written the supreme law of the land placed even his genuine claims under suspicion. He was a leader of the fight to get South Carolina to ratify the new Constitution and served as governor of the state from January 1789 to December 1792, capably overseeing the transition to the new mode of government and presiding over the state constitutional convention in 1790. At first a Federalist like his cousins Charles Cotesworth Pinckney and Thomas Pinckney, he began to fall away from the party during the 1790s, partly because of disappointment at not being offered a suitable diplomatic post, and by 1796, when he was elected governor for a third time, and 1798, when he was elected one of South Carolina's U.S. senators, representing the back- or up-country districts, he was clearly a Democratic Republican supporter of Thomas Jefferson, whom he helped to win the state in the 1800 presidential election. Named U.S. minister to Spain in March 1801, he at first seemed to be succeeding in his mission to resolve differences between the two countries, but he ultimately failed to bring about all that it was hoped he would accomplish, although the fault lay more with the administration than with him. His greatest disappointment was his failure to persuade Spain, in the aftermath of the Louisiana Purchase, to cede or sell Florida to the United States. Returning to Charleston in 1806, he was again elected governor and, by now a confirmed Democrat, he supported back-country claims to increased representation in the legislature and brought about the ratification of a constitutional amendment providing universal manhood suffrage. A member himself of the legislature from 1810 to 1814, he thereafter retired to his law practice until 1818, when he won election to the House of Representatives in a vituperative campaign against two Federalist candidates. His service as a congressman was marked by his staunch opposition to the Missouri Compromise of 1820, but, disliking life in Washington, he retired from public life at the conclusion of his first term in the House and returned to Charleston, where he died on October 29, 1824.

Pinckney, Charles Cotesworth (1746–1825), soldier and diplomat. Born in Charleston, South Carolina, on February 25, 1746, Charles Cotesworth Pinckney was a brother of Thomas Pinckney and a second cousin of Charles Pinckney. Taken to England in 1753 by his father, he was educated at the Westminister School, at Oxford, and at the Middle Temple, practiced law in England for a while, and after further studies on the Continent returned to South Carolina, where he was admitted to the bar in 1770. He immediately became involved in public affairs, serving in the provincial and later the state legislative bodies at various times between 1769 and 1778, and offering himself for military service at the outbreak of the Revolution. Captain of the 1st Regiment of South Carolina troops in 1775, he was soon a major and in September 1776 a colonel; he saw service in the Florida campaign of 1778 and in the siege of Savannah the next year. Taken prisoner upon the surrender of Charlestown in 1780, he was exchanged in 1782. He held the rank of brigadier general upon his discharge the next year. As delegate to the federal Constitutional Convention of 1787, he opposed religious tests for office, he suggested 1810 as the date to end the slave trade, and he proposed that the Senate ratify treaties in order to limit the power of the executive in foreign policy. He worked effectively for ratification of the new Constitution in his state. Having been offered the command of the army in 1791 by President George Washington and a seat on the Supreme Court in the same year, the secretaryship of war in 1794, and the secretaryship of state a year later, he declined all these posts but accepted an appointment as U.S. minister to France in July 1796, to succeed James Monroe. When he arrived in Paris in December, his credentials were refused by the Directory, whereupon he withdrew to Amsterdam. Returning to Paris the next year as a member of a commission that included John Marshall and Elbridge Gerry, he became involved in the XYZ Affair, which began with a request on the part of French negotiators (later referred to as "X, Y, and Z") for a gift to smooth the way to agreement. He replied angrily, "No! No! Not a sixpence!" This response was later improved in a toast by Robert Goodloe Harper, to "Millions for defense, but not a cent for tribute." The mission failed and war with France seemed imminent; Pinckney was made a major general by Washington and placed in charge of all forces south of Maryland. He was discharged in June 1800, and later that year he ran for vice-president on the Federalist ticket with John Adams. In 1804 and 1808 he was the unsuccessful Federalist candidate for president. He was not, however, abashed by these defeats—his position in South Carolina was secure, his law practice enormously successful, and his civic activities occupied his spare time. He was one of the founders of South Carolina College (later the University of South Carolina) in 1801, and he was first president of the Charleston Bible Society, serving from 1810 until his death in Charleston, South Carolina, on August 16, 1825.

Pinckney, Thomas (1750–1828), soldier and diplomat. Born in Charleston, South Carolina, on October 23, 1750, Pinckney was educated, like his brother Charles Cotesworth Pinckney, at Westminster School and at Oxford and the Middle Temple. He also took a year of training at the royal military academy in Caen, France. Admitted to the bar in England in 1774 and in South Carolina upon his return home later in the same year, he soon joined a company of rangers for service in the Revolution. He escaped capture in 1780 at the fall of Charleston, which he commanded during the siege. He went north to join Gen. George Washington's army, but soon returned south on the staff of Gen. Horatio Gates. He was badly wounded at Camden, South Carolina, in August 1780, and was captured; taken to Philadelphia, he stayed there on parole until his exchange, living with his brother, who was in like circumstances, and meeting the Marquis de Lafayette, whom he came to admire greatly. His country house having been burned by the British, he lived in Charleston after the war, practiced law successfully, and served as governor of the state for two terms between 1787 and 1789, when his cousin Charles Pinckney succeeded him in the office. President of the state convention that ratified the new federal Constitution in 1788, he was offered a federal judgeship the next year, which he declined, but accepted appointment as U.S. minister to Great Britain in 1791. Confirmed in January 1792, he carried out his duties with ability and tact during the next three years, but he was not notably successful in efforts to smooth relations between the two countries, mainly because of the unsettled conditions in Europe. Named envoy extraordinary to Spain in April 1795, he succeeded, over many obstacles, in negotiating the treaty of San Lorenzo el Real, better known as Pinckney's Treaty, signed October 27, 1795. The treaty settled amicably the boundaries of Florida and Louisiana, gave the United States the right of free navigation of the Mississippi River along with a port of entry and right of deposit at New Orleans, and pledged both nations to restraint of the Indians and to arbitration of future disputes. The Federalist candidate for vice-president in 1796, he was defeated (although John Adams, his party's candidate for president, was elected), but he swallowed his disappointment, ran for a seat in the House of Representatives from South Carolina, and took office in November 1797. During his service in the House, which lasted until 1801, he opposed the military buildup of the period and voted against the Sedition Act of 1798. For the rest of his life he devoted himself mainly to agriculture and to civic pursuits and also to practicing law. During the War of 1812 he was commissioned a major general; as such he was present at the end of the Creek War and negotiated the treaty of Fort Jackson in August 1813. He died in Charleston, South Carolina, on November 2, 1828.

Pinkerton, Allan (1819–1884), detective. Born on August 25, 1819, in Glasgow, the son of a police sergeant, Pinkerton emigrated to the United States in 1842 and, after a year in Chicago, opened a cooper's shop in Dundee, Illinois. Working on a desolate island one day, he discovered a gang of counterfeiters and later led in capturing them. Similar successful exploits followed and in 1846 he was elected deputy sheriff of Kane County. An abolitionist, he converted his shop into a way station for the Underground Railroad. He moved to Chicago when appointed deputy sheriff of Cook County, and joined the police force in 1850 as its first and only detective. In 1850, during a series of railway and express robberies, he opened his own firm, the Pinkerton National Detective Agency, a pioneer venture in the country. The agency solved many of the railroad crimes and in 1861 disclosed a plot to assassinate Abraham Lincoln while the President-elect was passing through Baltimore on the way to his inauguration. Plans for Lincoln's journey were changed and the plot failed. At Gen. George B. McClellan's request, Pinkerton organized a secret service in the area of McClellan's command and followed him to Washington to head a department of counterespionage, working in disguise as "Maj. E. J. Allen." He resigned from the department in 1862 and thereafter was an investigator of various claims and frauds against the government. After the Civil War he resumed control of his own detective agency, although after 1869 he relinquished the field work to subordinates. The agency became particularly prominent for its work against labor unions and labor movements, being widely regarded as a tool of the employers for strikebreaking, and the most famous "Pinkerton," James McParlan, was primarily responsible for the crushing of the Molly Maguires in the Pennsylvania coal fields. Pinkerton's files became invaluable to law-enforcement bodies and he published a number of popular accounts of his work, including *The Molly Maguires and the Detectives*, 1877; *Strikers, Communists, Tramps and Detectives*, 1878; *The Spy of the Rebellion*, 1883; and *Thirty Years a Detective*, 1884. He died in Chicago on July 1, 1884.

Pinkham, Lydia Estes (1819–1883), patent-medicine manufacturer. Lydia Estes was born on February 9, 1819, in Lynn, Massachusetts, where she spent her life. She was educated there, taught school there, in her young womanhood was an ardent member there of many reform groups—for abolition, Swedenborgianism, temperance, women's rights, and other causes—and in 1843 was married there to a young widower, Isaac Pinkham, to whom, together with her children, she devoted herself for the next 30 years. About 1865, however, she began to concoct a herb medicine that soon gained a local reputation as a remedy for "woman's weakness" and similar ills. Until 1875, when financial reverses reduced the family to want, Mrs. Pinkham gave the medicine away to anyone who wanted it, but thereafter she decided to sell it. Her contribution to the astounding success of the preparation, known from 1876, when she patented a label, as Mrs. Lydia E. Pinkham's

Vegetable Compound, was twofold—for years she prepared the brew herself on her own kitchen stove, and, more important, she quickly realized the value of advertising, writing most of the early advertisements herself in a quaint, homely style based largely on that of the reform movements of her youth. By 1900 the compound was the most widely advertised product in the United States. The medicine's therapeutic value, if any, was never ascertained, and at one time it was attacked by the American Medical Association (AMA) as a fraud, but it appears to have soothed the psyches, if not the bodies, of its millions of purchasers for two generations. The business eventually became enormously profitable, but Mrs. Pinkham lived to see only the promise of such results, for she died in Lynn on May 17, 1883, only eight years after the sale, also in Lynn, of the first bottle of her famous concoction.

Pinkney, William (1764-1822), lawyer, diplomat, and public official. Born in Annapolis, Maryland, on March 17, 1764, Pinkney had to leave King William's School in Annapolis (later St. John's College) when he was thirteen because of his family's lack of funds, but thereafter devoted himself to study on his own. Intending at first to pursue a medical career, he was heard in a debate among medical students in 1782 by Samuel Chase, who was so impressed that he offered to take Pinkney into his law office. Pinkney was admitted to the bar in 1786 and quickly attained fame both as a lawyer and as a politician, serving as a delegate to the state convention that ratified the Constitution in 1788 (when he voted against ratification) and in the legislature from 1788 to 1792. He was elected to the House of Representatives in 1790 but crustily declined to serve after winning a disputed point concerning his nonresidence in the district from which he was elected. Sent in 1796 to London as a joint commissioner with Christopher Gore to adjust U.S. claims under Jay's treaty, he spent eight difficult years there trying to get the British government to listen to him. At the same time he won a long-standing suit in chancery that restored large Maryland investments in the Bank of England, and thus returned to his native state a hero despite diplomatic failure. Soon afterward he was again sent to England, going with James Monroe to negotiate the questions of impressment and of reparations for shipping losses. Succeeding Monroe as U.S. minister in 1807, he was again largely unsuccessful in his mission, returning home in 1811 in full expectation that war would soon break out between the two countries. Appointed attorney general in President James Madison's cabinet at the end of the year, he strongly supported the War of 1812 and, after his resignation from the cabinet two years later, served in the Maryland militia, being badly wounded at the battle of Bladensburg on August 24, 1814. After a term in the House in 1815–1816 he was appointed minister to Russia, where he again suffered through difficult years of negotiations, but there, at least, he succeeded in establishing better relations between the two countries than had ever before obtained, although he failed to negotiate the commercial treaty that was his prime object. He returned to the United States in 1818 and was shortly elected to the U.S. Senate, in which he served until his death. His most notable achievement in the Senate was the passage of the Missouri Compromise of 1820, which he supported in a series of eloquent debates with Rufus King. Despite his many public services, he acquired his real fame as a lawyer, and was for many years, before the Supreme Court and other tribunals, recognized as the leader of the country's bar. In his appearances in such cases as *McCulloch* v. *Maryland* and *Cohens* v. *Virginia* he won the highest respect of such stern auditors as Justice Joseph Story and Chief Justice John Marshall. Notably vain, he was pompous and humorless in ordinary social intercourse, but when he rose to speak in court he became a different man, holding his audience spellbound with his eloquence and delivering speeches that were extolled years later by such men as Supreme Court justices Story and Roger B. Taney. None of his speeches was ever written down, however, and indeed he pretended always to be speaking extemporaneously, tossing in citations as it were by the way, when he had actually spent hours memorizing them. He died on February 25, 1822, in Washington, D.C.

Piston, Walter Hamor (1894–1976), composer and educator. Born in Rockland, Maine, on January 20, 1894, Piston moved to Boston when he was eleven. Intending to be an artist, he graduated from the Massachusetts Normal Art School in 1916, but he thereupon began to study music intensively on his own, served in the U.S. Navy Band during World War I, and by the end of the war had decided to become a musician. Entering Harvard in 1920 as a music major, he graduated summa cum laude four years later and won a fellowship that allowed him to spend two years in Paris, where he studied under Paul Dukas and Nadia Boulanger and, in 1926, enjoyed the first public performances of his work. He returned to Harvard in 1926 to become an assistant professor of music, rising to associate professor in 1938, to professor in 1944, and being named Walter W. Naumburg Professor of Music in 1948. He retired in 1960. In the course of his distinguished teaching career he produced four widely used textbooks, *Principles of Harmonic Analysis*, 1933; *Harmony*, 1941; *Counterpoint*, 1947; and *Orchestration*, 1955. The first U.S. performances of his music took place in 1928, with the playing by the Boston Symphony Orchestra under Serge Koussevitsky of his *Symphonic Piece*. Thereafter, few seasons went by without the premiere of an important new work by Piston. His *Suite for Orchestra* was first heard in 1930, his *Concerto for Orchestra* in 1934, his *Prelude and Fugue for Orchestra* in 1936, and his *First Symphony*, which he conducted himself in Boston, in 1938; in the meantime he had been producing much distinguished chamber music. His

music for the ballet *The Incredible Flutist* was his first major popular success; it was premiered in 1938. Subsequent works by Piston often won prizes and awards—New York Music Critics' Circle awards for his *Second Symphony*, 1944, and for his *Concerto for Viola and Orchestra*, 1958, and Pulitzer prizes for his *Third Symphony*, 1948, and his *Seventh Symphony*, 1958. His *Eighth Symphony* premiered in Boston in 1965, and three years later *Ricercare*, for orchestra, which had been commissioned for the 125th anniversary of the New York Philharmonic, was first performed under the baton of Leonard Bernstein. A neoclassical composer whose music was noted for its tunefulness, suavity, and charm as well as for its technical excellence, Piston was a member of many distinguished honor societies. He died in Belmont, Massachusetts, on November 12, 1976.

Pitcher, Molly, *see* McCauley, Mary Ludwig Hays

Pitkin, Walter Boughton (1878–1953), author. Born in Ypsilanti, Michigan, on February 6, 1878, Pitkin graduated from the University of Michigan in 1900 and thereafter studied for five years at the Hartford Theological Seminary. Graduate study and travel abroad during the next few years was interrupted by periods when he lectured on psychology at Columbia University; he finally joined the faculty of the Columbia School of Journalism in 1912, remaining there until his retirement in 1943. His restless energy found many other outlets as well: he worked on the editorial staff of the *New York Tribune*, 1907–1908, and of the *New York Evening Post*, 1909–1910; from 1927 he was an editor of *Parents' Magazine* and from 1935 to 1938 he was editorial director of *Farm Journal*; he served as American managing editor of *Encyclopaedia Britannica* in 1927–1928; and he wrote books in which he expressed an iconoclastic view of U.S. democracy and a high regard for big business. He came close to being a big businessman himself with the publication in 1932 of the famous *Life Begins at Forty*, which not only became one of the all-time best sellers but also provided Americans with a new household phrase. Sequels to this work included *Careers After Forty*, 1937, and *Making Good Before Forty*, 1939. He also wrote, among other books, *The Art of Rapid Reading*, 1929; *Capitalism Carries On*, 1935; *Careers for Youth*, 1936; and *Seeing Our Country*, 1939. He hoped to live to be eighty but died, in Palo Alto, California, on January 25, 1953, in his seventy-fifth year.

Pitney, Mahlon (1858–1924), justice of the Supreme Court. Born in Morristown, New Jersey, on February 5, 1858, Pitney was educated in the Morristown schools and at the College of New Jersey (now Princeton), from which he graduated in 1879. He read law in his father's office and was admitted to the bar, taking over his father's practice when the elder Pitney was appointed vice-chancellor of New Jersey in 1889. Pitney served in the House of Representatives as a Republican from

1895 to 1899, and from 1899 to 1901 in the state legislature, being elected president of the state senate in 1901. Also in that year he was named to the state supreme court and served on that bench until 1908, when he was elevated to chancellor of the court. On February 19, 1912, he was nominated by President William Howard Taft to succeed the elder John Marshall Harlan on the U.S. Supreme Court, and his nomination was confirmed the next month. His tenure on the Court was marked by conservatism and painstaking attention to detail in the writing of opinions. Several of his dicta, revealed his strong opposition to organized labor, for example his opinions in *Hitchman Coal & Coke Company* v. *Mitchell* and *Duplex Printing Press Company* v. *Deering*, which tended to limit sharply the right of workmen to function collectively. His opinion in *Eisner* v. *Macomber* held that Congress could not tax stock dividends, since they were capital gains, not income; his opinion in *Frank* v. *Mangum* earned the strong dissents of justices Oliver Wendell Holmes and Charles Evans Hughes, on the grounds that it validated mob law. Occasionally, however, Pitney wrote opinions for liberal majorities, as in *Mountain Timber Company* v. *Washington*. Exhausted by his work on the Court, he retired on December 31, 1922, and died less than two years later, in Washington, D.C., on December 9, 1924.

Pizi, *see* Gall

Platt, Orville Hitchcock (1827–1905), public official. Born in Washington, Connecticut, on July 19, 1827, Platt, the descendant of several old Connecticut families, was largely educated by his friend Frederick W. Gunn, founder of "The Gunnery" school. After a year of teaching in New Preston, Connecticut, and a further year as Gunn's assistant in a school in Towanda, Pennsylvania, he studied law in Litchfield, Connecticut, and in 1850 was admitted to the bar. He established a practice in Meriden, Connecticut, in that year, which soon flourished as he also began to make his mark in politics. Clerk of the state senate in 1855–1856 and secretary of state in 1857, he served in the legislature in 1864 and was speaker of the state house of representatives in 1869. Ten years later, in 1879, he was elected to the U.S. Senate and served until his death. His first important work was done in the field of patent legislation, and he was chairman of the committee on patents intermittently from 1881 to 1891; this post led to concern with the chaotic copyright laws of the day, and he managed to engineer through the Senate the copyright law of 1891 that ended most forms of literary piracy. He was chairman of the committee on territories from 1887 to 1893, and in that capacity oversaw the admission to the Union of six new Western states. He was one of the most powerful and influential protectionists in the Senate, and was also instrumental in the passage of the compromise Sherman Silver Purchase Act of 1890. He was best known, however, for his activities in connection with foreign relations, especially during the Spanish-American War. Hoping, like President William McKinley, that war could be avoided, he nevertheless supported the military aspect of the conflict when war broke out, laboring at the same time to retain the administration's freedom of movement and negotiation with Cuban rebels and Spanish authorities alike. At the end of the war he became an ardent expansionist, voting for annexation of Hawaii and using his great personal influence with McKinley in favor of retention of the Philippines. By this time one of the "Big Four" leaders of the Senate—with Nelson W. Aldrich, William B. Allison, and James C. Spooner—Platt was chairman of the committee on Cuban relations when, on behalf of Secretary of War Elihu Root, he introduced on February 25, 1901, the so-called Platt Amendment, attached to the army appropriation bill; when it was passed by the Senate, it provided for important guarantees by the Cuban government in return for U.S. withdrawal from the island. These included a promise by the Cubans not to enter into treaty relations with any "foreign" power that would impair their independence or grant concessions to other nations without U.S. consent, and a concession that the United States could intervene in the future to maintain order and Cuban independence—a right that the U.S. government exercised a number of times before most of the provisions of the Platt Amendment were abrogated in 1934. The amendment also gave the U.S. a naval station, later located at Guantanamo Bay, on the island. The terms of the amendment were later incorporated into the Cuban constitution and into a special treaty. Platt himself, though deeply conservative and a staunch supporter of business, defended Theodore Roosevelt when he became president after McKinley's assassination in 1901, believing him to be, as events later proved, quite "safe" on business matters. Platt continued to be the "grand old man" of the Senate, and served briefly as chairman of the judiciary committee, until his death in Meriden, Connecticut, on April 21, 1905.

Platt, Thomas Collier (1833–1910), public official and political leader. Born on July 15, 1833, in Owego, New York, Platt studied for a time at Yale and then became a druggist in his home town. He was elected county clerk as a Republican in 1859 and soon became chairman of the Tioga County Republican Committee, meanwhile extending his business interests into banking. From 1870 he was a close friend and political ally of Roscoe Conkling and with him became a leader of the "Stalwart" faction of the Republican party. He served in the House of Representatives from 1873 to 1877 without special distinction. In 1879 he became secretary and in the following year president of the United States Express Company, remaining in the latter post until his death. In March 1881 he joined Conkling in the Senate; in a dispute with President James A. Garfield over New York patronage—Garfield insisted on awarding the choice job of collector of customs for the port of New York to a "Half-Breed," as the Stalwarts' Republican opponents were termed—they both resigned in May of the same year. They then appealed to the state legislature for a reelection that would vindicate them, but were denied. Thereupon Conkling retired from politics, and Platt made a tactical retreat into private life until 1884. He reemerged to become the paradigm of a political boss, in control of the state's Republican machine. While his power within the state was enormous, his national influence declined. In 1896 he was again elected to the Senate and served there as an unobtrusive regular party man. He reluctantly supported Theodore Roosevelt for governor of New York in 1898, but soon became exasperated by his reformist notions and in 1900, in an attempt to remove Roosevelt from influence in the state, promoted his nomination for vice-president. But the assassination of President William McKinley elevated Roosevelt to the White House in 1901 and by 1903, when he was reelected to the Senate, Platt's power in New York was rapidly disappearing. He left the Senate in 1909 and died in New York City on March 6, 1910.

Plimpton, George Ames (1927–   ), author. Born in New York City on March 18, 1927, Plimpton was educated at Phillips Exeter Academy, where he worked on the *Exonian*, and at Harvard, where he was editor of the *Lampoon*. He graduated from Harvard in 1950 although he matriculated with the class of 1948. Three years in the army were followed by study at Cambridge University in England, from which he received a B.A. in 1952 and an M.A. in 1954. During a vacation in Paris in 1952, he planned with his friends H. L. Humes and Peter Matthiessen the first issue of the *Paris Review*, which appeared the next year and which he continued to edit thereafter. One of the more successful of the "little magazines," it was the first to publish such authors as Terry Southern and Philip Roth, and it featured interviews with such noted authors as Ernest Hemingway. These interviews were published as "Writers at Work" in 1958, 1963, and 1967. Plimpton did other magazine writing in the later 1950s, but his real career was launched in 1959 when he boxed three rounds with Archie Moore, the world's light-heavyweight champion, lost a set of tennis, 6-0, to Richard "Pancho" Gonzales, and was overwhelmed in a rubber of bridge by Oswald Jacoby; he undertook these contests, and a number of others later, just to show that he could do it, and also, more seriously, to get the feeling of competing with champions, a feeling he aimed to convey to his readers. And so he did in articles in *Sports Illustrated*, many of which were later made into books. His further experiences included pitching against stars of the American and National baseball leagues (from which grew the book *Out of My League*, 1961), playing quarterback for the Detroit Lions (*Paper Lion*, 1966), and performing in three golf tournaments on the regular professional tour (*The Bogey Man*, 1968). On television, in a series of "George Plimpton Specials" from 1968 to 1971, he also played several percussion instruments with

the New York Philharmonic under Leonard Bernstein and performed as a Hollywood bit-part actor, as a circus trapeze artist, and as a Las Vegas standup comedian.

Pocahontas (1595?–1617), Indian "princess." Given her royal title by analogy because she was a daughter of the head of the Powhatan Confederacy in Virginia, Pocahontas was apparently about twelve years old when the settlers at Jamestown first met her in 1607. Her name, meaning "the playful one" (in fact, her personal name was Matoaka), was appropriate not only among the Indians but also among the English, for she delighted in challenging the English boys of her own age to leave the fort and compete with her in turning handsprings in the marketplace. In 1608 Capt. John Smith was captured by Powhatan and was about to be executed when, according to his own account in his *General Historie of Virginia*, 1624, Pocahontas, "the king's dearest daughter, when no entreaty could prevail, got his head in her arms, and laid her own upon his to save him from death. Whereat the emperor was contented he should live to make him hatchets, and her bells, beads, and copper. . . ." This famous story has been in doubt, but the evidence neither proves nor disproves its validity. In fact, Pocahontas's charm was later confirmed historically. She was taken hostage in 1613 by the colonists and brought to Jamestown, where she was treated well, instructed in the Christian religion, baptized, and christened Rebecca. There John Rolfe, an English gentleman who introduced methods of regular cultivation of tobacco into Virginia, fell in love with her and asked the governor, Sir Thomas Dale, for permission to marry her. Permission was granted in the hope, later fulfilled, that the union would promote peace between the Indians and the settlers. The marriage took place in Jamestown in April 1614 and two years later Pocahontas accompanied her husband to England, where she was lionized and presented at Court. But she fell ill early the next year, 1617, and died as she was preparing to return to America. She was buried at Gravesend. Her son, Thomas Rolfe, later went to Virginia.

Poe, Edgar Allan (1809–1849), author, poet, and critic. Born in Boston on January 19, 1809, Poe was the son of actors and was left an orphan before he was three. He was taken into the home of John Allan of Richmond, Virginia; with the Allan family he lived in England and Scotland from 1815 to 1820 and attended school there and afterward in Richmond. During 1826 he attended the University of Virginia, but meager financial support by his foster father and his own gambling losses brought about the end of his formal education. Relations with Allan deteriorated seriously and in 1827 Poe went to Boston, where he published a slim volume, *Tamerlane and Other Poems*, which failed to attract attention and left him in extremely straitened circumstances. Later in the same year he enlisted in the army under the name Edgar A. Perry. In 1829, on the death of his foster mother, he and Allan were temporarily reconciled. With Allan's aid he secured a discharge from the army and sought appointment to West Point. While awaiting acceptance he published *Al Aaraaf, Tamerlane, and Minor Poems*, 1829. In 1830 he entered West Point, but after a few months another break with Allan prompted him to neglect his duties and early in 1831 he was dismissed. Traveling to New York City, he issued *Poems*, 1831, containing early versions of "Israfel" and "The Doomed City." For the next four years he was in Baltimore and began writing short stories; "Metzengerstein" appeared in 1832 and the next year "A Ms. Found in a Bottle" won a competition sponsored by the *Baltimore Saturday Visitor*. In 1835 he returned to Richmond as editor of the *Southern Literary Messenger*, which grew, under his guidance and because of the stories, poems, and criticism he contributed, into an influential periodical. He married Virginia Clemm, his thirteen-year-old cousin, in 1835; by late 1836 he had begun to drink heavily, was dismissed from the *Messenger*, and in 1837 went again to New York City. In 1838 he published *The Narrative of Arthur Gordon Pym* and engaged in free-lance journalism until becoming in 1839 editor of *Burton's Gentleman's Magazine*, in which he published "The Fall of the House of Usher" and other pieces. In the same year appeared *Tales of the Grotesque and Arabesque*. He resigned his editorial position in 1840 but in 1841 became editor of *Graham's Magazine*, in which appeared "The Murders in the Rue Morgue," credited with being the first detective story, and "The Masque of the Red Death." In 1842 drink and ill health cost him his job. In 1843 "The Gold Bug" was published in the *Philadelphia Dollar Newspaper*, winning a $100 prize and wide recognition for its author. "The Tell-Tale Heart" appeared in the same year. His reputation grew rapidly after his return to New York City in 1844 and the publication of his most famous poem, "The Raven." Holding positions with the *New York Evening Mirror*, 1844–1845, the *Broadway Journal*, 1845–1846, and *Godey's Lady's Book*, 1846, he established himself as a leading, if often contentious, literary critic. He published *The Raven and Other Poems* and *Tales*, both 1845, and during these years, 1844–1846, he produced "The Pit and the Pendulum," "The Premature Burial," "The Cask of Amontillado," "The Purloined Letter," and other stories that combined his power of cold analysis with his frenzied imaginations of horror and mystery. From 1847, the year his wife died, he fell deeper into poverty and became more erratic than ever. He sought solace in courting a succession of women and occasionally fell victim to alcohol; to the same period, however, belonged some of his best verse—"The Bells," "Ulalume," "Annabel Lee," "El Dorado," and others. After a relatively quiet summer in Richmond he traveled to Baltimore, where a final spree led to his death on October 7, 1849. His personal life had been almost continuously miserable, but his very misery found an answering chord in the great French poet Charles Baudelaire, who studied and translated many of his works in the 1850s, so that Poe became the first American author to be widely read and admired in France. Critical estimates of his work have ranged from great enthusiasm to outright dismissal, but in general he is held to have been one of a handful of true literary artists of his time. His extraordinary gifts for evoking melancholy or terror, or for charming with musical rhyme and dreamlike visions, have continued to fascinate both popular and critical audiences. He was elected to the Hall of Fame in 1910.

Poinsett, Joel Roberts (1779–1851), diplomat. Born in Charleston, South Carolina, on March 2, 1779, Poinsett was educated in Charleston and at various schools in Great Britain, including the medical department of the University of Edinburgh and the military academy at Woolwich. An unhappy few months spent studying law in Charleston in 1800 was followed by several years of European travel, in the course of which he met most of the great men of the age. Returning to the United States in 1808 in the hope of seeing action in the army, he was disappointed in this aim (war against England did not actually come for four years), and so went to Buenos Aires and to Chile, where for the next eight years he was deeply involved in the revolutionary activities in Spain's South American colonies. Returning to South Carolina, he served in the legislature from 1816 to 1818 and on the state board of public works from 1818 to 1820 and in the latter year was elected to the House of Representatives to succeed Charles Pinckney. Reelected in 1822 and 1824, he resigned in March 1825 to accept an appointment as the U.S. minister to Mexico, a post he held for four years. Returning to Washington in 1830, he found his friend President Andrew Jackson besieged by nullification threats from South Carolina, and for the next three years he ably led the Unionist faction in opposing nullification in his state; arms were placed at his disposal by Jackson in case of need, but Poinsett hoped for a peaceful resolution of the controversy and when it came in 1832 he retired to his plantation near Georgetown. Appointed secretary of war in 1837 by President Martin Van Buren, he served with great distinction in the post until 1841, greatly improving the facilities and the course of study at West Point, reorganizing the military forces and successfully directing the second Seminole War. He devoted the last ten years of his life to various agricultural and scholarly pursuits, helping, among other activities, to found the National Institute for the Promotion of Science and the Useful Arts. An amateur botanist of renown, he brought back with him from Mexico in 1829 several specimens of a subtropical plant of the euphorbia family. Named poinsettia in his honor, the winter-blooming plant became a traditional Christmas flower. Poinsett died near what is now Statesburg, Sumter County, South Carolina, on December 12, 1851.

Polk, James Knox (1795–1849), eleventh president of the United States. Born on November 2, 1795, in Mecklenburg County, North Carolina, the son of a wealthy farmer, Polk moved with his family to Tennessee in 1806. In frail health as a child, he was incapable of doing farm chores. Instead he labored in preparatory schools, and at the age of twenty he entered the University of North Carolina, where he did particularly well in mathematics and the classics. He graduated in 1818 as salutatorian of his class. He was admitted to the bar in 1820 and established a thriving practice in Columbia, Tennessee, becoming friendly with influential members of the Democratic party; this aided his advance in state politics, where, once established, he displayed an ardent loyalty to Democratic principles and the industry and efficiency of an executive. Andrew Jackson, already a prominent figure in the party, was especially impressed by Polk's ability to communicate with both politicians and the populace. With Jackson's support, he entered the House of Representatives in 1825, remained there for 14 years, and in 1835 was elected speaker. From the start of his congressional service he was the recognized spokesman for Jackson's administration in the House, and he rendered signal service in directing the legislative arm of the attack on the Bank of the United States. As speaker he was highly capable, in spite of being the target of considerable abuse by anti-Jackson representatives. Deferring to the wishes of his party in 1839, he accepted the nomination for governor of Tennessee and was elected. But his interest was in national politics, and after two unsuccessful tries for a second term as governor, he turned his thoughts to Washington. He allied himself once again with Jackson on two burning issues of the day: the annexation of Texas, and the acquisition of the Oregon territory from Great Britain, which occupied it with the United States under the terms of a joint convention. After President Martin Van Buren became known, via a published letter, as an opponent of the annexation of Texas, Jackson and much of the rest of the Democratic party vowed to prevent his renomination. It became clear that Polk, who had been under consideration for the vice-presidential nomination, was the most able and articulate advocate of expansionism in the party. Jackson therefore endorsed him for the presidential nomination over Van Buren in 1844. The country applauded him for his aggressive stance, and he was nominated as the party's first dark-horse candidate, opposing the Whigs' Henry Clay. At the age of forty-nine, he was the youngest man yet to be elected president. Although the Democrats had campaigned on Polk's expansionism and on the slogan "Fifty-four forty or fight," he approached the Oregon boundary question with a mind open to compromise, and by dint of firm diplomacy secured agreement in 1846 to a boundary between U.S. and Canadian territory along the 49th parallel. By that time, however, relations with Mexico had deteriorated, an attempt to settle outstanding claims and to buy California had been rebuffed by the Mexican government late in 1845 and Polk had immediately ordered U.S. troops under Gen.

Zachary Taylor into the disputed border area between the Rio Grande and the Nueces in the newly annexed state of Texas. The president was already considering war when news was received in Washington that Mexican forces had crossed the Rio Grande and skirmished with U.S. troops. War was declared on May 13, 1846. Although it was a military success, the two-year-long Mexican War was heavily criticized at home, particularly by abolitionists, who saw it as a way of extending the domain of slavery. With the signing of the treaty of Guadalupe Hidalgo on February 2, 1848, the United States solidified its hold on Texas and came into possession of California and nearly all of the territory of the present Southwest. Despite having thus fulfilled the major promises of his campaign—and having achieved other principal objectives with the Walker Tariff Act, 1846, which reduced tariffs, and the revival of the Independent Treasury Act in 1846—Polk lost popular support steadily during his administration, largely through his opposition to extremists of both sides on the slavery issue. A highly efficient and competent president, and one who was remarkably effective in handling Congress, Polk was nonetheless long underrated as a chief executive. Exhausted by his labors, he retired from the White House to Nashville, Tennessee, where he died three months later, on June 15, 1849.

Polk, Leonidas (1806–1864), religious leader and soldier. Born in Raleigh, North Carolina, on April 10, 1806, Polk, a cousin of James K. Polk, attended the University of North Carolina but left it in 1823 to go to West Point. There, for his first three years, he was a good student and a carefree soul; in his last year he was publicly converted by the new chaplain, Charles P. McIlvaine (afterward bishop of Ohio). Polk graduated in June 1827 but resigned his commission six months later and entered Virginia Theological Seminary. He was ordained in the Protestant Episcopal church on April 9, 1830, and a year later advanced to the priesthood. Assistant rector of a church in Richmond, Virginia, for a time, he traveled in Europe for his health during the early 1830s and not until 1838, when he was appointed missionary bishop of the Southwest—his thinly inhabited territory including Louisiana, Alabama, Mississippi, Arkansas, and part of Indian Territory—did he take up the religious duties that were to make him famous. Made bishop of Louisiana in 1841, he at first devoted himself to the paternalistic care of his rich wife's many slaves, establishing a large plantation and conducting Sunday school for blacks. The plantation failed, however, whereupon Polk set himself another task, that of founding a great Episcopalian educational institution in his region that would eventually lead to the emancipation of the slaves and to the training of the white aristocracy in their responsibilities toward what he called the "subject race." On October 9, 1860, Polk laid the cornerstone of the University of the South, at Sewanee, Tennessee, having in the previous four years gathered $500,000 in contributions and secured a grant of 9500 acres of land. Delayed by the Civil War, the University finally opened for classes in 1868. With the outbreak of the Civil War, Polk was offered a commission as major general in the Confederate army by his West Point classmate, President Jefferson Davis. He accepted after some hesitation and served ably, despite his lack of military experience. He saw action mainly in the Mississippi River defenses, for a time under his West Point roommate, Gen. Albert Sidney Johnston; he defeated Gen. U.S. Grant in a small engagement at Belmont, Missouri, on November 7, 1861. He commanded the right flank at Shiloh, where he performed gallantly, and for his conduct as second in command to Gen. Braxton Bragg at Perryville in September 1862 he was promoted to lieutenant general. He later saw action at Murfreesboro and at Chickamauga, but his record there was somewhat clouded by disputes with Bragg. He died of wounds suffered at Pine Mountain, Georgia, on June 14, 1864.

Pollock, Jackson (1912–1956), painter. Born on January 28, 1912, in Cody, Wyoming, of Scotch-Irish ancestry, Pollock grew up with the Western landscape, but eventually became fascinated with the movement and activity of big cities. After completing his secondary schooling he went to New York City, where he enrolled in the Art Students League under the tutelage of Thomas Hart Benton, a leading proponent of regionalism, who introduced him to the work of the Italian masters. From 1938 to 1942 he was enrolled in the Federal Arts Project. He held his first one-man show in 1944 at the Art of This Century Gallery in New York City. Pollock reacted against the realism then current in American painting, turning instead to his own form of artistic expression. Leaning more and more to the abstract, Pollock moved in new directions experimenting with daring methods. He began splashing and weaving lines and splotches of many colors, textures, rhythms, and hues onto his canvases, explaining that his work was personal, controlled by his moods and unconscious forces. Later he worked on whole rolls of canvas; from these vast canvases, portions were cut and shown as individual paintings. This innovation in technique, although rejected by conservative critics, helped mark the founding of the school of "action painting" and the movement known as Abstract Expressionism, a movement that became dominant after World War II and radically altered the path of American art. Several shows followed, and Pollock was recognized as a leader of the new movement. He died in an automobile accident in East Hampton, Long Island, New York, on August 11, 1956. His paintings became much sought after, and in 1973 one was sold by a private owner to the Australian government for some $2 million.

Pollock, Oliver (1737?–1823), merchant and Revolutionary financier. Born in northern Ireland, probably in 1737, Pollock emigrated with his father to Pennsylvania in 1760. Within a year or two he had established trade ties with merchants in the West Indies, and while doing so had learned Spanish and become a friend of Alexander O'Reilly, second in command of the Spanish army in Cuba. Pollock moved to New Orleans in 1768 and the next year, when O'Reilly appeared with an army to take formal possession of Louisiana in conformity with the treaty of 1762 and to put down pro-French agitation, Pollock was able to provide him with supplies. As a reward he was given freedom of trade in Louisiana by the Spanish, a grant that he utilized in the next few years in becoming one of the leading traders of the region. Upon the outbreak of the Revolution, his wealth and his trading contacts, as well as his intimacy with the Spanish authorities, proved of great value to the Americans. Obtaining 10,000 pounds of gunpowder from the Spaniards on his own credit, he forwarded it to the Continental army in Philadelphia. In 1778, after the capture of Kaskaskia, George Rogers Clark, military commander in Illinois country, prevailed upon Pollock to serve as commercial agent and to pay in silver all bills rendered against the credit of Virginia. All of Clark's needs—provisions, powder, cannon—were bought on Pollock's credit. In the course of the war he advanced some $300,000, which placed him so heavily in arrears in his business that, in 1783, he was arrested by his creditors and held in custody for 18 months, Virginia having refused to concede the existence of any formal arrangement with him and Congress being slow to pay its obligations. He was awarded $90,000 by Congress in 1785, although the money was not paid for many years, and his claims against Virginia were also finally settled. In the meantime he had taken measures to restore his fortune. Obtaining a vessel and a cargo on his own credit, he reentered the New Orleans–West Indies trade and, by 1790, was able to satisfy all of his creditors; within another few years he was again one of the wealthiest merchants in the region. He returned for a while to Cumberland County, Pennsylvania, where he bought a large estate, but he spent his last years in Pinckneyville, Wilkinson County, Mississippi, where he died on December 17, 1823. One of the most valiant fighters in behalf of the United States, he went largely without recognition in his time.

Ponce de León, Juan (1460?–1521), explorer. Born in Tierra de Campos, Spain, about 1460, Ponce de León fought against the Muslims (Moors) in Spain as a youth and accompanied Columbus on his second voyage to Hispaniola, in 1493. In 1502–1504 he served in the conquest of Higüey (today the Dominican Republic) and was appointed governor of the province. In 1508 he was approached by an Indian who had come from Borinquén (now Puerto Rico) by canoe; the Indian brought him gold and said there was much more where he came from. Ponce de León immediately set sail for Puerto Rico. Although Columbus had earlier discovered the island, Ponce de León was the first to explore it and find gold. Upon his return, he was appointed governor of the island, but his appointment, which was lucrative, was contested by a son of Columbus, who won out after a lengthy altercation. Ponce de León next became fascinated by Indian tales about an island called Bimini, where, Indians said, there was not only gold in abundance and everything else a man might desire, but also a spring the water of which could make an old man young again. In February 1512 he was commissioned to find the island. He set sail in March 1513 from Puerto Rico, touched at the present Grand Turk Island and at San Salvador and, turning westward, reached the coast of Florida, which he named for the season in which he found it (*Pascua Florida*, Easter time), at a point some 175 miles south of the present St. Augustine. Capturing an Indian and using him as a pilot, he coasted southward, passed the present site of Miami and threaded the Florida Keys at Key West, then turned northward along Florida's west coast to the present Cape Romano. But he had not yet found the fabled Bimini, so he turned southward again, discovered the island of Eleuthera, and then returned to Puerto Rico. On a visit to Spain in 1514 to report on his findings, he was appointed governor of Bimini and of the "island" of Florida, which he was directed to colonize. For the next several years however, he was engaged in putting down resistance by the Indians of the Caribbean region. But in February 1521 he set out again for Florida with colonists and supplies. Arriving at either Charlotte Harbor or Tampa Bay, he was attacked by a band of Indians and died from wounds several days later, in Havana, Cuba. He was buried in San Juan, Puerto Rico. He is remembered as the discoverer of Florida, which he hoped someday to be able to explore to determine whether or not it was an island.

Pontiac (1720?–1769), Indian leader. Born, probably about 1720, near the Maumee River in northern Ohio, Pontiac was the son of an Ottawa father and an Ojibwa mother. By 1755 he was chief of the Ottawa. After the victory of the English in the French and Indian Wars, he and the loosely knit confederation of tribes that he headed in the Old Northwest grew resentful of the British who, unlike the French before them, cheated the Indians in trading, did not welcome them into their forts, and planted and settled Indian lands. In 1762 he enlisted in his confederacy nearly all of the tribes of the trans-Appalachian region in a plan for what came to be known as Pontiac's Rebellion. British forts along the frontier were to be attacked simultaneously and frontier settlements destroyed. In May 1763 Pontiac himself led a surprise attack on the garrison of Detroit, which was under the command of Maj. Henry Gladwin. The siege that followed lasted for a year, and when British reinforcements finally gained control of the region, it was discovered that nearly every other Western fort had been ransacked and that settlements from Niagara to Virginia had been burned. Fort Pitt and Fort Ligonier were among the posts that successfully resisted, both being relieved by a force under Col. Henry Bouquet, who defeated the Indians again in 1764 and forced them to sue for peace. Pontiac himself and a small number of followers refused to consider surrender at that time, but by the following year Pontiac saw that there was no hope of raising a sufficient Indian force to meet the increasing strength of the British. After a preliminary truce arranged by George Croghan in 1765, Pontiac attended peace talks with Sir William Johnson in 1766 and signed a treaty, to which he thereafter adhered. The figure of Pontiac as a symbol of Indian resistance became almost legendary in his own lifetime, yet his actual role in the war and the scope of his influence became a subject of debate. There are various accounts of his death in 1769, but he was probably killed in Illinois by another Indian who had been bribed by an English trader.

Poole, Elijah, *see* Muhammad, Elijah

Poor, Henry Varnum (1812–1905), railroad historian and economist. Born in East Andover (now part of Andover), Maine (then part of Massachusetts), on December 8, 1812, Poor graduated from Bowdoin College in 1835 and thereafter studied and practiced law. In 1849 he accompanied his brother John to New York City; John bought the *American Railroad Journal* and made Henry editor. Retaining the post until 1862, Henry Poor not only made the journal a commercial success but also compiled railroad statistics from all over the country that led to the publication in 1860 of his *History of the Railroads and Canals of the United States of America.* As an editorial writer for the *New York Times* during the Civil War he continued to advocate railroad expansion, and in 1864 he was appointed the first secretary of the Union Pacific Railroad Company. Three years later he and his son, Henry William, founded the firm of H.V. & H.W. Poor to import railway supplies, and as a sideline began to publish railroad manuals that came to be considered the prime source of information about American railroads in the late nineteenth century. The *Manual of the Railroads of the United States* first appeared in 1868; commonly called "Poor's Manual" of railroads, it was published under different titles but always under his personal supervision until 1900, and it continued thereafter until 1924 under the supervision of others. The firm also published an annual *Poor's Directory of Railway Officials,* 1886–1895, and *Poor's Handbook of Investment Securities,* 1890—1892. Poor also wrote widely on other economic questions, publishing, among other books, *Money and Its Laws,* 1877; *Resumption and the Silver Question,* 1878; *Twenty-two Years of Protection,* 1888; and *The Tariff: Its Bearing upon the Industries and Politics of the United States,* 1892. He died in Brookline, Massachusetts, on January 4, 1905.

Popé (?–1690), medicine man and Pueblo Indian revolutionary leader. It is not known when Popé was born but he was of the Tewa, or San Juan, Pueblo. He seems to have first come to the attention of the Spanish authorities in Santa Fe, New Mexico, in 1675, when he led the resistance that year against the imprisonment, enslavement, and frequent execution of 47 medicine men being punished by the Roman Catholic Church for practicing their traditional religion. Moving to Taos, he began to plan a large-scale revolt, the success of which seemed assured because of constant quarreling between the religious and secular arms of the Spanish colonial government. The rebellion was scheduled to break out on August 13, 1680, but Popé advanced the date to August 10 when he learned that the plot had been revealed to the Spaniards. On that day some 400 Spaniards throughout the region were killed by the Indians. On August 14 a confrontation occurred between about 500 Indian warriors and 1000 remaining colonists at Santa Fe; the Spaniards refused to accept an ultimatum to leave, but, after a furious fight, began to retreat southward on August 21, regrouping eventually at El Paso, on the Rio Grande. Meanwhile the rebels were devastating most of the region from Taos to Isleta. For the next ten years, as a result of the most successful Indian uprising ever to occur on the North American continent, Popé and his warriors held absolute sway over Santa Fe and its environs; old ways of life were restored and all evidences of the Spanish language and of Christianity were obliterated. But Popé himself was no less a tyrant than the Spaniards had been, a fearful drought ensued, the Apaches and Utes raided the Pueblo settlements, and by 1690, when Popé died, the Pueblo population had decreased from 29,000 to 9000. The Spanish reconquest was complete by 1692.

Pope, Albert Augustus (1843–1909), bicycle and automobile manufacturer. Born in Boston on May 20, 1843, Pope was forced to leave school at fifteen in order to help support his family, which had suffered financial reverses; one of his first jobs was in a shoe store. He enlisted in the Union army in 1862, served creditably throughout the Civil War, ranking as a lieutenant colonel before being discharged in 1865. Returning to Boston, he went into the business of manufacturing supplies for shoe manufacturers and soon had made a sizable fortune. In 1877 he organized the Pope Manufacturing Company in Hartford, Connecticut, which concentrated on producing bicycles; Pope had seen his first bicycle at the Centennial Exposition in Philadelphia the year before and thought that the contraption had a promising future. By 1898 Pope, known as "the founder of American bicycle industries," had a large establishment in Hartford employing more than 3000 workers and turning out thousands of bicycles a year. In order to promote his product, he underwrote the costs of legal cases brought to test city ordinances forbidding the use of bicycles on public roads. He also founded the *Wheelman* in 1882, with Samuel S. McClure as editor; the magazine was combined with *Outing* the next year, and he continued to publish the

combined *Outing and the Wheelman* until 1885, when he sold it to Poultney Bigelow, who reorganized it under the name *Outing*. In the 1890s, as the bicycle craze diminished, Pope shifted to automobiles, producing the gasoline-powered Pope-Toledo and Pope-Hartford vehicles in Toledo, Ohio, and in Hartford, respectively, and built the electric Pope-Waverly automobiles in Indianapolis. But his machines predated the development of the great demand for automobiles, and this fact, combined with the decreasing market for his Columbia and Hartford brands of bicycles, forced his wide-ranging enterprises into receivership. Exhausted by efforts to recoup his fortunes in the next few years, he died in Cohasset, Massachusetts, on August 10, 1909.

Porter, Cole (1893–1964), lyricist and composer. Born in Peru, Indiana, on June 9, 1893, Porter had learned to play the violin at the age of six and the piano at eight. His first song, "The Bobolink Waltz," was published when he was ten. He attended Worcester Academy and Yale (where he wrote "Bingo Eli Yale" and "Bulldog," a football song), graduating in 1913. Despite his manifest talents, he entered Harvard Law School in 1914 but, at the dean's suggestion, he transferred to the school of music; there he wrote, with his classmate T. Lawrason Riggs, the musical *See America First*, which was presented on Broadway unsuccessfully in 1916. In 1919 he contributed to the score of the New York review *Hitchy Koo* and in 1924, to the *Greenwich Village Follies*. In 1928 five of his songs were used in a musical play, *Paris*; one of them, the amusing "Let's Do It," enjoyed much popularity and launched his career. The first of his successful Broadway musicals, *Fifty Million Frenchmen* ("You Do Something to Me") and *Wake Up and Dream* ("What Is This Thing Called Love") appeared in 1929, followed by *The New Yorkers*, 1930 ("Love for Sale"); *Gay Divorce*, 1932 ("Night and Day"), which in its later film version, 1934, was renamed *Gay Divorcée*; *Anything Goes*, 1934 ("I Get a Kick Out of You," "You're the Top," "All Through the Night," "Blow, Gabriel, Blow," and the title song); *Jubilee*, 1935, ("Begin the Beguine," "Just One of Those Things"); and *Red, Hot and Blue*, 1936 ("It's Delovely"). In 1937 he was injured in a fall from a horse and, despite numerous operations, was confined to a wheel chair for the rest of his life. He continued writing, however, and in 1938 appeared *Leave It to Me* ("My Heart Belongs to Daddy," "From Now On"); in 1939 *Du Barry was a Lady* ("Do I Love You"); in 1940 *Panama Hattie*; in 1941 *Let's Face It*; and in 1943 *Something for the Boys*. The greatest of his artistic and financial successes came in 1948 with *Kiss Me Kate*, derived from Shakespeare's *The Taming of the Shrew*, containing songs that combined his own and Shakespeare's idioms ("I've Come to Wive It Wealthily in Padua," "I Am Ashamed that Women Are So Simple," "I Hate Men," "Were Thine That Special Face," "Wunderbar"). In 1953 appeared *Can-Can* ("I Love Paris," "C'est Magnifique," "It's All Right with Me") and in 1955 *Silk Stockings*. He also contributed songs to many films: for *Born to Dance*, in 1936, he wrote "I've Got You Under My Skin" and "Easy to Love;" for *Rosalie*, 1937, "In the Still of the Night" and "Rosalie;" for *Broadway Melody*, 1940, "I Concentrate on You;" and for *Something to Shout About*, 1943, "You'd Be So Nice to Come Home To." In the genre of urbane, witty lyrics and sinuous music that came to be known as "the Cole Porter song," other memorable hits among his hundreds of compositions included "Don't Fence Me In," "From This Moment On," "Miss Otis Regrets," and "True Love." He died in Santa Monica, California, on October 15, 1964.

Porter, David (1780–1843), naval officer. Born in Boston on February 1, 1780, Porter was the grandson of a merchant captain and the son and namesake of a naval hero of the Revolution. He went to sea with his father in 1796, and entered the navy as a midshipman in 1798. He was on board the *Constellation* when she captured the French frigate *Insurgente* in the chief naval engagement of the undeclared war with France that began in 1798. Promoted to lieutenant in 1799, he commanded the *Enterprise* during the Tripolitan War and was wounded and captured in 1803; he was held until 1805. Promoted to master-commandant in 1808 and to captain on July 2, 1812, he sailed the next day on the *Essex* on a cruise during which he took nine prizes, including the *Alert*, the first British naval vessel captured in the War of 1812. The next year he took his ship into Pacific waters, thus making the *Essex* the first U.S. naval vessel to cruise those waters. He managed to maintain the *Essex* for more than a year by capturing British whalers and using their supplies, ammunition, and money. During this famous voyage he took possession of Nuku Hiva, one of the Marquesas Islands, renaming it Madison Island and becoming the first naval imperialist in U.S. history, but the United States never confirmed his action. Early in 1814 he learned that the British had sent a fleet into the Pacific to stop his raiding of whalers; he finally encountered the enemy ships off Valparaiso, Chile, and was defeated in a fierce engagement in which he was captured and 155 of his 225 men were lost. Paroled later in the year, he returned home in time to participate in naval operations around Washington, D.C., before the end of the war. By that time he was relatively wealthy, having married well and having taken many prizes, and on being named commissioner of the Navy Board in 1815—in which capacity he was apparently the first to propose a U.S. voyage to Japan—he bought a farm on the heights overlooking the White House that was to become a social center of official Washington. But his restless spirit was dissatisfied with shore duty, and he resigned from the board in 1823 to take command of the West India squadron, with which for two years he fought to suppress pirates. Impetuous and short-tempered, he responded to what he considered discourteous treatment by Spanish authorities in Puerto Rico by landing an armed force and demanding an apology; but relations between Spain and the United States were then friendly, and as a result he was court-martialed and sentenced to a suspension from duty. Furious, he resigned from the navy and went to Mexico, where he had been offered a post as commander in chief of the Mexican navy. But a two-year stay in Mexico was marked by grave disappointments, and he returned to the United States in 1828 seeking appointment as U.S. minister to Mexico so that he could avenge himself on enemies there; he settled in 1830 for the post of consul-general in Algiers, later becoming chargé d'affaires and in due course minister to Turkey in 1839. He died in Constantinople on March 3, 1843. Naval hero David Glasgow Farragut was his adopted son, and his son David Dixon Porter was also a distinguished naval officer.

Porter, David Dixon (1813–1891), naval officer. Born on June 8, 1813, in Chester, Pennsylvania, Porter was the son of David Porter. He received little formal education and at the age of ten made his first sea cruise, a pirate-hunting expedition commanded by his father. When the elder Porter became commander in chief of the Mexican navy in 1826, Porter joined also, serving as a midshipman for three years. In 1829, having been imprisoned by Spanish authorities following the capture of his ship, he was released and commissioned a midshipman in the U.S. navy; he then served with the Coastal Survey, the Naval Observatory, and on various routine cruises. In 1841 he was promoted to lieutenant. During the Mexican War he participated in the naval bombardment of Veracruz and for a time commanded the *Spitfire*. After the war he returned to his earlier duties but, dissatisfied with his failure to advance, soon left to enter the merchant service. He rejoined the navy in 1855, made two voyages to the Mediterranean to obtain camels for the army's use in the Southwest, and from 1857 to 1860 was assigned to the Portsmouth, New Hampshire, Navy Yard. He was on the verge of resigning again when he was ordered to command the *Powhatan* on a relief mission to Fort Pickens, Florida, in April 1861. Promoted to commander, he performed Civil War blockade duty along the Gulf Coast and made a short cruise in the West Indies. From November 1861 until April 1862 he helped plan a naval offensive against New Orleans; he recommended his foster brother, Captain David G. Farragut, for chief command, and was himself placed in charge of the mortar flotilla. The bombardment inflicted by Porter's command on Fort Jackson on April 24 opened the mouth of the Mississippi and aided the taking of New Orleans by Union forces. In October Porter was made acting rear admiral in command of the Mississippi Squadron and during 1863 he provided the necessary naval support for Union victories on the river at Arkansas Post, Grand Gulf, and most importantly at Vicksburg; for his actions in the Vicksburg Campaign he was given the official thanks of Congress. After further campaigns on the Western rivers, including the unsuccessful Red River campaign in conjunction with Gen. Nathaniel P. Banks, he was called in 1864 to command the North Atlantic Blockading Squadron. He was in command of the naval forces at the reduction of Fort Fisher, defensive stronghold of Wilmington, North Carolina, and was again formally thanked by Congress. From 1865 to 1869 he was superintendent of the U.S. Naval Academy and there introduced many improvements in organization and training. In 1866 he was promoted to vice-admiral. During 1869–1870, as adviser to the secretary of the navy, Porter was in virtually complete command of the navy. In 1870, upon the death of Farragut, he became an admiral and the senior officer of the service. Despite his eminence he found himself powerless and frustrated in these last years; his duties were virtually limited to membership on the Board of Inspection. He died in Washington, D.C. on February 13, 1891.

Porter, Gene Stratton (1863–1924), author. Born in Wabash County, Indiana, on August 17, 1863, Geneva Stratton attended school in the town of Wabash, to which the family moved in 1874. Her early life in a rural area gave her the appreciation for and insight into nature that permeated her writings. In 1886 she married Charles D. Porter of Geneva, Indiana, and when she began her writing career she hyphenated her maiden and married names into Stratton-Porter. She and her husband made their home in Geneva, and she continued her nature studies from their log-cabin home, which they called Limberlost, after a nearby swamp area. With the success of a short story published in *Metropolitan* magazine in 1901, Mrs. Porter decided on a career in fiction. Her first successful novel was *Freckles*, 1904, the story of an abandoned child who is eventually found by his wealthy family. Her other most popular works were *Girl of the Limberlost*, 1907, and *The Harvester*, 1911. She also wrote a series of nonfiction nature works and a long narrative poem entitled *The Fire Bird*. Her novels, which also included *Laddie*, 1913; *Michael O'Halloran*, 1915; *A Daughter of the Land*, 1918; *The White Flag*, 1923; and *The Keeper of The Bees*, 1925, were sentimental romances reflecting her nature studies and stood in sharp contrast to those of the naturalistic authors of the period—Stephen Crane, Frank Norris, Theodore Dreiser, and Edith Wharton—whose works she disliked intensely. Her books had sold some ten million copies by the time of her death. In about 1919 she and her family moved to California, and the first novel she wrote there, *Her Father's Daughter*, 1921, reflected her new surroundings, dealing with the anti-Japanese sentiment current on the West Coast at that time. She died on December 6, 1924, as the result of an automobile accident in Los Angeles.

Porter, Katherine Anne (1890–1980), author. Born in Indian Creek, in Brown county, Texas, on May 15, 1890, Miss Porter was a distant cousin of William Sydney Porter (O. Henry). Educated at convent schools in the South, she began to write early in life but did not publish any serious work until about 1925. In the meantime she supported herself with newspaper and literary hackwork. Her first collection of stories, *Flowering Judas*, appeared in 1930 and immediately established her as one of the leading American short-story writers; the purity and clarity of her style was hailed by critics. Slow to produce the small body of work by which she is known (although she wrote quickly when finally ready to set words to paper), she produced during the 1930s only three books—*Hacienda, a Story of Mexico*, 1934, based on the Mexican experiences of Soviet film maker Sergei Eisenstein; *Noon Wine*, 1937; and *Pale Horse, Pale Rider*, 1939, a collection of three novellas that included a reprint of *Noon Wine* and included also the title story and a story called *Old Mortality*. Although her reputation was firmly established none of her books sold widely, and she supported herself primarily by serving as writer-in-residence at a succession of colleges and universities. Although she had published in 1944 *The Leaning Tower*, stories, and in 1952 *The Days Before*, essays and prefaces, the entire literary world awaited with excited anticipation the appearance of her only full-length novel, on which she had been working since 1941. When *Ship of Fools* finally was published in 1962 it pleased most critics and gained Miss Porter her first large readership. A best-seller, and a major film in 1965, it told of the ocean voyage of a group of Germans back to their homeland from Mexico in 1931, on the eve of Hitler's takeover of Germany. Her style was perfectly suited to the allegorical exploration of the collusion of good and evil that was her theme, and the penetrating psychological insight that had always marked her work was evident in the book. Her *Collected Short Stories*, 1965, won a Pulitzer Prize and a National Book Award. Miss Porter died in Silver Spring, Maryland, on September 18, 1980.

Porter, William Sydney (1862–1910), "O. Henry," author. Born on September 11, 1862, in Greensboro, North Carolina, Porter left his poverty-stricken home after brief schooling and settled in Texas, trying his hand at various odd jobs, including publishing a humorous weekly and writing a column for a Houston newspaper. In 1896 he was charged with embezzling funds from an Austin bank where he had worked from 1891 to 1894. He fled to Honduras rather than be tried and returned only upon reports of his wife's serious illness. She died in Austin, and he was thereafter convicted and sentenced to prison for five years. He began to write short stories in prison, publishing them under the pseudonym "O. Henry." Released after three years for good behavior, he went to New York City in 1902 to devote himself to writing. Fascinated with the city, he called it "Bagdad on the Subway," he concerned himself with the intricacies of the lives of anonymous people in the bustle of the urban environment. His episodic short stories, a genre he never abandoned, employed irony, fate, sentiment, and coincidence. His most famous works, like "The Gift of the Magi" and "The Furnished Room" (both collected in *The Four Million*, 1906), typically pictured the dull lives of ordinary people and then often surprised the reader with trick endings. He wrote prolifically, delivering a story every week to the *New York World*, as well as writing for other periodicals. Collections of his stories appeared in book form regularly from 1904, and included *Cabbages and Kings*, 1904; *Heart of the West*, 1907; *The Trimmed Lamp*, 1907; *The Gentle Grafter*, 1908; *The Voice of the City*, 1908; *Roads of Destiny*, 1909; and *Whirligigs*, 1910. Several posthumous volumes also appeared, among them *Sixes and Sevens*, 1911; *Rolling Stones*, 1913; and *Waifs and Strays*, 1917. He died in New York City on June 5, 1910.

Portolá, Gaspar de (1723?–1784?), explorer. Born in Catalonia, Spain, about 1723, Portolá came of a noble family and served in the army in Italy and Portugal. He was named governor of the Californias in 1767 and given responsibility for removing the Jesuits from their missions and replacing them with Franciscans; but his principal task was to establish Spanish hegemony in the region in the face of threatened encroachments by England and Russia. Arriving at La Paz, Lower (Baja) California, on July 6, 1768, he immediately set about planning land and sea expeditions that were to meet at the site of present-day San Diego, California, and then continue on to Monterey, a harbor that had been described enthusiastically by Sebastián Vizcaíno in 1602. After a four-month journey overland he reached San Diego on July 1, 1769, to find that his ships and another land party had already arrived; he is nevertheless honored as the founder of San Diego. He established a presidio there and a mission was founded at the same time by Fr. Junípero Serra, who was accompanying the expedition to oversee the founding of Franciscan missions throughout California. Setting out two weeks later, on July 14, he and his men struggled northward through the region of Los Angeles and the ranges of mountains to the northward, arriving at Monterey Bay on October 1. But they did not recognize the bay from the earlier description and therefore forged on to San Francisco Bay, naming many places around the Golden Gate in the course of their journey. Realizing he had gone too far, Portolá returned to San Diego, where he arrived on January 24, 1770. But conversations with a sea captain convinced him that he had indeed been at Monterey Bay in October, so he set out again on April 17 and reached his destination five weeks later, on May 24, 1770. He took formal possession of the area, founded the mission of San Carlos Barromeo and established a presidio for Upper (Alta) California, then sailed away to San Blas, Mexico, his mission completed. Much of what is known of the expedition was recorded in the diary of Fr. Juan Crespi, another Franciscan who took part. Portolá was named governor of the city of Puebla in 1777 and in 1784 received a payment of money to return to Spain, but it is not known if he actually went, nor is anything known of him after that year.

Post, Charles William (1854–1914), breakfast-food manufacturer. Born in Springfield, Illinois, on October 26, 1854, Post attended the University of Illinois for a time and during his twenties worked at various occupations in many parts of the West. His health was uncertain during these years, and he became interested in healing by mental suggestion; arriving in Battle Creek, Michigan, in 1891, he established La Vita Inn, an institution devoted to that practice. It did not do very well, and within three years Post had struck off in still another direction, experimenting with various prepared food products, the first of which was a coffee substitute, Postum. This was a great success, partly as a result of his aggressive advertising, and it was soon followed by a line of breakfast foods that within a few years had gained him a fortune. His policies toward his employees were generous though paternal, but he was a bitter—almost hysterical—opponent of organized labor, and he devoted much of his time, energy, and money during his last years to campaigns, usually heavily advertised, to destroy what he called "the most tyrannical and dangerous trust this country has ever seen." He founded several organizations designed to substitute for labor unions and was a power in the National Association of Manufacturers (NAM). He lived on a grand scale, maintaining homes in Washington, D.C., and in Santa Barbara, California, as well as a 200,000–acre ranch in Texas, but, always highly nervous, he committed suicide in a fit of depression at his Santa Barbara home on May 9, 1914.

Post, Christian Frederick (1710?–1785), missionary. Born in Konitz, East Prussia (now Chojnice, Poland) about 1710, Post was by trade a cabinetmaker. He emigrated to Bethlehem, Pennsylvania, in 1742 and, although a layman, immediately set about doing missionary work on behalf of the Moravians among the Pennsylvania Germans. His efforts to establish a church confederation were unsuccessful and he went with several other missionaries to the region east of Poughkeepsie, New York, known as the "Oblong." There he worked ably, learning the language of the Mohican Indians and marrying an Indian girl. War the next year between the Indians and the settlers made his position untenable, however, and he was ordered out of the state. The year 1747 found him in the Wyoming Valley of the Susquehanna River in Pennsylvania, again undertaking missionary work among the Indians and in the process learning many of their ways. An expedition to Labrador in 1751 ended in disaster when an Indian attack decimated a group of which he was a member, and he returned to the Wyoming Valley. In 1758 he was commissioned by the Pennsylvania authorities to arrange a conference with the Indians in the western part of the state, in the hope of confirming their allegiance to the British. In this Post was highly successful, and in the end the French abandoned Fort Duquesne as a result of his efforts. He thereupon set out for the Ohio country, again doing missionary work among the Indians of the region; his restless spirit driving him always on, he was found to be continuing his work in Nicaragua in 1764. He visited Bethlehem, Pennsylvania, in 1767 and offered his assistance, which was refused, to the Moravian authorities; he thereupon returned to Nicaragua. He died in Germantown, Pennsylvania, on May 1, 1785.

Post, Emily Price (1873–1960), author. Born in Baltimore on October 30, 1873, the daughter of an architect, Emily Price was educated in private schools in New York City, among them Miss Graham's Finishing School for Young Ladies. A popular debutante, she was feted by Ward McAllister, the social arbiter who coined the term "the Four Hundred." In 1892 she married Edwin M. Post, a banker, from whom she was divorced in 1905. At the turn of the century financial circumstances compelled her to begin to write and she produced newspaper articles, on architecture and interior decoration, and light novels, in one of which she unfavorably compared American social customs with those of Europeans. At the request of her publisher, she brought out *Etiquette—The Blue Book of Social Usage* in 1922. Immediately popular, her charming and lively presentation differed from other guides to manners in being directed to popular audiences rather than merely to the upper classes. It laid down fundamental rules that remained unchanged through the book's many printings, although she took care to remain abreast of the times in dealing with broad changes in society. Proper behavior, she believed, was a manifestation of consideration of other people. Sections of the first edition reflected the period of her own upbringing (Chaperons and Other Conventions) and were later modified to reflect changing customs (The Vanishing Chaperon and Other New Conventions). She added to later editions guides to television, telephone, airplane, and business etiquette. After 1931 she spoke on radio programs and wrote a column on good taste for the Bell Syndicate; it appeared daily in some 200 newspapers after 1932. Her other books included *The Personality of a House*, 1930, which also appeared in several editions; *Children are People*, 1940; and *Motor Manners*, 1950. At her death in New York City on September 25, 1960, *Etiquette* was in its 10th edition.

Post, Wiley (1899–1935), aviator. Born near Grand Saline, Texas, on November 22, 1899, Post grew up there and in Oklahoma. He exhibited a marked ability for mechanics from his youth and in the early 1920s, after working for several years in the oil fields, he followed his early interest in airplanes into the barnstorming circuit, performing as a stunt parachutist while learning to fly himself. In 1926 he returned to the oil fields out of financial necessity, but he soon lost an eye in a drilling accident. With money received as compensation he bought an airplane with which he barnstormed the Texas backcountry. Post was hired as a private

pilot in 1928 by F. C. Hall, a wealthy Oklahoma oilman, and in 1930, flying Hall's plane *Winnie Mae*, he entered and won the Los Angeles–Chicago Bendix Trophy race. In 1931 he and his navigator, Harold Gatty, flew the *Winnie Mae* eastward to the British Isles, across Europe and Russia, and back to the United States, circling the globe in 8 days, 15 hours, and 51 minutes; later in the year they published *Around the World in Eight Days*. Post repeated the feat alone two years later, trimming nearly a full day off his earlier record in returning to New York City after 7 days, 18 hours, and 49 minutes, having clearly demonstrated the value of the automatic pilot and other instruments and having become the first solo flyer to circle the earth. Convinced that the future of aviation lay in large part in the development of techniques for high-altitude flight, he designed a pioneer version of the pressure suit and made extensive experiments with it. In 1935 he set out on a pleasure flight to the Orient, carrying as a passenger his close friend Will Rogers; their plane crashed near Point Barrow, Alaska, on August 15, 1935, and both were killed.

Potter, Henry Codman (1835–1908), religious leader. Born in Schenectady, New York, on May 25, 1835, Potter, the son and nephew of bishops of the Protestant Episcopal church, discovered his own religious vocation at nineteen, when he underwent a religious experience. He immediately enrolled in the Protestant Episcopal Theological Seminary in Virginia, at Alexandria, and graduated in 1857, being ordained by his father, Alonzo Potter, in that year; he advanced to the priesthood in 1858. Parish work during the next few years in Troy, New York, and in Boston was followed by his call to be the rector of Grace Church in New York City, where, for the next 15 years, he was one of the leading clergymen of the city. Elected bishop coadjutor of New York on September 27, 1883, and consecrated on October 20, he was for the next few years in charge of the diocese, the bishop, his uncle Horatio Potter, being retired from active work. Upon Horatio's death in 1887, Henry became bishop in his stead. A skillful diplomat, he resolved a number of difficult controversies and disputes within his church, and soon became one of the most influential clergyman in the country. Author of several popular books on religion, he delivered effective sermons and was an excellent administrator; but he also desired to know at first hand the condition of the poor in his diocese, and he therefore spent the summer of 1895 working in a mission on Stanton Street, on the Lower East Side, then one of the worst areas of the city. He was outspoken on the topics of honesty in government and the duties of citizenship and on more than one occasion became the focus of national attention for his attacks on corruption in government; his denunciation of police involvement in vice led to the election of a reform city administration in 1899. Among his books were *The Citizen in His Relation to the Industrial Situation*, 1902, and *The Modern Man and His Fellow Man*, 1903. Perhaps his most lasting achievement was undertaking the building of the Cathedral of St. John the Divine, on Morningside Heights near Columbia University. The cornerstone of this great building, one of the largest Gothic cathedrals in the world, was laid in 1892, and Potter devoted the rest of his life to overseeing the work of construction (in the early 1970s the edifice remained unfinished) and to obtaining the enormous funds required for it. He died in Cooperstown, New York, on July 21, 1908.

Pound, Erza Loomis (1885–1972), poet and critic. Born on October 30, 1885, in Hailey, Idaho, Pound grew up near Philadelphia and studied romance philology at the University of Pennsylvania and at Hamilton College, from which he graduated in 1905. He returned to the University of Pennsylvania for an M.A. in 1906. He taught briefly at Wabash College but was dismissed despite his academic brilliance because he would not bow to academic regulations. He went abroad to live in 1908, first in Italy, where he published his first book, *A Lume Spento*, then in London from 1908 to 1920, in Paris from 1920 to 1924, and in Italy from 1925 to 1945. In 1909 he published *Personae* and *Exultations*; more volumes followed, including *Ripostes*, 1912, and *Hugh Selwyn Mauberley*, 1920. For a period of years starting in 1917 he served as foreign editor of Margaret Anderson's *Little Review* and he contributed much to the success of *Poetry: A Magazine of Verse*. His verse quickly attracted attention. It was personal both in content and treatment and highly unorthodox in style. His knowledge of medieval literature, Provençal singers, and troubadour ballads was much reflected in his work, which often dwelt on obscure lore. He defined a poet's duty as interpreting his knowledge for his contemporaries, and he gave invaluable support and help to such poets, then unknown, as Robert Frost and T. S. Eliot. He fought for publication of James Joyce's controversial *Portrait of the Artist As a Young Man* and *Ulysses*, and Wyndham Lewis's *Tarr*, and he edited *The Wasteland* out of Eliot's massive manuscript. He produced many notable works of translation, among them *Cathay*, 1915, from notes and studies left by Ernest F. Fenollosa. He translated also from Anglo-Saxon, Italian, Greek, Egyptian, and other languages, although his renderings were more poetic and inspired than scholarly. His lifetime project, *The Cantos*, a huge, rambling work dealing with historical themes and current events, was begun in 1917 and by 1959 had attained a total of 109 cantos. Its concept of individual morality rested on Confucian thought, its concept of social mores, on Pound's interpretation of Jeffersonian economics. Often highly esoteric, the work even utilized Chinese ideographs, and despite its difficulty, it had a profound and liberating influence on modern poetry. The first volume of the *Cantos*, *A Draft of XVI Cantos*, appeared in 1925. Cantos 72 to 84 were published as *The Pisan Cantos*, 1948, which was awarded the Bollingen Prize amidst a storm of controversy because of Pound's conduct during World War II. Pound's own theory of poetry, which came to dominate first Imagism and later Vorticism, attempted to place verse in relationship to the other arts. In 1945 he was arrested by U.S. military forces in Italy and indicted for treason for his pro-Fascist and anti-Semitic propaganda broadcasts from Italy during World War II. Back in the United States, he was judged mentally unfit to stand trial and was confined to St. Elizabeth's Hospital in Washington, D.C., in 1946. Released in 1958, he returned to Italy. In his later years he traveled extensively and was said to be revising *The Cantos*. Among his critical and other prose works were *The Spirit of Romance*, 1910; *Pavannes and Divisions*, 1918; *Instigations*, 1920; *Indiscretions*, 1923; *ABC of Economics*, 1933; *Jefferson and/or Mussolini*, 1935; *Guide to Kulchur*, 1938; *Patria Mia*, 1950; and *Impact, Essays on Ignorance and the Decline of American Civilization*, 1960. His last years were passed in pain and virtual silence. Acclaimed, despite his pronounced and controversial quirks, as one of the greatest figures in English letters and as possibly the central moving force in the creation of modern poetry, Pound died in Venice on November 1, 1972.

Pound, Roscoe (1870–1964), educator and legal scholar. Born in Lincoln, Nebraska, on October 27, 1870, Pound studied at the University of Nebraska, from which he received a degree in botany in 1888. Continuing his studies in botany, he received an M.A. from Nebraska in 1889, then went to Harvard to study law. But he stayed only one year, returned to Nebraska, passed the bar examination in 1890 without a law degree, and practiced law until 1907. In 1890 he also resumed his work in botany at the University of Nebraska, earned a Ph.D. in 1897, and directed a botanical study of the state from 1892 to 1903; he was the discoverer of the rare lichen *Roscopoundia*. He taught law at the university from 1899 to 1903, was dean of the law department from 1903 to 1907, and was a legal adviser to the state government from 1904 to 1907, holding the post of commissioner of uniform state laws. The bifurcation of his career came to an end, for all practical purposes, in 1907, when he joined the law faculty at Northwestern; he taught law at the University of Chicago in 1909–1910, and then joined the Harvard law faculty; he was dean of the Harvard law school from 1916 to 1936. Resigning the deanship in 1936, he was given a "roving professsorship" as University Professor and taught a variety of subjects until his retirement in 1947. After his retirement, at the age of seventy-seven, he continued to be active in many legal, editorial, and educational positions. Among other activities, he spent several years in Taiwan reorganizing the Nationalist Chinese government's judicial system. During his long career he studied, taught, and wrote in many different fields of law. Among his many books were *Readings on the History and System of the Common Law*, 1904; *Readings on Roman Law*, 1906; *Outlines of Lectures on Jurisprudence*, 1914; *The Spirit of the Common Law* (perhaps his best-known book), 1921; *Law and*

Morals, 1924; *Criminal Justice in America*, 1930; *The Formative Era of American Law*, 1938; *Administrative Law, Its Growth, Procedure and Significance*, 1942; *New Paths of the Law*, 1950; *Justice According to the Law*, 1951; *The Lawyer from Antiquity to Modern Times*, 1953; *The Ideal Element in Law*, 1958; *Jurisprudence*, 5 volumes, 1959; and *Law Finding through Experience and Reason*, 1960. During his later years he shared with Learned Hand the reputation of being the nation's leading jurist outside the U.S. Supreme Court bench. He died in Cambridge, Massachusetts, on July 1, 1964.

Powderly, Terence Vincent (1849–1924), labor leader and public official. Born in Carbondale, Pennsylvania, on January 22, 1849, of Irish immigrant parents, Powderly went to work on the railroad at thirteen. Four years later he was apprenticed to a machinist and from 1869 to 1877 he followed that trade. His involvement in labor organization began in 1871, when he joined the Machinists' and Blacksmiths' National Union, of which he became president the next year; later he joined the Industrial Brotherhood and worked as an organizer in Pennsylvania. In 1874 he joined the Knights of Labor, at that time still a secret organization. He rose quickly in the Knights, serving on the committee on constitution at the first General Assembly in 1878, and in 1879 became Grand Master Workman, a position he held until 1893 (the last ten years as General Master Workman). His leadership of the Knights thus spanned the period of the organization's public and major influence, after about 1880. Powderly was at the same time active politically; from 1878 to 1884 he was the Greenback-Labor mayor of Scranton, Pennsylvania, and he stumped often and in many states for candidates sympathetic to labor. He resisted always, however, efforts of others to form a labor party. More idealistic and optimistic than many other labor leaders, Powderly sought through the Knights to create a union for all workers, skilled and unskilled, to discard the use of the strike and other coercive measures, and to establish labor-management relations on a basis of cooperation and arbitration. He opposed trade unionism as divisive of the working class and as devoted to short-term interests only. The Knights of Labor was at the time the largest and most powerful labor organization ever established, its membership reaching nearly a million in 1886. In that year, however, Samuel Gompers led his cigar-makers' union out of the Knights to join in establishing the American Federation of Labor (AFL), and the Knights declined steadily thereafter, to a large extent because of the conflict with the AFL over the issue of craft unionism. Powderly was admitted to the Pennsylvania bar in 1894; in 1897 he was appointed by President William McKinley, for whom he had campaigned, commissioner general of immigration. Removed from the post by President Theodore Roosevelt in 1902, he became four years later a special representative of the Department of Commerce and Labor, commissioned to study the causes of European immigration. From 1907 to 1921 he headed the Division of Information of the Bureau of Immigration. He wrote many articles and pamphlets on the problems of labor and immigration, of which the most notable was *Thirty Years of Labor*, 1889. He died in Washington, D.C., on June 24, 1924. His autobiography, *The Path I Trod*, was published in 1940.

Powell, *see* Osceola

Powell, Adam Clayton, Jr. (1908–1972), reformer and public official. Born in New Haven, Connecticut, on November 29, 1908, the son of the pastor of the Abyssinian Baptist Church in Harlem, New York City, Powell was educated at Colgate, from which he graduated in 1930, and at Columbia, from which he received an M.A. in 1932; he obtained a doctorate in divinity from Shaw University in 1938. Succeeding his father as pastor in 1936, he quickly established himself as an enormously effective leader, both political and religious, in Harlem, one of the nation's major black communities. His sermons before his church's congregation—the membership eventually grew to more than 14,000, making it one of the largest Protestant congregations in the country—were spellbinding; and his identification with the more militant elements in the black community led to his election to the New York city council in 1941, the first black man to serve on that body. He was first elected to the House of Representatives in 1944, becoming in time chairman of the House's Education and Labor Committee, a post in which he wielded great power over legislation. He was a highly active and visible leader in the fight against racial segregation and during his years in Congress authored some 50 pieces of social legislation. At the same time, however, his manner of life was flamboyant and, in the eyes of many observers, morally if not legally questionable. Reelected for the 11th time in the fall of 1966, he was the following January barred from his seat in the House and accused of misusing some $45,000 in public funds. Undaunted, he returned to his district, ran in a special election to fill his seat, and won overwhelmingly, but was again barred from the House. By that time his position was becoming exceptionally difficult in New York City. He had been sued for libel by a woman whom he had named on a television program as a "bagman," or collector of gambling proceeds. She had won her suit, in which he refused to defend himself, and a large jury award was growing, because of interest charges, every year. Whenever he was in New York, he was subject to subpoena for contempt of court; he therefore spent most of his time in the Bahamas, where he had a home, as he was safe from legal action there and while on the floor of the House. He nevertheless ran again in 1968, was again elected, and this time was seated, but by a vote of his colleagues was fined $25,000 and deprived of his seniority and therefore of his committee chairmanship. In June 1969, in a landmark decision, the Supreme Court decided that the action of the House in depriving him of his seat in 1967 had been unconstitutional, but by that time his health was already failing. After defeat in a Democratic primary election in the fall of 1970 he resigned as pastor of the Abyssinian Baptist Church in 1971 and retired to the island of Bimini in the Bahamas. Powell became ill there the next year and died in Miami, Florida, on April 4, 1972.

Powell, John Wesley (1834–1902), geologist and ethnologist. Born in Mt. Morris, now part of New York City, on March 24, 1834, Powell made with his family successive moves to Ohio, Wisconsin, and finally to Wheaton, Illinois. He attended Wheaton College, Illinois College, and Oberlin College, but took no degree. Although he had intended to follow his father into the ministry, an interest in natural science deepened and soon displaced the earlier ambition; he made long observing and collecting trips throughout the eastern Great Plains and became secretary of the Illinois Society of Natural History. He enlisted in the army at the beginning of the Civil War, served with distinction with an artillery company and emerged in 1865 as a major of artillery and with his right arm amputated at the elbow as a result of a wound sustained at Shiloh. He was soon appointed professor of geology at Illinois Wesleyan College and in a short time became lecturer and museum curator at Illinois State Normal University (now Illinois State University) as well. In 1867 he made the first of many exploratory journeys into the Rocky Mountain region; the earlier trips were intended as field work and training for students, but in 1869 he led a fully professional expedition, financed by the Smithsonian Institution and by Congress, down the Colorado River and through the Grand Canyon by boat. His report of the dangerous 900-mile journey and of his explorations of nearby areas appeared in 1875 as *Explorations of The Colorado River of the West and Its Tributaries*, which was revised as *Canyons of the Colorado*, 1895. He continued to make government-sponsored explorations and in 1875 was placed in charge of the United States Geographical and Geological Survey of the Rocky Mountain Region. In 1878 he published his now classic monograph, *Report on the Lands of the Arid Region of the United States*, in which he carefully explicated the limited uses for which the high plains region was suited and urged government involvement in reclamation and regulatory activities. In addition to his work in geology, Powell had made on his many trips close scientific observations of the Indians of the West and was the first to establish a definitive scheme of classification of Indian languages. In 1879 he became the first director of the Smithsonian's Bureau of American Ethnology; in the same yar his survey group was merged into the newly organized U.S. Geological Survey, of which he became the second director two years later. For both the Bureau of Ethnology and the Geological Survey he was an able and farsighted administrator, and in both agencies he inaugurated a program of regular publication of proceedings and activities

that greatly enhanced the scope and significance of the scientific work being done and did much to interest the public in the human and natural history of the continent. He resigned from his Survey post in 1894 but continued to direct the work of the Bureau until his death on September 23, 1902, in Haven, Maine.

Powell, Lewis Franklin, Jr. (1907–   ), justice of the Supreme Court. Born in Suffolk, Virginia, on September 19, 1907, Powell moved to Richmond with his family as a boy and spent most of his subsequent life there. He graduated from Washington and Lee University in 1929 and continued his studies at that institution, gaining his law degree in 1931; he received a master's degree in law from Harvard in 1932. He returned to Richmond in that year to join one of Virginia's oldest law firms and in 1938 became a partner. After service in the Army Air Forces during World War II he took up his law practice again and began to serve in a number of civic posts, always with distinction. His achievement, while a member of the Richmond Board of Education, 1952–1961, in peacefully integrating the city's schools, while other school districts in Virginia were experiencing great distress as a result of the 1954 Supreme Court racial-desegregation order, was especially notable. He was president of the American Bar Association (ABA), 1964–1965, of the American College of Trial Lawyers, 1969–1970, and of the American Bar Foundation, 1969–1971. He was one of two men, the other being William H. Rehnquist, who were nominated by President Richard M. Nixon on October 21, 1971, to fill the seats on the Supreme Court vacated by the retirement of justices Hugo Black and John Marshall Harlan. Rehnquist's nomination was controversial, but the choice of Powell was widely applauded and he was confirmed by the Senate, in a vote of 89–1, on December 6.

Powers, Hiram (1805–1873), sculptor. Born on a farm near Woodstock, Vermont, on July 29, 1805, Powers received little schooling because of the poverty of his family, and, as they and he moved westward, first to New York state and then to Ohio, he worked at odd jobs and in whatever employment he could find. Six years in a clock and organ factory in Cincinnati were followed by five more, from 1829 to 1834, in the waxworks department of a Cincinnati museum. He began there by installing clockwork mechanisms in the exhibits in the Chamber of Horrors, but soon found that he was adept at modeling the wax figures and thus became a sculptor. He began to receive commissions for portrait busts in Cincinnati, but by 1834 he was aware that a more fruitful field existed in Washington for such work, and so he moved to the capital in that year, making busts there from life of John Marshall (later placed in the U.S. Capitol), President Andrew Jackson, John C. Calhoun, Daniel Webster, and other notables. In 1837 he went to Florence, then the center of artistic activity in the Western world, and lived there for the rest of his life. He continued to do portrait busts but also began work on a life-size figure, "Eve before the Fall," which was highly praised, and followed it by his marble sculpture entitled "The Greek Slave," 1843. This work became probably the most discussed, admired, and disputed sculpture of the middle of the nineteenth century. Displayed at the Crystal Palace Exposition in London in 1851, it was sold in England for an undisclosed sum; a marble copy was later obtained for the Corcoran Gallery in Washington, D.C. Easy to understand—it depicted a lovely Greek girl captured by the Turks, and the Greek Revolution was then in everyone's mind and mouth—it was also controversial in the United States because of the undraped figure; a panel of clergymen finally decided it was acceptable. Poets wrote odes to it, and Edward Everett and Nathaniel Hawthorne lauded it in prose; it made Powers the best-known American artist, and probably the country's most highly regarded. Other full-size figures he completed included "Il Penseroso," 1856; "California," a nude, 1858; "Eve Disconsolate," 1871; and "The Last of the Tribe," an Indian girl, 1872. Powers's statue of Daniel Webster was placed on the terrace of the Boston State House in 1859, and he did other monumental sculptures as well, but his best work was probably his many marble portrait busts of men, which he continued to produce from his large studio in Florence until his death. In 1863 his statues of Benjamin Franklin and Thomas Jefferson were placed in the U.S. Capitol. His portrait busts of women, although numerous, were considered deficient in conveying character. Powers died in Florence on June 27, 1873, and was buried there.

Powhatan (1550?–1618), Indian leader. Born about 1550—Capt. John Smith thought he was about sixty years old in 1610—Powhatan, whose Indian name was Wa-hun-sen-a-cawh, or Wahunsonacock, was usually referred to by his official title as chieftain of the Powhatan Confederacy, which occupied the territory of the Virginia tidewater, from the Potomac south almost to Albemarle Sound. He was the son of a chief of a Southern tribe— thus Powhatan may have been born in Florida— who was driven northward by the Spanish and who conquered some six Algonquian tribes, welding them into a confederacy of which his son inherited the chieftainship. The son greatly extended the confederacy; he eventually ruled 30 tribes living in some 128 villages and containing 9000 or more people at the time that the English came to Jamestown in 1607. A stern ruler, Powhatan at first opposed the presence of the settlers along the James River, and in 1608, according to legend, was about to execute the captured Smith when one of his daughters, Pocahontas, saved him. Sporadic fighting between the Indians and the colonists, much of it arising from the settlers' seizure of the best lands, continued until the marriage between Pocahontas and John Rolfe in April 1614, after which Powhatan, who had been crowned "emperor" by the English in 1609, maintained friendly

relations with the colonists. Powhatan died in April 1618, and thereafter the peace deteriorated under his successors; an uprising in 1622 resulted in the massacre of 347 white settlers and marked the beginning of 14 years of war in which hundreds were killed.

Pratt, William Henry, *see* Karloff, Boris

Preminger, Otto Ludwig (1906–   ), director and producer. Born in Vienna on December 5, 1906, Preminger became interested in the stage at an early age and made his acting debut at seventeen in Max Reinhardt's production of *A Midsummer Night's Dream*. During the 1920s he continued his interest in theater, and for a time even had his own company in Vienna during vacations from his law studies at the University of Vienna; he received his Ll.D. in 1928. In that year he was engaged by Reinhardt to produce and direct a series of plays ranging from Greek tragedies to current U.S. hits. Emigrating to the United States in 1935, he made his Broadway debut that year with his production of *Libel* for Gilbert Miller. A relatively unsuccessful sojourn in Hollywood was followed by a series of Broadway hits: *Outward Bound*, 1938; *Margin for Error*, 1939, in which he also took the leading role; *My Dear Children*, 1940; and *In Time to Come*, 1941. He taught at the Yale School of Drama from 1938 to 1941. In 1941 he signed a long-term contract with Twentieth Century–Fox, directing a number of films for the company in the next few years and playing the part of a Nazi in some of them, capitalizing on his persistent German accent. He became a U.S. citizen in 1943. His first real hit was *Laura*, 1944, which won an Academy Award nomination. The year 1947 saw the release of the controversial *Forever Amber*, considered daring for the time, and 1953 that of the even more controversial *The Moon Is Blue*. He had directed the stage version of this work on Broadway, where its somewhat risqué language occasioned no comment; but when the play was transferred to the screen there was wide objection. A Supreme Court decision in 1955 led to the release of the film to local movie houses and also brought about a general liberalization of the motion-picture code the next year. Other celebrated Preminger films were the all-Negro *Carmen Jones*, 1954; *The Man with the Golden Arm*, 1955, still another controversial film, dealing with drug addiction; *Saint Joan*, 1957, starring the seventeen-year-old Jean Seberg; *Bonjour Tristesse*, 1958; *Porgy and Bess*, 1959; *Anatomy of a Murder*, 1959; *Exodus*, 1960; *Advise and Consent*, 1962; and *Hurry Sundown*, 1967.

Prescott, Samuel (1751–1777?), Revolutionary patriot. Born in Concord, Massachusetts, on August 19, 1751, Prescott was the son and grandson of physicians and was evidently a physician himself, although he could have had little time to practice his profession. On the evening of April 18, 1775, while returning by horseback from Lexington to his home in Concord, he met Paul Revere and William Dawes on the road and learned that they were carrying news of the British approach, which they had just imparted to John Hancock and Samuel Adams. Prescott was asked by Revere and Dawes to accompany them in their further efforts to rouse the sleeping countryside. Near the village of Lincoln, Revere was accosted by two British officers, who were soon joined by two others; Dawes was forced to flee back toward Lexington, but Prescott, after an unsuccessful attempt to dismount the officers, jumped his horse over a stone wall to the left of the road, shouting to Revere to go to the right. Revere was captured soon afterward, and the task of alerting the colonials thus devolved on Prescott. Giving the alarm first to Samuel Hartwell, of the Lincoln minutemen, he then rode on to Concord and roused the citizenry, his warning giving the minutemen there time to conceal their military stores. Prescott later served at Ticonderoga in 1776 but was captured by the British and taken to Halifax, Nova Scotia, where he is believed to have died in jail in 1777.

Prescott, William (1726–1795), Revolutionary soldier. Born in Groton, Massachusetts, on February 20, 1726, Prescott saw military service during King George's War and other phases of the French and Indian Wars, afterward becoming a farmer in Pepperell, Massachusetts. Colonel of a body of minutemen, he led them to Concord on April 19, 1775, but arrived too late for the fighting. His chance for action came two months later. Ordered to fortify Bunker Hill in Boston, he left Cambridge on June 16 but upon his arrival decided to fortify Breed's Hill instead, since it commanded the town more effectively. As soon as the British saw the Americans in position on the morning of June 17 they opened fire, training their muskets especially on Prescott himself, who walked up and down the battlements paying no attention to the hail of bullets, several of which pierced his clothing. It was a warm day, and he took off his uniform and replaced it with a jacket and a broad-brimmed hat, in which guise he is depicted in a statue on Bunker Hill. His extraordinary coolness under fire inspired his men, and he is remembered as the major hero of the battle erroneously named for Bunker Hill. He served in the Continental army in the campaign around New York City in 1776 and the Saratoga campaign in 1777, but his years were beginning to tell and an old injury made sitting on a horse almost impossible. Retiring to his farm, he undertook various civic duties in the remaining years of his life and died at Pepperell on October 13, 1795. The historian William H. Prescott was his grandson.

Prescott, William Hickling (1796–1859), historian. Born in Salem, Massachusetts, on May 4, 1796, Prescott was of a wealthy New England family; his grandfather had commanded the patriot troops at the battle of Bunker Hill and his father was a well-known lawyer. After entering Harvard College in 1811, he suffered an accident that affected his entire later life. While dining in commons, another student threw a crust of bread across the table; it struck and blinded him in one eye. In spite of this he completed his studies, graduating with honors in 1814. For two years, 1815–1817, he traveled in Europe. He hoped to enter his father's law office, but his doctors warned that the sight would dim in his other eye—it was already weakening—and he instead chose a literary career. He worked in a darkened study while assistants read to him; he took notes by means of a noctograph, a device which guided his hand; an assistant then read the notes back and he committed them to memory. His first book, the *History of the Reign of Ferdinand and Isabella the Catholic*, three volumes, 1837, established his reputation as a historian. Profoundly interested in Spanish history, he followed this with the *History of the Conquest of Mexico*, three volumes, 1843, which was translated into many languages and became one of the most widely read histories in the world. In 1845 appeared *Biographical and Critical Miscellanies*, a collection of his essays originally published in the *North American Review*. His *History of the Conquest of Peru*, which was published in 1847, was almost as popular as his work on Mexico. He then embarked on a *History of the Reign of Philip the Second, King of Spain*; two volumes were published in 1855, another in 1858, but the work was incomplete at his death in Boston on January 28, 1859. Possessing a vivid historical imagination, Prescott dramatized, sometimes to excess, the lives and achievements of the early Spanish explorers of America, and he was occasionally verbose and inattentive to details. But despite later findings, all minor, of anthropological research, his accounts have generally stood the test of time, and they remain wonderfully readable.

Presley, Elvis Aaron (1935–1977), entertainer. Born on January 8, 1935, in Tupelo, Mississippi, Presley first sang in a church choir and at revival meetings, and on his twelfth birthday began teaching himself to play the guitar (he never learned to read music). In 1953, having moved to Memphis, he graduated from high school and began driving a truck, while attending school at night to become an electrician. As a surprise for his mother, he cut a personal record that year at the Sun Record Company that was accidentally heard by the company's president. Signed to a recording contract as a result, he made his first commercial record in 1954 —"That's All Right, Mama" and "Blue Moon of Kentucky"—and achieved considerable local success. That year he toured the South as The Hillbilly Cat, performed on the "Louisiana Hayride" show over a Shreveport radio station, and in 1955, after singing at a disc jockeys' convention in Nashville, made a lucrative agreement with RCA-Victor, which released five of his records simultaneously. His first national television appearance was in 1955 on the Jackie Gleason "Stage Show." A later appearance on the Ed Sullivan show was notable for refusal to allow Presley to be shown full-length, a reflection of reactions to Presley's mannerisms, which included much gyration of the hips. In fact,

Presley was sometimes referred to as "Elvis the Pelvis." In 1956 he signed a seven-year movie contract, making *Love Me Tender* in that year. Presley became a veritable industry, with innumerable products bearing his name, picture, or the titles of his songs, bringing billions of dollars in international sales. His music combined strains of the country-and-western and rhythm-and-blues traditions into a more emotional, if sometimes less lyrical, style that came to be known as "rockabilly" and then as "rock and roll." As rock and roll grew to the proportions of a national mania among teen-agers, Presley remained for years the dominant figure, calling up scores of imitators and eliciting the same responses from audiences (and from disapproving elders) that, in earlier decades, had greeted Bing Crosby and Frank Sinatra. In the 1970s he reemerged from a semi-retirement to become a successful night-club performer. His most popular records included "Blue Suede Shoes," "Hound Dog," "All Shook Up," and "Love Me Tender." He died in Memphis, Tennessee, on August 16, 1977.

Price, Leontyne (1927–), singer. Born in Laurel, Mississippi, on February 10, 1927, Mary Leontyne Price sang in her church choir as a girl, but it was not until she graduated from Central State College in Wilberforce, Ohio, that she finally determined to seek a career as a singer. Financial aid provided by a friend, Elizabeth Chisholm of Laurel, helped her to study for four years at the Juilliard School of Music in New York City, where she worked under the former concert singer Florence Page Kimball, who remained her coach in later years. Her singing debut took place in April 1952, in a Broadway revival of Virgil Thomson's *Four Saints in Three Acts*; this led to Ira Gershwin's choosing her to sing Bess in his revival of *Porgy and Bess*, which played in New York City for two years, from 1952 to 1954, and also toured the United States and Europe. The year 1955 saw her triumphant performance of the title role in the National Broadcasting Company's television production of *Tosca*, and she sang leading roles in other operas on television in the next few years. Her operatic stage debut, however, did not take place until 1957, at the San Francisco Opera, where she sang each year until 1960. By that time she was one of the most popular lyric sopranos in the country and had also made triumphant appearances in Vienna in 1959 and at Milan's La Scala the next year, where her performance was applauded by an Italian critic who declared that Verdi would have found her the ideal Aïda. Despite this great success, however, her debut at the Metropolitan Opera in New York was deferred until 1961, when she appeared there in the difficult role of Leonora in *Il Trovatore*. After a brilliant performance she became one of the Met's leading sopranos. Later roles there included Cio-Cio-San in *Madame Butterfly*, Donna Anna in *Don Giovanni*, and Liù in *Turandot*. She won some 15 Grammy awards from the American Society of Recording Arts and Sciences.

Procofieff-Seversky, Alexander Nicolaievitch, *see* De Seversky, Alexander Procofieff

Prophet, The, *see under* Tecumseh

Pulaski, Kazimierz (1747–1779), Revolutionary soldier. Born at Winiary, Mazovia, Poland, on March 4, 1747, Pulaski was the oldest son of Count Jozef Pulaski, Polish patriot and one of the organizers of the Confederation of Bar. Casimir (the common anglicized spelling) and his two brothers all took part in the military activities of the confederation, and Casimir's defense of Czestochowa against the Russians in 1770–1771 brought him fame throughout Europe. But when the Russians were joined by Austrian and Prussian forces in 1772 further resistance seemed useless, and Pulaski went into exile, first in Turkey, then in Paris. There, after four years of restless inactivity, he was introduced to Silas Deane and Benjamin Franklin, who together arranged for him to go to America in behalf of the Revolution. Arriving in June 1777, he served with Gen. George Washington at Brandywine and was made a brigadier general by Congress and put in charge of the Continental cavalry. After service at Germantown and with the army at Valley Forge during the winter campaign of 1777–1778, differences with Gen. Anthony Wayne, under whom he refused to serve, led to his resigning his command, but he was soon given permission to organize a mixed corps of cavalry and light infantry, the Pulaski Legion, with which he waged guerrilla warfare against the British. None of his efforts were especially fruitful, however; he found himself once more mired in disputes with his fellow officers, and had it not been for his heroic death at the siege of Savannah in 1779 his American career would probably have been remembered, if at all, as a failure. Having joined the command of Gen. Benjamin Lincoln, at Savannah on October 9 he gallantly charged the British lines at the head of his cavalry, his sword waving and ribbons flying from his cap, but he was mortally wounded and died two days later, on October 11, 1779, on board the warship *Wasp* in Savannah Harbor.

Pulitzer, Joseph (1847–1911), editor and publisher. Born on April 10, 1847, in Makó, Hungary, Pulitzer was educated in Budapest and emigrated to Boston in 1864. He served in the Union army until 1865, then held various minor jobs until becoming a reporter in 1868 for the *St. Louis Westliche Post*, a German-language daily owned in part by Carl Schurz. He became active in politics, winning election to the Missouri legislature in 1869 in spite of the fact that he was short of the statutory age, and was a leading figure in the Liberal Republican movement. After the disastrous defeat of Horace Greeley's presidential campaign of 1872, in which he took a prominent part, he joined the Democratic party. In order to support his study of law, he earned money by purchasing the *Staats-Zeitung*, a defunct St. Louis newspaper, and selling its Associated Press (AP) subscription to the *St. Louis Daily Globe*. Admitted to the District of

Columbia bar in 1876, after two years of study, he nevertheless chose a career in journalism, purchasing the bankrupt *St. Louis Dispatch* in 1878, combining it with the *Post*, and becoming the sole owner of the *Post-Dispatch* by 1880. His editorial targets were soft money, high tariffs, and corrupt politicians. The paper was immediately successful, but a scandal involving its chief editorial writer turned the public against Pulitzer; profits declined and he sought other enterprises. In 1883 he purchased the *New York World* from Jay Gould and soon developed it into a successful and aggressive paper, espousing the Democratic party and the rights of the working class. In 1885 he made his last attempt at politics, winning election from New York to the House of Representatives; he served only a few months before resigning, however. In 1887 he founded the *New York Evening World* and later a Sunday edition was added. Failing eyesight forced him to abandon management of his newspapers in 1887 and in 1890 he gave up the editorship; he continued to exercise close watch on his papers' policies, however, and when a fierce competition began between the *World* and William Randolph Hearst's *New York Morning Journal*, involving outrageous sensationalism to which the term "yellow journalism" came to be applied, Pulitzer resumed direct control and went back to the original conservative and responsible format. At his death the *World* was noted for concise, intelligent, accurate reporting, political independence, and fearlessness in exposing corruption. In 1903 he announced that his will would provide for the endowment of the Columbia School (now Graduate School) of Journalism, opened in 1912, and the establishment of the Pulitzer Prizes, which have been awarded since 1917 for achievements in journalism, letters, and music. He died in Charleston, South Carolina, on October 29, 1911. At that time his eldest son, Joseph Pulitzer, Jr. (1885–1955), became publisher and editor of the *St. Louis Post-Dispatch*, holding the position until his death. The *World* and *Evening World* were sold to the Scripps-Howard chain in 1931.

Pullman, George Mortimer (1831–1897), inventor and industrialist. Born on March 3, 1831, in Brocton, New York, Pullman left school at fourteen to become a store clerk. In 1848 he was apprenticed to his brother, a cabinetmaker, and in the course of seven years undertook independent construction contracting work. He found such work more lucrative in Chicago and moved there in 1855. Working on streets and buildings, he accumulated enough capital to carry out his earlier ideas for building railroad cars with sleeping facilities. In 1858 he contracted with the Chicago & Alton Railroad to remodel two day coaches into sleeping cars, using his principle of hinging an upper berth to the sides of the car, and in 1859 he built a third car. Although passengers were delighted with the new accommodations, the railroads were reluctant to adopt them. He moved to Colorado in 1859 and ran a store for four years, in the meantime improving his design, ultimately developing plans for

the first Pullman car. In 1863 he returned to Chicago and applied for and received a patent on the folding upper berth and in 1865 on the lower berth, converted from a pair of facing seats used for nonsleeping accommodations, both inventions remaining unchanged in principle in today's cars. In 1865 the first Pullman car—The Pioneer—was introduced. Again public response was enthusiastic and this time several railroad companies ordered cars, despite their high cost and their large size, which necessitated adjustments in bridges and station platforms. In 1867 he organized and became president of the Pullman Palace Car Company, which grew to be the greatest railroad-car manufacturer in the world. In the same year the first combined sleeping and restaurant car was completed, followed by the first dining car in 1868, the first chair car in 1875, and the first vestibule car in 1887. He opened his first manufacturing plant in Palmyra, New York, then moved it to Detroit and added plants in St. Louis; Elmira, New York; Wilmington, Delaware; San Francisco; and Pullman, Illinois, the latter being a controversial town south of Chicago (from 1889 part of that city), built by the company for the accommodation of the factory and its employees. He was forced by the state to relinquish control of the town after the residents had voted for its merger with Chicago. In 1894 the Pullman workers went on strike and were soon joined by Eugene V. Debs's American Railway Union, which boycotted Pullman cars and tied up railroads across the nation. Besides the Pullman company, he owned the Eagle Wire Works in New York and was president of the Metropolitan Elevated Railroad in New York City. At his death in Chicago on October 19, 1897, he left $1 million for the founding of a free manual-training school in Pullman.

Pumpelly, Raphael (1837–1923), geologist and explorer. Born in Owego, New York, on September 8, 1837, Pumpelly, who was descended from a French Huguenot family that had originally spelled the name Pompilie, was about to enter Yale in 1854 when, on an impulse, he prevailed upon his mother to sail with him to Europe. There he spent two years traveling and learning languages, and after a four-month stay alone in Corsica, then very wild, during which his mother gave him up for lost, he entered the Royal School of Mines in Freiberg, Germany, from which he graduated in 1859. His first job was in Arizona, then Apache country, overseeing the development of silver mines; from there he went to Japan, in 1861, as a consulting geologist to the Japanese government. His stay was cut short in 1863 by political disturbances, but instead of coming home he journeyed up the Yangtze River in China and then made his way overland to St. Petersburg, Russia, studying especially coal deposits and the loess of China along the way and making the first extensive survey of the Gobi. He eventually published *Geological Researches in China, Mongolia, and Japan*, 1867, and *Relation of Secular Rock-Disintegration to Loess, Glacial Drift, and Rock*

Basins, 1879. Both were distinguished contributions to his field, as, indeed, were all of his writings. Returning to the United States after the Civil War, he was appointed the first professor of mining at Harvard in 1866, holding the post for seven years. From 1866 he spent ten years studying (and also investing in the development of) copper and iron deposits in the Lake Superior region; in both enterprises he was successful, laying the foundations of a fortune that became considerable and publishing two monographs on copper-bearing rocks of the Michigan peninsula in 1873 and 1878. State geologist of Michigan from 1869 to 1871 and of Missouri from 1871 to 1873, he resigned in 1873 and in 1875 moved to Boston, where he began a series of investigations of water pollution that were fully appreciated only in later years. In 1875 he was appointed to study the mineral resources of the United States for the 10th Census. Surveying work for Henry Villard on the route of the Northern Pacific railway occupied him from 1881 to 1884, whereupon he spent five years as head of the New England division of the U.S. Geological Survey, studying the geology of the Green Mountains and publishing a monograph on the subject in 1894. A consulting geologist, mainly in the Lake Superior region, from 1895 to 1902, he set out the next year—at the age of sixty-five—on the first of a series of expeditions to Central Asia sponsored by the Carnegie Institution of Washington, which resulted in two more important monographs, *Archaeological and Physico-Geographical Reconnaissance in Turkestan,* 1903, and *Ancient Anau and the Oasis World,* 1908. Pumpelly's *My Reminiscences* appeared in two volumes in 1918. His last years were spent in New England and at his home in Roseland, Georgia; he died in Newport, Rhode Island, on August 10, 1923.

Pupin, Michael Idvorsky (1858–1935), physicist and inventor. Born on October 4, 1858, in Idvor, the Banat region of Austria-Hungary (now in Yugoslavia), Pupin was the son of poor and illiterate parents who nonetheless encouraged him to seek an education. Having received his elementary schooling in his native town, in nearby Pančevo, and in Prague, he emigrated to the United States, landing in New York City in March 1874. For the next several years he worked at various jobs while devoting his spare time to mastering English and qualifying himself for college. In 1879 he entered Columbia, where he distinguished himself in mathematics; after graduation in 1883, the year in which he became a U.S. citizen, he continued his studies at Cambridge University and, as the first John Tyndall fellow, at the University of Berlin, where he studied under Herman von Helmholtz. He took his Ph.D. at Berlin in 1889 and the following year was appointed instructor in mathematical physics at Columbia. In 1892 he became adjunct professor of mechanics and in 1901 professor of electromechanics. Among his major achievements were his invention in 1894 of a system of multiplex telegraphy and later of an electrical resonator for determining the harmonic

structure of an alternating electrical current, and his thorough analysis of the wave pattern in a vibrating string. The latter work, applied by analogy to the behavior of electrical waves, led to his development of a system of spaced inductance coils that greatly increased the efficiency of long-distance telephony and that was quickly put into operation in the United States and in Europe. Soon after W. C. Roentgen announced his discovery of X rays in 1895, Pupin began experimenting with the new form of radiation and the next year, having constructed a machine with which he produced the first X-ray photograph in the United States, developed a method of greatly reducing the exposure time required for such a picture; he also discovered the phenomenon of secondary X-radiation. Later he worked on problems of radio transmission. Among his published works were *Thermodynamics of Reversible Cycles in Gases and Saturated Vapors,* 1894; *Electro-Magnetic Theory,* 1895; *The Serbian Orthodox Church,* 1918; *The New Reformation,* 1927; and *Romance of the Machine,* 1930. Pupin's autobiography, *From Immigrant to Inventor,* 1923, won a Pulitzer Prize, and his numerous inventions made him a wealthy man. He retired from Columbia in 1931 and died in New York City on March 12, 1935.

Purcell, Edward Mills (1912–   ), physicist. Born in Taylorville, Illinois, on August 30, 1912, Purcell received his B.S. from Purdue in 1933 and his M.A. in 1936 and his Ph.D. in 1938 from Harvard. An instructor at Harvard from 1938 to 1940, he worked on developing radar during World War II at the Radiation Laboratory of the Massachusetts Institute of Technology (MIT), returning to Harvard as an associate professor in 1946 and being promoted successively to full professor, 1949, Donner Professor of Science, 1958, and Gerhard Gade University Professor, 1960. While head of an advanced group studying radar problems at MIT he met Felix Bloch, who for some time had been working on nuclear magnetic resonance, and after the war Bloch returned to Stanford and Purcell to Harvard to continue their investigations independently. Employing a second magnetic field at right angles to the magnetic field of the atomic nucleus, Purcell was able to construct a complex but accurate measure of the precession frequency of protons in different substances, leading to a whole new field of physics: magnetic resonance spectroscopy. Bloch achieved similar results and their work led to their jointly receiving the 1952 Nobel Prize for Physics. The work yielded important information not only on nuclear magnetic moments but also on chemical bonds and atomic binding in liquids and solids. Purcell's investigation of nuclear magnetism was completed in 1949, whereupon, again building on his experience with radar during the war, he turned his attention to radio astronomy, in 1952 detecting (jointly with Harold I. Ewen) the 21-centimeter spectral line of neutral atomic hydrogen in the cosmos. This made possible the charting of the distribution of hydrogen in the universe, revealing hitherto invisible clouds of hydrogen within and between galaxies and laying the groundwork for the great expansion of radio astronomy in the following years. A member of many scientific societies, Purcell was also a member of the President's Science Advisory Committee from 1957 to 1960 and again from 1962.

Putnam, Herbert (1861–1955), librarian. Born in New York City on September 20, 1861, Putnam graduated from Harvard in 1883 and then studied law at Columbia, being admitted to the Minnesota bar in 1886 and later practicing law in Boston for a few years in the 1890s. His real career began, however, in Minneapolis, where he served as librarian of the Athenaeum from 1884 to 1887 and of the Minneapolis Public Library from 1887 to 1891. After moving to Boston in the latter year and spending four years in the practice of law, he served as librarian of the Boston Public Library from 1895 to 1899, in which year he was named Librarian of Congress, a post he held until his retirement in 1939. His long career in that position marked the transition of the institution, which was merely a reference collection for congressmen when he took it over, into the great national library, one of the world's best, that it is today. Besides showing a remarkable talent for library administration, Putnam also established many new methods and services, including the publishing of bibliographies and of the Library of Congress system of classification, the distribution of catalog cards, the establishment of an interlibrary loan service, the development of a photoduplication service, the publication seriatim of the National Union Catalog, and a book service for the blind. A member of many library and bibliographical boards and commissions, Putnam was president of the American Library Association (ALA) in 1898 and again in 1904. Librarian emeritus after 1939, Putnam died at his home in Woods Hole, Massachusetts, on August 14, 1955, in his ninety-fourth year.

Putnam, Israel (1718–1790), Revolutionary soldier. Born in Salem Village (now in Danvers), Massachusetts, on January 7, 1718, Putnam received little if any formal education as a youth—he was always close to illiterate—but instead learned in "the school of hard knocks," undergoing many harrowing experiences as a boy and young man that later led, when they were embellished by mythmakers, to his great reputation for self-reliance and bravery. It was said, for example, that he once entered the den of a wolf and captured it barehanded; the story may not be true, but it was typical of the tales that circulated about this rough-and-ready colonial soldier. Moving to Pomfret (now Brooklyn), Connecticut, about 1740, he soon became a prosperous farmer there. He volunteered for military service at the outbreak of the last of the French and Indian Wars and soon became one of Rogers' Rangers, seeing service at Ticonderoga in 1758. In the same year he was captured by Indians and was about to be burned alive—he was tied to a tree and the pyre was already built—when a French officer prevailed upon the Indians

to release him. He was promoted to major in 1758 and to lieutenant colonel the next year. In 1762 he joined an expedition to capture Havana, but his ship was wrecked off the Cuban coast and he was one of a handful who survived the wreck and the subsequent struggle to return to the mainland. After serving with the Connecticut forces at Detroit in Pontiac's Rebellion, 1763–1765, he settled down until the outbreak of the Revolution. In 1766 and 1767 he served in the legislature. In 1773 he joined an expedition that sailed through the West Indies and the Gulf of Mexico and explored the Mississippi River. In April 1775, as lieutenant colonel of the 11th Regiment of Connecticut militia, he was called into action at Lexington and Concord and, so the story goes, hastened from his plow to the battlefield without even changing his clothes. Named a brigadier general of Connecticut forces, he was one of the heroes of the battle of Bunker Hill, in June 1775, and soon thereafter was promoted to major general in the Continental army. But he was much less capable as a general officer than he had been as a ranger and scout and regimental commander, and his record during the Revolution was on the whole not one of success. He commanded in New York City for a while, was blamed for the Continental defeat in the battle of Long Island in 1776, was dilatory in responding to Gen. George Washington's orders in the campaign around Princeton in January 1777, and again disobeyed his commander while stationed in the Hudson Highlands in May of that year. The loss of forts Montgomery and Clinton to the British led to a court of inquiry in October 1777, which exonerated Putnam. During 1778–1779 he was engaged in recruiting duty in Connecticut and played other noncombat roles. Washington was greatly relieved when Putnam's military service was brought to an end by a paralytic stroke in December 1779. He nevertheless retained his wide reputation for military bravery. He died in Pomfret, Connecticut, on May 29, 1790.

Putnam, Rufus (1738–1824), soldier and Ohio pioneer. Born in Sutton, Massachusetts, on April 9, 1738, Putnam received scant formal education but studied various subjects on his own and at the age of sixteen was apprenticed to a millwright. In 1757 he enlisted for service in the last French and Indian War and remained in the army until 1760, seeing action around Lake Champlain. He took up farming near New Braintree, Massachusetts, in 1761 and moved to Brookfield four years later. In addition to farming he worked occasionally as a surveyor and as a millwright. In 1773 he was a member of a committee sent to inspect lands in Florida and along the Yazoo River granted by the Crown to veterans of the French and Indian War. Shortly after the battles of Lexington and Concord in 1775 he entered the Continental army as a lieutenant colonel, and during the first winter of the Revolution he organized the batteries on Dorchester Heights that forced the British to evacuate Boston. In 1776 he was engaged in the construction of fortifications around New York City and in August he was appointed by Congress chief engineer of the army, with the rank of colonel. Unable to win provision for a separate corps of engineers, he resigned and was promptly commissioned in the Massachusetts militia. He took command of the 5th Regiment, with which he served with distinction under Gen. Horatio Gates in the Saratoga Campaign. During 1778 he built new fortifications at West Point and in 1779 served under Gen. Anthony Wayne. In 1783 he was promoted to brigadier general. He had in 1780 bought a farm near Rutland, Massachusetts, and there he settled after the war, serving several terms in the legislature and taking part in putting down Shays's Rebellion. In 1785 he was appointed by Congress a surveyor of Western lands and out of that post grew his interest in the Ohio country. The next year, with Benjamin Tupper, Manasseh Cutler, and others, he formed in Boston the Ohio Company of Associates with the aim of obtaining a land grant in the Ohio country for settlement by Revolutionary veterans. Cutler took charge of negotiations with Congress and at length obtained the right for the company to purchase 1.5 million acres at a very low price. Putnam, appointed a director of the company and superintendent of its colonizing activities, set out in the spring of 1788 at the head of the first party of settlers. On April 7 he established the first settlement in the Northwest Territory, at present-day Marietta. In 1790 President George Washington appointed him a judge of the Northwest Territory and in 1792 he was commissioned a brigadier general in the regular army, in which capacity he concluded a treaty at Vincennes, Indiana, with eight Indian tribes of the region. He resigned his commission in 1793. In 1796 Washington named him surveyor general of the United States, but his work was less than satisfactory, owing to his deficiency in mathematics, and in 1803 he was dismissed by President Thomas Jefferson. In 1802 he was a member of the first Ohio constitutional convention. Putnam remained an influential figure in Ohio until his death in Marietta on May 4, 1824.

Pyle, Charles C. (1882?–1939), "Cash and Carry," promoter. The lack of formality exhibited in Pyle's business dealings, as indicated by his nickname, is paralleled by the paucity of information about his early years; it is a fair guess that he was born about 1882, but the place is not known. He was the manager of a movie theater in Urbana, Illinois, when he first came to national prominence by inducing the great University of Illinois football star, Harold "Red" Grange, to turn professional and join the Chicago Bears in 1925. Beginning with a much ballyhooed barnstorming tour of the nation in 1925, Grange is said to have earned more than a million dollars during the years that Pyle managed him, an enormously larger sum than that earned by any football player previously. Having succeeded with Grange, Pyle turned to tennis, and is thought to have been the one who induced such stars as Suzanne Lenglen, Vincent Richards, and

even William T. "Big Bill" Tilden to desert the amateur ranks, much to the consternation of the staid officials of American amateur tennis. Among the many sports events that were staged by Pyle was the "Bunion Derby" of 1928, in the course of which a number of famous athletes walked across the United States. A second transcontinental marathon the next year was a financial failure, with Pyle ending up on the wrong end of $50,000 in court judgments. He recouped with the "Believe It or Not" concession at the 1933–1934 Century of Progress Exposition in Chicago. He died in Los Angeles on February 3, 1939.

Pyle, Ernest Taylor (1900–1945), journalist. Born on August 3, 1900, near Dana, Indiana, Ernie Pyle studied journalism at Indiana University and in 1923 took a job with a local newspaper shortly before graduation. He served in many journalistic capacities in Washington and New York City, finally securing an assignment as aviation editor for the Scripps-Howard newspaper chain in 1928. From 1932 to 1935 he was managing editor of the Washington *Daily News*, but in 1935 he returned to the life of roving reporter. His daily experiences were recorded in a column that was enthusiastically received and eventually syndicated to nearly 200 newspapers. His columns attracted wide readership by their focus on and sympathy for the minor and often obscure figures behind the news. His sensitive reports of the bombing of London in 1940 prompted further World War II writing assignments, which led him on campaigns with U.S. troops into North Africa, Sicily, Italy, and France. His columns became immensely popular, in large part because of his comradeship with and understanding of the ordinary soldier in war. In 1944 he won a Pulitzer Prize for the stories he sent back home. Collections of his pieces were published as *Ernie Pyle in England*, 1941; *Here is Your War*, 1943; and *Brave Men*, 1944. During the Pacific campaign on the islands of Iwo Jima and Okinawa, he visited a neighboring island, Ie Shima. There on April 18, 1945, he was felled by enemy machinegun fire. He became a national hero, his last articles being published posthumously in *Last Chapter*, 1946. A collection of his prewar columns appeared in 1947 as *Home Country*.

Pyle, Howard (1853–1911), illustrator and author. Born on March 5, 1853, in Wilmington, Delaware, Pyle did not attend college but studied art with a private teacher in Philadelphia. Some years passed before he seriously undertook art as a career, but in 1876 he moved to New York City, pursued further study at the Art Students League, and by 1878 had begun contributing illustrations regularly to various magazines, particularly *Harper's Weekly* and other Harper publications. In 1880 he returned to Wilmington and was soon established as one of the country's leading illustrators. In 1883 he published *The Merry Adventures of Robin Hood*, an account of the outlaw's legend written and illustrated by himself; it was the first of a long series of highly popular children books, most of them dealing with medieval England or with pirates. Among them were *Pepper and Salt*, 1886; *Otto of the Silver Hand*, 1888; *Men of Iron*, 1892; *The Story of Jack Ballister's Fortunes*, 1894; *The Ruby of Kishmoor*, 1908; and, his best known works, a series of books on Arthurian legend, including *The Story of King Arthur and His Knights*, 1903; *The Story of the Champions of The Round Table*, 1905; and *The Story of Sir Lancelot and His Companions*, 1907. At the same time he provided illustrations for works by Woodrow Wilson, Henry Cabot Lodge, Oliver Wendell Holmes, and James Branch Cabell; his renderings of American historical subjects were particularly noteworthy. He taught classes in illustration at the Drexel Institute in Philadelphia from 1894 until 1900, when he established a free art school in Wilmington; among his many students there were Maxfield Parrish and N. C. Wyeth. Late in his life he turned to mural decoration and executed works for the Minnesota state capitol and other public buildings. In 1910 he decided to make a trip to Italy to study the old masters. Pyle died soon after in Florence on November 9, 1911.

Q

Quanah (1845?–1911), Indian leader. Born probably in north Texas about 1845, Quanah was the son of a Comanche chief and of Cynthia Ann Parker, a white captive who was recaptured in 1860 by the Texas Rangers and returned to civilization; in later life he adopted the name Quanah Parker. In his youth a bold fighter and leader, he was made chief of the Comanche in 1867 and for the next eight years led an alliance of Comanche, Kiowa, Apache, and Southern Cheyenne warriors in a series of raids on frontier settlements that culminated in 1874 in an attack on Adobe Walls, a fort on the South Canadian River in the Texas Panhandle. The Indians were defeated there but continued their resistance to white incursions until the next year, when all surrendered to the army authorities, Quanah being the last chief to do so. Somehow escaping the "accidental death" that was the fate of so many Indian warriors in captivity, he instead immediately set about learning the ways of the victors, became fluent in Spanish and fairly fluent in English, studied the agricultural methods employed by the whites in the arid Southwest, and soon had gained a reputation as a "white man's Indian." He was not only persuaded of the benefits of civilization himself, but also was widely successful in persuading his fellow Indians, especially after he managed to lease to cattlemen the surplus tribal pasturelands on his reservation for some $100,000 a year, greatly increasing tribal income. Believing that the only chance for survival of the Indians lay in education in the white man's way of life, he established Indian schools and saw to it that all of his own children were well educated. A shrewd businessman, he was said to be the wealthiest Indian in the country and for the last 25 years of his life was the general manager of almost all business dealings of the Comanche, Kiowa, and Apache tribes. He traveled widely and rode in the inaugural procession of president Theodore Roosevelt in 1905, seated next to Geronimo. He died in his large house near Fort Sill, Oklahoma, on February 23, 1911.

Quantrill, William Clarke (1837–1865), guerrilla leader. Born in Canal Dover (now Dover), Ohio, on July 31, 1837, Quantrill taught school briefly in Ohio, Indiana, and Illinois, but by the age of twenty he was determined to seek a more adventurous life. He went to Kansas in 1857 and filed a land claim, but farming did not suit his restless spirit and he joined an army provision train bound for Utah. At Fort Bridger and Salt Lake City during the next few years he was a professional gambler under the pseudonym of Charley Hart. He returned to Kansas in the fall of 1859 and although he taught school again that year, he was by that time a thoroughly bad character, living with Indians near Lawrence after the end of the school term, again under the name of Hart, and getting in trouble often and severely enough to be charged with horse stealing, theft, and murder. Posing as an abolitionist, he wormed his way into the confidence of a group of whites who were plotting to free some slaves in Missouri; but he then betrayed the whites to the slaves' owner, and three of the plotters were shot. His sympathies were with the South when the Civil War began, and as early as 1861 he was already the chief of a band of guerrilla fighters, only irregularly attached to the Confederate army, that raided communities in Kansas and Missouri, robbed mail coaches, and summarily executed supposed Union partisans. He was declared an outlaw by Union authorities in 1862 and a price was put upon his head. After he had aided the Confederates in the capture of Independence, Missouri, in August 1862, he, as captain, and his men were formally mustered into the Confederate service. His most notorious action occurred at Lawrence, Kansas, on August 21, 1863, when he rode into town at dawn at the head of some 450 men and sacked the place, killing some 180 men, women, and children and burning most of the buildings. On October 6 of the same year he defeated a Union detachment at Baxter Springs, Kansas, and afterwards executed all of his captives, including many noncombatants. In 1864 he lost control of his band, which broke up into several groups, and he went to Kentucky; on May 10, near Taylorsville, Kentucky, he was surprised by a Union force and captured after being severely wounded. He died in a Louisville, Kentucky, prison on June 6, 1865. His reputation of "the bloodiest man in American history" lived after him.

Quay, Matthew Stanley (1833–1904), political leader and public official. Born in Dillsburg, Pennsylvania, on September 30, 1833, Quay received a good classical education and delighted throughout his life in reading Horace and other Latin poets in the original and in discussing literature with friends in the infrequent intervals between political fights. He graduated in 1850 from Jefferson College (now part of Washington and Jefferson College) and thereafter studied law in Pittsburgh, being admitted to the bar upon his twenty-first birthday, in 1854. His first public office was that of prothonotary of Beaver County, but he soon found wider scope for his political talents, aiding Andrew G. Curtin in his successful bid for the Pennsylvania governorship in 1860. For the next several years he enjoyed Curtin's patronage and filled a number of state offices. At the same time Quay served effectively in the Union army during the Civil War, serving in various capacities, holding for a time the rank of colonel, and winning the Congressional Medal of Honor for his bravery at the battle of Fredericksburg in December 1862. For more than 20 years after his discharge in 1865 his field of battle was Pennsylvania Republican politics, and he acquitted himself there with consummate skill, winning almost every fight in which he was engaged and serving in the legislature, 1865–1867; as secretary of the commonwealth, 1872–1878 and again in 1879–1882 after a short stint as recorder of Philadelphia (an enormously lucrative office); and as state treasurer, 1885–1887. In 1887 he was elected by the legislature to the U.S. Senate, where he served for the rest of his life, with the exception of a short period in 1900, when the Senate voted him unqualified to occupy the seat to which the Pennsylvania legislature had failed to reelect him but to which the governor had appointed him to fill the vacancy. The state legislature at length broke the deadlock and reelected him. He was first named chairman of the Pennsylvania Republican committee in 1878 and thereafter, although he did not always possess the title, was the effective political boss of the state. A strong supporter of Benjamin Harrison for the presidency in 1888, he managed his victorious campaign as chairman of the Republican National Committee, but had broken with Harrison by 1892; his refusal to work for the Republicans in the 1892 campaign was probably the greatest single cause of their defeat by Grover Cleveland that year. It was owing largely to Quay that Theodore Roosevelt was nominated for the vice-presidency on the Republican ticket in 1900, and he supported Roosevelt after his accession to the presidency in 1901. Ranked as one of the great tactical politicians in U.S. history and possessing in his day a reputation for such mercilessness in political infighting that he was one of the most hated men of his time, he nevertheless was also known for his generosity to those in distress. He died in Beaver, Pennsylvania, on May 28, 1904.

Queen, Ellery, see Dannay, Frederic

Quincy, Josiah (1772–1864), public official and educator. Born on February 4, 1772, in the part of Braintree that later became Quincy, Massachusetts, the son of a prominent lawyer, known for his defense (with John Adams) of British soldiers accused of murder in the Boston Massacre of 1770, young Quincy graduated from Harvard in 1790. He was admitted to the bar in Boston in 1793 and began a career of politics, first in the state senate in 1804 and then as a Federalist member of the House of Representatives from Massachusetts in 1805. As minority leader, 1805–1813, he stressed free trade and open communication among nations and strongly opposed the Embargo Act of 1807. He shocked the country early in 1811 by declaring, in a speech opposing the admission of Louisiana to the Union, that the accession of new territory, if not unanimously agreed upon by the 13 original states, would invalidate and in effect dissolve the American union. His violent opposition to the country's involvement in the War of 1812, although manifesting party loyalty, was unpopular with his constituents, and he resigned from Congress in 1813. He returned home to devote himself to the affairs of Boston, serving also during the following decade in the state senate and the lower house. During 1821–1823 he was a municipal judge in Boston. He was elected mayor of Boston in 1823 and reelected five times. He was a great reformer and instituted many changes in municipal government. Defeated for reelection in 1828, he was named president of Harvard, in which post he served from 1829 to 1845. There, faced by a potent conservative element, he upheld the liberal traditions of the university, bringing the law school up to a professional level, building an observatory, and hiring outstanding faculty, including Henry Wadsworth Longfellow and Benjamin Pierce. However, his tenure was marked by student protests and riots, and he was burned in effigy in 1841. His works were voluminous; *The History of Harvard University,* two volumes, 1840, is perhaps the best known, but he also published *The History of the Boston Athenaeum,* 1851; *A Municipal History of the Town and City of Boston,* 1852; and *Memoir on the Life of John Quincy Adams,* 1858. Quincy spent the last 20 years of his long life in retirement, although after 1850 he wrote numerous political pamphlets in which he expressed his deep dislike (shared by other New England conservatives) of the West, of industrialism, and of democracy. But in his last public address, delivered at the age of ninety-one, he strongly supported President Abraham Lincoln and the Union that he had once attacked. Although he had been drummed out of the party in 1820, he called himself a Federalist until his death, in Boston, on July 1, 1864.

Quine, Willard Van Orman (1908–   ), philosopher. Born in Akron, Ohio, on June 25, 1908, Quine graduated summa cum laude from Oberlin College in 1930 and received his M.A. in 1931 and his Ph.D. in 1932 from Harvard. After study abroad he joined the philosophy department of Harvard in 1936; he remained there, after 1955 as Edgar Pierce Professor of Philosophy, for the rest of his academic career. He was a visiting professor at universities throughout the world, and a fellow of Balliol College, Oxford, 1953–1954. He served in the U.S. navy in World War II. He was a fellow of the Institute for Advanced Study in Princeton, New Jersey, in 1956–1957, and in 1958–1959 a fellow of the Center for Advanced Study in the Behavioral Sciences, Palo Alto, California. A contributor to many learned journals, he was also the author of a number of books, some of them quasipopular in nature, among them *A System of Logistic,* 1934; *Mathematical Logic,* 1940; *Elementary Logic,* 1941; *Methods of Logic,* 1950; *From a Logical Point of View,* 1953; *Word and Object,* 1960; *Set Theory and Its Logic,* 1963; *The Ways of Paradox,* 1966; and *Selected Logic Papers,* 1966. He was also the coauthor of studies of Alfred North Whitehead and Rudolf Carnap.

R

Rabi, Isidor Isaac (1898–   ), physicist. Born in Rymanów, Austria (now in Poland), on July 29, 1898, Rabi was brought to the United States in infancy. He received his B. Chem. from Cornell in 1919 and a Ph.D. from Columbia in 1927, whereupon he spent two years abroad, doing postgraduate work in Munich, Copenhagen, Hamburg, Leipzig, and Zurich. Until he went to Europe almost all of his work had been done in chemistry—he never formally studied physics, he once said, because that was the subject that most interested him, and he did not have to study it—although he had taught physics at the College of the City of New York (CCNY) from 1924 to 1927. In 1929, upon returning to the United States, he joined the Columbia physics department, where he remained, becoming a full professor in 1937, until 1964, when he became a university professor, without departmental responsibilities and able to teach whatever he pleased. His major contribution to physics was made in 1937, when he invented the atomic and molecular beam magnetic resonance method for observing spectra in the radio-frequency range. By this means the spectra of atoms and molecules could be observed and details of the mechanical and magnetic properties of atomic nuclei deduced. The development, subsequently by many other workers, of several different kinds of spectroscopic methods over a wide range of frequencies, depended greatly on his pioneering studies, for which he received the Nobel Prize for Physics in 1944. After 1940 he became deeply involved in the administration of research, serving from 1940 to 1945 as associate director of the Radiation Laboratory of the Massachusetts Institute of Technology (MIT), and after 1945 on many government commissions, including the general advisory committee of the Atomic Energy Commission (AEC), from 1952 to 1956. He was a delegate to the United Nations Educational, Scientific, and Cultural Organization (UNESCO) in 1950 and vice-president of the 1955 Geneva conference on the peaceful uses of atomic energy. In 1957 he was named chairman of the President's Science Advisory Committee, and in 1962 he became a member of the general advisory committee of the U.S. Arms Control Disarmament Agency. He was a visiting professor at many universities and institutions, received numerous honors and awards, and was involved to some degree with almost all of the advances in his field of atomic and nuclear physics in his time. He published an autobiography, *My Life and Times as a Physicist*, in 1960.

Rabinowitz, Jerome, see Robbins, Jerome

Radin, Paul (1883–1959), anthropologist. Born on April 2, 1883, in Lódz, Poland, Radin was brought to the United States as an infant and grew up in New York City. He graduated from the College of the City of New York (CCNY) in 1902 and, after studying in Munich and at the University of Berlin making studies of the culture of various South American Indian tribes, he received his Ph.D. in 1911 from Columbia, where James Harvey Robinson and Franz Boas were his teachers. From 1910 to 1912 he worked as an ethnologist for the Bureau of American Ethnology and after 1912 for the Geological Survey of Canada; he was also a visiting lecturer or professor at a number of universities, including California, Chicago, and Brandeis, as well as Kenyon College. His distinguished studies of the Winnebago Indians, whose language he knew better than any other white man, were summed up in a number of important books: *The Winnebago Tribe*, 1915–1916; *The Autobiography of a Winnebago Indian*, 1920 (republished as *Crashing Thunder*, 1926); and *Culture of the Winnebago as Described by Themselves*, 1949. In the last two books he employed autobiographical documents. A student not only of the Winnebago but also of a number of other peoples, he became especially interested in the Indians' religious beliefs and ceremonies. Several books resulted from his researches in this field, among them *Description and Significance of the Winnebago Medicine Dance*, 1909; *The Peyote Cult of the Winnebago*, 1913; and *Some Myths and Tales of the Ojibwa of Southeast Ontario*, 1913. More general analyses of Indian religion were contained in such works as *The Religion of the North American Indians*, 1914; *Literary Aspects of North American Mythology*, 1915; and—perhaps his most important book—*Primitive Religion*, 1937. Other works include *Primitive Man as a Philosopher*, 1927 (rev. ed., 1958); *Method and Theory of Ethnology*, 1933, a major work of theory and criticism; and *The World of Primitive Man*, 1953. Radin returned to some earlier themes in *The Road of Life and Death*, 1945. He died in New York City on February 21, 1959.

Radisson, Pierre Esprit (1636?–1710?), fur trader and explorer. Born probably in 1636 and probably in Paris, Radisson first came to Canada about 1651. In 1652 he was captured by the Iroquois while hunting near Three Rivers, Quebec, and spent some time with them, being apparently well treated and learning their language and ways. He escaped in 1653. In 1657, after one or two trips back to France, he joined his brother-in-law, Médard Chouart, Sieur des Groseilliers, on a colonizing and trading expedition to the Onondaga country; two years later the two men journeyed west and may have reached the upper Mississippi. It was about this time that Radisson and Groseilliers became aware—they were perhaps the first Europeans to do so—of the huge economic potential of the beaver-fur trade in inland North America. Their attempts, however, to exploit the fur trade for their own exclusive advantage were frustrated by the French authorities; their lack of a proper license, together with their refusal to share their profits with the governor of New France, led to the confiscation of all their furs and heavy fines for both of them. Thereupon they entered the English service, joining, as one report suggests, in the conquest of New Amsterdam and journeying before 1665 to Hudsons Bay. In 1665 they went to England, where their enthusiastic reports on the northern region led, in 1670, to the chartering of the Hudson's Bay Company. In 1668 Groseilliers built Fort Charles on the shore of James Bay and in 1670 he returned with Radisson to build another fort on the Nelson River. From 1674 to 1683 Radisson was back in the French service in Quebec and elsewhere, serving in raids on English posts in the West Indies, but in 1683, having married the daughter of an English knight, he rejoined the English. He probably spent most of his last years in the New World and died about 1710. Vigorous but confusing manuscript narratives of his experiences in the North were edited and published as *Voyages of Peter Esprit Radisson*, 1885.

Radnitz, Gerty, *see under* Cori, Carl Ferdinand

Rafinesque, Constantine Samuel (1783–1840), botanist. Born in a suburb of Constantinople, Turkey, on October 22, 1783, Rafinesque was of French and German parentage and grew up in France and Italy. Until 1814 he used the name Rafinesque-Schmaltz, the latter portion being his mother's maiden name. Educated largely by tutors, he evinced an early interest in languages and botany. In 1802 he came with his brother to the United States and settled in Philadelphia. Although he was employed in a countinghouse, he made many trips to the frontier in search of natural-history specimens; his botanical work came to the attention of Benjamin Rush and other American scientists as well as President Thomas Jefferson. He spent the years 1805–1815 in Palermo, Sicily, where he pursued business and scientific interests. While returning to the United States in 1815 he narrowly escaped death by drowning in a shipwreck off Fisher's Island in Long Island Sound that claimed his entire collection of specimens. Difficult times followed, but in 1819 he secured a position as professor of botany, materia medica, and modern languages at Transylvania University in Lexington, Kentucky. He continued to make collecting trips far afield during his tenure there, and established a botanical garden shortly before his departure for Philadelphia in 1826. A recognized if somewhat controversial botanist, he lec-

tured at the Franklin Institute and continued to travel widely in search of specimens. He published close to 1000 titles, the most important among his botanical works being *Autikon Botanikon*, 1815–1840; *Ichthyologia Ohioensis*, 1820; *Medical Flora of the United States*, two volumes, 1828–1830; *New Flora and Botany of North America*, in four parts, 1836–1838; and *American Manual of the Mulberry Trees*, 1839. He died in poverty in Philadelphia on September 18, 1840, having made a notable contribution to pre-Darwinian biology. He is chiefly remembered for his speculations concerning the origin of species, so similar to Darwin's later theory that he has been described as an unheralded genius.

Rainey, Henry Thomas (1860–1934), public official. Born near Carrollton, Illinois, on August 20, 1860, Rainey graduated from Amherst College in 1883. After taking a law degree in 1885 from Union College of Law in Chicago he returned to Amherst for an M.A. in 1886. He subsequently returned to Carrollton to practice law and until 1895 held minor political offices in Greene County. Increasingly active in the Democratic party after 1896, he was elected to the House of Representatives from Illinois in 1902, where he served, with one interruption (1921–1923) until his death. Rainey remained relatively inconspicuous in the Republican-controlled House until 1911. An able speaker, he early established a reputation as an expert on tariff measures and was actively involved in the preparation of the Underwood Tariff Act of 1913. A member of the Committee on Ways and Means after 1911, he served as its chairman during World War I and again in 1931–1933. Prominent among the members of the progressive wing of his party, he was a proponent of free silver and of tariff reform, and during the war, he was instrumental in the passage of war-revenue bills and he supported President Woodrow Wilson, who refused his request for assignment to military service. Democratic floor leader during 1931–1933, Rainey became speaker of the House after the Democratic sweep accompanying the election of Franklin D. Roosevelt to his first term as president in 1932. He served the Roosevelt administration well during 1933–1934 by securing the passage of numerous New Deal measures. He died in St. Louis, of complications following an attack of pneumonia, on August 19, 1934.

Rand, Ayn (1905–1982), author. Born in St. Petersburg, Russia (now Leningrad, U.S.S.R.), in 1905, Miss Rand graduated from the University of Leningrad in 1924, emigrated to the United States in 1926, married Frank O'Connor in 1929, and became a U.S. citizen in 1931. According to her own account, she decided to become an author at the age of nine and never changed her mind thereafter. But many years passed before she learned her craft to a degree satisfactory to her, and she did not sell any of her work—instead supporting herself by odd jobs—until the early 1930s, when she placed her first screen play. A screen writer from 1932 to 1934 and again from 1944 to 1949, she saw her first play, *The Night of January 16th*, produced in New York City in 1935, and she published her first book, *We, the Living*, the next year. From that date she wrote steadily and published often, *Anthem* appearing in 1938; *The Fountain-head* in 1943; *Atlas Shrugged* in 1957; *For the New Intellectual* in 1961; *The Virtue of Selfishness* in 1965; *Capitalism: The Unknown Ideal* in 1966; and *Introduction to Objectivist Epistemology* in 1967. Another play, *The Unconquered*, was produced in 1940, and from 1962 she was editor of *The Objectivist Newsletter*. From time to time, especially after 1960, she also lectured at various universities, among them Yale, Princeton, Columbia, and Harvard, and from 1961 she made regular appearances as a lecturer at the Ford Hall Forum in Boston. In all of her works, and especially her novels, she presented an earnest and persuasive defense of political conservatism, maintaining that enlightened self-interest is the ideal and attacking democratic selflessness and sacrifice for the common good. This doctrine was in the course of her work elaborated into a philosophical system to which she gave the name Objectivism. In her later years Miss Rand was a controversial figure in American intellectual life, but she retained a faithful audience of admirers and followers. She died on March 6, 1982, in New York City.

Rand, Sally (1904–1979), dancer. Born in Elkton, Missouri, on January 2, 1904, Miss Rand performed as an acrobatic dancer at carnivals and for a while in the Ringling Brothers–Barnum and Bailey circus while still in her teens. By the time she was twenty she was in Hollywood, where she appeared in a number of films, among them *The Dressmaker from Paris*, 1924; *Manbait*, 1926; *Getting Gertie's Garter*, 1927; and *King of Kings*, 1927, but never became a star. With the onset of the Depression of the 1930s she found herself stranded in Chicago and improvised a dance routine with fans that she performed in a speakeasy for $75 a week. Her great opportunity came with the opening in Chicago of the Century of Progress Exposition of 1933–1934. She tried to find a job but failed at first; however, after riding to the fair on a white horse, attired as Lady Godiva (more or less), she received star billing at the "Streets of Paris" concession on the Midway and is credited with having made the whole fair a financial success. Her act consisted of a slow dance, with ostrich plumes as her only costume, to the music of Debussy's *Clair de Lune*. Nudity, she conceded, was not new, but she insisted that she had made it financially successful with a new "sales" method: the difference between a mere performer and a star, she maintained, was merchandising. She continued to merchandise her act for more than 30 years, starring at the California Pacific International Exposition at San Diego in 1935–1936, San Francisco's Golden Gate International Exposition of 1939–1940, and at many other places and on many other occasions. In 1965 she

was the mistress of ceremonies of the hit Broadway review, *This Was Burlesque*, and she was still presenting her fan dance in the 1970s. She died on May 16, 1979, in New York City.

Randall, Samuel Jackson (1828–1890), public official. Born in Philadelphia on October 10, 1828, Randall attended University Academy in his native city. Soon established in the wholesale iron and coal business, he served on the city council (1852–1856) and in the state senate (1858) before he was elected to the House of Representatives as a Democrat from Pennsylvania in 1862. He repeatedly won reelection until his death. Randall's early career in the House was inconspicuous, but in early 1875 he achieved prominence, primarily as a result of filibusters against the Civil Rights Act of 1875 and the various Force Acts of the period. Later that year he also emerged in firm control of Pennsylvania's Democratic organization. Now a national figure, he was appointed chairman of the powerful House Appropriations Committee and late in 1876 was elected speaker of the House. During 1876–1877 he was involved in the bargaining that eventually awarded the disputed presidential election to Rutherford B. Hayes in return for the withdrawal of troops from the South. His tenure as speaker is remembered chiefly for his codification and condensation of the House rules. He was forced to relinquish the post of speaker after the Republican victory in 1880, and his support of a protective tariff, in opposition to a party majority, cost him the party leadership when the Democrats recaptured control of the House in 1882. He nonetheless remained powerful and influential as chairman of the appropriations committee. Although he had been an ardent supporter of President Grover Cleveland in 1884, his protectionism led in 1887 to a rift with the president that resulted in his loss of control over federal patronage in his state and ultimately over the Democratic party in Pennsylvania. His influence in Congress waned after 1888 and he died in Washington, D.C., on April 13, 1890.

Randolph, Asa Philip (1889–1979), labor leader. Born on April 15, 1889, in Crescent City, Florida, the son of a minister, A. Philip Randolph attended grade school and the Cookman Institute for Men in Jacksonville before traveling to New York City to gain a college education. He had worked as an attendant in his family's tailor shop, as errand boy for a grocer, and as a section hand on a railroad. In New York he held various minor jobs while studying political science, economics, and philosophy at the City College of New York (CCNY). While working as a waiter on a steamer of the Fall River Line, he organized a protest against the filthy living quarters of the crew and was fired and blackballed by other shipping lines. During the early years of World War I, when Negroes were physically beaten for participating in any movements toward unionization, he attempted to unionize shipyard workers in Virginia. In 1917 he organized a small local union of elevator operators in New York City. In the same year he was a founder of the *Messenger*, a magazine published to inform Negroes of their importance to war production and to encourage them to take advantage of it by demanding higher wages. After the war he addressed Negroes working in laundries, motion-picture theaters, and the garment industry, expressing his belief that unionization alone would create pride among black workers and bring about their equal treatment and recognition in industry. In 1925 he began his campaign to organize sleeping-car porters. Having discovered that dues collected from Negroes for a purported "benefit association" were actually paid to spies who were assigned to identify "union agitators," he waged a daring fight with the Pullman Company, through the *Messenger*, the press, public lectures and debates, and appearances before the Interstate Commerce Commission (ICC), the Federal Mediation Board, and several courts. Against all odds, and in the face of the porters' fear that supporting the movement would cause them to lose their jobs, he won recognition for the Brotherhood of Sleeping Car Porters, of which he served as president from 1925 until 1968, when he became president emeritus. In 1934 he secured an amendment to the Railroad Labor Act by which Negroes were included under its provisions. By 1937 the Brotherhood was strong enough to win long-overdue wage increases and other concessions from the Pullman Company. In 1941 Randolph threatened President Franklin D. Roosevelt with a march on Washington of 50,000 Negroes to protest unfair employment practices in war industries and the government. This, together with persistent lobbying, helped win establishment of the Fair Employment Practices Committee (FEPC). In 1942 he was awarded the Spingarn Medal by the National Association for the Advancement of Colored People (NAACP), He conferred in 1948 with President Harry S. Truman and stimulated the executive order of that year that desegregated the armed forces. In 1957 Randolph was named a vice-president of the recently merged AFL–CIO, and in 1960 he established a branch of the AFL–CIO, the Negro American Labor Council, to clarify Negro grievances for the larger organization. In 1963 he directed the 200,000–strong March on Washington to protest the lack of jobs and freedom, the largest of such demonstrations in the history of the United States. He died on May 16, 1979, in New York City.

Randolph, Edmund Jennings (1753–1813), public official and lawyer. Born near Williamsburg, Virginia, on August 10, 1753, Randolph (whose middle name was also spelled Jenings) came of a prominent colonial family. He was educated at the College of William and Mary and then took up the study of law under his father. At the outbreak of the Revolution in 1775 his family, Loyalists, returned to England while he became an aide-de-camp to Gen. George Washington. The next year he returned to Virginia to attend to the estate of a deceased uncle and was promptly elected to the

state constitutional convention; he was also elected mayor of Williamsburg and became attorney general under the new state government. He was sent to the Continental Congress in 1779, serving until 1782, and was elected governor of Virginia in 1786, the year in which he also led the Virginia delegation to the Annapolis Convention. He was sent the next year to the federal Constitutional Convention, where he proposed the Virginia Plan—also called the Randolph Plan and the "large state" plan—for the government of the states. He also served on the committee on detail, charged with writing the final draft of the Constitution. Considering the frame of government outlined in the final document to be insufficiently republican, he refused to sign his name to it; by the time of the Virginia ratifying convention in 1788, however, he had reconciled himself to it and joined James Madison in urging its adoption. When the new national government was organized, he was made the first attorney general; caught in the growing feud between Thomas Jefferson and Alexander Hamilton, he remained strictly neutral, and when at length Jefferson resigned in December 1793 Randolph succeeded him as secretary of state. Maintaining a middle course between the warring France and Great Britain, and at the same time between the Democratic Republicans and the Federalists, he was rewarded only with harsh criticism from both parties. He drafted the instructions for John Jay's mission to London; the resulting Jay's Treaty, 1794, demonstrated that his instructions had been ignored, and he was faced with the difficult task of mollifying both France and the Federalists. In neither case was he entirely successful. Before he left the cabinet, negotiations were begun with Spain that culminated in the treaty of San Lorenzo, or Pinckney's Treaty, guaranteeing, among other things, free use of the Mississippi to the United States. Charges of impropriety stemming from an intercepted message to the French government from its minister to the United States—in which it was hinted falsely that Randolph might be susceptible to bribery—led him to resign in August 1795. He returned to Virginia and became a leader of the bar in that state; his most notable case was the defense of Aaron Burr in his treason trial in 1807. He died at his home, Carter Hall, near Millwood, Clarke County, on September 12, 1813.

Randolph, John (1773–1833), "of Roanoke," public official. Born on June 2, 1773, at Cawsons, a plantation in Prince George County, Virginia, Randolph came of a prominent family and counted Pocahontas among his ancestors. He studied for brief periods at the College of New Jersey (now Princeton), Columbia, and the College of William and Mary, and for a time was tutored in law by his relative Edmund Randolph, then attorney general of the United States. Until 1799 he was a carefree young aristocrat; in that year, however, he was persuaded to run for the House of Representatives from Virginia and was elected. His rise to leadership was amazingly rapid, and at the opening of Congress in 1801 he was made chairman of the Committee on Ways and Means and thus became leader of the House Democratic Republicans. A brilliant orator, with a sharp and acerbic wit that often became biting sarcasm, Randolph was at the same time a master of parliamentary procedure. His Democratic Republicanism was never strictly regular and, although he supported the Louisiana Purchase, he eventually broke with the administration over the constitutional issues, in which he was a strict-constructionist, involved in President Thomas Jefferson's secret attempts to obtain Florida and in the Embargo Act of 1807. From his unsuccessful management of the impeachment trial of Supreme Court justice Samuel Chase in 1805 and his opposition to Jefferson's attempts to obtain West Florida from Spain, until the end of his long career, he was a political maverick, a "tertium quid," standing firmly on principle. About 1810, in order to distinguish himself from a distant and despised relation, he began to add "of Roanoke," after his Charlotte County plantation, to his name. An aristocrat and a strong defender of states' rights, he opposed all nationalizing legislation in Congress; his opposition to the War of 1812 lost him reelection in 1813, but he was back in the House two years later for the session in which he denounced the tariff enacted in 1816 and the chartering of the Second Bank of the United States. He declined reelection in 1817 because of poor health, but returned to the House in 1819 and remained for three more terms. In 1820 he roundly denounced the Missouri compromise as a cowardly surrender of principle by both North and South. From 1825 to 1827 he filled an unexpired term in the Senate and, defeated for reelection to that body by John Tyler, he returned to the House for a final term, from 1827 to 1829. During the 1820s Randolph, who had always tended to be erratic, became at times unstable almost to the point of insanity; his rhetoric remained brilliant, but he often drifted into irrelevance. In 1826, as a result of his intemperate comments on the election of 1824, he fought a duel with Henry Clay in which neither man was wounded. In 1829 he served prominently in the Virginia constitutional convention and the next year was appointed special minister to Russia by President Andrew Jackson. His health broke shortly after his arrival in St. Petersburg and he returned to Virginia in April 1831. He continued to decline mentally and physically until his death on May 24, 1833, in Philadelphia.

Rankin, Jeannette (1880–1973), suffragist and first woman member of Congress. Born near Missoula, Montana, on June 11, 1880, Miss Rankin graduated from the University of Montana in 1902. She subsequently attended the New York School of Philanthropy (later the New York, then the Columbia, School of Social Work) before embarking on a career of social work in Seattle in 1909. Caught up in the rising tide of sentiment for woman suffrage, she effectively campaigned on the West Coast on its behalf after 1910. In 1914 she became legislative secretary of the National American Woman Suffrage Association and in that same year led a successful campaign for woman suffrage in her native state. Two years later Montana voters elected her, as a Republican, to the House of Representatives, the first woman elected to that body. Continuing the suffrage fight in Congress, she also opposed U.S. entry into World War I in 1917, a stand that cost her the Republican nomination for the Senate in 1918 and a further bid as an independent for the same seat. She was active as a lobbyist and was also a social worker between 1918 and 1940, and then, running as an isolationist, she won another seat in Congress from Montana in 1940. On December 8, 1941, the day after the Japanese attack on Pearl Harbor, she created a furor by becoming the only legislator to vote against declaration of war on Japan. Declining to run for reelection in 1942, she retired from public life. She remained an ardent feminist and continued to lecture on social reform long before the beginning of the women's liberation movement of the early 1970s. In the 1960s she founded a cooperative homestead for women in Georgia. On January 15, 1968, at the age of eighty-seven, she led the Jeannette Rankin Brigade of 5000 women in a march on Capitol Hill to protest U.S. involvement in the Vietnam War. She died in Carmel, California, on May 18, 1973.

Ransom, John Crowe (1888–1974), poet and critic. Born on April 30, 1888, in Pulaski, Tennessee, Ransom graduated from Vanderbilt University in 1909 and was a Rhodes scholar at Oxford from 1910 until 1913. He taught English at Vanderbilt from 1914 to 1937, holding a professorship from 1927 to 1937. At Vanderbilt he gathered around him a remarkable group of colleagues and students, including Allen Tate, Robert Penn Warren, and Donald Davidson, with whom he published *The Fugitive*, a magazine of verse, from 1922 to 1925. This group, outspoken in their criticism of modern industrial society, also published a ringing manifesto on Jeffersonian agrarianism entitled *I'll Take My Stand*, 1930. Ransom left Vanderbilt in 1937, accepting an appointment as professor of poetry at Kenyon College. Two years later he founded the influential *Kenyon Review*, which he edited until 1958, when he retired. His typically sardonic criticism appeared in many periodicals and reviews and was collected in, among other books, *The World's Body*, 1938, and *The New Criticism*, 1941, the title of which gave its name to a school of criticism that emphasized close reading of poetic texts. *Poems About God*, his first book of verse, appeared in 1919, and was followed by *Chills and Fever*, 1924, *Two Gentlemen in Bonds*, 1926, and *Selected Poems*, 1945. A revised and enlarged edition of *Selected Poems* appeared in 1963. His total output was relatively small, but he was an important literary figure, not least because of the distinction achieved by a succession of his students at Vanderbilt and Kenyon. He died in Gambier, Ohio, on July 3, 1974.

Rauschenberg, Robert (1925–   ), painter. Born in Port Arthur, Texas, in 1925, the grandson of a German immigrant who had married a Cherokee Indian, Rauschenberg studied pharmacy at the University of Texas before World War II, but after serving in the navy during the war decided to become a painter. He entered the Kansas City Art Institute and then, in 1947, went to Paris, returning to the United States the next year to enter Black Mountain College, where he studied under Josef Albers. Further studies followed at the Art Students League in New York City in 1949 and 1950, a period when he came under the influence of such Abstract Expressionists as Robert Motherwell and Franz Kline. He enjoyed his first one-man show in New York City, at the Betty Parsons Gallery, in 1951, and then went to North Africa and Italy, where he made experiments with new artistic devices and produced his first constructions. Although not yet thirty, he had already stirred up controversy and even shock among art lovers; he expanded his reputation in 1958 when he produced what is considered the first Pop art painting—a semiabstraction with a hole into which he had inserted four Coca-Cola bottles. In the next few years Rauschenberg produced many works combining commercial objects—the detritus of urban civilization, as he allowed—with paint and canvas. He answered critics who thought these things ugly by saying that he was sorry for them, since these were the objects most commonly encountered in everyday life. From 1960, paintings and collages interested him more than constructions, his reputation became worldwide, and he became a major force in modern art. He won first prize at the Venice Biennale in 1964, only two other Americans, James McNeill Whistler and Mark Tobey, having done so, and he won first prize in the Corcoran Biennial of Contemporary Art the next year. At the same time he was a great financial success. However unpredictable, it seemed highly foreseeable that Rauschenberg would continue to suggest new departures in art.

Rauschenbusch, Walter (1861–1918), religious leader. Born on October 4, 1861, in Rochester, New York, Rauschenbusch was the son of an immigrant German minister. After schooling in Rochester he was sent to study in Germany, and in 1884, a year after his return, was granted a degree from the University of Rochester. Two years later he graduated from the Rochester Theological Seminary, was ordained, and assumed the pulpit of the Second German Baptist Church in New York City. The living conditions of the poor working-class people to whom he ministered made a deep impression on him, as did the writings of Leo Tolstoi, Karl Marx, Edward Bellamy, and Henry George, with whom he was acquainted. With two colleagues he founded the Society of Jesus—later renamed the Brotherhood of the Kingdom—and began in 1889 to publish *For the Right*, a Christian Socialist periodical that continued for a little more than a year. During 1891–1892 he was again in Europe studying, this time with an emphasis on economics and social problems, and he returned to New York in time to witness, and be reinforced in his developing Socialist beliefs by, the hardships of the economic depression beginning in 1893. In 1897 he left the pulpit to become a professor of New Testament exegesis at the Rochester Theological Seminary; in 1902 he became professor of church history, a position he retained until his death. His first book, *Christianity and the Social Crisis*, was published in 1907 and made him almost immediately a prominent national figure, the acknowledged leader of the Social Gospel movement that, though never organized, sought in various ways the amelioration of social problems through the workings of individual and social conscience and the establishment of a social order that Rauschenbusch called "the Kingdom of God." Subsequent books maintained and further developed this position: *Prayers for the Social Awakening*, 1910; *Christianizing the Social Order*, 1912; *The Social Principles of Jesus*, 1916; and *A Theology for the Social Gospel*, 1917. The outbreak of World War I was a profound shock to Rauschenbusch; before it ended he died, on July 25, 1918, in Rochester.

Ray, Man (1890–1976), painter and photographer. Born in Philadelphia on August 27, 1890, the son of Russian immigrants, Ray changed his name. He ended his formal education after high school because of his belief that he could study art better on his own. Frequent visits to Alfred Stieglitz's 291 Gallery in New York City introduced him while still in his teens not only to the artistic innovations and trends of the day but also to photography. From then until after World War I he continued to produce all sorts of experimental works, in many cases parodying and even anticipating "movements" of the time; but since his works did not sell, he also became a successful commercial photographer. He came to know Marcel Duchamp well during World War I, and partly because of him went to Paris in 1921; there he soon found himself at the center of the Dadaist and Surrealist movements in art. It was in 1922 that he discovered what he called his Rayograph process, in which he placed objects on photographic paper and then exposed the paper to light, creating the same "cameraless photographs" that are now imitated by children in many kindergartens. During the 1920s and 1930s he continued to work as a commercial photographer, making a series of photographs of the Parisian haut monde that were later highly valued. At the same time he continued to produce his strange, suggestive, surprising works—paintings, constructions, abstract photographs, films—which came to be greatly admired not only for their shock value and for their ironic commentary on the work of other artists, but also in their own right as genuine, memorable, and valuable works of art. Fleeing France in 1940 upon the outbreak of World War II, Ray spent the next decade in the United States, mostly in Los Angeles, and then returned to Paris in 1951. In the 1950s and 1960s he enjoyed a number of retrospective exhibitions that won much critical praise, but he persisted in feeling that critics were on the whole expendable, and he remained unpredictable and innovative. In 1963 he published *Self Portrait*, an autobiography. Ray died on November 18, 1976, in Paris.

Rayburn, Samuel Taliaferro (1882–1961), "Mr. Sam," public official. Born on January 6, 1882, in Roane County, Tennessee, of Scotch-Irish parents, Rayburn grew up on a farm in north Texas. He attended a one-room schoolhouse in Flag Springs, later traveling to Commerce to attend East Texas Normal School (now East Texas State University), from which he graduated in 1903. Having decided to enter politics, and with the stated ambition of one day becoming speaker of the House of Representatives, he studied law at the University of Texas and after being admitted to the bar in 1908 practiced law in Bonham, Texas. He was elected as a Democrat to the Texas house of representatives in 1907 and became speaker in 1911. The following year he was elected to the U.S. House of Representatives and was reelected 24 times, for a total service of 48 years and 8 months, a record. During 1931–1937 he helped mold much controversial New Deal legislation, including the Federal Securities Act of 1933, the Securities Exchange Act of 1934, and the Wheeler-Rayburn Holding-Company Act of 1935. His homespun demeanor and remarkable aptitude advanced him in the House; elected Democratic leader in 1937, he became speaker of the House three years later and retained the post until his death except for two periods, 1947–1949 and 1953–1955, when a Republican majority organized the House and he served instead as minority leader. His total of 17 years as speaker also set a record. Firmly devoted to his party and his country, "Mr. Sam" proclaimed himself to be a Democrat "without prefix, without suffix, and without apology." In the belief that he was no orator, he made few political speeches, but he won members of both parties to his policies through personal contacts. He was considered one of the most powerful speakers of the House in the history of the country, and he was a master of the legislative process. His patriotism and honesty made him a trusted adviser beyond the bounds of party; his confidants included presidents Franklin D. Roosevelt, Harry S. Truman, Dwight D. Eisenhower, and John F. Kennedy. He died in Bonham, Texas, on November 16, 1961.

Raymond, Henry Jarvis (1820–1869), newspaper editor and public official. Born near Lima, New York, on January 24, 1820, Raymond graduated from the University of Vermont in 1840 and taught briefly before taking up journalism as a career in New York City. He was employed by Horace Greeley on the old *New Yorker* and accompanied him when Greeley founded the *New York Tribune* in 1841. He also worked on the *Morning Courier and New York Enquirer*. As his reputation

as a competent newspaperman grew he began to formulate plans for a paper of his own. Short of funds, he bided his time and entered politics as a Whig. He was elected to the New York assembly in 1849 and became speaker in 1851, a post he again filled in 1862. Meanwhile, with George Jones as business manager and Raymond as editor and chief proprietor, the *New York Daily Times* (the *New York Times* after 1857) was launched on September 18, 1851. The paper strove for a bipartisanship that was uncharacteristic of the journalism of the time; deliberately passionless in reporting the news, it proved an immediate success. Raymond remained active in state politics, supporting the antislavery segment of the Whig party. Thurlow Weed's choice of Raymond over Greeley for lieutenant governor and Raymond's election in 1854 left Greeley bitter, and eventually led to the dissolution of the famous political alliance of William H. Seward, Weed, and Greeley. As the Whigs began to disintegrate, Raymond took a leading part in the formation of the Republican party, drafting its statement of principles at the Republican national convention in Pittsburgh in 1856. At the 1860 convention he initially supported Seward, while Greeley backed Abraham Lincoln. Upon Lincoln's nomination he threw the weight of the *Times* behind the Republicans, and he supported Lincoln strongly throughout the Civil War. In 1861 he was again elected to the state legislature, and the next year was again chosen speaker. In 1864 he figured prominently in shaping the Republican platform and himself won a seat in the House of Representatives from New York. Highly touted as a talented freshman congressman, he proved to be inexperienced and ineffectual against the Radical Republicans, whom he opposed. With the Radicals gaining strength by 1866, his political influence waned and he was expelled from the Republican National Committee, of which he had been appointed chairman in 1864. He retired from public life in 1867 to devote himself to the *Times*, in the pages of which he wrote vigorously in favor of civil-service reform, sound money, and tariff reduction, and played a major role in the campaign against the Tweed Ring. He died in New York City on June 18, 1869, having notably elevated the style and tone of newspapers in his day and having exerted a lasting influence on the editorial policy of the *New York Times*.

Read, George (1733–1798), Revolutionary patriot and public official. Born on September 18, 1733, in Cecil County, Maryland, Read grew up in New Castle, Delaware. He attended school in Pennsylvania, studied law privately in Philadelphia, and in 1754 began to practice in New Castle. A respected lawyer, he was appointed attorney general of the Lower Counties of Delaware in 1763, a post he held for 11 years. Outspoken against the Stamp Act in 1765, he was elected to the provincial assembly that year and later to the First Continental Congress. A moderate in the Second Continental Congress, he did not vote for the Declaration of Independence in 1776 but signed it after its adoption. He subsequently remained a prominent figure in Delaware politics. Presiding officer of the state constitutional convention in 1776, he became first speaker of the legislative council and, as such, was thrust into the chief executive office of Delaware after the state president became a prisoner of the British in 1777. He resigned the post of acting president in March 1778, returning to the council. In 1779 he urged acceptance in Delaware of the Articles of Confederation and in 1782 accepted election as a judge of the court of appeals in admiralty cases. A staunch supporter of the movement for a new federal constitution, he was a member of the Annapolis Convention in 1786 and headed the Delaware delegation to the federal Constitutional Convention in May 1787. He was instrumental in the rapid ratification of the new Constitution by Delaware, the first state to act upon it. Read was elected one of Delaware's first two senators in 1788, to serve for two years. Reelected in 1790, he resigned his seat in 1793 to become the chief justice of Delaware. He remained in that post until his death in New Castle on September 21, 1798.

Read, Opie Percival (1852–1939), author. Born in Nashville, Tennessee, on December 22, 1852, Read embarked on a career in journalism after attending Neophegen College in nearby Gallatin. At twenty-six he secured a post as city editor of the *Daily Arkansas Gazette* in Little Rock, but left after three years for a job with the *Cleveland Leader*. Aided by his brother-in-law, he returned to Little Rock in 1882 to launch the *Arkansaw Traveler*, a humorous weekly to which he contributed satirical sketches. Read was a born storyteller, and the magazine was a success; in 1887 he moved it to Chicago. Popular approval of his first novel, *Len Gansett*, 1888, led him to give up the journal, and after 1891 he devoted himself to writing fiction and lecturing. For the next 15 years he wrote about two books a year and lectured extensively. His *The Jucklins*, 1896, reportedly sold more than a million copies. Other popular titles included *A Kentucky Colonel*, 1890; *My Young Master*, 1896, a novel of the Civil War; *In the Alamo*, 1900; *The Starbucks*, 1902; and *An American in New York*, 1905. He died in Chicago on November 2, 1939.

Reagan, Ronald Wilson (1911–   ), fortieth president of the United States. Born in Tampico, Illinois, on February 6, 1911, Reagan grew up in a succession of towns in rural northern Illinois, finally settling in Dixon when he was nine. After graduating from Eureka College in 1932, Reagan worked as a sports announcer for radio stations in the Midwest. Discovered by a Hollywood agent, he was signed by Warner Brothers as a contract movie actor. He made his film debut in *Love Is On the Air*, 1937. Although many of his films were undistinguished, notable exceptions were *Brother Rat*, 1938; *Dark Victory*, 1939; *Kings Row*, 1941; and especially *Knute Rockne—All American*, 1940, in which he played the football hero George Gipp. During World War II he made

air force training films. Returning to Hollywood after the war, he made such films as *The Voice of the Turtle*, 1948; *Bedtime for Bonzo*, 1951; *Cattle Queen of Montana*, 1954; and *Hellcats of the Navy*, 1957. In all he made 52 theatrical features. From 1952 to 1962 he was employed by the General Electric Company, and he hosted and occasionally performed on the "General Electric Theater," a weekly television series. Afterwards he performed the same chores for the series "Death Valley Days" for three seasons. While he was associated with G.E., Reagan gradually evolved from a liberal to a conservative, and in 1962 he switched from the Democratic to the Republican party. His first active participation in politics was the Goldwater presidential candidacy in 1964. With Goldwater's defeat, he thenceforward assumed leadership of Republican conservatism. Two years later he successfully ran for the California governorship and served two terms. The first term agenda included a freeze in state hiring and consequent restraining of the growth of the state bureaucracy, the increasing of taxes to eliminate the state deficit, and a reduction of social services. The second term was marked by a welfare reform act that reduced the case load but increased the payments to families with dependent children. In 1976 he made his first serious bid for the U.S. presidency, losing the Republican nomination to Gerald Ford by a narrow margin. In 1980 he handily won his party's nomination and went on to defeat decisively the Democratic incumbent, Jimmy Carter. Reagan's first term was marked by substantial tax cuts, reduced spending for domestic programs, and major increases in military expenditures. His economic policies were credited with reducing the rate of inflation.

Red Cloud (1822–1909), Indian leader. Born in north-central Nebraska in 1822, Mahpiua Luta, or Red Cloud, grew to be an outstanding warrior and chief of the Bad Face band of Oglala Sioux and by 1860 had become a chief of the whole Oglala nation. He was one of the most awesome Indian warriors that the white men ever faced; in fact, it can be said of Red Cloud that he was the one chief who won a war with the United States. More correctly, perhaps, he won a series of battles, for in the long run he, like all Indians, lost, and his lands were overrun. He spent the decade of the 1860s defending the Powder River country from white invaders and his resistance made useless the army's Powder River Road, over the route of the Bozeman Trail, for several years. In June 1865 U.S. officials were sent to Fort Laramie to negotiate a treaty with the Sioux and Cheyenne leaders for the construction of forts and the opening of an emigrant route through Nebraska and Wyoming into Montana. When the Indians learned that a large military party with supply wagons had already started for the territory before any treaty could be negotiated, they followed Red Cloud's leadership and left Laramie to begin an unremitting guerrilla warfare against whites who passed over the proposed route. Red Cloud's War went on until 1868, and during it the Oglala chief led raids that included the well-known Fetterman Massacre on December 21, 1866, near Fort Phil Kearny, Nebraska, and the standoff Wagon Box Fight on August 2, 1867. The resistance of Red Cloud and his followers to the presence of forts Phil Kearny, C. F. Smith, and Reno was effective; the government agreed to abandon the Bozeman Trail during the negotiating of the Treaty of Fort Laramie in November 1868. Red Cloud held back from signing the treaty until 1869, after the garrisons had been withdrawn and the forts burned. He then agreed to lay down his arms and live at the Red Cloud Agency in Nebraska. He became an advocate of peace with the whites and frequently traveled East to visit Washington, D.C., and speak to white audiences in other cities. He took no part in the hostilities of the 1870s that culminated in Col. George A. Custer's defeat at the Little Bighorn and the eventual conquest of the Sioux. Belligerent leadership in that decade fell to others, such as Crazy Horse and Sitting Bull, as Red Cloud's prestige among his people declined. In 1878 he and his people moved to the Pine Ridge Agency in South Dakota, where he died on December 10, 1909.

Redfield, Robert (1897–1958), anthropologist and sociologist. Born in Chicago on December 4, 1897, Redfield was associated with the University of Chicago throughout much of his life. He received his Ph.B. from the institution in 1920, his J.D. in 1921, and his Ph.D. in 1928. He was married to Margaret Park, the daughter of sociologist Robert Park, in 1920 and thereafter did much of his field research in association with her. A visit to Mexico in the early 1920s first interested him in anthropology, and his 1928 doctoral dissertation, published as *Tepotzlan*, 1930, gained recognition as a pioneer study of a "folk" community. He thereafter spent much of his time in Yucatán doing field work on peasant communities and showing how, when they developed into more organized and urban communities, there was a progressive social disorganization of what he called the "moral order," for which formal, legalistic institutions had to be substituted. Combining the contributions of sociologists who studied primitive and folk societies, Redfield was able to present a coherent analysis of social change, particularly the social change forced or influenced by outside contacts, and he evolved a complementary theory of the interaction of a "great tradition" (urban) and a "little tradition" (rural or peasant) in stable societies. One of the leading figures at the University of Chicago during the 1930s and 1940s, Redfield became highly influential in his field through his studies not only of South and Central Americans and Chinese and Indian cultures, but also through his writings on U.S. society. Among his other works were *Chan Kom*, 1934; *The Folk Culture of Yucatan*, 1941; *A Village That Chose Progress*, 1950; *The Primitive World and Its Transformations*, 1953; *The Little Community*, 1955; and *Peasant Society and Culture*, 1956. He died in Chicago on October 16, 1958. His *Papers*

were edited by his wife and issued in two volumes in 1962–1963.

Red Jacket (1756?–1830), Indian leader. Born about 1756 in upper New York State, at or near Canoga, Seneca County, Red Jacket, whose real name was Otetiani, changed to Sagoyewatha on his elevation to chief, was a member of the Seneca tribe of the Iroquois federation. At the time of the American Revolution he, along with other Seneca warriors, fought for the British against the colonies. But once the war was over he became an advocate of peace with the new American nation. Having fought against the Americans, the Iroquois federation found itself at a disadvantage, but so long as the new nation was militarily weak and the British still occupied posts in the trans-Appalachian region, the tribes of New York had to be dealt with carefully. By the late 1780s Red Jacket had become one of the Seneca chiefs and, by virtue of his oratory and political skill, a forceful leader among his people. Although remaining a staunch advocate of peace with the Americans, he was a vehement opponent of white civilization, particularly of Christian missions among the Indians, a position he modified somewhat during a visit to George Washington in 1792. Before that, however, he also fought, unsuccessfully in the long run, to keep white settlers away from Indian lands, and strove for cooperation among the various tribes to halt land sales to whites and other actions that aided encroachment. But he would not cooperate with the Indians of the Ohio Valley who attempted, during the War of 1812, to fight off white domination. In fact, during the war, Red Jacket joined U.S. forces in battles against the British in northwestern New York. By 1815 he was the most powerful spokesman for the Seneca. His one great problem, however, was intemperance, and this, along with the growing influence of Christianity among the Indians, gradually subverted his leadership. In 1827 he was deposed as chief, and although he was later restored, he never regained his influence. He died at his Seneca village on land that was later part of Buffalo, New York, on January 20, 1830.

Reed, John (1887–1920), journalist and political radical. Born in Portland, Oregon, on October 22, 1887, Reed belonged to a wealthy family of considerable social standing, and after completing his secondary education in Portland had a successful career at Harvard, graduating in 1910. The next year he joined the staff of the *American Magazine*, in which he published poems that were highly regarded at the time. He met Lincoln Steffens and Ida M. Tarbell in the course of his journalistic work and was drawn by them to an interest in social problems; but he quickly went beyond them and, in 1913, joined the staff of the radical magazine, the *Masses*. The first of his many arrests occurred in 1914 when he attempted to speak in behalf of some strikers in the silk mills in Paterson, New Jersey. In the same year he was sent by the *Metropolitan* magazine to Mexico to report on Francisco ("Pancho") Villa's revolution; four months spent with Villa's army resulted in a series of brilliant articles that brought him a national reputation as a left-wing writer, and the articles were reprinted as *Insurgent Mexico*, 1914. When World War I broke out in Europe, *Metropolitan* sent him to Germany, and articles recounting his experiences on the Eastern Front with the German, Serbian, Bulgarian, Romanian, and Russian armies were collected in *The War in Eastern Europe*, 1916. He returned to the United States for an operation, married, and left again in August 1917, to arrive in Russia in time to observe the October Revolution in Petrograd (now Leningrad). An enthusiastic supporter of the Bolsheviks, he became a close friend of V. I. Lenin, wrote much of the Bolshevist propaganda intended for the Germans, and wired articles and reports to the *Masses* that led to an indictment of himself, Max Eastman, and others connected with the magazine for sedition. He returned to the United States to help in the defense, was acquitted in two successive trials, but was arrested several times for making "incendiary" speeches, and published, in 1919, the book by which he is best known—*Ten Days That Shook the World*, an account of events in Russia in 1917. Others of his books included *Sangar*, 1912, a privately printed volume of verse; *The Day in Bohemia*, 1913, a similar volume; *Tamburlaine and Other Poems*, 1916; and *Red Russia*, 1919. A member of the left wing of the Socialist party, he was expelled from the party for his radical views in August 1919, whereupon he helped to found the Communist Labor party (as distinguished from the Communist party, which in fact was bitterly opposed to his faction). He headed the party, wrote its statements of policy, and edited its journal, *Voice of Labor*. The "Red Scare" of 1919–1920 was by now in full swing, and he was indicted for sedition. By means of a forged passport he made his way to Finland, where he was imprisoned, but he managed to reach Russia, where he was making speeches at the same time that a nationwide search for him was going on in the United States. He died in Moscow on October 17, 1920.

Reed, Stanley Forman (1884–1980), justice of the Supreme Court. Born on December 31, 1884, in Maysville, Kentucky, Reed attended Kentucky Wesleyan College, where he took a B.A. in 1902. He subsequently studied law at the University of Virginia, at Columbia University, and at the Sorbonne in Paris. Admitted to the Kentucky bar in 1910, he practiced at Maysville, was a member of the Kentucky legislature from 1912 to 1916, and served as a lieutenant in army intelligence during World War I. He went to Washington after his appointment by President Herbert Hoover as general counsel for the Federal Farm Board in 1929. Impressed with his abilities, Franklin D. Roosevelt retained him as general counsel for the Reconstruction Finance Corporation (RFC) in 1932. He provided unspectacular but important legal counsel during the formulation of early New Deal measures designed to meet the national financial crises, and in 1935 he was rewarded with an appointment as U.S. solicitor general. He thus became responsible for presenting the government's arguments to the Supreme Court in cases testing the constitutionality of the economic powers extended to the government by the National Industrial Recovery Act (NIRA), the National Labor Relations Act, and the legislation creating the Tennessee Valley Authority (TVA). He compiled a creditable record, winning most of his cases. He became a logical choice to fill the vacancy on the Supreme Court created by the retirement of George Sutherland and was quickly confirmed. Reed served as an associate justice from January 1938 to February 1957, retiring at the age of seventy-two. Often called upon to cast the tie-breaking vote in split decisions, he usually sided with what was then a liberal majority on the Court. After his retirement he was called upon occasionally to sit on the U.S. Court of Claims. Reed died on April 3, 1980, in Huntington, New York.

Reed, Thomas Brackett (1839–1902), public official. Born in Portland, Maine, on October 18, 1839, Reed graduated from Bowdoin College in 1860 and took up the study of law. In 1861 he went to California and was there admitted to the bar two years later; he returned to Portland and was admitted to the Maine bar in 1865. He quickly entered politics. He was elected as a Republican to the state house of representatives in 1867 and 1868 and to the senate in 1869; from 1870 to 1873 he was state attorney general and in 1876 he was elected to the House of Representatives, where he served until 1899. In 1882 he was appointed to the Committee on Rules and was soon the acknowledged leader of the House Republicans. He began a long campaign for reform of House procedural rules as a member of the minority, and not until the Republican victory of 1888 was he able to succeed. The next year he was chosen speaker of the House and, with fellow representatives William McKinley and Joseph Cannon, devised a new set of rules for the more expeditious handling of business: the most significant changes were the redefinition of a quorum in terms of members present rather than members voting, and the grant to the speaker of discretionary powers in refusing to hear dilatory motions. He introduced the changes suddenly, assuming and wielding powers of his position so vigorously as to earn the title "Czar" Reed from opponents. After a little more than two weeks in use, the "Reed Rules" were formally adopted on February 14, 1890. Expedited by the rules, there followed a flood of Republican legislation, including the McKinley Tariff Act, 1890, that brought the Democrats back into power in that year's election. After a brief period under the old regime, the Reed Rules were again adopted with Reed's resumption in 1895 of the speakership, a post he held until his resignation from Congress in 1899. He died on December 7, 1902, in Washington, D.C.

Reed, Walter (1851–1902), physician. Born on September 13, 1851, in Gloucester County, Virginia, Reed was educated at the University of Virginia, where he was granted an M.D., and at Bellevue Hospital Medical College in New York City, where he received a second M.D. After working for several years for the boards of health of New York City and Brooklyn, he gained a commission in the Army Medical Corps in 1875. For more than 20 years he served as an army surgeon in New York, Arizona, and Baltimore and as professor of bacteriology and clinical microscopy at the Army Medical College and as curator of the Army Medical Museum, both in Washington, D.C. In 1890, while stationed temporarily in Baltimore, he undertook postgraduate study in clinical medicine and bacteriology at The Johns Hopkins Medical School. In 1898 he headed a committee directed to investigate an outbreak of typhoid fever in army camps; the commission's report contributed significantly to understanding the modes of infection and thus the means of control of the disease. The following year he and an associate published the results of their investigation of yellow fever; they had demonstrated the falsity of the belief, then widely accepted, that the disease agent was a specific bacillus. In 1900, when yellow fever broke out among U.S. troops in Cuba, he was sent to head the army's Yellow Fever Commission to do research into the cause and means of transmission of the disease. The idea that a particular species of mosquito served as the exclusive carrier of yellow fever had been proposed some time previously; Reed's observations led him to consider this possibility. In a long series of carefully controlled experiments with human subjects he demonstrated that yellow fever was spread only by the *Aëdes aegypti* mosquito (then known as *Stegomyia fasciata*), and only under certain conditions. The researches were complete by February 1901; several co-workers had died of yellow fever during the course of the investigations, but the disease could now be completely controlled. A program to wipe out the mosquito was instituted by army sanitary engineers under Maj. William C. Gorgas and had spectacular results: in 1900 there had been 1400 reported cases of yellow fever in Havana alone, but by 1902 there were none in all of Cuba. Dr. Reed returned to Washington, D.C., in 1901 to resume his teaching position and there died suddenly of appendicitis on November 23, 1902. The great army hospital and medical center in Washington, D.C., was later named in his honor. He was elected to the Hall of Fame in 1945.

Reeve, Tapping (1744–1823), lawyer, judge, and educator. Born in Brookhaven, Long Island, New York, in October 1744, Reeve graduated from the College of New Jersey (now Princeton) in 1763. He subsequently taught school and returned for a while to his alma mater as a tutor. He then turned to law, studying privately in Hartford, Connecticut, and on his admission to the bar in 1772 opening a practice in nearby Litchfield. He soon gained prominence in his profession and to supplement his income during the Revolution began to teach law informally in his office. Reeve is chiefly remembered for the law school that he launched formally in 1784. Preceded in the United States only by the department of law at the College of William and Mary, the Litchfield Law school soon outdistanced its rival to become the leading institution of its kind in the new nation. Attracting students from virtually every state, it graduated such later noteworthy political figures as John C. Calhoun and Horace Mann as well as other prominent men. Initially Reeve was the sole administrator and teacher. Appointed judge of the Connecticut superior court in 1798, he enlisted the aid of a graduate of his school, James Gould, to whom much of the credit for the school's continued prominence belongs. Reeve was a strong Federalist and remained politically active through much of his career on the bench. He was made chief justice of the Connecticut supreme court of errors in 1814, at the age of sixty-nine, but served only briefly. He retired from public life in 1816, the same year in which he published his successful *The Law of Baron and Femme; of Parent and Child; of Guardian and Ward; of Master and Servant....* Another work, *A Treatise on the Law of Descents*, concerning which he was an expert, appeared posthumously in 1825. He withdrew completely from the affairs of the law school in 1820; it continued to operate under Gould until 1833. Reeve died in Litchfield, Connecticut, on December 13, 1823.

Rehan, Ada (1857–1916), actress. Born on April 22, 1857, in Limerick, Ireland, Ada Crehan grew up in Brooklyn, New York, where her family settled shortly after the Civil War. She followed her older sisters to the stage, making her debut in *Across the Continent* at the age of thirteen, in Newark, New Jersey. Mistakenly billed as Rehan for her first appearance at Louisa Lane Drew's Arch Street Theatre in Philadelphia, she thereafter retained the misspelling as her stage name. She continued her apprenticeship in stock companies, playing in Louisville, Albany, and Baltimore, then invited to join the company of Augustin Daly, she made her debut in New York City in *L'Assomoir* in May 1879. Later that year Daly opened his Daly's Theatre in New York and Miss Rehan shortly became the company's leading lady, playing often opposite John Drew. Her repertory with the Daly company, which lasted until Daly's death in 1899, included plays by Shakespeare as well as several European comedies adapted by Daly for the American stage. She was already a star when she first appeared to general acclaim in London in 1884; her reception in Paris and other European capitals was equally enthusiastic. Her greatest role, first played in New York City in 1887, was Katherine in *The Taming of the Shrew*; other well received roles were those of Rosalind, Beatrice, Viola, and Portia. In 1893 she became a partner in Daly's London theater and there, in addition to successes in Shakespearean parts, she met with favor in *The School for*

Scandal. She appeared in San Francisco in 1896 as part of an American tour of that year, but she frequently returned to London during her last years on the stage. Her career effectively came to a close at the death of Daly in Paris. Increasingly criticized as artificial, her revivals of her basic repertory after 1900 seemed dated and unglamorous and she gave her final performance in New York City in 1905. She had prospered as an actress, however, and she subsequently lived in comfortable circumstances in England and the United States until her death in New York City on January 8, 1916.

Rehnquist, William Hubbs (1924–   ), justice of the Supreme Court. Born in Milwaukee on October 1, 1924, Rehnquist graduated from Stanford University in 1948, having served in the air force from 1943 to 1946. After a year of further study at Harvard he attended Stanford Law School and earned his degree in 1952. For the next 18 months he served as law clerk to Supreme Court Justice Robert H. Jackson. In 1953 he moved to Phoenix, Arizona, to open a law practice. While in Phoenix he became active in politics, becoming a member of the conservative wing of the Republican party. He took part in the 1964 presidential campaign as a supporter of Senator Barry M. Goldwater and aided Richard M. Nixon's successful campaign in 1968. When the Nixon administration took office in 1969, Rehnquist was appointed head of the Office of Legal Counsel for the Department of Justice. In that post he showed himself to be a staunch advocate of greatly enlarged police powers, such as wiretapping, "no-knock" entries into the premises of suspected persons, and pretrial detention, and was generally hostile to civil-rights legislation. On October 21, 1971, President Nixon nominated Rehnquist to be an associate justice of the Supreme Court. After extended Senate committee hearings, in which liberals attempted to defeat the nomination, he was finally confirmed by the Senate on December 10. He took his seat on the Court on January 7, 1972.

Reid, Ogden Mills, *see under* Reid, Whitelaw

Reid, Whitelaw (1837–1912), newspaper editor, publisher, and diplomat. Born near Xenia, Ohio, on October 27, 1837, Reid graduated from Miami University (Ohio) in 1856 and immediately began lifelong efforts in behalf of the Republican party, speaking throughout the state in support of the party's presidential candidate that year, John C. Frémont. After the election, which Frémont lost, Reid began to write occasional articles and then became a correspondent in Columbus for several papers, including the *Cincinnati Gazette*, of which he was made city editor in 1861. He reported on the Civil War for the *Gazette* in 1861–1862 and was its Washington correspondent from 1862 to 1868. Horace Greeley of the *New York Tribune* had observed Reid's career with interest, and in 1868 prevailed upon him to join the *Tribune* as second in editorial command. In 1869 Reid became

managing editor. A loyal friend and supporter of Greeley, he tried to persuade him not to enter the presidential race in 1872; but when Greeley insisted, and was nominated by the Liberal Republicans, Reid, who took over the paper temporarily during the campaign, supported him ably. After his defeat Greeley returned to head the *Tribune* again, but he soon died, and after a short but bitter struggle for financial control of the paper Reid emerged victorious. At the age of thirty-five he was thus the head of the most powerful newspaper in the United States. He maintained its reporting at a consistently high level, which was all the more remarkable in an era when his great competitors—Charles A. Dana, Joseph Pulitzer, and William Randolph Hearst— were in varying degrees depending on sensationalism for their success. He spent liberally to gather a glittering staff, and once proclaimed: "In making a newspaper, the heaviest item of expense used to be the white paper. Now it is the news. By and by, let us hope, it will be the brains." The *Tribune* continued Republican in its politics, although after the election in 1880 of Reid's friend, James A. Garfield to the presidency, Reid abandoned his earlier attempts to harmonize the opposing factions of the party and came out for thorough civil-service reform over the objections of the Republican Stalwarts. He was a strong supporter of Benjamin Harrison in 1888 and was rewarded after Harrison's election with appointment as U.S. minister to France. Reid spent three happy years in Paris, entertaining lavishly, making many important friends, and doing his country's business quietly and well. He was the Republican vice-presidential nominee in 1892, and his and Harrison's defeat by Grover Cleveland embittered him, although he had supported Cleveland's reform administration in New York State previously. He was an early supporter of William McKinley who, as president, gave him such diplomatic assignments as that of special ambassador to England at Queen Victoria's jubilee and membership in the Spanish-American War peace commission in 1898. He later became a loyal supporter of Theodore Roosevelt, after some initial suspicion. He was named ambassador to Great Britain in 1905, and before sailing for London, in May of that year, relinquished his editorial (although not financial) control of the *Tribune*. In the course of his eventful career, Reid published a number of books, including *After the War, a Southern Tour,* 1867; *Ohio in the War,* 1868; *The Scholar in Politics,* 1873; *Newspaper Tendencies,* 1874; *Our New Duties,* 1899; *A Continental Union,* 1900; and *Problems of Expansion,* 1900. He died in London after a brief illness on December 15, 1912. During his last years he enjoyed the esteem of most of his compatriots, and he is still regarded as one of the most distinguished journalists of his time. His son, Ogden Mills Reid (1882–1947), became editor and publisher of the *Tribune* in 1913. In 1924 he purchased the *New York Herald* and combined the two papers to form the *Herald Tribune*, which he edited until his death.

Reizenstein, Elmer, *see* Rice, Elmer Leopold

Remington, Eliphalet (1793–1861), inventor and firearms manufacturer. Born in Suffield, Connecticut, on October 27, 1793, Remington grew up after 1800 on his father's farm near Utica, New York. Moving to Herkimer County in 1816, the elder Remington established a smithy and forge for the manufacture of small agricultural implements. Eliphalet immediately took to forging and in 1816 made himself a flintlock rifle barrel. It was admired by the gunsmith who fitted the stock; orders for similar guns were soon received, and within a short time rifle barrels became the main product of the forge. At the death of his father in 1828 Remington built a sizable factory on the Erie Canal at the present site of Ilion, New York, and expanded his business to include rifling and stocking of the barrels. Demand for the Remington rifle, prized for its accuracy, increased and the business proved more successful each year. Aided by his son Philo, Remington devised improvements in the manufacturing process, inventing a lathe for cutting gunstocks and pioneering in the cast-steel drilled barrel. In 1845 he bought out Ames & Company of Springfield, Massachusetts, and soon after won a contract to supply the government with rifles. In 1847 Remington introduced a pistol that proved enormously popular and that same year supplied the navy with its first breech-loading rifle, the Jenks carbine. In the late 1850s the business was expanded to include the manufacture of agricultural implements. The outbreak of the Civil War brought Remington large orders from the government for rifles and small arms. Eliphalet died in Ilion on August 12, 1861, in the midst of plans for increasing the production of firearms. Philo Remington (1816–1889), who had been born in Litchfield, Herkimer County, New York, on October 31, 1816, and who had played a leading role in the manufacturing side of the business since 1840, took charge of the company upon his father's death. An important supplier of arms throughout the war, the company faced financial difficulties at the end of hostilities. Philo reorganized the firm for the manufacture of agricultural equipment in 1865, and formed a new firm, E. Remington and Sons, to take over the arms business, retaining control of this independent corporation until shortly before his death. In firearms he concentrated on the pistol, eventually marketing more than a dozen models, and on a breech-loading rifle that found reception in Europe as well. In 1870 he converted much of the old gunmaking machinery to the manufacture of sewing machines and met with some measure of success. Three years later he acquired the right from Christopher L. Sholes to produce the typewriter he had developed with Carlos Glidden and Samuel W. Soulé, and also gained control of the patents. The Remington typewriter was introduced to the public in 1876 at the Centennial Exposition in Philadelphia, but the financial condition of the nation was not favorable for the introduction of a new product, however promising, and within six years he stopped trying

to market it. By 1886 he had sold his interest in the typewriter. A last effort to save the sewing machine business by organizing the Remington Sewing Machine Company in 1882 also proved fruitless, and in 1887 he was forced to sell the agricultural firm as well. He retired to Silver Springs, Florida, where he died on April 4, 1889.

Remington, Frederic (1861–1909), painter, sculptor, and illustrator. Born on October 4, 1861, in Canton, New York, Remington was educated at the School of Fine Arts at Yale (where he was on the football team with Walter Camp) and the Art Students League in New York City. He traveled West, became a cowboy, and worked on a mule and sheep ranch. He sketched constantly and resolved to become an illustrator. All the time and money he could muster were used for traveling and illustrating: he visited Germany, Russia, North Africa, and Cuba—where he was an artist and correspondent for the Hearst newspapers during the Spanish-American War—and he spanned the North American continent. He chose for subjects men living close to nature—cowboys, Indians, soldiers, and frontiersmen. He painted bucking broncoes and modeled them in bronze sculptures; his human beings, like his animals, were alive with motion and all his works were remarkable for capturing the action and mood of a moment. Dedicated to accuracy in the smallest detail, he kept a reference collection of cowboy, Indian, and army garb in his studio. Notable examples of his sculpture were "The Bronco Buster" and "The Wounded Bunkie." His output of paintings and drawings totaled in the thousands and included illustrations for leading magazines. His sculptures and paintings have been extensively reproduced. His books were illustrated profusely, written in a concise, journalistic style, and dealt with the subject matter of his art. They included *Pony Tracks,* 1895; *Men with the Bark On,* 1900; and *The Way of an Indian,* 1906. He died in his home in Ridgefield, Connecticut, on December 26, 1909.

Remington, Philo, *see under* Remington, Eliphalet

Remsen, Ira (1846–1927), chemist and educator. Born in New York City on February 10, 1846, Remsen attended the Free Academy (subsequently the College of the City of New York) and then pursued medical studies at the College of Physicians and Surgeons, receiving his M.D. in 1867. He abandoned medicine to study chemistry in Germany, where the leading research in that field was then in progress. He received a Ph.D. from the University of Göttingen in 1870 and for two additional years served as assistant to Rudolf Fittig at Tübingen. On returning to the United States in 1872 he accepted a post as professor of chemistry at Williams College, where he continued to pursue the experimental studies begun in Europe. In 1876 he was chosen to organize the first department of chemistry at The Johns Hopkins University. Instituting at Hopkins many of the laboratory methods he had learned as a student in Germany, he also established and became director of the Hopkins Chemical Laboratory. Attracted by the ideal of pure research, many students came to Hopkins for training and for more than 30 years Remsen exercised a tremendous influence on American chemistry, both as a teacher and as a writer of textbooks. His *Principles of Theoretical Chemistry* first appeared in 1877, and he published several textbooks on organic and inorganic chemistry between 1885 and 1890. In 1879 he founded the *American Chemical Journal*, which he edited until it merged with the *Journal of the American Chemical Society* in 1914. He made notable discoveries: along with a pupil, C. Fahlberg, he discovered the properties of a new sweetening compound, subsequently marketed as saccharin; and he enunciated Remsen's law, concerning the prevention of oxidation in methyl and other groups. In 1901 he was chosen to succeed Daniel Coit Gilman as president of Johns Hopkins. During his tenure the university continued to be a center of research in many fields and also launched a school of engineering. He remained active head of the chemistry department until his retirement in 1913. Increasingly honored for his accomplishments in his later years he served as president of several professional chemical societies as well as of the National Academy of Sciences. After his retirement he served as an industrial consultant and did work for the government in connection with pure-food laws. Remsen died in Carmel, California, on March 5, 1927.

Renwick, James (1818–1895), architect. Born in New York City on November 1, 1818, Renwick graduated from Columbia in the class of 1836. He followed in the footsteps of his father, a noted engineer, working on the engineering staffs of the Erie Railroad and later the Croton Aqueduct, until 1843, when the selection of his design for the new Grace Church in New York City launched him on a career as an architect, a profession for which he was self-trained. The prestige accompanying this prize brought him several commissions for churches, culminating in 1853 with his selection as architect of the new St. Patrick's Cathedral, also in New York City. Begun in 1853 and delayed by the Civil War, the cathedral was essentially completed in 1879 and remains an outstanding example of Gothic Revival architecture. He continued to design churches into the 1870s, but other important projects came his way early in his career, notably the Smithsonian Institution in Washington in 1846 and the Free Academy (subsequently College of the City of New York) about the same time. Other Gothic buildings of his designing included hotels, banks, and a facade for the New York Stock Exchange. He embraced the French Renaissance style for Vassar College in Poughkeepsie, New York, in 1865 as well as for the Booth Theatre, 1869, in New York City. The Corcoran Gallery in Washington, begun in 1859 and opened in 1872, is perhaps the best example of his work in that style. As architect for the Board of Governors of Charities and Correction of New York he was responsible for several buildings that were erected

in the 1860s on Blackwell's, Ward's, and Randall's islands in the East River, including a workhouse, three hospitals, and an asylum for the mentally ill. Always in demand for private residences, he continued to design luxurious homes of quiet distinction until the very end of his career, and was a noted collector of Oriental art. At the peak of a flourishing practice in the 1870s he entered a partnership with Joseph Sands; later the firm became Renwick, Aspinwall & Renwick, later still Renwick, Aspinwall & Russell. His office trained several future architects of note, including John W. Root and Bertram G. Goodhue. He died in New York City on June 23, 1895.

Reston, James Barrett (1909–   ), journalist. Born in Clydebank, Scotland—hence his nickname, "Scotty"—on November 3, 1909, Reston came to the United States with his parents at the age of ten. He attended public schools in Dayton, Ohio, and graduated from the University of Illinois in 1932. He took a reporter's job with the *Springfield (Ohio) Daily News*, then left journalism briefly before joining the Associated Press (AP) as a sportswriter in New York City in 1934. His apprenticeship with the news service included assignments as a theater critic before he was sent to London in 1937 to cover both sports and foreign news. In 1939 he joined the London office of the *New York Times*, with which he remained associated throughout a long and distinguished career. Assigned to the *Times's* Washington bureau in 1941, he steadily gained stature as a reporter of national news during World War II. His polemical *Prelude to Victory* appeared about seven months after Pearl Harbor and urged the nation to an all-out effort to defeat the Fascists. In 1942 he organized and briefly headed the London office of the Office of War Information (OWI). Awarded a Pulitzer Prize for national reporting in 1945, he received Overseas Press Club awards in 1949, 1951, and 1955 for his interpretations of national news, and he won a second Pulitzer for national reporting in 1957. In 1953 Reston was advanced to chief Washington correspondent and political columnist, a position he held until promoted to associate editor of the *Times* in 1964. When made executive editor of the *Times* in charge of daily and Sunday news operations in 1968, Reston was one of the most respected members of his profession. He became vice-president of the paper in 1969 and from 1970 served on the board of advisers of the American Press Institute of Columbia University. He published *Foreign Policy* in 1967, and *Sketches in the Sand*, a collection of his columns, appeared in 1969. In 1971 Reston traveled to Communist China and, as one of the most influential of U.S. political analysts, was permitted a long personal interview with Premier Chou En-lai.

Reuther, Walter Philip (1907–1970), labor leader. Born in Wheeling, West Virginia, on September 1, 1907, Reuther became an apprentice tool-and-die-maker in Wheeling when he was sixteen, but was soon discharged for organizing a workers' protest against Sunday and holiday work. Moving to Detroit, he worked for the Briggs Manufacturing Company, for General Motors (GM), and for Ford, from 1927 to 1932, the last two years as a foreman at Ford. During those years he finished high school and completed three years of night classes at Wayne State University. Fired from Ford for union activities, from 1932 to 1935 he toured Europe by bicycle and also visited the Soviet Union and the Far East, observing the work in automobile plants and in tool and machine shops. He returned to the United States determined to further the organization of automobile workers. In 1935 he founded and served as the president of Local 174 of the United Automobile Workers (UAW); he was associated with the UAW for the rest of his career, serving as director of the GM Department from 1939 to 1946 and as president of the international union after 1946. In 1936 he led the first of the UAW's sit-down strikes that, in spite of considerable violence directed particularly at him, led by 1937 to recognition of the union by GM and Chrysler; Ford held out for another four years. During World War II he made a notable contribution to the war effort by proposing a plan to produce aircraft by mass-production methods in automobile plants, and he served on various government manpower and production boards during the conflict. From November 1945 to March 1946 he led the 113-day UAW strike against GM, a strike which ended with his union winning important wage increases and improvements in working conditions. He succeeded Philip Murray as president of the Congress of Industrial Organization (CIO) in 1952 and in 1955 he played a major role in engineering the merger of the CIO with the American Federation of Labor (AFL). He headed the Industrial Union Department of the new AFL-CIO and gained a wide reputation as a staunch opponent of corruption and of Communist influence in organized labor. He served as vice-president of the anti-Communist International Confederation of Free Trade Unions (ICFTU). An outspoken and fearless advocate of many social and political causes, including civil rights, improved medical care and health insurance, consumer protection, aid to developing nations, and the eradication of poverty, as well as of far-seeing labor policies, Reuther was a widely known and respected figure. During the 1960s a breach developed between him and George Meany, conservative president of the AFL-CIO, and in 1968 Reuther led the UAW out of the AFL-CIO, forming the Alliance for Labor Action with the Teamsters Union in the next year. A member of many government and philanthropic boards, he was also active in civic work in Detroit. He authored numerous articles and published *Selected Papers of Walter Reuther*, 1961, and *Education and the Public Good* (with Edith Green), 1963. He died in an airplane crash near Pellston, Michigan, on May 10, 1970.

Revels, Hiram Rhoades (1822–1901), religious leader, educator, and first black member of Congress. Born of free parents on September 1, 1822, in Fayetteville, North Carolina, Revels studied in a Quaker seminary in Liberty, Indiana, and at Knox College in Galesburg, Illinois, before being ordained a minister of the African Methodist Episcopal church. He preached in several states and then became pastor of a church in Baltimore and principal of a Negro school. After the Civil War broke out he recruited Negro troops, two regiments in Maryland and a third after moving to St. Louis in 1863. He also founded a school for freedmen in St. Louis, and while serving as chaplain to a Negro unit in Mississippi in 1864 he organized several churches in Jackson. Moving to Natchez, Mississippi, after the war, he became pastor of a large congregation and, despite misgivings, entered politics. He was appointed alderman by the Union military governor in 1868 and won election to the state senate the following year. In January 1870 he was elected to serve for the portion of Jefferson Davis's term that remained when he withdrew from the Senate in 1861; Revels occupied the seat from February 1870 until the following March. He was in an awkward position as Senator, but he maintained the delicate balance between the interests of his race and those of white Southerners. In his maiden speech in March 1870 he said, "They [black freedmen] aim not to elevate themselves by sacrificing one single interest of their white fellow citizen," and he could point to his support, while a state senator, of legislation that would have restored the right to vote and to hold office of disenfranchised white Southerners. He served creditably and upon leaving the Senate was appointed president of Alcorn University (later Alcorn Agricultural and Mechanical College), a recently launched school for Negroes near Lorman, Mississippi. Except for a brief term as interim secretary of state of Mississippi in 1873, he never sought or occupied political office again. His dismissal as president of Alcorn in 1874 was politically motivated and he was returned to office again in 1876 by the Democrats, after he helped to displace the Republicans. He devoted most of the remainder of his life to developing Alcorn and remained active in religious work until his death in Aberdeen, Mississippi, on January 16, 1901.

Revere, Paul (1735–1818), silversmith and Revolutionary patriot. Born on January 1, 1735, in Boston, the son of a silversmith, Revere attended local schools and pursued his father's trade. In 1756 he joined a military expedition against Crown Point, a French fort where major fighting occurred during the French and Indian War. By 1765 his silver shop was also a purveyor of copper engravings of portraits, music sheets, surgical instruments, crude political cartoons bolstering the patriot cause, carved picture frames, many for John Singleton Copley's portraits, and dental plates. Active in local patriotic activities, especially in recruiting volunteer political workers, he was appointed one of three advisers in the crisis caused by the Tea Act of 1773 and was a leader of the Sons of Liberty in holding the Boston Tea Party. He was the principal express rider for the Boston Committee of Safety and, when formally appointed a messenger to Congress for the Massachusetts provincial assembly, he was already a celebrated figure in the colonies. In 1773 he carried news of the Boston Tea Party to New York City and in 1774 the "Suffolk Resolves" to Philadelphia. His ride from Charlestown to Lexington on April 18, 1775, warning John Hancock and Samuel Adams that the British were seeking them and, with two other riders, alerting the entire Middlesex countryside to the approach of British troops, was immortalized in Longfellow's poem, *Paul Revere's Ride*. A master craftsman, he engraved the first Continental money and the official seal of the colonies. He was a member of the Massachusetts Committee of Correspondence, and his military services included command for a time of Castle William, a fortification in Boston Harbor, and participation in the ill-fated expeditions to Rhode Island in 1778 and Penobscot Bay in 1779. After the Revolution he returned to his many crafts. His silverware was among the finest in the colonial and post-Revolutionary periods and is highly prized today. He was also involved in the manufacture of gunpowder, copper bells, and cannons; in copper plating; and in making hardware for frigates, including the *Constitution*—"Old Ironsides." He worked with Robert Fulton in developing copper boilers for steamboats. He daily wore uniforms of the Revolution until his death in Boston on May 10, 1818.

Rhett, Robert Barnwell (1800–1876), public official. Born into the once-prominent Smith family in Beaufort, South Carolina, on December 21, 1800, Rhett was known by his family name, Smith, until 1837, when he adopted the surname of one of his distinguished ancestors, Col. William Rhett. Forced by financial circumstances to leave school at seventeen, he studied law privately and began practice in 1821. He entered politics as a member of the state legislature in 1826, and during the controversy over the Tariff of Abominations of 1828 evolved a states'-rights stance that he consistently maintained for the rest of his political career. His eloquence on state independence and his advocacy of open resistance against the protective tariff quickly won him a following that secured his prominence in state politics throughout the Civil War. Elected state attorney general in 1832, he went to the U.S. House of Representatives in 1837, where he served until 1849. Initially he sided with John C. Calhoun's efforts to unite the dissident groups within the Democratic party, and he labored to dedicate the party to states' rights and to agricultural interests as a barrier against federal centralization. Rhett himself, as the owner of a considerable number of slaves, sought protection against abolitionist intrusions into the South in the late 1830s. Although protectionist duties had been reduced by the 1840s the tariff principle still stood, and after 1844 Rhett defied Calhoun to lead a movement for separate state action on the tariff, but the effort failed. He opposed the Wilmot Proviso in 1846 and the Compromise of 1850. At the Nashville Convention of 1850 he emerged as a leader of the "fire-eaters,"

extremists who advocated secession. From then on secession appeared to be his principal aim; he was reputed to hope that the initiative taken by a single state would prompt others to join in a peaceful movement for an independent confederacy. At the death of Calhoun in 1850, Rhett succeeded him in the Senate, but his chief interest remained the fight for secession in South Carolina. He resigned his Senate seat in May 1852 after the compromise in South Carolina that enunciated the right of secession but withdrew from the deed. Rhett held elective office only once after that, but remained a force in the state. Through the *Charleston Mercury*, which he owned, he gave only nominal support to the Democrats and continued to work for his goal. Success came finally in 1860 at the South Carolina secession convention, where he wrote the "Address to the Slaveholding States." As a member of the provisional congress of the Confederate States of America in 1861, he was chairman of the committee that presented for adoption the Confederate constitution, but he failed to receive a prominent post in the new government. He embraced the war when it came but remained a staunch critic of Jefferson Davis and his prosecution of the war. Repudiated at the polls in 1863, he continued his attacks in the *Mercury*. After the war he moved to Louisiana, and in 1868 was a delegate to the Democratic national convention held in New York City. He died in St. James Parish, Louisiana, on September 4, 1876.

Rhine, Joseph Banks (1895–1980), parapsychologist. Born in Waterloo, Juniata County, Pennsylvania, on September 29, 1895, Rhine spent part of his youth in Ohio and saw service in the Marine Corps during World War I before enrolling at the University of Chicago in 1919. He studied botany, receiving a B.S. in 1922, an M.S. in 1923, and a Ph.D. in 1925. He taught botany briefly at West Virginia University from 1924 to 1926 but, sparked by an interest in extrasensory phenomena, he sought out William McDougall, the noted experimental psychologist, who since 1920 had held a chair at Harvard. He followed McDougall, an outspoken critic of American behaviorist theory and proponent of a theory of mind-body interaction, to Duke University in 1927. Appointed a fellow and promoted to instructor in 1928, he rose steadily to full professor of psychology in 1937. Initially undertaking an evaluation of mediumistic claims, McDougall, Rhine, and two associates launched the Parapsychology Laboratory in 1930. Using a specially designed deck of cards, they conducted experiments in telepathy, clairvoyance, and precognition. Rhine's book *Extra-Sensory Perception*, 1934, brought their work widespread attention and a more popular presentation, *New Frontier of the Mind*, 1937, became a best seller. The work of the laboratory remained the best known in its field and Rhine persisted in his investigations despite considerable criticism from established psychological circles. He also was attacked by mathematicians who argued that Rhine had not fully grasped the subtleties of probability theory on which the demonstration of his results depended. Sometimes charged with trading on the superstition latent in everyone, he countered that opposition to his conclusions was inevitable, given the scientific temper of the times. After McDougall's death in 1938, Rhine became director of the laboratory in 1940 and extended his inquiries to psychokinesis, perhaps the most ambitious and potentially crucial evidence for the existence of what are called "psi phenomena." He again obtained results that were unlikely to have occurred through chance; but, unlike those of the earlier experiments, the significance of his results was blurred by the inability to find subjects with persisting psychokinetic powers. He continued to publish and attract attention with *The Reach of the Mind*, 1947, *New World of the Mind*, 1953, and other books. Rhine left Duke in 1965; from 1964 to 1968 he directed the Institute of Parapsychology in Durham, North Carolina. He died on February 20, 1980, in Hillsborough, North Carolina.

Rhodes, James Ford (1848–1927), businessman and historian. Born in Cleveland on May 1, 1848, Rhodes studied for a year, 1865–1866, at the University of the City of New York (now New York University) and the next year at the University of Chicago. During a European sojourn he attended lectures at the Collège de France and studied metallurgy in Berlin. He returned to Cleveland in 1870 and entered the coal, iron, and steel business. Four years later he joined his father and brother and his brother-in-law, Mark (Marcus A.) Hanna, in Rhodes & Company, which proved a highly successful iron and coal enterprise and earned him a fortune sufficient to enable him to retire in 1885. Long interested in history, he then began to study it in earnest and began publishing articles in historical journals by way of preparation for his major work, *History of the United States from the Compromise of 1850*. The first two volumes appeared in 1893; subsequent single volumes followed in 1895, 1899, and 1904, and two appeared in 1906. Encompassing the period from 1850 to the restoration of home rule in the South in 1877, the monumental work was imbued with his balanced and detached historical judgment. It was warmly received by critics and professional historians alike and earned Rhodes a place in the academic and literary circles of Cambridge, Massachusetts, where he had moved in 1891. In 1898 he was elected president of the American Historical Association. His later books included *Historical Essays*, 1909; *History of the Civil War, 1861–1865*, 1917; *History of the United States from Hayes to McKinley, 1877–1896*, 1919; and *The McKinley and Roosevelt Administrations*, 1922. Failing to reflect the depth and detail of his earlier work, they were less well received, and his reputation continued to rest on his great seven-volume work. Rhodes died in Brookline, Massachusetts, on January 22, 1927.

Rice, Dan (1823–1900), clown. Born in New York City on January 25, 1823, Daniel McLaren took the name Dan Rice at a time and for reasons unknown; the later addition of Colonel was honorary. He left home early and spent several years working with and around horses. In 1841 he launched a performing career with an act that included a pig with purported intellectual abilities. He shortly began appearing in circuses as a strong man and was with P. T. Barnum as an acrobat and strong man in New York City and on a European tour in the early 1840s. He first appeared as a clown in 1844, and although his versatile act combined the abilities of several performers, he never relinquished that role. As equestrian acrobat, cracker-barrel humorist, speechmaker, strongman, and song-and-dance man, he became the most celebrated clown of his day. Truly a one-man show, he was several times the proprietor of his own circus and over the years was associated with most of the major circus masters. His use of Shakespearian material earned him the epithet "the Shakespeare Clown," and his best-known costume was one that resembled that of Uncle Sam. He earned several fortunes and gave much of his money away, often to Negro churches. In 1852 he experimented with electrically lighting his circus but abandoned the attempt because of the injurious effect upon "persons predisposed to pulmonary complaints" and upon "the tender brains of children." At the peak of his career in 1868 he launched a campaign for the Republican nomination for the presidency, but without success. In later years his passion for drink made inroads into his performances. He remained active, however, into his sixties, giving his last circus performances in 1885. An attempt to give up liquor led to his stumping the temperance circuit after 1878, but his reformation was never complete. For 15 years after his retirement he lived in seclusion in Long Branch, New Jersey, where he died on February 22, 1900.

Rice, Elmer Leopold (1892–1967), playwright. Born in New York City on September 29, 1892, Elmer Reizenstein graduated from New York Law School in 1912 and practiced law briefly. After the successful Broadway production of his first play, *On Trial*, in 1914, he abandoned the legal profession and his original name. Except for writing an occasional novel, Rice devoted the rest of his life to the theater. Several subsequent plays, chiefly works for the Morningside Players, were hardly noticed; but *The Adding Machine*, an expressionistic drama about the stagnating effect of mechanization on modern life, established him as a force in the American theater in 1923. It had a short run but was generally recognized as an important achievement and has often been revived. Over the next five years he spent more than half of the time in Europe, often ruminating about his role as a dramatist. His *Street Scene*, 1929, a naturalistic play about life in New York City's tenements, was awarded a Pulitzer Prize and set the tone for most of his work during the next decade. Eager now to convey significant commentary on society, in 1931 he produced and directed his *Left Bank* and *Counsellor-at-Law*. *We, the People*, 1933, about the Depression of the 1930s, and *Judgment Day*, 1934, attacking the Fascists, had some measure of success. His ideological plays continued with *Between Two Worlds*, 1934, and *American Landscape*, 1939. He also wrote numerous comedies and melodramas. *Dream Girl*, 1945, about the fantasies of a young girl, was one of his most successful plays and was a vehicle for his wife, actress Betty Field. In 1947 *Street Scene* became the basis for a successful musical by Kurt Weill and Langston Hughes. One of the founders of the Playwrights Company in 1938, he continued to direct plays for the company into the 1940s. *The Living Theatre*, a collection of essays on the social role of the theater, appeared in 1959, and his autobiography, *Minority Report*, was published in 1963. Rice died on May 8, 1967, in Southampton, England.

Rice, Grantland (1880–1954), sportswriter. Born in Murfreesboro, Tennessee, on November 1, 1880, Rice graduated from Vanderbilt University in 1901. A respectable baseball player, he also played football while in college. He took his first job as a reporter for the *Nashville News* in 1901 and worked as a sportswriter for other prominent Southern newspapers before joining the *New York Mail* in 1911. In 1914 he switched to the *New York Tribune*, subsequently the *Herald Tribune*, where he soon became established as one of the nation's leading sportswriters. A frequent composer of verses, he published his first book, *Songs of the Stalwart*, in 1917. He served in the U.S. forces in France in 1918–1919 and then returned to the *Tribune*, where he remained until 1930. Two additional books of verse appeared in 1924. At the death of Walter Camp, whose annual selections for the All-American football team had long commanded universal acceptance, *Collier's* magazine engaged Rice to carry on the selections. Faced with the difficulty of evaluating a rapidly increasing number of good teams across the nation, Rice and *Collier's* based their choices upon the findings of a country-wide board of the American Football Coaches' Association; Rice, now pre-eminent among football writers, served as chairman of the selection board until his death. After 1930 Rice wrote a widely syndicated column, "The Sportlight," and was the commentator in a series of short films, produced by his own firm, that had a large following in movie houses throughout the nation until World War II. *Only the Brave and Other Poems*, a collection from his syndicated column, appeared in 1941, and during the war he was a frequent lecturer on sports at military training camps. The Grantland Rice fellowship in journalism was established anonymously at Columbia University in 1951. Rice died in New York City on July 13, 1954. His autobiographical *The Tumult and the Shouting* was published later in the same year.

Rice, Thomas Dartmouth (1808–1860), "Jim Crow," entertainer. Born on May 20, 1808, in New York City, Rice was reared in poverty. He learned the wood-carver's trade, but became fascinated by the theater, working for a time at the Park Theatre in New York City and going on to Louisville, Kentucky, to Smith's Southern Theatre, where he was employed as a carpenter, lamplighter, and handyman. Always persistent, he convinced the theater manager that he could perform 'bit' parts; he demonstrated his talent, and was allowed to create and put on solo skits between scenes. One of these, a song-and-dance act called "Jim Crow," was first played to a receptive audience in 1828. The routine was based on Rice's observations of a Negro stable boy, jumping about and whistling as he groomed the horses. His impression of the boy's manner, dress, and shuffling dance established a stereotype that helped launch and maintain the highly popular minstrel shows of the nineteenth century. Rice's subsequent blackface characters included jovial or shiftless plantation workers and Negro dandies. The tune of "Jim Crow" became a hit in the United States and England and hundreds of stanzas were added to its original chorus to suit various locales and occasions. Rice brought "Jim Crow" to New York City in 1832, played in other major cities, and during 1836–1837 made a highly successful appearance in London. He wrote plays, among them *Long Island Juba*, 1833, *Jumbo Jim*, *Ginger Blue*, and *Jim Crow in London*, 1837, and Negro opera burlesques, one on "Othello." Joining in few of his company's productions, he preferred to perform alone. He earned a fortune as a box-office star, but his lavish style of life and erratic behavior led him into poverty. He died in New York City on September 19, 1860.

Richards, Dickinson Woodruff (1895–1973), physician. Born in Orange, New Jersey, on October 30, 1895, Richards attended Yale, receiving his B.A. in 1917. He served with the American Expeditionary Force (AEF) in France during World War I before enrolling at the College of Physicians and Surgeons of Columbia University; there he took an M.A. in physiology before receiving an M.D. degree in 1923. He chose research over practice after his internship and residency, continuing his work as a Columbia fellow and at the National Institute for Medical Research in London during 1927–1928. He joined the Columbia faculty in 1928, becoming Lambert Professor of Medicine in 1947 and holding that post until his retirement in 1961. In addition to a lifelong association with Presbyterian Hopital, affiliated with Columbia, he worked at Bellevue Hospital, where he met André F. Cournand, a graduate of the University of Paris who had come to the United States in 1930 seeking specialized training in treating chest ailments. During a collaboration of about 25 years in studies of diseases of the lungs and heart, it was necessary for them to develop new techniques to make more precise measurements of lung and heart function. They learned of the experiment of Werner Forssmann, who in 1929 had passed a flexible tube through a vein into the right chamber of the heart in order to find a safe means of injecting drugs, and adapted this method to determine the amount of blood the heart pumped and the pressures under which it functioned. Their perfection of this technique, subsequently termed cardiac catheterization, exposed the conditions under which the human heart labors and greatly improved the ability to diagnose and study diseases and physical defects of the heart. Their work opened a new era in heart research. During World War II Richards and Cournand conducted research at Bellevue, using the catheterization method, on victims of shock; their work led to the discovery that shock had to be treated with whole blood. Richards, Cournand, and Forssmann shared the Nobel Prize for Physiology and Medicine in 1956. His *Circulation of the Blood: Men and Ideas*, edited with A. P. Fishman, was published in 1964, and *Medical Priesthoods and Other Essays* appeared in 1970. Richards died in Lakeville, Connecticut, on February 23, 1973.

Richards, Ivor Armstrong (1893–1979), critic. Born in Sandbach, England, on February 26, 1893, I. A. Richards was educated at Clifton College and at Magdalene College, Cambridge, from which he graduated in 1915. From 1922 to 1929 he was a lecturer in English and moral science at Magdalene and in 1926 was named a fellow of the college. This period happened to coincide with a very extensive revision of the syllabus of the college, and his principal interests—psychology, linguistics, and social and intellectual history—found free play in the new atmosphere. In 1921, with Charles Kay Ogden and James Wood, he published *Foundations of Aesthetics* and two years later, again with Ogden, he published *The Meaning of Meaning*, a central document in the development of rationalist criticism. *The Principles of Literary Criticism*, 1924, and *Science and Poetry*, 1926, further developed his position and *Practical Criticism*, 1929, made a notable contribution to pedagogy by illustrating vividly the shortcomings of ordinary training in the interpretation of poetry. His insistence that criticism pay strict attention to its true object, the actual words on the page, and that historical and cultural studies be preceded by a close analysis of the text, helped establish a major critical school, known in the United States as "the New Criticism." Richards was also deeply interested in the development of basic English, a skeletal vocabulary of 850 words with simple grammatical rules which, Richards and Ogden believed, would function as a simple, unambiguous, international language. Richards worked on it while serving as director of the Orthological Institute of China during 1936–1938 and after moving to the United States and joining the Harvard faculty as lecturer in literary criticism in 1939. He advanced to professor in 1944 and remained at Harvard until his retirement in 1963. He served as director of Language Research, Inc., a group devoted to the promulgation of Basic English, Basic Chinese, and other proposed international languages. Other books by Richards included *Basic Rules of Reason*, 1933; *Coleridge on Imagination*, 1934; *Philosophy of Rhetoric*, 1936; *Interpretation and Teaching*, 1938; *Basic English and Its Uses*, 1943; *Nations and Peace*, 1947; *Speculative Instruments*, 1955; *Goodbye Earth*, 1958, a

volume of verse; *The Screens*, 1960, a second volume of verse; *So Much Nearer*, 1968; *Design for Escape*, 1968; *Poetries and Sciences*, 1970; and *Complementarities*, 1975. He died on September 7, 1979, in Cambridge, England.

Richards, Laura Elizabeth Howe, *see under* Howe, Julia Ward

Richards, Theodore William (1868–1928), chemist. Born on January 31, 1868, in Germantown, Pennsylvania, Richards graduated from Haverford College in 1885 and then enrolled at Harvard, where he took a second bachelor's degree in 1886 and his doctorate in 1888. After another year of study in Europe he returned to Harvard as an assistant, became an instructor in 1891, and by 1912 had risen to the Erving chair in chemistry. As a graduate student he had become interested in the precise determination of the atomic weights of chemical elements, and this line of work occupied the major portion of his career. In making his investigations he insisted upon the utmost possible accuracy; he was particularly ingenious at discovering hidden sources of error in the purification of samples, in the conducting of reactions, and in the measurements required throughout the process, and he devised a number of experimental tools and procedures to guard against such errors. Among the innovations were the use of quartz weighing apparatus, the "bottling process" to prevent contamination of samples by moisture, and the nephelometer to measure the concentration of particulate substances in suspension. From his work resulted a great refinement in the atomic-weight values for a large number of elements (his measurements of lead helped confirm the existence of isotopes); and, perhaps more importantly, his work was a great contribution to the development of chemistry into a precisely quantitative science. In 1914 Richards was awarded the Nobel Prize for Chemistry. In later researches he concentrated on studying the physical properties of solids, with special attention to thermochemistry and thermodynamics, atomic volumes, and compressibilities, and to each of these subjects he made notable contributions. His published papers numbered nearly three hundred. He continued to hold the Erving Professorship until his death in Cambridge, Massachusetts, on April 2, 1928.

Richardson, Henry Hobson (1838–1886), architect. Born on September 28, 1838, in St. James Parish, Louisiana, the son of a cotton-industry executive, Richardson attended public and private schools in New Orleans, where he excelled in mathematics, and graduated from Harvard in 1859. He had intended to become a civil engineer, but his interest had turned to architecture in college, and his family sent him to study at the École des Beaux-Arts in Paris, where he worked in architectural offices during the day and attended classes in the evening. He settled in New York City in 1866, by which time he had already achieved a reputation with his individual style. He won two competitions in that year, for the First Unitarian Church in Springfield, Massachusetts, and the Episcopal Church in West Medford. Two more awards, for the Brattle Street Church in 1870 and Trinity Church in 1877, both in Boston, established his nationwide fame. The design for Trinity was a combination of French and Spanish Romanesque that came to be called "Richardsonian." In 1878, owing to the frequency of his commissions in Boston, he moved his office there. In 1882 he toured Europe and studied further the Romanesque style of northern Spain, which he had incorporated in his designs. He tempered his own sense of daring with a functional approach in his most successful buildings and his work was marked by engineering as well as architectural innovations. This was seen, for example, in the Pittsburgh Jail and Court House, 1880, the Marshall Field warehouse building in Chicago, 1887, and in the Boston and Albany Railroad stations at Auburndale and Wellesley, Massachusetts. His shingled country houses, among them the Stoughton house in Cambridge, Massachusetts, relied on simple mass for their effect. Characteristic of his style was the use of graceful, expansive arches, interior ornamentation, and materials with inherent beauty, such as quarry-faced stone, which he had laid according to the texture and shape of each piece. Other architects, such as Charles F. McKim and Stanford White, both of whom worked for a time in his office, John Wellborn Root, and especially Louis H. Sullivan, were inspired by the originality and spontaneity of his work; through them his influence extended into the twentieth century. He was of assistance to the sculptor Augustus Saint-Gaudens and used many of his designs for interior figures in Trinity Church; he also made use of stained-glass work of John La Farge. Others of his major works included Sever Hall, 1878, and Austin Hall, 1881, at Harvard; the Ames and Pray wholesale-house buildings in Boston, 1882 and 1886; the Browne summer cottage in Marion, Massachusetts, 1881; and stone houses for J. J. Glessner and Franklin MacVeagh in Chicago, 1885. Having worked vigorously for many years despite weakening health, Richardson died in Boston on April 27, 1886.

Rickard, George Lewis (1871–1929), "Tex," boxing promoter. Born on January 2, 1871, in Kansas City, Missouri, Rickard grew up in Texas. Left fatherless at ten, he worked as a cowboy to help support his family. A good rider, he was elected marshal of Henrietta, Texas, in 1894. Addicted to gambling, he opened gaming houses, made a fortune, and then lost it in land speculation in the Klondike shortly before the turn of the century. He experienced further financial reverses in San Francisco and later in Nevada mining towns; but he was quick to realize the great potentialities of boxing as a spectacle after staging the world's lightweight championship bout between Joe Gans and Battling Nelson to publicize the mining town of Goldfield, Nevada, in 1906. A natural showman as well as a gambler, Rickard was eminently suited to become a fight promoter. Secure in his knowledge of popular prejudice, he offered James J. Jeffries and Jack Johnson more than $100,000 each for a fight in Reno, Nevada, in 1910. Johnson, the first black man to become the heavyweight titleholder, had won the crown from Tommy Burns in a bout in Sydney, Australia, in 1908. Rickard skillfully used the press to augment the clamor for a "white hope" to regain the title that had arisen after Johnson's victory, and talked Jeffries into coming out of an undefeated retirement. The Reno fight, which Johnson won, was a huge financial success for everyone, and Rickard took his money to South America to speculate in beef. He returned penniless to the United States in 1916 and again took up fight promoting. He profited from the Jess Willard-Frank Moran fight that year but lost money with the Willard-Jack Dempsey title bout in 1919. During the 1920s Rickard became a master in promoting the notion that it was fashionable to be at ringside at major bouts. Cleverly manipulating the press for the Dempsey–Georges Carpentier contest in 1921—characterizing Dempsey as an alleged "slacker" and Carpentier as a French war hero—he built the fight into the first boxing match to gross $1 million. He repeated the ploy—American against foreigner—in the Dempsey–Luis Firpo bout in 1923. The receipts approached $2 million when Dempsey first fought Gene Tunney, in 1926, dropping considerably but remaining over a million when Dempsey met Jack Sharkey in July 1927. This proved a banner year when Dempsey's unsuccessful attempt to regain the heavyweight title from Tunney two months later grossed more than $2 million. Rickard's fortunes declined after Dempsey retired, and he lost money in Tunney's title defense against Tom Heeney in 1928. He died on January 6, 1929, while promoting a fight in Miami Beach, Florida.

Rickenbacker, Edward Vernon (1890–1973), "Eddie," aviator and businessman. Born on October 8, 1890, in Columbus, Ohio, Rickenbacker adopted his middle name and dropped the Germanic spelling of his surname, Rickenbacher, during World War I. With little formal schooling and a succession of jobs behind him, he began working for a railroad-car manufacturing firm in 1905 and there discovered a deep interest in internal-combustion engines and engine-powered vehicles. He began driving racing cars at sixteen. By the time the United States entered World War I, he was internationally famous as a daredevil speed driver with a world speed record of 134 miles per hour, and was ranked third among American drivers. In 1917 he enlisted in the army and went to France as a member of Gen. John J. Pershing's motor-car staff. With help from Col. William (Billy) Mitchell he took pilot's training and was assigned to the 94th Aero Pursuit Squadron, which adopted the famous hat-in-the-ring insignia. It was the first U.S. flying unit to participate actively on the Western Front, fighting the "flying circus" commanded by the German ace, Baron Manfred von Richthofen. By the end of the war the 94th had

downed 69 enemy craft, of which Captain Rickenbacker accounted for 26. He earned nearly every
decoration possible, including the Congressional
Medal of Honor. His account, *Fighting the Flying
Circus*, appeared in 1919. Returning to the United
States a hero, he organized the Rickenbacker
Motor Company; the company was dissolved in
1926, and the next year he bought a controlling
interest in the Indianapolis Speedway, which he
retained until 1945. He began working for the
Cadillac division of General Motors Corporation
and then was associated with a number of aircraft
manufacturers and airlines. In 1935 he became
general manager and vice-president of Eastern
Airlines, and three years later became president
and director of the line. His technical knowledge,
to which he added throughout his career, prompted
his appointment as special representative of the
secretary of war to inspect air bases in the Pacific
theater of war in 1942. On his second mission over
the Pacific, his B-17 was forced down and he and
seven men (one of whom died) were set adrift on
rubber rafts with only fish and rain water to sustain them. After 23 days he was rescued and, after
a two-week rest, resumed his tour of the war
theater. In 1943 he published *Seven Came
Through*. A film biography, *Captain Eddie*, was
released in 1946. After the war he returned to
Eastern Airlines, where he served until his retirement in 1963. He died in Zurich, Switzerland, on
July 23, 1973.

Rickey, Branch Wesley (1881–1965), baseball executive. Born in Stockdale, Pike County, Ohio, on
December 20, 1881, Rickey grew up on a farm. He
taught in a rural school before enrolling at Ohio
Wesleyan University, where he took his B.A. in
1906, delayed somewhat because he pursued a
professional career in football and baseball concurrently with his studies. He coached briefly
before studying law at the University of Michigan,
where he also coached baseball, and after receiving
his law degree in 1911 he began to practice law
in Boise, Idaho. From 1913 to 1916 he was associated with the St. Louis Browns baseball club,
initially as a talent scout and subsequently as
manager of the team. In 1917 he was hired as
president of the St. Louis Cardinals, and after the
end of World War I he also served as manager.
In 1919 he inaugurated the farm system as a device
for acquiring and training young players, a revolutionary step that eventually became a permanent feature of professional baseball. When St.
Louis won its first pennant and World Series in
1926, Rickey was no longer manager, but his role
in the achievement was unquestioned. During his
tenure as vice-president and business manager of
the team prior to World War II, St. Louis went
on to win five more pennants and three more
world championships. Primarily for financial
reasons, he left St. Louis to become president of
the Brooklyn Dodgers in 1942. Active in promoting baseball in the Negro leagues after the war,
Rickey made sports history in 1946 by signing
Jackie Robinson to one of the Dodger farm teams.

Robinson thus, in 1947, became the first Negro to
play in the major leagues, opening the way for
scores of other black athletes. The step proved
important ideologically, soon having a small but
noticeable effect on race relations in the United
States. Brooklyn went on to win pennants in 1947
to 1949. Rickey, now the "Grand Old Man" of
baseball, traveled to Pittsburgh in 1950 as executive vice-president and general manager of the
Pirates and rebuilt the team, which won the 1960
championship. After failing in a two-year attempt
to activate the newly formed Continental League
(the move led, however, to the expansion of the
existing leagues), he returned as consultant to the
Cardinals, from 1962 to 1964. He died in Columbia,
Missouri, on December 9, 1965.

Rickover, Hyman George (1900–   ), naval officer. Born in Maków, Russia (now in Poland) on
January 27, 1900, Rickover came to Chicago with
his parents in 1906. He attended Chicago public
schools and the U.S. Naval Academy, becoming
an ensign after graduation in 1922. He had at first
an unspectacular career, serving at sea in various
types of ships and qualifying for submarine duty
in 1930. Meanwhile he pursued graduate studies
in electrical engineering at Annapolis and at
Columbia, where he took an M.S. in 1929. He was
appointed commander of a minesweeper in 1937;
his specialized knowledge led then to a post with
the electrical division of the Navy Department's
Bureau of Ships, of which he served as chief
during World War II. Rickover's subsequent importance in U.S. naval history is analogous to that
of George W. Melville, who played such an important role during the navy's transition to steam
power at the end of the nineteenth century. After
a six-month tour as assistant director of operations
of the Manhattan Engineering District at Oak
Ridge, Tennessee, during the second half of 1946,
Rickover became convinced of the feasibility and
the military necessity of developing an atomic-
powered submarine. Securing appointment as head
of the atomic submarine division of the Bureau
of Ships in 1947, during the next several years
he worked unceasingly, often in the face of apathy
and never without criticism, to achieve this goal.
When the *Nautilus*, the world's first nuclear-
powered submarine, went to sea in January 1954 it
was Rickover, more than any other single man,
who was responsible for its over-all design and
development. He also supervised the construction
of the subsequent *Seawolf*, and was instrumental
in the development of an atomic reactor for powering an aircraft carrier. During this time from 1947,
he also held a civilian post in charge of naval
reactor development for the Atomic Energy Commission (AEC) and in that capacity he helped
develop the experimental nuclear electric-power
plant at Shippingport, Pennsylvania, in 1956–1957.
When he was passed over for promotion in the
early 1950s, public outcry and Congressional pressure led to his advancement to rear admiral in
1953, to vice-admiral in 1958, and to extension of
his active service beyond the mandatory retire-

ment age in 1961. In the late 1950s Rickover established nuclear-power schools for the navy in Connecticut and California and in 1959 published *Education and Freedom*. Long a controversial figure in naval circles for his outspokenness and his devotion to the use of nuclear power, upon the publication of the book he attracted widespread attention as a critic of American educational practices. Further publications followed in the 1960s, including *Swiss Schools and Ours; Why Theirs are Better*, 1962, and *American Education; A National Failure*, 1963, as he contributed to the discussion of the need to train more and better engineers and scientists for the sake of the national defense. In 1964 he was retired on active duty, and in 1965 he received the AEC's Fermi Award for his work in atomic science. In 1973 he was promoted to the rank of admiral.

Ridgway, Mathew Bunker (1895–   ), soldier. Born in Fort Monroe, Virginia, on March 3, 1895, Ridgway graduated from West Point in 1917. Before World War II his tours of duty had the variety typical of a regular-army career, including posts in China, Nicaragua, the Panama Canal Zone, and the Philippines; an instructorship at West Point; and graduation in 1937 from the Army War College. In 1939 he was attached to the War Plans Division of the War Department and the next year was promoted to lieutenant colonel. Shortly after the war broke out he was promoted to temporary brigadier general; then, appointed commanding general of the 82nd Division in 1942, he oversaw its conversion into the 82nd Airborne and was responsible for the planning and execution of the first major airborne assault in the history of the U.S. army, the attack on Sicily in July 1943. He parachuted with his troops into Normandy on D-Day in 1944 and subsequently led the 18th Airborne Corps in action in the Netherlands, Belgium, and Germany. His troops played a significant role in stemming the German offensive known as the Battle of the Bulge. In 1945 he became temporary lieutenant general. He received important assignments after the war; his most extended tour of duty was on the Military Staff Committee of the United Nations from 1946 to 1948. During the Korean War he assumed command of the 8th Army during the overpowering Chinese offensive in late 1950 and directed the successful counteroffensive. After Gen. Douglas MacArthur's dismissal from supreme command in 1951, Ridgway was promoted to general and succeeded him as United Nations commander in Korea and Allied commander in Japan. He saw the fighting to its conclusion in Korea and then in 1952 replaced Gen. Dwight D. Eisenhower as supreme commander in Europe. Eisenhower, by then president, appointed him chief of staff of the army on August 15, 1953, and he served in that post until his retirement with the rank of general on June 30, 1955. Ridgway published *Soldier*, his war memoirs, in 1956.

Riesman, David, Jr. (1909–   ), sociologist. Born in Philadelphia on September 22, 1909, Riesman attended William Penn Charter School before going to Harvard, where he majored in biochemistry. After taking his B.A. in 1931, he studied at the Harvard Law School, from which he received an Ll.B. in 1934. He served as a clerk to Justice Louis D. Brandeis of the Supreme Court for two years before beginning an academic career as professor of law at the University of Buffalo, where he remained from 1937 to 1941. During World War II he was a deputy assistant district attorney of New York County and subsequently served as a legal adviser to the Sperry Gyroscope Company. In 1946 he launched another career at the University of Chicago, where in 1947 he became a professor of social sciences. In 1950, after a year's leave to carry out research, he published *The Lonely Crowd*, written with Reuel Denney and Nathan Glazer. *Faces in the Crowd: Individual Studies in Character and Politics*, subsequently written with Glazer, presented some of the original research on which the earlier volume was based. *The Lonely Crowd* attracted widespread attention outside academic circles; issued as a paperback volume in 1953, it was often reprinted and went on to become one of the most influential sociological studies of the decade. Its analysis of three characters—the inner-, other-, and outer-directed—was soon established as conventional typology. Reisman joined the graduate department of sociology at Chicago in 1954 and in 1958 accepted an appointment as Henry Ford II Professor of Social Sciences at Harvard. In 1967 he served as a member of the Carnegie Commission for the Study of Higher Education, and in 1968–1969 he was a fellow of the Center for Advanced Study in the Behavioral Sciences. Riesman also published *Individualism Reconsidered*, 1954, collected essays on a wide variety of subjects; *Constraint and Variety in American Education*, 1956; *Abundance for What? and Other Essays*, 1963; and *The Academic Revolution*, written with Cristopher Jencks, 1968. His constructive criticism of American culture earned him a following among scholars in several disciplines as well as among the general public.

Riis, Jacob August (1849–1914), journalist and social reformer. Born in Ribe, Denmark, on May 3, 1849, Riis was educated by his father and by a private tutor. He came to the United States in 1870 and after wandering from job to job for several years secured a position as a reporter for the *New York Tribune* in 1877. Eleven years later he joined the *New York Evening Sun* as a police reporter and remained on the staff until 1899. He followed detectives into tenement districts and photographed children in rags, garbage-filled alleyways, and rat- and insect-infested halls of tenement houses. His stories concentrated on the utter horror of slum conditions and exposed the institutions that perpetuated them. In 1890 Riis published *How the Other Half Lives*, a book that shocked the nation's conscience and led to the first organized efforts to wipe out the worst aspects of tenement life. He made many foes among politicians and landlords but crusaded with great success among the people. Among his most influential supporters was Theodore Roosevelt, during his tenure as head of the New York City police board, who responded to his work with enthusiasm. He carried on his crusade in several later books—*The Children of the Poor*, 1892, and *Children of the Tenements*, 1903, among them— and in a steady stream of articles and lectures. His work bore fruit in improvements in schools as well as housing and recreational facilities; it anticipated and in part stimulated the "muckraking" period of American journalism, and his photographs have remained classics of their kind. He contributed in a more direct fashion to the solution of social problems in the city by founding in 1888 a settlement house, the next year named the Jacob A. Riis Neighborhood House, in the infamous Mulberry Bend district. In 1901 he published an autobiography, *The Making of an American*. He died at Barre, Massachusetts, on May 26, 1914.

Riley, James Whitcomb (1849–1916), poet. Born on October 7, 1849, in Greenfield, Indiana, Riley left school at sixteen and worked at various jobs, from house painting to assisting in patent-medicine shows, at the same time becoming familiar with the habits, speech, and outlook of rural and small-town Indiana folk. As editor of Greenfield's local newspaper, he began writing poetry, and after joining the *Indianapolis Journal* in 1877 he achieved great popularity with a series of whimsical, friendly verses published in its columns, written in Hoosier dialect and purportedly composed by "Benj. F. Johnson, of Boone." The series, which included "When the Frost Is on the Punkin," was collected in *The Old Swimmin' Hole and 'Leven More Poems*, 1883. Although they were often obtrusively sentimental, the poems constituted a significant contribution to American letters in depicting rustic life and characters and helped earn Riley the sobriquet of "The Hoosier Poet." Among his most popular verses were "Little Orphant Annie," "Knee-Deep in June," "The Raggedy Man," and "The Old Man and Jim." Others among his numerous collections included *Afterwhiles*, 1887; *Pipes o' Pan at Zekesbury*, 1888; *Rhymes of Childhood*, 1890; *Flying Island of the Night*, 1891; *Green Fields and Running Brooks*, 1892; *Poems Here at Home*, 1893; *Armazindy*, 1894; *A Child World* 1896; *The Rubaiyat of Doc Sifers*, 1897; and *Home Folks*, 1900. In 1885 he retired from the *Journal*. Throughout his career he was sought after to read his verse in public and often shared the podium with humorist Edgar Wilson "Bill" Nye. He died in Indianapolis on July 22, 1916.

Rimmer, William (1816–1879), painter and sculptor. Born on February 20, 1816, in Liverpool, England, Rimmer grew up in Nova Scotia and, after the age of eight, near or in Boston. He showed an early talent for painting and carving and during his late teens supplemented the family income by working as a draftsman and sign painter. In his early twenties he earned modest fees for portraits, but shortly turned to medicine for a steadier income. Studying privately with a friend, he excelled at anatomy. From about 1845 to 1860 he was a practicing physician, but he never totally abandoned his artistic interests during this time. After 1855 he began to work in granite and in 1860 he carved his first significant work, a head of St. Stephen that is now in the Boston Athenaeum. "The Falling Gladiator," completed shortly afterward, showed him to be a master of anatomy and established his reputation as a sculptor. He subsequently devoted full time to his art. He opened his own art school in Boston and in 1863 lectured at the Lowell Institute. A successful teacher, he published his *Elements of Design* in 1864. His best-known works of this period are three nudes: "Chaldean Shepherd," "Endymion," and "Osiris," in addition to a less successful draped figure of Alexander Hamilton. The closing half of the decade was spent at the Cooper Union in New York City, where he was the leading instructor in the School of Design for Women. At the peak of his fame in 1870 he returned to Boston, where he continued to lecture and occasionally to teach. He taught at the Massachusetts Normal Art School for the year 1875–1876, and in 1877 he published *Art Anatomy*. Its success led to a post as instructor in anatomy at the Boston Museum of Fine Arts in 1877. He died in Boston on August 20, 1879. In addition to the "Gladiator," the Metropolitan Museum of Art in New York City also houses his "The Fighting Lions" and "Dying Centaur."

Rinehart, Mary Roberts (1876–1958), author. Born in Pittsburgh on August 12, 1876, Mary Roberts married Stanley M. Rinehart, a physician, shortly after completing nurses' training at the age of nineteen. She immediately began to raise a family and took up writing only as a result of difficulties created by financial losses in 1903. Her first story appeared in *Munsey's Magazine* that year, and her stories continued to be published. *The Circular Staircase*, 1908, her first mystery, was an immediate success and the following year *The Man in Lower Ten*, serialized earlier, reinforced her popular success. Thereafter she wrote steadily, averaging about a book a year. A long series of comic tales about the robust, redoubtable "Tish," Miss Letitia Carberry, appeared in the *Saturday Evening Post* and as novels over a number of years after 1911. She served as a war correspondent during World War I and later described her experiences in several books of travel. She produced as well a number of romances and some nine plays. Most of the plays were written in collaboration with Avery Hopwood; her greatest success was *The Bat*, derived from *The Circular Staircase*, in 1920. She remained best known, however, as a writer of mysteries and the growing American interest in that genre after World War II led to frequent republication of her works. Her most memorable tales combined murder, love, and humor in a style that was distinctly her own. Among her most popular books were *The Amazing Interlude*, 1917; *The Breaking Point*, 1922; *Lost Ecstasy*, 1927; *The Romantics*, 1929; *The Door*, 1930; *The Wall*, 1938; *Haunted Lady*, 1942; *The Yellow Room*, 1945; *A*

Light in the Window, 1948; and *The Frightened Wife*, 1953. She wrote her autobiography, *My Story*, in 1931 and revised it in 1948. New mysteries were still appearing in the early 1950s. At her death in New York City on September 22, 1958, her books had sold more than 10 million copies.

Ringling, Charles (1863–1926), circus owner. Born in McGregor, Iowa, on December 2, 1863, Charles Ringling, and his brother John, born in Baraboo, Wisconsin, in 1866, were the sons of a harness maker named Rüngeling—the brothers Ringling later changed their name for show-business purposes. They grew up in Iowa and in 1882 joined three older brothers, Albert (1852–1916), Otto (1858–1911), and Alfred (1861–1919) in forming the Classic and Comic Concert Company, a song-and-dance troupe that soon met with success and began to travel. Within a year or so they had expanded their act to include several circus specialties; John played the clown. They launched their first real circus in 1884, taking to the road in a wagon with a bear—the horse not only drew the wagon but performed in the ring. Charles soon emerged as the guiding spirit of the group, whose success was in large part owing to his management. The U.S. circus business in the late nineteenth century was highly competitive, and small circuses often went under or were absorbed by more successful ones. The Ringling Brothers' circus began to expand after 1888, a year marked also by the acquisition of their first elephant. They began to load their wagons on railway cars, thus making possible a much longer tour, about 1890, and during the next decade they experienced steady growth. Between 1900 and 1907 they acquired numerous other circuses, including that of John Robinson, plus the Forepaugh-Sells show. With the purchase in 1907 of Barnum and Bailey's "Greatest Show on Earth," for more than $400,000, they took over Barnum's camp in Bridgeport, Connecticut, and became the leading circus in the country. Charles entered other business ventures, especially real estate, after establishing winter quarters for Ringling Brothers–Barnum and Bailey in Sarasota, Florida, but continued actively to manage the circus until his death in Sarasota on December 3, 1926. The other Ringling brothers who had been active with the circus being by then dead, the leadership fell to John. He outlived Charles by ten years to the day—he died in Sarasota on December 3, 1936—and was responsible for the purchase in 1929 of the Circus Corporation of America, bringing a total of some 11 major circuses under Ringling control. The move essentially eliminated all competition. Employing more than 5000 people, the circus moved about the country in no fewer than 240 railroad cars and boasted a "big-top" main tent seating 10,000. The circus also pioneered later in indoor or arena performances. At its peak the Ringlings' version of "the Greatest Show on Earth" had three rings and five stages surrounded by a hippodrome track; it included spectacular processions and aerial ballets as well as the traditional contrast of ingeniously managed wild animals with the comic and sometimes tragic buffoonery of the clowns. John Ringling's home in Sarasota, built at a cost of more than $1 million and containing extensive collections of European art, was given to the state at his death, as was the nearby Venetian-Gothic Palace at Sarasota Bay, built in 1925 and lavishly furnished. The Museum of the Circus, also in Sarasota, was erected as a memorial to the Ringlings in 1948. The circus continued under the management of a nephew, John Ringling North, from 1936 until 1943; for three years another nephew, Robert E. Ringling, took charge, but North returned in 1946 and remained until 1967, when it was sold.

Ripley, George (1802–1880), editor, critic, and social reformer. Born in Greenfield Massachusetts, on October 3, 1802, Ripley graduated from Harvard in 1823, entered the Harvard Divinity School, and was ordained a Unitarian minister of the Purchase Street Church in Boston in 1826. During 1830–1840 he wrote ten articles for the *Christian Examiner* in which he displayed an attitude even more liberal than the broad Unitarian doctrine. Criticism led him to resign his ministry in 1841. In 1838, with F. H. Hedge, he began to edit *Specimens of Foreign Standard Literature* (eventually 14 volumes), which contained the translations of works by such theologians and philosophers as F. D. E. Schleiermacher that provided the New England Transcendentalists—among them Ralph Waldo Emerson, Bronson Alcott, Orestes A. Brownson, Theodore Parker, and Margaret Fuller—with their basic doctrine, a belief that intuition rather than experience or logic reveals the most profound truths. Ripley was a founder, editor, and contributor to the organ of the Transcendentalist movement, the *Dial*, published between 1840 and 1844. In 1841 he helped organize the Brook Farm community at West Roxbury, Massachusetts, which attempted to put Transcendentalist social ideals into practice. One of several nineteenth-century communal experiments, Brook Farm, which existed until 1847, achieved lasting fame because of its school's modern educational methods and because almost all of the Transcendalists taught or lived there at some point or contributed to its weekly journal, the *Harbinger*. In 1844 Brook Farm was reorganized as a Fourierist phalanx, and Ripley was editor of the *Harbinger* between 1845 and 1849 and president of the community throughout its existence. When its finances were finally exhausted in 1847, he moved to Flatbush, Long Island, and continued publishing the *Harbinger*. He also succeeded in paying off the remaining debts left by the experiment. From 1849 until his death he was literary critic of the *New York Tribune*, and during that time recognized and commented upon the most significant books published in the United States, among them Charles Darwin's *The Origin of Species* and Nathaniel Hawthorne's *The Scarlet Letter*. He was a founder of *Harper's New Monthly Magazine* in 1850 and editor of the magazine's literary department until 1854. Between 1858 and 1863 he produced with Charles A. Dana the 16-volume *New American Cyclopaedia*. From 1872 to 1880 he was president of the Tribune Association. He died in New York City on July 4, 1880.

Ripley, Robert LeRoy (1893–1949), cartoonist. Born in Santa Rosa, California, on December 25, 1893, LeRoy Ripley (he added the Robert later) left high school before graduating to help support his family. He had already shown a knack for drawing, and at the age of fourteen he sold his first cartoon to the old *Life* humor magazine. After various jobs, including a stint as a minor-league baseball pitcher, he was hired as a sports cartoonist by the *San Francisco Bulletin* in 1910. Later he went over to the *San Francisco Chronicle* and in 1913 he moved to New York City and joined the *New York Globe*. There he began using the name Robert, which his employers felt was more athletic-sounding than LeRoy. One day late in 1918, at a loss for a subject for the daily cartoon, he sketched some figures representing seven men who had set unusual records—for running backward, broad jumping on ice, and the like—and titled the cartoon "Believe It or Not!" The enthusiastic reader response encouraged him to continue to depict athletic oddities in a weekly illustrated column; soon he was using bizarre facts of all kinds. In 1923 he moved to the *New York Evening Post*, and the column was soon syndicated to 30 other newspapers. In 1928 he published a collection of his illustrated columns as *Believe It or Not*, a book that enjoyed a huge sale and that brought Ripley lucrative contracts from Warner Brothers–Vitaphone, for 26 movie shorts, and from the King Features Syndicate, through which the column eventually reached 38 countries, 326 newspapers, and untold millions of readers. For Chicago's Century of Progress Exposition in 1933 Ripley organized an exhibit of some of the oddities he had collected over the years, displaying them in his "Odditorium;" he repeated the exhibit in New York City in 1939 and elsewhere. Several more collections of columns were published, and from 1930 Ripley had a popular radio program in which he pioneered in the use of remote live pickups in order to broadcast from Niagara Falls, the Grand Canyon, and other faraway places. His column was credited with helping to establish "The Star-Spangled Banner" as the national anthem; in 1931 he pointed out that it was not officially so designated, whereupon public opinion was quickly mobilized and Congress took the necessary steps. Ripley died in New York City on May 27, 1949, and his large staff of assistants carried on the column.

Rittenhouse, David (1732–1796), astronomer and instrument maker. Born on April 8, 1732, near Germantown, Pennsylvania, Rittenhouse grew up on his father's farm. Largely self-taught, the boy was mathematically precocious and reportedly mastered Sir Isaac Newton's *Principia* with little assistance. He displayed very early an aptitude for mechanical contrivances; at nineteen he established himself as a clockmaker and later made refinements in the design of pendulum clocks. His subsequent interests followed Newton's own early predilection for optics and he was engaged in constructing telescopes in his early twenties. He later, in 1785, invented a collimating telescope and introduced the use of cross hairs (he used spider webs) in his transit telescope, a refinement that he is generally credited with originating. Self-schooled also in astronomy, he became, with the aid of his own instruments, a regular observer of the heavens. He was highly regarded as a surveyor, and William Penn enlisted his aid in settling the long-standing dispute over the Pennsylvania–Maryland boundary. He established in 1763 the arc of 12 miles' radius centered at New Castle, Delaware, which was used by Mason and Dixon in locating their line, the boundary between the two provinces and, by extension, between North and South. This was Rittenhouse's first public service and the beginning of wider recognition as a practical astronomer, he eventually was consulted on and made surveys for boundary disputes involving seven of the original colonies. About 1770 he constructed two celebrated orreries that displayed the planetary motions "for a period of 5000 years, either forward or backward." Only one, displayed at the Franklin Institute, in Philadelphia, is extant. In 1769, at an observatory built on his farm, he made excellent observations of the transit of Venus across the sun, using instruments he built especially for the purpose. His computation of the sun's parallax compares favorably with modern figures. He moved to Philadelphia, the intellectual center of the colonies, in 1770, and from 1771 until shortly after his death his researches were published in the *Transactions of the American Philosophical Society*. His work included the solution of notable mathematical problems, numerous planetary observations, including the discovery of a comet, and experiments on magnetism and electricity. A movement to publicly finance an observatory under his direction was thwarted by the outbreak of the Revolution. In 1775 he was appointed engineer of the Philadelphia Committee of Safety and charged with responsibility for overseeing the manufacture of arms and munitions. In 1776 he became vice-president and in 1777 president of the committee. He served also for a time on the Board of War. He was a member of the state convention that brought forth the radical Pennsylvania constitution of 1776 and from 1777 to 1789 he served as state treasurer. He taught astronomy at the University of Pennsylvania from 1779 to 1782 and later became a trustee, served on the commission that organized the First Bank of the United States in Philadelphia in 1791, reluctantly became the first director of the U.S. Mint from 1792 to 1795, held many offices in (and in 1791 succeeded Benjamin Franklin as president of) the American Philosophical Society, and in 1795 was elected a fellow of the Royal Society. He died in Philadelphia on June 26, 1796, the foremost American astronomer of his time. Benjamin Rush's *A Eulogium . . . to . . . David Rittenhouse* of that year was typically extravagant in ascribing to Rittenhouse the independent discovery of the "method of fluxions," or differential calculus, in the 1750s, but he was not far off the mark; for the pattern of Rittenhouse's intellectual interests and accomplishments, and even that of his public offices, marked him as a brilliant child of Newton.

Robbins, Frederick Chapman (1916–   ), physician. Born in Auburn, Alabama, on August 25, 1916, Robbins grew up in Missouri as a member of a family noted for its achievements in botany and chemistry. He earned two degrees at the University of Missouri before receiving his M.D. from Harvard Medical School in 1940. After two years at the Children's Hospital in Boston he entered the army and became chief, with the rank of major, of the section devoted to viral and rickettsial diseases at the 15th Medical General Laboratory stationed in the Mediterranean theater. His work centered on attempts to isolate the causes of infectious hepatitis, typhus, and Q (for Queensland) fever. He returned to Boston's Children's Hospital to complete his residency in 1946 and remained there as a researcher with a National Research Council grant in 1948. He joined John F. Enders and Thomas H. Weller in two years of research on techniques for cultivating poliomyelitis virus in tissue cultures. Their work later contributed to the development of poliomyelitis vaccine by Jonas E. Salk, to the development of a measles vaccine, to new diagnostic methods, and to the isolation of many unknown viruses. In 1950 he became an associate in pediatrics at Harvard Medical School but left two years later to become director of the department of pediatrics and contagious diseases at Cleveland City Hospital, and professor of pediatrics at Western Reserve University School of Medicine. In 1954 he shared the Nobel Prize for Physiology and Medicine with Enders and Weller for their work on the polio virus. In 1966 he left Cleveland General Hospital and assumed the duties of dean of the School of Medicine of Case Western Reserve University.

Robbins, Jerome (1918–   ), dancer and choreographer. Born in New York City on October 11, 1918, Jerome Rabinowitz changed his name to Robbins after achieving success as a choreographer in the early 1940s. He began to study dance while still a student at Woodrow Wilson High School. After graduating in 1935 he attended New York University briefly but continued to dance, appearing in several Broadway shows and, after 1937, in productions at the Gluck Sandor–Felicia Sorel dance center. He had already tried his hand at choreography by 1940, when he joined the Ballet Theatre, a recently organized group that included some of the most distinguished American dance artists. He toured with them, appearing eventually as a featured dancer in *Petrouchka*, *Romeo and Juliet*, and *Helen of Troy*. Encouraged by the Ballet Theatre's interest in promoting

American choreographers, he collaborated with the stage designer Oliver Smith and composer Leonard Bernstein in staging his first ballet, *Fancy Free*, in April 1944. The success of this production and its subsequent expansion into the musical *On the Town*, which opened on Broadway in December 1944, established Robbins as a new and important talent in theatrical dance. His next ballet was *Interplay*, and in 1946 he choreographed and danced in *Facsimile*, with music by Bernstein. After World War II Robbins contributed to the further development of theatrical dancing in choreographing *Billion Dollar Baby*, 1945; *High Button Shoes*, 1947; *Look Ma, I'm Dancin'*, 1948; *Miss Liberty*, 1949; *Call Me Madam*, 1950; *The King and I*, 1951 (together with its film version, 1956); and *The Pajama Game*, 1954. His Broadway shows were marked by the careful integration of the dancing with the action of the play and it was inevitable that he would graduate to more complete control of the entire production. In 1954 he adapted, choreographed, and directed *Peter Pan* and two seasons later choreographed and staged *The Bells Are Ringing*. *West Side Story*, produced in collaboration with Smith and Bernstein in 1957, triumphantly displayed the way in which dance could achieve equal partnership with the other elements of a production. He was codirector of a subsequent film version, 1961, that also won numerous awards. In 1948 he had joined George Balanchine as dancer and choreographer with the New York City Ballet and the following year became the associate artistic director. He continued to win acclaim as a dancer with that company until the early 1950s, but his chief contribution was in staging original ballets, among them *The Guests*, 1949; *Age of Anxiety*, 1950, with music again by Bernstein; *The Cage*, 1951; and *The Concert*, 1956. While still associated with Balanchine he launched his own company, Ballets, USA, which made its debut at the Festival of Two Worlds at Spoleto, Italy, in 1958. In 1959 he directed and choreographed the Broadway musical *Gypsy*, and in 1964 he opened the smash hit *Fiddler on the Roof*, based on stories by Shalom Aleichem. In 1971 *Fiddler* was made into a motion picture, for which he provided the choreography. In 1965 he returned to the Ballet Theatre for its 25th anniversary, with a ballet set to *Les Noces*, a late work of Igor Stravinsky. In 1969 the New York City Ballet, which he had left in 1963, presented his *Dances at a Gathering* to an enthusiastic reception.

Robert, Henry Martyn (1837–1923), engineer and parliamentarian. Born in Robertville, Jasper County, South Carolina, a descendant of the founder of the town, on May 2, 1837, Robert graduated from West Point in 1857 and, after spending a year as an instructor in military engineering there, was commissioned a second lieutenant of engineers and assigned to duty in the Northwest. He supervised the construction of defenses for Washington, D.C., and other places during the Civil War, being promoted twice. In 1867, being again promoted (to major), he was assigned once more to the Northwest, overseeing the making of river and harbor improvements in Oregon and Washington during the next four years. He was involved thereafter in various Corps of Engineers projects for the army in many parts of the country, rising eventually to the position of president of the U.S. Board of Fortifications during the Spanish-American War and retiring, in 1901, as a brigadier general and chief of engineers. He continued to be a consulting engineer after his retirement, receiving important commissions, including the supervision of the building of the sea wall for Galveston, Texas. He wrote several books describing his engineering work, but none is as famous as a little volume he quickly wrote when he was about twenty-five and several times enlarged and revised. About 1862 he was asked to preside over a meeting. He did not know how, and so he looked for a simple book or manual that would describe his duties. He soon discovered that none existed and decided to write one himself. *Pocket Manual of Rules of Order* was first published (although it had previously circulated in manuscript) in 1876, was revised in 1893 and 1904, and was greatly enlarged and systematized in 1915 and reissued under the title *Robert's Rules of Order Revised*. In time the book became the authority on parliamentary procedures for almost all organizations in the United States. Robert also published *Parliamentary Practice*, 1921, and *Parliamentary Law*, 1923, both standard works. He died in Hornell, New York, on May 11, 1923.

Roberts, Elizabeth Madox (1881–1941), author. Born on October 30, 1881, at Perryville, Kentucky, Miss Roberts suffered all throughout her life from ill health. She lived during part of her youth in Colorado and later spent intervals in New York and California, but she lived mostly in Springfield, Kentucky, and her native state provided the setting for her fiction. Illness interrupted her formal education and she did not complete work for her bachelor's degree at the University of Chicago until 1921. The Fiske Prize, awarded by the university that year, recognized her ability as a poet, a career that already had been launched with the publication of *In the Great Steep's Garden* in 1915. *Under the Tree*, published initially in 1922 and expanded in 1930, long continued to be praised as a book of verse exquisitely suited for children. Her final collection of verse, *Song in the Meadow*, appeared in 1940. But her principal importance was as a novelist, and after the immediate success of her first book, *The Time of Man*, in 1926, she remained a presence in American letters for the next 15 years. Subsequent novels that were well received included *My Heart and My Flesh*, 1927; *Jingling in the Wind*, 1928; *The Great Meadow*, 1930; *A Buried Treasure*, 1931; and *Black Is My Truelove's Hair*, 1938. Her only failure, with *He Sent Forth a Raven*, 1935, was attributed to her inability to handle the larger theme of world war. She also published two collections of short stories about Kentuckians: *The Haunted Mirror*, 1932,

and *Not by Strange Gods*, 1941. Sometimes misunderstood or not understood at all, it was nevertheless generally agreed that she was a serious writer with a unique voice. The philosophical profundity of her work was especially appreciated by the more thoughtful critics. Miss Roberts died in Orlando, Florida, on March 13, 1941.

Roberts, Glenn (1927–1964), "Fireball," automobile racer. Born in Tavares, Florida, in 1927, Roberts began racing modified stock cars in 1948 while he was still a student at the University of Florida and became a professional stock-car racer in 1950. In a blazing 15-year career, during which he acquired the nickname "Fireball," he won 32 races and some $400,000, set more records than any other member of the National Association for Stock Car Racing, and survived a number of serious accidents. He did not, however, survive the last one, which occurred during the running of the World 600–Mile race at Charlotte, North Carolina, on May 24, 1964; in a bad three-car crash he was burned severely and died in a Charlotte hospital on July 2. His most lasting achievement was probably his invention of "drafting." In this perilous maneuver a driver powers his car so close behind another that the semivacuum behind the first vehicle carries the second along, improving its speed in relation to fuel consumption. Many other drivers employed drafting in later years, despite its danger and the need for total trust in the ability of the leading driver to maintain his pace and direction.

Roberts, Oral (1918–   ), evangelist. Born near Ada, Oklahoma, on January 24, 1918, Granville Oral Roberts was the son of a Pentecostal preacher and was descended on his mother's side from Cherokee Indians. Hindered by poverty from receiving much formal education and beset as a youth by various physical ills, he underwent a religious experience in 1935 that convinced him that he should become a preacher. As an evangelist and pastor in a number of small Southern towns for the next 12 years, he began to build up and develop his Pentecostal Holiness Church, which by 1960 was said to have some 2 million members. During 1943–1945 he pursued studies at Oklahoma Baptist University, and in 1965 he became a Methodist. The recipient several times during his life, according to his own account, of direct oral communications from God, he began in 1947, shortly after one of these experiences, to engage in faith healing—or, as he insisted, to pray for God's help in healing the ill and deformed, who were then healed by God Himself. By 1955 his entourage required eight truck trailers to transport and included a cathedral tent, the largest in the world, that could seat 14,000 people. His Healing Waters, Inc., which he had established in Tulsa, Oklahoma, in 1948, soon became the Oral Roberts Evangelistic Association, Inc., and was the parent corporation of a large number of organizations, including a publishing firm that distributed some 25 million pieces of religious literature a year. *Abundant Life*, a periodical, reached a million subscribers, and his books, including *If You Need Healing, Do These Things*, 1952; *Faith Against Life's Storms*, 1957; and *God Is a Good God*, 1960, reached similarly large audiences. From the early 1950s onward his radio and television programs, which showed him—or God—healing the sick and disabled, in mind or body, were broadcast over 150 stations in the United States and other countries and attracted audiences in the millions. Oral Roberts University was founded in Tulsa in 1963. Roberts's manner of life was luxurious, as befitted a man who maintained that "Christ has no objection to prosperity."

Roberts, Owen Josephus (1875–1955), justice of the Supreme Court. Born in Philadelphia on May 2, 1875, Roberts was educated at the University of Pennsylvania, graduating from its college in 1895 after majoring in Greek, and from its law school in 1898. A brilliant student, he was immediately retained by the law school as a teacher, rising to professor within a few years. He retired from teaching in 1918, by which time his private practice had come to occupy much of his time. An assistant district attorney in Philadelphia from 1901 to 1904, he was a special deputy attorney general during World War I, when he prosecuted cases under the Espionage Act of 1917. He came to national attention during the 1920's when he was one of two attorneys appointed by President Calvin Coolidge to prosecute the "oil cases" growing out of the Teapot Dome scandal of the Harding administration. Making haste slowly—he was charged by liberals with refusing to act aggressively enough—he at last brought to justice the notorious Albert B. Fall, the former secretary of the interior, and at the same time created for himself a great reputation. Nominated to the Supreme Court by President Herbert Hoover in 1930 as a substitute for John J. Parker, who had been refused Senate confirmation, Roberts was confirmed unanimously and set to work with characteristic energy; he wrote more opinions than any other justice during 15 years on the Court. On balance a conservative, Roberts nevertheless was often a swing member of the Court, providing the key vote in many early anti–New Deal decisions and, after the liberalization of the Court about 1937, in many cases providing the key vote the other way. Early critical votes helped kill the Agricultural Adjustment Act, 1933, and the Railroad Retirement Act, 1934, but later votes upheld the Wagner-Connery National Labor Relations Act, 1936, and the Social Security Act, 1935. An ardent opponent of U.S. isolationism during the 1930s, he was appointed by President Franklin D. Roosevelt to head a commission charged with investigation of the Pearl Harbor disaster of December 7, 1941; his report, issued the next year, was highly critical of the military. Believing that members of the Court should retire at a statutory age, he retired himself on July 31, 1945. He was dean of the University of Pennsylvania Law School from 1948 to 1951 and until his death was a strong supporter of world government. Among his published works was *The Court and the Constitution*, 1951. He died in Chester Springs, Pennsylvania, on May 17, 1955.

Robeson, Paul Bustill (1898–1976), singer and actor. Born on April 9, 1898, in Princeton, New Jersey, of African and Indian descent, Robeson attended Rutgers University, where he was named to the All-American football team as an end in 1917 and 1918 and, where, for his scholastic achievement, he was elected to Phi Beta Kappa in his junior year. He graduated in 1919 and entered the Columbia University law school, taking his law degree in 1923. He had been seen the year before by Eugene O'Neill in a YMCA stage production and in 1922 O'Neill offered him a part in *The Emperor Jones*. He at first refused this role but accepted another, in *Taboo*; his performances with the Provincetown Players in 1923 in *The Emperor Jones* and in *All God's Chillun Got Wings* established him as an actor. With apparently more opportunity open to him in the theater than in the law, where he had experienced racial discrimination, he remained in acting. He became prominent as a singer as well, although he had never taken a voice lesson. In 1925–1926 he gave successful concerts of spirituals and gospel songs at the Greenwich Village Theatre and in New York City's Town Hall, employing his remarkable bass voice to good effect. In 1926 he also appeared in the Jerome Kern–Oscar Hammerstein production of *Show Boat*. His rendition of "Ol' Man River" was one of the high points of the show. He subsequently appeared in concert in Boston, Philadelphia, and Baltimore, and played as well in *Black Boy*, 1926, *Porgy*, 1928, and *The Hairy Ape*, 1931. In 1930 he went to England, where he appeared in *Show Boat*, *Othello*, and *The Hairy Ape*, and in 1934 returned to Broadway an international star. For the next five years he traveled throughout Europe, appearing in concert, making the first of many visits to the Soviet Union, and visiting the battlefield in the Spanish Civil War, singing to the Loyalist soldiers. In 1943–1944 he performed on Broadway in *Othello*, establishing the longest Shakespearian run in the U.S. theater. In 1950 he was denied a passport by the U.S. Department of State for refusing to sign an affidavit stating whether he was or ever had been a member of the Communist party. In 1958 the government's action was disallowed by the Supreme Court. He appeared in concert that year in San Francisco and at Carnegie Hall in New York City and in 1959 again played *Othello* at Stratford-upon-Avon. He thereafter lived in England and made concert tours of Europe and the Soviet Union until returning to the United States in 1963. He also appeared in motion pictures, among them *Emperor Jones*, *Showboat*, *Sanders of the River*, *King Solomon's Mines*, *Dark Sands*, *Jericho*, and *Song of Freedom*. He died in Philadelphia on January 23, 1976.

Robinson, Bill (1878–1949), "Bojangles," dancer. Born in Richmond, Virginia, on May 25, 1878,

Robinson was brought up by his grandmother after the death of his parents when he was still a baby. He was christened Luther, a name he did not like; he suggested to his younger brother Bill that they should exchange names; when Bill objected, Luther applied his fists, and the exchange was made. (The new "Luther" later adopted the name Percy and became a well-known drummer.) Bill began dancing for a living when he was about six years old, but he "retired" soon after and later supported himself as a waiter for a number of years. He returned to dancing in 1906, gained great success as a nightclub and musical comedy performer, and during the next 25 years became one of the toasts of Broadway. Upon the closing of the show *Brown Buddies* in 1930, he went to Hollywood, where he starred in some 14 films during the next decade, including most memorably *The Little Colonel*, 1935, *The Littlest Rebel*, 1935, and *Rebecca of Sunnybrook Farm*, 1937, all with Shirley Temple. He returned to Broadway in *The Hot Mikado* in 1939 and was one of the greatest hits at the New York World's Fair of 1939–1940. Thereafter he confined himself mainly to occasional performances, but he could still dance in his late 60s almost as well as he ever could, to the continuous astonishment of his millions of admirers. He explained his extraordinary versatility—he once danced for more than an hour before a dancing class without repeating a step—by insisting that his feet responded directly to the music, his head having nothing to do with it. Whatever the reason for his ability, the "Satrap of Tap," as he was once called, was one of the most attractive entertainers of his time; but he was also generously spendthrift, and he died penniless on November 25, 1949, in New York City, despite having earned more than $2 million in his lifetime. He was renowned for a second, though less useful, talent for running backwards; he set a world's record of 8.2 seconds for the 75-yard backward dash. His best-known and most enduring creation in dance was his "stair tap," which he claimed to have invented on the spur of the moment when he was receiving some honor (he could never remember exactly what) from the King of England. The King was standing at the top of a flight of stairs, and Bojangles's feet just danced up to be honored.

Robinson, Edwin Arlington (1869–1935), poet. Born on December 22, 1869, in Head Tide, Maine, Robinson was a collateral descendant of the poet Anne Bradstreet. He grew up in Gardiner, Maine, and from 1891 to 1893 studied at Harvard. He spent six years in Boston and in Gardiner working at various jobs and attempting to find an audience for his poetry. At his own expense he published *The Torrent and the Night Before*, 1896, and the next year appeared *The Children of the Night*, both of which were unsuccessful. In 1899 he moved to New York City and continued to lead a precarious existence until President Theodore Roosevelt, who had favorably reviewed *The Children of the Night*, offered him a job in the New York custom

house in 1905. He relinquished the post four years later, and from 1911 he spent most of his summers at the MacDowell Colony in Peterborough, New Hampshire. In 1910 he issued *The Town Down the River*, which included "Miniver Cheevy," and in 1916, *The Man Against the Sky*, which included "Cassandra" and "Ben Jonson Entertains a Man from Stratford" and which attracted more notice than his earlier poetry. Much of his early verse was in the form of brief dramatic lyrics and concerned the residents of "Tilbury Town," a provincial New England village modeled on his native Gardiner. Robinson's acute psychological portraits of narrow, occasionally perverse, often despairing people were stark dramatic monologues drawn from life and rendered without romanticizing. Later verse included long narratives and philosophical and theological reflections. With finely wrought structure and abundant evidence of wide learning, his poetry often seemed dark and pessimistic. His *Collected Poems*, 1921, won a Pulitzer Prize. With *Merlin*, 1917, he had entered the realm of Arthurian legend, and from it he also drew *Lancelot*, 1920, and *Tristram*, 1927, the last a popular success and another Pulitzer Prize winner. Other later volumes, which were primarily blank-verse narratives of considerable skill, included *The Three Taverns*, 1920, which contained "Rembrandt to Rembrandt"; *Roman Bartholow*, 1923; *The Man Who Died Twice*, 1924 (a third Pulitzer Prize winner); *Dionysus in Doubt*, 1925, including "Demos and Dionysus"; *Cavender's House*, 1929; *Matthias at the Door*, 1931; *Amaranth*, 1934; and *King Jasper*, 1935. He also wrote plays, including *Van Zorn*, 1914, and *The Porcupine*, 1915. Robinson died in New York City on April 6, 1935.

Robinson, Jack Roosevelt (1919–1972), "Jackie," baseball player. Born in Cairo, Georgia, on January 31, 1919, Jackie Robinson moved to California with his family when he was still a child. Growing up in and around Pasadena, he early manifested great athletic skill in several sports; he was a track, football, basketball, and baseball star at John Muir Technical High School in 1933–1937 and at Pasadena Junior College in 1938–1939. He continued to star in all four sports at the University of California at Los Angeles (UCLA), which he left in 1941. He was drafted the next year and served in the army throughout World War II, receiving a medical discharge (because of "football ankles") as a first lieutenant in 1945. An astounding year with the Kansas City Monarchs of the Negro National League in 1945 brought him to the attention of Branch Rickey, president of the Brooklyn Dodgers of baseball's National League, who determined, with Robinson's agreement, to make him the first black major leaguer. A season with the minor-league Montreal Royals, a Dodger farm team, during which Robinson led the league in hitting with a .349 average, stole 40 bases, and scored 113 runs as well as fielding superbly, confirmed Rickey's hopes, and when the Dodgers opened their season at Ebbets

Field in 1947 Jackie was at second base. He quickly established himself as one of the best and most exciting ball players in the league, winning rookie of the year honors in his first season and going on in 1949 to win the batting championship with a .342 average and also winning designation as the most valuable player. He retired from the Dodgers after the 1956 season with a .311 lifetime average and was elected to the National Baseball Hall of Fame in 1962, the first Negro to be so honored. He was probably best known as a player for stealing home plate—it was said that the presence of Robinson on third base, especially with Sal Maglie, star pitcher of the Dodgers' arch-rivals, the New York Giants, on the mound, was the most dramatic situation baseball could produce in his time. Possessing a fiery temper, Robinson showed heroic restraint in ignoring, or at least enduring, the taunts and sometimes the violent racial epithets of other players, some of them on his own team, and his example paved the way into the major leagues for dozens of other black players in after years. Upon his retirement from baseball he became a vice-president of the Chock Full O'Nuts Corporation in New York City and served on various civic boards and commissions and as a special assistant on community relations to the governor of New York. He was especially honored at the opening of the 1972 World Series, the 25th anniversary of his entry into the major leagues, but he died suddenly two weeks later, in Stamford, Connecticut, on October 24, 1972.

Robinson, James Harvey (1863–1936), historian and educator. Born in Bloomington, Illinois, on June 29, 1863, Robinson was descended from Dr. John Robinson, pastor of the Pilgrims before they left Holland for Massachusetts Bay. His education was eclectic; he attended the Bloomington public schools, then after a year abroad, the Illinois state normal school; then Harvard, from which he received his B.A. in 1887 and his M.A. the next year; then various German universities—he received his Ph.D. from Freiburg in 1890, after working under H. E. von Holst. Four years of teaching European history at the University of Pennsylvania were followed by nearly 25 years at Columbia University as professor of history, 1895–1919. Leaving Columbia after World War I he joined Charles A. Beard, Alvin S. Johnson, John Dewey, Thorstein Veblen, and others in founding the New School for Social Research, but after two years there as chairman of the executive board and a lecturer in history he resigned in 1921 to devote himself to writing. In that year he published his best-known and most influential book, *The Mind in the Making.* A popular success, the book was to a large extent based on his famous course at Columbia, "History of the Intellectual Classes of Europe," and dealt with intellectual history in terms of what he saw as man's growing ability to think critically and well about the human condition. His optimism about man's future became less marked in later years, however, and *The Ordeal of Civilization,* 1926, was both less hope-

ful and less popular. He had earlier produced a number of widely used textbooks in history, notably *Introduction to the History of Western Europe,* 1903, and *The Development of Modern Europe,* two volumes, 1907, a work written in collaboration with Beard; and he had also published a work on historiography, *The New History,* 1911, which testified to his belief—shared by many others in his time and since—that history henceforth would have to deal with social, cultural, scientific, and intellectual matters as well as with political and economic events. But *The Mind in the Making* was the book by which he continued to be known. He died at his home in New York City on February 16, 1936.

Robinson, Ray (1920–   ), "Sugar Ray," boxer. Born in Detroit on May 3, 1920, Walker Smith adopted the name by which he was thereafter known from another boxer about 1938 and was somewhat later dubbed "Sugar Ray" by a sportswriter who admired his "sweet style" as a pugilist. He was one of many Detroit youngsters who delighted in watching the young Joe Louis train, and on moving to New York City in 1932 he soon began engaging in amateur fights, winning 89 of them without a defeat and becoming Golden Gloves featherweight champion in 1939 and intercity lightweight champion the next year. He made his professional debut at New York's Madison Square Garden in October 1940, beating Joe Echevarria, and won 122 of his first 123 professional fights, his only defeat coming at the hands of Jake LaMotta on February 5, 1943—but he beat LaMotta in five other fights. After war service from 1943 to 1945, he returned to win his first world title, the welterweight championship, from Tommy Bell at Madison Square Garden in 1946. Universally hailed as one of the best fighters, pound for pound, who had ever lived (there were many who believed him the best), he defended his title a number of times before relinquishing it upon becoming middleweight champion in 1951, acquiring the title from LaMotta in Chicago on February 14, 1951, in one of the great boxing matches of the century. There then occurred a sequence of events unparalleled in ring history. Robinson lost his middleweight title to Randy Turpin on July 10, 1951, but regained it on September 12 of that year, and then, after two successful defenses, against Bobo Olson and Rocky Graziano, relinquished it to try for the lightheavyweight crown. On June 25, 1952, in New York's Yankee Stadium, he almost beat Joey Maxim for the title, although outweighed by some 25 pounds. Although he was ahead on points, he had to retire because of heat prostration after the 13th round; the temperature in the ring was measured at 105°. Returning from retirement on December 9, 1955, he won the middleweight title from Olson (assuming it for the third time and becoming the first boxer ever to regain a world title after retiring). He lost it to Gene Fullmer on January 2, 1957, regained it for a fourth time, from Fullmer, on May 2 of that year, lost it again, to Carmen

Basilio, on September 23, and then, on March 25, 1958, won it for a record fifth time by outpointing Basilio in a 15-round split decision at Chicago Stadium. Robinson fought a number of other fights and finally retired for good in 1965, after which he was involved in various business activities.

Rochambeau, Comte de (1725–1807), soldier. Born at Vendôme, France, on July 1, 1725, Jean Baptiste Donatien de Vimeur, Comte de Rochambeau, entered the army at seventeen and, after service in the War of the Austrian Succession, was made a colonel at the age of twenty-two. Further service in the Seven Years' War led to his promotion to brigadier general and, later, to major general and to lieutenant general, his rank in 1780 when he was placed in command of the troops sent by France to the thirteen Colonies to aid the Revolution. After languishing in Newport, Rhode Island, for nearly a year waiting for French naval vessels to be available for support, he led his 5500 soldiers to meet up with Gen. George Washington's forces at White Plains, New York. Washington and Rochambeau, after planning their campaign, led the combined force swiftly southward to Yorktown, where they joined other Continental forces and the French troops led by the Marquis de Lafayette, who had been harassing the British in the vicinity. Aided by a blockade by French naval forces under Admiral de Grasse, the force of allies settled down to the siege of Yorktown on September 28, forcing British Gen. Charles Cornwallis to surrender on October 19, 1781, an event that, to all intents and purposes, ended the Revolutionary War. Unlike many other European officers who served in the Revolution, Rochambeau was distinguished by the grace with which he accepted Washington's authority as commander in chief, at the same time maintaining commendable discipline among his own troops. For his services he was given the thanks of Congress. Remaining in Virginia until 1783, Rochambeau returned in that year to France, where he was successively appointed military commander of several districts. Made a marshal of France during the French Revolution, he fell out with the Robespierre regime and only escaped the guillotine because of the death of Robespierre himself, in 1794. He was later pensioned by Napoleon and died on May 10, 1807.

Rockefeller, John Davison (1839–1937), industrialist and philanthropist. Born on July 8, 1839, in Richford, Tioga County, New York, Rockefeller moved with his family successively to Moravia and Owego, New York, and in 1853 to Cleveland, Ohio, where he completed his formal education with high school. In 1855 he entered the office of a Cleveland mercantile firm and by 1859 felt competent to strike out independently in business as a partner in Clark & Rockefeller, a commodity-trading operation that, with the Civil War economic boom, did well. In 1863, with the four-year-old petroleum industry already thriving, he organized a new company with four partners to build an oil refinery in Cleveland; two years later he left his earlier business, bought out three of his oil partners, and devoted himself to Rockefeller & Andrews, within months Cleveland's largest refinery. Bringing his brother William and Henry M. Flagler into the business, John built a second refinery that in 1867 was merged with the first in Rockefeller, Andrews & Flagler; within three years the company had expanded vertically to include timber tracts, cooperage plants, sulfuric-acid factories, warehouses, and tanker cars and wagon fleets; it had grown to such an extent that it required reorganization. A joint stock company, the Standard Oil Company of Ohio, with Rockefeller as president, was incorporated on January 10, 1870. The fierce competition among oil companies at that time manifested itself largely in the juggling of transportation agreements and the playing off of one railroad against another in order to obtain preferential shipping rates and rebates. Standard Oil, efficiently organized, managed with great foresight, and wielding tremendous economic leverage, secured highly favorable freight rates and was in a position to consolidate the greater part of the industry under a single unified management. Able to survive temporary depressions as smaller or less efficient companies could not, Standard Oil, under Rockefeller's guidance, set about buying up other companies, driving many others out of business by sheer economic weight, and extending its vertical structure to include pipeline systems, oil terminals, and direct-marketing facilities. By 1878 Rockefeller dominated the entire oil industry. In 1882, in a move to circumvent state corporation laws, the various Standard Oil subsidiary companies were entrusted to a nine-man directorate that was itself incorporated; the result was the Standard Oil trust, the first of many such industrial combinations that caused public antipathy to monopolies to change to hostility, leading finally to passage of the Sherman Anti-Trust Act of 1890. The trust, which controlled about 95 percent of the petroleum industry in the United States, had extensive holdings in mining, manufacturing, and transportation, and was an economic power of global proportions, was ordered dissolved by the Ohio Supreme Court in 1892, but seven years later a new holding company was established under the name of the Standard Oil Company of New Jersey. By this time, although the public, highly critical of Standard Oil and its founder, was unaware of it, Rockefeller had retired from active business, although he retained the title of president of Standard of New Jersey until 1911, in which year that firm too was dissolved, by the Supreme Court, and was devoting himself to philanthropy. To this he brought the same organizational skills that had built an industrial empire; at first he gave to specific institutions, such as the University of Chicago, founded in 1891 and ultimately the recipient of $35 million of Rockefeller money, but soon he turned to the idea of endowed philanthropic foundations. Assisted and advised by Frederick T. Gates, he established four such organizations: the Rockefeller Institute for Medical Research (now Rockefeller University) in 1901, the General Education Board in 1902, the Rockefeller Foundation in 1913, and the Laura Spelman Rockefeller Memorial Foundation, named for his late wife, in 1918. His total benefactions during his lifetime came to more than $500 million. In his later years he kept much to himself, although he was not then so averse to publicity as he had been during his early days. He died at ninety-seven, in Ormond Beach, Florida, on May 23, 1937. His autobiographical *Random Reminiscences of Men and Events* had appeared in 1909. His son, John D. Rockefeller, Jr. (1874–1960), was born in Cleveland on January 29, 1874, and, after graduating from Brown in 1897, entered his father's business and participated as well in his various philanthropic activities. Among his notable achievements were the restoration of colonial Williamsburg, Virginia, the planning of Rockefeller Center in New York City, the donation of the site for the United Nations headquarters building in New York, the creation of forest and wild life preserves, and the establishment of the United Services Organization (USO) during World War II. He married Abby Greene Aldrich, daughter of Nelson W. Aldrich, in 1901 and by her had a daughter, Abby Aldrich (Mrs. Jean Mauzé), and five sons: John D., 3rd, (1906–1978) who entered the family businesses and philanthropies (and whose son, John D., 4th, successfully entered politics in West Virginia in the 1960s); Nelson Aldrich; Laurence Spelman (1910–   ), a businessman with special interests in conservation who developed a number of resort properties in the Caribbean and gave large tracts of land to the U.S. government for parks; Winthrop (1912–1973) who served two terms as governor of Arkansas in the later 1960s; and David (1915–   ), who, as head of the Chase Manhattan Bank in New York City, became one of the most powerful financiers in the world. John D. Rockefeller, Jr., died on May 11, 1960, at the age of eighty-six.

Rockefeller, Nelson Aldrich (1908–1979), public official. Born in Bar Harbor, Maine, on July 8, 1908, the grandson of John D. Rockefeller, Nelson Rockefeller graduated from Dartmouth College in 1930, and, after an apprenticeship in various branches of the family businesses and philanthropies, entered public service. A Republican, he served as an assistant secretary of state during World War II, concentrating mainly on the affairs of Central American and South American countries; in 1950 he was named head of the International Development Advisory Board, established as part of the Point Four Program. With the election of President Dwight D. Eisenhower in 1952 he was appointed chairman of the President's Advisory Committee on Government Organization and, a year later, undersecretary of Health, Education and Welfare. He retired from national service in 1956 to concentrate on affairs in New York State. After service on a number of state boards and commissions he was elected New York's governor in 1958 by a plurality of nearly 600,000

votes in an otherwise Democratic year, and he was reelected in 1962, 1966, and 1970. He made a try for the Republican presidential nomination in 1960, but when it became apparent early in the maneuvering for the nomination that Vice-President Richard M. Nixon could not be stopped, Rockefeller concentrated his efforts on liberalizing Nixon's platform; he loyally supported Nixon during the race. His best chance seemed to come in 1964, with Nixon apparently out of the running because of his defeat in the California gubernatorial election in 1962. Rockefeller, as a leader of the party's liberal wing, found himself opposed for the nomination by the conservative Senator Barry M. Goldwater of Arizona. The climax of the preconvention campaigning occurred in the California primary in June 1964; the polls predicted that Rockefeller would win, but he lost by a slim margin. Again Rockefeller gave his support to his party's candidate, albeit rather reluctantly. He failed a third time in 1968, when Nixon was again chosen. In 1973 he resigned the governorship, a move widely believed to presage a fourth try for the nomination. In 1974, however, he was chosen by President Ford to serve as vice-president; after confirmation by Congress he was sworn into office on December 19. He served until January 1977. He died on January 26, 1979, in New York City.

Rockhill, William Woodville (1854–1914), diplomat and Orientalist. Born in Philadelphia in April 1854, Rockhill graduated from the French military academy at St.-Cyr-l'École in 1873 and thereafter spent three years in the French army in Algeria. He spent the next few years in travel and then, in 1884, joined the U.S. diplomatic service. Serving first in Peking, he moved to Seoul, Korea, as chargé d'affaires in 1886. While still in Paris he had begun to study Oriental culture—his specialty was Tibet—and he continued his researches while in Peking and Seoul, publishing a French translation of the *Prâtimoksha Sutra* in 1884, and, in English and in the same year, *The Life of the Buddha*. Between 1888 and 1893 he made two journeys to Mongolia and Tibet for the Smithsonian Institution, his researches concentrating mainly on early Chinese trade with the West. He returned to the diplomatic service in 1893, as chief clerk of the Department of State, and was promoted to third assistant secretary of state the next year; he was assistant secretary of state in 1896–1897 and minister and consul-general to Greece, Romania, and Serbia from 1897 to 1899. He resigned from the service in 1899 to become director of the International Bureau of the American Republics, but he continued to provide valuable counsel to the Department of State, especially during the crucial period of the Boxer Rebellion in China. Secretary of State John M. Hay's announcement of the Open Door policy in 1900 was couched in phrases drawn almost verbatim from a memorandum from Rockhill to Hay of the year before, and it was evidently largely owing to Rockhill that the penalties imposed on the Chinese by the Western powers after the rebellion were considerably less harsh than they might have been. Rock-hill was sent as U.S. minister to China in 1905, remaining until 1909, when he was named ambassador to Russia; he was ambassador to Turkey in 1911–1913. In 1914 he again journeyed to China and Mongolia and later in the year was appointed personal adviser to the president of China, but he died en route, on December 8, 1914, in Honolulu. Concurrently with his important diplomatic activities he continued to study and to publish works on Oriental history and culture; among his books were *The Land of the Lamas*, 1891; *China's Intercourse with Korea from the XVth Century to 1895*, 1905; and *Conventions and Treaties with or concerning China and Korea*, two volumes, 1904–1908.

Rockne, Knute Kenneth (1888–1931), football coach. Born on March 4, 1888, in Voss, Norway, Rockne emigrated with his family to the United States in 1893. He grew up and attended school in Chicago and, after working for several years at various jobs, entered the University of Notre Dame in 1910. He starred on the Notre Dame football team in 1913 as captain, and his brilliant use of the forward pass against Army in that year is generally held to mark a turning point in the evolution of the game. Upon graduation in 1914 he became an instructor in chemistry and assistant football coach at Notre Dame and four years later was made head coach. During the next 13 years he fielded teams that amassed an overall record of 105 wins, 12 losses, and 5 ties. Rockne developed an approach to football that featured speed, agility, and deception rather than sheer brute force, and he strongly emphasized offensive play. He perfected the "Notre Dame shift" backfield maneuver and he instituted the practice of substituting entire teams—his "shock troops"—during a game. He was widely renowned for the fervor of his exhortations to his players. In one famous pep talk he invoked the memory of George Gipp, a talented player who had died in mid-career, and the line "Win one for the Gipper" became a national catch phrase. His backfield of 1924—Harry Stuhldreher, Don Miller, Jim Crowley, Elmer Layden—was immortalized by sportswriter Grantland Rice as the "Four Horsemen." The success of his teams, combined with Rockne's own colorful and ebullient personality, attracted a huge national following. He published a number of books on football, notably *Coaching, the Way of the Winner*, 1925. His career was cut short by death when an airplane in which he was traveling crashed in Kansas on March 31, 1931. His *Autobiography* appeared later that year. As a coach, as a trainer of other coaches, and as a personality, Rockne had an effect on college football second to none and equaled only by that of Walter Camp.

Rockwell, Norman (1894–1978), painter and illustrator. Born in New York City on February 3, 1894, Rockwell began to study painting when he was thirteen and left high school at sixteen to study at the Art Students League under George Bridgeman and Thomas Fogarty. Fogarty got him his first commissions, which led within a year or so to a regular position as an illustrator with *Boys' Life*; he supplemented his income by doing illustrations for books and for such other magazines as *St. Nicholas* and *American Boy*. He submitted his first cover painting to the *Saturday Evening Post* in 1916; it was not accepted, but other covers and illustrations soon were, and from that date until the *Post* ceased publication in 1969 Rockwell sold it an average of ten covers a year plus many illustrations for inside pages. During these years he also painted covers and supplied illustrations to other magazines, notably the *Ladies' Home Journal*, *McCall's*, and the old *Life*, and illustrated books as well, notably Mark Twain's *Tom Sawyer* and *Huckleberry Finn*, but it was his *Post* covers that brought him his greatest popularity—a fame, it was later felt, that was greater than that of any artist who ever lived, at least in terms of numbers of people whose hearts and minds were touched. Frankly sentimental, his illustrations were done in a style of amiable realism that constituted an American genre school all its own. For many years, however, he was looked down upon by the cognoscenti and by most other artists as "just an illustrator" (which, in fact, was all that he himself ever claimed to be); but, with the publication of such books as *Norman Rockwell, Illustrator*, 1946; *My Adventures as an Illustrator*, 1959; *The Norman Rockwell Album*, 1961; and especially *Norman Rockwell, Artist and Illustrator*, 1970—which sold some 57,000 copies in six weeks at $60 a copy—he progressively gained the respectful attention of the critics as well as more admiration from his huge public. In his later years he was generally regarded not only as an enormously effective commercial illustrator but also as an American painter of genuine importance. Among his best-known paintings were four illustrating the Four Freedoms, completed in 1943. Rockwell died on November 8, 1978, in Stockbridge, Massachusetts.

Rodgers, John (1773–1838), naval officer. Born near the present Havre de Grace, Maryland, in 1773, Rodgers was the son of John Rodgers, a Scotsman who had emigrated to America about 1760 and who founded one of the most celebrated naval families in U.S. history. After spending some 11 years in the merchant marine, the younger John was appointed second lieutenant aboard the *Constellation* in 1798 and served as executive officer of the ship during her victorious engagement with the *Insurgente* that year. He was rewarded by being promoted to captain, the first lieutenant to be raised to this rank in the new navy under the Constitution. From 1802 to 1806 he performed notably against the Barbary pirates and in the Tripolitan War, and he was named commander of the New York flotilla in 1807. In May 1811, cruising off Cape Henry aboard the frigate *President*, he engaged the smaller British sloop *Little Belt* and inflicted heavy damage and many casualties. The action was commended by his superiors and made him a popular hero. During the War of

1812 he was the ranking officer of the navy, and again he performed effectively, particularly against British merchant shipping. In 1815 he was chosen by President James Madison to head the Board of Naval Commissioners, a newly established body that ranked after the cabinet in official Washington. He retained the post until 1837, except for the period 1824–1827, when he was again on sea duty in the Mediterranean. He was senior officer of the navy from 1821, and in 1823 he served for a short period as secretary of the navy. He resigned his commission in 1837 and died in Philadelphia on August 1, 1838. His younger brother, George Washington Rodgers (1787–1832), was also a naval officer. He performed ably in various commands, particularly during the War of 1812.

Rodgers, John (1812–1882), naval officer. Born near Havre de Grace, Maryland, on August 8, 1812, Rodgers was the son of naval hero John Rodgers (1773–1838). Appointed midshipman in 1828, he saw his first service aboard the *Constellation* in the Mediterranean. Varied service in a number of naval posts and as a naval surveyor and explorer during the next 30 years was followed by notable achievements during the Civil War, when he was promoted first to captain and then to commodore for his service as aide to Adm. Samuel F. Du Pont, as commander of gunboat flotillas operating on the Savannah and James rivers, and as commander of the monitor *Weehawken*, which defeated the Confederate ironclad *Atlanta* in June 1863. After the war he continued in the navy, being promoted to rear admiral in 1869. From 1870 to 1872 he commanded the Asiatic Squadron, and in the latter year he became president of the navy's examining and retiring boards. During 1877–1882 he was superintendent of the Naval Observatory. He served also on various other boards and commissions until his appointment in the late 1870s as president of the First Naval Advisory Board, which planned the new navy. When he died in Washington, D.C., on May 5 1882, he was senior rear admiral on the active list. He had a son, William Ledyard Rodgers, who rose to the rank of rear admiral.

Rodgers, Richard (1902–1979), composer. Born on June 28, 1902, in Hammels, Long Island, now a part of New York City, Rodgers learned to play the piano at four and wrote his first song, "My Auto Show Girl," at fourteen. He entered Columbia College and in his freshman year wrote the annual varsity show, *Fly With Me*, meeting Lorenz Hart, a recent Columbia graduate, shortly thereafter. They agreed to collaborate on songs with Rodgers as composer and Hart as lyricist. Their first song was "Any Old Place With You" for Lew Fields's production of *A Lonely Romeo*, 1919. Rodgers left Columbia in 1921 and studied under Walter Damrosch for two years at the Institute of Musical Art in New York City. In 1920 he had contributed to Sigmund Romberg's score for *The Poor Little Ritz Girl*. After a number of amateur productions, he and Hart created the Theatre Guild's *Garrick*

Gaieties of 1925, for which they wrote "Manhattan" and "Sentimental Me." Their success was repeated in 1925 in *Dearest Enemy* ("Here in My Arms") and in *The Second Garrick Gaieties* ("Mountain Greenery"), then in *The Girl Friend* and *Peggy Ann*, 1926; *Connecticut Yankee* ("Thou Swell," "My Heart Stood Still") and *She's My Baby*, both in 1927; *Present Arms*, 1928; *Spring Is Here* ("Spring Is Here," "With a Song in My Heart") and *Heads Up*, 1929; *Simple Simon*, 1930 ("Ten Cents a Dance"); *America's Sweetheart*, 1931; *Jumbo*, 1935; *On Your Toes*, 1936; *I'd Rather Be Right*, 1937; *Babes in Arms*, also 1937 ("Where or When," "The Lady Is a Tramp," "My Funny Valentine"); *I Married an Angel*, 1938; *The Boys from Syracuse*, also 1938 ("This Can't Be Love," "Falling in Love with Love"); *Too Many Girls*, 1939 ("I Didn't Know What Time It was"); and *Pal Joey*, 1940 ("Bewitched, Bothered, and Bewildered"). Hart died in 1943, and in that year Rodgers began working with lyricist Oscar Hammerstein II. Together they produced *Oklahoma!*, 1943, a landmark in the musical theater, containing, besides the title song, "Oh What a Beautiful Mornin'," "People Will Say We're in Love," "The Surrey with the Fringe on Top" and for which they won a special Pulitzer Prize in 1944. They followed with *Carousel*, 1945 ("If I Loved You," "You'll Never Walk Alone," "June is Bustin' Out All Over"); *South Pacific*, 1949 ("Some Enchanted Evening," "Younger Than Springtime"), which also won a Pulitzer Prize; *The King and I*, 1951 ("Getting to Know You," "Hello, Young Lovers"); *Flower Drum Song*, 1958; and *The Sound of Music*, 1959 ("Climb Every Mountain," "My Favorite Things"). They also wrote the Academy Award–winning score for *State Fair*, 1945, containing "It Might As Well Be Spring" and "It's a Grand Night for Singing." After Hammerstein's death in 1960, Rodgers wrote both words and music for the musical *No Strings*, 1962. He also composed the motion-picture score for *Victory at Sea*, 1952, later shown also as a television series. His last show was *I Remember Mama*, 1979. He died in New York City, on December 30, 1979.

Roebling, John Augustus (1806–1869), engineer. Born on June 12, 1806, in Mühlhausen, Germany, Roebling studied engineering and philosophy (under G. W. F. Hegel) at the Royal Polytechnic Institute in Berlin and graduated in 1826. He emigrated to the United States in 1831 and purchased a large farm in Pennsylvania, but in 1838 he obtained a position as an engineer on state canal projects. He became a U.S. citizen in 1837. After developing machinery for making twisted wire cable to replace hemp ropes in hoisting canal boats onto barges, in 1841 he established a factory in Saxonburg, Pennsylvania, to produce the wire rope, the first made in America. In 1845 he constructed a wooden aqueduct over the Allegheny River; the next year he built a suspension bridge, his first, over the Monongahela at Pittsburgh. Thereafter he concentrated on designing suspension bridges, using wire rope from his new factory in Trenton,

New Jersey, instead of chain cable. His great Niagara Falls double-roadway railroad and vehicular bridge, completed in 1855, demonstrated the reliability of his methods, which subsequently were adopted by bridge builders throughout the world. In 1867 he completed a large span over the Ohio River at Cincinnati that firmly established his reputation. His most famous design was for the Brooklyn Bridge in New York City, connecting Brooklyn and Manhattan over the East River. Its great length and its long open span, which presented no obstacle to navigation, were both revolutionary and, to some, unbelievable. His plans, which were originally submitted to city officials in 1857, were finally approved in 1869 and work was begun immediately under his supervision. At the bridge site, he sustained a relatively minor injury, but contracted tetanus, and died on July 22, 1869.

Roebling, Washington Augustus (1837–1926), engineer. Born in Saxonburg, Pennsylvania, on May 26, 1837, Roebling was the son of John Augustus Roebling. He graduated from Rensselaer Institute (now Rensselaer Polytechnic Institute) in 1857 and after a year in his father's wire-rope factory in Saxonburg, he joined his father in the construction of bridges. He served in the army as an engineer for four years during the Civil War, attaining the rank of colonel. He then assisted his father in building the Ohio River bridge at Cincinnati and then spent a year studying new engineering techniques in Europe. He was a principal assistant on the Brooklyn Bridge project from its beginning in 1869 and on the death of the elder Roebling shortly thereafter he succeeded him as chief engineer. He insisted upon overseeing every detail of the work and by 1872 overexertion and caisson disease had ruined his health. He was confined to his home near the Brooklyn end of the span, and from there he continued to direct the project until the opening of the bridge in 1883. From 1869 he was also president of John A. Roebling's Sons, the manufacturing firm, in Trenton. After four years in Troy, New York, he retired permanently to Trenton, New Jersey in 1888 and lived quietly until his death there on July 21, 1926.

Roethke, Theodore (1908–1963), poet. Born in Saginaw, Michigan, on May 25, 1908, Roethke received his B.A. in 1929 and his M.A. in 1936 from the University of Michigan, and did further graduate work at Harvard in 1930–1931. He disliked both universities, although he did like certain people he met there, notably Robert Hillyer, who was the first to recognize his poetic gift. Roethke taught English at Lafayette College from 1931 to 1935, and was a teacher or poet in residence at Pennsylvania State University from 1936 to 1943, at Bennington College from 1943 to 1947, and at the University of Washington from 1947 until his death. His first volume of poems, *Open House*, was published in 1941; it was followed by *The Lost Son and Other Poems*, 1948; *Praise to the End*, 1951; *The Waking*, 1953, which won a Pulitzer Prize; *Words for the Wind*, 1958; and *I Am!*

Says the Lamb, 1961. The poems in all of these books—mostly short, sharp lyrics, although toward the end he wrote some longer works—were marked by a remarkable control of language combined with a kind of restrained violence that led some to compare Roethke to William Butler Yeats. He was only beginning to achieve a national reputation when he died on August 1, 1963, on Bainbridge Island, Washington.

Rogers, Bruce (1870–1957), book designer. Born in Lafayette, Indiana, on May 14, 1870, Rogers graduated from Purdue University in 1890 and almost immediately began a long and illustrious career as a designer of beautiful limited editions. His first job was with the *Indianapolis News*, 1891–1892; for the next year or so he worked as a designer with the Indiana Illustrating Company, and in 1894 he went to Boston to accept a similar position with L. Prang & Co. In 1895 he became a typographer and designer of limited editions for the Riverside Press, Cambridge, Massachusetts, remaining until 1912, when he went into the design business on his own. By this time very well known in the United States and England, not least because of his Centaur type, a design that was widely hailed as a masterpiece, he received many commissions to design books. He went to England in 1917 to join the firm of Emery Walker, Ltd., and also to be printing adviser to the Cambridge University Press; returning to the United States three years later, he was printing and design adviser to the Harvard University Press from 1920 to 1934. During the 1920s he was also associated with the American printer William Edwin Rudge and in 1928–1931 was again with Emery Walker, Ltd. After about 1930 he devoted much of his time to designs for the Limited Editions Club. He was widely honored for his work, being the first recipient of the Aldus Award of the Limited Editions Club and an honorary life member of the American Institute of Graphic Arts (AIGA). He died on May 18, 1957, in New Fairfield, Connecticut.

Rogers, John (1648–1721), religious leader, founder of the Rogerenes. Born on December 1, 1648, in Milford, Connecticut, Rogers spent most of his life in nearby New London. Converted by the Seventh Day Baptists in 1674, he soon, largely through independent study of the Bible, began to develop novel religious opinions. He opposed a salaried clergy, any use of meeting houses, formal prayers, and the use of medicine, and he strongly urged nonresistance and pacifism and the total separation of church and state, including the abolition of the marriage ceremony; he also enfranchised all his slaves. Not surprisingly, these views got him into serious and continuing trouble with the conservative Congregationalists of Connecticut. He was imprisoned seven times during his life, twice publicly whipped, and many times fined, together with other Rogerenes (their numbers were never great), for such crimes as nonattendance at meeting, working on the Sabbath (according to Rogers, this was lawful), refusing to pay ministers' salaries, refusing to engage in military training, and mingling with Quakers. The persecution was unremitting, but in fact Rogers did not suffer as much as he might have, for, his neighbors sympathizing if not agreeing with him, it seems to have been hard to find juries to convict him and officers to collect fines; in addition, he was elected to several offices in New London. In 1670 he married but, under the influence of his deep religious feelings, confessed a prior sexual experience to his wife; she thereupon accused him of all sorts of sexual crimes and obtained a divorce. He next married—refusing to have a ceremony performed—a maidservant, between whose family and Rogers intense litigation later developed. She herself was imprisoned for having a child "out of wedlock" and later, with Rogers's permission, married someone else. He later married a third time and died in New London, Connecticut, of smallpox on October 17, 1721. The Rogerenes became extinct in the nineteenth century.

Rogers, John (1829–1904), sculptor. Born in Salem, Massachusetts, on October 30, 1829, Rogers attended public schools in Boston and then clerked in a dry-goods store to obtain money to further his education in engineering. But trouble with his eyes ended his studies and he became a machinist, working in New Hampshire and Missouri and arriving in Chicago toward the end of the 1850s. For years he had experimented with modeling small figures in clay, and had even spent a few months in 1858 studying in Rome in the studio of the sculptor Benjamin Spence, but he was by no means an accomplished or professional artist when he was asked, in 1859, to provide some kind of sculpture for a local charity fair. The result was "Checkers up at the Farm," the first of the famous "Rogers groups" and in some ways the most successful of all, at least in his homely genre line. He went to New York City later in 1859 with "The Slave Auction," which created a sensation but was hard to sell because of fear on the part of dealers that it would offend their Southern customers. Rogers himself sold copies of this and other groups door to door, and by the end of the Civil War, during which he produced many groups depicting scenes from the conflict, he was prosperous. He exhibited several bronze figures and groups at the International Exposition of 1867 in Paris, 29 groups at Philadelphia's Centennial Exhibition in 1876, and a large number of his works at the World's Columbian Exposition in Chicago in 1893, where he won a gold medal. During these years he won an enormous reputation in the United States and even some international recognition. After about 1895, however, the critics began to be patronizing and to call him "just a folk sculptor." He was indeed never really more than that—nor did he claim to be—but the accuracy of his portraits (of Abraham Lincoln, for example), and the charm and humor of his genre groups ("Charity Patient," "Coming to the Par-

son," "Fetching the Doctor," "Checkers up at the Farm," among many others) were in later years greatly admired. During his lifetime he sold some 80,000 copies of his patented original models, many of which are now in the New York Historical Society. Rogers's hands became crippled after 1893 and he could work no more. He died in New Canaan, Connecticut, where he had long had a studio, on July 26, 1904.

Rogers, Robert (1731–1795), frontiersman and soldier. Born in Methuen, Massachusetts, then a frontier village, on November 7, 1731, Rogers obtained what education he had from Indians and from his companions on hunting and exploring expeditions. He got into his first trouble in New Hampshire about 1755, when he was charged with counterfeiting; he got out of it in a way that he would many times later adopt, by volunteering for the expedition against the French at Crown Point, at the resumption of the French and Indian Wars. His daring and ingenuity in various scouting forays recommended him to his commander, Sir William Johnson, and he was made a captain of a ranger unit in the British regular army the next year and was promoted to major in charge of nine such units—the famed Rogers's Rangers—two years later, in 1758. He was at Halifax in 1757; at Ticonderoga in 1758, a campaign in which, in the Battle on Snowshoes, on March 13, 1758, at Lake George, he sustained heavy losses and escaped only by deceiving the Indians at what became known as Rogers' Rock; at Crown Point again in 1759; and at Montreal the next year, which also saw his acceptance of the surrender of Detroit. All in all, with his many daring raids and his sweeping excursions into enemy territory to obtain information and to ambush small detachments of troops, he emerged from the last French and Indian War the most renowned and romantic military figure in the colonies. But his troubles returned with the return of peace: he was a bad administrator in the various frontier appointments given him by South Carolina and New York, and a greedy trader who engaged in illicit dealings with the Indians, and when his debts reached unmanageable proportions he fled to England, in 1765. There he published his *Journals* and his *Concise Account of North America,* both more renowned for their descriptions of frontier experience and adventure than for their accuracy, and a play, *Ponteach: or the Savages of America,* 1766. Lionized as a hero, he was appointed commander of the fort at Maclanac (Michilimackinac) in present-day Michigan and lived there for two years, during which he dispatched Jonathan Carver to explore the country that became Minnesota. His maladministration and outright dishonesty in his post led to charges being made against him by Johnson and Gen. Thomas Gage, and he was thrown into debtors' prison in England after making further vain pleas for a lucrative position in the service. He was arrested by George Washington soon after his return to America in 1775, but he escaped and organized two Loyalist ranger companies; neither had any military success, however, and, plagued by his own dishonesty and dissipation, he sailed back to England in 1780 and lived out the rest of his life in dire poverty. He died in London on May 18, 1795.

Rogers, Will (1879–1935), humorist, entertainer, and actor. Born on November 4, 1879, near Oologah in the Indian Territory (later in Oklahoma), William Penn Adair Rogers grew up in cattle country and became highly adept with the lasso. Sent to a succession of boarding schools, he found formal education confining and finally gave it up entirely in 1898. After a time as a cowboy in Texas he took to travel and in 1902, in South Africa, joined Texas Jack's touring Wild West Circus as a rope artist. Two years later he returned to the United States and continued to perform in various Wild West and vaudeville shows, gradually introducing into his act humorous patter that, spoken with a distinct Southwestern drawl and delivered in an offhand and rather diffident manner, proved a delight to his audiences. He first appeared in New York at Hammerstein's Roof Garden in 1905. Rogers rose quickly to stardom on Broadway, appearing in a number of musical revues and, after 1915, regularly in the Ziegfeld Follies. His wry humor—homely and good-natured but often with a sharply satirical point underneath—became even more popular as he turned to political topics and comments on the social scene. In 1922 he began writing a weekly column for the *New York Times* that was soon syndicated nationally; in 1926, while touring Europe as President Calvin Coolidge's unofficial goodwill ambassador, he began submitting daily reports to his readers and reached an audience estimated at 40 million. He wrote a number of books as well, including *The Cowboy Philosopher on Prohibition*, 1919; *The Illiterate Digest*, 1924; *There's Not a Bathing-Suit in Russia*, 1927; and *Ether and Me*, 1929. As early as 1918 Rogers appeared in motion pictures, but it was after about 1929 that he achieved real success in that medium; among his most popular films were *A Connecticut Yankee*, 1931; *State Fair*, 1933; and *David Harum*, 1934. Rogers died with pilot Wiley Post in an airplane crash near Point Barrow, Alaska, on August 15, 1935.

Rölvaag, Ole Edvart (1876–1931), author and educator. Born on April 22, 1876, on the island of Dönna in Helgeland, Norway, Rölvaag grew up in a small settlement where fishing was the only means of livelihood. From the time he was fifteen until after he turned twenty, he sailed in the open boats that worked the fishing grounds off the Lofoten Islands. At twenty he emigrated to the United States, arriving in 1896. For three years he worked on an uncle's farm in South Dakota. Then, being determined to get an education, he attended Augustana Academy at Canton, South Dakota, from 1899 to 1901. He graduated from St. Olaf College in 1905, and after a year of further study at the University of Oslo, returned to the college as professor of Norwegian language and literature.

He remained on the faculty until his death. Rölvaag was a strong devotee of Norwegian culture and a perceptive student of immigrant life in America. As he watched the natives of Scandinavia becoming assimilated into American society, he became an advocate of what came to be called "cultural pluralism." He urged his fellow Norwegians to retain their language, customs, and religion, feeling they would make a better contribution to their new country in so doing. He opposed the work of the "Americanizers" whose efforts during World War I were generated by the myth of the melting pot. In 1925 he was a founder and first secretary of the Norwegian American Historical Association. Rölvaag, whose novels were written in Norwegian, is best known for two novels, *I de Dage*, 1924, and *Riketgrundlægges*, 1925, translated and published together in English as *Giants in the Earth*, 1927, an epic of immigrant life on the prairies of South Dakota in the 1870s. The first of a trilogy, it was followed by *Peder Victorious*, 1929, and *Their Fathers' God*, 1931. Rölvaag's first published novel, *Amerika Breve*, 1912, was based on his own experiences in coming to the United States. It was translated in 1971 as *The Third Life of Per Smevik*. His next novel, *The Forgotten Path*, 1914, has fallen into obscurity. In 1920 he wrote a bitter account of two uncouth immigrants who were driven only by the desire for wealth. Its original title meant "two fools," but it was translated as *Pure Gold* in 1930. *The Boat of Longing*, 1921, translated 1933, took up the theme of the immigrant in the city. In 1926 Rölvaag suffered a heart attack which permanently impaired his health. In August 1931 he resigned his teaching duties to spend his full time writing, but he died suddenly on November 5, in Northfield, Minnesota.

Romanoff, Michael (1892?–1971), "Prince Mike," impostor and restaurant owner. Possibly born in Vilna, Lithuania, then a part of Russia, about 1892, Harry F. Gerguson—which may have been his real name—seems to have grown up in modest, if not poor, circumstances in the United States, although when he arrived, and in what circumstances, is lost in the miasma that he intentionally created in after years. According to one of his own accounts (they varied with each questioner) he stowed away to England about 1910 and attended Eton, Oxford, and Cambridge, although there is no evidence for this or numerous other claims of the same sort. He may have served the Allies in some military capacity during World War I, but in any event he first came to public notice in 1919, when, taking careful note of the well-publicized vacancies in the Russian imperial family, he announced that he was Prince Michael Alexandrovich Dmitri Obolensky Romanoff, nephew (later he said half-brother) of the last Czar of all the Russias. He ran up large bills at hotels, restaurants, and stores in Paris and London, declaring grandly that the Russian nobility settled its accounts only once a year, but when he failed to pay he was thrown into jail. Returning to the

United States, he applied as an engineering student to Harvard, explaining that his previous academic records had been lost in the Revolution. Further escapades were followed by a sojourn in Hollywood, where he fit in well with the other impostors who peopled the film capital. But it was not until the late 1930s that he was able to open his first restaurant, which catered aggressively and successfully to celebrities and celebrity watchers. The original Romanoff's grew to a chain of California establishments, and Mike retired in 1962 with a comfortable fortune. He died in Los Angeles on September 1, 1971. His lifelong pursuit of American citizenship—he was deported at least once and was always viewed with suspicion by the U.S. immigration service—had been capped with success in 1958, when in the course of the naturalization ceremonies and with a broad smile, he renounced his "titles."

Romberg, Sigmund (1887–1951), composer. Born in Szeged, Hungary, on July 29, 1887, Romberg early began the study of music, learning to play several instruments, but during his youth music became something of a pastime as he entered an engineering school in Vienna. He nonetheless attracted attention with his compositions. After military service he emigrated to the United States in 1910 and soon found work as a pianist in a New York City restaurant. Later, while leading his own café orchestra, he was engaged to compose the score for *The Whirl of the World*, produced in 1914 at the Winter Garden by the Shubert brothers. The show was a hit and Romberg went on to write all or part of the music for seven of the Shuberts' *Passing Show* productions over the next decade; in addition, he collaborated on a number of musical comedies, first achieving great success with *Maytime*, 1917 (with lyrics by R. J. Young and Cyrus Wood). *Blossom Time*, 1921, with lyrics by Dorothy Donnelly, ran for more than 500 performances and firmly established Romberg as one of the country's most popular composers and a worthy representative of the Viennese tradition. Subsequent operettas, some of them perennial favorites, included *The Student Prince*, 1924 ("Serenade," "Golden Days," "Deep in My Heart," "Drinking Song," lyrics by Donnelly); *The Desert Song*, 1926 ("Blue Heaven," "One Alone," lyrics by Oscar Hammerstein II and Otto Harbach); *My Maryland*, 1927 ("Silver Moon," "Your Land and My Land," lyrics by Donnelly); *The New Moon*, 1928 ("One Kiss," "Softly, As in a Morning Sunrise," "Stout-Hearted Men," "Lover, Come Back to Me," lyrics by Hammerstein and others); *May Wine*, 1938 (lyrics by Hammerstein); and *Up in Central Park*, 1945 (lyrics by Herbert and Dorothy Fields). From 1929 Romberg also composed for motion pictures. At various times he had his own radio program, and he conducted a number of highly successful concert tours. In all he wrote the scores for nearly 80 stage productions, many of which enjoyed regular revivals and were made into motion pictures. Others of his more than 2000 songs included "Auf Wiedersehen," 1915; "You Will Remember Vienna," 1930; and "When I Grow Too Old to Dream," 1935. He died in New York City on November 9, 1951.

Roosevelt, Eleanor (1884–1962), author, diplomat, and humanitarian. Born in New York City on October 11, 1884, Anna Eleanor Roosevelt came of a prominent, well-established family. Her parents died during her childhood and she grew up in the home of her grandmother, who sent her to be schooled in England. In 1905 she married a distant cousin, Franklin Delano Roosevelt, and was given away by her uncle, President Theodore Roosevelt. She provided constant support and aid to her husband in his career, particularly after a crippling attack of polio in 1921 and during his long convalescence. While rearing six children she cultivated an interest in social causes, politics, and public affairs that she maintained and widened after Roosevelt was elected governor of New York in 1928. With his election to the presidency in 1932 she began 12 years as First Lady, during which she shattered many precedents, set many more, and made her position one of great, if unofficial, influence. She held the first press conference by a first lady in 1933, and she conducted a regular column in the *Ladies Home Journal*. Her syndicated newspaper column "My Day," which she wrote for many years, changed in emphasis from women's affairs to public affairs about 1939; in that year she used it to announce her resignation from the Daughters of the American Revolution (DAR) in consequence of that organization's refusal to allow Negro singer Marian Anderson the use of its Constitution Hall for a concert. She actively promoted liberal causes, youth movements, and social betterment and worked effectively for civilian defense early in World War II, succeeding in becoming nearly as controversial a figure as her husband. During the war she traveled to virtually every war front to visit troops. Soon after President Roosevelt's death in 1945 she was named a delegate to the United Nations by President Harry S. Truman. As chairman of the UN Commission on Human Rights from 1946 she took a central role in drafting and securing the adoption of the Universal Declaration of Human Rights in 1948. She resigned her post in 1953 and for the next ten years traveled constantly, promoting her chosen causes, particularly the work of the UN. She was welcomed by heads of state around the world and was widely acknowledged to be the world's most admired woman. She remained active in Democratic politics, speaking at party conventions and campaigning in the party's behalf, and she was influential in the party's liberal and reform wings, particularly in New York State. She wrote prolifically, both books and articles; among her books were *This Is My Story*, 1937; *My Days*, 1938; *The Moral Basis of Democracy*, 1940; *This I Remember*, 1949; *On My Own*, 1958; *You Learn by Living*, 1960; and *The Autobiography of Eleanor Roosevelt*, 1961. In 1961 she was reappointed to the U.S. delegation to the United

Nations by President John F. Kennedy. Mrs. Roosevelt died in New York City on November 7, 1962.

Roosevelt, Franklin Delano (1882–1945), "FDR," thirty-second president of the United States. Born on January 30, 1882, in Hyde Park, New York, Roosevelt came of a wealthy family. He was educated at Groton and Harvard, where he took his B.A. in 1904. He studied at the Columbia University School of Law, was admitted to the bar in 1907, and entered the office of a distinguished New York City law firm. In 1905 he married Eleanor Roosevelt, a niece of President Theodore Roosevelt and his own distant cousin. His political career began in 1910 with his unexpected victory as a Democrat in a campaign for the state senate; during his tenure in that body he became identified with the interests of upstate farmers and with progressive legislation and reform generally; he was active among the insurgents who opposed New York City's Tammany Hall. During the 1912 campaign he was easily re-elected but his term was cut short when, in reward for his strong support, President Woodrow Wilson appointed him assistant secretary of the navy in 1913. He held this post until 1920, when he was nominated for vice-president at the Democratic national convention; defeated, with James M. Cox, in the Republican sweep with Warren G. Harding and Calvin Coolidge that year, he entered private business until, in 1921, he was stricken with poliomyelitis. From 1924 he frequently visited the mineral waters at Warm Springs, Georgia, where in 1927 he established the Warm Springs Foundation to provide care for other polio victims. He maintained his political interests and connections during his long and difficult convalescence—he attended the Democratic National Conventions of 1924 and 1928 and at both nominated Al Smith—and, although he had very little use of his legs (he remained crippled throughout his life), he accepted the nomination for governor in 1928. He outpolled Al Smith, the outgoing governor and unsuccessful Democratic candidate for president, and embarked on a progressive administration that won him easy re-election in 1930. His most notable programs as governor were tax relief for farmers, reduced public utilities rates, and the creation of a state power authority. He reacted swiftly and vigorously to the onset of the Depression of the 1930s and in 1931 secured the establishment of the nation's first state relief agency. He was the leading contender for the presidential nomination in 1932 and, with the skillful management of his close political associate James A. Farley, won it on the third ballot. In the November election, which turned solely on the Depression issue, he won easily over Herbert Hoover and carried Democratic majorities into both houses of Congress. Between election and inauguration Roosevelt and his advisers—dubbed the "brain trust" and including such men as Raymond Moley, Rexford G. Tugwell, Louis M. Howe, Harry L. Hopkins, and Adolf A. Berle—made detailed plans to carry out what had until then been a relatively vague intent to relieve and reform the economy. On March 4, 1933, he was inaugurated president of a nation on the verge of panic. His address that day stirred new confidence with his assertion that "the only thing we have to fear is fear itself." He followed with decisive action, declaring a national bank holiday to stop disastrous runs, and on the same day began the famous "hundred days" during which the sweeping, though unintegrated, program of legislation known as the New Deal was enacted. Government assumed new functions and powers for the reorganization of agriculture, industry, and finance, and the nation was confronted by a proliferation of agencies that came to be known by their initials —the "alphabet agencies." The already existing Reconstruction Finance Corporation (RFC) was strengthened, banking was reformed and underwritten by the Federal Deposit Insurance Corporation (FDIC), and the Federal Emergency Relief Administration (FERA) began the work of alleviating human suffering among the 13 million unemployed. Other primary agencies established included the Tennessee Valley Authority (TVA), the Civilian Conservation Corps (CCC), the Farm Credit Administration (FCA), and the Home Owners' Loan Corporation (HOLC). Most important of all were the Agricultural Adjustment Administration (AAA), and the twin agencies of the National Recovery Administration (NRA) and and the Public Works Administration (PWA). Although viewed as radical by many, the New Deal was planned as much for its psychological effect as for its economic consequences. The first step in providing protection against "economic royalists" for the ordinary citizen was the restoration of confidence, and to that end Roosevelt bent every effort, from legislation to his famed "fireside chats" on radio. A second major legislative program, with its emphasis on reform, was enacted in 1934–1935 and is often referred to as the "second New Deal." Major new agencies established then included the Federal Housing Administration (FHA), the Securities and Exchange Commission (SEC), the Works Progress Administration (WPA), later the Work Projects Administration, the Social Security Administration (SSA), and the National Labor Relations Board (NLRB), established under the Wagner (Wagner-Connery) Act, 1935. Roosevelt won reelection by a landslide in 1936, carrying all but two states, in defeating Alfred M. Landon. (The election ended Maine's reputation as national political bellwether and occasioned Farley's famous variation on an old saw: "As Maine goes, so goes Vermont.") FDR's second administration was beset by serious difficulties. The Supreme Court had invalidated NRA in 1935 and AAA in 1936 and seemed likely to cripple the New Deal still further; Roosevelt thus proposed a plan to reform the Court by, among other things, adding up to six more members. This "court-packing" plan aroused great opposition among already alienated conservatives and others, and only the Court's late approval of Social Security and of the Wagner Act in 1937 averted a head-on collision between the President and the Congress as Roosevelt allowed his Court plan to die. The Wagner Act, "labor's Magna Carta," was also a source of trouble, for the guarantees of one section prompted a wave of union activity that often came to violence; many charged Roosevelt with responsibility for such occurrences. The continued popularity of the New Deal among farmers and workers was never, however, threatened. The New Deal encouraged recovery, but to a degree impossible to determine; a cutback in government spending in 1937 caused a sharp recession and the resumption of spending brought about improvement in 1938, but within a year foreign policy was engaging more attention than domestic problems, and complete economic recovery became ultimately a function of war mobilization. Roosevelt's foreign policy since 1933 had been one of amiable isolation; beyond the "good neighbor" policy toward other American nations, he spoke little on relations with other countries, pursuing his program of economic nationalism and endorsing the several Neutrality acts of the 1930s. Japanese aggression in China, the rise of Adolf Hitler in Germany (and his alliance with the Fascist regime of Benito Mussolini in Italy) brought about a slow deterioration of U.S. relations with both countries, but until 1939 Roosevelt held firmly to a neutral policy. In that year, however, following the invasion of Poland by Germany, he called for a "cash-and-carry" plan to modify the ban on arms sales to belligerents contained in the Neutrality acts of 1935 and 1937, of which he had approved at the time of their passage. In 1940, by executive authority, he traded 50 overage naval destroyers to Britain for military bases in British possessions and finally, in 1941, the Lend-Lease Act, providing for the arms aid supplied first to Britain and later to other U.S. allies, was enacted at his request. Roosevelt accepted the nomination for and won election over Wendell L. Willkie to an unprecedented third term in 1940, although by a much diminished margin; in the campaign both parties opposed U.S. entry into the war, but made no issue of Roosevelt's assistance to the Allies. During 1941 the international situation worsened steadily as Germany overran nearly all of Europe and Japan approached the establishment of absolute hegemony in the Pacific. Opposition to Roosevelt passed from the hands of economic conservatives to isolationists as he persisted in his aim of rendering to the Allies "all aid short of war." In August 1941 he met on a naval vessel at sea with British Prime Minister Winston Churchill, and the two issued jointly the Atlantic Charter, proclaiming what were in effect war aims. Finally, on December 7, Japanese aircraft attacked the U.S. naval base at Pearl Harbor in Hawaii; the President obtained a declaration of war from Congress the next day and similar declarations against Germany and Italy a few days later. Even more rapid economic mobilization was the first imperative, and authority for it was given to the War Production Board (WPB) and the Office of War Mobilization (OWM). Roosevelt concerned himself primarily with securing close cooperation

among the Allies, and the course of the war was marked by a series of meetings with heads of state —primarily Churchill and Joseph Stalin of the Soviet Union—to plan overall war strategy (as at Casablanca and at Quebec in 1943) and the structure of the postwar world (at Teheran, 1943, and Yalta, 1945). Roosevelt was most eager to establish good working relations with the Soviet Union, both during the war and afterward, but was disappointed in this aim, especially when, soon after Yalta, it appeared that the U.S. and the U.S.S.R. placed differing interpretations on the agreements reached there. By this time he was in poor health; his health had been an issue in the election of 1944, when he nonetheless won a fourth term over the Republican Thomas E. Dewey, and it was now a serious problem. He traveled to Warm Springs, Georgia, to rest for the forthcoming meeting in San Francisco to draft the charter of the United Nations, for whose establishment he had striven successfully. Two weeks before the scheduled meeting he died suddenly, on April 12, 1945. A year later his Hyde Park Estate, containing his home and the Franklin D. Roosevelt Library, was dedicated as a national historic site. Roosevelt was probably the most ardently admired, even loved, and the most heartily hated and feared president in American history. Evaluations of his role range from savior of the nation to would be dictator. Doubtless his administration was highly effective in many ways, and he provided a style of leadership seldom matched. A skilled politician, an engaging campaigner, a bold and pragmatic president, and a farsighted world leader, he left a permanent mark on the nation and the world.

Roosevelt, Theodore (1858–1919), "Teddy," twenty-sixth president of the United States. Born in New York City on October 27, 1858, Roosevelt came of a well-to-do family long established in New York. In his youth he set about overcoming his physical weakness and developed his lifelong taste for the vigorous, rugged life. He graduated from Harvard in 1880 after winning election to Phi Beta Kappa and entered the Columbia University School of Law but soon withdrew to run successfully for the state assembly in 1881. During three terms in that body he was nominally a Republican, but he acted and voted as an outspoken independent. During these years he also undertook the writing of history as a serious and continuing avocation, beginning with *The Naval War of 1812*, 1882. With the defeat of his progressive faction that opposed James G. Blaine at the Republican national convention of 1884, and upon the death of his wife in the same year, Roosevelt retired to a ranch in the Dakota Territory where he remained until called back to New York City for the mayoral election of 1886, in which he ran third to the Democratic candidate, Henry George, and the victorious Abram S. Hewitt. He again retired from politics and devoted himself largely to writing, publishing *Hunting Trips of a Ranch Man*, 1885; *Ranch-Life and the Hunting*

Trail, 1888; biographies of Thomas Hart Benton and Gouverneur Morris; and in 1889 the first two volumes of *The Winning of the West* (the third and fourth volumes followed in 1894 and 1896). In 1889 he was appointed civil-service commissioner by President Benjamin Harrison and served in that position until 1895, when he became president of New York City's Board of Police Commissioners. Continuing to battle corruption whenever he found it, he maintained his reputation as a reformer and this, together with his strong support of William McKinley in the 1896 presidential election, won him appointment in 1897 as assistant secretary of the navy. In that post he advocated a strong military stance for the United States and acted to achieve his aim, sometimes undercutting or assuming the authority of his superior. In May 1898 he resigned to join Col. Leonard Wood in organizing the 1st U.S. Volunteer Cavalry for service in Cuba during the Spanish-American War; as commander of the "Rough Riders" he cut a spectacular figure, and the much-publicized charge up Kettle Hill (not San Juan Hill, as is often stated) near Santiago de Cuba made him a national hero. (Of his book *The Rough Riders*, 1899, "Mr. Dooley" said it ought to have been called "Alone in Cubia.") Immediately upon his return home he was nominated for and elected governor of New York. In two years in Albany his reformist views and insistence on competence in officeholders so exasperated Senator Thomas C. Platt and other Republican machine leaders that, in order to remove him from New York politics, they pushed for his nomination for vice-president in 1900. He accepted the bid but soon after the election found himself bored with the job and considered returning to the study of law or joining a university faculty. Six months after his inauguration, on September 14, 1901, McKinley died of an assassin's bullet and Roosevelt became president. While pledging a continuation of his predecessor's policies, he in fact pursued a course more in line with Western populist ideas than with the business-oriented views of the late protégé of Mark Hanna. Faced with a conservative, hostile Congress, however, the President, an excellent administrator, chose to work through an expansion of the ill-defined power of executive authority. He began by revitalizing the Sherman Anti-Trust Act of 1890 and, through Attorney General Philander C. Knox, hauled more than 30 corporations into court on antitrust charges. The most notable of the "trust-busting" cases were those against the Northern Securities Company and the Standard Oil Company of New Jersey, ordered dissolved by the Supreme Court in 1904 and 1911 respectively. When the anthracite miners' strike of 1902 began to cause massive coal shortages, he forced the recalcitrant operators to negotiate with the miners' union by threatening to use the army to work the mines. In 1903, on his recommendation, the cabinet-level Department of Commerce and Labor was created by Congress. In foreign affairs he exercised power even more vigorously. He supported Secretary of State John Hay's "Open Door"

initiatives in regard to China and was firm in his insistence that the United States be the dominant power in the Pacific. In 1902 and 1903, when first Venezuela and then the Dominican Republic were faced with intervention by European nations because of defaulted debts, he assumed for the United States responsibility for the payment of debts by Latin American nations; in 1904, with soon-to-be Secretary of State Elihu Root, he announced what came to be known as the "Roosevelt corollary" to the Monroe Doctrine, stating that the United States would be, in effect, the armed policeman and defender of the Western Hemisphere. In the Dominican Republic the United States took full control of national finance in 1905 through an appointed comptroller. In 1903 the government of Colombia rejected a treaty allowing construction of a canal through a U.S.–controlled section of the Isthmus of Panama; but Roosevelt saw to it that a revolutionary secession by the territory involved was encouraged and protected by the presence of U.S. warships, and shortly thereafter the Canal Zone was ceded to the United States by the new nation of Panama. The President maintained a close interest in the construction of the canal and, in visiting the site later, became the first incumbent president to leave U.S. soil. His later dispatch of a part of the U.S. navy's fleet on a world cruise in 1907–1909 perfectly exemplified his fundamental dictum in foreign policy: "Speak softly and carry a big stick." In 1904 he was reelected easily over Alton B. Parker; he subsequently announced that he would regard his first three years in the White House as constituting a first term and would therefore not run again in 1908. During his second term he secured passage of the Pure Food and Drug Act and the Hepburn Act, which greatly strengthened the Interstate Commerce Commission (ICC). In 1905 he took the initiative in arranging negotiations to end the Russo-Japanese War, a service for which he was awarded the Nobel Peace Prize in 1906. Throughout his seven years as president, he worked for an expanded government role in the conservation of natural resources, increasing the extent of national preserves nearly fivefold, and he was responsible for the Newlands Reclamation Act of 1902, providing for irrigation and reclamation projects. As 1908 approached he began to regret his promise not to run, but he promoted the nomination of William Howard Taft, then secretary of war, as his successor. Soon after leaving office he set out on an extended African safari, followed by a tour of Europe during which he consulted with many heads of state. Returning in 1910, he immediately resumed his political activity. As Taft slowly allied himself with the conservative wing of the Republican party, Roosevelt's views moved leftward and the breach between the two men was mirrored in the party ranks. He elaborated his earlier ideas of a "Square Deal" for all citizens, particularly for working men, and on a Western speaking tour that year delivered his famed "New Nationalism" address that enunciated the principles later found in his 1912 platform. As the 1912 Republican national convention approached he began to gather delegate votes for a showdown with Taft; he won several state primaries, but Taft controlled the party machinery and the convention. Rejected by the Republicans, Roosevelt immediately formed the Progressive party—soon dubbed the "Bull Moose" party after a comment by Roosevelt on his physical fitness—and, displacing Senator Robert M. La Follette, he accepted its nomination. The Republican split caused by the Progressive defection allowed Democrat Woodrow Wilson to win the election. Roosevelt took an active dislike to Wilson and his policies, particularly that of neutrality toward the European war, and in 1916, although he again lost the Republican nomination, campaigned against him. When the United States entered World War I Roosevelt unsuccessfully sought a military command and spoke widely in support of the war effort. He continued to publish books, among them *Progressive Principles*, 1913; *History as Literature*, 1913; *An Autobiography*, 1913; and *America and the World War*, 1915, as well as articles, for a total of more than 2000 titles. He still had hopes for the Republican nomination in 1920 when, weakened by a lingering illness contracted during a South American exploring journey in 1914, he died suddenly on January 6, 1919, at his home, Sagamore Hill, near Oyster Bay, Long Island, New York. He was elected to the Hall of Fame in 1950. One of the most colorful men ever to hold the presidency, Roosevelt was widely admired for his boundless gusto, his devotion to the "strenuous life," his nearly jingoistic nationalism, and his manifest integrity. Remarkably foresighted in seeing the need for political adjustment to a new economic age, he succeeded only in setting the stage for changes to come.

Root, Elihu (1845–1937), lawyer, public official, and diplomat. Born in Clinton, New York, on February 15, 1845, Root graduated from Hamilton College in 1864 and after a year teaching school entered the law school of the University of the City of New York (New York University). He graduated in 1867, was admitted to the bar, and, soon forming his own law firm in New York City, became within a few years one of the nation's leading corporation lawyers. Although not actively involved in politics, he was identifiably a Republican with leanings toward the party's conservative wing. He nonetheless became a close friend and adviser to Theodore Roosevelt while Roosevelt was in New York state politics, and he maintained the association for many years. In 1883 he was appointed U.S. attorney for the southern district of New York, serving until 1885. In 1894 he played a leading role in the state constitutional convention. He became secretary of war in 1899 at President William McKinley's invitation and in four years in that office directed the department's activities more effectively than had any of his predecessors since the Civil War. Charged with the administration of territories acquired in the Spanish-American War, Root quickly arranged for an effective, conservative management of Puerto Rico through the

Foraker Act of 1900, granting the island dependency much-needed tariff advantages, and turned to the more difficult problem in Cuba. He chose Gen. Leonard Wood as military governor and in 1901 drafted the Platt Amendment, outlining safeguards for U.S. interests in Cuba that were to be included in the island's new constitution, to take effect with independence the following year. In the Philippines there was open insurrection against U.S. occupation; Root dispatched more troops there and in 1900 sent a governing commission, headed by William Howard Taft, with detailed instructions that amounted to a constitution and a legal and judicial code. The instructions were affirmed by Congress in 1902. Of the War Department itself Root effected a reorganization that greatly improved its efficiency and the army's readiness; the general-staff concept was introduced for the army, along with rotation of staff and line assignments, the Army War College was established, and the state national guards were transformed into a national militia. He resigned from the cabinet in 1904 and returned to his law practice, only to be recalled by President Theodore Roosevelt to succeed the late Secretary of State John M. Hay in 1905. He managed, despite Roosevelt's "dollar diplomacy," to improve greatly U.S. relations with Latin America during a tour in 1906; U.S.–Japanese affairs were smoothed by the "gentleman's agreement" of 1907 and the Root-Takahira Agreement of 1908; and he negotiated numerous arbitration treaties with European nations. He brought the protracted dispute over North Atlantic fisheries to an end and strengthened U.S.–Canadian relations. For these accomplishments, and for his earlier success in constructing an enlightened policy for U.S. possessions, he was awarded the Nobel Peace Prize in 1912. In 1910 he had been named a member of the Permanent Court of Arbitration at the Hague. He also made considerable progress in professionalizing the diplomatic corps. Root resigned his post in 1909 and was immediately elected to the Senate, where he remained until 1915, a Taft Republican and a leading opponent of President Woodrow Wilson. His long friendship with Roosevelt ended in 1912 when he presided over the Republican national convention that ignored the bid of the former president and renominated Taft, to whom Root had earlier promised his backing. Out of the Senate, Root continued to oppose Wilson until the United States entered World War I. In April 1917 he was sent by Wilson to Russia in a futile attempt to bolster the government of Alexander Kerensky. He supported, with minor reservations, the Treaty of Versailles and the Covenant of the League of Nations, breaking with Henry Cabot Lodge on the issue. In 1920 he was appointed to a commission of jurists charged with framing the statute for the Permanent Court of International Justice (World Court) and in 1929 he helped revise the statute; he was a constant though unsuccessful advocate of U.S. membership in the Court. President Warren J. Harding appointed him one of the U.S. delegates to the 1921 Washington arms-limitation conference. In his later years he was active in the direction of a number of Andrew Carnegie's philanthropic activities, particularly the Carnegie Endowment for International Peace, of which he was president from 1910 to 1925. Among Root's published works were *Experiment in Government and the Essentials of the Constitution*, 1913; *Military and Colonial Policy of The United States*, 1916; *Russia and The United States*, 1917; and *Men and Policies*, 1924. He died in New York City on February 7, 1937.

Root, John Wellborn (1850–1891), architect. Born in Lumpkin, Georgia, on January 10, 1850, Root had his schooling interrupted by Gen. William T. Sherman in 1864—Union troops overran the town and burned the schoolhouse—and he was sent to England to continue his education. He returned to the United States in 1866, after a year at Oxford, and entered the University of the City of New York (now New York University), graduating with a degree in civil engineering in 1869. He entered the architectural office of James Renwick, remaining for a year, and in 1871 went to Chicago to take a job as a draftsman in an architectural firm. He met Daniel H. Burnham, who was employed in a similar capacity, in 1872 and the two young men established their own firm, Burnham & Root, in 1873. Their first years were spent in struggles to obtain commissions, but in 1880 they began, after having completed several private homes, a decade of commercial work that may be said to have marked the emergence of the "Chicago school" of architecture. The first of three influential buildings in Chicago that they designed before Root's untimely death was the Montauk Building, an early skyscraper, 1882; the second was the Rookery, 1884–1886; and the third—and by far the most important—was the Monadnock Building, 1889–1891, which broke completely with traditional styles of architecture by relying entirely on functional form and the most advanced techniques of steel framing and simplicity of construction. Root served on the planning commission for the World's Columbian Exposition of 1893, which he did not live to see, and wrote a number of influential papers on the new departures in architecture in Chicago. He died on January 15, 1891.

Rosecrans, William Starke (1819–1898), soldier and public official. Born in Kingston, Ohio, on September 6, 1819, Rosecrans graduated from West Point in 1842 and was commissioned in the engineers. He was assigned first to work on fortifications at Hampton Roads, Virginia, and later, after a period as an instructor at West Point, he served at various posts in New England. He resigned his commission in 1854 to enter business. The outbreak of the Civil War brought him back into the service as a brigadier general, and he served under Gen. McClellan and Gen. John Pope in various campaigns in the western theater at the beginning of the war. As commander of the Department of Western Virginia, he oversaw the operations that led to the complete expulsion of Confederate

forces and the formation of the state of West Virginia. During the summer of 1862, as commander of the Army of the Mississippi, he led his forces to victory at Iuka and Corinth, and then fought the indecisive Battle of Murfreesboro (Stones River) at the end of the year. He had been promoted to major general of volunteers and named commander of the Army of the Cumberland the previous October, and all during the spring of 1863 he troubled his superiors by his delay in employing his forces; finally, during the summer, he harried Gen. Braxton Bragg from Chattanooga to Chickamauga, catching up to him at the latter place on September 19, and there, that day and the next, suffering one of the most disastrous Union defeats of the war. Only the tactics of Gen. George H. Thomas averted total destruction of Rosecrans's army. Rosecrans was thereupon relieved of command by Gen. Ulysses S. Grant, who went on to victory in the Chattanooga Campaign, and he played no further role in the fighting. Sent to await orders in Cincinnati in 1864, he at length resigned his commission in 1867, having in 1865 received honorary promotion to major general in the regular army for his services at Murfreesboro. Later he was made U.S. minister to Mexico, 1868–1869, engaged in mining operations in Mexico and California for the next decade, and served as a member from California in the House of Representatives from 1881 to 1885. From 1885 to 1893 he was register of the U.S. treasury. He died near Redondo Beach, California, on March 11, 1898.

Rosenbach, Abraham Simon Wolf (1876–1952), rare-book dealer and collector. Born in Philadelphia on July 22, 1876, Rosenbach was a confirmed bibliomaniac by the time he was eleven, when he made his first purchase of a rare book—for more money than he had in his pocket, causing the auctioneer some distress. He made his first notable bibliographic discovery when he was eighteen, while still a sophomore at the University of Pennsylvania (from which he graduated in 1898 and received his Ph.D. in 1901). He was leafing through some books in the corner of an auction room and came upon a copy of Thomas Gray's 1757 volume of *Odes*. That was interesting in itself, but bound with it was Dr. Samuel Johnson's long-lost *Prologue* written for the reopening of London's Drury Lane Theatre in 1747. Trembling lest some other collector notice his find, Rosenbach carefully bid the book up in increments of ten cents and obtained it for $3.60; he later refused an offer of $5000 for it, although at the time he badly needed the money. He taught at the University of Pennsylvania from 1895 till 1901 and in 1902 established the Rosenbach Company, with his brother, to deal in rare books. When his uncle, Moses Polock, himself a noted dealer, died the next year, the brothers acquired his stock. Rosenbach soon established a reputation as the "terror of the auction rooms," making what others considered outrageous bids on his theory that no price was too high if a book was rare enough. A number of his successful bids established records in various categories, including $151,000 in 1947 for a copy of *The Bay Psalm Book*, 1640; he was said to have bid a total of some $75 million over the years, for which he obtained, among many other rare and choice books, eight Gutenberg Bibles and more than 30 first folios of Shakespeare. But he was as good a businessman as he was a bibliophile, and he always managed to come out ahead on his purchases. He is credited with having created the great collections of Henry E. Huntington and J. P. Morgan and had a hand in making almost every important American book collection of the twentieth century. He wrote three volumes of personal memoirs, *The Unpublishable Memoirs*, 1917; *Books and Bidders*, 1927; and *A Book Hunter's Holiday*, 1936. His bibliographic checklist, *Early American Children's Books*, 1933, remains a standard reference. He did not resell all that he purchased, either in the way of books or of antiques and objets d'art, and his homes in Philadelphia and New York City were held to be masterpieces in themselves, as a whole and in their parts. He died, the acknowledged giant in his field, on July 1, 1952, in Philadelphia. He had in 1930 established a fellowship in bibliography at his alma mater.

Rosenberg, Ethel, *see under* Rosenberg, Julius

Rosenberg, Julius (1918–1953), spy. Julius Rosenberg was born on the Lower East Side of New York City, of immigrant parents, in 1918. He attended the city's public schools, became a dedicated Communist while still a youngster, and in 1939 married Ethel Greenglass, who had been born in the same poor section of the city in 1915, and who had undergone the same ideological experiences. In the year of his marriage Julius graduated from the College of the City of New York (CCNY). After a short stay in Washington, D.C., the Rosenbergs returned to New York City, where Julius got an engineering job, as a civilian, with the army's Signal Corps. In 1943 Ethel's younger brother, David Greenglass, was inducted into the army and was stationed at the Los Alamos atomic-bomb laboratory as a machinist. In 1945 Julius was fired from the Signal Corps job because of his Communist affiliations and set up a small machinist's business. In mid-1950 Greenglass was arrested by the FBI and indicted in July for stealing top-secret information on the atomic bomb for the Soviet Union. On July 17 of the same year Julius Rosenberg was arrested on similar charges, and after his wife was also arrested, on August 11, both were indicted for, among other things, having recruited David into a spy ring headed by a Soviet consular official; David was named as a cocon-spirator, together with several other persons, all of whom (except Morton Sobell, a classmate of Julius's at City College) admitted their guilt and testified against the Rosenbergs at their trial. The trial was held in Federal District Court in March 1951, and on March 29 the jury found the Rosenbergs and Sobell guilty, although they had through-out insisted on their innocence; on April 5 Judge Irving R. Kaufman sentenced Julius and Ethel Rosenberg to death and Sobell to 30 years in prison. The next day David Greenglass, who had been the principal witness against them, and who had been tried separately, was sentenced to 15 years, with the possibility of parole after a few years. During the next two years the convicted defendants exhausted every avenue of appeal and the case became an international cause célèbre, with leading civil libertarians and humanitarians in many countries, as well as Communists everywhere, decrying what they considered a miscarriage of justice. The question was not so much whether the Rosenbergs were guilty, although they never admitted their guilt, but whether the death penalty was excessive, and whether Judge Kaufman's statement, at the sentencing, that their crime "was worse than murder" reflected undue prejudice against them because of their political beliefs. A plea for executive clemency was sent to the White House late in 1952, but President Harry S. Truman did not act; the incoming president, Dwight D. Eisenhower, after long consideration, refused the plea the following February. After a series of last-minute stays and a visit to them in Sing Sing prison by their sons, then ten and six, the Rosenbergs were electrocuted in Sing Sing on June 19, 1953. They were the first civilians ever to suffer the death penalty for wartime espionage and the first Americans ever to be executed in peacetime for that crime—the charge was not even treason, since the Soviet Union, at the time the events were supposed to have taken place, was an ally, not an enemy, of the United States.

Rosenwald, Julius (1862–1932), businessman and philanthropist. Born on August 12, 1862, in Springfield, Illinois, Rosenwald attended local public schools and began his career in 1879 with Hammerslough Brothers, wholesale clothiers in New York City. In 1885 he established and became president of Rosenwald and Weil in Chicago. He began a lifelong association with Sears, Roebuck and Company in 1895 as vice-president, becoming president in 1910 and chairman of the board in 1925. He had an outstanding ability to choose competent, efficient associates and he believed in the mail-order system of merchandising, which he actively promoted, and the business thrived. As the business grew his original investment of $35,000 became, in the course of 30 years, a fortune of $150 million. He became a generous and astute philanthropist. The Julius Rosenwald Fund, established in 1917 and endowed by 1928 with $40 million to be used for the welfare of mankind, was his largest benefaction. He refused to try to influence the enterprises he assisted; his faith was in men's ability to work out their destinies, and his purpose was to provide equipment and facilities where men could learn how to do so. He did not believe in permanent endowments—the Fund was charged with expending all of its assets within 25 years of his death—and insisted that matching funds and local self-help be contributed. He made sizable contributions to building 25 YMCAs and YWCAs in areas of cities with large Negro populations, and the Fund helped build more than 5000 public schools for Negroes in the South. He contributed to Jewish relief abroad and to the relief of German children after World War I. As a member of the American Jewish Committee, he fought both anti-Semitism and Zionism. Other principal beneficiaries of his wealth were the Museum of Science and Industry in Chicago and the University of Chicago. His gifts, exclusive of those made through the Fund, totaled more than $22 million. He died in Chicago on January 6, 1932.

Ross, Barnaby, *see* Dannay, Frederic

Ross, Betsy (1752–1836), patriot. Born in Philadelphia, the daughter of a master builder, on January 1, 1752, Elizabeth (Betsy) Griscom was brought up a Quaker and educated in Quaker schools. On her marriage to John Ross, an Episcopalian clergyman, in 1773, she was disowned by the Society of Friends; after his death in January 1776 she took over the upholstering business he had founded. Her late husband's uncle, George Ross, was a noted patriot and a friend of George Washington, and according to the traditional account, Washington, Ross, and Robert Morris came to Mrs. Ross's house in June 1776 and asked her to make a flag for the new country that was on the verge of declaring its independence. She suggested a design to Washington, he made a rough pencil sketch on the basis of it, and she thereupon made the famous flag in her back parlor. There is no written contemporary record of the story, which rests entirely on Mrs. Ross's own evidence, but there is no conflicting testimony or evidence, either, and the story is now widely accepted by historians. It is at least admitted by all that secrecy in the enterprise would have been mandatory at the time. Betsy Ross married Joseph Ashburn in 1777 and, after his death in a British prison in 1782, was married for a third time in 1783 to John Claypoole. She continued the business, which became very profitable, until 1827, when she turned it over to her daughter. She died in Philadelphia on January 30, 1836.

Ross, Harold Wallace (1892–1951), editor. Born in Aspen, Colorado, on November 6, 1892, Ross attended high school in Salt Lake City but did not go to college. He first went to work as a reporter for the *Salt Lake City Tribune* in 1906, at the age of thirteen. In 1910 he moved to California and worked as a reporter for the *Marysville Appeal*. He joined the *Sacramento Union* in 1911, then went to the Republic of Panama to work for the *Panama Star and Herald* in 1912; he then worked for the *New Orleans Item*, the *Atlanta Journal*, and the *San Francisco Call*. In 1917 he enlisted in the Railway Engineer Corps of the U.S. army but did not do much railroading. Instead, he became an editor of *Stars and Stripes*, the army newspaper, and is said to have discovered his ability

to recognize good humorous writing. After the war he worked for a time for the Butterick Publishing Company, was editor of the *American Legion Weekly* from 1921 to 1923, and in 1924 was editor of *Judge* magazine. The *New Yorker* began publication in February 1925, with Ross as editor, Raoul Fleischmann as publisher, and, for a time, with James Thurber as managing editor. The new magazine quickly caught on and ultimately had great influence on the development of American reporting, humorous writing, and cartooning over the next quarter-century. Ross was an unpredictable but brilliant editor who always knew exactly what he wanted although he was not always able to make this absolutely clear to contributors. Emphasis was on the content of stories and articles, not on authors' names, which appeared only at the end of their contributions, and the magazine carried no table of contents until the later 1960s. The *New Yorker* nevertheless helped to make the reputations of many writers, among them Thurber, Clifton Fadiman, Edmund Wilson, John O'Hara, and Truman Capote. Reporting was on a high level, for Ross demanded proof of every statement. Biography became a bold art in the innovative series of "profiles." One of the glories of the magazine was its cartoons. The *New Yorker* was the inventor, or reinventor, of the one-line joke, and Ross insisted obsessively that all his cartoonists make their point mainly in the drawing, ruling out lengthy, complex captions. A number of cartoonists were made famous by their work in the magazine, among them Gluyas Williams, Mary Petty, Charles Addams, and Peter Arno. The magazine printed a weekly review of events in New York City, fine poetry, excellent book and entertainment reviews, and enjoyed from about 1940 the highest advertising revenues of any periodical in the nation. Ross devoted himself completely to it, and did almost nothing else but worry about it, edit all of the copy, and plan for the future. He died in Boston on December 6, 1951. Thurber, probably his greatest discovery, wrote an entertaining biography of him, *The Years with Ross*, in 1959.

Ross, John (1790–1866), Indian leader. Born near Lookout Mountain, Tennessee, on October 3, 1790, Ross, who bore the Indian name Coowescoowe (Kooweskoowe), was the son of a Scotsman who had gone to live among the Cherokee during the Revolution and of a Scotswoman who was one-fourth Cherokee. He received a good secondary education and in 1809 was sent by the U.S. government as an Indian agent to the western Cherokee, in Arkansas, then largely wilderness. He was adjutant of a Cherokee regiment under Gen. Andrew Jackson in the War of 1812 and saw action in 1814 in the battle of Horseshoe Bend (Tohopeka) against the Creek Indians. A member of the national council of the Cherokee from 1817, he was president of the council from 1819 to 1826; in 1827 he was made assistant chief of the eastern Cherokee nation and the next year principal chief, a position he held until 1839. He had helped to write the 1827 Cherokee constitution, and during the next decade he made many efforts to resist the pressure of the state of Georgia to remove his tribe westward from their fertile lands; his resistance finally proving futile in 1838, when President Martin Van Buren ordered Gen. Winfield Scott to enforce the removal. He led his people to Indian Territory (now Oklahoma), a removal that took a year to effect and that resulted in the death of many from starvation and exposure on the "trail of tears." The eastern and western Cherokee were now united under a constitution he helped draft in 1839, and Ross was chosen chief of the entire nation, a position that he held until his death. Of an aristocratic bent, he possessed many slaves and a large plantation, and his efforts to resist alliance with the Confederacy during the Civil War were futile; the tribe signed a treaty of alliance with the Confederates in 1861, but repudiated it two years later. When Union forces invaded Indian Territory in 1862 Ross went to Philadelphia and died in Washington, D.C., in the midst of negotiations for a new Cherokee treaty, on August 1, 1866.

Ross, Nellie Tayloe (1880?–1977), public official. Born in St. Joseph, Missouri, on a date that she adamantly refused to divulge—it was probably about 1880—Nellie Tayloe married William Bradford Ross about 1900 and went with him in 1902 to Cheyenne, Wyoming, where he established a law practice. He was elected governor of Wyoming in 1922, but when he died in the middle of his term Mrs. Ross was elected to serve out its remaining two years, from January 1925 to January 1927. "Ma" Ferguson was elected governor of Texas on the same day in 1924, but because Mrs. Ross was inaugurated two weeks before Mrs. Ferguson, she is credited with having been the first woman ever to be elected governor of a U.S. state. Failing of reelection in 1926, Mrs. Ross devoted herself thereafter to Democratic politics, serving in the state legislature and as the leader of Democratic women in the presidential campaigns of 1928 and 1932. She was rewarded for her campaign efforts in behalf of President Franklin D. Roosevelt by being appointed director of the U.S. Bureau of the Mint in 1933, thereby becoming the first woman ever to hold the office. At the Mint she inherited an organization that had been cut to the bone because of Depression economies, but she administered it with skill until her retirement in 1953, upon the election of Dwight D. Eisenhower. From 1940 she headed the Treasury Assay Committee and was the first woman to have her likeness on a mint medal; her name also appears on the cornerstone of the U.S. gold depository at Fort Knox, Kentucky. She died in Washington, D.C., on December 19, 1977.

Rossby, Carl-Gustaf Arvid (1898–1957), meteorologist. Born in Stockholm on December 28, 1898, Rossby was educated at the University of Stockholm, the Geophysical Institute in Norway, and the University of Leipzig. In 1925 he came to the United States on a Swedish-American Foundation fellowship and joined the Daniel Guggenheim Fund for the Promotion of Aeronautics as a research meteorologist. In 1931 he moved to the Massachusetts Institute of Technology (MIT), where, as a professor, he became the head of the nation's first department of meteorology; also in 1931 he became associated with the Woods Hole Oceanographic Institution. From 1931 to 1941 he served as assistant chief for research and education of the U.S. Weather Bureau and during World War II, by which time he had left MIT to become head of the meteorology department of the University of Chicago, he was a consultant on meteorology to the War Department and to the Army Air Forces. Rossby's researches were of a general and theoretical nature and found application not only to meteorology but also to other dynamic fluid systems. He made significant advances in the understanding of the thermodynamics of air masses and atmospheric turbulence, identified and developed theoretical explanations for the "Rossby waves" and the "jet streams" of the upper air, and contributed such useful tools as the Rossby number and the thermal Rossby number to the study of rotating-fluid mechanics. He also devoted time to developing mathematical models of weather systems by which computational weather prediction might be made possible. In 1947 he returned to the University of Stockholm and founded the Institute of Meteorology, with which he was mainly associated for the rest of his life. In later years he organized worldwide studies of atmospheric chemistry and radioactivity. Rossby died in Stockholm on August 19, 1957.

Roth, Philip Milton (1933–   ), author. Born in Newark, New Jersey, on March 19, 1933, Roth was educated in Newark schools, at Bucknell University, from which he received his B.A. in 1954, and at the University of Chicago, from which he received an M.A. in English literature in 1955. After a short period of military service he returned to the University of Chicago for further graduate study and to teach literature. His first stories began to appear in "little magazines" during the later 1950s and were collected in his first book, *Goodbye, Columbus*, 1959. The work was a minor sensation, winning a National Book Award for fiction, and the title story became a popular film in 1969. Roth's first full-length novel, *Letting Go*, appeared in 1962 and was followed five years later by another novel, *When She Was Good*. All of his works up to this time had been for the most part "dark" and "brooding," in Roth's estimation, and he now determined to try to write something "extravagant and funny." As writer in residence at the University of Pennsylvania he was teaching a course on Franz Kafka, and he conceived the idea of trying to rewrite Kafka in the vein of the Marx Brothers comedies. The result was *Portnoy's Complaint*, which was published in 1969. An enormous commercial success, it sold some half a million copies in hard-cover in its first year and gained Roth more than a million dollars before publication, in advances and movie-sale proceeds; the book was also highly praised by the critics, who saw in its savage frankness about such subjects as masturbation and oral sex a new freedom from traditional novelistic restraints. *The Breast*, a weird and again Kafkaesque tale of a man who wakes up to find himself transformed into a huge female breast, appeared in 1972 and was also successful.

Rothko, Mark (1903–1970), painter. Born Marcus Rothkovich in Daugavpils (Dvinsk), Russia, on September 25, 1903, Rothko was brought to the United States in 1913 and grew up in Portland, Oregon, where as a youth he wanted to be a labor leader. He attended Yale from 1921 to 1923, leaving without a degree, and after a period of wandering spent a few months at the Art Students League in New York City, where he studied under Max Weber; but aside from this brief period in 1925 he was entirely self-taught as an artist. His first mythological and, later, surrealistic paintings were exhibited in group shows in the early 1930s, and he enjoyed his first one-man show at the Contemporary Arts Gallery in New York City (where he lived for most of the time after 1925) in 1933. He worked on the Federal Arts Project of the Works Progress Administration (WPA) during 1935–1937 but continued painting steadily and by 1947, when his style had become decidedly abstract, he was already beginning to attract the approval of critics. In that year he began annual one-man shows at the Betty Parsons Gallery, shifting to the Sidney Janis Gallery in 1954. During the 1950s his simple rectangles of glowing color began to be internationally acclaimed, and he was recognized as one of the leading figures—perhaps the leading figure—in Abstract Expressionism, the most distinctively American art movement of the middle of the twentieth century. His importance was signalized by a retrospective exhibition of 54 of his works at New York City's Museum of Modern Art in 1961, an honor previously accorded only to such artists as Pablo Picasso and Joan Miró. Two more major shows, at the Metropolitan Museum of Art and at the Museum of Modern Art, were held in 1970, but that year, on February 25, in New York City, Rothko committed suicide in a fit of depression. He had earlier expressed his artistic credo in a letter to the *New York Times* published on June 13, 1943. The letter, written by Rothko and another Abstract Expressionist, Adolph Gottlieb, stated their belief that "Art is an adventure into an unknown world, which can be explored only by those willing to take the risk." "We favor," they said, "the simple expression of the complex thought."

Rothkovich, Marcus, *see* Rothko, Mark

Rous, Peyton (1879–1970), pathologist. Born in Baltimore on October 5, 1879, Francis Peyton Rous attended The Johns Hopkins University, receiving his B.A. and M.A. in 1900 and his M.D. in 1905. After a year of residency at The Johns Hopkins Hospital he accepted a position as instructor in pathology at the University of Michigan, transferring in 1909 to the Rockefeller Institute for Medical Research (now Rockefeller University) in New York City, where he remained for the rest of his long career. He became a full member of the faculty in 1920 and, although he was made an emeritus member in 1945, continued his research at the institution for many years thereafter. The work for which he was best known began in 1909, when he was given a Plymouth Rock hen with a cancer that he soon diagnosed as a sarcoma. It was known that cancer could spread from one animal to another, but at the time it was assumed that this could only happen because of the transfer of cancer cells. Rous established as early as 1910, to his own satisfaction at least, that the spread of the disease was owing to a virus, and he wrote a landmark paper, "Transmission of a Malignant New Growth by Means of a Cell-free Filtrate," that was published in the *Journal of Experimental Medicine* in 1912. But prevailing medical opinion could not accept what it believed to be an impossibility, Rous's laboratory methods were criticized, and it was not until 1923 that independent researchers confirmed his results. He was first proposed for a Nobel Prize for his investigations in 1926, but even then the prevailing opinion was that his work applied only to chickens. As the years passed, however, other investigators discovered viral causes for a number of cancers in animals and possibly of some in man, and Rous's work loomed more and more important, a fact that was reflected by his winning the Nobel Prize for Physiology and Medicine in 1966; he shared the prize that year with Charles B. Huggins, who had done much later work on the effect of hormones on cancer in humans. Rous worked during World War I on blood banks, which he is credited with having helped to establish, and later on the physiology of the liver and gall bladder. But from time to time, and increasingly after 1940, he returned to his first researches in cancer and continued to make significant discoveries. Rous died in New York City on February 16, 1970.

Rowland, Henry Augustus (1848–1901), physicist. Born in Honesdale, Pennsylvania, on November 27, 1848, Rowland broke a long family line of Yale-educated clergymen by taking his degree in civil engineering at Rensselaer Polytechnic Institute in 1870. After teaching for a short time at the University of Wooster (now The College of Wooster) he returned to Rensselaer as an instructor in physics in 1872. In 1875 he was invited to become professor of physics at the newly founded Johns Hopkins University and he retained that position for the rest of his life. His earliest researches were in the field of magnetism and electromagnetism. His paper on magnetic lines of force and magnetic permeability was published in

England in 1873 by James Clerk Maxwell and two years later, while working in H. L. F. von Helmholtz's laboratory in Berlin, he demonstrated the similarity in magnetic effect of an electric current and a high-speed electrostatic charge. Later he made new and precise determinations of the mechanical equivalent of heat, of the value of the ohm, and of the ratios of electrical units. His interest turned to spectrometry, and he constructed an apparatus for ruling diffraction gratings on a curved surface at a density of 14,000 to 20,000 lines per inch, a great improvement over plane gratings. He made several detailed studies of various spectra and improved the determinations of spectral line wave lengths. He became a leading expert on both the theoretical and practical aspects of alternating currents and was consulted on the installation of electrical generators at Niagra Falls. In all his work he combined the mathematical knowledge of the pure scientist with great engineering skill, and his mechanical devices were of a value equal to his theoretical contributions. In 1899 he was elected to the Royal Society and during 1899–1900 he served as first president of the American Physical Society. He died in Baltimore on April 16, 1901.

Rowlands, John, *see* Stanley, Henry Morton

Rowson, Susanna Haswell (1762?–1824), author, actress, and educator. Born about 1762 in Portsmouth, England, Miss Haswell spent childhood days in Nantasket Beach, Massachusetts, where her father, a naval lieutenant, was stationed. In 1778 they returned to England. Her education consisted of wide reading in Shakespeare, the poetry of Edmund Spenser, and the Pope and Dryden translations of Homer and Virgil. She published her first novel, *Victoria*, in 1786, and the next year married William Rowson. Several other works, including a book of theatrical criticism, *A Trip to Parnassus*, 1788, appeared before her greatest success, *Charlotte, a Tale of Truth*, 1791, entitled *Charlotte Temple* in later editions. Reprinted in Philadelphia in 1794, this sentimental story of Charlotte Temple was the first best seller in the United States. Later in 1791 appeared her essays on education, *Mentoria, or the Young Lady's Friend*, and in 1792 a semiautobiographical work, *Rebecca, or the Fille de Chambre*. The failure of her husband's business led the couple to seek theatrical careers. During 1792–1793 they played in Edinburgh and other cities, and in 1793 came to the United States. They appeared in Baltimore, Annapolis, and Philadelphia, where she wrote a comic opera, *Slaves in Algiers*, 1794, and a light musical, *The Volunteers*, 1795. Her preoccupation with American patriotism in these and other works led to a much-publicized interchange in which William Cobbett, in *A Kick for a Bite*, intimated that she was guilty of betrayal of England, and she responded in *Trials of the Human Heart*, also 1795, calling him "a kind of loathsome reptile." She retired from the theater in 1797 and from that year until her death on March 2, 1824, operated

a successful boarding school for young ladies in Massachusetts. She wrote texts, songs, and poetry for her pupils, edited the *Boston Weekly Magazine* during 1802–1805, wrote for its successor, the *Boston Magazine*, and other publications, and completed several novels, among them *Sarah, the Exemplary Wife*, 1813, and a sequel to the story of Charlotte Temple, concerning a certain Lucy Temple. The book was titled *Charlotte's Daughter, or The Three Orphans*, and it was published posthumously in 1828.

Royall, Anne Newport (1769–1854), author and journalist. Born in Maryland on June 11, 1769, Miss Newport endured an unsettled childhood and while still a girl entered the employ of William Royall, a Virginia gentleman farmer and Revolutionary War veteran, as a domestic servant. Royall became interested in her, saw to it that she was reasonably well educated, and married her in 1797. He died 16 years later and left her most of his property, but after ten difficult years of litigation his other heirs succeeded in breaking the will, leaving Mrs. Royall penniless at the age of fifty-four. Ill as well, she spent several months struggling to gain a pension as the widow of a Revolutionary veteran, but although she had the assistance of John Quincy Adams her quest was not successful until 1848; even then, the pension turned out to be a mere pittance. But she was a woman of great courage, and in 1824 she began to travel and write to earn her living. Between 1826 and 1831 she published ten volumes of travel accounts, of which the first, *Sketches of History, Life and Manners in the United States, by a Traveler*, 1826, is the best known; but all remain valuable sources of information about the life of the period. She espoused many causes and attacked many others, and her anti-Presbyterianism resulted in 1829 in a conviction on the charge of being a common scold; she soon thereafter settled in Washington, D.C., and began, in 1831, to publish two papers, *Paul Pry*, 1831–1836, and the *Huntress*, 1836–1854, which ran more or less unbrokenly until shortly before her death. A vigorous and effective lobbyist for measures of which she approved and an equally effective opponent of measures of which she did not, she became in time the conscience of Washington and was a dangerous enemy of any corrupt politician, no matter how highly placed. She was, in effect, the first of the great muckrakers, although she anticipated them by some 50 years. During her last years she suffered greatly from illness and poverty, and she died in Washington on October 1, 1854, at the age of eighty-five. She had published in 1827 her only novel, *The Tennessean*, said by one of her biographers to be one of the worst ever to be written in America. But her travel books and newspaper articles, complete with more than 2000 "pen portraits" which she drew of the personalities of her day, survive.

Royce, Josiah (1855–1916), philosopher. Born on November 20, 1855, in Grass Valley, California, of English immigrant parents who had joined the Gold Rush, Royce grew up from the age of eleven in San Francisco and graduated from the University of California, at Berkeley, in 1875. For a year he studied philosophy at the universities of Leipzig and Göttingen and in 1876 accepted an invitation to be one of the first group of fellows at The Johns Hopkins University, where two years later he took his Ph.D. He returned to the University of California for four years as an instructor in English. Although literature had been the primary focus of his undergraduate studies, he was drawn more and more to philosophy and in 1881 published *Primer of Logical Analysis for the Use of Composition Students*, neatly bridging the two subjects. The opportunity to follow his chosen field came in 1882 when he was invited to substitute temporarily for William James at Harvard. Royce remained at Harvard for the rest of his life, becoming assistant professor in 1885 and professor in 1892. The bulk of his thought and writings fell into two general areas—logic and mathematics, on which he published a number of important papers, and religion and metaphysics, the subjects of his major books. An ethical idealist in his philosophy, he gradually evolved a system based on his conception of the Absolute, the single mind and will that encompasses all others; that, as the principle of unity and relation in the universe, is the ground of all consciousness and knowledge; and that, as the ultimate being, is the proper object of worship. In his later thought he elaborated the parallel and supplementary idea of the "beloved community," consisting of all humanity, the object of ultimate personal loyalty and the source of ethical values. He argued his position with great dialectical skill, drawing often upon his deep knowledge of logic and scientific method. William James, long his colleague and friend, once commented that Royce's brand of idealism was the only idealistic philosophy that tempted him to relinquish his own pluralistic pragmatism. His major works were many: *The Religious Aspect of Philosophy*, 1885; *The Spirit of Modern Philosophy*, 1892; *The Conception of God*, 1897; *Studies of Good and Evil*, 1898; *The World and the Individual*, two volumes, 1900–1901 (from his Gifford Lectures at the University of Aberdeen, 1899–1900); *The Conception of Immortality*, 1903; *Race Questions, Provincialism, and Other American Problems*, 1908; *The Philosophy of Loyalty*, 1908; *The Sources of Religious Insight*, 1912; *The Problem of Christianity*, 1913; and *The Hope of the Great Community*, 1916, published posthumously. In 1914 he succeeded to the Alford chair of philosophy at Harvard; he died in Cambridge, Massachusetts, on September 14, 1916.

Rubinstein, Arthur (1889–1982), pianist. Born in Lódź, Poland, on January 28, 1889, Rubinstein was a musical prodigy, beginning study of the piano when he was four and making his debut at six and his formal debut in Berlin, with a symphony orchestra conducted by Joseph Joachim, at eleven.

By the year 1905, when he was still only sixteen, he was an acknowledged virtuoso in Europe, but his U.S. debut in January of the next year was not a success, the coolness and precision of his playing repelling American audiences, who were accustomed to the grand manner. In Europe, however, he continued to be acclaimed, especially in Spain after 1916, when he first began to perform the music of such modern Spanish composers as Manuel de Falla, Enrique Granados, and Isaac Albéniz; for the same reason he was a great hit in South America. A second tour of the United States in 1919 was again relatively unsuccessful, and he remained in Europe for the next ten years, living a carefree cosmopolitan life and giving many concerts. In 1934, however, realizing that he had become careless (he always hated to practice) and was, as he said, "missing too many notes," he devoted six months to intensive study of the piano literature that he had already been performing for nearly 40 years, and emerged the accomplished perfectionist that he was later recognized to be. Three years later he had his first real American success, and upon the outbreak of World War II he moved his family to California, performing in a number of films, either in person or as a "ghost" for actors taking the parts of Schumann, Liszt, and Brahms, over the next few years. He became a U.S. citizen in 1946. He had signed a recording contract with RCA–Victor in 1938 and over the years made more records than any pianist in history, his sales of long-playing discs approaching the four-million mark by 1972. His most popular records were the Rachmaninoff *Second Piano Concerto* and Tchaikovsky's *Concerto No. 1*, but he was most renowned for his playing of Chopin, almost all of whose works he recorded at one time or another. He made the first of his famous marathon series of concerts in 1953, when he gave five concerts in less than two weeks; he played ten recitals in ten weeks in the fall of 1961 and in January 1966, at the age of seventy-seven, gave three recitals in Carnegie Hall devoted to works of Mozart, Beethoven, and Brahms. These concerts, as well as others that he gave from time to time (often wholly for charity), were sell-outs, and tickets were always at a premium. In his later years Rubinstein was almost universally accounted one of the greatest pianists of his time. In 1973 he published the autobiographical *My Young Years*. He died in Geneva, Switzerland, on December 20, 1982.

Ruffin, Edmund (1794–1865), agriculturalist. Born on January 5, 1794, in Prince George County, Virginia, Ruffin entered the College of William and Mary in 1809 but remained only briefly. He served for six months in the army during the War of 1812 and in 1813 returned home to take charge of his late father's farm. As was true of much of Virginia at the time, the soil on Ruffin's farm had been depleted by one-crop cultivation and overuse. He set about experimenting with various treatments and methods to revitalize the soil; by 1818 he was able to announce considerable success in using marl (an earth containing a large proportion of calcium carbonate) on the soil, together with fertilizing, crop rotation, and improved patterns of plowing and drainage. A published article detailing his results grew into a widely influential book, *An Essay on Calcareous Manures*, in 1832 and continued to expand through several editions. He was elected as a Whig to the Virginia senate in 1823 and remained in that body for three years. From 1833 to 1842 he published the *Farmer's Register*, a journal promoting scientific agriculture. In 1842 he became agricultural surveyor for the state of South Carolina; two years later he refused to become the first president of the Virginia State Agricultural Society but accepted the presidency in 1852. He continued to publish articles and books on the improvement of agriculture and was a much-sought lecturer. In his later years he changed his political affiliation from the Whigs to the Democratic party as, with the crisis between North and South worsening, he became an outspoken defender of slavery and states' rights and an early advocate—a "fire-eater"—of Southern secession; his views were given wide circulation in Southern newspapers, in *De Bow's Review*, and in his many pamphlets. Finally, as a member of the Palmetto Guards of Charleston, he was granted the honor of firing the first shot on Fort Sumter on April 12, 1861. He served sporadically in the Confederate army during the Civil War; despondent over the South's defeat, he took his own life on June 18, 1865, at his plantation, Redmoor, in Amelia County, Virginia.

Rugg, Harold Ordway (1886–1960), educator. Born in Fitchburg, Massachusetts, on January 17, 1886, Rugg graduated from Dartmouth College in 1908, took an engineering degree from Dartmouth's Thayer School of Civil Engineering the next year, and in 1909 was appointed an instructor at James Millikin (now Millikin) University. Two years later he joined the faculty of the University of Illinois and there continued his studies, turning to the field of education and acquiring a Ph.D. in 1915. He then accepted a post at the University of Chicago. In 1920 he moved to Teachers College of Columbia University, becoming professor of education and retaining that position until his retirement in 1951. Rugg was a prolific writer of high-school textbooks, and his selection and organization of materials for them, reflecting his belief in the value of frank, open discussion of all questions and in the avoidance of rote or dogmatic teaching, often caused considerable controversy. At various times his texts were removed from certain schools after being vehemently attacked by right-wing spokesmen, who accused him of promoting Communism by discussing it in objective terms. Among his texts, which remained nonetheless in wide use, were the 12-volume Social Science Pamphlets, 1921–1928, and the 14-volume Man and His Changing Society series, 1929–1945. He also wrote *The Child-Centered School*, 1928; *Culture and Education in America*, 1931; *American Life and the School Curriculum*, 1936; *That Man* *May Understand*, 1941; *Now Is the Moment*, 1943; *Foundations for American Education*, 1947; *The Teacher in School and Society*, 1950; and *Imagination*, published posthumously in 1963. Rugg edited the *Journal of Educational Psychology* from 1920 to 1931 and *Frontiers of Democracy* from 1939 to 1943; he was on the editorial board of *Social Frontier* from 1934 to 1939 and was social-studies editor of *Scholastic Magazine* from 1930 to 1940. He was founder in 1950 and thereafter editor of the New World Education Series. Rugg died in Woodstock, New York, on May 17, 1960.

Rumford, Benjamin Thompson, Count, *see* Thompson, Benjamin

Rumsey, James (1743–1792), inventor. Born in Cecil County, Maryland, in March 1743, Rumsey had but scant education before becoming a blacksmith and, it is believed, serving in the Revolution. In 1782 he was operating a grist mill at Sleepy Creek, Maryland, but the business failed—as most of his enterprises were to do—and he went to nearby Bath, Virginia (Berkeley Springs, West Virginia), to open a general store and engage in the building trade. There he met Gen. George Washington, who owned lands in the neighborhood, and Rumsey built a house and stables for him in 1784. But he was not really interested in building or in business; for some time he had been working in secret on a mechanically propelled boat, and he now, with Washington's help, acquired a monopoly for his proposed vessel on Virginia waters. But he could not raise any capital, despite being given a job with Washington's Potomac Navigation Company, and in 1785 he therefore began to work on another plan, for a steamboat. John Fitch was gaining considerable publicity in Philadelphia for a steam-powered craft, and Washington and his other friends urged Rumsey to announce his plans. He therefore demonstrated, on the Potomac River near Shepherdstown, Virginia (now in West Virginia), in December 1787, a boat that was propelled by jets of water forced out the stern by a force pump run by a steam engine. It was probably the first jet-propelled vehicle in history, but the world was not ready for it, and Rumsey was again unable to raise any capital to further his experiments or to manufacture more boats. The American Philosophical Society became interested in 1788 and tried to help, going so far as to form a "Rumseian Society" and sending him to England to obtain patents on the boat and on his other inventions, including an improved steam boiler, an improved grist mill and saw mill, and a steam-driven pump; but although he acquired the patents on some of these items (U.S. patents were also issued to him in 1791), he failed to obtain the capital he so desperately needed to finish his work. He seemed close to his goal early in the winter of 1792, but just a few months short of completing his improved steamboat, which he had named *Columbia Maid*, he died in London, on December 20, 1792.

Runyon, Damon (1884–1946), journalist and author. Born in Manhattan, Kansas, on October 4, 1884, the son of an itinerant newspaperman, Alfred Damon Runyon ran away from home to serve in the Spanish-American War at fourteen and, on returning, decided to become a newspaperman. From 1900 to 1911, when he settled down as a sportswriter with the *New York American*, he worked for a number of papers in Denver, San Francisco, and other cities; for the *American* he covered not only sports (his favorite events being heavyweight championship fights) but also the revolution in Mexico in 1912, Gen. John J. Pershing's Mexican Border expedition of 1916, and World War I in Europe. His sports column, "Both Barrels," was distributed by International News Service, the Hearst syndicate, from 1918 and was replaced by a more general column, "The Brighter Side," which was distributed by King Features Syndicate from 1937. He published two small volumes of bad verse in 1911 and 1912 but did not begin to write his famous stories of New York City low life until about 1930. Concentrating on the block of Broadway between 40th and 50th Streets—which included Lindy's restaurant, his favorite New York hangout, called "Mindy's" in his stories—he ranged the area from nightfall to dawn, talking to anybody and everybody and making mental note of the "slanguage" (metamorphosed in his stories into the even more picturesque "Runyonese") and crochets of the colorful crew of characters that he met—men and women who, like him, hardly ever saw the light of day. The stories were published in leading magazines and later collected in a series of books: *Guys and Dolls*, 1931 (later turned into a hit Broadway musical and a movie by Frank Loesser); *Blue Plate Special*, 1934; *Money from Home*, 1935; and *The Best of Runyon*, 1938; in 1938 also appeared, in England, *Take It Easy*, a collection of Runyon tales with a glossary of American slang by E. C. Bentley. In the meantime, Runyon had been writing movie scripts in Hollywood, some of his best-known productions being *Lady for a Day*, *Little Miss Marker*, *A Slight Case of Murder* (adapted from a play he had written with Howard Lindsay in 1935), *Lemon Drop Kid*, and *Butch Minds the Baby*. Pieces from "The Brighter Side" were also collected in such books as *My Old Man*, 1939, *My Wife Ethel*, 1940, and *In Our Town*, 1946. Runyon died in New York City on December 10, 1946, and for the next few years seemed to be fading very quickly into oblivion; but the production of Loesser's *Guys and Dolls* in 1950 (and later revivals) reestablished his reputation.

Rush, Benjamin (1745–1813), physician and educator. Born near Philadelphia on December 24 (old style), 1745, Rush graduated from the College of New Jersey (now Princeton) in 1760. He studied for six years in the office of a Philadelphia physician and then spent two years at the University of Edinburgh, taking his M.D. in 1768. He returned to Philadelphia the following year and immediately began the practice of medicine. At the same time he became professor of chemistry at the College of Philadelphia, later part of the University of Pennsylvania, and in 1770 he published *A Syllabus of a Course of Lectures on Chemistry*, the first such text to appear in America. In addition to following his scientific pursuits, he maintained a keen interest in politics and reform. He strongly supported the colonial side in the growing dispute with Great Britain and in 1776 was elected to the Second Continental Congress in time to become a signer of the Declaration of Independence. In 1777 he was appointed surgeon general of the Continental army, but his involvement in the so-called Conway Cabal, aimed at the removal of George Washington as commander in chief, led to his leaving the position a year later. He began to lecture at the University of the State of Pennsylvania (later the University of Pennsylvania) in 1780. He enjoyed a large practice and increasing popularity as a teacher. He established the nation's first free dispensary in 1786, and strongly urged the abolition of slavery and capital punishment, prison reform, the broadening of educational opportunities for women and the poor, the rational and humane treatment of the mentally ill, but, unfortunately, held a simplistic view of disease that insisted upon the great value of bleeding and purging under most circumstances. He was a leading member of the Pennsylvania convention for the ratification of the Constitution and the movement that led to the state constitution of 1790. In 1791 he joined the medical faculty of the newly unified University of Pennsylvania taking the lead in organizing the medical school. During the yellow-fever epidemic in Philadelphia in 1793 he performed devoted service, although despite his adoption of certain valuable techniques discovered by John Mitchell of Virginia, he lessened their impact by insisting also on his own therapeutic method of heavy bleeding. His *Account of the Bilious Remitting Yellow Fever As It Appeared in the City of Philadelphia in the Year 1793*, 1794, was a graphic and valuable description of the disease that won recognition in Europe. Despite his dogmatic approach to medicine, he made valuable contributions to the science, particularly with his observations of cholera infantum, dengue, and focal infection of the teeth. In 1797 he was appointed treasurer of the Mint of the United States by President John Adams and retained the position until his death. It was through his mediation that Adams and another old friend, Thomas Jefferson, were reconciled after both had retired from active politics. Among his other notable written works were *Medical Inquiries and Observations*, five volumes, 1789–1798, his collected *Essays, Literary, Moral, and Philosophical*, 1798, and *Medical Inquiries and Observations Upon the Diseases of the Mind*, 1812, the first systematic treatment of the subject in America. He died in Philadelphia on April 19, 1813.

Rush, Richard (1780–1859), lawyer, public official, and diplomat. Born in Philadelphia on August 29,

1780, the son of the physician Benjamin Rush, Richard Rush graduated from the College of New Jersey (now Princeton) in 1797, studied law, and was admitted to the bar in 1800. His law practice was unspectacular and he gained prominence but slowly. In 1811 he was appointed attorney general of Pennsylvania and, later in the same year, comptroller of the U.S. Treasury (his father was at the time treasurer of the Mint of the United States). He accepted President James Madison's invitation to become U.S. attorney general in 1814. With the inauguration of President James Monroe in March 1817 he became interim secretary of state until John Quincy Adams's return from Europe in September; during this time he negotiated the Rush-Bagot Convention providing for mutual American and British disarmament on the Great Lakes. In October of that year he was appointed U.S. minister to Great Britain. During eight years in the post he discharged his duties well, negotiating several agreements of which the most notable was the convention of 1818, which extended the U.S.–Canadian border westward from the Lake of the Woods along the 49th parallel and provided for joint U.S.–British occupation of Oregon. His reports of conversations with the British foreign minister in 1823, relating to British and French policy in Latin America, contributed directly to the enunciation of the Monroe Doctrine in December of that year. In 1825 he returned home to become secretary of the treasury under President Adams; he was Adams's running mate in the election of 1828 and with him was soundly defeated. For the next eight years he practiced law and dabbled briefly in politics. He supported Andrew Jackson in the controversy over the Bank of the United States in 1832. In 1836 he went to England to take part in the litigation surrounding the bequest of James Smithson of his large estate to the United States; two years later the case was cleared and Rush brought back the money that was used, according to the terms of the will, to establish the Smithsonian Institution. During his last years his final public service was as minister to France from 1847 to 1849. Rush wrote *Memoranda of a Residence at the Court of London*, 1833 and 1845, and *Occasional Productions, Political, Diplomatic, and Miscellaneous*, 1860. He died in Philadelphia on July 30, 1859.

Rush, William (1756–1833), sculptor and woodcarver. Born in Philadelphia on July 5, 1756, Rush was apprenticed to a wood-carver and soon was making ornamental carvings and figureheads for ships. He served in the army during the Revolution and after the war he established a shop in Philadelphia, where he carved figureheads for the frigates *America*, *Constellation*, and *United States*, as well as many other vessels; but none of his figureheads, which were said to be his masterpieces, survive. One of the founders of the Pennsylvania Academy of the Fine Arts in 1805, he served for many years on the city council of Philadelphia. Some of his wood carvings are preserved in various Philadelphia institutions, including a rugged self-portrait carved out of pine, in the Academy of the Fine Arts, and a life-sized statue of George Washington, in Independence Hall, that may have been intended as a figurehead but was never installed on a ship. He executed numerous other portrait busts, including those of William Bartram, Henry M. Mühlenberg, William Penn, and Benjamin Franklin, of which none survive. Accounted the first American-born sculptor, Rush died in Philadelphia on January 17, 1833.

Russell, Charles Taze (1852–1916), "Pastor Russell," religious leader. Born in Pittsburgh on February 16, 1852, Russell was educated in the city's common schools. Although he was raised in the Congregational church, he at length rejected its teachings, particularly the doctrine of eternal punishment, and began to study the Bible closely for verification of his own beliefs. In 1872 he published a booklet, *The Object and Manner of Our Lord's Return*, in which he announced that the second coming of Christ would occur, without mankind's awareness, in the fall of 1874. After a 40-year "millennial age" the ascension to the throne and the end of the "Gentile times" would come in 1914 and, after a period of world-wide strife marked by class warfare and consequent chaos, Christ's kingdom on earth would begin. Pastor Russell (commonly so called, although he was never ordained in any church) organized the International Bible Students' Association in Pittsburgh in 1872 and in 1879 began publishing the *Watch Tower and Herald of Christ's Presence*, later known as *Zion's Watch Tower* and finally simply as the *Watch Tower*. In 1881 he published his most influential book, *Food for Thinking Christians*, in which he outlined a pattern of unworldly devotion and warned against political and social allegiances or involvements on the part of true Christians. The book was reissued in 1886 as the first volume of *Millenial Dawn*, six volumes, 1886–1904, and still later became part of his six-volume *Studies in the Scriptures*. In 1884 he founded the Watch Tower Bible and Tract Society to publish his books, pamphlets, and periodicals. The original congregation in Pittsburgh was augmented by branches throughout the country, in Canada, England, and in Europe. In 1909 the organization's headquarters were moved to Brooklyn, New York. He traveled and preached all over the world; on one such trip he died, in Pampa, Texas, on October 31, 1916. The International Bible Students' Association—the Russellites—continued to grow and in 1931 the association was renamed the Jehovah's Witnesses by Russell's successor, Joseph Franklin "Judge" Rutherford.

Russell, Henry Norris (1877–1957), astronomer. Born in Oyster Bay, New York, on October 25, 1877, Russell graduated from Princeton cum laude in 1897. Then, after obtaining his Ph.D. from Princeton in 1900, he traveled to England and studied at King's College, Cambridge, until 1905, doing novel work on the determination of stellar parallax by photography. He returned to Princeton in 1905 to teach astronomy, becoming professor in 1911 and director of the observatory the next year; he retired in 1947. From 1947 to 1952 he was a research associate at the Harvard Observatory. His early work concerned double stars, and he developed a method for determining the orbits, masses, sizes, and densities of certain types of eclipsing binaries. Some of these results were arrived at independently by the Danish astronomer Ejnar Hertzsprung, and from about 1910 Russell and Hertzsprung often worked together or on parallel courses. The best-known result of their joint labors is the Hertzsprung-Russell (or H-R) diagram, first formulated in its modern form by Russell in 1913. The diagram illustrates the relationship between the spectral classes and absolute magnitudes of stars, placing the majority of stars on a so-called main sequence and grouping certain stars, including red giants and supergiants above the line formed by the sequence, and white dwarfs below it. Russell's own speculations about the evolution of stars, as suggested by the diagram, are now considered to be incorrect, but the H-R diagram continues to be a fundamental tool of research into stellar evolution. Russell was one of the first to postulate the existence of millions of solar systems like our own, with planets capable of supporting life, and was also one of the first to recognize the dominance of the element hydrogen in the universe; later, the development of radio astronomy confirmed his hypothesis on solar systems. His investigations ranged over almost every field of astronomy, and he published a number of books, including such technical works as *Astronomy: Analysis of Stellar Spectra*, 1928, with J. Q. Stewart; *On the Composition of the Sun's Atmosphere*, 1929; and *The Masses of the Stars*, 1940. His more popular books included *Fate and Freedom*, 1927, and *The Solar System and Its Origin*, 1935. At various times president of the American Philosophical Society, the American Astronomical Society, and the American Association for the Advancement of Science, and the recipient of many honors and awards, Russell died in Princeton, New Jersey, on February 18, 1957.

Russell, Lillian (1861–1922), singer and actress. Born on December 4, 1861, in Clinton, Iowa, Helen Louise Leonard adopted the stage name Lillian Russell while appearing at Tony Pastor's variety theater in New York City in 1880. From the age of four she lived in Chicago; she attended a convent, where she sang in the choir, and a finishing school. Her early training in voice and violin was supplemented by a year of opera study in New York City under Leopold Damrosch. Her first stage role was in the chorus of a company performing *H.M.S. Pinafore* in 1879. After appearing as a ballad singer at Tony Pastor's theater, she continued her studies in voice and acting, and then toured California as the lead in *Babes in the Wood*. Returning to New York City, she attained stardom as D'Jemma in Edmond Audran's comic

opera, *The Great Mogul: or, the Snake Charmer*, in October 1881, and then played in Gilbert and Sullivan's *Patience* and *The Sorcerer*. By 1883 she was the prima donna of the McCaul Opera Company. She made her London debut at the Gaiety Theatre in July 1883 in Edward Solomon's *Virginia and Paul*. Returning to the United States in 1884, she was in the news frequently because of her flamboyant personal life—her marriage to Solomon in 1884 was annulled nine years later, two of her three marriages ended in divorce, and she was for 40 years a frequent companion of Diamond Jim Brady—and numerous contract disputes; at one time she sought an injunction to prevent any theater manager from requiring her to appear in silk tights. Celebrated for her beauty and her clear, pleasant, soprano voice, not so highly trained as to be beyond popular audiences, she was dubbed "airy, fairy Lillian." Her most difficult roles were in two Offenbach operas, as Fiorella in *The Brigands*, in 1889, and in the title role in *The Grand Duchess* in 1890. She joined Weber and Fields's company in 1890 and sang in *Fiddle-dee-dee* and *Whoop-dee-doo*. With *Barbara's Millions* in 1906 she essayed straight comedy and was successful thereafter in this genre in *Wildfire* and *Hokey-Pokey*. After 1912 she appeared only rarely on the stage. She wrote articles on beauty for the women's pages of the *Chicago Herald* and the *Chicago Tribune* and in 1913 toured the country delivering a lecture on "How to Live a Hundred Years." During World War I she was active in the Red Cross and Liberty Loan campaigns. She died in Pittsburgh on June 6, 1922, 40 years short of her goal.

Russell, William Felton (1934–   ), basketball player and coach. Born in Monroe, Louisiana, on February 12, 1934, Bill Russell was brought up in Oakland, California, and did not begin playing basketball seriously until his senior year in high school. As a result he did not receive the plethora of scholarship offers that would ordinarily have been made to a player of his ability, and he therefore enrolled at the University of San Francisco, a school not previously noted for its basketball teams. Russell soon made it notable. After a sophomore year in which he polished his skills, he led the school to 55 straight victories and to National Collegiate Athletic Association (NCAA) championships in his junior and senior years—1955 and 1956—and in 1956 starred on the gold-medal-winning U.S. Olympic team. The first draft choice of the Boston Celtics of the National Basketball Association (NBA) in 1956, he led what was already a good team in the most astonishing winning streak ever recorded by a U.S. professional team, capturing the NBA title in each of his first eight years and winning it two more times—in 1968 and 1969—before retiring in the latter year. From 1965 to 1969 he was also the coach of the Celtics, the first black to coach a major professional team in the history of U.S. sport. Never a high scorer—he left that to others on his team—Bill Russell while in college had already developed his defensive skills to a degree never before attained by any big man in basketball, and he went on in the NBA literally to revolutionize the game, concentrating on blocking shots by opponents and on rebounding, and specializing in the long pass downcourt that made the Celtics' fast break the terror of the league. After his retirement as player and coach he worked as a radio and television sports commentator and devoted himself to various business activities.

Russwurm, John Brown (1799–1851), journalist and public official. Born in Port Antonio, Jamaica, on October 1, 1799, Russwurm was the son of a Jamaican woman and of a white American. When his father left Jamaica he put the boy in school in Canada, but his second wife, a white, later adopted the boy and insisted that he take the father's name. Russwurm was educated in schools in Maine and was sent to Bowdoin College, from which he graduated in August 1826; he was long thought to be the first Negro to graduate from an American college, but it seems now that a certain Edward A. Jones, graduated from Amherst College a few days before Russwurm's commencement. After graduating Russwurm made his way to New York City, where, on March 16, 1827, he and John Cornish brought out the first number of the first Negro paper in the United States, *Freedom's Journal.* Shortly concluding, however, that it was "a mere waste of words to talk of ever enjoying citizenship in this country," he emigrated in 1828 or 1829 to Liberia. He was immediately named superintendent of public schools and from 1830 to 1834 was colonial secretary, editing at the same time the *Liberia Herald.* In 1836 he was appointed governor of the Maryland Colony in Liberia and served effectively and courageously in that post until his death there on June 17, 1851.

Ruth, George Herman (1895–1948), "Babe," baseball player. Born in Baltimore on February 6, 1895, Ruth grew up amid poverty and had an irregular family life. From the age of seven he spent much time in St. Mary's Industrial School and there, encouraged by an interested priest, he developed a passionate love of baseball. In 1914 he was signed by the Baltimore Orioles and later in the year was sold to the Boston Red Sox of the American League. By 1919 he was the best lefthanded pitcher in the league, indeed one of the best ever—his record 29⅔ scoreless innings amassed in the 1916 and 1918 world series was one of his proudest accomplishments—but his obvious potential for even more spectacular achievements with a bat led to his transfer to the outfield. In that year he broke the major-league home-run record with 29. In 1920 he was sold to the New York Yankees, then a struggling team that rented the New York Giants' Polo Grounds for home games. The Babe, also known as "the Bambino," hit 54 home runs that year and 59 the next, and the Yankees won their first pennant. Beyond boosting his own team into prominence, he was credited with helping greatly to save baseball from a fatal loss of popularity that some feared might follow the "Black Sox" scandal of 1919–1920. Yankee Stadium, opened in 1923, was aptly dubbed "the house that Ruth built" and in that year he was voted the league's most valuable player. He slumped somewhat during 1924 and 1925, in the latter year drawing a $5000 fine for "misconduct off the ball field," but soon gave up the high life and rededicated himself to baseball and his legion of fans. In 1927 the "Sultan of Swat" set the standing record for home runs in a 154-game season with 60. The highest paid player of the day, he earned a salary of $80,000 in 1930 and 1931. With Ruth on the team the Yankees won pennants in 1921, 1922, 1923, 1926, 1927, 1928, and 1932. In 1935 he moved to the Boston Braves and ended his playing career in June of that year. In addition to his home-run record he held 53 more, including records for career home runs (714), runs batted in (2209), bases on balls (2056), and strikeouts (1330). He played in 10 World Series and in 1928, when the Yankees swept the Series in 4 games, he scored 9 runs. In 1936 he was one of the first five men elected to the National Baseball Hall of Fame in Cooperstown, New York. During the 1938 season he coached the Brooklyn Dodgers, but he never realized his ambition to manage a major-league team. In his later years he devoted much time to charity and his last home run, hit in 1942 against Walter Johnson, was in a benefit exhibition in Yankee Stadium for war-service organizations. During World War II, U.S. marines fighting in the Pacific were startled to hear Japanese soldiers shouting "To hell with Babe Ruth!" as a battle cry; the fact was a tribute, however, to both his worldwide fame and his heroic stature in the United States. He established the Babe Ruth Foundation for underprivileged children and it was the beneficiary of a major portion of his estate. He died in New York City on August 16, 1948.

Rutledge, John (1739–1800), justice of the Supreme Court. Born in or near Charleston, South Carolina, in September 1739, Rutledge became a leading member of the segment of the Southern planter aristocracy that supported independence so valiantly during the Revolution but afterwards opposed the democratization of the national government. Trained for the law in England, he was called to the English bar in 1760 and, returning the next year to Charleston, was almost immediately elected to the Commons House. He was a delegate to the Stamp Act Congress in 1765 and to the first and second Continental Congress, and, having served as chairman of the committee that in 1776 wrote South Carolina's new constitution, was elected the state's first president the same year. When the state constitution was liberalized in 1778—against his wishes—he was nonetheless chosen governor, and he did courageous service during the overrunning of the state by the British forces and the Carolina Campaign that followed. He served again in Congress in 1782–1783 and in 1787 was one of four South Carolina delegates to the federal Constitutional convention, where he championed slavery and argued unsuccessfully for a more conservative and aristocratic governmental organization than was finally agreed upon. In 1778 he was a member of the South Carolina ratifying convention and argued for ratification. He had been elected to the state chancery court in 1784, and in 1789, after having received South Carolina's first electoral vote for vice-president, was named by President George Washington senior associate justice of the U.S. Supreme Court, but he resigned this post in 1791 to become chief justice of South Carolina, in which position he remained until 1795. In that year he wrote Washington that he would like to be named chief justice of the Supreme Court to succeed John Jay, and Washington immediately proposed him; but Rutledge was so bitter in his denunciation of the Federalists when the text of Jay's Treaty was revealed later in the year that, after he had already presided over the Court's August term, the Senate refused to confirm him in December 1795. His last years were clouded by insanity, and he died in Charleston on July 18, 1800.

Rutledge, Wiley Blount, Jr. (1894–1949), justice of the Supreme Court. Born in Cloverport, Kentucky, on July 20, 1894, Rutledge attended Maryville College, and then transferred to the University of Wisconsin, from which he graduated in 1914. He spent the next seven years teaching in high schools in Indiana, New Mexico, and Colorado and in studying law, receiving his law degree from the University of Colorado in 1922. After two years of private practice he became an associate professor of law at the University of Colorado in 1924, becoming professor of law at Washington University in St. Louis in 1926 and dean of its law school in 1931; in 1935 he became professor of law and dean of the College of Law of the State University of Iowa, where he remained until his appointment to the federal Court of Appeals in the District of Columbia in 1939. He was appointed by President Franklin D. Roosevelt to the Supreme Court in 1943, the last of Roosevelt's appointees and the first from west of the Mississippi. Almost immediately upon his taking his seat he was presented with the problem of casting the deciding vote in important cases on which the court had previously split four-to-four. One of them involved the right of Jehovah's Witnesses to refuse to salute the flag (*West Virginia State Board of Education* v. *Barnette*) and another the case of a California Communist, William Schneiderman, whose naturalization had been revoked because of his political beliefs (*Schneiderman* v. *U.S.*), and, as expected, Rutledge threw in his lot with the Court's liberal bloc. In his later years on the bench he wrote a number of noted and to some extent controversial dissents, for example in *In re Yamashita*, 1946, when he dissented from the Court's validation of a military trial in which Gen. Tomoyuki Yamashita of the defeated Japanese army had been tried on charges of violating the laws of war; Rutledge objected strenuously to the way in which evidence and hearsay had been ac-

cepted in the trial with little reservation and to the general laxity of procedure that had prevailed. His defense of the right to a fair trial of even a defeated enemy won wide approbation. His generally liberal voting record was maintained until his death while vacationing in York, Maine, on September 10, 1949.

Ryan, Thomas Fortune (1851–1928), promoter and financier. Born in Lovingston, Virginia, on October 17, 1851, to a family of Irish Roman Catholic stock, Ryan was orphaned at the age of fourteen. When he was seventeen he went to Baltimore and, penniless, walked the streets for days before landing a job as an errand boy in a dry-goods commission house. His progress thereafter was rapid. Moving to New York City in 1872, he married the daughter of his boss, founded a brokerage firm in New York, and, with his father-in-law's financial help, had by 1874 bought a seat on the New York Stock Exchange. The next decade was one of quiet success. His first real opportunity came in 1884, when he formed a syndicate with William C. Whitney and Peter A. B. Widener and, over the next ten years, using every legal, extra-legal, and illegal trick in the book and with the canny advice of Elihu Root, managed to acquire control of New York City street-railway lines through the Metropolitan Traction Company, organized by the syndicate in 1886, and considered the first holding company in the United States. He and his associates in the Metropolitan Traction Company made a fortune, but the transit lines suffered; in 1905, when this was becoming apparent to all, Ryan joined with August Belmont (organizer of the Interborough Rapid Transit Company and previously a financial foe) to create an even more overcapitalized super-transit system, the Interborough Metropolitan Traction Company. After Ryan withdrew in 1906, the company failed and the city had to take it over; investigations showed that "the Ryan crowd" had gotten away with at least $100 million, but they were never even charged, to say nothing of being convicted. In the meantime Ryan had been engaged in other piratical financial operations. In the early 1890s he, Whitney, and others joined James B. Duke to organize the American Tobacco Company; by 1911, when it was ordered dissolved by the Supreme Court in a famous antitrust case, it had acquired monopolistic control of the entire industry. Ryan's control also extended over a number of important New York banks; into railroads, including in 1903 the Seaboard Air Line; public utilities; and into insurance, his efforts in this field resulting in virtual control from 1905 of the Equitable Life Assurance Society of New York and its $400 million in assets for an investment of only $2.5 million made at a time when scandal over management of the company had depressed the price of its stock. Ryan did not confine himself to the exploitation of U.S. companies. Beginning about 1900 he led a syndicate, at the invitation of Leopold II of Belgium, to engage in the exploitation of the Belgian Congo. The original goal was rubber production but, when that proved unfeasible, the syndicate settled for diamonds, gold, and copper. Once again fortunes were made by all. An aggressive meddler in politics who had always believed it was easier to buy a politician than persuade him, Ryan attempted to control the 1912 Democratic national convention but was formally banned from it by indignant delegates led by William Jennings Bryan. In his later years Ryan largely retired from business to devote himself to his magnificent Fifth Avenue mansion and to his collections of Limoges enamels, tapestries, bronzes, and other objects. During his lifetime he is reported to have given more than $20 million to the Roman Catholic church, but when he died, on November 23, 1928, in New York City, he left a fortune of more than $200 million.

Ryder, Albert Pinkham (1847–1917), painter. Born on March 19, 1847, in the seaport town of New Bedford, Massachusetts, Ryder was haunted all his life by the sea. He attended school locally and painted from an early age, but grew frustrated at his inability to recreate nature on the canvas. The family moved to New York City in 1868 and he studied art with William E. Marshall and at the school of the National Academy of Design. His paintings brought him a very small income; being totally naive in money matters, he left checks about the house and frequently gave what little he had to a beggar. Content to live in a dusty attic studio, he traveled abroad once but returned to New York City unaffected by his exposure to Europe; he had no taste for travel and felt that an artist should dedicate himself totally to his work. He often walked in solitude in the park or visited Cape Cod, where he made sketches of his famous "lunar landscapes." To achieve fresh, brilliant color he piled layer upon layer of rich, heavy paint; he finished only some 150 paintings in his lifetime. Many were small; all were worked and reworked with patience and care. Ranging in mood from romantic to mystical, from literary to allegorical, his paintings, mainly heavy impastos, were masterworks of design even when not of execution. Outstanding among his works were "The Race Track" (sometimes called "Death on a Pale Horse"), "Toilers of the Sea," and "The Flying Dutchman." His death after a long illness occurred in a friend's home at Elmhurst, Long Island, New York, on March 28, 1917. His marine and pastoral paintings and several still lifes were hailed as the work of a genius after his death; but because of his unfortunate lack of technical concern, many of his works have deteriorated seriously. Numbers of his canvases hang in major museums.

S

Saarinen, Eero (1910–1961), architect. Born on August 20, 1910, in Kyrkslatt (Kirkkonummi), Finland, the son of Eliel Saarinen, Eero accompanied his father to the United States in 1923. He graduated from the Yale School of Architecture in 1934 and worked with his father from that time until the elder Saarinen's death. He was naturalized in 1940 and in that year collaborated with Charles Eames in the design of a plywood chair. Highly innovative in his own right, he designed structures having a sculptural quality that inspired, he said, an endless "search for form." Examples of his stainless-steel and glass buildings with curving rooftops and convex walls are the Davis S. Ingalls hockey rink at Yale, 1958; the Trans World Airlines (TWA) Terminal at John F. Kennedy International Airport in New York City, 1962; and the Dulles International Airport near Washington, D.C., 1962. His winning design for the Jefferson National Expansion Memorial in St. Louis, a stainless-steel arch, was shown in 1948 and finally executed in 1964. Others of his buildings included the General Motors Technical Center, Warren, Michigan, 1948-1956; Kresge Auditorium and the chapel, Massachusetts Institute of Technology (MIT), 1955; U.S. embassies in Oslo, 1959, and London, 1960; Bell Laboratories, Holmdel, New Jersey, 1962; and the Vivian Beaumont Theatre, Lincoln Center, New York City, 1963. Often called the most creative architect of his day, he died in Ann Arbor, Michigan, on September 1, 1961.

Saarinen, Eliel (1873–1950), architect. Born on August 20, 1873, in Rantasalmi, Finland, Gottlieb Eliel Saarinen was educated at the Polytechnic Institute in Helsinki. Projects such as the design for the Finnish pavilion at the 1900 Paris Exposition and for the League of Nations building in Geneva had made him his country's foremost architect by the time he emigrated to the United States in 1923; public buildings such as the Helsinki railroad station, 1905–1914, and urban housing and development projects for Revel, Estonia (now Tallinn, U.S.S.R.), and Canberra, Australia, had also contributed to his reputation. In 1922 he entered the competition for the design of a building for the *Chicago Tribune*. His design did not win the prize—a Gothic tower was erected instead —but it nevertheless exerted a strong influence on the development of the skyscraper in the United States. He designed the buildings of the Cranbrook Foundation in Michigan, where he headed the Cranbrook Academy of Art and supervised its departments of architecture and city planning. His Tabernacle Church of Christ in Columbus, Indiana, 1942, and Christ Lutheran Church in Minne-

apolis, 1950, were especially notable. Together with his son Eero he received awards from the American Institute of Architects in 1948 for a design for a new annex to the Smithsonian Institution in Washington, D.C. His writings included *The City: Its Growth, Its Decay, Its Future*, 1943, and *Search for Form*, 1948. He died at Bloomfield Hills, near Detroit, on July 1, 1950.

Sabin, Albert Bruce (1906–   ), immunologist. Born on August 26, 1906, in Bialystok, Russia (now Poland), Sabin came to the United States with his family in 1921 and settled in Paterson, New Jersey. He was naturalized in 1930. He graduated from New York University in 1928, took his M.D. degree there in 1931, and interned at Bellevue Hospital, where he also carried on research that led to his isolation of virus B. During 1934–1935 he held a National Research Council fellowship and pursued further studies at the Lister Institute of Preventive Medicine in England. On his return in 1935 he was appointed an assistant at the Rockefeller Institute for Medical Research (now Rockefeller University). Then in 1939 Sabin joined the faculty of the University of Cincinnati College of Medicine as a professor of pediatrics, becoming at the same time a fellow of the Cincinnati Children's Hospital Research Foundation. He had already begun by that time the research project that occupied him for nearly 25 years—the development of a vaccine for the prevention of poliomyelitis. His work was interrupted by World War II, during which he served as a major and then a lieutenant colonel in the army medical corps and produced vaccines effective against dengue fever and Japanese encephalitis. Returning to Cincinnati in 1946 as research professor of pediatrics, he continued to work on his polio vaccine. Although Jonas E. Salk had by 1954 perfected his killed-virus vaccine, Sabin worked on the much more difficult but ultimately more fruitful task of preparing a vaccine from live virus that had been attenuated, or inactivated. Finally, in 1956, he released his vaccine for use by other researchers. Their results, and those gathered by the World Health Organization (WHO), which began using the Sabin vaccine on a worldwide basis in 1957, confirmed his belief that the attenuated-virus vaccine had many advantages over the killed-virus type: it was cheap to manufacture, could be stored for very long periods of time, could be administered orally, and provided long immunity for up to life. For his accomplishment Sabin was widely honored, his prizes including the Lasker Award in 1965. Although the Sabin vaccine had an undramatic impact in the United States—its licensing was delayed until 1961, by which time the Salk vaccine had virtually wiped out polio—it was of great importance in many other nations, notably the Soviet Union, where it had been administered to some 90 million persons by 1962. In 1960 Sabin was named Distinguished Service Professor at the University of Cincinnati. He moved to Israel in 1970 to become president of the Weizmann Institute of Science.

Sacagawea (1787?–1812?), Indian guide. Born about 1787 either in western Montana or eastern Idaho, Sacagawea (or Sacajawea) was a member of the Snake tribe of Shoshone Indians. Late in the year 1800 she was captured by a party of Hidatsas, or Minnetaree Indians, and taken to their village in the upper Missouri region, in present-day North Dakota. There she was sold to a French Canadian trapper, Toussaint Charbonneau, who had been living among the Indians. In 1804, when Sacagawea was eighteen, Charbonneau married her. In the fall of 1804, the Lewis and Clark expedition arrived among the Mandan Indians near present-day Bismarck, North Dakota, to spend the winter. Lewis and Clark engaged Charbonneau and his wife as interpreters and guides to travel with them for the rest of their journey of exploration to the Pacific Coast; they were particularly desirous of having Sacagawea along to help them make contact with the Shoshone in Montana and Idaho. On February 11, 1805, Sacagawea gave birth to a baby boy who was taken along when the expedition set out again on April 7. On August 17 they made their first contact with the Shoshone. Through the goodwill of Sacagawea's brother, who had become chief of the tribe, Lewis and Clark were enabled to obtain horses with which to continue their trek. Charbonneau and Sacagawea stayed with the expedition to the coast, and on its return, remained in North Dakota. There is some evidence that the pair traveled to St. Louis in 1809 to leave their son with Clark to be educated. Sacagawea died, according to contemporary sources, on December 20, 1812, probably at Fort Lisa, near present-day Omaha. The date of her death was later brought into doubt, however, for in 1875 an old Indian woman claiming to be Sacagawea was found among the Wind River Shoshone in Wyoming. This woman died in 1884, which would have made Sacagawea nearly 100 years old.

Sacco, Nicola (1891–1927) and Bartolomeo Vanzetti, (1888–1927), anarchists. Born in Apulia, in southern Italy, on April 22, 1891, Sacco emigrated in 1908, settling in Milford, Massachusetts, where he worked in a shoe factory for the next dozen years except for going to Mexico in 1917–1918 to escape the wartime draft. Vanzetti was born at Villafalletto, Cuneo province, in the Piedmont of northern Italy on June 11, 1888. He also came to the United States in 1908 but did not settle in one place until 1915, when he moved to Plymouth, Massachusetts, and became a fish peddler. Like Sacco, he left the country for Mexico during the U.S. involvement in World War I in order to avoid the draft. Of the two, Vanzetti was the better educated, a philosophical anarchist well read in the works of St. Augustine, Karl Marx, Leo Tolstoi, Prince Kropotkin, and Ernest Renan, among others. Both had become interested in Socialism and in working-class movements. On April 15, 1920, in South Braintree, Massachusetts, two men robbed and killed the paymaster and guard of a local shoe-manufacturing firm and subsequently escaped. The two were said to be dark "Italian-looking" types. On May 5, in Brockton, Sacco and Vanzetti were arrested and charged with the crime. Their reputations as draft-dodgers, radicals, and anarchists, plus their appearance and the fact they were both armed at the time of arrest, made them prime suspects. Their arrest occurred in the atmosphere of the 1919–1920 "Red Scare" and in an era of strong nativism, with anti-Italian sentiment running strong in Massachusetts. Their trial, before Judge Webster Thayer of the state superior court, began on May 31, 1921, and ended on July 14 with both defendants being found guilty of murder in the first degree. All the evidence tying them to the crime was circumstantial, and such was the hostility of the jury that it refused to believe any testimony of the 18 Italian-born witnesses who were called; it was apparent that they were convicted as much for their radical beliefs and for being Italian as for any connection with the crime. After they were given the death sentence they appealed for a new trial, but Judge Thayer denied their motion in November 1924. A year later, another convict, already sentenced for murder, confessed to having helped perpetrate the crime. Nevertheless, Sacco and Vanzetti were scheduled to die in April 1927. Mounting protests from Italian-American groups and from many other groups and individuals throughout the world influenced the state's governor to call for an independent investigation. A committee headed by A. Lawrence Lowell, president of Harvard, issued a report early in August 1927 declaring that the trial had been fair and without prejudice. With the publication of the report and the governor's subsequent refusal to stay the sentence, protests mounted throughout the nation and the world, and the premier of Italy, Benito Mussolini, made a special plea that the lives of the two convicted men be spared. But to no avail: Sacco and Vanzetti were electrocuted on August 23, 1927. Debate over the case was not ended by their execution, however, and as late as 1959 Massachusetts considered —and rejected—an act of retroactive pardon.

Sachs, Curt (1881–1959), musicologist. Born in Berlin on June 29, 1881, Sachs attended the University of Berlin, receiving his Ph.D. in 1904. He at first divided his studies between art and music, but soon gave full attention to music. His first endeavors in the field of musicology were devoted to tracing the history of musical instruments. The results of this early work were published in his first book, a dictionary of musical instruments entitled *Reallexikon de Musikinstrumente*, in 1913. This volume established him as an authority in the field. In 1919 he was appointed professor of musicology at the University of Berlin, where he remained until 1933, when the rise of the Nazi regime forced him to leave the country; during the same period he also taught at the National Academy of Music and worked for the Berlin State Museum. After leaving Berlin in 1933, Sachs went to Paris as a member of the staff of the ethnography museum, the Musée de l'Homme, for four years. While in Paris he produced a series of recordings, *Anthologie Sonore*, for use in studying the history of music. In 1937 he came to the United States and joined the faculty of New York University, where he taught until his retirement in 1957. He served as a consultant to the New York Public Library from 1937 to 1952 and also taught at Columbia University from 1953 until 1957. Among his other works in the field of musicology were *History of Musical Instruments*, 1940; *The Rise of Music in the Ancient World, East and West*, 1943; and *The Evolution of Piano Music*, 1944. Sachs died on February 5, 1959, in New York City.

Sage, Margaret Olivia Slocum, *see under* Sage, Russell

Sage, Russell (1816–1906), financier and public official. Born at Shenandoah in Oneida County, New York, on August 4, 1816, Sage grew up in Durhamville and Troy, New York. After a few years of schooling, he went to work in his brother's grocery store at Troy in 1828. By 1837 he had accumulated sufficient money to buy the store. In 1840 he opened a wholesale grocery business which prospered sufficiently so that he could pursue a short-term political career; from 1844 to 1851 he was treasurer of Rensselaer County and from 1845 to 1848 was an alderman in Troy. After an unsuccessful campaign for the House of Representatives in 1850, he was elected as a Whig to the House in 1852 and served two terms. He retired from Congress in 1857 to spend the rest of his life building up his fortune. He became associated with Jay Gould in a number of successful ventures on the stock market and in railroading, banking, and other enterprises, helping to develop the Chicago, Milwaukee, and St. Paul Railroad and serving as its vice-president. From 1863 until his death he lived in New York City and on Long Island and was active in the stock market. He served as a director of numerous corporations and through shrewd investments, stock manipulation, and money-lending amassed a fortune of more than $70 million. He died in Lawrence, Long Island, on July 22, 1906, leaving his whole fortune to his second wife, Margaret Olivia Slocum Sage (1828–1918). Born in Syracuse, New York, on September 8, 1828, Miss Slocum graduated from Troy Female Seminary (now Russell Sage College) in 1847. For as long a time as her family's affluence permitted, she lived comfortably at Syracuse, but when her father's fortune failed she turned to teaching school for a living. In 1869 she married Russell Sage and lived thereafter in New York

City. It was she who devoted much of her husband's wealth to philanthropy. After his death she used his fortune to subsidize numerous charities, giving generously to further education for women and church missions. In 1907 she endowed the Russell Sage Foundation to study and devise means of improving social and living conditions in the United States. The foundation represented the largest of her bequests, and at the time it was organized her founding gift of $10 million was considered the largest single such example of philanthropy. At her death it received an additional bequest of $5 million. Mrs. Sage died in New York City on November 4, 1918. The Russell Sage Foundation accumulated a great library in industrial development, social work, the professions, social statistics, and related fields, and continued to encourage study and research.

Sagoyewatha, *see* Red Jacket

St. Clair, Arthur (1736–1818), soldier and public official. Born in Thurso, Scotland, on March 23 (old style), 1736, St. Clair entered the British army in 1757 and served in the American colonies and Canada until 1762. He then resigned his commission to settle on an estate in western Pennsylvania, where he engaged in farming and the fur trade. From 1771 to 1775 he served the colonial government of Pennsylvania as justice of Westmoreland County and as captain of the militia. Between 1775 and 1777 he was in the Continental army, took part as a colonel in the retreat from the invasion of Canada, and served as a brigadier general under Gen. George Washington in New Jersey. The fall of Fort Ticonderoga in 1777 while he was in command there with the rank of major general earned him a reputation as militarily incompetent (although a court-martial freed him of blame), and he saw little useful service for the rest of the Revolutionary War. After the war he settled again in Pennsylvania and became involved in state politics. For two years, 1785 to 1787, he was a delegate to Congress under the Articles of Confederation, serving as president of the body in 1787. When the Northwest Ordinance of 1787 created the Northwest Territory, he was made its governor and held that post, governing from Cincinnati, until 1802. He established his headquarters in 1790 on the Ohio River at Losantiville, which he renamed Cincinnati. His tenure in office worked neither to his advantage nor to that of the Territory. He was particularly unfortunate in his dealings with the Indians. The tribes west of the Alleghenies had been in a state of agitation since the Seven Years' War because of the accelerating loss of their lands. The advance of white men into the Ohio Valley after the Revolution heightened their fears, and they were determined, with the aid of their British allies, to resist further encroachments. In 1789 St. Clair presided over the signing of the treaty of Fort Harmar, which was highly unfavorable to the Indians. Within the year the treaty, plus raids made by frontier whites, had started a new Indian war. St. Clair's attempt, as military commander, to put down the Indians turned out disastrously when his forces were surrounded and defeated on November 4, 1791, near present-day Fort Wayne, Indiana. With this victory the Indians redoubled their efforts to drive the whites out of Ohio, and the war was not ended until their defeat by Anthony Wayne's troops in 1794. Although exonerated of blame for the defeat, he resigned from the army in 1792, continuing to serve as governor, however. In addition to failing against the Indians, St. Clair did little to win the confidence of settlers in the Territory. He was an aristocrat and a Federalist, while most of the frontiersmen were poor and inclined toward Jeffersonian democracy. He also intrigued for several years to prevent statehood for Ohio, but the move for statehood nevertheless suceeded in 1802. When he denounced the enabling act, President Thomas Jefferson removed him from office. The rest of his life was spent at his home near Ligonier, Pennsylvania, where, after losing his wealth, he passed his last years in poverty. He died there on August 31, 1818.

St. Denis, Ruth (1878–1968), and Ted Shawn (1891–1972), dancers and choreographers. Born in Newark, New Jersey, on January 20, 1878, Ruth Dennis studied dancing as a child and made her first public appearance at sixteen. For several years thereafter she danced in vaudeville and in musical shows. In 1898 she was engaged for the London cast of David Belasco's *Zaza* and she toured with this and other shows until 1905, when she became interested in devising dance forms of her own. She studied the cultures, religions, and dances of ancient Egypt and India and choreographed and produced her first ballet, *Radha*, in 1906. On the occasion of its performance she changed her last name to St. Denis. She toured with the ballet in Europe for three years and, after her return to the United States, produced *Egypta* in 1910. In 1913 she created a Japanese dance-drama, *O-Mika*. She met and married Ted Shawn the next year. Born on October 21, 1891, in Kansas City, Missouri, Edwin Myers Shawn attended the University of Denver to study theology, but a siege of diphtheria that partially paralyzed his legs forced him to drop out of college in his third year. To recover full use of his legs, it was recommended that he take ballet lessons, and by 1910 he had decided to make a career of dancing; his first public performance took place in Los Angeles in 1912. In 1913–1914 he made a coast-to-coast tour ending in New York City, where he met Miss St. Denis. After their marriage they went to Los Angeles and founded the Denishawn School of Dancing and the Denishawn Dancers, and for the next 16 years operated the school (which was moved to New York City in 1921) and toured the United States, Europe, and the Orient with their company. During this period Shawn created a number of ballets and dance routines, most of them based on American Indian themes and motifs, including *Invocation to the Thunderbird*, 1918; *Xochitl*, 1919; *Osage-Pawnee*, 1930; and *Zuni Indian*, 1931; his *Jurgen*,

based on the novel by James Branch Cabell, was produced in 1928. Meanwhile Miss St. Denis had also been doing independent work, from 1917 developing her idea of "musical visualization," in which she set symphonic dances to the works of major composers, and in 1925 attempting dance without music in *Tragica*. In 1930 Shawn and St. Denis separated, although they were never divorced. She continued to live in New York City for several years, experimenting with innovative dance forms and becoming more and more involved in the religious aspects of her art and, through the Society of Spiritual Arts, which she founded in 1931, attempting to demonstrate the potential of dance as a form of worship. In 1940 in New York she founded with La Meri, her partner, the School of Natya. During World War II she lived in Los Angeles, where for a while she worked in an aircraft plant. In 1947 she established the Church of the Divine Dance. Shawn moved to Lee, Massachusetts, in the early 1930s and started a school for male dancers there in 1933, creating during the following seven years a number of ballets for men, including *John Brown, O Libertad!* and *Labor Symphony*, which he presented on tours with his male company. The school was disbanded with the onset of World War II, but in October 1941 he founded the Jacob's Pillow Dance Fesival, in Massachusetts, which operated under his direction as a "university of dance" and gained international fame. Starting in 1945 Miss St. Denis began to appear with him at the festival in dances they had developed earlier in their careers. In 1949 they presented a series titled "Around the World with Dance and Song" for the Museum of Natural History in New York City and in 1964 they appeared together at Jacob's Pillow to celebrate the fiftieth anniversary of their wedding. The previous year Miss St. Denis had toured the country in a program entitled "American Dances" and revived her *Incense* in New York City. Besides his teaching, dancing, and presentations of leading foreign ballet companies in the United States, Shawn also wrote a number of books on the dance, including *The American Ballet*, 1925; *Gods Who Dance*, 1929; and *Dance We Must*, 1940. Miss St. Denis, whose autobiographical *An Unfinished Life* had appeared in 1939, died in Los Angeles on June 21, 1968; Shawn was living in Eustis, Florida, when he became ill and died, in Orlando, Florida, on January 9, 1972.

Saint-Gaudens, Augustus (1848–1907), sculptor. Born in Dublin on March 1, 1848, Saint-Gaudens was brought by his parents to New York City later in the same year. He was apprenticed to a cameo cutter at thirteen and from 1861 to 1865 spent his evenings studying art at Cooper Union; he then studied for another year at the school of the National Academy of Design. In 1867 he went to Paris, and after a few months of travel enrolled in the École des Beaux-Arts. Three years later he moved to Rome, where he continued to study and develop his skill in sculpture while supporting himself by cameo cutting. His "Hiawatha" was the major work of these years. Except for a brief visit to New York City in 1872–1873 he remained in Rome until 1875; by the time of his return he was an established sculptor. He became associated with a number of leading architects, notably Henry H. Richardson, Charles F. McKim, and Stanford White, and the artist John La Farge; for La Farge he carved "Adoration of the Cross by Angels," a relief reredos for St. Thomas's Church, New York City, in 1877. In the same year he executed a memorial statue of Adm. David G. Farragut, mounted on a pedestal designed by White, and placed in Madison Square, New York City. A flood of major works followed, most notable among which were "The Puritan," 1885, in Springfield, Massachusetts; "Amor Caritas," 1887; the standing Abraham Lincoln for Lincoln Park, Chicago, 1887; the hooded figure on the memorial to Mrs. Henry Adams in Rock Creek Cemetery, Washington, D.C., 1891; the "Diana" for Madison Square Garden, in New York City, 1892; and the equestrian statue of Gen. William T. Sherman at 5th Avenue and 59th Street, New York City. He was an active member of the Society of American Artists from its founding in 1877, taught from 1888 to 1897 at the Art Students League in New York City, and was a staunch supporter of McKim in establishing and fostering the American Academy in Rome. From 1885 he spent much of his time at a home and studio he established near Cornish, New Hampshire. In addition to his large pieces, he produced a great number of smaller busts, portraits, plaques, and medallions, and in 1907 he designed the U.S. $20 gold piece and the head on the $10 gold piece. In 1901 he served with Charles F. McKim, Daniel H. Burnham, and Frederick Law Olmsted on a commission appointed to make recommendations on the development of Washington, D.C. Saint-Gaudens died on August 3, 1907, in Cornish, New Hampshire. He was elected to the Hall of Fame in 1920.

St. John, J. Hector, see Crèvecoeur, Michel Guillaume Jean de

St. Vrain, Ceran de Hault de Lassus de (1802–1870), fur trader and merchant. Born near St. Louis, on May 5, 1802, St. Vrain was the son of a former French naval officer who had come to the American frontier to engage in land speculation. When his father's hopes ended in misfortune, St. Vrain, at sixteen, went to live in the home of merchant-trader Bernard Pratte. In 1824, with Charles and William Bent, he explored and trapped the upper Arkansas. In 1825, with assistance from Pratte, he began to engage in the overland trade with Santa Fe, New Mexico. He settled at Taos and opened a store to supply trappers and miners, and for several years went on fur-trapping expeditions himself. In 1831 he, Charles and William Bent, and other associates formed the Bent & St. Vrain company, fur traders. As a part of their enterprise they built Bent's Fort on the Arkansas River near present-day La Junta, Colorado. The fort, completed in 1832, became a way

station and supply source for all parties going west along the Santa Fe trail and a gathering place for fur trappers and Indians who brought in furs to exchange for other goods. St. Vrain himself remained at Taos with a branch of the business, a supply station for trappers, and a flour mill. By 1840 the Bent & St. Vrain company had established a very strong economic position in the Southwest and was second in size only to John Jacob Astor's American Fur Company. As a resident of Taos, St. Vrain was a Mexican citizen, but one of what was called the "American party" in New Mexico. In 1834 he was named U.S. consul at Santa Fe. He and other Americans had begun the economic invasion of New Mexico from the east, and they soon had agents and traders traveling as far as northern Mexico buying and selling. In 1844 he and another resident received a land grant of four million acres. Politically and economically he and other Americans were in competition for control of New Mexico, and after the U.S. takeover brought about by the Mexican War, 1846–1848, he and his partners found themselves in a most fortunate position. Soon after the death of Charles Bent in 1847, however, St. Vrain retired from active participation in the business. The Santa Fe trade prospered even more, and it lasted until the railroads came into New Mexico in 1879. In addition to his profitable business ventures in Taos, St. Vrain also served in a military capacity when the need arose. In 1854–1855 he was an officer with the volunteers who fought off Indian raids in the territory, and at the start of the Civil War he was appointed a colonel in the New Mexico cavalry. He resigned his commission late in 1861 and spent his last years in retirement. He died at Mora, New Mexico, on October 28, 1870.

Salinger, Jerome David (1919–   ), author. Born in New York City on January 1, 1919, Salinger attended public schools in New York City and a military academy in Pennsylvania, and attended classes at New York University and Columbia. He began writing when he was fifteen and published his first short story in 1940 in *Story* magazine. From 1942 to 1946 he was in the army, his experiences inspiring such stories as the poignant "For Esmé—with Love and Squalor," 1950. With his first novel, *Catcher in the Rye,* 1951, he won a legion of admirers, young and old, who found aspects of their lives reflected in that of the hero, sixteen-year-old Holden Caulfield. As Salinger described it—in free-associative language, replete with adolescent slang—Holden's flight from the "phonies" to the good, the pure, and the true, was everyone's quest. In 1953 he published *Nine Stories,* which included "For Esmé," "A Perfect Day for Bananafish," "Uncle Wiggly in Connecticut," and others, followed by *Franny and Zooey,* 1961; *Raise High the Roof Beam, Carpenters;* and, *Seymour: An Introduction,* 1963 (earlier published in the *New Yorker*), on the life and activities of the Glass family. In his work, children—as possessors of an innocence lost too soon—were precisely, almost eerily described, with painstaking accuracy, and, particularly in the Glass family, they were possessed of a precocious wisdom usually far beyond the grasp of adults. His stories were published in the *New Yorker, Harper's, Saturday Evening Post, Esquire,* and other popular magazines.

Salk, Jonas Edward (1914–   ), immunologist. Born in New York City on October 28, 1914, Salk earned his B.S. degree in 1934 from the City College of New York (CCNY), his M.D. in 1939 from New York University's College of Medicine, where he stayed on briefly as a fellow in bacteriology, and was an intern for two years at the Mount Sinai Hospital in New York City. In 1942, on a fellowship in epidemiology from the University of Michigan, he began studies of the influenza virus with Dr. Thomas Francis, Jr., under whom he had studied at New York University, in order to produce vaccines in commercial quantities. He became a research fellow in 1943, research associate in 1944, and assistant professor of epidemiology in 1946 in the university's School of Public Health. In 1947 he went to the University of Pittsburgh as research professor of bacteriology and director of the Virus Research Laboratory. He continued his research on the influenza virus, but by 1949, when he became a research professor, was interested in developing a serum against poliomyelitis. He was made a director of a three-year project to investigate the polio virus sponsored by the National Foundation for Infantile Paralysis. The problem was complicated by the fact that there were three strains of virus capable of producing the disease, all of which had to be neutralized by a single vaccine if it were to be considered effective. Using this foundation, as well as technical accomplishments of others, notably John F. Enders, which made it possible to cultivate polio virus in the kidney tissue of monkeys, he was able to produce a killed-virus vaccine. He announced its successful use in experiments in 1953, just one year after a polio epidemic had struck more than 50,000 and killed 3300 in the United States. Mass inoculation of school children was undertaken by the National Foundation in 1954, and by the end of 1955 the Salk vaccine had been proven effective in large-scale use. In 1953 he also published the results of experimental inoculations of 20,000 persons with a flu vaccine which had produced immunity for as long as two years; that vaccine also went into wide use. A winner of numerous honors and awards, he became Commonwealth Professor of Preventive Medicine at Pittsburgh in 1956, of experimental medicine in 1957, and was a founder, fellow, and director of the Salk Institute for Biological Studies in La Jolla, California, after 1963. He retained an association with the University of Pittsburgh, with the title of professor at large. In 1970 he also became adjunct professor of health sciences at the University of California at San Diego. A major part of his later work was concerned with the development of a vaccine against cancer.

Salomon, Haym (1740?–1785), Revolutionary patriot and banker. Born in about 1740 in Leszno, Poland, Salomon received a university education and had traveled widely in Europe before emigrating to New York in 1772. He opened a brokerage and a dry-goods business in New York City and early in the Revolutionary War was given the task of provisioning Continental troops in upper New York State. He traveled with the army in the summer of 1776, and returned to the city shortly before the British captured it on September 15. He collaborated with other patriots in a plan to fire the British ships in New York harbor, but when the plot was discovered, he was arrested by the British as a spy. Because of his linguistic ability, Salomon was used by his captors as an interpreter for a time, then released. In 1778 he was again arrested and was condemned to death, but a timely bribe to the jailer secured his release. He promptly fled to Philadelphia and offered his services to the Second Continental Congress. He was asked by Robert Morris of the Bank of North America to sell government bonds to help finance the war. In this assignment he was so effective that he was called the "most successful of the war brokers;" he became, in effect, the Revolution's foremost banker after Morris. He succeeded at one point in negotiating a loan of $400,000 for Gen. George Washington's army in 1779, and it is possible a sizable amount of the loan came from him personally. How much of his own funds he used to further the Revolution has never been determined and is still a matter of debate—a figure of over $350,000 was later often quoted by his heirs and advocates—for there are no records extant; but it is most likely that the several hundred thousand dollars that went through his account from 1778 to 1782 represented the bond sales he had made. Although he had reestablished himself as a successful banker on his own account after the war, he lost much of his money in the recession that occurred after 1783. While living in Philadelphia he also devoted himself to obtaining equal treatment for his fellow Jews, both in employment and government service, and in December 1783 he petitioned the Board of Censors to do away with the religious oath required of public servants. He died in Philadelphia on January 6, 1785.

Samoset (?–1653?), Indian leader. Nothing is known of the early life of Samoset. He was a sachem, or minor chief, of the Pemaquid, also known as the Monhegan. His name, from Osamoset, means "he (who) walks over much." From English fishermen who worked the banks off the coast of Maine from about 1614 onward, he learned a smattering of English. It was thus that, in March 1621, he approached the Pilgrims at Plymouth with the words "Welcome, Englishmen!" He then introduced them to Massasoit, chief of the Wampanoag and to Squanto, who also spoke English, and thus began their warm acquaintance with the local tribe that proved very beneficial to the settlers. In 1625 Somoset, with Unongoit, signed the first deed of transfer between Indian and Englishman, selling some 12,000 acres of Pemaquid land to John Brown of New Harbor, Maine. No record of him survives for the period from 1625 to 1653, but in the latter year he executed another sale of land, this time of 1000 acres to three colonists. It is believed that he died shortly after the sale had been accomplished. He was buried on the site of present-day Bristol, Maine.

Samuelson, Paul Anthony (1915–   ), economist. Born in Gary, Indiana, on May 15, 1915, Samuelson graduated from the University of Chicago in 1935 and thereafter pursued graduate studies in economics at Harvard University, earning his doctorate in 1941. In 1940 he began teaching economics at the Massachusetts Institute of Technology (MIT) and in 1947 was made a full professor; he was named Institute Professor in 1966. His best-known and most influential book, *Foundations of Economic Analysis*, was published in 1947, although the original version of it had been written ten years before, when Samuelson was twenty-two. In that earlier work Samuelson had attempted to derive theorems that were operationally meaningful in the sense that they represented hypotheses about empirical data that could be tested and proved. In the process he discovered analogous features in many different areas of economics; he then brought them together into a unifield theory embracing such apparently diverse elements as price theory, income theory, taxation, business cycles, money, and international trade. For this important work, expressed not only in *Foundations of Economic Analysis* but also in more than 200 papers, he was awarded the Nobel Memorial Prize for Economics in 1970 by the Swedish National Bank; the citation asserted that he had "done more than any other contemporary economist to raise the level of scientific analysis in economic theory." Samuelson also published a textbook, *Economics: An Introductory Analysis*, that, by its eighth edition in 1970, was reported to have sold more than three million copies in some fourteen languages; there was no doubt that most beginning students of economics in the period after World War II cut their teeth on this work. Recognized from his early thirties as one of the nation's leading economic theorists, he served frequently as a consultant to various government agencies and was a special economic adviser to presidents John F. Kennedy and Lyndon B. Johnson.

Sandburg, Carl (1878–1967), poet and folklorist. Born on January 6, 1878, in Galesburg, Illinois, the son of a Swedish immigrant blacksmith, Sandburg worked from the age of eleven, combining schooling with various jobs, then went to fight in the Spanish-American War, seeing service in Puerto Rico. Upon his return he worked his way through Lombard College in Galesburg, graduating in 1902. His wanderings continued; he was a hobo, an itinerant newspaper man, and, briefly, an editor of a Chicago magazine. Later he recruited members for the Social-Democratic party in Wisconsin

and served as secretary to the Socialist mayor of Milwaukee from 1910 to 1912. He moved to Chicago in 1913. Although he had published poems as early as 1904, his work did not gain much attention until it began to appear in *Poetry* magazine in 1914. Including "Fog" and "I Am the People, the Mob," his first book, *Chicago Poems*, 1916, was immediately successful. His style was compared to Walt Whitman's for freedom and authenticity, but it was apparent that his knowledge of the land was deeper and born of personal experience. He used conspicuous colloquialisms, portraying everyday people and common things, embracing both the delicate and the crude. He turned to journalism, becoming feature editor of the *Chicago Daily News* by 1919, and issued subsequent volumes of poetry, including the Pulitzer Prize–winning *Cornhuskers*, 1918, which also won a share of the Poetry Society prize; *Smoke and Steel*, 1920, which also shared in a Poetry Society prize; and *Slabs of the Sunburnt West*, 1922. His six-volume biography of Abraham Lincoln, 1926–1939, was begun as a study for young people, but it expanded far beyond that and he received another Pulitzer Prize, in 1940, for the last volume of the work. His faith in the wisdom of the people pervaded *The People, Yes*, 1936, and his interest in American lore, especially that of his native Midwest, prompted him to give folk-song recitals throughout the country. Important collections of such songs appeared as *The American Songbag*, 1927, and *New American Songbag*, 1950. He wrote several charming children's books, notably *Rootabaga Stories*, 1922; *Rootabaga Pigeons*, 1923; and *Potato Face*, 1930. His later publications included *Remembrance Rock*, 1948, a novel of the history of the nation from Plymouth Rock through the events of World War II; *Complete Poems*, 1950, which won him a third Pulitzer Prize the next year; *Always the Young Stranger*, 1953, a volume of autobiography and reminiscence; and *The Sandburg Range*, 1957, selections from previous works, with many photographs. He died at his home in Flat Rock, North Carolina, on July 22, 1967.

Sanford, Edward Terry (1865–1930), justice of the Supreme Court. Born in Knoxville, Tennessee, on July 23, 1865, Sanford graduated from the University of Tennessee in 1883. In 1889 he received his law degree from Harvard Law School. He was admitted to the Tennessee bar in 1888 and two years later began practice in his home town. His public career did not begin until 1907, when President Theodore Roosevelt appointed him assistant attorney general of the United States. The following year he became a judge of the U.S. District Court in Tennessee, and in January 1923 President Warren G. Harding named him an associate justice of the U.S. Supreme Court. One of the notable cases for which he wrote the opinion for the court was *Gitlow* v. *New York*, a 1925 case dealing with the issue of freedom of expression. Probably his most important contribution to constitutional law was his opinion in the "pocket veto" case in 1929, in which he declared that a bill passed by Congress within ten working days of adjournment and subsequently unsigned or returned by the president was, in effect, vetoed. His interpretation of the ten-day period as being calendar rather than legislative days confirmed the construction that had prevailed in the past. Sanford died on March 8, 1930, in Washington, D.C.

Sanger, Margaret Higgins (1883–1966), social reformer. Born on September 14, 1883, in Corning, New York, Margaret Higgins completed nurse's training at the White Plains Hospital in New York and at the Manhattan Eye and Ear Clinic. In 1900 she married William Sanger, retaining that surname, by which she was well known, after they were divorced; she remarried in 1922. In New York City she contributed articles on health to the Socialist party's organ, the *Call*, later collected in *What Every Girl Should Know*, 1916, and *What Every Mother Should Know*, 1917. In her nursing career she ministered primarily to maternity cases from the city's crowded Lower East Side, coming directly into contact with her patients' desperate financial and emotional conditions and seeing many deaths from self-induced abortions. She gave up nursing in 1912 to devote herself to the cause of birth control. Gathering and disseminating information, however, was nearly impossible because of the federal Comstock Act of 1873, which classified contraceptive data with obscene matter and forbade its passage in the mails. Late in 1913 she traveled in Scotland and France as an observer of conditions there. In 1914 she returned to the United States and began publishing the *Woman Rebel*, a magazine addressed to her cause, and was indicted for sending an obscene publication through the mails. Her case was dismissed before coming to trial. Also in 1914 she founded the National Birth Control League. Soon after setting up the nation's first birth-control clinic in the Brownsville district of Brooklyn, she was sent to the workhouse in 1917 for 30 days on charges of creating a public nuisance. But her appeal, bolstered by mounting public sympathy, led to a favorable decision from the New York Court of Appeals, granting doctors the right to give advice about birth control to their patients. In 1936 a further modification granted doctors the right to import and prescribe contraceptive devices. She organized numerous conventions in the United States and abroad, beginning with the Birth Control Conference in New York City in 1921. That same year she established the American Birth Control League, serving as its president until 1928, after which she founded the National Committee on Federal Legislation for Birth Control. In 1939 the league combined with the education department of the Birth Control Research Bureau and became the Birth Control Federation of America, renamed in 1942 the Planned Parenthood Federation. As first president of the International Planned Parenthood Federation, organized in 1953, she furthered the cause of family planning in the Far East, notably in India and Japan. In 1935 she began the *Journal of Contraception* (later called

Human Fertility). Her many books included *The Case for Birth Control*, 1917; *Women, Morality, and Birth Control*, 1922; *Happiness in Marriage*, 1926; *Motherhood in Bondage*, 1928; *My Fight for Birth Control*, 1931; and *Margaret Sanger: An Autobiography*, 1938. She died in Tucson, Arizona, on September 6, 1966.

Santayana, George (1863–1952), philosopher, poet, novelist, and critic. Born in Madrid on December 16, 1863, Santayana was at first brought up by his father in Ávila joining his mother in Boston when he was eight, in 1872. Educated at the Boston Latin School and at Harvard, from which he graduated in 1886, he then studied in Germany, returning to Harvard in 1888 for his doctorate. He joined the Harvard philosophy department the next year, becoming a full professor in 1907 and remaining a member of its distinguished faculty—which included William James and Josiah Royce—until 1912, when a small inheritance allowed him to retire. He lived in England for several years, then in Paris, and in 1925 finally settled in Rome. His first major philosophical work, *The Sense of Beauty*, had appeared in 1896; in it he had attempted to set forth a complete aesthetic theory, which he later developed further in *Reason in Art*, 1905, Vol. IV of *The Life of Reason*. The other parts of this five-volume treatise published in 1905–1906 dealt with reason in common sense, in society, in religion, and in science. *The Life of Reason*, subtitled *The Phases of Human Progress*, was "a presumptive biography of the human intellect" that reflected Santayana's intense interest in psychology and also his desire to avoid the errors of the German idealists and transcendentalists. In 1923 appeared *Scepticism and Animal Faith*, in which he undertook an extensive recasting of his whole system of thought. Developed in the four volumes of *Realms of Being*, 1927–1940, his system took the form of a careful and detailed analysis of the four major modes of being—essence, matter, truth, and spirit—that emerge from the skeptical investigation of consciousness. Santayana's philosophy was basically personal and idiosyncratic, although he doubtless owed more to his contemporaries than he liked to admit. A graceful and intelligent writer, he produced, besides his philosophical studies, many works of criticism both philosophical and aesthetic, a novel, poems, and an autobiography. His criticism included *Three Philosophical Poets*, 1910; *Winds of Doctrine*, 1926; *Character and Opinion in the United States*, 1920; and *Some Turns of Thought in Modern Philosophy*, 1933. In these works he expressed his often quite individualistic opinions in a style that helped even the objects of his attacks to forgive him. His novel, *The Last Puritan*, 1936, a "memoir" of considerable psychological interest, was a best seller. His poetry, written mostly during his years at Harvard, is classical in tone and approach, and runs counter to most of the prevailing schools of the time. His three-volume autobiography, *Persons and Places*, 1944–1953, is one of his most delightful though crusty works. In it he revealed himself as a confirmed opponent of democracy and liberalism; instead of these he advocated a return to the "natural" aristocratic societies of the past while at the same time admitting that he did not expect such a turn of events to come about. As he grew older, he became more and more alienated from the modern world, and during World War II he took refuge in the convent of an order of English nuns in Rome. He died there on September 26, 1952.

Sapir, Edward (1884–1939), anthropologist and linguist. Born at Lauenburg, Germany (now Lębork, Poland), on January 26, 1884, Sapir came to the United States with his family in 1889. He grew up in Richmond, Virginia, and in New York City, graduating from Columbia College in 1904. In 1909 he took his doctorate in anthropology at Columbia University, where he studied under Franz Boas. From 1908 to 1910 he taught anthropology at the University of Pennsylvania, then was on the staff of the Canadian National Museum in Ottawa until 1925. From 1925 until 1931 he taught at the University of Chicago and from 1931 to 1939 taught anthropology and linguistics at Yale, chairing the department of anthropology from 1937. Although Sapir worked in the whole field of anthropology and human culture, his area of concentration was linguistics. He had a phenomenal grasp of the Indo-European languages and of the languages of the American Indian as well. He wrote a great many specialized studies on linguistics and culture and one general survey, *Language: An Introduction to the Study of Speech*, 1921. Other books included *Time Perspective in Aboriginal American Culture*, 1916; *Folk Songs of French Canada*, 1925; and the *Southern Paiute Language*, 1931. He also published verse in various magazines. He was a pioneer in descriptive linguistics, and he regarded language as part of the overall development of human culture, and in his work on American Indians was able to make significant contributions to understanding their societies. He was able to define six major language groupings to include all the Indians of North America. Sapir died in New Haven, Connecticut, on February 4, 1939.

Saraceni, Gene, *see* Sarazen, Gene

Sarazen, Gene (1901–   ), golfer. Born in Harrison, New York, on February 27, 1901, Gene Saraceni—he changed his name so that people could pronounce it more easily—dropped out of school to help support his family while in his early teens and was already a hard-working golf caddy before World War I. The transition from caddying to playing golf was natural enough, and by the time he was eighteen he was a redoubtable competitor. He played in the U.S. Open in 1920 and 1921 and won the tournament in 1922, when he was only twenty, with a brilliant 68 on the last round. He also won the Professional Golfers Association (PGA) tournament that year and repeated his PGA win the next year, beating the great Walter Hagen in the final round. He won no major

tournaments for nine years, although he was always a competitor, but he came back to win his second U.S. Open in 1932, shooting the last 28 holes of the tournament in an astonishing 100 strokes, and then won the PGA for the third time in 1933. He won the British Open in 1932, making that year one of the most successful of his long and distinguished career. His greatest triumph, however, occurred in 1935, when he won the Masters at Augusta, Georgia—the tournament had been established the preceding year—with a breathtaking double eagle on the 12th hole to make up a three-stroke deficit on the leader, Craig Wood, whom he went on to defeat in a playoff the next day. As time passed, that famous double eagle loomed more and more certainly as the greatest single hole in the history of golf in the United States. Sarazen also won dozens of other tournaments and was six times a member of U.S. Ryder Cup teams. As late as 1958 he was the winner of the PGA's Seniors tournament. During the height of his career he was a top money winner as well as a popular showman on the course. One of his enduring contributions to the game was his invention, about 1930, of the sand wedge. In the early 1960s, still a popular figure in golf, he went on television as host of "The Wonderful World of Golf."

Sargent, John Singer (1856–1925), painter. Born on January 12, 1856, in Florence, of American parents, Sargent received lessons in the Academy of Fine Arts at Florence and sketched profusely as the family traveled through Italy, France, and Germany during his childhood. His formal studies began at the École des Beaux-Arts in Paris in 1874. In 1876 he visited the United States and acquired U.S. citizenship, which he never relinquished, but he then returned to Paris. In 1877 he made his debut at the Salon, and there the next year he won an honorable mention for "En Route pour la Pêche." Confidently painting his subjects from life in oils, he developed a style marked by understated tones with brilliant highlights. For years he could not find patrons; his style was in advance of the academic painting fashionable in Paris and London. He nevertheless continued to work in his own way; his brilliantly conceived portrait of "Madame X," exhibited at the Salon in 1884, created a scandal in Paris. In 1885 he moved to London. His work continued to be poorly received; the unorthodox composition of "The Misses Vickers" was criticized with particular savagery. In 1887 he exhibited a painting of two children in a flower garden, "Carnation, Lily, Lily, Rose," which warmed the public toward his work. He was thereupon deluged with portrait commissions. His renderings, which mirrored the elegance of the Edwardian age, were not psychologically profound, but his remarkable brushwork gave directness and spontaneity to his style. Recognized as the leading portraitist of the day, he nonetheless tired of portraiture and switched to decorative work and landscapes. In 1887 he traveled to the United States and was lionized in

Boston, where a major exhibition of his works was held late in the year. He painted a series of large murals in the Boston Public Library, 1890–1910, and executed the interior design for the Boston Museum of Fine Arts. He traveled constantly between Europe and the United States, and in 1897 was elected to the Royal Academy. After 1910 he spent his summers in Italy and the Alps working freely in watercolors. In 1918 he was commissioned an official war artist by the British government; as such he produced "Gassed" and "General Officers of the Great War." In spite of being considered merely a "society painter" by modernists, he was seriously devoted to his work and received numerous honors for his painting during his lifetime. He died in London on April 15, 1925.

Sarnoff, David (1891–1971), engineer and businessman. Born near Minsk, Russia, on February 27, 1891, Sarnoff was brought to the United States at the age of nine. He was educated in public schools in Brooklyn, New York, and studied electrical engineering at the Pratt Institute. He began to work with wireless communications systems as early as 1906, when he was only fifteen. He joined the Marconi Wireless Company in 1906 and became a telegraph operator two years later. In 1912 he earned wide notice when, the first to pick up distress signals from the *Titanic,* he remained at his post for 72 hours through the dramatic sinking. He was promoted to chief radio inspector and assistant chief engineer, and rose through the ranks of the company until it was absorbed in 1919 by the Radio Corporation of America (RCA). At that time commercial manager of Marconi, he was employed in the same capacity in the new organization. He was elected general manager of RCA in 1921, vice-president and general manager in 1922, executive vice-president in 1929, president in 1930, and chairman of the board in 1947. An imaginative and innovative businessman, General Sarnoff, as he liked to be called—he had been commissioned in the army signal corps in 1924 and during 1944–45 on active duty as consultant to Gen. Dwight D. Eisenhower, he was promoted to brigadier general—made at least three important and far-reaching decisions in the course of his career, to each of which he stuck despite tremendous pressures both from within his company and from outside. In the 1920s RCA was the leading manufacturer of radio sets, and he insisted upon the founding of the National Broadcasting Company (NBC) as a subsidiary, in order to insure that something could be heard over the radios RCA was selling. NBC lost money at first but eventually justified his faith in it, becoming one of the nation's two largest radio and television networks. In the 1930s he was one of the first to see that television would replace radio as the popular medium, and he invested large sums for research in the new medium. World War II intervened, and television sets could not be manufactured; but after the war his faith was again confirmed. Finally, in the late 1940s, he decided that color television would eventually replace black and white. RCA began to manufacture color sets, and the NBC network transmitted broadcasts in color as often as possible. But for several years other manufacturers did not join in, nor did the other networks. RCA was said to have lost nearly half a billion dollars during the period. But Sarnoff triumphed again when his competitors were obliged to follow in his footsteps and color became almost universal. He retired as chairman of the board in 1970 and died in New York City on December 12, 1971.

Saroyan, William (1908–1981), author and playwright. Born in Fresno, California, on August 31, 1908, Saroyan spent about five years of his childhood in an orphanage following the death of his father. While he was still in his teens he decided to become a writer, although he was at least twenty-five before he sold his first story to a magazine. Using the pseudonym Sirak Gorgan, he published his short story, "The Broken Wheel," in an Armenian-American paper, *Hairenik,* in Boston; it was soon picked up for inclusion in *Best Short Stories of 1934.* The story that brought him his first literary fame, however, was "The Daring Young Man on the Flying Trapeze," 1934, which became the title for a collection of his stories published later the same year. After traveling abroad for a year, he published another collection, *Inhale and Exhale,* in 1936. A prolific writer, he continued to produce stories for national magazines over the next several years, and most of them were collected into books, among which were *Love, Here Is My Hat,* 1938, and *The Trouble with Tigers,* also 1938. In 1939 his play *My Heart's in the Highlands* was produced, a not very successful effort. But in 1940 he won the Pulitzer Prize and the New York Drama Critics' Circle Award for *The Time of Your Life,* a virtually plotless play consisting of conversation among the patrons and the owner in a saloon. Other Saroyan plays were *Love's Old Sweet Song,* 1939; *The Beautiful People,* 1941; and *The Cave Dwellers,* 1957. His first novel, *My Name Is Aram,* 1940, reflected his own youth in dealing with the childhood days of an Armenian-American boy growing up in the San Joaquin Valley. Saroyan occasionally worked in Hollywood as a script writer; there he wrote the scenario for *The Human Comedy,* 1942, later a book. After serving in the army during World War II, he returned to San Francisco to live, although he traveled frequently. Among his later works were *I Used To Believe I Had Forever, Now I'm Not So Sure,* 1968, and *Escape to the Moon,* 1970. He wrote two volumes of memoirs, *Here Comes, There Goes, You Know Who,* 1961, and *Places Where I've Done Time,* 1972. He died in Fresno, California, on May 18, 1981.

Sarton, George Alfred Leon (1884–1956), historian of science. Born at Ghent, Belgium, on August 31, 1884, Sarton graduated from the University of Ghent, in 1906. In 1911 he earned his doctorate in science. The following year he founded *Isis,* a review of the philosophy and history of science.

When World War I broke out in 1914 he went to England and a year later emigrated to the United States; he became a U.S. citizen in 1924. He brought with him the journal *Isis*, which he continued to publish until 1952. For a year, 1915–1916, he was a lecturer on the history of science at George Washington University, and from 1916 to 1918 he taught at Harvard. He continued to lecture at Harvard intermittently until 1940, when the university appointed him professor of history of sciences, a post he held until 1951. From 1918 to 1948 he was an associate of the Carnegie Institution of Washington, under whose auspices he published his multivolume *Introduction to the History of Science*, 1927–1947. In 1936 he founded the journal *Osiris* to publish papers on the philosophy and history of science. His *History of Science* was published by Harvard in 1952. Sarton died in Cambridge, Massachusetts, on March 22 1956.

Saunders, Richard, *see* Franklin, Benjamin

Say, Thomas (1787–1834), naturalist. Born in Philadelphia, on June 27, 1787, Say studied pharmacy and for a time ran his own shop until the business failed. But his real interest was in the natural sciences, to which he had taken a liking through acquaintance with his great-uncle, William Bartram. After 1810 he devoted most of his time to entomology and conchology, and on the basis of his published works has been called the "father of descriptive entomology." Between 1818 and 1829 he went on several expeditions: twice as a zoologist to the Rocky Mountains, once to the upper Midwest, to Florida and Georgia, and to Mexico. From 1821 to 1827 he was curator of the American Philosophical Society, and from 1822 to 1828 he was professor of natural history at the University of Pennsylvania. Say's principal published work was *American Entomology: or Descriptions of the Insects of North America.* He started the work in 1818 and the first two volumes were published in 1824 and 1825; the third volume came out in 1828. In 1825 he joined Robert Dale Owen at Owen's experimental colony in New Harmony, Indiana. Even after the utopian community failed Say remained; and it was while living there that he published his *American Conchology,* issued in six parts from 1830 to 1834. He died in New Harmony on October 10, 1834.

Schaff, Philip (1819–1893), theologian and church historian. Born on January 1, 1819, in Chur, Switzerland, Schaff studied at the universities of Tübingen, Halle, and Berlin, receiving the degree of licentiate in theology from Berlin in 1841. He remained to teach at Berlin and had already attracted considerable attention as a brilliant scholar when he accepted a call from the theological seminary of the German Reformed church at Mercersburg, Pennsylvania, in 1844. At his inauguration as professor of church history and biblical literature he delivered an address on "The Principle of Protestantism" in which he described the Protestant movement as an inspired evolution of the Church out of the best strains of Catholicism rather than as a revolutionary (or reactionary) development. His further statements looking toward the eventual possible unification among Christian sects raised charges of heresy, of which he was cleared by the Eastern Synod of the German Reformed Church the following year. He remained at the Mercersburg Seminary for 19 years, during which he founded *Der Deutsche Kirchenfreund,* a theological journal, in 1846; published, among other works, *What is Church History? A Vindication of the Idea of Historical Development,* 1846; and began his massive *History of the Christian Church,* seven volumes, 1858–1890. His 25-volume edition of Johann Peter Lange's *Commentary* began to appear in 1864; the following year he resigned his professorship and moved to New York City. From 1864 to 1870 he was secretary of the New York Sabbath Association and in 1870 joined the faculty of Union Theological Seminary, where he remained until his death. He published his *Bibliotheca Symbolicae Ecclesiae Universalis: The Creeds of Christendom* in 1877 and edited the *Schaff-Herzog Encyclopedia of Religious Knowledge,* 1884, a translation of J. J. Herzog's work in German. From 1881 to 1885 he headed the American committee engaged in the international work on revision of the English Bible. He founded and was first president of the American Society of Church History in 1888. He wrote or edited more than 80 published works and became known the world over as a great theological scholar. He died in New York City on October 20, 1893.

Schechter, Solomon (1847–1915), religious leader and educator. Born in Focşani, Romania, on December 7, 1847, Schechter studied at the universities of Vienna and Berlin and completed his rabbinical studies in Vienna in 1879. In 1882 he went to England and during the 1890s became a reader in rabbinics at Cambridge University. From 1899 to 1901 he was professor of Hebrew at University College, London. In 1896 he had excavated the Geniza, or archive, in the old synagogue in Cairo, Egypt, and recovered some 50,000 manuscripts, many of great importance for rabbinical and biblical research. Among them was a copy of the original Hebrew text of Ecclesiasticus, containing lost chapters. Schechter also identified another manuscript as relating to an ancient pre-Christian Jewish sect; his identification was questioned at the time but was triumphantly confirmed 50 years later with the discovery of the Dead Sea Scrolls. Schechter came to the United States in 1902 and settled in New York City as president of the Jewish Theological Seminary, developing it, before his death, into the country's foremost institution for Jewish studies and the training of rabbis and teachers. During these early years of the twentieth century, he was the leading spokesman for Conservative Judaism, and he founded the United Synagogue of America in 1913 to advance this cause. By the 1970s the Synagogue had grown to more than 800 congregations. He was editor of the first edition of the *Jewish Encyclopaedia*, 1901, and was an editor of the *Jewish Quarterly Review*, and he wrote, among other books, *The Wisdom of Ben Sira*, 1899; *Studies in Judaism*, 1896 and 1908; *Some Aspects of Jewish Theology*, 1909; and *Documents of Jewish Sectaries*, 1910. He died in New York City on November 19, 1915.

Schick, Béla (1877–1967), physician. Born on July 16, 1877, in Boglár, Hungary, Schick attended school in Graz, Austria, and in 1900 graduated with a medical degree from Karl Franz University in that city. In 1902 he joined the medical faculty of the University of Vienna, advancing to professor in 1918. From the beginning of his career he interested himself primarily in the diseases of children. In 1905, with Dr. Clemens von Pirquet, he published the results of a long study of "serum sickness" and laid down the basic principles of the medical study of allergy. Later he contributed also to the study of scarlet fever, infantile tuberculosis, and other diseases. In 1913 he announced his major accomplishment, the development of the Schick test for susceptibility to diphtheria. The test consisted of a subcutaneous injection of a small amount of diphtheria toxin; redness and swelling at the spot indicated a lack of immunity. At a time when diphtheria was a scourge of childhood around the world, and when the crude serums available for immunization had such serious side effects that physicians were reluctant to use them, the Schick test provided a safe, reliable means to eliminate unnecessary use of the serums. In later years, when new serums were developed that could be used freely, the Schick test continued to be useful as a check on retained immunity through life. Schick was widely honored for his achievement. In 1923 he was invited to New York City to deliver the Harvey lectures at the New York Academy of Medicine; while there he accepted the post of chief pediatrician at Mount Sinai Hospital, with which he continued to be associated until his retirement in 1942. He was naturalized in 1929. Schick was a consultant to many other hospitals as well and from 1936 to 1943 was clinical professor of the diseases of children at Columbia University's College of Physicians and Surgeons. From 1942 he was a consultant at Mount Sinai, director of the pediatrics service at Beth-El Hospital in Brooklyn, and a member of the faculty of the Béla Schick department of pediatrics of Yeshiva University's Albert Einstein College of Medicine in New York City. He was a founding member of the American Academy of Pediatrics and in 1932 published *Child Care Today*. Schick died in New York City on December 6, 1967.

Schirmer, Gustav (1829–1893), music publisher. Born at Königsee, in the German state of Saxony, on September 19, 1829, Schirmer emigrated to the United States with his family in 1840 and settled in New York City. For a number of years he worked in music-publishing firms and then, in 1861, with Bernard Beer, acquired his own music business. In 1866 he bought out Beer and named his company G. Schirmer, music publishers, importers, and dealers. An able musician himself, he succeeded well as a publisher by maintaining personal contacts with many composers in Europe whose work he published, particularly Richard Wagner, to whose Festspielhaus in Bayreuth he contributed. Schirmer also encouraged native American talent. Through his many acquaintances and through the talent he discovered, he built his publishing firm into one of international reputation in the world of music. Schirmer died in Eisenach, Germany, on August 6, 1893. The firm was then incorporated and his sons Rudolph Edward and Gustave headed the company.

Schlesinger, Arthur Meier (1888–1965), historian and educator. Born in Xenia, Ohio, on February 27, 1888, Schlesinger graduated from Ohio State University in 1910 and took his doctorate at Columbia University in 1918. He taught history at Ohio State from 1912 until 1919 and at the State University of Iowa from 1919 until 1924. In 1924 he became professor of history at Harvard, where he remained until his retirement in 1954. One of the most influential teachers of American history in the first half of the twentieth century, he was said to have helped train more of the nation's historians than any other person during that time. Among his many published works were *The Colonial Merchants and the American Revolution*, 1918; *New Viewpoints in American History*, 1922; *The Rise of the City, 1878–1898*, 1933; *Learning How to Behave*, 1946; *Paths to the Present*, 1949; *The American Reformer*, 1950; and his autobiography, *In Retrospect: The History of a Historian*, 1963. He was coeditor of the *Harvard Guide to American History*, 1954, and, with Dixon Ryan Fox, of the 13-volume *History of American Life*, 1927–1948, of which his own volume on the city was outstanding. In the early 1940s Schlesinger served on the Harvard committee that issued in 1945 the much-publicized report, *General Education in a Free Society*, that led to changes in the college's curriculum. He served twice, 1951–1955 and 1961–1965, on the National Historical Publications Committee. He died in Boston on October 30, 1965.

Schlesinger, Arthur Meier, Jr. (1917–   ), historian. Born in Columbus Ohio, on October 15, 1917, Schlesinger was the son of Arthur M. Schlesinger (1888–1965). He graduated from Harvard in 1938 and after a year of further study at Cambridge University in England he returned to Harvard as a fellow, remaining until 1942. During these years he researched and wrote the Pulitzer Prize–winning *The Age of Jackson*, 1945. In 1942–1943 he worked for the Office of War Information (OWI) in Washington, D.C., and from 1943 to 1945 he served in the army with the Office of Strategic Services (OSS) in Europe. Returning from the war in 1946, he was appointed to the faculty at Harvard, where he taught history until 1961, becoming a full professor in 1954. In 1946, also, he received a Guggenheim award that made it possible for him to begin work on a projected four-volume history of the era of Franklin D. Roosevelt. Three of the four volumes were published by 1960: *The Crisis of the Old Order*, 1957, *The Coming of the New Deal*, 1958, and *The Politics of Upheaval*, 1960. Other books he wrote during the same period included *The Vital Center*, 1949, and *The General and the President*, with Richard H. Rovere, 1951. Frequently active in politics, Schlesinger was a founder of Americans for Democratic Action (ADA) and served as a speechwriter for Adlai E. Stevenson in the presidential campaigns of 1952 and 1956 and for John F. Kennedy in 1960. When Kennedy was elected, he appointed Schlesinger a special presidential assistant for Latin American affairs. He served in that position until 1964. Following Kennedy's death he wrote a history of his administration entitled *A Thousand Days*, 1965, which won a Pulitzer Prize and a National Book Award. In 1967 he became a Schweitzer Professor of Humanities at the City University of New York.

Schlesinger, Bruno Walter, *see* Walter, Bruno

Schmucker, Samuel Simon (1799–1873), religious leader and educator. Born in Hagerstown, Maryland, on February 28, 1799, Schmucker graduated from the University of Pennsylvania in 1819 and from Princeton Theological Seminary in 1820. He was ordained in 1821 and served as pastor at New Market, Virginia, for more than five years. A man of unusual theological learning and familiar with all aspects of church life, Schmucker soon became one of the leading figures of nineteenth-century Lutheranism in the United States. With his father, also a clergyman, he aided in founding the General Synod of Lutheran churches in October 1820 at Hagerstown; and when it appeared in 1823 that the organization might collapse for lack of support, it was Schmucker's efforts that saved it from dissolution. One of his goals for the Synod was starting a theological school, for up to this time the church in the United States had depended on European schools or private tutors for training its clergy. In 1826 Gettysburg Theological Seminary (now Lutheran Theological Seminary) was opened, with Schmucker as its first professor. He held the post until 1864. In 1831 Gettysburg College was chartered as Pennsylvania College and Schmucker served as its president until 1834. Schmucker's theological outlook was a blend of traditional Lutheranism and American puritanism. His studies at Princeton had brought him into contact with men of other denominations, a fact which gave him a broader outlook on church practice and relationships than many of his fellow Lutherans possessed. Until after the Civil War he was considered, as the leader of the General Synod, a strong influence for conservatism in his church. But he also showed an ecumenical spirit in his willingness to cooperate with other denominations, and gradually he became a proponent of what was called "American Lutheranism," which aimed partially to divest the church of its distinctive traits and to conform to the prevailing religious attitudes of the country, particularly the puritan spirit. In 1838 Schmucker issued a "Fraternal Appeal to the American Churches" calling for reunion of churches. Slowly his position began to lose ground as the Lutheran churches were reinvigorated by a new conservative spirit emanating especially from Scandinavians and Germans in the Middle West. Other leaders, especially C. F. W. Walther in St. Louis, called for a strictly confessional church. In 1855 Schmucker published anonymously a *Definite Platform, Doctrinal and Disciplinarian, for Evangelical Lutheran District Synods*, a revision of the Augsburg Confession, pointing out errors in the latter. This attempt to revise the creed was passed over in the next four years, and Lutheran orthodoxy prevailed throughout most churches of the denomination. In addition to his role in the controversy over "American Lutheranism" Schmucker wielded wide influence as a professor at the Gettysburg seminary and as a leader in liturgical reform and church polity. He involved himself with social issues, believing the church to be the agent of betterment in society. He favored the abolition of slavery and helped organize emancipation societies and as a proponent of prohibition, was the organizer of one of the first temperance groups in the nation. His published works included also *Biblical Theology of Storr and Flatt, Translated from the German*, two volumes, 1826, and *Elements of Popular Theology*, 1834, the first English-language book on Lutheran theology to be published in America. Schmucker died in Gettysburg on July 26, 1873.

Schoenberg, Arnold, *see* Schönberg, Arnold

Schofield, John McAllister (1831–1906), soldier. Born in Gerry, New York, on September 29, 1831, Schofield graduated from West Point in 1853. After service in Florida against the Seminole, he taught at West Point from 1855 to 1860. In the later year he went to Washington University in St. Louis to teach and was there when the Civil War broke out. He was commissioned a major in the 1st Missouri Volunteer Infantry regiment and spent most of the war, rising to major general, in this border state, where both the political and the military situations remained tense. In February 1864 he was put in command of the Department of the Ohio and of the XXIII Corps to participate in Gen. William T. Sherman's campaign in the South. In this campaign, Schofield's troops defeated Confederate forces under Gen. John B. Hood at the battle of Franklin, Tennessee, and, with Gen. George H. Thomas's command, again defeated Hood at the battle of Nashville. He served under Sherman until the end of the war. For a few months in 1865–1866 Schofield served in France as a confidential agent of the Department of State, negotiating the withdrawal of French interventionist forces from Mexico. On his return to the United States he was for several years involved in implementing Reconstruction in the South, and served in 1868–1869 as secretary of war. In 1869 he became a major general and took command of the Department of the Missouri. Later, while commander of the Division of the Pacific, he traveled to Hawaii in 1872 to investigate its military value to the United States; his recommendations led to the acquisition of a naval base at Pearl Harbor. From 1876 to 1881 he served as commandant of West Point and in 1888 he became the army's commanding general, holding the post until his retirement in 1895. He died in St. Augustine, Florida, on March 4, 1906.

Schönberg, Arnold (1874–1951), composer. Born in Vienna on September 13, 1874, Schönberg (who later in life spelled his name Schoenberg) was virtually a self-taught composer. He began studying violin at eight and a few years later taught himself how to play the cello. As a musical exercise he would compose pieces for himself to play. When he was sixteen his father's death forced him to end his formal schooling, and he worked for a few years as a bank clerk, at the same time keeping up with his music. Once he had decided on a musical career, he spent many years orchestrating the works of other composers simply to make a living. His early compositions were modeled on those of his predecessors, especially Richard Wagner and Johannes Brahms. His first noteworthy composition was *Verklärte Nacht,* a string sextet, 1899. In 1901 he began working on *Gurrelieder,* a cantata for chorus and orchestra that was not completed until 1911 and not performed until 1913. In his early compositions, Schönberg worked within fairly traditional musical forms, but by 1909 he had abandoned tonality altogether for what he called pantonality. By that time he had begun a career of teaching music, mainly in Vienna and Berlin, to support himself. In 1909 he composed three piano pieces and five orchestral pieces in his new pantonality that shortly became famous; they established Schönberg as a major innovator in the field of music, although his works were much criticized at the time. During World War I his composing ceased because of two periods of military service. After 1920 he moved on to a device he called serialism, in which a whole composition could be derived from a series of notes, generally the 12 tones of the chromatic scale, in an order especially chosen for the work. His range of compositions was wide—among his operas, symphonies, chamber music, tone poems, and songs were the comic opera *Von Heute auf Morgen,* 1928, and the unfinished opera *Moses und Aron,* 1930, not produced until 1957; *Kammersymphonie,* 1935; *Ode to Napoleon,* 1942; *Theme and Variations,* 1943; and *A Survivor from Warsaw,* 1947. As early as 1904 Schönberg had begun taking private students, and throughout his life he remained an influential teacher. Outstanding among his students were Anton Webern and Alban Berg. From 1926 to 1933 he taught composition at the Prussian Academy of Fine Arts in Berlin, but with the rise of the Nazis in Germany was discharged because he was Jewish. For a while thereafter he lived in Paris, then, in 1934, he came to the United States to teach music in Boston and New York City. On March 16, 1934, he made his debut as a conductor with the Boston Symphony Orchestra in a performance of his 1905 symphonic poem, *Pelleas und Melisande.* From 1936 to 1944 Schönberg taught at the University of California at Los Angeles (UCLA). He retired in 1944 because of ill health, but continued composing until his death in Los Angeles on July 13, 1951. His work as a composer, as a pioneer in new modes of musical expression, and as a teacher, had made Schönberg one of the great figures of modern music.

Schoolcraft, Henry Rowe (1793–1864), explorer and ethnologist. Born in Albany County, New York, on March 28, 1793, Schoolcraft was educated at Union and Middlebury colleges, where his studies included geology and mineralogy. After leaving college he went on a collecting trip through the Indian country of Missouri and Arkansas. One of the fruits of this trip was a book, *A View of the Lead Mines of Missouri,* 1819; another was an appointment as geologist on an expedition led by Lewis Cass to the copper country in the upper Mississippi Valley and Lake Superior regions. There he became increasingly interested in Indian life, and in 1822 he was appointed Indian agent to the tribes of the Lake Superior region. Shortly afterward he married a girl of Indian extraction, a member of a tribe, the Ojibwa, which soon became his special study. He sat in the Michigan state legislature from 1828 to 1832 and was superintendent of Indian affairs for Michigan from 1836 to 1841. In this capacity he supervised a treaty, promulgated March 28, 1836, whereby the Ojibwa ceded much of northern Michigan to the United States. In the meantime he had written *Narrative Journal of Travels Through the Northwestern Regions of the United States . . . to the Sources of the Mississippi River,* 1821, after his return from the Cass expedition. A later exploring trip to the same area, in the course of which he discovered Lake Itasca, which he and others believed to be the source of the Mississippi, was described in *Narrative of an Expedition . . . to Itasca Lake,* 1834. *Algic Researches* appeared in 1839; a study of Indian psychology and spirituality, it was reissued in 1856 as *The Myth of Hiawatha,* and in this form was the inspiration, although not the source, of Henry Wadsworth Longfellow's poem. Schoolcraft's principal contribution to ethnology was *Historical and Statistical Information Respecting the History, Condition, and Prospects of the Indian Tribes of the United States.* Issued in six parts from 1851 to 1857, and illustrated by engravings from paintings by Seth Eastman, the work was almost impossible to use because of its lack of organization, but it contained much valuable lore. An index prepared by the Bureau of American Ethnology and published in 1954 made its information accessible. Schoolcraft died in Washington D.C., on December 10, 1864.

Schrieffer, John Robert (1931–), physicist. Born in Oak Park, Illinois, on May 31, 1931,

Schrieffer attended the Massachusetts Institute of Technology (MIT) before earning a Ph.D. from the University of Illinois in 1957. He subsequently did post-doctoral work in physics in England and in Denmark before returning to a post at the University of Chicago. In 1959 he joined the faculty of the University of Illinois, where as a graduate student he had collaborated on a theory of superconductivity with his professor, John Bardeen, a 1956 Nobel laureate in physics for the development of the transistor. The phenomenon of superconductivity, marked by an abrupt disappearance of resistance to an electrical current in certain metals at extremely low temperatures, had been discovered in 1911. In 1950 new discoveries of an isotope effect in the electrical behavior at cryogenic temperatures of mercury, tin, and lead led to the separation of the isotopes of these metals. That same year the assumption of another investigator that superconductivity was a function of the crystal–lattice vibrations of the atoms of a given metal proved correct. Theoretical work proceeded at a rapid pace after that and in 1957 Schrieffer, Bardeen, and a third colleague, Leon N. Cooper, were able to construct a theoretical model in which free electrons, which normally migrate randomly in metals, coupled in pairs and interacted with the lattice vibrations. The interpretation of the model satisfied in large measure the observed features of the superconducting state, and thus for the first time an adequate theory of the mechanism of the phenomenon became known. The theory led to a vast amount of further scientific exploration and to practical developments of great importance, such as very powerful electromagnets constructed of superconducting materials. Schrieffer left Illinois for an appointment at the University of Pennsylvania in 1962. Appointed Mary Amanda Wood Professor of Physics in 1964, he received numerous other honors, including a share of the Comstock Prize of the National Academy of Sciences in 1968. His *Theory of Superconductivity* appeared in 1964. In 1972 he shared, with Bardeen and Cooper, the Nobel Prize for Physics for their work on superconductivity.

Schuller, Gunther (1925–   ), musician. Born in New York City on November 22, 1925, Schuller grew up in a family with strong musical traditions. His musical ability became evident during childhood; he was put to studying the flute at the age of twelve, and two years later he took up the French horn. When he was fifteen he made his professional orchestral debut with the New York Philharmonic, conducted by Arturo Toscanini. His musical career soon took precedence over his formal education, so he left high school to continue playing regularly with the Philharmonic. In 1943 he joined the Ballet Theatre's orchestra for a tour, and from late 1943 to 1945 he played the French horn for the Cincinnati Symphony. From 1945 to 1959 he was a member of the New York Philharmonic, then left the orchestra to devote his time to composing and teaching. Schuller took a pronounced interest in jazz as well as classical

music, and in his compositions he effected a synthesis of the two forms, to which he gave the name "third stream" music. Examples of this style were his orchestral compositions *Spectra*, 1958, and *Seven Studies on Themes of Paul Klee*, 1960. In 1961 his ballet, *Variants*, was produced by the New York City Ballet Company. Beside composing and conducting, Schuller taught French horn and composition to both jazz and classical musicians. In 1965 he became head of the composition department at the Berkshire Music School at Tanglewood, Massachusetts. Among his later compositions were *Aphorisms for Flute and String Trio*, commissioned for the Carlton College centennial in 1967, and *Fanfare for St. Louis*, 1968.

Schultz, Dutch, *see* Flegenheimer, Arthur

Schulz, Charles Monroe (1922–   ), cartoonist. Born in Minneapolis on November 26, 1922, Schulz determined while still in grade school that he would become a cartoonist. From 1940 to 1943, he took a correspondence course from Art Instruction in Minneapolis. He served in the army from 1943 to 1945, and upon his return from service took a position with his former correspondence school. Some of his cartoons were published occasionally by local papers, and in 1948 he was hired to do a weekly series for the *St. Paul Pioneer Press*. Some of his work was also published in the *Saturday Evening Post*. In 1950 his idea for the comic strip *Peanuts* was accepted by the United Features Syndicate, launching Schulz on one of the most successful careers any cartoonist has ever enjoyed. The *Peanuts* characters, among them Charlie Brown, Lucy, Linus, Schroeder, and the irrepressible canine Snoopy, became familiar to newspaper readers everywhere as the strip's syndication grew from 8 newspapers in 1950 to more than 900 papers 20 years later. In addition, many *Peanuts* books were published from 1952. The characters derived their charm from being children but their humor and deeper appeal came from their very adult problems, viewpoints, maladjustments, rationalizations, and, occasionally, wisdom. As the comic strip picked up readers, a *Peanuts* vogue developed which prompted the manufacture of greeting cards, sweat shirts, dolls, records, and other products. Several *Peanuts* television specials appeared, including the award-winning *A Charlie Brown Christmas* in 1966; in March 1967, the musical *You're a Good Man, Charlie Brown* opened in New York City; it was later revived and was also produced on television. In 1955 and 1965 Schulz was honored as cartoonist of the year by the National Cartoonists' Society. He was also the author of the best-selling cartoon book *Happiness Is a Warm Puppy*, 1962. The *Peanuts* comic strip was the subject of much speculation concerning its "hidden" meaning, and although Schulz denied that anything more was embodied than a general satire on human foibles, a book entitled *The Gospel According to Peanuts*, published in 1965, attempted to extract a theological message from the cartoons.

Schuman, William Howard (1910–   ), musician and composer. Born in New York City on August 4, 1910, Schuman attended the Malkin Conservatory of Music and Teachers College of Columbia University, from which he took his B.S. in 1935 and his M.A. in 1937. From 1935 to 1945 he taught music at Sarah Lawrence College. In 1945 he became president of the Juilliard School of Music, and during his tenure there established the famed Juilliard String Quartet, updated the curriculum, and took part in the planning for the Lincoln Center for the Performing Arts in New York City. In 1962 he became president of Lincoln Center, a post he held until 1969. In addition to his teaching and administrative duties Schuman was a highly acclaimed composer; in 1943 his cantata, *A Free Song,* won him the first Pulitzer Prize ever awarded for music. He composed in a wide variety of forms, producing works that included symphonies; string quartets; another cantata, *This Is Our Time;* shorter orchestral works, including *American Festival Overture,* 1939, *William Billings Overture,* 1943, and *Prayer in Time of War,* 1943; songs; and several scores for theater and film productions. He also composed the ballets *Undertow,* 1945, *Night Journey,* 1948, and *Judith,* 1950, which was choreographed by Martha Graham; and an opera, *The Mighty Casey,* 1953.

Schumann-Heink, Ernestine (1861–1936), singer. Born at Libern, Austria, near present-day Prague, Czechoslovakia, on June 15, 1861, Ernestine Rössler grew up in poverty; she had little opportunity for formal musical training. After 1874, however, she was able to take singing lessons, and in 1876 she made her first public appearance. Her opera debut, in Dresden in 1878, was in *Il Trovatore,* but the first real success that launched her career as an opera star and solo artist was her appearance as the lead in *Carmen* in 1888 in Hamburg. By that time Miss Rössler had been married to Ernest Heink for six years. She divorced him in 1892, and married Paul Schumann, thus arriving at the hyphenated name she used for most of her professional career; she later married a third time. She appeared in London in 1892; six years later she made her American debut with the Metropolitan Opera in a Chicago performance of *Lohengrin.* Between 1896 and 1906 she appeared regularly in the Richard Wagner productions at Bayreuth. During her years in grand opera she was more famous for Wagnerian roles than for any others she sang. Mme Schumann-Heink spent five years with the Metropolitan Opera Company, then in 1904 went on the concert stage and sang frequently in light operas. She became a U.S. citizen in 1905. After a few seasons of concertizing, she returned to grand opera, both in the United States and Europe. In 1909 she appeared as Klytemnestra in Richard Strauss's *Elektra* in Dresden, Germany. During World War I she remained in the United States, although her sons fought on both sides. Her stage appearances after the war were infrequent, but when radio became popular she often sang on the air. Her farewell appearances for the

Metropolitan Opera in New York City, early in 1932, were in Wagnerian roles. Later she made a movie entitled *Here's to Romance,* 1935, and looked forward to continuing as a film actress. But she died in Hollywood, California, on November 17, 1936, after a remarkably long career. At her prime she had been considered the greatest contralto in the world, and in addition to her operatic work she had been a notable interpreter of German lieder.

Schumpeter, Joseph Alois (1883–1950), economist. Born in Trest, Moravia (now in Czechoslovakia), on February 8, 1883, Schumpeter was schooled in Vienna and received a doctorate in law from the University of Vienna in 1906. He began the practice of law the next year and in 1909 became a lecturer at the University of Vienna and professor of economics at the University of Chernovtsy (Czernowitz); he moved to the University of Graz in 1911 and remained there until the outbreak of World War I. War service was followed by appointment as Austrian minister of finance, a post he occupied in 1919–1920; he then returned to the private practice of law but again entered the academic ranks in '1925, becoming professor of economics at the University of Bonn. He had journeyed to the United States in 1913 as an exchange professor at Columbia University, and with the rise of Hitler's regime in Germany he emigrated to the United States. Upon his arrival in 1932 he was appointed to a chair in economics at Harvard University which he occupied until his death. His influential *Theory of Economic Development,* the work by which he is best known, had appeared in 1911 and was translated into English in 1934; others among his books were *Business Cycles, a Theoretical, Statistical and Historical Analysis of the Capitalist Process,* 1939, also an influential work, and *Capitalism, Socialism and Democracy,* 1942. Schumpeter died on January 8, 1950, in Taconic, Connecticut.

Schurman, Jacob Gould (1854–1942), educator and diplomat. Born in Freetown on Prince Edward Island, Canada, on May 22, 1854, Schurman graduated from the University of London in 1877. He pursued further studies at the universities of Edinburgh, Heidelberg, Göttingen, Berlin, and Paris as well as in Italy until 1880; then he taught at colleges in Canada until 1886. From 1886 until 1892 he was a professor of philosophy at Cornell; in 1890 he became dean of the newly endowed school of philosophy and in 1892 he became president of the university. As a philosopher deeply interested in the problem of ethics, he published several books on the topic, including *Kantian Ethics and the Ethics of Evolution,* 1881; *The Ethical Import of Darwinism,* 1888; *Belief in God,* 1890; and *Agnosticism and Religion,* 1896. In 1892 he helped found and became first editor of the *Philosophical Review.* Under his presidency Cornell grew rapidly and adopted high academic standards. He remained at Cornell until 1920, in the intervening years serving the federal government in a number of diplomatic assignments. In 1899 President William McKinley appointed him a member of the U.S. Philippines Commission, and in that post he helped draw up the charter under which the islands were governed by the United States. In 1912–1913 Schurman served as U.S. minister to Greece and Montenegro. In 1921 President Warren G. Harding appointed him ambassador to China, where he served until 1925, when President Calvin Coolidge made him ambassador to Germany. He returned to the United States in 1930 and spent 1931–1932 as a guest lecturer on foreign relations at the California Institute of Technology. He then retired, and spent several years as a world traveler and lecturer. Schurman died in New York City on August 12, 1942.

Schurz, Carl (1829–1906), soldier, political leader, editor, and public official. Born in Liblar, near Cologne, Germany, on March 2, 1829, Schurz studied at the University of Bonn. His deep involvement in the revolutionary movement of 1848–1849 forced him to flee to France and then to Switzerland; he returned to Germany briefly in 1850 to carry out the daring rescue of an imprisoned former teacher and revolutionary comrade. After a stay in England he came to the United States in 1852, living in Philadelphia until 1855, then moving to Watertown, Wisconsin. He was admitted to the Wisconsin bar in 1859. His reformist spirit led him to embrace the abolitionist cause and to join the Republican party; he campaigned in both English and German for John C. Frémont for president in 1856, for Abraham Lincoln for the Senate in 1858, and for Lincoln again in the presidential election of 1860. After Lincoln's election he was named minister to Spain, but he remained in Spain only until January 1862; he resigned in April and was commissioned a brigadier general in the Union army. He saw action at the second battle of Bull Run (Manassas), at Chancellorsville, at Gettysburg, and at Chattanooga, and was promoted to major general in 1863. Although without military training, Schurz was thoroughly competent and one of the best of the politically appointed generals. Soon after the war's end he was asked by President Andrew Johnson to tour the South and report on conditions; his report, containing strong recommendations for Negro suffrage and civil rights, was shelved by the President and published only at congressional insistence. After a brief time as Washington correspondent for Horace Greeley's *New York Tribune*, Schurz became editor of the newly founded *Detroit Post* in 1866; the next year he moved to St. Louis and became coeditor of the *St. Louis Westliche Post*. In 1869 he was elected to the Senate from Missouri and served a single term, during which he was an outspoken critic of Ulysses S. Grant's administration, the official corruption that accompanied it, and the effort to annex Santo Domingo; he also sought the establishment of a merit-based system of civil service. Such was his disgust with the regular Republican

party that in 1872 he was the chief organizer of the Liberal Republican party and campaigned vigorously for its ticket, despite its unfortunate nomination of Horace Greeley for president. In 1876, by then out of the Senate, Schurz returned to the regular Republican ranks and supported Rutherford B. Hayes, who, as President, appointed him secretary of the interior. In that post he followed an enlightened policy toward the Indians and continued his efforts at civil-service reform. From 1881 to 1883 he was an editor of the *New York Evening Post* and of the *Nation*. His consistently lofty approach to politics led him to bolt the Republican party twice more, in 1884 as leader of the "mugwump" revolt against the nomination of James G. Blaine, and in 1900 when he reluctantly supported William Jennings Bryan against William McKinley on the issue of imperialism. From 1892 to 1901 he was president of the National Civil Service Reform League and during about the same period was an editorial writer for *Harper's Weekly*; he ended his connection with the magazine because he refused to support agitation for war with Spain. Among his published works were a two-volume *Life of Henry Clay*, 1887, and the three volumes of *Reminiscences of Carl Schurz*, published posthumously in 1907–1908. He died in New York City on May 14, 1906.

Schuyler, Philip John (1733–1804), soldier and public official. Born in Albany, New York, on November 20, 1733, Schuyler was a member of one of the wealthy upstate New York families; after his father's death he eventually inherited sizable estates in the Mohawk Valley and a substantial income. As much as possible he lived the life of a country squire, overseeing his estates and promoting commerce and trade. But in the turbulent decades from 1755 to the end of the century he was frequently called upon for public service. During the last of the French and Indian Wars, 1755–1760, he was a commissioned officer and saw some action, but his main responsibility was provisioning troops. After the war he spent two years, 1761–1763, in England trying to settle some of the colonial claims resulting from the conflict. He then spent most of his time until the outbreak of the Revolution improving his estates, engaging in the lumber business and ocean commerce, and in 1764 building the first flax mill in the colonies. He was elected to a term in the New York assembly in 1768, and from 1775 to 1777 he served as a delegate to the Second Continental Congress. When the Revolutionary War began, Schuyler was named one of the four major generals to serve under George Washington's command; he was put in command of the northern, or New York, department. His wartime experiences were not entirely beneficial to his reputation; the Continental invasion of Canada, over which he was given supervision in 1775, proved a failure, and two years later he was blamed in part for Arthur St. Clair's surrender of Fort Ticonderoga. Thus in 1777 he was replaced by Gen. Horatio Gates. He immediately requested a court-martial to examine his actions in the loss of Ticonderoga, and as a result, the next year he was completely exonerated. From 1778 to 1781 he was again in the Continental Congress. Elected a state senator in New York, he served from 1780 to 1784 and again from 1786 to 1790. A staunch supporter of the new Constitution in 1787, he helped gain its ratification in New York; and when the new federal government began functioning, he was one of New York's first U.S. senators, serving as a Federalist from 1789 to 1791. During this short first term Schuyler strongly supported the monetary policies and other measures of benefit to large landholders proposed by his son-in-law, Alexander Hamilton. Then, defeated for reelection to the U.S. Senate, Schuyler returned to the state senate, from 1792 to 1797, during which period he helped found Union College, Schenectady, New York. In 1797 he was again elected to the U.S. Senate but was only able to serve for less than a year. Poor health led to his resignation in January 1798. He died in Albany, New York, on November 18, 1804.

Schwab, Charles Michael (1862–1939), industrialist. Born on February 18, 1862, in Williamsburg, Pennsylvania, Schwab grew up in the village of Loretto, Pennsylvania. After finishing high school, he entered the Carnegie-owned Edgar Thomson Steel Works in Braddock, Pennsylvania, as a laborer. His gift for handling people and his receptiveness to new industrial methods elevated him rapidly in the business: he was made general superintendent of the Thomson plant in 1889, became manager of both the Thomson and Homestead works three years later, and in 1897 was appointed president of the Carnegie Steel Company. As such he stimulated and negotiated the sale of the Carnegie properties to a group headed by J. P. Morgan and after the merger, he became, at thirty-nine, the first president of Morgan's United States Steel Corporation. In the meantime he had purchased a controlling interest in the small Bethlehem Steel Company and merged it with the defunct U.S. Shipbuilding Company; in 1903 he resigned from U.S. Steel to preside over the new enterprise. Firmly devoted to profit sharing and incentive wages and to giving freedom of action to his executives, he built the company into U.S. Steel's most formidable rival. He became chairman of the board in 1913. With lucrative contracts during World War I, he saw production rise to levels that made Bethlehem a prime arsenal for the Allies. He himself served in 1918 as director general of shipbuilding for the United States Shipping Board's Emergency Fleet Corporation. At its height, his fortune was estimated at $200 million. Unsound ventures outside the steel industry depleted his resources, however, and he died insolvent on September 18, 1939, in New York City.

Schwinger, Julian Seymour (1918–   ), physicist. Born in New York City on February 17, 1918, Schwinger showed extraordinary ability in mathematics and physics even before he had entered high school. At fourteen he entered the College of the City of New York (CCNY) but subsequently transferred to Columbia, from which he graduated in 1936 and earned his doctorate in 1939. For the next two years he studied under J. Robert Oppenheimer at the University of California at Berkeley and worked as a research assistant. After two years of teaching at Purdue University he worked for a few months in 1943 at the Metallurgical Laboratory of the University of Chicago. From late 1943 to 1945 he worked at the radiation laboratory of Massachusetts Institute of Technology (MIT), then moved to Harvard, where he became a full professor at the age of twenty-nine. Schwinger's studies in quantum mechanics led him to the formulation of a theory of quantum electrodynamics that was consistent with Einstein's theory of relativity and that proved useful in measuring and explaining the behavior of atomic and subatomic particles. In 1958 he edited *Quantum Electrodynamics*, containing basic articles relating to the subject, and in 1969 he published *Particles and Sources*. Along with fellow physicists Richard P. Feynman and Shinichiro Tomonaga, Schwinger was awarded the Nobel Prize for Physics in 1965. In 1966 he became Higgins Professor of Physics at Harvard.

Scott, James Brown (1866–1943), educator and lawyer. Born in Kincardine, Ontario, on June 3, 1866, Scott graduated from Harvard in 1890 and remained at the university for the next four years, pursuing studies in international law. For the next two years he studied in Paris, Berlin, and Heidelberg. He returned to the United States in 1892, moved to California, and opened a law office two years later. In 1896 he organized the Los Angeles Law School (later part of the University of Southern California), of which he was dean from 1896 to 1899. He also served as dean of the University of Illinois Law School, 1899–1903, and as professor at Columbia, 1903–1906, and George Washington, 1906–1911, universities. In addition to publishing a number of books, Scott contributed notably to the field of international law. He founded the American Society of International Law in 1906, acting as its secretary until 1924; he also founded and edited its *American Journal of International Law*, from 1907 to 1924. He launched the American Institute of International Law in 1912, and was its first president, and he helped to establish the Academy of International Law in 1914, and the Permanent Court of International Justice (the World Court) at The Hague in 1921. From 1906 to 1910 he served as solicitor for the U.S. Department of State, and from 1910 until his retirement in 1940 he was a trustee of the Carnegie Endowment for International Peace. After World War I he attended the Versailles Peace Conference, and two years later was an adviser to the Washington Arms Limitation Conference. In 1927 he served as chairman of the U.S.–Pan American Committee of Jurists for the preparation of codes of international law. Among his many books were *An International Court of Justice*, 1916; *Peace Through Justice*, 1917; *The U.S. of A.*, 1920; *Roger*

Bacon: His Life and Letters, 1923; and *Law, the State, and the International Community*, 1939. He died in Annapolis, Maryland, on June 25, 1943.

Scott, Walter Edward (1872–1954), "Death Valley Scotty," adventurer. Born in 1872, Scott first emerged into the light of history as a cowboy with Buffalo Bill's Wild West Show and arrived in Los Angeles in 1905, where, without any visible means of support, he began to spend large sums of money. He produced $5500 in cash to charter an Atchison, Topeka, and Santa Fe Railroad train that, he said, would take him from Los Angeles to Chicago in 45 hours, then well under the record. And, in fact, on July 9–11, 1905, the three-car train made the 2265–mile run in 44 hours, 54 minutes, averaging an astounding 50.4 miles per hour and, over one short stretch, attaining a speed of 106 miles per hour. The record stood until 1934. Subsequently Scott built a $2 million Moorish castle at Stovepipe Wells in Grapevine Canyon in Death Valley, where he lived for the last 30 years of his life. The castle remained a tourist attraction after his death there on January 5, 1954. "Death Valley Scotty" had claimed to own a secret gold mine, but it was later revealed that his activities had been financed by Albert Mussey Johnson (1872–1948), a onetime railroad worker who had risen to be chairman of the board of the National Life Insurance Company of Chicago. Johnson's support of Scott was one of the strangest, and most expensive, hobbies ever recorded, but he explained it simply: "He paid me back in laughs."

Scott, Winfield (1786–1866), soldier. Born on June 13, 1786, near Petersburg, Virginia, Scott attended the College of William and Mary briefly in 1805 and then studied law. In 1807, following the *Chesapeake-Leopard* impressment incident that almost brought on war with Britain, he enlisted in a local cavalry troop; he soon returned to law but the next year was commissioned a captain of light artillery and remained a military man thereafter. During 1810–1811 he served a one-year suspension imposed by a court martial called by Gen. James Wilkinson, of whom Scott had made disparaging remarks in relation to the trial of Aaron Burr. Subsequently, in the War of 1812, he was made a lieutenant colonel and saw action on the Niagara frontier, where he was captured by British forces at Queenston Heights. Soon after his release he participated, as adjutant to Gen. Henry Dearborn, in the attack on Fort George and in 1813 took command of the captured stronghold. In 1814, promoted to brigadier general, he fought at the battles of Chippewa and Lundy's Lane; he was wounded twice at Lundy's Lane, but his success there made him a national hero and his evident ability made him outstanding among the U.S. commanders. He was then made a department commander and made his headquarters in New York City. He made several trips to Europe to study military tactics, wrote or revised a number of military manuals, and took a deep interest in maintaining a well-trained and disciplined U.S.

army. He was passed over for command of the army in 1828 in favor of a former junior officer. Protesting in vain, he submitted his resignation, which was not accepted. In 1832 he saw active duty in Black Hawk's War, although an epidemic of cholera limited his and his troops effectiveness. Later in the year President Andrew Jackson commissioned him personally to observe and report on the activities of the Nullifiers in South Carolina. During 1835–1837 he was in command of the war against the Seminole and Creek Indians of Florida. In 1837 Jackson relieved him of command and placed him before a court of inquiry, which completely exonerated him of a charge of laxity in the prosecution of the war. In 1838 he was charged with overseeing the pacification and removal of the Cherokee Indians to reservations beyond the Mississippi River; immediately afterward President Martin Van Buren sent him to the far Northeast, where he successfully smoothed the border conflict with Canada known as the Aroostook War. In 1841 he succeeded to the command of the entire army. With the outbreak of the Mexican War he recommended Zachary Taylor for command of the U.S. forces. When Taylor appeared to be making little progress, however, Scott set out himself with a supplementary force; he captured Veracruz in March 1847, and six months later, after a series of victories, including those at Cerro Gordo, Contreras, Churubusco, Molino del Rey, and Chapultepec, entered Mexico City. He remained there until April 1848, governing the city with notable justice and humanity; unfounded charges by two subordinate officers led President James K. Polk to call a board of inquiry to investigate his conduct of the war, but soon after his return to the United States the charges were dropped amid the national celebration of his great success. Despite—or perhaps because of—the fact that he was by far the most capable military leader of his time, Scott was beset by political opposition from the beginning of his military fame; and although he was highly popular with his men, his insistence upon fine points of military etiquette earned him the nickname "Old Fuss and Feathers." In 1852 he received the Whig nomination for president but was soundly beaten by the Democratic candidate, Franklin Pierce. In 1855 he was promoted to lieutenant general, the first man since George Washington to hold that rank. In 1859, at the age of 73, he again served as a mediator between Great Britain and the United States, traveling to the Northwest to settle a dispute over possession of San Juan Island in Puget Sound. In 1860, forseeing trouble between the North and South, he began recommending reinforcement of army posts and arsenals in the South, but was ignored. He was still commander in chief when the Civil War began in 1861; but his advice was largely ignored and his proposed "anaconda" strategy of splitting the Confederacy—the plan eventually adopted—was widely ridiculed. In the fall of that year he retired, pleading age and infirmity. He died at West Point on May 29, 1866, the foremost U.S. military figure between the Revolution and the Civil War.

Scripps, Edward Wyllis, see under Scripps, James Edmund

Scripps, Ellen Browning, see under Scripps, James Edmund

Scripps, James Edmund (1835–1906), newspaper publisher. Born in London on March 19, 1835, James Scripps emigrated with his family to the United States and settled near Rushville, Illinois; it was there that his younger half-brother Edward Wyllis Scripps was born on June 18, 1854. Coming from a family with a tradition in the publishing business, James began his newspaper career in Chicago in 1857 with a paper that merged with the *Chicago Tribune* a year later. In 1859 he moved to Detroit and went to work for the *Daily Advertiser*. By the time it merged with the *Detroit Tribune* in 1862, Scripps was already its part owner. In 1873 he founded the *Detroit Evening News*, which soon outran its rivals in circulation. Edward Scripps had begun his newspaper career in 1872 by taking a job with the *Detroit Tribune*, for which James was the business manager and an editor. In 1873, when James started the *Evening News*, Edward joined the staff and remained for four years. After a year of European travel, he returned and settled in Cleveland to found, with James's help and that of another half-brother, George, the *Penny Press* (later the *Press*) in 1878. Two years later the Scripps brothers acquired the *Evening Chronicle* in St. Louis, and in 1880 they bought the *Cincinnati Post*, creating the first chain of daily newspapers in the nation. Differences over editorial policy—Edward was generally liberal on political and economic questions, while James was staunchly Republican—led to a split in 1889 and thereafter James took no active role in the management of the Scripps chain. He retained his interest in the *Detroit Evening News*, however, and in 1891 purchased the *Detroit Tribune*. He remained active in local civic and political affairs and in 1902 was elected to a term in the Michigan state legislature. He died in Detroit on May 29, 1906. Edward earlier had given up control over all the other papers in the chain but the *Cincinnati Post*. In 1895, with his half-brother, George, and Milton A. McRae, he began the Scripps-McRae League of Newspapers. Two years later they formed the Scripps-McRae Press Association to gather and disseminate news by telegraph. In 1904 the association took over the rival Publishers Press, becoming Scripps-McRae Publishers Press, and in 1907 the association became known as the United Press Association (which in 1958 became United Press International, UPI). In 1902, Edward established the Newspaper Enterprise Association (NEA) to syndicate newspaper columns and other features, and in 1920 he established the Science Service. During the 1890s he began acquiring a series of West Coast newspapers in major cities—he made his home in San Diego, California—and in 1908 established a regional press association to service them with news. In 1914 he and McRae split and his son James George Scripps took over direction

of the chain. Father and son quarreled in 1920, the year of Edward's complete retirement, and control of the main group of Scripps' papers passed to a second son, Robert Paine Scripps, who in 1922 entered into partnership with Roy W. Howard to form the Scripps-Howard Newspapers. Edward Scripps died on March 12, 1926, at Monrovia Bay, Liberia. He had in 1901, with his half-sister Ellen Browning Scripps, established the Scripps Institution for Biological Research at La Jolla, California; it was later renamed the Scripps Institution of Oceanography and became a part of the University of California. Ellen (1836–1932) had been involved with the newspaper business since 1873, had written for the Detroit and Cleveland papers, and had had financial interests in her brothers' holdings. She helped organize and finance the Scripps-McRae chain and later invested heavily in California real estate. A noted philanthropist, in 1926 she founded Scripps College, now part of the Claremont Colleges, in Claremont, California.

Seaborg, Glenn Theodore (1912–   ), chemist. Born on April 19, 1912, in Ishpeming, Michigan, Seaborg grew up there and, after 1922, near Los Angeles. He graduated from the University of California at Los Angeles (UCLA) in 1934 and moved to the University of California's Berkeley campus for graduate work, taking his Ph.D. in 1937. He remained there as a research associate and in 1939 was appointed an instructor. Until 1940 his work was concerned primarily with the production of isotopes of common elements. In that year Edwin M. McMillan produced at Berkeley the first synthetic transuranium element, neptunium (atomic number 93), by bombarding uranium with neutrons by means of a cyclotron; Seaborg joined him and by the next year they had isolated plutonium (atomic number 94). An isotope of plutonium, Pu-239, promised a higher energy yield from nuclear fission than uranium and in 1942 Seaborg moved to the Metallurgical Laboratory of the Manhattan Engineering District at the University of Chicago in order to seek means of producing and isolating usable quantities of plutonium for the atomic-bomb project. During the course of his work he and his staff discovered that extremely minute quantities of neptunium and plutonium occur in nature as the result of natural radioactive processes in uranium. His group also discovered two new elements, americium (95) and curium (96), in 1944, and confirmed his hypothesis that the transuranium elements form part of a transition series (the actinide series) similar to the lanthanide series of rare earths. In 1946 he returned to Berkeley as professor of chemistry and associate director of the Lawrence Radiation Laboratory. During the next 12 years he and his team of researchers discovered 6 more elements: berkelium (97) in 1949, californium (98) in 1950, einsteinium (99) in 1952, fermium (100) in 1953, mendelevium (101) in 1955, and nobelium (102) in 1958. In 1951 Seaborg was awarded the Nobel Prize for Chemistry jointly with McMillan for their discoveries concerning transuranium elements. In 1954 he became director of the Radiation Laboratory and in 1958 he gave up research to become chancellor of the Berkeley campus. In 1959 he won the Fermi Award of the Atomic Energy Commission (AEC) for his work in nuclear chemistry and with atomic energy, and in 1961 he left the university to become, at President John F. Kennedy's request, chairman of the AEC, the first scientist to hold the position. He represented the United States at international conferences on atomic energy and was a member of numerous scientific and educational organizations and advisory boards. In 1971 he left the AEC to return to the University of California at Berkeley.

Seabury, Samuel (1729–1796), religious leader. Born on November 30, 1729, in Groton, Connecticut, Samuel Seabury graduated from Yale in 1748, studied medicine at the University of Edinburgh, and was ordained a priest of the church of England by the bishop of London in 1753. He was sent as a missionary to New Brunswick, New Jersey, and later served in Jamaica and Westchester, New York. A Loyalist, just before the American Revolution he wrote several pamphlets and circulated them in New England under the pen name "A. W. Farmer," the middle initial standing for "Westchester." In them he encouraged Americans to accept British authority and forgo ideas of independence. He and his pamphlets became notorious and he was answered by Alexander Hamilton, then a student at King's College (Columbia) in New York City. He was imprisoned for a time in Connecticut in 1775 for working to prevent the choosing of delegates to the Continental Congress and to provincial bodies; after his release he returned to Westchester. He served British forces as a chaplain and as a guide around the southern part of New York. Through most of the Revolution he resided in New York City. In 1783 the Anglican clergy of Connecticut met to choose a candidate for bishop; when their first choice declined appointment, they turned to Seabury, who subsequently sailed to England to be consecrated. Problems were raised there—church authorities believed themselves unable legally to perform the rite—and he turned instead to the prelates of Scotland, by whom he was consecrated bishop of Connecticut and Rhode Island late in 1784. Upon his return to the United States he became rector of St. James's Church in New London, Connecticut. When other bishops from the former Middle and Southern colonies were consecrated in England in 1787, a movement was begun to reunite the English and Scottish factions of the Anglican church in the United States. At the General Convention of 1789 the reunification came about and in 1792 the four American bishops of the new Protestant Episcopal body met to conduct the first American consecration. Seabury continued as rector of St. James's and as bishop until his death in New London, Connecticut, on February 25, 1796.

Seaman, Elizabeth Cochrane (1867–1922), "Nellie Bly," journalist. Born at Cochrane Mills, Armstrong County, Pennsylvania, on May 5, 1867, Miss Cochrane began her career in journalism in the mid-1880s, working for the *Pittsburgh Dispatch*. It was on this paper that she began using her pen name "Nellie Bly." Her first articles, on the conditions among working girls in Pittsburgh, were indicative of the sensational, exposé and reform-oriented reporting that made her famous during the 1890s. In 1887 she traveled through Mexico, sending back travel reports to her paper. She subsequently published her articles in a book, *Six Months in Mexico*. In 1888 she left Pittsburgh for New York City and went to work for Joseph Pulitzer's *New York World*. One of her first undertakings for the paper was to get herself committed to the asylum on Blackwells (now Welfare) Island by pretending insanity, in order to write an exposé of conditions among the patients. Her accounts, published in the *World* and later (1887) collected in the book *Ten Days in a Mad House*, evoked a grand-jury investigation of the asylum and brought about some improvements in patient care. The high point of her career came in 1889–1890, when she traveled alone around the world in the record time of 72 days, 6 hours, and 11 minutes, in order to beat the time of Phileas Fogg, the hero of Jules Verne's novel *Around the World in Eighty Days*. The resulting work, *Nellie Bly's Book: Around the World in Seventy-two Days*, was her greatest success. In 1895 she married Robert L. Seaman and after his death nine years later attended to his business interests—he manufactured iron and steel—in Brooklyn for some years. But eventually she returned to journalism, working for the *New York Journal*. She died in New York City on January 27, 1922.

Sears, Isaac (1730–1786), merchant and Revolutionary patriot. Born in West Brewster, Massachusetts, about July 1, 1730, Sears engaged in merchant shipping and privateering until after the last of the French and Indian Wars (the Seven Years' War). When the Stamp Act crisis erupted in the colonies in 1765 he was living in New York City, and although he did not hold public office he became a leader in the Sons of Liberty and was one of the guiding forces behind most of the mob activities in the city directed against British rule. No sooner had the Stamp Act agitation died down than the Townshend Acts aroused new indignation in 1768–1769, resulting in non-importation agreements being made by the colonists at several ports. Even after the Townshend Act revenues were repealed, "King Sears," as he was called, fought to maintain the non-importation agreements; he was defeated on this issue in June 1769, and the New York agreement was revoked. For the next few years, Sears and the Sons of Liberty were inactive, but the 1773 Tea Act brought them to life again. As a followup to the Boston Tea Party, Sears led his followers in a similar exploit in New York City in 1774. On May 15, 1774, he was a signer of a letter to the Boston Committee of Correspondence calling for a "congress of deputies from the colonies" to be assembled. By September the First

Continental Congress had convened at Philadelphia. Once the war had started, in April 1775, Sears and his followers drove out Loyalist officials and took control of the city. They prepared for military action and carried on raids in the New York area against British positions. From 1777 Sears sailed out of Boston as a privateer, not returning to New York City until the war was over. He resumed his mercantile business and he was twice elected to the New York State legislature, in 1784 and 1786. In 1786 he set sail for China to trade. During the course of this venture, he died in China on October 28, 1786.

Sears, Richard Warren (1863–1914), businessman. Born on December 7, 1863, in Stewartville, Minnesota, Sears began working in Minneapolis in the offices of the Minneapolis and St. Louis Railway about 1880, and then was transferred to Redwood Falls, Minnesota; there he pursued various occupations, including selling lumber and coal. In 1886 a shipment of watches was left abandoned in the station and Sears obtained the right to sell them. He promoted them in letters, offering them at bargain rates, and sold the lot rapidly. He renewed his supply of watches, advertised them in St. Paul newspapers, and by 1886 was secure enough to leave railroading and start the R. W. Sears Watch Company, a mail-order business, in Minneapolis. Within a year he had issued a catalogue, moved to Chicago, and engaged Alvah C. Roebuck, a watchmaker, to fix watches that were returned for adjustments. Sears sold out in 1889 and agreed to refrain for three years from selling watches in Chicago, settling in Iowa as a banker. But this career did not suit his entrepreneurial temperament and he returned to Mineapolis, again engaged Roebuck, and started another mail-order watch and jewelry outlet. In 1893 they established themselves in Chicago and the firm was renamed Sears, Roebuck and Company. Its catalogue, which at first offered a choice of 25 watches, progressively expanded to an enormous variety of general merchandise at prices that reflected the economy of large-scale purchasing, efficient handling, and sales by mail. The bulk of their early customers were in rural areas inadequately served by retail outlets; they were later to acquire millions of city-dwelling customers as well. Sears's catalogue advertising, which he wrote himself, was liberally sprinkled with adjectives and was "folksy" enough to be readable as popular fare. The success of his business, however, was due to firm policies—fixed prices, guarantees, and a liberal adjustment plan—standards which, in themselves, fostered quality merchandise and helped bring about improvement in the conduct of competitive retailers. In 1897 Julius Rosenwald, who had bought out Roebuck's interest, became vice-president of the company. He rose to president in 1910, succeeding Sears, who had retired the year before to his farm north of Chicago. Sears died in Waukesha, Wisconsin, on September 28, 1914.

Sedges, John, see Buck, Pearl

Sedgwick, Theodore (1746–1813), public official and judge. Born in West Hartford, Connecticut, on May 9, 1746, Sedgwick attended Yale College, receiving a deferred degree in 1772 for the class of 1765. Admitted to the bar in 1766, he practiced law first in Great Barrington, Massachusetts, then at nearby Sheffield. He saw military service early in the Revolution in Gen. John Thomas's expedition to Canada. He served several terms in the Massachusetts legislature between 1780 and 1788; he was speaker of the Massachusetts House in 1788, and was a state senator in 1784–1785. From 1785 to 1788 he was also a member of the Continental Congress. In 1787 he played a prominent role in the suppression of Shays's Rebellion. As a supporter of the new Constitution, Sedgwick was a delegate to the state ratifying convention in 1788. When the new federal government began functioning he was elected to the House of Representatives, where he served as a Federalist from March 1789 until June 1796; he then resigned to take a Massachusetts seat in the U.S. Senate to fill out an unexpired term. He returned to the House in March 1799, and was elected speaker on December 2. After his term of office expired he was named in 1802 a justice of the Massachusetts Supreme Court. He held this post until his death in Boston on January 23, 1813.

Seeger, Pete (1919–   ), folk singer and song writer. Born in New York City on May 3, 1919, into a musical family, Peter Seeger attended Harvard from 1936 to 1938, and then began to travel. By 1940 he had passed through the 48 conterminous states, mostly by freight train and hitchhiking. He had acquired along the way a vast repertoire of songs—ballads, blues and country songs, hymns and spirituals, work songs, and dance tunes—and new ways of playing his favorite instrument, the five-string banjo. In 1940 he organized the Almanac Singers, with Millard Lampell, Lee Hays, and Woody Guthrie, and they toured the country in 1941, entertaining in accordance with their interest in social issues, primarily in union halls and at farmers' and factory workers' meetings, with industrial ballads and songs that he and Guthrie wrote. He made overseas broadcasts for the Office of War Information (OWI) during World War II, and after the war briefly rejoined the Almanac Singers. In 1948 he organized the Weavers, a singing group that achieved great popularity, with Hays, Fred Hellerman, and Ronnie Gilbert, and himself singing and playing banjo. In 1958 he left the group; he thereafter played and sang in high schools and colleges, churches, taverns, backyard theaters, New York City's Town Hall and Carnegie Hall, and on hundreds of radio and television programs. He was in the short film *To Hear My Banjo Play* in the 1940s and in a Los Angeles Repertory Theatre revival of the folk play *Dark of the Moon*. In the 1950s he appeared in the National Folk Festival in St. Louis and gave six concerts with commentary on "American Folk Music and Its World Origins" at Columbia University. In 1963–1964 he undertook a global singing tour with his family. A virtuoso and authority on the five-string banjo, he published an instructional manual replete with anecdotes, history, and biographical sketches, *How to Play the 5-String Banjo*, 1948, revised 1954. Among the songs he wrote or collaborated on were "Where Have All the Flowers Gone," "If I Had a Hammer," "Kisses Sweeter than Wine," and "Turn, Turn, Turn." An inspiration to countless young artists, he was one of the most beloved figures in the folk-music world and in the early 1970s was active in behalf of movements for conservation and environmental improvement.

Segal, George (1924–   ), sculptor. Born in New York City on November 26, 1924, Segal received his B.S. degree from the New York University School of Education in 1949. He also attended Cooper Union's art school, the Pratt Institute, and Rutgers, where he earned his M.F.A. degree in 1963. He began his art career as a painter in the early 1950s, but, dissatisfied with his work, he turned to sculpture in 1958. In 1960 he began executing life-size tableaux, doing plaster casts of living people, mostly friends and relatives. His first such work was "Man at a Table," 1961. Other early works were "Man on a Bicycle," "Lovers on a Bench," and "Woman Leaning Against a Chimney." Segal sometimes combined a flair for vivid color with his sculptures, although they were more often colorless and featureless, and occasionally he introduced lighting and sound effects, as in "Cinema," 1963, "Woman Listening to Music," 1965, and "The Subway," 1968. His 1966 tableau, "The Truck," won the Logan Medal of the Art Institute of Chicago. He had a number of one-man shows, mostly in New York City, where his works were usually praised by the critics. Among his larger tableaux were "Artist in His Studio," 1968, "The Parking Garage," 1968, and "The Aerial View," 1970.

Segar, Elzie Crisler (1894–1938), cartoonist. Born in Chester, Illinois, on December 8, 1894, Segar worked variously as a motion-picture projectionist, house and sign painter, and photographer, before taking up comic-strip drawing. After failing in his first cartooning efforts, he took a correspondence course, then succeeded in getting a job with the *Chicago Herald* drawing *Charley Chaplin's Comic Capers.* He also worked for the *Chicago Evening American* as a reporter and cartoonist before going to New York City in 1919 to initiate the comic strip *Thimble Theater.* It was an unusual strip, presented as a one-act play in cartoon form and starring the Oyl family, among whom the daughter, Olive, was the best known. In January 1929 Segar added to the cast of characters his most famous creation, Popeye, a one-eyed "old salt" complete with corncob pipe, bulging muscles, and a strong sense of chivalry. From that time on the comic strip, which eventually was renamed for the new central character, Popeye, consisted largely of the adventures of his new hero, along with Olive Oyl and Wimpy, the hamburger eater.

Popeye, who gave spinach a national reputation (it was the secret of his strength), became one of the world's most popular comic-strip characters and soon became a movie star in innumerable animated cartoons, many of which were later revived on television. Another of Segar's creations, an orchid-eating creature known, from the sound it made, as the "jeep," may have given its name to the famed army vehicle. Segar died in Santa Monica, California, on October 13, 1938, but Popeye's adventures continued in the hands of other artists.

Segrè, Emilio Gino (1905–   ), physicist. Born in Tivoli, Italy, on February 1, 1905, Segrè entered the University of Rome to study engineering, but he changed his field to physics and earned his doctorate in 1928. After a year of military service he returned to the university to teach physics and to do research in collaboration with Enrico Fermi. Segrè remained at the University until 1935, when he accepted an appointment at the University of Palermo as professor of physics and director of research. In 1938 he emigrated to the United States and became a research associate at the University of California's Lawrence Radiation Laboratory in Berkeley. He became a U.S. citizen in 1944. From 1943 to 1946 he worked on the atomic-bomb project at the secret Los Alamos laboratory in New Mexico, then, after World War II, returned to Berkeley as professor of physics. His early work at the University of Rome had dealt with X rays and atomic spectroscopy, but in 1934 he turned his attention to the study of nuclear physics. In collaboration with Fermi, Segrè produced in 1937 the first laboratory-made element, technetium (atomic number 43), by bombarding molybdenum with deuterons and neutrons. Technetium, although not a transuranium element, probably does not exist in nature. Working with Edwin M. McMillan and Glen T. Seaborg at Berkeley during 1938 to 1943, he became a codiscoverer of the isotope plutonium-239. He also shared in the discovery of the element astatine. His experiments in nuclear fission and radioactivity were a significant contribution to the U.S. development of atomic weapons. His researches at Berkeley while working with Owen Chamberlain and others, led to the confirmation in 1955 of the existence of the antiproton, a negatively charged particle having the same mass as the proton. The existence of the antiproton had been suspected for almost 30 years, but had never been proved; the discovery of the particle led to intense speculation during the subsequent decade concerning the actual existence and characteristics of antimatter. In 1959 Segrè and Chamberlain shared the Nobel Prize for Physics for their discovery of the antiproton.

Selden, George Baldwin (1846–1922), inventor and lawyer. Born in Clarkson, Monroe County, New York, on September 14, 1846, Selden attended the University of Rochester from 1861 to 1864 and also saw military service during the Civil War.

After the war he attended Yale College, but by 1867 he was forced to return home due to his father's illness. Thereupon he studied law in his father's firm and was admitted to the bar in 1871; his interest in technology led him to become a patent attorney. Over the years he worked on a number of minor inventions, but during the late 1870s he devoted his attention to designing an engine for road locomotion, or a "horseless carriage." He designed engines that could be run on ammonia, steam, and carbon bisulphite, and one that was propelled by a mixture of kerosene and nitrous oxide (laughing gas); but none of them were adequate. By 1879 he had made a vehicle with a workable engine that was basically a modification of one designed earlier by George Brayton of Boston. Selden applied for a patent on his engine which used a hydrocarbon petroleum fraction fuel—crude kerosene or gasoline—on May 8, 1879. Realizing that there was little enthusiasm at the time for a motor-driven vehicle and that money to produce the machines would be hard to raise, he managed to hold off having the patent issued until 1895 because his 17-year monopoly on the product would begin the year the patent was issued, not when it was applied for. By 1895, while Selden had gotten nowhere raising money to manufacture his car, other inventors were getting their vehicles on the road; therefore in 1899 he granted rights to his patent to the Columbia Motor Company and the Electric Vehicle Company in exchange for a royalty fee. Other manufacturers were notified that the patent existed and that they had to pay royalties. A court suit by the Electric Vehicle Company against the Winton Motor Carriage Company in 1900 settled the issue for a time in Selden's favor, and most of the companies organized as The Association of Licensed Automobile Manufacturers, began to pay Selden. One of the few companies that did not come to terms was Ford. Ford was sued in 1903 by the Columbia Motor Company and in 1909 the Selden patent rights were sustained, but on an appeal the verdict was overturned in 1911 on the grounds that the motors made by Ford (and by most other companies as well) were not covered by the patent. Royalty payments to Selden stopped immediately, but in any case his patent would have run out in 1912. In 1906 he had used some of his royalties to start his own motor-car company, but he was not successful as a businessman and the venture failed. He died in Rochester, New York, on January 17, 1922.

Seldes, Gilbert Vivian (1893–1970), author and critic. Born in Alliance, New Jersey, on January 3, 1893, Gilbert Seldes graduated from Harvard in 1914. For two years he worked as music critic for the *Philadelphia Evening Ledger*, then went to Europe as a foreign correspondent until the United States entered World War I. In 1918 he was American political correspondent in Washington, D.C., for *L'Echo de Paris*, and he served briefly in the army. In 1919–1920 he was associate editor of *Collier's* magazine and from 1920 to 1923, editor of the *Dial*. For the most part after the mid–1920s Seldes followed an independent career as critic and author. His best known early work was *The Seven Lively Arts*, 1924, a discourse on comic strips, movies, vaudeville, musical comedy, radio, popular music, and dancing. His other works of criticism included *The Movies and the Talkies*, 1929; *The Movies Come from America*, 1937; *The Great Audience* (of radio, movies, and television), 1950; and *The Public Arts*, 1956. He wrote a play, *The Wise-Crackers*, 1925; did an adaptation of Aristophanes's *Lysistrata*, 1930; wrote a novel, *The Wings of the Eagle*, 1929; and did scripts for a number of radio and television programs; and he published detective stories under the pseudonym "Foster Johns." From 1931 to 1937 Seldes was a columnist for the *New York Journal*, and from 1937 to 1945 he was a program director for the Columbia Broadcasting System (CBS). He was a teacher and dean of the Annenberg School of Communications of the University of Pennsylvania from 1959 until his retirement in 1963. He died in New York City on September 29, 1970.

Selfridge, Harry Gordon (1857?–1947), merchant. Born in Ripon, Wisconsin, in about 1857, Selfridge went to work at the age of twelve and within a few years had moved to Chicago and found a job with the retail store of Field, Leiter and Company. He rose rapidly in the firm, which in 1881 became Marshall Field and Company, eventually becoming a junior partner and manager of the great Field retail store on State Street. By the time he retired in 1904 he had accumulated a sizable fortune, increased by his purchase and profitable resale to Carson, Pirie, Scott and Company of another Chicago retail outlet. He moved to England in 1906 and in two years had organized Selfridge and Company, Ltd., wholesale and retail merchants. In the spring of the following year Selfridge's store opened on Oxford Street; it was from the outset one of the largest retail establishments in all of Europe and it soon became, by dint of his ingenuity in advertising, one of the best known. Selfridge took British citizenship in 1937. By 1939 his financial extravagances had led to his being removed from management of the business, and he died in London on May 8, 1947.

Seligman, Edwin Robert Anderson (1861–1939), economist. Born on April 25, 1861, in New York City, Seligman was a son of Joseph Seligman. He graduated from Columbia College in 1879 and for nearly four years thereafter studied abroad, in Berlin, Heidelberg, and Paris, before returning to Columbia to take his doctorate in 1885. He remained at Columbia, as professor of political economy after 1891 and from 1904 as the first McVickar Professor of Political Economy until his retirement in 1931. In 1885, along with Richard T. Ely and John Bates Clark, he helped to found the American Economic Association. In a time of rapid social and industrial change and growth, when new demands were being placed upon government, Seligman became one of the nation's foremost experts on public finance and taxation. He frequently served as an adviser to the federal government and was one of the formulators of the personal income tax base and of the banking system detailed in the act creating the Federal Reserve System. On the problems of taxation he wrote several books and articles, including *Progressive Taxation in Theory and Practice*, 1894, *Essays in Taxation*, 1895, and *The Income Tax*, 1911. Others of his books were *The Economic Interpretation of History*, 1902; *Principles of Economics with Special Reference to American Conditions*, 1905; *Essays in Economics*, 1925; *Studies in Public Finance*, 1925; *The Economics of Farm Relief*, 1929; and *Price Cutting and Price Maintenance*, 1932. From 1912 to 1915 he was president of the National Tax Association and in 1918–1919 helped draw up the New York State income-tax law. Much concerned with the public issues of his time, he was realistic enough to accept the need for some federal regulation of the economy. Although basically a conservative in outlook, Seligman favored the labor movement and regarded as necessary some workable means for an equitable distribution of wealth to prevent society from being torn by class warfare. In his concern for social issues he worked to promote reform government at the local level and devoted time to a variety of social service institutions. He was one of the founders of the Educational Alliance in New York City, which worked with Jewish immigrants, and he served for three years as chairman of the National Urban League. From 1886 he edited the *Political Science Quarterly* and also served as editor-in-chief of the *Encyclopaedia of the Social Sciences*, published from 1930 to 1935. He died at Lake Placid, New York, on July 18, 1939.

Seligman, Joseph (1819–1880), financier. Born in Baiersdorf, Germany, on November 22, 1819, Joseph Seligman emigrated to the United States in 1837 and settled in Pennsylvania. As soon as he could, he sent for his brothers. For a time the Seligman brothers operated a dry-goods business in Alabama, but by 1848 most of them had settled in New York City, where they operated a clothing store and an importing firm. Jesse Seligman, born in Baiersdorf on August 11, 1827, however, opened a dry-goods store in Watertown, New York. In 1850 Jesse went to San Francisco with the Gold Rush and started a department store that prospered rapidly; nevertheless, in 1857 he decided to join his brothers in New York City. In 1862 the Seligmans converted their enterprises into an international banking firm, J. & W. Seligman & Company. Joseph was president of the firm and various of his brothers ran branch offices. During the Civil War the firm was very successful in selling government bonds in Europe, a service which made the Seligmans influential in subsequent Republican administrations in Washington. Later, during the 1870s, the Frankfurt, London, and New York offices of the firm handled the conversions and refunding of government obligations. During Ulys-

ses S. Grant's terms of office, Joseph was one of the President's closest advisers on fiscal policy, and was, in fact, asked to become secretary of the treasury, but he declined the post. Joseph also played an active role in the affairs of city government in New York and was instrumental in the reform movement that ousted the Tweed Ring in 1871. He died in New Orleans on April 25, 1880, and was succeeded as head of the banking house by Jesse. Like Joseph, Jesse was active in civic affairs and philanthropies, but he reputedly twice turned down the opportunity to run for mayor of New York City on the Republican ticket. He also acted as a financial adviser to President Grant and other Republicans who occupied the White House, and he was recognized as one of the nation's foremost financiers. Jesse died in Coronado, California, on April 23, 1894.

Selznick, David Oliver (1902–1965), motion-picture producer. Born in Pittsburgh on May 10, 1902, Selznick attended Columbia University. His father had been a motion-picture producer in the early days of the movies, and Selznick followed him into the business. He worked in New York City in the early 1920s, but by 1925 had gone to Hollywood to work for Select Studios. From 1926 to 1935, he worked successively for M-G-M, Paramount, RKO, and for MGM again from 1933 to 1935. In 1935, with substantial financial backing, he formed his own company, Selznick-International Pictures, Inc. In 1940 his studio was dissolved and he joined United Artists. As a producer, Selznick turned out some of Hollywood's most memorable films, including *Little Women*, 1933; *King Kong*, 1933; *Anna Karenina*, 1935; *The Prisoner of Zenda*, 1937; *A Star Is Born*, 1937; *Intermezzo*, 1939; *Rebecca*, 1940; *Spellbound*, 1945; *Duel in the Sun*, 1946; *Portrait of Jennie*, 1949; and *A Farewell to Arms*, 1958. But his most outstanding production was the 1939 film of *Gone with the Wind*, at the time the most expensive, lavish, and lengthy movie ever shown. He won Academy Awards, given by the Academy of Motion Picture Arts and Sciences, in 1939 for *Gone with the Wind* and in 1940 for *Rebecca*. In 1939 he also received the Academy's Irving Thalberg Memorial Award for his contributions to film-making. Selznick died in Hollywood on June 22, 1965.

Semmes, Raphael (1809–1877), naval officer and lawyer. Born in Charles County, Maryland, on September 27, 1809, Semmes was appointed a midshipman in the navy in 1826. He saw occasional sea duty in the next dozen years, but also found enough free time to study law and be admitted to the bar. He was given the rank of lieutenant in 1837 and spent the next nine years on routine tours of duty. Then, during the Mexican War, he participated in the landing of U.S. troops at Veracruz and joined Gen. Winfield Scott's forces as they marched inland to Mexico City. From the end of the Mexican War until the start of the Civil War, Semmes spent most of his time awaiting orders at his home near Mobile, Alabama, and practicing law. He was raised to the rank of commander in 1855 but resigned his commission early in 1861 when Alabama seceded from the Union. With the start of the Civil War he was given a commander's commission by the Confederacy and placed in command of the *Sumter* to harass Union shipping. He scoured the Caribbean and South Atlantic with the first of the Confederate raiders, capturing and burning Union merchant ships until he was blockaded at Gibraltar. By then the *Sumter* had fallen into disrepair; he abandoned her and returned to the Confederacy in April 1862. Four months later, now with the rank of captain, he was given command of the British-built Confederate cruiser *Alabama*, with which he resumed his attacks on Union vessels in the Atlantic from Canada to Brazil. In 1863 he took the ship around the world via Capetown and the Indian Ocean in his quest. In all he captured or destroyed 64 ships before, in June 1864, the *Alabama* met the Union Warship *Kearsarge* in the English Channel near Cherbourg, France, and was defeated and sunk. Semmes was rescued by the British and returned to the Confederacy a hero. He was put in charge of the warships on the James River in defense of Richmond in January 1865, and promoted to rear admiral; when Richmond fell, he burned his ships. With the end of the war he returned to Mobile. He was arrested and spent a few months as a prisoner in Washington, D.C., but was released and returned to Mobile to the practice of law. He taught briefly in 1866 at Louisiana State Seminary (now Louisiana State University) and for a time edited the *Memphis Daily Bulletin*. He was a popular lecturer as well and made numerous tours of the South. During his career, Semmes wrote books and articles based on his war experiences, including *Service Afloat and Ashore During the Mexican War*, 1851, and *Memoirs of Service Afloat During the War Between the States*, 1869. He died at Point Clear, on Mobile Bay, Alabama, on August 30, 1877. His Civil War exploits with the *Alabama* provided a focus for a complex of claims by the United States against Great Britain, which had violated neutrality laws by supplying the Confederacy with ships and other aid. The whole claim became known as the "Alabama claims," for, although it was only one of eleven vessels involved, it had inflicted some $6.5 million of the total $19 million in damages to U.S. shipping. Eventually, in 1872, the U.S. government was awarded $15.5 million in damages by a joint U.S.-British tribunal.

Sennett, Mack (1884–1960), motion-picture producer and director. Born on January 17, 1884, in Richmond, Quebec, Michael Sinnott moved to New York City at the age of twenty from East Berlin, Connecticut, where he had been an ironworker. Intent upon a stage career, he changed his name and performed in burlesque and circuses. In addition, he secured minor parts in Broadway plays, including *The Boys of Company B*. In 1909 he began working for D. W. Griffith at the Biograph studios. Late in 1911 he opened his own studio, the Keystone Company, where three years later *Tillie's*

Punctured Romance, with Charles Chaplin and Marie Dressler, the first American feature-length comedy, was produced. Between 1919 and 1924 the company turned out a number of biting satires and parodies of industrialism, but Sennett became most famous for the broad comedy and burlesque known as slapstick. The legend "A Mack Sennett Comedy" signified incredible chases, the Mack Sennett Bathing Beauties, and custard pies flying through the air. (The original custard pie was flung spontaneously into the face of Ben Turpin by actress Mabel Normand.) At first Sennett acted in his films, but later he devoted himself to directing such stars as Chaplin, W. C. Fields, Gloria Swanson, Miss Dressler, Harold Lloyd, Wallace Beery, Buster Keaton, Miss Normand, and Turpin. He created the bumbling Keystone Kops, whose hilarious antics were frequently improvised at the scenes of actual events—fires or parades—that would have been too expensive to stage. The Kops featured such performers as Harry Langdon, Edgar Kennedy, Slim Summerville, and Roscoe ("Fatty") Arbuckle. The studio had turned out some 1000 short films before it closed in 1933 because of the Depression and the advent of talking pictures and double-feature film shows. Sennett was honored by the Academy of Motion Picture Arts and Sciences in 1937 and drifted gradually into obscurity. He died in Woodland Hills, California, on November 5, 1960.

Sequoya (1770?–1843), Indian leader. Born about 1770 in a Tuskegee village on the Tenessee River, within the present Loudon County, Tennessee, Sequoya (or Sequoyah) was probably the son of an English trader, Nathaniel Gist, and a part-Cherokee woman. Raised by his mother, he never learned English, although he was also known by the English name George Guess. He was a silversmith, a hunter, and a fur trader, and served with the army in the Creek War in 1813–1814. Wounds incurred either in battle or on a hunting trip left him lame in one leg. He began work about 1809 on an alphabet for the Cherokee language, having always been fascinated by the "talking leaves" or papers bearing the written language of the white man. He first experimented with pictographs, but by 1821 arrived at a syllabary of 86 characters adapted from the English, Greek, and Hebrew alphabets, which he studied in mission school books. His people had thought him foolish or a wizard—at one time they burned all his records—but his successful demonstration of the alphabet with his six-year-old daughter won the approval of the chieftains and in time thousands of his tribesmen learned to read and write. In 1822 he visited the western Cherokee in Arkansas and sent written communications from them to the tribe in the East. He settled with the western Cherokee and moved with them to the Indian Territory, later Oklahoma, in 1828 and became a teacher in schools that were established there; he was also a political envoy, traveling in 1828 to Washington, and he visited other Indian villages to compare their grammar and speech. In 1824 parts of the Bible were printed in Cherokee and in 1828 appeared the *Cherokee Phoenix*, a weekly newspaper printed in English and Cherokee, which continued to appear until suppressed by Georgia authorities in 1835. In 1841 the legislature of the Cherokee Nation voted him an allowance and two years later, a lifetime pension—the first in an Indian tribe. In 1843 he set out to find a band of Cherokee thought to have crossed the Mississippi at the time of the Revolution. On this journey, probably while in Tamaulipas, Mexico, he died. A national park in California, and the sequoia, a genus of giant redwood trees, were named for him. A statue of him was placed in Statuary Hall in the U.S. Capitol by the state of Oklahoma.

Serra, Junípero (1713–1784), missionary. Born in the village of Petra on the island of Majorca on November 24, 1713, Serra was christened Miguel José, and grew up in peasant surroundings. He studied at the cathedral school in Palma and on September 14, 1730, was invested with the Franciscan habit. A year later, on September 15, 1731, he made his religious profession and took the name Junípero, after the companion of St. Francis, founder of the order. He became a priest in December 1737 and took the degree of doctor of theology in 1743. For the rest of his years in Palma he occupied the chair of theology at the university. In spite of the reputation earned by his lecturing and preaching over a period of 17 years, Serra wanted to become a missionary; thus in 1749 he seized the opportunity to go to Mexico with several lifelong companions to work among the Indians. The group arrived at Veracruz on December 9, 1749, and Serra determined to walk the entire distance to Mexico City's College of San Fernando. One night during the journey he was bitten on his left leg; the wound eventually ulcerated and caused the "walking friar" great difficulty throughout his life. Serra arrived in Mexico City on January 1, 1750, and six months later was sent to work among the Pame Indians in the Sierra Gorda in the state of Querétaro. Headquartered at the village of Jalpan, he stayed among the Indians until 1758, when he was ordered back to Mexico City where he worked for nine years. On June 25, 1767, by order of Charles III, all Jesuits were expelled from the Spanish colonies in the New World. With the expulsion, the Franciscans were ordered to take up the Jesuit mission posts in Lower (Baja) California. Serra and his companions left Mexico City on July 14, 1767, and after some difficulties and confusion over orders, arrived at Loreto in Lower California on April 1, 1768. Meanwhile, the Visitador General of New Spain, José Gálvez, had formulated a plan for the Spanish conquest of Upper (Alta) California to ward off any Russian or British threat to colonize the region. The Franciscans had hardly begun their work in Lower California when Serra and several of his fellow friars were made part of the expedition to the north. With a company of soldiers under Gaspar de Portolá, Serra arrived at present-day San Diego on July 1, 1769. Serra remained there in great hardship to found Mission San Diego de Alcalá, while Portolá undertook an unsuccessful journey north in search of the bay of Monterey. Severe shortages of food and reluctance on the part of the Indians to work with the friars threatened the mission until the supply ship *San Antonio* arrived to save it on March 19, 1770. On Portolá's second venture to find Monterey Bay, Serra went along. The bay was found and Mission San Carlos Borromeo was founded on June 3, 1770. Serra spent most of the next 14 years at the San Carlos mission, which was soon moved to Carmel. A total of 21 California missions were founded by the Franciscans; those Serra saw constructed before his death included, besides San Diego and San Carlos, San Antonio de Padua, 1771; San Gabriel Arcángel, 1771; San Luís Obispo de Tolosa, 1772; San Francisco de Asís, 1776; San Juan Capistrano, 1776; Santa Clara de Asís, 1777; and San Buenaventura, 1782. Serra supervised all the missions of Upper California, and received a special papal dispensation allowing him to perform the rite of confirmation. In 1773 he journeyed to Mexico City to confer with the viceroy over mission problems and to explore the possibilities of an overland supply route to California. In 1774 Juan Bautista de Anza succeeded in establishing such a route. During his years as a missionary, Serra, always in frail health, walked thousands of miles performing his religious functions; by July 1784 he had confirmed 5307 persons and baptized an even larger number. He died on August 28, 1784, at Mission San Carlos, where he was buried.

Sessions, Roger Huntington (1896–   ), composer. Born in Brooklyn, New York, on December 28, 1896, Sessions received his B.A. from Harvard in 1915 and his Mus. B. from the Yale School of Music in 1917. He began that year as a music teacher, went to Smith College as an instructor in music in 1919–1921, and to the Cleveland Institute of Music as a teacher of theory in 1921–1925. For the next eight years he lived mainly in Europe, although from 1928 to 1931 he presented an important series of concerts in New York City in association with Aaron Copland. Returning permanently to the United States in 1933, he was from then until 1935 an instructor at Boston University, a lecturer at New Jersey College for Women (now Douglass College), 1935–1937, and then a member of the music faculty of Princeton University, where he remained until 1945. In that year he went to the University of California at Berkeley as professor of music, but returned to Princeton in 1953 as William Shubael Conant Professor of Music. He retired from Princeton in 1965, after which he served on the faculty of the Juilliard School of Music in New York City and as visiting professor of music at a number of universities in the United States and abroad. His first important composition, an orchestral suite developed by him from the incidental music he wrote for Leonid Andreyev's play *The Black Maskers*, 1923, was rhapsodic and remained probably his most popular work. His five symphonies (1927, 1946, 1957, 1958, and 1963), two string quartets (1936, 1950), a string quintet (1957), two piano sonatas (1930, 1946), a violin concerto (1940), a piano concerto (1956), and choral preludes for organ (1925) were all marked by a considerable severity and employed polyphonic techniques and asymmetrical rhythms; as a result, although they greatly influenced other composers of his time they were often not warmly received by audiences. He composed two operas, *The Trial of Lucullus*, 1947, and *Montezuma*, 1964, and a work for soprano and orchestra, *Idyll of Theocritus*, 1954, and published two important critical books, *The Musical Experience of Composer, Performer, Listener*, 1950, and *Reflections on the Music Life in the United States*, 1956.

Seton, Elizabeth Ann Bayley (1774–1821), religious leader. Born in New York City on August 28, 1774, Elizabeth Bayley married William M. Seton in 1794. She was much preoccupied with the problems of the poor and devoted a good deal of time to working among them. In 1797 she helped to found the first charitable institution in New York City, the Society for the Relief of Poor Widows with Small Children. In 1803 she and her family traveled to Italy for her husband's health, but he died there the same year. She returned to New York City and joined the Roman Catholic church in March 1805. In 1809, at the suggestion of Louis G. B. Dubourg, she opened a free Catholic elementary school in Baltimore, the beginning of parochial-school education in the United States. Within a year, she and four other women had organized the Sisters of St. Joseph, the first such order in the country, patterned after the Sisters of Charity of St. Vincent de Paul, and founded St. Joseph College for women. In 1810 they relocated the order and the college at Emmitsburg, Maryland. Two years later the order changed its name to the Sisters of Charity of St. Joseph. Mother Seton was early named superior of the community, which devoted itself to education and social welfare. She continued to teach and work for the community until her death there on January 4, 1821, by which time the order had 20 communities. In 1856 Seton Hall College (now University) was named in her honor. In 1959 she was declared venerable, her beatification followed in 1963, and on September 14, 1975, she became the first native American to be canonized.

Dr. Seuss *see* Geisel, Theodor Seuss

Sevier, John (1745–1815), frontiersman, soldier, and public official. Born near the present New Market, Virginia, on September 23, 1745, Sevier grew up on the frontier; what formal education he received was largely at the academy in Fredericksburg. As was common with pioneer families, he moved from place to place, mainly as a farmer and land speculator. In 1772 he settled on the Watauga River and in that year joined in forming the Watauga Association; in 1773 he took his family to the Holston River region in what is now eastern Tennessee. He served as a captain of militia in the campaign against the Indians called Lord Dunmore's War, 1773–1774, in addition to serving on the local Committee of Safety and in the provincial legislature of North Carolina. From 1777 to 1780 he was a county clerk and a district judge. In 1780 he led a battalion of frontiersmen at the battle of Kings Mountain, a victory over Loyalist forces that made him one of the heroes of the war. For the next two years he conducted raids against the Cherokee Indians, and after defeating them, forced them to cede more tribal lands. After the Revolution, North Carolina, among other seaboard states that claimed land in the West, ceded its claims to the federal government. With news of the North Carolina cession, frontiersmen met at Jonesboro to plan for an independent state in August 1784. North Carolina hurriedly repealed its act of cession, but the Westerners disregarded it and proclaimed the State of Franklin. Sevier joined the statehood movement, seeing in it a chance for profiting by land speculation, using a scheme he had for developing a colony at Muscle Shoals. He was chosen governor of the new state. But Congress refused to recognize Franklin and reversed some of the national policy toward the Indians in favor of the tribes. Gradually the State of Franklin began to disintegrate, and by 1788 it was defunct. Sevier was discredited and lived for a time almost as an outlaw. He soon became involved in what is known as the "Spanish Conspiracy" as a means of fostering his old plans for Muscle Shoals. The conspiracy was a grandiose but ill-conceived series of plots in which a number of Americans cooperated secretly with Spanish colonial officials to detach the West from the United States, with the goal of protecting Florida and Louisiana from encroachments by Americans. But nothing ever came of the affair and Sevier soon lost interest. He returned to respectability, was pardoned for his involvement in the Franklin fiasco, and was elected to the North Carolina senate in 1789. He also took part in the state's convention to ratify the Constitution, and when the new national government began to function he was elected to the House of Representatives from the state's western district. In 1790, when the trans-Allegheny lands became a territory (the Southwest Territory), Sevier was made a brigadier general of militia; when Tennessee became a state five years later, he became its first governor and served three consecutive terms, 1796–1801. In 1798–1799, during the undeclared war with France, he was a brigadier general in the army. From 1803 to 1809 he served again as governor of Tennessee, and in 1810–1811 he was a member of the state senate. He was elected to Congress again in 1810 and served in the House from March 1811 until his death. In 1812 he spoke in favor of a declaration of war against Britain and thereafter urged the vigorous prosecution of war, particularly against Indians. In 1815 he was appointed one of the commissioners to survey the boundary between Georgia and the Creek Indian territory in Alabama. While engaged in that expedition, Sevier died near Fort Decatur, Alabama, on September 24, 1815.

Sewall, Samuel (1652–1730), merchant and judge. Born on March 28, 1652, in Bishopstoke, England, to parents from New England, Sewall traveled with them back to Boston in 1661. He graduated from Harvard in 1671 and five years later married the daughter of wealthy shipowner John Hull, thereby acquiring a sizable fortune. A member of the Massachusetts General Court, he also held a position on the governor's advisory council from 1684 to 1686 and again from 1689 to 1725. Although he had not been trained specifically for the law, he was named a judge of the superior court of the colony and in 1718 became its chief justice. Noted throughout the colony for clarity and compassion in his rulings, he stood alone before the people in Boston's Old South Church five years after the 1692 Salem witchcraft trials to confess the error of his decisions, which had sent many to the gallows, while the other nine judges who had sat on the bench during the trials remained silent. His essay, *The Selling of Joseph,* 1700, was one of the first American appeals for an end to slavery. His diary, first published in three volumes, by the Massachusetts Historical Society in 1878–1882, covers the period from 1673 to 1729, with the omission of eight years from 1677 to 1685, and is unique and of great historical interest in its depiction of the values and character of a typical New England Puritan of his time. Sewall died in Boston on January 1, 1730.

Seward, William Henry (1801–1872), public official. Born in Florida, New York, on May 16, 1801, Seward graduated from Union College, in Schenectady, New York, in 1820, was admitted to the bar two years later, and began the practice of law in Auburn, New York. He soon became actively interested in politics and began what was to be a lifelong association with Thurlow Weed; he allied himself with the rising Anti-Masonic party and was elected to the state senate in 1830. As the Anti-Masonic movement subsided and opposition to the Jacksonian Democrats coalesced in the Whig party, Seward followed suit. Defeated for governor on the Whig ticket in 1834, he was elected in 1838 and again in 1840. During four years in office he took boldly liberal stands on several issues, advocating the employment of foreign-born and Roman Catholic teachers in the New York City public-school system, proposing public expenditures for internal improvements, and, most significantly, advising resistance to the extradition of fugitive slaves. In 1843 he returned to his law practice but maintained his political interests and connections and in 1848 was elected to the U.S. Senate from New York. His national political career began with his opposition to the Compromise of 1850 and his controversial appeal —later retracted in some confusion—to "a higher law than the Constitution." He strongly opposed the Kansas-Nebraska Bill in 1854 and led the remnants of the shattered Whig party into the new Republican party shortly afterward. He supported the admission of Kansas as a free state and denounced the Dred Scott decision of 1857; and it was he who, in a speech the next year, referred to the "irrepressible conflict" between the slave and free sections of the country. As the preeminent figure among Republicans, he had justifiable hopes for the presidential nomination in 1856 and 1860, but in both years was passed over for candidates with less previous political identification. Abraham Lincoln chose Seward as his secretary of state, and he took office confident that he would dominate the President and the government; he suggested to Lincoln that a war with one or more European nations would unite the country, and, conferring with Southern emissaries, made unauthorized statements to the effect that Fort Pickens and Fort Sumter would be surrendered to state authorities. He attempted to interfere in the Sumter expedition but to no avail; soon brought to heel by Lincoln, Seward performed the functions of his office with great skill thereafter, although, with Secretary of War Edwin M. Stanton, he continued to dominate the Cabinet. He successfully handled the problem of maintaining European neutrality during the Civil War and secured valuable advantages from the *Trent* and *Alabama* affairs. His diplomatic conduct concerning French intervention in Mexico was masterful, succeeding at length in obtaining the withdrawal of French forces. On April 14, 1865, simultaneously with the assassination of Lincoln by John Wilkes Booth, Seward was attacked by a coconspirator; already in poor health from an injury sustained some days earlier, he nonetheless survived the attack and regained his powers sufficiently to remain in office under President Andrew Johnson. In 1867 he negotiated the purchase of Alaska—"Seward's Folly"—from Russia, and looked forward to the annexation of Santo Domingo and Hawaii. He fell from political grace by siding with Johnson against the Radical Republicans in the battle over Reconstruction, and left office with him in 1869. After a world tour he returned to his home in Auburn, New York, and died there on October 10, 1872.

Seymour, Horatio (1810–1886), public official. Born in Onondaga County, New York, on May 31, 1810, Seymour was educated in a military academy, then studied law and was admitted to the bar in 1832, but rarely practiced law. He was military secretary to Governor William L. Marcy of New York from 1833 to 1839 and in that post entered the inner councils of the state Democratic party. In the split that took place in the party when Martin Van Buren was in the White House, Seymour aligned himself with the conservative "Hunker" faction. He moved to Utica in 1839 and became mayor in 1842, the same year that he served his first term in the state legislature. He served again in that body in 1844 and 1845, forcing through bills that set the state's policy on canals for decades, and was elected speaker in 1845. In 1850 he ran for governor and lost, but in 1852 he was elected and served one term before being defeated because of his veto of a prohibition measure. When out of office he usually lived in Utica, devoting himself to business and following the course of state politics. As a states'-rights Democrat, he was eager to work in or for the state government, but persistently refused to run for federal office until, much later, he was nominated for the presidency. Although he opposed the election of Abraham Lincoln and denounced many of Lincoln's extraconstitutional war powers, Seymour supported the Union cause during the Civil War. He was again elected governor of New York in 1862, when the war was going badly for the Union. He opposed the federal conscription law, feeling that troops should be raised by the states, and worked effectively to fill the New York army quotas. His uncertain attitude during the bloody draft riots of July 1863 in New York City lost him much support, and although he aided in putting down the disorders, the story that he had encouraged them lasted long after his death. Following the war, when he was out of office, he devoted his time to rebuilding the Democratic party, which had been fragmented during the conflict. He presided over the Democratic national convention in 1864 and again four years later; in 1868, as one of the leading Democrats in the East, he was nominated to oppose Ulysses S. Grant for the presidency. In the election, Seymour lost by only slightly more than 300,000 popular votes. He did not hold public office again, but continued to be active in state politics, helping in the fight to oust William M. ("Boss") Tweed from power in New York City. He declined to run both for U.S. senator and for governor during the 1870s. He died in Utica, New York, on February 12, 1886.

Shafter, William Rufus (1835–1906), soldier. Born in Kalamazoo County, Michigan, on October 16, 1835, Shafter enlisted in the Union army at the start of the Civil War and was commissioned a first lieutenant. He saw service throughout the war, taking part at Ball's Bluff, Fair Oaks (Seven Pines), where he won the Medal of Honor, Thompson's Station, and Nashville. By the end of hostilities he had attained the rank of colonel with a temporary promotion to brigadier general of volunteers. Mustered out in 1865, he entered the regular army in 1867 as a lieutenant colonel. For the next 30 years on frontier duty in the West, but when the Spanish-American War began he was promoted to major-general of volunteers and put in charge of troops. On May 30, 1898, he was directed to embark his troops at Tampa, Florida, and head for Santiago de Cuba to seize the garrison and help disable the Spanish fleet. The U.S. fleet finally sailed on June 14 and Shafter's troops landed at Daiquiri on June 22. During most of his stay in Cuba, Shafter, who weighed about 300 pounds, suffered from gout and from the heat, but he managed nevertheless to keep in touch with his forces. After the destruction of their fleet, the Spanish defenders of Santiago de Cuba surrendered the city to Shafter on

July 17. Shafter then returned to his former command in the Far West, with headquarters at San Francisco. He retired from active service in October 1899, but continued in command until June 1901. In July 1901 he was given the rank of major general on the retired list. Thereafter he remained in California and died in Bakersfield, on November 12, 1906.

Shahn, Benjamin (1898–1969), "Ben," painter and graphic artist. Born on September 12, 1898, in Kaunas (Kovno), Lithuania (then part of Russia), the son of a carpenter, Shahn came to New York at the age of eight and grew up in a Brooklyn slum. Beginning his training as a lithographer at fifteen, he worked while taking evening courses at the City College of New York, New York University, and the National Academy of Design. He was naturalized in 1918. He traveled through France, Italy, North Africa, and Spain in 1925 and 1927–1929. He devoted his art to social and political causes, changing his Expressionistic painting style to a realism that was highly personal and that often bordered on Surrealism. In 1931–1932 he completed a series of 23 small gouache paintings and two large panels on the trial and execution of Sacco and Vanzetti, and a year later executed 15 paintings and a panel on the trial of labor leader Tom Mooney in California. Between 1933 and 1943 he worked under the government's Federal Arts Project, completing eight temperas on life during Prohibition, and several epic murals, among them a fresco for a housing project for garment workers in New Jersey, a 13-panel mural in the Bronx Central Annex post office depicting American city and country life, and the story of American welfare under social security in the Social Security building in Washington D.C. These and other murals were influenced by the concepts of the Mexican artist Diego Rivera, whom Shahn assisted on the murals for Rockefeller Center in New York City in 1933. He designed posters in 1943 for the Office of War Information (OWI), in 1944 for the Political Action Committee of the Congress of Industrial Organizations (CIO), and in his later career for the presidential campaign of Eugene J. McCarthy. Simultaneously with his mural and poster work he completed paintings of urban life, including "Handball," 1939, and "Girl Jumping Rope," 1943, and others with pro-labor messages or views of social significance, such as "The Red Stairway," 1944, and "Liberation," 1945; "Hunger" and "The World's Greatest Comics," both 1946; and "Death of a Miner," "The Violin Player," and "East Twelfth Street," all in 1947. In 1956 he delivered the Charles Eliot Norton lectures at Harvard, published as *The Shape of Content*, 1957. Shahn was noted also for his graphics and book illustrations, and he experimented boldly in incorporating words and whole written messages into his paintings. Many of his works were acquired by museums, galleries, and universities throughout the United States and in Europe. Shahn died in New York City on March 14, 1969.

Shapiro, Karl Jay (1913–), poet and critic.
Born in Baltimore on November 10, 1913,
Shapiro attended the University of Virginia for
a year in 1932–1933, then worked at various jobs
before attending The John Hopkins University
from 1936 to 1939. In 1940 he studied library
science at the Enoch Pratt Free Library in Baltimore. He served in the army from 1941 to 1945,
and while in the service had the distinction of
having three books of poetry published: *Person,
Place, and Thing*, 1942, *The Place of Love*, 1942,
and *V-Letter and Other Poems*, which won the
Pulitzer Prize for poetry in 1944. He had begun
writing poetry while at Virginia, and his first
book, *Poems*, had been issued in 1935. Within a
few years his poems had appeared in several
journals, and by the end of the war, with publication of *Essay on Rime*, 1945, he was recognized
by critics as one of the best of the modern poets.
In 1946–1947 he served as consultant in poetry to
the Library of Congress. From 1947 to 1950 he
taught writing at Johns Hopkins, and from 1950
to 1956 he edited *Poetry* magazine. In 1956 he
joined the English faculty at the University of
Nebraska, where he remained for ten years. After
a semester at the Chicago Campus of the University of Illinois in 1966, he became professor
of English at the University of California at Davis.
His later volumes of poetry included *Trial of a
Poet*, 1947; *Poems, 1940–1953*; *Poems of a Jew*,
1958; *The Bourgeois Poet*, 1964; and *Selected
Poems*, 1968, for which he shared (with John
Berryman) the 1969 Bollingen Award. He also
wrote a novel, *Edsel*, 1971, and several books of
critical essays, including *Beyond Criticism*, 1953,
In Defense of Ignorance, 1960, and *To Abolish
Children*, 1968.

Shapley, Harlow (1885–1972), astronomer. Born in
Nashville, Barton County, Missouri, on November
2, 1885, Shapley graduated from the University of
Missouri in 1910 and received his M.A. in 1910
and his Ph.D. in 1911 from Princeton. He joined
the staff of the Mt. Wilson Observatory in 1914,
remaining until 1921, when he became a professor of astronomy at Harvard. He was director of
the Harvard Observatory, succeeding Edward C.
Pickering, from 1921 to 1952, continued as a professor until 1956, and was subsequently a professor emeritus at Harvard and a visiting lecturer at
several other institutions. A bold and imaginative
researcher and theorist, he did much important
work, the first of which concerned eclipsing binary
stars. As early as 1913, with Henry N. Russell,
he devised a method of determining the dimensions of the component stars of these systems
from measurements of the light variation during
eclipse. He was the first to show that Cepheid
variables cannot be eclipsing binaries and was also
the first to propose the theory, now accepted, that
they are instead single pulsating stars. He then
went on to study star clusters, especially globular
clusters, and was one of the first to employ variable stars (Cepheids and RR Lyrae stars) as indicators of distance. He was thus able to make a

map of star clusters by distance, and on the basis
of this he constructed the novel hypothesis, later
substantiated, that the globular clusters form a
fairly symmetrical swarm around the center of
earth's galaxy and that our sun must therefore be
in the outer regions of the galaxy, some tens of
thousands of light years from the center. He
studied the Milky Way galaxy, of which earth's
solar system is a part, in relation to other nearby
galaxies, such as the galaxy in the constellation
of Andromeda, and was able to show that galaxies
themselves tend to occur in clusters and that the
Milky Way is a member of one such cluster. He
wrote a number of books and articles, most of
them of a highly technical nature, but also including such more or less popular works as *Star
Clusters*, 1930; *Flights from Chaos*, 1930; *Galaxies*,
1943; *Inner Metagalaxy*, 1957; *Of Stars and Men*,
1958; and *The View from a Distant Star*, 1964. He
was the recipient of many honors and awards,
and was the president of the American Academy
of Arts and Sciences from 1939 to 1944 and of
the American Association for the Advancement
of Science in 1947. After his retirement in 1956 he
lived mainly in Peterborough, New Hampshire; he
remained active in scientific circles until his death
in Boulder, Colorado, on October 20, 1972.

Shaw, Henry Wheeler (1818–1885), "Josh Billings,"
humorist. Born on April 21, 1818, in Lanesborough,
Massachusetts, Shaw briefly attended Hamilton
College and led an unsettled life for his first 40
or more years, being at various times a farmer,
explorer, real-estate salesman, riverboat man, and
auctioneer. In 1858 he settled in Poughkeepsie,
New York. Then he began writing burlesques of
news items, featuring misspelled words, distorted
syntax, anticlimax, and numerous other humorous
devices. He joined the staff of Street and Smith's
New York Weekly in 1867 and won a national
reputation for his work, but he had made his first
great hit in 1860, with his "Essa on the Muel,"
which began: "The muel is half Hoss and half
Jackass, and then kums tu a full stop, natur dis-
kovering her mistake." His books included *Josh
Billings, His Sayings*, 1865; annual *Josh Billings'
Farmers' Allminax* published from 1869 to 1880;
Josh Billings on Ice, and Other Things, 1868;
Everybody's Friend, 1874; and *Josh Billings Struggling with Things*, 1881. He also contributed for a
time to the *Century* magazine as "Uncle Esek."
Shaw was also in great demand as a lecturer.
Unlike other contemporary humorists, he did not
base his work on current events but intended it
to be universal. He died in Monterey, California,
on October 14, 1885.

Shaw, Lemuel (1781–1861), judge. Born on January
9, 1781, in Barnstable, Massachusetts, Shaw graduated from Harvard in 1800, studied law in
Boston, and was admitted to the bar in 1804. A
distinguished career followed as a civic official
and as counsel to many important commercial
interests. In 1822, with few or no precedents to
guide him, he wrote Boston's first city charter,

which endured for more than 90 years. By 1830, when he was offered the post of chief justice of the Massachusetts supreme court, he was making upwards of $20,000 a year, an immense sum for the time. He accepted the post and served for 30 years, until his retirement in 1860. His long tenure on the bench coincided with the rise of important social and economic issues, and generally leaning in favor of the public interest, he left his mark on the structure and development of the law, not only of Massachusetts, but also of the nation. Two cases were particularly notable. In the first, *Commonwealth* v. *Hunt*, 1842, he ruled in favor of a striking labor union, thus freeing unions generally of the abusive application of the law of conspiracy; in the second, *Roberts* v. *City of Boston*, 1849, although he was personally opposed to slavery, he ruled that racial segregation in the city's schools did not create constitutional inequalities. This "separate but equal" doctrine was later extended nationwide by the Supreme Court in *Plessy* v. *Ferguson*, 1896, but in Massachusetts it had the effect of stimulating the passage of a state desegregation law, the only one to be enacted by a state until the twentieth century. Shaw aided many charitable institutions and was a fellow and overseer of Harvard. He died in Boston on March 30, 1861. His only daughter, Elizabeth, was the wife of Herman Melville.

Shaw, Robert Lawson (1916–   ), choral director and conductor. Born on April 30, 1916, in Red Bluff, California, Shaw graduated from Pomona College in 1938. Because of the expertise he had shown in choral conducting, he was immediately hired to reorganize and direct the Fred Waring Glee Club. He remained with the Waring organization until 1945, when he resigned to study music and to teach at the Juilliard School of Music in New York City. From 1946 to 1949 he was also director of choral music at the Berkshire Music Center in Tanglewood, Massachusetts. In 1941, while still with Waring, he had started the Collegiate Chorale, a choir of young people at the Marble Collegiate Church in New York City. He conducted the Chorale until 1954 in several seasons of highly acclaimed concerts. His own Robert Shaw Chorale made its debut in 1948, and through numerous tours, record albums, and radio and television concerts, earned a reputation as the most competent professional choral group in the country. The Chorale performed the best known of the classic choral works as well as those by contemporaries. Under the auspices of the Department of State, the Chorale made successful tours abroad. In addition to his work with the Chorale, Shaw became a noted orchestra conductor. He was much in demand as a guest conductor, working with symphony orchestras in such large urban centers as San Diego, California, Chicago, and Cleveland, as well as other cities, and in 1967 he became the principal conductor of the Atlanta (Georgia) Symphony Orchestra. He also expended a great deal of his time and effort in the promotion and teaching of choral music in general.

Shawn, Ted, *see under* St. Denis, Ruth

Shays, Daniel (1747?–1825), Revolutionary soldier and post-Revolutionary rebel. Shays was born, probably in Hopkinton, Massachusetts, about 1747, although the town's records do not mention his name. Little is known of his early life, but he responded to the call for volunteers at the outbreak of the Revolution and served with distinction at Bunker Hill, Ticonderoga, Saratoga, and Stony Point, being commissioned captain in the 5th Massachusetts at the beginning of 1777. He was a popular and effective officer and was rewarded, toward the end of the war, with a handsome sword that was presented to him by the Marquis de Lafayette; but poverty later forced him to sell it. He resigned from the army in 1780 and settled in Pelham, Massachusetts, where he held several town offices. The post-Revolutionary prosperity soon gave way to a severe countrywide depression. The Massachusetts legislature ignored demands for redress of grievances arising from the economic situation, demands which were especially urgent in western Massachusetts, and the situation deteriorated there in 1786 to the point of armed rebellion. Shays was but one of several leaders, but his name became associated with the revolt, mainly because of a confrontation in Springfield on September 26 between a group of about 800 armed farmers and about the same number of militia. The immediate question was whether the state supreme court should be allowed to sit, for the farmers feared that it would return indictments against them. An agreement was reached and the court adjourned, but a period of chaotic relations between the two sides ensued, and actual fighting broke out during the winter when the rebels marched on the arsenal at Springfield and were scattered by state troops. After confused rallyings, a band under Shays was defeated at Petersham, on February 2, 1787. He fled to Vermont and was one of the few who were exempted from a general pardon issued later in the year. He was condemned to death in absentia, but in February 1788 he petitioned for pardon and was granted it, on June 13. He later moved to New York State, where he lived until his death, in Sparta, on September 29, 1825. In his later years he was given a pension for his service in the Revolution; and he always insisted that he had fought then and in the rebellion for exactly the same principles. Shays's Rebellion had the effect of hastening not only the specific reforms in taxation and judicial procedure demanded by the rebels, but also the movement for a stronger central government capable of dealing swiftly with such uprisings.

Sheeler, Charles (1883–1965), painter and photographer. Born in Philadelphia on July 16, 1883, Sheeler attended the School of Industrial Art from 1900 to 1903 and then spent three years at the Pennsylvania Academy of the Fine Arts. For most of the next three years he traveled in Europe studying art. In 1910 he settled in Philadelphia to begin a career as a painter, although he did most of his actual work at a farm in nearby Bucks County. By 1912 he had also developed a serious interest in photography, particularly its industrial-commercial aspects, and this second vocation was later to have a strong influence on his painting style. In 1913 six of his paintings, all showing the influence of French Cubism, were exhibited at the influential Armory Show in New York City. His style alternated between abstractionism and an intense realism. In the late 1920s and 1930s, when he turned to painting industrial subjects, he gave meticulous attention to detail to heighten the realistic effect. One of his finest examples of this genre was "Upper Deck," painted in 1929. Between 1918 and 1960 he had more than 20 one-man shows, but it was not until his works were exhibited at New York City's Museum of Modern Art in 1939 that Sheeler was accepted as one of the nation's leading artists. In 1918 he had a one-man show of his photography at the Modern Gallery in New York City. Two years later he was one of Paul Strand's collaborators on the motion picture *Mannahatta*. He exhibited at the Zayas Gallery in New York City until 1923, when he joined Edward Steichen to do fashion photography for *Vogue* magazine. In 1927 he was commissioned to execute a series of photographs of the Ford Motor Company's River Rouge plant near Detroit, and in 1939 he was commissioned to do a series of industrial paintings for *Fortune* magazine. During the 1920s he also painted a series of cityscapes, and by the end of the decade he had effected a compromise in his work between realism and Cubism. His 1938 painting "The Upstairs" was shown at the Cincinnati Museum's 45th anniversary exhibit; and in 1945 his "Water" won an award at the Art Institute of Chicago. In 1960 Sheeler suffered a stroke that ended his painting career. In 1962 he was given the Award of Merit by the American Academy of Arts and Letters. He died in Dobbs Ferry, New York, on May 7, 1965.

Sheen, Fulton John (1895–1979), religious leader. Born in El Paso, Illinois, on May 8, 1895, Sheen graduated from St. Viator College, Bourbonnais, Illinois, in 1917. After earning his master's degree there in 1919, he studied at St. Paul Seminary in Minnesota, and was ordained on September 20, 1919. He continued his studies for the next several years, earning his S.T.B. and J.C.B. degrees at the Catholic University of America, Washington, D.C., and his Ph.D. at the University of Louvain in Belgium in 1923. He received a D.D. from the Collegio Angelico in Rome in 1924 and the following year was made Agrégé en Philosophie at Louvain. Returning to the United States, Sheen served in St. Patrick's parish in Peoria, Illinois, until the end of 1926, when he was appointed an instructor in religion at the Catholic University of America. He remained attached to the university until 1950. Because of his exceptional abilities as lecturer and preacher, he became a public figure whose reputation spread far beyond the confines of the Roman Catholic church. He maintained, in

fact, two careers, a public one and an ecclesiastical one, although the two were tied together. Beginning in 1930 he became the regular preacher on the NBC network radio program, "The Catholic Hour," and continued on radio until the advent of television. In 1952 his weekly television series, "Life Is Worth Living," made him one of the best-known personalities in the country. The program had consistently high ratings and remained on the air until 1965. As a churchman he was considered one of the most compelling and influential spokesment for Roman Catholicism in the United States, bringing many converts into the church. He was made a papal chamberlain and given the rank of monsignor in 1934, and on June 11, 1951, was consecrated an auxiliary bishop of the New York archdiocese; from 1966 to 1969 he was bishop of Rochester, New York, and in 1969 he was made a titular archbishop of Newport, Wales. From 1950 to 1966 he was the director of the U.S. activities of the Society for the Propagation of the Faith. As a proponent of the Christian faith, Sheen also became one of its staunchest apologists in opposing Communism and materialism. Among his many books were several that reached best-seller status, including *Peace of Soul*, 1949; *Three to Get Married*, 1951; *Life Is Worth Living*, five volumes, 1953–1957; *The Priest Is Not His Own*, 1963; *Missions and the World Crisis*, 1964; and *That Tremendous Love*, 1967. He died on December 9, 1979, in New York City.

Shelby, Isaac (1750–1826), soldier and public official. Born in Washington County (then part of Frederick County), Maryland, on December 11, 1750, Shelby grew up in a frontier environment. In 1773 he and his family moved to the Holston River region of what is now eastern Tennessee. For the next eight years he was engaged mainly in soldiering, taking part in Lord Dunmore's War, and in surveying the western lands for settlement. He saw continuous service during the Revolutionary War, mostly against various Indian tribes in the Kentucky and Tennessee regions and in 1779 served in the Virginia legislature as well. In the fall of 1780, by then a colonel of North Carolina militia, he and John Sevier led the frontiersmen who defeated a force of British Loyalists at the battle of Kings Mountain, and in January 1781 he took part in the battle of Cowpens. In 1781 and 1782 he served in the North Carolina legislature. After the war Shelby settled in Kentucky and took part in making the political arrangements that led to statehood. In 1792 he was a delegate to the convention that drew up Kentucky's constitution, and later in the year he was elected the state's first governor. He served one four-year term, then retired to private life until being elected governor again in 1812. His main duties during this term of office had to do with the prosecution of the War of 1812. He assembled and led several thousand volunteers in Gen. William Henry Harrison's invasion of Canada and took part in October 1813 in the battle of the Thames, at which the British were defeated. After his term of office expired Shelby was offered in 1817 the post of secretary of war in President James Monroe's Cabinet, but declined. In 1818 he joined Gen. Andrew Jackson in negotiating a treaty with the Chickasaw Indians. He died on July 18, 1826, at his home, Traveller's Rest, in Lincoln County, Kentucky.

Sheridan, Philip Henry (1831–1888), soldier. Born on March 6, 1831, Sheridan gave his birthplace variously as Albany, New York; Boston; and Somerset, Ohio. It is certain, at least, that he grew up and received his rather scanty schooling in Somerset. In 1848 he entered West Point and graduated in 1853, having been suspended for a year for fighting. He served in several Indian campaigns in the West and at the outbreak of the Civil War was a captain and quartermaster officer in Missouri. His much-desired opportunity for combat came in May 1862 when he was appointed colonel in command of the 2nd Michigan Cavalry. On July 1 he performed brilliantly at Booneville, Mississippi, was commended by Gen. William S. Rosecrans, and was promoted to brigadier general of volunteers. At the head of the 11th Division, of the Army of the Ohio, he shared in the victories at Perryville and Murfreesboro (Stones River) and was made a major general in recognition of his brilliant leadership. Taking command of the 20th Corps, Army of the Cumberland, in 1863, he fought at Chickamauga and then climaxed his service in the Western theater with the famous charge, under Gen. George H. Thomas, up Missionary Ridge that contributed in large measure to Gen. Ulysses S. Grant's victory at Chattanooga. When Grant went east to take over the Army of the Potomac, Sheridan followed to command the cavalry. During the Wilderness Campaign and the fighting around Richmond in 1864 his troopers destroyed Confederate supplies and lines of communication and constantly harassed the enemy. In August he took command of the Army of the Shenandoah with the object of denying the Shenandoah Valley's supplies to the Confederates defending Richmond; he defeated Jubal Early at Winchester, Fisher's Hill, and Cedar Creek—at the time of Early's attack at Cedar Creek, Sheridan was twenty miles away and was forced to make a desperate ride, later celebrated in verse, to rally his men—and was made successively a brigadier and then a major general in the regular army. In March 1865 he began cavalry actions around the enemy's rear at Petersburg; after victories at Dinwiddie Courthouse and Five Forks led to the fall of Petersburg, he cut off Gen. Robert E. Lee's line of retreat from Appomattox and Lee's surrender to Grant followed. Sheridan was sent after the war to command troops along the Gulf of Mexico and on the Mexican border. Early in 1867 he was made military governor of Louisiana and Texas, but his harsh administration of Reconstruction measures led to his removal soon thereafter. He returned to the campaigns against the Indians in the West and in 1869 became lieutenant general in command of the Division of the Mis-

souri. He was sent to accompany the Prussian armies as an observer during the Franco-Prussian War in 1870–1871. In 1883 he became commander in chief of the army, succeeding General William T. Sherman, and on June 1, 1888, was promoted by act of Congress to general of the army. He died shortly thereafter, on August 5, 1888, in Nonquitt, Massachusetts. His *Personal Memoirs of P. H. Sheridan* appeared in two volumes that year. As a military leader Sheridan had no great skill in strategy, but the confidence he inspired in his men, his meticulous care in gathering intelligence, and above all his aggressive nature made him a successful commander.

Sherman, James Schoolcraft (1855–1912), vice-president of the United States. Born in Utica, New York, on October 24, 1855, Sherman graduated from Hamilton College in 1878. He earned his law degree in 1879 and was admitted to the bar the next year. He soon took an active role in politics, and as a Republican was elected mayor of Utica in 1884. Two years later he was elected to the House of Representatives, where he served until March 1909, missing only one term, 1891-1893. Although he was an outstanding parliamentarian, his legislative record was generally undistinguished; he was a reliable party man in and out of Congress. In 1908 he was selected as William Howard Taft's running mate, and upon their election served as vice-president of the United States from 1909 until his death, in Utica, New York, on October 30, 1912.

Sherman, John (1823–1900), public official. Born in Lancaster, Ohio, on May 10, 1823, a younger brother of William Tecumseh Sherman, John Sherman studied law with an uncle in Mansfield, Ohio, and was admitted to the bar in 1844, establishing a law practice in Mansfield. He quickly achieved prominence as a lawyer and involved himself in Whig politics, although he did not run for public office until 1854, when he was elected to the House of Representatives primarily because of his opposition to the Kansas-Nebraska Bill of that year. Having moved easily into the Republican party as the Whigs disintegrated, he remained in the House until 1861. In 1856 he drafted the report of a committee investigation into the situation in Kansas, torn by strife over the question of slavery, and from 1859 he was chairman of the Ways and Means Committee. In 1861 he entered the Senate and in 1867 became chairman of the Senate finance committee; Sherman considered finance to be his special field of competence and, as a generally conservative Republican from a largely agrarian region, he attempted constantly to mediate between inflationist and sound-money factions, usually by compromise, although occasionally by wavering. He was persuaded to hold out against the cancellation of Civil War greenbacks, whose issue he had supported, until 1875, when he played a central role in the passage of the Resumption Act, providing for the redemption of the greenbacks in gold. Two years later he became President Rutherford B. Hayes's secretary of the treasury and skillfully administered the program leading to specie resumption and the revaluation of greenbacks to par in 1879. In 1881 he returned to the Senate. His next 16 years in that body were marked most notably by the Sherman Anti-Trust Act and the Sherman Silver Purchase Act, both in 1890, which were compromise measures having only his partial approval. In 1880, 1884, and 1888 his name was mentioned as a possibility for the Republican presidential nomination, but he attracted little real support. In 1897 President William McKinley appointed him secretary of state in order to create a Senate vacancy for Marcus (Mark) Hanna. Sherman, whose powers had been failing, found the duties of this office beyond him; he was, moreover, in profound disagreement with popular expansionist clamor, and when the decision for war with Spain was made he resigned. *John Sherman's Recollections of Forty Years in the House, Senate, and Cabinet* had appeared in two volumes in 1895. He died in Washington, D.C., on October 22, 1900.

Sherman, Roger (1721–1793), Revolutionary patriot and public official. Born on April 19, 1721, in Newton, Massachusetts, Sherman grew up in Stoughton, working on his father's farm and learning the trade of shoemaker. His formal education was scant, but on his own he was an avid student of theology, mathematics, and law. In 1743 he moved to New Milford, Connecticut, and opened a cobbler's shop. In 1745 he was appointed county surveyor and began to accumulate what eventually amounted to considerable wealth. He served in a succession of local offices while carrying on a mercantile business and publishing a series of almanacs. In 1754 he was admitted to the bar and during the next several years served on the county court; in the legislature in 1755, 1758–1761, and 1764–1766; as judge of the superior court 1766–1785; and in other public capacities. In 1761 he moved to New Haven, where he became a benefactor and for several years treasurer of Yale College. His public duties increased continually until he was forced to retire from business in 1772 to attend to them. In 1774 he was elected to the First Continental Congress and, a staunch though conservative supporter of the colonial cause, there signed the Articles of Association that pledged members to eschew the importation and consumption of British goods; he remained in Congress until 1781 and served again in 1783–1784. He was a member of the drafting committee and a signer of the Declaration of Independence and helped later to draft the Articles of Confederation, which he also signed. He was an indefatigable worker in committee and became an experienced and highly adroit legislator. During the Revolution he was several times a member of the Connecticut Council of Safety and in 1783 helped revise and codify the state laws. In 1787 he was a delegate to the federal Constitutional Convention and there introduced, with Oliver Ellsworth, the famous Connecticut Compromise that provided for the

dual system of representation in Congress—one house to have equal representation from each state, and one to have representation proportionate to population. By signing the Constitution he became the only person to have signed the Articles of Association, the Articles of Confederation, the Declaration of Independence, and the Constitution. He returned to Connecticut to campaign for ratification. He was held in high regard by his contemporaries, among whom he was known as a man of unimpeachable honesty; he was in the House of Representatives from 1789 to 1791 and in the Senate from 1791 until his death on July 23, 1793, in New Haven, Connecticut.

Sherman, William Tecumseh (1820–1891), soldier. Born on February 8, 1820, in Lancaster, Ohio, Sherman was the son of a state supreme court judge and was an elder brother of John Sherman. Left fatherless at nine, he grew up in the home of Thomas Ewing, a prominent Ohio politician and later the first secretary of the interior, who procured for him an appointment to West Point in 1836. Graduating in 1840, he served in Florida and other places in the South until the outbreak of the Mexican War; after holding several staff positions despite his eagerness for line duty during the conflict, he became adjutant to the commander of the Division of the Pacific and thereby effectively chief administrative officer of California until the state government was organized in 1848. In 1853 he resigned his commission and joined a St. Louis banking firm, managing its San Francisco branch; he was later in New York City for a short time and after the failure of the firm in 1857 he practiced law briefly in Leavenworth, Kansas. In 1859 he obtained the position of superintendent of a new military college in Alexandria, Louisiana, a post he held until 1861, when the secessionist movement in the South caused him to move to St. Louis. In May of that year he was appointed colonel of the 13th Infantry; he led a brigade at the first battle of Bull Run (Manassas) and soon was made brigadier general of volunteers and sent to Kentucky. He held command there, charged with keeping the state in the Union, only briefly; he was replaced by Gen. Don Carlos Buell and sent west to serve under Gen. Henry Halleck. Sherman then joined Gen. Ulysses S. Grant's command and took part in the battles of Shiloh and Corinth. He was promoted to major general of volunteers and sent to fortify Memphis in preparation for the Vicksburg Campaign; after an earlier failure, he played a conspicuous part in bringing about the fall of Vicksburg in July 1863 and was promoted to brigadier general in the regular army. When Grant was placed in charge of all Western forces, Sherman succeeded to command of the Army of the Tennessee. He took part in late 1863 in the Chattanooga Campaign; in February 1864 he took the Confederate arsenal in Meridian, Mississippi, and burned the town. In March, when Grant went east to assume command of all Union forces, Sherman again succeeded him in the West, becoming commander of the Division of the Mississippi. In May he assembled his armies—numbering about 100,000 men—and began the invasion of Georgia. By July he had forced Confederate Gen. Joseph E. Johnston back to Atlanta; he continued to pressure his outnumbered opponent, and on September 1, Gen. John B. Hood, who had replaced Johnston, abandoned Atlanta. After the evacuation of the civilian population, the city was burned. Sherman, who had been promoted to major general, moved in November; leaving behind a force to deal with Hood, he cut loose from his supply base and led 60,000 men through Georgia to Savannah, living off the land and destroying public buildings, supplies, and everything else of military value. The "march to the sea" through Georgia, intended to deprive the Confederate armies of their most important supply source and to bring the war home to the Southern citizenry, aroused bitter controversy, but was undeniably effective; looting along the route of march inevitably took place, but, despite Southern memories of the matter, was in fact held remarkably in check, although discipline failed to restrain stragglers accompanying the army. Sherman's army reached Savannah on December 21, and in January turned northward through the Carolinas, continuing to spread devastation. In February Columbia, capital of South Carolina, was burned, but Sherman denied responsibility for the act. Johnston was called east to oppose him but could offer little resistance; the Confederate general accepted Sherman's liberal terms at Durham Station, North Carolina, and surrendered on April 26, 1865, 17 days after Gen. Robert E. Lee had surrendered to Grant at Appomattox. Certain political points in the surrender were later repudiated by Congress. Sherman returned to St. Louis in command of the Division of the Mississippi and in that post, while restraining the Western Indians, aided in the construction of the transcontinental railroad. In 1866 he undertook a mission to Mexico that, while ostensibly a matter of escorting a U.S. minister to meet President Benito Juarez, was in fact designed to pressure the French to leave that nation. He became a lieutenant general in 1866 and in 1869, when Grant became president, assumed command of the entire army. He held this post until November 1883 and a few months later retired from active duty. His famed statement that "war is hell" occurred in a speech in Columbus, Ohio, in 1880. In 1884 he was proposed to the Republican national convention as a presidential possibility; he ended all speculations by sending a message to clarify his position: "If nominated, I will not accept. If elected, I will not serve." His *Memoirs* appeared in two volumes in 1885. He moved to New York City in 1886 and died there on February 14, 1891. He was elected to the Hall of Fame in 1905.

Sherwood, Robert Emmet (1896–1955), author and playwright. Born on April 4, 1896, in New Rochelle, New York, Sherwood attended Milton Academy and Harvard, where he showed more interest in the *Lampoon* and in various theatrical productions than in his studies. He left college in 1917 to enlist in the Canadian army and was discharged two years later, having fought in France and received a dose of poison gas. He returned to New York City and became drama editor of *Vanity Fair*. There his coworkers, Dorothy Parker and Robert Benchley, introduced him to the members of the New York circle with whom he subsequently associated at the famous "Round Table" at the Algonquin Hotel, the meeting place of wits and the center of literary society. He was an editor of the old *Life*, a humor magazine, from 1920 to 1928. His first play, *The Road to Rome*, 1927, was followed by *The Queen's Husband*, 1928; *Waterloo Bridge*, 1929; and *Reunion in Vienna*, 1931. *The Petrified Forest*, 1935, and *Idiot's Delight*, a 1936 Pulitzer Prize winner, both focused on selfish heroes who find that their lives become meaningful only when they sacrifice themselves for other people. *Abe Lincoln in Illinois*, 1938, and *There Shall Be No Night*, 1940, also won Pulitzer Prizes. His play about Lincoln so impressed Eleanor Roosevelt that she introduced him to her husband, President Franklin D. Roosevelt, with whom he became closely associated. He eventually became Roosevelt's chief speech writer, and his sensitivity in interpreting the President's views helped to end the disfavor in which speech writing had been generally held. He won a fourth Pulitzer Prize for the biographical *Roosevelt and Hopkins*, 1949, based on his friendship with both Roosevelt and Harry L. Hopkins. Between 1940 and 1945 he served in various government posts, including assistant to the secretary of war and to the secretary of the navy and director of the overseas division of the Office of War Information (OWI). He wrote little for the stage after the war, but a screenplay, *The Best Years of Our Lives*, 1946, won him an Academy Award. He died in New York City on November 14, 1955.

Shiras, George (1832–1924), justice of the Supreme Court. Born on January 26, 1832, in Pittsburgh, Shiras attended Ohio University, at Athens, and graduated from Yale in 1853; he studied law at Yale (although he did not graduate from its law school) and in a Pittsburgh law office and was admitted to the bar in 1855. He practiced first in Iowa but soon returned to Pittsburgh, where during the next 25 years he acquired a reputation as an extremely capable corporation lawyer. In 1892 President Benjamin Harrison nominated him as an associate justice of the U.S. Supreme Court, and he was confirmed in July. Though able, he never became widely known for his work on the Court except on one occasion, which was probably misconstrued. In the famous income-tax case of 1895, *Pollock* v. *Farmers' Loan and Trust Co.*, the decision was at first five to four in favor of the constitutionality of the income-tax statute, but later, on reargument, one justice changed his mind, and the statute was therefore declared unconstitutional. For many years Shiras was considered to be the justice who had changed his mind, and he was severely criticized for this, although it was of course a perfectly proper action. Shiras never answered his critics, but as late as 1928 Chief Justice Charles Evans Hughes indicated that it was in fact another justice, not Shiras, who had changed his vote. Shiras retired from the Court in 1903 and died in Pittsburgh on August 2, 1924, at the age of ninety-two.

Shirer, William Lawrence (1904–   ), journalist and author. Born in Chicago on February 23, 1904, Shirer graduated from Coe College in 1925. After traveling in Europe for a year, he took a job in the Paris office of the *Chicago Tribune.* From 1929 to 1932 he headed the *Tribune's* central European office, in Vienna, then left the paper to spend a year living and writing in Spain; in 1934 he joined the Paris office of the *New York Herald Tribune.* From 1937 to 1939 he worked for the Columbia Broadcasting System (CBS) in Vienna, until he was forced out by the Nazi takeover in Austria; he then went to London and then to Prague. When World War II began in September 1939, Shirer relocated in Berlin to broadcast news over CBS, but the imposition of censorship by the Germans in 1940 caused him to leave Europe and return to the United States. In 1941 he published *Berlin Diary: The Journal of a Foreign Correspondent,* which became an immediate best seller. He remained a commentator for CBS until 1947 and wrote a column for the *Herald Tribune* from 1942 to 1948, specializing in war coverage and the postwar trials of Nazis at Nuremberg. From 1947 to 1949 he was a news commentator for the Mutual Broadcasting System. From 1950 Shirer occupied himself with free-lance writing for a number of magazines and, in addition, published several books. His fiction works included *Traitor,* 1950; *Stranger, Come Home,* 1954; and *The Consul's Wife,* 1956. In 1960 his monumental history of Nazi Germany, *The Rise and Fall of the Third Reich,* was published after five years of intensive research. In spite of its length, more than a thousand pages, it immediately became a best seller and remained one of the most popular and critically acclaimed books on the war era. It won a National Book Award in 1961. As a sequel to this book, and continuing his coverage of World War II, Shirer published in 1969 *The Collapse of the Third Republic: An Inquiry into the Fall of France in 1940.*

Shirley, William (1694–1771), public official. Born in Preston, Sussex, England, on December 2, 1694, Shirley graduated from Cambridge in 1715. He studied law and was admitted to the bar in 1720. He practiced law in London for 11 years, but, unable to make much of a success at it, he emigrated to Massachusetts in 1731 to improve his fortune. An inveterate office seeker once he arrived in America, he succeeded in winning appointment as an admiralty judge in 1733 and as advocate general in 1734. Ever loyal to the interests of the king, he succeeded in gaining the governorship of Massachusetts in 1741 and held the post until 1756. While governor he enforced a sound-money policy in the colony, where depreciation of paper legal tender had been occurring rapidly. He also improved the defenses of Massachusetts by building a warship, strengthening Castle William in Boston Harbor, and garrisoning forts in Maine. When King George's War (the American phase of the War of the Austrian Succession and one of the series of French and Indian Wars) began, Shirley conceived the bold strategy of taking Louisbourg on Cape Breton Island from the French. The legislature, after some persuasion, voted money for the venture, and New England supplied more than 4000 volunteers. It was the single largest such expedition undertaken by the united colonies, and was brought off with success on June 17, 1745. When Britain reimbursed Massachusetts for money spent on the war, the colony received enough to stabilize its currency. From 1749 to 1753 Shirley was in England and France, serving on a commission appointed to settle the boundary between New England and French North America. Upon returning to Boston, he was sure that war with France would soon break out again, and he made plans to strengthen colonial defenses. In 1755 he was appointed a major-general of British forces, in addition to his duties as governor, and becoming, on the death of Gen. Edward Braddock, commander of all British forces in North America, he was put in charge of the expedition against Niagara in the last French and Indian War. This military venture was a failure, and Shirley's reputation suffered accordingly. Because of this and other matters he was recalled to England, but charges brought against him were ultimately dropped. He remained in England from 1756 to 1761, when he was appointed governor of the Bahama Islands. He held that post until 1767, and returned to Massachusetts in 1769. He died in Roxbury on March 24, 1771.

Shockley, William Bradford (1910–   ), physicist. Born in London on February 13, 1910, Shockley grew up in California and graduated from the California Institute of Technology in 1932. Four years later he earned his doctorate in physics at Massachusetts Institute of Technology (MIT). He joined the technical staff of the Bell Telephone Laboratories, doing research on semiconductors. From 1942 to 1944 he was assigned by the navy to the Columbia University division of war research to work on antisubmarine warfare. He also served from 1942 to 1945 as a consultant for the War Department. Following the war Shockley resumed his position at Bell Labs, remaining there until 1954. While at Bell he conducted research in cooperation with physicists John Bardeen and Walter H. Brattain that resulted in the invention in 1947 of the transfer resistor, soon dubbed the "transistor." The original point-contact type of transistor was improved upon in 1951 by Shockley's invention, the junction transistor. The transistor has come to replace the vacuum tube throughout the whole range of electronic equipment, including telephone equipment, radios, television sets, radar, airplanes, and computers. For their work on the transistor, Shockley, Bardeen, and Brattain were awarded the Nobel Prize for Physics in 1956. From 1955 to 1958 Shockley worked for Beckman Instruments, Inc., and in 1958 he became president of the Shockley Transistor Corporation. From 1960 to 1963 he was director of the Shockley Transistor Unit of the Clevite Corporation; thereafter he joined the faculty of Stanford University as A. N. Poniatoff Professor of Engineering Science. During the 1950s and 1960s he continued to serve as an adviser to the U.S. Department of Defense and to the army and the air force.

Shoemaker, William Lee (1931–   ), "Willie," jockey. Born on August 19, 1931, in Fabens, Texas, Shoemaker grew up there and in El Monte, California. He left school at sixteen to work on a ranch at Puente, and his acquaintance there with horses, coupled with his diminutive size, prompted him to become a jockey. He won his first race, at Golden Gate Park, on April 20, 1949, and rode 219 winners in his first year of racing. In 1951 he was the season's leading money winner among jockeys, a feat that he repeated in many racing seasons thereafter. He rode and won in every major race and at every major track in the United States, and although he never won the Triple Crown (the Kentucky Derby, Preakness Stakes, and Belmont Stakes in one season), he won each of the separate events several times. He first won the Kentucky Derby in 1955, on Swaps. He won it again in 1959, on Tomy Lee, and in 1965 on Lucky Debonair. His first Preakness victory came in 1963 on Candy Spots and his second in 1967 on Damascus. He won the Belmont Stakes four times: in 1957 on Gallant Man, in 1959 on Sword Dancer, in 1962 on Jaipur, and in 1967 on Damascus. In 1953 he ended the season with 485 wins, a record at that time. In January 1964 Shoemaker became the leading lifetime money winner among jockeys when he won at Santa Anita riding Braganza. By 1972 he had ridden in more than 24,000 races and won more than $46 million in purses for the owners of his mounts. In a 1971 Labor Day race at Del Mar, California, he rode to his 6033rd victory, on a horse named Dares J., a record number of wins for any jockey.

Sholes, Christopher Latham (1819–1890), printer, journalist, and inventor. Born on February 14, 1819, in Mooresburg, Montour County, Pennsylvania, Sholes grew up there and in Danville, where he served a four-year apprenticeship on the staff of the local newspaper to learn the printing trade. When he was eighteen his family moved to Green Bay, Wisconsin, and Sholes went to work as a printer. In 1839 he went to Madison to work as an editor on his brother's newspaper, the *Wisconsin Enquirer*. By 1841 he was living in present-day Kenosha and editing the *Southport Telegraph*, but when he was appointed postmaster in 1845 he left the newspaper business for 15 years to follow a political career. During the 1850s Sholes served three terms in the Wisconsin legislature; then in 1860 he settled in Milwaukee, where he edited both the *Milwaukee News* and the *Milwaukee Sentinel* until receiving an appointment as collector for the city's lake port. Sholes's work as a printer and newspaperman gave him occasion to use his mechanical abilities in an inventive way. He devised a means for addressing newspapers mechanically for mailing, and by 1866 he had built a machine that would number pages in a book. At the suggestion of one of his coworkers, Carlos Glidden, Sholes improved on this machine by building a primitive but workable typewriter, receiving with Glidden and a third partner, Samuel W. Soulé, the first patent on it in 1868. For several years he kept working to improve the typewriter, trying to make a model that would be marketable at a reasonable cost without being too cumbersome. By 1873 he had realized that perfecting the machine was beyond his means, so he sold the patent rights (his partners had relinquished their shares) to the Remington Arms Company of Ilion, New York, for $12,000. By 1876 Remington was marketing the typewriter under its own name. Sholes continued for several years to work on modifications and improvements for the typewriter. During those years he passed on all his new information to the Remington company. After 1881 he was in poor health, suffering from tuberculosis. He died nine years later, in Milwaukee, on February 17, 1890.

Shreve, Henry Miller (1785–1851), riverboat captain. Born in Burlington County, New Jersey, on October 21, 1785, Shreve grew up in the frontier environment of Fayette County, Pennsylvania, where his family had moved in 1788. At the age of fourteen he began working on keelboats and barges in the river commerce of the Ohio and Mississippi valleys. By 1810 he had worked his way up to being captain of his own vessel and had developed a prosperous carrying trade between New Orleans and various Midwestern cities. During the War of 1812 he operated the steamship *Enterprise* on the lower Mississippi, bringing supplies to Andrew Jackson's forces at New Orleans. His second steamboat, the *Washington*, with its shallow draft and deck-mounted engine, demonstrated the practicality of using steam vessels for river commerce, and a lawsuit he won against the steamboat monopoly that had been granted in 1811 to Robert Fulton and Robert R. Livingston opened the rivers to competitive carrying. In 1827 President John Quincy Adams appointed Shreve superintendent of river improvements in the West, a post he held until 1841. He designed and operated the first snagboat used to clear rivers of debris and thus open them for navigation. As part of this project he cleared a huge natural raft of logs and fallen trees from the Red River in the country of the Caddo Indians in northwest Louisiana, and in 1835 founded a camp that four years later took the name Shreveport and that grew to play a leading role in the economic development of the area. In his later years Shreve lived in retirement near St. Louis, where he died on March 6, 1851.

Shubert, Lee (1875–1953), theatrical manager and producer. Born in Syracuse, New York, on March 15, 1875, Lee and his brother Jacob J. (J. J. Shubert), born in Syracuse on August 15, 1880, as young men entered the theater business. With a third brother, Sam S. (1876–1905), they began by organizing several touring companies in Syracuse for the comedies of the playwright Charles H. Hoyt. At the time—the late 1890s—the Theatrical Syndicate, originally Charles Frohman's booking agency but later headed by Marc Klaw, A. L. Erlanger, and others, owned and operated most of the New York theaters and many playhouses outside the city. This trust had enormous power and was able—and was charged with desiring—to discriminate against some independent producers. In 1900 the Shuberts leased the Herald Square Theatre in New York City and thereupon began to acquire, by lease and purchase, control of other theaters both inside and outside the city. For about ten years the war between the Shuberts and the Syndicate was waged relentlessly, but in the end —by about 1910—the Shuberts emerged triumphant. At first, the Shuberts rented their theaters to producers against whom the Syndicate was discriminating; but soon they became producers themselves, putting on their own shows in their own houses, and once again this had the effect of limiting the availability of theaters for the productions of the independents. Thus the Shuberts came to be hated as monopolists, as the Syndicate had been; they were charged with demanding exorbitant rentals and with insisting on harsh contracts, particularly with neophyte producers. In 1950 the U.S. government filed a civil antitrust suit against the Shubert Theatre Corporation, charging the brothers with monopolistic practices, but the suit was dropped before coming to trial. At that time, the Shubert combine was said to control some 37 theaters (including 17 in New York City) and a large share of the theatrical bookings of the nation. These revelations were hardly news to those within the theater, but they led to a series of charges that the Shuberts were stifling American theatrical creativity. Sam S. Shubert died in 1905; a New York theater was later named after him by his surviving brothers. Lee died in New York City on Christmas Day, 1953, whereupon J. J. Shubert became head of all the family enterprises, which included, besides theaters, a company controlling production rights to a large number of plays, a music-publishing company, and one of the leading purveyors of stage costumes. Known as "the man who produced a thousand shows," J. J. included among his credits the staging of vast open-air operettas in cities from Miami to Los Angeles, and, as a principal backer of Florenz Ziegfeld's lavish musical spectacles, produced annually as the *Ziegfeld Follies*, the introduction to American audiences of such stars as Al Jolson, Eddie Cantor, Ed Wynn, Fanny Brice, the Dolly sisters, Ray Bolger, Bert Lahr, and many more. J. J. Shubert died in New York City ten years and a day after his brother Lee, on December 26, 1963.

Sibley, Hiram (1807–1888), businessman. Born in North Adams, Massachusetts, on February 6, 1807, Sibley received little education, but learned the cobbler's trade as a youth and in 1828 opened his own machine shop. Ten years later he had sold his business and moved to Rochester, New York, to engage in real estate and banking. On a visit to Washington, D.C., he met Samuel F. B. Morse and helped him gain congressional backing to build a telegraph line, the nation's first, in 1844. Telegraph lines and companies began proliferating throughout the East, and in 1851 Sibley himself organized the New York and Mississippi Valley Printing Telegraph Company, which brought together several small lines. In 1856, Sibley, in cooperation with Ezra Cornell, combined the company with others and renamed the unified organization the Western Union Telegraph Company. Sibley became president, and under his supervision the company greatly expanded its facilities, in 1861 completing the first transcontinental telegraph line. After Cyrus W. Field failed in a first attempt in 1858 to lay a transatlantic cable, Sibley determined to reach Europe with a telegraph line through Alaska, under the Bering Strait, and through Russia, connecting with a system the Russians had already announced their intention to build. In the winter of 1864–1865 he went to St. Petersburg to negotiate with the Russian government the details of building a line. On March 21, 1865, an agreement was signed. Sibley was also asked by the Russians if Western Union would be interested in purchasing Alaska; he turned down the offer, but made it known to the U.S. government, and in 1867 the United States agreed to buy Alaska from the Russians. Late in 1865 difficulties over arrangements for the telegraph line halted progress toward getting the work started, and in 1866 Cyrus Field finally succeeded in laying a cable across the Atlantic; therefore the deal with Russia was canceled. Sibley himself had become ill during the trip to St. Petersburg, and was forced to resign as president of Western Union in 1869. Thereafter he engaged in a variety of business ventures throughout the Southwest, including railroad financing, and also accumulated vast land holdings for farming and experimental agriculture. He died in Rochester, New York, on July 12, 1888. Among his many benefactions were a gift to Cornell University, of which he had been an incorporator, for the establishment of the Sibley College of Mechanic Arts (now Mechanical Engineering) and the building of Sibley Hall at the University of Rochester.

Siciliano, Angelo, *see* Atlas, Charles

Sickles, Daniel Edgar (1825–1914), soldier and public official. Born in New York City on October 20, 1825, Sickles attended the University of the City of New York (now New York University) and later studied law. Admitted to the bar in 1846, he was soon involved in politics, being elected to the state legislature for a term in 1847. As corporation counsel for New York City in 1853 he was part of the commission that acquired the site of Central Park for the city. From 1853 to 1855 he was in London serving as secretary of the U.S. legation. He served terms in the New York state senate in 1856 and 1857 and was also elected to the House of Representatives in 1856, serving there until 1861. In 1859, on the then-novel grounds of temporary insanity, he was acquitted of a charge of murder arising from his shooting to death the son of Francis Scott Key for what he believed were improper attentions to his wife. With the start of the Civil War, Sickles received a colonel's commission, raised troops in New York, and served throughout the war, taking part in the Peninsular Campaign and in the battles of Fredericksburg, Chancellorsville, and Gettysburg, and rising in 1863 to the rank of major general. His service on the battlefront ended when a wound at Gettysburg made it necessary to amputate his right leg. He remained in the army until 1869, however, and served as military governor of North and South Carolina in 1866–1867. From 1869 until 1875 he was U.S. minister to Spain, and after resigning from that post he remained in Europe for seven years. Back in the United States, he made his home in New York City, where he held various local offices during the 1880s. In 1892 he was elected again to the House, and served one term. Having lost in the congressional election of 1894, Sickles retired to private life. He died in New York City on May 3, 1914.

Sigourney, Lydia Howard Huntley (1791–1865), author and poet. Born in Norwich, Connecticut, on September 1, 1791, Lydia Huntley was a school teacher in her native town from 1811 to 1819. In June 1819 she married Charles Sigourney, a Hartford businessman, and from that time she turned to writing for a career. She had already published a book, *Moral Pieces in Prose and Verse*, 1815, by her students. Now she began to turn out poetry and essays for a number of magazines, as well as additional books. Her work soon became well known, and she was probably the nation's most widely read poet during her lifetime. Sentimental, elegant, frequently concerned with death, her writings had little literary merit. Among the 67 books she published were *How to Be Happy*, 1833; *Pocahontas, and Other Poems*, 1841; *Poems, Religious and Elegaic*, 1841; *The Faded Hope*, 1853; and her posthumous autobiography, *Letters of Life*, 1866. She died in Hartford, Connecticut, on June 10, 1865.

Sigsbee, Charles Dwight (1845–1923), naval officer. Born in Albany, New York, on January 16, 1845, Sigsbee graduated from the U.S. Naval Academy in 1863. After nearly two years of Civil War duty along the Atlantic and Gulf coast, he was assigned to the Asiatic Squadron from 1865 to 1869. Apart from sea duty over the next two decades, he taught at Annapolis in 1869–1871, 1882–1885, and 1887–1890. From 1875 to 1878 he worked with Alexander Agassiz doing a deep-water survey of the Gulf of Mexico. In the course of this work Sigsbee invented a number of devices to improve the accuracy of deep-water sounding and coastal surveying. The Sigsbee Deep, 12,425 feet below sea level in the center of the Gulf, was named in his honor. From 1893 to 1897 he was chief hydrographer for the U.S. Navy Department. His next sea duty was as commander, with the rank of captain, of the battleship *Maine*; the vessel was under his command when it blew up mysteriously in the harbor of Havana, Cuba, on February 15, 1898, giving impetus to the popular clamor for war with Spain. Despite the mishap, Sigsbee served in the Caribbean throughout the Spanish-American War, winning several engagements with Spanish vessels. He was advanced to the rank of rear admiral in 1903 and put in command of the Caribbean Squadron. On this tour of duty he commanded the squadron that brought the remains of John Paul Jones back to the United States from France in 1905. He published *Deep Sea Sounding and Dredging*, 1880, and *The Maine: an Account of her Destruction in Havana Harbor*, 1899. Sigsbee retired from the navy in 1907. He died on July 19, 1923, in New York City.

Sikorsky, Igor Ivan (1889–1972), aeronautical engineer. Born in Kiev, Russia, on May 25, 1889, Sikorsky was educated in Russia and in Paris. Interested in aviation from his youth, he gained his earliest ideas from drawings of flying machines by Leonardo da Vinci. He went to France and Germany before he was twenty and studied the accomplishments of Louis Blériot and the work being done on Count Ferdinand von Zeppelin's dirigible. In 1909 he designed and built his first aircraft, a helicopter. He turned to construction of fixed-wing aircraft and by 1911 was not only an experienced pilot, but had produced five successful airplanes. His S-5 made a world-record flight in 1911 with three men on board, flying 30 miles cross-country at 70 miles per hour. During 1912–1918, as head of engineering of the aviation plant at Russo-Baltic Railroad Car Works, he designed, built, and piloted planes of unsurpassed flying range and size. The most important of these, built and flown by him in 1913, was the first successful multimotored plane in the world. Leaving Russia during the Revolution, he stayed briefly in London and Paris before emigrating to the United States in 1919 (he was naturalized in 1928). Settling in New York City, he taught mathematics at a school for Russian immigrants until, in 1923, he was financially able to found his own aircraft manufacturing firm, the Sikorsky Aero Engineering Corporation. The enterprise turned out a variety of aircraft for commercial and military uses. Among these was the S-29, a twin-engine 14-passenger plane with a speed of 115 miles per hour. In 1925 he formed the Sikorsky Manufacturing Corporation on Long Island, New York, which built his S-38 flying boat, and in 1928 he organized Sikorsky Aviation Corporation, located in Stratford, Connecticut. The next year the company became the Sikorsky Aircraft Division of the United Aircraft and Transport

Corporation (now United Aircraft Corporation). In 1931 he unveiled his S-40 *American Clipper*, the first of the *Clipper* series of four-engine amphibian craft that pioneered transoceanic commercial routes in the 1930s. He resumed work on the helicopter in 1939, and in that year built and flew the first workable direct-lift machine in the country. Able to take off and land vertically, to hover in the air, and to move in any direction, the helicopter was quickly recognized as a highly versatile craft with a multitude of uses in civil and military operations. As a cargo, airbus, and rescue vehicle, it soon became the workhorse of the air. Sikorsky continued to produce and improve helicopters until retiring from United Aircraft in 1957, after which he served on a consulting basis. He was named to the International Aerospace Hall of Fame in 1966 and the next year received the federal government's National Medal of Science. He wrote *The Winged S*, 1938; *The Message of the Lord's Prayer*, 1942; and *The Invisible Encounter*, 1947. He died in Easton, Connecticut, on October 26, 1972.

Silliman, Benjamin (1779–1864), chemist, geologist, and educator. Born in North Stratford (now Trumbull), Connecticut, on August 8, 1779, Silliman graduated from Yale in 1796. Two years later he returned to New Haven to study law and in 1799 became a tutor at Yale; in 1802, after his admission to the bar, he was appointed Yale's first professor of chemistry and natural history. For two years he pursued further studies in chemistry, medicine, and related topics with prominent American scientists and in 1804 assumed his teaching duties. In 1805 he sailed to Europe for further studies; at that time he became interested in geology. He later published a popular account of his travels and associations in 1810 as *A Journal of Travels in England, Holland and Scotland*. He began to lecture in 1808 on topics in chemistry and geology. Eventually his lectures were in great demand throughout the nation, and much later, in 1839–1840, he delivered the first Lowell Institute lectures in Boston. Meanwhile he played a leading role in the establishment of the Yale Medical School in 1813 and served thereafter as professor of chemistry. In 1818 he issued the first number of the *American Journal of Science and the Arts*; remaining under his editorship until passed on to his son, "Silliman's Journal," as it was popularly known, became one of the world's leading scientific periodicals. In addition to American editions of standard English texts in chemistry and geology, he published in 1830 his own *Elements of Chemistry*. In 1847 he secured the establishment at Yale of the Department of Philosophy and the Arts that became in time the Yale, and finally the Sheffield, Scientific School. He was also instrumental in the founding of Yale's Trumbull Gallery. In 1849 he turned over his post as professor of natural history to James D. Dana, but he continued to teach chemistry for four more years. He retired in 1853 and ten years later was, with his son, an original member of the National Academy of Sciences. He died in New Haven, Connecticut, on November 24, 1864.

Silliman, Benjamin, Jr. (1816–1885), chemist and educator. Born in New Haven, Connecticut, on December 4, 1816, Silliman was the son of Benjamin Silliman (1779–1864). Graduating from Yale in 1837, he immediately became his father's assistant. The younger Silliman aided in the founding of the forerunner of Yale's Sheffield Scientific School and gradually took over from his father editorship of the *American Journal of Science and the Arts* ("Silliman's Journal"), serving in that capacity until his death. During 1845–1846 he conducted what is believed to have been the first course on agricultural chemistry, a series of lectures in New Orleans. In 1846 he was appointed professor of chemistry at Yale; from 1849 to 1854 he lectured at the University of Louisville, and then returned to Yale to succeed to his father's professorships of chemistry in Yale College and in the Yale Medical School. In 1855 he published his *Report on the Rock Oil, or Petroleum, from Venango County, Pennsylvania*, in which he described the first analysis of crude oil, the method of fractional distillation of oil into several components, and the superior usefulness of various fractions for lubrication, illumination, and the manufacture of paraffin, thus outlining the economic potential of the great industry that was to begin in Pennsylvania four years later. Others of Silliman's publications included *First Principles of Chemistry*, 1846, and *First Principles of Physics, or Natural Philosophy*, 1858. He retired from Yale College in 1870, but continued to lecture at the Medical School until his death in New Haven, Connecticut, on January 14, 1885.

Silverman, Sime (1873–1933), newspaper publisher. Born in Cortland, New York, on May 18, 1873, Silverman was educated there and also attended a business college in Syracuse. After working for his father for a few years he moved to New York City and worked for the *New York Morning Telegraph*, a daily newspaper concerned primarily with sports and theater news, from 1898 to 1905. In 1905 he started his own paper, the show-business weekly, *Variety*, for which he served as both editor and publisher. Under Silverman *Variety* became a show-business institution, noted for the fairness of its reviews and criticisms and for the flamboyant style of its writing. *Variety* reporters used language freely and innovatively, coined terms, used colloquialisms, transposed nouns into verbs and verbs into nouns, picked up the jargon of Broadway and added it to the American language. In 1933 the Funk & Wagnalls Company, publisher of dictionaries, named Silverman one of the ten most creative slang-makers in the United States. Many expressions born in *Variety* did not endure, but others, such as "disc jockey," coined in 1937, became permanent parts of the language. In addition to the weekly New York *Variety*, Silverman started a daily *Variety* in Hollywood, California, in 1933. He died in Los Angeles on

September 22, 1933, just three weeks after his West Coast edition began publication.

Simms, William Gilmore (1806–1870), author. Born on April 17, 1806, in Charleston, South Carolina, Simms grew up motherless and, after his father left to serve under Andrew Jackson in the campaigns against the Creek Indians and at New Orleans in the War of 1812, he was reared by his grandmother. He was a precocious student and, having mastered four languages by the age of ten, he entered the College of Charleston. Two years later he was apprenticed to a druggist. During the next few years he contributed poetry to Charleston newspapers, did editorial work, and took up the study of law. Although he was admitted to the bar in 1827 he had by that time decided to devote his energies to literature. He became editor of the Charleston *City Gazette* in about 1828, but lost the job when he took a highly unpopular stand against nullification in 1832. Following the death of his wife in the same year, he traveled to New York City, where he formed valuable friendships with William Cullen Bryant and other literary figures and wrote his first novel, *Martin Faber*, 1833. *Guy Rivers*, 1834, and *The Yemassee*, 1835, his best-known work, followed. In 1835 he returned to Charleston and the next year married the daughter of a wealthy plantation owner. Until about 1842 he continued to produce romantic novels, including *The Partisan*, 1835; *Mellichampe*, 1836; *Richard Hurdis*, 1838; and *The Kinsmen*, 1841. The larger portion of his fiction dealt with various periods of Southern history and, while his major characters tended to be formulaically aristocratic, in his secondary figures he presented accurate and engaging portraits of a wide range of Southern types—backwoodsmen, Indians, slaves, adventurers, outlaws, and gamblers. Simms's work as a whole suggested a Southern parallel, remarked at the time, to that of James Fenimore Cooper in the North. His reputation, at least during the early part of his career, was higher in the North than in the South, primarily because his social station was such as to retard recognition in conservative Charleston. During the 1840s he wrote a history and a geography of his native state, biographies of several Southern figures, and a good deal of criticism. He returned to the historical novel with *Katherine Walton*, 1851, and followed with *The Sword and the Distaff*, 1853 (revised as *Woodcraft*, 1854); *The Forayers*, 1855; and *Eutaw*, 1856. His collected poems appeared in 1853, the most notable of his 19 volumes of verse. He threw himself vigorously into the growing sectional dispute over slavery and secession, becoming a noted lecturer on the South and editing from 1849 to 1856 the proslavery *Southern Quarterly Review*. During the Civil War he suffered the loss of his second wife and two of his children and the burning of his home and library. In his last years he wrote little of note; a novel, *Joscelyn*, appeared in 1867 and in the same year he edited the *War Poetry of the South*. In all he produced some 82 volumes during his lifetime. He died in Charleston on June 11, 1870.

Simon, Neil (1927–   ), playwright. Born in New York City on July 4, 1927, Simon attended New York University under an Air Force Reserve program in engineering from 1943 to 1945. In 1945–1946 he was stationed at Lowry Air Force Base in Colorado. After his discharge he took a clerical job at the offices of Warner Brothers in New York City until an opening as a comedy writer for radio came in 1947. From 1948 to 1960 he wrote for television, working on such programs as "The Phil Silvers Show," "The Jackie Gleason Show," "The Sid Caesar Show," "Sergeant Bilko," and "The Garry Moore Show." In 1960, while working in Hollywood, he wrote his first play, *Come Blow Your Horn*, which opened on Broadway in 1961 and ran for two seasons. After this first effort Simon had a succession of hit comedies, most of which also became movies. He had the unusual distinction in 1966 of having four plays running on Broadway at the same time: *Barefoot in the Park*, which opened in 1963; *The Odd Couple*, 1965; *Sweet Charity*, 1966, a musical; and *Star Spangled Girl*, 1966. Of them all, *The Odd Couple* was probably the best known, having become a movie, then the basis of a successful television comedy series. In 1968 *Plaza Suite*, three short plays in one, opened in New York City. Another musical, *Promises, Promises*, with music by Burt Bacharach, followed in 1969. Then in 1970 Simon wrote the screenplay for the motion picture *The Out-of-Towners*. His output of plays continued unabated: *Last of the Red Hot Lovers*, 1969; *The Gingerbread Lady*, 1970; *The Prisoner of Second Avenue*, 1971; *The Sunshine Boys*, 1972; *God's Favorite*, 1974; *California Suite*, 1976; *Chapter Two*, 1977; *They're Playing Our Song* (a musical), 1978; *I Ought To Be in Pictures*, 1980; *Fools*, 1981; *Brighton Beach Memoirs*, 1983. His screenplays include: *Murder by Death*, 1976; *The Goodbye Girl*, 1977; and *Seems Like Old Times*, 1980.

Simonson, Lee (1888–1967), set designer. Born in New York City on June 26, 1888, Lee Simonson graduated from Harvard in 1908 (although he received his diploma in 1909). From 1908 to 1912 he studied in France with the intention of becoming a mural painter. After his return to the United States he painted for a few years, until he was hired in 1915 by the Washington Square Players to design the sets for *Love of One's Neighbor*. Over the next few years he did several more set designs for this group, but his career was interrupted by army service during World War I. Returning to his profession in 1919, he joined a small group of directors, actors, and stage designers of the disbanded Washington Square Players to form the Theatre Guild. He remained a director of the Guild until 1940, and during 21 years on its board was responsible for designing, among others, the settings for *The Power of Darkness*, 1920; *Heartbreak House*, 1920; *Peer Gynt*, 1923; *Volpone*, 1928; *Faust*, 1928; *Idiot's Delight*, 1936; and *Amphytrion*, 1937. Some of his productions outside the Theatre Guild were *Road to Rome,* 1927; *As You Like It,* 1931; *The Good Earth,* 1932; *Foxhole in the Parlor,* 1945; and *Joan of Lorraine,* 1946. After resigning from the Theatre Guild in 1940, he continued stage designing and worked to encourage community theaters throughout the nation. In 1947 he executed the sets for four operas in Wagner's Ring cycle for the Metropolitan Opera Company. Through lecturing and writing, Simonson influenced many people throughout the country concerned with play production and the architecture of theaters and auditoriums. In 1932 he had published *The Stage Is Set,* which contained many of his ideas on scenic design; in 1939 and 1940 he had served as consultant to several colleges that were building new auditoriums; and in 1944–1948 he served as consultant on costume exhibitions for the Metropolitan Museum of Art in New York City. *The Art of Scenic Design* was published in 1949. From the 1950s he lived in retirement in New York City, doing occasional lecturing, writing, and consulting; he died in Yonkers, New York, on January 23, 1967.

Simpson, George Gaylord (1902–), paleontologist. Born in Chicago on June 16, 1902, Simpson attended the University of Colorado but transferred to Yale, where he graduated in 1923 and took his doctorate in 1926. He then spent a year at the British Museum on a National Research Council fellowship. Returning to the United States, he joined the staff, as assistant curator of vertebrate paleontology, of the American Museum of Natural History in New York City, where he remained until 1959. From 1945 to 1959 he was also a professor of vertebrate paleontology at Columbia University. In his years with the Museum of Natural History Simpson traveled on numerous scientific expeditions, including two extensive research trips through Patagonia in 1930–1931 and in 1933–1934, and many trips to Mexico, all in search of fossil remains. In 1959 he accepted a professorship of vertebrate paleontology at Harvard's Museum of Comparative Zoology, and in 1967 he became professor of geology at the University of Arizona, while maintaining his connection with Harvard. Through his work in biology, paleontology, and taxonomy, Simpson came to be one of the world's foremost authorities on evolutionary theory. He wrote a large number of both scientific and popular works, including *The Meaning of Evolution,* 1949; *Principles of Animal Taxonomy,* 1961; *The Geography of Evolution,* 1965; and *Biology and Man,* 1969. His lifelong study and love of horses led to a fascinating handbook entitled *Horses,* 1951.

Simpson, Jeremiah (1842–1905), "Sockless Jerry," public official. Born March 31, 1842, in Westmorland County, New Brunswick, Simpson grew up there, in Ontario, and in Oneida, New York. With little formal schooling, he became a sailor on the Great Lakes and eventually, in 1856, became a ship's captain. He followed this career until 1879, except for brief service in the Union army during the Civil War. He then settled on a farm in Jackson County, Kansas, near Holton, and operated a sawmill. In 1884 he moved to Barber County and started a cattle ranch near Medicine Lodge. The ranch failed when an extremely cold winter destroyed his herd, and he became preoccupied with the problems of the farmers in the West, whose resources were rarely adequate to meet their expenses and mortgage payments. He entered politics as a Populist although his leanings had been Republican, and he ran unsuccessfully for state office in 1886 and 1888. But in 1890 he was elected to the House of Representatives after a campaign that gave him the nickname "Sockless Jerry." He served two terms in the House, from 1891 to 1895. Defeated in 1894, he was reelected for one term in 1896 with the aid of fusion-minded Democrats. After he was defeated for office in 1898 he settled in Kansas City, where he published his journal, *Jerry Simpson's Bayonet,* in 1899–1900. Remaining a Populist and a single-taxer, Simpson was never as effective in office as he was in campaigns. After living for a while in Roswell, New Mexico, he moved to Wichita, Kansas, where he died on October 23, 1905.

Simpson, Matthew (1811–1884), religious leader and educator. Born in Cadiz, Ohio, on June 21, 1811, Simpson was primarily self-educated as a child, but later attended Madison College in Unionville, Pennsylvania, and for a few years studied and practiced medicine. Having been active most of his life in the Methodist church, he decided to become a minister, and in 1836 was admitted to the Pittsburgh Conference. From 1835 to 1837 he served parishes near Cadiz and Pittsburgh, and in Williamsport. From 1837 to 1839 he taught natural science at Allegheny College and in 1839 was elected president of Indiana Asbury University (now DePauw) in Indiana, a Methodist institution, and remained in the post until 1848. Through his administrative ability and talent as a preacher he became well known in Methodist circles in the Midwest, and in 1848 the General Conference of the church chose him to edit its magazine, the *Western Christian Advocate.* Four years later he was consecrated a bishop. Through his travels in Europe and the United States, Simpson gained a reputation as a gifted and influential speaker and he was soon widely known outside his church. An opponent of slavery and a strong supporter of the Union cause during the Civil War, he was frequently in touch with President Abraham Lincoln and the highest officials of his administration. He delivered the eulogy at Lincoln's burial in Springfield, Illinois, in 1865. Apart from his episcopal duties, he was active also in such interchurch efforts as the Evangelical Alliance and in 1881 was called upon to deliver the opening sermon at the Ecumenical Methodist Conference in London. He died on June 18, 1884, in Philadelphia.

Simpson, Wallis Warfield, *see* Windsor, Wallis Warfield, Duchess of

Sims, James Marion (1813–1883), physician. Born in Lancaster County, South Carolina, on January 25, 1813, Sims graduated from South Carolina College (now the University of South Carolina) in 1832. He studied at Charleston Medical College and transferred in 1834 to Jefferson Medical College in Philadelphia, graduating the following year. For five years he practiced medicine at Mt. Meigs, Alabama, but in 1840 moved to Montgomery. During the 1840s he became an expert in the diseases of women, and in 1849, after an agonizing series of failures, he combined his knowledge with an excellent surgical technique to remove a bladder fistula. This and subsequent successes in curing this condition, which he described in the *American Journal of the Medical Sciences* in 1850, brought him international fame in medical circles within a few years; Sims, along with Ephraim McDowell, is credited with being one of the originators of operative gynecology. In 1853 he moved to New York City. There, after several years of a successful surgical practice and training surgeons in his methods, he promoted the founding, in 1855, and chartering, in 1857, of the Woman's Hospital. Because of his sympathy for the Confederacy, Sims spent the Civil War years in Europe, where he continued to practice medicine and widened the area of acceptance for his methods among European physicians. In 1866 he published *Clinical Notes on Uterine Surgery.* The years 1870–1872 were also spent in Europe, during part of the Franco-Prussian War as surgeon in chief of the Anglo-American Ambulance Corps. Apart from another visit abroad in 1882, Sims lived in New York City until his retirement to Washington, D.C. He died on November 13, 1883, shortly after moving there. His autobiography, *The Story of My Life,* was edited by his son and published in 1884.

Sims, William Sowden (1858–1936), naval officer. Born on October 15, 1858, in Port Hope, Ontario, of an American father, Sims moved with his family to Pennsylvania in 1872. In 1876, after one rejection, he was admitted to the U.S. Naval Academy and graduated four years later. From 1880 to 1897 he was almost continuously on sea duty; during that period he wrote a navigation text that was long used by both the navy and the merchant marine. From 1897 to 1900 he was naval attaché at the U.S. embassies in Paris and, briefly, St. Petersburg. By the time he resumed sea duty on the China Station in 1900 he had become convinced of the relative inferiority of the U.S. navy in matters of ship design, tactics, and gunnery, the victories of the Spanish-American War notwithstanding. In the Orient he met Capt. Percy Scott of the Royal Navy, developer of the new technique of continuous-aim firing; he wrote a series of memoranda to the Navy Department describing and advocating the adoption of this method, but received no satisfactory reply. Finally, in 1901 and again in 1902, he wrote directly to President Theodore Roosevelt—technically an act of insubordination—and as a result was brought to

Washington as inspector of target practice. Remaining in that post until 1909, and, after 1907 serving additionally as naval aide to the President, he brought about an almost revolutionary improvement in the state of naval gunnery. At his instigation a commission was appointed to investigate and make recommendations on the organization of the Navy Department, but this, like an earlier congressional investigation into faulty battleship design for which he was also indirectly responsible, led to no important reform. In 1910, while captain of the battleship *Minnesota,* he made an unauthorized speech in England pledging the full support of the United States in the event of an attack on the British Empire and was reprimanded by President William Howard Taft. From 1913 to 1915 he was commander of the Atlantic Torpedo Flotilla and developed a tactical doctrine for the deployment of the newly introduced naval destroyers. In 1917 he was promoted to rear admiral, appointed president of the Naval War College, and, later the same year, promoted again to vice admiral. When the United States entered World War I in April of that year he was placed in command of U.S. naval operations in European waters. Working closely with the naval departments of Allied nations, he secured the adoption of the convoy system. In 1918 he was made full admiral, and in 1919, on being relieved as commander of U.S. naval forces in Europe, he reverted to permanent rank of rear admiral and returned to the Naval War College. Because of the award of honors in a manner he considered arbitrary, he refused to accept the Distinguished Service Medal. His long and detailed report on mismanagement in the conduct of naval affairs during the war led to another congressional investigation, but 1920, like 1908, was an election year and the results were partisan and inconclusive. Despite such disappointments, Sims was acknowledged to be the most influential officer in U.S. naval history. His *The Victory at Sea,* 1920, written with Burton J. Hendrick, was awarded a Pulitzer Prize for history. He retired as rear admiral in 1922, but continued to write and speak on topics of public and military interest until his death in Boston on September 28, 1936.

Sinatra, Frank (1917–   ), singer and actor. Born in Hoboken, New Jersey, on December 12, 1917, Sinatra decided to become a singer about the time he was twenty-one. In 1937 he and some friends won first prize on the radio show "Major Bowes' Amateur Hour," and they then toured the country briefly. Until 1939, he sang at a roadhouse near his home and did a few local radio broadcasts. In that year Harry James hired him as a vocalist with the orchestra he was putting together, but in less than a year Sinatra had left James for the Tommy Dorsey band. He remained with Dorsey for more than three years, gaining for himself nearly as much renown as the bandleader. In 1942 he broke his contract with Dorsey and struck out on his own. An eight-week engagement at New York City's Paramount Theatre earned him a prominent spot on the popular radio musical show, "Your Hit Parade." Sinatra became the idol of what were then called "bobby-soxers," teen-age girls who bought his records and flocked to his personal appearances. Billed as "The Voice" or "The Crooner," he gained an enormous personal following throughout the 1940s. In 1943 he appeared in his first movie, *Higher and Higher*; this film was followed by several more over the next six years. By the early 1950s it seemed that his career was finished; the public was losing interest in him and the vagaries of his personal life were gaining more public attention than his talent. In 1951 he divorced his first wife and married actress Ava Gardner, but this marriage also ended in divorce, in 1957. Starting in 1953 Sinatra began a remarkable comeback in show business. He was given a supporting dramatic role in the movie *From Here to Eternity*, and his performance won him an Acadamy Award. He followed that film with a variety of roles, some singing and some dramatic, in many more successful movies, among them *Guys and Dolls*, 1955; *The Man with the Golden Arm*, 1956; *Pal Joey*, 1957; and *Ocean's Eleven*, 1962. During these years he became more technically expert in his singing than he had been previously, and he began to appeal to a much wider audience. He revived his nightclub career, primarily in Las Vegas, and continued his public appearances until the early 1970s. Enormously popular among his fellow entertainers, a number of whom formed a much publicized "clan" or "rat-pack," Sinatra was frequently the subject of press reports commenting on his personal, business, and political activities. In April 1971 Sinatra appeared as a guest at the Academy Award ceremony and announced his retirement from show business. He subsequently gave his official farewell appearance on June 14, but he soon tired of retirement and returned to performing.

Sinclair, Harry Ford (1876–1956), businessman. Born in Wheeling, West Virginia, on July 6, 1876, Sinclair grew up there and in Independence, Kansas. During 1887–1888 he studied pharmacy at the University of Kansas and upon receipt of his certificate he went to work in his father's drugstore. In 1901 he abandoned pharmacy for the exciting new petroleum business. Beginning as a lease broker, he gradually became an independent producer of oil; in 1905 his first well came in and before he was thirty-five he had ridden the oil boom in Kansas and Oklahoma to become a millionaire. In 1916 he broadened his participation in the industry by organizing the Sinclair Oil and Refining Corporation, a vertically integrated enterprise that controlled oil from wellhead to retail outlet. The firm grew rapidly and in 1919 became Sinclair Consolidated Oil Corporation. An avid sportsman, Sinclair was an organizer in 1914 of the short-lived Federal League of professional baseball teams; he owned a racing stable that included Zev, winner of the 1923 Kentucky Derby, and from 1928 was a part owner of the St. Louis Browns baseball team. Sinclair came to wide public

notice in 1923, when the scandals of the administration of President Warren G. Harding broke into the headlines. It was revealed by a Senate investigation that he had organized the Mammoth Oil Corporation to take a lease in 1922 on the naval oil reserve at Teapot Dome, Wyoming. The lease had been given by Albert B. Fall, secretary of the interior, who in the same year also leased the Elk Hills naval oil reserve in California to Edward L. Doheny, another major oil entrepreneur. In the welter of investigations and court suits that followed over a period of years, both leases were invalidated by the Supreme Court; Sinclair, Doheny, and Fall were indicted and Fall was sent to prison after conviction for accepting bribes, although neither Sinclair nor Doheny was convicted of giving any; and Sinclair was acquitted in 1928 of a charge of conspiracy to defraud the government. In 1929, however, he was found guilty of contempt of court, for having jurors in the 1928 trial followed, and of contempt of Congress, for refusing to cooperate in a Senate investigation of the scandal, and he served a term in prison. The affair had little effect on Sinclair's career; he remained president of Sinclair Oil until his retirement in 1949 and was a member of the board until 1954. He was also in later years chairman of the board of Richfield Oil Corporation. During World War II he served as a member of the Petroleum Industry War Council. Sinclair died in Pasadena, California, on November 10, 1956.

Sinclair, Upton Beall (1878–1968), author and social reformer. Born on September 20, 1878, in Baltimore, Maryland, of an eminent but financially straitened family, Sinclair earned money by writing from the age of fifteen. He graduated from the City College of New York (CCNY) in 1897, then did graduate work at Columbia while supporting himself by doing various kinds of literary hackwork. He published several novels, none of which won much attention. His first success came with his sixth novel, *The Jungle*, 1906, an account of immigrant workers in the Chicago stockyards. Commissioned by a Socialist weekly, it was intended to bring laborers under the Socialist party wing; but, ironically, the wheels of democracy began to turn in response to the book's horrifying revelations of conditions in meat-packing plants, and subsequent congressional investigations led to the passage of the Meat Inspection Act of 1906, a milestone in consumer protection. "I aimed at the public's heart," Sinclair said of the book, "and hit it in the stomach." With the income from the book he established a short-lived Socialist colony, Helicon Hall, in New Jersey. He repeatedly tried to expose the falseness of American society and, going beyond the usual limits of muckraking journalism, to show a Socialist alternative, as in *King Coal*, 1917; *The Profits of Religion*, 1918, an interpretation of religion as a capitalist instrument; *Oil!*, 1927, about the political scandals of the 1920s; and *Boston*, 1928, covering events of the Sacco and Vanzetti case. His Lanny Budd series, 11 novels written between 1939 and 1949 but involving the hero in national and international affairs in the period 1913–1949, stressed social reform, but did not propose Socialism as the remedy. The Lanny Budd volume covering 1930–1934, *Dragon's Teeth*, won a Pulitzer Prize in 1942. Sinclair ran five times unsuccessfully on the Socialist party ticket between 1906 and 1930—for the House of Representatives, the Senate, and the governorship of California. He finally formulated the EPIC program—"End Poverty in California" and on this platform he narrowly missed winning the governorship of California (he appeared on the ballot on the Democratic ticket) in 1934. However, he succeeded in uniting unemployed workers with liberals and paved the way for a Democratic victory in 1938; he also was instrumental in establishing the American Civil Liberties Union (ACLU) in California. An autobiography, revised and enlarged from an early version of 1932, appeared in 1962. Sinclair died in Bound Brook, New Jersey, on November 25, 1968.

Singer, Isaac Bashevis (1904–   ), author. Born on July 14, 1904, in Radzymin, Poland, Singer was the son and grandson of rabbis, and his family intended that he become a rabbi. At four he moved to Warsaw, where his family lived in the Jewish ghetto and his father had a beth din, or rabbinical court, where the people came for discussion and settlement of problems in their religious and worldly lives. He began a traditional Jewish education, attending the Tachkemoni Rabbinical Seminary in Warsaw, but in the early 1920s followed the example of his older brother and became a journalist. He wrote first in Hebrew but soon turned to Yiddish. His stories and book reviews appeared in the Warsaw Yiddish journals *Literarishe Bleter* and *Globus*, the last of which he co-edited from 1932 until 1935, when he came to New York City. His articles, book reviews, and stories were published in the original Yiddish in the *Jewish Daily Forward* (regularly after 1943), and in other Yiddish papers throughout the world. He was soon established as the leading Yiddish writer of his time and a story teller in the tradition of Shalom Aleichem. His work, permeated by traditional Jewish folklore, legend, and mysticism, was sympathetic to the foibles and temptations of his fellow men, and frequently depicted life as he had known it in the Jewish towns of eastern Europe. Popular English versions of his novels included *The Family Moskat*, 1950; *The Magician of Lublin*, 1960; *The Manor*, 1967; and *The Estate*, 1969. English translations of his stories were collected in *Gimpel the Fool and Other Stories*, 1957; *The Spinoza of Market Street*, 1961; *Short Friday and Other Stories*, 1964; and *The Seance and Other Stories*, 1968. Among his children's books were *Mazel and Schlimazel; or, The Milk of a Lioness*, 1967, and *When Schlemiel Went to Warsaw and Other Stories*, 1968. In *My Father's Court*, 1966, was a volume of childhood reminiscences. He also contributed to popular English-language magazines. In 1978 Singer was awarded the Nobel Prize for Literature.

Singer, Isaac Merrit (1811–1875), inventor and manufacturer. Born on October 27, 1811, in Rensselaer County, New York, of German immigrant parents, Singer attended public schools in Oswego until he was twelve, then ran away from home and became an apprentice in a machine shop in Rochester. Between 1830 and 1850 he was a roving actor and occasional mechanic. Among his early inventions were a rock-boring device and a carver. In 1851 he had an opportunity to study a sewing machine and in 11 days built a greatly improved model, which he patented in August of that year. Powered by a foot treadle, it employed a horizontal table on which the material was spread, with a toothed rotating feed mechanism projecting through the table top. A vertical spring presser foot secured the material as the wheel fed and the vertically held needle stitched. The model made possible continuous sewing, both straight and curved, and also made it possible to stitch at any place on the material. But the needle he used, with the eye near its point, and also the lockstitch his machine used, had been patented in 1846 by Elias Howe, who in 1856, after three years of involved litigation, won the right to royalty payments from the four major sewing-machine producers, one of whom was Singer. Singer had gone into partnership in 1851 with an attorney, Edward Clark, and by 1860 they were the world's foremost sewing-machine manufacturers. Clark supervised advertising and marketing of the machine, introducing traveling salesmen, installment buying, and trade-in allowances to stimulate domestic buying. Singer continued to make and patent improvements on the machine. In 1863 the Singer Manufacturing Company was incorporated and Singer retired. He moved to England, to live in a palace (called the Wigwam), which he had built on the English coast. By the time he died, on July 23, 1875, in Torquay, England, his sewing machine had not only helped women with the chores of family sewing, but had also fostered a major industry.

Sinnott, Michael, *see* Sennett, Mack

Sinte-galeshka, *see* Spotted Tail

Sitting Bull (1831?–1890), Indian leader. Born about 1831 into the Hunkpapa Sioux, a Dakota Sioux tribe, on the Grand River in what is now South Dakota, Tatanka Iyotake, or Sitting Bull, son of Jumping Bull, was a warrior by the age of fourteen, and in about 1856 he became head of the Strong Heart warrior society. He was involved in conflict with the U.S. army after the so-called Minnesota Massacre of 1862, in which a band of Sioux under Little Crow protested white encroachments by killing more than 350 settlers. In 1866 he became chief of the northern hunting Sioux, with Crazy Horse, leader of the Oglala Sioux, as his vice-chief. In 1868 he accepted peace with the U.S. government on the basis of a guaranteed reservation north of the North Platte River, with the right to hunt off the reservation. But in 1874 gold was discovered in the Black Hills region, and miners and settlers poured into the Indian territory. Enraged by the incursions, Sioux, Arapaho, and Cheyenne assembled at Sitting Bull's encampment in Montana, eventually growing to a force estimated at 2500 to 4000 men, and in 1875 he was made head of the war council of the confederacy. He defied the army's order that the Sioux return to their reservations by the end of January 1876; he was said to have beheld visions of the subsequent battles in a Sun Dance that he performed in June 1876. On the 17th of that month, forces under the command of Gen. George Crook were defeated by Crazy Horse at the battle of the Rosebud; on the 25th, Col. George A. Custer was killed and his immediate command destroyed at the battle of the Little Bighorn, by warriors led by Crazy Horse and Gall, Sitting Bull's chief lieutenant and war chief. Sitting Bull, as was his function, "made medicine" during the battle and took no part in the fighting. When the Indians' encampment at Little Bighorn broke up, Sitting Bull led his remaining people to Canada in May 1877, but could not obtain assistance from the Canadian government. Suffering from famine and disease, he and 187 tribesmen returned to the United States and finally surrendered to the army in July 1881. He was imprisoned at Fort Randle for two years, then in 1883 moved to the Standing Rock Reservation. For a year he toured in Buffalo Bill's Wild West Show and became a legendary figure, but he never acquiesced to white rule or considered himself other than leader of the Sioux. He encouraged the religious agitation that swept a number of tribes about 1889 and led to the Ghost Dance uprising of the Sioux, and was ordered arrested. As Sioux warriors attempted to rescue him, he was shot by Indian police at Grand River on December 15, 1890. A few days later, the U.S. 7th Cavalry engaged in the so-called "battle," in reality a massacre of Sioux, at Wounded Knee, ending the resistance fostered by the Ghost Dance.

Skinner, Burrhus Frederic (1904–), psychologist. Born in Susquehanna, Pennsylvania, on March 20, 1904, B. F. Skinner graduated from Hamilton College in 1926. After taking his doctorate at Harvard in 1931, he remained at the university doing research until 1936. From 1936 to 1945 he taught at the University of Minnesota and during World War II did specialized research, training pigeons to guide missiles, for the Office of Scientific Research and Development. He taught psychology at the University of Indiana from 1945 to 1948 and then returned to Harvard. During his tenure at Harvard, Skinner became one of the most influential American psychologists through his work in behavioral psychology and his contributions to education. He invented the teaching machine and is considered to be the 'father' of programmed instruction. He endeavored to turn the study of behavior into an objective science. He wrote several books, two of which in particular attracted a wide audience outside academic circles: *Walden Two*, 1948, developed the idea of a utopian community operated according to the principles of behavioral engineering; *Beyond Freedom and Dignity*, 1971, asserted that freedom, as traditionally understood, is obsolete and that society should be based on a technology of behavior such that the individual's actions would be forced to serve the interest of the group, with the result that society could live without a continuation of crises. In the mid–1960s Skinner ceased his research activities to devote his full time to writing and lecturing. Among his other, more technical, books were *Science and Human Behavior*, 1953; *The Analysis of Behavior*, 1961; and *The Technology of Teaching*, 1968.

Skinner, Otis (1858–1942), actor. Born in Cambridge, Massachusetts, on June 28, 1858, Skinner worked as a clerk in Hartford until a visit to a New York City theater convinced him that he wanted to be an actor. After studying acting and working with amateur groups he made his professional debut in October 1877 playing the part of an elderly Negro in a play at the Philadelphia Museum. After a year he went to the Walnut Street Theater, then continued in other stock companies, making his New York City debut in 1879 at Niblo's Gardens and playing a season with Edwin Booth in 1880. From 1881 to 1884 he took juvenile roles with the Lawrence Barrett company, after which he spent five years with Augustin Daly's company. With Daly he visited England and the Continent in 1886, on the first of many tours abroad. From 1890 to 1902 he worked with Edwin Booth and Helena Modjeska, appearing opposite Mme Modjeska in several Shakespearean roles. Becoming one of the greatest character actors in the history of the American theater, Skinner eventually played more than 325 parts, in addition to his Shakespearean roles. By the turn of the century he was an established star, and went on to some of his greatest successes at the head of his own company. One of his most notable performances was in *Kismet*, 1911–1914, which he made into a movie in 1930. He also appeared in *A Celebrated Case*, 1914–1915; *Mister Antonio*, 1916–1918; *Blood and Sand*, 1921; *Sancho Panza*, 1923–1925; *Captain Fury of the Holy Innocents*, 1925, written by his daughter, Cornelia Otis Skinner; *The Merry Wives of Windsor*, 1927–1928; and *The Merchant of Venice*, 1931–1932, playing Shylock opposite Maude Adams. He last appeared on the stage in 1940. He had earlier published an autobiography, *Footlights and Spotlights* in 1924, and *Mad Folk of the Theatre* in 1928. He died in New York City on January 4, 1942.

Skouras, Spyros Panagiotes (1893–1971), motion-picture executive. Born in Skourokhóri, Greece, on March 28, 1893, Skouras emigrated to the United States in 1910 and settled in St. Louis. He was naturalized in 1913. For a few years he and his brothers, Charles and George, worked as busboys in a local hotel until they had saved enough money to buy into a movie theater that was not doing too well. By 1915 they owned the theater and it began to prosper. After service in World War I, Skouras returned to St. Louis, and by 1926 he and his brothers were operating 37 theaters there and in Kansas City and Indianapolis. The Warner Brothers movie studios bought their chain of theaters and put Spyros in charge of their operation. In 1931 he left Warners to work for Paramount, but in 1932 he moved to New York City to take over the failing chain of Fox-Metropolitan theaters. He returned the organization to a profit-making enterprise and became one of the creators of the Twentieth Century–Fox movie company, which was organized in 1935 as the result of a merger. In 1942 he became president of the company, a post he held until 1962. During his presidency he made Twentieth Century–Fox one of the dominant movie studios in Hollywood, in cooperation with Darryl F. Zanuck, who was in charge of production. Among the outstanding films made during his tenure were *The Ox-Bow Incident*, 1943; *Winged Victory*, 1944; *State Fair*, 1945; *Miracle on 34th Street*, 1947; *A Letter to Three Wives*, 1949; *All About Eve*, 1950; *Twelve O'Clock High*, 1950; *Gentlemen Prefer Blondes*, 1953; *Carousel*, 1956; *South Pacific*, 1958; *The Diary of Anne Frank*, 1959; and *The Hustler*, 1961. In the early 1950s, as movie audiences dwindled under the onslaught of television, Skouras countered with the slogan "Movies are better than ever" and attempted to illustrate the point by producing *The Robe*, 1953, the first CinemaScope wide-screen epic, taken from the novel by Lloyd C. Douglas. In 1962 the financial disaster wrought by *Cleopatra*, another costly production, cost Skouras the presidency of the studio. From 1962 until 1969 he was chairman of the board, and Zanuck took over as operating head. Twentieth Century–Fox later went heavily into the making of television films. Skouras left the studio in 1969 to look after other business interests. He died in Mamaroneck, New York, on August 16, 1971.

Slater, Samuel (1768–1835), inventor and manufacturer. Born on June 9, 1768, in Belper, Derbyshire, England, the son of a farmer, Slater was apprenticed in a factory making textile machinery in 1783. During his apprenticeship and later, as a supervisor of machinery construction in a mill, he learned of the need in the new United States for skilled mechanics and efficient textile machinery and he sailed for America in 1789 with the intricate plans for a modern cotton mill in his mind. Since trained mechanics were forbidden to leave England, nor in fact could machinery be exported, his departure was necessarily surreptitious. When he arrived in New York City, he was employed by the New York Manufacturing Company. Then he communicated with the Almy and Brown textile manufacturing firm in Providence, Rhode Island and was offered a consultantship which he accepted. Beginning in 1790, he reworked their machinery, reproducing the designs of Sir Richard Arkwright, inventor of the spinning frame, from the smallest tools to the most complex carding and spinning devices, and trained mechanics to execute

his intricate designs. The new mill was completed by 1793; under the firm name of Almy, Brown and Slater, it marked the beginning of the modern American textile industry. Meanwhile, Slater's wife had developed a fine thread from cotton that was more usable than linen thread, and Samuel Slater & Company opened a factory to manufacture it. With other relatives, Slater opened a textile plant near Pawtucket. By 1812 he controlled 12 companies—mills or factories—in New England. An eager teacher and a willing consultant to other industrialists, he was active in the cotton industry until his death in Webster, Massachusetts, on April 21, 1835.

Slidell, John (1793–1871), public official and Confederate diplomat. Born in New York City in 1793, Slidell graduated from Columbia College in 1810. He operated a business for a few years, and after it failed moved to New Orleans and practiced law from 1819 to 1835. After serving a term in the Louisiana state legislature he ran unsuccessfully for the House of Representatives on the Jackson ticket in 1828. From 1829 to 1833 he was district attorney for New Orleans. In 1842 he was elected to the House, was reelected in 1844, and served through most of the first year of his second term before being selected in 1845 by President James K. Polk as minister to Mexico in the critical weeks after the U.S. annexation of Texas. The main point of contention which Polk hoped to resolve was the boundary between Mexico and the United States, but Polk also was determined to gain California and New Mexico for the United States, peaceably if possible. Because the Mexican government was very unstable, the acting president, José Herrera, dared not receive Slidell for fear of seeming to make concessions; but Herrera's government fell anyway, and the new leader, Gen. Mariano Paredes, also refused to see Slidell. The start of the Mexican War soon negated the purpose of his mission. He returned to the United States and spent the next few years trying to win a seat from Louisiana in the Senate. Finally successful in 1853, he served until 1861. As a states'-rights Democrat, he devoted much effort to helping James Buchanan win the nomination for the presidency in 1856 and managed his successful campaign. As a consequence of his efforts he was highly influential in the Buchanan administration and helped select the Cabinet. He left the Senate in 1861 when the Southern states seceded from the Union and was chosen as the Confederate States' commissioner to France. Sailing in November 1861 aboard the British mail ship *Trent*, Slidell and James M. Mason, the Confederate commissioner to Great Britain, were both taken from the ship by the U.S. cruiser *San Jacinto*, captained by Charles Wilkes, and conveyed to Boston. The incident—the *Trent* Affair—caused tension between England and the United States that nearly led to war. But the two men were released in January 1862 and allowed to go to Europe. Slidell's mission at the court of Napoleon III was to win diplomatic recognition for the Confederacy and gain material help for the war, but his efforts were unsuccessful. After the Civil War he remained in France until 1870. Slidell died in Cowes, on the Isle of Wight, on July 29, 1871.

Slipher, Vesto Melvin (1875–1969), astronomer. Born on November 11, 1875, near Mulberry, Indiana, Slipher graduated from Indiana University in 1901 and took his Ph.D. there eight years later. In 1901 he joined the staff of the Lowell Observatory in Flagstaff, Arizona, with which he remained associated for the rest of his career, becoming director soon after the death of Percival Lowell in 1916. Much of Slipher's research concerned spectroscopic observations; in 1905 he obtained the first spectrographic records of the atmospheres of Jupiter and the other giant planets, a feat that soon led to the complete chemical analysis of the atmospheres of those planets, and in 1911–1912, working with Lowell, he used the spectroscope to determine the rotational period of Uranus. In 1912 he obtained evidence that many diffuse nebulas shine by reflected light rather than by incandescence or excitation. During the close approach of Mars in 1924 he made pioneering experiments in monochromatic photography, revealing many previously unnoticed surface features of the planet. He also organized and directed the search for the ninth planet, Pluto, whose existence William H. Pickering and Lowell had predicted earlier and which was finally discovered at the Lowell Observatory in 1930. Other advances made by Slipher included his discoveries of the phenomenon of the permanent sky, the presence of sodium and calcium in interstellar space, and, most notably, the rapid rotations and very great space velocities of nebulas, a finding that constituted the first direct observational evidence in favor of the theory of the expanding universe. Slipher retired as director of the observatory in 1952 and died in Flagstaff, Arizona, on November 8, 1969.

Sloan, John French (1871–1951), painter. Born in Lock Haven, Pennsylvania, on August 2, 1871, Sloan began studying art at sixteen in the evening classes of the Pennsylvania Academy of the Fine Arts, part of the time under Robert Henri. He did sketches for the *Philadelphia Press*, and sometimes drew the Sunday puzzles and cartoons for the paper. He produced illustrations for major magazines, including *Harper's*, *Scribner's*, *Everybody's*, and *Collier's*, and contributed to the *Masses* before the United States entered World War I. In 1904 he went to New York City; establishing himself in a Greenwich Village studio that was a gathering place of artists for three decades. His first fame—a kind of notoriety—was achieved in 1908 in an historic showing with Henri and seven other painters—the Eight, also dubbed the "Ashcan School" and "the apostles of ugliness." Although they did not share a style or constitute a formal movement, their common themes were city life—waterfronts, slums, and other scenes—depicted with uncompromising veracity. Several of the "Ashcan" painters helped organize the epoch-mak-

ing Armory Show of 1913, which introduced new trends in European art to the United States. Sloan also painted scenes of Santa Fe, New Mexico, the site of his summer studio, New England, and Philadelphia. He painted in both watercolors and oils, was an etcher and a book illustrator, and a teacher at the Art Students League from 1914 to 1930 and from 1932 to 1938. His notable paintings included "The Coffee Line," "Madison Square in a Dust Storm," "Bleecker Street on Saturday Night," "Scrubwomen in the Old Astor Library," "McSorley's Bar," "Sunday, Women Drying Their Hair," "Backyards, Greenwich Village," and "Spring in Washington Square." In 1939 he published the autobiographical critique, *The Gist of Art*. He also helped to organize the Society of Independent Artists and was its president for many years. He died in Hanover, New Hampshire, on September 8, 1951.

Sloat, John Drake (1781–1867), naval officer. Born in Goshen, New York, on July 26, 1781, Sloat joined the navy at nineteen and was appointed a midshipman. After brief service in the Caribbean during the undeclared naval war with France (1798–1800), he was discharged from the navy in 1801. For the next 11 years he was captain of a merchant vessel, but during the War of 1812 he was called back into the navy. He served on the *United States* under Stephen Decatur, and in 1813 was raised to the rank of lieutenant. After the war he spent a year in France, then returned to the United States and sea duty for most of the next 30 years. He received his first command in 1823, when he sailed on the schooner *Grampus* to suppress piracy in the region of the Windward Islands. In 1844 he became commander of the Pacific Squadron. From November 1845 until June 1846 he cruised off the west coast of Mexico; during that time he received orders from Secretary of the Navy George Bancroft to proceed to California if hostilities should break out with Mexico. On May 16, 1846, he learned from the U.S. consul at Mazatlán that fighting had begun along the Rio Grande in Texas (war had actually been declared by Congress on May 13). On June 7 Sloat ordered his squadron to sail for Monterey, California, where they arrived on July 2. Meanwhile settlers in the Sacramento Valley had carried out their Bear Flag Revolt against Mexico and set up the short-lived Republic of California at Sonoma. Col. John C. Frémont's forces had then taken over, declared California to be under martial law, and added the insurgents to his command, naming the combined force the California Battalion. After several days of uncertainty, and unaware of most of what was going on in California, Sloat decided to occupy Monterey, which he did on July 7. He also dispatched one of his officers to occupy San Francisco. He announced that he was taking possession of California for the United States, since the nation was at war with Mexico. He also notified Frémont of what he had done, and when Frémont arrived at Monterey, Sloat dismissed him and refused to accept his forces as a U.S. military unit.

Sloat, in poor health, was relieved of command at Monterey by Commodore Robert Stockton on July 23, and returned to Washington, D.C., arriving in November 1846. His conduct in California was variously praised, notably by Secretary of the Navy George Bancroft, and condemned on the contradictory grounds that he was dilatory in taking action and that he exceeded his authority. He spent the next nine years of his navy service on shore duty as commander of the navy yard at Norfolk, Virginia, and at Hoboken, New Jersey. He retired from the service in 1855 and while on the reserve list was promoted to the rank of rear admiral in 1866. He died on Staten Island, New York, on November 28, 1867.

Smalls, Robert (1839–1915), naval hero and public official. Born a slave in Beaufort, South Carolina, on April 5, 1839, Smalls had the benefit, uncommon for slaves, of rudimentary schooling. In 1851 he followed his master to Charleston, where he worked for wages and, in a short time, married. Impressed into the Confederate navy at the outbreak of the Civil War, he served as wheelman on the *Planter,* an armed frigate stationed in Charleston harbor. Smalls gained widespread fame in the North when during the early hours of May 13, 1862, taking advantage of the absence of white crewmen, he commandeered the *Planter,* slipped through the Confederate fortifications, and delivered the ship into Union hands. He thus gained freedom for himself and his wife, two children, and a dozen slave crewmen who accompanied him, in addition to prize money for his exploit. Appointed a pilot in the Union navy by President Abraham Lincoln, he later earned the rank of captain for his bravery under fire. From 1863 to 1866 he served as the highest-ranking black officer in the Union navy. After the war, his fame and moderate views helped him launch a successful career in South Carolina politics. Elected as a Republican to the state house of representatives in 1868, he went to the South Carolina senate in 1871 and to the U.S. House of Representatives in 1875. He served in the House, except during 1880–1881, until 1887, achieving some prominence as an advocate of civil-rights legislation. Smalls spent his last years in Beaufort, where he held the appointed post of collector of the port during 1889–1893 and 1897–1913; the lapse was owing to the incumbency of a Democrat, Grover Cleveland, as president. As a delegate to the state constitutional convention in 1895 he unsuccessfully fought the final erosion of the black political rights that had been won during Reconstruction. He died on February 22, 1915, in Beaufort, South Carolina.

Smibert, John (1688–1751), painter. Born in Edinburgh in 1688, Smibert was apprenticed as a house painter for seven years before moving to London, where, while working as a coach painter and copyist, he was able to study art for a few years. Failing to make a living at portrait painting after returning to Edinburgh, he went to Italy in 1717 to study in Florence and Rome. Returning to England in 1720, Smibert set to work as a portrait painter in London. In 1728 he was persuaded by his friend, the philosopher George Berkeley, later Bishop Berkeley, to go to the New World on the promise of teaching art in a college to be established in Bermuda. Smibert arrived in Newport, Rhode Island, with Berkeley early in 1729, but the next year settled in Boston. The teaching position having failed to materialize, he married and made his home permanently in Boston. He was moderately successful as a portrait painter, doing canvases of many of the colony's notable citizens. To supplement his income he opened a store to sell art supplies and prints by famous artists; by selling copies of European masters, Smibert contributed significantly to the art education of colonial Boston. By 1749, when the failure of his eyesight forced him to give up painting, he had executed about 200 works, mostly portraits of individuals. One of his best-known paintings was a group portrait, however: "Bishop Berkeley, Family, and Friends," painted in 1729 after landing at Newport. In 1742 he drew up the designs for Boston's Faneuil Hall. From 1749 he lived in retirement until his death on April 2, 1751, in Boston.

Smith, Alfred Emanuel (1873–1944), "Al," public official. Born in New York City on December 30, 1873, Smith received little formal education and worked at the Fulton Street fish market until he was taken into the fold of Tammany Hall in 1895. Given a minor political job that year, he supplemented his meager formal education with experience at close hand in the city's Democratic politics, and in 1903 he was elected to the state assembly, where he remained until 1915. He served as speaker during his last two years. In 1915 he became sheriff of New York County and two years later president of the New York City board of aldermen. In 1918 he ran for governor and won an upset victory over the Republican candidate. He was defeated for reelection in 1920, although he ran far ahead of the Democratic presidential candidate. He turned to business for a time, as head of the United States Trucking Corporation, but in 1922 again entered the governor's race and was elected; reelected in 1924 and 1926, he was the first man to serve four terms as governor of New York in modern times. His administrations were honest and efficient government operations. Al Smith himself was a colorful character with picturesque, low-key speech and ever-present derby hat and cigar; as a Roman Catholic and an outspoken opponent of Prohibition, however, he was hampered in his ambition for national office. He was a contender for the presidential nomination at the 1924 Democratic national convention and was deadlocked with William G. McAdoo until John W. Davis was selected as a compromise candidate on the 103rd ballot. In 1928 Smith won the nomination on the first ballot and, dubbed "the Happy Warrior" by his protégé, Franklin D. Roosevelt, conducted a vigorous campaign; antipathy to his religious affiliation, his big-city political background, and his stand on Prohibition lost him support in rural areas and, combined with the continuing "Republican prosperity," led to his defeat by Herbert Hoover. His later years were unhappy, marked by financial setbacks and a major break with Roosevelt over the policies of the New Deal. In 1929 he published a volume of memoirs, *Up to Now*. He died on October 4, 1944, in New York City.

Smith, Bessie (1898?–1937), singer. Born in Chattanooga, Tennessee, probably on April 15, 1898 (but perhaps 1894), Miss Smith grew up in poverty and obscurity. She may have made a first public appearance at the age of ten. When she was thirteen she was discovered by "Ma" Rainey, one of the first of the great blues singers, from whom she received some training. For several years she traveled through the South singing in bars and theaters in such small towns and in cities as Birmingham, Atlanta, Selma, Memphis, and Savannah. After 1920 she made her home in Philadelphia, and it was there that she was first heard by the recording director of Columbia Records. In 1923 she made her first record, "Down Hearted Blues," which became an enormous success, selling more than 2 million copies. She continued her stage appearances in the cities of the North, and enjoyed a successful recording career, being often accompanied by some of the great jazz musicians of the time, including Benny Goodman and Louis Armstrong. Her idiom was the classic material of blues singers—poverty, oppression, stoic perseverance, and love. As the kind of music she sang began to diminish in popularity, her career waned in the late 1920s. This, combined with excessive drinking and the breakup of her marriage, nearly destroyed her career. When a revival of jazz during the Depression of the 1930s gave hope of a renewed career, she planned on making more records. But she was injured in an automobile accident near Clarksdale, Mississippi, and refused admittance to a segregated hospital for whites only, she bled to death on September 26, 1937. It was only decades after her death that, through the few precious recordings she left, she was recognized as one of the greatest of blues singers.

Smith, Charles Henry (1826–1903), "Bill Arp," author. Born on June 15, 1826, in Lawrenceville, Georgia, Smith attended Franklin College in Athens until 1848, studied law, and was admitted to the Georgia bar in 1849. A staunch partisan of the South and a keen political observer, he left his practice to enlist in the Confederate army in 1861. During the first year of the Civil War, a series of letters began to appear in the Rome, Georgia, newspaper, the *Southern Confederacy*, addressed to "Mr. Abe Linkhorn" from a "Bill Arp." They purportedly expressed the opinions of a foolhardy Northerner and sympathized with Yankee aims, but in fact, by means of a contrived ineptitude, they shrewdly satirized the North. As the letters continued and appeared in other papers, including the *Atlanta Constitution* and the *Louisville Home and Farm*, they gradually dropped the comic devices of dialect and misspelling and began to rely on acute commentary and direct satire to express their author's opinions on women's rights, Negroes in America, the income tax, agricultural policies, and other issues. The character of Arp evolved at the same time into that of a benign cracker-barrel philosopher. The letters were popular and eagerly anticipated by many ordinary folk, who found their own views reinforced by Bill Arp's homespun philosophizing. Smith was elected to the Georgia state senate in 1865 and became mayor of Rome in 1868. He continued his law practice until 1877, after which he devoted the rest of his life to writing. His works were compiled in such books as *Bill Arp, So Called*, 1866; *Bill Arp's Peace Papers*, 1873; *Bill Arp's Scrap Book*, 1884; *The Farm and Fireside*, 1891; and *Bill Arp: From the Uncivil War to Date*, 1903. He died in Cartersville, Georgia, on August 24, 1903.

Smith, David (1906–1965), sculptor. Born in Decatur, Indiana, on March 9, 1906, Smith attended Ohio University and the George Washington University. From 1922 to 1932 he studied in New York City at the Art Students League. It was during summer jobs as a riveter and spot-welder for the Studebaker plant in South Bend that he found his career as an artist working with metal. He had intended to be a painter, but in 1933 he abandoned painting for sculpture. He rented space in a machine shop in Brooklyn, New York, and began turning out abstract metal sculptures in the style of Picasso. In 1935 he traveled through Europe studying art. In 1940 he moved to Bolton Landing, New York, where for 25 years he operated his "sculpture farm." He worked mostly with iron and steel, forging, welding, and riveting them into increasingly more abstract works, and also developing "line-drawing" sculptures made from strips of flat steel welded together. In the late 1950s he went from executing small table-top sculptures to much larger pieces, several feet high. His first one-man show was in 1938 at the East River Gallery in New York City. Others followed in cities throughout the country, and his works are in the collections of major museums and galleries. Smith also taught art at several institutions, including Sarah Lawrence College, Indiana University, and the University of Mississippi. He died on May 24, 1965, in Albany, New York, following an automobile accident.

Smith, Francis Marion (1846–1931), miner and financier. Born in Richmond, Walworth County, Wisconsin, on February 2, 1846, Smith lived on the family farm until he was twenty-one, except for his high-school years. In 1867 he went to the Far West to follow the mining boom, and in 1872 while working in Columbus, Nevada, he and his partner, William Tell Coleman, discovered deposits of a mineral from which borax is derived, subsequently named colemanite. They gained control of the deposits, organized the Pacific Coast Borax Company, and gained a virtual world monopoly on the manufacture and marketing of borax. Smith also acquired borax deposits in Death Valley, California. The hauling of the mineral in huge mule-drawn wagons gave the product a brand trade-mark by which it became nationally known: "Twenty-Mule Team Borax." With his fortune from borax, Smith invested heavily in utilities and real estate in the San Francisco Bay area, but mis-management of these affairs had led him to bank-ruptcy by 1920. He attempted to build up his re-sources again during the 1920s, but died, on August 27, 1931, at Oakland, before he could succeed.

Smith, Gerrit (1797–1874), philanthropist and social reformer. Born into a wealthy family in Utica, New York, on March 6, 1797, Smith grad-uated from Hamilton College in 1818. He studied law, but spent the greater part of his life managing the family fortune and disbursing much of it to various philanthropies for the benefit of the poor. As a reformer he supported most of the liberal movements of the day, such as temperance, wom-en's rights, and in particular the antislavery crusade. He was active in the Underground Rail-road, helping slaves to escape into Canada. Re-garding politics as an avenue of obtaining reform, he was part of various third-party movements prior to the Civil War. He helped to start the anti-slavery Liberty party in 1840, and was its candi-date for governor of New York that year. In 1852 he was elected to the House of Representatives for one term on an ultra-abolitionist, independent tick-et. He was admitted to the bar in 1853, the same year his term in the House of Representatives began; in August 1854 he resigned from the House to take up a law practice at Peterboro, Madison County, New York. He advocated the use of force against the proslavery forces in Kansas and in 1858 he became involved with John Brown and gave him financial support; he may have had knowledge (although he denied it later) of the plan that eventuated in Brown's raid on the federal arsenal at Harpers Ferry in October 1859. During the Civil War Smith became a Republican and supported Abraham Lincoln for reelection in 1864. Smith took a moderate position on Reconstruction, advocating Negro suffrage and reconciliation. In 1872 he was a delegate to the Republican national convention, where he supported Ulysses S. Grant. He died in New York City on December 28, 1874.

Smith, Gladys Mary, *see* Pickford, Mary

Smith, Hoke (1855–1931), public official. Born in Newton, North Carolina, on September 2, 1855, Smith studied law in Atlanta and was admitted to the bar in 1873. He practiced law and also en-gaged in state Democratic politics, which gradually captured most of his interest. In 1887 he bought the *Atlanta Journal* and controlled the paper until 1900. Although a white supremacist on the race issue, he espoused most of the reform and pro-gressive movements of the time and vented his opinions freely through the columns of his paper. His strong support for Grover Cleveland in the

campaign of 1892 brought him the post of Cleve-land's secretary of the interior from 1893 to 1896. He resigned in the latter year to support William Jennings Bryan's presidential candidacy, despite Bryan's stand on the silver issue. He then went back to his law practice and to the *Journal* (which, although he sold it in 1900, remained under his influence), until 1906, when he ran for governor of Georgia. The main exception to Smith's progressive views was his vehement anti-Negro position; like many other Southerners, he urged the disenfranchisement of blacks. He was elected to the governorship in 1906 and in 1910, two nonconsecutive terms. During his tenure he was successful in getting much of his reform pro-gram enacted in Georgia, particularly in educa-tion, internal improvements, railroad regulation, prohibition, and prison reform. He also got a voting law that in effect took the suffrage away from blacks. At the start of his second term in July 1911, Smith was elected to fill an unexpired term in the U.S. Senate. He served in the Senate until March 1921, winning election to a full term in 1914. He was defeated for renomination by Thomas E. Watson in 1920. While in the Senate he furthered the same kind of progressive legisla-tion that he had espoused as a governor, making great contributions to the spread of vocational education throughout the country and into rural districts, but in foreign policy he disagreed with President Woodrow Wilson on the League of Nations. After he left office he maintained a law practice in Washington, D.C., and in Atlanta, until his death in the latter city on November 27, 1931.

Smith, Jedediah Strong (1799–1831), explorer and fur trader. Born on January 6, 1799, in Jericho (now Bainbridge), New York, Smith received a basic elementary education before going to work in the Lake Erie trade. At a date unknown he went to St. Louis to join a fur-trading expedition into the West; his first journey was made in 1822 as part of the William H. Ashley–Andrew Henry Rocky Mountain venture that effectively brought under American control the vast fur territory out-side of the English-dominated Oregon country. He ascended the Missouri again with the Ashley-Henry party in 1823, and early the next year, with Thomas Fitzpatrick, rediscovered the South Pass, a major gateway to the Northwest in what is now Wyoming (the original discovery, made some years earlier, had not been adequately re-ported). In 1826, after further explorations and trading expeditions in the mountains, Smith and two partners bought out Ashley's interests and formed a trading company at Great Salt Lake, Utah. That year he led a party from Great Salt Lake across the deserts into Southern California; from San Gabriel he then journeyed northward to the American River (just east of Sacramento), and in May 1827 crossed the Sierra Nevada and the deserts of the Great Basin back to Great Salt Lake, the first man to follow that route. Later in the year he retraced his path to San Gabriel, sur-viving an attack by Mojave Indians, and up to the Sacramento Valley; the next spring, contrary to the wishes of the Mexican government, he continued northwest, then north along the coast to Fort Vancouver on the Columbia River in Oregon, opening up the coastal route to that territory and remaining until the spring of 1829. In 1830 he and his partners sold their fur-trading interests to a new company organized by Jim Bridger, Fitzpatrick, and others and in 1831 he joined the Santa Fe trade. Smith was killed by Comanche Indians on the Cimarron River on May 27, 1831, en route to Santa Fe. His explorations were exceeded in importance only by those of Lewis and Clark; but his geographical discoveries were passed on orally among other mountain men and long remained unknown to others, while his maps were published in obscure works and also remained virtually unknown for years. As westward migration increased Smith's achievements became more widely known; he was the first American explorer to enter California from the east, the first to explore on land the northern California–Oregon coast, and he was the first to cross the Sierra Nevada from west to east.

Smith, John (1580?–1631), explorer and colonizer. Born about 1580 in Willoughby, Lincolnshire, England, Smith attended school until the age of fifteen, then was apprenticed to a wealthy merchant. He began to travel in Europe at the age of sixteen and four years later joined the fighting in Transylvania, where he was taken prisoner and made a slave by the Turks. He escaped, traveled further in Russia and Europe, and returned to England in 1604. In London he learned of the London (or South Virginia) Company and actively promoted its plan to found a colony in America. He sailed in 1606 and arrived with the first settlers in 1607, helping to found Jamestown, Virginia. He was appointed to the governing council and began to explore the region. He ventured alone many times into Indian territory to obtain food. On one occasion he was captured by Indians and was sentenced to death by their chief, Powhatan, and escaped death only by the intervention of Powhatan's daughter, Pocahontas. On his return to Jamestown in 1608 he found the government in the hands of personal enemies, and he was sentenced to be hanged for having lost the men of his exploring party. New settlers and needed supplies arrived at the straitened colony shortly thereafter and he was released and restored to his position on the council. In that year he published in England his *True Relation of Such Occurrences and Accidents of Noate as Hath Hapned in Virginia since the First Planting of That Colony.* In 1608 he was elected president of the colony and with great resourcefulness brought if through many hardships. He was constantly involved in quarrels over leadership, and, principally because of a severe injury, he finally returned to England in 1609. In 1614 he returned to America and for Sir Fernando Gorges and the Plymouth (North Virginia) Company, explored the coast of the region he named New England, returning to

Britain with a cargo of fish and furs. He became a strong advocate of colonization of New England and publicized its attractions widely. In 1615, on his way again to New England, he was captured by pirates, with whom he was forced to remain for several months. During this time he wrote *A Description of New England*, published in 1616, which included in its pages the most accurate map of the region yet produced. It provided a rosy picture of New England and was later instrumental in attracting settlers. When released, he returned to England and offered his services as a guide to the Pilgrims, but they felt his books and maps would give sufficient guidance. He remained in England thereafter, actively promoting colonization and persuading settlers to emigrate. In 1624 he published a *Generall Historie of Virginia, New England and the Summer Isles* and in 1630 *The True Travels, Adventures, and Observations of Captaine John Smith in Europe, Asia, Africa and America.* He died in London in June 1631.

Smith, Joseph (1805–1844), religious leader and founder of the Church of Jesus Christ of Latter-Day Saints. Born in Sharon, Vermont, on December 23, 1805. Smith moved with his parents to Palmyra, New York, in 1816. Little is known of his childhood; by his own account he was subject from about 1820 onward to visions in which God or Jesus Christ would grant revelations of true Christianity to him. In one of these visions he was directed to a hill near Manchester, New York, where he found golden plates on which was inscribed the history of the true church in America, as carried by ancient Indian descendants of lost Hebrew tribes. He deciphered the inscriptions, written in "reformed Egyptian," by magical means, and published them as *The Book of Mormon* in 1830. The book reflected the current social, political, and religious ferment of Smith's time and region and combined these elements with Indian legend in a work of quasi-biblical style that is remarkable, considering Smith's presumably rudimentary education. On April 6, 1830, he organized the Church of Jesus Christ of Latter-Day Saints and began immediately to win converts. The next year he led his congregation to Kirtland, Ohio. Church polity, as outlined in *A Book of Commandments for the Government of the Church of Christ*, 1833, and *Doctrine and Covenants of the Church of the Latter-Day Saints*, 1835, involved church ownership of all property, exercised for the communal good; the vesting of all power in the church; and the ultimate authority of the church's president—Smith—to whom alone was vouchsafed direct revelation. In 1838 the Mormons journeyed to western Missouri, but friction with other settlers forced them to leave and they established themselves anew in Illinois, at Commerce, a settlement renamed Nauvoo by Smith. There the church was granted considerable autonomy by the state, even to the point of maintaining its own courts and militia. Again there was constant trouble with non-Mormon neighbors—termed "Gentiles" by the Mormons—generated particularly by rumors of polygamy (Smith apparently followed this practice pursuant to a revelation in 1831, and his report of a second revelation in 1843 contributed to the start of a schism, but the doctrine of multiple marriage was not publicly proclaimed until 1852 by his successor, Brigham Young), and by the communalism and the impressive size of the colony. By 1844 Nauvoo held about 18,000 Mormons and Smith's ambitions had grown to include the presidency, for which he declared his candidacy in February of that year. In June of 1844 a group of dissenting Mormons published an attack on Smith and he ordered their press destroyed. He and his brother Hyrum were imprisoned in Carthage, Illinois, and on June 27, 1844, were dragged from the jail by a mob of non-Mormons and shot. There followed a schism in Mormon ranks, and control of the major group passed to Brigham Young, who led the subsequent Mormon emigration to the West in 1846. Many others followed James Jesse Strang, but disillusionment with his leadership led in 1852 to the organization of the Church of Jesus Christ of Latter-Day Saints (to which the word Reorganized was added in 1869) and the election in 1860 of Joseph Smith III (1832–1914), a son of the founder, as president.

Smith, Kate (1909–   ), entertainer. Born in Greenville, Augusta County, Virginia, on May 1, 1909, Kathryn Elizabeth Smith started singing before audiences as a child, and by the time she was seventeen had decided on a career in showbusiness. She went to New York City in 1926 and landed a role in a musical, *Honeymoon Lane,* the same year. In a succession of Broadway shows she had little chance to sing, however; she was wanted mainly for comic "fat-girl" parts, roles she despised, but they were better than not acting at all. Her chance as a full-time singer came when she met Ted Collins, an executive with Columbia Records, in 1930. He became her manager and guided her career until his death in 1964. She appeared at the Palace Theater in New York City for a record engagement, then in 1931 made her radio debut. It was on this program that she adopted her theme song, "When the Moon Comes over the Mountain." In 1936 she moved to a weekly half-hour evening show hosted by Collins, and in 1938 added a daytime talk program, broadcast three times a week. During the 1930s her evening show became one of the most popular; in the 1940s she was known as the First Lady of Radio. In 1938 she had acquired the exclusive right to sing Irving Berlin's "God Bless America" over the air, and it was this song, more than any other, with which her name was thereafter associated. In 1943 she appeared in the movie version of *This Is the Army,* an Irving Berlin musical. During World War II she performed notable service by selling more war bonds than anyone else —$600 million worth—and she entertained troops continuously. Miss Smith remained on daytime radio until 1954, and in 1950 went on television with "The Kate Smith Hour," also a daytime

show. In the 1952–1953 season she added an evening hour-long show. After 1956 she retired from television, although she did return for a season in 1960.

Smith, Nathan (1762–1829), physician and educator. Born in Rehoboth, Massachusetts, on September 30, 1762, Smith grew up in Chester, Vermont. As a youth he decided to go into medicine, and after private study under a physician and two years of practice in Cornish, New Hampshire, he studied further at Harvard's medical school in 1789–1790 and then resumed practice at Cornish. As his practice expanded during the 1790s, he became aware of the need for more and better medical training in the United States. Having resolved to teach medicine himself, he studied in England and Scotland for a year, and in 1797 began to give a course of lectures at Dartmouth College. He remained at Dartmouth until 1813, then accepted an appointment as professor of theory and practice of medicine, surgery, and obstetrics at Yale. During most of his teaching career, Smith kept up his medical practice in New England and gained a reputation as a leading and pioneering surgeon and as a diagnostician. In 1821 he performed what he believed was the first ovariotomy in the United States; it was later learned that he had been preceded by Ephraim McDowell of Kentucky. His fame increased after his death, however, for he was much ahead of his time in the classification and treatment of diseases and laid great stress on experiment and observation as a counter to widely accepted, traditional, but often untenable theories. In large part the founder of the Yale Medical School, he also helped to establish medical departments at Bowdoin College, where he lectured each summer from 1821 to 1826, and at the University of Vermont. Among his written works were *A Treatise on Febrile Diseases,* 1816, and his classic *Practical Essay on Typhous Fever,* 1824. From 1824 to 1826 he edited the *American Medical Review.* He remained at Yale until his death in New Haven, Connecticut, on January 26, 1829. He had four sons, all of whom became physicians.

Smith, Red, *see* Smith, Walter Wellesley

Smith, Robert Barnwell, *see* Rhett, Robert Barnwell

Smith, Samuel Francis (1808–1895), author and poet. Born in Boston on October 21, 1808, Smith graduated from Harvard College in 1829 and from Andover Theological Seminary in 1832. After being ordained in 1834, he served as pastor at Waterville, Maine, until 1842 and also taught at the institution that is now Colby College. From 1842 to 1854 he served a Baptist parish at Newton Center, Massachusetts, then became editorial secretary of the American Baptist Missionary Union. But Smith's fame rests less on his activities as a clergyman than on his accomplishments as a writer. He was an author of poetry and of prose works and a composer of hymns. For the missionary efforts of his church he wrote one of the best-known hymns by an American composer, "The Morning Light Is Breaking." In 1883 he published *Rambles in Mission Fields*, based on his tours of countries where the Baptists had foreign missions. His collected verse appeared as *Poems of Home and Country* in 1895. He is most of all remembered as the composer of the national hymn, "America," written in 1832, while he was still a seminary student. Asked to write a song for a children's choir, Smith took a tune from a German hymnbook and set down the familiar stanzas that begin "My country 'tis of thee." In spite of the fact that the music was also that of the British national anthem, the song gained immediate and enduring popularity. Smith died in Boston on November 16, 1895.

Smith, Seba (1792–1868), "Major Jack Downing," journalist and humorist. Born in Buckfield, Maine, on September 14, 1792, Smith graduated from Bowdoin College in 1818. He taught school for a few months, then traveled to Europe. Returning to Maine in 1820, he became an editor for the *Eastern Argus* at Portland, remaining in the position until 1826. In 1829 he founded his own newspaper, the nonpartisan *Portland Courier*, Maine's first daily. It was in the columns of the *Courier* in 1830 that he began publishing his satirical letters purportedly written by "Major Jack Downing." Downing was pictured as a rustic, commonsensical type who, as an adviser to President Andrew Jackson, was able to make shrewd, humorous, but nonpartisan comments on the workings of democracy. The popularity of the Downing letters led other writers to adopt both the character of Downing and Smith's humorous devices, but the imitators, especially Charles Augustus Davis, were usually more partisan in their sentiments. In 1833 Smith published his Downing letters in book form as *The Life and Writings of Major Jack Downing of Downingville*. In 1847 Smith began another series of letters for the *Daily National Intelligencer* and in 1859 these were published, along with some earlier ones, in *My Thirty Years Out of the Senate*; the title was a satirical allusion to Senator Thomas Hart Benton's autobiography, *Thirty Years' View*. Another popular work of Smith's was *Way Down East*, 1854, a series of stories depicting the New England Yankee character. Business losses caused Smith to move temporarily to South Carolina in 1839, but he was soon back in New York City as an editor and writer. He worked on several magazines, including the *Rover* and the *United States Magazine*, and had a journal of his own called the *Great Republic* in 1859–1860. During the 1860s he lived in retirement in Patchogue, Long Island, New York, where he died on July 28, 1868.

Smith, Theobald (1859–1934), pathologist. Born in Albany, New York, on July 31, 1859, Smith graduated from Cornell University in 1881 and from Albany Medical College in 1883. In 1884 he became director of the pathological laboratory of the U.S. Bureau of Animal Industry at Washington, D.C., and in 1886 he organized the nation's first department of bacteriology and from then until 1895 was professor of bacteriology at Columbian (now The George Washington) University. From 1895 to 1915 he was simultaneously professor of pathology at Harvard Medical School and director of the pathological laboratory of the Massachusetts State Board of Health. In 1915 he went to Princeton, New Jersey, as director of the department of animal pathology of the Rockefeller Institute for Medical Research (now Rockefeller University), a post he held until his retirement in 1929. A specialist in the causes and transmission of infectious diseases, Smith was also a pioneer in the field of immunology and did pioneering work on swine plague and hog cholera. One of his notable achievements was establishing the distinction between the bacillus of human tuberculosis and that of the bovine strain. In his work on animal pathology he demonstrated how Texas fever among cattle was carried by parasites from one animal to another. His work also pointed the way to later discoveries of the carriers of such diseases as malaria, typhoid fever, and yellow fever. He also demonstrated the value for immunology of killed cultures of the bacteria of a disease. He died in Princeton, New Jersey, on December 10, 1934.

Smith, Walker, *see* Robinson, Ray

Smith, Walter Bedell (1895–1961), soldier. Born in Indianapolis on October 5, 1895, Smith began his military career in the Indiana National Guard. In 1917 he attended officers' training school and was commissioned a second lieutenant. After service in Europe during World War I, he returned to duty with the Bureau of Military Intelligence at Washington, D.C., and then was stationed at various training camps and held staff appointments; from 1929 to 1931 he did a tour of duty in the Philippines. During the 1930s he both studied and taught at the Infantry School at Fort Benning, Georgia, and in 1937 he graduated from the Army War College. In 1939 he was promoted to the rank of major and assigned to the General Staff of the War Department. From February to September 1942 he served as secretary to the Combined Chiefs of Staff, and in the latter month went to Europe as Gen. Dwight D. Eisenhower's chief of staff, holding that post until 1946. Reaching the rank of major general in August 1945, Smith took part in both the Italian and German surrender ceremonies. In December 1945 President Harry S. Truman appointed him ambassador to the Soviet Union, in which post he served for three years. On the basis of his experiences in the postwar Soviet Union he wrote the book, *My Three Years in Moscow*, 1950. From March 1949 Smith commanded the First Army, with headquarters at Governors Island in New York City. President Truman appointed him director of the newly formed Central Intelligence Agency (CIA) in 1950. He served as director until Eisenhower became president in January 1953, at which time Smith became under secretary of state. In October 1954 he retired from government service and entered the business world; he continued to serve as a government consultant during the two Eisenhower administrations, however, and in 1956 he published *Eisenhower's Six Great Decisions*. Smith died in Washington, D.C., on August 9, 1961.

Smith, Walter Wellesley (1905–1982), "Red," journalist. Born in Green Bay, Wisconsin, on September 25, 1905, Smith graduated from Notre Dame in 1927 and, after working for the *Milwaukee Sentinel* for a year, went to St. Louis to join the staff of the *St. Louis Star*. It was while he was with the *Star* that he first began to write on sports, and sportswriting soon became his career. He left the *Star* in 1936 and moved to the *Philadelphia Record*, remaining until 1945, in which year he was hired by the *New York Herald Tribune* to write the column "Views of Sport," which was soon syndicated throughout the nation. One of the first sports journalists to discard the traditional sentimental and hero-worshiping attitude toward his subjects, Smith, with sardonic humor and obviously profound knowledge of various games, soon came to be considered one of the best sportswriters in the United States, if not absolutely the best. He was the recipient of numerous journalistic honors, including the Grantland Rice Memorial Award in 1956. When the *Herald Tribune* finally died in 1967, his column continued to be syndicated. He died on January 15, 1982, in Stamford, Connecticut.

Smith, William (1727–1803), educator. Born in Aberdeen, Scotland, on September 7, 1727, Smith graduated from the University of Aberdeen in 1747. He emigrated to New York City in 1751 to work as a tutor and was soon involved in the planning of a proposed college in New York. His educational proposals won the interest of Benjamin Franklin and a position on the faculty of the Philadelphia Academy, but before beginning his duties there he returned to London and was ordained a priest in the Church of England. He began teaching at the academy in 1754, and the following year, when the school became the College and Academy of Philadelphia under a new charter he had helped draw up, he became its first provost, a position he held until 1779. As a man with a wide range of interests, social and political, Smith became active in the affairs of Pennsylvania. He helped to establish schools among the Germans of the province, in order to facilitate their becoming loyal British subjects. As a churchman, he advocated an American episcopate to direct ecclesiastical affairs in the colonies. A staunch supporter of Britain during the last French and Indian War (the Seven Years' War), he sharply criticized the laxness of Pennsylvania officials in military matters. For one year, 1757–1758, he edited the *American Magazine and Monthly Chronicle*, published to support the interests of the king and the Penn family but also one of the best literary periodicals in colonial America. In 1758 he got into political difficulties in Pennsylvania, was accused of seditious libel, and was twice jailed. To vindicate himself he sailed for England, and the charge was voided. He returned to his position at the college in 1759, and three years later returned to England on a successful fund-raising trip for the college. From 1766 to 1777, in addition to his other duties, he served as rector of a parish in Oxford, Pennsylvania. In 1777, when British forces were about to seize Philadelphia, he was detained as a suspected Loyalist, so he left the city and lived for a year on the island of Barbados in the West Indies. When in 1779 the Pennsylvania legislature revoked the charter of the College of Philadelphia and founded the University of Pennsylvania, Smith moved to Chestertown, Maryland, as rector of a parish. He founded there a school, later chartered (1782) as Washington College, of which he became the first president. He also remained active in the affairs of the Protestant Episcopal church, as it came to be called in 1789. In 1789 the charter of the College of Philadelphia was restored, and Smith returned to his post as provost. When the college became part of the University of Pennsylvania in 1791, Smith retired; he died in Philadelphia on May 14, 1803.

Smohalla (1815?–1907), Indian religious leader. Born in the present state of Washington about 1815, Smohalla was a Wanapum Indian whose people lived near the Columbia River in the present Yakima County. His fame as a medicine man earned him the jealousy and enmity of the chief of a nearby band, and in an encounter Smohalla was believed by his people to have been killed. He survived, however, and spent several years wandering through the Southwest and northern Mexico. His sudden reappearance among his tribesmen had the effect of a miracle, and he was regarded as one brought back from the dead. He used his newfound prestige during the early 1870s to spread what has been called the Dreamer religion among the Indians of the Northwest. A hostile reaction to white civilization, Smohalla's tenets encouraged his followers to believe that one day all whites would be defeated and driven from the region and nature would be restored to what it was when the Indians occupied the land. Making use of hypnotic drumbeats and dancing, the religion had many points in common with the more widespread Ghost Dance religion promulgated by Wovoka in 1889–1890. Smohalla promised a general resurrection of the Indian dead and devised a ritual drawn from both tribal mythology and Christian sources. Probably the single greatest effect of the Dreamer religion was the Nez Percé revolt of 1877, led by Chief Joseph. Among the Indians of the Northwest Smohalla's beliefs served to hinder for a long time the acceptance of white society and its customs. Smohalla died in 1907.

Snead, Samuel Jackson (1912–   ), golfer. Born in Hot Springs, Virginia, on May 27, 1912, Sam

Snead grew up on the family farm. He was an all-round athlete in high school, but working as a caddy at the local golf course predisposed him to becoming a professional golfer. He entered the ranks of the professionals in 1935, and by 1937 had become the biggest attraction in Professional Golfers' Association (PGA) tournaments. By 1938 he was the game's biggest money winner, drawing large crowds wherever he played. He repeated as leading money winner in 1949 and 1950. In 1938, 1940, and 1941 he won the Canadian Open. Of the major tournaments, the only one Snead did not win was the United States Open, although he was several times a runner-up. In 1938 he also won the Harry Vardon Trophy, awarded each year to the player with the lowest average score in PGA-sanctioned tourneys. He won the PGA championship in 1942, 1949, and 1951, and the Masters in 1949, 1952, and 1954. In 1946 he was the first American golfer in 13 years to win the British Open. Snead earned the Vardon Trophy again in 1949, 1950, and 1955. Credited with having the finest natural swing in golf while he was active in tournaments, "Slammin' Sammy" as he was nicknamed, won more than 100 championships altogether. In 1960 and 1962 he teamed with Arnold Palmer to win the Canada Cup, a trophy he also won in 1961, with Jimmy Demaret as partner. In 1963 Snead played in his first seniors' tournament at Palm Beach Gardens, Florida, and won the Teacher Trophy. In 1953 he was elected to the PGA Hall of Fame. He retired from tournament play in the late 1960s and thereafter lived in Florida and taught golf.

Sorin, Edward Frederick (1814–1893), religious leader and educator. Born in Ahuillé, near Laval, France, on February 6, 1814, Sorin was ordained a priest in 1838. In 1840 he joined the newly formed Congregation of the Holy Cross, under whose auspices he and six others were sent to the region of present-day Vincennes, Indiana, to promote Roman Catholic missions. Arriving in Indiana in October 1841, he started his work in Daviess County, but within a year had been sent to South Bend with instructions to found a college. He began his work at South Bend in November 1842, and two years later the Indiana legislature granted a charter for the University of Notre Dame. Sorin became the first president of the new school and remained in that post until 1865, at which time he became chairman of the board of trustees. In 1868 he became superior general of his order. In addition to his work in founding Notre Dame, Sorin brought to the United States a group of the Sisters of the Holy Cross, whose community he located at Bertand, Michigan, in 1844 and moved to South Bend in 1854. The sisters, headed by the famed Mother Angela (Eliza Maria Gillespie), founded the academy which in 1903 became St. Mary's College. In 1865 Father Sorin began the publication of the magazine *Ave Maria* for Catholic laymen. He died on October 31, 1893. In after years his statue on the Notre Dame campus was stolen annually by the students, earning it the title of "peripatetic statue."

Sorokin, Pitirim Alexandrovitch (1889–1968), sociologist. Born in Touria, Russia, on January 21, 1889, Sorokin attended the teachers college in Kostroma Province and the Psycho-Neurological Institute in St. Petersburg before earning his doctorate at the University of Petrograd (St. Petersburg) in 1922. The years from 1917 to 1922 were hectic ones for Sorokin, for he played an active role in the Russian Revolution, in which he opposed the Bolshevik party of V. I. Lenin and Leon Trotsky. In 1917 he edited the pro-Revolutionary paper *Volia Naroda* (Free People) and was secretary to Alexander Kerenski after the Provisional Government was organized. Twice during 1918 he was arrested for anti-Bolshevik activity and was only saved from execution by Lenin's orders. From 1919 to 1922 he taught at the University of Petrograd and at the Agricultural Academy. With the publication of his *System of Sociology* in 1921 he was censured by the government, forbidden to teach, and finally, banished from the country. He spent 1922–1923 teaching in Berlin and Prague, and in November 1923 came to the United States to lecture at American universities. From 1924 until 1930 he was professor of sociology at the University of Minnesota. He became a U.S. citizen in 1930. In 1931 he became the first chairman of the sociology department at Harvard, where he remained until his retirement in 1955. Sorokin, who combined sociology with the study of civilization, theorized that there were two basic types of culture: idealistic and sensate. His conclusion—somewhat reminiscent of the view of Oswald Spengler—was that Western society had become a sensate culture and was heading for a complete breakdown. He felt the only way to reverse the trend was by "creative altruism." To implement his theories, he was given a grant in 1948 to start the Harvard Research Center in Creative Altruism. He was the author of more than 30 books, including *General Theory of Law*, 1920; *Leaves from a Russian Diary*, 1924; *Principles of Rural-Urban Sociology*, 1929; *Social and Cultural Dynamics*, four volumes, 1937–1941, probably his most important work; *Man and Society in Calamity*, 1942; *Reconstruction of Humanity*, 1948; *Sociological Theories of Today*, 1966; and his autobiography, *A Long Journey*, 1963. He died in Winchester, Massachusetts, on February 10, 1968.

Sothern, Edward Hugh (1859–1933), actor. Born in New Orleans on December 6, 1859, Sothern was the son of the English actor Edward Askew Sothern. He first appeared, without much success, with his father's company at the Park Theatre in New York City in 1879. After studying acting for a few years he joined the John McCullough company after touring England in 1882–1883 subsequent to his father's death. From 1886 until 1900 he was a member of Daniel Frohman's company in New York City. The most prominent role he achieved as a romantic actor in Frohman's company was as the star of *The Prisoner of Zenda*, in which he toured. In 1900 he formed his own company with Virginia Harned, whom he had married in 1896, as his leading lady. They were divorced in 1910. Other outstanding roles were in *Hamlet*, 1900, *Richard Lovelace*, 1901, and *If I Were King*, 1902–1903. In 1904 he began to co-star with Julia Marlowe, who became his second wife in 1911. They played together in *Romeo and Juliet*, as well as in several other Shakespearean productions and popular romances, and were an enormously popular team. She retired from the stage in 1916, but he continued to appear until 1927. Following his retirement he continued to tour, giving lectures and public readings. His autobiography, *The Melancholy Tale of Me*, appeared in 1916. He died in New York City on October 28, 1933.

Soulé, Pierre (1801–1870), public official and diplomat. Born in Castillon-en-Couserans, France, on August 31, 1801, Soulé studied at the Jesuit College of Toulouse and the college at Bordeaux, intending to enter the church. But at fifteen he rebelled against ecclesiastical authority and decided on a political career. Embracing republicanism, he advocated what were considered revolutionary policies in monarchical France. In 1819 he graduated at Bordeaux and studied law in Paris, earning his degree in 1822. In 1825 his anti-government activities caused his arrest, whereupon he escaped to the United States, by way of England and Haiti. He lived in several places before finally settling in New Orleans, where he was admitted to the bar and began to practice law. He prospered there, engaging in public affairs and gradually becoming active in the Democratic party. He was a delegate to the party's national convention in 1844, and two years later was elected to the state senate. In December 1846 he was elected as a states'-rights Democrat to fill an unexpired term in the U.S. Senate, serving until March 3, 1847. In 1848, with Whig support, he was elected to a full term and served until 1853, when he resigned to become U.S. minister to Spain. As a politician, Soulé was a curious combination of ardent democrat and exponent of slavery. He believed in self-government, yet was an advocate of U.S. imperialism. As minister to Spain he seemed particularly tactless; his anti-monarchical sentiments were ill-concealed, and he advocated revolutionary causes in European countries. His handling of U.S. policy with regard to Cuba was offensive to Spain, for he urged obtaining Cuba from Spain by various extralegal expedients if efforts to purchase the island failed. When James Buchanan, John Y. Mason, and Soulé, all U.S. ministers abroad, met at Ostend, Belgium, to confer on policy regarding Cuba, it was Soulé who composed the famous Ostend Manifesto—advocating the use of force, if necessary, to secure U.S. possession of Cuba—which was repudiated by the administration of Franklin Pierce in Washington. Soulé resigned as minister to Spain in December 1855 and returned to New Orleans and the practice of law. During the Civil War he was arrested in 1862 by Gen. Benjamin F. Butler, who occupied New Orleans, and imprisoned for a few months. On returning to Louisiana late in 1863 he saw some military service for the Confederacy under Gen. P. G. T. Beauregard. After the war he lived for a while in Havana, but returned eventually to New Orleans, where he died on March 26, 1870.

Sousa, John Philip (1854–1932), conductor and composer. Born on November 6, 1854, in Washington, D.C., Sousa early showed a marked aptitude for music. He studied violin and in 1867 took up the trombone. For about five years he played with the United States Marine Band, but in 1872 he returned to the violin and played in and conducted a number of theater orchestras during the next few years. In 1876 he played in Jacques Offenbach's orchestra at the Centennial Exposition in Philadelphia, and in 1880 he became conductor of the U.S. Marine Band, considerably improving its standards until he left in 1892 to form his own band. During this period with the Marine Band he began to compose the marches that won him the title of "the March King"—"Semper Fidelis" in 1888, "The Washington Post March" in 1889, and "The Liberty Bell" in 1893. He toured the United States and Europe with his own band and met outstanding success. In 1897 he wrote "The Stars and Stripes Forever," his most popular piece, and in 1899 "Hands Across the Sea." During the Spanish-American War he was music director for the Sixth Army Corps and during World War I became director of all navy bands. After the war's end he resumed his tours. In all he composed more than 100 marches, celebrated for their rhythm and ingenious orchestration, ten comic operas, the most successful of which were *El Capitan*, 1896, and *The Bride-Elect*, 1897, and many other songs and miscellaneous works. He compiled a potpourri of songs of foreign nations for the U.S. Navy Department, wrote three novels, dissertations on the trumpet and violin, and an autobiography, *Marching Along*, 1928. He died in Reading, Pennsylvania, on March 6, 1932.

Southworth, Emma Dorothy Eliza Nevitte (1819–1899), author. Born in Washington, D.C., on December 26, 1819, Emma Nevitte grew up there and in Boston. In 1840 she married Frederick H. Southworth and they settled in Prairie du Chien, Wisconsin. She taught school in a nearby town for two years, but then, her husband having left her, she returned East and lived in Georgetown, D.C. She continued teaching school for about six years and in her spare time took up writing as a hobby. After several of her short stories had been published, her first novel, *Retribution*, came out in 1849. Using the signature E.D.E.N. Southworth, she embarked on a full-time writing career during which she published many short stories and more than 60 novels, sentimental romances and melodramas of no lasting literary merit. Her more popular books were *The Curse of Clifton*, 1852; *The Missing Bride*, 1855; *The Hidden Hand*, 1859; *The Fatal Marriage*, 1869; *The Maiden Widow*, 1870; and *Self-Raised*, 1876. She is also credited with telling poet John Greenleaf Whittier the story of Barbara Fritchie, which Whittier turned into a popular Civil War ballad in 1863. Mrs. Southworth died in Georgetown, D.C., on June 30, 1899.

Spaatz, Carl (1891–1974), air-force officer. Born in Boyertown, Pennsylvania, on June 28, 1891, Spaatz graduated from West Point in 1914. After a short tour of duty in Hawaii, he took pilot training at the Aviation School in San Diego, becoming in 1916 one of the first army pilots. During World War I he saw service in France as commander of the 31st Aero Squadron and was an aviation instructor; he received the Distinguished Service Cross in 1918. He spent part of 1919 touring the United States with the army's famed Flying Circus. During the next decade he served at air bases in Texas and Michigan and studied at the Air Corps Tactical School at Langley Field, Virginia. In 1929 he commanded the airplane *Question Mark* that stayed in the air for a record 150 hours, and for this feat was awarded the Distinguished Flying Cross. He spent the 1930s on duty at bases in California and at Langley Field, Virginia. In 1939 he went to the office of the chief of the air corps as executive officer. During several months in 1940 Spaatz, by that time a brigadier general, was in England observing both British and German air combat methods during the battle of Britain. In 1941 he became chief of the Army Air Forces staff, under Gen. Henry H. ("Hap") Arnold. In 1942 he went to Europe to command the U.S. air forces in the European theater, overseeing as well the Northwest African Air Force in the North African and Sicily campaigns. In 1942 he was promoted to major general. In January 1944 he was named commander of the U.S. Strategic Air Force in Europe, and in that year he carried out the strategic daylight bombing of Germany. After the end of the war in Europe he was transferred to the Pacific to take charge of the strategic bombing of Japan that culminated in the dropping of atomic bombs on Hiroshima and Nagasaki. In 1945 he was promoted to full general, and in 1946 he became commanding general of the U.S. air forces; in 1947 he was named chief of staff of the air force upon its becoming an independent branch of the service. In 1948 he retired and after serving as chairman of the Civil Air Patrol, entered business and did occasional writing. He died in Washington, D.C., on July 14, 1974.

Spahn, Warren Edward (1921–   ), baseball player. Born in Buffalo, New York, on April 23, 1921, Spahn learned to play baseball early in life and by his junior year at South Park High School had decided to concentrate on pitching. His outstanding ability attracted the attention of major-league scout Billy Myers, whose report induced the Boston Braves to sign him to a contract in 1940. For two years he played on minor-league teams at Bradford, Pennsylvania, Evansville, Indiana, and Hartford, Connecticut. After an impressive record in the minors he was called up by the Braves late in the 1942 season, but appeared in only four

games. He was then drafted into the army, where he served for four years and saw action in the war in Europe, winning a battlefield commission and the Bronze Star for bravery. In 1945 he returned to the Braves and began what was to become one of the great pitching careers in baseball. In the 1947 season Spahn won more than 20 games, a pace he continued for the next three years, and helped bring the Braves the National League pennant. In the early 1950s his fast ball began to lose some effectiveness, so he developed a variety of other pitches that helped to keep him in the 20-game winning category for several more years. In 1953, 1957, 1958, and 1961, he was named most valuable pitcher in the National League by *Sporting News*, and in 1957 he received the Cy Young Award as the outstanding pitcher in both leagues. But the high point of his career came in a game against the Chicago Cubs on August 11, 1961, when he posted his 300th win, a feat that had been attained by only six other pitchers since 1900. At that time he was the highest-paid pitcher in baseball. But after 20 years in the majors his career began to slow down, and after a poor season in 1963–1964 he was traded to the New York Mets, and from there he went to the San Francisco Giants in the winter of 1965–1966. At the time of his release from the Giants in 1966 he had set a new National League career record of 363 major-league wins.

Spalding, Albert (1888–1953), violinist and composer. Born in Chicago on August 15, 1888, Spalding was the son of Albert G. Spalding. He began to study the violin at the age of seven under Ulpiano Chiti in Florence, Italy. He continued his studies in New York City and Paris and made his concert debut in Paris in 1905. His first American appearance came in 1908 at Carnegie Hall with the New York Symphony Orchestra under Walter Damrosch. He toured Europe and the United States extensively until World War I interrupted his career. During the war he served in Italy with the U.S. Air Service. Following the war he resumed concert appearances and began to devote a good deal of time to composing. In 1922 he became the first American violinist to play regularly at the Société des Concerts du Conservatoire in Paris. Among his compositions were numerous works for the violin and for piano and violin. In World War II Spalding again saw service, this time with the Office of War Information (OWI), for which he was in charge of Radio Rome. His autobiography, published in 1943, was entitled *Rise to Follow*, and ten years later he published a novel, *A Fiddle, a Sword and a Lady*. Spalding retired from his concert activities in 1950. He died on May 26, 1953, in New York City, where he had made his home.

Spalding, Albert Goodwill (1850–1915), baseball player and sporting-goods manufacturer. Born on September 2, 1850, near the town of Byron in northern Illinois, Spalding attended schools there and in nearby Rockford. In the mid-1860s he learned to play baseball and soon became an outstanding pitcher and hitter on the local Forest City team at Rockford. As professional teams of national renown began to appear after 1865, a few teams, one at Rockford among them, began putting players on salary. With the rise of professionalism, Spalding joined the Boston team of the National Association in 1871. In 1876 the National Association was replaced by the National League of Professional Baseball Clubs, formed by William A. Hulbert with the assistance of Spalding. In that same year, Spalding and his brother James organized the sporting-goods manufacturing firm that still bears their name. He maintained his close connection with baseball through the Chicago team of the National League, for which he became pitcher, manager, and captain. He served as team president from 1882 until 1891, when he retired to devote himself to his business interests and to promoting and popularizing baseball in the United States and abroad. In 1888–1889 he took a team on a tour around the world to show off the game. He founded and edited, from 1878 to 1880, *Spalding's Official Baseball Guide* and in 1911 published a history of baseball entitled *America's National Game*. He was one of the great early influences in shaping the professional nature of the game, and he fought to keep the sport untainted by gambling and corruption. From 1900 until his death there on September 9, 1915, he lived at Point Loma, near San Diego, California. He was elected to the National Baseball Hall of Fame in 1939.

Sparks, Jared (1789–1866), editor, historian, and educator. Born on May 10, 1789, in Willington, Connecticut, Sparks grew up in poverty and had few opportunities for schooling. His efforts at self-education, however, finally won him a scholarship to Phillips Exeter Academy and from there he went on to Harvard in 1811. Graduating four years later, he continued his studies at the Harvard Divinity School, took his master's degree in 1819, and in the same year became pastor of the First Independent Church (Unitarian) of Baltimore. His ministry lasted four years, during which time he traveled extensively in the South and served for a year, 1821, as chaplain of the House of Representatives. In 1823 he purchased the *North American Review* and edited it for seven years, during which time it became the nation's leading literary journal. About 1827 he began seeking out and collecting materials—original documents, correspondence, and first-hand accounts—for his projected historical works. After *The Life of John Ledyard*, 1828, appeared *The Diplomatic Correspondence of the American Revolution*, in 12 volumes, 1829–1830; the 3-volume *Life of Gouverneur Morris*, 1832; the 12-volume *Writings of George Washington*, 1834–1837; and *The Works of Benjamin Franklin*, 10 volumes, 1836–1840. Sparks also edited and contributed to *The Library of American Biography*, 25 volumes, 1834–1847, and founded and edited, 1830–1861, the *American Almanac and Repository of Useful Information*. He uncovered and published a great deal of valu-

able historical material in the course of his researches, which extended to European as well as American archives, and his work as a whole fostered a new interest in American history and historiography. The enduring value of his efforts was severely impaired, however, by his methods of editing his materials; he amended, omitted, and rewrote whole passages, often to prevent giving offense to any person or government and sometimes simply to polish the finished product. In 1839 he was named McLean Professor of History at Harvard, becoming the first professor of secular history in the United States. Ten years later he was chosen president of Harvard. Beset by heavy administrative duties and ill health, he remained in this position only four years, and his administration, with its somewhat reactionary academic policy, was not markedly successful. After his retirement in 1853 he lived in Cambridge, Massachusetts, until his death there on March 14, 1866.

Spellman, Francis Joseph (1889–1967), religious leader. Born in Whitman, Massachusetts, on May 4, 1889, to parents of Irish descent, Spellman chose the priesthood as his vocation shortly before receiving his B.A. degree from Fordham University in 1911. Completing his doctorate at the North American College in Rome, he was ordained on May 14, 1916, in Rome. In 1918, after two years as an assistant at All Saints' Parish in Roxbury, Massachusetts, he joined the staff of the Cathedral of the Holy Cross in Boston and supervised literature for the diocese, later editing the weekly *Boston Pilot*. Four years later he was appointed vice-chancellor of the archdiocese of Boston and in 1925 became the first American attaché in the office of the secretary of state of the Vatican. There he was responsible for translating papal broadcasts and encyclicals into English and for issuing foreign-language translations to Roman Catholics around the world. His abilities elevated him rapidly in the hierarchy; consecrated titular bishop of Sila on September 8, 1932, he soon afterward became auxiliary bishop of Boston, and in 1939 was named archbishop of New York by Pope Pius XII. In the same year he was designated military vicar for the United States, a post that took him throughout the world to wherever U.S. troops were stationed in World War II, the Korean War, and the Vietnam War. Having achieved in his early years a reputation for social and political conservatism, he remained preoccupied with the welfare of Roman Catholics in the years of new ecumenical and socially oriented Catholicism, preferring to deal with individuals rather than social issues. In 1946 he was created a cardinal of his church. In 1953 he defended Senator Joseph R. McCarthy's investigations into alleged Communist infiltration of the government, and in later years supported the U.S. military presence in Vietnam. He strongly advocated state aid to church schools, and engaged in public controversy with opponents of such aid. His administration of the huge New York diocese was the epitome of efficiency and discipline. Successful in doubling his flock between 1939 and 1967, he erected churches, schools, and hospitals. He wrote numerous articles for newspapers and popular magazines, as well as books, including *The Road to Victory*, 1942; *The Risen Soldier*, 1944; *The Foundling*, 1951; and *What America Means to Me and other Poems and Prayers*, 1953. One of the most influential Roman Catholic prelates in U.S. history, he died in New York City on December 2, 1967.

Sperry, Elmer Ambrose (1860–1930), inventor and engineer. Born in Cortland, New York, on October 12, 1860, Sperry attended the State Normal and Training School there prior to spending a year at nearby Cornell University. His early interest in mechanics was strongly reinforced by a visit to Philadelphia's Centennial Exposition in 1876. From that time on, he devoted himself to a wide range of pursuits in electronics and engineering. During the early 1880s, he worked on modifications and improvements of the dynamics of lighting systems. He founded the Sperry Electric Company in 1880 in Chicago to manufacture appliances, dynamos, and an improved type of arc lamp. From the mid 1880s until the end of the century he turned his attention to a variety of devices, including mining machinery, streetcar equipment, locomotives, storage batteries, and electric automobiles. In 1900 he opened a research laboratory in Washington, D.C., in partnership with C. P. Townsend, for work in electrochemistry, which he continued for about ten years. But Sperry is best remembered for his contributions to sea and air navigation. Beginning in 1890 he applied electronics and mechanics to the principle of the gyroscope and devised over a number of years a series of inventions that greatly improved the safety of water and air travel. His gyrocompass, entirely nonmagnetic, was first installed in the battleship *Delaware* in 1910 and was soon adopted as standard equipment by the U.S. navy and by many steamship lines. He formed the Sperry Gyroscope Company in Brooklyn, New York, in 1910 and headed the firm until 1929. He manufactured the gyroscopic stabilizer for ships in 1913, and within a year produced a similar device for airplanes. He also contrived an aerial torpedo with gyrocontrol that was used in World War I, and in 1918 he invented the arc searchlight. Sperry combined good business sense with his talent for inventing—during his lifetime he organized eight different companies to manufacture and market his inventions and obtained more than 400 separate patents. For his contributions to technology he received numerous honors and awards, both in the United States and abroad, including decorations from Russia, Japan, and France. He was also one of the founders of the American Institute of Electrical Engineers and of the American Electrochemical Society. After 1910 he made his home in Brooklyn, New York, where he died on June 16, 1930.

Spillane, Frank Morrison, *see* Spillane, Mickey

Spillane, Mickey (1918–   ), author. Born March 9, 1918, in Brooklyn, New York, where he attended Erasmus Hall High School, Frank Morrison Spillane continued his education briefly with a year at Fort Hays State College in Kansas in 1939. He began writing while in high school but began his professional career in 1940 shortly after leaving college. He got a job as a comic-strip writer, a line of work which was interrupted by service in the army air forces during World War II. He continued the comic-strip work for a while after the war, but in 1946 he wrote the first of his Mike Hammer detective stories, *I, the Jury*, an immediate best seller. His novels were in the tradition of private-eye fiction created by Raymond Chandler and Dashiell Hammett, but laid a good deal more emphasis on violence, sex, sadism, and death. Both Spillane's style and content received a cool reception from the critics, who preferred the more typical detective-mystery fiction of such authors as Ellery Queen, John Dickson Carr, and Agatha Christie. But critics notwithstanding, the Mike Hammer stories were an immediate and lasting success among readers. By 1951, *I, the Jury*, plus *My Gun Is Quick, Vengeance Is Mine, One Lonely Night*, and *The Big Kill*, had sold more than 40 million copies, mostly in paperback. By 1961 Spillane's seven early novels had sold 70 million copies. In the early 1950s Spillane joined the Jehovah's Witnesses and announced his retirement from writing. But in the early 1960s he resumed his writing career with *The Deep* and with another Hammer novel, *The Girl Hunters*. Several of the Mike Hammer books were also made into successful motion pictures. Spillane's novels appeared with relative regularity during the 1960s and early 1970s; *The Erection Set* was published in 1971.

Spingarn, Joel Elias (1875–1939), Critic, author, and social reformer. Born in New York City on May 17, 1875, Spingarn graduated from Columbia College in 1895 and, after a year of graduate study at Harvard, received his Ph.D. from Columbia in 1899. He was appointed in that year an assistant in the department of comparative literature at Columbia and was promoted to professor in 1909, but he was dismissed from the faculty in 1911 after a heated dispute with Columbia president Nicholas Murray Butler on a point of administrative procedure. Spingarn, who possessed an independent fortune, was unfazed by this setback and continued in after years the scholarly and critical studies that he had initiated while at Columbia. His *History of Literary Criticism in the Renaissance* appeared in 1899 and was followed by *The New Criticism*, 1911, and by *Creative Criticism*, 1917. He also published, among other books, *The New Hesperides, and Other Poems*, 1911; *Poems*, 1924; and *Poetry and Religion*, 1924; and was the editor of several important collections of literary materials. In 1919 he helped found the publishing firm of Harcourt, Brace and Company, and was its literary adviser from then until 1932. In his later years he became a well-known horticulturalist and was accounted the country's leading expert on the clematis. But he is remembered primarily for his work with the National Association for the Advancement of Colored People (NAACP), which he helped to found in 1909—the name was adopted a year later—and which he served in various capacities, including that of president from 1930 until his death; he was succeeded by his brother Arthur. In 1914 he established the award of the Spingarn Medal, given annually to a Negro in recognition of great service to his race. Spingarn died in New York City on July 26, 1939.

Spock, Benjamin McLane (1903–   ), physician, author, and social reformer. Born in New Haven, Connecticut, on May 2, 1903, Spock attended Phillips Academy in Andover, Massachusetts, took his B.A. degree from Yale in 1925, attended medical school there, and took his M.D. at Columbia in 1929. He interned at St. Luke's Hospital in New York City, served residencies in pediatrics at the New York Nursery and Children's Hospital (1931–1932) and in psychiatry at the New York Hospital (1932–1933), and completed six years of training at the New York Psychoanalytic Institute. During 1933–1943 he practiced in New York City and taught pediatrics at Cornell University's Medical College. During the next two years he was on active duty as a psychiatrist in the U.S. Naval Reserve and completed, in this period, *The Common Sense Book of Baby and Child Care,* 1946 (later *Baby and Child Care*), which became so popular—it was one of the all-time best sellers—that "Dr. Spock" became a household word. His attitude toward child rearing was kindly and understanding, in contrast to that of the traditional parents' manuals of stern, inflexible edicts. He reassured parents—"You know more than you think you know"—emphasized the fact that babies' personalities differ and that parental flexibility is thus required in addition to affectionate firmness, and provided insights into child psychology. In 1947 he taught psychiatry at the University of Minnesota and was professor of child development at the University of Pittsburgh from 1951 to 1955 and at Western Reserve University from 1955 until he retired in 1967. Articles collected in *Dr. Spock Talks with Mothers,* 1961, and *Problems of Parents,* 1962, first appeared in the *Ladies' Home Journal,* where his column on child rearing was published regularly during 1954–1963, his articles after that time appearing in *Redbook.* He worked on behalf of the National Committee for a Sane Nuclear Policy (SANE), warning of the effects of radioactive pollution, and was cochairman of the committee from 1963 to 1967. In 1963 he became publicly identified with the opposition to the Vietnam War. He appeared at numerous protest rallies and marches in U.S. cities. In 1968 he was indicted with four other prominent members of the peace movement for conspiring to violate selective-service laws. He was found guilty, fined, and given a two-year prison sentence; the conviction was reversed, however, by the U.S. Court of Appeals in 1969. Out of this controversy he produced *Decent and Indecent,* 1969, which elucidated his concerns for the fate of adults and of the country. A hero of the young and the radical during the late 1960s, he became anathema to many of their elders, who saw in him the symbolic source of the so-called "permissiveness" that they felt to be at the heart of the nation's problems at the time.

Spooner, John Coit (1843–1919), lawyer and public official. Born in Lawrenceburg, Indiana, on January 6, 1843, Spooner lived there until 1859, when his family moved to Madison, Wisconsin. There he attended the University of Wisconsin, from which he received his degree in 1864, while serving in the Union Army during the Civil War. In 1867 he was admitted to the bar and three years later settled at Hudson, in western Wisconsin, where he began his law practice. A successful legal career afforded him an entry into politics and eventually led to a lucrative position as counsel for the Chicago and North Western Railway. Spooner was politically conservative, Republican, a talented constitutional lawyer, and a lobbyist for business interests. He served a term in the U.S. Senate from 1885 until 1891, but was defeated for reelection when the Democrats took control of state offices. In 1897, however, he was returned to the Senate after the Republican sweep led by William McKinley; and he served there until March 1907. During this decade he became a nationally known figure, in company with such other distinguished senators of the time as William B. Allison, Nelson W. Aldrich, Orville H. Platt, with whom he formed the central conservative Republican group known as The Four, as well as George F. Hoar, Henry Cabot Lodge, and Chauncey M. Depew. But Spooner was, at that time, perhaps the ablest man in Congress. His tenure in the Senate coincided with the rise of Progressivism nationally, and there developed an insurgent Republican movement in Wisconsin led by Robert M. La Follette that made Spooner's position as an advocate of corporations and conservative politics rather uncomfortable. At the 1904 Republican national convention, La Follette, as governor of Wisconsin, led the regular delegation, and Spooner, the conservative, found himself in the position of leading a delegation whose credentials were being challenged. The Spooner delegation was eventually seated, but the consequent alienation of the Wisconsin Progressives was to prove harmful both to the Republican party and to Theodore Roosevelt in the years to come. In 1905 La Follette was elected to the Senate, and Spooner decided to retire at the end of his term, unable to accept the spectacle of traditional Republicanism being enveloped by a tide of progressivism and liberalism. He left his seat in the Senate in March of 1907, and he then settled in New York City, carrying on a successful law practice that he continued until his death there on June 11, 1919.

Spotted Tail (1833?–1881), Indian leader. Born near Fort Laramie, Wyoming, about 1833, Spotted Tail, whose Indian name was Sinte-galeshka, possessed great abilities as a warrior that advanced him to the position of head chief of the Brulé, a tribe of Sioux. His talents both on the battlefield and in council sessions maintained him in a position of leadership all his life; nevertheless, he tended to live in the shadow of the more famous Sioux of his time—his nephew Crazy Horse, Red Cloud, and Sitting Bull. Spotted Tail was nevertheless one of the shrewdest of the Sioux leaders in his perception of the overall invincibility of the invading white men; he knew that Indian wars would be destructive to the tribes, and became therefore an advocate of compromise to avoid conflict. He felt that the best chance for his people lay in a general accommodation with white society, and he often found himself opposing the stands of other Sioux chiefs who opted for war to defend their hunting grounds and their ancestral lands in the Black Hills. When the Black Hills were overrun by settlers and gold prospectors in the 1870s over the protest of the Indians, he succeeded in keeping most of his followers out of the warfare of 1876, including the battle of Little Bighorn, that occurred as a consequence. He also played a role, along with Red Cloud, in persuading Crazy Horse to surrender to the army in 1877. It turned out, of course, that his expectations of fair treatment by the government were too sanguine, and he lived to see his people forced off their traditional hunting lands and onto reservations where repeatedly promised food and supplies were rarely forthcoming. In 1881, when Red Cloud was deposed as chief of the Oglala, Spotted Tail was recognized as chief of that Sioux group as well. On August 5, 1881, Spotted Tail was assassinated on the Rosebud Reservation by Crow Dog, one of his fellow Sioux. The Indians were inclined to view the murder as an attempt to break the power of the chiefs over the Sioux and make the tribes more compliant in dealings with the agents of the Bureau of Indian Affairs.

Sprague, Frank Julian (1857–1934), engineer and inventor. Born in Milford, Connecticut, on July 25, 1857, Sprague lived after 1866 in North Adams, Massachusetts. He graduated in 1878 from the U.S. Naval Academy, where he had developed a keen interest in physics, particularly electricity, and between assignments to sea duty over the next three years he continued to experiment with various forms of dynamos and motors. In 1882 he overstayed by several months a leave of absence in order to serve on the awards jury for an electrical exhibition in England. The next year he resigned from the navy and became an assistant to Thomas A. Edison, whose ideas on electrical-power distribution he had been promoting. In 1884 he left Edison's employ and formed the Sprague Electric Railway and Motor Company, exhibiting later in that year his newly devised constant-speed electric motor. After extensive experiments on the New York Elevated Railway, in 1887,

Sprague contracted to construct for the city of Richmond, Virginia, the first major electric-trolley system in the United States. His success there led to more than a hundred other such contracts both in the United States and abroad. In 1890 he sold his firm to the Edison General Electric Company and in 1892 entered a new field by forming the Sprague Electric Elevator Company. He built that enterprise into a prosperous operation before selling it to the Otis Elevator Company. From 1887 he had experimented with a method of "multiple-unit" control for traction systems, whereby the train could be composed of independently powered units all operating under a central control from any of several points. By this means quick acceleration, high speed, uniform braking, and easy breakup into shorter trains were possible. Perfected in 1895 and first installed in Chicago in 1897, his multiple-unit system was thereafter widely adopted. His Sprague Electric Company was sold to General Electric in 1902. In later years he developed electric motors for various small tools and appliances, experimented with an automatic train-control system, contributed to the electrification of Grand Central Terminal in New York City, coinvented the protected electrical third rail employed by the New York Central Railroad, and served as chairman of the committees on electricity and ship construction of the Naval Consulting Board during World War I. The recipient of numerous honors and awards, Sprague was widely known as "the father of electric traction." He died on October 25, 1934, in New York City.

Spreckels, Claus (1828–1908), businessman and manufacturer. Born at Lamstedt in the province of Hanover, Germany, on July 9, 1828, Spreckels emigrated to the United States in 1846. For the next ten years he engaged in the retail and wholesale grocery business, first in Charleston, South Carolina, then for a short time in New York City. He was encouraged by his brother Bernard to move in 1856 to San Francisco, where new fortunes were being made as a result of the Gold Rush. Again he took up the grocery business, then went into brewing; in 1863 he started the Bay Sugar Refining Company. After intensive study of sugar manufacturing in Europe, he returned to the West Coast and opened the California Sugar Refinery, the enterprise that was to earn him the title of "Sugar King." He improved the processing of cane sugar from the Hawaiian Islands and ventured into the refining of beet sugar at Salinas, California, near sugar-beet farms that he had established. By 1883 Spreckels had the largest sugar refinery on the West Coast and a near-monopoly of the refining and marketing of sugarcane there, and he also obtained a large land concession in Hawaii for his sugar industry. Apparently unabashed by his own monopoly control of sugar, Spreckels did not hesitate to fight monopoly in other enterprises. He financed competition against the entrenched utilities at San Francisco and opposed the Southern Pacific Railroad, whose transportation monopoly was a constant financial threat to men engaged in agriculture or manufacturing on account of the arbitrary setting of rates in a region where there was no other means of hauling goods. His Hawaiian Commercial Company and its prosperous island plantations eventually became a source of intrafamily squabbles, with two of his sons wresting control of the Hawaiian enterprise from their father and the other two sons in 1899. A family reconciliation a few years later left Claus's son Rudolph in charge of his father's business affairs. The elder Spreckels died on January 10, 1908, in San Francisco.

Springs, Elliot White (1896–1959), businessman and author. Born in Lancaster, South Carolina, on July 31, 1896, Springs graduated from Culver Military Academy in 1913 and from Princeton University in 1917. He became a noted fighter pilot during World War I, credited with downing 11 enemy aircraft. In 1919, still a pilot, he flew in the first cross-country air race, from New York City to Toronto. He then turned down the opportunity to work in the family-owned textile mills in favor of settling in New York City to pursue a career as an author. Over the next ten years he produced many short stories and several novels, the best known of which was the best-selling *Warbirds— The Diary of an Unknown Aviator,* 1926; others were *Nocturne Militaire,* 1927; *Warbirds and Ladybirds,* 1931; and *Clothes Make the Man,* 1948. When his father died in 1931, Springs took over and consolidated the family's cotton mills in North and South Carolina. The way he ran the Springs Cotton Mills Company made him known as an innovative, daring, and occasionally eccentric entrepreneur. He made the business an unqualified success, so much so that he never had to close down even during the Depression of the 1930s, and he turned the task of running it into a source of considerable enjoyment for himself, using advertising that was considered startling for its time—so much so that some ads, with their racy pictures and double-entendre captions, were banned by major magazines. But he made "Springmaid" sheets virtually a household word and a popular product. By the end of his life, Springs had made his company one of the largest of its kind in the nation, with a work force of more than 12,000 in 1958. He died on October 15, 1959, in New York City.

Spruance, Raymond Ames (1886–1969), naval officer. Born in Baltimore on July 3, 1886, Spruance grew up there, in East Orange, New Jersey, and in Indianapolis. He graduated from the Naval Academy in 1906. Between graduation and 1939 he saw 18 years of sea duty, including a tour on the navy's around-the-world cruise ordered by President Theodore Roosevelt in 1907. From 1921 to 1929 he worked with the Naval Bureau of Engineering, spent a year as assistant to the commander of U.S. naval forces in Europe, studied at the Naval War College, and spent two years with naval intelligence. During the 1930s he

taught at the Naval War College and saw occasional sea duty. In 1939 he became a rear admiral. In 1940 he commanded the 10th Naval District in the Caribbean, and in 1941 was assigned to the Pacific fleet under Adm. Chester B. Nimitz. During World War II Spruance took part in several crucial engagements against the Japanese, showing himself to be one of the navy's ablest tacticians. His first major action was as commander of one of two task forces in the battle of Midway in June 1942, a four-day engagement that wrought havoc with the Japanese fleet, inflicting on Japan its first naval defeat in modern times and canceling the advantage that had been gained by the bombing of Pearl Harbor in 1941. The battle was a major factor in halting the Japanese in the Pacific. Spruance was awarded the Distinguished Service Medal and named chief of staff by Nimitz. In May 1943 he was promoted to vice admiral and he then was appointed commander of the Central Pacific area. He continued to direct naval forces in a succession of important offensives throughout the war, notably the attack on the Gilbert Islands in November 1943, the invasion of the Marshall Islands in January 1944, the bombardment of Truk in February 1944, the attacks on Tinian, Guam, and Saipan later in 1944, the battle of the Philippines in June 1944, and the final assault on Okinawa in April 1945. In February 1944 he had been promoted to full admiral and in April he took command of the U.S. Fifth Fleet. In November 1945 he succeeded Nimitz as commander in chief of the entire U.S. Pacific Fleet. In 1946 he returned to the United States as president of the Naval War College at Newport, Rhode Island, and on July 1, 1948, retired from the service. From 1952 to 1955 he was the U.S. ambassador to the Philippines. He died in Pebble Beach, California, on December 13, 1969.

Squanto (? –1622), Indian friend of the Pilgrims. Born sometime before 1590 (he was known to have been an adult by 1605), Squanto (also called Tisquantum) was a member of the Pawtuxet tribe of New England. He was probably the Indian who was taken to England in 1605 by George Weymouth and returned to America by Capt. John Smith some years later. In Smith's expedition to explore and map the New England coast in 1614–1615, Capt. Thomas Hunt, in command of one of the ships, seized a party of 30 Indians to sell as slaves in Malaga, Spain. One of these was Squanto. He made his escape and reached England, where he remained for two years. In 1619 he set out for North America in an expedition under the auspices of Sir Ferdinando Gorges, one of the most ardent English proponents of colonization of the New World. When Squanto reached his home, he found his whole tribe had been wiped out by a plague, probably of smallpox brought by English ships. He went to live with the Wampanoag tribe, about 40 miles from his native place, the present-day Plymouth. In 1620, when the Pilgrims arrived at Plymouth on the *Mayflower,* Squanto soon befriended them and taught them much about surviving in their new wilderness home, and he acted as interpreter and intermediary with the Wampanoag and their chief, Massasoit. Through the assistance of Squanto and another Indian, Samoset, the Pilgrims and Indians were able to make a treaty of mutual assistance that endured for some 40 years. Because Squanto had no tribal connections he passed much of his time with the Pilgrims, showing them how to plant corn and where to fish. It is likely that he took part in the celebration of the first Thanksgiving, or harvest festival, held by the colonists. For a time Squanto jeopardized his relations with other Indians by his friendship with the English, and it seemed the Wampanoag might try to do away with him. But late in 1622, while guiding Gov. William Bradford's expedition around Cape Cod, he took sick and died at Chatham Harbor on Cape Cod.

Squibb, Edward Robinson (1819–1900), physician and manufacturer. Born on July 4, 1819, in Wilmington, Delaware, Squibb was reared in the Quaker tradition and tutored privately. He earned his medical degree from Jefferson Medical College in Philadelphia in 1845. For two years he practiced medicine and taught anatomy at the college and then became an assistant surgeon in the navy. While serving at sea he discovered that many of the drugs supplied to him were impure or of poor quality. Objecting strongly and bringing the situation to the attention of the authorities, he gained permission in 1851 to establish a laboratory in the naval hospital in Brooklyn, New York, to produce chemicals and drugs for the armed forces. There he worked for six years, until the failure of the army to provide funds forced him to resign. He took a position with the Louisville Chemical Works in Kentucky, but in 1858, in the expectation that the army would purchase his products, he opened his own laboratory in Brooklyn. Fire demolished the premises soon after he moved in, but another laboratory was built to his specifications in 1859. Massive orders for drugs during the Civil War made the business a success, but even during the boom the high standards he set for his products were never compromised. He continually scored unlicensed medical practitioners, medical advertising, and ineffectual commercial preparations, and was a leading advocate of and contributor to the revision and improvement of the official *U.S. Pharmacopeia*. After 1882 he published sporadically *An Ephemeris*, a pharmaceutical journal. He drafted the model for the first pure food and drug laws in New York and New Jersey. When his sons entered the business in 1892 the company became E. R. Squibb & Sons. He retired in 1895 and died in Brooklyn, New York, on October 25, 1900. The company grew into one of the country's leading pharmaceutical houses and in the 1950s was purchased by the Mathieson Chemical Company, later the Olin Mathieson Chemical Company.

Stagg, Amos Alonzo (1862–1965), football coach. Born in West Orange, New Jersey, on August 16, 1862, Stagg attended Yale and while studying for the ministry played both baseball and football. In 1888, the year he pitched the Yale team to a victory over the Boston Braves, he turned down six offers from professional baseball teams. In 1889 he was selected by Walter Camp for the first All-American football team, and the next year, having graduated from Yale, he went to Springfield (Massachusetts) College, where he coached and played on the football team. Two years later he became coach at the University of Chicago; he remained there for 41 years, molding the "Giants of the Midway" into one of the football powerhouses of the early part of the century and developing such innovations as the huddle, the shift, the man-in-motion, the end-around play, and the hidden-ball trick, since outlawed. In addition to his coaching success—5 undefeated seasons, 6 conference championships, and an overall record of 268 wins and 141 losses—Stagg was the first college athletic director to hold full faculty status. In 1933, at the age of seventy, he refused promotion to the largely honorary position of superintendent of athletics and instead resigned from Chicago to assume the coaching job at the College (now University) of the Pacific in Stockton, California. In 1946 he went to Susquehanna (Pennsylvania) College in an advisory capacity and in 1953 returned to Stockton, where he was an adviser at the city junior college until his retirement in 1960. Known affectionately as the "grand old man of football," Stagg was elected to the Football Hall of Fame in 1951, one of the first men chosen and the only one honored both as a player and a coach. From 1904 until his death he was a member of the football rules committee. He published several books, including *Touchdown!*, 1927, with W. W. Stout. He died in Stockton on March 17, 1965, at the age of a hundred and two.

Standish, Burt L., *see* Patten, Gilbert

Standish, Miles (1584?–1656), soldier and colonist. Born about 1584 in Lancashire, England, Miles (or Myles) Standish carved out a military career for himself as a soldier of fortune in the Netherlands during the Dutch wars for independence from Spain. While in Holland, he met the English Pilgrims who were living in exile in Leiden. In 1620 he was hired by them to join their colonizing expedition to the New World, a fortunate move for them, for he became one of the mainstays of their small colony during its early years of near-starvation and illness. Standish became the military leader of the Plymouth Colony and the chief negotiator with the New England Indian tribes. He was the first of the colonists to learn the Indian languages, and he was the chief strategist of defense against attack. His expertise in Indian relations was such that after the first few years, the colony had no real Indian troubles for 50 years. In 1625–1626 he went to England as agent for the colony to secure new loans and purchase supplies. In 1627 he was one of a group of colonists that bought out the London merchants who had invested in the venture, thus enabling the Pilgrims to assume title to their land in New

England. In 1628 Standish led the expedition that arrested Thomas Morton at his unpuritanical Merrymount colony and sent him back to England. In 1631 Standish and John Alden founded the town of Duxbury, where Standish settled in 1637 and remained until his death on October 3, 1656. Until his death he remained one of the influential men in the growing colony, serving in various posts and amassing considerable property. He is probably best known to amateurs of American history through Henry Wadsworth Longfellow's narrative poem, *The Courtship of Miles Standish*, but there is no historical evidence for his purported offer of marriage through John Alden to Priscilla Mullins.

Stanford, Leland (1824–1893), railroad builder and public official. Born on March 9, 1824, in Watervliet, New York, Amasa Leland Stanford was educated in local schools, at the Clinton Liberal Institute, and at Cazenovia Seminary. In 1845 he took up the study of law and was admitted to the bar three years later. He moved to Port Washington, Wisconsin, to begin practice and remained there for four years before following the example of his brothers and moving to California. There he engaged in retail trade, became involved in Republican politics, and in 1861 was elected governor. In the same year he joined Collis P. Huntington, Charles Crocker, and Mark Hopkins in organizing the Central Pacific Railroad Company, of which he served as president for the rest of his life. During the next two years he freely employed his official position to aid the company's undertakings to build the western portion of a transcontinental line, and after leaving office in 1863 he devoted himself to the railroad and, because of his political connections, was primarily responsible for its finances and for maintaining good relations with California governmental bodies. The Central Pacific was completed and joined to the Union Pacific in 1869, and the partners began looking toward the extension of the line through Southern California and, ultimately, toward the construction of a second transcontinental route. The Southern Pacific Railroad was built through Southern California and in 1884 was absorbed along with the Central Pacific in a holding company, the Southern Pacific Company, of which Stanford was president until 1890. In 1885, in memory of his son who had died the year before at the age of fifteen, he founded Leland Stanford, Jr., University (now Stanford University) near Palo Alto, with a gift of 9000 acres of land and $21 million in endowment. Also in 1885 he was elected to the U.S. Senate by the California legislature and was reelected in 1890. He died at his home in Palo Alto, California, on June 21, 1893.

Stanley Brothers, inventors and automobile manufacturers. The Stanley brothers, Francis Edgar (1849–1918) and Freelan (1849–1940), were twins. Born in Kingfield, Maine, on June 1, 1849, they attended local schools. Francis did his college work at Farmington State Normal and Training School, graduating in 1871, and Freelan went to Bowdoin

College. Francis combined teaching school with an interest in portraiture that led him to give up teaching in 1874 and concentrate on art. In a few years his interest brought him to photography, and by the early 1880s he was considered one of the best portrait photographers in New England. In 1883 the brothers invented a process for manufacturing photographic dry plates and founded a manufacturing firm in Lewiston, Maine. Within a few years their plates were in general use throughout the United States and Europe and in 1905 they sold their business to the Eastman Kodak Company. The Stanley brothers had meanwhile turned their attention to the automobile, and in 1897 they made one of the first successful cars powered by a steam motor, an early version of the famous "Stanley Steamer." In 1898 they went into production on the car, but in a few months they sold the business. In 1902, however, they repurchased their patents and formed the Stanley Motor Carriage Company, which they operated until 1917. In 1906 one of their cars made the fastest one-mile run up to that time, in slightly over 28 seconds. In addition to their work on the automobile, the brothers also investigated the development of steam-operated cars on interurban rail lines. They even devised a process for the mass production of violins. In their later years Francis and Freelan turned their attention to such matters as economics, politics, and literature, and both of them lectured and wrote on topics of interest to them. Francis died on July 31, 1918, the result of an auto accident; Freeland lived on until his death in Boston on October 2, 1940.

Stanley, Henry Morton (1841–1904), explorer and journalist. Born in Denbigh, Wales, on January 31, 1841, Stanley was the illegitimate son of a certain John Rowlands and bore his name for his first 17 years. The treatment he received at the hands of his family and relatives during his early years ranged from hostile to cruel; what formal schooling he obtained was at the St. Asaph Union Workhouse, run by a tyrannical headmaster. At the age of fifteen he ran away from the workhouse, staying with various relatives until 1858, when he sailed from Liverpool as cabin boy on a ship bound for New Orleans. There he went to work for a merchant, Henry Morton Stanley, who adopted him in 1859 and gave him his name. The next several years were very unsettled for Stanley. In 1861, with the start of the Civil War, he enlisted in the Confederate army. He was captured in 1862 and interned at Camp Douglas in Chicago, whereupon he joined the Union army. Poor health resulting from his imprisonment soon caused him to be released from service, however, and he returned to England for a short time. Back in the United States in 1863, he enlisted in the Union navy. After the war he went West and began to work as a newspaper reporter. He wrote articles on life in the West, particularly on the Indian wars. Twice during the 1860s he went to the Middle East as a journalist, first in 1866, then again in 1868 to cover troubles involving Turkey, Crete, and Greece; he also reported from Spain and Ethiopia. In 1868 he was hired as a correspondent for the *New York Herald* by the younger James Gordon Bennett. It was Bennett who launched him on his career as the foremost explorer of Africa by giving him the assignment of going in search of the famous missionary David Livingstone, who had gone into the interior of Africa in 1866 to seek the source of the Nile. Stanley set out on his expedition in 1869, reaching Zanzibar on January 6, 1871. Two and a half months later he started for the interior and on November 10, after great difficulties, he found Livingstone at Ujiji, a village on the eastern shore of Lake Tanganyika. His greeting, "Dr. Livingstone, I presume?" became a catch-phrase of unequaled fame. Together they explored the region for some months, and in 1872 Stanley returned to England with the news of his encounter, publishing *How I Found Livingstone* in that year. A difficult man with an abrasive personality, he encountered much resentment and jealousy when he broke the news, and many asserted he had never made the trip at all. The Royal Geographical Society was especially peeved by having an upstart step in and win glory in a field it considered its own. Although he was vindicated easily enough, it took nearly 20 years and three major expeditions before Stanley was well received in his native land. Receipt of word of the death of Livingstone in 1873 prompted Stanley to take up the exploration of Africa where the missionary had left it. He returned for an epoch-making journey from 1874 to 1877. His major achievements in these years were many, but two were outstanding: ascertaining that Lake Victoria was a single body of water, not five separate ones, and therefore the largest lake in Africa; and tracing the course of the great and until then unknown Congo River. His explorations failed to interest Britain in colonizing the Congo region, but King Leopold II of Belgium took a definite interest and hired Stanley for further exploration of the area, which he carried out from 1879 to 1884. He established more than a score of steamer stations along the Congo and its major tributaries. His efforts resulted in the founding of the Congo Free State in 1884–1885 by Leopold. In 1885 he published *The Congo and the Founding of Its Free State.* During 1884–1887 he lectured widely, stirring up interest in the vast potential of Africa. A two-year expedition in 1887–1889 was led by Stanley in search of Mehmed Emin Pasha, the German-born governor of the equatorial province of Egypt, whose territory had been severed from the rest of the country in 1885 by the Mahdi revolt; in his journeyings Stanley discovered, besides other important geographical features, the Mountains of the Moon (Mt. Ruwenzori). Altogether, his explorations were enormously valuable, both for the light they shed on Africa and for their stimulation of colonization by European nations. He published the results of his travels for all to read, the most noted of his several books being *Through the Dark Continent*, two volumes, 1878, the title of which gave Africa the cognomen by which it has been known ever since. In 1892 Stanley again became a British subject and in 1895 won election to Parliament. But politics interested him little and he spent most of his time traveling and lecturing in various parts of the world. In 1897 he toured South Africa on what was to be his last visit to the continent that he, perhaps more than any other European, had helped the world to know. In 1899 he was knighted and retired to a country estate near Pirbright, Surrey. On May 10, 1904, he died at his home in London. His *Autobiography of Sir Henry Morton Stanley*, unfinished at his death, was edited by his wife, Dorothy Stanley, and published in 1909.

Stanley, Wendell Meredith (1904–1971), biochemist. Born on August 16, 1904, in Ridgeville, Indiana, Stanley attended Earlham College at Richmond, where the family had moved in 1920. Upon receiving his B.S. degree in 1926, he rejected his original intention of becoming a football coach in favor of enrolling in the graduate school of the University of Illinois. There he majored in organic chemistry, earning his Ph.D. in 1929. His work at Illinois awakened his interest in solving medical problems by means of chemistry. In 1931, after a year of further study in Munich, he became associated with the Department of Plant and Animal Pathology of the Rockefeller Institute for Medical Research, where he remained until 1948. His work at the Institute concentrated on the nature of viruses, and by 1935 he was able to demonstrate that viruses were of a proteinaceous nature, in contradiction to the prevailing belief that they were submicroscopic organisms. After 1941 he and his colleagues devoted themselves to problems relating to the war effort. For the Committee on Medical Research of the Office of Scientific Research and Development he studied the influenza virus and developed a vaccine that was far more effective than any previously produced. In 1946, for his work on viruses, he shared the Nobel Prize for chemistry with John H. Northrop and James B. Sumner. His work on viruses led him to a thesis he announced in a lecture at Yale University in 1947: that the hereditary pattern of organisms might one day be altered by chemistry. Late the same year he was appointed to establish and direct a laboratory for virus research at the University of California at Berkeley, where he lived after taking up the appointment in 1948. He also was chairman of the department of biochemistry from 1948 to 1953, was professor and chairman of the department of virology during 1958–1964, and in 1964 became professor of molecular biology. Stanley's work in biochemistry brought him international renown, as well as many awards, citations, and honorary degrees. He was a member of the expert advisory panel on virus diseases for the World Health Organization (WHO) from 1951, and a member of the advisory commission to the director of the National Institutes of Health from 1966. He died on June 15, 1971, in Salamanca, Spain.

Stanton, Edwin McMasters (1814–1869), lawyer and public official. Born in Steubenville, Ohio, on December 19, 1814, Stanton entered Kenyon College in 1831 but was forced by financial difficulties to withdraw before graduating. He turned to the law and was admitted to the bar in 1836, entering practice in Cadiz, Ohio. He soon won recognition as an industrious and highly capable attorney; he moved to Pittsburgh in 1847 and to Washington, D.C., in 1856, gaining constantly in prominence and coming to national notice in the early 1850s, when he represented Pennsylvania in a suit against the Wheeling & Belmont Bridge Company before the Supreme Court. In 1858 he represented the United States in a series of California cases involving land claims based on allegedly fraudulent Mexican titles. In December 1860 President James Buchanan reorganized his cabinet and named Stanton attorney general. Stanton opposed the evacuation of Fort Sumter after South Carolina's secession and was so fearful of the ineffectiveness of Buchanan's responses to secession that he secretly met with Radical Republican leaders in Congress to inform them of cabinet matters. He left the cabinet upon Abraham Lincoln's inauguration in March 1861, but soon afterward, although a Democrat, became legal adviser to Secretary of War Simon Cameron; when Cameron was dismissed, Stanton succeeded him, in January 1862. As the civilian head of the Union armed forces through the remainder of the Civil War, he applied his energy and ability with great effect, although his abrasive personality brought him often into conflict with other civil and military leaders and his brusque and summary conduct of his office made him widely unpopular. He was on several occasions accused of outright meddling in military operations. His original antipathy to Lincoln mellowed over three years of association. For President Andrew Johnson, by whom he was retained in office, he had little regard. He again collaborated with congressional leaders against a president, this time against Johnson's moderate Reconstruction policies, and on many occasions usurped his executive authority. An advocate of a punitive course of Reconstruction, he attempted by various means to erect a barrier to effective presidential or other civilian—except for himself —control of the army occupying the South. Finally, in August 1867, Johnson, convinced that instances of insubordination among military commanders were traceable to Stanton, requested his resignation. Stanton refused, claiming the protection of the Tenure of Office Act that had earlier been passed over Johnson's veto (ironically, Stanton had helped write the veto message). Johnson then suspended him, but in January 1868 the Senate refused to confirm Stanton's suspension and he returned to his office. A month later Johnson dismissed him outright; Stanton, still with the support of the Senate, barricaded himself in the War Department, posted a guard, and remained until the trial of the impeachment charges against Johnson, based on his dismissal of Stanton, failed in May; he was then forced to resign. In 1869 President Ulysses S. Grant nominated him to the Supreme Court, but four days after his confirmation by the Senate he died, on December 24, 1869, in Washington, D.C.

Stanton, Elizabeth Cady (1815–1902), social reformer. Born on November 12, 1815, in Johnstown, New York, the daughter of an eminent lawyer, Elizabeth Cady received a superior education— she attended the Troy Female Seminary—and often sat with her father observing his work. Many times she heard him explain to tearful women the details of laws that deprived them of their property and even their children. She resolved at an early age to reform those statutes that placed women in a lower status in church, state, and society. In 1840 she married Henry Brewster Stanton, a prominent abolitionist, insisting that the word "obey" would be dropped from the ceremony. Later that year they attended the World's Anti-Slavery Convention in London and she was outraged at being refused official recognition because of her sex. With Lucretia C. Mott she organized the first women's-rights convention in Seneca Falls, New York, in 1848. For it she drew up a Declaration of Sentiments, modeled on the Declaration of Independence, that detailed the inferior status of women and that, in calling for extensive reforms, launched the women's-rights movement. The convention was followed by several more; as the movement gained momentum, Mrs. Stanton remained in the forefront. Her suffrage proposals met with great opposition, even among women, and her reputation as a "radical" was later established when she suggested that a husband's drunkenness or brutality be made grounds for divorce. From 1851 she worked closely with Susan B. Anthony and together they remained active for 40 years after the first convention, planning campaigns, speaking before legislative bodies, and addressing gatherings in conventions, lyceums, and on the streets. By 1860 New York laws had been amended to grant women joint guardianship of their children, the right to sue in court, to receive and keep wages, and to own real and personal property. With Miss Anthony as her business manager, Mrs. Stanton edited and wrote militant articles for the *Revolution*, 1868–1870, a women's-rights newspaper. Almost continuously from its founding in 1869 until 1890 she presided over the National Woman Suffrage Association, and when in 1890 the organization merged with the American Woman Suffrage Association, she was elected first president of the new National American Woman Suffrage Association, a post she held until 1892. She helped to compile the first three volumes (1881–1886) of the six-volume *History of Woman Suffrage*, 1881–1922, contributed articles to newspapers and periodicals, and published an autobiography, *Eighty Years and More*, in 1898. She died in New York City on October 26, 1902.

Stark, John (1728–1822), soldier. Born on August 28, 1728, in Londonderry, New Hampshire, Stark grew up on the New England frontier, in an environment that prepared him well for the services he would perform in the last French and Indian War and in the American Revolution. During the former conflict he saw service with Rogers's Rangers, several units of frontiersmen led by Maj.

Robert Rogers that carried out raids and took part in a number of the hardest-fought battles of the war, including Ticonderoga. The strength of the Rangers, apart from their being sharpshooters, lay in their ability to adopt the most useful features of Indian warfare; they were hardy, mobile, and self-sufficient. All these traits served Stark well during his years of fighting the British in the Revolution. As soon as news of the fighting at Lexington and Concord came in April 1775, Stark set out for Boston. He was appointed colonel of a New Hampshire regiment and fought at Bunker Hill. He participated in the defense of New York City, the American retreat from Canada, and in the battles of Trenton and Princeton in New Jersey. Early in 1777 he resigned his commission and returned home, but by July he was back in the fray when Gen. John Burgoyne's British forces invaded New York and threatened Vermont. The General Court of New Hampshire appointed Stark to command a force, with the rank of brigadier general. In Vermont on August 16 he attacked a contingent of 700 Hessian soldiers and Tories under Lt. Col. Friedrich Baum, later reinforced by another 600 near Bennington and captured most of them in an important victory of the Saratoga Campaign. He was commended for his action by the Continental Congress and given the rank of brigadier general in the Continental army. Later he helped bring about the surrender of Burgoyne in New York, and twice he was put in command of the Northern Department. He also saw service in Rhode Island and at the battle of Springfield in 1780 and sat on the court martial of Major André. In 1783 he became a major general. Following the war Stark retired to his home in New Hampshire and declined several opportunities to hold office. He died in Manchester, New Hampshire, on May 8, 1822, at the age of ninety-three.

Stassen, Harold Edward (1907–   ), lawyer and public official. Born on April 13, 1907, in West Saint Paul, Minnesota, a few miles south of St. Paul, Stassen graduated from the University of Minnesota in 1927. During his college career, along with many other extracurricular activities, he took an interest in politics, and was instrumental in founding the Young Republican League. He went on to the university's law school, from which he graduated in 1929. Admitted to the bar the same year, he began practice in South St. Paul, a stockyard town with a population of immigrants and laborers. Almost immediately he went into politics, winning election in 1930 as county attorney, a post he held until 1938. During these eight years Stassen and his fellow young Republicans gradually gained the ascendancy over the old guard in the state party, and he became the Republican candidate for governor in 1938. He faced the strong opposition of an entrenched Farmer-Labor party, but by tireless campaigning in nearly every town of the state he won the contest in a landslide, obtaining a good deal of labor support in the process. At thirty-one, he was the youngest governor in the nation. He won reelection twice, in 1940 and 1942 (Minnesota had biennial gubernatorial contests at that time), and gained national prominence for his reforms and his brand of liberal Republicanism. In 1940 he was selected to give the keynote address at the Republican national convention, although he was still too young to be a presidential contender. While still governor, Stassen was commissioned a lieutenant commander in the navy, and during his third term he resigned to go on active duty in World War II. He served on the staff of Adm. William F. Halsey in the Pacific from June 1944 to January 1945. In the spring of 1945 he was appointed one of the U.S. delegates to the founding conference of the United Nations at San Francisco. Discharged from the service in November 1945, he immediately began making plans to run for the Republican presidential nomination in 1948. With the backing of the Minnesota Republicans he announced for the race in December 1946 and spent the following year speaking in all parts of the country on what he felt were the issues the United States faced. He lost the nomination to Thomas E. Dewey, but won a good deal of public approbation for his campaign. In July 1948 Stassen accepted the presidency of the University of Pennsylvania, serving until 1953. He unsuccessfully sought the Republican nomination again in 1952 and in 1964, but without a political base from which to work, there was never much chance of his obtaining it. During the administrations of Dwight D. Eisenhower Stassen served the federal government in several capacities, as director of the Mutual Security Agency (MSA) for a period in 1953, as director of the Foreign Operations Administration (FOA) from 1953 to 1955, and from 1955 to 1958 as special assistant to the President, with cabinet rank, to direct studies on disarmament. After 1958 he was a member of a law firm in Philadelphia.

Statler, Ellsworth Milton (1863–1928), hotel owner. Born in Somerset County, Pennsylvania, in 1863, Statler grew up there and in Bridgeport, Ohio. Through most of his childhood he had to work because of his family's poverty and at thirteen he got a job as a bellboy in a hotel in Wheeling, West Virginia. He advanced to hotel clerk and studied hotel management and bookkeeping. Within a few years he was running his own lunch room and billiard hall in Wheeling. In 1896 he moved to Buffalo, New York, and took over the restaurant concession at the Ellicott Square Building. Two years later, when Buffalo was designated as the site of the Pan-American Exposition to be held in 1901, Statler built his first hotel, a temporary building of 2100 rooms, near the exposition grounds. The reputation he earned from this venture won him the task of building the Inside Inn at the Louisiana Purchase Exposition in St. Louis in 1904. The same year he built the Statler Hotel in Buffalo, and his holdings were soon expanded into a chain of hotels in Detroit, Cleveland, St. Louis, and New York City. The slogan of his hotel business was "The customer is always right," and he took pains to provide for comfort and convenience in his hotels. The Statler Hotel in Buffalo was the first in the country in which each room had running water and a private bath. The name of the Statler chain became synonymous with efficient, customer-oriented service. By the mid–1920s the Statler hotel properties were the largest in the nation owned by a single individual. In 1927 he opened his last hotel, in Boston. He died the following year, on April 16, 1928, in New York City.

Staunton, Schuyler, *see* Baum, Lyman Frank

Stefansson, Vilhjalmur (1879–1962), explorer. Born in Arnes, Manitoba, on November 3, 1879, Stefansson graduated from the University of Iowa in 1903 and later studied at Harvard. He twice journeyed to Iceland, his parents' native country, once in 1904 and on an archaeological expedition sponsored by Harvard in 1905. He then embarked on his career in Arctic exploration and research. He visited the Arctic for the first time in 1906–1907; appointed ethnologist of an expedition to the Mackenzie River delta, he traveled overland alone to the meeting point and, when the ship was held up by the ice and never arrived, spent over a year living with the Eskimos. He learned their language and culture and formed the belief, which he later put into practice, that Europeans could live off the land in the Arctic if they lived like the Eskimos. From 1908 to 1912 he joined Rudolph M. Anderson of the University of Iowa in ethnological studies of the Eskimos of the Mackenzie delta and of the Copper Eskimos of Coronation Gulf; it was during these expeditions, undertaken under the auspices of the Canadian government and the American Museum of Natural History, that he discovered blond Eskimos whose existence had not been suspected. His greatest achievement in the Arctic was the expedition on which he spent five years between 1913 and 1918 continuously north of the Arctic Circle, exploring the western part of the Canadian Arctic and the far north of Alaska, discovering several islands, and living for considerable periods of time on nothing but raw meat and fat (blubber)—a restricted diet that, he later asserted, caused him no discomfort whatsoever and was indeed necessary in the extreme conditions that he faced. It was on that expedition that Robert A. Bartlett, captain of the *Karluk*, made his famed rescue trek from Wrangell Island to Siberia and back. Stefansson lived in various places in Canada and the United States during the 1920s, and from 1932 to 1945 was a consultant to Pan American World Airways on the planning of Arctic routes. During World War II he was an adviser to the U.S. government, with duties that included instructing troops in Arctic survival techniques. From 1947 he was a consultant to the Northern Studies program at Dartmouth College, which came into possession of his famous collection of books and materials on the Arctic, and he died in Hanover, New Hampshire, on August 26, 1962. He wrote a number of books and many articles and monographs; among his principal works were *My Life with the Eskimo*, 1913; *The Friendly Arctic*, 1921; *The Northward Course of Empire*, 1922, reflecting his abiding belief in the economic potential of the Arctic regions; *The Adventure of Wrangell Island*, 1925; *Unsolved Mysteries of the Arctic*, 1939; *Greenland*, 1942; *Arctic Manual*, 1945; *Cancer: Disease of Civilization*, 1960, in which he argued for a high-protein diet; and the posthumous *Discovery*, 1964.

Steffens, Lincoln (1866–1936), journalist and social reformer. Born in San Francisco on April 6, 1866, Joseph Lincoln Steffens grew up there and in Sacramento. In 1889 he graduated from the University of California and for three years traveled and studied in Europe. Upon his return late in 1892 he became a reporter for the *New York Evening Post;* in the course of his work he observed exposures of corruption in the police department and during the investigations met Theodore Roosevelt, then president of the board of police commissioners, with whom he remained friends for many years. From 1897 to 1901 he was city editor of the *New York Commercial Advertiser* and in 1901, after a brief and abortive attempt to write a novel, he became managing editor of *McClure's Magazine.* With his staff colleagues Ida M. Tarbell and Ray Stannard Baker he inaugurated the era of journalistic "muckraking"—so called by Roosevelt—by publishing a series of exposés of corruption in business and politics. Beginning with "Tweed Days in St. Louis," written with Claude Wetmore, Steffens contributed articles on corruption in municipal governments across the country that were later collected as *The Shame of the Cities*, 1904. In that book, in his subsequent *The Struggle for Self-Government*, 1906, and *Upbuilders*, 1909, and on many successful lecture tours, he avoided the often empty sensationalism of lesser muckrakers and confronted his audiences with factual studies in order to clarify the conflict of public and private interests, leaving the solution to enlightened public action. In 1906 he left *McClure's* and, with Miss Tarbell, Baker, Finley Peter Dunne, William Allen White, and others, bought the *American Magazine;* together they made it into the nation's leading journal of reform. He resigned in 1907 and, except for a part-time editorial association with *Everybody's Magazine*, 1906–1911, thereafter worked as a free-lance journalist. In 1909, at the invitation of Edward A. Filene, he undertook investigations of government and business activities in Boston. He gradually lost faith in the efficacy of spontaneous popular reform movements and turned more and more toward the notions of revolution and charismatic leadership, in the process losing most of his audience. In 1914 he traveled with Venustiano Carranza, the Mexican revolutionary leader, and in 1917 and 1919 visited Soviet Russia. On the second trip he met V. I. Lenin and returned much impressed; he wrote a friend, "I have seen the future, and it works." From 1919 to 1927 he lived in Europe; upon his return he settled in Carmel, California. In 1931 he published his *Autobiography*, which was highly successful, and for several years he was again a popular lecturer. He died on August 9, 1936, in Carmel.

Steichen, Edward Jean (1879–1973), photographer. Born in Luxembourg on March 27, 1879, Edouard Jean Steichen later changed the spelling of his first name. He emigrated with his parents to Hancock, Michigan, at the age of three, and in 1889 they settled in Milwaukee. At fifteen he left school to begin a four-year apprenticeship in a lithography house. He bought his first camera at sixteen and made profitable hobbies of photography and painting. His early camera work was impressionistic; he was preoccupied with conveying mood and used soft focus and such techniques as raindrops on his camera lens. "The Lady in the Doorway" was shown in a Philadelphia salon in 1889 and brought him early attention; he also exhibited in a Chicago salon in 1900. On the way to Paris that year, he stopped in New York City to show examples of his work to Alfred Stieglitz, who encouraged him to continue. In London he created a stir with several photographs in a show in 1900, and in Paris he became associated with the movement in modern art. There he photographed many notable Europeans, including Auguste Rodin, whom he studied for a year before producing "Rodin—Le Penseur," 1902, which won first prize in a 1904 competition at The Hague. He returned to New York City in 1902 and opened a studio at 291 Fifth Avenue, where in 1905 Stieglitz and the "photo-secessionists," among whom was Steichen, opened the famed 291 Gallery, devoted to winning for photography recognition as an art form. From 1906 until the beginning of World War I he was in France, conducting experiments in plant breeding, painting, and photography. In 1917 he became a lieutenant colonel in the photography section of the Air Service of the army and did important work in aerial photography. Returning to New York City in 1923, he became head of photography for Condé Nast Publications. His portraits of such people as Greta Garbo, Rudolph Valentino, Charlie Chaplin, and the Barrymores appeared regularly in *Vanity Fair*, and his fashion photography glorified *Vogue*. In 1938 he closed his New York City studio and spent much time at his farm in West Redding, Connecticut, cultivating and hybridizing delphiniums, upon which he was an acknowledged authority. In 1941 he entered the navy as a lieutenant commander and rose to captain by 1946, having supervised all navy combat photography during World War II. He produced the film *The Fighting Lady*, 1944, and published *The Blue Ghost: A Photographic Log and Personal Narrative of the Aircraft Carrier U.S.S. Lexington in Combat Operation*, 1947, and compiled two pictorial exhibitions, "Road to Victory," 1942, and "Power in the Pacific," 1945, for the Museum of Modern Art in New York City. He was appointed director of the museum's photography department in 1947 and remained in that position until 1962. Of the many outstanding exhibitions he organized for the museum, the most acclaimed was "The Family of Man," 1955, which he created in association with his brother-in-law, Carl Sandburg, and which toured widely. He retired in 1962. Steichen died in West Redding, Connecticut, on March 25, 1973.

Stein, Gertrude (1874–1946), author and critic. Born on February 3, 1874, in Allegheny, Pennsylvania, Miss Stein grew up in Oakland, California, and in San Francisco. She attended Radcliffe from 1893 to 1897, where she studied psychology under William James, and the Johns Hopkins Medical School from 1897 to 1902. In 1903 she moved to Paris, where she lived on an independent income, and returned to the United States only once, on a lecture tour in 1934. She became famous as the center of the American expatriate movement of the 1920s; she dubbed its members the "lost generation" and was quoted to that effect in the epigraph to Ernest Hemingway's *The Sun Also Rises*. An early patron of such artists as Pablo Picasso, Georges Braque, Henri Matisse, and Juan Gris, she built up a fabulous collection of their works before they became famous. Among numerous others who frequented her home were Hemingway, Sherwood Anderson, Wyndham Lewis, André Gide, Carl Van Vechten, Ezra Pound, Ford Madox Ford, Paul Robeson, Clive Bell, John Reed, Elliot Paul, and Jo Davidson. Her writing was for the most part unintelligible, but to many readers fascinating nevertheless. Concerned with sound and the rhythm of words rather than their conventional meanings, it was, she claimed, a literary counterpart of cubism, and was characterized by such sentences as "Rose is a rose is a rose is a rose." A second famous phrase, "Pigeons in the grass, alas," was from her libretto for the opera *Four Saints in Three Acts* (which neither concerned four saints nor had three acts), with music by Virgil Thomson, first produced in the United States in 1934 and many times revived. Her books included *Three Lives*, 1908; *Tender Buttons*, 1915; *The Making of Americans*, 1925; *Lucy Church Amiably*, 1930; *Before the Flowers of Friendship Faded Friendship Faded*, 1931; and *The Autobiography of Alice B. Toklas*, 1933, which was in reality her autobiography rather than that of Miss Toklas, her secretary and companion from 1907. Among her critical and other nonfiction works were *Composition as Explanation*, 1926; *How to Write*, 1931; *Narration*, 1935; *The Geographical History of America*, 1936; *Picasso*, 1938; *Paris France*, 1940; *Wars I Have Seen*, 1945; and *Brewsie and Willie*, 1946. She died in Paris on July 27, 1946.

Stein, William Howard (1911–1980), biochemist. Born in New York City on June 25, 1911, Stein attended Harvard (B.S. 1933) and Columbia University, where he took a Ph.D. in 1938. On completing his graduate studies he joined the staff of the Rockefeller Institute for Medical Research (subsequently Rockefeller University). Appointed full professor in 1952, he gained prominence for his work on cellular protein synthesis. Concentrating, along with his colleague Stanford

Moore, on a chemical analysis of the enzyme ribonuclease, Stein contributed to explaining the chemical processes essential for the existence of a cell. By the mid–1960s the problem of how the living cell synthesizes protein had been all but completely elucidated. The detailed analysis of this important process involved showing the way in which amino acids became attached to ribonuclease and are then linked together by peptide bonds in a sequence ultimately determined by DNA, the genetic material of the cell. The result is the synthesis of a unique polypeptide structure—a protein—characteristic of the cell that made it. In essence their work amounted to a chemical analysis at the molecular level of cell metabolism and reproduction. Stein and Moore shared, along with Christian B. Anfinsen, the 1972 Nobel Prize for Chemistry for their fundamental contributions to enzyme chemistry. Shortly before the announcement of the award, the two published their analysis of the action of deoxyribonuclease. The recipient of the Electrophoresis Award of the American Chemical Society, he was editor of the *Journal of Biological Chemistry* from 1968 to 1971. He died on February 2, 1980, in New York City.

Steinbeck, John Ernst (1902–1968), author. Born on February 27, 1902, in Salinas, California, Steinbeck grew up near Monterey and attended Stanford University off and on from 1920 to 1925. He moved to New York City and worked there as a newspaper writer and a bricklayer; returning to California in 1926, he lived on an estate in the High Sierra as a caretaker, completing in the course of two winters his first novel, *Cup of Gold*, published in 1929. The following two novels, *The Pastures of Heaven*, 1932, and *To a God Unknown*, 1933, although promising, attracted little notice. *Tortilla Flat*, however, published in 1935, became a best seller, was adapted to the stage and sold to Hollywood, and was criticized by the Monterey Chamber of Commerce as a possible deterrent to the tourist trade. Concerned with the colorful and unique Spanish-speaking "paisanos" in Monterey, it was a humorous depiction of life among raffish idlers who later reappeared in *Cannery Row*, 1945, *The Wayward Bus*, 1947, and *Sweet Thursday*, 1954. His distinguished collection of stories, *The Long Valley*, 1938, included those published separately in 1937 as *The Red Pony*. Its theme of leadership was foreshadowed by *In Dubious Battle*, 1936, a chilling, vivid portrayal of a California strike in the 1930s. His celebrated allegory of self-determination and need, *Of Mice and Men*, 1937, was initially conceived as a stage drama but was only later adapted for the theater following its completion as a novel; the play won the 1937 New York Drama Critics' Circle Award. Steinbeck was at that time accompanying several migrant workers to California on a journey that he described in *The Grapes of Wrath*, 1939, a novel that provoked almost as wide and shocked reaction as had Harriet Beecher Stowe's *Uncle Tom's Cabin*. Appearing at the end of the Depression of the 1930s, the story of the dispossessed Joad family of "Okies" became symbolic of the hardships of every victim of the Dust Bowl or of hard times. The book won a 1940 Pulitzer Prize and was made into a motion picture. During World War II he wrote *Bombs Away* and *The Moon is Down*, both in 1942, and was a correspondent for the *New York Herald Tribune*, his dispatches later being collected in *Once There Was a War*, 1958. He wrote movie scripts for *The Red Pony*, *The Pearl* (published as a novel in 1947), and *The Forgotten Village*. Although his critical reputation had declined somewhat, his later realistic novels, *East of Eden*, 1952, and *The Winter of Our Discontent*, 1961, and the autobiographical *Travels with Charley* (Charley being his dog), 1962, were significant additions to the corpus of his work, for which he won the 1962 Nobel Prize for Literature. The naturalism and sociological preoccupation of much of his early work gave way in his mature years to a deeper view of human life, and renewed critical interest revealed elements of allegory and even mythopoeic qualities in his finest work. He died in New York City on December 20, 1968.

Steinberg, Saul (1914–   ), painter and cartoonist. Born in Rîmnicu-Sărat, Romania, on June 15, 1914, Steinberg graduated from high school in Bucharest in 1932. After a year at the university there, he went to Milan, Italy, to pursue studies in architecture at the Reggio Politecnico, where he received his doctorate in 1940. He spent the years from 1939 to 1941 as a practicing architect in Milan, but gradually turned toward art and cartooning. These fields opened a career for which he became celebrated. Even while living in Europe his drawings began appearing in the United States in *Life* and *Harper's Bazaar*. Italy's involvement on the Axis side in World War II influenced Steinberg to leave for the United States; he arrived in 1942 after a short stay in the Dominican Republic. In 1943, although an alien, he was granted a commission in the U.S. navy and was then naturalized as a citizen. In the same year he had his first one-man show in the United States, at the Wakefield Gallery in New York City. During the war he served in the Far East, in the India-Burma-China theater, then was transferred to Italy to serve with the Office of Strategic Services (OSS). Returning to the United States after the war, he was recognized as a major artist by the inclusion of his drawings and watercolors in the "Fourteen Americans" show at New York City's Museum of Modern Art in 1946. His works were also exhibited at the Metropolitan Museum of Art in New York City, the Detroit Institute of Arts, and the Victoria and Albert Museum in London. Shows of his work in major U.S. cities increased his national reputation, and his cartoons and especially his remarkable magazine covers, enigmatic and allegorical and unfailingly fascinating in delicate detail, were familiar to readers of the *New Yorker* for three decades. In addition to making drawings and cartoons, Steinberg painted murals for which he achieved some fame. He was commissioned in 1948 to do a 1080-square-foot mural in the Skyline

Room in Cincinnati's Terrace-Plaza Hotel, and he worked for years on what he considered his masterpiece, a huge work entitled *Parades*, a panorama of nations and eras, that was a lifetime project. Much of it was acquired by the Metropolitan Museum of Art in New York City. In 1966 Steinberg became artist in residence at the Smithsonian Institution for two years, and in 1968 he was inducted into the National Institute of Arts and Letters. His extraordinary and totally unpredictable imagination made him one of the very few unique and inimitable artists of the twentieth century.

Steinitz, William (1836–1900), chess player. Born on May 17, 1836, in Prague, Bohemia (now Czechoslovakia), Wilhelm Steinitz (he later changed the spelling of his first name) studied at the Polytechnicum in Vienna, and while a student acquired an interest in chess. Within a few years he had become adept enough at the game to decide to devote full time to it. In 1861 he won a local championship in Vienna, and the following year placed sixth in an international meet at London. By 1866 he was generally recognized as the world chess champion, due to his defeat of Adolph Anderssen. In 1868 Steinitz won first prize in the British chess association handicap and in 1872 took top honors in the London grand tourney. He held his world title for 28 years—18 years longer than any previous champion—until he was defeated by Emanuel Lasker in 1894. From 1862 until 1882 Steinitz lived in England, playing in matches and editing a chess column for an English magazine. In 1883 he emigrated to the United States and eventually became a U.S. citizen. Over the next dozen years he wrote chess columns for several newspapers, edited the *International Chess Magazine*, and wrote a text on the game, *The Modern Chess Instructor*, two volumes, 1889–1895. His defeat for the championship in 1894 unsettled him mentally, and he was at various times after that committed to mental institutions. Still he continued to play chess, hoping to regain the championship. Intermittent mental breakdowns led to his confinement at Manhattan State Hospital in New York City, where he died on August 12, 1900.

Steinman, David Barnard (1886–1960), engineer. Born in New York City on June 11, 1886, Steinman graduated from City College of New York (CCNY) in 1906 and took his doctorate at Columbia University in 1911. From 1910 to 1914 he taught at the University of Idaho, then was invited to return to New York City to assist in the design and construction of the Hell Gate Bridge, which was opened in 1917. From 1917 to 1920 he taught engineering at City College before becoming an independent designer and consultant. During the next 40 years he was responsible for the design of some of the world's great bridges. He created the design and supervised the construction of the Florianópolis Bridge in Brazil, opened in 1926; the Carquinez Strait Bridge in California, 1927; the Mount Hope Bridge in Rhode Island, 1929; the St.

John's Bridge at Portland, Oregon, 1931; the Sydney Harbor Bridge in Australia, 1932; and the Triborough Bridge in New York City, 1936. He was one of the designers of the George Washington Bridge, 1931, connecting Manhattan with New Jersey across the Hudson River, and in 1938 his Thousand Islands International Bridge connecting Canada and the United States was opened. He was also responsible for the design and construction of bridges in the Far East, the Caribbean, the Middle East, and Europe. The Mackinac Bridge in Michigan designed by Steinman and spanning 3800 feet, was at the time of its construction (1954–1957) the third longest suspension bridge in existence. He also projected a bridge across the Strait of Messina to connect Italy and Sicily, which, if it were built, would become the longest suspension bridge in the world. In the 1950s he did preliminary design work for the Verrazano-Narrows Bridge across the Narrows at the entrance to New York Harbor. This, the longest span in the world at the time of its construction (1959–1964), stretched 4260 feet. Steinman did not live to see its completion; he died in New York City on August 21, 1960. Among his published works were *Suspension Bridges, Their Design, Construction and Erection*, 1923; *Bridges and Their Builders*, 1941; *Famous Bridges of The World*, 1953; and *Miracle Bridge at Mackinac*, 1957.

Steinmetz, Charles Proteus (1865–1923), engineer. Born on April 9, 1865, in Breslau, Germany (now Wroclaw, Poland), Steinmetz was originally named Karl August Rudolf. In 1883 he entered the University of Breslau and undertook a rigorous course in mathematics, the physical sciences, and electrical engineering. He studied there and at Berlin until his editorship of a Socialist newspaper brought him into conflict with the authorities in 1888 and he was forced to flee before receiving the Ph.D. he had earned. After a year in Switzerland, during part of which he attended the University of Zurich, he came to New York City in 1889 and took a job as a draftsman with an electrical-engineering firm in Yonkers. When he applied for citizenship he anglicized Karl to Charles and adopted as a middle name Proteus, a nickname from his university days. His great knowledge of electricity and mathematics quickly won him advancement from draftsman, and he began to undertake independent research. His first major accomplishment was the derivation of the law of hysteresis, the residual magnetism in the electromagnets of electrical generators and motors that causes power loss; his quantification of this hitherto little-understood phenomenon made possible great progress in the design of generators and motors. His papers on hysteresis were presented in 1892 and firmly established his reputation; in the same year his employer's firm was merged into the General Electric Company and he soon became a consulting engineer with the new company in Schenectady, New York. In 1893 he announced the results of his theoretical studies of alternating currents, a symbolic method of calculation that eventually brought this highly complex field within reach of the average practicing engineer and helped make the use of alternating current (AC) commercially feasible. His *Theory and Calculation of Alternating Current Phenomena*, 1897, and subsequent texts, including *Theory and Calculation of Transient Electric Phenomena and Oscillations*, 1909; *Radiation, Light and Illumination*, 1909; *Engineering Mathematics*, 1911; *Theory and Calculation of Electric Circuits*, 1917; and *Theory and Calculations of Electric Apparatus*, 1917, were long standard works. He later turned to the investigation of lightning, a line of research that led to the production of artificial lightning in the laboratory and his development of lightning arresters for the protection of electric-power lines. From 1902 until his death he supplemented his work at General Electric by serving as professor of electrical engineering and later of electrophysics at Union College in Schenectady. In addition to his theoretical contributions to electrical engineering, he also made many practical innovations and held some 200 patents in his field. He died in Schenectady, New York, on October 26, 1923.

Steinway, Henry Englehard (1797–1871), piano manufacturer. Born in Wolfshagen, Germany, on February 15, 1797, Steinway (originally Heinrich Engelhard Steinweg) grew up in the time of war and social upheaval that was the Napoleonic era. Several of his family were killed during the invasion of Germany, and in 1815 he was drafted into the army. After the war he settled at Seesen where, in spite of his lack of musical training, he went to work for an organ builder. In 1820 he took up piano making and built a successful business for himself over the next three decades. But when the European revolutions of 1848 destroyed his livelihood, he resolved to move to the United States and begin his work again. The family arrived in New York City in June 1851, but it was two years before he and his sons could get enough money together to begin their own piano shop. The Steinweg piano was almost immediately recognized for its quality, and over the next several years the family diversified by manufacturing upright and grand pianos as well as the then standard square pianos. In 1861 Henry Steinweg entered a formal partnership with his sons. In 1864 he changed his name legally to Steinway. He died in New York City ten years later, on February 7, 1871. His fourth son, William Steinway (1835–1896), had come to the United States with his family in 1851 and become an apprentice piano maker. Born at Seesen, Germany, on March 5, 1835, he studied at Jacobsohn College there and showed a definite interest in music. But once in the United States he turned down a musical career in favor of staying with his father's business and in 1853 he joined his father in the piano shop opened that year. The death of two of William's brothers in 1865 prompted him to devote himself increasingly to the commercial side of the business, and he gradually took over the promotion and selling of the firm's pianos. He urged the building of Steinway

Hall (1867) on 14th Street in New York City, and encouraged visits by European musicians to the United States. The firm gained, through William's efforts, an international reputation as noted musicians were persuaded to use Steinway pianos. In 1876 William was elected president of the firm. For the next 20 years he remained in charge, and also took an active part in the affairs of New York City as chairman of the Rapid Transit Commission that planned the city's first subway. In 1880 he founded the town of Steinway, Long Island (now a part of Long Island City) across from Manhattan, and moved the piano factories there. William died in New York City on November 30, 1896.

Steinweg, Heinrich Engelhard, *see* Steinway, Henry Engelhard

Stella, Frank Philip (1936–   ), painter. Born on May 12, 1936, in Malden, Massachusetts, Stella became interested in painting early in his school years and continued to paint through his years at Phillips Academy at Andover, Massachusetts, and at Princeton University. While still in school he found that traditional representational art was not for him, and during his studies at Andover he turned toward Abstract Expressionism. But in his senior year at Princeton (from which he did not graduate) he began to seek for a simpler, more direct style. After that time he employed a large number of modes, emphasizing color, shape, and structure without any attempt at illusionism. From Abstract Expressionism he moved into a transitional style in 1958, producing paintings that consisted of stripes or box forms. Later that year he undertook a series of "black" paintings, patterns of stripes on canvas that brought him his first popular acclaim with showings in 1959 and inclusion in the Museum of Modern Art's "Sixteen Americans" exhibition in 1959–1960. One of the youngest artists to receive such wide acceptance, from 1960 he exhibited his paintings throughout the country. His work also appeared in several shows abroad. After 1960 Stella worked through a number of successive series of paintings, each series distinctive for its use of color or emphasis on shapes, which ranged even into three dimensions. Because of his primary, almost exclusive, interest in color and structure and also because of the variety of his work, Stella came to be recognized as a leader of the "Minimal Art" movement.

Stengel, Charles Dillon (1891–1975), "Casey," baseball player and manager. Born on July 30, 1891, in Kansas City, Missouri (hence his nickname—KC, or Casey), Stengel attended Western Dental College there for a time, playing baseball during the summer. He dropped his dental course in 1910 in favor of playing professional ball with teams in Kankakee, Illinois, and Maysville, Kentucky. He played for various minor-league teams until halfway through the 1912 season, when he was drafted by the Brooklyn Dodgers of the National League. He stayed with the Dodgers until the end of the 1917 season, playing in one World

Series. He was traded to the Pittsburgh Pirates in 1917, to the Philadelphia Phillies in 1919, and to the New York Giants in 1921. With the Giants he attained a batting average of .368, the highest of his career, and took part in two World Series, 1922 and 1923. In 1923 he was traded to the Boston Braves and played for that team until 1925, when he became manager of their farm team at Worcester, Massachusetts. After one season he went to the Toledo team of the American Association, where he remained until 1931 and closed out his playing career. He ended his playing days with a total of 1277 games, a fielding average of .964, and a career batting average of .284. From 1932 on Stengel was exclusively a manager and coach. He was with the Brooklyn Dodgers from 1932 to 1937 and with the Boston Braves until 1943. Then for five years he managed minor-league teams and in 1948 led the Oakland team to the Pacific Coast championship. Late in 1948 Dan Topping and George Weiss, who had just purchased the New York Yankees, hired Stengel as manager. In that position until the end of the 1960 season, he led the Yankees to ten American League pennants and seven World Series championships. In the five seasons from 1949 to 1953 the Yankees won both the pennant and the Series every year, a feat never before accomplished by any other team (although the Yankees did win pennants five years in a row again, from 1960 to 1964). After the 1960 season Stengel was dropped as manager of the Yankees, but in 1962 he was back at work as the first manager of the newly organized New York Mets of the National League. After three and a half seasons of failing to get the club out of last place, he retired in the summer of 1965. Whether in or out of a managing position, Casey Stengel was acknowledged to be one of baseball's authentic "characters," whose humor and quotable malapropisms became nationally known through the sports columns. He was elected to the National Baseball Hall of Fame on March 8, 1966. At the age of eighty, in August 1970, he appeared at Old Timer's Day at Yankee Stadium on the occasion of his uniform number 37 being retired. Only four Yankees had previously been so honored: Babe Ruth, Lou Gehrig, Joe DiMaggio, and Mickey Mantle. Stengel died on September 29, 1975, in Glendale, California.

Stephens, Alexander Hamilton (1812–1883), public official. Born on February 11, 1812, in present-day Taliaferro County, Georgia, Stephens, who was orphaned at fourteen, graduated from the University of Georgia in 1832 and, after a time spent teaching school and reading law, was admitted to the bar in 1834. He began his practice in Crawfordville, Georgia. Two years later he was elected to the Georgia legislature; he was a member of the state house of representatives until 1841, and in 1842 was elected to the state senate. As the shifting political alignments in Georgia stabilized, he emerged as a leading Southern Whig and as such was elected to the House of Representatives in 1843. At the outset of his career he had opposed

the doctrine of nullification but had upheld the theoretical right of secession; he continued to hold to his position on secession while counseling all possible forbearance short of surrendering states' rights altogether. He strongly opposed the Mexican War even though he had supported the annexation of Texas as a means of increasing Southern representation in Congress, and in 1850 not only supported but placed great hope in Henry Clay's "omnibus bill" (the Compromise of 1850). In that year he joined in the organization of the short-lived Constitutional Union party, rejoining the Whigs upon the failure of the new party to attract wide support. Two years later he broke with the Whig party when it nominated for the presidency Gen. Winfield Scott, who refused to endorse the compromise. Stephens moved into the Democratic party and retained his seat in the House. He was instrumental in securing passage of the Kansas-Nebraska Bill in 1854. As the conflict over slavery deepened, he became more and more a defender and even an advocate of the institution, although he still hoped secession could be prevented. He left Congress in 1859 and returned to Georgia; there he continued to preach patience, but when secession was voted by the legislature early in 1861 he acquiesced. He was sent as a Georgia delegate to the Southern states' convention at Montgomery, Alabama, and was chosen vice-president of the Confederacy on February 9, 1861. His official duties were minimal and, a firm believer in the precedence of principle over expediency, he was frequently at odds with President Jefferson Davis over infringements of personal and states' rights in such matters as conscription, martial law, and suspension of habeas corpus. During the war he constantly urged a program of prisoner exchange, and in February 1865 he headed the Confederate delegation to the unsuccessful armistice conference with President Abraham Lincoln at Hampton Roads, Virginia. On May 11, shortly after the Confederate surrender, he was arrested at his home by Federal troops and until October was imprisoned in Boston. Returning home, he was elected to the U.S. Senate in 1866 but was refused his seat. He wrote *A Constitutional View of the Late War Between the States*, 1868–1870, which caused much debate, and reprinted and rebutted the comments of many of his critics in *The Reviewers Reviewed*, 1872; he also published in 1875 *A Compendium of the History of the United States*. In 1872 he was returned to the House of Representatives and remained there for ten years; in 1882 he was elected governor of Georgia but died after only a few months in office, on March 4, 1883, in Atlanta.

Stephens, Uriah Smith (1821–1882), labor leader. Born on August 3, 1821, in Cape May, New Jersey, Stephens was unable to prepare for a career in the Baptist clergy because of his family's financial plight following the panic of 1837. He was apprenticed instead to a tailor to learn a trade, and while working as a tailor he set himself to learning about merchandising and economics. From

1853 until 1859 he traveled extensively, spending some five years in California, and then went to Philadelphia and began to take an active part in the labor movements of the day. There were at the time numerous legal and social barriers against labor activities, and in many places unions were regarded as criminal conspiracies; nevertheless, after the Civil War began, unionism revived, and in 1862 Stephens was one of the organizers of the Garment Cutters' Association. Local difficulties and pressure from employers in Philadelphia led to the dissolution of the association in 1869, whereupon Stephens joined with other laboring men to form the Noble Order of the Knights of Labor as a secret society. For the first troubled decade of its existence, the Knights of Labor organization was largely under the influence of Stephens. He was emphatic on the importance of secrecy and ritual, which, he felt, would help bind the diverse elements of the organization together. He also urged education as a means of obtaining cooperation among laborers and tradesmen. He ran for the House of Representatives in 1878 on the Greenback ticket, but was defeated. By this time he was in open conflict with Terence V. Powderly over the secrecy issue, and he resigned as Grand Master Workman of the Knights in 1879, after which his influence over the organization was greatly lessened. The Knights repudiated the rule of secrecy in 1881. Stephens died in Philadelphia the next year, on February 13, 1882, but the Knights of Labor went on, under Powderly, to become the largest and most powerful union of its time, with nearly a million members by 1886.

Stern, Isaac (1920–   ), violinist. Born in Kremenets, Russia, on July 21, 1920, Stern was brought by his family to the United States the following year; they settled in San Francisco, where he grew up. His family was well trained in music, and it was natural for his parents to guide his interests along the same lines. At the age of eight he began studying the violin, and from 1930 until 1937 was a student at the San Francisco Conservatory. When he was eleven, he made his debut with the San Francisco Symphony Orchestra. During the next several years he made appearances with several orchestras in West Coast cities, and in 1937 made his New York City debut. Dissatisfied with his New York concert, Stern returned home for more study. He continued his concert appearances, and by the time of his first appearance at New York City's Carnegie Hall in January 1943 he was reckoned among the world's greatest violinists and the only outstanding violinist whose development and training had been exclusively American. Giving as many as 90 concerts a year, he toured the United States and virtually every part of the world. He took part in major music festivals, including appearances in 1950–1952 at the Prades Festivals founded by cellist Pablo Casals. In 1953 he appeared in the movie *Tonight We Sing.* He was president for many years of Carnegie Hall in New York City.

Stern, Otto (1888–1969), physicist. Born in Zary, Poland (then Sorau, Germany), on February 17, 1888, Stern received his doctorate in physical chemistry from the University of Breslau (Wroclaw) in 1912. He worked with Albert Einstein at the universities of Prague and Zurich until 1914, when he joined the faculty of the University of Frankfurt; he remained there until 1921. After a short period at the University of Rostock, he was appointed to the chair of physical chemistry at the University of Hamburg in 1923. He remained there until 1933, but with the coming of Adolf Hitler to power in Germany, he resigned his position and came to the United States. He joined the staff of the Carnegie Institute of Technology in Pittsburgh, to which the Buhl Foundation contributed $25,000 to provide him a laboratory in which to do research in nuclear physics. Whereas Stern's early endeavors had been in theoretical physics, after 1919 he had turned to experimental work, primarily on the development of the molecular-beam method for investigating the properties of atoms and their nuclei. His researches confirmed the magnetic moment of atoms and many aspects of quantum theory. In 1933 he was able to measure the magnetic moment of the proton and in 1943 he won the Nobel Prize for Physics for his work on atomic structure. In 1945 he became professor emeritus at the Carnegie Institute and accepted an invitation to be guest lecturer in physics at the University of California at Berkeley. He remained there for 15 years, until his death in Berkeley on August 18, 1969.

Sternberg, George Miller (1838–1915), bacteriologist and physician. Born at Hartwick Seminary in Otsego County, New York, on June 8, 1838, Sternberg attended the seminary, of which his father was the principal, interspersing his years of study with teaching in local rural schools. He also spent some time studying anatomy and physiology privately at Cooperstown. He then entered upon the study of medicine, and received his M.D. degree in 1860 from the College of Physicians and Surgeons in New York City. As an assistant surgeon in the Union army during the Civil War he was present at several battles, was captured and escaped, but after contracting typhoid fever he spent the remainder of the war serving in military hospitals. By 1865 he was in charge of the U.S. General Hospital at Cleveland. From 1866 to 1879 he served at army posts throughout the United States, frequently in the West during the Indian wars that marked the period. A three-year tour of duty at Fort Barrancas in Florida, from 1872–1875, brought him into close contact with yellow fever (he contracted the disease himself in 1875), and afforded him the opportunity to study means of preventing infection. During the period he published two important articles on the disease. In 1879 he was given an assignment on the Havana Yellow Fever Commission to study the nature and cause of the disease. In those studies he made pioneering use of the technique of photomicrography. The results of the commission's work were inconclusive, suggesting that further advances in the field of bacteriology were needed before progress on the problem could be made. Over the next few years Sternberg succeeded in identifying the malaria plasmodium and the bacilli of tuberculosis and typhoid fever, and as early as 1881, the same year as Louis Pasteur's announcement, he published his discovery of the pneumococcus, the bacterium that causes pneumonia. Along with his researches on disease, Sternberg also experimented on disinfection, work in which he paralleled the efforts of Robert Koch. In 1892 he served as consultant to the receiving station for immigrants in New York City to inspect new arrivals for communicable diseases. In 1893 he became surgeon general of the army, with the rank of brigadier general, a post he held until 1902 and his retirement from active service. His tenure saw the expansion of medical research facilities through the addition of laboratories to the larger army hospitals. The Army Medical School was started in 1893, the Typhoid Fever Board in 1898, and the Yellow Fever Commission in 1900, and he also prompted the organization of the army nurse corps and the dental corps. He was intent on using research to remedy the current deficiencies of knowledge in the fields of bacteriology and epidemiology, and in many ways his efforts were successful, for they paved the way for later measures for coping with dread diseases. His *Manual of Bacteriology*, 1892, was the first complete treatise of its kind published in the United States. Sternberg spent his retirement in Washington, D.C., where he died on November 3, 1915.

Stetson, John Batterson (1830–1906), hat manufacturer. Born in Orange, New Jersey, on May 5, 1830, Stetson was apprenticed in the family trade of hatmaking, but on coming of age he left the family business to go out on his own. After spending a few years in the Midwest and in Colorado for reasons of health, he returned east and settled in Philadelphia, where he opened his own small hat factory in 1865. A poor early showing in sales led him to make notable innovations in styles and models, and these soon brought him success. He made it a point to manufacture varied styles of hats that would be in vogue in different parts of the country, and he relied on the popularity of his product to do its own advertising. He achieved particular success with a line of wide-brimmed, high-crowned headgear based on western models, and these became known simply as "Stetsons." By about 1900 the John B. Stetson Company was the largest hat factory in the world, employing more than 3000 persons. Stetson was strongly opposed to unions but was nevertheless generous to his employees, providing bonuses, stock allotments, and other benefits. He also underwrote the building of a hospital to serve his employees' needs. Among his other philanthropic activities was his support of De Land University, renamed in 1889 John B. Stetson University, at De Land, Florida. He died at his home in De Land on February 18, 1906.

Steuben, Baron von (1730–1794), soldier. Born in Magdeburg, Prussia (now Germany) on September 17, 1730, Friedrich Wilhelm Ludolf Gerhard Augustin von Steuben was the son of a lieutenant of engineers in the army of Frederick William I. About his early years very little is known; at seventeen he entered military service and served throughout the Seven Years' War, emerging with the rank of captain. The professional military competence he acquired during this period was later demonstrated while he served on Gen. George Washington's staff. He was discharged from the Prussian army in 1763, and thereafter served as chamberlain in the court of Hohenzollern-Hechingen. Sometime between 1764 and 1775 it appears that he was raised to the rank of baron, but no documents survive to confirm this. After trying unsuccessfully from 1775 to 1777 to resume his military career in Europe, he learned of the American war for independence while in Paris. He obtained letters of introduction to General Washington from the American agents in France, one of whom was Benjamin Franklin. For the sake of gaining recognition in America he promoted himself to "lieutenant general in the King of Prussia's service" (although captain had been his highest rank) and set sail for the United States, where he arrived in December 1777; he reported to Washington at Valley Forge on February 23, 1778. Impressed with von Steuben's credentials, Washington had him appointed inspector general of the Continental army and put him in charge of training the Continental troops. As drillmaster, von Steuben proved extremely effective, bringing to the colonial citizen army a discipline and effectiveness it had hitherto lacked. His work in instilling necessary discipline into the ragged Continental Army brought him promotion to major general at Washington's urging, in May 1778, and he later proved his worth in the field as well by performing valuable service at Monmouth Court House. During the following winter he devised a manual of military regulations that remained in use until 1812. Although anxious for a field command, and occasionally exasperating to Washington on that topic, he nonetheless worked faithfully in his staff post, continuing his training duties and instituting a system of accounting for supplies. Finally, in 1780, he was sent to the Southern theater of war to get the Virginia militia into fighting shape, and he there became Gen. Nathanael Greene's aide. During Greene's absence in the Carolina campaign, von Steuben was in command in Virginia. In 1781 he served under the Marquis de Lafayette during Gen. Charles Cornwallis's invasion of South Carolina. At Yorktown he successfully commanded a division, and remained a divisional commander until the war's end. Following the war he continued as a military adviser to General Washington by whom he was publicly commended, until he was finally discharged from the army on March 24, 1784. He had, by act of the Pennsylvania legislature, become an American citizen in 1783. Von Steuben then took up residence in New York City, where an extravagant social life brought him to the verge of bankruptcy. He had served throughout the Revolution without pay, but in 1790 Congress granted him a lifetime annual pension of $2800. He divided his time between the city and his farm, granted him by the State of New York, near Remsen, New York. He maintained his membership in the Society of the Cincinnati; a founder in July, 1783, he served as president of the New York branch. He died at his Remsen farm on November 28, 1794.

Stevens, Edwin Augustus (1795–1868), inventor and businessman. Born in Hoboken, New Jersey, on July 28, 1795, Stevens was the son of John Stevens. He frequently participated in the engineering projects of his father and his brother Robert, but Edwin was basically the businessman of the family. He managed his father's estate and was overseer of the family's commercial ventures. In 1821 he invented a plow that was widely used for many years. In 1825 he became manager of the Union Line freight and passenger service between Philadelphia and New York City, and within two years the Stevens family owned the business. In 1830 he was named manager and treasurer of the family-organized Camden & Amboy Railroad and Transportation Company. He made the road a success and continued as its manager for the next 35 years. He participated with his brother Robert in the design of armored naval vessels, an idea he had nurtured since 1814, and in 1842 he won congressional approval of a trial of the idea. Construction of his *Stevens Battery* did not begin until 1854 and, after Robert's death in 1856, he struggled to keep the project before the government, although he was never able to induce the navy to take an interest in such vessels, even as the Civil War broke upon the country. At his death he left both land and money in his will for the founding of the Stevens Institute of Technology in Hoboken, New Jersey. He died in Paris on August 7, 1868.

Stevens, John (1749–1838), engineer and inventor. Born in New York City in 1749, Stevens grew up in Perth Amboy, New Jersey, and attended nearby Kenersley's College. After the family moved back to New York City he enrolled at King's College (now Columbia), from which he graduated in 1768. He served as treasurer of New Jersey during the Revolution, rising to the rank of colonel, and as surveyor-general for eastern New Jersey in 1782–1783. He turned then from an earlier interest in law and politics to the study of steam navigation, then in an experimental stage. He designed boilers and engines, and in order to protect his inventions petitioned Congress on the need for a patent law. The first such law, generally as he outlined it, was passed by Congress in April 1790 and the following year he received his first patent. After some years of unsuccessful experiments, Stevens built a small steamboat, the *Little Juliana*, powered by a multitubular boiler he had patented in 1803 and operated by screw propellers, that crossed the Hudson River in 1804. He next designed an engine for a paddle-wheel steamboat, hoping to inaugurate ferry service from New Jersey to Manhattan and also service on the Hudson between New York City and Albany. But before his 100-foot vessel, the *Phoenix*, was completed, Robert Fulton's boat, the *Clermont*, had made a successful trip from New York to Albany in 1807. Since steam navigation rights on New York rivers were held by Fulton and by Robert R. Livingston, who was Stevens's brother-in-law and who had earlier been in partnership with him in his experiments, Stevens sent the *Phoenix* on a trial run to Philadelphia in June 1809, the world's first sea voyage made by a steamship. In 1811 he built the *Juliana*, which was used as a ferry on Long Island Sound. After 1810 he turned his attention to the use of steam locomotion in land transportation. He spent the next several years trying to convince the public and state legislatures of the feasibility of rail transportation and its superiority over canal boats, and in 1815 he received from New Jersey the first railroad charter in America. A similar charter in 1823 from the Pennsylvania legislature led to his organization of the Pennsylvania Railroad, which soon lapsed for lack of funds. In 1825 he constructed the first steam locomotive in the United States and by the next year was operating it on a circular track on his estate in Hoboken, New Jersey. It was not until 1830, however, when he was more than eighty years old, that he succeeded in forming the Camden & Amboy Railroad and Transportation Company. John Stevens died in Hoboken, New Jersey, on March 6, 1838. During most of his active career, two of his sons, Robert Livingston Stevens and Edwin Augustus Stevens, had been associated with him in his work.

Stevens, John Paul (1920–   ), justice of the Supreme Court. Born in Chicago on April 20, 1920, Stevens graduated from the University of Chicago in 1941. After naval service in Washington, D.C., he entered Northwestern University Law School, graduating and winning admission to the bar in 1947. He clerked for Justice Wiley Rutledge in 1947–1948 and then joined a Chicago law firm. A specialist in antitrust law, Stevens also lectured at Northwestern and the University of Chicago and in various commission assignments gained experience in public affairs. In 1970 he was appointed a judge of the Seventh Circuit Court of Appeals by President Richard M. Nixon. On the bench he acquired a reputation for scholarship, legal acumen, and fairness. On the retirement of Justice William O. Douglas he was appointed to the Supreme Court in November 1975 by President Gerald R. Ford. He was quickly confirmed and took his seat the next month.

Stevens, Robert Livingston (1787–1856), inventor and ship builder. Born in Hoboken, New Jersey, on October 18, 1787, Stevens was the son of John Stevens. He assisted his father in the construction of the *Little Juliana* and the *Phoenix*, and he captained the *Phoenix* on her maiden voyage and in subsequent years operated her as a ferry on the Delaware River. His particular interest became naval architecture, and over the years he designed and built more than 20 ferries and steamboats, constantly endeavoring to increase both the safety and the speed of his vessels, and incorporating many of his own inventions in them. Later in life, as a yachtsman, he designed the *Maria*, 1844, for 20 years the fastest sailing ship of its time. The War of 1812 turned his attention to the possibilities of armored naval vessels and plans for harbor defense, but the Navy Department showed little interest in his plans until the 1840s. He received a contract to build an armored ship in 1842, but changes in plans coupled with improved weaponry caused delays for more than 12 years and he died before the work could be completed. Besides following his interest in ship building, he joined his father in promoting rail transportation. In 1830 he went to England to study locomotives and bring back iron rails. He designed the "T" rail which is in standard use today and he discovered that rails laid on wooden ties over gravel provided a safer and more comfortable roadbed than other types of construction. When the Stevens family organized the Camden & Amboy Railroad and Transportation Company in 1830, Robert Stevens became the president and chief engineer, and with the locomotive *John Bull*, purchased in England, he inaugurated the first steam railroad service in New Jersey in 1831. He died in Hoboken, New Jersey, on April 20, 1856.

Stevens, Thaddeus (1792–1868), lawyer and public official. Born in Danville, Vermont, on April 4, 1792, Stevens graduated from Dartmouth College in 1814 and two years later, having moved to Pennsylvania, was admitted to the bar and began the practice of law in Gettysburg. As he gradually attained success as a lawyer he invested in real estate and the iron business and developed an interest in politics. In 1833 he was elected on an Anti-Masonic platform to the Pennsylvania legislature; he remained in that body until 1842, supporting measures for public education and internal improvements and staunchly opposing all proposals that to him smacked of privilege or class distinction. He was then, as later, an advocate of high tariffs. After a few years in private law practice he returned to politics and was elected as a Whig to the House of Representatives in 1848. During two terms in the House he furthered his reputation for harsh, uncompromising views while opposing the Compromise of 1850 and particularly the Fugitive Slave Law of the same year. In 1853, exasperated with the Whigs for their refusal to take a strong stand on issues, he again retired from office but not from politics; he was soon deeply involved in organizing the new Republican party and in 1859 returned to the House as a Republican to begin the major phase of his career. He was a skilled parliamentarian, but more important was his stern, absolute, and sometimes blind devotion to democratic principles and his great power in debate. A master of sarcasm and invective and by far the fiercest of the abolition-ists, he lavished abuse on Southern congressmen and moderate Northerners alike, on numerous occasions bringing the House to near-violence with his oratory. During the Civil War he urged an impossibly vigorous prosecution of military operations and on this subject was often in conflict with President Abraham Lincoln. As chairman of the Ways and Means Committee of the House, however, he rendered invaluable aid to the administration in securing the fiscal legislation—notably the issue of greenbacks—necessary to carry on the war. Viewing secession as treason, he advocated confiscation of rebel-owned property, wholesale arrest and execution of the leaders of the secession movement and the Confederate government and military establishment, and the arming of slaves; as the war came to a close he declared the South to be a "conquered province" to which the Constitution had no application. Against Lincoln's moderate plan for Reconstruction he proposed much more rigorous measures, and when President Andrew Johnson indicated his intention to continue moderate policies, Stevens moved into open and complete opposition. The acknowledged leader of Radical Republicans in the House, he obtained the exclusion of newly elected Southern congressmen in 1866 and established the joint committee on Reconstruction, becoming its dominant member. He secured passage of the Civil Rights and Freedmen's Bureau acts over Johnson's vetoes, directed the preparation and passage of the Fourteenth and Fifteenth amendments, and used Republican gains in the 1866 election to force through the Reconstruction measures of 1867, establishing military rule to guarantee Negro suffrage in the South. Early in 1868 he introduced a resolution for the impeachment of Johnson, helped draw up the articles of impeachment, and helped manage the subsequent trial; the charges were flimsy and when Johnson was acquitted in May, Stevens was deeply disappointed. His health had failed by that time and he died in Washington on August 11, 1868. He was buried in Lancaster, Pennsylvania, amid the graves of Negroes, in order, he explained in an epitaph he had composed himself, "that I might illustrate in my death the principles which I advocated through a long life —Equality of Man before his Creator."

Stevens, Wallace (1879–1955), poet. Born in Reading, Pennsylvania, on October 2, 1879, Stevens spent three years at Harvard and was a reporter for the *New York Herald Tribune* before graduating from New York Law School in 1904 and being admitted to the bar. About that time he began writing poetry and began a general law practice in New York City. His poems were first published in *Poetry* magazine in 1914 and then appeared in other similar publications. In 1916 he joined the Hartford Accident and Indemnity Company in Connecticut and rose steadily in its ranks, becoming vice-president in 1934. In 1923, when he was forty-four years old, he published his first book of poetry, *Harmonium*, which was followed by numerous volumes, including *Ideas of Order* and *Owl's Clover*, both 1936; *The Man with the*

Blue Guitar, 1937; Parts of a World, 1942; and The Auroras of Autumn, 1950. He was a subtle, intellectual, but at the same time lively and engaging poet whose writings relied on the rhythm and sound of words as much as on their conventional meanings. The intent of his work, elucidated in his critical study, The Necessary Angel, 1951, was to contrast reality with imagination, an aim perhaps best achieved in one of his best-known poems, "The Emperor of Ice Cream." He won the Bollingen Prize for Poetry in 1950, and the National Book Award in 1951 for The Auroras of Autumn and in 1954 for his Collected Poems, which also won a 1955 Pulitzer Prize. He died in Hartford, Connecticut, on August 2, 1955.

Stevenson, Adlai Ewing (1835–1914), lawyer and public official. Born in Christian County, Kentucky, on October 23, 1835, Stevenson spent the first 16 years of his life there, until his family moved to Bloomington, Illinois, in 1852. He attended Illinois Wesleyan University and Centre College of Kentucky. His father's death forced him to leave college, so he took up the study of law privately and was admitted to the bar in 1857. His first practice was in Metamora, Illinois; but ten years later he returned to Bloomington and opened an office there. For most of his adult life he was politically active, and, as a staunch Democrat, he campaigned for the party's ticket in each election year. He was appointed to his first public office, that of master in chancery, in 1860. After four years in that position he was elected state's attorney in 1865. In 1874, for the first time, Stevenson gained national office by his election to the House of Representatives. He lost his seat in 1876, but was returned in 1878, with Greenback party support. He failed to win reelection in 1880. During Grover Cleveland's first term in the White House, 1885–1889, Stevenson served as assistant postmaster general. It was a post of dubious honor, for he found himself having to arrange the patronage affairs of his party by ousting Republicans from post-office jobs and replacing them with Democrats. This task probably cost him a federal judgeship in the District of Columbia in 1889, for the nomination required the approval of the Senate, which in 1888 had gained a Republican majority. Four years later, he was presiding over the Senate as vice-president during Cleveland's second term. President William McKinley appointed him to serve on a monetary commission to Europe in 1897. This brief venture was his last public office. Stevenson ran for the vice-presidency as William Jennings Bryan's running mate in 1900, and was an unsuccessful candidate for governor of Illinois in 1908. He died in Chicago on June 14, 1914.

Stevenson, Adlai Ewing (1900–1965), lawyer, public official, and diplomat. Born on February 5, 1900, in Los Angeles, Stevenson was the son of a newspaper executive and the grandson of Adlai E. Stevenson (1835–1914). Raised after 1906 in Bloomington, Illinois, the family home, he at-

tended Choate Preparatory School, graduated from Princeton in 1922, and entered Harvard Law School. After two years of study, he rejoined his family in Bloomington and became assistant managing editor of the Bloomington Pantagraph, a local newspaper that had been in the family for several generations. Returning to law school at Northwestern University, he graduated in 1926 and was admitted to the bar that year. He opened a practice in Chicago. In 1933 he was one of the many lawyers called to Washington to help plan and implement the New Deal of Franklin D. Roosevelt. For two years he was an adviser to the Agricultural Adjustment Administration (AAA), touring the country to interview farmers and relay their problems back to the administration. In 1935 he returned to Chicago, but his law practice was destined to be interrupted by further public service in various posts. Called back to Washington in 1941 as legal assistant to the secretary of the navy, he served in 1943 as head of a foreign-aid mission to Italy planning for military occupation. In 1945 he was an adviser to the San Francisco conference for the organization of the United Nations, and in 1946–1947 was a senior adviser to the U.S. delegation to the UN General Assembly. He returned to Chicago in 1947 and was nominated for governor on a reform Democratic ticket. He won the 1948 election by a large majority and, as governor, secured the passage of 78 "clean-up" measures. In 1952 he was chosen as the Democratic candidate for the presidency, despite his previous refusal to seek the nomination. But he waged a vigorous campaign that was marked by eloquent speeches whose wit and civility were often memorable. He lost the election to Gen. Dwight D. Eisenhower, but he gained national prominence. In 1956 he formally declared his candidacy and once again gained the Democratic nomination. His second campaign against Eisenhower was conducted on more conventional principles than the first, as he simplified and sharpened his oratory and platform; but he could not escape his identity as the "intellectual's candidate," and to some extent this cost him the race. He returned to his law practice, traveled extensively, and in 1960 received strong support for a third nomination, but John F. Kennedy was chosen on the first ballot. In 1961 Kennedy appointed him U.S. ambassador to the United Nations, with cabinet rank. In this role he was unsurpassed as a speaker and was widely respected by the delegates. He died in London while visiting friends on July 14, 1965. Among his writings were A Call to Greatness, 1954; What I Think, 1956; The New America, 1957; Friends and Enemies, 1959; Putting First Things First, 1960; and Looking Outward: Years of Crisis at the U.N., 1963.

Stevenson, Andrew (1784–1857), public official. Born in Culpeper County, Virginia, on January 21, 1784, Stevenson studied at the College of William and Mary. After reading law he was admitted to the bar and began practice in Richmond. He served in the Virginia House of Delegates from

1809 to 1816 and from 1818 to 1821; he was speaker from 1812 to 1815. He tried unsuccessfully for election to the U.S. House of Representatives in 1814 and 1816, and was finally elected to the House in 1820. Reelected for the next six terms, he served as speaker of the House from 1827 to 1834. He was a staunch supporter of Andrew Jackson and Martin Van Buren, and as speaker during Jackson's administration earned the enmity of the opposition party because he assigned committee membership on a partisan basis. During the nullification crisis in 1832–1833 he was a staunch Unionist. His partisan extremism deterred the Senate from confirming his appointment as U.S. minister to Great Britain in 1834, although he was finally confirmed two years later after Jackson refused to appoint anyone else in his stead. He served as minister until 1841, when William Henry Harrison and the Whig party took over the national administration. He spent the remainder of his life in Virginia, serving in various official capacities. He died at Blenheim, his estate in Albemarle County, on January 25, 1857.

Stewart, Alexander Turney (1803–1876), merchant and philanthropist. Born of Scottish parents in Lisburn, County Antrim, Ireland, on October 12, 1803, Stewart emigrated to the United States at the age of seventeen. After teaching school for a few years, he was enabled by an inheritance to go into business in New York City. He opened a small dry-goods shop in 1823 on lower Broadway, and within a few years had proved himself a shrewd and successful businessman. By 1850 A. T. Stewart and Company was the largest wholesale and retail dry-goods establishment in New York City and in 1862 he built, on the entire block bounded by Broadway and Fourth Avenue between 9th and 10th streets, what was then the largest retail store in the world. It employed more than 2000 persons. In addition to his retail business he acquired control of several textile mills in the surrounding states and also imported fabrics from Europe. In New York City he owned a number of hotels and theaters, including Niblo's Garden. Although notorious as a difficult and tight-fisted employer, Stewart contributed widely to charities, particularly in disaster-ridden areas: he aided famine victims in Scotland, mill operatives in England, and Chicagoans after the 1871 fire. In 1869 he founded Garden City, Long Island, as a planned community for families of moderate income. He died in New York City on April 10, 1876. After his death the A. T. Stewart and Company holdings were acquired by John Wanamaker.

Stewart, Potter (1915–   ), justice of the Supreme Court. Born in Jackson, Michigan, on January 23, 1915, Stewart attended Yale, graduating in 1937. After a year studying international law at Cambridge University in England, he entered Yale's law school. He received his law degree in 1941, and was admitted to the bar in Ohio and New York. His first practice, in New York City, was cut short by service in the navy for three years

during World War II. Following the war, he returned to his New York practice for a time, but in 1947 settled in Cincinnati. Stewart's first public office was as a member of the Cincinnati city council from 1949 to 1953. He was vice-mayor in 1952 and 1953. He was then appointed to the U.S. Court of Appeals, Sixth District, covering Ohio, Michigan, Kentucky, and Tennessee, assuming the post on June 1, 1954. During the administration of Dwight D. Eisenhower Stewart was a member of the committee for the White House Conference on Education, 1954–1955, and he served on the committee on court administration for the Judicial Conference of the United States. On October 14, 1958, President Eisenhower appointed him an associate justice of the U.S. Supreme Court, to succeed Harold H. Burton. The appointment was confirmed by the Senate on May 5, 1959. Over the next decade Stewart tended, on the whole, to vote with the conservative bloc on the Court and was the author of several notable dissents. In 1962 he was the lone dissenter against the Court's decision, in *Engel* v. *Vitale*, holding that the daily reading of a prayer in the New York public schools violated the constitutional prohibition against the establishment of religion. In 1965 he joined Justice Hugo L. Black in dissenting against the Court's decision, in *Griswold*. v. *Connecticut*, to the effect that the Connecticut statute forbidding the disseminating of birth-control information was unconstitutional; Stewart held, on the contrary, that the decision was defective because there was no specific "right of marital privacy" in the Constitution. However, two dissents in 1966 seemed to be contradictory in tenor. In one, he more or less predictably joined justices Clark, Harlan, and White in dissenting against the Court's controversial decision in *Miranda* v. *Arizona*, which was widely interpreted as limiting the power of police forces too sharply in order to assure to the accused the privilege against self-incrimination. On the other hand, he was one of four justices who dissented against the Court's decision in *Ginzburg* v. *United States*, 1966, which upheld a lower-court conviction of publisher Ralph Ginzburg for having sent obscene matter through the mails. Stewart's argument was to the effect that the majority was really expressing its disapproval of the material Ginzburg had published and mailed—a disapproval that it had no business under the Constitution, according to Stewart, to turn into a decision at law.

Stewart, William Morris (1827–1909), lawyer and public official. Born in Galen, Wayne County, New York, on August 9, 1827, Stewart spent a little more than a year at Yale before the California Gold Rush lured him to the West Coast in 1850. He did some mining in Nevada County, California, until he had accumulated a few thousand dollars. He then took up law and was admitted to the bar in 1852. Throughout the rest of his life he successfully combined his interests in law and mining with politics. He served as district attorney of Nevada County in 1852 and as attorney general of California in 1854. In 1859 the discovery of silver in the Nevada Territory influenced him to move to Carson City, and in the next few years he earned half a million dollars in legal fees by his successful representation of the original claimants to the Comstock Lode. His fame as an expert in mining law brought him as clients some of the largest mining companies in the West. With the admission of Nevada to the Union in 1864, Stewart was elected to the U.S. Senate, where he served from 1864 to 1875, and from 1887 to 1905. In 1869 he was the author of the Fifteenth (Equal Rights) Amendment to the Constitution. From 1875 to 1887 he worked at his Nevada law practice, but in 1887 he was once again elected to the Senate. These were the years of controversy over the issue of remonetization of silver, and Stewart faithfully aligned himself with the silver interests of the West during the 1890s. He broke with the Republican party in 1892 over its stand on silver, and was reelected to the Senate in 1893 and 1899 as a candidate of the Silver party. In the campaign of 1896 he endorsed William Jennings Bryan for the presidency. By the end of the decade, however, he had abandoned the silver issue and returned to the Republican party. He was an early, perhaps the first, congressional advocate of federal funds for reclamation of arid western lands. Having declined to be a candidate for reelection in 1905, Stewart retired. He died in Washington, D.C., on April 23, 1909.

Stiegel, Henry William (1729–1785), glass and iron manufacturer. Born near Cologne, Germany, on May 13, 1729, Stiegel emigrated to the British colonies in America in 1750 and settled in Pennsylvania. He went to work for an ironmaster named Jacob Huber, in Lancaster County. Two years later he married Huber's daughter and in 1758 was able to buy out the business. Stiegel showed a distinct talent for manufacturing and promoting, and by 1760 his ironworks had made him prosperous enough to buy up a large tract of land and develop his own town, Manheim. His foundry turned out iron castings, kettles, and stoves that were widely and eagerly sought after. In 1764 he brought from England several expert glassmakers and opened a glass factory at Manheim that also became highly successful; its products were window and sheet glass as well as the Stiegel glassware that later became a collector's item. In 1769 a second glassworks, known from 1772 as the American Flint Glass Manufactory, was opened in Manheim. Stiegel's very success was his downfall, however, for if he had one fault, it was a penchant for high living that earned him the sobriquet "Baron von Stiegel." His extravagant living and overextended business ventures combined to bring him to bankruptcy by 1774. He sold his property and even spent a few months in debtors' prison. Deprived of his wealth, he became dependent on relatives and friends, and he then turned to teaching to make a living. On January 10, 1785, Stiegel died in poverty in Berks County, Pennsylvania.

Stieglitz, Alfred (1864–1946), photographer and editor. Born in Hoboken, New Jersey, on January 1, 1864, the son of a wool merchant, Stieglitz moved to New York City with his family at the age of seven. He attended private and public schools and studied engineering at the City College of New York (CCNY) from the age of seventeen. In 1881 he went abroad and enrolled at the Polytechnic Institute in Berlin. He soon became interested in photography and began at once to experiment and take pictures under conditions then considered prohibitive—at night, in the snow and rain, and when subjects were reflected in windows—earning a reputation as a "revolutionary." His pictures of a trip to the Italian Tyrol won top honors and international acclaim in London three years before he returned to the United States, in 1890, and began pioneer experiments in three-color photoengraving. He produced a collection of prints on New York City, containing the classic "Winter—Fifth Avenue" (showing a horsecar moving up a hill in a blizzard) and "The Terminal—Streetcar Horses" (of steaming horses being watered at a train depot after the storm). He was the first to photograph skyscrapers, clouds, and views from an airplane. Beyond sheer technical virtuosity, however, was his pioneering role in turning the camera into a tool of art, a means of aesthetic expression equal to brush and palette. He used no retouching, would not make mechanically duplicated prints, or use eccentric camera angles; all of his effects relied on artistic vision, timing, and perfect focusing. He edited the *American Amateur Photographer* during 1892–1896 and *Camera Notes*, which he also published, from 1897 to 1903. In 1905, with a group of photographers that he dubbed the "photo-secessionists," and that included Edward Steichen, he opened a gallery at 291 Fifth Avenue in New York City—the famous 291 Gallery. In its first three years, the gallery showed only photographs. In 1908 he began to show and promote experimental paintings and sculpture of the burgeoning modern-art movement. He gave the first U.S. showings of the work of Henri Matisse, Constantin Brancusi, Henri Rousseau, Pablo Picasso, and Henri Toulouse-Lautrec, and other European artists, defended them to the outraged press and public, and introduced African sculpture as an art form. Then he began exhibiting the work of John Marin, Charles Demuth, Georgia O'Keeffe (his wife after 1924), Arthur Dove, Max Weber, and other previously unknown American artists whose contemporary styles were slow to be accepted by the art public. The 291 Gallery closed in 1917 and was followed by the Intimate Gallery in 1925 and in 1929 by An American Place. He edited and published *Camera Work*, 1903–1917. He died in New York City on July 13, 1946.

Stiles, Ezra (1727–1795), scholar and educator. Born in North Haven, Connecticut, on November 29, 1727, the son of the pastor of the Congregational Church, Stiles was educated at home and at Yale, from which he graduated in 1746. In May

1749 he was both licensed to preach and named a tutor at Yale, where he remained for six years, teaching, studying, and corresponding with such notables as Benjamin Franklin. He was called to Newport, Rhode Island, as pastor of the Second Congregational Church in 1755, and there embarked on the happiest and most active part of his life. He served as librarian of the Redwood Library, made a number of important scientific observations, took up the study of Hebrew at the age of forty and also studied Arabic, Syriac, and Armenian, and all in all was able to attain, by the time the Revolution broke out, a reputation as the most learned man in New England. He played a leading role in the founding in 1764 of Rhode Island College (now Brown University). He was made a member of the American Philosophical Society in 1768 and was elected a councilor of the society in 1781. His sympathies were as wide as his intellectual interests. He was a prominent abolitionist and freed the single slave he owned, and he was tolerant in his religious views, consorting with Jews and Christians alike and only drawing the line at the Anglican church, which he never could learn to accept. A staunch supporter of the Revolution, he had to flee Newport when the war began. He lived for a while in Dighton, Massachusetts, and in Portsmouth, New Hampshire, and served parishes briefly in other New England towns, including Boston. He was elected president of Yale in September 1777 but did not accept the post until March 1778; he served until his death in New Haven, Connecticut, on May 12, 1795. His presidency coincided with a difficult period in the college's history, largely owing to the disruptions caused by the Revolution. But he taught many of the courses himself and generally acquitted himself ably. He wrote a great deal during his lifetime but published little, the major works appearing as *The United States Elevated to Glory and Honor*, 1783, a sermon; *Account of the Settlement of Bristol*, 1785; and *History of Three of the Judges of King Charles I*, 1794. After his death various manuscripts were edited and published by others, notably his *Literary Diary*, three volumes, 1901, edited by F. B. Dexter.

Still, Andrew Taylor (1828–1917), founder of osteopathy. Born in Jonesville, Virginia, on August 6, 1828, the son of a Methodist minister, Still grew up in Tennessee and Missouri. Living on the frontier, he got what education he could from local schools and from his father. His early interest in medicine and cures probably came from his father. In 1853, a few years after he married, he went west to Kansas, settling at Wakarusa Mission, near Kansas City, where he treated Indians and studied anatomy by dissecting the bodies of Indians who died in the neighborhood. He also spent some time studying medicine at the Kansas City School of Physicians and Surgeons. He was active in the antislavery cause, fighting for a time with John Brown, and in 1857 he was elected to the legislature. After service in the Civil War as an officer with the

Kansas militia, Still returned to his medical practice and turned his attention to finding ways of treatment where other physicians had failed. The deaths in 1864 of three of his children from spinal meningitis led him to the theory that diseases are due to abnormalities—later called osteopathic lesions and spinal joint subluxations —in or near the joints in the body. Treatment, he concluded, should not be with drugs, which he considered poisons, but by correcting the abnormalities through manipulation of the body, thus enabling the body to bring to bear its own natural powers of healing. On this theory Still built the practice of osteopathy. For more than 25 years after the Civil War he moved about the country, teaching and practicing, and encountering a good deal of opposition from conventionally trained physicians. In 1875 he returned to Missouri, living in Kirksville, Hannibal, and other towns and continuing his practice. In 1892 he settled permanently in Kirksville and established the American School of Osteopathy. In 1894 he began publishing the *Journal of Osteopathy* and he wrote, among other works, *Philosophy of Osteopathy*, 1899; *Osteopathy, Research and Practice*, 1910; and *Autobiography*, 1897 and 1908. Still continued teaching at the school until his death on December 12, 1917, in Kirksville. The practice of osteopathy grew rapidly, spread to other nations, and in the United States eventually gained legal recognition equivalent to orthodox medical practice in most states.

Still, William Grant (1895–1978), composer. Born in Woodville, Mississippi, on May 11, 1895, Still attended Wilberforce University from 1911 to 1915 to study medicine, but left after three years to pursue his real interest, music. He stayed out of school for a few years, but at length was able to continue his musical education, attending the Oberlin College Conservatory of Music and later the New England Conservatory of Music. His first jobs were as an arranger of music for popular singers and jazz bands, including Paul Whiteman's, but grants from the Guggenheim and Rosenwald foundations enabled him to concentrate on orchestral composition. In 1926 the New York Guild of Composers first brought Still's work to public attention by presenting four of his songs in concert. In 1936 he became the first black American to conduct a major U.S. symphony orchestra when he led the Los Angeles Philharmonic at the Hollywood Bowl in playing his compositions. For the New York World's Fair in 1939 he was commissioned to write the tone poem that accompanied the visual presentation at Democracity in the Perisphere. His orchestral works, including *Darker America*, 1924; *Africa*, 1930; *Afro-American Symphony*, 1931; *Kaintuck* 1936; and *Festive Overture*, 1944, have been played by major symphony orchestras. His operatic works include *Blue Steel*, 1935; *Troubled Island*, 1938; *A Bayou Legend*, 1940; *Costaso*, 1949; and *Highway 1, U.S.A.*, 1963; and he composed such choral works as *And They Lynched Him on a Tree*, 1940, and *Those Who Wait*, 1943. He composed songs for Broadway musicals, created ballets, and wrote many songs, including "Levee Land," "Kaintuck," and "Log Cabin Ballads." He died on December 3, 1978, in Los Angeles.

Stilwell, Joseph Warren (1883–1946), soldier. Born on March 19, 1883, in Palatka, Florida, Stilwell attended West Point, graduating in 1904. After two years of active army duty in the Philippines he taught at West Point until 1917, except for a three-year tour of service, 1910–1913, divided between the Philippines and California. During World War I he went to Europe with the American Expeditionary Force (AEF) in 1917 and remained there with the army of occupation until 1919. Back in the United States, Stilwell began the studies that led to his becoming one of the nation's military and political experts on China. He spent most of the years from 1921 to 1945 in the Far East in one capacity or another, returning to the United States from time to time for further training, teaching, or consultation. He did two tours of duty in China during the 1920s, the second as chief of staff of U.S. forces there, coming back to the United States in 1928 with the rank of lieutenant colonel. He returned to China in 1932 as military attaché to the U.S. embassy in Peking and remained in that post until May 1939. His return to the United States at that time brought with it promotion to brigadier general, and he served assignments at Fort Sam Houston, Texas, Fort Ord, California, and the Presidio at Monterey, California. With the outbreak of the Pacific phase of World War II Stilwell returned to China, where he became chief of staff to China's Generalissimo Chiang Kai-shek and was also put in charge of all U.S. forces in China, Burma, and India. In 1942 the Japanese succeeded in taking Burma, thus breaking the overland supply route from India to China. The delivery of supplies to Chinese forces was thereafter done by air "over the hump," the towering Himalayas. In order to get more war supplies into China, he conceived the idea of the Ledo Road (later called the Stilwell Road) to run 478 miles from India through Burma to link up with the old Burma Road. The building of the road was one of the great episodes of the war. A counteroffensive led by Stilwell against the Japanese in 1944 had a telling effect, and by early 1945 the enemy had been driven from Burma. Apart from the problems of fighting a war on difficult terrain, Stilwell also had his troubles with Chiang's government, which, besides being afflicted with corruption, insisted on fighting a double war: one against the Japanese and one against Chinese Communists. Stilwell and Chiang fell to quarreling frequently, as the U.S. general expressed his views forthrightly on the situation in China and on the need to concentrate on the war against the Japanese. Stilwell's unequivocating attitude with Chiang led to friction that brought about his recall to the United States in October 1944. He was subsequently reassigned to the South Pacific under General Douglas MacArthur as commander of U.S. ground forces and then, from June 1945, as commander of the 10th Army, which fought with distinction in taking Okinawa in the last great amphibious campaign of the war. When the 10th Army was deactivated on September 27, 1945, after Japan had surrendered, Stilwell took command of the 6th Army at the Presidio in San Francisco. He died there on October 12, 1946.

Stimson, Henry Lewis (1867–1950), public official. Born on September 21, 1867, in New York City, Stimson graduated from Yale in 1888, took his M.A. at Harvard the next year, and after further study at the Harvard Law School was admitted to the New York bar in 1891. In 1893 he joined Elihu Root's law firm in New York City and remained with it until he was appointed U.S. attorney for the southern district of New York by President Theodore Roosevelt in 1906. In four years in this office he pursued a vigorous program of prosecutions of large companies, particularly for railroad rebate practices, and became a close associate of Roosevelt, who persuaded him to run, as a Republican, for governor of New York in 1910. The campaign was unsuccessful, but the following year Stimson was appointed secretary of war by President William Howard Taft and served until 1913. During World War I he served for a short time in France as a colonel of field artillery and then from 1918 to 1926 enjoyed a lucrative law practice. In 1926 he was sent to attempt a negotiation of the Tacna-Arica dispute between Chile and Peru and in the next year went to Nicaragua to arrange an armistice in that country's civil war. In 1927, despite his intention to retire from both business and public life, he was named to succeed Gen. Leonard Wood as governor general of the Philippines. After effectively dismissing for the time the question of Philippine independence and implementing a program of economic development, he returned to the United States in 1929 to become President Herbert Hoover's secretary of state. He headed the U.S. delegations to the London Naval Conference in 1930 and the Geneva Disarmament Conference in 1932. For his handling of the major problem of his four-year term, the Japanese invasion of Manchuria, he was widely criticized; eschewing both strong diplomatic measures and direct action, he proposed a policy of nonrecognition—the Stimson Doctrine—that, although adopted by the League of Nations, had no effect on Japanese aggression. In 1933, before leaving office, he supervised the transition from Hoover's administration to that of Franklin D. Roosevelt. In 1940, at the age of seventy-two, he was called back to service as Roosevelt's secretary of war, becoming one of two Republicans in the President's war cabinet. Stimson strongly advocated U.S. preparedness and aid to Britain in the early phases of World War II, then oversaw the mobilization, training, and operations of the U.S. armed forces throughout the war and also served as chief presidential adviser on atomic policy. In 1945 he made the final recommendation to President Harry S. Truman to use the atomic bomb against Japan. On September 21, 1945, he left office and retired to his Huntington, Long Island, estate, where he died on October 20, 1950. Among his published works were *American Policy in Nicaragua*, 1927; *The United States and Other American Republics*, 1931; *Pact of Paris*, 1932; *Far Eastern Crisis*, 1936; and the autobiographical *On Active Service in Peace and War*, 1948, with McGeorge Bundy.

Stockton, Frank (1834–1902), author. Born in Philadelphia on April 5, 1834, Francis Richard Stockton attended Central High School there and subsequently took up wood engraving. He worked at this trade until the late 1860s, when he began having some success selling short stories to magazines. He served on the staff of *Hearth and Home* magazine for a short time in 1869 and in 1873, when *Scribner's Monthly* was founded, he became assistant editor. Most of what he wrote during the 1870s consisted of children's stories, and from 1873 to 1881 he was assistant editor, under Mary Mapes Dodge, of *St. Nicholas* magazine, but with the success of a novel, *Rudder Grange*, in 1879, he turned more toward adult fiction. His best and most successful work was a novel of shipwreck in the South Pacific, *The Casting Away of Mrs. Lecks and Mrs. Aleshine*, published in 1886. Others included *The Dusantes*, 1888; *Pomona's Travels*, 1894; *The Adventures of Captain Horn*, 1895; and *Mrs. Cliff's Yacht*, 1896. But Stockton's best-known work is a short story, "The Lady or the Tiger," published in 1882. Ending with an unsolved dilemma, the story aroused a great deal of comment and went on to have a career of its own after the rest of Stockton's works passed from vogue. His novels were light, optimistic books of delightful nonsense that were amusing without possessing any notable content. Among his better books were such nonfiction works as *Personally Conducted*, 1889, on travel in Europe, and *Buccaneers and Pirates of Our Coasts*, 1898. He spent his last years living near Harpers Ferry, West Virginia, and died in Washington, D.C., on April 20, 1902.

Stockton, Robert Field (1795–1866), naval officer. Born on August 20, 1795, in Princeton, New Jersey, Stockton attended the College of New Jersey (now Princeton) for a short time before joining the navy in October 1811. During the War of 1812 he served in the North Atlantic and in the defenses of Baltimore and Washington, and later participated in the Algerine War against the Barbary pirates. He remained on duty with the navy until 1828, then was on inactive status until 1838. In this decade he settled at the family home in Princeton and followed civilian occupations. He invested a good deal of money in the construction of the Delaware and Raritan Canal and served as the canal company's president. He invested as well in the Camden & Amboy Railroad operated by the Stevens family of Hoboken, New Jersey.

One of Stockton's chief interests was in a short-lived colonization movement to return freed slaves to Africa in 1821. He had aided in the selection of the territory that became Liberia, and he helped found the New Jersey Colonization Society, of which he was the first president. In 1838 Stockton left the life of a country gentleman to return to active naval duty with the rank of captain. He sailed to the Mediterranean in command of the *Ohio* and later, in England, became involved with John Ericsson in the design of a steam vessel, commissioning on behalf of the navy the building of the *Princeton*, the navy's first screw-propeller driven ship. He stayed on sea duty for most of the next seven years, except for time off in 1840 to campaign for William Henry Harrison; he rejected an offer from President John Tyler in 1841 to become secretary of the navy. In 1845, when the U.S. annexation of Texas made war with Mexico seem inevitable, Stockton was sent to Texas with the resolution of annexation. The same year he commanded the ship *Congress* when it sailed to California to reinforce U.S. forces there. He arrived at Monterey on July 15, 1846, about a week after Commodore John D. Sloat's operations against the Mexican authorities had begun in California. He relieved Sloat, assumed command of both land and sea forces, including the men of the Bear Flag revolt and Capt. John C. Frémont's small command, and determined to bring all of California under U.S. sovereignty. Attacking several vital points along the coast including Los Angeles, San Diego, and Santa Barbara, he had won the whole Mexican province by August 13. Stockton then declared California a territory of the United States and set up a civil government, naming himself as temporary governor. His goal was the complete pacification of California before he would set off for the war zone in what is now Mexico and toward that end he appointed Frémont governor in his stead; but it was necessary to join Gen. Stephen W. Kearny in a battle in January 1847 to reconquer Los Angeles, and this diversion kept him from going south as he had planned. Shortly thereafter a heated dispute broke out between Stockton and Kearny as to supreme authority. Kearny was finally upheld by Washington, but the affair put an end to Frémont's career. He returned to the East in the fall of 1847 and spent three more years in the navy before resigning in 1850. Stockton served a brief term in the U.S. Senate, from March 1851 to January 10, 1853, during which he urged the improvement of harbor defenses and the abolition of flogging in the navy; he then returned to New Jersey and spent the last 13 years of his life as president of the Delaware and Raritan Canal Company. In 1850 the name of the town of Tuleburg, California, was changed to Stockton. He died in Princeton, New Jersey, on October 7, 1866.

Stoddard, Solomon (1643–1729), religious leader. Born about September 27, 1643, in Boston, Stoddard graduated from Harvard College in 1662. For a few years he was librarian of the college, and during 1667–1669 spent some months on the island of Barbados as a Congregational chaplain. In February 1672 he accepted a call to become pastor of the Congregational Church at Northampton, Massachusetts, in the Connecticut Valley. He held this pastorate until his death. Once in his parish, he was able to perceive the extent to which church life among the Puritan New Englanders had declined. Despite the liberalizing influence of the Half-Way Covenant, which he had accepted, attendance in the churches was low and piety was negligible. In response to these realities he reevaluated church polity and introduced into his congregation the practice that came to be called "Stoddardeanism." According to this practice, an individual's profession of faith was sufficient for church membership and admission to communion; the person need not witness to some experience of grace. This practice of Stoddard's received wide approval in his part of the state, although his own grandson, Jonathan Edwards, who joined him in Northampton as assistant pastor in 1727, later rejected it. Stoddard's views did not mean he was a religious liberal in any sense of the word. He was a strong advocate of clerical supremacy in the churches, an opponent of congregational autonomy, and a vehement moralist. He was also a devotee of revivalism, a trait he shared with his grandson, Edwards. He died on February 11, 1729. He published several tracts during the first decade of the eighteenth century, in which he defended Stoddardeanism.

Stoddert, Benjamin (1751–1813), public official. Born in Charles County, Maryland, in 1751, Stoddert was apprenticed to a merchant in his youth. In 1777 he joined a Pennsylvania militia regiment with the rank of captain, serving in the Revolution until April 1779, when he resigned over a question of seniority. In September of that year he was appointed secretary to the Board of War, a post he filled capably until 1781. He then settled in Georgetown, Maryland, and bought a partnership in a small mercantile firm. As he had foreseen, Georgetown soon flourished as a Potomac port and as his fortune grew he made extensive investments in real estate in the region around the city. When the area was chosen as the site for the proposed federal city Stoddert was asked confidentially by George Washington and others to act as agent in purchasing large tracts of land; his circumspect fulfillment of the commission prevented a frenzy of land speculation in what was to become the District of Columbia. In 1794 he helped found and later served as president of the Bank of Columbia. In 1798 President John Adams appointed Stoddert the first secretary of the navy. Stoddert brought all his considerable energy to the post and, prodded by an undeclared naval war with France, added some fifty vessels to the navy over the next two years. In July 1798 he drafted the bill that provided for the organization of the Marine Corps. After the Revolutionary War he pushed for the construction of dock and naval-yard facilities, acquiring properties for that

purpose in Washington, D.C.; Norfolk, Virginia; Portsmouth, New Hampshire; Philadelphia; Brooklyn, New York, and other places. He also promoted the construction of a naval hospital at Newport. He retired to private life in 1801. His later years were marked by serious financial difficulties as the Georgetown trade declined precipitously, and he was deeply in debt at his death in Bladensburg, Maryland, on December 18, 1813.

Stokowski, Leopold (1882–1977), conductor. Born in London on April 18, 1882, the son of a Polish anthropologist, Leopold Antoni Stanislaw Boleslawowicz Stokowski was a skilled performer on the violin, piano, and organ by the age of sixteen. Under teachers including Sir Edward Elgar he studied composition at Queens College, Oxford, from which he graduated in 1903. In 1905, after furthering his studies at the Conservatoire in Paris and in Germany, he arrived in the United States; he was naturalized in 1915. He played the organ and directed the choir for three years for New York's fashionable St. Bartholomew's Church before making his first appearance as a conductor in Paris in 1908 and leading a concert series that year in London. Returning to the United States in 1909, he became, at twenty-seven, the principal conductor of the Cincinnati Symphony. In three years in that post he gained national attention with his unorthodox and impassioned interpretations, especially of the music of Bach, Beethoven, Brahms, and Tchaikovsky. Invited in 1912 to become conductor of the Philadelphia Orchestra, he brought the group to prominence. In 1936 he became coconductor with Eugene Ormandy, finally resigning in 1938. During the next four years he conducted a number of radio concerts of the NBC (National Broadcasting Company) Symphony, supplementing the music with lectures. He founded the second New York Symphony, serving as its conductor in 1944 and 1945, and in 1945 he also led the Hollywood Bowl Symphony Orchestra. From 1947 to 1950 he conducted the New York Philharmonic, and in 1955 he became permanent conductor of the Houston Symphony. He formed the American Symphony Orchestra in New York City in 1962. He was one of the first symphonic conductors to pay heed to jazz and to employ young and female musicians. He introduced young people's concerts, with special rates and programs, in 1933, organized the All-American Youth Orchestra in 1940 and toured extensively with it in the United States, Canada, and Latin America, and in 1953 founded the Contemporary Music Society. A great success with his recordings, he also appeared in the motion pictures *The Big Broadcast of 1937,* 1936, *One Hundred Men and a Girl,* 1937, and Walt Disney's innovative *Fantasia,* 1940. He was praised and criticized alike for his "popularization" of the concert medium, as well as for his lush interpretations, his orchestral transcriptions, particularly of some of the organ works of J. S. Bach, and his introduction of contemporary and controversial music. He died on September 13, 1977, in Nether Wallop, Hampshire, England.

Stone, Barton Warren (1772–1844), religious leader. Born near Port Tobacco, Maryland, on December 24, 1772, Stone studied law before undergoing a religious conversion that determined him to become an evangelist. During the 1790s he studied theology privately and taught for a time at a Methodist school in Washington, Georgia. In 1798 he was ordained in the Presbyterian ministry, although he did not regard himself as a strict Calvinist. His first charge consisted of the parishes of Cane Ridge and Concord in Kentucky. The Great Revival of the early 1800s found Cane Ridge one of the centers of the awakening; and the forces there unleashed renewed the clash between "New Light" and conservative, or "Old Light," Presbyterians. In 1803 Stone and five of his fellow ministers withdrew from the Synod of Kentucky to found their own Springfield Presbytery. But a year later, convinced that all such ecclesiastical organizations were unbiblical, they dissolved their presbytery and explained their reasons in a document entitled "Last Will and Testament." Stone insisted that no word but "Christian" be used to describe church members, and he formed an entirely congregational polity. For the next two decades he was an evangelist in Ohio and Kentucky, organizing churches according to his principles. In 1824 he met and befriended Alexander Campbell, founder of the Disciples (later the Disciples of Christ). Finding much agreement with the Disciples, Stone urged his followers to cooperate with them. In 1832 Stone's Christians and Campbell's Disciples agreed to a virtual merger of forces, although both men were opposed to general ecclesiastical institutions. Differences between the two groups kept a complete union from being effected, however, and congregations of Christians persisted apart from the Disciples. In 1826 Stone founded a religious paper called *Christian Messenger*, which he edited for the rest of his life. He also continued his evangelistic work, following the frontier west first to Illinois, then to Missouri. He died in Hannibal, Missouri, on November 9, 1844.

Stone, Edward Durell (1902–1978), architect. Born on March 9, 1902, in Fayetteville, Arkansas, Stone early displayed a talent for design and won a prize for a bird cage overlaid with sassafras branches at the age of fourteen. In 1923, after three years as an art student at the University of Arkansas, he began his architectural career in Boston and, on a scholarship, furthered his studies at Harvard (1925–1926) and at the Massachusetts Institute of Technology (MIT, 1925–1927). For two more years he studied in Europe. In 1930 he moved to New York City to work for the Rockefeller Center Architects and Wallace K. Harrison, and with them he contributed to the designs for the Waldorf-Astoria Hotel, Rockefeller Center, and Radio City Music Hall. From 1935 to 1940 he taught advanced design at New York University and in 1936 founded his own architectural firm in New York City. During World War II he headed the army's planning and design section and in

1946 he became a professor of architecture at Yale, leaving in 1951 to devote himself to building. His plans with Philip L. Goodwin for New York City's Museum of Modern Art, 1937, exemplified the functional, clean lines of the International Style. As his career progressed, however, he exhibited a more traditional approach, frequently using central courtyards and gardens to unify interior and exterior designs. Experimental in his choice of materials and decorative elements, he achieved complex lighting effects and airy, serene moods with mesh, grillwork, skylights, pools, hanging gardens, and raised roofs. He designed, among many other buildings, the El Panama Hotel, Panama City, 1949; the Bay Roc Hotel, British West Indies, 1952; the Social Security Hospital, Lima, Peru, 1957; the U.S. Embassy, New Delhi, India, 1958, one of his most notable buildings; the Hotel Phoenicia, Beirut, Lebanon, 1958; and the American Pavilion at the Brussels World's Fair, 1958. In the United States he completed the Fine Arts Center at the University of Arkansas, 1951; Philadelphia's Commercial Museum, 1955; a pharmaceutical plant for the Stuart Company, Pasadena, California, 1958; the Huntington Hartford Museum, New York City; and the Kennedy Center for the Performing Arts, Washington, D.C. In 1962 he published *The Evolution of an Architect*. He died in New York City on August 6, 1978.

Stone, Harlan Fiske (1872–1946), justice of the Supreme Court. Born on October 11, 1872, in Chesterfield, New Hampshire, Stone enrolled in the Massachusetts Agricultural School, intending to become a scientific farmer. But his interest turned to medicine and he transferred to Amherst College, where instead of medicine he studied law, graduating in 1894. He earned his law degree at Columbia University in 1898. From 1899 to 1924 he practiced in New York City and taught at Columbia, becoming a professor of law in 1902. In 1910 he became dean of the Columbia Law School. There he attempted to extend to five the number of years required for earning a law degree, and to improve the quality and methods of teaching. Preaching simplification of the law, he attacked complex statutes that hindered social and economic progress. In 1924 he was appointed U.S. attorney general by President Calvin Coolidge, and in that post he oversaw the reorganization of the Federal Bureau of Investigation (FBI) in the aftermath of the scandals of the Harding administration, most notably Teapot Dome. He was named to the Supreme Court in 1925 and was appointed chief justice on July 1, 1941 by President Franklin D. Roosevelt. As a member of the liberal wing of the Court, along with justices Oliver Wendell Holmes and Louis D. Brandeis, he affirmed the far-reaching reforms instituted by many legislative acts of the New Deal. In 1934 he wrote the opinion upholding the Railway Labor Act of 1926, providing for collective bargaining with employees. In 1937 he supported the Social Security Act of 1935, upholding unemployment insurance, old-age pensions, and auxiliary state laws to enforce it. This led to the enactment of the Fair Labor Standards Act of 1938, providing minimum wages and maximum hours for adults engaged in production for interstate commerce and defining appropriate labor for children. In 1936, in *United States* v. *Butler*, he stood with the minority in support of the Agricultural Adjustment Act of 1933, which had provided farmers with government subsidies. He noted in his opinion that, unlike the legislative and executive branches of the government, whose actions were reviewed by the judicial branch, the judiciary had nothing but its own sense of restraint as a control upon its own actions; and it was said that Stone would not have voted for the act as a legislator, but that his obligation as a Supreme Court jurist led him to disregard personal philosophies. In 1940, in *Minersville* v. *Gobitis*, he was the only member of the Court to oppose a state's power to force a member of the Jehovah's Witnesses to salute the flag in contravention of his religious beliefs. The Court reversed its position in 1943 in *West Virginia State Board of Education* v. *Barnette*, and adopted Stone's earlier dissenting view. He upheld a traditional position of the Supreme Court in deciding against the power of a state to control interstate commerce in 1945 in *Southern Pacific Co.* v. *Arizona*, invoking the Court's power to invalidate local laws that affected the people of other states. In his last opinion, in *Girouard* v. *United States*, 1946, he reversed his 1931 opinion that a congressional act could not be so interpreted as to bar naturalization of an immigrant who refused to bear arms for religious reasons. In this case, the majority switched to the position in his original dissent but, in deference to legislative prerogative, he changed his opinion on the basis of further clarification by Congress of the act's intent. He died in Washington, D.C., on April 22, 1946, having written more than 600 opinions, a large number of them on constitutional questions of the first importance.

Stone, Isidor Feinstein (1907–), journalist. Born on December 24, 1907, in Philadelphia, I. F. Stone published his first newspaper, *The Progress*, at the age of fourteen. From 1924 to 1927 he studied at the University of Pennsylvania, at the same time working as a reporter for a series of newspapers in the Philadelphia area. In 1933 he became an editorial writer for the *Philadelphia Record*, but soon moved to New York City to join the *New York Post*. From 1938 to 1946 he was with the *Nation* as associate editor and was later its Washington editor. He had by this time established a reputation as a resourceful reporter and as a particularly hard-headed and lucid editorial writer. He was connected at various times during the 1940s and early 1950s with several other publications, notably the New York City newspaper *P.M.* In 1953 he severed his ties with all of them and in Washington began to write and publish his own four-page newsletter, *I. F. Stone's Weekly*. Beginning with a circulation of 5500, the small paper grew steadily, largely by word of mouth

recommendations, to reach a circulation of 45,000 by 1968, by which time it had become a biweekly. Generally thought of as a radical, Stone was nevertheless not to be labeled; his absolute independence led him to alienate some of his own avid readers by sternly criticizing Israel's policies in the Middle East, describing Soviet Russian society as "bourgeois," and ascribing to forms of paranoia the many denunciations of the Warren Commission's report on the assassination of President John F. Kennedy. He delighted in quoting official government pronouncements alongside contradictory quotes from the same sources of a week or a month or a year before, and his trenchant analyses of persons and policies won high praise from journalistic colleagues as well as from his readers. He was a regular contributor to the *New York Review of Books* and published several collections of essays, editorials, and reviews. Among his many books were *Business as Usual*, 1941; *This is Israel*, 1948; *The Hidden History of the Korean War*, 1952; *The Haunted Fifties*, 1964; and *In a Time of Torment*, 1967. He discontinued publication of *I. F. Stone's Weekly* in the fall of 1971 and thereafter wrote regularly for the *New York Review of Books*.

Stone, Lucy (1818–1893), social reformer. Born in West Brookfield, Massachusetts, on August 13, 1818, Miss Stone was graduated from Oberlin College in 1847. She had spent more than a dozen years in getting her education because she was forced to earn her own way from the age of sixteen. She came to the conviction early in life that women's rights were severely circumscribed in a male-dominated society; even her own family was unwilling for many years to support the then almost unthinkable notion that a girl should attend college. While in school, in addition to advocating women's rights, she also espoused the abolitionist and temperance movements. She soon became recognized as a gifted speaker and pamphleteer and was engaged in lecturing in various part of the country. She was instrumental in organizing the first national woman's rights convention, at Worcester, Massachusetts, in 1850 and the annual conventions that followed. She had intended to remain single all her life to devote herself to her work, but in 1855 she married a prominent Ohio abolitionist, Henry Brown Blackwell, who vowed to help her in the struggle for women's rights. After their marriage they agreed that she would keep the use of her maiden name, calling herself Mrs. Stone. They lived in New Jersey for ten years from 1858, continuing their reform efforts, and in 1868 moved to Boston to participate in the work of the New England Woman Suffrage Association. The following year Mrs. Stone chartered the American Woman Suffrage Association as a nationwide organization to promote woman suffrage through state legislation. In 1870 she founded the *Woman's Journal*, which remained until 1917 the leading magazine promoting woman suffrage and which she and Blackwell edited from 1872. She devoted the rest of her life to the women's-rights movement, lecturing, writing, and lobbying with state legislators to gain passage of favorable bills. Her last lecture was delivered in Chicago at the World's Columbian Exposition in 1893. She died on October 18, 1893, in Dorchester, Massachusetts.

Stone, Melville Elijah (1848–1929), journalist. Born in Hudson, Illinois, on August 22, 1848, Stone graduated from high school in Chicago in 1867 and took a job as a reporter on the *Chicago Republican*, after having, while a student, tried his hand at reporting for the *Chicago Tribune* in 1865. He left the *Republican* to run a machine shop and foundry from 1869 until 1871, when the Chicago fire destroyed the business; he then went back to newspaper work. In 1875 he helped organize the *Chicago Daily News*, the city's first penny daily, but after 13 years sold his interest and traveled to Europe. He returned to the United States in 1892 and became president of the Globe National Bank in Chicago, a position he held until the firm's merger with the Continental Bank in 1898. In 1893 he took over the general managership of the Associated Press (AP) of Illinois and remained with the AP until his retirement in 1921. In 1900 the AP left Illinois after an adverse court decision of two years earlier which affected its circulation of the news, and it was reorganized in New York City. Under Stone's guidance the AP succeeded in opening up foreign news sources until it became a worldwide news-gathering service. He felt that news could be gathered and circulated objectively, without partisanship or sensationalism, and he was thoroughly opposed to the "yellow journalism" purveyed by many of the large urban dailies of the time. Under his leadership was fought a series of legal battles, culminating in a Supreme Court decision in 1918 that news is a commodity. The publication of his *Fifty Years a Journalist*, 1921, revealed the central role he had played in 1905 in preventing the breakdown of the negotiations that led to the Treaty of Portsmouth ending the Russo-Japanese War. He retired in 1921 and died in New York City on February 15, 1929.

Story, Joseph (1779–1845), justice of the Supreme Court. Born on September 18, 1779, in Marblehead, Massachusetts, Story graduated from Harvard in 1798 and read law for a time in the office of Samuel Sewall, until he was admitted to the bar and began practice in Salem in 1801. Although he was a Jeffersonian Republican—a political rarity in the region—he was elected to the Massachusetts legislature for three terms, 1805–1807; in 1808–1809 he served out the final months of a term in the House of Representatives, and in 1810 he returned to the state legislature, where he became speaker of the house. In November 1811 President James Madison appointed him to the Supreme Court in the hope that his Republicanism would help offset the strongly Federalist views of Chief Justice John Marshall. Instead Story became an ally of the Federalists and during the course of his long career, which outlasted the chief justice's

by ten years, achieved a lasting influence on U.S. jurisprudence and became the closest challenger to Marshall's preeminence. His first major contribution, however, issued from his work on his circuit, in New England. The War of 1812 produced a flood of admiralty and prize cases, and he brought a scholarly mind to bear on them, creating for the first time a coherent body of opinion in this hitherto chaotic area of U.S. law. His first major opinion on the Supreme Court was in the 1816 case of *Martin* v. *Hunter's Lessee*, in which he ruled that the Supreme Court had appellate jurisdiction, hence supremacy, over state courts in civil cases arising from constitutional or federal law or treaties. Of his 286 opinions, only 14 were in dissent; in one of these, *Ogden* v. *Saunders*, 1827, he joined Marshall in the first opinion on constitutional law in which Marshall was in a minority. After Marshall's death in 1835, Story presided over the Court until the appointment of Roger B. Taney as chief justice. Taney, a Jacksonian, altered considerably the complexion of the Court, and Story found himself more and more in dissent, most notably in *City of New York* v. *Miln*, *Briscoe* v. *Bank of Kentucky*, and *Charles River Bridge* v. *Warren Bridge*, all in 1837. The last case was considered by Daniel Webster to have elicited Story's best opinion. In 1841 he spoke for the court in the *Amistad* case, involving a number of slaves who had mutinied, taken over their ship, and been brought to a U.S. port. He decided they were to be returned to Africa. In 1829 Story became, by explicit direction in the endowment, first Dane Professor of Law at Harvard. In this chair, which he held along with his justiceship until his death, he contributed greatly to the development of the Harvard Law School and the general improvement of legal education in the United States; his lectures led to the publication of his nine great *Commentaries* on various kinds of law between 1832 and 1845. Among his many other written works was *Constitutional Classbook*, 1834. He drafted several pieces of legislation and found time to act as adviser to numerous business firms and committees. He died on September 10, 1845, in Cambridge, Massachusetts. He was elected to the Hall of Fame in 1900.

Stowe, Harriet Elizabeth Beecher (1811–1896), author and social reformer. Born on June 14, 1811, in Litchfield, Connecticut, Harriet Beecher was a member of one of the nineteenth century's most remarkable families. The daughter of Lyman Beecher, whose Calvinist influence was offset somewhat by the liberalism of her sister Catharine and her brothers Henry Ward and Edward, she grew up in an atmosphere of learning and moral earnestness. She studied, and then taught, at Catharine Beecher's school in Hartford, and in 1832 accompanied Catharine and their father to Cincinnati, where he became president of Lane Theological Seminary and she taught in the Western Female Institute, which had been founded by Catharine. In 1836 she married Calvin E. Stowe, a professor at Lane. She supplemented their meager income by writing stories and sketches for periodicals, and published a collection, *The Mayflower*, in 1843. In 1850 the Stowes moved to Brunswick, Maine, where Calvin Stowe joined the faculty of Bowdoin College. Mrs. Stowe began writing a long tale of slavery, based on her observations in Ohio and Kentucky, and published it serially in the *National Era* in 1851–1852; in 1852 it appeared in book form as *Uncle Tom's Cabin, or, Life Among the Lowly*. It was an immediate sensation and was taken up eagerly by abolitionists while, along with its author, it was being vehemently denounced in the South, where reading or possessing the book became an extremely dangerous undertaking. With sales of 300,000 in the first year, the book exerted an influence equaled by few other novels in history; it helped solidify both pro- and antislavery sentiment and fanned the flames that were to erupt in the Civil War. The book was translated widely and several times dramatized, the first time, without Mrs. Stowe's permission, by George Aiken in 1852. Mrs. Stowe was enthusiastically received on a visit to England in 1853, and there she formed friendships with many leading literary figures. In the same year she published *A Key to Uncle Tom's Cabin*, a compilation of documentary evidence in support of disputed details of her indictment of slavery. Although firmly opposed to slavery, she found most abolitionists too extreme. In 1856 appeared *Dred: A Tale of the Great Dismal Swamp*, another antislavery novel. From 1852 to 1863 she lived in Andover, Massachusetts, and from 1863 onward in Hartford. She traveled widely in the United States and to Europe and continued to produce articles and stories, many of which appeared in the *Atlantic Monthly*, and novels, including *The Minister's Wooing*, 1859; *The Pearl of Orr's Island*, 1862; and *Oldtown Folks*, 1869. An article she published in 1869 in which she alleged that Lord Byron had had an incestuous affair with his half-sister created an uproar and cost her much of her popularity in England, but she remained a leading author and lyceum lecturer in the United States. (The charges concerning Byron later came to be widely accepted.) After the death of her husband in 1886 she remained in Hartford until her own death on July 1, 1896. She was elected to the Hall of Fame in 1910.

Strand, Paul (1890–1976), photographer. Born on October 16, 1890, in New York City, Strand graduated from the Ethical Culture School in 1909. While in school he had also studied photography under Lewis W. Hine, whose influence was significant in turning him toward a career in photography. In 1911 he went into business for himself as a commercial photographer, at the same time continuing to study and work out his own aesthetic motifs. In 1916 he had his first one-man show at the famous 291 Gallery of Alfred Stieglitz, thus becoming associated with such prominent photographers as Stieglitz, Edward Steichen, Frank Eugene, and Clarence White. After World War I Strand experimented with cinematography, and together with the painter Charles Sheeler produced the film *Manhatta, or New York the Magnificent*, a documentary issued in 1921. For the next decade he traveled about the country on photographing expeditions, finding New England, New Mexico, and Colorado particularly fruitful for the combinations of abstraction and realism that he wanted to attain. Photographic studies of Mexico led to his being appointed director of cinematography in Mexico's Secretariat of Education, and he produced the highly praised film, *The Wave*, dealing with a fisherman's strike at Veracruz. The years from 1932 to 1942 were primarily devoted to film-making. He assisted Pare Lorentz in producing *The Plow That Broke the Plains*, an epoch-making documentary for the federal Resettlement Administration. As a founder and president of Frontier Films, Strand did the photography for *Native Land*, released in 1942, a documentary based on materials furnished by the U.S. Senate's Civil Liberties Committee and dealing with labor problems of the 1930s. In 1943 he returned to still photography. He was noted for his refusal to alter his negatives for novel effect; his art lay in depicting the actual. He had a highly praised one-man show at New York City's Museum of Modern Art in 1945 and in 1950 published his first volume of pictures, *Time in New England*, comprising material he had put together in Vermont during the early 1940s. In 1950 he left the United States to make his home in France. His early impressions of France were published in *France de Profil* in 1952; a later collection of his works was *Living Egypt*, published in 1969. Strand died in Oregeval, France, on March 31, 1976.

Strang, James Jesse (1813–1856), religious leader. Born in Scipio, Cayuga County, New York, on March 21, 1813, Strang studied law and was admitted to the bar in 1836. A man of wide interests, he also edited a weekly newspaper and served as local postmaster. In 1843 he moved to Burlington, Wisconsin. Through his wife's brother-in-law, a Mormon, he visited Nauvoo, Illinois, and talked to Joseph Smith, founder of the Church of Jesus Christ of Latter-Day Saints (the Mormons). Strang soon became a convert and was ordained an elder in February 1844. Smith was murdered five months later, and Strang produced a letter, allegedly written by Smith but not in his handwriting, proclaiming Strang his successor as leader of the Mormons. Strang also claimed to have had a vision supporting the contents of the letter. He did not succeed in taking charge of the Mormons, for Brigham Young prevailed; but he did draw off a substantial following to form his own sect, the Strangites. He and his followers moved to Voree, Wisconsin, near Burlington, where they remained until 1847, when the whole group relocated on Beaver Island at the northern end of Lake Michigan, where in 1850 he had himself crowned King James I. Strang ran his sect with an iron hand and wrote a volume of revelations entitled *The Book of the Law of the Lord* to support his authority.

With a following numbering about 5000 after 1850, he became a local political power in Michigan and was twice elected to the state legislature. Nevertheless, his movement was harassed by state authorities and persecuted by private citizens. Dissension within the ranks of the sect caused his undoing. On June 16, 1856, he was shot by two followers, and, wounded, was taken to Voree, Wisconsin, where he died on July 9. After his death the group disintegrated.

Stratemeyer, Edward (1862–1930), author. Born in Elizabeth, New Jersey, on October 4, 1862, Stratemeyer worked as a clerk after graduating from high school and during the 1880s began writing juvenile fiction. He sold his first story in 1888 and quickly became a regular contributor to boys' magazines, editing several such magazines himself between 1893 and 1896. In 1894 he published his first book under the pseudonym "Arthur M. Winfield," and followed with a rapid succession of sequels to form the *Bound to Win* series. Other popular series ensued, including *Old Glory, Pan-American, Colonial, Mexican War, Frontier,* and *Civil War,* and in 1899 he began one of his most successful and long-lived series, *The Rover Boys,* which comprised some 30 volumes and eventually sold more than 6 million copies. Other series, including *Flag of Freedom* and *Frontier,* appeared under the name Capt. Ralph Bonehill. Combining the manner of Horatio Alger—whom Stratemeyer greatly admired and whose name he had borrowed for a few early books—with a facile, formulaic sense of adventure, he turned out volumes at a prodigious rate and was soon able to increase his productivity by founding the Stratemeyer Literary Syndicate in New York City in 1906. Hiring a stable of hack writers, he supplied characters (duly copyrighted), plot outlines, and authors' pseudonyms for what quickly became the largest juvenile-fiction publishing enterprise in the country. His productions ranged from the freewheeling *Motor Boys* series (by "Clarence Young"), selling upwards of four million copies, and the ingenious *Tom Swift* series (by "Victor Appleton," who was usually Stratemeyer's able assistant Howard Garis), selling well over six million, to the saccharine *Bobbsey Twins* series, written by "Laura Lee Hope," and the crime-fighting *Hardy Boys* series by "Franklin W. Dixon." Other syndicate series included *The Boy Scouts* ("Lieutenant Howard Payson") and, from 1930, the *Nancy Drew* books ("Carolyn Keene"). Stratemeyer himself wrote an estimated 160 books under his dozen or more pseudonyms, perhaps 60 under his own name, and outlined stories for about 800 more, supplying several generations of boys and girls with endless opportunities for harmlessly exciting escape. He died in Newark, New Jersey, on May 10, 1930.

Stratton, Samuel Wesley (1861–1931), physicist and educator. Born near Litchfield, Illinois, on July 18, 1861, Stratton graduated from the University of Illinois in 1884 with a degree in mechanical engineering. He became an instructor in mathematics at the university in 1885 and remained there until 1892, by which time he was a professor of physics. He taught physics at the newly established University of Chicago from 1892 until 1901, except for time out for service with the navy during the Spanish-American War. In 1900 he was engaged by the Department of the Treasury to draw up specifications for a federal bureau of standards and to prepare for Congress a bill pertaining to the establishment of such a bureau. When the bill was passed in 1901, Stratton became the first director of the new bureau, which, under his leadership, became a great research center of immense help to both the government and industry. In 1923 Stratton was invited to become president of the Massachusetts Institute of Technology (MIT). He accepted the position in the hope that he could make the school serviceable to industry and the government through research in theoretical and applied science. He remained president until 1930, when he became chairman of the corporation. He died on October 18, 1931, in Cambridge, Massachusetts.

Stratton-Porter, Gene, *see* Porter, Gene Stratton

Straus, Isidor (1845–1912), and Nathan Straus (1848–1931), merchants, philanthropists, and public officials. The Straus brothers were born in Otterberg, Germany, Isidor on February 6, 1845 and Nathan on January 31, 1848. Their father, Lazarus Straus, emigrated to the United States in 1852, settling at Talbotton, Georgia; the rest of the family, which included the youngest brother, Oscar Solomon Straus, joined him two years later. Isidor and Nathan were educated at the Collinsworth Institute in Talbotton. Shortly after the Civil War the family moved to New York City, where, in 1866, Isidor and his father formed the crockery firm of L. Straus & Son. In 1874 the firm took over the pottery and glassware department of Macy's department store. Seven years later the two other sons joined the family business, and in 1888 Isidor and Nathan became partners in Macy's. By 1896 they were its sole owners, and they made it into the world's largest department store. Isidor and Nathan also developed the Abraham & Straus department store. Apart from their involvement in retailing, the careers of the Straus brothers tended to diverge. Isidor remained with the business, and in addition took an interest in public affairs in New York. He was president of the Educational Alliance, a cultural-social-educational institution on the city's Lower East Side, from 1893 until his death. As a Democrat, he supported Grover Cleveland's presidential campaign in 1892, and he himself won election to the House of Representatives to fill a vacancy, serving from January 30, 1894 until March 3, 1895, but declined to serve as Cleveland's postmaster general. Isidor Straus and his wife sailed on the maiden voyage of the *Titanic* in 1912, and both of them went down with the ship on April 15. Nathan Straus maintained an active involvement with

Macy's until his retirement in 1914. But his leading interests became philanthropy and public service. He held various public offices, including those of parks commissioner, 1889–1893, and president of the board of health, 1898. Beginning in 1892 he spearheaded a drive, first in New York, then nationally, for the pasteurization of milk. Partly as a result of this effort the death rate among infants declined markedly. In the last 20 years of his life he devoted much time and money to the cause of Zionism. In 1923 he was selected as the individual who had done most for the welfare of New York City in the preceding 25 years. Nathan Straus died in New York City on January 11, 1931.

Straus, Oscar Solomon (1850–1926), lawyer, diplomat, and public official. Born in Otterberg, Germany, on December 23, 1850, Oscar Straus was the brother of Isidor and Nathan Straus. With his brothers, he was brought to the United States by his mother in 1854 to join his father, who had emigrated in 1852 and settled in Talbotton, Georgia. Oscar attended Columbia College and the Columbia Law School in New York City. He practiced law and was involved with his brothers in the family business, but the greater part of his adult life was devoted to public service. He was U.S. minister to Turkey from 1887 to 1889 and again from 1898 to 1900. He was a frequent consultant to the federal government during the administration of Theodore Roosevelt, and in 1902 Straus was appointed a member of the Permanent Court of Arbitration (the Hague Tribunal), a position to which he was reappointed three times. From 1906 until March 1909 he was secretary of commerce and labor in Theodore Roosevelt's administration; he was the first Jew to serve in the cabinet. From 1909 to 1910 he was again in Turkey, as U.S. ambassador. After an unsuccessful try for the governorship of New York on the Progressive ticket in 1912, Straus toured Europe and Africa for the Department of State. From 1915 to 1918 he served as chairman of the New York Public Service Commission, and following World War I he returned to diplomacy, assisting President Woodrow Wilson at the Versailles treaty talks. Like his brothers, he was a benefactor of Jewish charitable and cultural organizations. He was a founder of the American Jewish Historical Society in 1892, and later he supported the Zionist movement. After World War I he used his influence to help win guarantees of the rights of Jewish minorities in several European countries. Straus published a number of books, including *Reform in the Consular Service*, 1894; *The American Spirit*, 1913; and the autobiographical *Under Four Administrations: From Cleveland to Taft*, 1922. He died in New York City on May 3, 1926.

Strauss, Levi (1829?–1902), manufacturer. Other than that he was born about 1829, little is known of Strauss's early life. But when gold was discovered in California, he left his home in New York City to head west. Sailing around Cape Horn, he arrived in California in February 1850. To get

enough money to go to the gold fields, he sold several bolts of cloth he had brought from New York, keeping only a roll of canvas. When a miner friend of his complained of the quality of the work trousers that were available, Strauss had a pair of pants made from his tent canvas. Realizing that he had both a saleable commodity and a large market, he settled in San Francisco to manufacture the pants, to which the miners attached the name by which they are still known—"Levi's." He sent back to New York City for bolts of denim and duck cloth, and he was soon in business making a product for which there seemed to be an endless demand. Only two major changes were made during the first two decades of manufacturing Levi's: he began to use blue dye for uniformity of appearance, and he added copper rivets to reinforce the corners of the pockets. By the end of the 1860s the wearing of Levi's had expanded well beyond the mining areas—they had become the standard garment for the men on the cattle range, for example. Levi's continued to be the most popular work pants in the West, and eventually became so in the rest of the country because of the company's high standards of uniform quality. Strauss himself died in 1902, and the company was willed to two nephews. The business continued to expand, with new factories in various parts of the United States, until by the end of its first century more than 100 million pairs of Levi's had been sold worldwide. By the early 1970s the line of products had been expanded to cover, besides a number of styles of trousers and jackets for men and boys, an array of jeans and other types of pants for women and girls.

Stravinsky, Igor Fedorovich (1882–1971), composer. Born on June 5 (old style), 1882, in Oranienbaum (now Lomonosov), near St. Petersburg (now Leningrad), Russia, the son of the leading bass singer in the Imperial Opera, Stravinsky grew up in a musical environment but was intended for a law career. He began composing on the piano at the age of nine and later continued his studies in harmony while attending law school at the University of St. Petersburg. He graduated in 1905 and, abandoning the law, took up the study of orchestration and composition under the composer Nikolai Rimski-Korsakov, remaining in a close apprenticeship until Rimski-Korsakov's death in 1908. The romantic themes and lush orchestral usage of his mentor pervaded his early compositions, including *Symphony in E-flat*, 1905–1907, the symphonic poem *Fireworks*, 1908, and *The Firebird*, 1910, which was commissioned by impresario Sergei Diaghilev for the Ballet Russe, the major producer of Stravinsky's stage works for the next 20 years. The ballet *Petrouchka*, 1911, marked a change from Stravinsky's early romanticism to completely unconventional meters and syncopation and also introduced bitonality. It prefigured the style of the ballet *The Rites of Spring*, later recognized as the beginning of an epoch in twentieth-century music, a composition whose tumultuous rhythms and wild dissonances provoked violent demonstrations by the outraged audience at the premiere performance in Paris in 1913. By 1913 Stravinsky was considered an extremely gifted but controversial composer. The Russian Revolution deprived him of his home and property while he was visiting Switzerland, and he decided to remain in that country. During his years in that country he wrote the innovative stage works *Reynard*, 1915–1916, and *The Soldier's Tale*, 1918. After World War I he moved to France, becoming a citizen in 1934. His ballet *Pulcinella*, 1919–1920, marked a change from his dissonant mode to the predominant European musical tradition. He began a second career as a pianist and conductor, and composed *Capriccio* for piano and orchestra, 1929, and *Concerto* for two pianos, 1934–1935, for his own performances, and the *Violin Concerto*, 1931, for the violinist Samuel Dushkin. The last of his ballets to be produced by Diaghilev also was written in this period, *Apollo Musagetes*, 1928, as were *The Fairy's Kiss*, 1928, and *Persephone*, 1933–1934, both for Ida Rubinstein's ballet company, and *The Card Party*, 1936, for the American Ballet Company. The high points of his neoclassical period were the opera-oratorio *Oedipus Rex*, 1926–1927, and *Symphony of Psalms*, 1930. When World War II began Stravinsky moved to the United States, becoming naturalized in 1945. In 1939–1940 he held the Charles Eliot Norton chair of poetry at Harvard. A consolidation of all of his previous styles and techniques took place in *Symphony in C*, 1940; *Symphony in Three Movements*, 1945; the ballet *Orpheus*, 1947, reflecting his interest in jazz; the *Mass in C*, 1948; and an opera, *The Rake's Progress*, premiered in Venice, Italy, in 1951, with a libretto by W. H. Auden. To the amazement of listeners, he took up the twelve-tone system in numerous works, including *In Memoriam Dylan Thomas*, 1954; *Canticum Sacrum*, 1955; the ballet *Agon*, 1953–1957; and the completely atonal *Movements*, 1958–1959; *Noah and the Flood*, 1961–1962, choreographed by George Balanchine; and *Requiem Canticles*, 1965–1966. The range of his styles, forms, and techniques, while outrageous to many critics, marked him as one of the most fertile and influential of twentieth-century composers. He was the author of a number of books, including *Chronicles of My Life*, 1935; *Poetics of Music*, 1947; and, with Robert Craft, *Conversations*, 1959; *Memories and Commentaries*, 1960; *Expositions and Developments*, 1962; *Dialogues and a Diary*, 1963; and *Themes and Episodes*, 1966. Stravinsky died in New York City on April 6, 1971, and was buried in Venice, Italy.

Streisand, Barbra (1942–   ), entertainer. Born on April 24, 1942, in Brooklyn, New York, Miss Streisand graduated from Erasmus Hall High School there in 1959. Having determined at an early age to become an actress, she disdained going into less glamorous employment and immediately set out to achieve her goal. She interviewed producers, went to tryouts, held odd jobs, and studied acting for a short time. Her first break was as a singer in a Greenwich Village nightclub. An 11-week engagement at another club led to several local television appearances, a one-night stand in an off-Broadway play, and an engagement at the Blue Angel night club. It was at the Blue Angel that Broadway producer David Merrick saw her and signed her for a supporting role in the musical comedy *I Can Get It for You Wholesale*, 1962. Her outstanding performance in this show brought her to the verge of stardom. She went on immediately to national television guest appearances, recordings, and nightclub appearances. She opened on Broadway in 1964 in *Funny Girl*, a musical comedy based on the life of Fanny Brice. Playing the lead role, Miss Streisand won great acclaim and went on to star in the film version of *Funny Girl*, for which she won an Academy Award for 1968 (the first year in which two actresses were selected for best performance, the other being Katharine Hepburn). Miss Streisand had by now established herself as one of the biggest names in show business and enjoyed a nationwide following through records, nightclub appearances, and television specials. In 1967 she was signed to play the lead in the film version of *Hello Dolly!*, which was released in 1970, the year in which she received the Antoinette Perry (Tony) award as "star of the decade" for her stage work. Her more recent films included *On a Clear Day You Can See Forever*, 1970; *The Owl and the Pussycat*, 1970; *What's Up, Doc?*, 1972; *The Way We Were*, 1973; *Funny Lady*, 1975; *A Star is Born*, 1976; *The Main Event*, 1979; and *Yentl*, 1983.

Stroheim, Erich von (1885–1957), actor and motion-picture director. Born in Vienna on September 22, 1885, von Stroheim graduated from the Imperial Military Academy in 1902 and until 1909 was an officer in the Austrian cavalry. Then, on emigrating to the United States, he joined the U.S. army and saw service on the Mexican border. After leaving the army he worked at an assortment of jobs: railroad section hand, journalist, boatman, and vaudeville actor. In 1914 he arrived in Los Angeles; his first job there was in a series of roles in D. W. Griffith's film *Birth of a Nation*. Von Stroheim's talent commended itself to Griffith, and the newcomer became his assistant director. He worked with Griffith and other directors for a few years, particularly in war films. After World War I he was hired as a director by the Universal studios, where his first film was *Blind Husbands* in 1919. For the next ten years he was one of Hollywood's leading directors, although his success was in reality short-lived, the movies he directed (eight altogether) being what would have been called in the 1950s "art films," marked by realism and artistic integrity but with limited box-office appeal. They were not the light-hearted commercial ventures that the more "successful" directors of the time were making, but were instead executed with almost abrasive honesty, often portraying the darker sides of human life. *Blind Husbands* was followed by *The Devil's Passkey*, 1919; *Foolish Wives*, 1922; and *Merry-Go-Round*,

1923. Moving to Metro-Goldwyn-Mayer, he directed the movie generally considered von Stroheim's masterpiece, *Greed*, 1923, a film version of Frank Norris's novel *McTeague* that was an artistic success and a commercial failure. He followed it with *The Merry Widow* in 1925, a very successful film, but one in which he felt he had compromised his standards. His last two films were *The Wedding March*, 1928, and *Queen Kelly*. An index of his rapid rise and decline was the fact that in 1926 he was selected by *Film Daily* as one of Hollywood's ten best directors; the next year he was not even among the honorable mentions. By 1928 he was virtually finished in Hollywood. After a few years as a character actor he moved to France, where he became a top movie attraction, most memorably in Jean Renoir's *La Grande Illusion*, 1938. After World War II he returned to the United States and appeared in *Sunset Strip*, 1950, his last American film. By later generations of moviemakers and viewers he came to be looked upon as one of the true early geniuses of filmdom, whose abilities were sacrificed to commercialism. He returned to France after making *Sunset Strip*. He died near Paris on May 12, 1957.

Strong, Josiah (1847–1916), religious leader. Born on January 19, 1847, in Naperville, Illinois, Strong graduated from Western Reserve College in 1869, then attended Lane Theological Seminary and was ordained in 1871. Although he held many Congregational pulpits and was successful as a minister, he did not discover his true métier until he wrote *Our Country*, 1885, a revision of the manual for the Congregational Missionary Society of Cincinnati. His ideas were revolutionary, proposing religious solutions for social and industrial problems. His second book, *The New Era*, 1893, went further, affirming that it was God's intention that Christians aspire to the Kingdom of God through social work for the common good. His philosophy, called Christian Socialism, spread far beyond the Missionary Society, and he was in the forefront of the Social Gospel movement of the time. *The New Era* was translated into many languages, and Strong became celebrated internationally as a lecturer. He was made secretary of the American Evangelical Alliance, which he hoped to use to unite churches in a concerted response to what he considered their social responsibilities. Resistance from orthodox clergymen was vigorous, however, and he resigned from the Alliance and formed the League for Social Service in 1898, which became in 1902 the American Institute for Social Service. Under the auspices of the Institute, he wrote pamphlets and books, gave lectures, and initiated the "Safety First" movement for the prevention of accidents, which he extended to South American countries. He founded the Institute for Social Service in Great Britain, and in the United States he furthered the establishment of the Federal Council of the Churches of Christ, later merged into the National Council of the Churches of Christ in the United States. Strong died in New York City on April 28, 1916.

Strong, William (1808–1895), justice of the Supreme Court. Born in Somers, Connecticut, on May 6, 1808, Strong graduated from Yale in 1828 and pursued graduate work there until 1831. He then taught school and undertook the private study of law before attending Yale Law School for a few months. He was admitted to the bar in Philadelphia in 1832 and began practice the following year in Reading, Pennsylvania. He prospered in Reading and entered politics briefly, serving in the U.S. House of Representatives for two terms, from 1847 to 1851. In 1857 he was elected to the Pennsylvania supreme court and remained on the bench until 1868, when he resigned to return to private practice. On February 7, 1870, President Ulysses S. Grant nominated Strong and Joseph P. Bradley to the U.S. Supreme Court. After strong Senate opposition they were confirmed later that month. To many congressmen, and private citizens as well, the nominations appeared to be a court-packing scheme by Grant because of the Legal Tender Cases. Paper money ("greenbacks") issued during the Civil War by the federal government had been declared legal tender for all debts by Congress. The constitutionality of this declaration, the Legal Tender Act of 1862, was challenged and on February 7, 1870 the same day the Strong and Bradley nominations were made, the Supreme Court in a 5–3 decision in *Hepburn* v. *Griswold* had declared the Legal Tender Act unconstitutional. After the two new justices were confirmed, the newly constituted court at its next term agreed to a rehearing of the case, over the protests of the four remaining members who had pronounced the act unconstitutional. A year later, on May 1, 1871, in the cases of *Knox* v. *Lee* and *Parker* v. *Davis*, the Supreme Court reversed itself in a 5–4 decision overturning the *Hepburn* decision, with the two new justices swinging the balance and Strong writing the majority opinion. There is little doubt that Strong would have been appointed to the Court whether or not the Legal Tender Cases had arisen, for he was one of the noted jurists of his day and his views were well known. He served on the Court until his resignation on December 14, 1880. His term was generally considered one of the most distinguished of the nineteenth century. After his retirement he remained in Washington, D.C., lecturing and teaching, and working actively as a layman in the Presbyterian church. He died in Washington on August 19, 1895.

Stroud, Robert (1890–1963), ornithologist. Born in Seattle in 1890, Stroud grew up in a broken home and at the age of thirteen ran away to become a hobo. At age eighteen he was in Juneau, Alaska, living with a dancehall girl. One night he shot and killed a man who had beaten her, then surrendered to the local U.S. marshal. He pleaded guilty on August 3, 1909, and was sentenced to 12 years in the federal prison on McNeill Island in Puget Sound. It was the start of a prison life that would extend for 54 years, 42 of them in solitary confinement. In that time he became one of the nation's most famous convicts, known in the 1960s as the "Bird-Man of Alcatraz," from the 1955 biography of that title by Thomas Gaddes that was turned into a movie version of his life. Stroud's scholarly achievements in the study of birds were offset by a persistent, and at times vicious, antisocial attitude. But his attitude and actions may well have owed as much to his imprisonment as to any source. After two years at Puget Sound, he stabbed a fellow prisoner; six months were added to his sentence, and as a difficult prisoner he was transferred to Leavenworth Prison in 1912. There he showed an interest in studying and within three years had received diplomas from the extension service of Kansas State University in engineering, mechanical drawing, music, mathematics, and theology. In March 1916, in anger over not being able to see his brother who had visited the prison, Stroud killed one of the guards. He was tried and found guilty, and on June 28, 1918, was sentenced to hang; but on April 15, 1920, a few days before the execution date, President Woodrow Wilson commuted his sentence to life imprisonment. It was after this time that, in solitary confinement for the most part, he took up an interest in birds. He raised and sold canaries, and he obtained laboratory equipment for his cell to treat the birds when they were sick. He studied the diseases of birds and their cures and took up chemistry, pharmacology, veterinary medicine, and bacteriology. By 1931 he was an authority on the care and breeding of canaries and was corresponding with other bird breeders. Some of his articles were smuggled out of prison and published. In 1937 he applied for parole, but the parole board turned him down. His book, *Stroud's Digest of the Diseases of Birds*, was published in 1942 and soon came to be regarded as the definitive work in its field. Later that year he was transferred to Alcatraz, the maximum-security prison in San Francisco Bay, where he continued his research and writing, but was not allowed to publish. In 1959 he was transferred to the Medical Center for Federal Prisoners at Springfield, Missouri, where he spent the last four years of his life, out of solitary confinement, pressing his case for release from prison. He died there on November 21, 1963.

Struve, Otto (1897–1963), astronomer. Born on August 12, 1897, in Kharkov, Russia, Struve came of a family of German or Swiss origin that had for three generations produced distinguished astronomers. His education was interrupted by military service, and after graduating from the University of Kharkov in 1919 and seeing further service against the Bolsheviks during the Russian Revolution he left Russia, residing in Turkey until emigrating to the United States in 1921. He was naturalized in 1927. Entering the University of Chicago and joining the staff of its Yerkes Observatory, he took his Ph.D. in 1923 and the next year became an instructor in astronomy, advancing by 1932 to full professor and director of Yerkes. Seven years later he was named also director of the McDonald Observatory of the University of Texas and he held both posts, planning and co-

ordinating the work of the two installations, until 1947, when he became head of the astronomy department at Chicago. In addition he edited the *Astrophysical Journal* from 1932 to 1947. Under Struve's leadership a number of research projects were undertaken and significant discoveries made in the study of binary stars (a field of study that was a family tradition), eclipsing binaries, stellar spectroscopy (a method by which he found that a large proportion of very hot stars rotate at great speeds), and nebular spectroscopy, a field in which he was a pioneer and an innovator in the use of techniques by which the large-scale distribution of interstellar hydrogen clouds was discovered. The last finding was of great importance for the development of a comprehensive theory of galactic structure and stellar origins and for the refinement of the powerful new tool of radio astronomy, a subject in which Struve took an early interest. He was also a leading proponent of the theory that life, including intelligent life, exists throughout the universe. From 1950 to 1959 he was head of the department of astronomy at the University of California and director of its Leuschner Observatory and from 1959 to 1962 was the first director of the National Radio Astronomy Observatory in Green Bank, West Virginia. Widely honored as a stimulator of original research in a multitude of fields, Struve served as president of the American Astronomical Society in 1946–1949 and of the International Astronomical Union in 1952–1955. He died in Berkeley, California, on April 6, 1963.

Stuart, Gilbert Charles (1755–1828), painter. Born on December 3, 1755, in North Kingstown, Rhode Island, Stuart was raised and educated in Newport and was subsequently tutored by a Scottish painter living in Rhode Island. He traveled to Edinburgh with his teacher in 1771 and after the death of the master tried to earn his living by painting portraits, but he failed and returned to Newport the next year. In 1775 he sailed to England, where he lived in poverty for a year before approaching Benjamin West, who welcomed him to his studio as a pupil. He spent nearly six years with West, progressed rapidly in portraiture, and by 1777 he was exhibiting successfully at the Royal Academy. His painting "Portrait of a Gentleman Skating," 1782, won special favor and led to several commissions. Ranked among the leading portrait artists in England, he was nevertheless naive about money matters and fell into debt. In order to avoid prosecution he traveled to Ireland in 1787; there he painted with equal success but again met with financial disaster. He left for New York City in 1793, painted there for a brief time, and in late 1794 opened a successful studio in Philadelphia. He completed a famous series of portraits of women and two paintings from life of President George Washington, a profile in 1795, now in the National Gallery, and a full-length portrait in 1796, now in the Pennsylvania Academy of Fine Arts. Later that year he executed the famous unfinished "Athenaeum Head" of Washington, a highly romanticized version that has remained the most popular portrait of the Father of His Country. In 1803, in a new studio in Washington, D.C., he completed portraits of Thomas Jefferson, James Madison, and James Monroe, among other distinguished public figures. His paintings were noted for their elegance, perception, and vibrant colors. Living in Boston after 1805, he continued to be successful but was chronically in debt. He showed symptoms of paralysis after 1825 but continued to paint. Well mannered, happy, and congenial into his seventies, he died in Boston on July 9, 1828. He was elected to the Hall of Fame in 1900.

Stuart, James Ewell Brown (1833–1864), "Jeb," soldier. Born in Patrick County, Virginia, on February 6, 1833, Stuart attended Emory and Henry College for two years before entering West Point in 1850. He graduated in 1854, was commissioned in the cavalry, and for six years was assigned to duty in Texas and Kansas. During a visit to the East in 1859 he served as aide to Col. Robert E. Lee in the expedition against John Brown's raiding party at Harpers Ferry. In May 1861 Stuart, by then a captain, resigned his U.S. army commission and returned to Virginia, where he was commissioned a lieutenant colonel of infantry and, two weeks later, a captain of cavalry in the Confederate army. Jeb Stuart (the nickname derived from his initials) distinguished himself quickly at the first battle of Bull Run (Manassas) in July, and two months later was promoted to brigadier general. In command of the cavalry of the Army of Northern Virginia, he covered the retreat from the fighting of the Peninsular Campaign in the spring of 1862. In June he was sent to scout Gen. George B. McClellan's right just before the Seven Days' Battles; he completely circled the Union force and returned to Richmond with a quantity of captured supplies and a number of prisoners. In July he became a major general and all Confederate cavalry was placed under his command. He performed brilliantly at the second battle of Bull Run and at South Mountain, Antietam, and Fredericksburg, and was highly valued by Lee as an intelligence officer of foremost ability. When Gen. Thomas J. "Stonewall" Jackson was mortally wounded at Chancellorsville in May 1863, Stuart was given command of the 2nd Corps. The next month he made another daring raid, circling Federal forces in Pennsylvania and capturing more than 1000 horses. His conduct at Gettysburg in July 1863 was long a subject of controversy: ordered to deploy his cavalry as a screen and intelligence-gathering arm for the advancing Confederate army and to subordinate all other activity to this end, he nonetheless struck off on a raid, was delayed, and arrived at Gettysburg too late to provide Lee with vital information on the positions and movements of Union forces. In the Wilderness Campaign in 1864 he was invaluable in providing information on the advance of Gen. Ulysses S. Grant and as a shield against him, but by this time the Union cavalry under Gen. Philip H. Sheridan had been greatly improved and when Stuart met Sheridan at Yellow Tavern on May 11, his

heavily outnumbered force was routed and Stuart himself was mortally wounded. He died the next day, May 12, 1864, in Richmond, Virginia.

Studebaker, Clement (1831–1901), wagon and carriage manufacturer. Born in Pinetown, near Gettysburg, Pennsylvania, on March 12, 1831, Studebaker moved with his family to Ohio, where he attended school and worked in his father's blacksmith shop. He moved to South Bend, Indiana, in 1850 and taught school until 1852, when he and his brother Henry formed the H. & C. Studebaker blacksmith and wagonmaking company. The growing demand for wagons in the Midwest, combined with the brothers' scrupulously maintained high standards of quality, caused the business to prosper. Another brother, John M., replaced Henry in the firm in 1858, and soon government contracts occasioned by Civil War needs created further expansion. In 1868 Peter E., yet another brother, came into the company, which was reorganized as the Studebaker Brothers Manufacturing Company, with Clement as president. A fifth and final brother, Jacob F., joined them in 1870, the year in which a branch was opened in St. Joseph, Missouri, to provide wagons for westbound settlers. By this time the company was the world's largest manufacturer of wagons and other horse-drawn vehicles. Clement Studebaker became prominent in the Republican party and enjoyed personal friendships with presidents Ulysses S. Grant, Benjamin Harrison, and William McKinley; in 1889 he was appointed a delegate to the first Pan-American Conference by Harrison. About 1897 he began to experiment with self-propelled vehicles, the forerunners of a long line of Studebaker automobiles that became, after his death, the company's major product. During its history the Studebaker company produced more than 750,000 vehicles before turning to powered automobiles in 1902. Clement Studebaker died on November 27, 1901, in South Bend. John became president and in 1911 the firm was absorbed by the Studebaker Corporation. In 1954 a merger with the Packard Motor Car Company was effected, and the company continued to manufacture automobiles in South Bend until 1963.

Stutz, Harry Clayton (1876–1930), automobile manufacturer. Born near Ansonia, Ohio, on September 12, 1876, Stutz attended grade school there and then became an apprentice machinist. When he was twenty-one he opened his own machine shop in Dayton. He followed with great interest the development of the automobile and from 1903 to 1906 worked for various auto-parts companies. From 1906 to 1910 he was employed as an engineer and factory manager for the Marion (Ohio) Motor Car Company. About 1910, in association with Henry Campbell, he organized the Stutz Auto Parts Company and shortly thereafter the Ideal Motor Car Company. In 1913 he consolidated the two businesses into the Stutz Motor Car Company, which he served as president until 1919. It was during this six-year period that the famous Stutz racing and sports cars, including the Stutz Bearcat, were manufactured. In 1919 he sold his interest in the company and helped organize the H. C. S. Motor Car Company at Indianapolis to make tires and less expensive cars. Stutz spent a brief period in 1924–1925 developing a successful airplane engine. He died on June 26, 1930, in Indianapolis.

Stuyvesant, Peter (1610–1672), colonial official. Born in Scherpenzeel, the Netherlands, in 1610, Stuyvesant, whose first name was originally Petrus, came from a family of Dutch Reformed clergy, but chose for himself a military career. He had entered the service of the Dutch West India Company by 1635 and in 1643 became governor of the Caribbean islands of Curaçao, Bonaire, and Aruba (now the Netherlands Antilles). During his tenure in the islands, Stuyvesant suffered a wound in the right leg that led to its amputation and replacement with an ornamented wooden leg. After a brief recuperation in the Netherlands he was commissioned director general of the colony of New Netherland, with authority over the Caribbean islands as well. He arrived in New Amsterdam (now New York City) on May 11, 1647. The colony to which he came was in sore straits; it was nearly bankrupt and was hard pressed by neighboring Indians in a war with tribes that had previously been friendly. It was also a diversified, not to say motley, colony, with residents of various religious and national backgrounds who among them spoke at least 18 different languages. The measures adopted by Stuyvesant to impose social and religious uniformity and raise taxes were generally highhanded and unsuccessful. His high customs duties caused trade to wither away. His only great success, in the eyes of the Dutch West India Company, was in ending in 1655 the Swedish influence in North America by taking the defenses, near present-day Wilmington, Delaware, of New Sweden, which had offered commercial competition in the fur trade. Public reaction against his autocratic rule led to his appointment in 1647 of a nine-man advisory board to assist him, but in 1653 he was forced to grant New Amsterdam independent municipal government. At the end of his 17-year tenure in office, New Netherland had become neither prosperous nor politically peaceful, but it had served the purposes of the West India Company by paying its own way and serving as a port for the repairing and provisioning of ships. Stuyvesant's most notable achievement was probably his persistent fending off of English attempts to subjugate New Netherland, in which he succeeded until 1664. An English fleet anchored in the harbor that summer and demanded capitulation of the colony. The terms were generous, and the populace forced the director general to give in. He surrendered early in September, and from that time withdrew from public life. He died at his farm in present-day Manhattan in February 1672.

Sullivan, Anne Mansfield, see under Keller, Helen

Sullivan, Edward Vincent (1902–1974), journalist and entertainer. Born in New York City on Sep-

tember 28, 1902, Ed Sullivan grew up there and in Port Chester, New York. After graduating from high school, where he excelled in athletics, he was hired as a reporter for the *Port Chester Daily Item.* In 1920 he got a job on the *New York Evening Mail,* where he became a sports columnist. Over the next 12 years he was a sports writer for the *World,* the *Morning Telegraph,* and the *Evening Graphic,* all in New York City. In 1929 the *Graphic* made him its Broadway gossip columnist in competition with Walter Winchell, who had left the paper to go with the *New York Daily Mirror.* In 1932 Sullivan went to work for the *New York Daily News,* in which his column appeared thereafter. The same year he started a radio show on station WABC in New York City, and throughout the decade expanded his activities in show business by writing scripts, acting, and putting together his own vaudeville bills. During World War II he staged a number of benefit shows, and in 1942 the Columbia Broadcasting System (CBS) signed him to do a weekly radio show called "Ed Sullivan Entertains." In 1948, with the advent of television, he contracted to conduct a Sunday night variety show, known in its early years as "Toast of the Town." The program, eventually called "The Ed Sullivan Show," became the longest-running television show in the history of the medium; it went off the air at the end of the 1970–1971 season after 23 years. During those years Sullivan had introduced virtually every major show-business figure to television viewers, as well as bringing to national fame some hitherto little-known talents. After the show was dropped by CBS, Sullivan continued to make TV guest appearances and produced an occasional TV special. He died on October 13, 1974, in New York City.

Sullivan, Harry Stack (1892–1949), psychiatrist and educator. Born on February 21, 1892, in Norwich, New York, Sullivan graduated from the Chicago College of Medicine and Surgery in 1917 and studied psychiatry after 1919 under William Alanson White at St. Elizabeth's Hospital in Washington, D.C. From 1923 to 1930 he did clinical research at Sheppard and Enoch Pratt Hospital in Towson, Maryland, and taught at the medical schools of the University of Maryland and Georgetown University. In 1931 he moved to New York City to enter private practice. In 1934 he helped found and became president of the William Alanson White Foundation, under whose auspices in 1936 he helped to organize the Washington School of Psychiatry. He continued to head the foundation until 1943 and the school until 1947. A leader in the interpersonal school of psychiatry, he conceived of anxiety as a disturbance in interpersonal relations, having its first appearance in the relationship between a mother and child and then appearing in the response of an individual to life situations. He rejected the idea of an "individual personality" and contended that character traits were a result of cultural and personal interactions. By using group-treatment methods, he brought some forms of schizophrenia from the realm of incurable disorders to that of common mental diseases, showing them to be caused by anxiety and lack of self-esteem. At the beginning of World War II he was a consultant to the selective-service program. After the war he attempted to apply his theories to understanding international tensions. He was an editor of *Psychiatry* and published widely, including *Conceptions of Modern Psychiatry*, 1947; and the pieces collected posthumously in *The Interpersonal Theory of Phychiatry*, 1953; *The Psychiatric Interview*, 1954; *Clinical Studies in Psychiatry*, 1956; and *The Fusion of Psychiatry and Social Science*, 1964. He died in Paris on January 14, 1949.

Sullivan, James Edward (1860–1914), publisher and sports promoter. Born in New York City on November 18, 1860, Sullivan grew up there and attended the public schools. In 1878 he went to work for Frank Leslie's publishing firm and, as a result of that job, editing and publishing became his life work. He remained with Leslie's firm until 1889, when he became editor and manager of the *Sporting Times*. He bought that journal in 1891 and in 1892 became president of the American Sports Publishing Company. But if publishing was his vocation, it was sports that became his avocation and consuming interest. In 1877 Sullivan joined the Pastime Athletic Club and became, in a few years, proficient in a number of sports. As an athlete he became disturbed by the way the National Association of Amateur Athletics conducted amateur sports, and he accused the association of failing to distinguish properly between the amateur and the professional. In 1888 he formed the Amateur Athletic Union of the United States (AAU) to take over the responsibility of certifying athletes as amateurs. In 1889 the AAU claimed jurisdiction over 17 sports and divided the United States into districts for certification purposes. Sullivan remained an officer of the AAU from its founding until his death. He also prompted the founding of the Public School Athletic League in New York City and he started the first public playground-gymnasium in the city. For 25 years he officiated at U.S. championship track and field events. As the U.S. director of the Olympic Games he earned international fame; and as an uncompromising exponent of amateur status, it was he who disqualified Jim Thorpe after his unprecedented victories in the Olympics and took back his Olympic medals. Sullivan represented the United States as an official at the Olympic Games in 1900, 1904, 1908, and 1912. He died in New York City on September 16, 1914.

Sullivan, John (1740–1795), soldier and public official. Born in Somersworth, New Hampshire, on February 17, 1740, Sullivan studied law privately and began practice in the 1760s. In 1772, as trouble between the American colonies and Great Britain intensified, he was appointed a major in the colonial militia and later served as a delegate to the first and second Continental Congresses. Late in 1774 he commanded a band of New Hampshire militia that captured the forts at Portsmouth Harbour and secured the ordnance stored there. Once hostilities had begun in 1775, he put himself under George Washington's command. He served through the siege of Boston. Congress gave him the rank of brigadier general, and a year later, in August 1776, he was promoted to major general. For most of the Revolution he served in the Northern theater—New York, New Jersey, New England, and Pennsylvania. In August 1776 he was captured by the British at the battle of Long Island, but later was exchanged at Philadelphia for a British general. He participated in the New Jersey battles of Trenton and Princeton in 1776–1777, and in August of 1777 tried without success to dislodge the British from Staten Island. He spent the winter of 1777–1778 with Washington's forces at Valley Forge, and when spring came was assigned to capture Newport, Rhode Island. His failure in this mission was largely owing to the lack of support from the French navy when Sullivan needed it. Most of 1779 he spent in a highly successful drive to rid western New York State and Pennsylvania of the British and their Indian allies. On November 30, 1779, he resigned from the army because of poor health. He spent the remainder of his life in his native New Hampshire, holding a number of public offices after serving in the Continental Congress in 1780–1781. He participated in the New Hampshire constitutional convention, served as attorney general of the state from 1782 to 1786, and was a member of the state legislature in the same period. In 1788 he was chairman of the New Hampshire constitutional ratifying convention. He was elected to three terms as president (governor) of New Hampshire, in 1787, 1788, and 1789, and in 1789 was appointed a federal district judge. He remained on the bench until his death in Durham, New Hampshire, on January 23, 1795.

Sullivan, John Florence, see Allen, Fred

Sullivan, John Lawrence (1858–1918), boxer. Born in Boston on October 15, 1858, Sullivan studied briefly at Boston College and worked at various jobs before, at nineteen, he made his first appearance as a fighter. For several years he fought exhibition matches, gaining a reputation for great strength; in 1882, in Mississippi City, Mississippi, he knocked out Paddy Ryan for the world heavyweight championship. For a decade thereafter the "Great John L." reigned supreme in American boxing, attracting a large popular following and accumulating a small fortune that he as quickly lost by living on a spectacular scale. In 1887 he was lionized while visiting England and was eagerly sought out by the Prince of Wales. In 1889 in Richburg, Mississippi, he knocked out Jake Kilrain in the 75th round of the last bare-knuckle bout in professional boxing. Finally, on September 7, 1892, in New Orleans, the "Boston Strong Boy" was defeated in the 21st round by James J. "Gentleman Jim" Corbett in the first U.S. heavyweight title match fought with gloves and under the Marquis of Queensberry rules. From the ring Sullivan addressed the crowd: "I fought once too often. But I'm glad that it was an American who beat me and that the championship stays in this country. Very truly yours, John L. Sullivan." For a time he toured in plays and in vaudeville and later opened a bar in New York City. In 1905, after announcing his own reformation, he began lecturing on temperance. Sullivan died in near-poverty on February 2, 1918, in Abingdon, Massachusetts.

Sullivan, Louis Henry (1856–1924), architect. Born on September 3, 1856, in Boston, Sullivan was trained in architecture at the Massachusetts Institute of Technology (MIT), 1872–1873, the École des Beaux-Arts in Paris, 1874–1875, and in the offices of various architectural firms in Chicago, including that of William Le Baron Jenney. He had established a name as a competent draftsman in Chicago when he entered partnership with Dankmar Adler in 1881. Their firm, Adler and Sullivan, gained international fame upon completion of the Auditorium Theater building in Chicago in 1890. Its interior design, planned largely by Sullivan, was intricate and wholly magnificent, and the receding, elevated pattern of seat rows produced near-perfect acoustics. Among Sullivan's apprentices at this time was Frank Lloyd Wright, who regarded his ideas on design as gospel. Sullivan's firm completed several buildings based on his own structural theories: the Wainwright Building (1890) in St. Louis, generally thought to be the first true skyscraper; the Transportation Building at the World's Columbian Exposition (1893) and the Gage Building in Chicago; and the Guaranty Building in Buffalo, New York. After the dissolution of the partnership in 1895 Sullivan's financial resources diminished, primarily because his advanced ideas often bewildered potential clients. He was able, however, to erect the Carson, Pirie, Scott and Company department store in Chicago and several banks in small Midwestern towns. Through lectures, articles, and books, he expounded his theory that design should relate to use and materials and that architecture should be a response to the milieu—a principle made famous by the phrase "form follows function." This became the basis for all modern design. He was known as the founder of the "Chicago School" of architecture, a school diametrically opposed to useless tradition and devoted to modernism, uniquely represented by the skyscraper. He wrote, among other books, *The Autobiography of an Idea*, 1924. He died in Chicago on April 14, 1924. After his death the Auditorium Theater fell into disrepair and eventually into disuse, but it was refurbished and reopened in all its old magnificence in 1967.

Sullivan, Timothy Daniel (1862–1913), public official and political leader. Born in New York City on July 23, 1862, Sullivan grew up in an Irish tenement district on the Lower East Side of Manhattan. His schooling was limited because his family's needs made it imperative for him to be out selling papers and working at other jobs from the time he was eight years old. He became a

leader of the notorious Whyo Gang in the Five Points district of lower Manhattan, and his gang membership brought him into contact with local politicians. By the time he was twenty-one he had found a backer to set him up in the saloon business. Two years later he was elected to the state legislature as a member of a small anti-Tammany faction. Once in Albany he was soon convinced that any real political future would be found within the Tammany organization. In 1890 the Tammany leaders assigned "Big Tim," as he was known, to organize the Bowery, a tenement district fast filling up with new immigrants who had not yet been safely gathered within the organization's fold. He was eminently successful in his efforts and by 1900 was the dominant political figure on the Lower East Side. He had full control over all the vice in his district and had an enormous income from graft, the selling of "protection," and crime. But he remained one of the most beloved figures in New York City simply because he gave away most of the money he gained, bestowing it where it would be of the greatest benefit to the recipients. He also ran a number of businesses, including saloons, a chain of theaters, a vaudeville circuit, and sporting events. In 1892 Sullivan was elected to the state senate and served there until 1902, and was again a state senator from 1908 until 1912. He was in the U.S. House of Representatives for two terms, from 1902 until 1906, but national office did not particularly interest him; he preferred the challenge of local politics and the company of his friends in New York City. While in the state legislature he supported liberal social legislation, in contrast to many of the Tammany regulars. He supported woman suffrage, put through a bill for a shorter work week for women, made Columbus Day a legal holiday (to satisfy his Italian constituents), and was responsible for the Sullivan Law, which made the carrying of a handgun without a license a criminal offense. In 1912 his health began to fail and he died on August 31, 1913, near Eastchester, New York.

Sully, Thomas (1783–1872), painter. Born on either June 8 or 19, 1783, in Horncastle, England, the youngest son of actor parents, Sully came to the United States as a child, was raised in South Carolina, and moved to Virginia about 1799 to study art with his brother, a miniaturist. In 1801 he began indexing his work. By the end of his career, his portraits numbered nearly 2000 and his paintings of historical subjects over 500. In 1806 he moved to New York City. He studied briefly in Boston with Gilbert Stuart in 1807, and after establishing residence in Philadelphia in 1808 he spent a year in London, where he studied with Benjamin West and others. He was unmatched in portraiture after the deaths of Charles Willson Peale and Gilbert Stuart. His works included portraits of the Marquis de Lafayette, Thomas Jefferson, James Madison, and Andrew Jackson, and, in 1838, young Queen Victoria of England. The most famous of his historical works, "Washington Crossing the

Delaware," was executed about 1818. Throughout his later career, commissions and social acceptance were assured him. Although his portraits failed to capture the character of sitters in a way equal to Stuart's, they were warm and exquisite in color. He remained the leading portraitist in Philadelphia until his death there on November 5, 1872. The next year his *Hints to Young Painters and the Process of Portrait-Painting* was published.

Sulzberger, Arthur Hays (1891–1968), newspaper publisher. Born in New York City on September 12, 1891, Sulzberger graduated from Columbia University in 1913 with a degree in science. In 1917 he enlisted in the army and served until 1919. In 1911 Sulzberger had married the daughter of Adolph S. Ochs, publisher of the *New York Times*. When he was discharged from the army in 1919 he went to work for the *Times* to learn the newspaper business. His father-in-law encouraged him to become familiar with all aspects of newspaper publishing; his first task was to obtain an adequate supply of newsprint for the *Times*, an endeavor through which he became an expert on newsprint. One of Sulzberger's notable contributions to the newspaper field in the years of his "apprenticeship" was directing the development of a facsimile transmitter for photographs. Also through his efforts the *Times* acquired radio station WQXR in 1944. When Adolph Ochs died in April 1935, the *Times* board named Sulzberger the new publisher and he occupied the position until 1961. During this time he greatly expanded the services, facilities, and staff of the paper, which came to provide more space for news analysis and interpretation, more pictures, and specialized features. Sunday circulation nearly doubled and daily circulation rose 40 percent. The number of *Times* employees all over the world made the paper's staff the largest in existence. Politically the *Times* tried to steer an independent course, generally supporting liberal candidates from either major party. In 1943 Sulzberger was elected a director of the Associated Press (AP), a position he held for nine years. He was a trustee of Columbia University from 1944 to 1954 and was chairman of the university's bicentennial celebration. In April 1957 he became chairman of the *Times* board, and in 1961 he retired as publisher. He died on December 11, 1968, in New York City. He had been succeeded as publisher in 1961 by his son-in-law, Orville E. Dryfoos; Dryfoos, who died in 1963, was in turn succeeded by Sulzberger's son, Arthur Ochs Sulzberger.

Sumner, Charles (1811–1874), public official. Born in Boston on January 6, 1811, Sumner graduated from Harvard in 1830 and from Harvard Law School in 1833. He found the practice of law rather dull and in 1837 traveled to Europe, where he stayed for nearly three years, during which time he met prominent men of affairs and of letters and acquired a knowledge of European politics. He returned to his law practice and began lecturing at Harvard; he involved himself in several reform movements, notably those directed toward world peace, the improvement of education, and the abolition of slavery. He was a noted speaker, popular on the lyceum circuit, and attracted wide, if sometimes unfavorable, attention with his strongly stated views, notably his opposition to the Mexican War. After an unsuccessful campaign in 1848, he was nominated a second time in 1851 for the U.S. Senate by a coalition of Democratic and Free-Soil backers and, after several months of deadlock in the legislature, was elected. In his first major address, in August 1852, he reopened the issue of the Compromise of 1850 by proposing the repeal of the Fugitive Slave Law of that year. His oratory typically was of the nature of tirade; in vituperation he was peerless, and his uncompromising stand on slavery made him a favorite and most powerful abolitionist. He bitterly opposed the Kansas-Nebraska Bill in 1854 and in May 1856, in a debate on the admission of Kansas, made his most famous address, "The Crime Against Kansas." He scorned the Kansas-Nebraska Act as a "swindle" and he heaped invective upon its authors, senators Andrew P. Butler and Stephen A. Douglas, in the most vindictive terms. Two days later, while at his desk in the Senate chamber, he was set upon and severely beaten by Preston S. Brooks, a congressman from South Carolina who was a nephew of Butler. For three years Sumner was unable to resume his official duties, but the outraged Massachusetts legislature reelected him in 1857 despite his incapacitation. He took a leading role in organizing the Republican party and was its leader in the Senate when the party came into control in 1860. During the Civil War, as chairman of the foreign relations committee, he rendered service of great value in helping prevent intervention in the conflict by European powers; to this end he counseled the release of James M. Mason and John Slidell in the *Trent* Affair and prevailed over more reckless heads. His strong position against slavery and rebellion led him to assert the belief that the defeated South would be a conquered province outside the protection of the Constitution; against President Abraham Lincoln and later Andrew Johnson he worked in concert with Thaddeus Stevens to secure enactment of the Radical Reconstruction bills providing for military occupation of the South and making Negro suffrage a precondition for readmission of seceded states to the Union. Also with Stevens he sought the impeachment and conviction of Johnson. He opposed President Ulysses S. Grant's policies almost without exception and was instrumental in defeating Grant's plan to annex Santo Domingo in 1870, apparently in retaliation for which he was removed from the chairmanship of the foreign relations committee. In 1872 he supported Horace Greeley of the Liberal Republican party against Grant. His major accomplishments in his last years were the ratification of the 1871 Treaty of Washington, providing for arbitration of U.S.-British grievances (notably the *Alabama* claims), and a bill in 1872 that directed the removal from battle rolls and regimental flags of the names of all "battles with fellow-citizens." For the latter action he was at first censured by the Massachusetts legislature; in 1874, however, the censure was rescinded, but the day after the reversal was reported to the Senate, he died, on March 11, 1874, in Washington, D.C.

Sumner, James Batcheller (1887–1955), biochemist. Born in Canton, Massachusetts, on November 19, 1887, Sumner received his preparatory education at the Roxbury Latin School. A hunting accident in 1904 necessitated the amputation of his left arm, creating a severe handicap he had to overcome in his school years since he had been left-handed. He graduated from Harvard in 1910 and received his Ph.D. there in 1914. He had also taught chemistry in 1911 at Mt. Allison College in New Brunswick, and spent some months as research assistant at Worcester (Massachusetts) Polytechnic Institute in 1911–1912. In 1914 he joined the faculty of Cornell University Medical School, where he remained until his retirement in 1955, after 1929 as a professor. The research for which he is most noted was his work on enzymes. By 1926 he had concluded that enzymes were proteins, and succeeded in isolating and crystallizing the enzyme urease. His findings were not generally accepted, however, until 1930, when John H. Northrop crystallized three other enzymes. For his work on enzymes Sumner shared the Nobel Prize for Chemistry in 1946 with Northrop and Wendell M. Stanley. During his teaching career, Sumner had pursued further study at the universities of Brussels, Stockholm, and Uppsala. In 1937 he was awarded the Scheele Medal at Stockholm for achievements in the field of chemistry. Among his published works were *Biological Chemistry*, 1927; *Chemistry and Methods of Enzymes*, 1943, with G. F. Somers; and *The Enzymes: Chemistry and Mechanism of Action*, four volumes, 1950–1952, with Karl Myrbäck. He died on August 12, 1955, in Buffalo, New York.

Sumner, William Graham (1840–1910), social scientist and educator. Born on October 30, 1840, in Paterson, New Jersey, Sumner grew up in Hartford, Connecticut, and graduated from Yale in 1863. During the next three years he studied abroad, at Geneva, Göttingen, and Oxford, intent on entering the ministry. From 1866 to 1869 he was a tutor at Yale and in 1869 was ordained a minister in the Protestant Episcopal church. In 1870 he moved to Morristown, New Jersey, and led the church there until, no longer satisfied within the confines of clerical activity, he accepted an invitation to join the Yale faculty as professor of political and social science in 1872. In this position, which he held until his death and in which he won recognition as an outstanding teacher and a staunch proponent of broadening the classical curriculum, he became nationally influential, while devoting great energy to the study of social institutions from a viewpoint much like that of Herbert Spencer. In his economic and social outlook, Sumner was a Social Darwinist, holding that distinc-

tions of wealth and status among men were the direct result of inherently different capacities, that this stratifying tendency worked to the good of society by eliminating weaker and encouraging stronger strains (as natural selection does among animals and plants), and that this tendency should not be interfered with by sentimental, unintelligent attempts to hedge the free play of economic forces and personal abilities. Sumner thus championed laissez-faire as the only true principle of both economics and government; in lectures and written works with such titles as "The Absurd Attempt to Make the World Over" and *What Social Classes Owe to Each Other*, 1883, he decried any and all movements that pointed to a welfare state to the detriment of "The Forgotten Man" (an 1883 lecture title), the ordinary man of the middle class at whose expense government welfare programs were undertaken. He was throughout his life an opponent of inflationary fiscal policies and of the protective tariff. His interest in human institutions led him to study them at their deeper and more basic levels, and in 1906 he published his great work on customs and mores, *Folkways*. He died in Englewood, New Jersey, on April 12, 1910. Among his other published works were *A History of American Currency*, 1874; *American Finance*, 1875; biographies of Andrew Jackson, 1882, Alexander Hamilton, 1890, and Robert Morris, 1892; and posthumously edited collections of essays including *War and Other Essays*, 1911; *Earth Hunger and Other Essays*, 1913; and *The Challenge of Facts and Other Essays*, 1914. His notes and drafts for a major work on the entire range of sociology, left unfinished at his death, were edited and published in 1927–1928 as *The Science of Society*.

Sumter, Thomas (1734–1832), soldier and public official. Born in Hanover County, Virginia, near Charlottesville, on August 14, 1734, Sumter grew up on the frontier with little opportunity for schooling. During the last French and Indian War he served for a time under Gen. Edward Braddock and Gen. John Forbes. In 1765 he settled in South Carolina and opened a country store. In the early part of the Revolution he took part in a campaign against the Cherokee in Georgia and Florida, reaching the rank of colonel in the Continental army. He retired from the service in September 1778 and returned home. The British conquest of South Carolina in 1780 set off what amounted to a civil war within the region between Whigs and Tories. At that juncture, having fled to Charlotte, North Carolina, Sumter went back into military service, was commissioned a brigadier general in October 1780, and led partisan raids against the British and Tories throughout the remainder of the war, contributing materially to the eventual victory at Yorktown. After early setbacks, he defeated British forces under Col. Banastre Tarleton at Blackstock's Hill and was voted the thanks of Congress. He operated independently of the nearly nonexistent state government and, with considerable friction, of Gen. Horatio Gates, commander of the Southern theater of war. That conflict led to

Sumter's resignation early in 1782. Following the war Sumter founded the town of Stateburg, South Carolina, established his home, South Mount, nearby, engaging in tobacco raising, horse breeding, and land speculation. He served several terms in the state legislature and was an anti-Federalist at the South Carolina convention to ratify the Constitution. Under the new Federal government he served in the House of Representatives from 1789 to 1793, and again from 1797 to 1801. In 1801 he was elected to the U.S. Senate, where he remained until resigning on December 10, 1810. He then retired to his home near Stateburg, where he spent the rest of his life. Often harried by debts and creditors, he was finally relieved in 1830 when the state legislature granted him a lifetime moratorium from his debt to the state bank. He died at his plantation on June 1, 1832, in his ninety-eighth year. Fort Sumter, South Carolina, was named in his honor, as were the city and county of Sumter.

Sunday, William Ashley (1862–1935), "Billy," evangelist. Born in Ames, Iowa, on November 18 or 19, 1862, Billy Sunday grew up fatherless and in poverty. He completed high school and held a number of small jobs until he joined the Chicago White Sox baseball team in 1883. He played professional baseball in Chicago, Pittsburgh, and Philadelphia for eight years, during which time, in 1887, he underwent a religious conversion. In 1891 he began working with the Young Men's Christian Association (YMCA) in Chicago. After serving as assistant to another evangelist, he began traveling and preaching on his own as a revivalist in 1896. In 1903 he was ordained in the Presbyterian church. Sunday was a flamboyant preacher and much given to sensationalism. He preached a fundamentalist theology, denouncing among other things science and political liberalism. In tune with the prevailing mood of much of the rural United States, he quickly gained an enormous following and, from the offerings of his audiences, reputedly amassed a fortune. He is credited with having encouraged a number of local reform campaigns; his zealous advocacy of an essentially puritanic morality was of considerable effect in the popular agitation for Prohibition. He reached the peak of his career in the decade between 1910 and 1920; after that his popularity decreased, although he continued to preach until his death in Chicago on November 6, 1935.

Surratt, Mary Eugenia Jenkins (1820?–1865), alleged conspirator. Born in Waterloo, Maryland, probably in May 1820, Mary Jenkins married John H. Surratt in 1835. After her marriage she operated a tavern and post office at Surrattsville, Maryland. In 1864, by which time she was a widow, she moved to Washington, D.C., where she operated a boardinghouse. Her son John H. Surratt was co-opted by John Wilkes Booth late in 1864 in a plot to abduct President Abraham Lincoln and carry him to Richmond, Virginia, as hostage against the end of the Civil War. The failure of a trap laid by Booth, Surratt, and other conspirators on March 20, 1865, led to their temporary disbanding. Booth later changed his plan to the assassination of Lincoln. After the assassination on April 14, 1865, Booth himself was killed, but all of his accomplices were soon caught save for John Surratt, who had fled to Canada after the failed abduction. Amidst inflamed public opinion, a military trial of the conspirators was held from May 10 until June 29, 1865. As a trial it was irregular, replete with illegal procedures that included suppression of evidence by the prosecution, all designed to implicate Jefferson Davis and the Confederate government in the plot. All eight of those arrested were convicted (a foregone conclusion), and Mary Surratt, whose boardinghouse had been occasionally used as a meeting place for the conspirators, was sentenced to be hanged. The evidence against her was weak, and she may in fact have known nothing of the plot. She was nevertheless executed in Washington on July 7, 1865, along with three others whose complicity was certain. Her son John, arrested the next year and tried in 1867 by a civil court, was released in 1868 after the majority of the jury had voted for acquittal and the government had dropped further prosecution.

Sutherland, Earl Wilbur, Jr. (1915–1974), biochemist. Born in Burlingame, Kansas, on November 19, 1915, Sutherland decided to be a doctor when he read in high school about Louis Pasteur. But the Depression of the 1930s hindered his progress, and he had to work his way through Washburn College (now University) in Topeka, Kansas, and through Washington University Medical School in St. Louis, from which he received his M.D. in 1942. After service as an army doctor in World War II he returned to Washington University to work on hormones under Carl and Gerty Cori, Nobel Prize winners in 1947. He moved to Case Western Reserve University as a professor of pharmacology in the early 1950s and from there went to Vanderbilt University in 1963. All through the 1950s he worked, largely alone and without interest in his studies on the part of other researchers, on the mechanism by which hormones accomplish their task. At the time it was believed that hormones activated their target organs directly; but Sutherland was able to show that the active agent is cyclic adenosine 3', 5'–monophosphate (cyclic AMP for short); the hormones increase or decrease the organ's cellular level of cyclic AMP, and this in turn triggers or inhibits the cellular activity. The implications of the discovery were enormous, since cyclic AMP is found in every animal cell and affects "everything," as Sutherland said, "from your memory to your toes." For his work on cyclic AMP Sutherland won the 1970 Lasker Award and the 1971 Nobel Prize for Physiology and Medicine. The Nobel committee noted, in awarding him the prize, that "very seldom can a discovery be credited to a single person;" but the loneliness of Sutherland's work soon ended, for by the end of the 1960s there were thousands of scientists studying cyclic AMP. He died in Miami, Florida, on March 9, 1974.

Sutherland, George (1862–1942), justice of the Supreme Court. Born on March 25, 1862, in Buckinghamshire, England, Sutherland was brought to the United States by his family in 1864 and grew up in Springville, Utah. He attended Brigham Young University and the law school of the University of Michigan. Admitted to the bar in 1883, he opened a practice in Provo, Utah, and soon was involved in Republican party politics in the state. He ran unsuccessfully for mayor of Provo in 1890 and for the territorial legislature in 1892. Utah was admitted to the Union in 1896, and Sutherland won election to the state senate the same year. He served for four years, then was elected to the U.S. House of Representatives in 1900. He served one term, declining to run for reelection at its end, and was elected to the U.S. Senate in 1904. He served in the Senate until March 1917, being an unsuccessful candidate for reelection in 1916. He was president of the American Bar Association (ABA) in 1916–1917, and after a Republican administration took over the White House in 1921, he served as an adviser to President Warren G. Harding. In 1919 he published *Constitutional Power and World Affairs.* Sutherland had hoped to be appointed chief justice of the Supreme Court should the incumbent, Edward D. White, retire. But that position was given to William Howard Taft in 1921 when White died suddenly in May. Harding appointed Sutherland to the Court on September 5, 1922, after the resignation of John H. Clarke. As an associate justice, Sutherland was a staunch conservative and an advocate of the status quo, standing with those justices who would nullify social legislation. During the New Deal years he was vehemently opposed to most of President Franklin D. Roosevelt's program and wrote many of the opinions that hobbled it. His first important opinion was the decision in the 1923 case, *Adkins* v. *Children's Hospital,* outlawing the minimum wage. After Roosevelt's so-called court-packing scheme in 1937 had failed Sutherland decided to retire, and he left the bench early in the following year. He died in Stockbridge, Massachusetts, on July 18, 1942.

Sutro, Adolph Heinrich Joseph (1830–1898), mining engineer and public official. Born in Aachen, Germany, on April 29, 1830, Sutro emigrated to the United States with his mother, brothers, and sisters in 1850, his father having died three years earlier. Hearing of the Gold Rush to California, he headed West in 1851 and lived in San Francisco and Stockton for nine years. He went to Nevada in 1860 upon hearing of the silver strikes there and started an ore-reducing mill. Noting the slipshod and ineffective methods of mining in Nevada, Sutro devised a plan for a tunnel some three miles long to facilitate mining the Comstock Lode, with lateral branches to provide ventilation, drainage, and access. He formed a tunnel company in 1865 and received a charter for the work from the state legislature. He acquired financial backing in California for the tunnel, but the backers tried to gain control of the project; he then went to Europe for both financial aid and engineering advice. In 1868 he published *The Mineral Resources of the United States and the Importance and Necessity of Inaugurating a Rational System of Mining with Special Reference to the Comstock Lode and the Sutro Tunnel in Nevada.* Between European financiers and Nevada mine owners, he gathered enough money to begin work in 1869. The Sutro Tunnel into Mt. Davidson, near Virginia City, took nine years to complete and cost more than $6 million; its operation was both successful and rewarding to Sutro. In 1879 he sold his interest in the enterprise and moved to San Francisco, where he engaged in the real-estate business and land speculation, and in 1894 he was elected mayor of San Francisco for a two-year term. One of his avocations was the collecting of books. By the time of his death he had amassed one of the largest collections on the West Coast, more than 200,000 volumes. Nearly half of the books were destroyed in the 1906 San Francisco earthquake and fire, but the remainder became a part of the San Francisco Public Library collection. Sutro died on August 8, 1898, in San Francisco.

Sutter, John Augustus (1803–1880), California pioneer. Born on February 15, 1803, at Kandern in the Grand Duchy of Baden (now in Germany), Johann August Suter, as he was originally named, grew up there and in Basel Canton, Switzerland. Being of Swiss parentage, he was recognized as a Swiss citizen and served in the Swiss army. His childhood dream of traveling to the American West was delayed by an early marriage and a growing family. In 1834 he fled from Switzerland to avoid a bankruptcy suit, leaving his family behind, and headed for Le Havre, France. He sailed to New York and went directly to Missouri, where he engaged in the Santa Fe overland trade for two years. This venture proved financially disastrous, and again to escape creditors he went to the Rocky Mountains as an employee of the American Fur Company, then traveled on to Fort Vancouver, on the Columbia River. In 1839 he made his way to San Francisco by the roundabout means of sailing to Honolulu, from there to Sitka, Alaska, then to the Mexican province of California. He arrived on July 3, 1839, and a few days later paid a visit to the provincial governor, Juan Bautista Alvarado, at Monterey. The governor granted Sutter lands to start a settlement near the junction of the Sacramento and American rivers, where the city of Sacramento stands today. By becoming a Mexican citizen within a year of his arrival, Sutter gained title to his land grant in 1840. He took possession of a 50,000–acre tract he called New Helvetia and constructed a home and fort on the site. By the mid–1840s his ranch supported 4200 head of cattle, 2000 horses, and 2000 sheep. He also conducted a fur trade with the "mountain men" who trapped in the Rockies and the Sierra Nevada. New Helvetia, located on the main overland trail routes from the north and east, soon became a way station for U.S. settlers coming to California. When the Mexican War brought California under the sovereignty of the United States, Sutter seemed guaranteed a bright and prosperous future. His oldest son arrived to stay with him in 1844, and by 1851 the whole family had joined him. On January 24, 1848, one of Sutter's employees, James Wilson Marshall, discovered gold at a sawmill he was building for Sutter on the American River at present-day Coloma. From the time the great Gold Rush of 1849 began, Sutter's situation declined. His workmen all left to seek gold, his livestock was stolen, and prospectors overran his land looking for the precious metal; in three years he was bankrupt and, although the Supreme Court later confirmed his title to a portion of the lands he claimed, he had no way of paying for the necessary litigation to recover his property. From 1864 to 1878 he received a monthly pension from the state. In 1871 he moved to Lancaster County, Pennsylvania. After failing in several attempts to get financial relief from the federal government, Sutter died in Washington, D.C., on June 18, 1880.

Swayne, Noah Haynes (1804–1884), justice of the Supreme Court. Born in Frederick County, Virginia, on December 7, 1804, Swayne attended a Quaker academy at Waterford, Virginia, and then turned to the study of law after a brief introduction to medicine. Admitted to the bar in 1823, he moved to Ohio because of his antislavery views and settled at Coshocton. His practice was soon prosperous, and in 1826 he became county attorney. In 1829 he was elected to the state legislature for one term, and a year later President Andrew Jackson appointed him federal attorney for the Ohio district. Upon assuming this office Swayne moved to Columbus, where he lived and practiced law for the next 31 years. In January 1862 President Abraham Lincoln appointed him an associate justice of the U.S. Supreme Court to replace John McLean, who had been preparing to retire and who died suddenly late in 1861; it was probably through the influence of McLean, a fellow Ohioan, that Swayne received the appointment. As a member of the Court, he was an ardent nationalist and exponent of the growing power of the federal government. One of the notable opinions that he wrote (although the decision was later overturned) was a defense of the constitutionality of the federal income tax in *Springer* v. *United States*, in 1881. Swayne served on the court until his retirement in January 1881; a year later he moved from Washington, D.C., to New York City, where he died on June 8, 1884.

Swift, Gustavus Franklin (1839–1903), meat packer. Born on June 24, 1839, near Sandwich, Massachusetts, Swift was educated in public schools and at the age of fourteen joined his brother in the meat business. After butchering his own heifer and selling the meat door-to-door at a profit, he opened a butcher shop in 1859. First in Eastham, Massachusetts, and then in Barnstable, he established his trade by such innovations as displaying meat to the customer and packaging it in ways that made by-products like sausage look especially attractive. He opened meat markets in Freetown and Clinton and served customers in surrounding areas with meat wagons that traveled regular routes. Forming a partnership with James Hathaway in 1872, Swift moved three years later to Chicago, the new center of the cattle market. He there developed his idea of shipping dressed beef to Eastern cities in order to avoid the cost of shipping livestock. Anticipating failure, Hathaway sold his share of the business while Swift developed a refrigerator car to prevent the meat from deteriorating while in transit. Using a railroad that had not shipped livestock previously, since other lines asked exorbitant rates to compensate for the loss they would suffer owing to reduced tonnage, he sent his first meat shipment, to Boston, in 1877 and the new method of distribution was quickly accepted. He fought increasing competition from other Chicago firms that began shipping dressed meat by developing innumerable by-products such as margarine, soap, glue, fertilizer, and various pharmaceuticals. In 1885 Swift & Company was incorporated. Branch packing houses were established in other U.S. cities as well as in Great Britain and the Far East. Swift died in Chicago on March 29, 1903, and his five sons continued to manage and control the company, which by that time had increased its capital worth more than eightyfold to some $25 million.

Swope, Gerard (1872–1957), businessman. Born in St. Louis, on December 1, 1872, Swope graduated from the Massachusetts Institute of Technology (MIT) in 1895 with a degree in electrical engineering. While in school he had worked for the Western Electric Company, and after graduating he remained with the firm, working his way up to the position of vice-president and director. During World War I he served the federal government on the army's board of purchase, storage, and traffic. In 1919 he was named the first president of International General Electric (IGE), the foreign department of the U.S. parent firm. He built IGE into a large General Electric subsidiary, with worldwide offices, within three years. In 1922 he was elected president of General Electric. As president he greatly diversified the production of the company to make it a major competitor in the appliance business and kept the firm in the forefront of industrial research and technology. One of the most successful aspects of his administration was employee-company relations: he greatly enlarged employee benefits to include profit sharing and cost-of-living adjustments in wages, and made other improvements. The company's workers joined the CIO in 1936, but they received more from the company than the union contract provided: there was never a strike at GE during Swope's tenure, even during the troubled times for labor in the 1930s. On January 1, 1940, Swope retired as president of General Electric and became honorary president. A year later he became chairman of New York City's Housing Authority, and for a short time in 1942 he was also assistant to the secretary of the treasury. He left those positions in 1942 to return to the presidency of General Electric, serving until 1944. During the 1930s Swope had served the administration of President Franklin D. Roosevelt as a member of the Industrial Advisory Board for the National Recovery Administration (NRA). He wanted to arrive at national economic planning through the formation of trade associations, a scheme often called the "Swope Plan" and outlined in his *Stabilization of Industry*, 1931, and he felt that economic recovery problems should be turned over to business and taken out of the hands of the federal government. During the 1930s and early 1940s, he served on a great many governmental regulatory and advisory boards. After his second retirement from the presidency of General Electric in 1944 he again held the position of honorary president. He died in New York City on November 20, 1957.

Swope, Herbert Bayard (1882–1958), journalist. Born in St. Louis on January 5, 1882, Swope was a younger brother of Gerard Swope. After high school he found he had some writing talent and was hired as a reporter for the *St. Louis Post–Dispatch*. After a short term of employment there and on the *Chicago Tribune* he went to New York City, where he worked for the *New York Herald* and the *New York Morning Telegraph*, with occasional stints at the *New York World*; but it was with the *World* that he made a name as an enterprising crime reporter and with which he subsequently spent most of his journalistic career. He went with the *World* full-time in 1909, and through his perceptive, accurate reporting and investigations made a city-wide reputation for himself in a few years. He was a war correspondent for the *World*, reporting from Germany, in the early part of World War I and became a recognized authority on the war and on events in Germany; his articles, later collected as *Inside the German Empire*, 1917, brought him a Pulitzer Prize in 1917. Soon after U.S. entry into the war he was appointed to the War Industries Board. He covered the Versailles Peace Conference after the war and was the first reporter to publish the League of Nations covenant and the text of the reparations clauses in the treaty of Versailles. In 1920 he was made executive editor of the *World*, a post he held until he retired from newspaper work in 1929. During that decade the paper won three Pulitzer Prizes for its crusading reporting, one of them for an exposé of the Ku Klux Klan. During his newspaper career, one of Swope's leading interests and pleasures was horse racing, and with his reputation for integrity it was not unnatural that he was made chairman of the New York State Racing Commission in 1934, when betting was legalized. He stayed in this unpaid post for 11 years, until racing was shut down as a wartime measure early in 1945. Swope's familiarity with the important men and events of his time occasionally brought him into government service in an advisory capacity. During World War I he was commissioned a lieutenant commander in the navy and assigned to work as assistant to Bernard M. Baruch on the War Industries Board. In 1933 he went to the London Economic Conference with Raymond Moley, at President Franklin D. Roosevelt's behest. From 1942 to 1946 he was consultant to Secretary of War Henry L. Stimson. Following World War II he served with Baruch again on the U.S. delegation to the United Nations Atomic Energy Commission to draw up a plan for international control of nuclear power. He spent his retirement years at his home at Sands Point, Long Island, New York, where he died on June 20, 1958.

Sydenstricker, Pearl, *see* Buck, Pearl S.

Sylvis, William H. (1828–1869), labor leader and social reformer. Born in Armagh, Pennsylvania, on November 26, 1828, Sylvis learned the trade of ironfounding at an ironworks in Union County. He settled in Philadelphia in 1852 and followed his trade. In 1857 he was elected secretary of an ironworkers' moulders' union that had been organized two years previously. For the rest of his life he was heavily involved in union activities and politics, as well as in some of the reform movements of his day. He helped promote the first convention of the Iron-Moulders' International Union at Philadelphia in July 1859, and early in 1861 he called a national convention of workingmen to oppose the impending Civil War. During the war itself, he helped to reorganize the Iron-Moulders' Union, whose ranks had been severely depleted by the conflict. After the war he continued his labor-organizing activities, promoting the convening of the national Labor Congress at Baltimore in 1866 and the founding of the National Labor Union, of which he was elected president, in 1868. One of the activities of this 600,000-member union was maintaining lobbyists in Washington to work on behalf of legislation favorable to labor. Sylvis maintained contact with labor movements throughout the world, including Karl Marx's First International, and studied as well the work of cooperatives in other countries. He was one of the most articulate spokesman of the U.S. labor movement in his time, as evidenced by the large number of writings and speeches he produced on all issues touching labor and the economy. He was editor of the *Iron-Moulders' International Journal* for a time and in 1869 became part owner of the *Workingman's Advocate* at Philadelphia. He died at the age of forty on July 27, 1869.

Szell, George (1897–1970), conductor. Born in Budapest of Czech ancestry on June 7, 1897, Szell was a child prodigy in music. He began his musical education at the age of seven and graduated from the Academy of Music in Vienna. His first public appearance was at the age of ten with the Vienna Symphony as a pianist. Within a year he had also appeared in concerts in Dresden and London. His debut as a conductor was with the Berlin Philharmonic at the age of seventeen, leading the orchestra in a composition he had written when he was fourteen. He then spent two years as assistant conductor under Richard Strauss at the Royal

Opera House in Berlin. On the recommendation of Strauss, he was named first conductor of the Municipal Theater in Strasbourg in 1917. Between 1919 and 1929 he conducted at the Deutsches Landes Theater in Darmstadt, at Düsseldorf's Municipal Theater, and at the Berlin State Opera, and he also conducted the Berlin Broadcasting Symphony Orchestra and taught at the State Academy of Music in Berlin. From 1929 to 1939 he was a professor at the Academy of Music and Fine Arts in Prague. From 1930 to 1936 Szell conducted principally in Prague, but also served as guest conductor with numerous other orchestras, including the St. Louis Symphony in 1930 and 1931. From 1937 to 1939 he conducted orchestras in Scotland and in The Hague, but as war appeared to be drawing closer his musical activities in Europe diminished. In 1938 he went on a tour of Australia to conduct for the Australian Broadcasting Commission. In 1939, after the tour, he came to the United States, and for several years served as guest conductor with various symphony orchestras: the Los Angeles Philharmonic, the Detroit Symphony, the NBC (National Broadcasting Company) Symphony, the Ravinia Festival orchestra in Chicago, the Chicago Symphony, the Philadelphia Orchestra, and the Boston Symphony. He also conducted from time to time at the Metropolitan Opera between 1942 and 1946 and taught in New York City at the Mannes College of Music and the New School for Social Research. In 1946, the year he was naturalized, he became the conductor of the Cleveland Orchestra, a position he retained until his death. During his tenure the Cleveland Orchestra came to be ranked among the country's foremost symphony orchestras. During the next 20 years he also occupied the podiums of many of the world's great orchestras as guest conductor. He conducted at the Holland Festivals at Amsterdam, 1948–1966, the Salzburg Festivals, 1949–1968, and the Lucerne (Switzerland) Festivals, 1951–1967. He died in Cleveland on July 30, 1970.

Szent-Györgyi, Albert (1893–   ), biochemist. Born in Budapest on September 16, 1893, Szent-Györgyi studied medicine at the university there and received his medical degree in 1917, after service in the Austro-Hungarian army during World War I. After the war he held research posts at a large number of European universities, including Pozsony (Bratislava), Prague, Berlin, Hamburg, Leiden, and Groningen. In 1927 he moved his laboratory to Cambridge University in England, where he received his Ph.D. in the same year. Then, after a year in the United States, he returned to Hungary in 1932 to become professor of medical chemistry successively at Szeged and Budapest. During this period he concentrated his researches on hexuronic acid, a reducing agent found in the adrenal gland and also in fruit juices and, in a high concentration, in paprika. He was able to establish that hexuronic acid was the same as vitamin C, for which he proposed the name by which it is now known—ascorbic acid. He was awarded the 1937 Nobel Prize for Physiology and Medicine "for his

discoveries in connection with the biological combustion processes, with especial reference to vitamin C and the catalysis of fumaric acid." By 1939 his attention had turned to the studies of muscle tissue that were the main work of the rest of his life. In that year he established a laboratory in Budapest to study muscles but his work was interrupted by World War II, during which he was pursued by the Germans and forced to go into hiding. He came to the United States in 1947 and established the Institute for Muscle Research at the Marine Biological Laboratory at Woods Hole, Massachusetts, in that year; he became a U.S. citizen in 1955. His work on muscles led to his discovery of the effects of adenosine triphosphate (ATP) on muscular activity and, in turn, to important discoveries about the action of various muscles, notably the heart, under stress. For this work he received the Lasker Award in 1954. Working with other investigators, he also was the discoverer of a substance that he called vitamin P (no longer considered a vitamin), which prevents abnormal capillary breakdown in sufferers from scurvy and in persons who have been subjected to high levels of radiation, either in warfare or in the course of cancer therapy. Aside from his post as director of the Institute for Muscle Research he served as professor of biophysics at the Dartmouth Medical School from 1962 to 1966, and in the latter year he was named professor of biology at Brandeis University. The author of many technical research papers, he also wrote a number of books, including *On Oxidation, Fermentation, Vitamins, Health and Disease*, 1939; *Chemistry of Muscular Contraction*, 1947 and 1951; *Nature of Life*, 1948; *Chemical Physiology of Contraction in Body and Heart Muscle*, 1953; *Bioenergetics*, 1957; *Submolecular Biology*, 1960; *Science, Ethics, and Politics*, 1963; *Bioelectronics*, 1968; *The Crazy Ape*, 1970; and *What Next?*, 1971.

Szilard, Leo (1898–1964), physicist and biologist. Born in Budapest on February 11, 1898, Szilard studied at the Budapest Institute of Technology from 1916 to 1919 with the intention of becoming an engineer. But early in 1920 he transferred to the Technische Hochschule at Berlin-Charlottenburg. There, influenced by the work being done by Albert Einstein, Max Planck, and Max von Laue, he took up physics. He received his Ph.D. in 1922 from the University of Berlin and took a position at the university's Institute of Theoretical Physics, remaining at the university for 11 years. Early in 1933, when he was sure the Nazis would come to power in Germany, he literally kept his bags packed for an immediate flight from the country. Late in March 1933 he went to Vienna, and after six weeks there he went to London. In England he contemplated changing his field of study and beginning work in biology. But some of the work being pursued by other physicists brought to his attention the possibility that a nuclear chain reaction could be achieved, so he remained in physics. He conducted experiments in the physics laboratory at St. Bartholemew's Hospital in London, and his work brought him the offer of a fellowship at Oxford, which he accepted. He arranged to spend six months out of every year in the United States with the intention of living there if war came. He arrived in New York City in January 1938 and soon decided to remain. Hearing of Otto Hahn's demonstration of uranium fission, Szilard was certain it would be possible to sustain a chain reaction. He worked at Columbia University with Enrico Fermi, Walter Zinn, and other physicists. On March 3, 1939, they did experiments that led them to conclude they were on the right track. They realized the military significance of their work, and after failing to interest the Navy Department decided on a direct approach to President Franklin D. Roosevelt. Szilard and others drafted a letter, dated August 2, 1939, and signed by Albert Einstein, that was given to Roosevelt. By mid–1940 the physicists' work in nuclear fission was organized under the National Defense Research Committee. In 1942 the team of scientists moved their project from Columbia to the Metallurgical Laboratory under the stands of Stagg Field, the football stadium at the University of Chicago. Under the aegis of the Manhattan Engineering District project the first atomic pile was constructed there by Fermi, Szilard, and others, and it was there, on December 2, 1942, that the first sustained chain reaction was obtained. Then, once the atomic-bomb project was a success, Szilard and many of his fellow scientists turned their attention toward the problems it posed. In the postwar era they sought (vainly, it turned out) for international control of atomic weapons, the sharing of atomic secrets, and civilian control of nuclear energy. He remained with the atomic laboratory until 1946, then turned his attention to biology, while taking a position on the faculty of the University of Chicago. He did experimental work in molecular biology, out of which came theories of mutations and the aging process. In 1960 he received the Atoms for Peace award. He died on May 30, 1964, at La Jolla, California, where he had been for a short time a resident fellow at the Salk Institute for Biological Studies. Besides a number of technical papers, he published several science-fiction stories, notably the memorable *The Voice of the Dolphins*, 1961.

T

Taft, Lorado Zadoc (1860–1936), sculptor. Born in Elmwood, Illinois, on April 29, 1860, Taft graduated from the University of Illinois in 1879. Having taken an early interest in art, he went to Paris for three years to study sculpture at the École des Beaux-Arts. In 1886 he settled in Chicago and took a position as instructor and lecturer at the Art Institute of Chicago. He remained with the Institute until 1929, also lecturing at other schools from time to time. Basically a naturalist, Taft was one of the first American sculptors to work on large designs—group compositions or tableaux and fountains. He first came to prominence with his statuary groups for the Horticulture Building at the World's Columbian Exposition in Chicago in 1893. Some of his noteworthy works are the Fountain of Time in Chicago; the statue of Blackhawk, the Indian leader, at Oregon, Illinois; "Alma Mater" at the University of Illinois; the Columbus Memorial Fountain in Washington, D.C.; the Thatcher Memorial Fountain in Denver; and the two pylon groups of the state capitol at Baton Rouge, Louisiana, entitled "The Pioneers" and "The Patriots." In addition to executing his own sculptures and teaching, Taft promoted education in the arts by giving lectures (frequently in public schools), writing articles, serving on government fine arts commissions, and writing books, notably *History of American Sculpture*, 1903, and *Modern Tendencies in Sculpture*, 1921. He died in Chicago on October 30, 1936.

Taft, Robert Alphonso (1889–1953), public official. Born on September 8, 1889, in Cincinnati, a son of William Howard Taft, Robert Taft graduated from Yale in 1910 and from Harvard Law School in 1913. Admitted to the Ohio bar in the same year, he began practice in Cincinnati and, with several successful business investments and an inheritance, soon became a man of some wealth. In 1920 he was elected as a Republican to the Ohio legislature, where he served for six years, the last year as speaker of the house. From 1930 to 1932 he was in the state senate. In 1938 he entered the U.S. Senate and immediately became an outspoken critic of President Franklin D. Roosevelt's policies, both domestic and foreign. He labeled the New Deal "socialistic" and called for reduced and balanced government expenditures and an end to the concentration of power in Washington. In foreign affairs he was a firm isolationist until the Japanese attack on Pearl Harbor in December 1941, and he stoutly opposed Roosevelt's internationalist tendencies. In the period of Republican resurgence in the later 1930s that followed the party's defeats early in the Depression, Taft came

quickly to a position of power and leadership within the party; as his preeminence grew he eventually came to be known as "Mr. Republican." Reelected to his Senate seat in 1944 and 1950, he served until his death; in that body he held such influence over legislation that he incurred the special wrath of President Harry S. Truman for blocking measures that were part of Truman's Fair Deal. From 1946 Taft chaired the powerful Republican Policy Committee and served as the party's floor leader in the Senate. His principal legislative achievement was the 1947 Taft-Hartley Act, which restricted the activities of organized labor and nullified many of the concessions to labor embodied in the earlier Wagner (National Labor Relations) Act of the New Deal. He opposed U.S. membership in the North Atlantic Treaty Organization (NATO) alliance, attacked the administration for its "soft" response to Communist challenges, and lent support to Senator Joseph R. McCarthy's investigations of Communist infiltration and subversion in government and the military. Mentioned as a possible presidential candidate as early as 1940, Taft actively sought the nomination in that year and again in 1948 and 1952; in the latter year he was thought to be the strongest candidate, and he lost to Gen. Dwight D. Eisenhower only after a long and bitter struggle that threatened for a time to split the party. He remained a faithful Republican, however, supporting the Eisenhower ticket fully and becoming Senate majority leader in the new Congress. He died a few months later, on July 31, 1953, in New York City.

Taft, William Howard (1857–1930), twenty-seventh president of the United States and chief justice of the Supreme Court. Born in Cincinnati, Ohio, on September 15, 1857, Taft graduated from Yale in 1878 and two years later took a law degree at the Cincinnati Law School. Almost from the first he supplemented his law practice with involvement in local Republican politics, and in 1887, after holding a number of minor public offices, was appointed to fill an unexpired term on the superior court of Ohio. Elected to a full term in 1888, he served only until 1890, when he became U.S. solicitor general under President Benjamin Harrison. In 1892 he became presiding judge of the sixth federal circuit court of appeals (Tennessee, Kentucky, Ohio, and Michigan). During eight years on this bench Taft was a thorough and effective legal arbiter, but he acquired a reputation for conservatism that was not wholly deserved. His judgments against union activities were based not on antipathy to labor, whose right to organize and strike he never questioned, but on his view of the proper limits of such activities; in the major cases for which he was criticized for antiunion bias, his opinions were rendered against the use of secondary boycotts and the violence accompanying strikes. His use of the injunction power applied as well to businesses under the antitrust laws. In 1900 President William McKinley appointed Taft president of the Philippine Commission; arriving in the islands, he immediately set about organizing a civil government to replace military rule and he became civil governor in 1901. He effectively brought peace to the islands, negotiated a settlement with the Roman Catholic church for its property that had been confiscated, and began a program of economic development and internal improvements. While in the Philippines he twice declined offers from President Theodore Roosevelt of a seat on the Supreme Court because he felt his work as governor was incomplete, but in 1904 he accepted an offer to become secretary of war, a post that would allow him to remain in touch with the new Philippine government. In Washington he became Roosevelt's most trusted adviser and assistant, acting as troubleshooter to quell a potential rebellion in Cuba and to organize the construction of the Panama Canal, and he was chosen by Roosevelt to be nominated to succeed to the presidency in 1908. Taft was nominated and elected easily over William Jennings Bryan that year, but found the office trying and disappointing. Despite the influence of Roosevelt he allied himself more and more with the conservative wing of the party; pledged to tariff reduction, he nevertheless approved the Payne-Aldrich Tariff Act of 1909, with its negligible concessions to reduction, on the grounds that it was the best bill obtainable, and thus further alienated progressives. His administration was effective and efficient at the departmental level, but it functioned in a quiet way not calculated to win popular support. His major achievements, arbitration treaties with Britain and France and a trade agreement with Canada, failed of ratification, the first two through Senate recalcitrance. Although lack of publicity obscured the fact, the antitrust activities of the federal government under Taft were actually more extensive than had been the case under Roosevelt. After former President Roosevelt returned to the United States in 1910, the conservative-progressive split in the Republican party widened as Roosevelt articulated his "New Nationalism." Thus, in the 1910 congressional elections, the Democrats were able to win control of Congress. Taft, at the head of his party machinery, was the inevitable if reluctant nominee of the 1912 Republican national convention, but Roosevelt's challenge for the nomination led to charges that Taft had "stolen" it. Roosevelt's creation of the schismatic Bull Moose Progressive party made a Democratic victory certain; Taft ran a poor third behind candidates Woodrow Wilson and Theodore Roosevelt, finally amassing only eight electoral votes. He became Kent Professor of Constitutional Law at Yale on leaving the White House in 1913. During World War I he served as joint chairman of the National War Labor Board and afterward was a strong advocate of U.S. entry into the League of Nations. In 1921 President Warren G. Harding appointed him to succeed Edward D. White as chief justice of the Supreme Court, a position he found completely suited to his wishes, his temperament, and his abilities. Again, his most effective work for the Court was as an administrator; he successfully eliminated a large backlog of cases on the docket and in 1925 secured passage of the Judges' Act, providing for greater discretion by the Court in accepting cases and in considering them in order of national priority. His most important opinions included the majority opinion in *Bailey* v. *Drexel Furniture Co.*—the Child Labor Case—in 1922, holding that Congress had exceeded its authority in using the tax power for social reform to the destruction of state sovereignty; a dissent in *Adkins* v. *Children's Hospital*, 1923, in which he revealed his liberal side by arguing that a 1918 women's minimum wage law in the District of Columbia was in the public interest; and the majority opinion in *Myers* v. *United States*, 1926, extending and clarifying the president's power to remove executive officeholders. Poor health forced him to resign early in 1930; a month later, on March 8, he died in Washington, D.C.

Tah-gah-jute, *see* Logan, James (1725?–1780)

Tallchief, Maria (1925–   ), dancer. Born in Fairfax, Oklahoma, on January 24, 1925, Miss Tallchief was the daughter of an Osage Indian. She grew up on a reservation at Fairfax and later in Los Angeles. As a child she had decided upon a career as a concert pianist, but during her high-school years she determined instead to study ballet. She made her debut in 1942 with the Ballet Russe de Monte Carlo and remained with the company until 1947. In 1946 she married choreographer George Balanchine, and the following year both of them joined the newly organized New York City Ballet company. She danced to unanimous critical acclaim in the United States and Europe in a wide range of ballets including *Scheherazade, Danses Concertantes, Four Temperaments, Apollo, Black Swan, Orpheus, Serenade,* and especially the Stravinsky-Diaghilev-Balanchine *Firebird*. In 1965 she won the Capezio Award for distinguished service to the dance. Her marriage to Balanchine was dissolved in 1951 and she remarried in 1957. In 1967 she left the New York City Ballet and went into partial retirement, continuing, however, to teach dancing.

Tammen, Harry Heye, *see under* Bonfils, Frederick Gilmer

Taney, Roger Brooke (1777–1864), chief justice of the Supreme Court. Born in Calvert County, Maryland, on March 17, 1777, to a family of the region's landed aristocracy, Taney graduated from Dickinson College in 1795, was admitted to the bar in 1799, and two years later settled in Frederick, Maryland, to established a law practice.

While there, in 1806, he married Anne Key, the sister of Francis Scott Key. He became prominent in the Federalist party in his state, serving on occasion in the legislature, and in 1812 was the leader of the pro-war Federalists, called the "Coodies." As the division among the Federalists failed to heal, the party slowly disintegrated, and soon after moving to Baltimore in 1823 Taney switched his allegiance to the faction of the old Republican (later Democratic) party led by Andrew Jackson. A recognized leader of the Maryland bar, he was appointed state attorney general in 1827 and in 1831, by President Jackson's appointment, became U.S. attorney general. By this time he had come to view the Bank of the United States as a dangerous institution; although in many ways a useful instrument, it had abused its powers and was seeking an early renewal of its charter. Taney persuaded Jackson to veto the new charter passed by Congress and drafted much of the veto message; in the midst of the ensuing controversy he further pressed for a withdrawal of federal deposits from the Bank. Jackson agreed and when Secretary of the Treasury William J. Duane refused to withdraw the deposits Taney was appointed in September 1833 to replace him. The appointment came during a congressional recess, and nine months later the Senate, led by Whigs, refused to confirm him although the redistribution of federal money among selected state banks had already been effected. Taney returned to his law practice. In 1835 his nomination as an associate justice of the Supreme Court was also rejected by the Senate, but changes in that body enabled his appointment as chief justice to stand in March of the following year. Succeeding John Marshall, he immediately began to change the tenor of the Court by reversing the earlier trend toward strong centralization of government powers. In his first major opinion, *Charles River Bridge* v. *Warren Bridge*, 1837, he established a narrow construction of corporate charters granted by states, balancing charter powers and privileges against the public good. The reversal of Federalist tendencies by the Court under Taney was not so extreme as many had feared it might be; rather than being a spokesman for the radical states'-rights position, Taney held consistently—in *Bank of Augusta* v. *Earle*, 1839, the 1847 License Cases, and the 1849 Passenger Cases—that in the absence of federal legislation, states were competent to regulate commerce in any way that was not an invasion or violation of federal jurisdiction or law, a much more moderate view. On the other hand, he maintained the supremacy of federal over state courts and produced a masterly analysis of the power relations of federalism in *Ableman* v. *Booth*, 1859. In March 1857 he succumbed to the temptation to settle judicially the question of congressional authority over slavery. In his opinion for the Court in the case of *Dred Scott* v. *Sandford* he dismissed Scott's claim that he had been freed from slavery by residing in free territory by holding that a Negro could not be a citizen and therefore could not sue in federal court; he then went on, in what many

thought to be an ill-considered obiter dictum, to declare that Congress had never had the authority to ban slavery from the territories, thus in effect branding the 1820 Missouri Compromise unconstitutional. The decision roused a bitter controversy, and Republicans and abolitionists made it a major issue in the 1860 elections. The prestige of the Court dropped sharply, and during the Civil War the Court in general and Taney in particular were viewed with suspicion. He exacerbated such feelings by finding several governmental war measures unconstitutional, notably in *Ex Parte Merryman*, 1861, when, sitting as circuit judge, he overruled a military suspension of habeas corpus in Baltimore. He died, publicly unlamented, on October 12, 1864, in Washington, D.C.

Tanner, Henry Ossawa (1859–1937), painter. Born in Pittsburgh on June 21, 1859, Tanner was the son of Bishop Benjamin Tucker Tanner of the African Methodist Episcopal church. He showed an early inclination toward an artistic career, and when he was twenty-one began several years of study under Thomas Eakins at the Philadelphia Academy of the Fine Arts. He lived for a time in Atlanta, Georgia, where he continued his painting while trying to make a living from photography. In 1890 a showing of his works was arranged in Cincinnati in order to raise money for him to study in Europe. Early in 1891 Tanner arrived in Paris, the city where he would live the rest of his life. He studied at the Académie Julien under Benjamin Constant and Jean-Paul Laurens. In 1895 the Paris Salon recognized him by accepting one of his paintings. The success of his "Daniel in the Lions' Den" in 1896 inspired him to try his hand at other biblical themes. Through the generosity of Louis R. Wanamaker of Philadelphia, Tanner was able to tour the Holy Land and paint. By the turn of the century he had an international reputation, particularly for his paintings of biblical subjects and landscapes. From 1896 to 1915 he won numerous prizes and medals for his paintings, including several in the United States. His first one-man show in the United States took place in December 1908 at the American Art Galleries in New York City. His paintings were also shown in Buffalo, St. Louis, Washington, D.C., Chicago, and San Francisco, among other cities. Notable among his paintings were "Destruction of Sodom and Gomorrah" (now in the Metropolitan Museum of Art in New York City), "Disciples at the Tomb" (Art Institute, Chicago), and "Christ and Nicodemus" (Pennsylvania Academy of Fine Arts). During the 1920s Tanner's success as a painter gave strong inspiration to other black artists, particularly those in the movement known as the Harlem Renaissance. He died in Paris on May 25, 1937.

Tappan, Arthur (1786–1865), merchant, philanthropist, and social reformer. Born in Northampton, Massachusetts, on May 22, 1786, Arthur and his brother Lewis, born in Northampton on May 23, 1788, moved to Boston after finishing school and entered the dry-goods business. In about 1807 Arthur established his own silk-importing firm in Portland, Maine, moving it later to Montreal. In 1826 he founded a new company in New York City and was joined two years later by Lewis. The firm lasted until 1837; four years later Lewis opened the Mercantile Agency, the nation's first rating agency for commercial credit, and Arthur became a partner in 1849. Between the two, in various ventures, a considerable fortune was amassed, and they soon began to devote a major portion of their time to distributing it among worthy institutions and causes. Arthur founded the *New York Journal of Commerce* in 1827 to serve as a model of moral and reformist journalism; Lewis took over the paper after a year and continued it until 1831, when it was sold. They supported the revivalist Charles Grandison Finney and were primarily responsible for the construction of the Broadway Tabernacle for him. Money was contributed toward the establishment of Kenyon College, Auburn Theological and Lane Theological seminaries, and especially Oberlin College. They helped organize the American Anti-Slavery Society in 1833 with Arthur as its first president; the next year Lewis's house was sacked by a mob because of his abolitionist activities. Both men worked closely with William Lloyd Garrison until insistence on linking other reforms with abolitionism caused them to break with him and form the American and Foreign Anti-Slavery Society in 1840, again with Arthur as president. Arthur was deeply involved in the founding of several abolitionist journals, including the *Emancipator* in New York City and the *National Era* in Washington, D.C. In 1843 Lewis went to England to attend an international conference on the abolition of slavery and made valuable contacts for the U.S. group. In 1846 they helped found the American Missionary Association, in which both held high offices. Both Tappans were originally moderate abolitionists, hoping to achieve their goal by legal action and reform under the Constitution and within the Union, but after passage of the Fugitive Slave Law of 1850 their position became more radical as they openly defied the law and supported the Underground Railroad. By the late 1850s both found their activities were limited by the restraints of age. Arthur retired to New Haven, Connecticut, where he died on July 23, 1865; Lewis published a biography of his brother in 1870 and continued to work with the American Missionary Association until his death in Brooklyn, New York, on June 21, 1873.

Tappan, Lewis, see under Tappan, Arthur

Tarbell, Ida Minerva (1857–1944), author. Born on November 5, 1857, in Erie County, Pennsylvania, Miss Tarbell graduated from Allegheny College in Meadville, Pennsylvania. Intent on a career in journalism, she became an associate editor of the *Chautauquan* in 1883. She resumed her studies in Paris at the Sorbonne and the College de France, 1891–1894. From 1894 to 1906 she was an editor of the leading muckraking journal of the day,

McClure's Magazine, which in articles and editorials exposed political and industrial corruption and emphasized the need for reforms, thus giving impetus to the Populist and Progressive movements. Her own exhaustively researched articles for *McClure's* on the Rockefeller oil interests were collected in *The History of the Standard Oil Company,* two volumes, 1904. The articles and the book aroused public opinion and led to federal investigations into the activities of the Standard Oil Company of New Jersey, which was ultimately dissolved in 1911 under the Sherman Anti-Trust Act. In 1906 she left *McClure's* and with Lincoln Steffens, Ray Stannard Baker, and others, purchased the *American Magazine,* of which she was associate editor until 1915. She wrote biographies of business leaders and politicians, including Elbert H. Gary and Owen D. Young, and in all produced eight books on Abraham Lincoln. Other writings included *The Business of Being a Woman,* 1912; *The Ways of Women,* 1915; *The Nationalizing of Business, 1878–1898,* 1936; and an autobiography, *All in a Day's Work,* 1939. She died at her home in Bethel, Connecticut, on January 6, 1944.

Tarkington, Booth (1869–1946), author. Born in Indianapolis on July 29, 1869, Newton Booth Tarkington was educated at Phillips Exeter Academy, Purdue University, and Princeton. He lived in Maine and abroad at various times, but considered himself a Hoosier writer. His first book, *The Gentleman from Indiana,* 1899, was an immediate success, and was followed by *Monsieur Beaucaire,* 1900, which later in its stage adaptation provided Rudolph Valentino with one of his most memorable roles. Immensely versatile and prolific, producing some 40 popular novels in all, he was famous for stories of boyhood life, notably *Penrod,* 1914, its sequels, and *Seventeen,* 1916. His three portrayals of Midwestern life and character—*The Turmoil,* 1915; *The Magnificent Ambersons,* 1918, which won a Pulitzer Prize; and *The Midlander,* 1923—were published together as *Growth* in 1927; *The Plutocrat,* also about Midwesten life, was published the same year. His portrayals of female personalities—*Alice Adams,* 1921, which won him a second Pulitzer Prize; *Claire Ambler,* 1928; *Mirthful Haven,* 1930; and *Presenting Lily Mars,* 1933—added to his popularity as did numerous plays, many of which he adapted from his novels. He died in Indianapolis on May 19, 1946.

Tashunca-Uitco, see Crazy Horse

Tatanka Iyotake, see Sitting Bull

Tate, Allen (1899–1979), poet and critic. Born in Winchester, Kentucky, on November 19, 1899, John Orley Allen Tate graduated from Vanderbilt University in 1922. While in college he became associated with the group of poets, under the leadership of John Crowe Ransom, that came to be called the "Fugitives," the name derived from the literary journal, *Fugitive,* that they published from

1922 to 1925. Besides Tate, the group included such writers as Ransom, Robert Penn Warren, Cleanth Brooks, and others. In 1930 the members of the group made individual contributions to the book *I'll Take My Stand*, a plea for a regional return to agrarianism. Tate was awarded a Guggenheim fellowship in 1928 which enabled him to spend the following two years in Europe. While there he published a volume of poetry, *Mr. Pope and Other Poems*, 1928, and two biographies on which he had been working: *Stonewall Jackson—The Good Soldier*, 1928, and *Jefferson Davis—His Rise and Fall*, 1929. In 1930 he returned to the United States and settled in Tennessee to write. He taught at Southwestern University in Memphis from 1934 to 1936 and at North Carolina Woman's College from 1938 to 1939. He was a resident fellow at Princeton University in 1939–1942 and in 1943–1944 he held the chair of poetry at the Library of Congress. He edited the *Sewanee Review* from 1944 to 1946, worked as an editor for Henry Holt and Company from 1946 to 1948, and then, after four years as a lecturer at New York University, joined the English department of the University of Minnesota, where he remained until his retirement in 1968. Although probably best known as a poet—his "Ode to the Confederate Dead" was frequently anthologized—he had a much broader literary career, particularly as biographer and critic. His *Reactionary Essays on Poetry and Ideas* was published in 1936, and other critical works included *Reason in Madness*, 1941; *On the Limits of Poetry*, 1948; *The Hovering Fly*, 1949; *The Forlorn Demon*, 1953; and *Essays of Four Decades*, 1969. Volumes of verse included *Three Poems*, 1930; *The Mediterranean and Other Poems*, 1936; *Selected Poems*, 1937; *Winter Sea*, 1944; *Poems, 1922–1947*, 1948; and *Poems*, 1960. He wrote one novel, *The Fathers*, 1938. He died on February 9, 1979, in Nashville, Tennessee.

Tatum, Art (1910–1956), musician. Born in Toledo, Ohio, on October 13, 1910, Tatum was blind in one eye from birth and had very poor vision in the other. He nevertheless studied music as a child, taking up the violin at thirteen and switching to piano three years later. He played the piano in home town nightclubs and on the radio for a few years, then in 1932 he went to New York City as accompanist to singer Adelaide Hall. By the mid-1930s he had his own band in Chicago and was an internationally known jazz stylist. His fame was based on his solo playing, which was marked by originality of technique and by improvisation. Some of his most popular renditions were "Tea for Two," "Sweet Lorraine," and "Humoresque." After 1943 he played on radio and in nightclubs as part of a trio. He died in Los Angeles on November 5, 1956.

Tatum, Edward Lawrie (1909–1975), geneticist and biochemist. Born in Boulder, Colorado, on December 14, 1909, Tatum studied at the University of Chicago and completed his undergraduate work at the University of Wisconsin in 1931. He received a Ph.D. in biochemistry at Wisconsin in 1934.

After a year as a research assistant at the university, he studied bacteriological chemistry at the University of Utrecht in the Netherlands during 1936–1937. He then joined the faculty of Stanford University, where he taught and did research in biology from 1937 to 1945. From 1945 until 1948 Tatum was at Yale, where he taught botany and microbiology. He then returned to Stanford as professor of biochemistry, and was head of the department from 1956 to 1957. He subsequently became a professor at Rockefeller University (formerly Rockefeller Institute) in New York City. Much of Tatum's research in the 1930s and 1940s was done in association with Dr. George W. Beadle. Their experiments dealt with the metabolic activity of insects, particularly the *Drosophila melanogaster* fruit fly, and of a red bread mold, *Neurospora crassa*, and later with the chemical processes in genes. Their studies of nutritional requirements and genetic changes led them to conclude that genes act by regulating specific chemical processes in the organism, and further, that genes that are altered or impaired bring about hereditary changes in metabolic activity. Later research with Dr. Joshua Lederberg demonstrated that in *Escherichia coli* bacteria, exchanges of genetic material, amounting to a form of sexual reproduction, is a common occurrence. In 1958 Tatum was a corecipient of the Nobel Prize for Physiology or Medicine, along with Beadle and Lederberg. Tatum's early experiments led him into genetics, which remained his primary area of research. He died in New York City on November 5, 1975.

Taylor, Bayard (1825–1878), author. Born in Kennett Square, Pennsylvania, on January 11, 1825, James Bayard Taylor attended Bolnar's and Unionville academies before becoming an apprentice printer at seventeen. He had dabbled at writing poetry from his earliest years, and in 1844 he published a collection entitled *Ximena*. Having obtained advances for articles to be sent back to the *Saturday Evening Post*, the *United States Gazette*, and the *New York Tribune*, he quit his apprenticeship and set sail for Europe for two years of traveling, 1844–1846. This was the first of a series of journeys that would make Taylor perhaps the most widely known American traveler of his day and one of the most prolific travel-book writers. His first book, *Views Afoot*, 1846, was a great success. After his return he published his own newspaper for a while, worked for the *New York Literary World*, then took over the literary department of Horace Greeley's *New York Tribune* in 1848. When the California Gold Rush began, Taylor went West to observe, and returned to New York City in 1850 to publish *Eldorado*. From 1851 to 1853 he toured Asia Minor, the Middle East, India, and China, and also traveled to Japan. On his return he published more travel books and lectured throughout the country. He toured Europe again from 1856 to 1858, and after a few years of semiretirement in Pennsylvania returned to the *Tribune*, this time as Washington correspondent during the Civil War. In 1862 he was sent to St.

Petersburg as secretary of legation under Simon Cameron, the U.S. minister to Russia. Back in the United States in 1863, he spent the following seven years working on a verse translation of Goethe's *Faust*, published in two volumes in 1870–1871, the most lasting of his literary endeavors. From 1870 to 1877 he held a post as lecturer in German literature at Cornell. By this time, he was recognized as one of the country's outstanding writers. In 1876 he was commissioned to write the "Centennial Hymn" commemorating the 100th anniversary of the Declaration of Independence. Unfortunately, the work for which he wanted to be known—his poems and novels—were undistinguished efforts; it was his travel books that won him most of his fame. In 1878 he was named U.S. minister to Germany, and he died in Berlin on December 19, 1878.

Taylor, Bert Leston (1866–1921), "B.L.T.," journalist. Born in Goshen, Massachusetts, on November 13, 1866, Taylor grew up in New York City and attended City College of New York (CCNY) for a while. He worked on newspapers in Plainfield, New Hampshire, Montpelier, Vermont, and Duluth, Minnesota, before going to Chicago in 1899. After two years with the *Chicago Journal*, he went to work for the *Chicago Tribune*, where he published his column "A Line o' Type or Two." In 1903 he wrote for the *New York Morning Telegraph*, and from 1904 to 1909 he was assistant editor of *Puck*. The *Chicago Tribune* hired him back in 1909, and he remained with the paper for the rest of his journalistic career. He reestablished his column, a composite of contributions, excerpts from other papers, and his own remarks and satirical verse. It was to become one of the most noteworthy and widely read columns in the nation and was carried on by the *Tribune* for several decades after Taylor died. In addition to his columns, Taylor wrote short stories, two novels, *The Well in the Wood*, 1904, and *The Charlatans*, 1906, and published a series of collections of his journalism, including *Line-o'-Type Lyrics*, 1902; *A Line-o'-Verse or Two*, 1911; *Motley Measures*, 1913; *The So-Called Human Race*, 1922; and *The East Window, and the Car Window*, 1924. He died in Chicago on March 19, 1921.

Taylor, David Watson (1864–1940), naval officer and marine architect. Born in Louisa County, Virginia, on March 4, 1864, Taylor graduated from Randolph-Macon College in 1881. He then entered the U.S. Naval Academy and graduated in 1885 with the highest academic record ever achieved up to that time, a feat he repeated at the Royal Naval College in England, from which he graduated in 1888. Appointed an assistant naval constructor, he began work on designing new ships and quickly perceived the lack of scientific guidance that hindered the progress of the art. He became concerned in particular with the rule-of-thumb—even haphazard—approach to estimating the power requirements of ships, and from the publication of his first book, *Resistance of Ships and Screw Propulsion*, 1893, devoted himself to developing an experimental program to provide solid data. His campaign for a testing basin for ship models finally bore fruit in 1899, and from that year until 1914 he remained in charge of the testing facility. His systematic experiments with various hull configurations resulted in the publication of *The Speed and Power of Ships*, 1910, in which he outlined what became known internationally as the Taylor Standard Series, the first practical method of matching engine power to a given hull design. Named chief naval constructor and head of the navy's Bureau of Construction and Repair in 1914, Taylor, promoted to rear admiral two years later, oversaw the feverish and markedly successful shipbuilding program of World War I. At the same time he was concerned with the design of the navy's early aircraft, including the famed NC-4 seaplane built by Glenn H. Curtiss which became in 1919 the first aircraft to fly the Atlantic. From 1917 until his retirement from active naval service in 1923 he served on the National Advisory Committee for Aeronautics, and he was reappointed to that body as a civilian member in 1927, serving for three more years. During 1925–1932 he was also a member of a commercial shipbuilding firm. Widely honored both at home and abroad for his contributions to marine architecture, Taylor was a virtual invalid for several years before his death in Washington, D.C., on July 28, 1940.

Taylor, Deems (1885–1966), music critic and composer. Born in New York City on December 22, 1885, Joseph Deems Taylor graduated from New York University in 1906. His first intention was to be a newspaperman, but he was encouraged by Victor Herbert to try his hand at music. He studied composition and orchestration and first won recognition with *Siren Song*, a symphonic poem, 1913, and two cantatas, *The Chambered Nautilus* and *The Highwayman*, 1914. From 1912 to 1916 he worked at Western Electric Company in New York as assistant editor of their *Western Electric News*, and during World War I he became a foreign correspondent for the *New York Tribune*. From 1917 to 1919 he served as associate editor of *Collier's Magazine*, and from 1921 to 1925 he was music critic for the *New York World*. His 1918 orchestral suite *Through the Looking Glass* was well received and led to his being commissioned by Walter Damrosch to compose the symphonic poem *Jurgen*, 1925. Taylor resigned from the *World* in 1926 to compose the opera *The King's Henchman*, a romance with a libretto by Edna St. Vincent Millay that was performed for three seasons by the Metropolitan Opera, beginning in 1927. His second opera, *Peter Ibbetson*, 1931, was based on the 1899 novel by George du Maurier. From 1927 to 1929 Taylor served as editor of the magazine *Musical America*, and in 1931–1932 was music critic for the *New York American*. From 1936 to 1943 he was nationally known as the intermission commentator on the radio broadcasts of the New York Philharmonic and he remained a music consultant to the Columbia Broadcasting System (CBS) until his death. His later compositions included *Christmas Overture*, 1943, and *Restoration*, 1950, a suite for orchestra. His popular book, *The Well-Tempered Listener*, appeared in 1940; he also published *Music to My Ears*, 1949, *Some Enchanted Evenings*, 1953, and *The One Track Mind*, 1953. He died in New York City on July 3, 1966.

Taylor, Edward (1645?–1729), poet. Born about 1645 in England, in or near Coventry, Taylor is thought to have come from a family of religious dissenters. Unwilling to subscribe to the oath of conformity required of schoolteachers, he gave up his profession and emigrated to New England, where he arrived in 1668. Already twenty-three and a man of some education, he was immediately admitted by president Charles Chauncy as a sophomore at Harvard, and he graduated from the college in 1671. He then went to Westfield, Massachusetts, as physician and minister, and remained there until his death in 1729. He married twice and became the father of 13 children, most of whom he outlived. His grandson, Ezra Stiles, was president of Yale during the Revolution and was, in addition, the inheritor of his manuscripts and the greater part of his library, some 200 volumes. The manuscripts included a 400-page "Poetical Works" that, by its author's express desire, was not published by his heirs. But it came into the possession of Yale in 1883 by the gift of a descendant, and Taylor's poems first began to be published in the late 1930s. The occasion was a momentous one, for he was immediately recognized as the best American poet of the seventeenth century. The important poems fall into two main divisions. "God's Determinations Touching His Elect" is an extended verse sequence setting forth the drama of sin and redemption. "Sacramental Meditations," some 200 shorter poems on various subjects, were written over a period of 44 years, from 1682 to 1725; the author described them as "Preparatory Meditations Before My Approach to the Lord's Supper." The poems are interesting not only in themselves but also for the light they throw on the English poetic tradition; for Taylor was still writing in the fashion of the metaphysical poets he had read in his youth—John Donne, George Herbert, and Richard Crashaw, for example—long after the extravagant tropes that marked their work were completely passé, and sharply disapproved of, in England itself. *The Poetical Works of Edward Taylor*, edited by T. H. Johnson, a selection together with a biographical sketch, a critical introduction, and notes, appeared in 1939. *The Poems of Edward Taylor*, edited by Donald E. Stanford, 1960, is a comprehensive edition including the complete text of the "Meditations." *Christographia*, a collection of sermons delivered in 1701–1703, was published in 1962.

Taylor, Edward Thompson (1793–1871), "Father Taylor," religious leader. Born in Richmond, Virginia, on December 25, 1793, Taylor, left an orphan at an early age, spent much of his childhood and youth aboard ship as a cabin boy. In his late teens, while in Boston, he underwent a religious conversion. A few years later, in spite of his lack of education, he was licensed to preach by the Methodist church. His lack of formal training did not hinder his efforts as a preacher; he became known among those who heard him as an articulate, colorful, and honest speaker. In 1819 the New England Conference of the church admitted him to full clerical status, and for the next decade he preached in churches along the Massachusetts seaboard. In 1829, when the Methodists founded their Seamen's Bethel, a mission in Boston, Taylor, on account of his seagoing background, was chosen as its chaplain. This mission to sailors in port became his life work, and he became one of the most renowned preachers of his time, not just to the sailors, but to many others who learned of his reputation and came to his Bethel Chapel. "Father Taylor" as he was known among the sailors, was written of by many authors, including Ralph Waldo Emerson and Walt Whitman, and he was the figure upon whom Herman Melville patterned the preacher ("Father Mapple") and the sermon in Chapter 9 of *Moby Dick*. Taylor died in Boston on April 5, 1871.

Taylor, Elizabeth (1932–   ), actress. Born in London on February 27, 1932, Miss Taylor came to the United States with her family shortly before World War II and grew up in Pasadena, California. While still in grade school she had some professional training at the Universal movie studios. In 1943, largely because of her British accent, she was given a role in the film *Lassie Come Home*, but it was as the star of *National Velvet* two years later that she won popularity and critical praise as an accomplished child actress. For the next several years Miss Taylor appeared in roles that were basically transitional, as she was no longer a child star and not yet an adult actress. The critics seemed unable to decide whether she showed promise of becoming a polished performer or not, from her roles in *Life With Father*, 1947, *Little Women*, 1949, and *Father of the Bride*, 1950. But with the release of *A Place in the Sun*, 1951, based on Theodore Dreiser's *An American Tragedy*, there ceased to be any doubt that Elizabeth Taylor was an actress of talent. From that time she gave highly praised performances in a number of films, including *Giant*, 1956, *Cat on a Hot Tin Roof*, 1958, and *Suddenly Last Summer*, 1959. She won an Academy Award in 1960 as best actress for her performance in *Butterfield 8*, and again in 1966 for *Who's Afraid of Virginia Woolf?* After the filming of *Cleopatra*, 1963, she married British actor Richard Burton, with whom she starred in *Who's Afraid of Virginia Woolf?* and in *The Taming of the Shrew*, 1967. For two decades her marriages had kept her in the news nearly as much as her film performances. Her first two marriages, to Conrad "Nicky" Hilton and actor Michael Wilding, ended in divorce. Her third, to producer Mike Todd, ended with his death in an airplane crash in 1958. She married singer Eddie Fisher in 1959, but divorced him in 1964 to marry Burton. She and Burton appeared together in a number of films and on television.

Taylor, Frederick Winslow (1856–1915), inventor and industrial engineer. Born on March 20, 1856, in Germantown, Pennsylvania, Taylor intended to become a lawyer, but suffered from an eye defect that disrupted his plans to attend Harvard Law School. He was apprenticed to a pattern maker from 1874 to 1878 and later worked in several Philadelphia factories, then in a steel mill, all the while observing and sympathizing with his co-workers who frequently dropped of exhaustion trying to meet their employers' demands. For 12 years he remained in the steel company and rose to become its chief engineer. During this time, he attended night school at the Stevens Institute of Technology and graduated in 1883. From his position of authority in the steel plant he began investigations of the actual power of the machinery that was being used and related that information to the amount of work that could reasonably be expected of a man in one day. It became obvious that the demands being made were not reasonable. With two objectives in mind, to eliminate the hostility between labor and management and at the same time to increase daily output, he began to devise more powerful machinery and to study the amount of time that was involved in performing every operation in the plant. He invented the largest steel hammer in the United States in 1890; and his application of the data obtained from his "time and motion studies" led to reasonable work loads, better relations among employees and overseers, an incentive system of wages, and increased efficiency throughout the plant. "Taylorization," or industrial management, was adopted with great success in shops, offices, and industrial plants throughout the nation. In 1898 he was retained by the Bethlehem Steel Company to apply his theories and revise their entire manufacturing system. At that time he met Maunsel White; together they studied methods for tempering high-speed tool steels and in 1898 developed the Taylor-White heat-treating process that increased the cutting capacity of tool steels by as much as 300 percent. He resigned his post at Bethlehem Steel in 1901 to devote himself to spreading his ideas on industrial engineering. He offered his services to any company that was interested in Taylorization and completed, by 1911, *The Principles of Scientific Management* and a report to Congress on the fairness and reliability of his plan. His other works included *Notes on Belting*, 1893; *The Adjustment of Wages to Efficiency*, 1896; *Shop Management*, 1903; and *On the Art of Cutting Metals*, 1906. He died in Philadelphia on March 21, 1915.

Taylor, James Bayard, *see* Taylor, Bayard

Taylor, John (1753–1824), public official, political philosopher, and agriculturalist. Born, probably on December 19, 1753, in either Orange or Caroline County, Virginia, Taylor later lived in Caroline County and is usually identified with it, being commonly known as John Taylor of Caroline. Left an orphan at an early age, he was reared by his cousin, Edmund Pendleton. He studied for a time

at the College of William and Mary and after reading law began to practice in 1774. During the Revolution he served with the Continental army in Virginia, Pennsylvania, and New York, attaining the rank of major before resigning in 1779; two years later he was appointed lieutenant colonel of his home militia and served through the final campaigns in Virginia. He was elected to the Virginia house of delegates regularly, except for one year, from 1779 to 1785 and served again from 1796 to 1800. On three occasions he filled unexpired terms in the U.S. Senate, 1792–1794, 1803, and 1822–1824. It was through his political writings, however, that he became widely known; like so many Virginians of the time, he was an ardent democrat and staunchly opposed all efforts to establish a strong central government that, in his view, would inevitably usurp the rights and powers of the states and, ultimately, of the people. He joined Patrick Henry in opposing ratification of the Constitution in Virginia and then, having failed, attempted to stem the Federalist drift of the new government. *A Definition of Parties* and *An Enquiry into the Principles and Tendencies of Certain Public Measures*, both published in 1794, were directed against the fiscal policies of Alexander Hamilton; in 1798 he introduced into the legislature James Madison's Virginia Resolves against the Alien and Sedition Acts and in 1805 he published *A Defence of the Measures of the Administration of Thomas Jefferson*. His major writings came later: *An Inquiry into the Principles and Policy of the Government of the United States*, 1814, a rebuttal of John Adams; *Construction Construed and Constitutions Vindicated*, 1820, an attack on the growing power of the federal courts under John Marshall's leadership; *Tyranny Unmasked*, 1822, denouncing the protective tariff; and *New Views of the Constitution of the United States*, 1823. These works, despite their wordiness and infelicitous style, are among the best and most thorough expositions of the agrarian liberal democracy that remains one of the major strains in U.S. political thought. Taylor was, in addition, an agriculturalist of note and made significant experiments with crop rotation and other improved methods of cultivation. He published numerous essays on agriculture in newspapers; the collected articles were published in *The Arator*, 1813. He died on August 21, 1824, at his plantation, Hazlewood, in Caroline County, Virginia.

Taylor, John W. (1784–1854), public official. Born in Charlton, Saratoga County, New York, on March 26, 1784, Taylor graduated from Union College in Schenectady in 1806. After reading law for a year he was admitted to the bar in 1807 and began practice in Ballston Spa, New York. After serving a two-year term in the state legislature beginning in 1811, he was elected to the U.S. House of Representatives in 1812. Taylor served there for the next 20 years, until March 1833. He was speaker of the House for two periods, 1820–1821 and 1825–1827. Both times he was defeated for reelection to the speaker's post by a coalition of

New York Democrats and Southern congressmen —he was factional and vigorously opposed to slavery. His views on slavery brought him national attention. From early in 1819 the bill to admit Missouri to the Union was before Congress. When it was finally passed in March 1820, it was in large measure owing to the compromise solution of keeping the territory in the Louisiana Purchase north of the 36° 30' line free from slavery. This proposal—which was embodied in the Missouri Compromise—had been submitted to the House of Representatives by Taylor and to the Senate by Jesse B. Thomas of Illinois. It was Taylor's thesis that since Congress had the power of admitting new states, it consequently had the authority to set forth the conditions under which they would be admitted. Defeated for reelection in 1832, he returned to his law practice. He served a term in the New York senate, 1840–1842, but resigned because of poor health. In 1843 he moved to Cleveland, where he lived in retirement until his death on September 18, 1854.

Taylor, Joseph Deems, *see* Taylor, Deems

Taylor, William (1821–1902), missionary. Born in Rockbridge County, Virginia, on May 2, 1821, Taylor resolved to enter the Methodist ministry after undergoing experiences of religious conversion as a child and as a teen-ager. In 1847 he was ordained an elder of the Methodist Episcopal church and began preaching in Georgetown, D.C. In 1849, when the Gold Rush to California began, he was sent by his denomination to be an evangelist among the fast-growing populace of San Francisco. This enterprise began a missionary career that spanned half a century. After seven years on the Pacific Coast Taylor toured the major cities of the United States and Canada until 1861. Thereafter his work took in nearly every part of the world. He traveled to England, Australia, New Zealand, the Caribbean islands, South America, South Africa, and India. It was while in India in 1870–1875 that he developed a modified New Testament approach to missionary work: the missioner was to gain his livelihood from his congregation and by working himself, with the aim of making the mission self-supporting. Taylor supported his own family throughout most of his career by writing a large number of books recounting his experiences. Much of his mission work was done on his own, for he was impatient with ecclesiastical supervision and the slow process of decision-making in the church. A nonreligious benefit resulted from his work when he sent the seeds of eucalyptus trees from Australia to California in 1863, starting the present eucalyptus groves in the West. In 1884 he was elected missionary bishop for Africa, and for the next dozen years conducted a prodigious missionary enterprise on that continent, particularly in Liberia and the Congo. In 1896, after his health had weakened, the general conference of the Methodist church retired him. He lived thereafter in California, where he died, in Palo Alto, on May 18, 1902.

Taylor, Zachary (1784–1850), twelfth president of the United States. Born on November 24, 1784, in Orange County, Virginia, Taylor grew up near Louisville, Kentucky, where his family moved in 1785. He received little formal education. He first saw military service as a short-term volunteer in 1806; two years later he was commissioned a lieutenant in the regular army and by the end of the War of 1812, during which he served under Gen. William Henry Harrison, he had been promoted to captain and was serving in the rank of major. The reduction in forces that followed the war returned him to captain and he resigned from the army. In 1816 President James Madison recommissioned him as a major and for the next 21 years he saw garrison duty along the Western frontier from Louisiana to Wisconsin, where, in 1832, by then a colonel, he took part in the Black Hawk War. In 1837 he was ordered to Florida to help prosecute the war against the Seminole Indians; he won a major victory at the battle of Lake Okeechobee in December and was promoted to brigadier general. In May 1838 Taylor—now nicknamed "Old Rough and Ready"—became the army's departmental commander in Florida and for two years oversaw the frustrating and inconclusive campaign against the Seminole. Relieved at his own request in 1840, he returned to Louisiana and a year later became commander of a military department with headquarters at Fort Smith, Arkansas. In 1845 he was ordered to prepare for a possible invasion by Mexican forces of newly annexed Texas. Early in 1846 he advanced to the Rio Grande and in May, before war was declared, he won minor victories at Palo Alto and Resaca de la Palma and was promoted to major general and named commander of the Army of the Rio Grande. In September he captured Monterrey and granted the Mexicans an eight-week armistice; this action was repudiated by President James K. Polk, and Taylor began to suspect Polk and Secretary of War William L. Marcy of political intrigue aimed at his own growing popularity. This conviction was strengthened when Gen. Winfield Scott commandeered many of his seasoned troops for the Veracruz invasion, leaving him with orders to concentrate his forces at Monterrey and to pursue a strictly defensive policy. Instead he advanced southward and, although outnumbered four to one, forced General Santa Anna's army to withdraw from the battle of Buena Vista in February 1847. Now a national hero after ending the war on the northern front, he began to receive serious consideration by the Whigs as a presidential candidate; he was already something of a Whig by inclination, although he had never voted in a presidential election, and his status as a slaveholder was an advantage, as it would attract Southern support for a party suspected of Northern sympathies. At the 1848 Whig convention he was nominated over Henry Clay, Daniel Webster, and General Scott, and, aided by a Democratic split, was elected president over Lewis Cass and Martin Van Buren. He took office with virtually no knowledge of the political process but determined to preside over a neutral, nonpartisan administration; although he adapted himself to the patronage system, he soon came into conflict with other party leaders over the admission of California and New Mexico to the Union. He strongly resented opposition to his own policy of encouraging admission, and was himself opposed to the injection of sectionalism into the issue. He was contemptuous of Southern leaders who threatened secession should California enter the Union as a free state, and he referred with disdain to the proposals of the later Compromise of 1850 as the "Omnibus Bill." The signal achievement of his administration was the conclusion in 1850 of the Clayton-Bulwer Treaty with England, providing for joint control of any canal built across the Central American isthmus. In mid-1850 he was troubled by a scandal involving three of his cabinet advisers and decided to reorganize the entire cabinet; before any of these matters was resolved, however, he became seriously ill following a July 4th celebration and died on July 9, 1850, in Washington, D.C.

Teasdale, Sara (1884–1933), poet. Born in St. Louis on August 8, 1884, Miss Teasdale graduated from a private school near her home. She had early determined to write poetry, and to enlarge her experience she toured Europe and the Middle East from 1905 to 1907. Her first volume of poetry, *Sonnets to Duse and Other Poems*, 1907, established her reputation. In 1914 she married and went to New York City to live. *Rivers to the Sea* appeared in 1915. In 1918 she won the Columbia University Poetry Society prize, forerunner of the Pulitzer Prize for poetry, for her book *Love Songs*. Her poems were consistently classical in style, pure, straightforward, usually in such simple verse forms as quatrains or sonnets, and technically excellent. But from her earlier poems to her later work, *Flame and Shadow*, 1920, and *Dark of the Moon*, 1926, for example, an evident maturing process took place, with her poems evidencing an increasing subtlety of expression and sensitivity of reaction to the world. Her personal life was unhappy: her marriage ended in divorce in 1929, and she lived the life of a semi-invalid. In 1932, in London for some research work, she was overtaken by a bout of pneumonia. Back in New York City and still in frail health, she took an overdose of sleeping pills and died on the night of January 28, 1933, some 13 months after the suicide of Vachel Lindsay, who had courted her while she was living in St. Louis and of whom she had been extremely fond for many years. Her last book, *Strange Victory*, was published later that year.

Tecumseh (1768–1813), Indian leader. Born in March 1768 near what is now Oldtown, Greene County, Ohio, Tecumseh (Tecumtha or Tikamthi), chief of the Shawnee, was noted everywhere on the frontier for his courage and integrity. He wished to establish a powerful Indian confederation to halt white agricultural settlement in the Ohio Valley. He maintained that the frontier as a whole belonged to all the Indian tribes which throughout history had changed the location of their homelands without any concept of ownership of particular regions, and he held that land could not be sold by, or purchased from, individual tribes. He emphasized that the treaty of Greenville, 1795, had been negotiated with all Indian tribes, assuring them that unceded lands would be theirs. In 1805 he settled at Greenville and in 1808 he moved to the region of the Tippecanoe Creek in Indiana Territory. The governor of Indiana Territory, William Henry Harrison, who recognized the implications of the 1795 treaty, maneuvered individual tribes to sign cession treaties, frequently under conditions of trickery or deceit. Tecumseh, who was aided by his brother The Prophet (Tenskwatawa), traveled among the tribes, trying to unite them and to convince them that they should refuse white men's gifts, work in agriculture, make their own livelihood, and settle disputes with settlers peaceably. He acquired great influence and nearly perfected his confederation with the aid of the British, who supplied guns and ammunition. Despite his exertions, however, Governor Harrison continued to gain lands. In 1811, while he was absent, The Prophet was tricked by Harrison into a battle at Tippecanoe; the battle scattered Tecumseh's finest warriors, led to the destruction of the provisions he had stockpiled, and ended the confederation. When the War of 1812 broke out, Tecumseh joined the British forces as a brigadier general. They captured Detroit, and he rallied more warriors to fight on the British side. When he learned of the plan to burn Detroit and retreat eastward, he was angry and demanded arms so that he and his warriors could fight for the Western land or die upon it. He remained with the British troops, however, until the battle of the Thames, in Ontario, on October 5, 1813, in which he commanded the right wing of Gen. Henry A. Proctor's army opposing Harrison. He was killed in the battle, which reestablished U.S. supremacy in the Old Northwest. Tecumseh's attempt to create a pan-Indian movement with both political and cultural dimensions remained the most ambitious ever undertaken, and the most nearly successful.

Tekakwitha, Kateri (1656–1680), Indian religious. Born at present-day Auriesville in upper New York State in 1656, Kateri was the child of a Mohawk father and a mother who was a Christianized Algonkian. Her last name is sometimes given as Tegakwitha or Tegakovita. When she was four her parents died, and she was raised by her uncle, an anti-Christian Mohawk chief. In 1667 Jesuit missionaries came among the tribes and she appears to have been strongly influenced by them, although she must have had contacts with Christianized Indians from time to time as well. In 1675 she asked Father Jacques de Lamberville for baptism, and after instruction she was baptized on Easter Day the following year, being given then the name Catherine. Her conversion brought her a great deal of hostility, even persecution, from her fellow Indians, who were already suspicious of her pious ways and her refusal to marry. To escape possible torture and death in her home village she fled 200 miles to the mission of St. Frances Xavier at Sault St. Louis near Montreal. There she took her first communion in 1677. She lived a life of great spirituality and asceticism that impressed all who knew her at the mission. In 1678 she was enrolled in the Confraternity of the Holy Family. In 1680 she became seriously ill and died on April 17 at the mission, having become widely known as the "Lily of the Mohawks." After her death devotion to her spread among the French and the Indians of the region, and many miracles were credited to her intervention. In 1884 the third plenary council of the Roman Catholic church, meeting in Baltimore, petitioned Rome to initiate steps toward the canonization of Kateri Tekakwitha. With the formal presentation of her cause for beatification in 1932 she became the first North American Indian ever to be proposed for sainthood; in 1943 she was recognized as possessed of heroic virtue.

Télémaque, *see* Vesey, Denmark

Teller, Edward (1908–   ), physicist. Born in Budapest on January 15, 1908, Teller studied at the technological institute in Karlsruhe, Germany, and took his Ph.D. from the University of Leipzig in 1930. From 1931 to 1933 he was a research associate at the University of Göttingen, and in 1934 he studied with Niels Bohr in Copenhagen. In 1935 he fled the Nazi regime in Germany and, after a brief time as a lecturer at the University of London, moved to the United States, where he taught at The George Washington University. In 1941, the year he became a naturalized citizen, he moved to Columbia University to join Enrico Fermi in research on atomic fission and later in the year became a member of what was to become known as the Manhattan Engineering District project, the code name for a group working on development of the atomic bomb. For five years he was concerned with the project, first at Columbia and later at the University of Chicago, the University of California at Berkeley, and the Los Alamos National Laboratory in New Mexico. At the same time he began formulating the theoretical foundations for a hydrogen bomb, immensely more powerful than the atomic bomb, which explodes by a process of fusion, and was a major proponent of its development. In 1945 he returned to the Institute for Nuclear Studies at the University of Chicago and the following year became professor of physics there. In 1949 he was named assistant director of the Los Alamos facility and remained there until 1951, by which time the principal theoretical and practical problems of the H-bomb had been solved. After another year at the University of Chicago, Teller joined the staff of the Atomic Energy Commission's new laboratory in Livermore, California, operated by the University of California, and in 1953 he became professor of physics at the University of California at Berkeley. From 1954 he was associate director of the university's Lawrence Radiation Laboratory and during

1958–1960 was director of the Livermore laboratory; in 1960 he became professor at large at the university. He was a strong advocate of the continued testing and improvement of nuclear weapons and was critical of those favoring test moratoriums and bans; his view was in marked opposition to that of most of the scientific community. In 1954 he was a major figure in the security hearings concerning J. Robert Oppenheimer; he testified that Oppenheimer had, by lack of "moral support," delayed the development of the H-bomb by several years. Teller wrote a number of books on the history and future of nuclear weapons, including *Our Nuclear Future* (with A. L. Latter), 1958, and *The Legacy of Hiroshima*, 1962. In 1962 he received the Atomic Energy Commission's Fermi Award.

Temple, Shirley (1928–   ), entertainer. Born in Santa Monica, California, on April 23, 1928, Miss Temple began her acting career before she was four. Within a few years she was the most famous child star Hollywood films had produced; during the 1930s she was the most popular box-office attraction, child or adult, in the movies. She had had no dramatic training, apart from dancing lessons, before trying out for the movies, but her potential was immediately recognized and she was given a contract. When she was six years old, she received an Academy Award for her contribution to film entertainment. With her dimples and curly blonde hair, which inspired countless fads for dolls, hair styles, clothing, and such, she was the most photographed and probably the most recognized person in the world. Her first full-length movie was *Stand Up and Cheer*, in 1934, and it was followed by a succession of Shirley Temple hits, including *The Little Colonel*, 1935; *The Littlest Rebel*, 1935; *Captain January*, 1936; *Heidi*, 1937; *Little Miss Broadway*, 1938; and *Rebecca of Sunnybrook Farm*, 1938. In *Bright Eyes*, 1934, she sang her best-known song, "The Good Ship Lollipop." But at the age of thirteen, Shirley Temple was a former movie star. Attempted comeback roles in films from 1944 to 1949 did not succeed in reestablishing her movie career. In 1950 she married businessman Charles Black and thereafter lived near San Francisco. In the late 1950s she returned to entertainment with a television show, the "Shirley Temple Storybook." She took an active role in the social and political life of San Francisco; in 1967 she ran unsuccessfully in the Republican primary for a seat in Congress. In 1969 President Richard M. Nixon appointed her a delegate to the UN General Assembly. In 1974 she was named U.S. ambassador to Ghana, and in 1976 she became chief of protocol in the State Department.

Tennent, Gilbert (1703–1764), religious leader. Born on February 5, 1703, in County Armagh, Ireland, Tennent was the son of William Tennent, who brought him to America in about 1718. Educated by his father, he entered the ministry in 1725; the following year he accepted a pastorate in New Brunswick, New Jersey, and was ordained there. Associated there with the Dutch evangelist T. J. Frelinghuysen, Tennent soon developed into a zealous and rousing preacher. Joined by other students of his father's "log college," he became the central figure of the rapidly growing wave of revivalism that came to be known as the Great Awakening. In 1739 the group was joined by the great English revivalist George Whitefield, and during 1739–1740 Whitefield and Tennent traveled throughout the middle colonies and into New England, fervently preaching the awesome power and wrath of God and the imminent damnation of sinners. Tennent was harsh in his condemnation of what he saw as the empty formalism of the church, and he attacked with increasing bitterness the "hypocrisy" of much of the ministry. He flouted synodical regulations as to requirements for ordination, relying on evidences of inner conversion rather than theological training. The conservative majority of Presbyterian leaders was soon roused to concern, and in 1741 the church split into the traditional "Old Side" and the evangelistic "New Side." In 1743 Tennent became pastor of a New Side church organized by Whitefield in Philadelphia; he retained the position for the rest of his life and continued to be a controversial figure, although in later years, perhaps repenting his earlier contentiousness, he led the movement that resulted in the reunification of the Presbyterian church in 1758. In 1753 he traveled to England and Scotland with Samuel Davies and raised money for building Nassau Hall at the newly founded College of New Jersey (now Princeton). He died on July 23, 1764, in Philadelphia.

Tennent, William (1673–1746), religious leader. Born in Ireland in 1673, Tennent studied for the ministry at the University of Edinburgh, graduating in 1695. He was ordained in 1706 and served as a private chaplain for several years, but had no parish until he came to America. He and his family arrived in Philadelphia about 1718 and he was soon admitted to the Presbyterian ministry. Between 1718 and 1726 he served parishes in Eastchester and Bedford, New York. In 1726 he moved to Bucks County, Pennsylvania, where he settled at Neshaminy, the parish in which he spent the remainder of his life. At this period of colonial history, the Presbyterian clergy were generally educated at Yale or Harvard, or in England. The shortage of accessible educational institutions, plus the demand for clergymen in a rapidly expanding church, inspired Tennent to train his own sons—Gilbert, William, John, and Charles—for the ministry himself. In 1736 he opened a school for clergymen at his home. But Tennent's evangelical, revivalist zeal caused his school to be frowned upon by Presbyterians who were principally concerned with doctrinal purity and strict interpretation of the Westminister Confession. They derided his school as the "log college," and did not favor ordaining its graduates. But control of ordination was in the hands of the local presbyteries, not of the general synod; and the demand for clergy led to Tennent's students being accepted in the

churches. Within a few years, with a number of "log-college" graduates in Presbyterian pulpits and at the forefront of the "Great Awakening" revival movement, a rift developed within the church. One faction—the "Old Side" Presbyterians—wanted to keep things as they had been in Britain. The "New Side" ministers were largely native-born and had been educated under Tennent. With Tennent's death on May 6, 1746, the college ceased to function; but the divisions in the church remained and were soon widened by the sweeping revivalism of the Great Awakening. The College of New Jersey (now Princeton) was conceived immediately after his death to replace the log college.

Tenskwatawa, *see* Tecumseh

Terhune, Albert Payson (1872–1942), author. Born in Newark, New Jersey, on December 21, 1872, the son of a Presbyterian clergyman and of a successful novelist, Mary V. H. Terhune, who wrote under the name Marion Harland, Terhune was educated in Paris and Geneva, while his father was serving as chaplain of American churches abroad, and graduated from Columbia in 1893. After travels in Egypt and Syria he returned to New York City in 1894 to join the staff of the *Evening World.* His first book, *Syria from the Saddle,* appeared in 1896, and his first novel, *Dr. Dale,* written with his mother, in 1900; for the next 16 years he wrote constantly in an attempt to free himself from journalism, but he was finally able to leave the *World* in 1916 and become a freelance writer. He moved to a farm, Sunnybank, near Pompton Lakes, New Jersey, and there wrote his first great popular success, *Lad, a Dog,* 1919; it was also the first in a series of novels about dogs, which led to his being considered the dean of dogstory writers in America. He published nearly 25 novels after 1919, among them *Bruce,* 1920; *The Heart of a Dog,* 1926; *Lad of Sunnybank,* 1928; and *A Book of Famous Dogs,* 1937. The autobiographical *Now That I'm Fifty* appeared in 1925. When not writing, Terhune spent his time hunting, fishing, and breeding prize collies. He died in New Jersey, at Sunnybank, on February 18, 1942.

Terman, Lewis Madison (1877–1956), psychologist. Born in Johnson County, Indiana, on January 15, 1877, Terman graduated from Central Normal College at Danville in 1898. He received his Ph.D. in education and psychology from Clark University in 1905. From 1906 until 1910 he taught at the State Normal School in Los Angeles; and in 1910 he joined the faculty of education at Stanford University, where he remained until his retirement in 1942. From 1922 he was head of the psychology department. Terman contributed the term "IQ," or intelligence quotient, to the American language through his publication in 1916 of the first widely used test for measuring intelligence, the Stanford revision of the Binet-Simon intelligence scale, subsequently known as the Stanford-Binet test. The test, described in his book, *The Measurement of Intelligence,* 1916, was devised in such a way that the IQ of an average child of any age, computed as a ratio of intellectual age to chronological age, would be 100. During World War I, in which he served in the army, Terman also devised the Army Alpha and Army Beta intelligence tests, the first group intelligence tests. Most of his career was spent in studying the development of high-IQ children over a long period of years, and he emphasized the importance of providing greater educational opportunities for gifted children. He also found, in contrast to many popular beliefs, that children with high IQ's (over 140) tend to be healthier and emotionally more stable than children with average intelligence quotients. Among his books were *The Hygiene of the School Child*, 1914; *The Intelligence of School Children*, 1919; *Genetic Studies of Genius*, three volumes, 1925–1930; *The Gifted Child Grows Up*, 1947, with Melita Oden; and *The Gifted Group at Midlife*, 1959, also with Melita Oden. He died in Palo Alto, California, on December 21, 1956.

Terry, Alfred Howe (1827–1890), soldier. Born in Hartford, Connecticut, on November 10, 1827, Terry attended Yale Law School for a year and was admitted to the bar in 1849. He was clerk of the New Haven County Court from 1854 to 1860. When the Civil War started he was commissioned colonel of the 2nd Connecticut militia, a regiment he had commanded since 1854. He served with distinction throughout the whole war, from the first battle of Bull Run (Manassas) to the occupation of Wilmington, North Carolina. He took part in the capture of Port Royal, South Carolina, in 1861, and of Fort Pulaski, Georgia, in 1862, after which he was promoted to brigadier general of volunteers. Having also taken part in the fighting at Charleston in 1863, and Richmond and Petersburg in 1864, Terry was assigned the task of capturing Fort Fisher, at Wilmington, by Gen. Ulysses S. Grant in December 1864. He succeeded in doing so on January 15, 1865. As of that date, he was advanced to the rank of brigadier general in the regular army. After the occupation of Wilmington he joined forces with Gen. William T. Sherman, coming up through Georgia. After the war Terry was put in command of the Department of Dakota, with headquarters at St. Paul. Except for a three-year term of duty in the Department of the South from 1869 to 1872, he remained in the Northwest until 1886. This was the era of the fiercest Indian fighting in the West, and Terry saw much action against the Sioux tribes of the Dakotas and Montana. He was the general under whom Col. George A. Custer's force was serving when Custer met disaster at the Little Bighorn River in June 1876, and it was he who rescued Custer's harried fellow officers Marcus A. Reno and Frederick W. Benteen. In October 1877 Terry met with Sitting Bull at Fort Walsh in Canada in an unsuccessful attempt to persuade the Sioux leader to return to the reservation in South Dakota. During Terry's stay in the Northwest, the area underwent some of its important early development, with the building of railroads, the opening of the region for settlement, and the discoveries of minerals in the Black Hills and Montana. In March 1886 he was given the regular-army rank of major general and put in command of the Division of the Missouri. On April 5, 1888, he retired from the service. Terry, who was not a West Point graduate, was nevertheless highly regarded by his fellow officers and considered an exceptional student and practitioner of the science of war. He died in New Haven, Connecticut, on December 16, 1890.

Terry, Eli (1772–1852), clock manufacturer. Born in East Windsor, Connecticut, on April 13, 1772, Terry was apprenticed in the clockmaker's trade at the age of fourteen. In 1793 he went into business for himself in Plymouth, Connecticut. In 1800, to increase productivity, he began using machinery driven by waterpower to make his clock parts, instead of the traditional hand labor. His enterprise, an early form of the assembly line in that he used interchangeable parts, was quite successful. Most of the clocks made in this, the first clock factory in the United States, were wooden, both cases and works; Terry designed them himself. In 1807 he sold the factory to buy an even larger one in partnership with Seth Thomas and Silas Hoadley; he sold his share of the firm in 1810. In 1814 he designed a "perfected wood clock" that sold so well it dominated the market for several years, and production eventually reached more than 10,000 clocks a year. He also manufactured some brass clocks and tower clocks. Some of Terry's partners and employees—Chauncey Jerome, Seth Thomas, and Joseph Ives—remained in the clock business and gained even greater reputations than Terry, their names still being in use on clocks. Terry died in Plymouth, Connecticut, on February 26, 1852.

Terzaghi, Karl (1883–1963), engineer. Born in Prague, Bohemia (now Czechoslovakia), on October 2, 1883, Terzaghi graduated with an engineering degree from the Technische Hochschule in Graz, Austria, in 1904 and shortly thereafter went into professional practice with a Vienna engineering firm. During World War I he served with the Austrian air corps and in 1916 moved to Istanbul, becoming professor of foundation engineering at the École Impériale d'Ingénieurs; two years later he took a similar post at Robert College, an American institution in Istanbul, and retained it until coming to the United States in 1925. By that time his researches on various aspects of foundation engineering had resulted in his unification of much diverse information, both practical and theoretical, into the new field of soil mechanics, and his book *Erdbaumechanik*, 1925, firmly established the field as a fundamental part of mechanical and civil engineering studies. Terzaghi was professor of soil mechanics and foundation engineering at the Massachusetts Institute of Technology (MIT) from 1925 to 1929; from 1929 to 1938 he held the chair of soil mechanics at the Technische Hochschule in Vienna, working also as a consulting engineer in Europe, Africa, and Asia. From 1939 he was again in the United States, becoming a citizen in 1943, and from 1946 to 1956 serving as professor of civil engineering at Harvard and thereafter as a lecturer and consultant. Others of his books included *Theoretical Soil Mechanics*, 1943; *Soil Mechanics in Engineering Practice*, 1948; and *From Theory to Practice in Soil Mechanics*, 1960. President of the International Conference of Soil Mechanics and Foundation Engineering from its founding in 1936 until 1957, Terzaghi died in Winchester, Massachusetts, on October 25, 1963.

Tesla, Nikola (1856–1943), electrical engineer and inventor. Born on July 10, 1856, in Smiljan in what is now Yugoslavia, Tesla studied mathematics, physics, and engineering in Graz, Austria, for four years and then, from 1878 to 1880, was enrolled at the University of Prague, where he concentrated on philosophy. In 1881 he went to Paris to work as an electrical engineer and three years later came to the United States. For a time he was employed by Thomas A. Edison and later by George Westinghouse, but his preference was for independent research; his Tesla Electric Company, formed in 1887, soon failed, and he spent most of his life working alone. His was a fertile genius; he claimed some 700 inventions, beginning with his 1881 telephone repeater, but he never reaped the material rewards that might have been his. In 1888 he developed his idea of a rotating magnetic field and applied it to a practical induction motor run by an alternating electric current. The induction, synchronous, and split-phase motors were all of Tesla's invention, as were new and improved generators and transformers, together constituting a workable system for the production and distribution of alternating-current (AC) electric power. From about 1890 he devoted much time to the study of high-frequency current, developing several forms of oscillators and the famous Tesla coil. By 1893 he had worked out a method of transmitting information by wireless telegraphy. He became convinced that the power distribution system of the future would be by wireless transmission from tall, centrally located towers, and he concentrated his energies on developing this method for practical application. In 1899–1900 to test his idea, he built a gigantic Tesla coil, capable of generating 12 million volts, at Colorado Springs. He secured backing from J. P. Morgan to erect a power transmission tower on Long Island, but the financier's death interrupted the project; later he worked on designing such a system for the Niagara Falls power plant. As early as 1898 he developed a wireless guidance system for ships. A visionary as well as a practical engineer, he foresaw the harnessing of solar energy for man's use and about the turn of the century announced that he had been attempting wireless communication with other planets, which he was convinced were inhabited. He died in New York City on January 7, 1943.

Tevis, Lloyd (1824–1899), businessman. Born in Shelbyville, Kentucky, on March 20, 1824, Tevis studied law privately and practiced for a while, but his chief interest was business, and to it he devoted most of his life. He worked selling dry goods in Louisville and spent some time at the Bank of Kentucky. In 1849 the Gold Rush lured him to California, where he formed a business and law partnership in 1850 with James Ben Ali Haggin in Sacramento. They remained partners for the rest of Tevis's life, and both prospered greatly. At one time or another they had interests in nearly all the mining, communications, and transportation companies serving the West. They were among the principal backers of the telegraph system throughout California that was eventually taken over by Western Union. In 1853 they moved their office to San Francisco to be in closer touch with the other business interests of the state. Tevis was a promoter of the Southern Pacific Railroad and served as its president in 1869 and 1870. When it was apparent in 1868 that the transcontinental railroad would soon be finished, Tevis and his associates organized the Pacific Union Express Company as mail-carrying competition for Wells, Fargo & Company, which had failed to negotiate contracts with the railroads to carry the mail. The Tevis-backed express company drove down the price of Wells, Fargo stock, and Tevis and his partners bought enough of it to gain control of the company in 1869, when Wells Fargo was forced to end the competition by buying control of Pacific Union at an exorbitant price. Tevis served as president of Wells, Fargo from 1872 to 1892. He also had stock in the Sutro Tunnel built into the Comstock Lode; he controlled more than 1000 miles of stagecoach line in California alone; and he also owned ranch lands, gold and silver mines, and San Francisco's streetcar lines. In addition, he, and several associates, notably Marcus Daly, owned the huge Anaconda copper-mining company in Montana. Tevis died in San Francisco on July 24, 1899, leaving a large fortune.

Thalberg, Irving Grant (1899–1936), motion-picture executive. Born in Brooklyn, New York, on May 30, 1899, Thalberg was prevented from finishing high school by a bout with rheumatic fever. He took a secretarial course and in about 1918 went to work for the Universal Pictures Corporation in New York City as secretary to the president, Carl Laemmle. In 1919 he went to Hollywood on a business trip with his employer and remained there to learn more about the motion-picture business. He learned so quickly that he became acting head of the studio in four years, and in 1924 joined the newly formed Metro-Goldwyn-Mayer Studios (M-G-M) as vice-president in charge of production. His first major production was the epoch-making *The Big Parade*, 1925, the classic screen account of World War I. In 12 years at M-G-M he proved to have an exceptional eye for talent, story line, and dramatic content and effect—in fact all of the elements of production that go into the making of memorable and entertaining films, and introduced the multistar system for movies. During his career he produced such successful films as *Grand Hotel*, 1932; *Mutiny on the Bounty*, 1935; the Marx Brothers' *A Night at the Opera*, also 1935; and *The Good Earth*, 1937. He was stricken with pneumonia in 1936, for the second time in four years, and died on September 14, in Santa Monica, California. In 1937 the Academy of Motion Picture Arts and Sciences instituted the Thalberg Memorial Award for exceptional contributions to the film industry.

Thayendanegea, *see* Brant, Joseph

Thayer, Sylvanus (1785–1872), army engineer and educator. Born in Braintree, Massachusetts, on June 9, 1785, Thayer graduated from Dartmouth College in 1807. He spent one year at the U.S. Military Academy at West Point and was granted permission to graduate in 1808. For the next several years he worked on fortifications with the army's Corps of Engineers. During the War of 1812 he saw no combat, but served at Norfolk, Virginia, and along the Canadian border and reached the rank of major. After the war he and another officer went to Europe for two years on behalf of the government to study methods of military education and defense systems. Upon his return in 1817 he was appointed superintendent of West Point, with the rank of major, and it was Thayer's strong influence during the next 16 years that transformed the academy from a second-rate trade school into a first-class educational institution. He built up all academic departments, particularly engineering and science. West Point became a good four-year college, and in engineering it was without peer. He added to the faculty, restructured the student body, and instituted tough examinations and rigid student discipline. It was alleged by some that his discipline was too harsh, and it occasionally backfired; in 1818 there was a cadet revolt in which 200 students rejected his strict administration. Thayer's court-martial and dismissal of five ringleaders was upheld by Secretary of War John C. Calhoun and President James Monroe. Nevertheless, the cadets continued to resent what they deemed the arbitrary and rigid attitudes of the academy's administration; on at least one occasion, the Christmas of 1826, their resentment led to a riot. Eventually it was over the issue of discipline that Thayer left the academy: President Andrew Jackson several times went over Thayer's head by reinstating cadets who had been dismissed and, finally, indignant at such undermining of his position, Thayer was relieved at his own request on July 1, 1833. For the next 30 years he was the army's chief engineer in charge of New England coastal fortifications and harbor improvements, and in 1863 he retired from the army with the rank of brigadier general. In 1867 he endowed the Thayer School of Engineering at Dartmouth College. Known widely as the "Father of the Military Academy," Thayer lived in retirement in Braintree, Massachusetts, until his death there on September 7, 1872, at the age of eighty-seven. He was elected to the Hall of Fame in 1965.

Thomas, Christian Friedrich Theodore, *see* Thomas, Theodore

Thomas, George Henry (1816–1870), soldier. Born in Southampton County, Virginia, on July 31, 1816, a member of a wealthy Virginia family, Thomas graduated from West Point in 1840 and served in the artillery during the Seminole War in Florida and under Gen. Zachary Taylor in the Mexican War, distinguishing himself at Monterey and Buena Vista. In 1851 he was appointed an instructor at West Point and in 1855 was promoted to major in the 2nd Cavalry. When the Civil War broke out in 1861, he, unlike many of his Virginia contemporaries, remained faithful to the Union. After leading a brigade in some early movements in the Shenandoah Valley and being promoted to brigadier general of volunteers in August 1861, he was made commander of an independent force in eastern Kentucky, and at Mill Springs, on January 19, 1862, gained the first important Union victory in the West. He served under Gen. Don Carlos Buell at Nashville and Shiloh (Pittsburg Landing) and in April 1862 was promoted to major general of volunteers. He commanded the right wing at Corinth and was second in command under Buell at Perryville. In October 1862, when Buell was relieved, Thomas was offered the command but refused it; under Gen. W. S. Rosecrans, Buell's replacement, he was engaged at Murfreesboro (Stones River) early in 1863 and also in the early maneuvering in the Chattanooga Campaign. At the battle of Chickamauga, on September 19, he held Rosecrans's left wing against heavy odds, and gained the sobriquet "the Rock of Chickamauga." He succeeded to the command of the Army of the Cumberland shortly before that army's great victory at Chattanooga in late November. At the time Ulysses S. Grant was the chief Union officer in the West; when he departed for Washington as commander in chief of the Union armies, Gen. William T. Sherman replaced him in the West, but Thomas remained as second in command. In the autumn of 1864 Confederate Gen. J. B. Hood broke away from Atlanta and menaced Sherman's extended lines of communication, and Sherman left to Thomas the task of containing Hood. A delaying action at Franklin, Tennessee, checked Hood on November 30, and Thomas thereupon attacked him at Nashville on December 15–16, inflicting one of the worst defeats sustained in the open field by any army on either side during the war. Thomas was made a major general in the regular army, received the thanks of Congress, and continued in command in the Nashville region. After the war he commanded military departments in Kentucky and Tennessee; in 1869 he was placed in charge of the Military Division of the Pacific, with headquarters in San Francisco. He died there on March 28, 1870.

Thomas, Isaiah (1749–1831), printer and publisher. Born in Boston on January 19 (old style), 1749, Thomas had just six weeks of schooling and at the age of six began to learn printing from local printers, so that he was well qualified in the field by the age of seventeen. With his apprenticeship still in effect, he went to Nova Scotia in 1766 and obtained employment with the *Halifax Gazette*, hoping to go on to London and further his training. His refusal to comply with the Stamp Act, however, led him back to Boston, where he was released from his indenture. Then traveling south in the United States, hoping to reach England through the West Indies, he stopped in Charlestown and worked on the *South Carolina and American General Gazette*. With dim prospects for reaching England, he went back to Boston in 1770 and established with his former master, Zechariah Fowle, the *Massachusetts Spy*, a Whig paper. Soon becoming the sole owner of the paper, he took up the patriot cause and became notorious with the royal government and famous among the people. Driven from Boston by the British occupation in 1775, he sent his printing equipment to Worcester and on the way there was one of those who helped Paul Revere warn the countryside of the approach of the British on April 18. He then fought as a minuteman in the battles of Lexington and Concord. He set up offices in Worcester on April 20 and became the official printer for the patriots. In 1778, having spent a brief time in business in Salem, Massachusetts, he resumed issuing the *Spy*, now from Worcester. Opening offices throughout New England, he published textbooks (including Nicholas Pike's arithmetic book and William Perry's speller and dictionary), Blackstone's *Commentaries*, illustrated editions of children's books (including *Mother Goose's Melody* and *The History of Little Goody Two-Shoes*), a Bible, and almanacs, magazines, religious works, sheet music, and the first native American novel, William H. Brown's *The Power of Sympathy*, 1789. The books from his press were noted for their distinguished typography. He was the first postmaster of Worcester (1775–1801). He compiled his *History of Printing in America*, two volumes, 1810, which remained for more than a century the most authoritative treatment of the topic, and in 1812 he founded and incorporated the American Antiquarian Society, becoming its first president. He retired from active participation in business in 1802 and died in Worcester, Massachusetts, on April 4, 1831.

Thomas, Lowell Jackson (1892–1981), commentator and author. Born in Woodington, Darke County, Ohio, on April 6, 1892, Thomas graduated from Northern Indiana University at Valparaiso in 1911. He continued his education at the University of Denver, where he received both his B.A. and M.A. degrees in 1912. He then went to Chicago to work as a reporter for the *Chicago Journal* and to attend Kent College of Law (he also taught oratory at Kent for two years). Further graduate work at Princeton brought him another M.A. in 1915. In 1915 he made the first of innumerable trips to various parts of the world, journeying to Alaska, then a largely unknown territory for most Americans. The lectures he gave on his return were suc-

cessful enough to gain him a commission from President Woodrow Wilson to make an on-the-scene historical record of World War I. Subsequently, he was attached at one time or another to the armies of all the Allied nations. The contacts he made in Europe and the Middle East, especially with Gen. Edmund Allenby and Col. T. E. Lawrence (Lawrence of Arabia), became material for his lectures when he returned to the United States in 1919, as did his pictorial record of the German revolution. Following a successful lecture series, he toured the world in 1922. In 1924 he published his first and most popular book, *With Lawrence in Arabia*. During 1926–1927 he made a 28,000 mile flight around the world to study new developments in aviation. A series of other travels and other books followed. In 1930 he became a network newscaster for the Columbia Broadcasting System (CBS) and began a radio career that lasted more than 40 years. His radio duties did not deter him from continuing his world travels. In 1935 he filmed and narrated the first of many travelogues for Twentieth Century–Fox studios, and he continued writing books about his experiences and the places he had been—Australia, India, Burma, the Arctic, and many more lands and regions. During World War II he traveled to virtually all the war zones, from which he broadcast vivid reports. In 1949, at the invitation of the Dalai Lama, he traveled to Tibet, becoming one of the few Americans ever to do so. He did little television newscasting, preferring to work on radio, but from 1957 to 1959 he was the host of the TV travel series "High Adventure." His final broadcast of "Lowell Thomas and the News" was on May 14, 1976. He died on August 29, 1981, in Pawling, New York.

Thomas, Martha Carey (1857–1935), educator and feminist. Born in Baltimore on January 2, 1857, Miss Thomas graduated from Cornell University in 1877. After a year of graduate work at The Johns Hopkins University, she went to Europe to work on a doctorate in linguistics. After three years (1879–1882) at Leipzig, she was refused a degree because she was a woman, so she applied to Zurich, was accepted for examination, and received her Ph.D. in 1882. After a year of further work at the Sorbonne in Paris she returned to the United States and in 1884 was appointed professor of English and dean of the newly opened Bryn Mawr College for women; she was the first woman college faculty member in the country to hold the title "dean." At Bryn Mawr she organized the undergraduate studies program and started the first graduate program at any women's school. In 1885 she joined in founding the Bryn Mawr School for Girls in Baltimore. She also established scholarships for Europeans to study at Bryn Mawr, the first such graduate scholarships in the United States. In 1894 Miss Thomas became president of the college and held the post until her retirement in 1922. In addition to working for high educational standards for women, she championed the cause of woman suffrage and worked for the passage of the Nineteenth Amendment to the

Constitution. Serving the cause of women's rights in many ways, she was president of the National College Equal Suffrage League from 1906 to 1913, she organized the Summer School for Women Workers in Industry in 1921, and she prevailed upon the Johns Hopkins Medical School to accept woman students. She was a founder in 1900 of the Association to Promote Scientific Research by Women and of the International Federation of University Women. She died at her home in Philadelphia on December 2, 1935.

Thomas, Norman Mattoon (1884–1968), social reformer and political leader. Born on November 20, 1884, in Marion, Ohio, Thomas was educated at Bucknell University and at Princeton, where he graduated at the head of his class of 1905. After devoting some time to travel and to social-settlement work, he entered Union Theological Seminary. He graduated in 1911, was ordained in the Presbyterian church, and became pastor of the East Harlem Church in New York City. In his pastorate, and in his work with the American Parish, a settlement house, he was impressed with the problems of poverty; abandoning the conservatism of his youth, he gradually adopted the ideas of the Social Gospel as promulgated by Walter Rauschenbusch. The outbreak of World War I strengthened his conviction that the major political parties were incapable of solving the overriding problems of society. By 1918 he had moved from pacifism to socialism. Resigning from his pulpit (he left the ministry in 1931) and joining the Socialist party in that year, he also became secretary of the Fellowship of Reconciliation (FOR) and founded *The World Tomorrow*, which he edited until 1921. In 1920 he helped found the American Civil Liberties Union (ACLU). In 1921–1922 he was an associate editor of the *Nation* and from then until the mid-1930s was codirector of the League for Industrial Democracy. He was the Socialist party candidate for governor of New York in 1924, for mayor of New York City in 1925 and 1929, and, becoming the leader of the party after the death of Eugene V. Debs in 1926, ran for president in every election from 1928 to 1948. He was an indefatigable speaker and writer, and notable among his many books were *Is Conscience a Crime?*, 1927, on conscientious objection to military service; *As I See It*, 1932; *Socialism on the Defensive*, 1938; *We Have a Future*, 1941; *A Socialist's Faith*, 1951; *The Test of Freedom*, 1954; *The Prerequisites for Peace*, 1959; and *Socialism Reexamined*, 1963. He effectively shaped the policies of the Socialist party for more than 40 years, and, while offering the party's program as an alternative to capitalism, was remarkably successful in keeping it free of the taint of Communism in the minds of the American public. His staunch opposition to both Communism and Fascism, together with his deeply felt social concerns, made him a "conscience" candidate for many independent voters over the years. Many of his proposals—for low-cost housing, the five-day work week, minimum-wage laws, and the abolition of child labor—ultimately found their way into legislation. A brilliant speaker, he was constantly in demand and continued to lecture several times weekly until his death in New York City on December 20, 1968.

Thomas, Seth (1785–1859), clock manufacturer. Born in Wolcott, Connecticut, on August 19, 1785, Thomas was apprenticed as a carpenter and joiner in his early teens. For a number of years he worked in the building trades, but in 1807 he was invited by clockmaker Eli Terry to join him and Silas Hoadley in a manufacturing partnership at Plymouth, Connecticut. They fulfilled a three-year contract to make 4000 clocks, and in 1810 Thomas and Hoadley bought the business from Terry. Two years later Thomas sold his share of the factory and went into business for himself at Plymouth Hollow, now Thomaston. He paid Terry for the rights to manufacture his successful shelf clock, and the new factory flourished. In 1853 he organized the Seth Thomas Clock Company. He died in Plymouth, Connecticut, on January 29, 1859. His son, also named Seth, continued the business.

Thomas, Theodore (1835–1905), musician and conductor. Born in Esens, Germany, on October 11, 1835, Christian Friedrich Theodore Thomas showed a talent for music as a child and was trained by his musician father. He made his violin debut in Germany at the age of ten. In 1845 the Thomas family emigrated to the United States and settled in New York City. Young Theodore played the violin at social events and in theaters to supplement his family's meager income. At the age of fifteen he set off on his own on a performing tour of the South. Three years later he obtained a job as a violinist with an orchestra, and the experience aroused his interest in orchestra conducting. For the next several years he played with chamber music groups, including one he organized in 1855 with William Mason, as an accompanist, and with the orchestra at the Academy of Music in New York City. In 1860 he conducted the Academy orchestra for the first time, and the next year he became its regular conductor. For the next 30 years he was the conductor of orchestras in and around New York City. He founded in 1862 his own Thomas Orchestra, which gave concerts in the city and on tour all over the United States until 1878. In 1862 he also became coconductor of the Brooklyn Philharmonic Society, and fifteen years later, he was invited to become conductor of the New York Philharmonic. Except for an interlude spent in Cincinnati with the College of Music, 1878–1880, he remained with the Brooklyn and New York orchestras until 1891, when he accepted an offer to take over the Chicago Symphony. While in Chicago he also served as musical director for the World's Columbian Exposition of 1893. Thomas was an orchestra conductor at the time when urban cultural opportunities and patterns were just emerging in the United States; there were few symphony orchestras, and most Americans had never heard one. It was Thomas's goal to make good music available to more people by his tours, for which he arranged programs that were balanced and yet designed for wide acceptance. He remained with the Chicago Symphony until his death in Chicago on January 4, 1905.

Thompson, Benjamin (1753–1814), Count Rumford, colonial figure and scientist. Born in Woburn, Massachusetts, on March 26, 1753, Thompson combined a life of government service with strong scientific interests. He was apprenticed at thirteen to a merchant in Salem, and during three years there managed to study mathematics and science. He also studied medicine in Boston and taught school for a while. In 1772 he was commissioned a major in the 2nd New Hampshire regiment. With the onset of the American Revolution his loyalties were divided between Britain and the colonies, but when he was refused a commission in George Washington's army he went to England. He received an appointment in the Colonial Office and within a few months was secretary for the Georgia colony. In 1780 he became undersecretary of state for the Northern Department. From 1781 to 1783, with the rank of lieutenant colonel, he saw combat service with the British army on Long Island and in the Carolinas. Having returned to England in late 1783, he decided to tour Europe. In Strasbourg he met Prince Maximilian of Bavaria, who encouraged him to live in Bavaria and to work for the government there. Receiving permission to do so from the King of England, who also knighted him in February 1784, Thompson settled in Munich in 1784 and spent the next 11 years in the Bavarian civil service. By 1788 he was head of the war department and councilor of state to the Elector, and also held high military rank. He reorganized the Bavarian army and greatly improved the living conditions of the soldiers. He also instituted welfare measures for the impoverished and unemployed of the state. In 1791 he was created a count of the Holy Roman Empire by the Elector, and selected the name Rumford, after the New Hampshire home town of his wife (it is now Concord). After a year in England, 1795–1796, during which he published the first of his four volumes of *Essays, Political, Economical, and Philosophical,* 1796–1802, Thompson returned to Bavaria for two years as head of the regency council. In 1798 he was sent to Britain as minister from Bavaria, but English officials had changed their attitude about allowing British subjects to serve foreign governments, so he remained in London, relieved of diplomatic duties. For the next three years he occupied himself mostly with the founding and building of the Royal Institution, chartered by George III in 1800. In 1801 he visited Munich to help organize the Bavarian Academy of Arts and Sciences. In 1802, the year he published a volume of *Philosophical Papers,* he left England permanently and settled in France. From 1803 he was a member of the Institute of France, before which he delivered many of his scientific papers. Having separated from his first wife in 1775, he married the widow of the French chemist

Antoine Lavoisier in 1805. They separated four years later, and he went to live at Auteuil, now part of Paris. During his years as a public official Thompson's interest in science and mechanics never flagged, and he studied and experimented wherever he lived. He experimented with gunpowder, firearms, and especially with heat, and kept up a continuous correspondence with men of science in England, the United States, and Europe. As early as 1779 he had been elected to the Royal Society in London, and over the years he read several papers at its meetings. He established the society's Rumford Medal, as well as the Rumford Medal of the American Academy of Arts and Sciences, and he endowed the Rumford chair of science at Harvard. His most noteworthy study was the presentation to the Royal Society in 1798 of his paper "Enquiry Concerning the Source of Heat Which is Excited by Friction," in which he developed his theory, formed as a result of cannon-boring experiments in Munich in 1796, that heat is a mechanical phenomena, the result of and itself a form of motion. This theory, correct in all essential points, contrasted sharply with the prevailing notion of heat as a substance. Most of Rumford's greatest work was on the topic of heat. He studied convection currents, radiation and heat losses, and was the first to observe the anomalous expansion of water when cooled below $39°F$. Many practical advances resulted from his studies, including improved cooking methods, improved chimney flues, steam-heating systems, wide-rim carriage wheels, and improved lamps. Among his inventions were a calorimeter, a photometer, and the drip-coffee maker. He died at his home in Auteuil on August 21, 1814.

Thompson, David (1770–1857), explorer and geographer. Born in London on April 30, 1770, Thompson grew up in poverty and was apprenticed in 1784 to the Hudson's Bay Company as a fur trader. During his apprenticeship he developed a great interest in mathematics and astronomy. From 1789 until 1812 he made extensive explorations of all western Canada and the northwestern section of the present United States, traveling tens of thousands of miles alone and charting the best trade and travel routes in an enormous area. He kept careful journals, and he drew accurate maps of the regions he visited. In 1797 he left the Hudson's Bay Company and joined the North West Company, for which he continued his field service until 1812. In 1798 he located the source of the Mississippi and followed the St. Louis River through Minnesota into Lake Superior. He discovered the source of the Columbia River in 1807 and followed the river's whole course in 1811. In three years, from 1808 to 1810, he explored the territory comprising the present states of Montana, Idaho, and Washington, and established trading posts in the region. His explorations revealed an area of nearly 2 million square miles of Canada and northwestern United States, and during 1812–1814 he drew a great map, 5 feet by 10½ feet, of the region, and it remains remarkable in its detail and accuracy. He spent the ten years from 1816 to 1826 as a member of an official commission surveying the boundary between the United States and Canada from the St. Lawrence River to Lake of the Woods. He retired in 1836 and settled eventually in Longueuil, Quebec, where he died on February 10, 1857. Unfortunately, his journals were not published until 60 years later, and thus little was known during his lifetime of his enormous contributions to geography. With the publication of *David Thompson's Narrative of his Explorations*, 1916, however, he was recognized as one of the great land geographers of history.

Thompson, Dorothy (1894–1961), journalist. Born in Lancaster, New York, on July 9, 1894, Miss Thompson grew up there and in Chicago, where she attended the Lewis Institute. She graduated from Syracuse University in 1914 and for the next several years lived in New York City, doing social work and campaigning for woman suffrage. In 1920 she sailed for Europe and, while still on board ship, decided on a career in journalism. She spent the next nine years in Europe, establishing a name for herself as a reporter. She worked as a foreign correspondent for the *Philadelphia Ledger* and then for the *New York Post*, and from 1924 to 1928 she was chief of the *Post's* Berlin office. While in Europe Miss Thompson married a Hungarian author named Josef Bard in 1923, divorced him in 1927, and married novelist Sinclair Lewis in 1928. On returning to the United States after their marriage, they divided their time between Woodstock, Vermont, and New York City, although Miss Thompson traveled again to Europe in the early 1930s. They were divorced in 1942. From 1936 to 1941 she wrote the column "On the Record" for the *New York Herald Tribune;* the syndication of the column to other papers made her one of the most widely read journalists in the country. From 1937 she was a regular columnist for the *Ladies' Home Journal*. During the 1930s she took a vehemently anti-Nazi position in foreign affairs and lectured widely and effectively against the Hitler regime in Germany. Events in Germany drew her attention to the refugee problem, and she wrote articles urging the United States to admit refugees who were being driven out of Europe by Fascism. She continued her newspaper column, after 1941 for the Bell Syndicate. By that time she had published many books including *The New Russia*, 1928; *I Saw Hitler*, 1932; *Refugees*, 1938; *Political Guide*, 1938; *Let the Record Speak*, 1939; *Listen, Hans*, 1942; and *The Courage To Be Happy*, 1957. After the death that year of her third husband, Maxim Kopf, she retired to write her autobiography. She died in Lisbon, Portugal, on January 31, 1961.

Thompson, James Walter (1847–1928), advertising executive. Born in Pittsfield, Massachusetts, on October 28, 1847, Thompson grew up there and in Fostoria, Ohio. During the Civil War he joined the Union navy and took part in the blockade of Confederate shipping from 1863 until 1865. In 1867 he settled in New York City and went to work for William J. Carlton, an advertising agent. Thompson's job was to purchase space in magazines and retail the space to business firms, which used it for their own advertising. Thompson did not create ads as such; he merely marketed available copy space. By 1878 he had accumulated enough money to buy out Carlton and he changed the name of the firm to the J. Walter Thompson Company. As an agency, it was the Thompson company's task to sell both the magazines and businessmen on the idea of advertising, for many firms considered it demeaning and unethical to advertise their products, and some journals considered it undignified to give space to advertisements. Thompson's perseverance overcame both of these obstacles and turned his company into the most successful advertising firm of his time. Between 1880 and 1890 advertising in magazines increased by 300 percent and Thompson enjoyed a near-monopoly on such advertising, coming to represent the nation's 30 leading magazines as well as several dozen smaller ones. He also sold space in newspapers for ads. Some of his more famous promotions were for the Eastman Kodak Company, Pabst Blue Ribbon Beer, and Prudential Insurance (for which his company devised the famous "Rock of Gibraltar" slogan). By 1900 J. Walter Thompson was one of the three leading ad agencies in the United States, and the only one with an overseas branch. In 1896 the agency was incorporated and much of the public issue of stock was sold to employees of the firm. In 1916, convinced that the great days of advertising were past, Thompson sold his interest in the agency to the manager of one of his branch offices. He maintained an interest in advertising for the rest of his life, but occupied himself also with his hobbies, especially yachting. He died in New York City on October 16, 1928.

Thompson, Smith (1768–1843), justice of the Supreme Court. Born in Amenia, New York, on January 17, 1768, Thompson graduated from the College of New Jersey (now Princeton) in 1788. He subsequently studied law under James Kent and was admitted to the bar in 1792. He settled in Poughkeepsie, New York, and began practice, and was soon also active in state politics. After a term in the state legislature in 1800, he was appointed an associate justice of the state supreme court in 1802. He served on the court until 1818, and was the chief justice after 1814. President James Monroe appointed him secretary of the navy in 1818, and he held that post for more than four years, resigning in August 1823 to accept an appointment to the Supreme Court. He hesitated to take it at first because his political ambitions led him to hope to be nominated for the presidency in 1824. When he was sure the nomination would not be his, he accepted the position on the Court and remained there until 1843. He ran for the governorship of New York in 1828 but lost by a substantial margin, possibly owing to his decision not to resign from the Court before seeking the office. As a member of the Court, Thompson was generally an antinationalist and was therefore opposed to many of the views of Chief Justice John Marshall. One of his most noteworthy opinions was in *Kendall* v. *United States*, 1838, in one passage of which he rejected the theory that a president, by virtue of his authority to execute the laws, can enforce his own interpretation of the Constitution as against that of the Congress as expressed in legislation or the courts as expressed in mandates. It was a theory attributed to Andrew Jackson, but one that had roots in the writings of Thomas Jefferson. The offending statement, after its oral delivery, was expunged from the written opinion because of the attorney general's insistence that the theory it embodied had not been used in arguing the case. Other notable opinions were those in *Ogden* v. *Saunders*, 1827 (concurring); *Cherokee Nation* v. *Georgia*, 1831 (dissenting); and *Charles River Bridge* v. *Warren Bridge*, 1837 (dissenting). Thompson died in Poughkeepsie, New York, on December 18, 1843.

Thomson, Elihu (1853–1937), electrical engineer and inventor. Born in Manchester, England, on March 29, 1853, Thomson emigrated to the United States with his family five years later. He had an excellent record at Central High School in Philadelphia, and after graduation in 1870 he joined the faculty. Acquaintance with another faculty member, Edwin J. Houston, influenced Thomson to experiment almost exclusively with electricity, and together they studied dynamos and arc lighting. They designed improvements in both, and in 1879 they opened a factory for the manufacture of arc-lighting equipment. A year later Thomson left Philadelphia for New Britain, Connecticut, and a position as an electrical engineer with a new plant intended to develop the equipment he and Houston had designed and patented. The company was bought by businessmen who moved the factory to Lynn, Massachusetts, in 1883. Under Thomson's engineering guidance, it expanded into manufacturing virtually all types of electrical equipment then in general use. He discovered the alternating-current (AC) repulsion phenomenon, which laid the basis for alternating-current motors. He also developed the resistance electric welding process, the high-frequency generator, the high-frequency transformer, and the three-coil generator. In 1892 the Thomson-Houston Electric Company and the Edison General Electric Company combined to form General Electric (GE), with plant and offices in Schenectady, New York. Thomson remained with the company as a consultant, but continued to live and do research in Massachusetts. In 1894 he became a lecturer in electrical engineering at the Massachusetts Institute of Technology (MIT), a post he held for the rest of his life, and during 1920–1922 he served as acting president of MIT. The discovery of X rays in 1895 interested him, and he turned his attention to improving the design of X-ray apparatus. His entire career was an outstanding synthesis of pure and applied science; he was among the first to recognize the need for industrial research, and in the range of his investigation and invention he was without peer among the pioneers in electricity. He patented more than 700 inventions and designs. Thomson died at his home in Swampscott, Massachusetts, on March 13, 1937.

Thomson, Virgil Garnett (1896–   ), composer and music critic. Born in Kansas City, Missouri, on November 25, 1896, Thomson studied piano and organ from the age of five, and also studied musical theory and voice from an early age. He graduated from Kansas City Polytechnic Institute and Junior College and enlisted in the army in 1917. He entered Harvard and wrote his first piece, a song based on Amy Lowell's poem "Vernal Equinox," in 1920. In 1922 he studied under Nadia Boulanger in Paris. He graduated from Harvard in 1923 and studied counterpoint and conducting for a year in New York City at the Mannes Music School, afterward returning to Harvard as an instructor. In 1925 he settled in Paris, where he lived for ten years. There he wrote the dissonant but traditionally formed *Sonata da Chiesa* in 1926, the ultramodern *Symphony on a Hymn Tune* in 1928, and the more simply stated *Symphony Number 2* in 1931, both of the latter works drawing upon American folk themes. He based a cantata on Gertrude Stein's *Capitals, Capitals*, shortly after meeting her in 1926, and with her as librettist wrote the opera *Four Saints in Three Acts*, which premiered in 1934, and *The Mother of Us All*, an opera-collage of American historical, folk, and contemporary musical themes, depicting the life of Susan B. Anthony, which was first performed in 1947. He wrote scores for films that included *The Plow That Broke the Plains*, 1936; *The River*, 1937; *Louisiana Story*, 1948, for which he won a Pulitzer Prize; Paddy Chayefsky's *The Goddess*, 1958; and *Voyage to America*, 1964. In addition he wrote 100 musical "portraits" of such personalities as Pablo Picasso, Aaron Copland, Fiorello H. La Guardia, and Dorothy Thompson, and "landscapes" of Paris—*The Seine at Night*, 1947—and of Missouri—*Wheat Fields at Noon*, 1948. He also wrote liturgical music, including *Missa Pro Defunctis*, which premiered under his direction in 1960; the ballet *Filling Station*, 1937; organ music, piano sonatas, flute and cello concertos, and songs based on American folk themes and French, Spanish, and Latin texts. As music critic for the *New York Herald Tribune* from 1940 to 1954 he wrote articles that were gathered with other essays into *The Musical Scene*, 1945; *The Art of Judging Music*, 1948; and *Music Right and Left*, 1951. He also wrote *The State of Music*, 1939, which established him as a witty, opinionated commentator, and *Virgil Thomson on Virgil Thomson*, 1966.

Thoreau, Henry David (1817–1862), naturalist, philosopher, and author. Born in Concord, Massachusetts, on July 12, 1817, Thoreau was able to enter Harvard in 1833, despite his family's lack of means; he graduated four years later in the same week that Ralph Waldo Emerson, also of Concord and Thoreau's principal mentor, delivered his famous "American Scholar" address to the Harvard Phi Beta Kappa society. After a brief and unpleasant time teaching school in Concord —he resigned when his refusal to employ corporal punishment was objected to—he worked in the family business of pencil making until 1839 when, with his brother John, he opened a private school. The school lasted for two years, during which the two introduced an educational innovation—field trips for nature study. Henry then accepted an invitation to live with Emerson, nominally earning his keep as general handyman while devoting much of his time to reading, writing poetry and essays, talking with the members of the Transcendental Club that met with Emerson (he became one of the group's members), and rambling through the woods and fields. He assisted from time to time in editing the group's literary journal, the *Dial*, and occasionally published essays and verse in it. His reading from college days onward was concentrated in the English nature and mystical poets, Oriental philosophy, and the contemporary romantic literature of Europe; his writing was encouraged by Emerson, who proposed subjects, edited his pieces, and sought publication for them. In 1843 he went as tutor to the home of Emerson's brother William on Staten Island, New York, and during a year there confirmed his dislike for urban society by his visits to New York City. He returned to Concord in 1844 and resumed his pencil making. The following year he brought to fruition a project long planned. Moving to the shore of nearby Walden Pond, on land provided by Emerson, he built a house, planted a garden, and settled down to a two-year experiment in living the simple, self-reliant, contemplative life of a free spirit. While recording his experiences, observations, and reflections in his voluminous journals, he also wrote his first book, *A Week on the Concord and Merrimack Rivers*, which, while cast in the form of a record of a boat trip made with his brother in 1839, was largely drawn from his journals of that and subsequent years. His earlier failure to find a publisher for his work was repeated and in 1849 he issued the book at his own expense; few copies were sold. He was meanwhile at work on his second book, *Walden, or Life in the Woods*; this, too, depended upon several years of journal entries as well as the two years at Walden. Discouraged and in debt, he withheld it from publication until 1854. In 1849 he published his famous essay "Resistance to Civil Government" (later "On the Duty of Civil Disobedience") in a minor periodical. In it he told of his one-day imprisonment in 1846 for refusing, because of his antislavery views, to pay a poll tax levied to support the Mexican War; the essay was to be his most influential work, later impressing such people as Mahatma Gandhi and Martin Luther King, Jr. After a second period, 1847–1849, under Emerson's roof, he returned to his family home and remained there for the rest of his life, working in the pencil business and doing surveying for his living, and traveling occasionally to the Maine woods, Canada, and Cape Cod; records of these journeys were published posthumously in book form as *Excursions*, 1863, *The Maine Woods*, 1864, *Cape Cod*, 1865, and *A Yankee in Canada*, 1866. His vivid and fruitful *Journal* was published in 14 volumes in 1906. In all his works Thoreau urged the claim of the single, free individual determined to find and confront the world of reality; the civilization built on industry and commerce and their inauthentic concerns he viewed as a madness leading men blindly into "lives of quiet desperation." He prescribed no single alternative life; he counseled men only to examine themselves, to know nature, and to act and live truthfully in light of their own discoveries. He was confident, however, that a life lived in harmony with nature and itself would have as its first precept "Simplify, simplify." Through most of his life he had little contact, apart from his slight success at the local lyceum, with the public or public causes; during the 1850s, however, the movement to abolish slavery enlisted his sympathy, and he spoke often in its behalf. In 1859 he sprang to the defense of John Brown after the Harpers Ferry raid and did much to create the view of Brown as a martyr. Thoreau's last years were spent under the shadow of tuberculosis; he died in Concord, Massachusetts, on May 6, 1862. Thoreau's reputation as a writer and philosopher came late in his life and he remained a minor figure for decades after his death. Genuine appreciation of his achievements came with the twentieth century, when he came to be thought of as one of the great figures of American literary and intellectual history. He was elected to the Hall of Fame in 1960.

Thorfinn Karlsefni (980?– ?), explorer and colonist. Born in Iceland about 980, Thorfinn Karlsefni came from an aristocratic family and is mentioned in the *Vinland Sagas* as "a man of considerable wealth" on his arrival in Greenland in 1003. Norwegians in search of more land for stockfarming had begun migrating to Greenland about 986 under the leadership of Eric Thorvaldsson (Eric the Red). By the time Thorfinn arrived, the coast of North America had been sighted by Bjarni Herjolfsson, and Leif Ericsson had already made his exploratory voyage in about 1000. In hope of finding a milder climate and more arable land, Norse colonizing expeditions soon went out to the newly discovered Vinland. The second of these was led by Thorfinn, who after his arrival in Greenland had married Gudrid, the widow of Thorstein Ericsson, Leif's brother. Dates of departure for the expedition vary, but it may have been as early as 1004 or as late as 1020. They sailed in three ships with 250 men and women, in addition to cattle and household goods. They struck a coast they identified as the Helluland of Bjarni and Leif, sailed southward and landed first probably at a site visited by Leif on the northern tip of Newfoundland, possibly at L'Anse au Meadow, where Norse ruins have been found, and there Thorfinn's wife gave birth to a son, Snorri, the first white child born in America. After a severe winter, the settlers moved south to a better site—it may have been in what is now Massachusetts—where they passed one more winter. After several encounters with the native inhabitants, whom the Norsemen called Skrellings, the colonists became discouraged, and after one more winter, dissent growing among their ranks, they decided to return to Greenland. Thorfinn and his family spent one winter in Greenland, then returned to his home in Iceland. At this point he disappears from history.

Thorndike, Edward Lee (1874–1949), psychologist. Born on August 31, 1874, in Williamsburg, Massachusetts, Thorndike earned a B.A. from Wesleyan University in Connecticut in 1895, a second B.A. in 1896 from Harvard, and his M.A. in 1897, also from Harvard. His dissertation for a doctoral degree from Columbia in 1898 was in the area, then revolutionary, of animal psychology. He taught for one year at the women's college of Western Reserve University, and spent the rest of his career (after 1899) at Columbia's Teachers College, becoming a full professor in 1904. His theories of experimental psychology and his work in the quantitative measurement of intelligence and learning ability were of far-reaching influence in the development of learning theory. In the field of education, he wrote many basic textbooks. A pioneer in applying the results of animal experiments to human psychology, he devised such standard testing methods as the maze, the puzzle box, and signal or choice reaction. He applied scales of quantitative measurement to skills in reading, composition, language, and handwriting, and to behavior, intelligence, vocational aptitude, human nature, motivation, the effects of heredity on intelligence and character, and the interrelation of abilities. During World War I he helped to devise intelligence tests for the army. He retired from teaching in 1940 and continued writing, producing alone or in collaboration more than 500 articles and books, best known among which were his *Educational Psychology,* three volumes, 1913–1914; *Human Nature and Social Order,* 1940; and *Man and His Works,* 1943. He also compiled the *Thorndike-Century Senior Dictionary, The Thorndike-Century Junior Dictionary,* and *The Teacher's Book of 30,000 Words,* the last with Irving Lorge. Thorndike died on August 9, 1949, in Montrose, New York.

Thornton, William (1759–1828), architect and inventor. Born on the West Indian island of Tortola, now one of the British Virgin Islands, on May 20, 1759, Thornton attended the University of Edinburgh from 1781 to 1784 and graduated from Aberdeen University in 1784 with a degree in medicine. He did not follow the calling of physician, however, but found more to his interest a wide range of other activities that involved architecture, painting, linguistics, military arts, and abolitionism. He emigrated to the United States

in 1787, became a citizen the following year, and settled in Philadelphia. During the 1780s he experimented with John Fitch on paddle-wheel steamboats. While living on Tortola in 1792 he was informed of the competition for architectural designs for the U.S. Capitol, which was to be erected at Washington, D.C. One of his designs, after some modification, was accepted, and after some further changes and controversy, the exterior of the building was built according to Thornton's plans and in part under his supervision. Thornton had no training or experience in architecture, which led those more knowledgeable in the field to find flaws in his designs, and his lack of experience made it necessary for Benjamin H. Latrobe, who had designed the interior, to replace him as overseer of construction of the building. Thornton also designed a number of other buildings: The Library Company's building in Philadelphia, 1789, the Octagon House in Washington, and Tudor Place in Georgetown, D.C. He also supplied Thomas Jefferson with sketches for buildings at the proposed University of Virginia in 1817. In 1794 Thornton settled in Washington and was appointed a city commissioner. He remained in that post until 1802, when President Thomas Jefferson appointed him commissioner of patents. Among his own patents were those for improvements in boilers and firearms. Besides attending to a variety of business interests, he pursued his various avocations, and among other things promoted President George Washington's goal of a national university in the nation's capital. As early as 1788 he had taken an interest in the slavery issue and proposed a few years later the colonizing of ex-slaves in Africa. When the American Colonization Society was organized in 1817 he became an active member. He died in Washington on March 28, 1828.

Thorpe, James Francis (1888–1953), "Jim," athlete. Born on May 28, 1888, near Prague, Oklahoma, of Indian ancestry, Jim Thorpe received some early education and, mainly because of his athletic skills, was able to matriculate at Carlisle Indian School in Pennsylvania in 1907. There he devoted himself primarily to football, which he played extraordinarily well under the coaching of Glenn S. "Pop" Warner. He was named a halfback on Walter Camp's All-American teams in 1911 and 1912, and he helped make Carlisle a football power in the country. In 1912 he scored 25 touchdowns and 198 points. That same year he went to Stockholm to participate in track and field events at the Olympic Games, and achieved the unprecedented and never repeated feat of winning gold medals in both the decathlon and pentathlon. He could justifiably claim to be the world's greatest athlete on the strength of the performance, and he was so pronounced by Sweden's King Gustav V. Later, however, he admitted that he had played semiprofessional baseball during the summer vacation of 1911, thereby losing his amateur status, and his gold medals and his trophy were taken from him and his name was expunged from the Olympic record books at the insistence of the Amateur Athletic Union (AAU). In the meantime he had begun to play baseball seriously. He was signed by John J. McGraw in 1913 for $4500 per year, but he spent most of his time with the New York Giants on the bench. He stayed with the Giants for two years, moved to the Cincinnati Reds in 1915 then returned to the Giants during 1917–1919; he finished his baseball career in 1919 with the Boston Braves, where he played in 60 games and batted .327. He also played professional football, mostly for the Canton Bulldogs, who also were a power in the land because of his strength and skill. He was totally contemptuous of training rules and a terror on defense, wearing a "slightly illegal" shoulder pad with an outer covering of sheet metal that destroyed opposing ball carriers. Few records remain of his achievements before 1920, and by that year, when the American Professional Football Association was formed, his career was nearing its end, although as late as 1929 he made an appearance with the Chicago Cardinals. But he was the most famous football player in the country, and the association, later the National Football League (NFL), named him its first president. Lighthearted, erratic, and unpredictable, he was a bad executive, and he was replaced in 1921. In later years he fell on hard times. Often unable to find work except for occasional stunt roles for motion pictures, he lived the rest of his life in relative obscurity. He died in Lomita, California, on March 28, 1953. In 1950 an Associated Press (AP) poll had ranked him the outstanding American athlete of the twentieth century. The towns of Mauch Chunk and East Mauch Chunk, Pennsylvania, were joined and renamed Jim Thorpe in his honor in 1954. In 1973 the AAU voted to restore his amateur status for the period 1909–1912, thus removing a major obstacle to restoration of his Olympic records and medals.

Thorpe, Thomas Bangs (1815–1878), humorist and painter. Born in Westfield, Massachusetts, on March 1, 1815, Thorpe attended school in New York City and studied art under John Quidor. His painting "Ichabod Crane" was exhibited at the American Academy of Fine Arts in 1833 in New York City. He studied at Wesleyan University in Connecticut for slightly more than two years, but in 1836, for reasons of health, went to live in New Orleans. He remained there, editing several local newspapers, until 1853. While living in the South he became closely acquainted with what was then the western frontier, and he took to writing descriptive and humorous frontier pieces. His most famous story was "The Big Bear of Arkansas," published in 1841. His local-color articles were collected in a volume entitled *Mysteries of the Backwoods* in 1846, and *The Hive of the Bee Hunter*, 1854, contained humorous works and sketches. During the Mexican War Thorpe traveled with Gen. Zachary Taylor's army and subsequently wrote three books dealing with his experiences. In 1853 he moved back to New York City and continued his writing and for two years, from 1860 to 1862, he was co-owner and editor of the *Spirit of the Times*. During the Civil War he served in New Orleans as a colonel on the staff of Gen. Benjamin F. Butler. Back in New York City after the war, he worked at the customhouse and continued his painting and writing. He died in New York on September 20, 1878.

Thurber, James Grover (1894–1961), humorist and cartoonist. Born on December 8, 1894, in Columbus, Ohio, Thurber was the son of a tall, slender man who favored derby hats and lost continually in efforts to establish himself in politics, and a hearty woman who once aspired toward an acting career and staunchly refused to wear black when she passed eighty because she insisted it would make her look old. At the age of six, through an accident while playing with his brother, he lost the vision of his left eye. Although he continually bumped into furniture and missed doorways about the house, he made light of his injury and at a later age joked that if ever he wrote his memoirs they would surely be called "Long Time No See." He attended the Columbus public schools and matriculated at Ohio State University in 1913, where he was bookish and apparently rather mangy in appearance. There he met Elliott Nugent, a big man on campus, later to become a collaborator with him on plays, notably *The Male Animal*, 1940, and in other ventures. When World War I began, Thurber left school to enlist but was rejected because of his eyesight. Depressed but not daunted, he proceeded to France, where he obtained a job as a code clerk for the U.S. State Department. Returning to Columbus in 1922, he reported for the *Columbus Dispatch*, married, returned to Paris with his wife, and became a reporter for the European edition of the *Chicago Tribune* and for the *Paris Herald*. Unfortunately, his total salary was $12 a week and the Thurbers left Paris in financial straits. They went to New York City where he began writing for the *Evening Post*. Intrigued by the *New Yorker* magazine, which had recently begun publication, he began submitting stories and after 20 rejection notices was finally published. After that he became a leading contributor to the magazine. He met E. B. White, editor of the chatty "Talk of the Town" section of the magazine, at a social affair and convinced him that he should be made a staff member. When Thurber reported for work he found that he was to be managing editor of the magazine, under Harold W. Ross. But he did not like administration and shifted back to work with White on "Talk of the Town." With White he wrote *Is Sex Necessary?*, 1929, later reissued. He left the magazine in 1933 to devote full time to writing and completed numerous short stories, plays, and novels, including *My Life and Hard Times*, 1933; *Let Your Mind Alone!*, 1937; *Fables for Our Time*, 1940; *The Thurber Carnival*, 1945, later made into a successful Broadway musical; *The Beast in Me and Other Animals*, 1948; *The 13 Clocks*, 1950; *The Thurber Album*, 1952; and *The Years with*

Ross, 1959, a biography of his old boss at the *New Yorker*. His pen was equally facile and whimsical in writing or drawing, and many of his books consisted largely of cartoons. His most famous short story, "The Secret Life of Walter Mitty," pictured a humble little man with a vivid imagination which led him into scenes of passion and adventure. Constantly jolting him back to reality was his bombastic wife, who inevitably reminded him that he hadn't dumped the garbage or bought food for the dog. The character became a prototype and the story a part of American tradition. Its qualities typified Thurber's work, which poked fun at moderns who made tragedies out of their maladjustments. He treated the devilish aspects of life as if they were commonplace, and in his writing and drawing transformed them into so much quiet hysteria. He lived for many years in West Cornwall, Connecticut, and died in New York City on November 2, 1961.

Thurmond, James Strom (1902–), public official. Born in Edgefield, South Carolina, on December 5, 1902, J. Strom Thurmond graduated from Clemson College (now University) in 1923. For six years he taught high school, and from 1929 to 1933 was superintendent of education for Edgefield County. Having studied law privately and by correspondence course, he was admitted to the bar in 1930 and joined his father's law firm. From 1930 to 1938 he served as city and county attorney, and he was a member of the state senate from 1933 to 1938. He was appointed a judge of the circuit court in 1938. When the United States entered World War II, Thurmond took a leave of absence from the bench to go into the army. He saw duty in Europe until V-E Day in 1945, then was transferred to the Pacific theater. After his discharge in 1946 he resumed his duties on the court for a few months but resigned in the same year to run for governor of South Carolina. He was elected over a field of ten other candidates and served until 1951. His tenure as governor was a progressive one for the state, particularly in the field of education. The state appropriated money for libraries, adult education, colleges and universities, and school bus service. He also did a good deal to improve educational opportunities for blacks. At the 1948 Democratic national convention he led the Southern delegates opposed to President Harry S. Truman's civil-rights plank. The Southern Democrats who were disgruntled at the convention's results held their own gathering in Birmingham, Alabama, in July and Thurmond was chosen to be the presidential candidate of their States' Rights Democratic party. The unrealized hope of the "Dixiecrats," as they were also called, was to keep any one candidate from getting enough electoral votes to win the election; Thurmond won 39, but failed to deadlock the election. Thurmond ran unsuccessfully for the U.S. Senate in 1950, then retired to his law practice until 1954, when he was appointed to the Senate to fill a vacancy. He had actually been elected to the Senate in November 1954 as a write-in candidate (the first senator in U.S. history so elected), but he resigned in 1956 in compliance with a promise to the electorate. Elected to fill the vacancy thus created, he was reelected in 1960 and again in 1966, but then as a Republican. His advocacy of states' rights had led him to leave the Democratic party in 1964 when Barry M. Goldwater became the Republican nominee for the presidency, and Goldwater did succeed in carrying most of the South, in part because of Thurmond's backing. In 1968 Thurmond was influential in holding the Southern delegates for Richard M. Nixon at the Republican national convention, but in the November election nearly the whole region went for George C. Wallace. Thurmond was reelected in 1972, a year in which Richard M. Nixon won reelection, carrying all of the Southern states.

Thwaites, Reuben Gold (1853–1913), librarian, historian, and editor. Born in Dorchester, Massachusetts, now a part of Boston, on May 15, 1853, Thwaites grew up there and in Wisconsin. He was basically self-educated, but he did attend Yale for one year, 1874–1875, for postgraduate courses. He settled in Madison, Wisconsin, where he edited the *Wisconsin State Journal* from 1876 to 1886. In 1886 he became assistant to Lyman C. Draper, the secretary of the Wisconsin State Historical Society, and the next year was himself elected secretary. He remained with the society until his death, doing a prodigious amount of collecting, editing, and writing. He edited the society's *Proceedings* every year from 1888 until 1912, as well as the biennial *Collections* series. He also gathered a great deal of documentation for the study of colonial and frontier history. To house all the materials he was bringing together he superintended the building of a new library for the society on the Madison campus of the University of Wisconsin, which was dedicated in 1900. From 1895 to 1912, Thwaites and his assistants collected, edited, and published a number of important historical works, including the 73-volume *The Jesuit Relations and Allied Documents*, 1896–1901, and the 32-volume *Early Western Travels*, 1904–1907, as well as the *Original Journals of the Lewis and Clark Expedition*, 8 volumes, 1904–1905; Father Louis Hennepin's *New Discovery*, 2 volumes, 1903; the Baron de Lahontan's *New Voyages*, 2 volumes, 1905; biographies of Father Marquette and Daniel Boone, both in 1902; *France in America*, 1905, for the American Nation series; and numerous other books. He also edited, with L. P. Kellogg, the Draper Series of accounts of the early frontier and wrote a number of historical works, mostly on early America. He died in Madison, Wisconsin, on October 22, 1913.

Ticknor, George (1791–1871), educator and author. Born in Boston on August 1, 1791, Ticknor graduated from Dartmouth in 1807 and continued to study Latin and Greek privately; he read law for three years and was admitted to the bar in 1813. His interest in classical studies prevailed over the law, however, and in 1815 he sailed for Europe, remaining for two years at the University of Göttingen, where he devoted himself to learning German and studying Greek and German literature. During this time he was invited to fill the new post of Smith Professor of French and Spanish at Harvard; accepting in 1817, he spent the next two years in France, Italy, and Spain, acquainting himself with the languages and literatures of those countries. He assumed the professorship at Harvard in 1819 and remained there until 1835. His attempts to liberalize the organization of the university met stubborn resistance and eventually led to his resignation. But his influence on the school was great. He was successful in making modern-language studies respectable, and he consolidated all of the language courses into one department. Although criticized by his conservative peers, his lectures attracted large audiences from both inside and outside the university. Upon his resignation in 1835 his chair was filled by Henry Wadsworth Longfellow. During 1835–1838 he lived in Europe. For the next ten years he worked on his celebrated three-volume *History of Spanish Literature*, published in 1849. Written for general readers as well as for scholars, the study was the first to view the whole of Spanish letters and prompted continued research in the field. His other writings included *Remarks on Changes Lately Proposed or Adopted in Harvard University*, 1825; *Lecture on the Best Methods of Teaching the Living Languages*, 1833; and *Life of William Hickling Prescott*, 1864. Independently wealthy, he was prudent but generous in contributing to charities and various public institutions, including the Massachusetts General Hospital and the Boston Public Library, which he helped found in 1852 and to which he left his great collection of books on Spain. He died in Boston on January 26, 1871.

Tiffany, Charles Lewis (1812–1902), jeweler. Born on February 15, 1812, in Killingly, Connecticut, Tiffany spent two years at an academy in Plainfield, Connecticut, before joining the cotton-manufacturing business of his father, Comfort Tiffany. In 1837 he and a friend, John B. Young, began a small fancy-goods shop in New York City, which in 1841 became Tiffany, Young and Ellis. Eventually featuring jewelry, glass, and porcelain, the shop was known for superior standards of quality, beauty, and taste, a reputation enhanced when in 1851 they put English standards of silver quality into effect and consequently gained U.S. acceptance of the designation "sterling." In 1848 they began to manufacture their own jewelry in addition to importing it. Their collection of historic gems included those of Hungarian Prince Esterházy and the crown jewels of France's Second Empire. A Paris branch was opened in 1850 and three years later the firm was reorganized as Tiffany & Company. Tiffany did not restrict himself to expensive baubles and luxuries; in 1858 he sold as souvenirs pieces of a surplus section of the newly laid Atlantic cable, and during the Civil War he produced such items as medals and swords. In 1868 the company was incorporated and branches established in London and Geneva. Tiffany became the most prominent jeweler in the United States and in Europe, where he catered to European royalty and nobility, and in 1878 was made a chevalier of the French Legion of Honor. He was also a founder of the New York Society of Fine Arts. He died in Yonkers, New York, on February 18, 1902.

Tiffany, Louis Comfort (1848–1933), painter, craftsman, and decorator. Born on February 18, 1848, in New York City, Tiffany was the son of Charles L. Tiffany. He completed high school and studied art with several teachers, among them landscape artist George Inness; he also studied in Paris. In 1871 he was admitted as an associate to the National Academy of Design. In 1875 he began working with stained glass and three years later opened a factory to carry out his designs. His technique of adding color to glass while the glass was being made, rather than applying a stain or burning a pigment into already hardened glass, produced incomparably iridescent and beautifully colored results. He molded the pieces into free-form shapes and kneaded folds and other shapes and textural effects into the glass while still hot. His exhibit at the Paris Exposition in 1900 attracted great attention and he was recognized as the master practitioner of the "art nouveau" style. Among his many famous windows was the huge glass curtain in Mexico City's Palacio de Bellas Artes, 1911. He also designed vases, chandeliers, lamps, jewelry, and tiles made of his Favrile glass and won a great popular reputation for these pieces, which were the height of fashion during 1890–1915 and again after the 1960s, when they commanded high prices from collectors and interior decorators. He was vice-president and a director of Tiffany & Company, jewelers, and founded a New York interior decorating firm (later called Tiffany Studios), which served the elite, designed church interiors, and refurbished the reception areas of the White House. In 1919 he established the Louis Comfort Tiffany Foundation for art students at his estate at Oyster Bay on Long Island. He died in New York City on January 17, 1933.

Tilden, Samuel Jones (1814–1886), lawyer and public official. Born in New Lebanon, New York, on February 9, 1814, Tilden had a somewhat sketchy formal education that ended with a single term at Yale in 1834. But he learned a good deal about practical politics by serving for several years after 1834 as a writer of political tracts and treatises in support of the policies of his boyhood friend Martin Van Buren, president from 1837 to 1841. Tilden attended the law school of the University of the City of New York (later New York University) from 1838 to 1841 and was admitted to the bar in 1841. Suffering throughout his life from frail health, he nevertheless soon became a power in New York Democratic circles and by the time he was thirty-five had developed a lucrative law practice and gained a reputation as a corporation and railroad lawyer of great skill. A leader of the Barnburners, the Free-Soil element among New York Democrats, he supported the Union cause when the Civil War broke out, but he strongly opposed certain policies of Abraham Lincoln's administration, in particular disapproving of what he thought was a too great concentration of power in Washington. He was prominent nationally in the reorganization of the Democratic party after the war and, in his own state, was a leader in the successful effort to overthrow the notorious Tweed Ring. Nominated for governor in 1874, he ran on a reform ticket, was elected, and enjoyed notable success as a reforming administrator, among other achievements exposing and breaking up the so-called Canal Ring, a conspiracy of politicians and contractors that was defrauding the state in the course of canal repairs. In 1876, with an unbroken series of triumphs behind him, he was the obvious choice of the Democrats for the presidency, and he was nominated at the party's national convention in St. Louis in June. But the campaign was exceptionally bitter—memories of the Civil War were still vivid (Republican candidates who reminded voters of it were said to be "waving the bloody shirt"), and although Tilden won a majority of the popular vote, the Republicans disputed the returns from four states, Oregon, Florida, Louisiana, and South Carolina, claiming them for Rutherford B. Hayes. Tilden agreed to abide by the decision of a supposedly impartial electoral commission, composed of five members each from the Senate, the House of Representatives, and the Supreme Court, and appointed by Congress in early 1877. The commission included seven Democrats and seven Republicans and one supposed independent who, however, was in sentiment a Republican; the commission, after hearings, finally decided every disputed issue by consistent party-line votes of 8 to 7, giving Hayes the four disputed states and the presidency, by a margin of one electoral vote. Tilden is said to have failed to exert vigorous and direct leadership in the crisis; in any event, after it was over, he remarked: "I can retire to private life with the consciousness that I shall receive from posterity the credit of having been elected to the highest position in the gift of the people, without any of the cares and responsibilities of the office." In fact he accepted the verdict in order to prevent a possibly dangerous sectional dispute over the issue. He thereupon returned to New York City, taking up his law practice again and remaining until his death an important figure in his party. He died in Yonkers, New York, on August 4, 1886, leaving the bulk of the great fortune he had amassed to be used for establishing a free public library for the city. The Tilden Trust, joined with the Astor and Lenox libraries, formed the great New York Public Library in 1895.

Tilden, William Tatem, Jr. (1893–1953), "Big Bill," tennis player. Born on February 10, 1893, in Germantown, Pennsylvania, Tilden played tennis from his childhood and continued playing while attending the University of Pennsylvania, from which he graduated in 1922. In 1920 he won his first national singles championship; in the same year he became the first American to win the men's singles at Wimbledon, England. He won the national men's singles amateur championship each year through 1925 and won it again in 1930, while winning again at Wimbledon in 1921 and 1930. From 1920 through 1930 he played on the U.S. Davis Cup team, leading it to victory in seven consecutive years; in Davis Cup singles play he was unbeaten from 1920 to 1925 and lost only one doubles match. In 1928 he was captain of the team, but a minor infraction of rules led to his suspension by the U.S. Lawn Tennis Association (USLTA) shortly before the finals in France; the French were so incensed by the prospect of not having an opportunity to face him that at length the U.S. ambassador interceded and secured Tilden's reinstatement. In absolutely dominating world tennis from 1920 to 1925 he became one of the leading figures in the sports-conscious decade of the 1920s. Essentially a baseline player, he relied on strategy, devastating forehand and backhand drives, and a cannonball serve. In 1931 he turned professional and continued to play a powerful game. He was pro singles champion in 1931 and 1935, and with Vincent Richards won the pro doubles title in 1945 at the age of fifty-two. He made numerous short movies on tennis, wrote many books and pamphlets on the subject, including *The Art of Lawn Tennis*, 1923, and *Aces, Places, and Faults*, 1938, and for a time published and edited *Racquet* magazine. In 1950 an Associated Press poll voted him overwhelmingly the greatest tennis player of the first half of the twentieth century; and he was considered by many sportswriters to be the greatest athlete the United States had ever produced, in any sport. His autobiography, *My Story*, appeared in 1948. He died in Hollywood, California, on June 5, 1953.

Tillich, Paul Johannes (1886–1965), philosopher and theologian. Born in Starzeddel, Prussia (now Germany), on August 20, 1886, the son of a pastor, Tillich studied at the University of Berlin and other German universities, receiving his Ph.D. from Breslau in 1911 and the licentiate in theology from Halle in 1912. In the latter year he was ordained in the Evangelical Lutheran Church. He served in the German army as a chaplain during World War I. After the war he taught in the universities of Berlin, Marburg, Dresden, and Leipzig, and in 1929 became professor of philosophy at the University of Frankfurt (Frankfurt am Main). But his early writing and teaching were not calculated to endear him to the Nazis, and he was one of the first professors, and the first non-Jewish professor, to be removed from his post by Hitler's regime in Germany. He came to the United States in 1933 and was named professor of philosophical theology at the Union Theological Seminary in New York City. He remained there until 1955, when he became a university professor at

Harvard; from 1962 until his death he was Nuveen Professor of Theology at the divinity school of the University of Chicago. His thesis, published in Germany before World War I, was on Friedrich von Schelling, who, along with Jakob Böhme, was an important influence on his thought. During the 1920s, in the heyday of the Weimar Republic, Tillich was associated with the Religious Socialists, who sought to combine a spiritual revival with political reforms. He was an outspoken critic of the Nazis from their first appearance. In two books published shortly before he left Germany, *Religious Realization* and *The Religious Situation*, he analyzed with clarity and force the religious and cultural dilemmas of his time. The books that made his worldwide reputation, however, appeared after he arrived in the United States, and indeed after he had become a U.S. citizen in 1940. *The Protestant Era* was published in 1948, and *The Shaking of the Foundations*, a collection of sermons, appeared in the same year. Other theological works were *The Courage to Be*, 1952; *Love, Power and Justice*, 1954; *Biblical Religion and the Search for Ultimate Reality*, 1955; and *Dynamics of Faith*, 1957. More sermons were collected in *The New Being*, 1955, and *The Eternal Now*, 1963. Perhaps his major contribution, certainly the one on which he worked longest and hardest, was *Systematic Theology*, three volumes, 1951–1963. Including within its purview depth psychology, existentialism, and all kinds of artistic expression, it was an attempt to include in one system—primarily religious—all of the culture of man, or at least of Western man. Like his other works, it was infused with a deep and sometimes mystical piety; this made it difficult for some analytical theologians to read and appreciate him, but at the same time won him devoted disciples in many countries. Remarkable in his thought were the dynamic and fruitful tensions between skepticism and faith, or "ultimate concern," between religion and secular philosophy, and between tradition and modernism. A member of the United Church of Christ, Tillich died in Chicago on October 22, 1965.

Tillman, Benjamin Ryan (1847–1918), public official. Born in Edgefield County, South Carolina, on August 11, 1847, Tillman grew up on his family's plantation and studied in private schools. Illness prevented him from serving in the Civil War, and after his marriage in 1868 he worked his own land adjacent to the family estate for the next 18 years. In 1885 he began to turn his attention wholly to political issues, becoming a spokesman for the upcountry farmers and opposing the ruling powers of the state, particularly bankers and lawyers. His Populist approach won a large enough following in a few years to make him the Democratic nominee for governor in 1890, and he won the election handily. For the next 20 years Tillman was the most powerful politician in South Carolina, replacing such established figures as Sen. Wade Hampton, although in his later years in public office his personal ambition took precedence

over his Populism. He served two terms as governor, from December 1890 until November 1894, and his record was generally a good one. He founded Clemson College (now University) as an agricultural school for men, and Winthrop Normal and Industrial College (now Winthrop College) for women. He equalized tax rates, regulated railroads, and increased educational funding, and he gave the state a monopoly on liquor sales. One blemished aspect of his public career was his espousal of racism, which was so extreme as to embarrass his fellow legislators when he later went to the Senate; he disfranchised South Carolina's blacks and was an advocate of lynching and of repealing the Fifteenth Amendment. In 1894 he was elected to the U.S. Senate, where he served until 1918. In the Senate, "Pitchfork Ben" Tillman was an outspoken advocate of Southern agrarianism and was notably hostile to what he called the "interests." His very vehemence, in a speech to the national convention, lost him the Democratic presidential nomination in 1896. He continued to favor populist legislation and was one of the most influential senators in achieving the enactment in 1906 of the Hepburn Rate bill, strengthening the regulation of railroads. Strokes that he suffered in 1908 and 1910 curtailed his activities, and although he was reelected to the Senate in 1912, his influence in South Carolina had lessened noticeably. He died in Washington, D.C., on July 3, 1918.

Tillstrom, Burr (1917–   ), puppeteer. Born in Chicago on October 13, 1917, Tillstrom graduated from Senn High School and attended the University of Chicago for one semester. He had become interested in puppets and marionettes as early as his grade-school days, and even in high school had entertained with his puppets in the Chicago Park District Theater. He had learned to make his own puppets; his two most famous ones, Kukla, a doll-like little chap, and Ollie, a single-toothed dragon, were created in the late 1930s. Gradually, as he envisioned a whole troop of puppets, all of the characters of the "Kuklapolitan Players" of his later shows came into being. A television demonstration he witnessed in 1939 convinced him that the new medium was the perfect way to display his talents. He toured with an RCA demonstration show in 1939 and appeared at the 1940 World's Fair in New York. After World War II, when television began to come into general use, Tillstrom in 1947 originated the "Kukla, Fran and Ollie" program, one of the most successful shows television has ever presented, appealing to adults and children alike. The "Fran" of the show was Frances Allison, who had been a radio actress, and all other characters were puppets; they included an incompetent witch, a grande dame, a hare-brained rabbit, and certain relatives of Ollie, among others. The program was televised from WBKB in Chicago for two seasons, then in August 1949 it went onto national television over the National Broadcasting Company (NBC) network and remained on the air until 1957. The show returned to the air in 1961 as "Kukla and Ollie" and in the late 1960s was on National Educational Television (NET) under its original name and with Fran Allison back in the cast.

Tilyou, George Cornelius (1862–1914), inventor and amusement-park owner. Born in New York City on February 3, 1862, Tilyou grew up near the city on Coney Island, then a suburban resort area on the south shore of Long Island, where his father ran a hotel. When he was seventeen he launched a career as a real-estate operator at Coney Island. He laid out the area's "Bowery" amusement street and built a theater. In 1897 he opened Steeplechase Park, a large amusement area with rides and fun houses, many of which were his own inventions. He devised such amusements as the Human Roulette Wheel, the Electric Seat, the Barrel of Love, the Aerial Thrill, and numerous other attractions. It is said that Steeplechase Park also introduced a new edible concoction—a frankfurter sausage in a roll—that came to be known as the hot dog. The amusement park eventually expanded to cover 20 acres; fires twice destroyed it, but it was each time rebuilt. Competing amusement complexes sprang up around it, making Coney Island the greatest concentration of such enterprises in the world. Tilyou also operated amusement parks elsewhere on Long Island and in New Jersey, Connecticut, Massachusetts, St. Louis, and San Francisco. His original Steeplechase Park at Coney Island later gave way to urban "progress," as much of the Coney Island area was covered by high-rise buildings. Tilyou died on November 30, 1914.

Timrod, Henry (1828–1867), poet. Born in Charleston, South Carolina, on December 8, 1828, Timrod attended public school there and spent two years at Franklin College (now part of the University of Georgia). Throughout his life he suffered from poor health and an introverted personality. Finding himself unsuited to the study of law, he took up the work of a private tutor on a plantation in South Carolina during the 1850s. His verses were published occasionally, and in 1857 he joined a Charleston group in the publication of *Russell's Magazine*, which failed after a few months. A volume of his verses was published in 1860 but it escaped notice as the nation moved toward the outbreak of the Civil War. It was the war itself which brought out Timrod's best abilities. The dramatic events of the time inspired his best poetry, and he became for all practical purposes the poet of the Confederacy. Just prior to the war, in February 1861, he wrote what is probably his best poem, "Ethnogenesis," a studied interpretation of a new nation coming into being. Other wartime odes, "A Cry to Arms," "Charleston," and his postwar "Ode" to the Confederate dead at Magnolia Cemetery, 1867, all expressed the hopes and pathos of the Southern war effort. Timrod himself saw little military duty in the war. He enlisted in March 1861 but was discharged at the end of the year because of his poor health. The few years that were left to him were a time of disappointment and grief. In 1864 he settled in Columbia, South Carolina, where he helped edit the *South Carolinian*; but in February 1865 the city was burned by Gen. William T. Sherman and he lost his possessions. He and his family were reduced to a situation of abject poverty from which they never recovered. Later in the year his only son, less than a year old, died. His own health began to fail, and work came only intermittently. On October 6, 1867, he died in Columbia following an operation. Only after his death were his poems collected and published, in 1873. He regained posthumously his fame as laureate of the Confederacy and was recognized as one of the great poets of the nineteenth-century South.

Tiomkin, Dimitri (1899–1979), musician and composer. Born in St. Petersburg, Russia (now Leningrad, U.S.S.R.), on May 10, 1899, Tiomkin studied at the conservatory of music there. He became a concert pianist but at the age of twenty turned his attention to conducting and composing as well as performing. As a pianist he had successfully introduced a number of American piano works, such as George Gershwin's *Concerto in F*, to European audiences. He came to the United States in 1925 and continued his concert work. He was naturalized in 1937. With the advent of sound films, Tiomkin went to Hollywood, where he worked successfully at writing musical scores and conducting orchestras for movies. His first film score was for the 1933 movie *Alice in Wonderland*. Other well-known films for which he wrote the music were *Lost Horizon*, 1937; *Bridge of San Luis Rey*, 1944; *Mr. Smith Goes to Washington*, 1939; *Duel in the Sun*, 1949; and *The Great Waltz*, 1938. He was nominated for Academy Awards 24 times and received 4 Oscars, garnering two awards for *High Noon*, 1952, and one each for *The High and the Mighty*, 1954, and *The Old Man and the Sea*, 1958. Altogether he composed the scores for about 125 motion pictures and did some television work as well. The theme for the "Rawhide" show was probably his best-known work for television. In 1970 he was the executive producer of a multimillion-dollar film biography of Peter Ilich Tchaikovsky, made in the Soviet Union. He died in London on November 11, 1979.

Tisquantum, *see* Squanto

Titchener, Edward Bradford (1867–1927), psychologist. Born on January 11, 1867, in Chichester, England, Titchener earned his B.A. from Oxford in 1890 and took his doctorate under psychologist Wilhelm Wundt at the University of Leipzig in 1892. While residing in the United States, he submitted work to Oxford, earning his M.A. degree in 1894 and his D.Sc. degree in 1906. An instructor in psychology after 1893 at Cornell University, he became Sage Professor in 1895 and a research professor in the graduate school in 1909. A leader of the "structuralist" school of psychology, he emphasized the scientific aspects of his field and recognized as the only problem of psychology the contents of the mind. This introspective approach was opposed to that of functional or applied psychology, which, in the form of educational psychology and mental testing, was concerned only with manifest acts and functions. He completed a number of English translations of German texts, notably several seminal works by Wundt, and several original works in psychology, among them the monumental *Experimental Psychology*, two volumes 1901–1905; *A Textbook of Psychology*, two volumes, 1909–1910; and *A Beginner's Psychology*, 1915. He also wrote more than 200 papers and articles. From 1894 to 1921 he was the American editor of *Mind*, and was from 1895 to 1921 associate editor and from 1921 to 1925 editor of the *American Journal of Psychology*. In 1904 he founded the Society of Experimental Psychology. He died in Ithaca, New York, on August 3, 1927.

Titcomb, Timothy, see Holland, Josiah Gilbert

Tobey, Mark (1890–1976), painter. Born in Centerville, Trempealeau County, Wisconsin, on December 11, 1890, Tobey studied at the Art Institute of Chicago in 1908 and worked as a fashion illustrator. He also lived in New York City for a time from 1911 and studied portrait painting. In 1922 he settled in Seattle and taught school there until 1929, while continuing his painting and studying Chinese calligraphy. From 1931 until 1938 he was resident artist at Darlington Hall, England, an appointment which afforded him opportunities to travel. He spent some time in Mexico from 1931 to 1934 and in the Far East from 1934 until 1936. His experiences in the Far East, where he not only encountered art forms that were new to him but also investigated Oriental philosophy and religion, were a turning point in his career. From then on his art, described as "white line" or "white writing," derived from a synthesis of Oriental brushwork and American abstractionism. Tobey had numerous one-man exhibits after 1917 in America and Europe, and his paintings are included in the collections of the Chicago Art Institute, the Baltimore Museum of Art, the Boston Museum of Fine Arts, the Metropolitan Museum and the Museum of Modern Art in New York City, among others. He died on April 24, 1976, in Basel, Switzerland, where he had lived since 1960.

Todd, Thomas (1765–1826), justice of the Supreme Court. Born in King and Queen County, Virginia, on January 23, 1765, Todd studied law privately and was admitted to the bar in 1786, the year in which he settled in Danville, Kentucky. He early became associated with the movement to effect a separation of Kentucky from its parent state, Virginia, and served as clerk at several local conventions called for that purpose. Todd served as clerk of the court of appeals from the time Kentucky became a state in 1792 until 1801, when the governor appointed him a judge of the court. In 1806 he became chief justice of the state's court system. While on the state court his most notable decisions came in matters dealing with land titles, and his opinions formed the basis for Kentucky's subsequent land policies. In 1807 President Thomas Jefferson appointed Todd an associate justice of the U.S. Supreme Court, a position he held until his death. On the Court he was a fairly consistent adherent of the nationalism of Chief Justice John Marshall, differing with him on the Dartmouth College Case in 1819 but, being absent, rendering no dissent. In all he wrote only a dozen opinions in his nineteen years on the Court, none of particular note. As was true of the justices in that era, much of his time was spent riding the circuit of federal courts on the frontier, and this continual exertion took its toll on his health over the years. He died on February 7, 1826, in Frankfort, Kentucky.

Tompkins, Daniel D. (1774–1825), vice-president of the United States. Born in Fox Meadows (now Scarsdale), New York, on June 21, 1774, Tompkins graduated from Columbia College in 1795. He studied law, was admitted to the bar in 1797, and began practice in New York City. He very soon became involved in politics and in 1801 served as a delegate to the state constitutional convention. After one term in the state legislature, he was elected to the House of Representatives as a Democratic Republican in 1804, but resigned the office even before the term began in order to accept an appointment as associate justice of the New York supreme court. In 1807 he was elected governor of New York, a post to which he won reelection three times and in which he served until 1817. It was during his tenure at Albany that the United States became involved in the War of 1812. Owing to the military system prevailing at the time, Tompkins as governor was also commander in chief of the New York militia, and he had to see to the defense of the state and perform many military duties. In 1814, in order to field and supply troops, he was forced to borrow, often on his own credit, large sums for military spending. Although he had gone deeply into debt personally, there was a good deal of postwar confusion over accounting for all the money he had handled, until Congress finally authorized the payment of $95,000 to him in 1824. These financial entanglements and their slow resolution contributed to a decline in his health over the years. As a governor Tompkins was markedly liberal, taking positions that later generations might have called Populist. With moderate success he urged liberalizing the criminal laws and improving education, and he got the legislature to pass a bill outlawing slavery in New York. He was opposed to banking interests, but did not succeed in keeping the Bank of North America from being chartered in New York. In 1816 he was elected vice-president of the United States with James Monroe and he was reelected with Monroe in 1820, although he was often absent from Washington because of continuing frustrating efforts to clear up his affairs.

He left office in March 1825 and three months later, on June 11, died at his home on Staten Island, New York.

Tompkins, Sally Louisa (1833–1916), humanitarian and philanthropist. Born in Mathews County, Virginia, on November 9, 1833, Miss Tompkins grew up there and in Richmond. Coming from a wealthy family she devoted most of her time to philanthropic undertakings. When the Civil War began she turned a large house in Richmond into a hospital, at her own expense, and operated it as the Robertson Hospital throughout the war, until early April 1865. Late in the summer of 1861, President Jefferson Davis of the Confederate States issued an order discontinuing all non-military hospitals, but to circumvent his order in her case he commissioned Miss Tompkins a captain in the Confederate cavalry, making her the only woman to hold a Confederate commission. As "Captain Sally" (a title she carried the rest of her life), she was thereafter able to operate her hospital more efficiently than before and with the cooperation of the military. In the nearly four years her hospital was in operation, it cared for more than a thousand patients, of whom only 73 died. After the war she continued her various philanthropies until financial reverses destroyed the family fortune. She died in Richmond on July 25, 1916, and was buried with military honors.

Tonty, Henri de (1650–1704), explorer. Born in Paris in 1650, Tonty (or Tonti) was the son of a native of Naples. At the age of eighteen he joined the French army, and he lost his right hand in action. He replaced the limb with a metal hand and came to be known among the American Indians as "Iron Hand." In 1678 he met the French explorer René Robert Cavelier, Sieur de La Salle, while La Salle was in France seeking backing for an expedition into the interior of North America. La Salle had originally gone to New France (Canada) in 1666 and taken up a land grant near Montreal, but he had done much exploring in the Great Lakes region. Now he was back in France to get supplies and men for further explorations. He was granted permission to build forts in the Mississippi Valley and a monopoly of the fur trade there. Tonty enlisted in his service and returned with him to America. They arrived at Niagara late in 1678 and built a fort to guard Lake Ontario. Tonty took charge of building a ship, the *Griffon,* to sail the Great Lakes. They sailed to the region of Green Bay, Wisconsin, on Lake Michigan, where the boat was loaded with furs and sent back to Montreal, where it never arrived. Tonty left the party and sailed south in Lake Michigan and La Salle joined him at the mouth of the St. Joseph River. They entered the Illinois territory and built Fort Creve Coeur near Lake Peoria. La Salle set out to return to Fort Frontenac and Tonty was left in charge in the Illinois country. By the end of 1680 Tonty's men had mutinied and deserted him, and an Indian raid in which he was wounded forced him to move north. In June 1681 La Salle found him at Michilimackinac and from there they set out again. They traveled to the Mississippi, reaching it on February 6, 1682, and followed the course of the river until they reached its mouth in April. They took possession for France of the whole Mississippi Valley, about one-third of the present mainland United States, and named the region Louisiana. On their return late in 1682 they built a new post, Fort St. Louis, on the Illinois River at Starved Rock. The following year La Salle went to France to gain support for a colony in Louisiana and an expedition to the west to counter Spain's claims. Tonty never saw La Salle again, for after his return from France, La Salle was murdered in Texas by his own men after he had failed to find the mouth of the Mississippi. Tonty was traveling overland in 1686 to meet La Salle, but never found him; he did not hear of his death until September 1689, after which he tried unsuccessfully to find the colonists La Salle had left in Louisiana. Tonty remained in command of the Mississippi Valley for France for the following decade and a half. He was the founder of French settlements in the Illinois country and of trade in the Mississippi Valley. In 1700 he traveled to New Orleans, recently founded by Pierre Le Moyne, Sieur d'Iberville. Tonty died near the site of present-day Mobile, Alabama, in 1704.

Toombs, Robert Augustus (1810–1885), public official. Born in Wilkes County, Georgia, on July 2, 1810, Toombs graduated from Union College in Schenectady, New York, in 1828. After studying law at the University of Virginia, he was admitted to the bar in 1830 and began practice in Washington, Georgia. In 1837 he was elected to the state legislature, where he served, except for one term, until 1844. He then entered the House of Representatives, winning reelection three times. Toombs was a conservative, a Whig and then a states'-rights Democrat, and not unduly concerned over sectional matters, even in his early years in Congress. His main interest was fiscal responsibility and a balanced budget. In 1850, however, the crisis over the admission of slavery into the territories made Toombs an ardent states'-rights Southerner. He helped bring about the Compromise of 1850 and worked for its acceptance in Georgia. He founded the Constitutional Union party in his home state to support the states'-rights viewpoint and won election to the U.S. Senate in 1852 on its ticket. But when the party began to decline for lack of national support, Toombs again became a Democrat and won reelection to the Senate in 1858. The fever of the controversy over slavery, in his view, had been heightened under the influence of the new Republican party after 1854, and by 1860 he felt that a Republican election victory would dash the South's hopes for good. Thus upon Abraham Lincoln's election to the presidency and the failure of the Crittenden Compromise of 1860, which sought to resolve the issue of slavery through Constitutional amendment, Toombs declared in favor of secession and led the movement for a

Georgia convention to vote to secede from the Union. In February 1861 he resigned from the Senate and was a delegate to the Montgomery Convention, which established the Confederate States of America. Toombs became the Confederacy's secretary of state (he had hoped for the presidency). Within a few months he was so disillusioned with Jefferson Davis's leadership that he resigned from Davis's cabinet and accepted an army commission. Once the Civil War had started, Toombs was highly critical of the handling of both civilian and military affairs. His own military service was generally undistinguished, except for an exemplary display of bravery at the battle of Antietam in September 1862. After the battle, when he received no promotion, he resigned his commission as brigadier general. With the exception of some military duty again near the end of the war, he sat out most of the conflict and continued to criticize the domestic and military policies of the Davis administration, particularly conscription, the suspension of the writ of habeas corpus, and fiscal measures. At the war's end he fled to England, where he remained for two years, until the zeal to arrest and punish rebels had abated. He returned home in 1867 and reestablished his law practice. He spent most of the rest of his life combating the Reconstruction policies of the Republican party, and of the Radical Republicans in particular, and he himself never applied for a pardon. As time passed he regained much of his former influence, and in 1877 he presided over the convention that revised the state constitution. He died at his home in Washington, Georgia, on December 15, 1885.

Torrey, John (1796–1873), botanist. Born in New York City on August 15, 1796, Torrey graduated from the College of Physicians and Surgeons in 1818. He spent little time practicing medicine, for his true interest was botany. In 1817, while still a medical student, he and some classmates had founded in New York City the Lyceum of Natural History, forerunner of the New York Academy of Sciences. For several years after graduation he studied plant life in New York State and New England and published a number of scientific papers. In 1824 he accepted a position as professor of chemistry at West Point, and for the next 30 years continued to teach while pursuing his botanical studies. In 1827 he returned to New York City as professor at the College of Physicians and Surgeons, and three years later he took on the professorship of natural history and chemistry at the College of New Jersey (now Princeton), holding both posts until his retirement in 1854. In 1853 he was appointed chief assayer of the United States Assay Office in New York City, and he remained in that post until his death. As Torrey's reputation as a botanist increased, the various government-sponsored expeditions being made throughout the West began sending him the plant specimens they brought back so that he might do reports on them. Torrey prepared the botanical reports for Joseph N. Nicollet's ex-

peditions, John C. Frémont's trips of 1842 and 1843–1844, and many others. His first publication on such materials was a report on a collection of plants brought back from the northern Mississippi Valley in 1820. Some of the volumes that Torrey prepared or worked on were *A Flora of the Northern and Middle Sections of the United States*, 1823; *Flora of North America*, two volumes, with Asa Gray, 1838–1843; and *Flora of the State of New York*, 1843. His work in the Assay Office enabled him to travel occasionally and see the plants he had studied in their natural surroundings. During his career he put together a botanical library and herbarium which he turned over to Columbia University in 1860; the collections later went to the New York Botanical Garden. He died in New York City on March 10, 1873.

Toscanini, Arturo (1867–1957), conductor. Born in Parma, Italy, on March 25, 1867, the son of a tailor, Toscanini attended the Parma Conservatory from the age of nine, intending to become a cellist, and graduated at eighteen. In 1886 he was engaged as first cellist and assistant chorus master with Claudio Rossini's opera company, which was appearing in Rio de Janeiro. He was called upon to substitute for the conductor, and was so successful in leading *Aida* that he was engaged to conduct the performances for the rest of the season. For 12 years he conducted in opera houses in Genoa, Bologna, Treviso, and Turin. In 1898 he became the chief conductor and artistic director at La Scala in Milan, remaining there until 1908, when he arrived in New York City to become conductor of the Metropolitan Opera. He also made his first appearance as a symphonic conductor about this time. In 1915 he returned to Milan and conducted several benefit concerts during the remainder of World War I. He then organized his own orchestra and with it toured the United States during 1920 and 1921. From 1921 to 1929 he was again conductor and artistic director at La Scala, appearing in 1926 and 1927 as a guest conductor of the New York Philharmonic. In 1928 he was appointed conductor of the newly merged New York Philharmonic-Symphony Orchestra. He remained in this position until 1936, making a highly successful European tour in 1930. He also led the music festivals at Bayreuth, Germany, 1930–1931, Salzburg, Austria, 1934–1937, and Lucerne, Switzerland, 1938–1939, and conducted such prominent European orchestras as the Vienna Philharmonic Orchestra, the BBC (British Broadcasting Corporation) Orchestra, and the newly organized Palestine Orchestra. In 1937, at the age of seventy, he became conductor in New York City of the NBC Symphony, a group created especially for him by the National Broadcasting Company, with virtuoso players from many nations. They broadcast regularly until he retired in 1954, and also made tours in South America (1940) and the United States (1950), and recorded extensively. Toscanini came to be considered by many one of the world's greatest conductors. His reverence for music and his driving stamina evoked a similarly deep and vigorous musical response from his orchestra. He chose not to use a studied conducting technique, but employed intuitive gestures associated with the mood and tempo of each musical phrase. His tremendous feeling for the styles and traditions of the masters —notably Beethoven and Verdi—gave to his performances great vitality and emotional force. He died in New York City on January 16, 1957.

Touroff, Eleanor, *see under* Glueck, Sheldon

Town, Ithiel (1784–1844), architect. Born in Thompson, Connecticut, on October 3, 1784, Town pursued the study of architecture in Boston under Asher Benjamin. Little is known of his early years, and it is possible he had other training to qualify him for his later accomplishments. He made his reputation as an architect with the design and construction of Center Church, 1812, and Trinity Church, 1814, both in New Haven. Over the next two decades he was given the opportunity to design several public buildings, including the customhouse on Wall Street in New York City and the state capitol buildings in Indianapolis and in Raleigh, North Carolina. During the 1820s Town maintained offices in New York City, in partnership with Martin E. Thompson during 1827–1828 and with Alexander J. Davis in 1829–1843, as he found the city more productive of business contacts than New Haven, where he had his home. In addition to practicing as an architect he pursued a career of bridge building. In 1820 he patented a type of truss bridge, and he also built a number of covered bridges. With the money he made from bridge building he brought together in his New Haven house the best collection of books on art and architecture in the country. Town died in New Haven, Connecticut, on June 13, 1844.

Townes, Charles Hard (1915–   ), physicist. Born in Greenville, South Carolina, on July 28, 1915, Townes graduated from Furman University in 1935. He pursued graduate studies in physics at Duke University (M.A., 1937) and at the California Institute of Technology (Caltech), where he earned his Ph.D. in 1939. From 1939 to 1948 he was with the Bell Telephone Laboratories in New York City and New Jersey, working on radar and navigation devices. During World War II much of his research was for the U.S. air force. In 1948 Townes went to Columbia University, where he did microwave research and in 1950 became professor of physics. From 1959 to 1961 he was vice-president and director of research at the Institute for Defense Analyses in Washington, D.C., and in 1961 he became provost at the Massachusetts Institute of Technology (MIT). He became professor at large at the University of California at Berkeley in 1967 and conducted research in infrared and radio astronomy. The bulk of Townes's work concerned molecular wave and microwave experiments. In the early 1950s he investigated the idea of measuring time absolutely

and without reference to the motion of celestial bodies. By 1957 he had developed a method of microwave amplification by stimulated emission of radiation (maser, for short), which became the basis for the atomic clock, the most accurate of timing devices. The maser was later used by scientists to test Albert Einstein's theory of relativity, to obtain accurate measurements of the earth's rotation, to check the oscillation frequency of atoms and molecules, and to keep television and radio on precise frequencies. From his work with the maser came the development by others of the laser beam (light amplification by stimulated emission of radiation). For his microwave research and its subsequent developments Townes shared the Nobel Prize for Physics in 1964 with two Soviet physicists, A. M. Prokhorov and N. G. Basov.

Townsend, Francis Everett (1867–1960), physician and social reformer. Born in rural Livingston County, Illinois, on January 13, 1867, Townsend roamed the country as a young man, working at mining, farming, and teaching. In 1900 he enrolled at Omaha Medical College (from 1902 part of the University of Nebraska), and in 1903, upon graduation, settled in Belle Fourche, South Dakota, to practice medicine. He remained there for 17 years, until poor health forced him to move to Long Beach, California. There he continued his practice and also became involved in real-estate. When the Depression of the 1930s began he worked for a time as an assistant county health officer, but a change of local administrations in 1933 left him without employment. The feature of the Depression that impressed him the most was the plight of the aged, so many of whom had lost savings, jobs, and homes as economic conditions worsened. In September 1933 he devised the rudiments of what later became nationally known as the Townsend Plan. In its more polished form, the plan proposed to retire everyone over sixty and pay each retiree a monthly stipend of scrip worth $200, all of which was to be spent within a month; the pensions would be financed by a national sales tax. Townsend's real-estate associate, Robert E. Clements, helped organize the plan to appeal to a national audience, and in January 1934 they incorporated Old-Age Revolving Pensions, Ltd. (OARP). The movement became the most notorious phenomenon of 1935. Townsend clubs sprang up all over the country, and the Townsend organization conducted meetings for its millions of followers that had a revivalist flavor, including collections to finance the organization. In January 1935 the first bill incorporating the Townsend Plan was introduced into the House of Representatives. Congress managed to defeat the proposal without a vote, but not without difficulty. As the Townsend movement gained followers it loomed as a threat to both major political parties. Several more Townsend bills came before Congress. Congressional Democrats and Republicans worked together to stem the tide by an investigation of OARP in the spring of 1936. Clements, who had not scrupled to use the organization as a profit-making scheme for himself, resigned and gave some damaging testimony to the congressional committee; and in fact the organization's books were so confused that it was impossible to audit them and determine where the money had gone. Townsend himself refused to continue testifying when it became apparent the committee members were hostile, no matter what he said. He was cited for contempt of Congress, found guilty, but pardoned by President Franklin D. Roosevelt. With Clements out of the picture, Huey P. "Kingfish" Long's former associate Gerald L. K. Smith moved in and guided the Townsend organization along more political lines. In a tenuous political alliance with Father Charles E. Coughlin's National Union for Social Justice, the Townsendites supported third-party candidate William Lemke in the 1936 presidential election. Gradually, as economic conditions in the nation improved and with the passage of the Social Security Act in August 1935, public interest in the Townsend Plan abated; nevertheless Townsend retained a notable following for many years afterward. He died in Los Angeles on September 1, 1960.

Tracy, Spencer (1900–1967), actor. Born in Milwaukee on April 5, 1900, Tracy spent some time in the navy during World War I, and after the war graduated from high school. In 1922, after a year and a half at Ripon College, he went to New York City to join his childhood friend Pat O'Brien in pursuit of an acting career. His first nine years were rewarded with meager success, but in 1931, while in the play *The Lost Mile*, he was spotted by movie director John Ford and offered a job in Hollywood. Tracy's first movie assignments were in minor roles and it was not until 1933, with *The Power and the Glory*, that the studio became aware it had the makings of a major star. Four years later he won an Academy Award for his performance in *Captains Courageous*, and in 1938 he repeated as an Oscar winner for the role of Father Edward Joseph Flanagan in *Boys Town*. He played a number of other biographical roles: Henry M. Stanley in *Stanley and Livingstone*, 1939; *Edison the Man*, 1940; and Col. James H. Doolittle in *Thirty Seconds over Tokyo*, 1943. In 1942 Tracy costarred in *Woman of the Year* with Katharine Hepburn, the film marking the beginning of a lifelong professional and personal friendship. Some of Tracy's best-remembered films were those in which Hepburn and Tracy appeared together, among them *State of the Union*, 1948; *Adam's Rib*, 1949; *Pat and Mike*, 1952; *Desk Set*, 1957; and his last, *Guess Who's Coming to Dinner*, 1967. Altogether he appeared in more than 60 movies, giving memorable performances also in *Bad Day at Black Rock*, 1955; *The Old Man and The Sea*, 1958; *Judgment at Nuremberg*, 1960; *Inherit the Wind*, 1960; and many others. He maintained enormous popularity throughout his career; he was a solid box-office attraction for more than 35 years. He died in Beverley Hills, California, on June 10, 1967.

Train, George Francis (1829–1904), merchant and author. Born in Boston on March 24, 1829, Train was orphaned at the age of four while his family was living in New Orleans and was raised by his grandmother on a farm near Waltham, Massachusetts. He left home when he was fourteen and held odd jobs until 1844, when he found work in a shipping firm at Boston owned by a relative. In 1850 he went to Liverpool, England, to manage a branch office of the firm, and in 1853 he traveled to Australia and opened a shipping firm which proved successful. Throughout his life Train was a successful businessman and promoter as well as an eccentric who enjoyed drawing attention to himself. Among his feats to gain notoriety were trips around the world—he made four of them—to see how fast he could do it. He got his time down from 80 to 60 days, a nineteenth-century record. He built the Atlantic and Great Western Railway in Ohio in 1858, helped promote the Union Pacific Railway in the 1860s, and invested in streetcar lines in London and Liverpool as well as in other cities of Europe and Asia. In 1856 he turned author. Besides many pamphlets and articles over the years, he wrote a number of books, including such works as *Young America in Wall Street*, 1857, *An American Merchant in Europe, Asia and Australia*, 1857, and *Championship of Women*, 1867; an autobiography, *My Life in Many States and in Foreign Lands*, appeared in 1902. Early in the Civil War he made public addresses favoring the Union, and from 1869 until 1872 he conducted a sporadic and notably unsuccessful campaign for the presidency. In 1870, during the Franco-Prussian War, he was in Paris as a member of the Commune. He spent a few months in jail at Boston in 1872 on an obscenity charge growing out of a paper defending Victoria Claflin Woodhull in her charges that Henry Ward Beecher had committed adultery. The notoriety Train earned in the 1860s and afterward somewhat dimmed his business success, and he lived out his last years in near-solitude in New York City. He died there on January 19, 1904.

Travis, William Barret (1809–1836), lawyer and soldier. Born near Red Banks, Edgefield County, South Carolina, on August 9, 1809, Travis grew up there and in Conecuh County, Alabama, where the family moved when he was nine. He attended a military academy in South Carolina for a while, until he was expelled for inciting a student revolt. He then returned to Alabama and studied law privately. He was admitted to the bar before he was twenty years old. An unhappy marriage impelled him to leave Alabama in 1831, and he made his way to Texas and opened a law office in San Felipe. Almost from the day he arrived in Texas he was partial to the "war party," that minority of Anglo-Texans who wanted independence from Mexico and were willing to start a war to get their way. What is known about Travis's years in Texas suggest that he was often erratic and unstable. In May 1832 the Mexican authorities declared Anahuac, the port of Galveston in which

Travis was living, under martial law, and he was arrested along with other Anglo-Texans. After a near-rebellion the prisoners were released. The crisis in Texas affairs abated, although the war party remained active. In October 1835 the crisis was renewed when the president of Mexico, General Santa Anna, abolished all local legislatures, dissolved the Congress, and became a virtual dictator; he was determined on a strong central government and an end to U.S. migration into Texas. The war party redoubled its activities. When Anahuac was garrisoned in January 1835, Travis gathered two dozen followers and obtained the surrender of the Mexican soldiers on June 30. This unnecessary gambit on the part of the war hawks aroused much Mexican resentment and was denounced even by the majority of Anglo-Texans. Events moved toward a confrontation between the Anglo-Texan and Mexican forces, until on December 10 the Mexicans surrendered at San Antonio to the Texans. This surrender enraged Santa Anna, who moved northward with a large army to put an end to the Texas problem once and for all. Travis was now part of the Texas army, with the rank of lieutenant colonel. As the Texans prepared themselves for war, Travis was sent to the Alamo in San Antonio with reinforcements on February 3. Col. James Bowie commanded the volunteers at the Alamo and Travis the regulars, who numbered altogether slightly more than 150 men. For some reason both men were determined to hold out, even in the face of the overwhelming numbers of Santa Anna's approaching army. Since none of the Alamo defenders survived the siege, the situation is not well documented, but it is known that the entire garrison could have escaped even after Santa Anna's army arrived on February 23. Bowie fell ill shortly thereafter leaving Travis in full command. On March 6, 1836, the Alamo fell in a final assault and all the defenders died, Travis among them. The toll among the Mexican forces was far higher, with nearly 1600 dead and a large number wounded. The battle was lost, but Travis, in losing, had given the newly declared Republic of Texas desperately needed time to prepare for the defeat of Santa Anna, which was accomplished some weeks later at San Jacinto.

Trevellick, Richard F. (1830–1895), labor leader. Born on St. Mary's in the Scilly Isles off the coast of Cornwall, England, in May 1830, Trevellick was apprenticed to a ship's carpenter and worked for a time in Southampton. For several years he traveled, visiting all parts of the world, including Australia and New Zealand, where he both practiced his trade and was involved in labor agitation. He came to the United States in 1857 and settled in New Orleans, where he became president of the Ship Carpenters' and Caulkers' Union and gained for its members a nine-hour working day. When the Civil War began he moved north and settled in Detroit. He was immediately active in labor affairs and by 1864 was president of the Detroit Trades Assembly. During his next 30 years

as a labor leader, Trevellick held official positions in several unions; he was president of the International Union of Ship Carpenters and Caulkers in 1865, president of the National Labor Union in 1869, 1871, and 1872, an officer in the Michigan Grand Eight Hours League in 1867, and a labor lobbyist dealing with Congress in 1868. He also did organizational work for the Knights of Labor after the National Labor Union began to fail. He helped promote a bill before Congress giving federal workers the eight-hour day in 1868. In the late 1870s he joined the Greenback movement and was instrumental in the formation in 1878 of the short-lived Greenback-Labor party that ran James B. Weaver for the presidency two years later. He was a tireless worker and speaker throughout the nation in behalf of labor, constantly trying to organize new local unions and agitating in connection with the issues concerning hours, pay, working conditions, and blacklisting that were important to working people. He fearlessly opposed sentiments widespread among workingmen in favor of the exclusion of Chinese workers and the maintenance of the color line in unions. He died in Detroit on February 15, 1895.

Trevino, Lee (1939–   ), golfer. Born in Dallas, Texas, on December 1, 1939, Trevino left grade school to work at a country club near his home, and by the time he was seventeen he was a competent golfer. While serving in the marines from 1957 to 1961 he played in occasional amateur tournaments and from 1961 to 1965 worked as a pro at a Dallas course. In 1965, his first year on the professional tour, he played in an assortment of minor tournaments, and in 1966 he made his first appearance in a Class A Professional Golfers' Association (PGA) meet. This first year was disappointing, but in 1967 he won $28,000 and was named Rookie of the Year. His first major victory came in 1968, when he won the U.S. Open, setting a record as the first player to win it with four below-par rounds. His successful play continued unabated until the spring of 1970, when he went into a yearlong slump. But in the summer of 1971 he made a startling comeback, winning the U.S., Canadian, and British Opens within a month—the first player ever to win all three in one year—and taking first prize in several other tournaments as well. With his capture of the Sahara Invitational in Las Vegas late in the year he brought his total earnings for 1971 to $231,000, thereby becoming one of golf's greatest money winners as well as one of its most popular stars. Also in 1971 he teamed with Jack Nicklaus and Arnold Palmer to win the Ryder Cup against a strong British team, and he and Nicklaus won the World Cup at Palm Beach Gardens. He slumped again at the beginning of 1972 but came back once more to win the British Open.

Trilling, Lionel (1905–1975), critic and author. Born in New York City on July 4, 1905, Trilling graduated from Columbia College in 1925 and took his master's degree from Columbia a year later. Except for teaching English briefly at the University of Wisconsin and Hunter College, Trilling was associated with Columbia from 1932, when he was appointed instructor in English. He received his doctorate in 1938 and by 1948 was a full professor; he was named George Edward Woodberry Professor of Literature and Criticism in 1965. Over the years, during his career at Columbia, he was also associated with other institutions; he was one of the organizers of the Kenyon School of Letters at Kenyon College in Ohio, and he served as visiting professor at Oxford University in 1964–1965 and at Harvard in 1969–1970. Known to the reading public mainly through his critical works, essays, and reviews, he published as his first book his doctoral dissertation on Matthew Arnold. His *E. M. Forster*, 1943, made the British author well known to an American audience for the first time. Other critical works, mainly collections of essays, included *The Liberal Imagination*, 1950; *The Opposing Self*, 1955; *A Gathering of Fugitives*, 1956; *Beyond Culture*, 1965; *The Experience of Literature*, 1967; *Sincerity and Authenticity*, 1972; and *Mind in the Modern World*, 1973. He also edited volumes of works by Arnold, John Keats, and Sigmund Freud. His novel, *The Middle of the Journey*, 1957, dealt with the social-political conflicts in the United States during the 1930s and 1940s. He died on November 5, 1975, in New York City.

Trimble, Robert (1777–1828), justice of the Supreme Court. Born in Augusta County, Virginia, in 1777, Trimble grew up on the frontier in Clark County, Kentucky, where his family moved when he was very young. What formal education he got was obtained at Bourbon Academy and Kentucky Academy, but he did not graduate from either institution. He studied law privately and began practice about 1800 in Paris, Kentucky, although he was not admitted to the bar until 1803. He maintained a successful private practice until 1807, with time out in 1802 for a term in the state legislature. The governor of Kentucky appointed him a justice on the court of appeals in 1807, but he served for only two years before returning to his more profitable law office. He became district attorney in 1813 and held the post until President James Madison appointed him a justice of the federal court in 1817. In 1826 President John Quincy Adams nominated Trimble an associate justice of the U.S. Supreme Court, and he was confirmed with little opposition on May 9. On the Court he held generally to the nationalist positions of Chief Justice John Marshall, upholding the dominance of federal over state laws where the two conflicted. He broke with Marshall and wrote one of his finest opinions in concurring with the majority in *Ogden* v. *Saunders*, 1827. His service on the Court was brief, however, for only two years after taking his seat he died in Paris, Kentucky, on August 25, 1828.

Trist, Nicholas Philip (1800–1874), diplomat. Born in Charlottesville, Virginia, on June 2, 1800, Trist attended West Point, although he did not graduate, and studied law in the office of Thomas Jefferson, whose granddaughter he married. His first government post was as a clerk in the State Department in 1827. He retained the job even with the change in administrations in 1828, and, through the influence of President Andrew Jackson's nephew, came to know the President and acted as his private secretary. From 1833 until 1841 he served as U.S. consul in Havana. With the Whigs in power in Washington for four years, Trist was out of government service, but with the inauguration of President James K. Polk in 1845 he returned to the State Department as chief clerk. In April 1847 Polk appointed him a special secret commissioner to negotiate peace with Mexico, after the Mexican War had been fought to a standstill with the battle of Buena Vista and the U.S. victory at Veracruz early in the year. Trist arrived at Veracruz on May 6, but because Gen. Winfield Scott did not know he was coming, the two hit it off badly and it was weeks before they became mutually reconciled to each other's status. Trist made a promising contact with President Santa Anna of Mexico, but Santa Anna went back on his promises and hostilities resumed in August. By the middle of September Santa Anna had been defeated and forced to resign, and a new Mexican government was set up. When Polk heard of the breakdown in negotiations, he sent a letter recalling Trist, hoping to force even harsher terms on Mexico. (There were many in the government, including Secretary of State James Buchanan and Secretary of the Treasury Robert J. Walker, who wanted to annex all of Mexico.) Trist received his notice of recall on November 16, but Mexican officials urged him to stay and negotiate. He decided to ignore his recall and continue to work for a settlement. It was clearly an act of insubordination, but much to his credit General Scott supported Trist's decision. Trist knew better than the Washington officials the situation in Mexico, and he was convinced that he had to make peace with the moderates, lest the whole country dissolve into anarchy. He knew, too, that the proposals of the annexationists in the United States would lead to a protracted guerrilla war by the Mexicans and a U.S. campaign for the extinction of the Mexican people. By February 2, 1848, the two parties had worked out the treaty of Guadalupe Hidalgo, which Trist took back to Washington. It provided for a minimum of U.S. territorial demands, which nevertheless deprived Mexico of a vast area of the present Southwest, from Texas to California and including most of what is now Colorado, Utah, Nevada, New Mexico, and Arizona. In return the United States was to pay Mexico $15 million. President Polk was angry at Trist for ignoring his recall, but accepted the treaty because it conformed to his publicly announced goals for the war. The treaty was ratified by the Senate, with the exception of one article, on March 10, 1848; Mexico ratified it two months later. Trist returned to private life and his modest legal practice. His disobedience resulted, as he had forseen, in his fall from Polk's graces, and he was not even able to collect his unpaid salary for many years. His only other government post was as postmaster of Alexandria, Virginia, in 1870. He died there on February 11, 1874.

Truman, Harry S. (1884–1972), thirty-third president of the United States. Born in Lamar, Missouri, on May 8, 1884, Truman grew up on a farm near Independence and managed to finish high school, but there was no money for college. He went to Kansas City, Missouri, and became a bank clerk, but after five years he returned to the farm. World War I gave him his first opportunity. He had joined the National Guard; now he was called up and sailed for France as a first lieutenant of artillery. In action he was a capable officer, liked and respected by his men. He was promoted to captain, returned to the United States, and in June 1919 married Elizabeth Virginia (Bess) Wallace. Truman set up a clothing store in Kansas City with an army comrade, but the store failed after the depression of 1920–1921 and he was left with about $20,000 in debts. He refused to declare himself a bankrupt and eventually paid back every penny. In his search for a job, he got in touch with another comrade from his army days, who introduced him to Thomas J. Pendergast, boss of the Democratic machine in Kansas City, who appointed him overseer of highways and then, after a year, managed to get him elected to the county court of Jackson County. Truman served in the post from 1922 to 1924, was defeated for reelection, but won a second two-year term in 1926. This time he was elected presiding judge of the court, a post he held until 1934. Although state law did not require that he be a qualified lawyer, he studied at night from 1923 to 1925 at the Kansas City School of Law. His real opportunity came in 1934, when he was selected by Pendergast as Democratic nominee for the U.S. Senate. He won the primary and was duly elected. His first term was undistinguished, and it was predicted that he could not win reelection in 1940. (In the meantime, the Pendergast machine had collapsed: scores of Pendergast's associates had been convicted for voting frauds, and Pendergast himself was in federal prison for income-tax evasion.) But Truman won nevertheless; no one had ever even charged him with being involved in the corruption of his political mentor, and his personal integrity was unquestioned. During his second term in the Senate he began to make his mark. He was appointed chairman of a special Senate "watchdog" committee to investigate expenditures on national-defense projects. The Truman Committee did an excellent and impartial job, uncovering instances of waste and of collusion between corporations and certain army purchasing agents, and saving the government many millions of dollars. By now a nationally recognized figure, he was proposed to President Franklin D. Roosevelt as a running mate in the 1944 campaign, to replace Vice-President Henry

A. Wallace, who was thought to be too liberal for Southern voters. Truman was nominated on the second ballot at the Democratic national convention and was elected when Roosevelt won his fourth term. When Roosevelt died on April 12, 1945, Truman became president. As was customary with vice-presidents, he had not been taken into the President's confidence during the previous five months, and when he assumed office he knew almost nothing about confidential government policy; but he had little to do during his first few months as president except to oversee the military victories over Germany and Japan that had already been planned and prepared. At the Potsdam Conference in July 1945 Truman got his first real taste of diplomacy, meeting with Sir Winston Churchill and Josef Stalin to discuss the conclusion of the war with Japan and to make preliminary arrangements for reorganizing the postwar world. While at the conference he was informed of the successful first test of the atomic bomb, of the existence of which he had been completely unaware before assuming the presidency. His decision to use the bomb against the Japanese cities of Hiroshima and Nagasaki in August, although later questioned as to its necessity, was at the time a welcome expedient to avoid the estimated million casualties that would accompany an invasion of the Japanese homeland. With the war over, he presented his domestic program to Congress in September 1945. Called the Fair Deal, it proposed far-reaching reforms, including some unfinished New Deal business, but conservatives in both major parties blocked most of the measures, and Truman finally abandoned most of it. (Much of the legislation was later passed under President Lyndon B. Johnson.) The failure of many of his reconversion programs, particularly price controls, combined with adverse reaction to the long reign of the New Deal to produce a marked conservative shift in Congress. The Taft-Hartley Act, inimical to organized labor, was passed over his veto in 1947, but he alienated labor in intervening in railroad and coal strikes in 1946 and 1947. His dedication to civil rights, signalized by his order desegregating the armed forces in 1948, angered many in the Democratic South. Foreign affairs, however, soon became the dominant concern in his administration. In February 1947 Great Britain informed the U.S. government that it could no longer supply military and economic aid to Greece and Turkey in their fight against Communist revolutionaries aided by the Soviet Union. The Truman Doctrine was the U.S. answer, in which the President announced that this country would take over the responsibilities of aiding those nations. The first monies for Greece and Turkey were approved by Congress in May 1947. The step intensified what had been a trend since early 1946 of deteriorating relations between the former allies, the United States and the Soviet Union. In June, after an address by Secretary of State George C. Marshall at Harvard, the so-called Marshall Plan (the European Recovery Program—ERP) began to go into effect, involving the expenditure during 1948–1951 alone of over $12 billion. A broader program of foreign aid was announced in Truman's inaugural address in 1949 and became known as the Point Four program. The effort to rebuild Europe was born of equal portions of humanitarian concern and a desire to head off the appeal of Communist propaganda and subversion. More to that point were the negotiations that led by early 1949 to the formation of the North Atlantic Treaty Organization (NATO), a military defense alliance that assured a U.S. presence in Western Europe. The blockade of Berlin by the Soviet Union in May 1948, necessitating the massive airlift of supplies into the city, set the tone for what soon came to be called the Cold War. Meanwhile Truman faced an election at home, and his popularity was at a low ebb among even the most traditionally Democratic segments of the electorate. Thomas E. Dewey, governor of New York State and the defeated Republican candidate in 1944, was again the Republican standard-bearer, and all polls and most political observers predicted that Truman could not win. But he took his cause to the country, embarking on a vigorous "whistle-stop" campaign, and despite a challenge by the splinter States'-Rights Democratic party in the South, and the candidacy of Henry Wallace on the ultra-liberal platform of the Progressive party, Truman won. His "give 'em hell, Harry" campaign had relied largely on his attacks on the "do-nothing" 80th Congress, and his victory carried Democratic majorities into both houses of Congress. It was a remarkable upset; Truman captured 49.5 percent of the popular vote and 303 electoral votes to Dewey's 45.1 percent and 189. The major events of his second term were two: the Korean War and the right-wing challenge of Senator Joseph R. McCarthy of Wisconsin. The invasion of South Korea by North Korean armies in June 1950 created an international crisis of very grave potential, and was the first major challenge to the United Nations. With the UN slow to act, however, and the North Koreans advancing rapidly, the President intervened in Korea without Congressional approval, although he later received it, on the grounds that the authority of the UN was being directly attacked by the North Koreans. The Korean War was indecisive. Gen. Douglas MacArthur, U.S. and UN commander in the area, did not see matters as Truman did—he persisted in publicly calling for carrying the war into mainland China because of Chinese Communist support of the North Koreans—and the conflict between them was not resolved until April 1951, when MacArthur was recalled from his command. That action roused a storm of criticism of the President at home, for MacArthur was extremely popular, especially among conservatives and the more vocal anti-Communists. But Truman defended his act by pointing out the great importance of maintaining the principle of civil control of the military. On the domestic scene, the hysteria of McCarthyism was rampant, fired by the MacArthur affair, the elusiveness of a clearcut

victory in Korea, the success of the Soviet Union in developing their atomic bomb, and a rash of spectacular espionage cases, including those of Alger Hiss and the Rosenbergs. In March 1952 Truman announced his decision not to run again for the presidency. He retired to Independence, Missouri, where in 1957 the Harry S. Truman Library, a part of the national archives, was dedicated. His *Memoirs* were published in two volumes in 1955–1956. Truman remained an important figure in the Democratic party, and as the years passed and the passions of the time cooled he became a much beloved figure. The principal memories of his administration were of his integrity, his feistiness, his understanding of the common people, and his profound sense of responsibility, summed up in the sign that had adorned his presidential desk: "The buck stops here." Even into his eighties he continued his famous custom of taking a daily "constitutional;" he continued to live quietly at his home in Independence until his death, in Kansas City, Missouri, on December 26, 1972.

Trumbull, John (1750–1831), poet and lawyer. Born in a part of Westbury that is now in Watertown, Connecticut, on April 24, 1750, Trumbull, a cousin of Jonathan Trumbull and of the painter John Trumbull, graduated from Yale in 1767. Having passed the entrance examinations at seven, he matriculated at thirteen. He continued to study, taking an M.A. in 1770, and while tutoring at Yale he read law for a year before passing his bar examination in 1773. Before beginning practice in Boston, he studied law under John Adams for a year. Adams was influential in making Trumbull an ardent patriot during the Revolution and a Federalist thereafter. In August 1774 he returned to Connecticut and settled in New Haven to practice law; he followed his profession there and in Hartford for 50 years. Trumbull had two fairly distinct careers. From his college days until the mid-1780s he was a poet and essayist, but after that he devoted himself to law and public service until his retirement. His literary career centered around the times of crisis in which the United States became a nation and adopted its permanent form of government. Much of Trumbull's earlier work was critical of the educational system that prevailed at Yale. He wanted to see the curriculum liberalized and updated, and to that end he wrote his valedictory address, "An Essay on the Uses and Advantages of the Fine Arts," 1767, and *The Progress of Dulness*, 1772, a verse satire on the college education then being purveyed. In 1770 and 1773 he published a series of 38 essays in the *Connecticut Journal*. During the years of the Revolution and the making of a new constitution he turned to patriotic themes with his poem *An Elegy on the Times*, 1774, and his chief work, *M'Fingal*, a highly popular 3000–line mock epic satirizing British bungling during the Revolution. *M'Fingal* was published in several parts, the first canto coming out in 1776 and the work being completed in 1782. During the 15 years after the war when the federal government was being hammered out, Trumbull was a member of the group of writers called the Connecticut Wits or the Hartford Wits, which numbered among its members such writers as Joel Barlow, David Humphreys, and Timothy Dwight. In addition to their goals of reforming college education and achieving American literary independence from Europe, the Wits also favored the Federalist movement for a strong central government. To help achieve this goal they collectively wrote *The Anarchiad*, a 12-part satiric poem in heroic meter published anonymously in installments in 1786–1787. Trumbull's literary days were largely behind him by the mid-1780s, although he rendered some assistance to Noah Webster in the compilation of Webster's dictionary, and he settled into his law practice. In 1789 he held public office for the first time as Hartford County state's attorney. He was twice elected to the Connecticut legislature, in 1792 and 1800, and in 1801 he became a judge of the state superior court. In 1808 he was appointed to the state supreme court, and he held both judgeships concurrently until 1819. Following retirement from the bench he returned to his law office at Hartford until 1825, when he moved to Detroit, Michigan. He died there on May 11, 1831.

Trumbull, John (1756–1843), painter. Born on June 6, 1756, in Lebanon, Connecticut, the son of Jonathan Trumbull (1710–1785), Trumbull showed a talent for drawing at an early age. He graduated from Harvard in 1773, taught school in Lebanon, assisted his father by drawing maps of Connecticut's Western land claims, and dabbled in painting until the outbreak of the American Revolution. From 1775 to 1777 he served in the Continental army, first in a Connecticut regiment and later as an aide to Gen. George Washington and then as adjutant to Gen. Horatio Gates, and attained a colonelcy before he was twenty-one. He resigned his commission in 1777 but later served as a volunteer in the Rhode Island campaign of 1778; but for most of 1777–1778 he studied art in Boston. In 1780 he sailed to England to study with Benjamin West. In London he was seized and imprisoned for what was claimed to be suspicion of treason but may well have been a reprisal for the hanging of Major John André in the Benedict Arnold affair, but he used his time in prison profitably in the study of art and architecture. Upon his release (for which Edmund Burke was largely responsible) he went to Amsterdam and completed a full-length portrait of George Washington that was engraved and distributed throughout Europe, the first authentic likeness of Washington to be seen abroad. After an unproductive time back in the United States during 1782–1783, he returned to London and West's studio in 1784. A series of small-scale paintings including "The Battle of Bunker's Hill" and "The Death of General Montgomery at the Attack of Quebec" led Thomas Jefferson to encourage him to recreate in painting the scenes of the Revolution that he had witnessed. Trumbull returned again to the United States in 1789 to paint portraits, revisit the scenes of great battles, and study documents, uniforms, and equipment that related to his subjects. His most famous work, "The Declaration of Independence," begun in London but eight years in the completion, included 48 portraits, more than two-thirds of them painted from life, the others from portraits by others or from memory. In 1793 John Jay invited him to serve as his secretary during the negotiation of Jay's Treaty in England; he accepted and remained abroad as a member of the claims commission set up under the treaty until 1804. When his service was completed, he returned to portraiture, but his ten years spent away from painting had a considerable effect on the quality of his work. During 1804–1808 he was in New York City and for five years thereafter he again lived in London. In 1813 he again set up a studio in New York City. To the consternation of many young American painters, he was given in 1817 a congressional commission to execute four large historical scenes for the rotunda of the U.S. Capitol. The four pictures, already completed in miniature, took him seven years to transfer to large canvases; titled "The Surrender of Burgoyne," "The Surrender of Cornwallis," "Washington Resigning his Commission," and most notably an enlarged version of "The Declaration of Independence," they are Trumbull's best-known works. The large canvases were not, however, as well received as their originals had been—John Adams expressed himself as disappointed with them—and after four years they were removed because of the dampness of the walls. From 1817 to 1836 he was president of the American Academy of Fine Arts, and it was his dictatorial manner in that position that prompted a secession of younger artists, led by Samuel F. B. Morse, and the founding of the rival National Academy of Design. Long past his prime as a painter and receiving fewer and fewer commissions, Trumbull spent much of his old age in financial insecurity. Finally in 1831, through the agency of Benjamin Silliman, he donated his unsold paintings to Yale in exchange for an annuity. The university established the Trumbull Gallery, the first U.S. art gallery to be affiliated with an educational institution. He wrote an autobiography in 1841 and died in New York City on November 10, 1843.

Trumbull, Jonathan (1710–1785), merchant and public official. Born in Lebanon, Connecticut, on October 12, 1710, Trumbull graduated from Harvard College in 1727. He started studying for the ministry, but changed his mind when the death of his brother Joseph in 1731 influenced him to go into their father's business in Joseph's stead. He made a successful mercantile career for himself for about 35 years before the business all but ended in bankruptcy. But by that time Trumbull was well established in Connecticut politics. He served several terms in the legislature, once as speaker of the assembly. From 1740 to 1750 he was a member of the governor's council. In 1754 he was reelected to the council and remained a member until 1766, when he became deputy governor. In 1769 the general assembly elected him governor, and he remained in office until his retirement in 1784. Prior to assuming the governorship he had also served as judge of various Connecticut courts, and he was chief justice of the superior court from 1766 to 1769. Governor Trumbull was one of the first officials in the American colonies to foresee the possibilities of independence from England, and when the Revolution broke out he was the only governor openly to declare for the colonial cause. Because Connecticut was not one of the main war zones, Trumbull was able, in his position as governor, to make the state one of the major sources of supplies for the Continental army throughout the years of fighting. After the end of hostilities, he retired from office and died in Lebanon, Connecticut, on August 17, 1785.

Trumbull, Jonathan (1740–1809), soldier and public official. Born in Lebanon, Connecticut, on March 26, 1740, Jonathan was the son of Jonathan Trumbull (1710–1785) and the brother of artist John Trumbull. He graduated from Harvard in 1759. His first political office was on the Lebanon town council, from 1770 to 1775; he also served several terms in the Connecticut general assembly between 1774 and 1788. From 1775 to 1778 he was paymaster for the New York department of the Continental army, and from 1778 to 1779 he was first comptroller of the treasury. In 1780 he was appointed secretary to Gen. George Washington, a post he held until 1783. After the end of the Revolutionary War Trumbull retired from public life to pursue business interests. But he returned to public service in 1789 as a Federalist member of the first Congress under the Constitution and was speaker of the House during the second Congress, 1791–1793. After one more term in the House, he was elected to the U.S. Senate and served there from March 4, 1795, until June 10, 1796, when he resigned to become lieutenant governor of Connecticut. In December 1797 he became governor and was reelected to the office every year until his death in Lebanon, Connecticut, on August 7, 1809.

Truth, Sojourner (1797?–1883), abolitionist. Born a slave in Ulster County, New York, in the late 1790s, Sojourner Truth bore the legal name Isabella Van Wagener, her surname taken from the last of a series of masters who owned her prior to her emancipation, an event precipitated by the passage of the New York Emancipation Act of 1827. Little is known of her early life other than her claim that, from childhood, she had conversed with God. She subsequently lived and worked as a servant in New York City, where she became active as an evangelist. Adopting the new name Sojourner Truth, she took to the road as an itinerant preacher in 1843. Speaking out for woman suffrage as well as against slavery, she soon joined the abolitionist crusade as a featured speaker. Her usual opening, "Children, I talk to God and God talks to me!," had an electric effect

on her audiences in Connecticut, Massachusetts, Ohio, Indiana, Illinois, and Kansas. Repeated attempts by mobs or the law to silence her only spurred her on. Her remarkable power as a speaker led some to question if she were indeed a woman, to say nothing of the mother of five children, one of which she had recovered from slavery in a precedent-setting court suit. At times rivaling Frederick Douglass in eloquence, she often shared the podium with him. In their most famous encounter, when he moved a pre-Civil War black audience to seek justice in revolt, Sojourner broke the spell by asking, "Frederick, is God dead?" A large measure of her support came from widespread sales of *The Narrative of Sojourner Truth,* written by Olive Gilbert and with a preface by William Lloyd Garrison. Another edition after the Civil War was prefaced by Harriet Beecher Stowe. Her fame preceded her to Washington, where President Abraham Lincoln appointed her counselor to the freedmen in the capital. She remained active as a speaker on behalf of Negro causes even after the war and worked with the Freedmen's Bureau on behalf of former slaves. She died on November 26, 1883, in Battle Creek, Michigan, her last home.

Truxtun, Thomas (1755–1822), naval officer. Born on Long Island, New York, near Hempstead, on February 17, 1755, Truxtun had little formal schooling before he went to sea on a merchant ship at the age of twelve. His abilities were such that eight years later he was in command of his own ship. During the Revolution he fought for the United States by operating as a privateer against British shipping in the Atlantic. From 1776 to 1782 he commanded in turn the *Congress,* the *Independence,* the *Mars,* and the *St. James,* and was successful with all in capturing British ships. He returned to merchant shipping for 12 years after the war; he sailed in command of one of the first U.S. ships to engage in the China trade, the *Canton* out of Philadelphia in 1786. In 1794 he was appointed a captain in the U.S. navy. During the undeclared naval war with France, from 1798 to 1800, he captained the *Constellation* and took part, as commodore of a squadron, in several brilliant engagements in the West Indies that made him a popular hero, notably the victory over the *Insurgente* in 1799 and that over *La Vengeance* in 1800. During his period of service he nearly resigned in a dispute over rank with Richard Dale. After commanding the *President* for a few months in 1800 he returned home to Perth Amboy, New Jersey. When in 1801 he was refused a command in the Tripolitan War against the Barbary pirates, he considered himself to have resigned from the navy and stayed in general retirement in Perth Amboy and, from 1806, in Philadelphia. He ran unsuccessfully for a seat in the House of Representatives in 1810, but was elected sheriff of Philadelphia in 1816 for a four-year term. Truxtun contributed to the science of navigation with his books *Remarks, Instructions, and Examples Relating to Latitude and Longitude,* 1794, and *Instructions, Signals, and Explanations Of-*

fered for the U.S. Fleet, 1797. In 1806 he published an anthology of writings on naval tactics. He died in Philadelphia on May 5, 1822.

Tubman, Harriet (1820?–1913), abolitionist. Born a slave in Dorchester County, Maryland, about 1820, Harriet was first named Araminta, but later adopted her mother's name; the name Tubman came with a marriage forced upon her by her master in 1844. In her childhood and youth she was a field hand, but in 1849 she escaped from the plantation and made her way to the North with the aid of the Underground Railroad. During the next decade she became the most famous and successful of conductors on the Railroad; she made 19 trips into the South to aid escaped slaves and brought more than 300 to safety in the North and, after passage of the Fugitive Slave Law (1850), in Canada. In 1857 she even managed to rescue her aged parents. A woman of great strength, resourcefulness, and intelligence, she stoutly withstood spells of dizziness and unconsciousness stemming from a childhood head injury and maintained an iron discipline among her charges. She always evaded capture despite huge rewards offered for her, and she became known as the "Moses of her people." She met and worked with leading white abolitionists of the time—Ralph Waldo Emerson, William H. Seward, Wendell Phillips, and others—and was consulted by John Brown before his raid on Harpers Ferry. She made a number of speeches for the abolitionist cause. During the Civil War she attached herself to the Union forces operating in South Carolina as a cook, laundress, and nurse, and rendered valuable service as a guide and occasional spy. After the war she worked to establish schools in North Carolina for freedmen. She supported herself in part from sales of *Scenes in the Life of Harriet Tubman*, 1869, written for her by Sarah H. Bradford and later retitled *Harriet, the Moses of Her People*, 1886. Later she settled in Auburn, New York, where she founded the Harriet Tubman Home for Aged Negroes, maintained later by the town, and where she lived until her death there on March 10, 1913.

Tucker, Benjamin Ricketson (1854–1939), anarchist, journalist, and publisher. Born in South Dartmouth, Massachusetts, on April 17, 1854, Tucker attended Massachusetts Institute of Technology (MIT) from 1870 to 1873. Sometime during his second or third year at MIT he became a convert to social reform and to individualistic anarchism in particular. He traveled to France to study the writings of leading anarchists, especially Pierre Joseph Proudhon, and upon returning to the United States worked as associate editor of a journal called *The Word*, at Princeton, Massachusetts, in 1875–1876. In 1877 he founded and edited his own magazine, the *Radical Review*, but it was a short-lived venture. In 1878 he went to work for the *Boston Globe*, where he remained for 11 years. From 1892 until 1907 he was on the editorial staff of *Engineering News*, and was also associate

editor of the *New York Home Journal* from 1894 to 1899. During these years of making his living as a journalist, Tucker also published, in his spare time, a paper entitled *Liberty* which, from 1881 until 1908, served as a sounding board for anarchist theory. He was a champion of individual liberty and a philosophical anarchist, opposed to violence and to the theoretical and actual excesses of Socialism and Communism. During the heyday of radical thought in the United States, from the late 1870s until after 1900, when most leftist thought and action centered about organized labor and the working class, Tucker made the most significant anarchist and radical writings of Europeans available to American readers. He translated Proudhon's *What Is Property?*, M. A. Bakunin's *God and the State*, and other writings. And he published Walt Whitman's *Leaves of Grass* and Count Leo Tolstoi's *Kreutzer Sonata* in Boston, where they both had been banned. His own exposition of anarchism, entitled *Instead of a Book*, was published in 1893, and in 1899 he published *State Socialism and Anarchism*. His reputation was such that when the Chicago Civic Federation's Conference on Trusts met in September 1899, Tucker was one of the notables called to testify. In 1908 his publishing house burned down, and unable to afford to start again, he moved his family to France. He did not live in the United States again. Although he maintained many of his former contacts, he was never able to revive his publishing ventures; and World War I and its aftermath dealt severe blows to both anarchism and Socialism, especially in the United States. Tucker moved to Monaco in 1926 and lived there until his death on June 22, 1939.

Tucker, Sophie (1884–1966), entertainer. Born somewhere in Russia as her family was emigrating to the United States in 1884, Sophie Kalish grew up in Boston, where her mother ran a restaurant. Her father had changed the family name to Abuza during emigration. From her childhood she wanted to be an entertainer. After an unsuccessful teen-age marriage, which was ended by divorce by the time she was twenty, she saved enough money to leave home and headed for New York City. In 1906 she changed her name to Sophie Tucker and landed a few singing jobs. Her actual professional career began when, after a successful amateur appearance, she opened (in a blackface routine) at the old Music Hall in New York City, on December 9, 1906. That day she launched a show-business career that would span 60 years. She was in vaudeville for a little more than 25 years, from 1906 until the early 1930s. She worked at Tony Pastor's theater in New York City, then went into burlesque. While on tour in 1909 she was spotted by a talent scout and signed for the *Ziegfeld Follies*. After she was replaced in the *Follies* she engaged the William Morris Agency to manage her career, and from that time she was steadily successful. She traveled the U.S. vaudeville circuits from coast to coast for more than 20 years, and also made occasional appearances in England, where she gained a substantial following. It was in 1911 that she first sang "Some of These Days," which became her trademark. Her first appearance at the Palace Theater, in New York City, considered the summit of success in vaudeville, came in 1914. It was in 1928, at the Palace, that she was first billed as "The Last of the Red-hot Mamas." She also appeared in editions of Earl Carroll's *Vanities* and the Shuberts's *Gaieties*. In the early 1930s, when it became apparent that vaudeville was on the way out, Miss Tucker turned to nightclubs, while many of the other old vaudevillians either attempted the movies or slid into oblivion. She did make several films, none notable; but she preferred the live audiences a cabaret offered, and she played to them with great success for more than 30 years. She also made occasional television appearances, mainly on "The Ed Sullivan Show," during the 1950s and early 1960s. She was eighty-one years old when illness curtailed her performing late in 1965, but until then age had little diminished her ability to belt out a rousing blues or jazz rendition of one of her standards and to regale an audience with her racy patter. She died on February 9, 1966, in New York City.

Tugwell, Rexford Guy (1891–1979), economist and public official. Born in Sinclairville, New York, on July 10, 1891, Rexford Guy Tugwell grew up in the neighboring town of Wilson. In 1915 he graduated from the University of Pennsylvania's Wharton School of Finance and Commerce and in 1922 took his doctorate there. He taught economics at the university from 1915 to 1917 and at the University of Washington in 1917–1918. After two years abroad at the American University Union in Paris, he joined the economics faculty of Columbia University, with which he continued to be associated until 1937, after 1931 as a professor. Before and during the 1932 presidential campaign Tugwell was a member of Franklin D. Roosevelt's "brain trust," and when the Roosevelt administration took office he was appointed assistant secretary of agriculture. He remained with the Department of Agriculture until 1936, and during 1935–1936 administered the Resettlement Administration. He was one of the authors of the Agricultural Adjustment Act of 1933. An outspoken advocate of economic planning, social welfare, and the regulation of industry, he was often sharply criticized by opponents of the New Deal who accused him of trying to destroy the free-enterprise system. Tugwell maintained that he was only trying to help save capitalism from its own inherent defects. In 1938 Mayor Fiorello H. La Guardia of New York City appointed him chairman of the City Planning Commission. In 1940 he was sent by Secretary of the Interior Harold L. Ickes to Puerto Rico to investigate economic problems on the island, and the next year President Roosevelt appointed him governor of Puerto Rico. During five years in the post he worked closely with Luis Muñoz Marín, president of the Puerto Rican senate, to formulate plans for the agricultural and industrial development of the island. Their efforts resulted in the successful Operation Bootstrap that was inaugurated there under President Harry S. Truman. Out of his experiences as governor of Puerto Rico, Tugwell wrote the book, *The Stricken Land*, 1946. In 1946, after leaving the governorship, Tugwell joined the faculty of the University of Chicago, where he was professor of political science until his retirement in 1957. In the early postwar era he was a member of the committee at the university that drew up a proposed constitution for a world government. From 1961 to 1964 he served as consultant to the chancellor of the University of Puerto Rico and in 1964 he became associated with the Center for the Study of Democratic Institutions in Santa Barbara, California. Among his other books were *The Trend of Economics*, 1924; *Industry's Coming of Age*, 1927; *Soviet Russia in the Second Decade*, 1928; *The Battle for Democracy*, 1935; and *The Place of Planning in Society*, 1954. His autobiography, *The Light of Other Days*, was published in 1962. During the later 1960s he drafted at the Center a radically new version of the U.S. Constitution. He died in Santa Barbara on July 21, 1979.

Tunney, Gene (1898–1978), boxer. Born on May 25, 1898, in New York City, James Joseph Tunney attended a private school, the LaSalle Academy, there for two years before dropping out of school to work as a clerk for the Ocean Steamship Company from 1912 to 1917. While in his teens he had learned to box at a neighborhood recreational center and fought a number of amateur bouts in the city. He had just turned professional when the United States entered World War I, and he enlisted in the Marine Corps. He won the light-heavyweight championship of the American Expeditionary Forces (AEF) in Paris in 1919. After his discharge from the service he returned to professional boxing. In 1922 he won the U.S. light-heavyweight championship, only to be defeated later the same year by Harry Greb. In 1923 he regained the title from Greb, and in 1924 he began to fight as a heavyweight. In 1926, when Tunney challenged world champion Jack Dempsey, virtually all bets were on Dempsey; but Tunney demolished the champion, winning the decision after ten rounds before a record crowd on the night of September 23. In a rematch in Chicago the following year, again before a record crowd, Dempsey downed Tunney at one point but failed to go to a neutral corner immediately; the result was the famous "long count" by the referee during which Tunney revived and won a decision over Dempsey. On July 26, 1928, Tunney scored a 12th-round knockout over challenger Tom Heeney —it was Tunney's last fight; the following month he retired from the ring as undefeated champion. From that time he was a business executive, associated with a number of firms. He wrote *A Man Must Fight*, 1932, and *Arms for Living*, 1941. During World War II he was director of physical fitness for the navy. Tunney died in Greenwich, Connecticut, on November 7, 1978.

Tunney, James Joseph, *see* Tunney, Gene

Turner, Frederick Jackson (1861–1932), historian. Born on November 14, 1861, in Portage, Wisconsin, Turner graduated from the University of Wisconsin in 1884. After a short time working for a newspaper he returned to the university to pursue graduate studies in history; he took his master's degree in 1888 and then studied for a year at The Johns Hopkins University, where he formed a close friendship with Woodrow Wilson. In 1889 he joined the faculty at Wisconsin, received his Ph.D. from Hopkins the next year, and was made professor of American history at Wisconsin in 1892. In 1893, during the World's Columbian Exposition in Chicago, he presented a paper to a meeting of the American Historical Association in which he outlined a revolutionary interpretation of American history. Whereas earlier historians had focused on single issues and institutions—religious liberty, nationalism, slavery, or others—Turner, in "The Significance of the Frontier in American History," spoke from a new viewpoint in suggesting a complex of political and environmental forces as the key to the development of American civilization. He saw in the frontier the source of the individualism, restless energy, self-reliance, and inventiveness that are characteristically American. His paper was published in the *Proceedings of the State Historical Society of Wisconsin* and in the *Annual Report of the American Historical Association* in 1894. The "Turner thesis" sparked considerable controversy and was eagerly adopted by many of his colleagues and students, although often with less flexibility than he himself displayed in his continual revisions and modifications in light of other theories. His central idea remained nonetheless a major mode of interpretation in the study and teaching of American history. During 1909–1910 he was president of the American Historical Association, and in 1910 he moved to Harvard, where he remained for 14 years. In 1906 he wrote *Rise of the New West* for the American Nation series; in 1920 he published *The Frontier in American History,* and in 1932 *The Significance of Sections in American History,* which was awarded a Pulitzer Prize the next year. Following his retirement from Harvard in 1924 he became a research associate at the Henry E. Huntington Library and Art Gallery in San Marino, California. He died in Pasadena on March 14, 1932.

Turner, Nat (1800–1831), slave leader. Born on October 2, 1800, in Southampton County, Virginia, Nat Turner grew up a slave in a relatively permissive environment; recognized for his exceptional intelligence, he received instruction in reading, writing, and religion from the family of his first master, Benjamin Turner. In the early 1820s, in a period of financial straits, the Turners were forced to sell him to an almost illiterate farmer who gave him much work to do but no constructive outlet for his mental energy. He nourished an increasing religious ardor with trips into the woods, where he believed that he felt the presence of God and that he saw "white spirits and black spirits engaged in battle, and blood flowing in streams." Assuming the role of preacher to the slaves, he convinced many of his belief that he was chosen through divine inspiration to lead the Negro from slavery. In 1830 be became a slave of a craftsman, Joseph Travis. Shortly thereafter, in 1831, an eclipse of the sun convinced him the time for revolt was near. He secured the support of four other slaves, but the uprising was abandoned for the time. After a new sign was received, they set August 21, 1831, as the day of deliverance. With seven others he attacked the Travis family in their sleep and murdered them all. In company with about 75 undisciplined insurgent slaves he killed in two days and two nights more than 50 white persons on the way to Jerusalem, Virginia. The state militia and armed townsmen intercepted the raiders about three miles from Jerusalem. Turner escaped while the others were being dispersed and either captured or killed. An unknown but large number of slaves, including many who were innocent, were killed in the aftermath of the massacre. After six weeks he was found, tried, convicted, and sentenced to death. He was hanged in Jerusalem on November 11, 1831. *The Confessions of Nat Turner . . . to Thomas R. Gray* was published in 1832. Sixteen of his companions were also hanged. As a result of the Turner (or Southampton) Insurrection, nearly every Southern state passed more severe slave codes, and the fear of another rebellion remained among whites in the South through the time of the Civil War.

Twain, Mark, *see* Clemens, Samuel Langhorne

Tweed, William Marcy (1823–1878), public official and political leader. Born in New York City on April 3, 1823, Tweed received only elementary schooling before serving apprenticeships to a chairmaker and later a saddler. At seventeen he became a bookkeeper in his father's brush factory. His involvement in politics sprang from his work as a volunteer fireman, a not uncommon political stepping-stone at the time; he became foreman of his fire company in 1850 and the next year was elected an alderman on a notoriously thievish board. From 1853 to 1855 he served in the House of Representatives while retaining his aldermanic seat. He gradually strengthened his position in Tammany Hall, the New York City Democratic organization, and began to gather around himself the associates who would form the infamous Tweed Ring. In 1855 he was defeated for re-election as alderman, but his power in Tammany had increased to the point that he was able to force Fernando Wood out of the organization. In 1856 he was elected to the Board of Supervisors, a body created to stamp out corruption but which, with Tweed's help, became a center for graft. He became a sachem of Tammany and served as school commissioner, deputy commissioner of public works, and deputy street commissioner, at the same time elevating his friends to positions of influence. In 1860 he opened a law office to serve as a channel for graft payments from various corporate sources, among them the Erie Railroad, which he helped Jay Gould and Jim Fisk to plunder. In 1867 he was elected to the state senate; the next year he became grand sachem of Tammany, placed his own candidate, John T. Hoffman, in the governor's seat, elected A. Oakey Hall mayor, and was virtually dictator of politics in New York, both city and state. A systematic plundering of the city and state treasuries was instituted on a formula that eventually called for 85 percent padding in all bills charged to New York City; this program of fraud was aided by a new city charter in 1870 (procured at a cost of about a million dollars in bribes) that provided for a board of audit that quickly came under the control of the Tweed Ring. The amount of public money eventually diverted into the hands of Boss Tweed and his gang is estimated to have been between $45 million and $200 million. *Harper's Weekly* began an editorial campaign against the ring in 1870, counting among its most potent weapons the cartoons of Thomas Nast, who was offered half a million dollars to stop publishing them; the *New York Times* joined in the campaign later in the year, publishing evidence supplied by disgruntled officials. A Committee of Seventy was formed by concerned citizens and, prompted by Samuel J. Tilden, who brought civil suit against Tweed to recover stolen money, authorities arrested Tweed late in 1871 on charges of forgery and larceny. Convicted in 1873 at a second trial (there was a hung jury at the first), he was sentenced to a short term in prison and after his release in 1875 was rearrested in a civil action by the state to recover the loot. In December he escaped from jail and fled, disguised as a sailor, first to Cuba and then to Spain. There, with the aid of a Nast cartoon, he was recognized, apprehended, and returned to imprisonment in New York City, where he died on April 12, 1878.

Tyler, John (1790–1862), tenth president of the United States. Born in Charles City County, Virginia, on March 29, 1790, Tyler came of a family of aristocratic planters. He graduated from the College of William and Mary in 1807 and after studying law under his father, John Tyler, then governor of Virginia, began to practice in 1809. From 1811 to 1816 he served as a Jeffersonian Republican (Democratic Republican) in the state legislature, and in 1816 was elected to the House of Representatives, where he served until ill health forced his resignation in 1821. He was firm in his belief in a strict construction of the Constitution, with an emphasis on states' rights; he opposed the Bank of the United States, Henry Clay's nationalistic program of internal improvements and tariffs, and, although he disliked slavery and hoped to see it disappear, was especially harsh toward congressional attempts to regulate slavery, as in the Missouri Compromise of 1820. In 1823 he was returned to the Virginia legislature and from 1825 to 1827 served as governor, resigning

when he was elected to the U.S. Senate by the anti-Jacksonian element in the legislature. In 1828, however, he supported Andrew Jackson for president, preferring him to John Quincy Adams as the lesser of two evils. Tyler opposed the tariff bills of 1828 and 1832 and, while disagreeing with South Carolina's stand on nullification, stood also against Jackson by casting the only Senate vote against the Force Bill of 1833. It was upon Tyler's initiative that the Compromise Tariff of 1833 was negotiated and the tariff crisis ended. He supported Jackson's vetoes of the Maysville Road bill, 1830, and the rechartering of the Bank of the United States but, soon after his reelection in 1833, he joined in the Senate censure of Jackson for his removal of federal deposits from the Bank. In 1836 the Virginia legislature instructed Tyler to support Senator Thomas Hart Benton's resolution to expunge the censure from the record, but rather than do so he resigned his seat. His tenuous connection with his party (now called the Democrats) broken, he became loosely allied with the Whigs; in 1838 he was again in the state legislature, and two years later was elected vice-president on that ticket as William Henry Harrison's running mate. President Harrison died a month after the inauguration and Tyler, overcoming efforts to deny him the succession, became the first vice-president to succeed to the presidency. Clay, the Whig leader, immediately introduced a number of nationalistic measures for Senate approval; Tyler vetoed two successive bank bills that he considered detrimental to state sovereignty and, at Clay's behest, the entire cabinet (a carryover from Harrison) resigned except for Daniel Webster, secretary of state, who remained only long enough to negotiate the Webster-Ashburton Treaty settling the northeastern U.S.–Canadian border. Tyler now had no party. Nonetheless, his administration was not without achievements. The navy was reorganized and steps were taken toward the establishment of the Naval Observatory, the Seminole War and Dorr's Rebellion were ended, a trade agreement was reached with China, and Texas was annexed. Although Tyler had been working to acquire Texas through 1844, Congress had delayed; the Democratic national convention of that year endorsed expansion but passed over Tyler and chose James K. Polk for the nomination. Tyler was nominated by an irregular convention, but withdrew his name from the contest in favor of Polk. Tyler at last called for annexation by joint resolution of Congress, and this came just before he left the White House in March 1845. He retired to his Virginia plantation and remained out of active politics until the eve of the Civil War; he emerged in 1860 as a strong voice for moderation and deliberation in the South. He organized and presided over the unsuccessful Washington conference held to consider peaceful compromises in 1861, and only when all compromise seemed impossible did he endorse secession. He was elected to the provisional Confederate Congress and then to the permanent Congress but, before taking his seat, he died in Richmond, Virginia, on January 18, 1862.

Tyler, Moses Coit (1835–1900), educator and historian. Born in Griswold, Connecticut, on August 7, 1835, Tyler grew up in Detroit and attended the University of Michigan. In 1853 he transferred to Yale, from which he graduated in 1857. After pursuing seminary training for two years at Yale and Andover, he was ordained a minister of the Congregational church in 1859. He served a parish in Poughkeepsie, New York, but he resigned in 1862. He was never quite satisfied away from the ministry, however, and 20 years later, in the midst of an academic career, he was ordained a priest in the Protestant Episcopal church. After leaving his parish in Poughkeepsie, he was at loose ends for most of the 1860s. He took part in various reform activities and traveled abroad. In 1867 he accepted appointment as professor of English at the University of Michigan. He remained there until 1881, except for a one-year period, 1873–1874, when he worked on the editorial staff of Henry Ward Beecher's *Christian Union.* In 1881 Andrew D. White asked Tyler to accept the position of professor of American history at Cornell University, the first such professorship in any college in the United States. Tyler thus became one of the pioneer scholars in the field of American history, and one of the men who shaped the whole field of study in its early period. In 1884 he was one of the founders of the American Historical Association. His writings included *A History of American Literature During the Colonial Time, 1607–1765,* two volumes, 1878, *The Literary History of the American Revolution, 1763–1783,* two volumes, 1897, and *Three Men of Letters,* 1895, consisting of biographies of George Berkeley, Timothy Dwight, and Joel Barlow. He died in Ithaca, New York, on December 28, 1900.

Tyler, Royall (1757–1826), author and lawyer. Born in Boston on July 18, 1757, Tyler graduated from Harvard College in 1776. He saw intermittent service during the Revolution as a major in the Independent Company of Boston, and in 1787 he was a member of the force that put down Shays's Rebellion. Having studied law, he was admitted to the bar in 1780 and started a practice in Falmouth (now Portland), Maine, then a part of Massachusetts. He lived successively in Braintree, Massachusetts, and from 1785 in Boston before settling in Vermont in 1791. Throughout most of his life he continued to practice law, and while living in Vermont was attorney for Windham County from 1794 to 1801, a judge from 1801 to 1807, and chief justice of the Vermont supreme court from 1807 until 1813. From 1811 to 1814 he was also professor of jurisprudence at the University of Vermont. But it is not for law, but for his literary works, that Tyler is chiefly remembered. In 1787, after attending plays at the John Street Theater in New York City, he wrote a play of his own entitled *The Contrast.* It was a comedy of manners in which the American straightforward gentleman was contrasted with the English snob. The character Jonathan became the archetype of the stage Yankee. The first comedy written by a native American to be professionally produced, it was very successful at the time and has been produced often since. Of his other plays, none that were actually staged have survived; they included *May Day in Town; or New York in An Uproar,* a comic opera, and *The Georgia Spec, or Land on the Moon.* Apart from *The Contrast,* his best-known work was a novel, *The Algerine Captive,* 1797, a work satirizing the faults of both the North and the South. For a while in the mid-1790s Tyler cooperated with Joseph Dennie in writing a series of pro-Federalist satires in prose and verse that were published in various newspapers under the pseudonyms "Colon and Spondee," and collected in 1801 under the title *The Spirit of the Farmers' Museum.* From 1801 Tyler made his home in Brattleboro, Vermont, and he died there on August 26, 1826.

Typhoid Mary, *see* Mallon, Mary

U

Ulman, Douglas, *see* Fairbanks, Douglas

Uncle Sam, *see* Wilson, Samuel

Underhill, John (1597?–1672), colonial official and soldier. Born in England about 1597, Underhill grew up in the Netherlands, where his father was a mercenary soldier. He no doubt received military training himself, for when he came to Massachusetts Bay in 1630 it was to organize the colonial militia. In his first few years in America, he was readily accepted as a member of the colony; he was appointed a captain of the militia, voted arms and money, and granted a parcel of land. The only real annoyance he suffered was the colonists' general lack of interest in their own defense. He took part in the 1637 Pequot War against the Indians in Connecticut. His return to Boston afterward marked the beginning of 20 years of unsettled life, as he found himself thereafter on bad terms with the Massachusetts officials. In the religious controversy raging in the late 1630s he took the part of the Antinomians Anne Hutchinson and John Wheelwright against the Puritan administration. He was consequently charged with sedition and deprived of his militia rank and of his right to vote. After spending a few months in England in 1637–1638, during which he published *Newes from America*, 1638, an account of the Pequot War, he returned to Boston only to be put on trial for his religious attitudes and banished from the colony. After fleeing to Dover, New Hampshire, to avoid trial on charges of adultery, Underhill became governor of the Dover settlement and defied the Massachusetts authorities. He was excommunicated for a brief period during 1640, and was finally reconciled with the officials at Boston in 1641. About 1643, after living for a time at Stamford, Connecticut, he went into the service of the Dutch colony of New Netherland as an Indian fighter. But again his success as a soldier was negated by his political ineptitude. He risked being charged with sedition by criticizing Governor Peter Stuyvesant in 1653, for example. For the next several years he served as a British-commissioned privateer sailing out of Providence, Rhode Island. In 1658 he settled at Oyster Bay on Long Island, New York. During the Anglo-Dutch war in 1664–1665, he helped the British to extend their rule over New Amsterdam, and thereafter served in various public capacities in the colony, now called New York. He retired to his Long Island home in 1667 and lived there until his death on September 21, 1672.

Underwood, Oscar Wilder (1862–1929), public official. Born in Louisville, Kentucky, on May 6, 1862, Underwood grew up there and in St. Paul, Minnesota. He attended the University of Virginia for three years, 1881–1884, studied law, and was admitted to the bar in 1884. After practicing law briefly in Minnesota, he settled in Birmingham, Alabama. He served in the House of Representatives for about 18 months after apparently winning a contested election, but in June 1896 his opponent was declared the winner. Underwood ran again in 1896 and was elected. He served in the House through repeated reelections until March 1915, during the last four years as Democratic floor leader. In 1914 he won election to the U.S. Senate and served there until 1927. Underwood was a legislator of noted ability, unafraid to differ with his constituents or his fellow Democrats on matters he considered important. While in the House he became an expert on tariff problems, believing in tariffs for revenue only and not for protection. He assisted President William Howard Taft in working out reciprocal trade agreements with Canada, but he disagreed with Taft on his proposals for high protective tariffs. On this issue he sought the Democratic nomination for the presidency in 1912, but, although a strong contender, he lost out to Woodrow Wilson. With Wilson in the White House, Underwood was able to press for the kind of tariff reform he wanted. On April 22, 1913, he introduced into the House a bill that attempted to place U.S. industries on a competitive basis with those in other countries. Several commodities were put on the tariff-free list, and revenue rates were revised downward by an average of some ten percent. With some Senate amendments, the Underwood Tariff Act was passed; it was signed by Wilson on October 3, 1913. As chairman of the powerful Committee on Ways and Means, Underwood was also influential in the passage of the Federal Reserve Act (Glass-Owen Act). While in the Senate he aided Wilson in the battle for the League of Nations; and under President Warren G. Harding he served as one of the U.S. representatives to the arms-limitation conferences in London in 1921–1922. In 1924 he again sought the presidential nomination, but certain of the issues he espoused were not calculated to win his party's support at the time—although a Southerner, he mounted an attack on the Ku Klux Klan, and he denounced Prohibition. His anti-Klan plank failed of adoption by only one vote at the Democratic national convention, but Underwood himself could not muster enough support from his own region to get the nomination. He did not seek reelection to the Senate in 1926, instead retiring to his estate in Fairfax County, Virginia. He came out of retirement to serve on an international French-

American commission in 1927 and to attend the Pan-American Conference at Havana in 1928. He died at his Virginia home on January 25, 1929.

Unitas, John (1933–   ), football player. Born in Pittsburgh on May 7, 1933, Unitas graduated in 1955 from the University of Louisville, which he had attended on a football scholarship after being turned down by other schools, including Notre Dame and Indiana, for being too small to play football. He was drafted by the Pittsburgh Steelers in 1955, but was released by them even before the season started; so he spent the autumn playing for the minor-league Bloomfield (New Jersey) Rams. In February 1956 he was picked up in a rather haphazard way by the Baltimore Colts, and in the course of a long career with them became one of the game's outstanding quarterbacks. He led the team to the championship of the National Football League (NFL) in 1958, beating the New York Giants in a championship final that in after years came to be considered one of the greatest professional football games ever played. The team won the championship again in 1959, 1968, and 1970; the Colts repeated as NFL champions yet again in 1971 and went on to win the Super Bowl game that year. After only a few seasons with the Colts, Unitas was already the holder of many records. From 1957 to 1960 he completed passes for at least one touchdown in each of 47 consecutive games. In 1966 he broke the records for most touchdown passes and most yards gained in passing in a season. All told, he gained nearly 40,000 yards passing during his career—nearly 10,000 yards more than his nearest competitor— and recorded a lifetime pass-completion average of over 55 percent. In the mid–1960s his effectiveness was hampered by injuries and he considered retirement. He made a successful comeback in 1968, however, but the Colts decided to replace Unitas in 1972 with a much younger quarterback as the team worked to build for the future. Unitas remained a legendary figure in the game, however.

Untermyer, Samuel (1858–1940), lawyer. Born in Lynchburg, Virginia, on June 6, 1858, Untermyer grew up there and in New York City. He attended City College of New York (CCNY) for a year and graduated from Columbia Law School in 1878. Admitted to the bar in 1879, he opened a law office in partnership with an older half-brother. In a practice that lasted more than 50 years, Untermyer became one of the most esteemed trial lawyers of his time as well as one of the busiest and wealthiest. He handled an enormous variety of cases, but was most frequently in court because of problems growing out of corporation mergers and the conflict of public and private interests. For his first 20 years of practice he generally favored the interests of the corporations, and he himself invested in stocks, real estate, and business ventures. He also assisted in a number of great industrial consolidations. But during the "Progressive Era," from about 1900 to 1916, Untermyer began examining the social consequences of corporate power, particularly the abuse of the public interest

by trusts. During 1911 he delivered a number of addresses calling for the regulation of huge concentrations of capital. In 1912–1913 he served as counsel for the famed Pujo Committee, a subcommittee of the House Banking and Currency Committee that was charged with investigating what he and fellow lawyer Louis D. Brandeis called the "money trust." Untermyer had asserted that most of the economic power of the nation was concentrated in the hands of the largest banks through a series of interlocking directorates with major corporations. Out of the Pujo Committee's investigations came the Clayton Antitrust Act, the Federal Reserve Act (Glass-Owen Act), and the act setting up the Federal Trade Commission (FTC). A number of Untermyer's own court cases also influenced public policy. A suit for the control of the Equitable Life Assurance Society of New York led to a state investigation of the insurance business in 1905 and to the passage of reform laws in several states. During World War I he served as chairman of the federal board charged with formulating income-tax and excess-profits regulations and following the war he served as counsel in various international litigations, mostly involving the confiscation of property. In 1919–1920 he was counsel to the New York State legislative committee on housing that investigated the building-trades unions accused of profiteering conspiracies with builders. He represented William Randolph Hearst in a suit over the right to property in news. He aided Governor Alfred E. Smith of New York in defeating waterpower grants on the St. Lawrence River to private interests. In 1927 Untermyer, a moderate Zionist, served as counsel in the first libel suit against Henry Ford arising out of Ford's attacks on the Jews in his *Dearborn Independent*. Ford eventually printed a public apology and retracted his charges. Although he never held public office, Untermyer was an active lifelong Democrat, and he attended all the national conventions of the party from 1904 to 1936. He advocated public ownership of public utilities, a protective tariff, and a graduated income tax. He staunchly supported the New Deal of Franklin D. Roosevelt and was one of the first prominent Americans actively to oppose the Nazi regime in Germany. During the 1930s he went into semiretirement and spent the winters at Palm Springs, California. It was there that he died on March 16, 1940.

Updike, John Hoyer (1932–   ), author. Born in Shillington, Pennsylvania, on March 18, 1932, Updike graduated from Harvard in 1954. After a year of further studies at Oxford University in England, he went to work for the *New Yorker* magazine as a reporter. He left the magazine in 1957 to write full time. He published short stories, essays, and poetry, but he became most widely known for his novels. The first, *The Poorhouse Fair*, 1959, had as its setting a home for the aged in New Jersey, but much of his subsequent fiction was laid in a small Pennsylvania town, much like the town in which he grew up. *Rabbit, Run*, 1960, and its sequel, *Rabbit Redux*, 1971, had as their protagonist the unstable and irresponsible Harry "Rabbit" Angstrom, caught in the tedium of small-town life. Updike's other novels included *The Centaur*, 1963; *Of the Farm*, 1965; *Couples*, 1968; and *Bech: A Book*, 1970. His poems were collected in *The Carpentered Hen and Other Tame Creatures*, 1968; *Telephone Poles and Other Poems*, 1963; and *Midpoint*, 1969. Updike's short stories, like his poetry, often appeared in the *New Yorker*, and were subsequently collected in *The Same Door*, 1959; *Pigeon Feathers*, 1962; and *Museums and Women and Other Stories*, 1972.

Upjohn, Richard (1802–1878), architect. Born in Shaftesbury, England, on January 22, 1802, Upjohn was appenticed to a cabinetmaker and also became a draftsman. In 1829 he came to the United States and lived in New Bedford, Massachusetts. He took up architecture in the early 1830s and after moving to Boston in 1834 became an exponent of the Gothic Revival. In 1839 he made New York City his home. His design for Trinity Episcopal Church in New York, built between 1841 and 1846, established his reputation as a first-class architect, and he never lacked commissions afterward. Other churches of his design were the old St. Thomas's Episcopal in New York City, the Bowdoin College chapel, St. James Church in New London, Connecticut, Church of the Pilgrims in Brooklyn, New York, and Trinity Chapel in New York City. Although known primarily as a designer of churches, Upjohn also designed private houses and a number of public buildings, including the Corn Exchange Bank Building in New York City. In 1857 he was a founder of the American Institute of Architects (AIA), and he became its first president, serving until 1876. In 1852 he published *Upjohn's Rural Architecture*, basically a manual for poorer parishes, including plans for churches of simple design that could be built at minimal cost. He died in Garrison, New York, on August 17, 1878.

Urban, Joseph (1872–1933), architect and stage designer. Born in Vienna on May 26, 1872, Urban studied architecture and interior decoration at the Art Academy and the Polytechnicum there. Although he designed a number of buildings during his career and even the Tsar's Bridge in St. Petersburg, Russia (now Leningrad, U.S.S.R.), his chief work was interior decorating and set design for opera houses and theaters. He did the interiors of the Vienna town hall and the Austrian building at the Louisiana Purchase Exposition in St. Louis in 1904, the latter effort winning him the exposition's grand prize. He emigrated to the United States in 1911 under contract as art director for the newly formed Boston Opera Company. Three years later he moved to New York City after being offered the job of doing the sets for the *Ziegfeld Follies*; he also executed sets for the Metropolitan Opera Company. He was naturalized in 1917. Urban demonstrated great versatility by also designing a large array of houses, public buildings, and interiors, and such industrial products as automobiles and furniture. Among his better-known buildings were the Ziegfeld Theatre and the New School for Social Research, both in New York City. His excellent use of color brought him the opportunity to choose the color schemes to be used at the Century of Progress Exposition in Chicago in 1933–1934. Not an innovator, Urban was basically a popularizer of the best of a variety of styles. The great amount of work he accomplished, coupled with the variety of his styles and approaches, made him an influence on later designers, especially in the decoration of theaters. He died in New York City on July 10, 1933.

U'Ren, William Simon (1859–1949), lawyer and political reformer. Born in Lancaster, Wisconsin, on January 10, 1859, U'Ren grew up there and in Nebraska and Colorado. He studied law and was admitted to the Colorado bar in 1881. After practicing law for five years, he gave up the work for reasons of health and moved about the country a good deal, trying his hand at various jobs. He lived in Iowa and California and was foreman on a sugar plantation in Hawaii before settling in Milwaukie, Oregon. He opened a law office, later moving to Portland, and kept up at least a nominal practice until within a year of his death. As early as his law-student days he had learned something of the workings of machine politics and bossism, and he became determined to work for political reforms that would encourage wider popular participation in the affairs of government. Only once did he hold an elective office, serving a term in the Oregon legislature in 1896–1897. Most of his efforts were made through positions he held in such organizations as the Direct Legislation League (he was secretary from 1892 to 1902), the Direct Primary Nominations League, the People's Power League, the National Popular Government League, and the Anti-Monopoly League. Through concerted statewide efforts of the Populists and other groups, the initiative and referendum were passed by the Oregon senate in 1899. They were passed for a second time in 1901 and approved by the people in 1902. In June 1904 a bill for the direct primary was passed. U'Ren also promoted direct election of U.S. senators by persuading the Oregon legislature to vote for a candidate popularly chosen by the electorate. Oregon thus approximated the popular election of senators before the Seventeenth Amendment to the Constitution became law in 1913. Eventually the reforms that U'Ren brought about in Oregon were duplicated in other states. Others of his reforms included the passage of a state corrupt-practices act, and making it possible to amend the state constitution by popular vote. Probably his most enduring work was bringing about the direct election of senators and the direct presidential primary and increasing the potential for democracy in practice. He died in Portland, Oregon, on March 9, 1949.

Urey, Harold Clayton (1893–1981), chemist. Born on April 29, 1893, in Walkerton, Indiana, Urey overcame obstacles to gain his high school diploma. He taught in country schools in Indiana and Montana until he had saved enough to go to college, and he then matriculated at Montana State University in 1914. He received his B.S. in 1917. He worked for a chemical company in Philadelphia during World War I, taught chemistry at Montana State from 1919 to 1921, and then went to the University of California at Berkeley to study physical chemistry. He received his Ph.D. in 1923. He studied for a year under Niels Bohr in Copenhagen and returned to the United States to become an associate in chemistry at Johns Hopkins, but he moved from there to Columbia in 1929. He was a professor of chemistry at Columbia from 1934 until 1945, when he moved to the University of Chicago as a professor; in 1958 he was named professor at large at the University of California, La Jolla. In December 1931 he announced that, working with two other investigators, he had discovered the existence of heavy water (deuterium oxide), in which the molecules consist of an atom of oxygen and two atoms of deuterium, or heavy hydrogen, a rare isotope of hydrogen. This discovery is considered one of the most important in the history of modern science, and for it he was awarded the Nobel Prize for Chemistry in 1934. After his discovery he continued at Columbia to study the problem of isotope separation and developed the gas-diffusion process that was successfully used during World War II to separate fissionable uranium 235 from the much more common U238 for the construction of the first atomic bomb. By 1940 he was one of the first Americans to realize that such weapons could be made, and he was the director of an important section of the Manhattan Engineering District (Manhattan Project), which produced the bomb.

After atomic bombs had been dropped at Hiroshima and Nagasaki, however, he joined with other scientists in urging consideration of the ethical problems involved in the use of such weapons. Among his other significant contributions was a technique whereby a study of deposited oxygen isotope-bearing minerals could indicate the age of geological formations and make possible the measurement of water temperatures in ancient seas, important information for the understanding of geological and climatic evolution, and a now widely accepted theory of the origin of the solar system, which he advanced in *The Planets: Their Origin and Development*, 1952. After 1960 he served as an adviser to the U.S. space effort. He died in La Jolla, California, on January 5, 1981.

Uris, Leon Marcus (1924–   ), author. Born in Baltimore on August 3, 1924, Uris attended high school in Philadelphia but dropped out before graduating and joined the Marine Corps. He saw action during World War II in the Pacific theater, taking part in the battles of Guadalcanal and Tarawa. Out of his experiences came his first novel, *Battle Cry*, 1953, one of the more vivid narratives of the war. Probably his most successful and durable novel was *Exodus*, 1958, which later became a popular film. The novel, depicting the early years of the state of Israel, was extensively researched by Uris throughout Europe and the Middle East. He wrote the film scripts for the movies made from *Battle Cry* and *Exodus* and also turned out screenplays for other films. His later novels included *Armageddon*, 1964; *Topaz*, 1967; *QB VII*, 1970; *Ireland: A Terrible Beauty*, 1975; and *Trinity*, 1976.

V

Vail, Alfred Lewis (1807–1859), telegraphy pioneer and manufacturer. Born in Morristown, New Jersey, on September 25, 1807, Vail graduated from the University of the City of New York (now New York University) in 1836. As a youth he had become a competent mechanic, working at his father's Speedwell Iron Works. Seeing a demonstration of Samuel F. B. Morse's telegraph device in New York City in 1837, Vail persuaded the inventor to accept him as a partner in the production of telegraph instruments. With financial help from his father, he superintended production at the Speedwell Works and helped devise numerous improvements, and the new model telegraph was successfully demonstrated on January 6, 1838. Public exhibitions in New York City and Washington failed to win government support for a telegraph line, so Vail ceased working on it for several years and represented his father's company in Philadelphia. In 1843 Congress finally authorized an experimental telegraph line from Baltimore to Washington, and Vail returned to work for Morse. He served as Ezra Cornell's assistant in the construction of the line and was on the receiving end in Baltimore of Morse's famous message: "What hath God wrought!" on May 24, 1844. After four more years of working with Morse, during which he published *The American Electro Magnetic Telegraph*, 1845, Vail retired to his home in Morristown, New Jersey. He died there on January 18, 1859.

Vail, Theodore Newton (1845–1920), communications executive. Born in Carroll County, Ohio, near the town of Minerva, on July 16, 1845, Vail, a cousin of Alfred L. Vail, grew up in Morristown, New Jersey. Following high school, he learned telegraphy and went to work for the Western Union Company in New York City. In 1866 he moved with his family to Waterloo, Iowa, and settled down to farming. But by 1868 he was back with the telegraph company, in South Dakota. In 1869 he began to work for the railway mail service, and such was his efficiency that by 1876 he was general superintendent of the railway mails at Washington, D.C. In 1878 he was persuaded by Gardiner G. Hubbard to become general manager of the newly formed Bell Telephone Company in Boston. Vail spent the next years organizing the rapidly expanding Bell communications system, improving its finances and technology and consolidating the proliferating exchanges. He succeeded in connecting all the existing companies by a long-distance system. In 1885, when the American Telephone and Telegraph Company (AT&T) was incorporated in New York as part of the Bell system to build and maintain long-distance telephone lines, Vail became its first president. Two years later he resigned his position for reasons of health and retired to travel and spend time at his farm in Lyndonville, Vermont. From 1894 until 1907 he superintended the construction of transportation and communications systems in Argentina. In 1907 he was persuaded to return to the presidency of AT&T (now the parent company, the Bell company having dissolved by 1900) to bring some order and efficiency to the telephone business, which had fallen into chaos after the mid-1890s when the Bell patents had run out and independent and competing telephone companies had sprung up all over the nation. Over the following years Vail unified the telephone system, promoted the use of research to develop equipment, and inaugurated transcontinental service. In 1913 he inaugurated for AT&T employees the first pension plan in the United States. Vail resigned as president of AT&T in 1919 and became chairman of the board of directors. He died in Baltimore on April 16, 1920.

Valentino, Rudolph (1895–1926), actor. Born in Castellaneta, Italy, on May 6, 1895, Rodolpho d'Antonguolla arrived in the United States in 1913. He worked as a dishwasher and a gardener, and then broke into vaudeville as a dancer. He joined a musical-comedy company and went to San Francisco and later to Hollywood, where he became a bit player in films in 1918. He was promoted by a scenario writer, June Mathis, and received the role of Julio in the Metro Pictures production of *The Four Horsemen of the Apocalypse* in 1921. In this performance his dash and smoldering appeal transfixed countless female moviegoers and he was elevated to stardom. He played in *The Sheik*, 1921; *Blood and Sand*, 1922; *The Young Rajah*, 1922; *Moran of the Lady Letty*, 1922; *Monsieur Beaucaire*, 1924; *A Sainted Devil*, 1924; *Cobra*, 1925; *The Eagle*, 1925; and *The Son of the Sheik*, 1926. The paradigm matinee idol, he attracted a huge following, but at the height of his career he contracted a combination of pneumonia and peritonitis and died on August 23, 1926, in New York City. Skillful press agentry made his lying-in-state—attended by a crowd that stretched for 11 blocks—and his funeral into notable events of the decade.

Vallandigham, Clement Laird (1820–1871), public official and political leader. Born on July 29, 1820, in New Lisbon, Columbiana County, Ohio, Vallandigham studied for a time at Jefferson (now Washington and Jefferson) College in Pennsylvania and was admitted to the Ohio bar in 1842. He quickly became involved in politics and from 1845 to 1847 was a Democratic member of the Ohio legislature, the last year serving as speaker of the house. He returned to the practice of law in Dayton, edited a newspaper for a time, and served as a brigadier general of the state militia. After an earlier defeat he successfully contested the results of the election of 1856 and was finally seated in 1858 in the House of Representatives and served until 1863. He called for an end to sectionalism and denounced extremists on both sides of the growing controversy between North and South, but held Northern radicals especially responsible. He was particularly venomous in his indictment of the Republican party; he supported Stephen A. Douglas for president in 1860, and when Abraham Lincon's election was followed by secession and war he maintained a bitter opposition to the administration's war measures, claiming that Lincoln was destroying constitutional rule. The acknowledged leader of the faction called the Peace Democrats, or "Copperheads," he incurred the intense hatred of Republicans and War Democrats alike. He was defeated for reelection to the House in 1862 and returned to Ohio the next year; in defiance of an order issued by Gen. Ambrose E. Burnside, commander of the military Department the Ohio, he spoke out against the war and was arrested. Convicted by a military commission of expressing treasonable sentiments, he was imprisoned until Lincoln changed his sentence to banishment to the Confederacy. From the South, Vallandigham made his way to Canada. Later in 1863 the Ohio Peace Democrats nominated him in absentia for governor, but he lost the election. In 1864, after being elected commander of the Sons of Liberty, a secret organization of Copperheads and other Southern sympathizers, he returned to Ohio and was allowed to remain there; at the Democratic national convention of that year he wrote into the platform a denunciation of the war as a failure. After Lincoln's assassination he continued to oppose the Republicans on the issue of Reconstruction, but by 1870 he had concluded that the Civil War and its results had to be accepted and new issues found. Before he could develop a new position, he died, on June 17, 1871, in Lebanon, Ohio, as a result of an accidentally self-inflicted bullet wound.

Vallee, Rudy (1901–), entertainer. Born in Island Pond, Vermont, on July 28, 1901, Hubert Prior Vallee grew up there and in Westbrook, Maine. As a self-taught saxophonist he was good enough to work steadily in bands and combos during his college years. After one year, 1921–1922, at the University of Maine, he transferred to Yale, from which he graduated in 1927. His college career was interspersed with musical engagements, including nine months at the Savoy Hotel in London in 1924–1925, and a vaudeville tour in 1926. After graduation, having taken the name Rudy in the early 1920s, he went directly into show business, playing with the Vincent Lopez and Ben Bernie bands. In 1928 he formed his own group and opened at the Heigh-Ho Club in New York City. Within a month his music was being broadcast on radio, and he remained a regular performer on the air until 1947, except for a two-year hiatus during World War II. The nation's first "crooner," he had a singing style that became familiar to millions, as did some of the songs associated with him: "Vagabond Lover," the University of Maine "Stein Song," and his theme, "My Time Is Your Time." His informal radio variety hour also brought to the air a number of other entertainers who soon gained large followings of their own: Edgar Bergen and Charlie McCarthy, Alice Faye, and Burns and Allen, among others. During the years his show was broadcast, Vallee also toured the country with his ensemble and appeared as well in two Broadway musicals. During the nearly 30 years from 1929 to 1957 he also made many Hollywood films, mostly light comedies, and eventually proved himself to be one of filmdom's better comic actors. During World War II he enlisted in the Coast Guard, attaining the rank of lieutenant, senior grade, and in 1943–1944 was bandmaster for the Eleventh Naval District Coast Guard Band in California. After the war he made more than a dozen movies, including *I Remember Mama*, 1947, and *The Helen Morgan Story*, 1957; but he declined to go into television on a regular basis. He determined instead to become once again a nightclub comedian-singer, and from 1949 followed that career successfully. In 1961 he returned to Broadway in the long-running musical, *How to Succeed in Business Without Really Trying*. With his name again before the public, he made frequent television appearances and occasional nightclub appearances.

Vallejo, Mariano Guadalupe (1808–1890), soldier and California provincial official. Born in Monterey, California, on July 7, 1808, Vallejo took up soldiering at the age of fifteen. He served the Mexican provincial government in a military capacity until the United States took over California in 1846. Under the Mexican regime he was one of a generation of younger, native-born Californians affected by the ideas of the Enlightenment and hostile to the authority of the Roman Catholic church and of the far-away government at Mexico City. He favored the rule of native-born officialdom in the province and hoped to help bring about political independence for California comparable to its economic self-reliance. In 1827 he was stationed at the Presidio in San Francisco, and two years later helped put down an Indian uprising at the nearby San Jose mission. In 1831–1832 and 1835–1836 he supported revolts against authoritarian Mexican governors that succeeded in obtaining the appointment of governors more attuned to the political desires of Californians. In 1833–1834 he was put in charge of a military expedition to reconnoiter the Russian colony at Fort Ross to see if it posed a threat to the government at Monterey. Having decided that the Russians were too weak to be a danger, he proceeded to improve the defenses around Sonoma against hostile Indians of the area. His nephew, Juan Bautista Alvarado, who led the 1836 revolt that established California as a virtually free state, became governor of California and in 1838 appointed Vallejo military commandant of the provincial forces. He spent most of his time at Sonoma until the U.S. take-over of California in 1846. During the early 1840s, when "Anglos" from the East were arriving in California, Vallejo recognized the inevitability of the migration and aided the new arrivals in getting settled. He was ill rewarded for his goodwill; when the Bear Flag Revolt took place in 1846, Vallejo and his brother were both taken captive by the insurgents and held for two months. Soon after U.S. military forces claimed California for the United States he was released. In 1849 he was a delegate to the state constitutional convention and he was then elected to the senate of the first legislature. For many years after that, as the old Spanish-Mexican families saw their influence decline, he was involved in lawsuits to salvage some of his property. Land claims by newcomers took much of it, but he continued to live at Sonoma. In 1851 he offered the state a tract of land on his estate, site of the city of Vallejo, for a state capital. The offer was accepted, but the city was California's capital only briefly in 1852 and again for a short period in 1853. During the 1860s and 1870s he compiled materials for a history of California. He died at his home in Sonoma on January 18, 1890, at the age of eighty-one.

Van Allen, James Alfred (1914–   ), physicist. Born in Mount Pleasant, Iowa, on September 7, 1914, Van Allen graduated from Iowa Wesleyan College in 1935 and earned his Ph.D. in physics at the State University of Iowa in 1939. Until 1942 he did research in physics at the Carnegie Institution of Washington. During World War II, as a naval-reserve officer on active duty, he worked at the Ordnance Bureau on weapons and also saw action in the Pacific theater. After the war, from 1946 to 1951, he supervised high-altitude research at The Johns Hopkins University; in January 1951 he became head of the physics department at the State University of Iowa. Most of his research after 1946 was concentrated on the upper atmosphere. In this high-altitude research he used an invention called the "rockoon," a combination rocket and balloon; the launching was accomplished by the balloon, and a dozen miles or so above the earth the decreased air pressure released the rocket into space, providing a means of getting instruments into space that was much less expensive than rocket propulsion from the ground. In the early 1950s Van Allen was one of the scientists who proposed a period of concentrated study of the earth by many nations. The result was the International Geophysical Year, actually an 18-month period in 1957–1958. In this "year" were included, among other programs, the Explorer satellite program and the Pioneer moon probe. The Explorer I flight demonstrated the presence of two radioactive

zones of charged particles in the magnetosphere, trapped within the earth's magnetic field and extending from a few hundred miles to some 40,000 miles above the earth. Van Allen had predicted the presence of such zones, and after Explorer IV confirmed his theory the rings of radioactivity were named Van Allen Belts in his honor. His interest in the U.S. space program helped steer it away from entirely military objectives, and some of his criticisms and suggestions were influential when the National Aeronautics and Space Administration (NASA) was organized in 1958.

Van Buren, Abby, see Friedman, Esther Pauline and Pauline Esther

Van Buren, Martin (1782–1862), eighth president of the United States. Born on December 5, 1782, in Kinderhook, New York, Van Buren received no formal education beyond that provided by local schools. He read law for a number of years, however, and in 1803 began to practice in his native town. He was elected as a Democratic Republican to the state senate in 1812, campaigning as an opponent of the Bank of the United States; he served two four-year terms and from 1816 to 1819 was concurrently state attorney general. At the head of the "Bucktail" faction, Van Buren was in constant rivalry with De Witt Clinton (who had earlier been an ally) for the leadership of the New York Democratic Republicans and developed great skill in political organizing and maneuvering. After playing a major role in calling and expediting the state constitutional convention of 1821 he was elected to the U.S. Senate, leaving behind in New York a group of associates known as the Albany Regency to maintain his power in the state, where they had strong control of patronage. A staunch foe of the policies of John Quincy Adams, he led the supporters of William H. Crawford in the three-way presidential contest of 1824; later, having supported the tariff and opposed internal improvements measures, he drew close to Andrew Jackson. Reelected to the Senate in 1827, he managed the passage of the "Tariff of Abominations" the next year to bolster Jackson's popularity. Clinton having died, Van Buren resigned from the Senate to become governor of New York. A few months later he resigned this office to become Jackson's secretary of state. He was the President's most trusted adviser, and by this time his consummate political skill had earned him the title "Little Magician." At his urging, Jackson adopted the New York "spoils system" in staffing the executive branch. Van Buren stood firmly with Jackson on all issues, including the fight against rechartering the Bank of the United States. His conduct of foreign affairs was altogether creditable; a dispute with Great Britain over West Indian trade was settled, a commitment was secured from France for payment of spoliation claims dating from the Napoleonic wars, and a treaty was signed with Turkey, granting the United States most-favored-nation trade privileges and access to the Black Sea. In 1831, in a move calculated to force a reorganization of the cabinet to rid it of supporters of Vice-President John C. Calhoun, he resigned to become minister to Great Britain, but Senate confirmation of his appointment was blocked early the next year by Calhoun. By the time he returned to the United States from London he had been nominated for the vice-presidency. With his election and his effective support of the President through the nullification crisis and the next four years he became Jackson's clearly designated successor. Van Buren was duly nominated and, on a platform promising continuing enmity to the Bank and respect for the rights of slaveholding states, was elected president in 1836. He was faced immediately with the severe panic of 1837; while continuing Jackson's general fiscal policies, he proposed the establishment of an independent treasury as a depository for federal money that had been in state banks since its withdrawal from the Bank of the United States. This legislation—the Independent Treasury Bill—he finally secured in 1840. In the growing sectional controversy Van Buren maintained a middle ground, supporting slavery in the South but opposing its extension into the territories. Popular support by U.S. border residents of the small-scale Canadian rebellion against Britain created diplomatic difficulties with Great Britain, and subsequent armed clashes of local people along the Maine–Canada border—the "Aroostook War"—further complicated matters. He lost popularity by the second Seminole War in Florida and particularly by his refusal to annex Texas, a position he took in order to avoid war with Mexico (as secretary of state he had attempted to buy Texas) and to prevent the creation of another slave state. Renominated in 1840, he lost the election to the Whig candidate, Gen. William Henry Harrison, in a campaign marked by a great deal of emotionalism and ballyhoo. He was a leading contender for the Democratic nomination in 1844 but again his stand on Texas lost him needed support. In 1847 the antislavery faction of the New York Democrats—the "Barnburners"—proposed Van Buren for president; the next year he was also nominated by the Free-Soil party, a coalition of Barnburners, "conscience Whigs," and others. After a campaign which merely succeeded in depriving Lewis Cass, the Democratic candidate, of election, he continued to take an active interest, but little part, in politics until his death in Kinderhook, New York, on July 24, 1862.

Van Buren, Raeburn see Capp, Al

Vance, Zebulon Baird (1830–1894), public official. Born near Asheville, in Buncombe County, North Carolina, on May 13, 1830, Vance attended Washington College in Tennessee and studied law at the University of North Carolina. He was admitted to the bar in 1852 and became county attorney the same year. He took to politics immediately and was rarely out of office after his first term in the North Carolina state legislature, as a Whig, in 1854. He was elected in 1858 as a Know-Nothing to the House of Representatives to fill a vacancy

and served there until March 3, 1861. Although a Southerner, Vance was an ardent Unionist and counseled against secession. But once the Confederate States of America was formed and the Civil War had begun, he was solidly with the South. He served in the war for a year, rising to the rank of colonel and performing notably in the Seven Days' Battles. In 1862 he ran for governor of North Carolina and won by a large majority. During two terms as governor he was continually at odds with the rest of the Confederate leadership because they believed him pro-Union at heart. However, he carried out his duties in the prosecution of the war successfully and, in spite of criticism, won his second term by a larger majority than the first. Vance was hostile to proposals for conscription by the Confederacy, feeling it necessary to keep state units at full strength; and he engineered some successful blockade running to get shipments of matériel from England. Following the war he was imprisoned briefly and then returned to his law practice for a few years, while Reconstruction proceeded in the South. In 1870 he ran for the U.S. Senate and won, but was not allowed by the Radical Republicans to take his seat. In 1876 he was again elected governor of North Carolina in a successful effort to drive Republicans and carpetbaggers out of the state. His two-year term began the real work of economic recovery that had been left undone since 1865, and also saw much progress in public education. In 1879 he was elected to the U.S. Senate, and he served there until 1894. As a senator he did effective work for the South and for his state at a time when the whole region needed rebuilding. But on national issues such as the tariff, taxes, and civil-service reform, he usually found himself in a minority among his fellow Southerners. After 1891 his health began to deteriorate; he died in Washington, D.C., on April 14, 1894.

Van Cortlandt, Stephanus (1643–1700), merchant and colonial official. Born in New Amsterdam on May 7, 1643, Van Cortlandt had become a successful merchant by the time he was twenty-one. Even after the British took New Netherland in 1664 and New Amsterdam became New York, he maintained his wealth and position, and during the next 36 years served in a variety of official capacities. He was a colonel in the militia and a member of the governor's council. He was the first American-born mayor of New York, appointed in 1677, 1686, and 1687. And from 1677 until 1700 he served as judge on several local courts, becoming an associate justice of the provincial supreme court in 1691. Like several of the other Dutch-descended residents of long standing, Van Cortlandt managed, through his wealth and political influence, to build up a sizable estate along the Hudson River, north of Manhattan; in 1697 he was granted a royal patent for the manor of Cortlandt, and at the time of his death his properties totaled more than 85,000 acres. The only low point of his years of public service came during Jacob Leisler's rebellion against Governor Sir Edmund Andros in 1689–

1691. The governor's failure to announce the accession to the throne of William and Mary in January 1689 fostered rumors among the citizens about the colony being turned over to France. Existing factions, dissatisfied with the governance of New York, were willing enough for a change to be made when in May 1689 Leisler took over the fort at New York City and was proclaimed commander in chief of the province by his followers. Residents who opposed Leisler failed to challenge his actions, least of all Van Cortlandt. Already too closely associated with the hated Andros and the deposed Catholic King James II, he was forced to flee New York City until Leisler was deposed in March 1691. Van Cortlandt then reappeared and, on the council of the new governor, Henry Sloughter, was vigorous in pressing the prosecution of Leisler for treason. He then resumed his judgeship, becoming chief judge in 1700, served as commissioner of customs from 1698, and lived in New York City until his death on November 25, 1700.

Vandegrift, Alexander Archer (1887–1973), Marine Corps officer. Born in Charlottsville, Virginia, on March 13, 1887, Vandegrift attended the University of Virginia and was commissioned an officer in the Marine Corps in 1909. He served various tours of duty in the United States and many other parts of the world—Nicaragua in 1912, Vera Cruz in 1914, Haiti in 1915–1919, China in 1927–1929, among others—and had advanced to the rank of major general in 1942. He led the 1st Marine Division in the attack on Guadalcanal on August 7, 1942, beginning the first large-scale counteroffensive against the Japanese during World War II. With the 1st Division, later aided by other units from the marines and the army, he held the island against repeated and furious counterattacks by the Japanese until it was secured in February 1943. For that accomplishment he was awarded the Medal of Honor and the Navy Cross. In July 1943 he became a lieutenant general. He commanded the 1st Marine Amphibious Corps in the Bougainville landing in the fall of 1943 and on January 1, 1944, was appointed commandant of the Marine Corps. He was promoted to full general in March 1945, the first Marine Corps officer to hold that rank. He retired from active duty on January 1, 1948. Vandegrift died in Bethesda, Maryland, on May 8, 1973.

Vandenberg, Arthur Hendrick (1884–1951), public official. Born in Grand Rapids, Michigan, on March 22, 1884, Vandenberg matriculated at the law school of the University of Michigan after graduating from high school, but because of family financial problems remained only a year. He joined the staff of the *Grand Rapids Herald* and became its editor in 1906; an ardent Republican, he soon acquired considerable influence in the state party organization and in 1928 was appointed to fill an unexpired term in the Senate. He survived the Democratic election sweeps of the 1930s and held his seat until his death. He was a strong though not unreasonable critic of the New Deal, agreeing

with much of its purpose but differing on matters of method and efficiency. His major opposition to President Franklin D. Roosevelt was in the field of foreign affairs; he was a member of the Nye Committee of the Senate, investigating the operations of the munitions industry during World War I and was a leading spokesman for isolationism, or, as he called it, "insulationism." He was widely mentioned as a presidential possibility in 1936 and openly sought the Republican nomination in 1940. Although he had supported the series of Neutrality Acts of the late 1930s and had opposed their modification, he began to change his stand on neutrality after the Japanese attack on Pearl Harbor. He fully supported the U.S. war effort, becoming the central figure in the bipartisan stance adopted by Congress, and in January 1945 announced in a Senate speech the complete reversal of his earlier stand on U.S. participation in political and military alliances. He was a delegate to the San Francisco conference to organize the United Nations in 1945, and his support ensured Senate ratification of U.S. membership in the organization. He represented the United States at the first two meetings of the U.N. General Assembly in 1946. In 1948 he sponsored the Senate legislation establishing the Marshall Plan for European postwar recovery and introduced the Vandenberg Resolution by which the Senate approved foreign alliances; the next year he effectively supported the forming of the North Atlantic Treaty Organization (NATO). A leading member of the Senate Foreign Relations Committee and the committee's chairman from 1946 to 1948, he was the chief Republican architect of the bipartisan foreign policy of the post-World War II period. He died in Grand Rapids, Michigan, on April 18, 1951.

Van Depoele, Charles Joseph (1846–1892), inventor. Born in Lichtervelde, Belgium, on April 27, 1846, Van Depoele was apprenticed as a wood-carver in 1865. He also studied at the Imperial Lyceum in Lille, France, where he pursued his main interest, electricity. In 1869 he emigrated to the United States and settled in Detroit, where he became a manufacturer of church furniture; his avocational absorption in electricity, however, soon occupied most of his time. He was naturalized in 1878. He worked on electric lighting, motors, and generators, but most important, he demonstrated the feasibility of electric transportation—trolley cars operated by either street-level cables or overhead power. By about 1880 he had moved to Chicago, where in 1881 he had incorporated the Van Depoele Electric Lighting Company, and in 1883 he gave a public demonstration of his electric trolley at the Chicago Interstate Industrial Exposition. Within a few years electric streetcar systems designed by him were installed in more than a dozen U.S. cities. In 1888 he sold his electric railway patents to the Thomson-Houston Electric Company (later a part of General Electric) in Lynn, Massachusetts, and relocated there to work as an electrician and consultant. Among his other inventions were the carbon contact brush used in motor construction (1882) and a coal-mining machine (1891). He experimented with electrical refrigeration and in 1891 successfully produced color photographs. In all, he received some 250 patents during his lifetime; nearly 50 additional patents resulted from work left unfinished or unreported at his death. Van Depoele died in Lynn on March 18, 1892.

Vanderbilt, Cornelius (1794–1877), financier. Born on May 27, 1794, in Port Richmond, Staten Island, New York, the son of a farmer, Vanderbilt was a willful child and refused to attend school after the age of eleven. At sixteen he purchased a small sailboat with money borrowed from his parents and used it to carry passengers between Staten Island and New York City. He was authorized during the War of 1812 to transport provisions to regiments around the city and soon had a small fleet engaged in river and coastal trade. In 1818 he sold his boats and began working for Thomas Gibbons, a ferry-boat owner, whom he helped to compete against Robert Fulton, who claimed a monopoly right for mail, freight, and passenger service in the New York area. Operating for years illegally, Gibbons managed by 1824 to have Fulton's monopoly voided by the Supreme Court in *Gibbons* v. *Ogden*. Vanderbilt formed his own steamboat company in 1829. To the dismay of established firms on the Hudson River, he quickly came to dominate the business by charging lower fares than his competitors and converting his passenger boats into luxury vessels. He was paid royally to move his boats elsewhere and soon set up Long Island Sound lines to Boston and Providence. By 1846 "Commodore" Vanderbilt was a millionaire. He formed a company in 1847 to operate from New Orleans and New York City to Nicaragua, then overland to the Pacific part of the route, ending at San Francisco. The line capitalized on the traffic arising from the Gold Rush starting in 1849 and thrived by reducing the price of the trip. Two subordinates attempted to wrest control of the company from him in 1853 and they succeeded briefly. He skillfully regained control, however. They countered and enlisted the aid of William Walker, an American filibuster who made himself dictator of Nicaragua in 1855. Walker seized Accessory Transit's Nicaraguan facilities, claiming charter violations, and turned them over to Vanderbilt's rivals. Vanderbilt then organized a Central American coalition that in 1857 succeeded in driving Walker out. In 1858 Vanderbilt arranged with his competitors, whose businesses he had nearly ruined, to discontinue, for a monthly indemnity, all operations of Accessory Transit. Meanwhile in 1855 he had started to operate three vessels between New York and Le Havre, France. In 1861 he sold two for a large sum, and he donated the third, the *Vanderbilt*, to the government as a warship. He enlarged his fortune in great measure by buying old harbor vessels and selling them to the navy for blockade duty during the Civil War. He began purchasing stock in the New York & Harlem Railroad in 1862, and

by 1863 he controlled the line and used it to initiate New York streetcar service. He then acquired the Hudson River Railroad, for which he had, as over the Harlem, to fight Daniel Drew. They again clashed over the New York Central Railroad and on winning control, Vanderbilt, aided by Chauncey M. Depew, won legislative approval for consolidating it with the Hudson River Railroad in 1869. His attempt in 1868 to buy the Erie Railroad was thwarted by Daniel Drew, together with Jim Fisk and Jay Gould, who, in maneuvers that came to be called the "Erie War," flooded the market with a fraudulent stock issue. Vanderbilt's acquisition in 1873 of the Lake Shore & Michigan Southern Railroad completed the first New York-to-Chicago rail system. He later added the Michigan Central and the Canada Southern to his holdings. In every case he made large capital investments in improved roads, rolling stock, and facilities. He remained secure during the panic of 1873 and by ordering construction of Grand Central Terminal in New York City, opened jobs to thousands of unemployed. At his death in New York City on January 4, 1877, his wealth was estimated at $100 million. He made large gifts to Central University of Nashville, Tennessee, which became Vanderbilt University. His son William Henry Vanderbilt (1821–1885) inherited his financial empire.

Vanderbilt, Cornelius (1843–1899), *see under* Vanderbilt, William Henry (1821–1885).

Vanderbilt, George Washington, *see under* Vanderbilt, William Henry (1821–1885)

Vanderbilt, Harold Stirling (1884–1970), businessman and sportsman. Born in Oakdale, Long Island, New York, on July 6, 1884, the son of William Kissam Vanderbilt, Harold Stirling Vanderbilt graduated from Harvard in 1907. Like his father, he entered the family's railroad empire. In 1913 he became a director of the New York Central and remained on the railroad's board until 1954. But his interests were chiefly in the sports world. He became, during the 1920s and 1930s, one of the country's foremost yachtsmen. He won 11 major yacht races between 1922 and 1938, making successful defenses of the America's Cup in 1930 (on the *Enterprise*), 1934 (*Rainbow*), and 1937 (*Ranger*). In 1926, while on a sailing voyage, he developed the game of contract bridge, a merging of auction bridge with certain features of plafonde and with a new scoring schedule. The rules as he then established them still form the basis of the game today, and the Vanderbilt Cup, named in his honor, is one of the most sought-after trophies in the bridge world. Within two years of his devising the game, contract had replaced auction bridge as the leading game in club play in the United States. For many years, even in the heyday of Ely Culbertson, Vanderbilt was regarded as one of the world's top players. In 1942 he took up experimental farming in Virginia, and within a few years had established a model farm. He died in Newport, Rhode Island, on July 4, 1970.

Vanderbilt, William Henry (1821–1885), financier and railroad magnate. Born in New Brunswick, New Jersey, on May 8, 1821, Vanderbilt, while a youth, was considered by his father, Cornelius Vanderbilt (1794–1877), too ineffectual to cope with large financial responsibilities. So at age nineteen, when he married, the elder Vanderbilt bought him a farm on Staten Island and left him to run it. After making a success of the farm, William persuaded his father to have him appointed receiver of the bankrupt Staten Island Railroad in 1857. In a few years, to his father's surprise, he had shown enough business acumen to put the road on its feet, and in 1864 the elder Vanderbilt made him vice-president of the New York & Harlem Railroad. While he worked under his father, he showed great managerial ability, but after his father's death he demonstrated financial talents even beyond those of his parent. He had persuaded his father to acquire control of several railroads, including the Lake Shore & Michigan Southern and the Michigan Central; to those he added the Chicago and North Western, the New York, Chicago & St. Louis, and others. From 1877 he was president of the New York Central system, which he extended. Like his father but unlike some of the other railroad barons of the nineteenth century, Vanderbilt improved the roads he controlled and kept up the service on them. But like the others, he was frequently indifferent to the public interest when it involved increasing his own fortune. He participated in the rate wars and rate juggling of the 1870s; in fact, his cutting of charges to favor New York City merchants in 1876 set off the worst of the rate battles. Giving special rates to favored shippers was a common practice, increasing the power of the railroads to such an extent that they virtually became partners of some of the companies whose commodities they carried. State and federal officials were kept from adverse action or comment by outright bribery, a tactic which Vanderbilt openly admitted using. He fought railroad regulation vehemently; his attitude was, in his own words of 1882, "The public be damned." But regulation was inevitable and became a reality, however ineffectual, in the late 1880s. Vanderbilt himself did not live to see it. Poor health led him to resign his railroad presidencies in 1883. In the years since his father's death he had nearly doubled the Vanderbilt fortune, contributed to many philanthropic causes, and bequeathed a fortune to each of his eight children. He died suddenly in New York City on December 8, 1885. At William's death, the responsibilities as head of the Vanderbilt family and financial empire fell to his eldest son Cornelius Vanderbilt (1843–1899). Born on Staten Island, New York, on November 27, 1843, Cornelius Vanderbilt worked his way up in the business world under the watchful eye of his grandfather. In 1867 he was appointed assistant treasurer of the New York & Harlem Railroad, of which his father was vice-president. He soon became treasurer, and in 1880 was named vice-president. When his father died in 1885, Cornelius became chairman of the board of his father's

various corporations and was in charge of all family investments. He combined his business career with philanthropy and served on the boards of several social, religious, educational, and welfare institutions. His gifts to Yale University alone were estimated at $1.5 million, and he and his brothers built the Vanderbilt Clinic for the College of Physicians and Surgeons of Columbia University. He died in New York City on September 12, 1899. The directorship of the several Vanderbilt enterprises was then the responsibility of Cornelius's younger brother, William Kissam Vanderbilt (1849–1920). The youngest son of William Henry Vanderbilt, and the brother of Cornelius and William Kissam Vanderbilt, George Washington Vanderbilt (1862–1914), became particularly interested in architecture, landscaping, and forestry. Born near New Dorp, New York, on November 14, 1862, he was educated privately and in 1889 he began buying vast tracts of land near Asheville, North Carolina. He eventually created an estate of some 130,000 acres, on which he built a magnificent mansion, designed by Richard M. Hunt, and created extensive parks and gardens with the aid of Frederick Law Olmsted. He also carried on extensive experiments in scientific farming and stock breeding and hired Gifford Pinchot to manage the forests of "Biltmore." He died in Washington, D.C., on March 6, 1914.

Vanderbilt, William Kissam (1849–1920), businessman and sportsman. Born on Staten Island, New York, on December 12, 1849, the son of William Henry Vanderbilt, William went to work on his grandfather's Hudson River Railroad in 1868 and ten years later became a vice-president of the New York Central railroad system. When his father resigned his various railroad positions in 1883, William became president of the New York, Chicago & St. Louis Railroad and chairman of the board of the Lake Shore & Michigan Southern. From 1885 until his brother Cornelius's death in 1899, he cooperated with Cornelius in managing the Vanderbilt investments and enterprises, although he was much less interested in the problems of finance than either his father or his brother. In 1903 he withdrew from active direction of the railroads, while remaining on their boards of directors. He had various philanthropies and devoted much of his activity to sporting interests. As a yachtsman he sailed the vessel *Defender* in the 1895 race that retained the America's Cup for the United States. Art collecting, racehorses, theater, and opera consumed much of his time once he was relieved of running the railroads. With Otto Kahn he was deeply involved in running the Metropolitan Opera. His wife, Alva Smith, was a major figure in society; she divorced him in 1895 and later married Oliver H. P. Belmont. He died in Paris on July 22, 1920.

Vanderlyn, John (1775–1852), painter. Born in Kingston, New York, on October 15, 1775, Vanderlyn studied art under Archibald Robertson in New York and Gilbert Stuart in Philadelphia. Through the generosity of Aaron Burr, he was able to study painting in Paris from 1796 to 1801. After a two-year visit to the United States, Vanderlyn returned to Europe in 1803 and stayed until 1815, spending most of his time in Paris. It was in these years that he executed his best work, for the most part historical scenes or portraits. His "Marius amid the Ruins of Carthage" received a gold medal at the Paris Salon of 1808, and his "Ariadne" in 1812 created an even greater sensation. Back in the United States after 1815, he painted a number of portraits of such prominent persons as James Madison, Andrew Jackson, John C. Calhoun, Aaron Burr, and George Clinton. But his work was less popular in his homeland than in Europe, and his reputation suffered as well from the criticisms of other artists who considered his work undistinguished. In 1842 he obtained a commission to do a painting for the rotunda of the U.S. Capitol in Washington, D.C. He did this painting in Paris, but once back in the United States he found himself no longer in demand, even as a portraitist, and the last few years of his life were spent in poverty. He died in Kingston, New York, on September 23, 1852. His paintings were acquired by many major museums.

Van Der Rohe, Ludwig Mies, *see* Mies Van Der Rohe, Ludwig

Van Devanter, Willis (1859–1941), justice of the Supreme Court. Born in Marion, Indiana, on April 17, 1859, Van Devanter attended Asbury (now De-Pauw) University from 1875 to 1878. He enrolled at the Cincinnati Law School in 1879, graduating two years later. For nearly three years he worked with his father's law firm in Marion, but in July 1884 he went west and settled in Cheyenne, Wyoming. He quickly became involved in territorial politics, serving in 1886 on a commission to revise Wyoming's statutes and in 1887–1888 as Cheyenne city attorney. After one term in the territorial legislature in 1888, President Benjamin Harrison appointed him chief justice of the territorial supreme court, but when Wyoming became a state in 1890 Van Devanter retired to his law practice. From 1892 to 1894 he was chairman of the Republican state committee, and at the party's national convention in 1896 he was named to the national committee. From 1897 to 1903 he was an assistant U.S. attorney general, and in 1903 President Theodore Roosevelt appointed him a federal judge for the 8th Judicial Circuit. President William Howard Taft appointed Van Devanter an associate justice of the U.S. Supreme Court in 1910. In terms of opinions rendered, Van Devanter was never an outstanding member of the court, although he was an astute lawyer with a particular understanding of problems relating to land and admiralty law, water rights, corporation law, and Indian controversies. He was extremely conservative in his views, and by the early 1930s was a reactionary on a Court that was itself adamantly against social and economic change. He had intended to resign in 1932, but the prospect of

the New Deal policies of Franklin D. Roosevelt, which he could not abide, kept him on the Court for another five years; he remained firmly a part of the four-man conservative wing throughout that period. He retired on June 2, 1937, to his farm near Ellicott, Maryland, but presided occasionally over the U.S. District Court in New York. He died on February 8, 1941.

Van Doren, Carl Clinton (1885–1950), author and editor. Born on a farm near Hope, Illinois (a small town that, like its Vermilion County neighbors Faith and Charity, no longer exists), on September 10, 1885, Van Doren graduated from the University of Illinois in 1907, his doctor father having moved to Urbana in order to put his five sons through the university. Following his graduation he went to New York City to continue the study of literature. He received a Ph.D. from Columbia in 1911 and that year joined its English department, where he taught until 1930. He was involved in the revival of interest in American literature that marked Columbia in those years, was managing editor of the *Cambridge History of American Literature* from 1917 to 1921, and was literary editor of the *Nation*, 1919–1922, and of the *Century Magazine*, 1922–1925. He also wrote *The American Novel*, 1921 (revised edition 1940); *Contemporary American Novelists*, 1922; *American and British Literature Since 1890* (with his brother Mark), 1925 (revised edition 1939); and critical studies including *Thomas Love Peacock*, 1911; *James Branch Cabell*, 1925; *Swift*, 1930; and *Sinclair Lewis*, 1933. From 1926 to 1934 he was editor of the Literary Guild. In the 1930s he turned from literature to American history. A best-selling biography of Benjamin Franklin appeared in 1938, for which he received a Pulitzer Prize the next year, and which long remained the standard biography of Franklin. Among his other historical works were *Secret History of the American Revolution*, 1941; *Mutiny in January*, 1943; and *The Great Rehearsal*, 1948. The last was an account of the federal Constitutional Convention of 1787; its main thesis was that the creation of the Union, with its consequent giving up of sovereignty by the 13 original states, showed that the nations of the world could create a world government. From 1912 to 1935 he was married to Irita Bradford, for many years literary editor of the *New York Herald Tribune*. He died in Torrington, Connecticut, on July 18, 1950. His autobiography, *Three Worlds*, had appeared in 1936.

Van Doren, Mark (1894–1972), poet and critic. Born near Hope, Vermilion County, Illinois, on June 13, 1894, Mark Van Doren was a younger brother of Carl Van Doren. His career paralleled that of his brother for many years; he graduated from the University of Illinois in 1914, received his Ph.D. from Columbia in 1920, joined its English department (where he taught from 1920 to 1959, as professor of English from 1942), and was literary editor of the *Nation*, 1924–1928, and its motion picture critic, 1935–1938. He also wrote a number of works of literary criticism, among them studies of Henry David Thoreau, 1916; John Dryden, 1920; Shakespeare, 1939; and Nathaniel Hawthorne, 1949. *The Private Reader*, 1942, and *The Happy Critic*, 1961, were collections of occasional literary pieces. But Mark Van Doren's literary interests tended to diverge from those of his brother as the years wore on. Perhaps best known as a poet, he produced his first book of poems, *Spring Thunder*, in 1924. It was followed by a long series of others, culminating in *Collected Poems*, 1939, which won a Pulitzer Prize in 1940; *Selected Poems*, 1954; *Collected and New Poems, 1924–1963*, 1963, and *Narrative Poems*, 1964; the last included his *Winter Diary* (an account in verse of a year spent on a farm in the Connecticut foothills of the Berkshires) that had been issued separately in 1953. He became a permanent resident of the farm in 1959. Apart from poetry he also produced novels (*The Transients*, 1935; *Windless Cabins*, 1940); short stories, collections of which were published in 1962, 1965, and 1968; and plays (*The Last Days of Lincoln*, 1959; *Three Plays*, 1966). A book of new poems, *That Shining Place*, was published on his seventy-fifth birthday, in 1969, and his last, *Good Morning; Last Poems*, in 1973. He married Dorothy Graffe in 1922; she was also an editor of the *Nation* (1919–1936) and the author of a number of books. His autobiography was published in 1958. He died in Torrington, Connecticut, on December 10, 1972.

Van Dyne, Edith, *see* Baum, Lyman Frank

Van Hise, Charles Richard (1857–1918), geologist and educator. Born in Fulton, Rock County, Wisconsin, on May 29, 1857, Van Hise graduated from the University of Wisconsin in 1879, and was thereafter associated with the university for the rest of his life. He taught metallurgy and mineralogy, then geology, successively from 1879 until 1903, at which time he was named president of the university. He conducted investigations into the Precambrian formations of the Lake Superior region and assisted in surveys of the iron-producing capacity of the same area. From 1883 until his death he was also on the staff of the U.S. Geological Survey and contributed a number of studies to the Survey's annual reports. As president of the University of Wisconsin, he took the view that the school was meant to serve the state—a view that came to be called the "Wisconsin Idea"—and he greatly expanded its extension and research facilities and promoted a larger enrollment. In conjunction with his geological studies, Van Hise took up the cause of conservation after 1900. In 1908 he was appointed a member of the National Conservation Commission, and two years later he published an important book, *The Conservation of Natural Resources in the United States*. During World War I he worked as a consultant to the Food Administration in Washington and afterward he was a vigorous advocate of the concept of a league of nations. He died in Milwaukee on November 19, 1918.

Van Rensselaer, Stephen (1764–1839), soldier and public official. Born in New York City on November 1, 1764, Van Rensselaer graduated from Harvard in 1782. Since he had, at the age of five, inherited his father's entire estate—an enormous upstate manor of which he became the patroon—he was, on reaching maturity, one of the wealthiest residents of New York State and one of the state's major landholders. His military career was confined to service in the state militia, in which he rose, mostly by virtue of his social position, to the rank of major general. During the War of 1812 he was assigned to command the northern border of the state, but his only major action there—the attack on Queenston Heights, Ontario, in October 1812—turned into an unqualified defeat, largely due to his troops' lack of discipline. A Federalist in politics, Van Rensselaer had been a member of the state legislature in 1789–1791, in 1798, and again in 1818. He served in the state senate from 1791 to 1796. In 1795 he was elected lieutenant governor for one term. He sat in the state constitutional convention of 1801 and later in that of 1821. He strongly favored the building of a canal to connect the Hudson River with the Great Lakes, and he promoted this cause as a member of the state's canal commission in 1810 and 1816; from 1825, when the Erie Canal was opened, to 1839 he was president of the commission. He was a regent of the University of the State of New York from 1819 until 1839 and served as chancellor after 1835. In 1824 he founded at Troy, New York, the school that became Rensselaer Polytechnic Institute. He was elected to the House of Representatives from New York in 1822 to fill a vacancy and served until 1829. His most significant achievement during his congressional years was casting the deciding vote for the election of John Quincy Adams as president after the election of 1824 was thrown into the House. Van Rensselaer did not seek reelection in 1828 but instead retired to look after his huge manor. He died in Albany, New York, on January 26, 1839.

Van Sweringen, Oris Paxton (1879–1936), real-estate developer and railroad executive. Born in Wooster, Ohio, on April 24, 1879, Oris and his brother Mantis, born in Wooster on July 8, 1881, grew up there and in Cleveland. Both left school after the eighth grade and went to work as clerks in the same office. In 1900 they went into the real-estate business; five years later they bought a tract of land on the outskirts of Cleveland and turned it into the suburban development known as Shaker Heights. To improve the prospects of the new community, they saw to the building of a streetcar line connecting it to Cleveland. In 1916, while seeking the right-of-way for a streetcar line extension, they learned that the New York, Chicago, & St. Louis Railroad, the so-called Nickel Plate System, was for sale. With the help of backers and loans, the Van Sweringens bought the line and began a career as railroad executives. During the 15 years after World War I they acquired a number of other lines, including the Toledo, St.

Louis, and Western, the Chesapeake & Ohio, the Erie, the Pere Marquette, and the Missouri Pacific. In all, the Van Sweringens operated 21,000 miles of railroad at the height of their careers. In the Depression years of the early 1930s, this large rail empire, a pyramid of holding companies, became shaky, and when the brothers died, less than a year apart in the mid-1930s, their large holdings were divided up among their creditors. They died in Shaker Heights, Mantis on December 12, 1935, and Oris on November 23, 1936.

Van Wagener, Isabella, see Truth, Sojourner

Vanzetti, Bartolomeo, see under Sacco, Nicola

Varèse, Edgard (1883–1965), conductor and composer. Born in Paris on December 22, 1883, Varèse grew up there and in Turin, Italy. His schooling in mathematics and science was preparation for a career in engineering; but in his late teens he decided on music, and in 1904 he returned to Paris to study. For two years he attended the Schola Cantorum and in 1907 entered the Conservatoire. From about 1909 until the outbreak of World War I he was in Berlin, where he organized the Symphonischer Choir to perform polyphonic music. In 1914 he conducted the Prague Philharmonic Orchestra. In 1916, after brief service in the French army, he emigrated to the United States, becoming a citizen in 1926. As his musical style developed, Varèse combined some elements of his earlier interest in engineering and the sciences with music theory to devise new forms of sound, particularly by using electronic equipment. Some of his compositions, because of their dissonance and unconventionality, aroused the animosity of audiences and critics alike. Thought of as the father of electronic music, he used novel rhythmic and harmonic concepts as an elaboration of his assertion that music is organized sound and can be free from traditional confines or limitations. In 1921 he founded the International Composers' Guild, of which he remained director until 1927. In 1929 he founded the New Symphony Orchestra in New York City, and three years later he founded the first society devoted solely to the performance of modern music. Among his early works were *Hyperprism*, 1923, for wind instruments and percussion; *Amériques*, 1926, for a large orchestra; *Ionisation*, 1931, for two groups of percussion instruments; and *Espace*, 1937, for chorus and orchestra. His best-known later work was *Déserts*, 1954, an antiphonal composition in which standard instruments alternated with taped electronic sound. In 1958 he composed a "Poème Électrique" entitled *L'homme et la Machine* for the Brussels World's Fair; this composition was carried over 400 loudspeakers for a spatial-sound effect. Throughout his career Varèse had conducted in both the United States and Europe. He died in New York City on November 6, 1965.

Varnum, Joseph Bradley (1751–1821), public official. Born in Dracut, Massachusetts, on January 29, 1751, Varnum had little opportunity for education in the rural area where he grew up. He was born into a farm family, and he maintained the homestead throughout his life. Although he spent most of his adult life in politics, he saw service with "Dracut Minute Men" during the Revolutionary War, and on April 4, 1787, he was commissioned colonel of the 7th Regiment of the Massachusetts Militia. In June 1805 he became a major general. He entered politics as an anti-Federalist in 1780 when he was elected to the Massachusetts legislature; he remained there until 1795, for the last ten years as a state senator. In 1794 he was elected to the U.S. House of Representatives and took office on March 4, 1795, remaining there until June 29, 1811, and serving as speaker from October 1807 until March 3, 1811. Varnum was an early opponent of slavery and the slave trade; he likewise opposed the building of a federal military-naval establishment. In 1810 the Massachusetts legislature elected him to the U.S. Senate to fill a vacancy, and he served in the Senate from June 29, 1811 until March 3, 1817. He also served as chief justice of the Massachusetts court of general session from 1811 to 1815. His term in the Senate coincided in good part with the War of 1812, which he ardently supported; but because the war was very unpopular in New England, he also became unpopular with much of his constituency during this period. In 1813 he campaigned for the office of governor on a pro-war platform and was overwhelmingly defeated. In 1816, after the state legislature replaced him in the Senate, Varnum ran again for the state legislature, to which he was elected. He served in the state senate from 1817 until 1821 and in 1820 was a delegate to the state constitutional convention. He died on September 21, 1821, in Dracut, Massachusetts.

Vassar, Matthew (1792–1868), businessman and philanthropist. Born in East Tuddingham, Norfolk, England, on April 29, 1792, Vassar was brought to the United States four years later by his family, which settled near Poughkeepsie, New York. In 1808 he went to work in his father's brewery, and three years later opened one of his own, which he turned into a flourishing enterprise. Through the brewery, land speculation, and other enterprises, Vassar accumulated a handsome fortune, some of which he resolved to devote to philanthropy. In 1861 he founded and endowed Vassar Female College (now Vassar College) at Poughkeepsie and saw to it that the curriculum was as good as that at any men's school. He advertised the school, which opened in 1865, across the nation and attracted a large student body. The quality of Vassar education was a potent factor in helping to establish higher education for women throughout the United States. Vassar himself died in Poughkeepsie on June 23, 1868. A nephew carried on his philanthropic work.

Veblen, Oswald (1880–1960), mathematician. Born in Decorah, Iowa, on June 24, 1880, Veblen was a nephew of the economist Thorstein Veblen. He graduated from the State University of Iowa in 1898 and pursued further studies at Harvard before taking his Ph.D. at the University of Chicago in 1903. He stayed on at Chicago as a mathematics instructor before joining the faculty of Princeton University in 1905. He remained at Princeton until 1932, after 1910 as a professor, then transferred to the faculty of the Institute for Advanced Study, also at Princeton, New Jersey. He retired in 1950. Veblen's major field of study was geometry, and he first worked on topology. With the announcement of the theory of relativity in physics, he took up differential geometry and was one of the developers of generalized affine and projective geometry. He was one of the foremost theoreticians in abstract geometry in the United States. Among his published works were *Infinitesimal Analysis*, 1907, with N. J. Lennes; *Analysis Sitis*, 1922; *Invariants of Quadratic Differential Forms*, 1927; *Foundations of Differential Geometry*, 1932, with J. H. C. Whitehead; *Projektive Relativitätstheorie*, 1933; and *Geometry of Complex Domains*, 1936, with W. Givens. With J. W. Young he wrote a standard two-volume textbook, *Projective Geometry*, 1910–1918, a revised edition appearing in 1965. Veblen died in Brooklin, Maine, on August 10, 1960.

Veblen, Thorstein Bunde (1857–1929), social scientist. Born on July 30, 1857, in Manitowoc County, Wisconsin, Veblen came of Norwegian immigrant stock and was raised in an area of Minnesota where the rural patterns of life and the attitudes of transplanted Norwegian dwellers contrasted sharply, with those of more assimilated Americans. Only because of his father's passion for education did he arrive in 1874 at Carleton College in Northfield, Minnesota. He received his B.A. in 1880 and did graduate work at Johns Hopkins and at Yale, where he took a Ph.D. in philosophy in 1884, but he found, to his dismay, that no teaching post was open to him. He returned home and spent seven tortured years doing farm work for which he was no longer suited. In 1891 he finally obtained a special fellowship at Cornell. That same year he published his first essay, "Some Neglected Points in the Theory of Socialism," in a scholarly journal. Eager to study and teach, he accepted an offer from the University of Chicago and taught political economy there from 1892 to 1906 while privately pursuing studies in anthropology and psychology. He helped to launch in 1892, and edited until 1905, the *Journal of Political Economy*, in which appeared many of his essays, among them "The Economic Theory of Women's Dress," "The Instinct of Workmanship and the Irksomeness of Labor," and "The Barbarian Status of Women." His writings were marked by fantastic polysyllabic terminology and cryptic insinuations. In 1899 his first book, *The Theory of the Leisure Class*, brought him immediate fame. A bristling assault upon the mercenary business classes, it presaged *The Theory of Business Enterprise*, 1904, which further clarified his views concerning the

American economy. He had gained much notoriety by this time, and his unconventional conduct so enraged other Chicago faculty members, as well as the board of trustees, that he was forced to resign his post. He held a faculty position at Stanford from 1906 to 1909, but entanglements with women plagued his life and career and resulted in his leaving that university. From then on he was affiliated with a number of institutions, including Missouri and the New School for Social Research, of which he was a founding member, but he encountered many of the same problems, and his manner and writings became more revolutionary. *The Instinct of Workmanship*, 1914, was based on his course on economic factors in civilization; *An Inquiry Into the Nature of Peace*, 1917, attributed the lack of world peace to patriotism and big business; *The Higher Learning in America*, 1918, denounced the control by business of educational institutions; *The Vested Interests and the State of the Industrial Arts*, 1919, accused business of trying to stunt production to maximize profits; and *The Engineers and the Price System*, 1921, prophesied eventual business control of the whole country. In all his writing, little trace of the influence of other American authors could be found; he retained throughout his life the attitudes of his hard-bitten, rural heritage. Far from being simplistic, however, his ideas helped to jolt the nation away from a trend toward business domination to a more rational approach to the control of the economy. He died on August 3, 1929, in his cabin retreat near Palo Alto, California.

Veeck, William Louis, Jr. (1914–   ), sports promoter. Born in Chicago on February 9, 1914, Veeck grew up in Hinsdale, a nearby suburb. He attended Hinsdale High School for three years before transferring to Phillips Academy, Andover, from which he graduated in 1932. After a year at Kenyon College he dropped out of school to go to work for the Chicago Cubs baseball club, of which his late father had been president since 1919. He worked in the club's office for seven years, becoming treasurer in 1940. In June 1941 he and Charley Grimm purchased the Milwaukee Brewers, a Cub farm team in the American Association. For the next two decades Veeck was to be one of the most controversial club owners in the nation. In two years he and Grimm transformed the Brewers from a last-place, low-attendance team to winners of three consecutive American Association pennants, in 1943, 1944, and 1945. To do it they built up the team; but Veeck also showed a flair for promotion and entertainment to increase attendance, using tactics that other club owners denounced. (During these years Veeck also served in the marines, seeing action in the Pacific theater.) Critics notwithstanding, within five years the Milwaukee team was turned into the most valuable property in the minor leagues. In 1945 he sold his interest in the Brewers and in 1946 became part owner of the Cleveland Indians of the American League, another team with a woeful record. Again, by a combination of team-building and promotional gimmicks, such as sending a midget to the plate to the intense anguish of the opposing pitcher and the enormous delight of the home fans, he developed the Indians into a pennant winner by 1948, and they went on to win the World Series. In 1951 he bought the St. Louis Browns, also of the American League, but no pennant-winning miracles occurred this time. He relinquished the Browns two years later, and stayed out of baseball for more than five years. Then in 1959, after he had become owner of the Chicago White Sox, the team won its first American League pennant in 40 years. Whether a team owner or not, Veeck continued to be a controversial sports figure, roundly condemned by traditionalists who derided his promotion and reform schemes. But as an owner and later as a sportswriter he defended his views, even after leaving the White Sox in 1961. He sought to equalize teams by urging the right to draft any farm-club player, and he suggested dividing up television receipts among all teams equally. Veeck's conflicts with other owners eventually drove him from baseball altogether. From 1968 to 1970 he was president of Suffolk Downs racetrack near Boston. In 1975 he returned to baseball as owner of the White Sox again.

Very, Jones (1813–1880), poet. Born in Salem, Massachusetts, on August 28, 1813, Very was privately tutored. He taught at Fisk Latin School in order to earn enough money to attend Harvard, graduating in 1836 and continuing his studies at the Divinity School. During his theological training he turned into a deeply mystical transcendentalist, conjuring up for himself visions of the Holy Spirit and composing religious sonnets that he insisted were divinely inspired. The theological faculty, liberal as it was, found him somewhat incredible and questioned his sanity. Very was persuaded to spend a month in the autumn of 1836 in an asylum in Somerville, Massachusetts, but the experience did not change him noticeably. His religious enthusiasm remained intense, and he failed to graduate from the Divinity School. But from Ralph Waldo Emerson and others of the Transcendentalists he received sympathy and understanding as well as appreciation of his poetry. Under Emerson's supervision an edition of Very's writings, entitled *Essays and Poems*, was published in 1839 and was highly praised by other New England writers of the time. The poems, all in sonnet form, reflected a combination of pantheism and Asian mysticism and quietism; they were clear, well structured, and expressive, but rooted in the mystical inwardness of their author. In 1843 Very was licensed to preach by the Cambridge Association (Unitarian), and he temporarily served parishes at Eastport, Maine, and North Beverly, Massachusetts. But his introverted personality kept him from being a successful pastor, and about 1858 he retired from the church and went into virtual seclusion in Salem for the rest of his life. The works of his later years did not compare in quality with his published verses. He died in Salem, Massachusetts, on May 8, 1880. A volume entitled *Poems* appeared in 1883 and *Poems and Essays* was published in 1886.

Vesey, Denmark (1767?–1822), slave leader. Born probably on the island of St. Thomas in the West Indies about 1767, Vesey, also known as Télémaque Vesey, in 1781 became the property of a Captain John Vesey, a Bermuda slaver. Little is known of his early life. Reportedly an epileptic, he accompanied his master to Charleston, South Carolina, a city with a large population of black freedmen, in 1783. In the 1790s he assisted Captain Vesey in the relief of French colonials fleeing revolution in Haiti, and he was thus familiar with the events in the Caribbean that led to an independent Haiti. In 1800, the year of the abortive Gabriel Prosser slave uprising in Virginia, he won $1500 in a street lottery and used $600 of it to purchase his freedom. He subsequently prospered as a carpenter and shortly also became noted for his preaching. He was an outspoken critic of slavery on biblical grounds, and his views became well known in Charleston, even though his audiences were largely black. In the summer of 1822 rumors of a slave conspiracy came to the attention of the mayor of Charleston, and inquiries were begun. Suspicion became rampant after the original story was corroborated and ten slaves were arrested on June 16, the day upon which the uprising was expected. Secret hearings followed and led to the arrest of Denmark Vesey, to whom all evidence pointed as the leader of the plot. During his trial Vesey confessed to nothing other than knowing a white barber who allegedly had made a wig for Vesey to wear as a disguise. Impressive in his own defense, he questioned witnesses who had made charges against him but was unable to elicit a change in their story. In his closing speech he tried to convince the court that, being free, he would have had nothing to gain from such an attempt, and attributed the charges against him to the great hatred which he alleged the other blacks—he was the only Negro freedman among the leaders of the plot—had against him. Vesey and five other blacks were hanged on July 2, 1822, an event that only increased the hysteria and led to numerous other arrests and more than 30 later executions. The actual extent of the plot, believed at times to have involved thousands of blacks, remained something of a mystery, but the affair prompted a marked tightening of the slave codes of several Southern states.

Vespucci, Amerigo (1454–1512), navigator and explorer. Born in Florence, Italy, in 1454, Vespucci entered the service of the Medici banking interests about 1480. It was in the service of the Medici that he was sent to Seville, Spain, in 1491 to work in one of their enterprises whose business was outfitting ships. In 1496 Vespucci became head of the Seville ship chandlery, and it was sometime during these years that he made the acquaintance of Christopher Columbus and learned of his discoveries in the New World. Between 1497 and 1504 Vespucci made the voyages for which he has become famous, although it is unclear from surviving documents whether he made two or four voyages; the authenticity of conflicting letters remains unsettled. The larger number has been traditionally accepted because of a letter of his dated September 4, 1504, and Latin versions of this letter. The theory of two voyages, currently deemed more likely, rests on three private letters addressed to his employers, the Medici. If the contention is accepted that he made only two voyages, the first would have taken place between May 1499 and June 1500. He sailed, in a fleet of four ships commanded by Alonso de Ojeda, to the coast of Guiana, then left Ojeda and went south along the coast of Brazil to discover the mouths of the Amazon River. He returned north to the island of Trinidad, sighted the mouth of the Orinoco River, and then sailed north to Hispaniola and thence to Spain. Being unable to convince Spanish authorities of the need for another voyage, he hired out to Portugal for the second trip. This expedition left Lisbon on May 13, 1501, and again explored along the coast of Brazil, discovering the bay of Rio de Janeiro, then sailed south to the Río de la Plata, of which Vespucci is the undoubted discoverer. The ships were back in Portugal on June 22, 1502. It was the second voyage which convinced Vespucci and authorities in Portugal and Spain that the lands that had been encountered across the Atlantic were indeed a new world and not part of Asia. In 1507, in Lorraine, the scholar Martin Waldseemüller published Vespucci's 1504 letter in a Latin version and suggested that the new territories be named America in his honor. The name, at first applied only to South America, was eventually given to the whole hemisphere. In 1505 Vespucci went back into the service of Spain, working for the Commercial House for the West Indies at Seville. In 1508 he became chief pilot for the House, and among his duties were preparing maps of newly discovered land and organizing all data that the Spanish expeditions brought back. He made remarkably accurate calculations, from astronomical observations devised by himself, of the longitude of the New World and of the size of the earth. His postulate of two great oceans and a continent between western Europe and Asia proved true. He died in Seville in 1512.

Vick, James (1818–1882), horticulturist and publisher. Born in Chichester, England, on November 23, 1818, Vick emigrated to the United States in 1833. For four years he lived in New York City learning the printing trade; then in 1837 he settled in Rochester, New York, and worked for local newspapers. As he prospered in publishing, Vick turned his attention to his avocation—the growing of flowers. Within a few years he was able to combine his two interests into a career of horticultural publishing. He became one of the editors of the *Genesee Farmer;* and after the death of Andrew Jackson Downing in 1852, Vick bought Downing's magazine, the *Horticulturist,* and pub

lished it for three years. He edited the *Rural New Yorker* from 1857 until 1862, and in 1878 founded his own *Vick's Monthly Magazine.* But from the mid-1880s publishing was but a sideline, an auxiliary of his main business, that of importing and growing garden seeds and selling them to all parts of the country by mail order. He published a widely circulated annual catalog and employed a large staff to fill the thousands of orders he received. By the late 1860s Vick was the largest seed merchant in the nation, and his experiments in crossbreeding flowers and in gardening exerted a wide influence in U.S. horticulture. He died in Rochester on May 16, 1882.

Vidal, Gore (1925–   ), author and playwright. Born in West Point, New York, on October 3, 1925, Vidal graduated from Phillips Exeter Academy in 1943 and then enlisted in the army. He emerged from military service three years later as an author with a highly acclaimed first novel, *Williwaw,* based on his World War II experiences. He followed it in 1947 with another popular success, *In a Yellow Wood.* He wrote six novels in as many years thereafter, but they found fewer readers than his first two works. In the 1950s he wrote a number of television plays, of which the best known was "Visit to a Small Planet," subsequently turned into a Broadway production in 1957 and later a movie in 1960. He also wrote several film scripts, including *Suddenly Last Summer,* 1960, and the first half of the extravaganza *Ben Hur,* 1959. His second Broadway play, *The Best Man,* dealing with the forces at play during a political convention, opened in March 1960 and ran for two years. In 1964 it, too, was made into a movie. His third play, *Romulus,* was less successful. In the 1960s, after a ten-year hiatus, Vidal again turned to novel writing. In 1964 he published *Julian,* based on the life of the third-century apostate Roman emperor, and in 1967 came out with *Washington, D.C.* In 1968 he published the very successful, and sensational, *Myra Breckenridge,* in which the leading character went through a sex-change operation. The book was made into a lurid movie in 1970 from which Vidal dissociated himself. In addition to his writing he took an active interest in politics and social issues. In 1960 he ran for the House of Representatives from New York's 29th district, but lost. During the 1968 national political conventions, he and William F. Buckley, Jr., served as co-commentators, and often as near-combatants, on network television for the American Broadcasting Company (ABC). In the spring of 1972 Vidal returned to Broadway with a political satire entitled *An Evening with Richard Nixon,* and in 1973 he published *Burr,* a fictional and unorthodox treatment of Aaron Burr.

Villard, Henry (1835–1900), journalist, railroad executive, and financier. Born on April 10, 1835, in Speyer, Bavaria (now Germany), Ferdinand Heinrich Gustav Hilgard attended the universities of Munich and Würzburg and came to the United

States in 1853. He assumed the name Villard to avoid being called back to serve in the German army by his father, a Bavarian supreme-court jurist whose political philosophy had precipitated his son's emigration. He settled with relatives in Belleville, Illinois, and concentrated on mastering English. In 1858 he began a career in journalism with the *New York Staats-Zeitung*. In covering the Lincoln-Douglas debates in Illinois, he gained the confidence of Abraham Lincoln. Desirous of exploring the Pike's Peak region of Colorado, he secured a position with the *Cincinnati Daily Commercial* to cover the gold rush to Colorado in 1859. In 1860 he covered the Republican national convention in Chicago. He was selected by the *New Yord Herald* as a special correspondent in Springfield after Lincoln's election, and his stories to the *Herald* were also distributed through the New York Associated Press. The *Herald* and the *New York Tribune* printed his dispatches from the battlefields during the Civil War. In 1864 he organized his own news agency and served as its Washington correspondent through 1865. He then traveled as a free-lance writer in the United States and Europe through 1868, afterward becoming secretary of the American Social Science Association in Boston, where he studied the financial structure of banks and railroads. Visiting Germany in 1873, he met bondholders of the Oregon & California Railroad and agreed to go to Oregon in 1874 to represent their interests. He instituted reforms in the operations of the railway and became its president in 1876. He improved other local transportation companies and, also in 1876, became president of the Oregon Steamship Company. While representing the interests of stockholders in the Kansas Pacific Railroad in the 1870s, he saved the line from dissolution with his reforms, and was named receiver of it in 1876. In 1879 he bought the Oregon Steam Navigation Company, formed the Oregon Railway & Navigation Company, and proceeded to build a railway line along the Columbia River from Portland; when, in 1881, the approaching Northern Pacific, then under construction, threatened to break his monopoly on Northwest coastal outlets, he bought a controlling interest, securing from friends subscriptions amounting to millions of dollars with which to purchase stock. The Northern Pacific, with Villard as president, then completed its transcontinental line by way of the Portland route instead of the original route planned to Puget Sound, but by 1883 heavy expenses had put it deeply in debt and Villard was removed from the presidency in 1884. After a nervous breakdown and two years in Germany he became a New York City agent for a German bank. He was soon involved in railroads again, however, and in 1889 returned to the Northern Pacific as chairman of the board, a post he held until 1893. He gave financial support to Thomas Edison, and in 1890 merged two of Edison's companies into the Edison General Electric Company. He presided over this company until 1892, when it became part of the General Electric Company. He had purchased the controlling interest in the *New York Evening Post* in 1881 and hired Horace White, Carl Schurz, and E. L. Godkin as its editors; Godkin brought with him the *Nation*, a distinguished journal of current affairs which he had founded. Villard died in Dobbs Ferry, New York, on November 12, 1900. His widow, Helen Frances, the only daughter of abolitionist William Lloyd Garrison, was active in the formation of the National Association for the Advancement of Colored People (NAACP) in 1910, and organized the Women's Peace Society in 1919. Their son was Oswald Garrison Villard.

Villard, Oswald Garrison (1872–1949), editor and author. Born on March 13, 1872, in Wiesbaden, Germany, the son of Henry Villard and the grandson of William Lloyd Garrison, Villard graduated from Harvard in 1893 and began a career in journalism with the *Philadelphia Press*. In 1897 he joined the staff of his father's *New York Evening Post* and became its president and owner after the elder Villard's death in 1900. Under his control, the paper became a leading liberal organ with a nationwide circulation. Like his grandfather, Villard was a pacifist, and his feelings were reflected in the newspaper's editorial position. When his negative stance on U.S. entry into World War I adversely affected circulation, he sold the paper in 1918 but retained control of its weekly edition, the *Nation*, which he molded into a journal of social protest with astute commentary on politics and the arts. His controversial editorials, written at a time when pacifism was highly suspect, led to issues of the *Nation* being impounded by U.S. postal authorities, although they were finally released. Despite his feelings that the power to declare war should be placed in the hands of the people and that war would thereby be eliminated, his editors supported the government's defense program. Unable to sway them, he stepped down to the position of contributing editor of the *Nation* in 1932 and three years later sold the magazine. Thereafter he contributed articles and letters to many newspapers and magazines, protesting war and oppression in any form. With his mother he was a founder, in 1910, of the National Association for the Advancement of Colored People (NAACP) and was an active member of several antiwar organizations. He wrote a number of books, including *John Brown—A Biography Fifty Years After*, 1910; *Germany Embattled*, 1915; *Newspapers and Newspaper Men*, 1923; *Prophets—True and False*, 1928; *Our Military Chaos*, 1939; and *The Disappearing Daily*, 1944, which denounced the shift of emphasis in U.S. journalism from news coverage to entertainment. He also wrote an autobiography, *Fighting Years*, which was published in 1939. He died in New York City on October 1, 1949.

Vincent, John Heyl (1832–1920), religious leader and educator. Born in Tuscaloosa, Alabama, on February 23, 1832, Vincent grew up in Pennsylvania and after holding a number of jobs became a Methodist preacher in 1850. In 1852 he studied for a short time at the Wesleyan Institute in Newark, New Jersey, and in 1855 he was ordained a deacon; after several years in New Jersey he moved to Illinois and served a number of churches before assuming the pastorate of Trinity Church in Chicago in 1864. Setting himself the task of making over the institution of the Sunday school into one that was both effective and truly educational, he founded the Union Sunday School Institute for the Northwest and began publication of a journal to promote better organization and uniformity in lessons and standards. The journal became the monthly *Sunday School Teacher* in 1865. In 1866 he became general agent in New York City of the Sunday School Union of the Methodist Episcopal church, and during the next 20 years supervised the unified program and edited its publications, including the *Sunday School Journal*. Under his guidance uniform Sunday school teacher training, standards, and lessons spread throughout the nation. In 1874, in association with Lewis Miller, he organized a national assembly and training institute for Sunday-school teachers at Lake Chautauqua, New York. The great success of the idea caused the program to expand into a regular summer study and training institute, and in 1878 Vincent drew up proposals for the Chautauqua Literary and Scientific Circle, a four-year program of prescribed reading followed by an examination and the granting of a diploma. Soon hundreds of "chautauquas" were organized across the country and noted scholars, lecturers, and literary figures were touring the circuit, supplementing the program of adult home study. Vincent continued to direct both the Chautauqua movement and the Sunday School Union until 1888, when he was elected a bishop of his church; from 1888 to 1892 he was bishop of Buffalo, New York; from 1892 to 1900, of Topeka, Kansas; and from 1900 to his retirement in 1904, of Zurich, Switzerland, where he directed Methodist activities for all of Europe. His books included *Sunday School Institutes and Normal Classes*, 1872; *The Chautauqua Movement*, 1886; *The Modern Sunday School*, 1887; and *Our Own Church*, 1890. Vincent died in Chicago on May 9, 1920.

Vinson, Frederick Moore (1890–1953), chief justice of the Supreme Court. Born in Louisa, Kentucky, on January 22, 1890, Vinson graduated from Kentucky Normal College in 1908 and received his B.A. from Centre College of Kentucky in 1909. Two years later he took a law degree at Centre and opened a practice in his home town. He was soon active in local politics, and by 1914 was named city attorney. After service in World War I he returned to his law practice and in 1921 was appointed commonwealth attorney for the 32nd judicial district of the state. A Democrat, in 1923 he was named to fill a vacancy in the House of Representatives, taking his seat on January 12, 1924. He was reelected to the House through 1936 except for the Hoover landslide year of 1928, when he sat out one term. In Congress he became known as an expert in tax and fiscal matters. He was especially intent on removing inequities from the tax laws and was an early supporter of the pay-as-you-go income-tax plan that went into effect during World War II. In 1938 he resigned his seat in the House to accept appointment as an associate justice of the U.S. Court of Appeals for the District of Columbia. Five years later his fiscal expertise brought him appointment as director of the Office of Economic Stabilization. Vinson held this post until March 1945 and also served on other war emergency boards until President Harry S. Truman appointed him secretary of the treasury in July 1945. He had been in the President's cabinet for only a year when Truman appointed him 13th chief justice of the U.S. Supreme Court to succeed Harlan F. Stone in June 1946. As a member of the Court Vinson was an advocate of civil rights and an exponent of the liberal construction of the Constitution. He felt that the federal government had to have sweeping powers to deal with social problems and the changes taking place in society, and thus that the Court should play a fairly restrained role when dealing with governmental and particularly executive policy. For instance, when a majority of the Court held Truman's seizure of the steel mills unconstitutional in 1952 (*Youngstown Sheet and Tube Co.* v. *Sawyer*), Vinson issued a strong dissent. He served on the Court until his death in Washington, D.C., on September 8, 1953.

Von Braun, Wernher, *see* Braun, Wernher von

Von Kaltenborn, Hans, *see* Kaltenborn, Hans von

Von Kármán, Theodore, *see* Kármán, Theodore von

Vonnegut, Kurt, Jr. (1922–   ), author. Born in Indianapolis on November 11, 1922, Vonnegut attended Cornell University and the Carnegie Institute of Technology before entering the army for service in World War II. On his discharge in 1945 he began working as a reporter while continuing his studies at the University of Chicago, and in 1947 he joined the public-relations staff of the General Electric Company in Schenectady, New York. From 1950 he devoted his time to writing, producing short stories published in popular magazines, and in 1952 his first novel, *Player Piano*, a science-fictionalized rumination on the technocratic tendencies of modern society inspired by his experiences at General Electric. *The Sirens of Titan*, 1959, was again science fiction, but with *Mother Night*, 1961, *Cat's Cradle*, 1963, and *God Bless You, Mr. Rosewater*, 1965, Vonnegut began to concentrate his attention on exploring the social and moral conventions of American life, drawing with revealing perceptiveness the multitudinous foibles of men. During 1965–1967 he lectured at the Writer's Workshop of the University of Iowa. He subsequently moved to Massachusetts and published *Welcome to the Monkey House*, a collection of stories, 1968; *Slaughterhouse Five, or*

The Children's Crusade, 1969, a best-selling novel drawing upon his own experiences as a prisoner of war in Dresden during the Allied fire bombing of that city in World War II; and *Breakfast of Champions*, 1973, a macabre and mordant study of mental imbalance. A play, *Happy Birthday, Wanda June*, was produced in 1970, achieving some success off-Broadway and then on Broadway. By 1969 Vonnegut had emerged as one of the country's most popular authors; his satirical treatment of American culture and mores and his strong sympathy for the victimized and the gently mad clearly evoked responses from among a wide variety of readers.

Von Neumann, John, *see* Neumann, John Von

Von Stroheim, Erich, *see* Stroheim, Erich von

Vought, Chance Milton (1890–1930), aeronautical engineer. Born in New York City on February 26, 1890, Vought attended Pratt Institute, New York University, and the University of Pennsylvania. He left school in 1910 to work as a consulting engineer for a firm in Chicago, but within two years his interest had turned entirely toward aeronautics. He had learned to fly in 1910 under the Wright brothers' instruction, and soon became interested in airplane construction and design. In 1914 he established himself as an airplane designer by building a training plane that the British adopted for use in World War I. He worked for the Wright Aircraft Company in Dayton, Ohio, as chief engineer and designed the Model V military biplane for them. In 1917 he formed his own Lewis & Vought Corporation in Long Island City, New York. This company shortly became the Chance Vought Corporation, one of the leading designers and builders of military craft in the country. Among the firm's notable aircraft were the VE-7 trainer, introduced in 1919; the UO-1 convertible observation craft, 1922–1925; the FU-1 high-altitude fighter, 1925; and the O2U Corsair, a seaplane that set numerous speed and altitude records. In 1929 he merged his company into the United Aircraft and Transportation Corporation, but continued to direct the Vought division. (In 1961 the company again became independent.) He died on July 25, 1930, in Southampton, Long Island, New York.

W

Waddel, Moses (1770–1840), educator. Born in what is now Iredell County, North Carolina, on July 29, 1770, Waddel attended local schools until the age of fourteen and then himself began teaching. In 1788 he opened his own school in Greene County, Georgia, where he had moved with his family, but he soon abandoned the enterprise in order to attend Hampden-Sydney College, from which he graduated in 1791. A year later, after studying privately, he received a license to preach from the Presbyterian church, but his career as a clergyman was brief. He returned to schoolkeeping, establishing himself successively in Appling, Columbia County, Georgia, where his school was known for a time as Carmel Academy; in Vienna, South Carolina; and in 1804 in Willington, in what is now McCormick County, South Carolina. The school in Willington soon became famous throughout the South and made Waddel one of the best-known educators of his day. A stern disciplinarian, he helped mold virtually an entire generation of Southern leaders, numbering among his pupils such later prominent men as John C. Calhoun, whose sister Catherine he had married in 1795, William H. Crawford, Hugh S. Legaré, Augustus B. Longstreet, George McDuffie, and James L. Petigru. In 1819 he gave up his school to become president of Franklin College (now the University of Georgia) in Athens, Georgia. He returned to Willington upon his retirement in 1829, but in 1836 he moved back to Athens, where he died on July 21, 1840.

Waddell, James Iredell (1824–1886), naval officer. Born in Pittsboro, North Carolina, on July 13, 1824, Waddell joined the navy as a midshipman at seventeen. He saw action for about seven months in 1846 during the Mexican War, aboard the *Somers* in the Gulf of Mexico. For two years after the war he studied at the U.S. Naval Academy. He became a lieutenant in 1855, and sea duty took him to various parts of the world. Upon returning home from the Far East in 1862 he resigned his commission and went into the Confederate navy as a lieutenant. After a year's duty in the South he sailed for Europe, and in October 1864 took command of the Confederate cruiser *Shenandoah*, which had been purchased in England. He sailed for the Pacific and spent most of the ensuing year harassing Union shipping. He virtually wiped out the New England whaling fleet in the Pacific, capturing more than 30 prizes, commandeering some ships, and burning others. Not knowing that the Union had won the war in April 1865, he continued his depredations until August. He even planned an attack upon San Francisco, but when he found out from a British ship that the Civil War was indeed over he sailed instead for England, becoming the only Confederate commander to carry his flag around the world; he docked at Liverpool on November 6, 1865. Legally he and his crew had been engaged in acts of piracy since the end of the war, and they therefore remained in England until an amnesty was granted. After returning to the United States, Waddell sailed for private shipping companies for the rest of his life. He died in Annapolis, Maryland, on March 15, 1886.

Wade, Benjamin Franklin (1800–1878), lawyer and public official. Born in Springfield, Massachusetts, on October 27, 1800, Wade grew up amid the hardships of farm life and could attend school only in winter months. In 1821 the family moved to Andover, Ohio, where he undertook various jobs, including teaching school. In 1825 he settled down to the study of law in Canfield, Ohio, was admitted to the bar in 1827, and in 1831 became a partner of Joshua R. Giddings. He built a successful practice in northeastern Ohio and served a term, in 1835–1837, as prosecuting attorney for Ashtabula County until his election to the state senate. His outspoken stand against slavery cost him reelection in 1839, but he was returned to the senate for another term in 1841. He was chosen judge of Ohio's 3rd judicial district in 1847 and the Whig-controlled legislature elected him to the U.S. Senate in 1851. He was uncompromisingly opposed to the extension of slavery and vigorously fought the passage of the Kansas-Nebraska Bill (1854). Returned to the Senate as a Republican in 1857 and again in 1863, he stood with the Radical Republicans in their demands for decisive prosecution of the Civil War, emancipation of the slaves, and severe punishment of the Confederacy. He helped set up the Joint Congressional Committee on the Conduct of the War and as its chairman played a prominent and controversial role in investigating all aspects—some said meddlesomely—of the Union military effort. He worked closely with Secretary of War Edwin Stanton in attempting to undermine administration war policies. In 1864 his cosponsorship with Henry W. Davis of the Wade-Davis Bill, which declared Reconstruction of the Southern state governments a legislative and not an executive concern, brought him into direct conflict with President Abraham Lincoln. Beaten on the issue by Lincoln's pocket veto, Wade and Davis published a manifesto in the *New York Tribune* denouncing the President's "studied outrage on the legislative authority." They joined in the effort to replace Lincoln with

Salmon P. Chase as the Republican candidate in 1864, but the project failed and Wade finally supported the President's reelection. After Lincoln's assassination, Wade backed President Andrew Johnson until it was plain that he, following Lincoln, favored a lenient plan of Reconstruction. In 1867 Wade was elected president pro tempore of the Senate, a position that would have elevated him to the presidency had Johnson been removed after the impeachment trial of 1868. Sure of Johnson's conviction, Wade began selecting his cabinet while the trial was under way, and the acquittal of Johnson (Wade voted for conviction) bitterly disappointed him. A Democratic majority in the Ohio legislature denied him a fourth term in the Senate and the Republican national convention of 1868 nominated Schuyler Colfax instead of Wade to be Ulysses S. Grant's running mate. In 1869 Wade resumed his Ohio law practice; he became general counsel of the Northern Pacific Railway and served as a government director of the Union Pacific. In 1871 President Grant appointed him a member of the commission sent to investigate conditions in Santo Domingo, and he recommended its annexation. He died in Jefferson, Ohio, on March 2, 1878.

Wagner, George Raymond, see Gorgeous George

Wagner, Honus (1874–1955), baseball player. Born in Mansfield (now Carnegie), Pennsylvania, on February 24, 1874, John Peter Wagner, who was also known as Hans, started playing professional baseball in 1895 for minor-league teams. Two years later he was signed by the Louisville, Kentucky, team of the National League. After three seasons he went to the Pittsburgh Pirates and played with them for the rest of his career, retiring in 1917. Basically a shortstop, Wagner played other positions, he even pitched, as the situation demanded, and he is considered by many sports experts to have been the best all-round player in baseball history. He won the National League batting title eight times and ended his career with a lifetime average of .329 and record numbers of doubles and triples. A speedy runner despite his bulk—he was known as "the Flying Dutchman"—Wagner accumulated a total of 722 stolen bases, leading the National League five times. He was probably the best infielder who ever lived, scooping grounders out of the dirt with his huge hands and firing them across the diamond at his first basemen, who were sometimes hurt by the accompanying gravel. From 1933 until 1952 he was a member of the Pirates' coaching staff. When the National Baseball Hall of Fame was founded in 1936, Wagner was one of the first five players chosen, and the only infielder. He died in Carnegie, Pennsylvania, on December 6, 1955.

Wagner, John Peter, see Wagner, Honus

Wagner, Robert Ferdinand (1877–1953), public official. Born in Hesse-Nassau, Germany, on June 8, 1877, Wagner emigrated to the United States with his family in 1885 and settled in New York City. He graduated from the City College of New York (CCNY) in 1898 and from the New York Law School in 1900. Admitted to the bar in 1900, he opened a law practice but was immediately involved in politics as a member of Tammany Hall. In 1904 he was elected to the state assembly and in 1908 to the state senate, spending eight years as Democratic floor leader. He was appointed a justice of the state supreme court in 1919 and held the post until 1926. In 1926 he ran for the U.S. Senate and was elected. He was reelected in 1932, 1938, and 1944, serving in the Senate until he resigned on June 28, 1949, for reasons of health. In office Wagner proposed and supported some of the most far-reaching social and labor legislation of the first half of the twentieth century. In the New York assembly he brought about an investigation of working conditions in New York City following the disastrous Triangle Shirtwaist Company fire in 1911. He was also responsible for the passage of the state's Workmen's Compensation Law. In his first term in the U.S. Senate he consistently proposed legislation to benefit the workingman and the unemployed, but his proposals got nowhere until the administration of Franklin D. Roosevelt took over in 1933. Wagner helped draft several early New Deal measures, including the National Industrial Recovery Act (NIRA), 1933; the Federal Emergency Relief Administration bill (FERA), 1933; public-works legislation; and laws to ease the financial problems of farmers. He was the author of the 1935 National Labor Relations Act (or Wagner-Connery Act), which put the power of the federal government behind labor's right to bargain collectively and established the National Labor Relations Board (NLRB). He was the moving force behind the 1935 Social Security Act and the Wagner-Steagall Act of 1937, setting up the U.S. Housing Authority. His national health program and his anti-lynching legislation never were enacted, however. In 1945 he cosponsored a full-employment bill which, in a watered-down version, was passed and signed by President Harry S. Truman in 1946. After Wagner resigned from the Senate in 1949 he continued to make his home in New York City, where he died on May 4, 1953. His son, Robert F. Wagner, served as mayor of New York City for twelve years, 1953–1965.

Wahunsonacock, see Powhatan

Waite, Morrison Remick (1816–1888), chief justice of the Supreme Court. Born in Lyme, Connecticut, on November 29, 1816, Waite was the son of the chief justice of Connecticut. He graduated from Yale in 1837 and moved to Maumee, Ohio, the following year to enter a law firm. He was admitted to the bar in 1839 and after failing in a run for a seat in the House of Representatives in 1845 was elected to the state legislature in 1849. He moved to Toledo in 1850 and developed a substantial practice in railroad cases and other corporate matters that led him to argue frequently before the Ohio supreme court. In 1862 he ran as an independent Republican for the House and was again defeated. He declined appointment to the state supreme court in 1863. During the Civil War he was tireless in promoting the Union cause. In 1871 President Ulysses S. Grant appointed him one of the U.S. counsels in the international arbitration of the *Alabama* claims in Geneva; he wrote 5 of the 13 chapters of the U.S. *Argument*, and was noted for his "excellent tone and temper" with the British representatives. After returning from Geneva, he was elected as a delegate to the Ohio constitutional convention of 1873 and was made its president. While the convention was in session he learned of his nomination as chief justice of the U.S. Supreme Court by President Grant. Although Waite had no judicial experience, had argued no cases before the Court, and had little national reputation beyond that earned in the *Alabama* arbitration, the appointment was well received by the nation's bar and the Senate unanimously confirmed him the seventh chief justice on January 21, 1874. He immediately assumed a large share of the work of the Court and in 14 years on the bench wrote the opinion of the Court in more than 1000 cases. It was the main task of his Court to interpret the amendments to the Constitution, particularly the Fourteenth, that were adopted after the Civil War. His major contribution was his interpretation of the due-process clause of the Fourteenth Amendment: he held that businesses "clothed with a public interest" could be subject to regulation by states (*Munn* v. *Illinois*, 1877, the principal among the Granger Cases). While in general allowing the government great scope under the commerce clause and the notion of police power, Waite drew the line in *Stone* v. *Farmers' Loan and Trust Co.*, 1886, declaring that a state may not "do that which . . . amounts to taking of private property for public use . . . without due process of law." The two cases served the Court for decades in the application of the commerce clause. In *Reynolds* v. *U.S.*, 1878, in upholding the application of anti-polygamy laws to Mormons, he distinguished between freedom to hold a religious belief and freedom to engage in some practices. In *Santa Clara Co.* v. *Southern Pacific Railroad Co.*, 1886, he accepted the view that the word "person" in the Fourteenth Amendment included legal persons, that is, corporations, in its meaning. His decisions established or confirmed many of the accepted principles of constitutional law. Although active in civic affairs, he tried to disassociate his office from politics; he refused to allow his name to be considered among the presidential nominees of 1876 and he would not serve on the Electoral Commission appointed to resolve the presidential election disputed by Samuel J. Tilden and Rutherford B. Hayes. He died in Washington, D.C., on March 23, 1888.

Waksman, Selman Abraham (1888–1973), microbiologist. Born in Priluki, Russia, on July 22, 1888, Waksman emigrated to the United States in 1910 and was naturalized in 1916. He received his B.S.

from Rutgers in 1915, his M.S. in 1916, and he gained a Ph.D. from the University of California at Berkeley in 1918. After a few years of work as a bacteriologist and research biologist at commercial laboratories, he joined the Rutgers faculty. He was a lecturer in soil microbiology, 1918–1924, associate professor of that subject from 1924 to 1930, and professor from 1930 to 1942; he was professor of microbiology from 1942 to 1958. He was a microbiologist for the New Jersey agricultural experiment station at New Brunswick from 1921 to 1951 and he organized and headed a division of marine microbiology at Woods Hole Oceanographic Institution in Massachusetts, from 1930 to 1942. He was considered one of the world's leading authorities on soil microbiology and on antibiotics. His most important studies concerned certain filamentous bacteria, the actinomycetes, which include many antibiotic-producing organisms. With his coworkers he discovered the antibiotic streptomycin in 1943; it was the first specific agent found to be effective in the treatment of tuberculosis, and for its discovery he was awarded the 1952 Nobel Prize for Physiology and Medicine. Neomycin, derived, like streptomycin, from a species of the genus *Streptomyces*, is widely used in the treatment of infectious diseases of man, domestic animals, and plants. Apart from papers in technical journals and books describing his discoveries—such as *Principles of Soil Microbiology*, 1931; *Humus* 1938; and the massive *The Actinomycetes*, three volumes, 1959–1962—he also wrote two popular books, *My Life with the Microbes*, 1954, and *The Conquest of Tuberculosis*, 1964. Waksman died in Hyannis, Massachusetts, on August 16, 1973.

Walcott, Charles Doolittle (1850–1927), geologist and scientific administrator. Born in New York Mills, New York, on March 31, 1850, Walcott had no formal education in childhood beyond that provided by the public schools of Utica. He early developed an interest in natural history and by 1871 had decided to become a geologist. For five years he studied and collected fossils on his own, and in 1876 he was hired to be an assistant geologist for the New York State Survey. Then in 1879 he became a field assistant for the U.S. Geological Survey, working for two years under Clarence King and from 1881 until 1894 under J. Wesley Powell. In 1893 he became chief geologist. In 1894 Walcott himself was named director of the Survey, and under him the Survey and its activities were greatly expanded. He took part in establishing the Forest Service and the Bureau of Mines. He remained in the post until 1907, when he became secretary of the Smithsonian Institution. During his administration of the Smithsonian he was influential in obtaining the gift of the Freer Gallery of Art, given in 1906 by Charles L. Freer of Detroit and containing more than 9000 works of art. He also served as secretary of the Carnegie Institution of Washington from 1902 until 1905 and on its board of trustees from 1917 to 1922, and was influential in the founding of the

National Research Council and the National Advisory Committee for Aeronautics, of which he served as chairman during World War I. Although much of Walcott's career was devoted to administrative work, directing either the Geological Survey or the Smithsonian, he nevertheless found time to continue his geological researches into the rocks and fossil fauna of the Cambrian period. He did field work for as many years as he was able and wrote many papers and several books on his studies. His largest work was *Cambrian Brachiopoda*, published in two volumes in 1912. Walcott maintained an interest in air travel and in 1918 aided in the founding of the air-mail service. He drafted the Air Commerce Act that was passed by Congress in 1926. From 1917 to 1923 he was president of the National Academy of Sciences. He died in Washington, D.C., on February 9, 1927.

Wald, George (1906–   ), biologist. Born in New York City on November 18, 1906, Wald graduated from New York University in 1927. He pursued graduate studies in biology at Columbia University and took his Ph.D. there in 1932. He spent the next two years studying on a research fellowship, first in Germany, then at the University of Chicago. It was while in Germany in 1932 that he made his first important discovery, the presence of vitamin A in the retina of the eye. This laid the foundation for subsequent research demonstrating that the three retinal pigments are composed of a combination of different proteins and vitamin A. Most of his work after 1932 dealt with the retina of the eye and its composition, and with the formation and function of vitamin A, with the aim of learning more about how the eye changes light into sight. For his work in biology, much of which had been done in collaboration with his wife, Ruth Hubbard Wald, Wald shared the 1967 Nobel Prize for Physiology and Medicine with H. K. Hartline and with R. A. Granit of Sweden. In 1934 Wald joined the faculty of Harvard University, where he taught biology and conducted research; he was made a full professor in 1948. In early 1969 Wald came out of the confines of laboratory and classroom to become one of the most articulate spokesmen of the movement opposing the Vietnam War. He delivered a powerful antiwar speech in March 1969 to a faculty-student gathering at the Massachusetts Institute of Technology (MIT) entitled "A World to Win," and subsequently spoke to student groups and protest gatherings in all parts of the country.

Wald, Lillian D. (1867–1940), public-health nurse and social reformer. Born on March 10, 1867, in Cincinnati, Miss Wald grew up there and in Rochester, New York. She early became interested in nursing and in 1891 graduated from the New York Hospital Training School for Nurses. She later supplemented her training with courses at the Women's Medical College. In her work she observed at first hand the wretched conditions prevailing in New York City's Lower East Side, largely populated by immigrants, and in 1893,

with a companion, she moved to the neighborhood and offered her services as a visiting nurse. Two years later, with aid from philanthropist-banker Jacob H. Schiff and others, she took larger accommodations and opened the Nurses' Settlement, later known as the Henry Street Settlement House. As the number of nurses attached to the settlement grew, services were expanded to include nurses' training, educational programs for the community, and youth clubs. In 1902 nursing service was experimentally extended to a local public school; the project was so successful that the Board of Health soon instituted a city-wide public-school nursing program, the first such program in the world. The organization of nursing programs for their policyholders by insurance companies and of the district nursing service of the Red Cross were both at her suggestion, and in 1912 she helped found and became first president of the National Organization for Public Health Nursing. She also worked to establish educational, recreational, and social programs in underprivileged neighborhoods. In 1912 Congress established the U.S. Children's Bureau, also in no small part owing to her suggestion, and she was awarded the gold medal of the National Institute of Social Sciences. She was active in other areas of reform, particularly the National Women's Trade Union League and the American Union Against Militarism. She wrote *The House on Henry Street*, 1915, and *Windows on Henry Street*, 1934, both autobiographical. In 1933 ill health forced her to leave Henry Street. She settled in Westport, Connecticut, and died there on September 1, 1940. She was elected to the Hall of Fame in 1970.

Walgreen, Charles Rudolph (1873–1939), pharmacist. Born on October 9, 1873, in Knox County, Illinois, near Galesburg, Walgreen grew up there and in Dixon. In 1893 he moved to Chicago, where he worked in drugstores and studied pharmacy in his free time. Following service in the Spanish-American War he returned to Chicago and, as a registered pharmacist, worked in a drugstore that he was able to buy in 1902. In 1909 he organized the firm which in 1916 became known as the Walgreen Company. He added other stores to his enterprise and gradually built up the largest chain of drugstores in the nation. He was an innovator in merchandising, adding many lines of goods to his stores in addition to the stock of pharmaceuticals, and his stores popularized the drugstore lunch counter. It is said that the malted milk was first served in one of his stores. By the time he retired in 1934 there were more than 500 Walgreen stores coast-to-coast. He died in Chicago on December 11, 1939.

Walker, Amasa (1799–1875), economist and public official. Born in Woodstock, Connecticut, on May 4, 1799, Walker was raised in Brookfield, Massachusetts, attended the district school, and worked on the family farm and for a card manufacturer in Leicester until he was fifteen years old. For the next six years he clerked in a country store, farmed, and taught school in an unsuccessful attempt—mainly because of bad health—to gain admission to Amherst College. At twenty-one he bought a part interest in a store that he sold three years later in order to become a manufacturer's agent. In 1825 he and a partner opened a shoe store in Boston. In 1835 he wrote a series of articles for the *Boston Daily Advertiser and Patriot* calling for the building of a railroad from Boston to Albany. Four years later a St. Louis audience laughed when he told them that sleeping and dining cars would one day arrive at the Mississippi by rail from Boston. In 1840 he retired from business and visited Florida for his health. Influential in the founding of Oberlin College, he lectured there on political economy from 1842 to 1849. An advocate of world peace, he was vice-president of the International Peace Congress held in England in 1843 and of the Paris Peace Congress of 1849. He served in the Massachusetts house of representatives in 1848, the state senate in 1849, and as a Free-Soiler was secretary of state of Massachusetts, 1851–1853. He was examiner in political economy at Harvard from 1853 to 1860. His primary interest was the monetary system, and his study of the financial panic of 1837 led to a series of articles in *Hunt's Merchants' Magazine and Commercial Review* that were reprinted as *The Nature and Uses of Money and Mixed Currency* in 1857, the year of another financial panic. His advice to Boston businessmen to stop specie payments was ignored, only to be proved correct a short time later. He was elected to another term in the Massachusetts lower house in 1859 and was appointed to fill a vacancy in the U.S. House of Representatives, 1862–1863. He finally went to Amherst College as a lecturer from 1860 to 1869. His chief work, *The Science of Wealth: A Manual of Political Economy*, appeared in 1866 and was long a popular textbook of economics. He died in Brookfield, Massachusetts, on October 29, 1875. Francis Amasa Walker, the economist, was his son.

Walker, David (1785–1830), abolitionist. Born in Wilmington, North Carolina, on September 28, 1785, Walker was a free black by virtue of his mother's free status, although his father had been a slave. The facts of his early life are not known, except that he did somehow get an education and did travel a good deal throughout the South, where he was able to see the evils of the slave system. In the mid-1820s he settled in Boston, where he operated a used-clothing store near the waterfront. He became involved in the abolition movement that was taking shape in the North, and did much speaking before audiences of both blacks and whites in the Boston area. When *Freedom's Journal*, the nation's first Negro newspaper, began publication in New York City in March 1827, Walker became the Boston agent for the paper and began contributing articles. He soon became dissatisfied with reaching only the small audiences he spoke to or the readers of the *Journal*; he wanted somehow to get his message to the slaves themselves (most of whom, unfortunately, could

not read). In September 1829 he composed the pamphlet that launched the militant abolitionist crusade, his *Appeal to the Coloured Citizens of the World*, commonly known as *Walker's Appeal*. It was a powerful indictment of slavery and a call to the slaves to overthrow the system. The reaction to his appeal in the South was predictable—fear and hostility. In some places a price was put on Walker's head, and laws were passed to keep such "seditious" materials out of the hands of slaves. Even in the North many opponents of slavery found the *Appeal* a bit strong. Walker prepared two more editions of his pamphlet, the third appearing in June 1830. On June 28, 1830, he was found dead in the doorway of his shop under mysterious circumstances. But his *Appeal* went on to have a life of its own, and it is very possible that William Lloyd Garrison was sufficiently influenced by it to shift from a moderate to a militant position on abolition. Six months after Walker's death Garrison published his statement calling for immediate abolition.

Walker, Francis Amasa (1840–1897), economist, statistician, and educator. Born in Boston on July 2, 1840, the son of Amasa Walker, Francis entered Amherst College at fifteen, but his graduation was delayed until 1860 by his poor eyesight. After a year studying law in Worcester, Massachusetts, he joined the Union army as a private and rose to the temporary rank of brigadier general in 1865. Long after the war, in 1886, he published a *History of the 2nd Corps in the Army of the Potomac*. From 1865 to 1868 he taught Latin and Greek at Williston Seminary in Easthampton, Massachusetts, and spent the next year as an editorial writer for the *Springfield Republican*. In 1869 he was appointed to direct the U.S. Bureau of Statistics, with his primary task the supervision of the census of 1870. Difficulties with an appropriation for the bureau led President Ulysses S. Grant to appoint him U.S. Commissioner of Indian Affairs in November 1871; while in that post he continued and completed his work on the census. He nevertheless found time to perform his official duties in connection with Indian affairs, and his *Indian Question*, 1874, was notable for its common sense and honesty. While serving as a professor of economics at the Sheffield Scientific School at Yale, 1873–1881, he was appointed to direct the tenth U.S. census, the major work on which was done from 1879 to 1881. Many innovations in the census questions were made by Walker at this time, and he was also allowed greater freedom to employ good census takers, since a new law removed the department from the realm of political patronage. The work established his reputation as a statistician and was published in 22 volumes. The first of his important economic treatises, *The Wages Question*, 1876, earned him an international reputation and was widely adopted as a textbook in the United States and abroad. Notable among his other works were *Money*, 1878; *Political Economy*, 1833; *Land and Its Rent*, 1883; and *International Bimetallism*, 1896. One of his powerful theoretical insights was his notion of the importance of the entrepreneur, as opposed to the capitalist, in industrial development; and his influence was decisive in discrediting the myth that the total wage bill in the national economy was determined by the capital set aside for labor. He employed the wealth of statistics he had gathered in his years with the census in all of his work, and he emphasized the problems of immigration and population growth in his analyses of the economic circumstances of the country. He was a staunch advocate of international bimetallism, and of free trade. His contributions to economic theory and practice were more appreciated in Europe than in the United States, but he was generally recognized as the foremost economist in America and a major force in the abandonment of traditional Ricardian economics. He was named president of the Massachusetts Institute of Technology (MIT) in 1881 and served in this post until his death. His efforts at MIT resulted in the quadrupling of the student body, a great increase in facilities, and the solid grounding of instruction on a broadly practical and rigorously critical basis. He died in Boston on January 5, 1897.

Walker, James John (1881–1946), "Jimmy," public official. Born in New York City on June 19, 1881, Walker studied for a year at St. Francis Xavier College, then at the New York Law School, and was admitted to the bar in 1912. During his school days he was active in amateur theatricals and wrote several popular songs, including "Will You Love Me in December as You Do in May?" He early became involved in Democratic politics and in 1909 was a successful Tammany Hall candidate for assemblyman. Under the tutelage of Al Smith and others he was elevated in 1914 to the state senate, where seven years later he became leader of his party. He was noted for his liberal views, and not a little of his remarkable popularity stemmed from his sponsorship of a bill legalizing prizefighting in New York. In 1925 he was elected mayor of New York City. During his tenure in that office he became a world celebrity; equally at ease among workers and socialites, he delighted everyone with his ready wit and expansive, jovial manner. He was particularly fond of Broadway and the entertainment world and often referred to himself as the "night mayor." Under his administration the city's vast subway system was advanced, the hospital system unified, the Department of Sanitation created, and steps taken toward centralized city planning and management. Soon after his reelection in 1927 by a huge plurality over Fiorello La Guardia, charges of graft and corruption at many levels of city government prompted the state legislature to order a full investigation, headed by Judge Samuel Seabury. Walker himself was called on to explain certain financial transactions and was charged with several counts of impropriety. He denounced a hearing ordered before Governor Franklin D. Roosevelt and resigned as mayor on September 1, 1932, before the investigation had been completed. He spent several years in Europe

and returned to New York City to find his popularity undiminished. In 1940 La Guardia, by then mayor, appointed him arbiter of the National Cloak and Suit Industry. He died in New York City on November 18, 1946.

Walker, Joseph Reddeford (1798–1876), fur trapper, explorer, and guide. Born in Virginia on December 13, 1798, Walker grew up in Roane County, Tennessee. When he was twenty-one he went to Independence, Missouri, soon to become the eastern terminus of the Santa Fe Trail. Thereafter, Walker was to spend his whole life in the West. For most of the time up until 1840 he was a "mountain man," engaged in fur trapping and trading, living in the wilds and seeing few people other than the Indians for seasons on end. He took part in the 1822 Ashley-Henry expedition to the Upper Missouri country. Whether or not the fur trade was profitable, the mountain men learned to know the mountains, rivers, passes, and possible travel routes throughout the West; and they became familiar with the many Indian tribes. Consequently they were highly qualified to guide parties of American emigrants heading west. Walker himself served on several exploratory expeditions of the Far West between 1832 and 1860. In 1833 Benjamin Bonneville, for the time being in the fur trade, put Walker in charge of an expedition of 50 men sent to explore the territory west of the Great Salt Lake. The party journeyed from Bonneville's Green River camp in Wyoming across Utah and to the Humboldt River in Nevada and went south to the Walker River and Walker Lake, both named for him, 40 miles east of present-day Carson City. Then they turned southwest and to the mountains, going through the Sierra Nevada by way of Sonora Pass, Walker thus becoming the first white man to lead a party across the Sierra. They traveled into the San Joaquin Valley and on to Monterey, California, for the winter of 1833–1834. In the spring the expedition went south through the San Joaquin Valley and crossed the Sierra again at present-day Walker Pass, and then back across Nevada to Utah. Walker later served as guide to parties of emigrants who were going to California. In 1845–1846 he guided the third expedition of John C. Frémont to California. In the Gold Rush of 1849 he went again to California and remained there, guiding prospectors and selling cattle, for about 18 years. In 1861–1862 he led a party to Arizona, discovering in 1862 a number of gold deposits in the region of present-day Prescott. In 1867 he settled in Ignacio Valley, Contra Costa County, California, where he died on October 27, 1876.

Walker, Robert John (1801–1869), lawyer and public official. Born in Northumberland, Pennsylvania, on July 19, 1801, Walker, whose middle name is sometimes given as James, was educated in local schools and by private tutors and graduated first in his class at the University of Pennsylvania in 1819. Admitted to the bar in 1821, he joined the Jeffersonian movement and became the acknowledged Democratic (Democratic Republican) leader in Pennsylvania. In 1826 he moved to Natchez, Mississippi, to join his brother in a lucrative law practice. His speculations in plantations, slaves, and wild lands were huge, involving hundreds of thousands of dollars. In 1835 he was elected to the first of two terms in the U.S. Senate. He was an ardent supporter of Jacksonian and Democratic policies, particularly the annexation of Texas, and took charge of the 1844 Democratic presidential campaign. President James K. Polk thereafter appointed him secretary of the treasury, 1845–1849, and his report of 1845 on the economy was a classic exposition of free-trade economics. He was responsible for the Walker Tariff Act of 1846, which improved U.S.-British relations. His financing of the Mexican War was carried out with simplicity and success. He initiated the warehousing system for the handling of imports, and the creation of the Department of the Interior in 1849 was largely due to him. He worked to establish firmly the independent treasury system, and his administration, often considered the ablest in the history of the treasury, ended when Polk left office. Walker stayed on in Washington, practicing before the Supreme Court and managing his extensive business affairs. He visited England during 1852–1853 to sell securities for the Illinois Central Railroad. In 1853 he accepted the post of U.S. minister to China, but he finally rejected the appointment because of a disagreement with President Franklin Pierce. He supported James Buchanan in the 1856 presidential election and was appointed governor of the Kansas Territory in 1857. An enemy of slavery (he had earlier freed his own slaves), he resigned the same year when the President failed to back him in permitting the people of Kansas to decide the slavery issue themselves. His clear opposition to slavery and his refusal to acknowledge the pro-slavery Lecompton Constitution made him a distinct liability to the Democratic administration. During the Civil War, he served the Treasury Department abroad, selling federal bonds. He resumed his law practice after the war and played a part in getting through Congress the bill for the purchase of Alaska. He died in Washington, D.C., on November 11, 1869.

Walker, Sarah Breedlove (1867–1919), "Madam C. J. Walker," businesswoman. Born into a very poor black farm family in Delta, Louisiana, on December 23, 1867, Miss Breedlove was orphaned by the time she was six. At fourteen she married C. J. Walker, who left her a widow six years later; she kept his name and called herself Madam C. J. Walker. To make a living she moved to St. Louis and became a washerwoman, trying to educate herself as best she could in her spare time. In 1905 she devised a formula for the treatment and straightening of tightly curled hair. She became convinced of the commercial possibilities of her product, and started laboratories to manufacture it and a mail-order business to retail it. She moved her Madam C. J. Walker Company to Indianapolis in 1910 and made it into a thriving business. With-

in a few years she was one of the first women in the United States to have become a millionaire in her own right. With the business a success, she gave large amounts of money to charity and educational institutions, including an academy for girls she had founded in West Africa. She died on May 3, 1919, at her villa at Irvington, New York, leaving two-thirds of her fortune to charitable and educational institutions.

Walker, Thomas (1715–1794), land speculator, explorer, and public official. Born in King and Queen County, Virginia, on January 25, 1715, Walker probably attended the College of William and Mary. He became a physician in Fredericksburg after studying medicine privately, and also engaged in trade and ran a store. His marriage in 1741 changed the direction of his life, for his wife, a well-to-do widow from Albemarle County, brought to the union a large estate. Walker then turned more actively to trade and land speculation. In 1748 he, along with a few other influential Virginians, formed the Loyal Land Company and received an 800,000–acre grant of lands to the west of the mountains. Two years later he led an exploratory party to see the region, and during this expedition discovered the Cumberland Gap. This was to be the way through the mountains that would channel the course of western settlement for years. The party halted before the mountains and instead of passing on to the bluegrass region they laid claim to lands in the Clinch and Holston valleys; within four years 200 families were settled there. Walker was the first white man to keep a record of explorations in the Kentucky territory. He served for a short time in the Virginia House of Burgesses in 1752 before becoming deputy surveyor of Augusta County. In 1754–1755 he was commissary general to the Virginia soldiers serving under George Washington at the beginning of the last French and Indian War. He served again in the Virginia legislature from 1756 to 1761. He continued to be active in trade and in land acquisition and surveying during this time. His involvement with the Loyal Land Company put him in a position to become one of Virginia's delegates to the meeting at Fort Stanwix to negotiate a boundary with the Indians in 1768. It was to the interest of colonies and landholders who claimed western lands to get boundary lines drawn as far to the west as possible, and Walker helped in getting the line drawn in such a way that all the Loyal Land Company territory would be open for settlement. As difficulties with England threatened, Walker became part of the revolutionary effort in Virginia, and he was a member of the executive council from 1776 to 1781. He was frequently concerned with land claims and attempted to perpetuate Virginia's control over the western territory after the Revolution. After retiring from public life he lived at his estate in Albemarle County, where he died on November 9, 1794.

Walker, William (1824–1860), adventurer. Born in Nashville, Tennessee, on May 8, 1824, Walker graduated from the University of Nashville in 1838 and five years later took a medical degree from the University of Pennsylvania. After two years of study and travel in Europe he returned to the United States, became interested in the law, and was admitted to the bar in New Orleans. While practicing law he also dabbled in journalism as an editor and part owner of the *Daily Crescent*. In 1850 he moved to California and in San Francisco and later Marysville continued in law and journalism for three years. In 1853 he organized a party of American "colonists" and sailed to La Paz in the Mexican province of Baja (Lower) California; upon landing he proclaimed a republic with himself as president, and two months later announced the annexation of the Mexican state of Sonora. Needed reinforcements and supplies were held up in San Francisco by U.S. authorities, and in May 1854 Walker and his followers were forced to return to the United States, where he was acquitted of charges of violating neutrality laws. In 1855 he led a party to Nicaragua at the invitation of a revolutionary faction there. By the end of the year he was virtual dictator of the country; the new regime was recognized by the United States in May 1856, and two months later Walker became president. His grandiose but rather vague plans for Central American development, involving a military empire built on slave labor, agricultural development, and an isthmian canal, came to naught, for he entered into a scheme to wrest control of the Accessory Transit Company, which operated overland transportation facilities in Nicaragua, from Cornelius Vanderbilt. On the pretext of charter violations he seized the company's property in that country and turned it over to Vanderbilt's rivals. Vanderbilt then sent agents into other Central American nations to organize a joint effort to oust Walker. To avoid capture, Walker surrendered himself to a U.S. navy officer on May 1, 1857, and returned to the United States. Still claiming the presidency, he returned to Central America in November but was arrested near Greytown (San Juan del Norte) by Commodore Hiram Paulding, who, because of Southern sympathy for Walker's scheme, lost his command as a result of his action. Walker was returned to the United States. In 1860, shortly after the publication of *The War in Nicaragua*, he attempted to return to Nicaragua by way of Honduras; he was captured by a British naval officer and turned over to Honduran authorities. After a court-martial he was executed on September 12, 1860.

Wallace, De Witt (1889–1981), editor and publisher. Born in St. Paul, Minnesota, on November 12, 1889, Wallace attended Macalester College for two years (1907–1909) and the University of California at Berkeley from 1909 until 1912. He left school to return to St. Paul, where he worked as a book salesman for three years and then for an advertising and printing firm until he joined the army to serve in World War I. While working as a book salesman, he had conceived an idea for a digest form of magazine, and after returning from the war he prepared a sample copy of his *Reader's Digest*. After having offered it to several publishing companies without favorable response, he decided to publish the magazine himself. In 1921 he moved to New York City to begin his publication venture and there married Lila Bell Acheson. Born in Virden, Manitoba, on December 25, 1889, Miss Acheson grew up in various Midwestern towns in the United States, where her father served as a Presbyterian minister, and graduated from the University of Oregon in 1917. She went into social service, working for the Young Women's Christian Association (YWCA) during World War I. She had met De Witt Wallace in 1911 through her brother, one of his classmates at Berkeley. After the war she moved to New York City and married De Witt Wallace in October 1921. Together they launched the *Reader's Digest* in February 1922. The magazine succeeded quickly. Between 1922 and 1929 it went from 1500 subscribers to more than 200,000. For its first 11 years the *Digest* printed only articles excerpted from other magazines, but in 1933 it began to run original pieces. Increasingly successful, the *Digest* expanded into foreign-language editions in 1938. The only major change in policy came in 1955, when it began to accept advertising, a step the Wallaces attributed to the rising costs of publishing and the desire to keep the price of the magazine as low as possible. By 1981 the *Digest* had over 30 million U.S. readers and was published in many foreign-language editions. Its popularity was due to several factors: the breadth of its appeal—there was something in it for almost anyone—the brevity of the articles, its digest reprints of fiction, a variety of regular feature departments, and its unshakable tone of uplift. The Wallaces continued as owners and publishers of the *Digest*, making their headquarters in Pleasantville, New York, and in later years published books as well, with considerable success. Wallace died in Mount Kisco, New York, on March 30, 1981.

Wallace, George Corley (1919–   ), public official. Born in Clio, Alabama, on August 25, 1919, Wallace graduated from the University of Alabama law school in 1942. He joined the air force, hoping to become a pilot, but a bout of spinal meningitis curtailed his training. He spent World War II as a flight engineer on a B-29 in the Pacific theater. After discharge from service in December 1945 he returned to Alabama to practice law and soon became involved in state Democratic politics. In 1946 he was appointed assistant Alabama attorney general, and two years later, as a delegate to the Democratic national convention, put the name of Senator Richard B. Russell of Georgia in nomination for the vice-presidency on an anti-civil rights platform. In 1947 Wallace was elected to the first of two consecutive terms in the Alabama legislature. In 1953 he was elected a state judge of the 3rd judicial circuit, a post he held until 1959. He ran unsuccessfully for the governorship in 1958. Four years later he won, and it was during his first term as governor that he became a nationally known figure. The notoriety he earned between 1962 and 1966 arose from his opposition to the civil-rights movement and particularly to the racial integration of schools. One of the famous news photos of the 1960s showed the governor standing in the doorway of the University of Alabama administration building trying to block the registration of black students. But Wallace was not a traditional Southern racist (he denied that he was a racist at all); he was more of a populist, seizing on the issues that moved the majority of his constituents and profiting by them. The civil-rights issue gave him a national spotlight which he kept focused on himself, even while turning to other issues. He declined to run for president in 1964 in order not to attract votes away from the Republican nominee, Barry M. Goldwater. But in 1968 he did enter the presidential race. He was no longer governor, but in 1966 his wife, Lurleen, had run and was elected to succeed him, thus enabling him to maintain a political power base. Mrs. Wallace died in May 1968, however. In 1968, as the presidential candidate of the American Independent party, he won 13.5 percent of the U.S. popular vote, but it was a sectional candidacy: the only five states he won were in the South. In 1970 he was elected governor of Alabama for the second time. As 1972 approached he was running for the presidency again; he entered a number of primaries, winning several. But on May 15, 1972, at a campaign rally in Laurel, Maryland, he was shot by a would-be assassin. The next day he won both the Michigan and Maryland primaries, but was for all practical purposes out of the race. He returned to his duties as governor after an extended period of convalescence, but was confined to a wheelchair.

Wallace, Henry Agard (1888–1965), agriculturist and public official. Born in Adair County, Iowa, on October 7, 1888, Henry A. was the son of Henry C. Wallace, magazine editor and secretary of agriculture under Warren G. Harding and Calvin Coolidge. He graduated from Iowa State College in 1910 and joined his family's magazine, *Wallace's Farmer*, as associate editor. His study of farm prices produced the first hog-ratio charts and forecast the farm-price collapse of 1920. He also carried on experiments in developing hybrid corn, producing several high-yield strains that were marketed through his Pioneer Hi-Bred Corn Company. He became the magazine's editor in 1924 and in 1928 shifted from the Republican to the Democratic party. The magazine merged with another in 1929 to become *Wallace's Farmer and Iowa Homestead*; he remained editor until President Franklin D. Roosevelt appointed him secretary of agriculture in 1933. He helped formulate and administer the New Deal policies of soil conservation, controlled production, and higher farm prices. Roosevelt chose him as his running mate in 1940 and, as vice-president, Wallace became the U.S. goodwill ambassador to Latin America. During World War II he assumed many duties beyond those traditional to the vice-presidency, including chairmanship in 1942–1943 of the Board of Economic Warfare. Passed over for renomination as

vice-president in 1944 because his liberal views were unpopular with Southern Democratic leaders, he became secretary of commerce in 1945, a position he continued to hold, after Roosevelt's death, under President Harry S. Truman. His plans to revitalize the department were overshadowed by his criticism of the President's "get tough" policy toward the Soviet Union, and he was forced to resign in 1946. He edited the *New Republic* during 1946–1947. In 1948 he campaigned for president on the ultra-liberal Progressive ticket, calling in his platform for close cooperation with the Soviets, reduction of armaments, and United Nations supervision of foreign aid. He received more than a million popular votes but no electoral votes. He later broke with the Progressive party and retired from politics. His many books included *Agricultural Prices*, 1920; *America Must Choose*, 1934; *The Century of the Common Man*, 1943; *Sixty Million Jobs*, 1945; and *The Look Ahead*, 1960. Wallace died in Danbury, Connecticut, on November 18, 1965.

Wallace, Lewis (1827–1905), lawyer, soldier, diplomat, and author. Born in Brookville, Indiana, on April 10, 1827, Lew Wallace grew up there and in Indianapolis. He had some formal schooling but was basically self-taught. In 1846, when he was nineteen, he raised a volunteer company for the Mexican War and served with it in Mexico as part of Indiana's 1st Infantry. Following the war he returned to Indianapolis and, having read law in his father's law office, was admitted to the bar in 1849. By 1853 he had settled in Crawfordsville, where he kept his interest in the military by organizing and training a local militia company. He continued his law practice during the 1850s and was active in state politics. He was twice elected county attorney, in 1850 and 1852, and in 1856 he won election to the state senate. He served in the Union army throughout the Civil War, attaining the rank of major general in 1862 after his participation in the capture of Fort Donelson, serving with distinction at Shiloh, and emerging in 1865 as one of the Union heroes, having saved Cincinnati from capture in 1863 and in 1864 helping to defend Washington, D.C., against a much superior Confederate force under Gen. Jubal A. Early. In May and June of 1865 he sat on the military court that tried the conspirators in the assassination of Abraham Lincoln. After a brief period of service in Mexico in 1865 he returned to live in Indiana and resumed his law practice. In 1878 President Rutherford B. Hayes appointed him governor of the New Mexico Territory in the hope that he could settle the fierce "Lincoln County War" that was raging there. This cattle war, a complex feud between rival political and economic factions and involving Billy the Kid as a hired gunman, had been going on for some time, with a great deal of violence and little prospect of an end. After Wallace arrived in Santa Fe in August he issued a proclamation of amnesty, listened to the stories of the participants, and eventually restored order. (Billy the Kid, however, refused amnesty and continued his bloody career.) He remained in New Mexico until 1881, when

President James Garfield appointed him U.S. minister to Turkey. Leaving that post in 1885, he returned to live in Crawfordsville. Wallace's military and public careers notwithstanding, he is far better known for his novels. Early in life he had aspired to be an author, but it was not until after the Civil War that he wrote the books that made him famous. His first novel, *The Fair God*, 1873, dealt with the conquest of Mexico by Hernando Cortes and was based on William H. Prescott's history. *Ben Hur; A Tale of the Christ*, 1880, about Christians in the early Roman Empire, was one of the most popular novels ever published in the United States; continuously in print since its publication, it was twice made into film extravaganzas. Less well-known works were *The Boyhood of Christ*, 1888, and *The Prince of India*, 1893. Wallace died in Crawfordsville, Indiana, on February 15, 1905.

Wallace, Lila Bell Acheson, *see under* Wallace, De Witt

Wallack, James William (1795–1864), actor and theater manager. Born in London on August 24, 1795, Wallack was a member of a distinguished acting family whose members appeared on the stage in both England and the United States for two generations. His father, William, was a leading player at Astley's amphitheatre in London. His brother, Henry, five years his senior, had a long career in the United States after 1819, both as actor and stage manager. Wallack made his first professional appearance at the age of twelve at the Academic Theatre in London; his performance was impressive enough to earn him a place in the Drury Lane company. Except for two and a half years in Dublin, he remained at Drury Lane for ten years, playing classical roles for the most part. He made his American debut in New York City in September 1818. Over the next 35 years he crossed the Atlantic an average of once a year, keeping engagements both in London and New York City. On his first trip to the United States he toured Eastern cities, predominantly in Shakespearean roles. From 1837 to 1839 he managed the National Theatre in New York City, hiring his brother, Henry, as stage manager. From 1839 to 1852 he took to the road again, alternating between appearances in England and New York City. In 1852 he returned to New York as manager of Brougham's Lyceum, with his son, Lester, as stage manager. He renamed it Wallack's Theatre and operated it for nine years, appearing frequently on stage himself in lead roles. In 1861 he and his son, Lester Wallack, opened a new Wallack's Theatre at a new location, but since James's health was beginning to fail, the son actually managed the theater. James died on December 25, 1864, in New York City.

Wallack, John Johnstone, *see* Wallack, Lester

Wallack, Lester (1820–1888), actor, theater manager, and playwright. Born on January 1, 1820, in New York City, the son of James William Wallack, Lester was christened John Johnstone Wallack; he did not use the name Lester until he began managing the new Wallack's Theatre for his father in 1861. He began acting at nineteen in a play by Nathaniel P. Willis entitled *Tortesa the Usurer*, a vehicle written for his father and first produced in 1839. Most of his early stage work was in England and Ireland. His first appearance in the United States was in a comedy, *Used Up*, in 1847. He followed this with several other successes, including Shakespearean roles and the role of Dantès in *The Count of Monte Cristo*. When his father took over Brougham's Lyceum in 1852 Lester went to work for him as stage manager. And, like his father, he made frequent appearances in the plays that were performed at the Wallack theaters. When the new Wallack's was opened in 1861 Lester became its manager. There he appeared in a play of his own, *Rosedale, or The Rifle Ball*, in 1863. After 20 years the theater closed, and in 1882 still another Wallack's Theatre was opened on Broadway. Lester managed it until his retirement in 1887. A spectacular theatrical benefit was given in his honor in 1888—a performance of *Hamlet* that starred, among others, Mme Helena Modjeska and Edwin Booth. Wallack died near Stamford, Connecticut, on September 6, 1888. His *Memories of Fifty Years* was published in 1889.

Wallis, Hal Brent (1899–), motion-picture producer. Born in Chicago on September 14, 1899, Wallis left school at fourteen to go to work. For three years he clerked in an office, then in 1916 became an assistant sales and advertising manager at the General Electric Company. In 1922 he moved to Los Angeles, and for a year worked as manager of the Garrick Theater before becoming assistant publicity director for the Warner Brothers studios. In 1924 he became publicity director and within four years was promoted to studio manager and production executive. He was soon involved in the actual production of movies, at a time when the producer was becoming an increasingly important figure in the film world. As Hollywood became big business, it was the producer who was in overall charge of financing and budgets for pictures as well as determining who the director and cast would be and how the film story would be treated. Wallis's first production, in which he worked with Darryl F. Zanuck, was the enormously successful *Little Caesar*, 1930, the first of a long line of gangster movies. In 1933 he was put in charge of all production at Warner Brothers, and in 1944 he formed his own independent production company, Hal Wallis Productions. He was associated with more than 400 films. Among the more notable were *Green Pastures*, 1936; *Dark Victory*, 1939; *All This and Heaven Too*, 1940; *The Sea Hawk*, 1941; *The Man Who Came to Dinner*, 1941; *The Maltese Falcon*, 1941; *Sergeant York*, 1941; *Casablanca*, 1942; *Watch on the Rhine*, 1943; *Saratoga Trunk*, 1945; *Come Back, Little Sheba*, 1952; *The Rose Tattoo*, 1955; *Gunfight at the O.K. Corral*, 1957; *Becket*, 1964; and *True Grit*, 1969. He won Academy Awards in 1938 and 1943.

Walsh, Thomas James (1859–1933), public official. Born in Two Rivers, Wisconsin, on June 12, 1859, Walsh taught school and was principal of a high school in Sturgeon Bay, Wisconsin. He attended the University of Wisconsin and earned a law degree in 1884. Admitted to the bar, he practiced law in Redfield, South Dakota, until 1890, when he relocated in Helena, Montana. He maintained his law practice there until 1912, when he was elected to the U.S. Senate. In the Senate, as an expert on constitutional law, he was a liberal progressive Democrat who was ardently devoted to the public interest. He supported President Woodrow Wilson's domestic and foreign programs, including proposed U.S. membership in the League of Nations, contributed to the structure of the 1914 Clayton (anti-trust) Act, and was a strong supporter of the nomination of Louis D. Brandeis for the Supreme Court in 1916. But his signal contribution to the public weal was his investigation, at the head of a Senate committee, of the oil leases at Teapot Dome, Wyoming, and Elk Hills, California, which in 1923 erupted as the most disgraceful scandal of the Warren G. Harding administration. After a tedious 18 months of examining masses of conflicting evidence, Walsh began in October 1923 the hearings which showed among other things that Secretary of the Interior Albert B. Fall had accepted bribes to arrange leases of government oil properties to private interests. (Fall was later sent to prison after convictions on charges of bribery.) A contender for the Democratic presidential nomination in 1924, Walsh lost to John W. Davis and then declined the vice-presidential nomination. He served in the Senate until 1933, when President-elect Franklin D. Roosevelt named him attorney general. But he died on March 2, near Wilson, North Carolina, just two days before the new administration took office.

Walter, Bruno (1876–1962), conductor. Born Bruno Walter Schlesinger on September 15, 1876, in Berlin, Walter early dropped his surname to avoid confusion with others of the same name. He took to music as a child and was taught at home before attending the Stern Conservatory in Berlin. He was only seventeen when he made his first appearance as a conductor, in Cologne in 1893. He worked under Gustav Mahler for two years at Hamburg, then went on to conduct orchestras at Breslau (Wroclaw), Pressburg (Bratislava), Riga, and Berlin, until 1901 when, at the invitation of Mahler, he settled in Vienna, where he served for ten years as conductor of the Imperial Opera Company. In 1913 he accepted the post of conductor with the Munich Opera, and he remained there for a decade. By the early 1920s he was probably the most popular orchestra conductor in Europe and was in demand as a guest conductor in all the major cities. From 1922 until 1940 he also made frequent guest appearances in the United States. He went from Munich to the Berlin Städlische Opera in 1925, retaining the post until 1929, and annually conducted the Salzburg Music Festival from 1925 until 1938. From 1935 until 1938 he was also conductor at the Vienna State Opera. In 1938 he left Austria because of Nazi anti-Semitic activities and settled in Paris, taking French citizenship. After the outbreak of World War II in 1939, Walter came to the United States, where for two years he conducted various orchestras, including the National Broadcasting (NBC) Symphony, the Los Angeles Philharmonic, the New York Philharmonic, and the Minneapolis Symphony. He became a naturalized citizen in the early 1940s. He was also a frequent conductor at the Metropolitan Opera. From 1947 to 1949 he was conductor and musical adviser of the New York Philharmonic-Symphony Orchestra and in later years made regular appearances as a guest conductor with many orchestras in the United States and Europe. One of the great orchestra conductors of the twentieth century, he was known especially for his interpretations of the works of Mozart, Anton Bruckner, Schuman, Beethoven, and Mahler. Walter died in Beverly Hills, California, on February 17, 1962.

Walther, Carl Ferdinand Wilhelm (1811–1887), theologian and religious leader. Born at Langenschursdorf, near Waldenburg, in the German kingdom of Saxony, on October 25, 1811, Walther attended the Schneeberg Gymnasium from 1821 to 1829. He then enrolled at the University of Leipzig, where he completed theological studies in 1833. He taught for a few years before being ordained in the Lutheran Church, in 1837, and taking a pastorate in Bräunsdorf. But his church work there was of short duration, for by October 1838 he had resigned his parish to go to the United States. All the factors that led to his decision are not known, but the major influence was probably what he regarded as an unfavorable theological climate in Germany, especially the liberalism and rationalism enunciated by Friedrich Schleiermacher. He sailed for America in November 1838 along with a party of several hundred others leaving for religious reasons. Landing at New Orleans on January 5, 1839, he accompanied a major portion of the group north to St. Louis and soon settled into a parish in Perry County, Missouri. Later in the year he and other pastors started the Lutheran school that in 1850 was relocated in St. Louis as Concordia Theological Seminary. In 1841 Walther accepted a call to serve a congregation in St. Louis, and lived there the rest of his life. He soon became the most prominent Lutheran leader in Missouri, and with the launching of his biweekly paper, *Der Lutheraner,* in 1844, he emerged as one of the leading voices of his denomination in the United States. In order to bring the scattered German Lutheran congregations into one organization, the German Evangelical Lutheran Synod of Missouri, Ohio, and other states was formed in 1847 with Walther as its first president. He served as president until 1850 and again from 1864 to 1878. He became professor of theology at Concordia Theological Seminary in 1850 and president of the school in 1854, holding both positions until his death. Walther almost single-handedly shaped the development of the Missouri Synod and was the leading exponent of orthodox Reformation theology in the United States during the nineteenth century. His early views had leaned toward pietism, but later his staunch orthodoxy became the rallying point for clergy who opposed tendencies to "Americanize" their theology. It was his desire that all Lutherans eventually organize into one church body, but the diversity of their opinions (and national backgrounds) prevented it. And he himself came to be a divisive force because of the immutability of his later views. He was instrumental, however, in bringing some accord, albeit temporary, between the synods of his time. In 1872 the Synodical Conference of North America was founded with Walther as president. In 1877 the century's most severe controversy in U.S. Lutheranism broke out—the conflict over predestination—which split the Synodical Conference, leaving the Missouri Synod aligned only with the Wisconsin Synod. Walther's position on predestination—that election is prior to and the cause of faith—was at the heart of this controversy, which was not resolved within his lifetime. But he successfully maintained his leadership of the Missouri Synod. As theologian and church leader he wrote several works, the most significant being *The Proper Distinction Between Law and Gospel*, published posthumously in 1897; it was a collection of 39 lectures given at Concordia Seminary in 1884–1885. Walther died in St. Louis on May 7, 1887.

Wanamaker, John (1838–1922), businessman. Born in Philadelphia on July 11, 1838, Wanamaker started working at fourteen as a delivery boy for a bookstore and at eighteen entered the retail men's clothing business. During 1857–1861 he was secretary of the Philadelphia Young Men's Christian Association (YMCA). He returned to the clothing industry in 1861 with his brother-in-law, Nathan Brown. That year they founded Brown and Wanamaker, which became the leading men's retail clothier in the country. Brown died in 1868. Wanamaker then began to serve a more fashionable clientele at John Wanamaker and Company, which he established in 1869. He opened a clothing and dry-goods business in 1876 in the old freight depot of the Pennsylvania Railroad Company, inviting merchants in other lines to lease space from him. They did not, so in 1877 he himself established a number of small specialty shops under the depot's roof—a "new kind of store"—and thus founded one of the first major department stores in the country. In 1896 he purchased Alexander T. Stewart's huge retail store in New York City, renamed it Wanamaker's, broadened its general stock, created departments, and had a second department store. Innovation and continual reorganization were the basis of his success. He was one of the first American businessmen to use advertising and advertising agencies, and was one of the first to offer full refunds to dissatisfied customers. Paternalistic toward his employees, he created a program of employee benefits and started training classes for clerks which in 1896 evolved

into the John Wanamaker Commercial Institute. He chose reliable relatives and associates to manage his stores and consequently was free to become involved in religious and political work. He was an active temperance worker, several times sought public office (he was a Republican), and in 1888 led a fund-raising drive for Benjamin Harrison's presidential campaign and then served as postmaster general from 1889 to 1893. In that post he made various organizational improvements and advocated such advanced notions as postal savings and post-office control of telegraph and telephone service, but his effectiveness was compromised by his free use of the spoils system. He died in Philadelphia on December 12, 1922.

Ward, Aaron Montgomery, *see* Ward, Montgomery

Ward, Artemus, *see* Browne, Charles Farrar

Ward, John Quincy Adams (1830–1910), sculptor. Born in Champaign County, Ohio, near Urbana, on June 29, 1830, Ward left farming to go to Brooklyn, New York, to study sculpture. He studied privately there until 1856, then spent most of the next two years in Washington, D.C., working on portrait busts of public figures. In 1861 he opened a studio in New York City, where he was to live for the rest of his life. Ward was the first American sculptor whose training was obtained entirely in the United States, and his work was highly regarded for its quality and realism. Although he continued to do busts of prominent individuals, his best-known sculptures were outdoor statues in parks and other public places. Two of his early works, "Indian Hunter" now in Central Park, New York City, and "The Freedman," were shown in 1867 at the International Exhibition in Paris. These sculptures established Ward's reputation as an artist of the first rank, and thereafter he received numerous private and public commissions. Among his works during the next 40 years were "Good Samaritan," in the Boston Public Gardens; statues of Gen. John F. Reynolds in Gettysburg, Pennsylvania, and of Gen. Israel Putnam in Hartford, Connecticut; an equestrian statue of Gen. George H. Thomas in Washington, D.C.; statues of William Gilmore Simms in Charleston, South Carolina, of Henry Ward Beecher in Brooklyn, New York, and of the Marquis de Lafayette in Burlington, Vermont; and the 7th Regiment memorial figure in Central Park. In 1883, on Wall Street in New York City, he unveiled his statue of George Washington; it was judged to be one of the finest monuments to the first president. Also for New York City he executed likenesses of Peter Cooper and Horace Greeley, and in 1885 he unveiled "Pilgrim," a commemoration of early New Englanders, which was placed in Central Park. In 1903 Ward finished the massive New York Stock Exchange pediment. He served as president of the National Academy of Design in 1874 and was a founder and first president of the National Sculpture Society in 1899. He died in New York City on May 1, 1910.

Ward, Lester Frank (1841–1913), sociologist. Born in Joliet, Illinois, on June 18, 1841, Ward was raised in poverty on the Illinois and Iowa frontier and was largely self-taught. At seventeen he joined his brother, Cyrenus O. Ward, in Myersburg, Pennsylvania, in the manufacture of wagon hubs. In 1862, after four terms at the Susquehanna Collegiate Institute at Towanda, he enlisted in the Union army and as a result of wounds received at Chancellorsville was discharged in November 1864. He went to Washington, D.C., and in 1865 obtained a position with the Treasury Department; he continued his studies at Columbian College (now The George Washington University), graduated in 1869, earned his law degree in 1871, and received an M.A. degree in 1872. Instead of practicing law, however, he devoted himself to geology, paleontology, and botany, to which he contributed the theory of sympodial development. In 1881 he joined the U.S. Geological Survey, where he was appointed geologist in 1883 and paleontologist in 1892. In 1883 appeared his two-volume *Dynamic Sociology*, a pioneer work in evolutionary sociology that made him the leader in the field and that gave great impetus to the growth of modern sociology itself. He developed the theory of what he called "telesis," whereby man, through education and development of intellect, could direct the course of social evolution. A Hegelian, an evolutionist, and a Comtean in outlook, Ward saw sociology as the primary social science. He believed that its proper subject was social function as opposed to social structure, therefore its aim should be the development, through active involvement in education, of the higher society, the rational "Sociocracy." In 1903 he was president of the Institut International de Sociologie and in 1906 he became professor of sociology at Brown University. His books included *The Psychic Factors of Civilization*, 1893; *Outlines of Sociology*, 1898; *Pure Sociology*, 1903; *Applied Sociology*, 1906; and a "mental autobiography," *Glimpses of the Cosmos*, six volumes, 1913–1918. Ward died in Washington, D.C., on April 18, 1913.

Ward, Montgomery (1843–1913), businessman. Born on February 17, 1843, in Chatham, New Jersey, Aaron Montgomery Ward attended school until he was fourteen, then worked for various dry-goods firms, in St. Louis, Chicago, and St. Joseph, Michigan. Traveling for a St. Louis wholesale house, he became acquainted with the problems of farmers, who had to pay extremely high prices, relative to the money they earned in crop production, for a small selection of inferior goods. He thought of solving their needs with a retail outlet that would purchase goods wholesale in mass quantities and offer them by mail at a very small markup, eliminating the expense of running a store. In 1872 he opened a mail-order dry-goods business in Chicago and published a one-page catalog offering 30 items; his brother-in-law, George R. Thorne, joined the business a year later. The business was immediately successful and the catalog expanded rapidly; unquestioned

return of goods was allowed and the steadily increasing selection of previously unobtainable goods accounted for the growth of the firm, which was continually expanded and relocated, finally, in 1900, to the Ward Tower at Michigan Boulevard and Madison Street in Chicago. By 1888 annual sales of Montgomery Ward & Company totaled a million dollars. Giving up active management of the business in 1886, although remaining its president, Ward thereafter fought vigorously for an unobstructed lakefront for Chicago and for the preservation of Grant Park. He retired in 1901, although he still retained the title of president. He died in Highland Park, Illinois, on December 7, 1913. His fortune passed to his wife, by whom it was later distributed to various charities; the principal beneficiary was Northwestern University, which established a medical and dental school in his memory.

Ward, Nathaniel (1578?–1652), religious leader. Born in Haverhill, England, about 1578, into a notable Puritan family, Ward earned his B.A. in 1599 and his M.A. in 1603 at Emmanuel College, Cambridge. He was admitted to the bar, and he practiced law until, in Heidelberg in 1618, he met a noted theologian, David Pareus, who inspired him to join the Anglican ministry. Returning to England in 1624, he served in a parish in London until dismissed for nonconformity in 1633. The next year he emigrated to Massachusetts Bay and became minister at Agawam (now Ipswich), and endeavored to instill Puritan orthodoxy in the community. In 1638, having resigned his pulpit, he was engaged by the Massachusetts General Court to assist in compiling the first code of law for the state. The resulting Massachusetts Body of Liberties, enacted in 1641, constituted the first real bill of rights in America. Yet Ward's attitudes typified the conflict of the time between social and political liberalism and religious orthodoxy. He issued a booklet in 1647, on his return to England, that satirically but powerfully attacked religious toleration. It was called *The Simple Cobler of Agawam . . . Willing to Help 'mend his Native Country, Lamentably Tattered, Both in the Upper-leather and Sole, with All the Honest Stitches He Can Take.* Its putative author, the "cobler," known by the pseudonym of "Theodore de la Guard," also diverted his readers with offhand remarks on a variety of subjects. Ward settled in the ministry after 1648 in Shenfield, England, and died there in 1652.

Warfield, Wallis, *see* Windsor, Wallis Warfield, Duchess of

Warhol, Andy (1930?–   ), painter and film maker. Born about 1930, Warhol was secretive about the date and the place of his birth, which was recorded variously as Cleveland, Philadelphia, Pittsburgh, and McKeesport, Pennsylvania. He was early attracted to comic-strip pictures and studied art at the Carnegie Institute of Technology; he later worked as a window decorator in Pittsburgh.

Moving to New York City in his early twenties, he first worked as an advertising illustrator; he won the Art Directors' Club Medal in 1957 for a giant shoe ad. About 1959 his paintings of repeated rows of Campbell's soup cans, dollar bills, trading stamps, typewriters, telephones, Marilyn Monroe, and Dick Tracy heralded the start of a new movement called Pop art, whose other major exponents included Robert Rauschenberg, Roy Lichtenstein, and Claes Oldenburg. Different from the Abstract Expressionism that dominated the 1950s, Pop art, especially as Warhol exemplified it, was impersonal, was frequently reproduced in quantity like industrial goods, was often executed by studio assistants, and was significant in legitimizing commercial products as subject matter. The acknowledged leader of the movement by 1962, Warhol turned in 1964 to commercial silk-screen reproduction of paintings and photographs on canvas. Famous in this series were pictures of Elvis Presley, Jacqueline Kennedy, and an electric chair; an entire exhibition at New York City's Stable Gallery in 1964 contained his silk-screened paintings of Brillo soap-pad and Heinz tomato-catsup labels glued onto wooden boxes. His works were shown in major U.S. cities as well as abroad. In the 1960s he began making experimental movies that were popular with "underground" audiences, either because of or in spite of their often monumental length. They included *Eat, Kiss, Sleep,* all probably made in 1963; *Empire,* 1964; *My Hustler,* 1965; *The Chelsea Girls,* 1966; *I, A Man,* 1967; and, with Paul Morrissey, *Flesh,* 1968, *Trash,* 1969, *Heat,* 1970, and *L'Amour,* 1973. The Warhol films raised to a kind of dim stardom Joe Dallesandro, "Baby Jane" Holzer, Gerard Malanga, Edie Sedgwick, Ingrid Superstar, and Viva. Warhol also managed an electronic rock group, the Velvet Underground. Perennially controversial, Warhol reached mythic proportions in the 1960s largely because his motives were almost totally obscure; they may, however, have been no more than, as he once himself asserted, to bore his audiences and inculcate a sense of dehumanization.

Warner, Albert, see under Warner Brothers

Warner Brothers, moving-picture executives. The older two of the Warner brothers were born in Poland, Harry on December 12, 1881, and Albert on July 23, 1884. The family, whose original name was Eichelbaum, subsequently emigrated to London, Ontario, where Jack Warner was born on August 2, 1892. In 1894 the family relocated in Youngstown, Ohio. The brothers were together in business ventures most of their lives, including their boyhood days. They worked at odd jobs, helping support the family, until they decided on a new venture—showing motion pictures. Albert and another brother, Sam, started the business, and soon Harry and Jack were involved. After showing films in Youngstown for a few months, they moved to New Castle, Pennsylvania, in 1903. The general disarray of the motion-picture business at the time led them to form their own dis-tribution firm, the Duquesne Amusement Supply Company, in Pittsburgh. But the company was not a success since the movie producers disliked the idea of middlemen taking a percentage of their profits. Therefore the Warner brothers organized their own production company, using the Vitagraph studios in New York City. Jack, the youngest brother, went his own way for a few years, settling in California in 1914 and starting his own movie studio. The Vitagraph enterprise was only a moderate success until, in 1917, the Warners filmed Ambassador James W. Gerard's book *My Four Years in Germany,* which grossed enough money to make it possible for the two elder Warners to shift their operation to California in 1918 where they, along with Jack, opened studios in Hollywood. They incorporated as Warner Brothers Pictures and obtained control of a nationwide distributing system for their films. But success in not easily forthcoming in Hollywood, and in the mid-1920s the Warner studios were close to bankruptcy when the brothers decided to experiment with a novelty, a sound film. In 1926 they released the movie *Don Juan,* starring John Barrymore, with a completely synchronized musical score. The success of this film paved the way for two more such movies. In 1927 Sam Warner died as the Warner Brothers released the first "talking picture," *The Jazz Singer,* which revolutionized the movie industry. Within two years the "talkie" was the standard for motion pictures, and the Warners, with a head start, forged ahead in the field with a number of successful films, including *Kismet* and *Little Caesar,* both 1930. In 1929 Warner Brothers had acquired the Stanley Company of America, which controlled about 250 theater outlets around the nation. This, coupled with a distribution system, made the Warners financially secure. During the 1930s and 1940s the studio signed contracts with many stars, and with the services of such outstanding directors as Hal B. Wallis produced a series of successful films, including *Green Pastures,* 1936; *The Life of Emile Zola,* 1937; *Casablanca,* 1942; *Watch on the Rhine,* 1943; *This Is the Army,* 1943; *To Have and Have Not,* 1944; and *A Streetcar Named Desire,* 1951. Ever aware of media trends, Warner Brothers was the first of the Hollywood studios to go into television production, in the late 1940s. In 1954 Jack Warner won the Irving Thalberg Memorial Award for consistent excellence in movie production. In 1956 the Warners relinquished financial control of their studio to a banking firm, although Jack remained as president and largest single stockholder. Harry Warner died in Hollywood on July 25, 1958. Albert remained on the studio board of directors from 1956 until 1966; he died in Miami Beach, Florida, on November 26, 1967. In 1966 Jack Warner sold his interest in the studio. He died in Los Angeles, on September 9, 1978.

Warner, Charles Dudley (1829–1900), author and editor. Born in Plainfield, Massachusetts, on September 12, 1829, Warner graduated from Hamilton College in 1851. For the next several years he worked at various jobs before taking a law degree at the University of Pennsylvania in 1858. He practiced law in Chicago for nearly two years, but his lack of interest led him to abandon it and turn to his first choice, writing. In 1860 he settled in Hartford, Connecticut, to work on the editorial staff of the *Hartford Evening Press* (merged in 1867 with the *Hartford Courant*). He served as editor from 1861 and maintained a connection with the paper for the rest of his life, even after gaining success with his own literary endeavors. It was through articles he wrote for his newspaper and for magazines that he became known primarily as an essayist. A collection of essays published in 1871 under the title *My Summer in a Garden* was well received. He also produced a number of travel books based on several trips to Europe and the Middle East. The first of these, *Saunterings*, 1872, had also appeared as columns in the *Courant*. He followed with *My Winter on the Nile*, 1876, and *In the Levant*, 1877. Of all his writings his four novels were the least effective; but the first, published in 1873 and on which he collaborated with his neighbor Mark Twain, gave the name to an era—*The Gilded Age*. This novel, and his later three, were a departure from his earlier style of easy and quiet humor, for they dealt with social issues in a realistic way and were especially critical of the uses of great wealth. His trilogy, consisting of *A Little Journey in the World*, 1889, *The Golden House*, 1894, and *The Fortune*, 1899, was criticized for lack of literary distinction. However, Warner continued to publish collections of his essays, which remained popular throughout his life. They ranged in subject matter from reminiscences of earlier years to literary criticism and included *On Horseback*, 1888; *As We Were Saying*, 1891; *The Relation of Literature to Life*, 1896; and *Fashions in Literature*, 1902. He was also the general editor of the American Men of Letters series, 22 volumes of critical biographies issued between 1881 and 1904, and coeditor of the 30-volume *Library of the World's Best Literature*, 1896–1897. From 1884 to 1898 he was a contributing editor of *Harper's New Monthly Magazine*. Warner died in Hartford, Connecticut, on October 20, 1900.

Warner, Glenn Scobey (1871–1954), "Pop," football coach. Born in Springville, New York, on April 5, 1871, Warner graduated from Cornell University in 1894 with a degree in law. Having been an outstanding college athlete, especially in football, he chose to follow a career of coaching and accepted a job as football coach at the University of Georgia. He stayed there for two seasons, then returned to Cornell to coach in 1897–1898 before going to the Carlisle Indian School at Carlisle, Pennsylvania, where he coached until 1915, except for the period 1904–1906, when he was again at Cornell. It was at Carlisle that he became the nation's best-known football coach. He devised the double-wing formation with a seven-man line to outflank defensive tackles. The ability that his team gained at maneuvering and

deception opened up new avenues of attack and surprise plays that led to a great many victories over football giants for Carlisle. Perhaps the best-known of Warner's players was the exceptional all-round athlete Jim Thorpe. From 1915 until 1923 Warner coached at the University of Pittsburgh, where he had several undefeated seasons, then at Stanford University from 1924 until 1932. While at Stanford his teams won three Rose Bowl games, but it was at the bowl game on January 1, 1925, that he met his peer in coaching, Knute Rockne. Rockne's Notre Dame team beat Stanford 27-0. From 1933 until 1938 Warner coached at Temple University, then spent one year as an advisory coach at San Jose State College in California. His 46-year career ended with 312 games won, 104 lost, and 32 tied. In 1951 he was elected to the Football Hall of Fame. Warner died in Palo Alto, California, on September 7, 1954.

Warner, Harry, *see under* Warner Brothers

Warner, Jack, *see under* Warner Brothers

Warren, Earl (1891–1974), chief justice of the Supreme Court. Born in Los Angeles on March 19, 1891, Warren was raised in Bakersfield and graduated from the University of California at Berkeley in 1912 and from the law school of the University of California in 1914. Admitted to the California bar that year, he practiced law in San Francisco and Oakland for three years. He then served in the army as a first lieutenant in the infantry. He became clerk of a California state legislative committee in 1919 and was deputy city attorney for Oakland during 1919–1920, before serving Alameda County as deputy district attorney, 1920–1925, and district attorney, 1925–1939. For the next four years he was attorney general of California. With wide popular support from both parties, he was elected governor of California in 1943 and was twice reelected. As Republican candidate for vice-president in 1948, running with Thomas E. Dewey, he suffered the only political defeat of his career. In 1953 President Dwight D. Eisenhower named him chief justice of the Supreme Court, to succeed Frederick M. Vinson. In the following year the school segregation cases, principally *Brown* v. *Board of Education*, brought forth one of the most notable rulings of the Court in his time. "In the field of public education," he stated for the unanimous Court, "the doctrine of 'separate but equal' has no place. Separate educational facilities are inherently unequal." Warren also spoke for the Court in *United States* v. *Harriss*, 1954, in sustaining the constitutionality of the Federal Regulation of Lobbying Act of 1946; *Quinn* v. *United States*, 1955, and *Watkins* v. *United States*, 1957, in protecting the rights of witnesses before congressional investigation committees; *Pennsylvania* v. *Nelson*, 1956, in barring enforcement of state sedition laws that duplicated federal legislation on the same subject; *Trop* v. *Dulles*, 1958, in invalidating a federal statute revoking the citizenship of deserters; *Reynolds* v. *Sims*, 1964, in holding that state legislatures must be apportioned on the basis of population ("one man, one vote"); and *Miranda* v. *Arizona*, 1966, in upholding the rights of suspects held in custody by the police. He also served as chairman of the Presidential Commission to Investigate the Assassination of John F. Kennedy. Perhaps the most controversial judge of his time because of the combination of his devotion to civil liberties and his influential position, he resigned from the Court at the end of the 1968–1969 term, in June 1969. He continued to live in Washington, D.C., maintaining an office at the Supreme Court and working with retired Supreme Court Justice Tom C. Clark, director of the Federal Judicial Center, on ways to improve the federal judiciary. He died in Washington on July 9, 1974.

Warren, John (1753–1815), physician and educator. Born in Roxbury, Massachusetts (now part of Boston), on July 27, 1753, Warren, a younger brother of Joseph Warren, graduated from Harvard in 1771. He studied medicine privately for the next few years, took part in the Boston Tea Party in December 1773, and was about to open his own practice in Salem when the Revolutionary War began. He saw service in the medical department of the Continental army from 1775 until 1777, when he returned to Boston to start a private practice. Although Philadelphia and New York City had medical schools, no such training was available in Boston. Warren, therefore, began a series of lectures to a few select students in 1780 on the subjects of surgery and anatomy. The lectures were well received and were opened to a larger group during the following two years. Warren's lectures made it evident that a medical department was needed at Harvard. At the school's request he and Benjamin Waterhouse drew up a curriculum and the Harvard Medical School, formally established in 1782, opened in the autumn of 1783 with the two men as its first professors. While serving as professor of anatomy and surgery, Warren also kept up an extensive private practice, becoming one of the country's outstanding surgeons, and promoted public-health measures in the Boston area. He remained at Harvard until his death in Boston on April 4, 1815.

Warren, John Collins (1778–1856), surgeon. Born in Boston on August 1, 1778, the son of John Warren (1753–1815), Warren graduated from Harvard in 1797. After two years of private study, he spent the years from 1799 to 1802 studying medicine in London, Paris, and Edinburgh. In 1802 he joined his father's medical practice in Boston and in 1809 he became associate professor of anatomy and surgery at the Harvard Medical School; he became a full professor in 1815 and from 1816 to 1819 he served as dean of the medical school. A cofounder of the Massachusetts General Hospital, which opened in 1821, he was also its first surgeon. The hospital entered into a cooperative training program with the Harvard Medical School, which had moved its facilities to

Boston. Warren continued to serve both institutions while at the same time pursuing his own medical research. As the leading American surgeon of his day, he was in the forefront of medical progress and did not hesitate to experiment. In 1846 he lent his reputation to the first use of anesthesia for a surgical operation when William T. G. Morton administered ether to a patient before Warren's successful excision of a neck tumor. Warren also published a number of books in the field of medicine, the most important of which was *Surgical Observations on Tumors with Cases and Operations,* 1839. As one of the most prominent of Massachusetts' residents, he also devoted himself to a number of other interests including reform movements, experimental farming, and geology. He became professor emeritus at the medical school in 1847 but continued to occupy himself with his many interests until his death in Boston on May 4, 1856.

Warren, Joseph (1741–1775), Revolutionary soldier and physician. Born in Roxbury, Massachusetts (now part of Boston), on June 11, 1741, Warren, the eldest brother of John Warren (1753–1815), graduated from Harvard in 1759. He taught at the Roxbury Grammar School for a year before studying medicine. He established a good practice but his interest in the Whig cause led him to neglect medicine for politics. With the passage of the Stamp Act in 1765, he became active with other prominent Whigs in their political clubs. His frequent writings in the press and his speeches made him a leader of the popular party. He helped prepare the Suffolk Resolves of 1774 that denounced the coercive measures passed by Parliament after the Boston Tea Party, called Massachusetts to arms, and that recommended economic sanctions against Britain. Paul Revere carried the Resolves to the Continental Congress in Philadelphia, where they were endorsed. Warren was a member of the first three provincial congresses held in Massachusetts, was president of the third, and actively served the Committee of Safety. On April 18, 1775, he dispatched Paul Revere and William Dawes to Lexington to warn of the approach of British troops. Warren was named a major general of militia on June 14, 1775, but before receiving his commission he took part in the battle of Bunker Hill and was killed by enemy fire on June 17, 1775.

Warren, Mercy Otis (1728–1814), author. Born in Barnstable, Massachusetts, on September 14 (old style), 1728, Miss Otis was the sister of James Otis, who was early active in the anti-British agitation over the Stamp Act of 1765. She married James Warren, a Massachusetts political leader, in 1754. Knowing most of the leaders of the Revolution personally, she was continually in the center of events during the exciting years from 1765 to 1789. Her vantage point combined with a talent for writing to make her both a poet and historian of the Revolutionary era. She wrote several plays, including *The Adulateur,* 1773, a satire directed against Governor Thomas Hutchinson of Massachusetts, in which the war of revolution is foretold; and *The Group*, 1775, a satire conjecturing what would happen if the British king abrogated the Massachusetts charter of rights. In 1790 she published *Poems Dramatic and Miscellaneous*, a collection of her works. In 1805 she completed a three-volume history of the war entitled *A History of the Rise, Progress, and Termination of the American Revolution*, which is especially useful for its knowledgeable comments on the important personages of the day. Mrs. Warren died on October 19, 1814, in Plymouth, Massachusetts.

Warren, Robert Penn (1905–   ), author and poet. Born in Guthrie, Kentucky, on April 24, 1905, Warren graduated from Vanderbilt University in 1925. While in college he became associated with the group of poets known as the Fugitives which included John Crowe Ransom, Allen Tate, and others who were a part of the Southern literary renaissance. He worked with them on their literary magazine, the *Fugitive*, and joined with them in 1930, as one of the "Southern Agrarians," in publishing the defense of regionalism entitled *I'll Take My Stand*. After college he attended the University of California at Berkeley, where he earned an M.A. in 1927. Then he continued his studies with a year at Yale and two years at Oxford as a Rhodes scholar. For most of his career thereafter he taught literature at various institutions— in 1930–1931 at Southwestern College in Memphis, from 1931 to 1934 at Vanderbilt, from 1934 to 1942 at Louisiana State University, from 1942 to 1950 at the University of Minnesota, and from 1950 to 1956 at Yale. He returned to Yale in 1961 and taught there until his retirement in 1973. With Cleanth Brooks, Warren produced two distinguished and widely used textbooks, *Understanding Poetry*, 1938, and *Understanding Fiction*, 1943. As a writer, Warren showed a multifaceted talent, ranging from poetry, novels, and biography to criticism. A regional theme—life in the South— ran through most of his work. He is probably best known to the general public for his novels, particularly *All the King's Men*, 1946, which won the Pulitzer Prize for fiction in 1947. The book, based generally on the life of Louisiana's Huey "the Kingfish" Long, was made into an Academy Award–winning movie in 1949. He also won the Pulitzer Prize for poetry in 1958 for *Promises: Poems 1954–1956*, 1957; he was the first to win both the fiction and poetry awards. Warren's first book was *John Brown: The Making of a Martyr*, 1929. His first novel, *Night Rider*, published ten years later, dealt with the tobacco war in Kentucky at about the turn of the century. His other novels included *At Heaven's Gate*, 1943; *World Enough and Time*, 1950; *Band of Angels*, 1955; *The Cave*, 1959; *Wilderness: A Tale of the Civil War*, 1961; *Flood*, 1964, and *Meet Me In the Green Glen*, 1971. His poetry collections, in addition to *Promises*, included *Thirty-six Poems*, 1936; *Eleven Poems on the Same Theme*, 1942; *Selected Poems 1923–1943*, 1944; *Brother to Dragons*, 1953, a narrative verse

tale; *You Emperors, and Others: Poems 1957–1960*; *Incarnation Poems, 1966–1968*, and *Audubon: A Vision*, 1969. As a leading spokesman for the social values of the South, Warren wrote about the issues that troubled the region, especially racial problems. He had revealed himself as a segregationist in his essay *I'll Take My Stand* in 1930; but in 1956 he reversed himself in a volume called *Segregation, the Inner Conflict in the South*. And in 1965, in *Who Speaks for the Negro?*, he further elaborated ways in which the South would have to change. He was an editor (1935–1942) and founder of the *Southern Review*, and from 1938 to 1968 was advisory editor of the influential *Kenyon Review*. He published a number of essays in several journals, and in 1966 edited *Faulkner: A Collection of Critical Essays*.

Washakie (1804?–1900), Indian leader. Born in what is now Montana possibly as early as 1798, but certainly by 1804, Washakie was a friend and ally of the white men from the days of the fur trappers onward. As a youth among the Shoshone he took part in the customary "wars"—raids against enemy tribes such as the Sioux, Cheyenne, and Blackfeet. In the early 1840s he was recognized as chief of the Eastern Shoshone, a band that lived in the Green River Valley of eastern Utah and southern Wyoming. When the Indian wars began in the West following the Civil War, the white men were fighting those tribes, among others, with whom Washakie's people had long been in conflict. So the whites found natural allies in Washakie and his Shoshone, and a number of Shoshone warriors served under Gen. George Crook in the 1876 war against the Sioux and Cheyenne. As Washakie saw the number of white settlers moving West increase over the years, he recognized and accepted the inevitability of reservation life for his people; in 1868 he signed the treaty written at Fort Bridger that allowed the transcontinental railroad a right-of-way through the Green River Valley. The Shoshone agreed to move to the Wind River Reservation in Wyoming. Washakie continued as chief into his seventies, then was honored as an elder for the rest of his life. He died at Fort Washakie, Wyoming, the reservation headquarters, on February 21, 1900. His epitaph reads: "Always loyal to the Government and to his white brothers."

Washington, Booker Taliaferro (1856–1915), educator and social reformer. Born a slave on April 5, 1856, in Franklin County, Virginia, Washington, whose father is believed to have been white, was taken by his mother, with her two other children, to Malden, near Charleston, West Virginia, after the emancipation. There, poverty necessitated his working from the age of nine, first in a salt furnace and then a coal mine. He attended a school for Negroes where he identified himself as Booker Washington, only later to learn that his mother had named him Booker Taliaferro; he ultimately combined all three names. Having always been eager to accquire an education, he went to the Hampton Normal and Agricultural Institute in Virginia in 1872, and there studied for three years, working as a janitor to pay his expenses. Returning to Malden after graduation, he taught children in the daytime and adults in the evenings. During 1878–1879 he attended the Wayland Seminary in Washington, D.C. Then, summoned back to Hampton, he joined the faculty in a trial program of education for American Indians. The founding of Tuskegee Institute, a Negro normal and agricultural school in Tuskegee, Alabama, in 1881, and the choice of Washington as its first principal, began his major career. The school was provided with two unequipped buildings, a small appropriation, and a student body of 40 unschooled blacks from local farms. Thirty-four years later, at Washington's death, Tuskegee had more than 100 well-equipped buildings, a student body of over 1500, a faculty of almost 200, and an endowment of nearly $2 million. He was extremely successful in promoting goodwill and in raising funds for the school, and he won a national reputation as the most prominent Negro in the country. The school became famous for its hard-working, reliable graduates. A staunch believer in industrial training for Negroes rather than liberal-arts education, he was shunned by many black intellectuals, notably W. E. B. Du Bois, who saw in his philosophy the guarantee of continued Negro servility. Washington's most famous exposition of his position on race relations was his "Atlanta Compromise" speech of 1895, in which he said: "In all things that are purely social we can be as separate as the fingers, yet one as the hand in all things essential to mutual progress." Although his acceptance of racial segregation and discrimination counted on the success of self-help and of education on both sides to gradually break down the color line, he was viewed by more radical reformers as a temporizer whose power derived from white support. Among the organizations he established for uplifting and benefiting blacks was the National Negro Business League. He wrote numerous books, including the autobiographical *Up From Slavery*, 1901, and *My Larger Education*, 1911. Exhausted from overwork, he died at Tuskegee, Alabama, on November 14, 1915. He was elected to the Hall of Fame in 1945.

Washington, Bushrod (1762–1829), justice of the Supreme Court. Born in Westmoreland County, Virginia, on June 5, 1762, Bushrod Washington was a nephew of George Washington. He graduated in 1778 from the College of William and Mary, where he was one of the original members of the Phi Beta Kappa society, founded two years previously. After service in the Continental army during the Revolution, he studied law at Philadelphia under James Wilson. Admitted to the Virginia bar in 1786, he opened a law practice in Alexandria, but moved in 1790 to Richmond. He served a term in the Virginia house of delegates in 1787, and sat as a delegate in the state convention that ratified the federal Constitution in 1788. Washington continued his law practice until 1798, when President John Adams appointed him an associate justice of the Supreme Court. Within a few years, his fellow Virginian John Marshall became chief justice, and Washington, who generally agreed with Marshall in interpreting the Constitution, found himself involved in many of the Court's early important decisions. After the deaths of George and Martha Washington, Bushrod inherited Mount Vernon, their home, and became executor of his uncle's estate. In 1817 he became a founder and first president of the American Colonization Society for the repatriation of blacks to Africa, although he continued to own slaves himself. He continued to serve on the Supreme Court until his death in Philadelphia on November 26, 1829.

Washington, George (1732–1799), first president of the United States. Born on February 22, 1732, in Westmoreland County, Virginia, Washington grew up on the family plantation, Wakefield. Little is known of his childhood and much that was later written about it—notably Mason Locke Weems's cherry-tree story—is apocryphal. In 1743 his father died, and, after living for periods of time with various relatives, he came into the care of his older half-brother Lawrence, who was connected by marriage to the powerful Fairfax family and who owned a plantation known as Mount Vernon. His irregular schooling came to an end at fifteen and he turned to surveying as a profession; in 1748 he joined a surveying party sent by Lord Fairfax into the Shenandoah Valley, and the next year was appointed official surveyor of Culpeper County. In 1751 he accompanied Lawrence, then suffering from tuberculosis, to Barbados; the deaths of Lawrence and his daughter in 1752 left George in possession of Mount Vernon, one of the best estates in the colony, at the age of twenty. Shortly thereafter he was named adjutant for the southern district of Virginia by Governor Robert Dinwiddie. In 1753 he became adjutant of the Northern Neck and Eastern Shore and volunteered to carry a warning from Dinwiddie to French forces encroaching on the Ohio Valley region claimed by England. The winter journey was perilous and Washington's account of it, emphasizing the refusal of the French to leave after he finally reached Fort Le Boeuf, was published by the governor and widely read. In 1754 he was commissioned lieutenant colonel of a Virginia regiment and sent back to the Ohio territory, where Dinwiddie had meantime sent a party to build a fort at present-day Pittsburgh; near the fort, which the French had seized and named Fort Duquesne, he built Fort Necessity at Great Meadows and on May 28 he defeated a small French detachment. Promoted to colonel and given reinforcements, he was nonetheless compelled to surrender on liberal terms to a much superior enemy force in July; he and his men marched back to Virginia. In October he resigned his commission, largely because of conflicts with British regular officers who although of inferior rank, assumed authority because they held king's commissions. Early in 1755 Gen. Edward Braddock arrived in Virginia with a fresh army of regular troops and offered Washington a position as aide-de-camp. An expedition was mounted against Fort Duquesne and Washington, who had fallen ill, joined the vanguard just one day before the column was ambushed and dispersed by French and Indians on July 9. Braddock was wounded and Washington succeeded in turning the rout into an orderly retreat. After Braddock's death a few days later he returned home and was soon made commander of all Virginia forces. For the next three years of the last French and Indian War he was primarily concerned with defense of the frontier against constant raids, a mission in which he was given insufficient support by the colonial government. He commanded part of the force under Gen. John Forbes that built Fort Pitt on the site of the abandoned and razed Fort Duquesne in 1758. He resigned his commission shortly after his election to the Virginia house of burgesses in 1758. Early the next year he married Martha Dandridge Custis, a wealthy widow, and settled down to farming. He remained in the house of burgesses and from 1760 to 1774 was a justice of the peace; Mount Vernon and other properties waxed in value as he devoted himself to managing the estate and enjoying the social life of a country gentleman. As tension between the colonies and Britain grew he sided unequivocally with his native country; he took part in the unauthorized meetings of the burgesses at the Raleigh Tavern in Williamsburg in 1770 and 1774, declared himself in favor of armed resistance to unlawful authority, and in 1774 was elected to the First Continental Congress. He was also placed in command of the militia companies of several Virginia counties; he retained his Fairfax County militia uniform throughout the Revolutionary War. The next year he was a delegate to the Second Continental Congress and in June, as part of a compromise between Virginia and Massachusetts, leaders respectively of the Southern and Northern factions, he was chosen commander in chief of the Continental army. He arrived at Boston shortly after the battle of Bunker Hill (June 17, 1775) and spent several months training the ill-equipped troops, mostly short-term militia. In March 1776 he seized Dorchester Heights, brought in cannon captured earlier at Fort Ticonderoga by Ethan Allen, and forced Gen. Sir William Howe to evacuate the city. Washington then moved south to New York, where, outnumbered and outmaneuvered, he lost Long Island and Manhattan and, although he conducted a brilliant delaying retreat, was forced into New Jersey and across the Delaware into Pennsylvania. The British forces encamped at Trenton, Princeton, and elsewhere in New Jersey. On Christmas night of 1776 Washington ferried his troops back across the Delaware, overwhelmed the Trenton encampment, and slipped away in the night from a superior force that prevented his proceeding to take Morristown as he had intended. A few days later he captured Princeton and established himself at Morristown. The year 1777 was marked by the constant struggle to maintain the army despite short-term enlistments, desertions, and lack of congressional and state support in money and supplies, by the desperate battle at Brandywine (September 11) and the subsequent loss of Philadelphia, and by the Conway Cabal, an apparent plan by several of Washington's military rivals and their allies in Congress to have him replaced by Gen. Horatio Gates, who had been victorious at Saratoga. After a final unsuccessful attack on the British at Germantown in October, the army encamped at Valley Forge; the winter of 1777–1778 was perhaps the darkest moment of the Revolution, as the army starved and dwindled, Congress meddled, and only the personal strength of the commander held the tatters together. The efforts of Baron von Steuben to instill military discipline into the troops that winter, however, boded well for the renewed campaign. In early 1778 an alliance with France was sealed and, in anticipation of the arrival of a French fleet, the British abandoned Philadelphia and withdrew toward New York City. Washington met Sir Henry Clinton's army at Monmouth, New Jersey, and was kept from a major victory only by the incompetence and possible treachery of Gen. Charles Lee, commander of the American advance column. Clinton occupied New York City, the American forces surrounded the city, and, aside from Gen. John Sullivan's expedition against the Iroquois in 1779 and Gen. Anthony Wayne's capture of Stony Point on the Hudson, little action occurred in the northern department for the remainder of the war. In August 1781 Washington, reinforced by French troops that had arrived in Rhode Island in the previous year under the Count de Rochambeau and a fleet under Admiral De Grasse, marched south to face Gen. Charles Cornwallis, who entrenched himself at Yorktown, Virginia. On October 19, a month after arriving, the allied armies and the presence of the French fleet forced Cornwallis to surrender and the Revolutionary War was effectively ended. Washington remained in command of the army; he continued to plead with Congress to pay the soldiers, and he put down a scheme concocted by certain officers to displace Congress and make their commander king. He settled his army at Newburgh, New York, in 1782 and for more than a year awaited the peace. Articles of peace were signed in November, effective as of January 20, 1783; the treaty of peace was signed September 3, 1783. Soon after the occupation of New York City in November 1783 he bid his officers farewell there, resigned his commission, and on Christmas Eve returned to Mount Vernon. Much of his own money had gone into the war effort and he had accepted no compensation for the work of eight years; in addition, his properties had suffered greatly during the war, and he now devoted his energies to restoring them to prosperity. Washington shared in the rapidly growing concern that the Articles of Confederation were incapable of providing the unity and security necessary for the new nation. In 1785 a meeting was held at his home between representatives of Virginia and Maryland to settle problems concerning the navigation of the Potomac; the conference led to the larger Annapolis Convention of 1786, which in turn produced the Federal Constitutional Convention held in Philadelphia in 1787. Sent as a Virginia delegate, he was unanimously chosen to preside over the convention. He approved of the Constitution and played a prominent role in securing ratification in Virginia. When the state electors met early in 1789 to select the first president, they ratified without exception the long-obvious choice of George Washington, to which he acceded with reluctance. On April 30, 1789, he was inaugurated at Federal Hall in New York City. As the first president of a new and unsure government, not the least of his responsibilities was to avoid creating potentially harmful precedents. He constructed his cabinet with an eye to sectional and ideological balance, strove to the utmost to maintain cordial relations with and among all his governmental officers, and conducted himself with republican decorum and restraint. His first term passed without major crisis, but his second witnessed a heated and inevitable clash between Thomas Jefferson and Alexander Hamilton, the resignation of Jefferson, and the polarization of politics into party camps. While seeking to steer a middle course, Washington more often than not found himself aligned with the Hamiltonian Federalists, particularly when he issued his proclamation of neutrality upon the outbreak of war between England and France in 1793, when he sent troops under Hamilton to suppress the Whisky Rebellion in western Pennsylvania in 1794, and when he signed Jay's Treaty with England in 1795. The treaty provoked a particularly bitter attack from the opposition, and the President resisted an attempt by the House of Representatives to gain a share of the treaty-making power. In 1796 he firmly rejected pleas that he accept a third term (setting a precedent that endured for 144 years, until Franklin D. Roosevelt, and that was later made law) and in September he arranged the publication of his "Farewell Address," which owed much to Hamilton, and in which he advised his country on its future course. In March 1797 he returned once again to Mount Vernon. The apparent imminence of war with France in 1798 led to his appointment as lieutenant general in command of a provisional army, but the crisis passed without his having to take the field. He died at Mount Vernon, which eventually came into the possession of his nephew, Bushrod Washington, on December 14, 1799. He has remained in the century and three-quarters since his death, in the words of Henry Lee's famous eulogy, "First in war, first in peace, and first in the hearts of his countrymen." He was elected to the Hall of Fame in 1900.

Waterhouse, Benjamin (1754–1846), physician. Born in Newport, Rhode Island, on March 4, 1754, Waterhouse apprenticed himself to a surgeon at sixteen and went abroad in 1775 to complete his medical education. He studied in London and Edinburgh for three years before going to Leiden in 1778 for more training. There he stayed with the U.S. ambassador, John Adams, who arrived in 1780. In 1782 he returned to the United States and settled in Newport, but the opening of a medical school at Harvard led to his appointment in 1783 as professor of the theory and practice of physic there. The first part of his *Synopsis of a Course of Lectures on the Theory and Practice of Medicine* appeared in 1786. A discourse emphasizing experimental investigation was published in 1792 as *The Rise, Progress, and Present State of Medicine*. He publicized the work of Edward Jenner, the English discoverer of smallpox vaccination, in 1799 and the next year received some of the cowpox vaccine from England. Successfully vaccinating his five-year-old son and other members of the household, he became the first American physician to establish Jenner's method as a general practice. (Zabdiel Boylston, in 1721, had made crude inoculations using matter from smallpox pustules, but Jenner's vaccine method was vastly safer.) But in the anti-inoculation furor of the time, a serious epidemic that resulted from the use of impure vaccines by untrained persons was blamed on Waterhouse. He demanded that the Boston board of health investigate and their committee concluded that "the cow-pox is a complete security against the small-pox." Vaccination became known in the neighboring states, and President Thomas Jefferson had hundreds of persons inoculated with the cowpox vaccine Waterhouse sent him. Articles on vaccination written by Waterhouse appeared in many newspapers, and in 1810 he abstracted all previous publications to form *Information Respecting the Origin, Progress, and Efficacy of the Kine Pock Inoculation*. He was honored with memberships in various scientific societies in the United States, Britain, and France. His most popular book, *Shewing the Evil Tendency of the Use of Tobacco*, had already appeared in German and French translations when it was published in 1805; it ran through five American editions. His lectures on natural history, particularly mineralogy and botany, were also published, and he was a founder of the Massachusetts Humane Society. His relations with his Harvard colleagues became strained, however, mainly over the issue of moving the medical school to Boston, where facilities for clinical instruction were more easily available; he opposed the move as he had little inclination for clinical teaching. After an attempt to establish a rival school failed, a published attack on his colleagues led to his being forced to resign in 1812. He stayed on at the United States Marine Hospital, with which he had been connected since 1808, when he wrote their first *Rules and Orders*, and President James Madison appointed him medical superintendent of all military posts in New England in 1813. Of considerable note was his work in 1817 on the diagnosis and treatment of dysentery. Most of his later writings were not medical; in 1833 he edited and published a book on Oregon in order to deter immigration to the West. He died in his home in Cambridge, Massachusetts, on October 2, 1846.

Waterman, Lewis Edson (1837–1901), inventor and manufacturer. Born in Decatur, Otsego County, New York, on November 20, 1837, Waterman lived there until 1853, when his family moved to Kankakee County, Illinois. He had received enough formal education by the time he was sixteen to find teaching jobs in local schools. He divided his time between teaching and other jobs until 1862, when he began selling insurance. From 1864 until 1870 he worked in Boston for the Aetna Insurance Company. He had earned enough by 1870 to spend the next dozen years in semi-retirement and leisure. In the early 1880s he devoted his attention to developing a workable fountain pen. The problem with earlier pens had been controlling the ink flow. By late 1883 Waterman had perfected a method of using a hard-rubber insert with tiny channels cut into it to control the flow from the capsule of ink to the penpoint. Once his device was patented, he began manufacturing pens, and within three years was able to incorporate the L. E. Waterman Company in New York City. He operated the company until his death. After Waterman introduced what was the first really practical fountain pen, the pens sold by the millions for many years afterward. He died in Brooklyn, New York, on May 1, 1901.

Waters, Ethel (1896–1977), singer and actress. Born in Chester, Pennsylvania, on October 31, 1896, Miss Waters grew up there and in the Phila-delphia area amid conditions of extreme poverty. Married for the first time before she was thirteen, she worked as a chambermaid and scrubwoman. At the urging of friends she tried singing in a nightclub. At seventeen, billing herself as "Sweet Mama Stringbean," she was singing on stage at the Lincoln Theater in Baltimore. It was during her engagement there that she received permission from W. C. Handy to sing his "St. Louis Blues," thus becoming the first woman entertainer to perform the song. For years she worked in vaudeville and small clubs. In 1925 she sang at the Plantation Club in New York City's Harlem, and her performances there led to offers to appear on Broadway. In 1927 she appeared in the all-black review *Africana*, and thereafter divided her time between the stage, nightclubs, and eventually movies. In 1930 she was on the Broadway stage in *Blackbirds*, a revival of the popular 1924 musical; and the following year she starred in *Rhapsody in Black*. In 1933 she was in Irving Berlin's musical *As Thousands Cheer*, her first departure from shows with all-black casts. Her first straight dramatic role was in the 1938 pro-duction of *Mamba's Daughters*, and two years later she spent a season on Broadway in the musical *Cabin in the Sky*, later made into a movie. Probably her greatest dramatic success was in the stage version of Carson McCullers' *The Member of the Wedding* in 1950, a performance for which

she won the New York Drama Critics' Circle Award. She also starred in the movie version in 1952. Among Miss Waters's other films were *Cairo*, 1942; *Pinky*, 1949; and *The Sound and the Fury*, 1959. Her autobiography, *His Eye Is on the Sparrow*, 1951, conveying her deep spirituality, became a best seller. After the mid-1950s Miss Waters continued in show business but at a more relaxed pace, appearing frequently on television and occasionally in nightclubs. She died in Chats-worth, California, on September 1, 1977.

Watson, Elkanah (1758–1842), businessman and agriculturist. Born in Plymouth, Massachusetts, on January 22, 1758, Watson served an apprentice-ship to a Boston merchant from 1775 until 1779. Thereafter he traveled to France and set himself up in the mercantile business, remaining for about four years and becoming fairly affluent before a financial recession hit in 1783. His travels in Europe inspired in him an interest in canal trans-portation, and for the following 20 years, back in the United States, he attempted without suc-cess to promote the building of canals in both Virginia and New York. In 1785 he settled in Edenton, North Carolina, and conducted a success-ful business for four years, then having hit upon hard times again, he relocated in Albany, New York, and started the Bank of Albany. About 1800 he chartered the New York State Bank in Albany and operated it for four years until he was able to retire. Watson settled finally in Pitts-field, Massachusetts, where he took up experi-mental farming, the most successful venture of his long career. In order to disseminate informa-tion on agricultural improvements, he organized in cooperation with neighboring farmers a "Cattle Show" in 1810. In 1811 he organized the Berk-shire Agricultural Society, under the auspices of which the practice of holding an annual county-wide fair continued. At the fairs farmers exhibited their livestock and crops and their wives put on displays of homemade food and handiwork. The fairs were a means of enlivening competition among farmers and served an educational purpose at a time when there were no schools of agricul-ture. From Berkshire County the idea spread rapidly across the nation to become an enduring institution, and Watson is known as the father of county and state fairs in the United States. He continued his interest in agriculture for the re-mainder of his life. He died in Pittsfield, Mas-sachusetts, on December 5, 1842. His *History of Agricultural Societies on the Modern Berkshire System* appeared in 1820, and his autobiography, *Men and Times of the Revolution; or, Memoirs of Elkanah Watson*, was published posthumously by his son in 1856.

Watson, James Dewey (1928–   ), biochemist. Born in Chicago on April 6, 1928, Watson attended Chicago schools and then the University of Chicago, which he entered after only two years of high school; during four years there he earned a Ph.B. and a B.S., both conferred in 1947, when he was still only nineteen. Interested in bird study, he went to the University of Indiana, where he came under the influence of a brilliant group of researchers in genetics, including Salvador Luria and Hermann J. Muller. He received his Ph.D. at Indiana in 1950, and was granted a National Research Council fellowship which took him to Copenhagen for further work. After a year there he moved to Cambridge University, where he met Francis C. H. Crick, a nonconformist in science and a somewhat controversial geneticist. Having a small fellowship from the National Foundation for Infantile Paralysis, he joined with Crick in a series of genetic experiments carried out at Cambridge in a shabby building called The Hut. Obsessed with the problem of the molecular structure of deoxyribonucleic acid, or DNA, they worked for months on their three-dimensional jigsaw puzzle, making various models of the DNA molecule out of pieces of wire and colored beads and pieces of sheet metal. Finally they were successful in producing a model that met all requirements, and they described it in a now-classic one-page article in *Nature* on April 25, 1953. "We wish to suggest a structure for the salt of deoxyribose nucleic acid (DNA)," they modestly began. "This structure has novel features that are of considerable biological interest." The problem had been to build a model that would show how the genetic material in the cell could duplicate itself; and their model, of a helical ladder, one side of which determined the other side, was exactly what was needed. This, indeed, was the core of their discovery, which has been compared, for its importance in the history of science, with Isaac Newton's laws of motion, Charles Darwin's theory of evolution, and Albert Einstein's theory of relativity. In the next (May 30) issue of *Nature*, Watson and Crick developed some of the implications of their model, and researchers the world over immediately began to do experiments that soon confirmed it triumphantly. Watson and Crick shared the 1962 Nobel Prize for Physiology and Medicine with Maurice H. F. Wilkins, who had made studies in the same field. Meanwhile, Watson had joined the Harvard faculty in 1955, becoming a professor in 1961. He was also the recipient of many other awards and prizes, and was famous the world over by the time he was thirty. *The Molecular Biology of the Gene*, a highly technical study of the subject, appeared in 1965; in 1968 he published a best seller, *The Double Helix*, which, in candid and unsophisticated prose, told the story of his life and of his great discovery, in the process revealing much about the politics of science. Watson's later work was on the molecular structure of viruses and the mechanisms of molecular genetics and of protein biosynthesis, where once again he made notable contributions. In 1968 he became director of the Cold Spring Harbor Laboratory of Quantitative Biology.

Watson, John Broadus (1878–1958), psychologist. Born on January 9, 1878, in Greenville, South Carolina, Watson took his M.A. from Furman University in Greenville in 1900 and his Ph.D. from the University of Chicago in 1903. He remained at Chicago as an instructor in psychology for five years. In 1908 he became professor of experimental and comparative psychology at The Johns Hopkins University and remained there for 12 years. His principal contribution was founding the behaviorist school of psychology, whose principles were first formally stated in his paper of 1913, "Psychology as the Behaviorist Views It." Coming into direct opposition to the methods of introspective psychology, which had dominated the field, he based his "psychology of behavior" on extensive experiments at Johns Hopkins, many on animals, using the devices of Edward Lee Thorndike; and he concluded that personality and habits were results of training or conditioning rather than of inborn constitution. Contending that human beings could be trained to do or be anything, he denied the influence of instinct and heredity and stressed the effects of learning and environment. The only legitimate subject matter for behaviorist psychology was the strictly observable and measurable responses to outside stimuli. His books included *Animal Education*, 1903; *Behavior: An Introduction to Comparative Psychology*, 1914; *Psychology from the Standpoint of a Behaviorist*, 1919; *Behaviorism*, 1925; and *Psychological Care of Infant and Child*, 1928. In 1920 he was forced by the scandal of a divorce to resign his post at Hopkins. He entered the advertising business, became an agency vice-president in 1924, and retired in 1945. He died in New York City on September 25, 1958.

Watson, Thomas Augustus (1854–1934), telephone technician and shipbuilder. Born in Salem, Massachusetts, on January 18, 1854, Watson was apprenticed as an electrician in Boston in 1872. While working there he met Alexander Graham Bell and became his assistant in experiments on transmitting the sound of the human voice by wire. On June 2, 1875, they performed an almost accidentally successful experiment in which sound was transmitted by electricity by means of a "harmonic telegraph," an instrument with a reed mounted over a magnet and connected to a taut membrane. After further refinement by Bell and Watson this first telephone did carry the sounds of the human voice. But it was on March 10, 1876, using a different type of transmitter, that Bell succeeded in conveying a whole sentence by wire. Speaking to Watson, who was working in the basement of the building, Bell said: "Mr. Watson, come here, I want you." By October 1876 Watson and Bell were able to carry on a full conversation between Boston and suburban Cambridge. The new invention was soon put into use and in 1877 the Bell Telephone Company was organized with Watson as one of the partners and as head of research. He remained with Bell until 1881, then resigned and left for a year of travel abroad. In 1882 he settled at East Braintree, Massachusetts, and started a machine shop which grew into a shipyard. As his new company began to obtain government contracts for naval ships, it became a highly successful business and was incorporated in 1901 as the Fore River Ship & Engine Company. He built a number of destroyers and battleships, in addition to many commercial vessels. In 1904 he retired from the company to spend the rest of his life occupied with his personal interests. He attended Massachusetts Institute of Technology (MIT) and studied literature, drama, geology, art, and philosophy, all the while keeping up with developments in electronics and engineering. He died on December 13, 1934, in the Florida Keys.

Watson, Thomas Edward (1856–1922), public official and political leader. Born near Thomson, Georgia, on September 5, 1856, Watson attended Mercer University for two years. He taught school and studied law for another two years, was admitted to the bar in 1875, and began a highly successful practice. Shortly thereafter he began a political career that was to range over 40 years, although he held public office infrequently (he served a term in the Georgia legislature in 1882–1883; one term in the U.S. House of Representatives, from 1891 to 1893; and in 1920 was elected to a term in the U.S. Senate, but he died a year and a half after taking office). He was a man of strong, often extreme, positions, who early in his political life associated himself with the agricultural interests of the state as a Populist. He spoke against the industrialists and financiers of both North and South, and he urged Southern farmers to ally themselves with agriculturalists in all parts of the country. Watson was elected to the House of Representatives as a candidate of the Farmer's Alliance in 1890. In Congress he sponsored numerous reform bills and introduced the first resolution providing for rural free delivery of mail. But Populism did not make as much headway in the South as it did in other sections of the country, and in 1892, in a violent and thoroughly corrupt campaign, the Democrats succeeded in defeating Watson for reelection. Black field hands were hauled to the polls by wagonload and paid to vote and some "voters" were brought in from neighboring South Carolina, all with the result that the vote on election day in Watson's district was approximately twice the number of legally registered voters. After losing again in the election of 1894, he retired to his law practice for a time but remained active in Populist affairs. In 1896, when the Populist party met in convention at St. Louis, the delegates chose Watson as their vice-presidential candiate and accepted the Democratic candidate, William Jennings Bryan, as their presidential nominee. When this fusion ticket failed Watson retired from politics until 1904, when he ran unsuccessfully as the Populist candidate for the presidency, a race that he repeated in 1908 to no avail, for in the "Progressive Era" under Theodore Roosevelt the old Populist issues had lost most of their appeal. From 1893 until 1921 Watson devoted a great deal of time to writing and publishing. He wrote biographies of Thomas Jefferson, Andrew Jackson, and Napoleon Bona-

parte, and completed a history of France. For several years he published *Tom Watson's Magazine* in New York City. Then, moving back to Georgia, he started his *Watson's Jeffersonian Magazine* and *Weekly Jeffersonian* in 1911. Realizing that the Populist cause was a lost one, Watson moved into the ranks of the Democratic party in Georgia and dealt with the issues of the time through his publications and speeches. As he grew older, his attacks on persons and movements he opposed grew more extreme, and during the years 1910–1920 he adopted ardent nativist, anti-foreign, and racist views, fulminating in turn against blacks, Catholics, Jews, Socialists, participation in World War I, internationalism, and foreigners. Through violent editorials in his *Weekly Jeffersonian* he involved himself in the Leo M. Frank murder case in Atlanta, in terms of his extreme anti-Semitism; when Frank was lynched in August 1915, Watson reveled in the event. Finally, in 1917, the Post Office forbade him to send his paper through the mails. Apparently Watson's stands had pleased Georgians, for they elected him to the U.S. Senate in 1920 by a wide margin. He served only until September 26, 1922, when he died in Washington, D.C.

Watson, Thomas John (1874–1956), businessman. Born in Campbell, Steuben County, New York, on February 17, 1874, Watson was educated at the Addison (New York) Academy and at the Elmira School of Commerce. He did not receive a B.A., but he later garnered some 32 honorary degrees. He went to work in 1899 for the National Cash Register Company (NCR), serving successively as business manager, special representative, and general sales manager; in 1914 he left NCR to become president of the Computing-Tabulating-Recording Company, which in 1924 became International Business Machines (IBM). He was president and a director of IBM from then until 1949, when he became chairman of the board and chief executive officer. An astute and capable executive, he saw a revolution coming in the computing, tabulating, and recording of information. He was also a canny psychologist and felt that the constant reminder of duty would inspire employees—hence the internal IBM slogans that became famous, among them "Serve and Sell," "Make Things Happen," "Be Better Than Average," and, of course, "Think." He not only advocated thinking in human beings, but he also pioneered in the invention, development, and manufacture of machines that could "think," and thereby made the initials of his company almost synonymous with the so-called "second industrial revolution," which saw the computer and other cybernetic devices take over and perform many onerous business tasks quicker and better than humans. He died on June 19, 1956, in New York City. His son, Thomas John Watson, Jr., born in Dayton, Ohio, on January 8, 1914, at the age of five made his first tour of the IBM plants; at nine he visited the company's European installations; and at twelve he made his first speech to IBM salesmen. He graduated from Brown in 1937 and soon afterward joined the company as a salesman in its Manhattan district. He was astoundingly successful. His career was interrupted by World War II, during which he served in the Army Air Force, being discharged with the rank of lieutenant colonel. He returned to IBM in 1946 as assistant to the vice-president in charge of sales, a position he assumed himself in 1947, on the death of the incumbent. In 1949 he was named executive vice-president and in 1952 president of the company. He was chairman from 1961 to 1971. No less capable than his father, he oversaw the continued growth of the company and the expansion of IBM into new fields, including publishing.

Watterson, Henry (1840–1921), newspaper editor. Born in Washington, D.C., on February 16, 1840, Watterson, son of a U.S. congressman from Tennessee, had little formal education. Poor sight in his right eye, which later became blind, ended his musical studies and a possible career as a pianist. In 1858 he left Tennessee for New York City, where he was briefly a reporter on the *New York Times* before returning to Washington to join the staff of the *Daily States*. Although he was a Unionist and drawn to the views of Abraham Lincoln, his sectional sympathies led him to join the Confederate army in 1861. He was attached to the staffs of generals Nathan Bedford Forrest, John Bell Hood, and Leonidas Polk; was chief of scouts for Gen. Joseph E. Johnston in the Atlanta Campaign, and for a time in 1863–1864 he edited the *Rebel* in Chattanooga. At war's end he was running a newspaper in Montgomery, Alabama. After editorial stints in Cincinnati and Nashville, he became an editor of the *Louisville Daily Journal*, which in 1868 he merged with the competing *Courier* and *Democrat*. Under his editorship, the *Louisville Courier-Journal* became one of the nation's best-known newspapers. His editorials were carried by telegraph across the country and considered news in their own right. Watterson's complete integrity made the paper a leading influence in the South. In his editorials, he called for national reunification and to that end he advocated civil rights for Negroes and the restoration of home rule in the South; he joined Carl Schurz and Horace Greeley in the unsuccessful Liberal Republican campaign of 1872; and it was he who built up Samuel J. Tilden, "the ideal statesman," who won the Democratic presidential nomination in 1876. He filled a congressional vacancy in order to serve as Tilden's floor leader in the House, 1876–1877, until Rutherford B. Hayes was finally certified as president by the Electoral Commission after the disputed election. He sharply criticized Grover Cleveland, disapproved of William Jennings Bryan and free silver, crusaded against "the man on horseback" Theodore Roosevelt, and did not support Woodrow Wilson until 1916; he later disagreed with Wilson over the League of Nations. In 1917 he won a Pulitzer Prize for his editorials favoring U.S. entry into World War I. *"Marse Henry:" An Autobiography*, taking its title from the affectionate nickname by which Watterson in his later years was known nationwide, appeared in two volumes in 1919. In 1918 he sold his interest in the *Courier-Journal* and became "editor emeritus," a title he relinquished to retire completely the next year. He died in Jacksonville, Florida, on December 22, 1921. *The Editorials of Henry Watterson* were collected by Arthur Krock in 1923.

Watts, Alan Witson (1915–1973), philosopher. Born in Chislehurst, England, on January 6, 1915, Alan Watts attended King's School at Canterbury. Early in life he developed an interest in the cultures and religions of the Far East that led eventually to his becoming one of the foremost interpreters of Oriental thought in the United States. His first book, *The Spirit of Zen*, appeared in 1936, when he was twenty-one. He edited *The Middle Way* magazine in London from 1934 to 1938. In 1939 he came to the United States and attended Seabury-Western Theological Seminary in Evanston, Illinois, earning a master's degree in 1948. He was ordained in the Protestant Episcopal Church in 1944 and served as a chaplain at Northwestern University until 1950, when he left the church. He taught comparative philosophy and psychology at the College of the Pacific from 1951 to 1957. Except for brief institutional ties, Watts occupied himself thereafter in lecturing and writing. He was a research fellow at Harvard from 1962 to 1964, a visiting instructor at San Jose State College in California in 1968, and a research consultant at the Maryland Psychiatric Research Center in 1969; he also appeared as a guest lecturer at many other institutions. In his writings he continued to pursue his interest in the religions and philosophies of Asia, while refusing to tie himself dogmatically to any religious position. Among his books after 1950 were *The Wisdom of Insecurity*, 1951; *Myth and Ritual in Christianity*, 1954; *Nature, Man, and Woman*, 1958; *Two Hands of God*, 1963; *Beyond Theology*, 1964; and *The Book on the Taboo Against Knowing Who You Are*, 1966. Perhaps his most influential work was *The Way of Zen*, 1957, whose publication coincided with the emergence of the "beat generation." The "beats" took a definite, if often ill-formed, interest in Zen Buddhism, and this interest carried on into the youth culture of the 1960s. Watts thus found himself in the vanguard of an amorphous movement whose mantle of leadership he did not altogether welcome. In a critique of faulty understandings of Zen, he published in 1958 an essay, "Beat Zen, Square Zen, and Zen," in which he attempted to disentangle the authentic from the popular interpretations of Zen Buddhism. Watts died in Mill Valley, California, on November 16, 1973.

Wayland, Francis (1796–1865), educator. Born in New York City on March 11, 1796, Wayland graduated from Union College in Schenectady in 1813 and for the next four years studied medicine in Troy, New York, and theology at Andover

Theological Seminary. He was a tutor at Union College from 1817 until 1821, when he was ordained, and from that date until 1826 was pastor of the First Baptist Church of Boston. He returned to Union as professor of mathematics and natural philosophy for one year, but in 1827 was named president of Brown University, holding the position until his retirement in 1855. During his administration he greatly improved the curriculum at Brown, introducing electives, improving methods of teaching, developing the library, and emphasizing the teaching of science. He wrote popular textbooks on ethics and economics and also two influential works on educational theory, *Thoughts on the Present Collegiate System in the United States,* 1842, and *Report to the Corporation of Brown University,* 1850. These works urged and argued for educational reforms that were widely adopted, although not at Brown. He wrote the plan for the Rhode Island public school system, was a prime mover in the development of free public libraries, and interested himself in prison reform, a national university, and the work of the Baptist Church. During the short-lived Dorr's Rebellion of 1842 in Rhode Island, Wayland was one of the leaders of the "law-and-order" group that finally won out over the "People's Party" of Thomas Wilson Dorr. Wayland died in Providence on September 30, 1865; his son, also named Francis (1826–1904), served for 30 years as dean of the Yale Law School, 1873–1903.

Wayne, Anthony (1745–1796), soldier. Born at Wayneboro, in Chester County, Pennsylvania, on January 1, 1745, Wayne left school after two years at the Philadelphia Academy. He worked as a surveyor for several years and helped his father run the family farm and tannery. He served in the Pennsylvania assembly in 1774–1775, and when the Revolutionary War began was commissioned a colonel in the 4th Pennsylvania Battalion. In February 1777 he was commissioned a brigadier general. He saw duty throughout the whole of the war and was involved in many significant actions, including the battle of Three Rivers in Quebec during the American retreat from Canada, the defense of Philadelphia, the battles of Brandywine and Germantown in the autumn of 1777, the winter at Valley Forge in 1777–1778, and the battle of Monmouth in June 1778, in which he led the attack. Two particular exploits brought him fame during the war. In July 1779 he stormed and took Stony Point on the Hudson River, the northernmost British defense post, in a brilliantly executed maneuver that resulted in negligible casualties on either side but gave a huge boost in morale to the American army. And in September 1780 he forestalled British seizure of West Point, after Benedict Arnold's betrayal of the post, by moving in reinforcements. On account of his tactical boldness and his personal courage in the field (which some fellow officers called recklessness), Wayne was often called "Mad Anthony," but his worth

was recognized on all sides and for his Stony Point exploit he received the congratulations of Gen. George Washington and the Continental Congress and a medal was struck in his honor. From 1781–1783 he fought in the Southern theater of war under the Marquis de Lafayette and later under Gen. Nathanael Greene and was largely responsible for liberating Georgia from the British. He also helped pacify the Creek and Cherokee Indians of the region. Following the war he retired to private life and divided his time between Pennsylvania and Georgia, where the grateful state had given him an 847-acre rice plantation. He served in the Pennsylvania assembly during 1784–1785, then settled on his Georgia plantation, which proved to be a losing venture for him. He voted for the new Constitution as a member of the Pennsylvania ratifying convention in 1788 and, after moving South, was elected to the House of Representatives from Georgia in 1790 but served only until March 21, 1792, when his seat was declared vacant owing to irregularities in the election. In 1792 President Washington called Wayne back into military service, with the rank of major general, to deal with Indian troubles in the Ohio Valley. The Indians had been on the warpath there intermittently since the close of the last French and Indian War, and incitements to fresh hostilities were given them by the continued existence of British forts in the West. Wayne spent months preparing for his campaign. He marched his troops into the Ohio country in 1793 and built an outpost, Fort Greenville, where he wintered and trained his soldiers in 1793–1794. He did not enter into battle until the summer of 1794. In the first engagement Wayne's forces beat off an attack at Fort Recovery in June, after which Wayne moved north and built Fort Defiance on the Maumee River. The decisive engagement of the campaign was the brief battle of Fallen Timbers in Ohio on August 20; there much of the Indians' will to fight was lost when they realized the British would not aid them. Gradually Wayne pacified the whole region, built Fort Wayne in present-day Indiana, and in 1795 gathered together the chiefs of the several tribes and dictated the terms of the treaty of Greenville, which opened part of the old Northwest to settlement. He spent the winter of 1795–1796 in Philadelphia, then was sent West again to take possession for the United States of the forts the British were abandoning according to the terms of Jay's Treaty. He died at Presque Isle (now Erie), Pennsylvania, on December 15, 1796, while carrying out this mission.

Wayne, James Moore (1790–1867), justice of the Supreme Court. Born in Savannah, Georgia, in 1790, Wayne graduated from the College of New Jersey (now Princeton) in 1808. After two years of studying law he was admitted to the bar in 1810 and began practice in Savannah. During the War of 1812 he saw service with the Georgia Hussars, and following the conflict he was elected to a term in the state legislature for 1815–1816. From

1817 to 1819 he served as mayor of Savannah, and for the following three years was judge of the court of common pleas in the city. In 1822 he was appointed a judge of the superior court in Savannah, a post he held until his election to the House of Representatives in 1828. He was elected to the House as a Jackson Democrat and in his three terms was a staunch supporter of President Andrew Jackson on most issues. As a reward for his political loyalty, Jackson appointed him an associate justice of the U.S. Supreme Court in 1835. He remained on the Court for 32 years; when the Civil War came, although a Southerner, he declared for the Union and remained on the bench. He is remembered as a justice primarily for his opinions in admiralty cases. When he died in Washington, D.C., on July 5, 1867, he was the last surviving associate on the Supreme Court of Chief Justice John Marshall, and Wayne's death thus brought to an end one of the greatest eras in American judicial history.

Wayne, John (1907–1979), actor. Born in Winterset, Iowa, on May 26, 1907, Marion Michael Morrison grew up there and in Southern California. He attended the University of Southern California for two years on a football scholarship, and it was while in college that he obtained a summer job working as a prop man at the Fox movie studios. A football injury caused him to drop out of college, but he stayed on at the studio and in 1929 was given a part in a Western entitled *The Big Trail*. After making his first few pictures under the name Duke Morrison, he changed his name to John Wayne in the early 1930s. His first ten years in films were spent in making one "B" Western after another. He did not achieve star status until he was cast in John Ford's *Stagecoach*, 1939, the movie that lifted Westerns generally out of the "B" category. As he continued to appear in one picture after another, Wayne emerged in the early 1950s as one of Hollywood's main box-office attractions. Most often he played the role of a cowboy or a military man, and his typical movies had plots and characterizations that distinguished clearly between the "good guys" and the "bad guys," leaving little room for ambiguity. Among his better-known Westerns were *Tall in the Saddle* 1944; *Fort Apache*, 1948; *Red River*, 1948; *Rio Grande*, 1950; *Hondo*, 1954; *The Alamo*, 1960, which he directed; and *El Dorado*, 1966. He played military roles in *Flying Tigers*, 1942; *They Were Expendable*, 1945; *Sands of Iwo Jima*, 1949, for which he was nominated for an Academy Award; *Jet Pilot*, 1952; *Wings of Eagles*, 1956; *The Longest Day*, 1962; and *The Green Berets*, 1967. Among the many pictures he made that fitted neither of these categories were *The Long Voyage Home*, 1940; *Reap the Wild Wind*, 1942; *A Lady Takes a Chance*, a 1943 comedy; and *The Quiet Man*, 1952. In 1969 he won an Academy Award as best actor for his performance in *True Grit*, in which he played a hardbitten marshal in frontier Arkansas. His last film was *The Shootist*, 1976. He died on June 11, 1979, in Los Angeles.

A week before, Congress authorized a special gold medal in his honor.

Weaver, James Baird (1833–1912), political leader. Born in Dayton, Ohio, on June 12, 1833, Weaver was raised on farms amid the forests of Michigan and on the prairies of Iowa; he attended school in Bloomfield, Iowa, and worked as a mail carrier for four years. In 1853 he went to California but was cured of his "gold fever" in a few months. Returning to Iowa, he worked in a store in Bonaparte but refused a partnership in order to attend the Cincinnati Law School, 1855–1856. After graduation he began practicing law in Bloomfield. He had been a Democrat, but he was attracted to Free-Soil principles and from 1857 to the outbreak of the Civil War was active in local Republican circles. When President Abraham Lincoln called for troops in 1861 he volunteered. He fought at Fort Donelson, Shiloh, and Corinth, rising from the rank of first lieutenant to colonel. At the end of his enlistment in 1864 he returned to Iowa and was given the honorary rank of brigadier general the following year. He failed in an attempt to obtain the nomination for lieutenant governor in 1865. Although he was elected district attorney of the 2nd Iowa judicial district in 1866 and was a federal assessor of internal revenue from 1867 to 1873, he continued to lose ground with state Republican leaders, for he was an ardent prohibitionist, denounced the politically powerful railroads and predatory corporations, and strenuously objected to his party's stand on the currency question. He was outmaneuvered in an attempt to get the Republican nomination for a seat in the House of Representatives in 1874 and for governor in 1875. Running as a Greenbacker, he won election to the House in 1878 and was the presidential candidate of the Greenback party in 1880. Defeated for the House in 1882, he was reelected in 1884 and 1886. When the Farmers' Alliance succeeded the Greenbackers as the chief exponent of soft-money views, he led in transforming the Alliance groups into the Populist party. As the Populists' presidential candidate in 1892, he won more than a million popular votes and 22 votes in the electoral college. The fusion of the Populist party with the Democrats left him and other Populist leaders without a political future. In his *Call to Action*, 1892, he set forth his political principles as one of the first "progressives;" virtually all of the social and industrial legislation he called for was eventually enacted into law. In 1896 he supported William Jennings Bryan for the presidency and exerted his influence to give the Populist nomination to Bryan, the Democratic candidate. From 1904 to 1906 he was mayor of Colfax, Iowa. He died in Des Moines, Iowa, on February 6, 1912.

Weaver, Robert Clifton (1907–   ), economist and public official. Born in Washington, D.C., on December 29, 1907, Weaver graduated from Harvard in 1929 and took his Ph.D. in economics there in 1934. He was one of the many black advisers brought into the federal administration during the New Deal years by Harold L. Ickes, secretary of the interior. Weaver served in the administration of President Franklin D. Roosevelt from 1933 until 1944—an adviser to Ickes (1933–1937), with the U.S. Housing Authority (1937–1940), on the Advisory Commission to the Council of National Defense as assistant to Sidney Hillman (1940), and on various World War II government boards until 1944. As one of several members of Roosevelt's "black cabinet" Weaver kept the administration advised on racial issues in employment and housing. Following World War II he served with the United Nations Relief and Rehabilitation Administration (UNRRA) for a short time and also taught economics at several colleges. In 1949 he was appointed director of the opportunity fellowship program of the John Hay Whitney Foundation and served until 1955, when he was appointed New York State Rent Commissioner during the administration of Governor Averell Harriman. In December 1960 President-elect John F. Kennedy appointed Weaver to administer the Housing and Home Finance Agency; this was the highest post a black American had ever held in the executive branch of the government. Kennedy urged Congress to create a Department of Housing and Urban Development (HUD) with a head of cabinet rank, hoping to appoint Weaver to that post, but action on the proposal was blocked, largely by Southern congressmen, during Kennedy's term. Under President Lyndon B. Johnson, Congress finally did enact the bill setting up HUD and Weaver was appointed its first secretary, becoming the first Negro to serve in the cabinet; he retained the post until January 1969. With a change in administrations he left office to become president of Bernard M. Baruch College in New York City. Weaver was a civil-rights activist from his New Deal days, urging equal opportunity for blacks in employment, housing, and education. As a vocal opponent of gradualism or tokenism, he helped guide legislation favorable to the goal of equality through Congress and was influential in winning executive action on matters such as fair employment that did not require congressional approval. He wrote a number of books on the social and economic issues that confront blacks in the United States, among them *Negro Labor: A National Problem*, 1946; *The Negro Ghetto*, 1948; and *Dilemmas of Urban America*, 1965. He also wrote many articles.

Weber, Max (1881–1961), painter. Born in Bialystok, Russia (now in Poland) on April 18, 1881, Weber came with his family to the United States in 1891 and lived in Brooklyn, New York. He studied art at the Pratt Institute, graduating in 1900, and then taught art at the college level for a few years. In 1905 he left for a stay of several years in Europe to continue his own studies. There he became acquainted with some of the leading modernists, including Pablo Picasso and Henri Rousseau, and studied under Jean-Paul Laurens and Henri Matisse. He returned to the United States in 1908, an exponent of modern styles of painting, but it was many years before he received acclaim, neither the American public nor the critics showing any enthusiasm for his work. His first one-man show was in 1911 at Alfred Stieglitz's 291 Gallery, and it was almost unanimously denounced. He continued to paint, but for the next dozen years rarely exhibited his works. Weber taught at the Art Students League in New York City during 1920–1921 and 1926–1927. Only as the U.S. art world began to appreciate the works of other modernists did Weber gradually win recognition. No museum purchased a work of his until 1926, but within a few years after that several of his paintings were on display. In 1928 the Art Institute of Chicago awarded him the Potter Palmer Gold Medal and two years later the Museum of Modern Art in New York City had a retrospective exhibition of his work. During the 1930s Weber was gradually recognized as the pioneer and dean of modern art in the United States. His works were more frequently exhibited and purchased, and as he approached sixty he was finally able to make a living from his painting. In February 1941 the Associated American Artists honored him with the largest exhibit of his work to that time. As a painter, Weber's work was varied, ranging from still lifes to action paintings; often he depicted Hebraic religious scenes, and he was adept in the use of symbolism. His style changed over the years, moving from impressionism to cubism and fauvism to abstract. He was remarkably sensitive to new techniques and aesthetic doctrines and was influential in keeping American artists and art critics abreast of European developments. He published a number of books, including *Camera Work*, 1910; *Cubist Poems*, 1914; *Essays on Art*, 1916; *Primitives*, 1926; and *Woodcuts*, 1957. By the end of his life his paintings were in every major museum in the country and in many private collections. He died in Great Neck, New York, on October 4, 1961.

Webster, Daniel (1782–1852), lawyer and public official. Born in Salisbury, New Hampshire, on January 18, 1782, Webster received only rudimentary schooling, but his father, through great sacrifice, sent him to Phillips Exeter Academy and to Dartmouth College, where he graduated in 1801. While at Dartmouth he acquired, because of his swarthy complexion, the nickname "Black Dan." He studied law with a Salisbury firm and, after a time teaching in an academy in Fryeburg, Maine, was admitted to the Boston bar in 1805. Family obligations forced his return to New Hampshire and he began practicing law in Portsmouth in 1807. He promptly won distinction and developed a successful practice as champion of New England shipping interests during the war between England and France. He voiced the Federalist opposition to President Thomas Jefferson's policies in *Considerations on the Embargo Laws*, 1808. His speeches opposing the War of 1812—but opposing also the extremists who called for New England secession—earned him a seat in the House of Representatives as a Federalist from New Hampshire, 1813–1817. He afterward restricted himself to law practice in Boston and to delivering addresses on public occasions that earned him a reputation as one the great American orators of all time. He appeared before the Supreme Court in the Dartmouth College Case in 1818 ("It is, as I have said, a small college," he urged in his closing peroration, "and yet there are those who love it."); *McCulloch* v. *Maryland*, 1819; *Gibbons* v. *Ogden*, 1824; and *Ogden* v. *Saunders*, 1827. He returned to politics in 1823, representing Massachusetts in the House and voting for John Quincy Adams for president in 1824, and in 1827 was elected to the Senate. As the aggressive spokesman of Massachusetts industry, he clashed with Southern leaders who wanted low tariffs for the sake of their cotton-and-slave economy. He was, however, no sectionalist. In January 1830 he clashed with Robert Y. Hayne of South Carolina in a great debate on that point. Webster's speech known as the *Reply to Hayne* closed with the famed invocation: "Liberty *and* Union, now and forever, one and inseparable!" He thus set himself in direct opposition to John C. Calhoun, apostle of states' rights. Webster became a leading political figure, supporting President Andrew Jackson in the election of 1832 and standing with him against South Carolina's nullification of the tariff. But he had many disagreements with the President, particularly on fiscal policies and the issue of rechartering the Bank of the United States, a legal client of Webster, and with Henry Clay he became a leader of the Whig party. In 1836 he was the presidential candidate of the New England Whigs, but he won only the vote of the Massachusetts delegation. He returned to the Senate until President William Henry Harrison appointed him secretary of state in 1841. Webster, alone of the Whigs, stayed on in the cabinet after John Tyler became president that same year, after Harrison's death. He completed the negotiation of the Webster-Ashburton Treaty (1842), settling the northeast boundary between the United States and Canada, before resigning in 1843. He returned to the Senate in 1845, where he opposed the annexation of Texas and the war with Mexico and supported the Wilmot Proviso. His belief that the evil of disunion was worse than the evil of slavery finally led to his support of the Compromise of 1850, which lost him the support of antislavery advocates in his own party; they denounced the once-honored hero of New England as "Black Dan Webster." Passed over in favor of Zachary Taylor for the presidential nomination in 1848, he again became secretary of state in 1850, in which post he championed the government's right to recognize the new Hungarian republic and other popular governments. In 1852 poor health forced him to return to his home in Marshfield, Massachusetts, where he died on October 24. He was elected to the Hall of Fame in 1900.

Webster, Noah (1758–1843), lexicographer. Born in West Hartford, Connecticut, on October 16, 1758, Webster was the son of a farmer and descendant of a Connecticut governor. He entered Yale in 1774

and, after serving briefly in the Revolutionary War, graduated in 1778. He taught school and did clerical work while studying law and was admitted to the bar in 1781. In the following year, while teaching in Goshen, New York, his dissatisfaction with the existing texts for children led him to write *The American Spelling Book*, 1783, the first part of *A Grammatical Institute of the English Language*. He completed the *Institute* with a grammar, 1784, and a reader, 1785. Webster's principle that "grammar is formed on language, and not language on grammar" anticipated the modern doctrine of usage. A fervent nationalist, he instituted spelling reforms that were largely responsible for the differences between American and British spelling. The difficulty in copyrighting his work in 13 states led to his support of the Federalist cause and to his lobbying, from 1782 until its enactment in 1790, for a national copyright law. Other early writings included *Sketches of American Policy*, 1785, and *Dissertations on the English Language*, 1789. The *American Magazine*, which he founded in New York City in 1787, was short-lived, and after practicing law in Hartford he returned to New York City in 1793 to found and edit the *American Minerva*, a Federalist daily newspaper, and the *Herald*, a semiweekly, also Federalist. He sold both papers in 1803 when the income from his speller allowed him to retire from journalism. He had moved to New Haven in 1798 and there he brought out the *Compendious Dictionary of the English Language*, 1806, recording nonliterary words as well as "Americanisms" in a work that included 5000 words not included in previous dictionaries. But he considered it only preparatory to the *American Dictionary of the English Language*, on which he labored steadily for 20 years and which was finally published in 1828. The great work, containing entries for some 70,000 words, was received as a scholarly achievement of the first order in the United States and abroad. In 1833 he published for American readers a revision of the Authorized Version of the English Bible. Besides his many publications and revisions in the field of lexicography, other writings added to his reputation. His *Brief History of Epidemic and Pestilential Diseases*, 1799, was a standard medical work of the day. Webster's political writings included the "Curtius" articles on Jay's Treaty in 1795; the "Aristides" letter to Hamilton, 1800; *Ten Letters to Dr. Joseph Priestley*, 1800; and essays on economics, agriculture, and scientific topics. His *Experiments Respecting Dew*, 1809, a pioneer work in the physical sciences, foreshadowed work of later census and weather bureaus. In 1812 he moved to Amherst, Massachusetts. He served in the Massachusetts legislature in 1815 and again in 1819 and in 1821 he helped to found Amherst College. He was also a founder of the Connecticut Academy of Arts and Sciences. In 1822 he returned to New Haven, Connecticut, where he died on May 28, 1843. For generations his speller, popularly known as the "blue-backed speller," was used to teach children to read; annual sales passed the 1 million mark by 1850, and by 1890 more than 60 million had been sold. The rights to his dictionary were purchased from his estate by Charles and George Merriam, and their G. & C. Merriam Company continued thereafter to issue Webster's dictionaries. But, ironically, considering Webster's efforts to obtain a copyright law, his name went into the public domain and was later affixed to many reference works with which he had had nothing whatever to do.

Weed, Thurlow (1797–1882), journalist and political leader. Born on November 15, 1797, in Cairo, New York, Weed had little formal education but his newspaper work, which began when he was twelve, provided a thorough schooling in political affairs. For many years he was a journalist and printer and traveled throughout the state until he settled in a position with the *Rochester Telegraph* in 1822. Two years later he was sent as a lobbyist to the state capital at Albany and there set about effecting a union of political factions opposed to Martin Van Buren's "Albany Regency." Later he stumped western New York for John Quincy Adams and was himself elected to the legislature. He bought the *Telegraph* in 1825; a year later, however, he joined the rising tide of anti-Masonic sentiment and began a new journal, the *Anti-Masonic Enquirer*. He soon became the principal leader of the Anti-Masonic party and saw to it that its candidates were, when possible, drawn from the ranks of the National Republicans. In 1829 he was again elected to the legislature and in 1830 began publishing the *Albany Evening Journal* as a party organ. With William H. Seward he realized that the Anti-Masonic party was too narrowly based to become a national organization; accordingly he began slowly reorienting it along anti-Jacksonian lines and soon merged it into the newly formed coalition constituting the Whig party. He converted his newspaper to the new doctrine and his influence, preeminent in New York State, grew to national proportions. He eschewed office himself, preferring to manage affairs from the background; he took a liberal view of the corrupt methods of political maneuver and was a master of all of them, yet is said to have been himself personally incorruptible. He helped Seward win the governorship in 1838 and William Henry Harrison, the presidency in 1840. Weed began grooming Zachary Taylor for the White House as early as 1846, and he managed to install his long-time follower Millard Fillmore in the vice-presidency. After the Whigs split over the Compromise of 1850 he went with Seward, then in the Senate, into the new Republican party, formed in 1854, and six years later managed Seward's unsuccessful bid for the presidential nomination. Early in Abraham Lincoln's administration he was often consulted on appointments to government posts. In 1861 he was sent by Seward, then secretary of state, as a special agent to England to conciliate public opinion there and in France following the *Trent* affair. By 1863, with the Radicals ascendant, he found himself estranged from his party; he sold the *Evening Journal* and

retired from politics. His influence declined abruptly after the 1864 election and his support of Andrew Johnson's Reconstruction policies killed it outright. Moving to New York City in the same year, he edited for a time the *New York Commercial Advertiser* but remained out of public affairs. He died on November 22, 1882, in New York City.

Weems, Mason Locke (1759–1825), "Parson Weems," author and bookseller. Born in Anne Arundel County, Maryland, near Herring Bay, on October 11, 1759, Weems may have attended the University of Edinburgh as a medical student in 1777–1779, although little is known of his early years. He studied for the ministry in England and was ordained a priest in the Anglican church in September 1784. He served Episcopal parishes in Maryland from 1784 until 1792 but thereafter, although he preached occasionally and continued to consider himself a clergyman (he was known as "Parson Weems"), he was engaged in writing, publishing, and bookselling for the rest of his life. He edited and published the works of other clergymen and issued many of his own pamphlets on moral self-improvement. After 1795 he made his home in Dumfries, Virginia. In 1794 he went into business as agent for publisher Mathew Carey of Philadelphia and worked with him for the rest of his life. He traveled throughout most of the Atlantic seaboard from New York to Georgia, selling Carey's books and frequently purveying his own religious-patriotic-moralistic pamphlets and his almanacs, and eventually selling his own full-length books as well. His first and major work was *The Life and Memorable Actions of George Washington*, 1800, usually known as "Parson Weems' *Life of George Washington*," which has gone through numerous editions up to the present. It was a fictionalized and effusively laudatory biography of the first president, written to hold Washington up as a moral and political example for all Americans to emulate. It was in the book's fifth edition in 1808, under the revised title *The Life of George Washington*, that the famous account of the cherry tree and the hatchet appeared. This volume was Weems's most successful work; in spite of criticism it became a best seller at the time and remained so for the rest of the century; by his death it had gone through 29 editions. He also wrote biographies of Gen. Francis Marion, Benjamin Franklin, and William Penn, but none matched his *Washington* in popularity. He died in Beaufort, South Carolina, on May 23, 1825.

Weill, Kurt (1900–1950), composer. Born in Dessau, Germany, on March 2, 1900, Weill was the son of a Jewish cantor and occasional composer from whom he received his first musical training. At eighteen he entered the Staatliche Hochschule für Musik in Berlin, where his teachers included Engelbert Humperdinck. He left the school after a year to acquire practical experience as a theatrical coach in Dessau and as a director at the Ludenscheid Opera House, but in 1921 he returned to Berlin to resume formal musical studies under Ferruccio Busoni, with whom he remained for three years. Weill's early compositions were in the main instrumental works of a highly modernist, abstract nature, but his deep interest in the theater led to a collaboration with playwright Georg Kaiser on a one-act opera, *Der Protagonist*, which opened at the Dresden State Opera House in 1926 and was a considerable success. Two more similar works, *Na Und?*, 1926, and *Royal Palace*, 1927, were poorly received, but in the latter year he teamed with Bertolt Brecht on a one-act *Singspiel*, or song-play, entitled *Mahagonny*, which was a huge *succès de scandale* at the Baden-Baden Festival. The song-play, combining Brecht's sharp, satiric commentary on man and society with Weill's entrancing music full of jazz-inspired arrangements and exotic dance rhythms, firmly established Weill as a leading composer of theater music; it was revived in 1930 in an expanded three-act version as *Aufsteig und Fall der Stadt Mahagonny* ("The Rise and Fall of the City of Mahagonny"). In 1928 Weill and Brecht presented a startling new work, *Die Dreigroschenoper*, a musical transposition of John Gay's *The Beggar's Opera* into the social ferment of the Weimar Republic. Brilliant, rowdy, sardonic, the play featured musical styles ranging from the classical through foxtrot pieces to blues and even a shimmy number. It was a huge success all over Europe; in its first year it was performed more than 4000 times in over a hundred theaters. Lotte Lenya, whom Weill had married in 1926, starred in the role of Jenny. With *Die Dreigroschenoper* Weill was recognized as the leading composer of *Gebrauchmusik*, "practical music," and his vision of a musical theater that avoided both the pomposity of grand opera and the irrelevance of musical comedy was realized. With Brecht he also wrote *Der Jasager* ("The Yea-Sayer"), 1930, a students' opera, and *Der Lindberghflug* ("The Lindbergh Flight"), 1930, a cantata to which Paul Hindemith also contributed; with Casper Neher he wrote *Die Bürgschaft* ("The Surety"), 1933, and with Georg Kaiser, *Silver Lake*, 1933, which was performed only once before the new Nazi regime in Germany proscribed all of Weill's music. He and Lotte fled to Paris. There, for George Balanchine's Les Ballets company, he wrote the music for *Die sieben Todstunden* ("The Seven Deadly Sins"), 1933, which was successful in Paris and, under the title *Anna Anna*, in London. Weill later moved to London and in 1935 he came to the United States, where he remained for the rest of his life; he became a U.S. citizen in 1943. American audiences had already heard some of his work, notably in a poorly received 1933 production of *Die Dreigroschenoper* as *The Threepenny Opera*, but his first new works in the United States were only partially successful—music for Paul Green's *Johnny Johnson*, 1936, and for Franz Werfel's pageant of Jewish history, *The Eternal Road*, 1937. After a brief period in Hollywood writing music for such films as *Blockade*, 1938, and *You and Me*, 1938, Weill returned to Broadway to collaborate with Maxwell Anderson on

Knickerbocker Holiday, 1938, a hit musical in which Walter Huston introduced one of Weill's most popular songs, "September Song." Subsequently he worked with Moss Hart and Ira Gershwin on *Lady in the Dark*, 1941, with Ogden Nash on *One Touch of Venus*, 1943, and again with Gershwin on *Firebrand of Florence*, 1945, Weill's last attempt at standard musical comedy. Thereafter he returned to the musical-theater form he had created earlier, producing *Street Scene*, 1947, with Elmer Rice from Rice's 1929 play; *Love Life*, 1948, with Alan Jay Lerner; and *Lost in the Stars*, 1949, with Maxwell Anderson. A folk opera, *Down in the Valley*, 1948, gained a lasting popularity. Weill died in New York City on April 3, 1950. In 1954 a new English version of *The Threepenny Opera* by Marc Blitzstein began a record-breaking run in New York City; Weill's music continued to delight listeners and to exert a strong influence on many contemporary composers.

Weinstein, Nathan Wallenstein, *see* West, Nathanael

Weis, Isaac Mayer, *see* Wise, Isaac Mayer

Weiser, Conrad (1696–1760), Indian agent. Born near Herrenberg, Germany, on November 2, 1696, Johann Conrad Weiser emigrated with his family to the colony of New York in 1710 and settled at Livingston Manor on the Hudson River. There they lived among other Palatine Germans who had been brought to America by the British to become manufacturers of naval stores. When this enterprise failed, Weiser led many of the German families to the vicinity of Schoharie, New York, to become farmers. In 1729 he moved to Tulpehocken, in what later became Berks County, Pennsylvania, where he bought a farm that he maintained for the rest of his life. Weiser's experience on the frontier had frequently brought him into contact with the Indians, particularly the tribes of the Iroquois Confederacy. He learned their dialects, lived among, and traded with them; and by the time of his locating at Tulpehocken, he was an experienced interpreter; he was often called upon by Pennsylvania officials to help in dealings with the Indians. Weiser was especially aware of the need to maintain the friendship of the Iroquois for the English in order to halt attempts of the French to control the trans-Appalachian region. He arranged formal conferences in Philadelphia in 1731 and 1736 to form such an alliance, and he helped to negotiate several treaties with the Indians to maintain peace, help secure the colonial frontier, and gain accessions of land for white settlers. The support of the Iroquois was also gained for the English in King George's War. The treaty of Logstown in 1748 helped to open up the Western territories for trade as far as the Mississippi River. After 1748 his influence as an agent declined as Sir William Johnson and George Croghan shaped more of the colonial policy toward the Indians. But Weiser remained a valuable interpreter and local mediator and did assist at the treaty of Easton in 1758 by which the 1754 land cession by the Iroquois of the Susquehanna Valley to the British was negated and the region secured for the Delaware Indians. From the mid-1730s much of Weiser's time was devoted to the religious groups to which he belonged. He joined the community of Seventh-Day Baptists and lived with them at the Ephrata Cloisters for several years. In 1747 he became a Lutheran, after his daughter had married the influential Henry Melchior Mühlenberg. In the mid-1750s he switched to the German Reformed church. As a prominent member of the German community in Pennsylvania, Weiser served from time to time in various elected posts, including that of first president-judge of Berks County from 1752 to 1760 and as a colonel of militia, with which he served in the French and Indian War, when again he worked to gain the support of the Iroquois. He died in Womelsdorf, Pennsylvania, on July 13, 1760.

Weiss, Ehrich, *see* Houdini, Harry

Weissmuller, Johnny (1904–   ), swimmer and actor. Born in Windber, Somerset County, Pennsylvania, on June 2, 1904, Weissmuller grew up there and in Chicago. In the 1920s, during nearly ten years of competition, he became the best all-round swimmer the United States had produced and was undefeated in Amateur Athletic Union (AAU) contests in 1922 and 1923 and at the Olympics of 1924 and 1928. Before he retired, after the 1928 Olympics, he had won 52 national championships, 3 Olympic gold medals, and set 67 world records. He competed in events from the 50-yard free style to the 800-meter free-style relay, and many of his records endured for more than 20 years. After retiring from amateur competition as one of the notable sports figures of the 1920s, Weissmuller capitalized on his great fame by going into the movies in the role of Tarzan, Edgar Rice Burroughs's famous creation. He had a screen test in 1930 and a year later made his first film, *Tarzan the Ape Man.* He played the Tarzan role in 19 films over 18 years, and then in 1947, when the studio decided to cast a younger man in the part, switched to playing Jungle Jim; in that part he made 16 films over the next 7 years. In 1956 he retired from the movies to devote his time to various business ventures. In 1950 Weissmuller was selected by the Associated Press as the greatest swimmer of the half-century.

Welch, Joseph Nye (1890–1960), lawyer. Born in Primghar, Iowa, on October 22, 1890, Welch graduated from Grinnell College in 1914 and from the Harvard Law School three years later. Admitted to the Massachusetts bar in 1918, he became within a very few years a noted trial lawyer, dealing mostly in civil cases. Welch first gained national fame in 1954 as special counsel for the U.S. army in the congressional Army-McCarthy hearings of that year. He was appointed counsel

for the army on April 2, and the hearings continued from April 22 until June 17. With many of the sessions televised—a recent innovation for congressional committee proceedings—the hearings became one of the most engrossing and sensational spectacles ever offered the American public. Since early 1950 Senator Joseph R. McCarthy of Wisconsin had been making allegations of subversion and treason in places high and low in American life, particularly in the federal government. Early in 1954, by that time chairman of the Senate's permanent investigations subcommittee, he turned his attention to the military, charging that there was a spy ring at work in the Army Signal Corps installation at Fort Monmouth, New Jersey. Eventually the case boiled down to that of a New York City dentist who had been drafted during the Korean War, promoted to the rank of major and given an honorable discharge, in spite of his having taken the Fifth Amendment when questioned about alleged Communist activities at an earlier period. McCarthy leveled an attack upon the general in command at Fort Monmouth, then at the army itself, alleging that the secretary of the army had concealed evidence of spying. Countercharges against McCarthy and his aides were filed, and the hearings themselves ranged at large over the topic of supposed subversion. For television viewers the affair dissolved into a contest between Senator McCarthy and Joseph Welch. McCarthy revealed himself as a master of vicious invective, irresponsible charges, and pointless vituperation, while Welch remained for the most part calm, logical, and occasionally cutting. Only after McCarthy made a particularly nasty accusation against one of Welch's assistants did the lawyer respond with the most memorable statement to come out of the sessions: "Until this moment, Senator, I think I never really gauged your cruelty or recklessness. . . . Have you no sense of decency, sir, at long last? Have you left no sense of decency?" The hearings were McCarthy's undoing, although he and his staff were cleared of the charges against them. On December 2, 1954, the Senate, by a vote of 67 to 22, passed a resolution of condemnation against him for misconduct, and his influence rapidly faded thereafter. The charges against the dentist were forgotten, and Welch returned to his law practice in Boston a national figure. Five years later he returned to public view playing the part of a trial judge in the 1959 movie, *Anatomy of a Murder.* He died in Hyannis, Massachusetts, on October 6, 1960.

Welch, Robert H. W., Jr. (1899–   ), candy manufacturer and political activist. Born in Chowan County, North Carolina, on December 1, 1899, Welch graduated from the University of North Carolina in 1916. He then spent two years at the U.S. Naval Academy and two years at Harvard Law School. In 1922 he joined his brothers in the candy-manufacturing business in Boston and remained with the company until 1957, when he retired to devote his time to politics. He had, in

1956, begun publishing a monthly magazine, *American Opinion*, which embraced a wide range of extreme right-wing political views, notably an obsessive anti-Communism. In 1958, in Indianapolis, he founded what became known in 1961 as the John Birch Society. (John Birch had been an army captain, operating as an intelligence officer of the Office of Strategic Services (OSS) in China, who was killed by the Chinese Communists in August 1945, ten days after the end of World War II; the society later acclaimed him "the first casualty of World War III.") Of the society's inner workings and actual membership little is known save that there are chapters in nearly every state. Its working premise is that Communism is the most serious threat facing the United States, but the threat is internal, not external. Welch maintained that Communist influences had penetrated every aspect of American life, particularly the federal government. In his 1963 book, *The Politician*, he charged that dozens of prominent Americans, including former presidents Franklin D. Roosevelt, Harry S. Truman, and Dwight D. Eisenhower, were conscious agents of the Communist conspiracy. In its ostensibly patriotic drive to remake the nation, the John Birch Society advocated abandoning involvement in the North Atlantic Treaty Organization (NATO), and the United Nations, abolishing the graduated income tax, the Supreme Court, and Social Security, ending foreign aid, dismantling veterans' hospitals and all civil-rights programs, lowering defense spending, and impeaching a number of liberal public officials. The heyday of the society was from 1963 until 1969, particularly 1964, when Senator Barry M. Goldwater was running for the presidency and received much support from "John Birchers." After President Richard M. Nixon took office the society was much less in the news, although Nixon's trips to China and Russia in 1972 brought protests against his dealings with the leading Communist powers. Some of Welch's later views disconcerted his followers, especially his announcement in the late 1960s that the Western world had been dominated since 1777 by a well-concealed conspiracy centering around a group of Bavarian monks known as the Society of the Illuminati, supposedly affiliated in some way with the Masonic order.

Welch, William Henry (1850–1934), physician and educator. Born on April 8, 1850, in Norfolk, Connecticut, the son and grandson of doctors, Welch graduated from Yale in 1870, spent a year at the Sheffield Scientific School there, and earned his M.D. in 1875 from the College of Physicians and Surgeons in New York City. He broadened his knowledge of the sciences and was inspired by many of the latest advances while studying in Germany until 1878 under leading medical scientists. Becoming professor of pathology and anatomy at the Bellevue Hospital Medical College in 1879, he developed the first pathology laboratory in the country. In 1884, after a further year in Europe studying bacteriology under Robert

Koch, among others, he began a long and distinguished career at The Johns Hopkins University in Baltimore, as professor in the newly created department of pathology. There he earned a reputation as a stimulating educator, influencing numerous outstanding associates in his laboratory, where he discovered, with G. H. F. Nuttall, the so-called "gas bacillus," *Clostridium welchi*, of the group of bacilli that are the cause of gas gangrene. He was influential in the founding of The Johns Hopkins Hospital in 1889 and the Medical School in 1893, of which he was the first dean. He recruited prominent men, including William Osler and William S. Halsted, to staff both institutions, which he developed into major teaching, research, and clinical centers. In 1896 he founded the first journal to publish the results of major medical research projects, the *Journal of Experimental Medicine*, which he edited until 1906. From 1916 to 1926 he was director of the new Johns Hopkins school of hygiene and public health, and in 1926 became the university's first professor of the history of medicine. In 1931 he retired. One of the most important and influential figures in U.S. medicine, he was active in scientific and medical associations and served as a consultant to research foundations, notably the Rockefeller Institute of Medical Research (now Rockefeller University), which he helped to establish, and the Carnegie Foundation for the Advancement of Teaching. He received honorary degrees from universities in the United States and abroad and many other awards. His published works included *Thrombosis and Embolism*, 1899, the result of some early research work; *Public Health in Theory and Practice: an Historical Review*, 1925; and three volumes of *Papers and Addresses*, edited by Walter C. Burket and published in 1920 in honor of Welch's seventieth birthday. He died in Baltimore on April 30, 1934.

Weld, Theodore Dwight (1803–1895), social reformer. Born in Hampton, Connecticut, on November 23, 1803, Weld grew up near Utica in western New York. Converted by the Presbyterian revivalist Charles Grandison Finney, he joined Finney's "holy band" of crusaders and preached primarily among the young men of New York State for two years. About 1825 he entered the Oneida Institute in Whitesboro, New York, to prepare for the ministry, and scores of his followers entered too. During vacations he spoke on behalf of temperance and traveled around the country as a representative of the Society for Promoting Manual Labor in Literary Institutions, which was sponsored by the philanthropists Arthur and Lewis Tappan, also patrons of Finney. Weld was brought into the antislavery movement about 1830, primarily through the English reformer Charles Stuart, a friend and patron since childhood. His first converts to abolitionism were the Tappans. He persuaded them to contribute to the Lane Theological Seminary, then being built in Cincinnati, and they secured Lyman Beecher as president in 1832. Weld entered Lane, bringing a large enrollment from the participants in Finney's crusade. In 1834 he organized the famous anti-slavery debates at the school, in which the students and Beecher's children, including Henry Ward and Harriet, participated. In the meantime the Tappans founded the American and Foreign Anti-Slavery Society and incurred much ill will and misunderstanding in a campaign for "immediate emancipation." Under fire from the trustees of Lane, who now forbade students to discuss the abolition of slavery, Weld was dismissed in late 1834 and he then led the majority of the student body to Oberlin College and set out to rouse popular support for the Society. Large numbers of Lane students were sent out as agents for the Society, while Weld, using Finney's revival methods, preached emancipation and won to the cause hundreds of advocates and workers, among them Angelina Grimké, whom he married in 1838. His voice broken from constant preaching, he resigned from the Society soon after his marriage and with his wife opened a series of schools in New Jersey and Massachusetts. He wrote *The Bible Against Slavery*, 1837, and *Slavery As It Is*, 1839, the latter providing inspiration for a part of Charles Dickens's *American Notes* and for Harriet Beecher Stowe's *Uncle Tom's Cabin*. In 1841–1843 he was successful in establishing an antislavery bloc among insurgents in the Whig party, who then were able to defeat the "gag rule" in the House of Representatives, illustrating the value of the lobby to abolitionism; his lobbying work in Washington was later continued by Lewis Tappan. As the antislavery movement spread to the West, its leaders were almost without exception Weld's followers or pupils. Called the "greatest abolitionist," he published nothing under his own name during his life, and he refused to seek or even acknowledge public acclaim. He died in Hyde Park (now in Boston), Massachusetts, on February 3, 1895.

Welk, Lawrence (1903–   ), entertainer. Born in the German immigrant community of Strasburg, North Dakota, on March 11, 1903, Welk had little formal schooling or musical training but learned to play the accordion from his father. He left home at twenty-one to become an entertainer and in 1927 formed his own small band that was soon broadcasting to rural audiences from a radio station in Yankton, South Dakota. For several years he played at dances and in vaudeville theaters in the upper Midwest until he was able to hire a larger band. During the late 1930s through the early 1950s, the era of the "big bands," Welk's fame increased as his orchestra played in all parts of the nation and his "North Dakota German" accent became well known through public appearances and radio broadcasts. In 1938, while working on a nationwide radio show from Pittsburgh, he dubbed his style "Champagne Music," and the term became his trademark; his theme song, which he composed, was aptly titled "Bubbles in the Wine." In 1951 he moved his show to the Aragon Ballroom at Ocean Park, California, near Los Angeles, and he began to be telecast locally. The program became so popular that it was put on network television by the American Broadcasting Company (ABC) in 1955. The Welk show ran continuously on ABC until 1970 with a loyal following among those old enough to remember the big bands and prefer the easy and melodious dance music his orchestra played. After ABC dropped the show Welk kept the program on the air over independent stations. He also continued to make personal-appearance tours around the country.

Weller, Thomas Huckle (1915–   ), physician and biologist. Born in Ann Arbor, Michigan, on June 15, 1915, Weller graduated from the University of Michigan in 1936 and from the Harvard Medical School in 1940. For a year he interned and taught at Harvard, then during World War II served with the Army Medical Corps in Puerto Rico as a staff member of the Antilles Department Medical Laboratory studying tropical diseases and virology. Following the war he returned to Harvard to continue research, working mainly in the area of tissue culture and virus growth, in association with John F. Enders and Frederick C. Robbins. In 1949 they were able for the first time successfully to produce quantities of the virus of poliomyelitis by growing it in bits of tissue, and this led in turn to the development of a safe polio vaccine by Jonas E. Salk; their techniques made possible the isolation of many other viruses as well, and the development of appropriate vaccines. Weller shared the 1954 Nobel Prize for Physiology and Medicine with Enders and Robbins for their work with the polio virus. Also in 1954 he was appointed Richard Pearson Strong Professor and head of the department of Tropical Public Health at Harvard's School of Public Health.

Welles, George Orson, *see* Welles, Orson

Welles, Gideon (1802–1878), public official and political leader. Born in Glastonbury, Connecticut, on July 1, 1802, Welles attended the Episcopal Academy in Cheshire and the American Academy (now Norwich University) in Northfield, Vermont, before taking up the study of law in Hartford, Connecticut. In 1826, however, he became part owner and editor of the *Hartford Times* and made it the official spokesman for Jacksonian democracy in southern New England. He retained the editorship until 1836. He was also elected to the state legislature in 1826, where he remained for nine years and was responsible for legislation to end the debtor's prison, to free voting from property and religious requirements, and to establish Connecticut's model general incorporation law. He was elected state comptroller in 1835 and President Andrew Jackson appointed him postmaster of Hartford in 1836. Reelected as Connecticut comptroller in 1842 and 1843, he then served as chief of the Bureau of Provisions and Clothing for the navy from 1846 until 1849. He ran unsuccessfully for the U.S. Senate in 1850, as he had for the

House of Representatives in 1834. Breaking with the Democrats in 1854 on the slavery issue, he helped in organizing the Republican party. He became a founder of the *Hartford Evening Press*, one of the first Republican papers in New England, and was a major contributor to it; he wrote also for such journals as the *New York Evening Post* and the *National Intelligencer*. Although he had been defeated as the party candidate for governor in 1856, his party activities led President Abraham Lincoln to select him as New England's representative in the first Republican cabinet in 1861. As secretary of the navy, Welles was faced with an enormous task, and in it he succeeded beyond expectation. He swiftly reorganized a navy decimated by secession, launched a major program of shipbuilding, including the acquisition of iron-clad monitors that were ridiculed at first. He was effective in strategic and tactical planning, used generally excellent judgment in selecting advisers and commanders, and was impervious to criticism and temptation alike. Under him the navy grew from a negligible force of 90 ships and fewer than 9000 men to 670 ships and over 57,000 men. His execution of the blockade of Confederate ports was successful, and he oversaw in eight years what amounted to a revolution in naval warfare. Although he opposed Lincoln's suspension of habeas corpus and the suspension of newspapers critical of the Union, Welles nevertheless backed the Emancipation Proclamation as a war measure and, an advocate of moderate Reconstruction as proposed by Lincoln, stood behind President Andrew Johnson in the impeachment proceedings of 1868. He remained in the cabinet until 1869, completing the longest term of office up to that time for a navy secretary. He gave the Liberal Republicans his support in 1872, but voted for Samuel J. Tilden in 1876. Welles died in Hartford, Connecticut, on February 11, 1878. The *Diary of Gideon Welles*, one of the most important documents of the Civil War period, appeared in three volumes in 1911.

Welles, Orson (1915–   ), actor, director, and producer. Born in Kenosha, Wisconsin, on May 6, 1915, George Orson Welles grew up in an atmosphere of wealth and culture. After graduating in 1930 from the progressive Todd School for Boys in Woodstock, Illinois, he studied briefly at the school of the Art Institute of Chicago and made a sketching trip through Ireland. He won his first professional stage role at the age of sixteen at Dublin's famous Gate Theatre, as the Duke of Württemberg in *Jew Süss*. Returning to Woodstock in 1933, he coedited with Roger Hill, his former acting coach at Todd, a popular text, *Everybody's Shakespeare*, 1933, and illustrated acting editions of Shakespeare's *Julius Caesar*, *Twelfth Night*, and the *Merchant of Venice*, all published in 1934. He was engaged by the Katharine Cornell players, with whom he toured in 1933; he played Mercutio in *Romeo and Juliet*, made his Broadway debut in the same play in 1934 as both the Chorus and Tybalt, and later acted, opposite Miss Cornell, as Marchbanks in George Bernard Shaw's *Candida* and as Octavius Barrett in *The Barretts of Wimpole Street*. In 1934, again with Roger Hill, he organized and directed the Woodstock, Illinois, summer drama festival, and appeared as Hamlet. In 1934 he took part in a radio adaptation of Archibald MacLeish's *Panic*, and during 1934–1935 narrated the *March of Time* radio series. In 1936, under the aegis of the Federal Theatre Project (FTP), he codirected an extremely successful version of *Macbeth* at the Negro People's Theatre in Harlem. He and John Houseman also produced *Dr. Faustus* and Marc Blitzstein's controversial *The Cradle Will Rock* for the FTP and in 1937 founded the Mercury Theatre, which staged a modern-dress *Julius Caesar*, Thomas Dekker's *Shoemaker's Holiday*, Georg Büchner's *Danton's Death*, and G. B. Shaw's *Heartbreak House*. Welles also became known for his role as Lamont Cranston in the popular radio thriller *The Shadow*. In 1938 the Mercury company presented a series of radio dramatizations of famous novels. Notorious in this series was their October 1938 version of H. G. Wells's *War of the Worlds*, which was so realistic in its report of landings by Martians that near-panic resulted in many locales within range of the broadcast. In 1940 he went to Hollywood and embarked on the writing, producing, directing, and acting of the title role of his next triumph, *Citizen Kane*. Released in 1941, the allegory of a power-corrupted idealist (a thinly veiled portrait of William Randolph Hearst) marked an epoch in movie making in its powerful use of sound and editing technique. His movie adaptation of Booth Tarkington's *The Magnificent Ambersons*, 1942, was less successful. In 1941 he staged a highly praised adaptation of Richard Wright's *Native Son*. During World War II he wrote and delivered weekly *Hello, Americans* radio broadcasts, and wrote a syndicated column for the *New York Post*. In 1946 he adapted and staged a Broadway musical extravaganza, *Around the World*, from Jules Verne's *Around the World in Eighty Days*. For the next ten years he lived in Europe, where he produced and starred in films—*Macbeth*, 1948, and *Othello*, 1952—and acted in *The Third Man*, 1949; he played Othello in a 1951 London stage production. Returning to New York City in 1956 he starred on stage as King Lear and in 1958 appeared in *The Long Hot Summer*. He directed and designed Eugene Ionesco's *Rhinoceros* in London in 1960, and two years later directed a film adapted from Franz Kafka's *The Trial*. In 1966 he played Cardinal Wolsey in the movie *A Man for All Seasons*. Brilliant and controversial, his theatrical pursuits were largely confined in later years to television.

Wellman, Walter (1858–1934), journalist, explorer, and airman. Born in Mentor, Ohio, on November 3, 1858, Wellman grew up there and in Nebraska. At the age of fourteen he was in the newspaper business, publishing a weekly in Sutton, Nebraska. In 1879 he founded the *Cincinnati Post*, an evening paper, and from 1884 until 1911 worked as Washington correspondent for the *Chicago Herald* and the *Chicago Record-Herald*. In the early 1890s he became interested in travel and exploration, activities that he carried on intermittently for the next 20 years. His first major trip was in 1891, when he toured the Bahamas and claimed to have found the exact place where Columbus first landed, on Watling Island. In 1894 and in 1898–1899 he made two excursions into the Arctic regions. He determined to locate the North Pole from the air, and in 1907, sponsored by his newspaper, he set out from Spitsbergen in a dirigible-like motor-powered airship; but this expedition, as well as an attempt in 1909, were failures owing to mechanical difficulties and bad weather. In 1910 he proposed to cross the Atlantic Ocean in a 230-foot airship, the *America*. This venture also failed, but the ship did make a record-breaking flight of more than 1000 miles, and it sent back, while in transit, the first wireless transmission of radio messages. The *America* took off on October 15, 1910, but after a flight of 72 hours came down and had to be abandoned; the crew was saved, but the ship itself drifted off and was lost. He described the exploit in *The Aerial Age*, 1911. Wellman died in New York City on January 31, 1934.

Wells, David Ames (1828–1898), economist and author. Born in Springfield, Massachusetts, on June 17, 1828, Wells was a descendant of a colonial governor of Connecticut, Thomas Welles. He graduated in 1847 from Williams College, where he assisted in the publication of its *Sketches of Williams College*. He joined the staff of the *Springfield Republican* in 1848 and invented a device for folding paper that was attached to the power presses of the newspaper. In 1851 he graduated from the Lawrence Scientific School at Harvard, where he was a special student of Louis Agassiz. From 1850 until 1866 Wells and George Bliss published *The Annual of Scientific Discovery*. As a special partner in the publishing firm headed by G. P. Putnam in 1857–1858, he compiled and published *The Science of Common Things* and *Wells' Principles and Applications of Chemistry*. These books were followed by *Wells' First Principles of Geology*, 1861, and *Wells' Natural Philosophy*, which appeared in 1863 and went through 15 editions. He achieved international prominence in 1864 with the publication of his first work in economics, *Our Burden and Our Strength*. Demonstrating the economic dynamism of the North, the rapid capital accumulation and constantly improved labor-saving devices, the pamphlet reassured Northerners and foreign investors of the government's ability to pay the increasing debts caused by the Civil War. In 1865 President Abraham Lincoln appointed Wells chairman of the National Revenue Commission, and its report the following year made recommendations that were incorporated into law. The post of Special Commissioner of the Revenue was created for him, and his *Reports*, 1866–1869, thoroughly covering the subject of indirect taxes for the first time, recommended the use of stamps in collecting liquor and tobacco revenues. A visit to Europe in 1867, where he saw relatively backward methods of manufacturing, converted him from protectionism to free trade. His advocacy of tariff abolition cost him his job in 1869, when President Ulysses S. Grant abolished the office of special commissioner. Wells immediately became head of the New York State Tax Commission and its report on *Local Taxation*, 1871, was considered the first competent study of the subject. In 1875 he helped reorganize the Erie Railroad and in 1876 was one of the receivers for the Atlanta and Chattanooga Railroad. In 1878 he became a member of the board of arbitration of the Associated Railways, deciding on questions of pooling. Actively interested in politics, he was several times a delegate to Democratic national conventions. He was an adviser on tariff matters to presidents James A. Garfield and Grover Cleveland, and he ran unsuccessfully for the House of Representatives from Connecticut in 1876 and 1890. Others among his many books included *Robinson Crusoe's Money*, 1876 and 1896; *The Silver Question*, 1872; *Our Merchant Marine*, 1882; *A Primer of Tariff Reform*, 1884; *Practical Economics*, 1885; and *The Theory and Practice of Taxation*, 1900. He opposed the personal income tax and recognized the importance of "technological unemployment." He died in Norwich, Connecticut, on November 5, 1898.

Wells, Henry (1805–1878), express-company executive. Born in Thetford, Vermont, on December 12, 1805, Wells grew up there and in upper New York State. In 1821 he was apprenticed as a tanner and shoemaker at Palmyra, but by the mid-1830s he was working at shipping freight and passengers by way of the Erie Canal. In early 1841 he went to work for the Harnden Express Company but later in the year became a messenger and partner in Pomeroy & Company, operating an express service between Albany and Buffalo. The following year he met William G. Fargo, another Pomeroy messenger, based at Buffalo. Two years later Wells and Fargo, with another partner who soon dropped out, organized an express line to run from Buffalo to Detroit, and in 1845 the new concern, Wells & Company, later Livingston, Wells & Company, extended its services to Cincinnati, Chicago, and St. Louis. A year later Wells sold his interest in the company to William Livingston and moved to New York City to operate another express business, intending to expand services to Europe. But with the death in 1847 of Crawford Livingston, who had become a partner, Wells and Fargo both ended up as partners with William Livingston. Three years later Wells, Fargo, and John Butterfield (who operated Butterfield, Wasson & Company) merged their firms to form the American Express Company, with Wells as its first president. He held the position of president for the next 18 years. In 1850–1851, with the California Gold Rush, the officers of American Express considered the possibilities for a successful express service in the Far West. In 1852 they decided, instead of expanding the existing company, to incorporate a new concern in New York that would operate in the West. On March 18, 1852, Wells, Fargo & Company was organized to operate in California to carry mail, parcels, and, above all, gold. The field was already rife with competition, with Adams & Company the largest firm; but in 1855 Adams & Company folded in a financial recession, leaving Wells, Fargo nearly unopposed in the field. In 1861 Wells, Fargo purchased the Holladay Overland Mail & Express Company, thus bringing into its control nearly all the stage lines from the Missouri River to the Pacific; in the same transaction it acquired the Pony Express, which suspended operation in October 1861. The only major setback the company experienced came in 1869, when it failed to obtain a contract from the government to carry mail on the new transcontinental railroad. Charles Crocker and Lloyd Tevis, the former closely connected with the Central Pacific Railroad, beat Wells, Fargo to the contract by organizing the competing Pacific Union Express Company. This maneuver forced Wells, Fargo stock into a decline, and Tevis and Crocker bought enough stock to control the company, which was forced to buy Pacific Union Express for one-third of all Wells, Fargo stock. Tevis became president of Wells, Fargo in 1872. Wells, still living in New York, had seen American Express endure competition in the East from the Merchants Union Express Company; in 1868 the two companies merged to form the American Merchants Union Express Company and Wells retired as president. He lived in retirement for the next ten years, traveling and contributing to philanthropic causes. In 1868 he founded Wells Seminary (now Wells College) in his home town of Aurora, New York. He died in Glasgow, Scotland, on December 10, 1878.

Wells, Horace (1815-1848), dentist and pioneer anesthetist. Born in Hartford, Vermont, on January 21, 1815, Wells studied dentistry in Boston in 1834-1835. In 1836 he began dental practice in Hartford, Connecticut, and remained there for five years before going into partnership with another dentist, William G. T. Morton, in Boston. In 1840 Wells had become interested in the anesthetic properties of nitrous oxide—"laughing gas"—hoping to be able to extract teeth painlessly while patients were under the influence of the gas. Morton also favored the notion, but in his own experiments came to prefer ether, particularly in cases requiring protracted surgery. In 1844 Wells had one of his own teeth extracted under the influence of nitrous oxide and afterward used it successfully in his practice several times. Unfortunately, an experiment in 1845 with nitrous oxide by Wells at the Harvard Medical School in Boston failed. Morton successfully demonstrated the use of ether the next year, administering it for an operation performed at Massachusetts General Hospital. Wells promptly claimed prior use and success with both ether and nitrous oxide. He spent the rest of his life defending his claims and

maintaining his conviction that the gas was as effective as ether and less dangerous. But his contentions failed to prevent the general acceptance of ether for use during surgery. Wells continued experimenting and writing on anesthetics until 1848; in that year, while under the influence of chloroform, he was jailed in New York City. During the time he was in jail, he apparently became despondent over his failures, and he killed himself on January 24, 1848.

Wells, Ida Bell (1862-1931), journalist and social reformer. Born in Holly Springs, Mississippi, on July 16, 1862, Ida Wells was the daughter of slaves. She was educated in a freedmen's school in Holly Springs and at fourteen began teaching in a country school. She continued as a teacher after moving to Memphis, Tennessee, in 1884, attending Fisk University during several summer sessions. In 1891 she was removed from her teaching post by the Memphis school board as a result of a lawsuit, which she had pressed to the state supreme court and there lost, growing out of her refusal to give up a seat in a "whites only" railroad car. She thereupon turned to journalism, buying an interest in the *Memphis Free Speech* in 1891, and in 1892, after three friends of hers had been killed by a mob, she began a newspaper campaign against lynching that quickly led to the sacking of the newspaper's office. She moved to New York City, where she continued her antilynching crusade, first as a staff writer for the *New York Age* and then as a lecturer and organizer of antilynching societies. She traveled to speak in a number of major cities and twice visited Great Britain for the cause. In 1895 she married Ferdinand L. Barnett, a Chicago lawyer, editor, and public official, and she restricted her travels, but she was very active in Chicago affairs. She contributed to the *Conservator*, her husband's newspaper, and to other local journals, published a detailed look at lynching in *A Red Record*, 1895, and was active in organizing local black women in various causes from the antilynching campaign to the suffrage movement. From 1898 to 1902 she served as secretary of the National Afro-American Council and in 1910 she founded and became first president of the Negro Fellowship League. From 1913 to 1916 she served as a probation officer of the Chicago municipal court. She was militant in her demand for justice for black Americans and in her insistence that it was to be won by their own efforts; while she took part in the 1909 meeting of the Niagara Movement, she would have nothing to do with the less radical National Association for the Advancement of Colored People (NAACP) which sprang from it. Ida Wells, known after her marriage also as Ida Wells-Barnett, died in Chicago on March 25, 1931, having expended tireless effort in behalf of black Americans.

Welty, Eudora (1909-   ), author. Born in Jackson, Mississippi, on April 13, 1909, Miss Welty attended Mississippi State College for Women but transferred to the University of Wisconsin in 1929.

She spent a year (1930–1931) at Columbia University in preparation for a career in advertising, but abandoned thought of such work in order to return to her childhood love of writing. Her first short story was published in 1936, and thereafter her work began to appear regularly, first in "little magazines" such as the *Southern Review* and later in such general-circulation magazines as the *Atlantic Monthly* and *New Yorker*. A collection of her stories, *A Curtain of Green*, was published in 1941. The next year her short novel, *The Robber Bridegroom*, was issued, and in 1946 she published her first novel, *Delta Wedding*. Her 1954 story, "The Ponder Heart," won her the William Dean Howells Medal of the American Academy of Arts and Letters; the award is given every five years for the best work of fiction published within that period. "The Ponder Heart" was made into a Broadway play in 1956. Other books include *The Wide Net*, 1943; *The Golden Apples*, 1949; *The Bride of Innisfallen*, a 1955 collection of short stories; *The Shoe Bird*, 1964; and *The Optimist's Daughter*, 1972. The settings and characters of Miss Welty's books were usually rural Southern, but she was not simply a "regional" author, for her themes, like those of her fellow Mississippian William Faulkner, were universal.

West, Benjamin (1738–1820), painter. Born on October 10, 1738, near Springfield, Pennsylvania, West began drawing and painting before he started his formal education. Upon graduation in 1756 from the College of Philadelphia he opened a studio. Although he was a self-taught portrait painter, the number of commissions he received was encouraging, and he successfully solicited further work in New York City. With the help of friends he financed a trip to Italy in 1760, where, as the first American to study art in that country, he received much attention. The neoclassical movement was just becoming popular, and he was directed to the galleries and towns that exhibited the style. In extensive studies of Baroque and Renaissance painting, he was especially impressed by Titian and Raphael. Going to London in 1763, he soon became one of the foremost artists there; his interesting background and pleasant manner secured him friends and patrons in the highest circles. His work, "Agrippa with the Ashes of Germanicus," won the esteem of George III, who subsequently appointed him a charter member of the Royal Academy. His style leaned more and more toward the Italian neoclassical, featuring autumnal colors and modulated tones, while other British artists busied themselves with vigorous subjects and robust hues. In 1771 he flustered the Academy with his "Death of Wolfe," which placed contemporary figures in a classical composition. Although widely criticized, the painting pointed toward a growing realism in art and added impetus to that movement. The work won him appointment as painter to the King, and in that capacity he executed portraits of the royal family and other works that conformed to his patron's wishes. But his delicate brushwork and muted colors limited the impact of his canvases, which were typically large and well designed. He became president of the Royal Academy in 1792 and taught and otherwise assisted many American pupils, among them John Singleton Copley, Gilbert Stuart, John Trumbull, Robert Fulton, and Samuel F. B. Morse. About 1801 his position at court became less secure, and he left for France the next year. His sketches for "Death on a Pale Horse," 1817, exhibited in Paris, presaged the French romantic movement. He completed about 400 canvases in his career and dominated painting in both England and the United States for many years. Although he never returned to the United States, he stayed loyal to his Quaker heritage and rejected the knighthood that was offered him. When he died in London on March 11, 1820, his body lay in state in the Royal Academy before burial with great ceremony in St. Paul's Cathedral.

West, Mae (1892–1980), entertainer. Born in Brooklyn, New York, on August 17, 1892, Miss West was already acting in amateur theatricals by the time she was seven; at eight she became a member of a stock company and began playing juvenile roles. In 1906 she went into vaudeville as a partner in a song-and-dance team, and five years later, in 1911, she opened in the Broadway musical revue, *A la Broadway and Hello Paris*. For the next 15 years she alternated between vaudeville and Broadway shows and did an occasional nightclub act. Her first great success came in 1926 with the production of her original play *Sex*, which she starred in. From that time she appeared almost exclusively in vehicles which she herself wrote, whether for the stage or films. For all the variety of the scripts, the constant factor was her own personality and her ability to burlesque social attitudes, especially toward sex. Her plots, delivery, and frequent use of double-entendre lines often earned censure by conservative critics and some of her shows were closed by local authorities, but her loyal fans never failed to appreciate her talent and humor. In 1928 she starred in the play *Diamond Lil*, a characterization that virtually became her alter ego and public image. In 1931–1932 she appeared in the stage version of her book *The Constant Sinner*, then moved to Hollywood to begin the film career that brought her to national prominence. After starring with George Raft in *Night After Night* in 1932, she did a film version of *Diamond Lil* entitled *She Done Him Wrong*. It was in this film that she spoke to Cary Grant her most famous line: "Come up and see me sometime." For the next decade she worked almost solely in movies, making such comedies as *I'm No Angel*, 1933; *Klondike Annie*, 1934; *Go West Young Man*, 1936; and the classic *My Little Chickadee*, 1940, with W. C. Fields. During the 1930s Miss West became Hollywood's highest salaried star and invested heavily in real estate and business. In 1944 she returned to the stage with *Catherine Was Great* and she did revivals of *Diamond Lil* from 1948 to 1951. During the mid-1950s she toured with a nightclub act consisting of herself and a "chorus" of muscle men. Subsequently she performed less, although appearing occasionally on television; she also made records of some of her songs. After 1943 she did not make any movies until the 1970 filming of Gore Vidal's novel *Myra Breckenridge*. Miss West wrote her own part for it, received star billing, and proved its main attraction. Her speech, a provocative drawl, and her movements, a variety of languid drapes and swivels, were utterly hers, as was the shape that inspired World War II fliers to dub their pneumatic life-vests "Mae Wests." Her autobiography, *Goodness Had Nothing to Do with It*, was published in 1959. She died on November 22, 1980, in Los Angeles.

West, Nathanael (1903–1940), author. Born in New York City on October 17, 1903, Nathan Wallenstein Weinstein attended city schools and graduated from Brown University in 1924. He went to Paris, where he lived for 15 months, during which time he completed his first novel, *The Dream Life of Balso Snell*, which was published under the pen name of Nathanael West in 1931. It was one of four short novels that he wrote in a style derived from the Dadaist and Surrealist movement in the arts; all four ridiculed the superficial aspirations of contemporary men. *Miss Lonelyhearts*, 1933, was executed with extraordinary skill, and is considered his masterwork. It concerned a newspaper advice-to-the-lovelorn columnist who met and became involved with several of the people behind the letters. As if emphasizing the conclusion of *Miss Lonelyhearts*, his next work, *A Cool Million*, 1934, did not share the stark narrative or striking imagery of his other novels, but used broad humor to parody Horatio Alger's theme of fortitude in the face of frustration. His last book, *The Day of the Locust*, 1939, was a portrayal of the life and activities of Hollywood, which he had observed during his last five years while working as a motion-picture scriptwriter. The book pictured Hollywood as a center of luxury and wickedness, the underdogs of which were incited to destroy it in an attempt to satisfy their spiritual hunger. West was killed in an automobile accident near El Centro, California, on December 22, 1940. His writings, little noted on original publication, were reprinted with increasing frequency during the 1950s as critical estimation of his work rose sharply.

West, Thomas, *see* De La Warr, Thomas West, Baron

Westcott, Edward Noyes (1846–1898), banker and author. Born in Syracuse, New York, on September 27, 1846, Westcott left school at the age of sixteen to work in a bank. He spent the next 30 years in banking, except for a two-year period with a New York City insurance company in 1866–1868. In 1895 he contracted tuberculosis and during the following year and a half, while traveling and resting to recuperate, he worked on the novel *David Harum: A Story of American Life*, an account of a small-town New England banker. After several vain attempts to place the manuscript, Westcott finally found an interested publisher in 1898. He died on March 31, 1898, six months before the novel appeared and immediately became a best seller—nearly a half million copies were sold in the first two years. It remained one of the most popular books of the first part of the twentieth century; it was dramatized in 1900 and was twice made into a movie, the second time in 1934, when it starred Will Rogers.

Westinghouse, George (1846–1914), inventor and manufacturer. Born on October 6, 1846, in Central Bridge, New York, Westinghouse joined the Union army at the age of sixteen and later served in the navy as well. After his discharge in 1865 he attended Union College in Schenectady briefly and then returned home to a position in his father's agricultural-implement factory. At the age of nineteen he was granted, for a small rotary steam engine, the first of his 400-odd patents. Many of his early inventions were designed for use on railroads, and his major single development came in this field in 1869—the air brake. The device made it possible for the engineer to brake an entire train all at once, whereas previously it had been necessary to hand-set the brakes on each car individually; with the new system trains could begin to operate safely at high speeds. Westinghouse organized the Westinghouse Air Brake Company in Pittsburgh in 1869; subsequent improvements, notably automatic features introduced in 1872, led to the rapid adoption of the air brake by American railroads. He later turned his attention to developing an integrated automatic signaling system for railroad use and in 1882 began production of the system with the organization of the Union Switch & Signal Company in Pittsburgh. During the 1880s he also experimented with techniques for the transmission of natural gas. From about 1885 he became interested in the potential use of alternating current (AC) for the wide distribution of electrical power; aided by several brilliant engineers, among them Nikola Tesla, he eventually worked out a practical system of generation, transmission, and conversion of AC power and saw it develop over considerable opposition into the method used almost exclusively. During 1886 experimental power-distribution systems utilizing AC were built in Great Barrington, Massachusetts, and then in Lawrenceville, Pennsylvania. The Westinghouse Electric Company was founded in 1886 to produce the dynamos, transformers, and motors for alternating-current power systems, and the company's electrical equipment was used for the Niagara Falls power plant, in operation by 1895; and for the rapid-transit systems in New York City and London. In 1893 Westinghouse contracted to supply the lighting for the World's Columbian Exposition in Chicago. After 1907 he lost his control over most of the companies he had founded, but he remained president until retiring in 1911; he continued to invent and to improve earlier inventions until illness intervened in 1913. He died in New York City on March 12, 1914. He was elected to the Hall of Fame in 1955.

Westmoreland, William Childs (1914–), soldier. Born in Spartanburg County, South Carolina, on March 26, 1914, Westmoreland graduated from West Point in 1936. He was stationed in Hawaii on army duty before World War II, but once the war had begun was transferred to the European theater. He saw action in North Africa and Europe with the 9th Infantry Division. Following the war he took glider and paratroop training at Fort Benning, Georgia, and for the next several years taught at the Command and General Staff School at Fort Leavenworth, Kansas, and at the Army War College. In 1952, during the Korean War, he saw action with the 187th Airborne regimental combat team. From 1953 to 1958 he served in administrative posts in Washington, D.C., before returning to command duty with the 101st Airborne, or "Screaming Eagle," Division. In July 1960 President Dwight D. Eisenhower appointed Westmoreland superintendent of West Point; he served until 1963, when he became commanding general of the 18th Airborne Division at Fort Bragg, North Carolina. In 1964 President Lyndon B. Johnson appointed him senior U.S. military commander in Vietnam. It was under his command, and at his urging, that U.S. ground forces in the war there were increased to more than 500,000 by 1968. During his years in Vietnam he emphasized the use of massive "search and destroy" missions to draw the enemy into traditional forms of ground combat, and he sent back to the United States a series of optimistic reports about the course of the war. But after the Tet offensive by North Vietnam in February 1968, the progress of the war seemed stalled. Westmoreland was succeeded in command in 1968 by Gen. Creighton W. Abrams, and he returned to the United States to become army chief of staff. He retired in 1972 and in 1976 published *A Soldier Reports.*

Weston, Edward (1886–1958), photographer. Born in Highland Park, Illinois, on March 24, 1886, Weston grew up there and in Southern California. In 1904 he started a commercial photography business in Glendale, doing mostly portrait work, but in 1923 he gave up the business and spent three years living and traveling in Mexico. In 1926 he returned to California and began to do photographic nature studies. At first limiting himself to California, he gradually expanded his studies to the whole of the Far West as recognition was accorded him. An exceptional artist with a camera, he exhibited his nature studies in several one-man shows and his work came to be represented in museums in California and Mexico. A major showing of his work took place at the Museum of Modern Art in New York City in 1947. From 1947 until his death, Weston was on the faculty of the California School of Fine Arts at San Francisco. His photographic work was collected in several books, including *California and the West,* 1940; *The Cats of Wildcat Hill,* 1942; and *My Camera on Point Lobos,* 1950. He died in Carmel, California, on January 1, 1958.

Weston, Edward Paycon (1839–1929), long-distance walker. Born in Providence, Rhode Island, on March 15, 1839, Weston grew up there and in Boston. He developed the habit of walking as a means to better his health and developed it into a lifetime avocation. Most of his working time was spent as a newspaper reporter, but frequently he made news himself because of his cross-country jaunts. In February and March, 1861, he walked from Boston to Washington, D.C., in ten days. Six years later he walked from Portland, Maine, to Chicago, a distance of more than 1300 miles. Over the next several decades he took part in walking tours and races in the United States and England and in 1907 repeated his Maine-to-Chicago walk. In 1909–1910 he walked from New York City to San Francisco and back. His last major long-distance walk was in 1913, when at the age of seventy-five he walked from New York City to Minneapolis for the cornerstone-laying of the city's athletic club. He died in New York City on May 12, 1929, at the age of ninety; he never ceased to attribute his longevity to walking.

Wetzel, Lewis (1764–1808?), Indian fighter and scout. Born in Lancaster County, Pennsylvania, in 1764, Wetzel was one of five brothers, four of whom became noted Indian fighters, while the fifth was killed as a youth. In 1776 or 1777, after having moved to Virginia with his family, Lewis Wetzel and one of his brothers were captured by Indians; although they escaped shortly afterward, the experience evidently made an Indian hater out of Lewis, and he devoted himself henceforth to all the arts that would make him a more capable and efficient fighter and killer of Indians; among other things, he trained himself to load his rifle while running at full speed. From 1777 he was almost continuously employed as a scout, first in the neighborhood of his home, the present Wheeling, West Virginia, and then farther afield; he was a member of the party that raided an Indian village at the present-day Coshocton, Ohio, in 1781. He was known never to give quarter to the enemy and obtained a reputation as a cold, cruel, and remorseless killer. Once he even offended the white authorities by killing an old Indian who had earlier saved his life; Wetzel explained his conduct by saying that "He made me walk, and he was nothing but an Indian." In 1789 he murdered an important Indian and was apparently sentenced to be hanged, but he was saved by Ohio settlers who valued his scouting ability. He moved to New Orleans in the early 1790s and was there imprisoned for a time, perhaps for counterfeiting, and then went to Natchez, Mississippi, where, it is believed, he died about 1808. A county in West Virginia was named after him.

Weyerhaeuser, Frederick (1834–1914), businessman. Born at Niedersaulheim, near Mainz, Germany, on November 21, 1834, Weyerhaeuser emigrated to the United States in 1852. He lived in Erie County, Pennsylvania, for four years before moving to Rock Island, Illinois, where he went to work for a lumberyard. He worked his way up in the lumber business, eventually becoming a partner in the Denkman Company. About 1864 the company began investing heavily in timberlands, and within a few more years it owned three saw mills. In 1870 Weyerhaeuser formed a lumber syndicate by entering into marketing agreements with other lumbermen. In 1891 he moved his offices to St. Paul, Minnesota, and vastly increased his landholdings. In 1896 he bought another major company along with its 600 million board feet of standing timber. Eventually the Weyerhaeuser Company came to have the greatest holdings of standing timber of any company in the United States. As the fame of Weyerhaeuser, the "Lumber King," increased, opposition to the extent of his forest holdings grew among conservationists, businessmen, and others who, for various reasons, feared the consequences of such huge acreages being held by one man. In 1906 a committee of Congress investigated his lumber trust on the grounds that it operated to destroy competition. By the time of his death, Weyerhaeuser had accumulated more than 2 million acres of forest land from Wisconsin and Minnesota to the Pacific Northwest and a huge fortune. He died in Pasadena, California, on April 4, 1914.

Wharton, Edith (1862–1937), author. Born in New York City on January 24, 1862, Edith Newbold Jones came of a distinguished New York family. She was educated by private tutors and governesses at home and in Europe, and she read voraciously. She married Edward Wharton, a wealthy Boston banker, in 1885. Although she began publishing at sixteen, her first popular work was *The House of Mirth*, 1905, which analyzed the stratified society she knew and its reaction to social change. Her preoccupation with aristocratic values was also reflected in such works as *The Custom of the County*, 1913; *The Glimpses of the Moon*, 1922; *Hudson River Bracketed*, 1929; and *The Gods Arrive*, 1932, but she put it aside in her most famous work, a novelette of simple New England people, *Ethan Frome*, 1911, which eloquently expressed the anguish of individuals doomed to live within the barriers of convention. *The Age of Innocence*, 1920, which won her a Pulitzer Prize the next year, was considered her best-wrought novel. A work that explored hypocrisy and convention, it was infused with ironical observations on social affectation and foolishness. Other books included *The Reef*, 1912; *Summer*, 1917; *A Son at the Front*, 1923; *The Mother's Recompense*, 1925; *Twilight Sleep*, 1927; *The Children*, 1928; and collections of stories including *The Greater Inclination*, 1899; *Crucial Instances*, 1901; *The Hermit and the Wild Woman*, 1908; *Tales of Men and Ghosts*, 1910; *Here and Beyond*, 1926; *Certain People*, 1930; and *Human Nature*, 1933. In all she published more than 50 books, in-

cluding fiction, short stories, travel books, historical novels, and criticism, and published her early poetry in magazines. She lived in France from 1907, visiting the United States only occasionally. She was divorced from Wharton in 1913. In 1923, during her last visit to America, she became the first woman to receive an honorary doctorate from Yale University. She was a close friend in his last years of Henry James, with whose art her own had much in common. She died on August 11, 1937, at St. Brice-sous-forêt, near Paris.

Wheatley, Phillis (1753?–1784), poet. Born about 1753 in Senegal, Africa, Miss Wheatley was kidnapped and brought to Boston on a slaveship about 1761 and purchased by a tailor, John Wheatley, as a companion for his wife. In less than two years, under Mrs. Wheatley's tutelage, she had mastered English; she went on to learn Greek and Latin and caused a stir among Boston scholars by translating a tale from Ovid. From the age of thirteen she wrote exceptionally mature poetry, including "To the University of Cambridge in New England," "To the King's Most Excellent Majesty," and "On the Death of Rev. Dr. Sewall." When the authenticity of her work was challenged, she was defended by many people, including Thomas Jefferson, even though he did not fancy her work. She was escorted by Mr. Wheatley's son to London in 1773 and there her first book, *Poems on Various Subjects, Religious and Moral*, was published. She returned to Boston shortly thereafter because of the sickness of her mistress; both Mr. and Mrs. Wheatley died soon thereafter and Phillis was freed. In 1778 she married John Peters, an intelligent but irresponsible free Negro who eventually abandoned her. She died in Boston on December 5, 1784. Two books issued posthumously were *Memoir and Poems of Phillis Wheatley*, 1834, and *Letters of Phillis Wheatley, the Negro Slave-Poet of Boston*, 1864. Her work was used by abolitionists to combat notions of innate intellectual inferiority among Negroes and to promote educational opportunities for people of her race.

Wheaton, Henry (1785–1848), lawyer and diplomat. Born in Providence, Rhode Island, on November 27, 1785, Wheaton graduated from Rhode Island College (now Brown University) in 1802. After studying law in Providence and in France he was admitted to the bar in 1806 and began practice in Providence. In 1812 he moved to New York City, where he edited the *National Advocate*, a newspaper of the Jeffersonian (Democratic) Republicans, until 1815. After brief service during the War of 1812, as army judge advocate in 1814–1815, he was appointed a judge on the New York City marine court. He held that post until 1819. In 1816 he began 12 years as reporter for the U.S. Supreme Court, during which period he published the 12 volumes of U.S. Reports that are still referred to under his name. In 1821 he sat in the state constitutional convention and two years later he was elected to the legislature for one term.

After an unsuccessful campaign for the U.S. Senate he worked for two years, 1825–1827, on the revision of the laws of New York. From 1827 until 1835 he served as American chargé d'affaires in Denmark, where his interest in Scandinavian history resulted in the publication of numerous articles and of his *History of The Northmen*, 1831. His work eased the way for a treaty by which Denmark agreed in 1830 to indemnify U.S. merchants whose ships had been seized during the period of the Napoleonic Wars, when Denmark had taken strong measures against all shipping in its waters. From 1835 until 1837 he was chargé at the Prussian court in Berlin, and in 1837 was promoted to minister. Wheaton's public career was divided between law and diplomacy, and he brought to both a depth of knowledge and understanding that made him one of the foremost experts of his time on both American public law and international law. In addition to his 12 volumes of U.S. Reports, which were highly praised for their useful annotations, he was a prolific author on legal and historical subjects. His most important works were the *Elements of International Law*, 1836, which was widely translated and which remained in print for nearly a century, and his *History of the Law of Nations in Europe and America*, 1841. His diplomatic chores were also successfully accomplished. He was well liked by his colleagues in Europe, who had a high regard for his scholarly attainments and affability, and he cemented better relationships for the United States with both Denmark and Prussia. He was relieved of his post in Prussia in 1846 and returned to the United States in 1847, hoping to teach law, but poor health prevented him from doing so. He died in Dorchester, Massachusetts, on March 11, 1848.

Wheeler, Joseph (1836–1906), soldier and public official. Born in Augusta, Georgia, on September 10, 1836, Wheeler graduated from West Point in 1859. After two years of duty with the army he resigned his commission to fight for the Confederacy. After a little more than a year of infantry service, during which he saw action at Shiloh, he was given command of the cavalry of the Army of Mississippi in the Western (Tennessee–Kentucky) theater of the war, eventually, in February 1865, becoming a lieutenant general. He was engaged in the campaigns around Murfreesboro, Chickamauga, Chattanooga, and Knoxville, and was almost alone in opposing Sherman's March to the Sea after the fall of Atlanta. One of the most aggressive and popular of the Confederate generals, he saw continuous action during the war and earned the nickname "Fighting Joe;" he took part in more than 400 engagements, according to his own estimate. Following the war he lived for two years in New Orleans before settling, in 1868, in the Alabama town named in his honor, to practice law and take up cotton planting. He continued this comparatively sedate existence until Reconstruction ended in the South, then entered politics. He served most of one contested term as a Democrat in the House of Representatives in the 47th Congress (1881–1883), then was reelected in 1884 and remained in the House until 1900. There he interested himself in military affairs, was a leader in seeking reconciliation of North and South, and became chairman of the Committee on Ways and Means. When the Spanish-American War began, Wheeler again offered his services and President William McKinley appointed him a major general of volunteers in a cavalry division. He saw action in Cuba and after the war was sent to the Philippines to help put down the independence movement led by Emilio Aguinaldo. He rose to the regular-army rank of brigadier general before retiring from the service in September 1900. He died in Brooklyn, New York, on January 25, 1906.

Wheeler, Wayne Bidwell (1869–1927), lawyer and prohibitionist. Born in rural Trumbull County, Ohio, on November 10, 1869, Wheeler graduated from Oberlin College in 1895 and obtained his law degree there in 1898. As an exponent of prohibition, his purpose in becoming a lawyer was to work for the Anti-Saloon League. The League, founded in 1893, gave rise two years later to the Anti-Saloon League of America, which as a national body differed from the older Prohibition party in that it did not run candidates for public office but rather used its influence to promote anti-liquor candidates of either major party. Wheeler served the Anti-Saloon League of America in Ohio as attorney, then as general superintendent, from 1898 until 1915; he was national superintendent from 1915 until 1927. The League was one of the most intense and successful of political pressure groups in the nation, and Wheeler became one of the most astute and powerful of political manipulators and lobbyists. In the era of reform between about 1900 and 1917, prohibition made striking headway in the states. By 1920, the year the national prohibition amendment (Eighteenth Amendment) went into effect, 33 states had already enacted restrictive legislation. Wheeler played a major role in obtaining state-by-state legislation, in defeating candidates who were opposed to his program, and in obtaining adoption of the prohibition amendment. His opposition was much feared in local political campaigns, particularly in his home state of Ohio. Wheeler died in Battle Creek, Michigan, on September 5, 1927.

Wheeler, William Almon (1819–1887), public official. Born in Malone, New York, on June 30, 1819, Wheeler attended the University of Vermont for two years, then left to study law and was admitted to the bar in 1845. For several years he conducted a successful practice in his home town, and in 1853 went into banking. His political career began in 1846 when he became district attorney for Franklin County, New York, a post he held until 1849. He served two terms in the state legislature, one as assemblyman (1850–1851) and the second as state senator (1858–1859). He was elected to the House of Representatives in 1860 and served one term. He presided over the state constitutional convention of 1867–1868, then, in the Republican landslide of 1868 that carried Ulysses S. Grant to the White House, was again elected to the House serving there until 1877. His general political career was uneventful, except for his being that anomaly among officeholders of his period, an honest man. One of his notable actions during his congressional career was investigating a disputed election in Louisiana in 1874. The "Wheeler compromise" arrived at by his committee called for allowing the incumbent governor to remain in office, while 12 Democratic members of the legislature who had been denied seats be reinstated. The result was a Louisiana legislature with a Republican majority in the senate and a Democratic majority in the lower house. In 1876 Wheeler, almost a political unknown outside his state, was nominated for the vice-presidency on the Republican ticket headed by Rutherford B. Hayes. Upon the settlement of the famous disputed election that was thrown into the House of Representatives, Wheeler served with Hayes. After leaving office in 1881 Wheeler retired to private life. He died in Malone, New York, on June 4, 1887.

Wheelock, Eleazar (1711–1779), religious leader and educator. Born in Windham, Connecticut, on April 22, 1711, Wheelock graduated from Yale in 1733, studied theology for the next two years, and from 1735 until 1754 served as a Congregational pastor at Lebanon, Connecticut. He was an emotional preacher and thus was in tune with the fervor of the Great Awakening but he was loyal to established Congregational polity and took no part in schismatic activities. To add to his income, he took young men into his household to prepare them for college, and one such student, a Mohegan Indian named Samson Occom, made such excellent progress (he was later ordained and became a missionary) that Wheelock determined to found a free school where whites and Indians could be educated together. With aid from various sources, he founded such a school, known as Moor's Charity School after a leading local benefactor, at Lebanon in 1754; it lasted until 1768 but never enjoyed a large attendance and finally failed. Thereupon Wheelock accepted an offer from the governor of New Hampshire of a township of land along the Connecticut River; he went there in 1770 with 30 students and some other settlers and founded both the town of Hanover, New Hampshire, and Dartmouth College, whose charter dated from 1769. For the rest of his life he worked for the college, supervising building as well as preaching, teaching, and trying to raise money, which was difficult during the Revolutionary War. He died in Hanover on April 24, 1779. His son, John Wheelock (1754–1817), born in Lebanon, Connecticut, on January 28, 1754, graduated from Dartmouth in its first class of 1771. Upon his father's death in 1779 he became Dartmouth's second president. During his first 25 years in the position he served with distinction, adding to the

buildings of the institution, obtaining funds, teaching various subjects, and reviving his father's original program of educating Indians. From 1804, however, he was involved in increasingly bitter controversy with the board of trustees over his administrative policies. Pedagogical differences grew into a struggle for power and gradually political overtones crept in as well, Democratic sympathy falling to Wheelock and Federalist sympathy to the trustees. He was deprived of the presidency and his professorship in 1815 and thereupon wrote a history of the controversy that transformed it into a public issue that was widely debated throughout New England; as the Dartmouth College Case it was tried in the New Hampshire courts and ultimately, in 1819, reached the Supreme Court, where it contributed to the reputation of Daniel Webster. A truculent and dictatorial man in his last years, Wheelock died in Hanover on April 4, 1817.

Wheelock, John, see under Wheelock, Eleazar

Whipple, George Hoyt (1878–1976), physician and educator. Born in Ashland, New Hampshire, on August 28, 1878, Whipple graduated from Yale in 1900 and took his degree in medicine at The Johns Hopkins University in 1905. He taught at Johns Hopkins until 1914 and was resident pathologist at the university's hospital from 1910 to 1914. For the next seven years he was on the faculty of the University of California at Berkeley as professor of research medicine. He left there in 1921 to help organize and become first dean of the University of Rochester's School of Medicine and Dentistry, where he remained until his retirement in 1955. His research dealt primarily with the function of the liver in blood formation and the treatment of pernicious anemia. In 1934 he shared the Nobel Prize for Physiology and Medicine with George R. Minot and William P. Murphy for research on anemia. While at the University of Rochester he was instrumental in constructing the medical center there. Whipple's later research concerned phases of metabolism, blood plasma proteins, and related topics. He died on February 1, 1976, in Rochester, New York.

Whipple, Henry Benjamin (1822–1901), religious leader and social reformer. Born in Adams, New York, on February 15, 1822, Whipple attended Oberlin College, leaving school in 1839 to return home to work in his father's store. In 1848 he began studying for the Episcopal ministry and was ordained in 1850. He served a parish in Rome, New York, until 1857, then spent two years organizing a mission church in Chicago. In 1859 he was elected the first bishop of the Episcopal diocese of Minnesota, and thereafter made his home in Faribault. At that time Minnesota was still a frontier area, and there were many Indians, mainly Chippewa and Sioux, in Whipple's diocese. In 1859–1860 he toured the diocese and saw at first hand the demoralized condition of the Indians. His contact with the tribes and the evidence he gathered concerning the wretchedness of federal policy in regard to Indians and the injustices perpetrated under it led him to become one of the vocal proponents of reform of Indian policy in the nineteenth century. He warned the federal government to change its policy and stop corruption or else there would be an Indian war. As usual nothing was done, and the great Sioux uprising of August 1862 fulfilled his worst fears. By personal appeals to President Abraham Lincoln, Whipple helped mitigate some of the white savagery directed at the Sioux following the outbreak. In October 1868 he read a report on the condition of the Western tribes to a meeting of the U.S. Indian Commission, cataloguing the wrongs done to the tribes and the "blunders, frauds, and crimes" on the part of the federal government and urging complete overhaul of the Bureau of Indian Affairs, among other things giving it cabinet status. Most of Whipple's suggestions fell on deaf ears, as did the ideas of other reformers, for there was too much profit to be made by cheating the Indians, and the Bureau of Indian Affairs was not about to give up its hold on its wards. But some proposals concerning reservation policy were eventually adopted by Ulysses S. Grant's administration. Whipple wanted the Indians to be given inalienable land grants, schools, and a fairly run reservation system. Throughout his diocese he built up missions among the tribes and was successful in personal appeals for funds throughout the country to help the Indians. As one of the few white men the Indians were able to trust, he was called by them "Straight Tongue." As the years passed his reputation in the church grew, and he was called upon to travel to many parts of the United States and Europe to raise funds and fill speaking engagements. In 1871 he conducted the first Protestant service ever held in Havana, Cuba. He preached at the Lambeth Conference in England in 1881 and represented the United States at the Lambeth Conference in 1897 as senior bishop of the Protestant Episcopal church in the United States. In 1899 he published an autobiography, *Lights and Shadows of a Long Episcopate*. He died in Faribault, Minnesota, on September 26, 1901.

Whistler, James Abbott McNeill (1834–1903), painter and etcher. Born in Lowell, Massachusetts, on July 10, 1834, the son of a military engineer, Whistler lived in Russia, with brief visits to England, during 1843–1849, while his father directed the building of a railroad line for Czar Nicholas I. From 1851 to 1853 he was a cadet at West Point, but was obliged to leave because of his failure to understand chemistry. During 1854 he was a draftsman and map engraver for the U.S. Coast Survey in Washington, D.C. He left for Paris in 1855 (never to return to the United States) to become an artist. Of prime influence on him were the styles of Alphonse Legros and Henri Fantin-Latour, who relied on recollections of a scene, the realist Gustave Courbet, and Diego Velásquez. Such early paintings as "At the Piano" and "The

Blue Wave" showed the realist influence but their tonal treatment anticipated his later marked preoccupation with mood. In 1858 he published his first series of etchings; a second set, views of the Thames River, followed in 1860. In addition to his etchings, which have been compared to those of Rembrandt, Whistler did occasional remarkable work in dry paint, watercolor, and pastel. In 1859 he moved to London and began a controversial artistic career. His "White Girl," which had been rejected by the Paris Salon and by the British Royal Academy, was a huge success at the Salon des Refusés in Paris in 1863. He renamed the work "Symphony in White No. 1," the first in his series of "Symphonies" and "Nocturnes," which grew progressively more delicate and depended strongly on spatial relationships. His most famous painting in this genre was "Mrs. George Washington Whistler," 1872, which he also described as "Arrangement in Grey and Black No. 1" but which was universally known in after years as "Whistler's Mother." Subsequent portraits included "Thomas Carlyle," 1873; "Miss Cicely Alexander," 1873; "Yellow Buskin," 1878; and "Sarasate," 1884. In 1878 Whistler, with much publicity, sued the celebrated English art critic John Ruskin for libel after Ruskin, in the course of a criticism of "Nocturne in Black and Gold: The Falling Rocket," 1874, had made remarks about Whistler's character and artistic motives that seemed to him slanderous. At the trial, Whistler declared that a picture of a bridge was not that but instead a blending of colors based on his own personal feeling about the bridge. His sarcasm so upset the judge, however, that although he won the case, the damages were set at one farthing and the expense of the trial left him penniless. His book *The Gentle Art of Making Enemies*, about the suit, was published in 1890. During 1879–1880 he lived in Venice and produced his finest series of etchings. Returning to London, he enjoyed a new popularity and was sought as a portraitist. In his "Ten O'Clock" address of 1885 he summarized his feelings about art as they were manifested in his work. Always a step ahead of conservative academicians, however, he was never fully accepted by the critics, although by 1886 he was asked to preside over the Royal Society of British Artists; he also organized the newly founded International Society of Sculptors, Painters and Gravers during 1897. He settled again in Paris in 1892, but died in London on July 17, 1903. He was elected to the Hall of Fame in 1930.

White, Andrew Dickson (1832–1918), educator and diplomat. Born in Homer, New York, on November 7, 1832, White graduated from Yale in 1853 and then went to Europe to study. He stayed three years, spending part of the time as attaché to the U.S. legation in St. Petersburg, Russia, 1854–1855. He returned to the United States in 1856, spent a year in graduate study at Yale, and then accepted the post of professor of history and English literature at the University of Michigan. An effective teacher, he also devoted himself to developing a plan for a state university for New York that would, as he wrote a friend, exclude "no sex or color, [battle] mercantile morality and [temper] military passion, . . . [and] afford an asylum for science where truth shall be sought for truth's sake." Inheriting considerable wealth from his father, who died in 1860, he propagandized widely in support of his ideal. But his health broke down, and he took the first of many trips abroad in pursuit of the renewal of his strength in 1862. He returned late the next year to discover that he had been elected a New York State senator. As chairman of the senate committee on education in 1864 he helped to codify the state's school laws and to create a system of teacher-training schools, and in addition used the position to further his aim for a state university. He won over the philanthropist Ezra Cornell, who provided large sums of working capital, employed land given New York under the Morrill Act, and founded a university at Ithaca, New York, that bore Cornell's name. The charter, written by White, provided for the teaching of the sciences, humanities, and technical arts, for equal degrees based on various courses of study, for equal status for modern languages and history and political science with the classics, for the use of eminent scholars as "nonresident professors," and for the treatment of students as men, not boys. Upon Ezra Cornell's insistence, White resigned his professorship at Michigan and became president of the new institution, designating himself to assume the professorship of European history. The university opened in 1868 with a young faculty supplemented by distinguished nonresidents, among them Louis Agassiz and James Russell Lowell. Apart from teaching, White defended the university from attacks on its methods and saw it through a financial crisis when Cornell's gifts of securities and other property turned out to be less valuable than foreseen. He continued to struggle with these difficulties until 1885, when he resigned the presidency. In the meantime he had served as U.S. minister to Germany, 1879–1881, and in 1884 had helped to found the American Historical Association, of which he was elected the first president. After still another recuperative trip to Europe, 1885–1889, he resumed his researches and lecturing, was U.S. minister to Russia, 1892–1894, ambassador to Germany, 1897–1902, and the head of the U.S. delegation to the Hague Conference of 1899; he considered the last post the summit of his diplomatic career. Among his many books were the remarkable *History of the Warfare of Science with Theology in Christendom*, two volumes, 1896, *Seven Great Statesmen in the Warfare of Humanity with Unreason*, 1910, and an autobiography, 1905. He died in Ithaca, New York, on November 4, 1918, leaving his valuable library to Cornell University.

White, Byron Raymond (1917–   ), justice of the Supreme Court. Born in Fort Collins, Colorado, on June 8, 1917, White grew up in nearby Wellington. He attended the University of Colorado, where he achieved top academic honors and became one of the school's outstanding football players. As "Whizzer" White he gained a national reputation for passing, punting, and running; in leading his team to an undefeated season in 1937 he earned a spot on Grantland Rice's All-American team. After graduating in 1938 he played professional football for one season with the Pittsburgh Pirates (now the Steelers) to earn money for law school. He spent most of 1939 at Oxford University in England as a Rhodes scholar but returned in 1940 after war in Europe broke out. Back in the United States, he enrolled at the Yale Law School in 1940 and also played two seasons with the Detroit Lions. During the war he served in the navy in the South Pacific. White returned to Yale following the war and graduated in November 1946. After a year as law clerk for Chief Justice Frederick M. Vinson of the Supreme Court, he moved to Denver and joined a law firm. Having been acquainted with John F. Kennedy since 1939, White supported him when he ran for the presidency in 1960, heading the national Citizens for Kennedy committee. When the Kennedy administration took office in 1961, White became deputy attorney general under Robert F. Kennedy. He had served in the post a little more than a year when President Kennedy, on March 30, 1962, appointed him an associate justice of the U.S. Supreme Court. White was the first Kennedy appointee as well as the first Coloradan to serve on the Court. At the time of his appointment he was the Court's youngest member yet he was throughout the next decade more conservative than not in his opinions and dissents.

White, Canvass (1790–1834), engineer. Born in Whitesboro, Oneida County, New York, on September 8, 1790, White received no formal education beyond the age of seventeen, but he became one of the most expert engineers in the United States in his time. Between 1807 and 1816 he worked for his father, fought in the War of 1812, and worked his way to Russia and back on board a merchant ship. In 1816 he went to work for the Erie Canal Company as assistant to the men in charge of constructing the middle section of the canal (the project had been divided into three parts). At this time there were no professionally trained engineers in the United States; work was done by improvisation and experiment. In 1817–1818 White went to England and walked more than 2000 miles along canal routes, inspecting all details of construction and making drawings. Upon his return in 1818 he was the only one involved in the work on the Erie who knew European canal building. One of his chief contributions to the work was the discovery of the lime rock in New York State that could be converted into concrete for making the locks, thus saving the great expense of importing cement. He worked with the Erie Canal Company until 1825—the year of the canal's completion—designing locks and supervising construction. For the next nine years he worked on the building of several other canals, including the Delaware and Raritan Canal and the Lehigh Canal. He died in St. Augustine, Florida, on December 18, 1834, where he had gone to recover from a physical collapse.

White, David (1862–1935), paleobotanist and geologist. Born near Palmyra, New York, on July 1, 1862, White received his B.S. from Cornell in 1886. He went to work for the U.S. Geological Survey almost immediately and was associated with it for the rest of his life, from 1912 to 1922 as chief geologist. He was curator of paleobotany of the U.S. National Museum from 1903 to 1935 and was also an associate of the Carnegie Institution of Washington. His most important research was done before 1912; after that, administrative duties occupied most of his time. A keen observer, he supplemented the description of fossils with interpretations of their place in the time scale and their role in the formation of coal and petroleum. More precise in his methods than earlier scientists, he was able to disprove prevailing theories about the Appalachian coal basin and to show that coals could be classified according to their degree of deoxygenation. In 1915 he announced a generalization from this work—the so-called carbon-ratio hypothesis—that allowed the determination of the rank of a coal on the evolutionary scale. The idea soon became economically important when it became clear that it was now possible to predict the occurrence of liquid and gaseous hydrocarbons in association with certain kinds of coal. White was thus one of the founders of the twentieth-century petroleum industry. His theory of the carbon ratio was developed in a paper, "Metamorphism of Organic Sediments and Derived Oils," 1935. Among his books were *Fossil Flora of the Lower Coal Measures of Missouri*, 1899, and *Flora of the Hermit Shale, Grand Canyon, Arizona*, 1929. He died in Washington, D.C., on February 7, 1935.

White, Edward Douglass (1845–1921), justice of the Supreme Court. Born in Lafourche Parish, Louisiana, on November 3, 1845, White was educated at Catholic schools in New Orleans and Maryland and in 1857 entered Georgetown College (now University) in Georgetown, D.C. At fifteen he left college to join the Confederate army and was soon captured. Paroled, he settled in New Orleans, took up the study of law, and was admitted to the bar in 1868. He soon became involved in politics and was elected to the Louisiana state senate in 1874 and 1876. From 1879 to 1880 he served on the state supreme court, his tenure being cut short by the reorganization of the court under a new state constitution. For the next ten years he remained out of office, although maintaining his political ties, and aided in the founding of Tulane University. He was elected to the U.S. Senate, taking his seat in March 1891, and three years later was appointed to the Supreme Court by President Grover Cleveland. Although not a legal scholar, White achieved a high reputation on the Court, principally through dissents in the Income Tax Cases in 1895 and his opinions, both concurring and dissenting, in the early Insular Cases of 1901, arising from the territorial acquisitions of the Spanish-American War, in which he formulated the "White doctrine" of incorporated and unincorporated territories; by that doctrine it was held that the assumption of sovereignty over a territory did not automatically extend to it all the constitutional protections applying to a territory incorporated into the United States. In other major cases of the period he concurred with the majority in *United States* v. *E.C. Knight Co.*, 1895, by which the Sherman Anti-Trust Act was narrowly construed; *In re Debs*, 1895, in which the use of court injunctions against labor was upheld; and *Adair* v. *United States*, 1908, which struck down a law outlawing "yellow-dog" contracts in the railroad industry; and dissented in *Northern Securities Co.* v. *United States*, 1904, in which the Sherman Anti-Trust Act was rejuvenated; and *Lochner* v. *New York*, 1905, in which a New York State law regulating working hours for bakers was struck down. In 1910 he was named by President William Howard Taft to succeed the late Chief Justice Melville W. Fuller, becoming the first associate justice to be so promoted. In his remaining years on the bench his major contribution to jurisprudence was his "rule of reason" invoked to interpret the Sherman Anti-Trust Act in *Standard Oil Co.* v. *United States* in 1911. The "rule," as first employed by White in *United States* v. *Trans-Missouri Freight Association*, 1897, added to the "restraint of trade" test in the Sherman Anti-Trust Act the vague qualification of "reasonable" and "unreasonable," an interpretation of the law that was widely criticized but that remained a basic tool of the Court in dealing with antitrust cases thereafter. In all he wrote nearly a thousand opinions and was a strong conservative and nationalistic voice on the Court. He died in Washington, D.C., on May 19, 1921.

White, Elwyn Brooks (1899–   ), humorist and author. Born in Mount Vernon, New York, on July 11, 1899, E. B. White attended Cornell University and graduated in 1921 after military service in World War I. He worked as a reporter on the *Seattle Times* and as a ship's messboy on the Alaska run before he moved to New York City. While working for an advertising agency he wrote poems and pieces which he submitted to the *New Yorker* and which earned him a staff position with that magazine. For 11 years he wrote most of its "Talk of the Town" section. His collection of poems, *The Lady Is Cold*, appeared in 1929, as did his book written with James Thurber, *Is Sex Necessary?* His essays, editorials, and parodies on any subject—in prose or verse—led some critics to call him "a writer's writer." His "One Man's Meat" column appeared in *Harper's Magazine* from 1938 to 1943 and in book form under the same title in 1942 (revised and enlarged, 1944). His versatility was shown in *The Wild Flag*, 1946, a serious satire about world government, and "Across the River and into the Bar," a hilarious parody of Ernest Hemingway. The gentle fantasy of his three children's books, *Stuart Little*, 1945, *Charlotte's Web*, 1952, and *Trumpet of the Swan*, 1970, proved equally delightful to adults. Among his other books were *Every Day Is Saturday*, 1934; *The Fox of Peaback*, 1938; and *Quo Vadimus?*, 1939. *Here Is New York*, 1949, reprinted his famous *Holiday* magazine essay. *The Second Tree from the Corner* appeared in 1953, and *The Points of My Compass* in 1962. A notable anthology that he edited with his wife, *A Subtreasury of American Humor*, first appeared in 1941. In 1959 he published a revised edition of William Strunk, Jr.'s, 1918 manual, *The Elements of Style*.

White, George Leonard (1838–1895), choral conductor. Born in Cadiz, Cattaraugus County, New York, on September 20, 1838, White studied music at home and went on to teach it in schools and churches after moving to Ohio at the age of twenty. After serving with the Union army in the Civil War he worked for two years for the Freedmen's Bureau. In 1867 he became a teacher of vocal music at Fisk University in Nashville, Tennessee. In order to raise money for the financially pressed Negro school, White got the idea of taking a musical group on tour through Northern cities to sing and ask for contributions. He borrowed expense money from other teachers and from residents of Nashville and set out with his small troupe of Jubilee Singers in 1871. They sang in churches and public halls to great public acclaim, and on their first tour raised more than $20,000. For the next seven years the tours continued, and included trips to England, Germany, and other European countries. In all, the Jubilee Singers raised about $150,000 for Fisk University and for the education of black people. White remained at Fisk, serving also as treasurer and as a trustee, until 1885, when an accident forced him to give up his choral work. He taught for a few years at other institutions, then went into retirement in Ithaca, New York, where he died on November 8, 1895.

White, John (? –1593?), painter, cartographer, and colonial official. Aside from the role White played in the colonizing ventures promoted by Sir Walter Raleigh in the Chesapeake Bay regions, 1585–1590, almost nothing is known of his life. He was born in England and spent his later years in Ireland. His reputation derives from his work as painter and cartographer of the expedition and from his work as governor of Raleigh's second colony at Roanoke Island. He accompanied the first expedition sent out by Raleigh, which sailed from England on April 9, 1585, in ships under the command of Sir Richard Grenville. After stops in the West Indies, the ships arrived at Roanoke Island on July 3. A group with Governor Sir Ralph Lane in charge was left to spend the next 11 months, but White returned to England with the ships. On this first visit he executed a sizable number of paintings depicting the life of the Indians and the flora and fauna of the coast from Florida to Virginia. In addition he devised maps of the region which were widely reprinted and influential for later explorations and for European understanding of North America. The whole first colony returned to England in June 1586. For his second attempt at planting a colony, Raleigh selected White as governor. The ships sailed on May 8, 1587, with 117 people, including White's daughter, Eleanor (Mrs. Ananias) Dare, who would, shortly after arrival at Roanoke, give birth to Virginia Dare, the first English child born in North America. Instead of selecting a new site as Raleigh hoped they would, the expedition landed at Roanoke because the commander of the ships was anxious to disembark the colonists and go off privateering. When a ship was dispatched to England in late August to obtain supplies, White went along, hoping to promote the future of the colony there. Unfortunately for the stranded colonists, no relief ship was sent to them in 1588 or 1589, owing largely to war between England and Spain. When ships finally crossed over again in 1590, White went along. On arriving at Roanoke, they found that the only sign of the colony was an inscription that seemed to indicate that the settlers had fled from hostile Indians and taken refuge with the Croatan tribe. They were never found, and White returned to England. It is believed that he died in Ireland about 1593.

White, Margaret, *see* Bourke-White, Margaret

White, Stanford (1853–1906), architect. Born in New York City on November 9, 1853, White was the son of a well-known scholar and literary critic, Richard Grant White. After a rather desultory education, in the course of which he showed great artistic talent but was discouraged in his ambition to be a painter by John La Farge, a family friend, he joined the architectural firm of Gambrill & Richardson at the age of nineteen. H. H. Richardson was then the most influential architect in the United States and also a family friend, and he took young White under his wing, teaching him personally to draw and involving him in the work on one of his own major achievements, Boston's Trinity Church. In 1878 White went to Europe to study, to live with the Augustus Saint-Gaudens family in Paris, and to design the pedestal for the statue of Adm. David G. Farragut that the great sculptor was creating for Madison Square in New York City. The next year, together with two friends of long standing, Charles Fallen and W. R. Mead, White formed the famous firm of McKim, Mead & White, the most important architectural group in U.S. history until the later twentieth century. White was known as the Cellini, McKim as the Bramante, and Mead was popularly supposed to bear the burden of being associated with his two flighty friends, but in fact all three were exceptionally talented, although White was probably the most creative and imaginative. White worked in a large number of styles, always with great skill; he maintained throughout his career that any two or more things that were beautiful in themselves could be combined in a harmonious and beautiful whole, and he exemplified this eclecticism in, among other places, his own Long Island home, a made-over farmhouse embellished with gilded Spanish columns, Renaissance fireplaces, Persian rugs, Roman fragments, and Dutch tiles. Until about 1887 the firm specialized in enormous shingled buildings, exemplified by White's Casino at Newport, Rhode Island, 1881. Slowly, over the years, the firm turned from the romantic style of Richardson to classic modes and a Renaissance style that is best known to this day as that of White himself. Among the celebrated examples of his formal planning are the Villard Houses, completed in 1885, the Century and Metropolitan clubs, the New York Herald Building, the Madison Square Garden Presbyterian Church (torn down in 1919), and the old Madison Square Garden itself, all in New York City, as well as many luxurious homes in New York City, Newport, and the Berkshires. Among other buildings in different styles were the Judson Memorial church, on Washington Square in New York City, and White's restoration of the Rotunda and his designs for several accompanying buildings at the University of Virginia, where he worked reverently in the spirit of the original designer, Thomas Jefferson. Perhaps his most famous structure is the Washington Arch, at the foot of Fifth Avenue in New York City, which still stands, but his favorite was probably Madison Square Garden (1889), now long since gone, in the tower of which he built an apartment for himself. His dinners in this eyrie were famous, but after one of them, on the night of June 25, 1906, he was set upon by Harry K. Thaw, a wealthy playboy who was apparently jealous of White's former relationship with Mrs. Thaw, whom he had known when she was a chorus girl. White was shot to death. Thaw was adjudged insane.

White, Walter Francis (1893–1955), author and civil-rights leader. Born on July 1, 1893, in Atlanta, Georgia, White was by personal choice a Negro—his features and coloring were such that he could easily have passed for white if he had chosen to do so. He attended Atlanta Preparatory School and graduated from Atlanta University in 1916. In Atlanta he became active in organizing the local branch of the National Association for the Advancement of Colored People (NAACP), and his efforts were so successful that in 1918 he was called to New York City, to become assistant secretary of the NAACP. For the next ten years, passing as a white reporter while in the South, he investigated some 40 lynchings and eight race riots. He interviewed members of lynch mobs and many state officials. In 1930 he became secretary of the NAACP, and began to work for federal civil-rights legislation. His first-hand knowledge of the attitudes and conditions in the South gave impetus to his fight for legislations to bar lynching and racial segregation. He lobbied effectively to keep a North Carolina segregationist from being seated on the Supreme Court. In 1937 he was awarded the Spingarn Medal by the NAACP. He was consulted by presidents Franklin D. Roosevelt and Harry S. Truman, and was able to stimulate the formation of the Committee on Fair Employment Practice during World War II and to help secure a more liberal stance on civil rights in both administrations. In 1939, when singer Marian Anderson was refused the use of Constitution Hall in Washington, D.C., he arranged an open-air concert for her at the Lincoln Memorial that attracted 75,000 people. In 1945 and 1948 he served as a consultant to the U.S. delegations to the United Nations and he was a consultant to and a member of many state, national, and international civic and governmental organizations concerned with civil liberties. His books included two novels, *Fire in the Flint*, 1924, and *Flight*, 1926; *Rope and Faggot: A Biography of Judge Lynch*, 1929; *A Rising Wind: A Report of the Negro Soldier in the European Theater of War*, 1945; *A Man Called White*, 1948, an autobiography; and *How Far the Promised Land*, published posthumously in 1955. He died in New York City on March 21, 1955.

White, William (1748–1836), religious leader. Born in Philadelphia on April 4, 1748, White graduated from the College of Philadelphia (later the University of Pennsylvania) in 1765. He studied for the ministry and was ordained in the Anglican church in London in April 1772. During the whole of his long career he served a parish in Philadelphia, even while occupying the post of presiding bishop. During the years of conflict with England he remained loyal to the American cause and was appointed chaplain to the Continental Congress. Following the Revolutionary War he took the lead in "Americanizing" the Anglican church in the United States. The Church of England suffered more during the Revolution than other denominations because it was regarded as a British institution and its adherents were continually suspected of disloyalty. With national independence achieved, White among others realized the need for an American denomination with its own episcopate and not subject to the governance of Canterbury. In 1782 he published a pamphlet, *The Case of the Episcopal Church in the United States Considered*, which set forth a plan to form a national Episcopal church. He promoted a church convention at Philadelphia in 1785 which settled on a name, the Protestant Episcopal Church of America, and agreed upon a constitution. One of the principles of White's plan for the church was greater lay participation; the result was a general convention of the church, with both a house of bishops and a house of deputies. The convention also selected White to be one of the bishops. Thus White went to England and was consecrated bishop of Pennsylvania in February 1787. In 1789 he presided over the convention which finally united all former Anglican congregations in the Protestant Episcopal church. He continued his pastoral work in Philadelphia and in 1795 was named to succeed Samuel Seabury as presiding bishop of the church, a post he held until his death. In his work he was not limited by denominational lines, but cooperated with clergy of all churches while building up the parishes in his diocese. He assisted in the revision of the liturgy and the Book of Common Prayer to meet American circumstances. Apart from his ecclesiastical tasks, White took little part in public life, but did serve as chaplain for the U.S. Congress for a time. Among his published works were *Christian Baptism*, 1808; *Lectures on the Catechism*, 1813; and *Memoirs of the Protestant Episcopal Church in the United States of America*, 1820, a valuable source for the early history of the church. He died in Philadelphia on July 17, 1836.

White, William Allen (1868–1944), journalist. Born on February 10, 1868, in Emporia, Kansas, White attended the University of Kansas and held positions on the *El Dorado* (Kansas) *Republican* and the *Kansas City Star* before purchasing the *Emporia Daily and Weekly Gazette* in 1895. Through his editorials in the *Gazette* he became a rural spokesman for liberalism in the Republican party and in the nation. His paper had a small circulation, but his editorials were widely reprinted and "The Sage of Emporia" was quoted by papers throughout the nation. He first won recognition in August 1896 for "What's the Matter with Kansas?," an editorial that attacked the Populists and boosted William McKinley's campaign for the presidency. He won the Pulitzer Prize for editorial writing in 1923. Collections of his editorials were published in *The Editor and His People*, 1924, and *Forty Years on Main Street*, 1937. He was usually a loyal Republican, but he proved himself an individualist when in 1912 he actively promoted Theodore Roosevelt's Bull Moose Progressive party. He was at times associated with the loosely organized "muckraker" movement of investigative journalists, and in 1906 he joined with Ray Stannard Baker, Finley Peter Dunne, Ida M. Tarbell, and Lincoln Steffens in taking over the *American Magazine*. Others among his numerous books, some of them novels, were *Strategem and Spoils*, 1901; *In Our Town*, 1906; *A Certain Rich Man*, 1909; *In the Heart of a Fool*, 1918; and *Politics: the Citizen's Business*, 1924. He also published biographies of Woodrow Wilson and Calvin Coolidge. His *Autobiography* was published posthumously in 1946 and was awarded a Pulitzer Prize. He died in Emporia, Kansas, on January 29, 1944.

Whitefield, Charles T., *see* Doubleday, Frank Nelson

Whitehead, Alfred North (1861–1947), philosopher and mathematician. Born in Ramsgate, England, on February 15, 1861, Whitehead entered Trinity College, Cambridge, in 1880, remaining as student, fellow, and lecturer until 1910. From 1911 to 1914 he was a lecturer at University College, London, and from 1914 to 1942 was professor of mathematics and from 1921 to 1924 dean of the Imperial College of Science and Technology of the University of London. He was by then sixty-three years old and faced with the necessity of retiring if he remained in England. He therefore accepted a professorship of philosophy at Harvard, which he held from 1924 until his death, after 1936 as professor emeritus. He enjoyed the freedom that he found in the United States: "From twenty on I was interested in philosophy, religion, logic, and history," he once said. "Harvard gave me a chance to express myself." He was senior member of Harvard's Society of Fellows in his later years and was one of the intellectual monuments of the university community. He published his first important book in 1898, *A Treatise on Universal Algebra*; an attempt to house all mathematics under one roof, it recorded, in its introduction, a debt to a young student, one B. Russell. This was Bertrand Russell, then twenty-six, with whom Whitehead set to work to deduce the whole of mathematics from a few logical principles. The result was *Principia Mathematica*, three volumes, 1910–1913, a fundamental study of the structure of mathematical and logical thought that has been called one of the greatest contributions to logic since Aristotle and has been compared with Sir Isaac Newton's *Principia* for its mathematical power and innovation. Other books by Whitehead that were written before he left England were *An Introduction to Mathematics*, 1910; *The Organization of Thought*, 1916; *The Principles of Natural Knowledge*, 1919; *The Concept of Nature*, 1920; and *The Principle of Relativity*, 1922. But his most popular and widely read works appeared after he moved to Harvard. *Science and the Modern World* was published in 1925; he followed it with *Religion in the Making*, 1926; *The Aims of Education*, 1928; *Process and Reality*, 1929; and *Adventures of Ideas*, 1933. These and other books stressed individuality, creative interaction, and a pantheistic approach to religion, and were attempts to modify what Whitehead felt to be a contemporary overemphasis on science and deterministic philosophy. The works were often abstruse but included illuminating references to history and everyday life. The wise man showed through the thicket of technicalities and won Whitehead a large number of devoted disciples. One of the major philosophers of the twentieth century, he died in Cambridge, Massachusetts, on December 30, 1947.

Whiteman, Paul (1890–1967), conductor. Born in Denver, Colorado, on March 28, 1890, the young Whiteman received training in classical music at home and in school. As a teen-ager he played first viola for the Denver Symphony Orchestra and then for the San Francisco Symphony, and during World War I he served in the navy as a bandmaster. Following the war he discovered jazz music and in 1919 joined a jazz band. He regarded jazz, in his own words, as "simply a way of playing any music." The jazz he first knew was an intuitive music, usually played by musicians with little formal training doing individual improvisations around a common chord sequence. Whiteman took jazz elements such as blues notation and syncopated dance rhythms, elaborated them into music to be played by an orchestra, and at a time when jazz was not widely accepted, made it acceptable to at least avant-garde members of polite society. He gave jazz a style and form it had not had, and in doing so eventually captured a huge audience to become one of the most popular musician-entertainers of several decades. Beginning to appear with great success in California in 1919, he crossed the country and played in Atlantic City and New York City; in 1920 he opened the Palais Royale on Broadway. In a sense, his style and showmanship inaugurated the "Roaring Twenties" and the Jazz Age with that engagement. He organized other bands to play in clubs all over the nation, and in four years there were more than 50 Paul Whiteman bands. In 1924 he gave the first formal jazz concert, at Aeolian Hall in New York City. The featured piece, written for the occasion, was George Gershwin's epoch-making *Rhapsody in Blue*, and Gershwin appeared to play it as piano soloist. Whiteman toured the country, playing in vaudeville houses, giving concerts, appearing in nightclubs and in Broadway shows, and during the 1930s and 1940s made several movies. From 1932 until 1950 he had his own radio program, and during the 1950s he was frequently on television and continued his personal appearances. Renowned in both the United States and Europe, he introduced noted vocal and instrumental artists to the public, among them Bing Crosby, Bix Beiderbecke, Jack Teagarden, and Tommy and Jimmy Dorsey. Among the serious jazz compositions he introduced, in addition to Gershwin's work, was Ferde Grofé's *Grand Canyon Suite*. Whiteman's last public appearance was in 1962, after which he lived in retirement until his death in Doylestown, Pennsylvania, on December 29, 1967.

Whitlock, Brand (1869–1934), author, public official, and diplomat. Born in Urbana, Ohio, on March 4, 1869, Whitlock took up news reporting as soon as he was out of high school. He worked on a Toledo newspaper from 1887 until 1890, then moved to Chicago to become a reporter for the *Chicago Herald*. His interest in politics influenced him to study law, and he was admitted to the Illinois bar in 1894 and three years later to the Ohio bar. He opened a law office in Toledo and practiced until 1905, but he was torn between a career of full-time writing and political activism. Two acquaintances in public office—John P. Altgeld, governor of Illinois in the early 1890s, and Mayor Samuel M. "Golden Rule" Jones of Toledo —led him to turn to urban reform politics. He worked with Jones as legal adviser and secretary, and on Jones's death in 1904 decided to run for mayor himself on an independent ticket. He won the election of 1905 and was reelected mayor three times, but retired in 1911 without seeking another term because he was disillusioned with the possibilities of real reform in city politics. He returned

to writing and to his law practice, but in 1913 President Woodrow Wilson appointed him U.S. minister to Belgium. During World War I, he operated the Belgium Relief Commission, and he went with the Belgian government into exile when Belgium was invaded. He returned to Brussels in 1919 as U.S. ambassador. He remained in the post until February 1922, then went into retirement because of ill health, living the rest of his life in southern France. Whitlock's literary output, consisting of 18 books of fiction and nonfiction, was spread over a 30-year period from 1902 until 1933, apart from earlier magazine and newspaper pieces. About his own life and experiences in politics he wrote *Forty Years of It*, 1914, his autobiography, and *On the Enforcement of Law in Cities*, 1913, as well as the novels *The Thirteenth District*, 1902, and *The Turn of the Balance*, 1907, considered his best fictional work. His wartime experiences were described in *Belgium, a Personal Narrative*, 1919. Other novels included *Her Infinite Variety*, 1904; *The Happy Average*, 1904; *J. Hardin & Son*, 1923; *Uprooted*, 1926; *Transplanted*, 1927; and *Big Matt*, 1928. Whitlock died in Cannes, France, on May 24, 1934.

Whitman, Marcus (1802–1847), physician and frontier missionary. Born in Rushville, New York, on September 4, 1802, Whitman studied medicine privately and later attended the College of Physicians and Surgeons at Fairfield, Herkimer County, New York. For several years he practiced medicine, first in Canada and later in Wheeler, Steuben County, New York. In 1834, when missionaries were being recruited to work among the Indians of the Far West, Whitman offered his services and was accepted by the American Board of Commissioners for Foreign Missions, representing Congregational, Presbyterian, and Reformed churches. In 1835 he went West to verify the desire of the Indians to have missionaries among them, and when he became convinced of their earnestness, he returned to the East to get additional missionaries and supplies. His party traveled to the Oregon territory with a caravan of fur traders in 1836. For his mission station Whitman selected a spot named Waiilatpu, about nine miles east of present-day Walla Walla, Washington. Other members of the party established another mission, Lapwai, to the north in present-day Idaho. The Idaho missionaries ministered to the Nez Percé and Flathead Indians while Whitman worked among the Cayuse, Walla Walla, and Umatilla Indians. Waiilatpu was on the overland route that would soon become known as the Oregon Trail. The mission team worked there teaching the Indians the rudiments of modern farming, holding school, treating the sick, and giving religious instruction. Within a few years other missionaries arrived and other stations were opened in the Oregon country. In 1842 a letter came from the mission board at Boston ordering Whitman and his wife, the former Narcissa Prentiss, to close their station and settle at one of the other locations. Whitman was determined to keep the post open, both for its services to the Indians and because it was the first rest stop for caravans of immigrants coming into the Oregon territory. In October 1842 he set out on horseback for Boston and arrived there in April 1843. He convinced the board members that they should keep the mission open and also conferred with government officials about encouraging settlement in the region. He returned West as guide for a wagon train of more than 900 settlers. In Whitman's absence, the Indians among whom he worked had begun to grow uneasy. They heard rumours he was bringing back U.S. troops with him, and his arrival with a large party of white settlers did not assuage their anxieties. Their distrust mounted during the next three years as larger parties of settlers passed through, 3000 in 1845 alone. The Indians also began to distrust his medical ability, particularly his inability to deal effectively with outbreaks of smallpox and measles. Unfortunately the 1847 migration of whites brought with it a severe measles epidemic in which many Indians died, although whites generally recovered. They reasoned that Whitman was deliberately poisoning them. On November 29, 1847, a large number of Cayuse and other Indians were gathered at the mission; suddenly they attacked, killing 14 persons, including Whitman and his wife. The rest of the whites at the mission were held captive until ransomed by Peter Skene Ogden of the Hudson's Bay Company more than two weeks later. Out of the massacre came the Cayuse War of 1848–1850 and the eventual surrender of those who had done the killings; they were hanged at Oregon City in May 1850.

Whitman, Walt (1819–1892), poet. Born in West Hills, Long Island, New York, on May 31, 1819, Walter Whitman grew up there and, from the age of four, in Brooklyn. He attended school until he was twelve and then became a printer's devil, working on a succession of newspapers on Long Island and around New York City. He taught school occasionally as well until he established himself as a competent journalist. He held positions with and contributed to several leading magazines, including *Brother Jonathan*, *American Review*, and *Democratic Review*, and from 1846 to 1848 was editor of the *Brooklyn Eagle*, finally losing his position because of his Free-Soil inclinations. Of his early published prose and verse nothing was remarkable. He traveled to New Orleans, worked briefly there for the *New Orleans Crescent*, and returned to New York City. There, while supporting himself by newspaper writing and house-building, he began to experiment with radically new verse forms. Under the influence of Thomas Carlyle and Ralph Waldo Emerson, among others, his thoughts on man expanded into a triumphant vision of the robust individual and the robust democratic society; to keep pace with the vision, his poetry quickly lost all trace of convention and became a blend of rhythmically rambling discourse, mystical imagery, and epic cataloguery. In 1855 he assembled 12 poems, including those later titled "Song of Myself," "I Sing the Body Electric," and "There Was a Child Went Forth," prefaced by a lengthy introduction, and published them at his own expense as *Leaves of Grass*. The book featured an engraved likeness of himself in loose workman's clothes (he had once been something of a dandy about New York) with a jaunty, self-confident demeanor, and gave the author's name as Walt Whitman. It was a failure with the public and drew a mixed critical response; Emerson, however, to whom he sent a copy, wrote back that he found it "the most extraordinary piece of wit and wisdom that America has yet contributed. . . . I greet you at the beginning of a great career." Though Emerson later tempered his praise, Whitman seized upon the last sentence and had it stamped on the cover of the enlarged second edition in 1856. Not until the third edition, in 1860, did sales of the book become noticeable; by that time "By Blue Ontario's Shore," "Crossing Brooklyn Ferry," "Song of the Open Road," "Out of the Cradle Endlessly Rocking," and many other new poems had been added and the book was divided into more-or-less topical sections. Late in 1862 Whitman traveled to Virginia to seek his wounded brother on a Civil War battlefield, and then took up residence in Washington, D.C., where he devoted himself to caring for wounded soldiers. The publication of his war poems in 1865 as *Drum Taps*, to which "When Lilacs Last in the Dooryard Bloom'd" was appended and all of which was later incorporated into *Leaves of Grass*, marked the beginning of a mellower, maturer period during which his image was slowly transformed from that of the barbaric young man to that of the Good Gray Poet (the title of an 1866 pamphlet by a devoted disciple). Nonetheless, soon after obtaining a clerkship in the Department of the Interior in 1865 he was discharged for being the author of *Leaves of Grass*, a book supposedly replete with scandalously explicit sexual references. He found another position in the attorney general's office and remained in Washington until he suffered a paralytic stroke in 1873; then he moved to Camden, New Jersey. Larger and reorganized editions of *Leaves of Grass* continued to appear until the definitive "deathbed" version of 1892; he also published two remarkable works in prose, *Democratic Vistas*, 1871, and *Specimen Days*, 1882. His reputation grew more rapidly in Europe than in the United States during his lifetime, and his poetry was translated into many languages. His fame at home increased due to the efforts of younger champions, notably John Burroughs, but it did not begin to match his literary significance until after his death in Camden on March 26, 1892. He was elected to the Hall of Fame in 1930.

Whitney, Asa (1791–1874), inventor and manufacturer. Born in Townsend, Massachusetts, on December 1, 1791, Whitney learned the mechanical and technical trades while working for his father, a blacksmith, and in a number of machine shops. For most of the 1820s he worked as a wheelwright, then in 1830 went to work for the Mohawk & Hudson Railroad, constructing railroad cars and installing machinery. From 1833 to 1839 he was superintendent of the line. His mechanical abilities were such that he was appointed canal commissioner for New York State in 1839 and held the post for three years. In 1840 he received a patent for a steam locomotive and from 1842 to 1846 he was, in partnership with Matthias W. Baldwin, a locomotive builder in Philadelphia. In 1849 he formed his own manufacturing company, Asa Whitney & Sons, to turn out an improved cast-iron railroad car wheel that he had invented and patented. Within a few years he was the largest manufacturer of car wheels in the country. In 1860–1861 he served as president of the Philadelphia & Reading Railroad, but poor health forced him to retire. He continued to live in Philadelphia until his death on June 4, 1874.

Whitney, Eli (1765–1825), inventor. Born in Westborough, Massachusetts, on December 8, 1765, Whitney showed little fondness for school at first, but was particularly apt in his father's shop at making and repairing violins and had a business during 1781–1783 manufacturing nails and hatpins. He taught school in Pennsylvania to support his education at the Leicester Academy in Leicester, Massachusetts, and graduated from Yale in 1792. After traveling to Georgia, where he had been engaged as a tutor, he met Mrs. Nathanael Greene and her plantation manager, Phineas Miller; through them he learned of the pressing need in the South for a device that could be used to separate short-staple upland cotton from its seeds. Within a matter of weeks he designed and built a hand-operated cotton gin, which, by April 1793, he had improved so that one operator could use it to clean 50 pounds of cotton daily. He went into partnership with Miller to patent and manufacture cotton gins, and although they received a patent in 1794, throngs of others had seen the original and duplicated it; the subsequent infringements and litigation left them with practically no reward for the invention, although Whitney's claim was finally validated in 1807. He had anticipated financial problems and in 1798 obtained a government contract to supply 10,000 muskets on the basis of a system he had devised for manufacturing interchangeable parts. He purchased a factory site near New Haven, Connecticut, an area now known as Whitneyville, and built nearly all the tools and machinery for the factory, including what is believed to be the first successful milling machine. His system of using interchangeable parts manufactured and assembled by workers who required little skill was of vast significance in industrial development and eventually brought him liberal compensation. In the meantime, cotton growing had been revolutionized by his invention; by 1795 U.S. exports were more than 40 times greater than in the year before the invention of the cotton gin, and Whitney became one of the most celebrated inventors in American history. His only financial returns, however, came from his

musket factory, which prospered on numerous government contracts. He died in New Haven on January 8, 1825. He was elected to the Hall of Fame in 1900.

Whitney, Josiah Dwight (1819–1896), geologist. Born in Northampton, Massachusetts, on November 23, 1819, Whitney was educated at private schools, including George Bancroft's Round Hill School and Phillips Academy in Andover, Massachusetts, and he graduated from Yale in 1839. Intended by his father for a business career, he came under the influence of Benjamin Silliman while at Yale and after graduation studied chemistry and worked as an assistant to geologist Charles T. Jackson. After a period of indecision, during which he briefly read law, he traveled to Europe in 1842 to continue his scientific studies. Except for a few months in 1845, when he worked as a geologist for the Isle Royale Copper Company, he remained abroad until 1847, helping to support himself by publishing *The Use of the Blowpipe in Chemistry and Mineralogy*, 1845, a translation from an 1820 work in German by Jöns Berzelius. On his return to the United States in 1847 he was engaged to assist Jackson in a survey of ore deposits in the Upper Peninsula of Michigan. Jackson soon resigned, leaving Whitney and another assistant, John W. Foster, in charge; they completed the survey in 1849 and submitted a detailed report, which was published by Congress in two volumes in 1850–1851. For six years Whitney worked as an independent consulting mining geologist and during that time compiled *The Metallic Wealth of the United States*, 1854, a pioneering and highly influential treatment of the topic. During 1855–1858 he was a professor of geology at the University of Iowa while assisting James Hall on the state geological survey. He later served on the state surveys of Illinois and Wisconsin and in 1860 was appointed state geologist of California. In that post he immediately undertook an ambitious program of field work, utilizing various novel techniques and training on his staff a number of geologists who were later prominent, including Clarence King. In 1864 he headed a field expedition that measured the height of the highest peak in the state—also the highest peak in the United States outside of Alaska—which was subsequently named Whitney in his honor. While in California, in 1865, he was named Sturgis-Hooper Professor of Geology at Harvard, where he was to organize, on completing his work in California, a school of mines. In 1868 the California legislature suspended financial support for the state survey but retained Whitney in his post. He was able to prepare three volumes of his report on the work of the survey before appropriations ran out. He had already taken up his new duties at Harvard and begun field training for students when, in 1874, he at last relinquished his California post. The next year the school of mines was made a department of the Lawrence Scientific School at Harvard and Whitney's professorship was likewise transferred to Lawrence. He remained at Harvard for the rest of his life, publishing, among other works, *Climatic Changes of Later Geological Times*, 1882; *Names and Places*, 1888; and *The United States: Facts and Figures Illustrating the Physical Geography of the Country and Its Material Resources*, 1889, a collection of articles he had written for the *Encyclopaedia Britannica*. He also contributed to *The Century Dictionary*, 1889–1891, edited by his younger brother, William Dwight Whitney. Josiah D. Whitney died at Lake Sunapee, New Hampshire, on August 19, 1896.

Whitney, William Collins (1841–1904), businessman and public official. Born in Conway, Massachusetts, on July 5, 1841, Whitney graduated from Yale in 1863. He studied law at Harvard and was admitted to the New York bar in 1865. He soon became successful as a lawyer and active in New York City politics as an anti-Tammany Democrat. He was a supporter of Samuel J. Tilden and helped break up the notorious "Tweed Ring." From 1875 to 1882 he served as corporation counsel for the city, and spent much of his time contesting the large number of lawsuits brought against the city on account of the depredations of the Tweed Ring. Because of the strong and effective support he gave the Democratic ticket in the 1884 election, President Grover Cleveland appointed him secretary of the navy in 1885. During four years in this post, he was responsible for the revival and modernizing of the navy as a military force. Because the United States had no steel mills that could make armor plate or gun forgings, he gave Bethlehem Steel contracts large enough to enable them to build a new steel mill. Construction of war vessels increased and naval appropriations more than doubled. He built up the newly opened Naval War College at Newport, Rhode Island, and installed Alfred Thayer Mahan as its head in 1886. In 1889 Whitney returned to private life and to his business interests in New York City, which included operation of the Metropolitan Traction Company, chartered in 1886 to operate the streetcars and elevated trains of the city. In the traction business he was associated with the flamboyant Thomas F. Ryan. Whitney was active in Cleveland's 1892 campaign for the presidency, but declined to support William Jennings Bryan in 1896 because of the free-silver issue. The last few years of his life he devoted to raising racehorses and operating stables near Lexington, Kentucky. He died in New York City on February 2, 1904.

Whitney, William Dwight (1827–1894), linguist. Born in Northampton, Massachusetts, on February 9, 1827, Whitney, a younger brother of Josiah D. Whitney, graduated from Williams College in 1845. Turning from an original predilection for natural science to the field of linguistics, he began the study of Sanskrit privately, working at home for three years. In 1849–1850 he attended Yale, then continued his language studies at Berlin and Tübingen in Germany from 1850 to 1853. In 1854

he became professor of Sanskrit at Yale, adding in 1869 the title of professor of philology. Whitney was a pioneer in the field of linguistics and Sanskrit in the United States, and published a large number of studies as well as manuscripts and translations of Sanskrit texts. In 1879 he issued in Leipzig his *Sanskrit Grammar*, which became the standard work in the field, and he also published several edited and translated versions of classical Sanskrit texts, notably the *Atharva-Veda*. He also wrote texts for the study of German, French, and English and taught German and French both privately and at the college level. Upon the organization in 1861 of the Sheffield Scientific School at Yale he organized a department of modern languages and served as its head. During the 1880s he served as editor in chief of the six-volume *Century Dictionary*, 1889–1891. In the area of general linguistics he published *Language and the Study of Language*, 1867, and *The Life and Growth of Language*, 1875. He was long active in the American Oriental Society, serving as corresponding secretary, 1857–1884, and as president, 1884–1890, and in 1869 he led in founding and served as first president of the American Philological Association. He remained at Yale until his death in New Haven, Connecticut, on June 7, 1894.

Whittaker, Charles Evans (1901–1973), justice of the Supreme Court. Born on February 22, 1901, near Troy, Kansas, Whittaker left school at sixteen and for three years worked on his father's farm. He then made his way to Kansas City, Missouri, and, despite the lack of a high-school diploma, enrolled in the University of Kansas City Law School. He was admitted to the bar in 1923 and received his law degree the next year. As a member of a Kansas City law firm, of which he became a partner in 1930, Whittaker practiced corporation law in Kansas City for three decades, gaining a reputation as a diligent worker and eventually becoming president of the Missouri State Bar Association. In 1954 President Dwight D. Eisenhower appointed him to the U.S. District Court for western Missouri; after serving in that post for two years he was elevated in 1956 to the U.S. Court of Appeals for the Eighth Circuit. In 1957, on the retirement of Stanley F. Reed, he was named by President Eisenhower to the Supreme Court. In five years on the Court he again won respect for hard work and attention to detail, but in that time he wrote no major opinions and left little mark on the course of legal thought. He voted usually with the Court's conservative bloc and often cast the swing vote in 5–4 decisions. He resigned in 1962 for reasons of health and thereafter devoted himself to the private practice of law. Whittaker died in Kansas City on November 26, 1973.

Whittier, John Greenleaf (1807–1892), poet and abolitionist. Born on December 17, 1807, near Haverhill, Massachusetts, Whittier had little schooling as a child but was an avid reader and early developed a love of poetry. He was throughout life a devout Quaker. In 1826 his sister sent one of his poems, "The Exile's Departure," to William Lloyd Garrison, who printed it in his *Newburyport Free Press*. During 1827–1828 Whittier attended Haverhill Academy and continued to write poetry. From 1829 he engaged in journalism and from 1830 to 1832 was editor of the *New England Weekly Review*. His first book, *Legends of New England in Prose and Verse*, appeared in 1831 and was followed the next year by *Moll Pitcher*. After 1833 he devoted himself to the cause of abolitionism. He favored regular political action—an issue over which he broke with Garrison in 1840—and in 1835 sat in the Massachusetts legislature as a Whig. From 1840 he was active in the American and Foreign Anti-Slavery Society and in 1842 he ran for a seat in the House of Representatives on the Liberal party ballot. He was associated with several abolitionist periodicals, notably as editor of the *Pennsylvania Freeman* in 1838–1840 and for many years as contributing editor of the *National Era*. In 1857 he helped found the *Atlantic Monthly*, to which he became a regular contributor. Much of his poetry was concerned with the moral crusade against slavery and was collected in *Voices of Freedom*, 1846, which included "Massachusetts to Virginia." Other volumes—*Lays of My Home*, 1843; *Songs of Labor*, 1850; *The Chapel of the Hermits*, 1853; *The Panorama*, 1856, which included "Maud Muller" and "Barefoot Boy;" *Home Ballads*, 1860, with "Telling the Bees;" and *In War Time*, 1864, containing "Barbara Frietchie"—brought him to the front rank of American poets, as one of the "household poets," ranked by readers along with William Cullen Bryant and Henry Wadsworth Longfellow. Other notable single pieces of the period were "Ichabod," a denunciation of Daniel Webster's "Seventh of March" address, and "Laus Deo!" in celebration of the ratification of the Thirteenth Amendment in 1865. Living quietly in Amesbury and later Danvers, Massachusetts, after the Civil War, Whittier enjoyed an ever-growing popularity as a poet of homely faith and joy. In 1866 *Snow-Bound*, his most famous work, appeared; there followed *The Tent on the Beach*, 1867; *Among the Hills*, 1869; *Hazel-Blossoms*, 1875; and *At Sundown*, 1890, among many others. Although his poetry was later to suffer a decline in critical estimation, he was during the last years of his life a celebrated figure; his seventieth and eightieth birthdays were public events. He died in Hampton Falls, New Hampshire, on September 7, 1892. Whittier was elected to the Hall of Fame in 1905.

Wickersham, George Woodward (1858–1936), lawyer and public official. Born in Pittsburgh on September 19, 1858, Wickersham attended Lehigh University from 1873 to 1875 and graduated with a law degree from the University of Pennsylvania in 1880. He practiced law in Philadelphia until 1883, when he moved to New York City to join the firm of Strong and Cadwalader. He specialized

in corporation law and became counsel for a number of business interests in the East. His familiarity with the business world led President William Howard Taft to appoint him U.S. attorney general in 1909. In this post he used the powers of his office to prosecute an unprecedented number of antitrust suits. He moved in a wholesale way against business combinations and was an ardent opponent of monopoly. In his term of office he instituted 43 proceedings from which resulted 43 indictments. He succeeded in two important cases —against the American Tobacco Company and the Standard Oil Company—that became landmarks of anti-trust law, but he failed to obtain the dissolution of United States Steel and International Harvester. By the end of Taft's term the federal government had successfully established its power to suppress unfair trade practices and break up monopolies, thereby buttressing the competitive nature of the free-enterprise system. Wickersham also helped to strengthen the power of the Interstate Commerce Commission (ICC) with his drafting of a new interstate communications bill in 1909, which, after some amendment, was passed by Congress in 1910 as the Mann-Elkins Act. When Taft left the presidency in 1913, Wickersham went back to his law practice in New York City, but he continued to be active in Republican politics for the rest of his life. He served on the War Trade Board in 1918 and in 1919 was a member of President Woodrow Wilson's Second Industrial Conference. In 1919–1920 he ardently supported the League of Nations and campaigned against the Henry Cabot Lodge faction of the Republican party, which was determined to keep the United States out of the League. From 1924 to 1929 he was a member of the League's commission on the Progressive Codification of International Law. In 1929 President Herbert Hoover appointed him chairman of the National Commission on Law Observance and Enforcement (the Wickersham Commission), one of whose tasks was to ascertain the problems of enforcing Prohibition. The report of the commission, published in 1931, was somewhat inconclusive. While asserting that general law enforcement had virtually collapsed throughout the nation, particularly in controlling the sale and consumption of alcoholic beverages, the report nevertheless urged retaining the Eighteenth Amendment. The report of the commission satisfied no one, and after the brief furor it caused at the time it was soon relegated to obscurity. From 1932 to 1936 he was president of the International Arbitral Tribunal established under the Young Plan treaties. Wickersham died in New York City on January 25, 1936.

Wiener, Norbert (1894–1964), mathematician. Born in Columbia, Missouri, on November 26, 1894, Wiener had learned to read and write by the time he was three. He graduated from Tufts College in 1909 and pursued graduate work in mathematics at Harvard and Cornell, taking his Ph.D. from Harvard in 1913, before he was nineteen. After two years of further study at Cambridge, Göttingen, and Columbia, he lectured at Harvard and at the University of Maine, worked for a time for the *Encyclopedia Americana* and the *Boston Herald*, and in 1919 joined the faculty of the Massachusetts Institute of Technology (MIT), with which he was associated for 41 years. In his mathematical researches he was principally concerned with logic and the foundations of mathematics. During World War II he worked for the government, helping to develop and refine techniques in radar and missile guidance; this work, relying heavily on the use of automatic information processing and control by machine, led him to a deeper study of computers and their similarities to animal nervous systems. In 1948 he published *Cybernetics* (revised 1961), summarizing the results of his investigations into information control and communication; the book enjoyed wide popular attention despite its technical nature, and the title, a word he coined from the Greek for "steersman," came into common use as designating the whole field of automated machine control of information. Wiener continued to elaborate on the possibilities of cybernetics and also to warn of its dangers, particularly the danger that man, through intellectual laziness, would relinquish control to the machines of his creation. He made significant contributions to the study of harmonic functions and of random (stochastic) processes. Others among his books were *The Human Use of Human Beings*, 1950; *Non-Linear Problems in Random Theory*, 1958; *God and Golem, Inc.*, 1964; and two autobiographical works, *Ex-Prodigy*, 1953, and *I Am a Mathematician*, 1956. In 1960 he retired from MIT; he died in Stockholm on March 18, 1964.

Wiggin, Kate Douglas (1856–1923), educator and author. Born in Philadelphia on September 28, 1856, Kate Douglas Smith grew up there and in Hollis, Maine. In 1873 she moved with her family to Santa Barbara, California. For a year she studied to be a kindergarten teacher, and in 1878 she helped organize in San Francisco the first free kindergarten in the Far West. In 1880, with her sister, Nora A. Smith, she established the California Kindergarten Training School. Moving with her husband, Samuel B. Wiggin, to New York City in 1884, she stopped teaching, but kept up her interest in kindergartens for several years. Wiggin died in 1889 and in 1895 she married George C. Riggs. After moving East she devoted herself to a writing career, turning out a number of children's books in collaboration with her sister, and also writing several novels for adults. Among the children's books were *The Birds' Christmas Carol*, 1887; *Timothy's Quest*, 1890; *Polly Oliver's Problem*, 1893; *Mother Carey's Chickens*, 1911; and *Rebecca of Sunnybrook Farm*, 1903, which became one of the best-selling books of the twentieth century. It was made into an equally successful movie starring Shirley Temple in the 1930s. Her adult novels, originating in European travel experiences, were *A Cathedral Courtship*, 1893; *Penelope's Progress*, 1898; and *Penelope's Ex-*

periences, 1901. Her autobiography, *My Garden of Memory*, was published in 1923, the year of her death on August 24 in Harrow, England.

Wigglesworth, Michael (1631–1705), religious leader and poet. Born in Yorkshire, England, on October 18, 1631, Wigglesworth emigrated with his family to Massachusetts Bay in 1638. He grew up in New Haven, Connecticut, and attended Harvard College, graduating in 1651. He prepared himself for the ministry and preached intermittently in Cambridge churches and taught at Harvard until 1654. Ordained in 1656, he took a pastorate at Malden, Massachusetts, where he remained until his death. From 1663 on he took to practicing medicine in addition to his parish duties, possibly in an effort to restore his own perennially troubled health. Wigglesworth is remembered for his writings, particularly his long poem, *The Day of Doom: Or a Poetical Description of the Great and Last Judgment*, 1662. The poem is a dramatic exposition in ballad form of the grim Puritan theology of the Mathers and other New England divines. Yet it was so popular in its own way that many persons memorized all of the 224 stanzas, and it was used as well to catechize children. As poetry, the *Day of Doom* has not been viewed favorably by critics, but its aim was not so much literary as didactic: to encompass the body of strict Calvinist theology in readable form for the average church member. It sold a remarkable 1800 copies in its first year and appeared in many editions over the next century. He also wrote shorter theological treatises in verse form: "A Short Discourse on Eternity," "Vanity of Vanities," "God's Controversy with New England," and "Meat Out of the Eater, or Meditations Concerning the Necessity, End, and Usefulness of Affliction unto God's Children." From 1697 until 1705, in addition to his work at Malden, he again taught at Harvard. He died in Malden, Massachusetts, on May 27, 1705.

Wigmore, John Henry (1863–1943), lawyer and educator. Born on March 4, 1863, in San Francisco, Wigmore graduated from Harvard in 1883 and remained there to take a law degree four years later. After two years of practicing law in Boston he accepted the post of professor of Anglo-American law at Keio University, Japan, in 1889. Returning to the United States in 1892, he joined the law faculty of Northwestern University the following year and from 1901 to 1929 was dean of the Northwestern law school. He served also on the staff of the army judge advocate general during 1916–1919, advancing to the rank of colonel. An educator of outstanding ability, Wigmore achieved an international reputation as a scholar; his ten-volume *Treatise on the Anglo-American System of Evidence in Trials at Common Law* (1904–1905 and later editions) was quickly recognized as a contribution of the highest order to legal literature. Subsequent books included *Pocket Code of Evidence*, 1909; *Principles of Judicial Proof*, 1913; and *Panorama of the World's Legal Systems*, three volumes, 1928, as well as a great many works of which he was editor and hundreds of articles and notes for legal journals. He played a central role in the founding of the American Judicature Society, and from 1908 to 1924 and again from 1933 was a member of the Illinois Commission on Uniform State Laws. Wigmore died in Chicago on April 20, 1943.

Wigner, Eugene Paul (1902–   ), physicist. Born in Budapest on November 17, 1902, Wigner graduated from the Technische Hochschule in Berlin in 1924 and earned his doctorate in chemical engineering there the next year. For five years he taught at Berlin and Göttingen and in 1930 came to the United States; he was naturalized seven years later. He joined the faculty at Princeton University as professor of physics in 1931 and maintained his connection with Princeton in spite of frequent leaves of absence for work on government-connected projects and commissions. He was one of a number of scientists who, in the late 1930s, attempted to persuade the War Department to support research on nuclear fission. From 1942 to 1948 he worked on the Manhattan Engineering District project to produce an atomic bomb, and he was present in the laboratories at the University of Chicago on December 2, 1942, when the first self-sustaining nuclear reaction was effected. In 1946–1947 he was director of research and development at the "Clinton Engineer Works," laboratories working on nuclear fission in Oak Ridge, Tennessee, and from 1948 to 1952 worked with the National Bureau of Standards. He continued his involvement with the problems arising from atomic weapons by his efforts, along with other physicists, to seek workable international control of the weapons and to urge politicians to consider realistically the danger nuclear armaments posed. From 1952 to 1957 and from 1959 to 1964 Wigner served on the general advisory committee to the U.S. Atomic Energy Commission (AEC); he was a member of the National Research Council from 1952 to 1964. In 1958 he received the Fermi Award of the AEC, and in 1960 was the recipient of the Atoms for Peace Award. In 1963 he shared the Nobel Prize for Physics with J. H. D. Jensen, of Germany, and Maria G. Mayer. His early book, *The Group Theory and Its Application to the Quantum Mechanics of the Atom Spectrum,* 1931, became an advanced text in the teaching of physics.

Wilcox, Ella Wheeler (1850–1919), poet. Born in Johnstown Center, near Madison, Wisconsin, on November 5, 1850, Miss Wheeler took an early interest in literature, and with little formal education produced nearly 40 volumes of poetry. She was successful enough in getting her early poems published to be able to help support her family with the income. Her first volume of verse, *Drops of Water,* a collection of temperance poems, appeared in 1872. The success of *Poems of Passion,* 1883, owed much to its having been criticized as immoral. In 1884 she married Robert D. Wilcox

and went to live in Meriden, Connecticut, and she and her husband traveled widely in Europe and the Far East. As the years passed she became interested in such subjects as spiritualism and metaphysical religions, and her poems reflected her changing interests. Other books of poetry included *Poems of Pleasure, Poems of Sentiment, Poems of Power,* and *Poems of Problems.* She also wrote a novel, contributed many short stories and travel sketches to magazines, and for many years wrote a daily poem for a newspaper syndicate. Her autobiography, *The World and I,* was published in 1912. She spent several months during and after World War I touring Europe and visiting U.S. army camps as a lecturer. She became ill in Europe in 1919 and returned to the United States, where she died at Short Beach, near Branford, Connecticut, on October 31, 1919. She was anathema to serious critics because of her excessive sentimentality, but her millions of readers loved her. After her death her works faded quickly from view.

Wilder, Burt Green (1841–1925), zoologist. Born in Boston on August 11, 1841, Wilder graduated summa cum laude from Harvard's Lawrence Scientific School in 1862 and received his M.D. from Harvard four years later, after having served as a surgeon in the Union army throughout the Civil War. An assistant in anatomy at Harvard's Museum of Comparative Zoology from 1866 until 1868 and curator of herpetology at the Boston Society of Natural History in 1867–1868, he was in 1867 named professor of neurology and vertebrate zoology at Cornell University, in which position he remained until his retirement in 1910. He had wide interests, serving on such diverse bodies as the Simplified Spelling Board and the Non-Smokers' Protective League; he was an ardent advocate of temperance (as opposed to total abstinence) throughout his life, and in the 1860s he carried out some remarkable experiments in collecting and weaving spider silk into fabric. But he is remembered primarily for his studies of the brains of vertebrates, which he carried on at Cornell for more than 50 years, building up a remarkable collection of brains of animals and humans. At the time it was believed that the size and shape of the human brain reflected the intelligence and talents of the person who possessed it, and Wilder measured, weighed, and carefully described the hundreds of brains that he examined during his career. Bewailing the fact that the brains that other investigators had seen were those of the sick, the crippled, and the insane, he pleaded for "prominent people" to will their brains to his collection. He was thus able to acquire the brains of such persons as psychologist Edward B. Titchener, economist Jeremiah Whipple Jenks, pathologist Theobald Smith, feminists Rosica Schwimmer and Alice Chenoweth, and others. The largest brain he ever examined—and the second largest on record—was that of a compulsive criminal. His own brain joined the collection after his death and was examined by one of his associates; it was said to reflect his interest in music, which was manifested in his composition of several hymns and an orchestral rendering of Oliver Wendell Holmes's poem "Old Ironsides," 1912. Wilder wrote a number of books, including *What Young People Should Know*, 1874, and *The Brain of the Sheep*, 1903, as well as many scientific papers, mostly on the brain. He died on January 22, 1925.

Wilder, Thornton Niven (1897–1975), author and playwright. Born on April 17, 1897, in Madison, Wisconsin, Wilder was raised in China, where his father was stationed in the consular service, and the United States. He received his B.A. from Yale in 1920 and his M.A. from Princeton in 1925. He was an instructor in English at the Lawrence-ville School in New Jersey, taught at the University of Chicago from 1930 to 1937, and at Harvard in 1950 and 1951. His first book to win public attention was a novel, *The Bridge of San Luis Rey*, 1927, which was awarded a Pulitzer Prize. The action focused on five characters who were externally quite different but who shared the same fate in the destruction of the bridge of the book's title. The implication was that lives are essentially similar, regardless of race, class, time, or place; the idea reappeared in many of his works. His historical novels, *The Woman of Andros*, 1930, *Heaven's My Destination*, 1934, and *The Ides of March*, 1948, all stressed repeating or unchanging nature and events in different periods of time and history. His Pulitzer Prize-winning play *Our Town*, 1938, called for no scenery, suggesting that the action might occur anywhere, not only in the small New England town in which it was nominally placed. *The Skin of Our Teeth*, 1942, which won another Pulitzer Prize, contained intentional anachronisms and shifted characters from one time and place to other times and places in presenting a panoramic view of mankind's experience. In *The Match-maker*, 1956, stage characters addressed the audience, as though to bring the play's action as close as possible to real life. (The play formed the basis of the hit Broadway musical *Hello, Dolly!*, 1964.) His plays were widely popular and frequently revived. Later works by Wilder included *The Long Christmas Dinner*, 1961, and *The Eighth Day*, 1967, which won a National Book Award in 1968. He died in Hamden, Connecticut, on December 7, 1975.

Wiley, Harvey Washington (1844–1930), chemist and pure-food reformer. Born in Kent, Jefferson County, Indiana, on October 18, 1844, Wiley graduated from Hanover (Indiana) College in 1867 and received a medical degree from Indiana Medical College in 1871. He also pursued further studies at Harvard, in 1873, and in Germany in 1878. From 1874 to 1883 he taught chemistry at Purdue University and was Indiana state chemist from 1881 to 1883. In 1883 he was appointed chief chemist of the U.S. Department of Agriculture, in Washington, D.C., and filled that position until

1912. In his 30 years with the department he expanded its activities and services greatly; in 1883 there were not a half-dozen employees, but when he resigned in 1912 there were more than 500. Wiley dealt primarily with the chemical analysis of agricultural and food products. He studied the sugar crops of the United States, both beet and cane, and suggested the regions in which sugar beets could be grown most successfully. His chief contribution was his extensive analysis of foods to detect adulteration. His tests showed a large amount of additives and preservatives in food; he therefore campaigned for congressional action to correct the problem and to regulate the food-processing and meat industries. His efforts were aided by the work of the "muckrakers" in the early 1900s, particularly by the appearance in 1906 of Upton Sinclair's novel *The Jungle*, dealing with the Chicago stockyards. Public outrage, coupled with the efforts of Wiley and his assistants, moved Congress to pass the Pure Food and Drug Act that same year. For the next six years he administered the act despite much opposition from the food industry. In 1912 he resigned from the Department of Agriculture and for the next 17 years worked for *Good Housekeeping* magazine, writing articles on food and health, and also lectured in all parts of the country. From 1899 until 1914 he served as professor of agricultural chemistry at The George Washington University, and over the years wrote a number of books on various aspects of his work, including *The Sugar Industry of the United States*, 1885; *Foods and Their Adulteration*, 1907; *Not by Bread Alone*, 1915; *Health Reader*, 1916; *Beverages and Their Adulteration*, 1919; and *History of a Crime Against the Food Law*, 1929. He published an autobiography in 1930. He died in Washington, D.C., on June 30, 1930.

Wilkes, Charles (1798–1877), naval officer and explorer. Born in New York City on April 3, 1798, Wilkes entered the merchant service in 1815 and three years later was commissioned a midshipman in the navy. For several years he alternated routine sea cruises in the Mediterranean and the Pacific with periods of shore duty and study. In 1826 he was promoted to lieutenant and four years later was placed in charge of the navy's Depot of Charts and Instruments in Washington, D.C. In 1838, despite his junior rank, he was appointed to command a naval scientific expedition to the South Seas. Setting out in August with six ships, he was accompanied by a team of scientists in various fields. After stops in South America, islands of the South Pacific, and Australia, the squadron sailed through the Antarctic Ocean and made several successive sightings of land. Wilkes claimed on the basis of these observations to have discovered Antarctica as a continent; although long disputed, his claim was later substantiated and the large region he had seen was named Wilkes Land. The expedition sailed northward, visiting the Fiji and Hawaiian Islands, and made explorations along the North American coast that served to bolster U.S. claims to the Oregon Territory. After sailing westward to complete his circling of the globe, Wilkes and his party returned to the port of New York in 1842. In matters of discipline he was something of a martinet, and soon after his return he was court-martialed and publicly reprimanded for having improperly administered punishment to some of his crew, but in 1843 he was nonetheless promoted to commander. From 1844 to 1861 he was engaged in preparing the report of the expedition; of the 19 volumes, he edited all and himself wrote the five-volume *Narrative of the United States Exploring Expedition*, 1844, and the single volumes on *Meteorology*, 1851, and *Hydrography*, 1861. He was made a captain in 1855. In November 1861, in command of the *San Jacinto*, he stopped the British mail ship *Trent* and forcibly removed two Confederate commissioners en route to Europe, James M. Mason and John Slidell; although publicly acclaimed, his action in the Trent Affair was officially disavowed and Mason and Slidell were released to end tension between Britain and the United States. In 1862 he was promoted to commodore and placed in command of a squadron sent to suppress Confederate raiding on commerce in the West Indies; the mission was largely a failure and aroused considerable diplomatic difficulties. In 1864, after a period of considerable friction between him and the Navy department, he was court-martialed for insubordination and suspended from duty. He retired before the expiration of his suspension and in 1866 was given the rank of rear admiral (retired). He died in Washington, D.C., on February 8, 1877.

Wilkins, Mary Eleanor, *see* Freeman, Mary Eleanor Wilkins

Wilkins, Roy (1901–1981), social reformer. Born in St. Louis on August 30, 1901, Wilkins attended the University of Minnesota, where he was night editor of the school paper. Before his graduation in 1923 he was also editor of the St. Paul *Appeal*, a Negro weekly. For the next eight years he edited the country's leading Negro weekly, the Kansas City *Call*. In 1931 he began his long career with the National Association for the Advancement of Colored People (NAACP). He served as the organization's assistant secretary and in 1934 became editor of its official publication, the *Crisis*. In 1949 he became acting secretary, and in 1950 its administrator of internal affairs. He served as executive secretary, succeeding Walter F. White, from 1955 to 1965 and as executive director from 1965. He wrote for many publications, testified on many occasions before congressional hearings, and served in 1950 as chairman of the National Emergency Civil Rights Mobilization, a union of groups lobbying for civil-rights and fair-employment legislation. He never wavered in his determination to use all constitutional means at his disposal to help blacks achieve full citizenship within the democratic framework of American society. He continued, however, to work in the traditional channels used by the NAACP, those of political action, legal challenge, and public relations, and to oppose violence. In 1964 he received the Spingarn Medal of the NAACP and in 1969 the Presidential Medal of Freedom. He died on September 8, 1981, in New York City.

Wilkinson, James (1757–1825), soldier and adventurer. Born in 1757 in Calvert County, Maryland, Wilkinson was studying medicine in Philadelphia when the Revolution began. He was commissioned a captain in 1776, served under Benedict Arnold in the Montreal expedition that year, and then became aide-de-camp to Gen. Horatio Gates. He saw action at Trenton and Princeton, was appointed deputy adjutant general for the northern department, and later in 1777 he became a brigadier general. In 1778 he became secretary to the Board of War. He was a member of the Conway Cabal, a group planning to supplant George Washington as commander in chief; the exposure of the alleged plot forced his resignation. After a brief period as clothier general, a post he was forced to relinquish because of deficiencies in his accounting, he settled in Bucks County, Pennsylvania, was appointed brigadier general of militia, and in 1783 was elected to the legislature. The next year he moved to Kentucky and became a merchant. He gained considerable influence in the region, largely by playing on Westerners' fears of being cut off from the commercially vital Mississippi River and the port facilities of New Orleans. While agitating in Kentucky for separate statehood, he established valuable commercial connections in New Orleans and in 1787, in order to gain a trade monopoly, swore allegiance to Spain, promising to work for the secession of the Western settlements from the United States and for the extension of Spanish influence. For these services he collected until 1800 an annual $2000 pension from the Spanish authorities; he also secured several sizable loans and outright gifts to finance his activities. At the same time, however, he was actively working against the Spanish; his reports to them concerning his efforts in their behalf were greatly exaggerated. During the same time his schemes led him to work to discredit his principal rival for popular leadership in the West, George Rogers Clark. In 1791, his various business ventures having failed to prosper, he returned to the military service of the United States. The next year, as a brigadier general, he was placed under Gen. Anthony Wayne, against whom he intrigued until Wayne's death in 1796, after which he became the ranking officer in the army. He commanded at Detroit for two years and in 1798 he became military commander on the Southern frontier; his vague collusion with the Spanish in New Orleans, along with personal speculations in land and army contracts, continued until 1803, when he was one of the commissioners appointed to receive the Louisiana Territory from France. In 1804–1805 he met often with Aaron Burr and with him formed a plan, never clearly revealed—the so-called Burr conspiracy—supposedly to separate the

Western territory from the United States, invade Mexico, and establish an independent nation. In 1805 he became governor of a portion of the Louisiana Territory with headquarters in St. Louis. While conducting a highly unpopular administration, he sent out several expeditions, notably that of Zebulon M. Pike, to survey military routes into Spanish territories to the southwest, and also took part in the fur trade. In 1806 he was transferred to New Orleans; as numerous rumors about his and Burr's plans were confirmed by the admissions of an accomplice, Wilkinson, with characteristic bravado, first sent warning of a threatened rebellion to President Thomas Jefferson and then declared martial law and arrested scores of persons for alleged involvement with Burr. Burr himself traveled down the Mississippi with a party of followers who planned to settle on lands he had obtained, and Wilkinson had him arrested. At Burr's treason trial in Richmond, Virginia, in 1807, Wilkinson testified for the prosecution and barely escaped indictment; Burr was acquitted. Courts of inquiry and congressional investigations in 1807, 1809, and 1811 officially cleared Wilkinson of wrongdoing, although he was widely held in contempt, and in 1812 he was restored to his command in New Orleans. In 1813 he was promoted to major general and ordered to the St. Lawrence frontier. The spectacular failure of his Montreal campaign that year ended his military career; he was acquitted by another court of inquiry but in 1815 was honorably discharged. He returned to an estate near New Orleans. In 1821 he went to Mexico City and for several years sought a land grant in Texas. He died in Mexico City on December 28, 1825.

Willard, Emma Hart (1787–1870), educator. Born on February 23, 1787, in Berlin, Connecticut, Emma Hart was raised in a well-informed, communicative family and even as a child she became interested in world affairs. She graduated from the Berlin Academy, where she also taught while continuing her studies in other private schools. Subsequently she held teaching positions in Westfield, Massachusetts, and Middlebury, Vermont. She exhibited an unusual flair for her profession; but she married John Willard in 1809 and resigned her position. Her husband's nephew, a student at Middlebury College, lived with them for a time and acquainted her with the curriculum of his college. It included subjects, including geometry and philosophy, to which female students had never been exposed, and she studied his textbooks with interest. When her husband's business declined she opened her own school for females, the Middlebury Seminary. Its curriculum was designed to prepare the female graduate for college, an unheard-of idea at the time. In 1818 she wrote a letter to the governor of New York requesting funds for the establishment of schools for girls and outlining an ambitious course of study. She was met with some sympathy, but her proposals were dismissed by the majority of the legislature as being contrary to God's will for women. She moved her school to Waterford, New York, but was unsuccessful in finding financial support. At last, in 1821, a building was provided by the citizens of Troy, New York. Her students were as eager to learn as she was to teach, and the curriculum expanded rapidly. She developed new methods of teaching and published widely used and translated textbooks on geography and history. Stressing the importance of education, she trained many able female teachers. During a European journey in 1830 she aided in founding a teacher training school in Athens, and after her return she published *Journal and Letters from France and Great Britain*, 1833. She retired from the Troy Female Seminary (now the Emma Willard School) in 1838 to devote all of her time to improving public schools. She organized teachers' conventions, developed three model schools in Connecticut, and lectured in the South and the West on the significance of proper teaching, adequate salaries, and good textbooks and schoolhouses. Her attempts to provide equal educational opportunities for women led to many more female schools and eventually to the coeducational school system. Mrs. Willard died in Troy, New York, on April 15, 1870. She was elected to the Hall of Fame in 1905.

Willard, Frances Elizabeth Caroline (1839–1898), educator and reformer. Born on September 28, 1839, in Churchville, New York, Frances Willard moved with her family to Ohio and later to Wisconsin. Her parents were teachers and sternly religious, particularly her father. She entered the Milwaukee Female College at seventeen and after a year transferred to North-Western Female College in Evanston, Illinois. Following her graduation in 1859 she became a teacher at a succession of schools in Illinois, Pennsylvania, and New York. During 1868–1870 she traveled in Europe; in 1871 she accepted the presidency of the Evanston College for Ladies, becoming in 1873 dean of women at Northwestern University when the two schools merged. She had by this time already developed temperance sentiments and in 1874 she resigned her position to join the growing national crusade against liquor. She became corresponding secretary of the National Woman's Christian Temperance Union (WCTU), and five years later was named president, a post she held for the rest of her life. In 1883 she organized and was the first president of the World's Woman's Christian Temperance Union. A powerful speaker and an expert in mobilizing public and legislative support, she toured the country speaking on behalf of temperance and other reforms, notably woman suffrage. She attempted political action as well, becoming influential in the inner councils of the Prohibition party from 1882 and ten years later taking part in the Industrial Conference in St. Louis that became part of the Populist party. In 1888 she was elected president of the National Council of Women. Among her many writings were *Woman and Temperance*, 1883, and *Glimpses of Fifty Years*, 1889, her autobiography. She also edited, with Mary A. Livermore, *A Woman of the Century*, 1893. She died in New York City on February 18, 1898. She was elected to the Hall of Fame in 1910.

Williams, Bert (1876–1922), entertainer and songwriter. Born on New Providence Island in the Bahamas in 1876, Egbert Austin Williams grew up there and in California. In the early 1890s he began his show-business career with a touring vaudeville troupe, but teamed up in 1895 with George Walker. Upon their appearance in New York City in 1896, they soon became a successful song-and-dance team and worked vaudeville theaters for several years. In 1903 they were featured in the all-black musical *In Dahomey*, which played successfully on Broadway and in London. Williams, in his comedy roles, played the stereotype of the "shuffling" Negro, but was thoroughly conscious of the role's falseness as well as of the inability of white audiences of the time to appreciate any other form of Negro comedy. Walker and Williams appeared in other musicals during the next six years, but upon Walker's death in 1909 Williams went into the *Ziegfeld Follies* as the show's star comedian. He worked in the *Follies* for ten years and attained his greatest popularity as a stage personality there. He performed mostly his own material, including some of the songs he used. Of the latter, the popular and still performed "Nobody" is the best known. He left the *Follies* in 1919 to star in other Broadway reviews, and in 1922 opened in *Underneath the Bamboo Tree*. During the run of this show he became ill with pneumonia and died on March 4, 1922, in New York City.

Williams, Daniel Hale (1858–1931), surgeon. Born in Hollidaysburg, Pennsylvania, on January 18, 1858, Williams grew up there, in Rockford, Illinois, and in Janesville, Wisconsin. On his own from the age of twelve, when he was apprenticed to a shoemaker, he worked at that trade and held odd jobs until 1878, when he was able to begin the study of medicine. He graduated from Chicago Medical College (now part of Northwestern University) in 1883 and opened a practice on the south side of Chicago. Since black physicians were not permitted to work on the staff of the city's hospital at that time, Williams founded Provident Hospital in 1891, including in its organization the first nurses training school for black women in the United States. It was at this hospital in 1893 that he performed the operation which earned him immediate fame in U.S. medical circles. A street fighter with a knife wound in an artery near the heart was brought in, and Williams saved his life in what was the first instance of open-heart surgery. From 1893 to 1898 Williams served as surgeon in chief of Freedmen's Hospital in Washington, D.C., as an appointee of President Grover Cleveland; he reorganized the hospital and started there another school of nursing for Negroes. He returned to Chicago in 1898 to resume his association with Provident Hospital, and he served as well on the staff of Cook County Hospital (1900–

1906) and St. Luke's Hospital (1907–1931). In 1895 he founded the National Medical Association, an organization for black physicians, and over the years consistently worked to further the cause of civil rights. He was the only black charter member of the American College of Surgeons when it was founded in 1913. He also taught surgery intermittently at Meharry Medical College in Nashville from 1899 until his death. Williams died at his summer home in Idlewild, Lake County, Michigan, on August 4, 1931.

Williams, Edward Bennett (1920–   ), lawyer. Born in Hartford, Connecticut, on May 31, 1920, Williams graduated from the College of the Holy Cross in 1941. After two years of service with the air force in World War II he entered Georgetown University law school, from which he graduated in 1945. Admitted to the bar, he worked for a law firm in Washington, D.C., until 1949, when he opened his own office. He soon became one of the country's most publicized trial lawyers, gaining fame and often notoriety for taking unpopular cases. His defense of his clients was based on his determination to uphold the constitutional guarantees of fair trial and individual rights; he opposed trial by publicity or guilt by notoriety and dealt only with points of law, no matter how unpopular or well-liked a client might be. Among his better known cases were his representation of Senator Joseph R. McCarthy at the 1954 Senate hearings that ended with McCarthy's censure; his defense of mobster Frank Costello in 1957 deportation hearings; the acquittal of Teamsters' Union President James R. Hoffa in 1957 on a charge of bribing a government lawyer; his defense of Congressman Adam Clayton Powell, Jr., in a tax-evasion case in 1960; and his 1965 defense in Senate hearings of Robert G. Baker, formerly secretary to the Senate majority, against charges arising from the misuse of his position. Williams spelled out his ideas on trial law and constitutional rights in his 1962 book *One Man's Freedom*. As part owner of the Washington Redskins professional football team (he became president of the club in 1965), he maintained an active interest in sports.

Williams, Egbert Austin, see Williams, Bert

Williams, Eleazar (1789?–1858), missionary to the Indians. Born in Caughnawaga, Quebec, about 1789, Williams grew up there and in Longmeadow, Massachusetts. He was an Indian of the St. Regis band and was reputed to be descended from Eunice Willams, a white girl captured in the Indian raid on Deerfield, Massachusetts, in 1704. During the War of 1812 he served as a scout for U.S. forces in upper New York State. Following the end of hostilities he trained to become a lay preacher of the Episcopal church to serve as a missionary among the Oneida Indians, and he followed this career intermittently for the rest of his life. During the 1820s he promoted the settling of the Oneida in Wisconsin, and negotiated a treaty with Winnebago and Menominee tribesmen to obtain a land cession near Green Bay. A small band of Oneida went to Wisconsin with him in 1822; but the scheme eventually came to nothing, in part because the federal government would not approve his plans, and in the process he lost the confidence of the Oneida among whom he had worked. The whole experience apparently somewhat deranged him, for in the late 1830s he began claiming to be the lost Dauphin of France, the son of Louis XVI and Marie Antoinette, who had, he said, been saved from the excesses of the French Revolution. Williams maintained this claim for the rest of his life, and an 1853 magazine article about him gave him temporary notoriety. In 1850 he left Green Bay and settled at the St. Regis Reservation at Hogansburg, New York, where he preached to the Indians until his death there on August 28, 1858. Among his writings were *Good News to the Iroquois Nation*, 1813, *Prayers for Families and for Particular Persons, Selected from the Book of Common Prayer*, 1816, and various translations into the Mohawk written language, which he was credited with simplifying.

Williams, Roger (1603?–1683), religious leader and founder of Rhode Island. Born in London about 1603, Williams graduated from Pembroke College, Cambridge, in 1627 and was ordained probably in 1628. A religious nonconformist, he came to the Puritan colony at Massachusetts Bay in 1630, seeking free expression for his ideals. In 1631, when called to serve as pastor of a church in Boston, he refused, insisting upon open repudiation of the Church of England. At Plymouth, where the church was avowedly separatist, he was pastor from 1632 to 1633. He severely citicized the Puritans for enforcing religious principles with the power of civil government and for expropriating Indian lands. In 1634 the civil rulers of the colony denied him permission to become minister of the Salem church; in defiance of the General Court he took the pulpit anyway. In 1635 he was brought to trial and found guilty of spreading "dangerous opinions." Banished from the colony, he attempted to organize the Salem congregation into a separate colony at Narragansett Bay, but was pursued by Puritan leaders and compelled to leave Massachusetts. In 1636, with a group of followers, he founded the town of Providence and the colony of Rhode Island in the Narragansett Bay area. The colony became known for its democratic institutions, including a town government, the separation of church and state, and religious toleration. In 1639 he began to call himself a Seeker, identifying with no sect but believing in the basic tenets of Christianity. Although he mistrusted many new religions, he defended the right of all to worship as they pleased. He went to England in 1643 to obtain a patent to govern the four settlements that developed in Rhode Island. While in England he published *A Key into the Language of America*, 1643. He received a charter for the Providence Plantations in 1644, over the claims of the Puritan colonies, which had dispatched delegates to Lon-

don to negotiate for a Narragansett patent. In England he also wrote *The Bloudy Tenent of Persecution*, 1644, a famous defense of religious liberty issued to combat the Puritans' attempts to create a single church for the colonies. He also engaged in an exchange of pamphlets with John Cotton on the same topic. He went again to England in 1651 to have the charter confirmed, after William Coddington, a settler of Newport, had succeeded in splitting the colony and establishing himself as governor of a part; Williams was able to have him removed. In 1663 Charles II granted a royal charter for the colony of Rhode Island, containing provision for freedom in matters of religion. From 1654 to 1657, when Williams was the first president of Rhode Island, the colony harbored religious groups—Jews and Quakers—who were persecuted by the Puritans. He respected and was respected by the Narragansett Indians, and served as a peacemaker with them even on behalf of Massachusetts Bay. But his skepticism of existing churches made him abjure attempts at conversion. It was beyond his power to maintain peace in the colony in 1675; he reluctantly fought in King Philip's War, in which Providence and Warwick were burned. He remained in public office until his death early in 1683. Among his many writings on religion were *Christenings Make Not Christians*, 1645; *The Hireling Ministry None of Christ's*, 1652; and *George Fox Digg'd Out of His Burrows*, 1676, written against the Quaker leader.

Williams, Ted (1918–   ), baseball player. Born in San Diego, California, on August 31, 1918, Theodore Samuel Williams began to play baseball during his high-school days there and started his professional career in 1935 with the San Diego Padres of the Pacific Coast League. Two years later he was sold to the Boston Red Sox and, after a season with their farm club, the Minneapolis Millers, during which he led the American Association in batting, was brought up to the Red Sox in 1939 as an outfielder; during his first season with them he was named rookie of the year. He played his entire 19-year major-league career with the Red Sox, becoming one of the great hitters of all time and perhaps the greatest hitter of the modern era. His 1941 average of .406 was the highest since Rogers Hornsby hit .424 in 1924, and it marked the last time that anyone hit over .400 in either league. Had Williams not missed five seasons for service as an aviator in the Marine Corps during World War II and later during the Korean War, it is quite possible that he might have broken Babe Ruth's career home-run record of 714; as it was, Williams hit a total of 521 homers while compiling a lifetime batting average of .344 in 2292 games. He led the American League in batting six times, in 1941, 1942, 1947, 1948, 1957, and 1958, the last time when he was forty years old. He led in home runs four times, 1941 (37), 1942 (36), 1947 (32), and 1949 (43), and in runs batted in in 1939, 1942, 1947, and 1949. He was chosen the league's most valuable player in 1946, the year he led Boston to a pennant and dominated the All-Star game with five hits, two of them homers. He was chosen most valuable player again in 1949. Obsessed with the art of hitting, which he insisted was the most difficult skill to acquire in any sport, Williams retired on September 28, 1960, having hit a home run in his last time at bat. In February 1969, having been offered part ownership of the Washington Senators, he agreed to manage the club and was effective in his first season. But the Senators simply would not take hitting as seriously as he thought they should, and when the team moved to Texas and became the Texas Rangers in 1972, their hitting deteriorated even more; Williams resigned as manager at the end of the 1972 season and went back to fishing, his second love after batting. For many years there had existed in Boston a kind of civil war between Williams and the baseball writers of that city, but after he retired even the Boston writers joined the rest of the sports public in admiring Williams for his single-minded devotion to an art of which he was one of the greatest practitioners who ever lived. He was elected to the Baseball Hall of Fame in 1966.

Williams, Tennessee (1911–1983), playwright. Born in Columbus, Mississippi, on March 26, 1911, Thomas Lanier Williams came of a family of Tennesseans and himself chose the name by which he was known, "Tennessee." Raised in a Southern Puritan environment, largely by his grandfather, an Episcopalian minister, he and his family moved, when he was about thirteen, into a St. Louis slum. He worked for a shoe company in a job he detested, and attended the University of Missouri from 1931 to 1933, Washington University in St. Louis, 1936–1937, and the State University of Iowa, from which he graduated in 1938. Journeying throughout the country, he lived frugally on the proceeds of minor jobs and spent much time writing, producing several short plays that were performed by community theaters. His great success with his first Broadway play, *The Glass Menagerie,* 1944, which won the New York Drama Critics' Circle Award, was followed by three more Circle Awards—for *A Streetcar Named Desire,* 1947 (also a Pulitzer Prize winner), *Cat on a Hot Tin Roof,* 1955 (which won his second Pulitzer Prize), and *Night of the Iguana,* 1961. His other plays included *Summer and Smoke,* 1948; *The Rose Tattoo,* 1950; *Camino Real,* 1953; *Sweet Bird of Youth,* 1959; *The Two Character Play,* 1967; *Kingdom of Earth,* 1968; *In the Bar of a Tokyo Hotel,* 1969; and *Small Craft Warnings,* 1972. Many of his dramas were adapted for motion pictures, the medium for which *Suddenly Last Summer,* 1959, was directly written. His works included, besides major plays, numerous one-act plays, a book of poems, many short stories, and a novel, *The Roman Spring of Mrs. Stone,* 1950. Typically, the plays were set in the South, in which heat, exoticism, and languor barely hid the tensions and anxieties that lay below the surface. In this setting, his characters acted out a struggle between virtue and passion, frequently

being destroyed by the latter. His later plays were largely unsuccessful. He died on February 25, 1983, in New York City.

Williams, Theodore Samuel, *see* Williams, Ted

Williams, Thomas Lanier, *see* Williams, Tennessee

Williams, William Carlos (1883–1963), poet and physician. Born on September 17, 1883, in Rutherford, New Jersey, Williams attended small-town schools, traveled in France and Switzerland, attended secondary school in New York City, received a medical degree from the University of Pennsylvania in 1906, and interned in New York City hospitals. His graduate work in pediatrics at the University of Leipzig preceded a brief tour through Italy and Spain. In 1910 he settled once again in Rutherford and opened a medical practice. As his practice grew, he was inspired to write poetry. He had already published a small, imitative volume, *Poems,* 1909, but he grew more inventive and his works were solicited by avant-garde journals. At his best, his poetry was totally direct, realistic, and unembellished by traditional poetic formality either in language or structure. He referred to his practice of verse as "objectivism," which he viewed as a further development of the Imagism of Ezra Pound and others. Subsequent volumes included *The Tempers,* 1913; *Al Que Quiere!,* 1917; *Kora in Hell,* 1920; *Sour Grapes,* 1921; *Spring and All,* 1922; *An Early Martyr,* 1935; *Adam and Eve in the City,* 1936; and *The Wedge,* 1944. His most famous poem, *Paterson,* 1946, grew, with additions in 1948, 1949, 1951, and 1958, into an epic vision of modern America. He also wrote considerable prose, including a trilogy—*White Mule,* 1937, *In the Money,* 1940, and *The Build-up,* 1952; essays, collected in *The Great American Novel,* 1923, and *In the American Grain,* 1925; a number of plays; collections of stories, including *The Knife of the Times,* 1932, *Life Along the Passaic River,* 1938, *Make Light of It,* 1950, and *The Farmers' Daughters,* 1961; and an autobiography, published in 1951. His *Pictures from Brueghel and Other Poems,* 1962, won a Pulitzer Prize. Other of his awards included the Bollingen Prize in 1953. Williams died in Rutherford, New Jersey, on March 4, 1963.

Willis, Nathaniel Parker (1806–1867), journalist, editor, and author. Born in Portland, Maine, on January 20, 1806, Willis grew up there and in Boston. He graduated from Yale in 1827 and turned immediately to writing, which had already gained him some notice while in college. He became in his lifetime one of the most widely known and read of American authors, although his critics often attacked him for oversentimentality and affectation. His works are rarely reprinted or read today, however. He wrote poetry, a large number of travel letters and social commentaries, one unsuccessful novel, and a few plays. From 1829 until late 1831 he edited and published the *American Monthly* in Boston. When it failed he moved to

New York City and became associated with the *New York Mirror*, a daily newspaper, as a free-lance foreign correspondent. For five years, from 1832 to 1836, he traveled in Europe and the Middle East, sending back to the *Mirror* letters which were collected and published in book form as *Pencillings by the Way*, 1835, and *Loiterings of Travel*, 1840. He spent more than a year in England, during which he increased his income by writing for various British journals. While there he also published *Melanie and Other Poems*, 1835, and a series of sketches, under the pseudonym Philip Slingsby, entitled *Inklings of Adventure*, 1836. Willis spent the years 1836–1839 in the United States, writing for the *Mirror*, traveling, and writing the plays *Bianca Visconti*, 1837, and *Tortesa*, 1839, both of which were produced with fair success in New York City. After spending 1839–1840 in England as correspondent for the *Corsair*, a short-lived journal he had helped found, he returned to New York and became coeditor of the *New Mirror*, subsequently called the *Evening Mirror*. In 1845 he published a collection of short stories, *Dashes at Life with a Free Pencil*, before leaving for another year in Europe. While abroad he again sent back a series of travel letters which later were collected in two books, *Rural Letters*, 1849, and *Famous Persons and Places*, 1854. He returned to the United States in 1846 and became copublisher and editor of the *New York Home Journal*, with which he remained until the end of the Civil War. His novel, *Paul Fane*, came out in 1857. In 1857 he settled at a country estate on the Hudson River near Tarrytown, New York, and, except for the Civil War period when he was a news correspondent in Washington, continued to live there until his death on January 20, 1867.

Willkie, Wendell Lewis (1892–1944), lawyer and political leader. Born in Elwood, Indiana, on February 18, 1892, Willkie graduated from Indiana University in 1909 and earned his law degree there in 1916. After serving in World War I, he went into the practice of corporation law at Akron, Ohio. In 1929, when the Commonwealth and Southern Corporation was formed, he moved to New York City to become the utilities company's counsel. In 1933 he became president of the corporation, and he proved himself an astute businessman and manager in the building up of the company's holdings. He came into public prominence in the late 1930s as leader of the battle of the privately owned utilities against the federal government's Tennessee Valley Authority (TVA). Although he had long been a Democrat (in fact, he had been a delegate to the 1924 national convention), by 1939–1940 Willkie had become a leading spokesman for business interests in opposition to the New Deal economic policies. He had meanwhile switched his affiliation to the Republican party, and was looked upon as a possible nominee for the presidency in 1940. He had no political base, but support for him gradually grew throughout the nation among Republican voters, and some party leaders regarded him as the strongest opposition they could offer Franklin D. Roosevelt. At the Republican national convention in Philadelphia, in June 1940, he received the nomination on the sixth ballot. His campaign, however, had difficulty in developing clear-cut alternatives to Roosevelt's programs. Willkie was liberal, devoted to civil rights, and an internationalist. His basic attack was along economic lines; his proposals differed from the New Deal in means, not ends. Thus the Democrats touted him as the "me-too" candidate and counseled the people to stay with Roosevelt. They did, but Willkie still won more votes—some 22 million—than any previous Republican nominee. For the next four years he maintained the posture of loyal opposition to the administration, but to many conservative Republicans and isolationists he became indistinguishable from it as he attempted to bring the party's liberal wing into a position of leadership. At Roosevelt's behest he toured the world in 1942 visiting the nation's wartime allies and the battlefronts. On his return he wrote the best-selling book *One World*, pleading for an international peace-keeping organization after the war. Gradually he lost support within Republican ranks, and when he tried for the presidential nomination again in 1944 he was defeated by Governor Thomas E. Dewey of New York in the Wisconsin primary and withdrew from the race. In August 1944 he suffered a heart attack, which led to his death in New York City on October 8.

Wills, Helen Newington (1905–   ), tennis player. Born in Centerville, California, on October 6, 1905, Miss Wills began playing tennis when she was thirteen. She won her first girls' title in 1921, when she was fifteen, and her first women's singles title in 1923, when she was seventeen. Altogether she won the U.S. championship seven times, repeating in 1924, 1925, 1927–1929, and in 1931. She won her first Wimbledon championship—the unofficial world championship—in 1927, upon the retirement of the great French star Suzanne Lenglen, and repeated her victory seven times, in 1928–1930, 1932, 1933, 1935, and in 1938, when she was thirty-two. To her seven U.S. and eight Wimbledon singles championships she added four U.S. and three Wimbledon doubles titles, two U.S. and one Wimbledon mixed doubles titles, and four French singles and two doubles championships. In 1924 at Paris she won two gold medals in the only Olympic Games in which the United States entered a tennis team. Probably the most powerful woman player up to her time, and possessing extraordinary control as well, she long dominated women's tennis; from 1926, when she was beaten in the U.S. finals at Forest Hills by Molla Mallory, until 1932, when she had to default in the finals against Helen Hull Jacobs because of a painful back injury, she did not lose a single set in the United States, to say nothing of a match or a tournament. Miss Wills graduated from the University of California in 1927 and in 1929 married Frederick S. Moody, competing throughout the next decade as Helen Wills Moody; divorced in 1937, she married Aidan Roark in 1939 and continued thereafter to compete in senior tournaments as Mrs. Roark. She wrote two books on tennis—*Tennis*, 1928, and *Fifteen–Thirty*, 1937.

Willys, John North (1873–1935), automobile manufacturer. Born in Canandaigua, New York, on October 25, 1873, Willys dropped out of high school to go to work at fifteen. In a few years he had gone into the bicycle sales and repair business. In 1897 he moved to Elmira, New York, and the next year began manufacturing bicycles; by 1902 his company was extremely prosperous. He began selling Pierce automobiles as well, and he soon operated a thriving agency. In 1907, during a financial recession, he bought the Overland Automobile Company of Indianapolis, moved it to the old Pope-Toledo plant in Toledo, Ohio, and changed its name to Willys-Overland. As sales increased and the factory grew, he expanded his interests by acquiring auto accessory factories and a truck manufacturing plant, all of which he consolidated into the Willys Corporation in 1919. Business thrived until after World War I, but the economic downturn of 1919–1921, coupled with increased competition, led to the corporation being dissolved. He stayed with the auto manufacturing firm, Willys-Overland, through the period of reorganization directed by Walter P. Chrysler, until 1929, when he sold his stock and became chairman of the board. In 1930 President Herbert C. Hoover appointed him U.S. ambassador to Poland, and he served in that post for two years. On his return he took over as receiver the Willys-Overland Company, which had been failing badly in the Depression of the 1930s, and became its president in 1935. His tenure was short-lived, however, for he died on August 26, 1935, in Riverdale-on-Hudson, New York.

Wilmot, David (1814–1868), public official and judge. Born in Bethany, Pennsylvania, on January 20, 1814, Wilmot studied law privately and was admitted to the bar in 1834. He opened a law practice in Towanda, Pennsylvania, and remained active in it for about ten years, gradually becoming involved in Democratic party politics in the state. In 1844 he was elected to the House of Representatives, where he served through reelections from March 1845 to March 1851. The most notable action of his tenure in the House was the offering of an amendment to an appropriations bill for the settlement of Mexican boundary claims in August 1846, shortly after the start of the Mexican War. He proposed that "as an express and fundamental condition to the acquisition of any territory from the Republic of Mexico by the United States . . . neither slavery nor involuntary servitude shall ever exist in any part of said territory." The "Wilmot Proviso" brought to a head the issue that was inexorably dividing North and South. The Proviso passed the House by a vote of 87 to 64, but failed of action in the Senate. It was brought up in Congress again in 1847 but did not pass, and similar resolutions were proposed in subsequent years with equal futility. Debates over the Proviso aroused much discussion and emotion in the country and served to harden already well-defined positions with regard to slavery. It was out of the issue it raised that the Free-Soil party emerged for the election of 1848, and the Proviso provided the main basis for the founding of the Republican party in 1854. Wilmot himself joined the Free-Soil movement in 1848, although he did not run for the House again. From 1851 until 1861 he served as chief judge of the 13th judicial district of Pennsylvania, and during the 1850s became active in the new Republican party. He attended the party's national conventions in 1856 and 1860 and wrote the 1856 platform. In 1861 he was elected to the U.S. Senate to fill the vacancy caused by the resignation of Simon Cameron and he served in the Senate until March 1863. In June 1862 the substance of the Wilmot Proviso was finally approved by a Republican-controlled Congress in an act forbidding slavery in the territories. Wilmot did not run for reelection in 1862, but instead accepted the appointment by President Abraham Lincoln as a judge of the U.S. Court of Claims. He served on the court until his death in Towanda, Pennsylvania, on March 16, 1868.

Wilson, Alexander (1766–1813), ornithologist and poet. Born in Paisley, Scotland, on July 6, 1766, Wilson grew up in extreme poverty and in 1779 was apprenticed as a weaver. He worked at the trade for ten years, then turned to traveling as a peddler. He also took to writing verse, nature poems, and dialect ballads concerning the plight of the poor in Scotland. Finding himself unable to make a living in his homeland, Wilson emigrated to the United States in 1794 and settled in Philadelphia. For several years he taught school in the Philadelphia area until a chance meeting with naturalist William Bartram in 1802 enlivened an already keen interest in studying birds. He began to make studies and collect specimens of the birds in the eastern part of the United States, and over the next decade he ranged from upper New York State to Florida and Louisiana in search of new species. A job with a Philadelphia publishing firm in 1807 brought him increased income and a better opportunity to pursue his work, and in 1808 he was able to have published the first volume of his pioneering work, the remarkably complete *American Ornithology*, covering the eastern United States north of Florida. Over the next five years, six more volumes were published. Wilson himself died in Philadelphia on August 23, 1813, but George Ord, his assistant, carried on the work and the remaining volumes were published posthumously. A collection of his verse, *Poems, Chiefly in the Scottish Dialect*, was published in 1816. Wilson's other volume of poetry, *The Foresters*, issued in 1805, was a versified account of his wanderings through New York State.

Wilson, Charles Erwin (1890–1961), industrialist and public official. Born in Minerva, Ohio, on July 18, 1890, Wilson graduated in 1909 from the Carnegie Institute of Technology with a degree in engineering. He went to work for the Westinghouse Electric and Manufacturing Company, his speciality being the manufacture of electrical equipment for automobiles. In 1919 he became chief engineer for Delco Remy, a subsidiary of General Motors (GM), and after a merger in 1929 he became a GM vice-president. Executive vice-president in 1939–1940, he became president of GM early in 1941, upon the retirement of William S. Knudsen. "Engine Charlie," as he was called to distinguish him from "Electric Charlie" Wilson, president of General Electric (GE), remained in the GM presidency until 1953, presiding over the wartime growth of the company as it converted from car making to the manufacture of aircraft and armaments. The war and the postwar boom greatly expanded the size of General Motors and increased its production and earnings. During the period of postwar labor problems it was Wilson who devised the cost-of-living wage plan that was first written into GM's contracts with the auto workers' union in May 1948. In December 1946 President Harry S. Truman appointed him to chair the Advisory Commission on Civil Rights. The commission's report, issued in October 1947, was the widely publicized document, *To Secure These Rights*. During the Korean War, Truman called upon Wilson to head the Office of Defense Mobilization, to help increase the nation's industrial production. He held the post until March 1952, when he resigned in a disagreement over the President's resolution of a wage dispute in the steel industry. When Dwight D. Eisenhower was elected president in 1952 he named Wilson his secretary of defense. After making the much-debated remark, "What's good for the country is good for General Motors and vice versa," during Senate hearings, he was duly confirmed in his appointment. Wilson correlated his work at the Pentagon with the foreign policy of Secretary of State John Foster Dulles. He reduced appropriations and sought a cut in military manpower, while encouraging the buildup of nuclear and air defenses to create a massive retaliatory capability. He resigned from the Defense Department in mid-1957 and returned to General Motors as a director. He died in Norwood, Louisiana, on September 26, 1961.

Wilson, Edmund (1895–1972), author and critic. Born in Red Bank, New Jersey, on May 8, 1895, Wilson graduated from Princeton in 1916. He began as a reporter on the *New York Evening Sun*, but his career was interrupted by two years of service in U.S. army intelligence, in 1917–1919. He was managing editor of *Vanity Fair* in 1920–1921, associate editor of the *New Republic* from 1926 to 1931, and book reviewer for the *New Yorker* from 1944 to 1948. In the interims between these positions and after 1948 he was a free-lance writer, writing articles and books on subjects that interested him. Two collections of poetry and short plays appeared in the early 1920s; his first truly distinctive book was a novel, *I Thought of Daisy*, 1929. It was followed by, among others, *Axel's Castle*, 1931, a collection of critical pieces; *Travels in Two Democracies*, 1936; *The Triple Thinkers*, 1938; *To the Finland Station*, 1940, a study of

European revolutionary movements and of the career of V. I. Lenin up to the Russian Revolution; *The Wound and the Bow*, 1941, more literary criticism; *The Shock of Recognition*, 1943, an influential collection of literary pieces; *Memoirs of Hecate County*, 1946, a rambling fictional account that for a time was banned in some parts of the United States for indecency; *Europe Without Baedecker*, 1947; *The Shores of Light*, 1950; *Classics and Commercials*, 1952; *The Scrolls from the Dead Sea*, 1955, a best-selling account of then recent discoveries in the New East; *A Piece of My Mind: Reflections at Sixty*, 1956; *Apologies to the Iroquois*, 1959, a sympathetic history of the Indian tribes of upper New York State; and *Patriotic Gore*, 1962, a study of the Civil War and particularly of its influence on literature. He refused or at least failed to pay federal income taxes in the late 1950s and early 1960s and got into trouble with the Internal Revenue Service; an account of the affair appeared in 1963 as *The Cold War and the Income Tax*. *Bit Between My Teeth*, 1965, was a collection of later critical pieces, and *The Fruits of the MLA*, 1969, contained withering reviews of recent super-scholarly but unreadable editions of the classic American writers. Always truculent and almost always brilliant, he was recognized as one of the most distinguished American critics of the twentieth century and in 1963 was awarded the Presidential Medal of Freedom. He died in Talcottville, Lewis County, New York, on June 12, 1972.

Wilson, Harry Leon (1867–1939), author. Born in Oregon, Illinois, on May 1, 1867, Wilson left school at sixteen to go to work. He roamed over much of the country between Illinois and California, holding a variety of jobs, until 1887, when he started writing for a living. In 1892 he moved to New York City to become assistant editor of the weekly humor magazine *Puck*, then became editor in 1896 and remained in the post until 1902. During these years he wrote several novels, many with Western or rural settings: *The Spenders*, 1902; *The Seeker*, 1904; and *The Boss of Little Arcady*, 1905. From 1905 until 1912 he lived in Europe, collaborating with Booth Tarkington on plays. Their best-known work, *The Man from Home*, was first produced in 1907 and ran with great success for several years. In 1912 Wilson settled in Carmel, California, and once more took up writing short stories, which he contributed regularly to the *Saturday Evening Post*, and the novel. These later works were at once sentimental and comic and relied much on naive, timid protagonists for their appeal. In this period of fiction writing his best-known work was *Ruggles of Red Gap*, 1915, later made into a motion picture. Another novel, *Merton of the Movies*, 1922, was adapted for the stage by Marc Connelly and George S. Kaufman. Other novels included *Lions of the Lord*, 1903, on the Mormons in Utah; *Bunker Bean*, 1912; and *Cousin Jane*, 1925. Wilson died in Carmel on June 28, 1939.

Wilson, Henry (1812–1875), vice-president of the United States. Born in Farmington, New Hampshire, on February 16, 1812, Wilson was originally named Jeremiah Jones Colbath, but he changed his name by act of the state legislature when he reached twenty-one. He grew up in poverty with little formal schooling. From 1822 until 1833 he worked as a farm laborer; then, on reaching his majority, he left home and settled in Natick, Massachusetts, where he worked as a shoemaker for several years. He became fairly successful in business, building up a shoe factory employing as many as a hundred men, but he determined on a political career. A trip through Virginia in 1836 confronted him with the realities of slavery, with the result that abolitionism was to be the prime motive of his political life. His varied political affiliations depended on a particular party's attitude toward slavery at the time. Wilson entered politics as a Whig, and in 1840 was elected to his first term in the Massachusetts legislature. From 1844 to 1846 he served a term in the state senate. When the Whig convention of 1848 failed to affirm the Wilmot Proviso prohibiting slavery in the areas won from Mexico, he withdrew and became one of the founders of the short-lived Free-Soil party, editing a party organ, the *Boston Republican*, during 1848–1851. In 1850–1852 he was again in the state senate. When the Free-Soil party began to fail in the early 1850s he joined the new American, or Know-Nothing, party, although he disliked its nativist ideology. When this party also failed to live up to his antislavery beliefs, he withdrew from it in 1855. He had been elected to the U.S. Senate in January of 1855 to fill a vacancy, and he served in the Senate until March 1873. His election had been effected by a coalition of antislavery Democrats, Free-Soilers, and American party adherents. He soon joined the new Republican party and remained with it the rest of his life. In the Senate he served on the committee on military affairs and with the outbreak of the Civil War became committee chairman, a post in which he demonstrated exceptional ability in making necessary preparations for war. In his capacity as brigadier general of the Massachusetts militia, he worked effectively to promote recruitment in his state. Following the war he joined forces with the Radical Republicans to impose harsh Reconstruction terms on the South, although several visits to the South finally convinced him of the wisdom of a more conciliatory policy. He lost the Republican nomination for the vice-presidency in 1868 but won it four years later. He served as vice-president under Ulysses S. Grant from March 1873 until his death in office, in Washington, D.C., on November 22, 1875.

Wilson, Jack, *see* Wovoka

Wilson, James (1742–1798), justice of the Supreme Court. Born in Fifeshire, Scotland, on September 14, 1742, Wilson studied at St. Andrews, Glasgow, and Edinburgh universities until his father's death interrupted his education. He tried tutoring and bookkeeping before emigrating to America in 1765. Arriving in Philadelphia, after a brief stay in New York City, with a letter of introduction to an authority at the College of Philadelphia (now the University of Pennsylvania), he was made a Latin tutor in February 1766. Three months later he successfully petitioned for an honorary M.A. degree. After studying for a year in John Dickinson's law office, he was admitted to the bar. He practiced in Reading and in 1770 settled in Carlisle, where he soon developed a reputation as the best lawyer in Pennsylvania. For six years he also lectured on English literature at the College of Philadelphia. He was elected to the First Continental Congress in 1774. He then revised his *Considerations on the Nature and Extent of the Legislative Authority of the British Parliament*, 1774, for distribution to the other members of the Congress. The work, which concluded that there was no "power of Parliament over us," anticipated Britain's modern Commonwealth of Nations and exhibited an intellectual strength equal to that of John Adams and Thomas Jefferson. Wilson was elected to the Second Continental Congress, 1775–1777, and he signed the Declaration of Independence. He undertook many important committee assignments and served on the Board of War as well. He became advocate general for France in 1779 and represented that country in cases arising out of its alliance with the American colonies. He published an argument in favor of the establishment of the Bank of North America and supported the struggle for currency reform after 1781. He served as Pennsylvania's counsel in the dispute with Connecticut over the Wyoming Valley in 1782. During 1782–1783 and 1785–1787 he was again in Congress. His role at the 1787 Constitutional Convention was central; it was he who thought to the heart of the problem of establishing a central authority necessary to a union of states while, at the same time, preserving the local rights insisted upon by the states and by citizens. He staunchly maintained the position that sovereignty resided in, and a national government would draw its authority from, the people rather than the states. In addition to being a leading influence in framing the Constitution, he was also mainly responsible for its ratification by Pennsylvania and, in 1790, for writing that state's constitution. President George Washington appointed him one of the first associate justices of the U.S. Supreme Court in 1789. He also became the first professor of law at the College of Philadelphia, his lectures of 1790 being an attempt to interpret the national and state constitutions in the manner in which Blackstone had treated English law. His lectures enunciated the arguments Chief Justice John Marshall later used to declare an act of Congress unconstitutional; they remain landmarks in the history of American jurisprudence. Wilson participated in all the notable decisions of the Court and himself spoke for the majority in the case of *Chisholm* v. *Georgia*, which led to the Eleventh Amendment to the Constitution in 1798. Land speculations during the 1790s ruined him financially and undermined his health. He died in Edenton, North Carolina, on August 21, 1798.

Wilson, Samuel (1766–1854), "Uncle Sam," merchant. Born in what is now Arlington, Massachusetts, on September 16, 1766, Wilson fought in the Revolutionary War while still in his teens. In 1789 he settled in Troy, New York, where he worked at various jobs before starting a meat-packing plant. By the start of the War of 1812 he had a thriving business, and he acquired a large contract to supply meat to the army. All of the meat shipped from his plant for army use was stamped "U.S.," and when visitors to the plant in October 1812 asked what these initials stood for, they were jokingly told by workmen that they stood for the name of the owner—"Uncle Sam" Wilson. By the end of the war the term had come to symbolize the government itself, partly because Wilson enjoyed a reputation for hard work and integrity that it was supposed the nation shared. Wilson lived in Troy, operating his packing plant, until his death on July 31, 1854.

Wilson, Thomas Woodrow, see Wilson, Woodrow

Wilson, William Bauchop (1862–1934), labor leader and public official. Born in Blantyre, Scotland, on April 2, 1862, Wilson emigrated with his family to the United States in 1870 and settled at Arnot, in Tioga County, Pennsylvania. As a child he went to work in the coal mines and therefore had little formal schooling. For most of the years from 1872 until 1898 he worked in the mines and took part in attempts to unionize the miners. He met with the frustrations that occasionally overwhelmed union men who encountered the power of mine operators at the time, and he was often blacklisted. But he persisted in his efforts and was one of the founders of the United Mine Workers of America (UMW), organized on January 25, 1890, in Columbus, Ohio. He participated in the strikes of 1894, 1899, and 1902, by which hours were reduced and wages increased. From 1900 to 1908 he served as secretary-treasurer of the UMW. In 1906 he was elected to the House of Representatives as a Democrat and, twice reelected, served three terms, during which he promoted measures favorable to the labor movement, including inspection of mines for safety, the eight-hour day, and the organization of the U.S. Bureau of Mines. During 1911–1913 he was chairman of the House labor committee. He also advocated the creation of a separate cabinet-level Department of Labor, and when the department was established in March 1913 President Woodrow Wilson appointed him the first secretary of labor. The Democratic administration under President Wilson was more attuned to the interests of labor than previous administrations had been. While Wilson was secretary the La Follette Seaman's Act, sponsored especially by Andrew Furuseth, was passed by Congress in 1915. The Smith-Hughes Act of 1917 provided federal funds to vocational schools, and the immigration bill of 1917 (passed over a presidential veto) favored labor by imposing a literacy test on immigrants, thus limiting the number of those who could enter the country.

Wilson also undertook a complete reorganization of the Bureau of Immigration and Naturalization, and he established the U.S. Employment Service. During the "Red Scare" of 1919–1920, Wilson mitigated the offensive and unjust deportation procedures launched by Attorney General A. Mitchell Palmer against the foreign-born and against union members. During World War I he served on the Council of National Defense and from 1917 to 1921 was a member of the Federal Board for Vocational Education. He left office in March 1921, when the Republican administration of Warren G. Harding took over the White House. He ran for the U.S. Senate in 1926 but lost. He died near Savannah, Georgia, on May 25, 1934.

Wilson, Woodrow (1856–1924), twenty-eighth president of the United States. Born on December 28, 1856, in Staunton, Virginia, Thomas Woodrow Wilson, the son of a Presbyterian minister and teacher, grew up in Georgia and the Carolinas. After a year at Davidson College in North Carolina he went to the College of New Jersey (now Princeton) and graduated in 1879; he studied law briefly at the University of Virginia, entered upon a short and unsuccessful practice of law in Atlanta, and in 1883 took up graduate studies at The Johns Hopkins University. Three years later he was granted a Ph.D., his thesis being *Congressional Government*, 1885, a brilliant analysis of the power relations between the legislative and executive branches of the national government. Among his other writings were *The State: Elements of Historical and Practical Politics*, 1889; *Division and Reunion, 1829–1889*, 1893; *An Old Master and Other Political Essays*, 1893; *Mere Literature and Other Essays*, 1896; *George Washington*, 1897; *A History of The American People*, 1902; and *Constitutional Government in the United States*, 1908. From 1885 to 1888 he taught history and political economy at Bryn Mawr College; for two years thereafter he was on the faculty of Wesleyan University in Connecticut, and in 1890 he returned to Princeton as professor of jurisprudence and political economy. In 1902 he was elected president of the university. During eight years in this office he attempted to revolutionize the atmosphere of Princeton and to create what would truly be a community of scholars; his two avenues of approach, the preceptorial system and the quadrangle plan, were designed to encourage the growth of close personal contacts between students and teachers and to establish a collection of small communities much like those of Cambridge and Oxford. These ideas, strongly democratic in tendency, roused heated opposition at Princeton, long a club-dominated and class-conscious campus, but they were later adopted at many major universities. In 1910 Wilson, now with a national following and a reputation as a strong and incorruptible supporter of democracy, was offered the Democratic nomination for governor of New Jersey; he accepted and was easily elected. To the dismay of many of the Democratic professionals, he soon demonstrated that he took campaign promises seriously and actively pushed through the legislature a series of reform measures including a direct primary law, a corrupt practices act, and the creation of a public utilities commission, maintaining his leadership even after Republicans captured control of both houses of the state legislature. In 1911 he met Col. Edward M. House of Texas, who had been attracted by Wilson's high principles and liberalism and who saw in him presidential timber. House was a man of practical political wisdom and immediately set about building Wilson's political future. In 1912 Wilson was a prominent, though not leading, candidate for the Democratic presidential nomination; on the 46th ballot at the national convention, however, and after his public disavowal of Tammany Hall, he was nominated. The Taft-Roosevelt split in the Republican party enabled him to gain the largest electoral college victory up to that time, although he failed to win a majority of the popular vote. On the crest of progressive enthusiasm aroused by his "New Freedom" campaign he began his administration by carrying through a vigorous program of reform legislation, notably the Underwood Tariff (1913) that, in addition to lowering rates substantially, also included an income tax; the Federal Reserve Act, 1913; the establishment of the Federal Trade Commission, 1914; and the Clayton Antitrust Act, 1914, which, besides attacking monopoly, recognized the legality of labor unions and of their use of strikes and boycotts. In this work, which he predicated on the idea of returning power to the people, he worked closely with Congress; in April 1913 he made the first presidential address to a joint session of Congress in over a century and found that his mastery of oratory was as effective there as in mobilizing public opinion. In foreign affairs he faced more difficult problems. Certain outstanding conflicts were resolved quickly as "dollar diplomacy" was repudiated, the Panama Canal toll exemptions that had angered Britain were revoked, and a public position favoring the protection of the independence of smaller nations was clearly elaborated. But it became apparent that pacifism, high idealism, and moral uprightness failed to answer all the demands of international politics. Revolution and civil war in Mexico posed the thorniest question. Wilson refused on principle to recognize the new Mexican government of Adolfo de la Huerta and adopted a policy of "watchful waiting;" in April 1914, after a minor incident involving U.S. sailors in Tampico, Mexico, and with the approach of a shipment of German arms, the terminal facilities at Veracruz were seized by U.S. armed forces. War was averted by the mediation of Argentina, Brazil, and Chile (the "ABC powers") and the subsequent resignation of Huerta. In November U.S. forces were withdrawn and the new government was recognized; but friction developed again in 1916 when, after a raid into New Mexico by Pancho Villa and his guerrillas, Wilson ordered Gen. John J. Pershing to lead U.S. troops into Mexico in pursuit of the bandit. During 1915 U.S. protectorate governments had been established in

Haiti and Santo Domingo. By this time, however, world attention centered on the European war, and Wilson was embroiled in the problems of maintaining and defending U.S. neutrality. The first manifestations of the problem, brought about by Britain's blockade of Germany, were soon overshadowed by Germany's declaration of unrestricted submarine warfare. When loss of U.S. lives and property began, and particularly after the sinking of the *Lusitania* in May 1915, Wilson protested vigorously (so much so as to cause the resignation of William Jennings Bryan, secretary of state and a pacifist). Stronger protests followed until, early in 1916, a halt to such acts was secured; this victory was a major boon to the President's bid for reelection that year, and the slogan "He kept us out of war" helped him in a very close race. The Republicans, fielding Charles Evans Hughes against him, charged him with vacillation before Germany's threats and sharply criticized his pro-labor reforms. Only late returns from the agrarian and isolationist West ended Wilson's conviction that he had lost the election. In the meanwhile diplomatic maneuvers were being made in an attempt to bring the belligerents to the conference table. To bring public opinion to bear and to forestall a possible resumption of open submarine warfare by Germany, Wilson had already planned a public appeal for a peace conference when, in December 1916, Germany announced its willingness to negotiate. A week later Wilson made his proposal for a conference and in mid-January of 1917 outlined his ideas on the shape of the settlements to be made in a "peace without victory." But by this time German leaders had decided to resume unlimited submarine operations; relations with Germany were immediately broken and, on April 2, after several more ships were lost, Wilson requested a declaration of war against Germany from Congress, receiving it four days later. Throughout World War I Wilson's role was primarily that of moral leader and he enjoyed the overwhelming support of the people. Delegating much of the necessary practical work to others, he concerned himself with enlisting support for the war on his own terms—"making the world safe for democracy" in a moral crusade—and with planning the peace. To the latter end his major contribution was his formulation of the Fourteen Points announced in a speech in January 1918. Among these points, which were mostly concerned with adjustment of territorial and colonial claims, were proposals for freedom of the seas, arms reductions, open diplomacy, trade liberalization, and "a general association of nations." Wilson continued to advocate his peace program through 1918. In October of that year Germany suddenly accepted it as a basis for peace negotiations; until then the Allies had paid little attention to it, but now, faced with pressure from Washington and the prospect of shortening the war by several months, they also accepted and an armistice was signed on November 11, 1918. Wilson, now the preeminent figure in the world, committed a political blunder in trying to make the congressional elections of that month into a referendum on his policies. By that stroke he traded away much of the solid bipartisan support that underlay his influence abroad. He then compounded the error by failing to include representatives of the Republican party in his peace delegation. In December he sailed for Europe and was hailed almost as a savior by the people of the countries he visited; at the Versailles Peace Conference, however, he soon met major obstacles to his plans. Earlier secret agreements among the Allies came to light, and the idealism of the Fourteen Points paled before nationalistic fervor. He secured agreement to the League of Nations Covenant but, facing for the first time the necessity of resolving practical conflicts of right and interest, was forced into painful compromises on territorial matters and arms reduction. Despite the preliminary efforts of Colonel House to win European acceptance of the Fourteen Points, they turned out under pressure to be of little concrete value. In July he returned to the United States with the treaty of Versailles, which included the League covenant. Ill and disgusted with compromise, he soon made it clear that he had no intention of making concessions to the "reservationists" in the Senate. Instead he set off on a cross-country speaking tour to arouse public support for the treaty; but in September he suffered a collapse and was brought back to Washington, where his condition worsened to the point of virtual incapacitation. The Senate, under Henry Cabot Lodge's leadership, approved a number of reservations to be added to the treaty before ratification. More adamant than ever, Wilson refused to consider negotiating the reservations and called on his supporters to defeat ratification rather than accept any part of the Lodge policy. On November 19, 1919, and again on March 19, 1920, the treaty was voted down by the Senate. Wilson's hope of making the 1920 presidential election a "solemn referendum" on the treaty failed to materialize; he himself was too ill to take part in the campaign. In December he was awarded the 1919 Nobel Peace Prize. After the inauguration of Warren G. Harding, Wilson retired to a small house in Washington, D.C., where he remained, largely inactive and out of public life, until his death on February 3, 1924. He was elected to the Hall of Fame in 1950.

Winchell, Walter (1897–1972), journalist and broadcaster. Born in New York City on April 7, 1897, Winchell had a 12-year career in vaudeville before becoming a journalist. At the age of twelve he sang in a trio with George Jessel, and they were soon hired by impresario Gus Edwards as the Imperial Trio. For two years Winchell toured in reviews, then in 1915 teamed up with a partner for a song-and-dance act. During World War I he saw service with the navy and in 1919 returned to the stage. About 1920 he began contributing gossip-column material to *Billboard* and the *Vaudeville News*, and by 1922 he had his own column in the latter paper. Two years later he went to work for the *New York Evening Graphic*,

doing a column about show-business personalities and other celebrities. Soon he became a New York institution, his column, "On Broadway," gaining a wide local following. In 1929 Winchell left the *Evening Graphic* for the *New York Daily Mirror*, where his syndicated column appeared until 1963. He was regarded as one of the most audacious and entertaining reporters of his time. Not only was his gossipy information interesting, equally so was the idiom he used to express it. In 1933 Funk & Wagnalls lexicographers cited him as one of the ten most versatile American slang-makers; and H. L. Mencken, in *The American Language*, listed a number of terms Winchell had added to the language. He had a wide range of acquaintances among the public figures of the day, including show-business people, politicians, and even some of the gangsters of the Prohibition era. In 1939 it was Winchell who arranged for Louis Lepke, wanted on charges of narcotics smuggling, to turn himself in personally to J. Edgar Hoover of the FBI. From 1932 until the early 1950s Winchell had a weekly radio broadcast in which his rapid-fire delivery of frankly opinionated news became familiar to millions of listeners. In the 1930s, besides his preoccupation with celebrities, he took a political stand as an ardent supporter of Franklin D. Roosevelt's New Deal, a critic of the German Nazi Party and its U.S. supporters, and an opponent of the racial attitudes of many Southern politicians. It was Winchell who broke the news in 1940 that Franklin D. Roosevelt would seek an unprecedented third term. After Roosevelt's death, and with the onset of the Cold War, his politics took a decisive turn to the right as he became a critic of President Harry S. Truman and a vigorous anti-Communist (he was a staunch supporter of the Communist-hunting Senator Joseph R. McCarthy); he showed himself to be largely indifferent to the nation's racial problems. During his long and stormy journalistic career, one of Winchell's few close friends was the author Damon Runyon. Upon Runyon's death in 1946 Winchell founded the Damon Runyon Memorial Fund for Cancer Research, which over the next 25 years collected and disbursed more than $30 million. For a few years in the 1950s he was on television with his weekly broadcast, largely local in the New York area, and he was the unseen narrator for the network program "The Untouchables" from 1959 to 1963. In 1965 he retired to California. He died in Los Angeles on February 20, 1972.

Winchester, Oliver Fisher (1810–1880), firearms manufacturer. Born in Boston on November 30, 1810, Winchester was orphaned at an early age. He worked at various trades until settling in Baltimore in 1830; after several years of manual labor he operated a clothing store from 1837 until 1847, when he sold the business and settled in New York City. There he made a success in the shirt-manufacturing business and three years later set up a factory in New Haven, Connecticut. The success of his company enabled him to buy control of the Volcanic Repeating Arms Company of New

Haven, and by 1857 he was engaged full time in the manufacture of firearms, reorganizing the firm as the New Haven Arms Company, of which he was president. The Henry repeating rifle, put into production in 1860, was the first of a series of repeaters that proved themselves the best available at the time and were adopted by many state militia regiments during the Civil War and by large numbers of settlers in the Far West after the war. Over the next 20 years a number of improvements were made in the rifle, notably the incorporation of the side-loading magazine to produce the famed Winchester rifle, and the firm, reorganized again in 1867 as the Winchester Repeating Arms Company, bought out other firearms concerns and became a highly successful business. Winchester died in New Haven on December 11, 1880.

Windsor, Wallis Warfield, Duchess of (1896–   ), socialite. Born in Blue Ridge Summit, Pennsylvania, on June 19, 1896, Bessie Wallis Warfield, known as Wallis, grew up there and in Maryland. During World War I she married Earl W. Spencer, a navy pilot with the rank of lieutenant commander; they were divorced in the early 1920s. After living for a time in Warrenton, Virginia, she traveled to England, where she met Ernest A. Simpson, a U.S.-born British subject. They were married in 1928 and lived near London, where she became acquainted with many of the leading personalities of the day. In June 1931 she was introduced to the Prince of Wales and they were frequently seen together at social gatherings over the next few years. After his accession to the throne as Edward VIII on January 20, 1936, the possibility of romance between them became more than an occasion of social comment. In October 1936 Mrs. Simpson filed for divorce, and it soon became apparent that the king intended to marry her. This situation initiated an unprecedented constitutional crisis. On December 11, 1936, Edward VIII renounced his throne, and the next day made the famous radio address to the nation which concluded: "I have found it impossible to carry on the heavy burden of responsibility and to discharge the duties of king as I wish without the help and support of the woman I love." Immediately after his abdication, upon which he took the title of Duke of Windsor, he left England to live on the Continent. Her divorce became final in May 1937, and she had her name changed legally to Mrs. Wallis Warfield. He and Mrs. Warfield were married in France on June 3, 1937. They lived in France and traveled frequently until World War II broke out. In July 1940, his brother, King George VI, named him governor of the Bahama Islands, where the Duke and Duchess remained through most of World War II; he resigned his post in early 1945 and moved back to France. The couple were among the most prominent and newsworthy members of the "international set" of socialites and celebrities, traveling, entertaining, and being entertained a great deal. In 1956 the Duchess of Windsor published her autobiography, *The Heart Has Its Reasons.* The Duke of Windsor died in Paris on May 28, 1972, and the Duchess continued to live at her Paris home.

Winfield, Arthur M., *see* Stratemeyer, Edward

Winslow, Edward (1595–1655), colonial leader. Born in Droitwich, England, on October 18, 1595, Winslow grew up in a fairly affluent family. In the religious controversies of the day he became a Separatist Puritan, one who would not follow the practices of the Church of England. In 1617, while in Europe, he joined the Separatist congregation at Leiden, the Netherlands, and three years later sailed for North America with the Pilgrims on the *Mayflower.* As a man of better education than most, he served the Plymouth Colony in a variety of ways for more than 25 years. He was frequently chosen to deal with the Indians—he made the 1621 treaty of peace with Massasoit—and he made several trips back to England, serving as agent at the request of the colony to bring back supplies and negotiate with the investors in the venture. During one such assignment in 1624 he published *Good News from New England, or a True Relation of Things Very Remarkable at the Plantation of Plymouth in New England.* From 1624 to 1647 he was a member of the governor's council at Plymouth, except for his own three terms as governor, 1633–1634, 1636–1637, and 1644–1645. The accounts he wrote of Plymouth, which were published in London, were the first the English had of conditions and events in Massachusetts. In 1643 he served as one of the commissioners of the United Colonies of New England. In addition to farming, Winslow also engaged in trading with the Indians, an enterprise which made him one of the colony's chief explorers. In 1646 he sailed for England on the last of his several trips in behalf of the colony's interests. He engaged in considerable pamphlet controversy in later years and in 1649 published *The Glorious Progress of the Gospel among the Indians in New England.* He served in various offices under the Puritan government of Oliver Cromwell and gained Plymouth a license to trade with the Caribbean islands, thus enhancing their chance for prosperity. In 1655 Cromwell appointed him one of the leaders of an expedition against the Spanish islands in the West Indies. The fleet captured Jamaica for England, but on the return voyage Winslow died, on May 8, 1655.

Winslow, Josiah (1629?–1680), colonial leader. Born in Plymouth, Massachusetts, about 1629, the son of Edward Winslow, Josiah Winslow attended Harvard College but did not graduate. In his public career he was both military leader and officeholder. He commanded the militia in his home town of Marshfield, Massachusetts, and in 1659 he replaced Miles Standish as commander of colonial forces. He was a member of the governor's council from 1657 until 1673, when he became governor, the first American-born governor of any of the British North American colonies. During the Indian uprising known as King Philip's War, in 1675–1676, Winslow commanded the forces of the

United Colonies until February 1676. He served as governor until his death on December 18, 1680, in London, where he had gone to obtain a royal charter for the colony.

Winsor, Justin (1831–1897), historian and librarian. Born in Boston on January 2, 1831, Winsor attended Harvard but left before graduating and went to study in Europe. After spending the years 1852–1854 mainly in Germany and France he returned to Boston and devoted the next dozen years to writing articles, poems, and stories. In 1866 he was appointed a trustee of the Boston Public Library and two years later became its librarian. He remained with the Boston library until 1877, when he accepted an offer to become head librarian of Harvard. He did extensive work in promoting the development of libraries throughout the country and modernized the procedures in the libraries for which he was responsible. He was a founder and first president, from 1876 to 1888, of the American Library Association, serving again as president in 1897, and was a founder of the *Library Journal*. His work in libraries augmented his interest in historical research, and he made available much hitherto unread and unresearched documentation. Winsor was also a historian in his own right. He edited the four-volume *Memorial History of Boston*, 1880–1881, and completed the *Narrative and Critical History of America*, 1884–1889, in eight volumes. He also wrote a number of other historical works, including *Christopher Columbus*, 1891; *Cartier to Frontenac*, 1894; *The Mississippi Basin*, 1895; and *The Westward Movement*, 1897. He died in Cambridge, Massachusetts, on October 22, 1897.

Winthrop, John (1588–1649), lawyer, colonial leader, and first governor of Massachusetts Bay Colony. Born in England at Edwardstone, Suffolk, on January 12, 1588, Winthrop entered Trinity College, Cambridge, in 1603 but left after two years in order to marry. To augment the income from his lands, he studied law at Gray's Inn and established a law practice in London. In 1628 he was admitted to the Inner Temple. A Puritan of deep religious convictions, he was troubled by the future of religion and morals. In 1629 he joined other Puritans in the Cambridge Agreement, a pledge to settle in New England if the charter and the government of the colony were given entirely into their hands. He was active in organizing the Massachusetts Bay Company, which replaced the New England Company in 1628. He was chosen the colony's first governor and, with a royal charter, several shiploads of colonists sailed in March 1630, reaching Salem, where John Endecott had preceded them, in June. They went to the Shawmut Peninsula and founded the settlement that became Boston. Chosen as a governor of the colony from time to time for a total of 12 one-year terms, he was deputy governor in all other years. Winthrop strongly opposed democratic tendencies, such as the placing of sole legislative authority in the elected General Court, and he also resisted the efforts of the clergy to share control of the colony with the duly constituted officers. He took the lead in preparing the colony for the possibility of coercion by England. After being rebuked by the clergy for his leniency toward dissenters, he forcefully opposed the Antinomian beliefs of Anne Hutchinson and her followers, 1636–1638. In 1643 he headed the United Colonies of New England in their defense against the Indians, and he defended the colony from parliamentary interference in 1645–1646. Winthrop's influence on the history of colonial Massachusetts was enormous. He died in Boston on March 26, 1649. Two volumes of his richly informative *Journal* were published in 1790, and, with an additional volume, appeared in 1825–1826 as *The History of New England from 1630 to 1649*.

Winthrop, John (1714–1779), astronomer and mathematician. Born in Boston on December 19, 1714, Winthrop, a descendant of John Winthrop, (1588–1649), the first governor of the Massachusetts Bay Colony, graduated from Harvard in 1732. He devoted himself, by reading, observation, and experimentation, to the fields of mathematics, astronomy, and meteorology. In 1738 he became professor of mathematics and natural philosophy at Harvard, a position he held for the rest of his life. Most of his writings were descriptive of various phenomena which he observed—comets, an earthquake, the weather—and thus tended to be fragmentary works; and they were sent to the Royal Society in London for publication in its *Transactions* for other scientists to read, discuss, and comment on. He became a fellow of the Royal Society in 1766. But within the limitations imposed by colonial isolation from the centers of learning, Winthrop was an imposing and brilliant scholar, America's first thoroughgoing scientist. From 1742 until his death he kept a journal of the weather at Cambridge, Massachusetts, where he lived. The 1755 earthquake in New England led him to suggest the "wave" nature of earthquakes, the first scientist to do so. In his main area of study, astronomy, he traced the courses of the known planets, made observations of sunspots, investigated the transits of Venus and Mercury, and performed advanced calculations on the orbits of comets. In mathematics he introduced the study of algebra and calculus into the Harvard curriculum. In 1771 he was awarded an honorary doctorate by the University of Edinburgh, and two years later he received the first honorary doctorate ever awarded by Harvard. Winthrop died in Cambridge on May 3, 1779.

Winthrop, Robert Charles (1809–1894), public official. Born in Boston on May 12, 1809, a descendant of John Winthrop (1588–1649), the first governor of the Massachusetts Bay Colony, and a nephew of James Bowdoin, Winthrop graduated from Harvard in 1828. After studying law privately under Daniel Webster he was admitted to the bar in 1831 and opened a law practice in Boston. Coming from a family that had been both affluent and prominent in public affairs since the founding of Massachusetts, Winthrop was a patrician who entered public service because it was natural for him to do so. In the heated political climate of the two decades prior to the Civil War, he took no extreme positions and thus often found himself out of step with his more fervid colleagues. A Whig, he served for five years in the state legislature, from 1835 to 1840, and in 1840 was elected to the House of Representatives. He remained in the House until 1850, except for a few months during 1842. He was speaker of the House in 1847–1849. He lost popularity with his constituency by his moderate attitude toward slavery and toward the Free-Soil controversy after the Mexican War. In 1850 he was appointed to the U.S. Senate to fill the vacancy caused by Daniel Webster's resignation. But his term in the Senate was short, his lukewarmness on the issue of slavery caused him to be defeated for reelection in 1851 by Charles Sumner, one of the most ardent of antislavery Northerners. When the Whig party failed and the new Republican party emerged in the 1850s Winthrop did not join it, but instead continued to play the conciliatory role he felt was most beneficial when the country was being torn over the issue of slavery in the territories. After leaving the Senate, Winthrop did not hold public office again, and he was only sporadically involved in politics. For the most part he pursued scholarly interests and became involved in civic activities in the Boston area. He was for 55 years a member, and for 30 president, of the Massachusetts Historical Society. His published works were largely his addresses; he was one of the noted orators of his day. He died in Boston on November 16, 1894.

Winton, Alexander (1860–1932), automobile manufacturer. Born in Grangemouth, Scotland, on June 20, 1860, Winton emigrated to the United States in 1880. He worked at various jobs requiring mechanical ability before settling in Cleveland in 1884 and opening a bicycle-repair shop. In the ensuing years he developed it into a bicycle-manufacturing business, which prospered because of his ingenuity in making improvements and modifications in the vehicles. In the early 1890s he became interested in the internal-combustion engine and by 1896 had constructed an experimental motor car. Winton was one of the first men in the United States to build cars with a commercial market in mind, and he was the builder of the first big autos. In 1897 he built two cars of the phaeton type—touring cars—and organized the Winton Motor Carriage Company. Before the end of the next year he had received a patent for his vehicle and had built and sold nearly 30 cars. As his auto business grew he introduced the use of spare parts for his cars and started service stations to repair them once they were in the hands of private owners. He also pioneered in long-distance driving and auto racing. In 1897 Winton drove one of his own cars from Cleveland to New York City—a route covering some 800 miles over what were then considered roads. In 1903 one of his cars was the first to cross the United States, completing the trip in 63 days. His racer, the "Winton Bullet," set a speed record at Daytona Beach, Florida, in 1902, but in 1903 his car was defeated by a Ford driven by Barney Oldfield. Winton continued to improve his cars. Starting with four-cylinder engines, by 1907 he had switched to six cylinders, and he was the first of the automakers to experiment with eight cylinders. With the auto plant a success, he added to his interests in 1912 a company manufacturing Diesel engines. In 1924 he gave up the auto business in favor of producing Diesel engines. He retired a few years later. He died in Cleveland on June 21, 1932.

Wirt, William (1772–1834), lawyer, public official, and author. Born in Bladensburg, Maryland, on November 8, 1772, Wirt studied law and was admitted to the bar in 1792. He opened a law practice in Culpeper County, Virginia, where he lived for seven years before moving to Richmond. Although moderately successful as a lawyer, he was also drawn to writing. His first literary attempt was his most successful; in 1803 he published anonymously a series entitled "Letters of a British Spy" in the Richmond Argus that gained an immediate popular response. The letters were soon published in book form. His subsequent writings were less notable—two volumes of essays on Southern manners, The Rainbow, 1804, and The Old Bachelor, 1812. His most serious work was the 1817 publication, Sketches of the Life and Character of Patrick Henry, which drew together much of the existing material on Henry and remained for many years the definitive biography of the Virginia patriot. Wirt was elected clerk of the Virginia House of Delegates in 1800, and gained a reputation as a trial lawyer the same year when he served as defense counsel for James T. Callender in his trial under the Alien and Sedition Acts. In 1807 he was a counsel for the prosecution in the trial of Aaron Burr for treason. With his reputation as a lawyer established, he continued his practice and his writing at Richmond for nearly a decade. In 1816 President James Madison appointed him U.S. attorney for the Richmond district, and early the following year President James Monroe appointed him attorney general of the United States. He served in the cabinet for 12 years, until the end of John Quincy Adams's term of office as president. As attorney general, Wirt argued some of the great precedent-setting cases in U.S. constitutional history, including McCulloch v. Maryland, 1819, the Dartmouth College Case, 1819, and Gibbons v. Ogden, 1824, before a U.S. Supreme Court presided over by John Marshall. He also set the precedent of collecting and publishing the opinions of the attorney general. After leaving office in 1829 he settled in Baltimore to practice law, but in 1832 he was involved actively in politics as the reluctant candidate of the Anti-Masonic party for the presidency. Wirt died in Washington, D.C., on February 18, 1834.

Wise, Isaac Mayer (1819–1900), religious leader. Born on March 29, 1819, in Steingrub, Bohemia (then part of Austria, now Czechoslovakia), Isaac Mayer Weis attended Hebrew day schools, several rabbinical schools, the Prague Gymnasium, the University of Prague, and the University of Vienna. He became a rabbi at the age of twenty-three, and officiated at Radnice, Bohemia, where Jews were constantly and brutally harassed by non-Jews and by the government. In 1846 he came to the United States and was installed as a rabbi at Albany, New York. At this time he changed the spelling of his name. In 1854 he moved to the Bene Yeshurun congregation in Cincinnati, where he served for the rest of his life. Dismayed at the disunity among Jews across the nation, and feeling that the only way to defeat anti-Semitism was to develop pride in Judaism and to adapt its doctrines to American life, he espoused a gradual movement toward liberal, or reform, Judaism. By the time of his death, it had become a major branch of Judaism in the United States. He communicated with his followers through a newspaper, the *Israelite*, later the *American Israelite*, as well as a German language paper, *Die Deborah*. He also wrote a prayer book, *Minhag America*, as well as plays, novels, and several histories of Judaism. Among his published works were *History of the Israelitish Nation from Abraham to the Present Time*, 1854; *The Cosmic God*, 1876; and *Pronaos to Holy Writ*, 1891. A major step toward unity was taken in the founding of the Union of American Hebrew Congregations in 1873; at first only a regional organization, it grew to encompass the entire nation. From the time of his arrival in the United States he urged the founding of a theological seminary to provide U.S.-trained rabbis. This was realized in the establishment of the Hebrew Union College in Cincinnati in 1875, of which he was president until his death, and from which the first American rabbis were ordained. He also proposed a conference of rabbis, realized in 1889 in the Central Conference of American Rabbis held in Detroit. He is accepted as the founder of Reform Judaism in America; a universalist, he was strongly opposed to all manifestations of Jewish nationalism or separatism. He died in Cincinnati on March 26, 1900. His *Reminiscences* were published in 1901.

Wise, John (1652–1725), religious leader. Born in Roxbury, Massachusetts (now part of Boston), in August 1652, Wise graduated from Harvard College in 1673, the first son of an indentured servant to do so. For the next several years he preached in various parishes, then in 1680 accepted a call to a Congregational church in Ipswich, Massachusetts, where he served the rest of his life. His ordination took place in 1683. Throughout his career he was an articulate spokesman and pamphleteer on the rights of individuals and on the practice of democracy in church and state, and this at a time when democracy was not held in high repute by either political or ecclesiastical leaders. He was first involved in controversy in 1687, over a land tax imposed by the administration of Governor Sir Edmund Andros; the tax provoked dissension and resentment in every Massachusetts town, and Wise spoke for the resisters in terms

that would be echoed many decades later during the Stamp Act crisis: "No taxes should be levied upon the subject without the consent of an assembly chosen by freeholders for assessing the same." Wise was arrested, tried, and deprived of his church office; the deprivation was temporary, for in 1689 the Andros government collapsed in the wake of the Glorious Revolution in England and Wise was restored to his clerical duties. In 1690 he was appointed chaplain to the expedition against Quebec. In the first decade of the eighteenth century several of the New England clergy, led by Increase and Cotton Mather, favored organizing a synod of ministers that would give clergy control over the churches and regularize polity and discipline. Obviously a move to recover the waning authority of the Puritan clergy, it was promoted by Increase Mather in a tract, *Questions and Proposals*, in 1705. As pro and con arguments developed, the movement did not appear to be arriving at fruition, and in 1710 Wise demolished it with his carefully reasoned pamphlet *The Churches' Quarrel Espoused*. But his most memorable polemic, a document that would be quoted and republished frequently in the years before the American Revolution, was *A Vindication of the Government of New England Churches*, 1717, a plea for democracy in both church and civil affairs. In it he relied not only on traditional biblical arguments, but resorted as well to theories of natural law and rights derived from classical Greek and Roman authors. He asserted that democracy was a government "most agreeable with the light of nature" and that "the end of all good government is to cultivate humanity, and promote the happiness of all, the good of every man in his rights, his life, liberty, estate, honour, etc. without injury or abuse to any." His words would eventually be echoed in the Declaration of Independence. Wise died in Ipswich, Massachusetts, on April 8, 1725.

Wise, Stephen Samuel (1874–1949), religious leader. Born in Budapest on March 17, 1874, the descendant of seven generations of rabbis, Wise came to New York City with his father in 1875. He graduated from the City College of New York (CCNY) in 1892 and then attended Columbia University, from which he took a Ph.D. in Semitic languages in 1901. He studied religion with many private teachers. After serving as rabbi of the reform Congregation B'nai Jeshurun in New York City from 1893 to 1900, he moved to Temple Beth Israel in Portland, Oregon; while there he drafted the state's first child-labor laws and organized a conference on charities and correction. An ardent spokesman for Zionism, he was in demand as a lecturer and in 1898 founded the Federation of American Zionists, later known as the Zionist Organization of America (ZOA). In 1906 he declined a call to Temple Emanu-El in New York City, fearing censorship of his sermons by its conservative board of directors. He resigned his pulpit in Portland and returned to New York City in 1907, founding the Free Synagogue, where he served as rabbi. A staunch non-assimilationist, he declared that being a Jew and being an American were two separate things, of separate import. He spoke for civic reform, attacking Tammany Hall leaders from his pulpit and contributing to the downfall of Richard "Boss" Croker and, later, of Mayor James J. Walker. Perhaps his greatest desire was for the establishment of Palestine as a national home for Jews. In 1915–1916 he joined Louis D. Brandeis, Felix Frankfurter, and other leaders in the American Jewish Congress, later serving as its president, and, in 1919, as one of its spokesmen at the peace conference in Versailles at the end of World War I. He served as president of the World Jewish Congress, founded in 1922 the Jewish Institute of Religion to train young men for the reform rabbinate, founded and edited the magazine *Opinion*, and wrote numerous pamphlets and books, including *The Improvement of Moral Qualities*, 1902; *How to Face Life*, 1917; *Child Versus Parent*, 1922; and an autobiography, *Challenging Years*, 1949. He was one of the major spokesmen against Hitlerism in the 1930s. His Sunday services held for many years at Carnegie Hall in New York City attracted multitudes of Jews and non-Jews alike. He died in New York City on April 19, 1949.

Wister, Owen (1860–1938), author. Born in Germantown, Pennsylvania, on July 14, 1860, Wister was the favorite grandson of the great English actress Fanny Kemble. Brought up in an intellectual household, he graduated from Harvard in 1882, intending to devote himself to a musical career; but after two years of unproductive study in Paris he returned to the United States to restore his health and spent the summer of 1885 in Wyoming. There he came in contact with cowboys; their way of life, and the awesome beauty of the Western scenery, filled him with fascination. He nevertheless went back to Harvard to study law, was admitted to the bar in 1889, and practiced in Philadelphia for two years. But he continued to spend his summers in the West, and in 1891, after the acceptance by *Harper's* of two sketches about the region, he decided on a literary career. Two early books, *Red Men and White*, 1896, and *Lin McLean*, 1898, were moderately successful and contributed to the legends of the cunning horse thief, the chivalrous rancher, and the vanishing but noble red man. But his most memorable book, and one that is still read, was *The Virginian*, a humorous account of the misadventures of a "tenderfoot" in Wyoming that was published in 1902. It did as much as any single work to create the modern image of the cowboy, and it contained one line of dialogue—"When you call me that, *smile!*"—that is probably as often repeated as anything ever written by an American. Wister also wrote other novels, among them *Philosophy 4*, 1904, and *Lady Baltimore*, 1906; biographies of Ulysses S. Grant and of Theodore Roosevelt, a classmate at Harvard and lifelong friend; and political works on Anglo-American relations, but none approached the fame and popularity of *The Virginian*. His journals and let-

ters from 1885 to 1895 were published in *Owen Wister Out West*, 1958. He died in North Kingstown, Rhode Island, on July 21, 1938.

Witherspoon, John (1723?–1794), religious leader, educator, and public official. Born in Gifford, Scotland, on February 5 of 1722 or 1723, Witherspoon was educated at the University of Edinburgh, where he took his M.A. in 1739 and a divinity degree in 1743. He was licensed to preach by the Presbyterian church in 1743 and was ordained at Beith in 1745, remaining there until called to Paisley in 1757. A sternly conservative, orthodox churchman, he carried on for more than 20 years a running battle with what he saw as the decadence of the church in his day; in sermons and debates, and in diatribes like *Ecclesiastical Characteristics*, 1753, and *Essay on Justification*, 1756, he displayed a keenly logical mind and a marked talent for satire. After first refusing in 1766, in 1768 he answered a call to America to become president of the College of New Jersey (now Princeton). For eight years he devoted himself to enlarging and improving both the college and its curriculum, making of it much more than a training school for ministers; at the same time he came to a position of leadership among American Presbyterians, helping to heal the New Side –Old Side schism in the church. He stood firmly with the colonies in the growing dispute with Great Britain, and by 1776, when the Revolution forced the closing of the college, he had already served on a number of provincial committees and conventions. In that year he was elected to the Continental Congress and was the only clergyman to sign the Declaration of Independence; he served in Congress, until late 1779 and again from December 1780, with a brief interruption, until 1782, playing a prominent role in the work of a large number of committees. In 1782 he returned to Princeton to reopen and rebuild the college. He remained active in public affairs, serving twice in the New Jersey legislature and in the state's constitutional ratifying convention, 1787. At his suggestion, and after years of effort, the first General Assembly of the Presbyterian Church was held in 1789 with Witherspoon as moderator. He died near Princeton, New Jersey, on November 15, 1794.

Wolcott, Oliver (1726–1797), public official. Born in Windsor, Connecticut, on November 20, 1726, Wolcott was the son of Roger Wolcott and the father of Oliver Wolcott (1760–1833). He graduated from Yale in 1747 and studied medicine under his brother Alexander. Lands in the northwestern portion of the state were opened up for settlement in the late 1730s, and Oliver was made sheriff of the newly established Litchfield County in 1751 and practiced law in Litchfield. He was a member of the Governor's Council from 1774 to 1786 and was a delegate to the Continental Congress in 1775–1778 and 1780–1784. He was commissioner of Indian affairs for the Northern Department in 1775 and he helped to settle the

Wyoming Valley boundary dispute between Connecticut and Pennsylvania. He was a signer of the Declaration of Independence and during the Revolution was active in raising militia in Connecticut. In August 1776 he was in command of the Connecticut militia in the defense of New York City, and he served in the campaign against Gen. John Burgoyne in 1777 and in the defense of Connecticut when the British invaded it in 1779. In 1784, again as a commissioner of Indian affairs, he negotiated a treaty with the Iroquois signed at Fort Stanwix, and in 1789 he negotiated a treaty with the Wyandotte of the Western Reserve country. He was lieutenant governor of Connecticut from 1787 to 1796 and in 1787 was a member of the state convention that ratified the Constitution. He became governor in 1796 upon the death of Samuel Huntington and served until his own death, in Hartford, Connecticut, on December 1, 1797.

Wolcott, Oliver (1760–1833), public official. Born in Litchfield, Connecticut, on January 11, 1760, Wolcott, was the son of Oliver Wolcott (1726–1797) and the grandson of Roger Wolcott. He graduated from Yale in 1778, studied law at the Litchfield Law School of Tapping Reeve, and was admitted to the bar in 1781. He was appointed, with Oliver Ellsworth, a commissioner to adjust the claims of Connecticut against the United States in 1784. He served as auditor of the federal treasury, became comptroller of the treasury in 1791, and in 1795 succeeded Alexander Hamilton as secretary of the treasury. He resigned the post in 1800 after a particularly bitter attack on him in the press. He engaged in business in New York City, from 1803 to 1815, when he retired to Litchfield. He soon reentered politics as a leader of the Toleration Republicans and in 1817 was elected governor of Connecticut, serving ten years in the post. The third of his line to serve as governor, he pursued a moderate course in office, working to achieve economic growth in the state. In 1818 he presided over the state convention that adopted a new constitution. He died in New York City on June 1, 1833.

Wolcott, Roger (1679–1767), colonial official. Born on January 4, 1679, in Windsor, Connecticut, Wolcott was the third generation of Wolcotts to live in Windsor, his grandfather, Henry (1578–1655), having emigrated from England in 1628 and, in 1635, helped to found the town. He was apprenticed to a clothier and never attended school, but through his own efforts and those of his mother he obtained some education and wrote the first volume of verse produced in Connecticut (*Poetical Meditations*, 1725). He was a member of Connecticut's general assembly in 1709, a judge the following year, in 1711 commissary of the Connecticut forces in the expedition against Canada, and in 1714 a member of the state council. He was again a judge in 1721 and a justice of the superior court in 1732; in 1741 he became deputy governor, serving until 1750, and also chief

justice of the superior court. During King George's War, in the expedition of 1745 against the fortress of Louisbourg, in Canada, he was second in command of the land forces under William Pepperrell. He was elected governor of Connecticut in 1750 and served until 1754. He died in what is now East Windsor, Connecticut, on May 17, 1767. Among his other works were an epic poem about John Winthrop and a journal which recorded many of the events that took place during the siege of Louisbourg.

Wolfe, Thomas Clayton (1900–1938), author. Born on October 3, 1900, in Asheville, North Carolina, Wolfe was educated privately and entered the University of North Carolina at fifteen. He graduated in 1920, determined to be a dramatist. He had written and acted in several one-act plays, and he was encouraged to go to Harvard to study under George Pierce Baker in his famous 47 Workshop. There he wrote more plays, expanding his scope from his rural background to an urban setting, but none was particularly successful. He received an M.A. in English in 1922 and, to support himself, went to New York City, where he taught sporadically at New York University (NYU). In 1925 he went to Europe for a year, and on this trip he met a stage designer, Aline Bernstein, who gave him love and encouragement as well as monetary assistance and supported his growing interest in his personal background, which he thereupon decided to make the subject of an autobiographical novel. In 20 months he produced an enormous manuscript that was rejected by many publishers. But the chief editor at Charles Scribner's Sons, Maxwell Perkins, recognized its virtues, helped him to cut it drastically, and saw it through to publication in 1929 as *Look Homeward, Angel*. The book, quite literally autobiographical—the Gant family of the novel being in fact the Wolfe family of Asheville, and Eugene Gant being Wolfe himself—was a great critical success but was considered by Asheville to be a scandalous libel. Wolfe now decided to devote himself to a literary career, gave up his job at NYU, and set to work on another book. But though he could write vast amounts, he had extraordinary difficulty in arranging his productions, and it was six years before *Of Time and the River* appeared; and only then after extreme measures on the part of Perkins, who in the end felt it necessary to publish the work before Wolfe considered it finished. *The Story of a Novel*, 1936, was an account by Wolfe of the ordeal he had undergone to produce the book; it contained a generous description of Perkins's help. Wolfe embarked on a new work concerning another autobiographical character, George Webber, and his family. But he did not live to see it published; on a trip to the West Coast in 1938 he fell ill and died in Baltimore on September 15. Edward Aswell, his editor at Harper & Brothers, his new publishers, fashioned three books out of the manuscript Wolfe had left —*The Web and the Rock*, 1939, *You Can't Go Home Again*, 1940, and *The Hills Beyond*, 1941, the last a collection of stories and other short writings. *Look Homeward, Angel*, a play based on his first novel, was a hit on Broadway in the late 1950s and was adapted into a successful movie. Wolfe also wrote short stories, a collection of which was published under the title *From Death to Morning* in 1935. Selections of lyrical passages from his novels were published in 1939 and 1946 as *The Face of a Nation* and *A Stone, A Leaf, A Door*.

Wood, Fernando (1812–1881), public official. Born in Philadelphia on June 14, 1812, Wood grew up there and in New York City, where he worked at various jobs before going into the shipping business. While attaining a measure of prosperity as a ship chandler, merchant, and finally as an investor in New York City real estate, he entered politics via the Tammany Hall Democratic organization. His political career was one of alternating success and failure, for he was as adept at making enemies as he was at winning friends, and often his enemies were men of his own party. He served several terms in the House of Representatives, in 1841–1843, 1863–1865, and 1867–1881; and he was elected mayor of New York City in 1854, 1856, and in 1859. He also lost several elections in which he ran for one or the other of the two offices. He was a progressive mayor of New York City, but the graft of the Tammany machine alienated upstate Republicans in the legislature to the extent that they passed laws infringing upon his jurisdiction in several areas. His carelessness about awarding patronage to his own party members alienated them as well, with the result that he was defeated in 1858. With that, he formed his own political machine, named Mozart Hall, which, while it survived, proved a very effective organization. He regained the mayor's office in 1861, but soon became unpopular with his constituency because of his pro-Confederate sympathies. In January 1861 he proposed that New York City secede from the Union and become a free city, a move directed as much at Republican interference from Albany as it was against the Union itself. Early in the Civil War he supported the Union cause, but as the war dragged on he joined with Clement L. Vallandigham in organizing the "Peace Democrats," or "Copperheads," as they were called by those who deplored their divisive actions. As a member of Congress after the war he opposed Reconstruction measures but supported the Republicans in fiscal policy, again alienating fellow Democrats. When the Democrats won control of the House of Representatives in 1877 Wood became majority floor leader and chairman of the ways and means committee. He served in Congress until his death in Hot Springs, Arkansas, on February 14, 1881.

Wood, Grant (1892–1942), painter. Born on a farm near Anamosa, Iowa, on February 13, 1892, Wood showed an early talent for drawing with charcoal. Left fatherless at ten, he grew up in Cedar Rapids, Iowa, completed high school there, and after graduation attended the Minneapolis School of Design and Handicraft. He moved to Chicago in 1913; there he studied at the Art Institute during the evenings and worked as a craftsman on handmade jewelry at the Kalo silversmith shop. In 1918 and 1919 he was with the camouflage division of the army. For five years thereafter he taught art in the public schools of Cedar Rapids, spending the summer of 1920 in Europe and in 1923 attending the Académie Julien in Paris. Returning to Iowa, he met his first major patron and set up a studio and home in his garage. A commission in 1928 for a stained-glass window for the American Legion in Cedar Rapids took him to Munich in search of craftsmen. There he was influenced by the work of fifteenth-century Flemish and German primitives. His own painting style had been pseudo-impressionistic, but he now changed to an expressive, fine-lined realism. One of his initial works in this style was "Woman with Plants," 1929, a portrait of his mother. Another, and his most famous work, "American Gothic," 1930, portrayed his sister and his dentist as rural Iowa farm folk and helped launch the American native regionalist style, whose other major exponents were John Steuart Curry and Thomas Hart Benton. The painting, first shown at the Art Institute of Chicago, won the Harris bronze medal and prize, and was purchased for the museum by the Friends of American Art. His paintings and lithographs achieved high honors and great popularity; among them were "Daughters of the Revolution," "Dinner for Threshers," and "John B. Turner, Pioneer." After 1934 he was a professor of graphic and plastic arts at the State University of Iowa. Called the "Painter of the Soil," he died on February 12, 1942, in Iowa City.

Wood, James Rushmore (1813–1882), physician. Born in Mamaroneck, New York, on September 14, 1813, Wood attended the College of Physicians and Surgeons in New York City and graduated from the Vermont Academy of Medicine in 1834. He specialized in surgery and became one of the most adept, innovative, and renowned surgeons in the nation. He was particularly noted for his treatment of arterial aneurisms, for his often daring neurosurgical techniques, and for his work in bone repair and regeneration. In 1847 he cooperated in the founding of Bellevue Hospital in New York City, which became within a generation the leading hospital in the United States. The hospital expanded its facilities in 1856 to include Bellevue Hospital Medical College and in 1873 added the country's first training school for nurses. Wood was chief surgeon at Bellevue and taught in the medical school. He died in New York City on May 4, 1882.

Wood, Leonard (1860–1927), soldier and physician. Born on October 9, 1860, in Winchester, New Hampshire, Wood entered Harvard Medical School and took his M.D. in 1884. The following year he became a civilian contract surgeon with the army. Ordered to Arizona, he became involved in the campaign against the Apache leader Geronimo and for his participation in this action was later, in 1898, awarded the Medal of Honor. He was commissioned in the regular army in 1886 and in 1895 transferred to Washington, D.C., where he soon had President William McKinley as a patient. At the outbreak of the Spanish-American War he organized, with Theodore Roosevelt, the 1st U.S. Volunteer Cavalry—the Rough Riders—and was its colonel in Cuba. For his performance there he was promoted to brigadier and then major general of volunteers, while Roosevelt succeeded to command of the Rough Riders. In 1898 Wood became military governor of Santiago de Cuba and the next year of the entire island, and during the next three years he directed Cuban affairs with great skill and organized a new government. In 1903 he was made governor of Moro Province in the Philippines and given the rank of major general in the regular army. From 1906 to 1908 he was in command of the Philippine Division; returning to the United States, he became chief of staff in 1910. In that post he labored to reorganize the War Department along lines consistent with the General Staff system adopted in 1903. Four years later he was named for the second time commander of the Department of the East. The beginning of World War I in Europe prompted him to become an advocate of military preparedness, and he joined Theodore Roosevelt in organizing the training camp for volunteer officers at Plattsburgh, New York. Although he was the senior officer of the army, he was passed over for command of the American Expeditionary Force (AEF)—his advocacy of preparedness had offended the administration of President Woodrow Wilson—and was sent instead to supervise training at Camp Funston, Kansas. His work in the preparedness movement had made him a well-known and popular figure and, thought by many to be Roosevelt's political heir, he was a leading contender for the 1920 Republican presidential nomination; after eight deadlocked ballots at the national convention, however, the nomination went to the compromise candidate, Warren G. Harding. In 1921 he headed a special mission to the Philippines and he remained there as governor general until 1927. Wood died following surgery in Boston on August 7, 1927.

Wood, Robert Elkington (1879–1969), soldier and businessman. Born in Kansas City, Missouri, on June 13, 1879, Wood graduated from West Point in 1900. For five years he saw duty at various posts, including the Philippines during the rebellion led by Emilio Aguinaldo. From 1905 to 1914 he was in Panama, where from 1907 he served under Gen. George W. Goethals in directing the building of the Panama Canal. When the canal was finished, Wood returned home and resigned from the army to go into business. For two years he worked for the Du Pont Company, but when the United States entered World War I he rejoined the army, emerging at the end of the war with the rank of

brigadier general. He left the army again in 1919 and went to work for the mail-order firm of Montgomery Ward & Company in Chicago. In 1924 he joined the competing firm of Sears, Roebuck and Company, of which he became president in 1928. Under his leadership Sears expanded from a $200-million-a-year business to a $3-billion enterprise. He greatly diversified the firm's inventory, oversaw the building of retail outlets in all parts of the nation, and made Sears the first chain mail-order house to open stores in the suburbs, away from downtown centers. In 1931 he started the Allstate Insurance Company as an adjunct to the Sears chain. He also started a savings and profit-sharing plan that by 1969 had brought 23 percent of Sears ownership into the hands of its employees. By the time of his retirement in 1954 Wood had turned Sears into the largest merchandising company in the world. As time permitted he also was active in politics. During the 1930s he warmly supported Franklin D. Roosevelt's New Deal, but late in the decade, because of some of Roosevelt's economic and foreign policies, he switched his party affiliation to Republican and became increasingly conservative in political outlook. In 1940–1941 he was chairman of the America First Committee, working, along with Charles A. Lindbergh, to keep the country out of war and foreign involvements. When the United States entered World War II, however, he took a leave of absence from Sears and served as an adviser to the Army Ordnance Department and to the air force. After the war Wood returned to Sears. He died in Lake Forest, Illinois, on November 6, 1969.

Woodberry, George Edward (1855–1930), poet, critic, and educator. Born in Beverly, Massachusetts, on May 12, 1855, Woodberry graduated from Harvard in 1877. He taught English at the University of Nebraska from 1877 until 1882, except for the year 1879–1880. The next nine years were spent in research and writing. Then in 1891 he accepted an appointment as professor of literature at Columbia University, where he taught until 1904 and where he worked to broaden and liberalize the work of the graduate department. He spent the next several years traveling, writing, and teaching for short periods at schools as widely separated as Amherst College, the University of Wisconsin, and the University of California. The years after World War I he spent largely in retirement. He had begun his literary career in college, and during the 1880s he contributed to several periodicals and in 1885 published his first major critical book, a biography of Edgar Allan Poe. In 1890 he published a book of verse, *The North Shore Watch and Other Poems*, and a collection of essays, *Studies in Letters and Life*. His most successful volume of literary criticism, *Heart of Man*, appeared in 1899 and was followed a year later by *Makers of Literature*. Other critical works included *Nathaniel Hawthorne*, 1902; *America in Literature*, 1903; and *The Torch*, a collection of his Columbia lectures, 1905. Other volumes of poetry appeared later: *Ideal Passion*,

1917, and *The Roamer and Other Poems*, 1920. He also edited collections of the works of Percy Bysshe Shelley and Poe. A man of sound scholarship, Woodberry was in spirit one of the New England Transcendentalists. He saw that as America changed, so also was its literature changing during his lifetime; but he sympathized little with many of the writers of the late nineteenth and early twentieth centuries. He viewed with particular disfavor the realists—Herman Melville, Mark Twain, Walt Whitman, and their followers —whose works came to be widely read and accepted during his later years. Woodberry died in Beverly, Massachusetts, on January 2, 1930.

Woodbridge, Frederick James Eugene (1867–1940), philosopher. Born in Windsor, Ontario, on March 26, 1867, Woodbridge grew up in Kalamazoo, Michigan, where his family settled in 1868. He graduated from Amherst College in 1889 and earned a degree in theology at Union Theological Seminary in New York City in 1892. After pursuing additional studies in Berlin he joined the faculty of the University of Minnesota as an instructor in philosophy. In 1902 he accepted an appointment as professor of philosophy at Columbia University, where he spent the rest of his teaching career, retiring in 1939. In 1912 he took on the added task of dean of the graduate faculties, remaining in that position until 1929. At Columbia, Woodbridge was a colleague of John Dewey, but whereas Dewey's influence was widespread, particularly in education, Woodbridge's was confined to the area of professional philosophy. The two thinkers who most influenced his own work were Aristotle and Spinoza, and Woodbridge became responsible for the revival of Aristotelian thought in America in the first three decades of this century. He defined his own position in terms of "naturalism" and "realism." By nature he meant the "clearly identified subject-matter of all inquiry," that is, everything that is around us. Nature was thus presupposed in the quest for knowledge and did not derive from man's consciousness of it. Nature is the real, and is to be investigated without benefit of prior prejudices or value judgments. Woodbridge's philosophical points of view were elaborated in many essays and books, including *The Purpose of History*, 1916; *The Realm of Mind*, 1926; *Nature and Mind*, 1937; and *An Essay on Nature*. He was also a founder, in 1904, and editor for 36 years, of the *Journal of Philosophy*. He died in New York City on June 1, 1940.

Woodbury, Levi (1789–1851), justice of the Supreme Court. Born in Francestown, New Hampshire, on December 22, 1789, Woodbury graduated from Dartmouth in 1809. After studying law he was admitted to the bar in 1812 and conducted a law practice in his home town for five years. In 1817 he was appointed a judge of the state superior court, on which he served until being elected governor of New Hampshire in 1823. He failed to be elected to a second term in 1825, but served briefly in the state legislature before being elected to the U.S. Senate. He remained in the Senate from March 1825 until 1831, when President Andrew Jackson appointed him secretary of the navy. Three years later Jackson named him secretary of the treasury, and he served in this post until the end of Martin Van Buren's presidency in March 1841. As a member of Jackson's cabinet, Woodbury sided firmly with the President in opposition to the rechartering of the Bank of the United States and favored the removal from the bank of government deposits, which was effected in 1833. It was over the issue of the bank that the Senate had refused to confirm Roger B. Taney as secretary of the treasury, so in 1834 Woodbury was named instead. Woodbury continued the war on the bank, promoting instead the idea of an independent treasury; as a states'-rights man he insisted that Congress was without authority to charter a national bank. As a friend of New England business interests he was also a "hard-money" man and opposed the issuing of paper money to inflate currency. During the Panic of 1837 he was able to maintain the credit of the federal government, to the benefit of state banks as well. On other issues he differed from his New England associates; he was moderate on the issue of slavery, insisting that slavery was a state, not a federal matter; he had supported the War of 1812, which was held in great disfavor in New England; and he favored U.S. settlement and annexation of Oregon and Texas. After leaving the cabinet in 1841 he was again elected to the Senate. In 1845 he was appointed by President James K. Polk an associate justice of the U.S. Supreme Court. On the bench his most notable opinions were written in dissent—in *Waring* v. *Clarke*, 1847, he held that the application of admiralty law stopped at the shoreline of a nation; in *Luther* v. *Borden*, 1849, a case stemming from the Dorr Rebellion in Rhode Island, he broke with the Court's finding that it had no power to restrict the decision of Congress or the president to recognize either party in a state conflict over lawful government; and in the Passenger Cases, 1849, he held as constitutional laws in New York and Massachusetts that levied a head tax on aliens entering their ports. Usually taking a states'-rights, strict-constructionist view of the Constitution in his opinions and dissents, he served on the Court until his death in Portsmouth, New Hampshire, on September 4, 1851.

Woodhull, Tennessee, *see under* Woodhull, Victoria Claflin

Woodhull, Victoria Claflin (1838–1927), social reformer. Born on September 23, 1838, in Homer, Licking County, Ohio, into a poor and eccentric family, Victoria Claflin traveled with their medicine and fortune-telling show, giving demonstrations in spiritualism with her younger sister, Tennessee (1846–1923). She married Dr. Canning Woodhull before she was sixteen; they were divorced in 1864 and she subsequently twice remarried. The sisters traveled to New York City in 1868, where they met Cornelius Vanderbilt, who was interested in spiritualism. He set them up in a stock-brokerage firm, Woodhull, Claflin and Company, which was quite successful. With considerable profits, they founded in 1870 *Woodhull and Claflin's Weekly*, a women's-rights magazine that espoused a single moral standard for men and women, as well as free love. Much of each issue was written by Stephen Pearl Andrews, promoter of the social system he called "Pantarchy." Victoria's ardent speeches on women's rights, notably in 1871 before the House Judiciary Committee, won the acceptance of woman-suffrage leaders, who had been put off by her moral attitudes. In 1872 she became the first woman to be nominated for the presidency, being named by her own National Radical Reform party, known as the "Equal Rights Party;" the abolitionist and former slave Frederick Douglass was put on the ticket as her running mate, but he refused to take part in the campaign. Although she of course anticipated losing the election, she retained her enthusiasm for her movement and made a much-publicized though futile attempt to vote. In the most sensational scandal of the day she printed in the November 2, 1872, issue of the *Weekly* an exposé of an alleged affair between the prominent clergyman Henry Ward Beecher and a parishioner, the wife of her own former lover. Intended mainly to discredit Beecher's sisters, who opposed her stand on free love, the article led to Beecher's trial for adultery and subsequent exoneration and to libel charges being brought against Victoria and Tennessee. Charges of distributing improper materials through the mails were entered against them by Anthony Comstock, but they were acquitted in 1873. In 1872 the first American publication of the *Communist Manifesto* appeared in their weekly. In 1877, reportedly with money left in Vanderbilt's will, the sisters moved to England. Victoria continued to lecture, write books and pamphlets, and work for charities; after a marriage to a wealthy English banker, she was eventually received by London society. She wrote with her sister *The Human Body the Temple of God*, 1890, and by herself *Stirpiculture, or the Scientific Propagation of the Human Race*, 1888, and *Humanitarian Money*, 1892. From 1892 to 1910 she published with her daughter, Zulu Maud Woodhull, the *Humanitarian* magazine. Both sisters married well in England, Victoria to her banker, John B. Martin, and Tennessee to Francis Cook, later Baronet Cook. Although Victoria returned on occasion to the United States, she lived in England until her death at Norton Park, Bremons, Worcestershire, on June 10, 1927.

Woods, William Burnham (1824–1887), justice of the Supreme Court. Born in Newark, Ohio, on August 3, 1824, Woods attended Western Reserve College and graduated from Yale in 1845. After studying law for two years he was admitted to the bar in 1847 and joined a law firm in his home town. In the 1850s he became active in Democratic politics, serving a term as mayor of Newark in 1856–1857. From 1857 to 1861 he was a member of the Ohio assembly, and as a legislator strongly opposed Republican policies toward the South at the start of the Civil War. In 1862 he joined the Union army and served throughout the war, seeing action at Shiloh, Arkansas Post, Vicksburg, and in Gen. William T. Sherman's march to the sea, and rising to the rank of brigadier general. During the war his politics changed and he became a Republican; this enabled him to settle in Alabama in 1866 and take an active part in the Reconstruction policies of the federal government. He made his home thereafter in the South, and in 1869 was appointed by President Ulysses S. Grant to be a judge of the U.S. circuit court, based in Atlanta, Georgia. In 1880 President Rutherford B. Hayes appointed him an associate justice of the U.S. Supreme Court, as the "Southern member" of the Court. Although he served on the Court for only a little more than six years he wrote a large number of opinions, many of them in complex equity and patent cases where his ability and learning were revealed. He also spoke for the Court in *United States v. Harris*, 1883, in which the 1871 Ku Klux Klan Act was found unconstitutional on the grounds that the federal government had no power, under the Fourteenth Amendment or any other law, to regulate the activities of individuals; and in *Presser v. Illinois*, holding that the Bill of Rights was a limitation only upon the federal government, not upon state governments. Both of these positions, although shared by the majority of the Court, were later reversed. Woods died in Washington, D.C., on May 14, 1887.

Woodson, Carter Godwin (1875–1950), historian and educator. Born in New Canton, Buckingham County, Virginia, on December 19, 1875, Woodson grew up in such poverty that most of his formal schooling was postponed until he was almost twenty. He graduated from high school in 1896, but his college work and advanced studies were spread over the following 15 years as he earned enough money by teaching school to continue studying. He graduated from Berea College in 1903, earned a B.A. at the University of Chicago in 1907 and an M.A. in 1908, and, after traveling and studying abroad, took a doctorate at Harvard in 1912. For the next decade he continued to teach in order to support his own research and writing, and from 1909 to 1918 he taught high school in Washington, D.C. He was dean of the liberal arts college at Howard University for a year, 1919–1920, and from 1920 to 1922 was dean at West Virginia State College. Woodson is known as the father of Negro history in the United States, for, almost single-handedly, he freed black studies from the traditional biases and interpretations of white historians, and by extensive research into original sources made it into an academically respectable field of study. In 1915 he founded the Association for the Study of Negro Life and History, which began publication in 1916 of the

Journal of Negro History. In 1921 he organized Associated Publishers, Inc., to afford blacks the opportunity to publish works on Negro culture that other publishers would not readily accept. He himself wrote many books on black history, including *The Negro in Our History,* 1922, long a widely used textbook; *African Myths,* 1928; *The Rural Negro,* 1930; *The African Background Outlined,* 1936; and *African Heroes and Heroines,* 1939. In 1926, the year he was awarded the Spingarn Medal of the National Association for the Advancement of Colored People (NAACP), he inaugurated the observance of Negro History Week, and in 1937 began publication of the *Negro History Bulletin,* designed for use in schools. He devoted much time to urging other blacks to take up the study of the history of their people, thus laying the foundation for widespread adoption of black studies in schools in the 1960s. From 1944 until his death Woodson was engaged in editing the six-volume *Encyclopedia Africana.* He died in Washington, D.C., on April 4, 1950.

Woodward, Comer Vann (1908–   ), historian. Born on November 13, 1908, in Vanndale, Cross County, Arkansas, a town named after his mother's family, C. Vann Woodward graduated from Emory University in 1930, studied at Columbia University and took his M.A. there in 1932, and then obtained his Ph.D. from the University of North Carolina in 1937. His postgraduate studies were interrupted by teaching assignments at the Georgia Institute of Technology in 1930–1931 and 1932–1933; he taught history at the University of Florida, 1937–1939, at the University of Virginia, 1939–1940, and at Scripps College, 1940–1943, before serving in the navy during World War II. Returning from active service in 1946, he joined the faculty at The Johns Hopkins University that year and remained until 1961, when he became Sterling Professor of History at Yale. He was also from time to time a visiting professor at several American institutions and was Harmsworth Professor of American History at Oxford, 1954–1955. He was the author of a number of influential books which gained him a reputation as the dean of historians of the South. In 1968–1969 he became the first historian to serve concurrently as president of both the American Historical Association and the Organization of American Historians. His books included *Tom Watson: Agrarian Rebel,* 1938; *The Battle of Leyte Gulf,* 1947; *Origins of the New South, 1877–1913,* 1951, winner of the 1952 Bancroft Prize for history; *Reunion and Reaction: The Compromise of 1877 and the End of Reconstruction,* 1951; *The Strange Career of Jim Crow,* 1955; *The Burden of Southern History,* 1961; and *American Counterpoint: Slavery and Race in the North-South Dialogue,* 1971. In his later works, and especially in widely discussed magazine articles in the 1960s, he emphasized the necessity for American historians to reconsider Southern and especially Negro history in order to arrive at a truer understanding of the nation's past and also its future.

Woodward was also the editor of *The Comparative Approach to American History,* 1968.

Woodward, Robert Burns (1917–1979), chemist. Born in Boston on April 10, 1917, Woodward graduated from the Massachusetts Institute of Technology (MIT) in 1936 and one year later, at the age of twenty, took his doctorate in chemistry at the same institution. In 1938 he became a fellow of Harvard College, and two years later he became an instructor in chemistry there. He remained at Harvard throughout his teaching and research career, advancing to full professor in 1951 and to the Morris Loeb professorship in 1953. He also served as consultant to various companies, including the Pfizer Chemical and Polaroid companies. His main area of work was the laboratory synthesis of organic compounds. During World War II he and his associates successfully achieved a total synthesis of quinine, a substance in short supply because of the war. In 1947 he announced the synthesis of protein analogues, an attainment useful in medical research and in the manufacture of plastics and antibiotics. The first successful synthesis of a steroid, a highly complex type of organic molecule, was achieved in 1951. This led to the greater production and availability of rare drugs such as cortisone. During the next decade he and his coworkers were able to synthesize a great number of steroids and alkaloids, including strychnine (1954), lysergic acid (1954), reserpine (1956), chlorophyll (1961), and tetracycline (1962). Woodward also contributed to the understanding of the structures of such substances as penicillin and other antibiotics. In 1965 he was awarded the Nobel Prize for Chemistry for his work in chemical synthesis, the citation noting particularly his synthesis of chlorophyll. In 1972 he synthesized vitamin B-12, the most intricate molecule synthesized up to that time. He died on July 8, 1979, in Cambridge, Massachusetts.

Woollcott, Alexander (1887–1943), critic and actor. Born in Phalanx, Monmouth County, New Jersey, on January 19, 1887, Woollcott grew up there and in Kansas City, Missouri, and Philadelphia. He graduated from Hamilton College in 1909, and went to work as a reporter for the *New York Times.* In 1914 he became the drama critic of the *Times,* thus launching a career that saw him become one of the most influential arbiters of taste in theater and literature in the years between the World Wars. Except for service in Europe during World War I (where he worked on the staff of the army newspaper *Stars and Stripes*) he remained with the *Times* until 1922. He then successively worked as drama critic for the *New York Herald* (1922–1924), the *New York Sun* (1924–1925), and the *New York World* (1925–1928). Along with E. B. White and James Thurber, Woollcott was also a steady contributor to the *New Yorker* magazine in its early years. From 1929 to 1942 he was the "Town Crier" of network radio. This was an interview program with guests who discussed with Woollcott topics of literary and social importance and on which the moderator gave his own very definite views. As drama critic, Woollcott was also an actor at heart, and during the 1930s found several opportunities to appear on stage. His most memorable performance was in *The Man Who Came To Dinner*, 1939, written by George S. Kaufman and Moss Hart with Woollcott in mind as the lead character, Sheridan Whiteside. A prolific author of reviews and articles, he collected many of them in books, including *Shouts and Murmurs*, 1922, *Enchanted Aisles*, 1924, and *While Rome Burns*, 1934. He was a member of the famed literary "Round Table" at the Algonquin Hotel in New York City and a popular storyteller and molder of opinion. But primarily Woollcott was a "personality" who attracted a wide following as a popularizer of culture because of his wit and forceful opinions. He was stricken with a heart attack during a radio broadcast on January 23, 1943, and died in New York City later the same evening.

Woolman, John (1720–1772), social reformer and religious leader. Born on October 19, 1720, at Rancocas, in the present Burlington County, New Jersey, Woolman worked on his father's farm until moving to Mount Holly, New Jersey, in 1741. Deeply religious from his early youth, he had a Quaker education and read voraciously. At twenty-three he took up the Quaker ministry and opened a tailor shop to support himself, thereafter styling himself the "Tailor (or Quaker) of Mount Holly." During 1743–1771 he traveled throughout the colonies attending meetings of the Society of Friends, and spread the Quaker doctrine from North Carolina to New Hampshire. His principal mission was the ending of slavery, an institution that he viewed as utterly inconsistent with religion. Through his travels and writings—*Some Considerations on the Keeping of Negroes*, 1754 and 1762; *Considerations on Pure Wisdom and Human Policy, on Labour, on Schools, on the Right Use of the Lord's Outward Gifts*, 1758; and *Considerations on the True Harmony of Mankind, and How It Is to Be Maintained*, 1770—he had a wide influence; in fact, he was able to persuade the Philadelphia Yearly Meeting to forbid its members to own slaves. He aided Moravian missionaries in Indian camps on the Pennsylvania frontier in securing conversions, in stopping the sale of liquor to the Indians, and in attempting to secure more just land policies. He gave up his tailor shop because it was making more money than he needed and abandoned horseback riding as a vanity, making his later journeys on foot. He ate no sugar because it was produced by slaves, and wore clothing of undyed materials because fabric dyes were often injurious to workers. While working with the poor in England he contracted smallpox and died in York on October 7, 1772. His famous *Journal*, which he began when he was thirty-five, and continued until his death, was first published in 1774 and has often been republished.

Woolsey, Theodore Dwight (1801–1889), educator. Born in New York City on October 31, 1801,

Woolsey grew up there and in New Haven, Connecticut. He graduated from Yale in 1820, and during the next decade pursued theological studies at the Princeton Theological Seminary and at Yale and classical studies in Germany and France. In 1831 he was appointed professor of Greek language and literature at Yale; he became president of Yale in 1846. The years of his presidency saw great changes at the school, for it was a time of much agitation, ferment, and criticism in higher education in the United States. The older colleges were being expanded into universities with courses for advanced degrees, and the great state universities were being founded in the Midwest largely under the stimulus of the Morrill Land Grant Act of 1862. New fields of study, particularly those concerned with agriculture and technology, were being added to curriculums. In 1847 Yale established a department of philosophy and the arts to be responsible for graduate instruction in the arts and sciences and for undergraduate work in applied sciences. In the same year a school of applied chemistry was started, and in 1854 it was merged with the school of engineering as the Yale Scientific School. In 1861 it was renamed the Sheffield Scientific School after the philanthropist whose gifts had made it possible. The Yale curriculum was otherwise diversified, the campus enlarged, and endowment funds increased. In 1871 Woolsey retired as president of the university but remained as a member of the Yale Corporation until 1885. During the years he was president, he left the teaching of Greek and gave instruction instead in political science and international law. In his various fields of interest he also wrote a number of books, including *Introduction to the Study of International Law*, 1860; *Essay on Divorce and Divorce Legislation*, 1869; *Political Science*, 1878, and *Communism and Socialism*, 1880. After his retirement he served as chairman of the New Testament committee that aided in producing the American Standard Version of the Bible, published in 1901. Woolsey died in New Haven, Connecticut, on July 1, 1889.

Woolworth, Frank Winfield (1852–1919), merchant. Born on April 13, 1852, near Rodman, Jefferson County, New York, Woolworth attended country schools and studied for a brief time at a business school at Watertown, New York. He worked on his father's farm, although he craved a mercantile career and attempted to obtain jobs as a store clerk. Inexperienced and awkward, he consented to work for negligible wages in various concerns. By the time he was twenty-one, still on a tiny salary, he convinced his employer that a five-cent counter he had seen in another store would work. Goods that were slightly damaged or overstocked were placed on a special counter and priced at five cents. They sold immediately. In 1879 Woolworth began a store of his own in Utica, New York, which contained a variety of goods, all priced at five cents. The store was unsuccessful, but later in the year he opened another store in Lancaster, Pennsylvania, offering goods at prices up to ten cents, and was successful. Even frugal housewives bought such luxury items as toothpaste and cold cream. Subsequently he opened stores in Buffalo and Erie, New York, and Scranton, Pennsylvania; he acquired several partners, four of whom began their own chains of stores. In 1912 the four chains were merged into the F. W. Woolworth Company. As a business manager, he kept a careful watch on his stores, paying them unexpected visits and attempting to shoplift items to test his managers' keenness. By 1900 he had 59 stores and annual sales surpassed $5 million. He incorporated the business in 1905. In 1909 he opened his first store in England and by 1919 had a chain of more than 1000 stores in several countries and sales in excess of $107 million. The Woolworth Building in New York City, then (at 792 feet) the tallest in the world, was opened in 1913. He died in Glen Cove, Long Island, on April 8, 1919, leaving a fortune estimated at $65 million.

Worcester, Joseph Emerson (1784–1865), lexicographer. Born on August 24, 1784, in Bedford, New Hampshire, Worcester was delayed in his education by his family's limited means but finally graduated from Yale in 1811. For five years he taught school in Salem, Massachusetts (Nathaniel Hawthorne was one of his students), while preparing his *Geographical Dictionary, or Universal Gazetteer, Ancient and Modern,* published in 1817. After a brief stay in Andover he settled permanently in Cambridge and during the next nine years published several more books on geography and history. In 1828 appeared his edition of *Johnson's English Dictionary, . . . with Walker's Pronouncing Dictionary, Combined;* a year later it was followed by an abridgment of Noah Webster's *American Dictionary.* In 1830 he produced his first original dictionary, the *Comprehensive Pronouncing and Explanatory Dictionary of the English Language,* initiating the "Dictionary War" between Worcester and Webster. Webster charged plagiarism, a claim bolstered by the appearance of an English edition of Worcester's 1830 work with an unauthorized and false acknowledgment to Webster. While working on his next dictionary, Worcester served as editor of *The American Almanac and Repository of Useful Knowledge* from 1831 to 1842. *A Universal and Critical Dictionary of the English Language* appeared in 1846. In 1855 he published *A Pronouncing, Explanatory, and Synonymous Dictionary of the English Language,* a revision of the 1830 *Comprehensive,* which, in addition to the previously introduced "compromise vowel," midway between the *a* of *hat* and of *father,* featured the innovative use of synonymy and an etymological list of common surnames. Worcester's final and major dictionary was his illustrated *Quarto Dictionary of the English Language,* 1860. In this as in previous works he displayed a more conservative approach to spelling and etymology than did Webster, and his dictionaries were generally preferred for academic and literary use; lacking Webster's zeal and promotional ability, however, he could not

seriously compete in the popular market. He died in Cambridge, Massachusetts, on October 27, 1865; his dictionaries, unlike those of his rival, saw little subsequent publication.

Work, Henry Clay (1832–1884), songwriter. Born in Middletown, Connecticut, on October 1, 1832, Work moved with his family to Quincy, Illinois, where his father used their home as a station on the Underground Railroad. More than 4000 runaway slaves were helped to escape before his father's imprisonment. The family returned to Connecticut upon his father's release in 1845, and Henry finished his schooling in Hartford, where he became a printer's apprentice. Finding a melodeon above the shop, he practiced with it, studied harmony, and wrote songs for his friends. In 1854 he went to Chicago as a printer but continued to write songs. He finally achieved success with the song, "We're Coming, Sister Mary," written for the Christy Minstrels. His publisher encouraged him to compose for the Union cause and "Kingdom Coming!," 1861, was the result. Its success earned him a contract to write songs and he was able to stop working as a printer. Among the partisan songs he wrote during the Civil War were "Babylon Is Fallen!" 1863; "Wake Nicodemus," 1864; and "Marching Through Georgia," 1865. In 1864 his temperance song, "Come Home, Father," was published, and for years thereafter it was regularly included in performances of the popular temperance play *Ten Nights in a Barroom.* "Grandfather's Clock," 1876, is said to have sold 800,000 copies. The Chicago Fire of 1871 destroyed the plates of his songs and ruined his publisher. Work moved to Philadelphia and then to Vineland, New Jersey, where he joined his brother and uncle in land speculation that proved unsuccessful. By 1875 his publisher was reestablished and he returned to Chicago, resuming his career with songs that brought him even greater financial success than before. He died while visiting Hartford, Connecticut, on June 8, 1884.

Worth, Nicholas, *see* Page, Walter Hines

Wouk, Herman (1915–   ), author. Born in New York City on May 27, 1915, Wouk graduated from Columbia in 1934. For the next several years he wrote radio scripts for Fred Allen and other comedians. During World War II he served in the navy in the South Pacific, and it was during the war that he wrote his first novel, *Aurora Dawn,* 1947, a satire on radio advertising drawn from his own experiences in the medium. His next novel, *City Boy,* 1948, was a humorous treatment of growing up in a Bronx neighborhood in New York City. But it was with the publication of *The Caine Mutiny* in 1951 that Wouk emerged as one of the most successful novelists of mid-century. A superior war novel, it won the Pulitzer Prize for fiction in 1952 and subsequently became a successful Broadway play and a movie. Wouk's plays are less well known, although *The Traitor,* 1949, was moderately successful on Broadway, but

Nature's Way, 1957, did not do well. His next two novels, *Marjorie Morningstar,* 1955, and *Youngblood Hawke,* 1962, both reached the best-seller lists and were made into movies. In his 1971 novel, *Winds of War,* he again took up the theme of World War II but on a more epic scale than in the *Caine Mutiny.*

Wovoka (1858?–1932), Indian religious leader. Born near Walter Lake in what is now Esmeralda County, Nevada, about 1858, Wovoka was a member of the Paiute tribe and the son of a religious mystic. His father died when he was fourteen years old, and he was taken into the family of a local white rancher named David Wilson, to work as a farmhand. He became known as Jack Wilson to his white acquaintants. Late in the year 1888 Wovoka had a mystical religious experience or vision—possibly connected with an eclipse of the sun on January 1, 1889—from which he developed a teaching that he began proclaiming to his fellow Indians in 1889. In it were combined Indian hopes, traditions handed down through earlier visionaries, and bits of Christian doctrine that he had picked up from the Bible readings in the Wilson family. His message was a simple one: the earth was now old and worn, the hunting grounds were gone, the trees chopped down, and the Indians despoiled of their livelihood; but soon—in 1891—the earth would be reconstituted, the whites driven back whence they came, the buffalo and other game would return, and all dead Indians would be resurrected to join their living brethren. It was a message of great hope that slowly gained appeal among the Plains Indians and those of the Northwest. To prepare for the great event Wovoka instructed the Indians to live justly and peaceably and in anticipation of the resurrection to perform the Ghost Dance, a simple ritual to be danced while wearing "ghost shirts"—garments painted with religious symbols. Soon Indians from many tribes were visiting Wovoka, learning of the Ghost Dance, and accepting him as a messiah for all Indians. Nowhere did the new religion arouse a more enthusiastic following than among the Sioux; and against no tribe was the white reaction more fearful or vehement. Whites were convinced another uprising was in the making, and indeed the Ghost Dance enthusiasm became, for some Sioux, a promise of imminent victory over the hated whites. Sitting Bull, never one to follow the white man's instructions, seemed about to take over leadership of the movement among his people. Agitation on Sioux reservations grew, and many Indians broke confinement. The fervor of the Ghost Dance was matched by increased frenzy among white settlers and soldiers during 1890, eventuating in the murder of Sitting Bull on December 15 and in the massacre of Sioux by U.S. cavalry at Wounded Knee Creek in southwest South Dakota on December 29. That atrocity virtually ended the Ghost Dance enthusiasm, as the "Ghost Shirt," felt by many Indians to possess magical properties, seemed discredited by the deaths of so many of its wearers. But Wovoka kept a number of followers and during the next ten years he moderated his prophecies and counseled Indians to follow the white man's civilization. He died in Schurz, Nevada, on the Walker River Indian Reservation, in October 1932.

Wright Brothers, inventors, pioneer aviators, and manufacturers. Wilbur Wright, born on April 16, 1867, near Millville, Indiana, and his brother Orville Wright, born on August 19, 1871, in Dayton, Ohio, were sons of a minister who later became a bishop of the United Brethren church. Both early displayed great mechanical skill and ingenuity; while Orville was still in high school they built a large printing press and began publishing a local newspaper. In 1892 they opened a bicycle sales and repair shop in Dayton and were soon manufacturing their own bicycles. Their reading about the glider experiments of Otto Lilienthal in Germany and Octave Chanute in the United States kindled an interest in flying. They obtained all the information available on aerodynamics and set about constructing an improved glider. They first concentrated on the problem of control in three dimensions and came up with the method of "warping" or controlling the lift of the wings by twisting them; this method later evolved into the movable aileron. A model glider built in 1899 flew successfully as a kite. Through much of their experimental work they received advice and encouragement from Chanute. In 1900 they consulted the U.S. Weather Bureau to find a suitable location for extended glider flights, and that summer made their first trip to the sand hills near Kitty Hawk, North Carolina. Their glider experiments of that year revealed large errors in published tables of lift-pressures for various wing surfaces and wind speeds; and, back in Dayton in 1901, they devised the first wind tunnel and conducted a long series of experiments to construct their own tables. In 1902 they returned to Kitty Hawk with an improved glider and in the course of nearly a thousand flights perfected their control system. Now ready to attempt powered flight, they built a small but powerful four-cylinder engine and designed a highly efficient airscrew for propulsion. The new airplane was brought to Kitty Hawk in September 1903; bad weather delayed testing for many weeks, but on December 17 Orville climbed aboard and piloted the craft through a 12-second, 120-foot flight. Later in the day Wilbur flew for 59 seconds, covering 852 feet. After that flight the aircraft was badly damaged by wind and the brothers returned to Dayton. During the next two years they built two more airplanes, constantly improving their design and increasing the reliability and range of flight. In 1906 they were granted a U.S. patent for a flying machine. In the United States interest in flying was slow to develop, but the Wrights were soon negotiating with the British and French governments for the manufacture of aircraft. In 1908, however, the U.S. War Department awarded them a contract for a machine capable of flying 40 miles per hour for a distance of 125 miles carrying a pilot and a passenger. Later that year and into 1909 the brothers were busy demonstrating their airplanes to government officials and the public, Wilbur in Europe and Orville in the United States. In 1909 the American Wright Company was incorporated and both Wrights devoted themselves to the manufacture and improvement of their airplane and the training of pilots. Wilbur died of typhoid fever in Dayton on May 30, 1912, and for two years Orville continued to direct the American Wright Company. In 1914 he retired from the business to carry on his private research, and during World War I he served as a consultant to the Aviation Service of the Army Signal Corps. He died in Dayton on January 30, 1948. On December 17 of that year the original Kitty Hawk machine of 1903 was installed in the Smithsonian Institution. Wilbur Wright was elected to the Hall of Fame in 1955, and his brother Orville was elected in 1965.

Wright, Carroll Davidson (1840–1909), statistician and educator. Born in Dunbarton, New Hampshire. on July 25, 1840, Wright was the son of a Universalist minister. He grew up in Washington, New Hampshire, where he went to local schools and worked on his father's farm. After attending academies in the various New Hampshire and Vermont parishes to which his father moved, he began reading law in a Keene, New Hampshire, firm in 1860, paying his way by teaching in country schools. He moved to Boston to continue his legal studies, but in 1862 enlisted for Civil War service as a private in a regiment of New Hampshire volunteers. Rapidly promoted, he held assignments in Washington, D.C., before joining Gen. Philip H. Sheridan's staff in the Shenandoah Campaign of 1864 and becoming colonel of his own regiment in that year. In 1865 he returned to New Hampshire, was admitted to the bar, and finally established a successful practice in patent law in Boston. Living in Reading, he was elected in 1871 and 1872 to represent his district in the Massachusetts senate. In 1873 the governor appointed him chief of the Massachusetts Bureau of Statistics for Labor. In 1883 he organized the National Convention of Chiefs and Commissioners of Bureaus of Statistics of Labor and was its president for two decades. He stimulated objective research on labor problems and was an advocate of collective bargaining and of the sliding scale in wage adjustment. In 1885 President Chester A. Arthur appointed him the first commissioner of the Bureau of Labor, a post he retained until resigning in 1905. In 1894 he was chairman of the commission investigating the Pullman strike, and in 1902 he was recorder of the commission inquiring into the anthracite miners' strike. After 1895 he also taught, serving from then until 1904 as honorary professor of social economics at Catholic University and in 1900 as professor of statistics and social economics at Columbian (now The George Washington) University, and at Clark after becoming Clark's first president in 1902. He

planned and supervised the first volumes of the economic history of the United States financed by the Carnegie Institution of Washington. Among his own works were *The Industrial Evolution of the United States*, 1895, and the *Outline of Practical Sociology*, 1899. He was president of the American Statistical Association from 1897 until his death on February 20, 1909, in Worcester, Massachusetts.

Wright, Chauncey (1830–1875), philosopher and mathematician. Born in Northampton, Massachusetts, on September 30, 1830, Wright graduated from Harvard in 1852. He spent the rest of his life in research, writing, and lecturing, and taught mathematical physics at Harvard only in the last year of his life, 1874–1875. From 1852 to 1870 he worked as a mathematician for the *American Ephemeris and Nautical Almanac*. In 1860 he was elected a member of the American Academy of Arts and Sciences, and he served as its secretary from 1863 to 1870. In the early 1870s he presided over the Metaphysical Club at Cambridge, Massachusetts, which included among its members William James and Charles Sanders Peirce, both of whom were strongly influenced by Wright in the development of their philosophies. Wright contributed a large number of articles to various journals, particularly a series on philosophical subjects to the *North American Review* between 1864 and 1875. He was a supporter of the Darwinian theory of evolution and defended it in a series of articles, "The Limits of Natural Selection," 1870, "The Genesis of Species," 1871, and "Evolution by Natural Selection," 1872. He was probably the country's first outstanding philosopher of science, but did not set forth his views in books, only in articles in journals. In his philosophy he was a precursor of the pragmatism of Peirce, James, and John Dewey, and an exponent of the utilitarianism of John Stuart Mill. He died on September 12, 1875, in Cambridge, Massachusetts.

Wright, Elizur (1804–1885), social reformer and actuary. Born in South Canaan, Connecticut, on February 18, 1804, Wright grew up there and in what is now Tallmadge, Ohio, at the time part of Connecticut's Western Reserve. He graduated from Yale in 1826 and for the next three years taught at Groton Academy. In 1829 he joined the faculty of Western Reserve College. During three years there he was converted to the abolitionist cause by the preaching of Theodore Dwight Weld and joined the American Anti-Slavery Society. He remained active in the movement until 1840, editing the society's journal from 1835 to 1837 and acting as its secretary. In 1839 he edited the *Massachusetts Abolitionist*. For the next six years he struggled to make a living selling books, and finally returned to antislavery agitation in 1846 as editor of a Boston paper that was taken over in 1850 by the Free-Soil party's paper, the *Weekly Commonwealth*, with which he remained until 1852. In the early 1850s he was hired, in the capacity of mathematician, to prepare actuarial tables for various Massachusetts insurance companies. From that time he spent the rest of his life in attempts to standardize and improve the practices of life insurance companies in the state, both through public laws and company self-regulation. He was successful in gaining passage of a state law in 1858 compelling companies to maintain adequate reserves, for it was his conviction that the reserves belonged to the policyholders and could not be put to arbitrary use by the insurance companies. Wright prepared the tables by which the necessary reserves might be determined. He kept a check on the companies and was not hesitant about disclosing fraud and misuse of funds. He also promoted the successful passage of a non-forfeiture law in 1861 by which insurance companies were forbidden to appropriate reserve funds for their own uses. With the reforms and regulation of the insurance business in Massachusetts, other states began to follow suit. From 1858 to 1866 he served as a state commissioner of insurance. Thereafter he worked for a number of insurance companies and he acted as a public watchdog on insurance practices. He was often called, somewhat inaccurately, "the father of life insurance." He died on November 21, 1885, in Medford, Massachusetts.

Wright, Frances (1795–1852), social reformer. Born in Dundee, Scotland, on September 6, 1795, Miss Wright was the daughter of a well-to-do Scotch radical who had circulated the works of Thomas Paine. Her parents died and left her a fortune when she was two, and she was raised in London by conservative relatives. As soon as her legal status permitted, she returned to Scotland and, at eighteen, wrote *A Few Days in Athens*, 1822, a novelistic sketch of a disciple of Epicurus that contained the well worked-out materialistic philosophy to which she adhered throughout her life. Her guardians suggested a European tour to cap her education but she preferred to go to the United States. She arrived in New York City with her sister in 1818 and the following year saw the production and publication of her play *Altorf*, a tragedy of the Swiss struggle for independence. She toured the Northern and Eastern states, and the enthusiasm of her *Views of Society and Manners in America*, published in England in 1821, won her the friendship of the Marquis de Lafayette. She timed her return to New York on a second trip in 1824 with his triumphal tour of the country, and joined him in visits with Thomas Jefferson and James Madison. Slavery was discussed and they approved of her plan for gradual emancipation through purchase and colonization. She invested a large part of her fortune in a tract of land in western Tennessee that she called Nashoba. Slaves were purchased in 1825, established at the Nashoba community, and later colonized (1830) in Haiti, but Socialist-minded recruits in the Tennessee colony introduced free unions, as opposed to marriage, which contributed to its failure. She moved to New Harmony, Indiana, to edit the *New Harmony Gazette* with

Robert Dale Owen in 1828. She also lectured—an activity then considered scandalous for a woman—and her *Course of Popular Lectures* (1829 and 1836) attacked religion, church influence in politics, and authoritarian education, and defended equal rights for women and the replacement of legal marriage by a union based on moral obligation. In 1829 she settled in New York City, where with Owen she published the *Free Enquirer* and led the free-thinking movement there, calling for a reformed, free education run by the state and for the political organization of the working classes. Her sister died in 1831, and while on an extended trip to Europe she married William D'Arusmont, a Frenchman who had been a coworker in New Harmony and New York City. They were soon divorced. She returned to the United States in 1835 and continued writing and lecturing on modern causes, including birth control and a more equal distribution of property, as well as women's rights and the gradual emancipation of slaves and colonization of freemen outside the United States. In 1836 she supported Andrew Jackson's attack on the banking system and advocated an independent treasury. In her last years she lived in Cincinnati and continued her efforts at reform until her death there on December 13, 1852.

Wright, Frank Lloyd (1867–1959), architect. Born on June 8, 1867, in Richland Center, Wisconsin, Wright studied civil engineering at the University of Wisconsin from 1884 to 1888, was apprenticed to Louis H. Sullivan for five years in Chicago, and opened his own practice as an architect in 1893 in Oak Park, Illinois. His concepts of architectural design were highly unorthodox, unlike either the popular neoclassical and neo-Gothic styles of the nineteenth century or the twentieth century glass and steel high-rise structures. He used the colors, forms, and textures of nature in his buildings. His "prairie style" was intended to blend with the expansive, horizontal aspect of Western landscapes, and it featured houses of long, low proportions, wide windows, and open terraces. His windows curved around trees, and balconies perched in hollows in the wall. Interior space flowed from room to room, unifying the entire structure. He adapted his buildings to their environments as well as to the needs of the people who were to inhabit them, an aesthetic practice he called "organic architecture." Although his use of clean, simple lines was consonant with other expressions of modern design, his love of warm, earthy colors and materials and of decoration placed him in opposition to the dominant International Style. In designing commercial buildings, he used modern materials and introduced mechanical ventilation and steel furnishings. His engineering skill defied the doubts of his many skeptical critics; his Imperial Hotel in Tokyo, a controversial structure completed in 1922, was the only major building to survive the earthquake of 1923. Among his most famous creations were Fallingwater, a house in Mill Run, Pennsylvania, 1936; his own homes, Taliesin in Spring Green, Wisconsin, 1911, and Taliesin West in Phoenix, Arizona, 1938; the Johnson Wax Company administration building in Racine, Wisconsin, 1939; the Hanna House in Palo Alto, California, 1937; the First Unitarian Church in Madison, Wisconsin, 1951; and the Solomon R. Guggenheim Museum, a daring spiral structure, in New York City, opened in 1959. At Taliesin West he conducted a school for apprentices and he set down his ideas in several books, including *An Organic Architecture*, 1939, and *An American Architecture*, 1955. He died in Phoenix, Arizona, on April 9, 1959.

Wright, Harold Bell (1872–1944), author. Born in Rome, New York, on May 4, 1872, Wright grew up on a farm and had little formal schooling. From 1887 to 1892 he worked as a decorator and painter and for the next five years was a painter of landscapes. From 1897 to 1908, without benefit of theological training, he managed to serve as pastor for Christian Church congregations in several Missouri towns and at Redlands, California, averaging two years at each place. In 1903 he had published his first novel, *That Printer of Udell's*, based on his parish experiences. He then moved on to a very successful writing career and gave up the ministry altogether in 1908. His second novel, *The Shepherd of the Hills*, 1907, was a great success, as was *The Winning of Barbara Worth*, 1911, whose sales approached two million copies during the next quarter-century. Among his other novels were *When a Man's a Man*, 1916; *The Mine with the Iron Door*, 1923; *Exit*, 1930; and *The Man Who Went Away*, 1942. Most of his novels were set in the Far West, particularly California, and although not now highly regarded as literature they were popular for their direct and forceful style and their moral lessons. Wright died in La Jolla, California, on May 24, 1944.

Wright, Henry (1835–1895), "Harry," baseball player and manager. Born in Sheffield, England, on January 10, 1835, Wright was brought to the United States by his family the following year and lived in New York City. As a teen-ager he became proficient at cricket and baseball, and in 1856 began playing cricket professionally for a New York club. After ten years as a professional cricketer he moved to Cincinnati, where in 1866 he organized a baseball team with himself as player-coach. Baseball had been formalized as a game by the drawing of its first set of rules in 1845 by the Knickerbocker Club in New York City, but it continued to be a purely amateur sport until after the Civil War, when professionalism came in slowly with the paying of more expert players on a per-game basis. In 1868 Wright organized the Cincinnati Red Stockings, a new baseball team, on a semiprofessional basis; that is, the players did not make their living from baseball, but were hired only to play scheduled games. In 1869 the Cincinnati Red Stockings became a completely professional team and went on tour, the first team in baseball to do so. They were un-

defeated in 1869 (56 wins, 1 tie). The emergence of the Red Stockings inspired the development of other professional teams to compete with them. In 1871 the Cincinnati team disbanded and Wright left to become manager of the Boston club, which in 1876 became affiliated with the newly organized National League. He remained with Boston for five seasons before going to Providence, remaining from 1882 to 1883, and to Philadelphia as team manager from 1884 to 1893. For the next two seasons he was head umpire for the National League. He died in Atlantic City, New Jersey, on October 3, 1895.

Wright, Henry (1878–1936), architect and community planner. Born in Lawrence, Kansas, on July 2, 1878, Wright graduated from the University of Pennsylvania in 1901. He joined an architectural firm in Kansas City, Missouri, and over the next several years assisted in the landscaping of the Louisiana Purchase Exposition in St. Louis in 1904 and in the planning of parks and roadways in Kansas City, Denver, and Cincinnati. By 1909 he had achieved sufficient success to open his own office. In 1923 he moved to New York City and thereafter remained in the East. Wright approached the design of city parks and the planning of communities in the tradition of Frederick Law Olmsted, whom he had not known personally but whose influence he strongly felt. Included in Wright's early work, in addition to the laying out of parks and boulevards of larger cities, were notable examples of community development in several St. Louis suburban subdivisions. He regarded a community as an integration of all its features, public and private, into a whole, with no haphazard elements. He therefore opposed the usual zoning laws which derived often from political expediency and fostered economic segregation. It was his notion that community development be approached so as to make available good housing at reasonable cost for all strata of society, and to make each town livable for all its inhabitants through the allocation of parks and recreation facilities and the diversion of through traffic from residential neighborhoods. One of his significant innovations was the "superblock," with an internal park. Among the communities he planned in addition to subdivisions near St. Louis, were Sunnyside Gardens in Queens, New York; the Radburn community at Fair Lawn, New Jersey; and Chatham Village in Pittsburgh. Out of his work for the New York State Housing and Regional Planning Commission came the pioneering 1926 report, *A Plan for the State of New York*; he also published *Rehousing Urban America*, 1935. Wright died in Newton, New Jersey, on July 9, 1936.

Wright, Orville, *see under* Wright Brothers

Wright, Richard (1908–1960), author. Born near Natchez, Mississippi, on September 4, 1908, Wright was the grandson of slaves. Despite an underprivileged childhood in Memphis, he educated himself, and his first story was published when he was sixteen. In 1927 he moved to Chicago but could find only menial work. The Depression of the 1930s forced him to go on relief, and in 1932 he joined the Communist party. The publication of a second story in 1931 and a poem in 1934 finally enabled him to write full time as a member of the Federal Writers' Project. This resulted in his *Uncle Tom's Children,* four long stories of racial prejudice and brutality in the South, which were published in book form in 1938 and won the *Story* prize for the best book submitted by anyone from the Federal Writers' Project. He was then in New York City, where he had moved in 1937 to edit the Communist party's *Daily Worker;* in 1939 he received a Guggenheim Fellowship. The publication in 1940 of his novel *Native Son* brought him recognition as being more than the country's leading black author; it became a Book of the Month Club selection, and he was acclaimed as a major heir to the naturalistic tradition. The novel was dramatized successfully the following year by Wright and Paul Green, and Wright later made a film of it in Argentina, with himself playing the leading role. In 1941 he took part in producing *Twelve Million Black Voices,* a pictorial history of the American Negro. *Black Boy,* the story of his childhood and youth, appeared in 1945. After the war he broke with the Communists and, in protest against the treatment of Negroes in the United States, he became an expatriate in Paris. *The Outsider,* a sensational story of a Negro's life and his fatal involvement with the Communist party, appeared in 1953 and was hailed as America's first existential novel. A trip to the Gold Coast in Africa was recorded in *Black Power,* 1954. He reported the Bandung Conference in *The Color Curtain* in 1956, and an account of his life in *Pagan Spain* appeared in 1957. Lectures that he delivered in Europe from 1950 through 1956 were published in 1957 as *White Man, Listen!* His novel of corruption in the South, *The Long Dream,* appeared in the following year. Wright died in Paris on November 28, 1960. After his death were published *Eight Men,* 1961, and *Lawd Today,* 1963, a novel of the life of a Negro postal clerk in Chicago that had been written before *Native Son.*

Wright, Wilbur, *see under* Wright Brothers

Wrigley, William, Jr., (1861–1932), businessman. Born in Philadelphia on September 30, 1861, the son of a soapmaker, Wrigley began his own business in 1891 in Chicago, manufacturing and selling soap, baking powder, and chewing gum. Through salesmanship, organization, special-incentive offers to dealers, and sheer persistence, he developed a vast trade, eventually abandoning soap and baking powder and concentrating on the burgeoning market in chewing gum. In 1899 he announced an addition to his many gum flavors—"Spearmint" —which brought more than $1 million in sales in 1908, directly attributable to the previous year's advertising. In 1911 he purchased the Zeno Company, gum manufacturers, and consolidated it with the William Wrigley, Jr. Company. He

established many U.S. and foreign branches, and before his death had yearly sales of $75 million. Diversifying his interests, he held a controlling interest in the Chicago Cubs baseball team of the National League in 1916–1921, and bought the Los Angeles and Reading, Pennsylvania, baseball teams as well. He purchased and redeveloped Santa Catalina (or Catalina) Island in California, making it a major resort; directed banks, including the National Boulevard Bank of Chicago; and held interests in hotels and mines. The Wrigley Building, one of the most famous skyscrapers in Chicago, was completed in 1924. On January 26, 1932, Wrigley died in Phoenix, Arizona. Control of his enterprises passed to his son, Philip Knight Wrigley (1894–1977), who perpetuated the Wrigley name as the world's foremost manufacturer of chewing gum and continued to preside over the fortunes of the Cubs at Wrigley Field in Chicago.

Wyeth, Andrew Newell (1917–), painter. Born on July 12, 1917, in Chadds Ford, Pennsylvania, Wyeth received training in drawing and anatomy from his father, N. C. Wyeth. He was adept at drawing from memory, and his early watercolors were brisk and impressionistic in style. His first notable achievements were in illustrating the Brandywine edition of *The Merry Adventures of Robin Hood* at age twelve and Rob White's *The Nub* at fourteen. In 1936 he had his first one-man show at the Art Alliance in Philadelphia. The following year he exhibited his watercolors in New York City. The use of egg tempera, an exacting medium, disciplined his style, so much so that it has been called photographic. But visitors to scenes he painted were frequently disconcerted to find that what they saw differed substantially from what he drew. He created from the barns, fields, rooms, and people of his surroundings in Chadds Ford, Brandywine Valley, and Cushing, Maine, paintings that were painstakingly representational, yet were also both personal and richly symbolic. His watercolors included "The Coot Hunter," 1941; "Muddy Road by Adam Johnson's," 1943; and "Young Buck," 1945. Among the most notable of his tempera paintings were "Four Poster," 1946; "Wind from the Sea," 1947; "Young America," 1950; "Northern Point," 1950; "Faraway," 1952; "Nicholas," 1955; "Ground Hog Day," 1959; "Albert's Son," 1959; "Distant Thunder," 1961; "Day of the Fair," 1963; "Christina's World," 1963; and "Grape Wine," 1966. The recipient of many honors and awards, he was perhaps one of the most successful of American painters, his canvases bringing high prices and winning largely favorable critical opinion. His son, James (1946–), known as Jamie, became the third generation of Wyeths to win recognition as a painter.

Wyeth, Newell Convers (1882–1945), painter and illustrator. Born in Needham, Massachusetts, on October 22, 1882, N. C. Wyeth was educated in Boston. He attended art schools there and later studied with the noted illustrator Howard Pyle in

Wilmington, Delaware. Wyeth was known to millions of readers as the illustrator of popular editions of several novels of Robert Louis Stevenson —*Treasure Island*, *Kidnapped*, and *The Black Arrow*—as well as of works by James Fenimore Cooper and other widely-read authors, and of a celebrated illustrated edition of *The Merry Adventures of Robin Hood*, but he was also successful as a mural painter. Among his murals are panels in the Missouri state capitol, the Federal Reserve Bank in Boston, the Hubbard Memorial Building in Washington, D.C., the Metropolitan Life Insurance Building in New York City, and the National Cathedral in Washington, D.C. During much of his life he made his home in Chadds Ford, Pennsylvania, and he was killed there, with his grandson, on October 19, 1945, in an accident in which his car was struck by a train. Three of his children—Henriette, Carolyn, and Andrew—also became noted artists.

Wylie, Elinor Hoyt (1885–1928), author and poet. Born in Somerville, New Jersey, on September 7, 1885, Elinor Morton Hoyt grew up in Rosemont, Pennsylvania, and Washington, D.C. She was three times married. In 1910 she left her first husband and went to England with Horace Wylie, whose wife had not divorced him. They lived in England for four years, returning in 1914; her husband having died and Wylie having obtained a divorce, they married in 1915. They divided their time between New Jersey and Georgia until settling in Washington, D.C., in 1919 for two years. In 1921 she left Wylie to move to New York City, and it was there and while abroad occasionally during the next seven years that she did virtually all of her writing. In 1923, after divorcing Wylie, she married William Rose Benét, the critic and poet. She wrote almost continuously, still using the name Wylie. Her first book of poetry, *Nets to Catch the Wind*, was published in 1921. Three other collections of verse followed: *Black Armour*, 1923; *Trivial Breath*, 1928; and *Angels and Earthly Creatures*, 1929, a posthumous volume. During the same period she also completed four novels, the first, *Jennifer Lorn*, 1923, being a decided success. She wrote no realistic fiction; all of her novels were comic fantasies of a lively and colorful nature. Her second novel, *The Venetian Glass Nephew*, came out in 1925. *The Orphan Angel*, 1926, was a tale based on what might have happened to the English poet, Percy Bysshe Shelley had he not died at sea, but instead had come to America and lived on the frontier. *Mr. Hodge and Mr. Hazard*, 1928, also reflected her fascination with Shelley, but in an English setting. While in England in 1928 she had a stroke which led to her death in New York City on December 16, 1928. Benét edited her *Collected Poems*, 1932, and *Collected Prose*, 1933.

Wylie, Philip Gordon (1902–1971), author. Born in Beverly, Massachusetts, on May 12, 1902, Wylie spent three years at Princeton but left to become a journalist and professional writer. In addition to working as a press agent and as an editor for the *New Yorker* magazine in the 1920s he contributed articles to magazines and newspapers. His first novel, *Heavy Laden*, was published in 1928. Over the next dozen years he wrote several more novels, but it was not until 1942, with his nonfiction *Generation of Vipers*, that he attained national prominence as an author. The book was a survey of, and attack on, a whole array of cherished American institutions, including religion, education, and politics. But what caught most readers was his attack on "Mom," the American mother, and his use of the term "Momism." Five years later he also attacked organized religion in his *Essay on Morals*, 1947. But no other book of his received the attention, criticism, praise, or outraged blame that *Generation of Vipers* did, and it remained in print continuously. From 1937 Wylie made his home in Miami, Florida, where he pursued his hobby of deep-sea fishing and continued his writing. Fishing provided the occasion for some of his books: *Fish and Tin Fish*, 1944; *Stories of Florida Fishing*, 1948; and *Denizens of the Deep*, 1953, as well as his popular series of "Crunch and Des" fishing and adventure stories in the *Saturday Evening Post*. He devoted much of his time to work with conservation groups. Other books included *Opus 21*, 1949; *The Answer*, 1956; *The Innocent Ambassadors*, 1957; *Triumph*, 1963; and *The Spy Who Spoke Porpoise*, 1969. In his last nonfiction book he returned to the attack on "Momism" with *Sons and Daughters of Mom*, 1971. Wylie died in Miami, Florida, on October 25, 1971. His last novel, *The End of the Dream*, was published posthumously in 1972.

Wynn, Ed (1886–1966), entertainer. Born in Philadelphia, Pennsylvania, on November 9, 1886, Isaiah Edwin Leopold determined early in life on a stage career. At fifteen he ran away from home to join a repertory company, but when the company failed, he returned to Philadelphia. Soon he was off again, this time to New York City, where he teamed up with another comedian, Jack Lewis. They became an instant success and played at New York's top vaudeville house, the Colonial Theater, for nearly two years. By 1904 Ed Wynn—created out of his middle name—was a star. The team broke up and he worked for the next decade in vaudeville, apart from a 1910 Broadway review. In 1914 he joined the cast of the *Ziegfeld Follies* for a few seasons. In 1919 he was one of the leaders of an actors' strike and when he walked out on his contract was barred from Broadway by the Schubert brothers. But in 1920 he returned to the stage in a production written entirely by himself—*Ed Wynn's Carnival*. It was a smashing success, running for more than two years. His next two stage vehicles were also his own creations: *The Perfect Fool* (which gave him the cognomen by which he was known as long as he did comic roles), 1921, and *The Grab Bag*, 1924. On June 12, 1922, Wynn staged a radio broadcast of *The Perfect Fool*, the first time a Broadway production had been put on radio and the first time a radio show had been broadcast with a studio audience. When he went into radio in 1932 as the "Fire Chief," for Texaco, he insisted on having the performances done before studio audiences. In an era when radio comedians proliferated rapidly, Wynn's program was one of the most popular on the air and it ran until 1939. In that year, after suffering severe financial loss through the failure of a chain of radio stations he had invested in, he retired from show business. But his retirement was short-lived. He was persuaded to return to the stage in 1940 with *Boys and Girls Together*, which he had written. He had lost none of his comic genius, and the play was highly acclaimed by the critics and the public alike. He spent most of World War II entertaining troops and raising funds through benefits. He went into television in its early years, but soon found that his talent suffered from over-exposure. By 1950 he was virtually out of show business for lack of offers. But late in the decade he made a spectacular comeback, turning, after 55 years of comedy, to serious acting roles on television and in movies. In motion pictures he achieved great success in his roles in *The Great Man*, 1957, and *Marjorie Morningstar*, 1958, and was nominated for an Academy Award for his performance in *The Diary of Anne Frank*, 1959. He also returned to television briefly with the "Ed Wynn Show" and won a TV Emmy for his dramatic role in *Requiem for a Heavyweight* in 1956. His last film roles were in *Mary Poppins*, 1964, and *The Greatest Story Ever Told*, 1965. Wynn died on June 19, 1966, in Beverly Hills, California. His son Keenan Wynn also became a popular actor on the stage and in films.

Wythe, George (1726–1806), lawyer, public official, judge, and educator. Born in Elizabeth City County (now the city of Hampton), Virginia, in 1726, Wythe had had little formal education—he briefly attended the grammar school of the College of William and Mary—when he began the study of law. He was admitted to the bar in 1746 and began the practice of law. During 1754–1755 he served in the House of Burgesses and in 1758 began ten continuous years of membership in that body. By 1760, having devoted much time to the study of law and the classics, he was one of the leading lawyers and legal scholars in the colony, and from 1762 to 1767 Thomas Jefferson studied in his office. In 1764 he was charged with drafting the Virginia remonstrances to the House of Commons protesting the Stamp Act; his language was considered too strong and was much modified in the final version. In 1775 he was elected to the Continental Congress and remained there through 1776, becoming a signer of the Declaration of Independence. Upon his return to Virginia he was appointed, with Edmund Pendleton and Jefferson, to revise the laws of the commonwealth in the light of its recently achieved independence. After serving in the House of Delegates he was named a judge of the high court of chancery in 1778; he held this position until his death, and between 1788 and 1801 was the sole chancellor. Noted for his erudition and disinterested administration of justice, he was one of the first judges to enunciate the doctrine of judicial review, in *Commonwealth v. Caton*, 1782. Largely by the efforts of Jefferson, then governor, he was appointed in 1779 to the newly created professorship of law at the College of William and Mary, the first such chair in an American college. His judicial duties forced him to resign the chair in 1790, but in his ten years at the college he exerted a powerful influence on the course of American legal education, supplementing his lectures with moot courts and moot legislatures held by his students, among whom was John Marshall. He served in 1787 in the Federal Constitutional Convention and the next year in the Virginia ratifying convention. After leaving the College of William and Mary, he moved to Richmond, Virginia, to continue his duties on the bench and there opened a private law school; among his students was Henry Clay, who served also as his clerk. Wythe died in Richmond on June 8, 1806, after leaving instructions in his will to free his slaves.

Y

Yale, Linus (1821–1868), inventor and lock manufacturer. Born in Salisbury, Herkimer County, New York, on April 4, 1821, Yale originally intended to be a portrait painter, but instead followed his father into the lock-manufacturing business. In the 1840s he set up a small factory at Shelburne Falls, Massachusetts, to make bank locks. Through the 1850s he turned out a series of successively improved key-operated bank locks, then in the early 1860s began to market the Yale Monitor bank lock, a dial-operated combination lock. In 1863 he manufactured the first double-dial bank lock. In 1861 he patented a small cylinder lock with pin tumblers, operated by a key and meant for use in doors of houses and businesses. Four years later Yale obtained a patent on an improved cylinder lock, basically the type of Yale lock still in use today. His original shop was fully occupied making bank locks, so he formed a partnership with John H. Towne in 1868 under the name Yale Lock Manufacturing Company, and built a factory in Stamford, Connecticut, solely for the purpose of manufacturing the new cylinder locks. Yale died in New York City on December 25, 1868, shortly after the new plant of the Yale Lock Manufacturing Company had gone into operation.

Yamasaki, Minoru (1912–   ), architect. Born in Seattle on December 1, 1912, Yamasaki graduated from the University of Washington in 1934. He went to New York City to begin his career as an architect and from 1935 to 1945 was associated with various architectural firms. In 1945 he moved to Detroit and four years later joined the firm which later became Minoru Yamasaki and Associates. In building design, he turned away from the form-functional steel and glass-block structures to a more imaginative style that incorporated what he called "the delight of change and surprise." He was responsible for a number of award-winning designs, including the Lambert Field–St. Louis Municipal Airport building, 1955; the U.S. consulate general's office at Kobe, Japan, 1956; the American Concrete Institute, 1956, in Detroit; and the Macgregor Memorial Community Conference Center of Wayne State University, 1958. He also executed urban redevelopment plans in Detroit and St. Louis in the early 1950s. Other major structures designed by Yamasaki include the Michigan Consolidated Gas Company in Detroit, 1959; the U.S. Science Pavilion at the 1962 Century 21 Exposition in Seattle; the College of Education building at Wayne State University, 1963; the Northwestern Life Insurance Company building in Minneapolis, 1966; the Woodrow Wilson School of Public and International Affairs at Princeton, 1966; and, in the 1970s, the twin-towered World Trade Center in New York City.

Yancey, William Lowndes (1814–1863), public official. Born on August 10, 1814, in Warren County, Georgia, Yancey attended Williams College in Massachusetts. In 1833, in Greenville, South Carolina, he was a pro-Union editor of the *Greenville Mountaineer* during the furor over nullification. He also studied law in Greenville and in 1834 was admitted to the bar. He soon moved to Alabama and in 1838 became editor of the Cahawba *Southern Democrat*. In 1839 he purchased, with his brother, the *Wetumpka Commercial Advertiser* and the *Argus*. He soon rose to prominence in the state and was elected to the Alabama legislature in 1841 and became a state senator in 1843. He won election to the House of Representatives in 1844 and was reelected in 1845. He resigned on September 1, 1846, to devote himself to combating abolitionism. In response to the Wilmot Proviso, which sought to bar slavery in new territories, he drew up the Alabama Platform (or Yancey Platform) in 1848, calling for positive congressional action on behalf of the rights of slaveholders, particularly with respect to the territories, and calling upon the Democratic party to endorse pro-slavery presidential and vice-presidential candidates. At the party's national convention in Baltimore in 1848, he attempted unsuccessfully to have the statement included in the Democratic platform, and from then on he spoke widely on behalf of the Alabama platform. Following the Compromise of 1850, he openly advocated secession and organized nonpartisan Southern rights associations to take a united stand for Southern interests. He founded the League of United Southerners in 1858 and called for the repeal of laws against the slave trade. In 1860 he delivered the final statement of Southern delegates before their withdrawal from the Democratic national convention in Charleston. He then organized the splinter Constitutional Democratic party, which nominated John C. Breckinridge for president, and Yancey toured the country making campaign speeches for him. He personally drafted the ordinance of secession of the Alabama convention in 1861. Declining a cabinet post in Jefferson Davis's administration of the Confederate States of America, he went to England and France in 1861 and 1862 to try to secure recognition of the Confederacy. In 1862–1863 he served in the Confederate senate. He died in Montgomery, Alabama, on July 27, 1863.

Yang, Chen Ning (1922–   ), physicist. Born in Ho-fei in Anhwei Province, China, on September

22, 1922, Yang graduated from National Southwest Associated University at K'un-ming in 1942. He pursued graduate studies at Tsinghua University in the same city until coming to the University of Chicago on a scholarship in 1945 to study under physicist Enrico Fermi. He took his Ph.D. in physics at Chicago in 1948 and taught there for a year before joining the Institute for Advanced Study at Princeton, New Jersey. He remained at the Institute, becoming a full professor in 1955, until 1966, when he accepted appointment as Albert Einstein Professor of Physics at the Stony Brook campus of the State University of New York. Yang and his fellow physicist, Tsung-dao Lee of the Institute and later of Columbia University, investigated the theory of conservation of parity, important for the study of atoms and subatomic particles. Specifically, they suggested that in weak particle interactions there were certain decay paths that were preferred and that remained constant regardless of the reversal of other relevant parameters. They proposed experiments to test this simple but revolutionary hypothesis and in 1957 the experiments proved that the principle of parity was not valid in weak interactions. In upsetting the law their discoveries opened the way for deeper study of atomic structure while suggesting new philosophical questions on the possibility of defining absolute reference systems and of time reversal. For their discovery Yang and Lee shared both the Albert Einstein Award and the Nobel Prize for Physics in 1957. Among Yang's published works was *Elementary Particles*, 1962.

Yerby, Frank Garvin (1916–   ), author. Born in Augusta, Georgia, on September 5, 1916, Yerby graduated from Paine College in 1937. He did graduate work at Fisk University and the University of Chicago until 1939. From 1939 until 1945 he lived and taught in college English departments, in Florida and Louisiana, later moving to Detroit, and finally to New York City. It was while living in Detroit and working for the Ford Motor Company that he had his first short story, "Health Card," published in *Harper's* magazine in 1944. Other short stories appeared during the next two years, and his first novel, *The Foxes of Harrow*, was published in 1946. After the success of this first book he wrote more than 20 novels, many of which were on best-seller lists. Usually historical romances set in the Deep South, the novels were action stories with stock plots and characters, but were nevertheless carefully researched. Several were made into movies. Yerby's works included *The Vixens*, 1947; *Pride's Castle*, 1949; *Benton Row*, 1954; *Fair Oaks*, 1957; *Jarrett's Jade*, 1959; *An Odor of Sanctity*, 1965; *Heat Song*, 1967; *Speak Now*, 1969; *Dahomean*, 1971; and *The Girl from Storyville*, 1972. After the mid-1950s Yerby and his family lived in Spain.

Yerkes, Charles Tyson (1837–1905), financier. Born in Philadelphia on June 25, 1837, Yerkes left school in 1853 to go into the brokerage business. By 1859 he had opened his own firm and in 1862

he also opened a banking house. He became very adept at dealing in stocks and bonds and had attained a sizable fortune when business reverses hit him in 1871. Because his financial dealings were overextended and he could not properly account for certain municipal monies entrusted to him, he was tried, convicted, and sentenced to prison. Emerging from jail after seven months, he set about remaking his fortune and within a decade had reestablished himself financially with investments in railroads and Philadelphia transit companies. He moved to Chicago in 1882 and by 1886 had gained control of the streetcar lines on the north and west sides of the city. By a series of financial maneuvers and alignment with corrupt politicians he obtained transportation franchises and built up a complicated corporate empire. In 1895 he hoped to gain a 50-year renewal on his franchises through the cooperation of a pliant legislature, but Governor John P. Altgeld vetoed the project. Two years later Yerkes nearly succeeded, but public protests, aided by investigations of the Municipal Voters' League, pressured the Chicago city council into voting against him, although bribes had been passed around freely. The public turned against Yerkes and his "bought" politicians, and pressure mounted for municipal control of the transit lines. In 1899 he sold his interest in the city's transportation franchises and the next year moved to London to engage in transit operations there; he served as head of the syndicate that built the London subway system. He suffered financial reverses, however, and when he died in London on December 29, 1905, most of his fortune was gone. A gift by Yerkes to the University of Chicago in 1892 made possible the construction of the Yerkes Observatory, opened in 1897 in Williams Bay, Wisconsin. In 1912 novelist Theodore Dreiser published *The Financier*, the first volume of a trilogy based on the life of Yerkes. Subsequent volumes were *The Titan*, 1914, and *The Stoic*, 1947.

Yerkes, Robert Mearns (1876–1956), psychologist. Born in Breadysville, in Bucks County, Pennsylvania, on May 26, 1876, Yerkes received B.A. degrees from both Ursinus College and Harvard and took his M.A. in 1899 and his Ph.D. in 1902 from Harvard. He began research into animal behavior in 1901 at Harvard and was assistant professor of comparative psychology there from 1909 until 1917, when he left to take charge of the psychological testing of the nearly two million men who entered the army during World War I. During 1917–1919 he held the titles of professor of psychology and director of the psychology laboratory at the University of Minnesota. In 1916 he helped found the National Research Council and was chairman of its research information service from 1919 until 1924, when he joined the faculty of Yale University, where he was professor of psychology from 1924 to 1929 and professor of psychobiology from 1929 to 1944. He retired in 1944. In 1929 he organized and then directed the Yale Laboratories of Primate Biology at Orange

Park, Florida, which from 1942 were known as the Yerkes Laboratories, and it was there that he acquired a worldwide reputation as one of the leading authorities on the great apes, especially on the chimpanzee. He published many influential books and papers; among the books were *The Dancing Mouse; a Study in Animal Behavior,* 1907; *Introduction to Psychology,* 1911; *The Mental Life of Monkeys and Apes,* 1916; *Almost Human,* 1925; *The Great Apes: A Study of Anthropoid Life,* 1929, written with his wife, Ada W. Yerkes; and *Chimpanzees: A Laboratory Colony,* 1943. He also served as a consultant to army intelligence during World War II. The recipient of many awards and honors for his work with great apes, he died in New Haven, Connecticut, on February 3, 1956.

Yoelson, Asa, *see* Jolson, Al

York, Alvin Cullum (1887–1964), soldier. Born in Pall Mall, Fentress County, Tennessee, on December 13, 1887, York had little formal education, dropping out of school in the third grade to work in a blacksmith shop. In 1911 he underwent a religious conversion at a revival meeting and when the United States entered World War I he declared himself a conscientious objector. His petition for exemption from the draft was denied, however, and he was inducted into the army and served overseas in the 82nd Infantry Division. While taking part in the battle of the Argonne Forest on October 8, 1918, York demonstrated outstanding heroism by leading an attack on a German machine-gun nest. He and his men killed 25 of the enemy, and, acting almost alone, he captured 132 prisoners and 35 machine guns. When asked how he had done this all by himself, he replied: "I surrounded 'em." The act made him the major popular hero of the war. On November 1, 1918, shortly before the armistice, he was promoted to sergeant and later was awarded the Congressional Medal of Honor and the French Croix de Guerre. Altogether he received some 50 other decorations and became one of the most celebrated heroes of the war. After the war, however, he refused to capitalize on his fame; he returned to Tennessee to live on a farm granted him by the state. In 1928 he published his autobiography and in 1940 allowed the movie *Sergeant York,* starring Gary Cooper, to be made. Cooper won an Academy Award in 1941 for his performance. York himself lived very modestly, giving away the bulk of the proceeds from his book and the movie to a foundation organized to support an industrial school and a Bible school in Tennessee. He died in Nashville, Tennessee, on December 2, 1964.

Young, Brigham (1801–1877), religious leader. Born in Whitingham, Vermont, on June 1, 1801, Young was raised in western New York State and received only a few months of formal schooling in the towns where his poverty-stricken family drifted. He grew up to be a farmer, carpenter, painter, and glazier, and in 1829 he settled in Mendon, Monroe County, New York. Joseph Smith's *Book of Mormon* was published the following year in a nearby town, and Young was baptized into Smith's new Church of Jesus Christ of Latter-Day Saints (the "Mormon Church") on April 14, 1832. After several successful missionary tours for the church in the fall of 1833, he "gathered" with the Saints in Kirtland, Ohio, and joined in the march of Zion's Camp to Jackson County, Missouri, a fruitless effort to help dispossessed Mormons regain their lands. For his faith and works, he was named one of the Twelve Apostles when Smith organized this body in 1835. The failure of the Mormon bank along with the constant hostility of non-Mormons made it necessary for Young, like Smith and other Mormon leaders, to flee first, in 1838, to northwestern Missouri and by the following year, out of the state entirely. By that time two older apostles had died or left the church and Young became senior member of the quorum. A chief figure in the successful founding of Nauvoo, Illinois, he then went to England, where he preached for a year and established a mission that was to contribute many British converts to the church in the United States during the next half-century. Returning home in 1841, he lived quietly among the Saints in Nauvoo until the assassination of Smith in June 1844. At the time of the assassination he was absent in the East, but he quickly returned to Nauvoo. Young succeeded in his bid to head the church and early in 1846 the pressure of unfriendly neighbors forced him to lead the majority of the Saints out of Illinois. They spent the summer at the Missouri River and in 1847 he conducted a pioneer company to the West, where the site of Salt Lake City was chosen as a settling place for the Saints. He led the emigration of the whole church to Utah in 1848, and Salt Lake City became the base of a colonizing endeavor in which the Saints sought out irrigable land and settled every feasible locality, including areas in what are now the four surrounding states as well as in California. As the supreme authority in the cooperative Mormon theocracy, Young supervised the most minute details of the settlements, and the agricultural communities enjoyed phenomenal growth and prosperity and converts continued to arrive. When Congress changed the Mormons' provisional state of Deseret to the Territory of Utah in 1850, he continued as governor. He was appointed to a second term in 1854, but grinding friction between the Mormons and the federal judiciary over the Mormon practice of polygamy and their economic power finally led President James Buchanan to replace Young as governor in 1857. An army force under Gen. Albert S. Johnston was sent in 1857 to establish the primacy of federal rule in Utah, and Young passively resisted the incoming troops until the spring of 1858. His statesmanship avoided a real break with the United States, however. Although he never again held political office, he effectively ruled the people of Utah as president of the Mormon church. As a result of his foresight and firm command, Mormons held nearly all the choice and irrigable land in the region of Salt Lake and much land in surrounding states, and they early established a network of industrial and service operations that made them self-sufficient. Having accepted the doctrine of plural marriage, he took 27 wives—some merely "sealed" to him as ceremonial rather than conjugal partners—17 of whom survived him, along with 47 children, upon his death in Salt Lake City on August 29, 1877.

Young, Chic, see Young, Murat Bernard

Young, Clarence, see Stratemeyer, Edward

Young, Cy (1867–1955), baseball player. Born in Gilmore, Tuscarawas County, Ohio, on March 29, 1867, Denton True Young began playing baseball for a Canton team and was signed by the Cleveland team of the National League in 1890. In October of that year he demonstrated his amazing stamina by pitching and winning both ends of a double-header. He pitched for Cleveland through 1898, then successively for the St. Louis Cardinals, 1899–1900, the Boston Red Sox, 1901–1908, the Cleveland Indians (American League), 1909–1911, and the Boston Braves (National League) for part of the 1912 season. He retired in that year at the age of forty-five, too overweight to pitch well any more, and went into farming in Ohio. He pitched in 906 games, a record for his time that was later broken when the practice of using relief pitchers became common; but his records of 751 complete games, 7377 innings, and 511 victories seemed likely never to be broken. The last record was especially extraordinary; he was the first man ever to win 500 games. He pitched 76 shutouts and 3 no-hit games, including modern baseball's first "perfect" game—in which the pitcher faces 27 batters in 9 innings, none of whom reaches base—on May 5, 1904. He won more than 200 games in each of the major leagues and 16 times enjoyed seasons with 20 or more victories—and 5 times won over 30 games. He won 36 games in 1892, his best season. He was elected to the National Baseball Hall of Fame in 1937. He died in Newcomerstown, Tuscarawas County, Ohio, on November 4, 1955. After his death the Cy Young Award was established for the best pitcher in the major leagues each year, and later for the best pitcher in each major league.

Young, Denton True, see Young, Cy

Young, Murat Bernard (1901–1973), "Chic," cartoonist. Born in Chicago on January 9, 1901, Young grew up there and in St. Louis. He attended art schools in Chicago, New York City, and Cleveland before becoming a cartoonist for the Newspaper Enterprise Association in 1920. After a year he switched to the Bell Syndicate and in 1923 joined the King Features Syndicate, where he remained during the rest of his career. From 1924 to 1926 he drew a daily comic strip entitled *Dumb Dora*. In 1930 he originated *Blondie*, a comic strip about a jazz-age flapper who settled down to marry Dagwood Bumstead, playboy scion of a wealthy society family. After a halting and uncertain start the strip gained popularity, particularly as the social connections of the characters changed and it came to center on the problems of middle-class family life and the foibles of a cast of characters that grew to include two children, the dog Daisy and her puppies, Mr. Beasley, the postman, neighbors Herb and Tootsie Woodley, and the boss, Mr. Dithers, and his wife, Cora. Consistently a lighthearted, even slapstick, series, *Blondie* presented a comic allegory of the American family, with a bumbling, hard-working husband who strives continually to earn more money and a wife who cannot spend it fast enough. The plot lines revolved around situations familiar to nearly everyone. In the 1930s and 1940s there were *Blondie* movies and radio programs, and in the early 1950s a television series. *Blondie* became the most widely syndicated of all comic strips, appearing in more than 1600 newspapers in the United States and abroad. Dagwood's enormous sandwiches, created during evening raids on the refrigerator and consumed before going to bed, became an American institution and were widely known themselves as "dagwoods." Young died in St. Petersburg, Florida, on March 14, 1973.

Young, Whitney Moore, Jr. (1921–1971), civil-rights leader. Born in Lincoln Ridge, Shelby County, Kentucky, on July 31, 1921, Young graduated from Kentucky State College in 1941. After a year of high-school teaching he enlisted in the army and spent two years studying engineering at the Massachusetts Institute of Technology (MIT). After service in Europe he was discharged from the army and enrolled at the University of Minnesota for graduate study in social work, taking a master's degree in 1947. He worked for the St. Paul Urban League for three years and from 1950 to 1954 he was executive secretary of the Omaha Urban League and an instructor in the school of social work at the University of Nebraska. In 1954 he accepted appointment as dean of the school of social work at Atlanta University, where he remained until 1961, when he became executive director of the National Urban League, with offices in New York City. The League had been founded in 1911 as the National League on Urban Conditions, to ameliorate the economic situation of black Americans. At a time when thousands of blacks were emigrating from the rural South to Northern cities, the League strove to ease their adjustment by helping them to find jobs and housing. In the upsurge of the civil-rights movement in the 1960s, Young helped to broaden the program of the League by directing its activities into all the areas where blacks experienced deprivation and to transpose victories at law into actual improvements in housing, employment, and education. He called for a "Marshall Plan" for the nation's blacks to help them catch up after generations of discrimination. Many of Young's specific proposals were incorporated into

President Lyndon B. Johnson's antipoverty program in the mid-1960s. An articulate and powerful spokesman for civil rights, Young carried his message to platforms in all parts of the nation. He also elaborated his ideas in two books, *To Be Equal*, 1964, and *Beyond Racism*, 1969. While with the Urban League he also served on various commissions under presidents John F. Kennedy and Johnson. He died suddenly while in Lagos, Nigeria, on March 11, 1971.

Younger, Cole (1844–1916), bandit. Born in Jackson County, Missouri, near Lee's Summit, on January 15, 1844, Thomas Coleman Younger grew up during the years of the virtual civil war over slavery in Kansas. He took part in "border ruffian" raids into Kansas by those who sought through violence to make it a slave state. Shortly after the Civil War began Younger, along with Frank and Jesse James, joined William C. Quantrill's raiders, a band of irregulars who engaged in guerrilla warfare in Kansas and Missouri on behalf of the Confederacy. Their most notorious raid was an attack on Lawrence, Kansas, on August 21, 1863, when they captured and plundered the town, killing 180 people. Younger also served under "Bloody Bill" Anderson a year later in the assault on Centralia, Missouri, when between 150 and 200 civilians and Union soldiers were killed. After the war Younger, his brothers James and Robert, and the James brothers formed a gang to rob banks and trains.

Their first robbery, on February 14, 1866, at the Clay County Savings Association Bank in Liberty, Missouri, netted them about $70,000. For the next ten years they engaged in a series of robberies and killings. Their first attack on a railroad train came on July 21, 1873, in Iowa. Until 1876 they were never caught, much of their "luck" being actually the aid and protection of Confederate sympathizers. The gang was at the pinnacle of its notorious career when, on September 7, 1876, disaster overtook it. They arrived at Northfield, Minnesota, and attempted to hold up the bank. In the gun battle with local citizens that ensued, two of the gang members were killed and four captured. Frank and Jesse escaped, but Younger, along with two of his brothers, was taken. The Youngers were tried, convicted, and sent to prison in Minnesota. They had been sentenced to life imprisonment, but after several years pressure from friends in Missouri secured the parole of James and Cole Younger in July 1901. Robert Younger had died in prison in 1889. James committed suicide in 1902, and in 1903 Cole was pardoned and returned to Missouri. He never took up his lawless career again, but held various jobs, including one in a Wild West show, and lived as a respected citizen. In 1903 he published *The Story of Cole Younger, by Himself*, and at various times he lectured. He died in Jackson County, Missouri, on March 21, 1916.

Younger, Thomas Coleman, *see* Younger, Cole

Z

Zaharias, Mildred Ella Didrikson (1914–1956), athlete. Born in Port Arthur, Texas, on June 26, 1914, "Babe" Didrikson was an all-American basketball player in 1930, while she was still in high school. In 1932, at the women's national track and field tournament held by the Amateur Athletic Union (AAU), she entered eight of the ten events and won five of them. In the Olympic Games of 1932 at Los Angeles she won two gold medals, setting a new record of 143' 3-11/16" in the javelin throw and establishing a U.S. outdoor mark of 11.7 seconds in the 80-meter hurdles. Her record-breaking mark in the high jump was disallowed on a technicality. Shortly after the games she turned professional and gave athletic exhibitions throughout the country. In 1935 she took up golf and, regaining her status as an amateur, soon became the leading woman golfer in the United States. In 1947 she won 17 straight golf titles, including the British Women's Amateur, of which she was the first U.S. winner. She later became a professional golfer and continued to win most of the tournaments in which she played. In 1949 she was voted in an Associated Press (AP) poll the outstanding woman athlete of the century. But by 1952 it was obvious that she was very ill, and the next year she underwent an operation for cancer. She appeared to have recovered when she won the women's U.S. Open (for the third time) and the All-American Open in 1954. But she was operated on once again in 1956 and died that year in Galveston, Texas, on September 27. She married the wrestler George Zaharias in 1938 and published an autobiography, *This Life I've Led*, in 1955. The book revealed her as a delightful and courageous woman as well as one of the greatest woman athletes in history.

Zanuck, Darryl Francis (1902–1979), motion-picture executive. Born on September 5, 1902, in Wahoo, Nebraska, Zanuck grew up there and in Los Angeles. At fifteen he enlisted in the army, passing himself off as an eighteen-year-old, and saw action in France during World War I. When he got out of the service in 1920 he set out to become a short-story writer, and when he was able to sell some of his work to the Warner Brothers studios in 1924 he was hired as a script writer. Working in Hollywood, he learned how to direct, produce, and edit films, and by 1927 he had become an executive producer. One of his first efforts was the 1927 production of *The Jazz Singer*, starring Al Jolson, the first full-length movie in which sound dialogue was used. Among his other successes at Warner Brothers was *Little Caesar*, 1930, starring Edward G. Robinson. In 1933 he left Warners to help form Twentieth Century Pictures, which merged with the Fox studios in 1935 to become Twentieth Century–Fox. Having introduced audiences to sound films, Zanuck continued to innovate by his choice of scripts, giving audiences films that had social significance in addition to entertaining musicals, comedies, and Westerns. Among the movies he produced between 1935 and 1953 were *Grapes of Wrath*, 1940; *The Ox-Bow Incident*, 1943; *Wilson*, 1944; *Winged Victory*, 1944; *The Razor's Edge*, 1946; *Gentleman's Agreement*, 1947; *Twelve O'Clock High*, 1950; and *Snows of Kilimanjaro*, 1952. After World War II he also pioneered in the use of foreign locations for shooting films. When television began to make serious inroads into movie audiences Zanuck produced the first CinemaScope film, *The Robe*, in 1953. This was followed by more lavish productions, such as *The Egyptian*, 1954, and *Three Coins in the Fountain*, 1954. In 1956 he made *The Man in the Gray Flannel Suit* and in 1962 the notable movie about the Allied landings in France on D-Day, *The Longest Day*. In 1956 he became an independent producer, but in 1962, when Spyros Skouras left the presidency of Twentieth Century–Fox, Zanuck replaced him as operating head. He in turn was replaced by his son, Richard, in 1971. He died on December 22, 1979, in Palm Springs, California.

Zenger, John Peter (1697–1746), printer and editor. Born in Germany in 1697, Zenger emigrated to New York City in 1710 and was indentured to the printer, William Bradford, until 1719. For three years he lived in Maryland, returning to New York in 1720 and becoming a freeman of the city in 1723. He joined Bradford in partnership in 1725 and the next year started his own business, translating from the Dutch and publishing religious and polemic articles, and issuing *Arithmetica*, America's first mathematics text. In 1733, during the controversy over Governor William Cosby's dismissal of Chief Justice Lewis Morris, Zenger was installed as editor of an antigovernment paper, the *New-York Weekly Journal*, established by Morris, James Alexander, and William Smith. Its articles aggressively attacked the opinions and actions of the governor; certain especially hostile issues were confiscated and burned in 1734. Shortly thereafter Zenger was arrested for seditious libel, but the paper continued on his instructions under his wife's supervision. Zenger appeared before Chief Justice James De Lancey, Morris's successor, early in 1735, but his lawyers, Alexander and Smith, were disbarred by De Lancey and the trial was delayed. Zenger's defense at the trial in 1735 was handled by a noted Philadelphia lawyer, Andrew Hamilton, who, despite De Lancey's charge to the contrary, requested the jury to consider the truth of Zenger's statements as a defense against the charge of libel. On doing so the jury acquitted Zenger; while in fact no legal precedent was set by the action, popular sentiment was aroused in favor of both freedom of the press and a wider scope of responsibility for juries. Zenger's name thereafter was linked with the individual's right publicly to discuss and criticize his government and its officers. *A Brief Narrative of the Case and Tryal of John Peter Zenger* was prepared by Alexander and printed by Zenger in 1736. In 1737 Zenger was named public printer of New York and the next year of New Jersey. He died in New York City on July 28, 1746, and the paper continued under his wife's and his son's management until 1751.

Ziegfeld, Florenz (1869–1932), theatrical producer. Born in Chicago on March 21, 1869, Ziegfeld attended Chicago public schools and entered show business in 1892, engaging orchestras and musical attractions for the World's Columbian Exposition of 1893. He also managed Eugene Sandow, the strong man, at the fair and also later in country-wide appearances. In 1896 he introduced a French starlet, Anna Held, in *A Parlor Match*, and filling newspapers, magazines, and billboard advertisements with enticing pictures and with descriptions of the milk baths that were supposedly her beauty secret, Mme Held, whom Ziegfeld married in 1897 and divorced in 1913, became famous and appeared in his lavish musical-comedy productions of *Papa's Wife, The Little Duchess, The Parisian Model*, and *Mlle. Napoleon*, all of which were a prelude to *The Follies of 1907*, an experiment with a "revue," a type of musical production that was new to the United States. The first *Follies* were staged on the roof of the New York Theatre and were followed by editions seen, except for 1926, 1928, and 1929, every year on Broadway until 1931. They featured in the chorus line through the years the most beautiful women ever to walk across an American stage, all personally chosen by Ziegfeld, whose major aim was to "glorify the American girl." With a fine sense of the right effect, he also selected the music for the shows, approved the opulent costuming and stage effects, and directed the production of each number. His taste and standards popularized the revue and brought to the musical stage levels of artistry and production never before achieved. The ideal of slenderness in women, which replaced the popularity of ample figures, was attributed to the girls in the *Ziegfeld Follies*. Contributing to the scores of various productions, some of which cost more than $200,000, were such eminent composers as Irving Berlin, Jerome Kern, Rudolf Friml, and Victor Herbert. Featured entertainers wrote their own material; among the stars associated with the *Follies* were Eddie Cantor, Fannie Brice, W. C. Fields, Will Rogers, Ann Pennington, and Ed Wynn. Songs introduced in the *Follies* included "Shine On, Harvest Moon," sung by Nora Bayes in 1908; "By the Light of the Silvery Moon," by Lillian Lorraine in 1909; "A Pretty Girl Is Like a Melody," composed by Irving Berlin and used as the *Follies* theme song after 1919; "My Man," sung by Fannie Brice in 1921; and "My Blue Heaven," introduced by Eddie Cantor in 1927. Besides the *Follies* Ziegfeld produced *Sally* with Marilyn Miller in 1920, *Show Boat* and *Rio Rita*, which opened the specially designed Ziegfeld Theatre, both in 1927, and *Bitter Sweet* in 1929. From 1914 he was married to actress Billie Burke. He died in Hollywood, California, on July 22, 1932.

Zimmerman, Ethel, *see* Merman, Ethel

Zimmerman, Robert, *see* Dylan, Bob

Zinsser, Hans (1878–1940), physician and bacteriologist. Born in New York City on November 17, 1878, Zinsser graduated from Columbia College in 1899 and took his M.D. degree from Columbia's medical school in 1903. He had turned aside from a possible literary career to pursue medicine and bacteriology. He interned until 1905 at Roosevelt Hospital in New York City and then was a bacteriologist at Roosevelt, an assistant pathologist at St. Luke's, and taught bacteriology at Columbia. From 1910 until 1913 he taught bacteriology and immunology at Stanford University, then returned to Columbia's medical school. From 1923 until his death he was professor of bacteriology at Harvard Medical School in Boston. An expert in infectious diseases, he was one of the leading physicians in the development of immunology; and, with associates, he had contributed much by 1924 to the development of immunization against certain forms of typhus fever. During his years of teaching, Zinsser served occasionally in outside capacities; in 1915 he traveled to Serbia for the Red Cross to observe and combat an outbreak of typhus. During World War I he served with the U.S. armed forces in France as an epidemiologist, and in 1923 he went to the Soviet Union for the League of Nations to investigate a cholera epidemic. He wrote a large number of scientific papers and was coauthor of *Textbook of Bacteriology*, frequently revised, and a widely read "biography of typhus," *Rats, Lice, and History*, 1935. His autobiography, *As I Remember Him*, appeared in 1940. Zinsser died in New York City on September 4, 1940.

Zorach, William (1887–1966), sculptor and painter. Born in Eurburg, Lithuania (then part of Russia and now in the Soviet Union), on February 28, 1887, Zorach was brought to the United States by his parents at the age of four. He was raised in Cleveland, where he studied at the Cleveland School of Art. During 1908–1909 he studied at the National Academy of Design in New York City. First a painter, he was strongly influenced by the work of Henri Matisse and that of the Cubists, which he saw during a year in Paris in 1910–1911. So strong was their influence that he was numbered among the Fauvists, or wild young painters, who dominated the Paris art world at the beginning of the century, and who shocked art lovers elsewhere. He settled in New York City in 1912 and remained there, except for extended sojourns on a farm that he bought in 1923 in Robinhood, Maine, until his death. In 1913 he placed paintings in the famed Armory Show. In 1917 he did his first direct carving, hewing out the image that he perceived or conceived in the material without the aid of models, pointing machines, or other mechanical devices. Becoming fascinated by this traditional technique, he became at the same time more traditional, even conservative, in his approach and subject matter. In 1922 he gave up oils for sculpture, although he did watercolors sporadically for the rest of his life. His best-known work was monumental, strong, and simple in composition and in conception. He exerted an influence on many younger artists through his classes at the Art Students League in New York City, where he taught after 1929. He was honored in 1959 by a retrospective exhibition at the Whitney Museum of American Art. Among his works commissioned for public places were "Spirit of the Dance," at Radio City Music Hall in New York City, 1932; a figure of Benjamin Franklin, 1927, in a U.S. Post Office in Washington, D.C.; the Mayo Clinic reliefs at Rochester, Minnesota, 1954; and "The Spirit of the Sea" at Bath, Maine, 1962. He died in Bath on November 16, 1966.

Zworykin, Vladimir Kosma (1889–1982), engineer and inventor. Born in Mourom, Russia, on July 30, 1889, Zworykin graduated from the Institute of Technology in St. Petersburg in 1912 and then went to Paris to do graduate work at the Collège de France. After service in the Russian army in World War I he emigrated to the United States in 1919, becoming a naturalized citizen in 1924. He worked first as a researcher on the staff of the Westinghouse Electric Company in Pittsburgh, and in 1926 received his Ph.D. from the University of Pittsburgh. In 1929 he joined the Radio Corporation of America (RCA) as head of its electronic research laboratory, first at Camden, New Jersey, then at Princeton. From 1947 he was a vice-president and from 1954 an honorary vice-president of RCA and a consultant on various technical problems. From an early date Zworykin worked on the development of a system of electronic transmission of pictures. In 1923 he demonstrated a crude television system and six years later he introduced the kinescope picture tube for television receivers. Probably his greatest contribution was his invention in 1931 of the first iconoscope, the high-efficiency scanning camera tube that made possible the development of the all-electronic television system. But he also made many other contributions to the development of the television industry and is known as "the father of television." He made contributions to other fields of electronics and scientific instrumentation as well, among others the electron microscope. He was the recipient of a large number of prizes and awards, including the Rumford Medal of the American Academy of Arts and Sciences in 1941, and the National Medal of Science, awarded by President Lyndon B. Johnson in 1967. From 1954 to 1962 he was director of the medical electronics center of Rockefeller University (the Rockefeller Institute for Medical Research) in New York City. He lived for most of his later life in Princeton, New Jersey. Among his published works were *Television*, 1940; *Electron Optics and the Electron Microscope*, 1945; *Photoelectricity and Its Applications*, 1949; and *Television in Science and Industry*, 1958. He died in Princeton on July 29, 1982.

Geographical Index

Dyott, Thomas W.
Eliot, John
Endecott, John
Evans, George Henry
Fitzsimmons, Robert Prometheus
Gates, Horatio
Gompers, Samuel
Gosnold, Bartholomew
Grant, Cary
Guest, Edgar Albert
Gwinnett, Button
Hallam, Lewis
Harris, Benjamin
Harrison, Peter
Harvard, John
Harvey, Frederick Henry
Hitchcock, Alfred Joseph
Hooker, Thomas
Hope, Bob
Hudson, Henry
Hutchinson, Anne
Insull, Samuel
Iredell, James
Karloff, Boris
Keene, Laura
Kemble, Fanny
Latrobe, Benjamin Henry
Laurel, Stan
Lee, Ann
Lee, Charles
Le Gallienne, Eva
Leslie, Frank
McDougall, William
Mason, Charles, and Jeremiah Dixon
Mather, Richard
Meiklejohn, Alexander
Miller, Henry John
Mitchell, John
Montagu, Ashley
Morris, Robert
Murray, Lindley
Muybridge, Eadweard
Nizer, Louis
Oglethorpe, James Edward
Paine, Thomas
Parton, James
Penn, William
Richards, Ivor Armstrong
Rimmer, William
Rowson, Susanna Haswell
Scripps, James Edmund
Sewall, Samuel
Shirley, William
Shockley, William Bradford
Slater, Samuel
Smith, John
Standish, Miles
Stokowski, Leopold
Sully, Thomas
Sutherland, George
Taylor, Edward (1645?-1729)
Taylor, Elizabeth
Thompson, David
Thomson, Elihu
Titchener, Edward Bradford

Trevellick, Richard F.
Underhill, John
Upjohn, Richard
Vassar, Matthew
Vick, James
Wallack, James William
Ward, Nathaniel
Watts, Alan Witson
White, John
Whitehead, Alfred North
Wigglesworth, Michael
Williams, Roger
Winslow, Edward
Winthrop, John (1588-1649)
Wright, Henry (Harry, 1835-1895)

FINLAND

Saarinen, Eero
Saarinen, Eliel

FRANCE

Allouez, Claude Jean
Badin, Stephen Theodore
Barzun, Jacques Martin
Bonneville, Benjamin Louis Eulalie de
Brulé, Étienne
Cadillac, Antoine Laumet de la
    Mothe
Champlain, Samuel de
Chanute, Octave
Cournand, André Frédéric
Crèvecoeur, Michel Guillaume
    Jean de
Dubos, René Jules
Du Pont de Nemours, Eleuthère
    Irénée
Girard, Stephen
Lachaise, Gaston
Laclède, Pierre
Lafayette, Marquis de
Laffite, Jean
Lamy, Jean Baptiste
La Salle, Sieur de
L'Enfant, Pierre Charles
Loewy, Raymond Fernand
Marquette, Jacques
Marsh, Reginald
Merton, Thomas
Mitchell, William (Billy)
Mowatt, Anna Cora Ogden
Nicolet, Jean
Nicollet, Joseph Nicholas
Perrot, Nicolas
Radisson, Pierre Esprit
Rochambeau, Comte de
Sorin, Edward Frederick
Soulé, Pierre
Tonty, Henri de
Varese, Edgard

GERMANY

Adler, Dankmar
Adler, Felix
Albers, Josef

Altgeld, John Peter
Arendt, Hannah
Astor, John Jacob (1763-1848)
Baade, Walter
Beissel, Johann Conrad
Belmont, August
Berliner, Emile
Bethe, Hans Albrecht
Bierstadt, Albert
Bloch, Konrad
Boas, Franz
Braun, Wernher von
Busch, Adolphus
Carnap, Rudolf
Cornell, Katharine
Damrosch, Leopold
Damrosch, Walter Johannes
Delbrück, Max
Einstein, Albert
Erikson, Erik Homburger
Faber, John Eberhard
Fernow, Bernard Eduard
Fink, Albert
Fromm, Erich
Graupner, Gottlieb
Gropius, Walter Adolf
Hamilton, Edith
Hofmann, Hans
Jacobi, Abraham
Kahn, Otto Herman
Kalb, Johann
Kissinger, Henry Alfred
Kusch, Polykarp
Laemmle, Carl
Lasker, Albert Davis
Leisler, Jacob
Leutze, Emanuel Gottlieb
Leypoldt, Frederick
Lieber, Francis
Lipmann, Fritz Albert
Loeb, Jacques
Lovejoy, Arthur Oncken
Ludwick, Christopher
Mansfield, Richard
Marcuse, Herbert
Mayer, Maria Goeppert
Mergenthaler, Ottmar
Metz, Christian
Michelson, Albert Abraham
Mies Van Der Rohe, Ludwig
Minuit, Peter
Morgenthau, Henry (1856-1946)
Mühlenberg, Henry Melchior
Münsterberg, Hugo
Nast, Thomas
Nichols, Mike
Panofsky, Erwin
Pastorius, Francis Daniel
Post, Christian Frederick
Roebling, John Augustus
Sachs, Curt
Sapir, Edward
Schirmer, Gustav
Schurz, Carl
Seligman, Joseph

Spreckels, Claus
Steinmetz, Charles Proteus
Steinway, Henry Engelhard
Stern, Otto
Steuben, Baron von
Stiegel, Henry William
Straus, Isidor, and Nathan Straus
Straus, Oscar Solomon
Sutro, Adolph Heinrich Joseph
Sutter, John Augustus
Thomas, Theodore
Tillich, Paul Johannes
Villard, Henry
Villard, Oswald Garrison
Wagner, Robert Ferdinand
Walter, Bruno
Walther, Carl Ferdinand Wilhelm
Weill, Kurt
Weiser, Conrad
Weyerhaeuser, Frederick
Zenger, John Peter

GREECE

Hearn, Lafcadio
Skouras, Spyros Panagiotes

HAITI

Audubon, John James
Du Sable, Jean Baptiste Pointe

HUNGARY

Békésy, Georg von
Houdini, Harry
Kármán, Theodore von
Lugosi, Bela
Moholy-Nagy, László
Neumann, John von
Ormandy, Eugene
Pulitzer, Joseph
Romberg, Sigmund
Schick, Béla
Szell, George
Szent-Györgyi, Albert
Szilard, Leo
Teller, Edward
Wigner, Eugene Paul
Wise, Stephen Samuel

ICELAND

Leif Ericsson
Thorfinn Karlsefni

INDIA

Ashburner, Charles Edward
Barrymore, Maurice
Judd, Charles Hubbard
Khorana, Har Gobind

IRELAND

Barry, John
Barry, Leonora Marie Kearney
   (Mother Lake)
Bonner, Robert
Boucicault, Dion

Campbell, Thomas
Carey, Mathew
Colden, Cadwallader
Conway, Thomas
Croghan, George
Daly, Marcus
England, John
Fitzpatrick, Thomas
Flanagan, Edward Joseph
Fox, Richard Kyle
Gilmore, Patrick Sarsfield
Godkin, Edwin Lawrence
Grace, William Russell
Harnett, William Michael
Herbert, Victor
Hoban, James
Holland, John Philip
Hughes, John
Ireland, John
Johnson, Sir William (1715–1774)
Jones, Mary Harris (Mother Jones)
Logan, James (1674–1751)
McClure, Samuel Sidney
McParlan, James
Makemie, Francis
Montez, Lola
O'Reilly, John Boyle
Paterson, William
Pollock, Oliver
Rehan, Ada
Saint-Gaudens, Augustus
Stewart, Alexander Turney
Tennent, Gilbert
Tennent, William

ITALY

Andretti, Mario Gabriel
Atlas, Charles
Cabot, John
Cabrini, Frances Xavier (Mother
   Cabrini)
Capone, Alphonse
Capra, Frank
Columbus, Christopher
Crawford, Francis Marion
Fermi, Enrico
Kino, Eusebio Francisco
Luria, Salvador Edward
Mazzei, Philip
Menotti, Gian-Carlo
Sacco, Nicola, and Bartolomeo
   Vanzetti
Sargent, John Singer
Segrè, Emilio Gino
Toscanini, Arturo
Valentino, Rudolph
Vespucci, Amerigo

JAMAICA

Dallas, Alexander James
Garvey, Marcus Moziah
McKay, Claude
Russwurm, John Brown

JAPAN

Noguchi, Hideyo

LUXEMBOURG

Gernsback, Hugo
Steichen, Edward

MEXICO

Anza, Juan Bautista de
Oñate, Juan de

NETHERLANDS

Bok, Edward William
De Kooning, Willem
Matthes, François Émile
Stuyvesant, Peter

NETHERLANDS ANTILLES

De Leon, Daniel

NORWAY

Furuseth, Andrew
Onsager, Lars
Rockne, Knute Kenneth
Rölvaag, Ole Edvart

POLAND

Funk, Casimir
Glueck, Sheldon
Goldwyn, Samuel
Korzybski, Alfred
Kościusko, Thaddeus
Pulaski, Kazimierz
Radin, Paul
Rubinstein, Arthur
Salomon, Haym
Singer, Isaac Bashevis
Warner Brothers

ROMANIA

Culbertson, Ely
Schechter, Solomon
Steinberg, Saul

RUSSIA

Antin, Mary
Asimov, Isaac
Balanchine, George
Berenson, Bernard
Berlin, Irving
Cahan, Abraham
Cohen, Morris Raphael
De Seversky, Alexander Procofieff
Dobzhansky, Theodosius
   Grigorievich
Dubinsky, David
Gamow, George
Goldman, Emma
Heifetz, Jascha
Hillman, Sidney
Hillquit, Morris

Hurok, Solomon
Jolson, Al
Kaplan, Mordecai Menahem
Koussevitsky, Serge
Kuznets, Simon
Leontief, Wassily W.
London, Meyer
Mayer, Louis Burt
Nabokov, Vladimir Vladimirovich
Rand, Ayn
Rickover, Hyman George
Romanoff, Michael
Rothko, Mark
Sabin, Albert Bruce
Sarnoff, David
Shahn, Benjamin
Sikorsky, Igor Ivan
Sorokin, Pitirim Alexandrovitch
Stern, Isaac
Stravinsky, Igor Fedorovich
Struve, Otto
Tiomkin, Dimitri
Tucker, Sophie
Waksman, Selman Abraham
Weber, Max
Zorach, William
Zworykin, Vladimir Kosma

SCOTLAND

Bell, Alexander Graham
Bennett, James Gordon (1795–1872)
Blair, James
Brackenridge, Hugh Henry
Carnegie, Andrew
Garden, Alexander
Garden, Mary
Henderson, David Bremner
Jones, John Paul
Kidd, William
MacIver, Robert Morrison
McTammany, John
Muir, John
Murray, Philip
Owen, Robert Dale
Phyfe, Duncan
Pinkerton, Allan
Reston, James Barrett
St. Clair, Arthur
Smibert, John
Smith, William
Wilson, Alexander
Wilson, James
Wilson, William Bauchop
Winton, Alexander
Witherspoon, John
Wright, Frances

SENEGAL

Wheatley, Phillis

SPAIN

Benavides, Alonzo de
Columbus, Christopher
Coronado, Francisco Vásquez de

De Soto, Hernando
Meade, George Gordon
Menéndez de Avilés, Pedro
Ochoa, Severo
Peralta, Pedro de
Ponce de León, Juan
Portolá, Gaspar de
Santayana, George
Serra, Junípero

SURINAM

Matzeliger, Jan Ernst

SWEDEN

Alexanderson, Ernst Frederik Werner
Campanius, John
Ericsson, John
Garbo, Greta
Hill, Joe
Lindgren, Waldemar
Oldenburg, Claes Thure
Rossby, Carl-Gustaf Arvid

SWITZERLAND

Agassiz, Alexander
Agassiz, Louis
Bandelier, Adolph Francis Alphonse
Bloch, Ernest
Bloch, Felix
Delmonico, Lorenzo
Gallatin, Albert
Guggenheim, Meyer
Hassler, Ferdinand Rudolph
Piccard, Jean Félix
Schaff, Philip

THAILAND

Chang and Eng

TURKEY

Adams, Walter Sydney
Brewer, David Josiah
Grosvenor, Gilbert Hovey
Kazan, Elia
Rafinesque, Constantine Samuel

UNITED STATES

ALABAMA

Aaron, Henry Louis (Hank)
Bankhead, Tallulah Brockman
Bankhead, William Brockman
Belmont, Alva Ertskin Smith
   Vanderbilt
Black, Hugo LaFayette
Braun, Wernher von
Campbell, John Archibald
Carver, George Washington
De Soto, Hernando
Gorgas, Josiah
Gorgas, William Crawford
Handy, William Christopher
Iberville, Pierre Le Moyne, Sieur d'

Julian, Percy Lavon
Keller, Helen Adams
King, William Rufus de Vane
Louis, Joe
McGillivray, Alexander
McKinley, John
Mays, Willie Howard, Jr.
Morgan, John Hunt
Namath, Joseph William
Owens, Jesse
Paige, Leroy Robert (Satchel)
Robbins, Frederick Chapman
Semmes, Raphael
Sims, James Marion
Underwood, Oscar Wilder
Vincent, John Heyl
Wallace, George Corley
Washington, Booker Taliaferro
Wheeler, Joseph
Yancey, William Lowndes

ALASKA

Jackson, Sheldon
Seward, William Henry

ARIZONA

Benavides, Alonso de
Chavez, Cesar Estrada
Cochise
Coronado, Francisco Vásquez de
Earp, Wyatt
Gadsden, James
Geronimo
Goldwater, Barry Morris
Kay, Ulysses Simpson
Kino, Eusebio Francisco
Krutch, Joseph Wood
Lamy, Jean Baptiste
Lowell, Percival
Rehnquist, William Hubbs
Slipher, Vesto Melvin
Wright, Frank Lloyd

ARKANSAS

Adler, Cyrus
Cash, Johnny
Dean, Dizzy
De Soto, Hernando
Fulbright, J. William
Harvey, William Hope (Coin)
Hunt, Haroldson Lafayette
Johnson, John Harold
Joplin, Scott
MacArthur, Douglas
Pike, Albert
Read, Opie Percival
Stone, Edward Durell
Woodward, Comer Vann

CALIFORNIA

Adams, Ansel
Adams, Walter Sydney
Allen, Steve
Alvarez, Luis Walter
Anderson, Carl David

Anza, Juan Bautista de
Astaire, Fred
Austin, Mary
Baade, Walter
Bacharach, Burt
Baez, Joan
Ball, Lucille
Bancroft, Hubert Howe
Bara, Theda
Baum, Lyman Frank
Bayes, Nora
Beadle, George Wells
Beebe, Lucius Morris
Beery, Wallace
Belasco, David
Benny, Jack
Bergen, Edgar John
Berkeley, Busby
Berle, Milton
Bidwell, John
Bierce, Ambrose Gwinnett
Blanda, George Frederick
Bloch, Ernest
Bloch, Felix
Bogart, Humphrey DeForest
Bow, Clara
Brady, Alice
Brady, William Aloysius
Brando, Marlon
Brannan, Samuel
Bridges, Harry
Brubeck, David Warren
Budge, Don
Burbank, Luther
Burgess, Gelett
Burroughs, Edgar Rice
Bushman, Francis Xavier
Cage, John Milton, Jr.
Cagney, James
Calvin, Melvin
Campbell, William Wallace
Cantor, Eddie
Capra, Frank
Chamberlain, Owen
Chandler, Raymond Thornton
Chaney, Lon
Chaplin, Charles Spencer
Chavez, Cesar Estrada
Chessman, Caryl Whittier
Connolly, Maureen Catherine
Cooper, Gary
Corbett, James John
Cowell, Henry Dixon
Crabtree, Lotta
Crocker, Charles
Crosby, Bing
Davis, Bette
Davis, Sammy, Jr.
Dean, Man Mountain
De Forest, Lee
Delbrück, Max
DeMille, Cecil Blount
DiMaggio, Joseph Paul, Jr.
Disney, Walt
Doolittle, James Harold

Dressler, Marie
Duncan, Isadora
Durant, Will
Durante, Jimmy
Erikson, Erik Homburger
Erlanger, Joseph
Fairbanks, Douglas (1883–1939)
Fairbanks, Douglas, Jr. (1909–   )
Feynman, Richard Phillips
Field, Stephen Johnson
Fields, W. C.
Fisher, Harry Conway (Bud)
Fonda, Henry
Ford, John
Frémont, John Charles
Friml, Rudolf
Frost, Robert Lee
Gable, Clark
Garbo, Greta
Gardner, Erle Stanley
Gardner, John William
Garland, Judy
Geary, John White
Gell-Mann, Murray
George, Henry
Giannini, Amadeo Peter
Giauque, William Francis
Ginsberg, Allen
Gish, Lillian Diana and Dorothy
Glaser, Donald Arthur
Goldberg, Rube
Goldwyn, Samuel
Gonzales, Richard Alonzo (Pancho)
Grant, Cary
Griffith, D. W.
Grofé, Ferde
Haggin, James Ben Ali
Hale, George Ellery
Halleck, Henry Wager
Harlow, Jean
Harris, Roy Ellsworth
Hart, Moss
Hart, William Surrey
Harte, Bret
Hawks, Howard Winchester
Hayakawa, Samuel Ichiye
Hays, John Coffee (Jack)
Hearst, George
Hearst, William Randolph
Heifetz, Jascha
Heinlein, Robert Anson
Hepburn, Katharine
Hitchcock, Alfred Joseph
Hoffer, Eric
Hofstadter, Robert
Hoover, Herbert Clark
Hope, Bob
Hopper, Hedda
Howard, Sidney Coe
Hubble, Edwin Powell
Hughes, Howard Robard
Huntington, Collis Potter
Huntington, Henry Edwards
Huston, John
Huston, Walter

Hutchins, Robert Maynard
Jackson, Helen Hunt
Jeffers, Robinson
Jessel, George Albert
Johnson, Hiram Warren
Jordan, David Starr
Kaiser, Henry John
Karloff, Boris
Kármán, Theodore von
Kaye, Danny
Kazan, Elia
Kearny, Stephen Watts
Keaton, Buster
Kelly, Grace Patricia
Kelsen, Hans
Kino, Eusebio Francisco
Kornberg, Arthur
Koufax, Sanford (Sandy)
Kroeber, Alfred Louis
Kubrick, Stanley
Laemmle, Carl
Lahr, Bert
Lamb, Willis Eugene, Jr.
Lange, Dorothea
Lasky, Jesse Louis
Laurel, Stan, and Oliver Hardy
Lawrence, Ernest Orlando
Lederberg, Joshua
Lee, Gypsy Rose
Lewis, Gilbert Newton
Libby, Willard Frank
Lindsey, Benjamin Barr
Lloyd, Harold Clayton
Loesser, Frank Henry
London, Jack
Lowie, Robert Harry
Lugosi, Bela
McAdoo, William Gibbs
Mackay, Clarence Hungerford
McKenna, Joseph
McKuen, Rod Marvin
McMillan, Edwin Mattison
McPherson, Aimee Semple
Magnes, Judah Leon
Marcuse, Herbert
Markham, Edwin
Marshall, James Wilson
Martin, Glenn Luther
Marx, Groucho
Mather, Stephen Tyng
Mathias, Robert Bruce
Maxwell, Elsa
Mayer, Louis Burt
Mayer, Maria Goeppert
Mays, Willie Howard, Jr.
Meiggs, Henry
Menuhin, Yehudi
Miller, Henry Valentine
Millikan, Robert Andrews
Mix, Tom
Mizner, Addison
Monroe, Marilyn
Morgan, Thomas Hunt
Morse, Carlton Errol
Muir, John

Murieta, Joaquín
Murphy, Audie
Muybridge, Eadweard
Neutra, Richard Josef
Nichols, Mike
Nixon, Richard Milhous
Nizer, Louis
Noguchi, Isamu
Norris, Frank
Noyes, Arthur Amos
Odets, Clifford
Oppenheimer, J. Robert
Otis, Harrison Gray
Oxnam, Garfield Bromley
Parker, Dorothy
Parsons, Louella
Pattie, James Ohio
Patton, George Smith, Jr.
Pauling, Linus Carl
Perelman, Sidney Joseph
Pickford, Mary
Portolá, Gaspar de
Preminger, Otto Ludwig
Presley, Elvis Aron
Ripley, Robert LeRoy
Robinson, Bill (Bojangles)
Romanoff, Michael
Rosecrans, William Starke
Royce, Josiah
Rubinstein, Arthur
Russell, William Felton (Bill)
St. Denis, Ruth, and Ted Shawn
Salk, Jonas Edward
Saroyan, William
Schönberg, Arnold
Scott, James Brown
Scott, Walter Edward
Seaborg, Glenn Theodore
Segrè, Emilio Gino
Selznick, David Oliver
Sennett, Mack
Serra, Junípero
Shapiro, Karl Jay
Shaw, Robert Lawson
Shockley, William Bradford
Sinatra, Frank
Sinclair, Upton Beall
Skouras, Spyros Panagiotes
Sloat, John Drake
Smith, Francis Marion
Smith, Jedediah Strong
Spreckels, Claus
Stanford, Leland
Stanley, Wendell Meredith
Steffens, Lincoln
Steinbeck, John Ernst
Stern, Isaac
Stevenson, Adlai Ewing (1900–1965)
Still, William Grant
Stockton, Robert Field
Strauss, Levi
Streisand, Barbra
Stroheim, Erich von
Stroud, Robert
Struve, Otto

Sutro, Adolph Heinrich Joseph
Sutter, John Augustus
Tatum, Edward Lawrie
Taylor, Elizabeth
Taylor, William
Teller, Edward
Temple, Shirley
Terman, Lewis Madison
Tevis, Lloyd
Thalberg, Irving Grant
Tilden, William Tatem, Jr.
Tiomkin, Dimitri
Townes, Charles Hard
Townsend, Francis Everett
Tracy, Spencer
Valentino, Rudolph
Vallejo, Mariano Guadalupe
Walker, Joseph Reddeford
Wallis, Hal Brent
Warner Brothers
Warner, Glenn Scobey (Pop)
Warren, Earl
Watts, Alan Witson
Wayne, John
Weissmuller, Johnny
Welk, Lawrence
Welles, Orson
West, Mae
West, Nathanael
Weston, Edward
Whitney, Josiah Dwight
Wiggin, Kate Douglas
Wigmore, John Henry
Williams, Ted
Wills, Helen Newington
Wilson, Harry Leon
Wright, Harold Bell
Wynn, Ed
Zanuck, Darryl Francis

COLORADO

Bent, Charles
Bonfils, Frederick Gilmer
Chaney, Lon
Creel, George Edward
Dana, John Cotton
Dempsey, Jack
Evans, John
Fairbanks, Douglas (1883–1939)
Jackson, Helen Hunt
Lea, Homer
Libby, Willard Frank
Lindsey, Benjamin Barr
McParlan, James
Meeker, Nathan Cook
Parsons, Talcott
Ross, Harold Wallace
Tatum, Edward Lawrie
White, Byron Raymond
Whiteman, Paul

CONNECTICUT

Acheson, Dean Gooderham
Albers, Josef
Alcott, Amos Bronson

Allen, Ethan
Andrews, Charles McLean
Arnold, Benedict
Atwater, Wilbur Olin
Backus, Isaac
Baldwin, Henry
Barlow, Joel
Barnard, Henry
Barnum, Phineas Taylor
Bayley, Richard
Beach, Moses Yale
Beaumont, William
Beecher, Henry Ward
Beecher, Lyman
Beers, Clifford Whittingham
Bemis, Samuel Flagg
Benton, William
Bowles, Samuel (1797–1851)
Brace, Charles Loring
Brown, John
Buell, Abel
Burritt, Elihu
Bushnell, David
Bushnell, Horace
Camp, Walter Chauncey
Capp, Al
Church, Frederick Edwin
Clemens, Samuel Langhorne (Mark Twain)
Colt, Samuel
Comstock, Anthony
Cowles, Henry Chandler
Crandall, Prudence
Cutler, Manasseh
Dana, James Dwight
Deane, Silas
De Vinne, Theodore Low
Dow, Charles Henry
Dwight, Timothy
Earle, Ralph
Eaton, William
Edwards, Jonathan
Ellsworth, Henry Leavitt
Ellsworth, Oliver
Enders, John Franklin
Farrell, Eileen
Field, David Dudley
Field, Erastus Salisbury
Field, Stephen Johnson
Finney, Charles Grandison
Fisher, Irving
Fiske, John
Fitch, John
Foote, Andrew Hull
Fuller, Alfred Carl
Gallaudet, Thomas Hopkins
Gatling, Richard Jordan
Gesell, Arnold Lucius
Gibbs, Josiah Willard
Gilbert, Alfred Carlton
Gillette, William Hooker
Gilman, Daniel Coit
Goodhue, Bertram Grosvenor
Goodrich, Samuel Griswold
Goodyear, Charles

Graham, Sylvester
Grow, Galusha Aaron
Hadley, Arthur Twining
Hale, Nathan
Hall, Asaph
Harris, Louis
Harris, William Torrey
Harrison, Ross Granville
Heffelfinger, William Walter (Pudge)
Heifetz, Jascha
Hepburn, Katharine
Hersey, John Richard
Holbrook, Josiah
Holley, Alexander Lyman
Hooker, Thomas
Hopkins, Samuel
Howe, Elias
Hull, Isaac
Hull, William
Huntington, Collis Potter
Huntington, Ellsworth
Ives, Charles Edward
Ives, Frederic Eugene
Johnson, Philip Cortelyou
Johnson, William Samuel
Kendall, Edward Calvin
Korzybski, Alfred
Land, Edwin Herbert
Langer, Susanne
Lasswell, Harold Dwight
Leavenworth, Henry
Ledyard, John
Linton, Ralph
MacKaye, Benton
Marsh, Othniel Charles
Meigs, Josiah
Morgan, John Pierpont
Morse, Jedidiah
Moses, Robert
Murphy, Michael Charles
Nader, Ralph
Olmsted, Frederick Law
Onsager, Lars
Osborn, Henry Fairfield
Pinchot, Gifford
Platt, Orville Hitchcock
Pope, Albert Augustus
Powell, Adam Clayton, Jr.
Putnam, Israel
Reeve, Tapping
Remington, Eliphalet
Rogers, John (1648–1721)
Rogers, John (1829–1904)
Sapir, Edward
Seabury, Samuel
Sedgwick, Theodore
Sherman, Roger
Sigourney, Lydia Huntley
Sikorsky, Igor Ivan
Silliman, Benjamin (1779–1864)
Silliman, Benjamin, Jr. (1816–1885)
Smith, Nathan
Sparks, Jared
Spock, Benjamin McLane
Sprague, Frank Julian

Steichen, Edward
Stevens, Wallace
Stiles, Ezra
Stowe, Harriet Elizabeth Beecher
Strong, William
Sumner, William Graham
Terry, Alfred Howe
Terry, Eli
Thomas, Seth
Tiffany, Charles Lewis
Town, Ithiel
Trumbull, John (1750–1831)
Trumbull, John (1756–1843)
Trumbull, Jonathan (1710–1785)
Trumbull, Jonathan (1740–1809)
Tyler, Moses Coit
Waite, Morrison Remick
Walker, Amasa
Warner, Charles Dudley
Warren, Robert Penn
Webster, Noah
Welch, William Henry
Weld, Theodore Dwight
Welles, Gideon
Wells, David Ames
Wheelock, Eleazar
Whitney, Eli
Whitney, William Dwight
Wilcox, Ella Wheeler
Willard, Emma Hart
Williams, Edward Bennett
Winchester, Oliver Fisher
Wolcott, Oliver (1726–1797)
Wolcott, Oliver (1760–1833)
Wolcott, Roger
Woodward, Comer Vann
Woolsey, Theodore Dwight
Work, Henry Clay
Wright, Elizur
Yale, Linus
Yerkes, Robert Mearns

DELAWARE

Bayard, Thomas Francis
Campanius, John
Cannon, Annie Jump
Carothers, Wallace Hume
Clayton, John Middleton
Davies, Samuel
De La Warr, Thomas West, Baron
Dickinson, John
Du Pont, Samuel Francis
Du Pont de Nemours, Eleuthère
    Irénée
Evans, Oliver
Macdonough, Thomas
McKean, Thomas
Marquand, John Phillips
Minuit, Peter
Pyle, Howard
Read, George
Squibb, Edward Robinson

DISTRICT OF COLUMBIA

Abbe, Cleveland

Acheson, Dean Gooderham
Adams, Henry Brooks
Albee, Edward Franklin
Arnold, Thurman Wesley
Bailey, Gamaliel
Baird, Spencer Fullerton
Baugh, Samuel Adrian
Bell, Alexander Graham
Berliner, Emile
Billings, John Shaw
Blair, Francis Preston (1791–1876)
Block, Herbert Lawrence (Herblock)
Bowen, Norman Levi
Bulfinch, Charles
Colby, Frank Moore
Corcoran, William Wilson
Davis, Benjamin Oliver
Drew, Charles Richard
Dulles, John Foster
Eaton, Margaret O'Neale
Ellington, Duke
Force, Peter
Fortas, Abe
Franklin, John Hope
Frazier, E. Franklin
Gamow, George
Gannett, Henry
Gill, Theodore Nicholas
Gilliss, James Melville
Goldberger, Joseph
Greenhow, Rose O'Neal
Grosvenor, Gilbert Hovey
Hall, Asaph
Hastie, William Henry
Hay, John Milton
Hayes, Helen
Henry, Joseph
Hoban, James
Hollerith, Herman
Hoover, John Edgar
Howard, Oliver Otis
Hrdlička, Aleš
Hubbard, Gardiner Greene
Hyatt, Alpheus
Jameson, John Franklin
Johnson, Walter Perry
Just, Ernest Everett
Kelley, Oliver Hudson
Key, Francis Scott
Langley, Samuel Pierpont
Langston, John Mercer
Latrobe, Benjamin Henry
L'Enfant, Pierre Charles
Locke, Alain LeRoy
Lockwood, Belva Ann Bennett
McAuliffe, Anthony Clement
Meigs, Josiah
Mills, Robert
Nader, Ralph
Newcomb, Simon
Patterson, Eleanor Medill
Pearson, Drew
Pike, Albert
Powell, John Wesley
Putnam, Herbert

Reed, Walter
Royall, Anne Newport
Sheen, Fulton John
Sousa, John Philip
Southworth, Emma Dorothy Eliza
    Nevitte
Stanton, Edwin McMasters
Stoddert, Benjamin
Stone, Isidor Feinstein
Strong, William
Thornton, William
Walcott, Charles Doolittle
Walker, Robert John
Ward, Lester Frank
Watterson, Henry
Weaver, Robert Clifton
White, David
Wiley, Harvey Washington
Williams, Edward Bennett
Woodson, Carter Godwin

FLORIDA

Bethune, Mary McLeod
Cochran, Jacqueline
De Soto, Hernando
Fairchild, David Grandison
Flagler, Henry Morrison
Gadsden, James
Gorrie, John
Johnson, James Weldon
Lashley, Karl Spencer
Menéndez de Avilés, Pedro
Mizner, Addison
Osceola
Ponce de León, Juan
Randolph, Asa Philip
Ringling, Charles
Roberts, Glenn (Fireball)
Stilwell, Joseph Warren
Wylie, Philip Gordon
Yerkes, Robert Mearns

GEORGIA

Aaron, Henry Louis (Hank)
Abbott, Robert Sengstacke
Aiken, Conrad Potter
Baker, George (Father Divine)
Blalock, Alfred
Bond, Julian
Bozeman, John M.
Brown, James
Caldwell, Erskine
Campbell, John Archibald
Candler, Asa Griggs
Carter, James Earl
Cobb, Howell
Cobb, Tyrus Raymond (Ty)
Collier, John
Crawford, William Harris
Crisp, Charles Frederick
De Soto, Hernando
Dickey, James
Frémont, John Charles
Grady, Henry Woodfin
Gwinnett, Button

Harris, Joel Chandler
Hawkins, Benjamin
Hayes, Roland
Hope, John
Jones, Bobby
Kemble, Fanny
King, Martin Luther, Jr.
Lamar, Joseph Rucker
Lamar, Lucius Quintus Cincinnatus
Lamar, Mirabeau Buonaparte
Lanier, Sidney
Lee, Ivy Ledbetter
Long, Crawford Williamson
Longstreet, Augustus Bladwin
Low, Juliette Gordon
McAdoo, William Gibbs
McAllister, Ward
McCullers, Carson Smith
McDuffie, George
Meigs, Josiah
Mitchell, Margaret
Muhammad, Elijah
Oglethorpe, James Edward
Osceola
Robinson, Jack Roosevelt (Jackie)
Root, John Wellborn
Ross, John
Smith, Charles Henry (Bill Arp)
Smith, Hoke
Stephens, Alexander Hamilton
Toombs, Robert Augustus
Waddel, Moses
Watson, Thomas Edward
Wayne, Anthony
Wayne, James Moore
Wheeler, Joseph
White, Walter Francis
Yancey, William Lowndes
Yerby, Frank Garvin

HAWAII

Armstrong, Samuel Chapman
Dole, Sanford Ballard
Gulick, Luther Halsey
Jarves, James Jackson

IDAHO

Borah, William Edgar
Borglum, Gutzon
De Smet, Pierre Jean
Pound, Ezra Loomis
Sacagawea
Thompson, David

ILLINOIS

Abbott, Grace
Abbott, Robert Sengstacke
Adams, Franklin Pierce (F.P.A.)
Adams, Roger
Addams, Jane
Adler, Dankmar
Adler, Mortimer Jerome
Akeley, Carl Ethan
Albright, Ivan Le Lorraine
Alinsky, Saul David

Allouez, Claude Jean
Altgeld, John Peter
Anderson, Margaret
Anderson, Sherwood
Anson, Adrian Constantine (Cap)
Armour, Philip Danforth
Austin, Mary
Bandelier, Adolph Francis Alphonse
Bardeen, John
Barnard, Edward Emerson
Beecher, Edward
Bellow, Saul
Bendix, Vincent
Bennett, Edward Herbert
Benny, Jack
Bergen, Edgar John
Bettelheim, Bruno
Black, Greene Vardiman
Black Hawk
Blackmun, Harry Andrew
Blanda, George Frederick
Block, Herbert Lawrence (Herblock)
Bloomfield, Leonard
Borah, William Edgar
Bradbury, Ray Douglas
Breasted, James Henry
Brooks, Gwendolyn
Brundage, Avery
Bryan, William Jennings
Burnham, Daniel Hudson
Burroughs, Edgar Rice
Cabrini, Frances Xavier
Cannon, Joseph Gurney
Capone, Alphonse
Carnap, Rudolf
Cartwright, Peter
Chandler, Raymond Thornton
Chanute, Octave
Chase, Philander
Clark, George Rogers
Compton, Arthur Holly
Cowles, Henry Chandler
Cozzens, James Gould
Crothers, Rachel
Daley, Richard Joseph
Darrow, Clarence Seward
Davis, David
Davis, Miles Dewey, Jr.
Davisson, Clinton Joseph
Dawes, Charles Gates
Deere, John
De Forest, Lee
Dell, Floyd
Dewey, John
Dillinger, John
Dirksen, Everett McKinley
Disney, Walt
Doisy, Edward Adelbert
Dos Passos, John Roderigo
Douglas, Stephen Arnold
Dunham, Katherine
Dunne, Finley Peter (Mr. Dooley)
Duryea, Charles Edgar
Du Sable, Jean Baptiste Pointe
Du Vigneaud, Vincent

Earp, Wyatt
Ellsworth, Lincoln
Evans, John
Farrell, James Thomas
Fearing, Kenneth Flexner
Fermi, Enrico
Ferris, George Washington Gale
Field, Eugene
Field, Marshall
Fischer, Robert James
Fishbein, Morris
Fisher, Harry Conway (Bud)
Franklin, John Hope
Friedan, Betty Naomi Goldstein
Friedman, Milton
Fuller, Melville Weston
Garden, Mary
Garland, Hamlin
Gary, Elbert Henry
Gates, Frederick Taylor
Gates, John Warne
Glidden, Joseph Farwell
Goldberg, Arthur Joseph
Goodman, Benny
Goodnight, Charles
Goodspeed, Edgar Johnson
Gosden, Freeman Fisher and Charles
    J. Correll
Goudy, Frederic William
Gould, Chester
Grange, Harold Edward (Red)
Grant, Ulysses S.
Gray, Harold Lincoln
Gronlund, Laurence
Gropius, Walter Adolf
Gunther, John
Halas, George Stanley
Hale, George Ellery
Hall, James (1793–1868)
Hansen, Marcus Lee
Harlan, John Marshall (1899–1971)
Harper, William Rainey
Harvey, William Hope (Coin)
Hayakawa, Samuel Ichiye
Hecht, Ben
Hefner, Hugh Marston
Hemingway, Ernest Miller
Hennepin, Louis
Herskovits, Melville Jean
Hickok, James Butler (Wild Bill)
Hillman, Sidney
Hokinson, Helen
Holabird, William
Holley, Robert William
Hornsby, Rogers
Hough, Emerson
Hubbard, Elbert Green
Huggins, Charles Brenton
Hunt, Haroldson Lafayette
Huntington, Ellsworth
Hutchins, Robert Maynard
Ickes, Harold LeClair
Ingersoll, Robert Green
Insull, Samuel
Jackson, Jesse Louis

Jackson, Mahalia
Jenney, William Le Baron
Johnson, John Harold
Jolliet, Louis
Jones, Charles Jesse (Buffalo)
Judd, Charles Hubbard
Julian, Percy Lavon
Keokuk
King, Frank
Korzybski, Alfred
Laemmle, Carl
Landis, Kenesaw Mountain
Lardner, Ring
La Salle, Sieur de
Lasswell, Harold Dwight
Libby, Willard Frank
Lilienthal, David Eli
Lincoln, Abraham
Lindsay, Vachel
Livermore, Mary Ashton Rice
Lloyd, Henry Demarest
Logan, John Alexander
Lovejoy, Elijah Parish
Lowden, Frank Orren
McCormick, Cyrus Hall
McCormick, Robert Rutherford
McCoy, Joseph Geating
McCutcheon, John Tinney
McKay, Claude
MacLeish, Archibald
Marquette, Jacques
Marquis, Donald Robert Perry
Masters, Edgar Lee
Masterson, William Barclay (Bat)
Mather, Stephen Tyng
Mayer, Maria Goeppert
Mead, George Herbert
Medill, Joseph
Menard, Pierre
Michelson, Albert Abraham
Mies Van Der Rohe, Ludwig
Miller, Perry Gilbert Eddy
Millikan, Robert Andrews
Mitchell, Wesley Clair
Moholy-Nagy, László
Monroe, Harriet
Moody, Dwight Lyman
Moody, William Vaughn
Moore, Stanford
Moore, William Henry
Muhammad, Elijah
Mulliken, Robert Sanderson
Nagurski, Bronco
Neihardt, John Gneisenau
Nevins, Allan
Norris, Frank
Ogden, William Butler
Oldenburg, Claes Thure
Oliver, Joseph (King)
Owens, Jesse
Palmer, Potter
Park, Robert Ezra
Parker, Francis Wayland
Parrington, Vernon Louis
Parsons, Louella

Patterson, Eleanor Medill
Pearson, Drew
Perkins, George Walbridge
Perkins, Marlin
Pinkerton, Allan
Post, Charles William
Powell, John Wesley
Pullman, George Mortimer
Purcell, Edward Mills
Pyle, Charles C.
Rainey, Henry Thomas
Rand, Sally
Read, Opie Percival
Reagan, Ronald Wilson
Redfield, Robert
Rickover, Hyman George
Riesman, David, Jr.
Robinson, James Harvey
Root, John Wellborn
Rosenwald, Julius
Rossby, Carl-Gustaf Arvid
Sandburg, Carl
Schrieffer, John Robert
Sears, Richard Warren
Segar, Elzie Crisler
Selfridge, Harry Gordon
Sheen, Fulton John
Shirer, William Lawrence
Simpson, George Gaylord
Smith, Joseph
Spalding, Albert
Spalding, Albert Goodwill
Stagg, Amos Alonzo
Stevens, John Paul
Stevenson, Adlai Ewing (1835–
    1914)
Stevenson, Adlai Ewing (1900–
    1965)
Stone, Melville Elijah
Stratton, Samuel Wesley
Strong, Josiah
Struve, Otto
Sullivan, Louis Henri
Sunday, William Ashley (Billy)
Swift, Gustavus Franklin
Szilard, Leo
Taft, Lorado Zadoc
Taylor, Bert Leston (B.L.T.)
Teller, Edward
Thomas, Theodore
Tillstrom, Burr
Tonty, Henri de
Townsend, Francis Everett
Tugwell, Rexford Guy
Urey, Harold Clayton
Van Depoele, Charles Joseph
Van Doren, Carl Clinton
Van Doren, Mark
Veblen, Thorstein Bunde
Veeck, William Louis, Jr.
Vincent, John Heyl
Walgreen, Charles Rudolph
Wallis, Hal Brent
Ward, Lester Frank
Ward, Montgomery

Watson, James Dewey
Wells, Ida Bell
Weston, Edward
Weyerhaeuser, Frederick
Wigmore, John Henry
Willard, Frances Elizabeth Caroline
Williams, Daniel Hale
Wilson, Harry Leon
Wood, Robert Elkington
Work, Henry Clay
Wright, Frank Lloyd
Wright, Richard
Wrigley, William, Jr.
Yerkes, Charles Tyson
Young, Murat Bernard (Chic)
Ziegfeld, Florenz

INDIANA

Adams, Andy
Ade, George
Allport, Gordon Willard
Anderson, Margaret
Armstrong, John (1755–1816)
Badin, Stephen Theodore
Bass, Sam
Beard, Charles Austin
Beveridge, Albert Jeremiah
Billings, John Shaw
Burnside, Ambrose Everett
Carmichael, Hoagy
Chapman, John (Johnny Appleseed)
Coffin, Levi
Colfax, Schuyler
Davis, Elmer Holmes
Debs, Eugene Victor
Dillinger, John
Douglas, Lloyd Cassel
Dreiser, Theodore
Eads, James Buchanan
Eggleston, Edward
Evans, John
Ewry, Ray C.
Fairbanks, Charles Warren
Gary, Elbert Henry
Harrison, Benjamin
Harrison, William Henry
Hawks, Howard Winchester
Hay, John Milton
Hendricks, Thomas Andrews
Hoffa, James Riddle
Howe, Edgar Watson
Hubbard, Frank McKinney (Kin)
Jordan, David Starr
Kerr, Michael Crawford
Kinsey, Alfred Charles
Lane, James Henry
Lynd, Robert Staughton
McCutcheon, John Tinney
Marshall, Thomas Riley
Menard, Pierre
Miller, Joaquin
Minton, Sherman
Moody, William Vaughn
Mooney, James
Morton, Oliver Perry

Muller, Hermann Joseph
Nathan, George Jean
Owen, Robert Dale
Porter, Cole
Porter, Gene Stratton
Pyle, Ernest Taylor
Riley, James Whitcomb
Rockne, Knute Kenneth
Rogers, Bruce
Samuelson, Paul Anthony
Slipher, Vesto Melvin
Smith, David
Smith, Walter Bedell
Sorin, Edward Frederick
Spooner, John Coit
Stanley, Wendell Meredith
Studebaker, Clement
Stutz, Harry Clayton
Tarkington, Booth
Tecumseh
Terman, Lewis Madison
Urey, Harold Clayton
Van Devanter, Willis
Vonnegut, Kurt, Jr.
Walker, Sarah Breedlove
Wallace, Lewis
Wiley, Harvey Washington
Willkie, Wendell Lewis
Wright Brothers
Wright, Frances

IOWA

Allison, William Boyd
Anson, Adrian Constantine (Cap)
Becker, Carl Lotus
Beiderbecke, Leon Bismarck (Bix)
Borlaug, Norman Ernest
Carothers, Wallace Hume
Catt, Carrie Chapman
Cody, William Frederick (Buffalo Bill)
Coffin, Lorenzo S.
Cowles, Gardner
Cummins, Albert Baird
De Forest, Lee
Dodge, Grenville Mellen
Feller, Robert William Andrew
Friedman, Esther Pauline, and Pauline Esther
Gallup, George Horace
Henderson, David Bremner
Hoover, Herbert Clark
Hopkins, Harry Lloyd
Hough, Emerson
Hunsaker, Jerome Clarke
Keokuk
Leahy, William Daniel
Leopold, Aldo
Lewis, John Llewellyn
Martin, Glenn Luther
Maxwell, Elsa
Metz, Christian
Miller, Glenn
Miller, Samuel Freeman
Palmer, Daniel David

Ringling, Charles
Russell, Lillian
Sunday, William Ashley (Billy)
Van Allen, James Alfred
Veblen, Oswald
Wallace, Henry Agard
Wayne, John
Weaver, James Baird
Welch, Joseph Nye
Wood, Grant

KANSAS

Benton, Thomas Hart (1889–)
Brewer, David Josiah
Brooks, Gwendolyn
Browder, Earl Russell
Brown, John
Chaffee, Adna Romanza (1884–1941)
Chisholm, Jesse
Chrysler, Walter Percy
Coronado, Francisco Vásquez de
Curtis, Charles
Dalton, Robert
Earhart, Amelia Mary
Earp, Wyatt
Eisenhower, Dwight David
Fisher, Dorothy Canfield
Geary, John White
Haldeman-Julius, Emanuel
Harvey, Frederick Henry
Hickok, James Butler (Wild Bill)
Howe, Edgar Watson
Johnson, Hugh Samuel
Johnson, Walter Perry
Keaton, Buster
Kelly, Emmett
Landon, Alfred Mossman
Lane, James Henry
Lease, Mary Elizabeth Clyens
Leavenworth, Henry
McCoy, Joseph Geating
Masters, Edgar Lee
Masterson, William Barclay (Bat)
Menninger, Karl Augustus
Naismith, James
Parker, Charlie (Bird)
Quantrill, William Clarke
Runyon, Damon
Simpson, Jeremiah (Sockless Jerry)
Still, Andrew Taylor
Stroud, Robert
Sutherland, Earl Wilbur, Jr.
White, William Allen
Whittaker, Charles Evans
Wright, Henry (1878–1936)

KENTUCKY

Ali, Muhammad (Cassius Clay)
Applegate, Jesse
Atchison, David Rice
Audubon, John James
Badin, Stephen Theodore
Barkley, Alben William
Bean, Roy
Birney, James Gillespie

Chase, Samuel
Corcoran, William Wilson
Cushing, Harvey Williams
Davis, David
Decatur, Stephen
Dickinson, John
Douglass, Frederick
Dulany, Daniel
Duvall, Gabriel
Foxx, James Emory (Jimmy)
Frazier, E. Franklin
Galloway, Joseph
Gibbons, James
Gildersleeve, Basil Lanneau
Gilman, Daniel Coit
Gist, Christopher
Hall, Granville Stanley
Halsted, William Stewart
Hamilton, Edith
Hammett, Dashiell
Hanson, John
Harper, Robert Goodloe
Harris, Chapin Aaron
Harrison, Ross Granville
Hiss, Alger
Holiday, Billie
Hussey, Obed
Johnson, Reverdy
Johnson, Thomas
Johnson, Walter Perry
Key, Francis Scott
Kornberg, Arthur
Lake, Simon
Lanier, Sidney
Lovejoy, Arthur Oncken
McGraw, John Joseph
Machen, John Gresham
Marshall, Thurgood
Martin, Glenn Luther
Martin, Luther
Mason, Charles, and Jeremiah Dixon
Mencken, Henry Louis
Mergenthaler, Ottmar
Murray, John Courtney
Niles, Hezekiah
Nirenberg, Marshall Warren
Osler, Sir William
Peabody, George
Peale, Charles Willson
Pearl, Raymond
Pinkney, William
Post, Emily Price
Read, George
Remsen, Ira
Rodgers, John (1773–1838)
Rodgers, John (1812–1882)
Rous, Peyton
Rowland, Henry Augustus
Royall, Anne Newport
Rumsey, James
Ruth, George Herman (Babe)
Schmucker, Samuel Simon
Semmes, Raphael
Seton, Elizabeth Ann Bayley
Shapiro, Karl Jay

Shelby, Isaac
Sinclair, Upton Beall
Sparks, Jared
Spruance, Raymond Ames
Stoddert, Benjamin
Stone, Barton Warren
Surratt, Mary Eugenia Jenkins
Taney, Roger Brooke
Thomas, Martha Carey
Tubman, Harriet
Unitas, John
Uris, Leon Marcus
Watson, John Broadus
Weems, Mason Locke
Welch, William Henry
Wilkinson, James
Windsor, Wallis Warfield, Duchess of
Wirt, William
Woodward, Comer Vann

MASSACHUSETTS

Abbot, Francis Ellingwood
Abbott, Lyman
Adams, Abigail
Adams, Brooks
Adams, Charles Francis
Adams, Charles Francis, Jr.
Adams, Henry Brooks
Adams, Herbert Baxter
Adams, John
Adams, John Quincy
Adams, Roger
Adams, Samuel
Adams, William Taylor (Oliver Optic)
Agassiz, Alexander
Agassiz, Louis
Aiken, Conrad Potter
Alcott, Amos Bronson
Alcott, Louisa May
Alden, John
Aldrich, Thomas Bailey
Alger, Cyrus
Alger, Horatio
Allen, Fred
Allen, Frederick Lewis
Allport, Gordon Willard
Allston, Washington
Ames, Fisher
Ames, Oakes
Andrew, John Albion
Andrews, Stephen Pearl
Andros, Sir Edmund
Anthony, Susan Brownell
Antin, Mary
Arrow, Kenneth Joseph
Asimov, Isaac
Atkinson, Brooks
Attucks, Crispus
Ayer, Francis Wayland
Babbitt, Irving
Babbitt, Isaac
Babson, Roger Ward
Backus, Isaac
Bailey, F. Lee
Baker, George

Baker, George Pierce
Balch, Emily Greene
Baldwin, Loammi (1745–1807)
Baldwin, Loammi (1780–1838)
Ballou, Adin
Ballou, Hosea
Bancroft, Edward
Bancroft, George
Banks, Nathaniel Prentiss
Barnard, Frederick Augustus Porter
Barron, Clarence Walker
Bartlett, John (1820–1905)
Barton, Clara
Baskin, Leonard
Bates, Katharine Lee
Beach, Alfred Ely
Beach, Moses Sperry
Beebe, Lucius Morris
Beecher, Edward
Beecher, Lyman
Békésy, Georg von
Belcher, Jonathan
Bell, Alexander Graham
Bellamy, Edward
Bemis, Samuel Flagg
Benchley, Robert Charles
Benjamin, Asher
Berenson, Bernard
Berle, Adolf Augustus
Bernstein, Leonard
Bigelow, Erastus Brigham
Bigelow, Jacob
Billings, William
Birkhoff, George David
Blanchard, Thomas
Bloch, Konrad
Bond, George Phillips
Bond, William Cranch
Borden, Lizzie Andrew
Boring, Edwin Garrigues
Boutwell, George Sewall
Bowditch, Nathaniel
Bowdoin, James
Bowker, Richard Rogers
Bowles, Samuel (1797–1851)
Bowles, Samuel, II (1826–1878)
Boyden, Seth
Boyden, Uriah Atherton
Boylston, Zabdiel
Bradford, William
Bradley, Milton
Bradstreet, Anne
Brandeis, Louis Dembitz
Brattle, Thomas
Brewster, William
Bridgman, Laura Dewey
Bridgman, Percy Williams
Brooks, Phillips
Brown, Henry Billings
Brownson, Orestes Augustus
Bryant, William Cullen
Bulfinch, Charles
Bulfinch, Thomas
Bulkeley, Peter
Burbank, Luther

Burgess, Gelett
Burlingame, Anson
Burt, William Austin
Burton, Harold Hitz
Bush, George Herbert Walker
Bush, Vannevar
Butler, Benjamin Franklin
Cable, George Washington
Cannon, Annie Jump
Cannon, Walter Bradford
Carty, John Joseph
Carver, Jonathan
Chafee, Zechariah
Chandler, Charles Frederick
Channing, Edward
Channing, William Ellery
Chapman, John (Johnny Appleseed)
Chauncy, Charles
Child, Francis James
Child, Lydia Marie
Choate, Joseph Hodges
Choate, Rufus
Chomsky, Noam
Church, Benjamin
Ciardi, John Anthony
Clark, Alvan
Clarke, James Freeman
Cohn, Edwin Joseph
Conant, James Bryant
Conwell, Russell Herman
Coolidge, Calvin
Copley, John Singleton
Cotton, John
Cousy, Robert Joseph
Cram, Ralph Adams
Cummings, Edward Estlin
Curley, James Michael
Currier, Nathaniel
Curtis, Benjamin Robbins
Curtis, George Ticknor
Cushing, Caleb
Cushing, Harvey Williams
Cushing, William
Cushman, Charlotte Saunders
Cutler, Manasseh
Dana, Richard Henry
Davis, Bette
Davis, William Morris
Dawes, Henry Laurens
Day, Benjamin Henry
Dearborn, Henry
DeMille, Cecil Blount
Dennie, Joseph
Dickinson, Emily Elizabeth
Dix, Dorothea Lynde
Dodge, Grenville Mellen
Du Bois, William Edward Burghardt
Dudley, Thomas
Dunster, Henry
Durant, Thomas Clark
Durant, Will
Durant, William Crapo
Durocher, Leo Ernest
Duryea, Charles Edgar
Dwight, John Sullivan

Dwight, Timothy
Dyer, Mary
Earle, Ralph
Eaton, William
Eddy, Mary Morse Baker
Edwards, Jonathan
Eliot, Charles William
Eliot, John
Emerson, Ralph Waldo
Endecott, John
Enders, John Franklin
Erikson, Erik Homburger
Evarts, William Maxwell
Everett, Edward
Farmer, Fannie Merritt
Farmer, Moses Gerrish
Fenollosa, Ernest Francisco
Fessenden, Reginald Aubrey
Fewkes, Jesse Walter
Fiedler, Arthur
Field, Cyrus West
Field, Erastus Salisbury
Field, Marshall
Filene, Edward Albert
Fiske, John
Fitz, Reginald Heber
Flint, Austin
Flint, Timothy
Foster, William Zebulon
Fox, Gustavus Vasa
Foxx, James Emory (Jimmy)
Frankfurter, Felix
Franklin, Benjamin
Freeman, Mary Eleanor Wilkins
Frothingham, Octavius Brooks
Fuller, Buckminster
Fuller, Margaret, Marchioness Ossoli
Galbraith, John Kenneth
Garand, John Cantius
Gardner, Erle Stanley
Gardner, Isabella Stewart
Garrison, William Lloyd
Geisel, Theodor Seuss (Dr. Seuss)
Gerry, Elbridge
Gibbs, Oliver Wolcott
Gibson, Charles Dana
Gilbert, Henry Franklin Belknap
Gillett, Frederick Huntington
Gilmore, Patrick Sarsfield
Glidden, Charles Jasper
Glueck, Sheldon
Goddard, Robert Hutchings
Goodhue, Bertram Grosvenor
Goodrich, Samuel Griswold
Gorham, Nathaniel
Gosnold, Bartholomew
Graupner, Gottlieb
Gray, Asa
Gray, Horace
Greely, Adolphus Washington
Green, Hetty
Greenough, Horatio
Grew, Joseph Clark
Gropius, Walter Adolf
Gulick, Luther Halsey

Hale, Edward Everett
Hale, Lucretia Peabody
Hall, Granville Stanley
Hall, James (1811–1898)
Hancock, John
Handlin, Oscar
Hansen, Alvin Harvey
Harding, Chester
Harris, Benjamin
Hart, Albert Bushnell
Harvard, John
Hassam, Childe
Hawthorne, Nathaniel
Hayden, Ferdinand Vandeveer
Hayes, Roland
Higginson, Thomas Wentworth
   Storrow
Hoar, Ebenezer Rockwood
Hoar, George Frisbie
Hoar, Samuel
Hocking, William Ernest
Holbrook, Josiah
Holland, Josiah Gilbert
Holmes, Oliver Wendell (1809–1894)
Holmes, Oliver Wendell (1841–1935)
Homer, Winslow
Hooker, Joseph
Hooker, Thomas
Hooton, Earnest Albert
Hopkins, Mark
Hopkins, Samuel
Howe, Elias
Howe, Julia Ward
Howe, Samuel Gridley
Howells, William Dean
Hubbard, Gardiner Greene
Hudson, Manley Ottmer
Hull, William
Hunsaker, Jerome Clarke
Hunt, William Morris
Hutchinson, Anne
Hutchinson, Thomas
Hyatt, Alpheus
Jackson, Charles Thomas
Jackson, Helen Hunt
James, Henry (1811–1882)
James, Henry (1843–1916)
James, William
Jameson, John Franklin
Jarves, James Jackson
Jeffries, John
Jenney, William Le Baron
Johnson, Howard Deering
Judson, Adoniram
Kelley, Oliver Hudson
Kemble, Fanny
Kendall, Amos
Kennedy, Edward Moore
Kennedy, John Fitzgerald
Kennedy, Robert Francis
Kerouac, Jack
Khorana, Har Gobind
King, Rufus
Kissinger, Henry Alfred
Kittredge, George Lyman

Knox, Henry
Koussevitsky, Serge
Kuznets, Simon
Land, Edwin Herbert
Langdell, Christopher Columbus
Langer, William Leonard
Langley, Samuel Pierpont
Lashley, Karl Spencer
Lawrence, Abbot
Lawrence, Amos Adams
Leontief, Wassily
Levine, Jack
Lewis, Gilbert Newton
Lincoln, Benjamin
Lindgren, Waldemar
Lipmann, Fritz Albert
Lipset, Seymour Martin
Livermore, Mary Ashton Rice
Lodge, Henry Cabot (1850–1924)
Lodge, Henry Cabot (1902–   )
Longfellow, Henry Wadsworth
Lowell, Abbott Lawrence
Lowell, Amy
Lowell, Francis Cabot
Lowell, James Russell
Lowell, Percival
Lowell, Robert Traill Spence, Jr.
Luria, Salvador Edward
Luther, Seth
Lyon, Mary Mason
MacArthur, Arthur
McCormack, John William
McDougall, William
McIntire, Samuel
Mack, Connie
McKay, Donald
McKim, Charles Follen
MacLeish, Archibald
Mann, Horace
March, Francis Andrew
Marciano, Rocky
Marcuse, Herbert
Marcy, William Learned
Marquand, John Phillips
Martin, Joseph William, Jr.
Mason, Lowell
Massasoit
Mather, Cotton
Mather, Increase
Mather, Richard
Matzeliger, Jan Ernst
Mayer, Louis Burt
Mayhew, Jonathan
Mead, George Herbert
Meiklejohn, Alexander
Melville, Herman
Merriam, Charles
Miles, Nelson Appleton
Miller, Perry Gilbert Eddy
Miller, William
Minot, George Richards
Mitchell, Maria
Moody, Dwight Lyman
Moody, William Henry
Morison, Samuel Eliot
Morse, Samuel Finley Breese

Morton, Thomas
Morton, William Thomas Green
Motley, John Lothrop
Mott, Lucretia Coffin
Mulliken, Robert Sanderson
Münsterberg, Hugo
Murphy, Michael Charles
Murphy, William Parry
Naismith, James
Norton, Charles Eliot
Noyes, Arthur Amos
Olney, Richard
O'Neill, Thomas Philip, Jr.
O'Reilly, John Boyle
Otis, James
Paine, Robert Treat (1731–1814)
Paine, Robert Treat (1773–1811)
Palmer, Alice Elvira Freeman
Palmer, George Herbert
Parker, Francis Wayland
Parker, John
Parker, Theodore
Parkman, Francis
Parsons, Talcott
Parsons, Theophilus (1750–1813)
Parsons, Theophilus (1797–1882)
Parton, James
Peabody, Elizabeth Palmer
Peabody, George
Peirce, Benjamin
Peirce, Charles Sanders
Pepperrell, Sir William
Perkins, Frances
Philip
Phillips, Wendell
Phips, Sir William
Pickering, Edward Charles
Pickering, Timothy
Pike, Albert
Pinkham, Lydia Estes
Piston, Walter Hamor
Poe, Edgar Allan
Pope, Albert Augustus
Porter, David
Pound, Roscoe
Prescott, Samuel
Prescott, William
Prescott, William Hickling
Purcell, Edward Mills
Putnam, Herbert
Putnam, Israel
Putnam, Rufus
Quincy, Josiah
Quine, Willard Van Orman
Revere, Paul
Rhodes, James Ford
Richards, Ivor Armstrong
Richards, Theodore William
Richardson, Henry Hobson
Riesman, David, Jr.
Rimmer, William
Ripley, George
Robbins, Frederick Chapman
Rogers, Bruce
Rogers, John (1829–1904)
Rogers, Robert

Rossby, Carl-Gustaf Arvid
Rowson, Susanna Haswell
Royce, Josiah
Rugg, Harold Ordway
Russell, William Felton (Bill)
Ryder, Albert Pinkham
Sacco, Nicola, and Bartolomeo
   Vanzetti
St. Denis, Ruth, and Ted Shawn
Samoset
Samuelson, Paul Anthony
Santayana, George
Sargent, John Singer
Sarton, George Alfred Leon
Schlesinger, Arthur Meier (1888–
   1965)
Schlesinger, Arthur Meier, Jr.
   (1917–   )
Schumpeter, Joseph Alois
Schwinger, Julian Seymore
Sears, Isaac
Sedgwick, Theodore
Sewall, Samuel
Shapley, Harlow
Shaw, Henry Wheeler
Shaw, Lemuel
Shays, Daniel
Sherman, Roger
Shirley, William
Sibley, Hiram
Simpson, George Gaylord
Skinner, Burrhus Frederic
Skinner, Otis
Smibert, John
Smith, Nathan
Smith, Samuel Francis
Sorokin, Pitirim Alexandrovitch
Spahn, Warren Edward
Sparks, Jared
Spellman, Francis Joseph
Squanto
Standish, Miles
Stella, Frank Philip
Stoddard, Solomon
Stone, Lucy
Story, Joseph
Stratton, Samuel Wesley
Stuart, Gilbert Charles
Sullivan, John Lawrence (1858–1918)
Sullivan, Louis Henry
Sumner, Charles
Sumner, James Batcheller
Swift, Gustavus Franklin
Szent-Györgyi, Albert
Tappan, Arthur
Taylor, Bert Leston (B.L.T.)
Taylor, Edward
Taylor, Edward Thompson
Terzaghi, Karl
Thayer, Sylvanus
Thomas, Isaiah
Thompson, Benjamin, Count
   Rumford
Thompson, James Walter
Thomson, Elihu
Thoreau, Henry David

Thorfinn, Karlsefni
Thorndike, Edward Lee
Thorpe, Thomas Bangs
Thwaites, Reuben Gold
Ticknor, George
Tillich, Paul Johannes
Townes, Charles Hard
Train, George Francis
Tucker, Benjamin Ricketson
Turner, Frederick Jackson
Tyler, Royall
Underhill, John
Vail, Theodore Newton
Van Depoele, Charles Joseph
Varnum, Joseph Bradley
Very, Jones
Vonnegut, Kurt, Jr.
Wade, Benjamin Franklin
Wald, George
Walker, Amasa
Walker, David
Walker, Francis Amasa
Ward, Nathaniel
Warner, Charles Dudley
Warren, John (1753–1815)
Warren, John Collins (1778–1856)
Warren, Joseph
Warren, Mercy Otis
Waterhouse, Benjamin
Watson, Elkanah
Watson, James Dewey
Watson, Thomas Augustus
Webster, Daniel
Webster, Noah
Welch, Joseph Nye
Welch, Robert H. W., Jr.
Weller, Thomas Huckle
Wells, David Ames
Wells, Horace
Wheatley, Phillis
Whistler, James Abbot McNeill
Whitehead, Alfred North
Whitney, Asa
Whitney, Eli
Whitney, Josiah Dwight
Whitney, William Collins
Whitney, William Dwight
Whittier, John Greenleaf
Wiener, Norbert
Wigglesworth, Michael
Wilder, Burt Green
Williams, Roger
Williams, Ted
Wilson, Henry
Wilson, Samuel
Winchester, Oliver Fisher
Winslow, Edward
Winslow, Josiah
Winsor, Justin
Winthrop, John (1588–1649)
Winthrop, John (1714–1779)
Winthrop, Robert Charles
Wise, John
Woodberry, George Edward
Woodward, Robert Burns
Worcester, Joseph Emerson

Wright, Carroll Davidson
Wright, Chauncey
Wright, Elizur
Wright, Henry (Harry, 1835–1895)
Wyeth, Newell Convers
Wylie, Philip Gordon
Yale, Linus
Zinsser, Hans

MICHIGAN

Allouez, Claude Jean
Angell, James Burrill
Bagley, William Chandler
Bailey, Liberty Hyde
Baker, Ray Stannard (David Grayson)
Birkhoff, George David
Brown, Henry Billings
Brown, Olympia
Brundage, Avery
Bunche, Ralph Johnson
Burt, William Austin
Cadillac, Antoine Laumet de la Mothe
Cass, Lewis
Catton, Bruce
Chessman, Caryl Whittier
Chrysler, Walter Percy
Cobb, Tyrus Raymond (Ty)
Coffin, Howard Earle
Cooley, Charles Horton
Cooley, Thomas McIntyre
Corwin, Edward Samuel
Coughlin, Charles Edward
Couzens, James
Dewey, Thomas Edmund
Dow, Herbert Henry
Durant, William Crapo
Fairchild, David Grandison
Ferber, Edna
Flaherty, Robert Joseph
Ford, Gerald Rudolph, Jr.
Ford, Henry (1863–1947)
Geddes, Norman Bel
Glaser, Donald Arthur
Guest, Edgar Albert
Hershey, Alfred Day
Hoffa, James Riddle
Ingersoll, Robert Hawley
Joy, James Frederick
Kellogg, Will Keith
Kettering, Charles Franklin
Krehbiel, Henry Edward
Lardner, Ring
La Salle, Sieur de
Lindbergh, Charles Augustus
Louis, Joe
Marquette, Jacques
Murphy, Frank
Olds, Ransom Eli
Pitkin, Walter Boughton
Post, Charles William
Reuther, Walter Philip
Robinson, Ray (Sugar Ray)
Roethke, Theodore
Saarinen, Eero
Saarinen, Eliel
Schoolcraft, Henry Rowe

Scripps, James Edmund
Seaborg, Glenn Theodore
Shafter, William Rufus
Stewart, Potter
Strang, James Jesse
Trevellick, Richard F.
Vandenberg, Arthur Hendrick
Weller, Thomas Huckle
Wilson, Charles Erwin
Yamasaki, Minoru

MINNESOTA

Benton, William
Blackmun, Harry Andrew
Burger, Warren Earl
Butler, Pierce
Calvin, Melvin
Donnelly, Ignatius
Douglas, William Orville
Dylan, Bob
Fitzgerald, F. Scott
Fraser, James Earle
Garland, Judy
Getty, Jean Paul
Graham, Billy
Hansen, Alvin Harvey
Heffelfinger, William Walter (Pudge)
Hench, Philip Showalter
Hennepin, Louis
Hill, James Jerome
Humphrey, Hubert Horatio
Ireland, John
Kelley, Oliver Hudson
Kellogg, Frank Billings
Kendall, Edward Calvin
Langford, Nathaniel Pitt
Lewis, Sinclair
Lowden, Frank Orren
McCarthy, Eugene Joseph
Martin, Homer Dodge
Mayo, William James, and Charles
    Horace Mayo
Mondale, Walter Frederick
Nagurski, Bronco
Pegler, Westbrook
Perrot, Nicolas
Piccard, Jean Félix
Pillsbury, Charles Alfred
Putnam, Herbert
Rölvaag, Ole Edvart
Schulz, Charles Monroe
Sears, Richard Warren
Stassen, Harold Edward
Tate, Allen
Thompson, David
Wallace, De Witt
Weyerhaeuser, Frederick
Whipple, Henry Benjamin

MISSISSIPPI

Bienville, Jean Baptiste Le Moyne,
    Sieur de
Bilbo, Theodore Gilmore
Bodenheim, Maxwell
Bruce, Blanche Kelso
Davis, Jefferson

De Soto, Hernando
Evers, Charles
Faulkner, William Cuthbert
Iberville, Pierre Le Moyne, Sieur d'
Ingraham, Joseph Holt
Ingraham, Prentiss
Lamar, Lucius Quintus Cincinnatus
Lomax, John Avery
Longstreet, Augustus Baldwin
Meredith, James Howard
Presley, Elvis Aaron
Price, Leontyne
Revels, Hiram Rhoades
Still, William Grant
Walker, Robert John
Wells, Ida Bell
Welty, Eudora
Williams, Tennessee
Wright, Richard

MISSOURI

Ashley, William Henry
Atchison, David Rice
Bacharach, Burt
Baker, Josephine
Bates, Edward
Beery, Wallace
Benton, Thomas Hart (1782–1858)
Benton, Thomas Hart (1889–   )
Berra, Lawrence Peter (Yogi)
Berry, Charles Edward Anderson
    (Chuck)
Bingham, George Caleb
Blair, Francis Preston, Jr. (1821–1875)
Blair, Montgomery
Bonfils, Frederick Gilmer
Bradley, Omar Nelson
Brookings, Robert Somers
Brown, Benjamin Gratz
Burk, Martha Jane (Calamity Jane)
Burroughs, William Seward (1855–
    1898)
Burroughs, William Seward
    (1914–   )
Busch, Adolphus
Carnegie, Dale
Carver, George Washington
Chopin, Kate O'Flaherty
Chouteau, Pierre (1789–1865)
Chouteau, René Auguste (1749–1829)
Clark, Champ
Clark, William
Clemens, Samuel Langhorne (Mark
    Twain)
Compton, Arthur Holly
Cori, Carl Ferdinand
Creel, George Edward
Cronkite, Walter Leland, Jr.
Dalton, Robert
Dean, Dizzy
Doisy, Edward Adelbert
Dooley, Thomas Anthony
Durocher, Leo Ernest
Eads, James Buchanan
Eames, Charles
Eliot, Thomas Stearns

Erlanger, Joseph
Evans, Walker
Field, Eugene
Fishbein, Morris
Frank, Glenn
Fulbright, J. William
Gasser, Herbert Spencer
Glass, Hugh
Hall, Joyce Clyde
Harlow, Jean
Harris, William Torrey
Hatch, William Henry
Hearst, George
Heinlein, Robert Anson
Henry, Andrew
Hershey, Alfred Day
Holladay, Ben
Hornsby, Rogers
Hubble, Edwin Powell
Hudson, Manley Ottmer
Hughes, Langston
Huston, John
James, Jesse Woodson
Joplin, Scott
Kornberg, Arthur
Laclède, Pierre
Laws, Samuel Spahr
Lear, William Powell
Lewis, Meriwether
Lisa, Manuel
Macfadden, Bernarr
Mauldin, William Henry (Bill)
Merrick, David
Moore, Marianne Craig
More, Paul Elmer
Musial, Stanley Frank
Nation, Carry Amelia Moore
Neihardt, John Gneisenau
Nicollet, Joseph Nicolas
Niebuhr, Reinhold
Penney, James Cash
Perkins, Marlin
Pershing, John Joseph
Pulitzer, Joseph
Rand, Sally
Rickard, George Lewis (Tex)
Rickey, Branch Wesley
Ross, Nellie Tayloe
St. Vrain, Ceran de Hault de
    Lassus de
Schurz, Carl
Shapley, Harlow
Stengel, Charles Dillon (Casey)
Still, Andrew Taylor
Swope, Gerard
Swope, Herbert Bayard
Teasdale, Sara
Thomson, Virgil Garnett
Truman, Harry S.
Veeck, William Louis, Jr.
Walther, Carl Ferdinand Wilhelm
Wiener, Norbert
Wilkins, Roy
Wood, Robert Elkington
Wright, Henry (1878–1936)
Younger, Cole

MONTANA

Bozeman, John M.
Cooper, Gary
Crazy Horse
Custer, George Armstrong
Daly, Marcus
De Smet, Pierre Jean
Gall
Langford, Nathaniel Pitt
Rankin, Jeannette
Sacagawea
Sitting Bull
Thompson, David
Walsh, Thomas James
Washakie

NEBRASKA

Abbott, Grace
Astaire, Fred
Beadle, George Wells
Brando, Marlon
Bryan, William Jennings
Cather, Willa Sibert
Eiseley, Loren Corey
Flanagan, Edward Joseph
Fonda, Henry
Ford, Gerald Rudolph, Jr.
Gorgeous George
Hall, Joyce Clyde
Hanson, Howard Harold
Johnson, Alvin Saunders
Lloyd, Harold Clayton
Malcolm X
Morton, Julius Sterling
Neihardt, John Gneisenau
Norris, George William
North, Frank Joshua
Pound, Roscoe
Red Cloud
Zanuck, Darryl Francis

NEVADA

Stewart, William Morris
Sutro, Adolph Heinrich Joseph
Walker, Joseph Reddeford
Wovoka

NEW HAMPSHIRE

Aldrich, Thomas Bailey
Ballou, Hosea
Bissell, George Henry
Bridgman, Laura Dewey
Butler, Benjamin Franklin
Cass, Lewis
Chase, Philander
Chase, Salmon Portland
Chase, Stuart
Clarke, James Freeman
Clifford, Nathan
Coffin, Lorenzo S.
Cram, Ralph Adams
Dana, Charles Anderson
Dearborn, Henry
Dennie, Joseph
Dix, John Adams
Eddy, Mary Morse Baker

Alger, Horatio
Allen, Fred
Allen, Frederick Lewis
Allen, Horatio
Allen, John
Allen, Steve
Altman, Benjamin
Anderson, Carl David
Anderson, Marian
Anderson, Maxwell
Andrews, Roy Chapman
Andrews, Stephen Pearl
Andros, Sir Edmund
Anthony, Susan Brownell
Antin, Mary
Appleby, John Francis
Arden, Elizabeth
Arendt, Hannah
Arlen, Harold
Armour, Philip Danforth
Armstrong, Edwin Howard
Armstrong, John (1758–1843)
Arno, Peter
Arrow, Kenneth Joseph
Arthur, Chester Alan
Arthur, Timothy Shay
Ashmun, Jehudi
Astor, John Jacob (1763–1848)
Atkinson, Brooks
Atlas, Charles
Atwater, Wilbur Olin
Auden, Wystan Hugh
Axelrod, Julius
Babcock, Stephen Moulton
Baekeland, Leo Hendrik
Baer, Arthur (Bugs)
Baez, Joan
Bagley, William Chandler
Bailey, Liberty Hyde
Baker, George (Father Divine)
Baker, George Fisher
Balanchine, George
Baldwin, James
Ball, Lucille
Bandelier, Adolph Francis Alphonse
Bankhead, Tallulah Brockman
Bard, John
Bard, Samuel
Bard, William
Barnard, Frederick Augustus Porter
Barnard, George Grey
Barrymore, Ethel
Barrymore, John
Barrymore, Lionel
Barrymore, Maurice
Bartlett, John Russell (1805–1886)
Barton, Bruce
Baruch, Bernard Mannes
Barzun, Jacques Martin
Basie, William (Count)
Bateman, Hezekia Linthicum
Baum, Lyman Frank
Bayes, Nora
Bayley, Richard
Beach, Alfred Ely

Beach, Frederick Converse
Beach, Moses Sperry
Beach, Moses Yale
Beadle, Erastus Flavel
Beard, Charles Austin
Beard, Daniel Carter
Becker, Carl Lotus
Becker, George Ferdinand
Beebe, Lucius Morris
Beebe, William
Beecher, Catharine Esther
Beecher, Edward
Beecher, Henry Ward
Belasco, David
Bellows, George Wesley
Belmont, Alva Ertskin Smith
  Vanderbilt
Belmont, August
Benchley, Robert Charles
Bendix, Vincent
Benedict, Ruth Fulton
Benét, Stephen Vincent
Benét, William Rose
Bennett, Floyd
Bennett, James Gordon (1795–1872)
Bennett, James Gordon (1841–1918)
Bergh, Henry
Berle, Adolf Augustus
Berle, Milton
Berlin, Irving
Bernstein, Leonard
Berra, Lawrence Peter (Yogi)
Bethe, Hans Albrecht
Bidwell, John
Bierstadt, Albert
Bigelow, John
Bigelow, Poultney
Billings, John Shaw
Bissell, George Henry
Bitter, Karl Theodore Francis
Blackwell, Antoinette Louisa Brown
Blackwell, Elizabeth
Blakelock, Ralph Albert
Bland, James A.
Blanding, Sarah Gibson
Blatchford, Samuel
Blitzstein, Marc
Bloomer, Amelia Jenks
Boas, Franz
Bodenheim, Maxwell
Bogart, Humphrey DeForest
Bok, Edward William
Bonner, Robert
Bonney, William H. (Billy the Kid)
Booth, Edwin Thomas
Borden, Gail
Borglum, Gutzon
Boucicault, Dion
Bourke-White, Margaret
Bourne, Randolph Silliman
Bow, Clara
Bowker, Richard Rogers
Bowman, Isaiah
Brace, Charles Loring
Bradley, Joseph P.

Brady, Alice
Brady, James Buchanan (Diamond Jim)
Brady, Mathew B.
Brady, William Aloysius
Brando, Marlon
Brattain, Walter Houser
Brice, Fannie
Brisbane, Albert
Brisbane, Arthur
Bronk, Detlev Wulf
Broun, Heywood
Brown, Jacob Jennings
Browne, Charles Ferrar (Artemus Ward)
Bryant, William Cullen
Buckley, William Frank, Jr.
Bunche, Ralph Johnson
Burchfield, Charles Ephraim
Burleigh, Harry Thacker
Burlingame, Anson
Burnham, Daniel Hudson
Burns, Arthur Frank
Burr, Aaron
Burroughs, John
Burroughs, William Seward (1855–1898)
Butler, Nicholas Murray
Butterfield, John
Cabrini, Frances Xavier
Cage, John Milton, Jr.
Cagney, James
Cahan, Abraham
Callas, Maria
Cantor, Eddie
Capote, Truman
Cardozo, Benjamin Nathan
Carlson, Chester Floyd
Carnegie, Dale
Carty, John Joseph
Cary, Alice
Castle, Vernon Blythe
Cattell, James McKeen
Cerf, Bennett Alfred
Chadwick, Henry
Chandler, Charles Frederick
Chapman, Frank Michler
Chapman, John Jay
Chase, Stuart
Chayefsky, Paddy
Choate, Joseph Hodges
Church, Frederick Edwin
Clark, John Bates
Clark, Kenneth Bancroft
Clark, Mark Wayne
Cleveland, Grover
Clinton, De Witt
Clinton, George
Cohan, George Michael
Cohen, Morris Raphael
Cohn, Edwin Joseph
Colby, Frank Moore
Colden, Cadwallader
Cole, Thomas
Colfax, Schuyler

Colgate, William
Commager, Henry Steele
Comstock, Anthony
Conkling, Roscoe
Connelly, Marc
Cooley, Thomas McIntyre
Cooper, James Fenimore
Cooper, Leon N.
Cooper, Peter
Copland, Aaron
Corbin, Margaret
Corliss, George Henry
Cornell, Ezra
Cornell, Katharine
Cortelyou, George Bruce
Cournand, André Frédéric
Cousins, Norman
Cousy, Robert Joseph
Cowell, Henry Dixon
Cowles, Gardner
Cowley, Malcolm
Crabtree, Lotta
Crane, Hart
Crane, Stephen
Crater, Joseph Force
Crèvecoeur, Michel Guillaume
    Jean de
Crocker, Charles
Croly, Herbert David
Cronkite, Walter Leland, Jr.
Crothers, Rachel
Currier, Nathaniel
Curtis, George Ticknor
Curtis, George William
Curtiss, Glenn Hammond
Daft, Leo
Daly, Augustin
Damrosch, Leopold
Damrosch, Walter Johannes
Dana, Charles Anderson
Dana, James Dwight
Dannay, Frederic
Davidson, Jo
Davies, Arthur Bowen
Davis, Elmer Holmes
Davis, John William
Davis, Miles Dewey, Jr.
Davis, Richard Harding
Davis, Sammy, Jr.
Davis, Stuart
Davisson, Clinton Joseph
Day, Benjamin Henry
Day, Clarence Shepard, Jr.
Day, Dorothy
Dean, Man Mountain
De Kooning, Willem
Delamater, Cornelius Henry
De Lancey, James
De Leon, Daniel
Dell, Floyd
Dello Joio, Norman
Delmonico, Lorenzo
De Mille, Agnes George
Dempsey, Jack
Depew, Chauncey Mitchell

De Seversky, Alexander Procofieff
De Vinne, Theodore Low
De Voto, Bernard Augustine
Dewey, John
Dewey, Melvil
Dewey, Thomas Edmund
DiMaggio, Joseph Paul, Jr.
Dix, John Adams
Dobzhansky, Theodosius
    Grigorievich
Dodge, Mary Elizabeth Mapes
Donovan, William Joseph
Doubleday, Abner
Doubleday, Frank Nelson
Dove, Arthur Garfield
Dow, Charles Henry
Downing, Andrew Jackson
Drake, Edwin Laurentine
Draper, Henry
Draper, John William
Dreiser, Theodore
Drew, Daniel
Drew, John
Duane, William
Dubinsky, David
Dubos, René Jules
Dulles, John Foster
Dunham, Katherine
Dunlap, William
Dunne, Finley Peter (Mr. Dooley)
Durand, Asher Brown
Durant, Thomas Clark
Durant, Will
Durante, Jimmy
Durocher, Leo Ernest
Du Vigneaud, Vincent
Dylan, Bob
Eastman, George
Eastman, Max Forrester
Edelman, Gerald Maurice
Ederle, Gertrude Caroline
Eggleston, Edward
Ellington, Duke
Ellison, Ralph Waldo
Ely, Richard Theodore
Ericsson, John
Erskine, John
Evans, George Henry
Evans, Walker
Evarts, William Maxwell
Ewry, Ray C.
Faber, John Eberhard
Fadiman, Clifton Paul
Fairbanks, Douglas, Jr. (1909–   )
Fargo, William George
Farley, James Aloysius
Farrell, Eileen
Fearing, Kenneth Flexner
Ferber, Edna
Fernow, Bernhard Eduard
Feynman, Richard Phillips
Field, Cyrus West
Field, David Dudley
Fields, W. C.
Fillmore, Millard

Fink, Albert
Finney, Charles Grandison
Fischer, Robert James
Fish, Hamilton
Fisher, Irving
Fisk, James
Fiske, Haley
Fiske, Minnie Maddern
Fitch, Asa
Fitzgerald, Ella
Flagg, James Montgomery
Flagler, Henry Morrison
Flannagan, John Bernard
Flegenheimer, Arthur (Dutch Schultz)
Flint, Austin
Fonda, Henry
Ford, Paul Leicester
Forrest, Edwin
Forrestal, James Vincent
Fosdick, Harry Emerson
Fox, Margaret
Fox, Richard Kyle
Foy, Eddie
Fraser, James Earle
French, Daniel Chester
Freneau, Philip Morin
Frick, Henry Clay
Friedan, Betty Naomi Goldstein
Friedman, Milton
Friml, Rudolf
Frohman, Charles
Fulton, Robert
Funk, Casimir
Funk, Isaac Kauffman
Furman, Richard
Gallatin, Albert
Gardner, Isabella Stewart
Garvey, Marcus Moziah
Gasser, Herbert Spencer
Gates, Frederick Taylor
Geddes, Norman Bel
Gehrig, Lou
Gell-Mann, Murray
George, Henry
Gernsback, Hugo
Gershwin, George
Gibbs, Oliver Wolcott
Gibson, Althea
Gibson, Charles Dana
Gilbert, Cass
Gilbert, Grove Karl
Gilder, Richard Watson
Gill, Theodore Nicholas
Gillette, William Hooker
Gilpin, Charles Sidney
Ginsberg, Allen
Gish, Lillian Diana and Dorothy
Glackens, William James
Gleason, Jackie
Godey, Louis Antoine
Godfrey, Arthur Michael
Godkin, Edwin Lawrence
Goethals, George Washington
Goldberg, Rube
Goldman, Edwin Franko

Goldman, Emma
Goldwyn, Samuel
Gompers, Samuel
Goodhue, Bertram Grosvenor
Goodman, Benny
Goodyear, Charles
Goren, Charles Henry
Gorgeous George
Gorky, Arshile
Gottschalk, Louis Moreau
Goudy, Frederic William
Gould, Jay
Grace, William Russell
Graham, Martha
Gray, Asa
Greeley, Horace
Green, Hetty
Griffiths, John Willis
Grinnell, George Bird
Griswold, Rufus Wilmot
Grofé, Ferde
Gropper, William
Gulick, Luther Halsey
Hagen, Walter Charles
Hall, Abraham Oakey
Hall, James (1811–1898)
Hallam, Lewis
Halleck, Henry Wager
Halsted, William Stewart
Hamilton, Alexander
Hammerstein, Oscar, II
Hammett, Dashiell
Hampden, Walter
Hand, Learned
Handlin, Oscar
Handy, William Christopher
Hanson, Howard Harold
Harlan, John Marshall (1899–1971)
Harnett, William Michael
Harper Brothers
Harriman, Averell
Harriman, Edward Henry
Harris, Chapin Aaron
Harris, Louis
Harris, Townsend
Hart, Moss
Hart, William Surrey
Harte, Bret
Hartline, Haldan Keffer
Hassam, Childe
Hassler, Ferdinand Rudolph
Hayes, Helen
Hays, Arthur Garfield
Hearst, William Randolph
Heatter, Gabriel
Hecht, Ben
Hecker, Isaac Thomas
Held, John, Jr.
Hellman, Lillian
Helper, Hinton Rowan
Henri, Robert
Henry, Joseph
Hepburn, Katharine
Herbert, Victor
Herne, James A.

Herriman, George
Hersey, John Richard
Hershey, Alfred Day
Hewitt, Abram Stevens
Hiawatha
Hicks, Elias
Hillman, Sidney
Hillquit, Morris
Hine, Lewis Wickes
Hiss, Alger
Hitchcock, Thomas, Jr.
Hoard, William Dempster
Hoe, Richard March
Hoffer, Eric
Hofmann, Hans
Hofstadter, Richard
Hofstadter, Robert
Hokinson, Helen
Holabird, William
Holiday, Billie
Hollerith, Herman
Holley, Alexander Lyman
Holley, Robert William
Holt, Luther Emmett
Hone, Philip
Hope, Bob
Hopkins, Harry Lloyd
Hoppe, William Frederick
Hopper, DeWolf
Hopper, Edward
Houdini, Harry
House, Royal Earl
Howard, Roy Wilson
Howard, Sidney Coe
Howe, Julia Ward
Howells, William Dean
Hrdlička, Aleš
Hubbard, Elbert Green
Hudson, Henry
Hughes, Charles Evans
Hughes, John
Hughes, Langston
Huneker, James Gibbons
Hunt, Richard Morris
Hunt, Walter
Hunt, Ward
Huntington, Henry Edwards
Hurok, Solomon
Huston, Walter
Hutchins, Robert Maynard
Ingersoll, Robert Green
Ingersoll, Robert Hawley
Inman, Henry
Inness, George
Irving, Washington
Ives, Fredric Eugene
Jackson, Robert Houghwout
Jackson, Sheldon
Jacobi, Abraham
James, Henry (1811–1882)
James, Henry (1843–1916)
James, William
Jay, John
Jefferson, Joseph
Jessel, George Albert

Jessup, Philip Caryl
Johnson, Alvin Saunders
Johnson, Eastman
Johnson, James Weldon
Johnson, Philip Cortelyou
Johnson, Sir William (1715–1774)
Jolson, Al
Jordan, David Starr
Judson, Edward Zane Carroll (Ned
    Buntline)
Kahn, Otto Herman
Kaiser, Henry John
Kaltenborn, Hans von
Kaplan, Mordecai Menahem
Kaufman, George Simon
Kay, Ulysses Simpson
Kaye, Danny
Kazan, Elia
Kearny, Philip
Keene, Laura
Keeshan, Robert James (Captain
    Kangaroo)
Kellogg, Frank Billings
Kelly, Alvin A. (Shipwreck)
Kelly, Ellsworth
Kelly, Walter Crawford
Kemble, Gouverneur
Kennedy, Robert Francis
Kent, James
Kent, Rockwell
Kern, Jerome David
Kidd, William
Kilmer, Joyce
King, Richard
King, Rufus
Kline, Franz Joseph
Knopf, Alfred Abraham
Kornberg, Arthur
Koufax, Sanford (Sandy)
Krehbiel, Henry Edward
Kreisler, Fritz
Kress, Samuel Henry
Krutch, Joseph Wood
Kubrick, Stanley
Kusch, Polykarp
Lachaise, Gaston
Laemmle, Carl
La Farge, John
La Guardia, Fiorello Henry
Lahr, Bert
Lamb, Willis Eugene, Jr.
Landsteiner, Karl
Langer, Suzanne
Langford, Nathaniel Pitt
Langmuir, Irving
Lansing, Robert
Lardner, Ring
Lasker, Albert Davis
Lawes, Lewis Edward
Lazarus, Emma
Lease, Mary Elizabeth Clyens
Leavenworth, Henry
Lee, Ann
Lee, Gypsy Rose
Lee, Ivy Ledbetter

Lee, Tsung-Dao
Le Gallienne, Eva
Lehman, Herbert Henry
Leisler, Jacob
Leslie, Frank
Leypoldt, Frederick
Lichtenstein, Roy
Lieber, Francis
Lipmann, Fritz Albert
Lippmann, Walter
Lipset, Seymour Martin
Livingston, Edward
Livingston, Henry Brockholst
Livingston, Robert R.
Livingston, William
Lloyd, Henry Demarest
Locke, David Ross (Petroleum V.
  Nasby)
Lockwood, Belva Ann Bennett
Loeb, Jacques
Loeb, James Morris
Loesser, Frank Henry
Loewy, Raymond Fernand
Lombardi, Vincent Thomas
Lombardo, Guy Albert
London, Meyer
Low, Seth
Lowie, Robert Harry
Luce, Clare Boothe
Luce, Henry Robinson
Lunt, Alfred and Lynn Fontanne
Lynd, Robert Staughton
McAdoo, William Gibbs
McAllister, Ward
McCarthy, Mary Therese
McCloskey, John
McClure, Samuel Sidney
McCullers, Carson Smith
MacDowell, Edward Alexander
Macfadden, Bernarr
McGraw, John Joseph
MacIver, Robert Morrison
Mackay, Clarence Hungerford
McKay, Claude
MacKaye, Steele
Mackenzie, Ranald Slidell
McKim, Charles Follen
McMaster, John Bach
Magnes, Judah Leon
Mahan, Alfred Thayer
Mailer, Norman
Malamud, Bernard
Malcolm X
Mallon, Mary (Typhoid Mary)
Mansfield, Richard
Mantle, Mickey Charles
Marcuse, Herbert
Marcy, William Learned
Marin, John Cheri
Markham, Edwin
Marquis, Donald Robert Perry
Marsh, Othniel Charles
Marsh, Reginald
Marshall, Louis
Martin, Homer Dodge

Marx, Groucho
Masters, Edgar Lee
Masterson, William Barclay (Bat)
Mathewson, Christopher (Christy)
Maxwell, Elsa
Mays, Willie Howard, Jr.
Mead, Margaret
Meany, George
Meiggs, Henry
Melville, George Wallace
Melville, Herman
Mencken, Henry Louis
Menuhin, Yehudi
Merman, Ethel
Merrick, David
Merton, Robert King
Metz, Christian
Michener, James Albert
Millay, Edna St. Vincent
Miller, Arthur
Miller, Glenn
Miller, Henry John
Miller, Henry Valentine
Minuit, Peter
Mitchell, Wesley Clair
Mizner, Addison
Montagu, Ashley
Montez, Lola
Moore, Clement Clarke
Moore, Marianne Craig
Moore, Stanford
Moore, William Henry
More, Paul Elmer
Morgan, John Pierpont
Morgan, Lewis Henry
Morgan, Thomas Hunt
Morgan, William
Morgenthau, Henry (1856–1946)
Morgenthau, Henry, Jr. (1871–1967)
Morris, Gouverneur
Morse, Carlton Errol
Morse, Charles Wyman
Morse, Samuel Finley Breese
Morton, Julius Sterling
Morton, Levi Parsons
Moses, Anna Mary Robertson
  (Grandma Moses)
Moses, Robert
Mott, John Raleigh
Mount, William Sidney
Mowatt, Anna Cora Ogden
Muller, Hermann Joseph
Mumford, Lewis
Munro, George
Munsey, Frank Andrew
Murray, John Courtney
Murrow, Edward Roscoe
Nabokov, Vladimir Vladimirovich
Namath, Joseph William
Nash, Ogden
Nast, Thomas
Nathan, George Jean
Nelson, Samuel
Nevins, Allan
Nichols, Mike

Niebuhr, Reinhold
Nirenberg, Marshall Warren
Nizer, Louis
Nock, Albert Jay
Noguchi, Hideyo
Nordica, Lillian
Norris, Frank
North, Frank Joshua
Northrop, John Howard
Noyes, John Humphrey
Ochoa, Severo
Ochs, Adolph Simon
Odets, Clifford
Ogden, William Butler
O'Hara, John Henry
O'Keeffe, Georgia
Oldenburg, Claes Thure
Olmsted, Frederick Law
O'Neill, Eugene Gladstone
O'Neill, Rose Cecil
Oppenheimer, J. Robert
Osborn, Fairfield
Osborn, Henry Fairfield
O'Sullivan, Timothy H.
Otis, Elisha Graves
Outcault, Richard Felton
Owen, Robert Dale
Page, Walter Hines
Palmer, Alice Elvira Freeman
Palmer, Potter
Parker, Charlie (Bird)
Parker, Dorothy
Parrott, Robert Parker
Parsons, Elsie Worthington Clews
Parton, James
Parton, Sara Payson Willis
Pastor, Tony
Paulding, Hiram
Paulding, James Kirke
Payne, John Howard
Peale, Norman Vincent
Peckham, Rufus Wheeler
Pegler, Westbrook
Pennell, Joseph
Penney, James Cash
Perelman, Sidney Joseph
Perkins, Frances
Perkins, George Walbridge
Perkins, Maxwell Evarts
Peterson, Roger Tory
Phyfe, Duncan
Pitkin, Walter Boughton
Platt, Thomas Collier
Plimpton, George Ames
Poe, Edgar Allan
Pollock, Jackson
Poor, Henry Varnum
Porter, Cole
Porter, William Sydney
Post, Emily Price
Potter, Henry Codman
Powell, Adam Clayton, Jr.
Powell, John Wesley
Preminger, Otto Ludwig
Price, Leontyne

Pulitzer, Joseph
Pullman, George Mortimer
Pumpelly, Raphael
Pupin, Michael Idvorsky
Putnam, Herbert
Rabi, Isidor Isaac
Radin, Paul
Radisson, Pierre Esprit
Rand, Ayn
Randolph, Asa Philip
Rauschenberg, Robert
Rauschenbusch, Walter
Raymond, Henry Jarvis
Red Jacket
Reed, John
Reeve, Tapping
Rehan, Ada
Reid, Whitelaw
Remington, Eliphalet
Remington, Frederic
Remsen, Ira
Renwick, James
Reston, James Barrett
Rice, Dan
Rice, Elmer Leopold
Rice, Grantland
Rice, Thomas Dartmouth
Richards, Dickinson Woodruff
Rickey, Branch Wesley
Riis, Jacob August
Ripley, George
Ripley, Robert LeRoy
Robbins, Jerome
Robeson, Paul Bustill
Robinson, Bill (Bojangles)
Robinson, Edwin Arlington
Robinson, Jack Roosevelt (Jackie)
Robinson, James Harvey
Robinson, Ray (Sugar Ray)
Rockefeller, John Davison (1839–
    1937)
Rockefeller, Nelson Aldrich
Rockwell, Norman
Rodgers, Richard
Roebling, John Augustus
Roebling, Washington Augustus
Rogers, John (1829–1904)
Rogers, Will
Romberg, Sigmund
Roosevelt, Eleanor
Roosevelt, Franklin Delano
Roosevelt, Theodore
Root, Elihu
Rosenbach, Abraham Simon Wolf
Rosenberg, Julius
Ross, Harold Wallace
Rothko, Mark
Rous, Peyton
Rugg, Harold Ordway
Runyon, Damon
Russell, Charles Taze
Russell, Henry Norris
Russell, Lillian
Russwurm, John Brown
Ruth, George Herman (Babe)

Ryan, Thomas Fortune
Ryder, Albert Pinkham
Sachs, Curt
Sage, Russell
St. Denis, Ruth, and Ted Shawn
Saint-Gaudens, Augustus
Salinger, Jerome David
Salk, Jonas Edward
Salomon, Haym
Sanger, Margaret Higgins
Sarazen, Gene
Sarnoff, David
Schaff, Philip
Schechter, Solomon
Schick, Béla
Schirmer, Gustav
Schlesinger, Arthur Meier, Jr.
Schofield, John McAllister
Schoolcraft, Henry Rowe
Schuller, Gunther
Schuman, William Howard
Schumann-Heink, Ernestine
Schurman, Jacob Gould
Schurz, Carl
Schuyler, Philip John
Schwinger, Julian Seymore
Seabury, Samuel
Seaman, Elizabeth Cochrane (Nellie
    Bly)
Sears, Isaac
Seeger, Pete
Segal, George
Segar, Elzie Crisler
Selden, George Baldwin
Seldes, Gilbert Vivian
Seligman, Edwin Robert Anderson
Seligman, Joseph
Sennett, Mack
Sessions, Roger Huntington
Seton, Elizabeth Ann Bayley
Seward, William Henry
Seymour, Horatio
Shahn, Benjamin
Shaw, Henry Wheeler
Shaw, Robert Lawson
Sheen, Fulton John
Sheridan, Philip Henry
Sherman, James Schoolcraft
Sherwood, Robert Emmet
Shirer, William Lawrence
Shubert, Lee
Sibley, Hiram
Sickles, Daniel Edgar
Sigsbee, Charles Dwight
Sikorsky, Igor Ivan
Silverman, Sime
Simon, Neil
Simonson, Lee
Simpson, George Gaylord
Sims, James Marion
Singer, Isaac Bashevis
Singer, Isaac Merrit
Skinner, Otis
Skouras, Spyros Panagiotes
Slidell, John

Sloan, John French
Sloat, John Drake
Smith, Alfred Emanuel
Smith, David
Smith, Gerrit
Smith, Jedediah Strong
Smith, Joseph
Smith, Kate
Smith, Seba
Smith, Theobald
Smith, Walter Wellesley (Red)
Sothern, Edward Hugh
Spahn, Warren Edward
Spalding, Albert
Spellman, Francis Joseph
Sperry, Elmer Ambrose
Spillane, Mickey
Spingarn, Joel Elias
Sprague, Frank Julian
Springs, Elliot White
Squibb, Edward Robinson
Stanford, Leland
Stanton, Elizabeth Cady
Statler, Ellsworth Milton
Steffens, Lincoln
Steichen, Edward Jean
Stein, William Howard
Steinbeck, John Ernst
Steinberg, Saul
Steinitz, William
Steinman, David Barnard
Steinmetz, Charles Proteus
Steinway, Henry Engelhard
Stella, Frank Philip
Stengel, Charles Dillon (Casey)
Sternberg, George Miller
Steuben, Baron von
Stevens, John
Stewart, Alexander Turney
Stewart, William Morris
Stieglitz, Alfred
Still, William Grant
Stimson, Henry Lewis
Stokowski, Leopold
Stone, Edward Durell
Stone, Harlan Fiske
Stone, Isidor Feinstein
Stone, Melville Elijah
Strand, Paul
Strang, James Jesse
Stratemeyer, Edward
Straus, Isidor, and Nathan Straus
Straus, Oscar Solomon
Strauss, Levi
Stravinsky, Igor Fedorovich
Streisand, Barbra
Strong, Josiah
Stuyvesant, Peter
Sullivan, Edward Vincent
Sullivan, Harry Stack
Sullivan, James Edward
Sullivan, Timothy Daniel
Sulzberger, Arthur Hays
Sumner, James Batcheller
Swope, Gerard

Swope, Herbert Bayard
Tallchief, Maria
Tappan, Arthur
Tarbell, Ida Minerva
Tatum, Edward Lawrie
Taylor, Bayard
Taylor, Deems
Taylor, John W.
Teasdale, Sara
Tekakwitha, Kateri
Tesla, Nikola
Thalberg, Irving Grant
Thayer, Sylvanus
Thomas, Lowell Jackson
Thomas, Norman Mattoon
Thomas, Theodore
Thompson, Dorothy
Thompson, James Walter
Thompson, Smith
Thomson, Virgil Garnett
Thorndike, Edward Lee
Thorpe, Thomas Bangs
Thurber, James Grover
Tiffany, Charles Lewis
Tiffany, Louis Comfort
Tilden, Samuel Jones
Tillich, Paul Johannes
Tilyou, George Cornelius
Titchener, Edward Bradford
Tompkins, Daniel D.
Torrey, John
Toscanini, Arturo
Town, Ithiel
Townes, Charles Hard
Trilling, Lionel
Trumbull, John (1756–1843)
Truth, Sojourner
Truxtun, Thomas
Tubman, Harriet
Tucker, Sophie
Tugwell, Rexford Guy
Tunney, Gene
Tweed, William Marcy
Tyler, Moses Coit
Underhill, John
Untermyer, Samuel
Upjohn, Richard
Urban, Joseph
Urey, Harold Clayton
Vail, Theodore Newton
Vallee, Rudy
Van Buren, Martin
Van Cortlandt, Stephanus
Vanderbilt, Cornelius (1794–1877)
Vanderbilt, Harold Sterling
Vanderbilt, William Henry
Vanderbilt, William Kissam
Vanderlyn, John
Van Doren, Carl Clinton
Van Doren, Mark
Van Rensselaer, Stephen
Varèse, Edgard
Vassar, Matthew
Vick, James
Vidal, Gore

Villard, Henry
Villard, Oswald Garrison
Vincent, John Heyl
Vought, Chance Milton
Wagner, Robert Ferdinand
Walcott, Charles Doolittle
Wald, George
Wald, Lillian D.
Walker, James John
Wallace, De Witt
Wallack, James William
Wallack, Lester
Walter, Bruno
Wanamaker, John
Ward, John Quincy Adams
Warhol, Andy
Warner, Glenn Scobey (Pop)
Waterman, Lewis Edson
Waters, Ethel
Watson, Thomas John
Wayland, Francis
Weaver, Robert Clifton
Weber, Max
Webster, Noah
Weed, Thurlow
Weill, Kurt
Weiser, Conrad
Welch, William Henry
Weld, Theodore Dwight
Welles, Orson
Wells, Henry
West, Mae
West, Nathanael
Westcott, Edward Noyes
Westinghouse, George
Wharton, Edith
Wheaton, Henry
Wheeler, William Almon
Whipple, George Hoyt
Whipple, Henry Benjamin
White, Andrew Dickson
White, Canvass
White, David
White, Elwyn Brooks
White, George Leonard
White, Stanford
White, Walter Francis
Whiteman, Paul
Whitman, Marcus
Whitman, Walt
Whitney, William Collins
Wickersham, George Woodward
Wiggin, Kate Douglass
Wilder, Burt Green
Wilkes, Charles
Wilkins, Roy
Willard, Emma Hart
Willard, Frances Elizabeth Caroline
Williams, Bert
Williams, Eleazar
Williams, Tennessee
Willis, Nathaniel Parker
Willkie, Wendell Lewis
Willys, John North
Wilson, Edmund

Wilson, Harry Leon
Wilson, Samuel
Winchell, Walter
Wise, Stephen Samuel
Wolfe, Thomas Clayton
Wood, Fernando
Wood, James Rushmore
Woodberry, George Edward
Woodbridge, Frederick James
  Eugene
Woodhull, Victoria Claflin
Woollcott, Alexander
Woolsey, Theodore Dwight
Woolworth, Frank Winfield
Wouk, Herman
Wright, Frances
Wright, Harold Bell
Wright, Henry (1878–1936)
Wright, Richard
Wylie, Elinor
Wylie, Philip Gordon
Wynn, Ed
Yale, Linus
Yang, Chen Ning
Young, Whitney Moore, Jr.
Zenger, John Peter
Ziegfeld, Florenz
Zinsser, Hans
Zorach, William
Zworykin, Vladimir Kosma

NORTH CAROLINA

Albers, Josef
Atkinson, Henry
Benton, Thomas Hart (1782–1858)
Blount, William
Bragg, Braxton
Cannon, Joseph Gurney
Chang and Eng
Coffin, Levi
Coltrane, John William
Daly, Augustin
Dare, Virginia
Duke, James Buchanan
Gatling, Richard Jordan
Godfrey, Thomas (1736–1763)
Graham, Billy
Green, Paul Eliot
Hawkins, Benjamin
Helper, Hinton Rowan
Henderson, Richard
Iredell, James
Jackson, Andrew
Jackson, Jesse Louis
Johnson, Andrew
King, William Rufus de Vane
Koch, Frederick Henry
McDougall, William
Macon, Nathaniel
Means, Gaston Bullock
Moore, Alfred
Murrow, Edward Roscoe
Page, Walter Hines
Polk, James Knox
Polk, Leonidas

Porter, William Sydney
Revels, Hiram Rhoades
Rhine, Joseph Banks
Sevier, John
Smith, Hoke
Vance, Zebulon Baird
Waddel, Moses
Waddell, James Iredell
Walker, David
Welch, Robert H. W., Jr.
Wolfe, Thomas Clayton

NORTH DAKOTA

Flannagan, John Bernard
Koch, Frederick Henry
Sacagawea
Welk, Lawrence

OHIO

Abbe, Cleveland
Abbot, Francis Ellingwood
Allen, John
Allison, William Boyd
Anderson, Sherwood
Arcaro, George Edward (Eddie)
Armstrong, John (1755–1816)
Armstrong, Neil Alden
Babbitt, Irving
Bacon, Delia Salter
Bailey, Gamaliel
Baker, Newton Diehl
Bancroft, Hubert Howe
Bara, Theda
Beard, Daniel Carter
Beecher, Lyman
Bellows, George Wesley
Beveridge, Albert Jeremiah
Bierce, Ambrose Gwinnett
Birney, James Gillespie
Bloch, Ernest
Brant, Joseph
Bromfield, Louis
Browne, Charles Farrar
   (Artemus Ward)
Buell, Don Carlos
Burchfield, Charles Ephraim
Burton, Harold Hitz
Campbell, William Wallace
Caniff, Milton Arthur
Cary, Alice
Cass, Lewis
Chaffee, Adna Romanza (1842–
   1914
Chapman, John (Johnny Appleseed)
Chase, Philander
Chase, Salmon Portland
Chesnutt, Charles Waddell
Clarke, John Hessin
Coffin, Howard Earle
Coffin, Levi
Commons, John Rogers
Compton, Arthur Holly
Cooke, Jay
Cox, Jacob Dolson
Coxey, Jacob Sechler

Crane, Hart
Crook, George
Cushing, Harvey Williams
Custer, George Armstrong
Cutler, Manasseh
Darrow, Clarence Seward
Daugherty, Harry Micajah
Dawes, Charles Gates
Day, William Rufus
Dayton, Jonathan
Doherty, Henry Latham
Dow, Herbert Henry
Dunbar, Paul Laurence
Duveneck, Frank
Eaton, Cyrus Stephen
Edison, Thomas Alva
Emmett, Daniel Decatur
Evans, John
Fairbanks, Charles Warren
Feller, Robert William Andrew
Finney, Charles Grandison
Firestone, Harvey Samuel
Frohman, Charles
Funk, Isaac Kauffman
Funston, Frederick
Gable, Clark
Garfield, James Abram
Giddings, Joshua Reed
Gilbert, Cass
Gish, Lillian Diana and Dorothy
Gist, Christopher
Gladden, Washington
Glaser, Donald Arthur
Glenn, John Herschel, Jr.
Grant, Ulysses S.
Gray, Elisha
Green, William
Grey, Zane
Hall, Charles Martin
Hall, James (1793–1868)
Hanna, Mark
Harding, Warren Gamaliel
Harper, William Rainey
Harrison, Benjamin
Harrison, William Henry
Hayes, Rutherford Birchard
Hendricks, Thomas Andrews
Henri, Robert
Herrick, Myron Timothy
Herskovits, Melville Jean
Hocking, William Ernest
Howard, Roy Wilson
Howells, William Dean
Hubbard, Frank McKinney (Kin)
Hughes, Langston
Johnson, Philip Cortelyou
Johnson, Tom Loftin
Jones, Samuel Milton
Keifer, Joseph Warren
Kettering, Charles Franklin
King, Ernest Joseph
Krehbiel, Henry Edward
Landis, Kenesaw Mountain
Langston, John Mercer
LeMay, Curtis Emerson

Locke, David Ross
Logan, James (1725?–1780)
Longworth, Nicholas
McGuffey, William Holmes
McKinley, William
McLean, John
Matthews, Stanley
Medill, Joseph
Meeker, Nathan Cook
Morley, Edward William
Nicklaus, Jack William
Norris, George William
Oakley, Annie
Ochs, Adolph Simon
Oldfield, Barney
Olds, Ransom Eli
Otis, Harrison Gray
Outcault, Richard Felton
Owens, Jesse
Patterson, John Henry
Peale, Norman Vincent
Pontiac
Powers, Hiram
Putnam, Rufus
Quantrill, William Clarke
Quine, Willard Van Orman
Ransom, John Crowe
Reid, Whitelaw
Rhodes, James Ford
Rickenbacker, Edward Vernon
Rickey, Branch Wesley
Robbins, Frederick Chapman
Rockefeller, John Davison
   (1839–1937)
Rosecrans, William Starke
Sabin, Albert Bruce
St. Clair, Arthur
Schlesinger, Arthur Meier
   (1888–1965)
Schlesinger, Arthur Meier, Jr.
   (1917–   )
Sheridan, Philip Henry
Sherman, John
Sherman, William Tecumseh
Simpson, Matthew
Spock, Benjamin McLane
Stanton, Edwin McMasters
Stewart, Potter
Stutz, Harry Clayton
Swayne, Noah Haynes
Szell, George
Taft, Robert Alphonso
Taft, William Howard
Tatum, Art
Tecumseh
Thomas, Lowell Jackson
Thomas, Norman Mattoon
Thurber, James Grover
Vail, Theodore Newton
Vallandigham, Clement Laird
Van Sweringen, Oris Paxton
Veeck, William Louis, Jr.
Wade, Benjamin Franklin
Waite, Morrison Remick
Wald, Lillian D.

Ward, John Quincy Adams
Weaver, James Baird
Weld, Theodore Dwight
Wellman, Walter
Wetzel, Lewis
Wheeler, Wayne Bidwell
Whitlock, Brand
Willys, John North
Wilson, Charles Erwin
Winton, Alexander
Wise, Isaac Mayer
Woodhull, Victoria Claflin
Woods, William Burnham
Wright Brothers
Wright, Henry (Harry, 1835–1895)
Young, Cy

OKLAHOMA

Albert, Carl Bert
Berryman, John
Dalton, Robert
Ellison, Ralph Waldo
Franklin, John Hope
Gould, Chester
Guthrie, Woody
Harris, Roy Ellsworth
Jansky, Karl Guthe
Mantle, Mickey Charles
Quanah
Roberts, Oral
Rogers, Will
Ross, John
Sequoya
Tallchief, Maria
Thorpe, James Francis (Jim)

OREGON

Applegate, Jesse
De Smet, Pierre Jean
Gilbert, Alfred Carlton
Graves, Morris Cole
Gray, Robert
Joseph
Lee, Jason
McLoughlin, John
Markham, Edwin
Miller, Joaquin
Pauling, Linus Carl
Reed, John
U'Ren, William Simon
Villard, Henry
Wise, Stephen Samuel

PANAMA CANAL ZONE

Clark, Kenneth Bancroft
Goethals, George Washington
Gorgas, William Crawford

PENNSYLVANIA

Abbey, Edwin Austin
Adler, Cyrus
Agnew, David Hayes
Albright, Jacob
Alcott, Louisa May
Allen, Richard

Alter, David
Anderson, Marian
Anderson, Maxwell
Andretti, Mario Gabriel
Anfinsen, Christian Boehmer
Armstrong, John (1758–1843)
Arnold, Henry Harley (Hap)
Arthur, Timothy Shay
Ayer, Francis Wayland
Babbitt, Milton Byron
Bache, Alexander Dallas
Bache, Benjamin Franklin
Baer, Arthur (Bugs)
Baer, George Frederick
Baird, Spencer Fullerton
Baker, George (Father Divine)
Baldwin, Henry
Baldwin, Matthias William
Barber, Samuel
Bard, Samuel
Bard, William
Barnard, George Grey
Barry, John
Barrymore, Ethel
Barrymore, John
Barrymore, Lionel
Bartram, John
Bartram, William
Beissel, Johann Conrad
Benét, Stephen Vincent
Biddle, James
Biddle, Nicholas
Binney, Horace
Bissell, George Henry
Black, Jeremiah Sullivan
Blaine, James Gillespie
Blanda, George Frederick
Bliss, Tasker Howard
Blitzstein, Marc
Bond, Thomas
Boone, Daniel
Boring, Edwin Garrigues
Brackenridge, Hugh Henry
Brinton, Daniel Garrison
Brown, Charles Brockden
Brown, Jacob Jennings
Buchanan, James
Buchman, Frank Nathan Daniel
Burleigh, Harry Thacker
Calder, Alexander
Cameron, Simon
Campbell, Thomas
Carey, Henry Charles
Carey, Mathew
Carnegie, Andrew
Carson, Rachel Louise
Cassatt, Mary
Catlin, George
Cattell, James McKeen
Chamberlain, Wilt
Chomsky, Noam
Christy, Edwin P.
Commager, Henry Steele
Connelly, Cornelia
Connelly, Marc

Conwell, Russell Herman
Cooke, Jay
Cooper, Thomas
Corbin, Margaret
Cowley, Malcolm
Coxey, Jacob Sechler
Crater, Joseph Force
Croghan, George
Cummins, Albert Baird
Curtis, Cyrus Herman Kotzschmar
Dahlgren, John Adolphus Bernard
Dallas, Alexander James
Dallas, George Mifflin
Davis, Richard Harding
Davis, Stuart
Davis, William Morris
Decatur, Stephen
Delany, Martin Robinson
Demuth, Charles
Dennie, Joseph
Dickinson, John
Donnelly, Ignatius
Doolittle, Hilda (H.D.)
Drake, Edwin Laurentine
Drew, John
Duane, William
Duryea, Charles Edgar
Dyott, Thomas W.
Eakins, Thomas
Eiseley, Loren Corey
Ellet, Charles, Jr.
Espy, James Pollard
Fernow, Bernhard Eduard
Ferris, George Washington Gale
Fessenden, Reginald Aubrey
Fields, W. C.
Filson, John
Fink, Mike
Fitch, John
Forrest, Edwin
Forten, James
Foster, Stephen Collins
Foxx, James Emory (Jimmy)
Franklin, Benjamin
Frick, Henry Clay
Fry, Franklin Clark
Fulton, Robert
Furness, Horace Howard
Gallatin, Albert
Gallaudet, Thomas Hopkins
Galloway, Joseph
Geary, John White
George, Henry
Giddings, Joshua Reed
Girard, Stephen
Glackens, William James
Gladden, Washington
Godey, Louis Antoine
Godfrey, Thomas (1704–1749)
Godfrey, Thomas (1736–1763)
Goren, Charles Henry
Gorgas, Josiah
Graham, George Rex
Graham, Martha
Grange, Harold Edward (Red)

Grier, Robert Cooper
Gross, Samuel David
Grow, Galusha Aaron
Guggenheim, Meyer
Haldeman-Julius, Emanuel
Hale, Sarah Josepha Buell
Hall, Charles Martin
Hall, James (1793–1868)
Hancock, Winfield Scott
Harrison, Ross Granville
Hart, Albert Bushnell
Hartline, Haldan Keffer
Hayden, Ferdinand Vandeveer
Heinz, Henry John
Hench, Philip Showalter
Henri, Robert
Henry, Andrew
Hershey, Milton Snavely
Hicks, Edward
Hill, George Washington
Hires, Charles Elmer
Hopkinson, Francis
Hopper, Hedda
Humphreys, Joshua
Huneker, James Gibbons
Hutchins, Thomas
Ickes, Harold LeClair
Ives, Frederic Eugene
Jackson, Robert Houghwout
Jeffers, Robinson
Jefferson, Joseph
Jones, Rufus Matthew
Kane, Elisha Kent
Kaufman, George Simon
Kelly, Grace Patricia
Kelly, Walter Crawford
Kelly, William
Kerr, Michael Crawford
Kline, Franz Joseph
Knox, Philander Chase
Kress, Samuel Henry
Kuznets, Simon
Landon, Alfred Mossman
Langley, Samuel Pierpont
Latrobe, Benjamin Henry
Lease, Mary Elizabeth Clyens
Leidy, Joseph
Levy, Uriah Phillips
Linton, Ralph
Locke, Alain LeRoy
Logan, George
Logan, James (1674–1751)
Logan, James (1725?–1780)
Lorimer, George Horace
Ludwick, Christopher
McCauley, Mary Ludwig Hays
    (Molly Pitcher)
McClellan, George Brinton
McGuffey, William Holmes
Machen, John Gresham
Mack, Connie
McKean, Thomas
McKenna, Joseph
McKim, Charles Follen
McMaster, John Bach

McParlan, James
March, Francis Andrew
Marshall, George Catlett
Mason, Charles, and Jeremiah Dixon
Mathewson, Christopher (Christy)
Mead, Margaret
Mellon, Andrew William
Menotti, Gian-Carlo
Merton, Robert King
Michener, James Albert
Mifflin, Thomas
Mills, Robert
Mitchell, Silas Weir
Mix, Tom
Morgan, John
Morris, Robert
Mott, Lucretia Coffin
Muhlenberg, Frederick Augustus
Mühlenberg, Henry Melchior
Muhlenberg, John Peter Gabriel
Murphy, Michael Charles
Murray, Lindley
Murray, Philip
Musial, Stanley Frank
Namath, Joseph William
Neumann, John Nepomucene
Niles, Hezekiah
Odets, Clifford
O'Hara, John Henry
O'Neill, Rose Cecil
Ormandy, Eugene
Paine, Thomas
Palmer, Alexander Mitchell
Palmer, Arnold
Park, Robert Ezra
Parrish, Maxfield Frederick
Pastorius, Francis Daniel
Peale, Charles Willson
Peary, Robert Edwin
Peirce, Charles Sanders
Penn, William
Pennell, Joseph
Penrose, Boies
Pepper, William
Pickering, Timothy
Pinchot, Gifford
Porter, David Dixon
Post, Christian Frederick
Powderly, Terence Vincent
Quay, Matthew Stanley
Rafinesque, Constantine Samuel
Randall, Samuel Jackson
Ray, Man
Rhine, Joseph Banks
Richards, Theodore William
Riesman, David, Jr.
Rinehart, Mary Roberts
Rittenhouse, David
Roberts, Owen Josephus
Rockhill, William Woodville
Roebling, John Augustus
Roebling, Washington Augustus
Rosenbach, Abraham Simon Wolf
Ross, Betsy
Rowland, Henry Augustus

Rush, Benjamin
Rush, Richard
Rush, William
Russell, Charles Taze
St. Clair, Arthur
Salk, Jonas Edward
Salomon, Haym
Say, Thomas
Schaff, Philip
Schmucker, Samuel Simon
Schrieffer, John Robert
Schwab, Charles Michael
Seaman, Elizabeth Cochrane
    (Nellie Bly)
Selznick, David Oliver
Sheeler, Charles
Shiras, George
Sholes, Christopher Latham
Simpson, Matthew
Skinner, Burrhus Frederic
Sloan, John French
Smith, Bessie
Smith, William
Spaatz, Carl
Stassen, Harold Edward
Statler, Ellsworth Milton
Stein, Gertrude
Stephens, Uriah Smith
Stern, Otto
Stetson, John Batterson
Stevens, Thaddeus
Stevens, Wallace
Stiegel, Henry William
Stockton, Frank
Stokowski, Leopold
Stone, Isidor Feinstein
Strong, William
Stuart, Gilbert Charles
Studebaker, Clement
Sully, Thomas
Sylvis, William H.
Tanner, Henry Ossawa
Tarbell, Ida Minerva
Taylor, Bayard
Taylor, Frederick Winslow
Tennent, Gilbert
Tennent, William
Thomas, Martha Carey
Thorpe, James Francis (Jim)
Tilden, William Tatem, Jr. (Big Bill)
Truxtun, Thomas
Unitas, John
Updike, John Hoyer
Wagner, Honus
Walker, Robert John
Wanamaker, John
Warner, Glenn Scobey (Pop)
Waters, Ethel
Wayne, Anthony
Weiser, Conrad
Weissmuller, Johnny
West, Benjamin
Westinghouse, George
Wetzel, Lewis
White, William

Whitney, Asa
Wickersham, George Woodward
Wiggin, Kate Douglas
Williams, Daniel Hale
Wilmot, David
Wilson, Alexander
Wilson, James
Wilson, William Bauchop
Windsor, Wallis Warfield,
    Duchess of
Wister, Owen
Wood, Fernando
Wrigley, William, Jr.
Wyeth, Andrew Newell
Wyeth, Newell Convers
Wynn, Ed
Yerkes, Charles Tyson
Yerkes, Robert Mearns

PUERTO RICO

Muñoz Marín, Luis
Ponce de León, Juan
Tugwell, Rexford Guy

RHODE ISLAND

Abell, Arunah Shepherdson
Aldrich, Nelson Wilmarth
Angell, James Burrill
Baker, George Pierce
Ballou, Adin
Bartlett, John Russell (1805–1886)
Burnside, Ambrose Everett
Chafee, Zechariah
Channing, William Ellery
Church, Benjamin
Clark, John Bates
Cohan, George Michael
Cooper, Leon N.
Corliss, George Henry
Crandall, Prudence
Curtis, George William
Dorr, Thomas Wilson
Gray, Robert
Greene, Nathanael
Harrison, Peter
Hopkins, Esek
Hopkins, Samuel
Jackson, Helen Hunt
King, Clarence
La Farge, John
Lovecraft, Howard Phillips
Luther, Seth
McAllister, Ward
Mahan, Alfred Thayer
Malbone, Edward Greene
Massasoit
Patch, Sam
Perry, Matthew Calbraith
Perry, Oliver Hazard
Philip
Slater, Samuel
Stiles, Ezra
Stuart, Gilbert Charles
Waterhouse, Benjamin
Wayland, Francis

Weston, Edward Paycon
Wheaton, Henry
Williams, Roger

SOUTH CAROLINA

Allen, Horatio
Allston, Robert Francis Withers
Allston, Washington
Baruch, Bernard Mannes
Bee, Barnard Elliott
Bethune, Mary McLeod
Byrnes, James Francis
Calhoun, John Caldwell
Cheves, Langdon
Cooper, Thomas
De Bow, James Dunwoody Brownson
Delany, Martin Robinson
De Soto, Hernando
England, John
Furman, Richard
Gadsden, James
Garden, Alexander
Gibson, Althea
Gildersleeve, Basil Lanneau
Gorrie, John
Gregg, William
Grimké, Sarah Moore and
    Angelina Emily
Hampton, Wade
Harper, Robert Goodloe
Hayne, Robert Young
Heyward, DuBose
Hitchcock, Thomas, Jr.
Hoban, James
Jackson, Andrew
Johnson, William (1771–1834)
Just, Ernest Everett
Laurens, Henry
Legaré, Hugh Swinton
Lieber, Francis
Longstreet, James
McDuffie, George
Marion, Francis
Maverick, Samuel Augustus
Mills, Robert
Moultrie, William
Orr, James Lawrence
Petigru, James Louis
Pinckney, Charles (1757–1824)
Pinckney, Charles Cotesworth
    (1746–1825)
Pinckney, Thomas
Poinsett, Joel Roberts
Rhett, Robert Barnwell
Robert, Henry Martyn
Rutledge, John
Simms, William Gilmore
Sims, James Marion
Smalls, Robert
Springs, Elliot White
Sumter, Thomas
Thurmond, James Strom
Tillman, Benjamin Ryan
Timrod, Henry
Townes, Charles Hard

Travis, William Barret
Vesey, Denmark
Waddel, Moses
Watson, John Broadus
Westmoreland, William Childs

SOUTH DAKOTA

Burke, Martha Jane (Calamity Jane)
Chouteau, Pierre (1789–1865)
Gall
Glass, Hugh
Hansen, Alvin Harvey
Humphrey, Hubert Horatio
Lawrence, Ernest Orlando
McGovern, George Stanley
Sitting Bull
Spotted Tail

TENNESSEE

Agee, James
Andrews, Frank Maxwell
Barnard, Edward Emerson
Barton, Bruce
Bell, John
Blount, William
Bond, Julian
Boyd, Lynn
Brownlow, William Gannaway
Byrns, Joseph Wellington
Carter, Samuel Powhatan
Cash, Johnny
Catron, John
Chisum, John Simpson
Crockett, David
Farragut, David Glasgow
Forrest, Nathan Bedford
Fortas, Abe
Gregg, Josiah
Handy, William Christopher
Hastie, William Henry
Hays, John Coffee (Jack)
Henderson, Richard
Houston, Samuel
Hull, Cordell
Jackson, Andrew
Jackson, Howell Edmunds
Jarrell, Randall
Johnson, Andrew
Kefauver, Carey Estes
Krutch, Joseph Wood
Lindsey, Benjamin Barr
Lurton, Horace Harmon
McReynolds, James Clark
Murrell, John A.
Ochs, Adolph Simon
Polk, James Knox
Ransom, John Crowe
Rayburn, Samuel Taliaferro
Read, Opie Percival
Rice, Grantland
Ross, John
Sanford, Edward Terry
Sequoya
Sevier, John
Smith, Bessie

Sutherland, Earl Wilbur, Jr.
Walker, William
Wells, Ida Bell
White, George Leonard
Wright, Frances
York, Alvin Cullum

TEXAS

Adams, Andy
Austin, Stephen Fuller
Bass, Sam
Baugh, Samuel Adrian
Bean, Roy
Becknell, William
Blanda, George Frederick
Borden, Gail
Bowie, James
Buck, Frank
Chisholm, Jesse
Chisum, John Simpson
Clark, Tom Campbell
Crockett, David
Dies, Martin
Dobie, James Frank
Eisenhower, Dwight David
Farmer, James Leonard
Foyt, Anthony Joseph, Jr.
Garner, John Nance
Gates, John Warne
Goodnight, Charles
Hays, John Coffee (Jack)
Hogan, William Benjamin (Ben)
Hornsby, Rogers
House, Edward Mandell
Houston, Samuel
Hughes, Howard Robard
Hunt, Haroldson Lafayette
Johnson, Jack
Johnson, Lyndon Baines
Johnston, Albert Sidney
King, Richard
Lamar, Mirabeau Buonaparte
Lomax, John Avery
Maverick, Samuel Augustus
Menard, Michel Branamour
Murphy, Audie
Nimitz, Chester William
O'Connor, Sandra Day
Oñate, Juan de
Porter, Katherine Anne
Post, Wiley
Quanah
Rauschenberg, Robert
Rayburn, Samuel Taliaferro
Shoemaker, William Lee (Willie)
Struve, Otto
Travis, William Barret
Trevino, Lee
Zaharias, Mildred Ella Didrikson

UTAH

Adams, Maude
Browning, John Moses
De Voto, Bernard Augustine
Farnsworth, Philo Taylor

Gilbert, Grove Karl
Harris, Roy Ellsworth
Haywood, William Dudley (Big Bill)
Held, John, Jr.
Hill, Joe
Smith, Jedediah Strong
Sutherland, George
Walker, Joseph Reddeford
Young, Brigham

VERMONT

Allen, Ethan
Angell, James Burrill
Arthur, Chester Alan
Billings, Frederick
Brownson, Orestes Augustus
Coolidge, Calvin
Dana, John Cotton
Davenport, Thomas
Deere, John
Dewey, George
Dewey, John
Dillingham, William Paul
Douglas, Stephen Arnold
Edmunds, George Franklin
Fisher, Dorthy Canfield
Fisk, James
Griswold, Rufus Wilmot
House, Royal Earl
Howard, Oliver Otis
Hunt, Richard Morris
Hunt, William Morris
Marsh, George Perkins
Morrill, Justin Smith
Morton, Levi Parsons
Noyes, John Humphrey
Otis, Elisha Graves
Powers, Hiram
Smith, Joseph
Stevens, Thaddeus
Tyler, Royall
Vallee, Rudy
Wells, Henry
Wells, Horace
Willard, Emma Hart
Young, Brigham

VIRGINIA

Allen, Henry Watkins
Anderson, Joseph Reid
Andros, Sir Edmund
Armstrong, Samuel Chapman
Ashburner, Charles Edward
Ashe, Arthur Robert, Jr.
Ashley, William Henry
Austin, Stephen Fuller
Bacon, Nathaniel
Barbour, Philip Pendleton
Barron, James
Bates, Edward
Becknell, William
Berkeley, Sir William
Bingham, George Caleb
Blair, Francis Preston (1791–1876)

Blair, James
Blair, John
Bridger, James
Brownlow, William Gannaway
Bruce, Blanche Kelso
Byrd, Richard Evelyn
Byrd, William
Cabell, James Branch
Cartwright, Peter
Cather, Willa Sibert
Catron, John
Clark, George Rogers
Clark, William
Clay, Henry
Crawford, William Harris
Dale, Richard
Daniel, Peter Vivian
Davies, Samuel
De La Warr, Thomas West, Baron
Draper, Henry
Early, Jubal Anderson
Fitzgerald, Ella
Fitzhugh, George
Freeman, Douglas Southall
Gates, Horatio
Gildersleeve, Basil Lanneau
Gilpin, Charles Sidney
Glasgow, Ellen Anderson Gholson
Glass, Carter
Gosden, Freeman Fisher
Gosnold, Bartholomew
Harper, Robert Goodloe
Harrison, William Henry
Henderson, Richard
Henry, Patrick
Hill, Ambrose Powell
Houston, Samuel
Hunter, Robert Mercer Taliaferro
Jackson, Thomas Jonathan
    (Stonewall)
Jefferson, Thomas
Johnston, Joseph Eggleston
Jones, John Paul
Jones, John Winston
Langston, John Mercer
Laws, Samuel Spahr
Lee, Arthur
Lee, Charles
Lee, Fitzhugh
Lee, Henry (Light-Horse Harry)
Lee, Richard Henry
Lee, Robert Edward
Lewis, Meriwether
Lynch, Charles
McCormick, Cyrus Hall
McDowell, Ephraim
McGuffey, William Holmes
McKinley, John
Madison, James
Makemie, Francis
Marshall, John
Mason, George
Mason, James Murray
Maury, Matthew Fontaine
Mazzei, Philip

Mitchell, John
Monroe, James
Morgan, Daniel
Morgan, William
Mosby, John Singleton
Pendleton, Edmund
Pickett, George Edward
Pocahontas
Poe, Edgar Allan
Powell, Lewis Franklin, Jr.
Powhatan
Randolph, Edmund Jennings
Randolph, John (of Roanoke)
Reed, Walter
Ridgway, Mathew Bunker
Robinson, Bill (Bojangles)
Royall, Anne Newport
Ruffin, Edmund
Rumsey, James
Ryan, Thomas Fortune
Scott, Winfield
Sevier, John
Smith, John
Smith, Kate
Snead, Samuel Jackson
Stevenson, Andrew
Still, Andrew Taylor
Stuart, James Ewell Brown (Jeb)
Sumter, Thomas
Swayne, Noah Haynes
Taylor, David Watson
Taylor, Edward Thompson
   (1793–1871)
Taylor, John (of Caroline)
Taylor, William
Taylor, Zachary
Thomas, George Henry
Todd, Thomas
Tompkins, Sally Louisa
Trimble, Robert
Trist, Nicholas Philip
Turner, Nat
Tyler, John
Untermyer, Samuel
Vandegrift, Alexander Archer
Walker, Joseph Reddeford
Walker, Thomas
Washington, Booker Taliaferro
Washington, Bushrod
Washington, George
Weems, Mason Locke
White, John
Wilson, Woodrow
Wirt, William
Woodson, Carter Godwin
Wythe, George

WASHINGTON

Brattain, Walter Houser
Carlson, Chester Floyd
Crosby, Bing
De Smet, Pierre Jean
Faust, Frederick Schiller
Graves, Morris Cole
Lee, Gypsy Rose

McCarthy, Mary Therese
McLoughlin, John
Parrington, Vernon Louis
Roethke, Theodore
Smohalla
Stroud, Robert
Thompson, David
Tobey, Mark
Whitman, Marcus
Yamasaki, Minoru

WASHINGTON, D.C.

See DISTRICT OF COLUMBIA

WEST VIRGINIA

Baker, Newton Diehl
Bent, Charles
Buck, Pearl
Campbell, Thomas
Davis, John William
Delany, Martin Robinson
Gregg, William
Harvey, William Hope (Coin)
Jackson, Thomas Jonathan
   (Stonewall)
Lashley, Karl Spencer
Laws, Samuel Spahr
Morrow, Dwight Whitney
Reuther, Walter Philip
Sinclair, Harry Ford
Wetzel, Lewis

WISCONSIN

Aaron, Henry Louis (Hank)
Allouez, Claude Jean
Anderson, Rasmus Björn
Andrews, Roy Chapman
Appleby, John Francis
Babcock, Stephen Moulton
Bardeen, John
Berger, Victor Louis
Brown, Olympia
Cannon, Walter Bradford
Catt, Carrie Chapman
Commons, John Rogers
Cushing, William Barker
Ely, Richard Theodore
Frank, Glenn
Garland, Hamlin
Gasser, Herbert Spencer
Gesell, Arnold Lucius
Gillette, King Camp
Hansen, Marcus Lee
Hine, Lewis Wickes
Hoard, William Dempster
Hooton, Earnest Albert
Houdini, Harry
Juneau, Solomon Laurent
Kaltenborn, Hans von
Kennan, George Frost
Khorana, Har Gobind
King, Frank
La Follette, Robert Marion
Lederberg, Joshua
Leopold, Aldo

Lombardi, Vincent Thomas
Lunt, Alfred
MacArthur, Arthur
McCarthy, Joseph Raymond
Marquette, Jacques
Meiklejohn, Alexander
Murphy, William Parry
Nicolet, Jean
O'Keeffe, Georgia
Perrot, Nicolas
Rehnquist, William Hubbs
Selfridge, Harry Gordon
Sholes, Christopher Latham
Smith, Francis Marion
Smith, Walter Wellesley (Red)
Spooner, John Coit
Strang, James Jesse
Thwaites, Reuben Gold
Tobey, Mark
Tracy, Spencer
Turner, Frederick Jackson
U'Ren, William Simon
Van Hise, Charles Richard
Veblen, Thorstein Bunde
Walsh, Thomas James
Welles, Orson
Wilcox, Ella Wheeler
Wilder, Thornton Niven
Williams, Eleazar
Wright, Frank Lloyd

WYOMING

Arnold, Thurman Wesley
Bonneville, Benjamin Louis
   Eulalie de
Bridger, James
Crazy Horse
Fitzpatrick, Thomas
Gall
Pollock, Jackson
Red Cloud
Ross, Nellie Tayloe
Sitting Bull
Smith, Jedediah Strong
Spotted Tail
Van Devanter, Willis
Washakie

VIRGIN ISLANDS

Benjamin, Judah Philip
Thornton, William
Vesey, Denmark

WALES

See also ENGLAND, SCOTLAND
Jones, Samuel Milton
Stanley, Henry Morton

YUGOSLAVIA

Pupin, Michael Idvorsky
Tesla, Nikola

Careers and Professions Index

ABOLITIONISTS

See REFORMERS

ACTORS AND ACTRESSES

See also ENTERTAINERS

Adams, Maude
Aldridge, Ira Frederick
Astaire, Fred
Ball, Lucille
Bankhead, Tallulah Brockman
Bara, Theda
Barrymore, Ethel
Barrymore, John
Barrymore, Lionel
Barrymore, Maurice
Bayes, Nora
Beery, Wallace
Bogart, Humphrey DeForest
Booth, Edwin Thomas
Booth, John Wilkes
Booth, Junius Brutus
Boucicault, Dion
Bow, Clara
Brady, Alice
Brady, William Aloysius
Brando, Marlon
Brice, Fannie
Bushman, Francis Xavier
Cagney, James
Chaney, Lon
Chaplin, Charles Spencer
Cohan, George Michael
Cooper, Gary
Cornell, Katharine
Crabtree, Lotta
Crosby, Bing
Cushman, Charlotte Saunders
Davis, Bette
Dressler, Marie
Drew, John
Fairbanks, Douglas (1883–1939)
Fairbanks, Douglas, Jr. (1909–   )
Fields, W. C.
Fiske, Minnie Maddern
Fonda, Henry
Forrest, Edwin
Gable, Clark
Garbo, Greta
Garland, Judy
Gillette, William Hooker
Gilpin, Charles Sidney
Gish, Lillian Diana and Dorothy
Gosden, Freeman Fisher, and Charles J. Correll
Grant, Cary

Hallam, Lewis
Hampden, Walter
Harlow, Jean
Hart, William Surrey
Hayes, Helen
Hepburn, Katharine
Herne, James A.
Hopper, DeWolf
Hopper, Hedda
Huston, Walter
Jefferson, Joseph
Karloff, Boris
Kaye, Danny
Keaton, Buster
Keene, Laura
Keeshan, Robert James (Captain Kangaroo)
Kelly, Grace Patricia
Kemble, Fanny
Laurel, Stan, and Oliver Hardy
Le Gallienne, Eva
Lloyd, Harold Clayton
Lugosi, Bela
Lunt, Alfred, and Lynn Fontanne
MacKaye, Steele
Mansfield, Richard
Menken, Adah Isaacs
Merman, Ethel
Miller, Henry John
Mix, Tom
Monroe, Marilyn
Mowatt, Anna Cora Ogden
Murphy, Audie
Payne, John Howard
Pickford, Mary
Rehan, Ada
Robeson, Paul Bustill
Rogers, Will
Rowson, Susanna Haswell
Russell, Lillian
Sinatra, Frank
Skinner, Otis
Sothern, Edward Hugh
Streisand, Barbra
Stroheim, Erich von
Taylor, Elizabeth
Temple, Shirley
Tracy, Spencer
Valentino, Rudolph
Wallack, James William
Wallack, Lester
Waters, Ethel
Wayne, John
Weissmuller, Johnny
Welles, Orson
Wynn, Ed

AGRICULTURISTS AND AGRONOMISTS

Allston, Robert Francis Withers
Atwater, Wilbur Olin
Babcock, Stephen Moulton
Borlaug, Norman Ernest
Burbank, Luther
Carver, George Washington
Hoard, William Dempster
Kelley, Oliver Hudson
Morton, Julius Sterling
Ruffin, Edmund
Taylor, John (of Caroline)
Wallace, Henry Agard
Watson, Elkanah
Wiley, Harvey Washington

AIR MEN AND AIR WOMEN

See also ASTRONAUTS AND SPACE SCIENTISTS

Andrews, Frank Maxwell
Arnold, Henry Harley (Hap)
Bennett, Floyd
Byrd, Richard Evelyn
Chanute, Octave
Cochran, Jacqueline
Curtiss, Glenn Hammond
De Seversky, Alexander Procofieff
Doolittle, James Harold
Earhart, Amelia Mary
Hughes, Howard Robard
Hunsaker, Jerome Clark
Jeffries, John
Kármán, Theodore von
Langley, Samuel Pierpont
Lear, William Powell
LeMay, Curtis Emerson
Lindbergh, Charles Augustus
Lowe, Thaddeus Sobieski Coulincourt
Martin, Glenn Luther
Mitchell, William (Billy)
Piccard, Jean Félix
Post, Wiley
Rickenbacker, Edward Vernon
Sikorsky, Igor Ivan
Spaatz, Carl
Wellman, Walter
Wright Brothers

AMBASSADORS

See DIPLOMATS

ANTHROPOLOGISTS AND ARCHAEOLOGISTS

Albright, William Foxwell

Bandelier, Adolph Francis Alphonse
Benedict, Ruth Fulton
Boas, Franz
Breasted, James Henry
Brinton, Daniel Garrison
Dunham, Katherine
Eiseley, Loren Corey
Fewkes, Jesse Walter
Herskovits, Melville Jean
Hooton, Earnest Albert
Hrdlička, Aleš
Kroeber, Alfred Louis
Linton, Ralph
Lowie, Robert Harry
Mead, Margaret
Montagu, Ashley
Mooney, James
Morgan, Lewis Henry
Parsons, Elsie Worthington Clews
Powell, John Wesley
Radin, Paul
Redfield, Robert
Sapir, Edward
Schoolcraft, Henry Rowe

ARCHAEOLOGISTS

See ANTHROPOLOGISTS AND ARCHAE-
OLOGISTS

ARCHITECTS AND CITY PLANNERS

Adler, Dankmar
Benjamin, Asher
Bennett, Edward Herbert
Bulfinch, Charles
Burnham, Daniel Hudson
Cram, Ralph Adams
Downing, Andrew Jackson
Gilbert, Cass
Goodhue, Bertram Grosvenor
Griffiths, John Willis
Gropius, Walter Adolf
Harrison, Peter
Hoban, James
Holabird, William
Hunt, Richard Morris
Jenney, William Le Baron
Johnson, Philip Cortelyou
Latrobe, Benjamin Henry
L'Enfant, Pierre Charles
McIntire, Samuel
McKim, Charles Follen
Mies Van Der Rohe, Ludwig
Mills, Robert
Mizner, Addison
Neutra, Richard Josef
Olmstead, Frederick Law
Renwick, James
Richardson, Henry Hobson
Root, John Wellborn
Saarinen, Eero
Saarinen, Eliel
Stone, Edward Durell
Sullivan, Louis Henry
Taylor, David Watson

Thornton, William
Town, Ithiel
Upjohn, Richard
Urban, Joseph
White, Stanford
Wright, Frank Lloyd
Wright, Henry (1878–1936)
Yamasaki, Minoru

ARMY LEADERS AND SOLDIERS

Allen, Ethan
Allen, Henry Watkins
Anderson, Joseph Reid
Armstrong, John (1755–1816)
Armstrong, John (1758–1843)
Arnold, Benedict
Arnold, Henry Harley (Hap)
Atkinson, Henry
Banks, Nathaniel Prentiss
Beauregard, Pierre Gustave Toutant
Bee, Barnard Elliott
Bliss, Tasker Howard
Bonneville, Benjamin Louis Eulalie de
Bradley, Omar Nelson
Bragg, Braxton
Breckinridge, John Cabell
Brown, Jacob Jennings
Buckner, Simon Bolivar (1823–1914)
Buckner, Simon Bolivar, Jr. (1886–1945)
Buell, Don Carlos
Burnside, Ambrose Everett
Butler, Benjamin Franklin
Carson, Kit
Carter, Samuel Powhatan
Chaffee, Adna Romanza (1842–1914)
Chaffee, Adna Romanza (1884–1941)
Clark, George Rogers
Clark, Mark Wayne
Clark, William
Clinton, George
Conway, Thomas
Cox, Jacob Dolson
Crook, George
Custer, George Armstrong
Davis, Benjamin Oliver
Dearborn, Henry
Delany, Martin Robinson
Dix, John Adams
Dodge, Grenville Mellen
Donovan, William Joseph
Doubleday, Abner
Early, Jubal Anderson
Eaton, William
Eisenhower, Dwight David
Forrest, Nathan Bedford
Frémont, John Charles
Funston, Frederick
Gadsden, James
Gates, Horatio
Geary, John White
Goethals, George Washington
Gorgas, Josiah
Gorgas, William Crawford
Grant, Ulysses S.

Greely, Adolphus Washington
Greene, Nathanael
Hale, Nathan
Halleck, Henry Wager
Hampton, Wade
Hancock, Winfield Scott
Hays, John Coffee
Higginson, Thomas Wentworth Storrow
Hill, Ambrose Powell
Hood, John Bell
Hooker, Joseph
Houston, Samuel
Howard, Oliver Otis
Hull, William
Jackson, Andrew
Jackson, Thomas Jonathan (Stonewall)
Johnson, Hugh Samuel
Johnston, Albert Sidney
Johnston, Joseph Eggleston
Kalb, Johann
Kearny, Philip
Kearny, Stephen Watts
Keifer, Joseph Warren
Knox, Henry
Kosciusko, Thaddeus
Lafayette, Marquis de
Lamar, Mirabeau Buonaparte
Lane, James Henry
Lea, Homer
Leavenworth, Henry
Lee, Charles
Lee, Fitzhugh
Lee, Henry (Light-Horse Harry)
Lee, Robert Edward
Lewis, Meriwether
Lincoln, Benjamin
Logan, John Alexander
Longstreet, James
MacArthur, Arthur
MacArthur, Douglas
McAuliffe, Anthony Clement
McClellan, George Brinton
Mackenzie, Ranald Slidell
Marion, Francis
Marshall, George Catlett
Meade, George Gordon
Mifflin, Thomas
Miles, Nelson Appleton
Morgan, Daniel
Morgan, John Hunt
Mosby, John Singleton
Moultrie, William
Muhlenberg, John Peter Gabriel
Murphy, Audie
Otis, Harrison Gray
Parker, John
Patton, George Smith, Jr.
Pepperrell, Sir William
Pershing, John Joseph
Pickering, Timothy
Pickett, George Edward
Pike, Albert
Pike, Zebulon Montgomery
Pinckney, Charles Cotesworth
Pinckney, Thomas

Polk, Leonidas
Prescott, William
Pulaski, Kazimierz
Putnam, Israel
Putnam, Rufus
Quantrill, William Clarke
Ridgway, Matthew Bunker
Rochambeau, Comte de
Rogers, Robert
Rosecrans, William Starke
St. Clair, Arthur
Schofield, John McAllister
Schurz, Carl
Schuyler, Philip John
Scott, Winfield
Sevier, John
Shafter, William Rufus
Shays, Daniel
Shelby, Isaac
Sheridan, Philip Henry
Sherman, William Tecumseh
Sickles, Daniel Edgar
Smith, Walter Bedell
Standish, Miles
Stark, John
Sternberg, George Miller
Steuben, Baron von
Stilwell, Joseph Warren
Stuart, James Ewell Brown
Sullivan, John
Sumter, Thomas
Taylor, Zachary
Terry, Alfred Howe
Thayer, Sylvanus
Thomas, George Henry
Travis, William Barret
Trumbull, Jonathan (1740–1809)
Vallejo, Mariano Guadalupe
Walker, William
Wallace, Lewis
Warren, Joseph
Washington, George
Wayne, Anthony
Westmoreland, William Childs
Wheeler, Joseph
Wilkinson, James
Wood, Leonard
Wood, Robert Elkington
York, Alvin Cullum

ART COLLECTORS

Altman, Benjamin
Brundage, Avery
Corcoran, William Wilson
Gardner, Isabella Stewart
Getty, Jean Paul
Huntington, Henry Edwards
Jarves, James Jackson
Kahn, Otto Herman
Kress, Samuel Henry
Mellon, Andrew William
Rosenbach, Abraham Simon Wolf

ART CRITICS AND ART HISTORIANS

Berenson, Bernard

Fenollosa, Ernest Francisco
Jarves, James Jackson
Panofsky, Erwin

ASTRONAUTS AND SPACE SCIENTISTS

See also AIR MEN AND AIR WOMEN
Armstrong, Neil Alden
Braun, Wernher von
Glenn, John Herschel, Jr.
Goddard, Robert Hutchings

ASTRONOMERS

Abbe, Cleveland
Adams, Walter Sydney
Baade, Walter
Barnard, Edward Emerson
Bond, George Phillips
Bond, William Cranch
Bowditch, Nathaniel
Campbell, William Wallace
Cannon, Annie Jump
Clark, Alvan
Draper, Henry
Gilliss, James Melville
Hale, George Ellery
Hall, Asaph
Hubble, Edwin Powell
Langley, Samuel Pierpont
Lowell, Percival
Mason, Charles, and Jeremiah Dixon
Mitchell, Maria
Newcomb, Simon
Peirce, Benjamin
Pickering, Edward Charles
Rittenhouse, David
Russell, Henry Norris
Shapley, Harlow
Slipher, Vesto Melvin
Struve, Otto
Winthrop, John (1714–1779)

ATHLETES

See also SPORTS FIGURES
Aaron, Henry Louis
Ali, Muhammad
Anson, Adrian Constantine (Cap)
Arcaro, George Edward (Eddie)
Ashe, Arthur Robert, Jr.
Baugh, Samuel Adrian
Berra, Lawrence Peter (Yogi)
Blanda, George Frederick
Budge, Don
Button, Richard Totten
Chamberlain, Wilt
Cobb, Tyrus Raymond
Connolly, Maureen Catherine
Corbett, James John
Cousy, Robert Joseph
Dean, Dizzy
Dean, Man Mountain
Dempsey, Jack
DiMaggio, Joseph Paul, Jr.
Durocher, Leo Ernest
Ederle, Gertrude Caroline
Ewry, Ray C.

Feller, Robert William Andrew
Fitzsimmons, Robert Prometheus
Foxx, James Emory
Gehrig, Lou
Gibson, Althea
Gonzales, Richard Alonzo (Pancho)
Gorgeous George
Grange, Harold Edward (Red)
Hagen, Walter Charles
Halas, George Stanley
Heffelfinger, William Walter (Pudge)
Hitchcock, Thomas, Jr.
Hogan, William Benjamin (Ben)
Hornsby, Rogers
Johnson, Jack
Johnson, Walter Perry
Jones, Bobby
Koufax, Sanford (Sandy)
Louis, Joe
McGraw, John Joseph
Mack, Connie
Mantle, Mickey Charles
Marciano, Rocky
Mathewson, Christopher (Christy)
Mathias, Robert Bruce
Mays, Willie Howard, Jr.
Musial, Stanley Frank
Nagurski, Bronco
Namath, Joseph William
Nicklaus, Jack William
Owens, Jesse
Paige, Leroy Robert (Satchel)
Palmer, Arnold
Robinson, Jack Roosevelt (Jackie)
Robinson, Ray (Sugar Ray)
Russell, William Felton (Bill)
Ruth, George Herman (Babe)
Sarazen, Gene
Shoemaker, William Lee (Willie)
Snead, Samuel Jackson
Spahn, Warren Edward
Spalding, Albert Goodwill
Stengel, Charles Dillon (Casey)
Sullivan, John Lawrence
Thorpe, James Francis (Jim)
Tilden, William Tatem, Jr.
Trevino, Lee
Tunney, Gene
Unitas, John
Wagner, Honus
Weissmuller, Johnny
Weston, Edward Paycon
Williams, Ted
Wills, Helen Newington
Wright, Henry (Harry, 1835–1895)
Young, Cy
Zaharias, Mildred Ella Didrikson

AUTHORS

See also HUMORISTS; JOURNALISTS;
    PLAYWRIGHTS; POETS
Adams, Andy
Adams, Samuel Hopkins
Adams, William Taylor
Agee, James
Aiken, Conrad Potter

Alcott, Louisa May
Aldrich, Thomas Bailey
Alger, Horatio
Anderson, Sherwood
Antin, Mary
Applegate, Jesse
Arthur, Timothy Shay
Asimov, Isaac
Atkinson, Brooks
Austin, Mary
Babbitt, Irving
Bacon, Delia Salter
Baker, Ray Stannard
Baldwin, James
Barlow, Joel
Barth, John Simmons
Barton, Bruce
Bartram, William
Bates, Katherine Lee
Baum, Lyman Frank
Beard, Daniel Carter
Beebe, Lucius Morris
Beebe, William
Bellamy, Edward
Bellow, Saul
Benchley, Robert Charles
Benét, Stephen Vincent
Benét, William Rose
Bierce, Ambrose Gwinnett
Bigelow, John
Bodenheim, Maxwell
Bok, Edward William
Bourne, Randolph Silliman
Bowker, Richard Rogers
Brackenridge, Hugh Henry
Bradbury, Ray Douglas
Bromfield, Louis
Brooks, Van Wyck
Broun, Heywood
Brown, Charles Brockden
Brownson, Orestes Augustus
Buck, Pearl S.
Buckley, William Frank, Jr.
Bulfinch, Thomas
Burroughs, Edgar Rice
Burroughs, John
Burroughs, William Seward
    (1914–   )
Byrd, William
Cabell, James Branch
Cable, George Washington
Cahan, Abraham
Caldwell, Erskine Preston
Capote, Truman
Carey, Mathew
Carnegie, Dale
Carson, Rachel Louise
Cary, Alice
Cather, Willa Sibert
Catlin, George
Chandler, Raymond Thornton
Chapman, John Jay
Chesnutt, Charles Waddell
Child, Lydia Maria
Chopin, Kate O'Flaherty
Ciardi, John Anthony
Clarke, James Freeman

Clemens, Samuel Langhorne
Colby, Frank Moore
Connelly, Marc
Cooper, James Fenimore
Cousins, Norman
Cowley, Malcolm
Cozzens, James Gould
Crane, Stephen
Crawford, Francis Marion
Creel, George Edward
Crèvecoeur, Michel Guillaume Jean de
Croly, Herbert David
Curtis, George William
Dana, Richard Henry
Dannay, Frederic, and Manfred Ben-
    nington Lee (Ellery Queen)
Davis, Elmer Holmes
Davis, Richard Harding
Day, Clarence Shepard, Jr.
Dell, Floyd
Dennie, Joseph
De Voto, Bernard Augustine
Dickey, James
Dodge, Mary Elizabeth Mapes
Donnelly, Ignatius
Dos Passos, John Roderigo
Douglas, Lloyd Cassel
Douglas, William Orville
Dreiser, Theodore
Du Bois, William Edward Burghardt
Durant, Will
Dwight, Timothy
Eastman, Max Forrester
Eggleston, Edward
Eiseley, Loren Corey
Eliot, Thomas Stearns
Ellison, Ralph Waldo
Emerson, Ralph Waldo
Erskine, John
Fadiman, Clifton Paul
Farmer, Fannie Merritt
Farrell, James Thomas
Faulkner, William Cuthbert
Faust, Frederick Schiller
Fearing, Kenneth Flexner
Ferber, Edna
Field, Eugene
Filson, John
Fisher, Dorothy Canfield
Fitzgerald, F. Scott
Fitzhugh, George
Flint, Timothy
Frank, Glenn
Franklin, Benjamin
Freeman, Mary Eleanor Wilkins
Friedan, Betty Naomi Goldstein
Fromm, Erich
Frothingham, Octavius Brooks
Fuller, Margaret, Marchioness Ossoli
Gardner, Erle Stanley
Garland, Hamlin
Geisel, Theodor Seuss
Glasgow, Ellen Anderson Gholson
Goodrich, Samuel Griswold
Gregg, Josiah
Grey, Zane
Grinnell, George Bird

Griswold, Rufus Wilmot
Gronlund, Laurence
Gunther, John
Haldeman-Julius, Emanuel
Hale, Edward Everett
Hale, Lucretia Peabody
Hale, Sarah Josepha Buell
Hall, James (1793–1868)
Hamilton, Edith
Hammett, Dashiell
Harris, Joel Chandler
Harte, Bret
Hawthorne, Nathaniel
Hay, John Milton
Hearn, Lafcadio
Hecht, Ben
Heinlein, Robert Anson
Held, John, Jr.
Helper, Hinton Rowan
Hemingway, Ernest Miller
Hersey, John Richard
Heyward, DuBose
Higginson, Thomas Wentworth
    Storrow
Hillquit, Morris
Hines, Duncan
Holland, Josiah Gilbert
Holmes, Oliver Wendell (1809–1894)
Hone, Philip
Hopkinson, Francis
Hough, Emerson
Howe, Edgar Watson
Howells, William Dean
Hubbard, Elbert Green
Hughes, Langston
Huneker, James Gibbons
Ingraham, Joseph Holt
Ingraham, Prentiss
Irving, Washington
Jackson, Helen Hunt
James, Henry (1811–1882)
James, Henry (1843–1916)
Jewett, Sarah Orne
Johnson, James Weldon
Judson, Edward Zane Carroll
Kazan, Elia
Keller, Helen Adams
Kent, Rockwell
Kerouac, Jack
Kilmer, Joyce
Krutch, Joseph Wood
Lanier, Sidney
Lardner, Ring
Lazarus, Emma
Lee, Gypsy Rose
Lewis, Sinclair
Lippmann, Walter
Lloyd, Henry Demarest
Locke, Alain LeRoy
Lodge, Henry Cabot (1850–1924)
London, Jack
Longstreet, Augustus Baldwin
Lovecraft, Howard Phillips
Lowell, Amy
Lowell, James Russell
Lowell, Percival
Luce, Clare Boothe

McCarthy, Mary Therese
McCullers, Carson Smith
McKay, Claude
Mailer, Norman
Malamud, Bernard
Marquand, John Phillips
Marquis, Donald Robert Perry
Masters, Edgar Lee
Melville, Herman
Mencken, Henry Louis
Merton, Thomas
Michener, James Albert
Miller, Arthur
Miller, Henry Valentine
Miller, Perry Gilbert Eddy
Mitchell, Margaret
Mitchell, Silas Weir
More, Paul Elmer
Mowatt, Anna Cora Ogden
Mumford, Lewis
Nabokov, Vladimir Vladimirovich
Nathan, George Jean
Neal, John
Neihardt, John Gneisenau
Nock, Albert Jay
Norris, Frank
Norton, Charles Eliot
O'Hara, John Henry
O'Neill, Rose Cecil
O'Reilly, John Boyle
Owen, Robert Dale
Page, Walter Hines
Paine, Thomas
Parker, Dorothy
Parton, James
Parton, Sara Payson Willis
Patten, Gilbert
Paulding, James Kirke
Perelman, Sidney Joseph
Pitkin, Walter Boughton
Plimpton, George Ames
Poe, Edgar Allan
Porter, Gene Stratton
Porter, Katherine Anne
Porter, William Sydney
Post, Emily Price
Pound, Ezra Loomis
Pyle, Howard
Rand, Ayn
Ransom, John Crowe
Read, Opie Percival
Richards, Ivor Armstrong
Rinehart, Mary Roberts
Ripley, George
Robert, Henry Martyn
Roberts, Elizabeth Madox
Rölvaag, Ole Edvart
Roosevelt, Eleanor
Roth, Philip Milton
Rowson, Susanna Haswell
Royall, Anne Newport
Runyon, Damon
Salinger, Jerome David
Sandburg, Carl
Santayana, George
Saroyan, William
Seldes, Gilbert Vivian

Sherwood, Robert Emmet
Shirer, William Lawrence
Sigourney, Lydia Howard Huntley
Simms, William Gilmore
Sinclair, Upton Beall
Singer, Isaac Bashevis
Smith, Charles Henry
Smith, Samuel Francis
Smith, Seba
Southworth, Emma Dorothy Eliza
    Nevitte
Spillane, Mickey
Spingarn, Joel Elias
Springs, Elliot White
Stein, Gertrude
Steinbeck, John Ernst
Stockton, Frank
Stowe, Harriet Elizabeth Beecher
Stratemeyer, Edward
Tarbell, Ida Minerva
Tarkington, Booth
Tate, Allen
Taylor, Bayard
Terhune, Albert Payson
Thomas, Lowell Jackson
Thoreau, Henry David
Thorpe, Thomas Bangs
Thurber, James Grover
Ticknor, George
Train, George Francis
Trilling, Lionel
Tyler, Royall
Updike, John Hoyer
Uris, Leon Marcus
Van Doren, Carl Clinton
Van Doren, Mark
Vidal, Gore
Villard, Oswald Garrison
Vonnegut, Kurt, Jr.
Wallace, Lewis
Warner, Charles Dudley
Warren, Mercy Otis
Warren, Robert Penn
Weems, Mason Locke
Wells, David Ames
Welty, Eudora
West, Nathanael
Westcott, Edward Noyes
Wharton, Edith
White, Elwyn Brooks
White, Walter Francis
White, William Allen
Whitlock, Brand
Wiggin, Kate Douglas
Wilder, Thornton Niven
Willis, Nathaniel Parker
Wilson, Edmund
Wilson, Harry Leon
Wirt, William
Wister, Owen
Wolfe, Thomas Clayton
Woodberry, George Edward
Woollcott, Alexander
Wouk, Herman
Wright, Harold Bell
Wright, Richard
Wylie, Elinor

Wylie, Philip Gordon
Yerby, Frank Garvin

AUTO RACERS

See SPORTS FIGURES

AVIATORS

See AIR MEN AND AIR WOMEN

BACTERIOLOGISTS AND MICROBIOLOGISTS

See also BIOCHEMISTS; BIOPHYSICISTS
    AND MOLECULAR BIOLOGISTS;
    GENETICISTS; IMMUNOLOGISTS
Delbrück, Max
Dubos, René Jules
Enders, John Franklin
Hershey, Alfred Day
Luria, Salvador Edward
Noguchi, Hideyo
Smith, Theobald
Sternberg, George Miller
Waksman, Selman Abraham
Weller, Thomas Huckle
Zinsser, Hans

BALLET DANCERS

See CHOREOGRAPHERS AND DANCERS

BANKERS AND FINANCIERS

See also BUSINESSMEN AND BUSINESS-
    WOMEN
Baker, George Fisher
Baruch, Bernard Mannes
Belmont, August
Biddle, Nicholas
Brady, James Buchanan
Cheves, Langdon
Cooke, Jay
Corcoran, William Wilson
Crocker, Charles
Dawes, Charles Gates
Drew, Daniel
Durant, Thomas Clark
Eaton, Cyrus Stephen
Field, Cyrus West
Fisk, James
Gates, John Warne
Giannini, Amadeo Peter
Gould, Jay
Grace, William Russell
Green, Hetty
Harriman, Edward Henry
Hill, James Jerome
Holladay, Ben
Kahn, Otto Herman
Lehman, Herbert Henry
Loeb, James Morris
Mellon, Andrew William
Moore, William Henry
Morgan, John Pierpont
Morris, Robert

Morrow, Dwight Whitney
Morse, Charles Wyman
Peabody, George
Perkins, George Walbridge
Ryan, Thomas Fortune
Sage, Russell
Salomon, Haym
Seligman, Joseph
Vanderbilt, Cornelius (1794–1877)
Vanderbilt, William Henry
Villard, Henry
Westcott, Edward Noyes
Yerkes, Charles Tyson

BASEBALL PLAYERS

See ATHLETES

BASKETBALL PLAYERS

See ATHLETES

BIBLIOGRAPHERS AND LIBRARIANS

Bartlett, John Russell
Billings, John Shaw
Dana, John Cotton
Dewey, Melvil
Leypoldt, Frederick
Putnam, Herbert
Thwaites, Reuben Gold
Winsor, Justin

BILLIARD PLAYERS

See SPORTS FIGURES

BIOCHEMISTS

See also BACTERIOLOGISTS AND MICRO-
BIOLOGISTS; CHEMISTS; IMMU-
NOLOGISTS
Anfinsen, Christian Boehmer
Asimov, Isaac
Axelrod, Julius
Bloch, Konrad
Cori, Carl Ferdinand
Doisy, Edward Adelbert
Du Vigneaud, Vincent
Edelman, Gerald Maurice
Funk, Casimir
Holley, Robert William
Kendall, Edward Calvin
Khorana, Har Gobind
Kornberg, Arthur
Lipmann, Fritz Albert
Moore, Stanford
Nirenberg, Marshall Warren
Northrop, John Howard
Ochoa, Severo
Stanley, Wendell Meredith
Stein, William Howard
Sumner, James Batcheller
Sutherland, Earl Wilbur, Jr.
Szent-Györgyi, Albert
Tatum, Edward Lawrie
Watson, James Dewey

BIOLOGISTS

See AGRICULTURISTS AND AGRON-
OMISTS; BACTERIOLOGISTS AND
MICROBIOLOGISTS; BIOCHEMISTS;
BIOPHYSICISTS AND MOLECULAR
BIOLOGISTS; BOTANISTS AND HOR-
TICULTURISTS; CONSERVATIONISTS
AND NATURALISTS; GENETICISTS;
IMMUNOLOGISTS; PHYSIOLOGISTS;
ZOOLOGISTS

BIOPHYSICISTS AND MOLECULAR BIOLOGISTS

See also BACTERIOLOGISTS AND MICRO-
BIOLOGISTS; BIOCHEMISTS
Bronk, Detlev Wulf
Delbrück, Max
Glaser, Donald Arthur
Hartline, Halden Keffer
Hershey, Alfred Day
Szilard, Leo
Watson, James Dewey

BOTANISTS AND HORTI-CULTURISTS

See also CONSERVATIONISTS AND
NATURALISTS
Bailey, Liberty Hyde
Bartram, John
Bartram, William
Bigelow, Jacob
Borlaug, Norman Ernest
Burbank, Luther
Colden, Cadwallader
Cowles, Henry Chandler
Cutler, Manasseh
Downing, Andrew Jackson
Fairchild, David Grandison
Gray, Asa
Mitchell, John
Pound, Roscoe
Rafinesque, Constantine Samuel
Torrey, John
Vick, James
White, David

BOXERS

See ATHLETES

BRIDGE PLAYERS

Culbertson, Ely
Goren, Charles Henry
Vanderbilt, Harold Stirling

BUSINESSMEN AND BUSINESSWOMEN

See also BANKERS AND FINANCIERS
Alger, Cyrus
Altman, Benjamin
Ames, Oakes
Anderson, Joseph Reid
Anderson, Rasmus Björn
Arden, Elizabeth
Armour, Philip Danforth

Astor, John Jacob
Ayer, Francis Wayland
Baer, George Frederick
Baldwin, Matthias William
Bard, William
Barton, Bruce
Beach, Frederick Converse
Bendix, Vincent
Benton, William
Bigelow, Erastus Brigham
Billings, Frederick
Bissell, George Henry
Boyden, Seth
Bradley, Milton
Brattle, Thomas
Brookings, Robert Somers
Brundage, Avery
Busch, Adolphus
Butterfield, John
Candler, Asa Griggs
Carnegie, Andrew
Chrysler, Walter Percy
Clark, Alvan
Cochran, Jacqueline
Coffin, Howard Earle
Colgate, William
Colt, Samuel
Cooper, Peter
Corliss, George Henry
Cornell, Ezra
Cortelyou, George Bruce
Couzens, James
Coxey, Jacob Sechler
Crocker, Charles
Daly, Marcus
Deere, John
Delamater, Cornelius Henry
Delmonico, Lorenzo
Depew, Chauncey Mitchell
De Vinne, Theodore Low
Disney, Walt
Doherty, Henry Latham
Dow, Herbert Henry
Drake, Edwin Laurentine
Duke, James Buchanan
Du Pont de Nemours, Éleuthère
   Irénée
Durant, Thomas Clark
Durant, William Crapo
Duryea, Charles Edgar
Dyott, Thomas W.
Eastman, George
Evans, John
Faber, John Eberhard
Fargo, William George
Field, Cyrus West
Field, Marshall
Filene, Edward Albert
Firestone, Harvey Samuel
Fiske, Haley
Flagler, Henry Morrison
Ford, Henry
Forten, James
Frick, Henry Clay
Fuller, Alfred Carl
Gadsden, James

Gary, Elbert Henry
Getty, Jean Paul
Gilbert, Alfred Carlton
Gillette, King Camp
Girard, Stephen
Glidden, Charles Jasper
Gorham, Nathaniel
Grace, William Russell
Green, Duff
Gregg, William
Guggenheim, Meyer
Haggin, James Ben Ali
Hall, Charles Martin
Hall, Joyce Clyde
Hanna, Mark
Harriman, Averell
Harriman, Edward Henry
Harris, Townsend
Harvey, Frederick Henry
Hearst, George
Heinz, Henry John
Herrick, Myron Timothy
Hershey, Milton Snavely
Hewitt, Abram Stevens
Hill, George Washington
Hill, James Jerome
Hilton, Conrad Nicholson
Hires, Charles Elmer
Holladay, Ben
Hone, Philip
Hughes, Howard Robard
Humphreys, Joshua
Hunt, Haroldson Lafayette
Huntington, Collis Potter
Huntington, Henry Edwards
Ingersoll, Robert Hawley
Insull, Samuel
Johnson, Howard Deering
Johnson, Tom Loftin
Jones, Samuel Milton
Joy, James Frederick
Kaiser, Henry John
Kellogg, Will Keith
Kemble, Gouverneur
King, Richard
Kress, Samuel Henry
Landon, Alfred Mossman
Lasker, Albert Davis
Lawrence, Abbott
Lawrence, Amos Adams
Lee, Ivy Ledbetter
Low, Seth
Lowell, Francis Cabot
McAdoo, William Gibbs
McCormick, Cyrus Hall
McCoy, Joseph Geating
Mackay, Clarence Hungerford
McKay, Donald
Meiggs, Henry
Mizner, Addison
Morgenthau, Henry (1856–1946)
Ogden, William Butler
Olds, Ransom Eli
O'Neill, Rose Cecil
Otis, Elisha Graves
Palmer, Potter

Parrott, Robert Parker
Patterson, John Henry
Peabody, George
Penney, James Cash
Pepperrell, Sir William
Perkins, George Walbridge
Pillsbury, Charles Alfred
Pinkham, Lydia Estes
Pollock, Oliver
Pope, Albert Augustus
Post, Charles William
Pullman, George Mortimer
Remington, Eliphalet
Rhodes, James Ford
Rockefeller, John Davison
Romanoff, Michael
Rosenwald, Julius
Sarnoff, David
Schwab, Charles Michael
Sears, Isaac
Sears, Richard Warren
Selfridge, Harry Gordon
Sibley, Hiram
Sinclair, Harry Ford
Singer, Isaac Merrit
Slater, Samuel
Smith, Francis Marion
Spalding, Albert Goodwill
Spreckels, Claus
Springs, Elliot White
Squibb, Edward Robinson
Stanford, Leland
Stanley Brothers
Statler, Ellsworth Milton
Steinway, Henry Engelhard
Stetson, John Batterson
Stevens, Edwin Augustus
Stevens, Robert Livingston
Stewart, Alexander Turney
Stiegel, Henry William
Straus, Isidor, and Nathan Straus
Strauss, Levi
Studebaker, Clement
Stutz, Harry Clayton
Swift, Gustavus Franklin
Swope, Gerard
Tappan, Arthur
Terry, Eli
Tevis, Lloyd
Thomas, Seth
Thompson, James Walter
Tiffany, Charles Lewis
Tilyou, George Cornelius
Train, George Francis
Trumbull, Jonathan (1710–1785)
Vail, Alfred Lewis
Vail, Theodore Newton
Van Cortlandt, Stephanus
Vanderbilt, Cornelius
Vanderbilt, Harold Stirling
Vanderbilt, William Henry
Vanderbilt, William Kissam
Van Sweringen, Oris Paxton
Vassar, Matthew
Villard, Henry
Walgreen, Charles Rudolph

Walker, Sarah Breedlove
Wanamaker, John
Ward, Montgomery
Waterman, Lewis Edson
Watson, Elkanah
Watson, Thomas Augustus
Watson, Thomas John
Welch, Robert H. W., Jr.
Wells, Henry
Westinghouse, George
Weyerhaeuser, Frederick
Whitney, Asa
Whitney, William Collins
Willys, John North
Wilson, Charles Erwin
Wilson, Samuel
Winchester, Oliver Fisher
Winton, Alexander
Wood, Robert Elkington
Woolworth, Frank Winfield
Wrigley, William, Jr.
Yale, Linus

CARTOGRAPHERS, GEOGRAPHERS, AND SURVEYORS

Bowman, Isaiah
Davis, William Morris
Gannett, Henry
Hassler, Ferdinand Rudolph
Huntington, Ellsworth
Hutchins, Thomas
Mason, Charles, and Jeremiah Dixon
Matthes, François Émile
Mitchell, John
Morse, Jedidiah
Thompson, David
White, John

CARTOONISTS AND ILLUSTRATORS

See also PAINTERS
Abbey, Edwin Austin
Addams, Charles Samuel
Arno, Peter
Baker, George (1915–   )
Beard, Daniel Carter
Block, Herbert Lawrence
Caniff, Milton Arthur
Capp, Al
Davies, Arthur Bowen
Disney, Walt
Fisher, Harry Conway (Bud)
Flagg, James Montgomery
Geisel, Theodor
Gibson, Charles Dana
Glackens, William James
Goldberg, Rube
Gould, Chester
Gray, Harold Lincoln
Gropper, William
Held, John, Jr.
Herriman, George
Hokinson, Helen
Kelly, Walter Crawford

Kent, Rockwell
King, Frank
McCutcheon, John Tinney
Mauldin, William Henry (Bill)
Nast, Thomas
O'Neill, Rose Cecil
Outcault, Richard Felton
Parrish, Maxfield Frederick
Pennell, Joseph
Pyle, Howard
Remington, Frederic
Ripley, Robert LeRoy
Rockwell, Norman
Schulz, Charles Monroe
Segar, Elzie Crisler
Steinberg Saul
Thurber, James Grover
Wyeth, Newell Convers
Young, Murat Bernard (Chic)

CHEMISTS

See also BIOCHEMISTS
Adams, Roger
Atwater, Wilbur Olin
Babcock, Stephen Moulton
Baekeland, Leo Hendrik
Calvin, Melvin
Carothers, Wallace Hume
Chandler, Charles Frederick
Cohn, Edwin Joseph
Conant, James Bryant
Cooper, Thomas
Dow, Herbert Henry
Draper, Henry
Draper, John William
Giauque, William Francis
Gibbs, Oliver Wolcott
Hall, Charles Martin
Jackson, Charles Thomas
Julian, Percy Lavon
Langmuir, Irving
Lewis, Gilbert Newton
Libby, Willard Frank
Morley, Edward Williams
Mulliken, Robert Sanderson
Noyes, Arthur Amos
Onsager, Lars
Pauling, Linus Carl
Remsen, Ira
Richards, Theodore William
Seaborg Glenn Theodore
Silliman, Benjamin (1779–1864)
Silliman, Benjamin, Jr. (1816–1885)
Torrey, John
Urey, Harold Clayton
Wiley, Harvey Washington
Woodward, Robert Burns

CHESS PLAYERS

Fischer, Robert James
Morphy, Paul Charles
Steinitz, William

CHIROPRACTORS

See MEDICAL FIGURES

CHOREOGRAPHERS AND DANCERS

Astaire, Fred
Balanchine, George
Berkeley, Busby
Castle, Vernon Blythe
De Mille, Agnes George
Duncan, Isadora
Dunham, Katherine
Graham, Martha
Montez, Lola
Robbins, Jerome
Robinson, Bill (Bojangles)
St. Denis, Ruth, and Ted Shawn
Tallchief, Maria

CITY AND REGIONAL PLANNERS

See ARCHITECTS AND CITY PLANNERS

CIVIC LEADERS

See REFORMERS

CLERGYMEN

See RELIGIOUS LEADERS

COACHES

See SPORTS FIGURES

COLONIAL FIGURES

See also EXPLORERS; FRONTIER
FIGURES AND PIONEERS
Adams, Samuel
Alden, John
Andros, Sir Edmund
Anza, Juan Bautista de
Applegate, Jesse
Ashmun, Jehudi
Attucks, Crispus
Austin, Stephen Fuller
Bacon, Nathaniel
Belcher, Jonathan
Berkeley, Sir William
Bienville, Jean Baptiste Le Moyne,
Sieur de
Bowdoin, James
Bradford, William
Brent, Margaret
Brewster, William
Byrd, William
Cadillac, Antoine Laumet de la Mothe
Calvert, Charles
Calvert, George
Calvert, Leonard
Carroll, Charles
Champlain, Samuel de
Colden, Cadwallader
Coronado, Francisco Vásquez de
Croghan, George
Cutler, Manasseh
Dare, Virginia
Dayton, Jonathan
Deane, Silas
De Lancey, James

De La Warr, Thomas West, Baron
Dickinson, John
Dudley, Thomas
Dulany, Daniel
Endecott, John
Galloway, Joseph
Gosnold, Bartholomew
Hale, Nathan
Hutchinson, Thomas
Iberville, Pierre Le Moyne, Sieur d'
Johnson, Sir William
La Salle, Sieur de
Leisler, Jacob
Logan, James (1674–1751)
Ludwick, Christopher
McCauley, Mary Ludwig Hays
(Molly Pitcher)
Mazzei, Philip
Menéndez de Avilés, Pedro
Minuit, Peter
Morton, Thomas
Oglethorpe, James Edward
Oñate, Juan de
Pastorius, Francis Daniel
Pattie, James Ohio
Pendleton, Edmund
Penn, William
Pepperrell, Sir William
Peralta, Pedro de
Phips, Sir William
Pollock, Oliver
Prescott, Samuel
Read, George
Revere, Paul
Salomon, Haym
Sears, Isaac
Sherman, Roger
Shirley, William
Smith, John
Standish, Miles
Stuyvesant, Peter
Thompson, Benjamin, Count
Rumford
Thorfinn Karlsefni
Trumbull, Jonathan (1710–1785)
Underhill, John
Van Cortlandt, Stephanus
White, John
Williams, Roger
Winslow, Edward
Winslow, Josiah
Winthrop, John (1588–1649)
Wise, John
Witherspoon, John
Wolcott, Oliver (1726–1797)
Wolcott, Roger

COLUMNISTS

See JOURNALISTS

COMEDIANS

See ENTERTAINERS

COMMENTATORS

See JOURNALISTS

COMPOSERS AND SONGWRITERS

See also MUSICIANS
Arlen, Harold
Babbitt, Milton Byron
Bacharach, Burt
Barber, Samuel
Berlin, Irving
Bernstein, Leonard
Billings, William
Bland, James A.
Blitzstein, Marc
Bloch, Ernest
Brubeck, David Warren
Burleigh, Harry Thacker
Cage, John Milton, Jr.
Carmichael, Hoagland Howard
Cash, Johnny
Cohan, George Michael
Copland, Aaron
Cowell, Henry Dixon
Damrosch, Walter Johannes
Dello Joio, Norman
Dylan, Bob
Ellington, Duke
Emmett, Daniel Decatur
Foster, Stephen Collins
Friml, Rudolf
Gershwin, George
Gilbert, Henry Franklin Belknap
Gilmore, Patrick Sarsfield
Goldman, Edwin Franko
Gottschalk, Louis Moreau
Grofé, Ferde
Guthrie, Woody
Hammerstein, Oscar, II
Handy, William Christopher
Hanson, Howard Harold
Harris, Roy Ellsworth
Herbert, Victor
Hill, Joe
Ives, Charles Edward
Joplin, Scott
Kay, Ulysses Simpson
Kern, Jerome David
Kreisler, Fritz
Ledbetter, Huddie
Loesser, Frank Henry
MacDowell, Edward Alexander
McKuen, Rod Marvin
Mason, Lowell
Maxwell, Elsa
Menotti, Gian-Carlo
Morton, Jelly Roll
Oliver, Joseph (King)
Parker, Charlie (Bird)
Piston, Walter Hamor
Porter, Cole
Rodgers, Richard
Romberg, Sigmund
Schönberg, Arnold
Schuman, William Howard
Seeger, Pete
Sessions, Roger Huntington
Sousa, John Philip
Spalding, Albert

Still, William Grant
Stravinsky, Igor Fedorovich
Taylor, Deems
Thomson, Virgil Garnett
Tiomkin, Dimitri
Varèse, Edgard
Weill, Kurt
Williams, Bert
Work, Henry Clay

CONDUCTORS

See MUSICIANS

CONGRESSIONAL FIGURES

See PUBLIC OFFICIALS

CONSERVATIONISTS AND NATURALISTS

See also BOTANISTS AND
  HORTICULTURISTS
Agassiz, Louis
Akeley, Carl Ethan
Andrews, Roy Chapman
Audubon, John James
Baird, Spencer Fullerton
Beard, Daniel Carter
Beebe, William
Buck, Frank
Burroughs, John
Carson, Rachel Louise
Cowles, Henry Chandler
Fernow, Bernhard Eduard
Garden, Alexander
Grinnell, George Bird
Krutch, Joseph Wood
Langford, Nathaniel Pitt
Leopold, Aldo
MacKaye, Benton
Mather, Stephen Tyng
Muir, John
Osborn, Fairfield
Perkins, Marlin
Pinchot, Gifford
Thoreau, Henry David

CRAFTSMEN, DESIGNERS, AND GRAPHIC ARTISTS

See also PAINTERS; SCULPTORS
Albers, Josef
Baskin, Leonard
Bellows, George Wesley
Buell, Abel
Currier, Nathaniel
Durand, Asher Brown
Eames, Charles
Force, Peter
Franklin, Benjamin
Fuller, Buckminster
Geddes, Norman Bel
Goudy, Frederic William
Harper Brothers
Humphreys, Joshua
Leslie, Frank
Loewy, Raymond Fernand
McIntire, Samuel

Moholy-Nagy, László
Pennell, Joseph
Phyfe, Duncan
Revere, Paul
Rogers, Bruce
Rush, William
Shahn, Benjamin
Sholes, Christopher Latham
Simonson, Lee
Thomas, Isaiah
Tiffany, Louis Comfort
Urban, Joseph
Whistler, James Abbott McNeill
Zenger, John Peter

CRIMINALS AND OUTLAWS

See also INTELLIGENCE AGENTS AND
  SPIES
Bass, Sam
Bonney, William H. (Billy the Kid)
Booth, John Wilkes
Capone, Alphonse
Chessman, Caryl Whittier
Dalton, Robert
Dillinger, John
Flegenheimer, Arthur (Dutch
  Schultz)
James, Jesse Woodson
Kidd, William
Laffite, Jean
Means, Gaston Bullock
Murieta, Joaquín
Murrell, John A.
Stroud, Robert
Younger, Cole

CRIMINOLOGISTS AND PENOLOGISTS

See also LAW ENFORCEMENT AGENTS
Glueck, Sheldon
Lawes, Lewis Edward

CRITICS

See AUTHORS

DANCERS

See CHOREOGRAPHERS AND DANCERS

DENTISTS

See MEDICAL FIGURES

DESIGNERS

See CRAFTSMEN, DESIGNERS, AND
  GRAPHIC ARTISTS

DETECTIVES

See LAW ENFORCEMENT AGENTS

DIPLOMATS

See also POLITICAL LEADERS;
  PUBLIC OFFICIALS
Acheson, Dean Gooderham
Adams, Charles Francis (1807–1886)

Cahan, Abraham
Carey, Mathew
Cattell, James McKeen
Cerf, Bennett Alfred
Colby, Frank Moore
Cousins, Norman
Cowles, Gardner
Cowley, Malcolm
Creel, George Edward
Croly, Herbert David
Curtis, Cyrus Herman Kotzschmar
Curtis, George William
Dana, Charles Anderson
Day, Benjamin Henry
De Bow, James Dunwoody Brownson
Dell, Floyd
Dennie, Joseph
Dodge, Mary Elizabeth Mapes
Doubleday, Frank Nelson
Douglass, Frederick
Dow, Charles Henry
Du Bois, William Edward Burghardt
Eastman, Max Forrester
Evans, George Henry
Fadiman, Clifton Paul
Fishbein, Morris
Fox, Richard Kyle
Frank, Glenn
Franklin, Benjamin
Freeman, Douglas Southall
Freneau, Philip Morin
Funk, Isaac Kauffman
Furness, Horace Howard
Garrison, William Lloyd
Gernsback, Hugo
Gilder, Richard Watson
Godey, Louis Antoine
Godkin, Edwin Lawrence
Goodrich, Samuel Griswold
Grady, Henry Woodfin
Graham, George Rex
Greeley, Horace
Griswold, Rufus Wilmot
Grosvenor, Gilbert Hovey
Haldeman-Julius, Emanuel
Hale, Sarah Josepha Buell
Harper Brothers
Harris, Benjamin
Hearst, William Randolph
Hefner, Hugh Marston
Hines, Duncan
Hoard, William Dempster
Holland, Josiah Gilbert
Holley, Alexander Lyman
Howard, Roy Wilson
Howe, Edgar Watson
Howells, William Dean
Hubbard, Elbert Green
Johnson, Alvin Saunders
Johnson, James Weldon
Johnson, John Harold
Knopf, Alfred Abraham
Krutch, Joseph Wood
Leslie, Frank
Leypoldt, Frederick
Lieber, Francis
Lippmann, Walter

Lorimer, George Horace
Lovejoy, Elijah Parish
Lowell, James Russell
Luce, Henry Robinson
Lundy, Benjamin
McClure, Samuel Sidney
McCormick, Robert Rutherford
Macfadden, Bernarr
Medill, Joseph
Mencken, Henry Louis
Merriam, Charles
Monroe, Harriet
More, Paul Elmer
Munro, George
Munsey, Frank Andrew
Nathan, George Jean
Nevins, Allan
Niles, Hezekiah
Norton, Charles Eliot
Ochs, Adolph Simon
O'Reilly, John Boyle
Otis, Harrison Gray
Page, Walter Hines
Paine, Robert Treat (1773–1811)
Patterson, Eleanor Medill
Perkins, Maxwell Evarts
Pulitzer, Joseph
Raymond, Henry Jarvis
Reid, Whitelaw
Reston, James Barrett
Ripley, George
Ross, Harold Wallace
Schirmer, Gustav
Schurz, Carl
Scripps, James Edmund
Silverman, Sime
Sparks, Jared
Spingarn, Joel Elias
Stieglitz, Alfred
Stockton, Frank
Sullivan, James Edward
Sulzberger, Arthur Hays
Tarbell, Ida Minerva
Thomas, Isaiah
Thwaites, Reuben Gold
Tucker, Benjamin Ricketson
Van Doren, Carl Clinton
Vick, James
Villard, Oswald Garrison
Wallace, De Witt
Wallace, Henry Agard
Warner, Charles Dudley
Watterson, Henry
White, William Allen
Wilkins, Roy
Willis, Nathaniel Parker
Zenger, John Peter

EDUCATORS

Adler, Cyrus
Adler, Felix
Adler, Mortimer Jerome
Agassiz, Louis
Agnew, David Hayes
Albright, William Foxwell
Alcott, Amos Bronson

Anderson, Rasmus Björn
Angell, James Burrill
Armstrong, Samuel Chapman
Babbitt, Irving
Bache, Alexander Dallas
Bagley, William Chandler
Bailey, Liberty Hyde
Baker, George Pierce
Barnard, Frederick Augustus Porter
Barnard, Henry
Barzun, Jacques Martin
Bates, Katherine Lee
Beecher, Catharine Esther
Beecher, Edward
Bell, Alexander Graham
Bemis, Samuel Flagg
Bethune, Mary McLeod
Bettelheim, Bruno
Blair, James
Blanding, Sarah Gibson
Bowman, Isaiah
Bronk, Detlev Wulf
Brookings, Robert Somers
Butler, Nicholas Murray
Cattell, James McKeen
Conant, James Bryant
Cooley, Thomas McIntyre
Cooper, Thomas
Cox, Jacob Dolson
Crandall, Prudence
Davies, Samuel
Dewey, John
Dobie, James Frank
Du Bois, William Edward Burghardt
Dunster, Henry
Durant, Will
Duveneck, Frank
Dwight, Timothy
Eliot, Charles William
Erskine, John
Fernow, Bernhard Eduard
Finney, Charles Grandison
Flexner, Abraham
Flint, Austin
Frank, Glenn
Fulbright, J. William
Furman, Richard
Gallaudet, Thomas Hopkins
Gardner, John William
Gilman, Daniel Coit
Goodspeed, Edgar Johnson
Gulick, Luther Halsey
Hadley, Arthur Twining
Hall, Granville Stanley
Hamilton, Edith
Hanson, Howard Harold
Harper, William Rainey
Harris, William Torrey
Hayakawa, Samuel Ichiye
Holbrook, Josiah
Holmes, Oliver Wendell (1809–1894)
Holt, Luther Emmett
Hope, John
Hopkins, Mark
Howe, Samuel Gridley
Hudson, Manley Ottmer
Hutchins, Robert Maynard

Jackson, Sheldon
Jessup, Philip Caryl
Johnson, Alvin Saunders
Johnson, William Samuel
Jones, Rufus Matthew
Jordan, David Starr
Judd, Charles Hubbard
Kaplan, Mordecai Menahem
Kittredge, George Lyman
Koch, Frederick Henry
Langdell, Christopher Columbus
Langston, John Mercer
Laws, Samuel Spahr
Locke, Alain LeRoy
Longstreet, Augustus Baldwin
Low, Seth
Lowell, Abbott Lawrence
Lowell, James Russell
Lyon, Mary Mason
McGuffey, William Holmes
Magnes, Judah Leon
Mann, Horace
Mason, Lowell
Mather, Increase
Meigs, Josiah
Meiklejohn, Alexander
Norton, Charles Eliot
Noyes, Arthur Amos
Osborn, Henry Fairfield
Osler, Sir William
Palmer, Alice Elvira Freeman
Palmer, George Herbert
Parker, Francis Wayland
Parrington, Vernon Louis
Parsons, Theophilus (1797–1882)
Peabody, Elizabeth Palmer
Pepper, William
Pound, Roscoe
Quincy, Josiah
Reeve, Tapping
Remsen, Ira
Revels, Hiram Rhoades
Robinson, James Harvey
Rowson, Susanna Haswell
Rugg, Harold Ordway
Rush, Benjamin
Schmucker, Samuel Simon
Schurman, Jacob Gould
Scott, James Brown
Silliman, Benjamin (1779–1864)
Silliman, Benjamin, Jr. (1816–1885)
Simpson, Matthew
Smith, Nathan
Smith, William
Sorin, Edward Frederick
Sparks, Jared
Stiles, Ezra
Stratton, Samuel Wesley
Sullivan, Harry Stack
Sumner, William Graham
Thayer, Sylvanus
Thomas, Martha Carey
Thorndike, Edward Lee
Ticknor, George
Tyler, Moses Coit
Van Hise, Charles Richard

Vincent, John Heyl
Waddel, Moses
Walker, Francis Amasa
Warren, John
Washington, Booker Taliaferro
Wayland, Francis
Webster, Noah
Welch, William Henry
Wheelock, Eleazar
Whipple, George Hoyt
White, Andrew Dickson
Wiggin, Kate Douglas
Wigmore, John Henry
Willard, Emma Hart
Willard, Frances Elizabeth Caroline
Witherspoon, John
Woodberry, George Edward
Woodbridge, Frederick James Eugene
Woodson, Carter Godwin
Woolsey, Theodore Dwight
Wright, Carroll Davidson
Wythe, George

ENGINEERS AND INVENTORS

Alexanderson, Ernst Frederik Werner
Alger, Cyrus
Allen, Horatio
Appleby, John Francis
Armstrong, Edwin Howard
Ashburner, Charles Edward
Babbitt, Isaac
Baekeland, Leo Hendrik
Baldwin, Loammi (1745–1807)
Baldwin, Loammi (1780–1838)
Beach, Alfred Ely
Beach, Moses Sperry
Beach, Moses Yale
Bell, Alexander Graham
Bendix, Vincent
Berliner, Emile
Bigelow, Erastus Brigham
Blanchard, Thomas
Borden, Gail
Boyden, Seth
Boyden, Uriah Atherton
Braun, Wernher von
Browning, John Moses
Buell, Abel
Burroughs, William Seward (1855–1898)
Burt, William Austin
Bush, Vannevar
Bushnell, David
Carlson, Chester Floyd
Carty, John Joseph
Chanute, Octave
Coffin, Howard Earle
Colt, Samuel
Cooper, Peter
Corliss, George Henry
Curtiss, Glenn Hammond
Daft, Leo
Dahlgren, John Adolphus Bernard
Davenport, Thomas

Deere, John
De Forest, Lee
Delamater, Cornelius Henry
De Seversky, Alexander Procofieff
Dodge, Grenville Mellen
Duryea, Charles Edgar
Eads, James Buchanan
Eastman, George
Edison, Thomas Alva
Ellet, Charles, Jr.
Ellsworth, Lincoln
Ericsson, John
Evans, Oliver
Farmer, Moses Gerrish
Farnsworth, Philo Taylor
Ferris, George Washington Gale
Fessenden, Reginald Aubrey
Fink, Albert
Fitch, John
Ford, Henry
Franklin, Benjamin
Fuller, Buckminster
Fulton, Robert
Garand, John Cantius
Gatling, Richard Jordan
Gernsback, Hugo
Gillette, King Camp
Glidden, Joseph Farwell
Godfrey, Thomas (1704–1749)
Goethals, George Washington
Goodyear, Charles
Gorrie, John
Gray, Elisha
Hoe, Richard Marsh
Holland, John Philip
Hollerith, Herman
Holley, Alexander Lyman
House, Royal Earl
Howe, Elias
Hunsaker, Jerome Clark
Hunt, Walter
Hussey, Obed
Ives, Frederick Eugene
Jansky, Karl Guthe
Johnson, Tom Loftin
Kármán, Theodore von
Kelly, William
Kettering, Charles Franklin
Lake, Simon
Land, Edwin Herbert
Langley, Samuel Pierpont
Latrobe, Benjamin Henry
Lear, William Powell
Lowe, Thaddeus Sobieski Coulincourt
McCormick, Cyrus Hall
MacKaye, Steele
McTammany, John
Matzeliger, Jan Ernest
Maxim, Hiram Stevens
Maxim, Hudson
Melville, George Wallace
Mergenthaler, Ottmar
Mills, Robert
Morse, Samuel Finley Breese
Olds, Ransom Eli
Otis, Elisha Graves

Parrott, Robert Parker
Piccard, Jean Félix
Pullman, George Mortimer
Pupin, Michael Idvorsky
Remington, Eliphalet
Robert, Henry Martyn
Roebling, John Augustus
Roebling, Washington Augustus
Rumsey, James
Selden, George Baldwin
Sholes, Christopher Latham
Singer, Isaac Merrit
Slater, Samuel
Sperry, Elmer Ambrose
Sprague, Frank Julian
Stanley Brothers
Steinman, David Barnard
Steinmetz, Charles Proteus
Stevens, Edwin Augustus
Stevens, John
Stevens, Robert Livingston
Sutro, Adolph Heinrich Joseph
Taylor, Frederick Winslow
Terzaghi, Karl
Tesla, Nikola
Thomson, Elihu
Thornton, William
Tilyou, George Cornelius
Vail, Alfred Lewis
Van Depoele, Charles Joseph
Vought, Chance Milton
Waterman, Lewis Edson
Watson, Thomas Augustus
Westinghouse, George
White, Canvass
Whitney, Asa
Whitney, Eli
Wright Brothers
Yale, Linus
Zworykin, Vladimir Kosma

ENGRAVERS

See CRAFTSMEN, DESIGNERS, AND
GRAPHIC ARTISTS

ENTERTAINERS

See also ACTORS AND ACTRESSES;
MUSICIANS; SINGERS

Allen, Fred
Allen, Steve
Baker, Josephine
Benchley, Robert Charles
Benny, Jack
Bergen, Edgar John
Berle, Milton
Brice, Fannie
Cantor, Eddie
Cash, Johnny
Christy, Edwin P.
Cody, William Frederick
Davis, Sammy, Jr.
Durante, Jimmy
Emmett, Daniel Decatur
Fields, W. C.
Foy, Eddie

Gleason, Jackie
Godfrey, Arthur Michael
Hope, Bob
Houdini, Harry
Jessel, George Albert
Jolson, Al
Kaye, Danny
Keaton, Buster
Kelly, Emmett
Lahr, Bert
Lee, Gypsy Rose
Marx, Groucho
Nichols, Mike
Oakley, Annie
Pastor, Tony
Presley, Elvis Aaron
Rand, Sally
Rice, Dan
Rice, Thomas Dartmouth
Rogers, Will
Smith, Kate
Streisand, Barbra
Sullivan, Edward Vincent
Tillstrom, Burr
Tucker, Sophie
Vallee, Rudy
Welk, Lawrence
West, Mae
Williams, Bert
Wynn, Ed

ETHNOLOGISTS

See ANTHROPOLOGISTS AND ARCHAE-
OLOGISTS

EXPLORERS

See also COLONIAL FIGURES; FRONTIER
FIGURES AND PIONEERS

Andrews, Roy Chapman
Anza, Juan Bautista de
Armstrong, John (1755–1816)
Bartlett, Robert Abram
Becknell, William
Bienville, Jean Baptiste Le Moyne,
Sieur de
Bozeman, John M.
Brulé, Étienne
Byrd, Richard Evelyn
Cabot, John
Carver, Jonathan
Champlain, Samuel de
Clark, William
Columbus, Christopher
Coronado, Francisco Vásquez de
De Soto, Hernando
Ellsworth, Lincoln
Fairchild, David Grandison
Flaherty, Robert Joseph
Frémont, John Charles
Gosnold, Bartholomew
Gray, Robert
Greely, Adolphus Washington
Hennepin, Louis
Henry, Andrew
Hudson, Henry

Huntington, Ellsworth
Iberville, Pierre Le Moyne, Sieur d'
Jolliet, Louis
Kane, Elisha Kent
Kino, Eusebio Francisco
Langford, Nathaniel Pitt
La Salle, Sieur de
Ledyard, John
Leif Ericsson
Lewis, Meriwether
Marquette, Jacques
Melville, George Wallace
Menéndez de Avilés, Pedro
Nicolet, Jean
Nicollet, Joseph Nicolas
Oñate, Juan de
Peary, Robert Edwin
Perrot, Nicolas
Pike, Zebulon Montgomery
Ponce de León, Juan
Portolá, Gaspar de
Radisson, Pierre Esprit
Schoolcraft, Henry Rowe
Smith, Jedediah Strong
Smith, John
Stanley, Henry Morton
Stefansson, Vilhjalmur
Thompson, David
Thorfinn Karlsefni
Tonty, Henri de
Vespucci, Amerigo
Walker, Joseph Reddeford
Walker, Thomas
Wellman, Walter
Wilkes, Charles

FILMMAKERS AND
PHOTOGRAPHERS

Adams, Ansel
Bourke-White, Margaret
Brady, Mathew B.
Evans, Walker
Flaherty, Robert Joseph
Hine, Lewis Wickes
Lange, Dorothea
Moholy-Nagy, László
Muybridge, Eadweard
O'Sullivan, Timothy H.
Ray, Man
Sheeler, Charles
Steichen, Edward
Stieglitz, Alfred
Strand, Paul
Warhol, Andy
Weston, Edward

FINANCIERS

See BANKERS AND FINANCIERS

FIRST LADIES

See PRESIDENTS, VICE-PRESIDENTS,
AND FIRST LADIES

FOOTBALL PLAYERS

See ATHLETES

FORESTERS

See CONSERVATIONISTS AND
NATURALISTS

FRONTIER FIGURES AND PIONEERS

See also COLONIAL FIGURES;
EXPLORERS

Applegate, Jesse
Ashley, William Henry
Bean, Roy
Becknell, William
Bent, Charles
Bidwell, John
Boone, Daniel
Bozeman, John M.
Brannan, Samuel
Bridger, James
Burk, Martha Jane (Calamity Jane)
Carson, Kit
Chapman, John
Chisholm, Jesse
Chisum, John Simpson
Chouteau, Pierre
Chouteau, René Auguste
Clark, George Rogers
Cody, William Frederick (Buffalo Bill)
Crockett, David
Croghan, George
Du Sable, Jean Baptiste Pointe
Earp, Wyatt
Filson, John
Fink, Mike
Fitzpatrick, Thomas
Gist, Christopher
Glass, Hugh
Goodnight, Charles
Gregg, Josiah
Hays, John Coffee
Henderson, Richard
Henry, Andrew
Hickok, James Butler (Wild Bill)
Juneau, Solomon Laurent
Laclède, Pierre
Lee, Jason
Lisa, Manuel
McCoy, Joseph Geating
McLoughlin, John
Marshall, James Wilson
Masterson, William Barclay (Bat)
Maverick, Samuel Augustus
Menard, Michel Branamour
Menard, Pierre
North, Frank Joshua
Pattie, James Ohio
Perrot, Nicolas
Putnum, Rufus
Radisson, Pierre Esprit
Rogers, Robert
Sacagawea
St. Vrain, Ceran de Hault de Lassus de
Sevier, John
Shreve, Henry Miller
Smith, Jedediah Strong
Sutter, John Augustus
Vallejo, Mariano Guadalupe

Walker, Joseph Reddeford
Walker, Thomas
Weiser, Conrad
Wetzel, Lewis
Whitman, Marcus
Williams, Eleazar

GANGSTERS

See CRIMINALS AND OUTLAWS

GENETICISTS

Beadle, George Wells
Delbrück, Max
Dobzhansky, Theodosius Grigorievich
Hershey, Alfred Day
Kornberg, Arthur
Lederberg, Joshua
Luria, Salvador Edward
Morgan, Thomas Hunt
Muller, Hermann Joseph
Tatum, Edward Lawrie
Watson, James Dewey

GEOGRAPHERS

See CARTOGRAPHERS, GEOGRAPHERS,
AND SURVEYORS

GEOLOGISTS AND METEOROLOGISTS

Abbe, Cleveland
Agassiz, Louis
Becker, George Ferdinand
Bowen, Norman Levi
Dana, James Dwight
Davis, William Morris
Espy, James Pollard
Gilbert, Grove Karl
Hall, James (1811–1898)
Hayden, Ferdinand Vandeveer
Hyatt, Alpheus
Jackson, Charles Thomas
King, Clarence
Leidy, Joseph
Lindgren, Waldemar
Marsh, Othniel Charles
Matthes, François Émile
Maury, Matthew Fontaine
Osborn, Henry Fairfield
Powell, John Wesley
Pumpelly, Raphael
Rossby, Carl-Gustaf Arvid
Silliman, Benjamin (1779–1864)
Simpson, George Gaylord
Van Hise, Charles Richard
Walcott, Charles Doolittle
White, David
Whitney, Josiah Dwight

GOLFERS

See ATHLETES

GRAPHIC ARTISTS

See CRAFTSMEN, DESIGNERS, AND
GRAPHIC ARTISTS

HISTORIANS AND POLITICAL SCIENTISTS

Adams, Brooks
Adams, Charles Francis, Jr. (1835–1915)
Adams, Henry Brooks
Adams, Herbert Baxter
Adams, James Truslow
Allen, Frederick Lewis
Andrews, Charles McLean
Arendt, Hannah
Bancroft, George
Bancroft, Hubert Howe
Barzun, Jacques Martin
Beard, Charles Austin
Becker, Carl Lotus
Bemis, Samuel Flagg
Beveridge, Albert Jeremiah
Bradford, William
Breasted, James Henry
Brooks, Van Wyck
Catton, Bruce
Channing, Edward
Commager, Henry Steele
Corwin, Edward Samuel
Curtis, George Ticknor
De Voto, Bernard Augustine
Draper, John William
Du Bois, William Edward Burghardt
Dunlap, William
Durant, Will
Eggleston, Edward
Fiske, John
Force, Peter
Ford, Paul Leicester
Franklin, John Hope
Freeman, Douglas Southall
Handlin, Oscar
Hansen, Marcus Lee
Hart, Albert Bushnell
Hofstadter, Richard
Jameson, John Franklin
Kennan, George Frost
Kissinger, Henry Alfred
Langer, William Leonard
Lasswell, Harold Dwight
Lieber, Francis
Lodge, Henry Cabot (1850–1924)
Lomax, John Avery
Lowell, Abbott Lawrence
McMaster, John Bach
Mahan, Alfred Thayer
Miller, Perry Gilbert Eddy
Morison, Samuel Eliot
Motley, John Lothrop
Nevins, Allan
Paine, Thomas
Parkman, Francis
Parrington, Vernon Louis
Poor, Henry Varnum
Prescott, William Hickling
Rhodes, James Ford
Robinson, James Harvey
Sarton, George Alfred Leon
Schlesinger, Arthur Meier (1888–1965)
Schlesinger, Arthur Meier, Jr. (1917–   )

Sparks, Jared
Thwaites, Reuben Gold
Turner, Frederick Jackson
Tyler, Moses Coit
Winsor, Justin
Woodson, Carter Godwin
Woodward, Comer Vann

HISTORICAL FIGURES

Borden, Lizzie Andrew
Bowie, James
Bridgman, Laura Dewey
Chang and Eng
Corbin, Margaret
Jones, Casey
Jones, Charles Jesse (Buffalo)
Judson, Edward Zane Carroll (Ned
  Buntline)
Kelly, Alvin A. (Shipwreck)
Mallon, Mary (Typhoid Mary)
Morgan, William
Pocahontas
Ross, Betsy
Sacco, Nicola, and Bartolomeo Van-
  zetti
Scott, Walter Edward
Surratt, Mary Eugenia Jenkins
Turner, Nat
Vesey, Denmark

HORTICULTURISTS

See BOTANISTS AND HORTICULTURISTS

HUMORISTS

See also AUTHORS; ENTERTAINERS;
  POETS
Adams, Franklin Pierce (FPA)
Ade, George
Allen, Fred
Benchley, Robert Charles
Browne, Charles Farrar
Burgess, Gelett
Clemens, Samuel Langhorne
Dunne, Finley Peter
Hubbard, Frank McKinney (Kin)
Lardner, Ring
Locke, David Ross
Marquis, Donald Robert Perry
Marx, Groucho
Nash, Ogden
Rogers, Will
Runyon, Damon
Shaw, Henry Wheeler
Thurber, James Grover
White, Elwyn Brooks

ILLUSTRATORS

See CARTOONISTS AND ILLUSTRATORS

IMMUNOLOGISTS

See also BACTERIOLOGISTS AND MICRO-
  BIOLOGISTS; BIOCHEMISTS
Enders, John Franklin
Robbins, Frederick Chapman

Sabin, Albert Bruce
Salk, Jonas Edward
Schick, Béla
Smith, Theobald
Weller, Thomas Huckle
Zinsser, Hans

INDIAN LEADERS

Black Hawk
Brant, Joseph
Cochise
Crazy Horse
Gall
Geronimo
Hiawatha
Joseph
Keokuk
Logan, James (1725?–1780)
McGillivray, Alexander
Massasoit
Osceola
Philip
Pontiac
Popé
Powhatan
Quanah
Red Cloud
Red Jacket
Ross, John
Samoset
Sequoya
Sitting Bull
Smohalla
Spotted Tail
Squanto
Tecumseh
Tekakwitha, Kateri
Washakie
Wovoka

INDUSTRIALISTS

See BUSINESSMEN AND
  BUSINESSWOMEN

INTELLIGENCE AGENTS
AND SPIES

Bancroft, Edward
Church, Benjamin
Greenhow, Rose O'Neal
Hale, Nathan
Hiss, Alger
Rosenberg, Julius

INVENTORS

See ENGINEERS AND INVENTORS

JOCKEYS

See ATHLETES

JOURNALISTS

See also EDITORS AND PUBLISHERS
Adams, Franklin Pierce
Angell, James Burrill
Atkinson, Brooks

Bache, Benjamin Franklin
Baer, Arthur
Baker, Ray Stannard
Beach, Alfred Ely
Beach, Moses Sperry
Beach, Moses Yale
Beebe, Lucius Morris
Bierce, Ambrose Gwinnett
Bigelow, Poultney
Blair, Francis Preston (1791–1876)
Bowles, Samuel (1797–1851)
Brisbane, Arthur
Broun, Heywood
Cahan, Abraham
Catton, Bruce
Chadwick, Henry
Creel, George Edward
Cronkite, Walter Leland, Jr.
Dana, Charles Anderson
Davis, Elmer Holmes
Davis, Richard Harding
Day, Benjamin Henry
Day, Dorothy
Delany, Martin Robinson
Douglass, Frederick
Duane, William
Dunne, Finley Peter
Field, Eugene
Friedman, Esther Pauline and
  Pauline Esther
Garrison, William Lloyd
Godkin, Edwin Lawrence
Grady, Henry Woodfin
Green, Duff
Guest, Edgar Albert
Gunther, John
Harris, Joel Chandler
Heatter, Gabriel
Hecht, Ben
Hopper, Hedda
Johnson, Hugh Samuel
Kaltenborn, Hans von
Kendall, Amos
Krehbiel, Henry Edward
Lardner, Ring
Lippmann, Walter
Lloyd, Henry Demarest
Locke, David Ross
Masterson, William Barclay (Bat)
Maxwell, Elsa
Meeker, Nathan Cook
Mencken, Henry Louis
Murrow, Edward Roscoe
Parsons, Louella
Pearson, Drew
Pegler, Westbrook
Pyle, Ernest Taylor
Reed, John
Reston, James Barrett
Rice, Grantland
Riis, Jacob August
Royall, Anne Newport
Runyon, Damon
Russwurm, John Brown
Seaman, Elizabeth Cochrane
  (Nellie Bly)
Shirer, William Lawrence

Sholes, Christopher Latham
Smith, Seba
Smith, Walter Wellesley (Red)
Stanley, Henry Morton
Steffens, Lincoln
Stone, Isidor Feinstein
Stone, Melville Elijah
Sullivan, Edward Vincent
Swope, Herbert Bayard
Tarbell, Ida Minerva
Taylor, Bert Leston
Thomas, Lowell Jackson
Thompson, Dorothy
Tucker, Benjamin Ricketson
Villard, Henry
Weed, Thurlow
Wellman, Walter
Wells, Ida Bell
White, William Allen
Willis, Nathaniel Parker
Winchell, Walter

JUDGES AND LAWYERS

See also POLITICAL LEADERS; PUBLIC
   OFFICIALS; SUPREME COURT JUS-
   TICES

Acheson, Dean Gooderham
Arnold, Thurman Wesley
Atchison, David Rice
Baer, George Frederick
Bailey, F. Lee
Baker, Newton Diehl
Baldwin, Loammi (1780–1838)
Benjamin, Judah Philip
Berle, Adolf Augustus
Billings, Frederick
Binney, Horace
Black, Jeremiah Sullivan
Brackenridge, Hugh Henry
Bristow, Benjamin Helm
Chafee, Zechariah
Chesnutt, Charles Waddell
Choate, Joseph Hodges
Choate, Rufus
Conkling, Roscoe
Cooley, Thomas McIntyre
Crater, Joseph Force
Crittenden, John Jordan
Curtis, George Ticknor
Cushing, Caleb
Dallas, Alexander James
Dana, Richard Henry
Darrow, Clarence Seward
Davis, John William
De Lancey, James
Depew, Chauncey Mitchell
Dewey, Thomas Edmund
Dulany, Daniel
Dulles, John Foster
Edmunds, George Franklin
Evarts, William Maxwell
Field, David Dudley
Galloway, Joseph
Gardner, Erle Stanley
Gary, Elbert Henry

Haggin, James Ben Ali
Hall, James (1793–1868)
Hand, Learned
Harper, Robert Goodloe
Hastie, William Henry
Hays, Arthur Garfield
Hillquit, Morris
Hoar, Ebenezer Rockwood
Hoar, Samuel
Hopkinson, Francis
Hubbard, Gardiner Greene
Hudson, Manley Ottmer
Ingersoll, Robert Green
Jessup, Philip Caryl
Johnson, Reverdy
Kellogg, Frank Billings
Kelsen, Hans
Kent, James
Key, Francis Scott
Knox, Philander Chase
Landis, Kenesaw Mountain
Langdell, Christopher Columbus
Lansing, Robert
Legaré, Hugh Swinton
Lilienthal, David Eli
Lindsey, Benjamin Barr
Livingston, Edward
Livingston, Robert R.
Lockwood, Belva Ann Bennett
Logan, James (1674–1751)
London, Meyer
Longstreet, Augustus Baldwin
Lowden, Frank Orren
Lynch, Charles
McAdoo, William Gibbs
Marshall, Louis
Martin, Luther
Meigs, Josiah
Moore, William Henry
Morgenthau, Henry (1856–1946)
Morrow, Dwight Whitney
Nizer, Louis
Olney, Richard
Otis, James
Paine, Robert Treat (1731–1814)
Palmer, Alexander Mitchell
Parsons, Theophilus (1750–1813)
Parsons, Theophilus (1797–1882)
Pastorius, Francis Daniel
Petigru, James Louis
Pike, Albert
Pinkney, William
Pound, Roscoe
Randolph, Edmund Jennings
Reeve, Tapping
Root, Elihu
Rush, Richard
Scott, James Brown
Sedgwick, Theodore
Semmes, Raphael
Sewall, Samuel
Shaw, Lemuel
Spooner, John Coit
Stanton, Edwin McMasters
Stevens, Thaddeus
Stevenson, Adlai Ewing (1835–1914)

Stevenson, Adlai Ewing (1900–1965)
Stewart, William Morris
Straus, Oscar Solomon
Tilden, Samuel Jones
Travis, William Barret
Trumbull, John (1750–1831)
Tyler, Royall
Untermyer, Samuel
U'Ren, William Simon
Wade, Benjamin Franklin
Wallace, Lewis
Webster, Daniel
Welch, Joseph Nye
Wheaton, Henry
Wheeler, Wayne Bidwell
Wickersham, George Woodward
Wigmore, John Henry
Williams, Edward Bennett
Willkie, Wendell Lewis
Wilmot, David
Wirt, William
Wythe, George

LABOR LEADERS

Barry, Leonora Marie Kearney
Bridges, Harry
Chavez, Cesar Estrada
Debs, Eugene Victor
Dubinsky, David
Foster, William Zebulon
Furuseth, Andrew
Gompers, Samuel
Green, William
Haywood, William Dudley (Big Bill)
Hill, Joe
Hillman, Sidney
Hoffa, James Riddle
Jones, Mary Harris (Mother Jones)
Lewis, John Llewellyn
Meany, George
Murray, Philip
Powderly, Terence Vincent
Randolph, Asa Philip
Reuther, Walter Philip
Stephens, Uriah Smith
Sylvis, William H.
Trevellick, Richard F.
Wilson, William Bauchop

LAW ENFORCEMENT
AGENTS

See also CRIMINOLOGISTS AND PENOL-
   OGISTS

Hoover, John Edgar
McParlan, James
Masterson, William Barclay (Bat)
Means, Gaston Bullock
Pinkerton, Allan

LAWYERS

See JUDGES AND LAWYERS

LEGISLATORS

See PUBLIC OFFICIALS

LEXICOGRAPHERS, LINGUISTS, AND PHILOLOGISTS

Bloomfield, Leonard
Child, Francis James
Chomsky, Noam
Gildersleeve, Basil Lanneau
Hayakawa, Samuel Ichiye
Korzybski, Alfred
March, Francis Andrew
Marsh, George Perkins
Moore, Clement Clarke
Murray, Lindley
Sapir, Edward
Webster, Noah
Whitney, William Dwight
Worcester, Joseph Emerson

LIBRARIANS

See BIBLIOGRAPHERS AND
LIBRARIANS

LINGUISTS

See LEXICOGRAPHERS, LINGUISTS,
AND PHILOLOGISTS

LYRICISTS

See COMPOSERS AND SONGWRITERS

MANAGERS

See DIRECTORS, PRODUCERS, AND
THEATRICAL MANAGERS; SPORTS
FIGURES

MANUFACTURERS

See BUSINESSMEN AND
BUSINESSWOMEN

MARINE CORPS LEADERS

Vandegrift, Alexander Archer

MATHEMATICIANS AND STATISTICIANS

Babson, Roger Ward
Banneker, Benjamin
Birkhoff, George David
Bowditch, Nathaniel
Colden, Cadwallader
De Bow, James Dunwoody Brownson
Einstein, Albert
Fisher, Irving
Gallup, George Horace
Gibbs, Josiah Willard
Godfrey, Thomas (1704–1749)
Harris, Louis
Neumann, John von
Newcomb, Simon
Nicollet, Joseph Nicolas
Pearl, Raymond
Peirce, Benjamin
Peirce, Charles Sanders
Steinmetz, Charles Proteus
Veblen, Oswald

Walker, Francis Amasa
Whitehead, Alfred North
Wiener, Norbert
Winthrop, John (1714–1779)
Wright, Carroll Davidson
Wright, Chauncey
Wright, Elizur

MEDICAL FIGURES

See also BACTERIOLOGISTS AND MICRO-
BIOLOGISTS; BIOCHEMISTS; BIO-
PHYSICISTS AND MOLECULAR
BIOLOGISTS; GENETICISTS; IMMU-
NOLOGISTS; PHYSIOLOGISTS;
PSYCHIATRISTS, PSYCHOAN-
ALYSTS, AND PSYCHOLOGISTS

Agnew, David Hayes
Allen, John
Alter, David
Bard, John
Bard, Samuel
Barton, Clara
Bayley, Richard
Beaumont, William
Bigelow, Jacob
Billings, John Shaw
Black, Greene Vardiman
Blackwell, Elizabeth
Blalock, Alfred
Bond, Thomas
Boylston, Zabdiel
Church, Benjamin
Colden, Cadwallader
Cournand, André Frédéric
Cushing, Harvey Williams
Delany, Martin Robinson
Dooley, Thomas Anthony
Draper, Henry
Draper, John William
Drew, Charles Richard
Evans, John
Fishbein, Morris
Fitz, Reginald Heber
Flint, Austin
Garden, Alexander
Gesell, Arnold Lucius
Goldberger, Joseph
Gorgas, William Crawford
Gorrie, John
Gross, Samuel David
Halsted, William Stewart
Harris, Chapin Aaron
Hench, Philip Showalter
Holmes, Oliver Wendell (1809–1894)
Holt, Luther Emmett
Howe, Samuel Gridley
Huggins, Charles Brenton
Jacobi, Abraham
Jeffries, John
Kane, Elisha Kent
Long, Crawford Williamson
McDowell, Ephraim
Mayo, William James, and Charles
   Horace Mayo
Mazzei, Philip
Menninger, Karl Augustus

Minot, George Richards
Mitchell, John
Mitchell, Silas Weir
Morgan, John
Morton, William Thomas Green
Murphy, William Parry
Osler, Sir William
Palmer, Daniel David
Pepper, William
Reed, Walter
Richards, Dickinson Woodruff
Robbins, Frederick Chapman
Rous, Peyton
Rush, Benjamin
Sabin, Albert Bruce
Salk, Jonas Edward
Schick, Béla
Sims, James Marion
Smith, Nathan
Smith, Theobald
Spock, Benjamin McLane
Squibb, Edward Robinson
Sternberg, George Miller
Still, Andrew Taylor
Townsend, Francis Everett
Wald, Lillian D.
Walgreen, Charles Rudolph
Warren, John
Warren, John Collins
Warren, Joseph
Waterhouse, Benjamin
Welch, William Henry
Weller, Thomas Huckle
Wells, Horace
Whipple, George Hoyt
Whitman, Marcus
Williams, Daniel Hale
Williams, William Carlos
Wood, James Rushmore
Wood, Leonard
Zinsser, Hans

MERCHANTS

See BUSINESSMEN AND
BUSINESSWOMEN

METEOROLOGISTS

See GEOLOGISTS AND METEOROLOGISTS

MICROBIOLOGISTS

See BACTERIOLOGISTS AND
MICROBIOLOGISTS

MILITARY FIGURES

See AIR MEN AND AIR WOMEN; ARMY
LEADERS AND SOLDIERS; INDIAN
LEADERS; MARINE CORPS
LEADERS; NAVY LEADERS AND
SEAMEN

MISSIONARIES

See RELIGIOUS LEADERS

MOLECULAR BIOLOGISTS

See BIOPHYSICISTS AND MOLECULAR
BIOLOGISTS

Inness, George
Johnson, Eastman
Kelly, Ellsworth
Kent, Rockwell
Kline, Franz Joseph
La Farge, John
Leutze, Emanuel Gottlieb
Levine, Jack
Lichtenstein, Roy
Malbone, Edward Greene
Marin, John Cheri
Marsh, Reginald
Martin, Homer Dodge
Moholy-Nagy, László
Morse, Samuel Finley Breese
Moses, Anna Mary Robertson
   (Grandma Moses)
Mount, William Sidney
O'Keeffe, Georgia
Parrish, Maxfield Frederick
Peale, Charles Willson
Pollock, Jackson
Pyle, Howard
Rauschenberg, Robert
Ray, Man
Remington, Frederic
Rimmer, William
Rockwell, Norman
Rothko, Mark
Ryder, Albert Pinkham
Sargent, John Singer
Shahn, Benjamin
Sheeler, Charles
Sloan, John French
Smibert, John
Steinberg, Saul
Stella, Frank Philip
Stuart, Gilbert Charles
Sully, Thomas
Tanner, Henry Ossawa
Thorpe, Thomas Bangs
Tiffany, Louis Comfort
Tobey, Mark
Trumbull, John (1756–1843)
Vanderlyn, John
Warhol, Andy
Weber, Max
West, Benjamin
Whistler, James Abbott McNeill
White, John
Wood, Grant
Wyeth, Andrew Newell
Wyeth, Newell Convers
Zorach, William

PALEONTOLOGISTS

See GEOLOGISTS AND
   METEOROLOGISTS

PATHOLOGISTS

See MEDICAL FIGURES

PENOLOGISTS

See CRIMINOLOGISTS AND
   PENOLOGISTS

PHARMACISTS

See MEDICAL FIGURES

PHILANTHROPISTS

Baker, George Fisher
Baldwin, Matthias William
Brookings, Robert Somers
Busch, Adolphus
Candler, Asa Griggs
Carnegie, Andrew
Coffin, Lorenzo S.
Colgate, William
Cooper, Peter
Corcoran, William Wilson
Cornell, Ezra
Couzens, James
Curtis, Cyrus Herman Kotzschmar
Duke, James Buchanan
Eastman, George
Evans, John
Field, Marshall
Ford, Henry
Frick, Henry Clay
Gates, Frederick Taylor
Girard, Stephen
Harvard, John
Hershey, Milton Snavely
Huntington, Henry Edwards
Kahn, Otto Herman
Kellogg, Will Keith
Kress, Samuel Henry
Lasker, Albert Davis
Lawrence, Abbott
Lawrence, Amos Adams
Lehman, Herbert Henry
Loeb, James Morris
Ludwick, Christopher
Mackay, Clarence Hungerford
Morgan, John Pierpont
Peabody, George
Pulitzer, Joseph
Rockefeller, John Davison
Rosenwald, Julius
Smith, Gerrit
Stanford, Leland
Stetson, John Batterson
Stewart, Alexander Turney
Straus, Isidor, and Nathan Straus
Tappan, Arthur
Tilden, Samuel Jones
Tompkins, Sally Louisa
Vanderbilt, Cornelius (1794–1877)
Vanderbilt, William Henry
Vanderbilt, William Kissam
Vassar, Matthew

PHILOLOGISTS

See LEXICOGRAPHERS, LINGUISTS, AND
   PHILOLOGISTS

PHILOSOPHERS

Abbot, Francis Ellingwood
Adler, Mortimer Jerome
Andrews, Stephen Pearl
Carnap, Rudolf
Cohen, Morris Raphael

Dewey, John
Edwards, Jonathan
Emerson, Ralph Waldo
Fiske, John
Harris, William Torrey
Hocking, William Ernest
Hoffer, Eric
Hopkins, Mark
James, Henry (1811–1882)
James, William
Jordan, David Starr
Kelsen, Hans
Langer, Susanne
Lovejoy, Arthur Oncken
Marcuse, Herbert
Mead, George Herbert
More, Paul Elmer
Murray, John Courtney
Palmer, George Herbert
Peirce, Charles Sanders
Quine, Willard Van Orman
Royce, Josiah
Santayana, George
Thoreau, Henry David
Tillich, Paul Johannes
Watts, Alan Witson
Whitehead, Alfred North
Woodbridge, Frederick James Eugene
Wright, Chauncey

PHOTOGRAPHERS

See FILMMAKERS AND
   PHOTOGRAPHERS

PHYSICAL SCIENTISTS

See ASTRONOMERS; CHEMISTS;
   ENGINEERS AND INVENTORS;
   GEOLOGISTS AND
   METEOROLOGISTS; PHYSICISTS

PHYSICIANS

See MEDICAL FIGURES

PHYSICISTS

Alter, David
Alvarez, Luis Walter
Anderson, Carl David
Bache, Alexander Dallas
Bardeen, John
Békésy, Georg von
Bethe, Hans Albrecht
Bloch, Felix
Brattain, Walter Houser
Bridgman, Percy Williams
Chamberlain, Owen
Colden, Cadwallader
Compton, Arthur Holly
Condon, Edward Uhler
Cooper, Leon N.
Davisson, Clinton Joseph
Draper, John William
Einstein, Albert
Fermi, Enrico
Feynman, Richard Phillips
Gamow, George

Gell-Mann, Murray
Gibbs, Josiah Willard
Glaser, Donald Arthur
Goddard, Robert Hutchings
Henry, Joseph
Hofstadter, Robert
Kármán, Theodore von
Kusch, Polykarp
Lamb, Willis Eugene, Jr.
Lawrence, Ernest Orlando
Lee, Tsung-Dao
McMillan, Edwin Mattison
Mayer, Maria Goeppert
Michelson, Albert Abraham
Millikan, Robert Andrews
Morley, Edward Williams
Mulliken, Robert Sanderson
Oppenheimer, J. Robert
Pupin, Michael Idvorsky
Purcell, Edward Mills
Rabi, Isidor Isaac
Rowland, Henry Augustus
Schrieffer, John Robert
Schwinger, Julian Seymore
Segrè, Emilio Gino
Shockley, William Bradford
Stern, Otto
Stratton, Samuel Wesley
Szilard, Leo
Teller, Edward
Thompson, Benjamin, Count
    Rumford
Townes, Charles Hard
Van Allen, James Alfred
Wigner, Eugene Paul
Yang, Chen Ning

PHYSIOLOGISTS

See also MEDICAL FIGURES
Békésy, Georg von
Bronk, Detlev Wulf
Cannon, Walter Bradford
Cournand, André Frédéric
Erlanger, Joseph
Gasser, Herbert Spencer
Hartline, Haldan Keffer
Landsteiner, Karl
Loeb, Jacques
Wald, George

PIANISTS

See MUSICIANS

PIONEERS

See FRONTIER FIGURES AND PIONEERS

PIRATES

See CRIMINALS AND OUTLAWS

PLAYWRIGHTS

See also AUTHORS; HUMORISTS
Ade, George
Albee, Edward Franklin
Anderson, Maxwell
Baraka, Imamu Amiri

Belasco, David
Boucicault, Dion
Chayefsky, Paddy
Cohan, George Michael
Connelly, Marc
Crothers, Rachel
Daly, Augustin
Dell, Floyd
Dunlap, William
Ferber, Edna
Gillette, William Hooker
Godfrey, Thomas (1736–1763)
Green, Paul Eliot
Hart, Moss
Hecht, Ben
Hellman, Lillian
Herne, James A.
Howard, Sidney Coe
Kaufman, George Simon
Luce, Clare Boothe
McCullers, Carson Smith
MacKaye, Steele
Miller, Arthur
Moody, William Vaughn
Morse, Carlton Errol
Mowatt, Anna Cora Ogden
Odets, Clifford
O'Neill, Eugene Gladstone
Payne, John Howard
Rice, Elmer Leopold
Rinehart, Mary Roberts
Saroyan, William
Sherwood, Robert Emmet
Simon, Neil
Tarkington, Booth
Tyler, Royall
Vidal, Gore
Wallack, Lester
Wilder, Thornton Niven
Williams, Tennessee

POETS

See also AUTHORS; HUMORISTS;
    PLAYWRIGHTS
Aiken, Conrad Potter
Auden, Wystan Hugh
Baraka, Imamu Amiri
Barlow, Joel
Bates, Katherine Lee
Benét, Stephen Vincent
Benét, William Rose
Berryman, John
Bodenheim, Maxwell
Bradstreet, Anne
Brooks, Gwendolyn
Bryant, William Cullen
Ciardi, John Anthony
Cole, Thomas
Crane, Hart
Crane, Stephen
Cummings, Edward Estlin
Dickey, James
Dickinson, Emily Elizabeth
Doolittle, Hilda
Dunbar, Paul Laurence
Eliot, Thomas Stearns

Emerson, Ralph Waldo
Field, Eugene
Freneau, Philip Morin
Frost, Robert Lee
Ginsberg, Allen
Godfrey, Thomas (1736–1763)
Guest, Edgar Albert
Holmes, Oliver Wendell (1809–1894)
Howe, Julia Ward
Hughes, Langston
Jarrell, Randall
Jeffers, Robinson
Johnson, James Weldon
Key, Francis Scott
Kilmer, Joyce
Lanier, Sidney
Lazarus, Emma
Lindsay, Vachel
Longfellow, Henry Wadsworth
Lowell, Amy
Lowell, James Russell
Lowell, Robert Traill Spence, Jr.
McKay, Claude
McKuen, Rod Marvin
MacLeish, Archibald
Markham, Edwin
Masters, Edgar Lee
Menken, Adah Isaacs
Merton, Thomas
Millay, Edna St. Vincent
Miller, Joaquin
Monroe, Harriet
Moody, William Vaughn
Moore, Clement Clarke
Moore, Marianne Craig
Nash, Ogden
Neihardt, John Gneisenau
Paine, Robert Treat (1773–1811)
Parker, Dorothy
Poe, Edgar Allan
Pound, Ezra Loomis
Ransom, John Crowe
Riley, James Whitcomb
Roberts, Elizabeth Madox
Robinson, Edward Arlington
Roethke, Theodore
Sandburg, Carl
Santayana, George
Shapiro, Karl Jay
Sigourney, Lydia Howard Huntley
Smith, Samuel Francis
Stevens, Wallace
Tate, Allen
Taylor, Edward
Teasdale, Sara
Timrod, Henry
Trumbull, John (1750–1831)
Van Doren, Mark
Very, Jones
Warren, Robert Penn
Wheatley, Phillis
Whitman, Walt
Whittier, John Greenleaf
Wigglesworth, Michael
Wilcox, Ella Wheeler
Williams, William Carlos
Wilson, Alexander

Woodberry, George Edward
Wylie, Elinor

POLICEMEN

See Law Enforcement Agents

POLITICAL LEADERS

See also Presidents, Vice-Presidents,
   and First Ladies; Public
   Officials
Ames, Fisher
Austin, Stephen Fuller
Benton, Thomas Hart (1782–1858)
Berger, Victor Louis
Blaine, James Gillespie
Blair, Francis Preston (1791–1876)
Blair, Francis Preston, Jr. (1821–1875)
Blair, Montgomery
Borah, William Edgar
Browder, Earl Russell
Bryan, William Jennings
Burr, Aaron
Butler, Benjamin Franklin
Calhoun, John Caldwell
Cameron, Simon
Clark, Champ
Conkling, Roscoe
Coughlin, Charles Edward
Curley, James Michael
Daley, Richard Joseph
Debs, Eugene Victor
De Leon, Daniel
Douglas, Stephen Arnold
Farley, James Aloysius
Fessenden, William Pitt
Foster, William Zebulon
Frémont, John Charles
Goldman, Emma
Greeley, Horace
Hamilton, Alexander
Hanna, Mark
Henry, Patrick
Hewitt, Abram Stevens
House, Edward Mandell
La Follette, Robert Marion
Laurens, Henry
London, Meyer
Mather, Increase
O'Neill, Thomas Philip, Jr.
Penrose, Boies
Petigru, James Louis
Platt, Thomas Collier
Quay, Matthew Stanley
Reed, John
Schurz, Carl
Sullivan, Timothy Daniel
Thomas, Norman Mattoon
Tilden, Samuel Jones
Tweed, William Marcy
Vallandigham, Clement Laird
Watson, Thomas Edward
Weaver, James Baird
Weed, Thurlow
Welles, Gideon
Willkie, Wendell Lewis

POLITICAL SCIENTISTS

See Historians and Political
   Scientists

PRESIDENTS, VICE-PRESIDENTS, AND FIRST LADIES

Adams, Abigail
Adams, John
Adams, John Quincy
Agnew, Spiro Theodore
Arthur, Chester Alan
Barkley, Alben William
Breckinridge, John Cabell
Buchanan, James
Burr, Aaron
Calhoun, John Caldwell
Bush, George Herbert Walker
Calhoun, John Caldwell
Carter, James Earl
Cleveland, Grover
Clinton, George
Colfax, Schuyler
Coolidge, Calvin
Curtis, Charles
Dallas, George Mifflin
Dawes, Charles Gates
Eisenhower, Dwight David
Fairbanks, Charles Warren
Fillmore, Millard
Ford, Gerald Rudolph, Jr.
Garfield, James Abram
Garner, John Nance
Gerry, Elbridge
Grant, Ulysses S.
Hamlin, Hannibal
Harding, Warren Gamaliel
Harrison, Benjamin
Harrison, William Henry
Hayes, Rutherford Birchard
Hendricks, Thomas Andrews
Hobart, Garret Augustus
Hoover, Herbert Clark
Humphrey, Hubert Horatio
Jackson, Andrew
Jefferson, Thomas
Johnson, Andrew
Johnson, Lyndon Baines
Johnson, Richard Mentor
Kennedy, John Fitzgerald
King, William Rufus de Vane
Lincoln, Abraham
McKinley, William
Madison, James
Marshall, Thomas Riley
Mondale, Walter Frederick
Monroe, James
Morton, Levi Parsons
Nixon, Richard Milhous
Pierce, Franklin
Polk, James Knox
Reagan, Ronald Wilson
Roosevelt, Eleanor
Roosevelt, Franklin Delano
Roosevelt, Theodore
Sherman, James Schoolcraft

Stevenson, Adlai Ewing (1835–1914)
Taft, William Howard
Taylor, Zachary
Tompkins, Daniel D.
Truman, Harry S.
Tyler, John
Van Buren, Martin
Wallace, Henry Agard
Washington, George
Wheeler, William Almon
Wilson, Henry
Wilson, Woodrow

PRINTERS

See Craftsmen, Designers, and
   Graphic Artists

PRODUCERS

See Directors, Producers, and
   Theatrical Managers

PROHIBITIONISTS

See Reformers

PSYCHIATRISTS, PSYCHO-ANALYSTS, AND PSYCHOLOGISTS

Allport, Gordon Willard
Bettelheim, Bruno
Boring, Edwin Garrigues
Cattell, James McKeen
Clark, Kenneth Bancroft
Colden, Cadwallader
Dewey, John
Erikson, Erik Homburger
Fromm, Erich
Gesell, Arnold Lucius
Hall, Granville Stanley
James, William
Judd, Charles Hubbard
Lashley, Karl Spencer
McDougall, William
Mead, George Herbert
Menninger, Karl Augustus
Münsterberg, Hugo
Rhine, Joseph Banks
Skinner, Burrhus Frederic
Spock, Benjamin McLane
Sullivan, Harry Stack
Terman, Lewis Madison
Thorndike, Edward Lee
Titchener, Edward Bradford
Watson, John Broadus
Yerkes, Robert Mearns

PSYCHOLOGISTS

See Psychiatrists, Psychoanalysts,
   and Psychologists

PUBLIC OFFICIALS

See also Diplomats; Political
   Leaders; Presidents, Vice-
   Presidents, and First Ladies
Acheson, Dean Gooderham
Adams, Charles Francis (1807–1886)

PUBLISHERS

See EDITORS AND PUBLISHERS

REFORMERS

Bond, Julian
Brace, Charles Loring
Brisbane, Albert
Brown, John
Brown, Olympia
Brownson, Orestes Augustus
Burritt, Elihu
Catt, Carrie Chapman
Chafee, Zechariah
Child, Lydia Maria
Clay, Cassius Marcellus (1810–1903)
Coffin, Levi
Coffin, Lorenzo S.
Comstock, Anthony
Coxey, Jacob Sechler
Crandall, Prudence
Curtis, George William
Day, Dorothy
Delany, Martin Robinson
Dix, Dorothea Lynde
Donnelly, Ignatius
Dorr, Thomas Wilson
Douglass, Frederick
Dow, Neal
Du Bois, William Edward Burghardt
Evans, George Henry
Evers, Charles
Farmer, James Leonard
Field, David Dudley
Filene, Edward Albert
Finley, Robert
Forten, James
Friedan, Betty Naomi Goldstein
Fuller, Margaret, Marchioness Ossoli
Furuseth, Andrew
Gardner, John William
Garrison, William Lloyd
Garvey, Marcus Moziah
George, Henry
Graham, Sylvester
Greeley, Horace
Grimké, Sarah Moore and Angelina
  Emily
Gronlund, Laurence
Hale, Sarah Josepha Buell
Higginson, Thomas Wentworth
  Storrow
Hillquit, Morris
Howe, Julia Ward
Howe, Samuel Gridley
Jackson, Jesse Louis
Johnson, James Weldon
Johnson, Tom Loftin
Jones, Samuel Milton
Kelley, Oliver Hudson
King, Martin Luther, Jr.
Ladd, William
Lease, Mary Elizabeth Clyens
Livermore, Mary Ashton Rice
Lloyd, Henry Demarest
Lockwood, Belva Ann Bennett
Lovejoy, Elijah Parish
Low, Juliette Gordon
Low, Seth
Lundy, Benjamin
Luther, Seth
Malcolm X

Marshall, Louis
Meeker, Nathan Cook
Meredith, James Howard
Mott, Lucretia Coffin
Nader, Ralph
Nation, Carry Amelia Moore
Noyes, John Humphrey
Owen, Robert Dale
Parker, Theodore
Paul, Alice
Phillips, Wendell
Randolph, Asa Philip
Rankin, Jeannette
Riis, Jacob August
Ripley, George
Roosevelt, Eleanor
Sanger, Margaret Higgins
Sinclair, Upton Beall
Smith, Gerrit
Spingarn, Joel Elias
Spock, Benjamin McLane
Stanton, Elizabeth Cady
Steffens, Lincoln
Stone, Lucy
Stowe, Harriet Elizabeth Beecher
Sylvis, William H.
Tappan, Arthur
Tarbell, Ida Minerva
Thomas, Martha Carey
Thomas, Norman Mattoon
Townsend, Francis Everett
Truth, Sojourner
Tubman, Harriet
U'Ren, William Simon
Wald, Lillian D.
Walker, David
Washington, Booker Taliaferro
Weld, Theodore Dwight
Wells, Ida Bell
Wheeler, Wayne Bidwell
Whipple, Henry Benjamin
White, Walter Francis
Wilkins, Roy
Willard, Frances Elizabeth Caroline
Woodhull, Victoria Claflin
Woolman, John
Wright, Elizur
Wright, Frances
Young, Whitney Moore, Jr.

RELIGIOUS LEADERS

Abbot, Francis Ellingwood
Abbott, Lyman
Adler, Cyrus
Albright, Jacob
Allen, Richard
Allouez, Claude Jean
Asbury, Francis
Backus, Isaac
Badin, Stephen Theodore
Baker, George (Father Divine)
Ballou, Adin
Ballou, Hosea
Beecher, Edward
Beecher, Henry Ward
Beecher, Lyman

Beissel, Johann Conrad
Benavides, Alonzo de
Blair, James
Brooks, Phillips
Brown, Olympia
Brownlow, William Gannaway
Brownson, Orestes Augustus
Buchman, Frank Nathan Daniel
Bulkeley, Peter
Bushnell, Horace
Cabrini, Frances Xavier
Campanius, John
Campbell, Thomas
Carroll, John
Cartwright, Peter
Channing, William Ellery
Chase, Philander
Chauncy, Charles
Clarke, James Freeman
Connelly, Cornelia
Conwell, Russell Herman
Cotton, John
Coughlin, Charles Edward
Cutler, Manasseh
Davies, Samuel
De Smet, Pierre Jean
Douglas, Lloyd Cassel
Dunster, Henry
Dwight, Timothy
Dyer, Mary
Eddy, Mary Morse Baker
Edwards, Jonathan
Eggleston, Edward
Eliot, John
England, John
Finley, Robert
Finney, Charles Grandison
Flanagan, Edward Joseph
Flint, Timothy
Fosdick, Harry Emerson
Fox, Margaret
Frothingham, Octavius Brooks
Fry, Franklin Clark
Furman, Richard
Gates, Frederick Taylor
Gibbons, James
Gladden, Washington
Graham, Billy
Hale, Edward Everett
Hecker, Isaac Thomas
Hennepin, Louis
Hicks, Elias
Hooker, Thomas
Hopkins, Samuel
Hughes, John
Hutchinson, Anne
Ingraham, Joseph Holt
Ireland, John
Jackson, Sheldon
Jones, Rufus Matthew
Judson, Adoniram
Kaplan, Mordecai Menahem
King, Martin Luther, Jr.
Kino, Eusebio Francisco
Lamy, Jean Baptiste
Lee, Ann
Lee, Jason

McCloskey, John
Machen, John Gresham
McPherson, Aimee Semple
Magnes, Judah Leon
Makemie, Francis
Malcolm X
Marquette, Jacques
Mather, Cotton
Mather, Increase
Mather, Richard
Mayhew, Jonathan
Merton, Thomas
Metz, Christian
Miller, William
Moody, Dwight Lyman
Morse, Jedidiah
Mott, John Raleigh
Muhammad, Elijah
Muhlenberg, Frederick Augustus
Mühlenberg, Henry Melchior
Muhlenberg, John Peter Gabriel
Neumann, John Nepomucene
Niebuhr, Reinhold
Oxnam, Garfield Bromley
Parker, Theodore
Peale, Norman Vincent
Penn, William
Polk, Leonidas
Post, Christian Frederick
Potter, Henry Codman
Powell, Adam Clayton, Jr.
Rauschenbusch, Walter
Revels, Hiram Rhoades
Roberts, Oral
Rogers, John (1648–1721)
Russell, Charles Taze
Schaff, Philip
Schechter, Solomon
Schmucker, Samuel Simon
Seabury, Samuel
Serra, Junípero
Seton, Elizabeth Ann Bayley
Sheen, Fulton John
Simpson, Matthew
Smith, Joseph
Smohalla
Sorin, Edward Frederick
Spellman, Francis Joseph
Stoddard, Solomon
Stone, Barton Warren
Strang, James Jesse
Strong, Josiah
Sunday, William Ashley (Billy)
Taylor, Edward Thompson
  (1793–1871)
Taylor, William
Tekakwitha, Kateri
Tennent, Gilbert
Tennent, William
Vincent, John Heyl
Walther, Carl Ferdinand Wilhelm
Ward, Nathaniel
Wheelock, Eleazar
Whipple, Henry Benjamin
White, William
Wigglesworth, Michael
Williams, Roger

Wise, Isaac Mayer
Wise, John
Wise, Stephen Samuel
Witherspoon, John
Woolman, John
Wovoka
Young, Brigham

REPORTERS

See Journalists

REVOLUTIONARY LEADERS

See Colonial Figures

SAILORS

See Navy Leaders and Seamen

SCOUTS

See Frontier Figures and Pioneers

SCULPTORS

Akeley, Carl Ethan
Barnard, George Gray
Baskin, Leonard
Bitter, Karl Theodore Francis
Borglum, Gutzon
Calder, Alexander
Davidson, Jo
Eakins, Thomas
Flannagan, John Bernard
Fraser, James Earle
French, Daniel Chester
Greenough, Horatio
Kelly, Ellsworth
Lachaise, Gaston
Noguchi, Isamu
Oldenburg, Claes Thure
Powers, Hiram
Remington, Frederic
Rimmer, William
Rogers, John (1829–1904)
Rush, William
Saint-Gaudens, Augustus
Segal, George
Smith, David
Taft, Lorado Zadoc
Ward, John Quincy Adams
Zorach, William

SEAMEN

See Navy Leaders and Seamen

SEMANTICISTS

See Lexicographers, Linguists, and
Philologists

SENATORS

See Public Officials

SINGERS

See also Entertainers; Musicians
Anderson, Marian
Baez, Joan

Bayes, Nora
Berry, Charles Edward Anderson
Brown, James
Burleigh, Harry Thacker
Callas, Maria
Crosby, Bing
Dylan, Bob
Farrell, Eileen
Fitzgerald, Ella
Garden, Mary
Garland, Judy
Guthrie, Woody
Hayes, Roland
Holiday, Billie
Jackson, Mahalia
Ledbetter, Huddie
McKuen, Rod Marvin
Nordica, Lillian
Presley, Elvis Aron
Price, Leontyne
Robeson, Paul Bustill
Russell, Lillian
Schumann-Heink, Ernestine
Seeger, Pete
Sinatra, Frank
Smith, Bessie
Smith, Kate
Streisand, Barbra
Waters, Ethel

SOCIALITES

Belmont, Alva Ertskin Smith
  Vanderbilt
Bonaparte, Elizabeth Patterson
Eaton, Margaret O'Neale
Gardner, Isabella Stewart
McAllister, Ward
Windsor, Wallis Warfield, Duchess of

SOCIAL SCIENTISTS

See Anthropologists and
  Archaeologists; Cartog-
  raphers, Geographers, and
  Surveyors; Criminologists
  and Penologists; Economists;
  Educators; Historians and
  Political Scientists; Psychi-
  atrists, Psychoanalysts, and
  Psychologists; Sociologists

SOCIAL WORKERS

See Reformers

SOCIOLOGISTS

See also Criminologists and
  Penologists
Carey, Henry Charles
Clark, Kenneth Bancroft
Collier, John
Cooley, Charles Horton
Du Bois, William Edward Burghardt
Frazier, E. Franklin
Gallup, George Horace
Harris, Louis
Lipset, Seymour Martin
Lynd, Robert Staughton

MacIver, Robert Morrison
Merton, Robert King
Park, Robert Ezra
Parsons, Talcott
Redfield, Robert
Riesman, David, Jr.
Sorokin, Pitirim Alexandrovitch
Sumner, William Graham
Veblen, Thorstein Bunde
Ward, Lester Frank
Wright, Carroll Davidson

SOLDIERS

See Army Leaders and Soldiers

SONGWRITERS

See Composers and Songwriters

SPACE SCIENTISTS

See Astronauts and Space
Scientists

SPIES

See Intelligence Agents and Spies

SPORTS FIGURES

See also Athletes
Andretti, Mario Gabriel
Anson, Adrian Constantine (Cap)
Atlas, Charles
Bennett, James Gordon (1841–1918)
Brady, William Aloysius
Brundage, Avery
Camp, Walter Chauncey
Chadwick, Henry
Chandler, Albert Benjamin (Happy)
Cousy, Robert Joseph
Doubleday, Abner
Durocher, Leo Ernest
Foyt, Anthony Joseph, Jr.
Glidden, Charles Jasper
Gulick, Luther Halsey
Halas, George Stanley
Hoppe, William Frederick
Johnson, Walter Perry
Landis, Kenesaw Mountain
Lombardi, Vincent Thomas
McGraw, John Joseph
Mack, Connie
Murphy, Michael Charles
Naismith, James
Oldfield, Barney
Patch, Sam
Pyle, Charles C.
Rice, Grantland
Rickard, George Lewis (Tex)
Rickey, Branch Wesley
Roberts, Glenn (Fireball)
Rockne, Knute Kenneth
Russell, William Felton (Bill)
Stagg, Amos Alonzo
Stengel, Charles Dillon (Casey)
Sullivan, James Edward
Vanderbilt, Harold Stirling

Vanderbilt, William Kissam
Veeck, William Louis, Jr.
Warner, Glenn Scobey (Pop)
Wright, Henry (Harry, 1835–1895)

STATESMEN

See Diplomats; Political Leaders;
Presidents, Vice-Presidents,
and First Ladies; Public
Officials

STATISTICIANS

See Mathematicians and
Statisticians

SUFFRAGETTES

See Reformers

SUPREME COURT JUSTICES

Baldwin, Henry
Barbour, Philip Pendleton
Black, Hugo LaFayette
Blackmun, Harry Andrew
Blair, John
Blatchford, Samuel
Bradley, Joseph P.
Brandeis, Louis Dembitz
Brennan, William Joseph, Jr.
Brewer, David Josiah
Brown, Henry Billings
Burger, Warren Earl
Burton, Harold Hitz
Butler, Pierce
Byrnes, James Francis
Campbell, John Archibald
Cardozo, Benjamin Nathan
Catron, John
Chase, Salmon Portland
Chase, Samuel
Clark, Tom Campbell
Clarke, John Hessin
Clifford, Nathan
Curtis, Benjamin Robbins
Cushing, William
Daniel, Peter Vivian
Davis, David
Day, William Rufus
Douglas, William Orville
Duvall, Gabriel
Ellsworth, Oliver
Field, Stephen Johnson
Fortas, Abe
Frankfurter, Felix
Fuller, Melville Weston
Goldberg, Arthur Joseph
Gray, Horace
Grier, Robert Cooper
Harlan, John Marshall (1833–1911)
Harlan, John Marshall (1899–1971)
Holmes, Oliver Wendell (1841–1935)
Hughes, Charles Evans
Hunt, Ward
Iredell, James
Jackson, Howell Edmunds

Jackson, Robert Houghwout
Jay, John
Johnson, Thomas
Johnson, William (1771–1834)
Lamar, Joseph Rucker
Lamar, Lucius Quintus Cincinnatus
Livingston, Henry Brockholst
Lurton, Horace Harmon
McKenna, Joseph
McKinley, John
McLean, John
McReynolds, James Clark
Marshall, John
Marshall, Thurgood
Matthews, Stanley
Miller, Samuel Freeman
Minton, Sherman
Moody, William Henry
Moore, Alfred
Murphy, Frank
Nelson, Samuel
O'Connor, Sandra Day
Paterson, William
Peckham, Rufus Wheeler
Pitney, Mahlon
Powell, Lewis Franklin, Jr.
Reed, Stanley Forman
Rehnquist, William Hubbs
Roberts, Owen Josephus
Rutledge, John
Rutledge, Wiley Blount, Jr.
Sanford, Edward Terry
Shiras, George
Stevens, John Paul
Stewart, Potter
Stone, Harlan Fiske
Story, Joseph
Strong, William
Sutherland, George
Swayne, Noah Haynes
Taft, William Howard
Taney, Roger Brooke
Thompson, Smith
Todd, Thomas
Trimble, Robert
Van Devanter, Willis
Vinson, Frederick Moore
Waite, Morrison Remick
Warren, Earl
Washington, Bushrod
Wayne, James Moore
White, Byron Raymond
White, Edward Douglass
Whittaker, Charles Evans
Wilson, James
Woodbury, Levi
Woods, William Burnham

SURGEONS

See Medical Figures

SURVEYORS

See Cartographers, Geographers,
and Surveyors

THEATRICAL MANAGERS

See Directors, Producers, and
Theatrical Managers

THEOLOGIANS

See Philosophers; Religious
Leaders

UNION LEADERS

See Labor Leaders

VICE-PRESIDENTS

See Presidents, Vice-Presidents,
and First Ladies

VIOLINISTS

See Musicians

WOMEN'S RIGHTS LEADERS

See Reformers

WRESTLERS

See Athletes

WRITERS

See Authors; Humorists;
Journalists; Playwrights;
Poets

ZOOLOGISTS

See also Medical Figures;
Physiologists
Agassiz, Alexander
Bartram, William

Carson, Rachel Louise
Chapman, Frank Michler
Dana, James Dwight
Fitch, Asa
Gill, Theodore Nicholas
Harrison, Ross Granville
Hyatt, Alpheus
Jordan, David Starr
Just, Ernest Everett
Kinsey, Alfred Charles
Leidy, Joseph
Osborn, Henry Fairfield
Pearl, Raymond
Peterson, Roger Tory
Say, Thomas
Stroud, Robert
Wilder, Burt Green
Wilson, Alexander